A GUIDE BOOK OF
UNITED STATES COINS
MEGA RED™
7TH EDITION

George Washington was president of the United States when the
first U.S. Mint was established in Philadelphia, Pennsylvania, in 1792.

THE OFFICIAL RED BOOK®

A GUIDE BOOK OF
UNITED STATES COINS
MEGA RED™
7ᵀᴴ EDITION
EXPANDED DELUXE EDITION OF THE BEST-SELLING RED BOOK®

R. S. YEOMAN

Q. DAVID BOWERS, SENIOR EDITOR
JEFF GARRETT, VALUATIONS EDITOR
KENNETH BRESSETT, EDITOR EMERITUS

A Fully Illustrated Catalog of Useful Information on Colonial and Federal Coinage, 1556 to Date, With Detailed Photographs to Identify Your Coins and Retail Valuation Charts Indicating How Much They're Worth. Plus Illustrated Grading Instructions With Enlarged Images to Determine Your Coins' Conditions. Insider Tips on Treasures Waiting to be Discovered in Your Pocket Change; Advice on Smart Collecting; and More. Based on the Expertise of More Than 100 Professional Coin Dealers and Researchers. Also Featuring Entertaining Stories, Amazing Essays, and Astounding Facts and Figures About All Manner of Rare and Historical Coins of the United States of America.

A Guide Book of United States Coins™, Deluxe Edition
THE OFFICIAL RED BOOK OF UNITED STATES COINS™

THE OFFICIAL RED BOOK, MEGA RED, and
THE OFFICIAL RED BOOK OF UNITED STATES COINS
are trademarks of Whitman Publishing, LLC.

ISBN: 0794848974
Printed in the United States of America.

© 2021 Whitman Publishing, LLC
1974 Chandalar Drive, Suite D, Pelham, AL 35124

Correspondence concerning this book may be directed to Whitman Publishing, Attn: *Mega Red*, at the address above.

Whitman Publishing, LLC, does not deal in coins; the values shown herein are not offers to buy or sell but are included only as general information. Descriptions of coins are based on the most accurate data available, but could change with further research or discoveries.

Collect all the books in the Bowers Series. *A Guide Book of Morgan Silver Dollars* • *A Guide Book of Double Eagle Gold Coins* • *A Guide Book of United States Type Coins* • *A Guide Book of Modern United States Proof Coin Sets* • *A Guide Book of Shield and Liberty Head Nickels* • *A Guide Book of Flying Eagle and Indian Head Cents* • *A Guide Book of Washington Quarters* • *A Guide Book of Buffalo and Jefferson Nickels* • *A Guide Book of Lincoln Cents* • *A Guide Book of United States Commemorative Coins* • *A Guide Book of United States Tokens and Medals* • *A Guide Book of Gold Dollars* • *A Guide Book of Peace Dollars* • *A Guide Book of the Official Red Book of United States Coins* • *A Guide Book of Franklin and Kennedy Half Dollars* • *A Guide Book of Civil War Tokens* • *A Guide Book of Hard Times Tokens* • *A Guide Book of Mercury Dimes, Standing Liberty Quarters, and Liberty Walking Half Dollars* • *A Guide Book of Half Cents and Large Cents* • *A Guide Book of Barber Silver Coins* • *A Guide Book of Liberty Seated Silver Coins* • *A Guide Book of Modern United States Dollar Coins* • *A Guide Book of the United States Mint* • *A Guide Book of Gold Eagle Coins* • *A Guide Book of Continental Currency and Coins.*

For a complete listing of numismatic reference books, supplies, and storage products, visit Whitman Publishing online at www.whitman.com.

If you enjoy U.S. and related coins, join the American Numismatic Association. Visit www.whitman.com for membership information.

WHITMAN™

CONTENTS

CONTENTS

CONTENTS

CREDITS AND ACKNOWLEDGMENTS

CONTRIBUTORS TO THE SEVENTH *MEGA RED*

Senior Editor: Q. David Bowers. *Valuations Editor:* Jeff Garrett. *Editor Emeritus:* Kenneth Bressett.
Special Consultants: Philip Bressett, Maxwell Gregory, Robert Rhue, Troy Thoreson, Ben Todd, Jake Walker

The following coin dealers and collectors have contributed pricing information to this edition:

Gary Adkins	Michael Fey	Joseph Jones	Steve Roach
John Albanese	Gerry Fortin	Mike Joyce	Greg Rohan
Dominic Albert	Pierre Fricke	Donald H. Kagin	Maurice Rosen
Buddy Alleva	John Frost	Bradley S. Karoleff	Mark Salzberg
Richard M. August	Mike Fuljenz	Jim Koenings	Matthew Savanich
Mitchell Battino	Dennis M. Gillio	John Kraljevich	Gerald R. Scherer Jr.
Lee J. Bellisario	Ronald J. Gillio	Richard A. Lecce	Harry Schultz
Chris Berinato	Rusty Goe	Julian M. Leidman	Jeff Shevlin
Mark Borckardt	Ira Goldberg	Denis W. Loring	Roger Siboni
Larry Briggs	Lawrence Goldberg	Dwight N. Manley	James Simek
William Bugert	Kenneth M. Goldman	Syd Martin	David M. Sundman
H. Robert Campbell	Robert Green	David McCarthy	Barry Sunshine
Elizabeth Coggan	Thomas Hallenbeck	Jack McNamara	Anthony Terranova
Gary and Alan Cohen	James Halperin	Harry Miller	Rick Tomaska
Stephen M. Cohen	Ash Harrison	Lee S. Minshull	Frank Van Valen
Frank J. Colletti	Stephen Hayden	Scott P. Mitchell	Kevin Vinton
Steve Contursi	Brian Hendelson	Michael Moline	Fred Weinberg
Adam Crum	John W. Highfill	Charles Morgan	Douglas Winter
Raymond Czahor	Brian Hodge	Alex Nocerino	Mark S. Yaffe
John Dannreuther	Jack Howes	Paul Nugget	
Steven Ellsworth	Steve Ivy	Joseph Parrella	
Brant Fahnestock	Amandeep Jassal	Robert M. Paul	

Special credit is due to the following for contributions to the *Guide Book of United States Coins, Deluxe Edition*: Gary Adkins, David W. Akers, John Albanese, David Allison, Jeff Ambio, the American Numismatic Society, Marc Banks, Mitchell Battino, Jack Beymer, Doug Bird, Jon Alan Boka, Mark Borckardt, Nicholas P. Brown, Roger W. Burdette, David J. Camire, Julia Casey, Fonda Chase, Elizabeth Coggan, Greg Cohen, Ray Czahor, John W. Dannreuther, Beth Deisher, Dan Demeo, Richard Doty, Bill Eckberg, Michael Fahey, David Fanning, Bill Fivaz, Pierre Fricke, Ira Goldberg, Lawrence Goldberg, Ken Goldman, J.R. Grellman Jr., Ron Guth, James Halperin, Greg Hannigan, Steve Herman, Phil Hinkelman, Daniel W. Holmes Jr., Gwyn Huston, Walter Husak, Tom Hyland, Wayne Imbrogno, Steve Ivy, R.W. Julian, Brad Karoleff, David W. Lange, Julian Leidman, Jon Lerner, Denis W. Loring, John Lusk, Ron Manley, J.P. Martin, Jim Matthews, Chris Victor McCawley, Jim McGuigan, Jack McNamara, Harry Miller, Paul Minshull, Scott Mitchell, Charles Moore, Dan Moore, Jim Neiswinter, Eric P. Newman, Numismatic Guaranty Corporation of America (NGC), Joel J. Orosz, John M. Pack, D. Brent Pogue, Michael Printz, Jim Reardon, Tom Reynolds, Harry Salyards, Louis Scuderi, Thomas Scrfass, Neil Shafer, Michael Sherrill, Jeff Shevlin, Craig Sholley, the Smithsonian Institution, Rick Snow, Max Spiegel, Lawrence R. Stack, David M. Sundman, Barry Sunshine, David Sunshine, James Taylor, Saul

Teichman, R. Tettenhorst, Scott Travers, Rich Uhrich, the United States Mint, Frank Van Valen, Alan V. Weinberg, Fred Weinberg, Ken and Stephanie Westover, James Wiles, Ray Williams, Doug Winter, David Wnuck, and Winston Zack.

Special credit is due to the following for service and data in the 2022 regular edition of the *Guide Book of United States Coins*: Charles Davis, David Fanning, Robert W. Julian, George F. Kolbe, Christopher McDowell, P. Scott Rubin, and William Spencer.

Special credit is due to the following for service in past editions: Lee J. Bellisario, Stewart Blay, Roger W. Burdette, Frank J. Colletti, Tom DeLorey, Bill Fivaz, Chuck Furjanic, James C. Gray, Charles Hoskins, Richard Kelly, David W. Lange, G.J. Lawson, Andy Lustig, J.P. Martin, Eric P. Newman, Ken Potter, Paul Rynearson, Mary Sauvain, Richard J. Schwary, Robert W. Shippee, Craig Smith, Barry Sunshine, Jerry Treglia, Mark R. Vitunic, Holland Wallace, Weimar White, John Whitney, Raymond Williams, and John Wright.

Special photo credits are due to the following: Al Adams, David Akers, James Bevill, Heritage Auctions (ha.com), Ira & Larry Goldberg Coins & Collectibles, Ron Karp, Massachusetts Historical Society, Christopher McDowell, Tom Mulvaney, Ken Potter, John Scanlon, Roger Siboni, the Smithsonian Institution, Stack's Bowers Galleries, Richard Stinchcomb, and the United States Mint.

HOW TO USE THIS BOOK

Numismatics, in its purest sense, is the study of items used as money. Today in the United States, as around the world, the term embraces the activities of a diverse community of hobbyists, historians, researchers, museum curators, and others who collect and study coins, tokens, paper money, and similar objects.

Since 1946 the *Guide Book of United States Coins* has served this community as the preeminent annual reference for coin specifications, mintages, values, photographs, and other information important to collectors and students. With more than 23 million copies in print since the first edition, the *Guide Book* (commonly known as the *Red Book*) is well established as the most popular reference in numismatics—not to mention one of the best-selling nonfiction books in the history of American publishing. (In 1964 the 18th edition of the *Red Book* ranked number 5 on the national sales lists, at 1.2 million copies—higher than Dale Carnegie's *How to Win Friends and Influence People* at number 6, and John F. Kennedy's *Profiles in Courage* at number 9.)

Building on this strong foundation, *Mega Red* (the Deluxe Edition of the *Guide Book of United States Coins*) is an expanded and enlarged volume intended to serve not only beginning collectors, but also intermediate to advanced coin collectors, professional coin dealers and auctioneers, researchers, and investors. It features more photographs, detailed higher-grade valuations, additional listings of die varieties and rare early Proof coins, certified-coin population data, auction records, and other resources that provide a wealth of information on every coin type ever made by the U.S. Mint. *Mega Red* also expands on the regular edition's coverage of collectible die varieties, with close-up photographs, valuations, and chart notes. It is a handy single-source guide that educates its users in auction and certification trends, retail valuations, and similar aspects of the marketplace.

Like the regular-edition *Red Book*, *Mega Red* includes information on colonial and early American coins and tokens as well as all federal series (copper half cents through gold double eagles). It also covers private and territorial gold pieces; Hard Times tokens; Civil War tokens; Confederate coins; Hawaiian, Puerto Rican, and Philippine coins; Alaskan tokens; misstrikes and errors; numismatic books; Proof and Mint sets; commemorative coins from 1892 to date; silver, gold, and platinum bullion coins; and other topics.

Readers of *Mega Red* benefit from the following useful information.

The *Red Book* has become a popular collectible itself, with fans striving to acquire one of each edition dating back to number 1, published in November 1946 with a 1947 cover date. Rare early volumes can be worth $1,000 or more.

R.S. Yeoman, author of the original *Guide Book of United States Coins*, examining press proofs in 1969.

DENOMINATION INTRODUCTIONS

Each coinage denomination is discussed first in an overview of its history, major design types and sub-types, and general collectability by type. (The dollar denomination is divided into silver dollars, trade dollars, and modern dollars.) A second essay gives collectors a more in-depth analysis of specializing in that denomination. *These sections encapsulate decades of numismatic research and market observation, and they should be read in conjunction with the charts, photographs, and other information that follow.*

TYPE-BY-TYPE STUDIES

Within each denomination, each major coin type is laid out in chronological order. As with the *Red Book*'s regular edition, the type's designer and its specifications (weight, composition, diameter, edge treatment, and production facilities) are given. Coinage designs are pictured at actual size except commemorative designs, which are standardized (one Mint State example and one Proof example, when available). Each type section includes summary text on the type's history; aspects of its striking, sharpness, and related characteristics; and its market availability. In-depth grading instructions, with enlarged illustrations, show how to grade each coin type, covering circulation strikes as well as Proofs.

CHARTS

The data charts include these elements:

	Mintage	Cert	Avg	%MS	VF-20	EF-40	AU-50	MS-60	MS-62	MS-63	MS-64 / PF-60	MS-65 / PF-63	MS-66 / PF-65
1921, High Relief	1,006,473	15,809	58.8	74%	$110	$125	$150	$260	$350	$425	$850	$1,600	$5,000
	Auctions: $70,500, MS-67, August 2015; $5,875, MS-66, August 2016; $4,700, MS-66, January 2015; $2,820, MS-66, November 2016												
1921, High Relief, Line Through L (a)	(b)	57	60.7	79%			$225	$315	$400	$500	$900	$2,400	
	Auctions: $940, MS-63, June 2013												
1921, Satin Finish Proof	*10–20*	17	63.6								$15,000	$30,000	$75,000
	Auctions: $32,200, PF-64, July 2009												
1921, High Relief, Sandblast Finish Proof	*5–8*	3	64.0										$85,000
	Auctions: $99,875, PF-66, January 2014; $129,250, PF-64, August 2014												

a. A ray runs through the first L in DOLLAR, instead of behind it. b. Included in 1921, High Relief, mintage figure.

Mintages. Mintage data is compiled from official Mint records whenever possible, and in other cases from more than 70 years of active numismatic research. In instances where the Mint's early records are in question or have been proven faulty, the official numbers are provided and further information is given in chart notes. For some early Proof coins for which no official mintage records exist, an estimated mintage, or the number of coins known in collections, is given. For modern issues (usually those minted within the past five years), the Mint has released production and/or sales numbers that are not yet officially finalized; these are given in italics.

Note that Mint reports are not always reliable for estimating the rarities of coins. In the early years of the Mint, coinage dies of previous years often were used until they became worn or broken. Certain reported quantities, particularly for gold and silver coins, cover the number of pieces struck and make no indication of the quantity that actually reached circulation. Many issues were deposited in the Treasury as backing for paper currency and later were melted without ever being released to the public.

Gold coins struck before August 1, 1834, are rare today because from 1821 onward (and at times before 1821) the gold in the coins was worth more than their face values, so they were struck as bullion and traded at a premium. Many were exported and melted for their precious-metal value.

Mintage figures shown for 1964 through 1966 are for coins bearing those dates. Some of these coins were struck in more than one year and at various mints, both with and without mintmarks. In recent years, mintage figures reported by the Mint have been revised several times and precise amounts remain uncertain.

Mintage figures shown in italics are estimates based on the most accurate information available. Numismatic research is constantly ongoing, and listed figures are sometimes revised, when new information becomes available.

Certified Populations. For each coin of a particular date and mint, a summary is provided of (1) the number of coins certified, (2) the average grade, on the standard 1–70 scale, of those coins graded, and (3) for circulation-strike coins, the percentage certified in Mint State.

These summaries provide the collector and investor with working data useful in comparing coins offered for sale or bid.

Certified population data is provided courtesy of Numismatic Guaranty Corporation of America (NGC), one of the nation's leading professional third-party grading firms.

It should be noted that for most coins, especially rare dates and varieties, the number certified actually represents the quantity of *submissions*, rather than the number of individual coins submitted. For example, a particular 1801 silver dollar that is submitted for certification five times would be counted the same as five individual coins. Such resubmissions can sometimes result in numbers close to or higher than a coin's entire surviving mintage.

Note, too, that the grade number assigned to a "slabbed" (graded and encapsulated) coin does not tell anything about the strength of that particular coin's strike, the quality of its planchet, whether it has been cleaned or dipped, or its overall eye appeal. Such factors are important to a coin's value. Two rare coins of the same date and variety, each with the same amount of surface wear and graded, for example, MS-63, will find different values in the marketplace if one is eye-pleasing and well struck, and the other is dull and poorly struck.

Valuations. Coin values shown in *Mega Red* are retail prices compiled from data and market observations provided by active coin dealers, auctioneers, and other qualified observers, under the direction and analysis of Valuations Editor Jeff Garrett and Senior Editor Q. David Bowers and their consultants. In this guide book, values from under $1 up to several hundred dollars are for "raw" coins—that is, coins that have *not* been graded and encapsulated by a professional third-party grading service. Values near or above $500 reflect typical auction and retail prices seen for professionally certified coins. The valuations of professionally certified coins often are higher than what collectors normally pay for non-certified ("raw") coins. Values of certified coins may vary widely, depending on the grading service.

The coin market is so active in some categories that values can readily change after publication. Values are shown as a guide and are not intended to serve as a price list for any dealer's stock. A dash appearing in a valuations column indicates that coins in that grade exist even though there are no current retail or auction records for them. The dash does not necessarily mean that such coins are exceedingly rare. A number of listings of rare coins lack valuations or dashes in certain grades, indicating that they are not available, or not believed to exist, in those grades. Proof coins are usually not shown with values in circulated grades.

For wholesale pricing, the *Handbook of United States Coins* (popularly called the *Blue Book*, and published since 1942), by R.S. Yeoman, contains average prices dealers nationwide will pay for U.S. coins. It is obtainable through most coin dealers, hobby shops, bookstores, and the Internet.

Auction Records. Multiple recent auction records are provided for nearly every coin (some exceptions being coins that are too common to sell individually at auction). Each record indicates:

> the price paid for the coin (including any fees)

> the grade of the coin

> the date (month and year) of the auction

This combination of auction data gives valuable market information for each coin. It also serves as a springboard for further research. Many auction firms have online archives of coins sold, or else their auction catalogs can be studied using the information provided.

Chart notes. Additional information is provided for certain coins in chart notes. Historical background, die-variety diagnostics, notable market conditions, and other specific details are intended to further guide the collector and investor.

Abbreviations. These are some of the abbreviations you'll find in the charts.

> %MS—Percentage of coins certified in Mint State

> Avg—Average grade (on a 1–70 scale)

> BN—Brown; descriptive of the coloration or toning on certain copper coins

> Cam—Cameo

> Cert—Certified population

> DblDie—Doubled Die

> DCam—Deep Cameo

> DMPL—Deep Mirror Prooflike

> D/S—D Over S; a slash between words or letters represents an overdate or overmintmark

> Dt—Date

> Ex.—Extremely

> FB—Full Bands

> FBL—Full Bell Lines

> FH—Full Head

> FS—Full Steps

> FT—Full Torch

> Horiz—Horizontal

> Inv—Inverted

> Knbd—Knobbed-Top

> Lg—Large

> Ltrd—Lettered

> Ltrs—Letters

> Med—Medium

> Mintmk—Mintmark

> Obv—Obverse

> QuintDie—Quintupled Die

RB—Red and brown; descriptive of the mixture of mint red and brown coloration or toning on a copper coin

RD—Red; descriptive of the mint red color on an untoned copper coin

Rev—Reverse

RPD—Repunched Date

RPM—Repunched Mintmark

Sm—Small

SMS—Special Mint Set

Sq—Square

TransRev—Transitional Reverse

TripDie—Tripled Die

UCam—Ultra Cameo

Var—Variety

2021 COIN MARKET REPORT

by Valuations Editor Jeff Garrett

For several years, the general rare-coin market has been tepid at best. Trophy coins would grab headlines occasionally, but many series of United States coins drifted lower in price. This could be seen in high-profile series such as Morgan silver dollars, common-date gold coins, commemorative half dollars, and type coins. Much of the price depression was caused by inferior coins being sold onto the market at lower prices. Nothing seemed to inspire an uptick in the market.

Beginning in March of 2020, at the start of the COVID-19 pandemic, the financial markets and the rare-coin business were shaken to their cores by widespread lockdowns. The Dow Jones Industrial averages dropped more than 5,000 points in a matter of days. Companies around the country, including coin shops, were forced to send everyone home for an undetermined amount of time. Uncertainty ruled the day.

The first big test for the rare-coin market during COVID-19 occurred early as Stack's Bowers Galleries bravely staged another auction installment from the fabulous collection of D. Brent Pogue. No one knew what to expect, and the actual auction was touch-and-go as the restrictions in California were not fully understood or well defined. Only a handful of hardy souls made the trip to California to bid in person.

In a sign of what was to become the norm going forward, bidders flocked to the Internet to participate in this important sale. To the great relief of the coin owners and the auction firm, prices were not depressed, and in some cases record prices were achieved. The only surprising bargain was the sale of the extremely rare 1854-S half eagle for less than $2,000,000. The coin was purchased by Dell Loy Hansen (Salt Lake City) and is now part of his amazing collection.

For many years, all across the United States, commerce has been slowly moving to the Internet. The COVID-19 crisis has sped up that migration at warp speed. In the last year companies such as Amazon have been crushing traditional brick-and-mortar businesses. E-commerce companies now dominate in many areas of the economy. The dramatic shift is becoming clearly defined as we see many old-line companies go out of business.

The same phenomena are also occurring in the rare-coin market. Those rare-coin companies that have invested in a web presence have been doing wonderfully in 2020 and 2021. Many have seen sales rise by 50 to 100 percent as COVID-19 restrictions have forced Americans to be stuck at home with the constant attraction and entertainment of Internet access. Many companies that had a good stock of numismatic material when the pandemic began have seen record sales.

One terrible result of the COVID-19 pandemic has been the cancellation of nearly every major coin show through 2020 and into the first half of 2021. For more than 40 years my professional life, like that of many coin dealers, has revolved around attending two or three coin shows per month around the country. It's been very difficult for me and many of my fellow professionals to have these important rare-coin venues eliminated. Coin shows are a critical part of the rare-coin supply chain.

On the plus side: Although the pandemic has driven millions of people to stay home—with movie theaters closed, restaurants shut down, large public gatherings banned or discouraged, and other inconveniences—the need for safe distractions has drawn people to classic hobbies. Coin collecting has experienced a boom of interest in 2020 and 2021. Americans are discovering or rediscovering the hobby in large numbers. One tangible piece of evidence has been the 20 percent increase in membership in the American Numismatic Association, to nearly 30,000. For more than a decade membership had languished around 25,000. Hopefully, this trend will continue as the country heads to a reopening of the economy in the coming months.

Another important factor affecting the hobby has been political decisions made in Washington to combat the virus and its damage to the economy. Politicians of both parties have voted to spend vast sums to keep the economy afloat. Never have so many trillions of dollars been allocated so quickly. Instead of crashing, the stock market now flirts with record closes with regularity.

This enormous wealth creation and widespread government stimulus has clearly impacted the hobby. In the early months of 2021 trophy coins are once again taking center stage. An example of the world-famous 1787 Brasher doubloon sold for $9,300,000 to someone who had never bought a rare coin before. For several recent years colonial coinage had been slipping in price as the market found it difficult to absorb the many estate collections that were being sold. That trend has changed, and recent sales have seen new records being set. The Partrick Collection sale in March 2021 was a resounding success.

Trophy coins are not the only area of numismatics to shine in 2020 and 2021. Dealer inventories are being depleted at a rapid pace as sellers struggle to find new material. The aforementioned cancellation of coin conventions has been a huge blow to those who count on such buy-sell-trade venues to acquire new merchandise. The huge increase in web sales has created a sharp rise in demand for dealers looking for stock. They are being further squeezed by the increase in the number of online auction buyers who are making this traditional source of material nearly impossible for wholesalers to navigate. One major wholesale auction buyer told me he placed more than $3,000,000 in bids during a sale in early 2021. He was successful in spending only $25,000, and most of the coins he won, he thought cost too much.

Another driver for the hobby at the moment is the intense interest in precious metals. Silver ($27.50 per ounce) and gold ($2,000) spot prices have been stagnant lately, but the physical demand is off the charts. American Silver Eagles are selling for almost 30 percent above spot price, and that is if you can find them. There are millions of buyers for precious metals looking for ways to protect themselves from the consequences of trillions of dollars being spent by the federal government in the American Rescue Plan Act of 2021.

Historically, the hobby always benefits when large numbers of people flock to precious metals. Some of those newcomers will be attracted to the history and beauty of numismatics. It's a short leap from buying common-date silver dollars to wanting examples from different years and mints. A lot of great collections started this way, and I see no reason for that dynamic to change now.

2021 is also an important numismatic anniversary year. This year marks the 100th anniversary of the end of the 1878–1921 Morgan dollar series and the 100th anniversary of the start of the 1921–1935 Peace dollar series. Thanks to the considerable legislative efforts of numismatists Thomas Uram and

Michael Moran, the United States Mint will be issuing celebratory examples of each design in 2021. The anticipation of these new issues and the attention the two classic series will garner has pushed silver dollar prices up considerably. The 1921 Peace dollar has jumped 20 to 30 percent in most grades.

Common-date gold coins have also seen increased demand across the board. In 2019 many United States gold coin series were selling for not much more than their melt value. That has changed dramatically as supplies dried up and demand rose to new levels. MS-65 Saint-Gaudens double eagles are selling for more than $2,500 in early 2021, a 20 percent increase from two years ago. After suffering for years, generic-date gold coins are now back and in strong demand.

Coin collecting (and in fact many other collectible fields, such as baseball cards and comic books) are seeing the sharpest rise in demand in many years. Prices are only now beginning to show signs of life across the board. This is no longer restricted to trophy coins. If trends continue and the country can safely emerge from the pandemic, the remainder of 2021 could be the start of something great for numismatics.

COLLECTING U.S. COINS

Coins are meant to be enjoyed. This can be done by learning, going slowly, and becoming familiar with the many aspects of American numismatics. The following sections include an inside view of authenticity, cleaning, conservation, and more—elements that are known to most experienced professionals and long-time collectors.

In just about every other field of collectibles, prints, antiques, art, and related items there are problems with counterfeiting, cleaning, alterations, and the like. Fakes are so common in art that some dealers and auction houses now find it nearly impossible to have an impartial expert guarantee authenticity, as so many lawsuits against them have been filed by owners of paintings. In automobiles there are counterfeit classic cars made from a combination of old and new parts. Many other instances could be cited. And yet, art is popular to collect, classic cars ditto. In every field, caution and expertise are needed.

As a reader of *Mega Red* you know what leading dealers and other experts know. Knowledge is more readily available in numismatics than in many other collectible fields. Indeed, knowledge is the key to enjoyment.

The inside view you will get of some of the challenges contains elements rarely present in sales presentations, investment programs, and the like, for fear that knowledge of negative things can influence buyers to turn elsewhere. Over a long period of years the Whitman Publishing staff and key consultants have learned just the opposite: the more knowledge someone has, the more confident they are and the longer they will be immersed in numismatics. Indeed, countless informed people have made coins and related numismatic areas an integral part of their lives.

Carefully building a fine collection of coins by studying their art, history, and romance and by buying carefully can add a lot to the enjoyment of life. The vast majority of *experienced* numismatists active today were active a decade ago.

Eric P. Newman, who began collecting at the age of 11 years, maintained his interest to the time of his passing at 106. Emery May Holden Norweb began her interest as a pre-teenager when she attributed Massachusetts silver coins for her father, using E*arly American Coins*, published in 1875. She collected for the rest of her life and was a member of the American Numismatic Association for more than 70 years. Harry W. Bass Jr. (1927–1998), entrepreneur oil man and founder of the Beaver Creek ski resort, discovered rare coins in 1976 and by the time of his passing built one of the finest collections ever.

Others still living have focused their energy and received enjoyment from the history and lore of numismatics.

A great numismatic future awaits you!

A SEMINAR IN THE GRADING OF COINS

Grading is an art, not a science.

Repeat: Grading is an art, not a science.

Welcome to a "seminar" on the subject, giving information on various elements of one of the most important considerations when buying or selling coins.

COIN PRODUCTION AND STORAGE AND ITS EFFECTS ON MINT STATE GRADES

The grading of a coin is dependent on the amount of *wear* it has received. A mint-fresh coin, like new, is called Mint State. (Until recent generations the term "Uncirculated" was used most of the time, and Mint State rarely.) When struck, the typical coin was ejected mechanically from the press and dropped into a bin or hopper. Mixed with other coins, it was run through a mechanical counting device and then in most instances put into a cloth bag. A bag of silver dollars contained 1,000 coins; in the twentieth century a bag of Lincoln cents contained $50 face value (5,000 coins). Morgan silver dollars minted from 1878 to 1904 and later in 1921 were mostly stored in vaults. Hundreds of millions more were minted than could be used in commerce, so they were stored in Treasury and bank vaults. In Treasury vaults the bags were opened and mechanically counted at intervals, such as after a change in the presidential administration. In their day, before 1934, gold coins were made and bagged the same way. In no instance did any of the mints spend even the slightest effort to create mark-free circulating coins for numismatists.

As a result, a Mint State coin today can have nicks, minor scratches, and other defects and can thus be "low end," even though just taken from an original bag. Many other coins received light handling and can be nearly mark-free.

A WORD OF CAUTION REGARDING CERTIFIED MINT STATE COINS

Today as you read these words, certified grading services have endeavored to separate low-end and high-end Mint State coins into 21 categories using numbers adapted (but not copied from) the Sheldon Scale published in 1949 in *Early American Cents.* According to certain third-party grading (TPG) services, the lowest Mint State is MS-60, proceeding in single digits up to the highest grade of MS-70, representing absolute perfection. In the twenty-first century the TPGs added + marks, indicating better than average quality, after all grades from 60 to 69 (not to 70, as a coin cannot be better than perfect). This gives MS-60, MS-60+, MS-61, MS-61+, and so on, for a total of 21 different Mint State grades.

There is no way that such precise designations can be assigned in a way that can be consistently and accurately replicated. Grading strives to be scientific but is subjective and open to interpretation. There are no published written standards or photographic images to guide a buyer of a coin graded by Professional Coin Grading Service (PCGS) or Numismatic Guaranty Corporation (NGC) to understand how, for example, MS-65+ is defined and differentiated from MS-65 or MS-66. Moreover, if, say, 10 professionally graded Mint State coins with regular number and also + designations were taken from their holders and sent back for regrading, they most likely would not all be replicated in the exact same grades.

Both PCGS and NGC have population reports that list the number of "certification events" for each coin in each grade over the years. Such certification data must be studied and interpreted carefully. For example, a data point of 120 Mercury dimes, 1916-D, graded MS-66 might represent that 120 such coins were submitted for grading. However, it's more likely there were only 20 or 30 coins submitted, four to six times each, with their owners hoping to attain higher grades.

If at, say, MS-68 there are only three coins graded and none higher, it will be nicknamed "top pop" or top of the population. Both PCGS and NGC sponsor and maintain registry-set competitions. These are online competitions that register who has the best set of, for example, Peace silver dollars in PCGS holders or NGC holders. There is no crossover, so if the highest NGC grade for a particular date is MS-68 and PCGS has graded a 68+ this counts for the PCGS registry-set competition but has no relevance to someone being an NGC winner.

When it comes to market values, an uninformed collector might assume that the fewer coins have been certified for a particular date or variety in a particular grade, the more valuable it is. However, in many instances that is false security.

On March 16, 2021, these mid-range Morgan silver dollar listings (there were many higher) were posted by PCGS for the 1881-S dollar, one of the more common issues of that series:

1881-S $1

MS-64	109,379 coins
MS-64+	2,052 coins

This might lead a buyer to think that an MS-64+ coin is far rarer than a regular MS-64. The truth is that MS-64+ is a fairly recently developed designation, and tens of thousands of regular MS-64 coins were certified before the + was used. In actuality, MS-64+, a popular twenty-first-century grade, may or may not be *slightly* rarer and only slightly more valuable.

Let us explore the 1886-O, a Morgan dollar that is common in worn grades but rare in high Mint State levels. Here are the highest-graded PCGS coins, and their current prices in the seventh edition of *Mega Red*:

1886-O $1

MS-63	684 coins	$2,600
MS-63+	31 coins	
MS-64	228 coins	$8,000
MS-64+	28 coins	
MS-65	2 coins	$150,000
MS-65+	1 coin	

As Mint State levels are not precisely defined and as "gradeflation" (defined below) has been endemic since the early 1990s, a smart buyer seeking a high-grade 1886-O Morgan dollar, and being able to afford one, would likely opt to examine several certified MS-64 coins and buy a high-end one at the MS-64 price rather than an average MS-65 at the MS-65 price. In this case study, the coin's optimum collecting grade would be MS-64. A well-informed buyer would consider it to be a good value for the price paid.

CIRCULATED GRADES

After a coin is taken from a bag or roll or other holder and placed into circulation it begins to acquire wear. This takes the form of friction on the higher parts (which can also be found on some carefully graded low-end Mint State coins), and this is *definitive* loss of luster in the fields. On the obverse of a coin with a Liberty Head, this luster begins to be removed from the fields to the left and right. On some designs that are intricate the motifs protect the fields, so for example the luster can start disappearing from the obverse while it remains more intact on the reverse.

With circulation wear a coin's grade moves from Mint State down to About Uncirculated (AU), then with further wear to Extremely Fine (EF), then down to Very Fine (VF), Fine, Very Good (VG), Good (G), About Good (AG), Fair, and Poor.

THE SHELDON GRADING SCALE

Dr. William H. Sheldon, the originator of the numbering system proposed in 1949, laid out a simple grading arrangement. He applied it to early U.S. copper coins.

Basal State 1

Fair 2

Very Fair 3

Good 4

Fine 12

Very Fine 20

Extremely Fine 40

About Uncirculated 50

Mint State 60, 65, and 70

This was understandable enough to most specialists at the time. MS-70 or perfection was unusable, so for practical purposes that was satisfactory to all involved. When I first discovered numismatics at the age of 13 in 1952 most grading was by adjectives, but the Sheldon system was used for early cents and some other early coppers. Uncirculated was simply Uncirculated.

On November 12, 1957, Stack's sold the Empire Collection, one of the finest cabinets of American coins from colonials to silver dollars ever to cross the auction block. The firm was a leader in the auction business, was highly respected, and had a clientele that included most of the leading buyers. Here are some descriptions reflecting the *simplicity* of grading in effect at that time—adjectives with an occasional descriptor to clarify:

Half cent: 1828 The 13 star variety. Uncirculated. Brown but has some handling marks.

Cent: 1877 About Uncirculated. Chocolate brown.

Cent: 1909-S V.D.B. Lincoln. Brilliant Uncirculated, red.

Silver three cents: 1851 Uncirculated.

Nickel: 1885 Brilliant Proof.

Nickel: 1926-D Uncirculated, weak strike.

Dime: 1892-O Brilliant Uncirculated.

Quarter: 1901-S Perfect Brilliant Uncirculated Gem.

Half dollar: 1923-S Brilliant Uncirculated, however weakly struck.

Silver dollar: 1895 Brilliant Proof. Superb.

CHERRYPICKING FOR QUALITY

Not long after the Empire Sale I went to visit Arthur W. Conn, one of the largest advertisers in *The Numismatic Scrapbook Magazine*, at the office in his home in Melrose, Massachusetts. He specialized in commemorative coins and had each type in 2x2-inch paper envelopes in its own box. He had dozens of 1900 Lafayette dollars, each marked "Unc." and each priced the same. He offered me the usual typical dealer's discount. I went through his Lafayettes and picked out nearly a dozen that were almost perfect. I did the same with others.

Cherrypicking for quality was practiced by many collectors at the time. Both Emery May Holden Norweb and John J. Pittman, fine customers of mine at the time, would look through dealers' stocks and only buy top-level Uncirculated and Proof coins. These cost no more than less pristine examples.

This changed after the rare-coin boom that started in 1960. In 1970 James F. Ruddy published *Photograde*, which became a sensation. Later in the decade Abe Kosoff (data gathering), Kenneth Bressett (descriptions describing each grade number), and I (introductory narrative) created the *Official American Numismatic Association Grading Standards for United States Coins*. This was adopted by the ANA board of governors and published as a book. The American Numismatic Association Certification Service was set up in Colorado Springs to grade coins for a fee and return each with a certificate and photograph.

Both books were widely used. Responding to pressure from dealers (in particular) the ANA kept adding intermediate grades, including 11 grades from MS-60 to 70. In 1986 PCGS was formed, followed by NGC in 1987 and dozens of other third-party grading firms ("third party" meaning they are neither the owner nor the prospective buyer of graded coins). Later, most faded.

Coins graded by PCGS and NGC in the 1980s that still survive in their original holders are found to be very conservatively graded by today's market-accepted standards.

GRADEFLATION

Established standards notwithstanding, grading was anybody's game even in the 1980s and beyond. Gradeflation became endemic. Coins graded AU-55 and AU-58, if removed from their holders and resubmitted for certification later, might the next time around be graded as MS-60 to MS-62 or even 63. Grades of MS-65 were not common in the late 1980s, and there were very, very few higher in the population reports. Later they became as common as fleas on a stray dog. Anyone who in 1990 was proud of his MS-65 Red 1909-S V.D.B. cent and considered it to be top of the line became increasingly befuddled as coins not as nice were graded higher.

By definition a Mint State coin cannot have wear from circulation. Never mind—nearly all early gold coins certified today as MS-60 to MS-62 show *wear* in the fields, this being just one of many examples of "relaxed" application of the grading standards. An 1853 double eagle graded AU-58 and sold by Christie's in 1999 was sent to the same grading service a few days after the sale and was returned as MS-62. Magically, the coin had become Mint State. And so have thousands of others.

Circulated coins have undergone gradeflation as well. By *Photograde* and *Official ANA Standards* an Indian Head cent in VG-8 grade can have several letters in LIBERTY missing. For VF-20 all letters have to be full and *sharp*. A survey taken in 2018 of more than 100 Indian Head cents certified as VF-20 by the leading services showed *many* with some letters in LIBERTY *missing*, never mind full.

It used to be that a grading service could say "This is our interpretation of the standards." However, there is no way that a circulated 1807 $5 gold coin can be called Mint State by traditional standards or an 1877 Indian Head cent with letters in LIBERTY missing can be called VF-20.

In a phrase, *there are no widely accepted, definable, and strictly applied grading standards for United States coins today.*

STRATEGY FOR THE INFORMED BUYER

Good news for the educated, intelligent buyer: If you are a collector of rare books you can buy with confidence from dealers and auction houses that basically use these definitions: Mint (as new or close; if original dustjacket is present, that should be noted); Very Fine or Extremely Fine (a nice used copy without tears, stains, writing, or other problems); Reading copy (a book that has problems, is marked up, etc.).

Further good news for numismatists: You can follow in the footsteps of generations of earlier connoisseurs and examine multiple coins and pick one that is high end at no extra cost. As to value, this will require some homework. Basic references such as the *Guide Book of United States Coins*, the *Coin Dealer Newsletter*, *Coin World*, *Numismatic News*, and others list many prices. These are not consistent with each other but do give approximate values.

Before long you will able to cherrypick for high-end coins by instinct. I have collected 1785–1788 Vermont copper coins for a long time and wrote a book on them. There are some I would like to upgrade, such as my 1785 Vermont IMMUNE COLUMBIA muling. I would like a nice VF or EF. If offered one I will not care if it is certified, or, if it is, what grade has been assigned. I will look at the coin itself to see if it is pleasing in all respects. *Nearly all* advanced collectors of colonial coins, early copper coins, tokens, medals, foreign coins, and ancient coins are not the slightest bit interested in or concerned with minute differences in grading.

Buying coins from common to rare today does require study if you want to build a choice collection. Probably fewer than 10 percent of buyers care about this, so you are in the minority. You will also be able to cherrypick for quality at no extra price, if you know what to look for. The other 90 percent won't know about this.

Enjoy the pursuit!

RARE COINS AS AN INVESTMENT

The rare-coin market combines some aspects of commodity trading with peculiarities seen more often among markets such as those for fine art, real estate, cut gemstones, and similar investments and collectibles. Armed with knowledge and experience, a seasoned investor can have a very rewarding experience buying and selling rare coins. An uneducated investor can just as easily see substantial losses and many if not most do.

The "History of Coins in America" section that follows this gives many specifics concerning success or lack thereof. Success stories are very inspirational, but each includes knowledge, care, and patience. Today in the third decade of the twenty-first century there are many opportunities.

The regular edition of the *Guide Book of United States Coins* includes this bit of guidance, which bears repeating here: "The best advice given to anyone considering investing in rare coins is to use common sense."

Any collector with common sense would think twice about buying a silver dollar at a flea market for less than half of its *Red Book* or *Mega Red* value. A common-sense collector who is offered a $1,000 coin from an "unsearched estate," or from a non-specialist who claims to know nothing of its provenance, would refuse it at $500—at least until a diligent examination was possible, and only with an iron-clad return policy and guarantee of authenticity.

Profitable investment requires careful selection of one or several names from the large membership list of qualified dealers such as those who belong to the International Association of Professional Numismatists (www.iapn-coins.org) and/or the Professional Numismatists Guild (www.PNGdealers.org) and *your* careful personal attention. Very, very few significant success stories involve advisors whose clients are not themselves numismatically knowledgeable.

ASPECTS OF AUTHENTICITY

In the marketplace there are many counterfeit coins, or coins that have been altered so that they appear to be something other than what they really are. Many of these are sold by vendors who are not aware of their false nature. Others are deliberately, fraudulently sold. If a coin is found to be counterfeit, getting your money back may be difficult or impossible. Exceptions are coins certified by third-party grading services that have guaranteed authenticity.

Authenticity refers only to a coin being genuine and struck at the place and in the era as expected. As an example, a rare 1893-S Morgan dollar is expected to be a coin made by the San Francisco Mint in the year 1893. A 1916-D Mercury dime is expected to be a coin made at the Denver Mint in the year 1916. A one-ounce 2011-W American Gold Eagle is expected to be a one-ounce .9167 fine gold coin struck at the West Point Mint in the year 2011.

Authenticity does not refer to the grade of a coin, such as to whether it is MS-63 or MS-65, or to the character of its surface (i.e., whether it is Mint State, prooflike, or Proof). Authenticity refers only to originality.

Your risk of purchasing a spurious coin can be minimized if you are aware of certain factors. If a coin is priced significantly below market value, beware. If the seller will not give in writing a guarantee of authenticity, beware. If the seller is not a recognized professional numismatist, such as being a member of the Professional Numismatists Guild, at least be careful (many fine dealers do not belong to this group).

FALSE COINS

False coins can include these:

Struck copies from false dies. Many are crude, but in modern generations there have been a lot of fakes that almost defy detection. Many have come from China and include coins from common to rare as well as American Silver and Gold Eagles. Beth Deisher, former editor of *Coin World*, worked with the Anti-Counterfeiting Educational Foundation's Anti-Counterfeiting Task Force to combat these. EAC (Early American Coppers) is doing research as well, led by Jack Young.

Electrotypes made by using a genuine coin to create molds of the obverse and reverse and then electrodepositing metal into each mold. The two pieces are then smoothed and joined together. Most can be detected by a microscopic seam on the edge. Many rare copper half cents and cents, early medals, and other issues have been electrotyped. Both the British Museum and the American Numismatic Society furnished electrotypes years ago to collectors to have for display, these being offered openly as such.

Alterations are made by adding a mintmark to a Philadelphia Mint coin, reengraving a date to change it to another year, or changing another feature. One researcher reported that in the late 1950s more than half of the "1916-D" Mercury dimes seen at a leading convention had added D mintmarks. At a convention in 2018 I was shown a "1934-S" dollar with an added S. Many alterations can often be detected by examination under a high-power stereomicroscope.

Coins of the wrong weight. Silver and gold coins if in Mint State should conform to their authorized weights. Worn coins can show a slight reduction. Any off-weight coins should be viewed with suspicion.

Replicas of colonial and other coins have been made in quantity and sold as souvenirs including at historical sites maintained by the Department of the Interior. Many of these have changed hands to new owners not aware of their status. Some are marked COPY, but not all are, and some have had that word removed.

SURFACE ALTERATIONS OF GENUINE COINS

For genuine coins there are other elements that can decrease value.

Whizzing, or the treatment of the surface of a coin with a high-speed polishing wire brush, can give false luster. This problem was endemic in the late nineteenth century and the American Numismatic Association and others took action that nearly eliminated whizzing and forced the closing of a "factory" that produced such coins. Today newly whizzed coins are rare, but some older ones linger in the marketplace.

The alteration of a coin's surface can be done by plugging a hole, removing stamped initials or cuts, strengthening the hair details of Miss Liberty, etching to remove wear, or other doctoring. Such actions might improve a damaged or worn coin's visual appeal, but they are detectable, and will nearly always decrease rather than increase its value.

Cyanide, a lethal chemical, if applied to a silver coin will remove friction and a give an acceptable grainy surface. Decades ago James F. Kelly, a leading Ohio dealer, demonstrated this to me. A generation earlier, on June 24, 1922, J. Sanford Saltus, a well-to-do numismatist and benefactor of the American Numismatic Society, died while using cyanide to clean ancient silver coins (a tragedy widely reported at the time).

RECOMMENDATIONS AND CAVEATS

Buying coins from a trusted source is the best way to ensure authenticity, as many of the most obvious fakes (as described above) are recognized and not sold by reputable professionals and firms. However, even the most experienced expert can be fooled.

The UCC (Uniform Commercial Code) and various state regulations limit the time in which the buyer of a false coin has recourse against the seller, statutes of limitations.

As of press time certain elements of the guarantees of authenticity of *American coins* offered by several third-party grading firms are *excerpted* below. For *complete* information consult their web sites; this is extremely important. Guarantees for foreign and ancient coins can be much different. Guarantee provisions can be very complex, and herein we only give partial information.

Also be aware that the provisions of guarantees can change from time to time. Certain coins are excluded from guarantees, examples being private and territorial gold coins that were considered genuine in the twentieth century but for which research has found them to be fakes. Restrike vs. original status is not covered as well. Guarantees do not include obvious typographical errors made on the holders, such as the wrong date or mintmark or attribution. Guarantees involving *grading* can be widely different.

> **Professional Coin Grading Service (PCGS):** If a coin certified by PCGS is felt to be counterfeit and if PCGS agrees that it is, current market value as determined by PCGS will be paid, but PCGS will then own the coin. Or the coin will be returned and PCGS will pay the difference between the buyer's cost and the market value.

> **Numismatic Guaranty Corporation (NGC):** If a coin certified by NGC is felt to be counterfeit and if NGC agrees that it is, NGC will pay the lesser of the fair market price as determined by NGC or the price the owner paid. NGC can elect to retain the coin and replace it with a genuine example in the same assigned grade.

> **ANACS (years ago known as the American Numismatic Association Certification Service when it was owned by the ANA; later sold several times and known today as ANACS, with no affiliation with the ANA):** The guarantee applies only to coins certified by ANACS since January 1, 2008, the inception of current ownership. ANACS will purchase the coin at the fair market value as determined by ANACS or will pay the difference between that and the owner's original cost.

Most leading collectors and dealers today agree that buying a coin certified for its authenticity is the best protection against counterfeits and altered coins. Other services than PCGS, NGC, and ANACS offer guarantees and their guarantees should be checked if you are offered their coins. The counter to this is that it can be expensive to have modern coins and coins of low value certified, and their bulk adds to challenges of how to store and enjoy them.

To the above, Beth Deisher has contributed the following.

CHINESE COUNTERFEITS

by Beth Deisher

For two centuries large-scale counterfeiting of U.S. coins was virtually unheard of, because those who tried to manufacture fakes rarely had access to the die-making equipment or production presses necessary to succeed.

However, the landscape changed dramatically in the early years of the twenty-first century. By 2005 most sovereign mints around the world had begun embracing computer technology and robotics in their die-making and coin-production processes. It was not a matter of simply installing and adapting modern manufacturing methods. Rather, competition—especially in the commemorative coin sector—demanded cost-effective manufacturing and innovative features in design and metallurgy.

The U.S. Mint, content to produce its two lowest-denomination circulating coins at a loss, was directed by Congress to look for lower-cost alloys for the one-cent and five-cent coins. Also, increasingly innovative commemorative coins on the world stage led to questions of why the United States could not produce equally interesting and visually attractive coins.

The search for both efficiency and innovation led to the U.S. Mint's transition in 2008 to digital technology in its die-making operation, producing never-before-experienced efficiencies and precision. During the same period, the Mint moved to increase use of computer-controlled processes and robotics throughout its manufacturing and packaging operations.

Ironically, rather than making counterfeiting more difficult, the transition to computers and digital technology opened new doors of opportunity for counterfeiters, because rapid leaps in technology and knowledge of how to use it that have spread throughout the world at levels unprecedented in human history. The same is true for the accessibility of computer hardware and production equipment used in the various stages of coin production. Costs and availability are no longer barriers to entry for counterfeiters.

For example, software programs used by designers and engravers at government mints are both commercially available and easily acquired. Computer-savvy operators can bypass years of training and experience by simply scanning high-resolution digital images and manipulating them to produce the desired product. Equipment to laser-cut master dies can be purchased at manufacturers' trade shows. The same is true for each step of the coining process, from blanking, to burnishing, to metal-plating, to producing the finished coin.

During 2007 and 2008, it became apparent to the numismatic community that the numbers of counterfeit coins in the American marketplace were increasing at a rapid pace. Specialists in early American copper coins, trade dollars, and Morgan dollars were among the first to sound the alarm. The weekly *Coin World* joined the *New York Times* in a year-long investigation, resulting in *Coin World*'s publication of a December 2008 series that revealed more than 100 thriving coin-counterfeiting operations in China. Most were small, cottage-type operations. The largest, owned by a 26-year-old entrepreneur, relied on vintage 1870s U.S. coin presses salvaged from "scrap metal" sold by the Chinese government. (The U.S. government in the 1920s sold old coining presses to China, which after using them stored them in the 1950s and had recently sold them as scrap.)

The proprietor of this operation claimed in 2008 that he had the capacity to produce 100,000 coins a month, most of which were older Chinese coin types and sold in China. However, he was expanding a new line of counterfeit U.S. coins and selling about 1,000 per month in the United States via eBay. His business plan called for locating and establishing "wholesale" buyers in the United States who would buy in bulk and help him to identify the most popular sellers. Most of his "replica" coins could be identified because he used iron-based planchets plated with silver or with the proper alloy to match the authentic coin. He also accepted orders for counterfeits made of 90 percent silver and gold, but for those pieces his prices reflected the cost of the higher-quality planchets. They constituted a very small portion of his business.

By 2021, dozens of Chinese counterfeiters were claiming production capacities of more than 500,000 per month of highly sophisticated and dangerous gold and silver counterfeits of various types of U.S. coins. They proudly show on their websites images taken of lines of coin presses in operation within their modern manufacturing facilities in various locations throughout China. They brag of their extensive use of digital technology, including lasers and 3-D printing. And they also assure fast delivery, less than a week, depending on payment arrangements.

A prime factor in the accelerating growth of Chinese coin counterfeiters was their ability to market their wares worldwide via Alibaba, the e-commerce company that in 1999 entered the marketplace to connect Chinese manufacturers with overseas buyers. In April 2016 Alibaba became the world's largest retailer and one of the largest Internet companies, reaching into more than 200 countries. By 2021, independent websites (with American names) began popping up online in the United States selling Chinese counterfeit coins and precious-metal bars, indicating a switch in marketing strategy to avoid U.S. law enforcement and U.S. tariff restrictions imposed on China. However, the larger-volume venues continue to be highly saturated with fakes.

In addition to using Alibaba, counterfeiters continue to sell "replica" U.S. coins not properly marked with the word COPY online through companies such as AliExpress, DHgate, Wish, TopHatter, Amazon, and eBay. Counterfeits are also prevalent on Craigslist and Instagram. In America eBay takes steps to cancel proven sellers of counterfeits, but many continue to escape the attention of specialists who monitor eBay listings.

Usually, Chinese counterfeiters focus on products with high brand-name recognition. However, no U.S. coin is too cheap or too common for the Chinese to counterfeit. Conventional wisdom, long held in the numismatic community, was that "the coin has to be real since it is not worth faking"; this simply no longer applies. The Chinese counterfeiters make their money principally on the volume and the wide range of counterfeit coins they manufacture. For U.S. coins, the categories include:

- Historic collectible coins—every design type and denomination made by the U.S. Mint since 1793.
- Commemorative coins—specially made collector coins, usually of silver and gold, issued in limited quantities to honor a person, place, or event; early commemoratives, 1892 through 1954, and modern commemoratives, 1982 through the current year.
- Bullion coins—investment coins made of silver, gold, platinum, and palladium, traded on exchanges and sold based on the world market price for the coin's precious metal.
- Circulating (transactional) coins—the coins in your pocket used in daily commerce.

Chinese counterfeiters are also producing fakes of the most trusted brands of grading-service holders. Since the mid-1980s, independent third-party grading services have authenticated, graded, and encapsulated high-value collectible and bullion coins. Essentially from the beginning the grading services' plastic holders have incorporated anti-counterfeiting devices. However, during the past decade counterfeiters have become increasingly adept at mimicking the new anti-counterfeiting devices within months of their introduction.

In response, the numismatic community is mounting a multi-pronged defense.

In 2020 Professional Coin Grading Service introduced a number of new and enhanced technologies—including Near Field Communication (NFC)—on all of its coin and banknote holders to thwart counterfeiting. (See https://www.pcgs.com/security for details.)

Also in 2020, *Coin World* introduced a service for third-party graded coins that "tags" each coin holder with an NFC label designed to digitally authenticate and access product-related content with the tap of an NFC-enabled smartphone (iPhone 7 running iOS 11 or later and Android devices running Ice Cream Sandwich or later). It operates within a radius of about 1 to 2 inches and allows for two-way communication, with both devices involved being able to send and receive information.

With a *Coin World+* tag, each coin has its own unique, encrypted ID number securely fixed on the surface of the holder, enabling coins to be better safeguarded as they move through the numismatic market's distribution network (from mints to authorized purchasers to wholesalers to dealers to collectors) to protect them from counterfeiting, combat gray markets, and provide communication with a coin's owner directly, in a targeted manner. (See www.CoinWorldPlus.com for details.)

FAKE COINS, FAKE HOLDERS

When the holder makes it difficult to inspect the coin directly, go to the source for confirmation—and buy only from reputable companies that guarantee the authenticity of their products. *(top)* Fake 2011-W American Buffalo gold bullion coin in a fake NGC slab. Use Verify NGC Certification at NGCcoin.com to check for authenticity. The certification number should match the coin and the number on the holder. *(bottom)* Fake 1856-S Liberty Head $20 gold coin in a fake PCGS holder. Use Cert Verification at PCGS.com; if the coin in the holder isn't shown, use the CoinFacts link for images of the real thing.

In mid-2021 the United States Mint expects to introduce new silver and gold American Eagle bullion coin reverse designs that will incorporate new anti-counterfeiting features—a major step in the Mint's efforts to thwart the counterfeiters. Since approximately 2015, gold and silver American Eagles have been among the most widely counterfeited bullion coins in the world. Although Mint officials have not revealed the technology that will be used, they have indicated it will be implemented at the production stage. The anticipated sale date for American Eagle bullion coins for investment markets is June 28, 2021, and the anticipated sale date for American Eagle numismatic products is July 1, 2021.

Leaders from throughout the numismatic community in the United States, recognizing the danger and urgency of the threat posed by the growing numbers of highly deceptive counterfeit coins entering the marketplace, came together in January 2017 to create the Anti-Counterfeiting Task Force (ACTF), which in November of 2018 transitioned to the nonprofit Anti-Counterfeiting Educational Foundation (www.acefonline.org). The foundation and task force are funded entirely by donations.

ACEF's primary focus is educating law-enforcement authorities and policy makers about the continuing threat of counterfeiting. Simultaneously, it has sought to mobilize law enforcement to attack counterfeiters where they are most vulnerable. Equally important, the ACEF has committed to assisting law enforcement with expertise and other resources in the investigation and prosecution of counterfeiters and those involved at all levels of their distribution networks.

ACEF's mission and programs support all who work in and earn their livings from businesses related to numismatic, bullion, and circulating coins. Equally important is protecting collectors and investors who fall victim to counterfeiters. Above all, ACEF seeks to ensure that decades of consumer confidence are not eroded by the increasing threat posed by the counterfeiters. As a part of its education mission, ACEF presents anti-counterfeiting educational seminars and forums at major coin shows and has developed guidelines for both collectors and dealers on how to deal with counterfeit coins and fake bullion bars encountered in the marketplace. Among the most important is an understanding of individual responsibilities.

U.S. COUNTERFEITING LAWS AND COMPLIANCE

It is a federal crime to knowingly possess, buy, sell, or import into the United States counterfeit coins or precious metals bars (U.S. Code, Title 18, Part I, Chapter 25, Sections 485 through 492). There are no exceptions for possessing counterfeit coins for "educational" purposes.

Many collectors and coin dealers mistakenly believe they have a special dispensation to keep a "reference collection" of counterfeits. While such has been longstanding practice in the hobby, be aware that such "reference collections" could be confiscated and you could be charged with federal crimes punishable by fines and sentences ranging from 5 to 15 years in federal prison. Also, don't get caught up in purchasing so-called "replica" coins online from a seller in a foreign country because you are curious as to how deceptive the coins may be. Knowingly importing counterfeit coins into the United States is a federal crime punishable by up to 15 years in federal prison.

CLEANING, CONSERVATION, AND PRESERVATION

TONING ON COINS

Silver coins left in the atmosphere, especially in air that contains traces of sulfur (as from a furnace), will tone, sometimes attractively. Slow toning such as this is often described as *natural*. Cardboard album pages that contain sulfur, such as the National pages once marketed by Wayte Raymond, tend to give light rainbow toning from the edge of a coin inward, often imparting great beauty and, in today's marketplace, additional value.

In contrast, fast toning such as by deliberately applied heat and chemicals is often called *artificial*. Vast quantities of artificially toned coins have been encapsulated by the third-party grading services, but many others, even of similar appearance, have been sent back ungraded and marked "artificial toning." There are no rules. One leading dealer simply sends such coins to another grading firm and, often, they are returned graded, with no negative comment.

Toned silver coins enjoy a wide market. The exact definition of "artificial" has eluded definition. Silver coins placed in old National holders (with sulfur content in the cardboard) and heated slightly over a period of time can develop beautiful iridescent toning. Morgan silver dollars in original bags were often toned on one side—the side that contacted the canvas. In the 1960s no specialists had ever seen or heard of a coin with vivid rainbow toning on *both* sides. Today these are common. Some of this toning is accomplished by heat and chemicals.

Just as coins can be artificially toned, they can also be deliberately brightened. As described above, a silver coin if left in the atmosphere will gain toning over a period of time. Ancient silver coins found in hoards are routinely brightened by collectors using various processes, a practice well accepted in numismatics. Old silver American coins with the exception of long-stored silver dollars in bags have all gained toning to one degree or another. Sometimes the toning is dark gray or brown and other times it is attractively lightly iridescent. Such coins can be brightened by dipping into a liquid made for silverware, and other products. If no friction is used and coins are rinsed in cold water afterward, there is no numismatic problem. Every Capped Bust or Liberty Seated coin that is fully brilliant today has been dipped. (However, "dipped" is a nasty word within the hobby community, with an implication of dishonest or deceptive alteration, and is hardly ever used.)

Dipped copper coins become bright, but often of unnatural color. Such pieces tend to retone, often with spots. *Never dip a copper coin.* If a coin has been dipped it can often be restored by rubbing it lightly with powdered sulfur, then wiping it with mineral oil. A related process is described by Dr. William H. Sheldon in *Early American Cents*. Lightly rubbing a toned copper coin with a camel's-hair brush has been practiced for generations by collectors and museum staff (the American Numismatic Society being an example).

Grime on gold coins can be removed by acetone or ammonia without disturbing any original mint luster that may be present. The latter chemical may lighten the surface, as will the use of silver dip. Continued use of silver dip will microscopically etch the surface and in time lower the grade.

I received a brilliant Proof silver medal a few years ago and opened it from its packaging, but a visitor was about to enter the office, so I carefully placed in it the top drawer of a Conant Ball oak side table recently received. I forgot about it. About a month later I found it. The down-side was lightly toned the most gorgeous light blue I had ever seen. Was this natural toning or was it artificial?

As can be seen, the nature of toning is in the eye of the beholder. Refunds are not likely to be given if you have a certified coin and you and others consider it to be artificially toned (whatever that means).

CLEANING VS. CONSERVATION

In February 1901 in *The Numismatist* Augustus G. Heaton gave this good advice:

> Coins of all metals require the greatest care. They should be handled with clean fingers only by the edge, should not rest on colored material of any kind or on wood not thoroughly seasoned, or come in any contact with rubber bands and should be kept in a dry place and never exposed to dust, dandruff, damp or foul air or even human breath. All these influences will in time discolor them and much impair their value. Attempts at cleaning are also very dangerous to fine coins. Uncirculated pieces or Proofs

should be let alone. If really soiled or dirty, copper coins may be put in olive oil a while and then wiped (not rubbed) dry with a soft rag, and silver coins may be carefully washed, using a mild soap, but all methods of polishing are abhorrent and have made many coins worthless.

This brings up the subject of conservation, or the improvement of the appearance of a coin. And what defines a "cleaned" coin? Nearly all other hobbies have conservation as an essential activity. The Smithsonian Institution conserves many things (including the original Star Spangled Banner). The National Archives as well as dealers and collectors conserve documents and other items by removing stains, repairing folds and tears, and the like. Art is routinely cleaned and brightened. Antique furniture is improved. In numismatics, the filling of holes, removal of scratches, and similar actions, are not envisioned as being good practice, but many coins with "environmental damage," "cleaning," etc., would benefit from some conservation.

Bill Fivaz, longtime numismatist and author, says this: "When someone asks me the difference between conservation and cleaning, I tell them that in my opinion when you conserve a coin you are not altering the *original surface* of that coin. If there was original luster, there still should be original luster, etc. If you clean a coin the original surface(s) are altered in some way, affecting the luster, etc."

In general, the use of friction, such as rubbing a coin with baking soda under the pressure of a fingertip, will cause minute hairlines. Using silver polish or paste will leave many hairlines that cannot be removed. Such use was once recommended, including in pages of *The Numismatist*. As a result, more than 95 percent of all nineteenth-century and early twentieth-century mirror Proof coins have hairlines. Were it not so, all would be in ultra-high grades.

In *The Numismatist*, August 1903, Farran Zerbe told of visiting the Mint Cabinet collection in Philadelphia:

> I found many of the silver Proof coins of late years partially covered with a white coating. On inquiry I learned that an overzealous attendant during the last vacation months when the numismatic room was closed took it on himself to clean the tarnished coins, purchase some metal polish at a department store, and proceeded with his cleaning operation. Later a coating of white appeared on the coins, which was now slowly disappearing. I expressed my displeasure at this improper treatment of Proof coins, and the custodian explained, "that is nothing. I have been here eight years and they have been cleaned three or four times in my time."

Zerbe speculated that should this cleaning continue, in the future one would have nothing left except plain planchets and badly worn coins!

We cannot undo the past, but in the future all numismatists should refrain from *cleaning* coins.

The above said, many coins can be professionally conserved to improve their appearance and value. The National Conservation Service (NCS) branch of NGC does this for a fee. Researcher Bob Evans used chemicals and scientific procedures to remove stain, rust, and discoloration from gold coins and ingots from the SS *Central America* treasure without altering the original surfaces.

Some basic conservation of coins can be done at home. In any and all instances, experiment with common coins of low value before working with expensive ones. Also, this information reflects what many others have done with success, but there is no implication or guarantee that it will work for you. *You are on your own.*

Examples of household solutions include:

> *Acetone*, a chemical that must be used with adequate ventilation and away from flames, will remove PVC contamination, varnish, and other substances. A coin bathed in acetone should be lightly dried by touching with a piece of cotton or a swab. Avoid friction.

Ammonia is ideal for removing vault grime from silver and gold coins. It will often discolor copper coins, so should not be used with copper. It will also slightly lighten the color of gold.

Plain soap and water will often remove dirt.

CARE OF YOUR COINS AND COLLECTION

Coins require care in order to preserve them in the condition in which they were acquired.

Coins not in holders should always be handled carefully, by the edge. Avoid talking when handling a coin, as bits of moisture may fall on it and in time develop into black spots. Hold coins over a soft surface such as cloth or a pad.

Except on rare occasions with another knowledgeable collector or dealer, do not let anyone handle your valuable coins.

Keep coins in a dry place and avoid heat. Both of these cautions are very important. Dampness can facilitate spotting and corrosion. Heat can facilitate corrosion and change the color of a coin. Keep coins protected in a holder of some kind, not in the open air. Coastal areas often have microscopic salt particles in the air that can discolor copper coins in particular.

Effective holders include 2x2-inch paper envelopes with flaps; indeed these were the way that nearly all coins were stored prior to 1930. Many still are. Some specialists in colonial and early copper coins add a small cotton-lined inner envelope.

Albums and folders made specifically to hold coins are convenient. All old ones and many new ones contain traces of sulfur that over time can cause copper coins in particular to tone. 2x2-inch cardboard holders with clear Mylar interiors, stapled (carefully) at the edges, are a very effective way to store coins and study them at the same time. These require little space for storage.

Airtight plastic holders are very effective, but the small amount of air within can cause toning on copper coins and even spotting. For this reason the leading third-party certification services do not guarantee that copper will not change color or develop spots within their slabs.

PVC (polyvinyl chloride) envelopes must be avoided completely as they will deposit "goo" on the surface of copper and nickel coins and often will cause corrosions. For silver coins there will be goo but no corrosion. Gold coins are usually not affected by PVC. Envelopes made with PVC are clear and supple, durable, not brittle; this is what makes them attractive, and convenient for short-term storage. However, the irreversible nature of the damage the chemical causes over time makes it unacceptable.

The careful application of clear fingernail polish to brilliant Mint State copper coins will usually preserve the color perfectly. The polish can be removed instantly with acetone. This is an effective but little-used method of benefit for coins in folders and albums.

Each of the basic metals of federal coinage has its own characteristics:

Copper or *bronze* as used for cents, two-cent pieces, and some patterns is a very chemically active. Such coins should be kept away from heat, moisture, sunlight, and exposure to open air.

Silver is less sensitive but will tone, sometimes attractively, when exposed to heat or sulfur. It is best to keep silver coins away from such elements.

Gold is inert. Over a period of time, such as when stored in bulk in bank vaults, they will develop grime. This can be easily removed with acetone (with great care as the vapors should not be breathed or near flame) or alcohol. As noted above, ammonia can be used as well but will slightly lighten the color.

Security is an important aspect of coin preservation. For this reason many numismatists collect in private and do not want their names published, including when they sell their coins. Others, with care, will keep numismatists informed. It is not good practice to discuss coin values with non-collecting friends or the general public, as tales are often multiplied and could put you and your coins in danger.

The best protection is to keep coins in a safe deposit box in a local or regional bank. The facility should be checked to be sure it is never subject to flooding. It is good practice to select boxes or a vault a foot or two above the floor level.

Today photography and scanning are very sophisticated, and images of coins, tokens, medals, and paper money are often sharper than the pieces are themselves when examined under low magnification. Images of your collection can easily be stored on a personal computer or even an iPhone.

It is good practice to keep an inventory of your coins and to preserve original invoices. It is also good practice, if relationships and circumstances permit, to share the information with your immediate family so they will be aware in case for some reason you become incapacitated. If you have a trusted dealer or other advisor make him or her known to your family. This advisor should be reviewed from time to time.

More advice on security, storage, conservation, toning, and other important topics can be found in the *Whitman Guide to Coin Collecting* (Bressett), *Cash In Your Coins: Selling the Rare Coins You've Inherited* (Deisher), *Grading Coins by Photographs* (Bowers), and other Whitman Publishing books.

THE HISTORY OF COINS IN AMERICA, 1607 TO DATE

*This introduction to U.S. coins is the work of Whitman Publishing numismatic director (and **Mega Red** senior editor) **Q. David Bowers**.*

Settlers in America from the Jamestown Colony in 1607 and the landing of the Pilgrims in Plymouth in 1620, continuing with immigrants from many lands, were mostly of European stock.[1] The New World promised land for settlement and the pursuit of hunting and agriculture for most. For others such as settlers in what became Pennsylvania and Rhode Island, religious freedom prompted their settling on the far side of the Atlantic Ocean.

An NE (New England) shilling from the first coinage series struck in what is now the United States, by the Massachusetts Bay Colony in 1652.

The landing of the Pilgrims in the New World in 1620. In time the emigrants founded the Massachusetts Bay Colony.

During most of the seventeenth century, the first century of permanent North American colonization by Europeans, coins were scarce. To fill the demand for media of exchange many commodities and commercial products were used. In Maryland and Virginia tobacco, powder, and shot traded at set rates. As an example, on March 4, 1635, the Massachusetts General Court adopted legislation that provided: "It is likewise ordered

Cattle served as currency in certain areas of colonial America as did other perishable goods such as agricultural products.

that musket bullets of a full bore shall pass currently for a farthing apiece, provided that no man be compelled to take above XII [one shilling] at a time in them."

In the early days in some colonies grain (a general term for corn, peas, and wheat), oat meal, cattle, furs, and fish were also used in payment of debt. Each of these had a utility value. Tobacco could be smoked, or if the recipient did not indulge, a neighbor might. Fish could be eaten, fur could be made into caps and clothing. Such commodities were often referred to as "country pay," or barter items.

In New Hampshire dried and salted fish, lumber, and agricultural products saw service as currency as did gunpowder and cattle. Citizens of the Carolinas often used tobacco, corn, peas, rice, and even pine tar for the same purpose. In New York beaver skins were sometimes specified as payment in contracts. Each of these things required effort to find or produce. Accordingly, the market could not be disturbed by an unexpected flood of animal skins or musket balls. This is the labor theory of value, originally developed by Adam Smith (and later extensively expanded by Karl Marx). Counterfeiting was not a problem. Unfortunately, tobacco depreciated so badly from overproduction in Virginia that, in 1640 (21 years after tobacco was made the official currency), all the "bad" and half the "good" was ordered burned. This was not successful in decreasing the flood of tobacco on the market, so in 1666 both Virginia and Maryland banned the planting of tobacco entirely for a year. Prices in 1683 were so low from overproduction that there were riots when Virginia refused to order another one-year ban. Beaver skins fluctuated also.

In the meantime and since the earliest days gold and silver coins of all nations were accepted in normal dealings by the colonists who in turn used them to purchase imported goods. English silver coins were familiar and desirable, but of equal value were the German thalers, Dutch silver Lyon (lion) dollars and gold ducats, French louis, and of course, the ever-present gold doubloons and silver pieces-of-eight and their fractions from Spain as well as mints from Mexico to South America. English copper coins served the need for small change, but even these were scarce and rarely adequate for commercial needs.

On November 15, 1637, the Massachusetts General Court ordered that particular shell beads called wampum (shortened from the Algonquin *wampumpeage*, or "white beads") should pass at six per penny for any sum under 12 pence. From that year to 1661, Indian wampum became a standard medium of exchange for trade with the Native Americans. Strings of wampum were highly coveted and could be exchanged for furs. Six white beads or three blue beads equaled one English penny. All financial records were kept in the traditional English pounds, shillings, and pence, but debts and taxes were often paid in corn, beaver, peas, or whatever foreign coins were available.

A Dutch silver Lyon dollar of 1589 representative of many European crown- or dollar-size coins in circulation in America in the early years of colonization.

Harvard College was founded in 1636. Tuition of £1 6s 8d could be paid several ways, including by about 1,900 beads of white whelk and blue (purple) quahog wampum. On October 7, 1640, the General Court directed that white wampum should pass at four per penny and blue at two per penny, with no more than 12 pence worth to be used at one time unless the receiver desired more. Wampum had its problems, for it developed that similar glass beads could be made cheaply in factories, and wampum of quahog clam shells counterfeited from seashells. What had become an accepted medium of exchange among Indians became devalued when interfered with by white settlers.

Although country pay faded in the early 19th century and was largely replaced in cities and larger settlements by coins, the barter system endured. There are many nineteenth-century accounts of businesses in rural areas of America taking goods and services in trade for merchandise.[2]

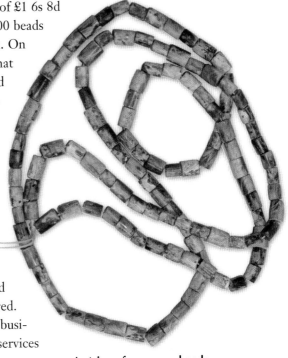

A string of wampum beads.

COINS USED IN THE COLONIES

Prior to establishment of the United States Mint in Philadelphia in 1792 and its subsequent production of coinage for circulation in 1793, metallic money in the American colonies came in many forms. Foreign coins comprised a wide variety of copper, silver, and gold issues from Spanish America, England, Portugal, Holland, France, Germany, and elsewhere. Many of these were made legal tender by federal law.

As a general rule, in the eighteenth century copper coins used for small change were apt to be British. Silver and gold issues, used in larger transactions, were typically struck by Spanish-American mints in Mexico (in particular), Chile, Peru, and elsewhere. These were denominated in reales (sometimes given as *reals*), with eight reales equaling a Spanish dollar. Gold coins were reckoned in escudos, with 8 escudos equaling a gold doubloon, worth about 16 Spanish dollars. Deeds, contracts, and other documents involving money were usually drawn in English or Spanish money. Brazilian gold coins were important as well as were scattered other European issues.

The popular Spanish milled dollar, or eight-reales piece, was divided into eighths or bits, the one-real worth 12-1/2¢. From this, the term "two bits" for a 25¢ coin passed into the modern idiom.

Indeed, long after the Philadelphia Mint and its several branches were in operation, most silver coins in circulation in the United States were still the Spanish-American types. In New York City, Boston, or Philadelphia in the 1850s, silver two-reales coins were much more common than federal

1745 Peru eight escudos or doubloon, one of many issues of Spanish-American gold coins that facilitated trade in early America.

Liberty Seated coins. From 1821 until August 1834 there were no United States gold coins in circulation as the value of that metal had risen to the point that it cost more than face value to mint a $5 gold coin.

These continued to be struck to the order of those who deposited sufficient gold to make them. After they were delivered, the coins were used in international trade where the face value made no difference. A $5 gold coin containing, for example, $5.05 worth of precious metal would be valued at $5.05 at a destination such as London, Paris, or Vienna. In the meantime, Spanish-American doubloons and other gold coins were widely used.

Spanish-American two-reales coins were the most plentiful silver coins in day-to-day commerce into the 1850s, by which time most were worn nearly smooth, as was this 1781 Mexico City Mint coin counterstamped in the 1850s in New York City to advertise a hair product.

Selected foreign silver and gold coins remained legal tender until after the Act of February 21, 1857, mandated their retirement. An extension was granted for two years, then another for six months, making them useful in commerce well into the year 1859. In 1857 the Treasury began large-scale redemption of foreign silver and gold issues, exchanging them for federal coins.

It was difficult, if not impossible, for the average merchant or banker to know the exchange value of an eight-escudo gold doubloon from Mexico, as compared to one from Peru or Chile, or to figure the trade worth of a French silver five-franc coin. Exchange-rate tables published in newspapers and almanacs were a help as were charts and publications known as cambists. Most city newspapers had a "prices current" column giving values of popular gold and silver coins as well as market values for commodities. A wide class of publications known as counterfeit detectors and bank-note reporters developed. These told the value of paper money in particular (in addition to endeavoring to identify counterfeits), but often gave exchange values for foreign coins.

Beyond that, values of coins varied from colony to colony. A Mexican doubloon had one value in New York City and a slightly different value in Charleston.

From time to time paper currency issues were produced by the various colonies, the earliest being the issue of Massachusetts dated December 10, 1690, on the old calendar (in which the year began on March 25). Because of this, other Massachusetts bills dated "February 3, 1690" were printed before March 25, 1691, as authorized by the "order of February 3, 1690/91," the double date used by historians to explain this transitional period. Although dated earlier, the February 3, 1690, bills were actually printed later than the December 10, 1690, currency. Confusing? Under the old Julian calendar in use in Protestant England before 1752, New Year's Day came on March 25. The day before March 25, 1691, was thus March 24, 1690, in the old calendar. In 1752 England and her American colonies changed to the Gregorian calendar and to adjust for doing so dropped 11 days from the month of September. To make the conversion beginning in 1752, the year 1751 was a "short" year beginning

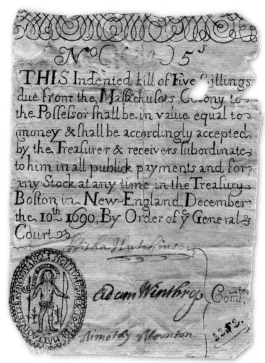

A December 10, 1690, 5-shilling note of Massachusetts, the first paper money printed in North America.

March 25, 1751, and ending December 31. Thus today we celebrate Benjamin Franklin's birthday on January 17 (1706) but the old-style date was January 6 (1705). Looking back from today, we use the double date to correct the Julian year to Gregorian but usually ignore the 11 days. The double date was not used in the eighteenth century.

Paper issues printed for colonial monies of account usually were reckoned in British pounds, shillings, and pence, or in Spanish dollars. For example, an early note of Pennsylvania bore the inscription: "This bill shall pass current for five shillings within the Province of Pennsylvania according to an Act of Assembly made in the 31st year of the reign of King George II. Dated May 20, 1758."

A note of Delaware was inscribed: "This indented bill shall pass current for Fifteen Shillings within the Government of the Counties of New Castle, Kent, Sussex on Delaware, according to an Act of Assembly of the said Government made in the 32nd Year of the Reign of our Sovereign Lord King George II. Dated the 1st Day of June, 1759."

A New Hampshire 10-shilling note of 1734. Most colonial bills traded within the colonies that issued them and were not accepted in distant places.

When the first issues of the Continental Congress appeared in 1775 they specified payment in Spanish coins. For example, a typical note reads: "This Bill entitles the Bearer to receive EIGHT Spanish milled DOLLARS, or the Value thereof in Gold or Silver, according to the Resolutions of the CONGRESS, held at Philadelphia the 10th of May, 1775."

Paper money of various kinds, issued in large amounts during the eighteenth century, was often viewed with distrust. Counterfeiting was rife, notes or bills good in one area were often valueless or deeply depreciated in another, and many other problems surfaced. Bills were often altered by removing one denomination and inking in a higher value. Counterfeits were made by various processes, including carefully drawing notes by hand as well as the more expedient making of a false printing plate. Because of counterfeits, official designs were often changed at short intervals, at which time earlier currency was called in, inspected for genuineness, and exchanged for the new. Very few people could tell counterfeits from the genuine, some of which were so clever that numismatists today need to look for secret privy marks and other signs. Despite the warning "To Counterfeit Is Death" printed on many notes, the game continued. In practice, very few makers of false notes were ever executed, as juries were reluctant to apply the ultimate penalty.

Moreover, much paper money became devalued. It took ever-increasing amounts of paper to buy a given item. Such currency generally stayed within the colony of issue, or, if taken across borders, was apt to sell at a deep discount. Older paper money of higher value was often referred to as "old tenor," as were earlier coins of higher weight. The quality and acceptance of paper varied from colony to colony—with some keeping tighter rein than others.

Making matters even more difficult, the value of a given note varied from colony to colony, much more so than changing values of silver and gold coins for paper had no intrinsic or melt-down worth.

The saying, "never keep a paper dollar in your pocket till tomorrow," popularized by Aaron White in a token he issued in 1857, was just as applicable in colonial days. A citizen holding Spanish coins worth five pounds and an equivalent amount of paper money with the same value would nearly always spend the paper money first.

Continental currency was authorized by the Continental Congress and was issued in five series with 11 different authorization dates, in denominations from fractions of a dollar up to, eventually, $80. Although these notes were payable in Spanish milled dollars, as related above, the federal treasury was empty. Accordingly, the bills depreciated rapidly from their first issue in 1775 to the last in 1779. In January 1777 it took $105 in Continental paper money to buy $100 in Spanish

A February 17, 1776, $8 Continental currency note. Each bill was signed by hand.

silver dollars at an exchange office. By February 1781 it took $7,500! After this time, the bills became virtually worthless. Some smart speculators made a market in them and were rewarded when on August 4, 1790, Congress passed an act providing that Continental currency would be received at the Treasury until September 1, 1791, at the rate of $100 in bills to $1 in silver or gold coins. Among those profiting on a large scale seems to have been "Lord" Timothy Dexter, a wealthy entrepreneur in Newburyport, Massachusetts, who decorated his front lawn with statues of prominent historical figures.

The Act of May 8, 1792, extended the redemption period of March 7, 1792, after which time the bills were repudiated, the status they retain today, although in all instances a well-preserved note has a numismatic value higher than its face value. Later paper-money issues of the various states, similar in design to certain Continental notes, were guaranteed by the state governments. It is an arguable point as to the legal-tender status today of signed, unredeemed bills. Again, that problem is solved by their numismatic worth.

In April 1782 the Commonwealth of Pennsylvania affirmed the charter of the Bank of North America, the first such institution authorized by a state, although banks and money-exchange offices were hardly new. Soon the bank issued paper money with its imprint, redeemable in specie (gold and silver coins) at its office. This set the pace for more than 3,000 banks to gain state charters and issue paper money from that time until the mid-1860s. In addition many private notes were issued by merchants and towns, particularly in times of economic stress, such as after the War of 1812 and following the Panic of 1837.

The failure of Continental notes had warned the public, and it was thought that federal paper money would be questioned.

Front of the mansion of "Lord" Timothy Dexter on High Street in Newburyport, Massachusetts. He speculated in Continental currency. The building (without statues) still stands today.

As it developed, bills of banks ranged from worthless to fully redeemable in gold or silver, depending on the reputation and capital of the institution involved. It was not until 1861 that the federal government again issued currency in quantity for public use. During the entire colonial era, and extending well into the mid-nineteenth century, gold and silver coins were always preferable to paper money. Anyone with a $5 gold coin and a $5 bill would spend the bill first.

EUROPEAN COINAGE FOR AMERICA

In the eighteenth century, as part of the flood of European coins brought to America, such low-denomination coins as Mark Newby farthings and half-pence featuring St. Patrick and British coppers were used here, although they were not made specifically for this side of the Atlantic, nor did they bear any inscriptions relating to the colonies. Mark Newby's coppers were legal tender for a time in West Jersey (largely today's New Jersey), but no such mantle was ever placed on other English or Irish coppers. The legislature of the colony made them legal tender.

Various coins were produced in England for specific distribution in America.

In 1688 Richard Holt, a British entrepreneur, caused a quantity of 1/24th-real tin coins to be made for the American plantations, but these never reached circulation this side of the Atlantic.

For Maryland, Cecil Calvert, the second Lord Baltimore, caused a series of silver coins ranging from the groat (fourpence) to the shilling to be struck. He also had struck a copper denarium or penny.

William Wood, under a royal patent, produced the distinctive Rosa Americana issues, these in addition to his Hibernia coppers made for circulation in Ireland, but some found their way to America. To the coins in circulation were added coins and tokens of private issuers.

St. Patrick halfpennies (illustrated here) and farthings made for circulation in Ireland were imported to West Jersey in America and declared legal tender.

Copper halfpence for Virginia were struck at the Tower Mint in London in 1773 and shipped to that colony.

Mention is made of the brass pieces produced in England circa 1616 for the Sommer Islands (Bermuda). At the time these were under the authority of the Virginia Company, but that division was separate from the colony on the American mainland. The authorization provided that these little coins, each depicting a wild hog, only be used on those islands. These are detailed in the present text by "numismatic tradition" although they are not part of coinage made for land that later became the United States. The main "currency" of the Sommer Islands during that time was tobacco.

Silver sixpence struck in England for circulation in the colony of Maryland.

Curiously, the many other issues that were legal tender on this side of the Atlantic—various foreign gold and silver issues—are *not* collected as part of the American colonial series. Many are of significant related interest, however. Extensive collections could be made of Spanish-American dollars and their fractional parts, as these were the main coins in American circulation in the eighteenth and early nineteenth centuries, and were given legal-tender status.

Rosa Americana coins intended for circulation in America were made under contract by William Wood beginning in 1722. Shown is a 1722 penny.

Halfpence for circulation in America were made in London and circulated widely.

EARLY COINAGE IN AMERICA

It was not until 1652, during the reign of Oliver Cromwell, three years after King Charles was removed from the British throne, that the Massachusetts Bay Colony faced and attempted to correct the shortage of circulating coins. A mint was established in Boston to provide a coinage that could be used to satisfy local needs and to counteract debased-alloy Spanish-American silver coins. The coins that were made at that historic facility were produced over the next 30 years in defiance of British law. The date 1652 was continued in use on them by convention, representing the date of authorization by the colony. Designs included the NE (New England), Willow Tree, Oak Tree, and Pine Tree motifs.

In Simsbury, Connecticut, in 1737, Dr. Samuel Higley struck copper threepence pieces made from metal taken from local mines, a coinage that was continued after his death the same year. The first issues were denominated as three pence. Objection arose among locals who disputed the value of the tokens, and later varieties said VALUE ME AS YOU PLEASE. Today all such coins are very rare.

In 1783 John Chalmers, an Annapolis, Maryland, silversmith, issued his own high-quality coins that were readily accepted in regional commerce. The dies were made by Thomas Sparrow, who also engraved plates for bank notes.

After the Declaration of Independence made the case for American freedom from British rule, the first of the emerging states to consider the subject of coinage was New Hampshire. The State House of

The 1652 Pine Tree shilling is perhaps the most famous American colonial coin. Nathaniel Hawthorne once wrote a story about it.

Higley coppers were struck in Simsbury, Connecticut, in 1737 and 1739. This early issue is lettered THE VALUE OF THREE PENCE.

Representatives authorized a limited quantity of pure-copper coins. Silversmith William Moulton was empowered to make them; he prepared cast patterns featuring a pine tree and a harp, and the date 1776. Historians believe these patterns were not accepted by the public, and few of them entered circulation. Still, they marked the beginning of a new period in American money.

During the pre-federal period each die was made of distinctive character, so the finished coins would indicate the authority of the issuer and be familiar as to value. By the time that state coinage commenced in 1785 (by Connecticut and Vermont) the most familiar foreign copper coins in circulation were British halfpence. These depicted the king on the obverse and the seated figure of Britannia, the personification of Great Britain, on the reverse. It was logical that Connecticut and Vermont (beginning in 1786, after its "landscape" coinage) placed a portrait on the one side of their coins and a seated figure on the other. Such motifs gave instant familiarity and credibility to new issues and implied that they were worth as much as a British halfpenny.

Other coppers of the 1780s had IMMUNIS COLUMBIA, NON VI VIRTUTE VICI, E PLURIBUS UNUM, LIBER NATUS LIBERTATEM DEFENDO, and other Latinized inscriptions, the meanings of which were probably unknown to the majority of the overall population. INDE ET LIB on the reverse of Connecticut and Vermont coppers meant "Independence and liberty," from Latin, later also related to 'Indépendence Et Liberté" used on certain French coins of the nineteenth century.

1783 silver shilling made in Annapolis, Maryland, by silversmith John Chalmers. Two birds compete for a worm, while behind a fence a dangerous snake (an allegory for Britain) lurks unnoticed amidst their squabble.

British halfpence and counterfeits thereof were the most often seen copper coins in circulation in the United States in the late eighteenth century. Shown is a genuine 1771 halfpenny.

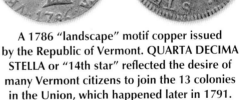

A 1786 "landscape" motif copper issued by the Republic of Vermont. QUARTA DECIMA STELLA or "14th star" reflected the desire of many Vermont citizens to join the 13 colonies in the Union, which happened later in 1791.

To facilitate their use in commerce the design of Vermont coppers was changed to the portrait of King George III and the figure of Britannia, now with Vermont-related legends translating to "By the Authority of Vermont" and "Independence and Liberty."

Copper coins for Connecticut were struck under contract from 1785 to 1788 and circulated widely. Most bore portraits of King George II or, as seen here, III.

TOWARD A FEDERAL COINAGE

Fugio coppers, struck under the authority of Congress under contract with the Connecticut mint, made their appearance in 1788 but were back-dated 1787, and used a sundial motif earlier found on certain Continental paper-money issues. Taken together, these diverse coinages and others are often referred to as "colonials" by numismatists today. As to when the colonial era ended can be debated. The Declaration of Independence, dated July 4, 1776, proclaimed that the colonies were henceforth independent. Therefore, they were no longer colonies. The Battle of Yorktown, 1781, marked the end of the war. The Treaty of Paris, signed in 1783, resulted in all countries, including Britain, recognizing the independence of the United States of America.

In 1782 Robert Morris, the Confederation's superintendent of finance, proposed to Congress a curious money system of 1,440 "units" making up a dollar. This was calculated to figure (to the smallest fraction) into the many different valuations of the Spanish dollar, which varied throughout the states. Thomas Jefferson favored a simpler dollar unit and a decimal system. "The most easy ratio of multiplication and division is that of ten," he noted in 1784. George Washington referred to the decimal system as "a measure, which in my opinion has become indispensably necessary."

The 1787 Fugio copper cent.

In 1783 Morris submitted to Congress a series of patterns, designed by Benjamin Dudley, as a proposal along the decimal line. The largest piece, with a denomination of 1,000 "units" (each unit being a quarter grain of silver), he called a *mark*. The 500-unit piece was a *quint* and the 100-unit a *bit*. These silver patterns were proposed along with a copper 5-unit piece. The system never went beyond the experimental stage.

Actual statehood commenced when the various former colonies ratified the United States Constitution. Delaware was the first in 1787.

Silver 1783 pattern for 1,000 units or one mark.

Complicating the discussion is the issuance of paper money by the Continental Congress in the late 1770s, specifically marked "United States."

Coins and tokens of George Washington, mostly struck in England from 1783 through the mid-1790s, are often collected with colonial issues and are included herein.

In *American Gold and Silver: U.S. Mint Collector and Investor Coins and Medals, Bicentennial to Date*, numismatist Dennis Tucker quoted Benjamin Franklin: "There are three faithful friends: An old wife, an old dog, and ready money." Tucker went on to note:

> For many decades, Americans considered the best kinds of ready money to be *silver* and *gold*, prized above copper, paper currency, credit, and other financial instruments. As treasured as they were, in many periods of our nation's history silver and gold coins were the most difficult to obtain and keep.
>
> Britain's colonies in North America, unlike most of Spain's in Mexico and Central and South America, never were significant sources of native gold and silver. The British would have to mine their New World treasure not with pick axes and shovels, but with trade and commercial policy. Tariffs and other

regulations were designed to give every advantage to British producers, and America's colonists were forced into the dependent status of consumers. The effect was a draining of capital, and in particular silver and gold coins, from the New World back to the Old.

The advent of extensive federal coinage beginning with the Philadelphia Mint in 1792 was intended to help solve that.

FEDERAL COINAGE IN THE EARLY YEARS

By the late 1780s the individual states had ceased to issue their own coins and paper money. The sinews of commerce were secured by foreign silver and gold coins authorized as legal tender by Congress (the authorization of most did not expire until 1860, as noted earlier). Dominating the activity were coins of Spanish America, with those from the Mexico City Mint being the most prevalent. Coins of Great Britain, France, the Netherlands, and certain other European countries were legal tender as well. Joining the legitimate silver and copper issues was a flood of copper coins, mostly genuine and counterfeit British halfpence that had no legal-tender status but were widely accepted in commerce. The value of such coppers in quantity fluctuated, and in the late 1790s there had been a deep depression. However, the coins singly and in small groups continued to pass readily.

Alexander Hamilton.

In planning for a federal coinage Alexander Hamilton, who would become the nation's first secretary of the Treasury, agreed fundamentally with the decimal concept and urged that gold and silver be used in the nation's standard money. On March 3, 1791—during George Washington's first presidential term—Congress authorized the president to hire artists and acquire machinery for coinage in order to establish a federal mint. Some initial steps were taken, and that October, in his annual address, Washington stated, "The disorders in the existing currency, and especially the scarcity of small change, a scarcity so peculiarly distressing to the poorer classes, strongly recommend the carrying into immediate effect the resolution already entered into concerning the establishment of a mint."

Philadelphia in the 1790s, when it was the seat of the United States government.

Five months later, the Mint Act of April 2, 1792, provided that "the money of account of the United States should be expressed in dollars or units, dismes or tenths, cents or hundredths, and milles or thousandths; a disme being the tenth part of a dollar, a cent the hundredth part of a dollar, a mille the thousandth part of a dollar. . . ." The Mint Act also established the metal content of the coins, and their imagery; identified the "seat of government," Philadelphia, as the site of the new mint; and guaranteed that silver and gold would be made into coins free of charge to those who brought the metal in.

> The latter provision would save the Mint from having to source its own raw gold and silver. It also offered banks, merchants, and others a way to transform bullion and miscellaneous foreign specie into official, spendable U.S. coins, and thereby inject larger-denomination coins into commerce. (The conversion, while convenient, was not automatic; refining and coining took time. Alternately, one could deliver bullion to the Mint and exchange it immediately for equivalent U.S. coins, with one-half of 1 percent deducted for expenses.) The act also provided for a coinage of copper small-change coins.[3]

Copper coinage was extremely important for the early Mint. There was no profit to be made on coining silver and gold, but copper half cents and cents yielded any profit that could be made between the cost of copper stock and the face value of the coins. It was more expedient to coin a single cent than two half cents, with the result that cents were made in large quantities as compared to sporadic lower quantities for half cents.

The coins specified in the Mint Act of 1792 included these:

Denomination	Value	Fineness	Denomination	Value	Fineness
eagle	$10.00	91.7% pure gold (22k)	quarter dollar	$0.25	89.2% pure silver
half eagle	$5.00	91.7% pure gold (22k)	disme	$0.10	89.2% pure silver
quarter eagle	$2.50	91.7% pure gold (22k)	half disme	$0.05	89.2% pure silver
dollar	$1.00	89.2% pure silver	cent	$0.01	100% pure copper
half dollar	$0.50	89.2% pure silver	half cent	$0.005	100% pure copper

COINAGE OF THE 1790s

On July 31, 1792, the cornerstone was laid for the Philadelphia Mint, the second building created by the United States government (the first was a lighthouse). In attendance were President George Washington, Mint Director David Rittenhouse, and others. At the time Rittenhouse, a maker of clocks and scientific apparatus, was one of the Americans most skilled in mechanics and was an ideal choice. Philadelphia was the seat of the federal government, and the president resided just a short walk away.

By that time there was a coining press and some other equipment on hand, stored in an old carriage house on Sixth Street, above Chestnut, owned by John Harper, a saw maker and mechanic. Thomas Jefferson, in his Memorandum Book July 11, 1792, entry, noted that he took $75 in silver to the Mint to be coined. His July 13, 1792, entry records receiving 1,500 half dismes from the Mint. In the autumn the Mint was in operation, and additional silver half dismes were produced.

Thomas Jefferson's memorandum book states that he personally purchased and distributed 1,500 1792 half dismes.

In December some pattern one-cent pieces and other proposals were made. Dies for some early patterns were made by Robert Birch, and Joseph Wright created a quarter-dollar pattern.

Copper one-cent pieces were first made for circulation in February 1793. The earliest versions had a head of Miss Liberty on the obverse and a chain of 15 links on the reverse, one for each state (by this time Vermont had joined the Union, in 1791, and Kentucky in 1792). To some the design was less than pleasing. One newspaper account described Miss Liberty as being "in a fright," and the chain on the reverse as an ill omen for a land of freedom. The motif was changed to a different face of Miss Liberty, and, on the reverse, a wreath. That summer, copper half cents were made for the first time. Some early dies were made by Joseph Wright (who died of yellow fever that September), and possibly by Henry Voigt, an engraver on the Mint staff. In the autumn Robert Scot, a British immigrant who was important as a local maker of copper plates for bank-notes, maps, and illustrations, was hired as engraver. In the first year the fledgling Mint struck 35,334 half cents and 111,512 cents, a creditable output. Sources of copper were erratic and problematical and ranged from new sheets to old roofing, some acquired through local advertisements.

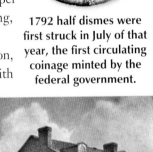

1792 half dismes were first struck in July of that year, the first circulating coinage minted by the federal government.

On October 15, 1794, the first silver dollars were struck for circulation, comprising 1,578 coins that were found satisfactory and some others with defects that were held back for recoinage of the metal. Half dollars were also struck in the autumn. Dies dated 1794 for the half dime were made, but were not used until 1795. It was not until 1795 that a press of sufficient size to strike dollars properly was installed. These were of the Flowing Hair design from dies by Robert Scot.

A view of the first Mint as envisioned by painter Edwin Lamasure in 1914. The front structure was two joined buildings that had earlier served as a brewery and for other purposes. The rear buildings are depicted with some artistic license on Lamasure's part. This facility was used through the year 1832.

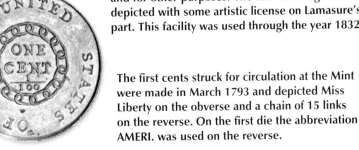

The first cents struck for circulation at the Mint were made in March 1793 and depicted Miss Liberty on the obverse and a chain of 15 links on the reverse. On the first die the abbreviation AMERI. was used on the reverse.

David Rittenhouse, in poor health, resigned as Mint director in June 1795 and was replaced by Henry William de Saussure, who served only to the following November. Replacing him in the same month was Elias Boudinot, who remained in the post until July 1805.

The Draped Bust design was introduced on the dollar in autumn 1795 and was later used on half cents (starting in 1800) and on cents and other silver coins (1796). This was from a portrait of socialite Mrs. William Bingham drawn by Gilbert Stuart.

In July of 1795 the first federal gold coins, half eagles ($5 gold pieces), were delivered, soon followed by eagles ($10), the largest denomination. Designs changed and evolved over the years. It was general practice to have copper coins bear one common design, silver coins another standard motif, and gold coins to share still another, although sometimes there was overlapping. The Draped Bust obverse was first used on silver coins of 1795 as noted, while gold coins of that and succeeding years into the next century depicted Miss Liberty wearing a conical cloth cap.

In 1796 the first silver dimes and quarter dollars were struck and also the first quarter eagles ($2.50 gold coins), completing all of the denominations authorized by the 1792 Mint Act. While half cents and cents were struck for the account and profit of the Mint, silver and gold coins were made only on the request of depositors of such precious metals. This was usually deposited in the form of foreign coins, but sometimes in other forms, including worn-out utensils and old ornaments.

In the early days dies for all denominations were cut by hand, with separate punches used to add numerals, letters, stars, and devices such as eagles and Liberty heads. No two dies were ever precisely alike, creating a wide panorama of varieties usually differing from each other slightly. However, more than just a few had interesting errors or blunders, such as having a word spelled as IINITED instead of UNITED, or having a fraction read 1/000, which is mathematically meaningless, instead of 1/100. While 13 stars, or one for each of the original colonies, has been the standard count on federal silver and gold coins up to the modern day, some of 1796 were given 15 stars, representing the current number of states

The first silver dollars were of the Flowing Hair type and were struck in one day on October 15, 1794.

The Draped Bust design was first used on silver dollars in 1795 and was later the motif on other copper and silver coins.

Half eagles first made in July 1795 were the first federal gold coins.

A famous reverse die for an 1801 cent had three errors: the left stem at the bottom of the wreath was missing, UNITED was spelled as IINITED, and the fraction was a meaningless 1/000 instead of 1/100.

in the Union. Tennessee joined in this year, raising the count to 16, and some coins were made with this number of stars. Soon, the idea was abandoned, and 13 became the standard.

During the 1790s continuing into the new century epidemics of yellow fever swept Philadelphia on several occasions, resulting in many deaths (including of engraver Joseph Wright in 1793). The Mint was closed during these periods and the dies stored in the vaults of a local bank. The Bank of America and the Bank of Pennsylvania were especially important in the early years of the Mint and made deposits of foreign gold and silver coins and received quantities of newly made federal issues.

Most dies of the era continued to be made by Robert Scot, with the assistance in earlier years of Henry Voigt and John Smith Gardner. Copper cents in circulation were augmented by many private tokens imported from England, mostly notably those bearing the advertisement of Talbot, Allum & Lee, New York City merchants in the India trade. In the spring of 1795 about 52,000 of them were bought by the Mint, and planchets for half cents were cut from them. Later, an arrangement was made for Boulton & Watt in Birmingham, England, to supply ready-made copper planchets, a practice that was maintained until the War of 1812. There were some schedule problems in 1799 that resulted in a smaller coinage of cents that year; no half cents were made in 1798 or 1799. In 1800 Johann (John) Matthias Reich was hired on contract to make medals, thus assisting engraver Robert Scot.

An engraver at the Philadelphia Mint.
(Concept by Marcia Davis, 1984)

"Despite the Mint's best efforts in its early years, its coinage remained scarce in circulation. Gold and silver in particular were rarely seen in commerce, but the problem extended to small change, as well. By 1799 only about $50,000 worth of copper cents and half cents had been pumped into the economy—roughly one coin for every citizen, not nearly enough for the nation's day-to-day business."[4] Filling the void, earlier tokens and coins of the colonies and states continued to circulate. Silver and gold coins were seldom seen in commerce, except in large cities. Many if not most silver dollars and gold $10 eagles were used in the export trade and never returned.

Legal-tender silver and gold coins of European and Central and South American countries continued to fill nearly all of the need for large denominations in circulation. The Spanish-American silver 8-reales, dollar sized, was the world's most popular trade coin. Vast quantities were purchased by American merchants and exported in exchange for goods. Whaling and merchant ships headed to the Pacific and Far East carried thousands of these coins as they were accepted at all foreign ports. A common arrangement for security was to store thousands of coins in a compartment near the captain's stateroom.

Despite the output of the Philadelphia Mint the Spanish-American 8-reales or piece-of-eight coin dominated domestic as well as world commerce well into the early nineteenth century. Shown is a 1761 Mexico City Mint 8-reales.

THE EARLY NINETEENTH CENTURY

At the beginning of the nineteenth century, officially 1801, these coins were being struck: cent, half dime, dime, and silver dollar, each with the Draped Bust obverse, and $5 and $10 gold of the Capped Bust motif. Yellow fever continued to be a problem, resulting in Mint closings. Another problem was the opposition of certain members of Congress to the Mint itself, and several proposals were made to close it and have coinage done under private contract. Those situations were resolved and the Mint continued operations.

Robert Maskell Patterson was appointed Mint director by President Thomas Jefferson on January 1, 1806. He served until July 1834, the longest tenure of anyone ever holding the office.

In 1806 John Reich was given a position on the Mint staff as assistant engraver. He created a version of Miss Liberty in a floppy mob cap, called the Capped Bust motif. This was first used on half dollars and half eagles of 1807 and later on the cent (1808), half cent (1809), half dime (1829), dime

Elias Boudinot, Mint director from 1795 to 1805.

(1809), and quarter (1815). Today Capped Bust half dollars, made in large quantities, are especially popular with numismatists. Reich also redesigned the reverses of silver and gold coins to incorporate a perched eagle holding arrows and an olive branch.

America was prosperous from the early 1790s until 1808, when the effects of Thomas Jefferson's 1807 Embargo Act were felt. By that time the French, then the British, had seized many American ships on the high seas, the British often kidnapping our sailors and forcing them to serve on their ships. The Embargo Act prohibited nearly all trade with foreign ports, in effect freezing the economy of most coastal cities. Many businesses failed, and other hardships were experienced. The War of 1812 created more chaos. The United States Navy was not strong, and to help fight the enemy, the government gave letters of

The Capped Bust design by John Reich was introduced on the 1807 half dollar (as shown) and half eagle and was used on certain coins as late as 1838.

Robert M. Patterson served as Mint director from 1806 to 1834.

marque, as they were called, to the captains of and owners of ships. They then engaged in privateering under the American flag, capturing whatever enemy prizes they could find and taking the ships to ports where they and their contents were sold at auction—with the money divided among the ship crews and owners. This was a rich undertaking for many, and more than a few family fortunes in Portsmouth, Baltimore, and other cities were augmented in this manner.

In a famous battle at sea in the War of 1812 the USS *Constitution* vanquished the HMS *Guerriere*. (Anton Otto Fischer)

The monetary situation in the United States was tumultuous. The supply of copper planchets from England was exhausted in 1814, and no copper coins were made in 1815. Deposits of silver and gold coins were small, and relatively few coins of these metals were struck in mid-decade. In 1816 only copper cents were made.

Gold and silver coins were in circulation in some periods in the 1810s, then one or another of these metals would rise in value, and many coins would disappear. Meanwhile, a flood of paper bills was issued by banks, merchants, and others.

John Reich left the Mint in 1817 to pursue other opportunities. Engraving was primarily continued by Robert Scot, in service since 1793, but his eyesight was failing. There were no new designs to be created for the next several years, and the design hubs and punches on hand remained in use for new dies. Economic times were difficult in 1818 and 1819, what would be called a recessionary period by later economists.

By this time only a few dozen collectors and museums pursued the art and history of numismatics. In coming years their numbers would increase.

The 1816 cent of the new Matron Head design was the only federal coinage of this year.

A $1 note issued by the Owl Creek Bank of Mount Vernon, Ohio, in 1816, a time of monetary crisis.

THE 1820s AND 1830s

The financial matters improved in the 1820s, in part spawning the creation historical societies, athenaeums, and libraries that often included coins in their holdings and exhibits.

The first professional numismatist in the United States seems to have been John Allan, born in Scotland. In 1820 he was just one of three American subscribers to Mudie's set of National Medals, published in England. Philip Hone, a wealthy New Yorker who served as mayor of the city in 1826, is known to have been an active coin collector in New York City circa 1822–1827.[5] The private collection of Benjamin H. Watkins, auctioned in Salem, Massachusetts, on June 12 and 13, 1828, is thought to be the first significant cataloged sale of coins in the United States, although the descriptions were poor by later standards.

In the meantime the international price of gold rose in relation to silver, and gold coins became worth more in melt value than face value. Large quantities were coined to the order of depositors who shipped them overseas, where they were received on the basis of weight, with the stamped value being of no importance. In the United States anyone desiring gold coins had to pay a premium for them to a money broker or exchange office. There were no federal gold coins in domestic circulation after 1820. Mintages of half eagles were nearly all to the order of merchants and others who exported them to Europe, where they were melted.

Robert Scot continued as engraver at the Mint until his death on November 3, 1823. William Kneass, a local engraver of copper plates for bank notes and other items, was appointed engraver in 1824. Christian Gobrecht, who did some contract work in the 1820s, hoped to be appointed but was not considered. Beginning about this year Adam Eckfeldt and perhaps one or two others working at the Philadelphia Mint began saving current coinage.[6] It is said that copper cents and other items were kept on hand for sale or exchange with interested collectors. Interesting rare coins were

From 1821 to June 1834 all newly minted federal gold coins such as this half eagle cost more than face value to make. Depositors were charged a premium for them. Nearly all were shipped overseas and melted for bullion value, as the face value made no difference.

picked out of incoming deposits and saved. Many old dies were still at the Mint, and on occasion restrikes would be made to supply pieces needed by collectors. No records were kept of such activities, and today we can only speculate as to what occurred.

On July 4, 1829, the cornerstone was laid for a new Philadelphia Mint building. For the occasion, half dimes of the Capped Bust type were struck for the first time, there having been no coinage of this denomination since 1805.

Andrew Jackson, elected president in 1828, took office on March 4, 1829. The first Bank of the United States had operated from 1791 to 1811, after which its 20-year charter was not renewed. The second Bank of the United States was chartered in 1816, to operate until 1836. This bank was mainly owned by private stockholders, although the government had a significant interest. It had many branches in the East and Midwest and issued paper money. Great resistance to it was made by the politicians of many states whose state-chartered banks felt it was unfair competition.

Jackson disliked the bank and resolved to veto any charter extension. His opponents in Congress passed a bill well in advance, in 1830, to assure that renewal would take place in 1836. Jackson kept his word, and in the 1830s the bank wound down its operations to the point that most activity ended in 1835. This was the great political issue of the era. From that time onward, politicians, newspapers, and others were largely divided into two groups: pro-Jackson and anti-Jackson. As if that was not enough, John C. Calhoun, senator from South Carolina, frequently suggested that South Carolina withdraw from the Union, and other Southern states do so as well, as the commercial interests of the South (cotton, tobacco, and other agricultural products) were so different from those of the North (manufacturing, banking, etc.). In particular, high tariffs had diminished exports of cotton, to the detriment of the South, while restricting imports from Europe and thus bringing great prosperity to factories in the North.

The charter to renew the second Bank of the United States was vetoed by President Andrew Jackson in 1830, after which the institution wound down its business, closing in 1836.

Extensive gold strikes were made in Georgia and North Carolina in the 1820s, the first time that significant quantities of that metal were discovered in the United States. In 1830 Templeton Reid issued his own $2.50, $5, and $10 gold coins, and in Rutherfordton, North Carolina, Christopher Bechtler and his family operated a private mint that would remain in business until the early 1850s and would make $1, $2.50, and $5 coins. In 1833 the new Philadelphia Mint went into operation and would remain the center of coinage activity until 1901.

A $2.50 gold coin minted by Templeton Reid in Georgia following the most important gold strike to that date on United States soil.

Prosperity continued apace, aided by the enthusiasm for building canals and railroads, the opening up of new lands in the West and making them easy to buy, and a general atmosphere of well-being. The age of steam was beginning in a large way and would soon revolutionize industrial America.

The Act of June 28, 1834, reduced the amount of gold in coins, and the lightweight issues made beginning in August of that year circulated readily. Gold had not been seen in domestic commerce since 1820.

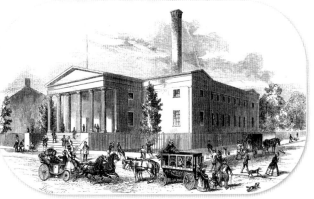

The second Philadelphia Mint operated from 1833 to 1901.

The expansion of America and continuing prosperity brought an increased need for coinage. In 1835 Congress authorized the opening of three branch mints. Each was opened for business several years later in 1838.

The New Orleans Mint was located near the mouth of the Mississippi River, the gateway to inland commerce. Mints at Charlotte, North Carolina, and Dahlonega, Georgia, were in gold-mining regions and provided convenient facilities for converting bullion to coins. The alternative would have been to ship it to distant Philadelphia. The mintmarks O, C, and D were added to each coin to signify their origin.

In August 1835, Chief Engraver Kneass was paralyzed by a stroke. In the next month Christian Gobrecht, a Philadelphia engraver of bank-notes, book plates, and other items, and an inventor, was hired as second engraver. A man of formidable artistic ability, Gobrecht did not want to be called "assistant," and thus the "second" in his title. As it turned out, he did most of the engraving work from that point onward, although Kneass retained the primary engravership until his death in 1840.

The New Orleans Mint operated from 1838 to 1861 and again from 1879 to 1909 and produced silver and gold coins. The facility houses a museum today.

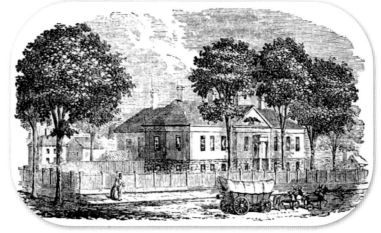

The Charlotte Mint coined gold from 1838 to 1861. Today the building, disassembled and moved to a park, is the Charlotte Art Museum.

Georgia's Dahlonega Mint produced gold coins from 1838 to 1861. The building burned in 1878. Today the Dahlonega Gold Museum Historic Site, housed in the historic Old Lumpkin County Courthouse, celebrates the region's importance in mining and private gold coinage.

An 1838-C quarter eagle, with Charlotte's C mintmark above the date.

Coinage presses were operated by hand. In 1836 steam power was introduced and in 1837 would be used on all presses for circulating coinage. Proofs made for collectors continued to be made on hand-operated equipment. Called "master coins" in the early days, Proofs would become increasingly important at the Mint, to the point in later years some coins were struck only in that format for collectors, and none for circulation (the earliest example may be the 1827 quarter dollar, for which information is incomplete, or may be the 1804 silver dollar, made in 1834 and backdated 20 years).

Prosperity continued in America through 1836, the year that the Bank of the United States charter expired. Speculation in real estate in the prairie beyond Pennsylvania was wildly out of control. Vast tracts were purchased through cred-

An early steam-powered knuckle-action coining press made for the Philadelphia Mint by a local manufacturer.

its and drafts, paper money of depreciated or uncertain value, and promissory notes. This set the scene for Andrew Jackson's Specie Circular, July 11, 1836, one of the most pivotal documents in American financial history. This decree mandated that lands be paid for in gold and silver coins, instead of paper money and credits, that buyers be bona-fide residents or settlers, and that the amount of acreage be restricted for each purchaser. Very few buyers of land had silver half dollars or gold half eagles, and speculation came to an abrupt halt. Loans were called, but debtors could not pay. By early 1837 there was a chill in the American economy, and European bankers, who held many investments, were becoming concerned.

In the same year, 1836, the Liberty Seated design made its debut on the silver dollar, the first of this denomination coined for circulation since 1804. By 1839 it was used on all silver denominations.

After the charter of the second Bank of the United States expired, many banks were formed with reckless abandon. The bank-note companies in New York and Philadelphia were eager to print as many bills as they could sell, with little notice taken as to whether the banks were chartered or legitimately established. The system of banks issuing large amounts of paper money worked perfectly fine in the heady days of 1835 and 1836. However, in early 1837 many people became wary of banks, and sought to redeem bills for gold and silver. It was quickly learned that while some banks could redeem a small percentage of their currency, no bank was able to exchange for all. On May 10, 1837, specie payments were suspended by most Eastern banks, and within weeks most banks in the South and West also stopped paying out coins.

A Liberty Seated half dime of 1837, the first year of use on this denomination as well as the dime. The motif first appeared on dollars of 1836 and later on quarters starting in 1838 and half dollars in 1839.

Soon, silver and gold coins disappeared completely from circulation, although copper cents remained. To facilitate commerce, countless cent-size Hard Times tokens (as we call them today) were issued, in a wide variety of designs, including advertisements for merchants, caricatures and comments about Jackson and his veto of the Bank of the United States, and more.

In 1837 coins became scarce and many Hard Times tokens were privately issued, such as this one mentioning the suspension of specie payments.

In June 1838 the Mint Cabinet was authorized by Congress—a display of American coins old and new, together with foreign and ancient coins and medals, and mineral specimens and ores. While a few coins were purchased, the main source of supply continued to be the extraction of interesting pieces from deposits made at the Mint. Veteran Mint employee Adam Eckfeldt supplied details of Mint history to interested visitors. Numismatics was becoming increasingly important, and there were at least several hundred serious collectors in America.

THE 1840s TO THE CIVIL WAR

By the early 1840s, Jacob Reese Eckfeldt and William DuBois were curators of the pieces on display in the Mint Cabinet. In 1842 a book by these two men, *A Manual of Gold and Silver Coins of All Nations*, was published by the Mint. The text did not contain numismatic text or comments of use to collectors, but dealt with the weights and designations of coins in these metals. The main audiences were banks and counting houses.

The gold districts of North Carolina and Georgia continued to supply the Charlotte and Dahlonega mints. The Bechtler family in North Carolina, which had begun producing $1, $2.50, and $5 gold coins from regional metal since the early 1830s, continued in business without interference from the Treasury Department, seemingly as their coins were of full weight and value and helped with commerce in the Southeast.

By 1844 the Hard Times era had ended, and American commerce was flourishing. Railroad stocks led the securities market. Year by year, towns and cities throughout the East and Midwest were connected. Many new lines were formed, many of which had banking support. Some even issued paper money. Meanwhile, canals, so important earlier, were fading from the scene with many old waterways and new projects abandoned. The Erie Canal connecting the Hudson River with Lake Erie remained important. On inland waterways and on the high seas sidewheel steamships carried most of the maritime passenger traffic and much cargo. Sailing vessels were still important on routes in which speed was important. In the 1850s fast-sailing clipper ships became important in long-distance freight.

In 1844 Christian Gobrecht, engraver at the Mint since autumn 1835 and responsible for the Liberty Seated design and other motifs, passed away. James B. Longacre, a highly accomplished engraver in the field of portraits and bank notes, was

Commerce on the Erie Canal.

Railroads were the growth industry of the 1840s and 1850s.

appointed in his place. He would serve until his death on January 1, 1869. During his tenure he would create many designs for pattern and regular coinage. Interest in numismatics moved another step forward in 1846 with William DuBois's 138-page *Pledges of History*, a carefully prepared volume describing coins and other items in the Mint Cabinet. The War with Mexico in 1846 and 1847 resulted in victory for the United States. As had been the case with earlier wars, medals were struck to commemorate leaders and battles. The West was expanding in population, most notably by emigrants on the Oregon Trail.

America changed dramatically following the discovery of a gleaming flake of gold in California in the tail race at Sutter's Mill, on the American River, January 24, 1848. This ignited the California Gold Rush, the travel westward of Forty Niners the following year, and the establishment of California as a state in 1850. This transformed the boundaries and encouraged settlement more than any other single event in American history. Now the country extended from sea to shining sea.

The vast discoveries of precious metal engendered the establishment of several private mints in San Francisco, Sacramento, and elsewhere in 1849 and 1850. Large quantities of gold were sent to the East for coinage, usually by sidewheel steamship from San Francisco to Panama, then across land for about 48 miles, then connecting to another ship on the Atlantic side at the port of Aspinwall (today's Colón).

The dramatic influx of gold resulted in the Act of March 3, 1849, which introduced two new denominations—the gold dollar and $20 double eagle. The unprecedented quantity of new gold upset the traditional ratio

Sutter's Mill on the American River, the site of the first large-scale discovery of gold in California.

In 1849 the U.S. Mint introduced the gold dollar to facilitate the coining of gold arriving from California.

of 1 ounce of gold being equal to about 15.5 ounces of silver. Silver became relatively rarer than before, causing federal silver coins in circulation to increase in value to the point at which, by December 1849, they could be melted down to yield more in bullion value than face value. Nearly all disappeared from circulation. The situation would become even more acute.

The first California private gold coins were issued by Norris, Gregg, and Norris in Benecia City with the imprint of San Francisco.

In California beginning in spring 1849 and continuing through 1855 more than a dozen private companies and banks issued their own gold coins of varied design. Although these were not official legal tender they passed readily in commerce. From 1851 to 1853 Augustus Humbert, appointed by the Treasury Department as the official United States assayer of gold in California, supervised the striking of gold coins of denominations from $10 to $50, including at the United States Assay Office of Gold, the activity being conducted by arrangement and under the aegis of Moffat & Company, a firm which separately issued its own coins.

Octagonal $50 gold coins called slugs were issued under the supervision of Augustus Humbert in 1851 (as shown here) and 1852.

In 1850 the California state constitution was adopted. It forbid the use of paper money at face value in the channels of commerce. Only coins had legal-tender value. This would have important implications in the following decade of the 1860s.

In the early 1850s there was the strange situation that in the channels of commerce in the East and Midwest, Liberty Seated coins were nowhere to be seen as they had been gathered by hoarders and speculators in silver metal, and their place was nearly completely taken by Spanish-American silver coins, with the 2-reales coin being the denomination most often seen.

In 1850 double eagles were introduced and were struck at the Philadelphia and New Orleans mints. These coins became exceedingly popular, and during the next 75 years, more value was minted in this denomination than of all other United States gold coins combined.

Placer Operations at Foster's Bar, an 1851 oil by Ernest Narjot, depicted gold mining on the American River east of Sacramento. (Bancroft Library)

In 1850 Jacob Reese Eckfeldt and William DuBois, continuing assayers at the Mint and keepers of the Mint Cabinet, published a small book of 61 pages, *New Varieties of Gold and Silver Coins, Counterfeit Coins, Bullion with Mint Values.* Included was information on gold coins privately minted in California. This work was also issued in modified form in 1851 and 1852. The two later versions also included the text of DuBois's 1846 *Pledges of History* work, the latter being out of print at the time.

The first truly important American auction sale featuring rare coins was that of the late Dr. Lewis Roper, a Philadelphia physician who had gone west to seek his fortune in the gold fields, but died of cholera at sea off of Panama on his return voyage in 1850. The coins were offered on February 20, 1851, in the sale room of Moses Thomas & Son, Philadelphia, a popular location for the sale of antiques, books, and other items.

In 1851 with Liberty Seated coins still absent from circulation the silver three-cent piece, or *trime*, was issued. Of 75 percent silver and 25 percent copper (instead of the standard 90:10 ratio), these coins were not profitable to melt, and thus they circulated in commerce at a time when other federal silver coins were being hoarded or melted.

In 1852 *Uncle Tom's Cabin*, a novel by Harriet Beecher Stowe describing the life of slaves on Southern plantations, was published. By decade's end it was the best-selling novel in American history. Perhaps more than any other single factor the book influenced millions of Americans, mostly in the North, to condemn slavery and campaign for abolition. Relations of Northern politicians with those in the South worsened, with the result that the presidential administrations of Franklin Pierce (1853–1857) and James Buchanan (1857–1861) would be viewed as by historians as two of the most ineffective in American history. Each attempted to please both the North and South, to the dissatisfaction of all.

The silver coinage problem ended with the implementation of the Act of February 21, 1853, in which the authorized weights of the silver half dime, dime, quarter, and half dollar were reduced. Coins made under the new standard had arrowheads added to each side of the date to distinguish them. These lightweight coins circulated, thus ending the money problems that had plagued the market since 1850. The Liberty Seated dollar weight was unchanged and those coins remained available for bullion value, or more than face value, for those who acquired them for export, in which transactions the imprinted face value made no difference.

The three-cent piece or trime was introduced in 1851. With a silver content of only 75 percent (unlike the 90 percent of other denominations) it had less than face value in metal and was not attractive to speculators.

Slaves at work in a cotton field under the gaze of the plantation owner and his family. (Vignette from a bank note of the Farmers Banking Association, Demopolis, Alabama)

In 1853 the Treasury Department acquired the building and facilities of private coiner Moffat & Company and its associates and remodeled it to become the San Francisco Mint. It opened in March 1854 and commenced striking coins with S mintmarks. Commercial connections between the Atlantic and Pacific coasts were mainly by ship, interrupted by a land crossing at Panama or, less often, Nicaragua, or entirely by sea, around the tip of South America. In the same year the new $3 gold denom-

An 1853 quarter dollar with arrows at the date to indicate reduced silver content.

ination was introduced at the Philadelphia, Dahlonega, and Charlotte mints, but this met with only a lukewarm reception, as the value was too close to the long-established $2.50 quarter eagle. Over the years the mintage figures declined, and in 1889 it was discontinued.

The American economy was enjoying a new era of prosperity brought on by the gold excitement, the continued expansion of railroads (their shares dominated the stock exchanges), and excellent business conditions everywhere. Land investment and speculation was back in vogue, and real-estate agents were literally doing a land-office business in what was by then known as the Midwest, the term *West* being descriptive of the Rocky Mountains to the Pacific shore.

The Mint had been experimenting since 1850 with ways to reduce the size and weight of the large-diameter one-cent piece, to increase profits. The price of copper had been rising. In 1856, Engraver Longacre created a cent which was proposed for adoption. The obverse featured a flying eagle (adapted from the reverse of Gobrecht's silver dollar of 1836), and the reverse used an "agricultural wreath" from the $3 gold coin of 1854. An estimated 800 to 1,000 coins were struck in late 1856 and early 1857, all dated 1856, and sent to congressmen, newspaper editors, and others to acquaint them with the new design.

The Philadelphia Mint remained the primary facility for federal coinage. The director of the Mint had his office there

The San Francisco Mint as depicted in *Hutchings' California Magazine.* This facility operated until 1874 when it was replaced by a new structure.

and supervised the operations of the branches at Charlotte, Dahlonega, New Orleans, and San Francisco. Coins in circulation or currently being minted included the copper half cent and cent, the silver three-cents, half dime, dime, quarter dollar, half dollar, and dollar, and the gold $1, $2.50, $3, $5, $10, and $20. Gold from California was still arriving in quantity, although the peak year was 1853.

The Act of February 21, 1857, abolished the copper half cent and cent and mandated other changes, including the planned expiration of the legal-tender privilege for certain foreign silver and gold coins. New cents of the Flying Eagle design, of smaller diameter and made of copper-nickel, soon began rolling off the presses. On May 25, the first small cents were available to the public in exchange for old coppers and Spanish silver.

A gold ingot issued by the assaying firm of Harris & Marchand in Sacramento. Such ingots facilitated the shipment of gold in quantity.

The passion for coin collecting spread rapidly, with numismatologists, as they were called, seeking rare early cents such as 1793 and 1799, while noticing other interesting old coins as well. Within several years important reference books would be published on coins, dealers would set up shop in major cities, and coin auctions would be held frequently. Thus was born an active market for rare coins, tokens, and medals. The *Historical Magazine* was launched in January 1857 and went on to include many articles about coins, including, in August, the first installment of "The First Coinage of America," by Jeremiah Colburn, who in the same year wrote articles about old copper cents for the Boston *Evening Transcript*. In New York City, Augustus B. Sage and Charles I. Bushnell engaged in a lively debate about rare coins in the pages of the *New-York Dispatch*. In the autumn the first issue of *Norton's Literary Letter*, mostly about books, but with much information on coins, was welcomed by collectors. Thus was born a new market with many thousands of numismatists participating.

The economy had enjoyed good times since 1844 and the passing of the Hard Times era. That changed on August 24, 1857, when the Ohio Life Insurance & Trust Company failed. With offices in Cincinnati and New York, it had been a big player in loans, credit, and the processing of paper relating to real estate. By then there had been some shivers in the money market, and some people were apprehensive concerning seemingly unwise investments, but little was said. On the same day the Mechanics Banking Association suspended specie payments. Fear spread, and those holding stocks and investment paper rushed to cash it in at current rates, but found few buyers. Within days, several stock brokers and money dealers failed. This was disturbing but exciting news, and papers in major cities lost no time printing "scare" headlines, which sold more papers, but also helped spread fear. In a domino effect, one failure created another, and soon the Panic of 1857 was underway. In October all of the banks in New York City suspended specie payments, except for the Chemical Bank. Unlike previous economic disturbances, the Panic of 1857 had little effect on the production of federal coinage.

On January 1, 1858, the Philadelphia Numismatic Society was formed, becoming the first such group in the United States. In March, teenaged Augustus B. Sage and friends founded the American Numismatic Society in New York City. By late summer 1858 there were nearly a dozen coin dealers active in the United States, including, in New York City alone, the venerable John Allan, and at least three young men: Augustus Sage, Henry Bogert, and John Curtis. In the same year the first important American numismatic book was published, *An Historical Account of American Coinage*, by John H. Hickcox. The slim volume included 151 numbered pages plus five pages of illustrations by John Gavit, a well-known engraver of bank note plates. Hickcox had spent some time in research and had contacted historical societies and several numismatists as well as Mint Director James Ross Snowden. Only 200 regular copies were printed, and these were mostly sent to libraries and historical societies. For collectors there was no single readily available source for information, and many still sought the elusive copper cent of 1815, not realizing that none were minted that year.

The issuance of medalets depicting historical events achieved wide popularity in 1858 and 1859 with the creation of hundreds of different privately minted varieties, most in copper and about 32 mm diameter.

A copper medalet depicting Charles I. Bushnell, one of America's most prominent numismatists in 1859. (Augustus Sage's Numismatic Gallery No. 1)

Proof coins became popular in 1858, and an estimated 210 sets of silver denominations were sold, plus a larger number of copper-nickel Flying Eagle cents. Proof gold coins were available singly, and the dollar was the most popular denomination in this metal, probably with a sale of a few dozen or so.

In the meantime James Ross Snowden, Mint director since 1853, was receiving continuous requests for restrikes of earlier coins (heretofore usually granted) and new patterns. Snowden was a numismatist and decided to vastly expand the Mint Cabinet's holding of George Washington–related tokens and medals. He offered to exchange restrikes and rarities for needed pieces. In the spring of 1859 the coining of special coins went "underground," no information was released, and *The Nation*, a popular journal, later estimated that by 1860 Mint officials had pocketed at least $60,000 secretly and without benefit to the government. This largesse would continue unabated until the summer of 1885.

In a way numismatists can be grateful for this illegal activity, for probably at least 90 percent of the nineteenth-century pattern coins in existence today were produced secretly! The logic of this can be contemplated.

Meanwhile, coin auctions became more frequent, and in 1859 dealer Sage cataloged four sales in New York City, more than any other professional. In Philadelphia, Edward Cogan and William K. Idler became important in the coin trade. Henry Cook bought and sold coins in Boston, another shop was open in Baltimore, and a few more were scattered here and there. The first really large and impressive book for coin collectors was published that year, the *American Numismatical Manual*, by Dr. Montroville W. Dickeson.

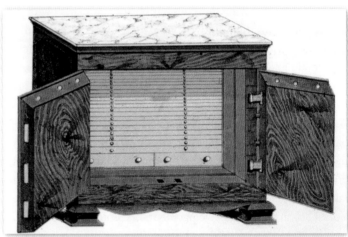

A wooden cabinet with sliding drawers was the standard way to store and display a rare-coin collection, as seen in this 1859 illustration in the *American Numismatical Manual*.

THE 1860s AND THE CIVIL WAR

In 1860 and 1861 in Denver the banking firm of Clark, Gruber & Co., headquartered in Leavenworth, Kansas, set up a private mint and bank, and coined $2.50, $5, $10, and $20 gold pieces from local bullion. The district was in the middle of the "Pikes Peak or Bust" gold boom. Such coins were also made in 1861.

The swelling number of incoming enthusiasts electrified the coin market. Most in demand were the old copper cents, but the hottest area in terms of rapid price appreciation was the specialty of Washington pieces. Collectors scrambled to buy them in competition with Director Snowden. Prices multiplied, and specimens were hard to find.

The Clark, Gruber & Co. bank and mint in Denver in 1861. In 1862 the facility
was acquired by the Treasury Department. It was renamed the Denver
Mint but functioned only as an assay office and did not produce coins.

The 1860 presidential election fielded four candidates: Abraham Lincoln, Republican Party from Illinois; John C. Breckinridge, Southern Democratic Party from Kentucky; John C. Bell, Constitution Union Party from Tennessee; and Stephen A. Douglas, Northern Democratic Party from Illinois. In the November contest Lincoln, who campaigned as a staunch abolitionist, won by a landslide. This prompted South Carolina to secede from the

An 1860 Lincoln token for the presidential campaign.

Union on December 20, followed by six other Southern states in short order. These formed the Confederate States of America (CSA) in January 1861, with its capital in Montgomery, Alabama (moved later in the year to Richmond, Virginia).

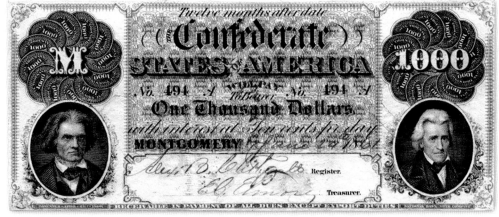

$1,000 note printed for the Confederate States of America by the
National Bank Note Company, New York City, in March 1861.

At first, many in the Confederacy hoped to have favorable relations with the Union as a separate nation and trading partner. The first CSA issues of paper money and the first bonds were printed to its order by the National Bank Note and American Bank Note companies in New York City. Lincoln was inaugurated on March 4, 1861. Relations deteriorated. In the second week of April CSA forces at Fort Moultrie on the shore of Charleston Harbor bombarded and destroyed federal Fort Sumter, but allowed the men there to escape under a white flag to board a steamship for the North.

The War of the Rebellion, later generally called the Civil War (or, in the South, the War of Northern Aggression), began. The Northerners or Yankees perceived this as a quick win—the mighty industrial North against the primarily agricultural South. President Lincoln called for 90-day enlistments, by which time it was thought the war would certainly be over. Reality proved otherwise, and it was not until late July that the first important battle took place, at Bull Run in Manassas, Virginia, not far from the Union capital of Washington, D.C. To the surprise of the North, the Confederate troops won.

Under the Act of July 17, 1861, the Treasury Department issued $50,000,000 in Demand Notes, the first widely circulated paper money since Revolutionary times. To facilitate their acceptance, they could be exchanged at par for gold coins. Additional Demand Notes were authorized in February 1862. The story of federal paper money from this point onward is extensive and complex, beyond the purview of *Mega Red*, although scattered mentions are included here.

Meanwhile, in the Confederate States of America, coins all but disappeared. The Confederacy contemplated issuing a new series of half dollars with a unique design, but the coinage amounted to only four patterns. The *Richmond Enquirer*, December 31, 1861, reported that entrepreneurs were paying 30 to 50 percent premium in paper money to buy silver and gold coins: "The present price of specie will be hereafter quoted through all time as a damning stigma upon the character of Southern merchants." By that time Confederate paper money circulated widely through the region. Such bills continued to be issued into 1864 and steadily depreciated in value.

The bombardment of federal Fort Sumter in the harbor of Charleston, South Carolina on April 12, 1861, by cannon at Fort Moultrie on the shore.

By December 1861 the war was not going well for either side. In the North, citizens became apprehensive and began to hoard gold and silver. By early 1862, such coins were worth a small premium in terms of paper money, the latter being in the form of bills issued by banks. Things went from bad to worse after the Act of February 25, 1862, authorized the issue of a new series of paper money, Legal Tender notes, not redeemable in coins, but only exchangeable for other paper money.

Jefferson Davis, president of the Confederate States of America. (portrait by Mathew Brady)

General Robert E. Lee, commander of the Confederate forces.

Union soldiers taking a break.

The Confederate ironclad CSS *Merrimac* (center) and the Union USS *Monitor*, in the first battle of ironclad ships, off of Norfolk, Virginia, ended in a draw but revolutionized naval warfare.

Legal Tender Notes authorized in early 1862 were exchangeable at par only for other bank notes and not for gold or silver coins. The monetary system became disruptive.

Coin hoarding increased, and by summer 1862 no silver or gold coins were to be seen anywhere in circulation in the East or Midwest. Money brokers conducted a lively exchange business with investors and speculators, and daily prices were quoted for silver and gold coins. Proof coins continued to be minted for collectors, but the Philadelphia Mint would not accept Legal Tender notes at par for them. Instead, numismatists had to go to money brokers and buy regular coins for a premium, then send these coins to the Mint, with extra coins for the proofing charge, to obtain such sets. As a result mintages were low.

Postage Currency notes with stamp designs, 5 cents to 50 cents, were issued by the Treasury in the summer of 1862 at a time when no coins were in circulation.

On the West Coast it was a different monetary story from the scenario in the East. The California State Legislature had made the use of paper money *illegal* in commerce, beginning in 1850. When the federal government started sending Legal Tender and other notes to the West, such as to pay soldiers and government employees, these bills were accepted only at a deep discount. "Hard money" in the form of silver and gold coins continued to trade there at face value during the conflict, continuing into the 1870s.

By the second week of July, 1862, even one-cent pieces were hoarded in the East and Midwest.

More than 30 merchants issued encased postage stamps beginning in the summer of 1862, using stamps from 1¢ to 90¢ values.

To facilitate commerce, a flood of paper scrip notes (3¢, 5¢, 10¢, and 25¢ were the most popular denominations) and even postage stamps was used as money. John Gault patented his encased postage stamps, with a regular stamp, from 1¢ to 90¢, mounted behind clear mica in a brass case—intended to be durable in circulation. Soon a flood of federal Postage Currency notes appeared, followed by Fractional Currency, eventually swelling to many millions of dollars in 3¢, 5¢, 10¢, 15¢, 25¢, and 50¢ denominations. Legal Tender notes rolled off the printing presses, and a new series of National Bank notes appeared.

Civil War tokens of bronze and brass were issued by the millions. Dates range from 1861 to 1864 but most bear the year 1863. These featured many different motifs, ranging from historical portraits to war heroes and scenes, to advertisements for more than 900 stores and services. Sutlers—licensed merchants who mostly traveled with the troops—issued tokens as well. At the very outset these became popular with numismatists and have remained a popular specialty ever since.

In 1862 the United States government purchased the private mint of Clark, Gruber & Co. and designated it as the Denver Mint in its reports for the next several decades, but no coins were struck there. Years later in 1906 another Denver Mint was opened and was the first facility there to make coins.

The Act of April 22, 1864, provided that bronze alloy be used for cents and the new two-cent denomination, and it made the cent legal tender up to the amount of 10¢ and the two-cent piece legal tender up to 20¢. Thus, for the first time, coins other than silver or gold became legal tender in the United States. It is a curious fact that the old copper half cents and cents (of 1793–1857) were not legal tender, and anyone had the right to refuse them in payment for debts. The motto IN GOD WE TRUST was employed on the two-cent piece, the first use of this for circulating coins. Later, it would be added to most other coins. After the spring of 1864 federal cents returned to circulation, including millions of hoarded pieces.

A Civil War token issued by
Sherwood & Hopson, Utica, New York.

In July 1864 in the East it took $285 in Legal Tender bills to buy $100 in gold coins from a money broker or exchange office, the all-time high for the Civil War period.[7] On the West Coast the situation was the opposite: coins were plentiful in stores, banks, and elsewhere; paper bills brought from the East remained illegal in commerce, but could be bought or sold to money brokers at a discount deep enough to equal the premium on gold and silver coins in the East. If at a particular time it took $285 in Legal Tender notes to buy $100 in gold coins in New York, then in San Francisco anyone with $100 in gold coins could go to an exchange dealer and buy $285 in Legal Tender notes.

A token issued by Harvey Lewis, sutler
to the 23rd Massachusetts regiment.

Silver and gold coins were anticipated to soon return to circulation when the Civil War ended in April 1865. However, the public remained wary of all of the paper bills in commerce, and silver and gold remained at a premium. It was not until years later, in April 1876, that silver coins were again exchangeable at par with paper, and not until December 1879 that gold and paper were equal. By those times in the 1870s a generation of children had grown into adulthood without seeing a single silver or gold coin in circulation!

In the meantime in the 1860s numismatics prospered. On February 22, 1860, the Washington Cabinet was opened at the Mint and featured the vastly

In 1864 the two-cent piece was introduced,
the first circulating coin to have the motto
IN GOD WE TRUST. These did not prove to
be popular and were discontinued in 1873.

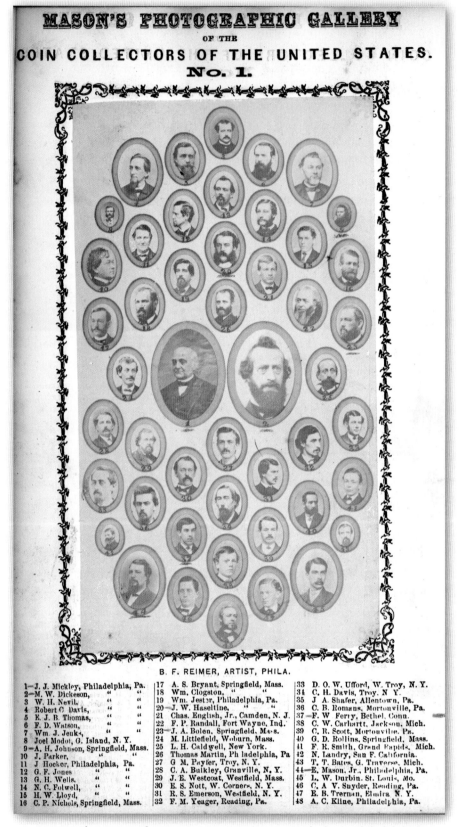

MASON'S PHOTOGRAPHIC GALLERY
OF THE
COIN COLLECTORS OF THE UNITED STATES.
No. 1.

B. F. REIMER, ARTIST, PHILA.

1—J. J. Mickley, Philadelphia, Pa.	17 A. S. Bryant, Springfield, Mass.	33 D. O. W. Ufford, W. Troy, N. Y.
2—M. W. Dickeson, " "	18 Wm. Clogston, " "	34 C. H. Davis, Troy, N. Y.
3 W. H. Nevil, " "	19 Wm. Jester, Philadelphia, Pa.	35 J. A. Shafer, Allentown, Pa.
4 Robert C. Davis, " "	20—J. W. Haseltine, " "	36 C. B. Romans, Mortonville, Pa.
5 E. J. B. Thomas, " "	21 Chas. English, Jr., Camden, N. J.	37—F. W. Ferry, Bethel, Conn.
6 F. D. Watson, " "	22 F. P. Randall, Fort Wayne, Ind.	38 C. W. Carhartt, Jackson, Mich.
7—Wm. J. Jenks, " "	23—J. A. Bolen, Springfield, Mass.	39 C. R. Scott, Mortonville, Pa.
8 Joel Modot, G. Island, N. Y.	24 M. Littlefield, Woburn, Mass.	40 G. D. Rollins, Springfield, Mass.
9—A. H. Johnson, Springfield, Mass.	25 L. H. Caldwell, New York.	41 F. R. Smith, Grand Rapids, Mich.
10 J. Parker, " "	26 Thomas Martin, Philadelphia, Pa	42 N. Landry, San F. California.
11 J Hocker, Philadelphia, "	27 G. M. Payfer, Troy, N. Y.	43 T. T. Bates, G. Traverse, Mich.
12 G. F. Jones, " "	28 C. A. Bulkley, Granville, N. Y.	44—E. Mason, Jr., Philadelphia, Pa.
13 G. H. Wells, " "	29 J. E. Westcoat, Westfield, Mass.	45 L. W. Durbin, St. Louis, Mo.
14 N. C. Folwell, " "	30 E. S. Nott, W. Corners, N. Y.	46 C. A. V. Snyder, Reading, Pa.
15 H. W. Lloyd, " "	31 R. S. Emerson, Westfield, N. Y.	47 E. B. Trernan, Elmira, N. Y.
16 C. P. Nichols, Springfield, Mass.	32 F. M. Yeager, Reading, Pa.	48 A. C. Kline, Philadelphia, Pa.

In 1869 Ebenezer Locke Mason Jr., a prominent coin dealer in Philadelphia,
published *Mason's Photographic Gallery of the Coin Collectors of the United States.*

expanded display gathered by Director James Ross Snowden. Auctions became a regular feature in the 1860s, and dozens of important sales were conducted by W. Elliot Woodward, Edward D. Cogan, and others. Usually, the sales were held in commercial auction rooms and conducted by a professional auctioneer, not the writer of the catalog. Such auction firms usually sold other things as well, including books, art, and furniture.

In 1865 the nickel three-cent piece was introduced to facilitate commerce, as silver coins were still being hoarded.

In 1866 the first regularly issued coin magazine, the *American Journal of Numismatics*, was published by the American Numismatic and Archaeological Society, successor in 1864 to the short-lived 1858–1859 American Numismatic Society. In the same decade Ebenezer Locke Mason Jr., a Philadelphia coin dealer, issued his own combined news magazine and price list. There were no grading standards and no single source to learn coin mintages and market prices. Accordingly, it devolved upon every successful collector and dealer to spend time to learn the intricacies of the hobby. This resulted in deep bonding with numismatics, and most serious numismatists remained in the field for many years.

The nickel five-cent piece made its debut in the summer of 1865 and largely replaced the three-cent piece. The larger denomination proved to be popular and has been made nearly continuously ever since.

THE 1870s AND 1880s

The Carson City Mint was opened in Nevada 1870 to coin silver and gold from Virginia City and the Comstock Lode. Each coin bore a CC mintmark. The facility produced silver and gold coins through 1885 and again from 1889 to 1893. The career of the mint was somewhat checkered—interlaced with politics. Much silver and gold was shipped from Virginia City to the distant San Francisco Mint instead of 15 miles away to the Carson City Mint. Today the Nevada State Museum is housed there. CC-mintmark coins are especially highly prized by numismatists.

In the 1870s the prices of most coins, tokens, and medals rose steadily, although Washington pieces, once the darlings of the market, fell from favor. Changes were in the wind, and among many other provisions, the Coinage Act of 1873 abolished the two-cent piece, silver three-cent piece, and half dime, provided for the new trade dollar denomination, and slightly increased the authorized weights of dimes, quarter dollars, and half dollars

The Carson City Mint.

(which subsequently were made with arrowheads at the date to indicate the different standard). The standard silver dollar was not treated in the act, and this denomination therefore lapsed.

Soon, there was a popular outcry that the act was unfavorable to silver-mining interests and citizens of Western states, and the legislation became known as the "Crime of '73." Some politicians said that the act was rushed through passage, they did not have time to study it, did not realize the standard dollar would be discontinued,

The Gould & Curry mine and mill in Virginia City, the largest producer of silver and gold in the Comstock Lode.

did not like the idea of the gold dollar becoming important by this default, would not have voted for it if they had been aware of its implications, etc. However, the *Congressional Record* shows very clearly that Western legislators studied and debated the bill at length before its passage. Later historians have been largely unaware of this.

In 1874 the San Francisco Mint was relocated to a new facility that would remain in operation until 1937. Modern equipment and the latest amenities were put in place. The cornerstone was laid in 1870 and included examples of the coinage of that year. Of the 1870-S half dime and $3 gold coin only one example of each is known today and of the 1870-S silver dollar only about a dozen.

In 1875 a new denomination, the 20-cent piece, was introduced with the expectation that it would be useful in the West, but the public confused the coins with quarter dollars, and in 1876 the mintage was sharply decreased. Only Proofs were made for collectors in 1877 and 1878, after which production was discontinued.

During the decade the price of silver declined on world markets. In the United States, increasing production in Nevada plus new discoveries,

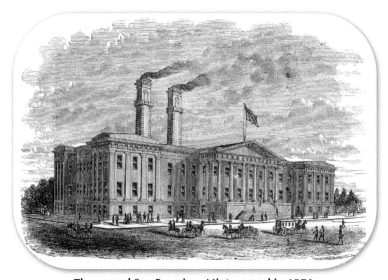

The second San Francisco Mint opened in 1874.

An 1875-S 20-cent piece.

including in the Leadville, Colorado, district, resulted in a glut of the metal. Free Silverites, as pro-silver advocates were called, pressured politicians to abandon gold and institute silver as the dominant coinage metal. From the late 1870s onward this was the overwhelming political question in America, and it remained so until the presidential election of 1896.

After about April 20, 1876, the price of silver coins reached parity with Silver Certificates and other paper money. Citizens, exchange brokers, and banks who had been hoarding quantities of coins since 1862 turned them loose, resulting in a large glut of coins from half dimes to half dollars flooding circulation. Because of this, most mintages of quarters and half dollars dropped to low levels through the end of the Liberty Seated design in 1891.

A notable political boondoggle to support the sagging market for silver bullion, the Bland-Allison Act of February 28, 1878, directed the government to purchase millions of ounces of silver each year and coin the metal into dollars. The talents of assistant engraver George T. Morgan were tapped for the design, based on an 1877 pattern half dollar. Hundreds of millions of these dollars were made through 1921 and mainly stored in bank vaults. Today Morgan silver dollars are the most popular nineteenth-century coins from a numismatic viewpoint, from the later release of millions of coins.

The new 1878 Morgan silver dollar.

In December 1879 the value of gold coins achieved parity with Legal Tender Notes on the markets, and long-stored gold coins came out of hiding and were once again seen in commerce. By this time the public had good faith in paper money with the result that the widespread use of gold in everyday transactions was mainly confined to the Western states.

A great speculation arose in gold dollars. All available supplies were bought, and the market price rose to a modest premium. New pieces produced at the Philadelphia Mint yielded instant profits for those who were lucky enough to obtain and resell them. Investment interest in gold dollars continued for the rest of the decade. As a result in today's market Mint State gold dollars of 1879 to 1889 are plentiful in relation to their low mintages, while most earlier dates are rare in this state of preservation. At the same time a "bubble" rose in the market for Proof silver trade dollars, a denomination that had not been made in circulation-strike form after early 1878. Speculators scrambled to order 1879 Proofs from the Mint, and the production jumped up to 1,541 pieces (as compared to only 900 Proofs in 1878). The excitement continued, and in 1880 the Mint set a record of 1,987 Proofs. The passion faded, and in 1881 just 960 Proofs were struck.

The New Orleans Mint, closed since early 1861, was refurbished in 1878 and reopened for business in 1879. Silver and gold coins would be made there until 1909, after which time the building was used for other purposes. Today it houses a museum.

In January 1883 the new Liberty Head nickel without CENTS on the reverse created a nationwide sensation. Sharpers gold-plated them and passed them off as $5 gold coins. It was stated in many newspaper articles that the Mint had made a terrible mistake and would be recalling all examples, after which they would have great value. Excitement prevailed, and thousands of newcomers entered the hobby. In the meantime, the coins

The first 1883 Liberty Head nickels had the denomination expressed only by the letter V, prompting some sharpers to gold-plate them and pass them as $5 gold coins.

never did become rare, as many were minted and large quantities were saved. Still, the craze was good for the hobby, as countless thousands of citizens went from the new nickels to collect other coins.

The market went into overdrive. Many dealers opened up shops, several issued their own magazines (Ed Frossard's *Numisma* and Scott Stamp & Coin Company's *Coin Collector's Journal* notable among them), and the field of auction catalogers grew as well. John W. Haseltine and the Chapman brothers (S. Hudson and Henry) created many memorable sales, with the 1882 Bushnell Collection by the Chapmans being the most exciting auction event of the decade.

T. Harrison Garrett, of Baltimore, and Lorin G. Parmelee, of Boston, became known as super-collectors, snatching up rarities. Rare coins furnished fodder for newspapers, and metropolitan dailies carried many accounts of rare 1804 silver dollars being sold at auction, or old Massachusetts Pine Tree shillings being found buried in the ground, and more. All during this scenario, the prices of scarce and rare early United States coins continued to rise. During the 1880s a dozen or more newspapers devoted to collecting coins, stamps, Indian relics, and other things were published, often with news on multiple fields of interest.

In 1888 *The Numismatist* began publication under the auspices of Dr. George F. Heath, a Monroe, Michigan, physician who was a deeply knowledgeable collector and a skilled writer. It has endured and today is the official publication of the American Numismatic Association, as it has been for many years.

The Coinage Act of 1889 discontinued the nickel three-cent piece and the gold $1 and $3.

The decade of the 1880s had been a golden era for many activities. More county and other history books were published than in any such period before, railroad and ocean-travel facilities were more elegant than ever, and the outlook was rosier than it had been in a long time. In the Midwest many towns rose from the land as boulevards, buildings, rail lines, and other construction took place.

Things changed. Late in the decade storm clouds rose on the economic horizon, mainly due to over-speculation in land and buildings in the prairie states. Bonds to furnish large-scale expansion had been issued at interest rates of 8 to 10 percent, several points more than comparable securities issued in the East paid. Large amounts of money flowed into Iowa, Nebraska, and other states. Then came reality. Municipalities and others were not able to maintain interest payments and there were many bankruptcies.

THE 1890s INTO THE 1900s

By 1890 there were coin dealers in most cities in the eastern part of the United States, with Boston, New York City, and Philadelphia the central points of activity. J.W. Scott. W. Elliot Woodward, the auction firm of Bangs, Merwin & Co., the Chapman brothers, John Haseltine, Lyman H. Low, Ed. Frossard, and Charles Steigerwalt were among the leading professionals of the day. In 1890 New York Coin & Stamp Co. conducted the sale of the Lorin G. Parmelee Collection, the second finest cabinet (after T. Harrison Garrett's) in private hands in America. Results were mixed, and Parmelee, hardly a motivated seller, bought many of the rarities back. The coin market was entering a chilly period as was the national economy. Difficult times lay ahead.

In November 1891 in Chicago the American Numismatic Association (ANA) was formed, thus providing a common meeting place for the exchange of ideas and values among collectors from all parts of the United States and elsewhere. Beginners and amateurs were encouraged to join, while some other societies preferred numismatists with experience. Charles E. Barber's Liberty Head silver dime, quarter, and half dollar, called "Barber coins" today, were first issued in 1892. Public and numismatic interest was lukewarm.

An 1894 proposal for the American Numismatic Association seal, and one later adopted.

An 1892-O Barber dime. Dimes, quarters, and half dollars designed by Chief Engraver Charles E. Barber were introduced in this year and remained in use until 1916 for the dime and quarter and 1915 for the half dollar.

The 1892 Columbian souvenir half dollar, as it was called, was produced in the year before the World's Columbian Exposition opened to the public. This was the first United States commemorative coin.

The World's Columbian Exposition was planned to open in Chicago in 1892 to celebrate the 400th anniversary of Christopher Columbus's landing in the New World. Progress was slower than anticipated, and it did not open to the public until 1893. Attractions included dozens of impressive buildings, the gigantic Ferris Wheel, and extensive exhibits of art, culture, and industry. America's first commemorative coins were issued for this event, initiating a numismatic specialty that eventually included hundreds of varieties and remains dynamic to the present day.

To this point numismatists had little interest in collecting coins by mintmark varieties. Whether a coin had an S, D, or other letter was of no importance. It was just the date of the coin that mattered. This began to change in 1893 when Augustus G. Heaton, a professional artist by trade and a numismatist by avocation, published a treatise on coins from the United States branch mints. In time such branch-mint rarities as the 1894-S dime and 1876-CC twenty-cent piece attracted notice. Interest in mintmarked gold coins developed much more slowly and did not become widely popular until decades later in the 1930s.

Speculation in prairie lands, unwise loans, and unbridled growth of the 1880s came together in the Panic of 1893. Times were difficult, many banks failed, and there was political unrest. Participants in the Free Silver movement, a political philosophy which had been gaining adherents since the 1870s, became especially vocal. It was felt by this faction that reliance on gold was hindering national growth and prosperity, and that American coinage and international trade should be based on silver, a metal in oversupply.

The government policy of coining large amounts of silver into dollar coins was part of the "Silver Question," the pivotal political debate of the era. As the poor economic climate continued, the supply of gold coins in the United States Treasury fell to $41 million due to large exports of double eagles. Foreign interests were fearful that the Silverites would convince the government to allow overseas debts to be paid in silver dollars (the intrinsic worth of which kept declining and were worth about 48 cents each) and demanded gold. Banker J.P. Morgan and his associates stepped in to augment the gold reserves, one of the most embarrassing points in American financial history.

Silver, in oversupply in relation to the market, continued to be produced in large quantities. Shown are silver ingots at the American Smelter in Leadville, Colorado, in 1893.

Several conventions were staged by advocates of free and unlimited coinage of silver to support the diminishing market. In an 1895 cartoon, "turtles" of silver dollars, marked "Real Value 50 Cents," are about to plunge into financial oblivion over a waterfall—suggesting what might happen to the American economy if such practice was continued. The presidential election of 1896 focused on silver and pitted Democrat William Jennings Bryan against Republican William McKinley. Bryan's "Cross of Gold" speech electrified the nation and gave momentum to the Free Silver movement and "easy money," promising Midwesterners and others in distress the ability to pay their debts more readily. McKinley won, and the silver movement faded sharply, although remnants lingered into the new century. Bryan ran for president on the Democratic ticket in 1900 and 1908 and lost both times.

In the 1890s gold strikes in the Cripple Creek District of Colorado starting early in the decade, followed by the Klondike Gold Rush of the late 1890s, yielded vast quantities of precious metals, much of which were coined into double eagles at the San Francisco Mint. Both events electrified the country with tales of adventures and fortunes and newspaper coverage knew no limits.

The discovery in the early 1890s of gold-bearing calaverite and telluride ore in the Cripple Creek District on the west side of Pikes Peak created a great rush that resulted in a population of more than 100,000 people by the turn of the century. An estimated $400 million in gold was extracted in an era in which the metal was worth $20.67 per ounce. The Cripple Creek District included Victor, Altman, and other communities. Shown is the panorama in 1895.

The Portland Mine on Battle Mountain, Victor, in 1896, the largest mine in the Cripple Creek District.

Main Street in Dawson City in 1898, the largest settlement in the Klondike district.

The Klondike on the Yukon River in British Columbia and Alaska yielded large amounts of gold late in the 1890s, much of which went to the San Francisco Mint to be coined into double eagles. Shown are adventurers in Chilkoot Pass, above Skagway, Alaska, on the way to the gold district.

In 1901 the third Philadelphia Mint was opened and would remain in use until 1966. All equipment and facilities were state of the art. The engraving and die-making departments continued to be centered there and served the branch mints.

In September of the same year President William McKinley was assassinated while attending the Pan-American Exposition in Buffalo, New York. Vice President Theodore Roosevelt succeeded him in the post.

In 1903 the United States began minting coins specifically for the Philippines, which had been a U.S. possession since the conclusion of the Spanish-American War in 1898. The coins featured the name UNITED STATES OF AMERICA and also the Spanish name FILIPINAS, along with designs by Filipino artist Melecio Figueroa.

The new Philadelphia Mint opened in 1901.

A silver peso minted for the Philippines under U.S. administration.

The Main Coining Room in the new Mint, with rows of electrically driven presses.

In 1904 the Louisiana Purchase Exposition opened in St. Louis. In connection with it two varieties of 1903 gold dollars were minted, the first U.S. commemoratives in that metal.

In 1906 the new Denver Mint opened for business and struck silver and gold coins. It was not until 1911 that copper coins were made there. Its coins bore a D mintmark, a letter that had been used earlier by the Dahlonega Mint from 1838 to 1861.

In April 1906 San Francisco was ravaged by a strong earthquake followed by a fire that leveled most of the commercial district of the city. The Mint was the only building remaining intact in its area and served as a headquarters for relief efforts as well as financial activity.

In 1904 President Roosevelt visited the Smithsonian Institution, a short distance from the White House, and was impressed with the beautiful artistry of ancient Greek coins on display. Not long afterward he determined to make American coins more attractive than ever before, replacing the current designs. He tapped Augustus Saint-Gaudens, America's most famous sculptor, to redesign the entire coinage spectrum from the cent to the double eagle. The artist's first effort was the $20 coin, the new design being in medallic high relief and the 1907 date in Roman numerals as MCMVII. On the obverse was *Victory* holding a palm branch, and on the reverse was a flying eagle. The sculptor redesigned he $10 eagle with an

The Denver Mint with the Colorado State Capitol in the distance. The facility was greatly expanded in 1937 and remains in use today.

Looking toward Market Street in San Francisco after the earthquake of April 18, 1906, with the fire beginning to consume most of the city.

After the fire the San Francisco Mint was the only building that remained standing. It served as a relief center and also assisted with banking.

Indian Head. Saint-Gaudens passed away in August 1907. The redesign of coinage by artists in the private sector was continued in later years with all other denominations.

The high relief of the MCMVII $20 caused production problems, and Chief Engraver Charles E. Barber changed the design to low relief and the date to regular numerals. Only 12,367 of the MCMVII coins were made, but they were so popular with the public and with numismatists that enough were saved that about half the mintage survives today.

In the same year the $2.50 and $5 gold coins were redesigned by Bela Lyon Pratt, with a recessed relief design. This met with uniformly negative reaction by collectors and dealers as expressed in pages of *The Numismatist*. Starting with each of the four gold denominations in 1908 the Sand Blast Proof finish took the place of the mirror style used in earlier years. These new Proofs were unpopular with collectors, and in the next year Satin Finish Proofs succeeded them. These also generated complaints, and in 1911 the Sand Blast Proofs were resumed, to continue in the gold series to 1915.

The MCMVII (1907) High Relief double eagle by Augustus Saint-Gaudens.

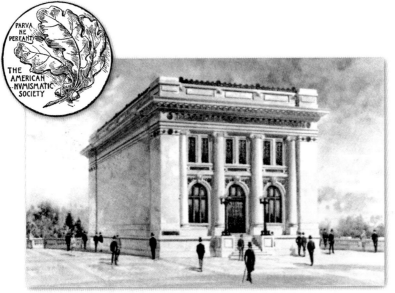

In 1908 Indian Head cents were struck at the San Francisco Mint, the first branch-mint coinage of a minor (non–precious metal) denomination. In the same year the American Numismatic Society ("and Archaeological" having been dropped from its name) moved into a handsome new stone building, largely financed by Archer M. Huntington (stepson of railroad magnate Collis P. Huntington), on Audubon Terrace, Morningside Heights, New York City. An additional gift from Huntington added an adjacent matching building in the early 1930s.

The 1908 $2.50 designed by Bela Lyon Pratt. $5 coins were made with the same motif.

The 1907 Indian Head $10 by Saint-Gaudens.

In August 1909 the new Lincoln design for the cent was issued, created by Victor D. Brenner, a sculptor and medalist of renown. It the latest in the series of motifs designed by artists in the private sector. The first issues had the initials V.D.B. on the reverse, but a controversy arose, and they were soon removed, by which time 27,995,000 had been made at the Philadelphia Mint. Only 484,000 were made of the San Francisco issue (1909-S V.D.B.), creating a numismatic rarity. Proofs for collectors were in the Matte style, not much different from circulation strikes upon quick glance, and were not popular.

The 1909-S V.D.B. Lincoln cent became the key to the series and remains a numismatic favorite today.

The rare-coin market had been very strong during the decade, with steady rises in the number of collectors and in values. Collecting coins by mintmarks had not become widely popular yet, but the 1909-S V.D.B. cent, which quickly went up in value to 5¢, then 10¢, then higher, prompted many more numismatists to pay attention to branch-mint issues.

The decade saw many innovations and expansions including the vastly increased popularity of the automobile and the dawn of the age of aviation. Prosperity was the order of the era, and the difficulties of the 1890s were largely forgotten.

Orville Wright and the first powered heavier-than-air craft at Kill Devil Hill on December 17, 1903, inaugurating the aviation age.

By 1910, automobiles were a familiar sight all across America. Shown is a Hupmobile of that year.

THE 1910s AND 1920s

In 1912 the first branch-mint nickel coins were struck at the Denver and San Francisco mints. This was the last year of the Liberty Head design (although a few 1913 coins were privately made the next year). In 1913 the Buffalo or Indian Head five-cent piece, by sculptor James Earle Fraser, was released and achieved wide popularity.

To observe the opening of the Panama Canal (in 1914) and the rebirth of the city after the fire and earthquake of 1906, the Panama-Pacific Exposition in San Francisco offered a grand "city" of elegant buildings with many displays and attractions. Coin dealer Farran Zerbe had charge of selling commemorative coins of the half dollar, gold dollar, $2.50, and two varieties of the $50 denominations. The American Numismatic Association held its annual convention in the same city this year, but attendance was very low, due in part to the unpopularity of Zerbe and certain questionable actions he had with the ANA earlier when he served as president (such as rigging an election).

Production of Sand Blast Proof gold coins ended in 1915, and 1916 was the last year for Matte Proof cents and nickels. These finishes were very unpopular with collectors, who preferred the older style "brilliant" or "mirror" field type. Protests to no avail had been made to the Mint by the New York Numismatic Club and others. It was not until 1936 that Proof coins, then of the popular mirror finish, were again available to collectors.

In 1916 the denominations of silver coins then being struck were given new designs, much to the enthusiasm and acclamation not only of the numismatic community but of the public as well. The new "Mercury" or Winged Liberty Head dime was created by Adolph A. Weinman, the Standing Liberty quarter dollar by Hermon A. MacNeil, and the Liberty Walking half dollar by Weinman. The 1916-D dime and the 1916 Standing Liberty quarter became rarities due to their low mintages.

The World War had been raging in Europe since August 1914. In 1916 many Americans joined the English and French and other forces opposing the German troops of Kaiser Wilhelm II and his allies.

In 1913 the Buffalo nickel, as it came to be called, was introduced with a design by sculptor James Earle Fraser. The obverse depicted a Native American and the reverse a bison. The motif was continued through 1938.

The 1916 Winged Liberty Head or "Mercury" dime by Adolph A. Weinman.

The 1916 Standing Liberty quarter by Hermon A. MacNeil.

The 1916 Walking Liberty half dollar by Adolph A. Weinman.

This was on a voluntary basis, such as service with the Red Cross and the airborne Lafayette Escadrille. In 1917 the United States declared war and many soldiers, sailors, and aviators volunteered for service. Liberty Bond campaigns were conducted across the land. Truce finally took place on November 11, 1918. The terms the victorious allies demanded of the Germans were very harsh, creating much turmoil during the next 15 years, including runaway inflation, which led to the rise of Adolph Hitler and the Nazi party in the early 1930s.

The war brought great prosperity to American industries supplying munitions, equipment, and other necessities of combat. Coin mintages reached record highs. The good times did not last, and from 1921 into 1923 the American economy took a nap. Coin mintages dropped precipitately. In 1922 no nickels, dimes, quarters, or regular-issue half dollars were made (although within the latter denomination there were some commemoratives).

In 1918 the Pittman Act resulted in the melting of 270,232,722 silver dollars in Treasury storage, to supply bullion to England to ship to India. None had been minted since 1904, and the denomination was believed to have been discontinued. At the Mint the models and master dies had been destroyed in 1910.

A Liberty Loan poster for the World War, 1917, designed by Howard Chandler Christy.

In February 1918 the Philippine Legislature passed an appropriations bill for construction of machinery for a new mint. The Philippines in that era was still under the administration of the United States, but moving steadily toward independence. The Manila Mint opened on July 15, 1920. Earlier U.S./Philippine coins had been struck in Philadelphia, San Francisco, and Denver. Now the islands had a domestic source for coinage, which would continue to operate until the Japanese military invaded in 1941.

In 1921 the Treasury gave a hurry-up call to mint more silver dollars to provide backing for Silver Certificates. The old Morgan design was remodeled slightly, and more than 85 million new dollars were struck at the Philadelphia, Denver, and San Francisco mints. The Treasury hoped for a new design, but that was not ready until December 1921, when 1,006,473 coins of the Peace design by sculptor Anthony de Francisci were struck. The Peace dollar design was continued to 1928 and again in 1934 and 1935.

Florida experienced a wild boom in real estate in 1924 and 1925, but the end came soon, in 1926. Acres of vacant home lots were left in planned communities. Not to worry, as overall the American economy experienced boom times—the "Roaring Twenties." Many skyscrapers were built in cities, luxury automobiles were all the rage, mansions were constructed—an era epitomized by novelist F. Scott Fitzgerald in *The Great Gatsby* and in a later retrospective history, *Only Yesterday*, by Frederick Lewis Allen. Riding along with the crest, in the next several years, rare books, art, and common stocks became investment sensations.

An official commemorative medal popularly known as the "Wilson Dollar" was struck to celebrate the 1920 opening of the Manila Mint.

The rare-coin market did not participate in the boom economy and remained very quiet. New York City dealer Thomas L. Elder lamented that the great collectors of yesteryear had not been replaced by a new generation of moneyed buyers. This had a bright side, in a way. When other markets collapsed in 1929, coins held their values fairly well. Several wealthy people who were hurt by the economic conditions of the early 1930s found comfort in the value of their coin collections—Waldo C. Newcomer of Baltimore being one. Great numismatic rarities sold slowly, but not at significant discounts.

In 1929 small-size bills replaced the large-size federal paper money in use since 1861.

Architect's illustration of the Empire State Building in New York City. Envisioned and designed during the late 1920s, it was built on the site of the first Waldorf-Astoria Hotel and opened in 1931. The top featured a mooring mast for passenger zeppelins but was never used for that purpose.

The Peace design silver dollar designed by Anthony de Francisci was first issued in 1921. With the design modified to lower relief in 1922, the motif continued in use through 1935.

THE 1930s AND THE DEPRESSION ERA

In the early 1930s the rare-coin market continued on a consistent basis. The only notable bankruptcy was the firm of Guttag Brothers, leading coin dealers in the 1920s whose main business was investment securities. In 1929 they moved into their new multi-story building in New York City. The business ran into trouble early that year and collapsed in early 1930, sustaining a loss reported as $9 million. In contrast other leading dealers such as B. Max Mehl in Texas, who had been prominent since the early 1900s, Thomas L. Elder, Wayte Raymond, John Macallister, and others continued to be profitable. Coin prices softened, as noted, but demand remained fairly strong.

Franklin D. Roosevelt entered the presidential race in 1932, running against incumbent Herbert Hoover. The latter promised that "recovery is just around the corner," but economic conditions worsened. Roosevelt promised the "New Deal," a change in policies. In November he won in a landslide. Inaugurated on March 4, 1933, he set about creating many new programs. He prohibited the further issuance of gold coins by the Treasury, although mintage of $10 and $20 gold coins continued for a while. Next came the demand that all citizens turn in gold coins, those of numismatic value and a small allowance per person excepted. In January 1934 America

The $10 and $20 denominations were the only gold coins struck in 1933.

abandoned the gold standard, resulting in runaway inflation of the prices of goods and services, particularly starting in the late 1930s when the Depression wound down.

The change in gold regulations had a dramatic effect on the numismatic market. All of a sudden collectors who had not paid much attention to gold coins set about forming sets and collections. Floyd Starr of Philadelphia and Louis E. Eliasberg of Baltimore were among the best known. Thomas L. Elder issued a premium guide he sent to bank tellers and others advising that many varieties of gold coins turned in to banks by the public had significant numismatic value. Countless thousands of scarce and rare coins were thus saved from destruction.

In New York City in 1933 Morton and Joseph Stack relocated from Wheeling, West Virginia, to set up a rare-coin dealership that soon expanded by leaps and bounds. In 1935 the firm held its first auction. In the meantime Thomas L. Elder and Wayte Raymond held many public auctions, and in Fort Worth, Texas, B. Max Mehl turned out a stream of mail auctions. He also published the *Star Rare Coin Encyclopedia* with buying prices, suggesting that treasures such as a 1913 Liberty Head nickel might be found in pocket change.

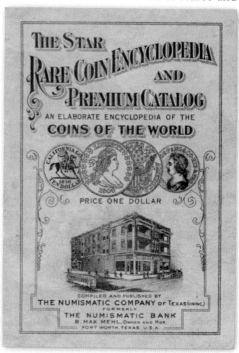

The *Star Rare Coin Encyclopedia* published by B. Max Mehl offered premiums for rare coins, including certain issues in circulation. In the 1930s the book was promoted by print advertising as well as a weekly radio program.

As curious as the scenario may seem to an economist or historian without numismatic knowledge, the 1930s saw the greatest market boom in coin-collecting history!

In the early 1930s the Scott Stamp & Coin Company under the direction of Wayte Raymond published the National line of cardboard coin-album pages. These had openings faced on the front and back with cellulose acetate slides, permitting coins to be easily stored and the obverse and reverse to be viewed. Dates and mintages were printed below each opening. This revolutionized numismatics. Now, instead of storing coins in wooden cabinets with trays, collectors could house them in convenient pages that fit into a notebook binder, and could examine the coins from both sides.

The race was on! In the depth of the Depression the hope was held to find in pocket change many coins that had numismatic value, such as the 1877 and 1909-S Indian Head cents, 1909-S V.D.B. and 1914-D Lincoln cents, and many others. The recently issued 1931-S cent with a low mintage of 866,000 coins created excitement, and nearly all were bought by dealers and collectors. Barber dimes, quarters, and half dollars could be found dating back to 1892, usually in About Good or Good grades, well-worn but exciting to collect and enjoy as hole after hole was filled in albums.

Helping matters was that hobbies were all the rage during this era. Crossword puzzles, games, hunting and fishing, and other pursuits drew many new participants. Many towns had shops that sold or rented jigsaw puzzles. Collecting scenic postcards achieved unprecedented popularity.

The National Coin Album line published by Scott Stamp & Coin Company, later by Wayte Raymond, Inc., did much to popularize the collecting of coins by dates and mintmarks.

Meanwhile in 1932 the new Washington quarter design by John Flanagan replaced the Standing Liberty motif in use since 1916 (excepting 1922 and 1931). It was intended as a circulating commemorative coin to honor the 200th anniversary of Washington's February 22, 1732, birth, but the Treasury Department decided to continue it as a regular design. Due to economic conditions, relatively few 1932 coins were saved by the general public and not many by numismatists either.

J.K. Post of Neenah, Wisconsin, in 1934 launched the Penny Collector board, a cardboard sheet with openings for each date and mintmark of Lincoln cent from 1909 to date. Western Publishing of Racine, Wisconsin, acquired the product and expanded it to include the Whitman line of boards and, in time, folders and albums.

While the preceding innovations were still in progress the commemorative-coin boom came next. This was launched by one man, Frank Dunn of Lexington, Kentucky, who was in charge of ordering and selling half dollars for the Boone Bicentennial in 1934. From his second-floor office in the Phoenix Hotel he sold 10,000 pieces for $1.60 each. At the time such coins could be ordered by various commissions (some of which were very questionable) who persuaded Congress to pass authorization. Coins were sent to the commissions for face value plus a small charge. The commissions were in charge of setting prices and policies—like coining your own money!

The year 1935 began in a normal way when 10,010 Boone halves were struck in Philadelphia in March and 5,005 each at the Denver and San Francisco mints in May. These were dated 1935 on the reverse of the coin, representing the issue date. Philadelphia coins were offered for $1.10 each, and $1.50 was charged for each Denver and San Francisco coin. A 1935 Boone set of three coins cost a total of $4.10. So far the only problem was that it was no longer the bicentennial of Boone's birthday, and there was no reason to continue celebrating a 1934 anniversary in 1935.[8]

Unexpectedly, in October 1935 at the Philadelphia Mint 10,008 more 1935-dated Boone half dollars were made but with the addition of 1934 / PIONEER YEAR in small numerals on the right side of the reverse. No excitement here, but why create the variety? Then came excitement that knew no bounds. In November the Denver and San Francisco mints produced the very small quantity of just 2,003 and 2,004, respectively, of the modified design. News releases calling attention to the rare issues were sent

A 1932-S
Washington quarter.

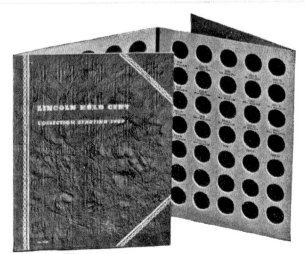

WHITMAN PUBLISHING CO.

Whitman Publishing entered the coin-supply business in 1934 and soon offered a line of boards, later followed by folders, as seen here. More people entered numismatics through the use of Lincoln cent folders than by any other method.

out by Dunn. New York City newspapers, among others, carried the information that a pair of low-mintage Boone half dollars had been created at the Denver and San Francisco mints and could be ordered for $3.70 by sending remittances to Dunn. This equaled $1.85 per coin—a truly affordable rarity. These were also advertised in *The Numismatist*. As might be expected for such an incredibly low mintage, orders rushed in. Not so fast! There was a problem. So far as is known (per research conducted years ago by Lee F. Hewitt) *everyone* who ordered received a "Sorry, sold out" letter. No exceptions! Dunn said that they had all been sold to those who had read newspaper accounts.

Detail of the reverse of the 1935-S Boone Bicentennial half dollar with small 1934, of which 2,000 were offered.

No collection was complete without these two coins. In an undisclosed way, some came on to the market, and the price rose to $50 per pair! Not long afterward it was discovered that most of the coins had been retained by Dunn! He was accused of fraud, and transferred many assets to his wife. However, he was never prosecuted, and he continued selling three-coin Boone sets yearly through 1938!

Thus was set the scene for much excitement, with the details of various issues being given later in this book. Many abuses took place. In late 1936, after *dozens* of new varieties had been introduced in that year, the market cooled. In 1939 Congress ended the largess by prohibiting further issues.

After the commemorative slump of late 1936 the overall coin market remained robust. A new monthly publication, *The Numismatic Scrapbook*, was launched by Lee F. Hewitt. Unlike *The Numismatist*, the *Scrapbook* emphasized the human interest side of numismatics rather than technical points and history. Reports of rare coins found in circulation, collector and dealer activities, and such make up most of the content. Quickly, it gained the largest subscription base of any numismatic publications. In the meantime *Hobbies* magazine had a monthly coin section.

In 1937 the third San Francisco Mint opened, replacing the facility in use since 1974. The building, with modernization in the intervening years, is still in use today.

In the same year the Federal Bullion Depository opened on the grounds of the Fort Knox military base in Kentucky. Double eagles and other federal gold coins dating back many years that had been stored in the Philadelphia Mint were melted and the metal was cast into gold ingots and shipped to Fort Knox. During this procedure some Mint employees substituted common-date $20 and other coins for those scheduled for melting, thus rescuing them for numismatic posterity. New York City dealers of the era eagerly purchased most of these coins, including 1933 $10 and $20 issues.

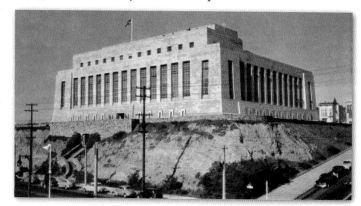

The third San Francisco Mint opened in 1937 on a prominent site overlooking the city.

The Federal Bullion Depository at Fort Knox, Kentucky.

In 1938 Felix O. Schlag entered a nationwide competition of about 300 artists vying to create a new design to replace the Buffalo nickel. His design won, and the obverse was selected. His reverse was considerably modified at the Mint.

In 1939 Nazi Germany went to war and overran Czechoslovakia. Other countries fell to the Nazis. Once again, American industries rose to supply forces opposing the Germans. The Depression ended, and the economy recovered, to go on to new highs.

The Jefferson nickel was introduced in 1938. Revised versions are still coined today.

The B-17 Flying Fortress bomber was developed in the 1930s and saw extensive use in Europe during World War II, especially with the 8th Air Force.

THE 1940s AND 1950s

In Europe World War II, as it was called, expanded as Adolf Hitler's Nazi troops overran France, Holland, Belgium, and other countries, meanwhile persecuting Jews, religious figures, and others, sending many to confinement and eventual death in concentration camps. Those who were fortunate fled, many finding asylum in America, including scientist Albert Einstein and professional numismatist Hans M.F. Schulman (whose other family members in Amsterdam perished). The Battle of Britain took place in 1940 with German bombers laying waste to large portions of London and with destruction in other areas (such as the famous cathedral in Coventry). America rushed to help with the Lend-Lease Act providing ships, exports of munitions, and more, including American men and women volunteers.

The United States officially entered the war after the "day of infamy," so called for Japan's unprovoked surprise attack on Pearl Harbor on December 7, 1941. War was also declared against other members of the Axis Powers—Germany and Italy (under dictator Benito Mussolini). In the Pacific Theater, more than a quarter million Filipino volunteers joined the American armed forces to fight off the Japanese. Then followed four more years of domestic and worldwide sacrifices, the details of which are well-known and beyond the scope of the present text.

After Proof sets were sold in 1942, production was stopped so as not to detract from the Mint's activity in providing record quantities of coins for circulation. To save copper, Lincoln cents were made of zinc-coated steel in 1943. The coins quickly tarnished and spotted, and bronze was resumed

In 1943 Lincoln cents were made of zinc-coated steel while copper was directed toward the war effort.

in 1944. The alloy of five-cent pieces was changed to eliminate nickel and to make silver the main metal, a policy continued through 1945.

By 1943 cash was plentiful, but consumer goods were scarce. Inflation was everywhere, despite federal efforts to control it. On September 10 and 11, 1943, New York City dealer Abe Kosoff conducted an auction of the Michael F. Higgy Collection. A bidding frenzy took place, and many coins sold for 5 to 10 times their pre-sale estimates! From that point, prices went onward and upward all across the market. Common-date double eagles were in particular demand, a place to put extra money, and sold for about $65 each.

In 1944 and 1945, the San Francisco, Denver, and Philadelphia mints were used to produce coins for the Philippines. These were then brought over by American military transport to aid commerce during the liberation of the islands from Japanese control.

In November 1946 *A Guide Book of United States Coins*, written by Richard S. Yeo (under the pen name of "R.S. Yeoman") with the technical assistance of Stuart Mosher, was published with a 1947 cover date. It went on to be published annually, selling tens of millions of copies over the ensuing decades. Although World War II was over, consumer goods were still scarce. There was much uncertainty as to the future of the economy—would it be booming, or would it bust? The rare-coin market continued to be a refuge for spare cash.

President Franklin D. Roosevelt, in office since 1933, died of natural causes while at Warm Springs, Georgia, in early 1945. The Treasury decided to honor him by changing the Mercury dime to his portrait as modeled by Chief Engraver John R. Sinnock. The 10-cent denomination was chosen because Roosevelt, stricken with a paralytic illness as young man, was the spokesperson for many years for the March of Dimes, a non-profit organization that raised money to combat polio (this was finally accomplished in 1955 with the vaccine of Dr. Jonas Salk).

Before long the coin market went into a slump. By 1947 consumer goods were becoming widely available. Money went to buy appliances,

A World War II centavo of the Philippines, minted in the United States.

In 1946 Whitman Publishing launched *A Guide Book of United States Coins* with the cover date of 1947. It went on to become the best-selling book in numismatic history.

The Roosevelt dime made its debut in 1946.

new homes springing up in vast developments, and other goods, and automobiles were beginning to be available. In this year and in 1948, prices of coins dropped across the board. Common-date double eagles that sold for $65 during the war now wholesaled below $40. Convention attendance dwindled. In retrospect, if there was ever a good time to *buy* coins in the postwar era it was now!

The very bottom was probably in early 1949.

Levittown, New York, in 1947, one of many communities and developments that sprung up to provide affordable housing for returning veterans and other buyers.

Not related to market prices at all, but in terms of numismatic history, 1949 is one of the most memorable years for it saw the publication of *Early American Cents*, by Dr. William H. Sheldon. The author, a psychologist and medical professor, billed himself as a scientist with the ability to analyze and make changes. With an office at Columbia University he had developed a new version of somatotypology by classifying people as *endomorphic*, *mesomorphic*, and *ectomorphic*, based on many photographs and measurements of nude figures taken at Ivy League schools. (Today this is dismissed as pseudo-science.) In numismatics he was a grand figure and respected for his knowledge.

For years the grading of coins was a problem, with no firmly established and globally recognized standards, and establishing market values involved a lot of guesswork. In the August 1949 issue of *The Numismatist* Abe Kosoff, one of America's leading coin dealers, told about Sheldon's forthcoming book, *Early American Cents*:

> Now comes one book that is complete within itself and is not only a list—it is a new treatment of the series. Order and system were applied to the identification, grading, and valuing of every known variety of early cent. Reference to the plates and tables makes it simple for even a novice to accurately identify and appraise the value of any of the early copper cents.

Guesswork was now replaced by science! His grading system, discussed earlier in the present text, was expanded beyond early cents to include coins in all series. (Unfortunately today it is in confusion.)

B. Max Mehl's sale of April 26, 1949, the Dr. Charles W. Green Collection, billed as the greatest gold coin sale ever held, broke price records left and right. Among the greatest rarities was a 1926-S double eagle, of which only three were said to be known. It realized $1,525, or more than double expectations.

All bets were off, and the room was up for grabs. All of a sudden, many collectors who had been inactive during the slump jumped back into the market with vigor. The

Early American Cents by William H. Sheldon, published in 1949, contained a market value and grading system that in time completely transformed American numismatics.

market became dynamic—more so than ever before when considered on a widespread basis from colonial coinage onward.

Secretly, James F. Kelly, a prominent Dayton, Ohio, dealer, had enlisted Paul Wittlin, a professional numismatist from California, to go to Europe and investigate reports of hoards of American gold coins shipped there before 1933, with some said to be intact. Wittlin struck gold—literally and figuratively—in bank vaults, primarily in Switzerland. Success attended his efforts. Surprisingly, banks in France also yielded many coins, especially double eagles that had been kept "underground" during the war. The rare became common. This set the scene for a broad and enthusiastic market in double eagles which exists to the present day.

In 1949 it was thought that only three examples existed of the 1926-S double eagle. This led to a treasure hunt in Europe and elsewhere to find coins shipped to foreign banks and governments earlier in the century. Today several hundred 1926-S $20 coins are known.

In the 1950s thousands of newcomers entered the market and, following the tradition of years earlier, bought blue Whitman folders, and started looking for treasures in pocket change—the 1909-S V.D.B. cent, 1916-D dime, and 1916 Standing Liberty quarter being targets. Some Indian Head cents and Liberty Head nickels were in circulation, and there were many Barber silver coins, particularly half dollars.

Bank-wrapped rolls, gold coins, copper coins, and just about all other federal series were in unprecedented demand. The Philadelphia Mint, which had stopped making Proofs in 1942, resumed the tradition in 1950 and produced 51,386 Proof sets. In 1950 the Denver Mint produced only 2,630,030 nickels—the smallest nickel five-cent piece coinage since 1931. When the mintage figures were released, excitement prevailed! These and the new Proofs gave a further boost to the market.

The Franklin half dollars introduced in 1948 remained the standard design through 1963.

In 1951, 57,500 Proof sets were made. As production climbed year by year there began to be considerable interest in Proof sets from an investment viewpoint. In this decade buy and sell prices were posted of these and for bank-wrapped rolls of modern circulation coins.

In Iola, Wisconsin, in 1952, Chet Krause started *Numismatic News* as a monthly publication devoted to classified advertisements. In time the emphasis changed, and news articles and announcements were carried. Later, in the early 1960s, it went to a weekly. Krause Publications, as it became called, included Cliff Mishler as a key executive. The parent company became one of America's most important publishers of magazines and reference books in many hobby and sports areas, one of the largest in the world.

Beginning with the 1952 ANA Convention sale (the work of a combination of four dealers with different specialties), the New Netherlands Coin Co. of New York City, owned by Charles M. Wormser (business manager) and John J. Ford Jr. (numismatic expert), with Walter Breen as a key employee, produced catalogs with extremely detailed descriptions. Coins came to life, the New Netherlands sales had an almost cult following, and the combination of salesmanship, history, market and coin-collecting gossip and remarks, and detailed descriptions of the offered pieces initiated a new trend. This methodology was later adopted by several other auction firms. In the meantime most retail sales were through shops, price lists, and advertisements.

In 1954 a Proof set of 1936 had a market value of $100, increasing to $300 in 1955, onward and upward to $500, then to $600. At several large coin shows, Cincinnati dealer Sol Kaplan posted "bid" and "ask" prices for sets from 1936 to 1942, and 1950 to date, and prices sometimes changed hourly. A 1956 Proof set, available from the Mint that year for $2.10, was worth $2.50 to those who did not want to wait for sets to arrive in the mail. In that year a record 669,384 sets were struck, nearly doubling the preceding year's total and exceeding by more than a dozen times the number struck six years earlier in 1950. In 1957 the market for Proof sets crashed. The 1936 set dropped all the way back to $300, with scarcely a buyer in sight. Latecomers to the market racked up large losses, and many left in a hurry—perhaps muttering that coin investment was for gullible people only. While the market for Proof sets busted in 1957, time healed the wounds, recovery took place in succeeding years, and today a gem 1936 Proof set is worth well into five figures!

In the meantime, anyone who diversified their holdings did well—as large copper cents, silver dollars, paper money, territorial gold, and Liberty Head nickels, along with just about everything else, continued to rise in price. Many records were set. In the autumn of 1957 in Stack's Empire Sale a rare 1894-S dime sold for an amazing $4,750, an event publicized in newspapers nationwide. The coin was later acquired by Emery May Holden Norweb, a leading collector of the era.

An 1894-S dime, one of only 24 minted and of only 10 or so known today.

The Professional Numismatists Guild, formally organized in 1955, would go on to become America's leading organization of dealers in numismatic items. The Guild (online today at www.PNGdealers.org) has helped with many educational, authentication, and other matters of interest to the collecting community.

In 1955 the San Francisco Mint struck only cents and dimes, after which the Treasury Department stated that coinage there would end and it would become known as the San Francisco Assay Office. That changed in the 1960s when it again was designed as a mint, and was kept busy striking coins.

In 1955 at the Philadelphia Mint an obverse die was impressed twice, slightly off-register, by a hub die. The result was that the date was blurred and appeared as 11995555. Your editor inquired at the Philadelphia Mint and learned that, on a particular day in 1955, several presses were coining cents, dumping the coins into a box where they were then collected and mixed with the cents from other coining presses. Late in the afternoon, a Mint inspector noticed the bizarre doubled cents and removed the offending die. By that time, somewhat more than 40,000 cents had been produced, about 24,000 of which had been mixed with normal cents from other presses. The decision was made to destroy the cents still in the box, and to release into circulation the 24,000 or so pieces that were mixed with other cents. The Mint had no reason to believe that these would attract attention or have value with collectors. They were simply viewed as defective coins. It is likely that about 3,000 to 4,000 1955 Doubled Die cents exist. This variety launched in a large way the numismatic passion, today dynamic, for unusual die errors and varieties. The *Cherrypickers' Guide to Rare Die Varieties of United States Coins*, published in staggered multiple volumes covering half cents through gold, commemoratives, and bullion, is the main guide.

The obverse of the 1955 Doubled Die Lincoln cent.

Coin collecting in the 1950s was becoming an increasingly popular pastime, conventions enjoyed record attendance (the 1955 ANA show in

Omaha totaled an unprecedented 49 dealers and 510 total registrants), and dealers enjoyed excellent business as well. Proof sets, bank-wrapped rolls of Mint State coins, and commemoratives were especially popular with investors, as they were easy to understand—quite unlike esoteric colonial or pattern coins.

The 1959 cent introduced the Lincoln Memorial reverse by Frank Gasparro, an engraver at the Mint.

Without earlier notice to the numismatic periodicals—the *Numismatic Scrapbook Magazine*, *The Numismatist*, and *Numismatic News*—the Treasury Department announced in December 1958 that the traditional wheat-ears reverse of the Lincoln cent in use since 1958 would be replaced by the Lincoln Memorial design in 1959. The new motif by Frank Gasparro drew mixed reviews, with numismatic writer Don Taxay saying that it looked like a trolley car. The design was continued through 2008.

1958 and 1959 were good years for the collector, investor-speculator, and dealer alike. Interest in early coins expanded, and colonial coins, copper cents and half cents, Capped Bust half dollars, and other series attracted many specialists, in time generating new reference books. Thousands of citizens took up the pursuit of numismatics, usually starting by filling in holes in blue Whitman folders. Coin clubs with monthly meetings expanded. Many regional associations were formed while others expanded. A short list includes the Central States Numismatic Association, Empire State Numismatic Association, Florida United Numismatists, Mid-Atlantic Numismatic Association, New England Numismatic Association, Penn-Ohio Coin Clubs, and Southern California Numismatic Association.

The Rittenhouse Society was organized in the late 1950s as an organization of young numismatic researchers (including Q. David Bowers, Kenneth Bressett, Walter Breen, George Fuld, Ken Rendell, and others). It would continue as an honorary society to the present day, with its original age limitation for membership removed.

Coin shows varied in attendance. The most dynamic American Numismatic Association convention for me was in 1957 with a line of five to ten people waiting their turn to examine coins. The slowest was a Penn-Ohio show in Akron in which neither I nor neighboring dealer William Fox Steinberg sold even a single coin, so each agreed to buy $300 worth from the other.

By 1959 the market was very strong in all areas from colonial coins to private and territorial gold and all series in between.

THE 1960s AND 1970s

1960 was a watershed year in the coin market, leaving behind the older scenario of collectors and dealers, plus a limited number of investors, participating in a relatively small market. *Coin World* was launched by the Sidney Printing and Publishing Co. (now Amos Media), an entrepreneurial company that sought to establish a weekly paper in a hobby field. The choice was narrowed to antiques, bowling, and coins, with the latter winning out.

Coin World became an instant success, fueled greatly by the nationwide publicity given to the 1960 Small Date Lincoln cents. Television and newspaper coverage reported on lucky people getting $50 bags of these new cents and selling them for $10,000 to $12,000 each. To put matters in perspective, in 1960 $12,000 was about twice the price of a new Cadillac Seville convertible, one of America's most popular top-of-the-line automobiles. The cost of the average American home was $11,900. Within this year the coin market probably doubled or tripled the number of participants.

Fueled by the launch of *Coin World* in 1960 and the excitement of the Small Date Lincoln cents of that year, the coin market took off like a rocket. Hundreds of thousands of new participants entered, and the circulation of *Coin World* alone crossed the 150,000 mark at one time, with D. Wayne ("Dick") Johnson as founding editor, soon followed in the post by Margo Russell (who went on to nearly 25 years of service). The *Coin World* "Trends" column, conducted by James F. Kelly, gave coin-market prices on a *weekly* basis—the first time ever. Teletype systems linked several hundred dealers by 1962–1963, and at one time the Professional Numismatists Guild even had its own network. Dealers posted bid and ask prices as well as market news and lots of gossip, printed out by noisy, clacking keys on rolls of yellow paper. To many, this was like the stock exchange—instant price information from Chicago could be printed out in New York or Los Angeles.

The Coin Dealer Newsletter was started in 1963, listing bid and ask prices for rolls, Proof sets, and other items, using Teletype data as a basis. The great silver dollar bonanza of 1962 to 1964 added more excitement. Leading the market activity were bank-wrapped rolls of coins (with the 1950-D nickel being the hottest item of all, a 40-coin roll rising during the period from below $200 to over $1,200), Proof sets 1936 to date, common-date gold coins

The first issue of *Coin World,* April 21, 1960.

(owning a common-date Mint State double eagle for less than $50 was very exciting), 1,000-coin bags of silver dollars, and more. The Coin and Currency Institute featured its new "Library of Coins" albums, more compact and attractive than any on the market at the time. Many interesting and attractive holders and albums were produced by others.

Many traditional market areas such as tokens, medals, colonials, copper half cents and cents, paper money, and just about any other area requiring study and knowledge, were ignored by investors and speculators not interested in numismatic art, science, and history. At the same time the interest in such specialties was growing, surely but slowly, aided by an unprecedented interest in numismatic history, tradition, and die varieties, and with special-interest groups adding to the growing excitement. The Token and Medal Society, Civil War Token Society, Early American Coppers, Liberty Seated Collectors Club, and other groups formed during the decade went on to become very important to the hobby.

The *Colonial Newsletter* was established in 1960 by Alfred D. Hoch, of Lexington, Massachusetts, to "provide in permanent form an exchange of information, opinions and discoveries concerning early American numismatics." Later in the decade the editorship passed to Jim Spilman, a true rocket scientist (he worked at the NASA facility in Huntsville, Alabama). From that time to the present, under several editors, the publication became the standard source for research on colonial and early American coins. Today under editor Christopher McDowell it is known as the *Journal of Early American Numismatics* and is published by the American Numismatic Society. Early American Coppers launched *Penny-Wise* under the editorship of Warren Lapp, in time succeeded by Harry Salyards, both medical doctors. Other specialized societies attracted editors and members of a generally high degree of education and intellectual curiosity. Most have remained in numismatics for their entire lives.

Large (top) and small dates on 1960 Philadelphia Mint Lincoln cents. The Small Date cents were perceived as rarities and created nationwide attention.

In November 1962 a long-sealed (since 1929) vault at the Philadelphia Mint was opened in order to tap reserves of silver dollars, popular for banks to pay out during the holiday season. A few hundred 1,000-coin bags of sparkling new 1903-O Morgan dollars were casually given out, this being the rarest and most famous of all coins in the series—so rare that it was estimated that no more than a dozen or two Mint State coins existed! The 1903-O listed for $1,500 in the *Red Book*, the top price level. This was like finding money in the streets, a nationwide silver rush occurred, and several hundred million silver dollars were paid out from Treasury and bank vaults.

In Washington at the Treasury Building people formed long lines with wheelbarrows and sacks for silver dollars to wait their turn to get coins from the Cash Room. Coins had been stored there for generations, including large quantities of dollars brought from the closed Carson City Mint in 1911.

Finally, in March 1964, the supply ran out, at which time the Treasury took stock of its remaining pieces and found about 3,000,000 CC dollars on hand—Mint State, low-mintage issues that were later auctioned over a period of time. This dollar bonanza inspired tens of thousands of people to discover numismatics and become serious collectors, while hundreds of thousands more developed a casual interest—perhaps setting aside a few dozen or even a bag or two of dollars.

About the same time the Kennedy half dollar made its debut. After the assassination of President John F. Kennedy in November 1963, the Treasury

Prior to November 1962 the 1903-O was considered to be the rarest Morgan silver dollar in Mint State. Most dealers had never seen or handled one.

The United States Treasury in Washington, D.C.

One of the Treasury Building silver dollar vaults as photographed in 1904.

abandoned the Benjamin Franklin motif and replaced it with a Kennedy portrait made by Chief Engraver Gilroy Roberts and a Heraldic Eagle reverse by Frank Gasparro, an assistant engraver on the Mint staff. Not long afterward Roberts resigned to take a position with the Franklin Mint, a private coiner of medals, and Gasparro became chief engraver, a position he held until his resignation in 1982.

In 1965 the coin-investment market, mostly driven by speculators with little interest in the hobby of coin collecting, ran out of new players. Rolls of 1950-D nickels seem to have stopped in their tracks at the $1,200 level or so, and holders of quantity could find few buyers at this figure. Rolls, Proof sets, 1960 Small Date Lincoln cents, and the number of subscribers to coin newspapers and magazines slumped. In the meantime, other areas that did not participate in the investment boom were doing just fine—colonials, paper money, early copper, and more. Silver dollars continued their popularity as the majority of the nearly 125 different dates and mintmarks of Morgan and Peace dollars could be obtained in Mint State for just a few dollars up to $50. It was realized that the vaults were empty, and there would be no more "surprise" bags of rarities coming on the market. Many dealers set up as to specialize in these coins.

The Kennedy half dollar was released in March 1964.

One of the most dramatic changes in both coin production and in numismatics took place in 1965. The price of silver rose on international markets, and in that year the Treasury Department abandoned this traditional metal for use in the dime and quarter, and created a reduced-silver version of the half dollar (until 1970). New copper-nickel–clad metal compositions were used instead. The price of silver continued to rise, and all silver coins in circulation became worth more than face value—and profitable to melt down, a repeat of the 1850 to 1853 situation in American history. Copper-nickel coins have remained standard for circulation since.

Within a short time most silver coins disappeared from circulation. No longer was it possible to fill a folder or album with Mercury and Roosevelt dimes, Standing Liberty and Washington quarters, or Walking Liberty and Franklin half dollars, as no more were to be found in change. The idea of finding a 1916-D or 1942, 2 Over 1, dime or a 1932-D or -S quarter "treasure" in pocket change was gone forever. Henceforth, coins had to be purchased from dealers or found here and there by chance.

For some illogical reason, as silver coins were quickly withdrawn from circulation the general public decided to hoard cents and nickels. These became scarce in circulation, and some stores offered to pay a premium for quantities of "pennies"! Mint Director Eva Adams blamed this on coin collectors, and "punished" them by removing mintmarks from branch-mint (Denver) coins and also discontinuing the making of Proof sets. Later, Miss Adams "got religion," realized it was really the fault of the general public, became interested in numismatics, and actually sought and was elected to the office of governor of the American Numismatic Association.

In 1968 Proof sets were again made available for collectors. For the first time they were struck at the San Francisco Mint and bore S mintmarks. Interest in collecting and investing in coins entered a new period of growth. Investors had been absent from the market for several years. In 1969 and 1970 and again in 1973 and 1974 the stock market was weak—at a period when the coin market exhibited great strength, making coins all the more attractive as an alternate investment. In particular, gold was a hot item.

A 1968-S Proof cent, the first Proof of this denomination ever to bear an S mintmark.

Silver dollars had not been issued for circulation since 1935. The Treasury decided that a new issue of dollars would be desirable, now of copper-nickel metal. These would find use on gaming tables but, much more importantly, as a substitute for the paper dollar. Paper bills lasted only about 18 months in circulation while a metal dollar was expected to be used for 20 years or more. The Eisenhower dollar designed by Chief Engraver Frank Gasparro was introduced in 1971. While collectors were enthu-

A 1971-S Eisenhower dollar, designed by Frank Gasparro, a Proof from the set of this year.

siastic, the coins found little use in commerce and were discontinued in 1978. In 1979 a new mini-dollar was introduced, again by Gasparro, this time with the portrait of Susan B. Anthony. It was hoped that at last the public would use them due to their convenient small size. The relatively few used in circulation were often confused with quarters of just slightly smaller size. These coins were discontinued in 1981, followed by a curious additional coinage of the same design in 1999.

The government provisions of 1933 and 1934 prohibiting citizens from holding non-numismatic gold coins (and a small personal allowance) did not include Proofs of various countries, and an exception was made for modern Krugerrands from South Africa, first minted in 1967. Pegged at $35 per ounce, gold had remained at this level for decades, until the 1960s, when it began going upward. In the early 1970s, the price of gold bullion continued to rise steadily. In America where investors could not buy bulk, they could and did buy quantities of Krugerrands. In 1974 there was great excitement as the restriction was to end on December 31. The prices of common gold coins escalated. The price of bulk gold varied.

In 1975 there was not much joy in the coin market. Many dealers had been caught up, and profitably so, in the boom market for Krugerrands, double eagles, and other gold-coin investments, and, to the public "coin investment" was still a bad term, with memories of the boom-and-bust of the early 1960s. Even serious collectors pulled in their horns, with the result that many fine-quality coins, including such things as Proof gold, slumped during this time.

The 1776–1976 Bicentennial coins, which would have been as hot as a pistol in normal "up" periods of the investment cycle, laid an egg, and the Mint had a hard time pushing Proofs and special strikings out the door—and had a supply on hand for several years afterward. Serious collectors and alert investors with a contrarian turn of mind bought quietly during this period, and were to reap great profits later. Harry W. Bass Jr., who later formed one of the greatest coin collections ever, began his numismatic interest this year.

In 1978 and 1979 there was a mad rush to speculate in silver and gold bullion, sparked by the Hunt brothers, wealthy Texans seeking to buy all the silver and silver futures they could. Coin dealers who had shops and stores bought large quantities of worn silver coins, tableware, and other items, as well as scrap silver and gold jewelry, to make profits by selling to refiners. Many profited handsomely and used their gains to buy trophy coins and rarities in the coin market, which was as hot as a firecracker. Runaway inflation in the

Numismatists found artistic fault with the Bicentennial half dollar and dollar, but the quarter dollar, shown here, was widely acclaimed. The market was in the doldrums and many fewer coins were distributed than had been hoped.

American economy and high interest rates made homes and other items less affordable than before, prompting many people to invest in tangible assets, hoping to yield more than bank interest. The first of four sessions of the Garrett Collection was auctioned by Bowers and Ruddy Galleries in November 1979 and set many records.

A uniform patch for the Apollo 11 mission that on July 20, 1969, achieved the first landing of humans on the Moon. Adaptations of this insignia were used on several coin types.

The 1960s and 1970s also saw vast changes in American society, including the gaining of improved civil rights by African-Americans and others, the popularization of passenger-jet aircraft that facilitated travel to foreign countries, and the space race between the United States and the Soviet Union. With the assassination of President John F. Kennedy in 1963, the resignation of President Richard M. Nixon in 1974, the election of former movie actor Ronald Reagan as president in 1979, and other events it was a time to remember. That was done and in spades by books and articles written by many people who had served in the White House and elsewhere in government. Detroit was still the epicenter of the automobile industry with Cadillac and Lincoln being the favorite marques for those who wanted an expensive vehicle. Volvo, Volkswagen, Toyota, Honda, Citroen, Mercedes, and other foreign makes were mostly in the shadows, but expanding rapidly. The Volkswagen "beetle" was the car of choice for many who desired transportation at low cost.

The Boeing 707 revolutionized air travel in the 1960s and was joined by the much larger 747 jumbo jet in the early 1970s.

The American Numismatic Association underwent transition as well. In the early 1960s members of the Professional Numismatist Guild and others in the field raised donations to build a permanent headquarters for the ANA. In 1965 the Home and Headquarters Committee interviewed representatives from cities desiring to be the location. In early 1965 Chairman Charles Johnson reported that one or more of the three committeemen had visited most of the 16 locations from which bids were received prior to February 1. For the record, the cities offering free sites or other inducements for the headquarters were Abilene, Kansas; Amarillo, Texas; Canton, Ohio; Colorado Springs, Colorado; Dubuque, Iowa; Evansville, Indiana; Kansas City, Missouri; Linton, Indiana; Oklahoma City, Oklahoma; Omaha, Nebraska; Prairie du Chien, Wisconsin; Salina, Kansas; Stafford, Virginia; Texarkana, Arkansas; Wichita, Kansas; and Yuma, Arizona. Evanston, Illinois; Minneapolis, Minnesota; and Philadelphia, Pennsylvania, contacted the committee but did not make firm offers.

Omaha was selected as the preferred site, with Colorado Springs, Oklahoma City, and Kansas City following in that order. This was reconsidered, and not long afterward the committee started negotiations for an ANA site at Colorado Springs. Satisfactory progress was being made for a site offered the Association on the campus of Colorado College. The site included in excess of 30,000 square feet of choice space and was offered on a 99-year lease at $1 annual rental. The proposed agreement included an option for renewal of the lease prior to its expiration. This was finalized, and the Home and Headquarters had its dedication on June 10, 1967.

During most of the period Edward C. Rochette was executive director.

In the late 1970s dealer Abe Kosoff was commissioned to set up what was published as *The Official ANA Grading Standards for United States Coins.* Kenneth Bressett, by that time editor of *A Guide Book of*

United States Coins, was tapped to write the grade descriptions and Q. David Bowers the general narrative. The American Numismatic Authentication Service (ANACS) was set up to examine coins for a fee and determine their authenticity or lack thereof. Soon, this evolved into the grading of coins as well. Each coin was assigned a separate grade for the obverse and reverse in accordance with the official standards. It is a matter of fact that each side can be different. Most Morgan silver dollars 1878 to 1921 are a point or two less on the obverse than on the reverse, as the head of Liberty on the obverse is in high relief and is more prone to receiving marks and wear. In the interest of simplification, this was later changed throughout the hobby to a single grade reflecting the average of both sides.

THE 1980s AND 1990s

Going into 1980 the coin market was still riding a crest. The price of bullion gold peaked at $873 an ounce in January 1980. The price of silver topped out at $50.35 per ounce on January 18. On the same day Allen Harriman, editor of the *Coin Dealer Newsletter*, said this: "With both silver and gold bullion soaring into new uncharted ranges, trading in many areas of the coin market becomes more uncertain each day—if not each hour! Most strongly affected, of course, is the bullion-related material. . . ." In early 1980 a longtime client, Dr. Collier, told me that he had been offered $15,000 *per coin* for the set of Barber Proof half dollars, 1892–1915, purchased from me a few years earlier for less than $2,000 per coin. In

March 1980, some say even during the Central States convention itself, the speculation-driven market for rare coins collapsed, and the prices of many "investment grade" coins (generally, MS-65 and Proof-65 or finer silver and gold coins) fell sharply. Many other areas of numismatics, such

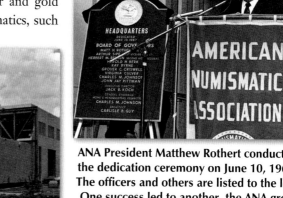

ANA President Matthew Rothert conducted the dedication ceremony on June 10, 1967. The officers and others are listed to the left. One success led to another, the ANA grew and prospered, and in 1982 a second story was added to the building, dedicated on June 10 (15th anniversary of the first event).

The expanded ANA headquarters in 1982.

The plaque for the 1982 dedication.

The American Numismatic Association headquarters building in 1967.

as copper coins, tokens, medals, etc., were not affected. Allen Harriman reported on March 21: "This week's unprecedented drop in the price of both silver and gold bullion has as yet had little or no effect on the numismatic market. In fact, plus signs are very liberally scattered across virtually all of the various pricing charts once again this week. . . ." Not helping matters was a nationwide recession that year in which the GDP (Gross Domestic Product) lost 2.2 percent followed the next year by a 2.6 percent loss.

That did not hold, and most series that were the darlings of speculators dropped sharply in price. The *investment market* for coins was in a blue funk for the next several years. In the meantime, scarce and rare Capped Bust and Liberty Seated silver coins, large copper cents, colonials, Charlotte and Dahlonega mint gold, and other collector-oriented series continued to play to a solid market. Established dealers in rare coins persevered and expanded as the decade progressed, and most auctions were very successful. Much dealer-to-dealer business was conducted on Teletype machines.

A perspective on what happened was given by David Hall in the Monthly Summary of the *Coin Dealer Newsletter*, January 1981 (excerpted):

> January 1 to April 17, 1980: dealers called it "stone heat" as prices went up virtually across-the-board every week! At coin shows, choice material was trading 30%, 40%, even 50% over CDN bid/ask levels. At auctions it wasn't unusual for coins to sell for double bid and then some! During the first four months of 1980, bid levels for choice Proof and choice Brilliant Uncirculated type coins increased over 100%! And MS-65 gold bid levels increased over 50%. CDN summary bids increased an average 86.9% for Buffalo nickels, 66.6% for Mercury dimes, 88.5% for Standing Liberty quarters and 75.6% for Walking Liberty half dollars. Though substantial, the 30% average price gain for MS-65 Morgan and Peace dollars was overshadowed by the explosive gains in other areas. Never before had coin prices increased so quickly!
>
> The prices realized by the coins sold by Bowers and Ruddy Galleries as "Part II" of the Garrett Sale in late March gives us a perfect example of the true hysteria of the "stone heat" market. The total price realized at that sale was in excess of $11 million. The average price per lot was an incredible $20,526! Twenty single coins sold in excess of $100,000 each.
>
> "Black Friday": The April 1980 Central States Numismatic Society convention was like no other coin show in history. At that show the four-year bull market literally "stopped on a dime." In retrospect, undoubtedly there were several reasons for the sudden slowdown. Dealers had become very sloppy with their purchase policies and many dealers were financially overextended. Bullion prices were crashing. Interest rates had soared to 20%. And those huge Garrett Sale payments were due on April 18th. In looking back, it's also evident that there were rumblings of a market slowdown, subtle hints if you will, in the weeks preceding the Central States Show. However, no one expected it to happen when it did and every dealer I know was stunned at how incredibly sudden and incredibly hard the brakes came on. If you weren't there, it may be hard to comprehend, but I was there and believe me on April 17th it was business as usual and on April 18th no one would even look at coins!
>
> April 19 to October 17 1980: For six months the rare coin market went through a period of sluggish activity and declining prices. At first, there were no buyers at *any* price, but, as prices continued to drop and dealer cash positions improved, the market began to firm up. Coins began to trade at 20% or 30% or 40% below bid. By mid-October many issues were again trading in the bid/ask range—or slightly below—with a lot of Teletype "bargain hunting" bids (in the 5% to 15% under bid range) for commemoratives, early Proof sets, Walking Liberty rolls, cheaper type coins, etc. It's important to note that this is an overview of the entire market and not all series followed the general pattern. For example, Morgan and Peace dollars started heating up after the rest of the market fell flat.

As a reader of *Mega Red* you can study much market information such as the above that has been largely forgotten.

The market recovered, and today just about all coins are worth more than they were in April 1980. As to the Garrett Collection, it was cataloged by me and my staff. This was an old-time holding started in 1864 by T. Harrison Garrett, scion of the family that controlled the Baltimore & Ohio Railroad. Items that were hot investment items in 1980 comprised only a tiny part of that collection. By the fourth sale in 1981 the Garrett Collection, appraised at $8.9 million, yielded $25 million. Today the collection would probably sell for more than $100 million.

Due to rising copper prices the Mint in 1982 changed the composition of Lincoln cents from bronze to copper-coated zinc, the standard still used today. In the same year the Treasury Department resumed the issuance of commemorative coins, the first since 1954. The Washington commemorative half dollar, designed by Chief Engraver Elizabeth Jones, recent successor to Frank Gasparro, accompanied by publicity and enthusiasm generated by Mint director Donna Pope, was issued to observe the 250th anniversary of the birth of our first president. The pieces, made with Proof finish by the San Francisco Mint and with Mint State finish by the Denver Mint, were very well received, and within a year or so most were sold. This set the scene for hundreds of later commemoratives, production of which continues to be important today. During the decade the Marketing Department of the Mint was expanded, put new policies in place, and became more interactive with the numismatic community than ever before.

The first commemorative coin issued since 1954 was the 1982 half dollar observing the 250th anniversary of George Washington's birth.

The United States Silver Bullion Depository, often referred to as the West Point Bullion Depository and today as the West Point Mint, officially opened on June 13, 1938. Its purpose was to store silver bullion, while at Fort Knox, Kentucky, the recently opened building stored most of the nation's gold reserve. In 1980 Lincoln cents were made at the Depository. Lacking mintmarks, they appeared similar to Philadelphia coins.

In the same year the facility began striking gold pieces for the American Arts Commemorative Series gold medallion program. Produced were half-ounce and one-ounce gold medals depicting famous American painters, writers, performers, and other artists. Marketing was encumbered by frequent changes of price in step with bullion values and a complex procedure to order. The program went through its legislated run, ending in 1984, and wasn't renewed. "In hindsight," writes Dennis Tucker in *American Gold and Silver: U.S. Mint Collector and Investor Coins and Medals, Bicentennial to Date*, "it might be tempting to label the American Arts initiative a failure. . . . But the American Arts medals were a crucial part of the nation's learning curve, and seen in this light the program was if not entirely *successful*, certainly *important*. Congress and the Treasury Department were feeling their way toward what would become the world's best-selling gold-bullion series."

A 1980 one-ounce gold American Arts Gold Medallion depicting artist Grant Wood.

Beginning in 1984, the W mintmark was first used on coins—$10 gold commemoratives for the Olympic Games. Since that time many W-mintmarked coins have been struck there.

The 1984-W commemorative $10 gold piece made the first use of the W mintmark on a legal-tender coin.

When it came to grading, many dealers felt that the main Mint State grades of 60, 63, 65, 67, and 70 were not enough. Many advertisers used plus marks, such as MS-65++. The *Coin Dealer Newsletter* reported this on July 4, 1986:

> This past weekend, the ANA Board of Governors met, debated, and unanimously accepted the 11 point grading scale—MS-60, 61, 62 . . . 70. Originally intended to discuss the feasibility of the MS-64 grade, the ANA Governors showed their leadership in the hobby by going the whole route and accepting all 11 grades. They felt this was a necessary action for the future as well as today. MS-64 has been used for the last couple of years in the marketplace and eventually all in-between grades will be followed. By accepting the new system, the ANA is looking to the future when grading can, at least in terminology, be standardized. There will probably always be debates over how a coin grades, but at least now, the industry will be talking the same language—numerals.

As it developed the 11-point scale would be defined but not consistently applied.

Investing in gold and silver bullion became very important. The market fall in 1980 was history, and in 1986 there were many new players buying Krugerrands, Canadian Maple Leafs, common-date double eagles, and other coins. The U.S. Mint entered the field with its own bullion coins—the American Eagle made in one-ounce silver and tenth-ounce to one-ounce gold formats. The date for the American Silver Eagle was 1986 but for the American Gold Eagle it was in Roman numerals the first year, MCM-LXXXVI, later changed to Arabic for each year. Bullion strikes were produced for mass sale and Proofs for collectors. The 1995-W Proof American Silver Eagle was a special issue sold at a premium and set the stage for many "special" Proof coins and West Point coins that would be made in various series in the twenty-first century, new varieties that met with mixed reviews from buyers. The basic program was an immediate success and continues as such to the present day.

In 1986 David Hall and a group of dealer associates formed the Professional Coin Grading Service (PCGS), which offered for a fee to receive coins, give an opinion of grade via several experts, and soni-cally seal the coin in a hard plastic holder, which became known as a "slab." In 1987 John Albanese, earlier with PCGS, established the Numismatic Guaranty Corporation of America (NGC), which also became spectacularly successful. Other services were founded, and some enjoyed niches in the marketplace. ANACS with its paper certificates and photographs faded in importance and was later sold by the ANA, eventually reestablishing itself among the most popular professional certification services.

1986 American Silver Eagle.

Certified grading did wonders for the invest-ment market as sellers found that newcomers to numismatics would readily buy coins in holders and not worry about the grade. An ugly or poorly struck coin that might be virtually unsaleable except at a deep discount now could be readily sold for the full "bid" price. This made many ugly ducklings marketable. It was further beneficial to dealers in that cli-ents rarely returned coins certified by a third-party grading service.

MCMLXXXVI (1986) American Gold Eagle.

The market for so-called investment-grade coins, 65 and higher, rose sharply as a part of the largely unquestioned numbers applied by grading services. *The Coin Dealer Newsletter* in April 1988 included this:

> The past two years have seen a growing interest, by the public, in certified coins. Experienced business entrepreneurs learned in the early stages of their training "to give the public what they want." Therefore, there has also been an increase in the marketing of certified coins, so much so, that the year 1987 may be remembered as the year of "overkill."

The CDN added that the public remained confused as to why different services would grade the same coin differently. Not making matters simpler, "there have been significant grading changes."

Several mutual funds were formed to simplify the buying of coins, including one by Merrill Lynch (it was later dissolved and participants reimbursed).

The market for investment coins reached a high in 1989 and early 1990, at which time commemoratives (most of which in the market are in Mint State) and related coins were trading to speculators (or the more popular term, investors) at prices far beyond what any seasoned collector would pay. Finally, the runaway train ran out of steam, and in early 1990 few investors wanted to get on board. The market crashed, and prices fell back to basic or foundational levels reflecting collector demand. Today, as you read these words in *Mega Red*, if you check the *Coin Dealer Newsletter* prices of early 1989 you will see that *most* MS-65 and higher commemorative silver coins and countless other high-grade speculators' favorites are far cheaper now than they were then.[9] Hardly anything about this crash has been mentioned in numismatic magazines and newspapers.

A 1926 Sesquicentennial of American Independence commemorative half dollar in MS-65 had a market value of $14,500 in the spring of 1990. Years later in the 2019 edition of *A Guide Book of United States Coins* it was listed as $600.

Most but hardly all areas of the market recovered as the years progressed. Along the way the interest in specialties increased. Although many 1989 investments were great disasters, most high-grade federal coins have increased in value since that time, and many high-level Mint State coins of the mid-nineteenth century and earlier have multiplied in price.

In June 1989 Edward C. Rochette retired from 20 years of service as the executive vice president (term for what is known as the executive director today) of the American Numismatic Association. Under his leadership the association had grown and prospered as never before. He went on to serve the ANA in other roles including as president and as interim executive director when changes were being made.

In 1990 the World Wide Web was initiated, but few people paid attention to the news.

The market regained strength by 1996 when the second part of the Louis E. Eliasberg Collection crossed the auction block. A Gem Proof 1913 Liberty Head nickel sold for $1,485,000, the first time in world numismatic history that any coin sold for more than a million dollars.

In 1997 the price of gold tumbled. On November 27 an ounce fell to $295.95, its lowest price since March 1985. In numismatic circles the precious metal remained popular and more than a few dealers based their marketing programs

The Eliasberg 1913 Liberty Head nickel, the finest of five known specimens.

on rosy expectations (which in time proved to be correct). In that year the Mint began making platinum bullion coins for collectors and investors. With mixed results these have been continued to the present day.

In 1999 the State quarter program was launched. It was one of the most dramatic programs ever instituted by the Treasury Department, largely based on congressional testimony given by Harvey Stack of Stack's, New York City. Five different states would be honored each year, in the order in which they ratified the Constitution, the first being Delaware. The program was planned to continue for ten years, until all states had been covered. The plan called for designs to be created within the individual states, by artists, members of the public, and others who were to submit ideas, to be reviewed and then finalized by the governors of the states. The eventual result was fifty different designs, no two alike, which delighted numismatists who gave many reviews and opinions concerning the beauty or lack thereof.

Each of the quarters had a special launch ceremony covered with fanfare. Great excitement prevailed from beginning to end, and much was done for the entire numismatic hobby, with books published about the coins, and folders, albums, maps, and other holders and display cases made for eager collectors.

In the same year the euro became the standard currency of many European nations.

New hobby organizations formed after the 1960s included the Colonial Coin Collectors Club and the John Reich Collectors Society. The older specialized groups continued to do well, publishing new research and encouraging new collectors.

As time went on, writers in the popular numismatic press told of gradeflation, or the assigning of higher numbers by certification services than given to the same coins earlier, a subject detailed elsewhere in this book. By the last year of the twentieth century, 2000, the hobby was quite strong in most areas. Personal computers were gaining in popularity, and by this time there were many numismatic applications. Chat rooms and message boards were set up and provided many exchanges as well as instant information.

The 1999-P Delaware quarter, the first in the State quarter program.

The American Numismatic Association remained the leading worldwide organization of numismatists and had slightly more than 30,000 paid members. In the United States the American Numismatic Society in New York City was a smaller group mostly devoted to advanced collectors and research. Its Coinage of the America Conference programs were held yearly with leading presenters discussing and displaying coins, tokens, and medals of the Western Hemisphere, followed by a reference book. This illustrious series ran into the early twenty-first century, after which time most conferences related to ancient coins. Across the nation several hundred local and regional coin clubs met monthly.

The American Numismatic Association headquarters in Colorado Springs on the campus of Colorado College.

An 1807 Capped Bust half dollar, designed by John Reich.

2000 TO DATE

The years from 2000 to date including the official start of the twenty-first century in 2001 have seen countless changes and events on the national and international scenes. A short list includes the Y2K monetary excitement of 2000, the NASDAQ stock-market crash, the World Trade Center disaster and its vast effects on security and travel, CDs and DVDs, presidential administrations from the end of Bill Clinton to that of Donald Trump and the election of Joe Biden, Enron, artificial intelligence, home theaters, space shuttles, federal budget, interest rates, LGBTQ, the rebirth of Apple, iPhones and other electronic devices, electronic credit and bill paying, domestic shootings, robots, Uber and Lyft, racial equality, the securities market and the rise and fall of various companies and industries, nanotechnology, video streaming, the fighting of multiple wars in countries that do not like America, global warming, self-driving cars, weather and natural disasters, the global COVID-19 pandemic and its aftershocks, and more.

The present chapter is nearly completely devoted to numismatics, and readers are referred to other sources for details concerning the above. The year 2000 began with a healthy, indeed dynamic rare-coin market mainly driven by speculator interest in coins common and rare certified in ultra-high grades. More broadly spread, and on a much more permanent basis, was well-studied *collector* interest in copper, silver, and gold coins.

The year started with the launch of the first "golden dollar," a mini-dollar in manganese-brass alloy. The obverse design featured Sacagawea, a translator who traveled with the Lewis and Clark expedition in the upper reaches of the Missouri River, carrying her baby, Pomp. The design was by artist Glenna Goodacre. The reverse depicted a flying eagle by Mint engraver Thomas D. Rogers Sr.

The Sacagawea "golden dollar" was launched in 2000 and proved to be a numismatic favorite. Circulation strikes were made at the Philadelphia and Denver mints. Proofs (as shown) were struck in San Francisco.

The Mint was eager to promote public interest and acceptance of the new dollar. It arranged with General Mills, Inc., the Minneapolis manufacturer of cereals and other foods, to supply 5,500 coins struck in late summer or early autumn 1999 with a 2000-P obverse and the prototype reverse. The difference in the reverse details was not disclosed to the numismatic community at the time. General Mills advertised a "treasure hunt"—one in every 2,000 boxes of Cheerios would contain a new Sacagawea dollar, not yet in general release, and a 2000-dated Lincoln cent. "The only place to get either coin is in a box of Cheerios." Further, one box in every 4,400 had a certificate redeemable for 100 Sacagawea dollars (finders who redeemed them received the dollars with the later-type reverse). It was not until February 2005 that the differences distinguishing this variety was noticed by a numismatist and publicized. The first one auctioned sold for nearly $35,000. More were found, and today somewhat more than 100 have been identified.[10]

Detail of the tail feathers with cross-vanes used only on the rare 2000-P "Cheerios" dollar, the "poster rarity" of the turn of the century.

In August 2000 the ANA World's Fair of Money convention was held in Philadelphia and drew more than 20,000 attendees, an all-time record.[11] Across the front of the bourse area the California Gold Marketing Group set up the 50-foot-wide Ship of Gold display. This was a reproduction of the *SS Central America*, the treasure-laden ship that sank on September 12,

The regular reverse with plain tail feathers (no vanes), as used on all regular Sacagawea dollars 2000 to 2008.

1857, and from which the Columbus-America Discovery Group recovered gold coins and ingots in the late 1980s. Shown were many items recovered, and a mini-theater projected films of the find. A program by treasure-finding scientist Bob Evans had an attendance of more than 400 visitors. Marketing of the treasure had begun in 1999 and continued for several years, by which time about $100 million was realized. The treasure and its publicity electrified the market and were called by *Coin World* "the story of the year."

How many people collect coins? How many are serious numismatists? Beth Deisher, editor of *Coin World*, provided comments on this in the issue of March 12, 2001. She suggested that most numismatists and related organizations define a collector as "one who spends time and money to systematically gather coins for the purpose of forming a collection. Using that definition, we can begin to build a total that has some facts behind it." She suggested that about 450,000 people were serious about numismatics but noted that the United States Mint had 1,800,000 names on its mailing list.[12] Further, "The U.S. Mint reports that its marketing surveys show that up to 110 million adults are actively collecting the State quarters."

More than 7,400 mint-fresh 1857-S double eagles have been recovered from the wreck of the SS *Central America*.

As to how many people in 2001 went beyond collecting State quarters and modern Mint products and were serious enough to spend, say, $500 to $1,000 each year on Morgan dollars, Indian Head cents, colonial copper coins, and the like, and to attend coin shows and bid in auctions, your editor's guess is about 250,000. That would have been a solid base for any collecting hobby that involves art, history, romance, and methodology of acquisition.

The numismatic collection of the late Harry W. Bass Jr., one of the finest ever formed, was sold at auction in several sales beginning in 1999. Christine Karstedt and Q. David Bowers worked with the Bass and Calhoun families in Dallas as they created the Bass Gallery at American Numismatic Association headquarters in Colorado Springs.

The SS *Central America* sidewheel steamship was in service to and from Panama and New York City in 1857. (*Frank Leslie's Illustrated Newspaper*, September 26, 1857)

A small part of the Harry W. Bass, Jr. Gallery at ANA headquarters in Colorado Springs.

The formation of registry sets, a collecting concept pioneered by PCGS and picked up by NGC, went into high gear. The challenge was to have the highest-graded coin or set of coins certified. In *COINage*, April 2003, editor Ed Reiter reported:

> Recently, one of these "modern rarities" brought $39,100 at an auction at the Florida United Numismatists convention in Orlando. The coin was a 1963 Lincoln cent graded Proof-70 Deep Cameo by the Professional Coin Grading Service (PCGS). It is said to be the only Proof Lincoln cent of that date ever to receive a perfect grade from one of the leading coin-certification services.[13]

Registry set participation would eventually involve more than 10,000 people at the various services and would be responsible in coming years for many coins that are common in, say, MS-65 grade and priced at below $10 to sell for thousands of dollars in ultra-grades. Sets have contributed much to the strength of the market in recent years. Multiple losses have occurred when an ultra-grade coin that was once rare "becomes common" when more are certified. All of this part of numismatics, and the key is to become as informed as possible before buying.

To this must be added the reality than in many older series such as colonials and early nineteenth-century copper, silver, and gold coins, coins from Good-4 to Mint State (never mind non-existent ultra-high grades) have enjoyed a strong market as well.

A renaissance in numismatic research and publishing was kindled in the early 2000s under the management and inspiration of Anderson Press. By 2003 Whitman Coin Products, after many years as a division of Western Publishing Company in its hometown of Racine, Wisconsin, and after later sales to various other firms, was operated by St. Martin's Press in New York City. Whitman had continued to publish the *Red Book* (its guide to retail coin prices) and the *Blue Book* (its guide to wholesale coin prices) under the editorial direction of Kenneth Bressett, but in recent years had done little in the way of new titles. This changed dramatically when H.E. Harris & Co., an Anderson Press company, bought Whitman from St. Martin's. Under new management and ownership, the combined firm took the name of the present-day Whitman Publishing, LLC. Since then Whitman has published more than 300 new books for collectors, investors, and researchers, including more than two dozen volumes in the Bowers Series (on various U.S. coin types, denominations, and related subjects); the *Cherrypickers' Guide to Rare Die Varieties of United States Coins*; the "100 Greatest" library of books; and many others ranging from 96-page monographs to multiple-volume encyclopedias, and the present 1,504-page *Mega Red*. These books cover American and world coins, ancient coins, paper currency, medals, tokens, bullion, and other numismatic and historical topics. Whitman has also dramatically increased its line of folders, albums, display cases, magnifiers, and other storage, display, and research products for collectors.

Whitman purchased the Baltimore Coin and Currency Convention and rebranded it as the Whitman Coin & Collectibles Expo, expanding the show and adding new features, with three events held annually in Baltimore. The company has supported many hobby organizations and programs, funding the ANA's annual Young Numismatists literary competition, sponsoring the Rittenhouse Society's annual breakfast, donating books and collector supplies to the Boy Scouts of America and other groups, assisting Women In Numismatics (www.womeninnumismatics.com), and facilitating communications and cooperation among researchers, specialty groups, museums, archives, government agencies, and others.

In 2003 the United States Mint implemented the novel Artistic Infusion Program, an effort to bring the talents of private-sector artists under the wing of the government. Eighteen "master" designers and six "associate" designers were selected from applications received, to create motifs for American coins and medals. By this time State quarters at the rate of five per year plus new medals put pressure on the Engraving Department. The program worked out well, and over the years various early artists departed and new ones were selected. The AIP has injected new artistry and creativity into American coinage and medal design.

Also in 2003, the Citizens Coinage Advisory Committee (www.CCAC.gov) was established by Act of Congress to advise the secretary of the Treasury on themes and design proposals for circulating coinage, bullion coins, Congressional Gold Medals, and national and other medals.

The Whitman Publishing exhibit at a Whitman Coin & Collectibles Expo in Baltimore, an event held three times a year.

In 2004 the American Numismatic Society relocated from its two stone bank-like buildings on Audubon Terrace in New York City, its home since 1908, to a multi-story structure at 140 William Street in the Financial District that included the expansive Harry W. Bass Jr. Memorial Library. The new building was sold at a handsome profit, and the ANS later moved to leased quarters on the 11th floor of the former New York Tribune printing plant on Varick Street.

In 2004 and 2005 Westward Journey nickel five-cent pieces were made at the mints to honor the Lewis and Clark expedition. Beyond the coins themselves, special sets including medals were marketed, not to the pleasure of some collectors who believed that coin issues should be simple and straightforward.[14] The portrait of President Thomas Jefferson was changed in 2005 from that created in 1938.

A reflection of the market was given by Mike Gumpel in *COINage*, January 2005 (excerpted):

> This past year saw the strength of the rare-coin market continue at a faster pace than the previous year while broadening at the same time. 2003 was a great year for collector coins, especially rare and better dates, and also a great year for more modern pieces in super-high grades. 2004 continued to be even better in those two areas, but the health of the market moved in several other sections also. Key date coins of Bust, Seated and Barber series all saw surprising demand. Common date, high-grade Barber coins; commems; common and rare date gold; circulated type coins; bullion-related coins, and just about everything was more in demand in 2004 than the previous years. Things like a weaker dollar overseas helped by influencing the advancing price of gold. A lackluster Wall Street also helped, as a number of investors decided to invest outside of the stock market with some of that money going into rare coins.

The *Coin Dealer Newsletter*, January 21, 2005, reported that at the recent Florida United Numismatists Convention many dealers lowered their "bid" and other prices as money was scarce for some, and there were auction expenses and other bills to be paid.

Year in and year out market commentaries appeared in the various numismatic magazines. Coverage of the same events often varied widely. Many shows routinely issued news releases saying that activity was

The two reverse designs for the 2004 Westward Journey nickels and the shared obverse.

The two reverse designs for the 2005 Westward Journey nickels
and the shared obverse with a revised portrait of Jefferson.

robust, although some were slow. Meanwhile, the Internet took away much business that formerly took place at conventions, and onerous security procedures at airports deterred some collectors from traveling.

At the same time grading became increasingly difficult to figure out. In *Penny-Wise*, journal of the Early American Coppers group, editor Harry Salyards commented that certified grades on large copper cents were often far higher than the grades assigned by longtime specialists who belonged to EAC. "For years, it has been recognized that the slabbed '62' may be an EAC '45,' or the slabbed '50' an EAC '30.'" This led to a new practice of auction listings giving both the EAC and certified grades. With accompanying pictures buyers were able to bid confidently.

The Mint reported in early 2005 that sales of platinum coins were sagging. The program had never caught on with enthusiasm, and a redesign of the series was being considered. High prices were a deterrent to buying, but for the Mint the coins produced a nice profit.[15]

Around this time increased numbers of sophisticated Chinese counterfeits of United States coins began appearing in quantity on the market, including on eBay.[16] Buying coins that were professionally certified as authentic became a necessity for many advanced collectors.

In 2005 the Mint announced that "Satin Finish" would be available on circulating coins included in Mint sets sold to collectors. In *Coin World*, May 23, 2005, editor Beth Deisher asked if this meant that coin albums needed to be redesigned to accommodate two versions of current circulating coins. Increasingly the Mint offered various packaging opinions and special finishes rather than single coins.

The ANA World's Fair of Money held in San Francisco in July 2005 was reported as one of the slowest such events in recent years and nearly all reports were negative. The reasons suggested were that a 300-mile circle drawn around the city was 50 percent ocean and in the land part there lived only a tiny percentage of ANA members, that parking cost $15 to $20 per day, and that the show was held on two floors, not well marked so that some visitors were not aware that there were two large separate levels of activities.[17] The ANA also held smaller shows at other times of the year. Convention scheduling caused great debate among members. Some thought it a good idea to constantly move events around the country so that various regions, even with low populations, would be represented, and others suggested that they be held only in large cities such as Chicago that had easy air connections.

The United States Mint regularly sets up displays at coin conventions. This one with information on the Westward Journey nickels was on view at the 2015 ANA convention. Many images of proposed 2006 nickels, none of which ever reached reality, were shown.

For a number of years Solomon Brothers, a leading Wall Street securities firm, published the results of rare-coin investment along with other fields. The "basket" of coins contributed by Stack's included these 20 coins:

1794 half cent, EF; 1873 two-cent piece, Brilliant Proof; 1866 nickel, Brilliant Proof; 1862 three-cent silver, Mint State; 1862 half dime, Mint State; 1807 dime, Mint State; 1866 dime, Mint State; 1876 20-cent piece, Mint State; 1873 With Arrows quarter, Mint State; 1886 quarter, Mint State; 1916 Standing Liberty quarter, Mint State; 1815, 5 Over 2, half dollar, Mint State; 1834 half dollar, Mint State; 1855-O half dollar, Mint State; 1921 half dollar, Mint State; 1795 Draped Bust dollar, Mint State; 1847 dollar, Mint State; 1884-S dollar, Mint State; 1881 trade dollar, Brilliant Proof; and 1928 Hawaiian commemorative half dollar, Mint State.

The index did not include colonials or gold coins. It did provide a bellwether of prices. David L. Ganz reported this in *Numismatic News*, March 7, 2006:

> Over a 67-year period of time, 1938 to 2005, rare coins increased an average of 13.56 percent, compared to 8.39 percent for the Dow Jones Industrial Average. Both the Dow Jones and the index compilation for rare coins use a market-basket approach, measuring selected coins designed to represent the whole marketplace, and selected stocks that are broadly representative of the industrial sector of the American economy.
>
> Components of the Dow Jones have changed during the period (though the results have not); the coin list is static. Dow Jones statistics are calculated daily, and based on actual components and prices published in many periodicals. The coin list was first compiled by Solomon Brothers going back to 1978, and carried through 1990, and was always done on an annualized basis [later it was done semi-annually].

In late 2006 extending to August 19, 2007, the American Museum of Natural History in New York City mounted a large exhibit, "Gold." The display included coins from ancient times to present, mostly on loan from the American Numismatic Society, and ingots and coins from the SS *Central America*, among many other sections.

On January 2, 2007, in *Coin World* market analyst Mark Ferguson discussed certified coins, including this:

Theoretically, there is very little difference between a coin grading Proof or Mint State 69 in comparison to the same design coin grading a perfect Proof or Mint State 70. In fact, a loupe is often required to find the minute blemishes in a 69-graded coin that keep it from a perfect grade. To the naked eye, these coins should look virtually identical. So, why are there wide variations in prices between these two grades, and even for the same grades? The answer partially lies in people's preferences for coins endorsed as "perfect" by third-party grading services. . . .

What we know about the coin in terms of rarity and availability is still evolving, resulting in vast price variations at this time. . . .

The American Museum of Natural History mounted the spectacular "Gold" exhibit in 2006 and 2007, advertised on banners in the city, including on the front of the museum.

At the time the American Numismatic Association was in a growth stage and had about 32,000 members. Overall attendance at auctions and conventions declined in the early 2000s as buying and selling via the Internet was much more comfortable and convenient. The association had proposed to establish a numismatic museum in Washington, D.C., but that was scrapped in October 2007. Such would have been redundant in any event, as the National Numismatic Collection at the Museum of American History building of the Smithsonian Institution, with curators Dr. Vladimir Clain-Stefanelli and his wife Elvira, succeeded by Dr. Richard Doty, had extensive exhibits of coins, tokens, medals, and paper money from all eras. Collectors and researchers were warmly welcomed and many special events were held.

In 2007 the Mint issued a Proof $20 gold coin of the Saint-Gaudens design with the date as MMVII on the 100th anniversary of the original MCMVII (1907) issue, much to the acclaim of the numismatic community. It was of smaller diameter than the 1907 original but was thicker, thus maintaining the same weight. During this era Mint Director Edmund C. Moy was very involved in numismatic activities and was a regular attendee of major coin conventions.

In 2007 the Presidential series of "golden dollars" was introduced, overlapping slightly with the Sacagawea dollar series that ended in 2008. Presidents were featured from George Washington onward, living presidents excluded. The obverse designs featured a portrait (by various artists) and the reverse the Statue of Liberty (by Mint sculptor-engraver Don Everhart).

The Presidential series of "golden dollars" was introduced in 2007 with the dates and mintmarks on the edge, a curious change.

In 2009 the Sacagawea obverse was continued in a new series with Native American reverse motifs. Both of these new series had a major numismatic liability, according to nearly everyone: the dates and mintmarks were placed on the *edges* of the coins, where they could not be seen in holders or albums! Other new series included 24-karat American Buffalo gold bullion coins and First Spouse coins. It cost more than $20,000 in Mint-issue prices to keep current with every legal-tender coin variety produced in a given year. Sales of platinum coins continued to fall below Mint expectations and there was discussion as to what to do, such as changing the designs.

The State quarter program wound down in 2008, after which in one year six quarters for the District of Columbia and U.S. territories were made, followed in 2010 by the new America the Beautiful quarters. The latter program features national parks, national historic sites, wildernesses, forests, and other "national" locations. In connection with these a parallel series of five-ounce silver bullion coins is being produced.

In 2009 the golden dollar was continued, now with a *dateless* obverse, combined with a yearly change of reverse in the Native American series. Dates and mintmarks were placed on the edge.

The 2008 ANA World's Fair of Money had a registered attendance of 9,717, including dealers and their helpers. The American economy was entering a recession, with the second week in October being the worst week in the 112-year history of the Dow-Jones Industrial Average, but this and the collapse of several major Wall Street firms had no measurable effect on the numismatic market.

Conventions were increasingly becoming "virtual" with no in-person attendance necessary. In 2008 American Numismatic Rarities held the sale of the Dice-Hicks Collection. A shareholder in the company called (on a cell phone of course) to check on progress. "How many people are attending?" I replied, "There were nine, but one went to the rest room, so now there are eight." Even with such a light crowd, the sale brought three times its estimate because nearly all of the bidders participated in real time on the Internet.

It is not unusual for a leading auction company to hold a public sale at a large convention and have fewer than a dozen people in attendance while at the same time setting many records. Bidders participate from all over the world from the comfort and convenience of their homes and offices.

Despite repeated predictions that "pennies" were no longer needed in commerce, the Mint continued to turn out billions, including four commemorative reverse designs in 2009 observing the bicentennial of Abraham Lincoln's 1809 birth. At this time the recession resulted in erratic distribution through the Federal Reserve Banks and less public interest than might have been the case in good times.

In 2010 the Union Shield design (by AIP artist Lyndall Bass, modeled by Mint medallic sculptor Joseph Menna) became the cent's new reverse motif.

In "Making the Grade" in *Numismatic News*, December 22, 2009, F. Michael Fazzari, longtime professional grader and columnist, discussed the fact that many coins called About Uncirculated–55 and 58 earlier were now being certified as Mint State. Many coins jumped five to seven or eight grade points higher over time, although the coins themselves did not change. Mint State and Proof coins saw gradeflation as well—for example, an 1804 dollar jumping from EF-45 to Proof-62.

In 2009 the price of gold bullion ranged from a low of $810.00 per ounce on January 15 to a high of $1,212.50 on December 2. American Eagle silver and gold issues remained very popular. In 2010 the year started on a high note with nearly 10,000 hobbyists attending the Florida United Numismatists convention in Orlando. Meanwhile, the ANA was striving to increase attendance at the World's Fair of Money show, and the board of governors voted to let the Professional Numismatists Guild have a pre-show day (which had been done in some earlier years). The Whitman Coin & Collectibles Expo conventions in Baltimore remained a strong drawing card three times a year— March, June, and November. On the West Coast the Long Beach shows were popular. Regional conventions were held by some clubs. Early American Coppers had its own stand-alone gathering each year, complete with "happenings" in which members shared particular coin types or years and compared them with others.

The four reverse designs used on Lincoln cents in 2009.

With increased hassles in air transportation (long security lines, extra charges for baggage, reduced comfort and amenities on board) more and more people were "attending" conventions in virtual reality. In the meantime the number of coin shops in America was smaller than ever. In 1963 Chester L. Krause told the editor that he estimated there were at least 6,000 walk-in coin, hobby, and other shops offering displays of coins for sale.

A 2010-D cent with the new reverse adopted as standard that year.

Obverse design 1 · Obverse design 2 · Obverse design 3 · Obverse design 4
Obverse design 5 · Obverse design 6 · Obverse design 7 · Obverse design 8
Obverse design 9 · Obverse design 10 · Obverse design 11 · Obverse design 12

How should Abraham Lincoln be depicted on new coinage? Here are proposals studied by the CCAC for the obverse of the proposed 2009 Lincoln bicentennial commemorative dollar. Many choices!

Throughout this era the Citizens Coinage Advisory Committee met several times a year at the U.S. Mint's executive offices in Washington, D.C., and at other venues. Proposed coinage and medallic designs were reviewed and discussed in depth. For example, on March 23, 2010, the CCAC overwhelmingly and enthusiastically endorsed a motif featuring a modern woman as Justice on the reverse of the Proof platinum series that year. The committee in its two-hour session had a prolonged discussion on the lack of interest by *collectors* in these and other non-circulating coins.[18]

In 2007 Mint Director Edmund C. Moy stated, "I want and intend to spark a neo-renaissance of coin design and achieve a new level of design excellence that will be sustained long after my term expires." Advances were made but overall this did not happen. "We are getting pictorial decorative art," said CCAC member Donald Scarinci. "We aren't getting anything bold or inspiring or new or innovative. The only time those four words get used are in Director (Ed) Moy's speeches. And the speeches have no bearing with reality."[19]

Elsewhere in Mint news it was noted that its customer mailing list had slipped below one million names in recent months. Apart from the CCAC quite a few people wondered why the Mint kept using early twentieth-century motifs instead of creating new classics. However, the recycled early-twentieth-century designs of James Earle Fraser (1913 Buffalo nickel)

The obverse of the 2010 Lincoln Presidential dollar, as chosen by the secretary of the Treasury. An attractive portrait?

**Mint Director Edmund C. Moy at a launch
ceremony for the John Adams Presidential dollar.**

and Adolph A. Weinman (1916 Walking Liberty half dollar) were considered by many numismatists to be the most beautiful designs used by the Mint in the early twenty-first century.

In the marketplace PCGS and NGC "officially" recognized adding + signs to grades. "Secure plus" and "star" additions were also used. More logical than any of this, the Certified Acceptance Corporation (CAC) led by John Albanese did not grade coins at all, but viewed coins graded by others and gave them a green sticker if they were high-end or attractive.[20]

There was not much of an aftermarket for modern Mint commemoratives, and dealers were often paying just melt value or slightly less in the secondary market. Hobbyists who were building collections and desired to buy coins for little more than melt value had a great opportunity, commented editor Steve Roach in *Coin World*, March 7, 2011. He observed that 38 varieties of commemorative silver dollars were thus available.

That situation did not change in later years. Of course, this strategy was and is not risk-free from a resale viewpoint. On April 25, 2001, the closing price of silver was $48.70, its highest in 31 years. Anyone who bought silver dollars at bullion value then would have lost money. In late February 2019, an ounce of silver was $16.

The market price of silver and gold bullion only affects certain common coins for which the bullion price is a component. This includes worn common-date Morgan and Peace silver dollars, common-date double eagles, pre-1965 common silver coins, etc. It has no impact on the vast majority of collectible coins. It is not important to the value of scarce and rare coins. The melt value of a Liberty Seated quarter or a gold dollar is irrelevant. Probably the best advice concerning modern commemoratives is to acquire one each for your collection, as in terms of the overall value of your holdings variations in metal prices will have little effect.

It was reported that Presidential dollars had proved to be a dud with regard to public acceptance, and with many numismatists they achieved low marks as well. In the three and a half years since the program started, 1,252,000,000 unwanted coins were placed in Treasury storage, and $650,000 was to be spent at the Federal Reserve Bank of Dallas to store them, with the expectation that there would be two billion coins by the time the program ended.[21] The main reason for this seemingly illogical

The price of a common 1884 Morgan dollar in Very Fine grade varies with the value of silver metal as a commodity.

The ANA Hall of Fame Gallery.

situation is that the Treasury booked a handsome profit on each coin—the difference between the low cost of metal and coinage and the face value—a fact rarely discussed.

As to numismatics, in 2011 it cost $23,500 for a completist to buy every 2011 coin variety offered by the Mint, a figure that did not include every packaging option.[22]

In 2011 the Hall of Fame Gallery was opened in the indoor atrium at American Numismatic Association headquarters in Colorado Springs. Each honoree has a special plaque with a portrait and about 100 words of biographical information.[23] At the World's Fair of Money held by the ANA in Rosemont, Illinois, in August the price of gold was $1,913 per ounce on the commodities market, and common-date double eagles in worn grades started at over $2,000. This enthusiasm spurred record sales volume of gold coins at the show. In November the price of an ounce of gold fell (below $1,700), as did the desire for common-date double eagles.[24]

In my "Joys of Collecting" column in *Coin World* on August 1, 2011, I stated, "Today, certified coins, electronic sources and more make it possible for anyone to be a coin dealer. No knowledge or experience is needed." A reader wrote in, "I look forward to and expect an apology from Q. David Bowers."

I am reminded of a telemarketer who called and upon questioning revealed he had never heard of the Professional Numismatists Guild.

In 2010 Edmund Moy announced his resignation as director of the Mint, effective January 2011. No successor was immediately appointed. Several deputy directors filled the leadership position as acting director or principal deputy director over the next few years. Deputy Director Richard Peterson acted as director for a time. Rhett Jeppson served as principal deputy director, and David Motl and Dave Croft were acting deputy directors in turn, by dint of their positions as senior career officials within the Mint management structure. Finally in 2017 David J. Ryder, who had served as Mint director in 1992 and 1993, was nominated to again take the post of director. He was confirmed by the Senate in March 2018.

There has been no presidentially appointed and Senate-confirmed chief engraver at the Mint since the highly accomplished Elizabeth Jones, successor to Frank Gasparro, resigned in 1991. The position of chief engraver, which had started under Director David Rittenhouse in the 1790s, remained vacant for several years. Then it was officially abolished in an organizational restructuring in 1996. In 2006 John Mercanti, who had worked as a sculptor-engraver at the Mint since 1974, was elevated to the new position of supervisory design and master tooling development specialist. In 2009 Director Moy under his own authority named Mercanti chief engraver. After Mercanti retired in 2010, the position of chief engraver was vacant until early 2019, when medallic sculptor Joseph Menna, of the Mint's Philadelphia staff, was named to the office.

In 2010 the Mint decided to discontinue most launch ceremonies for the America the Beautiful quarters. Public interest had reached a low, and the cost of sending Mint officials to distant locations was not effective. Launches were resumed later. Tom Jurkowsky, the Mint's director of corporate communications, working with Deputy Director Richard Peterson, interfaced with the numismatic community and helped with much research, including for multiple Whitman Publishing projects.

Mint products for numismatists such as Reverse Proofs and special issues with W mintmarks drew mixed reviews, and the continued placement of dates and mintmarks on the edge of dollars remained unfortunate. The Presidential dollars program received few glowing comments. The Sacagawea and Native American dollars earned complimentary notices and were and are well liked for their designs.

In 2013 the American Numismatic Association appointed Kimberly Kiick to the post of executive director. Kiick had been hired by the ANA in 1982 and over the years gained experience in many posts, starting as receptionist, progressing to senior manager and director of operations.

Chinese counterfeits continued to plague the hobby. These extended to coins such as common Morgan dollars in grades of Extremely Fine and About Uncirculated as well as to common large copper cents and other coins. Gold ingots and American Gold Eagles were faked and fooled many people. One American importer offered Eagles at a third of bullion value. It became a dangerous procedure to buy gold coins and ingots and store them without having them examined or assayed. Beth Deisher, who retired from *Coin World* in 2012, held seminars on the subject. Leading third-party grading services guaranteed authenticity, making the premium for encapsulation a worthwhile precaution for many buyers.

In the market for rare and expensive federal coins, certification was the rule, not the exception. In the marketplace certified coins attracted many buyers and bidders who lacked experience and would not otherwise participate. CAC stickers became more popular than ever for selected rarities.

In 2014 on the 50th anniversary of the Kennedy half dollar the Mint struck Proof dual-dated 1964–2014 coins in gold. Distribution began on August 4, including at the World's Fair of Money in Chicago, for the issue price of $1,240. Some enterprising dealers hired several hundred unemployed individuals to wait in line in a queue extending out the doors, to buy sets that were limited, in the process causing

**Mint Deputy Director Richard Peterson emcees the 2013
White Mountain New Hampshire quarter dollar launch.**

a great distraction and inconvenience. The first set acquired at the show was sold by the buyer for $6,240, then certified as the first by PCGS and resold for $100,000 to a buyer who had been purchasing other coins on a TV marketing program.[25] The coins met with a warm reception by the numismatic community. Several other variations of the anniversary coin were made, including a Reverse Proof from West Point and an "enhanced" Uncirculated coin from San Francisco, 13 different varieties in all.[26]

The 1964–2014 gold
Proof Kennedy half dollar.

In 2014 Bob Evans, the scientist who led the earlier discovery of the long-lost *SS Central America*, returned to the site off of the coast of North Carolina in a new expedition. The recovery of gold coins, ingots, and other items was substantial, in the tens of millions of dollars in numismatic value, but much less than the first find.

Several important collections were marketed in this era, including selections from the cabinets of Eugene Gardner, Donald Partrick, Eric P. Newman, D. Brent Pogue, and Bernard Edison, each one playing to a wide audience with strong bidding and many record prices. However, the overall prices for many series were lower as supply in the marketplace exceeded numismatic demand. (See Jeff Garrett's 2020 Market Report in the sixth edition of *Mega Red* for more information.)

In 2016 the Mint issued tribute coins of the 1916 dime, quarter, and half dollar, in gold with a 2016 date. This time, sales were orderly. These coins, like the 2014 Kennedy gold half dollar, were well received.

One of 45 gold ingots recovered
from the SS *Central America* in
2014, adding to the over 400
recovered in the 1980s.

The three different gold denominations struck in 2016 on the 100th
anniversary of the release of the silver coins of the same motifs in 1916.

The American Liberty series of $100 denomination one-ounce gold coins was launched in 2015. Shown are the 2017 obverse, designed by Justin Kunz and sculpted by Phebe Hemphill; and reverse, designed by Chris Costello and sculpted by Michael Gaudioso.

A 2017 American Palladium Eagle with imprinted value of $25, much lower than its bullion value. Apparently Congress felt the best choice for a design was not to tap the current Mint Engraving Department staff but to resurrect the Mercury dime motif created by Adolph A. Weinman in 1916, and a high-relief version of his 1907 American Institute of Architects gold medal reverse.

In 2008 Representative Michael Castle, longtime congressional friend of numismatists and the legislator who facilitated the 1999 and later special quarter issues, introduced a bill for palladium coins. That gained no traction, but years later in 2017 Eagles were made in that metal. Comments concerning palladium coins as well as platinum coins were mixed among numismatists.[27] Neither metal had anything to do with regular American circulating coins (although in 1815 an experimental platinum half dollar had been struck from regular dies). As to whether coins in either metal appealed more to numismatists or to speculators in bullion metal was debatable.

In the twenty-first century the Internet and computer have wrought major structural changes in the market. Today as you read these words, a large percentage of the membership of the American Numismatic Association, about 25,000 people, receive *The Numismatist* in virtual form on the Internet. *Coin World* and other magazines are far thinner than they were a generation ago as most dealers no longer list coins for sale in print. The Internet is faster, and cheaper, and allows instant transactions.

In recent years many sales of scarce and rare coins that might have been made privately by dealers to clients have been consigned to public auction instead. On eBay an unprecedented number of rarities from different vendors can be found, some of questioned authenticity. This has resulted in a rearrangement of retail practices that were in effect a generation ago.

Books in print remain important (*Mega Red* has had record sales), but information on the Internet offers competition to traditional numismatic publishing.

Instant communications bring the world of numismatics to everyone, even on cell phones when traveling. More data are available than ever before. On the negative side, anyone collecting a popular coin series such as Morgan dollars and who has a modest budget can complete most of their collection on the Internet in a day—and with the coin budget exhausted, the fun of months or years of measured collecting might not lie ahead. On the other hand, for tokens, medals, die varieties, and other specialties, many items are inexpensive. A budget of $10,000 can build a memorable display in certain token, medal, and die variety series. Many modern series are very affordable in, say, MS-65 or Gem Mint State—such as modern dollars, Eisenhower to date, State quarters, and America the Beautiful quarters. Current Mint products such as commemoratives, Proofs, and modern medals are interesting to own and contemplate, with many beautiful and historic designs.

A working library of interesting and useful numismatic books can be a treasure and resource. As an example, it is enjoyable to read about numismatic treasures, from hoards to shipwrecks, without owning any of the coins. The Newman Numismatic Portal on the Internet, coordinated by Leonard Augsburger, provides free and unlimited access to thousands of magazines, newspapers, price lists, auction catalogs, and other material, an unprecedented incredible asset for research, effectively taking the place of a library that would require a lifetime and hundreds of thousands of dollars to form—and even then it would not match the NNP. The Internet is a gateway to explore many numismatic side roads and to gain knowledge on any coin or series.

The March 2020 American Numismatic Association's National Money Show in Atlanta was one of the last big conventions before the COVID-19 pandemic shut down all such venues for a time. The pandemic's effects on the numismatic scene are still being felt and analyzed. Beyond the human toll of numismatists lost to the virus, businesses have been disrupted and normal hobby events and activities have been curtailed. At the same time, the hobby community has found ways to survive and in some ways even flourish. Videoconferencing has been a boon for club meetings and educational programs in a time when large in-person gatherings are prohibited. (Online meetings will undoubtedly continue to be a large factor in the numismatic landscape even after society "opens up" again.) Book sales have been strong, with Whitman Publishing reporting early sellouts of print runs, and increased demand for popular titles. (The *Red Book* celebrates its 75th anniversary in 2021, and the sale of more than 25 million copies since its first edition.) In the coin market, dealers and collectors have found creative ways to respond to restrictions caused by the coronavirus pandemic. Online trading, already strong, has become a flourishing market for many buyers and sellers unable to physically attend coin shows. The bullion markets have brought new attention to coins as collectibles and investments. In the past year, modern coinage has become an even more exciting and innovative arena, with the introduction of 2021 "centennial" coins honoring the Morgan and Peace dollars and the promise of remarkable, unprecedented new coinage programs on the horizon. All of these dynamic forces and factors combine at a time when numismatics is poised for change and growth.

As has always been true, a collecting instinct is needed to be a longtime numismatist and an intellectual curiosity is essential to keep exploring the endless byways of numismatics to discover new things. In recent years the number of leading buyers building large collections has been greater than ever before in numismatic history. The hobby is alive and well. At Whitman Publishing all of us are enthusiastic about the future.

Colonial Issues

FOREIGN COINS IN THE COLONIES

Money had a rich history in America prior to the advent of the United States' national coinage in 1793. When coins tumbled off the presses from the first Philadelphia Mint the country was much more accustomed to coins from other lands. Prior to 1652 there was no local coinage and the only money in circulation was whatever came here from Europe through trade or travel. People were content to use currency, both old and new, whose value was based more on the metal content than on the issuer's reliability. Foreign money in America during the colonial period had become so embedded that it continued to be accepted as legal tender until discontinued by the Coinage Act of February 21, 1857. Coins of this era are so fundamental to American numismatics that every collection should include at least a sampling.

From the very beginning of commerce in America "hard money" was needed for trade with overseas nations. The largest quantity of coinage consisted of English crowns, shillings, and pence, and Spanish and Spanish-American silver pieces of eight, all of which circulated throughout colonial settlements until being sent back to England for critically needed supplies. Additional quantities of coins came from trading furs, lumber, and other exports that provided a limited but much needed supply of hard currency. Of equal importance to commerce were similar coins of other European countries. The large silver Dutch *leeuwendaalder* (Lyon or Lion dollar) and French *écu* saw extensive circulation, as did the Brazilian gold *peças*. Some New York bills of 1709 were even denominated in Lyon dollars. Distinguishing between the relative values of the multitude of different foreign currencies was not a simple task. To facilitate conversions, books and tables showed comparison prices for each currency.

The most familiar currencies in Colonial America were the Spanish-American piece of eight, the Dutch Lion Dollar, and Native American wampum.

The popular Spanish-American silver eight reales, Pillar dollar, or piece of eight, which was a radical departure from denominations in terms of English pounds, shillings, and pence, became a model for the American silver dollar, and its fractional parts morphed into the half-dollar and quarter-dollar coins that are now considered decimal fractions of the dollar. The American quarter dollar, which was similar in size and value to the Spanish two-real coin, took on the nickname "two bits"—a moniker that remains today. Similarly, the American one-cent coin has never totally lost its association with the English penny, and is still called that by anyone indifferent to numismatic accuracy.

Coins, tokens, paper money, and promissory notes were not the only media of exchange used during the early formation of the country. Many day-to-day transactions were carried on by barter and credit. Mixed into this financial morass were local trade items such as native wampum, hides, household goods, and tools. Records were kept in the traditional English pounds, shillings, and pence, but debts and taxes were paid in corn, beaver pelts, or money—money being whatever foreign coins were available. The terms "country pay" or "corn" referred to a number of different kinds of grain or even peas. Standard exchange rates were established and country pay was lawfully received at the colonial treasury for taxes.

Beyond these pre-federal considerations are the many kinds of private and state issues of coins and tokens that permeate the colonial period from 1616 to 1776. These are items that catch the attention and imagination of everyone interested in the history and development of early America. Yet, despite their enormous historical importance, forming a basic collection of such items is not nearly as daunting as one might expect.

The coins and tokens described in the next three sections of this book are fundamentally a major-type listing of the metallic money used throughout the pre-federal period. Many collectors use this as a guide to forming a basic set of these pieces. It is not encyclopedic in its scope. Beyond the basic types are numerous sub-varieties of some of the issues, and a wider range of European coins. Some collectors aim for the finest possible condition, while others find great enjoyment in pieces that saw actual circulation and use during the formative days of the country. There are no rules about how or what to collect other than to enjoy owning a genuine piece of early American history.

SPANISH-AMERICAN COINAGE IN THE NEW WORLD

Values shown for these silver coins are for the most common dates and mintmarked pieces of each issue. Similar pieces were struck at Spanish-American mints in Bolivia, Chile, Colombia, Guatemala, Mexico, Panama, Peru, and Santo Domingo.

COB COINAGE – KING PHILIP II (1556–1598) TO KING CHARLES III (1760–1772)

| 1 real cob of Mexico from the reign of Philip III. | 1668 2 reales cob struck in Potosi, from the reign of Charles II. |

	VG	F	VF	EF
Cob Type, 1/2 Real (1556–1773)	$40	$90	$150	$400
Cob Type, 1 Real (1556–1773)	$60	$125	$200	$450
Cob Type, 2 Reales (1556–1773)	$90	$175	$300	$625
Cob Type, 4 Reales (1556–1773)	$125	$300	$450	$950
Cob Type, 8 Reales (1556–1773)	$150	$300	$500	$900

Values are for coins with partial or missing dates. Fully dated coins are valued much higher. Some cobs were also issued beyond these dates and until as late as 1773 in Bolivia.

PILLAR TYPE – KING PHILIP V (1732–1747), KING FERDINAND VI (1747–1760), AND KING CHARLES III (1760–1772)

1734 8 reales Pillar dollar from the reign of Philip V.	**1761 2 reales "pistareen" from the reign of Charles III.**	

	VG	F	VF	EF
Pillar Type, 1/2 Real (1732–1772)	$30	$50	$100	$175
Pillar Type, 1 Real (1732–1772)	$40	$90	$125	$200
Pillar Type, 2 Reales (1732–1772)	$50	$100	$150	$300
Pillar Type, 4 Reales (1732–1772)	$150	$300	$500	$900
Pillar Type, 8 Reales (1732–1772)	$120	$225	$475	$750
Spanish 2 Reales "pistareen" (1716–1771)	$30	$60	$135	$210

BUST TYPE – KING CHARLES III (1772–1789), KING CHARLES IV (1789–1808), AND KING FERDINAND VII (1808–1825)

1807 8 reales Bust dollar from the reign of Charles IV.

	VG	F	VF	EF
Bust Type, 1/2 Real (1772–1825)	$15	$25	$40	$110
Bust Type, 1 Real (1772–1825)	$20	$35	$60	$125
Bust Type, 2 Reales (1772–1825)	$35	$60	$100	$200
Bust Type, 4 Reales (1772–1825)	$100	$250	$475	$800
Bust Type, 8 Reales (1772–1825)	$50	$75	$110	$225

The New World began its first coinage in 1536 in Mexico City. By 1732 the first round coins were made and the columnario. or Pillar coinage, became the coin of trade internationally. In 1772 the Bust dollars with the effigy of the king of Spain were placed in circulation. These coins and the Republican style of later Latin American countries circulated legally in the United States until 1857. Parallel issues of Spanish-American gold coins were made during this period. They saw extensive use for international trade and somewhat lesser use in domestic transactions in America. The Spanish silver pistareen was also a popular and convenient coin in circulation.

TYPICAL WORLD COINAGE USED IN COLONIAL AMERICA
NETHERLANDS SILVER COINAGE, 1601–1693

1640 1/2 Leeuwendaalder.

	VG	F	VF	EF
Netherlands, 1/2 Leeuwendaalder (1601–1653)	$100	$250	$500	$1,000
Netherlands, Leeuwendaalder "Lion Dollar" (1601–1693)	$70	$175	$300	$600

FRENCH SILVER COINAGE OF KING LOUIS XV (1715–1774) AND KING LOUIS XVI (1774–1792)

1791 écu from the reign of Louis XVI.

	VG	F	VF	EF
France, 1/2 Écu (1715–1792)	$25	$80	$150	$350
France, Écu (1715–1792)	$50	$100	$225	$400

See additional listings of French coins authorized for use in North America on pages 139–142.

BRITISH SILVER COINAGE OF KING CHARLES I (1625–1649) TO KING GEORGE III (1760–1820)

1639 6 pence from the reign of Charles I.   1787 shilling from the reign of George III.

	VG	F	VF	EF
England, Threepence (1625–1786)	$15	$25	$60	$100
England, Sixpence (1625–1787)	$25	$40	$90	$120
England, Shilling (1625–1787)	$35	$60	$125	$225
England, Half Crown (1625–1750)	$90	$160	$350	$625
England, Crown (1625–1730)	$225	$450	$800	$1,200

English copper coins and their imitations circulated extensively in early America and are described on page 157.

Other items frequently used as money in early America included cut fractions of various silver coins. These were cut by private individuals. The quarter 8-reales coin was "two bits." Worn and cut portions of coins usually passed for change according to their weight.

BRITISH NEW WORLD ISSUES

SOMMER ISLANDS (BERMUDA)

This coinage, the first struck for the English colonies in the New World, was issued circa 1616. The coins were known as *Hogge Money* or *Hoggies*, from the wild hogs depicted on their obverses.

The Sommer Islands, as Bermuda was known at the time, were under the jurisdiction of the Virginia Company, a joint-stock mercantile venture formed under a British royal patent and headquartered in London. (This venture was actually undertaken by two companies: the Virginia Company of Plymouth, for what is now New England; and the Virginia Company of London, for the American South.)

English government of the islands had started a few years before the coins were issued—by accident! In 1609 Admiral Sir George Somers led a fleet bound from England to the New World, laden with relief supplies for the Virginia settlement of Jamestown. Somers and his ship were separated from the rest of the fleet in a strong storm, and they ran onto the reefs of the Bermuda Islands, some 700 miles from Virginia. (The islands were named for Juan de Bermúdez, who is believed to have stopped there some hundred years earlier.) For ten months Somers and his party were able to live on wild hogs and birds, local plants, and fish, building houses and a church. During this time they also constructed two small ships, in which, in May 1610, most of the shipwrecked colonists continued their interrupted journey to Virginia.

Bermuda became a separate entity of the Virginia Company of London, from November 1612 until June 29, 1615, when "the Governour and Company of the City of London for the Plantacon of the Somer Islands" (often called the Bermuda Company by historians) was officially incorporated under royal charter. This incorporation granted the right of coinage. The coins did not arrive in the islands until May 16, 1616, at the earliest, a year after Bermuda was under its new charter.

The pieces were struck on thin planchets of brass or copper, lightly silvered, in four denominations: shilling, sixpence, threepence, and twopence, each indicated by Roman numerals. A wild hog is the main device and appears on the obverse side of each coin. SOMMER ISLANDS is inscribed (misspelling both the English admiral's name and the corporation's) within beaded circles on the larger denominations. The reverse shows a full-rigged galleon, or carrack, with the flag of St. George on each of four masts. Many examples of these coins show signs of oxidation or pitting.

"In an era when British silver shillings and fractions traded in commerce based on their intrinsic value," writes Q. David Bowers, "the Bermuda pieces were tokens of little value, a fiat currency that circulated in the manner that paper money would later be used worldwide—good as long as both parties had confidence in the value. As might be expected, these coins had little or no trade value other than within the islands, where they were mostly used at the company storehouse, exchanged for supplies" (*Whitman Encyclopedia of Colonial and Early American Coins*).

These coins of Bermuda did not circulate in North America, but they have traditionally been considered part of early "American" coinage. Sylvester S. Crosby, writing in his 1875 masterwork *Early Coins of America*, insisted that the Bermuda coins laid claim to being "the first ever struck for the English colonies in America," this despite the fact that the islands were not a part of the Virginia colony proper. The regular edition of the *Guide Book of United States Coins* has included them in its pre-federal coverage since the first edition, published in 1946.

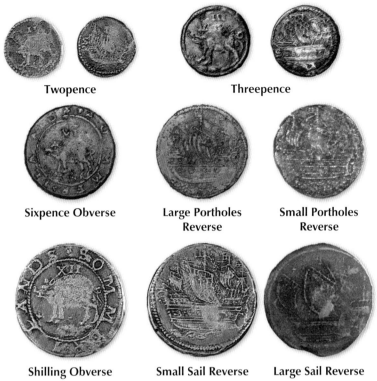

Twopence

Threepence

Sixpence Obverse

Large Portholes Reverse

Small Portholes Reverse

Shilling Obverse

Small Sail Reverse

Large Sail Reverse

	AG	G	VG	F	VF	EF
Twopence, Large Star Between Legs	$4,500	$10,000	$15,000	$17,500	$35,000	$65,000
Twopence, Small Star Between Legs	$4,500	$10,000	$15,000	$20,000	$40,000	$65,000
Threepence	—	—	$35,000	$65,000	$90,000	—
Sixpence, Small Portholes	$3,500	$7,500	$10,000	$20,000	$30,000	$50,000
Sixpence, Large Portholes	$3,750	$10,000	$15,000	$20,000	$55,000	$80,000
Shilling, Small Sail	$4,750	$6,500	$10,000	$30,000	$55,000	$75,000
Shilling, Large Sail	$8,000	$15,000	$40,000	$70,000	$90,000	—

MASSACHUSETTS
"NEW ENGLAND" COINAGE (1652)

The earliest authorized medium of exchange in the New England settlements was wampum. The General Court of Massachusetts in 1637 ordered "that wampamege should passe at 6 a penny for any sume under 12 d." Wampum consisted of shells of various colors, ground to the size of kernels of corn. A hole was drilled through each piece so it could be strung on a leather thong for convenience and adornment.

Corn, pelts, and bullets were frequently used in lieu of coins, which were rarely available. Silver and gold coins brought over from England, Holland, and other countries tended to flow back across the Atlantic to purchase needed supplies. The colonists, thus left to their own resources, traded with the friendly Native Americans in kind. In 1661 the law making wampum legal tender was repealed.

Agitation for a standard coinage reached its height in 1651. England, recovering from a civil war between the Puritans and Royalists, ignored the colonists, who took matters into their own hands in 1652.

The Massachusetts General Court in 1652 ordered the first metallic currency—the New England silver threepence, sixpence, and shilling—to be struck in the English Americas (the Spaniards had established a mint in Mexico City in 1535). Silver bullion was procured principally in the form of mixed coinage from the West Indies. The mint was located in Boston, and John Hull was appointed mintmaster; his assistant was Robert Sanderson (or Saunderson). At first, Hull received as compensation one shilling threepence for every 20 shillings coined. This fee was adjusted several times during his term as mintmaster.

The planchets of the New England coins were struck with prepared punches twice (once for the obverse, and once for the reverse). First the letters NE were stamped, and then on the other side the numerical denomination of III, VI, or XII was added.

These are called "NE coins" today.

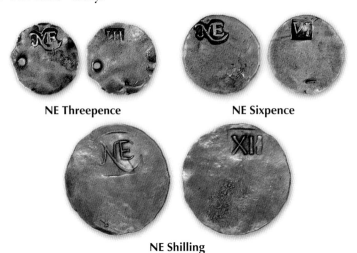

NE Threepence   NE Sixpence

NE Shilling

Early American coins in conditions better than those listed are rare and are consequently valued much higher.

	G	VG	F	VF	EF	AU
NE Threepence (a)				—		
NE Sixpence (b)	$55,000	$90,000	$135,000	$250,000	$350,000	$650,000
NE Shilling	$55,000	$75,000	$100,000	$125,000	$160,000	$250,000

a. Unique. **b.** 8 examples are known.

WILLOW TREE COINAGE (1653–1660)

The simplicity of the designs on the NE coins invited counterfeiting, and clipping or shaving of the edges by charlatans who sought to snip a little bit of metal from a lot of coins and thereby accumulate a pile of silver. Therefore, they were soon replaced by the Willow Tree series.

All of the Willow Tree coins bore the date 1652, when Oliver Cromwell was in power in Britain, after the English civil war and during the Interregnum government. In fact they were minted from 1653 to 1660. The date 1652 may have been used simply because this was the year the coinage was authorized. Output increased over the years, and the coins were plentiful in circulation.

These pieces, like all early American coins, were produced from handmade dies that are often individually distinctive. The tree in the design is known as a "willow" not from any official legislative records, and certainly not from lifelike resemblance to an actual willow tree, but from terminology dating from 1867 in an auction catalog of the Joseph Mickley Collection. To make the coins, a worker likely placed a silver planchet into a rocker press, which forced a curved upper die against a curved or flat bottom die. This would explain the slight elongation and gentle bend of many Willow Tree coins.

NEW ENGLAND is spelled out, instead of being abbreviated, as on the earlier NE coinage.

Among the four classes of Massachusetts silver coins—NE, Willow Tree, Oak Tree, and Pine Tree—the Willow Tree pieces are far and away the rarest today. The die varieties that can be found and identified are of interest to collectors who value each according to individual rarity. Values shown for type coins are for the most frequently seen die variety.

Threepence   Sixpence

Shilling

	G	VG	F	VF	EF
1652 Willow Tree Threepence (a)	—	—	—		
Auctions: $587,500, VF, March 2015					
1652 Willow Tree Sixpence (b)	$17,500	$30,000	$60,000	$100,000	$200,000
Auctions: $282,000, AU-58, March 2015					
1652 Willow Tree Shilling	$17,500	$30,000	$55,000	$100,000	$150,000
Auctions: $282,000, VF-35, November 2013					

a. 3 examples are known. **b.** 14 examples are known.

Oak Tree Coinage (1660–1667)

The Oak Tree coins of Massachusetts were struck from 1660 to 1667, following the Willow Tree coinage. The 1662-dated twopence of this type was the only coin of the Willow Tree, Oak Tree, and Pine Tree series that did not bear the date 1652. Numismatists are divided on whether the twopence date of 1662 is an error, or a deliberate use of the year that the new denomination was authorized.

The obverse of these coins features a tree traditionally described by numismatists as an oak tree. Although it is deciduous, it does not closely resemble a specific species. On the reverse, NEW ENGLAND is spelled out, surrounding the date and denomination.

In 1660 the Commonwealth of England was dissolved and the British monarchy was restored under King Charles II. At the time, following longstanding tradition and law, the right to produce coins was considered to be a royal sovereign prerogative. Sylvester Crosby in *Early Coins of America* suggested that during the Massachusetts silver coinage period, numerous tributes—including ship masts, 3,000 codfish, and other material items—were sent to the king to placate him and postpone any action on the Massachusetts coinage question. As with many situations involving early American coinage, facts are scarce.

As with other types of Massachusetts silver, a number of die varieties of Oak Tree coinage can be collected and studied. In the marketplace they are seen far more often than are the two earlier types. They are valued according to their individual rarity. Values shown here are for the most frequently seen die varieties.

Twopence

Threepence

Sixpence

Shilling

	G	VG	F	VF	EF	AU	Unc.
1662 Oak Tree Twopence, Small 2	$600	$850	$1,200	$2,700	$4,500	$6,500	$10,000
1662 Oak Tree Twopence, Large 2	$600	$850	$1,200	$2,700	$4,500	$6,500	$10,000
1652 Oak Tree Threepence, No IN on Obverse	$700	$1,100	$2,500	$5,000	$10,000	$17,500	$30,000
1652 Oak Tree Threepence, IN on Obverse	$650	$1,100	$2,800	$6,500	$12,000	$18,000	$45,000
1652 Oak Tree Sixpence, IN on Reverse	$800	$1,300	$2,500	$6,000	$10,000	$15,000	$35,000
1652 Oak Tree Sixpence, IN on Obverse	$800	$1,300	$3,000	$6,000	$10,000	$14,000	$32,000
1652 Oak Tree Shilling, IN at Left	$700	$1,200	$2,200	$6,000	$9,000	$12,500	$25,000
1652 Oak Tree Shilling, IN at Bottom	$750	$1,250	$2,500	$6,000	$9,000	$13,500	$27,500
1652 Oak Tree Shilling, ANDO	$750	$1,500	$3,000	$6,500	$10,000	$15,000	$30,000
1652 Oak Tree Shilling, Spiny Tree	$750	$1,250	$2,500	$5,500	$9,000	$15,000	$30,000

PINE TREE COINAGE (1667–1682)

The first Pine Tree coins were minted on the same-size planchets as the Oak Tree pieces, in denominations of threepence, sixpence, and shilling. Subsequent issues of the shilling were narrower in diameter and thicker. Large Planchet shillings ranged from 27 to 31 mm in diameter; Small Planchet shillings ranged from 22 to 26 mm in diameter.

The design of the Pine Tree coins borrowed from the flag of the Massachusetts Bay Colony, which featured a pine tree. On the reverse, NEW ENGLAND is spelled out, surrounding the date and a Roman numeral indicating the denomination (III, VI, or XII).

Large quantities of Pine Tree coins were minted. The coinage was abandoned in 1682. A proposal to renew coinage in 1686 was rejected by the General Court of Massachusetts.

As with other types of Massachusetts silver, a number of die varieties of Pine Tree coins are available for collecting and study. In the marketplace, they are valued according to their individual rarity. Values shown here are for the most often seen die varieties.

Threepence

Sixpence

Shilling, Large Planchet (1667–1674)

Shilling, Small Planchet (1675–1682)

	G	VG	F	VF	EF	AU	Unc.
1652 Threepence, Pellets at Trunk	$625	$950	$1,600	$2,500	$4,500	$7,500	$17,000
1652 Threepence, Without Pellets	$625	$950	$1,500	$2,500	$4,500	$7,500	$17,000
1652 Sixpence, Pellets at Trunk	$800	$1,000	$1,750	$3,000	$4,250	$6,500	$18,000
1652 Sixpence, Without Pellets	$900	$1,350	$2,500	$4,200	$5,250	$8,500	$22,000
1652 Shilling, Large Planchet (27–31 mm)							
Pellets at Trunk	$850	$1,250	$2,500	$4,500	$7,000	$11,000	$22,000
Without Pellets at Trunk	$700	$1,000	$2,500	$4,000	$6,500	$10,500	$22,000
No H in MASATUSETS	$800	$1,400	$2,700	$6,000	$10,000	$15,000	—
Ligatured NE in Legend	$750	$1,100	$2,500	$4,500	$7,000	$11,000	$22,000
1652 Shilling, Small Planchet (22–26 mm)	$600	$925	$2,000	$3,000	$4,500	$10,000	$20,000

MARYLAND
LORD BALTIMORE COINAGE

Cecil Calvert, the second Lord Baltimore, inherited from his father nearly absolute control over Maryland. Calvert believed he had the right to coin money for the colony, and in 1659 he ordered shillings, sixpences, and groats (four-penny pieces) from the Royal Mint in London and shipped samples to Maryland, to his brother Philip, who was then his secretary for the colony. Calvert's right to strike coins was upheld by Oliver Cromwell's government. The whole issue was small, and while his coins did circulate in Maryland at first, by 1700 they had largely disappeared from commerce.

Calvert's coins bear his portrait on the obverse, with a Latin legend calling him "Lord of Mary's Land." The reverses of the larger denominations bear his family coat of arms and the denomination in Roman numerals. There are several die varieties of each. Some of these coins are found holed and repaired. The copper penny, or denarium, is the rarest denomination, with only nine reported specimens, including some found in recent times by detectorists using electronic devices.

The silver groats (fourpence), sixpence, and shillings were used extensively in commerce, and today most examples show considerable wear. Typical grades include VG, Fine, and VF, often with surface marks or damage. Those graded AU or higher are major rarities. The silver pieces have an engrailed edge.

Penny (Denarium)	Fourpence (Groat)	Sixpence	Shilling

	G	VG	F	VF	EF	AU
Denarium copper (a)	—	—	$75,000	$125,000	$150,000	—
	Auctions: $199,750, MS-62BN, January 2015					
Fourpence	$4,000	$7,000	$13,000	$20,000	$30,000	$50,000
Fourpence, Small Bust						—
	Auctions: $63,250, MS-62, May 2008					
Sixpence	$1,700	$2,500	$4,500	$6,000	$10,000	$15,000
Shilling	$2,500	$4,500	$6,500	$12,000	$17,000	$30,000

a. Extremely rare.

NEW JERSEY
ST. PATRICK OR MARK NEWBY COINAGE

Mark Newby was a shopkeeper in Dublin, Ireland, in the 1670s and came to America in November 1681, settling in West Jersey (today's New Jersey). He brought with him a quantity of copper pieces, of two sizes, believed by numismatists to have been struck in Dublin circa 1663 to 1672. These are known as *St. Patrick coppers*. (Alternatively, they may have been struck for circulation in Ireland by Pierre Blondeau to fill an order made by the duke of Ormonde, but this has not been confirmed.) The larger-sized piece, called by collectors a *halfpenny*, bears the arms of the City of Dublin on the shield on the reverse. The smaller-sized piece, called a *farthing*, does not. Although neither bears a denomination, these are designations traditionally assigned by numismatists. Both sizes have reeded edges.

Newby became a member of the legislature of West Jersey, and under his influence the St. Patrick coinage was made legal tender by the General Assembly of New Jersey in May 1682. The legislature did not specify which size piece could circulate, only that the coin was to be worth a halfpenny in trade and that no one would be obliged to accept more than five shillings' worth (120 coins) in one payment. Some numismatists believe the larger-size coin was intended. However, many more farthing-size pieces are known than halfpennies, and numerous coins of the farthing size have been excavated by detectorists in New Jersey, while none of the larger coins have been found this way. Most numismatists believe that the smaller-sized piece was the one authorized as legal tender. Copper coins often circulated in the colonies at twice what they would have been worth in England.

The obverses show King David crowned, kneeling and playing a harp. The legend FLOREAT REX ("May the King Prosper") is separated by a crown. The reverse side of the halfpence shows St. Patrick with a crozier in his left hand and a trefoil in his right, and surrounded by people. At his left side is a shield. The legend is ECCE GREX ("Behold the Flock"). The farthing reverse shows St. Patrick driving away serpents and a dragon as he holds a metropolitan cross in his left hand. The legend reads QUIESCAT PLEBS ("May the People Be at Ease").

The decorative brass insert found on the coinage, usually over the crown on the obverse, was put there to make counterfeiting more difficult. On some pieces this decoration has been removed or does not show. Numerous die variations exist (more than 140 of the smaller coins, and 9 of the larger). The silver strikings, and a unique gold piece, were not authorized as legal tender, although many of the silver coins are heavily worn, suggesting that they were passed many times from hand to hand in commerce, perhaps at the value of a shilling.

St. Patrick "Farthing"   St. Patrick "Halfpenny"

	G	VG	F	VF	EF	AU
St. Patrick "Farthing"	$200	$400	$600	$1,650	$3,500	$12,500
Similar, Halo Around Saint's Head	$1,000	$2,500	$7,000	$18,000	$45,000	—
Similar, No C in QUIESCAT	$1,000	$5,000	$10,000	$20,000	—	—
St. Patrick "Farthing," Silver	$2,500	$4,000	$8,000	$17,500	$25,000	$40,000
St. Patrick "Farthing," Gold (a)						—
	Auctions: $184,000, AU, January 2005					
St. Patrick "Halfpenny"	$350	$600	$800	$2,500	$7,500	$15,000

a. Unique.

COINAGE AUTHORIZED BY BRITISH ROYAL PATENT

AMERICAN PLANTATIONS COINS (1688)

These tokens, struck in nearly pure tin, were the first royally authorized coinage for the British colonies in America. They were made under a franchise granted in August 1688 to Richard Holt, an agent for the owners of several tin mines. Holt proposed that the new issues be made with a Spanish monetary designation to increase their acceptance in the channels of American commerce, where Spanish-American coins were often seen. Thus the tokens are denominated as 1/24 part of a Spanish real.

The obverse shows an equestrian portrait of King James II in armor and flowing garments. The reverse features four heraldic shields (English, Scottish, French, and Irish) connected by chains. The edge is decorated with dots.

Numismatist Eric P. Newman has identified seven different obverse dies and an equal number of reverse dies. Most American Plantation tokens show black oxidation of the tin. Bright, unblemished original specimens are more valuable. (Around 1828 a London coin dealer acquired the original dies and arranged for restrikes to be made for sale. In high grades these pieces are seen more frequently in the marketplace than are originals. They are valuable but worth less than original strikes.)

	G	VG	F	VF	EF	AU	Unc.
(1688) James II Plantation 1/24 Real coinage							
1/24 Part Real	$200	$400	$900	$2,000	$3,000	$5,000	$7,500
1/24 Part Real, ET. HB. REX	$250	$400	$900	$2,000	$3,000	$7,000	$10,000
1/24 Part Real, Sidewise 4 in 24	$500	$1,000	$2,000	$4,000	$5,500	$7,500	$20,000
1/24 Part Real, Arms Transposed	$500	$1,500	$2,750	$7,000	$10,000	$15,000	
1/24 Part Real, Restrike					$500	$1,000	$2,000

COINAGE OF WILLIAM WOOD (1722–1733)

William Wood, an English metallurgist, experimented with the production of several pattern coins (of halfpenny, penny, and twopence size) in 1717. In 1722 he was granted royal patents to mint coins for America and Ireland. At the time his productions were largely unpopular as money, but later generations of coin collectors have sought his Rosa Americana coins for their connections to colonial America. The Hibernia coins are similar in some respects; they have no connection with America but are sought as companion pieces.

ROSA AMERICANA COINS (1722–1723, 1733)

On July 12, 1722, William Wood obtained a patent from King George I to make coins for the American colonies. At the time the colonies were facing a serious shortage of circulating coins.

The first pieces Wood struck were undated. Later issues bear the dates 1722, 1723, 1724, and 1733. The Rosa Americana pieces were issued in three denominations—half penny, penny, and twopence—and were intended for America. This type had a fully bloomed rose on the reverse with the words ROSA AMERICANA UTILE DULCI ("American Rose—Useful and Sweet").

The obverse, common to both Rosa Americana and Hibernia pieces, shows the head of George I and the legend GEORGIUS D:G MAG: BRI: FRA: ET. HIB: REX ("George, by the Grace of God, King of Great Britain, France, and Ireland") or abbreviations thereof.

Despite Wood's best efforts, these Rosa Americana coins circulated in the colonies only to a limited extent. They eventually did see use as money, but it was back in England, and likely at values lower than their assigned denominations. (Each was about half the weight of its English counterpart coin.)

The 1733 twopence is a pattern that bears the bust of King George II facing to the left. It was issued by the successors to the original coinage patent, as William Wood had died in 1730.

The coins are made of a brass composition of copper and zinc (sometimes mistakenly referred to as *Bath metal*, an alloy proposed by Wood that would have also included a minute portion of silver). Planchet quality is often rough and porous because the blanks were heated prior to striking. Edges often show file marks.

	VG	F	VF	EF	AU	Unc.
(No date) Twopence, Motto in Ribbon *(illustrated)*	$200	$400	$700	$1,000	$2,000	$4,000
(No date) Twopence, Motto Without Ribbon (a)		—	—	—		

a. 3 examples are known.

	VG	F	VF	EF	AU	Unc.
1722 Halfpenny, VTILE DVLCI	$900	$2,000	$3,500	$6,250	$10,000	
1722 Halfpenny, D.G.REX ROSA AMERI. UTILE DULCI	$125	$200	$400	$800	$1,250	$3,250
1722 Halfpenny, DEI GRATIA REX UTILE DULCI	$150	$200	$400	$700	$1,100	$2,700

	VG	F	VF	EF	AU	Unc.
1722 Penny, GEORGIVS	$2,500	$5,000	$12,000	$17,500	$20,000	$30,000
1722 Penny, VTILE DVLCI	$170	$300	$500	$850	$2,250	$5,000
1722 Penny, UTILE DULCI	$150	$200	$300	$600	$1,000	$2,500

	VG	F	VF	EF	AU	Unc.
1722 Twopence, Period After REX	$100	$200	$300	$700	$1,250	$2,000
1722 Twopence, No Period After REX	$175	$300	$600	$1,100	$1,800	$3,500

	VG	F	VF	EF	AU	Unc.
1723 Halfpenny, Uncrowned Rose	$1,000	$1,800	$3,600	$5,500	$8,500	$12,500
1723 Halfpenny, Crowned Rose	$125	$200	$375	$600	$1,000	$2,700

	VG	F	VF	EF	AU	Unc.
1723 Penny *(illustrated)*	$100	$125	$275	$500	$800	$2,000
1723 Twopence	$85	$150	$250	$350	$700	$1,600

	EF	AU	Unc.
1724, 4 Over 3 Penny (pattern), DEI GRATIA		$20,000	$27,500
1724, 4 Over 3 Penny (pattern), D GRATIA	$8,750	$20,000	$31,000
(Undated) (1724) Penny, ROSA: SINE: SPINA. (a)	$18,000	$25,000	$31,200

a. 5 examples are known.

1724 Twopence (pattern)
Auctions: $31,200, SP-61, October 2018

1733 Twopence (pattern), Proof

Auctions: $63,250, Gem PF, May 2005

WOOD'S HIBERNIA COINAGE (1722–1724)

Around the same time that his royal patent was granted to strike the Rosa Americana coins for the American colonies, William Wood received a franchise to produce copper coins for circulation in Ireland. This was ratified on July 22, 1722. The resulting coins, likely struck in Bristol, England, featured a portrait of King George and, on the reverse, a seated figure with a harp and the word HIBERNIA. Their edges are plain. Denominations struck were farthing and halfpenny, with dates of 1722, 1723, and 1724. These Hibernia coins were unpopular in Ireland and faced vocal public criticism, including from satirist Jonathan Swift. "It was asserted that the issues for Ireland were produced without Irish advice or consent, that the arrangements were made in secret and for the private profit of Wood, and that the pieces were seriously underweight" (*Whitman Encyclopedia of Colonial and Early American Coins*). As a result, King George reduced the number of coins allowed by Wood's patent, and the franchise was retired completely in 1725 in exchange for Wood receiving a £24,000 pension over eight years. Some of the unpopular Hibernia coins, meanwhile, may have been sent to the American colonies to circulate as small change. Their popularity with American numismatists stems from the similarity of their obverses to those in the Rosa Americana series.

Numerous varieties exist.

| 1722, Hibernia Farthing | 1722, Hibernia Halfpenny, First Type | 1722, Hibernia Halfpenny, Second Type | 1723, 3 Over 2, Halfpenny |

| 1724, Hibernia Farthing | 1724, Hibernia Halfpenny |

	G	VG	F	VF	EF	AU	Unc.
1722 Farthing, D: G: REX	$500	$2,500	$3,500	$5,000	$7,500	$10,000	$15,000
1722 Halfpenny, D: G: REX, Rocks at Right (pattern)	—	—	$5,000	$8,000	$12,000	$20,000	$40,000
1722 Halfpenny, First Type, Harp at Left	$50	$80	$125	$250	$450	$700	$1,400
1722 Halfpenny, Second Type, Harp at Right	$45	$70	$100	$200	$400	$700	$1,200
1722 Halfpenny, Second Type, DEII (blunder)	$80	$150	$375	$800	$1,400	$1,800	$3,000
1723 Farthing, D.G.REX	$125	$300	$400	$650	$1,000	$1,250	$2,000
1723 Farthing, DEI. GRATIA. REX	$25	$50	$80	$125	$225	$400	$600
1723 Farthing (silver pattern)	$400	$600	$1,200	$2,500	$4,000	$5,000	$7,500
1723 Halfpenny, 3 Over 2 (a)	$40	$60	$125	$350	$500	$900	$1,750
1723 Halfpenny	$25	$45	$75	$125	$250	$375	$700
1723 Halfpenny (silver pattern)			—	—	—	—	—
1724 Farthing	$50	$125	$200	$600	$1,250	$1,450	$3,600
1724 Halfpenny	$45	$100	$150	$350	$600	$900	$2,000
1724 Halfpenny, DEI Above Head					—	—	

a. Varieties exist.

VIRGINIA HALFPENNIES (1773–1774)

In 1773 the British Crown authorized coinage of copper halfpennies for the colony of Virginia, not to exceed 25 tons' weight. "This was the first and only colonial coinage authorized and produced in Britain for use in an American colony, thereby giving the Virginia pieces the unique claim of being the only true American colonial coinage" (*Whitman Encyclopedia of Colonial and Early American Coins*). The designs included a laurelled portrait of King George III and the royal coat of arms of the House of Hanover. The coins were struck at the Tower Mint in London. Their edges are plain.

Most Mint State pieces available to collectors today are from a hoard of some 5,000 or more of the halfpennies held by Colonel Mendes I. Cohen of Baltimore, Maryland, in the 1800s. Cohen came from a prominent banking family. His cache was dispersed slowly and carefully from 1875 until 1929, as the coins passed from his estate to his nieces and nephews. Eventually the remaining coins, numbering approximately 2,200, the property of Bertha Cohen, were dispersed in one lot in Baltimore. These pieces gradually filtered out, in groups and individually, into the wider numismatic marketplace.

The Proof patterns that were struck on a large planchet with a wide milled border are often referred to as pennies. The silver pieces dated 1774 are referred to as shillings, but they may have been patterns or trials for a halfpenny or a guinea.

Red Uncirculated pieces without spots are worth considerably more.

	G	VG	F	VF	EF	AU	Unc.
1773 Halfpenny, Period After GEORGIVS	$25	$50	$100	$150	$350	$500	$1,250
1773 Halfpenny, No Period After GEORGIVS	$35	$75	$125	$250	$400	$650	$1,400

1773, "Penny"   1774, "Shilling"

	PF
1773 "Penny"	$27,000
1774 "Shilling" (a)	$110,000

a. 6 examples are known.

EARLY AMERICAN AND RELATED TOKENS

ELEPHANT TOKENS (CA. 1672–1694)

LONDON ELEPHANT TOKENS

The London Elephant tokens were struck in London circa 1672 to 1694. Although they were undated, two examples are known to have been struck over 1672 British halfpennies. Most were struck in copper, but one was made of brass. Their legend, GOD PRESERVE LONDON, may have been a general plea for divine aid and not a specific reference to the outbreak of plague in 1665 or the great fire of 1666.

These pieces were not struck for the colonies, and they probably did not circulate widely in America, although a few may have been carried there by colonists. They are associated, through a shared obverse die, with the 1694 Carolina and New England Elephant tokens. They have a plain edge but often show the cutting marks from planchet preparation.

	VG	F	VF	EF	AU	Unc.
(1694) Halfpenny, GOD PRESERVE LONDON, Thick Planchet ‡	$350	$600	$900	$1,300	$2,000	$3,200
(1694) Halfpenny, GOD PRESERVE LONDON, Thin Planchet ‡	$750	$1,250	$2,500	$5,000	$7,500	$12,500
Similar, Brass ‡ (a)					—	
(1694) Halfpenny, GOD PRESERVE LONDON, Diagonals in Center of Shield ‡	$700	$1,800	$4,000	$7,500	$11,000	$25,000
(1694) Halfpenny, Similar, Sword in Second Quarter of Shield ‡	—	—	$20,000	—	—	—
(1694) Halfpenny, LON DON ‡	$1,000	$2,000	$3,500	$7,500	$15,000	$24,000

‡ All Elephant Tokens are ranked in the *100 Greatest American Medals and Tokens*, as a single entry. **a.** Unique.

CAROLINA ELEPHANT TOKENS

Although no law is known authorizing coinage for Carolina, two very interesting pieces known as Elephant tokens were made with the date 1694. These copper tokens are of halfpenny denomination. The reverse reads GOD PRESERVE CAROLINA AND THE LORDS PROPRIETERS 1694.

The second and more readily available variety has the last word spelled PROPRIETORS. The correction was made on the original die, for the E shows plainly beneath the O. On the second variety the elephant's tusks nearly touch the milling.

The Carolina pieces were probably struck in England and perhaps intended as advertising to heighten interest in the Carolina Plantation. Another theory suggests they may have been related to or made for the Carolina coffee house in London.

	VG	F	VF	EF	AU	Unc.
1694 PROPRIETERS ‡	$7,000	$16,000	$22,000	$35,000	$45,000	$70,000
1694 PROPRIETORS, O Over E ‡	$3,000	$6,000	$9,000	$15,000	$22,000	$45,000

‡ All Elephant Tokens are ranked in the *100 Greatest American Medals and Tokens*, as a single entry.

NEW ENGLAND ELEPHANT TOKENS

Like the Carolina tokens, the New England Elephant tokens are believed to have been struck in England, possibly as promotional pieces to increase interest in the American colonies, or perhaps related to the New England coffee house in London

	VG	F	VF	EF	AU
1694 NEW ENGLAND ‡ *(3 known)*	$50,000	—	$75,000	$100,000	

‡ All Elephant Tokens are ranked in the *100 Greatest American Medals and Tokens*, as a single entry.

NEW YORKE IN AMERICA TOKENS (1660S OR 1670S)

The New Yorke in America tokens are farthing or halfpenny tokens intended for New York, issued by Francis Lovelace, who was governor from 1668 until 1673. The tokens use the older spelling with a final "e" (YORKE), which predominated before 1710. The obverse shows Cupid pursuing the loveless butterfly-winged Psyche—a rebus on the name Lovelace. The reverse shows a heraldic eagle, identical to the one displayed in fesse, raguly (i.e., on a crenellated bar) on the Lovelace coat of arms. In weight, fabric, and die axis the tokens are similar to certain 1670 farthing tokens of Bristol, England, where they may have been struck. There is no evidence that any of these pieces ever circulated in America. Fewer than two dozen are believed to now exist.

	VG	F	VF	EF
(Undated) Brass or Copper ‡	$10,000	$15,000	$25,000	$50,000
(Undated) Pewter ‡		$20,000	$30,000	$65,000

‡ All New Yorke in America Tokens are ranked in the *100 Greatest American Medals and Tokens*, as a single entry.

GLOUCESTER TOKENS (1714)

Sylvester S. Crosby, in his book *The Early Coins of America*, stated that these tokens appear to have been intended as a pattern for a shilling—a private coinage by Richard Dawson of Gloucester (county), Virginia. The only specimens known are struck in brass, although the denomination XII indicates that a silver coinage (one shilling) may have been planned. The building depicted on the obverse may represent some public building, possibly the courthouse.

Although neither of the two known examples shows the full legends, combining the pieces shows GLOVCESTER COVRTHOVSE VIRGINIA / RIGHAVLT DAWSON. ANNO.DOM. 1714. This recent discovery has provided a new interpretation of the legends, as a Righault family once owned land near the Gloucester courthouse. A similar, but somewhat smaller, piece possibly dated 1715 exists. The condition of this unique piece is too poor for positive attribution.

	VF
1714 Shilling, brass ‡ (a)	$180,000

‡ Ranked in the *100 Greatest American Medals and Tokens*. **a.** 2 examples are known.

HIGLEY OR GRANBY COPPERS (1737–1739)

Dr. Samuel Higley owned a private copper mine near Granby, Connecticut, in an area known for many such operations. Higley was a medical doctor, with a degree from Yale College, who also practiced blacksmithing and experimented in metallurgy. He worked his mine as a private individual, extracting particularly rich copper, smelting it, and shipping much of it to England. He also made his own dies for plain-edged pure-copper "coins" that he issued.

Legend has it that a drink in the local tavern cost three pence, and that Higley paid his bar tabs with his own privately minted coins, denominated as they were with the legend THE VALUE OF THREEPENCE. When his supply of such coppers exceeded the local demand, neighbors complained that they were not worth the denomination stated, and Higley changed the legends to read VALUE ME AS YOU PLEASE and I AM GOOD COPPER (but kept the Roman numeral III on the obverse).

After Samuel Higley's death in May 1737 his older brother John continued his coinage.

The Higley coppers were never officially authorized. There were seven obverse and four reverse dies. All are rare. Electrotypes and cast copies exist.

	AG	G	VG	F	VF
1737 THE VALVE OF THREE PENCE, CONNECTICVT, 3 Hammers ‡	$12,000	$18,000	$30,000	$50,000	$100,000
1737 THE VALVE OF THREE PENCE, I AM GOOD COPPER, 3 Hammers ‡ (a)	—	$35,000	$50,000	$80,000	$175,000
1737 VALUE ME AS YOU PLEASE, I AM GOOD COPPER, 3 Hammers ‡	$12,000	$18,000	$30,000	$50,000	$100,000
1737 VALVE • ME • AS • YOU • PLEASE, I • AM • GOOD • COPPER, 3 Hammers ‡ (a)			$75,000		
(1737) VALUE • ME • AS • YOU • PLEASE, J • CUT • MY • WAY • THROUGH, Broad Axe ‡	$12,000	$18,000	$30,000	$50,000	$100,000
(1737) THE • WHEELE • GOES • ROUND, Reverse as Above (b) ‡					$350,000
1739 VALUE • ME • AS • YOU • PLEASE, J • CUT • MY • WAY • THROUGH, Broad Axe ‡	$15,000	$20,000	$37,500	$60,000	$125,000

‡ All Higley Coppers are ranked in the *100 Greatest American Medals and Tokens*, as a single entry. **a.** This issue has the CONNECTICVT reverse. 3 examples are known. **b.** Unique.

HIBERNIA–VOCE POPULI COINS

These coins, struck in the year 1760, were prepared by Roche, of King Street, Dublin, who was at that time engaged in the manufacture of buttons for the army. Like other Irish tokens, some could have found their way to colonial America and possibly circulated in the colonies with numerous other counterfeit halfpence and "bungtown tokens." There is no evidence to prove that Voce Populi pieces, which bear the legend HIBERNIA (Ireland) on the reverse, ever circulated in North America. Sylvester S. Crosby did not include them in *The Early Coins of America*, 1875. Nor were they covered in Wayte Raymond's *Standard Catalogue of United States Coins* (until Walter Breen revised the section on colonial coins in 1954, after which they were "adopted" by mainstream collectors). Various theories exist regarding the identity of the bust portrait on the obverse, ranging from kings and pretenders to the British throne, to the provost of Dublin College.

There are two distinct issues. Coins from the first, with a "short bust" on the obverse, ranged in weight from 87 to 120 grains. Those from the second, with a "long bust" on the obverse, ranged in weight from 129 to 154 grains. Most of the "long bust" varieties have the letter P on the obverse. None of the "short bust" varieties bear the letter P, and, judging from their weight, they may have been contemporary counterfeits.

Farthing, Large Letters

Halfpenny

Halfpenny, VOOE POPULI

Halfpenny, P in Front of Face

	G	VG	F	VF	EF	AU	Unc.
1760 Farthing, Large Letters	$200	$300	$500	$1,250	$2,000	$3,000	$5,500
1760 Farthing, Small Letters			$8,000	$10,000	$15,000	$20,000	$25,000
1760 Halfpenny	$80	$110	$180	$300	$500	$700	$1,250
1760 Halfpenny, VOOE POPULI	$90	$150	$200	$400	$550	$1,000	$3,000
1760 Halfpenny, P Below Bust	$110	$200	$300	$600	$900	$1,600	$4,500
1760 Halfpenny, P in Front of Face	$90	$175	$250	$500	$800	$1,400	$4,000

PITT TOKENS (CA. 1769)

William Pitt the Elder, the British statesman who endeared himself to America, is the subject of these brass or copper pieces, probably intended as commemorative medalets. The so-called halfpenny (the larger of the type's two sizes) served as currency during a shortage of regular coinage. The farthing-size tokens are rare.

The reverse legend (THANKS TO THE FRIENDS OF LIBERTY AND TRADE) refers to Pitt's criticism of the Crown's taxation of the American colonies, and his efforts to have the Stamp Act of March 22, 1765, repealed in 1766. The obverse bears a portrait and the legends THE RESTORER OF COMMERCE and NO STAMPS.

"Little is known concerning the circumstances of issue. Robert Vlack suggests that the pieces may have been designed by Paul Revere. Striking may have been accomplished around 1769 by James Smither (or Smithers) of Philadelphia" (*Whitman Encyclopedia of Colonial and Early American Coins*).

Farthing   Halfpenny

	G	VG	F	VF	EF	AU	Unc.
1766 Farthing ‡	$2,500	$5,000	$10,000	$20,000	$25,000	$35,000	
1766 Halfpenny ‡	$300	$450	$650	$1,100	$1,700	$2,700	$8,000
1766 Halfpenny, silvered ‡				$1,600	$3,500	$5,000	$12,000

‡ All Pitt Tokens are ranked in the *100 Greatest American Medals and Tokens*, as a single entry.

RHODE ISLAND SHIP MEDALS (CA. 1779)

The circumstances of the issue of these medals (or tokens) are mysterious. They were largely unknown to American coin collectors until 1864, when a specimen was offered in W. Elliot Woodward's sale of the Seavey Collection. It sold for $40—a remarkable price at the time.

The obverse shows the flagship of British admiral Lord Richard Howe at anchor, while the reverse depicts the American retreat from Rhode Island in 1778. The inscriptions show that the coin was meant for a Dutch-speaking audience. The word *vlugtende* ("fleeing") appears on the earlier issues below Howe's flagship—an engraving error. After a limited number of pieces were struck with this word, it was removed on all but two surviving examples by adding a wreath over the word on the dies or physically obliterating the word by grinding it off. It is believed the medal was struck in Holland as a jetton, but some think it was struck in England as a propaganda piece. Specimens are known in brass, pewter, and with a silvered (actually tin) wash.

Rhode Island Ship Medal (1778–1779)   Legend "vlugtende"   Wreath Below Ship
                                                Below Ship

	VF	EF	AU	Unc.
With "vlugtende" (fleeing) Below Ship, Brass ‡		$90,000		
Wreath Below Ship, Brass ‡	$1,350	$2,250	$3,250	$4,500
Without Wreath Below Ship, Brass ‡	$900	$1,700	$2,700	$5,000
Similar, Pewter ‡	$3,000	$4,500	$6,500	$10,000

‡ All Rhode Island Ship Tokens are ranked in the *100 Greatest American Medals and Tokens*, as a single entry.

JOHN CHALMERS ISSUES (1783)

John Chalmers, a Maryland goldsmith and silversmith, struck a series of silver tokens of his own design in Annapolis in 1783. The dies were by Thomas Sparrow, another silversmith in the town. The shortage of change in circulation and the refusal of the American people to use underweight cut Spanish coins prompted the issuance of these pieces. (Fraudsters would attempt to cut five "quarters" or nine or ten "eighths" out of one Spanish silver dollar, thereby realizing a proportional profit when they were all spent.)

On the Chalmers threepence and shilling obverses, two clasped hands are shown, perhaps symbolizing unity of the several states; the reverse of the threepence has a branch encircled by a wreath. A star within a wreath is on the obverse of the sixpence, with hands clasped upon a cross utilized as the reverse type. On this denomination, the designer's initials TS (for Thomas Sparrow) can be found in the crescents that terminate the horizontal arms of the cross. The reverse of the more common shilling varieties displays two doves competing for a worm underneath a hedge and a snake. The symbolic message is thought to have been against the danger of squabbling with brethren over low-value stakes while a dangerous mutual enemy lurked nearby. The edges of these tokens are crudely reeded. There are only a few known examples of the shilling type with 13 interlinked rings, from which a liberty cap on a pole arises.

Threepence	Sixpence, Small Date	Sixpence, Large Date

Shilling, Birds, Short Worm	Shilling, Rings

	VG	F	VF	EF	AU
1783 Threepence	$2,000	$4,000	$7,500	$15,000	$25,000
1783 Sixpence, Small Date	$2,600	$7,500	$12,500	$17,500	$25,000
1783 Sixpence, Large Date	$2,600	$6,000	$10,000	$15,000	$22,500
1783 Shilling, Birds, Long Worm	$1,100	$2,000	$5,000	$8,500	$16,000
1783 Shilling, Birds, Short Worm (*illustrated*)	$1,100	$2,000	$5,000	$8,000	$15,000
1783 Shilling, Rings (a)	$50,000	$100,000	$200,000	—	—

a. 5 examples are known.

FRENCH NEW WORLD ISSUES

None of the coins of the French regime relate specifically to territories that later became part of the United States. They were all general issues for the French colonies of the New World. The coinage of 1670 was authorized by an edict of King Louis XIV dated February 19, 1670, for use in New France,

Acadia, the French settlements in Newfoundland, and the French West Indies. The copper coinage of 1717 to 1722 was authorized by edicts of 1716 and 1721 for use in New France, Louisiana, and the French West Indies.

COINAGE OF 1670

The coinage of 1670 consisted of silver 5 and 15 sols and copper 2 deniers (or "doubles"). A total of 200,000 of the 5 sols and 40,000 of the 15 sols was struck at Paris. Nantes was to have coined the copper, but did not; the reasons for this may never be known, since the archives of the Nantes Mint before 1700 were destroyed. The only known specimen is a pattern struck at Paris. The silver coins were raised in value by a third in 1672 to keep them circulating, but in vain. They rapidly disappeared, and by 1680 none were to be seen. Later they were restored to their original values. This rare issue should not be confused with the common 1670-A 1/12 écu with reverse legend SIT. NOMEN. DOMINI. BENEDICTUM.

The 1670-A double de l'Amerique Françoise was struck at the Paris Mint along with the 5- and 15-sols denominations of the same date. All three were intended to circulate in France's North American colonies. Probably due to an engraving error, very few 1670-A doubles were actually struck. Today only one is known to survive.

Copper Double   Silver 5 Sols

	VG	F	VF	EF	Unc.
1670-A Copper Double (a)			$225,000		
1670-A 5 Sols	$750	$1,000	$2,000	$3,000	$7,500
1670-A 15 Sols	$13,000	$35,000	$75,000	$125,000	—

a. Unique.

COINAGE OF 1717–1720

The copper 6 and 12 deniers of 1717 were authorized by an edict of King Louis XV (by order of the six-year-old king's regent, the duke of Orléans) dated December 1716, to be struck at Perpignan (mintmark Q). The order could not be carried out, for the supply of copper was too brassy, and only a few pieces were coined. The issues of 1720, which were struck at multiple mints, are popularly collected for their association with the John Law "Mississippi Bubble" venture.

1720 6 Deniers

1717-Q 12 Deniers

1720 20 Sols

			F	VF	EF
1717-Q 6 Deniers, No Crowned Arms on Reverse (a)					—
1717-Q 12 Deniers, No Crowned Arms on Reverse					—
1720 Liard, Crowned Arms on Reverse, Copper			$350	$500	$900
1720 6 Deniers, Crowned Arms on Reverse, Copper			$550	$900	$1,750
1720 12 Deniers, Crowned Arms on Reverse, Copper			$400	$750	$1,500
1720 20 Sols, Silver			$375	$700	$1,500

a. Extremely rare.

Billon Coinage of 1709–1760

The French colonial coins of 30 deniers were called *mousquetaires* because of the outlined cross on their reverse, evocative of the design on the short coats worn by French musketeers. These coins were produced at Metz and Lyon. The 15 deniers was coined only at Metz. The sou marque and the half sou were coined at almost every French mint, those of Paris being most common. The half sou of 1740 is the only commonly available date. Specimens of the sou marque dated after 1760 were not used in North America. A unique specimen of the 1712-AA 30 deniers is known in the size and weight of the 15-denier coins.

30 Deniers "Mousquetaire"   Sou Marque (24 Deniers)

	VG	F	VF	EF	AU	Unc.
1711–1713-AA 15 Deniers	$150	$300	$500	$1,000	$1,750	$4,000
1709–1713-AA 30 Deniers	$75	$100	$250	$400	$675	$1,500
1709–1713-D 30 Deniers	$75	$100	$250	$400	$675	$1,500
1738–1748 Half Sou Marque, various mints	$60	$100	$200	$350	$575	$1,200
1738–1760 Sou Marque, various mints	$50	$80	$125	$175	$300	$500

Coinage of 1721–1722

The copper coinage of 1721 and 1722 was authorized by an edict of King Louis XV dated June 1721. The coins were struck on copper blanks imported from Sweden. Rouen and La Rochelle struck pieces of nine deniers (one sou) in 1721 and 1722. New France received 534,000 pieces, mostly from the mint of La Rochelle, but only 8,180 were put into circulation, as the colonists disliked copper. In 1726 the rest of the issue was sent back to France.

In American coin catalogs of the 1800s, these coins were often called "Louisiana coppers."

	VG	F	VF	EF
1721-B (Rouen)	$500	$1,000	$3,500	$10,000
1721-H (La Rochelle)	$100	$175	$1,000	$2,500
1722-H	$100	$175	$1,000	$2,500
1722-H, 2 Over 1	$175	$275	$1,200	$4,000

FRENCH COLONIES IN GENERAL (1767)

These copper coins were produced for use in the French colonies and only unofficially circulated in Louisiana along with other foreign coins and tokens. Most were counterstamped RF (République Française) for use in the West Indies. The mintmark A signifies the Paris Mint. The edge is decorated with a double row of dots.

	VG	VF	EF	AU
1767 French Colonies, Sou	$120	$250	$600	$1,400
1767 French Colonies, Sou, counterstamped RF	$100	$200	$250	$600

Post-Colonial Issues

The coins explored in this section are classified as "post-colonial" because they came after the colonial period (some during the early months of rebellion; most after the official declaration of independence) but before the first federal Mint was established in Philadelphia in 1792.

Early American coins were produced from hand-engraved dies, which are often individually distinctive. For many types, the great number of die varieties that can be found and identified are of interest to collectors who value each according to its individual rarity. Values shown for type coins in this section are for the most common die variety of each.

CONTINENTAL CURRENCY PIECES (1776)

The Continental Currency dollars (as they are known to numismatists) were made to serve in lieu of a paper dollar, but the exact nature of their monetary role is still unclear. They were the first dollar-sized coins ever attributed to the United States. One obverse die was engraved by someone whose initials were E.G. (thought to be Elisha Gallaudet) and is marked EG FECIT ("EG Made It"). Studies of the coinage show that there may have been two separate emissions made at different mints, one in New York City. The link design on the reverse was suggested by Benjamin Franklin and represents the former colonies.

Varieties result from differences in the spelling of the word CURRENCY and the addition of EG FECIT on the obverse. These coins were struck in pewter, brass, and silver. Pewter pieces served as a dollar, taking the place of a Continental Currency paper note. Brass and silver pieces may have been experimental or patterns. The typical grade encountered for a pewter coin is VF to AU. Examples in original bright Uncirculated condition are worth a strong premium.

Numerous copies and replicas of these coins have been made over the years. Authentication is recommended for all pieces.

CURRENCY   CURENCY

	G	F	VF	EF	AU	Unc.
1776 CURENCY, Pewter † (a)	$7,750	$12,000	$25,000	$35,000	$50,000	$70,000
	Auctions: $93,000, MS-63, August 2018; $90,000, MS-62, October 2018; $51,700, EF-45, March 2017					
1776 CURENCY, Brass † (a)	$25,000	$35,000	$65,000	$115,000		
	Auctions: $299,000, MS-63, July 2009					
1776 CURENCY, Silver † (b)			$850,000	$1,250,000		
	Auctions: $1,527,500, EF-40, January 2015; $345,000, VF-30, January 2005					
1776 CURRENCY, Pewter †	$8,000	$13,000	$25,000	$35,000	$50,000	$75,000
	Auctions: $127,075, MS-64, September 2011; $57,600, MS-62, October 2018; $61,688, AU-58, March 2015					
1776 CURRENCY, EG FECIT, Pewter †	$8,500	$15,000	$27,500	$40,000	$55,000	$85,000
	Auctions: $75,000, MS-62, February 2019; $48,000, Unc., April 2020; $45,600, AU-58, October 2018					
1776 CURRENCY, EG FECIT, Silver † (b)	—	—	—	—	—	$1,500,000
	Auctions: $1,410,000, MS-63, May 2014					
1776 CURRENCEY, Pewter †	—	—	$65,000		$175,000	—
1776 CURRENCY, Pewter, Ornamented Date † (c)				$276,000	$329,000	
	Auctions: $276,000, EF-45, July 2009					

† All varieties of Continental Currency dollars are ranked in the *100 Greatest U.S. Coins* (fifth edition), as a single entry. **a.** 2 varieties. **b.** 2 examples are known. **c.** 3 examples are known.

SPECULATIVE ISSUES, TOKENS, AND PATTERNS
NOVA CONSTELLATIO COPPERS (1783–1786)

The Nova Constellatio coppers, dated 1783 and 1785 and without denomination, were struck in fairly large quantities in Birmingham, England, and were shipped to New York where they entered circulation. Apparently they resulted from a private coinage venture undertaken by Constable, Rucker & Co., a trading business formed by William Constable, John Rucker, Robert Morris, and Gouverneur Morris as equal partners. The designs and legends were copied from the denominated patterns dated 1783 made in Philadelphia (see page 179). A few additional coppers dated 1786 were made by an inferior diesinker.

"The Nova Constellatio coppers were well received and saw extensive use in commerce, as evidenced by the wear seen on typically specimens today," writes Q. David Bowers in the *Whitman Encyclopedia of Colonial and Early American Coins*. "Later, they were devalued, and many were used as undertypes (planchets) for Connecticut and, to a lesser extent, New Jersey and Vermont coppers."

**1783, CONSTELLATIO,
Pointed Rays, Small U.S.**

**1783, CONSTELLATIO
Pointed Rays, Large U.S.**

	VG	F	VF	EF	AU	Unc.
1783, CONSTELLATIO, Pointed Rays, Small U.S.	$100	$200	$375	$750	$1,500	$3,000
1783, CONSTELLATIO, Pointed Rays, Large U.S.	$100	$500	$750	$2,000	$4,500	$10,000

1783, CONSTELATIO, Blunt Rays

1785, CONSTELATIO, Blunt Rays   1785, CONSTELLATIO, Pointed Rays

	VG	F	VF	EF	AU	Unc.
1783, CONSTELATIO, Blunt Rays	$100	$225	$550	$1,000	$2,500	$7,000
1785, CONSTELATIO, Blunt Rays	$100	$225	$550	$1,000	$2,500	$6,000
1785, CONSTELLATIO, Pointed Rays	$100	$200	$375	$750	$1,500	$3,000
1785, Similar, Small, Close Date	$300	$500	$1,800	$3,500	$5,500	$15,000
1786, Similar, Small Date	$2,500	$5,000	$7,500	$15,000		

IMMUNE COLUMBIA PIECES (1785)

These pieces are considered private or unofficial coins. No laws describing them are known. There are several types bearing the seated figure of Justice. These pieces are stylistically related to the Nova Constellatio coppers, with the Immune Columbia motif with liberty cap and scale replacing the LIBERTAS and JUSTITIA design.

1785, Silver, 13 Stars   1785, Pointed Rays, CONSTELLATIO

	F	VF	EF
1785, Copper, 13 Stars	$15,000	$27,000	$45,000
1785, Silver, 13 Stars	$25,000	$50,000	$75,000
1785, Pointed Rays, CONSTELLATIO, Extra Star in Reverse Legend, Copper	$15,000	$25,000	$45,000
1785, Pointed Rays, CONSTELLATIO, Gold (a)			—
1785, Blunt Rays, CONSTELLATIO, Copper (b)		$50,000	—

Note: The gold specimen in the National Numismatic Collection (now maintained by the Smithsonian) was acquired in 1843 from collector Matthew A. Stickney in exchange for an 1804 dollar. **a.** Unique. **b.** 2 examples are known.

1785, George III Obverse

	G	VG	F	VF
1785, George III Obverse	$5,500	$8,500	$12,500	$25,000
1785, VERMON AUCTORI Obverse, IMMUNE COLUMBIA	$6,000	$10,000	$15,000	$30,000

1787, IMMUNIS COLUMBIA, Eagle Reverse

	VG	F	VF	EF	AU	Unc.
1787, IMMUNIS COLUMBIA, Eagle Reverse	$600	$1,000	$3,000	$4,500	$9,000	$25,000

Note: Believed to be a prototype for federal coinage; some were coined after 1787.

CONFEDERATIO AND RELATED TOKENS

The Confederatio and associated coppers have patriotic motifs and were made in small quantities for circulation. The 1785, Inimica Tyrannis America, variety may owe its design to a sketch by Thomas Jefferson. In all, 12 dies were presumed struck in 13 combinations. No one knows for certain who made these pieces. The combination with a standard reverse die for a 1786 New Jersey copper is especially puzzling.

America

Americana

Washington

Immunis

Eagle

Libertas et Justitia

Large Circle

Small Circle

Pattern Shield

The 1786, Immunis Columbia, with scrawny-eagle reverse is a related piece probably made by a different engraver or mint.

	VG	F	VF	EF	AU
1785 Inimica Tyrannis America, Large Circle (a,b)	$40,000	$70,000	$100,000	$150,000	$225,000
1785 Inimica Tyrannis Americana, Small Circle (c,d)	$30,000	$40,000	$50,000	$125,000	$200,000
1785 Inimica Tyrannis Americana, Large Circle, Silver (e,f)		$50,000 **(g)**			
1785 Gen. Washington, Large Circle (h,i)	$50,000	$75,000	$125,000	$250,000	
1786 Gen. Washington, Eagle (j,k)		$40,000			
(No Date) Gen. Washington, Pattern Shield (l,m)		$75,000	$100,000		$300,000
1786 Immunis, Pattern Shield (n,o)		$25,000	$50,000	$75,000	$95,000
1786 Immunis, 1785 Large Circle (p,k)					$100,000
1786 Eagle, Pattern Shield (q,f)					$200,000
1786 Eagle, 1785 Large Circle (r,k)		$50,000	$85,000		
1785 Libertas et Justitia, 1785 Large Circle (s,f)	$25,000				
1785 Small Circle, 1787 Excelsior Eagle (t,k)		$35,000			
1786 Immunis Columbia, Scrawny Eagle (m)			$50,000	$90,000	

a. America obverse, Large Circle reverse. **b.** 7 examples are known. **c.** Americana obverse, Small Circle reverse. **d.** 9 examples are known. **e.** Americana obverse, Large Circle reverse. **f.** 1 example is known. **g.** Damaged. **h.** Washington obverse, Large Circle reverse. **i.** 6 examples are known. **j.** Washington obverse, Eagle reverse. **k.** 2 examples are known. **l.** Washington obverse, Pattern Shield reverse. **m.** 3 examples are known. **n.** Immunis obverse, Pattern Shield reverse. **o.** 17 examples are known. **p.** Immunis obverse, Large Circle reverse. **q.** Eagle obverse, Pattern Shield reverse. **r.** Eagle obverse, Large Circle reverse. **s.** Libertas et Justitia obverse, Large Circle reverse. **t.** Small Circle obverse, 1787 Excelsior Eagle reverse. Image of the 1787 Excelsior eagle (facing right) is on page 157.

COINAGE OF THE STATES AND VERMONT

REPUBLIC OF VERMONT (1785–1788)

The Republic of Vermont was not formally part of the Union in the 1780s. However, it considered itself American and allied with the original 13 colonies, having declared independence from Britain in January 1777 and having fought in the Revolutionary War. After the war Vermont sought political connection with the United States. Territorial disagreements with New York delayed its entry into the Union, but this was finally accomplished in 1791, when it was admitted as the 14th state. In the meantime, Vermont had already embarked on its own experiments in local coinage.

Reuben Harmon Jr., a storekeeper and entrepreneur of Rupert, Vermont, was granted permission by the Vermont House of Representatives to coin copper pieces for a period of two years beginning July 1, 1785. The well-known Vermont "Landscape" coppers were first produced in that year. The franchise was extended for eight years in 1786.

Harmon's mint was located in the northeast corner of Rupert near a stream known as Millbrook. Colonel William Coley, a New York goldsmith, made the first dies. Some of the late issues were made near Newburgh, New York, by the Machin's Mills coiners.

Most coppers made in Vermont were struck on poor and defective planchets. These included the landscape and Draped Bust Left varieties. Well-struck coins on smooth, full planchets command higher prices. Later pieces made at Machin's Mills are on high-quality planchets but usually have areas of weak striking.

1785, IMMUNE COLUMBIA

1785, VERMONTS   1785, Reverse   1785, VERMONTIS

1786, VERMONTENSIUM   1786, Baby Head

1786, Bust Left   1786, Reverse   1787, Reverse

	AG	G	VG	F	VF	EF	AU
1785, IMMUNE COLUMBIA	$4,000	$7,500	$12,500	$15,000	$30,000	$50,000	$75,000
1785, VERMONTS	$150	$275	$450	$800	$2,500	$6,000	$15,000
1785, VERMONTIS	$175	$325	$600	$1,300	$3,500	$12,000	$20,000
1786, VERMONTENSIUM	$110	$200	$450	$750	$1,750	$5,000	$10,000
1786, Baby Head	$150	$275	$400	$800	$3,000	$7,500	
1786, Bust Left		$300	$500	$750	$1,250	$2,000	
1787, Bust Left			$15,000	$20,000	$35,000	—	

1787, BRITANNIA

	AG	G	VG	F	VF	EF	AU
1787, BRITANNIA (a)	$45	$90	$120	$200	$400	$1,000	$2,500

a. The reverse of this coin is always weak.

1787, 1788, Bust Right (Several Varieties)

	AG	G	VG	F	VF	EF	AU
1787, Bust Right, several varieties	$60	$110	$150	$250	$800	$2,000	$3,500
1788, Bust Right, several varieties	$50	$90	$120	$225	$500	$1,250	$2,500
1788, Backward C in AUCTORI		$5,000	$10,000	$25,000	$40,000	$55,000	$85,000
1788, *ET LIB* *INDE	$175	$300	$550	$1,250	$4,000	$10,000	$15,000

1788, GEORGIVS III REX / INDE+ ET•LIB+

	AG	G	VG	F	VF	EF	AU
1788, GEORGIVS III REX (a)	$300	$500	$900	$2,000	$4,000	$10,000	

a. This piece should not be confused with the common English halfpence with similar design and reverse legend BRITANNIA.

NEW HAMPSHIRE (1776)

New Hampshire was the first of the states to consider the subject of coinage following the Declaration of Independence. On March 13, 1776, by which time the colonies were in rebellion but had not yet formally declared their independence, the New Hampshire House of Representatives established a committee to consider the minting of copper coins. The committee recommended such coinage as a way to facilitate small commercial transactions.

William Moulton was empowered to make a limited quantity of coins of pure copper authorized by the State House of Representatives in 1776. Although cast patterns were prepared, it is believed that they were not approved. Little of the proposed coinage was ever actually circulated.

Other purported patterns are of doubtful origin. These include a unique engraved piece and a rare struck piece with large initials WM on the reverse.

	VF
1776 New Hampshire Copper	$100,000
Auctions: $96,000, VF-25, January 2021	

MASSACHUSETTS
MASSACHUSETTS UNOFFICIAL COPPERS (1776)

Presumably, in 1776, the year the colonies proclaimed their independence from Britain, three types of Massachusetts coppers were created. Very little is known about their origins or the circumstances of their production. Numismatic historians deduced them to be patterns until recent scholarship cast doubt on their authenticity as coppers of the Revolutionary War era.

The obverse of one of these coppers has a crude pine tree with "1d LM" at its base and the legend MASSACHUSETTS STATE. The reverse has a figure probably intended to represent the Goddess of Liberty, seated on a globe and holding a liberty cap and staff. A dog sits at her feet. The legend LIBERTY AND VIRTUE surrounds the figure, and the date 1776 is situated beneath.

Sylvester S. Crosby, writing in 1875 in *The Early Coins of America*, traced the provenance of this unique copper back to a grocer who sold it to a schoolboy around 1852. The grocer was from "the northerly part" of Boston, and he had "found it many years before while excavating on his premises, in the vicinity of Hull or Charter Street."

	VF
1776 Pine Tree Copper (a)	—

a. Unique, in the Massachusetts Historical Society collection.

A similar piece, probably from the same source as the Pine Tree copper, features a Native American standing with a bow on the obverse, with a worn legend that may read PROVINCE OF MASSA or similar. On the reverse is a seated figure and globe, visible partially visible legend (LIBERTATIS), and the date 1776 at bottom. The only known example was overstruck on a 1747 English halfpenny, and is holed.

	VG
1776 Indian Copper (a)	—

a. Unique.

A third Massachusetts piece is sometimes called the *Janus copper*. On the obverse are three heads, facing left, front, and right, with the legend STATE OF MASSA. 1/2 D. The reverse shows the Goddess of Liberty facing right, resting against a globe. The legend is GODDESS LIBERTY 1776.

	F
1776 Halfpenny, 3 Heads on Obverse (a)	—
Auctions: $44,650, Fine, January 2015; $40,000, Fine, November 1979	

a. Unique.

MASSACHUSETTS AUTHORIZED ISSUES (1787–1788)

An "Act for establishing a mint for the coinage of gold, silver and copper" was passed by the Massachusetts General Court on October 17, 1786. The next year, the council directed that the design of the copper coins should incorporate ". . . the figure of an indian with a bow & arrow & a star on one side, with the word 'Commonwealth,' the reverse a spread eagle with the words—'of Massachusetts A. D. 1787'—" (this wording would be slightly different in the final product).

The coinage of Massachusetts copper cents and half cents in 1787 and 1788 was under the direction of Captain Joshua Witherle of Boston. These were the first coins bearing the denomination *cent* as would be later established by Congress. They were produced in large quantities and are fairly plentiful today. The wear seen on many of the Massachusetts cents and half cents indicates that they enjoyed long circulation in commerce. Many varieties exist, the most valuable being that with arrows in the eagle's right talon.

Most of the dies for these coppers were made by Joseph Callender. Jacob Perkins of Newburyport also engraved some of the 1788 dies.

The mint was abandoned early in 1789, in compliance with the newly ratified U.S. Constitution, and because its production was unprofitable.

1787 Half Cent

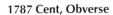  

1787 Cent, Obverse   Arrows in Right Talon   Arrows in Left Talon

	G	VG	F	VF	EF	AU	Unc.
1787 Half Cent	$100	$125	$225	$450	$650	$1,250	$2,500
1787 Cent, Arrows in Right Talon	$10,000	$16,000	$25,000	$50,000	$75,000	$100,000	$200,000
1787 Cent, Arrows in Left Talon	$75	$100	$150	$350	$800	$1,600	$3,500
1787 Cent, "Horned Eagle" (die break)	$110	$135	$235	$650	$1,100	$2,250	$6,000

1788 Half Cent

1788 Cent, Period After
MASSACHUSETTS

	G	VG	F	VF	EF	AU	Unc.
1788 Half Cent	$100	$125	$225	$500	$700	$1,400	$4,000
1788 Cent, Period After MASSACHUSETTS	$100	$110	$200	$600	$1,250	$2,500	$6,000
1788 Cent, No Period After MASSACHUSETTS	$100	$110	$200	$600	$1,250	$2,500	$6,000

CONNECTICUT (1785–1788)

Authority for establishing a mint near New Haven was granted by the state of Connecticut to Samuel Bishop, Joseph Hopkins, James Hillhouse, and John Goodrich in October 1785. They had petitioned the state's General Assembly for this right, noting the public need—small coins were scarce in circulation and many of those seen were counterfeits. Under the Assembly's grant, the four minters would pay the state's treasury an amount equal to 5 percent of the copper coins they produced. To make a profit, the minters would deduct this royalty, plus their other expenses (including materials, labor, and distribution), from the face value of the coins they struck.

Available records indicate that most of the Connecticut coppers were coined under a subcontract, by Samuel Broome and Jeremiah Platt, former New York merchants. Abel Buell was probably the principal diesinker. Many others were struck by Machin's Mills in Newburgh, New York, and were not authorized by Connecticut. These are as highly prized by collectors as are regular issues.

The Connecticut coppers were often struck crudely and on imperfect planchets. Numerous die varieties exist; over the years, collectors have given many of them distinctive nicknames.

1785 Copper, Bust Facing Left   1785 Copper, Bust Facing Right

1785 Copper, African Head

	G	VG	F	VF	EF	AU
1785 Copper, Bust Facing Left	$200	$325	$650	$1,750	$3,750	$8,000
1785 Copper, Bust Facing Right	$50	$90	$150	$500	$1,250	$3,500
1785 Copper, African Head	$100	$175	$500	$1,250	$3,000	$6,500

1786 Copper, ETLIB INDE　　**1786 Copper, Large Head Facing Right**

1786 Copper, Mailed Bust Facing Left　　**1786 Copper, Draped Bust**　　**1786 Copper, Mailed Bust Facing Left, Hercules Head**

	G	VG	F	VF	EF	AU
1786 Copper, ETLIB INDE	$70	$140	$325	$850	$2,500	$7,000
1786 Copper, Large Head Facing Right	$750	$1,500	$3,500	$5,500	$10,000	$15,000
1786 Copper, Mailed Bust Facing Left	$40	$75	$140	$400	$800	$2,200
1786 Copper, Draped Bust	$125	$200	$500	$1,200	$3,000	$5,000
1786 Copper, Mailed Bust Facing Left, Hercules Head	$110	$200	$450	$1,350	$3,250	

1787 Copper, Small Head Facing Right, ETLIB INDE　　**1787 Copper, Muttonhead Variety, Topless Liberty**

	G	VG	F	VF	EF	AU
1787 Copper, Small Head Facing Right, ETLIB INDE	$110	$200	$400	$1,300	$2,500	$5,000
1787 Copper, Liberty Seated Facing Right (a)		—		$125,000		
1787, Mailed Bust Facing Right, INDE ET LIB	$100	$180	$400	$2,200	$5,000	
1787 Copper, Muttonhead	$125	$200	$400	$1,700	$4,000	$7,500

a. 2 examples are known.

1787 Copper, Mailed Bust Facing Left　　**1787 Copper, Laughing Head**　　**1787 Copper, Reverse**

	G	VG	F	VF	EF	AU
1787 Copper, Mailed Bust Facing Left	$40	$65	$120	$350	$900	$2,200
1787 Copper, Mailed Bust Facing Left, Laughing Head	$65	$125	$250	$550	$1,000	$2,250

1787 Copper,
Horned Bust

	G	VG	F	VF	EF	AU
1787 Copper, Mailed Bust Facing Left, Horned Bust	$40	$65	$120	$375	$750	$1,750
1787 Copper, Mailed Bust Facing Left, Hercules Head (see 1786 for illustration)	$500	$900	$1,700	$5,000	$8,500	—
1787 Copper, Mailed Bust Facing Left, Dated 1787 Over 1877	$80	$180	$600	$1,400	$4,200	—
1787 Copper, Mailed Bust Facing Left, 1787 Over 88	$175	$235	$600	$1,500	$4,500	—
1787 Copper, Mailed Bust Facing Left, CONNECT, INDE	$50	$100	$175	$475	$1,200	$2,500
1787 Copper, Mailed Bust Facing Left, CONNECT, INDL	$375	$700	$1,500	$3,000	$6,500	

1787 Copper, Draped Bust Facing Left

	G	VG	F	VF	EF	AU
1787 Copper, Draped Bust Facing Left	$30	$50	$90	$250	$650	$1,200
1787 Copper, Draped Bust Facing Left, AUCIORI	$40	$65	$125	$350	$850	$1,500
1787 Copper, Draped Bust Facing Left, AUCTOPI	$50	$100	$200	$600	$1,400	$2,500
1787 Copper, Draped Bust Facing Left, AUCTOBI	$50	$90	$180	$500	$1,250	$2,000
1787 Copper, Draped Bust Facing Left, CONNFC	$40	$60	$125	$400	$750	$1,500
1787 Copper, Draped Bust Facing Left, CONNLC	$75	$150	$250	$700	$2,500	—
1787 Copper, Draped Bust Facing Left, FNDE	$40	$65	$150	$400	$1,300	$2,400
1787 Copper, Draped Bust Facing Left, ETLIR	$40	$60	$125	$300	$800	$1,400
1787 Copper, Draped Bust Facing Left, ETIIB	$40	$60	$125	$300	$800	$1,400
1787 Copper, GEORGIVS III Obverse, INDE•ET Reverse	$1,500	$3,250	$4,000	—	—	—

1788 Copper, Mailed Bust Facing Right

	G	VG	F	VF	EF	AU
1788 Copper, Mailed Bust Facing Right	$75	$125	$250	$650	$1,500	$3,000
1788 Copper, GEORGIVS III Obverse (Reverse as Above)	$100	$210	$500	$1,400	$2,800	—
1788 Copper, Small Head (see 1787 for illustration)	$1,500	$3,750	$4,500	$11,000	$20,000	—

1788 Copper, Mailed Bust Facing Left	**1788 Copper, Draped Bust Facing Left**

	G	VG	F	VF	EF	AU
1788 Copper, Mailed Bust Facing Left	$45	$70	$175	$350	$1,000	
1788 Copper, Mailed Bust Facing Left, CONNLC	$55	$130	$200	$500	$1,500	$2,800
1788 Copper, Draped Bust Facing Left	$55	$85	$200	$450	$1,350	
1788 Copper, Draped Bust Facing Left, CONNLC	$85	$200	$350	$800	$2,000	$3,000
1788 Copper, Draped Bust Facing Left, INDL ET LIB	$80	$140	$250	$700	$1,800	$3,400

NEW YORK AND RELATED ISSUES (1780S)

No official state coinage for New York is known to have been authorized. However, a number of issues in copper and gold were made relating to the state, by a variety of different issuers.

BRASHER DOUBLOONS (1786–1787)

Among the most famous early American pieces coined before establishment of the U.S. Mint at Philadelphia were those produced by the well-known New York City silversmith, goldsmith, and jeweler Ephraim Brasher, who was a neighbor and friend of George Washington's when that city was the seat of the federal government.

The gold pieces Brasher made weighed about 408 grains and were valued at $15 in New York currency. They were approximately equal to the Spanish doubloon, which was equal to 16 Spanish dollars.

Pieces known as *Lima Style doubloons* were dated 1742, but it is almost certain that they were produced in 1786, and were the first efforts of Brasher to make a circulating coin for regional use. Neither of the two known specimens shows the full legends; but weight, gold content, and hallmark are all identical to those for the 1787-dated Brasher coins. An analogous cast imitation Lima style doubloon dated 1735 bears a hallmark attributed to Standish Barry of Baltimore, Maryland, circa 1787.

The design used on the 1787 Brasher doubloon features an eagle on one side and the arms of New York on the other. In addition to his impressed hallmark, Brasher's name appears in small letters on each of his coins. The unique 1787 gold half doubloon is struck from doubloon dies on an undersized planchet that weighs half as much as the larger coins. It is in the National Numismatic Collection in the Smithsonian Institution.

It is uncertain why Brasher produced these pieces. He may have produced them for his own account, charging a nominal fee to convert metal into coin. He was later commissioned by the government to test and verify other gold coins then in circulation. His hallmark EB was punched on each coin as evidence of his testing and its value. In some cases the foreign coins were weight-adjusted by clipping.

	MS
"1742" (1786) Lima Style gold doubloon (a)	$2,000,000
Auctions: $2,100,000, MS-61, January 2021	

a. 2 examples are known.

	EF
1787 New York gold doubloon, EB on Breast	$5,000,000
Auctions: $2,990,000, EF-45, January 2005	
1787 New York gold doubloon, EB on Wing	$4,500,000
Auctions: $9,360,000, MS-65, January 2021	
1787 New York gold half doubloon (a)	—
Various foreign gold coins with Brasher's EB hallmark	$5,000–$100,000

a. Unique, in the Smithsonian Collection.

NEW YORK COPPER COINAGE

Several individuals petitioned the New York Legislature in early 1787 for the right to coin copper for the state, but a coinage was never authorized. Instead, a law was passed to regulate the copper coins already in use. Nevertheless, various unauthorized copper pieces were made privately and issued within the state.

One private mint known as Machin's Mills was organized by Captain Thomas Machin, a distinguished veteran of the Revolutionary War, and situated at the outlet of Orange Pond near Newburgh, New York. Shortly after this mint was formed, on April 18, 1787, it was merged with the Rupert, Vermont, mint operated by Reuben Harmon Jr., who held a coinage grant from the Republic of Vermont. The combined partnership agreed to conduct their business in New York, Vermont, Connecticut, or elsewhere if they could benefit by it (though their only known operation was the one at Newburgh).

The operations at Machin's Mills were conducted in secret and were looked upon with suspicion by the local residents. They minted several varieties of imitation George III halfpence, as well as counterfeit coppers of Connecticut and New Jersey. Only their Vermont coppers had official status.

Mints located in or near New York City were operated by John Bailey and Ephraim Brasher. They had petitioned the legislature on February 12, 1787, for a franchise to coin copper. The extent of their partnership, if any, and details of their operation are unknown. Studies of the state coinage show that they produced primarily the EXCELSIOR and NOVA EBORAC pieces of New York, and possibly the "running fox" New Jersey coppers.

*Believed to be the bust
of George Washington.*

	G	VG	F	VF	EF	AU
1786, NON VI VIRTUTE VICI	$3,500	$7,500	$12,500	$25,000	$50,000	$85,000

**1787 EXCELSIOR Copper,
Large Eagle on Obverse**

**1787 EXCELSIOR Copper,
Eagle on Globe Facing Left**

	G	VG	F	VF	EF
1787 EXCELSIOR Copper, Eagle on Globe Facing Right	$2,750	$4,000	$8,500	$25,000	$50,000
1787 EXCELSIOR Copper, Eagle on Globe Facing Left	$2,750	$3,500	$8,000	$20,000	$35,000
1787 EXCELSIOR Copper, Large Eagle on Obverse, Arrows and Branch Transposed	$4,100	$6,750	$18,000	$35,000	$70,000

1787, George Clinton

1787, Indian and New York Arms

1787, Indian and Eagle on Globe

1787, Indian and George III Reverse

	G	VG	F	VF	EF
1787, George Clinton	$10,000	$20,000	$50,000	$100,000	$165,000
1787, Indian and New York Arms	$10,000	$18,000	$40,000	$65,000	$125,000
1787, Indian and Eagle on Globe	$10,000	$20,000	$40,000	$70,000	$135,000
1787, Indian and George III Reverse (a)		—			

a. 4 examples are known.

BRITISH COPPER COINS AND THEIR IMITATIONS
(INCLUDING MACHIN'S MILLS AND OTHER UNDERWEIGHT COINAGE OF 1786–1789)

The most common copper coin used for small transactions in early America was the British halfpenny. Wide acceptance and the non–legal-tender status of these copper coins made them a prime choice for unauthorized reproduction by private individuals.

Many such counterfeits were created in America by striking from locally made dies, or by casting or other crude methods. Some were made in England and imported into this country. Pieces dated 1781 and 1785 seem to have been made specifically for this purpose, while others were circulated in both countries.

Genuine regal British halfpence and farthings minted in London and dated 1749 are of special interest to collectors because they were specifically sent to the North American colonies as reimbursement for participation in the expedition against Cape Breton, and circulated extensively throughout New England.

Genuine British halfpenny coppers of both George II (dated 1729–1754) and George III (dated 1770–1775) show finely detailed features within a border of close denticles; the 1 in the date looks like a J. They are boldly struck on good-quality planchets. Their weight is approximately 9.5 grams; their diameter, 29 mm.

British-made lightweight imitation halfpence are generally smaller in diameter and thickness, and weigh less than genuine pieces. Details are crudely engraved or sometimes incomplete. Inscriptions may be misspelled. Planchet quality may be poor.

	G	VG	F	VF	EF
1749, George II British farthing	$20	$40	$75	$175	$250
1749, George II British halfpenny	$25	$50	$100	$200	$300
1770–1775, George III British halfpenny (a)	$15	$20	$50	$100	$250
1770–1775, British imitation halfpenny (a)	$15	$20	$25	$100	$250

a. Values shown are for the most common variety. Rare pieces are sometimes worth significantly more.

During the era of American state coinage, New York diemaker James F. Atlee and/or other coiners minted unauthorized, lightweight, imitation British halfpence. These American-made false coins have the same or similar devices, legends, and, in some cases, dates as genuine regal halfpence, but they contain less copper. Their details are often poorly rendered or missing. Identification of American-made imitations has been confirmed by identifying certain punch marks (such as letters and numerals) and matching them to the distinct punch marks of known engravers.

There are four distinct groups of these halfpence, all linked to the regular state coinage. The first group was probably struck in New York City prior to 1786. The second group was minted in New York City in association with John Bailey and Ephraim Brasher during the first half of 1787. The third group was struck at Machin's Mills during the second half of 1787 and into 1788 or later. A fourth group, made by the Machin's Mills coiners, consists of pieces made from dies that were muled with false dies of the state coinages of Connecticut, Vermont, and New York. Pieces with very crude designs and other dates are believed to have been struck elsewhere in New England.

Georgivs/Britannia
"Machin's Mills" Copper Halfpennies Made in America

Dates used on these pieces were often "evasive," as numismatists describe them today. They include dates not used on genuine pieces and, sometimes, variations in spelling. They are as follows: 1771, 1772, 1774, 1775, and 1776 for the first group; 1747 and 1787 for the second group; and 1776, 1778, 1787, and 1788 for the third group. Pieces generally attributed to James Atlee can be identified by a single outline in the crosses (British Union) of Britannia's shield and large triangular denticles along the coin circumference. The more-valuable American-made pieces are not to be confused with the similar English-made George III counterfeits (some of which have identical dates), or with genuine British half-pence dated 1770 to 1775.

Group I coins dated 1771, 1772, 1774, 1775, and 1776 have distinctive bold designs but lack the fine details of the original coins. Planchets are generally of high quality.

Group II coins dated 1747 and 1787 are generally poorly made. The 1 in the date is not J-shaped, and the denticles are of various sizes. There are no outlines to the stripes in the shield.

Group III coins dated 1776, 1778, 1787, and 1788, struck at Machin's Mills in Newburgh, New York, are similar to coins of Group II, with their triangular-shaped denticles. Most have large dates and berries in the obverse wreath.

	AG	G	VG	F	VF	EF	AU
1747, GEORGIVS II. Group II	$150	$350	$600	$1,500	$3,500	$8,500	
1771, GEORGIVS III. Group I	$150	$350	$600	$1,500	$3,500	$8,500	
1772, GEORGIVS III. Group I	$150	$350	$1,000	$1,500	$3,500	$6,000	
1772, GEORGIUS III. Group I	$85	$200	$300	$750	$2,300	$4,500	—
1774, GEORGIVS III. Group I	$50	$100	$250	$750	$1,500	$3,500	
1774, GEORGIUS III. Group I	$100	$250	$800	$2,000	$4,000	$6,500	
1775, GEORGIVS III. Group I	$50	$100	$200	$750	$1,500	$3,500	
1776, GEORGIVS III. Group III	$100	$200	$500	$1,000	$3,000	$7,000	
1776, GEORCIVS III, Small Date	$1,000	$2,000	$4,500	$9,000	$18,000	$25,000	$35,000
1778, GEORGIVS III. Group III	$40	$70	$125	$275	$700	$2,000	$3,200
1784, GEORGIVS III	$150	$400	$1,000	$2,500	$4,500	$6,500	
1787, GEORGIVS III. Group II	$30	$75	$100	$200	$600	$1,200	$2,500
1787, GEORGIVS III. Group III	$30	$75	$100	$200	$600	$1,200	$2,500
1788, GEORGIVS III. Group III	$50	$100	$200	$650	$1,200	$2,750	

Note: Values shown are for the most common varieties in each category. Rare pieces can be worth significantly more. Also see related George III combinations under Connecticut, Vermont, and New York.

The muled coins of Group IV are listed separately with the Immune Columbia pieces and with the coins of Connecticut, Vermont, and New York. Other imitation coppers made by unidentified American makers are generally very crude and exceedingly rare. Cast copies of British coins probably circulated along with the imitations without being questioned. Counterfeits of silver Spanish-American coins and Massachusetts tree coins may have also been coined by American minters.

NOVA EBORAC COINAGE FOR NEW YORK

An extensive issue of 1787-dated copper coins appeared, each with a bust on the obverse surrounded by NOVA EBORAC ("New York"). The reverse showed a seated goddess with a sprig in one hand and a liberty cap on a pole in the other hand, with the legend VIRT. ET. LIB. ("Virtue and Liberty") surrounding, and the date 1787 below. The letter punches used on this issue are identical to those used on the Brasher doubloon die. It is likely that John Bailey and Ephraim Brasher operated a minting shop in New York City and produced these and possibly other issues.

1787, NOVA EBORAC, Reverse:
Seated Figure Facing Right

1787, NOVA EBORAC, Reverse:
Seated Figure Facing Left

1787, NOVA EBORAC, Small Head

1787, NOVA EBORAC, Large Head

	AG	G	F	VF	EF	AU
1787, NOVA EBORAC, Seated Figure Facing Right	$50	$110	$300	$700	$1,200	$2,000
1787, NOVA EBORAC, Seated Figure Facing Left	$50	$125	$300	$600	$1,000	$1,500
1787, NOVA EBORAC, Small Head	$3,000	$6,500	$25,000	$45,000		
1787, NOVA EBORAC, Large Head	$500	$900	$2,000	$4,250	$8,000	

NEW JERSEY (1786–1788)

On June 1, 1786, the New Jersey General Assembly granted to businessman and investor Thomas Goadsby, silversmith and assayer Albion Cox, and minter Walter Mould authority to coin three million coppers weighing six pennyweight and six grains (150 grains total, or 9.72 grams) apiece, to be completed by June 1788, on condition that they deliver to the state treasurer "one Tenth Part of the full Sum they shall strike." These coppers were to pass current at 15 to the shilling. Revolutionary War hero and New Jersey state legislator Matthias Ogden also played a significant financial and political role in the operation.

In an undertaking of this kind, the contractors purchased the metal and assumed all expenses of coining. The difference between these expenses and the total face value of the coins issued represented their profit.

Later, Goadsby and Cox asked authority to coin two-thirds of the total independently of Mould. Their petition was granted November 22, 1786. Mould was known to have produced his coins at Morristown, while Cox and Goadsby operated in Rahway. Coins with a diameter of 30 mm or more are generally considered Morristown products. Coins were also minted in Elizabethtown by Ogden and, without authority, by Machin's Mills.

The obverse shows design elements of the state seal, a horse's head with plow, and the legend NOVA CÆSAREA (New Jersey). The reverse has a United States shield and, for the first time on a coin, the legend E PLURIBUS UNUM (One Composed of Many). More than 140 varieties exist. The majority have the horse's head facing to the right; however, three of the 1788 date show the head facing left. Other variations have a sprig beneath the head, branches below the shield, stars, cinquefoils, a running fox, and other ornaments.

**1786, Date Under
Plow Beam**

**1786, Date Under
Plow, No Coulter**

**1786 and 1787,
Pattern Shield**

	AG	G	F	VF	EF
1786, Date Under Plow Beam			$85,000	$125,000	$200,000
1786, Date Under Plow, No Coulter		$600	$1,100	$2,000	$5,500
1787, Pattern Shield (a)		$200	$400	$900	$2,000

a. The so-called Pattern Shield reverse was also used on several speculative patterns. See page 146.

**1786, Straight
Plow Beam,
Protruding Tongue**

1786, Wide Shield

**1786, Curved Plow
Beam, Bridle Variety**

	AG	G	F	VF	EF	AU
1786, Straight Plow Beam (common varieties)		$60	$200	$500	$850	$1,250
1786, Curved Plow Beam (common varieties)		$60	$220	$650	$1,000	$1,750
1786, Protruding Tongue	$50	$90	$275	$600	$1,750	$6,000
1786, Wide Shield		$70	$240	$675	$2,000	$4,000
1786, Bridle variety		$100	$300	$700	$1,500	$5,000

1787, PLURIBS Error

1787, Second U Over S
in PLURIBUS

1787, PLURIRUS Error

	AG	G	F	VF	EF	AU
1786, PLUKIBUS error		$120	$500	$750	$2,000	$5,500
1787, PLURIBS error	$150	$300	$2,000	$3,500	$9,000	$12,500
1787, Second U Over S in PLURIBUS	$40	$160	$470	$1,000	$2,700	$5,000
1787, PLURIRUS error	$100	$250	$900	$1,800	$3,500	$7,000

1787, Sprig
Above Plow

1787, WM
Above Plow

1787, Hidden WM

	AG	G	F	VF	EF	AU
1787, Sprig Above Plow (common varieties)		$80	$275	$600	$1,200	$2,500
1787, No Sprig Above Plow (common varieties)		$65	$200	$550	$800	$1,250
1787, WM Above Plow (a)				—		
1787, Hidden WM in Sprig		$90	$350	$850	$2,200	$4,500

a. Unique.

1787, Camel Head

1787, Serpent Head

1787, 1787 Over 1887

	AG	G	F	VF	EF	AU
1787, 1787 Over 1887		$800	$4,000	$9,000	$20,000	—
1787, Camel Head (snout in high relief)	$40	$85	$250	$600	$1,000	$2,250
1787, Serpent Head	$50	$120	$400	$1,200	$2,500	$6,000
1787, Goiter Variety		$120	$500	$1,500	$3,500	$7,500

**1788, Running
Fox Before Legend**

**1788, Indistinct
Coulter**

**1788, Running
Fox After Legend**

1788, Braided Mane

**1788, Horse's
Head Facing Left**

	AG	G	F	VF	EF	AU
1788, Horse's Head Facing Right, several varieties		$60	$200	$500	$1,100	$2,400
1788, Horse's Head Facing Right, Running Fox Before Legend	$75	$150	$500	$1,400	$3,500	$8,000
1788, Similar, Indistinct Coulter	$150	$650	$2,500	$6,500	$15,000	—
1788, Horse's Head Facing Right, Running Fox After Legend				$50,000	$75,000	
1788, Braided Mane	$250	$600	$3,000	$5,500	$10,000	$15,000
1788, Horse's Head Facing Left		$250	$1,200	$3,500	$12,000	$22,000

PRIVATE TOKENS AFTER CONFEDERATION

The formal ratification of the Articles of Confederation—the document signed amongst the original 13 colonies, which established the United States of America as a confederation of sovereign states and served as its first constitution—was accomplished in early 1781. A number of private coinages sprang up after confederation, intended to facilitate local commerce. These were not the products of the federal government, but were tokens issued by businesses and other private concerns.

NORTH AMERICAN TOKENS (DATED 1781)

These tokens were struck in Dublin, Ireland. The obverse shows the seated figure of Hibernia, the personification of Ireland, facing left. The date of issue is believed to have been much later than that shown on the token (1781). Like many Irish tokens, this issue found its way to America in limited quantities and was accepted in commerce near the Canadian border.

	VG	F	VF	EF	AU
1781, Copper or Brass	$60	$100	$200	$600	$1,250

BAR COPPERS (CA. 1785)

The Bar coppers are undated and of uncertain origin. They have 13 parallel and unconnected bars on one side. On the other side is the large roman-letter USA monogram. The design is virtually identical to that used on a Continental Army uniform button.

The significance of the design is clearly defined by its extreme simplicity. The separate 13 states (bars) unite into a single entity as symbolized by the interlocking letters (USA).

These pieces are believed to have first circulated in New York during November 1785, as mentioned in a report in the *New Jersey Gazette* of November 12, 1785. They may have been made in England. Although they are scarce, examples enter the marketplace with regularity, and nearly all are in higher grades.

John Adams Bolen (1826–1907), a numismatist and a master diesinker in Springfield, Massachusetts, struck copies of the Bar copper around 1862. On these copies, the letter A passes under, instead of over, the S. Bolen's intent was not to deceive, and he advertised his copies plainly as reproductions. But his skills were such that W. Elliot Woodward, a leading auctioneer of tokens and medals in the 1860s, vacillated between selling Bolen's copies and describing them as "dangerous counterfeits." Bolen copies of the Bar copper are highly collectible in their own right, but they are less valuable than the originals.

	G	VG	F	VF	EF	AU	Unc.
(Undated) (Circa 1785) Bar Copper ‡	$1,000	$1,800	$3,000	$6,000	$8,000	$12,000	$20,000

‡ Ranked in the *100 Greatest American Medals and Tokens*.

AUCTORI PLEBIS TOKENS (1787)

These tokens are sometimes included with the coins of Connecticut, as they greatly resemble issues of that state. (The obverse features a draped male bust, possibly King George II, wearing laurels and facing left.) They were struck in England by an unknown maker, possibly for use in America.

	G	VG	F	VF	EF	AU	Unc.
1787, AUCTORI PLEBIS	$75	$100	$175	$350	$550	$1,000	$5,500

MOTT STORE CARDS (DATED 1789)

These 19th-century store cards have long been included in Early American coin collections because of the date they bear (1789). Most scholars believe these were produced no earlier than 1807 (and possibly in the Hard Times era of the late 1830s) as commemoratives of the founding of the Mott Company, and served as business cards. The firm, operated by Jordan Mott, was located at 240 Water Street, a fashionable section of New York at that time.

The obverse of the token features an eagle with wings spread and an American shield as a breastplate. The eagle holds an olive branch and arrows in his talons. Above is the date 1789, and around the rim is the legend CLOCKS, WATCHES, JEWELRY, SILVERWARE, CHRONOMETERS. The reverse of the token features a regulator clock with the legend MOTT'S N.Y. IMPORTERS, DEALERS, MANUFACTURERS OF GOLD & SILVER WARES.

	VG	F	VF	EF	AU	Unc.
"1789," Mott Token, Thick Planchet	$80	$175	$300	$400	$500	$1,000
"1789," Mott Token, Thin Planchet	$80	$200	$350	$600	$1,200	$2,200
"1789," Mott Token, Entire Edge Engrailed	$80	$300	$450	$900	$1,400	$3,000

STANDISH BARRY THREEPENCE (1790)

Standish Barry, of Baltimore, was a watch- and clockmaker, an engraver, and, later, a silversmith. In 1790 he circulated a silver threepence of his own fabrication. The tokens are believed to have been an advertising venture at a time when small change was scarce. The precise date on this piece may indicate that Barry intended to commemorate Independence Day, but there are no records to prove this. The head on the obverse is probably that of James Calhoun, who was active in Baltimore politics in the 1790s. The legend BALTIMORE TOWN JULY 4, 90, appears in the border. An enigmatic gold doubloon is also attributed to Barry (see pages 155–156).

Nearly all examples of the silver threepence show significant wear, suggesting that they circulated for a long time.

	VG	F	VF	EF	AU
1790 Threepence	$10,000	$20,000	$40,000	$65,000	$80,000

ALBANY CHURCH PENNIES (1790)

The First Presbyterian Church of Albany, New York, authorized an issue of 1,000 copper uniface tokens in 1790. These passed at 12 to a shilling. They were used to encourage parishioner donations (at that time, there was a scarcity of small change in circulation). They were also intended to stop contributions of worn and counterfeit coppers (in the words of the church elders' resolution, "in order to add respect to the weekly collections"). Two varieties were made, one with the addition of a large D (the abbreviation for *denarium*, or penny, in the British monetary system) above the word CHURCH. All are rare, with fewer than a dozen of each variety known.

	VG	F	VF	EF
(Undated) (1790) Without D ‡	$10,000	$12,500	$25,000	$40,000
(Undated) (1790) With D Added ‡	$10,000	$15,000	$35,000	$50,000

‡ Both Albany Church Penny varieties are ranked in the *100 Greatest American Medals and Tokens*, as a single entry.

KENTUCKY TOKENS (CA. 1792–1794)

These tokens were struck in England circa 1792 to 1794. Their obverse legend reads UNANIMITY IS THE STRENGTH OF SOCIETY; the central motif is a hand holding a scroll with the inscription OUR CAUSE IS JUST. The reverse shows a pyramid of 15 starbursts surrounded by rays. Each star in the triangle represents a state, identified by its initial letter. These pieces are usually called *Kentucky cents* or *Kentucky tokens* because the letter K (for Kentucky) happens to be at the top. Some of the edges are plain; others are milled with a diagonal reeding; and some have edge lettering that reads PAYABLE IN LANCASTER LONDON OR BRISTOL, PAYABLE AT BEDWORTH NUNEATON OR HINKLEY, or PAYABLE AT I. FIELDING, etc.

These are not known to have circulated in America. Rather, they were made as produced as collectibles, popular among English numismatists and others at the time. Likely more than 1,000 Kentucky tokens are in the hands of numismatists today.

	VF	EF	AU	Unc.
(1792–1794) Copper, Plain Edge	$175	$275	$450	$850
(1792–1794) Copper, Engrailed Edge	$500	$800	$1,200	$2,000
(1792–1794) Copper, Lettered Edge, PAYABLE AT BEDWORTH, etc.	—	—	—	—
(1792–1794) Copper, Lettered Edge, PAYABLE IN LANCASTER, etc.	$225	$300	$500	$700
(1792–1794) Copper, Lettered Edge, PAYABLE AT I. FIELDING, etc.	—	—	—	—

FRANKLIN PRESS TOKENS (1794)

These were English tradesman's tokens of the kind collected by English numismatists in the late 1700s and early 1800s. (As a group, they were popularly called Conder tokens, after James Conder, the man who first cataloged them for collectors.) The Franklin Press tokens did not circulate as money in America, but, being associated with a London shop where Benjamin Franklin once worked, they have long been included in American coin collections.

The obverse features a wood-frame printing press of the style that Benjamin Franklin would have operated by hand as a printer in England in 1725. He had left Philadelphia at the age of 18 to buy printing supplies in London and look for work. Around the central design is the legend SIC ORITOR DOCTRINA SURGETQUE LIBERTAS ("Thus Learning Advances and Liberty Grows"), and below is the date, 1794. The reverse legend reads PAYABLE AT THE FRANKLIN PRESS LONDON.

Most are plain-edged, but rare lettered-edge varieties exist, as well as a unique piece with a diagonally reeded edge.

	VG	VF	EF	AU	Unc.	MS-63
1794 Franklin Press Token	$100	$250	$350	$550	$750	$1,000
Similar, Edge Reads AN ASYLUM FOR THE OPPRESS'D OF ALL NATIONS	*(unique)*					
Similar, Edge Diagonally Reeded	*(unique)*					

TALBOT, ALLUM & LEE CENTS (1794–1795)

Talbot, Allum & Lee was a firm of importers engaged in the India trade and located at 241 Pearl Street, New York. It placed a large quantity of English-made coppers in circulation during 1794 and 1795.

ONE CENT appears on the 1794 issue, and the legend PAYABLE AT THE STORE OF on the edge. The denomination is not found on the 1795 reverse but the edge legend was changed to read WE PROMISE TO PAY THE BEARER ONE CENT. Rare plain-edged specimens of both dates exist. Exceptional pieces have edges ornamented or with lettering CAMBRIDGE BEDFORD AND HUNTINGDON.X.X.

It is estimated that more than 200,000 of these tokens were minted, though no original records have been located. Varieties and mulings are known; the values shown here are for the most common types.

Many undistributed tokens were sold to the Philadelphia Mint in a time of copper shortage. These were cut down and used by the Mint as planchets for coining 1795 and 1797 half cents.

1794 Cent, With NEW YORK   **1795 Cent**

	VG	F	VF	EF	AU	Unc.
1794 Cent, With NEW YORK ‡	$65	$80	$225	$350	$500	$1,000
1794 Cent, Without NEW YORK ‡	$500	$850	$1,500	$2,500	$4,500	$9,000
1795 Cent ‡	$50	$75	$150	$250	$350	$550

‡ All Talbot, Allum & Lee cents are ranked in the *100 Greatest American Medals and Tokens*, as a single entry.

MYDDELTON TOKENS (1796)

Philip Parry Price Myddelton was an Englishman who bought land in America after the Revolutionary War. He hoped to begin a vibrant farming community along the Ohio River and entice English craftsmen and workers to move there. To this end he contracted the design of a promotional token and had examples made in copper and silver. These tokens were struck at the Soho Mint of Boulton and Watt near Birmingham, England. Although their obverse legend reads BRITISH SETTLEMENT KENTUCKY, and Myddelton planned to order large quantities of the copper version for shipment to the United States, they were never actually issued for circulation in Kentucky. The entrepreneur was arrested in August 1796 and convicted in London for the crime of convincing hundreds of workers to leave England for America. He was jailed in Newgate prison for three and a half years, which ended his Kentucky plans.

The obverse of Myddelton's token shows Hope presenting two "little genii" (his description) to the goddess Liberty. She welcomes them with an open hand. At her feet is a flourishing sapling and a cornucopia representing America's bounty, and she holds a pole with a liberty cap. On the reverse, seated Britannia leans wearily on a downward-pointing spear, looking at the broken scale and fasces—symbols of unity, justice, and liberty—scattered at her feet.

Sylvester S. Crosby, in *The Early Coins of America*, remarked that "In beauty of design and execution, the tokens are unsurpassed by any piece issued for American circulation."

	PF
1796, Proof, Copper ‡	$20,000
1796, Proof, Silver ‡	$25,000

‡ Both Myddelton Token varieties are ranked in the *100 Greatest American Medals and Tokens*, as a single entry.

COPPER COMPANY OF UPPER CANADA TOKENS (EARLY 1800s)

These pieces were struck some time in the early 1800s. The obverse is the same as that of the Myddelton token. The new reverse refers to a Canadian firm, the Copper Company of Upper Canada, with the denomination ONE HALF PENNY. These tokens may have been made for numismatic purposes (for sale to collectors), or as part of the coiner's samples. Their maker is unknown. Restrikes were made in England in the 1890s.

	PF
1796, Proof, Copper	$15,000

CASTORLAND MEDALS (1796)

These medals, or "jetons," are dated 1796 and allude to a proposed French settlement known as Castorland. This was to be located on the Black River, in northern New York, not far from the Canadian border. Peter Chassanis of Paris had acquired land that he and others intended to parcel into large farms, with Chassanis heading the settlement's government, two commissaries residing at its seat, Castorville, and four commissaries headquartered in Paris. The medals were to be given as payment ("in recognition of the care which they may bestow upon the common concerns") to the Parisian directors of the colonizing company for their attendance at board meetings.

Some 20 French families, many of them aristocratic refugees from the French Revolution, moved to the settlement between 1796 and 1800. Challenges including sickness, harsh northern New York winters, loss of livestock, and theft of finances proved too much for the company, and Castorland was dissolved in 1814. Many of the surviving settlers moved to more prosperous American communities or returned to Europe.

The obverse of the Castorland medal features a profile portrait of the ancient goddess Sybele, associated with mountains, town and city walls, fertile nature, and wild animals. She wears a *corona muralis* ("walled crown"), laurels, and a draped head covering. The legend reads FRANCO-AMERICANA COLONIA, with CASTORLAND 1796 below. On the reverse the goddess Ceres, patroness of agriculture, stands at a maple with a sap drill while the tree's bounty flows into a waiting bucket. Ceres holds a cornucopia; at her feet are a sickle and a sheaf of wheat. A beaver at the bottom of the reverse further symbolizes Castorland and its resources (*castor* is French for "beaver," an animal crucial to the very profitable North American fur trade in the early 1800s). The legend, in Latin, is SALVE MAGNA PARENS FRUGUM—"Hail, Great Mother of Crops" (from Virgil).

Copy dies of the Castorland medal are still available and have been used at the Paris Mint for restriking throughout the years. Restrikes have a more modern look than originals; their metallic content (in French) is impressed on the edge: ARGENT (silver), CUIVRE (copper), or OR (gold).

	EF	AU	Unc.
1796, Original, Silver (reeded edge, unbroken dies) ‡	$3,000	$4,500	$7,500
1796, Original, Silver (reverse rusted and broken) ‡	$300	$600	$1,500
1796, Original, Bronze (reverse rusted and broken) ‡	$200	$300	$700
(1796) Undated, Restrike, Silver (Paris Mint edge marks) ‡		$30	$70
(1796) Undated, Restrike, Bronze (Paris Mint edge marks) ‡		$20	$40

‡ All Castorland Token varieties are ranked in the *100 Greatest American Medals and Tokens*, as a single entry.

THEATRE AT NEW YORK TOKENS (CA. 1798)

These penny tokens were issued by Skidmore of London and illustrate the New Theatre (later known as the Park Theatre) in Manhattan, as it appeared circa 1797. The theater was New York City's attempt at a prestigious new level of entertainment, as the famous John Street Theatre (the "Birthplace of American Theater") was suffering from poor management and physical decay in the 1790s. The building's cornerstone was laid on May 5, 1795, and the theater opened on January 29, 1798, with a presentation of entertainments including Shakespeare's *As You Like It*.

The obverse of this copper token features a view of the playhouse building with the legend THE THEATRE AT NEW YORK AMERICA. The reverse shows an allegorical scene of a cornucopia on a dock, with bales, an anchor, and sailing ships. The legend reads MAY COMMERCE FLOURISH. The edge is marked I PROMISE TO PAY ON DEMAND THE BEARER ONE PENNY.

All known examples are struck in copper and have a Proof finish. They were made for collectors, not for use as advertising. Today examples are scarce, with about 20 known.

	EF
	PF
Penny, THE THEATRE AT NEW YORK AMERICA	$10,000
Penny, THE THEATRE AT NEW YORK AMERICA, Proof ‡	$22,500

‡ Ranked in the *100 Greatest American Medals and Tokens*.

NEW SPAIN (TEXAS) JOLA TOKENS (1817–1818)

In 1817 the Spanish governor of Texas, Colonel Manuel Pardo, authorized Manuel Barrera to produce 8,000 copper coins known as jolas. These crudely made pieces show the denomination 1/2 [real], the maker's initials and the date on the obverse, and a five-pointed star on the reverse.

The 1817 coins were withdrawn from circulation the following year and replaced by a similar issue of 8,000 pieces. These bear the date 1818 and the initials, JAG, of the maker, José Antonio de la Garza. Several varieties of each issue are known. All are rare.

	F	VF	EF
1817 1/2 Real	$12,000	$22,000	$40,000
1818 1/2 Real, Large or Small Size ‡	$15,000	$27,500	$42,500

‡ Ranked in the *100 Greatest American Medals and Tokens*.

NORTH WEST COMPANY TOKENS (1820)

Holed Brass Token

These tokens were probably valued at one beaver skin and struck in Birmingham, England, in 1820 by John Walker & Co. All but two known specimens are holed. Most have been found in Oregon in the region of the Columbia and Umpqua river valleys. They feature a portrait of King George IV on the obverse, with the legend TOKEN and the date 1820. The reverse shows a beaver in the wild, with the legend NORTH WEST COMPANY.

James A. Haxby, in the *Guide Book of Canadian Coins and Tokens*, writes, "The pieces actually issued for circulation were pierced at the top for suspension or stringing. Unholed copper strikes are known with plain or engrailed edge and are very rare. A number of pieces have been found buried in western Canada and as far south as central Oregon."

Unholed Copper Token

	AG	G	VG	F	VF
1820, Copper or Brass, holed ‡	$375	$800	$2,000	$3,500	$7,500
1820, Copper, unholed, plain or engrailed edge ‡	—	—	—	—	—

‡ All North West Company Token varieties are ranked in the *100 Greatest American Medals and Tokens*, as a single entry.

WASHINGTON PIECES

Medals, tokens, and coinage proposals in this interesting series dated from 1783 to 1795 bear the portrait of George Washington. The likenesses in most instances were faithfully reproduced and were designed to honor the first president. Many of these pieces were of English origin and, although dated 1783, probably were made in the 1820s or later.

The legends generally signify a strong unity among the states and the marked display of patriotism that pervaded the new nation during that period. We find among some of these tokens an employment of what were soon to become the nation's official coin devices, namely, the American eagle, the United States shield, and stars. The denomination ONE CENT is used in several instances, while on some of the English pieces HALFPENNY will be found. Several of these pieces were private patterns for proposed coinage contracts.

GEORGIVS TRIUMPHO TOKENS

Although the head shown on these tokens bears a strong resemblance to that on some coins of King George III, many collectors consider the Georgivs Triumpho ("Triumphant George") tokens a commemorative of America's victory in the Revolutionary War.

The reverse side shows the Goddess of Liberty behind a framework of 13 bars and fleurs-de-lis. Holding an olive branch in her right hand and staff of liberty in her left, she is partially encircled by the words VOCE POPOLI ("By the Voice of the People") 1783. An example is known used as an undertype for a 1787 New Jersey copper.

	VG	F	VF	EF	AU
1783, GEORGIVS TRIUMPHO	$110	$225	$500	$700	$1,000

WASHINGTON PORTRAIT PIECES (1780S TO EARLY 1800S)

Military Bust. "The 1783-dated Washington Military Bust coppers bear a portrait, adapted (with a different perspective on the coin and a wreath added to the head) from a painting by Edward Savage," writes Q. David Bowers in the *Whitman Encyclopedia of Colonial and Early American Coins*. "These seem to have circulated in England as well as America. . . . Many varieties exist, but they are not well known outside of a circle of specialists. Accordingly, the opportunity exists to acquire rare die combinations for little premium over a regular issue."

The reverse features a seated female figure holding an olive branch and a pole topped by a liberty cap.

Values shown are for the most common varieties.

1783, Large Military Bust, Point of Bust Close to W

1783, Small Military Bust

	F	VF	EF	AU	Unc.
1783, Large Military Bust			$250	$500	$1,500
1783, Small Military Bust, Plain Edge	$80	$175	$450	$650	$1,800
1783, Small Military Bust, Engrailed Edge	$100	$200	$550	$1,000	$2,750

Draped Bust. Draped Bust coppers dated 1783 depict Washington with the top of a toga draped over his shoulder. One variety includes a button at the folds in front of the toga. Another variety has no button, and has the initial "I" (for Ingram) in the toga, above the right side of the numeral 3 in the date. Both varieties feature a similar reverse design with a female figure seated on a rock, holding an olive branch and a pole surmounted by a liberty cap.

1783, Draped Bust, No Button **With Button**

	F	VF	EF	AU	Unc.	PF
1783, Draped Bust, No Button *(illustrated)*	$80	$160	$300	$500	$1,500	
1783, Draped Bust, With Button (on Drapery at Neck)	$125	$225	$350	$700	$3,200	
1783, Draped Bust, Copper Restrike, Plain Edge, Proof	$125	$225	$350	$550	$650	$850
1783, Draped Bust, Copper Restrike, Engrailed Edge, Proof						$750
1783, Draped Bust, Silver Restrike, Engrailed Edge, Proof						$3,500

Unity States. The 1783-dated coppers with the legend UNITY STATES OF AMERICA were likely coined in the early 1800s at the Soho Mint in Birmingham, England. The obverse features a portrait of Washington in a toga and wearing laurels. The reverse is a copy of the wreath design on the copper cent produced by the Philadelphia Mint from 1796 to 1807, with UNITED spelled UNITY, perhaps as a way to evade charges of counterfeiting.

Despite the American denomination of this piece, they likely circulated in England (at the value of a halfpenny), as reflected by examples being found there in quantity in later years. They were imported into the United States as well, for use as a cent, and are mentioned in several counterfeit-detector publications in the 1850s.

1783, Unity States

	VG	F	VF	EF	AU	Unc.
1783, UNITY STATES	$100	$200	$250	$450	$500	$1,250

Double Head. Although the Washington Double Head cents are undated, some numismatists assign them a date of 1783, given their resemblance to the Military Bust coppers that bear that date (even though those were probably struck years later). They were likely struck in Birmingham, England, by Edward Thomason sometime in the 1820s or later. They were made in England, as evidenced by many having been found there, but long after the Conder token era. They are denominated ONE CENT and, when exported to the United States, circulated along with Hard Times tokens of the 1830s.

Undated Double-Head Cent

	F	VF	EF	AU	Unc.
(Undated) Double-Head Cent	$100	$250	$425	$500	$2,000

Ugly Head. The so-called Ugly Head token is a medalet struck in copper and white-metal varieties, possibly satirical, and presumably of American origin. The token's legend reads WASHINGTON THE GREAT D.G. The abbreviation "D.G." on English coins stands for Dei Gratia ("By the Grace of God"), and the portrait appears to be wigless and possibly toothless, leading some numismatists to opine that the token is a satire on George Washington. Bowers notes that the token's date, 1784, has no particular significance in Washington's life. By that year the American Revolution was over and the general had retired his commission as commander-in-chief of the Continental Army. He would not assume the presidency until 1789. The reverse of the token features a design of linked rings with abbreviations for the British colonies, reminiscent of the 1776 Continental dollar.

1784, Ugly Head

	VF	EF
1784, Ugly Head, Copper	$50,000	$75,000
Auctions: $20,000, Crude Good, December 1983		
1784, Ugly Head, Pewter		(unique)

Small and Large Eagle. Small Eagle and Large Eagle one-cent tokens dated 1791 were made in Birmingham, England, sponsored by merchants W. and Alex Walker of that city as proposals for official American coinage. Bowers writes in the *Whitman Encyclopedia of Colonial and Early American Coins* that the Walker firm "shipped a cask filled with these cents, estimated to be about 2,500 Large Eagle and 1,500 Small Eagle coins, to Thomas Ketland & Sons, a Philadelphia contact, to be distributed to legislators. The depiction of Washington was contrary to the president's own desires, who felt that having his image on coins would appear to have the 'stamp of royalty.'"

1791 Cent, Small Eagle Reverse, Edge Lettered UNITED STATES OF AMERICA

1791 Cent, Large Eagle Reverse

	VG	F	VF	EF	AU	Unc.
1791 Cent, Small Eagle (Date on Reverse)		$475	$650	$800	$1,200	$2,500
1791 Cent, Large Eagle (Date on Obverse)	$150	$350	$550	$750	$1,100	$2,250

Liverpool. The Liverpool Halfpenny tokens were most likely made around 1793. They were intended for circulation as small change in England, although numismatists of the time also sought them for their collections. The obverse shows a uniformed bust of George Washington, as used on the Large Eagle one-cent tokens of 1791. The reverse features a sailing ship and the legend LIVERPOOL HALFPENNY, a design used on various English Conder tokens.

1791 Liverpool Halfpenny

	VG	F	VF	EF	AU	Unc.
1791 Liverpool Halfpenny, Lettered Edge	$700	$900	$1,250	$1,500	$2,500	—

1792. An extensive series of 1792-dated Washington pieces was produced in many varieties, bearing no denomination. These apparently were made in England, and were collected by numismatists in addition to circulating as coinage substitutes in America.

1792 Cent, Eagle with 13 Stars Reverse

	VG	F	VF	EF
1792, WASHINGTON PRESIDENT, Eagle With 13 Stars Reverse				
PRESIDENT at Side of Bust, Copper				—
PRESIDENT, Silver			$125,000	—
PRESIDENT, Gold (a)			—	
PRESIDENT Extends Below Bust, Copper (a)				$125,000

a. Unique.

1792, WASHINGTON PRESIDENT   Legend Reverse

	VG	F	VF	EF
1792, WASHINGTON PRESIDENT, Legend on Reverse				
Plain Edge, Copper	$2,750	$7,500	$18,000	$50,000
Lettered Edge, Copper	—	—	—	—

**(1792) Undated,
WASHINGTON
BORN VIRGINIA**

	VG	F	VF	EF
(1792) Undated, WASHINGTON BORN VIRGINIA, Eagle With 13 Stars Reverse *(reverse illustrated on previous page)*, Copper ‡ (a)		—		
(1792) Undated, WASHINGTON BORN VIRGINIA, Legend on Reverse				
Copper ‡	$1,000	$1,500	$3,000	$5,000
Copper, Edge Lettered UNITED STATES OF AMERICA *(1 known)* ‡				
Silver ‡	—	—	—	—

‡ All WASHINGTON BORN VIRGINIA copper pieces are ranked in the *100 Greatest American Medals and Tokens*, as a single entry.
a. 3 examples are known.

Peter Getz. Dies engraved by silversmith, mechanic, and inventor Peter Getz of Lancaster, Pennsylvania, are believed to have been made to produce a half dollar and a cent as a proposal to Congress for a private contract coinage before the Philadelphia Mint became a reality. These feature George Washington, in a military bust portrait, and a heraldic eagle.

1792, Small Eagle Reverse **Large Eagle Reverse**

	VG	F	VF	EF	AU	Unc.
1792, Small Eagle, Silver	—	—	—	$150,000		
Auctions: $312,000, AU-58, January 2021						
1792, Small Eagle, Copper	$6,000	$12,000	$30,000	$50,000	$75,000	$100,000
Auctions: $165,000, MS-64BN, November 2014						
1792, Small Eagle, Ornamented Edge (Circles and Squares), Copper	—	—	—	$150,000		
Auctions: $207,000, AU, November 2006						
1792, Small Eagle, Ornamented Edge, Silver (a)	—	—	$100,000	$175,000		
Auctions: $360,000, MS-63, January 2021						
1792, Large Eagle, Silver			—	—		
Auctions: $34,500, EF, May 2004						

a. 4 examples are known.

Roman Head. The 1792-dated Roman Head cents show Washington in the style of an ancient Roman dignitary. These copper pieces were struck in England for collectors, as opposed to being intended for circulation. Their edge is lettered UNITED STATES OF AMERICA.

1792 Cent, Roman Head

	PF
1792 Cent, Roman Head, Lettered Edge UNITED STATES OF AMERICA, Proof	$75,000

Ship Halfpenny. The 1793 Ship Halfpenny tokens were struck from an overdated (3 Over 2) reverse die. These copper pieces were intended for collectors, but nearly all of them ended up in circulation in England. The more common lettered-edge variety reads PAYABLE IN ANGLESEY LONDON OR LIVERPOOL.

1793 Ship Halfpenny

	VG	F	VF	EF	AU	Unc.
1793 Ship Halfpenny, Lettered Edge	$100	$200	$400	$600	$850	$3,250
1793 Ship Halfpenny, Plain Edge (a)			—	—		

a. Rare.

1795 Copper. Copper tokens dated 1795 were made in large quantities as promotional pieces for the London firm of Clark & Harris, dealers in stoves and fireplace grates. The die work is attributed to Thomas Wyon, and numismatists believe the pieces were struck in Birmingham, England, for circulation in the British Isles (although collectors saved them as well).

The obverse features a right-facing portrait of George Washington in military uniform. Two varieties exist, Small Buttons and Large Buttons (describing the coats on his frock). The legend reads G. WASHINGTON: THE FIRM FRIEND TO PEACE & HUMANITY.

The reverse shows a fireplace with a coal grate, with legends PAYABLE BY CLARK & HARRIS 13. WORMWOOD St. BISHOPSGATE and LONDON 1795.

Most have a diagonally reeded edge, although some are edge-lettered as PAYABLE AT LONDON LIVERPOOL OR BRISTOL.

1795, Large Buttons   **1795, Small Buttons**

	F	VF	EF	AU	Unc.
1795, Large Buttons, Lettered Edge	$180	$300	$650	$1,000	$1,500
1795, Large Buttons, Reeded Edge	$80	$175	$300	$400	$700
1795, Small Buttons, Reeded Edge	$80	$200	$400	$550	$1,250

Liberty and Security. The Liberty and Security halfpenny and penny tokens were made in England in 1795 as collectibles, although the halfpence also circulated widely there as small change. Their designs consist of a portrait of George Washington, identified by name, and a heraldic eagle surmounting a stylized American shield, holding a sprig of olive and several arrows. Some of their edges are plain, and some are lettered with various phrases such as AN ASYLUM FOR THE OPPRESS'D OF ALL NATIONS and BIRMINGHAM REDRUTH & SWANSEA.

Varieties exist in copper and white metal, and with mulings of different reverses.

The common name of this series derives from the reverse legend, LIBERTY AND SECURITY.

1795, Liberty and Security Halfpenny

	F	VF	EF	AU	Unc.
1795 Halfpenny, Plain Edge	$110	$200	$500	$850	$2,500
1795 Halfpenny, LONDON Edge	$100	$210	$500	$700	$2,500
1795 Halfpenny, BIRMINGHAM Edge	$125	$250	$500	$900	$2,500
1795 Halfpenny, ASYLUM Edge	$200	$400	$1,000	$1,500	$3,000
1795 Penny, ASYLUM Edge	$2,500	$7,500	$10,000	$15,000	$25,000

(1795) Undated, Liberty and Security Penny, ASYLUM Edge

	F	VF	EF	AU	Unc.
(1795) Undated, Liberty and Security Penny	$275	$450	$600	$1,000	$1,700
Same, Corded Outer Rims	$600	$1,000	$2,500	$4,000	$6,000

North Wales. "The undated North Wales halfpenny issues, believed to have been struck in England in the early 1790s (usually listed as 1795, although this may be two or three years after they were coined), are part of the 'evasion halfpence' series. Accordingly, unlike Conder tokens, they were not created for collectors. None are known to have survived with sharp features and in high grades, as is characteristic of cabinet pieces" (*Whitman Encyclopedia of Colonial and Early American Coins*).

(1795) Undated, NORTH WALES Halfpenny

	G	F	VF	EF	AU
(1795) Undated, NORTH WALES Halfpenny	$90	$200	$500	$750	$1,000
(1795) Undated, Lettered Edge	$450	$1,200	$4,000	$6,000	$7,500
(1795) Undated, Two Stars at Each Side of Harp	$2,000	$5,000	$7,500	$25,000	

Success Tokens. Small and large types exist of these mysterious pieces of unknown date and purpose. Today known as Success tokens, they may have been souvenirs, perhaps struck to commemorate George Washington's second inauguration (March 1793), or 19th-century gaming tokens. They were struck in copper or brass and most likely were made in the mid-1800s. Specimens with original silvering are rare and are valued 20% to 50% higher than others. Varieties exist.

(Undated) SUCCESS Token, Large   (Undated) SUCCESS Token, Small

	F	VF	EF	AU	Unc.
(Undated) SUCCESS Token, Large, Plain or Reeded Edge	$250	$450	$750	$1,400	$2,750
(Undated) SUCCESS Token, Small, Plain or Reeded Edge	$300	$500	$800	$1,250	$3,000

Contract Issues and Patterns

NOVA CONSTELLATIO PATTERNS (1783)

These Nova Constellatio pieces represent the first official patterns for a coinage of the United States. They were designed by Benjamin Dudley for Gouverneur Morris to carry out his ideas for a decimal coinage system. The 1,000-unit coin is a mark, the 500 a quint. These denominations, together with the small 100-unit piece, were designed to fit in with the many different values for foreign coins that constituted money in America at the time. These pattern pieces represent the first attempt at a decimal ratio, and were the forerunners of our present system of money values. Neither the proposed denominations nor the coins advanced beyond the pattern stage. These unique pieces are all dated 1783. There are two types of the quint. The copper "five" was first brought to the attention of collectors in 1980. Electrotype and cast copies exist.

5 Units	Quint, Plain Obverse	Quint, Legend on Obverse	Quint Reverse

Bit (100 Units)   Mark

1783 (Five) "5," Copper		*(unique)*
1783 (Bit) "100," Silver, Decorated Edge		*(2 known)*
	Auctions: $97,500, Unc., November 1979	
1783 (Bit) "100," Silver, Plain Edge		*(unique)*
	Auctions: $705,000, AU-55, May 2014	
1783 (Quint) "500," Silver, Plain Obverse		*(unique)*
	Auctions: $1,175,000, AU-53, April 2013	
1783 (Quint) "500," Silver, Legend on Obverse		*(unique)*
	Auctions: $165,000, Unc., November 1979	
1783 (Mark) "1000," Silver		*(unique)*
	Auctions: $190,000, Unc., November 1979	

FUGIO COPPERS (1787)

The first coins issued under U.S. authority for which contract information is known today were the Fugio pieces, which were valued at one cent each. They were made under contract with James Jarvis, owner of a controlling interest in the Connecticut mint, which was then striking Connecticut coppers in New Haven. Jarvis obtained the federal contract with a $10,000 bribe to Col. William Duer, then head of the Board of Treasury. The contract called for Jarvis to deliver 345 tons of copper coins to the federal government. Congress, which was ignorant of the bribe, directed on July 7, 1787, "that the Board of Treasury direct the contractor for the copper coinage to stamp on one side of each piece the following device, viz: thirteen circles linked together, a small circle in the middle, with the words 'United States,' around it; and in the centre, the words 'We are one'; on the other side of the same piece the following device, viz: a dial with the hours expressed on the face of it; a meridian sun above on one side of which is the word 'Fugio,' ["time flies"] and on the other the year in figures '1787,' below the dial, the words 'Mind Your Business.'"

Jarvis was only able to mint 11,910 pounds of Fugios (equal to around 554,741 coins). Not all of these were shipped to the government, which cancelled the contract for failure to meet the delivery schedule.

All Fugios were minted in 1788 and back-dated 1787. The dies were engraved by Abel Buell.

1787, WITH POINTED RAYS

The 1787, With Pointed Rays, was later replaced by the With Club Rays variety.

American
Congress Pattern

Cross After Date

Label With
Raised Rims

	G	VG	F	VF	EF	AU	Unc.
Obverse Cross After Date, No Cinquefoils							
Reverse Rays and AMERICAN CONGRESS †				$200,000	$300,000	$450,000	
Reverse Label with Raised Rims † (a)			$14,000	$20,000	$35,000		
Reverse STATES UNITED †	$300	$650	$1,100	$2,700	$6,500	$13,000	—
Reverse UNITED STATES †	$275	$500	$900	$2,200	$5,000	$10,000	—

† All non-restrike Fugio Coppers are ranked in the *100 Greatest U.S. Coins* (fifth edition), as a single entry. **a.** Extremely rare.

Cinquefoil After Date
*These types, with pointed rays, have
regular obverses punctuated with four
cinquefoils (five-leafed ornaments).*

	G	VG	F	VF	EF	AU	Unc.
STATES UNITED at Sides of Circle, Cinquefoils on Label †	$200	$375	$600	$1,000	$1,500	$2,000	$3,500
UNITED STATES at Sides of Circle †	$200	$375	$650	$1,100	$1,600	$2,200	$3,800
STATES UNITED, 1 Over Horizontal 1 †	$275	$500	$1,000	$5,000	$8,500	$20,000	
UNITED STATES, 1 Over Horizontal 1 †	$300	$525	$1,100	$6,000	$11,000	$24,000	
STATES UNITED, Label With Raised Rims, Large Letters in WE ARE ONE †	$225	$400	$900	$2,000	$4,000	$8,500	$20,000
STATES UNITED, 8-Pointed Star on Label †	$200	$400	$700	$1,200	$2,000	$4,000	$9,000
UNITED Above, STATES Below †	$850	$1,750	$3,750	$7,500	$10,000	$15,000	$22,500

† All non-restrike Fugio Coppers are ranked in the *100 Greatest U.S. Coins* (fifth edition), as a single entry.

1787, WITH CLUB RAYS

The 1787, With Club Rays, is differentiated between concave and convex ends.

Rounded Ends **Concave Ends**

	G	VG	F	VF	EF	AU
Club Rays, Rounded Ends †	$225	$400	$800	$1,250	$2,250	$4,250
Club Rays, Concave Ends to Rays, FUCIO (C instead of G) † (a)	$1,750	$3,500	$7,500	$15,000	$25,000	
Club Rays, Concave Ends, FUGIO, UNITED STATES †	$2,200	$5,000	$10,000	$30,000	$40,000	$90,000
Club Rays, Similar, STATES UNITED Reverse †		—	—		—	—

† All non-restrike Fugio Coppers are ranked in the *100 Greatest U.S. Coins* (fifth edition), as a single entry. **a.** Extremely rare.

The so-called New Haven "restrikes" were made for Horatio N. Rust from dies recreated in 1859. These are distinguished by narrow rings on the reverse. At the time the fanciful story was given that teenaged C. Wyllys Betts discovered original dies in 1858 on the site of the Broome & Platt store in New Haven, where the original coins had been made.

New Haven Restrike
Note narrow rings.

	EF	AU	Unc.
New Haven restrike, Gold (a)		—	—
New Haven restrike, Silver	$3,200	$4,750	$7,500
New Haven restrike, Copper or Brass	$500	$600	$900

a. 2 examples are known.

1792 PROPOSED COINAGE

Some members of the House of Representatives favored a depiction of the president's head on the obverse of each federal coin; others considered the idea an inappropriately monarchical practice. George Washington himself is believed to have expressed disapproval of the use of his portrait on American coins. The majority considered a figure emblematic of Liberty more appropriate, and the Senate finally concurred in this opinion. Robert Birch was an engraver employed to design proposed devices for American coins. He, perhaps together with others, engraved the dies for the disme and half disme. He also cut the dies for the large copper patterns known today as *Birch cents*. Most 1792 half dismes circulated and were considered to be official coinage, rather than patterns; they are summarized here and discussed in more detail under "Half Dismes."

1792 SILVER CENTER CENT

The dies for the 1792 cent with a silver center may have been cut by Henry Voigt. The coins are copper with a silver plug in the center. The idea was to create a coin with an intrinsic or melt-down value of a cent, but of smaller diameter than if it were made entirely of copper. On the obverse is a right-facing portrait of Miss Liberty, the legend LIBERTY PARENT OF SCIENCE & INDUSTRY, and the date 1792.

	F	VF	EF	AU
Cent, Silver Center † (a)	$200,000	$275,000	$350,000	$600,000
Auctions: $1,997,500, MS-64, August 2014; $705,000, MS-61+, September 2014; $336,000, AU, April 2019				
Cent, Without Silver Center (b)	$250,000	$375,000	$475,000	$650,000
Auctions: $603,750, VF-30, January 2008				

† Ranked in the *100 Greatest U.S. Coins* (fifth edition). **a.** 14 examples are known, including one unique specimen without plug. **b.** Six or 7 examples are known.

1792 BIRCH CENT

On the large-diameter copper Birch cent, the portrait of Miss Liberty is "bright-eyed and almost smiling," as described in *United States Pattern Coins* (10th edition). The legend LIBERTY PARENT OF SCIENCE & INDUSTRY surrounds the portrait. BIRCH is lettered on the truncation of her neck, for the engraver. On the reverse is a ribbon-tied wreath with the legend UNITED STATES OF AMERICA and the denomination in fractional terms of a dollar: 1/100. The edge of some examples is lettered TO BE ESTEEMED BE USEFUL (with punctuating stars).

G★W.PT.

	F	VF	EF
Copper, Lettered Edge, TO BE ESTEEMED * BE USEFUL* † (a)	$225,000	$550,000	$675,000
Auctions: $564,000, MS-61, January 2015			
Copper, Plain Edge † (b)		$700,000	
Copper, Lettered Edge, TO BE ESTEEMED BE USFFUL * † (b)		—	
Auctions: $2,585,000, MS-65H, January 2015			
White Metal, G★W.PT. (George Washington President) Below Wreath † (c)			—

† All varieties of 1792 Birch Cents are ranked in the *100 Greatest U.S. Coins* (fifth edition), as a single entry. **a.** Six or seven examples are known. **b.** Two examples are known. **c.** Unique.

1792 HALF DISME

About 1,500 silver half dismes were struck in mid-August 1792 in the shop of John Harper, using equipment ordered for the Philadelphia Mint (the foundation stones of which would be laid on July 31). Nearly all were placed into circulation. In his annual address that autumn, President George Washington noted that these had been so distributed. Their obverse design is a portrait of Miss Liberty similar to the Birch cent's, but facing left. Its legend is abbreviated as LIB. PAR. OF SCIENCE & INDUSTRY. The reverse shows an eagle in flight, with UNI. STATES OF AMERICA around the top, and HALF DISME below.

	Mintage	AG	G	VG	F	VF	EF	AU	Unc.
Silver †	1,500	$9,500	$22,000	$27,500	$40,000	$80,000	$110,000	$175,000	$300,000
	Auctions: $1,145,625, MS-68, January 2013; $440,625, MS-64, May 2015; $240,000, MS-63, October 2018; $58,750, F-15, June 2013								

† Ranked in the *100 Greatest U.S. Coins* (fifth edition).

1792 DISME

The 1792 pattern disme occurs in one silver variety and two copper varieties (plain-edged and the more readily available reeded-edge). The obverse legend is abbreviated as LIBERTY PARENT OF SCIENCE & INDUST., with the date 1792 below Miss Liberty's neck. The reverse features an eagle in flight, different in design from that of the half disme, with UNITED STATES OF AMERICA around the top of the coin and the denomination, DISME, below.

	F	EF	AU	Unc.
Silver † (a)	$300,000	$450,000	$850,000	
	Auctions: $998,750, AU-50, January 2015			
Copper *(illustrated)* † (b)	$135,000	$225,000	$450,000	$950,000
	Auctions: $360,000, AU-58, October 2018; $211,500, VF-25, February 2014; $186,000, EF, April 2019; $63,000, VG-8, August 2019			

† Both 1792 Disme Pattern varieties are ranked in the *100 Greatest U.S. Coins* (fifth edition), as a single entry. **a.** 3 examples are known. **b.** Approximately 15 examples are known.

1792 QUARTER DOLLAR

Little is known of this pattern coin's origins, except that it was added to the Mint Cabinet by Chief Coiner Adam Eckfeldt. In the 19th century it was often called a "cent," but the eagle design is more appropriate for a silver or gold issue than a copper. It is commonly called a "quarter" today. Unique uniface trials of the obverse and reverse also exist.

	EF
1792, Copper *(illustrated)* † (a)	$750,000
Auctions: $2,232,500, MS-63, January 2015	
1792, White Metal † (b)	$325,000

† Both 1792 Quarter Dollar Pattern varieties are ranked in the *100 Greatest U.S. Coins* (fifth edition), as a single entry. **a.** 2 examples are known. **b.** 4 examples are known.

THE LIBERTAS AMERICANA MEDAL (1782)

The Liberty Cap coinage of the fledgling United States was inspired by the famous Libertas Americana medal, whose dies were engraved by Augustin Dupré in Paris in 1782 from a concept and mottoes proposed by Benjamin Franklin. To Franklin (then U.S. minister to France), the infant Hercules symbolized America, strangling two serpents representing the British armies at Saratoga and Yorktown. Minerva, with shield and spear, symbolized France as America's ally, keeping the British Lion at bay. Franklin presented gold examples of the medal to the French king and queen and silver strikings to their ministers, "as a monumental acknowledgment, which may go down to future ages, of the obligations we are under to this nation."

Between 100 and 125 original copper medals exist, and two dozen or more silver; the location of the two gold medals is unknown. Over the years the Paris Mint has issued additional medals that are appreciated and collected at a fraction of the cost for originals.

	PF-50	PF-60	PF-63	PF-65
Libertas Americana medal, Proof, Copper ‡ (a)	$10,000	$15,000	$27,500	$50,000
Libertas Americana medal, Proof, Silver ‡ (b)	$60,000	$100,000	$175,000	$300,000

‡ Both Libertas Americana varieties are ranked in the *100 Greatest American Medals and Tokens*, as a single entry. **a.** 100 to 125 examples are known. **b.** At least 24 examples are known.

Half Cents
1793–1857

AN OVERVIEW OF HALF CENTS

Building a type set of the six different major designs in the half cent series can be a challenging and rewarding pursuit. The first design, with Liberty Head facing left with pole and cap, minted only in 1793, is scarce in all grades and will be the most difficult to locate. However, hundreds exist of this American classic, and many are fairly attractive.

The second type, with a *large* Liberty Head facing right with pole and cap, made only in 1794, is scarce with good eye appeal. Most are dark and rough. The next type, the *small* Liberty Head facing right, with pole and cap, is scarce, but enough are on the market that a collector can find a specimen without difficulty.

The Draped Bust half cents, struck from 1800 to 1808, are easily available as a type, including in higher grades. The Classic Head (1809–1836) and Braided Hair (1840–1857) are plentiful as types.

For the earlier half cent types there is ample opportunity for connoisseurship, for quality often varies widely, and every coin is apt to have a different appearance and "personality," even within the same grade.

FOR THE COLLECTOR AND INVESTOR: HALF CENTS AS A SPECIALTY

Collecting half cents by dates and major varieties has been a popular niche specialty for a long time. Some key issues in the series are the 1793; 1796, With Pole to Cap; 1796, Without Pole to Cap, (the most famous of all the rarities); 1802, 2 Over 0, With Reverse of 1800, (a single leaf at each side of the wreath apex, rare but somewhat obscure); 1831; and the Proof-only issues of 1836, 1840 through 1848, Small Date, and 1852.

As there are so many Proof varieties, and each of these is rare as well as expensive, many collectors opt to acquire only the circulation strikes. However, the Proofs are not nearly as expensive as one might think, probably because with so many different dates and varieties needed to complete a Proof collection, the prospect is daunting to many buyers. Proofs of most dates are available in both original and restrike forms. Although this rule is not without exceptions, the original strikings of the 1840–1848 and 1849, Small Date, half cents are usually described as having the Large Berries reverse, while restrikes are of the Small Berries reverse (within the Small Berries issues there are two dies—one with diagonal die striae below RICA, and the other with doubling at the ribbon wreath). Assembling Proofs by reverse varieties is a somewhat esoteric pursuit.

For an exhaustive study of die varieties of circulation strikes and Proofs, *Walter Breen's Encyclopedia of United States Half Cents, 1793–1857*, is definitive. Roger S. Cohen Jr.'s study, *American Half Cents, The "Little Half Sisters,"* gives detailed information on circulation strikes, but omits Proofs.

Die varieties are especially abundant among half cents of the first several types, 1793 to 1808. The year 1804 offers a panorama of dies, some of which have been studied as to die states, referring to the progression of use of a die as it develops wear, cracks, etc. Varieties of 1795 exist with and without the pole to the liberty cap, the Without Pole half cents being the result of a die being relapped (reground to dress the surface), during which process the pole was removed. On the other hand, the 1796, Without Pole, half cent was the result of a die-engraving error—the diecutter forgot to add it. Some half cents of 1795 and 1797 were struck on planchets cut from copper tokens issued by the New York City firm of Talbot, Allum & Lee. Upon close inspection, some of the design details of the tokens can still be seen.

One curious and readily available variety of the 1828 half cent has 12 stars instead of the standard 13. However, in choice Mint State the 12-stars issue becomes a rarity, for, unlike the 13-stars issue, none were ever found in hoards.

The Early American Coppers Club is a special-interest group emphasizing copper half cents and large cents. Its journal, *Penny-Wise*, provides much research, social, and collecting news and information.

LIBERTY CAP, HEAD FACING LEFT (1793)

Designer: *Henry Voigt.* **Weight:** *6.74 grams.* **Composition:** *Copper.* **Diameter:** *21.2 to 24.6 mm.*
Edge: *Lettered TWO HUNDRED FOR A DOLLAR.* **Mint:** *Philadelphia.*

Bowers-Whitman–4,
Cohen-4, Breen-4.

History. Among U.S. coinage, the Liberty Cap, Head Facing Left, design belongs to the small class of one-year-only types. Its design was inspired by Augustin Dupré's Libertas Americana medal. The Liberty Cap dies are often credited to Joseph Wright, who also cut the dies for the related cent, but they were more likely done by Henry Voigt.

Striking and Sharpness. Good-quality copper was used in these half cents, so they are often found light brown and on fairly smooth planchets. Unlike in later types, the borders on both sides are raised beads; certain of these beads can be weak, though this is not the norm. Some varieties are lightly defined at HALF CENT on the reverse, due to a combination of striking and shallow depth of letters in the die. This feature cannot be used in assigning a grade, as in lower grades (up to and including VG-8) these words may be completely missing.

Availability. Most half cents of 1793 are AG-3 to F-12. EF and AU examples are rare, and MS very rare (most being MS–60 to 63). Market grading is often liberal. Early American Coppers Club (EAC) "raw" grades often are lower than those of the certification services.

GRADING STANDARDS

MS-60 to 65 (Mint State). *Obverse:* In the lower ranges, MS–60 and 61, some light abrasions can be seen on the higher areas of the portrait. Luster in the field is incomplete, particularly in the center of the open areas. At the MS-63 level, luster should be complete, with no abrasions evident. In higher levels, the luster is deeper, and some original mint color may be seen. *Reverse:* In the lower ranges some abrasions are seen on the higher

1793; Bowers-Whitman–3, Cohen-3,
Breen-3. Graded MS-60BN.

areas of the leaves. Generally, luster is complete in all ranges, as the open areas are protected by the lettering and wreath. Otherwise, the same comments apply as for the obverse.

Illustrated coin: Well struck and nicely centered on the planchet, this example shows no sign of wear. Its color is a rich orange-brown overall, with a bit of darker gray-brown on the lower-right edge and field of the obverse. The faint roughness on the obverse is a flaw of the original planchet, and is not related to wear.

AU-50, 53, 55, 58 (About Uncirculated). *Obverse:* Friction is seen on the higher parts, particularly on the rounded cheek and on the higher strands of the hair. Friction and scattered marks are in the field, ranging from extensive at AU-50 to minimal at AU-58. Luster may be seen in protected areas, minimal at AU-50, but sometimes extensive on an AU-58 coin. Border beads, if well struck, are separate and boldly defined. *Reverse:* Friction

1793; BW-3, C-3, B-3. Graded AU-58.

is seen on the higher wreath leaves and (not as easy to discern) on the letters. The fields, protected by the designs, show friction, but not as noticeably as on the obverse. At AU–55 and 58 little if any friction is seen. The reverse may have original luster, toned brown, minimal on lower About Uncirculated grades, sometimes extensive at AU-58. Border beads, if well struck, are separate and boldly defined. Grading at the About Uncirculated level is mainly done by viewing the obverse.

Illustrated coin: Two tiny rim bruises can be seen, and some nicks can be seen as well under low magnification, none of which immediately draw the eye. This coin is about as good as can be found in this grade, as many examples of the date are porous.

EF-40, 45 (Extremely Fine). *Obverse:* Wear is seen on the portrait overall, with reduction or elimination of some separation of hair strands on the highest part. The cheek is ever so slightly flat on the highest part. Some leaves will retain some detail, especially where they join the stems. Luster is minimal or non-existent at EF-40 and may survive in traces in protected areas at EF-45. *Reverse:* Wear is seen on the highest wreath and rib-

1793; BW-3, C-3, B-3. Graded EF-45.

bon areas and the letters. Luster is minimal, but likely more noticeable than on the obverse, as the fields are protected by the designs and lettering.

Illustrated coin: The devices are crisp for the grade. Note the glossy golden-tan surfaces and the lack of meaningful contact marks.

VF-20, 30 (Very Fine). *Obverse:* Wear on the portrait has reduced the hair detail to indistinct or flat at the center on a VF-20 coin, with slightly more detail at VF-30. The thin, horizontal (more or less) ribbon near the top of the hair is distinct. The border beads are blended together, with many blurred or missing. No luster is seen. *Reverse:* The leaf details are nearly completely worn away at VF-20, and with slight detail at

1793; BW-3, C-3, B-3. Graded VF-30.

VF-30. The border beads are blended together, with many indistinct. Some berries in the sprays may be worn away, depending on the strike (on strong strikes they can be seen down into Very Good and Good grades). No luster is seen. HALF CENT may be weak, but is fully readable, on certain coins (such as BW-1, C-1, B-1) in which this feature was shallowly cut into the dies.

Illustrated coin: A small planchet crack at 8 o'clock on the obverse rim appears as struck. This planchet crack explains the softness of detail at the borders both in that area at 10 o'clock on the reverse.

F-12, 15 (Fine). *Obverse:* The hair details are mostly worn away, with about one-third visible, mainly at the edges. Border beads are weak or worn away in areas. F-15 shows slightly more detail. *Reverse:* The wreath leaves are worn flat, but their edges are distinct. HALF CENT may be missing on 1793 (Bowers-Whitman–1)—also true of lower grades given below. Border beads are weak or worn away in areas. F-15 shows slightly more detail.

1793; BW-3, C-3, B-3. Graded F-15.

Illustrated coin: Under magnification the surfaces are seen to be lightly porous.

VG-8, 10 (Very Good). *Obverse:* The portrait is well worn, although the eye can be seen, and the hair tips at the right show separation. Border beads are worn away, and the border blends into the field in most if not all of the periphery. LIBERTY and 1793 are bold. VG-10, not an official ANA grading designation, is sometimes applied to especially nice Very Good coins. *Reverse:* The wreath, bow, and lettering are seen in outline

1793; BW-4, C-4, B-4. Graded VG-8.

form, and some leaves and letters may be indistinct in parts. Border beads are worn away, and the border blends into the field in most if not all of the periphery.

Illustrated coin: The scratch from the E of LIBERTY to the base of the cap behind Liberty's head is less evident at the coin's unmagnified size.

G-4, 6 (Good). *Obverse:* The portrait is worn smooth and is seen only in outline form, although the eye position can be discerned. LIBERTY and 1793 are complete, although the date may be weak. *Reverse:* Extensive wear is seen overall. From half to two-thirds of the letters in UNITED STATES OF AMERICA and the fraction numerals are worn away. The reverse shows more evidence of wear than does the obverse, and is key in assigning this grade. G-6 is often assigned to finer examples in this category.

1793; BW-2, C-2, B-2. Graded G-6.

AG-3 (About Good). *Obverse:* Wear is more extensive than on the preceding. The portrait is visible only in outline. LIBERTY is weak but usually fully discernible. 1793 is weak, and the bottoms of the digits may be worn away. *Reverse:* Parts of the wreath are visible in outline form, and all but a few letters are gone. Grading of AG-3 is usually done by the reverse.

1793; BW-3, C-3, B-3. Graded AG-3.

Fair-2 (Fair). *Obverse:* Worn nearly smooth. Date is partly visible, not necessarily clearly. Head of Miss Liberty is in outline form. Some letters of LIBERTY are discernible. *Reverse:* Worn nearly smooth. Peripheral letters are nearly all gone, with only vestiges remaining. Wreath is in outline form. HALF CENT ranges from readable to missing (the latter on certain die varieties as struck).

1793; BW-2, C-2, B-2. Graded Fair-2.

	Mintage	Cert	Avg	%MS	AG-3	G-4	VG-8	F-12	VF-20	EF-40	AU-50	MS-60BN	MS-63BN
1793	35,334	178	31.2	10%	$2,500	$3,500	$5,000	$8,000	$11,000	$17,000	$25,000	$60,000	$95,000
	Auctions: $176,250, MS-64, February 2016; $108,688, MS-64, April 2016; $47,000, MS-62, November 2016; $49,200, AU-58, April 2018												

LIBERTY CAP, HEAD FACING RIGHT (1794–1797)

Designer: *1794—Robert Scot; 1795–1797—Possibly Scot, John Smith Gardner, or other.*
Weight: *1794, thick planchet—6.74 grams; 1795–1797—5.44 grams.* **Composition:** *Copper.*
Diameter: *23.5 mm.* **Edge:** *1794, some of 1795, some of 1797—Lettered TWO HUNDRED*
FOR A DOLLAR; 1795, 1796, most of 1797—Plain; some of 1797—Gripped. **Mint:** *Philadelphia.*

1795, Lettered Edge,
With Pole; BW-1, C-1, B-1.

History. The design of the half cent changed in 1794 to a depiction, by Robert Scot, of Miss Liberty facing right. A smaller-headed portrait was used from 1795 on.

Striking and Sharpness. Half cents of 1794 usually are dark, with rough surfaces, and of low aesthetic quality. Most 1795's are on high-quality planchets, smooth and attractive, this being truer of the later plain-edge type than the early thick-planchet issue. Striking can be weak in areas. Often the denticles are incomplete on one or both sides. Many Small Head coins, particularly of 1795 to 1797, have very little detail on the hair, even in higher grades. Half cents of 1796 vary in quality; higher-grade pieces are usually attractive. Half cents of 1797 are usually seen in low grades and on poor planchets; striking varies widely, but is usually weak in areas. Denticles can be weak or can be prominent in various circulated grades, down to the lowest; on certain varieties of 1795 they are prominent even on well-worn coins. Grades must be assigned carefully, and expertise is recommended—combining knowledge of a given die variety and its relief or sharpness in the die, with observations of actual circulation wear. Grades of certified coins can vary widely in their interpretations.

Availability. As a general type, this issue is scarce, but available. Most are in lower grades, but VF and EF coins appear in the market with regularity.

GRADING STANDARDS

MS-60 to 70 (Mint State). *Obverse:* On MS–60 and 61 coins there are some traces of abrasion on the higher areas of the portrait. Luster in the field is incomplete, particularly in the center of the open areas. At MS-63, luster should be complete, and no abrasion is evident. At higher levels, the luster is deeper, and some original mint color may be seen. At MS-65 there are some scattered contact marks and possibly some traces of fingerprints or discoloration, but these should be minimal and not at all distracting. Above MS-65, a coin

1794; BW-9, C-9, B-9. Graded MS-65.

should approach perfection. *Reverse:* In the lower ranges some abrasions are seen on the higher areas of the leaves. Generally, luster is complete in all ranges, as the open areas are protected by the lettering and wreath. Otherwise, the same comments apply as for the obverse.

Illustrated coin: A spectacular coin of a year seldom seen in Mint State. Both sides have rich, brown surfaces. On the obverse the luster is light, while on the reverse it is not as noticeable. Note that the obverse die is in very high relief and of the Large Head style, while the reverse is in shallower relief.

AU-50, 53, 55, 58 (About Uncirculated).
Obverse: Friction is seen on the higher parts, particularly the center of the portrait. Friction and scattered marks are in the field, ranging from extensive at AU-50 to minimal at AU-58. To reiterate: knowledge of the die variety is important. For certain shallow-relief dies (such as those of 1797) an About Uncirculated coin may appear to be in a lower grade. Luster may be seen in protected

1794; BW-1a, C-1a, B-1a. Graded AU-50.

areas, minimal at AU-50, but sometimes extensive on an AU-58 coin. *Reverse:* Friction is seen on the higher wreath leaves and (not as easy to discern) on the letters. The fields, protected by the designs, show friction, but not as noticeably as on the obverse. At AU–55 and 58 little if any friction is seen. The reverse may have original luster, toned brown, minimal on lower About Uncirculated grades, sometimes extensive on higher. Grading at the About Uncirculated level is mainly done by viewing the obverse.

Illustrated coin: Note faint ruddy highlights in the protected areas. The devices are boldly impressed. On this variety the 179 in the date was punched low into the die, partly effaced, then repunched in a higher position. On the reverse, a natural planchet fissure, small and as struck, runs from the rim through the M of AMERICA, and a smaller fissure runs from the rim to the E of AMERICA.

EF-40, 45 (Extremely Fine). *Obverse:*
Wear is seen on the portrait overall, with some reduction or elimination of the separation of hair strands on the highest part. This varies by die variety, as some are better delineated than others. The cheek shows light wear. Luster is minimal or nonexistent at EF-40, and may survive in traces in protected areas (such as between the letters) at EF-45. *Reverse:* Wear is seen on the highest wreath and ribbon areas and the letters. Luster is minimal, but likely

1795, Pole to Cap, Lettered Edge;
BW-1, C-1, B-1. Graded EF-45.

more noticeable than on the obverse, as the fields are protected by the designs and lettering. Sharpness will vary depending on the die variety. Expect certain issues of 1794 and 1797 to be lighter.

Illustrated coin: This coin has bold details and excellent centering.

VF-20, 30 (Very Fine). *Obverse:* Wear on the portrait has reduced the hair detail to indistinct or flat at the center. The border denticles are blended together, with many indistinct. No luster is seen. Again, knowing details of the die variety is important. A VF–20 or 30 1797 is very different in appearance from a 1794, Large Head, in the same grade. *Reverse:* The leaf details are nearly completely worn away at VF-20, with slight

1797; BW-2, C-2. Graded VF-30.

detail at VF-30. The border denticles are blended together, with many indistinct. No luster is seen. The sharpness of details depends on the die variety. Half cents of 1797 require special care in their study.

Illustrated coin: Minor roughness is apparent at the center of both sides, undoubtedly a trace of microporosity from the blank planchet, although the devices are overall bold from a well executed strike.

F-12, 15 (Fine). *Obverse:* The hair details are mostly worn away, with about one-third visible, mainly at the edges. Border denticles are weak or worn away in areas. F-15 shows slightly more detail. *Reverse:* The wreath leaves are worn flat, but their edges are distinct. Border denticles are weak or worn away in areas. F-15 shows slightly more detail.

Illustrated coin: This late-die-state variety has a noticeable die crack in the E of UNITED.

1794, High-Relief Head; BW-7, C-7, B-7. Graded F-15.

VG-8, 10 (Very Good). *Obverse:* The portrait is well worn, although the eye can be seen, and the hair tips at the left show separation. Border denticles are worn away on some issues (not as much for 1795 coins), and the border blends into the field in most if not all of the periphery. LIBERTY and the date are bold. VG-10, not an official ANA grading designation, is sometimes applied to especially nice Very Good coins. *Reverse:* The

1794, High Relief Head; BW-9, C-9, B-9. Graded VG-8.

wreath, bow, and lettering are seen in outline form, and some leaves and letters may be indistinct in parts. Border denticles are worn away, and the border blends into the field in most if not all of the periphery. In certain die varieties and die states, especially of 1797, some letters may be very weak or missing.

Illustrated coin: This coin exhibits roughness in the fields, but the same does not apply to the devices.

G-4, 6 (Good). *Obverse:* The portrait is worn smooth and is seen only in outline form, although the eye position can be discerned. LIBERTY and the date are complete, although the date may be weak. Denticles are gone on some, but not all, die varieties. *Reverse:* Extensive wear is seen overall. From half to two-thirds of the letters in UNITED STATES OF AMERICA, and the fraction numerals, are worn away. Certain shallow-relief dies

1794; BW-2a, C-2a, B-2a. Graded G-4.

may have letters missing. G-6 is often assigned to finer examples in this category.

Illustrated coin: On this coin the surfaces are heavily worn, yet with considerable boldness of detail remaining on the obverse.

AG-3 (About Good). *Obverse:* Wear is more extensive than on the preceding. The portrait is visible only in outline. LIBERTY is weak but usually fully discernible. The date is weak, and the bottoms of the digits may be worn away. *Reverse:* Parts of the wreath are visible in outline form, and all but a few letters are gone. Grading of AG-3 is usually done by the reverse, as the obverse typically appears to be in a slightly higher grade. If split grading were used, more than just a few half cents of this type could be designated as G-4 / AG-3 or even G-6 / AG-3.

1795, Plain Edge, Punctuated Date; BW-5, C-4, B-4. Graded AG-3.

1794, Normal Head   **1794, High-Relief Head**   **1795, With Pole**   **1795, No Pole**

1795, Punctuated Date

	Mintage	Cert	Avg	%MS	AG-3	G-4	VG-8	F-12	VF-20	EF-40	AU-50	MS-60BN	MS-63BN
1794, All kinds	81,600												
1794, Normal Head		41	34.3	12%	$425	$575	$950	$1,800	$2,250	$5,000	$11,000	$26,500	$85,000
Auctions: $88,125, MS-63BN, April 2014													
1794, High-Relief Head		20	34.0	5%	$475	$600	$975	$1,750	$2,500	$6,000	$12,000	$27,500	$85,000
Auctions: $1,586, VF-20, October 2013													
1795, All kinds	139,690												
1795, Lettered Edge, With Pole		69	31.0	12%	$325	$600	$825	$1,300	$2,250	$4,500	$8,000	$17,500	$65,000
Auctions: $3,525, EF-40, September 2013; $2,820, VF-30, March 2015													
1795, Lettered Edge, Punctuated Date		8	28.1	25%	$350	$675	$875	$1,250	$2,250	$5,000	$11,000	$24,000	$75,000
Auctions: $12,925, AU-55, August 2013													
1795, Plain Edge, Punctuated Date		14	30.7	21%	$275	$550	$725	$1,250	$2,350	$5,500	$9,500	$25,000	$85,000
Auctions: $1,501, VF-20, August 2011													
1795, Plain Edge, No Pole (a)		46	27.4	2%	$220	$500	$675	$1,250	$2,000	$4,000	$7,500	$14,000	$26,500
Auctions: $7,638, AU-55, June 2014													

a. Many of this date/variety were struck on cut-down cents (coins that had been rejected for circulation by Mint workers), or on planchets cut from English-made Talbot, Allum & Lee tokens (see the *Whitman Encyclopedia of Colonial and Early American Coins*).

| | | | | 1796, "Dr. Edwards" Copy | | | 1797, 1 Above 1 | | 1797, Low Head | | |

	Mintage	Cert	Avg	%MS	AG-3	G-4	VG-8	F-12	VF-20	EF-40	AU-50	MS-60BN	MS-63BN
1796, With Pole † (b)	1,390	24	40.7	50%	$10,500	$20,000	$25,000	$37,500	$50,000	$70,000	$95,000	$175,000	
Auctions: $76,375, EF-40, August 2013													
1796, No Pole †	(c)	3	45.7	67%	$22,500	$35,000	$45,000	$105,000	$150,000	$210,000	$300,000	$450,000	
Auctions: $891,250, MS-65BN, January 2014; $382, VG-8, September 2013													
1797, All kinds	127,840												
1797, 1 Above 1, Plain Edge		0	n/a		$250	$500	$650	$1,100	$1,800	$4,000	$6,500	$15,000	
Auctions: $7,931, AU, March 2014													
1797, Plain Edge, Low Head		7	15.7	0%	$350	$575	$975	$2,000	$4,000	$14,000	—		
Auctions: $1,495, VG-10, February 2012													
1797, Plain Edge		65	21.2	5%	$275	$500	$750	$1,250	$3,500	$6,000	$8,500	$16,000	
Auctions: $3,055, AU-50, April 2013; $823, F-12, August 2015; $400, VG-8, September 2015; $505, G-6, January 2015													
1797, Lettered Edge		7	19.6	0%	$700	$1,400	$2,500	$6,000	$15,000	$50,000			
Auctions: $7,638, VG-10, November 2013; $3,995, VG-10, March 2016													
1797, Gripped Edge		1	8.0	0%	$40,000	$90,000		—	—	—			
Auctions: $195,500, G-6, September 2011													

† Both 1796 half cent varieties are ranked in the *100 Greatest U.S. Coins* (fifth edition), as a single entry. **a.** Many of this date/variety were struck on cut-down cents (coins that had been rejected for circulation by Mint workers), or on planchets cut from English-made Talbot, Allum & Lee tokens (see the *Whitman Encyclopedia of Colonial and Early American Coins*). **b.** The deceptive "Dr. Edwards" struck copy of this coin has a different head and larger letters, as pictured. **c.** Included in 1796, With Pole, mintage figure.

DRAPED BUST (1800–1808)

Designer: *Robert Scot.* **Weight:** *5.44 grams.* **Composition:** *Copper.*
Diameter: *23.5 mm.* **Edge:** *Plain.* **Mint:** *Philadelphia.*

1804, Crosslet 4, Stems to Wreath;
BW-9, C-10, B-9.

History. By the turn of the century the Draped Bust design was already familiar to Americans from its use on cents and silver coins. The motif was introduced to the half cent in 1800, and was used through 1808.

Striking and Sharpness. Striking varies. Weakness is often seen at the center of the obverse and on the wreath leaves on the reverse. Planchet quality is often porous and dark for 1802, 1803, 1807, and 1808 due to the copper stock used.

Availability. As a type, Draped Bust half cents are available in any grade desired, up to and including Mint State, the latter usually dated 1806 (occasionally 1800 and, less often, 1804). The year 1804 includes many different die varieties and die states. Apart from aspects of strike, cherrypicking for planchet quality is essential for 1802, 1803, 1807, and 1808.

GRADING STANDARDS

MS-60 to 70 (Mint State). *Obverse:* In the lower grades, MS–60 and 61, some slight abrasions can be seen on the higher areas of the portrait. Luster in the field is incomplete, particularly in the center of the open areas, which on this type are very extensive. At the MS-63 level, luster should be nearly complete, and no abrasions evident. In higher levels, the luster is complete and deeper and some original mint color may be seen. MS-64

1800; BW-1, C-1, B-1. Graded MS-62.

coins may have some slight discoloration or scattered contact marks. A well-graded MS-65 or higher coin has full, rich luster; no marks visible except under magnification; and a blend of brown toning or nicely mixed (not stained or blotchy) mint color and natural brown toning. *Reverse:* In the lower Mint State ranges some abrasions are seen on the higher areas of the leaves. Generally, luster is complete in all ranges, as the open areas are protected by the lettering and wreath. Sharpness of the leaves can vary by die variety, so check this aspect. Otherwise, the same comments apply as for the obverse.

AU-50, 53, 55, 58 (About Uncirculated). *Obverse:* Friction is seen on the higher parts, particularly the hair of Miss Liberty. Friction and scattered marks are in the field, ranging from extensive at AU-50 to minimal at AU-58. Luster may be seen in protected areas, minimal at AU-50, with more at AU-58. At AU-58 the field may retain some luster, as well. In all instances, the luster is lesser in area and in "depth" than on the reverse of this type.

1800; BW-1, C-1, B-1. Graded AU-58.

Reverse: Friction is evident on the higher wreath leaves and (not as easy to discern) on the letters. Again, the die variety should be checked. The fields, protected by the designs, show friction, but not as noticeably as on the obverse. At AU–55 and 58, little if any friction is seen. The reverse may have original luster, toned brown, minimal on lower About Uncirculated grades, often extensive at AU-58.

Illustrated coin: The motifs are very boldly rendered, except for partial weakness on the lower obverse and OF on the upper reverse, which is virtually missing due to the late die state.

EF-40, 45 (Extremely Fine). *Obverse:* Wear is seen on the portrait overall, with reduction or elimination of some separation of hair strands on the highest part. The cheek shows light wear. Luster is minimal or non-existent at EF-40, and may survive among the letters of LIBERTY at EF-45. *Reverse:* Wear is seen on the highest wreath and ribbon areas, and the letters. Luster is minimal, but likely more noticeable than on the obverse, as the fields are protected by the designs and lettering.

1800; BW-1, C-1, B-1. Graded EF-40.

VF-20, 30 (Very Fine). *Obverse:* Wear on the portrait has reduced the hair detail to indistinct or flat at the center. The border denticles are blended together, with many indistinct. No luster is seen. *Reverse:* The leaf details are nearly completely worn away at VF-20, and with slight detail at VF-30. The border denticles are blended together, with many indistinct. No luster is seen.

Illustrated coin: Struck from a later die state, the reverse shows a bisecting die crack.

1803; BW-1, C-1, B-1. Graded VF-20.

F-12, 15 (Fine). *Obverse:* The hair details are mostly worn away, with about one-third visible, mainly at the edges. Border denticles are weak or worn away in areas. F-15 shows slightly more detail. *Reverse:* The wreath leaves are worn flat, but their edges are distinct. HALF CENT may be missing on weakly struck varieties (also true of lower grades given below). Border denticles are weak or worn away in areas. F-15 shows slightly more detail.

1804, "Spiked Chin"; BW-5, C-8, B-7. Graded F-15.

Illustrated coin: This is the "Spiked Chin" variety, so called because of a thorn-like projection from the chin. The variety does not affect the grade.

VG-8, 10 (Very Good). *Obverse:* The portrait is well worn, although the eye can be seen, as can hints of hair detail (some at the left shows separation). Curls now appear as mostly solid blobs. Border denticles are worn away on most varieties, and the rim, although usually present, begins to blend into the field. LIBERTY and the date are bold. VG-10, not an official ANA grading designation, is sometimes applied to especially nice Very Good coins. *Reverse:* The wreath, bow, and letter-

1804, Plain 4, Stems to Wreath; BW-12, C-11, B-12. Graded VG-10.

ing are seen in outline form, and some leaves and letters may be indistinct in parts. The border may blend into the field on some of the periphery.

Illustrated coin: This coin is has many scratches, which detract from overall eye appeal.

G-4, 6 (Good). *Obverse:* The portrait is worn smooth and is seen only in outline form, although the eye position can be discerned. LIBERTY and the date are complete, although the date may be weak. The border blends into the field more extensively than on the preceding, but significant areas are still seen. *Reverse:* Extensive wear is seen overall. From one-half to two-thirds of the letters in UNITED STATES OF AMERICA and the

1808, 8 Over 7; BW-2, C-2, B-2. Graded G-4.

fraction numerals are worn away. G-6 is often assigned to finer examples in this category.

Illustrated coin: A slightly off-center strike has allowed areas of heavier wear to creep in near the borders. There are many noticeable scratches on the obverse.

AG-3 (About Good). *Obverse:* Wear is more extensive than on the preceding. The portrait is visible only in outline. LIBERTY is weak but usually discernible. The date is weak, and the bottoms of the digits may be worn away, but must be identifiable. *Reverse:* Parts of the wreath are visible in outline form, and all but a few letters are gone.

1802, 2 Over 0; BW-2, C-2, B-2. Graded AG-3.

1st Reverse
(Style of 1800)

2nd Reverse
(Style of 1802)

1803, Normally Spaced 3

1803, Widely Spaced 3

1804, Plain 4

1804, Crosslet 4

Stems to Wreath

Stemless Wreath

1804, "Spiked Chin"

	Mintage	Cert	Avg	%MS	AG-3	G-4	VG-8	F-12	VF-20	EF-40	AU-50	MS-60BN	MS-63BN
1800	202,908	240	42.0	28%	$55	$110	$150	$175	$300	$675	$850	$2,250	$4,000
	Auctions: $282, VF-35, May 2015; $329, VF-25, January 2015; $4,113, VF-20, June 2013												
1802, 2 Over 0, Reverse of 1800	(a)	3	11.3	0%	$10,000	$22,000	$32,500	$55,000	$75,000	$115,000	—		
	Auctions: $35,938, VG-8, April 2009; $4,935, AG-0, March 2016												
1802, 2 Over 0, Reverse of 1802	20,266	53	9.2	0%	$475	$950	$2,250	$4,750	$11,000	$20,000	—		
	Auctions: $4,406, F-12, February 2013; $940, G-6, June 2015; $940, G-6, March 2016; $940, G-6, August 2016; $960, G-6, January 2018												
1803	(b)	239	28.5	9%	$45	$95	$120	$175	$325	$950	$1,500	$3,250	$7,000
	Auctions: $646, VF-35, August 2015; $376, VF-25, June 2015; $235, VF-30, February 2015; $153, VG-8, February 2015; $79, G-4, March 2018												
1803, Widely Spaced 3	92,000	31	32.1	10%	$50	$100	$135	$185	$325	$950	$1,500	$3,500	$7,500
	Auctions: $1,840, AU-55, April 2012												
1804, All kinds	1,055,312												
1804, Plain 4, Stems to Wreath		17	31.4	0%	$55	$100	$125	$200	$475	$1,300	$2,200	$4,000	
	Auctions: $4,994, AU-58, October 2013; $1,410, EF-45, March 2016; $823, VF-30, August 2015												
1804, Plain 4, Stemless Wreath		230	42.8	16%	$40	$85	$125	$145	$225	$385	$675	$1,300	$2,800
	Auctions: $940, AU-58, June 2015; $646, AU-55, October 2015; $588, AU-55, August 2015; $259, AU-50, May 2015												
1804, Crosslet 4, Stemless		64	53.1	42%	$40	$85	$125	$145	$225	$385	$675	$1,300	$3,000
	Auctions: $5,141, MS-64BN, September 2013; $376, EF-40, January 2015												
1804, Crosslet 4, Stems		144	42.4	14%	$40	$85	$125	$145	$225	$400	$675	$1,300	$2,800
	Auctions: $705, AU-55, March 2015; $470, EF-45, October 2015; $364, EF-40, April 2015; $282, VF-35, August 2015												
1804, "Spiked Chin"	472	41.7	11%	$40	$05	$125	$225	$350	$600	$950	$2,000	$3,750
	Auctions: $764, AU-53BN, September 2015; $646, AU-50, February 2015; $423, EF-45, June 2015; $247, EF-40, July 2015												

a. Included in 1800 mintage figure. b. Included in 1802, 2 Over 0, Second Reverse, mintage figure.

1805, Medium 5

1805, Small 5

1805, Large 5

1806, Small 6

1806, Large 6

1808, Normal Date

1808, 8 Over 7

	Mintage	Cert	Avg	%MS	AG-3	G-4	VG-8	F-12	VF-20	EF-40	AU-50	MS-60BN	MS-63BN
1805, All kinds	814,464												
1805, Medium 5, Stemless		56	38.0	13%	$40	$85	$125	$145	$225	$400	$750	$1,350	$3,000
Auctions: $4,113, MS-64BN, April 2014; $517, EF-45, January 2015; $447, EF-40, January 2015													
1805, Small 5, Stems		11	14.0	0%	$500	$1,000	$1,600	$4,000	$8,000	$17,000	$45,000		
Auctions: $1,116, VG-8, August 2015; $1,175, G-6, March 2016													
1805, Large 5, Stems		40	33.8	0%	$40	$85	$125	$145	$225	$425	$850	$1,700	$3,750
Auctions: $1,293, AU-55, July 2015; $353, VF-35, June 2015; $223, VF-30, July 2015													
1806, All kinds	356,000												
1806, Small 6, Stems		29	26.0	0%	$100	$235	$425	$750	$1,650	$3,500	$6,500	$15,000	
Auctions: $646, F-15, September 2016; $505, F-12, July 2016; $400, VG-10, March 2016; $188, G-6, August 2016													
1806, Small 6, Stemless		151	44.0	16%	$40	$85	$125	$145	$175	$325	$675	$1,200	$2,900
Auctions: $823, AU-58, January 2015; $564, AU-50, September 2015; $517, AU-50, August 2015; $329, EF-45, February 2015													
1806, Large 6, Stems		99	49.0	40%	$40	$85	$125	$145	$175	$325	$675	$1,200	$2,900
Auctions: $5,581, MS-63RB, June 2014; $780, AU-55, April 2018													
1807	476,000	343	34.9	7%	$40	$85	$125	$145	$200	$500	$1,000	$2,000	$3,750
Auctions: $1,175, AU-58, February 2013; $212, VF-20, May 2015													
1808, All kinds	400,000												
1808, Normal Date		169	28.2	3%	$40	$85	$125	$145	$220	$525	$1,200	$2,500	$6,500
Auctions: $823, AU-50, June 2014; $447, EF-45, January 2015; $200, VF-25, June 2015; $660, EF-45, January 2018													
1808, 8 Over 7		55	18.6	0%	$80	$150	$350	$750	$2,000	$4,000	$10,000		
Auctions: $2,585, EF-40, April 2013													

CLASSIC HEAD (1809–1836)

Designer: *John Reich.* **Weight:** *5.44 grams.* **Composition:** *Copper.*
Diameter: *23.5 mm.* **Edge:** *Plain.* **Mint:** *Philadelphia.*

Circulation Strike
1833; BW-1.

Proof
1836; BW-1.

History. The Classic Head design (by Mint engraver John Reich) made its first appearance on the half cent in 1809, a year after it was adopted for the one-cent coin. A very similar motif of Miss Liberty was used on the quarter eagles and half eagles of the 1830s.

Striking and Sharpness. Coins of 1809 to 1811 usually have areas of light or incomplete striking. Grading coins of the early years requires special care and expertise. Sometimes coins as high as MS appear "blurry" in areas, due to the dies and striking. Those of later years are often found well struck and are easier to grade. Areas to check include the denticles and rims on both sides, the star centers and hair detail on the obverse, and the leaf detail on the reverse.

Availability. As a type this issue is found easily enough, although 1811 is scarce and 1831 and 1836 are notable rarities. MS coins from old hoards exist for certain of the later dates, particularly 1828, 1833, and 1835, but often have spotting, and many seen in the marketplace are cleaned or recolored. Care is advised. Although 1809–1811 half cents are often seen with extensive wear, those of the 1820s and 1830s are not often seen less than VF, as they did not circulate extensively.

GRADING STANDARDS

MS-60 to 70 (Mint State). *Obverse:* In the lower grades, MS–60 and 61, some slight abrasions can be seen on the portrait, most evident on the cheek, as the hair details are complex on this type. Luster in the field is complete or nearly complete. At MS-63, luster should be complete, and no abrasions are evident. In higher levels, the luster is complete and deeper, and some original mint color may be seen. MS-64 coins may have

1810; BW-1, C-1, B-1. Graded MS-64BN.

some slight discoloration or scattered contact marks. A well-graded MS-65 or higher coin has full, rich luster, with no marks visible except under magnification, and has a nice blend of brown toning or nicely mixed (not stained or blotchy) mint color and natural brown toning. Coins dated 1809 to 1811 may exhibit significant weakness of details due to striking (and/or, in the case of most 1811's, porous planchet stock). *Reverse:* In the lower Mint State grades, some abrasions are seen on the higher areas of the leaves. Mint luster is complete in all Mint State grades, as the open areas are protected by the lettering and wreath. Sharpness of the leaves can vary by die variety, so check this aspect. Otherwise, the same comments apply as for the obverse. Coins dated 1809 to 1811 may exhibit significant weakness of details due to striking (and/or, in the case of most 1811's, porous planchet stock).

 Illustrated coin: Some surface marks on the coin holder obscure the reverse, but no such marks mar the surface of this sharply struck coin.

AU-50, 53, 55, 58 (About Uncirculated).
Obverse: Friction is seen on the higher parts, particularly the cheek and hair (under magnification) of Miss Liberty. Friction and scattered marks are in the field, ranging from extensive at AU-50 to minimal at AU-58. Luster may be seen in protected areas, minimal at the AU-50 level, with more showing at AU-58. At AU-58 the field may retain some luster as well. *Reverse:* Friction is seen on the

1828, 12 Stars; BW-3, C-2, B-3. Graded AU-58.

higher wreath leaves and (not as easy to discern) on the letters. Again, half cents of 1809 to 1811 require special attention. The fields, protected by the designs, show friction, but not as noticeably as on the obverse. At AU–55 and 58, little if any friction is seen. The reverse may have original luster, toned brown, minimal on lower About Uncirculated grades, often extensive at AU-58.

EF-40, 45 (Extremely Fine). *Obverse:* Wear is seen on the portrait overall, with reduction or elimination of some separation of hair strands. The cheek shows light wear. Luster is minimal or nonexistent at EF-40 but may survive among the letters of LIBERTY at EF-45. *Reverse:* Wear is seen on the highest wreath and ribbon areas and the letters. Luster is minimal, but likely more noticeable than on the obverse, as the fields are protected by the designs and lettering.

1831, Original; BW-1, C-1, B-1. Graded EF-45.

VF-20, 30 (Very Fine). *Obverse:* Wear on the portrait has reduced the hair detail, but much can still be seen (in this respect the present type differs dramatically from earlier types). *Reverse:* The wreath details, except for the edges of the leaves, are worn away at VF-20, and have slightly more detail at VF-30.

   Illustrated coin: This coin is lightly struck at the left-reverse border, despite overall bold striking elsewhere.

1811, Close Date; BW-3, C-3, B-2. Graded VF-30.

F-12, 15 (Fine). *Obverse:* The hair details are fewer than at the preceding level, but many are still present. Stars have flat centers. F-15 shows slightly more detail. *Reverse:* The wreath leaves are worn flat, but their edges are distinct. F-15 shows slightly more detail.

1809, Normal Date. Graded F-15.

VG-8, 10 (Very Good). *Obverse:* The portrait is well worn, although the eye and ear can be seen, as can some hair detail. The border is well defined in most areas. *Reverse:* The wreath, bow, and lettering are seen in outline form, and some leaves and letters may be indistinct in parts. The border is well defined in most areas.

1809, 9 Over Inverted 9; BW-6, C-5, B-5. Graded VG-10.

G-4, 6 (Good). *Obverse:* The portrait is worn smooth and is seen only in outline form. Much of LIBERTY on the headband is readable, but the letters are weak. The stars are bold in outline. Much of the rim can be discerned. *Reverse:* Extensive wear is seen overall. Lettering in UNITED STATES OF AMERICA ranges from weak but complete (although the ANA grading guidelines allow for only half to be readable; the ANA text

1811; BW-1, C-1, B-1. Graded G-6.

illustrates the words in full) to having perhaps a third of the letters missing. HALF CENT is usually bold.

Illustrated coin: While ultimately well-preserved for the grade, this coin is a bit rough in texture, with light pitting and traces of old, inactive surface build up.

AG-3 (About Good). *Obverse:* Wear is more extensive than on the preceding. The portrait is visible only in outline. A few letters of LIBERTY are discernible in the headband. The stars are weak or worn away on their outer edges. The date is light. *Reverse:* The wreath is visible in outline form. Most or even all of UNITED STATES OF AMERICA is worn away. HALF CENT is usually readable.

1811; BW-1, C-1, B-1. Graded AG-3.

PF-60 to 70 (Proof). Proofs were struck of various years in the 1820s and 1830s, with 1831 and 1836 being great rarities (these dates were also restruck at the Mint circa 1859 and later). Some prooflike circulation strikes (especially of the 1833 date) have been certified as Proofs. Except for the years 1831 and 1836, for which Proofs are unequivocal, careful study is advised when contemplating the purchase of a coin described as Proof.

1831, First Restrike; BW-1a, C-PR-2, B-2. Graded PF-66BN.

Blotchy and recolored Proofs are often seen, but hardly ever described as such. Probably fewer than 25 of the Proofs of this type are truly pristine—without one problem or another. *Obverse and Reverse:* Proofs that are extensively hairlined or have dull surfaces, this being characteristic of many issues (1831 and 1836 usually excepted), are graded PF–60 to 62 or 63. This includes artificially toned and recolored coins, a secret that isn't really secret among knowledgeable collectors and dealers, but is rarely described in print. To qualify as PF-65 or higher, hairlines should be microscopic, and there should be no trace of friction. Surfaces should be prooflike or, better, fully mirrored, without dullness.

Illustrated coin: Note the traces of mint red throughout and the blue iridescence of the reverse. The reverse die is severely cracked from the F in OF to the T of UNITED.

1809, Normal Date

1809, Small 0 Inside 0

1809, 9 Over
Inverted 9

1811, Wide Date

1811, Close Date

1828, 13 Stars

1828, 12 Stars

	Mintage	Cert	Avg	%MS	G-4	VG-8	F-12	VF-20	EF-40	AU-50	MS-60BN	MS-63BN	MS-63RB
1809, All kinds	1,154,572												
1809, Normal Date		508	42.0	21%	$55	$95	$115	$125	$150	$275	$750	$1,350	$2,000
Auctions: $588, MS-61BN, June 2015; $823, AU-58, January 2015; $388, AU-55, March 2015; $176, AU-50, January 2015													
1809, Small o Inside 0		19	37.6	0%	$65	$85	$135	$325	$450	$900	$3,250		
Auctions: $55, G-4, January 2013													
1809, 9 Over Inverted 9 (a)		260	49.7	17%	$65	$85	$125	$150	$375	$750	$1,300	$2,200	$3,000
Auctions: $1,116, AU-58, June 2015; $423, AU-50, January 2015; $306, EF-45, September 2015; $200, VF-30, May 2015													
1810	215,000	124	39.8	19%	$70	$100	$150	$270	$575	$1,000	$2,000	$3,200	$6,750
Auctions: $2,800, MS-63BN, April 2014; $376, VF-30, May 2015													
1811, All kinds	63,140												
1811, Wide Date		8	31.9	0%	$450	$850	$1,900	$2,750	$6,500	$10,000	$32,500	$75,000	
Auctions: $764, VF-20, December 2015; $494, VF-20, August 2016; $1,050, F-12, February 2018													
1811, Close Date		9	21.4	0%	$400	$725	$1,750	$2,500	$6,500	$10,000	$32,500	$75,000	
Auctions: $82,250, MS-63, April 2014; $26,450, AU-50, September 2011; $1,050, F-12, February 2018; $528, VG-8, February 2018													
1811, Reverse of 1802, Unofficial Restrike (b)		6	64.2						—	—	$16,000	$20,000	$25,000
Auctions: $23,000, MS-64BN, September 2008													
1825	63,000	337	46.2	22%	$55	$90	$100	$115	$200	$325	$900	$1,800	$3,000
Auctions: $529, MS-61BN, June 2015; $564, AU-55, May 2015; $282, AU-55, January 2015; $259, EF-45, June 2015													
1826	234,000	424	47.2	26%	$55	$90	$100	$115	$150	$300	$600	$1,000	$1,450
Auctions: $999, MS-63BN, August 2015; $764, MS-62BN, September 2015; $306, MS-61BN, May 2015; $165, EF-45, August 2015													
1828, All kinds	606,000												
1828, 13 Stars		154	49.2	38%	$50	$90	$100	$115	$120	$200	$325	$600	$1,000
Auctions: $1,028, MS-64RB, January 2015; $999, MS-64BN, January 2015; $590, MS-63BN, February 2015; $309, MS-62BN, September 2015													
1828, 12 Stars		235	50.3	27%	$50	$90	$115	$120	$250	$425	$1,150	$1,850	$3,500
Auctions: $2,468, MS-63BN, February 2014													
1829	487,000	414	49.6	40%	$50	$90	$100	$115	$140	$220	$400	$700	$1,100
Auctions: $482, MS-63BN, February 2015; $764, MS-61BN, June 2015; $517, AU-58, September 2015; $235, AU-53, September 2015													

a. Traditionally called 9 Over Inverted 9, but recent research shows it not to have an inverted digit. **b.** This coin is extremely rare.

1831, Proof, Restrike   **Reverse of 1831–1836**   **Reverse of 1840–1857**

	Mintage	Cert	Avg	%MS	VG-8	F-12	VF-20	EF-40	AU-50	MS-60BN / PF-60BN	MS-63BN / PF-63BN	MS-63RB / PF-65BN	MS-65RB
1831, Original (a)		0	n/a							$50,000	$75,000		
Auctions: No auction records available.													
1831, Original, Proof (b)	2,200	7	55.6							$85,000	$125,000		
Auctions: $57,281, PF-60BN, January 2014													
1831, Restrike, Large Berries, Proof (Reverse of 1836)	25–35	9	65.8							$10,000	$15,000	$25,000	
Auctions: $47,000, PF-65RB, February 2014													
1831, Restrike, Small Berries, Proof (Reverse of 1840–1857)	10–15	1	66.0							$14,000	$21,500	$42,500	
Auctions: $63,250, PF-66BN, July 2009													
1832 (c)	51,000	535	51.4	34%		$65	$90	$110	$125	$200	$325	$475	$875
Auctions: $999, MS-64BN, June 2015; $306, MS-62BN, January 2015; $282, MS-61BN, May 2015; $259, AU-58, August 2015													
1832, Proof	10–15	2	64.5							$7,000	$12,500	$17,500	
Auctions: $44,063, PF-64BN, January 2014													
1833 (c)	103,000	731	56.0	56%		$65	$90	$110	$125	$200	$325	$450	$750
Auctions: $940, MS-64BN, February 2015; $823, MS-64BN, June 2015; $410, MS-63BN, May 2015; $212, AU-58, January 2015													
1833, Proof	25–35	13	64.2							$5,000	$6,000	$10,500	
Auctions: $11,163, PF-65BN, March 2013													
1834 (c)	141,000	773	54.4	46%		$65	$90	$110	$125	$200	$300	$450	$750
Auctions: $541, MS-64BN, January 2015; $423, MS-63BN, September 2015; $353, MS-62BN, March 2015; $259, AU-58, January 2015													
1834, Proof	25–35	14	64.8							$5,000	$6,000	$11,000	
Auctions: $18,800, PF-64RB, August 2013													
1835 (c)	398,000	1,434	53.6	48%		$65	$85	$110	$125	$200	$325	$450	$750
Auctions: $823, MS-64BN, August 2015; $646, MS-64, March 2015; $353, MS-63BN, May 2015; $329, MS-62BN, April 2015													
1835, Proof	15–20	3	64.0							$5,000	$6,000	$10,500	
Auctions: $11,163, PF-64RB, January 2014													
1836, Original, Proof	140–240	14	63.9							$6,000	$8,000	$12,500	
Auctions: $12,925, PF-64BN, April 2013													
1836, Restrike, Proof (Reverse of 1840–1857)	8–15	3	64.7							$9,000	$17,000	$30,000	
Auctions: No auction records available.													

a. Circulation strike. **b.** Beware of altered date. **c.** The figures given here are thought to be correct, although Mint records report these quantities for 1833 through 1836 rather than 1832 through 1835.

1837 "HALF CENT" TOKEN

The last circulation-strike half cents of the Classic Head design were minted in 1835, and Proofs of the series were made in 1836 (see next section). No half cents of any format were minted in 1837, 1838, or 1839—it would be 1840 before the denomination started up again, with the Braided Hair type.

To help fill that gap for date-by-date collectors, in the 1930s Wayte Raymond included in his "National" brand of coin albums a slot for a half cent–sized Hard Times token dated 1837. The token had been privately struck in the thousands as a supply of small change in the midst of the country's financial stagnation of the 1830s and early 1840s. It joined several hundred types of larger, cent-sized copper tokens, all privately manufactured and put into circulation by enterprising businesspeople, as substitutes for the federal government's half cents and large cents that were no longer circulating in any quantity.

Raymond's dignifying of the 1837 token brought about a new numismatic tradition. Half-cent collectors began to include the token—despite its not being official federal coinage—in their collections, and today the "Half Cent Worth of Pure Copper" is often found among their treasured coins.

	G-4	VG-8	F-12	VF-20	EF-40	AU-50	MS-60BN
1837 Token *(not a coin)*	$45	$65	$75	$110	$200	$375	$700

BRAIDED HAIR (1840–1857)

Designer: *Christian Gobrecht.* **Weight:** *5.44 grams.* **Composition:** *Copper.*
Diameter: *23 mm.* **Edge:** *Plain.* **Mint:** *Philadelphia.*

Circulation Strike	Proof
1854; BW-1, C-1, B-1.	*1843; BW-1c, C-SR-13, B-3.*

History. The Braided Hair half cent debuted in 1840, a year after the same design was introduced on copper cents. There was scant commercial demand for this denomination, so only Proofs were struck from 1840 to 1848 and in 1852. (In 1849–1851 and 1853–1857 both Proofs and circulation strikes were made.) Ultimately the half cent was discontinued by the Act of February 21, 1857. After that point the coins were rapidly withdrawn from circulation, and by 1860 virtually all had disappeared from commerce.

Striking and Sharpness. Many if not most Braided Hair half cents are well struck, and nearly all are on good planchet stock. Check these points for sharpness: the denticles on both sides; the star centers and hair detail on the obverse; and the leaf detail on the reverse.

Availability. Because Braided Hair half cents were not struck for circulation until 1849 and they did not circulate after the 1850s, they never acquired extensive wear. Most coins grade EF-40 and finer. Lower grades are sometimes seen, but are not in demand.

GRADING STANDARDS

MS-60 to 70 (Mint State). *Obverse:* In the lower Mint State grades, MS–60 and 61, some slight abrasion can be seen on the portrait, most evidently on the cheek. Check the tip of the coronet as well. Luster in the field is complete, or nearly so. At MS-63, luster should be complete, and no abrasions evident. At higher levels, the luster is complete and deeper, and some original mint color may be seen. Mint frost on this type is usually

1849, Large Date; BW-3, C-1, B-4. Graded MS-63BN.

deep, sometimes satiny, but hardly ever prooflike. MS-64 coins may have some slight discoloration or scattered contact marks. A well-graded MS-65 or higher coin has full, rich luster; no contact marks visible except under magnification; and a nice blend of brown toning or nicely mixed (not stained or blotchy) mint color and natural brown toning. The late Walter Breen stated that he had never seen an 1853 (common date) half cent with extensive original mint color, but these are plentiful with brown-toned surfaces. *Reverse:* In the lower Mint State grades some abrasions are seen on the higher areas of the leaves. Mint luster is complete in all Mint State grades, as the open areas are protected by the lettering and wreath.

AU-50, 53, 55, 58 (About Uncirculated). *Obverse:* Wear is evident on the cheek, the hair above the forehead, and the tip of the coronet. Friction is evident in the field. At AU-58, luster may be present except in the center of the fields. As the grades go down to AU-50, wear is more evident on the portrait. Wear is seen on the stars, but is not as easy to discern as it is elsewhere. At AU-50 there is either no luster or only traces of luster close

1849, Large Date; BW-3, C-1, B-4. Graded AU-50.

to the letters and devices. *Reverse:* Wear is most evident on the highest areas of the leaves and the ribbon bow. Luster is present in the fields. As the grades go downward from AU–58 to 50, wear increases and luster decreases. At the AU-50 level there is either no luster or traces of luster close to the letters and devices.

Illustrated coin: This coin shows Full Details on both sides, and has eye-pleasing, light-brown surfaces.

EF-40, 45 (Extremely Fine). *Obverse:* Wear is more extensive on the portrait, including the cheek, hair, and coronet. The star centers are worn down slightly. Traces of luster are minimal, if at all existent. *Reverse:* The centers of the leaves are well worn, with detail visible only near the edges of the leaves and nearby, with the higher parts worn flat. Letters show significant wear. Luster, if present, is minimal.

1853; BW-1, C-1, B-1. Graded EF-40.

VF-20, 30 (Very Fine). *Obverse:* Wear is more extensive than at the preceding levels. Some of the strands of hair are fused together. The center radials of the stars are worn nearly completely away. *Reverse:* The leaves show more extensive wear, with details visible at the edges, and only minimally and not on all leaves. The lettering shows smooth, even wear.

1849, Large Date; BW-3, C-1, B-4. Graded VF-30.

Braided Hair half cents are seldom collected in grades lower than VF-20.

PF-60 to 70 (Proof). For the issues of 1840 to 1848, the 1849, Small Date, and the issues of 1852, only Proofs were made, without related examples for circulation. All were restruck at the Mint. Generally, the quality of these Proofs is very good, with excellent striking of details and nice planchet quality. *Obverse and Reverse:* Superb gems at PF–65 and 66 show hairlines only under high magnification, and at PF-67 none are seen. The

1843, First Restrike; BW-2, C-SR-5, B-2. PF-64RB.

fields are deeply mirrorlike. There is no evidence of friction. At lower levels, hairlines increase, with a profusion at PF–60 to 62 (and also a general dullness of the fields). Typical color for an undipped coin ranges from light or iridescent brown to brown with some traces of mint color. Except for issues in the 1850s, Proofs are nearly always BN or, less often, RB. The rare Proofs of the 1840s are sometimes seen with light wear and can be classified according to the About Uncirculated and Extremely Fine comments above, except in place of "luster" read "Proof surface."

Illustrated coin: Overall this coin's surfaces are smooth, and the dominant sandy-olive patina belies semi-reflective tendencies in the fields and gold, apricot and lilac undertones when viewed under direct light.

Large Berries	Small Berries
(Original Strike)	(Restrike)

	Mintage	Cert	Avg	%MS	VG-8	F-12	VF-20	EF-40	AU-50	MS-60BN	MS-63BN	MS-63RB	MS-65RB
											PF-60BN	PF-63BN	PF-65BN
1840, Original, Proof	125–150	12	63.9								$5,350	$6,500	$10,000
Auctions: $7,475, PF-62BN, August 2006													
1840, Restrike, Proof	21–25	10	64.5								$5,350	$6,500	$9,250
Auctions: $25,850, PF-65RB, June 2014													
1841, Original, Proof	150–250	18	64.1								$4,500	$5,500	$10,000
Auctions: $21,150, PF-65BN, September 2013; $4,700, PF-58, September 2015; $2,400, PF-40, February 2018													
1841, Restrike, Proof	15–19	10	64.5								$4,500	$5,500	$8,750
Auctions: $8,625, PF-66BN, June 2008													

**1849, Small Date
(Proof Only)**   **1849, Large Date**

	Mintage	Cert	Avg	%MS	VG-8	F-12	VF-20	EF-40	AU-50	MS-60BN	MS-63BN	MS-63RB	MS-65RB
											PF-60BN	PF-63BN	PF-65BN
1842, Original, Proof	*120–180*	7	63.9								$5,500	$7,000	$10,000
	Auctions: $15,275, PF-64BN, February 2014; $12,925, PF-64, January 2015												
1842, Restrike, Proof	*35–45*	13	64.7								$4,500	$5,500	$8,750
	Auctions: $20,700, PF-65RB, April 2010												
1843, Original, Proof	*125–200*	6	64.0								$4,500	$5,500	$10,000
	Auctions: $73,438, PF-65RD, April 2014												
1843, Restrike, Proof	*37–44*	8	64.8								$4,750	$5,700	$8,750
	Auctions: $9,988, PF-64BN, February 2014												
1844, Original, Proof	*120–180*	10	63.2								$5,000	$6,000	$12,500
	Auctions: $4,888, PF-50, May 2008												
1844, Restrike, Proof	*21–26*	6	64.3								$4,750	$5,750	$8,750
	Auctions: $1,777, PF, February 2014												
1845, Original, Proof	*110–170*	4	64.5								$5,000	$6,000	$15,000
	Auctions: $23,500, PF-64BN, April 2013												
1845, Restrike, Proof	*20–24*	11	64.5								$4,500	$5,400	$9,000
	Auctions: $9,200, PF-65BN, October 2011												
1846, Original, Proof	*125–200*	9	63.9								$5,000	$6,000	$12,500
	Auctions: $21,150, PF-64BN, January 2014												
1846, Restrike, Proof	*19–24*	9	65.6								$4,750	$5,750	$8,750
	Auctions: $23,630, PF-66BN, June 2014; $15,275, PF-66BN, October 2015												
1847, Original, Proof	*200–300*	11	64.2								$5,000	$6,000	$12,500
	Auctions: $5,288, PF-63BN, January 2014												
1847, Restrike, Proof	*33–44*	18	64.6								$4,500	$5,500	$8,500
	Auctions: $15,275, PF-66BN, January 2014												
1848, Original, Proof	*150–225*	5	64.4								$5,500	$6,250	$15,000
	Auctions: $10,350, PF-64RB, September 2003												
1848, Restrike, Proof	*40–47*	15	64.6								$4,500	$5,600	$8,500
	Auctions: $6,169, PF-64BN, February 2014												
1849, Large Date	39,864	355	57.0	55%	$60	$75	$90	$150	$240	$500	$700	$900	$2,700
	Auctions: $517, MS-63, August 2016; $353, AU-58, June 2016; $176, AU-55, October 2016; $336, AU-55, February 2018												
1849, Original, Small Date, Proof	*70–90*	4	64.0								$4,500	$5,500	$10,000
	Auctions: $8,813, PF-64RB, April 2014												
1849, Restrike, Small Date, Proof	*30–36*	4	64.3								$5,000	$5,750	$9,750
	Auctions: $7,344, PF-64BN, January 2014												
1850	39,812	304	56.5	52%	$60	$75	$125	$175	$275	$600	$800	$1,500	$3,500
	Auctions: $7,210, MS-65, February 2016; $1,998, MS-64, July 2015; $517, AU-55, March 2016; $528, AU-55, January 2018												
1850, Proof	*10–20*	11	62.9								$5,000	$7,000	$13,000
	Auctions: $17,625, PF-64, May 2015; $5,875, PF-63BN, January 2014												
1851	147,672	927	57.1	57%	$60	$75	$90	$115	$175	$275	$500	$650	$2,000
	Auctions: $1,175, MS-64RB, October 2015; $705, MS-64BN, August 2015; $441, MS-64, March 2015; $447, MS-63BN, January 2015												
1851, Proof	*10–20*	0	n/a								$7,500	$10,000	$35,000
	Auctions: No auction records available.												

	Mintage	Cert	Avg	%MS	VG-8	F-12	VF-20	EF-40	AU-50	MS-60BN	MS-63BN PF-60BN	MS-63RB PF-63BN	MS-65RB PF-65BN
1852, Original, Proof	*225–325*	0	n/a										—
Auctions: No auction records available.													
1852, Restrike, Proof	*110–140*	36	64.3								$4,000	$6,000	$9,000
Auctions: $9,400, PF-66BN, April 2016; $4,377, PF-64BN, January 2017; $4,320, PF-63BN, February 2018													
1853	129,694	1,101	60.2	74%	$60	$75	$90	$115	$175	$275	$500	$650	$1,700
Auctions: $940, MS-65BN, September 2015; $646, MS-64BN, August 2015; $329, MS-63BN, May 2015; $223, MS-61BN, May 2015													
1854	55,358	819	60.7	79%	$60	$75	$90	$115	$165	$275	$500	$650	$1,700
Auctions: $1,410, MS-65BN, August 2015; $541, MS-63RB, June 2015; $230, MS-62BN, September 2015; $161, MS-60, May 2015													
1854, Proof	*10–20*	5	64.4								$3,500	$4,500	$8,000
Auctions: $7,931, PF-65RB, February 2014; $7,344, PF-65RB, January 2015													
1855	56,500	1,141	61.3	82%	$60	$75	$90	$100	$165	$275	$500	$650	$1,600
Auctions: $940, MS-65BN, January 2015; $494, MS-64BN, September 2015; $376, MS-63BN, September 2015													
1855, Proof	*40–60*	19	64.2								$3,500	$4,500	$8,000
Auctions: $5,750, PF-64BN, August 2011													
1856	40,430	432	59.2	69%	$60	$75	$90	$125	$185	$275	$575	$675	$2,000
Auctions: $400, MS-63BN, August 2015; $306, MS-63BN, May 2015; $294, MS-63BN, June 2015; $153, AU-55, May 2015													
1856, Proof	*50–75*	19	64.3								$3,500	$4,500	$8,000
Auctions: $7,050, PF-65BN, January 2015; $8,519, PF, February 2014													
1857	35,180	650	60.0	77%	$95	$115	$130	$185	$260	$400	$650	$750	$2,500
Auctions: $823, MS-64BN, October 2015; $541, MS-63BN, July 2015; $376, MS-62BN, May 2015; $720, MS-63RB, April 2018													
1857, Proof	*75–100*	37	63.9								$3,500	$4,500	$8,000
Auctions: $14,100, PF-66RB, June 2014; $4,465, PF-64BN, January 2015													

Large Cents
1793–1857

AN OVERVIEW OF LARGE CENTS

Collecting one each of the major types of 1793–1857 copper cents can be a fascinating challenge. Early varieties were struck from hand-engraved dies, often on copper planchets of uncertain quality. It was not until 1836 that steam power was used to run coining presses at the Mint. All earlier issues were made by hand, by two men tugging on the weighted lever arm of a small screw-type press. As might be expected, this resulted in many variations in striking quality.

The first cents of 1793, the Chain varieties, are found with two major differences: AMERI. on the reverse, and the later version with AMERICA spelled out in full. These early issues have been highly desired from the beginning days of the numismatic hobby in America, and remain in the limelight today.

Wreath cents of 1793 occur with the edge displaying a vine and bars motif and also with lettering ONE HUNDRED FOR A DOLLAR. Liberty Cap cents of the 1793–1796 years have lettered edges (ONE HUNDRED FOR A DOLLAR) used in 1793, 1794, and part of 1795, and plain edges for most 1795 coins and all of 1796.

The Draped Bust type commenced partway through 1796 and was continued through 1807. This span includes the notably rare 1799, 9 Over 8, overdate and the 1799 as well as the somewhat rare 1804. Many interesting die varieties occur in this type, particularly with regard to errors on the reverse. The Classic Head cent, designed by John Reich, was introduced in 1808, and was continued through 1814. In 1815 no cents of this date were produced. Then in 1816 the Matron Head commenced, a new motif with a new reverse as well. With modifications this was continued through 1839, in which year the Braided Hair design by Christian Gobrecht made its appearance. Large cents were made continually through January 1857 and then discontinued.

FOR THE COLLECTOR AND INVESTOR: LARGE CENTS AS A SPECIALTY

For the enjoyment of copper cents 1793–1857 it is possible to go far beyond a type set. Today, varieties of the 1793–1814 cents are generally collected by Sheldon numbers (S-1, S-2, etc.), given first in *Early American Cents* and, later, in its revision, *Penny Whimsy*. Building upon this foundation, *Walter Breen's Encyclopedia of Early United States Large Cents, 1793–1814*, gives more information on this date range than available in any other single source.

Among dates and major varieties in the early range of the series, the 1793 issues Chain AMERI., Chain AMERICA, Wreath, and Liberty Cap, the 1799 (far and away the rarest date in the series), and the 1804 are key issues, each a part of an extensive series of more than 300 die varieties through and including 1814.

The most popular way to collect large cents is by basic varieties, mainly dates, overdates, and major varieties. Sometimes, a particular date is selected as a specialty for collecting die varieties by Sheldon numbers.

Generally, grades from Good to VF are popular objectives for the early series from 1793 to 1814, and for some varieties no better coins exist. EF, AU, and Mint State coins are available and are more likely to be sought by collectors of basic dates and major varieties, rather than by specialists seeing long runs of Sheldon numbers. Type-set collectors are also important in the market for high-grade pieces, where sights can be set high as there are fewer varieties to obtain. Accordingly, as a type-set collector one may aspire to own an AU or Mint State cent of the 1796–1807 Draped Bust type. However, for a specialist in die varieties, who wants to acquire more than 100 different specimens from this date range, such high grades might not be feasible to acquire.

Collecting cents of the later dates by basic varieties is an interesting pursuit, and one that is quite attainable in such grades as EF, AU, or even MS-60, most dates after the 1820s being readily available for relatively inexpensive prices. Key issues among 1816–1857 cents include 1823, 3 Over 2; 1823; 1824, 4 Over 2; 1839, 9 Over 6; and a few others. Collecting Braided Hair cents toward the end of the series, 1839 to 1857, is least expensive of all, and most major varieties can be obtained in such grades as MS–60 to 63, with lustrous brown surfaces, for reasonable figures.

FLOWING HAIR, CHAIN REVERSE (1793)

Designer: *Henry Voigt.* **Weight:** *13.48 grams.* **Composition:** *Copper.*
Diameter: *Average 26 to 27 mm.* **Edge:** *Vine and bars design.* **Mint:** *Philadelphia.*

Chain AMERI. Reverse
1793; Bowers-Whitman–1, Sheldon-1, Breen-1.

Chain AMERICA Reverse

Vine-and-Bars Edge

History. The first U.S. cents intended for circulation were struck at the Mint in Philadelphia from February 27 through March 12, 1793. These were of the Flowing Hair design, with a Chain reverse. Several varieties were struck, today these can be attributed by Bowers-Whitman numbers or Sheldon numbers. The first, or Bowers-Whitman–1, Sheldon-1, had AMERICA abbreviated as AMERI. A contemporary account noted that Miss Liberty appeared to be "in a fright," and that the chain motif on the reverse, 15 links intended to symbolize unity of the states in the Union, was an "ill omen" for a land of liberty; accordingly, the design was used for only a short time. The rims on both sides are raised, without denticles or beads.

Striking and Sharpness. The details of Miss Liberty's hair are often indistinct or missing, including on many higher-grade specimens. For all grades and varieties, the reverse is significantly sharper than the obverse. The portrait of Miss Liberty is shallow and is often weak, especially on the BW-1, S-1, variety (which is often missing the date). Note that early copper coins of all kinds may exhibit "tooling" (engraving done outside the Mint in order to simulate details that were worn away or weakly struck to begin with). Also, these old coppers have sometimes been burnished to smooth out areas of porosity. These alterations are considered to be damage, and they significantly decrease a coin's value.

Availability. Demand is higher than supply for all varieties, with fewer than 1,000 or so examples surviving today. Most are in lower grades, from Fair-2 to VG-8. Even heavily worn coins (still identifiable by the chain device) are highly collectible. VF and EF coins are few and far between, and AU and MS are very rare.

GRADING STANDARDS

MS-60 to 70 (Mint State). *Obverse:* In the lower Mint State grades, MS–60 and 61, some slight abrasions can be seen on the higher areas of the portrait. The large open field shows light contact marks and perhaps a few nicks. At MS-63 the luster should be complete, although some very light abrasions or contact marks may be seen on the portrait. At MS-64 or higher—a nearly impossible level for a Chain cent—there is no sign of abrasion anywhere. Mint color is not extensive on any known Mint State coin,

1793; Bowers-Whitman–4, Sheldon-3, Breen-4. Graded MS-66BN.

but traces of red-orange are sometimes seen around the rim and devices on both sides. *Reverse:* In the lower Mint State grades some abrasions are seen on the chain links. There is some abrasion in the field. At MS-63, luster should be unbroken. Some abrasion and minor contact marks may be evident. In still higher grades, luster is deep and there is no sign of abrasion.

Illustrated coin: This coin is sharply struck with full hair detail. It is the Cleneay-Jackman-Ryder specimen mentioned in Sheldon's *Penny Whimsy* as the unrivalled, finest-known example of this variety.

AU-50, 53, 55, 58 (About Uncirculated). *Obverse:* Light wear is seen on the highest areas of the portrait. Some luster is seen in the large open fields at the AU-58 level, less at AU-55, and little if any for AU–53 and 50. Scattered marks are normal and are most evident in the field. At higher levels, some vestiges of luster may be seen among the letters, numerals, and between the hair tips. *Reverse:* Light wear is most evident on the chain, as

1793; BW-4, S-3, B-4. Graded AU-53.

this is the most prominent feature. The letters show wear, but not as extensive. Luster may be seen at the 58 and 55 levels, usually slightly more on the reverse than on the obverse. Generally, the reverse grades higher than the obverse, usually by a step, such as an AU-50 obverse and an AU-53 reverse (such a coin would be listed as the lower of the two, or AU-50).

EF-40, 45 (Extremely Fine). *Obverse:* The center of the portrait is well worn, with the hair visible only in thick strands, although extensive detail remains in the hair tips at the left. No luster is seen. Contact marks are normal in the large expanse of open field, but should be mentioned if they are distracting. *Reverse:* The chain is bold and shows light wear. Other features show wear, as well— more extensive in appearance, as the relief is

1793; BW-4, S-3, B-4. Graded EF-45.

lower. The fields show some friction, but not as much as on the obverse.

VF-20, 30 (Very Fine). *Obverse:* More wear is seen on the portrait, with perhaps half or slightly more of the hair detail showing, mostly near the left edge of the hair. The ear usually is visible (but might not be, depending on the sharpness of strike). The letters in LIBERTY show wear. The rim remains bold (more so than on the reverse). *Reverse:* The chain shows more wear than on the preceding, but is still bold. Other features show more wear and may be weak in areas. The rim may be weak in areas.

1793; BW-5, S-4, B-5. Graded VF-30.

F-12, 15 (Fine). *Obverse:* The hair details are mostly worn away, with about one-third visible, that being on the left. The rim is distinct on most examples. The bottoms of the date digits are weak or possibly worn away. *Reverse:* The chain is bold, as is the lettering within the chain. Lettering around the border shows extensive wear, but is complete. The rim may be flat in areas.

    Illustrated coin: The surface is generally

1793; BW-5, S-4, B-5. Graded F-15.

smooth and even under close scrutiny reveals only minor roughness. Note the shallow reverse rim bruise outside the letters AM in AMERICA and some mild encrustation around the letter C in CENT and the nearby chain links.

VG-8, 10 (Very Good). *Obverse:* The portrait is well worn, although Miss Liberty's eye remains bold. Hair detail is gone at the center, but is evident at the left edge of the portrait. LIBERTY is always readable, but may be faded or partly missing on shallow strikes. The date is well worn, with the bottom of the numerals missing (published standards vary on this point, and it used to be the case that a full date was mandatory). *Reverse:* The chain remains

1793; BW-4, S-3, B-4. Graded VG-10.

bold, and the center letters are all readable. Border letters may be weak or incomplete. The rim is smooth in most areas.

    Illustrated coin: The coin is smooth in appearance with the worn areas showing lighter copper, while the fields have trace roughness and the classic black olive texture. Note the planchet flaw right of ONE, which appears as a void in the metal.

G-4, 6 (Good). *Obverse:* The portrait is worn smooth and is seen only in outline form, although the eye position can be discerned. LIBERTY may be weak. The date is weak, but the tops of the numerals can be discerned. *Reverse:* The chain is fully visible in outline form. Central lettering is mostly or completely readable, but light. Peripheral lettering is mostly worn away.

Illustrated coin: Natural obverse planchet

1793; BW-1, S-1, B-1. Graded G-4.

flaws, as struck, can be seen both at 12 o'clock on the rim and above and to the left of the date, with other faint fissuring seen on the reverse under low magnification.

AG-3 (About Good). *Obverse:* The portrait is visible as an outline. LIBERTY and the date are mostly or even completely worn away. Contact marks may be extensive. *Reverse:* The chain is fully visible in outline form. Traces of the central letters—or, on better strikes, nearly all of the letters—can be seen. Around the border all letters are worn away.

1793; BW-5, S-4, B-5. Graded AG-3.

	Mintage	Cert	Avg	%MS	AG-3	G-4	VG-8	F-12	VF-20	EF-40	AU-50	MS-60BN
1793, Chain, All kinds †	36,103											
1793, AMERI. in Legend †		35	23.3	6%	$7,500	$10,500	$21,000	$35,000	$45,000	$90,000	$150,000	$350,000
	Auctions: $25,850, F-12, August 2016; $18,800, F-12, August 2015; $3,173, Fair-2, March 2015											
1793, AMERICA, Periods †		18	22.5	0%	$4,800	$6,500	$13,500	$21,000	$35,000	$70,000	$125,000	$250,000
	Auctions: $22,325, AU-50, September 2013											
1793, AMERICA, No Periods †		141	21.2	4%	$4,800	$6,500	$13,500	$22,000	$35,000	$80,000	$135,000	$275,000
	Auctions: $998,750, MS-65BN, January 2013; $998,750, MS-65RB, February 2016; $199,750, AU-55, January 2014											

† All varieties of 1793 Flowing Hair, Chair Reverse Large Cents are ranked in the *100 Greatest U.S. Coins* (fifth edition), as a single entry.

FLOWING HAIR, WREATH REVERSE (1793)

Designer: *Henry Voigt.* **Weight:** *13.48 grams.* **Composition:** *Copper.*
Diameter: *26 to 28 mm.* **Edge:** *Vine and bars design, or lettered ONE HUNDRED*
FOR A DOLLAR followed by either a single or a double leaf. **Mint:** *Philadelphia.*

1793, Wreath Type, Vine and
Bars Edge; BW-11, S-5, B-6.

Vine-and-Bars Edge

**Lettered Edge
(ONE HUNDRED FOR A DOLLAR)**

History. Between April 9 and July 17, 1793, the U.S. Mint struck and delivered 63,353 large copper cents. Most of these, and perhaps all, were of the Wreath type, although records do not specify when the design types were changed that year. The Wreath cent was named for the new reverse style. Both sides have raised beads at the border, similar to the style used on 1793 half cents.

Striking and Sharpness. These cents usually are fairly well struck, although high-grade pieces often exhibit some weakness on the highest hair tresses and on the leaf details. (On lower-grade pieces these areas are worn, so the point is moot.) Planchet quality varies widely, from smooth, glossy brown to dark and porous. The lettered-edge cents are often seen on defective planchets. Consult Sheldon's *Penny Whimsy (1793–1814)* and photographs to learn the characteristics of certain varieties. The borders have raised beads; on high-grade pieces these are usually very distinct, but they blend together on lower-grade coins and can sometimes be indistinct. The beads are not as prominent as those later used on the 1793 Liberty Cap cents.

Availability. At least several thousand examples exist of the different varieties of the type. Most are in lower grades, from AG-3 to VG-8, although Fine and VF pieces are encountered with regularity. Choice EF, AU, and finer coins see high demand. Some in MS have been billed as "specimen" or "presentation" coins, although this is supposition, as no records exist.

GRADING STANDARDS

MS-60 to 70 (Mint State). *Obverse:* On MS–60 and 61 coins there are some traces of abrasion on the higher areas of the portrait, most particularly the hair. As this area can be lightly struck, careful inspection is needed for evaluation, not as much in Mint State (as other features come into play), but in higher circulated grades. Luster in the field is incomplete at lower Mint State levels, but should be in generous quantity. At MS-63, luster should

1793; BW-12, S-6, B-7. Graded MS-66.

be complete, and no abrasion evident. At higher levels, the luster is deeper, and some original mint color may be seen. At MS-65 there might be some scattered contact marks and possibly bare traces of fingerprints or discoloration. Above MS-65, a coin should approach perfection. A Mint State 1793 Wreath cent is an object of rare beauty. *Reverse:* In the lower Mint State grades some abrasion is seen on the higher areas of the leaves. Generally, luster is complete in all grades, as the open areas are protected by the lettering and wreath. In many ways, the grading guidelines for this type follow those of the 1793 half cent—also with sprays of berries (not seen elsewhere in the series).

Illustrated coin: Remarkably, this coin displays some original Mint orange.

AU-50, 53, 55, 58 (About Uncirculated).
Obverse: Friction is seen on the highest areas of the hair (which may also be lightly struck) and the cheek. Some scattered marks are normal in the field, ranging from more extensive at AU-50 to minimal at AU-58. *Reverse:* Friction is seen on the higher wreath leaves and (not as easy to discern) on the letters. The fields, protected by the designs (including sprays of berries at the center), show fric-

1793; BW-23, S-11c, B-16c. Graded AU-50.

tion, but not as noticeably as on the obverse. At AU–55 and 58, little if any friction is seen. Border beads, if well struck, are separate and boldly defined.

Illustrated coin: Note the clash marks on the obverse indicative of a late die state. Significant portions of the reverse wreath are clashed in the field from Liberty's nose to the base of the throat, below the bust around the leaf cluster, and between some of the strands of hair at the back of Liberty's head. Additionally, the letters MERICA in the word AMERICA are clashed in the right-obverse field, the letters becoming bolder toward the end of that word.

EF-40, 45 (Extremely Fine). *Obverse:* More extensive wear is seen on the high parts of the hair, creating mostly a solid mass (without detail of strands) of varying width in the area immediately to the left of the face. The cheek shows light wear. Luster is minimal or nonexistent at EF-40, and may survive in traces in protected areas (such as between the letters) at EF-45. *Reverse:* Wear is seen on the highest wreath and ribbon areas, and

1793; BW-17, S-9, B-12. Graded EF-40.

the letters. Luster is minimal, but likely more noticeable than on the obverse, as the fields are protected by the designs and lettering. Some of the beads blend together.

VF-20, 30 (Very Fine). *Obverse:* Wear on the hair is more extensive, and varies depending on the die variety and sharpness of strike. The ANA grading standards suggest that two-thirds of the hair is visible, which in practice can be said to be "more or less." More beads are blended together, but the extent of this blending depends on the striking and variety. Certain parts of the rim are smooth, with beads scarcely visible at all. No

1793; BW-12, S-6, B-7. Graded VF-25.

luster is seen. The date, LIBERTY, and hair ends are bold. *Reverse:* The leaf details are nearly completely worn away at VF-20, with slight detail at VF-30. The border beads are blended together, with many indistinct. Some berries in the sprays are light, but nearly all remain distinct. No luster is seen.

Illustrated coin: The surfaces are a bit rough overall with a few areas also revealing slight verdigris.

F-12, 15 (Fine). *Obverse:* The hair details are mostly worn away, with about one-third visible, mainly at the edges. The ANA grading standards suggest that half of the details are visible, seemingly applying to the total area of the hair. However, the visible part, at the left, also includes intermittent areas of the field. Beads are weak or worn away in areas. F-15 shows slightly more detail. By this grade, scattered light scratches, noticeable contact marks,

1793; BW-17, S-9, B-12. Graded F-12.

and the like are the rule, not the exception. These are not mentioned at all on holders and are often overlooked elsewhere, except in some auction catalogs and price lists. Such marks are implicit for coins in lower grades, and light porosity or granularity is common as well. *Reverse:* The wreath leaves are worn flat, but their edges are distinct. Border beads are weak or worn away in areas. F-15 shows slightly more detail.

Illustrated coin: Despite slight pock-marking on the obverse and scattered rim bruises, this coin features strong definition for an F-12 piece.

VG-8, 10 (Very Good). *Obverse:* The hair is well worn toward the face. Details at the left are mostly blended together in thick strands. The eye, nose, and lips often remain well defined. Border beads are completely gone, or just seen in traces, and part of the rim blends into the field. LIBERTY may be slightly weak. The 1793 date is fully visible, although there may be some lightness. Scattered marks are more common than on

1793; BW-23, S-11c, B-16c. Graded VG-8.

higher grades. *Reverse:* The wreath, bow, and lettering are seen in outline form, and some leaves and letters may be indistinct in parts. Most of the berries remain visible, but weak. Border beads are worn away, and the border blends into the field in most if not all of the periphery.

G-4, 6 (Good). *Obverse:* The hair is worn smooth except for the thick tresses at the left. The eye, nose, and lips show some detail. LIBERTY is weak, with some letters missing. The date is discernible, although partially worn away. The sprig above the date is usually prominent. The border completely blends into the field. *Reverse:* Extensive overall wear. The wreath is seen in outline form, with some areas weak. Usually ONE CENT remains

1793; BW-12, S-6, B-7. Graded G-4.

readable at the center. The border letters and fraction show extensive wear, with some letters very weak or even missing, although most should be discernible. Dark or porous coins may have more details on both sides in an effort to compensate for the roughness. Marks, edge bumps, and so on are normal.

Illustrated coin: Note minor surface roughness. Definition in the major devices is strong for this grade.

AG-3 (About Good). *Obverse:* Wear is more extensive than on the preceding. The eye, nose, and lips may still be discernible, and the sprig above the date can usually be seen. LIBERTY may be very weak or even missing. The date is gone, or just a trace will remain. *Reverse:* Parts of the wreath are visible in outline form. ONE CENT might be readable, but this is not a requirement. Most border letters are gone. If a coin is dark or porous

1793; BW-18, S-8, B-13. Graded AG-3.

it may be graded AG-3 and may be sharper than just described, with the porosity accounting for the lower grade.

Regular Sprig   **Strawberry Leaf**

	Mintage	Cert	Avg	%MS	AG-3	G-4	VG-8	F-12	VF-20	EF-40	AU-50	MS-60BN	MS-63BN
1793, Wreath, All kinds	63,353												
1793, Vine/Bars Edge		215	29.7	9%	$2,300	$3,800	$5,500	$9,000	$15,000	$23,000	$35,000	$70,000	$150,000
Auctions: $176,250, MS-65BN, June 2015; $78,000, MS-63BN, April 2018; $52,800, AU-58, January 2018													
1793, Lettered Edge		46	21.5	4%	$2,500	$4,200	$6,000	$10,000	$17,500	$25,000	$40,000	$80,000	$175,000
Auctions: $18,800, F-15, January 2014; $4,935, F-15, March 2016; $646, VG-8, December 2015													
1793, Strawberry Leaf †	(a)	1	12.0	0%	$350,000	$500,000	$650,000	$1,000,000					
Auctions: $381,875, G-4, January 2014													

† Ranked in the *100 Greatest U.S. Coins* (fifth edition). **a.** 4 examples are known.

LIBERTY CAP (1793–1796)

Designer: *1793–1795, thick planchet—Probably Joseph Wright; 1795–1796, thin planchet—John Smith Gardner.* **Weight:** *1793–1795, thick planchet—13.48 grams; 1795–1796, thin planchet—10.89 grams.* **Composition:** *Copper.* **Diameter:** *Average 29 mm.* **Edge:** *1793–1795, thick planchet—Lettered ONE HUNDRED FOR A DOLLAR; 1795–1796, thin planchet—Plain.* **Mint:** *Philadelphia.*

1794, Thick Hair, Close Date, Short Right Stem; BW-80, S-61, B-53.

Lettered Edge (1793–1795)

Reeded Edge (1795)

History. The Liberty Cap design was created in the summer of 1793 by artist and engraver Joseph Wright, who is also believed by some to have designed the 1793 half cent. On the cent, Miss Liberty faces to the right, rather than to the left (as on the half cent). Liberty Cap cents of 1793 have raised beaded borders. Other issues have denticles. Cents of 1794 and some of 1795 are on thick planchets with the edge lettered ONE HUNDRED FOR A DOLLAR, while those made later in 1795, and in 1796, are on thinner planchets and have a plain edge.

Striking and Sharpness. The depth of relief and striking characteristics vary widely, depending on the variety. Points to check are the details of the hair on Miss Liberty, the leaf details on the wreath, and the denticles on both sides. Generally, the earlier, thick-planchet issues are better strikes than are the thin-planchet coins. Plain-edge 1795 cents often have low or shallow rims. To determine the difference between lightness caused by shallow dies and lightness caused by wear, study the characteristics of the die variety involved (see in particular the reverses of 1793, BW-27, S-13, and 1793, BW-28/BW-29, S-15/S-12).

Availability. Cents of this type are readily available, although those of 1793 are rare and in great demand, and certain die varieties of the other dates are rare and can command high prices. Typical grades range from AG upward to Fine, VF, and, less often, EF. Attractive AU and MS coins are elusive, and when found are usually dated 1795, the thin planchet variety.

GRADING STANDARDS

MS-60 to 70 (Mint State). *Obverse:* On
MS–60 and 61 coins there are some traces of
abrasion on the higher areas of the portrait.
Luster is incomplete, particularly in the field.
At MS-63, luster should be complete, and no
abrasion evident. At higher levels, the luster is
deeper, and some original mint color may be
seen on some examples. At the MS-65 level
there may be some scattered contact marks and

1794; BW-12, S-22, B-6. Graded MS-62BN.

possibly some traces of fingerprints or discoloration, but these should be very minimal and not at all distracting. Generally, Liberty Cap cents of 1793 (in particular) and 1794 are harder to find with strong eye
appeal than are those of 1795 and 1796. Mint State coins of 1795 often have satiny luster. Above MS-65,
a coin should approach perfection, especially if dated 1795 or 1796. Certified Mint State cents can vary in
their strictness of interpretation. *Reverse:* In the lower Mint State grades some abrasion is seen on the
higher areas of the leaves. Generally, luster is complete in all grades, as the open areas are protected by the
lettering and wreath. Often on this type the reverse is shallower than the obverse and has a lower rim.

Illustrated coin: Boldly struck on both the obverse and reverse, with strong hair separation evident
on Liberty and some evidence of a central vein on each leaf. Note the small toning speck under the L
of LIBERTY.

AU-50, 53, 55, 58 (About Uncirculated).
Obverse: Very light wear is evident on the
highest parts of the hair above and to the left
of the ear. Friction is seen on the cheek and
the liberty cap. Coins at this level are usually
on smooth planchets and have nice eye
appeal. Color is very important. Dark and
porous coins are relegated to lower grades,
even if AU-level sharpness is present. *Reverse:*

1794; BW-98, S-71, B-63. Graded AU-50.

Very light wear is evident on the higher parts of the leaves and the ribbon, and, to a lesser extent, on the
lettering. The reverse may have original luster, toned brown, varying from minimal (at lower About
Uncirculated grades) to extensive. Grading at the About Uncirculated level is mainly done by viewing
the obverse, as many reverses are inherently shallow due to lower-relief dies.

Illustrated coin: Note the rough patch on and below Liberty's cap.

EF-40, 45 (Extremely Fine). *Obverse:* The
center of the coin shows wear or a small, flat
area, for most dies. Other hair details are
strong. Luster is minimal or nonexistent at
EF-40, and may survive in traces in protected
areas (such as between the letters) at EF-45.
Reverse: Wear is seen on the highest wreath
and ribbon areas and the letters. Luster is minimal, but likely more noticeable than on the

1794; BW-18, S-28, B-10. Graded EF-40.

obverse, as the fields are protected by the designs and lettering. Sharpness varies depending on the die variety but is generally shallower than on the obverse, this being particularly true for many 1795 cents.

VF-20, 30 (Very Fine). *Obverse:* Wear on the portrait has reduced the hair detail to indistinct or flat at the center, and on most varieties the individual strands at the left edge are blended together. One rule does not fit all. The ANA grading standards suggest that 75% of the hair shows, while PCGS suggests 30% to 70% on varieties struck from higher-relief dies, and less than 50% for others. Examples such as this reflect the artistic, rather than sci-

1794, Head of 1794; BW-74, S-57, B-55. Graded VF-30.

entific, nature of grading. *Reverse:* The leaf details are nearly completely worn away at VF-20, and with slight detail at VF-30. Some border letters may be weak, and ditto for the central letters (on later varieties of this type). The border denticles are blended together with many indistinct. No luster is seen. The sharpness of details depends on the die variety.

F-12, 15 (Fine). *Obverse:* The hair details are mostly worn away, with about one-third visible, mainly at the lower edges. Border denticles are weak or worn away in areas, depending on the height of the rim when the coin was struck. F-15 shows slightly more detail. *Reverse:* The wreath leaves are worn flat, but their edges are distinct. Border denticles are weak or worn away in areas. F-15 shows slightly more detail. At this level and

1794, Head of 1794; BW-98, S-71, B-63. Graded F-15.

lower, planchet darkness and light porosity are common, as are scattered marks.

VG-8, 10 (Very Good). *Obverse:* The hair is more worn than on the preceding, with detail present only in the lower areas. Detail can differ, and widely, depending on the dies. Border denticles are worn away on some issues (not as much for 1793 and 1794 coins), and the border will blend into the field in areas in which the rim was low to begin with, or in areas struck slightly off center. LIBERTY and the date are bold. VG-10 is sometimes applied

1796; BW-1, S-91, B-1. Graded VG-8.

to especially nice Very Good coins. *Reverse:* The wreath, bow, and lettering are seen in outline form, and some leaves and letters may be indistinct in parts. Border denticles are worn away, and the border blends into the field in most if not all of the periphery. In certain die varieties and die states, especially of 1797, some letters may be very weak, or missing.

G-4, 6 (Good). *Obverse:* The portrait is worn smooth and is seen only in outline form, although the eye and nose can be discerned. LIBERTY and the date are complete, although the date may be weak. Denticles are gone on varieties struck with low or shallow rims. *Reverse:* Extensive wear is seen overall. From half to two-thirds of the letters in UNITED STATES OF AMERICA and the fraction numerals are worn away. Certain

1794, Starred Reverse; BW-59, S-48, B-38. Graded G-4.

shallow-relief dies may have letters missing. G-6 is often assigned to finer examples in this category. Darkness, porosity, and marks characterize many coins.

Illustrated coin: This coin is an example of the highly sought 1794, Starred Reverse, variety.

AG-3 (About Good). *Obverse:* Wear is more extensive than on the preceding. The portrait is visible only in outline. LIBERTY will typically have some letters worn away. The date is weak, but discernible. *Reverse:* Parts of the wreath are visible in outline form, and all but a few letters are gone. Grading of AG-3 is usually done by the reverse, as the obverse typically appears to be in a slightly higher grade.

1794, Starred Reverse; BW-59, S-48, B-38. Graded AG-3.

Illustrated coin: This coin is closer to G-4 on the obverse, but weak on the reverse, prompting a more conservative grade. While the reverse is worn nearly smooth, almost a third of the stars at the denticles, which mark this cent as a 1794, Starred Reverse, are visible.

Head of 1793 (1793–1794)
Head in high, rounded relief.

Head of 1794 (1794)
Well-defined hair; hook on lowest curl.

Beaded Border (1793)

Denticle Border (1794–1796)

	Mintage	Cert	Avg	%MS	AG-3	G-4	VG-8	F-12	VF-20	EF-40	AU-50	MS-60BN	MS-63BN
1793, Liberty Cap	11,056	29	11.8	0%	$6,000	$12,000	$15,000	$22,500	$40,000	$100,000	$135,000		
	Auctions: $30,550, VF-20, January 2017; $20,400, F-12, April 2018; $19,389, VG-10, August 2016; $3,760, VG-8, January 2015												

1794, Normal Reverse

1794, Starred Reverse

Head of 1795 (1794–1796)
Head in low relief;
no hook on lowest curl.

1795, "Jefferson Head"

	Mintage	Cert	Avg	%MS	AG-3	G-4	VG-8	F-12	VF-20	EF-40	AU-50	MS-60BN	MS-63BN
1794, All kinds	918,521												
1794, Head of 1793		22	20.1	18%	$800	$1,800	$3,600	$5,000	$12,000	$20,000	$40,000	$100,000	$200,000
Auctions: $881,250, MS-64BN, January 2013													
1794, Head of 1794		349	31.3	4%	$350	$450	$800	$1,500	$2,750	$4,750	$12,000	$20,000	$35,000
Auctions: $45,600, MS-64+BN, January 2018; $12,925, AU-55, June 2015; $9,988, AU-55, June 2015; $13,200, EF-40, January 2018													
1794, Head in Low Relief		0	n/a		$350	$450	$750	$1,200	$2,200	$4,250	$10,000	$15,000	$30,000
Auctions: No auction records available.													
1794, Exact Head of 1795 (a)		63	30.6	6%	$350	$475	$800	$1,400	$2,750	$5,250	$12,000	$20,000	$45,000
Auctions: $1,292.50, VF-25, August 2016; $329, VF-20, July 2015; $447, F-15, July 2015; $376, F-12, November 2015													
1794, Starred Reverse †		9	12.9	0%	$15,000	$22,500	$32,500	$60,000	$125,000	$300,000			
Auctions: $99,875, VF-25, May 2015; $15,275, AG-3, October 2013													
1794, No Fraction Bar		7	33.3	29%	$350	$500	$900	$1,750	$3,000	$6,500	$16,000	$40,000	$75,000
Auctions: $381,875, MS-64BN, January 2014													
1795, Lettered Edge	37,000	77	25.3	10%	$300	$450	$800	$1,250	$2,750	$5,500	$8,500	$14,000	$27,500
Auctions: $79,313, MS-65BN, April 2013; $1,170, F-12, September 2017, $1,140, VG-10, February 2018													
1795, Plain Edge	501,500	312	23.4	10%	$300	$400	$700	$1,000	$2,000	$3,700	$7,000	$9,000	$22,000
Auctions: $21,150, MS-63BN, April 2013; $4,993.75, AU-58BN, August 2015; $548, G-6, July 2015; $780, F-12, January 2018													
1795, Reeded Edge	(b)	0	n/a		$100,000	$200,000	$400,000	$750,000					
Auctions: $646,250, VG-10, January 2014													
1795, "Jefferson Head" (c)		3	20.0	0%	$11,000	$25,000	$37,500	$55,000	$100,000	$150,000			
Auctions: $184,000, VF-25, March 2012													
1795, "Jefferson Head," Lettered Edge (c)	(d)	0	n/a		—	$55,000	$90,000	$200,000					
Auctions: $52,875, F-2, January 2014													
1796, Liberty Cap	109,825	203	19.0	7%	$400	$500	$1,000	$1,850	$3,800	$9,000	$15,000	$30,000	$40,000
Auctions: $141,000, MS-64RB, January 2014; $763.75, VG-8, April 2017; $400, AG-3, February 2015; $240, AG-3, December 2017													

† Ranked in the *100 Greatest U.S. Coins* (fifth edition). **a.** The 1794 coin with Head of 1795 has a hooked curl but is in low relief. **b.** 9 examples are known. **c.** The "Jefferson Head" is not a regular Mint issue, but a design struck privately in an attempt to win a federal coinage contract. **d.** 3 examples are known.

DRAPED BUST (1796–1807)

Designer: *Robert Scot.* **Weight:** *10.89 grams.* **Composition:** *Copper.*
Diameter: *Average 29 mm.* **Edge:** *Plain.* **Mint:** *Philadelphia.*

1797, Reverse of 1795, Gripped Edge;
BW-3b, S-121b, B-3b.

History. The Draped Bust cent made its debut in 1796, following a coinage of Liberty Cap cents the same year. The motif, from a drawing by Gilbert Stuart, was first employed on certain silver dollars of 1795. (Its use on half cents did not take place until later, in 1800.) In 1798 Miss Liberty's head was slightly modified in design.

Striking and Sharpness. Most Draped Bust cents were struck on high-quality planchets. (This high planchet quality is less predictable for varieties of 1796, and almost never present for those of 1799 and 1800.) Detail sharpness differs by die variety. Weakness, when present, is usually on the hair behind the forehead, on the leaves in the upper part of the wreath, and among the denticles. However, a weak strike can show up in other areas as well. Many if not most Draped Bust cents are imperfectly centered, with the result that denticles can be bold on one side of a coin and light or even missing on the opposite side; this can occur on obverse as well as reverse. Typically this does not affect value. Certain Draped Bust cents of 1796 have semi-prooflike surfaces. Those of 1799 often have rough or porous surfaces and are found in lower grades.

Availability. As a type, Draped Bust cents are readily available, although the 1799, 9 Over 8, and 1799 are the keys to the series, and the 1804 is elusive. A different scenario evolves when considering engraving errors, repunched dates, and recut letters and numerals; many of these varieties are very difficult to locate. The eye appeal of these rarities usually is below par. Other years are generally available in high grades, VF and finer, well struck (except for some reverse leaves, in instances), on high-quality planchets, and with excellent eye appeal. Dark and porous coins are plentiful among coins graded below VF. True MS coins tend to be MS–60 to 63, when found.

GRADING STANDARDS

MS-60 to 70 (Mint State). *Obverse:* In the lower Mint State grades, MS–60 and 61, some slight abrasion can be seen on the higher areas of the portrait, especially the cheek, and the hair behind the forehead. Luster in the field is incomplete, particularly in the center of the open areas, which on this type are very open, especially at the right. At MS–63, luster should be nearly complete, and no abrasions evident. In higher levels, the lus-

1803, Small Date, Large Fraction;
BW-12, S-258, B-17. Graded MS-63BN.

ter is complete and deeper, and some original mint color should be seen. MS–64 coins may have some slight discoloration or scattered contact marks. A well-graded MS–65 or higher coin will have full, rich luster; no marks visible except under magnification; and a nice blend of brown toning or nicely mixed (not stained or blotchy) mint color and natural brown toning. ***Reverse:*** In the lower Mint State ranges some abrasions are seen on the higher areas of the leaves. Generally, luster is complete in all Mint State ranges, as the open areas are protected by the lettering and wreath. Sharpness of the leaves can vary by die variety, so check this aspect. Otherwise, the same comments apply as for the obverse.

Illustrated coin: This example is quite attractive despite the scratch on Liberty's bust and another through the D of UNITED. However, the left side of the reverse has toned differently from the rest of the coin's surfaces.

AU-50, 53, 55, 58 (About Uncirculated).

Obverse: Friction is seen on the higher parts, particularly the hair of Miss Liberty and the cheek. Friction and scattered marks are in the field, ranging from more extensive at AU-50 to minimal at AU-58. Luster may be seen in protected areas, minimal at AU-50, more visible at AU-58. At AU-58 the field may retain some luster, as well. In many instances, the luster is smaller in area and lesser in "depth"

1803, Small Date, Large Fraction; BW-12, S-258, B-17. Graded AU-58.

than on the reverse of this type. Cents of this type can be very beautiful in About Uncirculated. ***Reverse:*** Friction is seen on the higher wreath leaves and (not as easy to discern) on the letters. Again, the die variety should be checked. The fields, though protected by the designs, show friction, but not as noticeably as on the obverse. At AU–55 and 58, little if any friction is seen. The reverse may have original luster, toned brown, minimal on lower About Uncirculated grades, often extensive at the AU-58 level. General rules for cents follow the half cents of the same type.

Illustrated coin: Note the die crack arcing through the lower-left obverse. This crack was also on the preceding coin, but is more noticeable here.

EF-40, 45 (Extremely Fine).

Obverse: Wear is seen on the portrait overall, with reduction or elimination of some separation of hair strands on the highest part. By the standards of the Early American Coppers society, if the "spit curl" in front of Liberty's ear is missing, the coin is not EF. The cheek shows more wear than on higher grades, and the drapery covering the bosom is lightly worn on the higher areas. Often weakness in the separa-

1804, Original; BW-1, S-266, B-1. Graded EF-40.

tion of the drapery lines can be attributed to weakness in striking. Luster is minimal or nonexistent at EF-40, and may survive in amongst the letters of LIBERTY at EF-45. ***Reverse:*** Wear is seen on the highest wreath and ribbon areas, and on the letters. Luster is minimal, but likely more noticeable than on the obverse, as the fields are protected by the designs and lettering. The ANA grading standards state that at EF-45 nearly all of the "ribbing" (veins) in the leaves is visible, and that at EF-40 about 75% is sharp. In practice, striking plays a part as well, and some leaves may be weak even in higher grades.

Illustrated coin: This coin features a few small patches of porosity.

VF-20, 30 (Very Fine). *Obverse:* Wear on the portrait has reduced the hair detail further, especially to the left of the forehead. The rolling curls are solid or flat on their highest areas, as well as by the ribbon behind the hair. The border denticles are blended together, with many indistinct. No luster is seen. *Reverse:* The leaf details are nearly completely worn away at VF-20, and with slight detail at VF-30. The ANA grading

1805; BW-1, S-267, B-1. Graded VF-35.

standards are a bit stricter: 30% remaining at VF-20 and 50% at VF-30. In the marketplace, fewer details can be seen on most certified coins at these levels. The border denticles are blended together with many indistinct. No luster is seen.

F-12, 15 (Fine). *Obverse:* Many hair details are worn away, with perhaps one-half to one-third visible, mainly at the edges and behind the shoulder. Border denticles are weak or worn away in areas. F-15 shows slightly more detail. Porosity and scattered marks become increasingly common at this level and lower. *Reverse:* The wreath leaves are worn flat, but their edges are distinct. Little if anything remains of leaf vein details. Border denticles

1807, 7 Over 6; BW-2, S-273, B-3. Graded F-12.

are weak or worn away in areas. F-15 shows slightly more detail.

    Illustrated coin: There are several distracting contact marks on the obverse of this coin. Note the 6 visible under the 7 in the date.

VG-8, 10 (Very Good). *Obverse:* The portrait is well worn, although the eye can be seen, as can hints of hair detail. Some hair at the left shows separation. Curls now appear as mostly solid blobs. Border denticles are worn away on most varieties, and the rim, although usually present, begins to blend into the field. LIBERTY and the date are bold in most areas, with some lightness toward the rim. VG-10 is sometimes applied to espe-

1807, Large Fraction. Graded VG-8.

cially nice Very Good coins. *Reverse:* The wreath, bow, and lettering are seen in outline form, and some leaves and letters may be indistinct in parts. The border may blend into the field on some of the periphery. The strength of the letters is dependent to an extent on the specific die variety.

G-4, 6 (Good). *Obverse:* The portrait is worn smooth and is seen only in outline form, although the eye position can be discerned and some curls can be made out. LIBERTY is readable, but the tops of the letters may fade away. The date is clearly readable, but the lower part of the numerals may be very weak or worn away. The border will blend into the field more extensively than on the preceding, but significant areas will still be seen. *Reverse:*

1799, 9 Over 8; BW-2, S-188, B-2. Graded G-6.

Extensive wear is seen overall. From one-half to two-thirds of the letters in UNITED STATES OF AMERICA and the fraction numerals are worn away. On most varieties, ONE CENT is fairly strong. G-6 is often assigned to finer examples in this category.

Illustrated coin: This coin shows evidence of a past cleaning, but it has retoned.

AG-3 (About Good). *Obverse:* Wear is more extensive than on the preceding. The portrait is visible only in outline. LIBERTY is weak, partially worn away, but usually discernible. The date is weak, and the bottoms of the digits may be worn away, but must be identifiable. *Reverse:* Parts of the wreath are visible in outline form, and all but a few letters are gone. ONE CENT is usually mostly or completely discernible, depending on the variety.

1796, Reverse of 1797; BW-53, S-100, B-24. Graded AG-3.

Illustrated coin: Early American Coppers has graded this same coin at Good.

Reverse of 1794 (1794–1796)
*Note double leaf at top right;
14–16 leaves on left,
16–18 leaves on right.*

Reverse of 1795 (1795–1798)
*Note single leaf at top right;
17–21 leaves on left,
16–20 leaves on right.*

Reverse of 1797 (1796–1807)
*Note double leaf at top right; 16
leaves on left, 19 leaves on right.*

1796, LIHERTY Error

1797, Wreath With Stems

1797, Stemless Wreath

Style 1 Hair
Found on all coins of 1796 and 1797, many 1798 varieties, and 1800, 1800 Over 1798.

Style 2 Hair
Found on coins of 1798–1807. Note the extra curl near shoulders.

1798, 8 Over 7

	Mintage	Cert	Avg	%MS	AG-3	G-4	VG-8	F-12	VF-20	EF-40	AU-50	MS-60BN	MS-63BN
1796, Draped Bust, All kinds	363,375												
1796, Reverse of 1794		36	14.1	0%	$400	$500	$1,000	$1,850	$3,800	$9,000	$15,000	$30,000	$40,000
Auctions: $11,750, AU-53, January 2014; $3,120, VF-20, January 2018; $540.50, G-4, July 2017													
1796, Reverse of 1795		25	21.3	4%	$300	$400	$700	$1,500	$3,000	$7,500	$13,500	$24,000	$35,000
Auctions: $20,563, AU-58, January 2014; $764, G-6, October 2015; $646, G-6, October 2015													
1796, Reverse of 1797		27	19.0	11%	$300	$400	$600	$1,250	$2,500	$5,500	$7,500	$15,000	$20,000
Auctions: $28,200, MS-64BN, April 2013													
1796, LIHERTY Error		15	21.3	7%	$450	$850	$1,600	$3,500	$7,500	$15,000	$40,000	$65,000	$90,000
Auctions: $2,350, VF-20, August 2013; $1,704, VG-10, March 2015													
1796, Stemless Reverse	(a)	0	n/a		$25,000								
Auctions: No auction records available.													
1797, All kinds	897,510												
1797, 1795-Style Reverse, Gripped Edge		21	18.1	0%	$150	$250	$450	$800	$1,500	$3,700	$10,000	$27,000	
Auctions: $1,351, VG-8, March 2013													
1797, 1795-Style Reverse, Plain Edge		13	11.9	0%	$150	$275	$500	$1,200	$2,500	$4,500	$12,000	$28,000	
Auctions: $940, EF-40, June 2014													
1797, 1797 Reverse, With Stems		250	29.5	15%	$125	$225	$400	$750	$1,500	$2,500	$5,000	$7,500	$12,000
Auctions: $41,125, MS-65RB, January 2013; $2,350, EF-45, March 2015; $1,440, VF-25, January 2018; $660, F-15, April 2018													
1797, 1797 Reverse, Stemless		26	20.1	0%	$150	$275	$650	$1,400	$3,000	$7,000	$13,000	$55,000	
Auctions: $1,645, VF-25, January 2014; $720, VG-10, March 2018													
1798, All kinds	1,841,745												
1798, 8 Over 7		25	21.4	4%	$200	$400	$650	$1,500	$3,500	$8,000	$16,500		
Auctions: $14,688, AU-58, February 2013													
1798, Reverse of 1796		13	15.5	0%	$250	$500	$1,250	$3,000	$5,500	$12,000	$23,000	$32,000	$50,000
Auctions: $3,290, VF-20, September 2013; $564, VG-8, August 2015													
1798, Style 1 Hair		92	22.0	1%	$100	$150	$275	$600	$1,100	$2,200	$5,000	$12,000	$22,500
Auctions: $494, EF-40, June 2015; $494, VF-20, May 2015; $494, F-12, January 2015; $132, G-6, March 2018													
1798, Style 2 Hair		248	28.9	3%	$100	$150	$250	$500	$850	$1,750	$4,000	$10,000	$17,500
Auctions: $823, VF-30, August 2015; $940, VF-25, June 2015; $541, VF-20, January 2015; $1,020, VF-30, February 2018													

a. 3 examples are known.

1799, 9 Over 8

1799, Normal Date

1800, 1800 Over 1798

1800, 80 Over 79

1800, Normal Date

1801, Normal Reverse

1801, 3 Errors: 1/000, One Stem, and IINITED

1801, Fraction 1/000

1801, 1/100 Over 1/000

	Mintage	Cert	Avg	%MS	AG-3	G-4	VG-8	F-12	VF-20	EF-40	AU-50	MS-60BN	MS-63BN
1799, 9 Over 8	(b)	10	11.0	0%	$4,000	$6,500	$11,500	$25,000	$40,000	$135,000	$350,000	$950,000	
Auctions: $70,500, VF-25, January 2014; $1,293, AG-3, March 2016													
1799, Normal Date	904,585	58	10.1	2%	$3,500	$5,500	$9,000	$20,000	$35,000	$120,000	$250,000	$500,000	
Auctions: $30,550, AU-58, May 2016; $99,875, VF-35, January 2013; $32,900, VF-30, March 2015													
1800, All kinds	2,822,175												
1800, 1800 Over 1798, Style 1 Hair		35	21.6	3%	$65	$130	$250	$550	$1,400	$3,850	$7,000	$10,000	$17,500
Auctions: $2,585, G-6, January 2014													
1800, 80 Over 79, Style 2 Hair		83	20.2	5%	$65	$125	$200	$500	$1,000	$2,500	$4,000	$8,000	$25,000
Auctions: $19,388, MS-62BN, June 2014; $288, VG-10, March 2018													
1800, Normal Date		189	21.8	8%	$65	$100	$200	$375	$800	$2,000	$3,500	$6,500	$14,000
Auctions: $70,500, MS-65BN, January 2013; $1,058, VF-25, June 2015; $705, VF-20, October 2015													
1801, All kinds	1,362,837												
1801, Normal Reverse		187	20.6	4%	$55	$85	$150	$275	$600	$1,500	$3,000	$7,500	$14,500
Auctions: $1,645, EF-40, February 2015; $112, VF-20, July 2015; $494, F-12, August 2015; $282, VG-10, July 2015													
1801, 3 Errors: 1/000, One Stem, and IINITED		27	14.0	4%	$150	$300	$600	$1,400	$3,000	$7,500	$25,000	$50,000	$115,000
Auctions: $3,525, EF-40, August 2013; $2,400, VG-10, February 2018													
1801, Fraction 1/000		53	20.4	4%	$120	$150	$325	$600	$1,300	$4,250	$6,000	$9,000	$22,000
Auctions: $4,406, EF-40, January 2014													
1801, 1/100 Over 1/000		12	19.1	8%	$120	$180	$375	$700	$1,600	$5,500	$10,000	$30,000	$55,000
Auctions: $1,528, EF-45, January 2014													

b. Included in Included in 1798, All kinds, mintage figure. Most of this figure represents coinage from 1798 dies still in use.

1802, Normal Reverse

1802, Fraction 1/000

1802, Stemless Wreath

1803, Small Date   **1803, Large Date**

*Note that Small Date varieties have a
blunt 1 in the date, and Large Date varieties
have a pointed 1 and noticeably larger 3.*

1803, Small Fraction

1803, Large Fraction

1803, 1/100 Over 1/000

1803, Stemless Wreath

	Mintage	Cert	Avg	%MS	AG-3	G-4	VG-8	F-12	VF-20	EF-40	AU-50	MS-60BN	MS-63BN
1802, All kinds	3,435,100												
1802, Normal Reverse		590	26.7	3%	$65	$100	$125	$250	$500	$1,200	$2,500	$4,500	$11,000
Auctions: $1,058, AU-50, January 2015; $881, EF-40, January 2015; $705, VF-35, January 2015; $617, VF-30, June 2015													
1802, Fraction 1/000		32	28.2	9%	$75	$125	$200	$375	$650	$1,750	$4,800	$7,250	$17,000
Auctions: $11,163, AU-55, January 2014													
1802, Stemless Wreath		64	26.9	2%	$60	$100	$150	$300	$550	$1,300	$2,750	$4,000	$12,000
Auctions: $2,938, AU-55, October 2013; $646, VF-25, January 2015; $470, VF-25, September 2015; $447, VF-25, August 2015													
1803, All kinds	3,131,691												
1803, Small Date, Small Fraction		198	28.0	5%	$55	$85	$140	$275	$500	$1,200	$2,500	$5,500	$11,000
Auctions: $423, EF-40, November 2015; $646, VF-30, July 2015; $541, VF-30, September 2015; $259, F-12, September 2015													
1803, Small Date, Large Fraction		121	28.5	6%	$55	$85	$140	$275	$500	$1,100	$2,250	$4,500	$9,000
Auctions: $18,800, MS-64BN, January 2014; $840, EF-40, April 2018													
1803, Large Date, Small Fraction		3	12.0	0%	$5,000	$8,500	$12,000	$25,000	$40,000	$85,000			
Auctions: $15,275, VF-20, January 2014													
1803, Large Date, Large Fraction		5	46.0	20%	$160	$265	$500	$900	$2,200	$3,700	$8,500		
Auctions: $353, VF-20, August 2013													
1803, 1/100 Over 1/000		19	26.1	5%	$90	$175	$300	$500	$1,000	$2,250	$4,000	$12,000	$25,000
Auctions: $2,820, EF-45, September 2013													
1803, Stemless Wreath		16	24.5	6%	$75	$150	$200	$400	$800	$1,800	$4,000	$10,000	$20,000
Auctions: $8,225, AU-58, January 2014; $180, VG-8, March 2018													

1804, Broken Dies
Bowers-Whitman–1c, Sheldon-266c.

Unofficial 1804 "Restrike"
Bowers-Whitman–3, Breen-1761, Pollock-6050.

Small 1807, 7 Over 6, Blunt 1

Large 1807, 7 Over 6, Pointed 1

1807, "Comet" Variety
Note the die break behind Miss Liberty's head.

1807, Small Fraction

1807, Large Fraction

	Mintage	Cert	Avg	%MS	AG-3	G-4	VG-8	F-12	VF-20	EF-40	AU-50	MS-60BN	MS-63BN
1804 (c)	96,500	113	14.2	0%	$1,500	$3,000	$4,500	$6,000	$10,000	$17,000	$40,000	$275,000	$650,000
Auctions: $223,250, AU-55, January 2013; $780, Fair 2, January 2018													
1804, Unofficial Restrike of 1860 (d)		91	61.1	86%						$1,000	$1,100	$1,200	$1,500
Auctions: $489, AU-55, August 2011													
1805	941,116	194	32.6	9%	$65	$85	$125	$250	$500	$1,200	$2,750	$5,250	$16,000
Auctions: $940, VF-35, January 2015; $447, VF-20, February 2015; $376, VF-20, May 2015; $129, VG-10, May 2015													
1806	348,000	108	25.3	6%	$75	$150	$225	$500	$800	$2,500	$3,500	$9,000	$28,000
Auctions: $3,819, AU-50, February 2013													

c. All genuine 1804 cents have a crosslet 4 in the date and a large fraction. The 0 in the date is in line with the O in OF on the reverse.
d. Discarded Mint dies were used, circa 1860, to create "restrikes" (actually novodels or fantasies) of the scarce 1804 cent for collectors. These combine two unrelated dies: an altered 1803 die was used for the obverse, and a die of the 1820 cent for the reverse. The resulting coins cannot be confused with genuine 1804 cents.

	Mintage	Cert	Avg	%MS	AG-3	G-4	VG-8	F-12	VF-20	EF-40	AU-50	MS-60BN	MS-63BN
1807, All kinds	829,221												
1807, Small 1807, 7 Over 6, Blunt 1		3	11.0	0%	$2,000	$3,500	$6,000	$9,500	$22,500	$65,000	$150,000		
Auctions: $2,585, F-15, January 2014													
1807, Large 1807, 7 Over 6, Pointed 1		99	22.8	6%	$65	$110	$225	$400	$700	$1,500	$3,000	$10,000	$23,500
Auctions: $70,500, MS-65BN, April 2014; $764, VF-25, January 2015													
1807, Small Fraction		39	23.1	8%	$65	$110	$225	$450	$600	$2,500	$4,000	$12,500	$22,500
Auctions: $1,763, AU-50, August 2013													
1807, Large Fraction		37	18.9	0%	$65	$110	$225	$350	$550	$1,250	$2,300	$4,600	$16,500
Auctions: $5,750, AU-58, August 2011; $541, VF-25, October 2015; $306, F-12, June 2015; $89, G-6, March 2018													
1807, "Comet" Variety		31	25.0	10%	$100	$200	$350	$550	$1,350	$2,850	$5,500	$13,000	$26,000
Auctions: $27,600, MS-61BN, February 2012													

CLASSIC HEAD (1808–1814)

Designer: *John Reich.* **Weight:** *10.89 grams.* **Composition:** *Copper.*
Diameter: *Average 29 mm.* **Edge:** *Plain.* **Mint:** *Philadelphia.*

1808; BW-1, S-277, B-1.

History. The Classic Head design, by U.S. Mint assistant engraver John Reich, debuted in 1808. This cent type was minted through 1814. The quality of the coins' copper was poor during the War of 1812; the hostilities had ended the importation of high-quality planchets from England.

Striking and Sharpness. Striking sharpness varies, but often is poor. The cents of 1809 are notorious for having obverses much weaker than their reverses. Points to look for include sharpness of the denticles (which are often mushy, and in *most* instances inconsistent), star centers (a key area), hair details, and leaf details. Classic Head cents often are dark and porous due to the copper stock used.

Availability. Examples are readily available in grades from well worn to VF and EF, although overall quality often leaves much to be desired. AU and MS coins are elusive. Grading numbers do not mean much, as a connoisseur might prefer a high-quality EF-45 to a poorly struck MS-63. Overall eye appeal of obverse and reverse is often sub-par, a characteristic of this type.

GRADING STANDARDS

MS-60 to 70 (Mint State). *Obverse:* In the lower Mint State grades, MS–60 and 61, some slight abrasions can be seen on the portrait, most evidently on the cheek, as the hair details are complex on this type. Luster in the field is complete or nearly complete; the field is not as open on this type as on the Draped Bust issues. At MS-63, luster should be complete, and no abrasion evident. In higher levels, the luster is complete and deeper, and some orig-

1812, Large Date; BW-1, S-288, B-3. Graded MS-64BN.

inal mint color may be seen. MS-64 coins may have some slight discoloration or scattered contact marks. A well-graded MS-65 or higher coin will have full, rich luster; no marks visible except under magnification; and a nice blend of brown toning or nicely mixed (not stained or blotchy) mint color and natural brown toning. Incomplete striking of some details, especially the obverse stars, is the rule. *Reverse:* In the lower Mint State grades, some abrasion is seen on the higher areas of the leaves. Mint luster is complete in all Mint State grades, as the open areas are protected by the lettering and wreath. Sharpness of the leaves can vary by die variety, so check this aspect. Otherwise, the same comments apply as for the obverse.

Illustrated coin: The central devices are sharply struck and well preserved though obverse stars 1 through 5 are somewhat flat, as is virtually always seen on this type, and the reverse denticles from 8 o'clock to 11 o'clock are soft, which is also typical. This is one of the highest-graded Classic Head cents in existence.

AU-50, 53, 55, 58 (About Uncirculated).
Obverse: Friction is seen on the higher parts, particularly the cheek. The hair will have friction and light wear, but will not be as obvious. Friction and scattered marks are in the field, ranging from more extensive at AU-50 to minimal at AU-58. Luster may be seen in protected areas, minimal at AU-50, but more visible at AU-58. At AU-58 the open field may retain some luster, as well.

1812, Large Date; BW-2, S-289, B-4. Graded AU-58.

Reverse: Friction is seen on the higher wreath leaves and on the letters. Fields, protected by the designs, show less friction. At the AU–55 and 58 levels little if any friction is seen. The reverse may have original luster, toned brown, minimal on lower About Uncirculated grades, often extensive at AU-58.

EF-40, 45 (Extremely Fine). *Obverse:* Wear is seen on the portrait overall, but most hair detail will still be present. The cheek shows light wear. Luster is minimal or nonexistent at EF-40, and may survive in among the letters of LIBERTY at EF-45. *Reverse:* Wear is seen on the highest wreath and ribbon areas and the letters. Leaf veins are visible except in the highest areas. Luster is minimal, but likely more noticeable than on the obverse, as the fields are protected by the designs and lettering.

1809; BW-1, S-280, B-1. Graded EF-40.

VF-20, 30 (Very Fine). *Obverse:* Wear on the portrait has reduced the hair detail, especially on the area to the right of the cheek and neck, but much can still be seen. *Reverse:* The wreath details, except for the edges of the leaves and certain of the tips (on leaves in lower relief), are worn away at VF-20, and with slightly more detail at VF-30.

1812, Large Date; BW-2, S-289, B-4. Graded VF-25.

F-12, 15 (Fine). *Obverse:* The hair details are fewer than on the preceding, but many are still present. The central hair curl is visible. Stars have flat centers. F-15 shows slightly more detail. The portrait on this type held up well to wear. *Reverse:* The higher areas of wreath leaves are worn flat, but their edges are distinct. F-15 shows slightly more detail.

Illustrated coin: This is a dark and somewhat porous example of what is considered to be the key issue of the Classic Head type.

1809; BW-1, S-280, B-1. Graded F-15.

VG-8, 10 (Very Good). *Obverse:* The portrait is well worn, although the eye and ear can be seen clearly. The hair is mostly blended, but some slight separation can be seen in areas. The border is raised in most or all areas. *Reverse:* The wreath is more worn than on the preceding grade, but there will still be some detail on the leaves. On most coins, ONE CENT is bold. Border letters are light or weak but are fully readable. The border is well defined in most areas.

1808. Graded VG-8.

G-4, 6 (Good). *Obverse:* The portrait is worn smooth and is seen only in outline form. Much or even all of LIBERTY on the headband is readable, but the letters are weak. The stars are weak, only in outline form, and several may be scarcely discernible. *Reverse:* Extensive wear is seen overall. Lettering in UNITED STATES OF AMERICA is weak, but completely discernible. The wreath is in outline, but still fairly bold, and ONE CENT is usually strong.

1808; BW-1, S-277, B-1. Graded G-6.

AG-3 (About Good). *Obverse:* Wear is more extensive than on the preceding. The portrait is visible only in outline. Most letters of LIBERTY are discernible, as this feature is in low relief. The stars are weak or worn away on their outer edges, and the date is light. *Reverse:* The wreath is visible in outline form but remains fairly strong. Most or even all of UNITED STATES OF AMERICA is worn away. ONE CENT is usually easily readable.

1808; BW-2, S-278, B-2. Graded AG-3.

1810, 10 Over 09

1810, Normal Date

1811, Last 1 Over 0

1811, Normal Date

1812, Small Date

1812, Large Date

1814, Plain 4

1814, Crosslet 4

	Mintage	Cert	Avg	%MS	AG-3	G-4	VG-8	F-12	VF-20	EF-40	AU-50	MS-60BN	MS-63BN
1808	1,007,000	132	29.3	11%	$85	$150	$250	$600	$1,200	$2,500	$5,000	$10,000	$25,000
Auctions: $25,850, MS-64BN, January 2013; $400, F-12, May 2015; $69, F-12, April 2015													
1809	222,867	80	27.4	9%	$250	$350	$700	$1,000	$1,700	$4,000	$7,500	$15,000	$50,000
Auctions: $28,200, MS-63BN, January 2013; $754, F-12, January 2015; $376, G-4, May 2015													
1810, All kinds	1,458,500												
1810, 10 Over 09		57	27.3	7%	$75	$125	$250	$600	$1,200	$2,500	$3,600	$9,500	$40,000
Auctions: $10,575, AU-55, April 2013													
1810, Normal Date		152	30.4	12%	$60	$100	$225	$500	$1,000	$2,000	$3,300	$9,000	$20,000
Auctions: $32,900, MS-64BN, January 2014; $376, EF-40, January 2015; $1,234, VF-35, January 2015; $940, VF-20, July 2015													
1811, All kinds	218,025												
1811, Last 1 Over 0		34	22.4	9%	$150	$275	$600	$900	$2,250	$7,000	$12,500	$32,500	$60,000
Auctions: $2,585, VF-25, March 2015; $1,410, VF-20, August 2016; $764, VG-10, August 2015													
1811, Normal Date		97	27.5	12%	$125	$250	$500	$800	$1,850	$3,500	$6,500	$12,500	$40,000
Auctions: $23,500, MS-64BN, January 2013; $336, VG-10, March 2018													
1812, All kinds	1,075,500												
1812, Small Date		36	29.3	6%	$60	$100	$200	$450	$900	$1,900	$3,300	$9,500	$20,000
Auctions: $44,063, MS-65RB, June 2014; $881, VF-30, August 2015; $94, F-12, March 2015; $153, VG-8, June 2015													
1812, Large Date		33	32.3	9%	$60	$100	$200	$450	$900	$1,900	$3,300	$9,500	$20,000
Auctions: $3,819, AU-55, January 2014													
1813	418,000	208	34.0	10%	$125	$250	$400	$750	$1,250	$2,500	$5,000	$10,000	$25,000
Auctions: $211,500, MS-65BN, January 2013; $940, AU-50, January 2015; $1,880, EF-40, March 2015; $1,116, VF-20, August 2015													
1814, All kinds	357,830												
1814, Plain 4		170	21.0	6%	$60	$100	$250	$450	$850	$2,000	$4,000	$9,000	$20,000
Auctions: $47,000, MS-65BN, April 2014; $223, VG-10, May 2015; $129, G-6, April 2015; $74, G-4, April 2015													
1814, Crosslet 4		132	24.9	11%	$60	$100	$250	$450	$850	$2,000	$4,000	$9,000	$20,000
Auctions: $1,028, VF-30, February 2015; $376, VF-20, November 2015; $188, VF-20, May 2015; $259, VG-10, May 2015													

MATRON HEAD (1816–1839)

Designer: *1816–1835, Matron Head—Possibly Robert Scot or John Birch;*
1835–1839, Matron Head Modified—Christian Gobrecht. **Weight:** *10.89 grams.*
Composition: *Copper.* **Diameter:** *1816–1835, Matron Head—28 to 29 mm;*
1835–1839, Matron Head Modified—27.5 mm. **Edge:** *Plain.* **Mint:** *Philadelphia.*

Matron Head (1816–1835),
Circulation Strike
1827; Newcomb-5.

Matron Head, Proof
1831; Newcomb-10.

Matron Head Modified (1835–1839),
Circulation Strike
1835; Newcomb-8.

Matron Head Modified, Proof
1837; Newcomb-9.

History. The term *Matron Head* describes cents of 1816 to 1835 (none were struck in 1815). Engraver Christian Gobrecht experimented with various "Matron Head Modified" portraits in the later 1830s.

Striking and Sharpness. Planchet quality is generally very good for Liberty Head cents. Color tends to be lighter on coins of the 1830s than on earlier dates. Striking can vary. Points to check include the obverse stars (in particular), the highest hair details, and the leaves on the reverse. Denticles can range from sharp to weak, and centering is often irregular. The reverse design is essentially the same as that used on the Classic Head of 1808 to 1814, and can be graded the same way. This motif stood up to circulation particularly well.

Availability. As a type, Liberty Head cents are easily available. The scarcest date by far is 1823 (and the related 1823, 3 Over 2, overdate). Cents of 1816 to 1820 (particularly 1818 and 1820) are readily available in MS. Other MS coins are generally scarce, although those of the 1830s are more easily obtainable than those of the teens and 1820s. Circulated examples exist in approximate relationship to their mintages. Planchet quality and striking sharpness vary in all grades.

GRADING STANDARDS

MS-60 to 70 (Mint State). *Obverse:* In the lower Mint State grades, MS–60 and 61, some slight abrasions can be seen on the portrait, most evidently on the cheek, which on this type is very prominent. Higher areas of the hair can be checked, particularly the top and back of Liberty's head, but do not confuse with lightness of strike. Luster in the

1817; N-2. Graded MS-63BN.

field is complete or nearly complete. At MS-63, luster should be complete, and no abrasion is evident.

In higher levels, the luster is complete and deeper, and some original mint color may be seen. MS-64 coins may have some minimal discoloration or scattered contact marks. A well-graded MS-65 or higher coin will have full, rich luster; no marks visible except under magnification; and a nice blend of brown toning or nicely mixed mint color and natural brown toning. Randall Hoard coins of the 1816 to 1820 years usually have much mint red and some black spotting. *Reverse:* In the lower Mint State grades some abrasion is seen on the higher areas of the leaves. Mint luster is complete in all Mint State grades, as the open areas are protected by the lettering and wreath. Sharpness of the leaves can vary by die variety, so check this aspect. Otherwise, the same comments apply as for the obverse.

Illustrated coin: Note the reverse die break running from NI of UNITED to OF A in OF AMERICA.

AU-50, 53, 55, 58 (About Uncirculated).
Obverse: Friction is seen on the higher parts, particularly the cheek. The hair has friction and light wear, usually most notable in the general area above BER of LIBERTY. Friction and scattered marks are in the field, ranging from extensive at AU-50 to minimal at AU-58. Luster may be seen in protected areas, minimal at the AU-50 level, more visible at AU-58. At AU-58 the field may retain some luster as well.

1820, 20 Over 19; N-10. Graded AU-58.

Reverse: Friction is seen on the higher wreath leaves and on the letters. Fields, protected by the designs, show friction. At the AU–55 and 58 levels little if any friction is seen. The reverse may have original luster, toned brown, minimal on lower About Uncirculated grades, often extensive at AU-58.

Illustrated coin: Flecks of darker patination spot both sides, but are particularly evident on the obverse.

EF-40, 45 (Extremely Fine). *Obverse:* Wear is seen on the portrait overall, but most hair detail is still present, except in higher areas. The cheek shows light wear. Luster is minimal or nonexistent at EF-40, and may survive in among the letters of LIBERTY at EF-45. *Reverse:* Wear is seen on the highest wreath and ribbon areas, and on the letters. Leaf veins are visible except in the highest areas. Luster is minimal, but likely more noticeable

1816. Graded EF-45.

than on the obverse, as the fields are protected by the designs and lettering.

VF-20, 30 (Very Fine). *Obverse:* Wear on the portrait has reduced the hair detail, especially on the area to the right of the cheek and neck, but much can still be seen. *Reverse:* The wreath details, except for the edges of the leaves and certain of the tips (on leaves in lower relief), are worn away at VF-20, and with slightly more detail at VF-30.

1823; N2. Graded VF-20.

F-12, 15 (Fine). *Obverse:* The hair details are fewer than on the preceding, but still many are present. Wear is extensive above and below the LIBERTY coronet, with the area from the forehead to the coronet worn flat. Stars have flat centers. F-15 shows slightly more detail. *Reverse:* The higher areas of wreath leaves are worn flat, but their edges are distinct. F-15 shows slightly more detail.

1816. Graded F-15.

VG-8, 10 (Very Good). *Obverse:* The portrait is well worn, although the eye and ear can be seen clearly. The hair is mostly blended, but some slight separation can be seen in lower areas. The border is raised in most or all areas. *Reverse:* The wreath is more worn than on the preceding, but still there is some detail on the leaves. On most coins, ONE CENT is bold. Border letters are light or weak but are fully readable. The border is well defined in most areas.

1831, Large Letters; N-9. Graded VG-8.

Illustrated coin: A die break caused the internal cud which connects stars 3 through 5, and that broken die would have been retired shortly after striking this piece.

G-4, 6 (Good). *Obverse:* The portrait is worn smooth and is seen only in outline form. Much or even all of LIBERTY on the headband is readable, but the letters are weak, and L may be missing. The stars are weak. The rim is usually discernible all around. *Reverse:* Extensive wear is seen overall. Lettering in UNITED STATES OF AMERICA is weak, but completely discernible. The wreath is in outline, but still fairly bold, and ONE CENT

1830; N-9. Graded G-4.

is usually strong. The rim is usually faded into the field in many areas (depending on the die variety).

Illustrated coin: Note the lovely golden brown and rose surfaces.

AG-3 (About Good). *Obverse:* Wear is more extensive than on the preceding. The portrait is visible only in outline. Most letters of LIBERTY remain discernible in the headband, as this feature is in low relief. The stars are weak or worn away on their outer edges, and the date is light. *Reverse:* The wreath is visible in outline form, but remains fairly strong. Most of UNITED STATES OF AMERICA is worn away. ONE CENT is usually readable, but light.

1818; N-6. Graded AG-3.

PF-60 to 70 (Proof). Proofs were made for cents from 1817 onward. Often, what are called "Proofs" are only partially mirrorlike, and sometimes the striking is casual, e.g., with weakness on certain of the stars. Complicating the situation is the fact that all but one of the same die pairs were also used to make circulation strikes. Many misattributions were made generations ago, some of which have been perpetuated. Except among large-cent

1831, Large Letters; N-9. Graded PF-63BN.

specialists, debate is effectively ended when a certification service seals a coin as a Proof (logic aside). True Proofs with deeply mirrored surfaces are in the small minority. ***Obverse and Reverse:*** Proofs that are extensively hairlined or have dull surfaces, this being characteristic of many issues (exceptions, when found, are usually dated in the 1830s) are graded PF-60 to 62 or 63. Artificially toned and recolored coins may be graded lower. To qualify as PF-65 or higher, hairlines should be microscopic, and there should be no trace of friction. Surfaces should be prooflike or, better, fully mirrored and without dullness.

Illustrated coin: This coin shows high quality for the grade. The surfaces are a light, reddish brown with areas of deep tan and hints of blue, green, gold and violet as well as considerable faded mint red on the reverse. This is one of two known Proof examples for the year.

1817, 13 Stars   **1817, 15 Stars**

	Mintage	Cert	Avg	%MS	G-4	VG-8	F-12	VF-20	EF-40	AU-50	MS-60BN / PF-63BN	MS-63BN / PF-64BN	MS-65BN / PF-65BN
1816	2,820,982	366	51.4	51%	$30	$40	$60	$120	$300	$475	$675	$1,000	$3,600
Auctions: $823, MS-63BN, October 2015; $259, AU-50, August 2015; $306, EF-45, April 2015; $69, EF-40, October 2015													
1817, All kinds	3,948,400												
1817, 13 Stars		546	48.8	46%	$30	$40	$60	$110	$225	$375	$625	$1,000	$2,800
Auctions: $1,293, MS-63BN, January 2015; $1,116, MS-63BN, January 2015; $1,175, MS-62BN, June 2015; $282, MS-60, June 2015													
1817, 15 Stars		48	47.4	21%	$50	$100	$200	$300	$800	$1,850	$4,000	$6,500	$35,000
Auctions: $9,400, VF-20, January 2014; $360, VF-20, April 2018													
1817, Proof	*2–3*	1	63.0	100%							$70,000	$100,000	$150,000
Auctions: $48,300, PF-66, July 2005													
1818	3,167,000	865	56.3	71%	$30	$40	$45	$85	$175	$300	$450	$600	$1,600
Auctions: $823, MS-64BN, September 2015; $764, MS-63RB, June 2015; $541, MS-62BN, October 2015; $494, MS-62BN, June 2015													

1819, 9 Over 8

1819, Large Date

1819, Small Date

1820, 20 Over 19
Note the 1 under the 2.

1820, Large Date
Note the plain-topped 2.

1820, Small Date
Note the curl-topped 2.

	Mintage	Cert	Avg	%MS	G-4	VG-8	F-12	VF-20	EF-40	AU-50	MS-60BN PF-63BN	MS-63BN PF-64BN	MS-65BN PF-65BN
1819, All kinds	2,671,000												
1819, Large Date, 9 Over 8		135	49.0	35%	$30	$40	$55	$100	$325	$375	$850	$1,300	$4,000
Auctions: $705, AU-58, October 2015; $259, EF-45, September 2015													
1819, Large Date (a)		71	47.8	27%	$30	$40	$45	$85	$175	$300	$550	$950	$3,000
Auctions: $940, MS-63BN, August 2015; $259, AU-55, May 2015; $202, EF-40, September 2015													
1819, Small Date		105	54.1	59%	$30	$40	$45	$85	$200	$350	$550	$1,000	$3,300
Auctions: $1,293, MS-63BN, June 2015; $646, AU-58, October 2015; $282, AU-50, August 2015; $212, EF-40, May 2015													
1819, Large Date, 9 Over 8, Proof	2–3	1	64.0									$75,000	
Auctions: $32,200, PF-64BN, June 2005													
1820, All kinds	4,407,550												
1820, 20 Over 19		57	38.3	23%	$30	$50	$55	$110	$400	$550	$1,350	$1,600	$4,500
Auctions: $764, AU-55, August 2015													
1820, Large Date		123	56.4	70%	$30	$40	$45	$85	$175	$300	$400	$650	$1,800
Auctions: $1,293, MS-63BN, August 2015; $705, MS-63BN, January 2015; $588, MS-63BN, January 2015; $494, MS-60, September 2015													
1820, Small Date		68	46.6	41%	$30	$40	$120	$180	$450	$850	$1,500	$2,250	$4,500
Auctions: $4,994, MS-64BN, January 2014													
1820, Proof	8–15	3	63.7								$40,000	$50,000	$60,000
Auctions: $46,000, PF-64, November 2008													
1821 (b)	389,000	162	28.8	6%	$70	$125	$250	$550	$1,500	$2,600	$9,000	$20,000	
Auctions: $564, AU-50, January 2015; $494, VF-25, August 2015; $400, VF-20, January 2015; $129, VF-20, May 2015; $312, VF-30, April 2018													
1821, Proof	4–6	3	63.0								$32,500	$40,000	$55,000
Auctions: $35,250, PF-62BN, August 2013													
1822	2,072,339	285	41.1	20%	$30	$45	$55	$150	$425	$700	$1,200	$2,300	$10,000
Auctions: $1,058, AU-58, June 2015; $793, AU-58, February 2015; $494, AU-55, January 2015; $517, AU-50, June 2015													
1822, Proof	4–6	1	62.0								$35,000	$50,000	
Auctions: $25,300, PF-63, March 2004													

a. The 1819, Large Date, is technically a 9 Over 8 similar to the preceding coin, but the underlying 8 is hardly visible. **b.** Wide and closely spaced AMER varieties are valued the same.

1823, 3 Over 2

1824, 4 Over 2

Unofficial 1823 "Restrike"
Newcomb-3, Breen-1823, Pollock-6220.

1826, 6 Over 5

**Date Size, Through 1828
(Large, Narrow Date)**

**Date Size, 1828 and
Later (Small, Wide Date)**

	Mintage	Cert	Avg	%MS	G-4	VG-8	F-12	VF-20	EF-40	AU-50	MS-60BN	MS-63BN	MS-65BN
											PF-63BN	PF-64BN	PF-65BN
1823, 3 Over 2	(b)	116	19.4	2%	$150	$300	$700	$1,500	$3,300	$6,500	$20,000		—
Auctions: $1,645, VF-30, January 2015; $564, F-15, February 2015; $259, VG-10, May 2015; $132, G-6, February 2018													
1823, Normal Date	(b)	68	18.7	3%	$150	$300	$800	$2,000	$4,400	$8,500	$23,000	$30,000	$115,000
Auctions: $3,584, VF-35, January 2014; $900, VF-20, February 2018; $132, G-4, March 2018													
1823, Unofficial Restrike (c)		63	63.3	97%				$550	$650	$950	$1,500	$2,000	$2,850
Auctions: $2,350, MS-64BN, December 2013													
1823, Proof	2–3	1	65.0										$90,000
Auctions: No auction records available.													
1823, 3 Over 2, Proof	5–8	2	64.5								$50,000	$60,000	
Auctions: $47,000, PF-64BN, June 2014													
1824, All kinds	1,262,000												
1824, 4 Over 2		48	33.6	8%	$50	$80	$125	$350	$1,200	$2,500	$6,000	$25,000	
Auctions: $423, VF-25BN, September 2015; $129, VG-10, May 2015; $94, VG-10, June 2015; $99, VG-8, May 2018													
1824, Normal Date		165	36.9	13%	$40	$70	$90	$250	$600	$900	$3,000	$4,600	$13,000
Auctions: $564, EF-45, June 2015; $235, EF-40, January 2015; $259, VF-30, September 2015; $235, VF-30, May 2015													
1825	1,461,100	195	41.8	23%	$35	$50	$60	$150	$450	$750	$1,750	$2,750	$7,500
Auctions: $6,463, MS-64BN, January 2014													
1826, All kinds	1,517,425												
1826, 6 Over 5		19	46.9	37%	$35	$80	$100	$275	$975	$1,500	$2,800	$5,500	$20,000
Auctions: $10,575, MS-62BN, January 2014													
1826, Normal Date		311	44.3	29%	$25	$70	$90	$150	$400	$600	$1,250	$1,500	$3,100
Auctions: $3,290, MS-64, March 2015; $1,234, AU-58, August 2015; $376, AU-53, September 2015; $329, EF-40, June 2015													
1827	2,357,732	294	39.1	21%	$30	$40	$60	$100	$225	$425	$775	$1,400	$3,250
Auctions: $881, AU-58BN, October 2015; $576, AU-55, March 2015; $376, AU-53, May 2015; $259, EF-45, May 2015													
1827, Proof	5–8	2	64.0								$20,000	$25,000	$40,000
Auctions: $20,125, PF-64, March 2004													
1828, All kinds	2,260,624												
1828, Large Narrow Date		83	50.0	29%	$30	$40	$50	$90	$210	$400	$1,250	$1,750	$4,250
Auctions: $3,672, MS-64, March 2015; $881, AU-58, October 2015; $141, VF-30, January 2015													
1828, Small Wide Date		20	46.9	35%	$30	$40	$50	$190	$275	$650	$1,950	$3,500	$20,000
Auctions: $7,638, MS-64BN, February 2013; $432, EF-45, May 2018													
1828, Proof	2–3	1	65.0										$80,000
Auctions: No auction records available.													

b. Included in 1824, All kinds, mintage figure. **c.** The unofficial 1823 "restrikes" (actually novodels or fantasies) were made at the same time (around 1860) and by the same people as those of 1804. The coins were made from a discarded obverse die of 1823 and an 1813 reverse die—both heavily rusted, producing surface lumps. Most examples have both dies cracked.

Large Letters (1808–1834)
*Note the size and proximity
of individual letters.*

Medium Letters (1829–1837)
*Note the isolation of the
letters, especially of STATES.*

	Mintage	Cert	Avg	%MS	G-4	VG-8	F-12	VF-20	EF-40	AU-50	MS-60BN / PF-63BN	MS-63BN / PF-64BN	MS-65BN / PF-65BN
1829, All kinds	1,414,500												
1829, Large Letters		49	45.2	31%	$30	$40	$50	$110	$200	$385	$650	$1,500	$5,200
Auctions: $646, AU-55, February 2015; $129, VF-25, February 2015													
1829, Medium Letters		17	39.1	12%	$30	$40	$110	$325	$800	$2,250	$6,500	$10,500	$20,000
Auctions: $7,050, AU-58, January 2014													
1829, Proof	2–3	1	64.0								$20,000	$25,000	$40,000
Auctions: $47,000, PF-64RB, January 2014													
1829, Bronzed, Proof	10–15	5	64.6	100%							$18,000	$26,000	$40,000
Auctions: $41,125, PF-65BN, August 2013													
1830, All kinds	1,711,500												
1830, Large Letters		101	47.3	34%	$30	$40	$50	$70	$190	$300	$550	$1,000	$2,700
Auctions: $562, AU-55, August 2015; $646, AU-53, October 2015; $235, EF-40, May 2015; $153, VF-25, May 2015													
1830, Medium Letters		9	26.3	11%	$30	$40	$160	$500	$2,000	$5,000	$15,000	$25,000	$32,000
Auctions: $3,055, EF-40, June 2013													
1830, Proof	2–3	1	64.0								$25,000	$35,000	$65,000
Auctions: $16,500, PF-64, November 1988													
1831, All kinds	3,359,260												
1831, Large Letters		91	51.5	49%	$30	$40	$50	$70	$150	$250	$400	$700	$1,800
Auctions: $212, AU-53, July 2015; $224, AU-50, March 2015													
1831, Medium Letters		46	50.4	39%	$30	$40	$50	$70	$200	$350	$750	$1,600	$3,500
Auctions: $3,290, MS-62BN, January 2014													
1831, Proof	10–20	8	64.1								$14,500	$24,500	$50,000
Auctions: $30,550, PF-65BN, January 2014													
1832, All kinds	2,362,000												
1832, Large Letters		33	53.9	52%	$30	$40	$50	$70	$150	$250	$375	$650	$2,300
Auctions: $3,525, MS-65BN, January 2014; $306, AU-58, June 2015													
1832, Medium Letters		34	56.6	56%	$30	$40	$50	$85	$200	$550	$900	$1,200	$2,900
Auctions: $940, MS-62BN, July 2014													
1832, Proof	2–4	1	64.0								$40,000	$50,000	$65,000
Auctions: No auction records available.													
1833	2,739,000	335	47.9	37%	$30	$40	$50	$70	$150	$250	$375	$750	$2,600
Auctions: $423, AU-58, May 2015; $294, AU-53, May 2015; $223, EF-40, August 2015; $206, EF-40, June 2015													
1833, Proof	(d)	0	n/a										
Auctions: No auction records available.													

d. Unique.

1834, Large 8,
Large Stars,
Large Letters
Newcomb-6.

1834, Large 8,
Large Stars,
Medium Letters
Newcomb-5.

1834, Large 8,
Small Stars,
Medium Letters
Newcomb-3.

1834, Small 8,
Large Stars,
Medium Letters
Newcomb-1.

	Mintage	Cert	Avg	%MS	G-4	VG-8	F-12	VF-20	EF-40	AU-50	MS-60BN PF-63BN	MS-63BN PF-64BN	MS-65BN PF-65BN
1834, All kinds	1,855,100												
1834, Large 8, Stars, and Reverse Letters		14	40.4	0%	$30	$40	$75	$200	$550	$1,200	$2,250	$4,000	$8,500
Auctions: $2,820, AU-58, January 2014													
1834, Large 8 and Stars, Medium Letters		6	51.3	33%	$250	$450	$600	$1,250	$3,500	$6,500	$9,000	$12,000	$22,000
Auctions: $58,750, MS-65BN, January 2014; $253, AU-50, June 2015; $165, EF-40, January 2015													
1834, Large 8, Small Stars, Medium Letters		40	46.2	30%	$30	$40	$60	$70	$150	$240	$500	$800	$2,000
Auctions: $1,528, MS-63BN, January 2014; $216, EF-45, April 2018; $240, EF-40, March 2018													
1834, Small 8, Large Stars, Medium Letters		87	52.0	45%	$30	$40	$60	$70	$150	$240	$350	$625	$1,500
Auctions: $4,994, MS-66BN, January 2014; $823, AU-58, September 2015													
1834, Proof	6–8	4	65.0								$15,000	$21,000	$40,000
Auctions: $52,875, PF-60BN, January 2014													

1835, Large 8,
Large Stars,
Matron Head

1835, Small 8,
Small Stars,
Matron Head

Medium Letters
(1829–1837)

Small Letters
(1837–1839)

1835,
Matron
Head

1835, Head of 1836

1837
Note the plain
hair cords.

1837, Head of 1838
*Note the slim bust
and the beaded hair cords.*

1839, 1839 Over 1836
*Note the closed 9 and
the plain hair cords.*

1839, Silly Head
*Note the prominent lock
of hair at the forehead.*

1839, Booby Head
Note the shoulder tip. Also note the absence of a line under CENT.

	Mintage	Cert	Avg	%MS	G-4	VG-8	F-12	VF-20	EF-40	AU-50	MS-60BN PF-63BN	MS-63BN PF-64BN	MS-65BN PF-65BN
1835, All kinds	3,878,400												
1835, Large 8 and Stars		16	45.3	31%	$30	$40	$60	$75	$225	$400	$750	$1,400	$3,750
Auctions: $16,450, MS-64BN, January 2013													
1835, Small 8 and Stars		52	46.5	29%	$30	$40	$60	$70	$175	$375	$475	$675	$1,750
Auctions: $3,819, MS-63BN, January 2014													
1835, Head of 1836		100	53.5	40%	$30	$40	$50	$65	$125	$250	$350	$550	$1,300
Auctions: $712, MS-62BN, August 2015; $646, AU-58, September 2015; $176, AU-50, October 2015; $106, AU-50, April 2015													
1836	2,111,000	274	50.1	41%	$30	$40	$50	$65	$125	$250	$350	$550	$1,300
Auctions: $881, MS-64BN, January 2015; $447, AU-58, September 2015; $259, AU-55, September 2015; $153, EF-45, August 2015													
1836, Proof	6–8	4	64.0								$15,000	$21,000	$40,000
Auctions: $47,000, PF-63RB, June 2014													
1837, All kinds	5,558,300												
1837, Plain Cord, Medium Letters		171	57.5	63%	$27	$35	$50	$65	$125	$250	$350	$550	$1,200
Auctions: $94, VF-35, February 2015													
1837, Plain Cord, Small Letters		25	52.6	44%	$27	$35	$50	$65	$125	$250	$375	$600	$1,500
Auctions: $411, AU-58, February 2014													
1837, Head of 1838		83	57.8	59%	$27	$35	$50	$65	$110	$200	$325	$500	$1,200
Auctions: $1,116, MS-64BN, January 2015; $646, MS-63BN, August 2015; $306, AU-58, August 2015; $235, AU-53, June 2015													
1837, Proof	8–12	7	64.0								$30,000		
Auctions: $27,025, PF-63BN, January 2014													
1838	6,370,200	1,037	53.0	50%	$27	$35	$50	$65	$120	$225	$335	$575	$1,325
Auctions: $1,028, MS-64BN, January 2015; $470, MS-63BN, January 2015; $223, AU-58, August 2015; $223, AU-55, May 2015													
1838, Proof	10–20	5	64.4								$14,000	$20,000	$38,000
Auctions: $64,625, PF-64RD, January 2014													
1839, All kinds	3,128,661												
1839, 1839 Over 1836, Plain Cords		67	13.0	0%	$600	$1,000	$2,500	$4,500	$9,000	$22,500	$60,000	$100,000	$225,000
Auctions: $5,581, VF-35, January 2014; $881, F-12, August 2016; $588, VG-10, September 2016; $564, VG-8, February 2018													
1839, Head of 1838, Beaded Cords		123	50.4	37%	$40	$50	$75	$125	$200	$350	$450	$650	$1,450
Auctions: $1,645, MS-64BN, September 2013; $176, EF-45, February 2015; $141, EF-45, July 2015; $143, VF-35, September 2015													
1839, Silly Head		152	49.1	40%	$40	$50	$75	$125	$275	$550	$800	$1,500	$2,700
Auctions: $12,925, MS-67BN, January 2014; $160, EF-40, July 2015; $1,800, MS-63BN, 2018													
1839, Booby Head		264	49.8	41%	$30	$50	$75	$125	$350	$500	$950	$1,600	$2,800
Auctions: $470, AU-53, August 2015; $329, EF-40, May 2015; $141, VF-35, June 2015; $660, MS-61BN, February 2018													

BRAIDED HAIR (1839–1857)

Designer: *Christian Gobrecht.* **Weight:** *10.89 grams.* **Composition:** *Copper.*
Diameter: *27.5 mm.* **Edge:** *Plain.* **Mint:** *Philadelphia.*

Circulation Strike	**Proof**
1845; N-11.	*1852; N-24.*

History. Christian Gobrecht's Braided Hair design was introduced in 1839. It loosely followed the design he had created for the 1838 gold eagle. On issues of 1839 through part of 1843, Miss Liberty's portrait is tilted forward, with the left tip of her neck truncation over the 8 of the date. For most issues of 1843 and all later dates her head is larger and aligned in a more vertical position, and the tip of her neck is over the first digit of the date. The reverse lettering was made larger beginning in 1844. The net result is that cents after 1843 are less delicate in appearance than are those of earlier dates. These coins were made in large quantities, except for their final year. They remained in circulation in the United States until the late 1850s, not long enough to be worn down to very low grades. (Some circulated in the eastern part of Canada through the 1860s, accounting for many of the more worn examples seen today.)

Striking and Sharpness. Sharpness can vary. On the obverse, the star centers can be weak, especially for dates in the 1850s, and, less often, there can be lightness on the front of the coronet and the hair. On the reverse the leaves can be light, but most are well struck. The denticles can be mushy and indistinct on either side, this being particularly true of dates in the early and mid-1850s. Flaky or laminated planchets can be a problem, again among coins of the 1850s, in which tiny pieces of metal fall away from the surface, leaving areas in the field that interrupt the luster on MS coins.

Availability. All dates of Braided Hair cents are readily available, with the 1857 somewhat less so (it was minted in January 1857 in low quantity; seemingly not all were released). The delicate-featured issues of 1839 to 1843 are becoming more difficult to find in EF or finer grades without surface problems. Cents dated in the 1850s are usually seen in VF or higher grades. Certain die varieties attributed by Newcomb numbers can be scarce or rare. For issues in the 1850s the differences can be microscopic, thus limiting their numismatic appeal and making them unattributable unless in high grades. Hoards were found of some dates, particularly 1850 to 1856, making MS coins of these years more readily available than would otherwise be the case. MS-64RD or higher coins with *original* color range from scarce to very rare for dates prior to 1850, but those of the 1850s are seen regularly (except for 1857). Coins below VF-20 are not widely collected and, for many issues, are too worn to attribute by die variety.

GRADING STANDARDS

MS-60 to 70 (Mint State). *Obverse:* In the lower Mint State grades, MS–60 and 61, some slight abrasions can be seen on the portrait, most evidently on the cheek. Check the tip of the coronet and the hair above the ear, as well. Luster in the field is complete or nearly so. At MS-63, luster should be complete, and no abrasion evident. If there is weakness on the hair it is due to light striking, not to wear; this also applies for the stars. In

1840, Large Date; N-7. Graded MS-64BN.

higher levels, the luster is complete and deeper, and some original mint color may be seen. Mint frost on this type is usually deep, sometimes satiny, but hardly ever prooflike. MS-64 coins may have some slight discoloration or scattered contact marks. A well-graded MS-65 or higher coin will have full, rich luster; no marks visible except under magnification; and a nice blend of brown toning or nicely mixed (not stained or blotchy) mint color and natural brown toning. MS-64RD or higher coins with original color range from scarce to very rare for dates prior to 1850, but those of the 1850s are seen regularly (except for 1857). *Reverse:* In the lower Mint State grades some abrasion is seen on the higher areas of the leaves. Mint luster is complete in all Mint State ranges, as the open areas are protected by the lettering and wreath. The quality of the luster is the best way to grade both sides of this type.

Illustrated coin: This coin is a light, golden olive with faint tints of pale green in places, with scattered red spotting on both the obverse and reverse. About half of the stars show their centers, but all of the stars are soft.

AU-50, 53, 55, 58 (About Uncirculated). *Obverse:* Wear is evident on the cheek, the hair above the ear, and the tip of the coronet. Friction is evident in the field. At AU-58, luster may be present except in the center of the fields. As the grade goes down to AU-50, wear becomes more evident on the cheek. Wear is seen on the stars, but is not as easy to discern as it is elsewhere and, in any event, many stars are weakly struck. At AU-50 there

1840, Large Date; N-8. Graded AU-58.

will be either no luster or only traces of luster close to the letters and devices. *Reverse:* Wear is most evident on the highest areas of the leaves and the ribbon bow. Luster is present in the fields. As grade goes down from AU–58 to 50, wear increases and luster decreases. At AU-50 there will be either no luster or just traces close to the letters and devices.

EF-40, 45 (Extremely Fine). *Obverse:* Wear is more extensive on the portrait, including the cheek, the hair above the ear, and the coronet. The star centers are worn down slightly (if they were sharply struck to begin with). Traces of luster are minimal, if at all existent. *Reverse:* The centers of the leaves are well worn, with detail visible only near the edges of the leaves and nearby, with the higher parts worn flat. Letters show significant wear. Luster, if present, is minimal.

1842, Large Date; N-6. Graded EF-45.

VF-20, 30 (Very Fine). *Obverse:* Wear is more extensive than on the preceding. Some of the strands of hair are fused together at the top of the head, above the ear, and on the shoulder. The center radials of the stars are nearly completely worn away. *Reverse:* The leaves show more extensive wear. Details are visible at the leaves' edges only minimally and not on all the leaves. The lettering shows smooth, even wear.

1842, Large Date; N-6. Graded VF-30.

F-12, 15 (Fine). *Obverse:* About two-thirds of the hair detail is visible. Extensive wear is seen below the coronet. On the coronet the beginning of the word LIBERTY shows wear, with L sometimes only partially visible. The hair behind the neck is flat. The stars are flat. *Reverse:* The leaves show more wear and are flat except for the lower areas. The ribbon has very little detail.

Braided Hair large cents are seldom collected in grades lower than F-12.

1839, 9 Over 6; N-1. Graded F-12.

PF-60 to 70 (Proof). Except for the Proof 1841 cent, Proof Braided Hair cents before 1855 range from rare to very rare. Those from 1855 to 1857 are seen with some frequency. Most later Proofs are well struck and of nice quality, but there are exceptions. Most pieces from this era that have been attributed as Proofs really are such, but beware of deeply toned "Proofs" that are actually prooflike, or circulation strikes with polished fields, and

1841, Small Date; N-1. Graded PF-64RB.

recolored. *Obverse and Reverse:* Superb gems PF–65 and 66 show hairlines only under high magnification, and at PF-67 none are seen. The fields usually are deeply mirrorlike on issues after 1843, sometimes less so on earlier dates of this type. Striking should be sharp, including the stars (unlike the situation for many Proofs of the Matron Head type). There is no evidence of friction. In lower grades, hairlines are more numerous, with a profusion of them at the PF–60 to 62 levels, and there is also a general dullness of the fields. Typical color for an undipped coin ranges from light or iridescent brown to brown with some traces of mint color. Except for issues after 1854, Proofs are nearly always BN or, less often, RB. Prooflike pieces are sometimes offered as Proofs. Beware deeply toned "Proofs" and those that do not have full mirrorlike fields.

Illustrated coin: Early Proofs from this period are scarce to extremely rare. This example retains some mint orange in protected areas, as well as exhibiting hints of lilac and electric blue on the obverse.

1840, Large Date

Small Letters (1839–1843)   **Large Letters (1843–1857)**   **1840, Small Date**

1840, Small Date Over Large 18   **1842, Small Date**   **1842, Large Date**

	Mintage	Cert	Avg	%MS	G-4	VG-8	F-12	VF-20	EF-40	AU-50	MS-60BN PF-63BN	MS-63BN PF-64BN	MS-65BN PF-65BN
1839	(a)	91	49.0	40%	$35	$50	$80	$110	$225	$440	$800	$1,600	$5,500 (b)
Auctions: $17,625, MS-65RB, January 2014; $1,293, MS-63BN, January 2015; $176, EF-40, May 2015; $360, AU-50, January 2018
1840, All kinds	2,462,700												
1840, Large Date		118	54.4	47%	$25	$35	$40	$60	$110	$250	$600	$1,150	$3,200
Auctions: $14,100, MS-64RD, January 2013
1840, Small Date		137	46.3	31%	$25	$35	$40	$60	$110	$250	$600	$1,150	$2,300
Auctions: $541, MS-61BN, August 2015; $259, MS-60, October 2015; $400, AU-58, February 2015
1840, Small Date Over Large 18		15	40.9	33%	$50	$125	$175	$250	$600	$1,250	$1,850	$2,500	$4,000
Auctions: $16,100, MS-65RB, September 2011
1840, Proof	15–20	6	64.2								$7,000	$10,500	$20,000
Auctions: $14,100, PF-63RB, January 2014
1841, Small Date	1,597,367	195	50.0	39%	$30	$50	$125	$175	$350	$700	$1,500	$2,500	$4,000 (c)
Auctions: $4,113, MS-66BN, June 2014
1841, Proof	30–50	20	64.3								$6,000	$9,500	$18,500
Auctions: $21,150, PF-65RB, August 2013
1842, All kinds	2,383,390												
1842, Small Date		61	47.9	36%	$25	$35	$60	$100	$150	$250	$1,850	$2,500	$3,500 (d)
Auctions: $23,500, MS-64RD, January 2014
1842, Large Date		184	48.6	40%	$25	$35	$60	$100	$150	$250	$750	$1,850	$3,500 (e)
Auctions: $1,175, MS-63BN, August 2015; $881, MS-63BN, June 2015; $259, AU-55, April 2015; $188, AU-55, June 2015
1842, Proof	10–20	5	64.2								$7,000	$11,000	$20,000
Auctions: $14,100, PF-64BN, January 2014

a. Included in 1839, All kinds, mintage figure on page 244. **b.** Value in MS-65RB is $8,000. **c.** Value in MS-65RB is $4,500. **d.** Value in MS-65RB is $4,000. **e.** Value in MS-65RB is $4,000.

1844, 44 Over 81

Head of 1840
("Petite Head," 1839–1843)

Head of 1844
("Mature Head," 1843–1857)

1847, 7 Over "Small 7"

1846, Small Date
Note the squat date and the closed 6.

1846, Medium Date
Note the medium date height and the ball-top 6.

1846, Tall Date
Note the vertically stretched date and the open-mouthed 6.

1851, 51 Over 81
These are not true overdates, but are three of the more spectacular of several date-punch blunders of the 1844–1854 period. The so-called overdates of 1844 and 1851 each have the date punched upside down, then corrected normally.

1855, Upright 5's

1855, Slanting 5's

1855, Knob on Ear

	Mintage	Cert	Avg	%MS	G-4	VG-8	F-12	VF-20	EF-40	AU-50	MS-60BN PF-63BN	MS-63BN PF-64BN	MS-65BN PF-65BN
1843, All kinds	2,425,342												
1843, Petite Head, Small Letters		200	52.0	52%	$25	$35	$60	$100	$150	$250	$750	$2,000	$3,500
Auctions: $1,293, MS-63BN, January 2015; $588, MS-63BN, August 2015; $494, AU-58, August 2015; $376, AU-58, August 2015													
1843, Petite Head, Large Letters		64	53.0	48%	$25	$35	$60	$100	$250	$350	$850	$1,650	$2,300
Auctions: $4,406, MS-64BN, January 2014													
1843, Mature Head, Large Letters		67	45.4	34%	$25	$35	$60	$80	$150	$275	$750	$1,750	$2,500
Auctions: $9,988, MS-64RB, January 2014													
1843, Proof	10–20	8	64.5								$7,000	$11,000	$20,000
Auctions: $25,850, PF-66RB, June 2014													
1844, Normal Date	2,398,752	250	48.8	38%	$25	$35	$60	$80	$150	$250	$600	$1,250	$2,500
Auctions: $8,225, MS-65BN, January 2014; $940, MS-62BN, June 2015; $141, AU-53, January 2015													
1844, 44 Over 81	(f)	47	41.4	21%	$75	$125	$165	$250	$550	$900	$3,000	$4,500	$7,500
Auctions: $1,175, MS-60BN, January 2014; $705, AU-50, September 2016; $212, VF-25, August 2015													
1844, Proof	10–20	7	64.6								$13,000	$20,000	$30,000
Auctions: $55,813, PF-65RD, January 2014; $31,725, PF-64, May 2015													
1845	3,894,804	424	51.9	48%	$25	$35	$40	$60	$150	$250	$500	$1,250	$2,500
Auctions: $881, MS-64BN, January 2015; $423, MS-63BN, March 2015; $353, MS-62BN, May 2015; $176, AU-53, January 2015													
1845, Proof	8–12	5	63.8								$8,000	$15,000	$25,000
Auctions: $16,450, PF-64BN, April 2013													

f. Included in 1844, Normal Date, mintage figure.

	Mintage	Cert	Avg	%MS	G-4	VG-8	F-12	VF-20	EF-40	AU-50	MS-60BN / PF-63BN	MS-63BN / PF-64BN	MS-65BN / PF-65BN
1846, All kinds	4,120,800												
1846, Small Date		361	50.7	48%	$25	$35	$40	$60	$125	$350	$850	$1,200	$2,500
	Auctions: $494, MS-64BN, February 2015; $329, MS-62BN, February 2015; $129, AU-53, February 2015; $119, AU-50, April 2015												
1846, Medium Date		55	49.9	42%	$25	$50	$100	$150	$275	$500	$700	$1,000	$2,500
	Auctions: $705, MS-61BN, March 2013												
1846, Tall Date		76	45.2	32%	$25	$50	$75	$100	$150	$250	$650	$1,000	$2,000
	Auctions: $56, VF-30, September 2011												
1846, Proof	*8–12*	2	66.0								$8,000	$15,000	$25,000
	Auctions: $30,550, PF-65BN, June 2014												
1847	6,183,669	944	53.5	52%	$25	$35	$50	$75	$100	$175	$350	$750	$2,000
	Auctions: $646, MS-64BN, August 2015; $881, MS-63BN, August 2015; $188, MS-62BN, June 2015; $223, MS-61BN, September 2015												
1847, 7 Over "Small 7"	(g)	24	42.7	25%	$50	$100	$175	$250	$500	$850	$2,000	$2,800	$7,000
	Auctions: $9,694, MS-65BN, January 2014												
1847, Proof	*8–12*	1	64.0								$8,000	$15,000	$25,000
	Auctions: $31,050, PF-65RB, February 2011												
1848	6,415,799	963	52.4	47%	$25	$35	$40	$60	$95	$150	$300	$450	$1,750
	Auctions: $1,175, MS-65BN, January 2015; $223, MS-62BN, January 2015; $259, AU-58, January 2015; $129, AU-55, October 2015												
1848, Proof	*15–20*	9	64.8								$10,000	$15,000	$25,000
	Auctions: $14,100, PF-64BN, August 2013												
1849	4,178,500	523	53.1	47%	$25	$35	$40	$60	$95	$150	$250	$450	$1,750
	Auctions: $317, MS-62, March 2015; $259, AU-58, October 2015; $353, AU-50, July 2015; $84, EF-40, May 2015												
1849, Proof	*6–10*	5	64.4								$8,500	$16,000	$25,000
	Auctions: $23,500, PF-65RB, August 2013												
1850	4,426,844	1,147	57.9	70%	$25	$35	$40	$60	$95	$150	$250	$450	$1,750 (h)
	Auctions: $1,058, MS-65BN, January 2015; $376, MS-64BN, January 2015; $286, MS-63BN, February 2015; $259, AU-58, June 2015												
1850, Proof	*6–10*	3	65.0								$10,000	$20,000	$30,000
	Auctions: $19,550, PF-64RB, February 2011												
1851, Normal Date	9,889,707	1,680	56.2	61%	$25	$35	$40	$60	$95	$150	$250	$450	$1,750 (h)
	Auctions: $1,058, MS-65BN, August 2015; $411, MS-64BN, May 2015; $306, MS-64BN, October 2015; $100, AU-50, April 2015												
1851, 51 Over 81	(i)	96	56.8	63%	$40	$95	$150	$250	$450	$650	$850	$1,500	$3,500
	Auctions: $1,763, MS-65BN, June 2014; $329, AU-55, May 2015												
1852	5,063,094	1,513	58.4	67%	$25	$35	$40	$60	$95	$150	$225	$450	$1,750 (j)
	Auctions: $881, MS-65BN, October 2015; $764, MS-65BN, January 2015; $353, MS-64BN, January 2015; $129, AU-55, February 2015												
1852, Proof	*4–6*	1	65.0									$45,000	$75,000
	Auctions: $47,150, PF-64BN, February 2011; $9,528, PF-64, November 2016; $12,925, PF-62, March 2016												
1853	6,641,131	2,429	57.7	65%	$25	$35	$40	$60	$95	$150	$225	$450	$1,750 (j)
	Auctions: $2,115, MS-65RD, January 2015; $588, MS-64RB, January 2015; $235, MS-63BN, January 2015; $212, MS-62BN, June 2015												
1854	4,236,156	1,344	57.0	59%	$25	$35	$40	$60	$95	$150	$225	$450	$1,750 (j)
	Auctions: $360, MS-64BN, October 2015; $282, MS-63BN, May 2015; $212, MS-62BN, January 2015; $141, AU-58, January 2015												
1854, Proof	*4–6*	5	64.6								$8,500	$10,000	$15,000
	Auctions: $28,200, PF-65RB, June 2014												
1855, All kinds	1,574,829												
1855, Upright 5's		503	56.3	56%	$25	$40	$60	$95	$125	$175	$275	$500	$2,250 (k)
	Auctions: $1,116, MS-65RB, January 2015; $400, MS-64BN, June 2015; $282, MS-63BN, July 2015; $200, MS-62BN, January 2015												
1855, Slanting 5's		305	55.3	44%	$25	$40	$60	$95	$125	$175	$275	$500	$2,250 (k)
	Auctions: $353, MS-62BN, November 2015; $200, MS-61BN, June 2015; $141, MS-60, January 2015; $153, AU-53, June 2015												
1855, Slanting 5's, Knob on Ear		170	54.4	38%	$50	$100	$125	$200	$300	$450	$700	$1,250	$3,000
	Auctions: $259, AU-50, July 2015; $153, EF-45, September 2015; $100, EF-40, August 2015												
1855, Proof	*15–20*	10	64.5								$5,500	$7,000	$10,000
	Auctions: $8,050, PF-64RB August 2011												

g. Included in 1847 mintage figure. **h.** Value in MS-65RB is $2,250. **i.** Included in 1851, Normal Date, mintage figure. **j.** Value in MS-65RB is $2,000. **k.** Value in MS-65RB is $3,000.

| **1856, Upright 5** | **1856, Slanting 5** | **1857, Large Date** | **1857, Small Date** |

	Mintage	Cert	Avg	%MS	G-4	VG-8	F-12	VF-20	EF-40	AU-50	MS-60BN / PF-63BN	MS-63BN / PF-64BN	MS-65BN / PF-65BN
1856, All kinds	2,690,463												
1856, Upright 5		321	57.0	55%	$25	$35	$60	$95	$125	$150	$275	$350	$850 (I)
	Auctions: $725, MS-65BN, January 2015; $705, MS-64RB, January 2015; $482, MS-64BN, January 2015; $165, AU-58, September 2015												
1856, Slanting 5		498	55.4	52%	$25	$35	$60	$95	$125	$150	$275	$350	$850 (I)
	Auctions: $999, MS-66BN, June 2015; $764, MS-65BN, February 2015; $259, MS-63BN, February 2015; $223, MS-62BN, February 2015												
1856, Proof	*40–60*	20	64.7								$5,000	$7,000	$10,000
	Auctions: $25,850, PF-66RB, November 2013												
1857, All kinds	333,546												
1857, Large Date		694	56.3	54%	$150	$250	$325	$475	$550	$650	$800	$1,500	$3,000
	Auctions: $823, MS-64BN, January 2015; $558, MS-62, March 2015; $141, AU-50, July 2015; $223, EF-45, October 2015												
1857, Small Date		320	53.7	37%	$150	$250	$325	$475	$550	$600	$750	$1,250	$3,000
	Auctions: $940, MS-64BN, January 2015; $646, MS-63BN, August 2015; $494, MS-62BN, January 2015; $353, AU-55, September 2015												
1857, Small Date, Proof	*15–20*	8	65.1								$5,000	$7,000	$10,000
	Auctions: $52,875, PF-65RD, April 2014												

Note: Numismatic anachronisms dated 1868 were struck in nickel and in copper, featuring the large cent design last used in 1857. These likely were quietly and unofficially sold by Mint employees to collectors. They are classified as Judd-610 and 611 in *United States Pattern Coins* (10th edition). **I.** Value in MS-65RB is $1,750.

THE PASSING OF THE LARGE CENT AND HALF CENT

By 1857 the U.S. Mint's costs for manufacturing and distributing its half cents and large cents had risen so high that Mint Director James Ross Snowden reported that the copper coins "barely paid expenses." Both denominations had become unpopular, and they rarely circulated outside the nation's larger cities. With this pressure, change was on the horizon. The Treasury Department had recent precedent to tinker with coinage sizes and compositions. For several years in the early 1850s the Mint had issued silver coins of reduced weight, as a way to discourage their melting and export (the coins' silver content had been greater than their face values). On the heels of this coinage reform, new legislation in 1857 replaced the large copper cent with a smaller copper-nickel coin of the same value, and terminated the half cent outright.

The coinage legislation of 1857 brought important benefits to the United States. Under its terms, Spanish coins were redeemed for melting at the Mint and exchanged for the new, small cents. The old-fashioned reckoning of business transactions in Spanish *reales* and *medios*, British shillings, and other currencies was (officially, at least) abandoned, and the American decimal system was popularized. Citizens found the new small cent to be convenient, and it quickly became a favored and useful means of retail trade. Tens of millions would be minted before the decade closed.

The hobby of coin collecting experienced a boom when the large cent and half cent passed away. Casual observers set aside the obsolete coins as mementoes of a time gone by, while more experienced collectors sought to assemble collections composed of one of each date. Over the ensuing decades the study and collecting of these old coppers has become more and more specialized while still attracting hobby newcomers. Their devoted enthusiasts appreciate the coins' historical connections and cultural significance.

Small Cents
1856 to Date

AN OVERVIEW OF SMALL CENTS

On May 25, 1857, the U.S. Mint debuted its new small-diameter Flying Eagle cent. Designed by Chief Engraver James B. Longacre, the obverse featured a flying eagle, copied after Christian Gobrecht's silver dollar of 1836. The reverse showed an agricultural wreath enclosing the denomination. Problems developed with striking the pieces up properly, and in 1859 a new type, the Indian Head cent, was introduced. With several variations this design was continued through 1909. In that year the Lincoln cent with Wheat Ears reverse was introduced. The series was continued for many years, until 1959, when the Memorial Reverse type was introduced, continuing the same Lincoln portrait on the obverse. Then in 2009 four different reverses were introduced to commemorate the 200th anniversary of the birth of Abraham Lincoln. In 2010 a new reverse symbolized President Lincoln's preservation of the Union.

Forming a type set of small cents is done easily enough, although the first two issues, the 1857 and 1858 Flying Eagles, as well as the 1859 Indian Head with laurel wreath reverse, can be expensive in higher grades. Striking quality is a consideration for all small cents from 1857 to the end of the Indian Head series in 1909, but enough exist that finding a needle-sharp piece is simply a matter of time. Lincoln cents are easy enough to find sharply struck, though some varieties are more difficult to find this way than others.

FOR THE COLLECTOR AND INVESTOR:
SMALL CENTS AS A SPECIALTY

Flying Eagle and Indian Head cents often are collected together by specialists, who usually aspire to add the pattern 1856 Flying Eagle to the series. Proof Flying Eagle and Indian Head cents form a separate specialty and are widely collected. The Flying Eagle and Indian Cent Collectors Society (www.fly-inclub.org) welcomes aficionados of these series. Its journal, *Longacre's Ledger*, serves as a forum for new discoveries, market information, and the exchange of ideas and research.

One of the foundations of modern American numismatics is the collecting of Lincoln cents, 1909 to date. Collectors have a wide variety of folders, albums, and holders to choose from; these have a tradition dating back to the

This 1857 pattern small cent (J-186) features a proposed head of Liberty, similar to the design that would eventually be used on the nation's nickel three-cent pieces.

1930s, when R.K. Post of Neenah, Wisconsin, launched his "penny boards" (made for him by Whitman Publishing Co., which later acquired the rights), and Wayte Raymond marketed a series of "National" album pages. Today, a search through pocket change might yield coins dating back to 1959, the first year of the Lincoln Memorial reverse, before which date even high-mintage issues are hardly ever seen. A generation ago it was possible to find cents from 1909 onward. However, key issues such as 1909-S V.D.B. (the most famous of all "popular rarities" in the U.S. series), 1914-D, 1924-D, 1926-S, 1931-S, and 1955 Doubled Die Obverse eluded most enthusiasts.

Lincoln cents can be collected casually, or a specialty can be made of them. A dedicated enthusiast may want to secure one each in a grade such as MS-65, also taking care that each is sharply struck. There are quite a few issues, including Denver and San Francisco varieties from about 1916 to the late 1920s, that are plentiful *except* if sharply struck (with full hair detail on the Lincoln portrait, no tiny marks on Lincoln's shoulder, and sharp details and a smooth field on the reverse). Die-variety specialists have dozens of popular doubled dies, overmintmarks, and other varieties to hunt down, using the *Cherrypickers' Guide* as their standard reference. With the Mint's rollout of four new reverse designs in 2009, and another in 2010, the Lincoln cent promises to intrigue another generation of Americans and continue to bring new collectors to the hobby.

FLYING EAGLE (1856–1858)

Designer: *James B. Longacre.* **Weight:** *4.67 grams.* **Composition:** *.880 copper, .120 nickel.*
Diameter: *19 mm.* **Edge:** *Plain.* **Mint:** *Philadelphia.*

Circulation Strike   **Proof**

History. The nation's large copper cents became increasingly expensive to produce, leading the U.S. Mint to experiment with smaller versions during the 1850s. Finally a new design and format were chosen: the Flying Eagle cent, of smaller diameter and 4.67 grams' weight (compared to nearly 11). Many patterns were made of this design in 1856 (for distribution to interested congressmen), and later restrikes (bearing that same date) were extensive, with the result that many numismatists collect the 1856 cent along with the regular series. Distribution of the new 1857 Flying Eagle cents for circulation commenced on May 25 of that year. Problems resulted from striking the design properly, and the motif was discontinued in 1858. Although attempts were made to create a modified, thinner eagle, the unattractive results were scrapped in favor of an entirely new design. The coins remained in circulation until the early 1900s, by which time any found in pocket change were well worn.

Striking and Sharpness. The heavy wreath on the reverse was opposite in the dies (while in the press) from the head and tail of the eagle on the obverse, and, accordingly, many Flying Eagle cents were weakly struck in these areas. Today, this lightness of strike is most visible at each end of the eagle and on the wreath, particularly the higher areas, and on the vertical separation at the middle of the ribbon knot. Striking weakness is most obvious (especially for novice collectors) on the eagle's tail feathers. Many Flying Eagle cents, however, are quite well struck. A first-class Proof should have a fully and deeply mirrored field on both sides, except for those of 1856, which are usually a combination of mirror-like and grainy in character.

Availability. As a type the Flying Eagle cent is easy to find, although some varieties, such as 1856 and 1858, 8 Over 7, range from scarce to rare. Most are seen in worn grades. In MS, many are in the marketplace, although dipping, cleaning, and recoloring (causing staining and spotting) have eliminated the majority from consideration by connoisseurs. Proof Flying Eagle cents dated 1856 are plentiful, surviving from the quantity of perhaps 2,000 to 2,500 or more restruck in 1859 and later. (Today's collectors do not distinguish, price-wise, between the 1856 originals and restrikes dated 1856.) Proofs of 1857 are very rare. Proofs of 1858 are rare, but are significantly more readily available than for 1857. Some prooflike Mint State coins have been called Proofs. Quality is a challenge for Proofs, and problem-free examples are in the minority.

GRADING STANDARDS

Caveat: These grading standards do not take sharpness of strike into account.

MS-60 to 70 (Mint State). *Obverse:* Contact marks, most obvious in the field, are evident at MS-60, diminishing at MS-61, 62, and higher. The eagle, the feathers of which usually hide marks, shows some evidence of contact as well. At Gem MS-65 or finer there is no trace of friction or rubbing. A few tiny nicks or marks may be seen, but none are obvious. At MS-67 and higher levels the coin will approach perfection. A theoretically perfect MS-70 will

1858; Snow-11. Graded MS-64.

have no marks at all evident, even under a strong magnifier. Although in practice this is not always consistent, at MS-66 and higher there should be no staining or other problems, and the coin should have good eye appeal overall. *Reverse:* Check the higher parts of the wreath for slight abrasions at MS–60 to 62. Otherwise, the above guidelines apply.

    Illustrated coin: The surfaces display a healthy satin luster, as well as an iridescent rose and golden-tan patina. The coin is sharply and evenly struck and offers razor-sharp definition.

AU-50, 53, 55, 58 (About Uncirculated). *Obverse:* At AU-50, light wear is seen on the breast of the eagle, the top edge of the closest wing, and, less so, on the head. As both the head and tail tip can be lightly struck, these are not reliable indicators of grade. Luster is present in traces among the letters. At higher About Uncirculated levels the evidence of wear diminishes. An AU-58 coin will have nearly full luster, but friction is seen in the fields, as

1858. Graded AU-53.

are some marks. *Reverse:* At AU-50, light wear is seen on the ribbon bow and the highest areas of the leaves. Some luster is seen (more than on the obverse). Friction is evident, as are some marks, but these will not be as distracting as those on the obverse, as the heavy wreath and lettering are more protective of the reverse field. In higher grades, wear is less, and at AU-58 nearly full luster—or even completely full luster—is seen.

    Illustrated coin: The reverse features a large rim cud.

EF-40, 45 (Extremely Fine). *Obverse:* Wear is more extensive, especially on the eagle's breast and the top of the closest wing. Wear will also show on the other wing in the area below OF. Marks may be more extensive in the field. The wear is slightly greater at EF-40 than at EF-45, although in the marketplace these two grades are not clearly differentiated. *Reverse:* More wear shows on the higher areas of the wreath, but most detail

1858, Small Letters. Graded EF-40.

will still be present. There may be tinges of luster in protected areas, more likely at EF-45 than at EF-40.

VF-20, 30 (Very Fine). *Obverse:* Wear is appreciable, with the breast feathers gone over a larger area and with more wear on the wings. The tail shows significant wear, negating the question as to whether it was well struck originally. Marks are more extensive, although across all grades the durable copper-nickel metal resisted heavy marks and cuts; any such should be separately described. Staining and spotting, not related to grade, is

1858, Small Letters. Graded VF-20.

common. Cherrypicking (examining multiple coins, all slabbed at the same grade level, and selecting the finest of them) at this and lower grades will yield nice coins in any given category. *Reverse:* The wreath is worn flat in the higher and medium–relief areas, although some detail is seen in the lower areas close to the field. ONE / CENT may be slightly weak, depending on the quality of the original strike. Marks are fewer than on the obverse.

F-12, 15 (Fine). *Obverse:* The eagle shows extensive wear, with about half of the feathers gone. Some detail is still seen, especially on the underside of the closest wing, above the breast. *Reverse:* Wear is even more extensive, with the wreath nearing flatness, but still with some detail in the lower areas.

1857. Graded F-12.

VG-8, 10 (Very Good). *Obverse:* On the obverse the eagle is clear in outline form, but only a small number of feathers can be discerned, mostly above the breast. Letters and the date show extensive wear but are complete and clear. *Reverse:* The wreath is now mostly an outline, although some lower-relief features can be differentiated. ONE / CENT may be weak (depending on the strike).

1858, Small Letters. Graded VG-10.

G-4, 6 (Good). *Obverse:* The eagle is nearly completely flat, with just a few feathers, if any, discernible. The rim is worn down, making the outer parts of the letters and the lower part of the date slightly weak, but all are readable. *Reverse:* The wreath is basically in outline form, with hardly any detail. ONE / CENT is weak, usually with CENT weakest. The rim is worn down.

1857. Graded G-4.

AG-3 (About Good). *Obverse:* Wear is extensive, but most of the eagle is visible in outline form. The letters are mostly worn away, with vestiges remaining here and there. The date is partially worn away at the bottom, but is distinct and readable. *Reverse:* The wreath is so worn that it cannot be distinguished from the field in areas, usually toward the top. ONE / CENT is mostly gone, but much of CENT can be discerned (unless the coin was a weak strike to begin with).

1857. Graded AG-3.

PF-60 to 70 (Proof). *Obverse and Reverse:* Gem PF-65 coins have very few hairlines, and these are visible only under a strong magnifying glass. At the PF-67 level or higher there should be no evidence of hairlines or friction at all. PF-60 coins can be dull from repeated dipping and cleaning (remember, hairlines on any Proof were caused by cleaning with an abrasive agent; they had no hairlines when struck). At PF-63 the mirrorlike fields should be attractive, and hairlines should be minimal, best seen when the coin is held at an angle to the light. No rubbing is seen. PF-64 coins are even nicer.

1858, Large Letters. Graded PF-65.

Illustrated coin: The fields of this coin are highly reflective for a nickel-alloy Proof cent.

1857, Reverse 25¢ Clash
FS-01-1857-901.

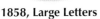

1857, Obverse $20 Clash
FS-01-1857-403.

1858, Large Letters

1858, Small Letters

1858, 8 Over 7
FS-01-1858-301.

	Mintage	Cert	Avg	%MS	G-4	VG-8	F-12	VF-20	EF-40	AU-50	MS-60BN	MS-63BN	MS-65
											PF-60	PF-63BN	PF-65BN
1856 † (a)	2,000	0	n/a		$7,000	$7,750	$9,750	$11,500	$13,000	$14,000	$15,500	$22,500	$65,000
Auctions: $32,900, MS-64, April 2013													
1856, Proof	*1,000–1,500* **(b)**	501	57.1								$14,000	$16,000	$32,500
Auctions: $37,691, PF-66, March 2011; $15,275, PF-64, August 2016; $11,750, PF-62, March 2016													
1857	*17,450,000*	4,587	50.2	52%	$25	$40	$50	$60	$140	$215	$475	$1,000	$3,000
Auctions: $21,150, MS-66, June 2014; $4,113, MS-65, November 2014; $2,468, MS-64+, November 2014													
1857, Obverse 50¢ Clash (c)	**(d)**	147	33.1	24%					$225	$450	$800	$1,250	$3,500
Auctions: $3,525, MS-65, October 2014; $5,816, MS-65, October 2013													
1857, Reverse 25¢ Clash ‡‡ (e)	**(d)**	48	44.0	31%					$250	$500	$1,000	$2,750	$8,500
Auctions: $223, EF-40, July 2014													
1857, Obverse $20 Clash (f)	**(d)**	21	18.4	0%					$2,500	$6,000	$20,000		
Auctions: $242, F-12, March 2011													
1857, Proof	*100*	33	63.9								$5,000	$8,000	$25,000
Auctions: $34,075, PF-65, October 2014; $8,813, PF-64, October 2014; $34,075, PF, January 2013													
1858, All kinds	*24,600,000*												
1858, Large Letters		1,968	46.6	42%	$25	$40	$50	$60	$140	$215	$450	$1,000	$3,000
Auctions: $9,988, MS-66, October 2014; $17,625, MS-66, June 2013; $3,290, MS-65, November 2014; $1,645, MS-64, October 2014													
1858, 8 Over 7 (g)		175	52.2	49%	$85	$115	$185	$400	$800	$1,350	$3,850	$11,000	$50,000
Auctions: $74,025, MS-65, October 2014; $764, AU-55, July 2014; $940, AU-50, January 2015; $504, EF-40, January 2018													
1858, Small Letters		2,180	44.9	36%	$25	$40	$50	$60	$150	$250	$550	$1,150	$3,500
Auctions: $24,675, MS-66, October 2014; $16,450, MS-66, August 2013; $3,525, MS-65, August 2014; $2,233													
1858, Large Letters, Proof	*100*	35	64.7								$5,000	$8,000	$23,500
Auctions: $20,563, PF-65, October 2014; $8,225, PF-64, October 2014; $28,200, PF, January 2013; $36,000, PF-66, January 2018													
1858, Small Letters, Proof	*200*	26	64.2								$5,000	$8,000	$20,000
Auctions: $32,900, PF-66, January 2014; $14,100, PF-64, October 2014; $7,638, PF-64, October 2014; $7,200, PF-64, February 2018													

† Ranked in the *100 Greatest U.S. Coins* (fifth edition). ‡‡ Ranked in the *100 Greatest U.S. Error Coins*. **a.** Actually a pattern, but collected along with the regular issue since it shares the same design. See *United States Pattern Coins* (10th edition). **b.** Most of those seen are Proofs; a small number have been designated circulation strikes. **c.** The obverse die was clashed with the obverse die of a Liberty Seated half dollar. This is most evident through AMERICA. **d.** Included in circulation-strike 1857 mintage figure. **e.** The reverse die was clashed with the reverse die of a Liberty Seated quarter dollar. The outline of the eagle's head is evident above ONE. **f.** The obverse die was clashed with the obverse die of a Liberty Head double eagle. **g.** The flag of the upper-right corner of a 7 can be seen above the second 8 in the date. There is a raised triangular dot in the field above the first 8. Late-die-state specimens are worth considerably less than the values listed, which are for early die states.

INDIAN HEAD (1859–1909)

Variety 1 (Copper-Nickel, Laurel Wreath Reverse, 1859):
Designer: *James B. Longacre.* **Weight:** *4.67 grams.* **Composition:** *.880 copper, .120 nickel.*
Diameter: *19 mm.* **Edge:** *Plain.* **Mint:** *Philadelphia.*

Copper-Nickel,
Laurel Wreath Reverse,
Without Shield (1859)

Copper-Nickel,
Laurel Wreath Reverse,
Without Shield, Proof

Variety 2 (Copper-Nickel, Oak Wreath With Shield, 1860–1864):
Designer: *James B. Longacre.* **Weight:** *4.67 grams.* **Composition:** *.880 copper, .120 nickel.*
Diameter: *19 mm.* **Edge:** *Plain.* **Mint:** *Philadelphia.*

Copper-Nickel,
Oak Wreath Reverse,
With Shield (1860–1864)

Copper-Nickel,
Oak Wreath Reverse,
With Shield, Proof

Variety 3 (Bronze, 1864–1909): **Designer:** *James B. Longacre.*
Weight: *3.11 grams.* **Composition:** *.950 copper, .050 tin and zinc.*
Diameter: *19 mm.* **Edge:** *Plain.* **Mints:** *Philadelphia and San Francisco.*

Bronze, Oak Wreath Reverse,
With Shield (1864–1909)

Bronze, Oak Wreath Reverse,
With Shield, Proof

History. After nearly a dozen varieties of patterns were made in 1858, in 1859 the Indian Head was adopted as the new motif for the cent. Observers of the time noted the incongruity of placing a Native American war bonnet on a bust which was meant to be both female and classically Greek; designer James B. Longacre's earlier use of a feathered tiara on the Indian Head three-dollar gold piece had been viewed as less strange. The reverse of the 1859 coin illustrates an olive (or laurel) wreath. In 1860 this was changed to a wreath of oak and other leaves with a shield at the apex, a design continued through the end of the series in 1909. From 1859 through spring 1864 cents were struck in copper-nickel, the alloy used earlier for Flying Eagle cents. In 1864 a new bronze alloy was adopted.

Indian Head cents remained in circulation through the 1940s, but by the early 1950s were rarely seen. In the 1930s, when Whitman and other coin boards and folders became widely available, collectors picked many key dates out of circulation. The typical grade for the scarce issues of the 1870s was Good or so, and the 1908-S and 1909-S could be found in VF.

Striking and Sharpness. The strike on Indian Head cents can vary widely. On the obverse the points to check include the details at the tips of the feathers and the diamonds on the ribbon. The diamonds *cannot* be used as a grading marker, and the feather tips can be used only if you have familiarity with how sharp the coin was struck to begin with. In general, the reverse is usually sharper, but check the leaf and shield details. On many bronze cents beginning in the 1870s the bottom of the N of ONE and the tops of the EN of CENT are light, as they were in the dies (this is not factored when grading). Check the denticles on both sides. Generally, copper-nickel cents of the early 1860s are candidates for light striking as are later issues in the bronze format, of the 1890s onward.

Availability. In worn grades Indian Head cents are available in proportion to their mintages, in combination with survival rates being higher for the later issues. (The low-mintage 1909-S was saved in larger quantities than the higher-mintage 1877, as an example.) MS coins survive as a matter of chance, with those of 1878 and before being much scarcer than those of 1879 and later, and some of the 1900s being readily available. Many if not most higher-grade MS coins have been dipped or recolored, unless they are a warm orange-red color with traces of natural brown. The search for quality among bronze cents is particularly challenging. Some tiny toning flecks are to be expected on many coins, and as long as they are microscopic they can often be ignored (except in grades on the far side of MS-65). A set of MS-65 coins in RB or RD can be formed quickly, but a collection with *original* color, sharp strike, and excellent eye appeal may take several years.

During the years these coins were in production, collectors who wanted single pieces each year often bought Proofs. In the late 1930s, many 1878–1909 Proof Indian Head cents began to be released from several estate hoards. These had vivid violet and blue iridescent toning from being stored for decades in tissue paper. They are highly sought-after today.

Proofs. Proof Indian Head cents were made of all dates 1859 to 1909. The 1864 bronze variety with a tiny L (for designer James B. Longacre) on the ribbon is a rarity, with only about two dozen known. Generally, Proofs are sharp strikes until the 1890s, when some can be weak. On bronze coins tiny carbon flecks are typical, but should be microscopic. If larger, avoid, and at PF-65 or higher, avoid as well. The majority of Proofs have been dipped, and many bronze pieces have been retoned. Most undipped coins are either rich brown (can be very attractive) or red and brown. The late John J. Pittman spent 50 years trying to find a Gem Proof 1907 Indian Head cent with brilliant original color! Cherrypicking is the order of the day. Extra value can be found in BN and RB, simply because investors won't buy them; instead, they are drawn to RD coins, most of which have been "improved" (dipped and retoned).

Proofs are generally designated BN if the surfaces are mainly brown or iridescent, or have up to perhaps 30% original mint red-orange color (there is little consistency, within the hobby community, in this determination). RB is the designation if the surface is a mixture of red-orange and brown, best if blended together nicely, but often with patches of mint color among brown areas. RD designates a coin with original (in theory) mint-red orange, always blending to slight natural brown toning unless the coin has been dipped. Likely, any RD coin with even a few hairlines has been cleaned (or at least mishandled) at one time; in most such cases, what appears to be mint-red color is not original. Certification services take no notice of this. For this reason, a connoisseur will prefer a gem BN coin with no hairlines to a PF-65 or 66, RD, coin with some hairlines. Proof copper-nickel Indian Head cents of 1859 to 1864 need no letter to indicate color, as their hue derives more from the nickel than the copper. As a general rule, these survive in higher grades and with greater eye appeal, as they stayed "brilliant" (the watchword for most collectors until recent decades) and did not need dipping. Moreover, when such pieces were cleaned and acquired hairlines, they tended to be fewer than on a bronze coin, due to the very hard nature of the copper-nickel alloy.

GRADING STANDARDS

Caveat: These grading standards do not take sharpness of strike into account.

MS-60 to 70 (Mint State). *Obverse:* Contact marks, most obvious in the field, are evident at MS-60, diminishing at MS–61, 62, and higher. This abrasion is most noticeable on copper-nickel cents, for it blends in with the background on bronze issues. The cheek of the Indian and the field show some evidence as well. Typical color is BN, occasionally RB at MS–63 and 64, unless dipped to be RD. At gem MS-65 or finer there is no trace of abra-

1860, Pointed Bust. Graded MS-63.

sion. A few tiny nicks or marks may be seen, but none are obvious. At MS-67 and finer the coin will approach perfection. Check "RD" coins for originality. A theoretically perfect MS-70 will have no marks at all, even under a strong magnifier. Although in practice this is not always consistent, at MS-66 and higher there should be no staining or other problems, and the coin should have good eye appeal overall. *Reverse:* Check the high parts of the wreath for abrasion. Otherwise the above comments apply.

Illustrated coin: The surfaces display satin luster and a lovely pinkish-tan patina.

AU-50, 53, 55, 58 (About Uncirculated). *Obverse:* At AU-50, wear is most noticeable on the hair above the ear, on the central portion of the ribbon, on the curl to the right of the ribbon, and near the feather tips, although the last is not a reliable indicator due to striking. Luster is present, but mostly in protected areas. At AU–53 and 55, wear is less. At AU-58 friction is evident, rather than actual wear. Luster, toned brown, is nearly complete at

1861. Graded AU-55.

AU-58, but may be incomplete in the field. *Reverse:* At AU-50, light wear is seen on the ribbon and the higher-relief areas of the leaves, while the lower areas retain their detail. Some luster may be present in protected areas. At AU–53 and 55, wear is less and luster is more extensive. An AU-58 coin will have nearly full luster and show only light friction.

EF-40, 45 (Extremely Fine). *Obverse:* Wear is more extensive, but all of LIBERTY is very clear. Wear is seen on the hair above and below the ear, on the central portion of the ribbon, and on the feather tips. Overall the coin is bold. Scattered marks are normal for this and lower grades, most often seen on the cheek and in the field. *Reverse:* The higher-relief parts of the leaves and ribbon bow show light wear, but details are sharp in lower

1861. Graded EF-45.

areas. Some tiny lines in the vertical stripes in the shield may be blended. Scattered marks may be present, but on all grades they are usually fewer on the reverse than on the obverse.

VF-20, 30 (Very Fine). *Obverse:* Wear is more extensive. LIBERTY shows significant wear on BE, but it is sharp overall. Most hair detail is gone. The feather tips show greater wear (the extent of which will depend on the original strike). The ribbon and hair no longer show separation. *Reverse:* Wear is more extensive than at the preceding level, and many tiny vertical lines are fused together. Detail is still good on lower levels of the leaves.

1870, Shallow N. Graded VF-30.

F-12, 15 (Fine). *Obverse:* Traditionally, the word LIBERTY should be fully readable, but weak on the higher letters of LIB. PCGS suggests this is true, but not if a coin was lightly struck. Full or incomplete, well-struck or lightly struck, no matter what the coin, most buyers still want the word to be discernible. Other areas have correspondingly more wear than on the next-higher grade. *Reverse:* The higher areas of the leaves and the bow show

1870. Graded F-15.

wear. The shield shows greater wear than at the preceding level. Overall, the reverse appears to be less worn than the obverse, this being generally true of all circulated grades.

VG-8, 10 (Very Good). *Obverse:* A total of at least three letters in LIBERTY must be visible. This can be a combination of several partial letters. PCGS does not adhere to this rule and suggests that wear on the feathers is a better indicator. The rim may blend into the field in areas, depending on striking. *Reverse:* Wear is even more extensive. Leaves on the left have hardly any detail, while those on the right may have limited detail. The rim is complete.

1870, Bold N. Graded VG-10.

G-4, 6 (Good). *Obverse:* The coin is worn flat, with the portrait visible mostly in outline form, with only slight indication of feathers. Lettering and date are complete. Part of the rim is usually gone. At G-6, the rim is clearer. *Reverse:* The wreath is nearly flat, although some hints of detail may be seen on the right side. All letters are readable, although the inscription is light at the center (on issues from the 1870s onward). The rim is discernible all around, but is light in areas. At G-6 the rim is clearly delineated.

1877. Graded G-6.

Illustrated coin: The date is actually quite sharp for this grade.

AG-3 (About Good). *Obverse:* Most letters are worn away, as is the rim. The portrait is in outline form. The date is clearly readable, but may be weak or missing at the bottom. *Reverse:* Extensive wear prevails, although the rim will usually be more discernible than on the obverse. Most lettering, or sometimes all, is readable.

1877. Graded AG-3.

PF-60 to 70 (Proof). *Obverse and Reverse:* Gem PF-65 coins will have very few hairlines, and these are visible only under a strong magnifying glass. At any level and color, a Proof with hairlines likely (though not necessarily) has been cleaned. At PF-67 or higher there should be no evidence of hairlines or friction at all. Such a coin is fully original. PF-60 coins can be dull from repeated dipping and cleaning and are often toned iridescent colors. At

1868. Graded PF-64RB.

PF-63 the mirrorlike fields should be attractive, and hairlines should be minimal. These are easiest to see when the coin is held at an angle to the light. No rubbing is seen. PF-64 coins are even nicer.

COPPER-NICKEL COINAGE

1860, Rounded Bust

1860, Pointed Bust

	Mintage	Cert	Avg	%MS	G-4	VG-8	F-12	VF-20	EF-40	AU-50	MS-60BN PF-63BN	MS-63BN PF-64BN	MS-65 PF-65BN
1859	36,400,000	2,502	55.7	57%	$15	$20	$25	$55	$110	$200	$285	$725	$2,500
Auctions: $23,500, MS-66+, November 2014; $11,750, MS-66, April 2013; $3,966, MS-65, September 2014													
1859, Proof	800	188	64.4								$1,600	$2,250	$4,000
Auctions: $13,513, PF-66Cam, June 2014; $4,700, PF-66, September 2014; $3,173, PF-64, October 2014; $2,585, PF-64, August 2014													
1859, Oak Wreath With Shield, experimental reverse (a)		0	n/a									$1,100	
Auctions: No auction records available.													
1860, Rounded Bust	20,566,000	1,490	57.9	66%	$10	$15	$20	$35	$70	$110	$185	$300	$1,100
Auctions: $8,813, MS-66, January 2014; $3,290, MS-66, October 2014; $2,938, MS-66, October 2014; $764, MS-64, December 2014													
1860, Pointed Bust	(b)	166	58.0	69%	$20	$25	$30	$50	$100	$165	$300	$575	$3,000
Auctions: $32,900, MS-67, February 2014; $7,931, MS-66, October 2014; $2,409, MS-65, August 2014; $1,469, MS-64, July 2014													
1860, Rounded Bust, Proof	1,000	58	64.7								$900	$1,850	$3,000
Auctions: $9,989, PF-66, April 2014; $5,875, PF-66, August 2014; $8,013, PF-66, October 2014; $4,137, PF-66, October 2014													

a. 1,000 pieces were made but never released for circulation. **b.** Included in circulation-strike 1860, Rounded Bust, mintage figure.

1863, Doubled
Die Reverse
FS-01-1863-801.

	Mintage	Cert	Avg	%MS	G-4	VG-8	F-12	VF-20	EF-40	AU-50	MS-60BN / PF-63BN	MS-63BN / PF-64BN	MS-65 / PF-65BN
1861	10,100,000	1,346	55.3	61%	$25	$35	$45	$65	$110	$175	$225	$400	$1,150
Auctions: $14,100, MS-67, October 2014; $4,113, MS-66, February 2014; $2,820, MS-66, September 2014													
1861, Proof	*1,000*	82	64.2								$1,200	$3,250	$5,500
Auctions: $24,675, PF-66, September 2013; $2,585, PF-64, October 2014; $1,763, PF-64, October 2014													
1862	28,075,000	2,246	60.2	77%	$10	$15	$20	$30	$50	$75	$120	$215	$900
Auctions: $15,275, MS-67, February 2013; $11,163, MS-67, October 2014; $8,813, MS-67, November 2014													
1862, Proof	*1,500–2,000*	320	64.6								$850	$1,250	$2,500
Auctions: $11,750, PF-67Cam, September 2014; $2,468, PF-66Cam, November 2014; $4,113, PF-66, June 2014													
1863	49,840,000	2,976	60.2	76%	$10	$15	$20	$30	$50	$75	$120	$215	$900
Auctions: $3,055, MS-66, August 2014; $1,998, MS-66, November 2014; $2,820, MS-66, August 2013; $969, MS-65, July 2014													
1863, Doubled Die Reverse (c)	**(d)**	2	62.5	100%					$200	$375	$450	$950	$3,000
Auctions: No auction records available.													
1863, Proof	*800–1,000*	140	64.3								$850	$1,250	$2,500
Auctions: $9,988, PF-67Cam, September 2014; $1,998, PF-65Cam, July 2014; $1,058, PF-64Cam, November 2014													
1864, Copper-Nickel	13,740,000	1,732	58.0	70%	$20	$30	$40	$55	$100	$150	$240	$400	$1,100
Auctions: $6,463, MS-66, April 2014; $3,055, MS-66, November 2014; $1,351, MS-65, October 2014; $676, MS-64, July 2014													
1864, Copper-Nickel, Proof	*800–1,000*	158	64.3								$850	$1,450	$2,500
Auctions: $8,813, MS-67Cam, September 2014; $12,925, PF-66DCam, July 2014; $1,880, MS-64Cam, August 2014													

c. Strong doubling is evident on the right leaves of the wreath, and, to a lesser degree, on the upper left leaves. **d.** Included in circulation-strike 1863 mintage figure.

BRONZE COINAGE

1864, No L   **1864, With L**

	Mintage	Cert	Avg	%MS	G-4	VG-8	F-12	VF-20	EF-40	AU-50	MS-60BN / PF-63BN	MS-63BN / PF-64BN	MS-65RB / MS-65RD / PF-65RD
1864, Bronze, All kinds	39,233,714												
1864, No L		1,564	58.9	78%	$15	$20	$25	$45	$70	$90	$115	$150	$400	$750
Auctions: $764, MS-66RB, September 2014; $881, MS-65RD, August 2014; $306, MS-64RB, October 2014; $7,050, VF-30, April 2013													
1864, With L		1,934	49.7	42%	$55	$80	$150	$200	$275	$375	$425	$575	$1,750	$4,750
Auctions: $2,115, MS-65RB, May 2013; $1,469, MS-64RD, November 2014; $1,293, MS-64RB, July 2014; $646, MS-62RB													
1864, No L, Proof	*150+*	117	64.6								$500	$1,750	$9,000
Auctions: $17,625, PF-67RB, April 2013; $2,585, PF-65RB, November 2014; $2,129, PF-65RB, October 2014; $1,980, PF-65RB, April 2018													
1864, With L, Proof	*20+*	5	64.4								$25,000	$55,000	
Auctions: $141,000, PF-65RD, September 2013; $45,600, PF-64RB, January 2018													

**1865, Die Gouge
in Headdress**
FS-01-1865-1401.

1865, Doubled Die Reverse
FS-01-1865-1801.

1869, 69 Over 69
FS-01-1869-301.

Shallow N

Bold N

	Mintage	Cert	Avg	%MS	G-4	VG-8	F-12	VF-20	EF-40	AU-50	MS-60BN	MS-63BN	MS-65RB	MS-65RD
												PF-63BN	PF-64RB	PF-65RD
1865	35,429,286	1,274	59.8	76%	$15	$20	$25	$30	$45	$65	$90	$150	$750	$1,750
Auctions: $1,998, MS-66RB, October 2014; $1,998, MS-65RD, March 2013; $270, MS-64BN, October 2014; $165, MS-64BN, September 2014
1865, Die Gouge in Headdress (a)	(b)	0	n/a								$500	$750	$1,200	
Auctions: No auction records available.
1865, Doubled Die Reverse	(b)	12	41.8	33%					$800	$1,100	$2,200	$5,500		
Auctions: $1,175, AU-55, April 2013
1865, Proof	500+	158	64.2									$375	$800	$7,500
Auctions: $14,100, PF-65Cam, August 2014; $15,275, PF-66RD, October 2014; $12,925, PF-65RD, June 2014; $3,055, PF-64RD, October 2014
1866	9,826,500	1,309	52.2	53%	$50	$65	$80	$100	$190	$250	$275	$380	$1,500	$2,750
Auctions: $1,087, MS-66BN, September 2014; $3,290, MS-65RD, June 2014; $499, MS-63RB, August 2014; $212, MS-62BN, October 2014
1866, Proof	725+	130	64.6									$400	$600	$4,000
Auctions: $21,150, PF-66Cam, June 2014; $2,820, PF-65Cam, October 2014; $999, PF-65RB, July 2014; $529, PF-64BN, November 2014
1867	9,821,000	1,366	50.2	52%	$50	$70	$90	$135	$230	$275	$300	$400	$1,600	$6,500
Auctions: $6,463, MS-65RD, February 2014; $1,293, MS-65RB, October 2014; $6,756, MS-65RD, October 2014; $780, MS-64RB, April 2018
1867, Proof	625+	192	64.3									$400	$600	$5,000
Auctions: $3,525, PF-66RB, July 2014; $6,463, PF-66RD, March 2014; $705, PF-64RB, August 2014; $306, PF-63BN, October 2014
1868	10,266,500	1,191	51.0	53%	$40	$50	$70	$125	$170	$220	$250	$360	$925	$2,500
Auctions: $1,880, MS-66RB, September 2014; $29,375, MS-66RD, April 2014; $3,525, MS-65RD, October 2014
1868, Proof	600+	135	64.4									$375	$550	$5,500
Auctions: $17,625, PF-66RD, June 2014; $6,756, PF-65RD, September 2014; $588, PF-63RB, October 2014; $5,040, PF-65RD, January 2018
1869	6,420,000	1,797	42.0	38%	$85	$120	$235	$335	$445	$550	$600	$700	$1,800	$2,750
Auctions: $3,290, MS-66RB, August 2013; $1,763, MS-64RB, October 2014; $499, MS-61BN, November 2014; $1,175, MS-60BN, July 2014
1869, 69 Over 69	(c)	446	39.9	33%	$125	$225	$450	$575	$725	$825	$975	$1,500	$2,400	
Auctions: $4,113, MS-66, March 2015; $1,645, MS-64RB, November 2014; $3,055, MS-64RD, August 2014
1869, Proof	600+	186	64.4									$380	$650	$3,000
Auctions: $4,847, PF-66Cam, June 2014; $11,750, PF-66RD, October 2014; $1,528, PF-65RB, October 2014; $558, PF-64RB, November 2014
1870, Shallow N	5,275,000	1,208	44.5	41%	$80	$100	$220	$320	$400	$500	$550	$900	$1,600	
Auctions: $1,265, MS-64RB, March 2012
1870, Bold N	(d)	(e)			$55	$75	$200	$280	$375	$450	$500	$850	$1,300	$4,000
Auctions: $23,500, MS-66RD, May 2013; $3,819, MS-65RD, October 2014; $1,880, MS-65RB, November 2014; $705, MS-65BN, July 2014

Note: Cents dated 1869 and earlier have a shallow N in ONE. Those dated 1870, 1871, or 1872 have either shallow N or bold N, except Proofs of 1872, which were struck only with the bold N, not the shallow N. Those dated 1873 to 1876 all have the bold N. Circulation strikes of 1877 have the shallow N, while Proofs have the bold N. **a.** Currently described as a die gouge in the *Cherrypickers' Guide to Rare Die Varieties, Vol. I* (sixth edition), the curved "gouge" is a mark from the Janvier reducing lathe. **b.** Included in circulation-strike 1865 mintage figure. **c.** Included in circulation-strike 1869 mintage figure. **d.** Included in circulation-strike 1870, Shallow N, mintage figure. **e.** Certified population figures included in 1870, Shallow N.

1870, Doubled Die Reverse	1873, Close 3	1873, Open 3	1873, Doubled LIBERTY
FS-01-1870-801.			*FS-01-1873-101.*

	Mintage	Cert	Avg	%MS	G-4	VG-8	F-12	VF-20	EF-40	AU-50	MS-60BN	MS-63BN / PF-63BN	MS-65RB / PF-64RB	MS-65RD / PF-65RD
1870, Doubled Die Reverse	(d)	9	62.6	89%					$575	$750	$850	$1,000	$2,500	
Auctions: $1,035, MS-64RB, January 2012														
1870, Shallow N, Proof	1,000+	182	64.3									$425	$525	$2,000
Auctions: $1,380, PF-65RB, April 2012														
1870, Bold N, Proof	(f)	(g)										$325	$725	$2,750
Auctions: $3,173, PF-67RB, August 2014; $10,575, PF-66RD, January 2014; $9,988, PF-66RD, July 2014; $1,528, PF-64RD, November 2014														
1871, Shallow N	3,929,500	1,268	43.9	39%	$130	$180	$325	$450	$575	$650	$775	$1,000	$2,600	
Auctions: $8,225, MS-66, January 2015; $2,585, MS-63RB, February 2013														
1871, Bold N	(h)	(i)			$70	$85	$250	$350	$475	$525	$550	$800	$2,350	$7,500
Auctions: $44,063, MS-66RD, January 2014; $999, MS-64BN, November 2014; $999, MS-62BN, October 2014														
1871, Shallow N, Proof	960+	215	64.3									$500	$875	$2,350
Auctions: $7,344, PF-65RD, January 2013														
1871, Bold N, Proof	(j)	(k)										$325	$600	$2,500
Auctions: $2,350, PF-65RD, June 2014; $499, PF-65BN, October 2014; $294, PF-62BN, November 2014; $282, PF-60BN, November 2014														
1872, Shallow N	4,042,000	1,574	40.6	31%	$100	$170	$370	$425	$575	$700	$950	$1,250	$4,500	
Auctions: $764, MS-63, March 2016; $881, AU-55, April 2013														
1872, Bold N	(l)	(m)			$90	$140	$300	$375	$500	$650	$785	$1,150	$3,750	$10,000
Auctions: $28,200, MS-65RD, June 2014; $3,819, MS-65RB, August 2014; $5,581, MS-64RD, October 2014; $588, AU-58BN, July 2014														
1872, Bold N, Proof (n)	950+	234	64.3									$400	$700	$4,300
Auctions: $7,050, PF-66RD, October 2014; $705, PF-65BN, November 2014; $705, PF-64RB, November 2014; $12,925, PF, October 2013														
1873, All kinds	11,676,500													
1873, Close 3		502	49.7	46%	$25	$35	$65	$125	$185	$235	$410	$550	$2,500	$5,500
Auctions: $6,463, MS-65RD, October 2014; $2,820, MS-65RB, December 2013; $1,293, MS-64RB, October 2014; $793, MS-63RB														
1873, Doubled LIBERTY		113	40.2	25%	$250	$350	$800	$1,500	$3,000	$4,750	$7,000	$12,500	$55,000	
Auctions: $15,275, MS-64, March 2015; $9,988, MS-63RB, October 2014; $7,050, MS-63BN, September 2014														
1873, Open 3		683	51.6	47%	$20	$30	$50	$85	$160	$190	$250	$325	$1,275	$3,500
Auctions: $4,406, MS-65RD, April 2014; $3,819, MS-65RD, October 2014; $470, MS-64RB, November 2014; $470, MS-63RB, July 2014														
1873, Close 3, Proof	1,100+	252	64.2									$265	$550	$2,050
Auctions: $1,293, PF-65RB, April 2013; $589, PF-64RD, October 2014; $470, PF-64RB, October 2014; $1,440, PF-64RD, April 2018														
1874	14,187,500	1,106	56.1	62%	$20	$25	$45	$65	$100	$150	$225	$250	$725	$2,450
Auctions: $1,880, MS-65RD, October 2014; $2,820, MS-65RD, April 2013; $1,116, MS-65RB, October 2014														
1874, Proof	700	173	64.4									$250	$400	$2,500
Auctions: $823, PF-66BN, July 2014; $1,175, PF-65RB, June 2013; $617, PF-64RD, October 2014; $470, PF-64RB, July 2014														

Note: Cents dated 1869 and earlier have a shallow N in ONE. Those dated 1870, 1871, or 1872 have either shallow N or bold N, except Proofs of 1872, which were struck only with the bold N, not the shallow N. Those dated 1873 to 1876 all have the bold N. Circulation strikes of 1877 have the shallow N, while Proofs have the bold N. **d.** Included in circulation-strike 1870, Shallow N, mintage figure. **f.** Included in 1870, Shallow N, Proof, mintage figure. **g.** Included in certified population for 1870, Shallow N, Proof. **h.** Included in circulation-strike 1871, Shallow N, mintage figure. **i.** Certified population figures included in 1871, Shallow N. **j.** Included in 1871, Shallow N, Proof, mintage figure. **k.** Included in certified population for 1871, Shallow N, Proof. **l.** Included in 1872, Shallow N, mintage figure. **m.** Certified population figures included in 1871, Shallow N. **n.** Proofs of 1872 were struck only with the bold N, not the shallow N.

1875, Dot Reverse
FS-01-1875-801.

1880, Doubled Die Obverse, Reverse Clash
FS-01-1880-101.

1882, Misplaced Date
FS-01-1882-401.

	Mintage	Cert	Avg	%MS	G-4	VG-8	F-12	VF-20	EF-40	AU-50	MS-60BN	MS-63BN	MS-65RB	MS-65RD
												PF-63BN	PF-64RB	PF-65RD
1875	13,528,000	1,025	54.9	64%	$20	$35	$60	$75	$120	$160	$235	$260	$900	$2,500
	Auctions: $1,763, MS-66RB, July 2014; $5,581, MS-65RD, December 2013; $881, MS-65RB, August 2014; $646, MS-64RB, August 2014													
1875, Dot Reverse (o)	(p)	3	64.3	100%								—		
	Auctions: $700, AU-50BN, April 2012													
1875, Proof	700	198	64.2									$250	$500	$5,500
	Auctions: $8,813, PF-65RD, June 2014; $306, PF-63RB, October 2014; $960, PF-64RD, January 2018													
1876	7,944,000	1,035	52.0	54%	$35	$40	$70	$135	$225	$240	$300	$390	$1,000	$2,750
	Auctions: $1,998, MS-65RD, October 2014; $1,880, MS-65RD, October 2013; $1,293, MS-65RB, November 2014; $270, MS-62RB, November 2014													
1876, Proof	1,150	222	64.5									$250	$450	$2,250
	Auctions: $15,275, PF-66Cam, January 2014; $2,585, PF-66RD, October 2014; $646, PF-64RD, October 2014; $823, PF-64BN, November 2014													
1877 (q)	852,500	3,710	22.2	10%	$500	$600	$1,100	$1,250	$2,150	$2,850	$3,800	$5,250	$15,000	$25,000
	Auctions: $32,900, MS-65RD, August 2014; $14,100, MS-65RB, January 2014; $14,100, MS-65, August 2016													
1877, Proof	900	268	63.7									$3,000	$4,500	$12,000
	Auctions: $9,988, PF-66RD, October 2014; $14,100, PF-66RD, June 2013; $3,525, PF-64RB, October 2014; $3,819, PF-63RB, November 2014													
1878	5,797,500	963	53.5	61%	$30	$45	$60	$110	$200	$275	$325	$380	$950	$2,250
	Auctions: $8,813, MS-66RD, September 2014; $1,645, MS-65RD, October 2013; $881, MS-65RB, August 2014; $388, MS-63RB, October 2014													
1878, Proof	2,350	349	64.3									$235	$450	$1,500
	Auctions: $7,638, PF-66Cam, June 2014; $1,763, PF-65Cam, August 2014; $1,116, PF-65Cam, November 2014; $588, PF-64RD, October 2014													
1879	16,228,000	987	60.5	81%	$8	$12	$20	$40	$70	$80	$90	$140	$425	$1,250
	Auctions: $2,233, MS-65RD, June 2014; $470, MS-65RB, November 2014; $259, MS-64RB, July 2014; $247, MS-63RB, August 2014													
1879, Proof	3,200	396	64.5									$150	$325	$1,200
	Auctions: $11,163, PF-67RD, July 2014; $2,115, PF-66Cam, August 2014; $1,645, PF-66RD, October 2014; $217, PF-64BN, November 2014													
1880	38,961,000	865	61.8	88%	$5	$7	$9	$12	$30	$60	$80	$130	$400	$1,150
	Auctions: $5,288, MS-66RD, June 2014; $940, MS-65RD, September 2014; $441, MS-65RB, November 2014; $129, MS-64BN, November 2014													
1880, Doubled Die Obverse, Reverse Clash (r)	(s)	10	61.1	80%						$390	$750	$1,500	$2,000	
	Auctions: $2,070, MS-65BN, June 2009													
1880, Proof	3,955	430	64.4									$150	$325	$1,200
	Auctions: $8,813, PF-67RD, June 2014; $969, PF-66RB, August 2014; $705, PF-65RD, July 2014; $646, PF-65RB+, July 2014													

Note: Cents dated 1869 and earlier have a shallow N in ONE. Those dated 1870, 1871, or 1872 have either shallow N or bold N, except Proofs of 1872, which were struck only with the bold N, not the shallow N. Those dated 1873 to 1876 all have the bold N. Circulation strikes of 1877 have the shallow N, while Proofs have the bold N. **o.** In 1875 Mint officials suspected a longtime employee was stealing Indian Head cents. They secretly modified a reverse die by making a small gouge in the N in ONE, and then put the die into production one morning. Later that morning the suspect employee was called aside. He was asked to empty his pockets, revealing 33 of the marked cents. At first he insisted his son gave him this pocket change, but when confronted with the secretly marked die, he admitted his guilt. He tendered his resignation, disgraced, after more than 50 years of service to the Mint. The market value for this variety is not yet reliably established. **p.** Included in circulation-strike 1875 mintage figure. **q.** Beware the numerous counterfeits and altered-date 1877 cents. The latter typically are altered from 1875- or 1879-dated cents. **r.** Doubling is visible on the obverse in higher grades, as a very close spread on LIBERTY. The primary diagnostic, though, is the misaligned die clash evident on the reverse, with obvious reeding running from the upper-right leaf tip, through the E of ONE, and down to the very top of the N of CENT. **s.** Included in circulation-strike 1880 mintage figure.

1886, Variety 1
*The last feather points between
the I and the C in AMERICA.*

1886, Variety 2
*The last feather points between
the C and the A in AMERICA.*

1887, Doubled Die Obverse
FS-01-1887-101.

	Mintage	Cert	Avg	%MS	G-4	VG-8	F-12	VF-20	EF-40	AU-50	MS-60BN	MS-63BN	MS-65RB	MS-65RD
												PF-63BN	PF-64RB	PF-65RD
1881	39,208,000	875	62.1	90%	$5	$6	$8	$10	$25	$35	$60	$90	$315	$1,150
Auctions: $1,645, MS-67RB, October 2014; $6,463, MS-66RD, October 2014; $1,528, MS-66RB, August 2014
1881, Proof	3,575	412	64.6									$150	$325	$1,200
Auctions: $2,115, PF-66RB, November 2014; $1,880, PF-66RD, June 2013; $1,234, PF-65Cam, July 2014; $881, PF-65RB, August 2014
1882	38,578,000	902	62.2	89%	$5	$6	$8	$10	$25	$35	$60	$90	$315	$1,150
Auctions: $294, MS-64RB, July 2014; $247, MS-64RB, October 2014; $3,525, EF-40, April 2013; $66, AU-55BN, October 2014
1882, Misplaced Date (t)	(u)	7	59.1	57%						$450	$875	$1,700	$6,000	
Auctions: $220, EF-45, February 2007
1882, Proof	3,100	421	64.6									$150	$325	$850
Auctions: $823, PF-66RB, September 2014; $734, PF-66BN, November 2014; $2,703, PF-65RD, January 2014; $323, PF-65BN, July 2014
1883	45,591,500	901	62.2	89%	$5	$6	$8	$10	$25	$35	$60	$90	$315	$1,150
Auctions: $2,585, MS-66RD, February 2014; $499, MS-65RB, July 2014; $241, MS-65BN, July 2014; $217, MS-64RB, October 2014
1883, Proof	6,609	621	64.6									$150	$325	$1,200
Auctions: $5,581, PF-67RB, August 2014; $2,938, PF-66RD, March 2013; $646, PF-66BN, November 2014; $441, PF-65RB, November 2014
1884	23,257,800	804	62.1	88%	$5	$7	$10	$14	$27	$40	$75	$120	$450	$1,350
Auctions: $4,994, MS-66RD, June 2014; $1,645, MS-65RD, September 2014; $257, MS-64RB, August 2014
1884, Proof	3,942	517	64.8									$150	$325	$1,200
Auctions: $7,050, PF-67Cam, June 2013; $4,113, PF-67RD, September 2014; $1,880, PF-66RD, July 2014; $306, PF-64RD, October 2014
1885	11,761,594	783	60.9	81%	$8	$9	$15	$30	$65	$80	$110	$200	$650	$1,750
Auctions: $12,925, MS-66RD, April 2013; $1,528, MS-66RB, November 2014; $1,645, MS-65RD, October 2014
1885, Proof	3,790	498	64.9									$150	$325	$1,200
Auctions: $4,994, PF-68BN, September 2013; $1,528, PF-66RB, July 2014; $2,115, PF-65RD, October 2014; $529, PF-65RB, October 2014
1886, All kinds	17,650,000													
1886, Variety 1		519	55.6	54%	$6	$8	$20	$50	$140	$175	$200	$250	$975	$3,500
Auctions: $8,813, MS-66RB, June 2013; $1,410, MS-64RD, July 2014; $764, MS-64RB, November 2014; $235, MS-63BN, September 2014
1886, Variety 2		565	56.8	63%	$7	$12	$25	$75	$175	$220	$325	$500	$2,900	$10,000
Auctions: $9,400, MS-65RD, January 2013; $2,115, MS-65RB, August 2014; $482, MS-60RB, July 2014; $247, AU-58BN, October 2014
1886, All kinds, Proof	4,290													
1886, Variety 1, Proof		151	64.6									$150	$325	$1,800
Auctions: $3,819, PF-66RD, June 2014; $1,880, PF-66RB, October 2014; $1,763, PF-65RD, October 2014; $558, PF-64RB, August 2014
1886, Variety 2, Proof		86	64.6									$350	$750	$11,500
Auctions: $1,116, PF-66BN, April 2013; $1,763, PF-64RB+, November 2014; $306, PF-64BN, November 2014
1887	45,223,523	797	60.4	85%	$3	$4	$5	$8	$18	$28	$55	$80	$575	$1,250
Auctions: $4,700, MS-66RD, November 2014; $8,813, MS-66RD, February 2013; $382, MS-65RB, November 2014
1887, DblDie Obverse	(v)	36	39.9	14%					$250	$490	$1,000	$2,500	$8,000	
Auctions: $881, MS-62BN, October 2013; $176, VF-25BN, October 2014
1887, Proof	2,960	340	64.4									$150	$300	$3,500
Auctions: $16,450, PF-66RD, June 2014; $823, PF-66BN, November 2014; $382, PF-64RB, October 2014; $3,120, PF-65RD, January 2018

t. The bases of at least four 1s are evident within the beads of the necklace. **u.** Included in circulation-strike 1882 mintage figure.
v. Included in circulation-strike 1887 mintage figure.

1888, Last 8 Over 7
FS-01-1888-301.

1891, Doubled Die Obverse
FS-01-1891-101.

1894, Doubled Date
FS-01-1894-301.

	Mintage	Cert	Avg	%MS	G-4	VG-8	F-12	VF-20	EF-40	AU-50	MS-60BN	MS-63BN PF-63BN	MS-65RB PF-64RB	MS-65RD PF-65RD
1888	37,489,832	897	58.7	81%	$3	$4	$5	$8	$22	$27	$65	$130	$725	$1,500
	Auctions: $11,750, MS-66RD, June 2014; $1,704, MS-65RD, July 2014; $1,880, MS-65RD, September 2014; $529, MS-64RD, October 2014													
1888, Last 8 Over 7	(w)	13	39.2	15%	$1,500	$2,000	$3,500	$4,500	$7,500	$12,500	$30,000	$50,000		
	Auctions: $99,142, MS-66, January 2016; $23,500, AU-58, April 2013													
1888, Proof	4,582	314	64.2									$150	$315	$3,500
	Auctions: $15,275, PF-66RD, October 2014; $382, PF-64RB, August 2014; $2,585, PF, February 2013; $294, PF-64BN, December 2014													
1889	48,866,025	961	61.4	88%	$3	$4	$5	$7	$18	$27	$60	$80	$400	$2,000
	Auctions: $13,513, MS-66RD, October 2014; $10,575, MS-66RD, October 2014; $4,113, MS-65RD, April 2014; $1,880, MS-65RD, October 2014													
1889, Proof	3,336	300	64.4									$150	$315	$1,750
	Auctions: $4,113, PF-66RD, February 2013; $499, PF-65RB, July 2014; $341, PF-64RB, July 2014; $282, PF-64BN, November 2014													
1890	57,180,114	871	62.1	91%	$3	$4	$5	$7	$16	$27	$60	$80	$410	$1,200
	Auctions: $4,113, MS-66RB, March 2014; $470, MS-64RD, July 2014; $170, MS-64RB, August 2014; $170, MS-63BN, July 2014													
1890, Proof	2,740	279	64.1									$150	$315	$1,650
	Auctions: $1,058, PF-65RD, October 2014; $1,293, PF-65RD, August 2013; $1,293, PF-64Cam, September 2014; $470, PF-64RD, November 2014													
1891	47,070,000	995	62.3	91%	$3	$4	$5	$7	$15	$27	$60	$80	$400	$1,200
	Auctions: $9,106, MS-66RD, November 2014; $1,528, MS-65RD, July 2014; $1,293, MS-65RD, August 2014; $135, MS-64RB, August 2014													
1891, Doubled Die Obverse	(x)	12	45.9	25%				$250	$450	$775	$1,150			
	Auctions: $138, VF-35, December 2011; $1,320, MS-64BN, February 2018													
1891, Proof	2,350	307	64.1									$150	$315	$1,375
	Auctions: $18,213, PF-65DCam, July 2014; $911, PF-64Cam, September 2014; $558, PF-64RB, November 2014; $176, PF-62RB, November 2014													
1892	37,647,087	889	62.5	92%	$3	$4	$5	$8	$20	$27	$60	$80	$375	$1,000
	Auctions: $8,813, MS-66RD, August 2013; $3,055, MS-65RD, October 2014; $1,293, MS-65RD, October 2014; $306, MS-64RD, October 2014													
1892, Proof	2,745	307	64.3									$150	$315	$1,200
	Auctions: $3,525, PF-67RD, November 2013; $2,585, PF-66Cam, November 2014; $2,233, PF-65RD, October 2014; $1,175, PF-64Cam, July 2014													
1893	46,640,000	1,068	62.6	93%	$3	$4	$5	$8	$20	$27	$60	$80	$320	$1,000
	Auctions: $6,463, MS-67RD, April 2013; $282, MS-64RD, October 2014; $176, MS-64RB, November 2014; $135, MS-63RB, November 2014													
1893, Proof	2,195	282	64.2									$150	$315	$1,300
	Auctions: $823, PF-65RB, November 2014; $499, PF-64RD, April 2013; $284, PF-64RB, October 2014; $247, PF-63RB, November 2014													
1894	16,749,500	1,075	58.8	79%	$5	$6	$15	$20	$50	$70	$85	$115	$385	$1,000
	Auctions: $3,290, MS-66RD, January 2014; $2,585, MS-66RD, October 2014; $2,174, MS-66RD, November 2014; $414, MS-64RB, July 2014													
1894, Doubled Date	(y)	115	44.9	49%	$50	$75	$100	$150	$250	$400	$675	$1,200	$4,000	$11,000
	Auctions: $5,875, MS-64RD, January 2013; $4,113, MS-64RB, September 2014; $1,116, MS-62, January 2015													
1894, Proof	2,632	315	64.1									$150	$315	$1,200
	Auctions: $5,581, PF-66RD, September 2013; $1,351, PF-65Cam, November 2014; $558, PF-65RB, November 2014													

w. Included in circulation-strike 1888 mintage figure. **x.** Included in circulation-strike 1891 mintage figure. **y.** Included in circulation-strike 1894 mintage figure.

	Mintage	Cert	Avg	%MS	G-4	VG-8	F-12	VF-20	EF-40	AU-50	MS-60BN	MS-63BN	MS-65RB	MS-65RD
												PF-63BN	PF-64RB	PF-65RD
1895	38,341,574	1,052	62.5	93%	$3	$4	$5	$8	$15	$25	$45	$65	$200	$800
	Auctions: $23,500, MS-67RD, November 2014; $7,050, MS-66RD, January 2014; $1,880, MS-66RD, October 2014; $206, MS-64RB, October 2014													
1895, Proof	2,062	302	64.4									$160	$315	$1,200
	Auctions: $9,988, PF-66Cam, June 2014; $1,880, PF-66RB, November 2014; $823, PF-64RB, November 2014; $260, PF-62RB, November 2014													
1896	39,055,431	800	62.4	91%	$3	$4	$5	$8	$15	$25	$45	$65	$220	$950
	Auctions: $1,528, MS-65RD, July 2014; $259, MS-64RD, July 2014; $182, MS-64RB, August 2014; $59, MS-63BN, October 2014													
1896, Proof	1,862	244	64.3									$150	$300	$1,500
	Auctions: $5,875, PF-65Cam, June 2014; $646, PF-65BN, November 2014; $295, PF-64RB, September 2014; $194, PF-64BN, November 2014													
1897	50,464,392	1,045	61.5	89%	$3	$4	$5	$8	$15	$25	$45	$65	$200	$800
	Auctions: $31,725, MS-67RD, August 2014; $7,050, MS-66RD, January 2014; $529, MS-64RD, September 2014; $118, MS-64RD, October 2014													
1897, Proof	1,938	268	64.5									$150	$300	$1,500
	Auctions: $6,169, PF-67RD, October 2014; $588, PF-65RB, July 2014; $411, PF-63RB, November 2014; $10,575, PF, January 2013													
1898	49,821,284	1,085	62.6	92%	$3	$4	$5	$8	$15	$25	$45	$65	$195	$500
	Auctions: $2,820, MS-66RD, April 2013; $368, MS-65RB+, November 2014; $458, MS-64RD+, October 2014; $212, MS-64RD, October 2014													
1898, Proof	1,795	278	64.7									$150	$300	$1,200
	Auctions: $7,931, PF-66Cam, June 2014; $27,025, PF-66RB, August 2014; $2,233, PF-66RD, August 2014; $353, PF-64RB, November 2014													
1899	53,598,000	1,747	63.0	93%	$3	$4	$5	$8	$15	$25	$45	$65	$195	$475
	Auctions: $3,525, MS-66RD, January 2014; $2,233, MS-66RD, September 2014; $1,351, MS-66RD, October 2014; $558, MS-65RD, October 2014													
1899, Proof	2,031	279	64.7									$150	$300	$1,200
	Auctions: $5,875, PF-67RD, June 2014; $764, PF-64Cam, November 2014; $823, PF-66RB, November 2014; $478, PF-65RB, October 2014													
1900	66,831,502	1,226	62.4	92%	$2	$3	$5	$6	$10	$20	$40	$60	$165	$475
	Auctions: $9,988, MS-67RD, December 2013; $2,115, MS-66RD+, July 2014; $1,998, MS-66RD, October 2014; $529, MS-65RD, December 2014													
1900, Proof	2,262	276	64.6									$150	$300	$1,200
	Auctions: $2,350, PF-66RB+, August 2014; $2,115, PF-66RD, October 2014; $5,581, PF-66RD, April 2013; $411, PF-64RD, October 2014													
1901	79,609,158	2,101	62.9	95%	$2	$3	$5	$6	$10	$20	$40	$60	$165	$450
	Auctions: $2,115, MS-67RB, November 2013; $1,293, MS-66RD, August 2014; $588, MS-65RD, August 2014; $194, MS-64RD, July 2014													
1901, Proof	1,985	286	64.7									$150	$300	$1,200
	Auctions: $2,500, PF-67RB, July 2014; $1,528, PF-66RD, October 2014; $999, PF-66RB, August 2014; $4,700, PF, March 2014													
1902	87,374,704	2,078	62.4	93%	$2	$3	$5	$6	$10	$20	$40	$60	$165	$525
	Auctions: $1,998, MS-66RD, July 2014; $2,585, MS-66RD, December 2013; $705, MS-65RD, November 2014; $165, MS-64RD, July 2014													
1902, Proof	2,018	299	64.5									$150	$300	$1,200
	Auctions: $7,344, PF-67RD, June 2014; $823, PF-66RB, November 2014; $1,146, PF-65RD, October 2014; $341, PF-64RB, July 2014													
1903	85,092,703	1,878	62.2	92%	$2	$3	$5	$6	$10	$20	$40	$60	$165	$450
	Auctions: $4,406, MS-67RD, July 2014; $1,998, MS-66RD, October 2014; $1,528, MS-66RD, November 2014; $411, MS-65RD, August 2014													
1903, Proof	1,790	270	64.6									$150	$300	$1,200
	Auctions: $2,820, PF-66RD, October 2014; $1,763, PF-66RB, November 2014; $499, PF-64RD, July 201412/29/2014 $10,575, PF, January 2013													
1904	61,326,198	1,651	62.5	92%	$2	$3	$5	$6	$10	$20	$40	$60	$165	$475
	Auctions: $2,585, MS-66RD, June 2014; $441, MS-65RD, November 2014; $183, MS-65RB, July 2014; $59, MS-63RB, November 2014													
1904, Proof	1,817	251	64.2									$150	$300	$1,200
	Auctions: $6,463, PF-67RB, October 2014; $4,994, PF-66Cam, June 2014; $2,585, PF-65Cam, October 2014; $7,931, PF-65RB, July 2014													
1905	80,717,011	1,885	62.5	92%	$2	$3	$5	$6	$10	$20	$40	$60	$165	$500
	Auctions: $19,975, MS-67RD, April 2013; $6,169, MS-66RD+, September 2014; $2,115, MS-66RD, September 2014; $456, MS-65RD, August 2014													
1905, Proof	2,152	262	64.4									$150	$300	$1,200
	Auctions: $411, PF-64RD, October 2014; $529, PF-64RB, November 2014; $8,225, PF, March 2014; $223, PF-63RB, October 2014													
1906	96,020,530	2,268	62.0	90%	$2	$3	$5	$6	$10	$20	$40	$60	$165	$450
	Auctions: $23,500, MS-67RD, June 2014; $2,585, MS-66RD, August 2014; $617, MS-65RD, September 2014; $247, MS-62BN, July 2014													
1906, Proof	1,725	249	64.4									$150	$300	$1,500
	Auctions: $21,150, PF-67Cam, June 2014; $2,820, PF-66RB+, November 2014; $1,704, PF-66RB, November 2014; $2,939, PF-64RB, July 2014													
1907	108,137,143	2,429	61.9	91%	$2	$3	$5	$6	$10	$20	$40	$60	$165	$450
	Auctions: $23,500, MS-67RD, December 2013; $364, MS-65RD, October 2014; $329, MS-65RB, October 2014; $247, MS-64RD, October 2014													
1907, Proof	1,475	224	64.5									$150	$300	$1,250
	Auctions: $4,113, PF-66RD, April 2014; $764, PF-65RD, October 2014; $306, PF-64RB, October 2014; $382, PF-62BN, November 2014													

	Mintage	Cert	Avg	%MS	G-4	VG-8	F-12	VF-20	EF-40	AU-50	MS-60BN	MS-63BN PF-63BN	MS-65RB PF-64RB	MS-65RD PF-65RD
1908	32,326,367	1,951	62.8	94%	$2	$3	$5	$6	$10	$20	$40	$60	$165	$450
Auctions: $19,975, MS-67RD, February 2013; $3,525, MS-66RD, August 2014; $4,113, MS-66RD+, October 2014; $1,293, MS-65RD, August 2014
1908, Proof	1,620	288	64.6									$150	$300	$1,200
Auctions: $1,293, PF-66RB, November 2014; $1,175, PF-65RD, January 2014; $382, PF-64RD, October 2014; $2,585, PF-62RB, July 2014
1908-S	1,115,000	3,977	42.7	28%	$90	$100	$125	$145	$175	$250	$290	$400	$850	$2,000
Auctions: $4,882, MS-66RD, August 2014; $1,763, MS-65RD, October 2014; $3,290, MS-65, March 2015
1909	14,368,470	2,636	61.8	91%	$12	$15	$17	$20	$25	$30	$45	$65	$175	$475
Auctions: $3,819, MS-67RD, January 2014; $11,163, MS-67RD, August 2014; $4,113, MS-66RD+, September 2014
1909, Proof	2,175	270	64.5									$150	$300	$1,300
Auctions: $12,925, PF-67RD, June 2014; $1,645, PF-66RD, August 2014; $1,645, PF-64Cam, November 2014; $206, PF-63RB, July 2014
1909-S	309,000	3,974	38.5	25%	$300	$325	$400	$475	$600	$700	$1,000	$1,200	$2,650	$5,000
Auctions: $9,989, MS-66RD, June 2014; $9,988, MS-66, September 2015; $5,875, MS-65RD, August 2014

LINCOLN, WHEAT EARS REVERSE (1909–1958)

Variety 1 (Bronze, 1909–1942): **Designer:** *Victor D. Brenner.* **Weight:** *3.11 grams.* **Composition:** *.950 copper, .050 tin and zinc.* **Diameter:** *19 mm.* **Edge:** *Plain.* **Mints:** *Philadelphia, Denver, and San Francisco.*

Variety 1, Bronze (1909–1942)

Mintmark location, all varieties 1909 to date, is on the obverse below the date.

Variety 1, Bronze, Matte Proof

Variety 2 (Steel, 1943): **Weight:** *2.70 grams.* **Composition:** *Steel, coated with zinc.* **Diameter:** *19 mm.* **Edge:** *Plain.* **Mints:** *Philadelphia, Denver, and San Francisco.*

Variety 2, Steel (1943)

Variety 1 Resumed (1944–1958): **Weight:** *3.11 grams.* **Composition:** *1944–1946—.950 copper and .050 zinc; 1947–1958—.950 copper and .050 tin and zinc.* **Diameter:** *19 mm.* **Edge:** *Plain.* **Mints:** *Philadelphia, Denver, and San Francisco.*

Variety 1 Resumed, Bronze (1944–1958)

Variety 1 Resumed, Bronze, Mirror Proof

History. The Lincoln cent debuted in 1909 in honor of the hundredth anniversary of the birth of Abraham Lincoln. Sculptor and engraver Victor David had been chosen to design the new cent because the artistry of Chief Engraver Charles Barber was under heavy criticism at the time. The new cent was released on August 2, 1909, and the earliest coins of the year's issue had Brenner's initials (V.D.B.) on the reverse; this was soon discontinued. (His initials would be restored in 1918, on the obverse, on Lincoln's shoulder.) This was the first U.S. cent to feature the motto IN GOD WE TRUST.

From 1909 to 1942 the coins were struck in bronze. In 1943, during World War II, zinc-coated steel was used for their planchets, as a way to reserve copper for the war effort. The bronze alloy would be resumed in 1944. (Although no bronze cents were officially issued in 1943, a few pieces struck on bronze or silver planchets are known to exist for that year; bronze examples have recently sold for more than $200,000. Such errors presumably occur when an older planchet is mixed in with the normal supply of planchets and goes through the minting process. Through a similar production error, a few 1944 cents were struck on steel planchets. Beware the many regular steel cents of 1943 that were later plated with copper, either as novelties or to deceive collectors; a magnet will reveal their true nature.) In 1944, 1945, and 1946, the Mint used salvaged gun-cartridge cases as its source metal for coining cents. In Mint State, the color of cents of these years can appear slightly different from other bronze Wheat Ears cents.

The Philadelphia, Denver, and San Francisco mints all produced Lincoln Wheat Ears cents, but not in all years. The Wheat Ears reverse design was used from 1909 until the coin's 50th anniversary in 1959, at which time it was replaced with a view of the Lincoln Memorial.

Striking and Sharpness. As a rule, Lincoln cents of 1909 through 1914 are fairly well struck. From 1915 through the end of the 1920s, many are weak, with Denver Mint coins particularly so. Issues of the 1930s onward are mostly well struck. With many different die pairs used over a long period of time, striking quality varies. On the obverse, check for details in Lincoln's hair and beard. Also check the lettering and the inner edge of the rim. Tiny marks on the shoulder of Lincoln indicate a weak strike there; this area cannot be used to determine wear on high-grade coins. (During striking, there was not enough die pressure to fill this, the deepest point of the obverse die; therefore, stray marks on the raw planchet remain evident in this spot.) On the reverse check the wheat stalks, letters, and inner rim. A weak strike will usually manifest itself on the O of ONE (the area directly opposite Lincoln's shoulder). Coins struck from overused or "tired" dies can have grainy or even slightly wavy fields on either side.

Availability. Of the earlier Lincoln Wheat Ears cents, those of 1909 are easily found in MS; later early dates are scarcer, although Philadelphia varieties were made in higher quantities and are more often seen. Beginning in the early 1930s, collectors saved bank-wrapped rolls of Mint State cents in large quantities (starting mainly in 1934, though the low-mintage 1931-S was also hoarded). Dates after this time all are plentiful, although some more so than others, and there are a number of scarce and rare varieties. The collector demand for scarcer Lincoln cents and higher-grade issues is intense, resulting in a strong market. Many Mint State coins before the 1930s have been dipped and recolored, this being particularly true of pieces listed as RD. Others are stained and blotchy.

Proofs. Matte Proof Lincoln cents of a new style were made from 1909 to 1916. These have minutely matte or pebbled surfaces caused by special treatment of the dies. The rims are square and sharp. Such pieces cannot easily be told from certain circulation strikes with similar borders. Certified holders usually list these simply as "Proof," not "Matte Proof." Buy only coins that have been verified by an expert. Most are brown, or brown with tinges of red. Nearly all full "red" coins have been dipped or recolored.

Exceptional specimens dated 1917 are reported to exist, although no records exist to indicate they are true Proofs.

Mirror-finish Proofs were made from 1936 to 1942 and again from 1950 to 1958. Proofs of this era are mostly from dies polished overall (including the portrait), although some later issues have frosted ("cameo") portraits. Quality can be a problem for the 1936 to 1942 issues. Check for carbon spots and recoloring. Proofs of later dates are easy to find.

Generally, Proofs below 63 are unattractive and are not desired by most collectors.

GRADING STANDARDS

Caveat: These grading standards do not take sharpness of strike into account.

MS-60 to 70 (Mint State). *Obverse and Reverse:* At MS-65 and higher, the luster is rich on all areas, except perhaps the shoulder (which may be grainy and show original planchet surface). There is no rubbing, and no contact marks are visible except under magnification. Coins with full or nearly full mint orange-red color can be designated RD; those with full or nearly full brown-toned surfaces can be designated BN; and those with a sub-

1909-S, V.D.B. Graded MS-64RB.

stantial percentage of red-orange and of brown can be called RB. Ideally, MS-65 or finer coins should have good eye appeal, which in the RB category means nicely blended colors, not stained or blotched. Below MS-65, full RD coins become scarce, and at MS–60 to 62 they are virtually non-existent, unless they have been dipped. Copper is a very active metal, and influences that define the grade—such as slight abrasions, contact marks, and so on—also affect the color. The ANA grading standards allow for "dull" and/or "spotted" coins at MS–60 and 61, as well as incomplete luster. In the marketplace, interpretations often vary widely. BN and RB coins at MS–60 and 61 are apt to be more attractive than (dipped) RD coins.

Illustrated coin: The rose-orange color of this cent is better than is usually expected for a coin graded Red Brown. Note some toning streaks on the obverse, lighter than the surrounding surfaces, across Lincoln's forehead and nose.

AU-50, 53, 55, 58 (About Uncirculated). *Obverse:* Slight wear shows on Lincoln's cheekbone to the left of his nose, and also on his beard. At AU–55 or 58 there may be some hints of mint red-orange. Most coins in About Uncirculated are BN, but they are seldom designated by color. *Reverse:* Slight wear is evident on the stalks of wheat to the left and right. Otherwise, the same standards apply as for the obverse.

1920-S. Graded AU-58.

EF-40, 45 (Extremely Fine). *Obverse:* Light wear is seen on Lincoln's portrait, and hair detail is gone on the higher areas, especially above the ear. *Reverse:* Light wear is seen overall, but the parallel lines in the wheat stalks are clearly separated.

1914-D. Graded EF-45.

VF-20, 30 (Very Fine). *Obverse:* Lincoln's portrait is worn all over, with most hair detail gone at the center. Hair separation is seen at the back and the top of the head, but hairs are blended together. The jaw outline is clear. The center of the ear is defined and the bowtie is clear. The date and lettering is sharp. *Reverse:* More wear is seen, but still the lines in the wheat stalks are separated. Lettering shows wear but is very clear.

1922-D, No D. Graded VF-20.

    Illustrated coin: This coin features even wear and few marks.

F-12, 15 (Fine). *Obverse:* More wear is seen overall. Hair definition is less. The center of the ear is partially visible. The jaw outline and bowtie are clear. *Reverse:* Most lines in the wheat stalks are either weak or blended with others, but more than half of the separating lines are clear.

1922-D, No D. Graded F-15.

    Illustrated coin: Other than one deep contact mark in the cheek, the surfaces are smooth.

VG-8, 10 (Very Good). *Obverse:* The portrait is more worn, with only slight hair strands visible (thick strands blended). The ear opening is visible. The bowtie and jacket show fewer details. *Reverse:* The lines in the wheat stalks are blended together in flat areas. Perhaps 40% to 50% of the separating lines can be seen. The rim may be weak in areas.

1909-S. Graded VG-10.

G-4, 6 (Good). *Obverse:* The portrait is well worn. Some slight details are seen at the top of the head and the bottom of the coat. LIBERTY is weak. The rim may touch or blend with the tops of the letters forming IN GOD WE TRUST. The date and mintmark (if any) are very clear. *Reverse:* The wheat stalks are flat, with just a few scattered details visible.

1914-D. Graded G-6.

AG-3 (About Good). *Obverse:* Wear is extensive. The portrait is mostly in outline form, with only scattered details visible. LIBERTY is weak and perhaps with some letters missing. IN GOD WE TRUST blends in with the rim, and several letters are very weak or missing. *Reverse:* The rim is worn down to blend with the outside of the wheat stalks in some areas, although some hints of the edge of the stalks can be seen. Lettering is weak, with up to several letters missing.

1913-D. Graded AG-3.

PF-60 to 70 (Matte Proof). *Obverse and Reverse:* At the Matte PF-65 level or higher there are no traces of abrasion or contact marks. Color will range from brown (BN)—the most common—to brown with significant tinges of mint red-orange (RB), or with much mint color (RD). Most RD coins have been dipped. Some tiny flecks are normal on coins certified as PF-65 but should be microscopic or absent above that. Coins in the PF-60 to

1909, V.D.B. Matte Proof. Graded PF-68RD.

63 range are BN or sometimes RB—almost impossible to be RD unless dipped. Lower-grade Proofs usually have poor eye appeal.

Illustrated coin: Most of the red tint is medium orange, but there is a faint pink tint to the upper-left obverse.

PF-60 to 70 (Mirror Proof). *Obverse and Reverse:* PF-65 and higher coins are usually RB (colors should be nicely blended) or RD, the latter with bright red-orange fading slightly to hints of brown. Some tiny flecks are normal on coins certified as PF-65 but should be microscopic or absent above that. PF–60 and 61 coins can be dull, stained, or spotted but still have some original mint color. Coins with fingerprints must be given

1936. Mirror Proof. Graded PF-66RD.

a low numerical grade. Lower-grade Proofs usually have poor eye appeal.

Illustrated coin: The mirrored surfaces are free of blemish.

Designer's initials, V.D.B. (1909 Reverse Only)	No V.D.B. on Reverse (1909–1958)	V.D.B. on Shoulder (Starting 1918)	1909-S, S Over Horizontal S FS-01-1909S-1502.

	Mintage	Cert	Avg	%MS	G-4	VG-8	F-12	VF-20	EF-40	AU-50	MS-60BN	MS-63BN	MS-65RD
											PF-63RB	PF-64RB	PF-65RD
1909, V.D.B.	27,995,000	15,260	63.3	95%	$6	$8	$10	$12	$16	$18	$25	$30	$165
Auctions: $881, MS-67RD, July 2014; $823, MS-67RD, September 2014; $1,763, MS-67RD, June 2013; $499, MS-66RD+, August 2014													
1909, V.D.B., Proof (a)		56	65.0								$11,500	$20,000	
Auctions: $258,500, PF-67RB+, August 2014; $55,813, PF-66RB, June 2014; $22,800, P-64RD, April 2018													
1909-S, V.D.B. † †† (b)	484,000	9,946	42.8	37%	$625	$700	$750	$825	$950	$1,100	$1,200	$1,550	$4,500
Auctions: $61,688, MS-67, February 2017; $33,600, MS-66, January 2018; $7,200, MS-66, February 2018; $1,800, MS-64, April 2018													
1909	72,702,618	2,083	63.4	97%	$3	$4	$5	$6	$7	$12	$17	$20	$160
Auctions: $1,880, MS-67RD, August 2014; $1,763, MS-67RD, November 2014; $4,406, MS-67RD, April 2013; $670, MS-66RD+, October 2014													
1909, Proof	2,618	253	64.5								$750	$1,150	$2,000
Auctions: $6,463, PF-66RB+, August 2014; $5,875, PF-66RD, April 2013; $1,782, PF-65RD, August 2014; $1,657, PF-64RD, August 2014													
1909-S	1,825,000	4,744	40.0	38%	$80	$90	$100	$130	$150	$225	$325	$350	$1,000
Auctions: $17,625, MS-67, January 2017; $3,760, MS-66+ RD, March 2016; $3,840, MS-66, April 2018; $312, MS-64, April 2018													
1909-S, S Over Horizontal S	(c)	645	48.2	59%	$95	$100	$120	$150	$200	$275	$350	$400	$1,250
Auctions: $1,880, MS-66RD, September 2014; $1,880, MS-66, August 2015; $969, MS-65RD, July 2014													
1910	146,801,218	1,447	63.0	94%	$0.45	$0.60	$1	$1.50	$4	$10	$18	$25	$230
Auctions: $4,406, MS-67RD, June 2014; $3,055, MS-67RD, September 2014; $2,938, MS-67RD, November 2014													
1910, Proof	4,118	255	64.2								$675	$1,100	$1,850
Auctions: $7,638, PF-67RB, August 2014; $1,764, PF-65RB, July 2014; $470, PF-63RB, August 2014; $3,290, PF, January 2013													
1910-S	6,045,000	1,615	54.9	70%	$12	$16	$22	$25	$50	$80	$100	$120	$650
Auctions: $15,275, MS-66RD, June 2014; $1,880, MS-66RD, August 2014; $1,998, MS-66RD, October 2014; $206, MS-64RB, November 2014													
1911	101,177,787	813	63.1	95%	$0.50	$0.70	$1.50	$2.50	$6	$11	$21	$50	$400
Auctions: $7,050, MS-67RD, April 2014; $1,645, MS-66RD, October 2014; $441, MS-65RD, August 2014; $165, MS-64RD, August 2014													
1911, Proof	1,725	222	64.2								$675	$1,050	$2,500
Auctions: $9,400, PF-66RD, June 2014; $14,688, PF-66RB, August 2014; $853, PF-65BN, October 2014; $705, PF-64RB, August 2014													
1911-D	12,672,000	937	57.6	73%	$6	$7	$10	$20	$50	$75	$95	$125	$900
Auctions: $8,225, MS-66RD, April 2014; $7,050, MS-66RD, October 2014; $6,169, MS-66RD, October 2014; $3,819, MS-65RD, September 2014													
1911-S	4,026,000	1,335	44.9	41%	$25	$35	$45	$60	$75	$110	$185	$295	$2,250
Auctions: $14,100, MS-66RD, October 2014; $881, MS-65RB, November 2014; $2,820, MS-65RD, August 2013; $505, MS-64RD, October 2014													
1912	68,153,060	761	62.8	93%	$1.25	$1.65	$2.25	$5.50	$13	$25	$35	$50	$500
Auctions: $18,800, MS-67RD, April 2013; $499, MS-65RD, December 2014; $441, MS-65RD, October 2014; $118, MS-64RD, July 2014													
1912, Proof	2,172	230	64.3								$675	$1,050	$3,000
Auctions: $3,966, PF-66RB, February 2014; $14,100, PF-66RB+, August 2014; $999, PF-65RB, October 2014; $940, PF-64RB, July 2014													
1912-D	10,411,000	704	55.6	65%	$7	$9	$11	$25	$75	$100	$170	$250	$1,150
Auctions: $8,238, MS-66RD, September 2014; $1,998, MS-65RD+, November 2014; $7,050, MS-65RD, February 2013													
1912-S	4,431,000	1,052	47.5	50%	$16	$20	$25	$40	$70	$110	$180	$255	$1,650
Auctions: $2,820, MS-65RD, October 2014; $4,406, MS-65RD, November 2013; $1,410, MS-64RD, August 2014													

Note: No early references (pre-1960s), Mint records, or reliable market listings have been found to confirm the existence of true 1917 Proofs. "Examples seen have had nice matte-like surfaces, sometimes on just one side, but have lacked the vital combination of broad, flat rims on both sides and a mirror Proof edge (when viewed edge-on from the side)" (*A Guide Book of Lincoln Cents*). The leading certification services do not recognize Proofs of this year. The editors of this book also do not believe that true Proofs of 1917 exist.
† Ranked in the *100 Greatest U.S. Coins* (fifth edition). †† Ranked in the *100 Greatest U.S. Modern Coins* (fourth edition). **a.** Of the 1,194 coins reported struck, an estimated 400 to 600 were issued. **b.** Many counterfeits exist—some die struck, some made by adding an "S" to a Philadelphia coin. **c.** Included in 1909-S mintage figure.

**1917, Doubled Die
Obverse
FS-01-1917-101.**

	Mintage	Cert	Avg	%MS	G-4	VG-8	F-12	VF-20	EF-40	AU-50	MS-60BN PF-63RB	MS-63BN PF-64RB	MS-65RD PF-65RD
1913	76,532,352	817	61.8	92%	$0.85	$1	$2	$4	$18	$27	$35	$55	$425
	Auctions: $19,975, MS-67RD, January 2013; $1,410, MS-66RD, July 2014; $529, MS-65RD, July 2014; $470, MS-65RD, August 2014											
1913, Proof	2,983	332	64.4								$675	$1,050	$1,750
	Auctions: $25,850, PF-67RD, January 2014; $8,225, PF-67RB, August 2014; $1,410, PF-65RB, November 2014; $1,058, PF-64RD, October 2014											
1913-D	15,804,000	695	57.0	72%	$3	$3.50	$4.50	$10	$50	$70	$110	$200	$1,350
	Auctions: $10,575, MS-66RD, January 2014; $8,225, MS-66RD, October 2014; $881, MS-64RD, August 2014; $705, MS-64RD, September 2014											
1913-S	6,101,000	933	48.0	51%	$10	$13	$18	$30	$60	$100	$200	$275	$2,750
	Auctions: $4,406, MS-65RD, June 2014; $676, MS-64RD, July 2014; $388, MS-63RD, September 2014; $823, MS-61BN, October 2014											
1914	75,238,432	854	60.1	85%	$0.85	$1.10	$2	$6	$20	$40	$55	$70	$500
	Auctions: $28,200, MS-67RD, August 2013; $2,585, MS-66RD, November 2014; $499, MS-65RD, July 2014; $270, MS-64RD, September 2014											
1914, Proof	1,365	161	64.7								$675	$1,100	$1,750
	Auctions: $3,525, PF-66BN, June 2014; $8,226, PF-66RB+, August 2014; $4,406, PF-66RB, October 2014; $1,410, PF-65RB, July 2014											
1914-D (d)	1,193,000	5,785	23.6	8%	$145	$165	$200	$240	$650	$1,400	$2,000	$3,000	$14,000
	Auctions: $152,750, MS-66, August 2017; $9,000, MS-66, April 2018; $4,080, MS-64, March 2018; $2,115, MS-62BN, August 2016											
1914-S	4,137,000	984	41.7	30%	$17	$23	$28	$40	$85	$150	$325	$460	$5,500
	Auctions: $5,875, MS-65RD, September 2014; $6,463, MS-65RD, September 2013; $1,528, MS-64RD, July 2014; $793, MS-64BN, October 2014											
1915	29,092,120	702	59.9	84%	$1.75	$2.75	$5	$18	$55	$70	$90	$105	$750
	Auctions: $10,575, MS-67RD, September 2014; $3,525, MS-66RD, January 2014; $1,293, MS-66RD, November 2014; $1,116, MS-65RD, August 2014											
1915, Proof	1,150	139	64.7								$600	$1,200	$3,500
	Auctions: $4,406, PF-66RB, July 2014; $22,325, PF-66RB+, August 2014; $17,625, PF-65RD, January 2014; $801, PF-64BN, October 2014											
1915-D	22,050,000	1,061	57.2	76%	$2	$3	$4	$7	$22	$45	$85	$120	$1,000
	Auctions: $4,465, MS-66RD, October 2014; $7,638, MS-66RD, June 2013; $1,063, MS-65RD, September 2014; $940, MS-65RD, November 2014											
1915-S	4,833,000	840	44.6	41%	$15	$20	$30	$35	$70	$125	$200	$450	$4,500
	Auctions: $23,500, MS-66RD, September 2013; $7,638, MS-65RD, November 2014; $3,055, MS-64RD, October 2014; $852, MS-63RB, July 2014											
1916	131,833,677	1,026	62.6	95%	$0.50	$0.60	$0.80	$2	$8	$13	$18	$35	$300
	Auctions: $2,350, MS-67RD, March 2014; $1,880, MS-67RD, August 2014; $2,820, MS-67RD, October 2014; $505, MS-66RD, July 2014											
1916, Proof	1,050	102	64.8								$1,250	$2,500	$10,000
	Auctions: $30,550, PF-66RB+, August 2014; $1,880, PF-64RB, October 2014; $7,931, PF-64RB, June 2014; $4,700, PF-63RB, July 2014											
1916-D	35,956,000	915	60.6	83%	$1	$1.75	$3	$6	$15	$35	$75	$125	$1,250
	Auctions: $17,625, MS-66RD, June 2014; $282, MS-65RB, August 2014; $823, MS-64RD+, July 2014; $441, MS-64RD, October 2014											
1916-S	22,510,000	899	57.7	70%	$1.75	$2.25	$3.50	$8	$25	$50	$105	$175	$7,000
	Auctions: $911, MS-65RB, July 2014; $7,638, MS-65RD, August 2013; $1,183, MS-64RD, October 2014; $1,410, MS-64RD, November 2014											
1917	196,429,785	1,031	57.3	82%	$0.35	$0.45	$0.55	$2	$4	$10	$16	$30	$375
	Auctions: $823, MS-66RD, September 2014; $1,586, MS-66RD+, November 2014; $2,585, MS-66RD, January 2013; $145, MS-64RD, September 2014											
1917, Doubled Die Obverse	(e)	97	30.3	13%	$150	$165	$225	$350	$1,100	$1,600	$3,250	$6,000	$19,500
	Auctions: $499, MS-65RB, October 2014; $329, MS-64RB, July 2014; $705, VF-35, January 2015; $6,600, MSF-64RD, January 2018											
1917-D	55,120,000	762	59.4	79%	$0.90	$1.10	$2.50	$4.50	$35	$50	$80	$125	$1,500
	Auctions: $9,400, MS-65RD, August 2014; $2,350, MS-65RD, August 2013; $1,116, MS-64RD, August 2014; $2,703, MS-64RD, November 2014											
1917-S	32,620,000	546	58.9	78%	$0.50	$0.70	$1.20	$2.50	$10	$25	$75	$160	$6,750
	Auctions: $11,750, MS-67RD, August 2014; $17,625, MS-67RD, November 2014; $881, MS-66RD, November 2014; $4,113, MS-65RD, December 2013											

d. Many counterfeits exist, including crude fakes, sophisticated die-struck forgeries, and altered 1944-D cents (the latter, unlike an authentic 1914-D cent, will have the designer's initials, V.D.B., on the shoulder). **e.** Included in 1917 mintage figure.

1922, No D
FS-01-1922-401.

1922, Weak D

	Mintage	Cert	Avg	%MS	G-4	VG-8	F-12	VF-20	EF-40	AU-50	MS-60BN / PF-63RB	MS-63BN / PF-64RB	MS-65RD / PF-65RD
1918	288,104,634	704	63.0	95%	$0.25	$0.35	$0.55	$1.50	$3	$8	$16	$27	$350
	Auctions: $423, MS-64BN, September 2014; $200, MS-63RB, August 2014; $74, MS-62BN, November 2014; $14,100, MS, March 2014												
1918-D	47,830,000	570	58.6	74%	$0.75	$1.25	$2.50	$4	$15	$35	$80	$140	$3,500
	Auctions: $25,850, MS-66RD, August 2013; $11,163, MS-65RD, October 2014; $1,528, MS-64RD, November 2014; $764, MS-64RB, August 2014												
1918-S	34,680,000	646	59.3	75%	$0.50	$1	$2	$3	$11	$35	$80	$185	$7,000
	Auctions: $823, MS-67RD, August 2014; $1,058, MS-67RD, October 2014; $499, MS-66RD, August 2014; $3,525, MS-64RD, February 2014												
1919	392,021,000	920	62.7	94%	$0.25	$0.35	$0.40	$1	$3.25	$5	$14	$28	$150
	Auctions: $8,225, MS-68RD, April 2014; $1,058, MS-67RD, October 2014; $499, MS-66RD, August 2014; $182, MS-65RD, September 2014												
1919-D	57,154,000	671	61.1	87%	$0.50	$0.75	$1	$4	$10	$32	$65	$110	$1,150
	Auctions: $1,763, MS-65RD, January 2014; $1,410, MS-65RD, October 2014; $353, MS-64RB, July 2014; $311, MS-64RB, August 2014												
1919-S	139,760,000	766	59.7	79%	$0.20	$0.40	$1	$2.50	$6	$18	$50	$115	$4,000
	Auctions: $7,638, MS-65RD, April 2014; $482, MS-64RB, July 2014; $259, MS-64RB, November 2014; $123, MS-63BN, December 2014												
1920	310,165,000	862	62.7	95%	$0.20	$0.30	$0.45	$0.75	$2.50	$6	$15	$28	$250
	Auctions: $940, MS-66RD, January 2013; $881, MS-66RD+, September 2014; $705, MS-66RD, September 2014; $200, MS-65RD, November 2014												
1920-D	49,280,000	576	60.3	82%	$1	$2	$3	$6.50	$15	$40	$80	$110	$2,000
	Auctions: $22,325, MS-66RD, June 2014; $283, MS-64RB, November 2014; $182, MS-63RB, October 2014; $45, MS-60BN, November 2014												
1920-S	46,220,000	590	58.5	71%	$0.50	$0.65	$1.50	$2.25	$10	$35	$110	$185	$12,500
	Auctions: $3,173, MS-64RD, October 2014; $2,115, MS-64RD, February 2013; $259, MS-63RB, November 2014; $79, MS-62BN, November 2014												
1921	39,157,000	662	62.5	92%	$0.50	$0.60	$1.30	$2.10	$9	$22	$50	$80	$350
	Auctions: $3,290, MS-66RD, January 2014; $411, MS-65RD, September 2014; $112, MS-64RD, October 2014; $16, MS-60RD, November 2014												
1921-S	15,274,000	852	55.4	57%	$1.50	$2.25	$3.50	$7	$35	$75	$135	$225	$11,500
	Auctions: $1,293, MS-65RB, September 2014; $499, MS-64RB, July 2014; $1,880, MS-64RD, August 2013; $282, MS-63RB, November 2014												
1922-D	7,160,000	2,683	34.4	29%	$20	$25	$28	$30	$40	$75	$110	$225	$1,350
	Auctions: $2,585, MS-65RD, August 2013; $499, MS-64RD, November 2014; $229, MS-63RD, July 2014; $106, MS-62RB, November 2014												
1922, No D (f)	(g)	3,799	20.5	2%	$450	$550	$600	$750	$1,500	$3,500	$8,500	$16,000	
	Auctions: $82,250, MS-65BN, April 2013; $20,563, MS-63, February 2015; $3,819, AU-55BN, August 2014; $1,080, EF-40, January 2018												
1922, Weak D (f)	(g)	715	16.2	3%	$25	$35	$50	$70	$160	$200	$350	$1,000	
	Auctions: $2,174, MS, April 2014; $376, AU-58BN, October 2014; $329, AU-58BN, October 2014; $153, AU-55BN, October 2014												
1923	74,723,000	650	62.9	96%	$0.35	$0.45	$0.65	$1	$5	$9.50	$15	$30	$350
	Auctions: $4,700, MS-67RD, June 2013; $1,645, MS-66RD+, September 2014; $247, MS-64RD+, July 2014; $84, MS-64RD, November 2014												
1923-S	8,700,000	552	54.6	54%	$5	$7	$8	$12	$45	$90	$220	$400	$25,000
	Auctions: $2,350, MS-65RB, June 2014; $3,055, MS-64RB, October 2014; $823, MS-64RB, November 2014; $353, MS-62RB, August 2014												
1924	75,178,000	501	62.7	94%	$0.20	$0.30	$0.40	$0.85	$5	$10	$24	$50	$400
	Auctions: $16,450, MS-67RD, April 2013; $12,925, MS-67RD, July 2014; $470, MS-65RD, November 2014; $259, MS-64RD, November 2014												
1924-D	2,520,000	1,514	40.8	32%	$30	$38	$50	$55	$115	$175	$300	$450	$12,500
	Auctions: $9,400, MS-65RD, January 2014; $2,820, MS-64RD, November 2014; $1,410, MS-64, March 2016												
1924-S	11,696,000	571	54.7	60%	$2	$2.50	$3.50	$5.50	$30	$75	$125	$300	$20,000
	Auctions: $9,400, MS-64RD, January 2014; $764, MS-64RB, November 2014; $529, MS-63RB, October 2014; $88, MS-60BN, November 2014												

f. 1922 cents with a weak or completely missing mintmark were made from extremely worn dies that originally struck normal 1922-D cents. Three different die pairs were involved; two of them produced "Weak D" coins. One die pair (no. 2, identified by a "strong reverse") is acknowledged as having struck "No D" coins. Weak D cents are worth considerably less. Beware of fraudulently removed mintmark.
g. Included in 1922-D mintage figure.

	Mintage	Cert	Avg	%MS	G-4	VG-8	F-12	VF-20	EF-40	AU-50	MS-60BN PF-63RB	MS-63BN PF-64RB	MS-65RD PF-65RD
1925	139,949,000	923	63.7	97%	$0.20	$0.25	$0.35	$0.60	$3	$6.50	$10	$20	$115
	Auctions: $1,410, MS-67RD, August 2014; $2,115, MS-67RD, September 2013; $110, MS-65RD, December 2014; $44, MS-64RD, September 2014												
1925-D	22,580,000	732	60.9	86%	$1	$1.30	$2.50	$5	$13	$30	$75	$100	$3,000
	Auctions: $4,113, MS-65RD, January 2014; $764, MS-64RD+, July 2014; $382, MS-64RD, September 2014; $129, MS-63RB, October 2014												
1925-S	26,380,000	581	58.7	73%	$1	$1.50	$2	$4	$12	$30	$90	$200	$20,000
	Auctions: $4,700, MS-65RB, February 2014; $852, MS-64RB, July 2014; $259, MS-63RB, October 2014; $200, MS-62BN, November 2014												
1926	157,088,000	1,152	63.8	97%	$0.20	$0.25	$0.30	$0.50	$2	$4	$8	$12	$65
	Auctions: $1,116, MS-67RD, January 2014; $353, MS-66RD, July 2014; $259, MS-65RD, October 2014; $84, MS-65RD, November 2014												
1926-D	28,020,000	555	59.7	80%	$1.35	$1.75	$3.50	$5.25	$14	$32	$85	$125	$1,750
	Auctions: $4,700, MS-65RB, February 2013; $353, MS-64RB, November 2014; $353, MS-64RB, December 2014; $364, MS-63RB, July 2014												
1926-S	4,550,000	1,118	52.2	44%	$9	$11	$13	$17	$35	$75	$165	$375	$90,000
	Auctions: $9,988, MS-65RB, October 2013; $1,058, MS-64RB, November 2014; $1,058, MS-63RB, August 2014; $259, MS-62BN, November 2014												
1927	144,440,000	871	63.2	95%	$0.20	$0.25	$0.30	$0.60	$2	$3.50	$10	$15	$125
	Auctions: $7,638, MS-67RD, February 2014; $1,880, MS-67RD, October 2014; $368, MS-66RD, September 2014; $115, MS-65RD, August 2014												
1927-D	27,170,000	668	61.0	84%	$1.25	$1.75	$2.75	$3.75	$7.50	$25	$62	$120	$1,500
	Auctions: $2,233, MS-65RD, January 2014; $617, MS-65RB, July 2014; $159, MS-64RB, September 2014; $212, MS-64RB, December 2014												
1927-S	14,276,000	491	59.6	76%	$1.50	$2	$3	$5	$15	$40	$85	$140	$8,500
	Auctions: $529, MS-64RB, July 2014; $1,763, MS-64RD, June 2013; $535, MS-63RD, November 2014; $86, MS-62BN, November 2014												
1928	134,116,000	939	63.5	97%	$0.20	$0.25	$0.30	$0.60	$2	$3	$9	$13	$120
	Auctions: $1,058, MS-67RD, September 2014; $3,408, MS-67RD, April 2013; $499, MS-66RD, July 2014; $120, MS-65RD, October 2014												
1928-D	31,170,000	623	61.6	86%	$0.75	$1	$1.75	$3	$5.50	$17	$37	$80	$1,000
	Auctions: $7,050, MS-66RD, November 2014; $1,410, MS-65RD, June 2014; $141, MS-64RD, September 2014; $51, MS-63RB, November 2014												
1928-S	17,266,000	432	60.2	80%	$1	$1.60	$2.75	$3.75	$9.50	$30	$75	$100	$4,500
	Auctions: $4,406, MS-65RD, September 2013; $764, MS-64RB, October 2014; $470, MS-64RB, November 2014; $382, MS-63RB, November 2014												
1929	185,262,000	1,121	64.1	98%	$0.20	$0.25	$0.30	$0.75	$2	$4	$8	$14	$100
	Auctions: $5,581, MS-67RD, April 2014; $1,528, MS-67RD, August 2014; $705, MS-67RD, September 2014; $382, MS-66RD+, August 2014												
1929-D	41,730,000	506	62.5	93%	$0.40	$0.85	$1.25	$2.25	$5.50	$13	$25	$37	$550
	Auctions: $4,113, MS-66RD, January 2014; $2,585, MS-66RD, August 2014; $1,645, MS-66RD, October 2014; $458, MS-65RD, July 2014												
1929-S	50,148,000	875	63.1	95%	$0.50	$0.90	$1.70	$2.35	$5.80	$14	$21	$29	$375
	Auctions: $4,700, MS-66RD, October 2014; $4,113, MS-66RD, March 2013; $411, MS-65RD, October 2014; $65, MS-64RD, October 2014												
1930	157,415,000	3,921	65.2	100%	$0.15	$0.20	$0.25	$0.50	$1.25	$2	$6	$10	$40
	Auctions: $3,525, MS-67RD, February 2014; $823, MS-67RD, August 2014; $108, MS-66RD, October 2014; $40, MS-65RD, October 2014												
1930-D	40,100,000	801	64.0	97%	$0.20	$0.25	$0.30	$0.55	$2.50	$4	$12	$28	$145
	Auctions: $1,645, MS-66RD, June 2014; $441, MS-66RD, October 2014; $142, MS-65RD, August 2014; $141, MS-65RD, September 2014												
1930-S	24,286,000	1,877	64.8	99%	$0.20	$0.25	$0.30	$0.60	$1.75	$6	$10	$12	$80
	Auctions: $6,463, MS-66RD, April 2014; $2,377, MS-66RD, August 2014; $499, MS-66RD, October 2014; $84, MS-65RD, November 2014												
1931	19,396,000	760	64.0	97%	$0.50	$0.75	$1	$1.50	$4	$9	$20	$35	$125
	Auctions: $5,288, MS-67RD, August 2013; $999, MS-66RD, August 2014; $153, MS-65RD, July 2014; $42, MS-64RB, October 2014												
1931-D	4,480,000	925	59.4	70%	$5	$6	$7	$8.50	$13.50	$37	$60	$70	$1,000
	Auctions: $4,113, MS-66RD, April 2013; $1,528, MS-65RD, August 2014; $270, MS-65RB, October 2014; $165, MS-64RB, July 2014												
1931-S	866,000	5,500	54.3	57%	$65	$75	$85	$100	$125	$150	$175	$195	$550
	Auctions: $2,350, MS-66RD, January 2014; $646, MS-65RD, October 2014; $646, MS-65, August 2015												
1932	9,062,000	825	64.4	97%	$1.50	$1.80	$2	$2.50	$4.50	$12	$20	$28	$100
	Auctions: $259, MS-66RD, November 2014; $940, MS-66RD, September 2013; $95, MS-65RD, October 2014; $34, MS-64RB, October 2014												
1932-D	10,500,000	586	63.5	92%	$1.50	$1.75	$2.50	$2.75	$4.50	$11	$19	$28	$175
	Auctions: $8,519, MS-67RD, November 2013; $206, MS-65RD, August 2014; $56, MS-64RD, September 2014; $49, MS-64RD, October 2014												
1933	14,360,000	762	64.6	98%	$1.50	$1.75	$2.50	$3	$6.25	$13	$20	$30	$105
	Auctions: $2,115, MS-67RD, October 2014; $3,557, MS-67RD, August 2013; $112, MS-65RD, July 2014; $32, MS-64RB, July 2014												
1933-D	6,200,000	1,191	64.2	97%	$3.50	$3.75	$5.50	$7.25	$12	$19	$23	$25	$135
	Auctions: $5,581, MS-67RD, February 2014; $764, MS-67RD, October 2014; $558, MS-66RD+, November 2014; $141, MS-65RD, August 2014												

1934, Doubled Die Obverse
FS-01-1934-101.

1936, Doubled Die Obverse
FS-01-1936-101.

	Mintage	Cert	Avg	%MS	G-4	VG-8	F-12	VF-20	EF-40	AU-50	MS-60BN PF-63RB	MS-63BN PF-64RB	MS-65RD PF-65RD
1934	219,080,000	2,551	65.5	99%	$0.15	$0.18	$0.20	$0.30	$1	$4	$7	$8	$35
Auctions: $1,058, MS-67RD, September 2014; $1,058, MS-67RD+, November 2014; $764, MS-67RD, December 2013													
1934, Doubled Die Obverse (h)	(i)	5	60.6	80%								$300	
Auctions: $1,600, MS-64RB, October 2011													
1934-D	28,446,000	1,118	64.7	98%	$0.20	$0.25	$0.50	$0.75	$2.25	$7.50	$20	$22	$65
Auctions: $11,163, MS-67RD, April 2014; $229, MS-66RD, July 2014; $123, MS-66RD, October 2014; $223, MS-66RD, December 2014													
1935	245,388,000	2,699	65.6	99%	$0.15	$0.18	$0.20	$0.25	$0.50	$1	$3	$5	$35
Auctions: $1,293, MS-67RD, March 2014; $106, MS-67RD, October 2014; $92, MS-67RD, November 2014; $106, MS-64RB, November 2014													
1935-D	47,000,000	1,692	65.6	100%	$0.15	$0.18	$0.20	$0.25	$0.50	$2	$5	$6	$40
Auctions: $823, MS-67RD, February 2014; $153, MS-67RD, August 2014; $141, MS-67RD, October 2014; $588, MS-67RD, November 2014													
1935-S	38,702,000	1,059	64.6	99%	$0.15	$0.18	$0.25	$0.50	$2	$5	$12	$17	$60
Auctions: $1,469, MS-67RD, October 2014; $3,055, MS-66RD+, July 2014; $1,175, MS-66RD, October 2014; $106, MS-65RD, December 2014													
1936	309,632,000	3,556	64.3	95%	$0.15	$0.18	$0.25	$0.50	$1.50	$2.60	$3	$4	$30
Auctions: $705, MS-67RD, February 2014; $353, MS-67RD, July 2014; $2,820, MS-67RD+, September 2014; $306, MS-67RD, October 2014													
1936, Doubled Die Obverse (j)	(k)	86	42.3	26%		$75	$125	$200	$350	$500	$1,500		
Auctions: $646, MS-62BN, August 2014; $259, AU-50, April 2014; $80, VF-30BN, November 2014; $76, VF-30BN, November 2014													
1936, Satin, PF	5,569	205	64.1								$185	$425	$2,000
Auctions: $2,585, PF-67RB, July 2017; $1,800, PF-65RD, November 2017; $336, PF-63RB, May 2018													
1936, Brilliant, PF	(l)	418	63.8								$200	$485	$1,750
Auctions: $18,600, PF-67RD, January 2018; $5,280, PF-66RD, January 2018; $1,527, PF-63RDCam, February 2017													
1936-D	40,620,000	1,927	65.9	100%	$0.15	$0.20	$0.30	$0.50	$1	$2	$3	$4	$20
Auctions: $646, MS-67RD, August 2013; $411, MS-67RD, October 2014; $145, MS-67RD, October 2014; $79, MS-67RD, December 2014													
1936-S	29,130,000	1,702	65.4	100%	$0.15	$0.25	$0.40	$0.55	$1	$3	$5	$6	$25
Auctions: $4,259, MS-67RD, February 2014; $2,703, MS-67RD, September 2014; $2,585, MS-67RD, November 2014													
1937	309,170,000	4,868	66.0	100%	$0.15	$0.20	$0.30	$0.50	$1	$2	$3	$4	$15
Auctions: $90, MS-67RD, August 2014; $94, MS-67RD, October 2014; $2,233, MS-67RD+, November 2013; $35, MS-66RD, November 2014													
1937, Proof	9,320	959	64.3								$65	$90	$350
Auctions: $21,150, PF-67Cam, September 2013; $5,288, PF-66Cam, August 2014; $1,763, PF-65Cam, October 2014; $3,643, PF-64RD, July 2014													
1937-D	50,430,000	3,234	66.1	100%	$0.15	$0.20	$0.25	$0.40	$1	$3	$5	$6	$17
Auctions: $135, MS-67RD, January 2014; $123, MS-67RD, August 2014; $106, MS-67RD, August 2014; $40, MS-66RD, August 2014													
1937-S	34,500,000	2,134	65.8	100%	$0.15	$0.20	$0.30	$0.40	$1	$3	$5	$8	$25
Auctions: $1,998, MS-67RD, January 2014; $881, MS-67RD+, July 2014; $764, MS-67RD+, July 2014; $55, MS-66RD, July 2014													
1938	156,682,000	3,128	66.0	100%	$0.15	$0.20	$0.30	$0.40	$1	$2	$4	$7	$15
Auctions: $2,585, MS-67RD+, September 2014; $106, MS-67RD, October 2014; $2,820, MS-67RD, November 2013; $27, MS-66RD, November 2014													
1938, Proof	14,734	1,137	64.5								$60	$80	$200
Auctions: $2,585, PF-66Cam, January 2014; $1,058, PF-66Cam, September 2014; $1,469, PF-66Cam, November 2014													
1938-D	20,010,000	2,437	66.1	100%	$0.20	$0.30	$0.50	$0.80	$1.25	$3	$4	$7	$15
Auctions: $3,055, MS-67RD, January 2014; $3,290, MS-67RD, August 2014; $100, MS-67RD, November 2014; $89, MS-67RD, December 2014													
1938-S	15,180,000	3,536	65.9	100%	$0.40	$0.50	$0.60	$0.75	$1.10	$3	$4	$6	$15
Auctions: $2,115, MS-67RD+, July 2014; $118, MS-67RD, July 2014; $92, MS-67RD, August 2014; $40, MS-66RD, August 2014													

h. The remains of a secondary 3 and 4 are evident below the primary digits. i. Included in 1934 mintage figure. j. FS-01-1936-101. k. Included in circulation-strike 1936 mintage figure. l. Included in 1936, Satin, Proof mintage figure.

	Mintage	Cert	Avg	%MS	G-4	VG-8	F-12	VF-20	EF-40	AU-50	MS-60BN	MS-63BN	MS-65RD
											PF-63RB	PF-64RB	PF-65RD
1939	316,466,000	3,666	65.8	99%	$0.15	$0.18	$0.20	$0.25	$0.50	$1	$2	$3	$10
	Auctions: $108, MS-67RD, August 2014; $106, MS-67RD, October 2014; $705, MS-67RD, June 2013; $38, MS-66RD, December 2014												
1939, Proof	13,520	1,102	64.6								$55	$70	$180
	Auctions: $2,820, PF-67RD, January 2014; $1,410, PF-67RD, October 2014; $270, PF-66RD, November 2014; $212, PF-65RD, September 2014												
1939-D	15,160,000	2,360	66.0	100%	$0.50	$0.60	$0.65	$0.85	$1.25	$3	$4	$5	$11
	Auctions: $529, MS-67RD, April 2014; $86, MS-67RD, October 2014; $100, MS-67RD, November 2014; $69, MS-67RD, December 2014												
1939-S	52,070,000	4,035	65.9	100%	$0.15	$0.20	$0.30	$0.75	$1	$2.50	$3	$4	$15
	Auctions: $1,175, MS-67RD+, July 2014; $1,116, MS-67RD+, August 2014; $3,966, MS-67RD, August 2013; $24, MS-66RD, November 2014												
1940	586,810,000	3,055	66.0	100%	$0.15	$0.18	$0.20	$0.40	$0.60	$1	$2	$3	$14
	Auctions: $3,819, MS-67RD, January 2014; $212, MS-67RD, July 2014; $147, MS-67RD, September 2014; $74, MS-65RD, November 2014												
1940, Proof	15,872	1,114	64.5								$45	$60	$150
	Auctions: $7,931, PF-67RD, June 2013; $4,700, PF-67RD, August 2014; $6,463, PF-67RD, October 2014; $764, PF-66RD, July 2014												
1940-D	81,390,000	1,624	66.1	100%	$0.15	$0.18	$0.25	$0.60	$0.75	$2	$3	$4	$15
	Auctions: $94, MS-67RD, August 2014; $68, MS-67RD, November 2014; $119, MS-67RD, December 2014; $159, MS-67RD, January 2013												
1940-S	112,940,000	3,194	66.0	100%	$0.15	$0.18	$0.20	$0.50	$1	$1.75	$3	$4	$15
	Auctions: $999, MS-67RD+, November 2014; $100, MS-67RD, November 2014; $79, MS-67RD, December 2014; $306, MS-67RD, June 2013												
1941	887,018,000	3,659	65.4	98%	$0.15	$0.18	$0.20	$0.30	$0.60	$1.50	$2	$3	$14
	Auctions: $147, MS-67RD, July 2014; $212, MS-67RD, August 2014; $259, MS-67RD, October 2014; $4,994, MS-65RD, November 2013												
1941, Proof	21,100	1,273	64.4								$40	$55	$150
	Auctions: $28,200, PF-67RD, November 2013; $705, PF-66RD, August 2014; $382, PF-66RD, October 2014; $705, PF-64RD, July 2014												
1941-D	128,700,000	1,987	66.3	100%	$0.15	$0.18	$0.20	$0.50	$1	$3	$4	$5	$15
	Auctions: $2,115, MS-67RD+, August 2014; $165, MS-67RD, August 2014; $63, MS-67RD, August 2014; $441, MS-67RD, August 2013												
1941-S	92,360,000	2,863	66.1	99%	$0.15	$0.18	$0.30	$0.50	$1	$3	$4	$5	$15
	Auctions: $646, MS-67RD, August 2014; $306, MS-67RD, October 2014; $119, MS-67RD, December 2014; $1,880, MS-67RD, November 2013												
1942	657,796,000	3,554	65.7	99%	$0.15	$0.18	$0.20	$0.25	$0.50	$0.75	$1	$2	$14
	Auctions: $3,290, MS-67RD+, July 2014; $112, MS-63RB, November 2014; $14,100, AU-58, November 2013; $282, Fair-2BN, November 2014												
1942, Proof	32,600	1,903	64.1								$40	$55	$150
	Auctions: $1,880, PF-66Cam, November 2014; $2,115, PF-66Cam, June 2013; $999, PF-65Cam, July 2014; $212, PF-64Cam, November 2014												
1942-D	206,698,000	3,896	66.0	100%	$0.15	$0.18	$0.20	$0.25	$0.50	$0.85	$1	$2	$14
	Auctions: $170, MS-67RD, August 2014; $141, MS-67RD, December 2014; $3,055, MS-67RD, November 2013; $20, MS-65RD, November 2014												
1942-S	85,590,000	2,484	65.9	99%	$0.20	$0.25	$0.30	$0.85	$1.25	$5.50	$7	$8	$20
	Auctions: $3,290, MS-67RD, February 2014; $2,350, MS-67RD+, September 2014												

	Mintage	Cert	Avg	%MS	F-12	VF-20	EF-40	AU-50	MS-63BN	MS-65	MS-66	MS-67	MS-68
1943, Steel (a)	684,628,670	20,562	65.8	100%	$0.30	$0.35	$0.40	$0.50	$2.50	$8	$35	$175	$2,000
	Auctions: $382, MS-67, July 2014; $182, MS-67, November 2014; $1,058, EF-45, September 2014; $1,763, VF-25, October 2014												
1943, Bronze † ‡‡ (a)	(b)	13	56.7	31%			$150,000	$200,000					
	Auctions: $218,500, AU-58, January 2010												
1943, Silver (a)	(b)	0	n/a				$4,500	$5,500					
	Auctions: $4,313, AU-58, March 2010												
1943-D	217,660,000	12,605	65.9	100%	$0.35	$0.40	$0.50	$0.75	$3	$10	$35	$225	$1,500
	Auctions: $1,175, MS-68, July 2014; $705, MS-68, July 2014; $2,820, MS-68, April 2013; $209, MS-67, October 2014												

† Ranked in the *100 Greatest U.S. Coins* (fifth edition). ‡‡ Ranked in the *100 Greatest U.S. Error Coins*. **a.** Due to a copper shortage in the critical war year 1943, the Treasury used zinc-coated steel for regular-issue cents. A handful were accidentally struck on old bronze and silver planchets, instead of the intended steel planchets. Today about a dozen are known to exist. Numerous regular steel cents have been plated with copper as novelties or with intent to deceive; their true nature is easily revealed with a magnet. **b.** Included in 1943 mintage figure.

1943-D, Boldly Doubled Mintmark
FS-01-1943D-501.

	Mintage	Cert	Avg	%MS	F-12	VF-20	EF-40	AU-50	MS-63BN	MS-65	MS-66	MS-67	MS-68
1943-D, Boldly Doubled Mintmark (c)	(d)	45	63.8	100%	$40	$50	$60	$70	$100	$1,000	$1,750	$8,000	
Auctions: $1,116, MS-65, December 2013; $411, MS-64, March 2015; $353, MS-63, November 2014													
1943-S	191,550,000	13,007	65.8	100%	$0.40	$0.65	$0.75	$1	$6	$20	$50	$225	$3,500
Auctions: $306, MS-67, August 2014; $153, MS-67, November 2014; $135, MS-67, December 2014; $165, MS-66, October 2014													

c. FS-01-1943D-501. **d.** Included in 1943-D mintage figure.

1944-D, D Over S
FS-01-1944D-511.

1946-S, S Over D
FS-01-1946S-511.

	Mintage	Cert	Avg	%MS	VF-20	EF-40	AU-50	MS-63RB	MS-65RB	MS-65RD	MS-67RD
									PF-65RD	PF-66RD	PF-67RD
1944	1,435,400,000	4,957	65.7	99%	$0.10	$0.20	$0.35	$1	$5	$12	$125
Auctions: $2,233, MS-67RD+, September 2014; $79, MS-67RD, November 2014; $30,550, AU-58, November 2013											
1944, Steel ‡‡		4	55.8	0%				$35,000			
Auctions: $26,400, AU-55, August 2019											
1944-D	430,578,000	4,885	64.5	94%	$0.10	$0.20	$0.35	$0.85	$4	$14	$100
Auctions: $141, MS-67RD, July 2014; $119, MS-67RD, September 2014; $58, MS-67RD, August 2014; $30,550, AU-53, November 2013											
1944-D, D Over S	(a)	112	52.3	46%	$100	$175	$235	$450	$700	$2,000	
Auctions: $1,116, MS-64RD, January 2014; $470, MS-64RB, September 2014; $517, MS-64, August 2016											
1944-S	282,760,000	6,989	65.9	100%	$0.15	$0.20	$0.35	$0.85	$4	$13	$75
Auctions: $141, MS-67RD, May 2014; $101, MS-67RD, July 2014; $96, MS-67RD, July 2014											
1945	1,040,515,000	3,809	65.6	100%	$0.10	$0.20	$0.35	$0.85	$2	$8	$185
Auctions: $764, MS-67RD, November 2014; $41, MS-66RD, August 2014; $36, MS-66RD, August 2014; $3,819, MS-68RD, November 2013											
1945-D	266,268,000	4,935	65.9	100%	$0.10	$0.20	$0.35	$0.85	$2	$9	$125
Auctions: $2,115, MS-67RD, June 2014; $165, MS-67RD, July 2014; $2,585, MS-67RD, September 2014; $99, MS-67RD, October 2014											
1945-S	181,770,000	5,387	66.2	100%	$0.15	$0.20	$0.35	$0.85	$2	$9	$75
Auctions: $106, MS-67RD, September 2014; $89, MS-67RD, December 2014; $84, MS-67RD, October 2014; $7,050, AU-58, November 2013											
1946	991,655,000	2,211	65.3	99%	$0.10	$0.20	$0.35	$0.60	$2	$14	$650
Auctions: $7,168, MS-67RD, January 2014; $2,585, MS-67RD, October 2014; $2,585, MS-67RD, November 2014; $470, MS-66RD+, August 2014											
1946-D	315,690,000	3,036	65.9	100%	$0.10	$0.20	$0.35	$0.60	$2	$10	$200
Auctions: $2,115, MS-67RD, March 2014; $176, MS-67RD, August 2014; $129, MS-67RD, November 2014; $182, MS-67RD, December 2014											
1946-S	198,100,000	5,961	65.8	99%	$0.15	$0.20	$0.35	$0.60	$2	$10	$185
Auctions: $470, MS-67RD, July 2014; $470, MS-67RD, December 2014; $940, MS-67RD, September 2013; $20, MS-66RD, November 2014											
1946-S, S Over D	(b)	19	61.9	84%	$35	$75	$125	$225	$400	$850	
Auctions: $541, MS-67, August 2016; $1,998, MS-66RD, June 2014											
1947	190,555,000	1,814	65.4	100%	$0.10	$0.20	$0.40	$1	$3	$12	$1,250
Auctions: $3,525, MS-67RD, July 2014; $4,113, MS-67RD, April 2013; $294, MS-66RD+, August 2014; $106, MS-66RD, November 2014											
1947-D	194,750,000	2,647	65.8	100%	$0.10	$0.20	$0.40	$0.60	$2	$10	$200
Auctions: $176, MS-67RD, October 2014; $764, MS-67RD, February 2013											
1947-S	99,000,000	3,947	65.9	100%	$0.20	$0.25	$0.50	$0.85	$2	$12	$175
Auctions: $1,704, MS-67RD, February 2014; $1,998, MS-67RD+, August 2014; $1,293, MS-67RD+, August 2014; $153, MS-67RD, November 2014											

‡‡ Ranked (along with the 1944-D and 1944-S steel cents) in the *100 Greatest U.S. Error Coins*. **a.** Included in 1944-D mintage figure. **b.** Included in 1946-S mintage figure.

1951-D, D Over S
FS-01-1951D-512.

	Mintage	Cert	Avg	%MS	VF-20	EF-40	AU-50	MS-63RB	MS-65RB	MS-65RD	MS-67RD
									PF-65RD	PF-66RD	PF-67RD
1948	317,570,000	1,904	65.6	100%	$0.10	$0.20	$0.35	$0.85	$2	$15	$1,850
	Auctions: $7,168, MS-67RD, January 2014; $441, MS-66RD+, September 2014; $135, MS-66RD, October 2014; $153, MS-66RD, November 2014										
1948-D	172,637,500	2,265	65.7	100%	$0.10	$0.20	$0.35	$0.60	$2	$11	$550
	Auctions: $353, MS-67RD, October 2014; $259, MS-67RD, November 2014; $188, MS-67RD, November 2014; $999, MS-67RD, August 2013										
1948-S	81,735,000	3,714	66.0	100%	$0.20	$0.30	$0.35	$1	$3	$9	$75
	Auctions: $1,998, MS-67RD+, August 2014; $212, MS-67RD, August 2014; $101, MS-67RD, August 2014; $306, MS-67RD, June 2013										
1949	217,775,000	1,533	65.6	100%	$0.10	$0.20	$0.35	$1	$3	$15	$1,000
	Auctions: $3,055, MS-67RD, July 2014; $247, MS-66RD, October 2014; $159, MS-66RD, October 2014; $4,406, MS, March 2014										
1949-D	153,132,500	2,201	65.6	100%	$0.10	$0.20	$0.35	$1	$3	$14	$450
	Auctions: $1,058, MS-67RD, October 2014; $1,164, MS-67RD, November 2014; $353, MS-67RD, December 2014; $1,763, MS-67RD, June 2013										
1949-S	64,290,000	3,791	66.0	100%	$0.25	$0.30	$0.35	$2	$4	$16	$175
	Auctions: $3,173, MS-67RD, March 2014; $247, MS-67RD, August 2014; $153, MS-67RD, September 2014; $41, MS-66RD, August 2014										
1950	272,635,000	1,654	65.5	100%	$0.10	$0.20	$0.35	$0.85	$2	$18	$650
	Auctions: $1,410, MS-67RD, August 2014; $1,293, MS-67RD, September 2014; $3,055, MS-67RD, August 2013; $96, MS-66RD, August 2014										
1950, Proof	51,386	1,958	65.3						$70	$100	$325
	Auctions: $5,141, PF-67DCam, January 2014; $12,925, PF-66DCam+, September 2014; $482, PF-66Cam, July 2014; $306, PF-65Cam, November 2014										
1950-D	334,950,000	2,368	65.6	99%	$0.10	$0.20	$0.35	$0.60	$2	$17	$600
	Auctions: $353, MS-67RD, November 2014; $282, MS-67RD, December 2014; $212, MS-67RD, December 2014; $15,275, MS-67RD, November 2013										
1950-S	118,505,000	2,609	65.9	100%	$0.15	$0.25	$0.35	$0.85	$2	$13	$275
	Auctions: $9,400, MS-67RD+, September 2014; $588, MS-67RD, October 2014; $529, MS-67RD, December 2014; $1,293, MS-67RD, June 2013										
1951	284,576,000	1,309	65.4	99%	$0.10	$0.25	$0.35	$0.70	$2	$18	$550
	Auctions: $2,291, MS-67RD, July 2014; $5,288, MS-67RD, August 2013; $353, MS-66RD+, August 2014; $411, MS-66RD+, October 2014										
1951, Proof	57,500	1,932	65.7						$65	$100	$225
	Auctions: $1,763, PF-67Cam, April 2013; $376, PF-67RB, September 2014; $206, PF-67RB, November 2014; $90, PF-66RB, September 2014										
1951-D	625,355,000	3,809	65.5	100%	$0.10	$0.12	$0.35	$0.60	$2	$9	$200
	Auctions: $282, MS-67RD, September 2014; $94, MS-67RD, November 2014; $1,410, MS-67RD, June 2013										
1951-D, D Over S	(c)	33	64.6	100%				$100			
	Auctions: $2,350, MS-67RD, April 2014; $82, MS-65RD, August 2014										
1951-S	136,010,000	2,149	65.8	100%	$0.25	$0.30	$0.50	$1	$3	$11	$300
	Auctions: $823, MS-67RD, January 2014; $170, MS-67RD, August 2014; $529, MS-67RD, September 2014; $617, MS-67RD, November 2014										
1952	186,775,000	1,600	65.6	100%	$0.10	$0.15	$0.35	$1	$3	$16	$1,250
	Auctions: $4,994, MS-67RD, April 2014; $2,350, MS-67RD, July 2014; $270, MS-66RD, August 2014; $135, MS-66RD, December 2014										
1952, Proof	81,980	2,034	66.0						$50	$75	$125
	Auctions: $1,528, PF-67Cam, April 2013; $306, PF-66Cam, July 2014; $646, PF-66Cam, October 2014; $646, PF-66RB, September 2014										
1952-D	746,130,000	4,131	65.6	100%	$0.10	$0.15	$0.25	$0.75	$2	$9	$350
	Auctions: $823, MS-67RD, September 2014; $646, MS-67RD, September 2014; $411, MS-67RD, November 2014; $1,058, MS-67RD, December 2013										
1952-S	137,800,004	2,843	66.0	100%	$0.15	$0.20	$0.35	$2	$4	$13	$150
	Auctions: $4,113, MS-67RD+, November 2014; $123, MS-67RD, November 2014; $999, MS-67RD, June 2013										

c. Included in 1951-D mintage figure.

1955, Doubled Die Obverse
FS-01-1955-101.

1955, Doubled Die Obverse, Closeup of Date

1956-D, D Above Shadow D
FS-01-1956D-508.

	Mintage	Cert	Avg	%MS	VF-20	EF-40	AU-50	MS-63RB	MS-65RB / PF-65RD	MS-65RD / PF-66RD	MS-67RD / PF-67RD
1953	256,755,000	1,701	65.4	99%	$0.10	$0.15	$0.20	$0.50	$1	$18	$2,000
	Auctions: $14,100, MS-67RD, January 2014; $8,813, MS-67RD, August 2014; $5,889, MS-67RD, August 2014; $4,700, MS-67RD, October 2014										
1953, Proof	128,800	3,091	66.3						$30	$40	$100
	Auctions: $2,585, PF-67Cam, February 2014; $499, PF-67Cam, July 2014; $1,293, PF-66DCam, October 2014; $223, PF-66Cam, November 2014										
1953-D	700,515,000	3,545	65.5	99%	$0.10	$0.15	$0.20	$0.50	$1	$11	$750
	Auctions: $2,115, MS-67RD, July 2014; $1,998, MS-67RD, November 2014; $3,525, MS-67RD, August 2013; $100, MS-66RD+, October 2014										
1953-S	181,835,000	3,769	66.0	100%	$0.10	$0.15	$0.20	$0.60	$2	$12	$185
	Auctions: $3,055, MS-67RD, March 2014; $306, MS-67RD, July 2014; $153, MS-67RD, November 2014; $69, MS-67RD, December 2014										
1954	71,640,050	2,235	65.4	100%	$0.25	$0.35	$0.45	$0.60	$2	$27	$4,500
	Auctions: $23,500, MS-67RD, March 2014; $1,175, MS-66RD+, July 2014; $1,645, MS-66RD+, August 2014; $881, MS-66RD+, October 2014										
1954, Proof	233,300	3,174	66.5						$20	$30	$60
	Auctions: $2,820, PF-68Cam, April 2013; $115, PF-66Cam, September 2014; $129, PF-66Cam, November 2014; $112, PF-66Cam, November 2014										
1954-D	251,552,500	4,712	65.7	100%	$0.10	$0.12	$0.20	$0.50	$1	$10	$450
	Auctions: $141, MS-67RD, October 2014; $123, MS-67RD, December 2014; $1,293, MS-67RD, June 2013; $36, MS-66RD+, October 2014										
1954-S	96,190,000	10,288	65.9	100%	$0.10	$0.12	$0.20	$0.50	$1	$8	$115
	Auctions: $70, MS-67RD, August 2014; $119, MS-67RD, December 2014; $1,880, MS-67RD, August 2013										
1955	330,958,200	9,325	62.5	77%	$0.10	$0.12	$0.15	$0.35	$1	$19	$800
	Auctions: $1,998, MS-67RD, September 2014; $3,819, MS-67RD, December 2013; $49, MS-66RD, July 2014; $60, MS-66RD, October 2014										
1955, Doubled Die Obverse	(d)	3,741	58.5	45%	$1,250	$1,350	$1,500	$4,000 (e)	$10,000	$30,000	
	Auctions: $17,625, MS-66RB, February 2014; $22,325, MS-64RD, March 2016; $6,463, MS-64RB, August 2016; $9,988, MS-64, April 2014										
1955, Proof	378,200	6,750	67.3						$18	$30	$50
	Auctions: $7,638, PF-68DCam, April 2013; $940, PF-67DCam, July 2014; $74, PF-67Cam, September 2014; $135, PF-67Cam, November 2014										
1955-D	563,257,500	5,637	65.4	99%	$0.10	$0.12	$0.15	$0.35	$1	$9	$750
	Auctions: $7,050, MS-67RD, April 2013; $165, MS-66RD+, September 2014; $130, MS-66RD+, October 2014										
1955-S	44,610,000	20,233	65.9	100%	$0.20	$0.30	$0.40	$0.85	$3	$8	$115
	Auctions: $2,115, MS-67RD, February 2014; $470, MS-67RD, July 2014; $270, MS-67RD, August 2014; $170, MS-67RD, October 2014										
1956	420,745,000	3,154	65.6	100%	$0.10	$0.12	$0.15	$0.35	$1	$13	$450
	Auctions: $3,819, MS-67RD, August 2013; $823, MS-67RD, September 2014; $823, MS-67RD, September 2014; $588, MS-67RD, November 2014										
1956, Proof	669,384	7,340	67.4						$10	$25	$30
	Auctions: $7,638, PF-68DCam, June 2013; $705, PF-67DCam, July 2014; $247, PF-66DCam, October 2014; $341, PF-68DCam, July 2014										
1956-D	1,098,201,100	5,924	65.4	98%	$0.10	$0.12	$0.15	$0.30	$1	$9	$275
	Auctions: $589, MS-67RD, July 2014; $705, MS-67RD, August 2014; $3,525, MS-67RD+, November 2014; $1,175, MS-67RD, November 2013										
1956-D, D Above Shadow D (f)	(g)	112	63.1	89%	$10	$25	$30	$35		$170	
	Auctions: $1,293, MS-67RD, February 2014										

d. Included in circulation-strike 1955 mintage figure. **e.** Value in MS-60BN, $2,250; in MS-63BN, $3,500; in MS-65BN, $8,000. Varieties exist with doubling that, while still strong, is weaker than that pictured; these command premiums, but are not nearly as valuable. Note that many counterfeit 1955 Doubled Die cents exist. On authentic pieces, there is a faint die scratch under the left horizontal bar of the T in CENT. **f.** The remains of a totally separated D mintmark are evident in the field below the primary D. **g.** Included in 1956-D mintage figure.

1958, Doubled Die Obverse
FS-01-1958-101.

	Mintage	Cert	Avg	%MS	VF-20	EF-40	AU-50	MS-63RB	MS-65RB	MS-65RD	MS-67RD
									PF-65RD	PF-66RD	PF-67RD
1957	282,540,000	2,908	65.7	100%	$0.10	$0.12	$0.15	$0.30	$1	$15	$1,500
	Auctions: $515, MS-67RD, September 2014; $470, MS, December 2013; $3,360, MS-67RD, April 2018										
1957, Proof	1,247,952	9,975	67.4						$10	$25	$30
	Auctions: $1,028, PF-68Cam, July 2014; $1,058, PF-68Cam, April 2013; $282, PF-67Cam, November 2014; $84, PF-67Cam, November 2014										
1957-D	1,051,342,000	6,488	65.6	99%	$0.10	$0.12	$0.15	$0.30	$1	$9	$225
	Auctions: $705, MS-67RD, August 2014; $558, MS-67RD, October 2014; $2,115, MS-67RD, June 2013										
1958	252,525,000	5,184	65.5	99%	$0.10	$0.12	$0.15	$0.30	$1	$9	$400
	Auctions: $194, MS-67RD, August 2014; $881, MS-67RD, October 2014; $1,528, MS-67RD, June 2013										
1958, Doubled Die Obverse (h,i)	(j)	0	n/a								
	Auctions: No auction records available.										
1958, Proof	875,652	9,102	67.5						$8	$20	$30
	Auctions: $1,293, PF-67DCam, June 2013; $1,293, PF-68Cam, July 2014; $74, PF-67Cam, November 2014; $62, PF-67Cam, November 2014										
1958-D	800,953,300	8,295	65.7	99%	$0.10	$0.12	$0.15	$0.30	$1	$8	$150
	Auctions: $1,939, MS-67RD, January 2014; $106, MS-67RD, August 2014; $2,585, MS-67RD+, September 2014; $212, MS-67RD, September 2014										

h. 3 examples are known. **i.** No specimens have been reported being found in circulation, Wheat cent bags, Uncirculated rolls, "or other means that would lead to credibility of a true accidental release from the mint," as per the *Cherrypickers' Guide to Rare Die Varieties, Vol. I* (sixth edition). **j.** Included in circulation-strike 1958 mintage figure.

LINCOLN, MEMORIAL REVERSE (1959–2008)

Copper Alloy (1959–1982): **Designer:** *Victor D. Brenner (obverse), Frank Gasparro (reverse).*
Weight: *3.11 grams.* **Composition:** *1959–1962—.950 copper, .050 tin and zinc; 1962–1982—*
.950 copper, .050 zinc. **Diameter:** *19 mm.* **Edge:** *Plain.* **Mints:** *Philadelphia, Denver, and San Francisco.*

Copper Alloy (1959–1982)   **Copper Alloy, Proof**

Copper-Plated Zinc (1982–2008): **Designer:** *Victor D. Brenner (obverse),*
Frank Gasparro (reverse). **Weight:** *2.5 grams.* **Composition:** *copper-plated zinc*
(core: .992 zinc, .008 copper, with a plating of pure copper; total content .975 zinc, .025 copper).
Diameter: *19 mm.* **Edge:** *Plain.* **Mints:** *Philadelphia, Denver, and San Francisco.*

Copper-Plated Zinc (1982–2008)   **Copper-Plated Zinc, Proof**

History. In 1959 a new cent design, by Frank Gasparro, was introduced to mark the 150th anniversary of Abraham Lincoln's birth. Victor Brenner's portrait of Lincoln was maintained on the obverse. The new reverse featured a view of the Lincoln Memorial in Washington, D.C., with Daniel Chester French's massive statue of the president faintly visible within. In 1969 the dies were modified to strengthen the design, and Lincoln's head on the obverse was made slightly smaller. In 1973 the dies were further modified, and the engraver's initials (FG) were enlarged. In 1974 the initials were reduced slightly. During 1982 the dies were modified again and the bust, lettering, and date were made slightly smaller. The Lincoln Memorial reverse was used until 2009, when a switch was made to four new reverse designs honoring the bicentennial of Lincoln's birth. Lincoln Memorial cents were struck for circulation at the Philadelphia, Denver, and San Francisco mints, with the latter in smaller numbers. Partway through 1982 the bronze alloy was discontinued in favor of copper-coated zinc. From 2005 to 2010, coins produced for Mint Sets were made with a Satin Finish instead of the traditional Uncirculated luster.

Striking and Sharpness. Striking varies and can range from "sloppy" to needle sharp. On the obverse, check Lincoln's hair and beard, although the sharpness of this feature varied in the dies; for more information see *A Guide Book of Lincoln Cents* (third edition). Tiny marks on the shoulder of Lincoln indicate a weak strike there. On the reverse the sharpness can vary, including on the tiny statue of Lincoln and the shrubbery. On the reverse there can be light striking on the steps of the Memorial, and at IBU and M of E PLURIBUS UNUM. The quality of the fields can vary, as well. Some early copper-coated zinc cents, particularly of 1982 and 1983, can have planchet blisters or other problems. All Proof Lincoln Memorial cents are of the mirror type, usually with cameo or frosted contrast between the devices and the fields. High quality is common. Special Mint Set (SMS) coins were struck in lieu of Proofs from 1965 to 1967, and in some instances these closely resemble Proofs.

Availability. Coins in this series are plentiful for standard dates and mintmarks. Collectible varieties exist, and are eagerly sought by specialists, who use the *Cherrypickers' Guide to Rare Die Varieties* as their standard reference. Some of the more popular varieties are illustrated and listed herein.

GRADING STANDARDS

Caveat: These grading standards do not take sharpness of strike into account.

MS-60 to 70 (Mint State). *Obverse and Reverse:* At MS-65 and higher, the luster is rich on all areas, except perhaps the shoulder (which may be grainy and show original planchet surface). There is no rubbing, and no contact marks are visible except under magnification. Coins with full or nearly full mint orange-red color can be designated RD; those with full or nearly full brown-toned surfaces can be designated BN; and those with a sub-

1998-D. Graded MS-68.

stantial percentage of red-orange and of brown can be called RB. Ideally, MS-65 or finer coins should have good eye appeal, which in the RB category means nicely blended colors, not stained or blotched. Below MS-65, full RD coins become scarce, and at MS–60 to 62 they are virtually non-existent, unless they have been dipped. Copper is a very active metal, and influences such as slight abrasions, contact marks, and so on that define the grade also affect the color. The ANA grading standards allow for "dull" and/or "spotted" coins at MS–60 and 61, as well as incomplete luster. In the marketplace, interpretations often vary widely. BN and RB coins at MS–60 and 61 are apt to be more attractive than (dipped) RD coins.

AU-50, 53, 55, 58 (About Uncirculated). *Obverse:* Same guidelines as for the preceding type except that tinges of original mint-red are sometimes seen on coins that have not been cleaned. *Reverse:* Slight wear is seen on the Lincoln Memorial, particularly on the steps, the columns, and the horizontal architectural elements above.

Illustrated coin: The doubling of the obverse die of this popular variety is easily visible to the naked eye.

1969-S, Double Die Obverse. Graded AU-58.

EF-40, 45 (Extremely Fine). *Obverse:* Light wear is seen on Lincoln's portrait, and hair detail is gone on the higher areas, especially above the ear. *Reverse:* Most detail is gone from the steps of the Lincoln Memorial, and the columns and other higher-relief architectural elements show wear.

Lincoln, Memorial Reverse, cents are seldom collected in grades lower than EF-40.

1962-D. Graded EF-40.

PF-60 to 70 (Proof). *Obverse and Reverse:* PF-65 and higher coins are usually RB (colors should be nicely blended) or RD, the latter with bright red-orange fading slightly to hints of brown. Some tiny flecks are normal on coins certified as PF-65 but should be microscopic or absent above that. PF–60 and 61 coins can be dull, stained, or spotted and still have some original mint color. Coins with fingerprints must be given a low numer-

1959. Graded PF-69RD Cameo.

ical grade. Lower-grade Proofs usually have poor eye appeal. Generally, Proofs below PF-64 are not desired by most collectors.

1960, Large Date	1960, Small Date	1960-D, D Over D, Small Over Large Date
		FS-01-1960D-101/501.

	Mintage	Cert	Avg	%MS	MS-63RB	MS-65RD	MS-66RD	MS-67RD
					PF-65RD	PF-67RD	PF-67Cam	PF-68DCam
1959	609,715,000	1,923	65.7	100%	$0.20	$0.30	$37	$350
1959, Proof	1,149,291	8,993	67.5		$3	$22	$55	$750
1959-D	1,279,760,000	1,842	65.6	99%	$0.50	$0.55	$25	$400

1969-S, Doubled Die Obverse
FS-01-1969S-101.

	Mintage	Cert	Avg	%MS	MS-63RB / PF-65RD	MS-65RD / PF-67RD	MS-66RD / PF-67Cam	MS-67RD / PF-68DCam
1960, Large Date (a)	586,405,000	2,437	65.5	100%	$0.20	$0.30	$30	
1960, Small Date (a)	(b)	1,640	65.5	100%	$3	$7	$38	
1960, Large Date, Proof	1,691,602	7,314	67.5		$2	$15	$25	$300
1960, Small Date, Proof	(c)	5,472	67.4		$22	$37	$55	$1,000
1960, Lg Dt Over Sm Dt, Proof (d)	(c)	142	66.7		—			
1960, Sm Dt Over Lg Dt, Proof (e)	(c)	91	67.0		—			
1960-D, Large Date (a,f)	1,580,884,000	2,539	65.4	99%	$0.20	$0.30	$30	
1960-D, Small Date (a)	(g)	1,934	65.5	99%	$0.20	$0.30	$30	$300
1960, D Over D, Small Over Large Date	(g)	321	64.1	97%	$150	$300	$800	
1961	753,345,000	1,110	65.3	100%	$0.15	$0.30	$50	
1961, Proof	3,028,244	7,986	67.3		$1.50	$23	$40	$300
1961-D	1,753,266,700	1,543	65.3	99%	$0.15	$0.30	$70	$100
1962	606,045,000	1,219	65.5	100%	$0.15	$0.30	$50	
1962, Proof	3,218,019	8,730	67.5		$1.50	$10	$15	$100
1962-D	1,793,148,140	1,149	65.3	99%	$0.15	$0.30	$75	$200
1963	754,110,000	1,631	65.3	100%	$0.15	$0.30	$60	
1963, Proof	3,075,645	9,526	67.6		$1.50	$10	$14	$55
1963-D	1,774,020,400	1,040	64.9	99%	$0.15	$0.30	$100	
1964	2,648,575,000	1,218	65.1	99%	$0.15	$0.30	$65	
1964, Proof	3,950,762	14,176	67.8		$1.50	$10	$11	$23
1964-D	3,799,071,500	732	65.0	96%	$0.15	$0.30	$42	
1965	1,497,224,900	592	65.6	99%	$0.20	$0.50	$27	
1965, Special Mint Set	2,360,000	2,409	66.4		$11	$55		
1966	2,188,147,783	470	65.1	97%	$0.20	$0.50	$60	
1966, Special Mint Set	2,261,583	3,406	66.8		$10	$25		
1967	3,048,667,100	498	65.3	98%	$0.20	$0.50	$90	
1967, Special Mint Set	1,863,344	3,386	66.8		$11	$42		
1968	1,707,880,970	547	65.2	99%	$0.25	$0.60	$33	
1968-D	2,886,269,600	1,085	65.2	98%	$0.15	$0.40	$27	
1968-S	258,270,001	1,350	65.4	99%	$0.15	$0.40	$29	
1968-S, Proof	3,041,506	1,330	67.2		$1	$12	$16	$50
1969	1,136,910,000	501	65.6	99%	$0.35	$0.70	$55	
1969-D	4,002,832,200	961	65.0	97%	$0.15	$0.30	$28	
1969-S	544,375,000	1,291	63.9	91%	$0.15	$0.50	$65	
1969-S, Doubled Die Obverse †† (h)	(i)	20	58.6	45%	$45,000			
1969-S, Proof	2,934,631	1,456	67.1		$1	$11	$13	$33

†† Ranked in the *100 Greatest U.S. Modern Coins* (fourth edition). **a.** The alignment of the 1 and 9 in the date can be used for a quick determination of Large versus Small Date. Large Date: the top of the 1 is significantly lower than the top of the 9. Small Date: the tops of the 1 and 9 are at the same level. **b.** Included in circulation-strike 1960, Large Date, mintage figure. **c.** Included in 1960, Large Date, Proof, mintage figure. **d.** FS-01-1960-101. **e.** FS-01-1960-102. A PF-68RD example sold in a 2009 auction for $2,300. **f.** A variety once called 1960-D, Large Date, D Over Horizontal D, has been disproved as such, and is now considered simply a triple-punched D. **g.** Included in 1960-D, Large Date, mintage figure. **h.** Beware of specimens that exhibit only strike doubling, as opposed to a true doubled die; these are worth only face value. See Appendix A of the *Cherrypickers' Guide to Rare Die Varieties, Vol. I* (sixth edition). **i.** Included in circulation-strike 1969-S mintage figure.

1970-S, Small
Date (High 7)

1970-S, Large Date
(Low 7)

1970-S, Proof, Doubled Die Obverse
FS-01-1970S-101.

1972, Doubled Die Obverse
FS-01-1972-101.

	Mintage	Cert	Avg	%MS	MS-63RB / PF-65RD	MS-65RD / PF-67RD	MS-66RD / PF-67Cam	MS-67RD / PF-68DCam
1970	1,898,315,000	556	65.6	100%	$0.30	$0.65	$25	$200
1970-D	2,891,438,900	786	65.1	99%	$0.15	$0.30	$70	$450
1970-S, All kinds	690,560,004							
1970-S, Small Date (High 7) ††		1,007	64.5	100%	$25	$55	$200	
1970-S, Large Date (Low 7)		1,948	64.6	96%	$0.20	$0.50	$30	$650
1970-S, Large Date, Doubled Die Obverse ††		36	63.7	92%	$3,250	$12,500	$35,000	
1970-S, All kinds, Proof	2,632,810							
1970-S, Small Date (High 7), Proof		719	66.6		$40	$65	$150	
1970-S, Large Date (Low 7), Proof		1,548	66.8		$1	$15	$25	$65
1971	1,919,490,000	860	65.2	98%	$0.25	$0.60	$25	
1971, Doubled Die Obverse	(j)	43	63.3	91%		$50		
1971-D	2,911,045,600	389	65.3	99%	$0.20	$0.50	$24	$350
1971-S	525,133,459	521	65.2	97%	$0.20	$0.50	$50	
1971-S, Proof	3,220,733	1,755	67.1		$1	$18	$30	$120
1971-S, Doubled Die Obverse, Proof ††	(k)	126	66.4		$500	$1,000	$1,500	
1972	2,933,255,000	4,670	64.3	97%	$0.15	$0.30	$32	
1972, Doubled Die Obverse †† (l)	(m)	2,625	64.2	98%	$400	$600	$950	$2,750
1972-D	2,665,071,400	342	64.9	96%	$0.15	$0.30	$28	
1972-S	376,939,108	399	64.7	97%	$0.25	$0.75	$78	$225
1972-S, Proof	3,260,996	1,073	67.2		$1	$15	$20	$35
1973	3,728,245,000	614	65.6	99%	$0.15	$0.30	$30	$250
1973-D	3,549,576,588	598	65.4	99%	$0.15	$0.30	$30	
1973-S	317,177,295	380	65.3	99%	$0.25	$0.85	$50	
1973-S, Proof	2,760,339	326	67.3		$1	$13	$16	$30
1974	4,232,140,523	546	65.7	99%	$0.15	$0.30	$27	$125
1974-D	4,235,098,000	590	65.5	99%	$0.15	$0.30	$20	$100
1974-S	409,426,660	271	65.0	99%	$0.25	$0.75	$100	$500
1974-S, Proof	2,612,568	374	67.3		$1	$13	$16	$30
1975	5,451,476,142	831	65.8	100%	$0.15	$0.30	$25	$125
1975-D	4,505,275,300	267	65.4	97%	$0.15	$0.30	$25	$250
1975-S, Proof	2,845,450	570	67.2		$3.50	$13	$16	$30
1976	4,674,292,426	323	65.8	100%	$0.15	$0.30	$25	$55
1976-D	4,221,592,455	172	65.1	98%	$0.15	$0.30	$35	$500
1976-S, Proof	4,149,730	857	67.1		$3.20	$13	$16	$30
1977	4,469,930,000	359	65.9	99%	$0.15	$0.30	$55	$130
1977-D	4,194,062,300	480	65.1	99%	$0.15	$0.30	$90	$175
1977-S, Proof	3,251,152	522	68.1		$2.50	$13	$16	$30

†† Ranked in the *100 Greatest U.S. Modern Coins* (fourth edition). **j.** Included in 1971 mintage figure. **k.** Included in 1971-S, Proof, mintage figure. **l.** Several less dramatically doubled varieties exist; these command premiums over the normal coin but are worth considerably less than the variety pictured. Counterfeits of the 1972 doubled die are frequently encountered. **m.** Included in 1972 mintage figure.

1980, Doubled Die Obverse
FS-01-1980-101.

1982, Large Date   **1982, Small Date**

1983, Doubled Die Reverse
FS-01-1983-801.

1984, Doubled Ear
FS-01-1984-101.

	Mintage	Cert	Avg	%MS	MS-63RB / PF-65RD	MS-65RD / PF-67RD	MS-66RD / PF-67Cam	MS-67RD / PF-68DCam
1978	5,558,605,000	322	65.3	99%	$0.15	$0.30	$80	$250
1978-D	4,280,233,400	278	65.3	99%	$0.15	$0.30	$75	$250
1978-S, Proof	3,127,781	569	67.6		$2.50	$13	$16	$30
1979	6,018,515,000	705	66.4	100%	$0.15	$0.30	$20	$70
1979-D	4,139,357,254	388	65.2	98%	$0.15	$0.30	$60	
1979-S, Type 1, Proof	3,677,175	787	68.3		$5	$11	$13	$17
1979-S, Type 2, Proof	(n)	1,187	68.3		$6	$17	$20	$30
1980	7,414,705,000	576	63.8	91%	$0.15	$0.30	$25	$100
1980, Doubled Die Obverse	(o)	239	61.8	79%	$225	$350		
1980-D (p)	5,140,098,660	369	65.1	99%	$0.15	$0.30	$40	$200
1980-S, Proof	3,554,806	1,059	68.5		$2.50	$10	$11	$15
1981	7,491,750,000	348	65.5	98%	$0.15	$0.30	$35	$100
1981-D	5,373,235,677	255	65.3	98%	$0.15	$0.30	$40	$175
1981-S, Type 1, Proof	4,063,083	1,482	68.5		$3	$10	$11	$15
1981-S, Type 2, Proof	(q)	914	68.0		$15	$28	$38	$55
1982, Large Date	10,712,525,000	1,022	65.4	98%	$0.20	$0.35	$25	$55
1982, Small Date	(r)	389	64.4	93%	$0.30	$0.50	$45	$100
1982-D, Large Date	6,012,979,368	385	64.1	89%	$0.15	$0.30	$20	$35
1982, Zinc, Large Date	(r)	661	66.3	99%	$0.35	$0.50	$35	$50
1982, Zinc, Small Date ††	(r)	586	66.3	99%	$0.50	$0.85	$35	
1982-D, Zinc, Large Date	(s)	419	66.3	100%	$0.20	$0.40	$25	$45
1982-D, Zinc, Small Date	(s)	418	65.8	98%	$0.15	$0.30	$15	$225
1982-S, Small Date, Proof	3,857,479	789	68.4		$2.50	$10	$11	$15
1983	7,752,355,000	1,562	65.0	98%	$0.15	$0.30	$15	$45
1983, Doubled Die Reverse †† (t)	(u)	1,054	64.9	98%	$250	$375	$500	$1,000
1983-D	6,467,199,428	379	66.1	99%	$0.15	$0.30	$15	$31
1983-S, Proof	3,279,126	1,077	68.7		$3	$10	$11	$15
1984	8,151,079,000	1,027	65.5	99%	$0.15	$0.30	$15	$35
1984, Doubled Ear †† (v)	(w)	649	65.3	99%	$175	$225	$325	$500
1984-D	5,569,238,906	334	66.1	99%	$0.15	$0.30	$15	$35
1984-S, Proof	3,065,110	714	69.0		$4	$10	$11	$15

†† Ranked in the *100 Greatest U.S. Modern Coins* (fourth edition). **n.** Included in 1979-S, Type 1, Proof, mintage figure. **o.** Included in 1980 mintage figure. **p.** A variety previously listed in the *Cherrypickers' Guide to Rare Die Varieties, Vol. I* as a 1980-D, D Over S, has since been delisted from that catalog. It should command no premium. **q.** Included in 1981-S, Type 1, Proof, mintage figure. **r.** Included in 1982, Large Date, mintage figure. **s.** Included in 1982-D mintage figure. **t.** All reverse lettering is strongly doubled, as are the designer's initials and portions of the Lincoln Memorial. **u.** Included in 1983 mintage figure. **v.** Values are for coins certified as the Doubled Ear variety (FS-01-1984-101). More than 1,500 certifications exist for all 1984 doubled-die varieties; this number certainly includes FS-01-1984-101, but it is unknown how many. **w.** Included in 1984 mintage figure.

1992, Normal AM

1992, Close AM

1995, Doubled Die Obverse
FS-01-1995-101.

	Mintage	Cert	Avg	%MS	MS-63RB / PF-65RD	MS-65RD / PF-67RD	MS-66RD / PF-67Cam	MS-67RD / PF-68DCam
1985	5,648,489,887	684	66.4	100%	$0.15	$0.30	$15	$35
1985-D	5,287,339,926	541	66.7	99%	$0.15	$0.30	$15	$29
1985-S, Proof	3,362,821	863	69.0		$5	$11	$12	$15
1986	4,491,395,493	406	66.4	100%	$0.15	$0.30	$15	$35
1986-D	4,442,866,698	476	66.8	100%	$0.15	$0.30	$15	$35
1986-S, Proof	3,010,497	746	69.0		$7	$11	$12	$15
1987	4,682,466,931	485	66.7	100%	$0.15	$0.30	$15	$29
1987-D	4,879,389,514	667	66.6	100%	$0.15	$0.30	$15	$32
1987-S, Proof	4,227,728	969	69.0		$5	$10	$11	$13
1988	6,092,810,000	296	66.2	98%	$0.15	$0.30	$20	$40
1988-D	5,253,740,443	421	66.5	100%	$0.15	$0.30	$15	$25
1988-S, Proof	3,262,948	695	69.1		$9	$11	$12	$13
1989	7,261,535,000	438	66.5	100%	$0.15	$0.30	$15	$25
1989-D	5,345,467,111	444	66.3	100%	$0.15	$0.30	$15	$30
1989-S, Proof	3,220,194	747	69.0		$9	$11	$12	$13
1990	6,851,765,000	314	66.4	99%	$0.15	$0.30	$19	$36
1990-D	4,922,894,533	390	66.8	99%	$0.15	$0.30	$15	$25
1990-S, Proof	3,299,559	1,014	69.1		$5	$10	$11	$13
1990-S, No S, Proof ††	(x)	91	67.8		$2,250	$2,500	$2,750	$3,750
1991	5,165,940,000	268	66.6	100%	$0.15	$0.30	$14	$25
1991-D	4,158,446,076	456	66.8	100%	$0.15	$0.30	$14	$25
1991-S, Proof	2,867,787	977	69.1		$12	$13	$14	$16
1992	4,648,905,000	661	66.8	99%	$0.15	$0.30	$14	$25
1992, Close AM †† (y)	(z)	9	60.4	67%				
1992-D	4,448,673,300	476	65.9	96%	$0.15	$0.30	$14	$25
1992-D, Close AM †† (y)	(aa)	36	60.6	69%				
1992-S, Proof	4,176,560	2,930	69.1		$5	$10	$11	$12
1993	5,684,705,000	326	66.8	100%	$0.15	$0.30	$14	$25
1993-D	6,426,650,571	506	66.8	100%	$0.15	$0.30	$14	$25
1993-S, Proof	3,394,792	2,302	69.0		$9	$10	$11	$12
1994	6,500,850,000	305	66.1	98%	$0.15	$0.30	$14	$25
1994-D	7,131,765,000	340	66.7	99%	$0.15	$0.30	$15	$27
1994-S, Proof	3,269,923	2,177	69.0		$9	$11	$12	$13
1995	6,411,440,000	19,561	67.2	100%	$0.15	$0.30	$15	$30
1995, Doubled Die Obverse ††	(bb)	19,169	67.2	100%	$35	$50	$90	$125
1995-D	7,128,560,000	406	66.7	99%	$0.15	$0.30	$15	$35
1995-S, Proof	2,797,481	2,707	69.1		$9	$11	$12	$13

†† Ranked in the *100 Greatest U.S. Modern Coins* (fourth edition). **x.** An estimated 100 to 250 Proofs of 1990 were struck without the S mintmark (apparently from a circulation-strike die, without a mintmark, which had been given a mirror finish). This error escaped the notice of at least 14 people during die preparation and coining. **y.** The reverse hub used for cents from 1974 to 1992 had the AM of AMERICA separated. A new reverse hub with the AM close together was used for all cents in 1993. At least one new reverse die of each type was used for 1992-P and -D cents made for circulation but it is not known if this usage was deliberate or accidental. Proof coinage reverted to the wide-AM design in 1994. In subsequent years a few dies from the circulation-strike hub were used for making Proof coins. **z.** Included in 1992 mintage figure. **aa.** Included in 1992-D mintage figure. **bb.** Included in 1995 mintage figure.

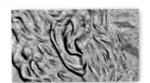

1997, Doubled Ear
FS-01-1997-101.

					MS-63RB	MS-65RD	MS-66RD	MS-67RD
	Mintage	Cert	Avg	%MS	PF-65RD	PF-67RD	PF-67Cam	PF-68DCam
1996	6,612,465,000	282	66.7	100%	$0.15	$0.30	$12	$18
1996 Wide AM (y)	(cc)	(dd)			—	—		
1996-D	6,510,795,000	469	66.9	100%	$0.15	$0.30	$12	$18
1996-S, Proof	2,525,265	1,997	69.1		$4.50	$9	$10	$12
1997	4,622,800,000	278	66.2	100%	$0.15	$0.30	$15	$42
1997, Doubled Ear	(ee)	55	65.1	100%	$275	$500		
1997-D	4,576,555,000	280	66.8	100%	$0.15	$0.30	$14	$30
1997-S, Proof	2,796,678	1,829	69.1		$10	$12	$13	$14
1998	5,032,155,000	589	65.5	98%	$0.15	$0.30	$12	$18
1998, Wide AM (y)	(ff)	340	64.8	97%	$12	$25	$40	$450
1998-D	5,225,353,500	279	66.7	100%	$0.15	$0.30	$17	$57
1998-S, Proof	2,086,507	2,565	69.0		$9	$10	$11	$12
1998-S, Close AM, Proof †† (gg)	(hh)	176	68.9		$150	$175	$185	$200
1999	5,237,600,000	490	65.0	97%	$0.15	$0.30	$13	$30
1999, Wide AM ‡ (y)	(ii)	196	64.2	92%		$500		$1,500
1999-D	6,360,065,000	314	66.7	99%	$0.15	$0.30	$12	$25
1999-S, Proof	3,347,966	7,864	69.0		$6	$9	$10	$12
1999-S, Close AM, Proof (gg)	(jj)	360	68.4		$80	$100	$125	$150
2000	5,503,200,000	2,404	65.7	100%	$0.15	$0.30	$12	$25
2000, Wide AM (y)	(kk)	1,031	65.5	100%	$10	$20	$35	$55
2000-D	8,774,220,000	232	66.5	100%	$0.15	$0.30	$12	$25
2000-S, Proof	4,047,993	6,157	69.1		$4	$7	$8	$10
2001	4,959,600,000	122	66.8	100%	$0.15	$0.30	$11	$18
2001-D	5,374,990,000	206	66.8	100%	$0.15	$0.30	$11	$18
2001-S, Proof	3,184,606	4,842	69.1		$4	$7	$8	$10
2002	3,260,800,000	137	67.3	100%	$0.15	$0.30	$11	$15
2002-D	4,028,055,000	171	67.2	100%	$0.15	$0.30	$12	$19
2002-S, Proof	3,211,995	5,306	69.2		$4	$7	$8	$10
2003	3,300,000,000	308	67.1	100%	$0.15	$0.30	$11	$15
2003-D	3,548,000,000	193	66.5	100%	$0.15	$0.30	$10	$15
2003-S, Proof	3,298,439	8,242	69.1		$4	$7	$8	$10

†† Ranked in the *100 Greatest U.S. Modern Coins* (fourth edition). **y.** The reverse hub used for cents from 1974 to 1992 had the AM of AMERICA separated. A new reverse hub with the AM close together was used for all cents in 1993. At least one new reverse die of each type was used for 1992-P and -D cents made for circulation but it is not known if this usage was deliberate or accidental. Proof coinage reverted to the wide-AM design in 1994. In subsequent years a few dies from the circulation-strike hub were used for making Proof coins. **cc.** Included in 1996 mintage figure. **dd.** Included in certified-population figure for 1996. **ee.** Included in 1997 mintage figure. **ff.** Included 1998 mintage figure. **gg.** Varieties were made in the circulation-strike style, with the A and the M in AMERICA nearly touching each other. On normal Proofs the two letters have a wide space between them. Included in 1999 mintage figure. **hh.** Included in 1998-S, Proof, mintage figure. **ii.** Included in 1999-S, Proof, mintage figure. **jj.** Included in 1999-S, Proof, mintage figure. **kk.** Included in 2000 mintage figure.

	Mintage	Cert	Avg	%MS	MS-63RB / PF-65RD	MS-65RD / PF-67RD	MS-66RD / PF-67Cam	MS-67RD / PF-68DCam
2004	3,379,600,000	200	66.6	100%	$0.15	$0.30	$10	$20
2004-D	3,456,400,000	160	66.4	100%	$0.15	$0.30	$10	$18
2004-S, Proof	2,965,422	5,663	69.1		$4	$7	$8	$10
2005	3,935,600,000	2,622	67.3	100%	$0.15	$0.30	$10	$25
2005, Satin Finish	1,160,000	2,421	67.2	100%	$5	$10	$15	$20
2005-D	3,764,450,500	2,521	66.9	100%	$0.15	$0.30	$20	$25
2005-D, Satin Finish	1,160,000	2,284	66.9	100%	$5	$10	$15	$20
2005-S, Proof	3,344,679	11,076	69.2		$4	$7	$8	$10
2006	4,290,000,000	1,512	67.0	100%	$0.15	$0.30	$10	$18
2006, Satin Finish	847,361	1,406	67.1	100%	$5	$10	$15	$20
2006-D	3,944,000,000	1,243	66.6	100%	$0.15	$0.30	$13	$25
2006-D, Satin Finish	847,361	1,092	66.8	100%	$5	$10	$15	$20
2006-S, Proof	3,054,436	5,423	69.2		$4	$7	$8	$10
2007	3,762,400,000	483	66.5	100%	$0.15	$0.30	$16	$30
2007, Satin Finish	895,628	291	66.9	100%	$5	$10	$15	$20
2007-D	3,638,800,000	364	66.1	100%	$0.15	$0.30	$16	$33
2007-D, Satin Finish	895,628	232	66.3	100%	$5	$10	$15	$20
2007-S, Proof	2,577,166	4,924	69.1		$4	$7	$8	$10
2008	2,558,800,000	271	67.2	100%	$0.15	$0.30	$10	$15
2008, Satin Finish	745,464	183	67.8	100%	$5	$10	$15	$20
2008-D	2,849,600,000	260	66.8	100%	$0.15	$0.30	$15	$30
2008-D, Satin Finish	745,464	158	67.4	100%	$5	$10	$15	$20
2008-S, Proof	2,169,561	3,862	69.1		$4	$7	$8	$10

LINCOLN, BICENTENNIAL REVERSES (2009)

Designer: *Victor D. Brenner (obverse); see image captions for reverse designers.*
Weight: *Regular-issue coins—2.5 grams; special coins included in collector sets—3.1 grams.*
Composition: *Regular-issue coins—copper-plated zinc (core: .992 zinc, .008 copper, with a plating of pure copper; total content .975 zinc, .025 copper); special coins included in collector sets—.950 copper, .050 tin and zinc.* **Diameter:** *19 mm.* **Edge:** *Plain.* **Mints:** *Philadelphia, Denver, and San Francisco.*

Circulation Strike

Birth and Early Childhood
Reverse designer: Richard Masters.

Formative Years
Reverse designer: Charles Vickers.

Professional Life
Reverse designer: Joel Iskowitz.

Presidency
Reverse designer: Susan Gamble.

Proof

Birth and Early Childhood, Proof

Formative Years, Proof

Professional Life, Proof

Presidency, Proof

History. The one-cent coins issued during 2009 pay unique tribute to President Abraham Lincoln, commemorating the bicentennial of his birth and the 100th anniversary of the first issuance of the Lincoln cent. Four different reverse designs were issued by the U.S. Mint, each representing a major aspect of Lincoln's life. The obverse retained the traditional profile portrait of previous years.

The reverse designs, released quarterly throughout 2009, are:

- Birth and Early Childhood (designer, Richard Masters; sculptor, Jim Licaretz), depicting a small log cabin like the one in which Lincoln was born in Kentucky.
- Formative Years (designer and sculptor, Charles Vickers), showing a youthful Abe Lincoln taking a break from rail-splitting to read a book, in Indiana.
- Professional Life (designer, Joel Iskowitz; sculptor, Don Everhart), with Lincoln standing in front of the Illinois state capitol in Springfield, symbolic of his pre-presidential career in law and politics.
- Presidency (designer, Susan Gamble; sculptor, Joseph Menna), depicting the partially completed U.S. Capitol dome in Washington, D.C., as it appeared when Lincoln held office.

The coins issued for general circulation were made of the exact same copper-plated composition used in the cent since 1982. Special versions struck for inclusion in collector sets were made of the same alloy as the first Lincoln cents of 1909—95 parts copper and 5 parts tin and zinc—and with a Satin finish.

Several die varieties (both circulation-strike and Proof) exist with minor doubling in the Formative Years reverse. Their values, which vary generally according to the severity of the doubling, are not yet firmly established with an active buy-and-sell market. These and other Lincoln cent die varieties are studied in greater depth in the *Cherrypickers' Guide to Rare Die Varieties*.

Striking and Sharpness. Striking is generally sharp. The quality of the fields can vary. Some 2009 cents, even from original rolls and bags, have surface marks that look like water spots. All Proof Lincoln Bicentennial cents are mirror Proofs, usually with cameo or frosted contrast between the devices and the fields.

Availability. Cents of this year were minted in quantities that, while large, were much smaller than for previous years (in the hundreds of millions, rather than multiple billions), if each of the four designs is considered individually. They are readily available in the numismatic marketplace, and are starting to be seen more frequently in circulation. High-quality Proofs (PF-69 and 70) are common in the secondary market.

GRADING STANDARDS

Caveat: These grading standards do not take sharpness of strike into account.

MS-60 to 70 (Mint State). *Obverse and Reverse:* At MS-65 and higher, luster is rich on all areas; there is no rubbing, and no contact marks are visible except under magnification. Coins with full or nearly full mint orange-red color can be designated RD; those with a substantial percentage of red-orange and of brown can be called RB; and those with full (or nearly full) brown-toned surfaces can be designated BN. Some 2009 cents, even from original rolls and bags, have surface marks that look like water spots.

2009-D, Formative Years. Graded MS-67RD.

Lincoln, Bicentennial Reverse, cents are seldom collected in grades lower than EF-40.

PF-60 to 70 (Proof). *Obverse and Reverse:* PF-65 and higher coins are RB (with colors nicely blended) or RD, the latter with bright red-orange color sometimes fading to hints of brown. Some tiny flecks are normal on coins certified as PF-65 but should be microscopic or absent above that level. PF–60 and 61 coins can be dull, stained, or spotted and still have some original mint luster. Proof coins with fingerprints are impaired and must be given a lower numerical grade. Lower-grade Proofs usually have poor eye appeal. Generally, Proofs of these types below PF-65 are not desired by most collectors.

**2009-S, Birthplace and Early Childhood.
Graded PF-70RD Deep Cameo.**

2009, Formative Years, Seven Fingers
FS-01-2009-801.
Other varieties exist.

2009, Formative Years, Seven Fingers
FS-01-2009-802.
Other varieties exist.

2009, Formative Years, Doubled Pinky
FS-01-2009-805.
Other varieties exist.

2009, Formative Years, Skeleton Finger
FS-01-2009-808.
Other varieties exist.

	Mintage	Cert	Avg	%MS	MS-63RB	MS-65RD	MS-66RD / PF-65RD	MS-67RD / PF-67RD	MS-68RD / PF-67Cam	MS-69RD / PF-68DCam
2009, Birth and Early Childhood	284,400,000	15,679	66.0	100%	$0.15	$0.30	$12	$20		
2009, Birth and Early Childhood, copper, Satin Finish	784,614	1,715	67.8	100%		$10			$15	$35
2009-D, Birth and Early Childhood	350,400,000	6,773	66.4	100%	$0.15	$0.30	$12	$20		
2009-D, Birth and Early Childhood, copper, Satin Finish	784,614	1,797	67.7	100%		$10			$17	$100
2009-S, Birth and Early Childhood, Proof	2,995,615	14,603	69.1				$4	$7	$8	$10
2009, Formative Years (a)	376,000,000	28,964	66.0	100%	$0.15	$0.30	$12	$20		
2009, Formative Years, copper, Satin Finish	784,614	1,612	67.6	100%		$10			$15	$35
2009-D, Formative Years (a)	363,600,000	4,347	66.5	100%	$0.15	$0.30	$12	$20		
2009-D, Formative Years, copper, Satin Finish	784,614	1,656	67.6	100%		$10			$15	$100
2009-S, Formative Years, Proof	2,995,615	14,500	69.1				$4	$7	$8	$10
2009, Professional Life	316,000,000	19,525	66.2	100%	$0.15	$0.30	$12	$20		
2009, Professional Life, copper, Satin Finish	784,614	1,982	67.8	100%		$10			$15	$35
2009-D, Professional Life	336,000,000	3,612	66.7	100%	$0.15	$0.30	$12	$20		
2009-D, Professional Life, copper, Satin Finish	784,614	1,615	67.6	100%		$10			$15	$100
2009-S, Professional Life, Proof	2,995,615	14,551	69.1				$4	$7	$8	$10
2009, Presidency	129,600,000	6,123	66.4	100%	$0.15	$0.30	$12	$20		
2009, Presidency, copper, Satin Finish	784,614	1,618	67.6	100%		$10			$15	$35

a. Several varieties exist with minor die doubling. Their values vary and their market is not yet firmly established.

| | Mintage | Cert | Avg | %MS | MS-63RB | MS-65RD | MS-66RD | MS-67RD | MS-68RD | MS-69RD |
							PF-65RD	PF-67RD	PF-67Cam	PF-68DCam
2009-D, Presidency	198,000,000	3,212	66.9	100%	$0.15	$0.30	$12	$20		
2009-D, Presidency, copper, Satin Finish	784,614	1,753	67.7	100%		$10			$15	$100
2009-S, Presidency, Proof	2,995,615	14,759	69.1				$4	$7	$8	$10

LINCOLN, SHIELD REVERSE (2010 TO DATE)

Designer: *Victor D. Brenner (obverse) and Lyndall Bass (reverse).* **Weight:** *2.5 grams.* **Composition:** *Copper-plated zinc (core: .992 zinc, .008 copper, with a plating of pure copper; total content .975 zinc, .025 copper).* **Diameter:** *19 mm.* **Edge:** *Plain.* **Mints:** *Philadelphia, Denver, San Francisco, and West Point.*

Circulation Strike   **Proof**

History. Symbolically capping the life story told by the Lincoln Bicentennial cents of 2009, today's cents feature a reverse design "emblematic of President Lincoln's preservation of the United States as a single and united country." This is the seventh reverse used on the Lincoln type since 1909.

The shield motif was designed by U.S. Mint Artistic Infusion Program Associate Designer Lyndall Bass, and engraved by Mint Sculptor-Engraver Joseph Menna. It was unveiled during the launch ceremony for the fourth and final 2009 Bicentennial cent, held at the Ulysses S. Grant Memorial at the Capitol Building in Washington, D.C., November 12, 2009.

In addition to a new reverse design, the Shield Reverse cents feature a modern update of Victor David Brenner's original portrait for the 1909 Lincoln cent.

Striking and Sharpness. Striking is generally sharp. All Proof Lincoln, Shield Reverse, cents are mirror Proofs, usually with cameo or frosted contrast between the devices and the fields.

Availability. Cents of this design are minted in large quantities. They are readily available in the numismatic marketplace, and have successfully entered circulation through normal distribution channels. High-quality Proofs (PF-69 and 70) are common in the secondary market.

GRADING STANDARDS

Caveat: These grading standards do not take sharpness of strike into account.

MS-60 to 70 (Mint State). *Obverse and Reverse:* At MS-65 and higher, luster is rich on all areas; there is no rubbing, and no contact marks are visible except under magnification. Coins with full or nearly full mint orange-red color can be designated RD; those with a substantial percentage of red-orange and of brown can be called RB; and those with full (or nearly full) brown-toned surfaces can be designated BN. Some 2009

2011-D. Graded MS-67RD.

cents, even from original rolls and bags, have surface marks that look like water spots.

Lincoln, Shield Reverse, cents are seldom collected in grades lower than MS-60.

PF-60 to 70 (Proof). *Obverse and Reverse:* PF-65 and higher coins are RB (with colors nicely blended) or RD, the latter with bright red-orange color sometimes fading to hints of brown. Some tiny flecks are normal on coins certified as PF-65 but should be microscopic or absent above that level. PF–60 and 61 coins can be dull, stained, or spotted and still have some original mint luster. Proof coins with fingerprints are impaired and must be given a lower numerical grade. Lower-grade Proofs usually have poor eye appeal. Generally, Proofs of this type below PF-65 are not desired by most collectors.

2012-S. Graded PF-70RD Deep Cameo.

	Mintage	Cert	Avg	%MS	MS-63RB PF-65RD	MS-65RD PF-67RD	MS-66RD PF-67Cam	MS-67RD PF-68DCam
2010	1,963,630,000	6,941	65.5	100%	$0.15	$0.30	$10	$15
2010, Satin Finish	583,897	285	67.0	100%	$5	$10	$15	$20
2010-D	2,047,200,000	2,824	66.1	100%	$0.15	$0.30	$10	$15
2010-D, Satin Finish	583,897	381	67.6	100%	$5	$10	$15	$20
2010-S, Proof	1,689,216	5,878	69.1		$4	$7	$8	$10
2011	2,402,400,000	503	66.2	100%	$0.15	$0.30	$10	$15
2011-D	2,536,140,000	294	66.8	100%	$0.15	$0.30	$10	$15
2011-S, Proof	1,673,010	6,497	69.1		$5	$7	$8	$10
2012	3,132,000,000	290	66.9	100%	$0.15	$0.30	$10	$15
2012-D	2,883,200,000	287	66.9	100%	$0.15	$0.30	$10	$15
2012-S, Proof	1,239,148	2,984	69.1		$5	$7	$8	$10
2013	3,750,400,000	568	66.2	100%	$0.15	$0.30	$10	$15
2013-D	3,319,600,000	852	66.9	100%	$0.15	$0.30	$10	$15
2013-S, Proof	1,274,505	2,631	69.1		$5	$7	$8	$10
2014	3,990,800,000	763	66.6	100%	$0.15	$0.30	$10	$15
2014-D	4,155,600,000	936	66.7	100%	$0.15	$0.30	$10	$15
2014-S, Proof	1,190,369	4,167	69.3		$5	$7.50	$8	$10
2015	4,691,300,000	401	65.6	100%	$0.15	$0.30	$10	$15
2015-D	4,674,000,000	234	66.3	100%	$0.15	$0.30	$10	$15
2015-S, Proof	1,099,182	4,073	69.3		$5	$7.50	$8	$10
2016	4,698,000,000	227	66.4	100%	$0.15	$0.30	$10	$15
2016-D	4,420,400,000	546	66.8	100%	$0.15	$0.30	$10	$15
2016-S, Proof	978,457	1,933	69.5		$5	$7.50	$8	$10
2017-P (a)	4,361,220,000	3,113	66.7	100%	$0.15	$0.30	$10	$15
2017-D	4,272,800,000	631	66.5	100%	$0.15	$0.30	$10	$15
2017-S, Enhanced Unc. (b)	210,419	11,130	69.9	100%		$7.50	$8	$10
2017-S, Proof	979,475	1,567	69.7		$5	$7.50	$8	$10
2018	4,066,800,000	553	66.8	100%	$0.15	$0.30	$10	$15
2018-D	3,736,400,000	984	66.8	100%	$0.15	$0.30	$10	$15
2018-S, Proof	899,739	13,502	69.8		$5	$7.50	$8	$10
2018-S, Reverse Proof (c)	199,116				$10	$15	$18 (d)	$20 (e)

a. All 2017-dated cents struck at the Philadelphia Mint bear a P mintmark in honor of the 225th anniversary of U.S. coinage. **b.** In 2017, to mark the U.S. Mint's 225th anniversary, the Mint released a special Enhanced Uncirculated set. **c.** In 2018, to mark the 50th Anniversary of the San Francisco Mint's first production of Proof coins, the Mint released a special silver Reverse Proof set. **d.** Value is for PF-67. **e.** Value is for PF-68

	Mintage	Cert	Avg	%MS	MS-63RB	MS-65RD	MS-66RD	MS-67RD
					PF-65RD	PF-67RD	PF-67Cam	PF-68DCam
2019	3,542,800,000	453	66.6	100%	$0.15	$0.30	$10	$15
2019-D	3,497,600,000	774	66.6	100%	$0.15	$0.30	$10	$15
2019-S, Proof	1,054,918	6,026	69.7		$5	$7.50	$8	$10
2019-W (f)	346,257	22,879	68.7	100%				
2019-W, Proof (f)	593,978	26,396	69.3		$10	$15	$18	$20
2019-W, Reverse Proof (f)	412,609	16,540	69.4		$10	$15	$18	$20
2020		270	66.5	100%	$0.15	$0.30	$10	$15
2020-D		249	66.5	100%	$0.15	$0.30	$10	$15
2020-S, Proof		6,032	69.8	100%	$5	$7.50	$8	$10
2021					$0.15	$0.30	$10	$15
2021-D					$0.15	$0.30	$10	$15
2021-S, Proof					$5	$7.50	$8 (d)	$10 (d)

d. Value is for PF-67. **e.** Value is for PF-68. **f.** In 2019, the Mint included special cents from the West Point Mint as premiums in each of three separate products: in the 2019 Uncirculated Mint Set, a 2019-W Uncirculated cent; in the 2019 Proof Set, a 2019-W Proof cent; and in the 2019 Silver Proof Set, a 2019-W Reverse Proof cent.

Two-Cent Pieces
1864–1873

AN OVERVIEW OF TWO-CENT PIECES

The two-cent piece was introduced in 1864. Made of bronze, it was designed by U.S. Mint chief engraver James B. Longacre, and was the first circulating U.S. coin to bear the motto IN GOD WE TRUST. At the time, coins were scarce in circulation because of the ongoing Civil War and the public's tendency to hoard hard currency, and silver and gold issues were entirely absent. Treasury officials felt that the two-cent piece would prove to be very popular as a companion to the Indian Head cent. However, the introduction of the nickel three-cent piece in 1865 negated much of this advantage, the production of two-cent pieces declined, and by 1873, when the denomination was discontinued, its only coinage consisted of Proofs for collectors.

A full "type set" of the two-cent piece consists of but a single coin. Most available in Mint State are the issues of 1864 and 1865, often seen with original mint orange color fading to natural brown. Proofs are available for all years.

The Coinage Act of 1873 eliminated not only the two-cent piece but also the three-cent silver and half dime.

FOR THE COLLECTOR AND INVESTOR: TWO-CENT PIECES AS A SPECIALTY

Two-cent pieces can be collected by date and variety. A basic display consists of an 1864, Large Motto; 1864, Small Motto (rare); 1873, Close 3; and 1873, Open 3, the latter two being available only in Proof format. Some specialists opt to include just one of the 1873 varieties.

Collectors should select both circulation strikes and Proofs with care, for the number of truly choice *original* (unprocessed, undipped, not retoned) coins is but a small percentage of the whole. As a type, though, the two-cent piece is readily available for collecting.

Several specialized studies of two-cent pieces have been published over a long span of years, the first of significance being "Two-Cent Pieces of the United States," by S.W. Freeman, published in the *Numismatist*, June 1954.

TWO-CENT PIECES (1864–1873)

Designer: *James B. Longacre.* **Weight:** *6.22 grams.*
Composition: *.950 copper, .050 tin and zinc.* **Diameter:** *23 mm.*
Edge: *Plain.* **Mint:** *Philadelphia.*

Circulation Strike

Proof

History. The two-cent piece, struck in bronze like the new Indian Head cents, made its debut under the Mint Act of April 22, 1864. Coins of all kinds were scarce in circulation at the time, due to hoarding. The outcome of the Civil War was uncertain, and Americans desired "hard money." Many millions of two-cent pieces were struck in 1864, after which the mintage declined, due to once-hoarded Indian Head cents becoming available again and to the new nickel three-cent coins being introduced in 1865. Continually decreasing quantities were made through 1872, and only Proofs were struck in the coin's final year, 1873.

Striking and Sharpness. Points to check for sharpness on the obverse include WE in the motto, the leaves, and the horizontal shield lines. On the reverse check the wreath details and the border letters. Check the denticles on both sides. Most coins are quite well struck.

Availability. Most MS coins are dated 1864 or 1865, after which the availability declines sharply, especially for the issue of 1872. Among 1864 coins most seen are of the Large Motto variety. Small Motto coins are elusive. Coins with much or nearly all *original* mint red-orange color are rare for the later years, with most in the marketplace being recolored. The 1864, Small Motto, Proof, is a great rarity, with fewer than two dozen estimated to exist. Coins of 1873 were made only in Proof format, of the Close 3 and Open 3 styles. Proofs of most dates are easily enough acquired. Very few have original color. Do not overlook the many nice brown and red-and-brown pieces on the market (some investors acquire only "red" copper coins, leaving many great values among others). Refer to the comments under Proof Indian Head cents.

GRADING STANDARDS

MS-60 to 70 (Mint State). *Obverse and Reverse:* At MS-65 and higher, the luster is rich on all areas. There is no rubbing, and no contact marks are visible except under magnification. Coins with full or nearly full mint orange-red color can be designated RD (the color on this is often more orange than red), those with full or nearly full brown-toned surfaces can be designated BN, and those with a substantial percentage of red-orange

1864, Large Motto, RPD; Leone-9. Graded MS-66RD.

and of brown can be called RB. Ideally, MS-65 or finer coins should have good eye appeal, which in the RB category means nicely blended colors, not stained or blotched, the latter problem mostly with dipped and irregularly retoned coins. Below MS-65, full RD coins become scarce, although MS-64RD coins can be attractive. These usually have more flecks and tiny spots, while the color remains bright. At MS–60 to 62, RD, coins are virtually nonexistent, unless they have been dipped. The ANA standards allow for "dull" and/or "spotted" coins at MS–60 and 61 as well as incomplete luster. As a rule, MS–60 to 63BN coins can be fairly attractive if not spotted or blotched, but those with hints of color usually lack eye appeal.

AU-50, 53, 55, 58 (About Uncirculated). *Obverse:* WE shows light wear, this being the prime place to check. The arrowheads and leaves also show light wear. At AU-50, level wear is more noticeable. At AU–53 and 55, wear is less. At AU-58, friction is evident, rather than actual wear. Luster, toned brown, is nearly complete at AU-58, but may be incomplete in the field. *Reverse:* At AU-50, light wear is seen on the ribbon and the higher-relief areas of the leaves and grains, while the lower areas retain their detail. Some luster may be present in protected areas. At AU–53 and 55, wear is lesser and luster is more extensive. An AU-58 coin will have nearly full luster and show only light friction.

1871. Graded AU-58.

EF-40, 45 (Extremely Fine). *Obverse:* Wear is more extensive. WE shows wear extensively, but still is clear. The leaves lack detail on their highest points. Some scattered marks are normal at this and lower grades. *Reverse:* The higher-relief parts of the leaves and ribbon bow show further wear, as do other areas.

1864, Small Motto. Graded EF-45.

VF-20, 30 (Very Fine). *Obverse:* WE is clear, but not strong. Leaves show more wear, as do all other areas. *Reverse:* Still more wear is seen, but the leaves still are separately defined. The wheat grains are very clear.

1864, Small Motto. Graded VF-20.

F-12, 15 (Fine). *Obverse:* WE is the defining factor and is very weak, but readable, if only barely. Other areas show more wear. The edges of some leaves are gone, blending them into adjacent leaves. *Reverse:* Wear is more extensive. Near the apex of the wreath the edges of some leaves are gone, blending them into adjacent leaves. The grains of wheat are clear, but some are slightly weak.

    Illustrated coin: WE is very weak.

1872. Graded F-15.

VG-8, 10 (Very Good). *Obverse:* WE is gone, although the ANA grading standards and *Photograde* suggest "very weak." IN GOD and TRUST are readable, but some areas may be weak. The inner edges of most leaves are gone. *Reverse:* The wear appears to be less extensive than on the obverse. All lettering is bold. A few grains of wheat may be well worn or even missing.

1872. Graded VG-8.

G-4, 6 (Good). *Obverse:* Wear is more extensive, and the leaf bunches are in flat clumps. IN GOD and TRUST are very worn, with a letter or two not visible. *Reverse:* All letters are clear. The wreath is mostly in outline on G-4. On G-6, perhaps half the grains are visible.

1864, Small Motto. Graded G-4.

AG-3 (About Good). *Obverse:* The motto shows only a few letters. The leaves are flat. Only a few horizontal shield stripes can be seen. *Reverse:* The wreath is in outline form. The letters are weak, with 20% to 40% worn away entirely.

1872. Graded AG-3.

PF-60 to 70 (Proof). *Obverse and Reverse:* Gem PF-65 two-cent pieces will have very few hairlines, and these visible only under a strong magnifying glass. At any level and color, a Proof with hairlines has likely been cleaned, a fact usually overlooked. At PF-67 or higher there should be no evidence of hairlines or friction at all. Such a coin is fully original. PF-60 coins can be dull from repeated dipping and cleaning and are often toned iridescent colors or have mottled surfaces. At PF-63, the mirrorlike fields should be attractive, and hairlines should be minimal, most easily seen when the coin is held at an angle to the light. No rubbing is seen. PF-64 coins are even nicer. As a general rule, Proofs of 1873 are of very high quality but, unless dipped or cleaned, are nearly always toned light brown.

1872. Graded PF-64RD.

1864, Small Motto   1864, Large Motto

1865, Plain 5   1865, Fancy 5

	Mintage	Cert	Avg	%MS	G-4	F-12	VF-20	EF-40	AU-50	MS-60BN	MS-63BN / PF-63BN	MS-64BN / PF-64BN	MS-65RD / PF-65RB
1864, Small Motto (a)	(b)	677	49.2	58%	$225	$350	$450	$600	$900	$1,100	$1,400	$1,500	$13,500
Auctions: $2,232, MS-65BN, January 2015; $29,375, MS-65, February 2015; $763, EF-45, October 2015; $540, EF-40, February 2018													
1864, Large Motto (c)	19,822,500	4,347	60.0	81%	$13	$20	$30	$50	$75	$110	$175	$200	$1,150
Auctions: $1,116, MS-66BN, June 2015; $305, MS-65BN, May 2015; $129, MS-63BN, January 2015; $111, AU-58, October 2015													
1864, Small Motto, Proof † (d)	(e)	7	64.9								$25,000	$30,000	$85,000
Auctions: $105,750, PF-66RD, June 2014													
1864, Large Motto, Proof	100+	122	64.6								$750	$1,150	$4,000
Auctions: $3,760, PF-66BN, October 2015; $3,642, PF-66BN, January 2015; $3,535, PF-65RB, August 2015; $646, PF-62BN, February 2015													
1865 (f)	13,640,000	2,882	59.4	78%	$13	$20	$30	$50	$75	$110	$175	$200	$1,150
Auctions: $540, MS-65RB, May 2015; $399, MS-65BN, February 2015; $646, MS-64RD, August 2015; $199, MS-64BN, January 2015													
1865, Proof	500+	158	64.7								$450	$550	$1,500
Auctions: $2,820, PF-66RB, October 2015; $3,290, PF-65RB, June 2015; $1,997, PF-65RB, January 2015; $1,178, PF-65BN, January 2015													
1866	3,177,000	601	57.3	70%	$13	$20	$30	$50	$75	$120	$175	$220	$2,000
Auctions: $1,692, MS-65RD, July 2015; $587, MS-64RD, January 2015; $517, MS-64RB, October 2015; $212, MS-64BN, April 2015													
1866, Proof	725+	169	64.6								$450	$550	$1,250
Auctions: $4,700, PF-66RB, July 2015; $1,527, PF-65RB, January 2015; $1,175, PF-65RB, September 2015; $470, PF-64BN, January 2015													

† Ranked in the *100 Greatest U.S. Coins* (fifth edition). **a.** The circulated Small Motto is distinguished by a wider D in GOD, and the first T in TRUST nearly touching the ribbon crease at left. **b.** Included in circulation-strike 1864, Large Motto, mintage figure. **c.** The circulated Large Motto is distinguished by a narrow D in GOD, and a 1 mm gap between the first T in TRUST and the ribbon crease. **d.** 20 to 30 examples are known. **e.** Included in 1864, Large Motto, Proof, mintage figure. **f.** Circulated varieties show the tip of the 5 either plain or fancy (curved).

1867, Doubled Die Obverse
FS-02-1867-101.

1869, Doubled Die Obverse
FS-02-1869-101.

	Mintage	Cert	Avg	%MS	G-4	F-12	VF-20	EF-40	AU-50	MS-60BN	MS-63BN / PF-63BN	MS-64BN / PF-64BN	MS-65RD / PF-65RB
1867	2,938,750	745	56.1	69%	$15	$25	$35	$50	$90	$130	$180	$235	$3,250
Auctions: $646, MS-64RB, August 2015; $423, MS-64RB, October 2015; $282, MS-64BN, February 2015; $141, MS-61BN, May 2015													
1867, Doubled Die Obverse (g)	(h)	87	41.4	26%	$125	$200	$375	$700	$1,200	$2,000	$3,200	$3,750	
Auctions: $22,325, MS-65RD, January 2014; $1,175, AU-55, March 2016													
1867, Proof	625+	201	64.7								$450	$550	$1,250
Auctions: $940, PF-65RB, August 2015; $763, PF-65BN, September 2015; $646, PF-64BN, January 2015													
1868	2,803,750	643	58.4	72%	$15	$35	$50	$75	$110	$150	$250	$375	$5,000
Auctions: $1,292, MS-65RB, January 2015; $1,057, MS-65RB, October 2015; $834, MS-64RB, June 2015; $211, MS-63BN, February 2015													
1868, Proof	600+	193	64.8								$450	$550	$1,250
Auctions: $470, PF-64BN, January 2015													
1869	1,546,500	563	57.9	73%	$20	$40	$55	$80	$125	$160	$250	$375	$2,850
Auctions: $2,820, MS-65RD, September 2015; $1,540, MS-65RB, January 2015; $763, MS-65BN, July 2015; $329, MS-64BN, June 2015													
1869, Doubled Die Obverse	(i)	0	n/a							$600	$900	$1,250	
Auctions: No auction records available.													
1869, Proof	600+	239	64.6								$450	$550	$1,300
Auctions: $2,820, PF-66RB, July 2015; $1,527, PF-66RB, October 2015; $1,881, PF-65RD, September 2015; $822, PF-65BN, January 2015													
1870	861,250	469	55.0	66%	$35	$55	$85	$150	$200	$275	$325	$575	$6,000
Auctions: $1,762, MS-65RB, August 2015; $329, MS-63RB, October 2015; $258, MS-62BN, May 2015; $62, EF-40, January 2015													
1870, Proof	1,000+	273	64.5								$450	$600	$1,350
Auctions: $3,290, PF-67BN, July 2015; $1,821, PF-65RD, February 2015; $1,116, PF-65RB, January 2015; $705, PF-65BN, September 2015													
1871	721,250	648	55.4	65%	$40	$75	$100	$155	$200	$275	$325	$600	$7,500
Auctions: $1,292, MS-64RD, January 2015; $1,008, MS-64RB, August 2015; $411, MS-64BN, June 2015; $282, MS-61BN, July 2015													
1871, Proof	960+	265	64.6								$450	$600	$1,375
Auctions: $8,233, PF-66RD, July 2015; $2,115, PF-65RB, August 2015; $1,057, PF-64RB, February 2015; $881, PF-64RB, January 2015													
1872	65,000	403	32.6	24%	$300	$450	$700	$1,000	$1,650	$2,800	$3,500	$4,000	$22,500
Auctions: $3,760, MS-65, March 2016; $2,350, MS-62, October 2016; $999, AU-50, December 2015													
1872, Proof	950+	351	64.5								$800	$1,000	$1,750
Auctions: $1,762, PF-66RB, June 2015; $1,410, PF-65BN, August 2015; $1,292, PF-65BN, February 2015; $2,820, PF-64BN, June 2015													
1873, Close 3, Proof	400	289	63.9	97%							$2,400	$2,750	$4,000
Auctions: $4,700, PF-66BN, June 2015; $5,141, PF-66, March 2015; $3,535, PF-65RB, October 2015													
1873, Open 3, Proof (Alleged Restrike)	200	128	63.8								$2,600	$3,750	$4,500
Auctions: $11,162, PF-66RB, October 2015; $5,640, PF-66BN, January 2015; $3,966, PF-65, February 2015													

g. This variety is somewhat common in low-end circulated grades, but is considered rare in EF and AU, and very rare in MS.
h. Included in circulation-strike 1867 mintage figure. i. Included in circulation-strike 1869 mintage figure.

Three-Cent Pieces
1851–1889

AN OVERVIEW OF THREE-CENT PIECES

SILVER THREE-CENT PIECES

The silver three-cent piece or *trime* is one of the more curious coins in American numismatics. The rising price of silver in 1850 created a situation in which silver coins cost more to produce than their face value. Mintages dropped sharply and older pieces disappeared from circulation. In 1851 a solution was provided by the three-cent piece. Instead of being made with 90% silver content, the fineness was set at 75%. Accordingly, the coins were worth less intrinsically, and there was no advantage in melting them. Large quantities were made through 1853. In that year, the standards for regular silver coins were changed, and other denominations reappeared on the marketplace, making the trime unnecessary. Mintages dropped beginning in 1854, until 1873, when production amounted to just 600 Proofs for collectors.

The term *trime* was first used by the director of the United States Mint, James Ross Snowden, at the time of the coins' production.

Of the three varieties of trimes, Variety 2 (1854–1858) is at once the scarcest and, by far, the most difficult to find with a sharp strike. In fact, not one in fifty Variety 2 coins is needle sharp. Curiously, when such pieces are found they are likely to be dated 1855, the lowest-mintage issue of the type. Trimes of the Variety 1 design (1851–1853) vary widely in striking, but can be found sharp. Variety 3 coins (1859–1873) often are sharp.

Mint State coins are readily found for Variety 1 and are usually in grades from MS–60 to 63 or so, although quite a few gems are around with attractive luster. Sharply struck gems are another matter and require some searching to find. Mint State Variety 2 trimes are all rare, and when seen are apt to be miserably struck and in lower grades. Variety 3 coins are readily found in Mint State, including in MS-65 and higher grades.

Proofs were made of all years, but not in quantity until 1858, when an estimated 210 were struck. For all dates after 1862, high-grade Proofs are much more readily available today than are Mint State coins. Circulated examples are available of all three varieties. While extensively worn coins of Variety 1 are available, most Variety 2 coins are Fine or better and most Variety 3 pieces are VF or better.

FOR THE COLLECTOR AND INVESTOR: SILVER THREE-CENT PIECES AS A SPECIALTY

Trimes cover a fairly long span of years and embrace several design types, but comprise no "impossible" rarities. Accordingly, it is realistic to collect one of each Philadelphia Mint coin from 1851 to 1873 plus the 1851-O. There are two overdates in the series, 1862, 2 Over 1 (which is distinct and occurs only in circulation-strike format) and 1863, 3 Over 2 (only Proofs, and not boldly defined), which some specialists collect and others ignore. A curious variety of 1852 has the first digit of the date over an inverted 2.

Typically, a high-grade set includes Mint State examples of all issues 1851 through 1857 and Proofs after that date. As noted, Variety 2 trimes usually are very poorly struck, save the occasionally encountered sharp 1855. As an example, a specialist in the series who found an 1856 with needle-sharp details, at three times the regular market price, might be well advised to buy it. After 1862, Mint State coins are rare for most dates. The formation of a choice Mint State set 1851 through 1872 plus a Proof 1873 would be a formidable challenge.

A set of circulated coins can be gathered through and including 1862, after which such pieces become very rare. Most later dates will have to be acquired on a catch-as-catch-can basis, perhaps by acquiring impaired Proofs for certain of the years.

NICKEL THREE-CENT PIECES

Nickel three-cent pieces were introduced in 1865 to help fill the need for coins in circulation. At the time, silver and gold issues were hoarded, and were available only at a premium. The nickel three-cent piece joined the Indian Head cent and the new (as of 1864) two-cent piece. The coin proved to be very popular in its time, and millions were struck. In 1866 the nickel five-cent piece was introduced, after which time the demand for the nickel three-cent piece diminished somewhat. However, pieces were made in quantity until 1876. In that year silver coins again returned to circulation, and mintages for the nickel three-cent piece dropped sharply. Only Proofs were made in 1877 and 1878. In later years, mintages ranged from small to modest, except for 1881.

Mint State coins are readily available for the early years, although many if not most have weak striking in areas or are from clashed dies. Pristine, sharp Mint State coins on the market are mostly of later years, in the 1880s, where such pieces are the rule, not the exception.

FOR THE COLLECTOR AND INVESTOR: NICKEL THREE-CENT PIECES AS A SPECIALTY

Nickel three-cent coins are interesting to collect by date sequence from 1865 to 1889. Varieties are provided by the 1873, Close 3, and 1873, Open 3, and the 1887, 7 Over 6, overdate. A set of Mint State coins is considerably more difficult to form than a run of Proofs. A hand-selected set of well-struck coins MS-65 or finer could take several years to complete.

Among Proofs, the rarest year is 1865, probably followed by the "perfect date" (not overdate) 1887. Proofs of the 1860s and early 1870s are scarce in PF-65 with excellent strike and eye appeal. Proofs of the latter decade of coinage are much more readily available and usually are choice.

SILVER THREE-CENT PIECES (TRIMES) (1851–1873)

Variety 1 (1851–1853): **Designer:** *James B. Longacre.* **Weight:** *0.80 gram.*
Composition: *.750 silver, .250 copper.* **Diameter:** *14 mm.*
Edge: *Plain.* **Mints:** *Philadelphia and New Orleans.*

Variety 1 (1851–1853)   **Variety 1, Proof**

Variety 2 (1854–1858): **Designer:** *James B. Longacre.* **Weight:** *0.75 gram.*
Composition: *.900 silver, .100 copper.* **Diameter:** *14 mm.* **Edge:** *Plain.* **Mint:** *Philadelphia.*

Variety 2 (1854–1858)   **Variety 2, Proof**

Variety 3 (1859–1873): **Designer:** *James B. Longacre.* **Weight:** *0.75 gram.*
Composition: *.900 silver, .100 copper.* **Diameter:** *14 mm.* **Edge:** *Plain.* **Mint:** *Philadelphia.*

Variety 3 (1859–1873)   **Variety 3, Proof**

History. In 1850 Americans began hoarding their silver coins, as the flood of gold from California made silver disproportionately valuable. To provide a small coin for commerce, the Mint introduced the silver three-cent piece, or *trime*. These were .750 fine (as opposed to the standard .900 fineness), and contained less than 3¢ of metal, so there was no incentive to hoard or melt them. Three different designs were made, Variety 1 of which was struck from 1851 to 1853. These coins were popular in their time and circulated widely. These are distinguished from the other two designs by having no outline or frame around the obverse star. The Act of February 21, 1853, reduced the amount of silver in other denominations (from the half dime to the half dollar, but not the dollar), which discouraged people from hoarding them. The tiny trime lost the public's favor, and mintages decreased.

In 1854 the design was changed considerably, creating Variety 2, which was made through 1858. The alloy was modified to the standard for other issues and the weight was lightened. A raised border was added to the obverse star plus two line frames around it. On the reverse an olive branch was placed above the III and a bundle of arrows below it. This new motif proved to be very difficult to strike up properly.

In 1859 the design was modified again, creating Variety 3. Demand for the denomination continued to be small, and after 1862 very few were made for circulation, as silver coins were hoarded by the war-weary public and began to trade at a premium. Under the Coinage Act of 1873 the trime was discontinued, and that year only Proofs were struck. Also in that year, nearly the entire production of non-Proof coins of 1863 to 1872 was melted.

Striking and Sharpness. On the Variety 1 obverse the tiny shield at the center of the star often lacks certain details. On the reverse check the details and strength of the III. On both sides check the rims. Needle-sharp coins are in the minority. Sharpness of strike has been nearly completely overlooked in the marketplace.

Trimes of Variety 2 are usually poorly struck, with some or all of these characteristics: obverse lettering weak in places; frames around the star of inconsistent strength or missing in certain areas; shield weak in places; reverse stars irregular and poorly formed; olive branch and arrows weak in areas; weak or irregular rims. Now and then a sharp 1855 is found.

Most Variety 3 trimes are sharply struck. Points to look for include full outlines around the star, full shield on the star, and full leaf details and sharp stars.

Most Proofs are needle sharp and have mirrored surfaces, although some of the late 1860s and early 1870s can have slightly grainy or satiny lustrous surfaces. Striking quality varies. Lint marks and surface problems are not unusual. Careful examination is recommended.

Availability. Circulated examples of the Variety 1 trimes are plentiful. MS coins are often seen, although the 1851-O is scarce in MS and high circulated grades. Most MS coins are lustrous and attractive, especially at 63 and above. Circulated Variety 2 coins are scarce in all grades, particularly so at MS-64 and higher. With a needle-sharp strike, MS-65 and higher are *rarities*. Among Variety 3 trimes, circulated coins of the years 1859 to 1862 are easy to find. All later dates range from scarce to rare in circulation-strike format. MS-63 and better coins 1865 and later are very rare. A few Proofs were made in the early 1850s and are great rarities today. After 1857, production increased to an estimated 210 or so in 1858, through 500 to 700 or so as a yearly average in the 1860s to 1873.

GRADING STANDARDS

MS-60 to 70 (Mint State). *Obverse and Reverse:* At MS-60, some abrasion and very minor contact marks are evident, most noticeably on the obverse star and the C ornament on the reverse. At MS-63, abrasion is hard to detect except under magnification. An MS-65 coin will have no abrasion. Luster should be full and rich (not grainy). Grades above MS-65 are defined by having fewer marks as perfection is approached. Most high-grade Mint State coins are of the Variety 3 design.

1853, Variety 1. Graded MS-66.

AU-50, 53, 55, 58 (About Uncirculated). *Obverse:* Light wear is most obvious on the star arms and shield on Variety 1, and on the points of the frames on Variety 2 and Variety 3. At AU-50, luster is evident, but only on part of the field. At AU-58 luster is nearly complete. *Reverse:* Light wear is seen on the C ornament and III. On Variety 2 and 3, light wear is seen on the leaves and arrows.

Illustrated coin: This is sharply struck, as are most Variety 3 trimes.

1863, Variety 3. Graded AU-50.

EF-40, 45 (Extremely Fine). *Obverse:* More wear is seen, most noticeable on the ridges of the star arms, this in addition to more wear on the frames (Variety 2 and Variety 3). Luster is absent, or seen only in traces. *Reverse:* More wear is seen on the C ornament and III. On Variety 2 and Variety 3 more wear is seen on the leaves and arrows.

1869, Variety 3. Graded EF-45.

VF-20, 30 (Very Fine). *Obverse:* Further wear reduced the relief of the star. On Variety 2 and Variety 3 the frames show further wear and begin to blend together. The center shield shows wear, and its border is indistinct in areas, but its horizontal and vertical stripes are fully delineated (unless the coin was weakly struck). *Reverse:* Still more wear is seen on the C ornament and III. On Variety 2 and Variety 3 the high-relief areas of the

1862, Variety 3. Graded VF-30.

leaves and the feathers of the arrow are partially worn away. Stars are flat at their centers (on sharply struck coins in addition to, as expected, on weak strikes).

F-12, 15 (Fine). *Obverse:* The star is worn so as to have lost most of its relief. On Variety 2 and Variety 3 the frames are mostly blended together. The center shield shows wear, and its border is flat (or else showing only slight separation of its two outlines), but its horizontal and vertical stripes still are delineated (unless the coin was weakly struck). *Reverse:* Still more wear is seen on the C ornament and III. On Variety 2 and Variety 3 the

1851, Variety 1. Graded F-12.

high-relief areas of the leaves, and the feathers of the arrow, have slight if any detail. Stars are flat. The designs within the C ornament are missing much detail.

VG-8, 10 (Very Good). *Obverse:* The border is incomplete in places, but all lettering is bold. The horizontal and vertical stripes within the shield begin to blend together, but most remain well delineated. *Reverse:* Still more wear is seen on all areas. The designs within the C ornament have more detail gone.

   Illustrated coin: The obverse of this coin shows VG wear, but if the dent in the star was considered it would grade lower.

1852, Variety 1. Graded VG-10.

G-4, 6 (Good). *Obverse:* The border is worn into the tops of the letters and the bottom of the date. The shield is blended into the star, and only traces of the shield outline remain. In this grade most coins seen are Variety 1. *Reverse:* The border is worn into the outer parts of the stars. Additional wear is seen in all other areas.

1851, Variety 1. Graded G-6.

AG-3 (About Good). *Obverse:* The star is flat. Strong elements of the shield are seen, but the tiny lines are mostly or completely blended together. Lettering and date are weak and partially missing, but the date must be identifiable. In this grade most coins seen are Variety 1. *Reverse:* The border is worn into the stars, with outer elements of the stars now gone. Additional wear is seen in all other areas. The designs within the C ornament are only in outline form.

1853, Variety 1. Graded AG-3.

PF-60 to 70 (Proof). *Obverse and Reverse:* Proofs that are extensively cleaned and have many hairlines, or that are dull and grainy, are lower level, such as PF–60 to 62. These are difficult to verify as Proofs. For a trime with medium hairlines and good reflectivity, an assigned grade of PF-64 is indicated, and with relatively few hairlines, gem PF-65. PF-66 should have hairlines so delicate that magnification is needed to see them. Above that, a Proof should be free of such lines.

1857, Variety 2. Graded PF-66.

Illustrated coin: Note the remarkable sharpness of strike, particularly evident on the obverse.

	Mintage	Cert	Avg	%MS	G-4	VG-8	F-12	VF-20	EF-40	AU-50	MS-60	MS-63	MS-65
											PF-63	PF-64	PF-65
1851	5,447,400	1,330	60.5	86%	$35	$40	$50	$65	$80	$165	$200	$275	$675
	Auctions: $3,055, MS-67, July 2015; $2,115, MS-66, June 2015; $1,292, MS-66, September 2015; $446, MS-64, January 2015												
1851, Proof (a)		0	n/a								—		
	Auctions: No auction records available.												
1851-O	720,000	490	57.5	69%	$45	$65	$75	$120	$200	$275	$550	$1,000	$2,500
	Auctions: $11,163, MS-67, July 2014; $12,925, MS-66, December 2013; $793, MS-62, October 2014; $317, AU-55, October 2014												

a. 1 or 2 examples are known.

1852, 1 Over Inverted 2	**1853, Repunched Date**	**1854, Repunched Date**
FS-3S-1852-301.	FS-3S-1853-301.	FS-3S-1854-301.

	Mintage	Cert	Avg	%MS	G-4	VG-8	F-12	VF-20	EF-40	AU-50	MS-60 / PF-63	MS-63 / PF-64	MS-65 / PF-65
1852, 1 Over Inverted 2 (b)	(c)	1	61.0										
Auctions: No auction records available.													
1852	18,663,500	1,773	56.0	75%	$35	$40	$50	$65	$80	$165	$200	$275	$675
Auctions: $2,643, MS-67, June 2015; $1,057, MS-66, July 2015; $1,028, MS-66, August 2015; $705, MS-65, January 2015													
1852, Proof (d)		0	n/a								—		
Auctions: No auction records available.													
1853	11,400,000	951	52.6	64%	$35	$40	$50	$65	$80	$165	$200	$275	$675
Auctions: $1,233, MS-66, June 2015; $587, MS-65, October 2015; $423, MS-64, January 2015; $152, AU-58, September 2015													
1853, Repunched Date (e)	(f)	1	15.0	0%					$100	$200	$260	$300	$1,000
Auctions: No auction records available.													
1854	671,000	408	58.4	69%	$45	$55	$60	$75	$120	$225	$350	$700	$2,500
Auctions: $3,290, MS-66, June 2015; $2,820, MS-65, January 2015; $646, MS-62, September 2015; $199, AU-53, April 2015													
1854, Repunched Date (g)	(h)	2	47.0	50%					$185	$325	$500	$800	$3,500
Auctions: No auction records available.													
1854, Proof	25–35	7	64.0								$10,000	$20,000	$35,000
Auctions: $32,900, PF-65, January 2015; $41,125, PF-65, June 2014; $14,688, PF-64, October 2014; $6,463, PF-63, August 2015													
1855	139,000	165	53.1	50%	$45	$65	$75	$125	$200	$350	$600	$1,450	$6,000
Auctions: $9,400, MS-66, August 2015; $1,645, MS-64, January 2015; $399, AU-55, April 2015; $305, EF-45, July 2015													
1855, Proof	30–40	23	64.7								$5,000	$8,500	$15,000
Auctions: $21,150, PF-66Cam, October 2014; $8,225, PF-64, October 2014; $14,400, PF-65, January 2018													
1856	1,458,000	375	57.3	66%	$45	$50	$55	$70	$120	$235	$360	$700	$2,250
Auctions: $1,292, MS-64, July 2015; $1,086, MS-64, October 2015; $329, MS-62, May 2015; $352, AU-58, April 2015													
1856, Proof	40–50	32	64.5								$5,000	$7,500	$12,500
Auctions: $22,325, PF-66, August 2016; $19,388, PF-66, February 2015; $9,988, PF-64, October 2015													
1857	1,042,000	369	57.5	73%	$45	$50	$55	$70	$120	$235	$360	$800	$3,000
Auctions: $5,405, MS-66, January 2015; $2,820, MS-65, September 2015; $940, MS-64, October 2015; $646, AU-58, April 2015													
1857, Proof	60–80	36	64.6								$3,500	$5,000	$10,000
Auctions: $15,863, PF-66, June 2014													
1858	1,603,700	678	56.4	64%	$45	$50	$55	$70	$120	$235	$360	$700	$1,650
Auctions: $5,875, MS-67, July 2015; $1,821, MS-65, February 2015; $1,116, MS-64, September 2015; $353, AU-58, April 2015													
1858, Proof	210	106	64.5								$2,500	$4,500	$6,500
Auctions: $12,925, PF-67, August 2015; $6,462, PF-65, October 2015													
1859	364,200	370	59.3	73%	$40	$50	$55	$60	$90	$175	$215	$300	$1,000
Auctions: $1,762, MS-66, January 2015; $1,645, MS-66, September 2015; $881, MS-65, October 2015; $763, MS-65, August 2015													
1859, Proof	800	114	64.1								$800	$1,100	$2,000
Auctions: $4,700, PF-66Cam, August 2015; $2,643, PF-66, June 2015; $1,880, PF-65, January 2015; $1,586, PF-64Cam, February 2015													
1860	286,000	372	57.3	60%	$40	$45	$55	$60	$90	$175	$215	$300	$1,000
Auctions: $434, MS-64, October 2015; $317, MS-63, April 2015; $211, MS-61, May 2015; $166, AU-55, January 2015													
1860, Proof	1,000	80	63.8								$900	$1,350	$3,750
Auctions: $4,935, PF-65, August 2015; $960, PF-64, January 2018													

b. An inverted 2 is visible beneath the primary 1. From the *Cherrypickers' Guide to Rare Die Varieties, Vol. I* (sixth edition): "A secondary date punch was obviously punched into the die In an inverted orientation and then corrected after some effacing of the die" **c.** Included in circulation-strike 1852 mintage figure. **d.** 1 example is known. **e.** Secondary digits are visible to the north of the primary 1 and 8. This repunched date can be detected on lower-grade coins. **f.** Included in 1853 mintage figure. **g.** Secondary digits are visible to the west of the primary digits on the 8 and 5. **h.** Included in circulation-strike 1854 mintage figure.

1862, 2 Over 1
FS-3S-1862-301.

	Mintage	Cert	Avg	%MS	G-4	VG-8	F-12	VF-20	EF-40	AU-50	MS-60 / PF-63	MS-63 / PF-64	MS-65 / PF-65
1861	497,000	934	60.1	73%	$40	$45	$55	$60	$90	$175	$215	$300	$875
	Auctions: $2,938, MS-67, June 2015; $1,410, MS-66, January 2015; $519, MS-64, August 2015; $164, AU-53, May 2015												
1861, Proof	1,000	93	64.1								$750	$1,100	$1,750
	Auctions: $3,055, PF-66, June 2015; $2,351, PF-66, September 2015; $1,175, PF-65, January 2015												
1862, 2 Over 1 (i)	(j)	358	63.2	88%	$45	$55	$60	$75	$95	$190	$240	$350	$1,050
	Auctions: $1,762, MS-66, June 2015; $881, MS-65, August 2015; $540, MS-64, February 2015; $329, AU-58, April 2015												
1862	343,000	1,561	62.5	86%	$35	$40	$50	$60	$90	$175	$215	$285	$875
	Auctions: $2,585, MS-67, September 2015; $1,116, MS-66, June 2015; $734, MS-65, January 2015; $223, AU-58, April 2015												
1862, Proof	550	140	64.0								$750	$1,100	$1,750
	Auctions: $2,127, PF-66, October 2015; $2,115, PF-65, January 2015; $1,527, PF-65, August 2015; $646, PF-63, June 2015												
1863	21,000	83	64.2	96%	$475	$550	$600	$650	$750	$1,000	$1,400	$1,800	$3,500
	Auctions: $7,050, MS-67, January 2015; $5,875, MS-67, October 2015												
1863, So-Called 3 Over 2, Proof	(k)	0	n/a								$2,850	$4,500	$7,500
	Auctions: $8,812, PF-67, January 2015; $12,925, PF-65, July 2015; $5,405, PF-64, October 2015; $2,640, PF-63, January 2018												
1863, Proof	460	142	64.2								$750	$1,100	$1,500
	Auctions: $3,995, PF-66Cam, January 2015; $1,703, PF-65Cam, January 2015												
1864	12,000	95	63.2	92%	$475	$525	$625	$650	$750	$900	$1,200	$1,400	$3,000
	Auctions: $13,513, MS-68, October 2014; $7,638, MS-67, January 2017; $3,760, MS-66, October 2015; $1,645, MS-64, August 2016												
1864, Proof	470	173	64.5								$750	$1,000	$1,500
	Auctions: $2,585, PF-66, August 2015; $3,055, PF-65Cam, January 2015; $1,116, PF-65, July 2015; $1,088, PF-64Cam, August 2015												
1865	8,000	114	62.4	85%	$475	$525	$575	$650	$800	$1,100	$1,700	$2,350	$4,500
	Auctions: $5,170, MS-67, August 2015; $4,230, MS-66, October 2015; $3,912, MS-64, September 2017; $2,232, MS-63, January 2015												
1865, Proof	500	165	64.4								$750	$1,000	$1,500
	Auctions: $3,642, PF-67, October 2015; $3,995, PF-66, June 2015; $1,645, PF-65, August 2015; $3,290, PF-64, January 2015												
1866	22,000	87	62.0	86%	$450	$525	$575	$625	$800	$1,100	$1,600	$2,000	$3,750
	Auctions: $9,400, MS-67, September 2016; $8,812, MS-66, October 2015; $2,468, MS-64, August 2014; $998, EF-40, January 2015												
1866, Proof	725	204	64.2								$750	$1,000	$1,500
	Auctions: $6,462, PF-67, January 2015; $1,762, PF-66, August 2015; $1,292, PF-64, September 2015; $705, PF-63, July 2015												
1867	4,000	51	61.0	84%	$450	$525	$575	$650	$850	$1,200	$1,700	$3,000	$12,500
	Auctions: $5,280, MS-66, April 2018; $14,100, MS-65, October 2015; $4,465, MS-64, August 2015; $3,643, MS-64, September 2015												
1867, Proof	625	264	64.4								$750	$1,000	$1,500
	Auctions: $1,762, PF-66, September 2015; $1,527, PF-65, August 2015; $998, PF-64, January 2015; $822, PF-64, July 2015												

i. A secondary 1 is evident beneath the 2 of the date. From the *Cherrypickers' Guide to Rare Die Varieties, Vol. I* (sixth edition): "This overdate is believed to be due more to economy (the Mint having used a good die another year) than to error. Circulated examples are about as common as the regular-dated coin." **j.** Included in circulation-strike 1862 mintage figure. **k.** Included in 1863, Proof, mintage figure.

	Mintage	Cert	Avg	%MS	F-12	VF-20	EF-40	AU-50	MS-60	MS-63	MS-64	MS-65	MS-66
											PF-63	PF-64	PF-65
1868	3,500	40	59.4	75%	$1,000	$1,350	$1,850	$2,500	$4,500	$6,000	$16,500	$22,500	$27,500
	Auctions: $21,150, MS-66, October 2015; $28,200, MS-66, May 2015; $5,405, AU-58, July 2015; $648, MS-66, February 2018												
1868, Proof	600	271	64.0								$750	$1,000	$1,500
	Auctions: $3,525, PF-66, October 2015; $1,410, PF-66, January 2015; $1,997, PF-65, August 2015; $940, PF-63, September 2015												
1869	4,500	49	61.4	86%	$600	$850	$1,200	$1,400	$1,750	$2,200	$4,000	$6,750	$8,000
	Auctions: $9,987, MS-65, October 2015; $4,230, MS-64, October 2015; $1,645, MS-62, August 2015; $940, EF-40, July 2015												
1869, Proof	600	186	64.4								$750	$1,000	$1,500
	Auctions: $7,050, PF-67, August 2015; $1,880, PF-66, January 2015; $1,645, PF-65, October 2015; $423, PF-62, June 2015												
1869, So-Called 9 Over 8, Proof (a)	**(b)**	0	n/a								$4,000	$6,750	$8,500
	Auctions: $9,987, PF-66, August 2015												
1870	3,000	91	61.5	78%	$550	$650	$750	$950	$1,200	$1,800	$3,000	$4,500	$7,500
	Auctions: $7,116, MS-66, October 2015; $470, EF-40, May 2015												
1870, Proof	1,000	252	64.0								$750	$1,000	$1,500
	Auctions: $1,880, PF-66, January 2015; $1,762, PF-65, September 2015; $1,762, PF-64, October 2015; $3,055, PF-63, October 2015												
1871	3,400	152	63.8	91%	$550	$650	$950	$1,050	$1,100	$1,200	$1,500	$2,000	$3,000
	Auctions: $3,290, MS-67, June 2015; $1,880, MS-66, February 2015; $1,645, MS-64, January 2015; $1,086, MS-63, November 2015												
1871, Proof	960	238	64.0								$750	$1,000	$1,500
	Auctions: $2,291, PF-66, January 2015; $1,527, PF-65, September 2015; $881, PF-63, July 2015; $646, PF-61, June 2015												
1872	1,000	47	61.2	83%	$1,000	$1,250	$1,800	$2,500	$2,750	$4,000	$7,000	$10,000	$15,000
	Auctions: $14,100, MS-67, August 2015; $54,050, MS-67, February 2015; $4,935, MS-65, October 2015; $13,200, MS-66, January 2018												
1872, Proof	950	258	64.1								$750	$1,000	$1,500
	Auctions: $11,750, PF-67Cam, January 2015; $2,585, PF-66, August 2015; $3,290, PF-65, October 2015; $1,645, PF-65, August 2015												
1873, Close 3, Proof (a)	600	377	64.1								$1,950	$2,500	$3,000
	Auctions: $12,220, PF-67, February 2015; $3,055, PF-66Cam, June 2015												

a. Proof only. b. Included in 1869, Proof, mintage figure.

NICKEL THREE-CENT PIECES (1865–1889)

Designer: *James B. Longacre.* **Weight:** *1.94 grams.* **Composition:** *.750 copper, .250 nickel.*
Diameter: *17.9 mm.* **Edge:** *Plain.* **Mint:** *Philadelphia.*

Circulation Strike   Proof

History. The copper-nickel three-cent coin debuted in the final year of the Civil War, 1865. The American public was still hoarding silver coins (a situation that would continue until 1876), including the silver three-cent piece. The highest-denomination coin remaining in circulation at the time was the recently introduced two-cent piece. After 1875, when silver coins circulated once again, the three-cent denomination became redundant and mintages dropped. The last pieces were coined in 1889.

Striking and Sharpness. On the obverse check the hair and other portrait details. On the reverse the tiny vertical lines in the Roman numeral III can be weak. Check the denticles on both sides of the coin. Among circulation strikes, clashed dies are common, particularly for the earlier high-mintage years. Generally, coins of the 1860s and 1870s have weakness in one area or another. Many if not most of the 1880s are well struck. Proofs from 1878 onward often have satiny or frosty fields, rather than mirrored surfaces, and resemble circulation strikes.

Availability. Circulated examples of dates from 1865 to the mid-1870s are readily available. MS coins, particularly from the 1860s, are easily found, but often have areas of weakness or lack aesthetic appeal. MS coins of the 1880s are readily found for most dates (except for 1883, 1884, 1885, and 1887), some of them probably sold as Proofs. Many Proofs of the era had slight to extensive mint luster. Proofs were struck of all dates and can be found easily enough in the marketplace. The rarest is the first year of issue, 1865, of which only an estimated 500 or so were made. The vast majority of 1865s have a repunched date. Second rarest (not counting PF-only date of 1877) is the 1887 (perfect date, not the overdate) with a production of about 1,000 coins. Proofs of the years 1865 to 1876 can be difficult to find as true gems, while later Proofs are nearly all gems.

GRADING STANDARDS

MS-60 to 70 (Mint State). *Obverse and Reverse:* Mint luster is complete in the obverse and reverse fields. Lower grades such as MS–60, 61, and 62 can show some evidence of abrasion. This is usually on the area of the hair to the right of the face (on the obverse), and on the highest parts of the wreath (on the reverse). Abrasion can appear as scattered contact marks elsewhere. At MS-63, these marks are few, and on MS-65

1865. Graded MS-61.

they are fewer yet. In grades above MS-65, marks can only be seen under magnification.

AU-50, 53, 55, 58 (About Uncirculated). *Obverse:* Light wear is seen on the portrait, most notably on the upper cheek and on the hair to the right of the face. Mint luster is present in the fields, ranging from partial at AU-50 to nearly complete at AU-58. All details are sharp, unless lightly struck. *Reverse:* Light wear is seen on the top and bottom horizontal edges of the III and the wreath. Luster is partial at AU-50, increasing

1881. Graded AU-55.

to nearly full at AU-58. All details are sharp, unless lightly struck.

EF-40, 45 (Extremely Fine). *Obverse:* More wear is seen on the cheek and the hair to the right of the face and neck. The hair to the right of the coronet beads shows light wear. *Reverse:* The wreath still shows most detail on the leaves. Some wear is seen on the vertical lines within III (but striking can also cause weakness). Overall the reverse appears to be very bold.

1889. Graded EF-40.

VF-20, 30 (Very Fine). *Obverse:* Most hair detail is gone, with a continuous flat area to the right of the face and neck, where the higher hair strands have blended together. The hair to the right of the coronet beads shows about half of the strands. *Reverse:* Higher details of the leaves are worn away; the central ridges are seen on some. Wear on the vertical lines in III has caused some to merge, but most are separate.

1880. Graded VF-25.

F-12, 15 (Fine). *Obverse:* Wear is more extensive. The forehead blends into the hair above it. About 10% to 29% of the hair detail to the right of the coronet remains, and much detail is seen lower, at the right edge opposite the ear and neck. Denticles are distinct. *Reverse:* The top (highest-relief) part of most leaves is flat. Many vertical lines in III are fused. Denticles are distinct.

1882. Graded F-15.

VG-8, 10 (Very Good). *Obverse:* Less hair detail shows. Denticles all are clear. *Reverse:* The leaves show more wear. The inner edges of some leaves are worn away, causing leaves to merge. Only about half, or slightly fewer, of the lines in III are discernible.

1865. Graded VG-10.

G-4, 6 (Good). *Obverse:* Most hair details are gone, but some remain at the lower right. The rim is worn smooth in areas, and many denticles are missing. The lettering is weak, but readable. *Reverse:* The leaves mostly are worn flat. Very few lines remain in III. The rim is worn smooth in areas, and many denticles are missing.

1867. Graded G-4.

AG-3 (About Good). *Obverse:* The rim is worn away and into the tops of most of the letters. The date remains bold. *Reverse:* The rim is worn away and into some of the leaves.

1867. Graded AG-3.

PF-60 to 70 (Proof). *Obverse and Reverse:* PF–60, 61, and 62 coins show varying amounts of hairlines in the field, decreasing as the grade increases. Fields may be dull or cloudy on lower-level pieces. At PF-65, hairlines are visible only under magnification and are very light; the cheek of Miss Liberty does not show any friction or "album slide marks." Above PF-65, hairlines become fewer, and in ultra-high grades are nonexistent, this mean-

1878. Graded PF-65.

ing that the coins have never been subject to wiping or abrasive cleaning. At PF-65 or better, expect excellent aesthetic appeal. Blotched, deeply toned, or recolored coins are sometimes seen at Proof levels from PF–60 through 65 or even 66 and should be avoided, but these are less often seen than on contemporary Proof nickel five-cent pieces.

1866, Doubled Die Obverse
FS-3N-1866-101.

	Mintage	Cert	Avg	%MS	G-4	VG-8	VF-20	EF-40	AU-50	MS-60	MS-63 / PF-63	MS-65 / PF-65	MS-66 / PF-66
1865	11,382,000	2,327	58.8	74%	$18	$20	$30	$40	$65	$100	$160	$550	$1,100
Auctions: $1,880, MS-66, January 2015; $399, MS-64, May 2015; $199, MS-61, November 2015; $111, AU-58, June 2015													
1865, Proof	*500+*	195	64.7								$1,500	$3,000	$4,000
Auctions: $4,583, PF-66, November 2016; $5,288, PF-65, July 2015; $4,113, PF-64, August 2016													
1866	4,801,000	916	59.1	78%	$18	$20	$28	$40	$65	$100	$160	$550	$1,500
Auctions: $7,637, MS-67, August 2015; $1,527, MS-66, June 2015; $111, MS-63, February 2015; $89, MS-62, April 2015													
1866, Doubled Die Obverse (a)	**(b)**	5	48.4	20%				$150	$250	$350	$450	$1,000	
Auctions: No auction records available.													
1866, Proof	*725+*	312	64.5								$325	$1,000	$1,450
Auctions: $2,820, PF-66, January 2015; $1,880, PF-66, September 2015; $1,527, PF-65, August 2015; $1,292, PF-65, June 2015													

a. Moderate doubling is visible on AMERICA and on portions of the hair. From the *Cherrypickers' Guide to Rare Die Varieties, Vol. I* (sixth edition): "The dies clashed midway through the obverse's life. Mid– and late–die-state coins exhibit the clash marks and die cracks as progression occurs. This variety has proven extremely scarce." **b.** Included in circulation-strike 1866 mintage figure.

	Mintage	Cert	Avg	%MS	G-4	VG-8	VF-20	EF-40	AU-50	MS-60	MS-63	MS-65	MS-66
											PF-63	PF-65	PF-66
1867	3,915,000	700	58.4	71%	$15	$20	$30	$40	$65	$100	$160	$650	$1,650
	Auctions: $238, MS-64, January 2015; $141, MS-63, February 2015; $111, MS-62, May 2015; $79, AU-58, August 2015												
1867, Proof	625+	314	64.7								$325	$850	$1,250
	Auctions: $9,400, PF-68, July 2015; $1,880, PF-66, January 2015; $1,527, PF-66, September 2015; $763, PF-65, August 2015												
1868	3,252,000	646	58.8	74%	$15	$20	$30	$40	$65	$100	$160	$625	$1,100
	Auctions: $881, MS-66, August 2015; $822, MS-65, January 2015; $111, MS-63, February 2015; $117, MS-62, April 2015												
1868, Proof	600+	295	64.8								$325	$900	$1,300
	Auctions: $1,065, PF-66, January 2015; $1,116, PF-65, September 2015; $705, PF-65, August 2015; $446, PF-64, January 2015												
1869	$1,604,000	452	59.5	76%	$15	$20	$30	$40	$65	$125	$185	$750	$1,500
	Auctions: $1,292, MS-66, August 2015; $141, MS-63, February 2015; $105, MS-62, February 2015; $129, MS-61, November 2015												
1869, Proof	600+	379	64.7								$325	$700	$950
	Auctions: $5,170, PF-67, July 2015; $881, PF-66, January 2015; $1,028, PF-65, October 2015; $705, PF-65, January 2015												
1870	1,335,000	475	59.5	76%	$20	$25	$30	$40	$65	$140	$195	$725	$1,450
	Auctions: $223, MS-64, March 2015; $164, MS-63, November 2015; $129, MS-62, May 2015; $84, AU-58, April 2015												
1870, Proof	1,000+	367	64.4								$325	$650	$950
	Auctions: $1,175, PF-66, January 2015; $763, PF-65, September 2015; $329, PF-64, April 2015; $235, MS-61, November 2015												
1871	604,000	266	58.6	77%	$20	$25	$30	$40	$65	$140	$195	$750	$1,500
	Auctions: $3,525, MS-67, January 2015; $2,723, MS-66, September 2015; $2,350, MS-66, February 2015; $282, MS-64, May 2015												
1871, Proof	960+	376	64.5								$325	$650	$950
	Auctions: $5,875, PF-67Cam, October 2015; $940, PF-66, February 2015; $763, PF-65, January 2015; $258, PF-63, November 2015												
1872	862,000	224	58.3	72%	$20	$25	$30	$40	$65	$150	$250	$1,200	$2,200
	Auctions: $881, MS-66, January 2015; $940, MS-65, October 2015; $211, MS-63, May 2015; $117, MS-62, July 2015												
1872, Proof	950+	443	64.5								$325	$650	$950
	Auctions: $4,700, PF-66, February 2015; $1,600, PF-66, July 2015; $505, PF-65, June 2015; $293, PF-63, November 2015												
1873, Close 3	390,000	133	54.2	63%	$20	$25	$30	$40	$65	$150	$250	$1,350	$2,750
	Auctions: $2,232, MS-66, August 2015; $423, MS-64, June 2015; $399, MS-64, October 2015; $237, MS-63, February 2015												
1873, Open 3	783,000	112	52.5	59%	$20	$25	$30	$40	$70	$160	$350	$1,500	$4,000
	Auctions: $3,055, MS-65, January 2015; $587, MS-64, June 2015; $223, MS-63, October 2015; $199, MS-63, May 2015; $780, MS-65, March 2018												
1873, Close 3, Proof	1,100+	461	64.5								$325	$650	$950
	Auctions: $969, PF-66, August 2015; $734, PF-65, June 2015; $540, PF-65, January 2015; $290, PF-64, November 2015												
1874	790,000	221	56.4	67%	$20	$25	$30	$40	$65	$150	$210	$975	$2,000
	Auctions: $2,115, MS-66, October 2015; $188, MS-63, August 2015; $176, MS-62, January 2015; $79, AU-58, February 2015												
1874, Proof	700+	343	64.6								$325	$600	$1,100
	Auctions: $601, PF-66, January 2015; $564, PF-66, October 2015; $587, PF-65, June 2015; $329, PF-64, April 2015												
1875	228,000	254	61.2	85%	$20	$25	$35	$45	$80	$175	$225	$800	$1,500
	Auctions: $646, MS-65, August 2015; $329, MS-64, November 2015; $446, AU-58, April 2015; $129, AU-55, May 2015												
1875, Proof	700+	257	64.4								$325	$950	$1,500
	Auctions: $998, PF-65, January 2015; $646, PF-65, June 2015; $470, PF-64, January 2015; $305, PF-64, October 2015												
1876	162,000	153	57.5	68%	$20	$25	$35	$65	$110	$200	$260	$1,600	$2,250
	Auctions: $1,880, MS-66, June 2015; $1,292, MS-65, February 2015; $940, MS-64, July 2015; $616, AU-58, May 2015												
1876, Proof	1,150+	412	64.5								$325	$650	$1,050
	Auctions: $1,057, PF-66, September 2015; $881, PF-66, July 2015; $517, PF-65, January 2015; $540, PF-64, May 2015												
1877, Proof (c)	900	468	64.8								$2,000	$3,250	$3,500
	Auctions: $5,280, PF-67, January 2018; $3,525, PF-65, May 2016; $2,585, PF-64, August 2017												
1878, Proof (c)	2,350	715	64.8								$775	$850	$1,000
	Auctions: $6,463, PF-68, January 2016; $1,320, PF-67, April 2018; $1,410, PF-66, March 2016; $690, PF-64, April 2018; $646, PF-63, January 2015												

c. Proof only.

1887, 7 Over 6, Proof
FS-3N-1887-302.

	Mintage	Cert	Avg	%MS	G-4	VG-8	VF-20	EF-40	AU-50	MS-60	MS-63 / PF-63	MS-65 / PF-65	MS-66 / PF-66
1879	38,000	202	54.7	63%	$60	$70	$100	$125	$175	$300	$400	$950	$1,200
Auctions: $998, MS-66, July 2015; $1,057, MS-65, August 2015; $575, MS-65, January 2015; $258, AU-53, May 2015													
1879, Proof	3,200	982	65.1								$325	$450	$600
Auctions: $2,820, PF-68, January 2015; $998, PF-67, July 2015; $675, PF-66Cam, August 2015; $411, PF-65, May 2015													
1880	21,000	224	56.0	72%	$100	$120	$155	$200	$220	$350	$500	$850	$1,250
Auctions: $705, MS-65, August 2015; $564, MS-64, January 2015; $296, MS-63, October 2015; $211, MS-60, May 2015													
1880, Proof	3,955	1,009	64.9								$325	$450	$600
Auctions: $540, PF-66, June 2015; $470, PF-66, January 2015; $376, PF-65, November 2015; $298, PF-64, April 2015													
1881	1,077,000	709	58.1	66%	$20	$25	$30	$40	$65	$125	$185	$650	$1,000
Auctions: $493, MS-65, July 2015; $152, MS-63, July 2015; $94, MS-62, August 2015; $89, AU-58, October 2015													
1881, Proof	3,575	1,039	65.1								$325	$450	$600
Auctions: $3,760, PF-68, February 2015; $1,057, PF-67, February 2015; $587, PF-66, January 2015; $282, PF-63, April 2015													
1882	22,200	148	47.7	36%	$135	$150	$215	$225	$275	$450	$600	$1,850	$2,750
Auctions: $587, MS-64, January 2015; $199, VF-30, February 2015; $164, VF-25, October 2015; $164, F-15, July 2015													
1882, Proof	3,100	1,083	65.2								$325	$450	$600
Auctions: $4,230, PF-68, January 2015; $446, PF-65, March 2015; $258, PF-62, August 2015; $199, PF-60, May 2015													
1883	4,000	57	51.6	47%	$300	$350	$500	$600	$850	$1,500	$2,750	$10,000	$15,000
Auctions: $7,638, MS-65, August 2016; $940, AU-50, May 2016; $588, EF-45, September 2016; $16,800, MS-66, April 2018													
1883, Proof	6,609	1,610	64.6								$325	$450	$600
Auctions: $5,287, PF-68, January 2015; $705, PF-66, February 2015; $376, PF-65, November 2015; $235, PF-64, January 2015													
1884	1,700	38	51.1	34%	$675	$1,000	$1,500	$2,000	$3,750	$4,750	$7,000	$17,500	$22,500
Auctions: $2,115, MS-61, December 2015; $1,998, EF-45, February 2015; $1,880, VF-30, July 2016													
1884, Proof	3,942	1,258	64.5								$325	$450	$600
Auctions: $998, PF-67, October 2015; $734, PF-66, August 2015; $376, PF-65, January 2015; $305, PF-64, February 2015													
1885	1,000	36	56.9	67%	$875	$1,150	$1,750	$2,500	$3,000	$4,500	$6,500	$12,500	$17,500
Auctions: $16,450, MS-66, June 2015; $8,225, MS-65, November 2016; $7,050, MS-64, August 2016; $3,408, AU-55, October 2016													
1885, Proof	3,790	1,050	64.5								$325	$450	$600
Auctions: $646, PF-66, June 2015; $340, PF-64, February 2015; $329, PF-64, January 2015; $258, PF-60, August 2015													
1886, Proof (c)	4,290	1,098	64.7								$400	$450	$750
Auctions: $900, PF-67, January 2015; $505, PF-66, January 2015; $517, PF-65, August 2015; $329, PF-64, February 2015													
1887	5,001	121	53.7	54%	$275	$325	$450	$525	$625	$750	$850	$1,500	$2,250
Auctions: $1,703, MS-66, August 2015; $1,763, MS-66, February 2015; $763, MS-63, July 2015; $705, EF-45, January 2015													
1887, Proof	2,960	860	64.6								$325	$465	$950
Auctions: $1,880, PF-67, June 2015; $540, PF-65, July 2015; $517, PF-65, January 2015; $423, PF-64, May 2015													
1887, 7 Over 6, Proof (d)	(e)	494	64.8								$450	$625	$900
Auctions: $2,585, PF-66, August 2015; $998, PF-66, October 2015; $517, PF-64Cam, January 2015; $376, PF-62, August 2015													
1888	36,501	360	58.0	61%	$50	$65	$75	$90	$150	$300	$400	$750	$1,250
Auctions: $1,527, MS-67, January 2015; $564, MS-65, September 2015; $305, MS-63, May 2015; $446, AU-58, February 2015													
1888, Proof	4,582	1,115	64.8								$325	$450	$600
Auctions: $3,055, PF-68, October 2015; $1,762, PF-67, February 2015; $600, PF-66, January 2015; $446, PF-65, February 2015													
1889	18,125	275	57.7	60%	$85	$120	$165	$235	$265	$350	$450	$800	$1,350
Auctions: $1,645, MS-66, January 2015; $795, MS-66, June 2015; $188, AU-55, May 2015; $176, AU-50, July 2015													
1889, Proof	3,436	1,100	64.9								$325	$450	$600
Auctions: $734, PF-67, January 2015; $646, PF-66, August 2015; $399, PF-65, September 2015; $282, PF-64, January 2015													

c. Proof only. **d.** Strong remnants of the underlying 6 are evident on either side of the lower portion of the 7, with the 1 and both 8's clearly repunched. This Proof overdate is relatively common; note that the regular date can be valued higher than the variety. **e.** Included in 1887, Proof, mintage figure.

Nickel Five-Cent Pieces
1866 to Date

AN OVERVIEW OF NICKEL FIVE-CENT PIECES

Five-cent pieces made of nickel were introduced in 1866, in an era in which the silver half dime as well as other silver denominations were not seen in circulation. More than a dozen designs and their variations have graced the "nickel" in the past 140-plus years.

While Shield nickels of both varieties are slightly scarce in upper Mint State levels, they are within the financial reach of most collectors. Proofs are available of each variety, but the 1866–1867, With Rays, and the 1913 Buffalo, Variety 1, issues are rare.

The quality of strike presents a challenge across the various types of nickel five-cent pieces, most particularly with the 1866–1867, With Rays, for there are fewer possibilities from which to choose. Although 1913–1938 Buffalo, Variety 2, nickels are often poorly struck, there are enough sharp ones that finding a choice example should present no great challenge for the collector.

FOR THE COLLECTOR AND INVESTOR: FIVE-CENT PIECES AS A SPECIALTY

Shield nickels of the 1866–1883 era are often collected by date sequence. A full set includes 1866 and 1867, With Rays, plus 1867 to 1883, Without Rays. In addition, there is the 1879, 9 Over 8, overdate, which is found only in Proof format but is readily available (constituting perhaps a third or so of the Proof mintage of 3,200 for the 1879 year) and the 1883, 3 Over 2 (scarce, and available only as a circulation strike).

Circulation strikes are available of all Shield nickel dates, 1866 to 1883, except 1877 and 1878, which were made only in Proof format. A set of Proofs can be completed except for the 1867, With Rays, which is exceedingly rare in Proof, with an estimated population of fewer than two dozen coins. Most 1878 Proofs are frosty and appear not much different from Mint State, but only Proofs were made this year.

In circulated grades, Shield nickels are available in proportion to their mintage figures. The dates 1879 to 1881 had high Proof mintages (in the context of Proof figures), but low circulation-strike mintages, and thus they are key dates in the latter format. In other words, a gem MS-65 1880 Shield nickel (16,000 coined, but few were saved, as collectors acquired Proofs instead) is exceedingly rare today. In the same year 3,955 Proofs were struck, all were preserved by collectors and dealers, and today the Proof 1880 is one of the most plentiful dates.

Liberty Head nickels of the 1883, Without CENTS (or "No CENTS"), variety are plentiful in Mint State and also in Proof. Later dates With CENTS, through 1912, are generally available in proportion to their mintages. The 1885 and 1886 are considered to be key dates. Proofs are readily collectible, although pristine high-quality examples can be hard to find. The 1912-D and 1912-S are scarce. In 1913 an estimated five Liberty Head nickels were made, and today stand as famous rarities.

Among Buffalo nickels, 1913 to 1938, the different dates and mints can be collected easily enough in circulated grades, although certain issues such as 1913-S, Variety 2; 1921-S; and 1926-S are on the scarce side. An overdate, 1918-D, 8 Over 7, is a rarity at all grade levels. Curious varieties are provided by the very rare 1916, Doubled Date; the scarce 1937-D, 3-Legged (the die was heavily polished, resulting in some loss of detail); and the fascinating and readily available 1938-D, D Over S, overmintmark.

In choice or gem Mint State most branch-mint Buffalo nickels, 1914–1927, are fairly scarce, and some are

Popularized in the 1890s and throughout the beginning of the 1900s, coin-operated machines took cents and other denominations, but the coin of choice was the nickel. Pictured is a postcard for Horn & Hardart restaurants, 1930s, where patrons would serve themselves with such coin-operated devices.

quite rare. Most branch-mint coins of the 1920s are lightly struck in one area or another, with the 1926-D being particularly infamous in this regard. Sharply struck examples of such varieties are worth much more than lightly struck ones, although the grading services take no particular note of such differences. Matte Proofs of dates 1913 to 1916 were struck, and mirror-finish Proofs were made in 1936 and 1937. These exist today in proportion to their mintages.

Jefferson nickels from 1938 to date are readily collectible in Mint State and Proof format. Many otherwise common varieties can be very rare if sharply struck.

SHIELD (1866–1883)

Designer: *James B. Longacre.* **Weight:** *5 grams.* **Composition:** *.750 copper, .250 nickel.*
Diameter: *20.5 mm.* **Edge:** *Plain.* **Mint:** *Philadelphia.*

Variety 1, Rays Between Stars (1866–1867)

Variety 1, Rays Between Stars, Proof

Variety 2, Without Rays (1867–1883)

Variety 2, Without Rays, Proof

History. The nickel five-cent piece was introduced in 1866. At the time, silver coins (except the trime) did not circulate in the East or Midwest. The new denomination proved popular, and "nickels" of the Shield variety were made continuously from 1866 to 1883. All 1866 nickels have rays between the stars on the reverse, as do a minority of 1867 issues, after which this feature was dropped. In 1877 and 1878 only Proofs were made, with no circulation strikes. The design, by Chief Engraver James B. Longacre, is somewhat similar to the obverse of the two-cent piece. Some Shield nickels were still seen in circulation in the 1930s, by which time most had been worn nearly smooth.

Striking and Sharpness. Sharpness can be a problem for Shield nickels in the 1860s through 1876, much less so for later years. On the obverse the horizontal shield stripes, vertical stripes, and leaves should be checked. The horizontal stripes in particular can be blended together. On the reverse the star centers can be weak. Check all other areas as well. Die cracks are seen on *most* circulation-strike Shield nickels, and do not affect value. Proof Shield nickels were struck of all dates 1866 to 1883, including two varieties of 1867 (With Rays, a great rarity, and the usually seen Without Rays). Fields range from deeply mirrorlike to somewhat grainy in character to mirror-surface, depending on a given year. Many of 1878, a date struck only in Proof format, have *lustrous* surfaces or prooflike surfaces combined with some luster, resembling a circulation strike. While most Proofs are sharp, some have weakness on the shield on the obverse and/or the star centers on the reverse. Lint marks or tiny recessed marks from scattered debris on the die faces are sometimes encountered, especially on issues of the 1870s, but not factored into the grade in commercial certification unless excessive.

Availability. Circulated coins generally are available in proportion to their mintage quantities (exceptions being the 1873, Open 3, and 1873, Close 3, varieties, which tend to be elusive in all grades despite their relatively high mintage). MS coins are similarly available, except that 1880 is a rarity. Those dated 1882 and 1883 are plentiful.

GRADING STANDARDS

MS-60 to 70 (Mint State). *Obverse and Reverse:* At MS-60 some abrasion and very minor contact marks are evident, most noticeably on high points of the shield on the obverse and the field on the reverse. Sometimes light striking on the shield and stars can be mistaken for light wear, and marks on the numeral 5 on the reverse can be from the original planchet surface not struck up fully. At MS-63 abrasions are hard to detect except

1873, Open 3. Graded MS-66.

under magnification. An MS-65 coin will have no abrasion. Luster should be full and rich (not grainy). Grades above MS-65 are defined by having no marks that can be seen by the naked eye. Higher-grade coins display deeper luster or virtually perfect prooflike surfaces, depending on the dies used.

    Illustrated coin: Note the faint golden toning along the obverse border.

AU-50, 53, 55, 58 (About Uncirculated). *Obverse:* Light wear is on the outside edges of the leaves, the frame of the shield, and the horizontal stripes (although the stripes can also be weakly struck). Mint luster is present in the fields, ranging from partial at AU-50 to nearly complete at AU-58. All details are sharp, unless lightly struck. *Reverse:* Light wear is seen on the numeral 5, and friction is seen in the field, identifiable as a change of color (loss of luster).

1867, Rays. Graded AU-58.

Luster is partial at AU-50, increasing to nearly full at AU-58. All details are sharp, unless lightly struck.

EF-40, 45 (Extremely Fine). *Obverse:* Nearly all shield border and leaf detail is visible. Light wear is seen on the shield stripes (but the horizontal stripes can be weakly struck). *Reverse:* More wear is seen on the numeral 5. The radial lines in the stars (if sharply struck to begin with) show slight wear. The field shows more wear.

1867, Rays. Graded EF-40.

VF-20, 30 (Very Fine). *Obverse:* The frame details and leaves show more wear, with much leaf detail gone. The shield stripes show more wear, and some of the vertical lines will begin to blend together. *Reverse:* More wear is seen overall, but some radial detail can still be seen on the stars.

1868. Graded VF-20.

F-12, 15 (Fine). *Obverse:* Most leaves are flat and have little detail, but will remain outlined. The shield frame is mostly flat. Most horizontal lines are blended together, regardless of original strike. Many vertical lines in the stripes are blended together. IN GOD WE TRUST is slightly weak. *Reverse:* All areas are in outline form except for slight traces of the star radials. Lettering is bold.

1867, Without Rays. Graded F-12.

VG-8, 10 (Very Good). *Obverse:* Many leaves are flat and blended with adjacent leaves. The frame is blended and has no details. Only a few horizontal lines may show. Vertical lines in the stripes are mostly blended. IN GOD WE TRUST is weak. *Reverse:* All elements are visible only in outline form. The rim is complete.

1879. Graded VG-10.

G-4, 6 (Good). *Obverse:* The shield and elements are seen in outline form except the vertical stripe separations. IN GOD WE TRUST is weak, and a few letters may be missing. *Reverse:* The rim is mostly if not completely worn away and into the tops of the letters.

Illustrated coin: Overall this coin is slightly better than G-4, but the 5 in the date is weak, making G-4 an appropriate attribution.

1881. Graded G-4.

AG-3 (About Good). *Obverse:* The rim is worn down and blended with the wreath. Only traces of IN GOD WE TRUST can be seen. The date is fully readable. *Reverse:* The rim is worn down and blended with the letters, some of which may be missing.

1880. Graded AG-3.

PF-60 to 70 (Proof). *Obverse and Reverse:* PF-60, 61, and 62 coins show varying amounts of hairlines in the reverse field in particular, decreasing as the grade increases. Fields may be dull or cloudy on lower-level pieces. At PF-65, hairlines are visible only under magnification and are very light and usually only on the reverse. Above PF-65, hairlines become fewer, and in ultra-high grades are nonexistent, this meaning that the coins have never been subject to wiping or abrasive cleaning. At PF-65 or better, expect excellent aesthetic appeal.

1882. Graded PF-66.

1866, Repunched Date
Several varieties exist.

	Mintage	Cert	Avg	%MS	G-4	VG-8	F-12	VF-20	EF-40	AU-50	MS-60 PF-63	MS-63 PF-65	MS-65 PF-66
1866, Rays	14,742,500	1,938	58.8	73%	$30	$45	$60	$90	$165	$240	$300	$500	$1,350
	Auctions: $2,056, MS-65, January 2015; $616, MS-64, February 2015; $176, MS-60, August 2015; $211, AU-58, May 2015												
1866, Repunched Date (a)	(b)	28	47.1	36%	$60	$100	$175	$250	$450	$1,000	$1,500	$3,250	
	Auctions: $12,925, MS-64, August 2014; $8,813, MS-64, October 2014; $1,293, AU-50, March 2013; $1,175, AU-50, August 2014												
1866, Rays, Proof	600+	267	64.8								$1,750	$3,000	$3,500
	Auctions: $2,585, PF-66, September 2015; $3,055, PF-65, January 2015; $1,997, PF-64, January 2015; $1,057, PF-61, October 2015												

a. There are at least five similar, very strong repunched dates for 1866; the values shown are typical for each. **b.** Included in circulation-strike 1866, Rays, mintage figure.

1873, Close 3	1873, Open 3	1873, Close 3, Doubled-Die Obverse

Several varieties exist. Pictured are
FS-05-1873-101 (left) and FS-05-1873-102 (right).

	Mintage	Cert	Avg	%MS	G-4	VG-8	F-12	VF-20	EF-40	AU-50	MS-60	MS-63	MS-65
											PF-63	PF-65	PF-66
1867, Rays	2,019,000	654	57.8	66%	$35	$50	$75	$120	$190	$285	$400	$500	$2,750
Auctions: $998, MS-64, January 2015; $705, MS-64, October 2015; $517, MS-63, June 2015; $117, EF-40, January 2015													
1867, Rays, Proof †	*25+*	30	64.5								$30,000	$37,500	$55,000
Auctions: $64,625, PF-66, January 2015; $25,850, PF-65, August 2015; $34,075, PF-64, August 2015													
1867, No Rays	28,890,500	1,070	59.0	70%	$25	$30	$35	$40	$70	$110	$140	$225	$750
Auctions: $1,116, MS-66, October 2015; $705, MS-65, January 2015; $305, MS-64, May 2015; $111, MS-60, February 2015													
1867, No Rays, Proof	*600+*	262	64.3								$475	$1,250	$2,500
Auctions: $3,760, PF-66, September 2015; $2,115, PF-66, October 2015; $1,410, PF-65, February 2015; $376, PF-63, January 2015													
1867, No Rays, Pattern Reverse, Proof (c)	**(d)**	6	65.2								$6,500	$10,000	
Auctions: $3,760, PF-66, June 2015													
1868	28,817,000	1,020	59.1	71%	$25	$30	$35	$40	$70	$110	$140	$225	$750
Auctions: $1,763, MS-66, October 2015; $940, MS-66, August 2016; $764, MS-65, October 2016; $164, MS-63, January 2015.													
1868, Proof	*600+*	213	64.7								$350	$900	$1,750
Auctions: $1,762, PF-66, September 2015; $1,116, PF-65, June 2015; $822, PF-65, January 2015; $270, PF-63, April 2015													
1869	16,395,000	595	59.3	76%	$25	$30	$35	$40	$70	$110	$140	$225	$750
Auctions: $587, MS-65, September 2015; $246, MS-64, May 2015; $176, AU-58, January 2015; $56, AU-50, February 2015													
1869, Proof	*600+*	360	64.6								$350	$700	$1,250
Auctions: $3,055, PF-67, June 2015; $1,116, PF-66, July 2015; $881, PF-65, January 2015; $646, PF-65, August 2015													
1870	4,806,000	258	57.2	71%	$30	$35	$60	$80	$95	$140	$225	$350	$1,350
Auctions: $7,638, MS-66, December 2015; $4,465, MS-66, February 2015; $1,292, MS-64, January 2015; $423, MS-64, August 2015													
1870, Proof	*1,000+*	331	64.3								$350	$750	$1,250
Auctions: $1,292, PF-66, October 2015; $763, PF-65, January 2015; $646, PF-65, October 2015; $258, PF-63, June 2015													
1871	561,000	133	52.3	57%	$80	$100	$150	$210	$285	$375	$525	$750	$2,350
Auctions: $4,230, MS-66, August 2016; $3,290, MS-66, August 2016; $3,055, MS-65, January 2015; $2,820, MS-66, October 2016													
1871, Proof	*960+*	331	64.5								$350	$850	$1,250
Auctions: $1,527, PF-66, September 2015; $1,410, PF-66, August 2015; $881, PF-65, October 2015; $646, PF-65, January 2015													
1872	6,036,000	336	56.8	66%	$40	$50	$85	$105	$130	$175	$235	$300	$1,350
Auctions: $3,525, MS-66, August 2016; $3,055, MS-66, May 2015; $1,997, MS-66, January 2015; $1,293, MS-65, October 2016													
1872, Proof	*950+*	365	64.7								$350	$675	$1,000
Auctions: $3,055, PF-67, July 2015; $2,585, PF-67, September 2015; $998, PF-66, January 2015; $493, PF-65, January 2015													
1873, Close 3	436,050	94	57.7	67%	$30	$40	$80	$100	$150	$200	$350	$750	$1,750
Auctions: $1,997, MS-65, August 2015; $822, MS-64, January 2015													
1873, Close 3, Doubled Die Obverse (e)	**(f)**	16	54.0	56%				$600	$1,000	$2,000	$3,000	$4,000	$10,000
Auctions: $1,880, MS-64, February 2015													
1873, Open 3	4,113,950	120	57.5	72%	$30	$40	$60	$80	$100	$145	$210	$300	$2,000
Auctions: $2,115, MS-66, July 2015; $1,880, MS-66, August 2015; $763, MS-64, October 2015; $600, MS-64, May 2015													
1873, Close 3, Proof	*1,100+*	373	64.5								$350	$675	$1,000
Auctions: $2,820, PF-67, January 2015; $1,292, PF-66, October 2015; $376, PF-64, February 2015; $258, PF-63, May 2015													

† Ranked in the *100 Greatest U.S. Coins* (fifth edition). **c.** These were made from a pattern (Judd-573) reverse die that is slightly different than the regular Without Rays design. **d.** 21 to 30 examples are known. **e.** There are several varieties of 1873, Close 3, Doubled Die Obverse. The values shown are representative of the more avidly sought varieties; others command smaller premiums. **f.** Included in circulation-strike 1873, Close 3, mintage figure.

1883, 3 Over 2
Several varieties exist, as well as pieces with a recut 3. Pictured are FS-05-1883-301 (left) and FS-05-1883-305 (right).

	Mintage	Cert	Avg	%MS	G-4	VG-8	F-12	VF-20	EF-40	AU-50	MS-60 / PF-63	MS-63 / PF-65	MS-65 / PF-66
1874	3,538,000	192	59.1	74%	$30	$40	$75	$95	$120	$170	$250	$325	$1,200
	Auctions: $5,170, MS-66, October 2015; $2,820, MS-66, August 2015												
1874, Proof	700+	303	64.6								$350	$725	$1,100
	Auctions: $3,290, PF-67, September 2015; $2,115, PF-66, January 2015; $340, PF-64, May 2015; $258, PF-63, January 2015												
1875	2,097,000	189	56.9	71%	$45	$65	$100	$130	$160	$220	$275	$360	$1,300
	Auctions: $5,640, MS-66, January 2015; $3,290, MS-66, October 2015; $229, AU-55, May 2015; $188, AU-50, January 2015												
1875, Proof	700+	295	64.3								$350	$1,100	$1,650
	Auctions: $3,290, PF-67, August 2015; $1,527, PF-66, January 2015; $881, PF-65, July 2015; $517, PF-64, March 2015												
1876	2,530,000	316	58.9	79%	$40	$55	$85	$130	$145	$200	$260	$325	$1,000
	Auctions: $940, MS-65, June 2015; $376, MS-64, August 2015; $105, AU-55, January 2015; $164, AU-50, January 2015												
1876, Proof	1,150+	410	64.5								$350	$750	$1,000
	Auctions: $2,350, PF-67, February 2015; $998, PF-66, July 2015; $763, PF-65, August 2015; $376, PF-64, January 2015												
1877, Proof (g)	900	428	64.3								$3,000	$4,500	$5,000
	Auctions: $9,987, PF-67, September 2015; $6,462, PF-66, July 2015; $4,230, PF-65, June 2015; $3,525, PF-64, January 2015												
1878, Proof (g)	2,350	634	64.3								$1,150	$1,250	$1,700
	Auctions: $1,880, PF-67, January 2015; $2,232, PF-66, July 2015; $1,233, PF-65, January 2015; $1,265, PF-64, June 2015												
1879	25,900	98	53.5	63%	$400	$500	$600	$660	$850	$1,075	$1,850	$2,250	$3,500
	Auctions: $10,575, MS-67, July 2015; $5,405, MS-66, August 2016; $4,935, MS-66, March 2016; $2,820, MS-65, July 2015												
1879, Proof	3,200	597	64.8								$350	$600	$750
	Auctions: $6,462, PF-68, January 2015; $564, PF-65, August 2015; $352, PF-64, May 2015; $282, PF-62, October 2015												
1879, 9 Over 8, Proof (h)	(i)	0	n/a								$500	$850	$1,100
	Auctions: $2,361, PF-67, June 2015; $646, PF-65, August 2015; $470, PF-64, January 2015; $305, AU-58, November 2015												
1880	16,000	41	44.8	24%	$1,850	$2,200	$2,600	$3,000	$6,000	$7,700	$13,000	$20,000	$55,000
	Auctions: $117,000, MS-66, January 2015; $8,233, AU-53, August 2016; $5,405, EF-45, March 2016; $3,995, AU-53, October 2015												
1880, Proof	3,955	968	63.7								$350	$600	$750
	Auctions: $6,462, PF-68, January 2015; $3,995, PF-67, October 2015; $505, PF-65, January 2015; $423, PF-64, May 2015												
1881	68,800	181	45.7	46%	$250	$350	$425	$510	$600	$775	$1,150	$1,350	$2,750
	Auctions: $3,173, MS-66, August 2016; $3,055, MS-66, December 2015; $2,350, MS66, October 2015; $822, AU58, January 2015												
1881, Proof	3,575	841	64.9								$350	$600	$750
	Auctions: $1,292, PF-67, July 2015; $616, PF-66, October 2015; $493, PF-65, January 2015; $250, PF-62, April 2015												
1882	11,472,900	1,213	58.0	78%	$25	$30	$35	$45	$65	$110	$150	$225	$650
	Auctions: $3,055, MS-67, July 2016; $734, MS-66, February 2015; $493, MS-65, January 2015; $235, MS-64, October 2015												
1882, Proof	3,100	947	65.1								$350	$600	$750
	Auctions: $15,275, PF-67, August 2015; $1,116, PF-66, August 2015; $705, PF-66, January 2015; $352, PF-64, May 2015												
1883	1,451,500	2,136	61.3	80%	$25	$30	$35	$45	$65	$110	$150	$225	$650
	Auctions: $2,938, MS-67, August 2015; $2,820, MS-67, January 2015; $1,057, MS-66, January 2015; $705, MS-66, August 2016												
1883, 3 Over 2 (j)	(k)	69	58.2	55%	$250	$325	$650	$950	$1,250	$1,500	$2,100	$2,500	$8,000
	Auctions: $7,050, MS-65, January 2015; $1,527, MS-63, January 2015; $1,292, MS-60, June 2015; $1,175, AU-58, January 2015												
1883, Proof	5,419	1,181	64.8								$350	$600	$850
	Auctions: $6,462, PF-68, January 2015; $470, PF-65, March 2015; $329, PF-64, August 2015; $282, PF-63, October 2015												

g. Proof only. **h.** This variety is confirmed only with Proof finish, although Breen mentions two circulation strikes and further mentions that there are "at least two varieties" (*Walter Breen's Complete Encyclopedia of U.S. and Colonial Coins*). In the *Guide Book of Shield and Liberty Head Nickels*, Bowers discusses research and theories from Breen, DeLorey, Spindel, and Julian, noting that the variety's overdate status is "not determined." **i.** Included in 1879, Proof, mintage figure. **j.** Several varieties exist. For more information, see the *Cherrypickers' Guide to Rare Die Varieties, Vol. I* (sixth edition): "Beware of 1882 Shield nickels with a filled-in, blobby 2, as these are very frequently offered as 1883, 3 Over 2. This is possibly the single most misunderstood coin in all U.S. coinage." (Howard Spindel, communication to Q. David Bowers, quoted in *A Guide Book of Shield and Liberty Head Nickels*.) **k.** Included in circulation-strike 1883 mintage figure.

LIBERTY HEAD (1883–1913)

Designer: *Charles E. Barber.* **Weight:** *5 grams.* **Composition:** *.750 copper, .250 nickel.*
Diameter: *21.2 mm.* **Edge:** *Plain.* **Mints:** *Philadelphia, Denver, and San Francisco.*

Variety 1, Without CENTS
(1883)

Variety 1, Without CENTS, Proof

Variety 2, With CENTS
(1883–1912)

Mintmark locations is on the reverse, to the left of CENTS.

Variety 2, With CENTS, Proof

History. Liberty Head nickels were popular in their time, minted in large quantities most years, and remained in circulation through the 1940s, by which time most were worn down to grades such as AG-3 and G-4. Stray coins could still be found in the early 1950s. Serious numismatic interest in circulated examples began in the 1930s with the popularity of Whitman and other coin boards, folders, and albums. Many of the scarcer dates were picked from circulation at that time. The five known 1913 Liberty Head nickels were not an authorized Mint issue, and were never placed into circulation.

Striking and Sharpness. Many Liberty Head nickels have areas of light striking. On the obverse, this is often seen at the star centers, particularly near the top border. The hair above the forehead can be light as well, and always is thus on 1912-S (the obverse die on this San Francisco issue is slightly bulged). On the reverse, E PLURIBUS UNUM can vary in sharpness of strike. Weakness is often seen at the wreath bow and on the ear of corn to the left (the kernels in the ear can range from indistinct to bold). Even Proofs can be weakly struck in areas. Mint luster can range from minutely pebbly or grainy (but still attractive) to a deep, rich frost. Some later Philadelphia coins show stress marks in the field, particularly the obverse, from the use of "tired" dies. This can be determined only by observation, as "slabbed" grades for MS coins do not indicate the quality of the luster or surfaces. Proof Liberty Head nickels were struck of all dates 1883 to 1912, plus both varieties of 1883 (with and without CENTS). The fields range from deeply mirrorlike to somewhat grainy character to mirror-surface, depending on a given year. While most Proofs are sharp, some have weakness at the star centers and/or the kernels on the ear of corn to the left of the ribbon bow. These weaknesses are overlooked by the certification services. Generally, later issues are more deeply mirrored than are earlier ones. Some years in the 1880s and 1890s can show graininess, a combination of mint luster and mirror quality. Lint marks or tiny recessed marks from scattered debris on the die faces are sometimes encountered, but not factored into third-party–certified grades unless excessive.

Availability. All issues from 1883 to 1912 are readily collectible, although the 1885 (in particular), 1886, and 1912-S are considered to be key dates. Most readily available are well-worn coins in AG-3 and G-4. As a class, VF, EF, and AU pieces are very scarce in relation to demand. MS coins are generally scarce in the 1880s, except for the 1883, Without CENTS, which is plentiful in all grades. MS pieces are less scarce in the 1890s and are easily found for most 20th-century years, save for 1909, 1912-D, and 1912-S, all of which are elusive.

GRADING STANDARDS

MS-60 to 70 (Mint State). *Obverse and Reverse:* Mint luster is complete in the obverse and reverse fields. Lower grades such as MS–60, 61, and 62 can show some evidence of abrasion, usually on the portrait on the obverse and highest parts of the wreath on the reverse, and scattered contact marks elsewhere. At MS-63 these marks are few, and at MS-65 they are fewer yet. In grades above MS-65, marks can only be seen under magnification.

1894. Graded MS-65.

AU-50, 53, 55, 58 (About Uncirculated). *Obverse:* Light wear is seen on the portrait and on the hair under LIB. Mint luster is present in the fields, ranging from partial at AU-50 to nearly complete at AU-58. All details are sharp, unless lightly struck. *Reverse:* Light wear is seen on the V, the other letters, and the wreath. Luster is partial at AU-50, increasing to nearly full at AU-58. All details are sharp, unless lightly struck.

1885. Graded AU-58.

EF-40, 45 (Extremely Fine). *Obverse:* Nearly all hair detail is visible, save for some lightness above the forehead. Stars show radial lines (except for those that may have been lightly struck). Overall bold appearance. *Reverse:* The wreath still shows most detail on the leaves. Denticles are bold inside the rim.

1885. Graded EF-40.

VF-20, 30 (Very Fine). *Obverse:* Letters in LIBERTY are all well defined. Hair detail is seen on the back of the head and some between the ear and the coronet. Denticles are bold. Some stars show radial lines. *Reverse:* Detail is seen in the wreath leaves. Lettering and denticles are bold, although E PLURIBUS UNUM may range from medium-light to bold (depending on the strike).

1888. Graded VF-20.

F-12, 15 (Fine). *Obverse:* All of the letters in LIBERTY are readable, although the I may be quite weak. The detail beginning at the front of hair is visible. Denticles are well defined. *Reverse:* Detail of the leaves begins to fade in the wreath. Denticles are well defined all around the border. E PLURIBUS UNUM has medium definition, and is complete.

1885. Graded F-15.

VG-8, 10 (Very Good). *Obverse:* Three or more letters in LIBERTY can be discerned. This can be a combination of two full letters and two or more partial letters. Some hair detail shows at the back of the head. The rim is well outlined and shows traces of most or even all denticles. *Reverse:* The wreath and lettering are bold, but in outline form. E PLURIBUS UNUM is readable, but may be weak. The rim is complete all around, with traces of most denticles present.

1885. Graded VG-8.

G-4, 6 (Good). *Obverse:* The rim is complete all around. Some denticles show on the inside of the rim. The date, Liberty head, and stars are in outline form. No letters of LIBERTY are visible in the coronet. *Reverse:* V and the wreath are visible in outline form. Most letters are complete, but may be faint. E PLURIBUS UNUM is very weak (this feature can vary, and on some G-4 coins it is better defined). The rim is complete in most areas, but may blend with the field in some parts.

1885. Graded G-6.

AG-3 (About Good). *Obverse:* The head is outlined, with only the ear hole as a detail. The date is well worn; the bottom of the digits can be weak or incomplete. The stars are solid, without detail; some may be incomplete. The rim is indistinct or incomplete in some areas. *Reverse:* Details are nearly all worn away, showing greater effects of wear than does the obverse. V is in outline form. The wreath is in outline form, and may be

1885. Graded AG-3.

indistinct in areas. Lettering ranges from faint to missing, but with some letters readable. The rim is usually worn down into the letters.

PF-60 to 70 (Proof). *Obverse and Reverse:* PF–60, 61, and 62 coins show varying amounts of hairlines in the field, decreasing as the grade increases. Fields may be dull or cloudy on lower-level pieces. At PF-65, hairlines are visible only under magnification and are very light; the cheek of Miss Liberty does not show any abrasion or "album slide marks." Above PF-65, hairlines become fewer, and in ultra-high grades are nonexistent, this meaning that the coins have never been subject to wiping or abrasive cleaning. At PF-65 or better, expect excellent aesthetic appeal. Blotched, deeply toned, or recolored coins can be found at most Proof levels from PF–60 through 65 or even 66, and should be avoided. Watch for artificially toned lower-grade Proofs colored to mask the true nature of the fields.

1883, With CENTS. Graded PF-66 Deep Cameo.

Illustrated coin: This Proof shows spotting in the fields.

	Mintage	Cert	Avg	%MS	G-4	VG-8	F-12	VF-20	EF-40	AU-50	MS-60 PF-63	MS-63 PF-64	MS-65 PF-65
1883, Without CENTS	5,474,300	8,127	63.0	92%	$7	$8	$9	$11	$15	$20	$35	$50	$225
Auctions: $3,525, MS-67, January 2015; $282, MS-66, June 2015; $164, MS-65, April 2015; $329, MS-64, October 2015													
1883, Without CENTS, Proof	5,219	1,048	64.6								$300	$450	$800
Auctions: $4,935, PF-67, August 2015; $3,055, PF-67, January 2015; $1,057, PF-66, January 2015; $379, PF-64, August 2015													
1883, With CENTS	16,026,200	1,214	59.9	79%	$20	$30	$35	$55	$85	$120	$150	$200	$550
Auctions: $5,875, MS-66, October 2015; $2,115, MS-66, January 2015; $1,292, MS-66, June 2015; $258, MS-64, February 2015													
1883, With CENTS, Proof	6,783	746	64.5								$275	$400	$700
Auctions: $881, PF-64, January 2015; $851, PF-66, September 2015; $822, PF-65, July 2015; $188, PF-63, May 2015													
1884	11,270,000	531	56.7	73%	$20	$30	$35	$55	$85	$130	$190	$300	$1,250
Auctions: $5,875, MS-67, August 2016; $8,225, MS-66, August 2015; $1,997, MS-66, February 2015; $1,351, MS-65, September 2015													
1884, Proof	3,942	829	64.5								$250	$375	$650
Auctions: $3,055, PF-67, June 2015; $763, PF-66, January 2015; $399, PF-65, April 2015; $376, PF-64, May 2015													
1885	1,472,700	1,033	24.1	22%	$275	$550	$750	$1,000	$1,200	$1,600	$2,000	$3,500	$6,000
Auctions: $30,000, MS-67, February 2018; $9,600, MS-66, January 2018; $5,875, MS-65, March 2016; $4,230, MS-64, January 2017													
1885, Proof	3,790	819	64.6								$1,150	$1,250	$1,350
Auctions: $2,232, PF-67, January 2015; $1,762, PF-66, June 2015; $1,292, PF-65, October 2015; $1,086, PF-64Cam, August 2015													
1886	3,326,000	958	26.2	23%	$200	$265	$375	$500	$700	$825	$1,250	$2,100	$4,250
Auctions: $33,600, MS-66, January 2018; $22,325, MS-66, February 2015; $3,760, MS-65, September 2016; $2,528, MS-64, February 2018													
1886, Proof	4,290	826	64.5								$650	$675	$950
Auctions: $2,115, PF-67, January 2015; $969, PF-65, February 2015; $793, PF-65, October 2015; $558, PF-64, May 2015													
1887	15,260,692	505	61.5	86%	$15	$20	$35	$50	$75	$110	$140	$195	$700
Auctions: $8,225, MS-67, December 2015; $7,638, MS-66, May 2015; $5,405, MS-66, January 2015; $1,293, MS-65, September 2016													
1887, Proof	2,960	604	64.3								$250	$345	$500
Auctions: $2,500, PF-67, January 2015; $705, PF-66, June 2015; $211, PF-63, October 2015; $141, PF-62, March 2015													
1888	10,167,901	458	55.3	74%	$30	$40	$65	$120	$175	$220	$275	$350	$1,000
Auctions: $7,050, MS-66, July 2016; $3,055, MS-66, September 2015; $1,763, MS-65, July 2016; $1,293, MS-65, December 2015													
1888, Proof	4,582	798	64.4								$250	$345	$500
Auctions: $3,642, PF-67, February 2015; $525, PF-66, January 2015; $423, PF-65, October 2015; $247, PF-64, May 2015													
1889	15,878,025	601	62.3	92%	$15	$20	$30	$55	$80	$120	$140	$175	$650
Auctions: $1,600, MS-66, January 2015; $705, MS-65, July 2015; $350, MS-64, October 2015; $141, MS 62, April 2015													
1889, Proof	3,336	631	64.5								$250	$345	$500
Auctions: $446, PF-66, January 2015; $493, PF-65, January 2015; $399, PF-65, October 2015; $182, PF-63, July 2015													

1899, Repunched Date,
Early Die State

1899, Repunched Date,
Late Die State

FS-05-1899-301.

	Mintage	Cert	Avg	%MS	G-4	VG-8	F-12	VF-20	EF-40	AU-50	MS-60 / PF-63	MS-63 / PF-64	MS-65 / PF-65
1890	16,256,532	364	61.6	88%	$10	$20	$25	$40	$70	$110	$160	$220	$800
	Auctions: $16,450, MS-67, October 2015; $9,400, MS-66, May 2015; $3,055, MS-66, October 2016; $705, MS-65, July 2015												
1890, Proof	2,740	483	64.1								$250	$345	$500
	Auctions: $2,467, PF-67, February 2015; $376, PF-65, January 2015; $376, PF-65, October 2015; $282, PF-64, May 2015												
1891	16,832,000	462	62.2	91%	$7	$12	$25	$45	$70	$125	$160	$220	$600
	Auctions: $4,406, MS-66, July 2016; $1,998, MS-66, October 2016; $1,058, MS-65, January 2015; $211, MS-64, October 2015												
1891, Proof	2,350	491	64.3								$250	$345	$500
	Auctions: $2,820, PF-67, February 2015; $705, PF-66, January 2015; $282, PF-64, November 2015; $141, PF-62, May 2015												
1892	11,696,897	503	61.6	89%	$6	$10	$20	$40	$65	$110	$145	$180	$750
	Auctions: $3,055, MS-66, January 2015; $1,645, MS-66, August 2015; $1,880, MS-66, July 2015; $822, MS-65, February 2015												
1892, Proof	$2,745	543	64.3								$250	$345	$500
	Auctions: $625, PF-66, January 2015; $517, PF-65, October 2015; $282, PF-64, August 2015; $184, PF-63, May 2015												
1893	13,368,000	500	62.2	91%	$6	$10	$20	$40	$65	$110	$140	$160	$700
	Auctions: $1,880, MS-66, January 2015; $1,527, MS-65, February 2015; $1,058, MS-66, July 2016; $176, MS-62, May 2015												
1893, Proof	2,195	481	64.5								$250	$345	$500
	Auctions: $1,292, PF-66, July 2015; $517, PF-65, September 2015; $458, PF-65, January 2015; $434, PF-65, October 2015												
1894	5,410,500	384	56.7	74%	$15	$35	$100	$165	$230	$300	$350	$425	$1,150
	Auctions: $2,526, MS-66, July 2016; $1,410, MS-66, October 2016; $1,527, MS-65, August 2015; $493, MS-64, October 2015												
1894, Proof	2,632	486	64.2								$250	$345	$500
	Auctions: $1,292, PF-67, October 2015; $564, PF-66, January 2015; $540, PF-65, July 2015; $117, PF-60, May 2015												
1895	9,977,822	387	61.7	91%	$6	$8	$22	$45	$75	$115	$140	$230	$1,000
	Auctions: $21,150, MS-67, July 2015; $4,994, MS-65, March 2015; 2,585, MS-65, January 2015; $2,233, MS-65, September 2016												
1895, Proof	2,062	459	64.2								$250	$345	$500
	Auctions: $3,995, PF-67, January 2015; $646, PF-66, August 2015; $399, PF-65, May 2015; $258, PF-64, February 2015												
1896	8,841,058	360	59.6	83%	$9	$20	$35	$65	$100	$150	$190	$265	$1,100
	Auctions: $8,813, MS-66, May 2015; $4,582, MS-66, June 2015; $2,350, MS-66, March 2016; $1,234, MS-65, October 2016												
1896, Proof	1,862	429	64.4								$250	$345	$500
	Auctions: $646, PF-66, October 2015; $587, PF-65, January 2015; $282, PF-64, February 2015; $139, PF-62, May 2015												
1897	20,426,797	507	61.8	91%	$4	$5	$12	$27	$50	$75	$100	$160	$650
	Auctions: $3,525, MS-66, October 2016; $3,055, MS-66, January 2015; $1,057, MS-65, July 2015; $616, MS-64, August 2015												
1897, Proof	1,938	474	64.7								$250	$345	$500
	Auctions: $4,022, PF-68, January 2015; $352, PF-65, November 2015; $176, PF-63, May 2015; $111, PF-60, February 2015												
1898	12,530,292	454	62.3	91%	$4	$5	$12	$27	$50	$75	$150	$190	$600
	Auctions: $2,350, MS-66, March 2015; $1,410, MS-66, August 2016; $763, MS-65, January 2015; $646, MS-65, August 2015												
1898, Proof	1,795	450	64.5								$250	$345	$500
	Auctions: $505, PF-66, January 2015; $364, PF-65, October 2015; $258, PF-64, September 2015; $164, PF-63, May 2015												
1899	26,027,000	817	62.4	92%	$2	$3	$8	$20	$30	$60	$90	$140	$500
	Auctions: $8,813, MS-67, August 2015; $4,230, MS-67, August 2016; $4,230, MS-66, January 2015; $705, MS-66, May 2016												
1899, Repunched Date (a)	(b)	0	n/a						$85	$150	$190	$240	$750
	Auctions: No auction records available.												
1899, Proof	2,031	479	64.7								$250	$345	$500
	Auctions: $1,410, PF-67, July 2015; $423, PF-65, January 2015; $258, PF-64, September 2015; $176, PF-63, May 2015												

a. From the *Cherrypickers' Guide to Rare Die Varieties, Vol. I* (sixth edition): "The loop of a 9, or possibly (but unlikely) an 8, is evident within the lower loop of the second 9. Some specialists believe this to be an 1899/8 overdate. However, we feel it is simply a repunched date, with the secondary 9 far to the south of the primary 9 at the last digit." **b.** Included in circulation-strike 1899 mintage figure.

1900, Doubled-Die Reverse
FS-05-1900-801.

	Mintage	Cert	Avg	%MS	G-4	VG-8	F-12	VF-20	EF-40	AU-50	MS-60 / PF-63	MS-63 / PF-64	MS-65 / PF-65
1900	27,253,733	920	62.8	94%	$2	$3	$8	$15	$30	$65	$90	$140	$500
	Auctions: $7,050, MS-67, January 2015; $4,700, MS-67, August 2016; $1,998, MS-66, July 2016; $117, MS-63, November 2015												
1900, Doubled-Die Reverse (c)	(d)	5	60.2	60%					$110	$160	$235	$310	$875
	Auctions: No auction records available.												
1900, Proof	2,262	486	64.8								$250	$345	$500
	Auctions: $5,640, PF-68, January 2015; $675, PF-66, August 2015; $387, PF-65, May 2015; $340, PF-64, March 2015												
1901	26,478,228	821	62.4	94%	$2	$3	$5	$15	$30	$60	$85	$125	$450
	Auctions: $8,812, MS-67, January 2015; $4,700, MS-67, August 2016; $1,399, MS-66, October 2015; $317, MS-65, May 2015												
1901, Proof	1,985	523	64.9								$250	$345	$500
	Auctions: $940, PF-67, January 2015; $587, PF-66, September 2015; $446, PF-65, October 2015; $305, PF-64, January 2015												
1902	31,480,579	813	62.2	92%	$2	$3	$4	$15	$30	$60	$85	$125	$450
	Auctions: $5,405, MS-67, January 2015; $1,645, MS-66, June 2015; $1,058, MS-66, August 2016; $881, MS-66, August 2016												
1902, Proof	2,018	491	64.6								$250	$345	$500
	Auctions: $1,028, PF-67, January 2015; $646, PF-66, June 2015; $399, PF-65, March 2015; $317, PF-64, October 2015												
1903	28,004,935	924	62.7	94%	$2	$3	$4	$15	$30	$60	$85	$125	$450
	Auctions: $4,230, MS-67, October 2016; $3,525, MS-67, November 2016; $1,645, MS-66, January 2015; $423, MS-65, August 2015												
1903, Proof	1,790	554	64.9								$250	$345	$500
	Auctions: $540, PF-66, October 2015; $376, PF-65, September 2015; $293, PF-64, January 2015; $129, PF-61, May 2015												
1904	21,403,167	766	62.7	93%	$2	$3	$4	$15	$30	$60	$85	$125	$450
	Auctions: $1,645, MS-66, June 2015; $999, MS-66, October 2016; $352, MS-65, August 2015; $176, MS-64, February 2015												
1904, Proof	1,817	493	64.2								$250	$345	$500
	Auctions: $998, PF-66, January 2015; $365, PF-65, October 2015; $258, PF-64, April 2015; $179, PF-63, May 2015												
1905	29,825,124	940	62.3	92%	$2	$3	$4	$15	$30	$60	$85	$125	$450
	Auctions: $4,935, MS-67, October 2016; $2,585, MS-66, January 2015; $852, MS-65, March 2015; $517, MS-64, September 2016												
1905, Proof	2,152	480	64.6								$250	$345	$500
	Auctions: $3,525, PF-67, June 2015; $2,585, PF-66, February 2015; $1,410, PF-66, October 2015; $285, PF-64, January 2015												
1906	38,612,000	714	61.2	85%	$2	$3	$4	$15	$30	$60	$85	$125	$450
	Auctions: $5,875, MS-66, January 2015; $423, MS-65, August 2015; $152, MS-64, May 2015; $211, MS-63, February 2015												
1906, Proof	1,725	474	64.6								$250	$345	$500
	Auctions: $3,290, PF-68, August 2015; $1,527, PF-67, October 2015; $1,292, PF-67, January 2015; $587, PF-66, June 2015												
1907	39,213,325	718	60.7	87%	$2	$3	$4	$15	$30	$60	$85	$125	$450
	Auctions: $7,931, MS-66, January 2015; $3,055, MS-66, August 2016; $1,645, MS-66, July 2015; $494, MS-65, October 2016												
1907, Proof	1,475	381	64.6								$250	$345	$500
	Auctions: $2,350, PF-67, February 2015; $616, PF-66, June 2015; $540, PF-66, January 2015; $253, PF-64, September 2015												
1908	22,684,557	618	60.8	87%	$2	$3	$4	$15	$30	$60	$85	$125	$450
	Auctions: $5,288, MS-66, August 2015; $1,293, MS-66, October 2016; $705, MS-65, August 2015; $176, MS-64, October 2015												
1908, Proof	1,620	451	64.6								$250	$345	$500
	Auctions: $8,225, PF-68, October 2015; $2,115, PF-67, January 2015; $763, PF-66, February 2015; $517, PF-65, June 2015												

c. Doubling on this very popular variety is evident on all reverse design elements, including the V, with a stronger spread on the lower quadrant of the reverse. **d.** Included in circulation-strike 1900 mintage figure.

1913, Liberty Head

	Mintage	Cert	Avg	%MS	G-4	VG-8	F-12	VF-20	EF-40	AU-50	MS-60 PF-63	MS-63 PF-64	MS-65 PF-65
1909	11,585,763	452	60.2	83%	$3	$4	$5	$18	$35	$75	$100	$140	$500
Auctions: $4,465, MS-66, October 2015; $2,585, MS-66, August 2016; $793, MS-65, August 2015; $705, MS-65, February 2015													
1909, Proof	4,763	1,367	64.9								$250	$345	$500
Auctions: $1,086, PF-67, October 2015; $493, PF-66, January 2015; $258, PF-64, February 2015; $117, PF-60, April 2015													
1910	30,166,948	732	61.0	85%	$2	$3	$4	$15	$30	$60	$85	$125	$450
Auctions: $3,760, MS-66, January 2015; $211, MS-64, September 2015; $130, MS-63, May 2015; $60, AU-58, June 2015													
1910, Proof	2,405	699	64.9								$250	$345	$500
Auctions: $6,462, PF-68, January 2015; $587, PF-66, June 2015; $399, PF-65, November 2015; $282, PF-64, April 2015													
1911	39,557,639	1,409	61.8	90%	$2	$3	$4	$15	$30	$60	$85	$125	$450
Auctions: $4,230, MS-66, May 2015; $646, MS-66, July 2016; $1,249, MS-65, January 2015; $141, MS-64, October 2015; $99, MS-63, May 2015													
1911, Proof	1,733	578	64.6								$250	$345	$500
Auctions: $600, PF-66, January 2015; $365, PF-65, October 2015; $258, PF-64, June 2015; $170, PF-63, February 2015													
1912	26,234,569	1,251	61.0	89%	$2	$3	$4	$15	$30	$60	$85	$125	$450
Auctions: $5,875, MS-66, January 2015; $446, MS-65, January 2015; $141, MS-64, April 2015; $94, MS-63, September 2015; $74, AU-58, June 2015													
1912, Proof	2,145	606	64.5								$250	$345	$500
Auctions: $2,232, PF-67, January 2015; $910, PF-66, July 2015; $489, PF-65, April 2015; $199, PF-63, October 2015													
1912-D	8,474,000	839	58.5	83%	$3	$4	$10	$40	$95	$180	$300	$400	$1,250
Auctions: $4,230, MS-66, January 2015; $1,703, MS-65, July 2015; $646, MS-64, September 2015; $305, MS-63, May 2015													
1912-S	238,000	1,600	28.4	33%	$135	$145	$175	$450	$850	$1,250	$1,500	$1,850	$2,850
Auctions: $3,360, MS-66, January 2018; $3,525, MS-65, January 2015; $2,585, MS-65, October 2015; $1,680, MS-64, February 2018													
1913 † (e)		2	47.5								$3,000,000	$3,750,000	
Auctions: $3,290,000, PF-64, January 2014; $3,172,500, PF-63, April 2013													

† Ranked in the *100 Greatest U.S. Coins* (fifth edition). **e.** An estimated five 1913 Liberty Head nickels were struck under uncertain circumstances at the Mint. Some researchers consider them all to be Proofs. Research published by John Dannreuther in 2021 suggests the 1913 nickels were executed with circulation-strike dies on regular unpolished planchets, leading Dannreuther to conclude that the coins should be classified as Specimens or other special strikes. They were dispersed and are now held in various public and private collections.

INDIAN HEAD OR BUFFALO (1913–1938)

Designer: *James Earle Fraser.* **Weight:** *5 grams.* **Composition:** *.750 copper, .250 nickel.*
Diameter: *21.2 mm.* **Edge:** *Plain.* **Mints:** *Philadelphia, Denver, and San Francisco.*

Variety 1, FIVE CENTS
on Raised Ground (1913)

*Mintmark location for all
varieties is on the reverse,
below FIVE CENTS.*

Variety 1, FIVE CENTS
on Raised Ground, Proof

Variety 2, FIVE CENTS
in Recess (1913–1938)

Variety 2, FIVE CENTS in Recess,
Matte Proof (1913–1916)

Variety 2, FIVE CENTS in
Recess, Satin Proof (1936)

Variety 2, FIVE CENTS in Recess,
Mirror Proof (1936–1937)

History. The Indian Head nickel five-cent piece today is almost universally known as the "Buffalo" nickel, after the American bison on the reverse. The design made its debut in 1913. James Earle Fraser, a sculptor well known in the private sector, was its creator. The obverse features an authentic portrait of a Native American, modeled as a composite from life, with three subjects posing. Unlike any preceding coin made for circulation, the Buffalo nickel had little in the way of open, smooth field surfaces. Instead, most areas on the obverse and reverse were filled with design elements or, especially on the reverse, an irregular background, as on a bas-relief plaque. Soon after the first coins were released, it was thought that the inscription FIVE CENTS, on a high area of the motif, would wear too quickly. The Mint modified the design to lower the ground under the bison, which had been arranged in the form of a mound (on what became known as Variety 1). The flat-ground design is called Variety 2.

Striking and Sharpness. Most circulation-strike Buffalo nickels are poorly struck in one or more areas, and for many Denver and San Francisco issues of the 1920s the striking is very poor. However, enough sharp strikes exist among common dates of the 1930s that one can be found with some patience. Certification services do not reflect the quality of strike on their labels, so examine carefully. The matter of striking sharpness on Buffalo nickels is an exceedingly important aspect for the connoisseur (who might prefer, for example, a sharply struck coin in AU-58 over a fully lustrous MS example with much shallower detail). Points to check on the obverse include the center of the coin, especially the area immediately above the tie on the braid. On the reverse check the fur on the head of the bison, and the fur "line" above the bison's shoulder on its back. On both sides, examine the overall striking of letters and other details.

Availability. Among circulated varieties of standard dates and mintmarks, availability is in proportion to their mintages. Among early issues the 1913-S, Variety 2, is the scarcest. The date wore away more quickly on the Variety 1 coins than on the modified design used from later 1913 through the end of the series. In the 1920s the 1926-S is the hardest to find. Collectors sought Buffalo nickels from circulation until the 1960s, after which most were gone. By that time the dates in the teens were apt to have their dates completely worn away, or be AG-3 or G-4. Among MS nickels, the issues of 1913 were saved in quantity as novelties, although 1913-S, Variety 2, is slightly scarce. Philadelphia Mint issues are readily available through the 1920s, while MS-63 and finer mintmarked issues from 1914 to 1927 can range from scarce to rare. From 1931 to 1938, all dates and mintmarks were saved in roll quantities, and all are plentiful today. Many Buffalo nickels in MS are very rare if with Full Details, this being especially true for mintmarked issues after 1913, into the early 1930s. Sharpness of strike is not noted on certification holders, but a connoisseur would probably rather own a Full Details coin in MS-65 than an MS-66 or higher with a flat strike.

Proofs. Proof Buffalo nickels are of two main styles. Matte Proofs were made from 1913 to 1916 and are rare. These have minutely granular or matte surfaces, are sharply struck with Full Details of the design on both sides, and have edges (as viewed edge-on) that are mirrored, a distinctive figure. These are easily confused with circulation strikes except for the features noted. Certified holders usually list these simply as "Proof," not "Matte Proof." Some early Proofs of 1936 have satiny rather than mirror-like fields. Later Proofs of 1936 and all of 1937 have a mirror surface in the fields. The motifs of the 1936 and 1937 mirror Proofs are lightly polished in the die (not frosty or matte).

GRADING STANDARDS

MS-60 to 70 (Mint State). *Obverse and Reverse:* Mint luster is complete in the obverse and reverse fields, except in areas not fully struck up, in which graininess or marks from the *original planchet surface* can be seen. Lower grades such as MS–60, 61, and 62 can show some evidence of abrasion, usually on the center of the obverse above the braid, and on the reverse at the highest parts of the bison. These two checkpoints are often areas of light

1937-D. Graded MS-67.

striking, so abrasion must be differentiated from original planchet marks. At MS-63 evidences of abrasion are few, and at MS-65 they are fewer yet. In grades above MS-65, a Buffalo nickel should be mark-free.

AU-50, 53, 55, 58 (About Uncirculated). *Obverse:* Light wear is seen on the highest area of the cheek, to the left of the nose, this being the most obvious checkpoint. Light wear is also seen on the highest-relief areas of the hair. Luster is less extensive, and wear more extensive, at AU-50 than at higher grades. An AU-58 coin will have only slight wear and will retain the majority of luster. *Reverse:* Light wear is seen on the shoulder

1925-S. Graded AU-53.

and hip, these being the key checkpoints. Light wear is also seen on the flank of the bison and on the horn and top of the head. Luster is less extensive, and wear more extensive, at AU-50 than at higher grades. An AU-58 coin will have only slight wear and will retain the majority of luster.

EF-40, 45 (Extremely Fine). *Obverse:* More wear is seen on the cheek (in particular) and the rest of the face. The center of the coin above the braid is mostly smooth. Other details are sharp. *Reverse:* More wear is evident. The tip of the horn is well defined on better strikes. The shoulder, flank, and hip show more wear. The tip of the tail may be discernible, but is mostly worn away.

1937-D. Graded EF-40.

VF-20, 30 (Very Fine). *Obverse:* The hair above the braid is mostly flat, but with some details visible. The braid is discernible. The feathers lack most details. On Variety 1 coins the date is light. *Reverse:* Wear is more extensive, with most fur detail on the high area of the shoulder gone, the tip of the tail gone, and the horn flat. Ideally the tip of the horn should show, but in the marketplace many certified coins do not show this. On some coins this is due to a shallow strike.

1937-D, 3-Legged. Graded VF-20.

Illustrated coin: On this highly desirable variety one of the buffalo's forelegs has been polished off of the die, probably as the result of an attempt to remove clash marks.

F-12, 15 (Fine). *Obverse:* Only slight detail remains in the hair above the braid. Some of the braid twists are blended together. LIBERTY is weak, and on some coins the upper part of the letters is faint. The rim still is separate. On all coins, the date shows extensive wear. On Variety 1 coins it is weak. *Reverse:* The horn is half to two-thirds visible. Fur details are gone except on the neck at the highest part of the back.

1918-D. Graded F-12.

VG-8, 10 (Very Good). *Obverse:* Hair details above the braid are further worn, as is the hair at the top of the head. Most braid twists are blended together. The rim is worn down to the tops of the letters in LIBERTY. The date is light on all coins and very weak on those of Variety 1. *Reverse:* The base of the horn is slightly visible. Fur details are worn more, but details can still be seen on the neck and top of the back. The hip and flank beneath are worn flat.

1913-D. Graded VG-8.

G-4, 6 (Good). *Obverse:* Scarcely any hair details are seen at the center, and the braid is flat. The rim and tops of the letters in LIBERTY are blended. The date is weak but readable, with at least the last two numerals showing on earlier issues. *Reverse:* The rim is worn to blend into the tops of some or all letters in UNITED STATES OF AMERICA (except for Variety 1). E PLURIBUS UNUM and FIVE CENTS are full, and the mint-mark, if any, is clear. The front part of the bison's head blends into the rim.

1918-D, 8 Over 7. Graded G-4.

AG-3 (About Good). *Obverse:* The head is mostly flat, but the facial features remain clear. LIBERTY is weak and partly missing. The date may be incomplete but must be identifiable. *Reverse:* Further wear is seen. On Variety 1 coins, UNITED STATES OF AMERICA is full and readable. On the Variety 2 the rim is worn further into the letters. The reverse of the Variety 1 nickels is bolder as the overall grade is defined by the date, which wore away more quickly than on the Variety 2.

1913-D, Variety 2. Graded AG-3.

PF-60 to 70 (Matte Proof). *Obverse and Reverse:* Most Matte Proofs are in higher grades. Those with abrasion or contact marks can be graded PF–60 to 62; these are not widely desired. PF-64 can have some abrasion. Tiny flecks are not common, but are sometimes seen. At the Matte PF-65 level or higher there will no traces of abrasion or flecks. Differences between higher-grade Proofs are highly subjective, and one certified at PF-65 can be similar to another at PF-67, and vice-versa.

1915. Graded Matte PF-67.

PF-60 to 70 (Mirror Proof). *Obverse and Reverse:* Most mirror Proofs are in higher grades. PF–60 to 62 coins can have abrasion or minor handling marks, but are usually assigned such grades because of staining or blotches resulting from poor cleaning. PF–63 and 64 can have minor abrasion and staining. Tiny flecks are not common, but are sometimes seen, as are dark stripe lines from the glued seams in the cellophane envelopes used by the Mint. PF-65

1937. Graded Mirror PF-66.

and higher coins should be free of stains, flecks, and abrasion of any kind. Differences between higher-grade Proofs are highly subjective, and one certified PF-65 can be similar to another at PF-67, and vice-versa.

**1913, Variety 1,
3-1/2 Legged**
FS-05-1913-901.

1914, 4 Over 3
FS-05-1914-101.

	Mintage	Cert	Avg	%MS	G-4	VG-8	F-12	VF-20	EF-40	AU-50	MS-60	MS-63	MS-65
											PF-63	PF-64	PF-65
1913, Variety 1	30,992,000	9,523	64.0	95%	$12	$15	$17	$20	$25	$35	$45	$60	$150
Auctions: $822, MS-67, February 2015; $211, MS-66, March 2015; $129, MS-65, January 2015; $84, MS-64, August 2015
1913, Variety 1, 3-1/2 Legged (a)	**(b)**	1	64.0	100%					$400	$500	$750	$1,500	$10,000
Auctions: $10,350, MS-64, April 2009
1913, Variety 1, Proof	1,520	308	65.4								$1,250	$2,000	$3,750
Auctions: $7,637, PF-67, July 2015; $4,230, PF-66, June 2015; $3,760, PF-66, January 2015; $2,115, PF-64, January 2015
1913-D, Variety 1	5,337,000	2,555	62.0	86%	$15	$20	$25	$35	$40	$60	$75	$80	$300
Auctions: $1,997, MS-67, June 2015; $329, MS-66, February 2015; $199, MS-65, August 2015; $84, MS-64, January 2015
1913-S, Variety 1	2,105,000	1,799	58.9	76%	$45	$50	$60	$70	$85	$110	$130	$150	$800
Auctions: $2,585, MS-66, January 2015; $998, MS-64, August 2015; $164, MS-63, October 2015; $152, MS-62, February 2015
1913, Variety 2	29,857,186	2,331	62.5	89%	$10	$12	$16	$20	$25	$30	$40	$65	$300
Auctions: $2,820, MS-67, January 2015; $564, MS-66, October 2015; $493, MS-66, July 2015; $223, MS-65, March 2015
1913, Variety 2, Proof	1,514	241	65.4								$1,000	$1,500	$2,000
Auctions: $3,525, PF-67, January 2015; $3,231, PF-66, October 2015; $1,762, PF-66, February 2015; $1,645, PF-65, January 2015
1913-D, Variety 2	4,156,000	1,597	48.9	46%	$120	$150	$175	$200	$235	$250	$300	$400	$1,100
Auctions: $1,997, MS-66, January 2015; $310, MS-63, June 2015; $211, AU-58, May 2015; $170, EF-45, February 2015
1913-S, Variety 2	1,209,000	2,092	44.1	39%	$225	$295	$350	$450	$500	$625	$800	$1,050	$2,750
Auctions: $28,200, MS-67, April 2014; $6,463, MS-66, April 2017; $3,055, MS-65, January 2015; $1,320, MS-64, February 2018
1914	20,664,463	1,761	57.5	76%	$20	$22	$25	$30	$35	$45	$60	$85	$425
Auctions: $8,225, MS-67, January 2015; $1,116, MS-66, October 2015; $705, MS-66, September 2016; $246, MS-64, February 2015
1914, 4 Over 3 (c)	**(d)**	0	n/a		$200	$250	$325	$525	$700	$1,000	$2,250	$5,000	$30,000
Auctions: $8,338, MS-64, April 2012
1914, Proof	1,275	438	65.5								$900	$1,300	$2,000
Auctions: $6,462, PF-67, February 2015; $2,820, PF-66, August 2015; $1,762, PF-66, January 2015; $1,527, PF-65, August 2015
1914-D	3,912,000	1,499	48.3	47%	$90	$125	$160	$220	$325	$350	$450	$550	$1,250
Auctions: $587, MS-64, January 2015; $376, MS-63, May 2015; $340, AU-58, February 2015; $211, EF-45, October 2015
1914-S	3,470,000	1,775	55.6	63%	$26	$38	$45	$65	$90	$160	$200	$425	$2,000
Auctions: $1,468, MS-65, July 2015; $305, MS-63, March 2015; $235, MS-62, November 2015; $123, AU-58, January 2015
1915	20,986,220	1,649	62.2	88%	$6	$8	$9	$15	$25	$45	$60	$100	$325
Auctions: $5,640, MS-67, January 2015; $540, MS-66, February 2015; $940, MS-65, August 2015; $823, MS-66, July 2016
1915, Proof	1,050	348	65.2								$1,000	$1,500	$2,000
Auctions: $8,812, PF-67, August 2015; $4,817, PF-67, June 2015; $3,760, PF-67, October 2015; $1,645, PF-66, January 2015
1915-D	7,569,000	1,181	56.1	56%	$20	$35	$40	$70	$130	$160	$270	$350	$1,400
Auctions: $376, MS-64, September 2015; $258, MS-63, January 2015; $236, MS-62, May 2015; $124, AU-58, February 2015
1915-S	1,505,000	983	45.2	45%	$45	$75	$100	$200	$400	$500	$650	$1,100	$2,800
Auctions: $3,525, MS-66, October 2015; $3,704, MS-65, August 2015; $1,527, MS-64, June 2015; $1,057, MS-63, January 2015

a. The reverse die was heavily polished, possibly to remove clash marks, resulting in a die with most of the bison's front leg missing. **b.** Included in circulation-strike 1913, Variety 1, mintage figure. **c.** The straight top bar of the underlying 3 is visible at the top of the 4. The start of the 3's diagonal is seen on the upper right, outside of the 4. On some coins, a hint of the curve of the lower portion of the 3 shows just above the crossbar of the 4. **d.** Included in circulation-strike 1914 mintage figure.

1916, Doubled Die Obverse FS-05-1916-101.	1916, Missing Designer's Initial FS-05-1916-401.	1918, Doubled Die Reverse FS-05-1918-801.	1918-D, 8 Over 7 FS-05-1918D-101.

	Mintage	Cert	Avg	%MS	G-4	VG-8	F-12	VF-20	EF-40	AU-50	MS-60 / PF-63	MS-63 / PF-64	MS-65 / PF-65
1916	63,497,466	2,481	60.4	82%	$6	$7	$8	$10	$15	$25	$50	$85	$275
Auctions: $7,050, MS-67, February 2015; $646, MS-66, August 2016; $235, MS-65, February 2015; $94, MS-64, November 2015													
1916, Doubled Die Obverse (e)	(f)	108	37.5	12%	$4,500	$6,000	$8,500	$12,000	$18,000	$30,000	$60,000	$150,000	
Auctions: $30,550, AU-55, January 2014; $28,200, AU-55, August 2014													
1916, Missing Initial (g)	(f)	13	51.8	31%				$135	$200	$280	$375	$600	
Auctions: $341, AU-55, February 2014													
1916, Proof	600	176	65.4								$1,500	$2,700	$3,500
Auctions: $4,230, PF-66, January 2015; $4,113, PF-66, October 2015; $2,820, PF-64, August 2015; $2,232, PF-64, January 2015													
1916-D	13,333,000	1,404	58.0	68%	$16	$28	$30	$45	$90	$120	$175	$260	$1,350
Auctions: $1,086, MS-65, January 2015; $493, MS-64, February 2015; $235, MS-63, April 2015; $158, MS-62, November 2015													
1916-S	11,860,000	1,083	57.6	65%	$10	$15	$20	$40	$90	$125	$200	$275	$2,000
Auctions: $3,290, MS-66, January 2015; $2,592, MS-65, February 2015; $1,880, MS-65, October 2015; $188, MS-62, July 2015													
1917	51,424,019	1,088	61.4	85%	$8	$9	$10	$12	$15	$35	$60	$150	$475
Auctions: $1,763, MS-66, November 2016; $705, MS-66, January 2015; $376, MS-65, August 2015; $176, MS-64, April 2015													
1917-D	9,910,000	1,104	49.7	50%	$18	$30	$50	$85	$150	$275	$375	$750	$2,000
Auctions: $1,880, MS-65, October 2015; $1,233, MS-64, October 2015; $793, MS-63, January 2015; $329, AU-58, February 2015													
1917-S	4,193,000	884	46.8	42%	$22	$45	$80	$120	$200	$325	$650	$1,550	$3,250
Auctions: $4,230, MS-66, January 2015; $1,527, MS-64, June 2015; $1,028, MS-63, August 2015; $616, MS-62, October 2015													
1918	32,086,314	697	59.7	78%	$6	$7	$8	$15	$35	$50	$125	$325	$1,000
Auctions: $3,055, MS-66, August 2015; $3,055, MS-65, December 2015; $1,645, MS-65, March 2016; $1,292, MS-65, January 2015													
1918, Doubled Die Reverse (h)	(i)	4	43.0	25%	$190	$260	$375	$525	$1,450	$2,300	$3,500	$7,000	
Auctions: $170, VF-20, August 2013													
1918-D, 8 Over 7 † (j)	(k)	910	18.3	5%	$800	$1,250	$2,500	$4,500	$8,500	$11,000	$35,000	$57,500	$265,000
Auctions: $1,292, VG-10, March 2015; $940, G-6, January 2015; $822, G-6, July 2015; $763, G-4, January 2015													
1918-D	8,362,000	1,781	30.8	21%	$22	$40	$70	$135	$225	$350	$550	$1,050	$3,250
Auctions: $5,875, MS-66, January 2015; $2,937, MS-65, July 2015; $575, AU-58, February 2015; $423, AU-58, October 2015													
1918-S	4,882,000	747	50.1	52%	$15	$30	$60	$110	$200	$325	$585	$2,500	$10,000
Auctions: $2,820, MS-63, February 2015; $998, MS-62, January 2015; $399, AU-55, June 2015; $235, EF-45, August 2015													
1919	60,868,000	1,281	61.9	88%	$2.25	$3	$3.50	$8	$15	$35	$55	$125	$450
Auctions: $6,463, MS-67, August 2015; $5,875, MS-67, January 2015; $1,645, MS-66, August 2015; $1,410, MS-65, June 2015													
1919-D	8,006,000	833	44.9	35%	$15	$30	$75	$135	$250	$450	$700	$1,500	$4,500
Auctions: $1,762, MS-64, January 2015; $1,410, MS-63, June 2015; $519, AU-58, October 2015; $305, AU-53, November 2015													
1919-S	7,521,000	902	47.8	40%	$9	$20	$50	$125	$250	$375	$675	$1,800	$10,000
Auctions: $2,585, MS-64, August 2015; $1,292, MS-63, February 2015; $493, AU-58, October 2015; $282, AU-55, January 2015													

† Ranked in the *100 Greatest U.S. Coins* (fifth edition). **e.** The date, chin, throat, feathers, and the tie on the braid are all doubled. From the *Cherrypickers' Guide to Rare Die Varieties, Vol. I* (sixth edition): "Beware of 1916 nickels with strike doubling on the date offered as this variety. . . . The true doubled die must look like the coin shown here." **f.** Included in circulation-strike 1916 mintage figure. **g.** The initial F, for Fraser—normally below the date—is clearly absent. Some dies exist with a partially missing or weak initial; these do not command the premium of the variety with a completely missing initial. **h.** Doubling is most obvious to the north on E PLURIBUS UNUM. Some coins show a die crack from the rim to the bison's rump, just below the tail. **i.** Included in 1918 mintage figure. **j.** From the *Cherrypickers' Guide to Rare Die Varieties, Vol. I* (sixth edition): "Look for the small die crack immediately above the tie on the braid, leading slightly downward to the Indian's jaw. The beginning of this die break can usually be seen even on lower-grade coins." **k.** Included in 1918-D mintage figure.

	Mintage	Cert	Avg	%MS	G-4	VG-8	F-12	VF-20	EF-40	AU-50	MS-60 / PF-63	MS-63 / PF-64	MS-65 / PF-65
1920	63,093,000	953	62.0	88%	$1.50	$2.50	$3	$7	$15	$30	$65	$145	$600
	Auctions: $8,225, MS-67, February 2015; $881, MS-66, November 2016; $764, MS-65, November 2016; $176, MS-64, January 2015												
1920-D	9,418,000	858	48.6	49%	$9	$18	$40	$120	$275	$350	$600	$1,400	$4,500
	Auctions: $3,525, MS-65, January 2015; $1,645, MS-64, June 2015; $881, MS-63, October 2015; $705, MS-62, February 2015												
1920-S	9,689,000	801	51.0	49%	$5	$14	$30	$100	$200	$300	$650	$1,750	$12,500
	Auctions: $8,812, MS-65, September 2015; $2,585, MS-64, January 2015; $1,410, MS-63, August 2015; $881, AU-58, February 2015												
1921	10,663,000	870	59.2	77%	$4	$6	$8	$24	$50	$75	$150	$320	$800
	Auctions: $7,050, MS-67, August 2015; $3,995, MS-67, November 2016; $3,055, MS-66, September 2015; $400, MS-64, March 2016;												
1921-S	1,557,000	1,474	29.7	17%	$65	$115	$155	$375	$950	$1,100	$1,750	$2,500	$10,000
	Auctions: $2,585, MS-64, October 2015; $646, AU-50, January 2015; $399, VF-30, August 2015; $199, VF-20, February 2015												
1923	35,715,000	1,083	62.2	87%	$2	$3	$4	$6	$15	$35	$65	$160	$500
	Auctions: $9,400, MS-67, August 2015; $1,880, MS-66, January 2015; $470, MS-65, April 2015; $176, MS-64, May 2015												
1923-S	6,142,000	1,350	49.3	52%	$8	$10	$30	$135	$250	$400	$600	$900	$5,500
	Auctions: $4,347, MS-65, January 2015; $1,086, MS-64, August 2015; $387, AU-58, May 2015; $282, AU-53, November 2015												
1924	21,620,000	745	61.8	87%	$1.50	$2	$5	$8	$25	$45	$75	$175	$750
	Auctions: $7,050, MS-67, March 2015; $1,645, MS-66, October 2016; $724, MS-65, September 2015; $352, MS-64, March 2015												
1924-D	5,258,000	927	45.6	46%	$8.50	$12	$30	$85	$235	$325	$450	$800	$4,500
	Auctions: $4,465, MS-65, January 2015; $1,880, MS-64, September 2015; $763, AU-58, April 2015; $223, EF-45, July 2015												
1924-S	1,437,000	1,431	26.5	13%	$17	$40	$110	$375	$850	$1,700	$2,500	$4,500	$14,000
	Auctions: $5,287, MS-64, July 2015; $1,292, AU-50, June 2015; $470, EF-40, January 2015; $105, F-15, September 2015												
1925	35,565,100	1,085	63.1	94%	$3	$3.50	$4	$8	$15	$35	$45	$100	$400
	Auctions: $7,344, MS-67, August 2015; $4,230, MS-67, June 2015; $2,468, MS-66, August 2016; $352, MS-65, March 2015												
1925-D	4,450,000	883	51.1	59%	$10	$20	$40	$80	$165	$300	$450	$800	$4,000
	Auctions: $940, MS-64, February 2015; $472, MS-62, January 2015; $470, MS-61, July 2015; $352, AU-58, July 2015												
1925-S	6,256,000	993	47.5	44%	$5	$10	$20	$80	$180	$275	$600	$1,850	$20,000
	Auctions: $1,762, MS-64, January 2015; $1,292, MS-63, July 2015; $188, AU-50, May 2015; $135, EF-40, February 2015												
1926	44,693,000	1,615	63.3	94%	$1.25	$1.75	$2.50	$5	$10	$20	$35	$75	$200
	Auctions: $6,463, MS-67, December 2015; $4,465, MS-67, November 2016; $646, MS-66, November 2016; $176, MS-65, October 2016												
1926-D	5,638,000	976	51.9	61%	$10	$18	$28	$90	$185	$300	$350	$600	$4,000
	Auctions: $3,995, MS-65, July 2015; $1,410, MS-64, January 2015; $376, MS-63, April 2015; $258, MS-62, November 2015												
1926-S	970,000	2,175	28.2	10%	$25	$45	$100	$225	$850	$2,500	$4,500	$8,500	$95,000
	Auctions: $11,700, MS-64, January 2018; $4,324, AU-58, April 2018; $1,920, AU-55, January 2018; $705, EF-45, September 2015												
1927	37,981,000	1,174	63.1	93%	$1.25	$1.75	$2.50	$5	$15	$20	$35	$80	$250
	Auctions: $4,935, MS-67, September 2016; $999, MS-66, January 2015; $881, MS-66, December 2015; $164, MS-65, September 2015												
1927, Presentation Strike, Proof (l)	(m)	5	65.0										$45,000 (n)
	Auctions: $43,125, SP-65, January 2012												
1927-D	5,730,000	857	58.2	78%	$2.50	$6	$10	$35	$80	$135	$165	$375	$5,000
	Auctions: $4,935, MS-65, January 2015; $646, MS-64, October 2015; $376, MS-63, May 2015; $188, AU-58, September 2015												
1927-S	3,430,000	747	53.5	50%	$1.50	$3	$5	$35	$95	$185	$850	$2,250	$12,000
	Auctions: $3,525, MS-64, January 2015; $1,116, MS-62, October 2015; $329, AU-58, August 2015; $282, AU-55, February 2015												
1928	23,411,000	1,005	63.1	90%	$1.25	$1.75	$2.50	$5	$15	$25	$35	$90	$280
	Auctions: $5,875, MS-67, June 2015; $1,528, MS-66, November 2016; $258, MS-65, October 2015; $258, MS-65, November 2015												
1928-D	6,436,000	1,618	62.9	96%	$1.50	$2.50	$5	$15	$45	$50	$60	$110	$600
	Auctions: $517, MS-65, September 2015; $481, MS-65, August 2015; $129, MS-64, January 2015; $99, MS-63, February 2015												
1928-S	6,936,000	799	59.1	74%	$1.75	$2	$2.50	$11	$26	$110	$260	$550	$2,850
	Auctions: $7,343, MS-65, October 2015; $2,115, MS-65, January 2015; $822, MS-64, August 2015; $458, MS-63, February 2015												

l. Some experts believe that certain 1927 nickels were carefully made circulation strikes; such pieces are sometimes certified as "Examples" or "Presentation Strikes." Professional numismatic opinions vary. See Bowers, *A Guide Book of Buffalo and Jefferson Nickels* (second edition). **m.** The mintage figure is unknown. **n.** Value in PF-66 is $75,000.

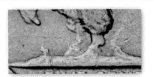

1935, Doubled Die Reverse
FS-05-1935-801.

1936-D, 3-1/2 Legged
FS-05-1936D-901.

	Mintage	Cert	Avg	%MS	G-4	VG-8	F-12	VF-20	EF-40	AU-50	MS-60 / PF-63	MS-63 / PF-64	MS-65 / PF-65
1929	36,446,000	1,338	62.7	93%	$1.25	$1.50	$2.50	$5	$15	$20	$40	$75	$275
	Auctions: $8,225, MS-67, September 2016; $5,402, MS-66, January 2015; $212, MS-65, October; $258, MS-64, August 2015												
1929-D	8,370,000	814	62.1	91%	$1.25	$2	$2.50	$7	$32	$45	$60	$130	$950
	Auctions: $763, MS-65, October 2015; $376, MS-64, February 2015; $282, MS-64, January 2015; $129, MS-63, May 2015												
1929-S	7,754,000	1,142	62.6	89%	$1.25	$1.50	$2	$4	$12	$25	$55	$90	$375
	Auctions: $340, MS-65, January 2015; $329, MS-65, October 2015; $129, MS-64, April 2015; $79, MS-63, May 2015												
1930	22,849,000	1,704	62.0	89%	$1.25	$1.50	$2.50	$4	$11	$20	$35	$75	$220
	Auctions: $3,525, MS-67, June 2015; $2,585, MS-67, October 2016; $1,763, MS-66, September 2016; $353, MS-65, October 2016												
1930-S	5,435,000	876	61.8	88%	$1.25	$1.50	$2.50	$4	$15	$35	$65	$120	$385
	Auctions: $1,880, MS-66, January 2015; $364, MS-65, February 2015; $188, MS-64, August 2015; $111, MS-63, May 2015												
1931-S	1,200,000	2,423	60.5	83%	$15	$16	$20	$25	$35	$55	$65	$100	$300
	Auctions: $616, MS-66, August 2015; $1,057, MS-65, January 2015; $517, MS-65, October 2015; $111, MS-64, May 2015												
1934	20,213,003	1,356	63.1	89%	$1.25	$1.50	$2.50	$4	$10	$18	$50	$65	$300
	Auctions: $9,988, MS-67, January 2015; $3,525, MS-67, August 2016; $1,880, MS-66, September 2016; $188, MS-65, August 2016												
1934-D	7,480,000	1,295	62.7	93%	$1.50	$2.50	$4	$9	$20	$45	$80	$125	$550
	Auctions: $1,880, MS-66, October 2015; $188, MS-64, August 2015; $152, MS-64, January 2015; $117, MS-63, April 2015												
1935	58,264,000	2,253	59.9	82%	$1	$1.50	$1.75	$2	$5	$10	$22	$45	$120
	Auctions: $3,995, MS-67, July 2016; $1,763, MS-67, October 2016; $229, MS-66, March 2015; $164, MS-66, September 2015												
1935, Doubled Die Reverse (o)	(p)	221	29.9	6%	$45	$65	$100	$135	$450	$1,300	$4,000	$6,000	$25,000
	Auctions: $329, EF-40, January 2015; $282, VF-35, January 2015; $95, VF-20, July 2015; $65, VG-10, August 2017												
1935-D	12,092,000	1,517	63.1	95%	$1	$1.50	$2.50	$6	$18	$42	$75	$90	$400
	Auctions: $2,232, MS-67, January 2015; $1,410, MS-66, September 2015; $352, MS-65, March 2015; $89, MS-64, May 2015												
1935-S	10,300,000	1,715	63.6	96%	$1	$1.50	$2	$2.50	$4	$18	$55	$70	$210
	Auctions: $2,585, MS-67, January 2015; $305, MS-66, October 2015; $164, MS-65, March 2015; $74, MS-64, May 2015												
1936	118,997,000	4,016	63.4	89%	$1	$1.50	$1.75	$2	$3	$9	$25	$40	$80
	Auctions: $646, MS-67, December 2015; $352, MS-67, May 2015; $153, MS-66, August 2016; $339, MS-64, August 2015												
1936, Proof, Both kinds	4,420												
1936, Satin Finish, Proof		643	65.8								$1,000	$1,250	$1,400
	Auctions: $6,462, PF-68, July 2015; $2,585, PF-67, June 2015; $1,527, PF-67, October 2015; $1,527, PF-66, January 2015												
1936, Brilliant Finish, Proof		590	65.5								$1,100	$1,500	$1,750
	Auctions: $5,875, PF-68, August 2015; $3,290, PF-67, July 2015; $1,762, PF-66, February 2015; $1,762, PF-65, January 2015												
1936-D	24,814,000	2,903	63.1	94%	$1	$1.50	$1.75	$2	$4	$12	$40	$45	$100
	Auctions: $1,527, MS-67, January 2015; $123, MS-66, November 2015; $117, MS-66, February 2015; $69, MS-65, April 2015												
1936-D, 3-1/2 Legged (q)	(r)	54	24.3	0%	$400	$600	$1,000	$1,500	$3,000	$4,250	$12,500		
	Auctions: $3,290, AU-50, January 2014												
1936-S	14,930,000	2,076	63.6	94%	$1	$1.50	$1.75	$2	$4	$12	$38	$45	$95
	Auctions: $822, MS-67, January 2015; $270, MS-66, February 2015; $188, MS-66, November 2015; $94, MS-65, May 2015												

o. Strong doubling is evident on FIVE CENTS, E PLURIBUS UNUM, and the eye, horn, and mane of the bison. This variety (FS-05-1935-801) is extremely rare above VF, and fewer than a dozen are known in MS. Do not mistake it for the more moderately doubled FS-05-1935-803, which commands much lower premiums. **p.** Included in 1935 mintage figure. **q.** The right front leg has been partially polished off the die—similar to the 1937-D, 3-Legged, variety, but not as severe. (This variety is not from the same die as the 1937-D.) Fewer than 40 are known in all grades. Incorrectly listed by Breen as 1936-P. **r.** Included in 1936-D mintage figure.

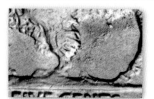

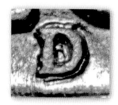

1937-D, 3-Legged
FS-05-1937D-901.

1938-D, D Over S
FS-05-1938D-511.

	Mintage	Cert	Avg	%MS	G-4	VG-8	F-12	VF-20	EF-40	AU-50	MS-60 / PF-63	MS-63 / PF-64	MS-65 / PF-65
1937	79,480,000	9,211	65.1	97%	$1	$1.50	$1.75	$2	$3	$9	$25	$40	$60
Auctions: $8,225, MS-68, August 2016; $2,820, MS-67, September 2015; $1,059, MS-67, October 2015; $999, MS-67, August 2016													
1937, Proof	5,769	1,653	65.6								$900	$1,100	$1,200
Auctions: $3,525, PF-68, August 2015; $3,055, PF-67, January 2015; $1,351, PF-66, July 2015; $1,292, PF-65, June 2015													
1937-D	17,826,000	12,119	55.3	54%	$1	$1.50	$1.75	$3	$4	$10	$35	$45	$60
Auctions: $540, MS-67, January 2015; $423, MS-67, February 2015; $69, MS-66, June 2015; $48, MS-65, March 2015													
1937-D, 3-Legged (s)	(t)	7,093	48.7	25%	$450	$475	$550	$600	$675	$850	$1,850	$4,000	$25,000
Auctions: $7,638, MS-64, January 2014; $1,560, AU-58, February 2018; $900, AU-55, April 2018; $646, EF-45, July 2015													
1937-S	5,635,000	4,405	65.0	99%	$1	$1.50	$1.75	$3	$6	$9	$32	$42	$65
Auctions: $881, MS-67, October 2015; $446, MS-67, January 2015; $62, MS-66, March 2015; $52, MS-64, June 2015													
1938-D	7,020,000	44,487	65.7	100%	$3.50	$4	$4.50	$4.75	$5	$8	$22	$35	$45
Auctions: $188, MS-67, October 2015; $129, MS-67, January 2015; $50, MS-66, February 2015; $28, MS-65, August 2015													
1938-D, D Over D	(u)	3,389	65.6	100%	$4.50	$6.50	$9	$11	$20	$25	$45	$50	$75
Auctions: $822, MS-67, October 2015; $564, MS-67, January 2015; $129, MS-66, February 2015; $60, MS-65, June 2015													
1938-D, D Over S (v)	(u)	2,305	65.2	98%	$5.50	$8	$10	$14	$20	$32	$55	$80	$150
Auctions: $646, MS-67, August 2015; $517, MS-66, November 2015; $188, MS-66, March 2015; $94, MS-65, January 2015													

s. The reverse die was polished heavily, perhaps to remove clash marks, resulting in the shaft of the bison's right front leg missing. Beware altered examples fraudulently passed as genuine. From the *Cherrypickers' Guide to Rare Die Varieties, Vol. I* (sixth edition): "Look for a line of raised dots from the middle of the bison's belly to the ground as one of the diagnostics on the genuine specimen." **t.** Included in 1937-D mintage figure. **u.** Included in 1938-D mintage figure. **v.** There are five different D Over S dies for this date. Varieties other than the one listed here (FS-05-1938D-511) command smaller premiums.

JEFFERSON (1938–2003)

Designer: *Felix Schlag.* **Weight:** *5 grams.* **Composition:** *1938–1942, 1946–2003—.750 copper, .250 nickel; 1942–1945—.560 copper, .350 silver, .090 manganese, with net weight .05626 oz. pure silver.* **Diameter:** *21.2 mm.* **Edge:** *Plain.* **Mints:** *Philadelphia, Denver, and San Francisco.*

Circulation Strike

Mintmark location, 1938–1941 and 1946–1964, is on the reverse, to the right of Monticello.

Mintmark location, 1942–1945, is on the reverse, above Monticello.

Proof

Wartime Silver Alloy (1942–1945)

Mintmark location, 1968–2004, is on the obverse, near the date.

Wartime Silver Alloy, Proof

History. The Jefferson nickel, designed by Felix Schlag in a public competition, made its debut in 1938, and has been a numismatic favorite since. The obverse features a portrait of Thomas Jefferson after the famous bust by Jean Antoine Houdon, and the reverse a front view of Jefferson's home, Monticello.

From partway through 1942 to the end of 1945 a copper-silver-manganese alloy replaced the traditional 75% copper and 25% nickel composition. This was to help save nickel for the war effort. These silver-content coins bear a distinctive P, D, or S mintmark above the dome of Monticello. Starting in 1966, Felix Schlag's initials, FS, were added below the presidential bust. The coinage dies were remodeled to strengthen the design in 1971, 1972, 1977, and 1982. The mintmark position, originally on the reverse to the right of Monticello, was moved to the obverse starting in 1968.

Striking and Sharpness. On the obverse, check for weakness on the portrait, especially in the lower jaw area. On the reverse, most circulation strikes have weak details on the six steps of Monticello, especially under the third pillar from the left, as this section on the reverse was opposite in the dies (in the press) from the high parts of the Jefferson portrait, and metal could not effectively flow in both directions at once. Planchet weight allowance was another cause, the dies being spaced slightly too far apart. Jefferson nickels can be classified as "Full Steps" (FS) if either five or six of Monticello's porch steps (with the top step counting as one) are clear. Notations of 5FS or 6FS can indicate the number of visible steps. It is easier to count the incuse lines than the raised steps. If there are four complete, unbroken lines, the coin qualifies as Full Steps (with five steps); five complete, unbroken lines indicate six full steps. There must be no nicks, cuts, or scratches interrupting the incuse lines. It is difficult to determine a full five-step count on the 1938 and some 1939 issues, as the steps are wavy and ill-defined; a great deal of subjectivity is common for these dates. Even if the steps are mostly or fully defined, check other areas to determine if a coin has Full Details overall. Interestingly, nickels of the 1950s and 1960s are among the most weakly struck. The silver-content coins of the 1940s usually are well struck. Some nickels of the 1950s to 1970s discolored easily, perhaps due to some impurities in the alloy. Proofs were struck from 1938 to 1942, 1950 to 1964, and 1968 to 2003. All have mirror fields. Striking is usually with Full Details, although there are scattered exceptions. Most survivors are in high grade, PF-64 and upward. Most since the 1970s have frosted or cameo contrast on the higher features. Special Mint Set (SMS) coins were struck in lieu of Proofs from 1965 to 1967; these in some instances closely resemble Proofs.

Availability. All basic dates and mintmarks were saved in roll quantities. Scarce issues in MS include 1939-D and 1942-D. The low-mintage 1950-D was a popular speculation in its time, and most of the mintage went into numismatic hands, making MS coins common today. Many different dates and mints are rare if with 5FS or 6FS; consult *A Guide Book of Buffalo and Jefferson Nickels* for details.

GRADING STANDARDS

MS-60 to 70 (Mint State). *Obverse and Reverse:* Mint luster is complete in the obverse and reverse fields, except in areas not fully struck up, in which graininess or marks from the *original planchet surface* can be seen. This may include the jaw, the back of Jefferson's head, and the higher-relief central features of Monticello. The highest parts of the design may have evidence of abrasion and/or contact marks in lower MS grades. Lower grades such

1939. Graded MS-66.

as MS-60, 61, and 62 can show some evidence of abrasion, usually on the same areas that display weak striking. At MS-63, evidences of abrasion are few, and at MS-65 they are fewer yet. In grades above MS-65, a Jefferson nickel should be mark-free.

AU-50, 53, 55, 58 (About Uncirculated). *Obverse:* The cheekbone and the higher points of the hair show light wear, more at AU-50 than at AU-58. Some mint luster will remain on some AU-55 and most AU-58 coins. *Reverse:* The central part of Monticello shows light wear, but is difficult to evaluate as this area often shows weakness of strike. Some mint luster will remain on some AU-55 and most AU-58 coins.

1943-P, 3 Over 2. Graded AU-58.

EF-40, 45 (Extremely Fine). *Obverse:* More wear is evident on the cheekbone. The higher parts of the hair are without detail. *Reverse:* Monticello shows wear overall. The bottom edge of the triangular area above the columns at the center are worn away.

1942-D, D Over Horizontal D. Graded EF-40.

VF-20, 30 (Very Fine). *Obverse:* Most hair detail is lost, except for the back of the head and lower area. The cheekbone is flat and mostly blended into the hair at the right. *Reverse:* Many shallow-relief architectural features are worn away. The windows remain clear and the four columns are distinct.

Jefferson nickels are seldom collected in grades lower than VF-20.

1945-P, Doubled-Die Reverse. Graded VF-20.

PF-60 to 70 (Proof). *Obverse and Reverse:* Most Proof Jefferson nickels are in higher grades. Those with abrasion or contact marks can be graded PF–60 to 62 or even 63; these are not widely desired by collectors. PF-64 can have some abrasion. Tiny flecks are sometimes seen on coins of 1938 to 1942, as are discolorations (even to the extent of black streaks); these flaws are from cellophane holders. You should avoid such coins. Undipped Proofs of

1975-S. Graded PF-70 Deep Cameo.

the early era often have a slight bluish or yellowish tint. At PF-65 or higher there are no traces of abrasion or flecks. Evaluation of differences between higher-grade Jefferson Proofs is highly subjective; one certified at PF-65 might be similar to another at PF-67, and vice-versa. Striking is typically with full details, although there are scattered exceptions. At PF–69 and 70 there are no traces of abrasion, contact marks, or other flaws.

Five Steps

Six Steps

1939, Doubled
Die Reverse
FS-05-1939-801.

	Mintage	Cert	Avg	%MS	VF-20	EF-40	AU-50	MS-60	MS-63	MS-65 PF-65	MS-65FS PF-66	MS-67 PF-67
1938	19,496,000	1,387	65.4	98%	$0.50	$1	$1.50	$3	$5	$16	$135	$150
Auctions: $188, MS-66, August 2015; $164, MS-66, May 2015; $141, MS-66, September 2015; $141, MS-66, October 2015												
1938, Proof	19,365	1,414	65.5							$100	$120	$350
Auctions: $1,997, PF-68, October 2015; $1,057, PF-68, January 2015; $399, PF-67, July 2015; $94, PF-66, August 2015												
1938-D	5,376,000	3,016	66.0	99%	$1.50	$2	$3	$7	$10	$15	$125	$100
Auctions: $881, MS-67, August 2015; $423, MS-67, January 2015; $141, MS-66, February 2015; $111, MS-66, September 2015												
1938-S	4,105,000	1,702	65.7	99%	$2.50	$3	$3.50	$4.50	$8	$16	$200	$225
Auctions: $282, MS-67, January 2015; $305, MS-66, February 2015; $258, MS-66, October 2015; $129, MS-65, May 2015												
1939	120,615,000	2,089	63.0	86%	$0.25	$0.50	$1	$2	$2.50	$12	$47	$175
Auctions: $1,116, MS-67FS, January 2015; $223, MS-66FS, February 2015; $36, MS-66, April 2015; $223, MS-65FS, February 2015												
1939, Doubled Die Reverse (a)	(b)	271	51.3	41%	$100	$135	$165	$200	$375	$900	$2,100	$2,500
Auctions: $89, EF-40, November 2014; $86, EF-40, November 2014; $70, EF-40, November 2014; $7,050, EF-40, August 2013												
1939, Proof	12,535	1,137	65.5							$120	$170	$400
Auctions: $2,115, PF-67, January 2015; $447, PF-67, February 2015; $129, PF-66, August 2015; $84, PF-65, October 2015												
1939-D	3,514,000	1,630	65.4	96%	$10	$13	$30	$60	$70	$80	$425	$250
Auctions: $282, MS-67, January 2015; $129, MS-67, May 2015; $188, MS-66, November 2015; $135, MS-66, January 2015												
1939-S	6,630,000	965	65.0	95%	$2	$5	$10	$18	$35	$70	$350	$275
Auctions: $1,528, MS-67, November 2013; $764, MS-66FS, June 2015; $247, MS-65FS, November 2014; $229, MS-65FS, September 2014												
1940	176,485,000	949	65.8	98%	$0.25	$0.40	$0.75	$1	$1.50	$15	$40	$100
Auctions: $1,645, MS-67FS, June 2015; $1,320, MS-67FS, July 2015; $969, MS-67FS, August 2016; $153, MS-67, July 2015												
1940, Proof	14,158	1,120	65.4							$100	$120	$350
Auctions: $6,463, PF-68, October 2015; $259, PF-67, January 2015; $94, PF-66, May 2015; $79, PF-65, June 2015												
1940-D	43,540,000	1,790	65.9	99%	$0.35	$0.50	$1	$2	$2.50	$15	$35	$115
Auctions: $229, MS-67FS, November 2013												
1940-S	39,690,000	622	65.4	99%	$0.35	$0.50	$1	$2.25	$3	$12	$60	$235
Auctions: $5,170, MS-67FS, June 2015; $282, MS-67FS, May 2015; $125, MS-66FS, February 2015; $69, MS-66FS, January 2015												
1941	203,265,000	858	65.6	99%	$0.20	$0.30	$0.50	$0.75	$1.50	$12	$55	$85
Auctions: $2,010, MS-67FS, December 2015; $1,410, MS-67FS, October 2016; $940, VF-20, October 2014												
1941, Proof	18,720	1,245	65.3							$75	$110	$400
Auctions: $200, PF-67, April 2015; $112, PF-66, May 2015; $106, PF-66, May 2015; $60, PF-65, August 2015												
1941-D	53,432,000	1,846	66.0	99%	$0.25	$0.40	$1.50	$2.50	$3.50	$12	$37	$65
Auctions: $1,058, MS-67FS, June 2015; $166, MS-67FS, February 2015; $69, MS-67, February 2015; $54, MS-67, February 2015												
1941-S (c)	43,445,000	630	65.0	97%	$0.30	$0.50	$1.50	$3	$4	$12	$70	$165
Auctions: $2,585, MS-66FS, April 2014; $282, MS-66FS, November 2014; $259, MS-66FS, January 2015; $106, MS-66FS, August 2015												

a. Very strong doubling is evident to the east of the primary letters, most noticeably on MONTICELLO and FIVE CENTS. Lesser doubling is also visible on UNITED STATES OF AMERICA and the right side of the building. **b.** Included in circulation-strike 1939 mintage figure. **c.** Large and small mintmark varieties exist.

1942-D, D Over Horizontal D
FS-05-1942D-501.

1943-P, 3 Over 2
FS-05-1943P-101.

1943-P, Doubled Die Obverse
The "Doubled Eye" variety. FS-05-1943P-106.

	Mintage	Cert	Avg	%MS	VF-20	EF-40	AU-50	MS-60	MS-63	MS-65 / PF-65	MS-65FS / PF-66	MS-67 / PF-67
1942	49,789,000	864	64.9	98%	$0.30	$0.45	$1.25	$4	$6	$15	$72	$150
Auctions: $4,700, MS-66FS, July 2015; $2,115, MS-67FS, September 2016; $1,763, MS-66FS, July 2015; $188, MS-66FS, August 2015												
1942, Proof	29,600	2,137	65.7							$90	$100	$175
Auctions: $1,410, PF-68, January 2015; $423, PF-67, June 2015; $118, PF-66, May 2015; $79, PF-66, January 2015												
1942-D	13,938,000	1,621	64.3	94%	$1	$2	$5	$28	$38	$60	$75	$150
Auctions: $541, MS-67FS, January 2015; $494, MS-67FS, July 2015; $100, MS-66FS, January 2015; $89, MS-66FS, February 2015												
1942-D, D Over Horizontal D (d)	(e)	96	46.2	22%	$75	$200	$500	$1,500	$3,000	$8,000		
Auctions: $15,275, MS-66, April 2013; $764, AU-58, October 2014; $329, AU-50, August 2014; $44, F-12, September 2014												
1942-P, Silver	57,873,000	5,903	66.2	99%	$2.50	$3	$4	$7	$12	$20	$60	$75
Auctions: $764, MS-67FS, September 2015; $153, MS-67, September 2015; $129, MS-66FS, January 2015												
1942-P, Proof, Silver	27,600	3,054	65.5							$110	$160	$275
Auctions: $230, PF-67, January 2015; $223, PF-67, January 2015; $100, PF-66, January 2015; $74, PF-64, March 2015												
1942-S	32,900,000	5,246	66.0	100%	$2.50	$3	$4	$7	$12	$25	$175	$100
Auctions: $2,820, MS-67FS, August 2015; $176, MS-66FS, January 2015; $153, MS-66FS, January 2015; $54, MS-65FS, September 2015												
1943-P, 3 Over 2 (f)	(g)	362	53.7	60%	$50	$100	$165	$225	$260	$700	$1,000	$1,500
Auctions: $588, MS-66, October 2015; $539, MS-65, January 2015; $376, MS-64, January 2015; $333, MS-63, June 2015												
1943-P	271,165,000	6,983	64.9	96%	$2.50	$3	$4	$6	$9	$20	$35	$65
Auctions: $881, MS-67FS, June 2015; $646, MS-67FS, January 2015; $118, MS-67, August 2015; $62, MS-66FS, June 2015												
1943-P, Doubled Die Obverse (h)	(g)	153	62.6	82%	$25	$40	$60	$90	$160	$650	$850	$1,100
Auctions: $1,293, MS-66FS, September 2015; $940, MS-66FS, July 2015; $823, MS-66, June 2015; $411, MS-65, October 2015												
1943-D	15,294,000	10,610	66.1	100%	$2.50	$4	$5	$7	$12	$20	$37	$50
Auctions: $3,760, MS-67FS, August 2015; $1,645, MS-67FS, July 2015; $62, MS-66FS, September 2015; $30, MS-66, September 2015												
1943-S	104,060,000	7,454	66.0	100%	$2.50	$3	$4	$6	$8	$20	$40	$85
Auctions: $1,645, MS-67FS, February 2015; $517, MS-67FS, January 2015; $94, MS-66FS, January 2015; $69, MS-66FS, June 2015												
1944-P (i)	119,150,000	4,583	65.8	99%	$2.50	$3	$4	$7	$12	$30	$70	$100
Auctions: $259, MS-67, February 2015; $223, MS-67, February 2015; $212, MS-67, February 2015; $106, MS-67, May 2015												
1944-D	32,309,000	6,997	66.2	100%	$2.50	$3	$3.50	$7	$12	$25	$30	$75
Auctions: $1,528, MS-67FS, July 2015; $1,410, MS-67FS, January 2015; $100, MS-66FS, January 2015; $79, MS-66FS, April 2015												
1944-S	21,640,000	6,260	66.2	100%	$2.50	$3	$3.50	$6	$11	$22	$135	$90
Auctions: $5,170, MS-67FS, July 2015; $2,350, MS-67FS, January 2015; $329, MS-66FS, January 2015; $188, MS-65FS, January 2015												

Note: Genuine examples of some wartime dates were struck in nickel, in error. **d.** The initial D mintmark was punched into the die horizontally, then corrected. From the *Cherrypickers' Guide to Rare Die Varieties, Vol. I* (sixth edition): "This is the rarest of the major Jefferson nickel varieties in Mint State." **e.** Included in 1942-D mintage figure. **f.** From the *Cherrypickers' Guide to Rare Die Varieties, Vol. I* (sixth edition): "This popular variety was created when the die was first hubbed with a 1942-dated hub, then subsequently hubbed with a 1943-dated hub. The diagonal of the 2 is visible within the lower opening of the 3. Doubling is also visible on LIBERTY and IN GOD WE TRUST. . . . There is at least one 1943-P five-cent piece that has a faint, short die gouge extending upward from the lower ball of the 3; this is often mistaken for the overdate." **g.** Included in 1943-P mintage figure. **h.** This variety is nicknamed the "Doubled Eye." Doubling is visible on the date, LIBERTY, the motto, and, most noticeably, Jefferson's eye. **i.** 1944 nickels without mintmarks are counterfeit.

1945-P, Doubled Die Reverse
FS-05-1945P-803.

	Mintage	Cert	Avg	%MS	VF-20	EF-40	AU-50	MS-60	MS-63	MS-65 / PF-65	MS-65FS / PF-66	MS-67 / PF-67
1945-P	119,408,100	4,921	65.5	99%	$2.50	$3	$3.50	$7	$9	$20	$110	$225
	Auctions: $9,988, MS-67FS, July 2015; $329, MS-67, October 2015; $223, MS-66FS, January 2015; $58, MS-66, January 2015											
1945-P, DblDie Reverse (j)	**(k)**	121	63.5	91%	$20	$30	$50	$75	$130	$800	$6,000	
	Auctions: $400, MS-65, January 2015; $353, MS-65, February 2015; $212, MS-65, January 2015; $176, MS-64, January 2015											
1945-D	37,158,000	6,979	66.2	100%	$2	$2.50	$3	$5	$8	$20	$35	$80
	Auctions: $705, MS-67FS, January 2015; $54, MS-66FS, May 2015; $50, MS-66FS, January 2015; $48, MS-66FS, May 2015											
1945-S	58,939,000	7,316	66.1	100%	$2	$2.50	$3	$5	$8	$20	$175	$175
	Auctions: $3,055, MS-67FS, August 2015; $1,116, MS-67FS, January 2015; $1,058, MS-66FS, January 2015											
1946	161,116,000	515	65.0	98%	$0.25	$0.30	$0.35	$0.75	$2.50	$15	$175	
	Auctions: $1,763, MS-67, December 2013; $1,528, MS-66FS, August 2016; $1,175, MS-66FS, November 2016; $259, MS-65FS, May 2015											
1946-D	45,292,200	1,413	65.5	99%	$0.35	$0.40	$0.45	$1	$2.50	$12	$30	$335
	Auctions: $2,350, MS-67FS, September 2015; $1,528, MS-67FS, January 2015; $1,175, MS-67FS, October 2015;											
1946-S	13,560,000	1,275	65.6	99%	$0.40	$0.45	$0.50	$1	$2	$11	$110	$120
	Auctions: $353, MS-66FS, December 2014; $306, MS-66FS, July 2015; $223, MS-66FS, October 2014; $529, MS-66FS, April 2014											
1947	95,000,000	722	65.5	100%	$0.25	$0.30	$0.35	$0.75	$1.75	$12	$57	$120
	Auctions: $3,760, MS-67FS, January 2015; $564, MS-66FS, July 2015; $153, MS-66FS, February 2015; $150, MS-66FS, January 2015											
1947-D	37,822,000	1,040	65.7	100%	$0.30	$0.35	$0.40	$0.90	$1.75	$11	$25	$115
	Auctions: $940, MS-67FS, October 2015; $79, MS-66FS, January 2015; $74, MS-66FS, May 2015; $69, MS-66FS, November 2015											
1947-S	24,720,000	797	65.6	99%	$0.40	$0.45	$0.50	$1	$1.75	$12	$43	$500
	Auctions: $2,056, MS-66FS, June 2014											

Note: Genuine examples of some wartime dates were struck in nickel, in error. **j.** There are several collectible doubled-die reverses for this date. Values are for the variety pictured (FS-05-1945P-801), with a strongly doubled reverse. The doubling spread increases from left to right. **k.** Included in 1945-P mintage figure.

1949-D, D Over S
FS-05-1949D-501.

	Mintage	Cert	Avg	%MS	MS-60	MS-63	MS-65	MS-65FS	MS-66	MS-66FS / PF-65	MS-67 / PF-66	MS-67FS / PF-67
1948	89,348,000	412	65.1	99%	$1	$1.50	$10	$175	$55	$650		
	Auctions: $1,646, MS-66FS, August 2016; $1,058, MS-66FS, October 2016; $112, MS-65FS, January 2015; $106, MS-65FS, July 2015											
1948-D	44,734,000	1,126	65.8	100%	$1.60	$4	$10	$25	$37	$70	$125	
	Auctions: $588, MS-67FS, January 2015; $112, MS-66FS, November 2015											
1948-S	11,300,000	1,398	65.9	100%	$1.50	$2.50	$9	$37	$35	$265	$170	
	Auctions: $7,050, MS-67FS, January 2015; $4,935, MS-67FS, July 2015; $517, MS-67, January 2015											
1949	60,652,000	540	65.3	99%	$2.50	$9	$15	$1,500	$30			
	Auctions: $1,880, MS-65FS, December 2015; $1,553, MS-65FS, February 2010											
1949-D	36,498,000	1,083	65.2	99%	$1.50	$6	$12	$42	$28	$125	$265	
	Auctions: $734, MS-67, January 2015; $411, MS-67, July 2014; $84, MS-67, December 2014											
1949-D, D Over S (a)	**(b)**	72	62.5	94%	$150	$225	$500	$1,450	$850			
	Auctions: $564, MS-66, January 2015; $541, MS-66, January 2015; $541, MS-66, July 2015; $494, MS-66, October 2015											
1949-S	9,716,000	497	65.4	99%	$1.75	$5	$10	$175	$55	$350		
	Auctions: $15,275, MS-67FS, January 2014; $235, MS-65FS, November 2014; $188, MS-65FS, November 2014											

a. The top serif of the S is visible to the north of the D, with the upper left loop of the S visible to the west of the D. From the *Cherrypickers' Guide to Rare Die Varieties, Vol. I* (sixth edition): "This variety is quite rare in Mint State and highly sought after. Some may still be found in circulated grades. Some examples have been located in original Mint sets." **b.** Included in 1949-D mintage figure.

1954-S, S Over D
FS-05-1954S-501.

	Mintage	Cert	Avg	%MS	MS-60	MS-63	MS-65	MS-65FS	MS-66	MS-66FS	MS-67	MS-67FS
										PF-65	PF-66	PF-67
1950	9,796,000	833	65.7	100%	$2	$3.25	$8	$170	$42	$335		
Auctions: $2,820, MS-67, September 2016; $106, MS-65FS, January 2015; $94, MS-65FS, July 2015												
1950, Proof	51,386	2,019	66.2							$75	$85	$125
Auctions: $329, PF-68, October 2015; $188, PF-68, August 2015; $141, PF-66Cam, November 2015; $50, PF-65, July 2015												
1950-D	2,630,030	9,907	65.5	100%	$14	$16	$27	$50	$53	$110	$190	$750
Auctions: $1,293, MS-67FS, August 2015; $250, MS-67, January 2015; $306, MS-66FS, February 2015; $118, MS-66FS, February 2015												
1951	28,552,000	465	65.4	100%	$3	$6.50	$15	$300	$70	$650		
Auctions: $1,410, MS-66FS, October 2016; $282, MS-66FS, August 2015; $259, MS-65FS, January 2015; $235, MS-65, August 2015												
1951, Proof	57,500	2,448	66.8							$65	$75	$120
Auctions: $823, PF-68Cam, January 2015; $705, PF-68Cam, October 2015; $129, PF-67Cam, June 2015; $58, PF-67, February 2015												
1951-D	20,460,000	1,119	65.8	100%	$4	$7	$15	$70	$30	$250	$235	
Auctions: $2,820, MS-66FS, June 2013												
1951-S	7,776,000	705	65.7	99%	$1.50	$2	$12	$175	$37	$550		
Auctions: $646, MS-67, August 2015; $194, MS-67, September 2015; $1,293, MS-66FS, January 2015; $881, MS-66FS, January 2015												
1952	63,988,000	358	65.5	100%	$1	$4	$9	$875	$135	$3,500	$375	
Auctions: $1,175, MS-67, August 2016; $1,058, MS-67, October 2016; $259, MS-66FS, July 2014; $259, MS-64FS, November 2014												
1952, Proof	81,980	2,656	67.1							$45	$60	$75
Auctions: $176, PF-67Cam, January 2015; $153, PF-67Cam, December 2015; $64, PF-66Cam, December 2015; $26, PF-66, March 2015												
1952-D	30,638,000	962	65.8	100%	$3.50	$6.25	$20	$150	$35	$290	$500	
Auctions: $16,450, MS-67FS, July 2015; $12,338, MS-67FS, January 2015; $329, MS-66FS, August 2015; $112, MS-65FS, January 2015												
1952-S	20,572,000	1,086	65.6	100%	$1	$1.50	$17	$265	$38	$1,600		
Auctions: $235, MS-65FS, August 2015; $212, MS-65FS, January 2015												
1953	46,644,000	450	65.2	99%	$0.25	$0.75	$8	$1,700	$38	$4,500		
Auctions: $129, PF-67Cam, December 2015; $26, PF-66Cam, August 2015; $54, PF-66, June 2015												
1953, Proof	128,800	3,529	67.2							$45	$50	$65
Auctions: $15,275, PF-68DCam, April 2013; $65, PF-68, September 2014; $135, PF-67Cam, November 2014; $35, PF-67, July 2014												
1953-D	59,878,600	926	65.6	100%	$0.25	$0.75	$9	$190	$38	$750	$385	
Auctions: $129, MS-67, January 2015; $1,880, MS-66FS, July 2015; $135, MS-65FS, August 2015; $141, MS-65, October 2015												
1953-S	19,210,900	904	65.2	100%	$0.75	$1	$15	$4,500	$75			
Auctions: $1,293, MS-64FS, June 2013												
1954	47,684,050	613	65.2	100%	$1	$1.50	$15	$215	$28	$1,000	$190	
Auctions: $999, MS-66FS, November 2014; $259, MS-65FS, January 2015; $207, MS-65FS, February 2010												
1954, Proof	233,300	3,654	67.3							$22	$40	$55
Auctions: $5,875, PF-68DCam, March 2013												
1954-D	117,183,060	498	64.6	98%	$0.60	$1	$30	$600	$100	$1,400	$265	
Auctions: $646, MS-65FS, January 2015; $282, MS-65FS, August 2015; $200, MS-65FS, August 2015; $176, MS-65FS, August 2015												
1954-S	29,384,000	1,308	64.5	98%	$1.75	$2	$25	$5,250	$100			
Auctions: $1,410, MS-64FS, January 2015; $764, MS-64FS, October 2015												
1954-S, S Over D (c)	(d)	196	62.9	94%	$35	$65	$150	$435	$425			
Auctions: $329, MS-66, January 2015; $159, MS-65, April 2015; $147, MS-65, February 2015; $84, MS-64, April 2015												

c. The overall strength of the strike is the important factor in this overmintmark's value. **d.** Included in 1954-S mintage figure.

1955-D, D Over S
FS-05-1955D-501.

	Mintage	Cert	Avg	%MS	MS-60	MS-63	MS-65	MS-65FS	MS-66	MS-66FS / PF-65	MS-67 / PF-66	MS-67FS / PF-67
1955	7,888,000	820	65.1	100%	$0.75	$1	$15	$675	$100			
Auctions: $3,643, MS-66FS, September 2016; $382, MS-65FS, April 2014												
1955, Proof	378,200	8,059	67.7							$18	$30	$45
Auctions: $1,175, PF-68DCam, October 2015; $646, PF-68DCam, August 2015; $69, PF-66, July 2015; $54, PF-63, May 2015												
1955-D	74,464,100	813	64.6	98%	$0.50	$0.75	$20	$4,000	$140			
Auctions: $165, MS-66, August 2014; $69, MS-66, November 2015; $999, MS-64FS, February 2013												
1955-D, D Over S (e)	(f)	204	64.3	97%	$36	$57.50	$175	$390	$750			
Auctions: $823, MS-66, August 2015; $165, MS-65, January 2015; $50, MS-63, November 2015												
1956	35,216,000	1,388	65.6	100%	$0.50	$0.75	$25	$67	$38	$165		$1,650
Auctions: $9,400, MS-67FS, June 2015; $1,293, MS-66FS, December 2015; $588, MS-66FS, June 2014												
1956, Proof	669,384	6,389	67.6							$5	$25	$40
Auctions: $47, PF-69, October 2014; $5,581, PF-68DCam, June 2013												
1956-D	67,222,940	859	65.7	100%	$0.50	$0.75	$25	$575	$34	$1,700	$285	
Auctions: $911, MS-65FS, February 2013												
1957	38,408,000	725	65.3	100%	$0.50	$0.75	$15	$80	$55	$1,500		
Auctions: $441, MS-66FS, April 2014; $400, MS-67, August 2016												
1957, Proof	1,247,952	7,770	67.5							$4	$12	$20
Auctions: $881, PF-68Cam, June 2013												
1957-D	136,828,900	946	65.4	100%	$0.50	$0.70	$15	$150	$30	$1,300		
Auctions: $1,087, MS-66FS, August 2015; $376, MS-66FS, August 2015; $259, MS-66FS, August 2015; $188, MS-66FS, January 2015												
1958	17,088,000	556	64.6	99%	$0.60	$0.80	$12	$900	$85			
Auctions: $1,116, MS-66FS, November 2014; $764, MS-65, January 2014; $42, MS-64FS, June 2015												
1958, Proof	875,652	6,329	67.5							$8	$12	$20
Auctions: $7,050, PF-68DCam, April 2013												
1958-D	168,249,120	1,031	65.4	99%	$0.40	$0.50	$12	$33	$45	$38	$125	$750
Auctions: $1,763, MS-67FS, December 2013												
1959	27,248,000	971	65.3	99%	$0.25	$0.50	$10	$55	$65	$475		
Auctions: $764, MS-66FS, August 2016; $617, MS-66FS, September 2016; $165, MS-66FS, August 2015; $165, MS-66FS, August 2015												
1959, Proof	1,149,291	6,075	67.6							$3	$10	$20
Auctions: $7,050, PF-69DCam, April 2013; $1,293, PF-68DCam, September 2014; $494, PF-67DCam, August 2015												
1959-D	160,738,240	799	65.3	99%	$0.25	$0.50	$8	$190	$65	$1,100		
Auctions: $306, MS-66FS, July 2015; $223, MS-66FS, January 2015; $118, MS-65FS, January 2015; $107, MS-65FS, September 2015												
1960	55,416,000	536	65.1	99%	$0.25	$0.50	$8	$2,000	$65			
Auctions: $1,495, MS-65FS, February 2010												
1960, Proof	1,691,602	6,646	67.5							$3	$10	$18
Auctions: $6,463, PF-69DCam, March 2013; $229, PF-69Cam, September 2014												
1960-D	192,582,180	628	65.4	99%	$0.25	$0.50	$15	$2,500	$130		$425	
Auctions: $223, MS-66, February 2013												

e. There are 10 or more different D Over S varieties for 1955. Values shown are for the strongest (FS-05-1955D-501); others command smaller premiums. f. Included in 1955-D mintage figure.

	Mintage	Cert	Avg	%MS	MS-60	MS-63	MS-65	MS-65FS	MS-66	MS-66FS	MS-67	MS-67FS
										PF-65	PF-66	PF-67
1961	73,640,100	617	65.5	100%	$0.25	$0.50	$20	$1,500	$47	$2,650		
Auctions: $2,530, MS-65FS, February 2010												
1961, Proof	3,028,144	7,021	67.4								$3	$10	$18
Auctions: $1,763, PF-69DCam, April 2013												
1961-D	229,342,760	537	65.0	99%	$0.25	$0.50	$20	$6,500	$200		$1,250	
Auctions: $11,163, MS-64FS, February 2013												
1962	97,384,000	613	65.3	99%	$0.25	$0.50	$15	$43	$40	$350	$285	
Auctions: $21,150, MS-67FS, August 2013												
1962, Proof	3,218,019	7,633	67.4								$3	$10	$18
Auctions: $823, PF-69DCam, September 2013												
1962-D	280,195,720	425	64.7	99%	$0.25	$0.50	$30		$300			
Auctions: $89, MS-63FS, November 2014; $118, MS-63FS, June 2013												
1963	175,776,000	838	65.4	100%	$0.25	$0.50	$15	$150	$43	$675	$650	
Auctions: $1,058, MS-66FS, July 2016; $705, MS-66FS, October 2016; $541, MS-66FS, July 2015; $79, MS-65FS, January 2015												
1963, Proof	3,075,645	9,547	67.5								$3	$10	$18
Auctions: $329, PF-69UCam, July 2015; $317, PF-69DCam, December 2014; $823, PF-69DCam, September 2013												
1963-D	276,829,460	302	64.5	98%	$0.25	$0.50	$25	$4,750				
Auctions: $7,475, MS-65FS, February 2010												
1964	1,024,672,000	598	65.0	98%	$0.25	$0.50	$10	$260	$33	$1,200		
Auctions: $881, MS-66FS, July 2015; $147, MS-65, January 2015; $129, MS-64, August 2015; $62, MS-64, August 2015												
1964, Proof	3,950,762	13,788	68.1								$3	$10	$18
Auctions: $176, PF-69DCam, January 2015; $112, PF-69DCam, January 2015; $94, PF-69UCam, July 2015												
1964-D	1,787,297,160	582	64.7	97%	$0.25	$0.50	$8	$575	$38	$1,450		
Auctions: $2,350, MS-66FS, January 2015; $969, MS-66FS, January 2015; $282, MS-65FS, January 2015												
1965	136,131,380	808	65.8	99%	$0.25	$0.50	$8	$60	$50	$250	$2,000	
Auctions: $165, MS-67, December 2014; $646, MS-66, August 2013												
1965, Special Mint Set	2,360,000	3,886	66.7								$55	$15	$40
Auctions: $5,288, PF-67DCam, July 2014; $123, PF-67Cam, September 2014; $79, PF-67Cam, January 2015												
1966	156,208,283	174	65.3	98%		$0.25	$5	$50	$25	$225	$175	
Auctions: $56, MS-66, July 2014; $322, MS-65DCam, February 2010												
1966, Special Mint Set	2,261,583	3,621	66.9								$65	$15	$30
Auctions: $329, PF-67Cam, July 2015; $94, PF-67Cam, January 2015												
1967	107,325,800	401	65.5	99%		$0.25	$5	$50	$25	$235	$185	
Auctions: $132, MS-66, February 2013												
1967, Special Mint Set	1,863,344	3,933	66.9								$60	$15	$30
Auctions: $188, PF-68Cam, August 2015; $823, PF-67DCam, July 2015; $40, PF-67Cam, February 2015												

	Mintage	Cert	Avg	%MS	MS-63	MS-64FS	MS-65	MS-65FS	MS-66	MS-66FS	MS-67	MS-67FS
										PF-66	PF-67Cam	PF-69DC
1968-D	91,227,880	810	65.6	100%	$0.25		$4		$35			
Auctions: No auction records available.												
1968-S	100,396,004	479	65.5	100%	$0.25	$475	$5	$1,250	$35	$4,000	$275	
Auctions: No auction records available.												
1968-S, Proof	3,041,506	1,655	67.7								$4	$16	$115
Auctions: $4,406, PF-65, August 2013												
1969-D	202,807,500	514	65.4	100%	$0.25	$10	$4		$115			
Auctions: $94, MS-66, February 2013												
1969-S	120,165,000	296	64.9	99%	$0.25		$2		$275			
Auctions: $188, PF-69DCam, January 2015												
1969-S, Proof	2,934,631	1,522	67.7								$4	$10	$350
Auctions: $282, PF-69DCam, November 2014; $1,116, PF-69DCam, June 2013												

	Mintage	Cert	Avg	%MS	MS-63	MS-64FS	MS-65	MS-65FS	MS-66	MS-66FS	MS-67	MS-67FS
										PF-66	PF-67Cam	PF-69DC
1970-D	515,485,380	658	65.0	100%	$0.25		$10		$180			
1970-S	238,832,004	355	64.9	99%	$0.25	$225	$8	$400	$225	$1,500		
1970-S, Proof	2,632,810	1,528	67.7								$4	$15	$300

Auctions: 1970-D: $200, MS-63, August 2013; $200, MS-62, July 2014; $176, MS-62, August 2015
Auctions: 1970-S: $999, MS-66FS, December 2013; $89, MS-64FS, November 2014
Auctions: 1970-S, Proof: $499, PF-69DCam, September 2013; $411, PF-69DCam, September 2014; $376, PF-69DCam, January 2015

	Mintage	Cert	Avg	%MS	MS-63	MS-64FS	MS-65	MS-65FS	MS-66	MS-66FS	MS-67	MS-67FS	MS-69FS
											PF-66	PF-67Cam	PF-69DC
1971	106,884,000	382	64.9	99%	$0.75	$10	$3	$30	$50	$100			
1971-D	316,144,800	812	65.9	100%	$0.30	$10	$3	$20	$30	$60		$350	
1971-S, Proof	1,655	1,589	67.6								$8	$20	$500
1971-S, No S, Proof ++ (a)	3,220,733	127	67.6								$1,100	$1,200	$3,250
1972	202,036,000	214	65.1	99%	$0.25	$10	$3	$40	$60	$300			
1972-D	351,694,600	299	65.0	99%	$0.25	$10	$3	$40	$75	$350			
1972-S, Proof	3,260,996	1,288	67.5								$8	$20	$120
1973	384,396,000	381	65.2	100%	$0.25	$10	$3	$30	$45	$150	$110		
1973-D	261,405,000	341	65.2	99%	$0.25	$10	$3	$25	$30	$60	$90		
1973-S, Proof	2,760,339	361	67.7								$7	$15	$30
1974	601,752,000	288	65.0	100%	$0.25	$40	$3	$175	$35	$675			
1974-D	277,373,000	214	65.1	99%	$0.25	$15	$3	$40	$45	$110		$1,550	
1974-S, Proof	2,612,568	435	67.1								$8	$12	$20
1975	181,772,000	415	65.3	100%	$0.50	$20	$3	$50	$55	$250			
1975-D	401,875,300	242	64.7	96%	$0.25	$15	$3	$60	$55	$225			
1975-S, Proof	2,845,450	608	67.8								$8	$12	$20
1976	367,124,000	139	64.8	99%	$0.45	$30	$3	$175	$37	$675		$3,250	
1976-D	563,964,147	334	65.2	100%	$0.45	$10	$3	$30	$40	$250			
1976-S, Proof	4,149,730	917	67.9								$8	$12	$20

Auctions: 1971: $127, MS-66FS, February 2010
Auctions: 1971-D: $646, MS-67FS, August 2013
Auctions: 1971-S, Proof: $1,704, PF-69Cam, August 2015; $881, PF-68Cam, October 2015; $1,175, PF-67Cam, January 2015; $940, PF-67, January 2015
Auctions: 1971-S, No S, Proof: $1,528, PF-69DCam, June 2013
Auctions: 1972: $141, MS-66FS, November 2014; $276, MS-66FS, March 2012
Auctions: 1972-D: $212, MS-63, November 2014; $823, MS-63, August 2013
Auctions: 1972-S, Proof: $58, PF-69DCam, November 2015; $52, PF-69DCam, November 2015; $42, PF-69DCam, October 2015
Auctions: 1973: $103, MS-66FS, February 2013
Auctions: 1973-D: $353, MS-65, February 2014
Auctions: 1973-S, Proof: $44, PF-69DCam, September 2009
Auctions: 1974: $1,116, MS-66FS, July 2016; $110, MS-65FS, March 2014; $54, MS-65FS, January 2015; $46, MS-65FS, November 2014
Auctions: 1974-D: $34, MS-66FS, November 2014; $200, MS-62, April 2013
Auctions: 1974-S, Proof: $25, PF-69DCam, March 2008
Auctions: 1975: $2,820, MS-67FS, January 2015; $129, MS-66FS, August 2015
Auctions: 1975-D: $176, MS-66FS, August 2015; $153, MS-64FS, August 2015
Auctions: 1975-S, Proof: $42, PF-68Cam, August 2013
Auctions: 1976: $1,265, MS-66FS, February 2012
Auctions: 1976-D: $235, MS-65, February 2014; $94, MS-64, July 2014
Auctions: 1976-S, Proof: $36, PF-70DCam, January 2010

++ Ranked in the *100 Greatest U.S. Modern Coins* (fourth edition). **a.** 1971-S, Proof, nickels without the S mintmark were made in error after an assistant engraver forgot to punch a mintmark into a die. The U.S. Mint estimates that 1,655 such error coins were struck.

**1979-S, Filled S
(Type 1), Proof**

**1979-S, Clear S
(Type 2), Proof**

**1981-S, Rounded S
(Type 1), Proof**

**1981-S, Flat S
(Type 2), Proof**

	Mintage	Cert	Avg	%MS	MS-63	MS-64FS	MS-65	MS-65FS	MS-66	MS-66FS	MS-67	MS-67FS	MS-69FS
											PF-66	PF-67Cam	PF-69DC
1977	585,376,000	201	65.2	100%	$0.25	$70	$3	$150	$48	$775			
Auctions: $705, MS-66FS, July 2016; $306, MS-65, September 2015; $881, MS-64, October 2014; $329, MS-63, September 2013													
1977-D	297,313,422	315	64.7	99%	$0.50	$10	$3	$35	$40	$250			
Auctions: $940, MS-68, August 2013													
1977-S, Proof	3,251,152	970	68.4								$7	$12	$20
Auctions: $1,116, PF-70DCam, April 2013													
1978	391,308,000	211	65.0	100%	$0.25	$35	$3	$175	$55	$750			
Auctions: $43, MS-64, July 2014; $259, MS-64, September 2013; $282, MS-63, October 2014													
1978-D	313,092,780	304	64.9	100%	$0.25	$15	$3	$40	$55	$75			
Auctions: $104, MS-66FS, February 2010													
1978-S, Proof	3,127,781	1,069	68.7								$7	$12	$20
Auctions: $165, PF-70DCam, February 2015; $153, PF-70DCam, February 2015; $129, PF-70DCam, July 2015													
1979	463,188,000	221	65.0	100%	$0.25	$40	$3	$300	$50	$650			
Auctions: $200, MS-63, January 2015; $129, MS-60, September 2015													
1979-D	325,867,672	408	64.9	100%	$0.25	$10	$4	$30	$37	$125			
Auctions: $182, MS-66FS, February 2013													
1979-S, Proof, Both kinds	3,677,175												
1979-S, Type 1, Proof		1,062	68.7								$7	$12	$22
Auctions: $1,763, PF-70DCam, June 2013													
1979-S, Type 2, Proof		1,382	68.9								$8	$13	$30
Auctions: $646, PF-70DCam, June 2013													
1980-P	593,004,000	229	65.3	99%	$0.25	$10	$4	$45	$30	$225			
Auctions: $329, MS-64, January 2015; $259, MS-65, January 2015; $240, MS-64, January 2015; $188, MS-60, January 2015													
1980-D	502,323,448	226	65.0	99%	$0.25	$10	$3	$20	$60	$250			
Auctions: $217, MS-66FS, February 2013													
1980-S, Proof	3,554,806	1,227	68.7								$7	$12	$20
Auctions: No auction records available.													
1981-P	657,504,000	295	65.4	100%	$0.25	$100	$3	$500	$50	$1,750			
Auctions: $282, MS-66, January 2015; $223, MS-62, January 2015													
1981-D	364,801,843	318	65.2	100%	$0.25	$10	$3	$30	$35	$150			
Auctions: $206, MS-66FS, June 2014													
1981-S, Proof, Both kinds	4,063,083												
1981-S, Type 1, Proof		1,702	68.8								$7	$12	$20
Auctions: $1,528, PF-70DCam, June 2013													
1981-S, Type 2, Proof		1,296	68.9								$10	$13	$30
Auctions: $3,525, PF-70DCam, April 2013													
1982-P	292,355,000	130	65.2	98%	$5	$12	$10	$50	$35	$275			
Auctions: $881, MS-67, February 2014; $2,350, MS-62, September 2014; $306, MS-62, February 2015													
1982-D	373,726,544	215	65.3	99%	$2	$25	$6	$55	$30	$325			
Auctions: $374, MS-66FS, February 2010													
1982-S, Proof	3,857,479	1,403	68.9								$8	$12	$20
Auctions: No auction records available.													

	Mintage	Cert	Avg	%MS	MS-63	MS-64FS	MS-65	MS-65FS	MS-66	MS-66FS	MS-67 / PF-66	MS-67FS / PF-67Cam	MS-69FS / PF-69DC
1983-P	561,615,000	110	64.6	95%	$2	$60	$9	$450	$60	$875			
	Auctions: $141, MS-64, January 2015; $64, MS-64, January 2015; $36, MS-64, August 2015												
1983-D	536,726,276	143	65.1	97%	$1.50	$15	$4	$175	$35	$675			
	Auctions: $863, MS-66FS, June 2010; $112, MS-65FS, November 2014												
1983-S, Proof	3,279,126	1,331	68.9								$8	$12	$20
	Auctions: $1,528, PF-70DCam, June 2013												
1984-P	746,769,000	230	65.5	100%	$1	$10	$3	$25	$40	$75			
	Auctions: $66, MS-66FS, February 2013												
1984-D	517,675,146	172	65.1	99%	$0.25	$10	$3	$30	$65	$135			
	Auctions: $36, MS-65FS, February 2013												
1984-S, Proof	3,065,110	816	68.7								$10	$12	$20
	Auctions: $705, PF-70DCam, June 2013												
1985-P	647,114,962	265	65.6	100%	$0.50	$25	$3	$50	$60	$135			
	Auctions: $89, MS-66FS, November 2014; $70, MS-66FS, November 2014; $259, MS-62, November 2013												
1985-D	459,747,446	197	65.4	99%	$0.50	$10	$3	$40	$45	$125		$1,250	
	Auctions: $196, MS-66FS, June 2010												
1985-S, Proof	3,362,821	968	69.0								$8	$12	$20
	Auctions: $1,528, PF-70DCam, June 2013												
1986-P	536,883,483	207	65.7	100%	$0.50	$10	$3	$50	$35	$175			
	Auctions: $705, MS-66FS, August 2015; $99, MS-66FS, February 2013; $47, MS-66FS, November 2014												
1986-D	361,819,140	197	65.4	100%	$1	$10	$3	$35	$50	$250			
	Auctions: $253, MS-66FS, February 2010												
1986-S, Proof	3,010,497	840	68.9								$9	$13	$20
	Auctions: $3,525, PF-70DCam, April 2013												
1987-P	371,499,481	482	66.0	100%	$0.25	$10	$2.75	$15	$60	$65		$225	
	Auctions: $329, MS-67FS, June 2014												
1987-D	410,590,604	462	65.6	100%	$0.25	$10	$3.50	$20	$30	$125			
	Auctions: $173, MS-67FS, April 2008												
1987-S, Proof	4,227,728	820	69.0								$8	$12	$20
	Auctions: $558, PF-70DCam, June 2013												
1988-P	771,360,000	238	65.8	100%	$0.25	$12	$3	$30	$35	$100			
	Auctions: $329, MS-67, August 2013; $79, MS-64, August 2015; $69, MS-64, July 2014												
1988-D	663,771,652	266	65.3	99%	$0.25	$10	$3	$35	$32	$125			
	Auctions: $165, MS-67, June 2014												
1988-S, Proof	3,262,948	673	68.8								$9	$13	$25
	Auctions: $823, PF-70DCam, June 2013												
1989-P	898,812,000	322	65.9	100%	$0.25	$10	$2.75	$20	$25	$35		$650	
	Auctions: $18, AU-50, August 2013												
1989-D	570,842,474	228	65.1	99%	$0.25	$12	$2.75	$40	$35	$180			
	Auctions: $188, MS-66FS, February 2013												
1989-S, Proof	3,220,194	710	69.1								$8	$12	$20
	Auctions: $82, PF-70DCam, May 2013												
1990-P	661,636,000	308	65.9	99%	$0.25	$10	$2.75	$20	$25	$40			
	Auctions: $24, MS-66FS, October 2009												
1990-D	663,938,503	217	65.2	100%	$0.25	$9	$2.75	$30	$45	$150			
	Auctions: $129, MS-67FS, June 2014												
1990-S, Proof	3,299,559	1,010	69.1								$8	$12	$20
	Auctions: $441, PF-69DCam, June 2014												
1990-S, Proof, Dbl Die Obverse ††	(b)	39	68.9										
	Auctions: $129, MS-67FS, June 2014												

†† Ranked in the *100 Greatest U.S. Modern Coins* (fourth edition). **b.** Included in 1990-S, Proof mintage figure.

	Mintage	Cert	Avg	%MS	MS-63	MS-64FS	MS-65	MS-65FS	MS-66	MS-66FS	MS-67	MS-67FS	MS-69FS
											PF-66	PF-67Cam	PF-69DC
1991-P	614,104,000	148	65.7	100%	$0.30	$10	$2.75	$45	$35	$150			
Auctions: $90, MS-66FS, February 2013													
1991-D	436,496,678	172	65.5	100%	$0.30	$10	$2.75	$25	$35	$125			
Auctions: $76, MS-66FS, February 2013													
1991-S, Proof	2,867,787	831	69.1								$10	$12	$20
Auctions: $64, PF-70DCam, August 2013													
1992-P	399,552,000	219	65.8	100%	$1.50	$10	$3	$20	$28	$50		$1,250	
Auctions: $88, MS-67FS, August 2013													
1992-D	450,565,113	186	65.3	100%	$0.25	$10	$2.75	$30	$40	$160			
Auctions: $72, MS-66FS, February 2013													
1992-S, Proof	4,176,560	2,662	69.1								$8	$12	$20
Auctions: $45, PF-70DCam, May 2013													
1993-P	412,076,000	190	65.9	100%	$0.25	$10	$1	$30	$35	$75			
Auctions: $68, MS-66FS, February 2013													
1993-D	406,084,135	225	65.5	100%	$0.25	$10	$1	$20	$30	$40	$450	$425	
Auctions: $374, MS-67FS, February 2010													
1993-S, Proof	3,394,792	2,133	69.1								$8	$12	$20
Auctions: $47, PF-70DCam, October 2009													
1994-P	722,160,000	214	65.8	100%	$0.25	$10	$2.50	$25	$30	$100	$35		
Auctions: $235, MS-70, January 2015; $881, MS-63, April 2013													
1994-P, Matte Finish †† (c)	167,703	2,919	69.1	100%	$35	$60	$85	$115	$115	$135	$185	$285	
Auctions: $123, MS-70, November 2014; $66, MS-69FS, March 2013; $40, MS-69, September 2014; $38, MS-69, November 2014													
1994-D	715,762,110	144	64.7	99%	$0.25	$10	$1	$30	$35	$100	$50		
Auctions: $92, MS-66FS, February 2013													
1994-S, Proof	3,269,923	2,118	69.1								$8	$12	$20
Auctions: $33, PF-70DCam, April 2013													
1995-P	774,156,000	261	66.1	100%	$0.25	$20	$1	$40	$20	$90	$25	$250	
Auctions: $499, MS-65, August 2013; $141, MS-63, July 2014													
1995-D	888,112,000	102	65.1	99%	$0.50	$10	$1	$25	$30	$175	$35	$850	
Auctions: $940, MS-67FS, April 2014													
1995-S, Proof	2,797,481	2,585	69.1								$10	$13	$20
Auctions: $79, PF-70DCam, February 2010													
1996-P	829,332,000	225	65.7	100%	$0.25	$18	$1	$20	$25	$30	$35	$350	
Auctions: $129, MS-64, January 2015; $69, MS-64, January 2015													
1996-D	817,736,000	262	65.3	100%	$0.25	$20	$1	$22	$25	$35	$40	$200	
Auctions: $161, MS-67FS, February 2010													
1996-S, Proof	2,525,265	2,099	69.1								$8	$12	$25
Auctions: $56, PF-70DCam, February 2010													
1997-P	470,972,000	142	65.8	99%	$0.50	$10	$2	$45	$25	$175	$50	$350	
Auctions: $306, MS-70FS, July 2015; $118, MS-69FS, February 2015													
1997-P, Matte Finish †† (c)	25,000	1,174	69.3	100%	$45	$65	$65	$75	$90	$105	$110	$135	
Auctions: $200, MS-70FS, October 2014; $499, MS-70FS, June 2014; $223, MS-69FS, November 2014; $118, MS-69FS, November 2014													
1997-D	460,640,000	136	65.1	99%	$1	$15	$1	$50	$20	$100	$25	$500	
Auctions: $33, MS-66FS, June 2014													
1997-S, Proof	2,796,678	1,949	69.3								$8	$12	$25
Auctions: $36, PF-70DCam, December 2009													

†† Ranked in the *100 Greatest U.S. Modern Coins* (fourth edition). **c.** Special "frosted" Uncirculated nickels were included in the 1993, Thomas Jefferson, commemorative dollar packaging (sold in 1994) and in the 1997, Botanic Garden, sets (see related listing in the "Government Commemorative Sets" section). They resemble Matte Proof coins.

	Mintage	Cert	Avg	%MS	MS-63	MS-64FS	MS-65	MS-65FS	MS-66	MS-66FS	MS-67 PF-66	MS-67FS PF-67Cam	MS-69FS PF-69DC
1998-P	688,272,000	138	65.2	100%	$0.35	$8	$1	$35	$45	$125	$110	$400	
Auctions: $176, MS-65, July 2014; $940, MS-64, August 2014; $42, MS-62, November 2014													
1998-D	635,360,000	197	64.4	98%	$0.35	$10	$1	$100	$60	$450	$150		
Auctions: $66, MS-65FS, November 2014; $90, MS-65FS, June 2014													
1998-S, Proof	2,086,507	2,530	69.3								$8	$12	$25
Auctions: $47, PF-70DCam, November 2009													
1999-P	1,212,000,000	245	65.2	96%	$0.25	$10	$1	$15	$25	$75	$35	$250	
Auctions: $56, MS-65FS, August 2015; $46, MS-64FS, August 2015; $40, MS-65FS, August 2015; $23, MS-63, August 2015													
1999-D	1,066,720,000	209	65.5	99%	$0.25	$8	$1	$15	$30	$300	$50		
Auctions: $106, MS-64, September 2015; $89, MS-64, August 2015													
1999-S, Proof	3,347,966	7,677	69.1								$9	$12	$25
Auctions: $42, PF-70DCam, September 2009													
2000-P	846,240,000	172	65.6	100%	$0.25	$10	$1	$12	$18	$35	$25	$500	
Auctions: $470, MS-67FS, August 2013													
2000-D	1,509,520,000	198	65.8	99%	$0.25	$10	$1	$12	$18	$50	$25	$500	
Auctions: $613, MS-67FS, July 2015; $36, MS-65, August 2015; $56, MS-64FS, August 2015; $56, MS-63, August 2015													
2000-S, Proof	4,047,993	6,757	69.1								$7	$12	$25
Auctions: $17, PF-69DCam, March 2014													
2001-P	675,704,000	118	65.8	98%	$0.25	$8	$1	$10	$12	$20	$25	$40	
Auctions: $50, MS-67FS, June 2013													
2001-D	627,680,000	126	65.5	98%	$0.25	$8	$1	$10	$12	$20	$25	$130	
Auctions: $138, MS-67FS, February 2010													
2001-S, Proof	3,184,606	5,238	69.2								$7	$12	$25
Auctions: $17, PF-69DCam, March 2014													
2002-P	539,280,000	110	65.6	100%	$0.25	$8	$1	$10	$12	$20	$30	$75	
Auctions: $72, MS-67FS, June 2014													
2002-D	691,200,000	78	65.3	96%	$0.25	$8	$1	$10	$12	$90			
Auctions: $74, MS-66FS, February 2013													
2002-S, Proof	3,211,995	5,559	69.1								$7	$12	$25
Auctions: $15, PF-69DCam, February 2013													
2003-P	441,840,000	224	65.7	100%	$0.25	$8	$1	$10	$12	$20	$22	$50	
Auctions: $1,058, MS-68FS, November 2013													
2003-D	383,040,000	154	65.1	100%	$0.25	$8	$1	$15	$12	$80			
Auctions: $86, MS-66FS, February 2013													
2003-S, Proof	3,298,439	9,438	69.2								$7	$12	$25
Auctions: $15, PF-69DCam, March 2014													

WESTWARD JOURNEY (2004–2005)

Designers: *See image captions for designers.* **Weight:** *5 grams.* **Composition:** *.750 copper, .250 nickel.* **Diameter:** *21.2 mm.* **Edge:** *Plain.* **Mints:** *Philadelphia, Denver, and San Francisco.*

| Westward Journey, Obverse (2004) *Designer: Felix Schlag.* | Peace Medal Reverse (2004) *Designer: Norman E. Nemeth.* | Keelboat Reverse (2004) *Designer: Al Maletsky.* | Westward Journey, Obverse (2005) *Designer: Joe Fitzgerald.* | American Bison Reverse (2005) *Designer: Jamie Franki.* | Ocean in View Reverse (2005) *Designer: Joe Fitzgerald.* |

| Westward Journey, Obverse, Proof | Peace Medal Reverse, Proof | Keelboat Reverse, Proof | Westward Journey, Obverse, Proof | American Bison Reverse, Proof | Ocean in View Reverse, Proof |

Mintmark location, 2005, is on the obverse, near the date (2004 location is the same as previous years).

History. In 2004 special designs commemorating the Westward Journey (Lewis and Clark expedition) were introduced. They utilized the previous obverse design paired with two different reverse designs, one representing the Peace Medals given out by Lewis and Clark, the other showing the keelboat that provided much of their transportation. Two new reverse designs were introduced for 2005, showing the American Bison and a representation of Clark's journal entry upon spotting what he thought was the Pacific Ocean (in actuality, they were still approximately 20 miles from the coast). They were paired with a new obverse, a tightly cropped profile of Jefferson facing right.

Striking and Sharpness. On the obverse, check for weakness on the portrait. Proofs were struck for each design. All have mirror fields. Most have frosted or cameo contrast on the higher features.

Availability. All basic dates and mintmarks were saved in roll quantities.

GRADING STANDARDS

MS-60 to 70 (Mint State). *Obverse and Reverse:* Mint luster is complete in the obverse and reverse fields. Check the higher parts of the obverse and reverse for abrasion and contact marks.

Westward Journey nickels are seldom collected in grades lower than MS-60.

2004-D, Peace Medal. Graded MS-66.

PF-60 to 70 (Proof). *Obverse and Reverse:* Evaluation of differences between higher-grade Jefferson Proofs is highly subjective; one certified at PF-65 might be similar to another at PF-67, and vice-versa. All Proof Westward Journey nickels have mirror fields. Striking is typically with full details, although there are scattered exceptions. Nearly all Westward Journey nickel Proofs are as issued, in PF–69 or 70.

2005-S, Ocean in View. Graded PF-70 Ultra Cameo.

	Mintage	Cert	Avg	%MS	MS-63	MS-65 / PF-65	MS-66 / PF-67	MS-67 / PF-69DC
2004-P, Peace Medal	361,440,000	2,151	63.7	97%	$0.25	$0.75	$8	$50
Auctions: $200, MS-67, February 2013								
2004-D, Peace Medal	372,000,000	560	65.6	99%	$0.25	$0.75	$5	$30
Auctions: $374, MS-68, February 2010								
2004-S, Peace Medal, Proof	2,992,069	12,502	69.2			$4	$12	$25
Auctions: $15, PF-69DCam, March 2014								
2004-P, Keelboat	366,720,000	316	65.6	100%	$0.25	$0.75	$5	$20
Auctions: $299, MS-68, February 2010								
2004-D, Keelboat	344,880,000	368	65.9	100%	$0.25	$0.75	$5	$20
Auctions: No auction records available.								
2004-S, Keelboat, Proof	2,965,422	12,258	69.2			$4	$12	$25
Auctions: $31, PF-70DCam, November 2013								
2005-P, American Bison	448,320,000	4,365	66.7	100%	$0.35	$1.25	$8	$30
Auctions: $28, MS-69, January 2010								
2005-P, American Bison, Satin Finish	1,160,000	3,713	67.0	100%	$0.50	$1	$3	$10
Auctions: No auction records available.								
2005-D, American Bison	487,680,000	4,724	66.1	100%	$0.35	$1.25	$8	$25
Auctions: $388, MS-66, June 2014; $170, MS-64, November 2014; $26, MS-64, November 2014; $84, MS-64, November 2014								
2005-D, American Bison, Satin Finish	1,160,000	3,233	66.6	100%	$0.50	$1	$3	$10
Auctions: No auction records available.								
2005-S, American Bison, Proof	3,344,679	19,642	69.2			$5	$14	$30
Auctions: $34, PF-70DCam, July 2013								
2005-P, Ocean in View	394,080,000	3,317	66.5	100%	$0.25	$0.75	$6	$25
Auctions: $19, MS-66, February 2010								
2005-P, Ocean in View, Satin Finish	1,160,000	3,054	66.7	100%	$0.50	$1	$3	$10
Auctions: No auction records available.								
2005-D, Ocean in View	411,120,000	3,530	66.5	100%	$0.25	$0.75	$5	$22
Auctions: $15, MS-65, August 2009								
2005-D, Ocean in View, Satin Finish	1,160,000	3,264	66.6	100%	$0.50	$1	$3	$10
Auctions: No auction records available.								
2005-S, Ocean in View, Proof	3,344,679	19,349	69.2			$4	$12	$25
Auctions: $21, PF-70DCam, November 2013								

JEFFERSON MODIFIED (2006 TO DATE)

Designers: *Jamie Franki (obverse) and Felix Schlag (reverse).* **Weight:** *5 grams.* **Composition:** *.750 copper, .250 nickel.* **Diameter:** *21.2 mm.* **Edge:** *Plain.* **Mints:** *Philadelphia, Denver, San Francisco, and West Point.*

Circulation Strike

Mintmark location, 2006 to date, is on the obverse, below the date.

Proof

History. 2006 saw the return of Felix Schlag's reverse design showing a front view of Jefferson's home, Monticello. It also featured the debut of another new Jefferson portrait on the obverse, this time in three-quarters profile.

Striking and Sharpness. On the obverse, check for weakness on the portrait. Jefferson nickels can be classified as "Full Steps" (FS) if either five or six of Monticello's porch steps (with the top step counting as one) are clear. Notations of 5FS or 6FS can indicate the number of visible steps. It is easier to count the incuse lines than the raised steps. If there are four complete, unbroken lines, the coin qualifies as Full Steps (with five steps); five complete, unbroken lines indicate six full steps. There must be no nicks, cuts, or scratches interrupting the incuse lines. Even if the steps are mostly or fully defined, check other areas to determine if a coin has Full Details overall. Proofs were struck; all have mirror fields. Striking is usually with Full Details, although there are scattered exceptions. Most survivors are in high grade, PF-64 and upward. Most have frosted or cameo contrast on the higher features.

Availability. All basic dates and mintmarks were saved in roll quantities.

GRADING STANDARDS

MS-60 to 70 (Mint State). *Obverse and Reverse:* Mint luster is complete in the obverse and reverse fields. Check the higher parts of the obverse and reverse for abrasion and contact marks.

Jefferson Modified nickels are seldom collected in grades lower than MS-60.

2011-P. Graded MS-67FS.

PF-60 to 70 (Proof). *Obverse and Reverse:* Evaluation of differences between higher-grade Jefferson Proofs is highly subjective; one certified at PF-65 might be similar to another at PF-67, and vice-versa. All Proof Jefferson Modified nickels have mirror fields. Striking is typically with full details, although there are scattered exceptions. Nearly all Jefferson Modified nickel Proofs are as issued, in PF–69 or 70.

2006-S. Graded PF-70 Deep Cameo.

	Mintage	Cert	Avg	%MS	MS-63	MS-65	MS-65FS	MS-66	MS-66FS	MS-67	MS-67FS / PF-65	MS-68FS / PF-67	MS-69FS / PF-69DC
2006-P, Monticello	693,120,000	1,589	66.5	100%	$0.25	$0.75	$4	$3	$9	$8	$12	$20	$35
Auctions: $705, MS-67FS, July 2014; $19, MS-64FS, January 2013													
2006-P, Monticello, Satin Finish	847,361	1,253	66.8	100%	$0.50	$1	$2	$3	$8	$10	—	—	—
Auctions: No auction records available.													
2006-D, Monticello	809,280,000	1,734	66.6	100%	$0.25	$0.75	$5	$4	$8	$9	$24	$30	$55
Auctions: $11, MS-67, July 2008													
2006-D, Monticello, Satin Finish	847,361	1,368	66.9	100%	$0.50	$1	$2	$3	$8	$10	—	—	—
Auctions: No auction records available.													
2006-S, Monticello, Proof	3,054,436	7,445	69.3								$4	$12	$25
Auctions: $32, PF-70DCam, April 2013													
2007-P	571,680,000	337	66.1	100%	$0.25	$0.50	$4	$3	$9	$8	$12	$20	$35
Auctions: $11, MS-68FS, July 2008													
2007-P, Satin Finish	895,628	271	66.3	100%	$0.50	$1	$2	$3	$8	$10	—	—	—
Auctions: No auction records available.													
2007-D	626,160,000	279	66.1	100%	$0.25	$0.50	$5	$4	$8	$9	$24	$30	$55
Auctions: $14, MS-68FS, July 2008													
2007-D, Satin Finish	895,628	235	66.3	100%	$0.50	$1	$2	$3	$8	$10	—	—	—
Auctions: No auction records available.													
2007-S, Proof	2,577,166	5,654	69.3								$4	$12	$30
Auctions: $15, PF-69DCam, May 2013													
2008-P	279,840,000	222	66.3	100%	$0.25	$0.50	$4	$3	$8	$8	$12	$20	$35
Auctions: No auction records available.													
2008-P, Satin Finish	745,464	118	67.0	100%	$0.50	$1	$2	$3	$8	$10	—	—	—
Auctions: No auction records available.													
2008-D	345,600,000	227	66.3	100%	$0.25	$0.50	$5	$4	$9	$9	$24	$30	$55
Auctions: No auction records available.													
2008-D, Satin Finish	745,464	147	67.1	100%	$0.50	$1	$2	$3	$8	$10	—	—	—
Auctions: No auction records available.													
2008-S, Proof	2,169,561	4,205	69.5								$4	$12	$30
Auctions: $56, PF-70DCam, June 2009													
2009-P	39,840,000	498	66.3	100%	$3	$5	$15	$6	$20	$10	$30	$35	$40
Auctions: No auction records available.													
2009-P, Satin Finish	784,614	268	67.1	100%	$0.50	$1	$2	$3	$8	$10	—	—	—
Auctions: No auction records available.													
2009-D	46,800,000	436	66.3	100%	$3	$5	$20	$7	$25	$12	$35	$40	$60
Auctions: No auction records available.													
2009-D, Satin Finish	784,614	258	67.2	100%	$0.50	$1	$2	$3	$8	$10	—	—	—
Auctions: No auction records available.													
2009-S, Proof	2,179,867	6,327	69.3								$4	$12	$30
Auctions: $79, PF-70UCam, November 2009													
2010-P	260,640,000	178	66.4	100%	$0.25	$0.50	$4	$3	$8	$8	$12	$20	$35
Auctions: $15, MS-67FS, June 2013													
2010-P, Satin Finish	583,897	89	66.9	100%	$0.50	$1	$2	$3	$8	$10	—	—	—
Auctions: No auction records available.													
2010-D	229,920,000	221	66.6	100%	$0.25	$0.50	$5	$4	$9	$9	$24	$30	$55
Auctions: No auction records available.													
2010-D, Satin Finish	583,897	109	67.4	100%	$0.50	$1	$2	$3	$8	$10	—	—	—
Auctions: No auction records available.													

	Mintage	Cert	Avg	%MS	MS-63	MS-65	MS-65FS	MS-66	MS-66FS	MS-67	MS-67FS	MS-68FS	MS-69FS
											PF-65	PF-67	PF-69DC
2010-S, Proof	1,689,216	4,248	69.3								$4	$12	$30
2011-P	450,000,000	199	66.5	100%	$0.25	$0.50	$4	$3	$8	$8	$12	$20	$35
2011-D	540,240,000	259	66.5	99%	$0.25	$0.50	$5	$4	$9	$9	$24	$30	$55
2011-S, Proof	1,673,010	5,774	69.3								$4	$12	$30
2012-P	464,640,000	122	66.7	100%	$0.25	$0.50	$4	$3	$8	$8	$12	$20	$35
2012-D	558,960,000	128	66.6	100%	$0.25	$0.50	$5	$4	$9	$9	$22	$27	$45
2012-S, Proof	1,239,148	2,425	69.5								$5	$12	$30
2013-P	607,440,000	116	66.4	100%	$0.25	$0.50	$4	$3	$8	$8	$12	$20	$35
2013-D	615,600,000	98	66.6	100%	$0.25	$0.50	$5	$4	$9	$9	$22	$27	$45
2013-S, Proof	1,274,505	2,305	69.4								$4	$12	$30
2014-P	635,520,000	158	67.0	100%	$0.25	$0.50	$4	$3	$8	$8	$12	$20	$35
2014-D	570,720,000	171	67.0	100%	$0.25	$0.50	$5	$4	$9	$9	$22	$27	$45
2014-S, Proof	1,190,369	2,791	69.3								$4	$12	$30
2015-P	752,880,000	40	66.2	100%	$0.25	$0.50	$4	$3	$8	$8	$12	$20	$35
2015-D	846,720,000	67	66.3	100%	$0.25	$0.50	$5	$4	$9	$9	$22	$27	$45
2015-S, Proof	1,099,182	1,166	69.5								$4	$12	$30
2016-P	786,960,000	119	66.5	100%	$0.25	$0.50	$5	$4	$9	$9	$22	$27	$45
2016-D	759,600,000	284	66.8	100%	$0.25	$0.50	$5	$4	$9	$9	$22	$27	$45
2016-S, Proof	978,457	586	69.8								$4	$12	$30
2017-P	710,160,000	99	66.7	100%	$0.25	$0.50	$5	$4	$9	$9	$22	$27	$45
2017-D	663,120,000	180	66.6	100%	$0.25	$0.50	$5	$4	$9	$9	$22	$27	$45
2017-S, Enhanced Unc.	210,419										$20	$25	$40
2017-S, Proof	979,475	224	69.9								$4	$12	$30
2018-P	629,520,000	171	67.0	100%	$0.25	$0.50	$5	$4	$9	$9	$22	$27	$45
2018-D	626,880,000	231	66.9	100%	$0.25	$0.50	$5	$4	$9	$9	$22	$27	$45
2018-S, Proof	*899,739*	390	69.7								$4	$12	$30
2018-S, Reverse Proof (a)	*199,116*										$8	$12	$20 **(b)**
2019-P	*567,854,400*	214	67.2	100%	$0.25	$0.50	$5	$4	$9	$9	$22	$27	$45
2019-D	*527,040,000*	224	67.1	100%	$0.25	$0.50	$5	$4	$9	$9	$22	$27	$45
2019-S, Proof	*1,054,918*	2,053	69.6								$4	$12	$30
2020-P		55	66.8	100%	$0.25	$0.50	$5	$4	$9	$9	$22	$27	$45
2020-D		25	66.4	100%	$0.25	$0.50	$5	$4	$9	$9	$22	$27	$45
2020-S, Proof	*802,035*	590	69.6								$4	$12	$30
2020-W, Proof (c)	*593,978*										$12		
2020-W, Reverse Proof (c)	*412,609*	11,330	69.5								$18		
2021-P		10,099	69.4		$0.25	$0.50	$5	$4	$9	$9	$22	$27	$45
2021-D					$0.25	$0.50	$5	$4	$9	$9	$22	$27	$45
2021-S, Proof													

a. In 2018, to mark the 50th Anniversary of the San Francisco Mint's first production of Proof coins, the Mint released a special silver Reverse Proof set. **b.** Value is for PF-69. **c.** In 2020, the Mint included special nickels from the West Point Mint as premiums in each of two separate products: in the 2020 Proof Set, a 2020-W Proof nickel; and in the 2020 Silver Proof Set, a 2020-W Reverse Proof nickel.

Half Dismes
1792

AN OVERVIEW OF HALF DISMES

Half dimes or five-cent silver coins were provided for in the Mint Act of April 2, 1792. The spelling was stated as *half disme*. The latter word (likely pronounced "dime," as in modern usage, but perhaps in some places as "deem," in the French mode) was used intermittently in government correspondence for years afterward, but on coins dated 1794 and beyond it appeared only as *dime*.

President George Washington, in his fourth annual message to the House of Representatives, November 6, 1792, referred to the half disme:

> In execution of the authority given by the Legislature, measures have been taken for engaging some artists from abroad to aid in the establishment of our Mint; others have been employed at home. Provision has been made of the requisite buildings, and these are now putting into proper condition for the purposes of the establishment.
>
> There has also been a small beginning in the coinage of half-dismes; the want of small coins in circulation calling the first attention to them. The regulation of foreign coins, in correspondence with the principles of our national Coinage, as being essential to their due operation, and to order in our money-concerns, will, I doubt not, be resumed and completed.

The 1792 half dismes are studied in *United States Pattern Coins* (the hobby's standard reference on pattern coins and experimental and trial pieces), and some numismatists have traditionally referred to them as patterns. It is true that they were struck at a private shop in Philadelphia while the official Mint buildings were still in planning. However, several factors point to their status as regular circulating coins. The half disme was authorized as a federal issue by congressional legislation. Its mintage was considerable—some 1,500 or so pieces—and, as noted by President Washington, the coins were meant to alleviate the national need for small change. Furthermore, nearly all surviving examples show signs of extensive wear.

The 1792 half dismes are not commonly collected, simply because they are not common coins; only 200 to 250 are estimated to still exist. However, their rarity, the romance of their connection to the nation's founding, and the mysteries and legends surrounding their creation make them a perennial favorite among numismatists.

The 1792 half dismes used to be considered patterns by some numismatists. However, the coins circulated as currency.

HALF DISME (1792)

Designer: *Unknown (possibly Robert Birch).* **Weight:** *1.35 grams.*
Composition: *.8924 silver, .1076 copper.* **Diameter:** *16.5 mm.*
Edge: *Reeded.* **Mint:** *John Harper's shop, Philadelphia.*

Judd-7, Pollock-7,
Logan-McCloskey–1.

History. Rumors and legends are par for the course with the 1792 half disme. Martha Washington was sometimes said to have posed for the portrait of Miss Liberty, despite the profile's dissimilarity to life images of the First Lady. Longstanding numismatic tradition said that President George Washington had his own silver tableware taken to the mint factory to be melted down, with these little coins being the result. That legend has been proven fanciful, most authoritatively by researchers Pete Smith, Joel J. Orosz, and Leonard Augsburger in *1792: Birth of a Nation's Coinage.* While the Philadelphia Mint was in the planning stage (its cornerstone would be laid on July 31, 1792), dies were being cut for the first federal coinage of that year. The designer may have been Robert Birch, a Mint engraver who created (or helped create) the dies for the half disme, the disme, and other coins. The half dismes were struck in a private facility owned by saw-maker John Harper, in mid-July and in October. It is believed, from Thomas Jefferson's records, that 1,500 were made. Most were placed into circulation. The coin's designs, with a unique head of Miss Liberty and an outstretched eagle, would not be revived when normal production of the half dime denomination started at the Mint's official facilities in 1795.

Striking and Sharpness. These coins usually are fairly strongly struck, but with some lightness on Miss Liberty's hair above her ear, and on the eagle's breast. Most were struck off center to some degree. Some have what appear to be adjustment marks (which come from a planchet being manually filed to adjust its weight prior to striking); these striations might actually be roller marks from the planchet-production process.

Availability. Most of the estimated 200 to 250 surviving coins show extensive wear. Some AU and MS coins exist, several in choice and gem state, perhaps from among the eight or nine examples that Mint Director David Rittenhouse is said to have reserved for himself.

Grading Standards

MS-60 to 70 (Mint State). *Obverse:* No wear is visible. Luster ranges from nearly full at MS-60 to frosty at MS-65 or higher. Toning often masks the surface, so careful inspection is required. *Reverse:* No wear is visible. The field around the eagle is lustrous, ranging from not completely full at MS-60 to deep and frosty at MS-65 and higher.

1792. Graded MS-64.

AU-50, 53, 55, 58 (About Uncirculated). *Obverse:* Light wear is seen on the cheek and on the hair (not as easily observable, as certain areas of the hair may be lightly struck). Luster ranges from light and mostly in protected areas at AU-50, to extensive at AU-58. Friction is evident in the field, less so in the higher ranges. *Reverse:* Light wear is seen on the eagle, but is less noticeable on the letters. Luster ranges from light and mostly in protected areas at AU-50, to extensive at AU-58. Friction is evident in the field, less in the higher ranges.

1792. Graded AU-55.

EF-40, 45 (Extremely Fine). *Obverse:* The hair shows medium wear to the right of the face and on the bust end. The fields have no luster. Some luster may be seen among the hair strands and letters. *Reverse:* The eagle shows medium wear on its breast and the right wing, less so on the left wing. HALF DISME shows wear. The fields have no luster. Some luster may be seen among the design elements and letters.

1792. Graded EF-40.

VF-20, 30 (Very Fine). *Obverse:* More wear is seen on the hair, including to the right of the forehead and face, where only a few strands may be seen. The hair tips at the right are well detailed. The bust end is flat on its high area. Letters all show light wear. *Reverse:* The eagle displays significant wear, with its central part flat and most of the detail missing from the right wing. Letters all show light wear.

1792. Graded VF-30.

F-12, 15 (Fine). *Obverse:* The portrait, above the neck, is essentially flat, but details of the eye, the nose, and, to a lesser extent, the lips can be seen. The bust end and neck truncation are flat. Some hair detail can be seen to the right of the neck and behind the head, with individual strands blended into heavy groups. Both obverse and reverse at this grade and lower are apt to show marks, minor digs, and other evidence of handling.

1792. Graded F-12.

Reverse: Wear is more advanced than on a Very Fine coin, with significant reduction of the height of the lettering, and with some letters weak in areas, especially if the rim nearby is flat.

VG-8, 10 (Very Good). *Obverse:* The head has less detail than a Fine coin and is essentially flat except at the neck. Some hair, in thick strands, can be seen. The letters show extensive wear, but are readable. *Reverse:* The eagle is mostly flat, and the letters are well worn, some of them incomplete at the borders. Detail overall is weaker than on the obverse.

1792. Graded VG-10.

G-4, 6 (Good). *Obverse:* There is hardly any detail on the portrait, except that the eye can be seen, as well as some thick hair tips. The date is clear. Around the border the edges of the letters are worn away, and some are weak overall. *Reverse:* The eagle is only in outline form. The letters are very worn, with some missing.

1792. Graded G-6.

AG-3 (About Good). *Obverse:* Extreme wear has reduced the portrait to an even shallower state. Around the border some letters are worn away completely, some partially. The 1792 date can be seen but is weak and may be partly missing. *Reverse:* Traces of the eagle will remain and there are scattered letters and fragments of letters. Most of the coin is worn flat.

 Illustrated coin: The scratches on the obverse should be noted.

1792. Graded AG-3.

	Mintage	Cert	Avg	%MS	AG-3	G-4	VG-8	F-12	VF-20	EF-40	AU-50	MS-60	MS-62
1792 †	1,500	41	46.7	37%	$17,500	$32,500	$50,000	$60,000	$80,000	$115,000	$135,000	$165,000	$190,000
	Auctions: $212,750, AU-58, March 2012												

† Ranked in the *100 Greatest U.S. Coins* (fifth edition).

Half Dimes
1794–1873

AN OVERVIEW OF HALF DIMES

The first half dimes, dated 1794 and of the Flowing Hair type, were not actually struck until 1795. In that year additional half dimes with the 1795 date were made. In 1796 and 1797 the short-lived Draped Bust obverse combined with the Small Eagle reverse was used, after which no half dimes were struck until 1801. From that year through 1805, excepting 1804, the Draped Bust obverse was used in combination with the Heraldic Eagle reverse. Then followed a long span of years without any coinage of the denomination. In 1829 the laying of the cornerstone for the second Philadelphia Mint precipitated a new issue, the Capped Bust design, some examples of which were made for the ceremony. Production was resumed for circulation, and half dimes of this motif were made through 1837. In that year the Liberty Seated motif, by Christian Gobrecht, was introduced, to be continued without interruption through 1873, although there were a number of design modifications and changes during that span.

Assembling a set of the different half-dime types is a challenge for the collector. The 1794 and 1795, Flowing Hair, half dimes are fairly scarce at all levels and are quite rare in choice Mint State. Then come the Draped Bust obverse, Small Eagle reverse half dimes of 1796 and 1797. In the late 1960s, researcher Jim Ruddy found that of the various silver types (including the more famous 1796–1797 half dollars), half dimes of this type were the hardest to complete a photographic set of, from the lowest grades to the highest.

Draped Bust obverse, Heraldic Eagle reverse half dimes of the 1800–1805 years are scarce in all grades, more so than generally realized. In Mint State they are very rare, although on occasion some dated 1800 turn up (not often for the others). Finding a *sharply struck* example is next to impossible, and a collector may have to give up on this aspect and settle for one that has some weakness in areas.

Capped Bust half dimes and the several variations of Liberty Seated half dimes will pose no problem at all, and with some small amount of patience a collector will be able to find a sharply struck example in nearly any grade desired.

FOR THE COLLECTOR AND INVESTOR: HALF DIMES AS A SPECIALTY

Collecting half dimes by early die varieties of 1794–1837, and/or by dates and mintmarks (beginning with the 1838-O), has captured the fancy of many numismatists over the years. As these coins are so small it is necessary to have a magnifying glass when studying the series—something the collector of silver dollars and double eagles does not need.

One of the earlier enthusiasts in the field was Philadelphia attorney and numismatist Harold P. Newlin, who in 1883 issued *A Classification of the Early Half Dimes of the United States*. Newlin's two

The new design upon the resumption of the denomination in 1829 was created by Chief Engraver William Kneass. It is thought to have been based upon an earlier design by John Reich.

favorite varieties were the 1792 half disme and the rare 1802, and after reading his enticing prose about the desirability of each, no doubt some collectors in 1883 put both coins on their "must have" lists.

Among early half dimes the rarest and most expensive is the 1802. In 1883 Newlin listed just 16 examples known to him. Although no one has compiled an up-to-date registry, it is likely that fewer than 30 exist. Most are well worn. Other early half dimes range from rare to very rare.

Capped Bust half dimes of the 1829–1837 years are all easily available as dates, but some of the die varieties are very rare. Today, most half dimes on the market are not attributed by varieties, making the search for such things rewarding when a rarity is found for the price of a regular coin.

In 1978 the numismatic world was startled to learn that Chicago dealer Edward Milas had located an 1870-S half dime, a variety not earlier known to exist and not listed in the annual Mint reports. Other than this coin, still unique today, the dates and mints in the Liberty Seated series 1837 to 1873-S are readily collectible by date and mint, with no great rarities. There are several very curious varieties within that span, the most interesting of which may be the 1858, Over Inverted Date. The date was first punched into the die upside down, the error was noted, and then it was corrected.

FLOWING HAIR (1794–1795)

Designer: *Unknown.* **Engraver:** *Robert Scot.*
Weight: *1.35 grams.* **Composition:** *.8924 silver, .1076 copper.*
Diameter: *Approximately 16.5 mm.* **Edge:** *Reeded.* **Mint:** *Philadelphia.*

Logan-McCloskey–8.

History. Half dimes dated 1794 and 1795, of the Flowing Hair type, were all struck in the calendar year 1795, although dies were ready by the end of 1794. The Flowing Hair motif was also used on half dollars and silver dollars of the same years, but not on other denominations.

Striking and Sharpness. Many Flowing Hair half dimes have problems of one sort or another, including adjustment marks (from the planchet being filed down to proper weight) and/or light striking in some areas. On the obverse, check the hair and stars, and on the reverse the breast of the eagle. It may not be possible to find a *needle-sharp* example, but with some extensive searching a fairly decent strike can be obtained. Sharp striking and excellent eye appeal add dramatically to the value.

Availability. Examples appear on the market with frequency, typically in lower circulated grades. Probably 250 to 500 could be classified as MS, most of these dated 1795. Some searching is needed to locate choice examples in any grade. As a rule, half dimes are more readily available than are half dollars and dollars of the same design, and when found are usually more attractive and have fewer problems.

GRADING STANDARDS

MS-60 to 70 (Mint State). *Obverse:* At MS-60 some abrasion and contact marks are evident, most noticeably on the cheek and in the fields. Luster is present, but may be dull or lifeless, and interrupted in patches. At MS-63, contact marks are very few, and abrasion is hard to detect except under magnification. An MS-65 coin has no abrasion, and contact marks are so minute as to require magnification. Luster should be full and rich. Coins

1795; LM-10. Graded MS-63.

graded above MS-65 are more theoretical than actual for this type—but they do exist, and are defined by having fewer marks as perfection is approached. *Reverse:* Comments apply as for the obverse, except that abrasion and contact marks are most noticeable on the eagle at the center. The field area is small and is protected by lettering and the wreath, and in any given grade shows fewer marks than on the obverse.

Illustrated coin: This coin reveals increased olive and blue iridescence under bright light. The central weakness is typical for the striking of this die marriage.

AU-50, 53, 55, 58 (About Uncirculated). *Obverse:* Light wear is seen on the hair area immediately to the left of the face and neck, on the cheek, and on the top of the neck truncation, more so at AU-50 than at AU-53 or 55. An AU-58 coin will have minimal traces of wear. An AU-50 will have luster in protected areas among the stars and letters, with little in the open fields or on the portrait. At AU-58, most luster is present in the fields, but is worn

1794; LM-3. Graded AU-55.

away on the highest parts of the motifs. *Reverse:* Light wear is seen on the eagle's body and right wing. At AU-50, detail is lost in most feathers in this area. However, striking can play a part, and some coins are weak to begin with. Light wear is seen on the wreath and lettering. Luster is the best key to actual wear. This will range from perhaps 20% remaining in protected areas at AU-50 to nearly full mint bloom at AU-58.

Illustrated coin: Liberty's hair displays impressive detail for this grade.

EF-40, 45 (Extremely Fine). *Obverse:* More wear is evident on the portrait, especially on the hair to the left of the face and neck; the cheek; and the tip of the neck truncation. Excellent detail remains in low-relief areas of the hair. The stars show wear, as do the date and letters. Luster, if present at all, is minimal and in protected areas. *Reverse:* The eagle, this being the focal point to check, shows more wear. Observe in combination with a knowl-

1794; LM-2. Graded EF-40.

edge of the die variety, to determine the sharpness of the coin when it was first struck. Some were flat at the center at the time they were made. Additional wear is on the wreath and letters, but many details are present. Some luster may be seen in protected areas, and if present is slightly more abundant than on the obverse.

VF-20, 30 (Very Fine). *Obverse:* The hair is well worn at the VF-20 level, less so at VF-30. The strands are blended so as to be heavy. The cheek shows only slight relief, and the tip of the neck truncation is flat. The stars have more wear, making them appear larger (an optical illusion). *Reverse:* The body of the eagle shows few if any feathers, while the wings have about half of the feathers visible, depending on the strike. The leaves lack

1795; LM-8. Graded VF-30.

detail and are in outline form. Scattered, non-disfiguring marks are normal for this and lower grades. Any major defects should be noted separately.

F-12, 15 (Fine). *Obverse:* Wear is more extensive than on a Very Fine coin, reducing the definition of the thick strands of hair. The cheek has less detail, and the stars appear larger. The rim is distinct and many denticles remain visible. *Reverse:* Wear is more extensive. Now, feather details are reduced, mostly remaining on the right wing. The wreath and lettering are more worn, and the rim is usually weak in areas, although some denticles can be seen.

1794; LM-1. Graded F-12.

Illustrated coin: Two light adjustment marks on the lower left of the portrait date from the time of striking.

VG-8, 10 (Very Good). *Obverse:* The portrait is mostly seen in outline form, with most hair strands gone, although the tips at the lower left are clear. The ear is discernible, as is the eye. The stars appear larger still, again an illusion. The rim is weak in areas. LIBERTY and the date are readable and usually full, although some letters may be weak at their tops. *Reverse:* The eagle is mostly an outline, although some traces of feathers may be seen

1795; LM-9. Graded VG-8.

in the tail and the lower part of the inside of the right wing. The rim is worn, as are the letters, with some weak, but the motto is readable.

G-4, 6 (Good). *Obverse:* Wear is more extensive, and some stars may be missing or only partially visible. The head is an outline, although a few elements of thick hair strands may be seen. The eye is visible only in outline form. The rim is well worn or even missing. LIBERTY is worn, and parts of some letters may be missing, but elements of all are readable. The date is readable, but worn. *Reverse:* The eagle is flat and discernible in outline

1795; LM-8. Graded G-6.

form. The wreath is well worn. Some of the letters may be partly missing. At this level some "averaging" can be done. If the letters are stronger than usual in one area, but some are missing in another area, the coin can still qualify as G-4.

Illustrated coin: There are several adjustment marks on the obverse, but this coin lacks the bisecting obverse die crack typical of later issues struck from this die pair. The reverse die on this coin was rotated 20 degrees out of the normal alignment.

AG-3 (About Good). *Obverse:* Wear is so extensive that the coin is barely identifiable. The head is in outline form, LIBERTY is mostly gone, and the date, while readable, may be partially missing. *Reverse:* The reverse is well worn with parts of the wreath and lettering missing.

1794; LM-4. Graded AG-3.

	Mintage	Cert	Avg	%MS	AG-3	G-4	VG-8	F-12	VF-20	EF-40	AU-50	MS-60
1794	(a)	142	48.3	34%	$1,000	$1,750	$2,200	$3,000	$4,000	$7,500	$11,000	$17,500
	Auctions: $129,250, MS-65, August 2014; $5,875, EF-45, March 2015; $6,463, EF-40, August 2014; $7,638, F-12, August 2016											
1795	86,416	410	48.5	32%	$650	$1,350	$1,600	$2,000	$3,000	$6,000	$7,750	$10,000
	Auctions: $73,438, MS-66, September 2015; $58,750, MS-65, March 2015; $734, F-12, September 2015; $494, F-12, September 2016											

a. Included in 1795 mintage figure.

DRAPED BUST, SMALL EAGLE REVERSE (1796–1797)

Designer: *Probably Gilbert Stuart.* **Engraver:** *Robert Scot.*
Weight: *1.35 grams.* **Composition:** *.8924 silver, .1076 copper.*
Diameter: *Approximately 16.5 mm.* **Edge:** *Reeded.* **Mint:** *Philadelphia.*

LM-2.

History. Although the Draped Bust obverse design was used on various copper and silver coins circa 1795 to 1808, it was employed in combination with the *Small Eagle* reverse only on silver coins of 1795 to 1798—for the half dime series, only in 1796 and 1797.

Striking and Sharpness. Most 1796–1797 half dimes are weak in at least one area. Points to check for sharpness include the hair of Miss Liberty, the centers of the stars, the bust line, and, on the reverse, the center of the eagle. Check for planchet adjustment marks (these are infrequent). Denticles around the border are usually decent, but may vary in strength from one part of the border to another. Sharp striking and excellent eye appeal add to the value dramatically.

Availability. This type is fairly scarce in *any* grade; in MS-63 and finer, no more than a few dozen examples have been traced. As is advisable for other early silver types, beware of deeply toned or vividly iridescent-toned pieces whose flawed surface characters are obscured by the toning, but which are offered as MS; in truth some of these are barely better than EF.

GRADING STANDARDS

MS-60 to 70 (Mint State). *Obverse:* At MS-60 some abrasion and contact marks are evident, most noticeably on the cheek, on the drapery, and in the right field. Luster is present, but may be dull or lifeless, and interrupted in patches. At MS-63, contact marks are very few, and abrasion is hard to detect except under magnification, although this type is sometimes graded liberally due to its rarity. An MS-65 coin has no abrasion, and contact

1797, 16 Stars; LM-2, Valentine-4. Graded MS-62.

marks are so minute as to require magnification. Luster should be full and rich. Coins graded above MS-65 are more theoretical than actual for this type—but they do exist, and are defined by having fewer marks as perfection is approached. *Reverse:* Comments apply as for the obverse, except that abrasion and marks are most noticeable on the eagle at the center, a situation complicated by the fact that this area was often flatly struck. Grading is best done by the obverse, then verified by the reverse. The field area is small and is protected by lettering and the wreath, and in any given grade shows fewer marks than on the obverse.

Illustrated coin: Note the clash marks in the right obverse field, which are typical for this die variety.

AU-50, 53, 55, 58 (About Uncirculated). *Obverse:* Light wear is seen on the hair area above the ear and extending to left of the forehead, on the ribbon, and on the bosom—more so at AU-50 than at AU-53 or 55. An AU-58 coin has minimal traces of wear. An AU-50 coin has luster in protected areas among the stars and letters, with little in the open fields or on the portrait. At AU-58, most luster is present in the fields, but is worn away on the high-

1796, LIKERTY; LM-1. Graded AU-50.

est parts of the motifs. *Reverse:* Light wear is seen on the eagle's body (keep in mind this area might be lightly struck) and edges of the wings. Light wear is seen on the wreath and lettering. Luster is the best key to actual wear. This ranges from perhaps 20% remaining in protected areas at AU-50 to nearly full mint bloom at AU-58.

Illustrated coin: This is the LIKERTY variety, its fanciful name derived from the top and bottom lines of the B being defective.

EF-40, 45 (Extremely Fine). *Obverse:* More wear is evident on the upper hair area and the ribbon and on the drapery and bosom. Excellent detail will remain in low relief areas of the hair. The stars show wear as will the date and letters. Luster, if present at all, is minimal and in protected areas. *Reverse:* The eagle shows more wear, this being the focal point to check. On most examples, many feathers remain on the interior areas of the wings.

1796, LIKERTY; LM-1. Graded EF-40.

Check the eagle in combination with a knowledge of the die variety to determine the sharpness of the coin when it was first struck. Additional wear is evident on the wreath and letters, but many details are present. Some luster may be seen in protected areas and, if present, is slightly more abundant than on the obverse.

VF-20, 30 (Very Fine). *Obverse:* The higher-relief areas of hair are well worn at VF-20, less so at VF-30. The drapery and bosom show extensive wear. The stars have more wear, making them appear larger (an optical illusion seen on most worn silver coins of this era). *Reverse:* The body of the eagle shows few if any feathers, while the wings have about half of the feathers visible, depending on the strike. The leaves lack most detail

1796, LIKERTY; LM-1. Graded VF-30.

and are in outline form. Scattered, non-disfiguring marks are normal for this and lower grades; any major distractions should be noted separately.

F-12, 15 (Fine). *Obverse:* Wear is more extensive than on a Very Fine coin. Wear is particularly noticeable on the hair, face, and bosom, and the stars appear larger. About half the hair detail remains, most noticeably behind the neck and shoulder. The rim may be partially worn away and may blend into the field. *Reverse:* Wear is more extensive. Feather details are diminished, with fewer than half remaining on the wings. The wreath

1797, 13 Stars; LM-4. Graded F-15.

and lettering are worn further, and the rim is usually weak in areas, although some denticles can be seen.

VG-8, 10 (Very Good). *Obverse:* The portrait is mostly seen in outline form, with most hair strands gone, although there is some definition at the back of the hair and behind the shoulder. The ear is discernible, as is the eye. The stars appear larger still, again an illusion. The rim is weak in areas. LIBERTY and the date are readable and usually full, although some letters may be weak at their tops. *Reverse:* The eagle is mostly an outline,

1796, LIKERTY; LM-1. Graded VG-8.

with parts blending into the field (on lighter strikes). The rim is worn, as are the letters, with some weak, but the motto is readable.

G-4, 6 (Good). *Obverse:* Wear is more extensive, and some stars may be partly missing. The head is an outline. The eye is visible only in outline form. The rim is well worn or even missing in areas. LIBERTY is worn, and parts of some letters may be missing, but elements of all should be readable. The date is readable, but worn. *Reverse:* The eagle is flat and discernible in outline form, and may be blending into the field. The wreath is well

1797, 16 Stars. Graded G-4.

worn. Some of the letters may be partly missing. At this level some "averaging" can be done. If the letters are stronger than usual in one area, but some are missing in another area, the coin can still qualify as G-4.

AG-3 (About Good). *Obverse:* Wear is so extensive that the coin is barely identifiable. The head is in outline form. LIBERTY is mostly gone, as are some of the stars. The date, while readable, may be partially worn away. *Reverse:* The reverse is well worn, with parts of the wreath and lettering missing.

1796, LIKERTY; LM-1. Graded AG-3.

1796, 6 Over 5	1796, LIKERTY

1797, 15 Stars	1797, 16 Stars	1797, 13 Stars

	Mintage	Cert	Avg	%MS	AG-3	G-4	VG-8	F-12	VF-20	EF-40	AU-50	MS-60	MS-63
1796, 6 Over 5	10,230	16	52.3	63%	$1,000	$2,500	$3,250	$4,000	$5,250	$10,000	$15,000	$25,000	$40,000
Auctions: $31,725, MS-63, August 2013													
1796	(a)	93	47.0	31%	$850	$1,700	$2,000	$3,500	$5,000	$8,500	$10,000	$18,500	$35,000
Auctions: No auction records available.; $4,440, VF-30, March 2018													
1796, LIKERTY (b)	(a)	59	44.4	22%	$850	$1,500	$2,000	$3,450	$4,750	$8,500	$10,500	$16,000	$35,000
Auctions: $17,625, MS-61, September 2013; $1,586, Fair-2, October 2014; $676, Fair-2, October 2014													
1797, 15 Stars	44,527	32	44.9	16%	$850	$1,500	$1,800	$3,450	$4,750	$8,750	$10,000	$15,000	$25,000
Auctions: $70,500, MS-64, June 2014; $7,638, AU-55, October 2014; $7,638, AU-53, March 2015; $494, G-4, September 2015													
1797, 16 Stars	(c)	27	42.0	30%	$1,000	$1,750	$2,000	$3,600	$4,750	$8,750	$10,500	$16,000	$25,000
Auctions: $54,344, MS-65, June 2014; $734, Fair-2, October 2014; $1,763, Fair-2, August 2014													
1797, 13 Stars	(c)	6	39.2	0%	$1,250	$2,250	$3,500	$5,000	$6,500	$13,500	$25,000	$45,000	$70,000
Auctions: $25,850, AU-55, February 2013													

a. Included in 1796, 6 Over 5, mintage figure. **b.** A die imperfection makes the B in LIBERTY somewhat resemble a K. **c.** Included in 1797, 15 Stars, mintage figure.

DRAPED BUST,
HERALDIC EAGLE REVERSE (1800–1805)

Designer: *Robert Scot.* **Weight:** *1.35 grams.* **Composition:** *.8924 silver, .1076 copper.*
Diameter: *Approximately 16.5 mm.* **Edge:** *Reeded.* **Mint:** *Philadelphia.*

LM-1.

History. The combination of Draped Bust obverse / Heraldic Eagle reverse was used in the silver half dime series from 1800 to 1805. The obverse style, standardized with 13 stars, is the same as used in 1796 and 1797. During this span the rare 1802 was produced, and none were minted with the date 1804.

Striking and Sharpness. Most 1800–1805 half dimes are lightly struck in one area or another. The obverse stars usually show some weakness. On many coins the central details of Miss Liberty are not sharp. On the reverse the upper right of the shield and the adjacent part of the eagle's wing are often soft, and several or even most stars may be lightly defined (sharp stars show sharply peaked centers); high parts of the clouds are often weak. The area on the reverse opposite the bosom of Miss Liberty may be flat or weak, due to the metal having to flow in both directions when the coins were struck. (The area curving obliquely up and to the right of the eagle's head—exactly mirroring the curvature of the bust on the obverse—is especially prone to weakness of strike.) Denticles are likely to be weak or missing in areas. Many have Mint-caused adjustment marks, from overweight planchets being filed down to proper specifications. In summary, *a sharply struck coin is a goal, not necessarily a reality*. In this series, sharp striking and excellent eye appeal will add to a coin's value dramatically, this being particularly true for all issues from 1801 to 1805.

Availability. This is a challenging type to find with nice eye appeal. Many toned pieces have been recolored to hide flaws or to improve eye appeal. Some are porous or have other problems. The majority of pieces surviving today are dated 1800, and nearly all of the AU or finer coins are of this date.

Grading Standards

MS-60 to 70 (Mint State). *Obverse:* At MS-60 some abrasion and contact marks are evident, most noticeably on the cheek, on the drapery, and in the right field. Luster is present, but may be dull or lifeless, and interrupted in patches. At MS-63, contact marks are very few, and abrasion is hard to detect except under magnification, although this type is sometimes graded liberally due to its rarity. An MS-65 coin will have no abrasion,

1800; LM-1, V-1. Graded MS-63.

and contact marks are so minute as to require magnification. Luster should be full and rich. Coins graded above MS-65 are more theoretical than actual for this type—but they do exist, and are defined by having fewer marks as perfection is approached. *Reverse:* Comments apply as for the obverse, except that abrasion and contact marks are most noticeable on the eagle's neck, the tips of the wing, and the tail. The field area is complex—with stars above the eagle, the arrows and olive branch, and other features, there is not much open space. Accordingly, marks will not be as noticeable as on the obverse.

AU-50, 53, 55, 58 (About Uncirculated). *Obverse:* Light wear is seen on the hair area above the ear and extending to left of the forehead, on the ribbon, and on the bosom, more so at AU-50 than at AU-53 or 55. An AU-58 coin will have minimal traces of wear. An AU-50 coin will have luster in protected areas among the stars and letters, with little in the open fields or on the portrait. At AU-58, most luster is present in the fields,

1803, Large 8; LM-2. Graded AU-58.

but is worn away on the highest parts of the motifs. *Reverse:* Comments as for Mint State coins, except that the eagle's neck, the tips and top of the wings, the clouds, and the tail show noticeable wear, as do other features. Luster ranges from perhaps 20% remaining in protected areas at AU-50 to nearly full mint bloom at AU-58. Often the reverse of this type retains much more luster than the obverse.

Illustrated coin: Note the areas of rich, blue toning.

EF-40, 45 (Extremely Fine). *Obverse:* More wear is evident on the upper hair area and the ribbon, and on the drapery and bosom. Excellent detail remains in low-relief areas of the hair. The stars show wear, as do the date and letters. Luster, if present at all, is minimal and only in protected areas. *Reverse:* Wear is greater than on an About Uncirculated coin, overall. The neck lacks feather detail on its highest points. Feathers lose some detail near

1800; LM-1. Graded EF-45.

the edges of the wings, and some areas of the horizontal lines in the shield may be blended together. Some traces of luster may be seen, more so at EF-45 than at EF-40.

Illustrated coin: The obverse cud break is as struck.

VF-20, 30 (Very Fine). *Obverse:* The higher-relief areas of hair are well worn at VF-20, less so at VF-30. The drapery and bosom show extensive wear. The stars have more wear, making them appear larger (an optical illusion seen on most worn silver coins of this era). *Reverse:* Wear is greater, including on the shield and wing feathers. Star centers are flat. Other areas have lost detail as well.

1800; LM-1. Graded VF-20.

F-12, 15 (Fine). *Obverse:* Wear is more extensive than on a Very Fine coin, particularly noticeable on the hair, face, and bosom, and the stars appear larger. About half the hair detail remains, most noticeably behind the neck and shoulder. The rim may be partially worn away and may blend into the field. *Reverse:* Wear is even more extensive, with the shield and wing feathers being points to observe. The incuse E PLURIBUS UNUM

1801; LM-2. Graded F-15.

may have a few letters worn away. The clouds all seem to be connected. The stars are weak. Parts of the border and lettering may be weak.

VG-8, 10 (Very Good). *Obverse:* The portrait is mostly seen in outline form, with most hair strands gone, although there is some definition at the back of the hair and behind the shoulder. The ear is discernible, as is the eye. The stars appear larger still, again an illusion. The rim is weak in areas. LIBERTY and the date are readable and usually full, although some letters may be weak at their tops. *Reverse:* Half or so of the letters in the

1800; LM-1. Graded VG-8.

motto are worn away. Most feather details are worn away, although separation of some of the lower feathers may be seen. Some stars are faint. The border blends into the field in areas, and some letters are weak.

G-4, 6 (Good). *Obverse:* Some stars may be partly missing. The head is an outline. The eye is visible only in outline form. The rim is well worn or even missing in areas. LIBERTY is worn, and parts of some letters may be missing, but elements of all should be readable. The date is readable, but worn. *Reverse:* The upper part of the eagle is flat, and feathers are noticeable only at the lower edge of the wings and do not have detail. The upper part of the

1801; LM-2. Graded G-6.

shield is flat. Only a few letters of the motto can be seen. The rim is worn extensively, and a few letters may be missing.

AG-3 (About Good). *Obverse:* Wear is so extensive that the coin is barely identifiable. The head is in outline form. LIBERTY is mostly gone; same for the stars. The date, while readable, may be partially worn away. *Reverse:* Extensive wear is seen overall, with the rim worn away and some areas worn smooth. The eagle can be discerned in outline form, but not necessarily completely. A few stray motto letters may remain.

1800. Graded AG-3.

1800, LIBEKTY

	Mintage	Cert	Avg	%MS	AG-3	G-4	VG-8	F-12	VF-20	EF-40	AU-50	MS-60	MS-63
1800	24,000	219	44.0	23%	$600	$1,100	$1,500	$2,000	$3,000	$6,000	$8,000	$12,500	$20,000
	Auctions: $25,850, MS-64, August 2014; $4,994, AU-50, October 2014; $2,350, EF-40, November 2014; $676, EF-40, October 2015												
1800, LIBEKTY (a)	16,000	42	44.7	31%	$600	$1,200	$1,750	$2,500	$3,250	$6,200	$8,500	$14,500	$22,000
	Auctions: $31,725, MS-64, April 2014; $3,086, VF-25, October 2014; $617, Fair-2, October 2014												

a. A defective die punch gives the R in LIBERTY the appearance of a K.

1803, Large 8   **1803, Small 8**

	Mintage	Cert	Avg	%MS	AG-3	G-4	VG-8	F-12	VF-20	EF-40	AU-50	MS-60	MS-63
1801	27,760	31	35.8	13%	$600	$1,450	$1,750	$2,500	$4,000	$6,500	$10,000	$17,500	$27,500
	Auctions: $5,581, EF-40, February 2014												
1802 †	3,060	3	50.0	0%	$45,000	$100,000	$135,000	$155,000	$170,000	$225,000	$350,000		
	Auctions: $61,688, AU-58, August 2015; $3,290, VF-25, August 2016; $823, VG-8, August 2016; $541, AG-3, September 2015												
1803, Large 8	37,850	11	33.7	18%	$750	$1,250	$1,500	$2,000	$3,000	$6,500	$9,000	$14,000	$25,000
	Auctions: $7,050, AU-50, February 2014												
1803, Small 8	(b)	4	43.8	0%	$1,000	$1,750	$2,500	$3,500	$5,000	$9,000	$17,500	$60,000	$95,000
	Auctions: $5,922, EF-35, April 2013; $646, VF-20, November 2016; $999, Fair-2, October 2014												
1805	15,600	29	27.4	0%	$800	$1,450	$2,000	$2,750	$3,750	$10,000	$25,000		
	Auctions: $1,998, VF-35, August 2015; $823, VF-20, November 2016; $1,058, F-15, February 2015; $646, VG-10, July 2016												

† Ranked in the *100 Greatest U.S. Coins* (fifth edition). **b.** Included in 1803, Large 8, mintage figure.

CAPPED BUST (1829–1837)

Engraver: *William Kneass, after a design by John Reich.* **Weight:** *1.35 grams (changed to 1.34 grams in 1837).* **Composition:** *.8924 silver, .1076 copper (changed to .900 silver, .100 copper in 1837).* **Diameter:** *Approximately 15.5 mm.* **Edge:** *Reeded.* **Mint:** *Philadelphia.*

Circulation Strike   **Proof**
LM-7.   *LM-4.*

History. Half dimes of the Capped Bust design were first struck the morning of July 4, 1829, to be included in the cornerstone time capsule of the new (second) Philadelphia Mint building and, presumably, to have some inexpensive coins on hand for distribution as souvenirs. Engraver John Reich's design was not new; it had been used on half dollars as early as 1807. It was logical to employ it on the new half dime, a coin that had not been made since 1805. The new half dimes proved popular and remained in circulation for many years.

Striking and Sharpness. Striking varies among Capped Bust half dimes, and most show lightness in one area or another. On the obverse, check the hair details to the left of the eye, as well as the star centers. On the reverse, check the eagle's feathers and neck. The motto, which can be a problem on certain other coins of this design (notably half dollars), is usually bold on the half dimes. Denticles range from well defined to somewhat indistinct, and, in general, are sharper on the obverse than on the reverse.

Proofs. Proofs were struck in small quantities, generally as part of silver Proof sets, although perhaps some were made to mark the Mint cornerstone event mentioned above; facts are scarce. True Proofs have fully mirrored fields. Scrutinize deeply toned pieces (deep toning often masks the true nature of a coin, e.g., if it is not a true Proof, or if it has been cleaned or repaired). Some pieces attributed as "Proofs" are not Proofs. This advice applies across the entire Capped Bust silver series.

Availability. Finding an example in any desired grade should not be a challenge. Finding one with Full Details will take more time. Connoisseurship is required at the MS level, given the high value of these coins.

GRADING STANDARDS

MS-60 to 70 (Mint State). *Obverse:* At MS-60 some abrasion and contact marks are evident, most noticeably on the cheek, on the hair below the left part of LIBERTY, and on the area near the drapery clasp. Luster is present, but may be dull or lifeless, and interrupted in patches. At MS-63, contact marks are very few, and abrasion is hard to detect except under magnification. An MS-65 coin has no abrasion, and has contact marks so

1830; LM-3. Graded MS-65.

minute as to require magnification. Luster should be full and rich, usually more so on half dimes than larger coins of the Capped Bust type. Grades above MS-65 are seen now and again, and are defined by having fewer marks as perfection is approached. *Reverse:* Comments apply as for the obverse, except that abrasion and contact marks are most noticeable on the eagle's neck, the top of the wings, the claws, and the flat band that surrounds the incuse motto. The field is mainly protected by design elements and does not show abrasion as much as does the obverse.

AU-50, 53, 55, 58 (About Uncirculated). *Obverse:* Light wear is seen on the cap, the hair below LIBERTY, the hair near the clasp, and the drapery at the bosom. At AU-58, the luster is extensive except in the open area of the field, especially to the right. At AU–50 and 53, luster remains only in protected areas. *Reverse:* Wear is visible on the eagle's neck, the top of the wings, the claws, and the flat band above the eagle. An AU-58 coin will have

1829; LM-4. Graded AU-58.

nearly full luster. At AU-50 and 53, there will still be significant luster, more than on the obverse.

   Illustrated coin: Note the rings of toning on the obverse, displaying russet, cobalt, and rosy iridescence.

EF-40, 45 (Extremely Fine). *Obverse:* Wear is most noticeable on the higher areas of the hair. The cap shows more wear, as does the cheek. Stars, usually protected by the rim, still show their centers (unless lightly struck). Luster, if present, is in protected areas among the star points and close to the portrait. *Reverse:* The wings show wear on the higher areas of the feathers, and some details are lost. Feathers in the neck are light. The eagle's claws and the

1837, Small 5 C.; LM-4. Graded EF-40.

leaves show wear. Luster may be present in protected areas, even if there is little or none on the obverse.

VF-20, 30 (Very Fine). *Obverse:* Wear has caused most of the hair to be combined into thick tresses without delicate features. The curl on the neck is flat. Most stars, unless they were weakly struck, retain their interior lines. *Reverse:* Wear is most evident on the eagle's neck, to the left of the shield, and on the leaves and claws. Most feathers in the wing remain distinct.

1834; LM-2. Graded VF-30.

F-12, 15 (Fine). *Obverse:* Wear is more extensive, with much of the hair blended together. The drapery is indistinct at its upper edge. Stars have lost some detail at the centers, but still have relief (are not flat). *Reverse:* Wear is more extensive, now with only about half of the feathers remaining on the wings. Some of the horizontal lines in the shield may be worn away.

1830; LM-6. Graded F-12.

VG-8, 10 (Very Good). *Obverse:* The hair is less distinct, with the area surrounding the face blended into the facial features. LIBERTY is complete, but weak in areas. The stars are nearly flat, although some interior detail can be seen on certain strikings. *Reverse:* Feathers are fewer and mostly appear on the right wing. Other details are weaker. All lettering remains easily visible.

1829. Graded VG-8.

G-4, 6 (Good). *Obverse:* The portrait is mostly in outline, with few interior details discernible. LIBERTY may still be readable or may be partially worn away, depending on the variety. Stars are flat at their centers. *Reverse:* The eagle mostly is in outline form, although some feathers can be seen in the right wing. All letters around the border are clear. E PLURIBUS UNUM may be weak, sometimes with a few letters worn away.

1829; LM-8. Graded G-6.

AG-3 (About Good). *Obverse:* The portrait is an outline, although traces of LIBERTY can still be seen. The rim is worn down, and some stars are weak. The date remains clear. *Reverse:* The reverse shows more wear overall than the obverse, with the rim indistinct in areas and many letters worn away.

1835, Small Date, Large 5 C. Graded AG-3.

PF-60 to 70 (Proof). *Obverse and Reverse:* Proofs that are extensively cleaned and have many hairlines, or that are dull and grainy, are lower level, such as PF–60 to 62. These are not of great interest to specialists unless they are of rare die varieties (such as 1829, LM–1 to 3, described in the image caption). With medium hairlines, an assigned grade of PF-64 may be in order, and with relatively few hairlines, gem PF-65. PF-66 should have

1829; LM-2, V-3. Graded PF-67+.

hairlines so delicate that magnification is needed to see them. Above that, a Proof should be free of such lines. Grading is highly subjective with early Proofs, and eye appeal also is a factor.

Illustrated coin: Stunning in sharpness of strike and attractiveness of toning, this coin is the finest-known Proof of this type.

	Mintage	Cert	Avg	%MS	G-4	VG-8	F-12	VF-20	EF-40	AU-50	MS-60 PF-60	MS-63 PF-63	MS-65 PF-65
1829	1,230,000	781	56.7	61%	$50	$75	$80	$125	$175	$275	$400	$925	$3,000
Auctions: $881, MS-63, October 2015; $705, MS-63, January 2015; $353, MS-60, June 2015; $329, AU-58, September 2015													
1829, Proof	20–30	8	64.4								$4,500	$10,000	$35,000
Auctions: $36,719, PF-65Cam, January 2014													
1830	1,240,000	693	56.0	62%	$50	$65	$85	$125	$175	$275	$400	$875	$2,500
Auctions: $852, MS-63, October 2015; $646, MS-62, February 2015; $400, MS-60, May 2015; $353, AU-58, August 2015													
1830, Proof	10–15	4	64.5								$6,500	$15,000	$37,000
Auctions: $49,938, PF-66, September 2013; $30,550, PF-64, August 2014													
1831	1,242,700	855	58.1	66%	$50	$65	$85	$125	$175	$250	$400	$875	$2,500
Auctions: $564, MS-62, June 2015; $376, MS-61, October 2015; $259, MS-60, March 2015; $212, AU-58, January 2015													
1831, Proof	20–30	1	67.0								$4,500	$12,500	$35,000
Auctions: $73,438, PF-67, January 2014													
1832	965,000	1,058	56.9	64%	$50	$65	$85	$125	$175	$250	$400	$875	$2,500
Auctions: $823, MS-63, June 2015; $541, MS-62, January 2015; $376, MS-61, March 2015; $247, AU-55, March 2015													
1832, Proof	5–10	2	64.0								$6,000	$12,500	$40,000
Auctions: $19,550, PF-64, March 2004													
1833	1,370,000	708	56.6	62%	$50	$65	$85	$125	$175	$250	$400	$875	$2,500
Auctions: $8,813, MS-67, January 2015; $764, MS-63, January 2015; $470, MS-62, January 2015; $282, MS-60, August 2015													

1834, 3 Over Inverted 3	1835, Large Date	1835, Small Date
FS-H10-1834-301.		

Large 5 C.	Small 5 C.

	Mintage	Cert	Avg	%MS	G-4	VG-8	F-12	VF-20	EF-40	AU-50	MS-60 PF-60	MS-63 PF-63	MS-65 PF-65
1834	1,480,000	719	57.0	61%	$50	$65	$85	$125	$175	$250	$400	$875	$2,500
Auctions: $6,463, MS-67, September 2015; $646, MS-63, October 2015; $517, MS-62, August 2015; $282, AU-55, June 2015													
1834, 3 Over Inverted 3	(a)	25	55.2	48%	$80	$100	$150	$175	$300	$500	$700	$1,200	$4,000
Auctions: $25,850, MS-67, May 2015; $5,640, MS-66, August 2016; $1,774, MS-65, February 2015; $376, AU-55, November 2015													
1834, Proof	25–35	14	65.0								$4,500	$10,000	$27,500
Auctions: $32,900, PF-66, November 2013; $12,925, PF-64, October 2014; $14,100, PF-64, August 2014													
1835, All kinds	2,760,000												
1835, Large Date and 5 C.		53	55.9	58%	$50	$65	$85	$125	$175	$250	$400	$850	$2,500
Auctions: $376, AU-58, March 2015; $188, AU-50, February 2015; $129, AU-50, July 2015; $89, EF-45, May 2015													
1835, Large Date, Small 5 C.		23	58.3	52%	$50	$65	$85	$125	$175	$250	$400	$850	$2,500
Auctions: $376, MS-62, September 2015													
1835, Small Date, Large 5 C.		31	55.4	58%	$50	$65	$85	$125	$175	$250	$400	$850	$2,500
Auctions: $165, MS-60, May 2015													
1835, Small Date and 5 C.		44	56.1	61%	$50	$65	$85	$125	$175	$250	$400	$850	$2,500
Auctions: $494, MS-62, June 2015; $400, MS-62, June 2015; $400, MS-61, July 2015													
1836, Small 5 C.	1,900,000	39	53.3	46%	$50	$65	$85	$125	$175	$250	$400	$850	$2,500
Auctions: $153, EF-45, May 2015													
1836, Large 5 C.	(b)	26	56.4	65%	$50	$65	$85	$125	$175	$250	$400	$850	$2,500
Auctions: $423, AU-58, October 2015; $201, AU-55, February 2015; $74, AU-50, February 2015; $129, EF-45, January 2015													
1836, 3 Over Inverted 3	(b)	35	52.8	51%	$80	$100	$150	$175	$300	$350	$675	$1,200	$3,750
Auctions: $329, AU-58, January 2015													
1836, Proof	5–10	2	65.5								$4,500	$10,000	$35,000
Auctions: $47,000, PF-66, February 2014													
1837, Small 5 C.	871,000	33	58.5	67%	$125	$150	$200	$275	$325	$375	$1,650	$2,500	$10,000
Auctions: $1,880, MS-63, June 2013; $660, AU-50, March 2018													
1837, Large 5 C.	(c)	30	51.5	47%	$60	$85	$125	$200	$225	$350	$450	$850	$3,500
Auctions: $5,288, MS-65, March 2015; $159, AU-50, March 2015; $118, AU-50, June 2015; $129, VF-35, February 2015													
1837, Proof (d)	5–10	0	n/a										
Auctions: No auction records available.													

a. Included in circulation-strike 1834 mintage figure. b. Included in 1836, Small 5 C., mintage figure. c. Included in 1837, Small 5 C., mintage figure. d. The 1837, Proof, coin is untraced.

LIBERTY SEATED (1837–1873)

Variety 1, No Stars on Obverse (1837–1838): **Designer:** *Christian Gobrecht.* **Weight:** *1.34 grams.* **Composition:** *.900 silver, .100 copper.* **Diameter:** *15.5 mm.* **Edge:** *Reeded.* **Mints:** *Philadelphia and New Orleans.*

Variety 1, No Stars
on Obverse (1837–1838)   Variety 1, No Stars
on Obverse, Proof

Variety 2, Stars on Obverse (1838–1853): **Designer:** *Christian Gobrecht.* **Weight:** *1.34 grams.* **Composition:** *.900 silver, .100 copper.* **Diameter:** *15.5 mm.* **Edge:** *Reeded.* **Mints:** *Philadelphia and New Orleans.*

Variety 2, Stars on
Obverse (1838–1853)   Variety 2, Stars
on Obverse, Proof

Variety 3, Arrows at Date, Reduced Weight (1853–1855): **Designer:** *Christian Gobrecht.* **Weight:** *1.24 grams.* **Composition:** *.900 silver, .100 copper.* **Diameter:** *15.5 mm.* **Edge:** *Reeded.* **Mints:** *Philadelphia and New Orleans.*

Variety 3, Arrows at Date,
Reduced Weight (1853–1855)   Variety 3, Arrows at Date,
Reduced Weight, Proof

Variety 2 Resumed, With Weight Standard of Variety 3 (1856–1859): **Designer:** *Christian Gobrecht.* **Weight:** *1.24 grams.* **Composition:** *.900 silver, .100 copper.* **Diameter:** *15.5 mm.* **Edge:** *Reeded.* **Mints:** *Philadelphia and New Orleans.*

Variety 2 Resumed, Weight
Standard of Variety 3 (1856–1859)   Variety 2 Resumed, Weight
Standard of Variety 3, Proof

Variety 4, Legend on Obverse (1860–1873): **Designer:** *Christian Gobrecht.* **Weight:** *1.24 grams.* **Composition:** *.900 silver, .100 copper.* **Diameter:** *15.5 mm.* **Edge:** *Reeded.* **Mints:** *Philadelphia, New Orleans, and San Francisco.*

Variety 4, Legend on
Obverse (1860–1873)   *Mintmark location,
1860–1869 and
1872–1873, is on the
reverse, below the bow.*   *Mintmark location,
1870–1872, is on the
reverse, above the bow.*   Variety 4, Legend
on Obverse, Proof

History. The Liberty Seated design without obverse stars, known as Variety 1, was used in the half dime and dime series only at the Philadelphia Mint in 1837 and the New Orleans Mint in 1838 (1838-O). The motif, by Christian Gobrecht, follows the obverse inaugurated on the 1836 silver dollar. Miss Liberty has no drapery at her elbow. In 1838 13 obverse stars were added, and in 1840 a restyling (drapery added to the elbow) by Robert Ball Hughes appeared. Arrows were added to the sides of the date starting in 1853, through 1855; these denoted the reduction of weight under the terms of the Act of February 21, 1853. The earlier design resumed in 1856. The reverse design stayed the same during these changes. In 1860 on the half dime the legend UNITED STATES OF AMERICA was moved to the obverse, in place of the stars. The reverse displayed a "cereal wreath" (as it was called in Mint records) enclosing the words HALF DIME.

Striking and Sharpness. For half dimes dated 1837 to 1838, check the highest parts of the Liberty Seated figure (especially the head and horizontal shield stripes) and, on the reverse, the leaves. Check the denticles on both sides. These coins are very attractive, and the starless obverse gives them a cameo-like appearance. For half dimes dated 1838 to 1859, strike quality varies widely. Most from 1838 to 1852 are sharper than later ones, but there are exceptions. (Coins with "mushy" details are especially common among the high-mintage dates of the mid- to late 1850s.) On the obverse, check the star centers, the head and center of Miss Liberty, and the denticles. On the reverse, check the wreath leaves and denticles. Excellent strike and deeply mirrored fields characterized nearly all Proofs. Points to check on coins dated 1860 to 1873 include the head of Miss Liberty on the obverse, the wreath details on the reverse (particularly at the inside upper left, above the H of HALF) and the denticles on both sides. Generally, MS coins have excellent luster, although some struck from relapped dies tend to be prooflike and with many striae. The word LIBERTY is not an infallible guide to grading at lower levels, as on some dies the shield was in lower relief, and the letters wore away less quickly. This guideline should be used in combination with other features. Generally, Proofs are well made, with deeply mirrored fields, although some of the late 1860s and early 1870s can have weak areas. Average quality in the marketplace is higher than for larger Liberty Seated denominations.

Availability. Liberty Seated half dimes are easily available as a type, but with many scarce varieties. The Philadelphia coins are easily available in all grades. The 1838-O is a rarity in true Mint State, often is over-graded, and typically has low eye appeal. Such issues as 1849-O and 1846 are extreme rarities at the true MS level. San Francisco coins, first made in 1863, are rare in MS for the first several years. Grades above MS-65 are seen with regularity, more often than the related No Stars dimes. Quality varies widely, and many MS coins are artificially toned.

Proofs. It is likely that at least several dozen Proofs were made of the 1837 half dime, although perhaps more were made of the related dime. Today, attractive examples exist and are rare. Nearly all designated as Proofs are, indeed, Proofs. If you aspire to acquire one, select an example with deep mirror surfaces. 1858 was the first year Proofs were widely sold to collectors, and an estimated 210 silver sets were distributed. (Proofs were made of earlier dates, but in much smaller numbers.) It is believed that 800 Proofs were struck of 1859, of which slightly more than 400 found buyers. From 1860 to 1873, Proof coins were made in fair quantities each year and are readily available today. The quality of Proofs on the market varies widely, mainly due to cleaning and dipping. Patience and care are needed to find a choice example.

GRADING STANDARDS

MS-60 to 70 (Mint State). *Obverse:* At MS-60 some abrasion and contact marks are evident, most noticeably on the bosom, thighs, and knees. Luster is present, but may be dull or lifeless, and interrupted in patches in the large open field. At MS-63, contact marks are very few, and abrasion is hard to detect except under magnification. An MS-65 coin has no abrasion, and contact marks are so minute as to require magnification. Luster

1844-O, Small O; V-2. Graded MS-64.

should be full and rich, except for Philadelphia (but not San Francisco) half dimes of the early and mid-1860s. Most Mint State coins of 1861 to 1865, Philadelphia issues, will have extensive die striae (from the dies being incompletely finished). Some low-mintage Philadelphia issues may be prooflike (and some may even be mislabeled as Proofs). Clashmarks are common in this era. Half dimes of this type can be very beautiful at this level. *Reverse:* Comments apply as for the obverse except that in lower Mint State grades abrasion and contact marks are most noticeable on the highest parts of the leaves and the ribbon, less so on HALF DIME. The field is mainly protected by design elements and does not show abrasion as much as does the open-field obverse on a given coin.

Illustrated coin: This coin was struck in medallic alignment, as is seen with multiple examples of 1844-O, V-2.

AU-50, 53, 55, 58 (About Uncirculated). *Obverse:* Light wear is seen on the thighs and knees, bosom, and head. At AU-58, the luster is extensive, but incomplete. Friction is seen in the large open field. At AU–50 and 53, luster is less. *Reverse:* Wear is noticeable on the leaves and ribbon. An AU-58 coin has nearly full luster—more so than on the obverse, as the design elements protect the small field areas. At AU–50 and 53, there still is significant luster, more than on the obverse.

1853, Arrows. Graded AU-50.

EF-40, 45 (Extremely Fine). *Obverse:* Further wear is seen on all areas, especially the thighs and knees, bosom, and head. Little or no luster is seen. *Reverse:* Further wear is seen on all areas, most noticeably at the leaves to each side of the wreath apex, and on the ribbon bow knot. Leaves retain details except on the higher areas.

1852-O. Graded EF-40.

VF-20, 30 (Very Fine). *Obverse:* Further wear is seen. Most details of the gown are worn away, except in the lower-relief areas above and to the right of the shield. Hair detail is gone on the higher points. *Reverse:* Wear is more extensive. The highest leaves are flat, particularly the larger leaves at the top of the wreath.

1846. Graded VF-35.

F-12, 15 (Fine). *Obverse:* The seated figure is well worn, but with some detail above and to the right of the shield. LIBERTY on the shield is fully readable, but weak in areas. *Reverse:* Most detail of the leaves is gone. The rim is worn but remains bold, and most if not all denticles are visible.

1844-O; V-6. Graded F-15.

VG-8, 10 (Very Good). *Obverse:* The seated figure is more worn, but some detail can be seen above and to the right of the shield. The shield is discernible. In LIBERTY at least three letters are readable but very weak at VG-8; a few more appear at VG-10. *Reverse:* Further wear has combined the details of most leaves. The rim is complete, but weak in areas. On most coins the reverse appears to be in a slightly higher grade than the obverse.

1846. Graded VG-10.

G-4, 6 (Good). *Obverse:* The seated figure is worn smooth. At G-4 there are no letters in LIBERTY remaining. At G-6, traces of one or two can be seen. *Reverse:* Wear is more extensive. The leaves are all combined and in outline form. The rim is clear but well worn and missing in some areas, causing the outer parts of the peripheral letters to be worn away in some instances. On most coins the reverse appears to be in a slightly higher grade than the obverse.

Illustrated coin: This is a No Stars variety.

1837, Small Date. Graded G-4.

AG-3 (About Good). *Obverse:* The seated figure is mostly visible in outline form, with no detail. The rim is worn away. The date remains clear. *Reverse:* Many if not most letters are worn away, as are parts of the wreath, though this and the interior letters are discernible. The rim can usually be seen, but is weak.

    Illustrated coin: This is a No Stars variety.

1837, Small Date. Graded AG-3.

PF-60 to 70 (Proof). *Obverse and Reverse:* Proofs that are extensively cleaned and have many hairlines, or that are dull and grainy, are lower level, such as PF–60 to 62. These are not widely desired, save for the rare (in any grade) date of 1846. Both the half dime and dime Proofs of 1837 were often cleaned, resulting in coins which have lost much of their mirror surface. With medium hairlines and good reflectivity, a grade of PF-64 is assigned, and with relatively few hairlines, gem PF-65. In various grades hairlines are most easily seen in the obverse field. PF-66 should have hairlines so delicate that magnification is needed to see them. Above that, a Proof should be free of such lines.

1873. Graded PF-66 Ultra Cameo.

1837, Small Date	1837, Large Date	No Drapery From Elbow	Drapery From Elbow
Note the flat-topped 1.	*Note the pointed-top 1.*	(1837–1840)	(Starting 1840)

	Mintage	Cert	Avg	%MS	G-4	VG-8	F-12	VF-20	EF-40	AU-50	MS-60	MS-63	MS-65
											PF-60	PF-63	PF-65
1837, Small Date	1,405,000	48	58.5	67%	$40	$55	$90	$145	$250	$450	$600	$950	$2,500
	Auctions: $7,050, MS-67, January 2015; $1,175, MS-64, July 2015; $705, MS-63, January 2015; $793, MS-62, June 2015												
1837, Large Date	(a)	37	60.8	76%	$40	$55	$80	$145	$250	$450	$600	$950	$2,500
	Auctions: $8,225, MS-67, January 2015; $3,290, MS-66, September 2015; $2,115, MS-65, September 2015; $541, MS-62, January 2015												
1837, Proof	15–20	9	64.1								$7,000	$12,500	$32,500
	Auctions: $105,750, PF-67, June 2014												
1838-O, No Stars	70,000	47	42.2	26%	$150	$215	$400	$750	$2,250	$3,250	$5,250	$10,750	$27,500
	Auctions: $21,150, MS-65, October 2015; $17,625, MS-64, October 2015; $7,050, MS-62, October 2015; $4,700, MS-62, July 2015												

a. Included in 1837, Small Date, mintage figure.

1838, Large Stars

1838, Small Stars

1840-O, No Drapery,
Normal Reverse
*Note four-leaf cluster
next to DIME.*

1840-O, No Drapery,
Transitional Reverse
*Note three-leaf cluster
next to DIME.*

	Mintage	Cert	Avg	%MS	G-4	VG-8	F-12	VF-20	EF-40	AU-50	MS-60	MS-63	MS-65
											PF-60	PF-63	PF-65
1838, No Drapery, Large Stars	2,225,000	761	59.7	71%	$24	$28	$34	$45	$125	$200	$280	$475	$1,350
Auctions: $5,523, MS-67, October 2015; $2,585, MS-66, January 2015; $999, MS-65, January 2015; $705, MS-64, January 2015													
1838, No Drapery, Small Stars	(b)	66	56.3	61%	$28	$40	$70	$175	$250	$375	$625	$1,000	$3,500
Auctions: $3,290, MS-66, October 2015; $2,820, MS-65, October 2015; $423, AU-58, October 2015; $306, AU-55, February 2015													
1838, Proof	4–5	2	64.5								$8,500	$10,500	$50,000
Auctions: $129,250, PF-67, October 2014; $182,125, PF-66, January 2014													
1839, No Drapery	1,069,150	332	59.5	70%	$25	$30	$35	$50	$100	$185	$275	$450	$1,600
Auctions: $5,405, MS-66, October 2015; $1,175, MS-65, February 2015; $400, MS-63, January 2015; $329, MS-60, October 2015													
1839, Proof	5–10	3	64.7								$12,000	$15,000	$37,500
Auctions: $27,600, PF-65Cam, April 2008; $24,000, PF-65, January 2018													
1839-O, No Drapery	1,291,600	96	50.1	34%	$25	$30	$40	$85	$200	$325	$850	$2,100	$8,000
Auctions: $16,450, MS-67, May 2015; $7,050, MS-65, October 2015; $1,998, MS-63, January 2015; $1,175, MS-62, August 2015													
1840, No Drapery	1,034,000	320	59.0	69%	$25	$30	$35	$45	$100	$185	$275	$450	$1,450
Auctions: $6,000, MS-67, August 2015; $2,585, MS-66, October 2015; $1,293, MS-65, October 2015; $470, MS-64, January 2015													
1840, No Drapery, Proof	5–10	2	65.5								$8,500	$10,500	$35,000
Auctions: $30,550, PF-64, April 2014													
1840-O, No Drapery	695,000	61	51.7	23%	$40	$55	$85	$125	$220	$475	$1,200	$3,750	$15,000
Auctions: $18,213, MS-66, June 2014; $11,163, MS-65, October 2015; $141, EF-45, July 2014; $80, VF-25, September 2014													
1840-O, No Drapery, Transitional Reverse (c)	100	0	n/a		$300	$500	$675	$800	$1,200	$2,000	$3,500	$12,000	
Auctions: $431, F-15, November 2011													
1840, Drapery	310,085	72	56.0	69%	$35	$50	$70	$140	$210	$360	$500	$900	$3,250
Auctions: $3,995, MS-65, October 2015; $1,763, MS-65, August 2015; $329, AU-55, April 2015													
1840, Drapery, Proof	(d)	0	n/a										
Auctions: No auction records available.													
1840-O, Drapery	240,000	47	45.9	13%	$45	$75	$150	$300	$750	$1,550	$10,000	$22,000	
Auctions: $9,988, AU-58, October 2015; $282, VF-30, September 2015													
1841	1,150,000	190	59.9	76%	$24	$28	$30	$35	$70	$150	$190	$325	$975
Auctions: $1,528, MS-66, January 2015; $1,175, MS-65, October 2015; $940, MS-65, October 2015; $141, AU-55, January 2015													
1841, Proof	10–20	3	64.0								$8,500	$12,500	$30,000
Auctions: $28,200, PF-65, October 2014; $46,000, PF-65, January 2008													
1841-O	815,000	67	46.1	21%	$60	$90	$140	$200	$325	$500	$1,000	$3,250	$8,000
Auctions: $8,225, MS-66, October 2015; $3,173, MS-64, October 2015; $470, AU-55, April 2015													

b. Included in 1838, No Drapery, Large Stars, mintage figure. **c.** From the *Cherrypickers' Guide to Rare Die Varieties, Vol. II* (sixth edition): "This rare transitional variety exhibits large letters and open or split buds on the reverse die, along with a small O mintmark. The key diagnostic of the variety is three-leaf clusters on either side of the word DIME, while the common reverse has four-leaf clusters." **d.** The mintage figure is unknown.

1848, Medium Date	1848, Large Date	1849, 9 Over Widely Spaced 6 FS-H10-1849-301.	1849, 9 Over 6 FS-H10-1849-302.

	Mintage	Cert	Avg	%MS	G-4	VG-8	F-12	VF-20	EF-40	AU-50	MS-60	MS-63	MS-65
											PF-60	PF-63	PF-65
1842	815,000	206	58.6	65%	$24	$26	$28	$35	$75	$150	$225	$400	$1,250
	Auctions: $3,055, MS-66, May 2015; $1,058, MS-66, October 2015; $652, MS-64, August 2015; $400, MS-63, July 2015												
1842, Proof	*10–20*	5	64.8								$8,000	$10,000	$20,000
	Auctions: $12,075, PF-64, January 2010												
1842-O	350,000	46	39.1	17%	$55	$75	$125	$215	$550	$900	$1,275	$2,250	$13,000
	Auctions: $18,800, MS-66, May 2015; $13,513, MS-66, October 2015; $1,998, MS-63, October 2015; $1,763, MS-63, October 2015												
1843	815,000	266	58.1	64%	$25	$35	$40	$60	$90	$160	$225	$400	$1,350
	Auctions: $1,645, MS-66, October 2015; $676, MS-63, October 2015; $259, MS-62, August 2015; $165, AU-58, April 2015												
1843, 1843 Over 1843, Proof	*10–20*	1	67.0								$8,000	$10,000	$20,000
	Auctions: $55,813, PF-67, January 2014												
1844	430,000	188	60.2	80%	$24	$28	$35	$55	$115	$200	$275	$500	$1,250
	Auctions: $1,058, MS-66, January 2015; $1,293, MS-65, October 2015; $823, MS-64, October 2015; $423, MS-63, October 2015												
1844, Proof	*15–25*	5	64.6								$8,000	$10,000	$22,500
	Auctions: $35,250, PF-67, February 2014; $12,925, PF-64, October 2014												
1844-O	220,000	48	33.3	10%	$80	$160	$300	$750	$1,250	$2,750	$5,000	$10,000	$25,000
	Auctions: $7,050, MS-64, October 2015; $1,293, EF-45, January 2015; $317, EF-40, January 2015; $494, VF-30, September 2015												
1845	1,564,000	273	57.3	62%	$24	$28	$30	$35	$60	$145	$225	$365	$1,150
	Auctions: $3,995, MS-67, May 2015; $1,175, MS-66, June 2015; $793, MS-64, October 2015; $306, MS-63, March 2015												
1845, Proof	*10–15*	6	65.3								$10,000	$15,000	$30,000
	Auctions: $64,625, PF-68, January 2014												
1846	27,000	68	26.0	1%	$850	$1,275	$1,650	$2,350	$4,250	$7,500	$12,500	$30,000	
	Auctions: $32,900, MS-62, October 2014; $3,840, EF-45, April 2018; $2,585, VF-30, January 2017; $1,320, VG-10, December 2017												
1846, Proof	*10–20*	8	65.5								$8,000	$12,500	$22,000
	Auctions: $35,250, PF-66, June 2014												
1847	1,274,000	248	57.1	62%	$24	$28	$35	$70	$95	$150	$225	$400	$1,000
	Auctions: $1,763, MS-66, January 2015; $940, MS-65, January 2015; $447, MS-64, April 2015; $259, MS-63, January 2015												
1847, Proof	*8–12*	2	64.5								$8,000	$10,000	$22,000
	Auctions: $38,188, PF-67, October 2014; $36,719, PF-66Cam, April 2014												
1848, Medium Date	668,000	5	53.0	60%	$25	$30	$40	$60	$95	$180	$285	$600	$3,000
	Auctions: $3,525, MS-65, May 2015; $1,293, MS-64, June 2015; $447, MS-63, February 2015; $329, AU-58, April 2015												
1848, Large Date	(e)	35	54.7	51%	$35	$50	$80	$150	$190	$350	$750	$2,500	$4,000
	Auctions: $14,100, MS-66, May 2015; $1,645, MS-62, September 2015; $470, AU-58, February 2015; $306, AU-53, February 2015												
1848, Proof	*6–8*	2	65.0								$9,000	$12,000	$22,500
	Auctions: $63,250, PF-66, July 2008												
1848-O	600,000	83	60.3	80%	$26	$30	$45	$85	$210	$325	$650	$1,400	$2,750
	Auctions: $12,338, MS-67, January 2014												
1849, All kinds	1,309,000												
1849, 9 Over 6 (f)		71	55.4	56%	$35	$50	$75	$120	$200	$350	$700	$1,200	$2,100
	Auctions: $2,585, MS-65, June 2014; $200, MS-60, September 2014												
1849, 9 Over Widely Placed 6 (g)		27	54.1	44%	$50	$70	$100	$150	$275	$380	$620	$1,400	$2,250
	Auctions: $5,405, MS-67, October 2015; $541, MS-62, March 2015; $306, MS-62, April 2015; $270, AU-58, April 2015												

e. Included in 1848, Medium Date, mintage figure. f. As noted in the *Cherrypickers' Guide to Rare Die Varieties, Vol. II* (sixth edition), Fivaz and Stanton contend that this is actually a 9 Over 8 overdate. g. The 4 of the date is at least triple punched, with one secondary 4 south and one east of the primary 4. There is also a secondary numeral east of the lower portion of the 9.

	Mintage	Cert	Avg	%MS	G-4	VG-8	F-12	VF-20	EF-40	AU-50	MS-60 / PF-60	MS-63 / PF-63	MS-65 / PF-65
1849, Normal Date		169	55.2	50%	$26	$30	$40	$58	$100	$175	$265	$750	$1,600
Auctions: $4,406, MS-67, June 2014; $270, MS-61, November 2014; $188, AU-58, November 2014													
1849, Proof	8–12	3	64.7								$8,000	$10,000	$22,500
Auctions: $22,325, PF-65, June 2014													
1849-O	140,000	58	44.6	33%	$45	$75	$145	$285	$625	$1,200	$2,175	$4,000	$8,500
Auctions: $4,465, MS-64, October 2015; $1,528, MS-61, September 2015; $1,293, AU-53, January 2015; $223, VF-30, February 2015													
1850	955,000	250	60.5	78%	$25	$30	$40	$60	$90	$180	$220	$375	$925
Auctions: $7,050, MS-67, October 2015; $1,116, MS-66, March 2015; $705, MS-65, July 2015; $494, MS-64, June 2015													
1850, Proof	8–12	3	63.7								$12,000	$20,000	$40,000
Auctions: $44,650, PF-67, May 2015; $61,688, PF-65, October 2015; $19,975, PF-64, May 2015; $17,626, PF-62, August 2016													
1850-O	690,000	75	53.3	47%	$30	$40	$60	$100	$200	$275	$675	$1,400	$5,250
Auctions: $11,456, MS-67, January 2015; $7,638, MS-66, October 2015; $1,293, MS-63, October 2015; $212, AU-50, September 2015													
1851	781,000	181	58.1	69%	$24	$26	$28	$40	$75	$140	$190	$325	$1,000
Auctions: $8,813, MS-67, May 2015; $4,171, MS-67, January 2015; $646, MS-64, October 2015; $235, MS-62, April 2015													
1851-O	860,000	128	53.9	51%	$25	$30	$35	$50	$110	$235	$450	$925	$4,200
Auctions: $5,170, MS-66, May 2015; $4,465, MS-65, October 2015; $588, MS-62, March 2015; $376, MS-61, February 2015													
1852	1,000,500	187	61.4	80%	$25	$28	$30	$40	$75	$140	$190	$325	$1,050
Auctions: $1,410, MS-66, October 2015; $705, MS-65, January 2015; $317, MS-63, March 2015; $141, AU-58, September 2015													
1852, Proof	10–15	9	64.2								$8,000	$10,000	$22,500
Auctions: $30,550, PF-65, January 2014; $19,975, PF-65, June 2015; $14,100, PF-64, October 2014													
1852-O	260,000	66	48.9	36%	$30	$40	$75	$150	$275	$500	$950	$2,250	$7,000
Auctions: $646, AU-58, August 2015; $353, AU-50, January 2015; $206, AU-50, June 2015; $84, VF-20, June 2015													
1853, No Arrows	135,000	146	58.1	74%	$60	$85	$140	$225	$325	$500	$750	$1,200	$2,000
Auctions: $2,510, MS-66, July 2015; $1,880, MS-65, September 2015; $1,175, MS-64, January 2015; $940, MS-63, January 2015													
1853-O, No Arrows	160,000	34	33.8	6%	$350	$600	$775	$1,200	$2,400	$3,850	$6,200	$12,500	$32,500
Auctions: $32,900, MS-65, October 2014; $25,850, MS-65, October 2014; $3,819, AU-55, April 2013; $1,175, VF-25, January 2015													
1853, With Arrows	13,210,020	1,451	55.7	55%	$25	$28	$30	$35	$70	$150	$200	$325	$950
Auctions: $7,638, MS-67, August 2015; $1,880, MS-66, August 2015; $470, MS-64, January 2015; $259, MS-63, January 2015													
1853, With Arrows, Proof (h)	3–5	2	62.5									$60,000	
Auctions: No auction records available.													
1853-O, With Arrows	2,200,000	120	50.5	42%	$26	$30	$40	$65	$100	$240	$350	$1,250	$3,750
Auctions: $15,275, MS-67, October 2015; $5,405, MS-66, October 2015; $376, MS-61, October 2015; $259, AU-58, September 2015													
1854	5,740,000	711	56.7	63%	$25	$28	$30	$35	$65	$150	$200	$300	$1,100
Auctions: $7,050, MS-67, October 2015; $1,645, MS-66, June 2015; $1,116, MS-65, January 2015; $494, MS-64, February 2015													
1854, Proof	15–25	10	64.6								$4,000	$7,500	$10,000
Auctions: $9,694, PF-65, August 2013													
1854-O	1,560,000	110	55.8	56%	$25	$28	$35	$45	$90	$200	$300	$900	$3,500
Auctions: $15,275, MS-67, October 2015; $4,465, MS-66, October 2015; $1,058, MS-64, October 2015; $999, MS-63, October 2015													
1855	1,750,000	264	58.4	70%	$25	$28	$30	$35	$75	$150	$210	$375	$1,650
Auctions: $8,813, MS-67, February 2015; $2,585, MS-66, July 2015; $1,293, MS-65, July 2015; $353, MS-63, August 2015													
1855, Proof	15–25	19	65.0								$4,000	$7,500	$11,500
Auctions: $21,150, PF-66, June 2014; $11,750, PF-65, October 2014; $8,519, PF-65, June 2015													
1855-O	600,000	83	57.6	61%	$30	$40	$55	$85	$200	$380	$850	$1,500	$5,000
Auctions: $4,230, MS-65, October 2015; $84, VF-35, April 2015													
1856	4,880,000	520	58.4	69%	$24	$26	$28	$35	$60	$115	$175	$285	$750
Auctions: $1,410, MS-66, October 2015; $846, MS-65, January 2015; $447, MS-63, May 2015; $212, MS-63, January 2015													
1856, Proof	40–60	22	64.7								$2,500	$4,000	$7,500
Auctions: $8,813, PF-65, October 2015; $4,230, PF-64, October 2015; $4,113, PF-64, July 2015; $3,800, PF-64, January 2018													
1856-O	1,100,000	108	53.9	31%	$24	$26	$28	$55	$135	$285	$550	$1,000	$2,250
Auctions: $3,408, MS-66, October 2015; $1,645, MS-65, October 2015; $470, AU-58, April 2015; $235, AU-55, January 2015													

h. This coin is extremely rare.

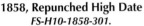

1858, Repunched High Date
FS-H10-1858-301.

1858, Over Inverted Date
FS-H10-1858-302.

1860, Obverse of 1859, Reverse of 1860
Transitional pattern, with stars (Judd-267).

	Mintage	Cert	Avg	%MS	G-4	VG-8	F-12	VF-20	EF-40	AU-50	MS-60	MS-63	MS-65
											PF-60	PF-63	PF-65
1857	7,280,000	919	58.5	71%	$24	$26	$28	$35	$60	$115	$175	$285	$700
Auctions: $6,463, MS-68, September 2015; $2,585, MS-67, September 2015; $1,058, MS-66, June 2015; $646, MS-65, January 2015													
1857, Proof	*40–60*	28	64.9								$2,000	$2,750	$4,000
Auctions: $21,738, PF-67Cam, January 2014; $7,050, PF-66, August 2014; $4,935, PF-66, May 2015													
1857-O	1,380,000	249	56.9	59%	$24	$26	$28	$45	$80	$175	$300	$500	$1,250
Auctions: $3,525, MS-67, June 2015; $1,293, MS-66, October 2015; $1,058, MS-65, October 2015; $329, MS-62, October 2015													
1858	3,500,000	827	59.1	73%	$24	$26	$28	$35	$60	$125	$170	$320	$700
Auctions: $2,800, MS-67, January 2015; $999, MS-66, September 2015; $881, MS-65, January 2015; $388, MS-64, March 2015													
1858, Repunched High Date (i)	(j)	8	44.9	13%	$35	$50	$80	$125	$200	$325	$650	$1,300	$4,000
Auctions: $135, AU-50, November 2014; $65, VF-30, July 2011													
1858, Over Inverted Date (k)	(j)	30	52.5	47%	$40	$60	$100	$150	$250	$350	$800	$1,600	$4,500
Auctions: $7,638, MS-65, February 2014													
1858, Proof	*300*	83	64.0								$750	$1,200	$3,000
Auctions: $3,055, PF-65Cam, October 2015; $823, PF-62, September 2015													
1858-O	1,660,000	256	58.4	72%	$24	$26	$30	$50	$80	$155	$240	$480	$1,150
Auctions: $517, MS-64, August 2015; $470, MS-64, October 2015; $435, MS-63, May 2015; $212, MS-61, April 2015													
1859	340,000	251	61.4	82%	$25	$26	$30	$45	$80	$135	$200	$425	$925
Auctions: $5,640, MS-68, January 2015; $3,290, MS-67, October 2015; $2,585, MS-67, August 2015; $329, MS-63, October 2015													
1859, Proof	*800*	233	64.0								$550	$1,100	$2,500
Auctions: $5,640, PF-66Cam, September 2015; $3,525, PF-66, October 2015; $2,585, PF-65, October 2015; $1,293, PF-64, March 2015													
1859, Obverse of 1859 (With Stars), Reverse of 1860, Proof (l)	*20*	6	63.5								$20,000	$35,000	$75,000
Auctions: $34,500, PF-63, August 2010													
1859-O	560,000	132	59.4	70%	$28	$35	$65	$90	$165	$225	$285	$500	$1,750
Auctions: $4,935, MS-66, October 2015; $881, MS-64, October 2015; $423, MS-63, August 2015; $282, MS-62, October 2015													
1860, Obverse of 1859 (With Stars), Reverse of 1860 (m)	*100*	55	64.4	100%					$2,500	$2,750	$3,500	$5,500	
Auctions: $5,750, MS-66, February 2012													
1860, Legend on Obverse	798,000	549	61.8	83%	$24	$25	$28	$35	$50	$85	$175	$300	$600
Auctions: $2,115, MS-67, January 2015; $881, MS-66, January 2015; $705, MS-65, January 2015; $447, MS-64, January 2015													
1860, Proof	1,000	111	64.3								$350	$550	$1,100
Auctions: $2,115, PF-66Cam, July 2014; $$3,290, PF-66Cam, April 2014; 1,528, PF-65Cam, July 2014													
1860-O	1,060,000	272	58.7	69%	$25	$28	$30	$45	$80	$120	$170	$320	$1,000
Auctions: $7,050, MS-67, August 2015; $1,116, MS-65, October 2015; $447, MS-64, June 2015; $259, MS-63, October 2015													

i. The date was first punched into the die very high, then corrected and punched into its normal location. The original high-date punch is clearly visible within the upper portions of the primary date. j. Included in circulation-strike 1858 mintage figure. k. The date was first punched into the die in an Inverted orientation, and then corrected. The bases of the secondary digits are evident above the primary digits. l. This transitional issue, made surreptitiously at the Mint for a private collector, has the new Liberty Seated die made in the old style of 1859, but with the date of 1860. The reverse is the regular die of 1860, with a cereal wreath. Classified as Judd-267 in *United States Pattern Coins* (10th edition). m. Classified as Judd-232 in *United States Pattern Coins* (10th edition), this features the obverse design of 1859 and the reverse of 1860.

1861, So-Called 1 Over 0
FS-H10-1861-301.

	Mintage	Cert	Avg	%MS	G-4	VG-8	F-12	VF-20	EF-40	AU-50	MS-60 PF-60	MS-63 PF-63	MS-65 PF-65
1861	3,360,000	701	58.1	65%	$25	$28	$30	$40	$70	$120	$160	$275	$650
	Auctions: $2,820, MS-67, October 2015; $1,763, MS-66, August 2015; $617, MS-65, August 2015; $329, MS-64, January 2015												
1861, So-Called 1 Over 0	(n)	2	63.5	100%	$35	$45	$50	$90	$200	$325	$525	$800	$1,750
	Auctions: $3,290, MS-66, October 2015; $1,645, MS-65, June 2015; $1,293, MS-64, January 2015; $588, MS-62, February 2015												
1861, Proof	1,000	91	64.4								$350	$550	$1,100
	Auctions: $6,169, PF-67, June 2014												
1862	1,492,000	781	61.6	83%	$26	$30	$45	$55	$70	$100	$160	$300	$650
	Auctions: $2,115, MS-67, January 2015; $494, MS-65, January 2015; $329, MS-64, January 2015; $259, MS-63, August 2015												
1862, Proof	550	186	64.3								$350	$550	$1,100
	Auctions: $3,760, PF-67Cam, June 2015; $1,293, PF-66Cam, October 2015; $960, PF-65, August 2015; $541, PF-63, September 2015												
1863	18,000	128	61.2	85%	$200	$280	$330	$425	$600	$750	$825	$975	$1,650
	Auctions: $9,988, MS-68, October 2015; $3,995, MS-67, January 2015; $1,645, MS-66, October 2015; $1,410, MS-66, July 2015												
1863, Proof	460	183	64.1								$350	$550	$1,100
	Auctions: $3,760, PF-67, October 2015; $4,700, PF-66Cam, October 2015; $1,293, PF-66, March 2015; $1,175, PF-65, January 2015												
1863-S	100,000	97	59.1	73%	$45	$60	$100	$200	$300	$400	$750	$1,175	$3,850
	Auctions: $4,935, MS-66, October 2015; $4,230, MS-65, October 2015; $1,645, MS-64, October 2015; $764, MS-60, June 2015												
1864	48,000	52	56.3	75%	$325	$440	$675	$850	$1,100	$1,200	$1,300	$1,475	$2,800
	Auctions: $2,585, MS-65, January 2015; $1,410, MS-64, July 2015; $646, MS-64, January 2015; $541, MS-63, June 2015												
1864, Proof	470	148	64.2								$350	$550	$1,100
	Auctions: $4,700, PF-67, August 2014; $4,259, PF-67, June 2014; $1,175, PF-66, September 2015												
1864-S	90,000	61	53.7	48%	$65	$100	$175	$250	$400	$750	$1,100	$1,850	$3,750
	Auctions: $4,935, MS-66, October 2015; $2,115, MS-64, October 2015; $224, VF-35, August 2015												
1865	13,000	59	57.1	71%	$400	$475	$550	$750	$900	$1,200	$1,300	$1,650	$2,150
	Auctions: $7,638, MS-67, October 2015; $376, G-6, February 2015												
1865, Proof	500	173	64.1								$350	$550	$1,100
	Auctions: $1,763, PF-66Cam, July 2015; $1,116, PF-65Cam, August 2015; $764, PF-64Cam, September 2015; $435, PF-63, March 2015												
1865-S	120,000	57	51.6	35%	$50	$80	$125	$200	$350	$550	$1,100	$2,450	$7,500
	Auctions: $881, AU-55, January 2015; $212, EF-40, June 2015												
1866	10,000	62	57.6	77%	$325	$400	$500	$650	$850	$1,000	$1,100	$1,225	$2,500
	Auctions: $5,640, MS-67, January 2015; $3,055, MS-66, October 2015; $940, MS-61, October 2015; $999, EF-45, January 2015												
1866, Proof	725	182	64.1								$350	$550	$1,100
	Auctions: $19,975, PF-67DCam, January 2015; $2,820, PF-65DCam, January 2015; $580, PF-64, June 2015; $541, PF-63, July 2015												
1866-S	120,000	77	57.5	57%	$45	$60	$90	$150	$225	$325	$500	$900	$4,250
	Auctions: $7,638, MS-66, May 2015; $3,760, MS-65, October 2015; $564, MS-61, April 2015; $482, AU-58, April 2015												
1867	8,000	87	59.3	82%	$450	$525	$625	$750	$850	$1,000	$1,200	$1,500	$2,250
	Auctions: $2,585, MS-66, October 2015; $8,813, MS-65, October 2015; $1,410, MS-63, September 2015												
1867, Proof	625	231	64.4								$350	$550	$1,100
	Auctions: $1,528, PF-66Cam, August 2015; $999, PF-65, January 2015; $823, PF-64Cam, July 2015; $705, PF-64, October 2015												
1867-S	120,000	70	55.7	51%	$30	$40	$60	$90	$250	$345	$575	$1,150	$3,250
	Auctions: $3,055, MS-66, February 2015; $2,585, MS-65, August 2015; $881, MS-63, January 2015; $458, AU-58, April 2015												

n. Included in circulation-strike 1861 mintage figure.

1872, Doubled Die Obverse
FS-H10-1872-101.

	Mintage	Cert	Avg	%MS	G-4	VG-8	F-12	VF-20	EF-40	AU-50	MS-60	MS-63	MS-65
											PF-60	PF-63	PF-65
1868	88,600	83	60.0	80%	$55	$65	$120	$185	$325	$475	$675	$800	$1,500
	Auctions: $4,230, MS-67, October 2015; $517, AU-58, April 2015												
1868, Proof	600	185	64.1								$350	$550	$1,100
	Auctions: $2,585, PF-66Cam, February 2015; $1,058, PF-65Cam, October 2015; $588, PF-64, September 2015; $376, PF-62, May 2015												
1868-S	280,000	161	60.3	65%	$25	$28	$40	$50	$85	$145	$320	$700	$1,650
	Auctions: $5,170, MS-66, October 2015; $1,410, MS-65, October 2015; $282, MS-62, April 2015; $212, MS-60, January 2015												
1869	208,000	110	62.3	85%	$30	$40	$50	$70	$110	$175	$275	$450	$1,100
	Auctions: $3,760, MS-67, May 2015; $1,880, MS-66, October 2015; $1,058, MS-65, July 2015; $999, MS-65, October 2015												
1869, Proof	600	222	64.2								$350	$550	$1,100
	Auctions: $2,585, PF-67Cam, June 2015; $2,115, PF-67, January 2015; $1,410, PF-66, January 2015; $588, PF-64, January 2015												
1869-S	230,000	85	59.8	75%	$30	$40	$50	$90	$150	$250	$335	$500	$3,500
	Auctions: $4,465, MS-67, May 2015; $3,290, MS-65, October 2015; $306, AU-58, April 2015; $282, AU-55, April 2015												
1870	535,000	323	59.8	76%	$24	$26	$28	$32	$45	$80	$175	$400	$900
	Auctions: $2,820, MS-67, September 2015; $949, MS-66, October 2015; $235, MS-62, February 2015; $129, MS-62, May 2015												
1870, Proof	1,000	192	64.1	98%							$350	$550	$1,100
	Auctions: $1,293, PF-66Cam, October 2015; $764, PF-64Cam, July 2015; $541, PF-63, September 2015; $259, PF-62, May 2015												
1870-S † (o)		1	63.0									$2,000,000	
	Auctions: $661,250, MS-63, July 2004												
1871	1,873,000	543	59.3	70%	$24	$26	$28	$32	$60	$80	$150	$250	$600
	Auctions: $1,410, MS-66, August 2015; $400, MS-64, May 2015; $361, MS-64, July 2015; $62, AU-55, January 2015												
1871, Proof	960	205	64.2								$350	$550	$1,100
	Auctions: $2,468, PF-67Cam, August 2015; $1,175, PF-65Cam, August 2015; $1,293, PF-66, January 2015; $823, PF-64, January 2015												
1871-S	161,000	132	60.3	65%	$25	$28	$32	$65	$80	$180	$250	$450	$1,350
	Auctions: $423, MS-64, January 2015; $235, MS-62, May 2015; $259, MS-61, April 2015; $208, AU-58, April 2015												
1872	2,947,000	468	58.6	68%	$24	$26	$28	$32	$45	$80	$150	$300	$675
	Auctions: $3,760, MS-67, May 2015; $1,469, MS-66, August 2015; $376, MS-64, May 2015; $106, AU-58, April 2015												
1872, DblDie Obv (p)	(q)	10	48.7	0%					$250	$350	$650	$1,500	
	Auctions: $89, EF-45, August 2011												
1872, Proof	950	180	64.2								$350	$550	$1,100
	Auctions: $3,525, PF-67Cam, March 2015; $1,058, PF-65Cam, October 2015; $999, PF-64Cam, October 2015												
1872-S, All kinds	837,000												
1872-S, Mintmark above bow		183	61.3	76%	$25	$28	$30	$45	$55	$100	$180	$300	$750
	Auctions: $2,468, MS-67, May 2015; $764, MS-66, July 2015; $529, MS-65, January 2015; $282, MS-63, April 2015												
1872-S, Mintmark below bow		188	61.3	76%	$25	$28	$30	$45	$55	$120	$160	$285	$675
	Auctions: $2,585, MS-67, January 2015; $1,058, MS-66, September 2015; $353, MS-64, January 2015; $282, MS-63, March 2015												
1873, Close 3 (r)	712,000	168	58.7	70%	$24	$26	$28	$32	$45	$80	$150	$350	$1,100
	Auctions: $2,820, MS-67, October 2015; $1,528, MS-66, January 2015; $165, MS-62, January 2015; $100, MS-60, May 2015												
1873, Proof	600	247	64.2								$350	$550	$1,100
	Auctions: $1,528, PF-66, March 2015; $1,469, PF-66, June 2015; $1,293, PF-65, January 2015; $580, PF-64, June 2015												
1873-S Close 3 (r)	324,000	277	61.6	81%	$24	$26	$28	$32	$65	$125	$150	$300	$675
	Auctions: $1,175, MS-66, October 2015; $646, MS-65, June 2015; $423, MS-64, August 2015; $376, MS-64, November 2015												

† Ranked in the *100 Greatest U.S. Coins* (fifth edition). **o.** The 1870-S coin is unique. **p.** From the *Cherrypickers' Guide to Rare Die Varieties, Vol. II* (sixth edition): "Doubling is evident on UNITED STATES OF AMERICA and on most elements of Miss Liberty. AMERICA is the strongest point." **q.** Included in circulation-strike 1872 mintage figure. **r.** Close 3 only.

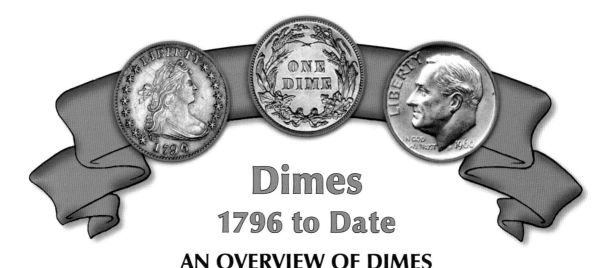

Dimes
1796 to Date

AN OVERVIEW OF DIMES

A collection of dimes ranging from 1796 to date includes many interesting issues. As a type, none are super-rare, but earlier types, combining low mintages with commonly weak striking, can be a challenge for the collector.

The 1796–1797 dime with Draped Bust obverse, Small Eagle reverse, is the rarest of the dime types by far, with fewer than 50,000 pieces minted. These hail from an era in which there was no numismatic interest in saving such coins. Finding a choice example in whatever grade desired will require time and effort.

Then comes the Draped Bust obverse, Heraldic Eagle reverse type, made from 1798 through 1807 (except for 1799). Today these are available easily enough in circulated grades, but are elusive in Mint State. Nearly all are lightly struck—another challenge. Capped Bust dimes of the 1809–1828 years also require connoisseurship to locate a sharply struck specimen. For all of these early types some compromise with perfection is required.

Later Capped Bust dimes of 1828 to 1837 can be found well struck, as can be the later variations within the Liberty Seated type. Barber, Mercury, and Roosevelt dimes are easy to find in just about any grade desired.

Proofs are most readily available from the Liberty Seated era to the present and are sometimes included in type sets, usually answering the call for sharply struck pieces, as most (but not all) were made with care.

FOR THE COLLECTOR AND INVESTOR: DIMES AS A SPECIALTY

Dimes have been a very popular denomination to collect on a systematic basis. Generally, interest is separated into different eras. Those of the early years, the Draped Bust and Capped Bust issues, 1796 to 1837, are enthusiastically sought not only for dates and major varieties (as, for example, those listed in the charts to follow), but also by more rarefied die varieties. Aficionados use the book *Early United States Dimes, 1796–1837*, whose listings are by JR numbers, for John Reich, the designer of the Capped Bust silver issues. The

Controversy over Chief Engraver John R. Sinnock's design arose after claims that Sinnock had borrowed his design from Selma Burke's bas relief, as seen at the Recorder of Deeds building in Washington, D.C.

John Reich Collectors Society (www.jrcs.org), publisher of the *John Reich Journal*, serves as a forum for the exchange of ideas and new information.

Among early varieties, the 1796; 1797, 16 Stars; and 1797, 13 Stars, are each rare in all grades. Dimes with the Heraldic Eagle reverse, 1798–1807, are generally scarce, but not prohibitively rare, although Mint State coins are elusive. Among the reverse dies some were shared with contemporary quarter eagles of like design and diameter—feasible as there is no indication of denomination on them. Indeed, there was no mark of value on any dime until 1809.

Among Classic Head dimes of the 1809–1828 years, the 1822 is the key date and is especially rare in high grades. Among the modified Classic Head dimes of 1829–1837, all varieties listed in this book are available without difficulty. An example of how a newly discovered variety can be considered unique or exceedingly rare, and later be recognized as plentiful, is provided by the 1830, 30 Over 29, overdate, first publicized by Don Taxay in 1970 in *Scott's Comprehensive Catalogue of United States Coinage* (cover-dated 1971). The overdate was then considered one of a kind, but since then dozens more have been identified.

Liberty Seated dimes of the various varieties have been a popular specialty over a long period of time. There are no impossible rarities except for the unique 1873-CC, Without Arrows, but certain other varieties are very hard to find, including the Carson City issues of the early 1870s.

Barber dimes can be collected by date and mint from 1892 to 1916, except for the 1894-S, of which only 24 are believed to have been struck, with only about 10 accounted for today. The other Barber varieties range from common to scarce. Mercury dimes, 1916–1945, have an enthusiastic following. The key issues are 1916-D (in particular); 1921; 1921-D; 1942, 2 Over 1; and 1942-D, 2 Over 1. Roosevelt dimes from 1946 to date can easily be collected by date and mint and are very popular.

DRAPED BUST, SMALL EAGLE REVERSE (1796–1797)

Designer: *Probably Gilbert Stuart.* **Engraver:** *Robert Scot.*
Weight: *2.70 grams.* **Composition:** *.8924 silver, .1076 copper.*
Diameter: *Approximately 19 mm.* **Edge:** *Reeded.* **Mint:** *Philadelphia.*

John Reich-2.

History. Dimes were first minted for circulation in 1796. There are no records of publicity surrounding their debut. The coins featured the Draped Bust obverse, as used on cents and other silver coins, combined with the Small Eagle reverse. Some 1796 dimes exhibit prooflike surfaces, suggesting that they may have been "presentation pieces," but no records exist to confirm this possibility.

Striking and Sharpness. Most dimes of this type have weakness or problems in one area or another, usually more so on those dated 1797. Points to check for sharpness include the hair of Miss Liberty, the drapery lines on the bust, the centers of the stars, and, on the reverse, the breast and wing feathers of the eagle. Also check for adjustment marks. A sharply struck coin is a goal, not necessarily a reality. Sharp striking and excellent eye appeal add dramatically to the value.

Availability. This is the rarest and most expensive type in the dime series. Within any desired grade, examples should be selected with great care, as many have problems of one sort or another. MS coins are especially rare; when seen they are usually dated 1796. Dimes of 1797 are much rarer in all grades, and nearly impossible to find in MS-63 or finer.

GRADING STANDARDS

MS-60 to 70 (Mint State). *Obverse:* At MS-60, some abrasion and contact marks are evident, most noticeably on the cheek, the drapery, and the right field. Luster is present, but may be dull or lifeless, and interrupted in patches. At MS-63, contact marks are very few, and abrasion is hard to detect except under magnification, although this type is sometimes graded liberally due to its rarity. An MS-65 coin has no abrasion, and contact

1796; JR-3. Graded MS-63.

marks are so minute as to require magnification. Luster should be full and rich. Coins graded above MS-65 are more theoretical than actual for this type—but they do exist, and are defined by having fewer marks as perfection is approached. *Reverse:* Comments apply as for the obverse, except that abrasion and marks are most noticeable on the eagle at the center, a situation complicated by the fact that this area was sometimes lightly struck. The field area is small and is protected by lettering and the wreath, and in any given grade shows fewer marks than on the obverse.

   Illustrated coin: This coin is one of only two known with this triangular rim break on the reverse. The dies were likely discarded shortly after the break occurred. Also note the die break from the rim break to the eagle's left wing.

AU-50, 53, 55, 58 (About Uncirculated). *Obverse:* Light wear is seen on the hair area above the ear and extending to left of the forehead, on the ribbon, and on the bosom, more so at AU-50 than at AU–53 or 55. An AU-58 coin has minimal traces of wear. An AU-50 coin has luster in protected areas among the stars and letters, with little in the open fields or on the portrait. At AU-58, most luster is present in the fields, but is worn

1796; JR-3. Graded AU-50.

away on the highest parts of the motifs. Generally, grading guidelines for this dime type follow those of the related half dimes. *Reverse:* Light wear is seen on the eagle's body (keep in mind that the higher parts of this area might be lightly struck) and the edges of the wings. Light wear is seen on the wreath and lettering. Luster is the best key to actual wear. This ranges from perhaps 20% remaining in protected areas (at AU-50) to nearly full mint bloom (at AU-58).

EF-40, 45 (Extremely Fine). *Obverse:* More wear is evident on the upper hair area and the ribbon, and on the drapery and bosom. Excellent detail remains in low-relief areas of the hair. The stars show wear as do the date and letters. Luster, if present at all, is minimal and in protected areas. *Reverse:* The eagle shows more wear, this being the focal point to check. Many feathers remain on the interior areas of the wings. Additional wear is

1796; JR-5. Graded EF-45.

on the wreath and letters, but many details are present. Some luster may be seen in protected areas, and if present is slightly more abundant than on the obverse.

Illustrated coin: Note the single adjustment mark running across the eagle's chest. Most examples of this die variety bear similar adjustment marks at varying angles.

VF-20, 30 (Very Fine). *Obverse:* The higher-relief areas of hair are well worn at VF-20, less so at VF-30. The drapery and bosom show extensive wear. The stars have more wear, making them appear larger (an optical illusion seen on most worn silver coins of this era). *Reverse:* The body of the eagle shows few if any feathers, while the wings have about half of the feathers visible, depending on the strike. At VF-30 more than half of the

1796; JR-6. Graded VF-30.

feathers may show. The leaves lack most detail and are in outline form. Scattered, non-disfiguring marks are normal for this and lower grades. Any major defects should be noted separately.

F-12, 15 (Fine). *Obverse:* Wear is more extensive than on a Very Fine coin, particularly noticeable on the hair, face, and bosom, and the stars appear larger. About half the hair detail remains, most noticeably behind the neck and shoulder. The rim may be partially worn away and blend into the field. *Reverse:* Wear is more extensive. Now, feather details are diminished, with fewer than half remaining on the wings. The wreath and lettering

1796; JR-4. Graded F-12.

are worn further, and the rim is usually weak in areas, although some denticles can be seen.

Illustrated coin: This coin falls at the low end of the Fine range.

VG-8, 10 (Very Good). *Obverse:* The portrait is mostly seen in outline form, with most hair strands gone, although there is some definition at the back of the hair and behind the shoulder. The ear is discernible, as is the eye. The stars appear larger still, again an illusion. The rim is weak in areas. LIBERTY and the date are readable and usually full, although some letters may be weak at their tops. *Reverse:* The eagle is mostly an outline

1796; JR-4. Graded VG-8.

with parts blending into the field (on lighter strikes). The rim is worn, as are the letters, with some weak, but the motto is readable.

G-4, 6 (Good). *Obverse:* Wear is more extensive, and some stars may be partly missing. The head is an outline. The eye is visible only in outline form. The rim is well worn or even missing in areas. LIBERTY is worn, and parts of some letters may be missing, but elements of all should be readable. The date is readable, but worn. *Reverse:* The eagle is flat and discernible in outline form, and may be blending into the field. The wreath is well

1796; JR-6. Graded G-4.

worn. Some of the letters may be partly missing. At this level some "averaging" can be done. If the letters are stronger than usual in one area, but some are missing in another area, the coin can still qualify as G-4.

AG-3 (About Good). *Obverse:* Wear is so extensive that the coin is barely identifiable. The head is in outline form. LIBERTY is mostly gone, same for the stars. The date, while readable, may be partially worn away. *Reverse:* The reverse is well worn with parts of the wreath and lettering missing.

1796; JR-2. Graded AG-3.

1797, 16 Stars

1797, 13 Stars

	Mintage	Cert	Avg	%MS	AG-3	G-4	VG-8	F-12	VF-20	EF-40	AU-50	MS-60	MS-63
1796	22,135	243	46.8	38%	$1,100	$2,750	$3,750	$5,000	$6,500	$9,500	$14,500	$18,000	$35,000 (a)
	Auctions: $793,125, MS-68, August 2014; $881,250, MS-67, June 2014; $32,900, MS-63, March 2015; $17,625, MS-62, September 2015												
1797, All kinds	25,261												
1797, 16 Stars		19	37.3	16%	$1,100	$2,750	$4,000	$5,000	$7,000	$9,500	$15,000	$27,500	$50,000
	Auctions: $35,250, MS-62, April 2014; $1,020, F-2, April 2018												
1797, 13 Stars		24	27.0	4%	$1,200	$2,850	$4,000	$6,500	$8,250	$16,000	$21,000	$35,000	$85,000
	Auctions: $38,188, AU-58, April 2014												

a. Value in MS-65 is $105,000.

DRAPED BUST, HERALDIC EAGLE REVERSE (1798–1807)

Designer: *Robert Scot.* **Weight:** *2.70 grams.* **Composition:** *.8924 silver, .1076 copper.*
Diameter: *Approximately 19 mm.* **Edge:** *Reeded.* **Mint:** *Philadelphia.*

JR-1.

History. Dimes of this style were minted each year from 1798 to 1807 (with the exception of 1799 and 1805). The designs follow those of other silver coins of the era.

Striking and Sharpness. Nearly all have one area or another of light striking. On the obverse, check the hair details and drapery lines, and the star centers. On the reverse, the upper right of the shield and the adjacent part of the eagle's wing often are soft, and several or even most stars may be lightly defined (sharp stars show sharply peaked centers); high parts of the clouds are often weak. Denticles are likely to be weak or missing in areas on either side. Expect to compromise on the strike; a sharply struck coin is a goal, not necessarily a reality. Certain reverse dies of this type were also used to coin quarter eagles. Sharp striking and excellent eye appeal dramatically add to a Draped Bust dime's value, this being particularly true for the dates most often seen in MS: 1805 and 1807 (which are usually weakly struck, especially 1807).

Availability. Although certain die varieties are rare, the basic years are available, with 1805 and 1807 being the most often seen. As a class, MS coins are rare. Again, when seen they are usually dated 1805 or 1807, and have areas of striking weakness. Coins of 1801 through 1804 are scarce in VF and higher grades, very scarce in AU and better.

GRADING STANDARDS

MS-60 to 70 (Mint State). *Obverse:* At MS-60 some abrasion and contact marks are evident, most noticeably on the cheek, the drapery at the shoulder, and the right field. Luster is present, but may be dull or lifeless, and interrupted in patches. At MS-63, contact marks are very few, and abrasion is hard to detect except under magnification. An MS-65 coin has no abrasion, and contact marks are so minute as to require magnifica-

1802; JR-4. Graded MS-62.

tion. Luster should be full and rich. Coins graded above MS-65 are more theoretical than actual for this type—but they do exist, and are defined by having fewer marks as perfection is approached. *Reverse:* Comments apply as for the obverse, except that abrasion and marks are most noticeable on the eagle's neck, the tips of the wing, and the tail. The field area is complex, without much open space, given the stars above the eagle, the arrows and olive branch, and other features. Accordingly, marks are not as noticeable as on the obverse.

    Illustrated coin: Attractive luster and toning increase the eye appeal and desirability of this coin, despite softer-than-average striking. More than one important 20th-century collector has called this the finest dime of its kind.

AU-50, 53, 55, 58 (About Uncirculated).

Obverse: Light wear is seen on the hair area above the ear and extending to left of the forehead, on the ribbon, and on the drapery at the shoulder, more so at AU-50 than at AU–53 or 55. An AU-58 coin has minimal traces of wear. An AU-50 coin has luster in protected areas among the stars and letters, with little in the open fields or on the portrait. At AU-58, most luster is present in the fields, but is worn

1800; JR-2. Graded AU-50.

away on the highest parts of the motifs. *Reverse:* Comments as preceding, except that the eagle's neck, the tips and top of the wings, the clouds, and the tail now show noticeable wear, as do other features. As always, a familiarity with a given die variety will help differentiate striking weakness from actual wear. Luster ranges from perhaps 20% remaining in protected areas (at AU-50) to nearly full mint bloom (at AU-58). Often the reverse of this type will retain much more luster than the obverse.

EF-40, 45 (Extremely Fine).

Obverse: More wear is evident on the upper hair area and the ribbon and on the drapery and bosom. Excellent detail remains in low-relief areas of the hair. The stars show wear, as do the date and letters. Luster, if present at all, is minimal and in protected areas. *Reverse:* The neck lacks feather detail on its highest points. Feathers have lost some detail near the edges of the wings, and some areas of the horizontal lines

1802; JR-2. Graded EF-45.

in the shield may be blended together, particularly at the right (an area that is also susceptible to weak striking). Some traces of luster may be seen, more so at EF-45 than at EF-40.

Illustrated coin: Note the die crack on the reverse from above OF to below the eagle's left foot. There is also some die clashing evident in the field behind the eagle. This reverse was used to coin dimes long after it was damaged.

VF-20, 30 (Very Fine).

Obverse: The higher-relief areas of hair are well worn at VF-20, less so at VF-30. The drapery and bosom show extensive wear. The stars have more wear, making them appear larger (an optical illusion seen on most worn silver coins of this era). *Reverse:* Wear is greater, including on the shield and wing feathers. Star centers are flat. Other areas have lost detail, as well. E PLURIBUS UNUM is complete (this incuse feature tended to wear away slowly).

1801; JR-1. Graded VF-20.

Illustrated coin: Here is a problem-free example with normal wear for this grade.

F-12, 15 (Fine). *Obverse:* Wear is more extensive than on a Very Fine coin, particularly noticeable on the hair, face, and bosom, and the stars appear larger. About half the hair detail remains, most noticeably behind the neck and shoulder. The rim may be partially worn away and blend into the field. *Reverse:* Wear is even more extensive, with the shield and wing feathers being points to observe. About half of the feathers are visible

1805; JR-2. Graded F-15.

(depending on striking). E PLURIBUS UNUM may have a few letters worn away. The clouds all seem to be connected. The stars are weak. Parts of the border and lettering may be weak.

Illustrated coin: There are some digs in the fields of both the obverse and reverse.

VG-8, 10 (Very Good). *Obverse:* The portrait is mostly seen in outline form, with most hair strands gone, although there is some definition at the back of the hair and behind the shoulder. The ear may be discernible. The eye is evident. The stars appear larger still, again an illusion. The rim is weak in areas. LIBERTY and the date are readable and usually full, although some letters may be weak at their tops. *Reverse:* Half or so of the

1798, 8 Over 7; JR-2. Graded VG-8.

letters in the motto are worn away. Most feathers are worn away, although separation of some may be seen. Some stars are faint. The border blends into the field in areas, and some letters are weak. Sharpness can vary widely depending on the die variety. At this level, grading by the obverse first, then checking the reverse, is recommended.

G-4, 6 (Good). *Obverse:* Some stars may be partly missing. The head is an outline. The eye is visible only in outline form. The rim is well worn or even missing in areas. LIBERTY is worn, and parts of some letters may be missing, but elements of all should be readable. The date is readable, but worn. *Reverse:* The upper part of the eagle is flat, and feathers are noticeable at the lower edge of the wing. Some scattered feather detail may or may not be seen. The

1807; JR-1. Graded G-4.

upper part of the shield is flat or nearly so, depending on the variety. Only a few letters of the motto can be seen, although this depends on the variety. The rim is worn extensively, and a few letters may be missing.

AG-3 (About Good). *Obverse:* Wear is very extensive, and some stars and letters are extremely weak or missing entirely. The date is readable. *Reverse:* Extensive wear is seen overall, with the rim worn away and some areas worn smooth. The eagle can be discerned in outline form, but not necessarily completely. A few stray motto letters may remain. Sometimes the obverse can be exceedingly worn (but the date must be readable) and the reverse with more detail, or vice-versa.

1803; JR-3. Graded AG-3.

1798, 8 Over 7

1798, 8 Over 7,
16 Stars on Reverse

1798, 8 Over 7,
13 Stars on Reverse

1798, Large 8

1798, Small 8

	Mintage	Cert	Avg	%MS	AG-3	G-4	VG-8	F-12	VF-20	EF-40	AU-50	MS-60	MS-63
1798, All kinds	27,550												
1798, 8 Over 7, 16 Stars on Reverse		53	50.9	55%	$350	$950	$1,450	$1,800	$2,450	$3,500	$5,000	$8,500	$18,000
	Auctions: $88,125, MS-65, November 2013; $960, G-6, January 2018												
1798, 8 Over 7, 13 Stars on Reverse		5	38.2	20%	$1,250	$2,000	$4,500	$6,500	$8,500	$12,500	$28,000	$50,000	
	Auctions: $58,750, MS-62, January 2014												
1798, Large 8		24	45.0	25%	$325	$1,000	$1,300	$1,650	$2,500	$3,750	$4,750	$9,500	$32,500 (a)
	Auctions: $70,500, MS-63, June 2014; $499, AG-3, August 2014												
1798, Small 8		4	26.8	0%	$500	$1,500	$2,500	$3,500	$6,500	$10,000	$16,000	$50,000	$70,000
	Auctions: $103,500, MS-64, January 2012												
1800	21,760	56	38.1	9%	$325	$1,000	$1,050	$1,650	$2,750	$4,000	$9,000	$20,000	$45,000
	Auctions: $352,500, MS-66, June 2014; $259, Fair-2, October 2014; $900, G-6, February 2018												
1801	34,640	37	29.1	11%	$325	$1,150	$1,250	$2,150	$3,750	$6,000	$11,000	$45,000	$60,000
	Auctions: $4,406, VF-25, February 2014; $411, Fair-2, August 2014												
1802	10,975	36	30.6	8%	$650	$1,500	$2,250	$3,000	$4,500	$7,500	$16,500	$35,000	
	Auctions: $67,563, MS-62, September 2013; $541, AG-3, September 2015												
1803	33,040	41	25.2	5%	$350	$1,100	$1,500	$1,800	$2,750	$6,000	$10,000	$60,000	
	Auctions: $35,250, AU-53, August 2013; $823, Fair-2, November 2014; $1,200, VG-10, January 2018												

a. Value in MS-65 is $85,000.

| 1804, 13 Stars on Reverse | 1804, 14 Stars on Reverse | 1805, 4 Berries | 1805, 5 Berries |

	Mintage	Cert	Avg	%MS	AG-3	G-4	VG-8	F-12	VF-20	EF-40	AU-50	MS-60	MS-63
1804, All kinds	8,265												
1804, 13 Stars on Reverse		2	54.0	0%	$2,000	$4,250	$6,000	$10,000	$15,000	$35,000	$70,000		
Auctions: $164,500, AU-55, May 2015; $48,175, EF-45, April 2013; $19,975, VF-35, August 2015														
1804, 14 Stars on Reverse		10	18.1	10%	$3,000	$6,500	$13,500	$22,500	$30,000	$55,000	$85,000		
Auctions: $367,188, MS-63, April 2013; $329,000, AU-58, May 2015; $99,875, AU-53, May 2015														
1805, All kinds	120,780												
1805, 4 Berries		301	38.5	33%	$250	$600	$1,000	$1,400	$1,850	$3,000	$3,500	$7,500	$9,000 (b)
Auctions: $49,938, MS-66, April 2014; $800, VG-10, February 2018														
1805, 5 Berries		45	29.7	18%	$250	$600	$1,000	$1,400	$1,900	$3,000	$3,750	$8,000	$17,500
Auctions: $1,998, VF-20, June 2013; $528, G-6, January 2018														
1807	165,000	290	41.6	34%	$250	$550	$850	$1,300	$1,750	$2,750	$3,250	$5,500	$9,500 (c)
Auctions: $55,813, MS-65, June 2014; $2,587, AU-53, August 2014; $317, G-4, October 2014; $643, VG-8, March 2018														

b. Value in MS-65 is $40,000. **c.** Value in MS-65 is $37,500.

CAPPED BUST (1809–1837)

Variety 1, Wide Border (1809–1828): **Designer:** *John Reich.*
Weight: *2.70 grams.* **Composition:** *.8924 silver, .1076 copper.*
Diameter: *Approximately 18.8 mm.* **Edge:** *Reeded.* **Mint:** *Philadelphia.*

Variety 1, Wide Border
(1809–1828)
JR-2.

Variety 1, Wide Border, Proof
JR-12.

Variety 2, Modified Design (1828–1837): **Designer:** *John Reich.*
Weight: *2.70 grams (changed to 2.67 grams, .900 fine in 1837).*
Composition: *.8924 silver, .1076 copper.*
Diameter: *Approximately 18.5 mm.* **Edge:** *Reeded.* **Mint:** *Philadelphia.*

Variety 2, Modified Design
(1828–1837)
JR-6.

Variety 2, Modified Design,
Proof
JR-1.

History. The wide-border dimes were struck intermittently from 1809 to 1828. The design, by John Reich, closely follows that inaugurated with the Capped Bust half dollars of 1807. New equipment at the U.S. Mint was used to make the 1828, Small Date, dimes, and those subsequent. The slightly modified design includes smaller denticles or beads in the border and other minor differences, and they are of uniform diameter. The 2 in the 1828, Small Date, dime has a square (not curled) base.

Striking and Sharpness. Many if not most Wide Border dimes have areas of light striking. On the obverse, check the star centers, the hair details, and the drapery at the bosom. On the reverse, check the eagle, especially the area in and around the upper right of the shield. Denticles are sometimes weak, but are usually better defined on the reverse than on the obverse. The height of the rims on both sides can vary, and coins with a low rim or rims tend to show wear more quickly. Most dimes of the modified design (Variety 2) are fairly well struck, with fewer irregularities of strike than those of 1809 to 1828. On the obverse, check the hair and the brooch. The stars usually are sharp, but don't overlook them. On the reverse, check the details of the eagle. The denticles usually are sharp.

Availability. There are no extremely rare dates in this series, so all are available to collectors, but certain die varieties range from rare to extremely rare. In MS, most are scarce and some rare. The dates of the early 1830s to 1835 are the most readily available. Those exhibiting a strong strike, with Full Details, command a premium, especially the earlier dates. Most have nice eye appeal.

Proofs. Proof Capped Bust dimes of 1809 to 1828 were struck in small numbers, likely mostly as part of presentation sets. As is the case with any and all early Proofs, you should insist on a coin with deeply and fully (not partially) mirrored surfaces, well struck, and with good contrast. Carefully examine deeply toned pieces (deep toning can mask the true nature of a coin, e.g., if it is not a true Proof, or if it has been cleaned or repaired). More than just a few pieces attributed as "Proofs" are not Proofs at all. Proofs were made of each year from 1828 to 1837 and are rare. Beware of "Proofs" that have deeply toned surfaces or fields that show patches of mint frost. Buy slowly and carefully.

GRADING STANDARDS

MS-60 to 70 (Mint State). *Obverse:* The rims are more uniform for the 1828–1837 variety than for the 1809–1828 variety, striking is usually very sharp, and any abrasion occurs evenly on both sides. At MS-60 some abrasion and contact marks are evident, most noticeably on the cheek and on the area near the drapery clasp. Luster is present, but may be dull or lifeless, and interrupted in patches. At MS-63, contact marks are very few, and

1831; JR-5. Graded MS-64.

abrasion is hard to detect except under magnification. An MS-65 coin has no abrasion, and contact marks are so minute as to require magnification. Luster should be full and rich. Grades above MS-65 are seen now and again, and are defined by having fewer marks as perfection is approached. *Reverse:* Comments apply as for the obverse, except that abrasion and contact marks are most noticeable on the eagle's neck, the top of the wings, the claws, and the flat band that surrounds the incuse motto. The field is mainly protected by design elements and does not show abrasion as much as does the obverse.

AU-50, 53, 55, 58 (About Uncirculated).
Obverse: The rims are more uniform for the 1828–1837 variety than for the 1809–1828 variety, striking is usually very sharp, and any abrasion occurs evenly on both sides. Light wear is seen on the cap, the hair below LIBERTY, the hair near the clasp, and the drapery at the bosom. At AU-58, the luster is extensive except in the open area of the field, especially to the right. At AU–50 and 53, lus-

1814; JR-5. Graded AU-55.

ter remains only in protected areas. As is true of all high grades, sharpness of strike can affect the perception of wear. *Reverse:* Wear is evident on the eagle's neck, the top of the wings, and the claws. An AU-58 has nearly full luster. At AU-50 and 53, there still is significant luster, more than on the obverse.

Illustrated coin: The stars on this coin are weakly struck.

EF-40, 45 (Extremely Fine). *Obverse:* The rims are more uniform for the 1828–1837 variety than for the 1809–1828 variety, striking is usually very sharp, and the wear occurs evenly on both sides. Wear is more extensive, most noticeable on the higher areas of the hair. The cap shows more wear, as does the cheek. Stars still show their centers (unless lightly struck, and *many* are). Luster, if present, is in protected areas among the star

1834, Large 4; JR-1. Graded EF-40.

points and close to the portrait. *Reverse:* The wings show wear on the higher areas of the feathers (particularly on the right wing), and some details are lost. Feathers in the neck are light. The eagle's claws show wear. Luster may be present in protected areas, even if there is little or none on the obverse.

VF-20, 30 (Very Fine). *Obverse:* The rims are more uniform for the 1828–1837 variety than for the 1809–1828 variety, striking is usually very sharp, and wear occurs evenly on both sides. Wear is more extensive, and most of the hair is combined into thick tresses without delicate features. The curl on the neck is flat. Unless they were weakly struck to begin with, most stars retain their interior lines. *Reverse:* Wear is most evident on the eagle's

1825. Graded VF-30.

neck, to the left of the shield, and on the leaves and claws. Most feathers in the wing remain distinct.

F-12, 15 (Fine). *Obverse:* The rims are more uniform for the 1828–1837 variety than for the 1809–1828 variety, striking is usually very sharp, and wear occurs evenly on both sides. (For both varieties the striking is not as important at this and lower grades.) Wear is more extensive, with much of the hair blended together. The drapery is indistinct along part of its upper edge. Stars have lost detail at the center and some may be flat. The height of

1821; JR-7. Graded F-15.

obverse rim is important in the amount of wear the coin has received. *Reverse:* Wear is more extensive, now with only about a third to half of the feathers remaining on the wings, more on the wing to the left. Some of the horizontal lines in the shield may be worn away.

VG-8, 10 (Very Good). *Obverse:* The hair is less distinct, with the area surrounding the face blended into the facial features. LIBERTY is complete, but weak in areas. Stars are nearly flat. *Reverse:* Feathers are fewer and mostly visible on the eagle's left wing. Other details are weaker. All lettering remains easily readable, although some letters may be faint.

1822; JR-1. Graded VG-8.

G-4, 6 (Good). *Obverse:* The portrait is mostly in outline, with few interior details discernible. LIBERTY may still be readable or may be partially worn away, depending on the variety (this varies due to the strike characteristics of some die marriages). Stars are flat at their centers. *Reverse:* The eagle is mostly in outline form, although some feathers can be seen in the right wing. All letters around the border are clear on a sharp strike;

1820, Large 0. Graded G-4.

some letters are light or missing on a coin with low rims. E PLURIBUS UNUM may be weak, often with some letters worn away.

Illustrated coin: This is an attractive, problem-free coin at this grade.

AG-3 (About Good). *Obverse:* The portrait is an outline, although traces of LIBERTY can still be seen. The rim is worn down, and some stars are weak. The date remains clear although weak toward the rim. *Reverse:* The reverse shows more wear overall than the obverse, with the rim indistinct in areas and many if not most letters worn away.

1811, 11 Over 09; JR-1. Graded AG-3.

PF-60 to 70 (Proof). *Obverse and Reverse:* Generally, Proof dimes of the 1828–1837 variety are of better quality than the 1809–1828 variety and have Full Details in almost all areas. Proofs of this type can have areas of light striking, such as at the star centers. Proofs that are extensively cleaned and have many hairlines, or that are dull and grainy, are lower level, such as PF–60 to 62. These are not of great interest to specialists unless they

1835; JR-4. Graded PF-65 Cameo.

are of rare die varieties. A PF-64 has fewer hairlines, but they are obvious, perhaps slightly distracting. A Gem PF-65 should have fewer still and full mirrored surfaces (no trace of cloudiness or dullness). PF-66 should have hairlines so delicate that magnification is needed to see them. Above that, a Proof should be free of such lines. Grading is highly subjective with early Proofs, and eye appeal also is a major factor.

Illustrated coin: Note the awkward mix of numerals in the date. Punches of different sizes were used, and the 3 in particular looks clumsy and large in comparison to the 8 and the 5.

1811, 11 Over 09	1814, Small Date	1814, Large Date	1814, STATESOFAMERICA

	Mintage	Cert	Avg	%MS	G-4	VG-8	F-12	VF-20	EF-40	AU-50	MS-60	MS-63	MS-65
											PF-60	PF-63	PF-65
1809	51,065	53	35.7	34%	$750	$1,000	$1,400	$2,250	$3,500	$4,500	$5,500	$8,000	$28,500
	Auctions: $940, VG-8, December 2015; $646, G-4, July 2015; $1,080, F-12, January 2018												
1811, 11 Over 09	65,180	65	39.5	26%	$225	$350	$1,000	$1,150	$1,700	$2,350	$4,000	$7,000	$27,500
	Auctions: $8,225, MS-64, February 2014; $1,058, VF-25, September 2016; $764, VF-20, November 2015; $960, F-15, January 2018												
1814, All kinds	421,500												
1814, Small Date		35	53.0	54%	$70	$115	$145	$275	$650	$1,200	$2,200	$4,250	$15,000
	Auctions: $5,875, MS-64, January 2014; $259, EF-40, October 2014; $176, F-12, August 2016												
1814, Large Date		32	46.7	47%	$65	$125	$135	$250	$650	$1,000	$2,000	$3,750	$12,500
	Auctions: $999, AU-50, June 2015; $588, EF-40, August 2015; $234, VF-25, May 2018												
1814, STATESOFAMERICA		17	42.1	41%	$225	$500	$750	$1,000	$1,650	$2,650	$4,500	$7,000	$25,000
	Auctions: $11,456, AU-58, March 2015; $1,234, VF-30, January 2015; $374, VG 10, February 2012												

1820, Large 0

1820, Small 0   1820, STATESOFAMERICA

1821, Large Date

1821, Small Date

1823, 3 Over 2

1823, 3 Over 2, Small E's

1823, 3 Over 2, Large E's

1824, 4 Over 2

1824 and 1827,
Flat Top 1

1824 and 1827,
Pointed Top 1

	Mintage	Cert	Avg	%MS	G-4	VG-8	F-12	VF-20	EF-40	AU-50	MS-60 / PF-60	MS-63 / PF-63	MS-65 / PF-65
1820, All kinds	942,587												
1820, Large 0		13	34.8	23%	$65	$115	$150	$225	$550	$675	$1,400	$2,750	$12,500
		Auctions: $1,939, AU-58, January 2015; $911, AU-53, July 2015; $764, AU-53, August 2015; $223, AU-50, May 2015											
1820, Small 0		61	38.9	23%	$65	$115	$150	$225	$650	$1,200	$1,500	$3,500	$15,000
		Auctions: $1,293, MS-60, February 2014; $564, EF-40, January 2018											
1820, STATESOFAMERICA		18	40.7	33%	$150	$300	$450	$700	$1,200	$2,000	$4,000	$6,000	$18,000
		Auctions: $1,176, EF-40, January 2015; $1,176, EF-40, February 2015; $306, F-15, August 2016; $441, F-12, August 2014											
1820, Proof	2–5	1	66.0								$12,000	$20,000	$95,000
		Auctions: $80,500, PF-66, February 2008											
1821, All kinds	1,186,512												
1821, Small Date		86	40.5	37%	$75	$115	$150	$225	$525	$1,000	$1,750	$4,000	$14,000
		Auctions: $5,581, MS-64, March 2013; $1,175, MS-60, August 2014; $764, EF-45, June 2015; $432, EF-45, March 2018											
1821, Large Date		165	32.2	18%	$75	$115	$150	$225	$525	$800	$1,700	$3,250	$12,500
		Auctions: $1,058, AU-55, July 2015; $823, AU-53, February 2015; $564, EF-45, January 2015; $153, EF-40, May 2015											
1821, Proof	5–8	3	64.0								$10,000	$20,000	$75,000
		Auctions: $55,200, PF-65, April 2005											
1822	100,000	53	27.7	26%	$2,250	$3,000	$4,250	$7,500	$9,500	$12,500	$20,000	$30,000	$70,000
		Auctions: $129,250, MS-66, February 2016; $30,550, MS-64, January 2014											
1822, Proof (a)	2–5	0	n/a								$25,000	$45,000	$150,000
		Auctions: $440,625, PF-66Cam, June 2014											
1823, 3 Over 2, All kinds	440,000												
1823, 3 Over 2, Small E's		9	34.8	22%	$100	$150	$225	$400	$700	$1,100	$1,650	$3,250	$16,500
		Auctions: $7,050, MS-65, April 2013; $288, VF-20, March 2018											
1823, 3 Over 2, Large E's		20	36.7	40%	$100	$150	$225	$400	$700	$1,100	$1,650	$3,250	$18,000
		Auctions: $7,050, MS-65, April 2013											

a. This coin is extremely rare.

1828, Large Date, Curl Base 2 (Variety 1)	1828, Small Date, Square Base 2 (Variety 2)	1829, Curl Base 2

1829, Small 10 C.	1829, Medium 10 C.	1829, Large 10 C.

	Mintage	Cert	Avg	%MS	G-4	VG-8	F-12	VF-20	EF-40	AU-50	MS-60 / PF-60	MS-63 / PF-63	MS-65 / PF-65
1824, 4 Over 2, Flat Top 1 in 10 C.	510,000	15	19.0	0%	$100	$150	$225	$400	$1,000	$1,500	$2,250	$4,000	$20,000
Auctions: No auction records available.; $168, VG-10, March 2018													
1824, 4 Over 2, Pointed Top 1 in 10 C.	(b)	2	14.5	0%	$325	$750	$1,500	$5,500	$7,500				
Auctions: No auction records available.													
1824, 4 Over 2, Proof	4–6	3	65.7								$10,000	$18,000	$50,000
Auctions: $42,550, PF-65, July 2005													
1825	(b)	148	40.2	34%	$65	$115	$150	$225	$525	$950	$1,800	$3,250	$15,000
Auctions: $823, AU-53, July 2015; $564, AU-50, June 2015; $341, VF-30, August 2015; $282, VF-20, February 2015													
1825, Proof	4–6	3	65.0								$8,000	$18,000	$40,000
Auctions: $18,400, PF-63, June 2011													
1827, Flat Top 1 in 10 C.	1,215,000	4	7.3	0%	$225	$375	$1,000	$1,800	$3,000	$4,500			
Auctions: No auction records available.													
1827, Pointed Top 1 in 10 C.	(c)	0	n/a		$65	$115	$165	$250	$525	$700	$1,400	$3,000	$12,500
Auctions: $517, AU-53, June 2015; $881, AU-50, October 2015; $541, AU-50, June 2015; $400, EF-45, October 2015													
1827, Proof	10–15	5	65.4								$8,000	$18,000	$40,000
Auctions: $120,750, PF-67, February 2008													
1828, Variety 1, Large Date, Curl Base 2	(d)	38	41.7	21%	$115	$175	$275	$650	$1,000	$1,200	$3,750	$6,000	$22,000
Auctions: $4,113, AU-58, November 2013													
1828, Variety 2, Small Date, Square Base 2	(e)	60	46.0	38%	$65	$100	$175	$250	$475	$750	$1,300	$2,500	$12,000
Auctions: $2,820, MS-63, April 2013													
1828, Proof	4–6	2	64.0								$8,500	$18,000	$35,000
Auctions: $29,900, PF-65, February 2008													
1829, All kinds	770,000												
1829, Curl Base 2 (f)		9	6.7	0%	$5,000	$7,500	$16,500	$20,000	$35,000				
Auctions: $7,638, VG-8, June 2014													
1829, Small 10 C.		60	38.6	28%	$45	$50	$55	$120	$375	$475	$1,200	$2,000	$9,000
Auctions: $764, AU-58, June 2015; $588, AU-53, July 2015; $329, AU-53, May 2015; $282, EF-45, April 2015													
1829, Medium 10 C.		9	34.2	33%	$45	$50	$55	$120	$350	$450	$1,000	$2,000	$8,500
Auctions: $717, AU-55, August 2013													
1829, Large 10 C.		19	42.2	26%	$45	$50	$55	$125	$400	$750	$2,000	$4,000	$9,000
Auctions: $259, F-12, November 2013													
1829, Proof	6–10	4	63.5								$7,500	$15,000	$35,000
Auctions: $37,375, PF-66, June 2002													

b. Included in 1824, 4 Over 2, Flat Top 1 in 10 C., mintage figure. **c.** Included in 1827, Flat Top 1 in 10 C., mintage figure. **d.** 1828, Variety 1 and Variety 2, have a combined mintage of 125,000. **e.** 1828, Variety 1 and Variety 2, have a combined mintage of 125,000. **f.** Only one working die for the 1829 dime coinage featured a curled 2, rather than the normal square-based 2. Nearly all known examples are in low grades.

1830, 30 Over 29

1830, Large 10 C.

1830, Small 10 C.

1833, Last 3 Normal

1833, Last 3 High

1834, Small 4

1834, Large 4

	Mintage	Cert	Avg	%MS	G-4	VG-8	F-12	VF-20	EF-40	AU-50	MS-60 / PF-60	MS-63 / PF-63	MS-65 / PF-65
1830, All kinds	510,000												
1830, 30 Over 29 (g)		42	50.8	40%	$55	$65	$100	$140	$400	$650	$1,300	$4,000	$20,500
Auctions: $23,500, MS-66, June 2014; $270, VF-35, December 2014; $212, VF-35, July 2015													
1830, Large 10 C.		0	n/a		$45	$55	$65	$100	$275	$500	$1,200	$2,500	$13,000
Auctions: $823, MS-61, June 2015; $200, AU-50, February 2015; $306, EF-45, July 2015; $123, EF-40, January 2015													
1830, Small 10 C.		7	43.3	57%	$45	$55	$85	$125	$375	$650	$1,200	$2,500	$10,500
Auctions: $1,221, MS-63, January 2012													
1830, Proof (h)	5–8	3	64.0								$7,500	$15,000	$50,000
Auctions: $18,800, PF-63, April 2014													
1831	771,350	437	49.1	45%	$40	$45	$50	$100	$275	$450	$1,000	$1,800	$6,000
Auctions: $999, MS-62, January 2015; $1,880, AU-58, January 2015; $646, AU-55, October 2015; $541, AU-55, June 2015													
1831, Proof	15–25	11	64.9								$7,500	$15,000	$40,000
Auctions: $58,750, PF-66Cam, January 2014; $1,560, PF-66, January 2018													
1832	522,500	403	47.5	42%	$40	$45	$50	$100	$275	$450	$1,000	$1,800	$6,000
Auctions: $646, AU-55, October 2015; $575, AU-55, October 2015; $223, EF-40, January 2015; $141, VF-30, May 2015													
1832, Proof (i)	2–5	0	n/a								—		
Auctions: No auction records available.													
1833, All kinds	485,000												
1833		478	44.8	37%	$40	$45	$50	$100	$275	$450	$1,000	$1,800	$6,000
Auctions: $1,543, AU-58, August 2015; $646, AU-55, February 2015; $353, AU-55, May 2015; $400, AU-53, February 2015													
1833, Last 3 High		33	43.6	30%	$35	$45	$50	$100	$275	$450	$1,000	$1,800	$8,500
Auctions: $17,625, MS-66, April 2013													
1833, Proof	5–10	5	65.6								$8,000	$15,000	$40,000
Auctions: $13,800, PF-64, January 2009													
1834, All kinds	635,000												
1834, Small 4		15	36.2	27%	$35	$45	$50	$100	$275	$450	$1,500	$2,250	$9,000
Auctions: $1,116, MS-62, June 2015; $940, AU-58, October 2015; $676, AU-55, July 2015; $447, AU-53, August 2015													
1834, Large 4		74	41.4	27%	$35	$45	$50	$100	$275	$450	$1,000	$1,800	$6,000
Auctions: $270, MS-60, February 2015; $447, AU-55, August 2015; $423, AU-53, May 2015													
1834, Proof	5–10	2	65.0								$7,500	$15,000	$30,000
Auctions: $35,250, PF-65, October 2014													

g. The tail of the 2 is evident to the right of the lower curve of the 3. The very top of the 9 is evident below the 0. Surface doubling from the initial 1829 punch is also evident on the 8. There are three of four known dies of this overdate; all are similar and command similar values. Today the variety is known to be more common than thought in the early 1970s, when it was first publicized. **h.** Values are for JR-6. A very few Proof versions of the 1830, 30 Over 29, dime are known. A PF-60, JR-4, sold at auction in January 2012 for $5,750. **i.** This coin is extremely rare.

	Mintage	Cert	Avg	%MS	G-4	VG-8	F-12	VF-20	EF-40	AU-50	MS-60	MS-63	MS-65
											PF-60	PF-63	PF-65
1835	1,410,000	732	45.2	37%	$35	$45	$50	$100	$275	$450	$1,000	$1,800	$6,000
Auctions: $1,058, AU-58, February 2015; $764, AU-58, January 2015; $282, EF-45, January 2015; $188, EF-40, May 2015													
1835, Proof	5–10	8	64.4								$10,000	$15,000	$35,000
Auctions: $41,125, PF-65Cam, April 2014													
1836	1,190,000	332	43.9	34%	$35	$45	$50	$100	$275	$450	$1,000	$1,800	$6,000
Auctions: $646, AU-58, July 2015; $376, EF-45, September 2015; $240, EF-45, August 2015; $200, EF-40, May 2015													
1836, Proof	2–5	2	63.5								$10,000	$15,000	$40,000
Auctions: $6,900, PF-66, September 1998													
1837	359,500	221	46.8	46%	$35	$45	$50	$100	$275	$450	$1,000	$1,800	$9,500
Auctions: $400, AU-50, May 2015; $125, VF-35, February 2015; $129, VF-25, January 2015; $123, VF-25, February 2015													
1837, Proof	2–5	1	64.0								$8,750	$15,000	$40,000
Auctions: $23,000, MS-64 Specimen, April 2010													

LIBERTY SEATED (1837–1891)

Variety 1, No Stars on Obverse (1837–1838): **Designer:** *Christian Gobrecht.*
Weight: *2.67 grams.* **Composition:** *.900 silver, .100 copper.* **Diameter:** *17.9 mm.*
Edge: *Reeded.* **Mints:** *Philadelphia and New Orleans.*

Variety 1, No Stars on Obverse
(1837–1838)

Variety 1, No Stars on Obverse,
Proof

Variety 2, Stars on Obverse (1838–1853): **Designer:** *Christian Gobrecht.*
Weight: *2.67 grams.* **Composition:** *.900 silver, .100 copper.* **Diameter:** *17.9 mm.*
Edge: *Reeded.* **Mints:** *Philadelphia, New Orleans, and San Francisco.*

Variety 2, Stars on Obverse
(1838–1853)

Mintmark location,
1837–1860 (Variety 2),
is on the reverse,
above the bow.

Variety 2, Stars on Obverse,
Proof

Variety 3, Stars on Obverse, Arrows at Date, Reduced Weight (1853–1855):
Designer: *Christian Gobrecht.* **Weight:** *2.49 grams.* **Composition:** *.900 silver, .100 copper.*
Diameter: *17.9 mm.* **Edge:** *Reeded.* **Mints:** *Philadelphia, New Orleans, and San Francisco.*

Variety 3, Stars on Obverse,
Arrows at Date, Reduced
Weight (1853–1855)

Variety 3, Stars on Obverse,
Arrows at Date, Reduced
Weight, Proof

Variety 2 Resumed, With Weight Standard of Variety 3 (1856–1860):
Designer: *Christian Gobrecht.* **Weight:** *2.49 grams.* **Composition:** *.900 silver, .100 copper.*
Diameter: *17.9 mm.* **Edge:** *Reeded.* **Mints:** *Philadelphia, New Orleans, and San Francisco.*

Variety 2 Resumed,
Weight Standard of Variety 3
(1856–1860)

Variety 2 Resumed, Weight
Standard of Variety 3, Proof

Variety 4, Legend on Obverse (1860–1873): **Designer:** *Christian Gobrecht.*
Weight: *2.49 grams.* **Composition:** *.900 silver, .100 copper.* **Diameter:** *17.9 mm.*
Edge: *Reeded.* **Mints:** *Philadelphia, New Orleans, San Francisco, and Carson City.*

Variety 4, Legend on Obverse
(1860–1873)

*Mintmark location,
1860 (Variety 4)–1891,
is on the reverse,
below the bow.*

Variety 4, Legend
on Obverse, Proof

Variety 5, Legend on Obverse, Arrows at Date, Increased Weight (1873–1874):
Designer: *Christian Gobrecht.* **Weight:** *2.50 grams.* **Composition:** *.900 silver, .100 copper.*
Diameter: *17.9 mm.* **Edge:** *Reeded.* **Mints:** *Philadelphia, New Orleans, San Francisco, and Carson City.*

Variety 5, Legend on Obverse,
Arrows at Date, Increased
Weight (1873–1874)

Variety 5, Legend on Obverse,
Increased Weight, Proof

Variety 4 Resumed, With Weight Standard Variety of 5 (1875–1891):
Designer: *Christian Gobrecht.* **Weight:** *2.50 grams.* **Composition:** *.900 silver, .100 copper.*
Diameter: *17.9 mm.* **Edge:** *Reeded.* **Mints:** *Philadelphia, New Orleans, San Francisco, and Carson City.*

Variety 4 Resumed,
Weight Standard Variety of 5
(1875–1891)

Variety 4 Resumed, Weight
Standard Variety of 5, Proof

History. The first of the Liberty Seated designs, with no stars on the obverse, was inspired by Christian Gobrecht's silver dollar of 1836. The reverse features a different motif, with a wreath and inscription. This variety was made only at the Philadelphia Mint in 1837 and at the New Orleans Mint in 1838. Liberty Seated dimes of the Stars on Obverse varieties were first made without drapery at Miss Liberty's elbow. These early issues have the shield tilted sharply to the left. Drapery was added in 1840, and the shield reoriented, this being the style of the 1840s onward. Variety 3 coins (minted in part of 1853, and all of

1854 and 1855) have arrows at the date, signifying the reduction in weight brought on by the Coinage Act of February 21, 1853. The earlier design resumed in 1856 at the new weight standard. Liberty Seated dimes were made in large quantities, and circulated widely. In 1860 the Liberty Seated design continued with UNITED STATES OF AMERICA replacing the stars on the obverse. A new reverse featured what the Mint called a "cereal wreath," encircling ONE DIME in two lines. In 1873 the dime was increased in weight to 2.50 grams (from 2.49); arrows at the date in 1873 and 1874 indicate this change, making Variety 5. Variety 4 (without the arrows) resumed from 1875 and continued to the end of the series in 1891.

Striking and Sharpness. Coins of these varieties usually are fairly well struck for the earlier years, somewhat erratic in the 1870s, and better from the 1880s to 1891. Many Civil War dimes of Philadelphia, 1861 to 1865, have parallel die striae from the dies not being finished (this being so for virtually all silver and gold issues of that period). Some dimes, especially dates from 1879 to 1881, are found prooflike. Check the highest parts of the Liberty Seated figure (especially the head and horizontal shield stripes), the star centers, and, on the reverse, the leaves. Check the denticles on both sides. Avoid coins struck from "tired" or overused dies, as evidenced by grainy rather than lustrous fields (on higher-grade coins). Issues of the Carson City Mint in the early 1870s, particularly 1873-CC, With Arrows, are often seen with porous surfaces (a post-striking effect).

Note that the word LIBERTY on the shield is not an infallible key to attributing lower grades. On some dies such as those of the early 1870s the shield was in low relief on the coins and wore away slowly, with the result that part or all of the word can be readable in grades below F-12.

Availability. The 1837 is readily available in all grades, including MS-65 and higher. The 1838-O is usually seen with wear and is a rarity if truly MS-63 or above. Beware coins with deep or vivid iridescent toning, which often masks friction or evidence of wear. Coins with uniformly grainy etching on both sides have been processed and should be avoided. The 1838 to 1860 dimes are plentiful as a rule, although certain dates and varieties are rare. Most MS coins on the market are dated in the 1850s and are often found MS–63 to 65. While certain issues of the 1860s through 1881 range from scarce to very rare, those from 1882 to 1891 are for the most part very common, even in MS-63 and finer.

Proofs. Examples of Proofs have deep-mirror surfaces and are mostly quite attractive. Proofs of 1837 (but not 1838-O) were struck in an unknown small quantity, but seemingly more than the related 1837 half dime. Proofs were made of most years and are mostly available from 1854 onward, with 1858 and especially 1859 being those often seen. Some Proofs of the 1860s and early 1870s can be carelessly struck, with areas of lightness and sometimes with lint marks. Those of the mid-1870s onward are usually sharply struck and without problems. Proof Liberty Seated dimes of this variety were made continuously from 1860 to 1891. They exist today in proportion to their mintages. Carefully examine deeply toned pieces to ensure the toning does not hide flaws.

GRADING STANDARDS

MS-60 to 70 (Mint State). *Obverse:* At MS-60, some abrasion and contact marks are evident, most noticeably on the bosom and thighs and knees. Luster is present, but may be dull or lifeless, and interrupted in patches in the large open field. At MS-63, contact marks are very few, and abrasion is hard to detect except under magnification. An MS-65 coin has no abrasion, and contact marks are so minute as to require magnification. Luster

1876-CC, Variety 1. Graded MS-64.

should be full and rich, except for Philadelphia (but not San Francisco) dimes of the early and mid-1860s. Most Mint State coins of the 1861 to 1865 years, Philadelphia issues, have extensive die striae (from not completely finishing the die). Some low-mintage Philadelphia issues may be prooflike. Clashmarks are common in this era. This is true of contemporary half dimes as well. Half dimes of this type can be very beautiful at this level. Grades above MS-65 are seen with regularity, more so than for the related No Stars dimes. *Reverse:* Comments apply as for the obverse, except that in lower Mint State grades abrasion and contact marks are most noticeable on the highest parts of the leaves and the ribbon, less so on ONE DIME. At MS-65 or higher there are no marks visible to the unaided eye. The field is mainly protected by design elements and does not show abrasion as much as does the open-field obverse on a given coin.

Illustrated coin: Note the blend of pink, lilac, and gold tones.

AU-50, 53, 55, 58 (About Uncirculated). *Obverse:* Light wear is seen on the thighs and knees, bosom, and head. At AU-58, the luster is extensive, but incomplete. Friction is seen in the large open field. At AU–50 and 53, luster is less. *Reverse:* Wear is evident on the leaves (especially at the top of the wreath) and ribbon. An AU-58 coin has nearly full luster, more so than on the obverse, as the design elements protect the small field areas. At AU–50 and 53, there still is significant luster, more than on the obverse.

1838-O, No Stars; F-101. Graded AU-58.

EF-40, 45 (Extremely Fine). *Obverse:* Further wear is seen on all areas, especially the thighs and knees, bosom, and head. Little or no luster is seen. *Reverse:* Further wear is seen on all areas, most noticeably at the leaves to each side of the wreath apex and on the ribbon bow knot. Leaves retain details except on the higher areas.

1838-O, No Stars; F-102. Graded EF-45.

VF-20, 30 (Very Fine). *Obverse:* Further wear is seen. Most details of the gown are worn away, except in the lower-relief areas above and to the right of the shield. Hair detail is mostly or completely gone. *Reverse:* Wear is more extensive. The highest leaves are flat.

1872-CC; F-101. Graded VF-30.

F-12, 15 (Fine). *Obverse:* The seated figure is well worn, with little detail remaining. LIBERTY on the shield is fully readable but weak in areas. On the 1838–1840 subtype Without Drapery, LIBERTY is in higher relief and will wear more quickly; ER may be missing, but other details are at the Fine level. *Reverse:* Most detail of the leaves is gone. The rim is worn but bold, and most if not all denticles are visible.

1874-CC. Graded F-15.

VG-8, 10 (Very Good). *Obverse:* The seated figure is more worn, but some detail can be seen above and to the right of the shield. The shield is discernible. In LIBERTY at least three letters are readable but very weak at VG-8; a few more visible at VG-10. On the 1838–1840 subtype Without Drapery, LIBERTY is in higher relief, and at Very Good only one or two letters may be readable. However, LIBERTY is not an infallible

1843-O; F-101. Graded VG-8.

way to grade this type, as some varieties have the word in low relief on the die, so it wore away slowly. *Reverse:* Further wear has combined the details of most leaves. The rim is complete, but weak in areas. The reverse appears to be in a slightly higher grade than the obverse.

G-4, 6 (Good). *Obverse:* The seated figure is worn smooth. At G-4 there are no letters in LIBERTY remaining on most (but not all) coins. At G-6, traces of one or two can be seen (except on the early No Drapery coins). *Reverse:* Wear is more extensive. The leaves are all combined and in outline form. The rim is well worn and missing in some areas, causing the outer parts of the peripheral letters to be worn away in some instances. On

1873-CC. Graded G-4.

most coins the reverse appears to be in a slightly higher grade than the obverse.

Illustrated coin: The scratch on the obverse lessens the desirability of this coin.

AG-3 (About Good). *Obverse:* The seated figure is mostly visible in outline form, with no detail. The rim is worn away. The date remains clear. *Reverse:* Many if not most letters are worn away, at least in part. The wreath and interior letters are discernible. The rim is weak.

1874-CC. Graded AG-3.

PF-60 to 70 (Proof). *Obverse and Reverse:* Proofs that are extensively cleaned and have many hairlines, or that are dull and grainy, are lower level, such as PF-60 to 62. These command less attention than more visually appealing pieces, save for the scarce (in any grade) dates of 1844 and 1846, and 1863 through 1867. Both the half dime and dime Proofs of 1837 were often cleaned, resulting in coins that have lost much of their mirror surface. With

1886. Graded PF-67.

medium hairlines and good reflectivity, an assigned grade of PF-64 is indicated, and with relatively few hairlines, Gem PF-65. In various grades hairlines are most easily seen in the obverse field. PF-66 should have hairlines so delicate that magnification is needed to see them. Above that, a Proof should be free of such lines.

1837, Large Date

1837, Small Date

No Drapery From Elbow, Tilted Shield (1838–1840)

Drapery From Elbow, Upright Shield (1840–1891)

1838, Small Stars

1838, Large Stars

1838, So-Called Partial Drapery

	Mintage	Cert	Avg	%MS	G-4	F-12	VF-20	EF-40	AU-50	MS-60 / PF-60	MS-63 / PF-63	MS-64	MS-65 / PF-65
1837, All kinds	682,500												
1837, Large Date		42	49.5	43%	$45	$100	$275	$500	$750	$1,100	$1,800	$4,000	$7,750
Auctions: $8,813, MS-66, March 2016; $1,586, MS-64, October 2016; $881, AU-58, July 2016													
1837, Small Date		40	53.3	48%	$50	$120	$325	$500	$750	$1,200	$2,000	$4,500	$8,500
Auctions: $1,645, MS-64, March 2016; $764, MS-63, November 2016; $447, AU-58, August 2016													
1837, Proof	25–35	26	64.0							$6,000	$12,000		$35,000
Auctions: $8,813, PF-62, January 2015													
1838-O, Variety 1	489,034	198	37.8	15%	$100	$180	$400	$800	$1,200	$3,600	$5,500	$8,500	$22,500
Auctions: $6,463, MS-64, January 2015; $999, AU-55, January 2015; $646, VF-35, January 2015; $376, VF-25, February 2015													
1838, Variety 2, All kinds	1,992,500												
1838, Small Stars		83	57.1	64%	$25	$55	$85	$175	$400	$700	$1,350	$2,000	$4,000
Auctions: $2,820, MS-65, June 2015													
1838, Large Stars		414	57.1	62%	$30	$40	$48	$150	$300	$500	$850	$1,200	$3,000
Auctions: $646, MS-62, December 2015; $282, AU-50, November 2015; $235, EF-45, March 2016													
1838, Partial Drapery (a)		21	60.7	71%	$30	$60	$100	$200	$500	$850	$1,500	$2,500	
Auctions: $1,293, MS-62, January 2015; $89, VF-20, February 2015													
1838, Proof (b)	2–3	0	n/a										$125,000
Auctions: $161,000, PF-67Cam, January 2008													

a. The so-called "partial drapery" is not a design variation; rather, it is evidence of die clashing from the E in DIME on the reverse.
b. The 1838, Proof, dime may be unique.

| 1839-O, Repunched Mintmark | 1841-O, Transitional Reverse, Small O | 1841-O, Transitional Reverse, Large O | Regular Reverse Style of 1841-O |

	Mintage	Cert	Avg	%MS	G-4	F-12	VF-20	EF-40	AU-50	MS-60	MS-63	MS-64	MS-65
											PF-60	PF-63	PF-65
1839	1,053,115	252	58.3	65%	$20	$30	$48	$145	$300	$475	$850	$1,100	$3,000
Auctions: $9,988, MS-67, May 2015; $1,410, MS-64, September 2015; $764, MS-63, February 2015; $388, AU-55, June 2015
1839, Proof	4–5	3	64.3								$10,000	$20,000	$45,000
Auctions: $39,950, PF-65, May 2015; $28,200, PF-64, May 2015; $12,925, PF-62, August 2016
1839-O	1,291,600	103	48.5	36%	$25	$75	$145	$240	$425	$800	$1,950	$3,000	$7,000
Auctions: $15,863, MS-67, May 2015; $823, AU-55, October 2015; $764, AU-50, June 2015; $470, AU-50, June 2015
1839-O, Repunched Mintmark	(c)	4	24.3	0%	$40	$100	$225	$325	$700	$750	$3,500		
Auctions: $13,800, MS-66+, February 2012
1839-O, Proof	2–3	1	65.0									$25,000	$70,000
Auctions: $74,750, PF-65, October 2008
1840, No Drapery	981,500	169	53.0	51%	$20	$30	$48	$150	$300	$425	$850	$1,200	$3,200
Auctions: $3,290, MS-65, August 2016; $1,998, MS-65, June 2015; $270, AU-55, February 2015
1840, No Drapery, Proof	4–5	5	64.8								$10,000	$15,000	$30,000
Auctions: $27,600, PF-65Cam, August 2007
1840-O, No Drapery	1,175,000	58	37.7	14%	$60	$120	$180	$480	$1,025	$7,000	$14,500	$22,500	$40,000
Auctions: $376, AU-50, June 2015; $206, AU-50, June 2015; $423, EF-45, September 2015; $188, VF-30, November 2015
1840, Drapery	377,500	28	40.7	25%	$90	$180	$300	$800	$1,300	$3,000	$12,000	$19,500	$30,000
Auctions: $27,025, MS-64, May 2015; $2,585, MS-62, January 2015; $84, VF-20, January 2015; $216, VF-20, March 2018
1841 (d)	1,622,500	86	56.9	62%	$20	$30	$35	$60	$140	$425	$775	$1,200	$3,600
Auctions: $223, AU-55, March 2015; $212, AU-55, January 2015; $141, AU-53, August 2015; $79, AU-53, January 2015
1841, Proof (d)	2–3	1	63.0									$55,000	
Auctions: $41,125, PF-63Cam, October 2014
1841, No Drapery, Proof	2–3	2	60.0									$65,000	
Auctions: $305,500, PF-67, November 2013
1841-O	2,007,500	116	40.8	17%	$25	$45	$100	$150	$325	$850	$1,400	$5,400	$9,000
Auctions: $353, AU-55, June 2015; $329, AU-53, January 2015; $259, AU-53, July 2015; $106, EF-45, June 2015
1841-O, Transitional Reverse, Small O (e)	(f)	4	9.3	0%									
Auctions: $940, G-6, June 2013
1841-O, Transitional Reverse, Large O (e)	(f)	5	9.8	0%		$1,250	$2,500						
Auctions: $2,611, F-12, January 2014
1842	1,887,500	107	51.7	56%	$20	$30	$35	$50	$125	$400	$650	$1,200	$3,000
Auctions: $4,700, MS-66, May 2015; $3,760, MS-66, January 2015; $3,290, MS-65, June 2015; $881, MS-64, August 2015
1842, Proof	6–10	4	63.8								$10,000	$15,000	$40,000
Auctions: $37,375, PF-65Cam, April 2008
1842-O	2,020,000	109	38.2	18%	$35	$90	$175	$475	$1,500	$2,750	$5,000	$7,500	$20,000
Auctions: $14,100, MS-65, May 2015; $306, AU-50, August 2015; $447, EF-45, February 2015; $141, VF-35, January 2015

c. Included in circulation strike 1839-O mintage figure. **d.** Two examples are known of 1841, No Drapery, Small Stars, Upright Shield. One is a Proof and the other is a circulation strike in VF. **e.** The 1841-O, Transitional Reverse, varieties were struck with a reverse die that was supposed to have been discontinued in 1840, but saw limited use into 1841. Note the closed buds (not open, as in the regular reverse die of 1841); also note that the second leaf from the left (in the group of four leaves to the left of the bow knot) reaches only halfway across the bottom of the U in UNITED. **f.** Included in 1841-O mintage figure.

	Mintage	Cert	Avg	%MS	G-4	F-12	VF-20	EF-40	AU-50	MS-60	MS-63	MS-64	MS-65
											PF-60	PF-63	PF-65
1843	1,370,000	94	53.7	48%	$20	$30	$35	$50	$125	$475	$800	$1,850	$3,500
Auctions: $881, MS-64, June 2015; $705, MS-63, August 2016; $141, AU-53, July 2015													
1843, Proof	*10–15*	9	64.3								$5,000	$10,000	$20,000
Auctions: $25,850, PF-66, June 2014													
1843-O	150,000	59	21.9	0%	$175	$600	$1,350	$3,500	$11,000	$70,000			
Auctions: $423, F-12, February 2015; $206, VG-10, January 2015; $84, G-3, June 2015													
1844	72,500	124	22.6	7%	$150	$375	$600	$1,000	$1,750	$4,000	$11,500	$15,000	$26,500
Auctions: $881, EF-45, August 2016; $705, VF-30, July 2015; $447, $235, VG-10, August 2016; $1,080, EF-45, January 2018													
1844, Proof	*4–8*	1	64.0								$12,500	$22,500	$40,000
Auctions: $44,063, PF-65, October 2014; $31,725, PF-64, May 2015													
1845	1,755,000	161	57.9	64%	$20	$30	$35	$50	$150	$400	$800	$1,250	$3,500
Auctions: $4,935, MS-66, May 2015; $3,290, MS-65, January 2015; $646, MS-63, June 2015; $141, AU-53, November 2015													
1845, Proof	*6–10*	5	64.8								$5,000	$8,500	$17,500
Auctions: $30,550, PF-66, May 2015; $19,975, PF-65, April 2013													
1845-O	230,000	50	28.5	2%	$90	$240	$550	$1,000	$3,000	$12,000	$25,000		
Auctions: $123,376, MS-69, May 2015; $541, AU-50, June 2015; $865, EF-40, January 2015; $364, VF-25, January 2015													
1846	31,300	64	23.5	2%	$325	$750	$1,150	$2,500	$7,000	$22,500	$50,000		
Auctions: $11,456, AU-58, January 2015; $2,115, EF-40, April 2016; $999, VF-30, January 2018; $1,058, VF-25, August 2016													
1846, Proof	*8–12*	7	63.9								$7,500	$12,000	$35,000
Auctions: $31,725, PF-65, March 2013													
1847	245,000	45	49.3	29%	$20	$40	$70	$180	$425	$1,550	$4,000	$6,500	$10,000
Auctions: $4,700, MS-63, October 2014; $229, EF-45, November 2014													
1847, Proof	*3–5*	1	66.0								$8,000	$13,000	$30,000
Auctions: $35,250, PF-66Cam, March 2013; $44,063, PF-66, October 2014													
1848	451,500	70	54.9	54%	$20	$32	$50	$85	$180	$725	$975	$2,200	$6,500
Auctions: $6,463, MS-65, May 2015; $400, AU-58, April 2015; $306, AU-58, July 2015													
1848, Proof	*10–15*	9	64.6								$5,000	$10,000	$17,500
Auctions: $18,800, PF-65, May 2015; $14,100, PF-65, August 2016; $15,275, PF-64, January 2015													
1849	839,000	90	53.2	53%	$20	$30	$40	$75	$180	$375	$900	$1,500	$3,500
Auctions: $14,100, MS-66, March 2015; $1,763, MS-65, August 2016; $46, VF-30, April 2015													
1849, Proof	*4–6*	2	65.0								$10,000	$12,500	$35,000
Auctions: $35,250, PF-65, August 2013; $21,150, PF-64, January 2015													
1849-O	300,000	90	43.8	20%	$25	$75	$150	$375	$950	$2,500	$5,500	$12,500	
Auctions: $5,288, MS-64, January 2015; $3,525, MS-63, June 2015; $617, AU-55, January 2015; $165, AU-50, July 2015													
1850	1,931,500	155	53.6	53%	$20	$30	$40	$60	$150	$300	$700	$1,500	$4,500
Auctions: $940, MS-64, June 2015; $881, MS-64, August 2016; $646, MS-63, January 2015													
1850, Proof	*4–6*	4	64.5								$10,000	$15,000	$35,000
Auctions: $44,650, PF-67, May 2015; $19,975, PF-64, May 2015													
1850-O	510,000	34	37.0	21%	$25	$100	$120	$300	$900	$2,000	$4,500	$6,000	$8,500
Auctions: $823, AU-58, January 2015; $1,058, AU-55, July 2015; $74, VF-20, August 2015													
1851	1,026,500	84	51.6	49%	$20	$30	$40	$70	$200	$425	$850	$1,800	$5,000
Auctions: $20,563, MS-67, June 2013; $8,225, MS-67, May 2015; $170, AU-53, October 2014													
1851-O	400,000	47	41.3	15%	$25	$40	$120	$300	$1,000	$2,500	$3,750	$6,000	$16,500
Auctions: $15,275, MS-65, May 2015; $165, EF-40, January 2015; $106, EF-40, June 2015													
1852	1,535,500	101	55.4	61%	$20	$30	$40	$60	$125	$300	$650	$1,000	$2,500
Auctions: $9,400, MS-67, July 2015; $1,058, MS-64, November 2016; $646, MS-64, September 2016													
1852, Proof	*5–10*	7	64.4								$5,000	$10,000	$25,000
Auctions: $20,563, PF-65, May 2015; $9,400, PF-65, September 2015; $8,225, PF-62, January 2014													
1852-O	430,000	64	49.6	44%	$30	$90	$180	$325	$550	$1,800	$3,600	$4,800	$12,500
Auctions: $259, EF-40, January 2015; $129, VF-20, January 2015													

	Mintage	Cert	Avg	%MS	G-4	F-12	VF-20	EF-40	AU-50	MS-60	MS-63	MS-64	MS-65
											PF-60	PF-63	PF-65
1853, No Arrows	95,000	120	52.2	68%	$110	$300	$500	$650	$800	$950	$1,500	$2,250	$3,000
	Auctions: $1,998, MS-64, February 2015; $1,880, MS-64, July 2015; $376, VF-20, August 2016												
1853, With Arrows	12,173,000	1,009	57.0	61%	$20	$25	$30	$50	$150	$325	$650	$950	$1,550
	Auctions: $764, MS-64, October 2016; $494, MS-62, August 2016; $141, AU-55, March 2016												
1853, Proof	5–10	5	64.6								$10,000	$20,000	$35,000
	Auctions: $37,600, PF-66, December 2015; $34,075, PF-65, October 2014												
1853-O	1,100,000	61	40.6	11%	$25	$85	$125	$300	$650	$2,000	$4,500	$6,500	$12,000
	Auctions: $1,880, AU-55, June 2015; $200, EF-40, July 2015; $89, VF-25, August 2015; $54, VF-25, January 2015												
1854	4,470,000	268	56.9	57%	$20	$25	$30	$50	$175	$325	$675	$950	$1,600
	Auctions: $3,055, MS-66, October 2016; $1,175, MS-65, September 2016; $764, MS-64, December 2015												
1854, Proof	8–12	9	65.0								$6,000	$8,500	$20,000
	Auctions: $19,975, PF-65, October 2014; $17,625, PF-65, January 2015; $11,163, PF-64, August 2016												
1854-O	1,770,000	98	55.6	67%	$20	$25	$45	$85	$225	$425	$1,000	$1,500	$4,500
	Auctions: $8,225, MS-66, May 2015; $646, MS-62, August 2015												
1855	2,075,000	120	58.2	66%	$20	$25	$30	$60	$185	$325	$850	$1,100	$3,000
	Auctions: $881, MS-64, March 2016; $705, MS-64, September 2016; $646, MS-63, June 2015												
1855, Proof	8–12	14	64.9								$6,000	$8,500	$20,000
	Auctions: $29,375, PF-67, October 2015; $14,100, PF-64, May 2015; $9,400, PF-64, September 2015												
1856, All kinds	5,780,000												
1856, Large Date		42	40.7	14%	$40	$90	$120	$180	$300	$600	$2,100	$3,600	$9,500
	Auctions: $6,463, MS-64, October 2015; $2,233, MS-63, October 2015; $114, EF-45, March 2018												
1856, Small Date		119	48.0	39%	$16	$20	$30	$60	$145	$300	$550	$950	$2,250
	Auctions: $1,880, MS-65, March 2016; $1,763, MS-65, January 2015; $494, MS-63, October 2015												
1856, Proof	40–50	21	64.6								$2,500	$3,500	$8,000
	Auctions: $14,100, PF-66, August 2016; $6,463, PF-65, October 2015; $5,405, PF-65, August 2015												
1856-O	1,180,000	76	45.8	36%	$20	$60	$90	$150	$360	$800	$1,350	$2,650	$6,000
	Auctions: $3,672, MS-65, October 2014; $1,469, MS-63, November 2013; $74, AU-50, February 2015; $147, EF-45, November 2014												
1856-S	70,000	32	37.4	13%	$250	$650	$1,200	$1,700	$2,500	$7,250	$15,000	$25,000	$45,000
	Auctions: $1,410, VF-30, January 2015; $341, G-6, January 2015												
1857	5,580,000	357	58.1	66%	$16	$20	$30	$50	$130	$300	$550	$850	$1,950
	Auctions: $2,080, MS-66, October 2015; $700, MS-64, July 2016; $705, MS-64, October 2016												
1857, Proof	45–60	34	64.5								$2,000	$3,000	$5,000
	Auctions: $7,638, PF-66, October 2015; $4,700, PF-65, August 2015; $2,233, PF-64, March 2016												
1857-O	1,540,000	191	57.5	62%	$18	$25	$35	$70	$200	$425	$750	$1,000	$2,000
	Auctions: $2,468, MS-66, May 2015; $1,998, MS-66, June 2015; $423, MS-62, February 2015; $212, AU-55, August 2015												
1858	1,540,000	152	57.3	63%	$16	$20	$30	$50	$130	$300	$550	$850	$1,850
	Auctions: $4,935, MS-67, June 2015; $2,585, MS-66, June 2015												
1858, Proof	(g)	72	64.5								$1,000	$1,750	$3,750
	Auctions: $7,051, PF-66, August 2016; $1,175, PF-64, March 2016; $1,293, PF-63, September 2016												
1858-O	290,000	55	52.4	33%	$25	$40	$85	$150	$360	$900	$2,000	$4,000	$7,500
	Auctions: $517, AU-58, January 2015; $188, EF-45, April 2015												
1858-S	60,000	38	32.7	8%	$200	$375	$825	$1,250	$2,000	$7,000	$17,000	$22,500	$32,500
	Auctions: $1,116, EF-40, January 2015; $999, VF-35, March 2015; $646, VF-20, January 2015; $306, F-12, February 2015												
1859	429,200	152	61.2	82%	$20	$22	$32	$60	$140	$300	$650	$850	$2,000
	Auctions: $2,174, MS-65, November 2015; $341, MS-62, March 2015; $40, AU-53, January 2015; $112, AU-50, September 2015												
1859, Proof	(g)	218	64.5								$900	$1,250	$2,000
	Auctions: $5,875, PF-67, March 2016; $2,115, PF-65, September 2016; $1,998, PF-65, March 2016												

g. The mintage figure is unknown.

**1859 Pattern Dime: Obverse of 1859,
Reverse of 1860, Proof**
Judd-233.

**1861, Six Vertical
Shield Lines**

	Mintage	Cert	Avg	%MS	G-4	F-12	VF-20	EF-40	AU-50	MS-60	MS-63	MS-64	MS-65
											PF-60	PF-63	PF-65
1859, Obverse of 1859, Reverse of 1860, Proof (h)	(i)	12	64.7								$10,000	$15,000	$20,000
Auctions: $5,875, PF-67Cam, October 2014; $4,113, PF-66Cam, July 2014; $3,672, PF-66Cam, October 2014; $2,585, PF-65, July 2014													
1859-O	480,000	126	56.6	63%	$20	$25	$60	$95	$275	$400	$850	$1,150	$2,250
Auctions: $5,405, MS-67, June 2015; $494, MS-63, February 2015; $329, MS-61, January 2015; $106, AU-50, February 2015													
1859-S	60,000	28	28.0	7%	$250	$475	$1,050	$2,750	$5,500	$18,000	$30,000	$47,500	$90,000
Auctions: $376, EF-40, February 2015; $200, F-12, January 2015; $447, G-6, February 2015													
1860-S, Variety 2	140,000	52	41.2	13%	$60	$150	$300	$480	$950	$2,500	$8,100	$12,500	$42,500
Auctions: $37,600, MS-65, May 2015; $1,998, MS-62, May 2015; $999, AU-58, March 2015; $823, AU-50, January 2015													
1860, Variety 4	606,000	125	61.8	86%	$16	$20	$32	$40	$100	$200	$325	$500	$1,000
Auctions: $11,163, MS-67, May 2015; $1,410, MS-66, June 2015; $1,880, MS-65, January 2015; $423, MS-64, June 2015													
1860, Variety 4, Proof	1,000	148	64.5								$350	$600	$1,200
Auctions: $5,405, PF-68, August 2015; $6,463, PF-67, October 2014; $1,646, PF-65+, September 2014; $734, PF-64, July 2014													
1860-O, Variety 4	40,000	53	27.7	6%	$650	$1,500	$2,500	$5,000	$8,500	$18,000	$35,000	$75,000	
Auctions: $64,625, MS-64, May 2015; $2,350, VF-35, February 2015; $999, VF-20, September 2015													
1861 (j)	1,883,000	164	58.5	73%	$16	$22	$30	$40	$100	$200	$325	$450	$1,150
Auctions: $3,290, MS-66, January 2015; $764, MS-65, January 2015; $376, MS-64, January 2015; $259, MS-63, January 2015													
1861, Proof	1,000	99	63.9								$350	$650	$1,200
Auctions: $4,935, PF-66, December 2015; $3,055, PF-65, August 2016; $705, PF-64, August 2015													
1861-S	172,500	33	41.5	21%	$175	$425	$650	$900	$1,200	$5,500	$18,000	$30,000	$45,000
Auctions: $51,700, MS-66, January 2015; $823, EF-40, February 2015; $764, VF-25, February 2015; $235, VF-20, January 2015													
1862	847,000	190	61.2	87%	$16	$25	$30	$40	$100	$185	$350	$500	$1,150
Auctions: $1,763, MS-66, July 2015; $1,175, MS-66, December 2015; $1,998, MS-65, August 2016													
1862, Proof	550	103	63.6								$350	$650	$1,200
Auctions: $1,293, PF-65, June 2015; $1,175, PF-65, August 2016													
1862-S	180,750	24	34.8	21%	$150	$300	$550	$1,000	$2,400	$4,250	$9,000	$12,500	$37,500
Auctions: $35,250, MS-65, October 2014; $646, AU-50, October 2014; $646, VF-30, April 2014; $388, VF-25, July 2014													
1863	14,000	42	56.0	81%	$800	$1,050	$1,150	$1,200	$1,300	$1,500	$2,400	$3,000	$4,000
Auctions: $5,170, MS-66, May 2015; $2,820, MS-63, January 2015; $881, G-6, August 2015													
1863, Proof	460	154	64.4								$325	$600	$1,200
Auctions: $1,821, PF-66, August 2016; $1,528, PF-65, December 2015; $1,175, PF-65, March 2016													
1863-S	157,500	40	43.5	25%	$120	$300	$480	$900	$1,200	$3,600	$9,500	$12,500	$35,000
Auctions: $30,550, MS-66, May 2015; $881, EF-45, January 2015; $153, F-15, January 2015													

h. In 1859 the Mint made a dime pattern, of which some 13 to 20 examples are known. These "coins without a country" do not bear the nation's identity (UNITED STATES OF AMERICA). They are transitional pieces, not made for circulation, but struck at the time that the dime's legend was being transferred from the reverse to the obverse (see Variety 4). For more information, consult *United States Pattern Coins* (10th edition). **i.** The mintage figure is unknown. **j.** The dime's dies were modified slightly in 1861. The first (scarcer) variety has only five vertical lines in the top part of the shield.

	Mintage	Cert	Avg	%MS	G-4	F-12	VF-20	EF-40	AU-50	MS-60	MS-63	MS-64	MS-65
											PF-60	PF-63	PF-65
1864	11,000	48	55.5	73%	$300	$650	$925	$1,000	$1,150	$1,200	$2,150	$2,750	$5,500
	Auctions: $23,500, MS-67, August 2016; $999, VF-25, February 2015; $1,293, F-15, September 2016												
1864, Proof	470	159	64.3								$325	$600	$1,200
	Auctions: $1,293, PF-65, August 2016; $1,058, PF-65, October 2016; $887, PF-64, September 2016												
1864-S	230,000	60	41.4	28%	$120	$240	$360	$800	$1,000	$1,300	$2,000	$7,000	$12,500
	Auctions: $1,528, MS-62, January 2015; $1,293, MS-61, March 2015; $1,058, AU-55, February 2015; $153, VF-30, January 2015												
1865	10,000	55	55.3	71%	$500	$950	$1,250	$2,000	$2,250	$3,000	$3,750	$4,000	$4,500
	Auctions: $3,916, MS-66, June 2015; $1,528, EF-40, October 2014												
1865, Proof	500	112	64.0								$350	$650	$1,200
	Auctions: $2,703, PF-66, October 2015; $646, PF-64, August 2016; $1,058, PF-63, November 2015												
1865-S	175,000	35	31.2	9%	$120	$360	$725	$1,200	$3,000	$7,000	$16,500	$25,000	$40,000
	Auctions: $5,875, MS-62, January 2015; $517, AU-50, January 2015; $823, VF-35, January 2015; $212, VF-30, January 2015												
1866	8,000	44	53.2	75%	$750	$1,100	$1,300	$1,600	$2,000	$2,500	$3,000	$3,250	$3,500
	Auctions: $4,465, MS-66, May 2015; $3,760, MS-66, June 2015												
1866, Proof	725	172	64.0								$325	$600	$1,200
	Auctions: $2,585, PF-66, August 2016; $2,585, PF-65, December 2015; $1,175, PF-65, August 2016												
1866-S	135,000	45	38.8	29%	$120	$240	$425	$625	$1,500	$3,500	$6,500	$8,500	$11,500
	Auctions: $14,100, MS-66, May 2015; $588, EF-40, August 2015; $541, EF-40, January 2015; $165, VF-20, June 2015												
1867	6,000	49	60.8	86%	$600	$925	$1,200	$1,300	$1,400	$1,500	$2,000	$3,250	$4,500
	Auctions: $2,468, MS-64, July 2014; $1,998, MS-63, August 2016; $1,763, MS-63, February 2015												
1867, Proof	625	134	64.1								$325	$600	$1,100
	Auctions: $6,169, PF-66, November 2016; $1,058, PF-65, March 2016; $881, PF-65, August 2016												
1867-S	140,000	41	38.9	24%	$120	$240	$400	$725	$1,550	$2,750	$4,250	$7,500	$10,000
	Auctions: $2,585, MS-62, January 2015; $2,233, MS-62, June 2015; $447, AU-50, April 2015; $376, VF-30, January 2015												
1868	464,000	42	56.0	74%	$20	$30	$40	$65	$150	$300	$850	$1,500	$4,000
	Auctions: $3,819, MS-65, March 2015; $118, EF-45, April 2015; $62, EF-40, January 2015												
1868, Proof	600	159	63.9								$325	$600	$1,000
	Auctions: $12,925, PF-67, September 2016; $3,055, PF-65, October 2015; $541, PF-64, August 2016												
1868-S	260,000	27	46.7	48%	$60	$150	$250	$550	$650	$1,250	$2,000	$3,500	$5,250
	Auctions: $541, AU-53, March 2015; $89, EF-40, March 2015												
1869	256,000	31	50.3	48%	$22	$40	$85	$150	$200	$400	$1,000	$1,750	$3,250
	Auctions: $7,638, MS-67, May 2015; $79, AU-50, January 2015; $125, VF-25, September 2015												
1869, Proof	600	178	64.1								$325	$600	$1,000
	Auctions: $823, PF-65, August 2016; $823, PF-64, June 2015; $475, PF-63, July 2015												
1869-S	450,000	62	59.6	74%	$18	$25	$50	$225	$250	$450	$800	$1,300	$3,000
	Auctions: $3,995, MS-66, May 2015; $2,585, MS-65, January 2015; $764, MS-62, March 2015; $306, AU-53, March 2015												
1870	470,500	79	59.6	75%	$16	$25	$30	$50	$100	$225	$450	$800	$1,650
	Auctions: $588, MS-64, January 2015; $176, MS-61, July 2015; $188, AU-58, July 2015												
1870, Proof	1,000	168	64.0								$325	$600	$1,000
	Auctions: $2,585, PF-66, October 2016; $1,528, PF-65, October 2015; $823, PF-64, August 2016												
1870-S	50,000	38	38.2	32%	$250	$575	$725	$900	$1,200	$1,800	$2,750	$3,750	$7,500
	Auctions: $1,116, AU-53, March 2015; $646, VF-30, July 2015; $223, VF-20, January 2015; $306, VG-8, February 2015												
1871	906,750	73	57.6	66%	$16	$25	$30	$50	$150	$250	$425	$850	$1,600
	Auctions: $3,995, MS-66, December 2015; $235, AU-58, January 2015; $141, AU-55, July 2015												
1871, Proof	960	153	63.9								$325	$600	$1,000
	Auctions: $1,645, PF-66, January 2015; $517, PF-64, August 2016; $423, PF-62, October 2016												
1871-CC	20,100	24	32.1	17%	$2,500	$5,250	$7,250	$14,500	$22,500	$45,000	$125,000	$175,000	$300,000
	Auctions: $270,250, MS-65, October 2014; $30,550, MS-61, August 2015; $6,463, AU-50, July 2014; $3,525, EF-40, January 2015												
1871-S	320,000	31	53.4	45%	$25	$120	$180	$375	$750	$1,600	$3,750	$5,000	$10,000
	Auctions: $4,230, MS-64, October 2015; $364, EF-45, March 2015; $69, VF-20, January 2015; $40, VF-20, February 2015												

1872, Doubled Die Reverse
FS-10-1872-801.

	Mintage	**Cert**	**Avg**	**%MS**	**G-4**	**F-12**	**VF-20**	**EF-40**	**AU-50**	**MS-60**	**MS-63**	**MS-64**	**MS-65**
											PF-60	**PF-63**	**PF-65**
1872	2,395,500	82	57.8	67%	$18	$25	$30	$40	$90	$175	$300	$650	$1,100
	Auctions: $17,625, MS-68, May 2015; $494, MS-64, February 2015; $69, MS-60, January 2015												
1872, Doubled Die Reverse (k,l)	(m)	2	37.5	0%	$100	$350	$550	$850	$1,500	$1,750			
	Auctions: $425, VF-20, May 2008												
1872, Proof	950	154	63.9								$325	$600	$1,000
	Auctions: $5,170, PF-67, September 2016; $823, PF-65, August 2016; $588, PF-64, July 2016												
1872-CC	35,480	39	27.2	0%	$1,450	$2,750	$4,500	$11,500	$17,500	$70,000	$200,000	$275,000	$450,000
	Auctions: $182,125, MS-63, May 2015; $5,288, AU-50, April 2014; $2,233, EF-40, January 2015; $1,293, VF-20, June 2015												
1872-S	190,000	25	47.9	36%	$25	$120	$180	$325	$500	$1,800	$3,500	$7,500	$25,000
	Auctions: $28,200, MS-65, May 2015; $1,647, MS-60, March 2015; $376, EF-40, January 2015; $69, VF-30, January 2015												
1873, No Arrows, Close 3	1,506,800	50	57.5	58%	$16	$30	$48	$70	$120	$240	$480	$950	$1,500
	Auctions: $6,463, MS-67, June 2014; $259, AU-58, October 2014												
1873, No Arrows, Open 3	60,000	38	48.9	34%	$20	$50	$75	$130	$200	$600	$1,500	$4,500	$15,000
	Auctions: $9,400, MS-64, August 2013; $353, AU-55, October 2014; $259, AU-55, October 2014; $259, AU-55, February 2015												
1873, No Arrows, Close 3, Proof	600	172	64.3								$325	$600	$1,000
	Auctions: $14,100, PF-68Cam, May 2015; $8,813, PF-67Cam, January 2015; $1,116, PF-65Cam, June 2015												
1873-CC, No Arrows † (n,o)	12,400	0	n/a										$2,500,000
	Auctions: $7,475, VF-20, January 2012												
1873, With Arrows	2,377,700	205	54.5	55%	$18	$25	$55	$150	$300	$550	$900	$1,650	$4,000
	Auctions: $11,750, MS-66, June 2015; $2,233, MS-65, January 2015; $400, MS-62, May 2015; $329, MS-61, March 2015												
1873, With Arrows, Doubled Die Obverse (p)	(q)	4	27.8	25%	$500	$1,200	$1,700	$3,300	$7,500	$20,000			
	Auctions: $3,220, VF-25, October 2011												
1873, With Arrows, Proof	500	103	64.1								$650	$850	$3,500
	Auctions: $9,988, PF-67Cam, September 2014; $9,988, PF-66Cam, September 2014; $16,450, PF-67, November 2013												
1873-CC, With Arrows	18,791	39	16.3	3%	$2,850	$5,000	$7,250	$14,000	$42,500	$60,000	$150,000	$250,000	$300,000
	Auctions: $199,750, MS-65, June 2014; $3,290, AU-50, January 2015; $9,400, AU-50, March 2014; $5,581, VF-20, August 2015												
1873-S	455,000	62	60.8	85%	$22	$35	$60	$175	$450	$1,000	$2,000	$3,500	$7,500
	Auctions: $3,890, MS-64, January 2015; $2,233, MS-64, January 2015; $1,058, MS-62, March 2015; $46, AU-50, January 2015												

† Ranked in the *100 Greatest U.S. Coins* (fifth edition). **k.** The first die hubbing was almost completely obliterated by the second, which was rotated about 170 degrees from the first. The key indicators of this variety are inside the opening of the D, and near the center arm of the E in ONE. **l.** This coin is considered rare. **m.** Included in circulation-strike 1872 mintage figure. **n.** Most of the mintage of 1873-CC, No Arrows, was melted after the law of 1873, affecting the statuses and physical properties of U.S. coinage, was passed. **o.** This coin is considered unique. **p.** Doubling is evident on the shield and on the banner across the shield. Although well known for decades, very few examples of this variety have been reported. **q.** Included in circulation-strike 1873, With Arrows, mintage figure.

1875-CC, Mintmark Above Bow	**1875-CC, Mintmark Below Bow**	**1876-CC, Variety 1 Reverse**	**1876-CC, Variety 2 Reverse** *FS-10-1876CC-901.*

	Mintage	Cert	Avg	%MS	G-4	F-12	VF-20	EF-40	AU-50	MS-60	MS-63 / PF-60	MS-64 / PF-63	MS-65 / PF-65
1874	2,940,000	284	56.4	61%	$18	$25	$55	$150	$310	$600	$1,000	$1,400	$4,500
	Auctions: $8,225, MS-67, December 2015; $2,820, MS-66, March 2016; $652, MS-63, October 2016												
1874, Proof	700	177	63.7								$650	$850	$3,500
	Auctions: $3,772, PF-65, October 2015; $764, PF-63, July 2015; $282, PF-58, August 2016												
1874-CC	10,817	13	31.3	8%	$8,000	$15,000	$20,000	$30,000	$45,000	$85,000	$150,000		
	Auctions: $152,750, MS-63, October 2014; $41,125, AU-53, April 2014; $6,463, EF-40, January 2015; $2,585, G-3, February 2015												
1874-S	240,000	52	57.7	67%	$25	$65	$110	$225	$500	$900	$2,000	$3,000	$6,500
	Auctions: $505, AU-58, March 2015; $306, AU-50, February 2015												
1875	10,350,000	442	60.5	82%	$15	$20	$25	$35	$80	$150	$250	$400	$700
	Auctions: $617, MS-66, July 2016; $588, MS-65, August 2016; $329, MS-64, May 2016												
1875, Proof	700	165	64.4								$300	$600	$1,000
	Auctions: $5,405, PF-67, October 2015; $764, PF-65, August 2016; $588, PF-64, August 2015												
1875-CC, All kinds	4,645,000												
1875-CC, Above Bow		181	51.7	50%	$45	$75	$95	$145	$220	$400	$950	$1,400	$3,250
	Auctions: $5,170, MS-67, September 2015; $3,760, MS-66, January 2015; $3,525, MS-65, October 2015; $823, MS-64, January 2015												
1875-CC, Below Bow		69	54.1	61%	$60	$95	$165	$250	$315	$550	$1,550	$2,000	$4,500
	Auctions: $4,230, MS-65, May 2015; $1,880, MS-65, August 2015												
1875-S, All kinds	9,070,000												
1875-S, Below Bow		78	56.7	65%	$15	$20	$25	$40	$95	$175	$285	$475	$1,200
	Auctions: $2,233, MS-66, May 2015; $999, MS-66, October 2015; $940, MS-65, August 2015; $600, MS-65, October 2015												
1875-S, Above Bow		37	62.3	78%	$15	$20	$25	$35	$85	$160	$275	$500	$1,400
	Auctions: $3,055, MS-66, May 2015; $1,880, MS-66, July 2015; $705, MS-63, August 2015; $400, MS-63, March 2015												
1876	11,460,000	372	60.7	82%	$15	$20	$25	$35	$80	$150	$250	$400	$800
	Auctions: $1,293, MS-67, October 2015; $764, MS-66, December 2015; $823, MS-65, September 2016												
1876, Proof	1,250	162	63.6								$300	$600	$1,000
	Auctions: $1,410, PF-66, October 2015; $764, PF-65, September 2016; $541, PF-64, August 2016												
1876-CC	8,270,000	481	50.0	54%	$30	$50	$70	$100	$150	$350	$700	$1,000	$1,750
	Auctions: $9,988, MS-67, January 2015; $2,056, MS-66, September 2015; $1,146, MS-65, January 2015; $353, MS-60, October 2015												
1876-CC, Variety 2 Reverse (r)	(s)	3	56.3	33%				$225	$450	$750	$1,200	$1,750	$3,000
	Auctions: $3,738, MS-64, February 2012												
1876-CC, Proof	3–4	5	65.2										$55,000
	Auctions: $38,188, PF-65, October 2014												
1876-S	10,420,000	105	58.9	73%	$15	$20	$25	$35	$80	$150	$250	$450	$1,500
	Auctions: $2,401, MS-66, June 2015; $2,056, MS-66, August 2015; $388, MS-64, March 2015; $100, MS-60, January 2015												
1877	7,310,000	165	60.8	83%	$15	$20	$25	$35	$80	$150	$250	$450	$850
	Auctions: $1,645, MS-66, October 2015; $764, MS-65, June 2015; $235, MS-62, February 2015												
1877, Proof	510	129	63.9								$300	$600	$1,000
	Auctions: $1,410, PF-66, September 2016; $1,880, PF-65, October 2015; $823, PF-65, August 2016												
1877-CC	7,700,000	503	55.0	66%	$30	$45	$60	$90	$130	$280	$650	$1,150	$2,000
	Auctions: $4,935, MS-67, January 2015; $2,115, MS-66, July 2015; $1,116, MS-65, January 2015; $881, MS-64, August 2015												
1877-S	2,340,000	95	61.2	83%	$15	$20	$25	$35	$80	$150	$300	$650	$2,750
	Auctions: $494, MS-64, May 2015; $353, MS-64, March 2015; $129, AU-58, January 2015												

r. The scarce Variety 2 reverse exhibits a single point to the end of the left ribbon; the common Variety 1 reverse has a split at the ribbon's end. **s.** Included in circulation-strike 1876-CC mintage figure.

	Mintage	Cert	Avg	%MS	G-4	F-12	VF-20	EF-40	AU-50	MS-60	MS-63	MS-64	MS-65
											PF-60	PF-63	PF-65
1878	1,677,200	96	61.0	84%	$15	$20	$25	$35	$80	$150	$250	$425	$1,000
	Auctions: $5,170, MS-67, May 2015; $1,645, MS-66, October 2015; $376, MS-63, May 2015; $188, MS-62, October 2015												
1878, Proof	800	172	64.0								$300	$600	$1,000
	Auctions: $2,233, PF-66Cam, August 2015; $1,058, PF-65Cam, August 2015; $881, PF-64, January 2015; $676, PF-64, March 2015												
1878-CC	200,000	81	47.7	57%	$200	$300	$330	$475	$1,000	$1,350	$2,500	$3,000	$5,000
	Auctions: $7,638, MS-67, May 2015; $541, EF-45, January 2015; $235, EF-40, January 2015; $353, VF-25, February 2015												
1879	14,000	217	62.9	92%	$200	$325	$400	$500	$550	$575	$650	$800	$1,100
	Auctions: $2,174, MS-67, January 2015; $3,525, MS-66, June 2015; $494, MS-63, January 2015												
1879, Proof	1,100	309	64.2								$300	$600	$1,000
	Auctions: $4,935, PF-68, May 2015; $2,115, PF-67Cam, January 2015; $1,116, PF-65Cam, July 2015; $999, PF-65, October 2015												
1880	36,000	153	60.1	83%	$150	$250	$350	$400	$500	$650	$700	$800	$1,200
	Auctions: $1,763, MS-67, January 2015; $646, MS-63, June 2015; $376, EF-45, June 2015; $223, F-12, January 2015												
1880, Proof	1,355	324	64.4								$300	$600	$1,000
	Auctions: $1,058, PF-65Cam, January 2015; $664, PF-64, March 2015; $646, PF-64, February 2015; $376, PF-60, May 2015												
1881	24,000	91	55.7	68%	$160	$260	$375	$425	$525	$675	$775	$950	$1,600
	Auctions: $8,225, MS-67, May 2015; $2,820, MS-67, August 2015; $823, MS-64, January 2015; $646, MS-62, July 2015												
1881, Proof	975	256	64.5								$300	$600	$1,000
	Auctions: $4,583, PF-67Cam, January 2015; $1,116, PF-66Cam, July 2015; $1,234, PF-66, February 2015; $1,012, PF-65, January 2015												
1882	3,910,000	415	62.7	91%	$15	$20	$25	$35	$80	$150	$250	$425	$650
	Auctions: $1,645, MS-67, January 2015; $600, MS-65, June 2015; $400, MS-64, November 2015; $176, MS-63, March 2015												
1882, Proof	1,100	355	64.6								$300	$600	$1,000
	Auctions: $2,586, PF-67, August 2015; $1,763, PF-66Cam, January 2015; $1,175, PF-66, January 2015; $705, PF-64, January 2015												
1883	7,674,673	505	60.7	85%	$15	$20	$25	$35	$80	$150	$250	$425	$650
	Auctions: $1,586, MS-67, September 2015; $1,234, MS-66, September 2015; $712, MS-65, August 2015; $329, MS-64, January 2015												
1883, Proof	1,039	307	64.4								$300	$600	$1,000
	Auctions: $2,350, PF-67, January 2015; $1,188, PF-66, August 2015; $3,760, PF-65, August 2015; $705, PF-64Cam, January 2015												
1884	3,365,505	406	62.6	88%	$15	$20	$25	$35	$80	$150	$250	$425	$650
	Auctions: $2,585, MS-67, May 2015; $1,528, MS-66, January 2015; $329, MS-64, June 2015; $212, MS-63, January 2015												
1884, Proof	875	315	64.9								$300	$600	$1,000
	Auctions: $3,290, PF-67Cam, August 2015; $1,763, PF-66Cam, September 2015; $1,116, PF-65Cam, October 2015; $1,002, PF-65, March 2015												
1884-S	564,969	63	58.4	68%	$20	$32	$60	$100	$300	$750	$1,100	$1,500	$5,000
	Auctions: $14,100, MS-66, October 2015; $1,175, MS-64, July 2015; $999, MS-63, March 2015; $705, MS-61, June 2015												
1885	2,532,497	369	62.5	89%	$15	$20	$25	$35	$80	$150	$250	$425	$650
	Auctions: $8,813, MS-67, August 2015; $764, MS-66, January 2015; $194, MS-63, January 2015; $129, MS-61, November 2015												
1885, Proof	930	294	64.7								$300	$600	$1,000
	Auctions: $5,640, PF-68Cam, August 2015; $4,465, PF-67Cam, May 2015; $1,351, PF-66Cam, October 2015; $1,293, PF-65Cam, August 2015												
1885-S	43,690	60	33.6	23%	$650	$1,100	$1,400	$2,250	$4,000	$5,500	$8,500	$15,000	$27,500
	Auctions: $1,645, VF-35, January 2015; $1,175, VF-25, January 2015; $505, F-12, October 2015; $499, VG-8, October 2015												
1886	6,376,684	645	61.7	85%	$15	$20	$25	$35	$80	$150	$250	$425	$650
	Auctions: $1,293, MS-67, July 2015; $1,116, MS-66, June 2015; $1,293, MS-65, January 2015; $353, MS-64, November 2015												
1886, Proof	886	285	64.5								$300	$600	$1,000
	Auctions: $1,998, PF-67, July 2015; $1,528, PF-66, June 2015; $999, PF-65, January 2015; $999, PF-65, January 2015												
1886-S	206,524	53	57.5	74%	$30	$50	$75	$135	$200	$550	$1,000	$2,000	$3,250
	Auctions: $8,813, MS-67, October 2014; $4,700, MS-66, September 2014; $6,463, MS-66, June 2013; $2,585, MS-65, October 2014												
1887	11,283,229	638	60.0	80%	$15	$20	$25	$35	$80	$150	$250	$425	$600
	Auctions: $2,820, MS-67, May 2015; $1,528, MS-66, January 2015; $588, MS-65, January 2015; $423, MS-64, February 2015												
1887, Proof	710	211	64.4								$300	$600	$1,000
	Auctions: $3,173, PF-67Cam, September 2015; $3,525, PF-66, October 2015; $1,058, PF-65Cam, May 2015; $999, PF-65, June 2015												
1887-S	4,454,450	285	59.3	76%	$15	$20	$25	$35	$80	$150	$300	$450	$1,000
	Auctions: $6,463, MS-67, June 2015; $1,586, MS-66, May 2015; $999, MS-65, October 2015; $423, MS-64, August 2015												

**1891-O, O Over
Horizontal O**
FS-10-1891o-501.

**1891-S, Repunched
Mintmark**
FS-10-1891S-501.

	Mintage	Cert	Avg	%MS	G-4	F-12	VF-20	EF-40	AU-50	MS-60	MS-63	MS-64	MS-65
										PF-60	PF-63	PF-65
1888	5,495,655	345	60.4	82%	$15	$20	$25	$35	$80	$150	$250	$425	$650
Auctions: $1,293, MS-66, August 2015; $423, MS-64, October 2015; $217, MS-63, October 2015; $89, AU-58, January 2015													
1888, Proof	832	213	64.4							$300	$600	$1,000
Auctions: $3,995, PF-67Cam, May 2015; $1,410, PF-66Cam, July 2015; $1,351, PF-65Cam, August 2015; $1,200, PF-65Cam, September 2015													
1888-S	1,720,000	71	56.8	62%	$15	$20	$25	$35	$100	$250	$850	$1,150	$3,250
Auctions: $501, MS-63, March 2015; $390, MS-62, October 2015; $56, AU-50, October 2015													
1889	7,380,000	381	61.0	83%	$15	$20	$25	$35	$80	$150	$250	$425	$650
Auctions: $3,819, MS-67, January 2015; $2,350, MS-66, January 2015; $517, MS-64, October 2015; $176, MS-63, July 2015													
1889, Proof	711	180	64.5							$300	$600	$1,000
Auctions: $4,700, PF-68, October 2015; $1,939, PF-67, July 2015; $1,175, PF-66, January 2015; $1,058, PF-65, October 2015													
1889-S	972,678	86	60.2	64%	$20	$30	$50	$80	$150	$450	$1,000	$1,650	$4,750
Auctions: $2,115, MS-65, January 2015; $329, MS-62, March 2015; $74, AU-55, January 2015; $129, AU-50, September 2015													
1890	9,910,951	612	60.7	83%	$15	$20	$25	$35	$80	$150	$250	$425	$600
Auctions: $4,700, MS-67, September 2015; $1,058, MS-66, October 2015; $588, MS-65, June 2015; $282, MS-64, February 2015													
1890, Proof	590	209	64.4							$300	$600	$1,000
Auctions: $1,939, PF-66Cam, August 2015; $1,410, PF-66, February 2015; $1,116, PF-66, July 2015													
1890-S, Large S	1,423,076	126	58.1	73%	$18	$25	$55	$85	$150	$350	$700	$1,000	$1,500
Auctions: $6,169, MS-66, May 2015; $676, MS-64, March 2015; $1,293, MS-63, September 2015; $270, MS-62, January 2015													
1890-S, Small S (t)	(u)	(v)						—	—	—			
Auctions: $1,208, MS-65, February 2006													
1891	15,310,000	1,064	61.3	83%	$15	$20	$25	$35	$80	$150	$250	$400	$650
Auctions: $1,645, MS-67, July 2015; $1,116, MS-66, March 2015; $588, MS-65, January 2015; $282, MS-64, October 2015													
1891, Proof	600	230	64.8							$300	$600	$1,000
Auctions: $6,463, PF-67Cam, November 2013													
1891-O	4,540,000	238	57.8	77%	$15	$20	$30	$50	$100	$175	$350	$550	$1,100
Auctions: $2,000, MS-66, September 2015; $1,528, MS-65, January 2015; $306, MS-63, August 2015; $60, AU-50, June 2015													
1891-O, O Over Horizontal O (w)	(x)	2	51.5	0%	$60	$120	$150	$225	$1,000	$3,000			
Auctions: $253, AU-58, May 2010													
1891-O, Proof (y)	2–3	1	66.0										$50,000
Auctions: No auction records available.													
1891-S	3,196,116	182	61.6	85%	$15	$20	$25	$35	$80	$175	$300	$450	$1,000
Auctions: $881, MS-66, August 2015; $764, MS-65, January 2015; $235, MS-63, March 2015; $141, MS-61, January 2015													
1891-S, Repunched Mintmark (z)	(aa)	4	61.5	75%	$20	$45	$55	$85	$115	$300			
Auctions: $5,750, MS-66, September 2010													

t. This coin is considered rare. u. Included in 1890-S, Large S, mintage figure. v. Included in certified population for 1890-S, Large S. w. The primary O mintmark was punched over a previously punched horizontal O. x. Included in circulation-strike 1891-O mintage figure. y. This coin is considered extremely rare. z. The larger primary S mintmark (known as the medium S) was punched squarely over the smaller S, which is evident within both loops. aa. Included in 1891-S mintage figure.

BARBER OR LIBERTY HEAD (1892–1916)

Designer: *Charles E. Barber.* **Weight:** *2.50 grams.* **Composition:** *.900 silver, .100 copper (net weight: .07234 oz. pure silver).* **Diameter:** *17.9 mm.* **Edge:** *Reeded.* **Mints:** *Philadelphia, Denver, New Orleans, and San Francisco.*

Circulation Strike

Mintmark location is on the reverse, below the bow.

Proof

History. This dime belongs to a suite of silver coins (including the quarter and half dollar) designed by U.S. Mint chief engraver Charles E. Barber. It features a large Liberty Head styled similarly to contemporary French coinage. The reverse of the dime continues the "cereal wreath" motif of the late Liberty Seated era.

Striking and Sharpness. Check the details of the hair on the obverse. The reverse usually is sharp. If weakness is seen, it is typically in the wreath details. The denticles usually are sharp on the obverse and reverse. The Proofs of 1892 to 1901 usually have cameo contrast between the designs and the mirror fields. Later Proofs vary in contrast.

Availability. With the exception of the rare 1894-S, of which fewer than a dozen are known, all dates and mintmarks are collectible. Probably 90% or more of the survivors are in lower grades such as AG-3 and G-4. The word LIBERTY in the headband, a key to grading, tended to wear away quickly. Relatively few are in grades from Fine upward. MS coins are somewhat scarce, this being especially true of the branch-mint issues. MS-63 and finer Barber dimes usually are from the Philadelphia Mint or, if from a branch mint, are dated after 1905. Proof Barber dimes survive in proportion to their mintages. Choice and Gem examples are more easily found among dimes than among quarters and half dollars of this type. All were originally sold in silver-coin sets.

GRADING STANDARDS

MS-60 to 70 (Mint State). *Obverse:* At MS-60, some abrasion and contact marks are evident, most noticeably on the cheek and the obverse field to the right. Luster is present, but may be dull or lifeless. Many Barber coins have been cleaned, especially of the earlier dates. At MS-63, contact marks are very few; abrasion still is evident, but less than at lower levels. An MS-65 coin may have minor abrasion on the cheek, but contact marks are so

1910. Graded MS-65.

minute as to require magnification. Luster should be full and rich. *Reverse:* Comments apply as for the obverse, except that in lower Mint State grades abrasion and contact marks are most noticeable on the highest parts of the leaves and the ribbon, less so on ONE DIME. At MS-65 or higher, there are no marks visible to the unaided eye. The field is mainly protected by design elements and does not show abrasion as much as does the obverse on a given coin.

   Illustrated coin: The striking on this example is razor sharp.

AU-50, 53, 55, 58 (About Uncirculated). *Obverse:* Light wear is seen on the head, especially on the forward hair under LIBERTY. At AU-58, the luster is extensive, but incomplete, especially on the higher parts and in the right field. At AU-50 and 53, luster is less. *Reverse:* Wear is seen on the leaves and ribbon. An AU-58 coin will have nearly full luster, more so than on the obverse, as the design elements protect the small field areas. At AU–50 and 53, there still is significant luster.

1910. Graded AU-53.

EF-40, 45 (Extremely Fine). *Obverse:* Further wear is seen on the head. The hair above the forehead lacks most detail. LIBERTY shows wear but still is strong. *Reverse:* Further wear is seen on all areas, most noticeably at the wreath and ribbon. Leaves retain excellent details except on the higher areas.

1895-O. Graded EF-40.

VF-20, 30 (Very Fine). *Obverse:* The head shows more wear, now with nearly all detail gone in the hair above the forehead. LIBERTY shows wear, but is complete. The leaves on the head all show wear, as does the upper part of the cap. *Reverse:* Wear is more extensive. The details in the highest leaves are weak or missing, but in lower levels the leaf details remain strong.

1914-S. Graded VF-30.

F-12, 15 (Fine). *Obverse:* The head shows extensive wear. LIBERTY, the key place to check, is weak, especially at ER, but is fully readable. The ANA grading standards and *Photograde* adhere to this. PCGS suggests that lightly struck coins "may have letters partially missing." Traditionally, collectors insist on full LIBERTY. *Reverse:* Much detail of the leaves in the higher areas is gone. The rim remains bold.

1901-S. Graded F-12.

   Illustrated coin: LIBERTY is readable, but letters ER are light.

VG-8, 10 (Very Good). *Obverse:* A net of three letters in LIBERTY must be readable. Traditionally LI is clear, and after that there is a partial letter or two. *Reverse:* Further wear has made the wreath flat; now only in outline form with only a few traces of details. The rim is complete.

1903-S. Graded VG-10.

G-4, 6 (Good). *Obverse:* The head is in outline form, with the center flat. Most of the rim is there. All letters and the date are full. *Reverse:* The leaves are all combined and in outline form. The rim is weak in areas.

1895-O. Graded G-6.

AG-3 (About Good). *Obverse:* The lettering is readable, but the parts near the border may be worn away. The date is clear. *Reverse:* The wreath and interior letters are partially worn away. The rim is weak.

1895-O. Graded AG-3.

PF-60 to 70 (Proof). *Obverse and Reverse:* Proofs that are extensively cleaned and have many hairlines, or that are dull and grainy, are lower level, such as PF–60 to 62. These are not widely desired, save for the rare (in any grade) year of 1895, and even so most collectors would rather have a lustrous MS-60 than a dull PF-60. With medium hairlines and good reflectivity, an assigned grade of PF-64 is indicated. Tiny horizontal lines on Miss Liberty's cheek, known

1911. Graded PF-67 Deep Cameo.

as *slide marks*, from National and other album slides scuffing the relief of the cheek, are endemic among Barber silver coins. With noticeable marks of this type, the highest grade assignable is PF-64. With relatively few hairlines, a rating of PF-65 can be given. PF-66 should have hairlines so delicate that magnification is needed to see them. Above that, a Proof should be free of any hairlines or other problems.

Illustrated coin: Proof dimes of 1911 are rare (only 543 minted), but one with a Deep Cameo finish, as displayed by this coin, is *extremely* rare. The coin is fully struck on both sides, and has neither a blemish nor a trace of toning.

1893, 3 Over 2   **1897, Repunched Date**
FS-10-1897-301.

	Mintage	Cert	Avg	%MS	G-4	VG-8	F-12	VF-20	EF-40	AU-50	MS-60 / PF-60	MS-63 / PF-63	MS-65 / PF-65
1892	12,120,000	1,470	61.2	82%	$7	$7.50	$18	$25	$30	$75	$125	$185	$375
Auctions: $8,813, MS-66, September 2016; $881, MS-64, November 2016; $447, AU-58, June 2016; $153, AU-58, March 2016													
1892, Proof	1,245	299	64.6								$300	$500	$950
Auctions: $8,225, PF-68, October 2016; $3,760, PF-67, March 2016; $1,821, PF-67, August 2016; $1,469, PF-66, September 2016													
1892-O	3,841,700	260	56.9	69%	$12	$15	$35	$55	$75	$95	$175	$350	$1,250
Auctions: $1,645, MS-65, August 2016; $676, AU-55, July 2016; $494, VF-20, March 2016													
1892-S	990,710	189	42.1	46%	$65	$115	$200	$240	$280	$330	$425	$775	$3,000
Auctions: $2,350, MS-65, August 2016; $940, AU-58, June 2016; $705, EF-40, August 2016; $306, VG-10, March 2016													
1893, 3 Over 2 (a)	(b)	0	n/a		$140	$155	$200	$250	$350	$650	$1,350	$1,950	$5,250
Auctions: $2,233, MS-63, January 2015; $1,763, MS-63, June 2015; $1,528, MS-62, February 2015; $1,351, AU-58, August 2016													
1893	3,339,940	317	58.2	76%	$8	$12	$20	$30	$45	$80	$150	$250	$900
Auctions: $999, MS-65, September 2016; $1,410, MS-64, August 2016; $823, MS-63, May 2016; $329, AU-55, October 2016													
1893, Proof	792	274	64.9								$300	$500	$950
Auctions: $3,995, PF-67, August 2016; $1,528, PF-66, March 2016; $1,293, PF-66, October 2016; $999, PF-65, September 2016													
1893-O	1,760,000	197	47.3	55%	$30	$45	$120	$150	$190	$230	$325	$500	$1,950
Auctions: $1,763, MS-65, October 2016; $223, AU-58, August 2016; $306, EF-40, July 2015; $141, VF-35, July 2015													
1893-S (c)	2,491,401	165	50.2	56%	$15	$25	$40	$60	$90	$150	$325	$750	$2,000
Auctions: $15,275, MS-65, August 2016; $1,528, AU-55, July 2016; $1,293, EF-45, October 2016; $100, G-6, November 2015													
1894	1,330,000	264	48.1	53%	$30	$45	$120	$160	$180	$220	$300	$400	$1,000
Auctions: $3,290, MS-66, March 2016; $999, MS-64, October 2016; $541, AU-58, July 2016; $165, EF-45, August 2016													
1894, Proof	972	318	64.9								$300	$500	$950
Auctions: $2,820, PF-67, March 2016; $793, PF-65, July 2016; $764, PF-65, October 2016													
1894-O	720,000	191	24.1	13%	$70	$95	$220	$300	$425	$750	$1,950	$3,000	$10,000
Auctions: $6,169, MS-66, November 2016; $10,869, MS-65, October 2016; $734, AU-53, August 2016; $447, EF-40, March 2016													
1894-S, Proof † (d)	24	5	64.2									$1,250,000	$1,500,000
Auctions: $1,552,500, PF-64, October 2007													
1895	690,000	216	37.3	36%	$80	$160	$350	$500	$550	$650	$725	$900	$1,500
Auctions: $5,640, MS-66, October 2015; $1,116, MS-64, June 2015; $764, MS-63, October 2015; $423, AU-50, September 2015													
1895, Proof	880	316	64.9								$300	$500	$950
Auctions: $4,465, PF-68Cam, September 2015; $1,058, PF-66Cam, September 2015; $1,175, PF-66, October 2015; $764, PF-63, October 2015													
1895-O	440,000	404	16.1	7%	$475	$600	$900	$1,350	$2,500	$3,500	$6,000	$11,000	$25,000
Auctions: $58,756, MS-67, January 2017; $35,250, MS-66, June 2017; $15,275, MS-64, January 2017; $3,720, AU-58, November 2017													
1895-S	1,120,000	252	40.9	44%	$42	$60	$135	$190	$240	$325	$500	$1,050	$3,500
Auctions: $3,760, MS-65, June 2015; $2,468, MS-65, October 2015; $1,175, MS-64, January 2015; $881, MS-62, February 2015													
1896	2,000,000	164	52.1	65%	$10	$22	$55	$80	$100	$125	$175	$375	$1,100
Auctions: $1,293, MS-66, October 2015; $1,528, MS-65, June 2015; $400, MS-64, January 2015; $353, MS-63, August 2015													
1896, Proof	762	249	64.9								$300	$500	$950
Auctions: $15,275, PF-68Cam, June 2014; $1,763, PF-67, March 2015; $676, PF-64, July 2014; $588, PF-64, July 2014													
1896-O	610,000	182	24.1	15%	$80	$160	$290	$375	$475	$800	$1,200	$2,400	$8,500
Auctions: $11,750, MS-65, October 2015; $4,935, MS-65, June 2015; $3,290, AU-58, July 2015; $676, EF-45, June 2015													
1896-S	575,056	180	31.8	33%	$85	$175	$280	$350	$400	$550	$750	$1,350	$3,200
Auctions: $5,875, MS-66, August 2015; $3,055, MS-65, October 2015; $2,820, MS-65, January 2015; $447, AU-53, April 2015													

† Ranked in the *100 Greatest U.S. Coins* (fifth edition). **a.** Overlaid photographs indicate this is not a true overdate. **b.** Included in circulation-strike 1893 mintage figure. **c.** Boldly doubled mintmark. **d.** The reason for the low mintage of the Proof 1894-S dime is unknown. Popular theories, among others, include a rounding out of the Mint's record books, or a special presentation to bankers visiting the San Francisco Mint. Fewer than a dozen examples are known to exist. Five of these coins were reserved for assay.

	Mintage	Cert	Avg	%MS	G-4	VG-8	F-12	VF-20	EF-40	AU-50	MS-60 PF-60	MS-63 PF-63	MS-65 PF-65
1897	10,868,533	501	60.2	80%	$4	$5	$8	$15	$32	$75	$135	$200	$400
Auctions: $2,585, MS-67, January 2015; $2,200, MS-67, August 2015; $541, MS-65, January 2015; $270, MS-64, January 2015													
1897, Repunched Date (e)	(f)	0	n/a						$80	$120	$200		
Auctions: No auction records available.													
1897, Proof	731	250	64.8								$300	$500	$950
Auctions: $5,889, PF-68Cam, January 2015; $3,819, PF-68, March 2015; $2,938, PF-67, January 2015; $999, PF-66, January 2015													
1897-O	666,000	177	29.4	27%	$65	$115	$300	$375	$475	$600	$1,100	$1,500	$3,250
Auctions: $5,640, MS-66, May 2015; $4,230, MS-66, June 2015; $1,998, MS-64, July 2015; $353, EF-40, August 2015													
1897-S	1,342,844	131	43.9	39%	$18	$40	$100	$120	$175	$300	$500	$800	$3,000
Auctions: $5,170, MS-66, May 2015; $2,585, MS-65, October 2015; $1,410, MS-64, August 2015; $259, MS-60, March 2015													
1898	16,320,000	549	59.4	76%	$4	$5	$8	$12	$26	$75	$130	$200	$400
Auctions: $1,028, MS-66, September 2015; $646, MS-65, January 2015; $306, MS-64, January 2015; $153, MS-63, February 2015													
1898, Proof	735	292	65.1								$300	$500	$950
Auctions: $1,998, PF-67, June 2015; $1,087, PF-66, July 2015; $1,058, PF-65, March 2015; $646, PF-64, January 2015													
1898-O	2,130,000	121	46.4	46%	$12	$30	$90	$150	$200	$300	$475	$1,050	$3,000
Auctions: $3,760, MS-65, January 2015; $2,115, MS-65, January 2015; $153, AU-50, July 2015; $107, VF-25, January 2015													
1898-S	1,702,507	82	49.0	48%	$8	$15	$32	$45	$85	$150	$500	$1,200	$2,250
Auctions: $2,115, MS-64, September 2015; $141, AU-53, July 2015; $89, AU-50, February 2015; $84, AU-50, January 2015													
1899	19,580,000	417	58.6	71%	$4	$5	$8	$12	$25	$75	$130	$200	$475
Auctions: $6,169, MS-68, September 2015; $1,645, MS-66, August 2015; $1,058, MS-66, October 2015; $230, MS-64, April 2015													
1899, Proof	846	244	64.6								$300	$500	$950
Auctions: $1,410, PF-66, October 2015; $999, PF-66, January 2015; $999, PF-65, January 2015; $646, PF-64, July 2015													
1899-O	2,650,000	153	43.1	37%	$10	$20	$75	$100	$150	$225	$400	$900	$4,000
Auctions: $1,998, MS-64, September 2015; $940, MS-63, June 2015; $764, MS-63, June 2015; $84, EF-40, January 2015													
1899-S	1,867,493	119	56.2	64%	$8.50	$16	$32	$35	$45	$110	$300	$650	$2,300
Auctions: $6,463, MS-67, January 2015; $100, AU-53, April 2015													
1900	17,600,000	323	59.6	74%	$4	$5	$8	$12	$25	$75	$125	$225	$575
Auctions: $5,405, MS-67, September 2015; $2,585, MS-66, June 2015; $482, MS-65, April 2015; $306, MS-64, October 2015													
1900, Proof	912	234	64.7								$300	$500	$950
Auctions: $2,350, PF-67Cam, January 2015; $1,146, PF-66Cam, July 2015; $999, PF-65, January 2015; $646, PF-64, January 2015													
1900-O	2,010,000	160	38.6	28%	$18	$38	$115	$160	$220	$350	$650	$1,000	$4,000
Auctions: $3,995, MS-66, May 2015; $2,115, MS-64, February 2015; $764, MS-61, February 2015; $141, AU-50, May 2015													
1900-S	5,168,270	178	55.7	48%	$5	$6	$12	$20	$30	$75	$175	$375	$1,500
Auctions: $4,230, MS-66, May 2015; $3,525, MS-66, June 2015; $764, MS-64, January 2015; $42, AU-50, January 2015													
1901	18,859,665	396	59.3	71%	$4	$5	$7	$10	$26	$75	$125	$200	$500
Auctions: $999, MS-66, February 2015; $423, MS-65, January 2015; $259, MS-64, January 2015; $176, MS-63, July 2015													
1901, Proof	813	251	64.6								$300	$500	$950
Auctions: $14,100, PF-68, May 2015; $1,645, PF-67, January 2015; $999, PF-66, January 2015; $940, PF-65, July 2015													
1901-O	5,620,000	145	51.1	39%	$4	$5.50	$16	$28	$75	$180	$600	$1,100	$2,200
Auctions: $1,763, MS-64, September 2015; $1,175, MS-64, October 2015; $423, MS-62, April 2015; $135, AU-55, January 2015													
1901-S	593,022	180	30.3	21%	$80	$135	$375	$500	$550	$750	$1,300	$2,100	$4,500
Auctions: $2,350, MS-64, September 2015; $377, AU-50, May 2015; $376, EF-40, November 2015; $259, VF-30, January 2015													
1902	21,380,000	310	55.2	55%	$4	$5	$6	$8	$25	$75	$125	$225	$550
Auctions: $259, MS-64, January 2015; $212, MS-64, August 2015; $200, MS-64, September 2015; $100, AU-58, March 2015													
1902, Proof	777	210	64.2								$300	$500	$950
Auctions: $1,116, PF-66, October 2015; $999, PF-65, January 2015; $646, PF-64, January 2015; $423, PF-63, November 2015													
1902-O	4,500,000	134	53.2	49%	$4	$6	$15	$32	$65	$175	$425	$750	$3,500
Auctions: $1,410, MS-64, September 2015; $1,399, MS-64, September 2015; $356, AU-58, January 2015; $123, AU-53, April 2015													
1902-S	2,070,000	111	46.0	44%	$9	$20	$55	$90	$140	$200	$400	$750	$3,100
Auctions: $235, AU-58, August 2015; $153, AU-55, January 2015; $106, AU-50, May 2015; $94, VF-35, February 2015													

e. More than one repunched date exists for 1897. This listing is for FS-10-1897-301, one of the most dramatic RPDs of the series. See the *Cherrypickers' Guide to Rare Die Varieties, Vol. II* (sixth edition). The secondary digits of the date are evident west of the primary digits. f. Included in circulation-strike 1897 mintage figure.

1905-O, Normal O   **1905-O, Micro O**

	Mintage	Cert	Avg	%MS	G-4	VG-8	F-12	VF-20	EF-40	AU-50	MS-60	MS-63	MS-65
											PF-60	PF-63	PF-65
1903	19,500,000	225	56.2	58%	$4	$5	$6	$8	$25	$75	$125	$225	$700
	Auctions: $1,998, MS-66, May 2015; $1,528, MS-66, October 2015; $259, MS-64, January 2015; $165, MS-63, January 2015												
1903, Proof	755	221	64.3								$300	$500	$950
	Auctions: $2,233, PF-67, October 2015; $1,058, PF-66, January 2015; $1,058, PF-66, July 2015; $329, PF-62, January 2015												
1903-O	8,180,000	209	53.8	40%	$5	$6	$14	$25	$55	$110	$275	$550	$2,750
	Auctions: $8,813, MS-67, May 2015; $2,350, MS-65, July 2015; $881, MS-64, February 2015; $306, AU-58, July 2015												
1903-S	613,300	166	27.0	16%	$85	$130	$375	$500	$675	$825	$1,100	$1,350	$2,500
	Auctions: $3,055, MS-66, May 2015; $2,820, MS-66, June 2015; $1,058, AU-58, January 2015; $282, AU-50, October 2015												
1904	14,600,357	240	57.3	66%	$4	$5	$6	$9	$25	$75	$125	$240	$800
	Auctions: $2,585, MS-66, May 2015; $1,763, MS-66, January 2015; $306, MS-64, January 2015; $50, AU-58, January 2015												
1904, Proof	670	229	64.2								$300	$500	$950
	Auctions: $2,233, PF-67Cam, March 2015; $1,821, PF-67, January 2015; $1,080, PF-66, October 2015; $1,146, PF-65Cam, January 2015												
1904-S	800,000	174	35.6	30%	$45	$75	$160	$250	$325	$500	$850	$1,800	$4,500
	Auctions: $10,117, MS-66, January 2015; $400, AU-55, August 2015; $376, AU-55, May 2015; $153, EF-40, January 2015												
1905	14,551,623	255	56.7	60%	$4	$5	$6	$10	$25	$75	$125	$200	$600
	Auctions: $1,528, MS-66, January 2015; $1,293, MS-66, September 2015; $517, MS-65, September 2015; $235, MS-64, September 2015												
1905, Proof	727	219	64.7								$300	$500	$950
	Auctions: $4,465, PF-68, January 2015; $2,800, PF-67, July 2015; $1,000, PF-65Cam, June 2015; $940, PF-65, July 2015												
1905-O	3,400,000	269	46.1	48%	$5	$10	$35	$60	$100	$150	$300	$425	$1,200
	Auctions: $1,998, MS-66, October 2015; $1,645, MS-65, October 2015; $564, MS-64, January 2015; $153, AU-58, August 2015												
1905-O, Micro O	(g)	55	29.0	13%	$60	$90	$150	$300	$725	$1,150	$2,700	$5,500	$10,000
	Auctions: $4,113, MS-62, June 2014; $282, VF-25, August 2014; $223, VF-25, October 2014												
1905-S	6,855,199	227	55.4	54%	$4	$6	$9	$20	$40	$95	$250	$325	$1,000
	Auctions: $1,528, MS-66, October 2015; $141, MS-61, January 2015; $69, MS-60, October 2015												
1906	19,957,731	495	58.2	65%	$4	$5	$6	$10	$25	$75	$125	$200	$400
	Auctions: $3,525, MS-67, July 2015; $259, MS-64, May 2015; $212, MS-64, July 2015; $165, MS-63, April 2015												
1906, Proof	675	187	64.6								$300	$500	$950
	Auctions: $1,645, PF-67, January 2015; $1,050, PF-65, January 2015; $646, PF-64, January 2015; $447, PF-63, October 2015												
1906-D	4,060,000	135	54.5	67%	$4	$5	$8	$15	$35	$80	$175	$350	$1,100
	Auctions: $3,055, MS-66, May 2015; $646, MS-64, July 2015; $182, MS-62, August 2015; $118, AU-58, October 2015												
1906-O	2,610,000	168	54.3	70%	$6	$14	$45	$75	$110	$130	$200	$380	$1,100
	Auctions: $4,935, MS-67, August 2015; $1,116, MS-66, January 2015; $764, MS-65, June 2015; $153, MS-60, February 2015												
1906-S	3,136,640	138	57.1	68%	$4	$6	$13	$25	$45	$130	$275	$450	$825
	Auctions: $4,465, MS-66, May 2015; $1,763, MS-66, August 2015; $999, MS-64, August 2015; $212, AU-58, August 2015												
1907	22,220,000	568	56.8	67%	$4	$5	$6	$10	$25	$55	$125	$190	$400
	Auctions: $705, MS-66, August 2015; $329, MS-65, May 2015; $259, MS-64, January 2015; $165, MS-63, May 2015												
1907, Proof	575	184	64.6								$300	$500	$950
	Auctions: $6,463, PF-68, May 2015; $2,115, PF-67, January 2015; $1,351, PF-66, January 2015; $600, PF-64, January 2015												
1907-D	4,080,000	102	54.9	61%	$4	$5	$10	$20	$45	$110	$250	$700	$1,800
	Auctions: $1,293, MS-65, June 2015; $1,175, MS-64, July 2015; $1,058, MS-64, July 2015; $494, MS-63, June 2015												
1907-O	5,058,000	185	55.4	69%	$4	$7	$30	$45	$70	$110	$200	$325	$1,050
	Auctions: $1,645, MS-66, January 2015; $400, MS-64, February 2015; $153, MS-63, May 2015; $212, MS-62, June 2015												
1907-S	3,178,470	120	54.6	48%	$4	$6	$15	$27	$75	$150	$400	$700	$2,000
	Auctions: $1,070, MS-64, July 2015; $482, MS-62, February 2015; $79, AU-55, January 2015; $106, AU-50, July 2015												

g. Included in 1905-O mintage figure.

	Mintage	Cert	Avg	%MS	G-4	VG-8	F-12	VF-20	EF-40	AU-50	MS-60	MS-63	MS-65
											PF-60	PF-63	PF-65
1908	10,600,000	398	58.9	75%	$4	$5	$6	$10	$25	$75	$125	$200	$400
Auctions: $1,293, MS-66, June 2015; $499, MS-65, January 2015; $259, MS-64, February 2015; $240, MS-64, July 2015													
1908, Proof	545	188	64.7								$300	$500	$950
Auctions: $1,528, PF-67, September 2015; $1,410, PF-66, June 2015; $940, PF-65, January 2015; $622, PF-64, June 2015													
1908-D	7,490,000	238	54.5	57%	$4	$5	$6	$10	$30	$75	$120	$250	$700
Auctions: $646, MS-65, July 2015; $588, MS-65, February 2015; $200, MS-63, July 2015; $60, AU-53, February 2015													
1908-O	1,789,000	140	52.3	60%	$6	$12	$45	$65	$95	$150	$300	$650	$900
Auctions: $1,528, MS-66, August 2015; $764, MS-64, June 2015; $447, MS-63, June 2015; $182, AU-58, April 2015													
1908-S	3,220,000	107	54.5	51%	$4	$6	$15	$25	$45	$170	$350	$650	$1,350
Auctions: $4,700, MS-67, August 2015; $153, AU-53, July 2015; $42, EF-45, January 2015													
1909	10,240,000	352	58.4	74%	$4	$5	$6	$10	$25	$75	$125	$225	$400
Auctions: $881, MS-66, May 2015; $212, MS-64, April 2015; $170, MS-63, July 2015; $118, MS-62, July 2015													
1909, Proof	650	251	64.6								$300	$500	$950
Auctions: $1,528, PF-67, October 2015; $1,058, PF-65Cam, February 2015; $881, PF-65, January 2015; $646, PF-64, January 2015													
1909-D	954,000	135	49.3	50%	$8	$20	$60	$90	$140	$225	$500	$800	$1,850
Auctions: $3,055, MS-66, May 2015; $212, AU-53, May 2015; $100, EF-40, July 2015													
1909-O	2,287,000	132	54.2	61%	$5	$8	$13	$25	$70	$160	$275	$600	$1,500
Auctions: $4,935, MS-66, May 2015; $2,820, MS-66, July 2015; $999, MS-64, February 2015; $235, AU-53, April 2015													
1909-S	1,000,000	120	47.6	57%	$9	$20	$80	$130	$180	$310	$475	$975	$2,300
Auctions: $9,400, MS-67, September 2015; $9,988, MS-66, May 2015; $517, MS-62, July 2015; $235, MS-60, October 2015													
1910	11,520,000	546	59.3	79%	$4	$5	$6	$10	$24	$75	$125	$225	$400
Auctions: $1,410, MS-66, October 2015; $646, MS-65, February 2015; $259, MS-64, February 2015; $188, MS-63, February 2015													
1910, Proof	551	217	64.7								$300	$500	$950
Auctions: $8,813, PF-68, May 2015; $1,880, PF-67, August 2015; $1,058, PF-66, October 2015; $646, PF-64, January 2015													
1910-D	3,490,000	109	56.1	67%	$4	$5	$10	$20	$48	$95	$220	$375	$1,500
Auctions: $3,643, MS-66, January 2015; $1,293, MS-64, June 2015; $588, MS-63, August 2015; $353, AU-58, October 2015													
1910-S	1,240,000	104	45.3	42%	$6	$9	$50	$70	$110	$180	$425	$600	$2,000
Auctions: $7,344, MS-67, June 2014; $2,820, MS-66, July 2014; $411, MS-62, July 2014													
1911	18,870,000	1,117	59.3	77%	$4	$5	$6	$10	$24	$75	$125	$200	$400
Auctions: $1,116, MS-66, September 2015; $401, MS-65, August 2015; $243, MS-64, February 2015; $165, MS-63, May 2015													
1911, Proof	543	222	64.9								$300	$500	$950
Auctions: $3,760, PF-67Cam, January 2015; $1,528, PF-66Cam, July 2015; $860, PF-65, September 2015; $646, PF-64, January 2015													
1911-D	11,209,000	290	56.8	70%	$4	$5	$6	$10	$24	$75	$125	$200	$400
Auctions: $3,525, MS-67, June 2015; $370, MS-65, September 2015; $306, MS-64, September 2015; $118, MS-62, May 2015													
1911-S	3,520,000	205	59.2	79%	$4	$5	$10	$20	$40	$100	$200	$375	$850
Auctions: $4,818, MS-67, September 2015; $1,410, MS-66, August 2015; $734, MS-65, July 2015; $529, MS-64, February 2015													
1912	19,349,300	1,121	58.8	75%	$4	$5	$6	$10	$24	$75	$125	$200	$400
Auctions: $2,056, MS-67, May 2015; $911, MS-66, January 2015; $400, MS-65, August 2015; $240, MS-64, January 2015													
1912, Proof	700	187	64.3								$300	$500	$950
Auctions: $2,350, PF-67, August 2015; $1,020, PF-65, September 2015; $999, PF-65, January 2015; $588, PF-64, January 2015													
1912-D	11,760,000	410	53.8	61%	$4	$5	$6	$10	$24	$75	$125	$200	$400
Auctions: $6,169, MS-67, August 2015; $6,169, MS-66, May 2015; $517, MS-65, September 2015; $306, MS-64, November 2015													
1912-S	3,420,000	198	58.2	67%	$4	$5	$6	$12	$32	$90	$170	$325	$1,100
Auctions: $1,293, MS-66, June 2013; $999, MS-65, May 2015; $206, MS-62, July 2014; $206, MS-62, August 2014													

	Mintage	Cert	Avg	%MS	G-4	VG-8	F-12	VF-20	EF-40	AU-50	MS-60	MS-63	MS-65
											PF-60	PF-63	PF-65
1913	19,760,000	998	56.8	70%	$4	$5	$6	$10	$24	$75	$125	$225	$400
	Auctions: $564, MS-66, October 2015; $999, MS-65, October 2015; $200, MS-64, April 2015; $118, MS-62, April 2015												
1913, Proof	622	200	64.1								$300	$500	$950
	Auctions: $4,935, PF-67Cam, May 2015; $3,290, PF-66Cam, July 2015; $2,056, PF-66, October 2015; $1,036, PF-65, September 2015												
1913-S	510,000	292	31.0	30%	$35	$55	$125	$190	$250	$325	$725	$1,200	$3,250
	Auctions: $2,967, MS-66, October 2015; $1,058, MS-63, June 2015; $881, MS-63, October 2015; $617, MS-61, June 2015												
1914	17,360,230	1,003	57.7	76%	$4	$5	$6	$10	$24	$75	$125	$200	$400
	Auctions: $2,703, MS-67, January 2015; $1,763, MS-66, June 2015; $564, MS-65, January 2015; $259, MS-64, October 2015												
1914, Proof	425	169	64.5								$300	$500	$950
	Auctions: $3,055, PF-67, January 2015; $650, PF-64, January 2015; $470, PF-63, October 2015												
1914-D	11,908,000	643	54.6	64%	$4	$5	$6	$10	$24	$75	$125	$200	$500
	Auctions: $823, MS-66, October 2015; $470, MS-65, January 2015; $165, MS-63, February 2015; $118, AU-58, May 2015												
1914-S	2,100,000	186	56.9	73%	$4	$5	$10	$18	$40	$80	$125	$250	$1,100
	Auctions: $1,645, MS-66, October 2015; $881, MS-65, August 2015; $646, MS-64, March 2015; $400, MS-64, February 2015												
1915	5,620,000	410	58.1	77%	$4	$5	$6	$10	$24	$75	$125	$225	$400
	Auctions: $1,880, MS-67, June 2015; $1,175, MS-66, May 2015; $235, MS-64, February 2015; $141, MS-62, January 2015												
1915, Proof	450	144	64.3								$300	$500	$950
	Auctions: $1,763, PF-67, January 2015; $999, PF-65, August 2015; $940, PF-64, October 2015; $153, PF-60, August 2015												
1915-S	960,000	178	51.5	55%	$7	$12	$35	$50	$70	$140	$275	$400	$1,450
	Auctions: $1,998, MS-66, January 2015; $1,200, MS-65, June 2015; $823, MS-64, August 2015; $517, MS-64, October 2015												
1916	18,490,000	1,485	58.5	76%	$4	$5	$6	$10	$24	$75	$125	$225	$400
	Auctions: $646, MS-66, January 2015; $588, MS-65, January 2015; $242, MS-64, January 2015; $120, MS-62, January 2015												
1916-S	5,820,000	383	58.6	74%	$4	$5	$6	$10	$24	$75	$125	$240	$400
	Auctions: $2,233, MS-66, January 2015; $1,058, MS-66, June 2015; $282, MS-64, May 2015; $188, MS-63, October 2015												

WINGED LIBERTY HEAD OR "MERCURY" (1916–1945)

Designer: *Adolph A. Weinman.* **Weight:** *2.50 grams.* **Composition:** *.900 silver, .100 copper (net weight .07234 oz. pure silver).* **Diameter:** *17.9 mm.* **Edge:** *Reeded.* **Mints:** *Philadelphia, Denver, and San Francisco.*

Circulation Strike

Mintmark location is on the reverse, at the base of the branch.

Proof

History. In 1916 a new dime, designed by sculptor Adolph A. Weinman (who also created the half dollar that debuted that year), replaced Charles Barber's Liberty Head type. Officially Weinman's design was known as the Winged Liberty Head, but numismatists commonly call the coin the *Mercury* dime, from Miss Liberty's wing-capped resemblance to the Roman god. The reverse depicts a fasces (symbolic of strength in unity) and an olive branch (symbolic of peaceful intentions). Production was continuous from 1916 to 1945, except for 1922, 1932, and 1933. The Mint also created a 2016 gold Mercury dime at a smaller dimension. See page 448.

Striking and Sharpness. Many Mercury dimes exhibit areas of light striking, most notably in the center horizontal band across the fasces, less so in the lower horizontal band. The bands are composed of two parallel lines with a separation or "split" between. The term Full Bands, abbreviated FB, describes coins with both parallel lines in the center band distinctly separated. *In addition,* some dimes may display weak striking in other areas (not noted by certification services or others), including at areas of Liberty's hair, the rim, and the date. Dimes of 1921 in particular can have FB but poorly struck dates. Proof dies were completely polished, including the portrait.

Availability. Certain coins, such as 1916-D; 1921-P; 1921-D; 1942, 2 Over 1; and 1942-D, 2 Over 1, are elusive in any grade. Others are generally available in lower circulated grades, although some are scarce. In MS many of the issues before 1931 range from scarce to rare. If with FB and also sharply struck in other areas, some are rare. MS coins usually are very lustrous. In the marketplace certain scarce early issues such as 1916-D, 1921, and 1921-D are often graded slightly more liberally than are later varieties. Proofs were minted from 1936 to 1942 and are available in proportion to their mintages.

GRADING STANDARDS

MS-60 to 70 (Mint State). *Obverse:* At MS-60, some abrasion and contact marks are evident on the highest part of the portrait, including the hair immediately to the right of the face and the upper left part of the wing. At MS-63, abrasion is slight at best, less so for MS-64. Album slide marks on the cheek, if present, should not be at any grade above MS-64. An MS-65 coin should display no abrasion or contact marks except under mag-

1928. Graded MS-66FB.

nification, and MS-66 and higher coins should have none at all. Luster should be full and rich. *Reverse:* Comments apply as for the obverse, except that the highest parts of the fasces, these being the horizontal bands, are the places to check. The field is mainly protected by design elements and does not show contact marks readily.

AU-50, 53, 55, 58 (About Uncirculated). *Obverse:* Light wear is seen on the cheek, the hair immediately to the right of the face, the left edge of the wing, and the upper right of the wing. At AU-58, the luster is extensive, but incomplete, especially on the higher parts and in the field. At AU–50 and 53, luster is less. *Reverse:* Light wear is seen on the higher parts of the fasces. An AU-58 coin has nearly full luster, more so than on the obverse, as the

1942, 2 Over 1. Graded AU-50.

design elements protect the field areas. At AU–50 and 53, there still is significant luster. Generally, the reverse appears to be in a slightly higher grade than the obverse.

EF-40, 45 (Extremely Fine). *Obverse:* Further wear is seen on the head. Many of the hair details are blended together, as are some feather details at the left side of the wing. *Reverse:* The horizontal bands on the fasces may be fused together. The diagonal bands remain in slight relief against the vertical lines (sticks).

1942-D, 2 Over 1; FS-10-1942D-101. Graded EF-45.

VF-20, 30 (Very Fine). *Obverse:* The head shows more wear, now with the forehead and cheek mostly blending into the hair. More feather details are gone. *Reverse:* Wear is more extensive, but the diagonal and horizontal bands on the fasces still are separated from the thin vertical sticks.

1942-D, 2 Over 1; FS-10-1942D-101. Graded VF-20.

F-12, 15 (Fine). *Obverse:* The head shows more wear, the hair has only slight detail, and most of the feathers are gone. In the marketplace a coin in F-12 grade usually has slightly less detail than stated by the ANA grading standards or *Photograde*, from modern interpretations. *Reverse:* Many of the tiny vertical sticks in the fasces are blended together. The bands can be barely discerned and may be worn away at the highest-relief parts.

1916-D. Graded F-12.

VG-8, 10 (Very Good). *Obverse:* Wear is more extensive on the portrait, and only a few feathers are seen on the wing. The outlines between the hair and cap and of the wing are distinct. Lettering is clear, but light in areas. *Reverse:* The rim is complete, or it may be slightly worn away in areas. Only a few traces of the vertical sticks remain in the fasces. Current interpretations in the marketplace are given here and are less strict than those

1921. Graded VG-8.

listed by the ANA grading standards and *Photograde*. Often, earlier issues are graded more liberally than are later dates.

G-4, 6 (Good). *Obverse:* Wear is more extensive, with not all of the outline between the hair and the wing visible. The rim is worn into the edges of the letters and often into the bottom of the last numeral in the date. *Reverse:* The rim is worn away, as are the outer parts of the letters. The fasces is flat or may show a hint of a vertical stick or two. The leaves are thick from wear. The mintmark, if any, is easily seen.

1916-D. Graded G-4.

AG-3 (About Good). *Obverse:* The rim is worn further into the letters. The head is mostly outline all over, except for a few indicates of edges. Folds remain at the top of the cap. The date is clearly visible. *Reverse:* The rim is worn further into the letters. The mintmark, if any, is clear but may be worn away slightly at the bottom. The apparent wear is slightly greater on the reverse than on the obverse.

1916-D. Graded AG-3.

PF-60 to 70 (Proof). *Obverse and Reverse:* Proofs that are extensively cleaned and have many hairlines, or that are dull and grainy, are lower level, such as PF–60 to 62. These are not widely desired, and represent coins that have been mistreated. With medium hairlines and good reflectivity, assigned grades of PF–63 or 64 are appropriate. Tiny horizontal lines on Miss Liberty's cheek, known as *slide marks*, from National and other album slides

1942. Graded PF-67.

scuffing the relief of the cheek, are common; coins with such marks should not be graded higher than PF-64, but sometimes are. With relatively few hairlines and no noticeable slide marks, a rating of PF-65 can be given. PF-66 should have hairlines so delicate that magnification is needed to see them. Above that, a Proof should be free of any hairlines or other problems.

Full Bands

	Mintage	Cert	Avg	%MS	G-4	VG-8	F-12	VF-20	EF-40	AU-50	MS-60	MS-63	MS-65
1916	22,180,080	3,185	62.0	93%	$4	$5	$7	$8	$15	$20	$35	$50	$125
	Auctions: $1,116, MS-67, October 2015; $106, MS-65, November 2015; $153, MS-64, July 2016; $541, AU-58, August 2016												
1916-D † (a)	264,000	5,162	9.6	4%	$850	$1,500	$2,500	$4,000	$6,000	$8,250	$12,500	$16,000	$25,000
	Auctions: $6,463, AU-53, July 2016; $3,995, VF-25, August 2016; $646, G-4, September 2016; $1,116, VG-8, October 2016												

† Ranked in the *100 Greatest U.S. Coins* (fifth edition). **a.** Beware of altered or otherwise spurious mintmarks.

	Mintage	Cert	Avg	%MS	G-4	VG-8	F-12	VF-20	EF-40	AU-50	MS-60	MS-63	MS-65
1916-S	10,450,000	1,182	57.7	84%	$4	$6	$9	$12	$20	$25	$42	$65	$215
	Auctions: $646, MS-65, July 2016; $165, MS-64, August 2016; $1,116, MS-66, October 2016; $400, MS-66, November 2016												
1917	55,230,000	980	62.0	87%	$3	$3.25	$3.50	$6	$8	$12	$30	$60	$170
	Auctions: $235, MS-65, March 2016; $564, MS-66, August 2016; $611, MS-66, September 2016; $1,998, MS-67, October 2016												
1917-D	9,402,000	665	60.2	77%	$4.50	$6	$11	$22	$45	$95	$145	$350	$900
	Auctions: -$1, MS-65, July 2015; $5,875, MS-65, October 2015; $118, AU-58, July 2016; $2,938, MS-65, October 2016												
1917-S	27,330,000	694	60.9	80%	$3	$3.25	$4	$7	$12	$30	$60	$180	$425
	Auctions: $1,293, MS-66, December 2015; $823, MS-65, March 2016; $1,410, MS-66, August 2016; $881, MS-66, September 2016												
1918	26,680,000	504	61.7	85%	$3	$4	$6	$12	$25	$40	$70	$125	$350
	Auctions: $1,175, MS-65, October 2015; $940, MS-65, December 2015; $1,058, MS-66, July 2016; $3,290, MS-66, October 2016												
1918-D	22,674,800	580	60.0	81%	$3	$4	$6	$12	$24	$50	$125	$250	$800
	Auctions: $1,880, MS-66, September 2015; $1,763, MS-62, December 2015; $165, AU-58, July 2016; $1,116, MS-62, September 2016												
1918-S	19,300,000	463	60.7	81%	$3	$3.25	$5	$10	$18	$40	$120	$275	$750
	Auctions: $1,528, MS-66, December 2015; $2,820, MS-64, September 2016; $881, MS-66, October 2016; $646, MS-65, November 2016												
1919	35,740,000	591	60.2	83%	$3	$3.25	$4	$6	$10	$30	$45	$150	$350
	Auctions: $1,058, MS-66, October 2015; $1,763, MS-66, December 2015; $141, MS-61, July 2016; $517, MS-65, August 2016												
1919-D	9,939,000	413	59.2	79%	$4	$7	$12	$24	$35	$75	$200	$450	$1,350
	Auctions: $646, MS-64, December 2015; $329, MS-62, May 2016; $3,290, MS-64, August 2016; $1,763, MS-65, October 2016												
1919-S	8,850,000	330	58.4	60%	$3.50	$4	$8	$16	$35	$80	$200	$450	$1,500
	Auctions: $1,645, MS-65, August 2015; $1,645, MS-66, October 2015; $764, MS-64, November 2015; $881, MS-64, August 2016												
1920	59,030,000	895	63.1	95%	$3	$3.25	$3.50	$5	$8	$15	$35	$75	$250
	Auctions: $646, MS-66, March 2016; $494, MS-66, July 2016; $881, MS-66, August 2016; $423, MS-66, September 2016												
1920-D	19,171,000	470	60.3	79%	$3	$3.50	$4.50	$8	$20	$45	$145	$350	$625
	Auctions: $2,115, MS-65, October 2015; $1,175, MS-64, September 2016; $2,585, MS-65, October 2016; $4,230, MS-66, November 2016												
1920-S	13,820,000	335	60.4	75%	$3.25	$4	$5	$8	$18	$45	$145	$350	$1,300
	Auctions: $5,170, MS-65, July 2015; $4,935, MS-65, August 2015; $4,700, MS-65, December 2015; $259, AU-58, July 2016												
1921	1,230,000	1,762	21.2	14%	$45	$75	$125	$250	$550	$850	$1,250	$2,250	$3,250
	Auctions: $538,286, VF-25, January 2016; $8,905, EF-45, April 2016; $1,763, AU-58, August 2016; $6,463, MS-66, November 2016												
1921-D	1,080,000	1,853	21.2	14%	$60	$130	$200	$350	$675	$1,200	$1,450	$2,500	$3,500
	Auctions: $423, EF-45, June 2016; $259, VF-20, July 2016; $564, AU-50, August 2016; $3,290, MS-64, October 2016												
1923 (b)	50,130,000	1,010	62.6	91%	$3	$3.25	$3.50	$5	$7	$15	$30	$45	$130
	Auctions: $1,116, MS-67, August 2015; $588, MS-66, November 2015; $259, MS-65, July 2016; $1,175, MS-67, November 2016												
1923-S	6,440,000	370	58.8	70%	$3	$4	$8	$18	$65	$105	$160	$400	$1,250
	Auctions: $1,704, MS-66, July 2015; $1,293, MS-65, August 2015; $2,115, MS-64, October 2015; $65, 0, September 2016												
1924	24,010,000	577	63.2	94%	$3	$3.25	$4	$6	$15	$30	$45	$100	$175
	Auctions: $2,115, MS-67, October 2015; $823, MS-66, November 2015; $2,115, MS-67, August 2016; $3,760, MS-67, September 2016												
1924-D	6,810,000	485	59.8	79%	$3.50	$4.50	$8	$24	$70	$110	$175	$500	$950
	Auctions: $1,175, MS-65, October 2015; $1,058, MS-65, March 2016; $764, MS-63, July 2016; $3,995, MS-65, October 2016												
1924-S	7,120,000	386	59.4	74%	$3.50	$4	$6	$10	$60	$110	$200	$525	$1,250
	Auctions: $7,638, MS-65, July 2016; $400, MS-61, August 2016; $14,100, MS-65, September 2016; $3,055, MS-65, October 2016												
1925	25,610,000	382	62.5	88%	$3	$3.25	$4	$5	$10	$20	$30	$85	$250
	Auctions: $588, MS-65, July 2016; $494, MS-65, September 2016; $447, MS-65, October 2016; $517, MS-65, November 2016												
1925-D	5,117,000	340	56.9	62%	$4	$5	$12	$45	$120	$200	$375	$750	$1,700
	Auctions: $664, MS-62, November 2015; $2,585, MS-65, December 2015; $165, AU-55, May 2016; $6,463, MS-66, July 2016												
1925-S	5,850,000	293	58.6	70%	$3.25	$4	$8	$18	$70	$110	$180	$500	$1,250
	Auctions: $341, MS-63, February 2015; $1,998, MS-64, September 2015; $2,585, MS-65, October 2015; $1,116, MS-64, December 2015												
1926	32,160,000	803	62.9	92%	$3	$3.25	$3.50	$5	$7	$15	$25	$65	$250
	Auctions: $1,645, MS-66, March 2016; $3,760, MS-67, August 2016; $823, MS-66, September 2016; $529, MS-66, November 2016												
1926-D	6,828,000	486	61.0	83%	$3.25	$4.50	$6	$10	$28	$50	$125	$275	$500
	Auctions: $1,763, MS-65, December 2015; $306, MS-64, May 2016; $3,290, MS-66, August 2016; $3,525, MS-66, September 2016												

b. Dimes dated 1923-D or 1930-D are counterfeit.

1928-S, Small S   **1928-S, Large S**   **1929-S, Doubled Die Obverse**
                FS-10-1928S-501.   FS-10-1929S-101.

	Mintage	Cert	Avg	%MS	G-4	VG-8	F-12	VF-20	EF-40	AU-50	MS-60	MS-63	MS-65
1926-S	1,520,000	460	43.4	28%	$13	$15	$26	$60	$250	$450	$1,100	$1,750	$3,500
	Auctions: $676, AU-58, July 2015; $705, AU-58, November 2015; $5,888, MS-65, September 2016; $5,170, MS-65, November 2016													
1927	28,080,000	611	61.9	90%	$3	$3.25	$3.50	$5	$7	$15	$30	$60	$150
	Auctions: $1,116, MS-66, August 2016; $2,585, MS-67, September 2016; $2,115, MS-67, October 2016; $494, MS-66, November 2016													
1927-D	4,812,000	318	57.7	66%	$3.50	$5.50	$8	$25	$80	$115	$200	$400	$1,200
	Auctions: $881, MS-65, August 2015; $1,410, MS-64, October 2015; $7,931, MS-64, August 2016; $8,813, MS-66, November 2016													
1927-S	4,770,000	274	58.6	71%	$3.25	$4	$6	$12	$28	$50	$275	$550	$1,350
	Auctions: $1,410, 63, August 2015; $6,463, MS-65, October 2015; $5,405, MS-65, August 2016; $5,640, MS-65, October 2016													
1928	19,480,000	595	63.7	95%	$3	$3.25	$3.50	$5	$7	$18	$30	$55	$130
	Auctions: $1,528, MS-67, October 2015; $999, MS-66, November 2015; $423, MS-66, August 2016; $494, MS-66, September 2016													
1928-D	4,161,000	318	58.4	74%	$4	$5	$8	$20	$50	$100	$175	$360	$850
	Auctions: $1,058, MS-64, September 2015; $1,645, MS-65, October 2015; $353, MS-62, August 2016; $1,293, MS-64, September 2016													
1928-S (c)	7,400,000	5	56.4	40%	$3	$3.25	$4	$6	$16	$40	$150	$320	$425
	Auctions: $2,820, MS-65, March 2016; $329, MS-62, July 2016; $3,878, MS-66, August 2016; $3,290, MS-66, October 2016													
1929	25,970,000	1,057	63.9	96%	$3	$3.25	$3.50	$5	$6	$10	$25	$35	$75
	Auctions: $212, MS-65, November 2015; $1,528, MS-67, July 2016; $1,293, MS-67, August 2016; $1,293, MS-67, October 2016													
1929-D	5,034,000	1,298	64.1	98%	$3	$3.50	$5	$8	$15	$24	$30	$36	$75
	Auctions: $470, MS-66, July 2016; $1,998, MS-67, August 2016; $1,293, MS-67, September 2016; $1,998, MS-67, October 2016													
1929-S	4,730,000	471	62.7	89%	$3	$3.25	$3.75	$5	$10	$20	$35	$45	$125
	Auctions: $2,585, MS-67, October 2015; $764, MS-66, December 2015; $2,056, MS-67, August 2016; $3,290, MS-67, September 2016													
1929-S, Doubled Die Obverse (d)	(e)	4	58.5	50%								$150	$200
	Auctions: $170, AU-58, December 2009													
1930 (b)	6,770,000	521	63.1	91%	$3	$3.25	$3.50	$5	$8	$16	$30	$50	$125
	Auctions: $2,115, MS-66, February 2015; $7,050, MS-67, June 2015; $3,055, MS-66, October 2015; $999, MS-66, November 2016													
1930-S	1,843,000	335	62.0	87%	$3	$4	$5	$7	$15	$45	$80	$150	$210
	Auctions: $5,170, MS-67, July 2016; $1,763, MS-66, August 2016; $1,645, MS-66, October 2016; $600, MS-67, November 2016													
1931	3,150,000	518	63.1	91%	$3	$3.10	$4	$6	$10	$22	$35	$70	$150
	Auctions: $823, MS-66, November 2015; $823, MS-66, July 2016; $494, MS-65, August 2016; $1,175, MS-66, October 2016													
1931-D	1,260,000	625	61.7	88%	$8	$10	$12	$20	$35	$60	$90	$140	$315
	Auctions: $1,175, MS-67, December 2015; $329, MS-66, June 2016; $881, MS-66, September 2016; $1,528, MS-67, October 2016													
1931-S	1,800,000	482	59.5	79%	$4	$5	$6	$10	$16	$45	$90	$150	$275
	Auctions: $2,233, MS-66, September 2015; $1,998, MS-65, October 2015; $15,275, MS-67, August 2016; $646, MS-64, November 2016													

b. Dimes dated 1923-D or 1930-D are counterfeit. **c.** Two mintmark styles exist: Large S (scarce) and Small S (common). About 80% of 1928-S dimes are of the Small S style. The scarcer Large S is worth about two to three times the values listed (which are for the Small S). **d.** Moderate doubling is evident on the date and IN GOD WE TRUST. **e.** Included in 1929-S mintage figure.

	Mintage	Cert	Avg	%MS	F-12	VF-20	EF-40	AU-50	MS-60	MS-63	MS-65	MS-65FB	MS-66
											PF-65	PF-66	PF-67
1934	24,080,000	1,206	64.4	96%	$2.75	$3	$3.25	$16	$25	$35	$50	$140	$65
	Auctions: $588, MS-67, March 2016; $129, MS-66, July 2016; $470, MS-67, August 2016; $470, MS-67, November 2016													
1934-D	6,772,000	793	64.1	95%	$2.75	$3	$8	$33	$50	$60	$85	$325	$230
	Auctions: $881, MS-67, October 2015; $1,175, MS-67, December 2015; $705, MS-66, August 2016; $646, MS-66, September 2016													

1936-S, Possible Overdate
FS-10-1936S-110.

	Mintage	Cert	Avg	%MS	F-12	VF-20	EF-40	AU-50	MS-60	MS-63	MS-65 / PF-65	MS-65FB / PF-66	MS-66 / PF-67
1935	58,830,000	1,847	65.0	96%	$2.75	$3	$3.25	$7	$10	$15	$35	$75	$60
Auctions: $705, MS-67, November 2015; $153, MS-66, March 2016; $223, MS-66, July 2016; $881, MS-67, September 2016													
1935-D	10,477,000	593	63.5	92%	$2.75	$3	$8	$26	$35	$50	$90	$525	$325
Auctions: $28,200, 0, March 2016; $2,174, MS-67, August 2016; $353, MS-65, October 2016; $940, MS-66, November 2016													
1935-S	15,840,000	852	64.5	95%	$2.75	$3	$5	$16	$22	$30	$40	$350	$80
Auctions: $65, MS-66, February 2015; $1,058, MS-67, November 2015; $1,998, MS-67, December 2015; $881, MS-66, August 2016													
1936	87,500,000	2,456	64.9	97%	$2.75	$3	$3.25	$7	$10	$18	$30	$90	$48
Auctions: $646, MS-67, November 2015; $940, MS-67, July 2016; $2,938, MS-68, August 2016; $646, MS-67, November 2016													
1936, Proof	4,130	1,120	64.9								$1,000	$1,150	$2,350
Auctions: $2,350, PF-67, March 2016; $1,469, MS-66, August 2016; $1,880, MS-67, October 2016; $705, MS-64, November 2016													
1936-D	16,132,000	692	64.0	92%	$2.75	$3	$6	$16	$25	$40	$55	$275	$80
Auctions: $1,351, MS-67, August 2015; $826, MS-67, November 2015; $1,645, MS-67, December 2015; $588, MS-67, September 2016													
1936-S	9,210,000	1,296	65.2	98%	$2.75	$3	$3.25	$13	$23	$30	$38	$95	$55
Auctions: $423, MS-67, September 2015; $705, MS-67, November 2015; $564, MS-67, December 2015; $505, MS-67, July 2016													
1936-S, Possible Overdate (a)	**(b)**	0	n/a								$600		
Auctions: $1,500, MS-65FB, November 2011													
1937	56,860,000	4,754	65.6	98%	$2.75	$3	$3.25	$7	$10	$15	$30	$60	$40
Auctions: $764, MS-68, January 2015; $541, MS-68, June 2015; $129, MS-67, August 2016													
1937, Proof	5,756	1,328	65.4								$525	$550	$750
Auctions: $1,528, PF-68, March 2016; $3,525, MS-68, August 2016; $646, MS-67, September 2016; $447, MS-67, October 2016													
1937-D	14,146,000	1,146	65.1	97%	$2.75	$3	$4	$12	$21	$30	$45	$100	$85
Auctions: $541, MS-67, January 2015; $353, MS-66, February 2015; $353, MS-67, July 2016; $2,820, MS-68, August 2016													
1937-S	9,740,000	1,284	65.1	96%	$2.75	$3	$3.25	$12	$20	$30	$40	$185	$80
Auctions: $2,233, MS-67, August 2015; $541, MS-67, November 2015; $552, MS-67, July 2016; $588, MS-67, August 2016													
1938	22,190,000	1,873	65.4	98%	$2.75	$3	$3.25	$7	$10	$15	$30	$85	$55
Auctions: $740, MS-67, June 2015; $940, MS-67, August 2015; $646, MS-67, November 2015; $482, MS-67, July 2016													
1938, Proof	8,728	1,949	65.5								$300	$325	$500
Auctions: $646, MS-67, November 2015; $4,113, MS-68, December 2015; $423, MS-67, August 2016; $1,293, MS-67, November 2016													
1938-D	5,537,000	2,295	65.5	99%	$2.75	$3	$4	$11	$18	$25	$35	$65	$75
Auctions: $4,230, MS-68, December 2015; $212, MS-67, June 2016; $1,058, MS-67, August 2016; $1,116, MS-67, November 2016													
1938-S	8,090,000	1,172	64.9	96%	$2.75	$3	$3.50	$12	$20	$28	$42	$160	$80
Auctions: $823, MS-67, August 2015; $588, MS-67, November 2015; $564, MS-67, July 2016; $1,763, MS-67, August 2016													
1939	67,740,000	4,028	65.6	98%	$2.75	$3	$3.25	$6	$8	$12	$26	$180	$40
Auctions: $764, MS-67, November 2015; $4,935, MS-68, August 2016; $5,170, MS-68, September 2016; $999, MS-67, November 2016													
1939, Proof	9,321	2,161	65.9								$225	$235	$400
Auctions: $470, PF-67, November 2015; $1,116, PF-68, March 2016; $1,058, PF-68, August 2016; $423, MS-67, September 2016													
1939-D	24,394,000	4,211	65.6	98%	$2.75	$3	$3.25	$6	$8	$12	$32	$55	$60
Auctions: $7,638, MS-69, December 2015; $259, MS-66, March 2016; $1,528, MS-68, August 2016; $376, MS-68, September 2016													
1939-S	10,540,000	952	64.7	95%	$2.75	$3	$4	$13	$23	$30	$42	$625	$110
Auctions: $1,293, MS-66, August 2015; $2,585, MS-67, September 2015; $999, MS-66, November 2015; $3,995, MS-67, August 2016													

a. From the *Cherrypickers' Guide to Rare Die Varieties, Vol. II* (sixth edition): "The secondary image of a 2 is evident beneath the 3 of the date. Most evident is the flat portion of the base of the underlying 2. Remains of what is likely a secondary 9 are evident to the left of the primary 9. Many die polish marks are also evident throughout the surface of the obverse. No doubling is evident on other elements. . . . The length of time between the striking of the last 1929-dated coins and this 1936 coin would seem to eliminate the possibility of a 2 underlying the 3. However, examination has matched the shapes on the image under the 3 to that of the 2 on 1929-dated dimes. Stranger things have happened. Keep in mind that 1936 was during the Great Depression, when Mint personnel wanted to save money whenever possible." **b.** Included in 1936-S mintage figure.

1941-S, Small S

1941-S, Large S
FS-10-1941S-511.

1942, 42 Over 41
FS-10-1942-101.

1942-D, 42 Over 41, Repunched Mintmark
FS-10-1942D-101.

	Mintage	Cert	Avg	%MS	F-12	VF-20	EF-40	AU-50	MS-60	MS-63	MS-65 / PF-65	MS-65FB / PF-66	MS-66 / PF-67
1940	65,350,000	4,230	65.5	98%	$2.75	$3	$3.25	$5	$7	$12	$30	$50	$45
Auctions: $400, MS-67FB, September 2015; $200, MS-67FB, August 2015; $165, MS-67FB, May 2015; $112, MS-67FB, February 2015													
1940, Proof	11,827	2,370	65.6								$180	$200	$325
Auctions: $1,293, MS-68, June 2015; $940, MS-68, December 2015; $141, PF-65, March 2016; $2,350, MS-68, October 2016													
1940-D	21,198,000	2,907	65.4	99%	$2.75	$3	$3.25	$5	$7	$14	$35	$50	$60
Auctions: $1,763, MS-68, February 2015; $999, MS-68, October 2015													
1940-S	21,560,000	3,157	65.5	99%	$2.75	$3	$3.25	$6	$8	$15	$35	$100	$40
Auctions: $617, MS-67, February 2015; $1,293, MS-67, November 2015; $470, MS-67, July 2016; $541, MS-67, August 2016													
1941	175,090,000	5,962	65.1	97%	$2.75	$3	$3.25	$5	$7	$12	$30	$50	$45
Auctions: $7,050, MS-68, July 2015; $646, MS-67, August 2015; $165, MS-67, March 2016; $999, MS-67, August 2016													
1941, Proof	16,557	3,022	65.5								$175	$200	$325
Auctions: $7,050, MS-68, October 2015; $141, PF-66, March 2016; $400, PF-67, August 2016; $2,468, MS-68, September 2016													
1941-D	45,634,000	4,223	65.1	97%	$2.75	$3	$3.25	$6	$8	$14	$25	$50	$32
Auctions: $24, MS-66, July 2015; $353, MS-67, November 2015; $212, MS-67, March 2016; $423, MS-68, August 2016													
1941-S	43,090,000	5,825	65.4	98%	$2.75	$3	$3.25	$5	$7	$12	$30	$50	$38
Auctions: $165, MS-67FB, May 2015; $259, MS-67FB, September 2015; $306, MS-67, March 2016; $400, MS-67, September 2016													
1941-S, Large S (c)	(d)	40	56.4	65%							$325		
Auctions: $217, MS-66, September 2015													
1942, 42 Over 41 (e)	(f)	1,990	39.3	6%	$450	$550	$650	$1,000	$2,500	$4,750 (g)	$15,000	$45,000	$20,000
Auctions: $76,375, MS-66, January 2016; $2,585, MS-62, August 2016; $1,320, AU-58, January 2018; $840, AU-55, February 2018													
1942	205,410,000	8,766	59.1	76%	$2.75	$3	$3.25	$4.50	$6	$12	$30	$50	$45
Auctions: $188, MS-67, March 2016; $646, MS-67, July 2016; $3,290, MS-68, August 2016; $3,525, MS-68, October 2016													
1942, Proof	22,329	4,395	65.7								$175	$200	$275
Auctions: $999, PF-68, March 2016; $940, MS-68, September 2016; $881, MS-68, October 2016; $4,113, MS-68, November 2016													
1942-D, 42 Over 41 (h)	(i)	1,138	35.8	8%	$425	$525	$600	$1,000	$2,500	$4,750 (j)	$10,000	$30,000	$12,000
Auctions: $940, AU-55, February 2015; $853, AU-50, January 2015; $588, EF-40, June 2015; $400, VF-25, February 2015													
1942-D	60,740,000	6,508	59.5	80%	$2.75	$3	$3.25	$4.50	$6	$12	$28	$48	$45
Auctions: $881, MS-68, October 2015; $141, MS-67, March 2016; $1,058, MS-68, August 2016													
1942-S	49,300,000	2,470	64.7	95%	$2.75	$3	$3.25	$6	$8	$20	$30	$150	$50
Auctions: $400, MS-67, January 2015; $2,820, MS-67, July 2015; $306, MS-67, March 2016; $3,525, MS-67, September 2016													
1943	191,710,000	6,923	65.2	97%	$2.75	$3	$3.25	$4.50	$6	$12	$27	$55	$35
Auctions: $129, MS-67, March 2016; $1,645, MS-67, August 2016; $1,293, MS-67, October 2016; $1,528, MS-67, November 2016													

c. This is the "Trumpet Tail" S mintmark, which is rare for this date. The upper serif points downward and the lower serif is rounded, like the bell of a trumpet. There are several dies known for the Large S dime, including one that is repunched. For more information, see the *Cherrypickers' Guide to Rare Die Varieties, Vol. II* (sixth edition). **d.** Included in 1941-S mintage figure. **e.** Doubling is evident in the 42 over 41 overdate, and slightly evident on IN GOD WE TRUST. Values for this variety fluctuate. **f.** Included in circulation-strike 1942 mintage figure. **g.** Value in MS-64 is $7,500. **h.** Doubling is evident in the 42 over 41 overdate, slightly evident on IN GOD WE TRUST, and as a D over D repunched mintmark (slanted west). Values for this variety fluctuate. **i.** Included in 1942-D mintage figure. **j.** Value in MS-64 is $8,500.

1943-S, Trumpet Tail Mintmark
FS-10-1943S-511.

1945-D, D Over Horizontal D
FS-10-1945D-506.

1945-S, S Over Horizontal S
FS-10-1945S-503.

1945-S, Normal S

1945-S, Micro S
FS-10-1945S-512.

	Mintage	Cert	Avg	%MS	F-12	VF-20	EF-40	AU-50	MS-60	MS-63	MS-65	MS-65FB	MS-66
											PF-65	PF-66	PF-67
1943-D	71,949,000	7,354	65.4	99%	$2.75	$3	$3.25	$4.50	$6	$15	$30	$50	$45
	Auctions: $1,116, MS-68, December 2015; $153, MS-67, March 2016; $447, MS-67, July 2016; $1,410, MS-68, September 2016												
1943-S	60,400,000	4,368	65.5	98%	$2.75	$3	$3.25	$5	$7	$16	$30	$70	$40
	Auctions: $1,351, MS-67, June 2015; $3,525, MS-68, October 2015; $646, MS-67, December 2015; $1,028, MS-67, July 2016												
1943-S, Trumpet Tail Mintmark (k)	(l)	8	62.9	75%							$450	$750	$500
	Auctions: $130, MS-62, December 2011												
1944	231,410,000	8,923	65.3	98%	$2.75	$3	$3.25	$4.50	$6	$12	$25	$80	$45
	Auctions: $12,925, MS-68, August 2015; $1,586, MS-67, October 2015; $1,293, MS-67, July 2016; $1,293, MS-67, September 2016												
1944-D	62,224,000	9,471	65.7	99%	$2.75	$3	$3.25	$5	$7	$15	$30	$50	$48
	Auctions: $94, MS-67, August 2016; $705, MS-68, September 2016; $881, MS-68, October 2016; $764, MS-68, November 2016												
1944-S	49,490,000	6,645	65.7	99%	$2.75	$3	$3.25	$5	$7	$15	$30	$55	$50
	Auctions: $1,763, MS-67, December 2015; $176, MS-67, March 2016; $188, MS-67, June 2016; $881, MS-67, November 2016												
1945	159,130,000	9,806	65.4	99%	$2.75	$3	$3.25	$4.50	$6	$12	$30	$15,000	$45
	Auctions: $100, MS-0, November 2015; $13,513, MS-65, December 2015; $494, MS-67, March 2016; $14,688, MS-66, November 2016												
1945-D	40,245,000	9,330	65.6	99%	$2.75	$3	$3.25	$4.50	$6	$12	$26	$45	$50
	Auctions: $200, MS-67FB, September 2015; $112, MS-67FB, November 2015; $353, MS-68, August 2016; $2,820, MS-67, August 2016												
1945-D, D Over Horizontal D (m)	(n)	6	44.3	0%							$900	$950	
	Auctions: No auction records available.												
1945-S	41,920,000	9,644	65.7	99%	$2.75	$3	$3.25	$4.50	$6	$12	$30	$125	$40
	Auctions: $423, MS-67, March 2016; $588, MS-67, July 2016; $881, MS-67, August 2016; $541, MS-68, September 2016												
1945-S, S Over Horizontal S (o)	(p)	1	30.0	0%							$900	$950	
	Auctions: No auction records available.												
1945-S, Micro S (q)	(p)	1,375	65.1	97%	$3.25	$3.50	$6	$18	$30	$40	$100	$650	$120
	Auctions: $441, MS-67, November 2015; $705, MS-65, December 2015; $1,116, MS-67, August 2016; $823, MS-66, October 2016												

k. This variety is considerably rarer than the 1941-S, Large S, which also features a Trumpet S mintmark. It is extremely rare in MS, and examples with FB command a significant premium. The top serif of the S points downward, with the lower serif rounded, much like the bell of a trumpet. **l.** Included in 1943-S mintage figure. **m.** The first D mintmark was punched into the die horizontally and then corrected. **n.** Included in 1945-D mintage figure. **o.** The first S mintmark was punched into the die horizontally and then corrected. **p.** Included in 1945-S mintage figure. **q.** The S mintmark is significantly smaller than that of the normal S punch. This variety has the only mintmark punch of this type and size known to have been used during the 1940s. It was originally used for Philippine coins of 1907 through 1920.

ROOSEVELT (1946 TO DATE)

Designer: *John R. Sinnock.* **Weight:** *Silver issue (1946–1964) and silver Proofs (1968–2018)—2.50 grams; clad issue (1965 to date)—2.27 grams; silver Proofs (2019 to date)—2.537 grams.* **Composition:** *Silver issue (1946–1964) and silver Proofs (1968–2018)—.900 silver, .100 copper (net weight: .07234 oz. pure silver); clad issue (1965 to date)—Outer layers of copper-nickel (.750 copper, .250 nickel) bonded to inner core of pure copper; silver Proofs (2019 to date)—.999 silver, .001 copper (net weight: .0728 oz. pure silver).* **Diameter:** *17.9 mm.* **Edge:** *Reeded.* **Mints:** *Philadelphia, Denver, San Francisco, and West Point.*

Circulation Strike   **Proof**

Mintmark location, 1946–1964, is on the reverse, to the left of the fasces.   Mintmark location, 1968 to date, is on the obverse, above the date.

History. After President Franklin D. Roosevelt died in 1945, the Treasury rushed to create a coin in his honor. The ten-cent denomination was particularly appropriate, given the president's active support of the March of Dimes' fundraising efforts to cure polio. The obverse of the coin bears Roosevelt's profile portrait, while the reverse features a torch flanked by branches of olive and oak.

Striking and Sharpness. Compared to earlier coinage series, collectors and dealers have paid relatively little attention to the sharpness of Roosevelt dimes. The obverse portrait is such that lightness of strike on the higher points is difficult to detect. On the reverse, check the leaves and the details of the torch. Some with complete separation on the lower two bands have been called Full Torch (FT) or Full Bands (FB), but interest in this distinction seems to be minimal in today's marketplace.

Availability. All are common, although some are more common than others. MS coins in higher grades are usually very lustrous.

Note: Values of common-date silver coins have been based on a silver current bullion price of $27.50 per ounce, and may vary with the prevailing spot price.

GRADING STANDARDS

MS-60 to 70 (Mint State). *Obverse:* At MS-60, some abrasion and contact marks are evident on the cheek, the hair above the ear, and the neck. At MS-63, abrasion is slight at best, less so for MS-64. An MS-65 coin should display no abrasion or contact marks except under magnification, and MS-66 and higher coins should have none at all. Luster should be full and rich. *Reverse:* Comments apply as for the obverse, except that the highest parts of the torch, flame, and leaves are the places to check. On both sides the fields are protected by design elements and do not show contact marks readily.

1955-D. Graded MS-68FB.

AU-50, 53, 55, 58 (About Uncirculated). *Obverse:* Light wear is seen on the cheek and higher-relief part of the hair. At AU-58, the luster is extensive, but incomplete, especially on the higher parts and in the field. At AU–50 and 53, luster is less. *Reverse:* Light wear is seen on the higher parts of the torch and leaves. An AU-58 coin has nearly full luster. At AU–50 and 53, there still is significant luster.

1962-D. Graded AU-58.

EF-40, 45 (Extremely Fine). *Obverse:* Further wear is seen on the head. Some details are gone in the hair to the right of the forehead. *Reverse:* Further wear is seen on the torch, but the vertical lines are visible, some just barely. The higher-relief details in the leaves, never strong to begin with, are worn away.

The Roosevelt dime is seldom collected in grades lower than EF-40.

1950-S. Graded EF-40.

PF-60 to 70 (Proof). *Obverse and Reverse:* Proofs that are extensively cleaned and have many hairlines, or that are dull and grainy, are lower level, such as PF–60 to 62. These are not widely desired, and represent coins that have been mistreated. Fortunately, only a few Proof Roosevelt dimes are in this category. With medium hairlines and good reflectivity, assigned grades of PF–63 or 64 are appropriate. PF-65 may have hairlines so delicate that magnification is needed to see them. Above that, a Proof should be free of any hairlines or other problems.

1983-S, No S. Graded PF-69 Deep Cameo.

Illustrated coin: The S mintmark is missing from this popular variety.

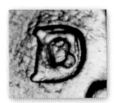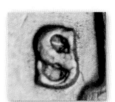

1950-D, D Over S	1950-S, S Over D
FS-10-1950D-501.	FS-10-1950S-501.

	Mintage	Cert	Avg	%MS	EF-40	MS-63	MS-65	MS-66	MS-67	MS-67FT
								PF-65	PF-66	PF-67
1946	255,250,000	2,129	65.9	99%	$3	$5	$12	$28	$55	$200
1946-D	61,043,500	2,556	66.1	100%	$3	$5	$14	$30	$50	$150
1946-S	27,900,000	3,115	66.1	99%	$3	$4.50	$20	$32	$75	$150
1947	121,520,000	1,586	65.7	97%	$3	$6	$12	$24	$60	$225

	Mintage	Cert	Avg	%MS	EF-40	MS-63	MS-65	MS-66	MS-67	MS-67FT
								PF-65	PF-66	PF-67
1947-D	46,835,000	1,433	66.1	100%	$3	$6.50	$12	$24	$45	$200
1947-S	34,840,000	2,453	66.2	100%	$3	$6	$12	$30	$45	$125
1948	74,950,000	1,372	65.9	100%	$3	$5	$12	$30	$100	$115
1948-D	52,841,000	1,567	66.2	100%	$3	$6	$12	$30	$55	$100
1948-S	35,520,000	1,982	66.2	100%	$3	$5.50	$12	$32	$55	$100
1949	30,940,000	1,441	65.8	99%	$4	$27	$38	$45	$100	$850
1949-D	26,034,000	2,042	66.1	100%	$4	$12	$20	$35	$55	$100
1949-S	13,510,000	2,705	66.2	99%	$5	$45	$55	$75	$85	$1,150
1950	50,130,114	1,556	65.9	99%	$4	$13	$16	$35	$125	$225
1950, Proof	51,386	2,017	66.4					$50	$65	$120
1950-D	46,803,000	2,094	66.2	100%	$2	$6	$12	$28	$55	$100
1950-D, D Over S (a)	**(b)**	0	n/a			$400	$650	$775	$1,050	
1950-S	20,440,000	1,674	66.1	99%	$5	$38	$55	$75	$85	$350
1950-S, S Over D (c)	**(d)**	0	n/a			$250	$400	$750	$900	$1,675
1951	103,880,102	1,894	66.0	99%	$3	$5	$10	$30	$65	$100
1951, Proof	57,500	2,433	66.8					$50	$65	$100
1951-D	56,529,000	1,122	66.0	99%	$3	$5	$10	$28	$85	$105
1951-S	31,630,000	1,892	66.2	100%	$4	$14	$25	$45	$55	$100
1952	99,040,093	1,260	65.9	100%	$3	$5	$10	$30	$75	$125
1952, Proof	81,980	2,236	66.9					$35	$50	$85
1952-D	122,100,000	1,402	66.0	99%	$3	$5	$9	$25	$65	$135
1952-S	44,419,500	1,986	66.2	100%	$4	$8	$12	$35	$50	$225
1953	53,490,120	1,026	65.9	100%	$3	$5	$8	$15	$75	$850
1953, Proof	128,800	2,862	66.8					$38	$55	$80
1953-D	136,433,000	1,458	66.0	100%	$3	$5	$9	$20	$55	$150
1953-S	39,180,000	3,154	66.2	100%	$4	$5	$9	$25	$55	$300
1954	114,010,203	1,620	65.9	100%	$3	$5	$8	$20	$55	$250
1954, Proof	233,300	3,559	67.1					$18	$25	$30
1954-D	106,397,000	1,291	65.8	100%	$3	$5	$9	$15	$115	$150
1954-S	22,860,000	2,883	66.0	100%	$3	$5	$9	$16	$55	$350
1955	12,450,181	3,177	65.9	100%	$3	$5	$8	$16	$75	$750
1955, Proof	378,200	7,317	67.6					$15	$20	$25
1955-D	13,959,000	2,101	65.5	100%	$3	$5	$8	$15	$100	$175
1955-S	18,510,000	4,314	65.9	100%	$3	$5	$8	$15	$55	$1,250
1956	108,640,000	2,602	66.1	100%	$3	$4	$7	$14	$45	$250
1956, Proof	669,384	6,366	67.7					$8	$10	$18
1956-D	108,015,100	1,303	66.0	100%	$3	$4	$7	$15	$35	$250
1957	160,160,000	2,632	66.1	100%	$3	$4	$7	$14	$35	$1,250
1957, Proof	1,247,952	7,619	67.7					$5	$8	$25
1957-D	113,354,330	1,871	66.0	100%	$3	$4	$7	$14	$35	$150
1958	31,910,000	2,589	66.2	100%	$3	$4	$8	$15	$25	$2,000
1958, Proof	875,652	6,285	67.5					$5	$8	$10
1958-D	136,564,600	2,057	66.1	100%	$3	$4	$8	$14	$25	$100
1959	85,780,000	1,803	65.8	99%	$3	$4	$7	$15	$125	$200
1959, Proof	1,149,291	7,006	67.7					$5	$8	$10
1959-D	164,919,790	1,375	65.9	99%	$3	$4	$7	$14	$40	$100

a. The diagonal stroke of the initially punched S mintmark is visible within the opening of the primary D mintmark. The lower curve of the S is evident on the lower right curve of the D. **b.** Included in 1950-D mintage figure. **c.** The S mintmark is punched squarely over a previously punched D. CONECA lists this coin as an S Over Inverted S, indicating that the line enclosing the lower loop is that of the long upper serif on an inverted S. However, Fivaz and Stanton, in the *Cherrypickers' Guide to Rare Die Varieties, Vol. II* (sixth edition), "believe this to be an [overmintmark] (actually S/S/D) because the long upper serif of an S would not enclose the lower opening. In addition, the curve of the face of a D is clearly evident in the upper opening." **d.** Included in 1950-S mintage figure.

1960, Doubled Die Obverse, Proof
FS-10-1960-102. Various die states exist.

1963, Doubled Die Reverse
FS-10-1963-805.

1963, Doubled Die Reverse, Proof
FS-10-1963-802. Other varieties exist

1963-D, Doubled Die Reverse
FS-10-1963D-801.

| | Mintage | Cert | Avg | %MS | EF-40 | MS-63 | MS-65 | MS-66 | MS-67 | MS-67FT |
								PF-65	PF-66	PF-67
1960	70,390,000	1,520	65.8	100%	$3	$4	$7	$14	$65	$300
1960, Proof	1,691,602	8,339	67.5					$5	$10	$18
1960, Doubled Die Obverse, Proof	(e)	90	66.4					$150	$200	
1960-D	200,160,400	1,166	65.9	100%	$3	$4	$6	$15	$75	$300
1961	93,730,000	1,402	65.8	100%	$3	$4	$6	$12	$85	$800
1961, Proof	3,028,244	8,082	67.4					$5	$8	$12
1961-D	209,146,550	1,053	65.7	99%	$3	$4	$6	$12	$25	$225
1962	72,450,000	1,716	65.8	100%	$3	$4	$6	$12	$35	$250
1962, Proof	3,218,019	8,074	67.4					$5	$8	$10
1962-D	334,948,380	1,237	65.9	99%	$3	$4	$6	$12	$30	$150
1963	123,650,000	1,499	65.7	99%	$3	$4	$6	$12	$30	$1,500
1963, Doubled Die Reverse (f)	(g)	11	63.3	91%		$25	$38	$100		
1963, Proof	3,075,645	10,745	67.5					$5	$8	$10
1963, Doubled Die Reverse, Proof (h)	(i)	127	67.5					$150	$250	
1963-D	421,476,530	1,391	65.6	99%	$3	$4	$6	$12	$30	$400
1963-D, Doubled Die Reverse (j)	(k)	14	63.6	93%		$125	$175	$250		
1964 (l)	929,360,000	2,358	65.3	98%	$3	$4	$6	$12	$30	$300
1964, Proof	3,950,762	19,229	67.8					$5	$8	$10

e. Included in 1960, Proof, mintage figure. **f.** Doubling is evident on UNITED, E PLURIBUS, the olive branch, and the stem. Lesser doubling is also visible on ONE DIME. **g.** Included in circulation-strike 1963 mintage figure. **h.** Several less-valuable 1963, Proof, DDRs exist. Values shown are for FS-10-1963-802. **i.** Included in 1963, Proof, mintage figure. **j.** Doubling is evident on all reverse lettering, with the most obvious doubling on AMERICA and on the top of the flame. Most MS examples are MS-63 and lower. **k.** Included in 1963-D mintage figure. **l.** The 9 in the date has either a pointed tail or a straight tail.

1964-D, Doubled Die Reverse
FS-10-1964D-801. Other varieties exist.

1967, Doubled Die Obverse
FS-10-1967-101.

1968-S, Doubled Die Obverse, Proof
FS-10-1968S-102.

1968-S, No S, Proof
FS-10-1968S-501.

1970, Doubled Die Reverse
FS-10-1970-801.

	Mintage	Cert	Avg	%MS	EF-40	MS-63	MS-65	MS-66	MS-67	MS-67FT
								PF-65	PF-66	PF-67
1964-D (l)	1,357,517,180	2,328	65.4	97%	$3	$4	$6	$12	$50	$225
1964-D, Doubled Die Reverse (m)	(n)	19	57.9	26%	$35	$100	$160	$235	$400	$750
1965	1,652,140,570	194	64.7	92%			$2	$15	$75	$850
1965, Special Mint Set	2,360,000	3,793	67.2					$3	$5	$17
1966	1,382,734,540	215	65.8	96%			$2.25	$6	$30	$800
1966, Special Mint Set	2,261,583	3,783	67.3					$3	$5	$20
1967	2,244,007,320	234	64.7	86%			$2	$5	$25	$250
1967, Doubled Die Obverse (o)	(p)	0	n/a				$400	$600	$850	
1967, Special Mint Set	1,863,344	3,809	67.2					$4	$6	$18
1968	424,470,400	296	65.4	98%			$2	$5	$25	$500
1968-D	480,748,280	823	66.2	100%			$2	$5	$20	$50
1968-S, Proof	3,041,506	1,359	67.9					$2	$4	$6
1968-S, Doubled Die Obverse, Proof (q)	(r)	8	66.9					$350	$500	$750
1968-S, No S, Proof †† (s)	(r)	14	68.0					$11,500	$13,000	$17,500
1969	145,790,000	141	65.0	99%			$3	$6	$30	
1969-D	563,323,870	846	66.0	100%			$2	$6	$25	$750
1969-S, Proof	2,394,631	1,083	68.1					$2	$4	$6
1970	345,570,000	247	64.4	96%			$2	$6	$35	
1970, Doubled Die Reverse (t)	(u)	4	62.3	75%			$300	$650	$1,000	
1970-D	754,942,100	738	65.1	99%			$2	$5	$35	$2,000
1970-S, Proof	2,632,810	1,441	67.7					$2	$4	$6

†† Ranked in the *100 Greatest U.S. Modern Coins* (fourth edition). **l.** The 9 in the date has either a pointed tail or a straight tail.
m. There are several varieties of 1964-D with a doubled-die reverse. The variety pictured and valued here is FS-10-1964D-801. For more information, see the *Cherrypickers' Guide to Rare Die Varieties, Vol. II* (sixth edition). **n.** Included in 1964-D mintage figure. **o.** This is a very rare doubled die. Its doubling is evident on IN GOD WE TRUST, the date, and the designer's initials. **p.** Included in circulation-strike 1967 mintage figure. **q.** There are several 1968-S, Proof, doubled-die obverse varieties. The one listed here is FS-10-1968S-102. See the *Cherrypickers' Guide to Rare Die Varieties, Vol. II* (sixth edition). **r.** Included in 1968-S, Proof, mintage figure. **s.** The S mintmark was inadvertently left off the coinage die; this defect was probably discovered before the end of the die's life. **t.** Doubling on this extremely rare variety is evident on all reverse lettering, especially on UNITED STATES OF AMERICA, with slightly weaker doubling on ONE DIME. **u.** Included in circulation-strike 1970 mintage figure.

1979-S, Filled S (Type 1), Proof	1979-S, Clear S (Type 2), Proof	1981-S, Rounded S (Type 1), Proof	1981-S, Flat S (Type 2), Proof

	Mintage	Cert	Avg	%MS	EF-40	MS-63	MS-65	MS-66 / PF-65	MS-67 / PF-66	MS-67FT / PF-67
1970-S, No S, Proof †† (s)	(v)	223	67.7					$800	$950	$1,100
1971	162,690,000	102	65.1	100%			$2.50	$6	$40	
1971-D	377,914,240	169	65.7	100%			$2.25	$6	$50	$1,000
1971-S, Proof	3,220,733	1,511	68.1					$2	$4	$6
1972	431,540,000	123	65.1	99%			$2	$6	$60	
1972-D	330,290,000	245	65.7	100%			$2	$6	$40	$800
1972-S, Proof	3,260,996	1,353	68.0					$2	$4	$6
1973	315,670,000	126	65.1	99%			$2	$5	$70	$1,200
1973-D	455,032,426	184	65.4	99%			$2	$6	$50	$500
1973-S, Proof	2,760,339	476	67.7					$2	$4	$6
1974	470,248,000	70	65.0	100%			$2	$5	$25	$3,000
1974-D	571,083,000	131	65.4	100%			$2	$5	$25	$1,000
1974-S, Proof	2,612,568	424	67.9					$2	$4	$6
1975	585,673,900	162	64.0	91%			$2	$5	$25	$2,000
1975-D	313,705,300	221	66.1	99%			$2	$5	$30	$600
1975-S, Proof	2,845,450	590	68.0					$2.50	$4	$6
1975-S, No S, Proof †† (s)	(w)	0	n/a						$350,000	$400,000
1976	568,760,000	149	65.9	99%			$2	$5	$25	$2,000
1976-D	695,222,774	159	65.8	97%			$2	$5	$40	$1,200
1976-S, Proof	4,149,730	999	68.2					$2.75	$4	$6
1977	796,930,000	231	65.8	100%			$2	$5	$25	$1,750
1977-D	376,607,228	141	65.5	100%			$2	$5	$35	$650
1977-S, Proof	3,251,152	908	68.6					$2.50	$4	$6
1978	663,980,000	127	65.5	98%			$2	$5	$27	$2,500
1978-D	282,847,540	112	65.5	99%			$2	$5	$25	
1978-S, Proof	3,127,781	847	68.9					$2.50	$4	$6
1979	315,440,000	218	65.5	100%			$2	$5	$30	
1979-D	390,921,184	199	65.5	100%			$2	$5	$30	$2,000
1979-S, Type 1, Proof	3,677,175	1,059	69.1					$2.50	$4	$6
1979-S, Type 2, Proof	(x)	1,513	69.2					$5	$6	$8
1980-P	735,170,000	198	65.9	99%			$2	$5	$25	
1980-D	719,354,321	132	65.4	98%			$2	$5	$30	
1980-S, Proof	3,554,806	1,236	68.6					$2.50	$4	$6
1981-P	676,650,000	309	66.0	99%			$2	$5	$40	$70
1981-D	712,284,143	423	66.6	100%			$2	$5	$20	$80
1981-S, Type 1, Proof	4,063,083	1,750	68.9					$2.50	$4	$6
1981-S, Type 2, Proof	(y)	752	69.1					$5.50	$7	$9

†† Ranked in the *100 Greatest U.S. Modern Coins* (fourth edition). **s.** The S mintmark was inadvertently left off the coinage die; this defect was probably discovered before the end of the die's life. **v.** Included in 1970-S, Proof, mintage figure. **w.** Included in 1975-S, Proof, mintage figure. **x.** Included in the 1979-S, Type 1, Proof, mintage figure. **y.** Included in the 1981-S, Type 1, Proof, mintage figure.

**1982, No S,
Strong Strike**
FS-10-1982-501.

**1982, No S,
Weak Strike**
FS-10-1982-502.

	Mintage	Cert	Avg	%MS	EF-40	MS-63	MS-65	MS-66	MS-67	MS-67FT
								PF-65	PF-66	PF-67
1982, No Mintmark, Strong Strike †† (z)	(aa)	566	64.4	93%			$200	$350	$550	$1,250
1982, No Mintmark, Weak Strike †† (z)	(aa)	16	65.1	100%			$65	$100	$250	
1982-P	519,475,000	245	66.0	98%			$7.50	$18	$50	$1,000
1982-D	542,713,584	164	65.5	95%			$2.50	$8	$25	$500
1982-S, Proof	3,857,479	1,021	69.1					$2.50	$4	$6
1983-P	647,025,000	132	65.3	95%			$6.50	$15	$30	$1,250
1983-D	730,129,224	86	65.6	97%			$3.25	$8.50	$25	$1,000
1983-S, Proof	3,279,126	1,116	69.2					$3	$4	$6
1983-S, No S, Proof †† (s)	(bb)	193	68.8					$500	$550	$675
1984-P	856,669,000	185	66.3	98%			$2	$5	$20	$50
1984-D	704,803,976	143	65.3	98%			$2.25	$5	$20	$125
1984-S, Proof	3,065,110	703	69.2					$2.50	$4	$6
1985-P	705,200,962	163	66.5	99%			$2.25	$5	$25	$150
1985-D	587,979,970	256	66.7	99%			$2.25	$5	$30	$100
1985-S, Proof	3,362,821	818	69.2					$3	$4	$6
1986-P	682,649,693	193	65.9	99%			$2.50	$5	$20	$1,000
1986-D	473,326,970	202	66.2	100%			$2.50	$5	$20	$850
1986-S, Proof	3,010,497	553	69.2					$4	$5	$7
1987-P	762,709,481	189	66.0	99%			$2	$5	$25	$800
1987-D	653,203,402	192	66.1	99%			$2	$5	$20	$350
1987-S, Proof	4,227,728	730	69.2					$3	$4	$6
1988-P	1,030,550,000	166	65.6	95%			$2	$5	$35	$225
1988-D	962,385,489	188	66.4	99%			$2	$5	$40	$100
1988-S, Proof	3,262,948	530	69.2					$4	$5	$7
1989-P	1,298,400,000	184	66.3	99%			$2	$5	$20	$50
1989-D	896,535,597	246	66.4	99%			$2	$6	$20	$50
1989-S, Proof	3,220,194	569	69.2					$3	$4	$6
1990-P	1,034,340,000	90	65.8	96%			$2	$6	$20	$1,000
1990-D	839,995,824	146	66.0	96%			$2	$4	$25	$2,000
1990-S, Proof	3,299,559	721	69.3					$2.50	$4	$6
1991-P	927,220,000	89	66.3	99%			$2	$4	$20	$2,000
1991-D	601,241,114	100	66.0	100%			$2	$4	$20	$200
1991-S, Proof	2,867,787	740	69.5					$4	$5	$7
1992-P	593,500,000	117	67.0	100%			$2	$5	$35	$150
1992-D	616,273,932	105	66.4	100%			$2	$4	$30	$175
1992-S, Proof	2,858,981	592	69.5					$3	$4	$6
1992-S, Proof, Silver	1,317,579	2,410	69.3					$6	$7	$8
1993-P	766,180,000	163	66.3	96%			$2	$4	$30	$200
1993-D	750,110,166	110	65.7	99%			$2	$4	$25	$1,000

†† Ranked in the *100 Greatest U.S. Modern Coins* (fourth edition). **s.** The S mintmark was inadvertently left off the coinage die; this defect was probably discovered before the end of the die's life. **z.** The P mintmark was omitted from this working die. There are two versions of this variety: one with a strong strike, and one with a weak strike. The strong strike is far more valuable and in demand than the weak. **aa.** Included in 1982-P mintage figure. **bb.** Included in 1983-S, Proof, mintage figure.

	Mintage	Cert	Avg	%MS	EF-40	MS-63	MS-65	MS-66 / PF-65	MS-67 / PF-66	MS-67FT / PF-67
1993-S, Proof	2,633,439	603	69.5					$5	$6	$7
1993-S, Proof, Silver	761,353	1,572	69.2					$7	$8	$9
1994-P	1,189,000,000	140	66.4	98%			$2	$4	$25	$200
1994-D	1,303,268,110	79	65.3	99%			$2	$4	$25	$150
1994-S, Proof	2,484,594	531	69.5					$5	$6	$8
1994-S, Proof, Silver	785,329	1,649	69.3					$8	$9	$10
1995-P	1,125,500,000	93	66.8	99%			$2	$4	$30	$300
1995-D	1,274,890,000	111	66.0	98%			$2	$5	$35	$600
1995-S, Proof	2,117,496	538	69.6					$10	$16	$20
1995-S, Proof, Silver	679,985	2,245	69.3					$14	$23	$30
1996-P	1,421,163,000	203	66.7	98%			$2	$4	$25	$45
1996-D	1,400,300,000	228	66.2	100%			$2	$4	$20	$75
1996-W †† (cc)	1,457,000	6,797	66.5	100%			$20	$30	$45	$70
1996-S, Proof	1,750,244	507	69.5					$3	$6	$8
1996-S, Proof, Silver	775,021	1,639	69.2					$8	$10	$15
1997-P	991,640,000	86	66.7	99%			$2	$6	$60	$100
1997-D	979,810,000	91	66.1	99%			$2	$6	$50	$100
1997-S, Proof	2,055,000	448	69.7					$8	$10	$15
1997-S, Proof, Silver	741,678	1,607	69.3					$12	$16	$24
1998-P	1,163,000,000	127	66.7	99%			$2	$3	$18	$100
1998-D	1,172,250,000	126	65.8	99%			$2	$3	$15	$125
1998-S, Proof	2,086,507	437	69.6					$4	$6	$8
1998-S, Proof, Silver	878,792	2,054	69.3					$6	$8	$10
1999-P	2,164,000,000	145	66.4	94%			$2	$3	$15	$30
1999-D	1,397,750,000	135	66.3	97%			$2	$3	$15	$40
1999-S, Proof	2,543,401	2,424	69.2					$4	$6	$8
1999-S, Proof, Silver	804,565	5,053	69.2					$7	$8	$12
2000-P	1,842,500,000	78	65.4	90%			$2	$3	$15	$30
2000-D	1,818,700,000	92	66.4	97%			$2	$3	$15	$30
2000-S, Proof	3,082,572	1,456	69.3					$2.50	$4	$7
2000-S, Proof, Silver	965,421	4,425	69.3					$5	$6	$8
2001-P	1,369,590,000	72	66.4	99%			$2	$3	$12	$30
2001-D	1,412,800,000	92	66.3	96%			$2	$3	$12	$30
2001-S, Proof	2,294,909	1,176	69.4					$2.50	$4	$7
2001-S, Proof, Silver	889,697	3,949	69.4					$5	$6	$8
2002-P	1,187,500,000	52	66.4	98%			$2	$3	$12	$30
2002-D	1,379,500,000	61	66.4	97%			$2	$3	$12	$30
2002-S, Proof	2,319,766	1,620	69.3					$2.50	$4	$7
2002-S, Proof, Silver	892,229	3,725	69.4					$5	$6	$8
2003-P	1,085,500,000	158	66.1	100%			$2	$3	$10	$30
2003-D	986,500,000	115	65.9	100%			$2	$3	$10	$30
2003-S, Proof	2,172,684	3,747	69.3					$2.50	$4	$7
2003-S, Proof, Silver	1,125,755	4,698	69.4					$4.50	$5	$8
2004-P	1,328,000,000	126	66.6	100%			$2	$3	$8	$30
2004-D	1,159,500,000	105	66.5	98%			$2	$3	$8	$35
2004-S, Proof	1,789,488	1,459	69.3					$3	$5	$7
2004-S, Proof, Silver	1,175,934	4,601	69.5					$5	$6	$8
2005-P	1,412,000,000	2,247	67.0	100%			$2	$3	$8	$65
2005-P, Satin Finish	1,160,000	2,200	67.0	100%	$1	$2	$3	$5	$7	$10

†† Ranked in the *100 Greatest U.S. Modern Coins* (fourth edition). **cc.** Issued in Mint sets only, to mark the 50th anniversary of the design.

	Mintage	Cert	Avg	%MS	EF-40	MS-63	MS-65	MS-66 / PF-65	MS-67 / PF-66	MS-67FT / PF-67
2005-D	1,423,500,000	2,408	66.9	100%			$2	$3	$8	$70
2005-D, Satin Finish	1,160,000	2,304	66.9	100%	$1	$2	$3	$5	$7	$10
2005-S, Proof	2,275,000	6,101	69.3					$2.50	$4	$7
2005-S, Proof, Silver	1,069,679	5,643	69.5					$5	$6	$8
2006-P	1,381,000,000	1,312	66.8	100%			$2	$3	$6	$22
2006-P, Satin Finish	847,361	1,190	66.9	100%	$1	$2	$3	$5	$7	$10
2006-D	1,447,000,000	1,254	66.8	100%			$2	$3	$6	$22
2006-D, Satin Finish	847,361	1,146	66.8	100%	$1	$2	$3	$5	$7	$10
2006-S, Proof	2,000,428	1,985	69.4					$2.50	$4	$7
2006-S, Proof, Silver	1,054,008	3,065	69.5					$5	$6	$8
2007-P	1,047,500,000	244	66.4	100%			$2	$3	$6	$22
2007-P, Satin Finish	895,628	214	66.5	100%	$1	$2	$3	$5	$7	$10
2007-D	1,042,000,000	446	66.5	100%			$2	$3	$6	$22
2007-D, Satin Finish	895,628	247	66.7	100%	$1	$2	$3	$5	$7	$10
2007-S, Proof	1,702,116	1,676	69.6					$2.50	$4	$7
2007-S, Proof, Silver	875,050	3,607	69.6					$5	$6	$8
2008-P	391,000,000	131	67.4	100%			$2	$3	$5	$22
2008-P, Satin Finish	745,464	102	67.8	100%	$1	$2	$3	$5	$7	$10
2008-D	624,500,000	246	67.4	100%			$2	$3	$5	$22
2008-D, Satin Finish	745,464	147	68.2	100%	$1	$2	$3	$5	$7	$10
2008-S, Proof	1,405,674	1,323	69.7					$2.50	$4	$7
2008-S, Proof, Silver	763,887	3,881	69.8					$6	$7	$9
2009-P	96,500,000	500	66.4	100%			$2	$3	$5	$22
2009-P, Satin Finish	784,614	150	67.6	100%	$1	$2	$3	$5	$7	$10
2009-D	49,500,000	451	67.2	100%			$2	$3	$5	$22
2009-D, Satin Finish	784,614	232	68.4	100%	$1	$2	$3	$5	$7	$10
2009-S, Proof	1,482,502	3,394	69.6					$2.50	$4	$7
2009-S, Proof, Silver	697,365	3,950	69.7					$6	$7	$9
2010-P	557,000,000	264	67.3	100%			$2	$3	$4	$20
2010-P, Satin Finish	583,897	133	68.0	100%	$1	$2	$3	$5	$7	$10
2010-D	562,000,000	244	67.2	100%			$2	$3	$4	$20
2010-D, Satin Finish	583,897	127	68.3	100%	$1	$2	$3	$5	$7	$10
2010-S, Proof	1,103,815	1,395	69.5					$2.50	$4	$7
2010-S, Proof, Silver	585,401	3,788	69.7					$6	$7	$9
2011-P	748,000,000	208	67.2	100%			$2	$3	$4	$20
2011-D	754,000,000	212	67.1	100%			$2	$3	$4	$20
2011-S, Proof	1,098,835	2,363	69.5					$2.50	$4	$7
2011-S, Proof, Silver	574,175	4,735	69.7					$6	$7	$9
2012-P	808,000,000	104	66.9	100%			$2	$3	$4	$20
2012-D	868,000,000	114	66.6	99%			$2	$3	$4	$20
2012-S, Proof	841,972	1,468	69.5					$4	$5	$7
2012-S, Proof, Silver	395,443	1,820	69.8					$20	$22	$24
2013-P	1,086,500,000	90	66.8	100%			$2	$3	$4	$20
2013-D	1,025,500,000	128	67.0	99%			$2	$3	$4	$20
2013-S, Proof	802,460	1,742	69.6					$4	$5	$7
2013-S, Proof, Silver	419,719	1,892	69.9					$10	$12	$14
2014-P	1,125,500,000	140	67.3	99%			$2	$3	$4	$20
2014-D	1,177,000,000	200	67.3	100%			$2	$3	$4	$20
2014-S, Proof	665,100	1,410	69.5					$5	$6	$7
2014-S, Proof, Silver	393,037	2,893	69.8					$6	$7	$8

	Mintage	Cert	Avg	%MS	EF-40	MS-63	MS-65	MS-66	MS-67	MS-67FT
								PF-65	PF-66	PF-67
2015-P	1,497,510,000	96	66.7	100%			$2	$3	$4	$20
2015-P, Reverse Proof, Silver	74,430	0	n/a					$30	$40	$50
2015-D	1,543,500,000	140	66.9	100%			$2	$3	$4	$20
2015-S, Proof	711,872	898	69.8					$4	$5	$7
2015-S, Proof, Silver	387,310	1,312	69.9					$6	$7	$8
2015-W, Proof, Silver	74,430	0	n/a					$30	$40	$50

In 2016 a special .9999 fine gold striking of Adolph A. Weinman's Winged Liberty Head or "Mercury" dime was created to celebrate the 100th anniversary of its introduction. It is smaller than the silver strikings, with a diameter of 16.5 mm and weighing 3.11035 grams (net weight .1 oz. pure gold). Struck at West Point, it has a reeded edge. Similar strikings were made for the 1916 quarter and half dollar designs.

	Mintage	Cert	Avg	%MS	SP-67	SP-70
2016-W, Mercury Dime Centennial Gold Coin ††	124,885	0	n/a		$325	$355

†† 2016 Centennial Gold Coins in all denominations are ranked in the *100 Greatest U.S. Modern Coins* (fourth edition), as a single entry.

Normally scheduled production of clad and silver Roosevelt dimes, in the same standards and specifications as previously, continued in 2016 and beyond, and was not disrupted by the gold Mercury dime.

	Mintage	Cert	Avg	%MS	EF-40	MS-63	MS-65	MS-66	MS-67	MS-67FT
								PF-65	PF-66	PF-67
2016-P	1,517,000,000	84	67.4	100%			$2	$3	$4	$20
2016-D	1,437,000,000	227	67.2	100%			$2	$3	$4	$20
2016-S, Proof	621,774	207	69.8					$4	$5	$6
2016-S, Proof, Silver	406,330	927	70.0					$15	$17	$19
2017-P	1,437,500,000	152	66.9	100%			$2	$3	$4	$20
2017-D	1,290,500,000	103	66.7	100%			$2	$3	$4	$20
2017-S, Enhanced Unc.	210,419							$8	$9	$12
2017-S, Proof	621,390	60	70.0					$5	$6	$7
2017-S, Proof, Silver	406,986	287	70.0					$10	$11	$12
2018-P	1,193,000,000	136	67.0	100%			$2	$3	$4	$20
2018-D	1,006,000,000	131	67.1	100%			$2	$3	$4	$20
2018-S, Proof	567,856	399	69.9					$5	$6	$8
2018-S, Proof, Silver	381,356	561	69.9					$6	$7	$8
2018-S, Reverse Proof	199,116							$12	$15	$18
2019-P	1,147,500,000	186	67.2	100%			$2	$3	$4	$20
2019-D	1,001,500,000	339	67.7	100%			$2	$3	$4	$20
2019-S, Proof (a)	642,309	1,038	69.9					$2.50	$4	$7
2019-S, Proof, Silver	458,685	5,439	70.0					$7	$8	$9
2020-P		0	n/a				$2	$3	$4	$20
2020-D		0	n/a				$2	$3	$4	$20
2020-S, Proof		180	69.8					$2.50	$4	$7
2020-S, Proof, Silver		1,799	69.8					$8	$9	$10
2021-P										
2021-D										
2021-S, Proof										
2021-S, Proof, Silver										

a. For its 225th anniversary, the Mint issued a special set of Enhanced Uncirculated coins from the San Francisco Mint; they are not included in the listings here.

Twenty-Cent Pieces
1875–1878

AN OVERVIEW OF TWENTY-CENT PIECES

The twenty-cent piece, made in silver, proved to be the shortest-lived denomination in American coinage history. The coins were struck in quantity in their first year of issue, 1875, after which it was learned that the public confused them with quarter dollars. Mintages dropped sharply, and in 1877 and 1878 coinage was limited to just Proofs for collectors.

Both sides of the twenty-cent piece were designed by U.S. Mint chief engraver William Barber. The obverse is simply an adaptation of the Liberty Seated motif earlier used on other denominations. The reverse is new and depicts a perched eagle (of the same general appearance as introduced by Barber on the 1873 silver trade dollar).

Only one twenty-cent piece is needed for inclusion in a type set. By far the most readily available in Mint State is the 1875-S, followed by the 1875-CC. These are often somewhat lightly struck on the reverse, particularly near the top of the eagle's wings. The 1875 and 1876 Philadelphia coins are occasionally encountered in Mint State and are usually well struck.

Proofs are readily available for all years, 1875 through 1878.

Senator John P. Jones was involved with the minting of the twenty-cent piece silver coin.

FOR THE COLLECTOR AND INVESTOR: TWENTY-CENT PIECES AS A SPECIALTY

A full date-and-mintmark set of twenty-cent pieces consists of the 1875, 1875-CC, 1875-S, 1876, 1876-CC, 1877, and 1878, the latter two years being available only in Proof format. The great challenge in forming a set is the 1876-CC, of which 10,000 were minted, but, seemingly, all but about two dozen were melted. Those that do survive are typically encountered in Mint State and are widely heralded when they are offered at auction.

LIBERTY SEATED (1875–1878)

Designer: *William Barber.* **Weight:** *5 grams.* **Composition:** *.900 silver, .100 copper.*
Diameter: *22 mm.* **Edge:** *Plain.* **Mints:** *Philadelphia, Carson City, and San Francisco.*

Circulation Strike

Mintmark location
is on the reverse,
below the eagle.

Proof

History. The twenty-cent coin debuted in 1875 as a convenient denomination to make change in the West (at the time silver coins did not circulate in the East or Midwest). The coins sometimes were confused with quarter dollars, given their similar Liberty Seated design on the obverse, and their similar size. The quantity minted dropped considerably in 1876, and in 1877 and 1878 only Proofs were struck. Despite the brief time of their production, these coins were still seen in circulation through the early 1900s, by which time they were often casually used as quarters. Proof coins were made of all years 1875 to 1878.

Striking and Sharpness. Areas of weakness are common. On the obverse, check the head of Miss Liberty and the stars. The word LIBERTY is *raised* on this coin, a curious departure from other Liberty Seated coins of the era, on which it is recessed or incuse (the Gobrecht silver dollars of 1836 and 1839 being exceptions). On the reverse, check the eagle's feathers, especially the top of the wing on the left, but other areas can be weak as well. Some 1875-S coins are highly prooflike. The 1877 and 1878 are Proof-only issues with no related circulation strikes. Most have been cleaned or even lightly polished. Many Proofs in the marketplace have been convincingly retoned to mask problems. Proofs are usually well struck, but more than just a few are somewhat flat on the hair details of Miss Liberty.

Availability. Most often seen is the high-mintage 1875-S, although the 1875 and 1875-CC are encountered with frequency. The 1876 is quite scarce and when seen is usually in high grades and well struck. The 1876-CC is a rarity, and only about two dozen are known, nearly all of which are MS. The eye appeal of MS coins can vary widely. The number of letters in LIBERTY on certain coins graded from VG through VF can vary widely in the marketplace. Proofs most often seen are those of 1875 and 1876. For some unexplained reason, high-quality Proofs of the series' final two years are very hard to find.

GRADING STANDARDS

MS-60 to 70 (Mint State). *Obverse:* At MS-60, some abrasion and contact marks are evident, most noticeably on the bosom and thighs and knees. Luster is present, but may be dull or lifeless. At MS-63, contact marks are very few, and abrasion is hard to detect except under magnification. An MS-65 coin has no abrasion, and contact marks are sufficiently minute as to require magnification. Check the knees of Liberty and the right field.

1875; BF-1. Graded MS-64.

Luster should be full and rich. *Reverse:* Comments apply as for the obverse, except that in lower–Mint State grades abrasion and contact marks are most noticeable on the eagle's breast and the top of the wing to the left. At MS-65 or higher, there are no marks visible to the unaided eye. The field is mainly protected by design elements and does not show abrasion as much as does the obverse on a given coin.

Illustrated coin: Semi-Proof surfaces contrast nicely against the frosted devices of this well-struck piece.

AU-50, 53, 55, 58 (About Uncirculated). *Obverse:* Light wear is seen on the thighs and knees, bosom, and head. At AU-58, the luster is extensive but incomplete, especially in the right field. At AU–50 and 53, luster is less. *Reverse:* Very light wear is evident on the eagle's breast (the prime focal point) and at the top of the wings. An AU-58 coin will have nearly full luster, more so than on the obverse, as the design elements protect the small field areas. At AU–50 and 53, there still are traces of luster.

1875-CC. Graded AU-55.

EF-40, 45 (Extremely Fine). *Obverse:* Further wear is seen on all areas, especially the thighs and knees, bosom, and head. Little or no luster is seen on most coins. From this grade downward, sharpness of strike of the stars and the head does not matter to connoisseurs. *Reverse:* More wear is evident on the eagle's breast and the top of the wings. Some feathers may be blended together, but most details are defined.

1875-S. Graded EF-45.

VF-20, 30 (Very Fine). *Obverse:* Further wear is seen. Most details of the gown are worn away, except in the lower-relief areas above and to the right of the shield. Hair detail is mostly or completely gone. As to whether LIBERTY should be completely readable, this seems to be a matter of debate. On many coins in the marketplace the word is weak or missing one to several letters. ANA grading standards and PCGS require full

1875-S. Graded VF-30.

LIBERTY. *Reverse:* Wear is more extensive, but at least three-quarters of the feathers in the breast and wings are distinct. At VF-30 the head is flat with distinct details; head details are less distinct at VF-20.

F-12, 15 (Fine). *Obverse:* The seated figure is well worn, but with some detail above and to the right of the shield. LIBERTY has at least three letters visible (per ANA grading standards). In the marketplace, some have more letters missing. *Reverse:* Wear is extensive, with about half of the feathers flat or blended with others and head details are indistinct except for the eye.

1875-CC. Graded F-15.

VG-8, 10 (Very Good). *Obverse:* The seated figure is more worn, but some detail can be seen above and to the right of the shield. The shield is discernible. In LIBERTY a letter or two may be visible per ANA grading standards. In the marketplace, many have no letters. *Reverse:* Further wear has flattened about half of the feathers. Those remaining are on the inside of the wings. The rim is full and shows many if not most denticles.

1875-S. Graded VG-10.

G-4, 6 (Good). *Obverse:* The seated figure is worn nearly smooth, but with some slight detail above and to the right of the shield. At G-4, there are no letters in LIBERTY remaining. On some at the G-6 level, there may be a trace of letters. *Reverse:* Most feathers in the eagle are gone. The border lettering is weak. The rim is visible partially or completely (depending on the strike).

1875-CC. Graded G-6.

AG-3 (About Good). *Obverse:* The seated figure is mostly visible in outline form, with only a hint of detail. Much of the rim is worn away. The date remains clear. *Reverse:* The border letters are partially worn away. The eagle is mostly in outline form, but with a few details discernible. The rim is weak or missing.

1875-CC. Graded AG-3.

PF-60 to 70 (Proof). *Obverse and Reverse:* Proofs that are extensively cleaned and have many hairlines, or that are dull and grainy, are lower level, such as PF–60 to 62. These are not widely desired. With medium hairlines and good reflectivity, an assigned grade of PF-64 is indicated, and with relatively few hairlines, Gem PF-65. In various grades hairlines are most easily seen in the obverse field. PF-66 should have hairlines so delicate that

1877. Graded PF-61.

magnification is needed to see them. Above that, a Proof should be free of such lines.

    Illustrated coin: Lovely frosted devices are complemented by indigo toning in the peripheries of the fields.

	Mintage	Cert	Avg	%MS	G-4	VG-8	F-12	VF-20	EF-40	AU-50	MS-60 / PF-60	MS-63 / PF-63	MS-65 / PF-65
1875	38,500	593	51.5		$220	$250	$300	$325	$400	$600	$875	$1,350	$4,500
Auctions: $1,292, MS-64, August 2015; $940, MS-62, July 2015; $881, MS-61, January 2015; $352, AU-50, February 2015													
1875, Proof	1,200	265	63.5	99%							$1,300	$2,750	$6,500
Auctions: $7,050, PF-65, August 2015; $4,465, PF-64Cam, July 2015; $3,995, PF-64, January 2015; $2,585, PF-63Cam, October 2015													
1875-CC	133,290	1,143	37.0	27%	$200	$250	$300	$425	$700	$1,000	$1,650	$2,750	$10,000
Auctions: $7,050, MS-65, August 2015; $2,820, MS-62, January 2015; $2,056, MS-62, September 2015; $1,116, AU-55, June 2015													
1875-S (a)	1,155,000	3,780	47.0	41%	$95	$105	$130	$150	$250	$350	$650	$1,050	$2,350
Auctions: $52,875, MS-68, August 2015; $6,462, MS-66, June 2015; $2,467, MS-65, March 2015; $540, MS-61, January 2015; $352, AU-53, April 2015													
1875-S, Proof	10–20	2	63.0								$20,000	$150,000	
Auctions: No auction records available.													
1876	14,750	475	57.4	61%	$235	$275	$350	$450	$525	$650	$850	$1,600	$4,250
Auctions: $15,275, MS-66, June 2015; $4,700, MS-65, July 2015; $4,465, MS-65, January 2015; $940, AU-58, October 2015													
1876, Proof	1,150	306	63.5								$1,300	$2,800	$7,500
Auctions: $25,850, PF-68, August 2015; $4,230, PF-64, February 2015; $3,995, PF-64, January 2015; $3,760, PF-63Cam, October 2015													
1876-CC †	10,000	7	64.6	100%						$175,000	$250,000	$350,000	$500,000
Auctions: $564,000, MS-65, January 2013													
1877, Proof	510	264	63.6								$6,500	$8,500	$14,500
Auctions: $7,637, PF-65, July 2015; $15,275, PF-64, August 2016; $3,995, PF-62, June 2015; $3,995, PF-62, October 2015													
1878, Proof	600	323	63.6								$3,500	$4,500	$8,000
Auctions: $28,200, PF-66, August 2016; $4,700, PF-64, March 2015; $3,290, PF-62, September 2016; $1,827, AU-50, September 2015													

† Ranked in the *100 Greatest U.S. Coins* (fifth edition). **a.** There are at least two misplaced-date die varieties of the 1875-S twenty-cent piece. These do not command a premium in the marketplace. A repunched mintmark is likewise common.

Quarter Dollars
1796 to Date

AN OVERVIEW OF QUARTER DOLLARS

In 1796 the first silver quarters were struck at the Philadelphia Mint. The Draped Bust obverse in combination with the Small Eagle reverse was produced only in this year, after which no pieces of this denomination were produced until 1804. At that time the Draped Bust obverse was continued, but now with the Heraldic Eagle reverse. The coinage proved to be brief and lasted only through 1807, after which no quarters were struck until 1815. The new quarters dated 1815 were of the Capped Bust style, by John Reich. These were produced intermittently through 1838. The Liberty Seated motif, by Christian Gobrecht, made its debut in 1838 and was produced continuously through 1891, with several modifications in design and metallic content over the years. The Liberty Head quarter, today called the Barber quarter after its designer, was introduced in 1892 and minted continuously through 1916. The obverse features the head of Miss Liberty, and the reverse a heraldic eagle. In late 1916 the Standing Liberty by Hermon A. MacNeil became the new design. This was produced through 1930, except for 1922. Some changes to both the obverse and reverse were made partway through 1917.

The Washington quarter dollar was struck in 1932 to observe the 200th anniversary of the birth of our first president. Washington quarters have been struck continuously since then, except for 1933, and with none dated 1975. In 1976 a special Bicentennial motif was introduced. Beginning in 1999 the State quarters were launched, issued at the rate of five per year, covering all 50 states, each coin having its own distinctive design. After this successful and popular program came quarter dollars with motifs celebrating the District of Columbia and U.S. territories. A similar program commemorating national parks started in 2010 and is slated to run through 2021.

While there are no super-rarities among the different *types* of quarter dollars, the first one, the 1796 with Draped Bust obverse and Small Eagle reverse, is hard to find and expensive in all grades. The values are, of course, justified by the great demand for this single-year type.

Quarter-dollar designers
Hermon A. MacNeil and John Flanagan.

The collector's greatest challenge in finding a decent strike is in the short-lived 1804–1807 type with the Heraldic Eagle reverse. Sufficient quantities were made that examples from these years are not rarities, but nearly all are weakly struck. Quarters of the 1815–1828 Capped Bust, large planchet, type are available easily enough in worn grades but are scarce to rare in Mint State. Some cherrypicking (close examination for high quality within a given grade) is needed to find a sharp strike.

Respite from the sharp-strike difficulty is at last found with the 1831–1838 type, Capped Bust, small diameter, and without E PLURIBUS UNUM. Most are quite nicely struck. Also, for the first time Mint State coins are generally available with frequency in the marketplace, although those with good eye appeal are in the distinct minority.

The Liberty Seated quarters of the several types made from 1838 to 1891 are generally available in proportion to their mintages, with an allowance for the earlier dates being scarcer than the later ones—as they had a longer time to become worn or lost. Many quarters of earlier dates were melted circa 1850 to 1853, when the price of silver rose on international markets, making such coins worth slightly more than 25 cents in melt-down value.

Barber quarters, 1892–1916, present no difficulty for the collector, except that there is a challenge to find an example with sharp striking overall, including in the telltale area on the reverse at and near the eagle's leg to the right. MS-65 and better Barber quarters are scarcer than generally known (the same can be said for Barber half dollars). Proofs were sold to collectors and saved, and thus they are available in proportion to their mintages, with probably 70% to 80% surviving today.

The Variety 1 Standing Liberty quarter is a rarity if dated 1916, for only 52,000 were struck, and not many were saved. The feasible alternative is the 1917, Variety 1, which is often seen in Mint State, sharply struck, and very beautiful. Standing Liberty quarters of the Variety 2 design, minted from partway through 1917 to 1930, often are weakly struck on the head of Miss Liberty and on the shield rivets, and sometimes other places as well. Diligent searching is needed to locate a nice example.

Washington quarters also present no difficulty for collectors. The State, D.C./Territorial, and America the Beautiful (National Park) reverses are appealing in their diversity and make a fascinating study in themselves.

For the Collector and Investor: Quarter Dollars as a Specialty

The formation of a specialized collection of quarter dollars from 1796 to date, by dates, mints, and major varieties, is a considerable challenge. As a class, quarters are considerably more difficult to acquire than are either dimes or half dollars. Relatively few numismatists have ever concentrated on the entire series.

The 1796 is rare and popular both as a date and a type. The 1804, although elusive in worn grades, is of commanding importance if in AU or Mint State. The 1823, 3 Over 2, is a classic rarity and is nearly always encountered well worn. From the same decade the 1827 is famous. Although Mint records indicate that 4,000 circulation strikes were produced in calendar-year 1827, they were probably struck from 1825-dated or earlier dies, as no unequivocal circulation strike has ever been located. There are, however, a dozen or so Proofs. Originals are distinguished by the 2 (in the 25 C. denomination) having a curved base, while restrikes, also very rare, have a square-base 2.

One of the unsolved mysteries in numismatics involves certain quarter dollars dated 1815 (the die variety known as Browning-1) and 1825, 5 Over 3 (Browning-2), which are often seen counterstamped, above the cap, with either an E or an L. Hundreds exist. As other quarter-dollar die varieties were made during this period, but only these two bear counterstamps, it may be that this was done either at the Mint or elsewhere before they were generally distributed.

Ard W. Browning's 1925 text, *The Early Quarter Dollars of the United States, 1796–1838*, remains the standard reference on the series, together with new information added here and there, including in issues of the *John Reich Journal*, the magazine of the John Reich Collectors Society, and in more recently published books.

The panorama of Liberty Seated quarters from 1838 to 1891 is highlighted by several rarities, notably the 1842, Small Date (known only in Proof format), and the 1873-CC, Without Arrows (of which only five are known, at least three being Mint State). The others are generally available, but some can be almost impossible to find in Mint State, the 1849-O, certain early San Francisco issues, and Carson City coins of the early 1870s being well known in this regard. From the mid-1870s onward Mint State coins are generally available, including choice and gem pieces. Proofs from 1858 onward can be found in proportion to their mintages, with later dates often being seen with higher numerical designations than are earlier ones.

Barber quarters are collectible by date and mint, although the "big three" rarities, the 1896-S, 1901-S, and 1913-S, are expensive and hard to find.

Standing Liberty quarters, 1916–1930, represent a short-lived series, one easy enough to collect in grades up to MS-63, except for the rare 1918-S, 8 Over 7, overdate. Finding higher-grade coins that are sharply struck is another matter entirely, and over the years few sets of this nature have been assembled.

Washington quarters are all collectible, with no great rarities. However, in relation to the demand for them, certain early issues are elusive, the 1932-D being a well-known example. Modern issues, including the Bicentennial, State, D.C./Territorial, and National Park coins, are at once plentiful, inexpensive, and interesting.

The Early Quarter Dollars OF THE United States 1796-1838

By A.W. Browning
Completely Updated by Walter Breen
New Foreword by Q. David Bowers

A copy of Ard W. Browning's 1925 text, *The Early Quarter Dollars of the United States, 1796–1838.*

DRAPED BUST, SMALL EAGLE REVERSE (1796)

Designer: *Probably Gilbert Stuart.* **Engraver:** *Robert Scot.*
Weight: *6.74 grams.* **Composition:** *.8924 silver, .1076 copper.*
Diameter: *Approximately 27.5 mm.* **Edge:** *Reeded.* **Mint:** *Philadelphia.*

Browning-2.

History. The Philadelphia Mint coined its first quarter dollar in 1796. Its design followed that of other silver U.S. coins. Only 6,146 were made, followed by a production hiatus until 1804, by which time a new reverse was used. Thus the 1796 was isolated as a single-year type.

Striking and Sharpness. On the obverse, check the hair details and the star centers. Most are well struck. On the reverse, most are well struck except for the head of the eagle, which can be shallow or flat, especially on the Browning-2 variety (there are two known die varieties for this year, Browning-1 being the rarer). Rarely is a Full Details coin encountered. The denticles are unusually bold and serve to frame the motifs. Check for planchet adjustment marks (from overweight planchets being filed down at the Mint to achieve proper weight). A few pieces have carbon streaks, which lower their value. Sharp striking (as on Browning-2) will add to the value. Most MS examples have excellent eye appeal.

Availability. Examples are available in all grades from well worn to superb MS. Nearly all of the latter are highly prooflike, but there are some exceptions. Although hundreds of circulated examples exist, demand for this famous coin exceeds supply in the marketplace, making public offerings a scene of excitement and strong bidding. Hundreds of higher-grade examples also survive, many of them prooflike and attractive. They attract great attention when offered for sale.

GRADING STANDARDS

MS-60 to 70 (Mint State). *Obverse:* At MS-60, some abrasion and contact marks are evident, most noticeably on the cheek, the drapery, and the right field. Luster is present, but may be dull or lifeless, and interrupted in patches. On prooflike coins the contact marks are more prominent. At MS-63, contact marks are very few, and abrasion is hard to detect except under magnification, although this type is sometimes graded liberally due to its

1796; Browning-2. Graded MS-62.

rarity. An MS-65 coin has no abrasion, and contact marks are so minute as to require magnification. Luster should be full and rich. Grades above MS-65 are defined by having fewer marks as perfection is approached. *Reverse:* Comments apply as for the obverse, except that abrasion and contact marks are most noticeable on the eagle at the center, a situation complicated by the fact that this area is typically flatly struck (except on the Browning-2 variety). Grading is best done by the obverse, then verified by the reverse. The field area is small and is protected by lettering and the wreath and in any given grade shows fewer marks than on the obverse.

Illustrated coin: This coin is well struck on the obverse, and the weak striking on the eagle's breast and head is typical of this issue.

AU-50, 53, 55, 58 (About Uncirculated). *Obverse:* Light wear is seen on the hair area above the ear and extending to left of the forehead, on the ribbon, on the drapery at the shoulder, and on the high points of the bust line, more so at AU-50 than at AU–53 or 55. An AU-58 coin has minimal traces of wear. An AU-50 coin has luster in protected areas among the stars and letters, with little in the open fields or on the portrait. At AU-58, most

1796; Browning-2. Graded AU-58.

luster remains in the fields, but is worn away on the highest parts of the motifs. *Reverse:* Light wear is seen on the eagle's body (keep in mind this area is nearly always lightly struck) and the edges of the wings. Light wear is seen on the wreath and lettering. Luster is the best key to actual wear. This ranges from perhaps 20% remaining in protected areas (at AU-50) to nearly full mint bloom (at AU-58).

EF-40, 45 (Extremely Fine). *Obverse:* More wear is evident on the upper hair area and the ribbon, and on the drapery and bosom. Excellent detail remains in low-relief areas of the hair. The stars show wear as do the date and letters. Luster, if present at all, is minimal and in protected areas. *Reverse:* The eagle shows more wear, this being the focal point to check. Most feathers remain on the interior areas of the wings. Additional wear is on

1796; Browning-1. Graded EF-40.

the wreath and letters, but many details are present. Some luster may be seen in protected areas and if present is slightly more abundant than on the obverse.

VF-20, 30 (Very Fine). *Obverse:* The higher-relief areas of hair are well worn at VF-20, less so at VF-30, although much detail remains on the areas below the ear. The drapery and bosom show extensive wear. The stars have more wear, making them appear larger (an optical illusion seen on most worn silver coins of this era). *Reverse:* The body of the eagle shows few if any feathers, while the wings have about half of the feath-

1796; Browning-2. Graded VF-30.

ers visible, mostly on the right wing, depending on the strike. The leaves lack most detail and are in outline form. Scattered, non-disfiguring marks are normal for this and lower grades. Any major defects should be noted separately.

F-12, 15 (Fine). *Obverse:* Wear is more extensive than on a Very Fine coin, particularly noticeable on the hair, face, and bosom. The stars appear larger. About half the hair detail remains, most noticeably behind the neck and shoulder. The denticles remain strong (while on most other silver denominations of this design they become weak at this grade level). *Reverse:* Wear is more extensive. Now feather details are diminished, with

1796; Browning-2. Graded F-12.

fewer than half remaining on the wings. The wreath and lettering are worn further, and the rim is slightly weak in areas, although most denticles can be seen.

VG-8, 10 (Very Good). *Obverse:* The portrait is mostly seen in outline form, with most hair strands gone, although there is some definition at the back of the hair and behind the shoulder. The ear is discernible, as is the eye. The stars appear larger still, again an illusion. The rim is weak in areas. Most denticles are seen, some of them even bold. LIBERTY and the date are readable and usually full, although some letters may be weak

1796; Browning-2. Graded VG-10.

at their tops (the high rim and denticles protect the design more on the quarter dollar than on other silver coins of this type). *Reverse:* The eagle is mostly an outline, with parts blending into the field (on lighter strikes), although some slight feather detail can be seen on the right wing. The rim is worn, as are the letters, with some weak, but the motto is readable. Most denticles remain clear.

G-4, 6 (Good). *Obverse:* Wear is more extensive. The head is an outline. The rim still is present, as are most of the denticles, most well defined. LIBERTY is worn, but complete. The date is bold. *Reverse:* The eagle is flat and discernible in outline form, blending into the field in areas. The wreath is well worn. Some of the letters may be partly missing. Some rim areas and denticles are discernible. At this level some "averaging" can

1796; Browning-1. Graded G-4.

be done. If the letters are stronger than usual in one area, but some are missing in another area, the coin can still qualify as G-4.

AG-3 (About Good). *Obverse:* Wear is so extensive that the coin is barely identifiable. The head is in outline form, LIBERTY is mostly gone, same for the stars, and the date, while readable, may be partially worn away. *Reverse:* The reverse is well worn, with parts of the wreath and lettering missing.

1796; Browning-2. Graded AG-3.

	Mintage	Cert	Avg	%MS	AG-3	G-4	VG-8	F-12	VF-20	EF-40	AU-50	MS-60	MS-63
1796 †	6,146	194	33.9	21%	$7,500	$11,000	$17,000	$25,000	$32,500	$48,500	$60,000	$80,000	$125,000
	Auctions: $105,750, MS-63, August 2016; $25,850, F-15, August 2016												

† Ranked in the *100 Greatest U.S. Coins* (fifth edition).

DRAPED BUST, HERALDIC EAGLE REVERSE (1804–1807)

Designer: *Robert Scot.* **Weight:** *6.74 grams.* **Composition:** *.8924 silver, .1076 copper.*
Diameter: *Approximately 27.5 mm.* **Edge:** *Reeded.* **Mint:** *Philadelphia.*

Browning-1.

History. Early on, the U.S. Mint's production of silver coins in any given year depended on requests made by depositors of silver; they were not made for the Mint's own account. After 1796 no quarters were struck until 1804. When production started up again, the Draped Bust obverse was used, but with the new Heraldic Eagle reverse—similar to that on other silver (and gold) denominations of the time. The Heraldic Eagle design was patterned after the Great Seal of the United States.

Striking and Sharpness. Virtually all examples are lightly struck in one area or another. On the obverse, check the hair details and the star centers. On the reverse, check the shield, stars, feathers, and other design elements. The denticles and rims on both sides often have problems. Quarters of 1807 are usually the lightest struck. Also check for planchet adjustment marks (where an overweight planchet was filed down by a Mint worker to reach acceptable standards). Sharp striking and excellent eye appeal add to a coin's value. This series often is misgraded due to lack of understanding of its strike anomalies.

Availability. All dates are collectible, with 1804 being scarcer than the others and a rarity in MS. Those of 1805, 1806, and 1807 are readily available in the marketplace, usually in circulated grades although MS examples are sometimes seen. Some die varieties are rare. High-grade coins with Full Details are very rare.

GRADING STANDARDS

MS-60 to 70 (Mint State). *Obverse:* At MS-60, some abrasion and contact marks are evident, most noticeably on the cheek, the drapery, and the right field. Luster is present, but may be dull or lifeless, and interrupted in patches. At MS-63, contact marks are very few, and abrasion is hard to detect except under magnification. An MS-65 coin will have no abrasion, and contact marks are so minute as to require magnification. Luster should be

1806; Browning-9. Graded MS-66.

full and rich. Coins graded above MS-65 are more theoretical than actual for this type—but they do exist, and are defined by having fewer marks as perfection is approached. As noted in the introduction, expect weakness in some areas. *Reverse:* Comments apply as for the obverse, except that abrasion and contact marks are most noticeable on the eagle's neck, the tips of the wing, and the tail. The field area is complex, without much open space, given the stars above the eagle, the arrows and olive branch, and other features. Accordingly, marks are not as noticeable as on the obverse.

    Illustrated coin: This coin is lightly struck on the right obverse stars and at the center of the reverse. Some planchet adjustment marks are mostly hidden. Some tiny carbon streaks are on the obverse (seemingly typical for Browning-9).

AU-50, 53, 55, 58 (About Uncirculated). *Obverse:* Light wear is seen on the hair area above the ear and extending to left of the forehead, on the ribbon, and on the drapery at the shoulder, more so at AU-50 than at AU–53 or 55. An AU-58 coin has minimal traces of wear. An AU-50 coin has luster in protected areas among the stars and letters, with little in the open fields or on the portrait. At AU-58, most luster is present in the fields, but is worn away on the highest parts of the motifs.

1804; Browning-1. Graded AU-58.

Reverse: Comments as preceding, except that the eagle's neck, the tips and top of the wings, the clouds, and the tail now show noticeable wear, as do other features. Luster ranges from perhaps 20% remaining in protected areas (at AU-50) to nearly full mint bloom (at AU-58). Often the reverse retains much more luster than the obverse, more so on quarter dollars than on other denominations of this design.

Illustrated coin: Lightly struck on the obverse stars. The reverse has some light areas but is sharp overall. A few planchet adjustment marks are visible. Abundant luster and good eye appeal rank this as an exceptional example of this date, the most difficult of the type to find in high grades.

EF-40, 45 (Extremely Fine). *Obverse:* More wear is evident on the upper hair area and the ribbon, and on the drapery at the shoulder and the bosom. Excellent detail remains in low-relief areas of the hair. The stars show wear, as do the date and letters (note: on most coins of this type the stars are softly struck). Luster, if present at all, is minimal and in protected areas. *Reverse:* Wear is greater than on an About Uncirculated coin, overall. The

1804; Browning-1. Graded EF-45.

neck lacks feather detail on its highest points. Feathers have lost some detail near the edges of the wings, and some areas of the horizontal lines in the shield may be blended together. Some traces of luster may be seen, more so at EF-45 than at EF-40.

VF-20, 30 (Very Fine). *Obverse:* The higher-relief areas of hair are well worn at VF-20, less so at VF-30. The drapery and bosom show extensive wear. The stars have more wear, making them appear larger (an optical illusion seen on most worn silver coins of this era). *Reverse:* Wear is greater, including on the shield and wing feathers, although more than half of the feathers are defined. Star centers are flat. Other areas have lost

1804; Browning-1. Graded VF-30.

detail as well. Some letters in the motto may be missing, depending on the strike.

F-12, 15 (Fine). *Obverse:* Wear is more extensive than on a Very Fine coin, particularly noticeable on the hair, face, and bosom. The stars appear larger. About half the hair detail remains with the tresses fused so as to appear thick, most noticeably behind the neck and shoulder. The rim may be partially worn away and blend into the field. *Reverse:* Wear is even more extensive, with the shield and wing feathers being points to observe.

1804; Browning-1. Graded F-12.

About half of the feathers can be seen. The incuse E PLURIBUS UNUM may have a few letters worn away. The clouds all seem to be connected. The stars are weak. Parts of the border and lettering may be weak. As with most quarters of this type, peculiarities of striking can account for some weakness.

VG-8, 10 (Very Good). *Obverse:* The portrait is mostly seen in outline form, with most hair strands gone, although there is slight definition at the back of the hair and behind the shoulder. The ear is discernible, as is the eye. The stars appear larger still, again an illusion. The rim is weak in areas. LIBERTY and the date are readable and usually full, although some letters may be weak at their tops. *Reverse:* Wear is more extensive. Half

1804; Browning-1. Graded VG-8.

or so of the letters in the motto are worn away. Most feathers are worn away, although separation of some of the lower feathers may be seen. Some stars are faint. The border blends into the field in areas (depending on striking), and some letters are weak.

G-4, 6 (Good). *Obverse:* Wear is more extensive, and some stars may be partly missing. The head is an outline. The eye is visible only in outline form. The rim is well worn or even missing in areas. LIBERTY is worn, and parts of some letters may be missing, but elements of all should be readable. The date is readable, but worn. *Reverse:* Wear is more extensive. The upper part of the eagle is flat, and feathers are noticeable only at some (but

1804; Browning-1. Graded G-4.

not necessarily all) of the lower edge of the wings, and do not have detail. The shield lacks most of its detail. Only a few letters of the motto can be seen (depending on striking). The rim is worn extensively, and a few letters may be missing.

AG-3 (About Good). *Obverse:* Wear is so extensive that the coin is barely identifiable. The head is in outline form, LIBERTY is mostly gone. Same for the stars. The date, while readable, may be partially worn away. *Reverse:* Extensive wear is seen overall, with the rim worn away and some areas worn smooth. The eagle can be discerned in outline form, but not necessarily completely. A few stray motto letters may remain. Some-

1804; Browning-1. Graded AG-3.

times the obverse appears to be more worn than the reverse, or vice-versa.

1806, 6 Over 5

	Mintage	Cert	Avg	%MS	AG-3	G-4	VG-8	F-12	VF-20	EF-40	AU-50	MS-60	MS-63
1804	6,738	134	16.5	4%	$2,500	$4,000	$6,500	$9,000	$13,000	$30,000	$50,000	$95,000	$175,000
Auctions: $6,463, F-15, August 2016; $1,351, Fair-2, January 2015													
1805	121,394	376	21.7	4%	$250	$500	$650	$950	$1,800	$3,250	$5,500	$11,000	$20,000
Auctions: $946, F-15, January 2015; $709, VG-10, June 2015; $564, VG-8, January 2015; $552, VG-8, March 2015													
1806, All kinds	206,124												
1806, 6 Over 5		155	23.0	6%	$300	$550	$700	$1,100	$2,000	$4,000	$6,000	$13,500	$25,000
Auctions: $152,750, MS-66, November 2013; $1,645, EF-40, March 2016; $1,293, VF-20, August 2016; $1,116, VG-10, October 2014													
1806		723	22.5	7%	$225	$500	$650	$950	$1,800	$3,250	$5,500	$11,000	$20,000
Auctions: $1,528, VF-20, March 2015; $764, VF-20, August 2015; $529, VF-20, January 2015; $470, F-12, February 2015													
1807	220,643	307	22.1	12%	$225	$500	$700	$1,000	$1,750	$3,500	$5,500	$11,000	$20,000
Auctions: $764, VG-10, June 2015; $676, VG-10, March 2015; $494, VG-8, July 2015; $424, G-6, June 2015													

CAPPED BUST (1815–1838)

Variety 1, Large Diameter (1815–1828): **Designer:** *John Reich.*
Weight: *6.74 grams.* **Composition:** *.8924 silver, .1076 copper.*
Diameter: *Approximately 27 mm.* **Edge:** *Reeded.* **Mint:** *Philadelphia.*

Variety 1, Large Diameter (1815–1828)
Browning-1.

Variety 1, Large Diameter, Proof
Browning-8.

Variety 2, Reduced Diameter, Motto Removed (1831–1838):
Designer: *William Kneass.* **Weight:** *6.74 grams (changed to 6.68 grams, .900 fine, in 1837).*
Composition: *.8924 silver, .1076 copper.* **Diameter:** *24.3 mm.* **Edge:** *Reeded.* **Mint:** *Philadelphia.*

Variety 2, Reduced Diameter,
Motto Removed (1831–1838)
Browning-1.

Variety 2, Reduced Diameter,
Motto Removed, Proof
Browning-1.

History. The Capped Bust design, by John Reich, was introduced on the half dollar of 1807 but was not used on the quarter until 1815. The difference between the Large Diameter and the Reduced Diameter types resulted from the introduction of the close collar in 1828. Capped Bust, Reduced Diameter, quarter dollars are similar in overall appearance to the preceding type, but with important differences. The diameter is smaller, E PLURIBUS UNUM no longer appears on the reverse, and the denticles are smaller and restyled using a close collar.

Striking and Sharpness. Striking sharpness of Capped Bust, Large Diameter, quarters varies. On the obverse, check the hair of Miss Liberty, the broach clasp (a particular point of observation), and the star centers. On this type the stars are often well defined (in contrast with half dollars of the same design). On the reverse, check the neck of the eagle and its wings, and the letters. The details of the eagle often are superbly defined. Check the scroll or ribbon above the eagle's head for weak or light areas. Examine the denticles on both sides. When weakness occurs it is usually in the center. Proofs were struck for inclusion in sets and for numismatists. Some deeply toned coins, and coins with patches of mint luster, have been described as Proofs but are mostly impostors, some of which have been certified or have "papers" signed by Walter Breen. Be careful! Nearly all coins of the Capped Bust, Reduced Diameter, Motto Removed, variety are very well struck. Check all areas for sharpness. Some quarters of 1833 and 1834 are struck from rusted or otherwise imperfect dies and can be less attractive than coins from undamaged dies. Avoid any Proofs that show patches of mint frost or that are darkly toned.

Availability. Most quarters of the Large Diameter variety range from slightly scarce to rare, with the 1823, 3 Over 2, and the 1827 being famous rarities. Typical coins range from well worn to Fine and VF. AU and MS coins are elusive (and are usually dated before the 1820s), and gems are particularly rare. All authentic Proofs are rarities. Examples of the Reduced Diameter, Motto Removed, variety are readily available of all dates, including many of the first year of issue. Mint frost ranges from satiny (usual) to deeply frosty. Proofs were struck of all dates for inclusion in sets and for sale or trade to numismatists; avoid deeply toned pieces, and seek those with deep and full (not partial) mirror surfaces and good contrast.

GRADING STANDARDS

MS-60 to 70 (Mint State). *Obverse:* At MS-60, some abrasion and contact marks are evident, most noticeably on the cheek, the hair below LIBERTY, and the area near the drapery clasp. Luster is present, but may be dull or lifeless, and interrupted in patches. At MS-63, contact marks are very few, and abrasion is hard to detect except under magnification. An

1831, Large Letters; Browning-5. Graded MS-62.

MS-65 coin has no abrasion, and contact marks are so minute as to require magnification. Luster should be full and rich. Grades above MS-65 are seen now and again and are defined by having fewer marks as perfection is approached. Grading for Reduced Diameter, Motto Removed, examples is similar, except the rims are more uniform, striking is usually very sharp, and the wear occurs evenly on both sides. *Reverse:* Comments apply as for the obverse, except that abrasion and contact marks are most noticeable on the eagle's neck, the top of the wings, the claws, and the flat band that surrounds the incuse motto. The field is mainly protected by design elements and does not show abrasion as much as does the obverse on a given coin.

AU-50, 53, 55, 58 (About Uncirculated).

Obverse: Light wear is seen on the cap, the hair below LIBERTY, the curl on the neck, the hair near the clasp, and the drapery. At AU-58, the luster is extensive except in the open area of the field, especially to the right. At AU–50 and 53, luster remains only in protected areas. Grading for Reduced Diameter, Motto Removed, examples is similar, except the rims are more uniform, striking is usually

1834; Browning-2. Graded AU-55.

very sharp, and the wear occurs evenly on both sides. *Reverse:* Wear is evident on the eagle's neck, the top of the wings, the claws, and the flat band above the eagle. An AU-58 coin has nearly full luster. At AU–50 and 53, there still is significant luster, more than on the obverse. Generally, light wear is most obvious on the obverse.

EF-40, 45 (Extremely Fine). *Obverse:* Wear

is more extensive, most noticeably on the higher areas of the hair. The cap shows more wear, as does the cheek. Most or all stars have some radial lines visible (unless lightly struck, as many are). Luster, if present, is in protected areas among the star points and close to the portrait. Grading for Reduced Diameter, Motto Removed, examples is similar, except the rims are more uniform, striking is

1831, Small Letters; Browning-4. Graded EF-40.

usually very sharp, and the wear occurs evenly on both sides. *Reverse:* The wings show wear on the higher areas of the feathers, and some details are lost. Feathers in the neck are light on some (but not on especially sharp strikes). The eagle's claws and the leaves show wear. Luster may be present in protected areas, even if there is little or none on the obverse.

VF-20, 30 (Very Fine). *Obverse:* Wear is more extensive, and most of the hair is combined into thick tresses without delicate features. The curl on the neck is flat. Details of the drapery are well defined at the lower edge. Unless they were weakly struck, the stars are mostly flat although a few may retain radial lines. Grading for Reduced Diameter, Motto Removed, examples is similar, except the rims are more uniform, striking is usually

1828. Graded VF-20.

very sharp, and the wear occurs evenly on both sides. *Reverse:* Wear is most evident on the eagle's neck, to the left of the shield, and on the leaves and claws. Most feathers in the wing remain distinct, but some show light wear. Overall, the reverse on most quarters at this level shows less wear than the obverse.

F-12, 15 (Fine). *Obverse:* Wear is more extensive, with much of the hair blended together. The drapery is indistinct at its upper edge. The stars are flat. Grading for Reduced Diameter, Motto Removed, examples is similar, except the rims are more uniform, striking is usually very sharp, and the wear occurs evenly on both sides. *Reverse:* Wear is more extensive, now with only about half of the feathers remaining on the wings. The claws on the right are fused at their upper parts.

1815. Graded F-15.

VG-8, 10 (Very Good). *Obverse:* The hair is less distinct, with the area above the face blended into the facial features. LIBERTY is complete, but can be weak in areas. At the left the drapery and bosom are blended together in a flat area. The rim is worn away in areas, and blends into the field. *Reverse:* Feathers are fewer and mostly on the eagle's wing to the left. Other details are weaker. E PLURIBUS UNUM is weak, perhaps with some letters missing. All border lettering remains easily readable.

1828, 25 Over 50 C.; Browning-3. Graded VG-10.

Illustrated coin: Gunmetal toning in the fields contrasts nicely with the lighter devices. The overpunched denomination shows signs of the 50 punched first into the die to the left of both 2 and 5.

G-4, 6 (Good). *Obverse:* The portrait is mostly in outline, with few interior details discernible. LIBERTY may still be readable or may be partially worn away, depending on the variety. Most or all of the border is worn away, and the outer parts of the stars are weak. *Reverse:* The eagle mostly is in outline form, although some feathers can be seen in the wing to the left. All letters around the border are clear. E PLURIBUS UNUM is mostly or completely worn away.

1815; Browning-1. Graded G-4.

AG-3 (About Good). *Obverse:* The portrait is an outline. Most of LIBERTY can still be seen. Stars are weak or missing toward what used to be the rim. The date remains clear, but may be weak at the bottom. *Reverse:* The reverse shows more wear than at G-4, but parts of the rim may remain clear.

1825, 5 Over 4; Browning-3. Graded AG-3.

PF-60 to 70 (Proof). *Obverse and Reverse:* Proofs that are extensively cleaned and have many hairlines, or that are dull and grainy, are lower level, such as PF–60 to 62. While any early Proof coin will attract attention, lower-level examples are not of great interest to specialists unless they are of rare die varieties. With medium hairlines, an assigned grade of PF-64 may be in order and with relatively few, Gem PF-65. PF-66 should have

1833; Browning-1. Graded PF-64 Cameo.

hairlines so delicate that magnification is needed to see them. Above that, a Proof should be free of such lines. Grading is highly subjective with early Proofs, and eye appeal also is a factor.

Illustrated coin: This coin features frosted devices and reflective fields, though the fields are marred by some light scratches.

1818, 8 Over 5   **1818, Normal Date**

	Mintage	Cert	Avg	%MS	AG-3	G-4	VG-8	F-12	VF-20	EF-40	AU-50	MS-60	MS-63
											PF-60	PF-63	PF-65
1815	89,235	199	40.1	32%	$150	$250	$400	$550	$850	$2,200	$3,000	$5,000	$7,500
	Auctions: $10,575, MS-64, March 2016; $999, VF-30, October 2014; $635, F-15, September 2014; $499, VG-8, September 2014												
1818, 8 Over 5	361,174	109	50.4	53%	$100	$125	$200	$350	$575	$1,700	$2,350	$4,000	$7,250
	Auctions: $176,250, MS-67, November 2013; $270, F-15, July 2014; $259, F-12, October 2014; $88, G-6, July 2014												
1818, Normal Date	(a)	586	37.2	25%	$70	$125	$200	$300	$550	$1,350	$2,250	$4,000	$7,250
	Auctions: $823, VF-35, February 2015; $764, VF-35, January 2015; $674, VF-35, October 2015; $517, VF-35, October 2015												

a. Included in 1818, 8 Over 5, mintage figure.

1819, Small 9   1819, Large 9   1820, Small 0   1820, Large 0

1822, 25 Over 50 C.   1823, 3 Over 2   1824, 4 Over 2

1825, 5 Over 2   1825, 5 Over 4

	Mintage	Cert	Avg	%MS	AG-3	G-4	VG-8	F-12	VF-20	EF-40	AU-50 / PF-60	MS-60 / PF-63	MS-63 / PF-65
1819, Small 9	144,000	28	35.8	11%	$70	$125	$200	$300	$550	$1,350	$2,250	$4,250	$8,500
Auctions: $646, EF-45, September 2014; $646, EF-40, June 2015; $353, VF-20, September 2014; $243, VF-20, May 2015													
1819, Large 9	(b)	43	21.4	9%	$70	$125	$200	$300	$550	$1,350	$2,450	$5,000	$10,000
Auctions: $23,501, MS-64, November 2013; $764, VF-25, July 2014; $676, VF-25, August 2016; $564, VF-20, August 2016													
1820, Small 0	127,444	18	36.3	17%	$70	$125	$200	$300	$550	$1,500	$2,450	$4,000	$6,000
Auctions: $3,055, AU-55, February 2014; $441, VF-20, September 2014; $176, G-6, July 2014; $94, G-6, July 2014													
1820, Large 0	(c)	34	39.4	18%	$70	$125	$200	$300	$550	$1,350	$3,250	$6,500	$10,000
Auctions: $41,125, MS-66, November 2013													
1820, Proof	6–10	2	65.5									$45,000	$125,000
Auctions: $188,000, PF-66, May 2015; $97,750, PF-64, May 2008													
1821	216,851	297	36.5	20%	$70	$125	$200	$300	$550	$1,350	$2,250	$3,500	$7,000
Auctions: $646, VF-30, January 2015; $1,293, VF-25, June 2015; $764, VF-25, July 2015; $112, G-6, November 2014													
1821, Proof	6–10	4	65.3									$40,000	$100,000
Auctions: $235,000, PF-67, May 2015; $82,250, PF-65, August 2015; $94,000, PF-65, October 2014; $51,750, PF-64, April 2009													
1822	64,080	158	33.8	15%	$200	$300	$375	$750	$1,100	$1,500	$3,000	$7,250	$11,500
Auctions: $25,850, MS-64, November 2013													
1822, 25 Over 50 C.	(d)	14	33.1	14%	$4,250	$5,500	$10,000	$16,500	$25,000	$33,000	$42,500	$55,000	$80,000
Auctions: No auction records available.													
1822, Proof	6–10	1	63.0									$50,000	$165,000
Auctions: $223,250, PF-65, May 2015; $229,125, PF-65, January 2014													
1823, 3 Over 2	17,800	6	39.5	0%	$25,000	$42,500	$60,000	$75,000	$95,000	$135,000	$165,000	$300,000	
Auctions: $17,625, G-4, February 2014													
1823, 3 Over 2, Proof	2–4	0	n/a									$250,000	
Auctions: $396,563, PF-64, June 2014													
1824, 4 Over 2	168,000	92	23.4	3%	$500	$800	$1,100	$1,750	$2,750	$5,250	$7,500	$25,000	$55,000
Auctions: $35,250, MS-62, June 2014; $1,293, VG-10, January 2015; $999, VG-8, August 2014													
1824, 4 Over 2, Proof	2–4	1	63.0									$50,000	
Auctions: No auction records available.													
1825, 5 Over 2	(e)	16	36.9	0%	$75	$125	$200	$300	$600	$1,600	$2,200	$3,500	$6,000
Auctions: $3,290, VF-30, February 2014; $159, G-6, July 2014; $94, G-4, July 2014													
1825, 5 Over 4	(e)	177	41.1	20%	$100	$200	$250	$500	$1,150	$1,750	$3,000	$6,500	$15,000
Auctions: $1,495, EF-45, April 2012													
1825, 5 Over 4 Over 3, Proof	6–10	0	n/a									$40,000	
Auctions: $4,313, PF-63, January 2010													

b. Included in 1819, Small 9, mintage figure. **c.** Included in circulation-strike 1820, Small 0, mintage figure. **d.** Included in circulation-strike 1822 mintage figure. **e.** Included in circulation-strike 1824, 4 Over 2, mintage figure.

1827, Original, Proof
Curl-Base 2 in 25 C.

1827, Restrike, Proof
Square-Base 2 in 25 C.

1828, 25 Over 50 C.

	Mintage	Cert	Avg	%MS	AG-3	G-4	VG-8	F-12	VF-20	EF-40	AU-50	MS-60	MS-63
											PF-60	PF-63	PF-65
1827, 7 Over 3, Original, Proof †	20–30	3	63.3								$125,000	$225,000	$550,000
Auctions: $411,250, PF-64, June 2014													
1827, 7 Over 3, Restrike, Proof	20–30	9	64.0									$65,000	$115,000
Auctions: $69,000, PF-66, July 2009													
1828	102,000	224	39.4	23%	$75	$115	$180	$300	$550	$1,350	$2,250	$3,500	$7,500
Auctions: $764, VF-35, January 2015; $400, VF-25, June 2015; $176, VG-10, May 2015; $106, G-6, August 2015													
1828, 25 Over 50 C.	(f)	25	32.9	16%	$750	$1,250	$1,750	$2,250	$3,500	$7,000	$10,000	$17,500	$90,000
Auctions: $352,500, MS-67, November 2013; $117,500, MS-63, August 2014													
1828, Proof	8–12	4	64.8								$15,000	$35,000	$80,000
Auctions: $82,250, PF-65, June 2014													

† Ranked in the *100 Greatest U.S. Coins* (fifth edition). *Note:* Although 4,000 1827 quarters were reported to have been made for circulation, their rarity today (only one worn piece is known, and it could be a circulated Proof) suggests that this quantity was for coins struck in calendar-year 1827 but bearing an earlier date, probably 1825. **f.** Included in circulation-strike 1828 mintage figure.

1831, Small Letters
Browning-2.

1831, Large Letters
Browning-6.

	Mintage	Cert	Avg	%MS	G-4	VG-8	F-12	VF-20	EF-40	AU-50	MS-60	MS-63	MS-65
											PF-60	PF-63	PF-65
1831, Small Letters	398,000	75	48.7	20%	$85	$115	$140	$165	$375	$750	$2,000	$3,750	$22,500
Auctions: $853, AU-50, July 2015; $341, AU-50, July 2015; $382, EF-45, April 2015; $376, EF-45, June 2015													
1831, Large Letters	(a)	49	47.6	24%	$85	$115	$140	$165	$400	$750	$2,400	$4,250	$27,500
Auctions: $6,463, MS-64, October 2015; $3,525, MS-63, January 2015; $1,175, MS-60, February 2015; $423, EF-45, September 2015													
1831, Large Letters, Proof	20–25	1	65.0								$15,000	$22,500	$75,000
Auctions: $141,000, PF-66, January 2014; $28,200, PF-63, October 2015													
1832	320,000	204	43.2	22%	$85	$115	$140	$165	$375	$750	$2,000	$3,750	$25,000
Auctions: $400, EF-45, May 2015; $212, EF-40, May 2015; $259, VF-35, July 2015; $176, VF-30, October 2015													

a. Included in 1831, Small Letters, mintage figure.

1834, O Over F in OF
FS-25-1834-901.

	Mintage	Cert	Avg	%MS	G-4	VG-8	F-12	VF-20	EF-40	AU-50	MS-60	MS-63	MS-65
											PF-60	PF-63	PF-65
1833	156,000	230	44.8	25%	$85	$125	$150	$215	$400	$850	$2,150	$4,000	$25,000
Auctions: $764, AU-50, June 2015; $646, AU-50, March 2015; $353, EF-45, August 2015; $306, VF-35, May 2015													
1833, O Over F in OF (b)	(c)	13	39.8	8%	$100	$135	$180	$250	$500	$900	$2,000	$5,000	$27,500
Auctions: No auction records available.													
1833, Proof	10–15	5	64.8								$15,000	$25,000	$90,000
Auctions: $46,000, PF-65Cam, April 2009													
1834	286,000	738	43.9	22%	$85	$115	$140	$165	$375	$750	$2,000	$4,000	$22,500
Auctions: $28,200, MS-66, January 2015; $8,519, MS-64, January 2015; $6,463, MS-64, August 2015; $4,230, MS-63, October 2015													
1834, O Over F in OF (b)	(d)	64	45.3	16%	$95	$135	$165	$215	$450	$850	$2,000	$5,000	$25,000
Auctions: $1,116, AU-58, November 2014; $588, AU-50, October 2014													
1834, Proof	20–25	6	64.5								$15,000	$22,500	$75,000
Auctions: $235,000, PF-66, November 2013													
1835	1,952,000	729	40.9	13%	$85	$115	$140	$165	$375	$750	$2,000	$3,750	$22,500
Auctions: $611, MS-60, January 2015; $823, AU-55, August 2015; $223, AU-55, July 2015; $764, AU-53, October 2015													
1835, Proof	10–15	5	64.2								$15,000	$30,000	$95,000
Auctions: $25,850, PF-63, August 2013													
1836	472,000	272	36.8	13%	$85	$115	$140	$165	$375	$750	$2,000	$3,750	$45,000
Auctions: $940, AU-53, January 2015; $823, AU-53, February 2015; $558, EF-45, November 2014; $329, EF-40, May 2015													
1836, Proof	8–12	2	65.5								$15,000	$25,000	$85,000
Auctions: $97,750, PF-67, January 2006													
1837	252,400	338	45.5	27%	$85	$115	$140	$165	$375	$750	$2,000	$3,750	$22,500
Auctions: $646, AU-55, November 2014; $823, AU-50, January 2015; $306, EF-40, November 2014; $200, VF-30, January 2015													
1837, Proof	8–12	1	65.0								$15,000	$25,000	$90,000
Auctions: $132,250, PF-67, August 2006													
1838	366,000	322	43.9	22%	$85	$115	$140	$165	$375	$750	$2,000	$3,750	$22,550
Auctions: $82,250, MS-67, September 2015; $646, EF-45, August 2015; $576, EF-45, March 2015; $423, EF-40, August 2015													
1838, Proof	8–12	2	66.0								$25,000	$35,000	$100,000
Auctions: $48,875, PF-64, July 2011													

b. The OF is re-engraved with the letters connected at the top, and the first A in AMERICA is also re-engraved. Other identifying characteristics: there is no period after the C in the denomination, and the 5 and C are further apart than normal. **c.** Included in circulation-strike 1833 mintage figure. **d.** Included in circulation-strike 1834 mintage figure.

LIBERTY SEATED (1838–1891)

Variety 1, No Motto Above Eagle (1838–1853): **Designer:** *Christian Gobrecht.*
Weight: *6.68 grams.* **Composition:** *.900 silver, .100 copper.* **Diameter:** *24.3 mm.*
Edge: *Reeded.* **Mints:** *Philadelphia and New Orleans.*

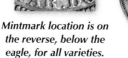

Variety 1 (1838–1853)

Mintmark location is on the reverse, below the eagle, for all varieties.

Variety 1, Proof

Variety 2, Arrows at Date, Rays Around Eagle (1853): **Designer:** *Christian Gobrecht.*
Weight: *6.22 grams.* **Composition:** *.900 silver, .100 copper.* **Diameter:** *24.3 mm.*
Edge: *Reeded.* **Mints:** *Philadelphia and New Orleans.*

Variety 2 (1853)   Variety 2, Proof

Variety 3, Arrows at Date, No Rays (1854–1855): **Designer:** *Christian Gobrecht.*
Weight: *6.22 grams.* **Composition:** *.900 silver, .100 copper.* **Diameter:** *24.3 mm.*
Edge: *Reeded.* **Mints:** *Philadelphia, New Orleans, and San Francisco.*

Variety 3 (1854–1855)   Variety 3, Proof

Variety 1 Resumed, With Weight Standard of Variety 2 (1856–1865):
Designer: *Christian Gobrecht.* **Weight:** *6.22 grams.* **Composition:** *.900 silver, .100 copper.*
Diameter: *24.3 mm.* **Edge:** *Reeded.* **Mints:** *Philadelphia, New Orleans, and San Francisco.*

Variety 1 Resumed, Weight   Variety 1 Resumed, Weight
Standard of Variety 2 (1856–1865)   Standard of Variety 2, Proof

Variety 4, Motto Above Eagle (1866–1873): **Designer:** *Christian Gobrecht.*
Weight: *6.22 grams.* **Composition:** *.900 silver, .100 copper.* **Diameter:** *24.3 mm.*
Edge: *Reeded.* **Mints:** *Philadelphia, San Francisco, and Carson City.*

Variety 4 (1866–1873)   Variety 4, Proof

Variety 5, Arrows at Date (1873–1874): **Designer:** *Christian Gobrecht.*
Weight: *6.25 grams.* **Composition:** *.900 silver, .100 copper.* **Diameter:** *24.3 mm.*
Edge: *Reeded.* **Mints:** *Philadelphia, San Francisco, and Carson City.*

Variety 5 (1873–1874)   Variety 5, Proof

Variety 4 Resumed, With Weight Standard of Variety 5 (1875–1891):
Designer: *Christian Gobrecht.* **Weight:** *6.25 grams.* **Composition:** *.900 silver, .100 copper.*
Diameter: *24.3 mm.* **Edge:** *Reeded.* **Mints:** *Philadelphia, New Orleans, and San Francisco.*

Variety 4 Resumed, Weight   Variety 4 Resumed, Weight
Standard of Variety 5 (1875–1891)   Standard of Variety 5, Proof

History. The long-running Liberty Seated design was introduced on the quarter dollar in 1838. Early issues lack drapery at Miss Liberty's elbow and have small lettering on the reverse. Drapery was added in 1840 and continued afterward. In 1853 a reduction in the coin's weight was indicated with the addition of arrows at the date and rays on the reverse (in the field around the eagle). The rays were omitted after 1853, but the arrows were retained through 1855. The motto IN GOD WE TRUST was added to the reverse in 1866. Arrows were placed at the date in the years 1873 and 1874 to denote the change of weight from 6.22 to 6.25 grams. The new weight, without the arrows, continued through 1891.

Striking and Sharpness. On the obverse, check the head of Miss Liberty and the star centers. If these are sharp, then check the central part of the seated figure. On the reverse, check the eagle, particularly the area to the lower left of the shield. Check the denticles on both sides. Generally, the earliest issues are well struck, as are those of the 1880s onward. The word LIBERTY is not an infallible guide to grading at lower levels, as on some dies the shield was in lower relief, and the letters wore away less quickly. This guideline should be used in combination with examining other features. Some Proofs (1858 is an example) have lint marks, and others can have light striking (particularly in the 1870s and 1880s). Avoid "problem" coins and those with deep or artificial (and often colorful) toning.

Availability. Coins of this type are available in proportion to their mintages. MS coins can range from rare to exceedingly rare, as they were mostly ignored by numismatists until the series ended. Quality can vary widely, especially among branch-mint coins. Proofs of the earlier years are very rare. Beginning with 1856, they were made in larger numbers, and from 1859 onward the yearly production was in the multiple hundreds. Proofs of the later era are readily available today; truly choice and gem pieces with no distracting hairlines are in the minority and will require diligent searching.

GRADING STANDARDS

MS-60 to 70 (Mint State). *Obverse:* At MS-60, some abrasion and contact marks are evident, most noticeably on the bosom and thighs and knees. Luster is present, but may be dull or lifeless. At MS-63, contact marks are very few, and abrasion is hard to detect except under magnification. An MS-65 coin has no abrasion, and contact marks are sufficiently minute as to require magnification. Check the knees of Liberty and the right

1853, Repunched Date, No Arrows or Rays; FS-25-1853-301. Graded MS-67.

field. Luster should be full and rich. Most Mint State coins of the 1861 to 1865 years, Philadelphia issues, have extensive die striae (from not completely finishing the die). *Reverse:* Comments apply as for the obverse, except that in lower Mint State grades abrasion and contact marks are most noticeable on the eagle's neck, the claws, and the top of the wings (harder to see there, however). At MS-65 or higher there are no marks visible to the unaided eye. The field is mainly protected by design elements and does not show abrasion as much as does the obverse on a given coin.

Illustrated coin: Note the delicate toning in the fields. In addition to hints of green, rose, and teal there is a good deal of luster as well.

AU-50, 53, 55, 58 (About Uncirculated). *Obverse:* Light wear is seen on the thighs and knees, bosom, and head. At AU-58, the luster is extensive, but incomplete, especially in the right field. At AU–50 and 53, luster is less. *Reverse:* Wear is evident on the eagle's neck, claws, and top of the wings. An AU-58 coin has nearly full luster, more so than on the obverse, as the design elements protect the small field areas. At AU–50 and 53, there still are traces of luster.

1891. Graded AU-53.

EF-40, 45 (Extremely Fine). *Obverse:* Further wear is seen on all areas, especially the thighs and knees, bosom, and head. Little or no luster is seen on most coins. From this grade downward, sharpness of strike of the stars and the head does not matter to connoisseurs. *Reverse:* Further wear is evident on the eagle's neck, claws, and wings. Some feathers in the right wing may be blended together.

1843. Graded EF-40.

VF-20, 30 (Very Fine). *Obverse:* Further wear is seen. Most details of the gown are worn away, except in the lower-relief areas above and to the right of the shield. Hair detail is mostly or completely gone. *Reverse:* Wear is more extensive, with more feathers blended together, especially in the right wing. The area below the shield shows more wear.

1860-S. Graded VF-20.

Illustrated coin: The surfaces of this coin are unusually smooth and problem free for the issue.

F-12, 15 (Fine). *Obverse:* The seated figure is well worn, but with some detail above and to the right of the shield. LIBERTY is readable but weak in areas. *Reverse:* Wear is extensive, with about half of the feathers flat or blended with others.

1854-O. Graded F-12.

VG-8, 10 (Very Good). *Obverse:* The seated figure is more worn, but some detail can be seen above and to the right of the shield. The shield is discernible. In LIBERTY at least the equivalent of two or three letters (can be a combination of partial letters) must be readable but can be very weak at VG-8, with a few more visible at VG-10. However, LIBERTY is not an infallible guide to grade this type, as some varieties had the word in low relief on

1872-CC. Graded VG-10.

the die, so it wore away slowly. *Reverse:* Further wear has flattened all but a few feathers, and the horizontal lines of the shield are indistinct. The leaves are only in outline form. The rim is visible all around, as are the ends of most denticles.

Illustrated coin: Note the faint red toning evident in areas of this otherwise pleasingly gray coin.

G-4, 6 (Good). *Obverse:* The seated figure is worn smooth. At G-4 there are no letters in LIBERTY remaining on most (but not all) coins; some coins, especially of the early 1870s, are exceptions. At G-6, traces of one or two can barely be seen. *Reverse:* The designs are only in outline form, although some vertical shield stripes can be seen on some. The rim is worn down, and tops of the border letters are weak or worn away, although the inscription can still be read.

1872-CC. Graded G-6.

AG-3 (About Good). *Obverse:* The seated figure is mostly visible in outline form, with only a hint of detail. Much of the rim is worn away. The date remains clear. *Reverse:* The border letters are partially worn away. The eagle is mostly in outline form, but with a few details discernible. The rim is weak or missing.

1862-S. Graded AG-3.

PF-60 to 70 (Proof). *Obverse and Reverse:* Proofs that are extensively cleaned and have many hairlines, or that are dull and grainy, are lower level, such as PF-60 to 62. These are not widely desired by connoisseurs. With medium hairlines and good reflectivity, an assigned grade of PF-64 is appropriate and with relatively few hairlines, Gem PF-65. In various grades hairlines are most easily seen in the obverse field. PF-66 should have hairlines so

1860. Graded PF-65.

delicate that magnification is needed to see them. Above that, a Proof should be free of such lines.

| 1839, No Drapery | 1840-O, Drapery | 1840-O, Drapery, Normal O | 1840-O, Drapery, Large O |

Coins designated Deep Cameo or Ultra Cameo bring a premium of 50% to 100% above listed values.

	Mintage	Cert	Avg	%MS	G-4	VG-8	F-12	VF-20	EF-40	AU-50	MS-60 PF-60	MS-63 PF-63	MS-65 PF-65
1838, No Drapery	466,000	211	50.6	40%	$50	$65	$75	$175	$450	$1,000	$1,700	$4,000	$35,000
Auctions: $3,055, MS-63, January 2015; $591, AU-53, January 2015; $794, AU-50, January 2015; $364, EF-45, March 2015													
1838, Proof	2–3	0	n/a								$250,000		
Auctions: No auction records available.													
1839, No Drapery	491,146	156	49.2	24%	$50	$65	$75	$175	$450	$1,050	$1,750	$4,250	$40,000
Auctions: $940, AU-58, June 2015; $1,116, AU-55, September 2015; $823, AU-53, January 2015; $764, AU-53, June 2015													
1839, Proof (a)	2–3	1	65.0										$350,000
Auctions: $270,250, PF-65, October 2014; $411,250, PF-65, April 2013													
1840-O, No Drapery	$382,200	168	44.6	21%	$50	$70	$100	$195	$450	$950	$2,000	$5,500	$35,000
Auctions: $199,750, MS-67, May 2015; $19,975, MS-65, May 2015; $3,533, MS-63, June 2015; $1,410, MS-62, September 2015													
1840, Drapery	188,127	44	50.0	30%	$60	$65	$75	$175	$425	$750	$1,650	$4,800	$18,000
Auctions: $17,625, MS-66, May 2015; $16,450, MS-64, October 2015; $423, AU-53, June 2015; $306, AU-53, May 2015													
1840, Drapery, Proof	5–8	2	64.5										$75,000
Auctions: $99,889, PF-65, August 2013													
1840-O, Drapery	43,000	91	47.2	31%	$45	$70	$115	$215	$450	$750	$1,400	$3,800	$20,000
Auctions: $16,450, MS-65, May 2015; $2,585, MS-63, March 2015; $1,410, MS-62, October 2015; $1,293, AU-58, October 2015													
1840-O, Drapery, Large O (b)	(c)	1	6.0	0%					$4,000	$6,500	$12,000		
Auctions: $18,600, MS-64, April 2018; $3,220, MS-63, December 2010; $2,115, VG-10, August 2015													

a. This piece is unique. **b.** The O mintmark punch is about 25% larger than normal. There are two known reverse dies for this variety, with one showing doubled denticles. **c.** Included in 1840-O, Drapery, mintage figure.

1842, Small Date	1842, Large Date	1842-O, Small Date	1842-O, Large Date

Philadelphia Small Date is Proof only.

	Mintage	Cert	Avg	%MS	G-4	VG-8	F-12	VF-20	EF-40	AU-50	MS-60 PF-60	MS-63 PF-63	MS-65 PF-65
1841	120,000	63	55.6	57%	$55	$100	$125	$225	$400	$800	$1,200	$2,250	$8,000
Auctions: $28,200, MS-66, May 2015; $8,225, MS-65, October 2015; $6,463, MS-65, October 2015; $1,528, AU-58, August 2015													
1841, Proof	3–5	1	66.0								$45,000	$65,000	
Auctions: $235,000, PF-66, April 2013; $42,300, PF-61, October 2015; $48,175, PF-61, January 2015													
1841-O	452,000	77	54.3	53%	$50	$65	$90	$165	$315	$425	$850	$1,900	$10,000
Auctions: $1,763, MS-63, August 2015; $646, AU-58, February 2015; $353, AU-53, June 2015; $306, AU-50, June 2015													
1842, Large Date (d)	88,000	47	49.4	30%	$65	$100	$150	$250	$450	$850	$1,600	$4,500	$12,500
Auctions: $1,175, AU-58, August 2015; $423, EF-45, July 2015; $423, EF-40, May 2015; $318, VF-30, January 2015													
1842, Small Date, Proof † (e)	3–5	2	65.0									$60,000	$135,000
Auctions: $164,500, PF-66, January 2015; $282,000, PF-65, October 2014; $258,500, PF-65, August 2013													
1842-O, All kinds	769,000												
1842-O, Small Date		22	19.7	5%	$600	$1,150	$1,600	$3,000	$7,500	$11,000	$35,000	$70,000	
Auctions: $12,925, AU-55, October 2015; $7,638, AU-53, December 2015; $1,763, F-12, August 2015; $940, VG-10, October 2016													
1842-O, Large Date		64	36.1	23%	$50	$65	$80	$125	$275	$600	$1,750	$4,500	
Auctions: $3,290, MS-63, November 2014; $423, MS-60, July 2015; $306, AU-53, November 2014; $141, AU-50, May 2015													
1843	645,600	106	56.7	50%	$50	$65	$75	$95	$200	$350	$675	$1,300	$4,500
Auctions: $4,935, MS-65, May 2015; $483, MS-61, May 2015; $188, AU-55, March 2015; $141, EF-45, May 2015													
1843, Proof	10–15	2	58.0								$12,500	$25,000	$75,000
Auctions: $64,625, PF-66, April 2013													
1843-O	968,000	71	39.6	10%	$50	$85	$150	$400	$1,000	$1,350	$3,000	$6,000	$22,500
Auctions: $19,975, MS-64, May 2015; $7,050, MS-64, May 2015; $3,290, EF-45, October 2015; $1,880, EF-40, February 2015													
1844	421,200	89	53.9	42%	$50	$65	$75	$80	$165	$325	$650	$1,650	$14,500
Auctions: $4,935, MS-64, June 2015; $940, MS-61, June 2015; $306, AU-53, May 2015; $100, AU-50, November 2014													
1844, Proof (f)	3–5	1	63.0										
Auctions: $276,000, PF-66, July 2009													
1844-O	740,000	72	42.0	21%	$50	$45	$80	$115	$250	$475	$1,250	$2,500	$10,000
Auctions: $1,880, MS-63, July 2015; $259, AU-50, July 2015; $141, VF-25, January 2015; $69, VF-20, November 2014													
1845	922,000	135	54.7	43%	$50	$65	$75	$80	$165	$235	$650	$1,250	$6,000
Auctions: $705, MS-62, September 2015; $517, MS-62, February 2015; $494, AU-58, August 2015; $423, AU-58, August 2015													
1845, Proof	6–8	7	64.9									$20,000	$32,500
Auctions: $31,725, PF-65, October 2015; $26,438, PF-64, September 2015; $25,850, PF-64, August 2015													
1846	510,000	91	52.3	36%	$55	$80	$100	$125	$225	$425	$800	$1,850	$12,500
Auctions: $22,325, MS-66, January 2014													
1846, Proof	15–20	10	64.4								$5,000	$8,500	$17,500
Auctions: $25,850, PF-65, April 2013													
1847	734,000	88	52.9	40%	$50	$65	$75	$95	$160	$275	$600	$1,650	$5,500
Auctions: $10,575, MS-65, May 2015; $1,410, MS-63, July 2015; $940, AU-58, May 2015; $705, AU-58, October 2015													
1847, Proof	6–8	3	65.0								$5,000	$10,000	$22,500
Auctions: $17,625, PF-66, October 2015; $28,200, PF-65, November 2013; $14,688, PF-64, July 2014													
1847-O	368,000	48	37.0	10%	$100	$175	$300	$600	$1,000	$1,750	$7,000	$12,500	
Auctions: $8,225, MS-62, October 2015; $4,230, AU-58, August 2015; $1,293, EF-45, June 2015; $376, VF-20, August 2015													

† Ranked in the *100 Greatest U.S. Coins* (fifth edition). **d.** The Large Date was used on the Philadelphia Mint's 1842 coins struck for circulation. **e.** For the Philadelphia Mint's quarters of 1842, the Small Date was used on Proofs only. **f.** 2 examples are known.

1853, Repunched Date, No Arrows or Rays
FS-25-1853-301.

1853, 3 Over 4 (Arrows at Date, Rays Around Eagle)
FS-25-1853-301.

	Mintage	Cert	Avg	%MS	G-4	VG-8	F-12	VF-20	EF-40	AU-50	MS-60	MS-63	MS-65
											PF-60	PF-63	PF-65
1848	146,000	49	44.6	27%	$55	$95	$150	$200	$450	$650	$1,250	$4,750	$12,000
	Auctions: $5,170, MS-64, January 2015; $4,230, MS-63, October 2015; $1,116, AU-55, January 2015; $494, EF-45, June 2015												
1848, Proof	5–8	2	65.0								$5,000	$10,000	$30,000
	Auctions: $64,625, PF-66, October 2014; $55,813, PF-66, August 2013; $22,325, PF-65, January 2015												
1849	340,000	100	52.2	29%	$50	$75	$95	$100	$250	$400	$1,000	$1,650	$9,500
	Auctions: $11,163, MS-65, August 2015; $8,813, MS-65, May 2015; $8,225, MS-65, August 2015; $1,116, MS-63, January 2015												
1849, Proof	5–8	3	64.3								$5,000	$10,000	$27,500
	Auctions: $32,900, PF-65, January 2014												
1849-O	(g)	39	32.7	13%	$1,250	$1,750	$2,250	$3,000	$7,000	$8,500	$17,500	$20,000	
	Auctions: $24,675, MS-64, May 2015; $17,625, MS-63, January 2015; $7,050, AU-55, August 2015; $7,050, AU-53, January 2015												
1850	190,800	38	55.0	53%	$45	$95	$135	$225	$400	$650	$1,500	$3,000	$11,000
	Auctions: $13,513, MS-65, October 2015; $3,055, MS-64, November 2014; $1,293, MS-60, November 2014; $306, AU-50, June 2015												
1850, Proof	5–8	2	63.5										
	Auctions: $258,500, PF-68, August 2013												
1850-O	412,000	74	49.1	39%	$65	$115	$150	$225	$500	$750	$1,600	$4,500	$13,500
	Auctions: $9,400, MS-64, October 2015; $3,525, MS-63, August 2015; $447, EF-40, February 2015; $212, VF-35, May 2015												
1851	160,000	49	45.1	22%	$100	$175	$275	$400	$700	$1,000	$1,450	$2,350	$6,500
	Auctions: $4,935, MS-65, October 2015; $646, EF-45, August 2015; $764, EF-40, January 2015; $517, VF-35, August 2015												
1851-O	88,000	41	26.9	7%	$375	$600	$900	$1,100	$2,500	$3,350	$8,500	$32,500	
	Auctions: $881, VF-20, June 2015; $823, F-12, August 2015; $764, VG-10, August 2015; $376, G-4, January 2015												
1852	177,060	59	54.5	54%	$125	$225	$325	$350	$600	$750	$1,100	$2,100	$5,500
	Auctions: $99,875, MS-68, May 2015; $18,800, MS-66, October 2015; $3,760, MS-65, July 2015; $646, EF-45, August 2015												
1852, Proof	5–8	0	n/a										$75,000
	Auctions: $105,750, PF-65, April 2013												
1852-O	96,000	31	28.6	6%	$350	$500	$850	$1,500	$2,250	$6,000	$9,500	$35,000	
	Auctions: $17,625, MS-63, November 2016; $21,150, MS-62, May 2015; $18,800, MS-62, October 2015; $2,820, MS-60, October 2016												
1853, Repunched Date, No Arrows or Rays (h)	44,200	47	47.5	47%	$1,250	$2,000	$2,500	$3,250	$4,000	$5,000	$6,250	$7,500	$12,000
	Auctions: $32,900, MS-67, June 2015; $19,975, MS-66, October 2015; $9,400, MS-65, October 2015; $3,760, EF-40, June 2015												
1853, Variety 2	15,210,020	1,494	48.2	30%	$30	$35	$40	$50	$175	$350	$950	$1,750	$10,000
	Auctions: $17,625, MS-65, August 2015; $11,163, MS-65, August 2015; $9,988, MS-65, February 2015; $7,638, MS-65, October 2015												
1853, Variety 2, 3 Over 4 (i)	(j)	56	41.2	20%	$55	$100	$175	$250	$350	$675	$1,850	$4,000	$30,000
	Auctions: $9,988, MS-64, October 2014; $617, EF-45, August 2015; $494, EF-45, October 2016; $423, VF-35, September 2015												
1853, Variety 2, Proof	10–15	5	65.2								$25,000	$45,000	$100,000
	Auctions: $141,000, PF-66Cam, August 2013; $41,125, PF-64, May 2015; $64,625, PF-64, October 2014												
1853-O, Variety 2	1,332,000	116	42.6	14%	$55	$70	$100	$150	$400	$1,100	$4,250	$10,000	$25,000
	Auctions: $17,625, MS-64, October 2015; $1,293, AU-53, August 2015; $1,058, EF-45, February 2015; $494, EF-45, March 2016												

g. Included in 1850-O mintage figure. **h.** The secondary 5 and 3 are evident south of the primary digits. In the past, this variety was erroneously attributed as a 53 Over 2 overdate. This is the only die known for 1853 that lacks the arrows and rays. **i.** In addition to the 3 punched over a 4, there is also evidence of the repunched 8 and 5 (weaker images slightly north and west of the primary digits). The right arrow shaft is also doubled, north of the primary. From the *Cherrypickers' Guide to Rare Die Varieties*, Vol. II (sixth edition): "On well-worn or late-die-state specimens, the doubling of the arrow shaft may be the only evidence of the overdate. This is the only quarter dollar date known to be punched over the *following* year!" **j.** Included in 1853, Variety 2, mintage figure.

1854-O, Normal O

1854-O, Huge O

1856-S,
S Over Small S
FS-25-1856S-501.

1857, Clashed
Reverse Die
FS-25-1857-901.

	Mintage	Cert	Avg	%MS	G-4	VG-8	F-12	VF-20	EF-40	AU-50	MS-60	MS-63	MS-65
											PF-60	PF-63	PF-65
1854	12,380,000	771	50.1	32%	$30	$35	$40	$45	$85	$250	$625	$1,100	$5,500
Auctions: $8,225, MS-65, October 2015; $4,230, MS-65, February 2015; $4,230, MS-65, June 2015; $1,998, MS-64, September 2015
1854, Proof	20–30	10	64.2								$8,500	$12,500	$30,000
Auctions: $30,550, PF-66, April 2013
1854-O, Normal O	1,484,000	184	33.5	17%	$50	$55	$60	$75	$125	$300	$1,100	$1,750	$15,000
Auctions: $23,500, MS-66, October 2015; $15,275, MS-65, January 2015; $14,100, MS-65, October 2015; $247, AU-50, October 2015
1854-O, Huge O (k)	(l)	77	19.5	0%	$650	$1,100	$1,350	$1,850	$3,500	$7,500			
Auctions: $4,994, EF-45, February 2013; $3,055, VF-30, August 2016; $793, VF-20, March 2015; $423, VG-8, September 2016
1855	2,857,000	202	51.9	34%	$30	$35	$40	$50	$125	$250	$625	$1,100	$6,500
Auctions: $27,025, MS-67, May 2015; $17,625, MS-66, October 2015; $23,406, MS-65, July 2015; $1,116, MS-63, March 2015
1855, Proof	20–30	10	64.6								$8,500	$15,000	$30,000
Auctions: $28,200, PF-66, October 2014; $21,150, PF-65Cam, April 2013; $8,225, PF-62, October 2015
1855-O	176,000	36	38.8	28%	$125	$185	$300	$550	$850	$2,000	$4,500	$12,500	
Auctions: $82,250, MS-67, May 2015; $12,925, MS-63, October 2015; $2,400, EF-45, September 2017; $646, VF-25, March 2016
1855-S	396,400	37	36.1	11%	$100	$225	$350	$600	$1,000	$1,450	$2,850	$7,500	$25,000
Auctions: $19,975, MS-65, January 2015; $15,275, MS-64, May 2015; $7,050, MS-63, October 2015; $423, EF-40, May 2015
1855-S, Proof	1–2	1	64.0										—
Auctions: $176,250, PF-64, August 2013
1856	7,264,000	305	51.7	40%	$28	$30	$35	$45	$75	$185	$350	$650	$2,750
Auctions: $3,525, MS-66, January 2015; $3,290, MS-66, July 2015; $5,288, MS-66, October 2015; $3,231, MS-66, June 2015
1856, Proof	40–50	27	64.0								$3,500	$4,500	$12,500
Auctions: $12,959, PF-66, August 2014; $11,750, PF-66, May 2015; $12,925, PF-65, January 2015; $9,400, PF-65, October 2015
1856-O	968,000	91	44.1	16%	$45	$55	$75	$125	$250	$475	$1,000	$2,500	$12,000
Auctions: $11,163, MS-65, March 2015; $4,230, MS-64, October 2015; $940, AU-58, January 2015; $259, AU-50, September 2015
1856-S, All kinds	286,000												
1856-S		29	32.7	7%	$300	$475	$600	$800	$2,000	$3,500	$7,500	$13,500	$45,000
Auctions: $9,988, MS-63, October 2016; $11,163, MS-62, August 2016; $441, EF-40, July 2015; $259, EF-40, June 2015
1856-S, S Over Small S (m)		7	14.9	0%	$500	$850	$1,350	$2,500	$7,500	$15,000			
Auctions: $28,200, AU-58, June 2014
1857	9,644,000	617	53.8	51%	$28	$30	$35	$45	$75	$185	$350	$600	$2,750
Auctions: $14,100, MS-67, June 2015; $12,925, MS-67, September 2015; $10,575, MS-67, August 2015; $10,575, MS-67, October 2015
1857, Clashed Rev Die (n)	(o)	5	50.2	40%	$100	$150	$250	$450	$800	$1,500			
Auctions: No auction records available.
1857, Proof	40–50	34	63.8								$3,000	$4,000	$11,000
Auctions: $7,050, PF-66, January 2015; $6,463, PF-66, June 2015; $2,820, PF-63, January 2015; $2,233, PF-62, June 2015
1857-O	1,180,000	93	47.8	19%	$45	$55	$100	$150	$300	$500	$1,200	$2,750	
Auctions: $7,050, MS-64, October 2015; $2,820, MS-63, October 2015; $2,585, MS-63, October 2015; $1,880, MS-63, August 2015
1857-S	82,000	46	47.5	20%	$200	$300	$425	$800	$1,150	$1,850	$3,500	$6,000	
Auctions: $11,163, MS-64, October 2015; $8,813, MS-64, October 2015; $940, EF-40, August 2015; $588, VF-30, July 2015

k. The Huge O mintmark is very large, extremely thick on the left side, and irregular, suggesting that it was punched into the die by hand. **l.** Included in 1854-O mintage figure. **m.** A larger S mintmark was punched over a much smaller S mintmark, the latter probably intended for half-dime production. **n.** The reverse clashed with the reverse die of an 1857 Flying Eagle cent. Images of the cent reverse die are easily visible on either side of the eagle's neck, within the shield, and below the eagle's left wing. **o.** Included in circulation-strike 1857 mintage figure.

	Mintage	Cert	Avg	%MS	G-4	VG-8	F-12	VF-20	EF-40	AU-50	MS-60 / PF-60	MS-63 / PF-63	MS-65 / PF-65
1858	7,368,000	484	52.4	45%	$28	$30	$35	$45	$75	$185	$350	$600	$2,500
	Auctions: $17,625, MS-67, May 2015; $3,760, MS-66, October 2015; $3,290, MS-66, October 2015; $2,703, MS-65, October 2015												
1858, Proof	300	70	63.7								$1,500	$2,000	$5,500
	Auctions: $28,200, PF-67, September 2015; $9,400, PF-66, October 2014; $7,638, PF-66, October 2015; $4,935, PF-65, February 2015												
1858-O	520,000	52	47.7	12%	$30	$40	$75	$125	$300	$650	$4,000	$10,000	$25,000
	Auctions: $14,100, MS-65, October 2015; $21,150, MS-64, May 2015; $7,638, MS-62, October 2015; $94, EF-45, September 2014												
1858-S	121,000	50	31.5	2%	$250	$400	$600	$1,000	$3,000	$5,000	$20,000		
	Auctions: $35,250, MS-62, May 2015; $28,200, MS-62, October 2015; $8,813, AU-58, October 2015; $1,645, VF-35, August 2015												
1859	1,343,200	175	53.9	43%	$28	$30	$45	$65	$90	$200	$425	$900	$4,000
	Auctions: $3,878, MS-65, January 2015; $3,819, MS-65, January 2015; $3,055, MS-65, September 2015; $1,645, MS-64, August 2015												
1859, Proof	800	153	64.1								$1,000	$1,500	$4,500
	Auctions: $17,625, PF-67, May 2015; $7,638, PF-66, October 2015; $4,583, PF-65Cam, September 2015; $1,998, PF-64Cam, January 2015												
1859-O	260,000	56	45.4	20%	$50	$75	$100	$150	$300	$850	$2,500	$7,500	$22,500
	Auctions: $793, AU-55, January 2015; $423, AU-53, August 2015; $329, AU-50, February 2015; $329, AU-50, March 2015												
1859-S	80,000	27	26.2	0%	$425	$625	$950	$1,450	$4,500	$11,000			
	Auctions: $9,988, AU-50, October 2015; $6,756, EF-45, January 2015; $940, VF-25, July 2015; $1,028, VG-10, August 2015												
1860	804,400	141	52.7	35%	$28	$30	$35	$65	$100	$195	$500	$850	$5,000
	Auctions: $200, MS-60, May 2015; $130, AU-50, May 2015; $118, EF-40, November 2015; $94, EF-40, August 2015												
1860, Proof	1,000	113	63.9								$700	$1,200	$4,000
	Auctions: $21,150, PF-68, May 2015; $7,050, PF-66, February 2015; $5,875, PF-66, October 2015; $3,525, PF-65, August 2015												
1860-O	388,000	89	52.8	34%	$50	$55	$60	$85	$250	$475	$1,000	$1,750	$12,500
	Auctions: $3,055, MS-64, July 2015; $1,350, MS-63, September 2015; $1,028, MS-62, June 2015; $176, AU-50, October 2015												
1860-S	56,000	22	27.6	0%	$1,000	$1,500	$3,000	$5,000	$9,000	$16,500	$50,000		
	Auctions: $45,825, MS-61, October 2016; $15,275, AU-50, January 2015; $8,225, EF-45, September 2015; $7,638, EF-40, March 2016												
1861	4,853,600	692	56.1	50%	$32	$37	$42	$65	$100	$200	$350	$725	$2,500
	Auctions: $12,925, MS-67, August 2015; $11,750, MS-67, September 2015; $3,760, MS-66, September 2015; $2,350, MS-65, September 2015												
1861, Proof	1,000	101	63.5								$700	$1,200	$4,000
	Auctions: $10,575, PF-67, October 2015; $6,169, PF-66, January 2015; $5,405, PF-66, October 2015; $1,410, PF-64, January 2015												
1861-S	96,000	37	28.4	0%	$650	$925	$1,250	$2,000	$4,500	$9,000			
	Auctions: $21,150, AU-58, May 2015; $1,293, VF-20, February 2015; $1,469, F-15, August 2015; $940, F-12, August 2015												
1862	932,000	188	56.1	59%	$30	$35	$50	$65	$100	$210	$425	$750	$2,750
	Auctions: $7,638, MS-67, June 2015; $3,995, MS-66, October 2015; $1,293, MS-64, October 2015; $999, MS-64, October 2015												
1862, Proof	550	133	63.7								$700	$1,200	$4,000
	Auctions: $9,988, PF-67Cam, October 2015; $6,463, PF-66, May 2015; $6,169, PF-66, October 2015; $1,998, PF-64, August 2015												
1862-S	67,000	48	41.8	21%	$175	$300	$450	$600	$1,250	$2,500	$4,250	$7,500	
	Auctions: $6,463, MS-62, October 2015; $3,525, MS-62, January 2015; $2,115, AU-53, July 2015; $447, VF-25, August 2015												
1863	191,600	72	54.8	60%	$65	$85	$115	$275	$400	$550	$800	$1,350	$5,000
	Auctions: $4,935, MS-65, October 2015; $1,586, MS-64, January 2015; $881, MS-62, June 2015; $823, MS-61, June 2015												
1863, Proof	460	153	63.6								$700	$1,200	$4,000
	Auctions: $8,519, PF-67, January 2015; $5,875, PF-66, October 2015; $2,585, PF-64, August 2015; $1,998, PF-64, June 2015												
1864	93,600	66	50.8	56%	$150	$215	$300	$425	$575	$700	$1,250	$2,500	$5,500
	Auctions: $35,250, MS-67, May 2015; $14,100, MS-66, October 2015; $494, AU-50, September 2015; $646, EF-45, August 2015												
1864, Proof	470	183	64.0								$700	$1,200	$4,000
	Auctions: $3,760, PF-65Cam, October 2015; $2,585, PF-64Cam, January 2015; $1,528, PF-64, January 2015; $1,410, PF-63Cam, July 2015												
1864-S	20,000	44	28.9	11%	$1,000	$1,100	$1,500	$2,000	$4,500	$6,000	$13,500	$20,000	
	Auctions: $28,200, MS-64, October 2015; $3,525, EF-40, August 2015; $1,998, VF-30, March 2016; $1,234, VG-10, August 2015												
1865	58,800	54	45.7	30%	$100	$165	$250	$350	$450	$750	$1,250	$1,850	$10,000
	Auctions: $32,900, MS-67, January 2015; $1,645, MS-62, August 2015; $400, VF-35, April 2015; $153, VF-20, October 2015												
1865, Proof	500	177	63.9								$700	$1,200	$4,000
	Auctions: $23,500, PF-68, May 2015; $12,925, PF-67Cam, October 2015; $5,405, PF-66Cam, October 2015; $8,225, PF-66, September 2015												
1865-S	41,000	42	48.4	38%	$225	$350	$475	$700	$1,100	$1,600	$3,500	$6,000	$22,500
	Auctions: $64,625, MS-66, February 2014; $999, EF-40, October 2014; $764, VF-35, February 2015; $200, G-4, September 2014												

	Mintage	Cert	Avg	%MS	G-4	VG-8	F-12	VF-20	EF-40	AU-50	MS-60 PF-60	MS-63 PF-63	MS-65 PF-65
1866	16,800	48	49.8	58%	$750	$1,000	$1,250	$1,500	$1,850	$2,450	$2,800	$3,150	$8,500
Auctions: $1,410, VF-25, August 2015; $1,175, VF-25, November 2015; $1,058, VF-25, August 2015; $999, VF-20, June 2015
1866, No Motto, Proof † (p)	1	0	n/a										—
Auctions: No auction records available.
1866, Proof	725	167	63.9								$500	$850	$2,500
Auctions: $19,975, PF-68, November 2013
1866-S	28,000	29	27.2	17%	$500	$900	$1,350	$1,650	$2,300	$3,500	$5,500	$13,500	$35,000
Auctions: $25,263, MS-65, October 2014; $5,405, MS-62, December 2015; $1,293, VF-30, September 2014; $1,146, VF-20, December 2015
1867	20,000	36	41.7	31%	$375	$550	$750	$1,000	$1,500	$1,850	$2,250	$4,500	$15,000
Auctions: $9,400, MS-64, October 2015; $6,463, MS-63, October 2015; $3,760, MS-63, October 2015; $1,528, AU-55, October 2015
1867, Proof	625	171	63.9								$500	$850	$2,250
Auctions: $3,525, PF-66, October 2015; $2,703, PF-64Cam, October 2015; $1,116, PF-64, October 2015; $764, PF-63, September 2015
1867-S	48,000	20	25.5	10%	$600	$850	$1,150	$1,750	$3,500	$7,250	$10,500	$15,000	
Auctions: $88,125, MS-67, May 2015; $17,625, MS-64, June 2015; $3,525, EF-45, June 2015; $1,410, VF-25, June 2015
1868	29,400	35	49.5	49%	$185	$325	$400	$500	$700	$850	$1,750	$3,500	$9,000
Auctions: $8,225, MS-65, October 2015; $7,050, MS-65, August 2015; $400, EF-40, May 2015; $354, EF-40, August 2015
1868, Proof	600	157	63.6								$500	$850	$2,250
Auctions: $4,465, PF-66, January 2015; $3,055, PF-66, October 2015; $2,820, PF-65, January 2015; $2,233, PF-65, September 2015
1868-S	96,000	44	38.7	25%	$125	$175	$350	$750	$1,000	$1,750	$5,500	$9,500	$20,000
Auctions: $82,250, MS-67, August 2015; $18,800, MS-66, August 2015; $14,100, MS-64, October 2015; $999, EF-40, July 2015
1869	16,000	30	39.9	37%	$500	$650	$850	$1,000	$1,250	$1,500	$2,250	$4,500	$10,000
Auctions: $1,028, VF-25, August 2015; $646, VF-20, July 2015; $764, F-12, August 2015; $541, G-6, April 2015
1869, Proof	600	174	63.5								$500	$850	$2,250
Auctions: $18,800, PF-67Cam, November 2013; $4,818, PF-67, October 2015; $3,290, PF-66, October 2015; $445, PF-53, September 2014
1869-S	76,000	37	33.2	14%	$175	$250	$425	$650	$1,250	$1,650	$4,500	$7,000	$17,500
Auctions: $9,988, MS-64, October 2015; $564, VF-25, July 2015; $400, F-15, August 2015; $447, F-12, February 2015
1870	86,400	41	47.0	32%	$65	$100	$150	$250	$450	$650	$1,000	$1,750	$5,000
Auctions: $8,813, MS-66, May 2015; $382, EF-45, November 2014; $306, EF-45, April 2015; $212, EF-40, May 2015
1870, Proof	1,000	168	63.5								$500	$850	$2,250
Auctions: $6,169, PF-67, October 2014; $3,290, PF-66, January 2015; $1,087, PF-64, January 2015; $1,763, PF-63, January 2015
1870-CC	8,340	26	26.9	4%	$10,000	$13,000	$18,000	$22,500	$45,000	$100,000			
Auctions: $188,000, AU-55, May 2015; $70,500, AU-53, January 2014; $35,250, EF-45, August 2015; $10,281, VG-8, August 2015
1871	118,200	50	49.4	48%	$50	$75	$125	$175	$325	$450	$750	$1,500	$7,000
Auctions: $32,900, MS-67, June 2014; $6,484, MS-65, October 2015; $1,175, MS-63, June 2015; $259, AU-50, May 2015
1871, Proof	960	153	63.5								$500	$850	$2,500
Auctions: $15,275, PF-68, May 2015; $4,706, PF-67, October 2015; $3,055, PF-66, August 2015; $2,820, PF-66, January 2015
1871-CC	10,890	14	18.9	0%	$8,000	$12,500	$16,500	$25,000	$37,500	$55,000			$350,000
Auctions: $352,500, MS-65, June 2014; $79,313, AU-55, October 2015; $25,850, VF-35, January 2017; $19,200, F-15, January 2018
1871-S	30,900	29	48.2	52%	$900	$1,400	$2,150	$3,200	$4,000	$5,500	$7,250	$10,000	$20,000
Auctions: $17,625, MS-65, October 2015; $4,406, AU-58, March 2015; $2,115, VF-25, August 2015; $2,527, F-12, September 2015
1872	182,000	63	48.7	40%	$50	$85	$125	$185	$350	$500	$900	$2,250	$7,500
Auctions: $6,025, MS-65, August 2015; $2,820, MS-64, February 2015; $2,115, MS-63, August 2015; $541, AU-58, August 2015
1872, Proof	950	174	63.8								$500	$850	$2,000
Auctions: $6,756, PF-67Cam, October 2015, $2,820, PF-66, June 2015; $2,585, PF-65Cam, March 2015; $1,528, PF-65, January 2015
1872-CC	22,850	32	17.8	0%	$2,250	$2,800	$4,500	$8,500	$13,500	$20,000	$65,000		
Auctions: $3,567, F-15, August 2015; $1,410, F-12, July 2015; $1,645, G-6, August 2015; $1,087, Fair-2, June 2015
1872-S	83,000	22	37.7	36%	$2,000	$2,600	$3,200	$4,750	$5,500	$7,000	$10,000	$14,000	$36,000
Auctions: $10,575, MS-63, October 2015; $8,225, AU-55, June 2015; $4,700, F-15, August 2015; $3,995, F-15, August 2015

† Ranked in the *100 Greatest U.S. Coins* (fifth edition). **p.** The unique 1866, Proof, quarter dollar without motto (as well as the half dollar and dollar of the same design) is not mentioned in the Mint director's report. From *United States Pattern Coins* (10th edition): "Not a pattern, but a muling created at a later date as a numismatic rarity." Saul Teichman dates its creation to the 1870s. It is classified as Judd-536.

1873, Variety 4, Close 3   **1873, Variety 4, Open 3**

	Mintage	Cert	Avg	%MS	G-4	VG-8	F-12	VF-20	EF-40	AU-50	MS-60 / PF-60	MS-63 / PF-63	MS-65 / PF-65
1873, Variety 4, Close 3	40,000	18	29.6	11%	$500	$700	$1,000	$1,300	$3,000	$4,500	$20,000	$35,000	
Auctions: $9,988, AU-58, April 2014													
1873, Variety 4, Open 3	172,000	39	52.2	54%	$30	$45	$85	$150	$300	$425	$675	$1,850	$5,500
Auctions: $7,638, MS-66, May 2015; $3,290, MS-64, February 2015; $1,939, MS-64, June 2015; $1,763, MS-63, June 2015													
1873, Variety 4, Proof	600	173	63.5								$500	$850	$2,000
Auctions: $11,750, PF-67Cam, August 2015; $5,170, PF-67Cam, July 2015; $4,700, PF-66Cam, October 2015; $1,880, PF-65, June 2015													
1873-CC, Variety 4 (q)	4,000	3	56.7	67%					$150,000			$400,000	$500,000
Auctions: $540,500, MS-64, August 2012; $431,250, MS-63, January 2009; $376,000, MS-63, May 2015													
1873, Variety 5	1,271,200	283	53.6	43%	$30	$35	$45	$60	$225	$425	$850	$1,650	$4,000
Auctions: $176,250, MS-64, May 2015; $76,375, AU-55, October 2015; $18,800, EF-45, August 2015; $4,465, G-6, July 2015													
1873, Variety 5, Proof	540	149	63.7								$900	$1,350	$5,500
Auctions: $14,100, PF-67, October 2015; $5,405, PF-66, September 2015; $2,820, PF-64Cam, January 2015; $2,585, PF-64, June 2015													
1873-CC, Variety 5	12,462	23	22.7	4%	$5,000	$9,500	$13,000	$19,000	$27,500	$45,000	$85,000	$125,000	
Auctions: $176,250, MS-64, May 2015; $76,375, AU-55, October 2015; $4,465, G-6, July 2015; $4,818, G-4, August 2015													
1873-S, Variety 5	156,000	68	47.5	32%	$100	$125	$175	$250	$450	$650	$1,750	$4,500	$16,500
Auctions: $18,800, MS-65, May 2015; $13,513, MS-65, October 2015; $11,163, MS-65, October 2015; $5,640, MS-64, October 2015													
1874	471,200	113	54.0	49%	$30	$35	$40	$65	$200	$450	$850	$1,100	$3,000
Auctions: $5,875, MS-66, November 2014; $1,528, MS-63, August 2014; $564, AU-58, May 2015; $89, EF-40, September 2015													
1874, Proof	700	246	63.9								$900	$1,350	$5,500
Auctions: $17,625, PF-67, May 2015; $7,050, PF-66, October 2015; $2,233, PF-64, February 2015; $1,998, PF-64, March 2015													
1874-S	392,000	162	58.6	72%	$30	$40	$65	$100	$265	$485	$850	$1,100	$3,000
Auctions: $18,800, MS-67, June 2015; $9,988, MS-67, October 2015; $4,465, MS-66, October 2015; $3,525, MS-65, June 2015													
1875	4,292,800	364	57.6	63%	$28	$30	$35	$45	$65	$160	$275	$550	$1,750
Auctions: $2,233, MS-66, October 2015; $1,528, MS-65, January 2015; $494, MS-63, September 2015; $376, MS-62, August 2015													
1875, Proof	700	171	63.8								$475	$750	$1,400
Auctions: $9,988, PF-68Cam, January 2015; $8,225, PF-67Cam, October 2015; $1,800, PF-65Cam, January 2015; $1,116, PF-64Cam, July 2015													
1875-CC	140,000	55	44.3	31%	$225	$325	$550	$850	$1,350	$2,500	$4,000	$7,500	$22,500
Auctions: $49,350, MS-66, February 2015; $30,550, MS-65, August 2015; $2,064, AU-55, August 2015; $1,311, EF-40, August 2016													
1875-S	680,000	113	54.1	53%	$45	$60	$95	$130	$250	$325	$600	$1,000	$3,000
Auctions: $6,580, MS-66, January 2015; $3,055, MS-65, October 2014; $68, EF-40, November 2014; $165, VF-35, May 2015													
1876	17,816,000	664	55.4	58%	$28	$30	$35	$45	$65	$160	$275	$550	$1,600
Auctions: $10,575, MS-67, May 2015; $8,225, MS-67, September 2015; $3,290, MS-66, October 2015; $999, MS-65, October 2015													
1876, Proof	1,150	231	63.7								$475	$750	$1,400
Auctions: $32,900, PF-68, May 2015; $10,281, PF-68, October 2015; $2,585, PF-66, January 2015; $1,645, PF-65Cam, July 2015													
1876-CC	4,944,000	460	44.8	37%	$45	$85	$115	$135	$175	$325	$500	$1,250	$4,000
Auctions: $9,400, MS-66, May 2015; $3,672, MS-65, August 2015; $646, MS-63, August 2015; $517, MS-62, September 2015													
1876-S	8,596,000	347	58.3	67%	$28	$30	$35	$45	$65	$160	$275	$550	$1,800
Auctions: $5,640, MS-66, May 2015; $4,230, MS-66, August 2015; $1,645, MS-65, August 2015; $541, MS-62, March 2015													

q. 6 examples are known.

1877-S, S Over
Horizontal S
FS-25-1877S-501.

	Mintage	Cert	Avg	%MS	G-4	VG-8	F-12	VF-20	EF-40	AU-50	MS-60	MS-63	MS-65
											PF-60	PF-63	PF-65
1877	10,911,200	458	58.7	71%	$28	$30	$35	$45	$65	$160	$275	$550	$1,300
Auctions: $3,055, MS-67, July 2015; $2,938, MS-67, September 2015; $2,056, MS-66, September 2015; $940, MS-64, February 2015													
1877, Proof	510	146	63.9								$475	$750	$1,400
Auctions: $22,325, PF-68Cam, May 2015; $4,700, PF-67, October 2015; $3,055, PF-66Cam, January 2015; $1,528, PF-65, January 2015													
1877-CC (r)	4,192,000	578	52.2	57%	$50	$90	$110	$125	$175	$275	$475	$1,150	$2,250
Auctions: $15,289, MS-67, July 2015; $5,640, MS-66, October 2015; $3,525, MS-66, July 2015; $1,410, MS-64, July 2015													
1877-S	8,996,000	456	57.8	67%	$28	$30	$35	$45	$65	$160	$275	$550	$1,300
Auctions: $3,055, MS-67, October 2015; $1,528, MS-66, October 2015; $1,293, MS-65, October 2015; $705, MS-64, October 2015													
1877-S, S Over Horizontal S (s)	(t)	47	58.5	57%	$30	$45	$85	$150	$285	$500	$850	$2,000	$4,000
Auctions: $23,500, MS-66, June 2014; $1,645, MS-63, July 2014; $217, EF-45, November 2014													
1878	2,260,000	125	56.3	64%	$28	$30	$35	$45	$65	$160	$275	$550	$2,250
Auctions: $3,055, MS-66, October 2015; $2,585, MS-66, August 2015; $2,233, MS-65, June 2015; $1,763, MS-65, October 2015													
1878, Proof	800	205	63.6								$475	$750	$1,400
Auctions: $21,150, PF-68, May 2015; $3,525, PF-67, October 2015; $3,525, PF-66Cam, August 2015; $3,760, PF-66, January 2015													
1878-CC	996,000	305	51.9	55%	$75	$95	$120	$150	$275	$425	$750	$1,650	$4,000
Auctions: $823, MS-62, September 2015; $306, AU-50, August 2015; $235, AU-50, October 2015; $282, EF-40, April 2015													
1878-S	140,000	37	53.2	57%	$300	$400	$600	$900	$1,250	$1,700	$3,500	$6,000	$12,500
Auctions: $14,100, MS-65, January 2015; $1,528, AU-50, June 2015; $882, EF-40, August 2015; $823, VF-30, July 2015													
1879	13,600	215	62.8	90%	$200	$275	$350	$425	$475	$550	$675	$850	$2,000
Auctions: $23,500, MS-68, May 2015; $4,700, MS-67, May 2015; $1,998, MS-66, September 2015; $1,410, MS-65, January 2015													
1879, Proof	1,100	300	63.9								$475	$750	$1,400
Auctions: $3,995, PF-67, August 2015; $3,525, PF-67, May 2015; $1,821, PF-66, January 2015; $1,294, PF-65, January 2015													
1880	13,600	134	62.3	86%	$200	$275	$350	$425	$475	$550	$675	$850	$2,250
Auctions: $4,935, MS-67, October 2015; $3,525, MS-67, October 2015; $2,115, MS-66, July 2015; $1,293, MS-64, March 2015													
1880, Proof	1,355	376	64.3								$475	$750	$1,400
Auctions: $21,150, PF-68, May 2015; $7,638, PF-68, January 2015; $3,055, PF-67, October 2015; $2,585, PF-66Cam, January 2015													
1881	12,000	103	59.4	82%	$200	$275	$350	$425	$475	$550	$675	$850	$2,100
Auctions: $4,465, MS-67, October 2015; $2,350, MS-66, October 2015; $494, MS-60, May 2015; $447, VF-20, August 2015													
1881, Proof	975	292	64.3								$475	$750	$1,400
Auctions: $7,638, PF-68Cam, January 2015; $8,225, PF-68, October 2015; $2,350, PF-66Cam, January 2015; $1,880, PF-66, June 2015													
1882	15,200	79	58.8	78%	$200	$275	$350	$425	$475	$550	$675	$850	$2,100
Auctions: $19,975, MS-68, September 2015; $14,100, MS-68, May 2015; $646, AU-50, August 2015; $517, EF-45, August 2015													
1882, Proof	1,100	312	64.1								$475	$750	$1,400
Auctions: $18,800, PF-68Cam, May 2015; $9,400, PF-67DCam, February 2015; $4,465, PF-67, October 2015; $6,463, PF-66DCam, August 2015													
1883	14,400	84	58.0	83%	$200	$275	$350	$425	$475	$550	$675	$850	$2,400
Auctions: $4,700, MS-66, October 2015; $2,820, MS-66, June 2015; $2,350, MS-65, July 2015; $1,236, MS-64, July 2015													
1883, Proof	1,039	352	64.2								$475	$750	$1,400
Auctions: $8,225, PF-68, October 2015; $7,638, PF-67, May 2015; $2,350, PF-66Cam, September 2015; $1,645, PF-65, January 2015													

r. The 1877-CC quarter with fine edge-reeding is scarcer than that with normally spaced reeding; in the marketplace, there is no price differential. **s.** This variety, known since the 1950s, was caused by an initial S mintmark being punched into the die horizontally, and then corrected with an upright S mintmark. **t.** Included in 1877-S mintage figure.

	Mintage	Cert	Avg	%MS	G-4	VG-8	F-12	VF-20	EF-40	AU-50	MS-60 PF-60	MS-63 PF-63	MS-65 PF-65
1884	8,000	98	57.4	79%	$300	$400	$500	$625	$725	$800	$900	$1,150	$2,100
Auctions: $8,519, MS-67, June 2015; $3,290, MS-66, October 2015; $881, AU-53, August 2015; $564, VF-35, August 2015													
1884, Proof	875	290	64.4								$475	$750	$1,400
Auctions: $3,643, PF-67, October 2015; $2,115, PF-66, July 2015; $1,800, PF-66, June 2015; $2,115, PF-65, March 2015													
1885	13,600	90	58.6	74%	$200	$250	$350	$500	$575	$700	$850	$1,100	$2,400
Auctions: $6,756, MS-67, May 2015; $3,055, MS-66, August 2015; $3,290, MS-65, October 2015; $705, MS-62, October 2015													
1885, Proof	930	262	64.2								$475	$750	$1,400
Auctions: $5,881, PF-67Cam, June 2015; $4,700, PF-67, October 2015; $2,820, PF-67, January 2015; $1,998, PF-66Cam, January 2015													
1886	5,000	46	56.2	76%	$400	$550	$750	$950	$1,100	$1,250	$1,500	$1,900	$2,600
Auctions: $6,169, MS-66, August 2015; $2,115, MS-65, October 2015; $1,410, MS-64, June 2015; $1,116, VF-30, August 2015													
1886, Proof	886	290	64.4								$475	$750	$1,400
Auctions: $11,750, PF-68, May 2015; $12,925, PF-67Cam, October 2015; $21,150, PF-67, August 2015; $4,230, PF-66Cam, March 2015													
1887	10,000	101	61.0	84%	$250	$350	$425	$500	$575	$625	$850	$1,150	$2,500
Auctions: $4,935, MS-67, October 2015; $2,585, MS-66, October 2015; $2,295, MS-66, January 2015; $999, MS-62, August 2015													
1887, Proof	710	234	64.3								$475	$750	$1,400
Auctions: $7,638, PF-68, January 2015; $3,760, PF-67, October 2015; $2,350, PF-66Cam, January 2015; $1,880, PF-66, August 2015													
1888	10,001	132	62.8	92%	$250	$350	$425	$500	$550	$600	$700	$900	$1,600
Auctions: $5,640, MS-67, May 2015; $3,760, MS-67, October 2015; $2,350, MS-66, January 2015; $1,351, MS-65, January 2015													
1888, Proof	832	232	64.1								$475	$750	$1,400
Auctions: $3,525, PF-67, January 2015; $3,055, PF-66Cam, August 2015; $1,528, PF-65, January 2015; $282, PF-60, August 2015													
1888-S	1,216,000	155	55.5	63%	$30	$35	$40	$45	$70	$200	$360	$750	$3,000
Auctions: $7,638, MS-66, May 2015; $6,463, MS-66, October 2015; $3,525, MS-65, September 2015; $1,528, MS-64, June 2015													
1889	12,000	179	62.6	88%	$200	$275	$425	$500	$550	$600	$700	$900	$1,950
Auctions: $4,700, MS-67, January 2015; $3,525, MS-66, October 2015; $1,880, MS-65, January 2015; $1,116, MS-64, June 2015													
1889, Proof	711	192	64.5								$475	$750	$1,400
Auctions: $15,275, PF-68, May 2015; $8,519, PF-68, October 2015; $1,880, PF-66, January 2015; $1,645, PF-65Cam, January 2015													
1890	80,000	188	62.2	85%	$95	$135	$180	$275	$325	$375	$485	$900	$1,400
Auctions: $10,589, MS-68, June 2015; $3,995, MS-67, January 2015; $2,233, MS-66, October 2015; $2,350, MS-65, October 2015													
1890, Proof	590	228	64.8								$475	$750	$1,400
Auctions: $4,700, PF-67Cam, September 2015; $3,643, PF-66Cam, January 2015; $1,500, PF-65, June 2015; $1,410, PF-64, August 2015													
1891	3,920,000	722	59.8	73%	$30	$35	$40	$45	$65	$160	$260	$550	$1,800
Auctions: $4,230, MS-67, May 2015; $1,998, MS-65, June 2015; $1,763, MS-66, September 2015; $1,645, MS-66, January 2015													
1891, Proof	600	245	64.6								$475	$750	$1,400
Auctions: $15,275, PF-67, October 2015; $3,760, PF-67, October 2015; $2,820, PF-66, January 2015; $1,528, PF-64Cam, October 2015													
1891-O	68,000	38	34.8	29%	$350	$550	$1,000	$1,650	$2,500	$3,350	$7,000	$12,500	$30,000
Auctions: $28,200, MS-65, May 2015; $22,325, MS-65, January 2015; $14,100, MS-63, August 2015; $852, VG-10, July 2015													
1891-S	2,216,000	213	58.2	69%	$30	$35	$40	$45	$70	$160	$260	$550	$2,000
Auctions: $3,055, MS-66, May 2015; $1,645, MS-65, October 2015; $823, MS-64, October 2015; $564, MS-63, June 2015													

BARBER OR LIBERTY HEAD (1892–1916)

Designer: *Charles E. Barber.* **Weight:** *6.25 grams.*
Composition: *.900 silver, .100 copper (net weight .18084 oz. pure silver).*
Diameter: *24.3 mm.* **Edge:** *Reeded.* **Mints:** *Philadelphia, Denver, New Orleans, and San Francisco.*

Circulation Strike

Mintmark location
is on the reverse,
below the eagle.

Proof

History. The Liberty Head design was by Charles E. Barber, chief engraver of the U.S. Mint. Barber quarters feature the same obverse motif used on dimes and half dollars of the era, with the designer's initial, B, found at the truncation of the neck of Miss Liberty. The reverse depicts a heraldic eagle holding an olive branch in one talon and arrows in the other, along with a ribbon reading E PLURIBUS UNUM.

Striking and Sharpness. On the obverse, check the hair details and other features. On the reverse, the eagle's leg at the lower right and the arrows can be weak. Also check the upper–right portion of the shield and the nearby wing. Once these coins entered circulation and acquired wear, the word LIBERTY on the headband tended to disappear quickly. Most Proofs are sharply struck, although more than just a few are weak on the eagle's leg at the lower right and on certain parts of the arrows. The Proofs of 1892 to 1901 usually have cameo contrast between the designs and the mirror fields. Later Proofs vary in their contrast.

Availability. Barber quarters in Fine or better grade are scarce. Today, among circulation strikes, 90% or more in existence are G-4 or below. MS coins are available of all dates and mints, but some are very elusive. The 1896-S, 1901-S, and 1913-S are the key dates in all grades. Proofs exist in proportion to their mintages. Choicer examples tend to be of later dates.

GRADING STANDARDS

MS-60 to 70 (Mint State). *Obverse:* At MS-60, some abrasion and contact marks are evident, most noticeably on the cheek and the obverse field to the right. Luster is present, but may be dull or lifeless. Many Barber coins have been cleaned, especially of the earlier dates. At MS-63, contact marks are very few. Abrasion still is evident, but less than at lower levels. Indeed, the cheek of Miss Liberty virtually showcases abrasion. An MS-65 coin

1896-S. Graded MS-65.

may have minor abrasion, but contact marks are so minute as to require magnification. Luster should be full and rich. *Reverse:* Comments apply as for the obverse, except that in lower Mint State grades abrasion and contact marks are most noticeable on the head and tail of the eagle and on the tips of the wings. At MS-65 or higher, there are no marks visible to the unaided eye. The field is mainly protected by design elements, and often appears to grade a point or two higher than the obverse.

Illustrated coin: This brilliant coin shows full satin luster.

AU-50, 53, 55, 58 (About Uncirculated). *Obverse:* Light wear is seen on the head, especially on the forward hair under LIBERTY. At AU-58, the luster is extensive but incomplete, especially on the higher parts and in the right field. At AU–50 and 53, luster is less. *Reverse:* Wear is evident on the head and tail of the eagle and on the tips of the wings. At AU–50 and 53, there still is significant luster. An AU-58 coin (as determined by the obverse) can have the reverse appear to be full Mint State.

1911-D. Graded AU-50.

EF-40, 45 (Extremely Fine). *Obverse:* Further wear is seen on the head. The hair above the forehead lacks most detail. LIBERTY shows wear, but still is strong. *Reverse:* Further wear is seen on the head and tail of the eagle and on the tips of the wings, most evident at the left and right extremes of the wings. At this level and below, sharpness of strike on the reverse is not important.

Illustrated coin: Note the subtle lilac and gold toning.

1913-S. Graded EF-40.

VF-20, 30 (Very Fine). *Obverse:* The head shows more wear, now with nearly all detail gone in the hair above the forehead. LIBERTY shows wear, but is complete. The leaves on the head all show wear, as does the upper part of the cap. *Reverse:* Wear is more extensive, particularly noticeable on the outer parts of the wings, the head, the shield, and the tail.

Illustrated coin: The dig and discoloration in Liberty's cheek decrease the appeal of this example.

1896-S. Graded VF-20.

F-12, 15 (Fine). *Obverse:* The head shows extensive wear. LIBERTY, the key place to check, is weak, especially at ER, but is fully readable. The ANA grading standards and *Photograde* adhere to this. PCGS suggests that lightly struck coins "may have letters partially missing." Traditionally, collectors insist on full LIBERTY. *Reverse:* More wear is seen on the reverse in the places as above. E PLURIBUS UNUM is light, with one to several letters worn away.

1913-S. Graded F-15.

VG-8, 10 (Very Good). *Obverse:* A net of three letters in LIBERTY must be readable. Traditionally, LI is clear, and after that there is a partial letter or two. *Reverse:* Further wear has smoothed more than half of the feathers in the wing. The shield is indistinct except for a few traces of interior lines. The motto is partially worn away. The rim is full, and many if not most denticles can be seen.

1914-S. Graded VG-10.

G-4, 6 (Good). *Obverse:* The head is in outline form, with the center flat. Most of the rim is there. All letters and the date are full. *Reverse:* The eagle shows only a few feathers, and only a few scattered letters remain in the motto. The rim may be worn flat in some or all of the area, but the peripheral lettering is clear.

1913-S. Graded G-4.

AG-3 (About Good). *Obverse:* The stars and motto are worn, and the border may be indistinct. Distinctness varies at this level. The date is clear. Grading is usually determined by the reverse. *Reverse:* The rim is gone and the letters are partially worn away. The eagle is mostly flat, perhaps with a few hints of feathers.

1901-S. Graded AG-3.

PF-60 to 70 (Proof). *Obverse and Reverse:* Proofs that are extensively cleaned and have many hairlines, or that are dull and grainy, are lower level, such as PF-60 to 62. These are not widely desired by collectors. With medium hairlines and good reflectivity, an assigned grade of PF-64 is appropriate. Tiny horizontal lines on Miss Liberty's cheek, known as slide marks, from National and other album slides scuffing the relief of the

1913. Graded PF-68 Cameo.

cheek, are endemic on all Barber silver coins. With noticeable marks of this type, the highest grade assignable is PF-64. With relatively few hairlines, a rating of PF-65 can be given. PF-66 should have hairlines so delicate that magnification is needed to see them. Above that, a Proof should be free of any hairlines or other problems.

Illustrated coin: Exceptional fields offset the bright devices to high advantage.

1892, Variety 1 Reverse   **1892, Variety 2 Reverse**
Note position of wing tip relative to E in UNITED.

Coins designated Deep Cameo or Ultra Cameo bring a premium of 50% to 100% above listed values.

	Mintage	Cert	Avg	%MS	G-4	VG-8	F-12	VF-20	EF-40	AU-50	MS-60 PF-60	MS-63 PF-63	MS-65 PF-65
1892 (a)	8,236,000	1,924	59.8	70%	$10	$12	$26	$45	$75	$130	$250	$375	$750
Auctions: $9,988, MS-68, January 2015; $2,820, MS-67, July 2015; $1,528, MS-66, August 2015; $1,058, MS-65, August 2015													
1892, Proof	1,245	402	64.6								$350	$650	$1,250
Auctions: $2,820, PF-65DCam, April 2015; $940, PF-64Cam, January 2015; $2,468, PF-64, August 2015; $560, PF-63, September 2015													
1892-O	2,460,000	501	58.7	64%	$15	$20	$45	$60	$95	$180	$320	$425	$1,450
Auctions: $14,100, MS-68, October 2015; $9,106, MS-67, October 2015; $3,055, MS-66, August 2015; $1,645, MS-65, August 2015													
1892-S	964,079	147	45.8	44%	$30	$65	$95	$135	$215	$450	$650	$1,150	$3,750
Auctions: $14,100, MS-66, January 2015; $3,055, MS-65, July 2015; $940, AU-58, June 2016; $447, AU-55, October 2015													
1893	5,444,023	363	57.1	65%	$10	$12	$20	$30	$55	$130	$240	$450	$1,000
Auctions: $1,058, MS-65, January 2015; $470, MS-64, October 2015; $259, MS-61, May 2015; $165, MS-60, May 2015													
1893, Proof	792	305	65.0								$350	$650	$1,250
Auctions: $8,813, PF-68, September 2015; $5,170, PF-67Cam, January 2015; $2,115, PF-66Cam, January 2015; $1,528, PF-65Cam, February 2015													
1893-O	3,396,000	235	55.9	60%	$10	$14	$35	$60	$110	$180	$300	$480	$1,500
Auctions: $8,225, MS-67, October 2015; $2,938, MS-66, February 2015; $1,412, MS-65, January 2015; $517, MS-64, September 2015													
1893-S	1,454,535	121	44.4	49%	$20	$35	$70	$120	$180	$325	$425	$1,000	$4,500
Auctions: $20,563, MS-67, October 2015; $4,700, MS-66, August 2015; $7,638, MS-65, September 2015; $223, EF-45, May 2015													
1894	3,432,000	206	56.0	68%	$10	$12	$35	$50	$95	$150	$240	$425	$1,050
Auctions: $3,760, MS-66, May 2015; $1,116, MS-65, June 2015; $60, EF-40, May 2015													
1894, Proof	972	337	64.7								$350	$650	$1,250
Auctions: $8,225, PF-68, May 2015; $3,055, PF-67, January 2015; $2,585, PF-66Cam, October 2015; $1,450, PF-65, January 2015													
1894-O	2,852,000	168	52.9	60%	$10	$20	$45	$80	$130	$230	$325	$600	$1,800
Auctions: $11,163, MS-67, May 2015; $9,988, MS-66, October 2015; $1,763, MS-65, January 2015; $259, AU-55, May 2015													
1894-S	2,648,821	221	56.5	66%	$10	$15	$40	$65	$150	$210	$325	$550	$1,900
Auctions: $17,625, MS-67, May 2015; $1,410, MS-65, January 2015; $2,820, MS-64, October 2015; $588, MS-62, August 2015													
1895	4,440,000	264	55.3	66%	$10	$14	$30	$45	$80	$140	$275	$450	$1,250
Auctions: $2,820, MS-66, October 2015; $1,175, MS-65, January 2015; $1,651, MS-64, March 2015; $411, MS-63, May 2015													
1895, Proof	880	275	64.9								$350	$650	$1,250
Auctions: $9,988, PF-68Cam, January 2015; $4,935, PF-67Cam, October 2015; $3,761, PF-66, March 2015; $588, PF-63, July 2015													
1895-O	2,816,000	146	49.3	49%	$12	$20	$50	$70	$140	$230	$400	$950	$2,000
Auctions: $1,528, MS-65, January 2015; $423, AU-58, May 2015; $470, AU-55, February 2015; $69, EF-40, May 2015													
1895-S	1,764,681	142	44.8	42%	$20	$35	$80	$120	$170	$275	$420	$950	$2,500
Auctions: $8,225, MS-68, January 2015; $2,585, MS-64, August 2015; $823, MS-63, August 2015; $705, MS-62, January 2015													
1896	3,874,000	219	54.7	71%	$10	$14	$30	$45	$80	$135	$250	$325	$875
Auctions: $3,760, MS-66, February 2015; $764, MS-65, June 2015; $541, MS-64, October 2015; $165, AU-55, May 2015													
1896, Proof	762	328	65.3								$350	$650	$1,250
Auctions: $8,225, PF-68Cam, February 2015; $4,465, PF-67Cam, January 2015; $1,645, PF-66, January 2015; $1,061, PF-64Cam, January 2015													
1896-O	1,484,000	232	26.8	21%	$60	$95	$200	$320	$600	$950	$1,100	$1,950	$6,000
Auctions: $9,988, MS-66, January 2015; $2,820, MS-64, July 2016; $1,410, MS-63, September 2015; $999, MS-62, August 2015													
1896-S	188,039	548	11.0	6%	$650	$1,200	$2,100	$3,500	$5,000	$6,500	$14,000	$21,000	$48,000
Auctions: $70,500, MS-65, November 2016; $20,400, MS-64, April 2018; $3,760, VF-25, April 2017; $1,175, VG-10, September 2015													

a. There are two varieties of the 1892 reverse. Variety 1: the eagle's wing covers only half of the E in UNITED; Variety 2: the eagle's wing covers most of the E. Coins of Variety 1 are somewhat scarcer.

	Mintage	Cert	Avg	%MS	G-4	VG-8	F-12	VF-20	EF-40	AU-50	MS-60	MS-63	MS-65
											PF-60	PF-63	PF-65
1897	8,140,000	328	54.5	63%	$9	$14	$26	$40	$70	$120	$240	$350	$800
	Auctions: $5,640, MS-67, May 2015; $2,350, MS-66, September 2015; $329, MS-62, January 2015; $79, EF-45, June 2015												
1897, Proof	731	280	64.7								$350	$650	$1,250
	Auctions: $9,988, PF-68Cam, August 2015; $9,988, PF-68, May 2015; $1,410, PF-65Cam, February 2015; $881, PF-64, February 2015												
1897-O	1,414,800	188	27.7	24%	$45	$85	$200	$350	$400	$650	$900	$1,750	$3,000
	Auctions: $14,100, MS-67, May 2015; $20,563, MS-66, October 2015; $3,055, MS-65, August 2015; $2,115, MS-64, March 2015												
1897-S	542,229	269	20.9	17%	$110	$160	$300	$600	$925	$1,300	$1,650	$2,400	$6,800
	Auctions: $21,150, MS-67, October 2015; $20,563, MS-66, October 2015; $6,463, MS-65, August 2016; $1,998, AU-58, January 2015												
1898	11,100,000	415	51.9	58%	$9	$10	$26	$45	$70	$125	$225	$350	$700
	Auctions: $4,700, MS-67, October 2015; $1,763, MS-66, October 2015; $764, MS-65, January 2015; $705, MS-64, August 2015												
1898, Proof	735	326	65.6								$350	$650	$1,250
	Auctions: $23,500, PF-69Cam, October 2015; $4,700, PF-67DCam, January 2015; $2,233, PF-66, October 2015; $1,469, PF-65, March 2015												
1898-O	1,868,000	103	44.5	40%	$15	$30	$85	$140	$300	$480	$950	$1,800	$6,000
	Auctions: $11,750, MS-66, January 2015; $764, AU-58, January 2015; $329, AU-50, January 2015; $212, EF-45, July 2015												
1898-S	1,020,592	88	50.8	49%	$11	$25	$45	$75	$140	$350	$1,050	$2,400	$6,500
	Auctions: $7,050, MS-65, June 2015; $4,935, MS-64, August 2015; $881, AU-58, January 2015; $541, AU-55, July 2015												
1899	12,624,000	448	50.3	54%	$9	$10	$26	$45	$75	$125	$240	$375	$750
	Auctions: $1,293, MS-66, January 2015; $823, MS-65, January 2015; $188, AU-58, September 2015; $165, AU-55, February 2015												
1899, Proof	846	203	64.8								$350	$650	$1,250
	Auctions: $5,876, PF-67Cam, July 2015; $1,998, PF-66Cam, August 2015; $494, PF-62, August 2015												
1899-O	2,644,000	116	53.7	56%	$12	$20	$35	$70	$130	$260	$500	$1,000	$2,750
	Auctions: $12,925, MS-67, August 2015; $4,818, MS-66, October 2015; $2,820, MS-65, January 2015; $1,058, MS-64, June 2015												
1899-S	708,000	73	47.1	40%	$28	$44	$95	$150	$180	$400	$1,200	$2,150	$4,800
	Auctions: $9,988, MS-67, June 2015; $940, AU-58, January 2015; $329, AU-55, January 2015; $376, AU-53, May 2015												
1900	10,016,000	332	56.3	68%	$9	$10	$26	$45	$75	$125	$240	$375	$1,200
	Auctions: $10,575, MS-67, May 2015; $1,184, MS-65, January 2015; $588, MS-64, July 2015; $317, MS-63, October 2015												
1900, Proof	912	275	64.8								$350	$650	$1,250
	Auctions: $7,344, PF-68, May 2015; $3,290, PF-67Cam, October 2015; $2,585, PF-66Cam, January 2015; $1,293, PF-65, January 2015												
1900-O	3,416,000	129	47.6	49%	$15	$28	$75	$120	$160	$390	$750	$1,100	$3,000
	Auctions: $17,626, MS-68, May 2015; $12,925, MS-67, October 2015; $7,050, MS-66, August 2015; $2,350, MS-65, June 2015												
1900-S	1,858,585	157	51.0	27%	$10	$15	$35	$55	$80	$200	$650	$1,200	$2,750
	Auctions: $10,575, MS-67, May 2015; $6,169, MS-66, August 2015; $341, MS-61, May 2015; $259, AU-58, January 2015												
1901	8,892,000	388	45.0	52%	$9	$10	$26	$45	$80	$135	$275	$425	$950
	Auctions: $2,115, MS-66, October 2015; $940, MS-65, January 2015; $423, MS-64, May 2015; $329, MS-63, May 2015												
1901, Proof	813	255	64.8								$350	$650	$1,250
	Auctions: $5,875, PF-68, July 2015; $3,995, PF-67, October 2015; $1,528, PF-66, March 2015; $1,293, PF-65, January 2015												
1901-O	1,612,000	122	25.2	15%	$55	$90	$200	$400	$800	$1,200	$1,900	$2,650	$7,200
	Auctions: $2,585, MS-63, January 2015; $940, AU-50, July 2015; $705, EF-40, June 2015; $212, F-15, February 2015												
1901-S	72,664	391	7.7	3%	$3,750	$8,000	$13,500	$20,000	$27,500	$32,500	$40,000	$50,000	$78,000
	Auctions: $70,500, MS-65, November 2016; $14,400, VF-20, April 2018; $12,925, F-12, July 2016; $7,800, VG-8, November 2017												
1902	12,196,967	367	52.3	54%	$9	$10	$26	$45	$65	$120	$240	$375	$850
	Auctions: $7,638, MS-67, May 2015; $2,233, MS-66, October 2015; $999, MS-65, January 2015; $656, MS-64, June 2015												
1902, Proof	777	227	64.2								$350	$650	$1,250
	Auctions: $2,820, PF-67, October 2015; $3,055, PF-66, October 2015; $1,410, PF-66, January 2015; $646, PF-63, January 2015												
1902-O	4,748,000	120	48.5	40%	$10	$16	$50	$85	$140	$240	$500	$1,100	$3,000
	Auctions: $28,200, MS-68, May 2015; $7,050, MS-66, October 2015; $1,763, MS-64, August 2015; $823, MS-63, July 2015												
1902-S	1,524,612	126	51.1	48%	$14	$22	$55	$90	$160	$250	$525	$900	$3,100
	Auctions: $3,995, MS-66, August 2015; $2,233, MS-65, January 2015; $1,410, MS-64, August 2015; $705, MS-63, September 2015												

	Mintage	Cert	Avg	%MS	G-4	VG-8	F-12	VF-20	EF-40	AU-50	MS-60 PF-60	MS-63 PF-63	MS-65 PF-65
1903	9,759,309	157	52.9	51%	$9	$10	$26	$45	$65	$120	$240	$450	$1,650
	Auctions: $9,400, MS-66, October 2015; $423, MS-64, May 2015; $353, MS-64, November 2015; $94, AU-53, April 2015												
1903, Proof	755	287	65.1								$350	$650	$1,250
	Auctions: $5,875, PF-68, May 2015; $3,290, PF-66, August 2015; $823, PF-64, February 2015; $589, PF-62, February 2015												
1903-O	3,500,000	116	46.8	35%	$10	$12	$40	$60	$120	$250	$475	$950	$3,250
	Auctions: $32,900, MS-67, May 2015; $3,055, MS-65, October 2015; $176, AU-50, July 2015; $101, EF-45, November 2014												
1903-S	1,036,000	94	55.3	67%	$15	$25	$45	$85	$150	$275	$600	$1,000	$2,400
	Auctions: $19,975, MS-67, May 2015; $4,230, MS-66, October 2015; $1,821, MS-65, September 2015; $1,000, MS-62, May 2015												
1904	9,588,143	189	54.0	56%	$9	$10	$26	$45	$70	$120	$240	$475	$1,300
	Auctions: $5,170, MS-66, October 2015; $141, AU-55, August 2015; $125, AU-55, May 2015; $64, EF-40, March 2015												
1904, Proof	670	268	64.7								$350	$650	$1,250
	Auctions: $5,405, PF-68, June 2015; $4,230, PF-67, January 2015; $1,528, PF-66, July 2015; $823, PF-64, October 2015												
1904-O	2,456,000	166	40.4	33%	$30	$40	$90	$160	$240	$400	$900	$1,350	$4,000
	Auctions: $41,125, MS-67, June 2014												
1905	4,967,523	250	45.1	48%	$30	$35	$50	$65	$70	$120	$240	$425	$950
	Auctions: $2,233, MS-66, October 2015; $1,293, MS-66, October 2015; $999, MS-65, July 2015; $353, MS-63, November 2015												
1905, Proof	727	248	64.6								$350	$650	$1,250
	Auctions: $3,878, PF-67, January 2015; $3,173, PF-66, September 2015; $1,293, PF-65, February 2015; $881, PF-64, August 2015												
1905-O	1,230,000	128	36.5	35%	$35	$60	$130	$220	$260	$350	$600	$1,300	$4,500
	Auctions: $11,750, MS-67, October 2015; $5,170, MS-65, September 2015; $2,585, MS-64, August 2015; $833, MS-62, January 2015												
1905-S	1,884,000	144	41.3	35%	$30	$40	$75	$100	$120	$225	$525	$1,000	$3,600
	Auctions: $3,055, MS-65, August 2015; $1,175, MS-64, September 2015; $646, MS-62, June 2015; $84, VF-30, July 2015												
1906	3,655,760	220	58.3	77%	$9	$10	$26	$45	$70	$120	$240	$375	$950
	Auctions: $2,820, MS-66, June 2014												
1906, Proof	675	207	64.9								$350	$650	$1,250
	Auctions: $16,450, PF-68, May 2015; $2,233, PF-66, August 2015; $1,410, PF-65, January 2015; $1,351, PF-65, September 2015												
1906-D	3,280,000	145	58.5	72%	$9	$10	$30	$50	$70	$145	$250	$425	$1,650
	Auctions: $9,400, MS-67, May 2015; $823, MS-64, January 2015; $235, AU-58, October 2015; $58, EF-40, April 2015												
1906-O	2,056,000	147	59.7	74%	$9	$10	$40	$60	$100	$200	$300	$500	$1,350
	Auctions: $11,750, MS-67, October 2015; $5,640, MS-67, May 2015; $2,233, MS-66, October 2015; $1,666, MS-65, September 2015												
1907	7,132,000	424	55.5	61%	$9	$10	$26	$40	$65	$120	$240	$375	$750
	Auctions: $6,463, MS-67, October 2015; $1,998, MS-66, October 2015; $705, MS-65, January 2015; $376, MS-64, May 2015												
1907, Proof	575	287	65.0								$350	$650	$1,250
	Auctions: $5,170, PF-67Cam, August 2015; $2,115, PF-66, July 2015; $1,293, PF-65Cam, September 2015; $940, PF-64Cam, October 2015												
1907-D	2,484,000	121	53.9	64%	$9	$10	$26	$48	$70	$200	$360	$650	$2,250
	Auctions: $1,058, MS-64, July 2015; $999, MS-64, July 2015; $150, AU-53, July 2015; $141, AU-50, May 2015												
1907-O	4,560,000	208	54.8	65%	$9	$10	$26	$45	$70	$135	$250	$450	$1,500
	Auctions: $9,988, MS-68, January 2015; $10,575, MS-67, October 2015; $1,293, MS-65, August 2015; $552, MS-64, July 2015												
1907-S	1,360,000	89	51.8	64%	$10	$20	$45	$75	$150	$280	$525	$1,300	$3,250
	Auctions: $6,463, MS-66, September 2015; $5,405, MS-66, October 2015; $3,564, MS-65, August 2015; $223, EF-45, July 2015												
1908	4,232,000	264	58.3	70%	$9	$10	$26	$45	$70	$120	$240	$375	$750
	Auctions: $1,116, MS-66, January 2015; $940, MS-65, June 2015; $447, MS-64, January 2015; $329, MS-63, January 2015												
1908, Proof	545	187	64.6								$350	$650	$1,250
	Auctions: $5,170, PF-67, October 2015; $1,528, PF-66, February 2015; $1,175, PF-65, June 2015; $823, PF-64, July 2015												
1908-D	5,788,000	295	51.4	54%	$9	$10	$26	$45	$70	$120	$240	$375	$750
	Auctions: $2,585, MS-66, October 2015; $1,058, MS-65, August 2015; $306, MS-62, February 2015; $94, AU-50, May 2015												
1908-O	6,244,000	284	52.9	64%	$9	$10	$26	$45	$65	$120	$240	$375	$850
	Auctions: $764, MS-65, October 2015; $235, MS-62, January 2015; $176, AU-58, April 2015; $112, AU-53, August 2015												
1908-S	784,000	152	41.3	48%	$30	$65	$130	$165	$325	$525	$950	$1,200	$3,500
	Auctions: $7,050, MS-67, October 2015; $2,963, MS-65, January 2015; $1,763, MS-64, January 2015; $1,293, MS-63, September 2015												

	Mintage	Cert	Avg	%MS	G-4	VG-8	F-12	VF-20	EF-40	AU-50	MS-60	MS-63	MS-65
											PF-60	PF-63	PF-65
1909	9,268,000	567	55.6	65%	$9	$10	$26	$45	$65	$120	$240	$375	$750
Auctions: $3,055, MS-66, May 2015; $999, MS-65, January 2015; $494, MS-64, September 2015; $247, MS-62, May 2015													
1909, Proof	650	271	64.7								$350	$650	$1,250
Auctions: $13,513, PF-68, May 2015; $1,704, PF-66, February 2015; $1,058, PF-64, January 2015; $719, PF-63Cam, June 2015													
1909-D	5,114,000	349	48.6	49%	$9	$10	$26	$45	$85	$150	$240	$375	$750
Auctions: $9,400, MS-67, May 2015; $1,293, MS-66, October 2015; $2,350, MS-65, October 2015; $705, MS-64, January 2015													
1909-O	712,000	155	25.2	25%	$55	$180	$475	$900	$2,000	$3,350	$4,000	$4,800	$7,200
Auctions: $21,150, MS-67, May 2015; $1,175, VF-35, February 2015; $1,116, VF-25, October 2015; $646, VF-20, December 2015													
1909-S	1,348,000	124	47.5	56%	$9	$10	$35	$55	$90	$225	$350	$750	$1,650
Auctions: $12,925, MS-67, May 2015; $2,585, MS-66, January 2015; $1,763, MS-65, January 2015; $182, AU-55, September 2015													
1910	2,244,000	219	54.6	70%	$9	$10	$26	$45	$80	$140	$240	$375	$750
Auctions: $1,528, MS-66, January 2015; $711, MS-65, January 2015; $676, MS-64, August 2015; $176, AU-58, June 2015													
1910, Proof	551	263	65.1								$350	$650	$1,250
Auctions: $2,703, PF-67Cam, September 2015; $1,998, PF-65Cam, January 2015; $911, PF-64Cam, October 2015; $881, PF-64Cam, October 2015													
1910-D	1,500,000	145	52.8	58%	$10	$11	$45	$70	$125	$240	$375	$800	$1,650
Auctions: $4,818, MS-67, October 2015; $447, MS-62, February 2015; $376, MS-61, April 2015; $212, AU-55, August 2015													
1911	3,720,000	321	58.3	71%	$9	$10	$26	$45	$70	$125	$240	$375	$750
Auctions: $3,055, MS-66, August 2015; $764, MS-65, February 2015; $470, MS-64, January 2015; $329, MS-63, October 2015													
1911, Proof	543	238	65.3								$350	$650	$1,250
Auctions: $7,050, PF-68Cam, February 2015; $3,290, PF-67Cam, October 2015; $2,585, PF-66Cam, October 2015; $1,704, PF-65Cam, October 2015													
1911-D	933,600	150	37.2	35%	$30	$45	$150	$300	$425	$675	$850	$1,200	$4,250
Auctions: $4,113, MS-65, June 2015; $764, MS-62, January 2015; $705, AU-58, January 2015; $353, EF-45, April 2015													
1911-S	988,000	177	57.2	74%	$9	$10	$55	$85	$180	$280	$475	$775	$1,500
Auctions: $37,600, MS-66, August 2017; $21,738, MS-64, August 2013; $15,000, MS-63, February 2018; $15,275, AU-58, April 2013													
1912	4,400,000	477	57.1	73%	$9	$10	$26	$45	$70	$120	$240	$375	$750
Auctions: $8,225, MS-67, May 2015; $1,410, MS-66, September 2015; $823, MS-65, January 2015; $235, MS-62, February 2015													
1912, Proof	700	216	64.6								$350	$650	$1,250
Auctions: $19,975, PF-68Cam, May 2015; $3,055, PF-67, February 2015; $2,820, PF-67, March 2015; $1,175, PF-64Cam, September 2015													
1912-S	708,000	126	45.3	53%	$20	$30	$65	$95	$125	$240	$480	$900	$1,750
Auctions: $11,163, MS-68, May 2015; $5,875, MS-67, June 2015; $1,763, MS-65, January 2015; $1,880, MS-64, August 2015													
1913	484,000	170	40.2	39%	$30	$45	$110	$180	$400	$525	$750	$900	$2,250
Auctions: $3,055, MS-65, October 2015; $2,585, MS-65, February 2015; $1,998, MS-65, October 2015; $588, AU-58, August 2015													
1913, Proof	613	241	64.5								$350	$650	$1,250
Auctions: $4,230, PF-67Cam, July 2015; $1,483, PF-66, January 2015; $2,585, PF-65, August 2015; $1,175, PF-64Cam, January 2015													
1913-D	1,450,800	204	52.9	60%	$12	$15	$35	$60	$85	$175	$360	$600	$1,000
Auctions: $6,756, MS-67, July 2015; $1,704, MS-66, October 2015; $705, MS-64, August 2015; $376, MS-63, May 2015													
1913-S	40,000	599	9.5	7%	$1,200	$2,000	$4,750	$7,200	$10,000	$12,500	$15,000	$18,500	$32,500
Auctions: $35,250, MS-66, June 2015; $3,995, F-12, July 2015; $2,350, VG-10, September 2016; $1,351, VG-8, September 2016													
1914	6,244,230	731	54.7	64%	$9	$10	$22	$40	$65	$120	$240	$375	$750
Auctions: $1,763, MS-66, October 2015; $823, MS-65, January 2015; $447, MS-64, June 2015; $329, MS-63, May 2015													
1914, Proof	380	197	64.8								$350	$650	$1,250
Auctions: $7,050, PF-68, October 2014; $3,525, PF-67, October 2015; $2,938, PF-67, November 2014; $1,763, PF-66, June 2015													
1914-D	3,046,000	372	55.1	65%	$9	$10	$22	$40	$65	$120	$240	$375	$750
Auctions: $4,700, MS-67, October 2015; $2,938, MS-66, June 2015; $676, MS-65, August 2015; $364, MS-63, August 2015													
1914-S	264,000	538	14.0	9%	$90	$170	$425	$525	$900	$1,200	$1,600	$2,500	$6,500
Auctions: $6,463, MS-66, August 2016; $3,290, MS-64, January 2015; $2,468, MS-63, July 2015; $1,880, AU-58, October 2016													

	Mintage	Cert	Avg	%MS	G-4	VG-8	F-12	VF-20	EF-40	AU-50	MS-60 PF-60	MS-63 PF-63	MS-65 PF-65
1915	3,480,000	543	55.8	70%	$9	$10	$22	$40	$65	$120	$240	$375	$750
	Auctions: $2,350, MS-66, May 2015; $881, MS-65, January 2015; $401, MS-64, August 2015; $376, MS-63, May 2015												
1915, Proof	450	180	64.2								$425	$750	$1,500
	Auctions: $15,275, PF-68, May 2015; $3,055, PF-67, January 2015; $1,234, PF-65, January 2015; $830, PF-64, June 2015												
1915-D	3,694,000	689	57.3	71%	$9	$10	$22	$40	$70	$120	$240	$375	$750
	Auctions: $4,935, MS-67, May 2015; $1,410, MS-66, August 2015; $999, MS-65, January 2015; $388, MS-64, October 2015												
1915-S	704,000	267	45.3	49%	$25	$40	$60	$85	$115	$200	$285	$425	$1,150
	Auctions: $8,225, MS-67, May 2015; $2,820, MS-66, January 2015; $2,468, MS-65, September 2015; $259, MS-62, August 2015												
1916	1,788,000	486	56.3	67%	$9	$10	$22	$40	$70	$120	$240	$375	$750
	Auctions: $3,055, MS-67, October 2015; $1,293, MS-66, August 2015; $940, MS-65, August 2015; $400, MS-64, March 2015												
1916-D	6,540,800	1,667	57.8	71%	$9	$10	$22	$40	$70	$120	$240	$375	$750
	Auctions: $3,525, MS-67, March 2015; $1,528, MS-66, January 2015; $1,058, MS-65, January 2015; $541, MS-64, January 2015												

STANDING LIBERTY (1916–1930)

Variety 1, No Stars Below Eagle (1916–1917): **Designer:** *Hermon A. MacNeil.*
Weight: *6.25 grams.* **Composition:** *.900 silver, .100 copper (net weight .18084 oz. pure silver).*
Diameter: *24.3 mm.* **Edge:** *Reeded.* **Mints:** *Philadelphia, Denver, and San Francisco.*

Variety 1, No Stars Below Eagle
(1916–1917)

Mintmark location is on the
obverse, at the top left of
the date, for both varieties.

Variety 2, Stars Below Eagle (1917–1930): **Designer:** *Hermon A. MacNeil.*
Weight: *6.25 grams.* **Composition:** *.900 silver, .100 copper (net weight .18084 oz. pure silver).*
Diameter: *24.3 mm.* **Edge:** *Reeded.* **Mints:** *Philadelphia, Denver, and San Francisco.*

Variety 2, Stars Below Eagle
(1917–1930)

History. The Standing Liberty quarter dollar, designed by sculptor Hermon A. MacNeil (whose initial, M, is located above and to the right of the date), was greeted with wide acclaimed from its first appearance. All of 1916 and many of 1917 are of the Variety 1 design, with the right breast of Miss Liberty exposed on the obverse and with no stars below the eagle on the reverse. Variety 2 of the Standing Liberty design was introduced in 1917 and continued to the end of the series. Miss Liberty is clothed in a jacket of chainmail armor, and the reverse is slightly redesigned, with stars below the eagle. These changes came at the suggestion of the designer, Hermon A. MacNeil. The Mint also created a 2016 gold Standing Liberty quarter at a smaller dimension. See page 529.

Striking and Sharpness. Many if not most 1916 quarters are somewhat lightly struck on the head and body of Miss Liberty. The 1917, Variety 1, quarters usually are quite well struck. When light striking is found, it is usually on the higher-relief parts of the head, the right knee (not as obvious), and the rivets on the left side of the shield. The 1917 Philadelphia Mint coins are usually sharper than the other varieties of this type. Most coins of the Variety 2 design have areas of light striking. On the obverse these are most notable on the head of Miss Liberty and on the shield, the latter often with the two lower-left rivets weak or missing and with the center emblem on the shield weak. The center of the standing figure can be weak as well, as can the upper-left area at and near the date. After 1924 the date was slightly recessed, eliminating that problem. On the reverse, check the eagle's breast. A misleading term, Full Head (FH), is widely used to describe quarters that have only *partial* head details; such coins often actually have the two lower-left shield rivets poorly struck or not visible at all. Most third-party grading services define these criteria for "Full Head" designation (in order of importance): a full, unbroken hairline from Liberty's brow down to the jawline; all three leaves on the head showing; and a visible ear hole.

Availability. The 1916 quarter is the key to the series. Examples tend to be liberally graded in the real-life marketplace, especially in EF and AU, this in contrast to more careful grading for the less valuable 1917 issues. Circulated coins of 1916 and 1917 often have the date worn partly away, due to the high position of this feature in the design. Among Variety 2 coins, the 1918-S, 8 Over 7, is recognized as the key issue, and the 1919-D, 1921, 1923-S, and 1927-S as quite scarce. MS coins are readily available for most issues, but Full Details coins can be *extreme* rarities. Circulated coins dated from 1917 through 1924 often have the date worn partly away, due to the high position of this feature in the design. On MS coins the luster usually is rich and attractive. No Proof coins of this type were officially issued, but specimen strikings dated 1917 are known to exist.

GRADING STANDARDS

MS-60 to 70 (Mint State). *Obverse:* At MS-60 some abrasion and contact marks are evident on the higher areas, which are also the areas most likely to be weakly struck. This includes the rivets on the shield to the left and the central escutcheon on the shield, the head, and the right leg of Miss Liberty. The luster may not be complete in those areas on weakly struck coins, even those certified above MS-65—the *original planchet surface*

1919. Graded MS-65FH.

may be revealed as it was not smoothed out by striking. Accordingly, grading is best done by evaluating abrasion and mint luster as it is observed. Luster may be dull or lifeless at MS–60 to 62 but should have deep frost at MS-63 or better, particularly in the lower-relief areas. At MS-65 or better, it should be full and rich. *Reverse:* Striking is usually quite good, permitting observation of luster in all areas. Check the eagle's breast and the surface of the right wing. Luster may be dull or lifeless at MS–60 to 62 but should have deep frost at MS-63 or better, particularly in the lower-relief areas. At MS-65 or better, it should be full and rich.

   Illustrated coin: See the subtle notes of gold, blue, and pink on this lustrous example.

AU-50, 53, 55, 58 (About Uncirculated). *Obverse:* Light wear is seen on the figure of Miss Liberty, especially noticeable around her midriff and right knee. The shield shows wear, as does the highest part of the sash where it crosses Miss Liberty's waist. At AU-58 the luster is extensive, but incomplete on the higher areas, although it should be nearly full in the panels of the parapet to the left and right, and in the upper field. At AU–50 and 53, luster is

1917-S, Variety 1. Graded AU-53.

less. *Reverse:* Wear is most evident on the eagle's breast, the edges of both wings, and the interior area of the right wing. Luster is nearly complete at AU-58, but at AU-50, half or more is gone.

EF-40, 45 (Extremely Fine). *Obverse:* Wear is more extensive, with the higher parts of Miss Liberty now without detail and the front of the right leg flat. The shield is worn. On coins dated from 1917 to 1924 the date shows wear at the top (on those of 1925 to 1930, with the date recessed, the numbers are bold). Little or no luster is seen, except perhaps among the letters. *Reverse:* The eagle shows more wear, with the surface of the right wing being mostly flat. Little or no luster is evident.

1927-S. Graded EF-45.

VF-20, 30 (Very Fine). *Obverse:* Wear is more extensive. The higher-relief areas of Miss Liberty are flat, and the sash crossing her waist is mostly blended into it (some sharply struck pieces being exceptions). The left side of the shield is mostly flat, although its outline can be seen. On quarters dated 1917 to 1924 the top of the date shows more wear. *Reverse:* The eagle shows further wear, with the body blending into the wing above

1919-S. Graded VF-20.

it. Much feather detail is gone from the wing to the left (on quarters dated 1925 to 1930; less so for those dated 1917 to 1924). Most detail is gone from the right wing.

F-12, 15 (Fine). *Obverse:* Miss Liberty is worn nearly flat. Most detail in her gown is gone, except to the left of her leg and below her knee to the right. The stars on the parapet are well worn, with some indistinct. The top of the date is weak. Quarters of the rare 1916 date are slightly weaker than those of 1917 in this and lower grades. On quarters of 1917 to 1924 the top of the date is weak. On those dated 1925 to 1930 the date remains strong.

1917-D. Graded F-12.

Reverse: The eagle shows further wear, this being greater on 1925 to 1930 issues than on the earlier dates.

VG-8, 10 (Very Good). *Obverse:* The obverse is worn further, with fewer details in the skirt, and part of the shield border to the left blended into the standing figure. The date is partially worn away at the top, and quarters from 1917 to 1924 have less detail. Those from 1925 to 1930 retain more detail, and the date is full. *Reverse:* The eagle is worn further, with only about a third of the feathers now discernible, these mostly on the wing to the left.

1921. Graded VG-10.

G-4, 6 (Good). *Obverse:* The wear is more extensive. Most coins have the stars missing, the standing figure flat, and much of the date worn away, although still clearly identifiable. Quarters of 1925 to 1930 show more detail and the date is clear. *Reverse:* The eagle is mostly in outline form, with only a few feather details visible. The rim is worn into the letters, and on quarters of 1916 to 1924, E PLURIBUS UNUM is very faint; it is clear on quarters of later dates.

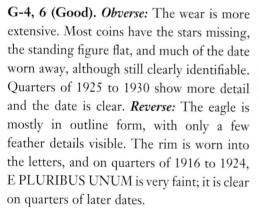

1927-S. Graded G-6.

AG-3 (About Good). *Obverse:* The obverse is worn nearly smooth, and the date is mostly gone. On some coins just one or two digits are seen. Fortunately, those digits are usually on the right, such as a trace of just a 6, which will identify the coin as a 1916. On quarters of 1925 to 1930 the wear is more extensive than for G-4, but most features are discernible and the date is clear. *Reverse:* The eagle is flat, and the border is worn down further.

1921. Graded AG-3.

On quarters of 1916 to 1924, E PLURIBUS UNUM is extremely faint or even missing in areas; it remains readable on quarters of later dates.

Full Head Details, Variety 1
Note the excellently defined cheek, facial features, and wreath.

Full Head Details, Variety 2
Note the full unbroken hairline from brow to neck, all three leaves clearly visible in Liberty's cap, and a visible ear hole.

Pedestal Date (1917–1924)

Recessed Date (1925–1930)

1918-S, 8 Over 7
FS-25-1918S-101.

	Mintage	Cert	Avg	%MS	G-4	VG-8	F-12	VF-20	EF-40	AU-50	MS-60	MS-63	MS-65FH
1916 †	52,000	938	44.1	47%	$3,000	$4,750	$6,000	$7,000	$9,000	$11,000	$12,500	$15,000	$35,000
	Auctions: $146,875, MS-67FH, January 2015; $52,875, MS-66FH, January 2015; $35,250, MS-66FH, May 2016; $18,800, MS-64FH, October 2015												
1917, Variety 1	8,740,000	7,504	58.5	75%	$25	$45	$50	$80	$110	$150	$225	$325	$900
	Auctions: $4,465, MS-67FH, August 2015; $8,225, MS-66FH, October 2015; $1,821, MS-65FH, January 2015; $646, MS-64FH, February 2015												
1917-D, Variety 1	1,509,200	2,105	57.9	69%	$30	$75	$95	$125	$175	$225	$300	$375	$1,350
	Auctions: $2,585, MS-67, July 2015; $2,585, MS-66FH, August 2015; $3,055, MS-65FH, February 2015; $1,058, MS-64FH, January 2015												
1917-S, Variety 1	1,952,000	1,363	52.1	59%	$35	$85	$115	$150	$200	$275	$350	$425	$2,500
	Auctions: $5,405, MS-66FH, February 2015; $2,703, MS-65FH, June 2015; $705, MS-64FH, June 2015; $364, MS-63, January 2015												
1917, Variety 2	13,880,000	1,731	59.5	73%	$20	$32	$45	$55	$75	$110	$150	$275	$950
	Auctions: $2,585, MS-67, January 2015; $3,525, MS-66FH, February 2015; $1,998, MS-65FH, August 2015; $353, MS-64, October 2015												
1917-D, Variety 2	6,224,400	947	57.4	63%	$30	$45	$65	$90	$110	$185	$225	$300	$2,500
	Auctions: $5,875, MS-66FH, October 2015; $3,995, MS-65FH, August 2015; $1,880, MS-64FH, August 2015; $646, MS-63, August 2015												
1917-S, Variety 2	5,552,000	884	57.9	65%	$35	$50	$75	$105	$125	$200	$235	$325	$3,000
	Auctions: $4,935, MS-66FH, February 2015; $3,525, MS-65FH, August 2015; $1,410, MS-66, October 2015; $400, MS-64, October 2015												
1918	14,240,000	1,016	59.6	70%	$20	$25	$30	$35	$55	$95	$150	$250	$2,000
	Auctions: $3,525, MS-67, June 2015; $7,638, MS-66FH, August 2015; $1,543, MS-65FH, August 2015; $282, MS-63, November 2015												
1918-D	7,380,000	851	56.5	57%	$22	$30	$60	$75	$120	$150	$200	$360	$3,500
	Auctions: $5,405, MS-66FH, June 2015; $8,813, MS-65FH, February 2015; $646, MS-64, August 2015; $282, MS-62, January 2015												
1918-S	11,072,000	1,418	51.0	49%	$20	$25	$35	$45	$60	$120	$180	$300	$11,500
	Auctions: $27,025, MS-67FH, August 2015; $22,325, MS-66FH, October 2015; $21,150, MS-65FH, May 2015; $2,350, MS-64FH, February 2015												
1918-S, 8 Over 7 † (a)	(b)	336	39.1	17%	$1,600	$2,200	$3,500	$4,500	$7,500	$10,000	$17,500	$27,500	$250,000
	Auctions: $188,000, MS-64FH, June 2014; $23,500, MS-64, August 2016; $24,675, AU-58FH, July 2014; $17,625, AU-58, January 2015												
1919	11,324,000	1,218	59.6	72%	$25	$40	$55	$65	$80	$105	$150	$210	$1,650
	Auctions: $8,520, MS-67FH, August 2015; $1,058, MS-66, August 2015; $1,939, MS-65FH, August 2015; $1,293, MS-64FH, August 2015												
1919-D	1,944,000	547	44.9	34%	$75	$125	$200	$350	$550	$700	$1,200	$1,800	$45,000
	Auctions: $6,463, MS-66, August 2015; $49,350, MS-65FH, August 2015; $18,800, MS-64FH, August 2015; $2,585, MS-63, June 2015												
1919-S	1,836,000	569	45.3	30%	$75	$115	$160	$300	$500	$600	$1,000	$2,000	$37,500
	Auctions: $6,463, MS-66, August 2015; $24,675, MS-64FH, June 2015; $1,880, MS-63, January 2015; $881, AU-58, October 2015												

† Ranked in the *100 Greatest U.S. Coins* (fifth edition). **a.** This clear overdate was caused by the use of two differently dated hubs when the die was made. From the *Cherrypickers' Guide to Rare Die Varieties, Vol. II* (sixth edition): "Because of the boldness of the 7, this variety can be confirmed easily in low grades. . . . This variety is extremely rare in high grades. We recommend authentication because alterations do exist. Genuine specimens have a small die chip above the pedestal, just to the left of the lowest star on the right." **b.** Included in 1918-S mintage figure.

	Mintage	Cert	Avg	%MS	G-4	VG-8	F-12	VF-20	EF-40	AU-50	MS-60	MS-63	MS-65FH
1920	27,860,000	1,930	60.1	74%	$12	$16	$25	$30	$45	$75	$125	$210	$1,450
Auctions: $9,400, MS-67, January 2015; $1,528, MS-66, February 2015; $3,290, MS-65FH, August 2015; $470, MS-64FH, October 2015													
1920-D	3,586,400	478	51.2	48%	$85	$115	$150	$175	$200	$285	$550	$1,000	$8,500
Auctions: $10,575, MS-67, June 2015; $16,450, MS-66FH, October 2015; $4,465, MS-64FH, February 2015; $999, MS-64, March 2015													
1920-S	6,380,000	641	56.9	60%	$20	$25	$35	$50	$70	$150	$275	$700	$22,500
Auctions: $8,813, MS-66, February 2015; $1,880, MS-65, August 2015; $4,818, MS-64FH, January 2015; $646, MS-63, October 2015													
1921	1,916,000	1,255	41.2	36%	$150	$250	$385	$550	$700	$900	$1,200	$1,900	$8,000
Auctions: $18,800, MS-66FH, May 2015; $6,463, MS-66, February 2015; $2,820, MS-65, October 2015; $3,055, MS-64FH, January 2015													
1923	9,716,000	1,725	60.7	79%	$12	$18	$25	$35	$45	$80	$150	$200	$2,750
Auctions: $2,350, MS-67, February 2015; $4,465, MS-65FH, August 2015; $329, MS-64, June 2015; $306, MS-62FH, February 2015													
1923-S	1,360,000	907	45.5	37%	$250	$350	$625	$875	$1,200	$1,700	$2,100	$3,000	$6,500
Auctions: $18,213, MS-66, September 2016; $4,935, MS-66, August 2015; $5,405, MS-65, November 2016; $3,290, MS-64, January 2015													
1924	10,920,000	1,264	59.8	76%	$12	$16	$22	$35	$45	$80	$150	$225	$1,200
Auctions: $20,563, MS-68, January 2015; $14,100, MS-67FH, October 2015; $2,820, MS-66FH, June 2015; $470, MS-65, March 2015													
1924-D	3,112,000	1,664	61.6	85%	$40	$45	$70	$110	$160	$195	$240	$350	$3,750
Auctions: $999, MS-67, September 2015; $18,800, MS-66FH, March 2015; $4,700, MS-65FH, August 2015; $364, MS-64, November 2015													
1924-S	2,860,000	657	57.1	65%	$18	$28	$35	$55	$110	$225	$300	$800	$5,500
Auctions: $3,760, MS-66, July 2015; $5,875, MS-65FH, March 2015; $1,116, MS-64, September 2015; $1,058, MS-63FH, August 2015													
1925	12,280,000	1,361	60.3	79%	$6	$8	$10	$20	$40	$70	$130	$200	$800
Auctions: $3,055, MS-67, August 2015; $5,405, MS-66FH, May 2015; $1,116, MS-65FH, August 2015; $235, MS-64, July 2015													
1926	11,316,000	1,409	60.9	78%	$6	$8	$9	$20	$40	$70	$130	$150	$1,200
Auctions: $3,760, MS-67, September 2015; $2,585, MS-66FH, October 2015; $353, MS-65, March 2015; $646, MS-64FH, October 2015													
1926-D	1,716,000	2,392	62.8	95%	$8	$11	$24	$38	$70	$110	$150	$225	$23,000
Auctions: $564, MS-66, January 2015; $400, MS-65, December 2015; $447, MS-64, November 2015; $270, MS-63, August 2015													
1926-S	2,700,000	501	53.0	54%	$6	$9	$15	$28	$90	$150	$375	$800	$30,000
Auctions: $4,700, MS-66, August 2015; $17,625, MS-65FH, January 2015; $2,350, MS-65, September 2016; $1,528, MS-64, October 2016													
1927	11,912,000	1,706	59.6	73%	$6	$8	$9	$17	$35	$70	$130	$200	$800
Auctions: $2,820, MS-67, August 2015; $7,050, MS-66FH, August 2015; $447, MS-65, August 2015; $764, MS-64FH, March 2015													
1927-D	976,000	1,073	59.1	84%	$15	$20	$30	$75	$140	$190	$225	$330	$2,250
Auctions: $6,463, MS-66FH, June 2015; $793, MS-66, August 2015; $2,585, MS-65FH, August 2015; $353, MS-64, May 2015													
1927-S	396,000	1,432	24.2	10%	$35	$45	$110	$325	$1,000	$2,250	$4,750	$7,000	$175,000
Auctions: $11,750, MS-66, August 2016; $9,988, MS-65, September 2016; $28,200, MS-64, November 2016; $6,463, MS-63, August 2016													
1928	6,336,000	1,093	60.6	78%	$6	$8	$9	$17	$35	$65	$120	$175	$1,400
Auctions: $1,058, MS-67, January 2015; $3,525, MS-66FH, September 2015; $1,410, MS-65FH, August 2015; $306, MS-64, June 2015													
1928-D	1,627,600	1,538	62.8	91%	$6	$8	$9	$17	$35	$65	$120	$175	$4,500
Auctions: $517, MS-66, January 2015; $423, MS-65, March 2015; $353, MS-64, July 2015; $223, MS-63, February 2015													
1928-S (c)	2,644,000	1,600	61.6	86%	$6	$8	$9	$22	$40	$70	$120	$190	$1,000
Auctions: $4,700, MS-67FH, January 2015; $1,410, MS-66, February 2015; $1,293, MS-65FH, October 2015; $400, MS-64, November 2015													
1929	11,140,000	2,059	60.8	78%	$6	$8	$9	$17	$35	$65	$120	$175	$700
Auctions: $1,528, MS-66FH, February 2015; $646, MS-65FH, August 2015; $423, MS-64FH, October 2015; $235, MS-64, April 2015													
1929-D	1,358,000	1,105	60.2	73%	$6	$8	$10	$17	$35	$65	$120	$175	$5,000
Auctions: $5,405, MS-67, July 2015; $1,116, MS-66, February 2015; $423, MS-65, November 2015; $329, MS-64, October 2015													
1929-S	1,764,000	1,519	60.9	81%	$6	$8	$9	$17	$35	$65	$120	$175	$700
Auctions: $4,935, MS-67FH, February 2015; $1,381, MS-66FH, July 2015; $353, MS-65, October 2015; $235, MS-64, May 2015													
1930	5,632,000	3,946	61.2	75%	$6	$8	$9	$17	$35	$65	$120	$175	$675
Auctions: $2,820, MS-67, February 2015; $1,175, MS-66FH, January 2015; $734, MS-65FH, August 2015; $423, MS-64FH, May 2015													
1930-S	1,556,000	1,165	61.2	82%	$6	$8	$10	$17	$35	$65	$120	$175	$700
Auctions: $2,820, MS-67FH, January 2015; $793, MS-66, January 2015; $494, MS-65, March 2015; $365, MS-64FH, August 2015													

c. Large and small mintmarks exist; their values are the same.

WASHINGTON, EAGLE REVERSE (1932–1998)

Designer: *John Flanagan.* **Weight:** *Silver issue—6.25 grams; clad issue—5.67 grams; silver Proofs—6.25 grams.* **Composition:** *Silver issue—.900 silver, .100 copper (net weight .18084 oz. pure silver); clad issue—outer layers of copper nickel (.750 copper, .250 nickel) bonded to inner core of pure copper; silver Proofs—.900 silver, .100 copper (net weight .18084 oz. pure silver).* **Diameter:** *24.3 mm.* **Edge:** *Reeded.* **Mints:** *Philadelphia, Denver, and San Francisco.*

Circulation Strike   Proof

Mintmark location, 1932–1964, is on the reverse, below the eagle.   *Mintmark location, 1965 to date, is on the obverse, to the right of the hair ribbon.*

Bicentennial variety: **Designers:** *John Flanagan and Jack L. Ahr.* **Weight:** *Silver issue— 5.75 grams; copper-nickel issue—5.67 grams.* **Composition:** *Silver issue—outer layers of .800 silver, .200 copper bonded to inner core of .209 silver, .791 copper (net weight .0739 oz. pure silver); copper-nickel issue—outer layers of .750 copper, .250 nickel bonded to inner core of pure copper.* **Diameter:** *24.3 mm.* **Edge:** *Reeded.* **Mints:** *Philadelphia, Denver, and San Francisco.*

Bicentennial variety   Bicentennial variety, Proof

History. The Washington quarter, designed by New York sculptor John Flanagan, originally was intended to be a commemorative coin, but it ultimately was produced as a regular circulation issue. The obverse is inspired by a famous bust by Jean Antoine Houdon. Flanagan's initials, JF, are at the base of Washington's neck. The reverse features a modernistic eagle perched on a quiver of arrows, with wings unfolding. In October 1973, the Treasury Department announced an open contest for the selection of suitable designs for the Bicentennial reverses of the quarter, half dollar, and dollar, with $5,000 to be awarded to each winner. Twelve semifinalists were chosen, and from these the symbolic entry of Jack L. Ahr was selected for the quarter reverse. It features a military drummer facing left, with a victory torch encircled by 13 stars at the upper left. Except for the dual dating, "1776–1976," the obverse remained unchanged. Pieces with this dual dating were coined during 1975 and 1976. They were struck for general circulation and included in all the U.S. Mint's offerings of Proof and Uncirculated coin sets. (The grading instructions below are for the regular Eagle Reverse variety.)

Striking and Sharpness. The relief of both sides of the Washington quarter issues from 1932 to 1998 is shallow. Accordingly, any lightness of strike is not easily seen. Nearly all are well struck. On all quarters of 1932 and some of 1934, the motto IN GOD WE TRUST is light, as per the design. It was strengthened in 1934.

Availability. The 1932-D and -S are key issues but not rarities. All others are readily available in high grades, but some are scarcer than others. Proof dates available are 1936 to 1942 and 1950 to 1964 (from the Philadelphia Mint) and 1968 to 1998 (from San Francisco). Certain later Proofs are available in clad metal as well as silver strikings. Special Mint Set (SMS) coins were struck in lieu of Proofs from 1965 to 1967; these in some instances closely resemble Proofs. The majority of Proofs made in recent decades are in high levels, PF–66 to 68 or higher.

Note: Values of common-date silver coins have been based on the current bullion price of silver, $27.50 per ounce, and may vary with the prevailing spot price.

GRADING STANDARDS

MS-60 to 70 (Mint State). *Obverse:* At MS-60, some abrasion and contact marks are evident on the hair above the ear and at the top of the head below the E of LIBERTY. At MS-63, abrasion is slight at best, less so for MS-64. An MS-65 coin should display no abrasion or contact marks except under magnification, and MS-66 and higher coins should have none at all. Luster should be full and rich. *Reverse:* Comments apply as for the

1939-D. Graded MS-64.

obverse, except that the eagle's breast and legs are the places to check. On both sides the fields are protected by design elements and do not show contact marks readily.

AU-50, 53, 55, 58 (About Uncirculated). *Obverse:* Light wear is seen on the cheek, the high areas of the hair, and the neck. At AU-58, the luster is extensive but incomplete, especially on the higher parts and in the field. At AU–50 and 53, luster is less. *Reverse:* Light wear is seen on the breast, legs, and upper edges of the wings of the eagle. An AU-58 coin has nearly full luster. At AU–50 and 53, there still is significant luster.

1932-S. Graded AU-55.

EF-40, 45 (Extremely Fine). *Obverse:* Further wear is seen on the head. Higher-relief details are gone in the hair. The higher-relief parts of the neck show wear, most noticeably just above the date. *Reverse:* Further wear is seen on the eagle. Most breast feathers, not strong to begin with, are worn away.

1932-D. Graded EF-40.

VF-20, 30 (Very Fine). *Obverse:* Most hair detail is worn away, except above the curls. The delineation between the temple and the edge of the hair is faint. The curl by the ear is worn flat. Tips of the letters in LIBERTY and the date digits touch the rim in some instances. *Reverse:* More details of the eagle are worn away, and the outlines of the feathers in the wing, while nearly all present, are faint. Tips of the letters touch the rim in some instances on this and lower grades, but this can vary from coin to coin depending on the strength of the rim.

1942-D, Doubled Die Obverse;
FS-25-1942D-101. Graded VF-30.

F-12, 15 (Fine). *Obverse:* Most of the hair is worn flat, with no distinction between the face and the beginning of the hair. There is some detail remaining just above and below the curls. *Reverse:* More feathers are worn away. The end of the branch at the left is worn so as to blend into the wing. The edge of the rim is barely visible and in some areas is worn away. (In this and the Very Good grade, opinions concerning the rim vary in the ANA grading standards and in *Photograde*; PCGS is silent on the matter.)

1932-D. Graded F-12.

VG-8, 10 (Very Good). *Obverse:* Further wear is seen on the head, with most of the upper part of the curls now blending into the hair above. *Reverse:* The rim is worn into the tops of the letters. There is no detail on the leaves. About half of the feathers are outlined, but only faintly.

1932-S. Graded VG-10.

G-4, 6 (Good). *Obverse:* Further wear is seen in all areas. On 1932 and some 1934 coins the IN GOD WE TRUST motto is so worn that some letters are missing. *Reverse:* The rim is worn further into the letters. Fewer details are seen on the eagle's wing. On both sides the coin appears to be "worn flat," with little in relief.

1932-D. Graded G-4.

AG-3 (About Good). *Obverse:* Wear is more extensive, with about half of the letters gone. *Reverse:* Wear is more extensive, with about half of the letters gone. Slight detail remains in the eagle's wings. The mintmark, if any, is very clear.

1942. Graded AG-3.

PF-60 to 70 (Proof). *Obverse and Reverse:* Proofs that are extensively cleaned and have many hairlines, or that are dull and grainy, are lower level, such as PF-60 to 62. These are not widely desired, and represent coins that have been mistreated. Most low-level Proofs are of the 1936 to 1942 dates. With medium hairlines and good reflectivity, assigned grades of PF-63 or 64 are appropriate. PF-66 should have hairlines so delicate that magnification is needed to see them. Above that, a Proof should be free of any hairlines or other problems.

1974-S. Graded PF-70 Deep Cameo.

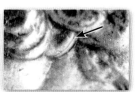

1932, Doubled Die Obverse
FS-25-1932-101.

	Mintage	Cert	Avg	%MS	VG-8	F-12	VF-20	EF-40	AU-50	MS-60	MS-62	MS-63	MS-65
1932	5,404,000	2,306	62.0	83%	$8	$10	$12	$14	$16	$25	$40	$60	$275
Auctions: $8,813, MS-67, June 2015; $1,763, MS-66, January 2015; $505, MS-65, January 2015; $64, MS-64, February 2015													
1932, DblDie Obv (a)	(b)	27	57.3	33%						$350	$400	$500	$1,000
Auctions: $235, MS-62, December 2013													
1932-D	436,800	4,563	38.1	24%	$90	$100	$135	$175	$300	$1,000	$1,200	$1,450	$7,500
Auctions: $74,400, MS-66, January 2018; $18,000, MS-65, January 2018; $4,800, MS-65, February 2018; $1,560, MS-64, January 2018													
1932-S	408,000	5,540	45.0	36%	$85	$95	$115	$135	$200	$400	$500	$600	$2,500
Auctions: $1,800, MS-65, March 2018; $780, MS-64, February 2018; $432, MS-63, January 2018; $210, AU-58, January 2018													

a. The doubling is evident on the earlobe, the nostril, and the braid of hair. **b.** Included in 1932 mintage figure.

1934, Doubled Die Obverse
FS-25-1934-101.

1934, Light Motto
FS-25-1934-401.

1934, Heavy Motto
FS-25-1934-403.

	Mintage	Cert	Avg	%MS	VG-8	F-12	VF-20	EF-40	AU-50	MS-60	MS-62	MS-63	MS-65
1934, All kinds	31,912,052												
1934, Doubled Die Obverse (c)		223	38.4	25%	$55	$85	$150	$225	$600	$1,000	$1,350	$1,700	$3,250
Auctions: $306, AU-55, May 2015; $329, AU-50, May 2015; $129, F-12, February 2015													
1934, Light Motto (d)		326	63.2	88%	$7	$8	$9	$10	$24	$60	$80	$135	$200
Auctions: $447, MS-66, August 2015; $259, MS-66, July 2015; $235, MS-65, January 2015; $176, MS-64, January 2015													
1934, Heavy Motto (e)		71	62.4	80%	$7	$8	$9	$10	$15	$30	$40	$50	$165
Auctions: $470, MS-66, September 2014; $100, MS-65, May 2015; $88, MS-65, August 2014; $118, MS-64, July 2014													
1934-D	3,527,200	1,523	60.8	74%	$7	$8	$12	$25	$85	$250	$280	$340	$475
Auctions: $1,058, MS-66, January 2015; $646, MS-65, June 2015; $447, MS-64, July 2015; $165, AU-55, October 2015													
1935	32,484,000	2,191	64.3	93%	$7	$8	$9	$11	$14	$22	$30	$35	$70
Auctions: $2,820, MS-67, January 2015; $2,115, MS-67, September 2015; $147, MS-66, August 2015; $69, MS-65, June 2015													
1935-D	5,780,000	1,388	61.3	78%	$7	$8	$10	$20	$125	$240	$265	$275	$425
Auctions: $517, MS-66, January 2015; $306, MS-64, August 2015; $213, MS-62, August 2015; $141, AU-58, October 2015													
1935-S	5,660,000	1,571	62.3	81%	$7	$8	$10	$15	$38	$100	$120	$135	$215
Auctions: $999, MS-67, January 2015; $282, MS-65, May 2015; $141, MS-64, September 2015; $79, MS-62, March 2015													

c. Very strong doubling is visible on the motto, LIBERTY, and the date. **d.** From the *Cherrypickers' Guide to Rare Die Varieties, Vol. II* (sixth edition): "Notice the considerable weakness in the letters of the motto. In addition, the center point of the W is pointed." **e.** The motto has very thick letters, and the central apex of the W is pointed, rising slightly above the other letters.

1937, Doubled Die Obverse
FS-25-1937-101.

	Mintage	Cert	Avg	%MS	EF-40	AU-50	MS-60	MS-63	MS-65 PF-64	MS-66 PF-65	MS-67 PF-67
1936	41,300,000	1,959	64.1	94%	$7	$10	$25	$35	$90	$130	$500
Auctions: $306, MS-67, May 2015; $247, MS-67, October 2015; $89, MS-66, July 2015; $79, MS-65, April 2015											
1936, Proof	3,837	999	64.3						$800	$1,000	$5,750
Auctions: $6,463, PF-67, June 2015; $1,528, PF-66, February 2015; $1,058, PF-65, October 2015; $541, PF-64, January 2015											
1936-D	5,374,000	1,314	60.2	73%	$55	$250	$525	$850	$1,000	$1,250	$3,500
Auctions: $1,528, MS-66, June 2015; $705, MS-64, January 2015; $646, MS-62, February 2015; $429, AU-58, May 2015											
1936-S	3,828,000	1,562	63.5	94%	$15	$50	$120	$140	$235	$350	$950
Auctions: $1,528, MS-67, September 2015; $517, MS-66, October 2015; $188, MS-65, February 2015; $106, MS-64, April 2015											
1937	19,696,000	1,401	62.6	92%	$7	$12	$25	$35	$95	$135	$525
Auctions: $6,463, MS-68, June 2015; $881, MS-67, January 2015; $148, MS-66, September 2015; $74, MS-65, August 2015											
1937, Doubled Die Obverse (a)	(b)	52	25.6	12%	$700	$1,500	$2,450	$3,200	$9,000	$16,000	
Auctions: $1,778, MS-63, April 2013; $494, VF-35, July 2015; $188, F-12, November 2014											
1937, Proof	5,542	1,038	65.1						$325	$425	$800
Auctions: $1,410, PF-67, January 2015; $412, PF-66, November 2015; $306, PF-65, October 2015; $141, PF-62, August 2015											
1937-D	7,189,600	1,301	63.9	94%	$15	$30	$70	$90	$135	$225	$825
Auctions: $1,116, MS-67, August 2015; $235, MS-66, July 2015; $106, MS-65, January 2015; $79, MS-64, July 2015											
1937-S	1,652,000	1,292	63.0	91%	$35	$95	$150	$250	$335	$535	$2,000
Auctions: $705, MS-66, June 2015; $295, MS-65, September 2015; $212, MS-64, May 2015; $200, MS-63, March 2015											

a. Very strong doubling is evident on the motto, LIBERTY, the date, and the end of the braid ribbons. From the *Cherrypickers' Guide to Rare Die Varieties, Vol. II* (sixth edition): "This variety is considered one of the most important in the series." **b.** Included in circulation-strike 1937 mintage figure.

1942-D, Doubled Die Obverse	**1942-D, Doubled Die Reverse**
FS-25-1942D-101.	*FS-25-1942D-801.*

	Mintage	Cert	Avg	%MS	EF-40	AU-50	MS-60	MS-63	MS-65 / PF-64	MS-66 / PF-65	MS-67 / PF-67
1938	9,472,000	1,212	63.4	89%	$15	$45	$95	$110	$190	$250	$675
Auctions: $734, MS-67, October 2015; $494, MS-67, June 2015; $212, MS-66, July 2015; $141, MS-65, January 2015											
1938, Proof	8,045	1,332	65.0						$170	$225	$900
Auctions: $1,058, PF-67, June 2015; $235, PF-66, October 2015; $153, PF-65, May 2015; $94, PF-63, February 2015											
1938-S	2,832,000	1,520	63.9	95%	$20	$55	$105	$140	$155	$275	$650
Auctions: $705, MS-67, August 2015; $188, MS-66, January 2015; $155, MS-65, March 2015; $129, MS-64, September 2015											
1939	33,540,000	2,198	65.0	96%	$7	$10	$15	$25	$60	$100	$225
Auctions: $1,293, MS-68, September 2015; $764, MS-67, June 2015; $64, MS-66, July 2015; $56, MS-65, August 2015											
1939, Proof	8,795	1,318	65.4						$145	$200	$525
Auctions: $3,055, PF-68, September 2015; $517, PF-67, January 2015; $165, PF-66, July 2015; $112, PF-64, February 2015											
1939-D	7,092,000	1,526	64.6	96%	$11	$20	$40	$50	$85	$135	$350
Auctions: $494, MS-67, May 2015; $129, MS-66, August 2015; $74, MS-65, January 2015; $36, MS-63, September 2015											
1939-S	2,628,000	1,265	63.5	91%	$20	$60	$95	$135	$250	$300	$750
Auctions: $764, MS-67, January 2015; $282, MS-66, September 2015; $223, MS-65, February 2015; $100, MS-62, March 2015											
1940	35,704,000	1,566	65.0	96%	$7	$10	$17	$35	$50	$80	$235
Auctions: $15,275, MS-68, January 2015; $705, MS-67, June 2015; $46, MS-66, May 2015; $28, MS-64, November 2015											
1940, Proof	11,246	1,597	65.4						$100	$125	$500
Auctions: $1,821, PF-68, June 2015; $541, PF-67, September 2015; $106, PF-66, January 2015; $100, PF-65, February 2015											
1940-D	2,797,600	1,402	64.0	94%	$24	$65	$120	$165	$250	$365	$900
Auctions: $564, MS-67, June 2015; $353, MS-66, January 2015; $147, MS-64, August 2015; $153, MS-63, February 2015											
1940-S	8,244,000	1,491	65.0	97%	$10	$16	$21	$32	$45	$80	$375
Auctions: $423, MS-67, January 2015; $69, MS-66, April 2015; $50, MS-65, August 2015; $28, MS-64, November 2015											
1941	79,032,000	2,373	65.0	97%	$7	$8	$10	$14	$33	$50	$225
Auctions: $259, MS-67, September 2015; $200, MS-67, January 2015; $38, MS-66, April 2015; $36, MS-65, May 2015											
1941, Proof	15,287	1,956	65.4						$90	$120	$250
Auctions: $329, PF-67, March 2015; $100, PF-66, November 2015; $79, PF-65, January 2015; $72, PF-64, September 2015											
1941-D	16,714,800	1,569	64.9	97%	$8	$14	$32	$55	$65	$110	$550
Auctions: $470, MS-67, June 2015; $112, MS-66, January 2015; $94, MS-66, November 2015; $69, MS-63, September 2015											
1941-S	16,080,000	1,484	64.2	93%	$7	$12	$28	$50	$65	$105	$425
Auctions: $705, MS-67, January 2015; $376, MS-67, October 2015; $106, MS-66, February 2015; $69, MS-65, March 2015											
1942	102,096,000	1,518	64.2	94%	$7	$8	$10	$11	$27	$105	$675
Auctions: $823, MS-67, October 2015; $282, MS-67, January 2015; $141, MS-66, September 2015; $79, MS-66, October 2015											
1942, Proof	21,123	2,446	65.2						$85	$110	$225
Auctions: $10,575, PF-68, June 2015; $235, PF-67, January 2015; $79, PF-65, May 2015; $56, PF-64, December 2015											
1942-D	17,487,200	1,653	63.3	94%	$7	$9	$17	$20	$27	$115	$425
Auctions: $223, MS-67, July 2015; $207, MS-67, January 2015; $69, MS-66, January 2015; $58, MS-66, November 2015											
1942-D, DblDie Obv (c)	(d)	67	30.4	6%	$350	$750	$1,800	$3,500	$7,000	$10,500	
Auctions: $823, MS-64, June 2014; $1,207, AU-55, April 2013; $188, AU-50, August 2014											
1942-D, DblDie Rev (e)	(d)	22	43.8	36%		$385	$500	$700	$1,150	$4,000	
Auctions: $5,875, MS-66, August 2013											
1942-S	19,384,000	1,521	63.7	90%	$12	$20	$70	$115	$150	$200	$525
Auctions: $400, MS-67, January 2015; $235, MS-66, April 2015; $118, MS-65, June 2015; $84, MS-64, September 2015											

c. Doubling is evident, with a very strong spread, on LIBERTY, the date, and the motto. **d.** Included in 1942-D mintage figure.
e. Doubling on this popular variety is most prominent on the eagle's beak, the arrows, and the branch above the mintmark.

1943, Doubled Die Obverse
FS-25-1943-103.
Other varieties exist.

1943-S, Doubled Die Obverse
FS-25-1943S-101.

	Mintage	Cert	Avg	%MS	EF-40	AU-50	MS-60	MS-63	MS-65	MS-66	MS-67
									PF-64	PF-65	PF-67
1943	99,700,000	3,334	64.5	96%	$6	$7	$10	$11	$37	$75	$250
	Auctions: $223, MS-67, September 2015; $165, MS-67, January 2015; $36, MS-66, January 2015										
1943, DblDie Obverse (f)	(g)	15	28.0	7%	$2,500	$3,500	$5,000	$7,500	$12,000	$14,500	
	Auctions: $30, VF-20, March 2012										
1943-D	16,095,600	1,316	65.0	97%	$9	$11	$28	$39	$55	$70	$450
	Auctions: $282, MS-67, August 2015; $217, MS-67, January 2015; $52, MS-66, January 2015; $32, MS-65, February 2015										
1943-S	21,700,000	1,631	62.9	92%	$10	$14	$26	$42	$55	$105	$500
	Auctions: $6,463, MS-68, July 2015; $734, MS-67, January 2015; $89, MS-66, May 2015; $62, MS-66, November 2015										
1943-S, DblDie Obv (h)	(i)	134	42.3	43%	$200	$350	$500	$1,000	$1,650	$3,800	$7,500
	Auctions: $1,293, MS-64, August 2015; $1,528, MS-64, June 2015; $705, MS-64, January 2015; $79, EF-40, August 2015										
1944	104,956,000	2,605	65.3	98%	$6	$7	$9	$10	$26	$48	$300
	Auctions: $282, MS-67, October 2015; $165, MS-67, July 2015; $36, MS-66, August 2015										
1944-D	14,600,800	2,197	65.6	99%	$6	$10	$17	$20	$37	$70	$275
	Auctions: $10,575, MS-68, August 2015; $235, MS-67, September 2015; $165, MS-67, January 2015; $50, MS-66, April 2015										
1944-S	12,560,000	2,209	65.6	99%	$6	$10	$14	$20	$30	$57	$225
	Auctions: $317, MS-67, February 2015; $176, MS-67, September 2015; $48, MS-66, August 2015; $129, MS-65, April 2015										
1945	74,372,000	1,922	64.9	98%	$6	$7	$9	$10	$33	$80	$500
	Auctions: $16,450, MS-68, January 2015; $2,350, MS-68, October 2015; $329, MS-67, August 2015; $58, MS-66, January 2015										
1945-D	12,341,600	1,480	65.3	99%	$6	$10	$18	$25	$40	$50	$575
	Auctions: $364, MS-67, September 2015; $329, MS-67, May 2015; $42, MS-64, April 2015										
1945-S	17,004,001	1,939	65.3	99%	$6	$7	$9	$13	$33	$75	$400
	Auctions: $353, MS-67, October 2015; $236, MS-67, May 2015; $69, MS-66, July 2015; $54, MS-66, May 2015										
1946	53,436,000	1,269	65.1	98%	$6	$7	$9	$10	$35	$80	$850
	Auctions: $353, MS-67, September 2015; $306, MS-67, July 2015; $74, MS-66, January 2015; $20, MS-64, September 2015										
1946-D	9,072,800	2,951	65.5	100%	$6	$7	$9	$10	$33	$42	$200
	Auctions: $306, MS-67, November 2015; $165, MS-67, January 2015; $34, MS-65, September 2015										
1946-S	4,204,000	7,093	65.5	100%	$6	$7	$9	$10	$30	$55	$350
	Auctions: $235, MS-67, March 2015; $223, MS-67, November 2015; $58, MS-66, October 2015; $46, MS-66, August 2015										
1947	22,556,000	1,908	65.4	99%	$6	$7	$11	$19	$32	$65	$265
	Auctions: $176, MS-67, August 2015; $153, MS-67, October 2015; $56, MS-66, September 2015										
1947-D	15,338,400	3,005	65.6	100%	$6	$7	$11	$17	$32	$42	$150
	Auctions: $147, MS-67, December 2015; $84, MS-67, May 2015; $52, MS-66, July 2015; $38, MS-65, April 2015										
1947-S	5,532,000	5,477	65.7	100%	$6	$7	$9	$15	$25	$38	$200
	Auctions: $646, MS-68, September 2015; $165, MS-67, December 2015; $40, MS-66, May 2015; $21, MS-65, July 2015										
1948	35,196,000	2,711	65.4	99%	$6	$7	$9	$10	$24	$42	$185
	Auctions: $135, MS-67, November 2015; $112, MS-67, January 2015; $69, MS-66, May 2015; $52, MS-66, October 2015										
1948-D	16,766,800	2,197	65.2	99%	$6	$7	$13	$18	$45	$65	$500
	Auctions: $2,585, MS-67, January 2015; $74, MS-66, February 2015; $52, MS-66, September 2015; $46, MS-65, May 2015										
1948-S	15,960,000	3,170	65.4	99%	$6	$7	$9	$10	$37	$70	$300
	Auctions: $153, MS-67, November 2015; $118, MS-67, January 2015; $129, MS-66, February 2015; $74, MS-66, October 2015										

f. Doubling is very strong on the motto, LIBERTY, and the date. **g.** Included in 1943 mintage figure. **h.** Very strong doubling is visible on the motto, LIBERTY, the designer's initials, and the date. From the *Cherrypickers' Guide to Rare Die Varieties, Vol. II* (sixth edition): "Values for this variety are generally firm, but do change with market conditions and demand fluctuations." **i.** Included in 1943-S mintage figure.

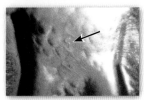

1950-D, D Over S
FS-25-1950D-601.
Other varieties exist.

1950-S, S Over D
FS-25-1950S-601.

1952, Die Damage, Proof
"Superbird" variety.
FS-25-1952-901.

	Mintage	Cert	Avg	%MS	EF-40	AU-50	MS-60	MS-63	MS-65 / PF-64	MS-66 / PF-65	MS-67 / PF-67
1949	9,312,000	1,714	65.1	98%	$11	$14	$35	$47	$65	$95	$275
	Auctions: $329, MS-67, August 2015; $282, MS-67, January 2015; $84, MS-66, April 2015; $74, MS-66, October 2015										
1949-D	10,068,400	1,795	65.2	99%	$6	$10	$16	$38	$55	$85	$235
	Auctions: $4,700, MS-68, September 2015; $223, MS-67, July 2015; $74, MS-66, January 2015; $74, MS-65, August 2015										
1950	24,920,126	1,693	65.4	99%	$6	$7	$9	$10	$32	$55	$315
	Auctions: $529, MS-67, September 2014; $282, MS-67, September 2015; $223, MS-67, January 2015; $52, MS-66, February 2015										
1950, Proof	51,386	2,565	66.0						$60	$65	$135
	Auctions: $881, PF-67Cam, January 2015; $106, PF-67, August 2015; $317, PF-66Cam, May 2015; $42, PF-66, August 2015										
1950-D	21,075,600	1,959	63.2	91%	$6	$7	$9	$10	$34	$65	$225
	Auctions: $206, MS-67, November 2015; $170, MS-67, May 2015; $56, MS-66, October 2015										
1950-D, D Over S (j)	(k)	153	46.7	26%	$150	$250	$350	$550	$2,900	$6,750	
	Auctions: $2,585, MS-64, July 2015; $400, MS-62, December 2015; $176, AU-58, June 2015; $100, EF-45, August 2015										
1950-S	10,284,004	2,019	63.7	92%	$6	$7	$12	$16	$35	$58	$265
	Auctions: $259, MS-67, September 2015; $235, MS-67, January 2015; $106, MS-66, September 2015; $74, MS-66, April 2015										
1950-S, S Over D (l)	(m)	120	50.5	50%	$150	$250	$350	$500	$1,150	$1,650	$6,000
	Auctions: $1,880, MS-66, September 2015; $705, MS-65, June 2015; $588, MS-64, February 2015; $306, AU-58, May 2015										
1951	43,448,102	1,887	65.3	98%	$6	$7	$9	$10	$26	$50	$235
	Auctions: $450, MS-67, September 2014; $282, MS-67, September 2014; $206, MS-67, November 2015; $176, MS-67, January 2015										
1951, Proof	57,500	2,542	66.1						$55	$65	$110
	Auctions: $1,645, PF-68Cam, June 2015; $1,293, PF-68Cam, June 2015; $1,234, PF-68Cam, November 2014; $176, PF-66Cam, February 2015										
1951-D	35,354,800	1,989	65.3	99%	$6	$7	$9	$10	$32	$55	$285
	Auctions: $284, MS-67, March 2015; $235, MS-67, July 2015; $76, MS-66, March 2015; $66, MS-66, October 2015										
1951-S	9,048,000	1,974	65.7	100%	$6	$7	$11	$15	$35	$70	$145
	Auctions: $2,115, MS-68, September 2015; $229, MS-67, February 2015; $176, MS-67, September 2015; $79, MS-66, February 2015										
1952	38,780,093	1,421	65.4	99%	$6	$7	$9	$10	$24	$50	$135
	Auctions: $494, MS-68, January 2015; $165, MS-67, January 2015; $141, MS-67, December 2015; $42, MS-66, December 2015										
1952, Proof	81,980	2,954	66.3	100%					$40	$45	$100
	Auctions: $69, PF-67, August 2015; $46, PF-66, March 2015; $42, PF-66, August 2015; $212, PF-65Cam, May 2015										
1952, Die Damage, Proof (n)	(o)	(p)	n/a						$200	$250	$500
	Auctions: $3,525, PF-66DCam, April 2014										
1952-D	49,795,200	1,235	64.9	98%	$6	$7	$9	$10	$28	$65	$1,350
	Auctions: $3,878, MS-67, September 2015; $3,055, MS-67, January 2015; $84, MS-66, February 2015; $69, MS-66, October 2015										
1952-S	13,707,800	2,218	65.7	99%	$6	$7	$14	$20	$36	$55	$200
	Auctions: $4,935, MS-68, October 2015; $153, MS-67, January 2015; $141, MS-67, September 2015; $94, MS-66, October 2015										

j. The upper left curve of the underlying S is visible west and north of the D mintmark. Most Mint State specimens have brilliant surfaces. **k.** Included in 1950-D mintage figure. **l.** Most Mint State specimens have a frosty luster, rather than the brilliant surface seen on most of this year's Mint State D Over S coins. **m.** Included in 1950-S mintage figure. **n.** From the *Cherrypickers' Guide to Rare Die Varieties, Vol. II* (sixth edition): "There is an unusual S-shaped mark on the breast of the eagle. The cause of this mark is unknown. The nickname for this well-known variety is, suitably, 'Superbird'!" **o.** Included in 1952, Proof, mintage figure. **p.** Included in certified population for 1952, Proof.

	Mintage	Cert	Avg	%MS	EF-40	AU-50	MS-60	MS-63	MS-65 / PF-64	MS-66 / PF-65	MS-67 / PF-67
1953	18,536,120	1,244	65.3	99%	$6	$7	$9	$10	$25	$60	$215
	Auctions: $447, MS-67, February 2015; $423, MS-67, January 2015; $52, MS-66, April 2015; $42, MS-66, June 2015										
1953, Proof	128,800	4,506	66.7						$40	$45	$75
	Auctions: $1,293, PF-69Cam, October 2015; $7,638, PF-68DCam, October 2015; $52, PF-67, September 2015; $40, PF-66, August 2015										
1953-D	56,112,400	1,295	64.9	98%	$6	$7	$9	$10	$32	$50	$700
	Auctions: $1,528, MS-67, January 2015; $1,058, MS-67, October 2015; $177, MS-66, October 2015; $54, MS-66, April 2015										
1953-S	14,016,000	2,989	65.6	100%	$6	$7	$9	$10	$25	$50	$185
	Auctions: $235, MS-67, January 2015; $129, MS-67, September 2015; $341, MS-66, February 2015; $62, MS-66, July 2015										
1954	54,412,203	2,760	65.3	99%	$6	$7	$9	$10	$24	$30	$180
	Auctions: $2,820, MS-67+, September 2014; $223, MS-67, October 2014; $200, MS-67, September 2015; $129, MS-67, January 2015										
1954, Proof	233,300	5,307	67.0						$17	$25	$60
	Auctions: $376, PF-69Cam, March 2015; $42, PF-68, August 2015; $411, PF-67DCam, January 2015; $42, PF-66, September 2015										
1954-D	42,305,500	1,606	65.2	100%	$6	$7	$9	$10	$25	$60	$900
	Auctions: $2,115, MS-67, January 2015; $705, MS-67, August 2015; $79, MS-66, November 2015; $54, MS-66, April 2015										
1954-S	11,834,722	5,397	65.5	100%	$6	$7	$9	$10	$23	$50	$250
	Auctions: $368, MS-67, November 2014; $200, MS-67, January 2015; $182, MS-67, November 2014; $182, MS-67, March 2015										
1955	18,180,181	3,195	65.3	99%	$6	$7	$9	$10	$25	$55	$450
	Auctions: $353, MS-67, September 2014; $282, MS-67, October 2014; $259, MS-67, June 2015; $212, MS-67, September 2015										
1955, Proof	378,200	8,382	67.4						$17	$25	$50
	Auctions: $1,175, PF-69UCam, January 2015; $764, PF-68UCam, August 2015; $200, PF-67DCam, April 2015										
1955-D	3,182,400	3,571	64.6	100%	$6	$7	$9	$10	$40	$90	$2,000
	Auctions: $2,350, MS-66, April 2012										
1956	44,144,000	3,959	65.7	100%	$6	$7	$9	$10	$18	$30	$100
	Auctions: $306, MS-67, May 2015; $129, MS-67, September 2015; $36, MS-65, September 2015; $588, MS-64, October 2014										
1956, Proof	669,384	10,477	67.6						$14	$20	$50
	Auctions: $1,293, PF-69DCam, September 2015; $329, PF-69Cam, August 2015; $89, PF-68UCam, May 2015; $32, PF-68, July 2015										
1956-D	32,334,500	1,330	65.3	99%	$6	$7	$9	$10	$25	$40	$600
	Auctions: $447, MS-67, September 2015; $423, MS-67, January 2015; $48, MS-66, September 2015; $26, MS-66, September 2015										
1957	46,532,000	2,760	65.6	99%	$6	$7	$9	$10	$20	$25	$70
	Auctions: $1,528, MS-68, July 2015; $79, MS-67, January 2015; $69, MS-67, September 2015; $22, MS-66, September 2015										
1957, Proof	1,247,952	10,675	67.4						$12	$17	$45
	Auctions: $188, PF-69Cam, January 2015; $588, PF-68UCam, July 2015; $353, PF-68, May 2015; $200, PF-67DCam, July 2015										
1957-D	77,924,160	2,133	65.5	99%	$6	$7	$9	$10	$23	$40	$150
	Auctions: $1,293, MS-68, September 2015; $259, MS-67, January 2015; $176, MS-67, November 2015; $36, MS-65, February 2015										
1958	6,360,000	4,865	65.7	100%	$6	$7	$9	$10	$18	$35	$85
	Auctions: $79, MS-67, February 2015; $69, MS-67, November 2015; $62, MS-67, August 2014; $69, MS-67, November 2014										
1958, Proof	875,652	7,699	67.3						$12	$17	$40
	Auctions: $1,528, PF-68DCam, September 2014; $764, PF-68DCam, November 2014; $235, PF-67DCam, October 2015										
1958-D	78,124,900	2,697	65.6	99%	$6	$7	$9	$10	$23	$35	$165
	Auctions: $353, MS-68, September 2015; $235, MS-67, June 2015; $118, MS-66, November 2015; $30, MS-65, September 2015										
1959	24,384,000	2,980	65.3	100%	$6	$7	$9	$10	$20	$40	$850
	Auctions: $2,585, MS-67, January 2015; $1,763, MS-67, September 2015; $282, MS-66, April 2015; $60, MS-65, August 2015										
1959, Proof	1,149,291	8,424	67.4						$12	$14	$35
	Auctions: $9,400, PF-69DCam, November 2014; $881, PF-68DCam, September 2014; $705, PF-68UCam, November 2015										
1959, Doubled Die Obverse, Proof (q)	(r)	116	66.5						$140	$185	
	Auctions: $150, PF-65, February 2012										
1959-D	62,054,232	1,669	65.1	99%	$6	$7	$9	$10	$20	$45	$1,000
	Auctions: $646, MS-67, August 2015; $470, MS-67, June 2015; $68, MS-66, November 2015; $16, MS-65, November 2014										

q. Dramatic doubling is evident on all obverse lettering, especially IN GOD WE TRUST. There are at least five different doubled-die obverses for this date; the one featured here is FS-25-1959-101. **r.** Included in 1959, Proof, mintage figure.

	Mintage	Cert	Avg	%MS	EF-40	AU-50	MS-60	MS-63	MS-65 / PF-64	MS-66 / PF-65	MS-67 / PF-67
1960	29,164,000	2,334	65.3	100%	$6	$7	$9	$10	$16	$40	$900
	Auctions: $1,058, MS-67, June 2015; $764, MS-67, September 2015; $100, MS-66, November 2015; $50, MS-66, August 2015										
1960, Proof	1,691,602	8,863	67.2						$11	$12	$30
	Auctions: $2,115, PF-69DCam, September 2014; $999, PF-69Cam, July 2015; $764, PF-69DCam, November 2014; $217, PF-68DCam, November 2014										
1960-D	63,000,324	1,103	65.1	99%	$6	$7	$9	$10	$18	$40	$2,000
	Auctions: $2,233, MS-67, January 2015; $2,115, MS-67, April 2014; $92, MS-66, September 2014										
1961	37,036,000	1,427	65.2	99%	$6	$7	$9	$10	$15	$45	$2,000
	Auctions: $3,995, MS-67, June 2015; $946, MS-67, June 2015; $940, MS-67, September 2015; $764, MS-67, January 2015										
1961, Proof	3,028,244	10,598	67.3						$11	$12	$30
	Auctions: $1,058, PF-69DCam, June 2015; $881, PF-69DCam, September 2015; $282, PF-69UCam, July 2015; $88, PF-68DCam, November 2014										
1961-D	83,656,928	1,040	64.8	98%	$6	$7	$9	$10	$17	$85	$4,000
	Auctions: $7,638, MS-67, July 2014; $7,638, MS-67, August 2014; $129, MS-66, November 2015; $112, MS-66, June 2015										
1962	36,156,000	1,969	65.4	99%	$6	$7	$9	$10	$15	$45	$2,500
	Auctions: $881, MS-67, February 2015; $353, MS-67, August 2015; $100, MS-66, August 2015; $52, MS-66, November 2015										
1962, Proof	3,218,019	9,927	67.2						$11	$12	$30
	Auctions: $823, PF-69DCam, June 2015; $447, PF-69UCam, July 2015; $94, PF-68DCam, September 2015										
1962-D	127,554,756	978	64.8	97%	$6	$7	$9	$10	$17	$110	$3,000
	Auctions: $4,759, MS-67, January 2015; $1,293, MS-67, June 2015; $212, MS-66, January 2015; $165, MS-66, June 2015										
1963	74,316,000	2,934	65.2	99%	$6	$7	$9	$10	$15	$40	$750
	Auctions: $1,410, MS-67, February 2015; $940, MS-67, July 2015; $18, MS-66, April 2015; $2,115, MS-62, September 2014										
1963, Proof	3,075,645	11,985	67.4						$11	$12	$30
	Auctions: $223, PF-69DCam, November 2014; $212, PF-69DCam, May 2015; $200, PF-69UCam, July 2015; $22, PF-67DCam, April 2015										
1963-D	135,288,184	1,066	64.8	97%	$6	$7	$9	$10	$17	$65	$850
	Auctions: $969, MS-67, October 2015; $435, MS-67, June 2015; $74, MS-66, June 2015; $69, MS-66, November 2015										
1964	560,390,585	3,209	64.9	97%	$6	$7	$9	$10	$15	$45	$700
	Auctions: $447, MS-67, January 2015; $353, MS-67, September 2015; $153, MS-66, October 2015										
1964, Proof	3,950,762	15,930	67.8						$11	$12	$30
	Auctions: $329, PF-69DCam, January 2015; $282, PF-69UCam, January 2015; $259, PF-69UCam, July 2015										
1964-D	704,135,528	3,272	64.4	93%	$6	$7	$9	$10	$15	$40	$450
	Auctions: $517, MS-67, June 2015; $447, MS-67, January 2015; $56, MS-66, February 2015										

1966, Doubled Die Reverse
FS-25-1966-801.

	Mintage	Cert	Avg	%MS	MS-63	MS-65 / PF-65	MS-66 / PF-67Cam	MS-67 / PF-68Cam
1965	1,819,717,540	531	63.9	92%	$2	$9	$30	$185
	Auctions: $317, MS-67Cam, August 2015; $141, MS-67Cam, January 2015; $223, MS-67, March 2015; $188, MS-67, January 2015							
1965, Special Mint Set ††	2,360,000	4,556	66.9	100%		$12	$375	$600
	Auctions: $505, MS-67Cam, January 2014; $588, MS-67Cam, September 2014; $441, MS-67Cam, October 2014							
1966	821,101,500	178	63.4	89%	$2	$7	$25	$125
	Auctions: $376, MS-67, January 2015; $259, MS-67, September 2014; $353, MS-63, January 2015; $212, MS-63, July 2015							
1966, Doubled Die Reverse (a)	(b)	2	58.0	50%	$900	$1,400	$2,250	
	Auctions: $920, EF-45, April 2012							
1966, Special Mint Set ††	2,261,583	4,276	66.9	100%		$12	$115	$1,450
	Auctions: $1,293, MS-68Cam, June 2014; $4,113, MS-68Cam, September 2014; $84, MS-67Cam, November 2014							

†† Ranked in the *100 Greatest U.S. Modern Coins* (fourth edition). **a.** Very strong doubling is visible on all reverse lettering. Note that this is not the 1966 Special Mint Set issue. **b.** Included in circulation-strike 1966 mintage figure.

1968-S, Doubled Die Reverse, Proof
FS-25-1968S-801.

1970-D, Doubled Die Obverse
FS-25-1970D-101.

	Mintage	Cert	Avg	%MS	MS-63 / PF-65	MS-65 / PF-67Cam	MS-66 / PF-68DC	MS-67
1967	1,524,031,848	179	65.2	96%	$2	$6	$35	$150
Auctions: $118, MS-68, January 2015; $188, MS-67, January 2015; $141, MS-67, November 2015; $95, MS-67, January 2015								
1967, Special Mint Set ††	1,863,344	4,987	67.0	100%		$12	$50	$200
Auctions: $212, MS-68Cam, September 2014; $188, MS-68Cam, August 2013								
1968	220,731,500	400	65.9	99%	$2	$8	$25	$100
Auctions: $159, MS-67, July 2014; $141, MS-67, January 2015; $123, MS-67, September 2014; $84, MS-67, July 2015								
1968-D	101,534,000	934	66.0	100%	$2	$6	$15	$55
Auctions: $123, MS-67, March 2013								
1968-S, Proof	3,041,506	1,307	67.3			$5	$15	$150
Auctions: $194, PF-64, May 2013								
1968-S, Doubled Die Reverse, Proof (c)	(d)	23	66.1			$200		
Auctions: $196, PF-66, March 2012								
1969	176,212,000	170	65.0	98%	$3	$10	$35	$350
Auctions: $3,290, MS-67, January 2015; $141, MS-66, January 2015; $135, MS-66, June 2014; $123, MS-66, September 2014								
1969-D	114,372,000	759	65.8	99%	$2.50	$10	$25	$75
Auctions: $1,998, MS-68, July 2014; $72, MS-67, July 2014; $69, MS-67, April 2015; $200, MS-63, July 2015								
1969-S, Proof	2,934,631	1,620	67.9			$5	$15	$100
Auctions: $617, PF-69DCam, December 2013								
1970	136,420,000	385	65.1	99%	$2	$10	$40	$100
Auctions: $153, MS-67, August 2014; $441, MS-67, September 2014; $2,115, MS-67, November 2013; $30, MS-66, July 2014								
1970-D	417,341,364	1,405	65.5	98%	$2	$6	$10	$35
Auctions: $2,926, MS-68, January 2014; $40, MS-67, December 2015; $182, AU-55, July 2014; $69, EF-45, September 2015								
1970-D, Doubled Die Obverse (e)	(f)	5	46.8	20%	$300	$375	$500	
Auctions: $2,875, MS-65, January 2012								
1970-S, Proof	2,632,810	1,339	67.9			$5	$15	$125
Auctions: $705, PF-69DCam, June 2013; $1,175, PF-67Cam, October 2014								
1971	109,284,000	219	64.4	97%	$1	$6	$50	$150
Auctions: $306, MS-66, August 2015; $212, MS-66, August 2015; $123, MS-66, September 2014; $89, MS-66, August 2015								
1971-D	258,634,428	377	65.6	98%	$1	$6	$20	$100
Auctions: $4,113, MS-68, September 2013; $86, MS-67, July 2014; $182, MS-67, September 2014; $235, MS-62, October 2015								
1971-S, Proof	3,220,733	1,535	67.8			$5	$15	$300
Auctions: $1,058, PF-69DCam, December 2013								
1972	215,048,000	297	65.6	100%	$1	$6	$25	$175
Auctions: $588, MS-67, November 2013								
1972-D	311,067,732	779	66.1	99%	$1	$6	$18	$30
Auctions: $3,055, MS-68, January 2014; $259, MS-65, October 2014								
1972-S, Proof	3,260,996	1,217	67.9			$5	$10	$30
Auctions: $411, PF-65Cam, August 2013								

†† Ranked in the *100 Greatest U.S. Modern Coins* (fourth edition). **c.** Doubling is evident on all reverse lettering around the rim and the left tips. **d.** Included in 1968-S, Proof, mintage figure. **e.** This extremely rare variety (fewer than a half dozen known) shows very strong doubling on the date, IN GOD WE TRUST, and the ERTY of LIBERTY. **f.** Included in 1970-D mintage figure.

1979-S, Filled S
(Type 1), Proof

1979-S, Clear S
(Type 2), Proof

| | Mintage | Cert | Avg | %MS | MS-63 | MS-65 | MS-66 | MS-67 |
					PF-65	PF-67Cam	PF-68DC
1973	346,924,000	195	65.1	98%	$1	$6	$25	$175
	Auctions: $1,116, MS-67, September 2013							
1973-D	232,977,400	206	65.1	99%	$1	$6	$25	$175
	Auctions: $1,410, MS-65, February 2014							
1973-S, Proof	2,760,339	487	68.0			$5	$10	$20
	Auctions: $96, PF-67, March 2013							
1974	801,456,000	172	65.1	98%	$1	$6	$25	$175
	Auctions: $382, MS-67, November 2013							
1974-D	353,160,300	231	65.1	98%	$1	$7	$25	$75
	Auctions: $1,763, MS-64, September 2013							
1974-S, Proof	2,612,568	501	68.1			$5	$10	$20
	Auctions: $7,015, PF-70DCam, April 2012							
1776–1976, Copper-Nickel Clad ††	809,784,016	738	65.3	97%	$1.25	$6	$15	$50
	Auctions: $306, MS-62, February 2014							
1776–1976-D, Copper-Nickel Clad	860,118,839	990	65.1	95%	$1.25	$6	$15	$60
	Auctions: $66, MS-67, March 2013							
1776–1976-S, Silver Clad	11,000,000	1,873	68.0		$5	$7	$15	$40
	Auctions: $129, MS-68, October 2014; $100, MS-68, January 2015; $78, MS-68, August 2014; $64, MS-68, January 2015							
1776–1976-S, Proof, Copper-Nickel Clad	7,059,099	1,757	66.1	100%		$5	$10	$20
	Auctions: $253, PF-70DCam, January 2015; $212, PF-70DCam, July 2015; $141, PF-70DCam, November 2015							
1776–1976-S, Proof, Silver Clad	4,000,000	4,628	68.2			$8	$12	$25
	Auctions: $376, PF-70DCam, January 2015; $282, PF-70DCam, July 2015; $235, PF-70DCam, October 2015							
1977	468,556,000	204	65.5	99%	$1	$6	$20	$100
	Auctions: $123, MS-67, September 2014; $52, MS-66, August 2015; $100, MS-60, September 2015							
1977-D	256,524,978	132	64.2	95%	$1	$6	$25	$125
	Auctions: $229, MS-67, September 2014							
1977-S, Proof	3,251,152	936	68.8			$5	$10	$20
	Auctions: $70, PF-70DCam, August 2014; $103, PF-70DCam, November 2014; $90, PF-70DCam, May 2013							
1978	521,452,000	240	65.5	99%	$1	$6	$20	$100
	Auctions: $165, MS-67, January 2015; $470, MS-65, February 2015; $247, MS-65, August 2015; $259, MS-60, July 2015							
1978-D	287,373,152	197	65.4	98%	$1	$6	$25	$175
	Auctions: $26, MS-66, August 2014							
1978-S, Proof	3,127,781	831	68.8			$5	$10	$18
	Auctions: $61, PF-70DCam, August 2014; $80, PF-70DCam, May 2013; $12, PF-70DCam, March 2015							
1979	515,708,000	239	65.4	97%	$1	$6	$25	$125
	Auctions: $411, MS-66, June 2014; $200, MS-64, February 2015; $176, MS-64, November 2014							
1979-D	489,789,780	199	65.1	97%	$1	$6	$25	$125
	Auctions: $441, MS-67, September 2013							
1979-S, Proof, All kinds (g)	3,677,175							
1979-S, Type 1 ("Filled" S), Proof		1,190	68.9			$5	$10	$18
	Auctions: $68, PF-70DCam, August 2014							
1979-S, Type 2 ("Clear" S), Proof		1,424	69.0			$6	$12	$25
	Auctions: $529, PF-70DCam, September 2014; $76, PF-70DCam, August 2014; $72, PF-70DCam, September 2014							

†† Ranked in the *100 Greatest U.S. Modern Coins* (fourth edition). **g.** The mintmark style was changed during 1979 Proof production, creating two distinctly different types. From the *Cherrypickers' Guide to Rare Die Varieties, Vol. II* (sixth edition): "The Type 2 is the rare variety, and is easily distinguished from the common Type 1. The Type 1 has a very indistinct blob, whereas the Type 2 shows a well-defined S."

		1981-S, Rounded S (Type 1), Proof			1981-S, Flat S (Type 2), Proof	

	Mintage	Cert	Avg	%MS	MS-63 / PF-65	MS-65 / PF-67Cam	MS-66 / PF-68DC	MS-67
1980-P	635,832,000	427	65.8	99%	$1	$6	$18	$85
Auctions: $74, MS-65, November 2015; $56, MS-62, August 2015; $141, AU-58, January 2015								
1980-D	518,327,487	207	65.3	99%	$1	$6	$20	$175
Auctions: $1,380, MS-67, February 2007								
1980-S, Proof	3,554,806	1,279	68.8			$5	$10	$18
Auctions: $79, PF-70DCam, May 2013								
1981-P	601,716,000	413	65.9	99%	$1	$6	$17	$100
Auctions: $176, MS-65, August 2013								
1981-D	575,722,833	434	65.6	99%	$1	$6	$22	$150
Auctions: $259, MS-67, September 2013								
1981-S, Proof, All kinds (h)	4,063,083							
1981-S, Type 1 ("Rounded" S), Proof		1,832	68.9			$4	$8	$16
Auctions: $70, PF-70DCam, May 2013								
1981-S, Type 2 ("Flat" S), Proof		1,033	69.0			$6	$12	$25
Auctions: $705, PF-70DCam, April 2013								
1982-P	500,931,000	224	64.9	97%	$14	$35	$85	$385
Auctions: $646, MS-67, January 2015; $282, MS-63, September 2015; $353, AU-50, January 2015								
1982-D	480,042,788	346	65.3	98%	$10	$25	$65	$325
Auctions: $30, MS-66, March 2013								
1982-S, Proof	3,857,479	1,295	69.0			$4	$8	$16
Auctions: $103, PF-70DCam, May 2014; $56, PF-70DCam, September 2014; $47, PF-70DCam, November 2014								
1983-P ††	673,535,000	1,079	64.9	98%	$30	$65	$200	$400
Auctions: $74, MS-66, July 2014; $74, MS-66, September 2014; $423, AU-58, January 2015								
1983-D	617,806,446	213	64.6	95%	$15	$45	$150	$500
Auctions: $1,058, MS-67, June 2014; $108, MS-66, August 2014; $92, MS-66, September 2014; $84, MS-66, January 2015								
1983-S, Proof	3,279,126	1,036	68.9			$4	$8	$16
Auctions: $72, PF-70DCam, September 2014; $90, PF-70DCam, August 2013								
1984-P	676,545,000	209	65.2	97%	$2	$10	$20	$125
Auctions: $1,058, MS-67, September 2013								
1984-D	546,483,064	99	64.6	98%	$2	$12	$65	$300
Auctions: $764, MS-67, September 2013								
1984-S, Proof	3,065,110	686	69.0			$4	$8	$16
Auctions: $80, PF-70DCam, May 2013; $55, PF-70DCam, August 2014; $50, PF-70DCam, August 2015								
1985-P	775,818,962	256	65.4	98%	$2	$15	$25	$100
Auctions: $764, MS-65, June 2014								
1985-D	519,962,888	267	65.7	99%	$1	$9	$25	$100
Auctions: $66, MS-66, March 2013								
1985-S, Proof	3,362,821	858	69.0			$4	$8	$16
Auctions: $86, PF-70DCam, May 2013								

†† Ranked in the *100 Greatest U.S. Modern Coins* (fourth edition). **h.** The mintmark style was changed during the 1981 Proof production, creating two distinct types. From the *Cherrypickers' Guide to Rare Die Varieties, Vol. II* (sixth edition): "The Type 2 is the rare variety, and is not easily distinguished from the common Type 1. For most collectors, the easiest difference to discern on the Type 2 is the flatness on the top curve of the S, which is rounded on the Type 1. Additionally, the surface of the Type 2 mintmark is frosted, and the openings in the loops slightly larger."

1989-D, Repunched Mintmark
FS-25-1989D-501.

1990-S, Doubled Die Obverse, Proof
FS-25-1990S-101.

	Mintage	Cert	Avg	%MS	MS-63	MS-65	MS-66	MS-67
						PF-65	PF-67Cam	PF-68DC
1986-P	551,199,333	252	64.9	98%	$2.50	$12	$30	$125
Auctions: $129, MS-64, October 2014; $103, MS-66, September 2014; $100, MS-66, August 2015; $30, MS-66, November 2014								
1986-D	504,298,660	302	65.6	99%	$6	$18	$25	$100
Auctions: $104, MS-66, November 2007								
1986-S, Proof	3,010,497	690	69.1			$4	$8	$16
Auctions: $39, PF-70DCam, August 2013								
1987-P	582,499,481	213	65.3	100%	$1	$9	$40	$200
Auctions: $59, MS-66, December 2007								
1987-D	655,594,696	216	65.5	98%	$1	$6	$20	$150
Auctions: $676, MS-67, January 2015; $66, MS-66, September 2014								
1987-S, Proof	4,227,728	893	69.0			$4	$8	$16
Auctions: No auction records available.								
1988-P	562,052,000	281	65.2	99%	$1.25	$15	$30	$175
Auctions: $66, MS-66, March 2013								
1988-D	596,810,688	200	65.5	100%	$1	$10	$20	$125
Auctions: $66, MS-66, November 2007								
1988-S, Proof	3,262,948	611	69.1			$4	$8	$16
Auctions: $55, PF-70DCam, August 2013								
1989-P	512,868,000	267	65.4	98%	$1	$12	$30	$150
Auctions: $216, MS-66, August 2009								
1989-D	896,535,597	244	65.6	99%	$1	$7	$25	$125
Auctions: $70, MS-66, March 2013								
1989-D, Repunched Mintmark (i)	(j)	0	n/a		$20	$25	$50	
Auctions: No auction records available.								
1989-S, Proof	3,220,194	690	69.0			$4	$8	$16
Auctions: $79, PF-70DCam, January 2010								
1990-P	613,792,000	288	65.9	99%	$1	$10	$20	$100
Auctions: $282, MS-64, June 2014								
1990-D	927,638,181	224	65.9	100%	$1	$10	$20	$125
Auctions: $646, MS-68, April 2014; $52, MS-67, August 2014								
1990-S, Proof	3,299,559	896	69.2			$4	$8	$16
Auctions: $53, PF-68DCam, April 2013								
1990-S, Doubled Die Obverse, Proof †† (k)	(l)	7	68.1			$225	$700	
Auctions: $4,888, PF-70DCam, April 2012								
1991-P	570,968,000	165	65.9	99%	$1	$12	$30	$100
Auctions: $90, MS-66, November 2007								
1991-D	630,966,693	159	65.6	100%	$1	$12	$30	$225
Auctions: $66, MS-66, March 2013								
1991-S, Proof	2,867,787	835	69.3			$4	$8	$16
Auctions: $69, PF-70DCam, January 2010								

†† Ranked in the *100 Greatest U.S. Modern Coins* (fourth edition). **i.** The secondary D mintmark is visible west of the primary D. **j.** Included in 1989-D mintage figure. **k.** Very strong doubling is visible on the date and the mintmark, with slightly less dramatic doubling on IN GOD WE TRUST. **l.** Included in 1990-S, Proof, mintage figure.

	Mintage	Cert	Avg	%MS	MS-63 PF-65	MS-65 PF-65	MS-66 PF-67Cam	MS-67 PF-68DC
1992-P	384,764,000	299	66.0	100%	$1.50	$16	$35	$250
Auctions: $242, MS-66, February 2008								
1992-D	389,777,107	200	65.4	98%	$1	$16	$35	$350
Auctions: $1,763, MS-67, November 2013; $47, MS-66, July 2014								
1992-S, Proof	2,858,981	675	69.3			$4	$8	$16
Auctions: $50, PF-70DCam, January 2010								
1992-S, Proof, Silver	1,317,579	2,446	69.2			$10	$12	$22
Auctions: $109, PF-70DCam, January 2010								
1993-P	639,276,000	249	66.1	98%	$1	$7	$20	$85
Auctions: $86, MS-67, August 2014; $306, MS-64, June 2014; $282, MS-64, February 2015								
1993-D	645,476,128	212	65.9	99%	$1	$7	$25	$100
Auctions: $1,298, MS-67, January 2015; $59, MS-67, August 2014; $101, MS-66, September 2014; $36, AU-58, July 2014								
1993-S, Proof	2,633,439	670	69.3			$4	$8	$16
Auctions: $58, PF-70DCam, May 2013								
1993-S, Proof, Silver	761,353	1,588	69.1			$10	$12	$22
Auctions: $70, PF-70DCam, August 2013								
1994-P	825,600,000	193	65.9	99%	$1	$10	$25	$100
Auctions: $70, MS-66, March 2013								
1994-D	880,034,110	216	65.0	94%	$1	$10	$30	$150
Auctions: $123, MS-66, September 2014; $212, MS-64, July 2014								
1994-S, Proof	2,484,594	638	69.4			$4	$8	$16
Auctions: $69, PF-70DCam, January 2010								
1994-S, Proof, Silver	785,329	1,634	69.1			$10	$14	$25
Auctions: $76, PF-70DCam, September 2014; $96, PF-70DCam, May 2013								
1995-P	1,004,336,000	180	66.5	99%	$1.25	$14	$20	$65
Auctions: $129, MS-67, March 2013								
1995-D	1,103,216,000	187	66.0	99%	$1	$13	$20	$75
Auctions: $165, MS-67, September 2014; $38, MS-64, July 2015								
1995-S, Proof	2,117,496	546	69.5			$8	$10	$20
Auctions: $69, PF-70DCam, January 2010								
1995-S, Proof, Silver	679,985	2,226	69.1			$10	$14	$25
Auctions: $68, PF-70DCam, September 2014; $69, PF-70DCam, November 2014; $135, PF-70DCam, May 2013								
1996-P	925,040,000	255	66.3	99%	$1	$10	$18	$30
Auctions: $441, MS-68, March 2013								
1996-D	906,868,000	298	66.1	99%	$1	$10	$18	$30
Auctions: $447, MS-68, March 2013; $165, MS-64, November 2014; $79, MS-63, January 2015								
1996-S, Proof	1,750,244	606	69.3			$5	$8	$18
Auctions: $84, PF-70DCam, January 2010								
1996-S, Proof, Silver	775,021	1,690	69.1			$10	$14	$25
Auctions: $76, PF-70DCam, May 2013								
1997-P	595,740,000	168	66.3	100%	$1	$11	$18	$40
Auctions: $15, MS-60, January 2013								
1997-D	599,680,000	165	66.0	98%	$1	$12	$18	$40
Auctions: $66, MS-67, March 2013								
1997-S, Proof	2,055,000	537	69.5			$5	$8	$18
Auctions: $69, PF-70DCam, January 2010								
1997-S, Proof, Silver	741,678	1,629	69.2			$10	$14	$25
Auctions: $89, PF-70DCam, January 2010								

| | Mintage | Cert | Avg | %MS | MS-63 | MS-65 | MS-66 | MS-67 |
					PF-65	PF-67Cam	PF-68DC
1998-P	896,268,000	226	66.5	99%	$1	$7	$18	$40
	Auctions: $364, MS-68, September 2014; $329, MS-68, June 2014; $306, MS-66, January 2015; $159, MS-64, November 2014							
1998-D	821,000,000	214	65.3	97%	$1	$7	$20	$100
	Auctions: $1,528, MS-67+, January 2015; $364, MS-67, September 2014; $32, MS-66, June 2014; $69, MS-63, August 2015							
1998-S, Proof	2,086,507	579	69.5			$6	$8	$18
	Auctions: $9,988, PF-65, August 2014							
1998-S, Proof, Silver	878,792	2,170	69.3			$10	$12	$22
	Auctions: $70, PF-70DCam, May 2013							

WASHINGTON, STATE, D.C., AND TERRITORIAL (1999–2009)

Designers: *John Flanagan (obverse); see image captions for reverse designers.* **Weight:** *Clad issue—5.67 grams; silver Proofs—6.25 grams.* **Composition:** *Clad issue—Outer layers of copper-nickel (.750 copper, .250 nickel) bonded to inner core of pure copper; silver Proofs—.900 silver, .100 copper (net weight .18084 oz. pure silver).* **Diameter:** *24.3 mm.* **Edge:** *Reeded.* **Mints:** *Clad issue—Philadelphia, Denver, and San Francisco.*

Circulation Strike   Proof

History. In 1999 the U.S. Mint introduced a new program of State quarters (officially called the United States Mint 50 State Quarters® Program). These were released at the rate of five new reverse designs each year, in combination with a restyled obverse, through 2008. Each design honored the state the coin was issued for, and they were released in public celebrations in the order in which the states joined the Union. The coins became very popular, adding millions of Americans to the ranks of everyday coin collectors, and are still widely collected with enthusiasm. In 2009 the Mint released a similar program of quarter dollars for Washington, D.C., and the five U.S. territories. Circulation strikes were made at the Philadelphia and Denver mints, and special silver-content and Proof issues at San Francisco. Each coin combines a modified obverse depicting George Washington, without a date. The reverses are distinctive and bear the date of issue, the date of statehood (for the State quarters), and other design elements. Each state or district/territory selected its own design.

Some State quarters were accidentally made with "disoriented" dies and are valued higher than ordinary pieces. Normal U.S. coins have dies oriented in coin alignment, such that the reverse appears upside down when the coin is flipped from right to left. Values for the rotated-die quarters vary according to the amount of shifting. The most valuable are those that are shifted 180 degrees, so that both sides appear upright when the coin is turned over (called *medal alignment*).

Striking and Sharpness. State quarters can have light striking on the highest area of the obverse. On the reverse there can be weak areas, depending on the design, seemingly more often seen on Denver Mint coins. Some in the State quarter series were struck through grease, obliterating portions of both the obverse (usually) and reverse designs.

Availability. All modern quarters are readily available in high grades. Typical MS coins are MS–63 and 64 with light abrasion. MS–65 and higher coins are in the minority, but enough exist that finding them is no problem. Around MS–68 many issues are scarce, and higher grades are scarcer yet.

Proofs. State and D.C./Territorial quarter dollar Proofs are made in San Francisco. For certain later issues of Washington quarters as well as State, D.C., and Territorial issues, Proofs are available in copper-nickel–clad metal as well as silver strikings. On some Proofs over-polishing of dies eliminated some details, as on part of the WC (for William Cousins) initials on certain 1999 Delaware pieces.

Grading Standards

MS-60 to 70 (Mint State). *Obverse:* At MS-60, some abrasion and contact marks are evident on the highest-relief parts of the hair and the cheek. At MS-63, abrasion is slight at best, less so at MS-64. An MS-65 coin should display no abrasion or contact marks except under magnification, and MS-66 and higher coins should have none at all. Luster should be full. *Reverse:* Check the highest-relief areas of the design (these differ from coin to coin). Otherwise, comments are as for the obverse.

2004-D, Wisconsin, Extra Leaf Low. Graded MS-66.

AU-50, 53, 55, 58 (About Uncirculated). *Obverse:* Light wear is seen on the cheek, the high areas of the hair, and the neck. At AU-58, the luster is extensive, but incomplete, especially on the higher parts and in the field. At AU–50 and 53, luster is less. About Uncirculated coins usually lack eye appeal. *Reverse:* Light wear is seen on the higher-relief areas. Otherwise, comments are as for the obverse.

2004-D, Wisconsin, Extra Leaf High. Graded AU-58.

State, D.C., and Territorial quarter dollars are seldom collected in grades lower than AU-50.

PF-60 to 70 (Proof). *Obverse and Reverse:* These coins are so recent, and as only a few have been cleaned, most approach perfection and can be designated PF–68 to 70, the latter only if no contact marks or other problems can be seen under magnification. A cleaned coin with extensive hairlines would not be collectible for most numismatists and would be classified at a lower level such as PF–60 to 63. Those with lighter hairlines qualify for PF–64 or 65.

2008-S, Alaska. Graded PF-70 Ultra Cameo.

1999, Delaware
Reverse designer: William Cousins.

1999, Pennsylvania
Reverse designer: John Mercanti.

1999, New Jersey
Reverse designer: Alfred Maletsky.

1999, Georgia
Reverse designer: T. James Ferrell.

1999, Connecticut
Reverse designer: T. James Ferrell.

	Mintage	Cert	Avg	%MS	AU-50	MS-63	MS-65 / PF-65	MS-66 / PF-66DC	MS-67 / PF-69DC
1999-P, Delaware	373,400,000	1,273	66.0	99%	$0.50	$2	$5	$25	$55
1999-D, Delaware	401,424,000	1,381	65.9	100%	$0.50	$2	$5	$25	$55
1999-S, Delaware, Proof	3,713,359	6,734	69.2				$7	$8	$20
1999-S, Delaware, Proof, Silver	804,565	14,517	69.0				$22	$27	$38
1999-P, Pennsylvania	349,000,000	1,137	66.1	100%	$0.50	$2	$5	$25	$55
1999-D, Pennsylvania	358,332,000	1,014	65.9	100%	$0.50	$2	$5	$25	$55
1999-S, Pennsylvania, Proof	3,713,359	6,503	69.2				$7	$8	$20
1999-S, Pennsylvania, Proof, Silver	804,565	13,999	69.1				$22	$27	$38
1999-P, New Jersey	363,200,000	1,081	66.1	100%	$0.50	$2	$5	$25	$55
1999-D, New Jersey	299,028,000	1,216	66.0	100%	$0.50	$2	$5	$25	$55
1999-S, New Jersey, Proof	3,713,359	6,499	69.2				$7	$8	$20
1999-S, New Jersey, Proof, Silver	804,565	14,073	69.1				$22	$27	$38
1999-P, Georgia	451,188,000	1,186	65.7	99%	$0.50	$2	$5	$25	$55
1999-D, Georgia	488,744,000	1,193	65.8	99%	$0.50	$2	$5	$25	$55
1999-S, Georgia, Proof	3,713,359	6,536	69.2				$7	$8	$20
1999-S, Georgia, Proof, Silver	804,565	14,253	69.1				$22	$27	$38
1999-P, Connecticut	688,744,000	1,369	65.6	99%	$0.50	$1.50	$5	$25	$55
1999-D, Connecticut	657,880,000	2,303	65.4	100%	$0.50	$1.50	$5	$25	$55
1999-S, Connecticut, Proof	3,713,359	6,573	69.3	100%			$7	$8	$20
1999-S, Connecticut, Proof, Silver	804,565	14,058	69.1				$22	$27	$38

2000, Massachusetts
Reverse designer: Thomas D. Rogers Sr.

2000, Maryland
Reverse designer: Thomas D. Rogers Sr.

2000, South Carolina
Reverse designer: Thomas D. Rogers Sr.

2000, New Hampshire
Reverse designer: William Cousins.

2000, Virginia
Reverse designer: Edgar Z. Steever.

	Mintage	Cert	Avg	%MS	AU-50	MS-63	MS-65 / PF-65	MS-66 / PF-66DC	MS-67 / PF-69DC
2000-P, Massachusetts	628,600,000	929	66.2	100%	$0.35	$1	$4	$15	$40
2000-D, Massachusetts	535,184,000	772	66.0	100%	$0.35	$1	$4	$15	$40
2000-S, Massachusetts, Proof	4,020,172	4,632	69.2				$3	$4	$15
2000-S, Massachusetts, Proof, Silver	965,421	10,222	69.2				$9	$12	$20
2000-P, Maryland	678,200,000	643	65.8	99%	$0.35	$1	$4	$15	$40
2000-D, Maryland	556,532,000	649	66.0	100%	$0.35	$1	$4	$15	$40
2000-S, Maryland, Proof	4,020,172	4,533	69.2				$3	$4	$15
2000-S, Maryland, Proof, Silver	965,421	10,358	69.2				$9	$12	$20

| | Mintage | Cert | Avg | %MS | AU-50 | MS-63 | MS-65 | MS-66 | MS-67 |
							PF-65	PF-66DC	PF-69DC
2000-P, South Carolina	742,576,000	616	66.0	100%	$0.35	$1	$4	$15	$40
2000-D, South Carolina	566,208,000	758	66.3	100%	$0.35	$1	$4	$15	$40
2000-S, South Carolina, Proof	4,020,172	4,586	69.2				$3	$4	$15
2000-S, South Carolina, Proof, Silver	965,421	10,016	69.2				$9	$12	$20
2000-P, New Hampshire	673,040,000	569	65.6	98%	$0.35	$1	$4	$15	$40
2000-D, New Hampshire	495,976,000	585	66.0	100%	$0.35	$1	$4	$15	$40
2000-S, New Hampshire, Proof	4,020,172	4,592	69.2				$3	$4	$15
2000-S, New Hampshire, Proof, Silver	965,421	10,001	69.1				$9	$12	$20
2000-P, Virginia	943,000,000	683	66.1	99%	$0.35	$1	$4	$15	$40
2000-D, Virginia	651,616,000	600	66.1	99%	$0.35	$1	$4	$15	$40
2000-S, Virginia, Proof	4,020,172	4,575	69.2				$3	$4	$15
2000-S, Virginia, Proof, Silver	965,421	10,152	69.2				$9	$12	$20

2001, New York
Reverse designer: Alfred Maletsky.

2001, North Carolina
Reverse designer: John Mercanti.

2001, Rhode Island
Reverse designer: Thomas D. Rogers Sr.

2001, Vermont
Reverse designer: T. James Ferrell.

2001, Kentucky
Reverse designer: T. James Ferrell.

| | Mintage | Cert | Avg | %MS | AU-50 | MS-63 | MS-65 | MS-66 | MS-67 |
							PF-65	PF-66DC	PF-69DC
2001-P, New York	655,400,000	407	66.1	100%	$0.35	$1	$4	$15	$40
2001-D, New York	619,640,000	476	66.2	100%	$0.35	$1	$4	$15	$40
2001-S, New York, Proof	3,094,140	3,672	69.2				$3	$8	$15
2001-S, New York, Proof, Silver	889,697	8,339	69.2				$10	$15	$20
2001-P, North Carolina	627,600,000	390	66.3	100%	$0.35	$1	$4	$15	$40
2001-D, North Carolina	427,876,000	419	66.3	100%	$0.35	$1	$4	$15	$40
2001-S, North Carolina, Proof	3,094,140	3,761	69.2				$3	$8	$15
2001-S, North Carolina, Proof, Silver	889,697	8,260	69.2				$10	$15	$20
2001-P, Rhode Island	423,000,000	334	65.9	100%	$0.35	$1	$4	$15	$40
2001-D, Rhode Island	447,100,000	379	65.9	100%	$0.35	$1	$4	$15	$40
2001-S, Rhode Island, Proof	3,094,140	3,361	69.2				$3	$8	$15
2001-S, Rhode Island, Proof, Silver	889,697	8,341	69.2				$10	$15	$20
2001-P, Vermont	423,400,000	1,889	65.7	100%	$0.35	$1	$4	$15	$40
2001-D, Vermont	459,404,000	390	66.3	99%	$0.35	$1	$4	$15	$40
2001-S, Vermont, Proof	3,094,140	3,534	69.3				$3	$8	$15
2001-S, Vermont, Proof, Silver	889,697	8,400	69.3				$10	$15	$20
2001-P, Kentucky	353,000,000	399	66.3	100%	$0.35	$1.25	$5	$16	$40
2001-D, Kentucky	370,564,000	311	66.1	100%	$0.35	$1.25	$5	$16	$40
2001-S, Kentucky, Proof	3,094,140	3,396	69.3				$3	$8	$15
2001-S, Kentucky, Proof, Silver	889,697	8,306	69.2				$10	$15	$20

2002, Tennessee
Reverse designer:
Donna Weaver.

2002, Ohio
Reverse designer:
Donna Weaver.

2002, Louisiana
Reverse designer:
John Mercanti.

2002, Indiana
Reverse designer:
Donna Weaver.

2002, Mississippi
Reverse designer:
Donna Weaver.

	Mintage	Cert	Avg	%MS	AU-50	MS-63	MS-65	MS-66	MS-67
							PF-65	PF-66DC	PF-69DC
2002-P, Tennessee	361,600,000	318	66.5	100%	$0.75	$1.75	$3	$18	$40
2002-D, Tennessee	286,468,000	321	66.4	100%	$0.75	$1.75	$3	$18	$40
2002-S, Tennessee, Proof	3,084,245	2,950	69.2				$3	$5	$15
2002-S, Tennessee, Proof, Silver	892,229	8,088	69.2				$9	$11	$20
2002-P, Ohio	217,200,000	353	66.7	100%	$0.35	$1	$1.50	$10	$30
2002-D, Ohio	414,832,000	301	66.2	100%	$0.35	$1	$1.50	$10	$30
2002-S, Ohio, Proof	3,084,245	2,936	69.3				$3	$5	$15
2002-S, Ohio, Proof, Silver	892,229	8,164	69.2				$9	$11	$20
2002-P, Louisiana	362,000,000	273	66.7	100%	$0.35	$1	$1.50	$10	$30
2002-D, Louisiana	402,204,000	227	66.3	100%	$0.35	$1	$1.50	$10	$30
2002-S, Louisiana, Proof	3,084,245	2,942	69.2				$3	$5	$15
2002-S, Louisiana, Proof, Silver	892,229	7,887	69.2				$9	$11	$20
2002-P, Indiana	362,600,000	319	66.5	99%	$0.35	$1	$1.50	$10	$30
2002-D, Indiana	327,200,000	257	66.3	100%	$0.35	$1	$1.50	$10	$30
2002-S, Indiana, Proof	3,084,245	2,967	69.2				$3	$5	$15
2002-S, Indiana, Proof, Silver	892,229	7,999	69.2				$9	$11	$20
2002-P, Mississippi	290,000,000	294	66.3	100%	$0.35	$1	$1.50	$10	$30
2002-D, Mississippi	289,600,000	237	66.4	100%	$0.35	$1	$1.50	$10	$30
2002-S, Mississippi, Proof	3,084,245	3,003	69.3				$3	$5	$15
2002-S, Mississippi, Proof, Silver	892,229	8,254	69.2				$9	$11	$20

2003, Illinois
Reverse designer:
Donna Weaver.

2003, Alabama
Reverse designer:
Norman E. Nemeth.

2003, Maine
Reverse designer:
Donna Weaver.

2003, Missouri
Reverse designer:
Alfred Maletsky.

2003, Arkansas
Reverse designer:
John Mercanti.

	Mintage	Cert	Avg	%MS	AU-50	MS-63	MS-65	MS-66	MS-67
							PF-65	PF-66DC	PF-69DC
2003-P, Illinois	225,800,000	268	65.9	100%	$0.50	$1.50	$2	$12	$32
2003-D, Illinois	237,400,000	2,082	65.2	100%	$0.50	$1.50	$2	$12	$32
2003-S, Illinois, Proof	3,408,516	5,615	69.3				$3	$5	$15
2003-S, Illinois, Proof, Silver	1,125,755	8,928	69.2				$9	$11	$20
2003-P, Alabama	225,000,000	287	65.7	100%	$0.35	$1	$1.50	$10	$30
2003-D, Alabama	232,400,000	2,083	65.1	100%	$0.35	$1	$1.50	$10	$30
2003-S, Alabama, Proof	3,408,516	5,701	69.3				$3	$5	$15
2003-S, Alabama, Proof, Silver	1,125,755	8,937	69.2				$9	$11	$20

	Mintage	Cert	Avg	%MS	AU-50	MS-63	MS-65 / PF-65	MS-66 / PF-66DC	MS-67 / PF-69DC
2003-P, Maine	217,400,000	257	65.8	100%	$0.35	$1	$1.50	$10	$30
2003-D, Maine	231,400,000	2,083	65.2	100%	$0.35	$1	$1.50	$10	$30
2003-S, Maine, Proof	3,408,516	5,567	69.2				$3	$5	$15
2003-S, Maine, Proof, Silver	1,125,755	8,739	69.2				$9	$11	$20
2003-P, Missouri	225,000,000	277	65.9	99%	$0.35	$1	$1.50	$10	$30
2003-D, Missouri	228,200,000	2,094	65.2	100%	$0.35	$1	$1.50	$10	$30
2003-S, Missouri, Proof	3,408,516	5,759	69.3				$3	$5	$15
2003-S, Missouri, Proof, Silver	1,125,755	8,921	69.2				$9	$11	$20
2003-P, Arkansas	228,000,000	247	65.8	100%	$0.35	$1	$1.50	$10	$30
2003-D, Arkansas	229,800,000	2,119	65.2	100%	$0.40	$1	$1.50	$10	$30
2003-S, Arkansas, Proof	3,408,516	5,707	69.3				$3	$5	$15
2003-S, Arkansas, Proof, Silver	1,125,755	8,920	69.3				$9	$11	$20

2004, Michigan
Reverse designer: Donna Weaver.

2004, Florida
Reverse designer: T. James Ferrell.

2004, Texas
Reverse designer: Norman E. Nemeth.

2004, Iowa
Reverse designer: John Mercanti.

2004, Wisconsin
Reverse designer: Alfred Maletsky.

2004-D, Wisconsin, Normal Reverse

2004-D, Wisconsin, Extra Leaf High
FS-25-2004D-WI-5901.

2004-D, Wisconsin, Extra Leaf Low
FS-25-2004D-WI-5902.

	Mintage	Cert	Avg	%MS	AU-50	MS-63	MS-65 / PF-65	MS-66 / PF-66DC	MS-67 / PF-69DC
2004-P, Michigan	233,800,000	2,362	65.2	100%	$0.35	$0.75	$3	$10	$30
2004-D, Michigan	225,800,000	411	67.3	100%	$0.35	$0.75	$3	$10	$30
2004-S, Michigan, Proof	2,740,684	3,861	69.3				$3	$5	$15
2004-S, Michigan, Proof, Silver	1,769,786	10,518	69.2				$9	$11	$20
2004-P, Florida	240,200,000	2,355	65.2	100%	$0.35	$0.75	$3	$10	$30
2004-D, Florida	241,600,000	317	66.9	100%	$0.35	$0.75	$3	$10	$30
2004-S, Florida, Proof	2,740,684	3,787	69.3				$3	$5	$15
2004-S, Florida, Proof, Silver	1,769,786	10,036	69.2				$9	$11	$20
2004-P, Texas	278,800,000	2,430	65.2	100%	$0.35	$0.75	$3	$10	$30
2004-D, Texas	263,000,000	377	66.7	100%	$0.35	$0.75	$3	$10	$30
2004-S, Texas, Proof	2,740,684	3,904	69.3				$3	$5	$15
2004-S, Texas, Proof, Silver	1,769,786	10,457	69.3				$9	$11	$20
2004-P, Iowa	213,800,000	2,334	65.1	100%	$0.35	$0.75	$3	$10	$30
2004-D, Iowa	251,400,000	295	66.8	100%	$0.35	$0.75	$3	$10	$30
2004-S, Iowa, Proof	2,740,684	3,942	69.4				$3	$5	$15
2004-S, Iowa, Proof, Silver	1,769,786	10,330	69.3				$9	$11	$20

	Mintage	Cert	Avg	%MS	AU-50	MS-63	MS-65	MS-66	MS-67
							PF-65	PF-66DC	PF-69DC
2004-P, Wisconsin	226,400,000	2,566	65.2	100%	$0.35	$0.75	$3	$10	$30
2004-D, Wisconsin	226,800,000	14,060	65.0	97%	$0.35	$0.75	$10	$15	$30
2004-D, Wisconsin, Extra Leaf High †† (a)	(b)	4,788	64.8	96%	$75	$170	$225	$325	$1,000
2004-D, Wisconsin, Extra Leaf Low †† (a)	(b)	6,465	64.9	97%	$50	$140	$175	$295	$800
2004-S, Wisconsin, Proof	2,740,684	3,932	69.3				$3	$5	$15
2004-S, Wisconsin, Proof, Silver	1,769,786	10,467	69.3				$9	$11	$20

†† Ranked in the *100 Greatest U.S. Modern Coins* (fourth edition). **a.** Some 2004-D, Wisconsin, quarters show one of two different die flaws on the reverse, in the shape of an extra leaf on the corn. **b.** Included in 2004-D, Wisconsin, mintage figure.

2005, California
Reverse designer:
Don Everhart.

2005, Minnesota
Reverse designer:
Charles Vickers.

2005, Oregon
Reverse designer:
Donna Weaver.

2005, Kansas
Reverse designer:
Norman E. Nemeth.

2005, West Virginia
Reverse designer:
John Mercanti.

	Mintage	Cert	Avg	%MS	AU-50	MS-63	MS-65	MS-66	MS-67
							PF-65	PF-66DC	PF-69DC
2005-P, California	257,200,000	3,307	66.8	100%	$0.30	$0.75	$5	$10	$30
2005-P, California, Satin Finish	1,160,000	2,843	67.0	100%			$3	$5	$12
2005-D, California	263,200,000	2,816	66.9	100%	$0.30	$0.75	$5	$10	$30
2005-D, California, Satin Finish	1,160,000	2,522	66.9	100%			$3	$5	$12
2005-S, California, Proof	3,262,960	8,624	69.3				$3	$4.50	$15
2005-S, California, Proof, Silver	1,678,649	11,340	69.4				$9	$11	$20
2005-P, Minnesota	239,600,000	3,334	66.9	100%	$0.30	$0.75	$5	$10	$30
2005-P, Minnesota, Satin Finish	1,160,000	2,965	67.2	100%			$3	$5	$12
2005-D, Minnesota	248,400,000	2,925	67.1	100%	$0.30	$0.75	$5	$10	$30
2005-D, Minnesota, Satin Finish	1,160,000	2,740	67.1	100%			$3	$5	$12
2005-S, Minnesota, Proof	3,262,960	8,587	69.3				$3	$4.50	$15
2005-S, Minnesota, Proof, Silver	1,678,649	11,088	69.4				$9	$11	$20
2005-P, Oregon	316,200,000	3,271	67.0	100%	$0.30	$0.75	$5	$10	$30
2005-P, Oregon, Satin Finish	1,160,000	3,009	67.2	100%			$3	$5	$12
2005-D, Oregon	404,000,000	2,888	67.1	100%	$0.30	$0.75	$5	$10	$30
2005-D, Oregon, Satin Finish	1,160,000	2,737	67.1	100%			$3	$5	$12
2005-S, Oregon, Proof	3,262,960	8,549	69.3				$3	$4.50	$15
2005-S, Oregon, Proof, Silver	1,678,649	11,066	69.4				$9	$11	$20
2005-P, Kansas	263,400,000	2,908	66.6	100%	$0.30	$0.75	$5	$10	$30
2005-P, Kansas, Satin Finish	1,160,000	2,559	66.8	100%			$3	$5	$12
2005-D, Kansas	300,000,000	2,878	67.0	100%	$0.30	$0.75	$5	$10	$30
2005-D, Kansas, Satin Finish	1,160,000	2,647	67.0	100%			$3	$5	$12
2005-S, Kansas, Proof	3,262,960	8,602	69.3				$3	$4.50	$15
2005-S, Kansas, Proof, Silver	1,678,649	11,207	69.3				$9	$11	$20
2005-P, West Virginia	365,400,000	3,135	66.8	100%	$0.30	$0.75	$5	$10	$30
2005-P, West Virginia, Satin Finish	1,160,000	2,833	67.0	100%			$3	$5	$12
2005-D, West Virginia	356,200,000	2,622	66.8	100%	$0.30	$0.75	$5	$10	$30
2005-D, West Virginia, Satin Finish	1,160,000	2,434	66.9	100%			$3	$5	$12
2005-S, West Virginia, Proof	3,262,960	8,616	69.3				$3	$4.50	$15
2005-S, West Virginia, Proof, Silver	1,678,649	11,209	69.4				$9	$11	$20

2006, Nevada	2006, Nebraska	2006, Colorado	2006, North Dakota	2006, South Dakota
Reverse designer:	*Reverse designer:*	*Reverse designer:*	*Reverse designer:*	*Reverse designer:*
Don Everhart.	*Charles Vickers.*	*Norman E. Nemeth.*	*Donna Weaver.*	*John Mercanti.*

	Mintage	Cert	Avg	%MS	AU-50	MS-63	MS-65 / PF-65	MS-66 / PF-66DC	MS-67 / PF-69DC
2006-P, Nevada	277,000,000	1,339	66.5	100%	$0.30	$0.75	$1	$10	$30
2006-P, Nevada, Satin Finish	847,361	1,057	66.6	100%			$3	$5	$12
2006-D, Nevada	312,800,000	1,650	66.8	100%	$0.30	$0.75	$1	$10	$30
2006-D, Nevada, Satin Finish	847,361	1,282	66.9	100%			$3	$5	$12
2006-S, Nevada, Proof	2,882,428	5,956	69.4				$3	$4.50	$15
2006-S, Nevada, Proof, Silver	1,585,008	10,021	69.5				$9	$11	$20
2006-P, Nebraska	318,000,000	1,490	66.9	100%	$0.30	$0.75	$2	$10	$30
2006-P, Nebraska, Satin Finish	847,361	1,343	67.0	100%			$3	$5	$12
2006-D, Nebraska	273,000,000	1,864	67.1	100%	$0.30	$0.75	$2	$10	$30
2006-D, Nebraska, Satin Finish	847,361	1,597	67.2	100%			$3	$5	$12
2006-S, Nebraska, Proof	2,882,428	5,960	69.4				$3	$4.50	$15
2006-S, Nebraska, Proof, Silver	1,585,008	9,907	69.5				$9	$11	$20
2006-P, Colorado	274,800,000	1,454	66.7	100%	$0.30	$0.75	$2	$10	$30
2006-P, Colorado, Satin Finish	847,361	1,190	66.8	100%			$3	$5	$12
2006-D, Colorado	294,200,000	1,951	67.0	100%	$0.30	$0.75	$2	$10	$30
2006-D, Colorado, Satin Finish	847,361	1,512	67.2	100%			$3	$5	$12
2006-S, Colorado, Proof	2,882,428	5,947	69.4				$3	$4.50	$15
2006-S, Colorado, Proof, Silver	1,585,008	10,012	69.5				$9	$11	$20
2006-P, North Dakota	305,800,000	1,331	66.6	100%	$0.30	$0.75	$2	$10	$30
2006-P, North Dakota, Satin Finish	847,361	1,145	66.8	100%			$3	$5	$12
2006-D, North Dakota	359,000,000	1,829	67.0	100%	$0.30	$0.75	$2	$10	$30
2006-D, North Dakota, Satin Finish	847,361	1,547	67.1	100%			$3	$5	$12
2006-S, North Dakota, Proof	2,882,428	5,957	69.4				$3	$4.50	$15
2006-S, North Dakota, Proof, Silver	1,585,008	9,994	69.5				$9	$11	$20
2006-P, South Dakota	245,000,000	1,502	66.8	100%	$0.30	$0.75	$2	$10	$30
2006-P, South Dakota, Satin Finish	847,361	1,322	66.9	100%			$3	$5	$12
2006-D, South Dakota	265,800,000	1,746	67.0	100%	$0.30	$0.75	$2	$10	$30
2006-D, South Dakota, Satin Finish	847,361	1,554	67.1	100%			$3	$5	$12
2006-S, South Dakota, Proof	2,882,428	5,968	69.5				$3	$4.50	$15
2006-S, South Dakota, Proof, Silver	1,585,008	9,990	69.5				$9	$11	$20

2007, Montana	2007, Washington	2007, Idaho	2007, Wyoming	2007, Utah
Reverse designer:	*Reverse designer:*	*Reverse designer:*	*Reverse designer:*	*Reverse designer:*
Don Everhart.	*Charles Vickers.*	*Don Everhart.*	*Norman E. Nemeth.*	*Joseph Menna.*

	Mintage	Cert	Avg	%MS	AU-50	MS-63	MS-65 / PF-65	MS-66 / PF-66DC	MS-67 / PF-69DC
2007-P, Montana	257,000,000	455	66.4	100%	$0.30	$0.75	$4	$10	$30

	Mintage	Cert	Avg	%MS	AU-50	MS-63	MS-65	MS-66	MS-67
							PF-65	PF-66DC	PF-69DC
2007-P, Montana, Satin Finish	895,628	338	66.6	100%			$3	$5	$12
2007-D, Montana	256,240,000	502	66.3	100%	$0.30	$0.75	$4	$10	$30
2007-D, Montana, Satin Finish	895,628	331	66.5	100%			$3	$5	$12
2007-S, Montana, Proof	2,374,778	3,433	69.5				$3	$4.50	$15
2007-S, Montana, Proof, Silver	1,313,481	8,522	69.4				$9	$11	$20
2007-P, Washington	265,200,000	467	66.3	100%	$0.30	$0.75	$4	$10	$30
2007-P, Washington, Satin Finish	895,628	316	66.4	100%			$3	$5	$12
2007-D, Washington	280,000,000	509	66.4	99%	$0.30	$0.75	$4	$10	$30
2007-D, Washington, Satin Finish	895,628	351	66.7	100%			$3	$5	$12
2007-S, Washington, Proof	2,374,778	3,221	69.5				$3	$4.50	$15
2007-S, Washington, Proof, Silver	1,313,481	8,451	69.4				$9	$11	$20
2007-P, Idaho	294,600,000	438	66.5	100%	$0.30	$0.75	$4	$10	$30
2007-P, Idaho, Satin Finish	895,628	359	66.6	100%			$3	$5	$12
2007-D, Idaho	286,800,000	471	66.4	100%	$0.30	$0.75	$4	$10	$30
2007-D, Idaho, Satin Finish	895,628	335	66.5	100%			$3	$5	$12
2007-S, Idaho, Proof	2,374,778	3,237	69.5				$3	$4.50	$15
2007-S, Idaho, Proof, Silver	1,313,481	8,504	69.4				$9	$11	$20
2007-P, Wyoming	243,600,000	386	65.9	100%	$0.30	$0.75	$4	$10	$30
2007-P, Wyoming, Satin Finish	895,628	298	66.2	100%			$3	$5	$12
2007-D, Wyoming	320,800,000	517	66.3	100%	$0.30	$0.75	$4	$10	$30
2007-D, Wyoming, Satin Finish	895,628	346	66.5	100%			$3	$5	$12
2007-S, Wyoming, Proof	2,374,778	3,163	69.4				$3	$4.50	$15
2007-S, Wyoming, Proof, Silver	1,313,481	8,351	69.3				$9	$11	$20
2007-P, Utah	255,000,000	454	66.1	100%	$0.30	$0.75	$4	$10	$30
2007-P, Utah, Satin Finish	895,628	313	66.3	100%			$3	$5	$12
2007-D, Utah	253,200,000	555	66.4	100%	$0.30	$0.75	$4	$10	$30
2007-D, Utah, Satin Finish	895,628	337	66.6	100%			$3	$5	$12
2007-S, Utah, Proof	2,374,778	3,183	69.5				$3	$4.50	$15
2007-S, Utah, Proof, Silver	1,313,481	8,531	69.4				$9	$11	$20

2008, Oklahoma
Reverse designer:
Phebe Hemphill.

2008, New Mexico
Reverse designer:
Don Everhart.

2008, Arizona
Reverse designer:
Joseph Menna.

2008, Alaska
Reverse designer:
Charles Vickers.

2008, Hawaii
Reverse designer:
Don Everhart.

	Mintage	Cert	Avg	%MS	AU-50	MS-63	MS-65	MS-66	MS-67
							PF-65	PF-66DC	PF-69DC
2008-P, Oklahoma	222,000,000	242	66.6	99%	$0.30	$0.75	$2	$10	$30
2008-P, Oklahoma, Satin Finish	745,464	135	67.3	100%			$3	$5	$12
2008-D, Oklahoma	194,600,000	240	66.7	100%	$0.30	$0.75	$2	$10	$30
2008-D, Oklahoma, Satin Finish	745,464	115	67.2	100%			$3	$5	$12
2008-S, Oklahoma, Proof	2,078,112	3,515	69.5				$3	$5	$18
2008-S, Oklahoma, Proof, Silver	1,192,908	8,894	69.5				$9	$11	$22
2008-P, New Mexico	244,200,000	222	66.3	100%	$0.30	$0.75	$2	$10	$30
2008-P, New Mexico, Satin Finish	745,464	118	67.1	100%			$3	$5	$12
2008-D, New Mexico	244,400,000	231	66.6	100%	$0.30	$0.75	$2	$10	$30
2008-D, New Mexico, Satin Finish	745,464	85	67.0	100%			$3	$5	$12

	Mintage	Cert	Avg	%MS	AU-50	MS-63	MS-65	MS-66	MS-67
							PF-65	PF-66DC	PF-69DC
2008-S, New Mexico, Proof	2,078,112	3,576	69.4				$3	$5	$18
2008-S, New Mexico, Proof, Silver	1,192,908	8,749	69.5				$9	$11	$22
2008-P, Arizona	244,600,000	296	66.6	100%	$0.30	$0.75	$2	$10	$30
2008-P, Arizona, Satin Finish	745,464	141	67.3	100%			$3	$5	$12
2008-D, Arizona	265,000,000	179	66.9	99%	$0.30	$0.75	$2	$10	$30
2008-D, Arizona, Satin Finish	745,464	98	67.4	100%			$3	$5	$12
2008-S, Arizona, Proof	2,078,112	3,661	69.6				$3	$5	$18
2008-S, Arizona, Proof, Silver	1,192,908	9,150	69.5				$9	$11	$22
2008-P, Alaska	251,800,000	244	66.7	100%	$0.30	$0.75	$2	$10	$30
2008-P, Alaska, Satin Finish	745,464	131	67.3	100%			$3	$5	$12
2008-D, Alaska	254,000,000	191	66.5	100%	$0.30	$0.75	$2	$10	$30
2008-D, Alaska, Satin Finish	745,464	96	67.0	100%			$3	$5	$12
2008-S, Alaska, Proof	2,078,112	3,495	69.5				$3	$5	$18
2008-S, Alaska, Proof, Silver	1,192,908	9,068	69.5				$9	$11	$22
2008-P, Hawaii	254,000,000	328	66.2	100%	$0.30	$1	$2	$10	$30
2008-P, Hawaii, Satin Finish	745,464	147	67.3	100%			$3	$5	$12
2008-D, Hawaii	263,600,000	194	66.5	100%	$0.30	$1	$2	$10	$30
2008-D, Hawaii, Satin Finish	745,464	108	67.0	100%			$3	$5	$12
2008-S, Hawaii, Proof	2,078,112	3,519	69.4				$3	$10	$25
2008-S, Hawaii, Proof, Silver	1,192,908	9,091	69.4				$10	$12	$22

2009, District of Columbia
Reverse designer: Don Everhart.

2009, Puerto Rico
Reverse designer: Joseph Menna.

2009, Guam
Reverse designer: Jim Licaretz.

2009, American Samoa
Reverse designer: Charles Vickers.

2009, U.S. Virgin Islands
Reverse designer: Joseph Menna.

2009, Northern Mariana Islands
Reverse designer: Phebe Hemphill.

	Mintage	Cert	Avg	%MS	AU-50	MS-63	MS-65	MS-66	MS-67
							PF-65	PF-66DC	PF-69DC
2009-P, District of Columbia	83,600,000	361	67.1	100%	$0.50	$1	$2	$10	$30
2009-P, District of Columbia, Satin Finish	784,614	260	67.5	100%			$3	$5	$12
2009-D, District of Columbia	88,800,000	400	67.3	99%	$0.50	$1	$2	$10	$30
2009-D, District of Columbia, Satin Finish	784,614	267	67.8	100%			$3	$5	$12
2009-S, District of Columbia, Proof	2,113,478	4,159	69.6				$3	$4.50	$15
2009-S, District of Columbia, Proof, Silver	996,548	6,519	69.7				$10	$12	$20
2009-P, Puerto Rico	53,200,000	304	66.9	100%	$0.50	$1	$2	$10	$30
2009-P, Puerto Rico, Satin Finish	784,614	189	67.4	100%			$3	$5	$12
2009-D, Puerto Rico	86,000,000	350	67.4	100%	$0.50	$1	$2	$10	$30
2009-D, Puerto Rico, Satin Finish	784,614	232	67.8	100%			$3	$5	$12
2009-S, Puerto Rico, Proof	2,113,478	4,149	69.6				$3	$4.50	$15
2009-S, Puerto Rico, Proof, Silver	996,548	6,695	69.7				$10	$12	$20

	Mintage	Cert	Avg	%MS	AU-50	MS-63	MS-65	MS-66	MS-67
							PF-65	PF-66DC	PF-69DC
2009-P, Guam	45,000,000	291	67.1	100%	$0.50	$1	$2	$10	$30
2009-P, Guam, Satin Finish	784,614	233	67.3	100%			$3	$5	$12
2009-D, Guam	42,600,000	296	67.3	100%	$0.50	$1	$2	$10	$30
2009-D, Guam, Satin Finish	784,614	204	67.5	100%			$3	$5	$12
2009-S, Guam, Proof	2,113,478	4,045	69.6				$3	$4.50	$15
2009-S, Guam, Proof, Silver	996,548	6,456	69.7				$10	$12	$20
2009-P, American Samoa	42,600,000	434	67.4	100%	$0.50	$1	$2	$10	$30
2009-P, American Samoa, Satin Finish	784,614	295	67.8	100%			$3	$5	$12
2009-D, American Samoa	39,600,000	492	67.8	100%	$0.50	$1	$2	$10	$30
2009-D, American Samoa, Satin Finish	784,614	336	68.2	100%			$3	$5	$12
2009-S, American Samoa, Proof	2,113,478	4,211	69.6				$3	$4.50	$15
2009-S, American Samoa, Proof, Silver	996,548	6,598	69.7				$10	$12	$20
2009-P, U.S. Virgin Islands	41,000,000	438	67.0	100%	$0.75	$1	$2	$12	$32
2009-P, U.S. Virgin Islands, Satin Finish	784,614	286	67.2	100%			$3	$5	$12
2009-D, U.S. Virgin Islands	41,000,000	446	67.4	100%	$0.75	$1	$2	$12	$32
2009-D, U.S. Virgin Islands, Satin Finish	784,614	320	67.8	100%			$3	$5	$12
2009-S, U.S. Virgin Islands, Proof	2,113,478	4,185	69.6				$3	$4.50	$15
2009-S, U.S. Virgin Islands, Proof, Silver	996,548	6,568	69.7				$10	$12	$20
2009-P, Northern Mariana Islands	35,200,000	468	67.5	100%	$0.50	$1	$2	$10	$30
2009-P, Northern Mariana Islands, Satin Finish	784,614	312	67.8	100%			$3	$5	$12
2009-D, Northern Mariana Islands	37,600,000	436	67.4	100%	$0.50	$1	$2	$10	$30
2009-D, Northern Mariana Islands, Satin Finish	784,614	293	67.7	100%			$3	$5	$12
2009-S, Northern Mariana Islands, Proof	2,113,478	4,188	69.6				$3	$4.50	$15
2009-S, Northern Mariana Islands, Proof, Silver	996,548	6,559	69.7				$10	$12	$20

WASHINGTON, AMERICA THE BEAUTIFUL™ (2010–2021)

Designers: *John Flanagan (obverse); see image captions for reverse designers.* **Weight:** *Clad issue—5.67 grams; silver Proofs (2010–2018)—6.25 grams; silver Proofs (2019 to date)—6.343 grams.* **Composition:** *Clad issue—Outer layers of copper-nickel (.750 copper, .250 nickel) bonded to inner core of pure copper; silver Proofs (2010–2018)—.900 silver, .100 copper (net weight .18084 oz. pure silver); silver Proofs (2019 to date)—.999 silver, .001 copper (net weight .182 oz. pure silver).* **Diameter:** *24.3 mm.* **Edge:** *Reeded.* **Mints:** *Clad issue—Philadelphia, Denver, San Francisco, and West Point.*

Circulation Strike   Proof

History. In 2010 the U.S. Mint introduced a new program of quarters honoring national parks and historic sites in each state, the District of Columbia, and the five U.S. territories. They were released at the rate of five new reverse designs each year, in combination with the obverse found on the State and D.C./Territorial quarters of previous years; the program concluded in 2021 with the Tuskegee Airmen National Historic Site (Alabama) quarter. Circulation strikes were made at the Philadelphia and Denver mints, and special silvercontent and Proof issues at San Francisco. Each coin features a modified obverse depicting

George Washington, without a date. The reverses are distinctive and bear the date of issue and a special design showcasing a national park in the state, district, or territory. The official title of the series was the America the Beautiful™ Quarters Program; popularly, they are known as National Park quarters.

In 2012, the U.S. Mint introduced a new innovation in the National Park quarters program. For the first time since the 1950s, the San Francisco Mint is being used to produce quarters in a non-Proof format. These Uncirculated coins are made in limited quantities for collectors. They can be purchased directly from the Mint for a premium above their face value, as opposed to being released into circulation like normal quarters. Unlike the Uncirculated S-mintmark Bicentennial quarters dated 1976, which were 40% silver and sold only in sets, the S-mintmark National Park quarters are of normal copper-nickel–clad composition and are sold in bags of 100 and rolls of 40 coins. Thus the 2012-S coins are considered the first circulation-strike quarters made at San Francisco since 1954. The S-mintmark coins have been made of each National Park design from 2012 to date.

Striking and Sharpness. These quarters can have light striking on the highest area of the obverse. On the reverse there can be weak areas, depending on the design, seemingly more often seen on Denver Mint coins.

Availability. All modern quarters are readily available in high grades. Typical MS coins are MS–63 and 64 with light abrasion. MS-65 and higher coins are in the minority, but enough exist that finding them is easy. Around MS-68 many issues are scarce; higher grades are scarcer yet. The S-mintmark coins are proportionally scarce compared to Philadelphia and Denver issues, and are not seen in circulation. They are available for direct purchase from the U.S. Mint in their year of issue, and from the secondary market after that.

Proofs. National Park quarter dollar Proofs are made in San Francisco. Through 2018, silver Proofs were .900 fine silver; as of 2019, all regular silver Mint products are .999 fine silver. Proofs are available in clad metal as well as silver strikings. On some Proofs over-polishing of dies has eliminated some details.

GRADING STANDARDS

MS-60 to 70 (Mint State). *Obverse:* At MS-60, some abrasion and contact marks are evident on the highest-relief parts of the hair and the cheek. At MS-63, abrasion is slight at best, less so at MS-64. An MS-65 coin should display no abrasion or contact marks except under magnification, and MS-66 and higher coins should have none at all. Luster should be full. *Reverse:* Check the highest-relief areas of the design (these differ from coin to coin). Otherwise, comments are as for the obverse.

2010-D, Hot Springs (AR). Graded MS-68.

America the Beautiful quarter dollars are seldom collected in grades lower than MS-60.

PF-60 to 70 (Proof). *Obverse and Reverse:* These coins are so recent, and as only a few have been cleaned, most approach perfection and can be designated PF–68 to 70, the latter only if no contact marks or other problems can be seen under magnification. A cleaned coin with extensive hairlines would not be collectible for most numismatists and would be classified at a lower level such as PF–60 to 63. Those with lighter hairlines qualify for PF–64 or 65.

2010-S, Grand Canyon (AZ).
Graded PF-69 Ultra Cameo.

2010, Hot Springs National Park (AR)
Reverse designer: Don Everhart.

2010, Yellowstone National Park (WY)
Reverse designer: Don Everhart.

2010, Yosemite National Park (CA)
Reverse designer: Joseph Menna.

2010, Grand Canyon National Park (AZ)
Reverse designer: Phebe Hemphill.

2010, Mt. Hood National Forest (OR)
Reverse designer: Phebe Hemphill.

	Mintage	Cert	Avg	%MS	AU-50	MS-63	MS-65 PF-65	MS-66 PF-66DC	MS-67 PF-69DC
2010-P, Hot Springs National Park (AR)	35,600,000	1,095	66.6	100%	$0.45	$0.50	$1	$10	$30
2010-P, Hot Springs National Park (AR), Satin Finish	583,897	372	67.5	100%			$3	$5	$12
2010-D, Hot Springs National Park (AR)	34,000,000	1,983	66.0	100%	$0.45	$0.50	$1	$10	$30
2010-D, Hot Springs National Park (AR), Satin Finish	583,897	410	67.5	100%			$3	$5	$12
2010-S, Hot Springs National Park (AR), Proof	1,402,889	4,051	69.5				$3	$4.50	$15
2010-S, Hot Springs, National Park (AR), Proof, Silver	859,417	11,250	69.6				$9	$11	$20
2010-P, Yellowstone National Park (WY)	33,600,000	800	66.6	100%	$0.45	$0.50	$2	$10	$30
2010-P, Yellowstone National Park (WY), Satin Finish	583,897	345	67.4	100%			$3	$5	$12
2010-D, Yellowstone National Park (WY)	34,800,000	1,134	66.3	100%	$0.45	$0.50	$2	$10	$30
2010-D, Yellowstone National Park (WY), Satin Finish	583,897	361	67.4	100%			$3	$5	$12
2010-S, Yellowstone National Park (WY), Proof	1,404,259	4,089	69.5				$3	$4.50	$15
2010-S, Yellowstone National Park (WY), Proof, Silver	859,417	11,260	69.7				$9	$11	$20
2010-P, Yosemite National Park (CA)	35,200,000	676	66.8	100%	$0.50	$0.75	$2	$12	$30
2010-P, Yosemite National Park (CA), Satin Finish	583,897	376	67.3	100%			$3	$5	$12
2010-D, Yosemite National Park (CA)	34,800,000	1,033	66.5	100%	$0.50	$0.75	$2	$12	$30
2010-D, Yosemite National Park (CA), Satin Finish	583,897	403	67.3	100%			$3	$5	$12
2010-S, Yosemite National Park (CA), Proof	1,401,522	4,015	69.5				$3	$4.50	$15
2010-S, Yosemite National Park (CA), Proof, Silver	859,417	11,159	69.6				$9	$11	$20
2010-P, Grand Canyon National Park (AZ)	34,800,000	768	66.9	100%	$0.45	$0.50	$1	$10	$30
2010-P, Grand Canyon National Park (AZ), Satin Finish	583,897	391	67.5	100%			$3	$5	$12
2010-D, Grand Canyon National Park (AZ)	35,400,000	1,073	66.7	100%	$0.45	$0.50	$1	$10	$30
2010-D, Grand Canyon National Park (AZ), Satin Finish	583,897	438	67.7	100%			$3	$5	$12
2010-S, Grand Canyon National Park (AZ), Proof	1,401,462	4,001	69.5				$3	$4.50	$15
2010-S, Grand Canyon National Park (AZ), Proof, Silver	859,417	11,181	69.6				$9	$11	$20
2010-P, Mt. Hood National Forest (OR)	34,400,000	560	66.9	100%	$0.45	$0.50	$2	$10	$30
2010-P, Mt. Hood National Forest (OR), Satin Finish	583,897	343	67.3	100%			$3	$5	$12
2010-D, Mt. Hood National Forest (OR)	34,400,000	859	66.6	100%	$0.45	$0.50	$2	$10	$30
2010-D, Mt. Hood National Forest (OR), Satin Finish	583,897	441	67.4	100%			$3	$5	$12
2010-S, Mt. Hood National Forest (OR), Proof	1,398,106	4,016	69.4				$3	$4.50	$15
2010-S, Mt. Hood National Forest (OR), Proof, Silver	859,417	11,354	69.6				$9	$11	$20

2011, Gettysburg National Military Park (PA)
Reverse designer: Joel Iskowitz.

2011, Glacier National Park (MT)
Reverse designer: Barbara Fox.

2011, Olympic National Park (WA)
Reverse designer: Susan Gamble.

2011, Vicksburg National Military Park (MS)
Reverse designer: Thomas Cleveland.

2011, Chickasaw National Recreation Area (OK)
Reverse designer: Donna Weaver.

	Mintage	Cert	Avg	%MS	AU-50	MS-63	MS-65 PF-65	MS-66 PF-66DC	MS-67 PF-69DC
2011-P, Gettysburg National Military Park (PA)	30,800,000	760	66.3	100%	$0.50	$0.75	$1.25	$12	$30
2011-D, Gettysburg National Military Park (PA)	30,400,000	307	66.5	100%	$0.50	$0.75	$1.25	$12	$30
2011-S, Gettysburg National Military Park (PA), Proof	1,273,068	2,760	69.5				$3	$4.50	$15
2011-S, Gettysburg National Military Park (PA), Proof, Silver	722,076	6,000	69.7				$10	$12	$20
2011-P, Glacier National Park (MT)	30,400,000	297	67.1	100%	$0.45	$0.50	$1	$10	$30
2011-D, Glacier National Park (MT)	31,200,000	462	65.9	100%	$0.45	$0.50	$1	$10	$30
2011-S, Glacier National Park (MT), Proof	1,269,422	2,758	69.6				$3	$4.50	$15
2011-S, Glacier National Park (MT), Proof, Silver	722,076	6,155	69.7				$10	$12	$20
2011-P, Olympic National Park (WA)	30,400,000	312	67.1	100%	$0.45	$0.50	$2	$10	$30
2011-D, Olympic National Park (WA)	30,600,000	560	66.2	100%	$0.45	$0.50	$2	$10	$30
2011-S, Olympic National Park (WA), Proof	1,268,231	2,772	69.6				$3	$4.50	$15
2011-S, Olympic National Park (WA), Proof, Silver	722,076	5,977	69.7				$10	$12	$20
2011-P, Vicksburg National Military Park (MS)	30,800,000	284	66.8	100%	$0.45	$0.50	$1	$10	$30
2011-D, Vicksburg National Military Park (MS)	33,400,000	481	66.3	100%	$0.45	$0.50	$1	$10	$30
2011-S, Vicksburg National Military Park (MS), Proof	1,268,623	2,765	69.5				$3	$4.50	$15
2011-S, Vicksburg National Military Park (MS), Proof, Silver	722,076	6,020	69.7				$10	$12	$20
2011-P, Chickasaw National Recreation Area (OK)	73,800,000	329	67.2	100%	$0.45	$0.50	$1	$10	$30
2011-D, Chickasaw National Recreation Area (OK)	69,400,000	435	66.2	100%	$0.45	$0.50	$1	$10	$30
2011-S, Chickasaw National Recreation Area (OK), Proof	1,266,825	2,752	69.5				$3	$4.50	$15
2011-S, Chickasaw National Recreation Area (OK), Proof, Silver	722,076	5,936	69.6				$10	$12	$20

2012, El Yunque National Forest (PR)
Reverse designer: Gary Whitley.

2012, Chaco Culture National Historical Park (NM)
Reverse designer: Donna Weaver.

2012, Acadia National Park (ME)
Reverse designer: Barbara Fox.

2012, Hawai'i Volcanoes National Park (HI)
Reverse designer: Charles L. Vickers.

2012, Denali National Park and Preserve (AK)
Reverse designer: Susan Gamble.

	Mintage	Cert	Avg	%MS	AU-50	MS-63	MS-65 PF-65	MS-66 PF-66DC	MS-67 PF-69DC
2012-P, El Yunque National Forest (PR)	25,800,000	568	66.1	100%	$0.45	$0.50	$2	$10	$30
2012-D, El Yunque National Forest (PR)	25,000,000	257	66.8	100%	$0.45	$0.50	$2	$10	$30
2012-S, El Yunque National Forest (PR) (a)	1,680,140	649	66.4	100%		$1	$8	$12	$35
2012-S, El Yunque National Forest (PR), Proof	1,012,094	2,069	69.4				$3	$4.50	$15
2012-S, El Yunque National Forest (PR), Proof, Silver	608,060	5,378	69.7				$10	$12	$20
2012-P, Chaco Culture National Historical Park (NM)	22,000,000	150	67.1	100%	$0.45	$0.50	$2	$10	$30
2012-D, Chaco Culture National Historical Park (NM)	22,000,000	360	66.2	100%	$0.45	$0.50	$2	$10	$30
2012-S, Chaco Culture National Historical Park (NM) (a)	1,389,020	672	66.5	100%		$2	$8	$12	$35
2012-S, Chaco Culture National Historical Park (NM), Proof	961,464	2,030	69.3				$3	$4.50	$15
2012-S, Chaco Culture National Historical Park (NM), Proof, Silver	608,060	5,124	69.7				$10	$12	$20
2012-P, Acadia National Park (ME)	24,800,000	346	65.6	100%	$0.45	$0.50	$1	$10	$30
2012-D, Acadia National Park (ME)	21,606,000	117	66.7	100%	$0.45	$0.50	$1	$10	$30
2012-S, Acadia National Park (ME) (a)	1,409,120	672	66.3	100%		$2	$8	$12	$35
2012-S, Acadia National Park (ME), Proof	962,038	2,033	69.3				$3	$4.50	$15
2012-S, Acadia National Park (ME), Proof, Silver	608,060	5,293	69.7				$10	$12	$20

a. Not issued for circulation. From 2012–2021, the San Francisco Mint made Uncirculated S-mintmark quarters of each design in the National Park series. These could be purchased by collectors directly from the U.S. Mint, in bags of 100 or rolls of 40 coins, for a premium above face value.

| | Mintage | Cert | Avg | %MS | AU-50 | MS-63 | MS-65 | MS-66 | MS-67 |
							PF-65	PF-66DC	PF-69DC
2012-P, Hawai'i Volcanoes National Park (HI)	46,200,000	139	67.0	99%	$0.45	$0.50	$1	$10	$30
2012-D, Hawai'i Volcanoes National Park (HI)	78,600,000	411	66.1	100%	$0.45	$0.50	$1	$10	$30
2012-S, Hawai'i Volcanoes National Park (HI) (a)	1,409,120	617	66.3	100%		$2	$8	$12	$35
2012-S, Hawai'i Volcanoes National Park (HI), Proof	962,447	2,036	69.3				$3	$4.50	$15
2012-S, Hawai'i Volcanoes National Park (HI), Proof, Silver	608,060	5,431	69.7				$11	$14	$20
2012-P, Denali National Park and Preserve (AK)	135,400,000	158	67.0	100%	$0.40	$0.50	$1	$10	$30
2012-D, Denali National Park and Preserve (AK)	166,600,000	447	66.2	100%	$0.40	$0.50	$1	$10	$30
2012-S, Denali National Park and Preserve (AK) (a)	1,409,220	536	66.2	100%		$1	$8	$12	$35
2012-S, Denali National Park and Preserve (AK), Proof	959,602	2,038	69.3				$3	$4.50	$15
2012-S, Denali National Park and Preserve (AK), Proof, Silver	608,060	5,319	69.7				$10	$12	$20

a. Not issued for circulation. From 2012–2021, the San Francisco Mint made Uncirculated S-mintmark quarters of each design in the National Park series. These could be purchased by collectors directly from the U.S. Mint, in bags of 100 or rolls of 40 coins, for a premium above face value.

2013, White Mountain National Forest (NH)
Reverse designer: Phebe Hemphill.

2013, Perry's Victory and International Peace Memorial (OH)
Reverse designer: Don Everhart.

2013, Great Basin National Park (NV)
Reverse designer: Ronald D. Sanders.

2013, Fort McHenry National Monument and Historic Shrine (MD)
Reverse designer: Joseph Menna.

2013, Mount Rushmore National Memorial (SD)
Reverse designer: Joseph Menna.

| | Mintage | Cert | Avg | %MS | AU-50 | MS-63 | MS-65 | MS-66 | MS-67 |
							PF-65	PF-66DC	PF-69DC
2013-P, White Mountain National Forest (NH)	68,800,000	557	66.5	100%	$0.45	$0.50	$1	$10	$30
2013-D, White Mountain National Forest (NH)	107,600,000	321	67.1	100%	$0.45	$0.50	$1	$10	$30
2013-S, White Mountain National Forest (NH) (a)	1,606,900	380	66.5	100%		$1.50	$8	$12	$35
2013-S, White Mountain National Forest (NH), Proof	989,803	1,893	69.5				$3	$4.50	$15
2013-S, White Mountain National Forest (NH), Proof, Silver	467,691	5,015	69.7				$10	$12	$20
2013-P, Perry's Victory and Int'l Peace Memorial (OH)	107,800,000	492	66.5	100%	$0.45	$0.50	$2	$10	$30
2013-D, Perry's Victory and Int'l Peace Memorial (OH)	131,600,000	300	67.1	100%	$0.45	$0.50	$2	$10	$30
2013-S, Perry's Victory and Int'l Peace Memorial (OH) (a)	1,425,860	306	66.4	100%		$1.50	$8	$12	$35
2013-S, Perry's Victory and Int'l Peace Memorial (OH), Proof	947,815	1,862	69.5				$3	$4.50	$15
2013-S, Perry's Victory and Int'l Peace Memorial (OH), Proof, Silver	467,691	4,898	69.7				$10	$12	$20
2013-P, Great Basin National Park (NV)	122,400,000	230	66.9	100%	$0.45	$0.50	$1	$10	$30
2013-D, Great Basin National Park (NV)	141,400,000	460	66.5	100%	$0.45	$0.50	$1	$10	$30
2013-S, Great Basin National Park (NV) (a)	1,316,500	373	66.9	100%		$1.50	$8	$12	$35
2013-S, Great Basin National Park (NV), Proof	945,777	1,862	69.5				$3	$4.50	$15
2013-S, Great Basin National Park (NV), Proof, Silver	467,691	5,071	69.7				$10	$12	$20
2013-P, Ft. McHenry Nat'l Monument / Historic Shrine (MD)	120,000,000	502	66.5	100%	$0.45	$0.50	$1	$10	$30
2013-D, Ft. McHenry Nat'l Monument / Historic Shrine (MD)	151,400,000	320	67.2	100%	$0.45	$0.50	$1	$10	$30
2013-S, Ft. McHenry Nat'l Monument / Historic Shrine (MD) (a)	1,313,680	610	67.1	100%		$1.50	$8	$12	$35
2013-S, Ft. McHenry Nat'l Monument / Historic Shrine (MD), Proof	946,380	1,860	69.5				$3	$4.50	$15
2013-S, Ft. McHenry National Monument / Historic Shrine (MD), Proof, Silver	467,691	5,028	69.7				$10	$12	$20

a. Not issued for circulation. From 2012–2021, the San Francisco Mint made Uncirculated S-mintmark quarters of each design in the National Park series. These could be purchased by collectors directly from the U.S. Mint, in bags of 100 or rolls of 40 coins, for a premium above face value.

	Mintage	Cert	Avg	%MS	AU-50	MS-63	MS-65	MS-66	MS-67
							PF-65	PF-66DC	PF-69DC
2013-P, Mount Rushmore National Memorial (SD)	231,800,000	210	66.8	100%	$0.45	$0.50	$1	$10	$30
2013-D, Mount Rushmore National Memorial (SD)	272,400,000	458	66.3	100%	$0.45	$0.50	$1	$10	$30
2013-S, Mount Rushmore National Memorial (SD) (a)	1,373,260	561	66.9	100%		$1.50	$8	$12	$35
2013-S, Mount Rushmore National Memorial (SD), Proof	958,853	1,863	69.5				$3	$4.50	$15
2013-S, Mount Rushmore National Memorial (SD), Proof, Silver	467,691	5,044	69.7				$10	$12	$20

a. Not issued for circulation. From 2012–2021, the San Francisco Mint made Uncirculated S-mintmark quarters of each design in the National Park series. These could be purchased by collectors directly from the U.S. Mint, in bags of 100 or rolls of 40 coins, for a premium above face value.

2014, Great Smoky Mountains National Park (TN) Reverse designer: Chris Costello.	**2014, Shenandoah National Park (VA)** Reverse designer: Phebe Hemphill.	**2014, Arches National Park (UT)** Reverse designer: Donna Weaver.	**2014, Great Sand Dunes National Park (CO)** Reverse designer: Don Everhart.	**2014, Everglades National Park (FL)** Reverse designer: Joel Iskowitz.

	Mintage	Cert	Avg	%MS	AU-50	MS-63	MS-65	MS-66	MS-67
							PF-65	PF-66DC	PF-69DC
2014-P, Great Smoky Mountains National Park (TN)	73,200,000	515	66.6	100%	$0.45	$0.50	$1	$10	$30
2014-D, Great Smoky Mountains National Park (TN)	99,400,000	396	67.1	100%	$0.45	$0.50	$1	$10	$30
2014-S, Great Smoky Mountains National Park (TN) (a)	1,360,780	547	66.7	100%		$2	$8	$12	$35
2014-S, Great Smoky Mountains National Park (TN), Proof	881,896	2,097	69.5				$3	$4.50	$15
2014-S, Great Smoky Mountains National Park (TN), Proof, Silver	472,107	4,331	69.7				$10	$12	$20
2014-P, Shenandoah National Park (VA)	112,800,000	455	66.5	100%	$0.45	$0.50	$1	$10	$30
2014-D, Shenandoah National Park (VA)	197,800,000	288	67.4	100%	$0.45	$0.50	$1	$10	$30
2014-S, Shenandoah National Park (VA) (a)	1,266,720	773	66.9	100%		$1.50	$8	$12	$35
2014-S, Shenandoah National Park (VA), Proof	846,441	2,092	69.5				$3	$4.50	$15
2014-S, Shenandoah National Park (VA), Proof, Silver	472,107	4,336	69.7				$10	$12	$20
2014-P, Arches National Park (UT)	214,200,000	265	67.3	100%	$0.45	$0.50	$1	$10	$30
2014-D, Arches National Park (UT)	251,400,000	323	67.3	100%	$0.45	$0.50	$1	$10	$30
2014-S, Arches National Park (UT) (a)	1,235,940	707	66.8	100%		$1.50	$8	$12	$35
2014-S, Arches National Park (UT), Proof	844,775	2,095	69.4				$3	$4.50	$15
2014-S, Arches National Park (UT), Proof, Silver	472,107	4,462	69.7				$10	$12	$20
2014-P, Great Sand Dunes National Park (CO)	159,600,000	197	67.4	100%	$0.45	$0.50	$2	$10	$30
2014-D, Great Sand Dunes National Park (CO)	171,800,000	250	67.5	100%	$0.45	$0.50	$1.50	$10	$30
2014-S, Great Sand Dunes National Park (CO) (a)	1,176,760	954	67.1	100%		$1.50	$8	$12	$35
2014-S, Great Sand Dunes National Park (CO), Proof	843,238	2,091	69.5				$3	$4.50	$15
2014-S, Great Sand Dunes National Park (CO), Proof, Silver	472,107	4,329	69.7				$10	$12	$20
2014-P, Everglades National Park (FL)	157,601,200	203	67.3	100%	$0.45	$0.50	$1	$10	$30
2014-D, Everglades National Park (FL)	142,400,000	317	67.6	100%	$0.45	$0.50	$1	$10	$30
2014-S, Everglades National Park (FL) (a)	1,180,900	595	67.1	100%		$1.50	$8	$12	$35
2014-S, Everglades National Park (FL), Proof	856,139	2,093	69.5				$3	$4.50	$15
2014-S, Everglades National Park (FL), Proof, Silver	472,107	4,328	69.7				$10	$12	$20

a. Not issued for circulation. From 2012–2021, the San Francisco Mint made Uncirculated S-mintmark quarters of each design in the National Park series. These could be purchased by collectors directly from the U.S. Mint, in bags of 100 or rolls of 40 coins, for a premium above face value.

| 2015, Homestead National Monument of America (NE) *Reverse designer: Ronald D. Sanders.* | 2015, Kisatchie National Forest (LA) *Reverse designer: Susan Gamble.* | 2015, Blue Ridge Parkway (NC) *Reverse designer: Frank Morris.* | 2015, Bombay Hook National Wildlife Refuge (DE) *Reverse designer: Joel Iskowitz.* | 2015, Saratoga National Historical Park (NY) *Reverse designer: Barbara Fox.* |

	Mintage	Cert	Avg	%MS	AU-50	MS-63	MS-65 PF-65	MS-66 PF-66DC	MS-67 PF-69DC
2015-P, Homestead National Monument of America (NE)	214,400,000	2,326	64.7	100%	$0.50	$0.75	$1	$10	$30
2015-D, Homestead National Monument of America (NE)	248,600,000	64	66.3	100%	$0.50	$0.75	$1	$10	$30
2015-S, Homestead National Monument of America (NE) (a)	1,153,840	1,025	67.0	100%		$2	$8	$12	$35
2015-S, Homestead National Monument of America (NE), Proof	831,503	1,406	69.5				$3	$4.50	$15
2015-S, Homestead National Monument of America (NE), Proof, Silver	490,829	3,157	69.5				$10	$12	$20
2015-P, Kisatchie National Forest (LA)	397,200,000	89	66.9	99%	$0.50	$0.75	$1	$10	$30
2015-D, Kisatchie National Forest (LA)	379,600,000	97	66.8	100%	$0.50	$0.75	$1	$10	$30
2015-S, Kisatchie National Forest (LA) (a)	1,099,380	599	67.0	100%		$2	$8	$12	$35
2015-S, Kisatchie National Forest (LA), Proof	762,407	1,340	69.5				$3	$4.50	$15
2015-S, Kisatchie National Forest (LA), Proof, Silver	490,829	3,172	69.5				$10	$12	$20
2015-P, Blue Ridge Parkway (NC)	325,616,000	62	66.3	98%	$0.50	$0.75	$1	$10	$30
2015-D, Blue Ridge Parkway (NC)	505,200,000	88	66.4	98%	$0.50	$0.75	$1	$10	$30
2015-S, Blue Ridge Parkway (NC) (a)	1,096,620	357	66.5	100%		$2	$8	$12	$35
2015-S, Blue Ridge Parkway (NC), Proof	762,407	1,340	69.5				$3	$4.50	$15
2015-S, Blue Ridge Parkway (NC), Proof, Silver	490,829	3,147	69.5				$10	$12	$20
2015-P, Bombay Hook National Wildlife Refuge (DE)	275,000,000	83	67.0	100%	$0.50	$0.75	$1	$10	$30
2015-D, Bombay Hook National Wildlife Refuge (DE)	206,400,000	118	67.0	100%	$0.50	$0.75	$1	$10	$30
2015-S, Bombay Hook National Wildlife Refuge (DE) (a)	1,013,920	279	66.8	100%		$2	$8	$12	$35
2015-S, Bombay Hook National Wildlife Refuge (DE), Proof	762,407	1,343	69.5				$3	$4.50	$15
2015-S, Bombay Hook National Wildlife Refuge (DE), Proof, Silver	490,829	3,167	69.5				$10	$12	$20
2015-P, Saratoga National Historical Park (NY)	223,000,000	66	66.7	100%	$0.50	$0.75	$1	$10	$30
2015-D, Saratoga National Historical Park (NY)	215,800,000	102	66.9	100%	$0.50	$0.75	$1	$10	$30
2015-S, Saratoga National Historical Park (NY) (a)	1,045,500	284	66.8	100%		$2	$8	$12	$35
2015-S, Saratoga National Historical Park (NY), Proof	791,347	1,344	69.5				$3	$4.50	$15
2015-S, Saratoga National Historical Park (NY), Proof, Silver	490,829	1,181	69.4				$10	$12	$20

a. Not issued for circulation. From 2012–2021, the San Francisco Mint made Uncirculated S-mintmark quarters of each design in the National Park series. These could be purchased by collectors directly from the U.S. Mint, in bags of 100 or rolls of 40 coins, for a premium above face value.

In 2016 a special .9999 fine gold striking of Hermon A. MacNeil's Standing Liberty quarter was created to celebrate the 100th anniversary of its introduction. It is smaller than the silver strikings, with a diameter of 22 mm, weight of 7.776 grams, and a net weight of 0.5 ounces pure gold. Struck at West Point, it has a reeded edge. Similar strikings were made for the 1916 dime and half dollar designs.

	Mintage	Cert	Avg	%MS	SP-67	SP-70
2016-W, Standing Liberty Centennial Gold Coin	91,752	0	n/a		$600	$700

Normally scheduled production of clad and silver America the Beautiful quarters, in the same standards and specifications as previously, continued in 2016 and beyond, and was not disrupted by the gold Standing Liberty quarter.

2016, Shawnee National Forest (IL)
Reverse designer: Justin Kunz.

2016, Cumberland Gap National Historical Park (KY)
Reverse designer: Barbara Fox.

2016, Harpers Ferry National Historical Park (WV)
Reverse designer: Thomas Hipschen.

2016, Theodore Roosevelt National Park (ND)
Reverse designer: Joel Iskowitz.

2016, Fort Moultrie at Fort Sumter National Monument (SC)
Reverse designer: Richard Scott.

	Mintage	Cert	Avg	%MS	AU-50	MS-63	MS-65 / PF-65	MS-66 / PF-66DC	MS-67 / PF-69DC
2016-P, Shawnee National Forest (IL)	155,600,000	231	66.9	100%	$0.50	$0.75	$1	$10	$30
2016-D, Shawnee National Forest (IL)	151,800,000	215	66.9	100%	$0.50	$0.75	$1	$10	$30
2016-S, Shawnee National Forest (IL) (a)	1,081,914	300	66.8	100%		$2	$3	$12	$35
2016-S, Shawnee National Forest (IL), Proof	696,564	297	69.7				$3	$4.50	$15
2016-S, Shawnee National Forest (IL), Proof, Silver	502,039	1,088	69.8				$10	$12	$20
2016-P, Cumberland Gap National Historical Park (KY)	215,400,000	275	67.1	100%	$0.50	$0.75	$1	$10	$30
2016-D, Cumberland Gap National Historical Park (KY)	223,200,000	293	67.3	100%	$0.50	$0.75	$1	$10	$30
2016-S, Cumberland Gap National Historical Park (KY) (a)	1,036,093	511	66.6	100%		$2	$3	$12	$35
2016-S, Cumberland Gap National Historical Park (KY), Proof	666,857	295	69.7				$3	$4.50	$15
2016-S, Cumberland Gap National Historical Park (KY), Proof, Silver	502,039	1,068	69.7				$10	$12	$20
2016-P, Harpers Ferry National Historical Park (WV)	434,630,000	207	66.7	100%	$0.50	$0.75	$1	$10	$30
2016-D, Harpers Ferry National Historical Park (WV)	424,000,000	167	66.8	99%	$0.50	$0.75	$1	$10	$30
2016-S, Harpers Ferry National Historical Park (WV) (a)	1,050,185	387	66.6	100%		$2	$3	$12	$35
2016-S, Harpers Ferry National Historical Park (WV), Proof	666,857	305	69.7				$3	$4.50	$15
2016-S, Harpers Ferry National Historical Park (WV), Proof, Silver	502,039	1,110	69.8				$10	$12	$20
2016-P, Theodore Roosevelt National Park (ND)	231,600,000	219	66.9	100%	$0.50	$0.75	$1	$10	$30
2016-D, Theodore Roosevelt National Park (ND)	223,200,000	200	66.9	100%	$0.50	$0.75	$1	$10	$30
2016-S, Theodore Roosevelt National Park (ND) (a)	1,073,092	213	66.6	100%		$2	$3	$12	$35
2016-S, Theodore Roosevelt National Park (ND), Proof	666,857	295	69.8				$3	$4.50	$15
2016-S, Theodore Roosevelt National Park (ND), Proof, Silver	502,039	1,065	69.7				$10	$12	$20

a. Not issued for circulation. From 2012–2021, the San Francisco Mint made Uncirculated S-mintmark quarters of each design in the National Park series. These could be purchased by collectors directly from the U.S. Mint, in bags of 100 or rolls of 40 coins, for a premium above face value.

	Mintage	Cert	Avg	%MS	AU-50	MS-63	MS-65	MS-66	MS-67
							PF-65	PF-66DC	PF-69DC
2016-P, Fort Moultrie (Fort Sumter National Monument) (SC)	154,400,000	233	66.9	100%	$0.50	$0.75	$1	$10	$30
2016-D, Fort Moultrie (Fort Sumter National Monument) (SC)	142,200,000	223	67.1	100%	$0.50	$0.75	$1	$10	$30
2016-S, Fort Moultrie (Fort Sumter National Monument) (SC) (a)	979,566	178	66.6	100%		$2	$3	$12	$35
2016-S, Fort Moultrie (Fort Sumter National Monument) (SC), Proof	683,741	296	69.7				$3	$4.50	$15
2016-S, Fort Moultrie (Fort Sumter National Monument) (SC), Proof, Silver	502,039	1,077	69.7				$10	$12	$20

a. Not issued for circulation. From 2012–2021, the San Francisco Mint made Uncirculated S-mintmark quarters of each design in the National Park series. These could be purchased by collectors directly from the U.S. Mint, in bags of 100 or rolls of 40 coins, for a premium above face value.

2017, Effigy Mounds National Monument (IA) *Reverse designer: Richard Masters.*	2017, Frederick Douglass National Historic Site (DC) *Reverse designer: Thomas Hipschen.*	2017, Ozark National Scenic Riverways (MO) *Reverse designer: Ronald D. Sanders.*	2017, Ellis Island (Statue of Liberty National Monument) (NJ) *Reverse designer: Barbara Fox.*	2017, George Rogers Clark National Historical Park (IN) *Reverse designer: Frank Morris.*

	Mintage	Cert	Avg	%MS	AU-50	MS-63	MS-65	MS-66	MS-67
							PF-65	PF-66DC	PF-69DC
2017-P, Effigy Mounds National Monument (IA)	271,200,000	100	66.9	100%	$0.50	$0.75	$1	$10	$30
2017-D, Effigy Mounds National Monument (IA)	210,800,000	169	66.9	99%	$0.50	$0.75	$1	$10	$30
2017-S, Effigy Mounds National Monument (IA) (a)	945,853	561	66.1	100%		$2	$3	$12	$35
2017-S, Effigy Mounds National Monument (IA), Enhanced Uncirculated	210,419	8,298	69.9				$6	$15	$25
2017-S, Effigy Mounds National Monument (IA), Proof	692,129	231	69.4				$3	$4.50	$15
2017-S, Effigy Mounds National Monument (IA), Proof, Silver	496,618	1,642	69.7				$10	$12	$20
2017-P, Frederick Douglass National Historic Site (DC)	184,800,000	94	66.8	100%	$0.50	$0.75	$1	$10	$30
2017-D, Frederick Douglass National Historic Site (DC)	185,800,000	104	66.8	100%	$0.50	$0.75	$1	$10	$30
2017-S, Frederick Douglass National Historic Site (DC) (a)	950,503	248	66.6	100%		$2	$3	$12	$35
2017-S, Frederick Douglass National Historic Site (DC), Enhanced Uncirculated	210,419	8,305	69.9				$6	$15	$25
2017-S, Frederick Douglass National Historic Site (DC), Proof	657,587	233	69.4				$3	$4.50	$15
2017-S, Frederick Douglass National Historic Site (DC), Proof, Silver	496,618	1,643	69.7				$10	$12	$20
2017-P, Ozark National Scenic Riverways (MO)	203,000,000	91	66.8	100%	$0.50	$0.75	$1	$10	$30
2017-D, Ozark National Scenic Riverways (MO)	200,000,000	102	66.5	99%	$0.50	$0.75	$1	$10	$30
2017-S, Ozark National Scenic Riverways (MO) (a)	921,747	453	66.4	100%		$2	$3	$12	$35
2017-S, Ozark National Scenic Riverways (MO), Enhanced Uncirculated	210,419	8,297	69.9				$6	$15	$25
2017-S, Ozark National Scenic Riverways (MO), Proof	657,587	231	69.4				$3	$4.50	$15
2017-S, Ozark National Scenic Riverways (MO), Proof, Silver	496,618	1,628	69.7				$10	$12	$20

a. Not issued for circulation. From 2012–2021, the San Francisco Mint made Uncirculated S-mintmark quarters of each design in the National Park series. These could be purchased by collectors directly from the U.S. Mint, in bags of 100 or rolls of 40 coins, for a premium above face value.

	Mintage	Cert	Avg	%MS	AU-50	MS-63	MS-65 PF-65	MS-66 PF-66DC	MS-67 PF-69DC
2017-P, Ellis Island (Statue of Liberty National Monument) (NJ)	234,000,000	108	66.9	100%	$0.50	$0.75	$1	$10	$30
2017-D, Ellis Island (Statue of Liberty National Monument) (NJ)	254,000,000	120	66.7	100%	$0.50	$0.75	$1	$10	$30
2017-S, Ellis Island (Statue of Liberty National Monument) (NJ) (a)	973,147	172	66.7	100%		$2	$3	$12	$35
2017-S, Ellis Island (Statue of Liberty National Monument) (NJ), Enhanced Uncirculated	210,419	9,932	69.9				$6	$15	$25
2017-S, Ellis Island (Statue of Liberty National Monument) (NJ), Proof	657,587	231	69.4				$3	$4.50	$15
2017-S, Ellis Island (Statue of Liberty National Monument) (NJ), Proof, Silver	496,618	1,516	69.7				$10	$12	$20
2017-P, George Rogers Clark National Historical Park (IN)	191,600,000	63	66.8	100%	$0.50	$0.75	$1	$10	$30
2017-D, George Rogers Clark National Historical Park (IN)	180,800,000	83	66.5	99%	$0.50	$0.75	$1	$10	$30
2017-S, George Rogers Clark National Historical Park (IN) (a)	933,150	349	66.4	100%		$2	$3	$12	$35
2017-S, George Rogers Clark National Historical Park (IN), Enhanced Uncirculated	210,419	3,671	69.9				$6	$15	$25
2017-S, George Rogers Clark National Historical Park (IN), Proof	675,757	232	69.4				$3	$4.50	$15
2017-S, George Rogers Clark National Historical Park (IN), Proof, Silver	496,618	1,649	69.7				$10	$12	$20

a. Not issued for circulation. From 2012–2021, the San Francisco Mint made Uncirculated S-mintmark quarters of each design in the National Park series. These could be purchased by collectors directly from the U.S. Mint, in bags of 100 or rolls of 40 coins, for a premium above face value.

2018, Pictured Rocks National Lakeshore (MI) *Reverse designer: Paul C. Balan.*	**2018, Apostle Islands National Lakeshore (WI)** *Reverse designer: Richard Masters.*	**2018, Voyageurs National Park (MN)** *Reverse designer: Patricia Lucas-Morris.*	**2018, Cumberland Island National Seashore (GA)** *Reverse designer: Donna Weaver.*	**2018, Block Island National Wildlife Refuge (RI)** *Reverse designer: Chris Costello.*

	Mintage	Cert	Avg	%MS	AU-50	MS-63	MS-65 PF-65	MS-66 PF-66DC	MS-67 PF-69DC
2018-P, Pictured Rocks National Lakeshore (MI)	186,714,000	83	67.1	100%	$0.50	$0.75	$1	$10	$30
2018-D, Pictured Rocks National Lakeshore (MI)	182,600,000	105	67.0	100%	$0.50	$0.75	$1	$10	$30
2018-S, Pictured Rocks National Lakeshore (MI) (a)	946,617	206	66.7	100%		$2	$3	$12	$35
2018-S, Pictured Rocks National Lakeshore (MI), Proof	636,806	380	69.7				$3	$4.50	$15
2018-S, Pictured Rocks National Lakeshore (MI), Proof, Silver	460,615	1,622	69.7				$10	$12	$22
2018-S, Pictured Rocks National Lakeshore (MI), Reverse Proof, Silver	199,116						$10		$15 (b)
2018-P, Apostle Islands National Lakeshore (WI)	223,200,000	97	67.2	100%	$0.50	$0.75	$1	$10	$30
2018-D, Apostle Islands National Lakeshore (WI)	216,600,000	59	66.8	100%	$0.50	$0.75	$1	$10	$30
2018-S, Apostle Islands National Lakeshore (WI) (a)	904,103	109	66.8	100%		$2	$3	$12	$35
2018-S, Apostle Islands National Lakeshore (WI), Proof	603,512	376	69.8				$3	$4.50	$15
2018-S, Apostle Islands National Lakeshore (WI), Proof, Silver	460,615	1,591	69.7				$10	$12	$22

a. Not issued for circulation. From 2012–2021, the San Francisco Mint made Uncirculated S-mintmark quarters of each design in the National Park series. These could be purchased by collectors directly from the U.S. Mint, in bags of 100 or rolls of 40 coins, for a premium above face value. **b.** Value is for PF-69; value in PF-70 is $35.

	Mintage	Cert	Avg	%MS	AU-50	MS-63	MS-65 PF-65	MS-66 PF-66DC	MS-67 PF-69DC
2018-S, Apostle Islands Nat'l Lakeshore (WI), Rev Pf, Silver	199,116						$10		$15 (b)
2018-P, Voyageurs National Park (MN)	237,400,000	103	67.2	100%	$0.50	$0.75	$1	$10	$30
2018-D, Voyageurs National Park (MN)	197,800,000	97	67.1	100%	$0.50	$0.75	$1	$10	$30
2018-S, Voyageurs National Park (MN) (a)	882,384	415	66.5	100%		$2	$3	$12	$35
2018-S, Voyageurs National Park (MN), Proof	603,512	377	69.8				$3	$4.50	$15
2018-S, Voyageurs National Park (MN), Proof, Silver	460,615	1,644	69.7				$10	$12	$22
2018-S, Voyageurs National Park (MN), Reverse Proof, Silver	199,116						$10		$15 (b)
2018-P, Cumberland Island Nat'l Seashore (GA)	138,000,000	114	67.3	100%	$0.50	$0.75	$1	$10	$30
2018-D, Cumberland Island Nat'l Seashore (GA)	151,600,000	104	67.1	99%	$0.50	$0.75	$1	$10	$30
2018-S, Cumberland Island Nat'l Seashore (GA) (a)	895,018	223	66.4	100%		$2	$3	$12	$35
2018-S, Cumberland Island Nat'l Seashore (GA), Proof	603,512	386	69.7				$3	$4.50	$15
2018-S, Cumberland Island Nat'l Seashore (GA), Proof, Silver	460,615	1,616	69.7				$10	$12	$22
2018-S, Cumberland Island Nat'l Seashore (GA), Rev Pf, Silver	199,116						$10		$15 (b)
2018-P, Block Island Nat'l Wildlife Refuge (RI)	159,600,000	81	66.9	100%	$0.50	$0.75	$1	$10	$30
2018-D, Block Island Nat'l Wildlife Refuge (RI)	159,600,000	54	66.8	100%	$0.50	$0.75	$1	$10	$30
2018-S, Block Island Nat'l Wildlife Refuge (RI) (a)	868,956	179	66.5	100%		$2	$3	$12	$35
2018-S, Block Island National Wildlife Refuge (RI), Proof	621,231	380	69.7				$3	$4.50	$15
2018-S, Block Island Nat'l Wildlife Refuge (RI), Proof, Silver	460,615	1,584	69.7				$10	$12	$22
2018-S, Block Island Nat'l Wildlife Refuge (RI), Reverse Proof, Silver	199,116						$10		$15 (b)

a. Not issued for circulation. From 2012–2021, the San Francisco Mint made Uncirculated S-mintmark quarters of each design in the National Park series. These could be purchased by collectors directly from the U.S. Mint, in bags of 100 or rolls of 40 coins, for a premium above face value. **b.** Value is for PF-69; value in PF-70 is $35.

2019, Lowell National Historical Park (MA) Reverse designer: Joel Iskowitz.	2019, American Memorial Park (Northern Mariana Islands) Reverse designer: Donna Weaver.	2019, San Antonio Missions National Historical Park (TX) Reverse designer: Joel Iskowitz.	2019, War in the Pacific National Historical Park (Guam) Reverse designer: Chris Costello.	2019, Frank Church River of No Return Wilderness (ID) Reverse designer: Emily Damstra.

	Mintage	Cert	Avg	%MS	AU-50	MS-63	MS-65 PF-65	MS-66 PF-66DC	MS-67 PF-69DC
2019-P, Lowell National Historical Park (MA)	165,800,000	157	66.6	100%	$0.50	$0.75	$1	$10	$30
2019-D, Lowell National Historical Park (MA)	182,200,000	138	66.7	100%	$0.50	$0.75	$1	$10	$30
2019-S, Lowell National Historical Park (MA) (a)	904,442	178	66.7	100%		$2	$3	$12	$35
2019-S, Lowell National Historical Park (MA), Proof	743,860	745	69.8				$3	$4.50	$15
2019-S, Lowell National Historical Park (MA), Proof, Silver	537,244	4,065	69.8				$10	$12	$20
2019-W, Lowell National Historical Park (MA) (c)	2,000,000					$10	$25	$50	$100
2019-P, American Memorial Park (Northern Mariana Islands)	142,800,000	253	67.2	100%	$0.50	$0.75	$1	$10	$30
2019-D, American Mem'l Park (Northern Mariana Islands)	182,600,000	378	67.6	100%	$0.50	$0.75	$1	$10	$30
2019-S, American Mem'l Park (Northern Mariana Islands) (a)	508,325	160	66.8	100%		$2	$3	$12	$35
2019-S, American Mem'l Park (Northern Mariana Islands), Proof	679,625	740	69.9				$3	$4.50	$15
2019-S, American Mem'l Park (Northern Mariana Islands), Proof, Silver	537,244	3,752	69.8				$10	$12	$20

a. Not issued for circulation. From 2012–2021, the San Francisco Mint made Uncirculated S-mintmark quarters of each design in the National Park series. These could be purchased by collectors directly from the U.S. Mint, in bags of 100 or rolls of 40 coins, for a premium above face value. **c.** Coinciding with National Coin Week (April 21–27, 2019), the United States Mint released into circulation 10 million 2019 quarters struck at the West Point Mint, each bearing a W mintmark. The coins were mixed into bulk bags of quarters at the Philadelphia and Denver mints and shipped and distributed to banks and financial institutions by the Federal Reserve starting in early April.

	Mintage	Cert	Avg	%MS	AU-50	MS-63	MS-65 / PF-65	MS-66 / PF-66DC	MS-67 / PF-69DC
2019-W, American Memorial Park (Northern Mariana Islands) (c)	2,000,000					$10	$25	$50	$100
2019-P, San Antonio Missions National Historical Park (TX)	142,800,000	190	67.4	100%	$0.50	$0.75	$1	$10	$30
2019-D, San Antonio Missions National Historical Park (TX)	129,400,000	299	67.4	100%	$0.50	$0.75	$1	$10	$30
2019-S, San Antonio Missions National Historical Park (TX) (a)	946,817	319	66.6	100%		$2	$3	$12	$35
2019-S, San Antonio Missions National Historical Park (TX), Proof	679,625	744	69.8				$3	$4.50	$15
2019-S, San Antonio Missions Nat'l Historical Park (TX), Proof, Silver	537,244	3,795	69.8				$10	$12	$20
2019-W, San Antonio Missions National Historical Park (TX) (c)	2,000,000					$10	$25	$50	$100
2019-P, War in the Pacific National Historical Park (Guam)	116,600,000	204	67.0	100%	$0.50	$0.75	$1	$10	$30
2019-D, War in the Pacific National Historical Park (Guam)	114,400,000	318	67.1	100%	$0.50	$0.75	$1	$10	$30
2019-S, War in the Pacific National Historical Park (Guam) (a)	939,799	177	66.7	100%		$2	$3	$12	$35
2019-S, War in the Pacific National Historical Park (Guam), Proof	679,625	740	69.8				$3	$4.50	$15
2019-S, War in the Pacific Nat'l Historical Park (Guam), Proof, Silver	537,244	3,828	69.8				$10	$12	$20
2019-W, War in the Pacific National Historical Park (Guam) (c)	2,000,000					$10	$25	$50	$100
2019-P, Frank Church River of No Return Wilderness (ID)	223,400,000	190	67.4	100%	$0.50	$0.75	$1	$10	$30
2019-D, Frank Church River of No Return Wilderness (ID)	251,600,000	410	67.5	100%	$0.50	$0.75	$1	$10	$30
2019-S, Frank Church River of No Return Wilderness (ID) (a)	915,336	307	66.8	100%		$2	$3	$12	$35
2019-S, Frank Church River of No Return Wilderness (ID), Proof	698,426	735	69.8				$3	$4.50	$15
2019-S, Frank Church River of No Return Wilderness (ID), Proof, Silver	537,244	3,761	69.8				$10	$12	$20
2019-W, Frank Church River of No Return Wilderness (ID) (c)	2,000,000					$10	$25	$50	$100

a. Not issued for circulation. From 2012–2021, the San Francisco Mint made Uncirculated S-mintmark quarters of each design in the National Park series. These could be purchased by collectors directly from the U.S. Mint, in bags of 100 or rolls of 40 coins, for a premium above face value. **c.** Coinciding with National Coin Week (April 21–27, 2019), the United States Mint released into circulation 10 million 2019 quarters struck at the West Point Mint, each bearing a W mintmark. The coins were mixed into bulk bags of quarters at the Philadelphia and Denver mints and shipped and distributed to banks and financial institutions by the Federal Reserve starting in early April.

2020, National Park of American Samoa (AS)
Reverse designer: Justin Kunz.

2020, Weir Farm National Historic Site (CT)
Reverse designer: Barbara Fox.

2020, Salt River Bay National Historical Park and Ecological Preserve (USVI)
Reverse designer: Thomas Hipschen.

2020, Marsh-Billings-Rockefeller National Historical Park (VT)
Reverse designer: Joel Iskowitz.

2020, Tallgrass Prairie National Preserve (KS)
Reverse designer: Richard Scott.

2020 obverse privy mark. (d)

2021, Tuskegee Airmen National Historic Site (AL)
Reverse designer: Chris Costello.

	Mintage	Cert	Avg	%MS	AU-50	MS-63	MS-65 / PF-65	MS-66 / PF-66DC	MS-67 / PF-69DC
2020-P, National Park of American Samoa (American Samoa)	286,000,000	477	66.9	100%	$0.50	$0.75	$1	$10	$30
2020-D, National Park of American Samoa (American Samoa)	212,200,000	358	67.6	100%	$0.50	$0.75	$1	$10	$30
2020-S, National Park of American Samoa (American Samoa) (a)	955,140	227	66.8	100%		$2	$3	$12	$35

a. Not issued for circulation. From 2012–2021, the San Francisco Mint has made Uncirculated S-mintmark quarters of each design in the National Park series. These could be purchased by collectors directly from the U.S. Mint, in bags of 100 or rolls of 40 coins, for a premium above face value. **d.** To recognize the 75th anniversary of the conclusion of World War II, the United States Mint released into circulation 2020 quarters struck at the West Point Mint, each bearing a W mintmark and a privy mark. The mark has the text "V75," signifying the allied victory in World War II, placed inside an outline representing the Rainbow Pool of the World War II Memorial in Washington, D.C., as seen from the air. The coins were mixed into bulk bags of quarters at the Philadelphia and Denver mints and shipped and distributed to banks and financial institutions by the Federal Reserve starting in early April.

	Mintage	Cert	Avg	%MS	AU-50	MS-63	MS-65 PF-65	MS-66 PF-66DC	MS-67 PF-69DC
2020-S, National Park of American Samoa (American Samoa), Proof	539,150	480	69.8				$3	$4.50	$15
2020-S, National Park of American Samoa (American Samoa), Proof, Silver	373,838	2,468	69.7				$10	$12	$20
2020-W, National Park of American Samoa (American Samoa) (d)	2,000,000					$10	$25	$50	$100
2020-P, Weir Farm National Historic Site (CT)	125,600,000	318	67.3	100%	$0.50	$0.75	$1	$10	$30
2020-D, Weir Farm National Historic Site (CT)	155,000,000	374	67.6	100%	$0.50	$0.75	$1	$10	$30
2020-S, Weir Farm National Historic Site (CT) (a)	893,347	584	65.6	100%		$2	$3	$12	$35
2020-S, Weir Farm National Historic Site (CT), Proof	514,174	448	69.8				$3	$4.50	$15
2020-S, Weir Farm National Historic Site (CT), Proof, Silver	373,838	2,468	69.7				$10	$12	$20
2020-W, Weir Farm National Historic Site (CT) (d)	2,000,000					$10	$25	$50	$100
2020-P, Salt River Bay National Historical Park and Ecological Preserve (USVI)	580,200,000	354	67.7	100%	$0.50	$0.75	$1	$10	$30
2020-D, Salt River Bay National Historical Park and Ecological Preserve (USVI)	515,000,000	396	67.8	100%	$0.50	$0.75	$1	$10	$30
2020-S, Salt River Bay National Historical Park and Ecological Preserve (USVI) (a)	865,999	560	66.4	100%		$2	$3	$12	$35
2020-S, Salt River Bay National Historical Park and Ecological Preserve (USVI), Proof	514,174	448	69.8				$3	$4.50	$15
2020-S, Salt River Bay National Historical Park and Ecological Preserve (USVI), Proof, Silver	373,838	2,467	69.7				$10	$12	$20
2020-W, Salt River Bay National Historical Park and Ecological Preserve (USVI) (d)	2,000,000					$10	$25	$50	$100
2020-P, Marsh-Billings-Rockefeller National Historical Park (VT)	304,600,000	312	67.5	100%	$0.50	$0.75	$1	$10	$30
2020-D, Marsh-Billings-Rockefeller National Historical Park (VT)	345,800,000	453	67.8	100%	$0.50	$0.75	$1	$10	$30
2020-S, Marsh-Billings-Rockefeller National Historical Park (VT) (a)	788,595	282	66.7	100%		$2	$3	$12	$35
2020-S, Marsh-Billings-Rockefeller National Historical Park (VT), Proof	514,174	448	69.8				$3	$4.50	$15
2020-S, Marsh-Billings-Rockefeller National Historical Park (VT), Proof, Silver	373,838	2,467	69.7				$10	$12	$20
2020-W, Marsh-Billings-Rockefeller National Historical Park (VT) (d)	2,000,000					$10	$25	$50	$100
2020-P, Tallgrass Prairie National Preserve (KS)	101,200,000	381	67.7	100%	$0.50	$0.75	$1	$10	$30
2020-D, Tallgrass Prairie National Preserve (KS)	142,400,000	439	67.8	100%	$0.50	$0.75	$1	$10	$30
2020-S, Tallgrass Prairie National Preserve (KS) (a)	684,034	0	n/a	100%		$2	$3	$12	$35
2020-S, Tallgrass Prairie National Preserve (KS), Proof	530,734	470	69.8				$3	$4.50	$15
2020-S, Tallgrass Prairie National Preserve (KS), Proof, Silver	373,838	2,467	69.7				$10	$12	$20
2020-W, Tallgrass Prairie National Preserve (KS) (d)	2,000,000					$10	$25	$50	$100
2021-P, Tuskegee Airmen National Historic Site (AL)									
2021-D, Tuskegee Airmen National Historic Site (AL)									
2021-S, Tuskegee Airmen National Historic Site (AL) (a)									
2021-S, Tuskegee Airmen National Historic Site (AL), Proof									
2021-S, Tuskegee Airmen National Historic Site (AL), Proof, Silver									

a. Not issued for circulation. From 2012–2021, the San Francisco Mint made Uncirculated S-mintmark quarters of each design in the National Park series. These could be purchased by collectors directly from the U.S. Mint, in bags of 100 or rolls of 40 coins, for a premium above face value. **d.** To recognize the 75th anniversary of the conclusion of World War II, the United States Mint released into circulation 2020 quarters struck at the West Point Mint, each bearing a W mintmark and a privy mark. The mark has the text "V75," signifying the allied victory in World War II, placed inside an outline representing the Rainbow Pool of the World War II Memorial in Washington, D.C., as seen from the air. The coins were mixed into bulk bags of quarters at the Philadelphia and Denver mints and shipped and distributed to banks and financial institutions by the Federal Reserve starting in early April.

WASHINGTON, GENERAL GEORGE WASHINGTON CROSSING THE DELAWARE (2021)

Designers: *John Flanagan and Benjamin Sowards.* **Weight:** *Clad issue—5.67 grams; silver Proofs— 6.343 grams.* **Composition:** *Clad issue—Outer layers of copper-nickel (.750 copper, .250 nickel) bonded to inner core of pure copper; silver Proofs—.999 silver, .001 copper (net weight .182 oz. pure silver).* **Diameter:** *24.3 mm.* **Edge:** *Reeded.* **Mints:** *Philadelphia, Denver, and San Francisco.*

| Circulation Strike | Proof |

History. The America's Beautiful National Parks Quarter Dollar Coin Act of 2008 specified what would happen to the coin after that program ended in 2021: "The reverse of the quarter dollar shall contain an image of General Washington crossing the Delaware River prior to the Battle of Trenton," and the obverse would "revert to the same design containing an image of President Washington" that was used before the State quarters program started in 1999.

GRADING STANDARDS

MS-60 to 70 (Mint State). *Obverse:* At MS-60, some abrasion and contact marks are evident on the highest-relief areas. At MS-63, abrasion is slight at best, less so at MS-64. An MS-65 coin should display no abrasion or contact marks except under magnification, and MS-66 and higher coins should have none at all. Luster should be full. *Reverse:* Check the highest-relief areas of the design. Otherwise, comments are as for the obverse.

General George Washington Crossing the Delaware quarter dollars are seldom collected in grades lower than MS-60.

PF-60 to 70 (Proof). *Obverse and Reverse:* These coins are so recent, and as only a few have been cleaned, most approach perfection and can be designated PF–68 to 70, the latter only if no contact marks or other problems can be seen under magnification. A cleaned coin with extensive hairlines would not be collectible for most numismatists and would be classified at a lower level such as PF–60 to 63. Those with lighter hairlines qualify for PF–64 or 65.

	Mintage	Cert	Avg	%MS	AU-50	MS-63	MS-65	MS-66	MS-67
							PF-65	PF-66DC	PF-69DC
2021-P, General George Washington Crossing the Delaware									
2021-D, General George Washington Crossing the Delaware									
2021-S, General George Washington Crossing the Delaware, Proof									
2021-S, General George Washington Crossing the Delaware, Proof, Silver									

FUTURE DESIGNS (2022–2030 and Beyond)

The Circulating Collectible Coin Redesign Act of 2020, signed into law January 13, 2021, brings wide-ranging changes that involve all of America's circulating coins. In particular it schedules the quarter dollar as the venue for several new educational coin programs.

From 2022 to 2025, the quarter will commemorate prominent American women and the ratification of the Nineteenth Amendment granting women the right to vote. Up to five coins will be issued per year, each featuring a new reverse design honoring a woman selected from fields and accomplishments such as "suffrage, civil rights, abolition, government, humanities, science, space, and arts."

In 2026, quarters will be issued with up to five different designs emblematic of the United States' 250th anniversary of independence. Of these, one design will represent "a woman's or women's contribution to the birth of the Nation or the Declaration of Independence or any other monumental moments in American History." (Other coins from the cent to the half dollar, plus a dollar coin, will also be used to celebrate the semiquincentennial.)

From 2027 to 2030, quarter dollars will be issued with new reverse designs, up to five per year, "emblematic of sports played by American youth."

Designs for these coin programs will be selected by the secretary of the Treasury, after consultation with the U.S. Commission of Fine Arts and review by the Citizens Coinage Advisory Committee.

The legislation gives the Treasury secretary authority to change the obverse of the quarter dollar. The coin still must bear a likeness of George Washington, but that likeness could be completely different from the traditional John Flanagan portrait. At the conclusion of the Youth Sports program, "the reverse of the quarter dollar shall be of a design selected by the Secretary after consultation with the Commission of Fine Arts and review by the Citizens Coinage Advisory Committee."

Half Dollars
1794 to Date
AN OVERVIEW OF HALF DOLLARS

Many hobbyists consider a collection of half dollars to be one of the most satisfying in the American series. The panorama of designs is extensive, ranging from the early Flowing Hair issues of 1794 and 1795 down to classic twentieth-century motifs and the presidential portrait of the present day. The large size of half dollar coins makes them convenient to view and easy to enjoy.

Among the types, the 1794–1795 Flowing Hair half dollar is readily available in circulated grades and rare in Mint State, but at any level is hard to find well struck and without adjustment marks (evidence of where a Mint worker filed an overweight planchet down to proper weight). Most on the market are dated 1795. Careful selection for quality is advised.

The next type, dated 1796–1797 with a Draped Bust obverse and Small Eagle reverse, is the scarcest in the American silver series excepting the 1839 Gobrecht dollar. (However, the latter is available in Proof restrike form, yielding choice and gem examples, so it can be considered in a different category from the circulation-strike 1796–1797 half dollar type.) It might not be possible to be particular, but, finances permitting, a collector should take some time and endeavor to find an example that is sharply struck on both sides. Needle-sharp striking is more of a theory than a practicality, and some compromise in this regard may be necessary.

Half dollars of the 1801–1807 type, with the obverse as preceding but now with the Heraldic Eagle reverse, are plentiful enough in worn grades but somewhat scarce in Mint State. Striking is seldom needle-sharp and ranges from average to very poor. However, there are enough coins in the marketplace that collectors can afford to take their time and seek a sharp strike.

Capped Bust half dollars with a lettered edge, 1807–1836, abound in just about any grade desired. Again, striking is a consideration, and some searching is needed for a high-quality strike. Generally, those in the late 1820s and the 1830s are better struck than are those of earlier dates, the earlier coins being scarcer and more expensive in any event.

The short-lived type of 1836–1837, Capped Bust with a reeded edge and with the denomination spelled as 50 CENTS, is available easily enough through the high-mintage 1837, but most have problems with the quality of striking. Then comes the 1838–1839 type of the same obverse style, its reverse modified with a slightly different eagle and with the denomination as HALF DOL. Generally these are fairly well struck.

Liberty Seated half dollars of the several styles within the series, 1839–1891, admit of no great rarities for the type collector, save for the 1839, No Drapery, in levels of MS-63 and finer. However, among the earlier types in particular, sharply struck pieces are in the minority. Curiously, the most readily available Mint State Liberty Seated half dollars also are the lowest-mintage issues, the dates 1879 and later, as these were recognized as desirable at the time of issue and were widely saved.

Barber half dollars were not popular in their time, and while Proofs exist in proportion to their production figures, few circulation-strike coins were saved by collectors and Mint State examples are quite scarce today. In fact, as a type, a Barber half dollar dated 1900 or later in Mint State is the scarcest of all silver issues of that century. Well-struck MS-63 and better Barber half dollars, with the upper-right corner of the shield and the leg at lower right showing full details, are significantly scarcer than generally realized.

Liberty Walking half dollars, minted from 1916 to 1947, are plentiful in all grades. Again, some attention should be made to striking sharpness, which makes the search become more intense. Fortunately there are countless thousands of MS-63 and finer coins of the 1940s on the market, giving collectors a wide choice. Then come Franklin half dollars, made only from 1948 to 1963, with representative coins easy enough to acquire in about any grade desired. Kennedy half dollars exist in several varieties, all of which are available without any problem. Among these and other modern coins care needs to be taken for value received versus price paid. Modern issues in, for example, MS–65 and 66, selected for quality, are for many collectors preferable to MS–69 or 70 coins offered at a much higher price.

The release of the Franklin half dollar was announced to the coin-collecting world on the front page of the *Numismatist*, June 1948.

FOR THE COLLECTOR AND INVESTOR: HALF DOLLARS AS A SPECIALTY

Many collectors over the years have pursued half dollars by date, mint, and variety. Except for the series of copper cents, half dollars are the most generally available coins over a nearly continuous span, making them possible to collect for reasonable cost. Also, enough die varieties exist that this can form another focus of interest and importance.

In general, the half dollars of the early era form a concentration in themselves. Die varieties can be attributed by Overton numbers, as listed by Al C. Overton in his immensely popular *Early Half Dollar Die Varieties 1794–1836*. Glenn R. Peterson's book, *The Ultimate Guide to Attributing Bust Half Dollars*, is also useful in this regard. The John Reich Collectors Society (www.jrcs.org) publishes the *John Reich Journal* and serves as a forum for the exchange of information, updates, news about die varieties, and the like.

Among rarities in the early years, the 1796 and 1797 half dollars with the Draped Bust obverse and Small Eagle reverse are perhaps the most famous, needed for variety collections as well as one example for a type set. Variety enthusiasts aspire to get two of 1796—one with 15 stars on the obverse and the other with 16 stars—plus the 1797.

Draped Bust half dollars from 1801 through 1807 have a number of rare die varieties (as listed by Overton), but the basic varieties are easy enough to find. The 1805, 5 Over 4, overdate is particularly popular, as there was no "perfect date" 1804, and this is the closest collectors can come to it.

A vast and interesting field in early American numismatics is that of the Capped Bust half dollar, 1807–1836, with a lettered edge. Several hundred different die combinations exist, and many collectors are active in their pursuit, using the Overton book as a road map. All the major varieties are readily collectible except the 1817, 7 Over 4, overdate, of which only about a half dozen exist. The 1815, 5 Over 2, is considered the key issue among the specific dates (rather than varieties of dates). The majority of these survive in VF grade, not often lower and not often higher either—an interesting situation. During the 1820s vast quantities of these were transferred among banks, not wearing down from as much hand-to-hand circulation as they might have otherwise. While many if not most of the varieties listed herein can be obtained in Mint

State, most collectors opt for VF or EF, these grades showing the necessary details but also permitting a budget to be stretched to include more varieties, rather than just a few high-grade pieces. Choice and gem examples can be found here and there, and are most plentiful among the later dates.

Among the Capped Bust half dollars of reduced size, 1836–1837, the 1836 is a key date, with fewer than 5,000 believed to have been minted. The next type, 1838 and 1839, Capped Bust, reeded edge, with a modified eagle on the reverse, includes the famous 1838-O rarity, of which only 20 are said to have been struck (per a note published in 1894 in the catalog of the Friesner Collection). These have a prooflike surface. Interestingly, they were not struck until 1839. In the same year, 1839-O half dollars were also struck, to the extensive quantity of 178,976 pieces; they are unusual as the mintmark is on the obverse, an odd placement for the era.

Within the series of Liberty Seated half dollars, collectors generally seek the varieties listed herein, although certain dedicated specialists will consult the *Complete Guide to Liberty Seated Half Dollars*, by Randy Wiley and Bill Bugert—a volume that delineates many interesting features, including the number of different reeds on the edges of certain coins.

Among Liberty Seated half dollars there is just one "impossible" rarity, that being the 1853-O coin without arrows at the date. Only three exist, and each shows extensive wear. At the San Francisco Mint, half dollars were first struck in 1855, and at the Carson City Mint in 1870. Generally, large quantities were minted of most dates and mintmark varieties of Liberty Seated half dollars, making them readily obtainable today. Except for the later dates, 1879 to 1891, Mint State pieces are generally scarce, gems especially so. Many specialists in half dollars belong to the Liberty Seated Collectors Club (LSCC, at www.lsccweb.org) and receive its magazine, *The Gobrecht Journal*.

Proof Liberty Seated halves can be collected by date sequence from 1858 onward. Survivors exist in proportion to their mintage quantities. Generally those before the mid-1870s often are found cleaned or hairlined, and more care is needed in selecting choice examples than is necessary for the later dates.

Barber half dollars were made continuously from 1892 through 1915, in such quantities that today there are no great rarities in the series. However, a number of issues are quite scarce, even in well-worn grades, and in MS-63 and better many are difficult to find. These coins had little honor in the era in which they were issued, and few numismatists saved them. Proofs were made each year from 1892 to 1915 and today can be obtained in proportion to their mintages. However, those of 1914 and 1915 are hard to find with choice, original surfaces—decades ago a collector hoarded these two dates and polished the ones in his possession.

Liberty Walking half dollars are popular to collect by date and mint. Scarce varieties include the 1917-S with obverse mintmark, the three issues of 1921, and the low mintage 1938-D, although the latter is not inordinately expensive. Mint State pieces are most readily available for 1916 and 1917, and then especially so in the 1930s and 1940s. Striking quality can be a problem, particularly for issues of the mid-1920s and also the later dates. For example, with a needle-sharp strike the 1923-S is an extreme rarity. Among later coins the 1940-S and 1941-S often are weakly struck.

Franklin half dollars minted from 1948 through 1963 have been very popular in recent decades. The complete series of dates and mintmarks is short and contains no scarce or rare pieces in higher grades such as MS–63 and 64. However, if you consider the element of sharp striking, usually defined as Full Bell Lines (FBL) on the reverse, certain otherwise common dates become elusive. Proofs of most years can also be readily collected.

Kennedy half dollars are easily enough collected, and so many have been made by this time that nearly 200 date-and-mintmark combinations extend from 1964 to present, including a gold version that marks the design's 50th anniversary. The wise collector will select coins that have a meeting point between a high grade such as MS–65 or 66 (or equivalent Proofs) and a reasonable price.

FLOWING HAIR (1794–1795)

Designer: *Robert Scot.* **Weight:** *13.48 grams.*
Composition: *.8924 silver, .1076 copper.* **Diameter:** *Approximately 32.5 mm.*
Edge: *FIFTY CENTS OR HALF A DOLLAR with decorations between the words.* **Mint:** *Philadelphia.*

Overton-104

History. The Flowing Hair design inaugurated the half-dollar denomination. They were immediately popular, as was evident in 1795, when many depositors of silver at the Philadelphia Mint asked for half dollars in return. The same motif was used on half dimes and silver dollars of the same years. Early half dollars have been extensively collected by die varieties, of which many exist for most dates. Valuations given below are in each case for the most readily available variety; scarcer ones, as listed by Overton, generally command higher prices.

Striking and Sharpness. Many have problems of one sort or another, including adjustment marks from the planchet being filed down to proper weight and mushy denticles. On the obverse, check the hair details and the stars. On the reverse, check the breast of the eagle in particular. As with other silver coins of this design, it may not be possible to find a *needle-sharp* example, but with some extensive searching a fairly decent strike can be obtained. Sharp striking and excellent eye appeal add to the value dramatically. However, very few 1794 and 1795 halves are uniformly sharp on both sides.

Availability. Probably 3,500 to 6,000 circulated Flowing Hair half dollars exist. Most are dated 1795, the 1794 being considered a rare date (though not among the great U.S. coin rarities). Typical grades are Good to Fine. EF and AU grades are elusive in regard to the total population. Probably 100 or so could be graded MS (nearly all of them 1795). Unlike half dollars of the 1796–1797 type, none of these are known to have been made with prooflike surfaces.

GRADING STANDARDS

MS-60 to 70 (Mint State). *Obverse:* At MS-60, some abrasion and contact marks are evident, most noticeably on the cheek and in the fields. This denomination, heavier than the half dime of the same design, was more susceptible to contact and other outside influences. A typical half dollar certified at MS–60 or 61 today might well have been designated as About Uncirculated a generation ago. Luster is present, but may be dull or lifeless, and

1795; Overton-110a. Graded MS-63.

interrupted in patches, perhaps as much from old cleaning as from contact the coin may have received. At MS-63, contact marks are very few, and abrasion is present, but not as noticeable. An MS-65 coin has no abrasion, and contact marks are very few. Luster should be full and rich. Higher grades are seldom seen in this type, but are defined in theory by having fewer marks as perfection is approached. *Reverse:* Comments apply as for the obverse, except that abrasion and contact marks are most noticeable on the eagle at the center. This area is often lightly struck, so in all grades do not mistake weak striking for actual wear. Knowledge of specific die varieties is helpful in this regard. The field area is small and is protected by lettering and the wreath, and in any given grade shows fewer marks than on the obverse.

Illustrated coin: This is a well-struck example with superb eye appeal.

AU-50, 53, 55, 58 (About Uncirculated). *Obverse:* Light wear is seen on the hair area immediately to the left of the face and above the forehead, on the cheek, and, to a lesser extent, on the top of the neck truncation, more so at AU-50 than at AU–53 or 55. An AU-58 coin has minimal traces of wear. An AU-50 coin has luster in protected areas among the stars and letters, with little in the open fields or on the portrait. At AU-58,

1795; O-116. Graded AU-55.

much luster is present in the fields but is worn away on the highest parts of the motifs. *Reverse:* Light wear is seen on the eagle's body and the upper part of both wings. On well-struck pieces the details of the wing features are excellent. At AU-50, detail is lost in some feathers in this area. However, striking can play a part, as some coins were weakly struck to begin with. Light wear is seen on the wreath and lettering, but is harder to discern. Luster is the best key to actual wear. This will range from perhaps 20% remaining in protected areas (at AU-50) to nearly full mint bloom (at AU-58), although among certified coins the amounts of luster can vary widely.

Illustrated coin: Significant luster remains in protected areas on this attractive early half dollar.

EF-40, 45 (Extremely Fine). *Obverse:* More wear is evident on the portrait, especially on the hair to the left of and above the forehead, and in the back below the LI of LIBERTY. The tip of the neck truncation shows flatness, and the cheek is worn. Excellent detail remains in low-relief areas of the hair. The stars show wear, as do the date and letters. Luster, if present at all, is minimal and in protected areas. *Reverse:* The eagle shows more

1794; O-101. Graded EF-40.

wear on the body and on the tops of the wings. Interior wing detail is good on most coins (depending on the variety and the striking), and the tail feathers can be discerned. Additional wear is on the wreath and letters, but many details are present. Some luster may be seen in protected areas and if present is slightly more abundant than on the obverse.

Illustrated coin: Note some lightness of the stars at the right and at the reverse center, as struck. The scrape on the reverse below the ribbon knot was mentioned by the cataloger in an auction offering.

VF-20, 30 (Very Fine). *Obverse:* The hair is well worn at VF-20, less so at VF-30, and is most noticeable in the upper part of the head, the area above the level of the eye, and extending to the back. The strands are blended as to be heavy. The cheek shows only slight relief, and the tip of the neck truncation is flat. The stars have more wear, making them appear larger (an optical illusion). Scattered marks are common on half dollars at this level

1795; O-109. Graded VF-20.

and below, and should be mentioned if particularly serious. *Reverse:* The body of the eagle shows few if any feathers, while the wings have perhaps a quarter or a third of the feathers visible depending on the strike, with sharper strikes having up to half visible (as PCGS suggests). *Photograde* and the ANA grading standards suggest half of the feathers on all, which may be the case on coins that were well struck to begin with. The leaves lack detail and are in outline form. Scattered, non-disfiguring marks are normal for this and lower grades. Any major defects should be noted separately.

Illustrated coin: On this variety in this grade, the denticles are especially prominent on each side. Such aspects vary from coin to coin.

F-12, 15 (Fine). *Obverse:* Wear is more extensive than on the preceding, with less hair visible. The ear position can be seen, as can the eye. The cheek is nearly flat, and the stars appear larger. The rim is distinct and most denticles remain visible. *Reverse:* Wear is more extensive. Now, feather details are fewer, mostly remaining on the wing to the left. The wreath and lettering are more worn, and the rim is usually weak in areas, although most denticles can be seen.

1795; O-107. Graded F-12.

VG-8, 10 (Very Good). *Obverse:* The portrait is mostly seen in outline form, with most hair strands gone save for an area centered behind the neck. The hair tips at the lower left are clear. The eye location is barely discernible. The stars appear larger still and often quite bold, again an illusion. The rim is weak in areas. LIBERTY and the date are readable and usually full, although some letters may be weak at their tops. *Reverse:* The

1795; O-109. Graded VG-8.

eagle is mostly an outline, although traces of the separation between the body and the right wing can sometimes be seen. The rim is worn, as are the letters, with some weak, but the motto is readable. On many coins the rim remains fairly prominent.

Illustrated coin: Note a spot, a tiny edge bruise, and some adjustment marks. A cataloger mentioned that "the top of the obverse is slightly soft due to axial misalignment"—a technical note. On any half dollar of this era, knowledge of the varieties and peculiarities of striking is useful.

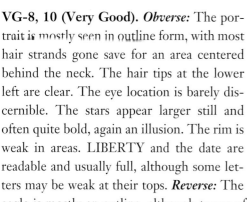

G-4, 6 (Good). *Obverse:* Wear is more extensive, and some stars may be missing or only partially visible. The head is an outline, although a few elements of thick hair strands may be seen. The rim is well worn or even missing. LIBERTY is worn, and parts of some letters may be missing, but elements of all should be readable. The date is readable, but worn. *Reverse:* The eagle is flat and discernible in outline form. The wreath is well

1794; O-106. Graded G-6.

worn. Some of the letters may be partly missing. At this level some "averaging" can be done. If the letters are stronger than usual in one area, but some are missing in another area, the coin can still qualify as G-4. Often on this type in lower grades the reverse is more detailed than the obverse.

AG-3 (About Good). *Obverse:* Wear is very extensive. The head is in outline form (perhaps partly blended into the field). LIBERTY is mostly gone. The date, while readable, may be partially worn away. Some stars are missing. *Reverse:* The reverse is well worn, with parts of the wreath and lettering very weak or even missing. The details that remain and those that do not is often dependent on the particular die variety.

1795; O-116. Graded AG-3.

| 1795, Normal Date | 1795, Recut Date | 1795, Two Leaves Under Each Wing | 1795, Three Leaves Under Each Wing |

	Mintage	Cert	Avg	%MS	AG-3	G-4	VG-8	F-12	VF-20	EF-40	AU-50	AU-55	MS-60
1794	23,464	346	21.6	2%	$2,500	$3,500	$4,500	$6,000	$12,000	$30,000	$70,000	$125,000	$300,000
Auctions: $152,750, MS-61, June 2014; $19,975, VF-30, March 2016; $18,800, VF-30, August 2014; $12,925, VF-20, August 2014													
1795, All kinds (a)	299,680												
1795, Normal Date		1,235	22.9	4%	$650	$1,100	$1,750	$2,500	$3,250	$7,500	$13,500	$16,500	$37,500
Auctions: $129,250, MS-62, November 2013; $1,998, F-12, March 2015; $881, G-6, September 2015; $705, AG-3, June 2015													
1795, Recut Date		45	23.4	0%	$750	$1,250	$1,750	$2,750	$4,750	$13,500	$20,000	$22,500	
Auctions: $1,651, F-12, March 2014; $1,645, VG-8, September 2014													
1795, 3 Leaves Under Each Wing		16	24.4	0%	$1,000	$2,500	$3,500	$5,500	$8,500	$20,000	$35,000	$45,000	$75,000
Auctions: $8,519, VF, March 2014													
1795, Small Head		19	13.1	0%	$750	$1,250	$2,000	$4,500	$7,500	$15,000	$25,000	$27,500	
Auctions: $1,620, G-6, January 2021; $3,738, VG-10, November 2009; $3,000, F-15, February 2018; $14,100, VF-35, January 2016													

a. Varieties of 1795 are known with the final S in STATES over a D; with the A in STATES over an E; and with the Y in LIBERTY over a star. All are scarce. Some 1794 and 1795 half dollars were weight-adjusted by insertion of a silver plug in the center of the blank planchet before the coin was struck.

DRAPED BUST, SMALL EAGLE REVERSE (1796–1797)

Designer: *Robert Scot.* **Weight:** *13.48 grams.*
Composition: *.8924 silver, .1076 copper.* **Diameter:** *Approximately 32.5 mm.*
Edge: *FIFTY CENTS OR HALF A DOLLAR with decorations between words.* **Mint:** *Philadelphia.*

O-101a.

History. Robert Scot's Draped Bust design is similar to that used on the half dime, dime, quarter, and silver dollar of this era. In 1796 and 1797 there was little demand for half dollars and the combined mintage for the two years was therefore low. Among design types of U.S. silver coins made in circulation-strike format this is the Holy Grail—a classic rarity, with no common date in the series.

Striking and Sharpness. On the obverse, check the hair details and the stars. On the reverse, first check the breast of the eagle, but examine other areas as well. Also check the denticles on both sides. Look especially for coins that do not have significant adjustment marks (from an overweight planchet being filed down to correct specifications). Coins of this denomination are on average better struck than are half dimes, dimes, quarters (which have reverse problems), and dollars in the Draped Bust suite.

Availability. Examples are rare in any grade—survivors likely number only in the hundreds of coins. MS examples are particularly rare, and when seen are nearly always dated 1796. Some of these have partially prooflike surfaces. Any half dollar of this type has strong market demand.

GRADING STANDARDS

MS-60 to 70 (Mint State). *Obverse:* At MS-60, some abrasion and contact marks are evident, most noticeably on the cheek, the drapery at the shoulder, and the right field. Also check the hair to the left of the forehead. Luster is present, but may be dull or lifeless, and interrupted in patches. At MS-63, contact marks are few, and abrasion is hard to detect, although this type is sometimes graded liberally due to its rarity. An MS-65 coin has

1797; O-101a. Graded MS-66.

no abrasion, and contact marks are so minute as to require magnification. Luster should be full and rich. Coins graded above MS-65 are more theoretical than actual for this type, although some notable pieces have crossed the auction block. These are defined by having fewer marks as perfection is approached. *Reverse:* Comments apply as for the obverse, except that abrasion and contact marks are most noticeable on the eagle at the center, a situation that should be evaluated by considering the original striking (which can be quite sharp, but with many exceptions). The field area is small and is protected by lettering and the wreath, and in any given grade shows fewer marks than on the obverse.

Illustrated coin: This superb gem has prooflike surfaces.

AU-50, 53, 55, 58 (About Uncirculated). *Obverse:* Light wear is seen on the hair area above the ear and extending to the left of the forehead, on the ribbon, and on the drapery at the shoulder, more so at AU-50 than at AU–53 or 55. An AU-58 coin has minimal traces of wear. An AU-50 coin has luster in protected areas among the stars and letters, with little in the open fields or on the portrait. At AU-58, most luster is present in the fields, but is worn away on the highest parts of the motifs. *Reverse:* Light wear is seen on the eagle's body and the edges of the wings. Light wear is seen on the wreath and lettering. Luster is the best key to actual wear. This ranges from perhaps 20% remaining in protected areas (at AU-50) to nearly full mint bloom (at AU-58).

1797; O-101a. Graded AU-50.

EF-40, 45 (Extremely Fine). *Obverse:* More wear is evident on the upper hair area, particularly to the left of the forehead and also below the LI of LIBERTY, in the ribbon, and on the drapery and bosom. Excellent detail remains in low-relief areas of the hair. The stars show wear as do the date and letters. Luster, if present at all, is minimal and in protected areas. *Reverse:* The eagle shows more wear, this being the focal point to check. Many feathers remain on the interior areas of the wings. Additional wear is on the wreath and letters, but many details are present. Some luster may be seen in protected areas and if present is slightly more abundant than on the obverse.

1796, 15 Stars; O-101. Graded EF-40.

VF-20, 30 (Very Fine). *Obverse:* The higher-relief areas of hair are well worn at VF-20, less so at VF-30. The drapery and bosom show extensive wear. The stars have more wear. *Reverse:* The body of the eagle shows few if any feathers, while the wings have about half or more of the feathers visible, depending on the strike. The leaves lack most detail and are outlined. Scattered, non-disfiguring marks are normal for this and lower grades; major defects should be noted separately.

1796, 16 Stars; O-103. Graded VF-20.

F-12, 15 (Fine). *Obverse:* Wear is more extensive than on a Very Fine coin, particularly noticeable on the hair, face, and bosom. The stars appear larger (an optical illusion). About half the hair detail remains, most noticeably behind the neck and shoulder. The rim may be partially worn away and blend into the field, but on many coins it remains intact. *Reverse:* Wear is more extensive. Now, feather details are diminished,

1797; O-101a. Graded F-15.

with fewer than half remaining on the wings. The wreath and lettering are worn further, and the rim is usually weak in areas, but most denticles can be seen.

VG-8, 10 (Very Good). *Obverse:* The portrait is mostly seen in outline form, with most hair strands gone, although there is some definition at the back of the hair and behind the shoulder. The ear is barely discernible and the eye is fairly distinct. The stars appear larger still, again an illusion. The rim is weak in areas, but shows most denticles. LIBERTY and the date are readable and usually full, although some letters may be weak at their

1796, 16 Stars; O-102. Graded VG-10.

tops. *Reverse:* The eagle is mostly an outline, with parts blending into the field (on lighter strikes). The rim is worn, as are the letters, with some weak, but the motto is readable.

G-4, 6 (Good). *Obverse:* Wear is more extensive, and some stars may be partly missing. The head is an outline. The eye is visible only in outline form. The rim is well worn or even missing in areas, but many denticles remain. LIBERTY is worn. The letters and date are weak but fully readable. *Reverse:* The eagle is flat and discernible in outline form, and may be blending into the field. The wreath is well worn. Some of the letters may

1797. Graded G-4.

be partly missing. At this level some "averaging" can be done. If the letters are stronger than usual in one area, but some are missing in another area, the coin can still qualify as G-4.

AG-3 (About Good). *Obverse:* Wear is so extensive that the coin is barely identifiable. The head is in outline form. LIBERTY is mostly gone; same for the stars. The date, while readable, may be partially worn away. *Reverse:* The reverse is well worn, with parts of the wreath and lettering missing. On most coins the reverse shows more wear than the obverse.

1797. Graded AG-3.

1796, 15 Stars

1796, 16 Stars

	Mintage	Cert	Avg	%MS	AG-3	G-4	VG-8	F-12	VF-20	EF-40	AU-50	AU-58	MS-60
1796, 15 Stars †	(a)	16	38.0	25%	$23,000	$35,000	$40,000	$47,500	$60,000	$125,000	$165,000	$235,000	$290,000
	Auctions: No auction records available.												
1796, 16 Stars †	(a)	14	34.2	29%	$23,000	$36,500	$42,000	$48,500	$62,500	$125,000	$170,000	$250,000	$300,000
	Auctions: $470,000, MS-63, November 2013												
1797, 15 Stars †	3,918	59	26.9	5%	$23,000	$37,500	$42,500	$50,000	$62,500	$125,000	$165,000	$235,000	$300,000
	Auctions: $1,680,000, MS-66, March 2021; $17,625, MS-64, August 2015; $8,225, AU-53, November 2015; $4,406, EF-40, August 2015												

† All Draped Bust, Small Eagle Reverse Half Dollars are ranked in the *100 Greatest U.S. Coins* (fourth edition). **a.** Included in 1797, 15 Stars, mintage figure.

DRAPED BUST, HERALDIC EAGLE REVERSE (1801–1807)

Designer: *Robert Scot.* **Weight:** *13.48 grams.*
Composition: *.8924 silver, .1076 copper.* **Diameter:** *Approximately 32.5 mm.*
Edge: *FIFTY CENTS OR HALF A DOLLAR with decorations between words.* **Mint:** *Philadelphia.*

O-101.

History. The half dollar's Draped Bust, Heraldic Eagle design is similar to that of other silver coins of the era. While dies were prepared for the 1804 half dollar, none were minted in that year, despite Mint reports that state otherwise.

Striking and Sharpness. Most have light striking in one area or another. On the obverse, check the hair details and, in particular, the star centers. On the reverse, check the stars above the eagle, the clouds, the details of the shield, and the eagle's wings. Check the denticles on both sides. Adjustment marks are sometimes seen, from overweight planchets being filed down to correct weight, but not as often as on earlier half dollar types. Typically, the earlier years are better struck; many of 1806 and nearly all of 1807 are poorly struck. Sharp striking and excellent eye appeal add to the value dramatically, this being particularly true for those of 1805 to 1807, which are often weak (particularly 1807).

Availability. Earlier years are scarce in the marketplace, beginning with the elusive 1801 and including the 1802, after which they are more readily available. Some die varieties are scarce. Most MS coins are dated 1806 and 1807, but all are scarce. Finding sharply struck high-grade coins is almost impossible, a goal more than a reality.

GRADING STANDARDS

MS-60 to 70 (Mint State). *Obverse:* At MS-60, some abrasion and contact marks are evident, most noticeably on the cheek, the drapery at the shoulder, and the right field. Luster is present, but may be dull or lifeless, and interrupted in patches. At MS-63, contact marks are very few, and abrasion is hard to detect except under magnification. An MS-65 coin has no abrasion, and contact marks are so minute as to require magnifica-

1803, Large 3; O-101. Graded MS-63.

tion. Luster should be full and rich. Coins grading above MS-65 are more theoretical than actual for this type—but they do exist, and are defined by having fewer marks as perfection is approached. Later years usually have areas of flat striking. *Reverse:* Comments apply as for the obverse, except that abrasion and contact marks are most noticeable on the eagle's neck, the tips of the wing, and the tail. The field area is complex, without much open space, given the stars above the eagle, the arrows and olive branch, and other features. Accordingly, marks are not as noticeable as on the obverse.

Illustrated coin: This is an extraordinary strike with superb eye appeal. A connoisseur might prefer this coin to an MS-65 example with flat striking.

AU-50, 53, 55, 58 (About Uncirculated). *Obverse:* Light wear is seen on the hair area above the ear and extending to left of the forehead, on the ribbon, and on the bosom, more so at AU-50 than at AU-53 or 55. An AU-58 coin has minimal traces of wear. An AU-50 coin has luster in protected areas among the stars and letters, with little in the open fields or on the portrait. At AU-58, most luster is present in the fields, but is worn

1806, Pointed 6, No Stem; O-109. Graded AU-50.

away on the highest parts of the motifs. *Reverse:* Comments as preceding, except that the eagle's neck, the tips and top of the wings, the clouds, and the tail now show noticeable wear, as do other features. Luster ranges from perhaps 20% remaining in protected areas (at AU-50) to nearly full mint bloom (at AU-58). Often the reverse of this type retains much more luster than the obverse.

Illustrated coin: This example has gray and lilac toning.

EF-40, 45 (Extremely Fine). *Obverse:* More wear is evident on the upper hair area and the ribbon, and on the drapery and bosom. Excellent detail remains in low-relief areas of the hair. The stars show wear, as do the date and letters. Luster, if present at all, is minimal and in protected areas. *Reverse:* Wear is greater than on an About Uncirculated coin, overall. The neck lacks feather detail on its highest points. Feathers have lost some detail

1807; O-105. Graded EF-40.

near the edges of the wings, and some areas of the horizontal lines in the shield may be blended together. Some traces of luster may be seen, more so at EF-45 than at EF-40.

Illustrated coin: Light striking at the obverse center is normal for this die variety.

VF-20, 30 (Very Fine). *Obverse:* The higher-relief areas of hair are well worn at VF-20, less so at VF-30. The drapery on the shoulder and the bosom show extensive wear. The stars have more wear, making them appear larger (an optical illusion seen on most worn silver coins of this era). *Reverse:* Wear is greater, including on the shield and wing feathers. Half to two-thirds of the feathers are visible. Star centers are flat. Other areas have lost detail as well.

1806, 6 Over Inverted 9; O-111a. Graded VF-30.

Illustrated coin: Note the cud break on the reverse rim over the E in UNITED.

F-12, 15 (Fine). *Obverse:* Wear is more extensive than on a Very Fine coin, particularly noticeable on the hair, face, and bosom. The stars appear larger. About half the hair detail remains, most noticeably behind the neck and shoulder, but the fine hair is now combined into thicker tresses. The rim may be partially worn away and blend into the field. *Reverse:* Wear is even more extensive, with the shield and wing feathers being

1805; O-109. Graded F-15.

points to observe. The incuse E PLURIBUS UNUM may have half or more of the letters worn away (depending on striking). The clouds all appear connected. The stars are weak. Parts of the border and lettering may be weak.

VG-8, 10 (Very Good). *Obverse:* The portrait is mostly seen in outline form, with most hair strands gone, although there is some definition at the back of the hair and behind the shoulder. The ear is discernible as is the eye. The stars appear larger still, again an illusion. The rim is weak in areas. LIBERTY and the date are readable and usually full, although some letters may be weak at their tops. *Reverse:* Wear is more extensive. Half

1805, 5 Over 4; O-103. Graded VG-8.

or more of the letters in the motto are worn away. Most feathers are worn away, although separation of some of the lower feathers may be seen. Some stars are faint (depending on the strike). The border blends into the field in areas and some letters are weak.

G-4, 6 (Good). *Obverse:* Wear is more extensive, and some stars may be partly missing. The head is mostly an outline, although some hair strand outlines may be visible on some strikings. The rim is well worn or even missing in areas. LIBERTY is worn, and parts of some letters may be missing, but elements should be readable. The date is readable, but worn. *Reverse:* Wear is more extensive. The upper part of the eagle is flat. Feathers are

1805; O-111. Graded G-4.

noticeable only at the lower edge of the wings, and do not have detail. The upper part of the shield is flat or mostly so (depending on the strike). Only a few letters of the motto can be seen. The rim is worn extensively, and a few letters may be missing.

AG-3 (About Good). *Obverse:* Wear is so extensive that the coin is barely identifiable. The head is in outline form. LIBERTY is mostly gone; same for the stars. The date, while readable, may be partially worn away. *Reverse:* Extensive wear is seen overall, with the rim worn away and some areas worn smooth. The eagle can be discerned in outline form, but not necessarily completely. A few stray motto letters may remain.

1801. Graded AG-3.

	Mintage	Cert	Avg	%MS	G-4	VG-8	F-12	VF-20	EF-40	AU-50	AU-55	MS-60	MS-63
1801	30,289	153	26.9	1%	$950	$1,500	$2,200	$2,600	$5,250	$15,000	$25,000	$75,000	$160,000
	Auctions: $329,000, MS-64, November 2013; $4,700, EF-40, March 2015; $576, G-4, October 2014; $517, AG-3, July 2015												
1802	29,890	102	31.0	0%	$1,200	$1,600	$2,400	$2,850	$5,750	$17,000	$26,500	$60,000	
	Auctions: $70,500, AU-58, August 2013; $3,173, VF-20, August 2014; $2,115, F-15, August 2014												

1803, Small 3

1803, Large 3

1805, 5 Over 4

1805, Normal Date

1806, 6 Over 5

1806, 6 Over Inverted 6

1806, Stem Not Through Claw

1806, Stem Through Claw

1806, Knobbed-Top 6, Large Stars
With traces of overdate.

1806, Knobbed-Top 6, Small Stars

	Mintage	Cert	Avg	%MS	G-4	VG-8	F-12	VF-20	EF-40	AU-50	AU-55	MS-60	MS-63
1803, All kinds	188,234												
1803, Small 3		40	36.5	3%	$350	$475	$650	$1,100	$2,700	$4,500	$9,500	$25,000	$100,000
Auctions: $49,938, MS-62, June 2014													
1803, Large 3		133	31.5	4%	$300	$425	$500	$750	$1,850	$3,000	$7,000	$22,500	$65,000
Auctions: $1,763, EF-40, March 2015; $881, VF-30, June 2015; $752, VF-25, March 2015; $552, VF-20, March 2015													
1805, All kinds	211,722												
1805, 5 Over 4		118	32.7	1%	$500	$850	$1,250	$1,800	$3,500	$8,500	$12,750	$35,000	$85,000
Auctions: $3,055, EF-40, March 2016; $2,233, VF-30, August 2015; $999, F-12, June 2015; $9,106, VG-8, March 2015													
1805, Normal Date		458	31.3	2%	$260	$350	$475	$850	$1,600	$4,500	$6,500	$22,500	$35,000
Auctions: $4,406, AU-50, March 2015; $2,350, EF-45, May 2015; $1,528, VF-25, September 2015; $617, F-15, August 2015													
1806, All kinds	839,576												
1806, 6 Over 5		232	31.8	3%	$300	$425	$600	$900	$2,300	$4,750	$6,500	$13,500	$45,000
Auctions: $21,150, MS-61, November 2013; $881, VF-30, September 2014; $794, VF-25, January 2015; $764, VF-20, July 2014													
1806, 6 Over Inverted 6		75	26.1	1%	$350	$450	$925	$1,500	$4,000	$8,000	$12,500	$27,500	$50,000
Auctions: $28,200, MS-61, November 2013; $999, F-12, September 2014; $940, F-12, August 2014; $999, Fair-2, August 2014													
1806, Knobbed 6, Large Stars (Traces of Overdate)		40	28.2	0%	$225	$275	$400	$700	$1,400	$4,000	$7,000		
Auctions: $2,364, EF-40, August 2013													
1806, Knobbed 6, Small Stars		45	29.9	0%	$250	$325	$500	$700	$1,500	$4,000	$7,000	$12,000	$35,000
Auctions: $2,350, EF-45, January 2014; $435, F-15, July 2014													
1806, Knobbed 6, Stem Not Through Claw		1	25.0	0%	$70,000	$75,000	$85,000	$125,000					
Auctions: $126,500, EF-40, January 2009													
1806, Pointed 6, Stem Through Claw		313	31.7	5%	$225	$275	$400	$700	$1,500	$2,500	$5,000	$8,000	$20,000
Auctions: $35,250, MS-64, November 2013; $7,638, AU-53, August 2014; $447, F-12, October 2015; $327, VG-10, February 2015													
1806, Pointed 6, Stem Through Claw, E Over A in STATES		8	21.3	0%	$550	$1,500	$2,500	$4,000	$10,000				
Auctions: $4,465, VF-20, January 2015; $2,280, VG-8, February 2018													
1806, Pointed 6, Stem Not Through Claw		118	35.6	6%	$225	$275	$400	$700	$1,500	$2,500	$5,000	$8,000	$20,000
Auctions: $12,925, MS-62, November 2013; $3,840, AU-55, August 2014; $1,293, EF-40, January 2015; $881, VF-30, July 2015													
1807	301,076	1,287	32.0	7%	$225	$275	$400	$700	$1,500	$2,500	$5,000	$8,000	$20,000
Auctions: $1,528, EF-40, March 2015; $588, VF-20, February 2015; $400, F-12, August 2015; $306, VG-10, May 2015													

CAPPED BUST, LETTERED EDGE (1807–1836)

Designer: *John Reich.* **Weight:** *13.48 grams.*
Composition: *.8924 silver, .1076 copper.* **Diameter:** *Approximately 32.5 mm.*
Edge: *1807–1814—FIFTY CENTS OR HALF A DOLLAR;*
1814–1831—star added between DOLLAR and FIFTY;
1832–1836—vertical lines added between words. **Mint:** *Philadelphia.*

First Style (1807–1808)
O-104.

Remodeled Portrait and Eagle
(1809–1836)
O-109.

Remodeled Portrait and Eagle, Proof
O-103.

History. The Capped Bust design was created by Mint assistant engraver John Reich; the motif was widely used, in several variations, on much of the era's coinage. Reich was the first artist to consistently include the denomination in his designs for U.S. gold and silver coins. The half dollar, minted continuously from 1807 to 1836, except 1816, was the largest silver coin of the realm at the time (silver dollars had not been struck since 1804).

Striking and Sharpness. On the obverse, check the hair and brooch details. The stars are often flatly struck on Capped Bust half dollars, much more so than on other denominations. On the reverse, check the motto band and the eagle's head, and the wing to the left, as well as other areas (the neck feathers, often lightly struck on other denominations of Capped Bust silver, are usually fairly sharp on half dollars). The E PLURIBUS UNUM band is often weak in the area left of its center; this does not normally occur on other Capped Bust silver coins. Inspect the denticles on both sides. Generally, later dates are better struck than are earlier ones. Many half dollars have semi-prooflike surfaces, or patches of mirror-like character interspersed with luster. Others can have nearly full prooflike surfaces, with patches of luster being in the minority (and often in the left obverse field); some of these have been mischaracterized as "Proofs." Some issues from the early 1830s have little digs or "bite marks" on the portrait, possibly from some sort of a gadget used to eject them from the press. Unlike the Capped Bust half dime, dime, and quarter dollar, the half dollar is particularly subject to very wide variations in striking quality.

True Proofs have deeply mirrored surfaces. Impostors are often seen, with deeply toned surfaces or with patches of mint luster. This situation is more prevalent with half dollars than with any other Capped Bust denomination. Proceed slowly, and be careful. There are some crushed-lettered-edge ("CLE")

Proofs of the 1833 to 1835 era that are especially beautiful and are more deeply mirrorlike than original issues. Some of these are restrikes (not necessarily an important consideration, but worth mentioning), believed to have been made at the Mint beginning in the spring of 1859.

Availability. Examples of most dates and overdates are easily found in just about any grade desired, from Fine and VF to MS. (As the largest silver coin struck between 1803 and 1836, these half dollars spent much of their time in bags, transferred from bank to bank, rather than wearing down in circulation.) The later years are the most readily available and are also seen in higher average grades. Many die varieties range from scarce to rare. Proofs were made in limited numbers for presentation purposes and for distribution to numismatists.

GRADING STANDARDS

MS-60 to 70 (Mint State). *Obverse:* At MS-60, some abrasion and contact marks are evident, most noticeably on the cheek, the hair below the left part of LIBERTY, the cap, and the front part of the bosom and drapery. These areas also coincide with the highest parts of the coin and are thus susceptible to lightness of strike. Complicating matters is that when an area is lightly struck, and the planchet is not forced into the deepest parts

1827, Square Base 2; O-104. Graded MS-60.

of the die, the *original planchet surface* (which may exhibit scuffing and nicks) is visible. A lightly struck coin can have virtually perfect luster in the fields, deep and rich, and yet appear to be "worn" on the higher parts, due to the lightness of strike. This is a very sophisticated concept and is hard to quantify. In practice, the original planchet surface will usually be considered as wear on the finished coin, which of course is not true. Such grades as high About Uncirculated and low Mint State levels are often assigned to pieces that, if well struck, would be MS–64 and 65. As a matter of practicality, but not of logic, you will need to do the same. If a coin has original planchet abrasions, but otherwise is a Gem, those abrasions must be taken into consideration. Apart from this, on well-struck coins in lower Mint State grades, luster is present, but may be dull or lifeless, and interrupted in patches. At MS-63, on a well-struck coin, contact marks are very few, and abrasion is hard to detect except under magnification. A well-struck MS-65 coin has no abrasion, and contact marks are so minute as to require magnification. Luster should be full and rich. Grades above MS-65 are seen now and again and are defined by having fewer marks as perfection is approached. *Reverse:* Comments apply as for the obverse, except that nearly all coins with weak striking on the obverse (so as to reveal original planchet surface) do not show such original surface on the reverse, except perhaps on the motto ribbon. Accordingly, market grading is usually by the obverse only, even if the reverse seems to be in much better preservation. On well-struck coins, abrasion and contact marks are most noticeable on the eagle's head, the top of the wings, the claws, and the flat band that surrounds the incuse motto. The field is mainly protected by design elements and does not show abrasion as much as does the obverse on a given coin.

Illustrated coin: This is an exceptional coin at the low Mint State level.

AU-50, 53, 55, 58 (About Uncirculated). *Obverse:* Light wear is seen on the cheek, the hair below the left part of LIBERTY, the cap, and the front part of the bosom and drapery. Some of this apparent "wear" may be related to the original planchet surface (as noted under Mint State, above), but at the About Uncirculated level the distinction is less important. On a well-struck coin, at AU-58 the luster is extensive except in the open area of the field, espe-

1820, Curl Base 2, Small Date; O-103. Graded AU-55.

cially to the right. At AU–50 and 53, luster remains only in protected areas. *Reverse:* Wear is evident on the eagle's head, the top of the wings, the claws, and the flat band above the eagle. An AU-58 coin has nearly full luster. At AU–50 and 53, there still is significant luster, more than on the obverse.

Illustrated coin: An attractive coin by any measure, this has light toning and ample areas of original luster.

EF-40, 45 (Extremely Fine). *Obverse:* Wear is more extensive, most noticeably on the higher areas of the hair. The cap shows more wear, as does the cheek. Luster, if present, is in protected areas among the star points and close to the portrait. *Reverse:* The wings show wear on the higher areas of the feathers, and some details are lost. The top of the head and the beak are flat. The eagle's claws and the leaves show wear. Luster may be present

1810; O-110. Graded EF-45.

in protected areas, even if there is little or none on the obverse.

Illustrated coin: This coin probably was lightly cleaned years ago so as to give a light silver color, which added some hairlines, but now it has halo toning around the borders that adds attractiveness.

VF-20, 30 (Very Fine). *Obverse:* Wear is more extensive, and most of the hair is combined into thick tresses without delicate features. The curl on the neck is flat. The cap shows significant wear at its top, and the left part of the drapery and bosom is nearly flat. Stars are flat at their centers (even if sharply struck to begin with). *Reverse:* Wear is most evident on the eagle's head, the tops of the wings, and the leaves and claws. Nearly all

1815, 5 Over 2; O-101. Graded VF-30.

feathers in the wing remain distinct.

Illustrated coin: The areas of wear appear exaggerated due to the light toning, a feature often observed on half dollars of this date but not as often among other years.

F-12, 15 (Fine). *Obverse:* Wear is more extensive, with much of the hair blended together. The drapery is indistinct on most of its upper edge. The stars are flat at their centers. LIBERTY remains bold. *Reverse:* Wear is more extensive, now with only about half of the feathers remaining on the wings, more on the right wing. The head shows the eye, nostril, and beak but no details. The claws show more wear. Other features are worn as well, but not as noticeable as the key points mentioned.

1827, Square Base 2; O-122. Graded F-12.

VG-8, 10 (Very Good). *Obverse:* The hair is less distinct, with the forehead blended into the hair above. LIBERTY is complete, but may be slightly weak in areas. The stars are flat. The rim is distinct, with most if not all denticles visible. *Reverse:* Feathers are fewer and mostly on the right wing, although sharp strikes can show detail in both wings. Other details are weaker. All lettering remains easily readable.

1831; O-120. Graded VG-8.

    Illustrated coin: This coin was cleaned and partially retoned. It is sharply struck on the reverse.

G-4, 6 (Good). *Obverse:* The portrait is mostly in outline, with few interior details discernible. LIBERTY may still be readable or may be partially worn away, depending on the variety. The rim is weak, but distinct in most areas. *Reverse:* The eagle is mostly in outline form, although some feathers can be seen in the right wing. All letters around the border are clear. E PLURIBUS UNUM may be weak. Overall, a typical coin has the reverse in a slightly higher grade than the obverse.

1808. Graded G-4.

AG-3 (About Good). *Obverse:* The portrait is an outline, although some of LIBERTY can still be seen. The rim is worn down, and some stars are blended into it. The date remains clear, but is weak at the bottom (on most but not all). *Reverse:* At this level the reverse shows more wear overall than the obverse, with the rim indistinct in areas and many letters worn away. This is an interesting turnabout from the situation of most G-4 coins.

1824. Graded AG-3.

PF-60 to 70 (Proof). *Obverse and Reverse:* Proofs of this type have confused experts for a long time (as have large copper cents of the same era). Proofs that were extensively cleaned and therefore have many hairlines, or that are dull and grainy, are lower level, such as PF–60 to 62. While any early Proof half dollar will generate interest among collectors, lower levels are not of great interest to specialists unless they are of rare die varieties. With medium

1836; O-108. Graded PF-64 Cameo.

hairlines, an assigned grade of PF-64 may be in order and with relatively few, Gem PF-65. PF-66 should have hairlines so delicate that magnification is needed to see them. Above that, a Proof should be free of such lines. Grading is highly subjective with early Proofs, with eye appeal being a major factor.

1807, Small Stars

1807, Large Stars

1807, Large Stars, 50 Over 20

1807, "Bearded" Liberty

1808, 8 Over 7

	Mintage	Cert	Avg	%MS	G-4	F-12	VF-20	EF-40	AU-50	AU-55	MS-60	MS-63	MS-65
											PF-63	PF-64	PF-65
1807, All kinds	750,500												
1807, Small Stars		43	32.8	7%	$200	$750	$950	$2,000	$4,000	$5,750	$20,000	$32,500	$100,000
Auctions: $28,200, MS-61, January 2014; $999, EF-40, August 2014; $1,058, VF-30, March 2016; $823, VF-25, January 2015													
1807, Large Stars		40	38.0	8%	$175	$600	$800	$1,850	$3,000	$6,000	$15,000	$32,500	$150,000
Auctions: $152,750, MS-65, November 2013; $646, VF-25, September 2016; $1,080, VF-35, March 2018													
1807, Large Stars, 50 Over 20		195	36.4	5%	$150	$450	$625	$1,100	$2,250	$3,750	$6,500	$11,000	$65,000
Auctions: $1,293, EF-45, January 2015; $940, VF-35, February 2015; $764, VF-35, January 2015; $282, VG-10, February 2015													
1807, "Bearded" Liberty (a)		38	29.2	0%	$1,000	$2,500	$3,800	$7,000	$27,500				
Auctions: $5,405, EF-45, February 2015; $4,700, VF-30, March 2015													
1808, All kinds	1,368,600												
1808, 8 Over 7		215	40.1	9%	$100	$225	$350	$650	$1,500	$2,250	$5,000	$10,000	$25,000
Auctions: $21,150, MS-65, November 2013; $676, EF-45, January 2015; $705, EF-40, July 2014; $388, VF-35, October 2014													
1808		892	39.2	12%	$75	$150	$250	$450	$1,150	$1,850	$3,500	$6,000	$19,000
Auctions: $1,175, AU-50, August 2015; $705, EF-45, March 2015; $259, VF-20, April 2015; $212, F-15, March 2015; $660, EF-45, March 2018													

a. Also called the Bearded Goddess variety; a die crack gives the illusion of long whiskers growing from Miss Liberty's chin.

1809, xxxx Edge
*Experimental edge has
"xxxx" between the words.*

1809, | | | | | Edge
*Experimental edge has
"| | | | |" between the words.*

1811, (18.11), 11 Over 10
The date is "punctuated" with a period.

1811, Small 8

1811, Large 8

1812, 2 Over 1, Small 8

1812, 2 Over 1, Large 8

**1812, Two Leaves
Below Wing**

**1812, Single Leaf
Below Wing**

	Mintage	Cert	Avg	%MS	G-4	F-12	VF-20	EF-40	AU-50	AU-55	MS-60 PF-63	MS-63 PF-64	MS-65 PF-65
1809, All kinds	1,405,810												
1809, Normal Edge		745	40.2	12%	$100	$175	$250	$650	$900	$1,500	$3,000	$8,500	$22,500
Auctions: $764, AU-55, February 2015; $494, EF-40, April 2015; $353, VF-35, August 2015; $165, F-15, January 2015; $900, AU-50, April 2018													
1809, xxxx Edge		70	33.9	3%	$150	$250	$425	$1,100	$2,000	$4,000	$8,500	$20,000	
Auctions: $1,645, AU-50, April 2014; $411, VF-25, July 2014													
1809, IIIII Edge		147	38.6	7%	$100	$175	$250	$650	$1,200	$2,500	$4,750	$12,500	$37,500
Auctions: $38,188, MS-66, April 2014; $780, EF-40, January 2018													
1810	1,276,276	832	41.2	11%	$75	$135	$200	$400	$800	$1,400	$2,750	$7,000	$35,000
Auctions: $646, AU-53, January 2015; $505, AU-50, June 2015; $447, EF-40, June 2015; $282, VF-35, October 2015; $1,200, AU-55, February 2018													
1811, All kinds	1,203,644												
1811, (18.11), 11 Over 10		135	41.2	10%	$100	$250	$400	$650	$1,400	$2,750	$5,500	$14,000	
Auctions: $9,988, MS-63, February 2016; $6,463, AU-58, January 2014; $423, VF-35, August 2015; $494, VF-30, June 2015													
1811, Small 8		241	44.3	16%	$75	$135	$200	$385	$950	$1,400	$3,000	$5,500	$20,000
Auctions: $999, AU-55, January 2015; $1,175, AU-53, February 2015; $494, VF-35, March 2015; $188, VF-20, June 2015													
1811, Large 8		69	44.2	3%	$75	$145	$225	$425	$1,100	$1,250	$2,750	$5,000	$17,250
Auctions: $1,880, AU-58, January 2015; $329, EF-45, June 2015; $494, EF-40, October 2015; $282, VF-35, March 2015													
1812, All kinds	1,628,059												
1812, 2 Over 1, Small 8		136	41.3	15%	$115	$200	$300	$600	$1,200	$2,000	$3,500	$8,500	$35,000
Auctions: $1,293, AU-55, July 2014; $306, VF-30, March 2015; $248, VF-25, October 2015; $182, F-15, October 2015; $1,320, AU-53, January 2018													
1812, 2 Over 1, Large 8		15	34.3	0%	$2,000	$5,000	$8,000	$13,000	$24,000	$30,000			
Auctions: $14,100, AU-58, August 2013; $8,225, VF-30, August 2014													
1812		1,307	44.4	21%	$75	$135	$175	$450	$750	$1,100	$2,200	$4,000	$15,000
Auctions: $44,063, MS-65, November 2013; $441, AU-50, October 2014; $470, EF-45, August 2014; $324, EF-40, October 2014													
1812, Single Leaf Below Wing		2	31.5	0%	$750	$1,300	$2,400	$3,750	$7,000	$12,000	$17,000	$30,000	
Auctions: $31,200, AU-53, February 2018													

1813, 50 C. Over UNI.

1814, 4 Over 3

1814, E Over A in STATES

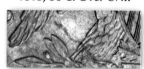

1814, Two Leaves Below Wing

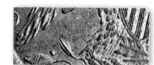

1814, Single Leaf Below Wing

1815, 5 Over 2

1817, 7 Over 3

1817, 7 Over 4

1817, Dated 181.7
The date is "punctuated" with a period between the second 1 and the 7.

1817, Two Leaves Below Wing

1817, Single Leaf Below Wing

	Mintage	Cert	Avg	%MS	G-4	F-12	VF-20	EF-40	AU-50	AU-55	MS-60 PF-63	MS-63 PF-64	MS-65 PF-65
1813, All kinds	1,241,903												
1813		856	43.5	15%	$75	$115	$160	$400	$750	$1,250	$2,500	$4,500	$16,000
Auctions: $881, AU-53, September 2015; $423, EF-45, January 2015; $353, EF-40, May 2015; $212, VF-30, October 2015													
1813, 50 C. Over UNI		81	45.5	15%	$125	$275	$425	$900	$1,400	$2,500	$4,000	$7,500	
Auctions: $24,675, MS-64, June 2014													
1814, All kinds	1,039,075												
1814, 4 Over 3		123	38.9	11%	$135	$300	$425	$875	$2,000	$2,650	$4,500	$8,500	$35,000
Auctions: $1,175, EF-45, June 2015; $823, EF-40, September 2015; $353, VF-35, March 2015; $482, VF-25, February 2015													
1814, E Over A in STATES		38	38.5	5%	$125	$275	$450	$1,500	$2,750	$5,500	$8,500	$15,000	
Auctions: $4,700, AU-55, January 2014; $505, VF-35, July 2014													
1814		871	43.8	17%	$85	$150	$225	$600	$800	$1,300	$2,750	$5,250	$20,000
Auctions: $22,325, MS-65, November 2013; $3,290, MS-62, August 2014; $705, AU-50, October 2014; $382, EF-45, September 2014													
1814, Single Leaf Below Wing		27	33.6	0%	$85	$150	$400	$1,000	$2,750	$3,500	$4,500	$8,000	
Auctions: $3,408, AU-50, August 2014; $705, EF-40, November 2013; $159, VF-20, October 2014													
1815, 5 Over 2	47,150	268	42.3	10%	$1,450	$3,500	$4,500	$5,500	$10,000	$13,000	$22,500	$50,000	
Auctions: $117,500, MS-64, November 2013; $7,931, EF-45, August 2016; $5,581, EF-40, March 2015													
1817, All kinds	1,215,567												
1817, 7 Over 3		175	38.8	13%	$200	$500	$750	$1,350	$3,500	$4,750	$8,500	$17,500	$60,000
Auctions: $28,200, MS-64, November 2013; $823, AU-50, January 2015; $541, F-15, October 2015; $499, F-15, July 2014													
1817, 7 Over 4 † (b)		2	40.0	0%			$140,000	$175,000	$275,000	$375,000			
Auctions: $184,000, VF-20, August 2010													
1817, Dated 181.7		36	42.4	6%	$125	$300	$400	$750	$2,000	$2,500	$4,000	$8,000	$40,000
Auctions: $3,055, AU-58, August 2013; $529, VF-30, July 2014; $540, VF-35, March 2018													
1817		895	40.6	12%	$100	$145	$200	$400	$750	$1,100	$2,500	$4,750	$24,500
Auctions: $508, AU-53, January 2015; $541, AU-50, June 2015; $325, EF-45, May 2015; $153, F-12, August 2015													
1817, Single Leaf Below Wing		15	38.1	7%	$115	$160	$250	$700	$1,250	$1,650	$2,750	$4,500	
Auctions: $3,055, AU-55, April 2013													

† Ranked in the *100 Greatest U.S. Coins* (fourth edition). **b.** 8 examples are known.

| **1818, First 8 Small, Second 8 Over 7** | **1818, First 8 Large, Second 8 Over 7** | **1819, Small 9 Over 8** | **1819, Large 9 Over 8** |

| **1820, 20 Over 19, Square Base 2** | **1820, 20 Over 19, Curl Base 2** | **1820, Curl Base, No Knob 2, Small Date** | **1820, Square Base, Knob 2, Large Date** |

1820, Square Base, No Knob 2, Large Date

1820, Broken Serifs on E's
Compare with normal serifs on 1834, Large Letters, reverse.

	Mintage	Cert	Avg	%MS	G-4	F-12	VF-20	EF-40	AU-50	AU-55	MS-60 / PF-63	MS-63 / PF-64	MS-65 / PF-65
1818, All kinds	1,960,322												
1818, 8 Over 7, Small 8		64	42.9	11%	$100	$165	$275	$550	$1,450	$2,000	$3,250	$8,500	$25,000
Auctions: $881, AU-53, August 2014; $499, EF-40, September 2014; $270, VF-35, March 2015; $165, F-15, October 2015													
1818, 8 Over 7, Large 8		87	41.9	9%	$90	$145	$225	$475	$1,250	$1,800	$3,250	$7,500	$25,000
Auctions: $1,645, AU-55, January 2015; $999, AU-50, September 2014; $764, EF-40, August 2014; $212, VF-25, October 2015													
1818		1,190	44.7	14%	$70	$100	$155	$300	$650	$1,400	$2,750	$4,500	$16,000
Auctions: $2,174, MS-62, May 2015; $1,528, AU-55, January 2015; $353, EF-45, January 2015; $235, EF-40, May 2015													
1818, Proof	3–5	3	65.3								$45,000	$60,000	$100,000
Auctions: $100,625, PF-65, April 2011													
1819, All kinds	2,208,000												
1819, Small 9 Over 8		63	38.9	0%	$85	$150	$225	$450	$1,000	$1,750	$3,000	$5,750	$22,500
Auctions: $588, AU-50, July 2015; $353, EF-45, May 2015; $235, VF-35, May 2015; $141, VF-20, May 2015; $432, EF-40, March 2018													
1819, Large 9 Over 8		157	44.7	6%	$75	$120	$175	$350	$750	$1,450	$3,000	$5,750	$25,000
Auctions: $734, AU-53, October 2014; $1,763, AU-50, September 2015; $329, EF-40, January 2015; $206, Fair-2, October 2014													
1819		1,047	43.3	12%	$75	$100	$150	$325	$650	$1,150	$2,500	$5,000	$20,000
Auctions: $823, AU-55, February 2015; $646, AU-53, July 2015; $259, EF-40, May 2015; $400, VF-35, October 2015													
1820, All kinds	751,122												
1820, 20 Over 19, Square 2		52	39.9	12%	$110	$175	$300	$750	$1,750	$3,250	$4,750	$10,000	$45,000
Auctions: $15,863, MS-63, January 2014; $3,819, AU-58, August 2014; $382, VF-30, July 2014													
1820, 20 Over 19, Curl Base 2		63	42.0	3%	$100	$150	$250	$600	$1,250	$2,750	$4,200	$10,000	$35,000
Auctions: $8,225, MS-63, January 2014; $1,028, AU-50, January 2015; $940, AU-50, March 2015; $470, VF-35, May 2015													
1820, Curl Base 2, Small Dt		37	50.7	19%	$100	$200	$275	$500	$1,000	$2,000	$3,800	$8,000	$25,000
Auctions: $823, AU-50, January 2015; $705, AU-53, January 2015; $376, VF-35, March 2015; $165, F-12, August 2015													
1820, Sq Base, Knob 2, Lg Dt		64	47.5	9%	$100	$175	$250	$600	$1,000	$1,600	$3,250	$6,000	$20,000
Auctions: $18,800, MS-64, January 2014; $517, MS-60, August 2015; $1,880, AU-55, October 2014; $411, EF-40, March 2015													
1820, Sq Base, No Knob 2, Large Date		65	45.8	11%	$100	$175	$250	$500	$950	$1,600	$3,250	$6,500	$20,000
Auctions: $61,688, MS-65, June 2014; $1,293, AU-53, March 2015; $259, AU-50, August 2015; $1,058, EF-45, July 2014													
1820, Broken Serifs on E's		12	38.3	17%	$1,000	$2,250	$4,000	$7,500	$12,500	$15,000	$25,000		
Auctions: $4,888, VF-35, December 2011													
1820, Proof	3–5	1	63.0								$45,000	$55,000	$65,000
Auctions: No auction records available.													

1822, So-Called 2 Over 1

| 1823, Normal Date | 1823, Broken 3 | 1823, Patched 3 | 1823, Ugly 3 |

1824, Normal Date   1824, 4 Over 1   1824, 4 Over Various Dates *Probably 4 Over 2 Over 0.*   1824, 4 Over 4 *4 Over 4 varieties are easily mistaken for the scarcer 4 Over 1. Note the distance between the 2's and 4's in each.*

	Mintage	Cert	Avg	%MS	G-4	F-12	VF-20	EF-40	AU-50	AU-55	MS-60	MS-63	MS-65
											PF-63	PF-64	PF-65
1821	1,305,797	778	44.9	15%	$70	$100	$145	$275	$650	$850	$2,000	$4,000	$15,000
	Auctions: $447, AU-50, May 2015; $282, EF-45, March 2015; $306, EF-40, August 2015; $84, VG-10, February 2015												
1821, Proof	3–5	2	64.5								$50,000	$65,000	$80,000
	Auctions: No auction records available.												
1822, All kinds	1,559,573												
1822		978	46.5	22%	$70	$100	$155	$300	$500	$800	$1,800	$3,500	$14,000
	Auctions: $823, AU-55, February 2015; $282, EF-40, April 2015; $153, VF-35, May 2015; $94, F-15, February 2015												
1822, So-Called 2 Over 1		115	47.6	18%	$100	$140	$225	$600	$1,100	$1,650	$2,500	$5,500	$20,000
	Auctions: $1,410, MS-60, November 2013; $1,645, EF-45, September 2014; $306, VF-30, October 2014												
1822, Proof	3–5	1	64.0								$45,000	$55,000	$95,000
	Auctions: $55,813, PF-64, June 2014												
1823, All kinds	1,694,200												
1823, Broken 3		50	39.0	12%	$120	$225	$400	$850	$2,250	$3,000	$5,500	$11,000	$40,000
	Auctions: $23,500, MS-64, November 2013; $720, VF-35, February 2018												
1823, Patched 3		53	47.8	28%	$100	$150	$275	$700	$1,600	$2,250	$4,250	$6,500	$22,500
	Auctions: $4,113, MS-63, March 2015; $1,410, AU-50, January 2015; $353, EF-45, February 2015; $165, VF-25, May 2015												
1823, Ugly 3		27	43.3	11%	$100	$150	$250	$650	$2,250	$3,500	$5,500	$12,500	$40,000
	Auctions: $4,113, AU-55, January 2014; $900, EF-45, February 2018												
1823, Normal		1,036	45.8	19%	$70	$100	$130	$250	$500	$800	$1,500	$3,400	$12,500
	Auctions: $94,000, MS-67, November 2013; $3,290, MS-64, August 2014; $2,115, MS-62, August 2014; $1,410, MS-62, August 2014												
1823, Proof	3–5	1	63.0								$50,000	$60,000	$75,000
	Auctions: $80,500, PF-63, April 2011												
1824, All kinds	3,504,954												
1824, 4 Over Various Dates		85	41.8	8%	$70	$145	$175	$350	$1,250	$1,750	$3,250	$5,500	$15,000
	Auctions: $11,163, MS-64, June 2014; $1,116, AU-53, August 2015; $306, VF-25, February 2015; $129, F-15, September 2015												
1824, 4 Over 1		99	47.8	32%	$75	$115	$200	$375	$800	$1,200	$2,500	$6,500	$20,000
	Auctions: $799, AU-53, September 2014; $529, AU-53, September 2014; $517, AU-50, January 2015; $353, EF-40, October 2015												
1824, 4 Over 4 (c)		174	46.2	17%	$75	$110	$200	$400	$1,000	$1,200	$2,000	$3,500	$12,000
	Auctions: $558, AU-50, August 2014; $550, AU-50, July 2014; $458, AU-50, January 2015; $235, VF-30, October 2015												
1824, Normal		1,302	45.5	19%	$75	$100	$115	$175	$500	$850	$1,150	$2,500	$14,000
	Auctions: $10,575, MS-65, January 2015; $2,820, MS-63, March 2015; $223, EF-45, March 2015; $94, F-15, August 2015												

c. 2 varieties.

1827, 7 Over 6

1827, Square Base 2

1827, Curl Base 2

1828, Curl Base, No Knob 2

1828, Curl Base, Knob 2

1828, Square Base 2, Large 8's

1828, Square Base 2, Small 8's

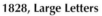

1828, Large Letters

1828, Small Letters

	Mintage	Cert	Avg	%MS	G-4	F-12	VF-20	EF-40	AU-50	AU-55	MS-60 / PF-63	MS-63 / PF-64	MS-65 / PF-65
1825	2,943,166	1,461	48.9	23%	$75	$100	$115	$175	$425	$500	$1,150	$2,500	$9,500
Auctions: $541, AU-58, January 2015; $176, EF-45, March 2015; $188, EF-40, March 2015; $112, VF-30, July 2015													
1825, Proof	3–5	1	66.0								$50,000	$60,000	$75,000
Auctions: $32,200, PF-62, May 2008													
1826	4,004,180	2,201	49.6	24%	$75	$100	$115	$175	$350	$525	$1,150	$2,000	$9,500
Auctions: $1,058, MS-61, January 2015; $881, AU-55, September 2015; $182, EF-40, March 2015; $89, VF-30, January 2015													
1826, Proof	3–5	2	65.0								$50,000	$60,000	$75,000
Auctions: $76,375, PF-65, September 2013													
1827, All kinds	5,493,400												
1827, 7 Over 6		200	49.3	21%	$100	$150	$200	$450	$800	$1,350	$2,350	$4,250	$15,000
Auctions: $18,800, MS-65, November 2013; $764, AU-55, October 2014; $810, AU-55, February 2018													
1827, Square Base 2		744	48.6	16%	$75	$100	$115	$175	$400	$525	$1,350	$2,500	$10,000
Auctions: $764, MS-60, June 2015; $494, AU-55, January 2015; $329, AU-50, May 2015; $165, EF-40, July 2015													
1827, Curl Base 2		67	48.7	9%	$75	$100	$130	$300	$550	$850	$1,800	$3,500	$17,500
Auctions: $8,813, MS-64, January 2014; $192, VF-30, March 2018													
1827, Proof	5–8	1	65.0								$50,000	$60,000	$75,000
Auctions: $21,150, PF-62, September 2013													
1828, All kinds	3,075,200												
1828, Curl Base, No Knob 2		87	49.0	14%	$70	$100	$130	$200	$450	$650	$1,350	$2,250	$10,000
Auctions: $5,875, MS-65, March 2015; $940, AU-58, June 2015; $764, AU-55, October 2015; $247, EF-45, April 2015													
1828, Curl Base, Knob 2		41	52.5	24%	$70	$115	$150	$250	$700	$950	$2,000	$4,500	$12,000
Auctions: $19,975, MS-65, April 2013; $382, AU-58, July 2014; $259, EF-45, May 2015													
1828, Square Base 2, Large 8's		54	48.7	9%	$70	$95	$115	$175	$400	$650	$1,500	$3,000	$11,000
Auctions: $32,900, MS-66, November 2013; $306, AU-50, October 2014; $112, EF-45, October 2014; $204, EF-45, March 2018													
1828, Square Base 2, Small 8's, Large Letters		338	48.6	17%	$65	$90	$115	$165	$350	$550	$1,150	$2,000	$9,000
Auctions: $329, AU-50, October 2015; $223, EF-45, January 2015; $192, VF-35, May 2015; $188, VF-30, October 2015													
1828, Square Base 2, Small 8's and Letters		28	48.5	4%	$75	$105	$150	$250	$600	$1,100	$2,500	$5,000	$17,000
Auctions: $30,550, MS-65, April 2014; $411, AU-50, July 2014; $1,020, AU-53, March 2018													

1829, 9 Over 7	1830, Small 0	1830, Large 0

1830, Large Letters

Experimental Edge of 1830
Raised segment lines angled to the right.

Experimental Edge of 1830–1831
Raised segment lines angled to the left.

Edge Adopted for Coinage, 1830–1836
Straight vertical lines.

1832, Large Letters Reverse
O-101a. Note the prominent die crack.

	Mintage	Cert	Avg	%MS	G-4	F-12	VF-20	EF-40	AU-50	AU-55	MS-60 / PF-63	MS-63 / PF-64	MS-65 / PF-65
1829, All kinds	3,712,156												
1829, 9 Over 7		254	49.8	21%	$70	$120	$165	$350	$750	$1,000	$1,500	$3,500	$22,500
Auctions: $2,115, MS-61, January 2015; $558, AU-53, September 2014; $353, EF-45, July 2014; $141, VF-25, October 2015													
1829		1,995	47.5	19%	$60	$80	$110	$180	$400	$500	$1,150	$2,000	$10,000
Auctions: $16,450, MS-66, March 2015; $1,058, AU-55, January 2015; $306, AU-50, June 2015; $153, EF-45, March 2015													
1829, Large Letters		31	54.1	26%	$65	$90	$120	$200	$400	$550	$1,200	$2,500	$10,500
Auctions: $194, AU-50, September 2013; $408, AU-55, May 2018													
1829, Proof	6–9	4	64.5								$50,000	$60,000	$75,000
Auctions: $102,813, PF-64, January 2014													
1830, All kinds	4,764,800												
1830, Small 0		594	46.7	12%	$65	$90	$120	$180	$375	$550	$1,100	$2,100	$10,000
Auctions: $1,410, MS-61, January 2015; $589, AU-58, August 2015; $217, EF-45, July 2015; $100, VF-25, September 2015													
1830, Large 0		155	49.7	15%	$65	$90	$120	$180	$375	$550	$1,000	$2,100	$10,000
Auctions: $41,125, MS-66, November 2013; $588, AU-58, July 2014; $482, AU-55, July 2014; $353, AU-53, July 2014; $2,280, AU-58, April 2018													
1830, Large Letters		12	33.3	8%	$1,200	$2,500	$3,250	$4,500	$6,000	$8,000	$12,000	$22,000	
Auctions: $2,990, VF-35, October 2011													
1830, Proof	3–5	2	64.5								$50,000	$60,000	$75,000
Auctions: $41,400, PF-64, January 2005													
1831	5,873,660	2,205	50.2	23%	$65	$90	$110	$180	$375	$500	$1,100	$2,000	$9,000
Auctions: $922, MS-61, January 2015; $541, AU-58, August 2015; $306, AU-53, October 2015; $153, EF-40, February 2015													
1831, Proof	3–5	2	64.5								$50,000	$60,000	$75,000
Auctions: $79,313, PF-65, April 2013													
1832, All kinds	4,797,000												
1832		2,873	49.5	18%	$65	$90	$110	$180	$375	$500	$1,100	$2,000	$9,000
Auctions: $999, MS-62, January 2015; $764, AU-58, January 2015; $212, EF-45, March 2015; $112, VF-35, October 2015													
1832, Large Letters		87	49.6	11%	$65	$90	$110	$180	$400	$550	$1,250	$2,250	$12,000
Auctions: $4,400, MS-64, November 2013; $364, AU-55, July 2014; $382, AU-50, August 2014; $420, AU-55, January 2018													
1832, Proof	6–9	3	64.7								$50,000	$60,000	$75,000
Auctions: $29,900, PF-63, January 2008													

| 1834, Large Date | 1834, Small Date | 1834, Large Letters | 1834, Small Letters |

1836, Over 1336

	Mintage	Cert	Avg	%MS	G-4	F-12	VF-20	EF-40	AU-50	AU-55	MS-60 PF-63	MS-63 PF-64	MS-65 PF-65
1833	5,206,000	1,980	49.6	20%	$65	$90	$110	$180	$375	$500	$1,100	$2,000	$10,000
	Auctions: $353, AU-55, February 2015; $317, AU-53, August 2015; $270, AU-50, May 2015; $188, EF-45, April 2015												
1833, Proof	1–2	2	63.0										
	Auctions: No auction records available.												
1833, Crushed Lettered Edge, Proof	3–5	2	64.5								$55,000	$75,000	$115,000
	Auctions: No auction records available.												
1834, All kinds	6,412,004												
1834, Large Date and Letters		155	49.6	17%	$60	$80	$110	$180	$375	$500	$1,100	$2,000	$9,000
	Auctions: $564, AU-58, January 2015; $135, EF-45, May 2015; $159, EF-40, July 2015; $153, VF-35, February 2015												
1834, Large Date, Small Letters		230	50.3	18%	$60	$80	$110	$180	$375	$500	$1,100	$2,000	$9,000
	Auctions: $823, AU-58, January 2015; $447, AU-55, August 2015; $376, AU-53, June 2015; $200, EF-45, April 2015												
1834, Small Date, Stars, Letters		456	48.7	13%	$60	$80	$110	$180	$375	$500	$1,100	$2,000	$9,000
	Auctions: $764, AU-58, February 2015; $350, AU-55, May 2015; $120, EF-40, January 2015; $94, VF-35, September 2015												
1834, Proof	8–12	6	64.2	100%							$40,000	$60,000	$75,000
	Auctions: $23,710, PF-63, November 2013												
1834, Crushed Lettered Edge, Proof	3–5	1	55.0								$40,000	$65,000	$100,000
	Auctions: No auction records available.												
1835	5,352,006	1,245	47.6	18%	$60	$80	$110	$180	$375	$500	$1,100	$2,000	$9,000
	Auctions: $881, AU-58, August 2015; $350, AU-55, February 2015; $212, EF-45, August 2015; $141, VF-35, October 2015												
1835, Proof	5–8	2	63.0								$40,000	$65,000	$100,000
	Auctions: $43,125, PF-64, August 2007												
1835, Crushed Lettered Edge, Proof	3–5	2	65.0								$40,000	$65,000	$100,000
	Auctions: No auction records available.												
1836, All kinds	6,545,000												
1836		2,206	47.4	18%	$60	$80	$110	$180	$375	$500	$1,100	$2,000	$9,000
	Auctions: $823, AU-58, August 2015; $282, AU-50, January 2015; $100, VF-30, August 2015; $94, VF-25, October 2015												
1836, 1836 Over 1336		72	48.6	14%	$80	$100	$130	$225	$475	$700	$1,200	$2,500	$10,000
	Auctions: $2,703, MS-64, August 2014; $499, AU-53, July 2014; $270, AU-50, March 2015; $194, VF-35, December 2014												
1836, 50 Over 00		49	50.4	20%	$125	$200	$350	$500	$925	$1,500	$2,750	$5,000	$30,000
	Auctions: $1,645, AU-55, February 2013; $384, EF-45, February 2018												
1836, Beaded Border on Reverse (d)		49	43.1	14%	$85	$120	$140	$250	$525	$675	$1,300	$3,000	$14,000
	Auctions: $494, AU-53, May 2015; $212, EF-45, February 2015; $153, VF-35, September 2015 $112, EF-40, November 2014												
1836, Lettered Edge, Proof	8–12	5	64.4								$40,000	$65,000	$85,000
	Auctions: $96,938, PF-66, November 2013												
1836, 50 Over 00, Proof	3–5	3	65.3								$50,000	$80,000	$115,000
	Auctions: $81,937, PF-65, October 2006												

d. The same beaded-border reverse die was used for Proofs of 1833, 1834, and 1835 with the crushed edge lettering; all are very rare.

CAPPED BUST, REEDED EDGE (1836–1839)

Designer: *Christian Gobrecht.* **Weight:** *13.36 grams.* **Composition:** *.900 silver, .100 copper.* **Diameter:** *30 mm.* **Edge:** *Reeded.* **Mint:** *Philadelphia and New Orleans.*

Reverse 50 CENTS (1836–1837)

Reverse 50 CENTS, Proof

Reverse HALF DOL. (1838–1839)

Mintmark location is on the obverse, above the date.

Reverse HALF DOL., Proof

History. This half dollar type features a slight restyling of John Reich's Capped Bust design, modified by Christian Gobrecht. It is of smaller diameter than the preceding type, and made with a reeded edge. The reverse is of two variations: the 1836–1837, with 50 CENTS; and the 1838–1839, with HALF DOL.

Striking and Sharpness. The key points for observation are the stars on the obverse. On the reverse, check the border letters and the details of the eagle. The 1839-O nearly always shows die cracks, often extensive (these have no effect on desirability or market value).

Availability. The 1836 is rare. The 1838-O is a famous rarity, and the 1839-O is scarce. The others are easily available in nearly any grade desired, with 1837 being the most common. Proofs are occasionally encountered of the year 1836 and are quite rare. Authentic Proofs of 1837 exist but for all practical purposes are unobtainable. Most 1838-O (a rarity) and a few 1839-O coins have been called branch-mint Proofs.

GRADING STANDARDS

MS-60 to 70 (Mint State). *Obverse and Reverse:* Grading guidelines are the same as for the 1807–1836 type, except on this type the rims are more uniform. On the 1836–1837 dates the reverse rim is generally lower than the obverse, causing the reverse to wear slightly more quickly. On the 1838–1839 type (with slightly different lettering) the wear occurs evenly on both sides, and light striking showing areas of the original planchet on the obverse does not occur here.

1837. Graded MS-62.

Illustrated coin: This example displays light gray toning with a sprinkling of gold over fully lustrous surfaces.

AU-50, 53, 55, 58 (About Uncirculated). *Obverse and Reverse:* Grading guidelines are the same as for the 1807–1836 type, except on this type the rims are more uniform. On the 1836–1837 dates the reverse rim is generally lower than the obverse, causing the reverse to wear slightly more quickly. On the 1838–1839 type (with slightly different lettering) the wear occurs evenly on both sides.

1836. Graded AU-53.

EF-40, 45 (Extremely Fine). *Obverse and Reverse:* Grading guidelines are the same as for the 1807–1836 type, except on this type the rims are more uniform. On the 1836–1837 dates the reverse rim is generally lower than the obverse, causing the reverse to wear slightly more quickly. On the 1838–1839 type (with slightly different lettering) the wear occurs evenly on both sides.

1836. Graded EF-40.

VF-20, 30 (Very Fine). *Obverse and Reverse:* Grading guidelines are the same as for the 1807–1836 type, except on this type the rims are more uniform. On the 1836–1837 dates the reverse rim is generally lower than the obverse, causing the reverse to wear slightly more quickly. On the 1838–1839 type (with slightly different lettering) the wear occurs evenly on both sides.

1836. Graded VF-20.

F-12, 15 (Fine). *Obverse and Reverse:* Grading guidelines are the same as for the 1807–1836 type, except on this type the rims are more uniform. On the 1836–1837 dates the reverse rim is generally lower than the obverse, causing the reverse to wear slightly more quickly. On the 1838–1839 type (with slightly different lettering) the wear occurs evenly on both sides.

1839-O. Graded F-15.

VG-8, 10 (Very Good). *Obverse and Reverse:* Grading guidelines are the same as for the 1807–1836 type, except on this type the rims are more uniform. On the 1836–1837 dates the reverse rim is generally lower than the obverse, causing the reverse to wear slightly more quickly. On the 1838–1839 type (with slightly different lettering) the wear occurs evenly on both sides.

1836. Graded VG-10.

G-4, 6 (Good). *Obverse and Reverse:* Grading guidelines are the same as for the 1807–1836 type, except on this type the rims are more uniform. On the 1836–1837 dates the reverse rim is generally lower than the obverse, causing the reverse to wear slightly more quickly. On the 1838–1839 type (with slightly different lettering) the wear occurs evenly on both sides.

1838. Graded G-4.

AG-3 (About Good). *Obverse and Reverse:* Grading guidelines are the same as for the 1807–1836 type, except on this type the rims are more uniform. On the 1836–1837 dates the reverse rim is generally lower than the obverse, causing the reverse to wear slightly more quickly. On the 1838–1839 type (with slightly different lettering) the wear occurs evenly on both sides.

1836. Graded AG-3.

PF-60 to 70 (Proof). *Obverse and Reverse:* Proofs in grades of PF–60 to 62 show extensive hairlines and cloudiness. At PF–63, hairlines are obvious, but the mirrored fields are attractive. PF–64 and 65 coins have fewer hairlines, but they still are obvious when the coin is slowly turned while held at an angle to the light. PF–66 coins require a magnifier to discern hairlines, and higher grades should have no hairlines.

1836. Graded PF-64 Cameo.

1839, Regular Letters Reverse   **1839, Small Letters Reverse**

	Mintage	Cert	Avg	%MS	G-4	F-12	VF-20	EF-40	AU-50	AU-55	MS-60 / PF-60	MS-63 / PF-63	MS-65 / PF-65
1836	*1,200+*	213	48.4	0%	$900	$1,600	$2,000	$3,000	$4,500	$7,000	$9,500	$19,000	$75,000
Auctions: $38,188, MS-64, October 2014; $423, AU-58, September 2015; $4,113, AU-53, March 2015; $3,290, EF-45, March 2015													
1836, Reeded Edge, Proof	*10–15*	10	63.7								$30,000	$42,500	$80,000
Auctions: $32,900, PF-63, April 2013													
1837	3,629,820	1,685	52.5	32%	$65	$100	$120	$220	$450	$575	$1,150	$2,500	$17,500
Auctions: $11,456, MS-64, March 2015; $1,645, MS-62, January 2015; $425, AU-55, June 2015; $247, EF-45, August 2015													
1837, Inverted G	(a)	0	n/a		$75	$110	$130	$255	$500	$625	$1,250	$2,750	
Auctions: No auction records available.													
1837, Proof	*4–6*	1	63.0								$50,000	$100,000	
Auctions: $32,200, PF-62, July 2008													
1838	3,546,000	1,312	51.7	25%	$65	$100	$125	$220	$450	$675	$1,150	$2,750	$18,000
Auctions: $17,625, MS-66, May 2015; $1,645, MS-62, January 2015; $588, AU-55, January 2015; $235, EF-45, June 2015													
1838, Proof	*3–5*	0	n/a									$50,000	$115,000
Auctions: $129,250, PF-64, April 2014													
1838-O		0	n/a					$300,000	$350,000		$425,000	$525,000	
1838-O, Proof † (b)	20	4	59.0								$325,000	$450,000	
Auctions: $193,875, PF-65, March 2015; $646,250, PF-64, May 2015; $293,750, PF-50, August 2015													
1839	1,392,976	579	49.6	22%	$75	$110	$140	$300	$500	$750	$1,400	$3,100	$30,000
Auctions: $5,288, MS-64, March 2015; $470, AU-55, January 2015; $259, EF-45, June 2015; $235, EF-40, June 2015; $600, AU-58, February 2018													
1839, Small Letters Reverse		2	52.5	0%	$15,000	$40,000	$50,000	$75,000	$95,000				$175,000
Auctions: $50,025, AU-50, January 2010													
1839, Reeded Edge, Proof (c)	n/a	0	n/a								—		
Auctions: No auction records available.													
1839-O	116,000	303	46.3	18%	$400	$900	$1,175	$1,800	$2,500	$3,500	$6,500	$11,500	$55,000
Auctions: $52,875, MS-65, July 2015; $1,528, VF-25, June 2015; $2,585, EF-40, August 2016; $1,293, F-12, August 2016													
1839-O, Proof	*5–10*	5	63.2								$65,000	$95,000	$225,000
Auctions: $92,000, PF-63, March 2012													

† Ranked in the *100 Greatest U.S. Coins* (fourth edition). **a.** Included in 1837 mintage figure. **b.** The 1838-O, Proof, was the first branch-mint half dollar, though it was not mentioned in the Mint director's report. The New Orleans chief coiner stated that only 20 were struck. **c.** Unverified.

LIBERTY SEATED (1839–1891)

Variety 1, No Motto Above Eagle (1839–1853): **Designer:** *Christian Gobrecht.*
Weight: *13.36 grams.* **Composition:** *.900 silver, .100 copper.* **Diameter:** *30.6 mm.*
Edge: *Reeded.* **Mints:** *Philadelphia and New Orleans.*

Mintmark location is on the reverse, below the eagle, for all varieties.

Variety 1 (1839–1853) **Variety 1, Proof**

Variety 2, Arrows at Date, Rays Around Eagle (1853): **Designer:** *Christian Gobrecht.*
Weight: *12.44 grams.* **Composition:** *.900 silver, .100 copper.* **Diameter:** *30.6 mm.*
Edge: *Reeded.* **Mints:** *Philadelphia and New Orleans.*

Variety 2 (1853) **Variety 2, Proof**

Variety 3, Arrows at Date, No Rays (1854–1855): **Designer:** *Christian Gobrecht.*
Weight: *12.44 grams.* **Composition:** *.900 silver, .100 copper.* **Diameter:** *30.6 mm.*
Edge: *Reeded.* **Mints:** *Philadelphia, New Orleans, and San Francisco.*

Variety 3 (1854–1855) **Variety 3, Proof**

Variety 1 Resumed, With Weight Standard of Variety 2 (1856–1866):
Designer: *Christian Gobrecht.* **Weight:** *12.44 grams.* **Composition:** *.900 silver, .100 copper.*
Diameter: *30.6 mm.* **Edge:** *Reeded.* **Mints:** *Philadelphia, New Orleans, and San Francisco.*

**Variety 1 Resumed, Weight Standard
of Variety 2 (1856–1866)** **Variety 1 Resumed, Weight Standard
of Variety 2, Proof**

Variety 4, Motto Above Eagle (1866–1873): **Designer:** *Christian Gobrecht.*
Weight: *12.44 grams.* **Composition:** *.900 silver, .100 copper.* **Diameter:** *30.6 mm.*
Edge: *Reeded.* **Mints:** *Philadelphia, San Francisco, and Carson City.*

Variety 4 (1866–1873)	Variety 4, Proof

Variety 5, Arrows at Date (1873–1874): **Designer:** *Christian Gobrecht.*
Weight: *12.50 grams.* **Composition:** *.900 silver, .100 copper.* **Diameter:** *30.6 mm.*
Edge: *Reeded.* **Mints:** *Philadelphia, San Francisco, and Carson City.*

Variety 5 (1873–1874)	Variety 5, Proof

Variety 4 Resumed, With Weight Standard of Variety 5 (1875–1891): **Designer:** *Christian Gobrecht.*
Weight: *12.50 grams.* **Composition:** *.900 silver, .100 copper.* **Diameter:** *30.6 mm.*
Edge: *Reeded.* **Mints:** *Philadelphia, San Francisco, and Carson City.*

Variety 4 Resumed, Weight Standard of Variety 5 (1875–1891)	Variety 4 Resumed, Weight Standard of Variety 5, Proof

History. Half dollars of the Liberty Seated type were struck every year from 1839 to 1891. The designs varied slightly over the years, but with the basic obverse and reverse motifs remaining the same (e.g., from 1842 to 1853 the coins bore a modified reverse with large letters in the legend, and in 1846 the date size was enlarged). Large quantities were made until 1879, at which time there was a glut of silver coins in commerce. After that mintages were reduced.

The earliest Liberty Seated half dollars, dated 1839, lacked drapery at Miss Liberty's elbow. In that year Robert Ball Hughes modified Christian Gobrecht's design by adding drapery, a feature that continued for the rest of the series.

Striking and Sharpness. On the obverse, first check the head of Miss Liberty and the star centers. On coins of the Arrows at Date variety, especially 1855, the word LIBERTY tends to wear faster compared to earlier and later varieties. On the reverse, check the eagle at the lower left. Afterward, check all other features. Generally, the higher-mintage issues are the least well struck, and many New Orleans Mint coins can be lightly struck, particularly those of the 1850s. The luster on MS coins usually is very attractive. Resurfaced dies often are prooflike, some with the drapery polished away (as with 1877-S, in particular). Above and beyond issues of strike, the Small Letters coins of 1839 to 1842 have narrower, lower rims that afforded less protection to the central devices of the reverse. In contrast, the No Motto, Large Letters, coins have wider, higher rims that tend to better protect the central devices. Many pre–Civil War dates, particularly of the 1840s, show evidence of extensive die polishing in the fields (especially evident in the open expanses of the obverse). From grades of EF downward, sharpness of strike of the stars and the head does not matter to connoisseurs. Quality is often lacking, with lint marks seen on some issues of the late 1850s and early 1860s. Light striking is occasionally seen on the star centers and the head of Miss Liberty; connoisseurs avoid coins with this detraction, but most buyers will not be aware. Slide marks (usually seen on the right knee) from coin albums can be a problem, more so on Liberty Seated halves than on lower denominations of this design.

Availability. Collecting these coins is a popular pursuit with many enthusiasts. Examples of the higher-mintage dates are readily available, with earlier years being much scarcer than later ones. Most often seen among MS coins are issues from the mid-1870s onward. Circulated coins from well worn through AU can be found of most dates and mintmarks; these are avidly sought. Proofs were made in most years, with production beginning in a particularly significant way in 1858, when an estimated 210 silver sets were sold. Today, Proofs from 1858 through 1891 are readily available.

GRADING STANDARDS

MS-60 to 70 (Mint State). *Obverse:* At MS-60, some abrasion and contact marks are evident, most noticeably on the bosom and thighs and knees. Luster is present, but may be dull or lifeless. At MS-63, contact marks are very few, and abrasion is hard to detect except under magnification. An MS-65 coin has no abrasion, and contact marks are sufficiently minute as to require magnification. Check the knees of Liberty and the right field. Luster

1856-O. Graded MS-63.

should be full and rich. Most Mint State coins of the 1861 to 1865 years, Philadelphia issues, have extensive die striae (from dies not being completely finished); note that these are *raised* (whereas cleaning hairlines are incuse). *Reverse:* Comments as preceding, except that in lower Mint State grades abrasion and contact marks are most noticeable on the eagle's head, neck, and claws, and the top of the wings (harder to see there, however). At MS-65 or higher there are no marks visible to the unaided eye. The field is mainly protected by design elements and does not show abrasion as much as does the obverse on a given coin.

AU-50, 53, 55, 58 (About Uncirculated). *Obverse:* Light wear is seen on the thighs and knees, bosom, and head. At AU-58, the luster is extensive, but incomplete, especially in the right field. At AU–50 and 53, luster is less. *Reverse:* Wear is evident on the eagle's neck, the claws, and the top of the wings. An AU-58 coin has nearly full luster, more so than on the obverse, as the design elements protect the small field areas. At AU–50 and 53, there still are traces of luster.

1841-O. Graded AU-55.

Illustrated coin: Gray toning is evident on this coin. The reverse is lightly struck, a characteristic that should not be mistaken for wear.

EF-40, 45 (Extremely Fine). *Obverse:* Further wear is seen on all areas, especially the thighs and knees, bosom, and head. Little or no luster is seen on most coins. From this grade downward, sharpness of strike of stars and the head does not matter to connoisseurs. *Reverse:* Further wear is evident on the eagle's neck, claws, and wings.

1839, No Drapery From Elbow. Graded EF-40.

VF-20, 30 (Very Fine). *Obverse:* Further wear is seen. Most details of the gown are worn away, except in the lower-relief areas above and to the right of the shield. Hair detail is mostly or completely gone. *Reverse:* Wear is more extensive, with some of the feathers blended together.

1839, No Drapery From Elbow. Graded VF-20.

F-12, 15 (Fine). *Obverse:* The seated figure is well worn, but with some detail above and to the right of the shield. LIBERTY is readable but weak in areas, perhaps with a letter missing (a slightly looser interpretation than the demand for full LIBERTY a generation ago). *Reverse:* Wear is extensive, with about a third to half of the feathers flat or blended with others.

1842-O, Small Date. Graded F-12.

VG-8, 10 (Very Good). *Obverse:* The seated figure is more worn, but some detail can be seen above and to the right of the shield. The shield is discernible, but the upper-right section may be flat and blended into the seated figure. In LIBERTY at least the equivalent of two or three letters (can be a combination of partial letters) must be readable, possibly very weak at VG-8, with a few more visible at VG-10. In the marketplace and among certified coins, parts of

1873-CC, Arrows at Date. Graded VG-8.

two letters seem to be allowed. Per PCGS, "localized weakness may obscure some letters." LIBERTY is *not* an infallible guide: some varieties have the word in low relief on the die, so it wore away slowly. *Reverse:* Further wear has flattened all but a few feathers, and many if not most horizontal lines of the shield are indistinct. The leaves are only in outline form. The rim is visible all around, as are the ends of most denticles.

G-4, 6 (Good). *Obverse:* The seated figure is worn nearly smooth. At G-4 there are no letters in LIBERTY remaining on most (but not all) coins; some coins, especially of the early 1870s, are exceptions. At G-6, traces of one or two can barely be seen and more details can be seen in the figure. *Reverse:* The eagle shows only a few details of the shield and feathers. The rim is worn down, and the tops of the border letters are weak or worn away, although the inscription can still be read.

1873, No Arrows, Open 3. Graded G-6.

AG-3 (About Good). *Obverse:* The seated figure is visible in outline form. Much or all of the rim is worn away. The date remains clear. *Reverse:* The border letters are partially worn away. The eagle is mostly in outline form, but with a few details discernible. The rim is weak or missing.

1873, No Arrows, Open 3. Graded AG-3.

PF-60 to 70 (Proof). *Obverse and Reverse:* Proofs that are extensively cleaned and have many hairlines, or that are dull and grainy, are lower level, such as PF–60 to 62. These are not widely desired, save for the low mintage (in circulation-strike format) years from 1879 to 1891. With medium hairlines and good reflectivity, an assigned grade of PF-64 is appropriate, and with relatively few hairlines, Gem PF-65. In various grades hairlines are

1889. Graded PF-65.

most easily seen in the obverse field. PF-66 should have hairlines so delicate that magnification is needed to see them. Above that, a Proof should be free of such lines.

		No Drapery From Elbow (1839)		Drapery From Elbow (Starting 1839)	

 No Drapery From Elbow (1839) Drapery From Elbow (Starting 1839)

	Mintage	Cert	Avg	%MS	G-4	VG-8	F-12	VF-20	EF-40	AU-50	MS-60 / PF-60	MS-63 / PF-63	MS-65 / PF-65
1839, No Drapery From Elbow	(a)	185	45.9	15%	$125	$250	$500	$750	$1,650	$2,850	$7,500	$27,500	$150,000
Auctions: $2,180, EF-40, January 2015; $881, VF-30, June 2015; $705, VF-25, August 2015; $595, VF-20, February 2015													
1839, No Drapery, Proof	4–6	6	63.2								$100,000	$135,000	$250,000
Auctions: $223,250, PF-64, November 2013													
1839, Drapery From Elbow	1,972,400	188	50.0	30%	$50	$75	$100	$200	$275	$450	$1,300	$2,300	$16,000
Auctions: $4,230, MS-64, January 2015; $541, AU-55, January 2015; $564, AU-53, January 2015; $541, AU-50, May 2015													
1839, Drapery, Proof	1–2	1	64.0									$95,000	$200,000
Auctions: $184,000, PF-64, April 2008													
1840, Small Letters	1,435,008	281	49.8	23%	$50	$75	$100	$150	$350	$400	$800	$1,400	$7,500
Auctions: $5,640, MS-65, October 2015; $329, AU-50, February 2015													

a. Included in circulation-strike 1839, Drapery From Elbow, mintage figure.

Small Letters in Legend (1839–1841)	1840 (Only), Medium Letters, Large Eagle	Large Letters in Legend (1842–1853)

1842, Small Date	1842, Medium Date

	Mintage	Cert	Avg	%MS	G-4	VG-8	F-12	VF-20	EF-40	AU-50	MS-60 / PF-60	MS-63 / PF-63	MS-65 / PF-65
1840, Medium Letters (b)	(c)	54	40.8	15%	$225	$375	$600	$900	$1,500	$2,250	$5,000	$10,000	$45,000
Auctions: $2,233, MS-62, February 2015; $1,028, AU-58, January 2015; $259, EF-45, May 2015; $188, VF-30, September 2015													
1840, Small Letters, Proof	4–8	7	64.0										$65,000
Auctions: $49,350, PF-65, May 2015; $30,550, PF-63, November 2013													
1840-O	855,100	132	45.3	17%	$60	$75	$100	$200	$325	$450	$1,650	$4,500	
Auctions: $2,350, MS-62, January 2015; $1,410, MS-60, June 2015; $212, EF-45, June 2015; $141, VF-30, June 2015													
1841	310,000	90	54.0	29%	$65	$110	$150	$250	$400	$600	$1,400	$2,800	$9,000
Auctions: $11,750, MS-65, May 2015; $4,230, MS-64, January 2015; $857, AU-58, June 2015; $364, EF-45, August 2015													
1841, Proof	4–8	7	63.6								$15,000	$20,000	$37,500
Auctions: $30,550, PF-64, September 2013													
1841-O	401,000	134	48.3	21%	$50	$75	$115	$200	$350	$600	$1,450	$3,500	$12,000
Auctions: $27,025, MS-66, May 2015; $447, AU-53, July 2015; $259, EF-45, May 2015; $153, VF-30, July 2015													
1842, Sm Date, Sm Letters	(d)	1	64.0	100%	$17,000			$30,000		$40,000			
Auctions: $99,875, MS-64, June 2014													
1842, Medium Date	2,012,764	180	49.1	16%	$50	$75	$100	$150	$225	$350	$975	$2,000	$7,000
Auctions: $2,585, MS-64, October 2015; $353, MS-60, August 2015; $360, AU-58, May 2015; $129, EF-40, September 2015													
1842, Sm Date, Lg Letters	(d)	62	51.5	24%	$65	$110	$135	$200	$300	$450	$1,300	$3,750	$15,000
Auctions: $21,150, MS-65, April 2014; $2,585, MS-63, January 2015; $306, EF-45, May 2015; $176, VF-25, August 2015													
1842, Sm Date, Lg Ltrs, Proof	4–8	4	64.3								$15,000	$25,000	$45,000
Auctions: $44,063, PF-66, June 2014													
1842-O, Sm Date, Sm Letters	203,000	37	33.6	3%	$750	$1,000	$1,500	$2,250	$3,500	$6,500	$16,500	$35,000	
Auctions: $35,250, MS-62, January 2014; ; $3,760, EF-40, January 2015; $764, VG-10, November 2014; $823, VG-8, September 2014													
1842-O, Med Date, Lg Letters	754,000	76	46.4	18%	$65	$75	$100	$200	$300	$700	$1,600	$4,500	$20,000
Auctions: $19,975, MS-65, January 2015; $517, AU-50, July 2015; $282, EF-45, July 2015; $212, VF-35, January 2015													
1843	3,844,000	269	49.4	25%	$50	$75	$100	$150	$200	$300	$900	$2,000	$8,500
Auctions: $4,935, MS-65, January 2015; $201, AU-50, January 2015; $212, EF-45, August 2015; $89, VF-25, March 2015													
1843, Proof	4–8	2	64.0								$15,000	$27,500	$60,000
Auctions: $70,500, PF-65Cam, August 2013; $44,063, PF-64, October 2014													
1843-O	2,268,000	136	50.1	32%	$50	$75	$100	$175	$300	$400	$1,400	$3,250	$25,000
Auctions: $3,290, MS-63, January 2015; $764, AU-58, August 2015; $646, AU-55, June 2015; $223, EF-40, January 2015													

b. The 1840, Medium Letters, half dollars were struck at the New Orleans Mint from a reverse die of the previous style, without mintmark. **c.** Included in circulation-strike 1840, Small Letters, mintage figure. **d.** Included in 1842, Medium Date, mintage figure.

1846, Medium Date

1844-O, Doubled Date
FS-50-1844o-301.

1846, Tall Date

1846-O, Medium Date

1846-O, Tall Date

1847, 7 Over 6
FS-50-1847-301.

	Mintage	Cert	Avg	%MS	G-4	VG-8	F-12	VF-20	EF-40	AU-50	MS-60 PF-60	MS-63 PF-63	MS-65 PF-65
1844	1,766,000	169	51.4	28%	$50	$75	$100	$150	$200	$300	$700	$1,700	$8,750
Auctions: $12,338, MS-65, May 2015; $223, AU-50, August 2015; $129, EF-45, May 2015; $247, EF-40, February 2015													
1844, Proof	3–6	1	62.0										$80,000
Auctions: $149,500, PF-66Cam, January 2008; $31,725, PF-64, May 2015													
1844-O	2,005,000	160	42.7	22%	$50	$75	$100	$175	$275	$400	$1,350	$3,000	$13,500
Auctions: $10,575, MS-64, May 2015; $764, AU-58, January 2015; $295, AU-50, October 2015; $376, EF-45, October 2015													
1844-O, Doubled Date (e)	(f)	21	37.2	0%	$650	$1,000	$1,500	$1,850	$3,250	$5,500	$8,500		
Auctions: $6,463, AU-55, February 2013; $115, VG-8, July 2014; $235, Fair-2, October 2014													
1845	589,000	62	49.4	21%	$75	$100	$150	$250	$325	$600	$1,000	$3,500	
Auctions: $3,055, MS-64, January 2015; $447, AU-55, June 2015; $536, AU-53, January 2015; $235, VF-30, January 2015													
1845, Proof	3–6	3	65.0								$15,000	$30,000	$65,000
Auctions: $57,500, PF-64, May 2008													
1845-O	2,094,000	191	42.6	18%	$50	$75	$100	$200	$250	$500	$1,000	$3,000	$9,000
Auctions: $329, AU-50, November 2015; $259, AU-50, November 2015; $353, EF-45, May 2015; $223, EF-40, August 2015													
1845-O, No Drapery (g)	(h)	21	48.7	19%	$100	$125	$150	$325	$480	$800	$1,400	$4,500	
Auctions: $6,463, MS-64, June 2014													
1846, All kinds	2,210,000												
1846, Medium Date		133	49.0	22%	$50	$75	$100	$175	$250	$350	$1,000	$2,600	$12,000
Auctions: $1,293, MS-63, January 2015; $705, AU-58, June 2015; $223, AU-50, May 2015; $165, EF-40, August 2015													
1846, Tall Date		126	50.6	25%	$75	$110	$175	$250	$325	$400	$1,300	$2,750	$25,000
Auctions: $881, AU-58, September 2015; $588, AU-53, October 2015; $423, AU-53, May 2015; $317, EF-45, April 2015													
1846, 6 Over Horizontal 6 (i)		40	46.6	15%	$225	$300	$500	$1,000	$1,650	$2,500	$4,750	$10,000	$20,000
Auctions: $7,050, MS-62, June 2014; $1,440, VF-30, February 2018													
1846, Med Letters, Proof	15–20	11	63.5								$11,000	$21,000	$50,000
Auctions: $28,200, PF-64, October 2014; $23,500, PF-63, January 2014; $14,100, PF-63, March 2015													
1846-O, Medium Date	2,304,000	133	39.9	13%	$50	$90	$175	$300	$400	$500	$1,500	$3,600	$20,000
Auctions: $2,820, MS-62, January 2015; $588, AU-55, January 2015; $376, AU-53, July 2015; $153, VF-35, March 2015													
1846-O, Tall Date	(j)	29	37.2	10%	$250	$450	$600	$900	$1,850	$2,500	$7,500	$15,000	
Auctions: $1,528, EF-45, January 2015; $881, VF-30, June 2015; $306, F-15, June 2015; $360, VG-10, January 2015													
1847, 7 Over 6 (k)	(l)	5	45.4	20%	$2,000	$2,850	$3,500	$5,000	$9,000	$12,000	$25,000		
Auctions: $17,038, AU-55, May 2015; $5,875, AU-50, August 2014; $8,225, VF-35, August 2014; $5,640, VF-35, January 2015													
1847	1,156,000	127	51.4	22%	$50	$75	$100	$150	$250	$350	$850	$1,650	$7,000
Auctions: $8,813, MS-65, May 2015; $1,410, MS-63, February 2015; $235, AU-53, May 2015; $165, EF-40, October 2015													
1847, Proof	15–20	9	63.6								$10,000	$20,000	$45,000
Auctions: $12,338, PF-63, August 2013													
1847-O	2,584,000	108	48.2	24%	$50	$75	$100	$150	$250	$450	$1,000	$2,750	$15,000
Auctions: $30,550, MS-66, May 2015; $1,880, MS-62, January 2015; $378, AU-53, February 2015; $176, EF-40, October 2015													

e. This rare variety shows all four numerals protruding from the rock above the primary date. f. Included in 1844-O mintage figure. g. The drapery is missing because of excessive polishing of the die. h. Included in 1845-O mintage figure. i. This variety can be detected in low grades. j. Included in 1846-O, Medium Date, mintage figure. k. Remains of an underlying 6 are visible below and between the primary 4 and 7. "The overdate might not be evident on later die states" (*Cherrypickers' Guide to Rare Die Varieties*, sixth edition, volume II). l. Included in circulation-strike 1847 mintage figure.

	Mintage	Cert	Avg	%MS	G-4	VG-8	F-12	VF-20	EF-40	AU-50	MS-60	MS-63	MS-65
											PF-60	PF-63	PF-65
1848	580,000	74	53.5	42%	$75	$125	$175	$250	$425	$650	$1,200	$2,500	$14,000
	Auctions: $7,638, MS-64, January 2015; $617, AU-55, March 2015; $341, EF-45, August 2015; $235, VF-35, May 2015												
1848, Proof	*4–8*	2	66.0								$10,000	$20,000	$45,000
	Auctions: $34,075, PF-64, June 2014												
1848-O	3,180,000	124	47.4	21%	$50	$75	$100	$150	$250	$450	$1,200	$2,200	$27,500
	Auctions: $940, AU-58, January 2015; $999, AU-55, June 2015; $306, EF-45, July 2015; $141, VF-35, August 2015												
1849	1,252,000	115	55.1	33%	$75	$100	$150	$200	$300	$450	$1,000	$2,250	$13,500
	Auctions: $10,575, MS-65, January 2015; $517, AU-58, June 2015; $400, AU-53, August 2015; $294, EF-45, March 2015												
1849, Proof	*4–8*	4	65.0								$10,000	$20,000	$45,000
	Auctions: $70,500, PF-66, January 2014; $38,188, PF-66, October 2014; $18,800, PF-63, October 2015												
1849-O	2,310,000	103	47.6	24%	$50	$75	$100	$150	$300	$750	$1,600	$2,700	$17,000
	Auctions: $793, AU-55, January 2015; $564, AU-53, January 2015; $153, VF-35, January 2015; $129, VF-30, August 2015												
1850	227,000	100	53.2	33%	$275	$375	$600	$800	$1,200	$1,450	$2,000	$3,500	$22,500
	Auctions: $117,500, MS-67, May 2015; $15,275, MS-65, November 2013; $764, EF-40, August 2015; $447, Fair-2, October 2014												
1850, Proof	*4–8*	4	63.8								$13,000	$27,500	$60,000
	Auctions: $20,125, PF-64, July 2009												
1850-O	2,456,000	99	52.3	39%	$50	$75	$100	$200	$300	$400	$1,000	$1,500	$15,000
	Auctions: $28,200, MS-66, May 2015; $329, AU-50, May 2015; $259, EF-40, November 2015; $165, VF-35, August 2015												
1851	200,750	51	56.3	55%	$750	$1,000	$1,500	$1,750	$2,350	$2,850	$3,500	$5,000	$12,500
	Auctions: $49,938, MS-66, June 2014; $2,820, AU-58, January 2015; $1,645, EF-45, September 2014; $881, Fair-2, October 2014												
1851-O	402,000	62	51.5	40%	$65	$110	$175	$325	$450	$850	$1,650	$3,250	$10,000
	Auctions: $999, AU-55, January 2015; $940, AU-53, September 2015; $588, EF-45, November 2015; $376, VF-35, August 2015												
1852	77,130	77	55.3	49%	$500	$750	$1,000	$1,250	$2,000	$2,350	$2,850	$3,500	$13,500
	Auctions: $12,338, MS-66, October 2014; $3,525, MS-62, January 2015; $2,115, AU-58, January 2015; $1,410, AU-53, July 2014												
1852, Proof	*3–6*	3	62.7									$35,000	$55,000
	Auctions: $74,750, PF-65, July 2008												
1852-O	144,000	48	45.5	10%	$275	$450	$600	$800	$1,100	$1,800	$3,500	$10,000	$35,000
	Auctions: $1,116, EF-40, June 2015; $940, VF-20, February 2015; $823, F-15, July 2015; $764, F-15, September 2015												
1852-O, Proof	*2–3*	1	62.0									$37,500	
	Auctions: $24,150, PF-62, May 2001												
1853-O, Variety 1 † (m)		0	n/a		$165,000	$185,000	$300,000	$500,000					
	Auctions: $368,000, VF-35, October 2006; $199,750, VG-8, August 2015												
1853, Variety 2	3,532,708	1,294	48.3	21%	$50	$75	$95	$125	$225	$450	$1,500	$3,000	$22,000
	Auctions: $73,438, MS-66, January 2015; $28,200, MS-66, May 2015; $282, EF-45, October 2015; $165, VF-35, August 2015												
1853, Variety 2, Proof	*5–10*	3	64.7									$50,000	$165,000
	Auctions: $117,500, PF-65, October 2014; $184,000, PF-65, January 2012; $94,000, PF-64, October 2014												
1853-O, Variety 2	1,328,000	254	41.5	13%	$60	$75	$95	$180	$400	$750	$2,750	$5,500	$40,000
	Auctions: $12,338, MS-64, January 2015; $1,058, AU-55, August 2015; $259, EF-40, January 2015; $176, VF-25, June 2015												
1854	2,982,000	574	50.8	25%	$50	$75	$95	$125	$175	$300	$625	$1,500	$8,750
	Auctions: $1,645, MS-63, February 2015; $282, AU-55, June 2015; $153, EF-40, January 2015; $79, VF-30, January 2015												
1854, Proof	*15–20*	14	64.8								$8,500	$13,500	$30,000
	Auctions: $70,500, PF-67, November 2013												
1854-O	5,240,000	876	48.5	25%	$50	$75	$95	$125	$175	$300	$650	$1,500	$7,500
	Auctions: $5,405, MS-65, January 2015; $470, MS-61, September 2015; $494, AU-58, August 2015; $94, VF-35, January 2015												

† Ranked in the *100 Greatest U.S. Coins* (fourth edition). **m.** 4 examples are known.

1855, 1855 Over 854
FS-50-1855-301.

	Mintage	Cert	Avg	%MS	G-4	VG-8	F-12	VF-20	EF-40	AU-50	MS-60 / PF-60	MS-63 / PF-63	MS-65 / PF-65
1855, All kinds	759,500												
1855, 1855 Over 1854		57	48.1	26%	$75	$90	$175	$360	$500	$1,200	$2,250	$3,600	$11,500
Auctions: $353, AU-50, November 2014; $588, EF-45, January 2015; $423, EF-45, July 2015; $411, VF-35, December 2014													
1855, Normal Date		166	53.7	33%	$50	$75	$100	$140	$200	$400	$800	$1,750	$12,500
Auctions: $881, AU-58, June 2015; $329, AU-53, January 2015; $176, EF-45, January 2015; $118, VF-35, August 2015													
1855, 55 Over 54, Proof	1–2	0	n/a								$10,000	$22,000	$60,000
Auctions: $30,550, PF-64, June 2014													
1855, Proof	15–20	8	64.5								$7,500	$12,500	$35,000
Auctions: $41,125, PF-66Cam, June 2014													
1855-O	3,688,000	629	50.6	26%	$50	$75	$95	$125	$175	$300	$650	$1,500	$9,500
Auctions: $705, MS-62, September 2015; $423, AU-58, May 2015; $172, EF-45, March 2015; $100, VF-35, May 2015													
1855-S	129,950	58	30.6	5%	$500	$1,000	$1,350	$1,750	$3,500	$7,000	$35,000	$50,000	
Auctions: $41,125, MS-61, October 2014; $14,688, AU-55, January 2015; $8,225, AU-53, July 2014; $423, G-4, October 2015													
1855-S, Proof	2–3	1	65.0									$85,000	$200,000
Auctions: $276,000, PF-65, August 2011													
1856	938,000	143	51.6	30%	$50	$75	$95	$125	$185	$250	$600	$1,200	$5,750
Auctions: $16,450, MS-66, May 2015; $376, AU-58, November 2015; $188, AU-50, March 2015; $176, EF-45, March 2015													
1856, Proof	20–30	20	64.3								$4,000	$6,500	$23,000
Auctions: $17,625, PF-65, October 2014; $17,625, PF-65, November 2013													
1856-O	2,658,000	334	50.4	35%	$50	$75	$95	$125	$185	$250	$500	$1,100	$6,000
Auctions: $4,818, MS-65, January 2015; $470, MS-61, September 2015; $282, AU-53, May 2015; $141, EF-45, July 2015													
1856-S	211,000	41	40.0	10%	$95	$150	$240	$450	$1,100	$2,250	$5,000	$13,000	
Auctions: $12,925, MS-63, May 2015; $3,055, AU-58, January 2015; $881, VF-35, August 2015; $499, VF-35, October 2014													
1857	1,988,000	270	51.1	28%	$50	$75	$95	$125	$185	$250	$600	$1,100	$4,800
Auctions: $3,525, MS-65, January 2015; $764, MS-63, September 2015; $400, AU-58, July 2015; $282, AU-55, August 2015													
1857, Proof	30–50	36	63.8								$3,000	$4,500	$20,000
Auctions: $23,500, PF-66, June 2013													
1857-O	818,000	102	47.2	10%	$50	$75	$100	$175	$300	$500	$1,350	$3,500	$12,000
Auctions: $517, AU-58, June 2015; $259, AU-53, May 2015; $212, EF-45, August 2015; $182, EF-40, June 2015													
1857-S	158,000	41	42.9	12%	$150	$180	$250	$425	$1,100	$2,000	$4,500	$13,500	$35,000
Auctions: $61,688, MS-66, June 2014; $400, EF-40, August 2014; $176, VG-8, October 2014													
1858	4,225,700	713	51.2	26%	$50	$75	$95	$125	$185	$250	$600	$1,100	$5,000
Auctions: $1,058, MS-63, January 2015; $423, AU-58, August 2015; $259, AU-55, October 2015; $147, EF-45, February 2015													
1858, Proof	300+	57	63.7								$1,400	$2,250	$6,500
Auctions: $7,050, PF-65, February 2015; $6,756, PF-65, January 2015; $6,463, PF-64, October 2015; $1,821, PF-63, October 2015													
1858-O	7,294,000	620	45.2	15%	$50	$75	$95	$125	$185	$250	$600	$1,200	$8,500
Auctions: $411, MS-61, June 2015; $470, AU-58, January 2015; $141, EF-45, September 2015; $123, EF-40, March 2015													
1858-S	476,000	86	47.7	19%	$60	$100	$150	$200	$350	$500	$1,700	$4,000	$13,500
Auctions: $505, AU-53, March 2015; $423, AU-50, August 2015; $400, EF-45, November 2015; $235, VF-30, February 2015													

1861-O, Cracked Obverse Die
FS-50-1861o-401.

	Mintage	Cert	Avg	%MS	G-4	VG-8	F-12	VF-20	EF-40	AU-50	MS-60	MS-63	MS-65
											PF-60	PF-63	PF-65
1859	747,200	230	52.6	29%	$50	$75	$95	$125	$185	$250	$500	$1,100	$5,250
	Auctions: $18,213, MS-67, May 2015; $1,293, MS-61, January 2015; $329, AU-55, October 2015; $153, EF-40, August 2015												
1859, Proof	800	148	63.5								$1,150	$1,600	$5,500
	Auctions: $12,925, PF-67, October 2015; $7,050, PF-66, January 2015; $4,004, PF-65, September 2015; $4,700, PF-64, August 2015												
1859-O	2,834,000	310	46.0	17%	$50	$75	$95	$125	$185	$250	$650	$1,800	$7,500
	Auctions: $9,988, MS-66, May 2015; $541, MS-62, September 2015; $376, AU-55, February 2015; $141, EF-40, September 2015												
1859-S	566,000	77	53.4	44%	$60	$100	$150	$200	$400	$600	$1,300	$3,000	$8,500
	Auctions: $47,000, MS-68, May 2015; $646, AU-55, February 2015; $329, EF-40, May 2015; $306, EF-40, August 2015												
1860	302,700	89	54.5	39%	$60	$75	$95	$125	$200	$300	$735	$1,450	$5,000
	Auctions: $940, MS-62, January 2015; $423, AU-55, October 2015; $400, AU-55, May 2015; $247, EF-45, March 2015												
1860, Proof	1,000	117	63.6								$750	$1,600	$5,000
	Auctions: $29,375, PF-67, May 2015; $2,585, PF-64, January 2015; $1,998, PF-63, July 2015; $1,410, PF-63, June 2015												
1860-O	1,290,000	290	50.9	33%	$50	$75	$100	$140	$250	$350	$650	$1,300	$5,000
	Auctions: $940, MS-63, January 2015; $306, AU-55, May 2015; $235, AU-50, May 2015; $206, EF-45, August 2015												
1860-S	472,000	82	51.5	29%	$60	$100	$150	$200	$300	$500	$1,400	$3,750	
	Auctions: $1,116, AU-58, July 2015; $646, AU-55, October 2014; $165, AU-50, November 2014; $282, EF-40, April 2015												
1861	2,887,400	531	54.3	42%	$50	$75	$95	$125	$185	$250	$575	$1,200	$5,000
	Auctions: $10,575, MS-66, January 2015; $306, AU-53, May 2015; $165, EF-45, February 2015; $112, VF-35, October 2015												
1861, Proof	1,000	107	63.5								$750	$1,600	$5,000
	Auctions: $1,351, PF-63, September 2015; $823, PF-61, July 2014; $764, PF-60, January 2015												
1861-O (n)	2,532,633	429	47.3	32%	$70	$90	$120	$180	$300	$900	$1,500	$2,800	$6,500
	Auctions: $2,820, MS-64, January 2015; $1,528, AU-53, June 2015; $259, EF-45, March 2015; $212, F-15, October 2015												
1861-O, Cracked Obv (o)	(p)	41	35.5	7%	$350	$600	$800	$1,250	$3,000	$4,250	$12,000	$22,500	
	Auctions: $16,450, MS-62, October 2014; $11,750, AU-58, September 2013; $4,700, EF-40, August 2014; $3,525, EF-40, August 2014												
1861-S	939,500	117	47.2	27%	$60	$75	$95	$200	$350	$500	$1,200	$3,000	$22,500
	Auctions: $3,760, MS-64, January 2015; $588, AU-55, June 2015; $259, EF-40, September 2015; $112, VF-20, August 2015												
1862	253,000	85	52.8	52%	$100	$150	$200	$350	$500	$650	$1,250	$1,950	$6,000
	Auctions: $18,800, MS-66, May 2015; $881, MS-62, July 2015; $282, EF-45, August 2015; $259, EF-40, February 2015												
1862, Proof	550	198	63.6								$750	$1,600	$5,000
	Auctions: $9,988, PF-65Cam, February 2015; $4,935, PF-65, February 2015; $4,230, PF-65, October 2015; $4,113, PF-65, March 2015												
1862-S	1,352,000	147	40.8	13%	$60	$90	$120	$180	$300	$425	$1,150	$2,700	$25,000
	Auctions: $42,300, MS-66, May 2015; $1,058, MS-61, February 2015; $793, AU-55, January 2015; $223, EF-40, August 2015												
1863	503,200	105	53.7	50%	$100	$125	$150	$200	$350	$600	$1,250	$1,750	$7,500
	Auctions: $24,675, MS-67, January 2015; $212, AU-50, February 2015; $329, EF-45, February 2015; $270, VF-30, December 2014												
1863, Proof	460	132	63.4								$750	$1,600	$5,000
	Auctions: $7,638, PF-66, October 2015; $4,700, PF-65, February 2015; $2,468, PF-64, March 2015; $2,233, PF-64, January 2015												
1863-S	916,000	149	51.3	34%	$60	$75	$95	$150	$300	$550	$1,300	$2,500	$12,000
	Auctions: $3,408, MS-64, January 2015; $588, AU-55, January 2015; $165, EF-40, September 2015; $84, VF-20, October 2015												

n. The 1861-O mintage includes 330,000 half dollars struck by the United States government; 1,240,000 struck for the State of Louisiana after it seceded from the Union; and 962,633 struck after Louisiana joined the Confederate States of America. All of these coins were made from federal dies, rendering it impossible to distinguish one from another with but one exception. **o.** In 1861, the New Orleans Mint used a federal obverse die and a Confederate reverse die to strike a handful of Confederate half dollars. That particular obverse die was also paired with a regular federal reverse die to strike some 1861-O half dollars, which today are popular among collectors, especially in higher grades. Their identifying feature is a die crack running from the denticles to the right of the sixth star down to Miss Liberty's nose (and to her shoulder below her jaw). **p.** Included in 1861-O mintage figure.

	Mintage	Cert	Avg	%MS	G-4	VG-8	F-12	VF-20	EF-40	AU-50	MS-60	MS-63	MS-65
											PF-60	PF-63	PF-65
1864	379,100	110	53.2	53%	$100	$125	$175	$300	$400	$750	$1,300	$1,800	$7,500
	Auctions: $999, MS-62, July 2015; $646, AU-53, August 2015; $376, AU-50, September 2015; $306, EF-40, February 2015												
1864, Proof	470	152	63.6								$750	$1,600	$5,000
	Auctions: $2,233, PF-64, September 2015; $1,175, PF-62, June 2015; $940, PF-62, September 2015; $676, PF-60, October 2015												
1864-S	658,000	96	36.9	16%	$100	$125	$175	$300	$400	$750	$1,800	$4,250	$15,000
	Auctions: $4,700, MS-63, February 2015; $940, AU-55, January 2015; $247, VF-30, August 2015; $235, VF-25, May 2015												
1865	511,400	91	49.0	36%	$100	$125	$175	$300	$450	$800	$1,400	$2,100	$5,500
	Auctions: $32,900, MS-67, May 2015; $3,290, MS-64, February 2015; $764, AU-53, June 2015; $282, EF-40, August 2015												
1865, Proof	500	195	64.0								$750	$1,600	$5,000
	Auctions: $7,050, PF-66, July 2015; $4,465, PF-65Cam, June 2015; $4,700, PF-65, January 2015; $2,115, PF-64, October 2015												
1865-S	675,000	106	39.2	13%	$100	$125	$175	$300	$400	$750	$2,000	$4,500	$50,000
	Auctions: $42,300, MS-65, May 2015; $705, AU-53, June 2015; $282, EF-40, May 2015; $247, VF-35, August 2015												
1866-S, Variety 1	60,000	73	28.2	11%	$450	$600	$875	$1,250	$2,300	$3,500	$9,500	$20,000	$70,000
	Auctions: $164,500, MS-67, November 2013; $2,585, EF-45, August 2014; $1,410, VF-35, July 2014; $676, F-12, July 2014												
1866, Variety 4	744,900	137	49.5	39%	$60	$100	$150	$200	$300	$500	$1,000	$2,100	$6,000
	Auctions: $5,170, MS-66, January 2015; $282, AU-53, May 2015; $200, EF-45, May 2015; $118, VF-25, August 2015												
1866, Variety 4, Proof	725	124	63.6								$700	$1,350	$3,200
	Auctions: $3,643, PF-66, January 2015; $3,525, PF-66, July 2015; $2,115, PF-64Cam, November 2014; $1,116, PF-63, October 2015												
1866, No Motto, Proof † (q)	1	1	62.0									—	
	Auctions: No auction records available.												
1866-S, Variety 4	994,000	95	42.6	20%	$60	$100	$175	$225	$350	$600	$1,150	$2,250	$12,000
	Auctions: $881, AU-55, January 2015; $259, EF-45, May 2015; $223, EF-40, August 2015; $176, VF-30, January 2015												
1867	449,300	71	49.0	31%	$100	$125	$150	$200	$300	$550	$1,150	$1,600	$5,000
	Auctions: $999, AU-58, January 2015; $235, EF-45, May 2015; $329, EF-40, May 2015; $259, VF-35, July 2015												
1867, Proof	625	161	64.0								$700	$1,500	$3,200
	Auctions: $8,225, PF-66Cam, October 2015; $3,995, PF-65Cam, February 2015; $3,290, PF-64Cam, January 2015; $793, PF-62, July 2015												
1867-S	1,196,000	122	46.9	19%	$60	$100	$150	$200	$300	$500	$1,250	$3,000	$12,500
	Auctions: $1,116, AU-58, January 2015; $306, AU-53, January 2015; $176, EF-45, October 2015; $188, VF-30, June 2015												
1868	417,600	57	48.0	32%	$100	$125	$175	$250	$450	$550	$1,000	$2,000	$7,000
	Auctions: $9,988, MS-65, May 2015; $1,175, MS-63, January 2015; $494, AU-55, July 2015; $259, VF-30, May 2015												
1868, Proof	600	168	63.7								$700	$1,250	$3,200
	Auctions: $4,230, PF-66, February 2015; $2,585, PF-65, August 2015; $823, PF-62, July 2015; $564, PF-61, March 2015												
1868-S	1,160,000	98	46.6	14%	$60	$100	$125	$175	$275	$450	$1,000	$2,100	$12,500
	Auctions: $17,625, MS-66, May 2015; $564, AU-55, January 2015; $353, AU-53, November 2015; $349, AU-53, March 2015												
1869	795,300	163	51.5	29%	$60	$100	$125	$175	$250	$300	$1,000	$2,000	$15,000
	Auctions: $1,293, MS-62, June 2015; $376, AU-55, October 2015; $200, EF-45, May 2015; $200, EF-40, May 2015; $408, AU-55, March 2018												
1869, Proof	600	154	63.6								$700	$1,250	$3,200
	Auctions: $7,638, PF-67, May 2015; $6,169, PF-67, September 2015; $1,410, PF-64, January 2015; $1,293, PF-64, February 2015												
1869-S	656,000	79	45.2	28%	$60	$100	$125	$175	$350	$475	$1,000	$2,600	$7,500
	Auctions: $259, AU-50, November 2015; $189, AU-50, August 2015; $141, EF-40, May 2015; $94, EF-40, February 2015												
1870	633,900	94	49.3	27%	$60	$75	$100	$150	$250	$325	$725	$1,500	$8,000
	Auctions: $1,058, MS-62, January 2015; $376, AU-53, November 2015; $212, EF-40, August 2015; $165, VF-30, January 2015												
1870, Proof	1,000	137	63.1								$700	$1,250	$2,500
	Auctions: $1,645, PF-64, March 2015; $1,528, PF-64, May 2015; $1,175, PF-63, September 2015; $1,058, PF-63, January 2015												
1870-CC	54,617	73	24.5	5%	$1,750	$2,750	$4,000	$5,500	$10,000	$30,000	$85,000	$225,000	
	Auctions: $28,200, AU-50, August 2016; $17,625, EF-45, January 2015; $11,750, EF-45, January 2015; $7,050, VF-30, January 2015												
1870-S	1,004,000	67	41.9	13%	$100	$125	$150	$300	$500	$650	$1,950	$4,500	$32,000
	Auctions: $1,293, AU-55, January 2015; $376, EF-45, January 2015; $306, EF-40, May 2015; $176, VF-25, February 2015												

† Ranked in the *100 Greatest U.S. Coins* (fourth edition). **q.** Classified as Judd-538 (*United States Pattern Coins*, tenth edition). This fantasy piece was deliberately struck for pharmacist and coin collector Robert Coulton Davis, likely around 1869 or in the early 1870s, along with the No Motto Proof quarter and dollar of the same date.

1873, Close 3   1873, Open 3

	Mintage	Cert	Avg	%MS	G-4	VG-8	F-12	VF-20	EF-40	AU-50	MS-60 PF-60	MS-63 PF-63	MS-65 PF-65
1871	1,203,600	187	51.7	32%	$60	$75	$100	$150	$250	$325	$725	$1,300	$4,750
	Auctions: $3,525, MS-64, May 2015; $223, AU-50, March 2015; $176, EF-45, October 2015; $91, VF-30, March 2015												
1871, Proof	960	165	63.2								$700	$1,250	$3,250
	Auctions: $4,230, PF-66, January 2015; $2,703, PF-65, January 2015; $1,410, PF-64, June 2015; $1,058, PF-63, January 2015												
1871-CC	153,950	66	27.0	5%	$500	$750	$1,250	$1,650	$3,250	$5,500	$30,000	$55,000	
	Auctions: $76,375, MS-64, May 2015; $3,055, EF-45, January 2015; $1,998, VF-30, January 2015; $259, AG-3, November 2015												
1871-S	2,178,000	161	46.4	19%	$60	$75	$100	$150	$250	$400	$1,000	$1,850	$8,000
	Auctions: $2,611, MS-64, May 2015; $294, AU-53, July 2015; $165, EF-45, November 2015; $112, EF-40, August 2015												
1872	880,600	99	48.0	24%	$60	$100	$150	$200	$300	$325	$725	$2,300	$5,500
	Auctions: $1,528, MS-62, February 2015; $329, AU-55, August 2015; $223, AU-50, May 2015; $153, AU-50, January 2015												
1872, Proof	950	162	63.6								$700	$1,250	$2,500
	Auctions: $5,523, PF-65Cam, June 2015; $4,935, PF-65Cam, January 2015; $4,465, PF-65Cam, February 2015												
1872-CC	257,000	124	26.8	1%	$300	$600	$750	$1,300	$2,250	$3,850	$25,000	$70,000	
	Auctions: $4,230, AU-53, January 2015; $2,115, EF-45, August 2016; $447, F-12, October 2015; $282, VG-8, May 2015												
1872-S	580,000	55	46.3	24%	$100	$150	$200	$300	$400	$700	$1,750	$3,000	$13,500
	Auctions: $2,820, MS-63, February 2015; $1,028, AU-55, June 2015; $353, EF-45, April 2015; $306, VF-30, May 2015												
1873, Close 3, Variety 4	587,000	98	45.9	17%	$60	$100	$175	$225	$350	$600	$1,000	$1,500	$6,000
	Auctions: $1,410, AU-58, July 2015; $212, AU-53, May 2015; $176, EF-45, July 2015; $94, EF-40, May 2015												
1873, Open 3, Variety 4	214,200	17	30.4	0%	$3,250	$4,500	$5,500	$6,750	$8,000	$13,500	$50,000	$95,000	
	Auctions: $55,813, MS-61, October 2014; $21,150, AU-58, January 2015; $4,230, VG-8, January 2015; $3,290, VG-8, August 2014												
1873, Variety 4, Proof	600	188	63.8								$700	$1,250	$2,500
	Auctions: $8,813, PF-66, June 2015; $3,290, PF-65, February 2015; $1,410, PF-64, September 2015; $618, PF-61, June 2015												
1873-CC, Variety 4	122,500	62	31.8	11%	$400	$725	$1,150	$1,650	$3,750	$6,000	$12,000	$32,500	$85,000
	Auctions: $5,053, AU-50, January 2015; $423, G-6, August 2015; $306, G-6, October 2015; $206, AG-3, November 2015												
1873-S, Variety 4 (r)	5,000	0	n/a										
	Auctions: No auction records available.												
1873, Variety 5	1,815,200	336	49.0	31%	$50	$60	$75	$150	$300	$475	$950	$1,800	$15,000
	Auctions: $1,293, AU-58, January 2015; $259, EF-45, November 2015; $159, VF-35, August 2015; $107, VF-25, February 2015												
1873, Variety 5, Proof	800	153	63.8								$1,000	$2,200	$8,500
	Auctions: $12,925, PF-66, September 2014; $6,463, PF-65, March 2015; $2,174, PF-63, June 2015; $1,763, PF-63, January 2015												
1873-CC, Variety 5	214,560	132	33.3	11%	$300	$475	$800	$1,150	$2,000	$3,500	$8,250	$18,500	$55,000
	Auctions: $2,497, EF-45, January 2015; $764, VF-20, June 2015; $376, VG-10, October 2015; $176, AG-3, November 2015												
1873-S, Variety 5	228,000	52	46.8	19%	$100	$150	$200	$350	$550	$1,000	$3,500	$8,000	$35,000
	Auctions: $705, AU-50, May 2015; $364, AU-50, November 2015; $208, EF-40, October 2015; $165, VF-20, May 2015												
1874	2,359,600	401	52.0	39%	$50	$60	$75	$150	$300	$450	$950	$1,875	$15,000
	Auctions: $25,850, MS-66, May 2015; $200, MS-60, October 2015; $364, AU-53, June 2015; $259, EF-45, August 2015												
1874, Proof	700	199	63.3								$1,000	$2,200	$8,500
	Auctions: $11,750, PF-66, January 2015; $6,169, PF-65, June 2015; $4,465, PF-64Cam, June 2015; $1,469, PF-62, August 2015												
1874-CC	59,000	76	31.6	14%	$1,150	$1,650	$2,350	$3,250	$5,750	$8,000	$14,000	$32,500	$95,000
	Auctions: $94,000, MS-65, May 2015; $44,650, MS-64, January 2015; $1,293, VG-10, October 2014; $1,410, VG-8, September 2014												
1874-S	394,000	63	48.9	43%	$100	$180	$225	$300	$450	$700	$1,700	$3,000	$25,000
	Auctions: $15,275, MS-65, January 2015; $4,406, MS-64, March 2015; $1,116, AU-55, June 2015; $282, VF-35, August 2015												

r. The 1873-S, No Arrows, half dollar is unknown in any collection.

1877, 7 Over 6
FS-50-1877-301.

	Mintage	Cert	Avg	%MS	G-4	VG-8	F-12	VF-20	EF-40	AU-50	MS-60	MS-63	MS-65
											PF-60	PF-63	PF-65
1875	6,026,800	422	52.2	45%	$50	$75	$100	$140	$200	$300	$475	$800	$3,000
	Auctions: $1,410, MS-64, January 2015; $1,116, MS-63, August 2015; $376, AU-58, April 2015; $129, EF-45, March 2015												
1875, Proof	700	147	63.7								$600	$1,150	$2,500
	Auctions: $12,925, PF-67, May 2015; $4,465, PF-66, February 2015; $3,055, PF-65Cam, January 2015; $810, PF-62, March 2015												
1875-CC	1,008,000	193	43.3	33%	$115	$135	$225	$325	$550	$1,000	$2,000	$3,000	$8,500
	Auctions: $881, AU-55, July 2015; $999, AU-53, January 2015; $881, AU-50, January 2015; $353, VF-30, May 2015												
1875-S	3,200,000	294	55.9	64%	$50	$75	$100	$140	$200	$300	$475	$800	$3,000
	Auctions: $2,820, MS-65, January 2015; $646, MS-63, August 2015; $329, AU-55, November 2015; $165, EF-45, August 2015												
1876	8,418,000	509	50.5	40%	$50	$75	$100	$140	$200	$300	$475	$800	$3,800
	Auctions: $3,055, MS-65, March 2015; $588, MS-62, February 2015; $176, AU-53, January 2015; $94, VF-35, January 2015												
1876, Proof	1,150	211	63.5								$600	$1,150	$2,500
	Auctions: $3,055, PF-65Cam, February 2015; $1,410, PF-64, November 2014; $1,116, PF-62Cam, August 2014; $646, PF-61, September 2014												
1876-CC	1,956,000	266	44.7	36%	$115	$135	$165	$200	$400	$700	$1,600	$2,400	$5,500
	Auctions: $1,528, AU-58, January 2015; $212, VF-35, August 2015; $212, VF-25, February 2015; $69, VG-10, March 2015												
1876-S	4,528,000	270	49.8	42%	$40	$45	$65	$80	$120	$225	$450	$800	$3,600
	Auctions: $3,173, MS-65, January 2015; $212, AU-55, July 2015; $176, AU-50, May 2015; $118, EF-45, June 2015												
1877	8,304,000	445	49.7	44%	$40	$60	$70	$80	$120	$225	$450	$800	$3,200
	Auctions: $6,463, MS-67, May 2015; $376, AU-58, July 2015; $200, EF-45, November 2015; $71, EF-40, March 2015												
1877, 7 Over 6 (s)	(t)	1	61.0	100%					$1,200	$2,200	$3,750	$12,000	
	Auctions: $3,335, MS-62, August 2009												
1877, Proof	510	171	63.4								$600	$1,150	$3,000
	Auctions: $11,750, PF-66Cam, February 2015; $3,290, PF-66, October 2015; $1,528, PF-64, January 2015; $881, PF-62, March 2015												
1877-CC	1,420,000	280	49.5	55%	$115	$135	$160	$225	$400	$550	$1,150	$2,350	$5,500
	Auctions: $7,931, MS-66, May 2015; $960, AU-58, January 2015; $212, VF-20, May 2015; $100, VG-10, June 2015												
1877-S	5,356,000	595	53.9	51%	$40	$45	$65	$80	$100	$225	$475	$800	$3,000
	Auctions: $19,975, MS-67, May 2015; $353, AU-58, March 2015; $206, AU-50, January 2015; $153, EF-45, August 2015												
1878	1,377,600	128	50.9	41%	$45	$90	$120	$135	$150	$240	$425	$1,100	$5,200
	Auctions: $705, MS-62, January 2015; $259, AU-50, November 2015; $119, VF-35, June 2015; $84, F-12, May 2015												
1878, Proof	800	235	64.0								$600	$1,150	$2,500
	Auctions: $35,250, PF-68, May 2015; $4,935, PF-66Cam, October 2015; $1,998, PF-64, January 2015; $969, PF-63, January 2015												
1878-CC	62,000	59	23.5	10%	$1,050	$1,450	$2,000	$3,000	$4,250	$5,500	$12,500	$25,000	$50,000
	Auctions: $64,625, MS-65, June 2014; $1,763, VG-10, September 2014; $881, G-4, November 2014												
1878-S	12,000	13	37.3	46%	$32,500	$40,000	$45,000	$55,000	$70,000	$75,000	$100,000	$150,000	$250,000
	Auctions: $199,750, MS-64, June 2014; $58,750, AU-50, August 2014												
1879	4,800	271	59.9	80%	$350	$450	$550	$650	$750	$900	$1,050	$1,300	$3,250
	Auctions: $2,938, MS-65, January 2015; $940, AU-55, June 2015; $881, AU-53, June 2015; $705, EF-40, January 2015												
1879, Proof	1,100	328	63.6								$600	$1,150	$2,500
	Auctions: $8,225, PF-67Cam, February 2015; $2,468, PF-65, March 2015; $1,410, PF-64, January 2015; $911, PF-62, March 2015												
1880	8,400	108	57.6	74%	$350	$450	$550	$650	$750	$900	$1,050	$1,500	$4,000
	Auctions: $8,225, MS-67, May 2015; $4,230, MS-66, January 2015; $1,293, AU-58, June 2015; $1,087, AU-55, June 2015												
1880, Proof	1,355	395	63.7								$600	$1,150	$2,500
	Auctions: $7,050, PF-66Cam, August 2015; $2,938, PF-66, January 2015; $1,645, PF 64, July 2015												

s. The top portion of a 6 is visible on the upper surface of the last 7.   **t.** Included in circulation-strike 1877 mintage figure.

	Mintage	Cert	Avg	%MS	G-4	VG-8	F-12	VF-20	EF-40	AU-50	MS-60 PF-60	MS-63 PF-63	MS-65 PF-65
1881	10,000	112	54.6	71%	$350	$450	$550	$650	$750	$900	$1,050	$1,500	$4,000
	Auctions: $9,400, MS-67, June 2014												
1881, Proof	975	342	63.8								$600	$1,150	$2,500
	Auctions: $9,400, PF-68, May 2015; $6,698, PF-67, July 2014; $2,820, PF-65Cam, July 2014; $2,938, PF-65, September 2014												
1882	4,400	84	56.9	70%	$350	$450	$550	$650	$750	$900	$1,050	$1,600	$4,750
	Auctions: $4,700, MS-65, January 2015; $2,291, MS-64, January 2015; $646, VF-25, October 2015; $470, VG-8, October 2015												
1882, Proof	1,100	319	64.0								$600	$1,150	$2,500
	Auctions: $15,275, PF-67Cam, November 2013; $6,463, PF-66DCam, August 2014; $6,169, PF-65DCam, August 2014; $1,763, PF-63DCam, August 2015												
1883	8,000	99	54.5	63%	$350	$450	$550	$650	$750	$900	$1,050	$1,500	$4,250
	Auctions: $5,640, MS-66, May 2015; $1,116, MS-61, June 2015; $911, AU-58, June 2015; $306, AG-3, October 2015												
1883, Proof	1,039	336	64.0								$600	$1,150	$2,500
	Auctions: $11,163, PF-67Cam, October 2014; $7,638, PF-67Cam, November 2014; $1,998, PF-64Cam, March 2015; $1,528, PF-63Cam, June 2015												
1884	4,400	100	60.1	84%	$425	$475	$550	$650	$775	$925	$1,100	$1,500	$4,500
	Auctions: $21,150, MS-67, January 2015; $15,275, MS-67, June 2014; $1,234, EF-45, July 2015; $517, VG-10, October 2015												
1884, Proof	875	231	63.8								$600	$1,150	$2,500
	Auctions: $7,931, PF-67, May 2015; $2,233, PF-65, September 2015; $1,528, PF-64, August 2015; $764, PF-61, January 2015												
1885	5,200	85	54.9	65%	$500	$550	$625	$725	$800	$925	$1,100	$1,500	$4,500
	Auctions: $4,230, MS-66, January 2015; $1,998, MS-63, January 2015; $1,058, AU-55, February 2015; $1,410, EF-45, January 2015												
1885, Proof	930	305	64.0								$600	$1,150	$2,500
	Auctions: $5,758, PF-67, September 2015; $2,585, PF-65Cam, September 2015; $1,351, PF-63Cam, March 2015; $823, PF-61, July 2015												
1886	5,000	97	56.0	71%	$500	$550	$625	$725	$800	$900	$1,100	$1,500	$4,250
	Auctions: $25,850, MS-67, May 2015; $617, AU-50, June 2015; $646, VG-10, August 2015; $517, VG-8, October 2015												
1886, Proof	886	251	63.9								$600	$1,150	$2,500
	Auctions: $11,163, PF-67Cam, August 2015; $3,290, PF-66, June 2015; $2,585, PF-65, January 2015; $1,116, PF-62, June 2015												
1887	5,000	116	57.0	72%	$525	$575	$650	$750	$950	$1,000	$1,100	$1,400	$4,250
	Auctions: $24,675, MS-67, June 2014; $1,116, AU-50, August 2014; $734, EF-40, October 2014												
1887, Proof	710	184	64.2								$600	$1,150	$2,500
	Auctions: $29,375, PF-68DCam, November 2013												
1888	12,001	130	55.9	69%	$350	$425	$550	$650	$750	$900	$1,000	$1,350	$4,000
	Auctions: $8,813, MS-67, January 2015; $4,230, MS-66, January 2015; $852, AU-50, March 2015; $447, VG-10, October 2015												
1888, Proof	832	223	63.8								$600	$1,150	$2,500
	Auctions: $8,225, PF-67, July 2015; $3,760, PF-66, February 2015; $2,820, PF-65, October 2015; $2,350, PF-64Cam, January 2015												
1889	12,000	117	54.0	65%	$325	$425	$550	$650	$750	$900	$1,000	$1,250	$4,250
	Auctions: $8,225, MS-66, May 2015; $2,115, MS-64, January 2015; $823, AU-55, June 2015; $588, VF-25, October 2015												
1889, Proof	711	205	63.8								$600	$1,150	$2,500
	Auctions: $2,820, PF-66, August 2015; $2,115, PF-65, March 2015; $2,233, PF-64, January 2015; $1,175, PF-63, June 2015												
1890	12,000	110	56.8	76%	$325	$425	$550	$650	$750	$900	$1,000	$1,150	$4,000
	Auctions: $676, MS-60, February 2015; $705, AU-50, September 2015; $676, AU-50, June 2015; $411, VG-8, October 2015												
1890, Proof	590	220	64.3								$600	$1,150	$2,500
	Auctions: $9,988, PF-67Cam, May 2015; $2,585, PF-65, January 2015; $1,645, PF-64Cam, February 2015; $823, PF-62Cam, January 2015												
1891	200,000	202	54.9	61%	$100	$150	$200	$350	$500	$700	$800	$1,200	$3,800
	Auctions: $423, AU-55, November 2015; $541, AU-53, May 2015; $141, VF-35, August 2015; $125, VF-30, October 2015												
1891, Proof	600	200	64.2								$600	$1,150	$2,500
	Auctions: $5,405, PF-67, January 2015; $4,230, PF-66, February 2015; $1,410, PF-64, January 2015; $1,175, PF-63, June 2015												

BARBER OR LIBERTY HEAD (1892–1915)

Designer: *Charles E. Barber.* **Weight:** *12.50 grams.* **Composition:** *.900 silver, .100 copper.*
Diameter: *30.6 mm.* **Edge:** *Reeded.* **Mints:** *Philadelphia, Denver, New Orleans, and San Francisco.*

Mintmark
location is
on the reverse,
below the eagle.

Circulation Strike **Proof**

History. Charles E. Barber, chief engraver of the U.S. Mint, crafted the eponymous "Barber" or Liberty Head half dollars along with similarly designed dimes and quarters of the same era. His initial, B, is at the truncation of Miss Liberty's neck. Production of the coins was continuous from 1892 to 1915, stopping a year before the dime and quarter of the same design.

Striking and Sharpness. On the obverse, check Miss Liberty's hair details and other features. On the reverse, the eagle's leg at the lower right and the arrows often are weak, and there can be weakness at the upper right of the shield and the nearby wing area. At EF and below, sharpness of strike on the reverse is not important. Most Proofs are sharply struck, although many are weak on the eagle's leg at the lower right and on certain parts of the arrows and/or the upper-right area of the shield and the nearby wing. The Proofs of 1892 to 1901 usually have cameo contrast between the designs and the mirror fields. Those of 1914 and 1915 are often with extensive hairlines or other problems.

Availability. Most examples seen in the marketplace are well worn. There are no rarities in the Barber half dollar series, although some are scarcer than others. Coins that are Fine or better are much scarcer—in particular the San Francisco Mint issues of 1901, 1904, and 1907. MS coins are available of all dates and mints, but some are very elusive. Proofs exist in proportion to their mintages. Choicer examples tend to be of later dates, similar to other Barber coins.

GRADING STANDARDS

MS-60 to 70 (Mint State). *Obverse:* At MS-60, some abrasion and contact marks are evident, most noticeably on the cheek and the obverse field to the right. Luster is present, but may be dull or lifeless. Many Barber coins have been cleaned, especially of the earlier dates. At MS-63, contact marks are very few; abrasion still is evident but less than at lower levels. Indeed, the cheek of Miss Liberty vir-

1909. Graded MS-62.

tually showcases abrasion. This is even more evident on a half dollar than on lower denominations. An MS-65 coin may have minor abrasion, but contact marks are so minute as to require magnification. Luster should be full and rich. *Reverse:* Comments apply as for the obverse, except that in lower Mint State grades abrasion and contact marks are most noticeable on the head and tail of the eagle and on the tips of the wings. At MS-65 or higher there are no marks visible to the unaided eye. The field is mainly protected by design elements, so the reverse often appears to grade a point or two higher than the obverse.

Illustrated coin: On this example, mottled light-brown toning appears over lustrous surfaces.

AU-50, 53, 55, 58 (About Uncirculated). *Obverse:* Light wear is seen on the head, especially on the forward hair under LIBERTY. At AU-58, the luster is extensive but incomplete, especially on the higher parts and in the right field. At AU–50 and 53, luster is less. *Reverse:* Wear is seen on the head and tail of the eagle and on the tips of the wings. At AU–50 and 53, there still is significant luster. An AU-58 coin (as determined by the obverse) can have the reverse appear to be full Mint State.

1915-D. Graded AU-53.

Illustrated coin: Areas of original Mint luster can be seen on this coin, more so on the reverse than on the obverse.

EF-40, 45 (Extremely Fine). *Obverse:* Further wear is seen on the head. The hair above the forehead lacks most detail. LIBERTY shows wear but still is strong. *Reverse:* Further wear is seen on the head and tail of the eagle and on the tips of the wings, most evident at the left and right extremes of the wings At this level and below, sharpness of strike on the reverse is not important.

1908. Graded EF-45.

VF-20, 30 (Very Fine). *Obverse:* The head shows more wear, now with nearly all detail gone in the hair above the forehead. LIBERTY shows wear, but is complete. The leaves on the head all show wear, as does the upper part of the cap. *Reverse:* Wear is more extensive, particularly noticeable on the outer parts of the wings, the head, the shield, and the tail.

Illustrated coin: This coin is seemingly lightly cleaned.

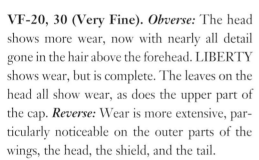

1897-S. Graded VF-30.

F-12, 15 (Fine). *Obverse:* The head shows extensive wear. LIBERTY, the key place to check, is weak, especially at ER, but is fully readable. The ANA grading standards and *Photograde* adhere to this. PCGS suggests that lightly struck coins "may have letters partially missing." Traditionally, collectors insist on full LIBERTY. *Reverse:* More wear is seen on the reverse, in the places as above. E PLURIBUS UNUM is light, with one to several letters worn away.

1909-O. Graded F-12.

VG-8, 10 (Very Good). *Obverse:* A net of three letters in LIBERTY must be readable. Traditionally LI is clear, and after that there is a partial letter or two. *Reverse:* Further wear has smoothed more than half of the feathers in the wing. The shield is indistinct except for a few traces of interior lines. The motto is partially worn away. The rim is full, and many if not most denticles can be seen.

1915-S. Graded VG-8.

G-4, 6 (Good). *Obverse:* The head is in outline form, with the center flat. Most of the rim is there and all letters and the date are full. *Reverse:* The eagle shows only a few feathers, and only a few scattered letters remain in the motto. The rim may be worn flat in some or all of the area, but the peripheral lettering is clear.

Illustrated coin: On this coin the obverse is perhaps G-6 and the reverse AG-3. The grade might be averaged as G-4.

1892-O. Graded G-4.

AG-3 (About Good). *Obverse:* The stars and motto are worn, and the border may be indistinct. Distinctness varies at this level. The date is clear. Grading is usually determined by the reverse. *Reverse:* The rim is gone and the letters are partially worn away. The eagle is mostly flat, perhaps with a few hints of feathers. Usually, the obverse appears to be in a slightly higher grade than the reverse.

1896-S. Graded AG-3.

PF-60 to 70 (Proof). *Obverse and Reverse:* Proofs that are extensively cleaned and have many hairlines, or that are dull and grainy, are lower level, such as PF–60 to 62; these are not widely desired. With medium hairlines and good reflectivity, an assigned grade of PF-64 is appropriate. Tiny horizontal lines on Miss Liberty's cheek, known as slide marks, from National and other album slides scuffing the relief of the cheek, are endemic on all Barber

1914. Graded PF-61.

silver coins. With noticeable marks of this type, the highest grade assignable is PF-64. With relatively few hairlines, a rating of PF-65 can be given. PF-66 should have hairlines so delicate that magnification is needed to see them. Above that, a Proof should be free of any hairlines or other problems.

Illustrated coin: This is an attractive coin at the relatively low PF-61 grade.

1892-O, Normal O **1892-O, Micro O**
FS-50-1892o-501.

	Mintage	Cert	Avg	%MS	G-4	VG-8	F-12	VF-20	EF-40	AU-50	MS-60	MS-63	MS-65
											PF-60	PF-63	PF-65
1892	934,000	1,072	58.0	69%	$24	$35	$80	$135	$200	$325	$550	$800	$1,675
	Auctions: $39,950, MS-68, October 2015; $1,116, MS-64, January 2015; $353, AU-55, May 2015; $247, EF-45, September 2015												
1892, Proof	1,245	380	64.4								$525	$1,000	$1,750
	Auctions: $7,639, PF-68, January 2015; $9,400, PF-67UCam, October 2015; $4,700, PF-66, January 2015; $2,585, PF-64DCam, August 2015												
1892-O	390,000	527	30.9	29%	$250	$450	$550	$625	$700	$825	$1,025	$1,650	$3,000
	Auctions: $47,000, MS-68, August 2015; $588, AU-55, October 2015; $725, AU-53, January 2015; $200, G-4, February 2015												
1892-O, Micro O (a)	(b)	17	22.3	24%	$3,650	$7,500	$10,000	$12,500	$15,500	$18,000	$32,000	$45,000	$100,000
	Auctions: $36,014, MS-63, June 2014; $3,055, G-4, March 2016; $3,055, AG-3, September 2016												
1892-S	1,029,028	390	24.9	19%	$275	$340	$400	$525	$700	$900	$1,200	$2,100	$5,500
	Auctions: $30,550, MS-67, October 2015; $646, EF-40, January 2015; $259, VG-8, June 2015; $188, G-6, November 2015												
1893	1,826,000	309	52.6	49%	$25	$30	$70	$140	$210	$350	$600	$1,000	$2,350
	Auctions: $28,200, MS-67, August 2015; $1,058, MS-64, October 2015; $212, EF-40, September 2015; $306, VF-35, January 2015												
1893, Proof	792	285	64.5								$525	$1,100	$1,750
	Auctions: $18,800, PF-68Cam, August 2015; $4,530, PF-67, February 2015; $1,265, PF-63Cam, June 2015; $564, PF-61, September 2015												
1893-O	1,389,000	240	45.8	51%	$40	$75	$135	$250	$350	$480	$850	$1,250	$9,500
	Auctions: $18,800, MS-66, July 2015; $1,880, MS-64, March 2015; $505, MS-60, September 2015; $588, AU-53, July 2015												
1893-S	740,000	323	19.1	15%	$150	$210	$550	$750	$1,200	$1,500	$2,250	$4,300	$15,000
	Auctions: $12,925, MS-65, February 2015; $1,763, AU-58, August 2015; $388, F-12, October 2015; $212, VG-10, February 2015												
1894	1,148,000	256	42.9	47%	$30	$50	$115	$200	$275	$375	$650	$1,000	$2,000
	Auctions: $17,625, MS-67, October 2015; $306, AU-55, May 2015; $223, EF-40, May 2015; $188, VF-30, January 2015												
1894, Proof	972	322	64.2								$525	$1,100	$1,750
	Auctions: $4,406, PF-67, June 2015; $4,113, PF-66, May 2015; $1,293, PF-64, July 2015; $3,055, PF-63, January 2015												
1894-O	2,138,000	232	47.7	53%	$25	$40	$100	$180	$300	$400	$700	$1,200	$5,350
	Auctions: $14,100, MS-66, August 2015; $999, AU-58, June 2015; $194, VF-20, August 2015; $106, F-15, January 2015												
1894-S	4,048,690	256	43.0	41%	$22	$35	$90	$180	$240	$400	$650	$1,300	$6,500
	Auctions: $8,813, MS-66, May 2015; $1,175, MS-63, June 2015; $329, AU-50, September 2015; $212, VF-25, June 2015												
1895	1,834,338	230	47.4	50%	$28	$40	$80	$140	$210	$350	$600	$900	$2,800
	Auctions: $5,170, MS-66, October 2015; $1,058, MS-64, January 2015; $517, AU-55, October 2015; $306, AU-50, May 2015												
1895, Proof	880	352	64.5								$525	$1,100	$1,750
	Auctions: $3,819, PF-67, March 2015; $3,290, PF-66, June 2015; $2,100, PF-65, November 2014; $1,755, PF-65, October 2015												
1895-O	1,766,000	207	34.0	30%	$50	$70	$160	$200	$260	$410	$750	$1,550	$6,000
	Auctions: $25,850, MS-67, October 2015; $541, AU-50, July 2015; $176, EF-45, January 2015; $79, VG-10, February 2015												
1895-S	1,108,086	205	47.3	55%	$30	$75	$160	$250	$450	$550	$775	$1,200	$4,800
	Auctions: $11,163, MS-66, August 2015; $794, AU-55, July 2015; $355, VF-30, January 2015; $94, F-12, May 2015												
1896	950,000	167	45.2	46%	$40	$60	$115	$175	$240	$400	$650	$1,050	$3,300
	Auctions: $25,850, MS-67, October 2015; $1,293, MS-64, September 2015; $852, MS-63, January 2015; $176, VF-25, January 2015												
1896, Proof	762	271	64.3								$525	$1,100	$1,750
	Auctions: $7,050, PF-67Cam, October 2015; $1,880, PF-64, August 2015; $940, PF-63, February 2015; $881, PF-62, June 2015												
1896-O	924,000	167	22.0	13%	$50	$95	$200	$500	$1,900	$3,250	$6,250	$12,000	$24,000
	Auctions: $88,125, MS-67, August 2015; $3,525, AU-55, July 2016; $3,525, AU-55, October 2015; $646, VF-30, January 2015												
1896-S	1,140,948	232	20.9	18%	$115	$165	$240	$480	$1,100	$1,450	$2,400	$3,750	$7,000
	Auctions: $23,500, MS-66, May 2015; $1,528, EF-45, September 2015; $881, VF-35, October 2015; $212, VG-8, February 2015												

a. This variety "was created when an O mintmark punch for quarters was used in place of the regular, larger mintmark intended for use on half dollar dies. . . . Many examples show strong strike doubling on reverse" (*Cherrypickers' Guide to Rare Die Varieties*, sixth edition, volume II). **b.** Included in 1892-O mintage figure.

	Mintage	Cert	Avg	%MS	G-4	VG-8	F-12	VF-20	EF-40	AU-50	MS-60	MS-63	MS-65
											PF-60	PF-63	PF-65
1897	2,480,000	273	49.9	49%	$25	$35	$65	$130	$240	$375	$600	$950	$2,700
	Auctions: $19,388, MS-67, August 2015; $212, EF-45, January 2015; $141, VF-30, May 2015; $52, F-15, September 2015												
1897, Proof	731	329	64.8								$525	$1,100	$1,750
	Auctions: $61,688, PF-69UCam, August 2015; $18,800, PF-68DCam, January 2015; $5,875, PF-67Cam, October 2015; $4,465, PF-65Cam, January 2015												
1897-O	632,000	372	14.3	8%	$160	$230	$450	$850	$1,200	$1,600	$2,750	$4,000	$8,000
	Auctions: $25,850, MS-67, October 2015; $8,813, MS-66, October 2016; $940, VF-25, January 2015; $259, VG-10, August 2015												
1897-S	933,900	328	19.4	16%	$175	$250	$400	$550	$1,200	$1,850	$2,800	$3,750	$7,000
	Auctions: $35,250, MS-67, May 2015; $4,230, AU-58, August 2015; $282, F-12, November 2015; $176, VG-8, May 2015												
1898	2,956,000	303	45.8	40%	$15	$20	$50	$130	$200	$325	$650	$950	$2,800
	Auctions: $37,600, MS-67, October 2015; $5,170, MS-66, January 2015; $482, AU-58, June 2015; $353, AU-53, January 2015												
1898, Proof	735	274	64.9								$525	$1,100	$1,750
	Auctions: $15,275, PF-68Cam, January 2015; $12,925, PF-67Cam, August 2015; $2,938, PF-66Cam, September 2015; $1,528, PF-64Cam, January 2015												
1898-O	874,000	173	27.8	23%	$38	$95	$210	$500	$675	$800	$1,500	$2,500	$7,200
	Auctions: $22,325, MS-67, October 2015; $2,233, AU-50, January 2015; $553, VF-30, July 2015; $212, F-12, August 2015												
1898-S	2,358,550	169	36.1	20%	$30	$50	$140	$185	$360	$540	$1,600	$2,500	$5,500
	Auctions: $4,700, MS-64, January 2015; $3,564, MS-64, September 2015; $823, AU-55, August 2015; $247, VF-30, January 2015												
1899	5,538,000	465	45.8	39%	$15	$20	$45	$120	$200	$325	$575	$800	$1,750
	Auctions: $19,975, MS-67, August 2015; $400, AU-58, April 2015; $376, AU-55, September 2015; $112, VF-30, February 2015												
1899, Proof	846	207	64.3								$525	$1,100	$1,750
	Auctions: $11,163, PF-68, August 2015; $3,290, PF-66Cam, October 2015; $1,234, PF-64Cam, March 2015; $646, PF-62, July 2015												
1899-O	1,724,000	168	37.5	35%	$25	$40	$85	$170	$270	$400	$1,000	$1,700	$6,000
	Auctions: $11,750, MS-66, May 2015; $3,760, MS-65, August 2015; $2,820, AU-58, January 2015; $141, VF-30, November 2015												
1899-S	1,686,411	150	44.5	35%	$25	$40	$100	$175	$300	$450	$850	$2,100	$4,500
	Auctions: $17,625, MS-67, August 2015; $764, AU-58, January 2015; $259, EF-45, June 2015; $141, VF-25, November 2015												
1900	4,762,000	417	49.6	48%	$15	$20	$45	$130	$180	$350	$625	$850	$2,800
	Auctions: $19,975, MS-67, October 2015; $4,700, MS-66, May 2015; $376, AU-58, August 2015; $147, VF-35, December 2015												
1900, Proof	912	304	64.4								$525	$1,100	$1,750
	Auctions: $10,869, PF-68Cam, October 2015; $7,638, PF-67Cam, August 2015; $2,115, PF-65, February 2015; $940, PF-63, January 2015												
1900-O	2,744,000	148	33.5	22%	$30	$45	$100	$180	$360	$500	$1,100	$2,850	$10,000
	Auctions: $37,600, MS-67, May 2015; $30,550, MS-66, August 2015; $5,170, MS-64, January 2015; $376, AU-50, May 2015												
1900-S	2,560,322	140	41.7	21%	$17	$35	$60	$160	$240	$325	$850	$2,200	$8,500
	Auctions: $22,325, MS-67, May 2015; $14,100, MS-66, October 2015; $470, AU-58, January 2015; $353, AU-53, February 2015												
1901	4,268,000	400	48.8	38%	$15	$20	$50	$130	$180	$280	$550	$850	$3,000
	Auctions: $17,625, MS-67, August 2015; $376, AU-58, January 2015; $165, VF-30, October 2015; $123, VF-25, April 2015												
1901, Proof	813	266	64.5								$525	$1,100	$1,750
	Auctions: $32,900, PF-69Cam, August 2015; $9,106, PF-68, September 2015; $1,175, PF-64, January 2015; $881, PF-63, March 2015												
1901-O	1,124,000	110	38.4	35%	$30	$45	$125	$290	$1,250	$1,575	$2,400	$4,200	$13,500
	Auctions: $6,169, MS-64, August 2015; $1,528, AU-55, September 2015; $470, VF-35, July 2015; $317, VF-20, August 2015												
1901-S	847,044	133	20.8	11%	$42	$75	$225	$475	$1,250	$1,700	$3,600	$6,900	$12,000
	Auctions: $11,750, MS-65, August 2015; $9,694, MS-65, October 2016; $2,703, AU-55, September 2015												
1902	4,922,000	349	46.7	38%	$15	$20	$48	$130	$200	$325	$500	$850	$1,550
	Auctions: $14,100, MS-67, October 2015; $517, MS-62, February 2015; $541, AU-58, February 2015; $84, VF-25, January 2015												
1902, Proof	777	235	64.1								$525	$1,100	$1,750
	Auctions: $4,113, PF-67, March 2015; $4,230, PF-66Cam, February 2015; $2,233, PF-65, January 2015; $1,293, PF-64, January 2015												
1902-O	2,526,000	166	42.0	33%	$15	$24	$65	$130	$270	$425	$950	$2,000	$6,500
	Auctions: $16,450, MS-67, August 2015; $1,763, MS-63, October 2015; $1,528, AU-58, June 2015; $129, VF-30, April 2015												
1902-S	1,460,670	100	39.9	37%	$25	$40	$110	$240	$425	$600	$1,500	$3,000	$4,500
	Auctions: $28,200, MS-67+, August 2015; $10,575, MS-66, October 2015; $5,170, MS-65, August 2015; $5,170, MS-64, October 2015												

	Mintage	Cert	Avg	%MS	G-4	VG-8	F-12	VF-20	EF-40	AU-50	MS-60	MS-63	MS-65
											PF-60	PF-63	PF-65
1903	2,278,000	139	45.6	40%	$15	$20	$48	$125	$180	$325	$600	$1,250	$5,000
	Auctions: $12,925, MS-66, May 2015; $4,230, MS-65, June 2015; $588, AU-58, June 2015; $165, VF-30, January 2015												
1903, Proof	755	255	64.3								$525	$1,100	$1,750
	Auctions: $12,925, PF-68, May 2015; $4,348, PF-66Cam, January 2015; $2,938, PF-66, June 2015; $1,382, PF-64, February 2015												
1903-O	2,100,000	197	48.6	50%	$15	$30	$70	$150	$230	$430	$875	$1,700	$4,500
	Auctions: $9,988, MS-66, May 2015; $4,230, MS-65, August 2015; $646, AU-55, January 2015; $353, EF-45, January 2015												
1903-S	1,920,772	139	41.9	46%	$25	$35	$80	$155	$300	$600	$1,000	$1,700	$3,500
	Auctions: $17,625, MS-67, May 2015; $1,763, AU-58, July 2015; $308, EF-40, January 2015; $153, VF-25, February 2015												
1904	2,992,000	250	46.1	41%	$15	$30	$45	$130	$200	$325	$550	$850	$3,600
	Auctions: $4,465, MS-66, August 2015; $250, AU-55, May 2015; $259, EF-45, May 2015; $89, VF-25, January 2015												
1904, Proof	670	264	64.3								$525	$1,100	$1,750
	Auctions: $12,925, PF-68, October 2015; $3,878, PF-67, October 2015; $2,820, PF-66, July 2015; $2,291, PF-65, January 2015												
1904-O	1,117,600	111	37.1	23%	$30	$55	$120	$350	$550	$1,000	$1,700	$3,900	$10,300
	Auctions: $12,925, MS-66, October 2015; $2,233, MS-60, June 2015; $705, AU-55, June 2015; $881, EF-45, January 2015												
1904-S	553,038	288	17.1	7%	$65	$175	$425	$1,150	$2,100	$7,000	$14,000	$19,000	$36,000
	Auctions: $91,063, MS-67, August 2015; $28,200, MS-64, March 2016; $3,055, EF-45, July 2015; $2,820, VF-35, January 2015												
1905	662,000	147	42.7	39%	$15	$20	$100	$185	$265	$425	$725	$1,250	$4,550
	Auctions: $16,450, MS-67, October 2015; $4,583, MS-65, January 2015; $823, AU-58, July 2015; $223, EF-45, February 2015												
1905, Proof	727	216	64.1								$525	$1,100	$1,750
	Auctions: $9,106, PF-68, August 2015; $2,585, PF-66, October 2015; $2,350, PF-65, March 2015; $1,645, PF-64, January 2015												
1905-O	505,000	156	41.3	52%	$40	$60	$150	$250	$400	$550	$1,050	$1,750	$4,000
	Auctions: $56,400, MS-68, January 2015; $8,813, MS-67, October 2015; $2,233, AU-58, June 2015; $118, F-12, January 2015												
1905-S	2,494,000	152	38.0	35%	$15	$20	$48	$140	$200	$400	$725	$1,600	$7,000
	Auctions: $14,100, MS-67, August 2015; $1,410, AU-58, August 2015; $259, EF-45, April 2015; $179, VF-30, May 2015												
1906	2,638,000	400	49.4	51%	$15	$20	$60	$130	$180	$325	$500	$900	$1,800
	Auctions: $15,275, MS-67, August 2015; $2,703, MS-65, March 2015; $329, AU-53, January 2015; $188, EF-45, May 2015												
1906, Proof	675	266	64.4								$525	$1,100	$1,750
	Auctions: $10,869, PF-68, May 2015; $4,230, PF-67, October 2015; $2,938, PF-66, July 2015; $2,176, PF-65, January 2015												
1906-D	4,028,000	347	45.6	41%	$15	$20	$60	$125	$180	$325	$500	$800	$1,900
	Auctions: $47,000, MS-67, May 2015; $423, AU-58, June 2015; $223, EF-45, August 2015; $118, VF-30, February 2015												
1906-O	2,446,000	161	36.6	28%	$15	$20	$45	$100	$180	$350	$900	$1,550	$5,500
	Auctions: $18,800, MS-67, May 2015; $7,050, MS-66, October 2015; $282, EF-45, September 2015; $94, F-15, June 2015												
1906-S	1,740,154	136	46.4	45%	$15	$25	$85	$140	$210	$425	$850	$1,600	$3,500
	Auctions: $15,275, MS-67, May 2015; $940, MS-62, February 2015; $1,058, AU-55, January 2015; $212, VF-25, January 2015												
1907	2,598,000	357	51.3	59%	$15	$25	$55	$95	$180	$300	$425	$700	$2,000
	Auctions: $3,995, MS-66, January 2015; $881, MS-63, October 2015; $282, AU-53, May 2015; $165, VF-35, February 2015												
1907, Proof	575	193	64.2								$525	$1,100	$1,750
	Auctions: $18,800, PF-68, June 2014												
1907-D	3,856,000	395	45.9	42%	$15	$25	$60	$130	$180	$300	$500	$850	$1,900
	Auctions: $3,055, MS-66, October 2015; $1,116, MS-63, August 2015; $353, AU-53, April 2015; $112, VF-30, May 2015												
1907-O	3,946,600	335	45.5	48%	$15	$20	$45	$105	$180	$300	$500	$900	$1,800
	Auctions: $16,450, MS-67, August 2015; $306, AU-50, January 2015; $153, EF-40, August 2015; $212, VF-35, May 2015												
1907-S	1,250,000	128	31.8	25%	$30	$50	$100	$240	$425	$850	$2,600	$5,500	$9,000
	Auctions: $17,625, MS-67, October 2015; $2,585, AU-53, January 2015; $450, VF-35, May 2015; $165, F-15, May 2015												
1908	1,354,000	236	49.1	53%	$15	$20	$40	$85	$180	$300	$425	$750	$2,100
	Auctions: $12,925, MS-67, August 2015; $2,233, MS-65, June 2015; $1,058, MS-64, March 2015; $911, MS-63, January 2015												
1908, Proof	545	181	64.3								$525	$1,100	$1,750
	Auctions: $7,050, PF-68, October 2015; $2,115, PF-65, June 2015; $823, PF-63, September 2015; $764, PF-62, June 2015												
1908-D	3,280,000	440	43.1	37%	$15	$20	$45	$85	$180	$300	$500	$800	$2,100
	Auctions: $22,325, MS-68, October 2015; $2,350, MS-65, March 2015; $306, AU-55, January 2015; $176, EF-45, September 2015												
1908-O	5,360,000	349	42.4	42%	$15	$20	$45	$85	$180	$300	$500	$1,000	$2,000
	Auctions: $15,275, MS-67, August 2015; $793, MS-63, June 2015; $646, AU-58, January 2015; $646, AU-53, May 2015												
1908-S	1,644,828	124	32.9	33%	$15	$20	$65	$160	$400	$675	$1,050	$2,300	$4,000
	Auctions: $7,050, MS-66, August 2015; $3,819, MS-65, March 2015; $3,055, MS-64, January 2015; $2,585, AU-58, August 2015												

1909-S, Inverted Mintmark
FS-50-1909S-501.

1911-S, Repunched Mintmark
FS-50-1911S-501.

	Mintage	Cert	Avg	%MS	G-4	VG-8	F-12	VF-20	EF-40	AU-50	MS-60 PF-60	MS-63 PF-63	MS-65 PF-65
1909	2,368,000	566	45.6	46%	$15	$20	$45	$85	$180	$300	$450	$825	$1,800
	Auctions: $3,760, MS-66, May 2015; $447, AU-55, February 2015; $306, AU-53, October 2015; $165, EF-40, January 2015												
1909, Proof	650	281	64.4								$525	$1,100	$1,750
	Auctions: $11,163, PF-68Cam, May 2015; $1,880, PF-64, January 2015; $940, PF-63, October 2015; $881, PF-62, June 2015												
1909-O	925,400	204	30.5	27%	$25	$45	$90	$175	$475	$700	$1,050	$1,900	$5,400
	Auctions: $$16,450, MS-66, May 2015; $2,820, MS-64, September 2015; $705, AU-50, July 2015; $106, F-15, August 2015												
1909-S	1,764,000	210	30.7	24%	$15	$35	$45	$80	$350	$400	$650	$1,150	$3,000
	Auctions: $17,625, MS-67, May 2015; $3,525, MS-65, January 2015; $329, EF-45, January 2015; $259, EF-40, February 2015												
1909-S, Inverted Mintmark (c)	(d)	3	24.7	0%							$425	$675	$1,550
	Auctions: $11,750, MS-67, October 2015; $4,406, MS-66, November 2014; $141, VF-35, June 2015; $206, VF-30, August 2014												
1910	418,000	194	42.3	44%	$30	$40	$100	$175	$320	$410	$600	$1,100	$3,000
	Auctions: $8,225, MS-66, August 2015; $646, MS-61, September 2015; $764, AU-58, October 2015; $188, VF-25, May 2015												
1910, Proof	551	261	64.5								$525	$1,100	$1,750
	Auctions: $15,275, PF-68, October 2015; $5,875, PF-67Cam, January 2015; $1,175, PF-64, August 2015												
1910-S	1,948,000	181	32.7	26%	$15	$24	$60	$125	$240	$450	$800	$1,800	$3,000
	Auctions: $15,275, MS-67, October 2015; $376, AU-50, January 2015; $147, VF-35, October 2015; $141, VF-30, May 2015												
1911	1,406,000	370	51.2	58%	$15	$25	$45	$130	$180	$300	$500	$775	$1,850
	Auctions: $4,702, MS-66, August 2015; $494, MS-62, January 2015; $306, AU-55, January 2015; $129, VF-30, January 2015												
1911, Proof	543	239	64.5								$525	$1,100	$1,750
	Auctions: $16,450, PF-67, October 2015; $1,175, PF-64, October 2015; $588, PF-62, September 2015; $541, PF-61, June 2015												
1911-D	695,080	171	48.8	54%	$20	$35	$80	$130	$240	$325	$500	$800	$2,500
	Auctions: $15,275, MS-67, October 2015; $2,115, MS-65, September 2015; $1,704, MS-64, June 2015; $1,177, MS-64, July 2015												
1911-S	1,272,000	156	33.9	26%	$18	$20	$48	$130	$240	$480	$1,150	$1,700	$3,200
	Auctions: $42,300, MS-67, August 2015; $3,532, MS-65, August 2015; $118, VF-30, April 2015; $106, VF-25, February 2015												
1911-S, Repunched Mintmark (e)	(f)	0	n/a								$475	$750	$1,600	$5,400
	Auctions: $4,888, MS-65, December 2009												
1912	1,550,000	459	47.4	49%	$15	$25	$45	$120	$180	$300	$500	$775	$1,900
	Auctions: $15,275, MS-66, May 2015; $2,233, MS-65, January 2015; $1,116, MS-64, January 2015; $423, AU-58, September 2015												
1912, Proof	700	200	63.8								$525	$1,100	$1,750
	Auctions: $8,813, PF-68, May 2015; $4,465, PF-67, January 2015; $1,763, PF-65, October 2015; $881, PF-63, June 2015												
1912-D	2,300,800	676	47.0	47%	$20	$35	$85	$140	$200	$350	$500	$775	$2,100
	Auctions: $4,700, MS-66, October 2015; $353, AU-58, February 2015; $176, EF-40, May 2015; $94, VF-20, July 2015												
1912-S	1,370,000	281	37.0	38%	$15	$25	$45	$150	$250	$375	$750	$1,100	$3,000
	Auctions: $12,338, MS-67, August 2015; $376, AU-50, October 2015; $200, EF-40, January 2015; $129, VF-25, January 2015												
1913	188,000	591	15.5	9%	$75	$90	$210	$400	$850	$1,400	$2,100	$2,400	$4,800
	Auctions: $8,225, MS-66, October 2015; $494, VF-20, June 2015; $79, VG-8, February 2015; $59, G-6, August 2015												
1913, Proof	627	205	64.0								$600	$1,100	$1,750
	Auctions: $3,055, PF-66, October 2015; $1,293, PF-64, August 2015; $940, PF-63, June 2015; $541, PF-62, June 2015												
1913-D	534,000	301	50.0	49%	$15	$25	$60	$130	$240	$375	$625	$900	$3,500
	Auctions: $7,050, MS-66, August 2015; $282, AU-55, July 2015; $353, AU-53, April 2015; $306, FF-40, November 2015												
1913-S	604,000	203	35.8	39%	$20	$35	$90	$150	$360	$475	$975	$1,700	$4,000
	Auctions: $21,150, MS-67, October 2015; $12,925, MS-66, September 2015; $1,763, MS-64, January 2015												

c. The S mintmark was punched into the die upside-down (with the top slightly wider than the base). **d.** Included in 1909-S mintage figure. **e.** The lower serif of the underlying mintmark is visible protruding from the primary serif. **f.** Included in 1911-S mintage figure.

	Mintage	Cert	Avg	%MS	G-4	VG-8	F-12	VF-20	EF-40	AU-50	MS-60 PF-60	MS-63 PF-63	MS-65 PF-65
1914	124,230	657	17.8	14%	$110	$140	$400	$550	$1,100	$1,200	$2,000	$2,400	$6,500
	Auctions: $9,988, MS-65, January 2015; $2,585, AU-58, September 2015; $294, F-15, May 2015; $129, VG-8, February 2015												
1914, Proof	380	175	64.5								$650	$1,250	$2,500
	Auctions: $5,875, PF-67, October 2015; $4,700, PF-66, June 2015; $2,056, PF-64, October 2015; $423, PF-58, June 2015												
1914-S	992,000	235	35.9	35%	$16	$20	$45	$130	$240	$450	$725	$1,300	$3,250
	Auctions: $22,325, MS-66, February 2015; $235, EF-40, January 2015; $118, VF-25, May 2015; $79, F-15, March 2015												
1915	138,000	696	14.1	6%	$85	$150	$300	$375	$650	$1,000	$1,600	$2,850	$5,000
	Auctions: $11,750, MS-66, August 2015; $6,463, MS-66, October 2016; $4,230, MS-65, July 2016												
1915, Proof	450	180	64.5								$700	$1,250	$2,500
	Auctions: $15,275, PF-68, May 2015; $2,703, PF-66, January 2015; $3,290, PF-65, October 2015; $1,528, PF-64, August 2015												
1915-D	1,170,400	755	49.8	50%	$20	$30	$70	$130	$200	$300	$550	$850	$1,800
	Auctions: $4,465, MS-66, July 2015; $188, AU-50, February 2015; $188, EF-45, October 2015; $165, EF-40, May 2015												
1915-S	1,604,000	577	44.6	47%	$20	$30	$70	$110	$200	$300	$550	$900	$1,800
	Auctions: $8,225, MS-67, August 2015; $588, AU-58, October 2015; $112, VF-25, May 2015; $52, F-12, February 2015												

LIBERTY WALKING (1916–1947)

Designer: *Adolph A. Weinman.* **Weight:** *12.50 grams.*
Composition: *.900 silver, .100 copper (net weight .36169 oz. pure silver).*
Diameter: *30.6 mm.* **Edge:** *Reeded.* **Mints:** *Philadelphia, Denver, and San Francisco.*

Circulation Strike   Proof

Mintmark location,   Mintmark location,
1916–1917, is on the   1917–1947, is on the
obverse, below the motto.   reverse, below the branch.

History. The Liberty Walking half dollar was designed by Adolph A. Weinman, the sculptor who also created the Mercury or Winged Liberty Head dime. His monogram appears under the tips of the eagle's wing feathers. Mintage was intermittent from 1916 to 1947, with none struck in 1922, 1924, 1925, 1926, 1930, 1931, and 1932. On the 1916 coins and some of the 1917 coins, the mintmark is located on the obverse, below IN GOD WE TRUST. Other coins of 1917, and those through 1947, have the mintmark on the reverse, under the pine branch. The Mint also created a 2016 gold Liberty Walking half dollar at a smaller dimension. See page 615.

Striking and Sharpness. Most circulation-strike Liberty Walking half dollars are lightly struck. In this respect they are similar to Standing Liberty quarters of the same era. On the obverse, the key points to check are Miss Liberty's left hand, the higher parts and lines in the skirt, and her head; after that, check all other areas. *Very few* coins are sharply struck in these areas, and for some issues sharp strikes might not exist at all. On the reverse, check the breast of the eagle.

Proofs were made beginning in 1936 and continuing through 1942. The entire die was polished (including the figure of Miss Liberty and the eagle), generating coins of low contrast. Proofs are usually fairly well struck. Most Proofs of 1941 are from over-polished dies, with the AW monogram of the designer no longer present. Striking sharpness can vary. Seek coins with full head and left-hand details.

Availability. All dates and mintmarks are readily collectible, although some, such as 1917-S (obverse mintmark), 1919-D, the three issues of 1921, and 1938-D, are scarce. Earlier years are often seen with extensive wear. MS coins are most often seen of the three issues of 1916, the 1917, and those of 1933 to 1947. Collectors saved the issues of the 1940s in large quantities, making the coins common today. As noted, coins with Full Details can range from scarce to extremely rare for certain dates. Half dollars dated 1928-D are counterfeit.

Note: Values of common-date silver coins have been based on the current bullion price of silver, $27.50 per ounce, and may vary with the prevailing spot price.

Grading Standards

MS-60 to 70 (Mint State). *Obverse:* At MS-60, some abrasion and contact marks are evident on the higher areas, which are also the areas most likely to be weakly struck. This includes Miss Liberty's left arm, her hand, and the areas of the skirt covering her left leg. The luster may not be complete in those areas on weakly struck coins (even those certified above MS-65)—the *original planchet surface* may be revealed, as it was not smoothed out by strik-

1917. Graded MS-65.

ing. Accordingly, grading is best done by evaluating abrasion as it is observed *in the right field*, plus evaluating the mint luster. Luster may be dull or lifeless at MS–60 to 62, but should have deep frost at MS-63 or better, particularly in the lower-relief areas. At MS-65 or better, it should be full and rich. Sometimes, to compensate for flat striking, certified coins with virtually flawless luster in the fields, evocative of an MS–65 or 66 grade, are called MS-63 or a lower grade. Such coins would seem to offer a lot of value for the money, if the variety is one that is not found with Full Details (1923-S is one of many examples). *Reverse:* Striking is usually better, permitting observation of luster in all areas except the eagle's body, which may be lightly struck. Luster may be dull or lifeless at MS–60 to 62, but should have deep frost at MS-63 or better, particularly in the lower-relief areas. At MS-65 or better, it should be full and rich.

Illustrated coin: This is a lustrous gem example.

AU-50, 53, 55, 58 (About Uncirculated). *Obverse:* Light wear is seen on the higher-relief areas of Miss Liberty, the vertical area from her head down to the date. At AU-58, the luster in the field is extensive, but is interrupted by friction and light wear. At AU–50 and 53, luster is less. *Reverse:* Wear is most evident on the eagle's breast immediately under the neck feathers, the left leg, and the top of the left wing. Luster is nearly complete at AU-58, but at AU-50 half or more is gone.

1921. Graded AU-50.

EF-40, 45 (Extremely Fine). *Obverse:* Wear is more extensive, with the higher parts of Miss Liberty now without detail, and with no skirt lines visible directly over her left leg. Little or no luster is seen. *Reverse:* The eagle shows more wear overall, with the highest parts of the body and left leg worn flat.

1919. Graded EF-40.

VF-20, 30 (Very Fine). *Obverse:* Wear is more extensive, and Miss Liberty is worn mostly flat in the line from her head to her left foot. Her skirt is worn, but most lines are seen, except over the leg and to the left and right. The lower part of her cape (to the left of her waist) is worn. *Reverse:* The eagle is worn smooth from the head to the left leg, and the right leg is flat at the top. Most feathers in the wings are delineated, but weak.

1921-S. Graded VF-20.

F-12, 15 (Fine). *Obverse:* Wear is more extensive, now with only a few light lines visible in the skirt. The rays of the sun are weak below the cape, and may be worn away at their tips. *Reverse:* Wear is more extensive, with most details now gone on the eagle's right leg. Delineation of the feathers is less, and most in the upper area and right edge of the left wing are blended together.

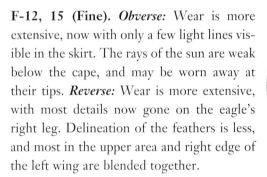

1918-S. Graded F-12.

VG-8, 10 (Very Good). *Obverse:* Wear is slightly more extensive, but the rim still is defined all around. The tops of the date numerals are worn and blend slightly into the ground above. *Reverse:* Wear is more extensive. On the left wing only a few feathers are delineated, and on the shoulder of the right wing most detail is gone. Detail in the pine branch is lost and it appears as a clump.

1921-D. Graded VG-8.

G-4, 6 (Good). *Obverse:* Miss Liberty is worn flat, with her head, neck, and arms all blended together. Folds can be seen at the bottom of the skirt, and nearly all gown lines are visible. The rim is worn done into the tops of some of the letters. *Reverse:* All areas show more wear. The rim is worn down into the tops of some of the letters, particularly at the top border.

1917-S, Obverse Mintmark. Graded G-4.

AG-3 (About Good). *Obverse:* Wear is more extensive. The sun's rays are nearly all gone, the motto is very light and sometimes incomplete, and the rim is worn down into more of the letters. *Reverse:* Wear is more extensive, with the eagle essentially worn flat. The rim is worn down into more of the letters.

1918. Graded AG-3.

PF-60 to 70 (Proof). *Obverse and Reverse:* Proofs that are extensively cleaned and have many hairlines, or that are dull and grainy, are lower level, such as PF–60 to 62. These are not widely desired, and represent coins that have been mistreated. With medium hairlines and good reflectivity, assigned grades of PF–63 or 64 are appropriate. Tiny horizontal lines on Miss Liberty's leg, known as slide marks, from National and other album slides scuffing the relief of the cheek, are common; coins with such marks should not be graded higher than PF-64, but sometimes are. With relatively few hairlines and no noticeable slide marks, a rating of PF-65 can be given. PF-66 should have hairlines so delicate that magnification is needed to see them. Above that, a Proof should be free of any hairlines or other problems.

1939. Graded PF-65.

Illustrated coin: This example is a brilliant gem Proof.

	Mintage	Cert	Avg	%MS	G-4	VG-8	F-12	VF-20	EF-40	AU-50	MS-60 PF-64	MS-63 PF-65	MS-65 PF-67
1916	608,000	1,729	50.2	63%	$50	$55	$90	$175	$250	$265	$450	$750	$2,000
	Auctions: $35,250, MS-67, August 2015; $588, MS-61, August 2015; $329, AU-55, May 2015; $118, F-15, February 2015												
1916-D, Obverse Mintmark	1,014,400	2,004	49.8	59%	$50	$60	$85	$135	$215	$240	$450	$725	$2,000
	Auctions: $4,935, MS-66, August 2015; $400, AU-58, October 2015; $200, EF-45, February 2015; $141, VF-25, February 2015												
1916-S, Obverse Mintmark	508,000	1,297	31.1	34%	$100	$140	$250	$450	$650	$950	$1,600	$2,500	$6,000
	Auctions: $9,988, MS-65, June 2015; $1,821, AU-58, August 2015; $411, VF-25, January 2015; $160, VG-10, December 2015												

	Mintage	Cert	Avg	%MS	G-4	VG-8	F-12	VF-20	EF-40	AU-50	MS-60 PF-64	MS-63 PF-65	MS-65 PF-67
1917	12,292,000	2,459	61.1	80%	$18	$19	$19.50	$21	$40	$70	$150	$210	$950
Auctions: $2,233, MS-66, June 2015; $353, MS-64, August 2015; $118, MS-61, April 2015; $94, AU-58, February 2015													
1917-D, Obverse Mintmark	765,400	1,082	50.8	54%	$25	$35	$80	$150	$240	$325	$800	$1,150	$7,000
Auctions: $32,900, MS-66, August 2015; $5,640, MS-65, September 2015; $705, AU-58, February 2015; $282, EF-45, April 2015													
1917-S, Obverse Mintmark	952,000	636	41.1	38%	$27	$50	$140	$375	$750	$1,300	$3,250	$5,500	$25,000
Auctions: $152,750, MS-67, August 2015; $21,150, MS-65, August 2015; $376, VF-35, February 2015; $112, F-12, January 2015													
1917-D, Reverse Mintmark	1,940,000	648	51.9	46%	$18	$19	$45	$145	$280	$515	$1,200	$2,200	$12,500
Auctions: $28,200, MS-66, August 2015; $1,410, AU-58, February 2015; $470, AU-53, November 2015; $141, VF-30, June 2015													
1917-S, Reverse Mintmark	5,554,000	941	55.9	62%	$18	$19	$20	$35	$70	$170	$700	$1,800	$12,500
Auctions: $37,600, MS-66, August 2015; $10,869, MS-65, January 2015; $541, AU-58, October 2015; $212, EF-45, February 2015													
1918	6,634,000	871	57.3	64%	$18	$19	$20	$65	$155	$265	$625	$1,100	$4,000
Auctions: $32,900, MS-66, August 2015; $4,230, MS-65, June 2015; $306, AU-55, May 2015; $84, VF-35, August 2015													
1918-D	3,853,040	842	51.8	53%	$18	$19	$38	$100	$250	$475	$1,500	$2,500	$25,000
Auctions: $99,875, MS-66, August 2015; $35,250, MS-65, August 2015; $84, VF-30, January 2015; $40, F-15, September 2015													
1918-S	10,282,000	1,016	55.2	60%	$18	$19	$20	$35	$80	$200	$600	$1,650	$15,000
Auctions: $18,800, MS-65, August 2015; $4,700, MS-64, March 2015; $376, AU-55, May 2015; $123, EF-45, January 2015													
1919	962,000	648	41.1	37%	$25	$32	$78	$265	$515	$950	$2,350	$3,500	$8,500
Auctions: $54,050, MS-67, August 2015; $32,900, MS-66, May 2015; $4,113, MS-64, January 2015; $1,116, AU-53, October 2015													
1919-D	1,165,000	721	37.1	33%	$26	$40	$115	$345	$825	$2,000	$4,750	$10,000	$225,000
Auctions: $32,900, MS-64, August 2016; $30,550, MS-64, August 2015; $5,170, MS-62, November 2016; $1,939, AU-50, July 2015													
1919-S	1,552,000	565	36.7	25%	$20	$30	$85	$275	$815	$1,750	$4,000	$8,750	$22,500
Auctions: $44,650, MS-66, August 2016; $42,300, MS-66, August 2015; $11,750, MS-64, January 2015; $2,233, AU-50, June 2015													
1920	6,372,000	919	58.9	72%	$18	$19	$20	$45	$80	$160	$425	$700	$3,500
Auctions: $7,050, MS-66, January 2015; $564, MS-63, August 2015; $329, AU-58, April 2015; $123, EF-45, August 2015													
1920-D	1,551,000	432	40.4	38%	$18	$20	$75	$250	$450	$925	$3,000	$5,500	$16,500
Auctions: $54,050, MS-66, August 2015; $2,585, AU-58, June 2015; $823, EF-45, June 2015; $235, VF-25, March 2015													
1920-S	4,624,000	562	50.0	49%	$18	$18.50	$23	$90	$230	$600	$1,200	$3,250	$15,000
Auctions: $58,750, MS-66, August 2015; $999, AU-58, January 2015; $376, EF-45, August 2015; $141, VF-35, April 2015													
1921	246,000	1,582	17.3	12%	$135	$200	$325	$775	$2,000	$2,900	$6,000	$8,000	$22,500
Auctions: $54,050, MS-66, August 2015; $10,575, MS-64, January 2015; $1,410, VF-35, August 2015; $176, VG-8, January 2015													
1921-D	208,000	1,929	15.5	10%	$200	$350	$550	$850	$2,850	$5,500	$9,250	$12,500	$40,000
Auctions: $94,000, MS-66, August 2015; $37,600, MS-65, August 2016; $3,290, EF-40, March 2015; $1,175, VF-20, January 2015													
1921-S	548,000	1,528	17.7	7%	$48	$80	$250	$800	$4,500	$8,000	$20,000	$32,000	$110,000
Auctions: $117,500, MS-65, August 2015; $70,500, MS-64, August 2016; $8,813, AU-53, March 2015; $3,055, EF-40, January 2015													
1923-S	2,178,000	509	47.5	44%	$13	$15	$30	$110	$365	$1,400	$2,750	$4,250	$15,000
Auctions: $25,850, MS-66, August 2015; $2,233, MS-62, September 2015; $1,645, AU-55, February 2015; $376, EF-40, September 2015													
1927-S	2,392,000	674	55.0	65%	$13	$15	$18	$50	$160	$450	$1,200	$2,500	$10,000
Auctions: $44,650, MS-66, August 2015; $969, AU-55, August 2015; $707, AU-53, June 2015; $259, EF-45, October 2015													
1928-S (a,b)	1,940,000	566	51.0	54%	$13	$15	$19	$75	$180	$500	$1,250	$3,000	$6,500
Auctions: $25,850, MS-66, August 2015; $8,813, MS-65, September 2015; $1,410, AU-58, June 2015; $940, AU-55, January 2015													
1929-D	1,001,200	978	56.9	57%	$12	$15	$18	$30	$100	$190	$450	$825	$2,000
Auctions: $5,405, MS-66, May 2015; $646, MS-63, August 2015; $282, AU-55, January 2015; $118, EF-45, August 2015													
1929-S	1,902,000	956	56.5	65%	$12	$15	$18	$35	$115	$230	$500	$1,150	$2,500
Auctions: $3,290, MS-66, January 2015; $1,293, MS-64, October 2015; $400, AU-58, September 2015; $106, EF-45, May 2015													
1933-S	1,786,000	1,139	56.1	53%	$12	$15	$18	$20	$60	$240	$750	$1,350	$3,250
Auctions: $25,850, MS-67, June 2015; $1,410, MS-63, September 2015; $705, AU-58, January 2015; $282, AU-55, May 2015													
1934	6,964,000	2,735	63.3	90%	$10	$11	$12	$15	$19	$26	$75	$100	$275
Auctions: $5,405, MS-67, August 2015; $118, MS-64, October 2015; $94, MS-63, August 2015; $79, MS-61, March 2015													
1934-D (a)	2,361,000	1,495	62.2	86%	$10	$11	$12	$15	$35	$85	$140	$250	$900
Auctions: $3,819, MS-66, August 2015; $306, MS-64, June 2015; $223, MS-63, September 2015; $141, AU-50, October 2015													
1934-S	3,652,000	972	59.6	66%	$10	$11	$12	$15	$30	$90	$365	$750	$2,000
Auctions: $30,550, MS-67, August 2015; $2,585, MS-65, July 2015; $1,001, MS-64, January 2015; $79, AU-53, January 2015													

a. Large and small mintmark varieties exist. **b.** Half dollars dated 1928-D are counterfeit.

1936, Doubled Die Obverse
FS-50-1936-101.

	Mintage	Cert	Avg	%MS	G-4	VG-8	F-12	VF-20	EF-40	AU-50	MS-60 / PF-64	MS-63 / PF-65	MS-65 / PF-67
1935	9,162,000	2,726	63.3	91%	$10	$11	$12	$15	$19	$25	$40	$70	$225
	Auctions: $11,750, MS-68, October 2015; $4,935, MS-67, August 2015; $200, MS-65, August 2015; $89, MS-64, February 2015												
1935-D	3,003,800	1,104	62.1	85%	$10	$11	$12	$15	$30	$65	$140	$300	$1,250
	Auctions: $8,225, MS-66, May 2015; $1,821, MS-65, August 2015; $259, MS-62, January 2015; $100, MS-60, November 2015												
1935-S	3,854,000	967	61.1	80%	$10	$11	$12	$15	$26	$95	$275	$465	$1,500
	Auctions: $5,640, MS-66, January 2015; $1,293, MS-64, October 2015; $564, MS-63, August 2015; $259, AU-58, March 2015												
1936	12,614,000	3,792	63.8	93%	$10	$11	$12	$15	$18	$25	$45	$75	$175
	Auctions: $1,528, MS-67, June 2015; $306, MS-66, September 2015; $212, MS-65, January 2015; $89, MS-64, August 2015												
1936, DblDie Obv (c)	(d)	0	n/a		$500	$600							
	Auctions: $235, MS-65, January 2015; $940, MS-65, December 2013												
1936, Proof	3,901	1,381	64.7								$1,850	$2,750	$9,000
	Auctions: $14,689, PF-67, June 2015; $4,348, PF-66, July 2015; $2,820, PF-65, January 2015; $2,820, PF-64, October 2016												
1936-D	4,252,400	1,849	63.2	92%	$10	$11	$12	$15	$20	$50	$85	$120	$350
	Auctions: $4,935, MS-67, August 2015; $2,585, MS-66, February 2015; $212, MS-64, September 2015; $79, MS-63, June 2015												
1936-S	3,884,000	1,411	62.9	92%	$10	$11	$12	$15	$22	$60	$130	$200	$600
	Auctions: $19,975, MS-67, August 2015; $881, MS-65, January 2015; $329, MS-64, May 2015; $217, MS-63, September 2015												
1937	9,522,000	3,372	63.6	92%	$10	$11	$12	$15	$18	$25	$40	$70	$150
	Auctions: $1,528, MS-67, June 2015; $270, MS-66, July 2015; $259, MS-65, January 2015; $84, MS-64, August 2015												
1937, Proof	5,728	1,590	65.2								$650	$850	$1,800
	Auctions: $5,640, PF-68, January 2015; $2,115, PF-67, August 2015; $564, PF-64, January 2015; $470, PF-63, October 2015												
1937-D	1,676,000	1,262	62.6	87%	$10	$11	$12	$18	$32	$100	$215	$265	$600
	Auctions: $5,170, MS-67, August 2015; $482, MS-65, October 2015; $235, MS-63, January 2015; $153, AU-58, January 2015												
1937-S	2,090,000	1,319	63.3	92%	$10	$11	$12	$15	$25	$60	$165	$210	$500
	Auctions: $8,813, MS-67, August 2015; $353, MS-65, October 2015; $247, MS-64, February 2015; $129, MS-62, July 2015												
1938	4,110,000	2,449	63.2	91%	$10	$11	$12	$15	$20	$45	$70	$160	$250
	Auctions: $2,585, MS-67, January 2015; $212, MS-65, September 2015; $123, MS-63, May 2015; $46, AU-55, May 2015												
1938, Proof	8,152	1,913	65.4								$500	$675	$1,500
	Auctions: $14,100, PF-68, January 2015; $764, PF-66, August 2015; $734, PF-65, June 2015; $430, PF-64, October 2015												
1938-D	491,600	3,311	40.3	36%	$10	$11	$12	$15	$20	$45	$70	$160	$1,000
	Auctions: $5,640, MS-67, June 2015; $1,110, MS-65, July 2015; $400, AU-58, February 2015; $176, EF-45, January 2015												
1939	6,812,000	3,896	64.1	93%	$10	$11	$12	$15	$18	$26	$40	$65	$155
	Auctions: $8,225, MS-68, August 2015; $194, MS-66, September 2015; $118, MS-65, January 2015; $84, MS-64, September 2015												
1939, Proof	8,808	2,056	65.6								$450	$600	$1,200
	Auctions: $4,935, PF-68, August 2015; $570, PF-66, March 2015; $646, PF-65, February 2015; $388, PF-64, July 2015												
1939-D	4,267,800	3,148	64.1	95%	$10	$11	$12	$15	$18	$25	$43	$75	$145
	Auctions: $4,700, MS-67, January 2015; $270, MS-66, October 2015; $165, MS-65, August 2015; $94, MS-64, February 2015												
1939-S	2,552,000	2,082	64.1	94%	$10	$11	$12	$15	$26	$70	$125	$150	$200
	Auctions: $12,925, MS-68, September 2015; $564, MS-66, October 2015; $153, MS-64, April 2015; $74, AU-58, June 2015												
1940	9,156,000	4,636	64.1	95%	$10	$11	$12	$15	$18	$22	$35	$55	$120
	Auctions: $7,050, MS-68, August 2015; $294, MS-66, January 2015; $89, MS-65, September 2015; $94, MS-64, April 2015												
1940, Proof	11,279	2,422	65.4								$450	$500	$1,000
	Auctions: $3,290, PF-68, January 2015; $517, PF-66, June 2015; $423, PF-65, October 2015; $376, PF-64, February 2015												
1940-S	4,550,000	3,221	63.7	97%	$10	$11	$12	$15	$18	$35	$45	$80	$280
	Auctions: $27,025, MS-67, June 2015; $823, MS-66, October 2015; $235, MS-65, August 2015; $112, MS-64, February 2015												

c. No examples have yet been discovered grading better than Fine. "Extremely strong doubling is evident on the date. Less doubling is evident on IN GOD WE TRUST, the skirt, and some other elements" (*Cherrypickers' Guide to Rare Die Varieties*, sixth edition, volume II). Several varieties exist; this one is FS-50-1936-101. **d.** Included in circulation-strike 1936 mintage figure.

1945, Missing Designer's Initials
FS-50-1945-901.

	Mintage	Cert	Avg	%MS	G-4	VG-8	F-12	VF-20	EF-40	AU-50	MS-60 / PF-64	MS-63 / PF-65	MS-65 / PF-67
1941	24,192,000	12,420	64.1	94%	$10	$11	$12	$15	$18	$22	$35	$55	$100
Auctions: $2,938, MS-68, January 2015; $588, MS-67, August 2015; $79, MS-65, February 2015; $46, MS-64, October 2015													
1941, Proof (e)	15,412	3,333	65.3								$450	$500	$950
Auctions: $7,050, PF-68, August 2015; $646, PF-67, October 2015; $400, PF-65, September 2015; $400, PF-64, February 2015													
1941-D	11,248,400	6,535	64.2	95%	$10	$11	$12	$15	$18	$22	$38	$65	$125
Auctions: $881, MS-67, January 2015; $176, MS-66, November 2015; $118, MS-65, July 2015; $67, MS-64, May 2015													
1941-S	8,098,000	6,138	63.1	90%	$10	$11	$12	$15	$18	$26	$75	$120	$500
Auctions: $35,250, MS-67, August 2015; $1,293, MS-66, January 2015; $141, MS-64, April 2015; $64, MS-61, June 2015													
1942	47,818,000	18,544	63.7	92%	$10	$11	$12	$15	$18	$22	$40	$60	$100
Auctions: $3,290, MS-67+, February 2015; $129, MS-66, July 2015; $84, MS-65, August 2015; $46, MS-64, October 2015													
1942, Proof	21,120	4,573	65.6								$450	$500	$750
Auctions: $4,465, PF-68, June 2015; $1,528, PF-67+, August 2015; $400, PF-65, October 2015; $470, PF-64, January 2015													
1942-D	10,973,800	4,772	64.1	95%	$10	$11	$12	$15	$18	$20	$40	$80	$175
Auctions: $834, MS-67, June 2015; $212, MS-66, January 2015; $165, MS-65, October 2015; $84, MS-64, February 2015													
1942-S (a)	12,708,000	4,783	63.6	95%	$10	$11	$12	$15	$18	$22	$40	$80	$275
Auctions: $1,116, MS-66, February 2015; $306, MS-65, January 2015; $94, MS-64, November 2015; $118, MS-63, February 2015													
1943	53,190,000	19,021	63.7	92%	$10	$11	$12	$15	$18	$20	$35	$50	$100
Auctions: $21,150, MS-68, August 2015; $1,293, MS-67+, January 2015; $74, MS-64+, April 2015; $40, MS-63, February 2015													
1943-D	11,346,000	5,475	64.5	96%	$10	$11	$12	$15	$18	$24	$48	$75	$175
Auctions: $4,935, MS-68, June 2015; $646, MS-67, February 2015; $94, MS-64, August 2015; $40, MS-62, October 2015													
1943-S	13,450,000	5,589	63.8	96%	$10	$11	$12	$15	$18	$25	$42	$60	$200
Auctions: $6,463, MS-67, August 2015; $4,465, MS-66+, February 2015; $200, MS-65, August 2015; $69, MS-64, May 2015													
1944	28,206,000	11,244	63.7	94%	$10	$11	$12	$15	$18	$20	$35	$50	$100
Auctions: $3,525, MS-67, August 2015; $76, MS-65, March 2015; $56, MS-64, October 2015; $32, MS-60, March 2015													
1944-D	9,769,000	6,747	64.5	97%	$10	$11	$12	$15	$18	$20	$40	$60	$100
Auctions: $1,528, MS-67+, September 2015; $183, MS-66, January 2015; $118, MS-65, March 2015; $89, MS-64, February 2015													
1944-S	8,904,000	6,532	63.8	98%	$10	$11	$12	$15	$18	$24	$40	$63	$250
Auctions: $3,290, MS-66+, June 2015; $376, MS-65, July 2015; $84, MS-64, February 2015; $44, MS-62, October 2015													
1945	31,502,000	15,375	63.8	95%	$10	$11	$12	$15	$18	$20	$35	$50	$100
Auctions: $1,645, MS-67, July 2015; $89, MS-65, October 2015; $94, MS-64, August 2015; $44, MS-63, February 2015													
1945, Missing Initials	(f)	44	57.4	68%							$100	$150	$250
Auctions: $705, MS-64, January 2014													
1945-D	9,966,800	9,820	64.7	98%	$10	$11	$12	$15	$18	$20	$35	$60	$120
Auctions: $14,100, MS-68, August 2015; $4,465, MS-67+, August 2015; $94, MS-65, May 2015; $64, MS-64, February 2015													
1945-S	10,156,000	8,133	64.2	98%	$10	$11	$12	$15	$18	$24	$38	$55	$120
Auctions: $6,463, MS-67, January 2015; $212, MS-66, August 2015; $106, MS-65, April 2015; $74, MS-64, February 2015													

a. Large and small mintmark varieties exist. **e.** The variety without the designer's initials was created by the over-polishing of dies. **f.** Included in 1945 mintage figure.

1946, Doubled Die Reverse
FS-50-1946-801.

	Mintage	Cert	Avg	%MS	G-4	VG-8	F-12	VF-20	EF-40	AU-50	MS-60 PF-64	MS-63 PF-65	MS-65 PF-67
1946	12,118,000	8,096	63.5	94%	$10	$11	$12	$15	$18	$20	$37	$50	$100
	Auctions: $3,525, MS-67, August 2015; $176, MS-66, April 2015; $112, MS-65, April 2015; $94, MS-64, September 2015												
1946, DblDie Rev (g)	(h)	224	51.5	35%	$20	$24	$28	$40	$65	$125	$275	$550	$2,000
	Auctions: $2,233, MS-64, January 2015; $188, AU-58, April 2015; $84, EF-45, August 2015; $79, F-15, April 2015												
1946-D	2,151,000	14,280	64.8	100%	$10	$11	$12	$15	$22	$32	$47	$60	$105
	Auctions: $3,760, MS-67, August 2015; $141, MS-66, January 2015; $60, MS-64, October 2015; $42, MS-62, October 2015												
1946-S	3,724,000	9,383	64.6	99%	$10	$11	$12	$15	$18	$25	$43	$58	$100
	Auctions: $8,225, MS-67, October 2015; $217, MS-66, February 2015; $100, MS-65, July 2015; $89, MS-64, May 2015												
1947	4,094,000	8,171	64.2	97%	$10	$11	$12	$15	$18	$25	$48	$60	$110
	Auctions: $9,400, MS-67, February 2015; $188, MS-66, November 2015; $123, MS-65, July 2015; $64, MS-64, October 2015												
1947-D	3,900,600	9,161	64.5	99%	$10	$11	$12	$15	$18	$30	$45	$60	$105
	Auctions: $5,640, MS-67, August 2015; $182, MS-66, April 2015; $129, MS-65, September 2015; $69, MS-64, July 2015												

g. Very strong doubling is visible on E PLURIBUS UNUM, the eagle's wing feathers and left wing, and the branch. **h.** Included in 1946 mintage figure.

FRANKLIN (1948–1963)

Designer: *John R. Sinnock.* **Weight:** *12.50 grams.*
Composition: *.900 silver, .100 copper (net weight .36169 oz. pure silver).*
Diameter: *30.6 mm.* **Edge:** *Reeded.* **Mints:** *Philadelphia, Denver, and San Francisco.*

Mintmark
location is
on the reverse,
above the beam.

Circulation Strike | Proof

History. U.S. Mint chief engraver John R. Sinnock developed a motif for a silver half dime in 1942; it was proposed but never adopted for regular coinage. In 1948, the year after Sinnock died, his Franklin half dollar was introduced, its design an adaptation of his earlier half dime motif. The Liberty Bell is similar to that used by Sinnock on the 1926 Sesquicentennial commemorative half dollar modeled from a sketch by John Frederick Lewis. The designs were finished by Sinnock's successor, chief engraver Gilroy Roberts. The coin-collecting community paid little attention to the Franklin half dollar at the time, but today the coins are widely collected.

Striking and Sharpness. Given the indistinct details of the obverse, sharpness of strike usually is ignored. On the reverse, if the bottom lines of the Liberty Bell are complete the coin may be designated as Full Bell Lines (FBL). Virtually all Proofs are well struck.

Availability. All dates and mintmarks are easily available in grades from VF upward. Lower-level MS coins can be unattractive due to contact marks and abrasion, particularly noticeable on the obverse.

High-quality gems are generally inexpensive, although varieties that are rare with FBL can be costly amid much competition in the marketplace. Most collectors seek MS coins. Grades below EF are not widely desired. Proofs were made from 1950 to 1963 and are available today in proportion to their mintages. Those with cameo-frosted devices are in the minority and often sell for strong premiums.

Note: Values of common-date silver coins have been based on the current bullion price of silver, $27.50 per ounce, and may vary with the prevailing spot price.

GRADING STANDARDS

MS-60 to 70 (Mint State). *Obverse:* At MS-60, some abrasion and contact marks are evident on the cheek, on the hair left of the ear, and the neck. At MS-63, abrasion is slight at best, less so for MS-64. An MS-65 coin should display no abrasion or contact marks except under magnification, and MS-66 and higher coins should have none at all. Luster should be full and rich. As details are shallow on this design, the amount and "depth" of luster is important to grading.

1951-S. Graded MS-65.

Reverse: General comments apply as for the obverse. The points to check are the bell harness, the words PASS AND STOW on the upper area of the Liberty Bell, and the bottom of the bell.

Illustrated coin: Satiny brilliance is seen on the obverse of this coin, light golden toning on the reverse.

AU-50, 53, 55, 58 (About Uncirculated). *Obverse:* At AU-50, medium wear is evident on the portrait, and most of the luster in the field is gone. At AU-53, wear is less and luster is more extensive. AU–55 and 58 coins show much luster. Wear is noticeable on the portrait and, to a lesser extent, in the field. *Reverse:* At AU-50, medium wear is evident on most of the Liberty Bell, and most of the luster in the field is gone. At AU-53, wear is

1949-D. Graded AU-50.

slightly less. AU–55 and 58 coins show much luster. Light wear is seen on the higher areas of the bell.

EF-40, 45 (Extremely Fine). *Obverse:* Wear is more extensive, and some hair detail (never strong to begin with) is lost. There is no luster. *Reverse:* Wear is seen overall. The inscription on the bell is weak, and the highest parts of the bottom horizontal lines are worn away. There is no luster.

The Franklin half dollar is seldom collected in grades lower than EF-40.

1955. Graded EF-40.

PF-60 to 70 (Proof). *Obverse and Reverse:* Proofs that are extensively cleaned and have many hairlines, or that are dull and grainy, are lower level, such as PF–60 to 62. These are not widely desired, and represent coins that have been mistreated. Fortunately, only a few Proof Franklin half dollars are in this category. With medium hairlines and good reflectivity, assigned grades of PF–63 or 64 are appropriate. PF-66 should have hairlines

1950. Graded PF-65 Cameo.

so delicate that magnification is needed to see them. Above that, a Proof should be free of any hairlines or other problems.

Full Bell Lines

1948, Doubled Die Reverse
FS-50-1948-801.

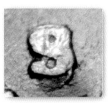

1949-S, Repunched Mintmark
FS-50-1949S-501.

	Mintage	Cert	Avg	%MS	VF-20	EF-40	MS-60	MS-63	MS-64	MS-65	MS-65FBL PF-64	MS-66 PF-65	MS-66FBL PF-65DC
1948	3,006,814	5,399	64.0	97%	$10	$11	$20	$27	$35	$70	$175	$265	$450
	Auctions: $3,760, MS-67FBL, September 2015; $1,410, MS-66FBL+, June 2015; $84, MS-65FBL, August 2015; $46, MS-64FBL, August 2015												
1948, Doubled Die Reverse (a)	(b)	35	63.8	100%				$75	$125	$190	$285	$235	
	Auctions: No auction records available.												
1948-D	4,028,600	5,291	64.0	98%	$10	$11	$20	$24	$30	$135	$175	$475	$750
	Auctions: $19,975, MS-67FBL, January 2015; $12,925, MS-67FBL, July 2015; $135, MS-65FBL, February 2015; $74, MS-64, January 2015												
1949	5,614,000	3,432	63.1	89%	$12	$18	$40	$75	$85	$130	$175	$315	$550
	Auctions: $1,469, MS-66FBL+, September 2015; $212, MS-65FBL, November 2015; $188, MS-65FBL, July 2015; $62, MS-64FBL, January 2015												
1949-D	4,120,600	3,428	63.2	95%	$12	$18	$45	$75	$90	$325	$500	$1,100	$1,000
	Auctions: $1,116, MS-66, July 2016; $1,058, MS-66, August 2016; $1,058, MS-66, September 2016; $5,640, MS-66, October 2016												
1949-S	3,744,000	4,062	63.9	95%	$12	$20	$65	$95	$115	$165	$450	$265	$750
	Auctions: $6,463, MS-67FBL, June 2015; $259, MS-66, September 2015; $200, MS-65FBL, May 2015; $74, MS-64, January 2015												
1949-S, Doubled Mintmark (c)	(d)	10	61.0	70%				$120	$170	$280	$350	$575	
	Auctions: $223, MS-65, January 2014												
1950	7,742,123	2,958	63.5	92%	$10	$11	$30	$35	$55	$100	$195	$275	$525
	Auctions: $18,213, MS-67FBL, August 2015; $1,528, MS-66FBL, January 2015; $259, MS-65, February 2015; $56, MS-64FBL, November 2015												
1950, Proof	51,386	4,497	64.9								$425	$750	$15,000
	Auctions: $4,230, PF-67, January 2015; $7,638, PF-66Cam, October 2015; $1,645, PF-65Cam, July 2015; $376, PF-64, June 2015												
1950-D	8,031,600	3,150	63.4	95%	$10	$11	$26	$40	$70	$200	$375	$850	$1,350
	Auctions: $2,585, MS-66FBL, January 2015; $1,058, MS-66FBL, June 2015; $235, MS-65FBL, May 2015; $46, MS-64FBL, August 2015												

a. Doubling is visible on E PLURIBUS UNUM, UNITED, HALF DOLLAR, the dots, and the Liberty Bell's clapper. "There are several similar, yet lesser, DDRs for this date" (*Cherrypickers' Guide to Rare Die Varieties,* sixth edition, volume II). The variety listed and pictured is FS-50-1948-801. **b.** Included in 1948 mintage figure. **c.** The secondary mintmark is visible south of the primary. CONECA lists two other repunched mintmarks for this date; the one illustrated and listed here is FS-50-1949S-501. **d.** Included in 1949-S mintage figure.

1951-S, Doubled Die Reverse
FS-50-1951S-801.

1955, Clashed Obverse Die "Bugs Bunny" variety
FS-50-1955-401.

	Mintage	Cert	Avg	%MS	VF-20	EF-40	MS-60	MS-63	MS-64	MS-65	MS-65FBL / PF-64	MS-66 / PF-65	MS-66FBL / PF-65DC
1951	16,802,102	3,435	63.8	95%	$10	$11	$14	$24	$35	$75	$200	$240	$550
	Auctions: $1,410, MS-66FBL, July 2015; $200, MS-66, July 2015; $235, MS-65FBL, September 2015; $44, MS-65, January 2015
1951, Proof	57,500	4,598	65.0								$300	$550	$3,500
	Auctions: $4,465, PF-68, June 2015; $3,290, PF-67Cam, February 2015; $494, PF-65Cam, July 2015; $259, PF-64, March 2015
1951-D	9,475,200	2,567	63.5	96%	$10	$11	$30	$45	$70	$140	$250	$500	$700
	Auctions: $764, MS-66FBL, January 2015; $141, MS-65FBL, July 2015; $84, MS-64FBL, April 2015; $28, MS-63FBL, July 2015
1951-S	13,696,000	3,688	64.0	97%	$10	$11	$25	$35	$45	$75	$450	$185	$1,200
	Auctions: $1,645, MS-67, October 2015; $588, MS-66FBL, July 2015; $176, MS-64FBL, January 2015; $46, MS-63, May 2015
1951-S, DblDie Rev (e)	(f)	11	64.5	100%			$80	$110	$250	$400	$500		
	Auctions: $188, MS-65, January 2014
1952	21,192,093	3,413	63.8	96%	$10	$11	$14	$23	$35	$75	$150	$185	$335
	Auctions: $4,935, MS-67FBL, July 2015; $200, MS-66FBL, February 2015; $94, MS-65FBL, February 2015; $48, MS-64FBL, November 2015
1952, Proof	81,980	5,523	65.5								$190	$275	$5,500
	Auctions: $3,821, PF-67Cam, August 2015; $8,813, PF-66DCam, June 2015; $260, PF-66, October 2015; $118, PF-64, January 2015
1952-D	25,395,600	3,359	63.6	97%	$10	$11	$14	$23	$32	$115	$250	$550	$700
	Auctions: $564, MS-66FBL, January 2015; $176, MS-65FBL, September 2015; $129, MS-65FBL, February 2015; $40, MS-64FBL, February 2015
1952-S	5,526,000	3,279	64.4	99%	$12	$17	$50	$70	$80	$110	$725	$175	$1,750
	Auctions: $21,150, MS-67FBL, February 2015; $1,645, MS-67, January 2015; $129, MS-66, July 2015; $423, MS-64FBL, January 2015
1953	2,668,120	2,937	64.0	98%	$10	$11	$14	$27	$40	$110	$750	$325	$1,800
	Auctions: $2,233, MS-66FBL, January 2015; $306, MS-66, March 2015; $646, MS-65FBL, October 2015; $129, MS-64FBL, May 2015
1953, Proof	128,800	7,351	65.6								$125	$190	$1,400
	Auctions: $4,230, PF-68Cam, August 2015; $2,585, PF-66DCam, January 2015; $165, PF-66, February 2015; $84, PF-64, May 2015
1953-D	20,900,400	4,722	63.8	98%	$10	$11	$14	$23	$38	$105	$145	$500	$450
	Auctions: $494, MS-66FBL, February 2015; $112, MS-65FBL, February 2015; $74, MS-65, May 2015; $56, MS-64FBL, October 2015
1953-S	4,148,000	6,458	64.7	99%	$10	$11	$25	$35	$48	$75	$20,000	$275	$55,000
	Auctions: $2,233, MS-67, January 2015; $447, MS-66, June 2015; $21,150, MS-65FBL, September 2015; $100, MS-65, September 2015
1954	13,188,202	6,210	64.1	99%	$10	$11	$14	$20	$30	$45	$150	$300	$550
	Auctions: $1,880, MS-66FBL, July 2015; $823, MS-66FBL, October 2015; $153, MS-65FBL, January 2015; $38, MS-64FBL, July 2015
1954, Proof	233,300	10,036	66.3								$65	$100	$600
	Auctions: $14,100, PF-68DCam, October 2015; $270, PF-67, May 2015; $129, PF-66Cam, May 2015; $34, PF-64, August 2015
1954-D	25,445,580	7,340	64.1	99%	$10	$11	$14	$24	$28	$75	$115	$400	$750
	Auctions: $588, MS-66FBL, June 2015; $353, MS-66, February 2015; $89, MS-65FBL, January 2015; $54, MS-65, May 2015
1954-S	4,993,400	10,118	64.6	100%	$12	$14	$16	$24	$30	$55	$300	$185	$950
	Auctions: $1,763, MS-67, July 2015; $194, MS-66, November 2015; $188, MS-65FBL, September 2015; $56, MS-64FBL, February 2015
1955	2,498,181	11,760	64.0	99%	$18	$22	$25	$30	$40	$55	$100	$135	$275
	Auctions: $1,763, MS-66FBL, January 2015; $52, MS-65, September 2015; $38, MS-64FBL, April 2015; $40, MS-63FBL, April 2015
1955, Clashed Obverse Die (g)	(h)	1,778	63.7	100%			$48	$65	$100	$150	$235	$750	
	Auctions: $423, MS-66FBL, February 2013; $129, MS-64FBL, September 2014; $76, MS-64FBL, September 2014
1955, Proof	378,200	17,856	67.1								$65	$75	$425
	Auctions: $4,700, PF-68DCam, October 2015; $212, PF-68, January 2015; $165, PF-67Cam, March 2015; $141, PF-66, August 2015

e. Doubling is evident on the eagle's tail feathers and left wing, as well as on E PLURIBUS UNUM. This variety is FS-50-1951S-801.
f. Included in 1951-S mintage figure. **g.** This variety, popularly known as the "Bugs Bunny," has evidence of clash marks that appear as two buckteeth on Benjamin Franklin. **h.** Included in circulation-strike 1955 mintage figure.

1956, Type 1, Low-Relief Eagle, Four Feathers Left of Perch
FS-50-1956-901.

1956, Type 2, Normal Eagle, Three Feathers Left of Perch

1957, Tripled Die Reverse, Proof
FS-50-1957-801.

1959, Doubled Die Reverse
FS-50-1959-801.

	Mintage	Cert	Avg	%MS	VF-20	EF-40	MS-60	MS-63	MS-64	MS-65	MS-65FBL PF-64	MS-66 PF-65	MS-66FBL PF-65DC
1956	4,032,000	12,601	64.3	100%	$10	$11	$14	$25	$28	$55	$90	$85	$175
Auctions: $353, MS-67, January 2015; $176, MS-66FBL, September 2015; $106, MS-66, July 2015; $60, MS-65FBL, December 2015													
1956, Proof, Type 1	**(i)**	0	n/a								$100	$150	$3,000
Auctions: No auction records available.													
1956, Proof, Type 2	669,384	32,181	67.3								$35	$45	$100
Auctions: $2,820, PF-69DCam, September 2015; $329, PF-69, February 2015; $118, PF-68, February 2015; $376, PF-67, July 2015													
1957	5,114,000	6,501	64.6	100%	$10	$11	$14	$19	$25	$55	$95	$85	$200
Auctions: $$1,763, MS-67FBL, October 2015; $329, MS-67, January 2015; $94, MS-66FBL, October 2015; $48, MS-66, October 2015													
1957, Proof	1,247,952	29,116	67.1								$25	$28	$250
Auctions: $2,585, PF-69Cam, September 2015; $112, PF-68, June 2015; $90, PF-67, July 2015; $84, PF-66Cam, February 2015													
1957, Tripled Die Reverse, Proof (j)	**(k)**	18	67.1								$75	$90	$800
Auctions: No auction records available.													
1957-D	19,966,850	7,133	64.3	99%	$10	$11	$14	$19	$23	$55	$75	$80	$200
Auctions: $3,055, MS-67FBL, October 2015; $764, MS-67, October 2015; $212, MS-66FBL, February 2015; $120, MS-65, August 2015													
1958	4,042,000	8,657	64.5	00%	$10	$11	$14	$19	$24	$55	$125	$70	$300
Auctions: $4,700, MS-67FBL, January 2015; $400, MS-67, February 2015; $353, MS-67, September 2015; $44, MS-66, April 2015													
1958, Proof	875,652	21,423	66.9								$18	$30	$675
Auctions: $705, PF-69Cam, July 2015; $2,115, PF-67UCam, July 2015; $153, PF-67Cam, March 2015; $20, PF-63, September 2015													
1958-D	23,962,412	9,148	64.3	99%	$10	$11	$14	$18	$19	$45	$75	$80	$225
Auctions: $1,175, MS-67FBL, October 2015; $588, MS-67, January 2015; $153, MS-66FBL, February 2015; $20, MS-64, May 2015													
1959	6,200,000	6,869	64.2	99%	$10	$11	$14	$18	$20	$60	$150	$550	$1,400
Auctions: $1,763, MS-66FBL, January 2015; $154, MS-65FBL, May 2015; $84, MS-65, November 2015; $46, MS-64, May 2015													
1959, Doubled Die Reverse (l)	**(m)**	76	63.9	97%			$85	$90	$150	$450	$1,125		
Auctions: $1,528, MS-66, October 2016; $431, MS-65FBL, March 2011													
1959, Proof	1,149,291	23,611	67.0								$18	$25	$2,250
Auctions: $1,529, PF-68Cam, January 2015; $423, PF-67Cam, February 2015; $341, PF-67Cam, March 2015; $235, PF-66Cam, October 2015													
1959-D	13,053,750	6,352	64.2	99%	$10	$11	$14	$10	$22	$75	$115	$600	$700
Auctions: $1,528, MS-66FBL, August 2015; $470, MS-66, January 2015; $118, MS-65FBL, February 2015; $89, MS-65FBL, September 2015													

i. Included in 1956, Proof, Type 2, mintage figure. **j.** A closely tripled image is evident on E PLURIBUS UNUM, portions of UNITED STATES OF AMERICA, and HALF DOLLAR. **k.** Included in 1957, Proof, mintage figure. **l.** Strong doubling is evident on the eagle; doubling is also visible on E PLURIBUS UNUM, UNITED, and portions of the Liberty Bell. **m.** Included in circulation-strike 1959 mintage figure.

1961, Doubled Die Reverse, Proof
FS-50-1961-801.

	Mintage	Cert	Avg	%MS	VF-20	EF-40	MS-60	MS-63	MS-64	MS-65	MS-65FBL	MS-66	MS-66FBL
											PF-64	PF-65	PF-65DC
1960	6,024,000	5,744	64.1	100%	$10	$11	$14	$18	$19	$80	$210	$575	$1,000
	Auctions: $1,293, MS-66FBL, January 2015; $1,058, MS-66FBL, September 2015; $176, MS-65FBL, February 2015; $153, MS-65FBL, November 2014												
1960, Proof	1,691,602	27,198	66.9								$18	$25	$150
	Auctions: $646, PF-69, January 2015; $1,369, PF-68UCam, July 2015; $176, PF-68Cam, March 2015; $46, PF-66, August 2015												
1960, Doubled Die Obverse, Proof (n)	(o)	93	66.4								$80	$95	$400
	Auctions: $160, PF-67, May 2012												
1960-D	18,215,812	4,801	63.9	99%	$10	$11	$14	$18	$30	$160	$400	$600	$1,500
	Auctions: $1,645, MS-66FBL, February 2015; $331, MS-65FBL, August 2015; $112, MS-65, July 2015; $28, MS-64FBL, January 2015												
1961	8,290,000	6,445	64.1	99%	$10	$11	$14	$18	$25	$50	$850	$500	$5,000
	Auctions: $8,225, MS-66FBL, July 2015; $881, MS-66, September 2015; $40, MS-65, July 2015; $84, MS-64FBL, May 2015												
1961, Proof	3,028,244	35,211	66.9								$18	$25	$125
	Auctions: $1,880, PF-68DCam, January 2015; $306, PF-68Cam, January 2015; $129, PF-68, July 2015; $84, PF-67Cam, May 2015												
1961, Doubled Die Reverse, Proof (p)	(q)	97	65.7								$2,200	$3,500	(r)
	Auctions: $4,935, PF-67, August 2015; $5,405, PF-67, July 2016; $2,350, PF-65, June 2014; $1,880, PF-64, July 2014												
1961-D	20,276,442	4,726	64.0	99%	$10	$11	$14	$18	$25	$100	$550	$575	$3,000
	Auctions: $3,302, MS-66FBL, February 2015; $1,175, MS-66, January 2015; $423, MS-65FBL, January 2015; $79, MS-65, October 2015												
1962	9,714,000	4,833	64.0	99%	$10	$11	$14	$18	$25	$80	$1,250	$800	$4,000
	Auctions: $7,638, MS-66FBL, October 2015; $1,645, MS-65FBL, January 2015; $200, MS-64FBL, February 2015; $36, MS-63FBL, July 2015												
1962, Proof	3,218,019	40,837	66.8								$18	$25	$75
	Auctions: $153, PF-68Cam, July 2015; $212, PF-67UCam, April 2015; $26, PF-67, September 2015; $56, PF-66Cam, April 2015												
1962, Doubled Die Obverse, Proof (s)	(t)	7	66.0								$25	$30	$150
	Auctions: No auction records available.												
1962-D	35,473,281	5,756	63.9	99%	$10	$11	$14	$18	$25	$80	$435	$800	$1,750
	Auctions: $4,230, MS-66FBL, January 2015; $60, MS-65, March 2015; $22, MS-64, October 2015; $38, MS-63FBL, March 2015												
1963	22,164,000	15,525	64.2	99%	$10	$11	$14	$18	$19	$45	$1,250	$625	$20,000
	Auctions: $$17,625, MS-66FBL, October 2015; $1,880, MS-65FBL, January 2015; $1,116, MS-65FBL, October 2015; $330, MS-64FBL, January 2015												
1963, Proof	3,075,645	40,295	67.0								$18	$25	$75
	Auctions: $364, PF-69, February 2015; $1,998, PF-68DCam, September 2015; $118, PF-68Cam, January 2015; $129, PF-67Cam, June 2015												
1963-D	67,069,292	12,887	63.9	98%	$10	$11	$14	$18	$19	$45	$160	$400	$875
	Auctions: $1,175, MS-66FBL, July 2015; $282, MS-65FBL, September 2015; $153, MS-65FBL, March 2015; $36, MS-64FBL, April 2015												

n. Doubling is visible on LIBERTY, TRUST, and the date. **o.** Included in 1960, Proof, mintage figure. **p.** Other reverse doubled dies exist for this date. The variety pictured and listed here (FS-50-1961-801) is by far the most dramatic. Very strong doubling is evident on the reverse lettering. **q.** Included in 1961, Proof, mintage figure. **r.** Value in PF-67 is $7,500. **s.** Doubling is visible on the 62 of the date and on WE TRUST. **t.** Included in 1962, Proof, mintage figure.

KENNEDY (1964 TO DATE)

Designers: *Gilroy Roberts and Frank Gasparro.* **Weight:** *1964, modern silver Proofs, and 2014 silver—12.50 grams; 1965–1970—11.50 grams; 1971 to date—11.34 grams.* **Composition:** *1964 and modern silver Proofs—.900 silver, .100 copper (net weight .36169 oz. pure silver); 1965–1970—outer layers of .800 silver and .200 copper bonded to inner core of .209 silver, .791 copper (net weight .1479 oz. pure silver); 1971 to date—outer layers of copper-nickel (.750 copper, .250 nickel) bonded to inner core of pure copper; 2014 gold—.9999 gold (net weight .75 oz. pure gold).* **Diameter:** *30.6 mm.* **Edge:** *Reeded.* **Mints:** *Philadelphia, Denver, and San Francisco.*

Circulation Strike   Proof

Mintmark location, 1964, is on the reverse, below the claw holding the branch.

Mintmark location, 1968 to date, is on the obverse, above the date.

Bicentennial variety: **Designers:** *Gilroy Roberts and Seth Huntington.* **Weight:** *Silver clad—11.50 grams; copper-nickel clad—11.34 grams.* **Composition:** *Silver clad—outer layers of .800 silver, .200 copper bonded to inner core of .209 silver, .791 copper (net weight .14792 oz. pure silver); copper-nickel clad—outer layers of copper-nickel (.750 copper, .250 nickel) bonded to inner core of pure copper.* **Diameter:** *30.6 mm.* **Edge:** *Reeded.* **Mints:** *Philadelphia, Denver, and San Francisco.*

Bicentennial variety   Bicentennial variety, Proof

50th Anniversary varieties: Designers: *Gilroy Roberts and Frank Gasparro.*
Weight: *Gold—23.33 grams; silver Proofs and Unc.—12.50 grams; copper-nickel clad—*
11.34 grams. **Composition:** *Gold—.9999 gold (net weight .75 oz. pure gold); silver—.900 silver,*
.100 copper (net weight .36169 oz. pure silver); copper-nickel clad—outer layers of copper-nickel
(.750 copper, .250 nickel) bonded to inner core of pure copper. **Diameter:** *30.6 mm.*
Edge: *Reeded.* **Mints:** *Philadelphia, Denver, San Francisco, and West Point.*

50th Anniversary variety, gold

50th Anniversary variety, Uncirculated

50th Anniversary variety,
Enhanced Uncirculated

50th Anniversary variety, Proof

50th Anniversary variety, Reverse Proof

History. Kennedy half dollars, minted from 1964 to date, were struck in 90% silver the first year, then with 40% silver content through 1970, and in later years in copper-nickel (except for special silver issues made for collectors and a gold issue in 2014). The obverse, by Chief Engraver Gilroy Roberts, features a portrait of President John F. Kennedy, while the reverse, by Frank Gasparro, displays a modern version of a heraldic eagle.

The 1976 Bicentennial coin shows Philadelphia's Independence Hall, a design by Seth G. Huntington. The obverse was unchanged except for the dual dating 1776–1976. The Bicentennial half dollars were struck during 1975 and 1976 and were used for general circulation as well as being included in Proof and Uncirculated sets for 1975 and 1976.

The year 2014 brought several special issues to mark the 50th year of the Kennedy half dollar: a .9999 fine gold version containing three-quarters of an ounce of pure gold; a Proof in silver; a Reverse Proof in silver; an Enhanced Uncirculated in silver; and an Uncirculated in silver. These coins are dual-dated 1964–2014 on the obverse. They were offered for sale by the U.S. Mint in a number of packages and options.

Striking and Sharpness. Nearly all are well struck. Check the highest points of the hair on the obverse and the highest details on the reverse.

Availability. All issues are common in high circulated grades as well as MS and Proof.

Proofs and Special Mint Set Coins. Proofs of 1964 were struck at the Philadelphia Mint. Those from 1968 to date have been made in San Francisco. All are easily obtained. Most from the 1970s to date have cameo contrast. Special Mint Set (SMS) coins were struck in lieu of Proofs from 1965 to 1967; in some instances, these closely resemble Proofs. Silver Proofs have been struck in recent years, for Silver Proof sets and for the 2014 50th Anniversary issue (which also includes a Reverse Proof). In 1998, a special Matte Proof silver Kennedy half dollar was struck for inclusion in the Robert F. Kennedy commemorative coin set.

Note: Values of common-date silver coins have been based on the current bullion price of silver, $27.50 per ounce, and may vary with the prevailing spot price.

GRADING STANDARDS

MS-60 to 70 (Mint State). *Obverse:* At MS-60, some abrasion and contact marks are evident on the cheek, and on the hair to the right of the forehead and temple. At MS-63, abrasion is slight at most, and less so for MS-64. An MS-65 coin should display no abrasion or contact marks except under magnification, and MS-66 and higher coins should have none at all. Luster should be full and rich. *Reverse:* Comments apply as for the

1964-D. Graded MS-66.

obverse, except that the highest parts of the eagle at the center are the key places to check.

AU-50, 53, 55, 58 (About Uncirculated). *Obverse:* Light wear is seen on the cheek and higher-relief area of the hair below the part, high above the ear. At AU-58, the luster is extensive but incomplete, especially on the higher parts and in the field. At AU–50 and 53, luster is less. *Reverse:* Light wear is seen on the higher parts of the eagle. At AU–50 and 53 there still is significant luster.

1964. Graded AU-55.

EF-40, 45 (Extremely Fine). *Obverse:* Further wear is seen on the head. More details are gone on the higher parts of the hair. *Reverse:* Further wear is seen on the eagle in particular, but also on other areas in high relief (including the leaves, arrowheads, and clouds).

The Kennedy half dollar is seldom collected in grades lower than EF-40.

1964. Graded EF-45.

PF-60 to 70 (Proof). *Obverse and Reverse:* Proofs that are extensively cleaned and have many hairlines, or that are dull and grainy, are lower level, such as PF–60 to 62. There are not many of these in the marketplace. With medium hairlines and good reflectivity, assigned grades of PF–63 or 64 are appropriate. With relatively few hairlines a rating of PF–65 can be given. PF-66 should have hairlines so delicate that magnification is needed to see them. Above that, a Proof should be free of any hairlines or other problems.

1964. Graded PF-66.

1964, Doubled Die Obverse
FS-50-1964-102.

1964, Heavily Accented Hair, Proof
FS-50-1964-401.

1964-D, Doubled Die Obverse
FS-50-1964D-101.

1964-D, Repunched Mintmark
FS-50-1964D-502.

	Mintage	Cert	Avg	%MS	MS-60	MS-63	MS-65 / PF-65	MS-66 / PF-67Cam	MS-67 / PF-68DC
1964	273,304,004	14,886	64.5	99%	$10	$12	$35	$90	$900
Auctions: $1,234, MS-67, October 2015; $118, MS-66, January 2015; $34, MS-65, April 2015; $37, MS-64, April 2015									
1964, Doubled Die Obverse (a)	(b)	22	64.6	100%			$35	$70	$275
Auctions: $69, MS-65, June 2015; $52, MS-64, August 2015; $34, MS-64, August 2015									
1964, Proof (c)	3,950,762	47,931	67.5	100%			$20	$75	$600
Auctions: $4,700, PF-70, August 2015; $4,230, PF-69DCam, August 2015; $364, PF-68DCam, January 2015									
1964, Heavily Accented Hair, Proof †† (d)	(e)	17,292	66.4	100%			$100	$400	$15,000
Auctions: $1,645, PF-69, June 2015; $212, PF-67, April 2015; $89, PF-65, September 2015; $40, PF-63, October 2015									
1964-D	156,205,446	9,523	64.3	99%	$10	$12	$45	$150	$1,200
Auctions: $2,291, MS-67, February 2015; $1,880, MS-67, January 2015; $69, MS-65, January 2015; $60, MS-65, August 2015									
1964-D, Doubled Die Obverse (f)	(g)	39	62.4	74%			$45	$110	$325
Auctions: $60, MS-66, November 2011; $89, MS-65, June 2015; $36, MS-64, August 2015									
1964-D, Repunched Mintmark (h)	(g)	46	63.4	93%			$45	$160	$850
Auctions: $130, AU-55, June 2010									

†† Ranked in the *100 Greatest U.S. Modern Coins* (fourth edition). **a.** There are several doubled-die obverses for the 1964 Kennedy half dollar. The one pictured and listed is FS-50-1964-102. **b.** Included in circulation-strike 1964 mintage figure. **c.** In August 2019, a 1964 Special Strike Kennedy half dollar sold for $156,000 in a Stack's Bowers auction, settting a new auction record for a modern U.S. issue. Ranked in the *100 Greatest U.S. Modern Coins* (fourth edition), such coins were struck for inclusion in a handful of rare 1964 sets that may have been atttempts to perfect the finish for the 1965–1967 Special Mint Sets. **d.** This variety "is identifiable by the enhanced hairline in the central area of the hair, just below the part. However, the easiest way to identify the variety is the weak or broken lower left serif of the I (in LIBERTY)" (*Cherrypickers' Guide to Rare Die Varieties*, sixth edition, volume II). **e.** Included in 1964, Proof, mintage figure. **f.** Doubling on this variety is evident on the date, IN GOD WE TRUST, the designer's initials, and the LI and TY of LIBERTY. "This is a very popular variety. It is extremely rare above MS-65" (*Cherrypickers' Guide to Rare Die Varieties*, sixth edition, volume II). There are other doubled-die obverses for 1964-D. The one pictured and listed is FS-50-1964D-101. **g.** Included in 1964-D mintage figure. **h.** There are several repunched mintmarks for 1964-D. The one listed is FS-50-1964D-502.

1966, Doubled Die Obverse, Special Mint Set
FS-50-1966-103.

1967, Quintupled Die Obverse, Special Mint Set
FS-50-1967-101.

	Mintage	Cert	Avg	%MS	MS-63	MS-65	MS-66	MS-67
					PF-65	PF-67Cam	PF-68DC
1965	65,879,366	2,548	64.6	99%	$6	$75	$350	$3,000
	Auctions: $470, MS-67, January 2015; $282, MS-67, October 2015; $259, MS-66, July 2015							
1965, Special Mint Set	2,360,000	17,123	66.6			$9	$550	
	Auctions: $999, MS-67, September 2016; $2,350, MS-66, October 2015; $823, MS-65, July 2015							
1966	108,984,932	2,385	64.5	98%	$6	$75	$350	$2,500
	Auctions: No auction records available.							
1966, Special Mint Set	2,261,583	20,516	66.8			$9	$175	
	Auctions: $376, MS-68, September 2015; $1,410, MS-67, October 2015; $94, MS-67, July 2015							
1966, Special Mint Set, Doubled Die Obverse (a)	(b)	242	66.7			$65	$550	
	Auctions: $176, MS-67, October 2015; $153, MS-67, September 2015; $940, MS-67, August 2016							
1967	295,046,978	2,737	64.4	96%	$6	$75	$350	$2,500
	Auctions: $17,625, MS-68, August 2015; $3,525, MS-67, October 2015; $100, MS-67, October 2015							
1967, Special Mint Set	1,863,344	17,047	66.7			$9	$90	
	Auctions: $200, PF-68, September 2014; $734, PF-67DCam, November 2014							
1967, Special Mint Set, Quintupled Die Obverse (c)	(d)	69	66.4			$135	$600	
	Auctions: $19,975, MS-69, August 2016; $176, MS-68, March 2016; $705, MS-67, July 2016							
1968-D	246,951,930	3,976	64.7	98%	$6	$30	$75	$950
	Auctions: $1,763, MS-67, January 2015; $1,293, MS-67, October 2015; $46, MS-66, April 2015							
1968-S, Proof	3,041,506	9,086	67.7			$8	$22	$100
	Auctions: $10,575, PF-70DCam, August 2015; $329, PF-69DCam, August 2015							
1969-D	129,881,800	3,238	64.5	99%	$6	$30	$200	$2,500
	Auctions: $1,116, MS-66, March 2016; $30,550, MS-65, August 2016; $823, MS-63, December 2015							
1969-S, Proof	2,934,631	12,922	67.9			$8	$23	$75
	Auctions: $224, PF-69DCam, January 2014							
1970-D ††	2,150,000	6,345	64.3	100%	$20	$75	$550	$4,000
	Auctions: $622, MS-66, November 2016; $235, MS-66, September 2015; $74, MS-65, October 2015							
1970-S, Proof	2,632,810	11,299	67.9			$15	$30	$100
	Auctions: $306, PF-69DCam, January 2015; $282, PF-69DCam, January 2015							
1971	155,164,000	324	64.3	94%	$3	$15	$45	$2,000
	Auctions: $170, MS-66, May 2014							
1971-D	302,097,424	1,295	64.9	94%	$3	$10	$22	$70
	Auctions: $235, MS-67, January 2015; $112, MS-67, March 2015; $100, MS-66, July 2015							
1971-S, Proof	3,220,733	6,669	67.8			$4	$20	$400
	Auctions: $1,821, PF-67, July 2013							

†† Ranked in the *100 Greatest U.S. Modern Coins* (fourth edition). **a.** There are several doubled-die obverse varieties of the 1966, Special Mint Set, half dollar. The one listed is FS-50-1966-103, with strong doubling evident on the profile, IN GOD WE TRUST, the eye, the hair, and the designer's initials. **b.** Included in 1966, Special Mint Set, mintage figure. **c.** "A prominent quintupled (at least) spread is evident on RTY of LIBERTY, with strong multiple images on all obverse lettering and portions of the hair" (*Cherrypickers' Guide to Rare Die Varieties*, sixth edition, volume II). **d.** Included in 1967, Special Mint Set, mintage figure.

1972, Doubled Die Obverse
FS-50-1972-101.

1972-D, Missing Designer's Initials
FS-50-1972D-901.

	Mintage	Cert	Avg	%MS	MS-63 / PF-65	MS-65 / PF-67Cam	MS-66 / PF-68DC	MS-67 / PF-68DC
1972	153,180,000	433	64.7	94%	$3	$15	$50	$1,000
Auctions: $36, MS-66, July 2014								
1972, Doubled Die Obverse (e)	(f)	3	55.3	0%	$140	$165	$225	$450
Auctions: $90, AU-50, March 2011								
1972-D	141,890,000	738	64.9	94%	$3	$10	$23	$150
Auctions: $153, MS-67, November 2015; $94, MS-67, October 2015; $17, MS-66, July 2015								
1972-D, Missing Designer's Initials	(g)	20	59.0	40%	$60	$80	$150	$250
Auctions: $380, EF-45, October 2009								
1972-S, Proof	3,260,996	5,229	68.0			$4	$16	$50
Auctions: $92, PF-69DCam, June 2014								
1973	64,964,000	309	64.7	96%	$3	$15	$45	$200
Auctions: $282, MS-67, August 2014; $153, MS-67, October 2015; $38, MS-66, October 2015								
1973-D	83,171,400	505	64.9	96%	$3	$11	$20	$170
Auctions: $329, MS-67, July 2014; $206, MS-67, October 2015								
1973-S, Proof	2,760,339	1,134	68.3			$3	$16	$35
Auctions: $2,350, PF-70DCam, December 2011								
1974	201,596,000	329	64.5	95%	$3	$20	$35	$1,000
Auctions: $3,290, MS-67, October 2015; $2,350, MS-67, August 2014; $37, MS-66, March 2008								
1974-D	79,066,300	985	64.0	94%	$3	$15	$35	$175
Auctions: $382, MS-67, August 2014; $259, MS-67, October 2015; $65, MS-65, June 2014								
1974-D, Doubled Die Obverse (h)	(i)	589	63.8	94%	$40	$100	$200	$450
Auctions: $411, MS-66, July 2014; $135, MS-65, July 2014; $28, MS-63, October 2014								
1974-S, Proof	2,612,568	1,236	68.3			$4	$9	$30
Auctions: $4,406, PF-70DCam, March 2014								
1776–1976, Copper-Nickel Clad	234,308,000	723	64.3	95%	$3	$15	$100	$1,000
Auctions: $1,998, MS-67, August 2014; $2,350, MS-62, February 2014								
1776–1976-D, Copper-Nickel Clad	287,565,248	1,007	64.8	98%	$3	$15	$25	$500
Auctions: $1,116, MS-67, October 2015; $79, MS-65, August 2015; $999, AU-58, August 2015								
1776–1976-S, Silver Clad	11,000,000	1,822	66.0	100%	$8	$10	$15	$30
Auctions: $217, MS-68, July 2014; $188, MS-68, October 2015; $153, MS-68, September 2015; $141, MS-68, May 2015								
1776–1976-S, Proof, Copper-Nickel Clad	7,059,099	2,512	68.0			$4	$13	$30
Auctions: $3,290, PF-70DCam, January 2015; $2,585, PF-70DCam, July 2015; $2,233, PF-70DCam, August 2015								
1776–1976-S, Proof, Silver Clad (j)	4,000,000	5,018	68.2			$12	$15	$35
Auctions: $881, PF-70DCam, January 2015; $881, PF-70DCam, July 2015; $750, PF-70DCam, August 2015								
1977	43,598,000	494	65.3	98%	$3	$12	$28	$150
Auctions: $1,116, MS-67, November 2014; $764, MS-67, June 2014; $259, MS-67, August 2014								
1977-D	31,449,106	259	64.6	95%	$3	$15	$22	$225
Auctions: $176, MS-67, August 2014; $153, MS-67, October 2015; $21, MS-66, August 2007								
1977-S, Proof	3,251,152	2,053	68.8			$4	$9	$15
Auctions: $141, PF-70DCam, February 2015; $129, PF-70DCam, March 2015; $106, PF-70DCam, August 2015								

e. Doubling is strongly evident on IN GOD WE TRUST and on the date. This variety is very rare above MS-65. **f.** Included in 1972 mintage figure. **g.** Included in 1972-D mintage figure. **h.** Strong doubling is visible on IN GOD WE TRUST, the date, and LIBERTY. **i.** Included in 1974-D mintage figure. **j.** Mintage figures for 1976-S silver coins are approximate. Many were melted in 1982.

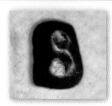

1979-S, Filled S (Type 1), Proof	1979-S, Clear S (Type 2), Proof	1981-S, Rounded S (Type 1), Proof	1981-S, Flat S (Type 2), Proof

	Mintage	Cert	Avg	%MS	MS-63	MS-65	MS-66	MS-67
					PF-65	PF-67Cam	PF-68DC	
1978	14,350,000	333	65.2	99%	$3	$12	$20	$300
Auctions: $411, MS-67, August 2014; $212, MS-67, October 2015; $19, MS-66, July 2008								
1978-D	13,765,799	308	65.3	100%	$3	$10	$23	$300
Auctions: $881, MS-67, August 2014; $18, MS-66, September 2008								
1978-S, Proof	3,127,781	2,191	68.9			$3	$12	$18
Auctions: $106, PF-70DCam, February 2015; $89, PF-70DCam, June 2015; $84, PF-70DCam, October 2015; $74, PF-70DCam, May 2015								
1979	68,312,000	399	65.2	98%	$3	$10	$25	$300
Auctions: $423, MS-67, July 2014; $306, MS-67, October 2015; $188, MS-64, September 2015; $764, AU-58, July 2015								
1979-D	15,815,422	377	65.3	100%	$3	$12	$25	$500
Auctions: $823, MS-67, October 2015; $764, MS-67, August 2014; $11, MS-66, September 2008								
1979-S, Proof, All kinds (k)	3,677,175							
1979-S, Type 1, Proof		2,987	69.0			$3	$11	$14
Auctions: $200, PF-70DCam, April 2012								
1979-S, Type 2, Proof		2,860	69.1			$25	$27	$30
Auctions: $588, PF-70DCam, February 2013								
1980-P	44,134,000	468	65.6	99%	$3	$10	$17	$50
Auctions: $129, MS-67, July 2014; $129, MS-67, October 2015; $42, MS-67, October 2015								
1980-D	33,456,449	249	64.9	98%	$3	$15	$55	$300
Auctions: $4,935, MS-68, October 2015; $212, MS-67, October 2015; $138, MS-66, September 2008; $65, MS-66, October 2015								
1980-S, Proof	3,554,806	2,745	68.9			$3	$12	$15
Auctions: $135, PF-70DCam, July 2015; $106, PF-70DCam, November 2015; $100, PF-70DCam, October 2015; $60								
1981-P	29,544,000	443	65.3	99%	$3	$12	$65	$400
Auctions: No auction records available.								
1981-D	27,839,533	210	64.5	98%	$3	$18	$40	$500
Auctions: $1,880, MS-67, August 2014; $50, MS-66, June 2014								
1981-S, Proof, All kinds (l)	4,063,083							
1981-S, Type 1, Proof		3,576	68.9			$3	$12	$15
Auctions: $259, PF-70DCam, June 2013								
1981-S, Type 2, Proof		1,701	69.0			$30	$35	$40
Auctions: $2,585, PF-70DCam, November 2013								
1982-P	10,819,000	385	64.9	97%	$7	$23	$70	$2,000
Auctions: $153, MS-66, October 2015; $74, MS-65, October 2015; $69, MS-65, August 2015; $42, MS-64, October 2015								
1982-D	13,140,102	597	65.5	99%	$7	$18	$40	$500
Auctions: $3,290, MS-67, November 2013; $999, MS-67, August 2014; $823, MS-67, October 2015; $141, MS-66, October 2015								
1982-S, Proof	3,857,479	2,504	69.1			$4	$12	$15
Auctions: $529, PF-70DCam, June 2013								

k. The mintmark style of 1979-S, Proof, coins was changed during production, resulting in two distinct types. The scarcer, well-defined Type 2 is easily distinguished from the more common blob-like Type 1. l. The mintmark style of the 1981-S, Proof, coins was changed during production, creating two different types. The scarcer Type 2 is not easily distinguished from the common Type 1. Type 2 is flat on the top curve of the S, compared to Type 1, which has a more rounded top. The surface of Type 2 is frosted, and the openings in the loops are slightly larger.

**1988-S, Doubled Die
Obverse, Proof**
FS-50-1988S-101.

	Mintage	Cert	Avg	%MS	MS-63 / PF-65	MS-65 / PF-67Cam	MS-66 / PF-68DC	MS-67
1983-P	34,139,000	516	65.2	99%	$8	$22	$45	$350
Auctions: $147, MS-65, April 2014								
1983-D	32,472,244	359	65.0	98%	$7	$15	$30	$350
Auctions: $1,645, MS-67, August 2014; $646, MS-67, October 2015; $13, MS-66, October 2008								
1983-S, Proof	3,279,126	2,195	69.1			$4	$12	$15
Auctions: $115, PF-70DCam, August 2013								
1984-P	26,029,000	268	65.4	98%	$3	$12	$38	$300
Auctions: $1,116, MS-67, August 2014; $940, MS-67, October 2015; $98, MS-66, September 2008								
1984-D	26,262,158	280	65.2	100%	$3	$17	$40	$1,250
Auctions: $3,290, MS-67, October 2015; $2,820, MS-67, August 2014; $11, MS-66, September 2008								
1984-S, Proof	3,065,110	1,468	69.0			$4	$12	$15
Auctions: $382, PF-70DCam, June 2013								
1985-P	18,706,962	356	66.0	100%	$5	$15	$25	$90
Auctions: $123, MS-67, July 2014; $62, MS-67, October 2015								
1985-D	19,814,034	518	66.1	100%	$5	$12	$15	$100
Auctions: $159, MS-67, July 2014; $112, MS-67, October 2015								
1985-S, Proof	3,362,821	1,775	69.1			$4	$12	$15
Auctions: $135, PF-70DCam, November 2015; $106, PF-70DCam, August 2013								
1986-P	13,107,633	365	65.9	99%	$6	$13	$28	$70
Auctions: $282, MS-67, July 2014; $118, MS-67, October 2015; $112, MS-67, August 2015								
1986-D	15,336,145	465	66.1	100%	$5	$11	$20	$45
Auctions: $57, MS-67, July 2014								
1986-S, Proof	3,010,497	1,377	69.1			$4	$12	$15
Auctions: $106, PF-70DCam, October 2015; $94, PF-70DCam, March 2015; $94, PF-70DCam, July 2015								
1987-P (m)	2,890,758	705	65.8	100%	$5	$15	$30	$100
Auctions: $4,113, MS-68, October 2015; $3,290, MS-68, August 2014; $223, MS-67, October 2015								
1987-D (m)	2,890,758	991	66.0	100%	$5	$12	$23	$50
Auctions: $3,055, MS-68, October 2015; $2,585, MS-68, August 2014; $21, MS-67, October 2008								
1987-S, Proof	4,227,728	2,081	69.1			$4	$12	$15
Auctions: $96, PF-70DCam, August 2013								
1988-P	13,626,000	309	65.9	100%	$5	$15	$28	$125
Auctions: $282, MS-67, July 2014; $153, MS-67, October 2015								
1988-D	12,000,096	468	66.2	100%	$4	$12	$25	$40
Auctions: $57, MS-67, July 2014								
1988-S, Proof	3,262,948	1,552	69.1			$4	$12	$15
Auctions: $113, PF-70DCam, May 2013								
1988-S, Doubled Die Obverse, Proof (n)	(o)	14	68.8			$110	$160	
Auctions: $260, PF-68UCam, February 2011								

m. Not issued for circulation; included with Mint and Souvenir sets. **n.** Clear doubling is visible on IN GOD WE TRUST, the date, and the mintmark. Some doubling is also evident on LIBERTY and the mintmark. **o.** Included in 1988-S, Proof, mintage figure.

	Mintage	Cert	Avg	%MS	MS-63	MS-65	MS-66	MS-67
						PF-65	PF-67Cam	PF-68DC
1989-P	24,542,000	441	65.8	100%	$4	$15	$23	$90
Auctions: $282, MS-67, October 2015; $259, MS-67, July 2014								
1989-D	23,000,216	503	66.1	100%	$3	$11	$18	$60
Auctions: $129, MS-67, July 2014; $74, MS-67, October 2015								
1989-S, Proof	3,220,194	1,421	69.1			$5	$12	$20
Auctions: $123, PF-70DCam, May 2013								
1990-P	22,278,000	318	65.9	99%	$3	$11	$22	$150
Auctions: $259, MS-67, October 2015; $200, MS-66, November 2015; $153, MS-66, November 2015; $106, MS-65, November 2014								
1990-D	20,096,242	337	65.7	100%	$3	$16	$32	$350
Auctions: $31, MS-66, October 2008								
1990-S, Proof	3,299,559	1,582	69.1			$5	$12	$18
Auctions: $82, PF-70DCam, May 2013								
1991-P	14,874,000	326	66.1	100%	$4	$12	$25	$200
Auctions: $217, MS-67, July 2014; $165, MS-67, October 2015								
1991-D	15,054,678	320	65.8	100%	$4	$15	$30	$300
Auctions: $920, MS-67, September 2008; $329, MS-67, August 2014; $294, MS-67, October 2015								
1991-S, Proof	2,867,787	1,374	69.3			$10	$14	$20
Auctions: $68, PF-70DCam, July 2013								
1992-P	17,628,000	274	66.0	100%	$3	$11	$22	$25
Auctions: $2,350, MS-68, August 2014; $11, MS-67, October 2008								
1992-D	17,000,106	206	66.1	100%	$3	$10	$18	$30
Auctions: $147, MS-67, August 2014; $30, MS-67, August 2014; $46, MS-67, July 2014								
1992-S, Proof	2,858,981	1,001	69.2			$5	$14	$20
Auctions: $35, PF-70DCam, May 2013								
1992-S, Proof, Silver	1,317,579	3,317	69.1			$17	$20	$25
Auctions: $92, PF-70DCam, July 2013								
1993-P	15,510,000	398	66.4	99%	$3	$11	$20	$40
Auctions: $58, MS-67, July 2014								
1993-D	15,000,006	663	66.0	100%	$3	$10	$22	$60
Auctions: $2,585, MS-68, August 2014; $11, MS-66, October 2008								
1993-S, Proof	2,633,439	1,036	69.3			$8	$17	$23
Auctions: $31, PF-70DCam, May 2013								
1993-S, Proof, Silver	761,353	2,145	69.1			$27	$30	$37
Auctions: $99, PF-70DCam, May 2014								
1994-P	23,718,000	471	65.8	100%	$3	$10	$20	$55
Auctions: $2,115, MS-68, August 2014; $10, MS-66, October 2008								
1994-D	23,828,110	236	65.8	100%	$3	$10	$20	$200
Auctions: $364, MS-67, July 2014; $141, MS-67, October 2015								
1994-S, Proof	2,484,594	1,015	69.3			$8	$17	$23
Auctions: $45, PF-70DCam, May 2013								
1994-S, Proof, Silver	785,329	2,218	69.2			$26	$33	$35
Auctions: $206, PF-70DCam, February 2013								
1995-P	26,496,000	306	66.1	99%	$3	$10	$17	$40
Auctions: $55, MS-67, July 2014								
1995-D	26,288,000	362	66.2	100%	$3	$10	$20	$50
Auctions: $2,585, MS-68, August 2014; $13, MS-67, October 2008								
1995-S, Proof	2,117,496	962	69.3			$16	$20	$25
Auctions: $66, PF-70DCam, August 2013								
1995-S, Proof, Silver	679,985	2,940	69.2			$38	$40	$45
Auctions: $135, PF-70DCam, May 2014								

	Mintage	Cert	Avg	%MS	MS-63	MS-65	MS-66	MS-67
						PF-65	PF-67Cam	PF-68DC
1996-P	24,442,000	408	66.2	100%	$3	$10	$17	$35
Auctions: $247, MS-68, July 2014; $165, MS-68, October 2015								
1996-D	24,744,000	400	66.0	99%	$3	$10	$17	$35
Auctions: $1,293, MS-68, August 2014; $999, MS-68, January 2015; $11, MS-67, October 2008								
1996-S, Proof	1,750,244	949	69.3			$10	$15	$22
Auctions: $66, PF-70DCam, August 2013								
1996-S, Proof, Silver	775,021	2,118	69.1			$30	$35	$40
Auctions: $135, PF-70DCam, August 2013								
1997-P	20,882,000	204	66.2	100%	$3	$12	$30	$80
Auctions: $60, MS-67, July 2014								
1997-D	19,876,000	324	65.9	100%	$3	$13	$30	$150
Auctions: $646, MS-68, June 2013; $123, MS-67, July 2014; $79, MS-67, October 2015								
1997-S, Proof	2,055,000	857	69.3			$12	$20	$25
Auctions: $76, PF-70DCam, August 2013								
1997-S, Proof, Silver	741,678	2,104	69.2			$30	$40	$50
Auctions: $96, PF-70DCam, August 2013								
1998-P	15,646,000	268	66.3	100%	$3	$15	$35	$70
Auctions: $76, MS-67, July 2014								
1998-D	15,064,000	276	65.8	99%	$3	$11	$20	$70
Auctions: $62, MS-67, July 2014								
1998-S, Proof	2,086,507	1,170	69.4			$10	$17	$23
Auctions: $56, PF-70DCam, August 2013								
1998-S, Proof, Silver	878,792	2,717	69.3			$18	$25	$35
Auctions: $88, PF-70DCam, August 2013								
1998-S, Matte Finish Proof, Silver †† (p)	*62,000*	2,681	69.2			$125		
Auctions: $113, PF-69, November 2014; $170, PF-69, March 2015; $165, PF-69, March 2015								
1999-P	8,900,000	277	66.3	100%	$3	$10	$20	$30
Auctions: $2,115, MS-69, June 2013; $823, MS-68, August 2014								
1999-D	10,682,000	302	66.2	100%	$3	$10	$16	$23
Auctions: $1,998, MS-68, August 2014; $10, MS-66, October 2008								
1999-S, Proof	2,543,401	3,877	69.3			$13	$16	$20
Auctions: $90, PF-70DCam, May 2013								
1999-S, Proof, Silver	804,565	6,987	69.1			$25	$30	$32
Auctions: $147, PF-70DCam, August 2013								
2000-P	22,600,000	174	66.1	100%	$3	$10	$17	$35
Auctions: $764, MS-68, August 2014; $48, MS-67, October 2008								
2000-D	19,466,000	267	66.0	100%	$3	$10	$20	$100
Auctions: $123, MS-67, July 2014; $94, MS-67, October 2015								
2000-S, Proof	3,082,483	3,361	69.3			$5	$12	$16
Auctions: $58, PF-70DCam, May 2013								
2000-S, Proof, Silver	965,421	6,895	69.2			$15	$18	$20
Auctions: $78, PF-70DCam, May 2013								
2001-P	21,200,000	440	65.6	100%	$3	$8	$15	$28
Auctions: $176, MS-68, September 2015; $60, MS-68, October 2015								
2001-D	19,504,000	484	65.8	100%	$3	$8	$13	$28
Auctions: $247, MS-68, July 2014; $153, MS-68, October 2015								
2001-S, Proof	2,294,909	2,633	69.3			$6	$10	$13
Auctions: $76, PF-70DCam, May 2013								
2001-S, Proof, Silver	889,697	5,281	69.2			$15	$21	$23
Auctions: $90, PF-70DCam, May 2013								

†† Ranked in the *100 Greatest U.S. Modern Coins* (fourth edition). **p.** Minted for inclusion in the Robert F. Kennedy commemorative set (along with an RFK commemorative dollar).

	Mintage	Cert	Avg	%MS	MS-63	MS-65	MS-66	MS-67
						PF-65	PF-67Cam	PF-68DC
2002-P (q)	3,100,000	263	65.7	100%	$3	$8	$15	$30
	Auctions: $182, MS-68, June 2014; $135, MS-68, January 2015; $129, MS-68, October 2015; $118, MS-68, July 2014							
2002-D (q)	2,500,000	281	65.8	100%	$3	$9	$20	$40
	Auctions: $2,115, MS-69, June 2013							
2002-S, Proof	2,319,766	2,537	69.2			$5	$13	$16
	Auctions: $60, PF-70DCam, May 2013							
2002-S, Proof, Silver	892,229	5,592	69.3			$15	$18	$20
	Auctions: $61, PF-70DCam, May 2013							
2003-P (q)	2,500,000	321	65.8	100%	$3	$9	$20	$30
	Auctions: $59, MS-67, July 2014							
2003-D (q)	2,500,000	311	65.8	100%	$3	$8	$16	$25
	Auctions: $51, MS-67, July 2014							
2003-S, Proof	2,172,684	4,521	69.3			$5	$12	$16
	Auctions: $62, PF-70DCam, August 2015; $35, PF-70DCam, May 2013							
2003-S, Proof, Silver	1,125,755	6,545	69.2			$15	$18	$20
	Auctions: $76, PF-70DCam, November 2014; $82, PF-70DCam, May 2014							
2004-P (q)	2,900,000	277	66.2	100%	$3	$8	$17	$50
	Auctions: $100, MS-67, October 2015; $86, MS-67, July 2014							
2004-D (q)	2,900,000	462	66.3	100%	$3	$8	$16	$25
	Auctions: $423, MS-68, July 2014; $235, MS-68, October 2015							
2004-S, Proof	1,789,488	2,292	69.3			$13	$17	$24
	Auctions: $66, PF-70DCam, August 2013							
2004-S, Proof, Silver	1,175,934	6,339	69.2			$20	$22	$23
	Auctions: $69, PF-70DCam, January 2013							
2005-P (q)	3,800,000	240	66.0	100%	$4	$18	$25	$200
	Auctions: $470, MS-67, October 2015; $42, MS-66, July 2014							
2005-P, Satin Finish (q)	1,160,000	2,565	67.0	100%			$8	$15
	Auctions: No auction records available.							
2005-D (q)	3,500,000	286	66.3	100%	$4	$15	$23	$100
	Auctions: $1,116, MS-68, August 2014; $11, MS-66, October 2008							
2005-D, Satin Finish (q)	1,160,000	2,210	66.7	100%			$8	$15
	Auctions: No auction records available.							
2005-S, Proof	2,275,000	7,428	69.2			$5	$12	$16
	Auctions: $66, PF-70DCam, August 2013							
2005-S, Proof, Silver	1,069,679	7,719	69.3			$12	$18	$20
	Auctions: $74, PF-70DCam, January 2013							
2006-P (q)	2,400,000	211	66.7	100%	$2	$9	$22	$26
	Auctions: $42, MS-69, January 2009; $764, MS-68, August 2014; $376, MS-68, October 2015							
2006-P, Satin Finish (q)	847,361	1,401	66.8	100%			$8	$15
	Auctions: No auction records available.							
2006-D (q)	2,000,000	206	66.3	100%	$2	$7	$15	$28
	Auctions: $82, MS-67, July 2014; $60, MS-67, October 2015							
2006-D, Satin Finish (q)	847,361	1,381	66.8	100%			$8	$15
	Auctions: No auction records available.							
2006-S, Proof	2,000,428	3,171	69.3			$5	$12	$16
	Auctions: $46, PF-70DCam, August 2013							
2006-S, Proof, Silver	1,054,008	4,567	69.4			$12	$18	$20
	Auctions: $76, PF-70DCam, August 2013							
2007-P (q)	2,400,000	242	66.6	100%	$2	$6	$11	$17
	Auctions: $270, MS-68, July 2014; $100, MS-68, October 2015							

q. Not issued for circulation. Sold directly to the public in rolls and small bags.

	Mintage	Cert	Avg	%MS	MS-63	MS-65	MS-66	MS-67
						PF-65	PF-67Cam	PF-68DC
2007-P, Satin Finish (q)	895,628	398	66.8	100%			$8	$15
	Auctions: No auction records available.							
2007-D (q)	2,400,000	202	66.3	100%	$2	$6	$15	$30
	Auctions: $15, MS-69, January 2009							
2007-D, Satin Finish (q)	895,628	412	66.9	100%			$8	$15
	Auctions: No auction records available.							
2007-S, Proof	1,702,116	3,195	69.3			$5	$12	$16
	Auctions: $64, PF-70DCam, January 2013							
2007-S, Proof, Silver	875,050	4,130	69.4			$14	$19	$22
	Auctions: $86, PF-70DCam, August 2013							
2008-P (q)	1,700,000	295	66.3	100%	$2	$8	$20	$40
	Auctions: $1,410, MS-68, August 2014; $12, SP-67, April 2012							
2008-P, Satin Finish (q)	745,464	127	67.1	100%			$8	$15
	Auctions: No auction records available.							
2008-D (q)	1,700,000	198	66.0	100%	$2	$8	$20	$300
	Auctions: $24, MS-66, June 2011							
2008-D, Satin Finish (q)	745,464	100	67.0	100%			$8	$15
	Auctions: No auction records available.							
2008-S, Proof	1,405,674	2,013	69.3			$5	$12	$16
	Auctions: $71, PF-70DCam, November 2013							
2008-S, Proof, Silver	763,887	4,170	69.4			$14	$20	$23
	Auctions: $66, PF-70DCam, August 2013							
2009-P (q)	1,900,000	218	66.2	100%	$2	$6	$12	$25
	Auctions: $1,998, MS-68, August 2014; $6, MS-66, November 2011							
2009-P, Satin Finish (q)	784,614	247	67.1	100%			$8	$15
	Auctions: No auction records available.							
2009-D (q)	1,900,000	170	66.2	100%	$2	$6	$12	$250
	Auctions: $27, MS-66, February 2012							
2009-D, Satin Finish (q)	784,614	285	67.4	100%			$8	$15
	Auctions: No auction records available.							
2009-S, Proof	1,482,502	3,845	69.3			$5	$12	$16
	Auctions: $31, PF-70DCam, May 2013							
2009-S, Proof, Silver	697,365	4,717	69.3			$14	$18	$20
	Auctions: $41, PF-70DCam, May 2013							
2010-P (q)	1,800,000	347	66.6	100%	$2	$6	$12	$25
	Auctions: $23, MS-67, July 2014							
2010-P, Satin Finish (q)	583,897	229	67.1	100%			$8	$15
	Auctions: No auction records available.							
2010-D (q)	1,700,000	228	66.2	100%	$2	$6	$12	$30
	Auctions: $3,995, MS-68, August 2015; $101, MS-67, July 2014; $48, MS-67, October 2015							
2010-D, Satin Finish (q)	583,897	337	67.6	100%			$8	$15
	Auctions: No auction records available.							
2010-S, Proof	1,103,815	1,547	69.3			$5	$12	$16
	Auctions: $48, PF-70DCam, August 2013							
2010-S, Proof, Silver	585,401	4,446	69.6			$14	$18	$20
	Auctions: $48, PF-70DCam, May 2013							
2011-P (q)	1,750,000	514	66.8	100%	$3	$6	$12	$25
	Auctions: $229, MS-68, July 2014; $176, MS-68, October 2015							
2011-D (q)	1,700,000	435	66.5	100%	$3	$6	$12	$25
	Auctions: $1,116, MS-68, August 2014; $1,058, MS-68, August 2014; $33, MS-67, January 2012							

q. Not issued for circulation. Sold directly to the public in rolls and small bags.

	Mintage	Cert	Avg	%MS	MS-63	MS-65	MS-66	MS-67
						PF-65	PF-67Cam	PF-68DC
2011-S, Proof	1,098,835	2,515	69.4	100%		$5	$12	$16
Auctions: $21, PF-70UCam, March 2012								
2011-S, Proof, Silver	574,175	5,146	69.7	100%		$14	$18	$20
Auctions: $39, PF-70DCam, August 2014; $36, PF-70DCam, April 2012								
2012-P (q)	1,800,000	279	66.8	100%	$3	$6	$12	$25
Auctions: No auction records available.								
2012-D (q)	1,700,000	323	66.7	100%	$3	$6	$12	$25
Auctions: No auction records available.								
2012-S, Proof	843,705	2,077	69.3			$5	$12	$16
Auctions: $51, PF-70DCam, May 2013								
2012-S, Proof, Silver	445,612	2,972	69.5			$50	$65	$75
Auctions: No auction records available.								
2013-P (q)	5,000,000	315	66.8	100%	$3	$6	$12	$25
Auctions: No auction records available.								
2013-D (q)	4,600,000	336	66.9	100%	$3	$6	$12	$25
Auctions: No auction records available.								
2013-S, Proof	854,785	2,036	69.3			$5	$12	$16
Auctions: No auction records available.								
2013-S, Proof, Silver	467,691	2,274	69.6			$14	$18	$20
Auctions: No auction records available.								
2014-P (q)	2,500,000	445	66.7	100%	$3	$6	$12	$25
Auctions: No auction records available.								
2014-P, High Relief †† (r)	197,608	9,641	67.0	100%	$15	$20		
Auctions: No auction records available.								
2014-P, Proof, Silver †† (s)	219,173	17,780	69.6			$15	$35	$40
Auctions: No auction records available.								
2014-D (q)	2,100,000	691	67.2	100%	$3	$6	$12	$25
Auctions: No auction records available.								
2014-D, High Relief †† (r)	197,608	9,209	67.0	100%	$15	$20		
Auctions: No auction records available.								
2014-D, Silver †† (s)	219,173	17,430	69.6	100%	$10	$15	$25	$30
Auctions: No auction records available.								
2014-S, Enhanced Uncirculated, Silver †† (s)	219,173	18,406	69.7	100%	$10	$15	$20	$25
Auctions: No auction records available.								
2014-S, Proof	767,977	2,643	69.3			$15	$18	$20
Auctions: No auction records available.								
2014-S, Proof, Silver	472,107	5,202	69.5			$15	$20	$23
Auctions: No auction records available.								
2014-W, Reverse Proof, Silver †† (s)	219,173	18,203	69.6			$20	$25	$35
Auctions: No auction records available.								
2014-W, 50th Anniversary, Proof, Gold †† (t)	73,772	10,132	69.7			$900	$1,000	$1,200
Auctions: No auction records available.								
2015-P (q)	2,300,000	323	66.0	100%	$3	$6	$12	$25
Auctions: No auction records available.								
2015-D (q)	2,300,000	438	66.1	100%	$3	$6	$12	$25
Auctions: No auction records available.								

†† All 2014 Kennedy 50th Anniversary Half Dollars are ranked in the *100 Greatest U.S. Modern Coins* (fourth edition), as a single entry. **q.** Not issued for circulation. Sold directly to the public in rolls and small bags. **r.** To celebrate the 50th anniversary of the Kennedy half dollar, in 2014 the U.S. Mint issued an Uncirculated two-coin set featuring a Kennedy half dollar from Philadelphia and one from Denver. **s.** Featured in the 2014 half dollar silver-coin collection released by the U.S. Mint to commemorate the 50th anniversary of the Kennedy half dollar. **t.** First gold half dollar offered by the U.S. Mint. It commemorates the 50th anniversary of the first release of the Kennedy half dollar in 1964. Dual-dated 1964–2014.

	Mintage	Cert	Avg	%MS	MS-63	MS-65	MS-66	MS-67
						PF-65	PF-67Cam	PF-68DC
2015-S, Proof	662,854	2,718	69.3			$5	$12	$16
Auctions: No auction records available.								
2015-S, Proof, Silver	387,310	1,950	69.5			$14	$18	$20
Auctions: No auction records available.								

q. Not issued for circulation. Sold directly to the public in rolls and small bags.

In 2016 a special .9999 fine gold striking of Adolf A. Weinman's Liberty Walking half dollar was created to celebrate the 100th anniversary of its introduction. It is smaller than the silver strikings, with a diameter of 27 mm and weighing 15.552 grams. Struck at West Point, it has a reeded edge. Similar strikings were made for the 1916 dime and quarter designs.

	Mintage	Cert	Avg	%MS	SP-67	SP-70
2016-W, Liberty Walking Centennial Gold Coin ††	65,509	0	n/a		$1,000	$1,150

†† 2016 Centennial Gold Coins in all denominations are ranked in the *100 Greatest U.S. Modern Coins* (fourth edition), as a single entry.

Normally scheduled production of clad and silver Kennedy half dollars, in the same standards and specifications as previously, continued in 2016 and beyond, and was not disrupted by the gold Liberty Walking half dollar.

	Mintage	Cert	Avg	%MS	MS-63	MS-65	MS-66	MS-67
						PF-65	PF-67Cam	PF-68DC
2016-P (q)	2,100,000	267	66.5	100%	$3	$6	$12	$25
2016-D (q)	2,100,000	344	66.6	100%	$2	$6	$12	$25
2016-S, Proof	621,774	450	69.5			$5	$12	$16
2016-S, Proof, Silver	406,330	1,517	69.6			$14	$18	$20
2017-P (q)	1,800,000	242	66.7	100%	$2	$6	$12	$25
2017-D (q)	2,900,000	245	66.6	100%	$2	$6	$12	$25
2017-S, Enhanced Uncirculated (u)	210,419	20,415	70.0			$15	$17	$20
2017-S, Proof	621,390	190	69.4			$5	$12	$16
2017-S, Proof, Silver	406,986	985	69.6			$14	$18	$20
2018-P (q)	4,800,000	388	66.6	100%	$2	$6	$12	$25
2018-D (q)	6,100,000	472	66.5	100%	$2	$6	$12	$25
2018-S, Proof	*567,856*	930	69.9			$5	$12	$16
2018-S, Proof, Silver	*381,356*	748	69.6			$14	$18	$20
2018-S, Reverse Proof, Silver (v)	199,116	0	n/a			$46	$50	$55
2019-P (q)	1,700,000	431	66.7	100%	$2	$6	$12	$25
2019-D (q)	1,700,000	2,196	67.3	100%	$2	$6	$12	$25
2019-S, Proof	*642,309*	3,710	69.9			$5	$12	$16
2019-S, Proof, Silver (w)	*458,685*	12,032	69.9			$14	$18	$20
2019-S, Enhanced Reverse Proof (w)		0	n/a				$25	$30
2020-P (q)	*2,300,000*	212	66.2	100%	$2	$6	$12	$25
2020-D (q)	*3,400,000*	105	66.0	100%	$2	$6	$12	$25
2020-S, Proof		2,079	69.9			$5	$12	$16
2020-S, Proof, Silver (x)						$14	$18	$20
2021-P (q)					$2	$6	$12	$25
2021-D (q)					$2	$6	$12	$25
2021-S, Proof						$5	$12	$16
2021-S, Proof, Silver						$14	$18	$20

q. Not issued for circulation. Sold directly to the public in rolls and small bags. **u.** Included in the 225th Anniversary Enhanced Uncirculated Set. **v.** Included in the 50th Anniversary Silver Reverse Proof Set. **w.** Beginning in 2019, the Mint changed its composition for silver Proofs to .999 fine. **x.** Included in the Apollo 11 50th Anniversary Proof Half Dollar Set.

Silver Dollars
1794–1935

This survey of U.S. silver dollars is based on the work of Q. David Bowers,
a numismatic professional and author in the field for more than 60 years.

AN OVERVIEW
OF SILVER DOLLARS

This seventh edition of *Mega Red* presents an expanded study of the silver dollar denomination, beginning with classic early silver coins and ending with the clad coinage of the modern era. The results rest on a foundation of many sources, including specialized references, auction results, historical documents, news reports, numismatic research, and more.

Congress authorized the production of coins struck in silver, alloyed with copper, with the Mint Act of April 2, 1792. Coins were first struck at the Philadelphia Mint in the 1790s; the first in this metal were the half dismes of 1792, followed by the 1794-dated half dime, half dollar, and dollar. Dimes made their appearance in 1796, as did quarters. As time went on, designs changed and evolved, as did weights and alloy standards. The silver three-cent piece ("trime"), a new denomination, appeared in 1851. In 1873 the silver trade dollar was born, but it lasted only until 1878 (plus later Proofs struck for collectors), followed by the even shorter-lived twenty-cent piece of 1875 and 1876 (plus two more years of Proofs for numismatists).

Generally, designs for early silver coins were similar, with most issues of 1794 and 1795 having the Flowing Hair design, later denominations having the Draped Bust style and then the Capped Bust motif, followed by the long-lived Liberty Seated design, then in 1892 the Barber dime, quarter, and half dollar. In the meantime, the twenty-cent piece (1875), the trade dollar (1873), and the new silver dollar (the Morgan dollar of 1878) had their own motifs.

In 1916, private-sector artists were commissioned to create the "Mercury" dime, Standing Liberty quarter, and Liberty Walking half dollar, each of which went on to become extremely popular with numismatists. In 1921 the Peace silver dollar, also designed by an outside sculptor, joined this illustrious group.

By 1964, silver was becoming expensive on international markets, and after that time the standard alloy of 90% silver and 10% copper was abandoned, although some silver-content half dollars were produced through 1970. Occasional special coins and commemoratives in silver have been made for sale to collectors, but for coins used in general circulation, clad alloys replaced silver in such denominations as the dime, quarter, half dollar, and dollar. In 2000 the dollar composition was changed to a manganese-brass outer layer over a copper core, giving them a distinctive golden appearance. The Sacagawea style was the first of the "golden" dollars, followed by the Native American, Presidential, and American Innovation designs.

Silver dollars are now among the most historic, interesting, and numismatically popular of all American coin denominations, and they include some of the most popular series in American numismatics—indeed, a significant percentage of all rare coin dealers' business involves coins of the dollar denomination. While the series includes the famous "King of American Coins" (the 1804 dollar) and a few other great rarities, most dates and mintmarks are readily collectible. Modern enthusiasts enjoyably pursue and collect Morgan silver dollars of 1878 to 1921, Peace dollars of 1921 to 1935, and the later clad coinage.

On January 5, 2021, the 1921 Silver Dollar Coin Anniversary Act was signed into law. It requires the Treasury Department to mint and issue coins in honor of the 100th anniversary of the transition from the Morgan to the Peace design. Appendix I delves more deeply into the story behind the law, while other appendices examine pattern silver dollars, modern dollar counterfeits, error and misstruck dollars, and more.

Note: Values of common-date silver coins listed in the seventh edition of **Mega Red** *have been based on a silver bullion price of $27.50 per ounce, and may vary with the prevailing spot price. To determine the intrinsic value of common silver coins, see page 1415.*

MAJOR DESIGN TYPES

American dollar coins have seen more changes to their basic format than any other federal denomination. The tiny gold dollar of 1849–1889 is collected as a class of its own and is not included in this chapter. The other dollars fall into two basic categories: classic silver dollars of 1794 through 1935 (the truly "silver" dollars), and modern dollars of 1971 to date. If a person references a "gold dollar," there's no question which denomination they mean; but if someone speaks of a "dollar" coin, they could mean any classic or modern dollar. A straightforward distinction for collectors, but a nomenclature headache!

Classic silver dollars were universally struck in .900 fine silver; from 1794 through 1839 their diameter was 39 to 40 millimeters, after which time they were standardized to 38.1 millimeters. Modern dollars began at 38.1 millimeters with the Eisenhower type—the last of the large-format dollar coins—then dropped to 26.5 millimeters thereafter. The Eisenhower and Susan B. Anthony dollars were struck on copper planchets clad in outer layers of copper-nickel; some Eisenhower planchets included silver in the central alloy and were clad in .800 silver. The "golden" dollars—Sacagawea, Presidential, Native American, and American Innovation—have a copper core clad in an outer layer of manganese brass. This wide array of types means there's something for every collector to delve into, regardless of their budget.

The U.S. Mint has also produced various commemorative silver dollars from 1900 to date, as well as one-ounce American Silver Eagle bullion coins denominated one dollar. (These coins are covered in the Commemoratives and Bullion chapters, respectively.)

Flowing Hair (1794 and 1795). Fewer than 150 silver dollars of 1794 exist, to which can be added several thousand or more dated 1795. Many interesting die combinations were made for the latter year. Examples are easy enough to obtain (given the proper budget) in grades from Very Fine through low Mint State. Striking usually ranges from poor to barely acceptable, and adjustment marks (from an overweight planchet being filed down to correct weight) are often seen. Accordingly, careful examination is needed to find a good example.

Draped Bust, Small Eagle (1795–1798). Although they were struck from 1795 to 1798, most examples with the Draped Bust obverse and the Small Eagle reverse are dated 1796 or 1797; both years exist in about the same numbers today. Although mintage figures refer to the quantities produced in the given calendar year, these figures do not necessarily refer to the dates on the coins themselves, as Mint workers would use coinage dies into the next calendar year. This is the scarcest of the early (1794–1804) types and is difficult to find in higher grades. Sharpness of strike presents a challenge to the collector, and usually there are weaknesses in the details, particularly on the reverse eagle. However, enough are around that finding an attractive Very Fine or Extremely Fine will be no problem.

Draped Bust, Heraldic Eagle (1798–1804). The type of 1798 to 1804 features the Draped Bust obverse paired with a Heraldic Eagle reverse. Many such coins exist, mostly in grades from Very Fine through lower Mint State levels. Dollars of this design are far and away the most plentiful of the early types, although "plentiful" is a relative term. Striking can be indifferent, but the population of surviving coins is such that collectors have more to choose from, and can select for quality.

Gobrecht (1836 and 1839). The Gobrecht silver dollars of 1836 (starless obverse, stars on reverse, plain edge) and 1839 (stars on obverse, starless reverse, reeded edge) present a special challenge in the formation of a type set. For quite a few years these were considered by numismatists to be patterns, and thus anyone forming a type set of regular-issue U.S. coins could ignore them. However, in recent decades, research by R.W. Julian (in particular), Walter Breen, and others has revealed that the vast majority of 1836 and 1839 silver dollars originally produced were put into circulation at face value.

The 1836 Gobrecht dollar is easy enough to find in today's marketplace, although it is expensive. The original production amounted to 1,600 coins, to which an unknown number of restrikes can be added. The main problem arises with the 1839, made only to the extent of 300 pieces. All were Proofs, but most were placed in circulation, and those that exist today nearly always have abundant signs of their time spent in commerce. This is the rarest of all major U.S. coin design types, outclassing even the 1796 and 1797 half dollar and the 1808 quarter eagle. Nearly all in existence today are Proof restrikes, which is probably a good thing, or they would be virtually uncollectible!

Liberty Seated (1840–1873). In 1840 the regular Liberty Seated dollar made its appearance, with the reverse depicting a perched eagle holding an olive branch and arrows. This style was continued through 1873, with minor modifications over the years; for example, in 1866 the motto IN GOD WE TRUST was added to the reverse. Generally, Liberty Seated dollars can be easily enough found in circulated grades from Very Fine on up, as well as low Mint State levels. MS-63 and higher-grade pieces are in the minority, particularly of the 1840–1865 No Motto type.

Forming a specialized collection of Liberty Seated dollars from 1840 through 1873 has been a pursuit of many collectors over the years. Generally, the Philadelphia Mint dates are available without difficulty, although the 1851 and 1852 are typically acquired as Proof restrikes—originals of both years being prohibitively rare. More difficult to find in higher grades are coins of the branch mints, including the famous 1870-S, of which only 10 are known to exist and for which no mintage figure has ever been found in official reports. Branch-mint pieces, starting with the 1846-O, were placed into circulation and used extensively. Beginning in 1870, dollars of this type were struck at Carson City; these also are seen with evidence of circulation. The only exceptions to this are certain dollars of 1859-O and 1860-O which turned up in very "baggy" Mint State preservation (showing contact marks from other coins) among Treasury hoards, to the extent of several thousand pieces of both dates combined.

Morgan (1878–1921). Morgan silver dollars are one of the most active and popular series in American numismatics. Approximately 100 different major varieties can be collected, although certain unusual varieties (not basic dates and mintmarks) can be dropped from a collection or added as desired. The vast majority of Morgan dollars can be found in Mint State. When these coins were first minted there was little need for them in circulation, and hundreds of millions of coins piled up in Treasury and other vaults. Although many were melted in 1918, enough remained that untold millions exist today in the hands of the public.

Made by the hundreds of millions from 1878 through 1921, Morgan dollars are abundantly available, with one of the most common of all coins in gem preservation, the 1881-S, being readily available with sharply struck details and exceptional eye appeal. Similar varieties are common and are normally seen in high grades with sharp strike, but others with high mintages, the 1886-O and 1896-O being examples, are quite rare in MS-63 and finer, and when seen usually have rather poor eye appeal. Accordingly, quite a bit of discernment is recommended for the savvy collector.

Peace (1921–1935). Peace silver dollars include the High Relief style of 1921 and the shallow-relief motif of 1922 to 1935. A basic set of 24 different dates and mintmarks is easily enough obtained, including in Mint State. The 1921 is plentiful in Mint State, but rarely is found sharply struck at the obverse and reverse center. Later Peace dollars with shallow relief abound in MS-63 and finer grades, although strike quality can be a problem. The most elusive is the 1934-S.

Eisenhower (1971–1978). The Peace dollar was the last of the United States' circulating .900 fine silver dollars. One final type of dollar coin was produced in the large 38.1 mm format—the Eisenhower dollar, often colloquially called a "silver dollar" even though its regular issues were made of copper and nickel. All are readily available in just about any grade desired, although some are elusive in the highest grades. Bicentennial Eisenhower dollars were struck with the dual date "1776–1976." The regular copper-nickel-clad issues are quite common, as are the silver-clad versions, which were sold to collectors.

Susan B. Anthony (1979–1999). The Susan B. Anthony dollars were the first circulating U.S. coins to bear the likeness of a female historical figure. Unfortunately, the coins were only two millimeters larger in diameter than the quarter dollar. That fact, plus their clad composition and edge reeding, meant they were easily mistaken for quarters. "Susies" were ignored by the public and made fun of by politicians and comedians, but numismatists loved them—and still do. Uncirculated examples are plentiful and inexpensive, but as with the Eisenhower dollars, the highest grades can be elusive.

Sacagawea (2000–2008). The "golden dollar" was meant to replace the paper bill but, like the Eisenhower and Anthony dollars before it, the Sacagawea fell flat with the public. First issued for circulation in 2000, the coin was struck only for collectors starting in 2002. They were supplanted by the Native American dollar, which uses the Sacagawea obverse, in 2009. Examples are well-struck, plentiful, and affordable.

Presidential (2007–2016, 2020). Another golden series, this one honoring U.S. presidents, commenced in 2007. Four obverse designs per year honored the nation's former presidents, in the order of their presidencies, through 2016. After the death of George H.W. Bush in 2018, the program was expanded to include his coin in 2020. This type was issued for circulation a bit longer than its predecessor, but in 2012 the Mint opted to issue the coins for collectors only. They are usually well struck and are affordable in even the highest grades.

Native American (2009 to date). Building on the original Sacagawea dollar, the golden Native American dollar use the same obverse (a portrait of Sacagawea and her infant son, Jean Baptiste)—but each year features a new, thematic reverse design that honors Native American history, culture, and contributions. Like the Sacagawea and Presidential dollars, they are plentiful and accessibly priced, and nearly all are in grades MS-68 to 70.

American Innovation (2018-2032). These coins honor quintessentially American traits of the willingness to explore, to discover, and to create one's own destiny.

COLLECTING SILVER AND MODERN DOLLARS

Building a complete date-and-mintmark set of modern dollars, beautifully struck and in high grades, is a satisfying and affordable pursuit, and depending on the collector's budget and patience, can be accomplished in a relatively short time. A complete date-and-mintmark set of classic silver dollars can be built affordably, excepting a few great rarities; but if the collector is choosy about quality this will take years or else an unlimited budget. Fortunately, there are other satisfying—and much less daunting—ways to collect silver dollars, including the following:

- Form a nice type set.
- Specialize in a single type and seek one of each date and mintmark.
- Collect the early coins by type and the later coins by date and mintmark.
- Form a basic collection of early dates and major varieties.
- Seek out beautifully toned coins.
- Include specific silver dollars within a broader collection—say, Liberty Seated coins, or designs by Christian Gobrecht, or coins of the New Orleans Mint.

Possibilities abound for the enthusiastic collector. The following considers two of the most popular: forming a representative collection of early dollars, and forming a type set.

COLLECTING EARLY DOLLARS, 1794–1803

Early silver dollars are generally collected by dates and major types. Perhaps as many as a few hundred numismatists today collect early dollars by die variety as described by Bolender (B) numbers and Bowers-Borckardt (BB) numbers. The number of early dollar devotees is but a fraction of those interested in, for example, early copper cents or Capped Bust half dollars, which means that scarce and rare die combinations of early dollars can often be purchased for little premium over more plentiful varieties. Although the 1794, of which an estimated 135 or so exist today, is famous and expensive, other early varieties are eminently affordable in such grades as Very Fine and Extremely Fine.

This rich panorama of die varieties is most extensively delineated in the 1993 two-volume study *Silver Dollars and Trade Dollars of the United States: A Complete Encyclopedia*. This built upon earlier works, including J.W. Haseltine's *Type Table of United States Dollars, Half Dollars and Quarter Dollars*, and, especially, the long-term standard work by M.H. Bolender, *The United States Early Silver Dollars from 1794 to 1803*.

If I were forming a basic collection of early dates and major varieties, I would want to include the following, although other collectors might emphasize different choices:

1794	1799, 9 Over 8 overdate
1795 Flowing Hair (with either two leaves or three leaves beneath each wing)	1799, 7 stars left, 6 right (normal arrangement)
1795 Draped Bust	1799, 8 stars left, 5 stars right
1796	1800
1797, 10 Stars left, 6 right	1801
1797, 9 Stars left, 7 right	1802, 2 Over 1 overdate
1798 Small Eagle reverse, 15 obverse stars	1802
1798 Small Eagle reverse, 13 obverse stars	1803
1798 Heraldic Eagle reverse	

COLLECTING A TYPE SET OF SILVER DOLLARS

Forming a type set of any denomination admits of personal options, and perhaps nowhere is this more relevant than whether to decide to include the 1839 Gobrecht silver dollar as a special type—or to ignore it. However, let me pursue the discussion in logical order:

- *Flowing Hair (1794–1795).* Examples of this type are easy enough to obtain in grades from Very Fine through low Mint State. The strike ranges from rather poor to barely acceptable, and planchet-adjustment marks are often seen, so cherrypicking will be needed to find a good example.

- *Draped Bust, Small Eagle (1795–1798).* Silver dollars of this type are fairly scarce. Sharpness of strike presents difficulty, and usually there are weaknesses in details, particularly on the reverse eagle.

- *Draped Bust, Heraldic Eagle (1798–1804).* Many examples of this type exist, mostly in grades from Very Fine through the lower Mint State ranges. The strike can be middling, but the population size presents more options to choose from.

- *Gobrecht (1836–1839).* Gobrecht dollars present a special challenge to the type-set collector. They were long considered to be patterns, exempting from the parameters of a type set of circulating coins. Research by R.W. Julian (in particular), Walter Breen, and others has revealed that the majority of 1836 and 1839 silver dollars originally produced went into circulation at face value. They were freely spent and are deserving of a place among regular coinage types. The 1836 is easy enough to find, although expensive. The 1839, however, was made only to the extent of 300 originals and perhaps a couple hundred restrikes. It is the rarest of all major United States silver design types, even outclassing the 1796 and 1797 half dollar. Whether to include this issue or to avoid it is up to the collector.

- *Liberty Seated (1840–1873).* The Liberty Seated design was produced with no motto from 1840 through 1865, and with the motto IN GOD WE TRUST on the reverse from 1866 through 1873. Both types are found easily enough in circulated grades from Very Fine up, as well as in the low Mint State ranges. Choice and gem Mint State pieces are in the minority, particularly of the 1840 to 1865 type.

- *Morgan (1878–1921).* Made by the hundreds of millions, Morgan dollars are easily found. The 1881-S in particular is the most common of issue existing today in gem condition and is usually seen with sharp strike and nice appearance.

- *Peace (1921–1935).* These are easy enough to obtain as examples abound. One can also consider the first year of issue, 1921, a separate type, as the design is in high relief. Plentiful in Mint State, the 1921 is rarely sharply struck. Later Peace dollars with shallow relief abound in choice and gem preservation, although striking can be a problem.

FLOWING HAIR (1794–1795)

Engraver: *Robert Scot.* **Weight:** *26.96 grams.* **Composition:** *.900 silver, .100 copper (net weight 0.78011 oz. pure silver).* **Diameter:** *Approximately 39–40 mm.* **Edge:** *Lettered HUNDRED CENTS ONE DOLLAR OR UNIT with decorations between the words.* **Mint:** *Philadelphia.*

BB-14, B-4.

Note: Values of common-date silver coins listed in the seventh edition of **Mega Red** *have been based on a silver bullion price of $27.50 per ounce, and may vary with the prevailing spot price. To determine the intrinsic value of common silver coins, see page 1415.*

BACKGROUND

The first U.S. silver dollars were of the Flowing Hair design. Although the Mint Act of April 2, 1792, specified the dollar as the largest silver denomination, no coins were struck in this metal until 1794, as there were problems in gaining surety bonds for certain Mint officials. At the time, the largest press at the Mint was intended for striking coins no larger than a half dollar. Surviving documents record Mint officials' lamenting the lack of a press suitable for coining silver dollars and medals. It was not until spring 1795 that one of sufficient capacity was installed.

In the meantime, a screw press suitable for coining cents and half dollars was put into service to make silver dollars. The initial coinage of the new denomination was accomplished in the first part of October 1794. The effort was not completely successful, as evidenced by surviving coins, which show areas of weak striking. Apparently, just one blow of the press was used (as evidenced by the lack of double-struck features on all this author has seen).

All known silver dollars dated 1794 are from a single pair of dies and are believed to have been made to the extent of perhaps 2,000 coins (per Walter H. Breen), of which 1,758 pieces deemed satisfactory were delivered by the coiner on October 15, 1794. The remaining impressions, possibly amounting to 242 coins, were rejected as being too weak and probably were kept on hand for later use as planchets. Supporting this theory is the existence of at least one 1795 silver dollar plainly overstruck on a 1794 dollar.

As with other early U.S. coins, the Mint took care to ensure that each planchet weighed a specific amount—in the case of the dollar, 29.96 grams. Overweight dollar planchets were filed as needed to bring them down to the proper weight. Underweight planchets were drilled or punched at the center and a small plug of silver was inserted into the hole. When the dies struck the planchet the plug merged into the surrounding silver, all but disappearing in many cases. Typically the plug is more visible on the back of the coin, where its spread is wider. Some coins show evidence of both planchet filing and plugging as the Mint workers attempted to perfect the planchet's weight. The Smithsonian's National Numismatic Collection includes a unique Specimen 1794 dollar, plugged.

The motif of the new dollars was the same as that used on the half dime and half dollar. On the obverse, the head of Miss Liberty faces to the right, with stars to each side, LIBERTY above, and the date below. On the reverse a delicate eagle perched on a rock is within a wreath, with UNITED STATES OF AMERICA around the border.

There seems to have been no ceremony launching the first American silver dollar, and none are known to have been preserved for collecting purposes. However, a few were preserved by chance, and today the handful existing in Mint State are exceedingly rare and highly prized.

In 1795, coinage of silver dollars was much more extensive, an adequate press having been installed. The mintage was 160,295, across many different die varieties and combinations.

ROBERT SCOT, ENGRAVER

Robert Scot (1740–1823) was born somewhere in the British Isles, but the exact location of his birth is unknown. He was first trained as a watchmaker in England but later learned the art of engraving. Scot was best known as an engraver of flat work, particularly of bank note plates. He came to America in 1777 and engraved plates for subsistence money. Just three years later he was appointed state engraver of Virginia.

In November 1793 Scot was commissioned as engraver of the U.S. Mint, by Mint director David Rittenhouse, to replace the recently deceased Joseph Wright. Although Scot has commonly been regarded incompetent as a die engraver, somehow the Mint was able to produce many beautiful dies in the decade to come. John Smith Gardner was hired as an assistant, and early in the nineteenth century, John Reich held a similar position. However, it seems likely that Scot, as the engraver in charge, did most of the important work. Punches for numbers and letters were obtained outside the Mint from the early days onward. Portrait engraving, wreaths, and other art was done at the Mint itself. At an early time, punches were devised for portraits and wreaths, with some decorative features such as berries added by hand.

Scot was less active in later years and is said to have been in poor health and with failing eyesight. He held the position of Mint engraver as a sinecure until his passing on November 3, 1823. Accordingly, it is difficult today to attribute certain work to Scot.

FLOWING HAIR (1794–1795): GUIDE TO COLLECTING

BEING A SMART BUYER

On the obverse, check the hair details. It is essential to check the die variety, as certain varieties were struck with very little detail at the center. Accordingly, high-grade examples can appear to be well worn on the hair. Check the star centers as well. On the reverse, check the breast and wings of the eagle. All 1794 dollars are lightly struck at the lower left of the obverse (often at portions of the date) and to a lesser extent the corresponding part of the reverse. Many coins of both dates have planchet adjustment marks (from overweight blanks being filed down to proper weight before striking), often heavy and sometimes even disfiguring; these are not noted by the certification services. Expect weakness in some areas on dollars of this type; a coin with Full Details on both sides is virtually unheard of. Sharp striking and excellent eye appeal add to the value dramatically. These coins are very difficult to find problem-free, even in Mint State.

AVAILABILITY

Finding a coin from a well-detailed die, and showing such features as hair details, sharp star centers, and sharp breast feathers on the eagle, will be a challenge—not in the league of the challenge facing you for the half dollar of the Flowing Hair type, but still requiring quite a bit of effort. The 1794 is rare in all grades, with an estimated 125 to 135 known, including a handful in Mint State. The 1795 is easily available, with an estimated 4,000 to 7,500 still existing, although some die varieties range from scarce to rare. Finding a coin without adjustment marks will be easier with the 1795 than the 1794. In addition, many have been dipped at one time or another, and many have been retoned, often satisfactorily. The existence of *any* luster is an exception between EF-40 and AU-58. Mint State coins are quite scarce (perhaps 150 to 250 existing, most dated 1795), especially at MS-63 or above.

Varieties listed herein are those most significant to collectors, but numerous minor variations may be found because each of the early dies was made individually. (Values of varieties not listed in *Mega Red* depend on collector interest and demand.) Coins with old adjustment marks from this filing process may be worth less than the values shown herein. Some Flowing Hair dollars were weight-adjusted through insertion of a small (8 mm) silver plug in the center of the blank planchet before the coin was struck.

FLOWING HAIR (1794–1795)

GRADING STANDARDS

**1794; BB-1, Bolender-1. Graded MS-64.
Fully brilliant and highly lustrous.**

MS-60 to 70 (Mint State). *Obverse:* At MS-60, some abrasion and contact marks are evident, most noticeably on the cheek and in the fields. Luster is present, but may be dull or lifeless, and interrupted in patches. At MS-63, contact marks are very few, and abrasion is light and not obvious. An MS-65 coin has little or, better yet, no abrasion, and contact marks are minute. Luster should be full and rich. Coins graded above MS-65 are more theoretical than actual for this type—but they do exist, and are defined by having fewer marks as perfection is approached. *Reverse:* Comments apply as for the obverse, except that abrasion and contact marks are most noticeable on the eagle at the center, although most dollars of this type are lightly struck in the higher points of that area. The field area is small and is protected by lettering and the wreath and in any given grade shows fewer marks than on the obverse.

Illustrated coin: Like all 1794 dollars, this coin is weak at the left obverse and the corresponding part of the reverse. Planchet flaws are seen at stars 3 and 5. The center obverse is very well struck.

AU-50, 53, 55, 58 (About Uncirculated). *Obverse:* Light wear is seen on the hair area immediately to the left of the face and neck (except for those flatly struck there), on the cheek, and on the top of the neck truncation, more so at AU-50 than at AU–53 or 55. An AU-58 coin has minimal traces of wear. An AU-50 coin has luster in protected areas among the stars and letters, with little luster in the open fields or the portrait. Some certi-

1795, Two Leaves; BB-21, Bolender-1. Graded AU-58.

fied coins have virtually no luster, but are considered high quality in other aspects. At AU-58, most luster is partially present in the fields. On any high-grade dollar, luster is often a better key to grading than is the appearance of wear. *Reverse:* Light wear is seen on the eagle's body and the upper edges of the wings. At AU-50, detail is lost for some of the feathers in this area. However, some coins are weak to begin with. Light wear is seen on the wreath and lettering. Again, luster is the best key to actual wear. This ranges from perhaps 20% remaining in protected areas (at AU-50) to two-thirds or more (at AU-58). Generally, the reverse has more luster than the obverse.

Illustrated coin: This coin shows above-average striking sharpness on the obverse.

EF-40, 45 (Extremely Fine). *Obverse:* More wear is evident on the portrait, especially on the hair to the left of the face and neck (again, remember that some varieties were struck with flatness in this area), the cheek, and the tip of the neck truncation. Excellent detail remains in low-relief areas of the hair. The stars show wear, as do the date and letters. Luster, if present at all, is minimal and in

1795, Three Leaves; BB-26, Bolender-12a. Graded EF-40.

protected areas. ***Reverse:*** The eagle shows more wear, this being the focal point to check. Most or nearly all detail is well defined. These aspects should be reviewed in combination with knowledge of the die variety, to determine the sharpness of the coin when it was first struck. Most silver dollars of this type were flat at the highest area of the center at the time they were made, as this was opposite the highest point of the hair in the press when the coins were struck. Additional wear is on the wreath and letters, but many details are present. Some luster may be seen in protected areas, and if present is slightly more abundant than on the obverse.

Illustrated coin: On the obverse, a massive die crack extends upward through the 7 of the date.

VF-20, 30 (Very Fine). *Obverse:* The hair is well worn at VF-20, less so at VF-30. On well-struck varieties the weakness is in the area left of the temple and cheek. The strands are blended as to be heavy. The cheek shows only slight relief. The stars have more wear, making them appear larger (an optical illusion). ***Reverse:*** The body of the eagle shows few if any feathers, while the wings have a third to half of the feathers visible, depending on the strike. The leaves

1795, Two Leaves; BB-21, Bolender-1. Graded VF-20.

lack most detail, but veins can be seen on a few. Scattered, non-disfiguring marks are normal for this and lower grades. Any major defects should be noted separately.

Illustrated coin: Light rim bumps should be noted. This coin features attractive medium toning.

F-12, 15 (Fine). *Obverse:* Wear is more extensive than on the preceding, reducing the definition of the thick strands of hair. The cheek has less detail, but the eye is usually well defined. On most coins, the stars appear larger. The rim is distinct in most areas, and many denticles remain visible. ***Reverse:*** Wear is more extensive. Now, feather details are fewer, mostly remaining on the wing to the left and at the extreme tip of the wing on the

1795, Three Leaves; BB-27, Bolender-5. Graded F-12.

right. As always, the die variety in question can have an influence on this. The wreath and lettering are worn further. The rim is usually complete, with most denticles visible.

Illustrated coin: This variety is flatly struck on the head, and examples in higher grades show no detail at the center. Note the smooth, even wear with some marks.

VG-8, 10 (Very Good). *Obverse:* The portrait is mostly seen in outline form, with most hair strands gone, although some are visible left of the neck, and the tips at the lower left are clear. The eye is distinct. The stars appear larger still, again an illusion. LIBERTY and the date are readable and usually full, although some letters may be weak at their tops. The rim is usually complete, and many denticles

1795, Two Leaves; BB-11, Bolender-3. Graded VG-10.

can be seen. *Reverse:* The eagle is mostly an outline, although some traces of feathers may be seen in the tail and the lower part of the inside of the right wing. The rim is worn, as are the letters, with some weak, but the motto is readable.

Illustrated coin: This coin shows some microscopic granularity overall. It is an interesting variety with a silver plug inserted at the center of the planchet prior to minting, to slightly increase the weight; this feature can barely be seen in outline form.

G-4, 6 (Good). *Obverse:* Wear is more extensive. LIBERTY and the stars are all there, but weak. The head is an outline, although the eye can still be seen. The rim is well worn or even missing. LIBERTY is worn, and parts of some letters may be missing, but elements of all should be readable. The date is readable, but worn. *Reverse:* The eagle is flat and discernible in outline form. The wreath is well worn. Some of the letters may be partly miss-

1795, Two Leaves; BB-11, Bolender-1. Graded G-6.

ing. At this level some "averaging" can be done. If the letters are stronger than usual in one area, but some are missing in another area, the coin can still qualify as G-4.

Illustrated coin: This is an attractive example with smooth, even wear and a few defects.

AG-3 (About Good). *Obverse:* Wear is extensive, but some stars and letters can usually be discerned. The head is in outline form. The date, while readable, may be partially worn away. *Reverse:* The reverse is well worn, with parts of the wreath and lettering missing.

1795, Three Leaves. Graded AG-3.

1794 Flowing Hair Dollar

1794 • **Circulation-Strike Mintage:** 1,758.

Availability: *Circulated state,* 140 to 160; *Mint State,* 5 to 7.

Commentary: In any grade a 1794 silver dollar attracts a lot of attention when offered for sale. All show some light striking at the lower left of the obverse and at the corresponding area of the reverse, as the die faces were not completely parallel in the coining press. PCGS lists two as MS-66!

BB-1, B-1.

	Cert	Avg	%MS	AG-3	G-4	VG-8	F-12	VF-20	EF-40	AU-50	MS-60	MS-63
1794	34	35.7	15%	$40,000	$67,500	$105,000	$135,000	$165,000	$325,000	$550,000	$1,000,000	$1,600,000

1794, Silver Plug • Circulation-Strike

Mintage: Part of 1,758.

Availability: These have not been carefully studied or described in listings. It is estimated that pieces with a silver plug are in the distinct minority, comprising less than 10% of the total.

Commentary: PCGS records exactly one 1794 coin with a silver plug, and it happens to be one of the most famous coins in all of American numismatics. Pictured above, the coin is known as the Neil/Carter coin (for two of its illustrious prior owners, Will W. Neil and Amon Carter Jr.), and it is the holder of many distinctions: Graded SP-66, it is the only one of the surviving 1784 dollars with prooflike fields, and in fact it may have been the first dollar ever struck. A peek at appendix D, "Top 250 U.S. Coin Prices Realized at Auction," reveals its status at the top of the list. In January 2013, the coin sold at auction for $10,016,875—a breathtaking sum.

BB-1, B-1.

	Cert	Avg	%MS	AG-3	G-4	VG-8	F-12	VF-20	EF-40	AU-50	MS-60	MS-63
1794, Silver Plug (unique)	1	66.0	100%									

1795 Flowing Hair Dollar

1795, Two Leaves • **Circulation-Strike**
Mintage: Part of 160,295.

Availability: *Circulated state,* 1,750 to 2,000; *Mint State,* 50 to 75.

Commentary: The upward-facing leaf clusters under each of the 1795 eagle's wings hold either two leaves or three, creating the two major varieties of this issue. In lower circulated grades the two varieties see little, if any, price differential, but when the condition approaches Mint State the Two Leaves variety has a slight edge.

BB-24, B-13.

Detail of the Two Leaves.

	Cert	Avg	%MS	AG-3	G-4	VG-8	F-12	VF-20	EF-40	AU-50	MS-60	MS-63
1795, Two Leaves	222	31.4	5%	$1,100	$2,250	$2,600	$4,000	$5,750	$12,500	$19,500	$65,000	$160,000

1795, Three Leaves • Circulation-Strike

Mintage: Part of 160,295.

Availability: *Circulated state*, 800 to 1,000; *Mint State*, 17 to 25

Commentary: See the commentary for the Two Leaves variety.

BB-18, B-7.

Detail of the Three Leaves.

	Cert	Avg	%MS	AG-3	G-4	VG-8	F-12	VF-20	EF-40	AU-50	MS-60	MS-63
1795, Three Leaves	199	34.1	2%	$1,100	$2,250	$2,500	$4,000	$5,250	$11,000	$18,000	$55,000	$150,000

1795, Silver Plug • Circulation-Strike

Mintage: Part of 160,295.

Availability: *Circulated state*, 80 to 110; *Mint State*, 2

Commentary: Coins with a silver weight-adjustment plug are seen in both the Two Leaves and Three Leaves varieties. At the low end of the condition spectrum, an AG-3 coin with silver plug commands a modest premium, but the gap widens with each successive grade, and a Mint State coin with silver plug can bring more than double what it would have without one.

BB-14, B-4.

	Cert	Avg	%MS	AG-3	G-4	VG-8	F-12	VF-20	EF-40	AU-50	MS-60	MS-63
1795, Silver Plug	1	61.0	100%	$1,500	$4,000	$6,500	$9,500	$16,000	$22,500	$45,000	$130,000	

DRAPED BUST, SMALL EAGLE REVERSE (1795–1798)

Designer: *Robert Scot.* **Weight:** *26.96 grams.* **Composition:** *.8924 silver, .1076 copper (net weight .77352 oz. pure silver).* **Diameter:** *Approximately 39–40 mm.* **Edge:** *Lettered HUNDRED CENTS ONE DOLLAR OR UNIT with decorations between the words.* **Mint:** *Philadelphia.*

BB-71, B-3.

Note: Values of common-date silver coins listed in the seventh edition of Mega Red have been based on a silver bullion price of $27.50 per ounce, and may vary with the prevailing spot price. To determine the intrinsic value of common silver coins, see page 1415.

BACKGROUND

The Draped Bust silver dollar with the Small Eagle reverse, inaugurated in 1795, brought the first appearance of this popular obverse portrait—a depiction of Miss Liberty that later was used on other silver denominations as well as copper half cents and cents. The design was said to have come from a Gilbert Stuart sketch of Ann Willing Bingham, a well-known society woman. The reverse design was modified slightly, with the eagle gaining a sturdier appearance, shorter wings, and clouds below its feet.

A 1785 sketch by Gilbert Stuart of Ann Willing Bingham, a 21-year-old socialite whose likeness the artist rendered several times over the years, both on paper and on canvas. The design of the Flowing Hair dollar may have come from a similar sketch by Stuart, passed along to Robert Scot ten years later.

This motif combination was continued on the dollar into 1798. Production of the Draped Bust silver dollars started at the end of the year on a new mint press that had first been used for striking Flowing Hair dollars that summer. Draped Bust dollars circulated widely, especially outside the United States, and in the Caribbean in particular.

DRAPED BUST, SMALL EAGLE REVERSE, DOLLARS (1795–1798): GUIDE TO COLLECTING

BEING A SMART BUYER

Striking on Draped Bust, Small Eagle, silver dollars is usually fairly decent, unless you take out a magnifying glass. Perfection is more of a goal than a possibility, but there are some nice examples out there, even if not every detail is needle-sharp. On the obverse, check the highest areas of the hair, the bust line, and the centers of the stars. On the reverse, check the feathers on the eagle's breast and wings. Examine the denticles. Planchet adjustment marks (from the filing down of overweight blanks) are common and should be avoided.

Studying die varieties can be helpful for accurate grading. For example, the Small Letters reverse, a long-lived die design used from 1795 to 1798, has shallow relief and is usually seen with a low rim, with the result that its grade is lower than that of the obverse. On some reverse dies the eagle has very little detail. Fairly sharp striking (not necessarily Full Details) and excellent eye appeal add to the value dramatically.

AVAILABILITY

These silver dollars are readily available as a type, although certain varieties range from scarce to very rare. Typical grades are Very Fine and Extremely Fine. About Uncirculated coins are rare; Mint State coins are elusive and when seen are usually of the 1795 date, sometimes with prooflike surfaces. Most coins have been dipped and/or retoned, some successfully so as not to impair the value. These coins acquired marks more readily than did smaller denominations, and such are to be expected (but should be noted along with the grade, if distracting). Careful buying is needed to obtain coins with good eye appeal. Many About Uncirculated examples are deeply toned and recolored.

The Smithsonian's National Numismatic Collection includes a unique Specimen 1797 dollar with 10 Stars Left, 6 Stars Right.

DRAPED BUST, SMALL EAGLE REVERSE (1795–1798)
GRADING STANDARDS

MS-60 to 70 (Mint State). *Obverse:* At MS-60, some abrasion and contact marks are evident, most noticeably on the cheek, the drapery at the shoulder, and the right field. Luster is present, but may be dull or lifeless, and interrupted in patches. At MS-63, contact marks are few, and abrasion is harder to detect. Many coins listed as Mint State are deeply toned, making it impossible to evaluate abrasion and even light wear; these are best avoided completely. An MS-65 coin has

1796, Small Date, Large Letters;
BB-61, Bolender-2. Graded MS-60.

no abrasion, and contact marks are so minute as to require magnification. Luster should be full and rich. Coins grading above MS-65 are more theoretical than actual for this type—but they do exist, and are defined by having fewer marks as perfection is approached. *Reverse:* Comments apply as for the obverse, except that abrasion and contact marks are most noticeable on the eagle at the center, a situation complicated by the fact that this area was often flatly struck, not only on the famous Small Letters dies used from 1795 to 1798, but on some others as well. Grading is best done by the obverse, then verified by the reverse. In the Mint State category the amount of luster is usually a good key to grading. The field area is small and is protected by lettering and the wreath, and in any given grade shows fewer marks than on the obverse.

Illustrated coin: Note the tiny dig near Miss Liberty's ear. This coin is fairly well struck overall, but with some lightness on the eagle's body and leg on the right. It has excellent eye appeal.

AU-50, 53, 55, 58 (About Uncirculated).
Obverse: Light wear is seen on the hair area above the ear and extending to left of the forehead, on the ribbon, and on the drapery at the shoulder, more so at AU-50 than at AU-53 or 55. An AU-58 coin has minimal traces of wear. An AU-50 coin has luster in protected areas among the stars and letters, with little in the open fields or on the portrait. At AU-58, most luster is present in the fields, but is worn away on the highest parts of the motifs. At this level

1797, Stars 9x7, Large Letters;
BB-73, Bolender-1. Graded AU-50.

there are many deeply toned and recolored coins, necessitating caution when buying. *Reverse:* Light wear is seen on the eagle's body (keep in mind this area might be lightly struck) and edges of the wings. Light wear is seen on the wreath and lettering. Luster is the best key to actual wear. This ranges from perhaps 20% remaining in protected areas (at AU-50) to nearly full mint bloom (at AU-58).

Illustrated coin: This coin has some lightness of strike, but is better than average. It has some dings and marks, but these are not immediately obvious; without them, the coin might grade higher. This illustrates the many variables on these large, heavy coins. No single rule fits all.

EF-40, 45 (Extremely Fine). *Obverse:* More wear is evident on the upper hair area and the ribbon, and on the drapery and bosom. Excellent detail remains in low-relief areas of the hair. The stars show wear, as do the date and letters. Luster, if present at all, is minimal and in protected areas. For any and all dollars of this type, knowledge of die variety characteristics is essential to grading. Once again, one rule does not fit all. *Reverse:* The eagle, this being the focal point to check, shows

1796, Small Date, Large Letters; BB-61, Bolender-4. Graded EF-40.

more wear. On most strikings, the majority of feathers remain on the interior areas of the wings. Additional wear is on the wreath and letters, but many details are present. Some luster may be seen in protected areas and if present is slightly more abundant than on the obverse.

Illustrated coin: Some marks are on the neck and a small pit is above the eagle's beak.

VF-20, 30 (Very Fine). *Obverse:* The higher-relief areas of hair are well worn at VF-20, less so at VF-30. The drapery and bosom show extensive wear, usually resulting in loss of most detail below the neck. The stars have more wear, making them appear larger. *Reverse:* The body of the eagle shows few if any feathers, while the wings have about half of the feathers visible, depending on the strike. The leaves lack most detail and are in outline form. Scattered, non-disfiguring marks are normal for this and lower grades. Any major defects should be noted separately.

1797, Stars 9x7, Small Letters; BB-72, Bolender-2. Graded VF-20.

Illustrated coin: This is the particularly famous Small Letters die (one of three Small Letters dies used for this type) first used in 1795 and last used in 1798. Used on 1795 BB-51, later 1796 BB-62, BB-63, and BB-66 now relapped, 1797 BB-72, and 1798 BB-81. The rims are low, and the eagle is in low relief. For coins struck from this particular reverse die, grading must be done by the obverse only.

F-12, 15 (Fine). *Obverse:* Wear is more extensive than on a Very Fine coin, particularly noticeable on the hair, face, and bosom. The stars appear larger. About half the hair detail remains, most noticeably behind the neck and shoulder. The rim shows wear but is complete or nearly so, with most denticles visible. *Reverse:* Wear is more extensive. Now, feather details are diminished, with relatively few remaining on the wings. The wreath and lettering are worn further, and

1796, Large Date, Small Letters; BB-65, Bolender-5. Graded F-12.

the rim is usually weak in areas, although most denticles can be seen.

Illustrated coin: This is not the long-lived Small Letters die discussed above; this Small Letters die was used only in 1796. It is distinguished by a piece out of the die at the lower right of the reverse.

VG-8, 10 (Very Good). *Obverse:* The portrait is worn further, with much detail lost in the area above the level of the ear, although the curl over the forehead is delineated. There is some definition at the back of the hair and behind the shoulder, with the hair now combined to form thick strands. The ear is discernible, as is the eye. The stars appear larger still, again an illusion. The rim is weak in areas. LIBERTY and the date are readable and usually full. The rim is worn away in areas, although

1796, Small Date, Large Letters;
BB-61, Bolender-4. Graded VG-10.

many denticles can still be discerned. *Reverse:* The eagle is mostly an outline, with parts blending into the field (on lighter strikes). The rim is worn, as are the letters, with some weak, but the motto is readable.

Illustrated coin: Note the vertical scratches on the cheek.

G-4, 6 (Good). *Obverse:* Wear is more extensive, and some stars may be partly missing. The head is an outline. The eye is visible only in outline form. The rim is well worn or even missing in areas. LIBERTY is worn, and parts of some letters may be missing, but elements of all should be readable. The date is readable, but worn. Usually the date is rather bold. *Reverse:* The eagle is flat and discernible in outline form, and may be blending into the field. The wreath is well worn. Some

1797, Stars 9x7, Large Letters;
BB-73, Bolender-1. Graded G-4.

of the letters may be partly missing (for some shallow-relief dies with low rims). At this level some "averaging" can be done. If the letters are stronger than usual in one area, but some are missing in another area, the coin can still qualify as G-4. This general rule is applicable to most other series as well.

Illustrated coin: This is a well-circulated coin with several edge bumps.

AG-3 (About Good). *Obverse:* Wear is very extensive, but most letters and stars should be discernible. The head is in outline form. The date, while readable, may be partially worn away. *Reverse:* The reverse is well worn, with parts of the wreath and lettering missing. At this level, the reverse usually gives much less information than does the obverse.

1796, Large Date, Small Letters;
BB-65, Bolender-5a. Graded AG-3.

1795 Draped Bust, Small Eagle Reverse, Dollar

1795 • **Circulation-Strike Mintage:** 42,738 estimated.

Availability: *Circulated state,* 2,200 to 3,400; *Mint State,* 35 to 45.

Commentary: The Draped Bust dollar in 1795 is seen in two major varieties, one with the bust of Liberty centered and one with the bust slightly offset to the left. The difference between the two is most evident at the ribbon in Liberty's hair, which is closer to the stars at left on the offset variety; and at the truncation of Liberty's bust, which is farther from the lower right star. Both varieties are readily available in the middle circulated grades. Although the Off-Center Bust variety (BB-51) is seen less frequently than the Centered Bust variety (BB-52), there is little price differential between them.

BB-52, B-15, Centered Bust.

Comparison of a Centered Bust (top) to an Off-Center Bust. Their relative positions are most obvious at the back of the bow in Liberty's hair.

	Cert	Avg	%MS	AG-3	G-4	VG-8	F-12	VF-20	EF-40	AU-50	MS-60	MS-63
1795	141	37.7	9%	$960	$1,850	$2,150	$3,500	$5,100	$9,500	$15,500	$55,000	$150,000

1796 Draped Bust, Small Eagle Reverse, Dollar

The 1796 Draped Bust coinage exists in three major varieties combining two different date sizes and two different letter sizes, plus a number of die varieties enjoyed by specialists. The Small Date, Small Letters variety is most commonly encountered.

1796, Small Date, Small Letters •
Circulation-Strike Mintage: Part of 79,920.

Availability: *Circulated state,* 175 to 300; *Mint State,* 1 reported; not confirmed.

BB-66, B-1.

Detail of the Small Date.   Detail of the Small Letters.

	Cert	Avg	%MS	AG-3	G-4	VG-8	F-12	VF-20	EF-40	AU-50	MS-60	MS-63
1796, Small Date, Small Letters	24	40.5	4%	$825	$1,850	$2,100	$3,800	$5,500	$9,500	$14,000	$62,500	$150,000

1796, Small Date, Large Letters •

Circulation-Strike Mintage: Part of 79,920.

Availability: *Circulated state*, 1,200 to 2,000; *Mint State*, 4 to 6.

BB-61, B-4.

Detail of the Small Date.   Detail of the Large Letters.

	Cert	Avg	%MS	AG-3	G-4	VG-8	F-12	VF-20	EF-40	AU-50	MS-60	MS-63
1796, Small Date, Large Letters	52	37.3	4%	$825	$1,850	$2,100	$3,800	$5,500	$9,500	$14,000	$75,000	$200,000

1796, Large Date, Small Letters •

Circulation-Strike Mintage: Part of 79,920.

Availability: *Circulated state*, 800 to 1,400; *Mint State*, 4 to 6.

BB-65, B-5.

Detail of the Large Date.   Detail of the Small Letters.

	Cert	Avg	%MS	AG-3	G-4	VG-8	F-12	VF-20	EF-40	AU-50	MS-60	MS-63
1796, Large Date, Small Letters	57	32.4	4%	$825	$1,850	$2,100	$3,400	$5,250	$9,500	$14,000	$62,500	$160,000

1797 Draped Bust, Small Eagle Reverse, Dollar

1797, 10 Stars Left, 6 Right •

Circulation-Strike Mintage: Part of 7,776.

Availability: *Circulated state*, 1,200 to 1,800; *Mint State*, 10 to 15.

BB-71, B-3.

	Cert	Avg	%MS	AG-3	G-4	VG-8	F-12	VF-20	EF-40	AU-50	MS-60	MS-63
1797, 10 Stars Left, 6 Right	124	37.3	5%	$850	$1,850	$2,000	$3,000	$5,000	$9,000	$13,750	$62,000	$125,000

1797, 9 Stars Left, 7 Right, Small Letters • Circulation-Strike Mintage: Part of 7,776.

Availability: *Circulated state,* 200 to 300; *Mint State,* 2 or 3.

BB-72, B-2.

Detail of the Small Letters.

	Cert	Avg	%MS	AG-3	G-4	VG-8	F-12	VF-20	EF-40	AU-50	MS-60	MS-63
1797, 9 Stars Left, 7 Right, Small Letters	32	31.7	0%	$1,200	$2,100	$2,750	$3,900	$8,200	$15,000	$32,500	$105,000	

1797, 9 Stars Left, 7 Right, Large Letters • Circulation-Strike Mintage: Part of 7,776.

Availability: *Circulated state,* 1,200 to 2,200; *Mint State,* 5 to 10.

BB-73, B-1.

Detail of the Large Letters.

	Cert	Avg	%MS	AG-3	G-4	VG-8	F-12	VF-20	EF-40	AU-50	MS-60	MS-63
1797, 9 Stars Left, 7 Right, Large Letters	88	34.7	5%	$850	$1,850	$2,000	$3,100	$6,000	$9,500	$13,500	$63,000	$135,000

1798 Draped Bust, Small Eagle Reverse, Dollar

1798, 15 Stars on Obverse • Circulation-Strike Mintage: Part of 327,536.

Availability: *Circulated state,* 599 to 900; *Mint State,* 6 to 12 (MS-60 or close).

BB-81, B-2.

	Cert	Avg	%MS	AG-3	G-4	VG-8	F-12	VF-20	EF-40	AU-50	MS-60	MS-63
1798, 15 Stars on Obverse	34	36.8	6%	$1,100	$2,150	$2,650	$3,800	$8,000	$15,000	$25,000	$82,500	$155,000

1798, 13 Stars on Obverse •

Circulation-Strike Mintage: Part of 327,536.

Availability: *Circulated state,* 700 to 1,200; *Mint State,* 1.

BB-82, B-1.

	Cert	Avg	%MS	AG-3	G-4	VG-8	F-12	VF-20	EF-40	AU-50	MS-60	MS-63
1798, 13 Stars on Obverse	30	38.4	7%	$1,000	$1,850	$2,100	$3,500	$7,750	$12,500	$20,000	$150,000	

DRAPED BUST, HERALDIC EAGLE REVERSE (1798–1804)

Designer: *Robert Scot.* **Weight:** *26.96 grams.* **Composition:** *.8924 silver, .1076 copper (net weight .77352 oz. pure silver).* **Diameter:** *Approximately 39–40 mm.* **Edge:** *Lettered HUNDRED CENTS ONE DOLLAR OR UNIT with decorations between the words.* **Mint:** *Philadelphia.*

BB-159, B-23.

Note: Values of common-date silver coins listed in the seventh edition of **Mega Red** *have been based on a silver bullion price of $27.50 per ounce, and may vary with the prevailing spot price. To determine the intrinsic value of common silver coins, see page 1415.*

BACKGROUND

The design of the silver dollar closely follows that of other silver coins of the era. The two earliest reverse dies of 1798 have five vertical lines in the stripes in the shield. All dollar dies thereafter have four vertical lines. Production of the Draped Bust dollar continued through early 1804, but in that year the 19,570 dollars struck were from earlier-dated dies, probably mostly 1803.

The 1804 issues were actually struck in 1834 from dies prepared that year with the 1804 date. Popularly known as the "King of American Coins," these Proof strikes are discussed in more detail in their catalog listing.

DRAPED BUST, HERALDIC EAGLE REVERSE (1798–1804): GUIDE TO COLLECTING

BEING A SMART BUYER

Very few of the Draped Bust, Heraldic Eagle, dollars have Full Details. On the obverse, check the highest points of the hair, the details of the drapery, and the centers of the stars. On the reverse, check the shield, the eagle details, the stars above the eagle, and the clouds. Examine the denticles on both sides. Planchet adjustment marks are often seen, from overweight blanks being filed down to proper specifications, but they usually are lighter than on the earlier silver dollar types. The relief of the dies and the height of the rims can vary, affecting sharpness. Sharp striking and excellent eye appeal add to the value dramatically. Top-grade Mint State coins, when found, usually are dated 1800.

AVAILABILITY

This is the most readily available type among the early silver dollars, with 1798 and 1799 being the dates most often seen. Many of the varieties are available in just about any grade desired (although MS-63 and 65 coins are elusive), while others are rare at any level. These silver dollars usually have problems, so—as with other early dollars—connoisseurship is needed to acquire high-quality coins. To evaluate one for the market it is necessary to grade it, determine its quality of striking, and examine the characteristics of its surface. Nearly all have been dipped or cleaned.

PROOFS

No Proofs of this type were issued in the normal course of Mint business. Years later, in 1834, the Mint created dies with the 1804 date and struck an unknown number of Proofs, perhaps a dozen or so, for inclusion in presentation Proof sets for foreign dignitaries. Today these are called Class I 1804 dollars. Eight examples are known, one of which shows evidence of circulation. The finest by far is the Sultan of Muscat coin, which approaches perfection. Circa 1858 or 1859 the Mint prepared a new obverse die dated 1804 and struck an unknown number of examples for private sale to collectors and dealers—the Class III dollars. No records were kept. These were artificially worn to give them the appearance of original dollars struck in 1804.

Sometime between about 1858 and the 1870s, the Mint prepared new obverse dies dated 1801, 1802, and 1803, and struck Proof coins for secret sale to the numismatic market. Many if not most were distributed through J.W. Haseltine, a Philadelphia dealer who had close connections with Mint officials. Today these are known as "Proof restrikes." All are rare, the 1801 being particularly so.

Class I 1804 dollars typically show hairlines and light abrasion. Grading is usually very liberal, in view of the fame of this rarity (not that this is logical). Circulated examples of Class I and Class III 1804 dollars have been graded using prefixes such as Extremely Fine and About Uncirculated. Proof restrikes of 1801 to 1803 generally survive in much higher grades, PF-64 or finer.

DRAPED BUST, HERALDIC EAGLE REVERSE (1798–1804)

GRADING STANDARDS

MS-60 to 70 (Mint State). *Obverse:* At MS-60, some abrasion and contact marks are evident, most noticeably on the cheek, the drapery, and the right field. Luster is present, but may be dull or lifeless, and interrupted in patches. At MS-63, contact marks are very few, and abrasion is hard to detect except under magnification. Knowledge of the die variety is desirable, but on balance the por-

1798, 10 Arrows; BB-108, Bolender-13. Graded MS-63.

traits on this type are usually quite well struck. An MS-65 coin has no abrasion, and contact marks are so minute as to require magnification. Luster should be full and rich. Coins grading above MS-65 are more theoretical than actual for this type—but they do exist and are defined by having fewer marks as perfection is approached. *Reverse:* Comments apply as for the obverse, except that abrasion and contact marks are most noticeable on the eagle's neck, the tips of the wing, and the tail. The field area is complex, without much open space, given the stars above the eagle, the arrows and olive branch, and other features. Accordingly, marks will not be as noticeable as on the obverse.

Illustrated coin: This coin is well struck, essentially problem free, and with superb eye appeal.

AU-50, 53, 55, 58 (About Uncirculated). *Obverse:* Light wear is seen on the hair area above the ear and extending to left of the forehead, on the ribbon, and on the drapery and bosom, more so at AU-50 than AU-53 or 55. An AU-58 coin has minimal traces of wear. An AU-50 coin has luster in protected areas among the stars and letters, with little in the open fields or on the portrait. At AU-58, much luster is present in the fields, but is worn away on the highest parts of the

1799, Irregular Date, 13-Star Reverse; BB-152, Bolender-15. Graded AU-50.

motifs. *Reverse:* Comments as preceding, except that the eagle's neck, the tips and top of the wings, the clouds, and the tail now show noticeable wear, as do other features. Luster ranges from perhaps 20% remaining in protected areas (at AU-50) to nearly full mint bloom (at AU-58). Sometimes the reverse of this type retains much more luster than the obverse, this being dependent on the height of the rim and the depth of the strike (particularly at the center).

Illustrated coin: This is an attractive and problem-free coin.

EF-40, 45 (Extremely Fine). *Obverse:* More wear is evident on the upper hair area and the ribbon, and on the drapery and bosom. The shoulder is a key spot to check for wear. Excellent detail remains in low-relief areas of the hair. The stars show wear, as do the date and letters. Luster, if present at all, is minimal and in protected areas. *Reverse:* Wear is greater than on an AU coin, overall. The neck has lost its feather detail on the highest points. Feathers have lost some detail near the edges of the

1802, Narrow Normal Date; BB-241, Bolender-6. Graded EF-45.

wings. Some traces of luster may be seen, more so at EF-45 than at EF-40.

Illustrated coin: This is an attractive example retaining some mint luster. It has above-average striking sharpness.

VF-20, 30 (Very Fine). *Obverse:* The higher-relief areas of hair are well worn at VF-20, less so at VF-30. The drapery at the shoulder and the bosom show extensive wear. The stars have more wear, making them appear larger (an optical illusion seen on most worn silver coins of this era). *Reverse:* Wear is greater, including on the shield and the wing feathers. Most of the feathers on the wings are clear. The star centers are flat. Other areas have lost detail as well.

1799; BB-157, Bolender-5. Graded VF-20.

Illustrated coin: Some scratches appear on the portrait. This coin was cleaned long ago and now is retoned. It is a typical early dollar at this grade.

F-12, 15 (Fine). *Obverse:* Wear is more extensive than on a Very Fine coin, particularly on the hair, face, and bosom. The stars appear larger. About half the hair detail remains, most noticeably behind the neck and shoulder. The rim may be partially worn away and blend into the field. *Reverse:* Wear is even more extensive, with the shield and wing feathers being points to observe. Half or slightly more of the feathers will remain clear. The incuse E PLURIBUS UNUM

1798, Pointed 9, Close Date; BB-122, Bolender-14. Graded F-12.

may have a few letters worn away. The clouds all seem to be connected except on varieties in which they are spaced apart. The stars are weak. Parts of the border and lettering may be weak.

Illustrated coin: This coin was cleaned long ago. Cleaning and retoning is common on dollars of this era, but often is not noted by the grading services.

VG-8, 10 (Very Good). *Obverse:* The portrait is mostly seen in outline form, with most hair strands gone, although there is some definition at the back of the hair and behind the shoulder. The ear is discernible, as is the eye. The stars appear larger still, again an illusion. The rim is weak in areas. LIBERTY and the date are readable and usually full, although some letters may be weak at their tops. *Reverse:* Wear is more extensive. Half

1799. Graded VG-8.

or more of the letters in the motto are worn away. Most feathers are worn away, although separation of some of the lower feathers may be seen at the edges of the wings. Some stars are faint or missing. The border blends into the field in areas and some letters are weak. As always, a particular die variety can vary in areas of weakness.

G-4, 6 (Good). *Obverse:* Wear is more extensive, and some stars may be partly missing. The head is an outline. The eye is visible only in outline form. The rim is well worn or even missing in areas. LIBERTY is worn, and parts of some letters may be missing, but elements of all should be readable. The date is readable, but worn. *Reverse:* Wear is more extensive. The upper part of the eagle is flat. The feathers are noticeable only at the lower

1799; BB-169, Bolender-21. Graded G-4.

edge of the wings, sometimes incompletely, and do not have detail. The upper part of the shield is mostly flat. Only a few letters of the motto can be seen, if any at all. The rim is worn extensively, and the letters are well worn, but the inscription should be readable.

Illustrated coin: This coin has some marks, but is respectable for the grade.

AG-3 (About Good). *Obverse:* Wear is so extensive that the coin is barely identifiable. The head is in outline form. LIBERTY is mostly gone; same for the stars. The date, while readable, may be partially worn away. *Reverse:* Extensive wear is seen overall, with the rim worn away and some areas worn smooth. The eagle can be discerned in outline form, but not necessarily completely. A few stray motto letters may remain.

1799. Graded AG-3.

PF-60 to 70 (Proof). *Obverse and Reverse:* For lower Proof levels, extensive abrasion is seen in the fields, or even evidence of circulation (the Mickley example of the 1804 Class I, earlier graded as AU-50, was certified as PF-62 by a leading certification service in 2008). Numbers assigned by grading services have been erratic. No rules are known, and grading has not been consistent.

1804, Class I. Proof.

1798 Draped Bust, Heraldic Eagle Reverse, Dollar

1798, Knob 9 • Circulation-Strike
Mintage: Part of 327,536.

Availability: *Circulated state,* 750 to 1,100; *Mint State,* 4 to 6.

Commentary: A total of 31 different die marriages are known for the date. All can be divided into one of two major date varieties: the earlier coins have a Knob 9, with a small knob or finial on the tail of the 9 in the date; the later and more common dies have a Pointed 9, with the tail of the digit tapering to a clean point. The Knob 9 is found with either four or five vertical lines in the shield on the reverse. Some of the 5 Lines coins have 10 Arrows (rather than 12) in the eagle's claw. Most of the 1798 varieties are valued similarly, with only small divergences in certain grades.

BB-96, B-6.

Detail of the Knob 9.

	Cert	Avg	%MS	G-4	VG-8	F-12	VF-20	EF-40	AU-50	MS-60	MS-63	MS-65
1798, Knob 9	77	37.3	4%	$850	$1,050	$1,450	$2,600	$4,000	$6,000	$25,000	$75,000	

1798, Pointed 9 • Circulation-Strike
Mintage: Part of 327,536.

Availability: *Circulated state,* 3,000 to 4,000; *Mint State,* 12 to 18.

Commentary: The 1798 with Pointed 9 in the date shares in the 31 known die marriages for the date. The Pointed 9, with the tail of the digit tapering to a clean point, is from the later and more plentiful dies. Like the Knob 9, the Pointed 9 is found with either four or five vertical lines in the shield on the reverse. Other desirable varieties are the 10 Arrows, the 4 Berries, and the Wide Date. None of the 1798 varieties stands dramatically apart from the others with respect to market value.

BB-105, B-23.

Detail of the Pointed 9.

	Cert	Avg	%MS	G-4	VG-8	F-12	VF-20	EF-40	AU-50	MS-60	MS-63	MS-65
1798, Pointed 9	436	34.7	3%	$850	$1,050	$1,450	$2,600	$4,000	$6,000	$22,000	$70,000	

1799 Draped Bust, Heraldic Eagle Reverse, Dollar

1799, 99 Over 98, 15-Star Reverse •
Circulation-Strike Mintage: Part of 423,515.

Availability: *Circulated state,* 300 to 500; *Mint State,* 20 to 30.

BB-141, B-3.

	Cert	Avg	%MS	G-4	VG-8	F-12	VF-20	EF-40	AU-50	MS-60	MS-63	MS-65
1799, 99 Over 98, 15-Star Reverse	46	39.4	7%	$960	$1,250	$1,800	$2,850	$4,250	$6,250	$23,000	$57,000	—

1799, 99 Over 98, 13-Star Reverse •
Circulation-Strike Mintage: Part of 423,515.

Availability: *Circulated state,* 500 to 800; *Mint State,* 6 to 12.

BB-143, B-2.

	Cert	Avg	%MS	G-4	VG-8	F-12	VF-20	EF-40	AU-50	MS-60	MS-63	MS-65
1799, 99 Over 98, 13-Star Reverse	36	36.8	8%	$950	$1,150	$1,750	$2,700	$4,000	$6,000	$22,400	$56,500	—

1799, Normal Date • Circulation-Strike
Mintage: Part of 423,515.

Availability: *Circulated state,* 3,000 to 4,500; *Mint State,* 15 to 25.

B-5a.

	Cert	Avg	%MS	G-4	VG-8	F-12	VF-20	EF-40	AU-50	MS-60	MS-63	MS-65
1799, Normal Date	2,158	34.5	4%	$900	$1,050	$1,550	$2,550	$4,000	$6,000	$22,400	$56,500	$185,000

1799, 8 Stars Left, 5 Right • Circulation-Strike Mintage: Part of 423,515.

Availability: *Circulated state,* 500 to 900; *Mint State,* 1 to 3.

BB-159, B-23.

	Cert	Avg	%MS	G-4	VG-8	F-12	VF-20	EF-40	AU-50	MS-60	MS-63	MS-65
1799, 8 Stars Left, 5 Right	38	38.7	5%	$1,000	$1,250	$1,900	$3,100	$5,000	$7,500	$32,500	$92,500	—

1800 Draped Bust, Heraldic Eagle Reverse, Dollar

1800 • Circulation-Strike Mintage:
Part of 220,920.

Availability: *Circulated state,* 5,000 to 7,400; *Mint State,* 28 to 35.

BB-193, B-13.

Commentary: The many varieties found in the 1800 coinage present Draped Bust afficionados with ample opportunities for enjoyment. Among them are the Very Wide Date, Low 8 variety; the 12 Arrows variety; the Dotted Date variety (with later die states showing rust dots not apparent on early states); and a variety with AMERICAI in the legend.

	Cert	Avg	%MS	G-4	VG-8	F-12	VF-20	EF-40	AU-50	MS-60	MS-63	MS-65
1800	999	36.2	3%	$900	$1,050	$1,600	$2,400	$4,000	$7,000	$24,000	$55,000	$185,000

1801 Draped Bust, Heraldic Eagle Reverse, Dollar

1801 • Circulation-Strike Mintage: 54,454.

Availability: *Circulated state,* 1,400 to 1,800; *Mint State,* 14 to 18.

BB-211, B-1.

	Cert	Avg	%MS	G-4	VG-8	F-12	VF-20	EF-40	AU-50	MS-60	MS-63	MS-65
1801	324	36.7	5%	$900	$1,050	$1,600	$2,400	$4,250	$6,500	$29,500	$82,500	$275,000

1801, Restrike, Proof • Proof Mintage: 2 known.

Availability: 2.

Commentary: In 1858, a handful of Draped Bust, Heraldic Eagle Proofs—the 1801, 1802, and 1803—were restruck at the Mint and tucked away. In the 1870s they were sold to collectors. Of these coins the rarest is the 1801, with just two examples known.

	Cert	Avg	%MS	PF-63	PF-64	PF-65
1801, Restrike, Proof	1	66.0		$750,000	$1,000,000	—

1802 Draped Bust, Heraldic Eagle Reverse, Dollar

1802, 2 Over 1 • Circulation-Strike Mintage: Part of 41,650.

Availability: *Circulated state,* 125 to 175; *Mint State,* 10 to 15.

Commentary: This overdate has Narrow Date and Wide Date subvarieties, with the Wide Date coins commanding a slight premium over the values listed here.

BB-232, B-4.

Narrow Date.　　　Wide Date.

	Cert	Avg	%MS	G-4	VG-8	F-12	VF-20	EF-40	AU-50	MS-60	MS-63	MS-65
1802, 2 Over 1	60	35.1	7%	$950	$1,100	$1,800	$2,500	$4,250	$6,500	$30,000	$65,000	—

1802 • Circulation-Strike Mintage: Part of 41,650.

Availability: *Circulated state,* 1,000 to 1,500; *Mint State,* 12 to 20.

Commentary: The 1802 issue without over-date, like the 1802, 2 Over 1, has both Narrow Date and Wide Date subvarieties. Here, too, the Wide Date coins command a slight premium in most grades over the values listed here; in MS-65, a Wide Date coin would bring around $300,000.

BB-241, B-6.

	Cert	Avg	%MS	G-4	VG-8	F-12	VF-20	EF-40	AU-50	MS-60	MS-63	MS-65
1802	67	39.8	10%	$950	$1,100	$1,700	$2,400	$4,250	$6,500	$23,500	$65,000	$185,000

1802, Restrike, Proof • Proof Mintage: 4 known.

Availability: 4.

Commentary: See the commentary for the 1801, Restrike, Proof.

BB-302, B-8.

	Cert	Avg	%MS	PF-63	PF-64	PF-65
1802, Restrike, Proof	3	64.0		$275,000	$450,000	$700,000

1803 Draped Bust, Heraldic Eagle Reverse, Dollar

1803 • Circulation-Strike Mintage: 85,634.

Availability: *Circulated state,* 2,000 to 3,000; *Mint State,* 15 to 20.

Commentary: Two different punches were used for the 3 in the date for 1803. One of these resulted in the date we know today as the Small 3 variety, while the other is known as the Large 3. The two are about equally represented among today's surviving examples, although the Small 3 has a slight edge over the other. Both varieties are quite rare in Mint State grades. As to pricing, little if any differential is seen in circulated grades; at about MS-63, the Small 3 begins to command a slight premium.

BB-254, B-4.
Small 3.

BB-255, B-6. Large 3.

Detail of the Small 3.

Detail of the Large 3.

	Cert	Avg	%MS	G-4	VG-8	F-12	VF-20	EF-40	AU-50	MS-60	MS-63	MS-65
1803	146	37.5	5%	$1,000	$1,050	$1,800	$2,650	$4,500	$6,500	$27,000	$70,000	—

1803, Restrike, Proof • Proof Mintage:
4 known.

Availability: 3.

Commentary: See the commentary for the 1801, Restrike, Proof.

BB-303, B-7.

	Cert	Avg	%MS	PF-63	PF-64	PF-65
1803, Restrike, Proof	6	65.7		$275,000	$450,000	$700,000

1804 Draped Bust, Heraldic Eagle Reverse, Dollar

The 1804 silver dollars were first struck in 1834 from dies prepared that year but dated 1804. (As a class these can be called *novodels*, rather than *restrikes*, as no originals were ever made in 1804.) The 1804 dollars were produced in Proof format. Later, probably circa 1859, a new reverse die was made up and combined with the earlier 1804 obverse (made in 1834). The coins made around that time are known today as Class I dollars, whereas those made with a different reverse, beginning in 1859 and continuing perhaps through the 1870s, are known as Class III. An intermediate variety, from the Class III die combination but with a plain rather than lettered edge, is in the Smithsonian Institution's National Numismatic Collection and is known as Class II. All varieties combined comprise 15 different specimens. The 1804 dollar has been called the "King of American Coins" for well over a century and has achieved great fame. Interested numismatists are directed to *The Fantastic 1804 Dollar, Tribute Edition* (2009).

1804, First Reverse, Class I, Proof •
Proof Mintage: 8 known.

Availability: 8.

BB-304.
Sultan of Muscat–Childs
Collection coin. Finest known.

	Cert	Avg	%MS	PF-63	PF-64	PF-65
1804, Class I, First Reverse (O Above Cloud)	4	56.0		$2,750,000	$3,000,000	$3,500,000

1804, Second Reverse, Restrike, Plain Edge, Class II, Proof • Proof Mintage: 1.
Availability: 1.

	Cert	Avg	%MS	PF-63	PF-64	PF-65
1804, Class II, Second Reverse (O Above Space Between Clouds)				*(unique, in Smithsonian collection)*		

1804, Second Reverse, Restrike, Class III, Proof • Proof Mintage: 6 known.

Availability: 6.

BB-306.

	Cert	Avg	%MS	PF-63	PF-64	PF-65
1804, Class III, Second Reverse (O Above Space Between Clouds)					(6 known)	

1804, Electrotype of Unique Plain-Edge Specimen • Specimen Mintage: 4.

Availability: 4.

GOBRECHT DOLLARS (1836–1839)

No Stars on Obverse, Stars on Reverse (1836): **Designer:** *Christian Gobrecht.*
Weight: *26.96 grams.* **Composition:** *.8924 silver, .1076 copper (net weight .77352 oz. pure silver).* **Diameter:** *39–40 mm.* **Edge:** *Plain.*

Judd-58.

Stars on Obverse, No Stars on Reverse (1838–1839): **Designer:** *Christian Gobrecht.*
Weight: *26.73 grams.* **Composition:** *.900 silver, .100 copper (net weight .77345 oz. pure silver).* **Diameter:** *39–40 mm.* **Edge:** *Reeded.*

J-104.

Note: Values of common-date silver coins listed in the seventh edition of **Mega Red** *have been based on a silver bullion price of $27.50 per ounce, and may vary with the prevailing spot price. To determine the intrinsic value of common silver coins, see page 1415.*

BACKGROUND

President Thomas Jefferson stopped the coinage of silver dollars in 1804—too many were being exported to foreign countries and not coming back. In 1831 the Mint director, Samuel Moore, sought to resume coinage, but the project ran aground when it became clear that the exportation of silver dollars was still a problem. It was not until 1835 that the first real steps were taken toward a resumption of dollar coinage. A limited number of Christian Gobrecht–designed dollars would be struck for circulation to test public demand before full-scale resumption of the denomination.

In autumn of 1836 all was set to commence the coinage of Liberty Seated dollars with Liberty on the obverse and a flying eagle on the reverse, designed by Mint engraver Christian Gobrecht, called Gobrecht dollars by numismatists today. In its final form for quantity coinage, the 1836-dated Gobrecht silver dollar appeared with a Liberty Seated figure on the obverse, Gobrecht's name placed inconspicuously on the base, with the eagle flying onward and upward on the reverse amid a galaxy of 26 stars, 13 large and 13 small. At the time there were 25 states in the Union, but soon afterward (in 1837) Michigan was officially made the 26th. Striking began on a hand-operated screw press in December 1836, with 1,000 coins in mirror Proof format and with plain edge. Although a knuckle-action Uhlhorn-type steam press designed by Franklin Peale had struck cents, quarters, and half dollars in that year, it would not be until after March 1837 that one would be installed with the capacity to strike silver dollars. Notices were sent to newspapers and were widely reproduced.

In 1835 Mint Director Patterson had Thomas Sully, a well-known artist, create sketches of Miss Liberty for use on coinage. She was depicted seated on a rock, her left hand holding a liberty pole with a liberty cap at the end, and her right hand resting on a shield emblazoned LIBERTY. (By 1835 the liberty cap, or *pileus*, was a very familiar motif, indeed "universally understood," dating back to at least the era of ancient coinage when it was featured on many coins. Such a cap was presented to slaves when they were given their freedom, and in colonial America the liberty cap was widely used to represent freedom from the shackles of British rule. Many towns and cities had liberty poles set up in prominent places—tall and with a cap at the top.) Titian Peale, one of several artistically inclined sons of local artist and museum proprietor Charles Willson Peale, was tapped to make sketches of the national bird, an eagle in flight, going "onward and upward"—modeled, it is said, after "Peter," an eagle who was kept as a mascot at the Mint.

On January 8, 1836, impressions of the Liberty Seated obverse design in fusible metal were sent to Secretary Woodbury in Washington, D.C., for him to show to President Andrew Jackson. On January 12 Woodbury advised Patterson that the president had approved of the design but suggested some modifications. In the same month Gobrecht started work on the reverse.

By April impressions of the dollar reverse were ready, with the eagle in flight and nothing in its claws—the branches and arrows omitted as a matter of "good taste." On June 18, 1836, Director Patterson wrote to Secretary of the Treasury Levi Woodbury, noting in part: "Mr. Gobrecht will commence the die for the reverse immediately." This silver dollar reverse die was completed by the last week in August. After other correspondence, Secretary Woodbury approved the final reverse design on August 27. Some type of reducing lathe, details of which are not known today, was employed in the process; it may have been a derivation of the improved engraving machine that Gobrecht had invented in 1817.

On September 22 Director Patterson instructed chief coiner Adam Eckfeldt, who had been at the Mint since the 1790s, to have hubs and working dies prepared and to strike dollars on a screw press using a "reeded or ground" collar. Accordingly, the coins were made with a plain edge. It was anticipated that a large-capacity, steam-powered press would be used for the regular-production coinage, but the press was not ready.

On November 8 the first coinage production of Capped Bust half dollars with reeded edges took place on the steam press. It was not until after March 1837 that a steam press capable of striking large-diameter silver dollars was completed by Franklin Peale and installed. Accordingly, the 1836-dated Gobrecht dollars were struck on a traditional screw press operated by three or four men, a fact not widely known until today. On December 31, 1836, 1,000 silver dollars, struck in mirror Proof finish, were delivered.

Thus began the Liberty Seated coinage.

An additional 600 Gobrecht dollars, struck from the same dies but oriented in a different direction (see below), were delivered on March 31, 1837. Nearly all were deposited in the Bank of the United

States of Philadelphia and paid out into commerce. A number were saved for presentation and numismatic purposes, with two given to President Andrew Jackson.

In 1839, additional Gobrecht silver dollars were minted for circulation (although in a Proof finish), but only to the extent of 300 pieces. The Liberty Seated motif now had 13 stars arranged around the obverse border, and no stars on the reverse; reeding was added to the edge.

Early in 1840, Director Patterson made the decision to resume regular mintage of silver dollars. Those struck in the 1830s had been at the whim of the director, but now the coinage would be at the behest of the depositor who brought silver bullion to the Mint and asked for dollars.

Gobrecht dollars in circulation traded among banks, bullion brokers, and exchange houses, but not for face value (at least, not for long). Beginning in the 1850s numismatics became a widely popular pursuit in America. Silver dollars did not circulate at the time, as the value of silver had risen to more than their face value. Most new dollars were exported, as detailed in the next chapter. The Gobrecht dollars were recognized as having a premium value to collectors, and these dealers and agents rescued hundreds of them and sold them to numismatists, accounting for most of the coins known today.

J. Hewitt Judd classified the Gobrecht dollar issues in his *United States Pattern Coins.* Although some are recognized as circulation strikes today, they are still identified by their Judd numbers. Professional Coin Grading Service (PCGS) lists them among the pattern coins, while Numismatic Guaranty Corporation (NGC) lists them with the circulating dollars.

One of the major indicators for the Gobrecht varieties is the relative alignment of the obverse and reverse dies. The varying die alignments are due to problems with the feeder mechanism during the coining process—the reverse die had to be periodically rotated during the striking run in an (unsuccessful) attempt to prevent damage to the rim. The four resulting die alignments are:

Die Alignment I: The reverse is aligned 180 degrees from the obverse ("coin turn"). The eagle is flying upward, and ONE DOLLAR is centered at the bottom. Most 1836-dated original strikings are of this format.

Die Alignment II: The reverse is the same as the obverse ("medal turn"). The eagle is flying upward, and ONE DOLLAR is centered at the bottom.

Die Alignment III: The reverse is inverted, nearly coin turn, but with the eagle flying horizontally, with the result that ONE DOLLAR is now at the lower right. This format was introduced in 1859 for restrikes and novodels.

Die Alignment IV: The reverse was inverted, medal turn or nearly, with the eagle being upside down. This alignment exists in several rotational variations.

In addition to the regular-issue Gobrecht dollars of 1836 and 1839, a number of different patterns and fancy pieces were made, including with the date 1838, in different die combinations, with plain edge or reeded edge, and in copper and silver. By tradition these have been given Judd numbers 60 and 104. Many varieties of patterns, novodels, restrikes, and off-metal strikes were made strictly for the numismatic trade. The full range of Judd attributions is as follows.

1836 (J-58 and 59). *Obverse:* The Liberty Seated design is placed on a starless field. C GOBRECHT. F. is in raised letters below the base and above the date. Made at a later date (see below). *Reverse:* The eagle is flying to the left, in a starry field of 13 small and 13 large stars. These are fantasies or novodels (not *restrikes,* as there were no originals) created at the Mint circa spring 1859.

1836 (J-60). This is the 1836 regular issue. *Obverse:* The Liberty Seated design is placed on a starless field. C GOBRECHT. F. is in recessed letters on base; the date is in the field below. *Reverse:* The eagle is flying upward to the left in a starry field. Judd-60 also includes some restrikes, made with die alignment III, circa the 1860s to 1870s.

1836 (J-61 and 62). The obverse and reverse dies of these restrikes are as preceding, but the eagle is flying level. Judd-61 (die alignment IV, original 1837 striking) is struck in silver and has a reeded edge. Judd-62 (die alignment III, circa 1876, with rust in field left of Liberty's face) is struck in copper and has a plain edge—*all* copper Gobrecht dollars are novodels, as no originals were struck in this metal.

1836 (J-63 and 64). *Obverse:* The Liberty Seated design is placed on a starless field. C GOBRECHT. F. is in raised letters below the base and above the date (the obverse of J-58). These strikes, created at the Mint in later years, are novodels, as no originals were made with a starless reverse fields. All other silver Gobrechts that have different die combinations from those originally used in 1836, 1838, and 1839 are novodels. *Reverse:* The eagle is flying to the left on a *plain* field (die first regularly used in 1838). These are later restrikes, all with plain edge and die alignment III, produced circa 1876. Judd-63 is struck in silver; J-64, in copper.

1836 (J-65 and 66). The obverse and reverse dies of these restrikes are as preceding, with die alignment III (circa 1876), rust in the field to the left of Liberty's face, and a plain edge. Judd-65 is struck in silver, J-66 in copper.

1838 (J-84, 85, and 87). *Obverse:* The Liberty Seated motif is situated on a field with stars. *Reverse:* The eagle flies to the left on a plain (starless) field. Issues are in silver with some originals (some J-84); others are restrikes. All copper issues are restrikes. Judd-84, struck in silver with a reeded edge, exists in alignments III and IV; J-85 (restrikes, alignment III) is struck in silver with a plain edge; and J-87 (restrikes, alignment III) is struck in copper with a plain edge.

1838 (J-88 and 89). *Obverse:* As preceding. *Reverse:* The eagle is flying to the left on a field of 26 stars (style of 1836). These are plain-edged restrikes with die alignment III; J-88 is silver, J-89, copper.

1839 (J-104, 105, and 107). *Obverse:* As preceding. *Reverse:* The eagle flies to the left on a plain field (style of 1838). Judd-104 (originals, alignment IV; restrikes, III and IV) is struck in silver and has a reeded edge, while J-105 (restrikes, alignment III), also silver, has a plain edge. Judd-107 (restrikes, alignment III) is struck in copper with a plain edge.

1839 (J-108 and 109). *Obverse:* As preceding. *Reverse:* The eagle flies to the left in a field of 26 stars (style of 1836). Restrikes were made with the die used to coin J-60 of 1836; the use of stars on both obverse and reverse is illogical. Both have die alignment III and a plain edge; J-108 is struck in silver, while J-109 is copper.

CHRISTIAN GOBRECHT, DESIGNER

Christian Gobrecht, born in Hanover, Pennsylvania, on December 23, 1785, had a strong interest and ability in art from an early age. In time, he became an engraver of illustrations for books and also produced plates for bank notes. He is said to have been the first to have invented a medal-ruling machine—a device incorporating a stylus that traces over the face of a medallion or plaque, and by means of a pantograph arm, transfers the image, reduced in size if desired, to a

Christian Gobrecht.

William Kneass.

two-dimensional surface, such as a copper plate for printing. He also created a talking doll and made improvements on the reed organ. As early as 1824 he did contract work for the Mint, producing medal dies and letter punches. By the time he joined the staff his talents were widely known and appreciated.

In 1835, Mint director Robert Maskell Patterson, who had been in office only since July (succeeding his brother-in-law Samuel Moore in the post), desired to make the American coinage more artistic. This was the era of Neoclassicism, and themes of art and architecture from the past were being revived. The Greek Revival craze swept America and resulted in the use of this style for the several mint buildings erected in that decade in Philadelphia, Charlotte, Dahlonega, and New Orleans, and for many banks and public buildings as well. On bank notes, gods and goddesses from mythology were seen in profusion, including Hebe (cup-bearer to the gods), Mercury (messenger with wings on his cap and feet), Minerva (goddess of wisdom), Ceres (goddess of agriculture), Justice (goddess usually shown standing, holding balance scales in one hand and, sometimes, a sword in the other), and, from the American idiom, many representations of Liberty as a goddess—seated, standing, caressing an eagle, gazing with admiration at a portrait of Washington, and so on.

By that time, Mint engraver William Kneass, in office since January 28, 1824, was recognized as a good technician and fine craftsman for reproducing and multiplying images from models, but not as a creative artist. In contrast, Gobrecht, who had worked for a decade or more on selected contracts with the Mint for medals (and possibly other things), was recognized as an artist of high caliber. Indeed, Gobrecht had submitted himself for the position of chief engraver in 1823, after the demise of Robert Scot, but Kneass got the job. This was a political appointment, as Gobrecht was the stronger candidate.

In August 1835 Kneass was incapacitated by a stroke. Gobrecht was made second engraver a month later, and was thus at the helm for the production of the new dollar coin. The chief engravership at the time was a lifetime proposition—a sinecure—and Kneass continued to draw his paycheck until his death on August 27, 1840, although a small part of his salary was transferred to Gobrecht. On December 21 of 1840, Gobrecht was appointed chief engraver, to remain in the post until his passing on June 23, 1844.

GOBRECHT DOLLARS (1836–1839): GUIDE TO COLLECTING

BEING A SMART BUYER

A complete set of Gobrecht dollars—each date, in every combination of die alignment and original/restrike status—would be difficult to assemble. A more manageable goal is to find one of each date (1836, 1838, and 1839); many collectors are happy to settle for a single representative of the series, usually the relatively plentiful 1836, or else skip the Gobrechts completely. Study the series carefully before committing to purchase. At the relatively affordable grade levels, expect wear on the high points of the obverse (the thighs, knees, bosom, and head) and the reverse (the eagle's breast and the tops of the wings). With the 1836 in particular, examples are prone to hairlines and dullness in the fields.

AVAILABILITY

The 1836 is easy enough to find, although expensive. The restrikes with Gobrecht's name on the base and a plain edge are most commonly seen at auction. The 1839 was made only to the extent of 300 originals and perhaps a couple hundred restrikes. It is the rarest of all major U.S. silver design types, outclassing even the 1796 and 1797 half dollar.

PROOFS

Gobrecht dollars of 1836 and 1839 are seen only in Proof format, although a generous portion of them saw circulation.

GOBRECHT DOLLARS (1836–1839)

GRADING STANDARDS

PF-60 to 70 (Proof). *Obverse and Reverse:* Many Proofs have been extensively cleaned and have many hairlines and dull fields. This is more applicable to 1836 than to 1839. Grades are PF–60 to 61 or 62. With medium hairlines and good reflectivity, an assigned grade of PF-64 is appropriate, and with relatively few hairlines, Gem PF-65. In various grades hairlines are most easily seen in the obverse field. PF-66 should have hairlines so

1839. Graded PF-65.

delicate that magnification is needed to see them. Above that, a Proof should be free of such lines.

Illustrated coin: This is a restrike made at the Mint in or after spring 1859.

PF-50, 53, 55, 58 (Proof). *Obverse:* Light wear is seen on the thighs and knees, bosom, and head. At PF-58, the Proof surface is extensive, but the open fields show abrasion. At PF–50 and 53, most if not all mirror surface is gone and there are scattered marks. *Reverse:* Wear is most evident on the eagle's breast and the top of the wings. Mirror surface ranges from perhaps 60% complete (at PF-58) to none (at PF-50).

1836. Graded PF-58.

Illustrated coin: This original 1836 Gobrecht dollar, of which 1,000 were coined in 1836, is nicely toned and has excellent eye appeal.

PF-40 to 45 (Proof). *Obverse:* Further wear is seen on all areas, especially the thighs and knees, bosom, and head. The center of LIBERTY, which is in relief, is weak. Most at this level and lower are the 1836 issues. *Reverse:* Further wear is evident on the eagle, including the back edge of the closest wing, the top of the farthest wing, and the tail.

1836. Graded PF-45.

PF-20, 25, 30, 35 (Proof). *Obverse:* Further wear is seen. Many details of the gown are worn away, but the lower-relief areas above and to the right of the shield remain well defined. Hair detail is mostly or completely gone. LIBERTY is weak at the center. *Reverse:* Even more wear is evident on the eagle, with only about 60% of the feathers visible.

1836. Graded PF-20.

1836 Gobrecht Dollar

1836, Name on Base (J-60) •
Proof Mintage: 1,000+.

Availability: Coins grading PF-60 or higher probably comprise fewer than 250 of the quantity of 600 to 750 mentioned above. Coin in PF-64 are rare, and in PF-65 are very rare.

1836,
Name on Base, J-60.

Characteristics of striking: This issue is sharply struck.

Commentary: Judd-60 is distinguished by the reverse eagle flying upward to the left, stars in the reverse field, and the designer's name on the base of the obverse device. Its edge is plain, and its obverse and reverse dies were aligned in "coin turn" (Die Alignment I).

Detail of the Name Below Base;
several varieties exist.

By the 1850s sharp-eyed bullion brokers, bankers, and others were retrieving these coins from circulation for face value, with the result that an estimated 600 to 750 of the Name on Base variety exist today. Indeed, they are the most commonly seen of all the Gobrecht dollars. Some are worn down to low grades, but most are Extremely Fine or finer. These are often given Proof grades such as PF-40, as all were struck with Proof finish. PCGS records 120 grading events for J-60, with about half of these clustering around PF-61 to PF-64. NGC records 149, with a similar distribution.

	Cert	Avg	%MS	PF-60	PF-62	PF-63	PF-65
1836 (J-60)	152	54.8	55%	$25,000	$27,000	$40,000	$125,000

1838 Gobrecht Dollar

1838 (J-84) • **Pattern Mintage:** 125 to 200 estimated.

Availability: Judd-84 is the most commonly seen of the 1838 varieties, usually in grades of PF-60 to 64 but occasionally higher. Up to about 100 are known. Worn PF-20 is known, as is a PF-35, and there are a handful of impaired Proofs in the 50 to 58 range.

J-84.

Characteristics of striking: This issue is sharply struck.

Commentary: Originals of J-84 were struck from perfect dies in Die Alignment IV. Restrikes have Die Alignment III or IV, and the reverse die for this issue was cracked. The two major grading services record slightly more than 60 certifications of J-84, largely in the range of PF-60 to PF-65.

	Cert	Avg	%MS	PF-60	PF-62	PF-63	PF-65
1838 (J-84)	23	62.0	96%	$55,000	$65,000	$75,000	$150,000

1839 Gobrecht Dollar

1839 (J-104) • **Proof Mintage:** 300.

Availability: About 200–500 coins of this issue exist in grades ranging from PF-20 to PF-66. Many if not most of these have problems and have not been certified. All are Die Alignment IV.

Characteristics of striking: This issue is well struck.

J-104,
Pollock-116.

Commentary: Originals of J-104 have Die Alignment IV; restrikes have Die Alignment III or IV. PCGS and NGC record 105 total grading events for J-104, most in the range of PF-62 to PF-65. The lowest graded is single PF-12 (PCGS); the highest is a single PF-66 (NGC).

	Cert	Avg	%MS	PF-60	PF-62	PF-63	PF-65
1839 (J-104)	52	61.9	88%	$29,000	$38,500	$55,000	$150,000

LIBERTY SEATED DOLLARS (1840–1873)

No Motto (1840–1865): **Designer:** *Christian Gobrecht.* **Weight:** *26.73 grams.*
Composition: *.900 silver, .100 copper (net weight .77344 oz. pure silver).*
Diameter: *38.1 mm.* **Edge:** *Reeded.* **Mints:** *Philadelphia, New Orleans, and San Francisco.*

Mintmark location
is on the reverse,
below the eagle,
for all varieties.

No Motto
(1840–1865)

No Motto, Proof

With Motto IN GOD WE TRUST (1866–1873): **Designer:** *Christian Gobrecht.*
Weight: *26.73 grams.* **Composition:** *.900 silver, .100 copper (net weight .77344 oz. pure silver).*
Diameter: *38.1 mm.* **Edge:** *Reeded.* **Mints:** *Philadelphia, Carson City, and San Francisco.*

With Motto
IN GOD
WE TRUST
(1866–1873)

With Motto
IN GOD
WE TRUST,
Proof

BACKGROUND

In 1840, after a six-year hiatus in the production of silver dollars, Mint director Robert M. Patterson decided it was time to relaunch the denomination. He selected the obverse design of the Gobrecht dollar, which had been given a trial run in 1836, to grace the obverse of the new coin, but with some light modifications.

Some of these changes may have been due to taste, but others were probably made in deference to the demands of the steam coinage press. Designed by Franklin Peale, the steam press was in use during the Gobrecht dollar era but was unable to accommodate the larger planchets at the time, so the Gobrecht dollars were struck on a manual screw press. By 1840, the steam press was ready for the big planchets—only now, the design wasn't ready for the new press. Peale, now chief coiner of the Mint, believed the relief of Gobrecht's original design was too high for the press to bring up, and that some modifications were needed.

Other developments in minting technology also affected production of the new dollars. Franklin Peale had visited several of the European mints in the 1830s and was impressed by what he saw there. As a result, in 1836, the Mint ordered a revolutionary new Contamin portrait lathe from its French manufacturer. No

British-American sculptor Robert Ball Hughes, as painted by John Trumbull, ca. 1835.

This 1928 Assay Commission medal depicts the first coining press at the U.S. Mint in Philadelphia—a screw press similar to the type in use during Christian Gobrecht's earlier years as a Mint engraver.

Franklin Peale's steam press at the Philadelphia Mint. This type of press required adjustments to older production methods.

longer was it necessary to engrave each hub by hand. Instead, an artist made a plaster model about four times the size of the desired punch; a hardened version called a *galvano* (usually in copper but sometimes in iron) was placed at one end of the portrait lathe. By a clever use of the pantograph principle and cutting tools, the device would turn out a positive hub of the proper size at the other end of the machine. The engraver then finished the details by hand. The use of a portrait lathe enabled more accurate copying of devices onto hubs for different denominations.

Also in the mid-1830s, William Kneass pioneered another change in die-making techniques. Prior to that time, each working die was made by hand with the separate original device hubs; the workman punched in the hubs and the lettering in separate operations. Kneass changed all of this by sinking a master die (incuse, complete except for date or mintmark), using original hubs and letter and star punches, and then raising from this a working hub (in relief).

The press operator put this working hub into the hubbing press opposite a die blank, the face of which was a shallow, raised cone. Each working die received several blows from the hub, with annealing between successive blows. Dates and mintmarks were punched in by hand.

Although Christian Gobrecht was still chief engraver at the time his silver dollar obverse design was adopted for the new coinage, it was a Philadelphia artist named Robert Ball Hughes whom Patterson hired to revise the design. Some have interpreted this situation as evidence that Gobrecht had some objection about it, but it is more likely that Hughes was simply better acquainted with the new die-making techniques and equipment required by the steam press.

THE NEW DESIGN

In Hughes's rendition of the Liberty Seated design, Miss Liberty's head is a bit larger, and her arms are rounder and less muscular. The drapery of her garment is a bit different, and a drape of fabric descends below her left elbow. At the lower left, the rock is less prominent, Liberty's hand is shown at a different angle, and LIBERTY on the shield's banner is incused instead of raised. The vertical bands on the shield are wider and have an alternating plain-and-striped pattern forming a total of 13 bands. Mint records contain no indication of the engraver's name.

The reverse with a perched eagle was adapted from Gobrecht's motif used on quarters beginning in 1838 and half dollars in 1839 which, in turn, was based on John Reich's half dollar reverse design of 1807. The one notable difference is the absence of the motto E PLURIBUS UNUM. Director Patterson felt the motto was inappropriate unless the Great Seal of the United States was displayed in the design.

The 1836 Gobrecht design was lightly reworked for the 1840 coinage, the most obvious change being the addition of drapery below Liberty's left elbow.

The incused LIBERTY on the new shield design (right) was better suited to mass production on the new steam press than the raised version the original Gobrecht shield (left).

John Reich's half dollar reverse design of 1807 was revived in 1838 for the quarter dollars (left), in 1839 for half dollars (center), and in 1840 for silver dollars (right).

COINAGE FOR CIRCULATION

Striking of the new design commenced in July 1840, with 12,500 pieces struck on spec at Peale's instruction to attract the attention of silver bullion depositors. By November enough bankers and bullion dealers were interested in the new coin to deposit the necessary silver. Coinage resumed in November 1840 with 41,000 pieces, followed by another 7,505 in December.

Most of the dollars struck in the early 1840s, and probably later in the decade as well, made their way into commerce, although many were stored in banks, and some may have been exported to the East or to the West Indies. Quite a few were melted after 1850, which accounts for their relative scarcity. There was little public demand for the dollar, which was equivalent to the better part of an average day's wage. They were bulky to carry, and most citizens would have been content to have a small collection of cents, half dimes, and dimes in their pockets instead. The *gold* dollar did circulate, and heavily, showing that the public would use coins of this denomination so long as they were not too bulky to carry around.

Silver dollar coinage in the 1840s fluctuated from as low as 15,000 pieces (1848) to more than 184,000 (1841). It all depended upon the state of the economy and how much silver was being imported (for American goods sent abroad) in comparison with exports of the same metal. In addition, each bullion owner would decide from year to year how their excess silver should be stored. Much of it wound up as bank reserves when the original owner of the dollars needed to earn interest from the coinage. There was also a limit to how many silver dollars could be absorbed by the mercantile community; if they were not in circulation, they had to be stored or invested.

In 1840 a dollar contained about its value in silver, and other silver denominations were of full intrinsic value as well; yet only a few dollars circulated in commerce. In 1841 a silver dollar had a premium value of about 3 percent to 6 percent in terms of paper money, the last being bills of state-chartered banks in sound financial condition. One reason for this extra value is that while gold coins were exported in quantity to foreign banks and merchants (bank notes were not wanted) and took up most of the trade, there was a demand for silver dollars as well, these being more convenient to handle than coins of smaller denominations. Most were shipped to Europe, particularly to England and to a lesser extent France. China was also an important export destination beginning in 1842. The Chinese strongly preferred silver to gold, including in large transactions. Silver dollars sent to Europe were often returned to America to purchase goods. Dollars that went to China were nearly all melted.

In 1846 the first branch-mint coinage took place, with the New Orleans Mint producing 59,000 dollars with the O mintmark. Most of the dollars in commerce at the time were Spanish-American eight-reales coins, of which there were millions. Unlike the U.S. dollar, the eight-reales were accepted in every port in the world and were instantly recognized as being full silver value.

In early 1848 came one of those seemingly minor events that would disrupt the economies and monetary systems of the world: the discovery of gold on the giant Sutter ranch in California. Frantic (and futile) efforts were made to keep the secret from reaching the outside world, as it soon did. The amount of gold produced from the streams and mines of the American West was enormous, and the United States could not absorb all of it. Massive gold discoveries in Australia in the early 1850s added to the monetary upheaval.

So much gold came onto the world market that silver was soon undervalued, and bullion dealers bought every American silver coin they could obtain. Between domestic hoarding and the sending of silver to Europe for melting, by the middle of 1849 the American monetary system was in serious trouble. By early 1850, little silver was to be seen in general commerce except for an occasional badly worn Spanish coin. Since the large half dollars and silver dollars were easier to handle than smaller coinage, they were the first to go. This accounts for the relative rarity of certain dates that ought to be more common based on their mintage, such as the 40,000 struck in New Orleans in 1850.

At that time it cost $1.013 in metal to make a dollar. This was not a deterrent to their coinage, as such pieces were made at the request of bullion depositors and circulated for slightly more than face value. After this point the price of silver rose further, and dollars in circulation, not plentiful at the time, were bought up by exchange and bullion brokers, as were other silver denominations, especially quarters and half dollars. Production of silver dollars fell sharply, almost but not quite to the vanishing point in 1851 and 1852. In the meantime gold dollars, which made their debut in 1849, were produced in large quantities for the next several years and satisfied domestic demand for a dollar coin.

The Act of February 21, 1853, remedied the lack of silver coins in commerce by reducing the weight of silver coins from the half dime to the half dollar. The new lightweight coins circulated very effectively afterward. The weight of the silver dollar was unchanged as it was viewed as a bullion or trade coin used only for export. Beginning in that year, production of dollars increased. Nearly all were struck to the order of bullion depositors who used them in international commerce, especially to Liverpool (in large shipments during the decade, sometimes more than 100,000 dollars at a time) and to China. Considering the large quantities involved, it may be that some "American dollar" shipments included other coins. It also seems that many were returned to the United States and used again in the export trade, such as from England back to America to buy bales of cotton. This accounts for the circulation seen on many dollars, especially those dated in the 1840s. Such coins were exchanged for their bullion value at their destinations, and the face value did not matter.

Silver dollars continued to be made for commerce each year except for 1858, when the production was limited to about 210 or more for the numismatic trade.

In God We Trust

In November 1861, Rev. M.R. Watkinson wrote a letter to the secretary of the Treasury in suggesting that a religious motto be placed on the coinage to reflect the growing awakening because of the war.

This struck a receptive chord in the administration, and the Mint began producing patterns in December 1861 with "God Our Trust" on the reverse of half dollars and eagles. The motto "In God We Trust" was officially adopted by Congress for the two-cent piece in 1864. A law of 1865 permitted the Treasury to put the motto on such coins as it thought proper, and this was done in 1866 for several gold and silver denominations and the new Shield nickel.

The first silver dollar patterns with the motto (as adopted in 1866) appear with a date of 1863, but the 1863–1865 pieces with IN GOD WE TRUST were apparently all coined in 1867–1868 under Mint director Henry Richard Linderman, an avid collector of patterns.

At the beginning of 1866, Longacre's new reverse with IN GOD WE TRUST went into service; it continued through the end of the Liberty Seated dollar series in March 1873. Two specimens exist without the motto and are sometimes called *transitional dollars*, but they were coined, probably under Linderman's orders, in 1867–1868. In reality they are fantasy coins, but still they have long drawn collector interest as something out of the ordinary. (One of the two specimens, from the Willis du Pont Collection, was stolen in 1967 and has never been recovered.)

This pattern silver dollar (J-347) with the motto IN GOD WE TRUST was likely struck in 1867 or 1868, *after* the motto first appeared on the Liberty Seated dollar in 1866.

The full story of the national motto is told in William Bierly's *In God We Trust: The American Civil War, Money, Banking, and Religion.*

PROOF LIBERTY SEATED DOLLARS

From 1840 through 1858 Proofs were issued to satisfy requests of collectors. (The Mint was very accommodating to numismatists.) Some were also issued as part of sets. There have been various theories on whether the Mint *re*-struck Proof dollars, and it seems likely that it did to accommodate collectors' needs. Note that one obverse die is known for each of the Proof years of the 1840s. For 1840 there are two reverse dies. A single reverse die was used from 1841 to 1850, then discarded. This has a tiny "pimple" or projection on the right side of the final A in AMERICA. If restrikes were made the original die pairs were used.

Specialists know that in 1851 no original Proofs were made. At a later time the Mint provided restrikes for collectors that were privately sold by officials, mainly to Philadelphia dealer William K. Idler and, later, to his son-in-law John W. Haseltine. The 1851 restrikes have the date centered, rather than high as on the originals. As the date numerals are identical it is not known whether the restrike die was made in 1851 and not used at that time, or made later.

No Proof silver dollars were coined in 1853. Years later restrikes were made and were said to be 12 in number, but facts are scarce. These were made to satisfy numismatists who were building sets of Proofs. This may reflect that by the early 1860s this was more or less the number of active specialists in that area. The 1851 and 1852 restrikes were made to fill the need of many more collectors who were assembling date sets, mostly of circulation strikes.

Almost without exception numismatists of the 1800s and early 1900s who built high-grade sets of Liberty Seated dollars acquired Proofs. In most instances circulation strikes, preserved by chance, were simply unavailable in choice and gem grades.

LIBERTY SEATED DOLLARS (1840–1873): GUIDE TO COLLECTING

Today, probably most buyers of high-grade Liberty Seated dollars desire one of each type—1840–1865, Without Motto, and 1866–1873, with IN GOD WE TRUST—to add to a type set. These are easily found. Circulation strikes are readily available in such grades as Very Fine to About Uncirculated, and in the upper ranges from MS-60 to 63. MS-64 coins are scarce and MS-65 examples are rare. Proofs are not hard to find with dates in the 1860s and 1870s, although gems are scarce.

Forming a complete collection by date and mintmarks is difficult to do and is limited by the 1870-S, of which only nine are confirmed to exist with a tenth reported. If this issue is ignored, then the most difficult in all grades are the 1851 and 1852 originals; the Proof-only 1858 among Philadelphia issues; and, among branch-mint coins, the 1873-CC. Next in rarity comes the 1871-CC, then 1872-CC. Other branch-mint issues such as 1846-O, 1850-O, 1859-S, 1870-CC, and 1872-S are somewhat elusive, particularly in higher grades. Among Carson City coins, 1870-CC is the most readily available and is also the best struck, often occurring (in better grades) with a prooflike surface. The 1859-O and 1860-O are readily obtainable in Mint State, the typical piece being MS-60 with heavy scarring from coin-to-coin contact in bags. Unlike the situation for lower denominations in the Liberty Seated series, coins below the grade of F-12 are rarely encountered and thus are not studied here. Most circulated coins range from VF-20 upward.

After 1858, through the end of the series in 1873, Proofs were made in quantities averaging about 500 to 1,000 per year. Although these quantities in an absolute sense are small, still the remaining coins from the Proof mintages survive in larger numbers than do Mint State coins of certain of the same dates. In terms of auction appearances, for some dates in the early 1860s, more Proofs appear in catalogs than do Very Fine, Extremely Fine, About Uncirculated, and Mint State coins combined! Impaired Proofs sell at a deep discount from attractive Proofs and provide the most feasible way to acquire high-grade examples of dates in the early 1860s.

Most probably, the commonest date among no-motto Liberty Seated dollars 1840–1865 is the 1847, with competition furnished by 1842 and 1843. Among later Liberty Seated dollars, with IN GOD WE TRUST (1866–1873), the 1871 is most often seen.

In general, Mint State Liberty Seated dollars are rare, exceptions being the 1859-O and 1860-O, many of which came to light during the Treasury release of silver dollars in 1962. At the same time many thousands of circulated Liberty Seated coins were released.

ASPECTS OF STRIKING

On circulating Liberty Seated dollars 1840 and later, the prominent relief of the shield caused the word LIBERTY to wear away much faster than on lower denominations in the Liberty Seated series, particularly the half dime and dime. These latter denominations can be considerably worn and still have LIBERTY showing, whereas on silver dollars the word begins to disappear after only slight wear.

Striking can vary, even on coins made from the same die pairs, because dies were handled thusly: First, the operator mounted the dies on a press and adjusted the separation. (The distance between the dies determines how deeply the metal will flow into the die recesses; the wider the distance, the poorer the strike, but the longer the dies will last.) The coins were struck and the dies were then removed, and stored if they were still serviceable. Later, the usable dies were put back on a press, adjusted again (perhaps differently from the first time), and used to strike additional coins.

On circulation strikes weakness can be present in several areas. On the obverse the prime places to look for weakness are the top of the head of Liberty and the stars. Weakness, when present, typically begins with stars eight and nine (counting from the left) and progresses gradually to the left and the right. There are some coins in which this varies, and stars to the left are sharply struck and stars to the right are weak, but in general the weakness begins or is centered around stars eight and nine.

On the reverse, typical areas of weakness are the top of the shield and the eagle's neck immediately above it, the top of the eagle's wing on the left, and the eagle's leg on the left.

BEING A SMART BUYER

Those who intend to make Liberty Seated dollars a specialty would do well to accept the fact that nearly all existing circulation strikes are in grades below Mint State. The typical incoming collector or investor has been led through advertising and promotion to believe that the only coins worth owning are choice and gem Mint State and Proof pieces. Of course, this is silly when it comes to Liberty Seated coins across all denominations: as with the early series, for certain dates and mintmarks worn coins are the rule rather than the exception. No one has ever completed a set of Mint State coins of the 1840s and 1850s.

Liberty Seated collectors should cherrypick for quality. Striking sharpness can vary, and a well-defined coin costs no more than one that is weakly struck. Avoid coins with dark or deep toning. Not only are they usually unattractive, but more than just a few have been recolored in order to mask friction or light wear. The most attractive coins are brilliant or lightly toned. In all instances it is probably best to use PCGS or NGC certified coins as a *starting point*. Examine such pieces carefully. As mentioned for other Liberty Seated denominations, a sharply struck MS-63 coin with great eye appeal is more worthwhile than an MS-65 with areas of light striking and/or dark or unattractive toning.

Take your time when buying. No one ever built a fine collection of Liberty Seated dollars quickly. Enjoy the experience over a period of a year or two or three.

LIBERTY SEATED (1840–1873)

GRADING STANDARDS

MS-60 to 70 (Mint State). *Obverse:* At MS-60, some abrasion and contact marks are evident, most noticeably on the bosom and thighs and knees. Luster is present, but may be dull or lifeless. At MS-63, contact marks are very few, and abrasion is minimal. An MS-65 coin has no abrasion in the fields (but may have a hint on the knees), and contact marks are trivial. Check the knees of Liberty and the right

1864. Graded MS-65.

field. Luster should be full and rich on later issues, not necessarily so for dates in the 1840s. Most Mint State coins of the 1861 to 1865 years, Philadelphia issues, have extensive die striae (from not completely finishing the die). *Reverse:* Comments apply as for the obverse, except that in lower Mint State grades, abrasion and marks are most noticeable on the eagle's head, the neck, the claws, and the top of the wings (harder to see there, however). At MS-65 or higher, there are no marks visible to the unaided eye. The field is mainly protected by design elements and does not show abrasion as much as does the obverse on a given coin.

Illustrated coin: The fields show striations from incomplete polishing of the dies, but this does not affect the grade.

AU-50, 53, 55, 58 (About Uncirculated). *Obverse:* Light wear is seen on the thighs and knees, bosom, and head. At AU-58, the luster is extensive but incomplete, especially in the right field. At AU-50 and 53, luster is less. *Reverse:* Wear is visible on the eagle's neck, the claws, and the top of the wings. An AU-58 coin has nearly full luster. At AU-50 and 53, there still are traces of luster.

1842. Graded AU-58.

Illustrated coin: This is an attractive example with much of the original luster.

EF-40, 45 (Extremely Fine). *Obverse:* Further wear is seen on all areas, especially the thighs and knees, bosom, and head. Little or no luster is seen on most coins. From this grade downward, strike sharpness in the stars and the head does not matter to connoisseurs. *Reverse:* Further wear is evident on the eagle's neck, claws, and the wings, although on well-struck coins nearly all details are sharp.

1846. Graded EF-40.

VF-20, 30 (Very Fine). *Obverse:* Further wear is seen. Many details of the gown are worn away, but the lower-relief areas above and to the right of the shield remain well defined. Hair detail is mostly or completely gone. The word LIBERTY is weak at BE (PCGS allows BER to be missing "on some coins"). *Reverse:* Wear is more extensive, with some feathers blended together, especially on the neck for a typical coin. Detail remains quite good overall.

1854. Graded VF-20.

F-12, 15 (Fine). *Obverse:* The seated figure is well worn, but with some detail above and to the right of the shield. BER in LIBERTY is visible only in part or missing entirely. *Reverse:* Wear is extensive, with about a third to half of the feathers flat or blended with others.

Illustrated coin: The reverse is stronger than the obverse on this coin.

1872-CC. Graded F-12.

VG-8, 10 (Very Good). *Obverse:* The seated figure is more worn, but some detail can be seen above and to the right of the shield. The shield is discernible, but the upper-right section may be flat and blended into the seated figure. In LIBERTY two or three letters, or a combination totaling that, are readable. *Reverse.* Further wear has flattened half or slightly more of the feathers (depending on the strike). The rim is visible all around, as

1871-CC. Graded VG-8.

are the ends of the denticles. A Very Good Liberty Seated dollar usually has more detail overall than a lower-denomination coin of the same design.

G-4, 6 (Good). *Obverse:* The seated figure is worn nearly smooth. The stars and date are complete, but may be weak toward the periphery. *Reverse:* The eagle shows only a few details of the shield and feathers. The rim is worn down. The tops of the border letters are weak or worn away, although the inscription can still be read.

1850-O. Graded G-6.

AG-3 (About Good). *Obverse:* The seated figure is visible in outline form. Much or all of the rim is worn away. The stars are weak and some may be missing. The date remains clear. *Reverse:* The border letters are partially worn away. The eagle is mostly in outline form, but with a few details discernible. The rim is weak or missing.

1872. Graded AG-3.

PF-60 to 70 (Proof). *Obverse and Reverse:* Proofs that are extensively cleaned and have many hairlines, or that are dull and grainy, are lower level, such as PF-60 to 62. These are not widely desired, except for use as fillers for the dates (most circulation-strike dollars are rare after 1849 and before 1870). The rarities of 1851, 1852, and 1858 are in demand no matter what the grade. With medium hairlines and good reflectivity, an assigned

1861. Graded PF-63.

grade of PF-64 is appropriate, and with relatively few hairlines, gem PF-65. In various grades hairlines are most easily seen in the obverse field. PF-66 should have hairlines so delicate that magnification is needed to see them. Above that, a Proof should be free of such lines.

Illustrated coin: The frosty cameo motifs on this example contrast with the deeply mirrored fields.

1840 Liberty Seated Dollar

1840 • Mintage: 61,005.

Availability in Mint State: Even though the 1840 is the first year of issue of this design, there seems to have been no particular notice of it by the general public. By then the 1836 Gobrecht dollars were well known to those interested, and the 1840 dollars attracted little

attention. Accordingly, surviving Mint State coins are those that were saved as a matter of chance, not intent. Among first-year-of-issue Liberty Seated denominations, dollars of 1840 are far and away rarer than any of the others. *MS-60 to 62:* 15 to 20. *MS-63:* 8 to 11. *MS-64:* 2 to 4. *MS-65 or better:* 0 or 1.

Availability in circulated grades: For some of the dollars in the 1840s an occasional example in lower grades is found, but most are Fine or better. *F-12 to AU-58:* 800 to 1,200.

Characteristics of striking: This issue is usually quite well struck with sharp stars and prominent, broad rims.

Notes: Striking of dollars with the revised design began in July 1840, with 12,500 pieces being delivered by chief coiner Franklin Peale. This was a speculative coinage ordered by Mint Director Robert M. Patterson to acquaint silver bullion depositors with their new option. Little happened for some months, but finally enough bankers and bullion dealers became interested in the new coins to deposit the necessary silver and order them. Coinage resumed in November 1840 with 41,000 pieces. A further 7,505 were minted the following month.

In the year 1840, silver dollars amounted to 61,005 pieces, while half dollars came to 2,290,108 coins with a face value of $1,145,054, or 19 times greater than the value of silver dollars minted during the same 12-month period. While there is no doubt that the Liberty Seated dollar did limited duty in American commerce during the 1840s, the vast majority went into the hands of bullion dealers, banks, and exchange brokers, or where used in the export trade. As previously noted, such coins traded at a premium from the outset. Throughout the Liberty Seated dollar era, half dollars were the coins of choice for circulation at face value within the United States.

The 1840 has always been in strong demand by type-set collectors seeking the first year of the design.

	Cert	Avg	%MS	VG-8	F-12	VF-20	EF-40	AU-50	MS-60	MS-63	MS-64	MS-65
1840	300	48.7	18%	$450	$500	$575	$850	$1,500	$5,500	$14,500	$27,500	—

1840, Proof • **Mintage:** 40 to 60.

Commentary and Availability: The number of issued Proofs of the 1840 dollar exceeded that of any other Proofs of the decade. Those that survive are mostly at lower levels, suggesting that many may have been presented to various officials rather than to interested numismatists, although a few were

included in sets. Two Proof reverse dies were created. The best known of these is the coin that was thereafter carefully preserved at the Mint, to be brought out on various occasions through 1850 to strike Proof dollars. This has a tiny raised area or "pimple" extending into the field from the final A in AMERICA. There is absolutely no evidence that the die was used at a later date for restriking. This die was used on most of the single dollars as well as those in all of the rare Proof sets seen from this decade. Another die used for Proof 1840 dollars, and apparently not later, was first identified on a coin offered by Heritage Auctions in the 2002 Central States sale: (1) The first horizontal line in the shield extends to the left into the eagle's wing; (2) The final element of vertical stripe two and the first and third elements of stripe three penetrate the innermost shield border; (3) The final two elements of stripe one penetrate solidity to horizontal line five; (4) The first element of stripe two penetrates to horizontal line two. Approximately 27 examples have been certified.

	Cert	Avg	%MS	PF-60	PF-63	PF-64	PF-65
1840, Proof	25	63.3		$12,500	$25,000	$45,000	$80,000

1841 Liberty Seated Dollar

1841 • **Mintage:** 173,000.

Availability in Mint State: As is true of other silver dollars of the 1840s, there is no record of any numismatic interest in newly coined circulation strikes. The survival of Mint State coins is a matter of rare chance. *MS-60 to 62:* 15 to 20. *MS-63:* 5 to 8. *MS-64:* 3 to 5. *MS-65 or better:* 1 or 2.

Availability in circulated grades: *F-12 to AU-58:* 1,000 to 1,500.

Characteristics of striking: Striking of this issue varies; some have flatness in areas, including stars and/or denticles.

Notes: The 1841 *Annual Report of the Director of the Mint* showed the main sources of silver were bullion from North Carolina, foreign bullion, Mexican dollars, dollars of South America, European coins, and silver plate. However, the total supply of bullion had little to do with silver *dollar* coinage. The number struck depended solely on the bullion deposited by those specifically asking for dollars. Few depositors did, as they were not useful for general circulation and sold at a slight premium.

	Cert	Avg	%MS	VG-8	F-12	VF-20	EF-40	AU-50	MS-60	MS-63	MS-64	MS-65
1841	302	49.2	19%	$400	$450	$550	$650	$1,000	$2,750	$8,000	$30,000	$90,000

1841, Proof • **Mintage:** 10 to 15.

Commentary and Availability: The 1841 Proof dollar is viewed today as one of the great Proof rarities in the series. Typically, a decade or more may elapse between auction offerings. Approximately four examples have been certified.

	Cert	Avg	%MS	PF-60	PF-63	PF-64	PF-65
1841, Proof	4	63.0		$30,000	$70,000	$125,000	$250,000

1842 Liberty Seated Dollar

1842 • **Mintage:** 184,618.

Availability in Mint State: Examples of the 1842 Liberty Seated dollar are occasionally available in grade levels of MS-60 to MS-63, but in higher grades the issue is a rarity. This is the first Liberty Seated dollar variety that has any claim to general availability in Mint State, but, even so, in absolute terms Mint State specimens are rare. *MS-60 to 62:* 40 to 55. *MS-63:* 20 to 25. *MS-64:* 15 to 20. *MS-65 or better:* 0 or 1.

Availability in circulated grades: *F-12 to AU-58:* 3,500 to 5,000+.

Characteristics of striking: This issue is usually seen well struck, but there are exceptions, including some light striking on stars four through six on the obverse and at the top of the shield and on the eagle's neck on the reverse.

	Cert	Avg	%MS	VG-8	F-12	VF-20	EF-40	AU-50	MS-60	MS-63	MS-64	MS-65
1842	688	47.9	13%	$400	$450	$525	$575	$850	$2,400	$5,000	$8,500	$90,000

1842, Proof • Mintage: 10 to 15.

Commentary and Availability: Approximately eight examples have been certified.

	Cert	Avg	%MS	PF-60	PF-63	PF-64	PF-65
1842, Proof	7	63.0		$15,000	$35,000	$55,000	$80,000

1843 Liberty Seated Dollar

1843 • **Mintage:** 165,100.

Availability in Mint State: *MS-60 to 62:* 20 to 25. *MS-63:* 8 to 12. *MS-64:* 1 or 2. *MS-65 or better:* 0 or 1.

Availability in circulated grades: *F-12 to AU-58:* 3,500 to 5,000+.

Characteristics of striking: Striking of this issue varies, but the topmost stars and head of Liberty are often lightly struck.

	Cert	Avg	%MS	VG-8	F-12	VF-20	EF-40	AU-50	MS-60	MS-63	MS-64	MS-65
1843	570	47.1	10%	$400	$450	$525	$575	$850	$2,400	$7,000	$20,000	$100,000

1843, Proof • Mintage: 10 to 15.

Commentary and Availability: Approximately seven examples have been certified, of which one is lightly circulated.

	Cert	Avg	%MS	PF-60	PF-63	PF-64	PF-65
1843, Proof	6	63.3		$15,000	$30,000	$50,000	$110,000

1844 Liberty Seated Dollar

1844 • **Mintage:** 20,000.

Availability in Mint State: What few Mint State coins the author has seen have all been very frosty, sometimes with prooflike reverse fields. *MS-60 to 62:* 15 to 20. *MS-63:* 2 or 3. *MS-64:* 1 or 2. *MS-65 or better:* 0 or 1.

Availability in circulated grades: *F-12 to AU-58:* 700 to 1,000.

Characteristics of striking: This issue is usually well struck with smooth surfaces.

Notes: The year 1844 was notable as the first of low-mintage silver dollars of this design. As before, most depositors of silver bullion wanted lower denominations that could be placed in the channels of commerce for face value. Only one delivery of silver dollars was made this year, that of 20,000 pieces on December 31. The China trade in particular demanded silver after certain ports, mainly Canton, were opened for the first time to Westerners in 1842. Europe remained the primary destination for exported dollars.

	Cert	Avg	%MS	VG-8	F-12	VF-20	EF-40	AU-50	MS-60	MS-63	MS-64	MS-65
1844	172	50.8	12%	$450	$500	$575	$800	$1,300	$5,000	$14,000	$35,000	$100,000

VARIETY: *1844, Four Stripes.* This issue is also known as "quad stripes." Circulation strikes of the year 1844 have four tiny vertical stripes composing each large vertical stripe on the obverse shield, whereas all other circulation strikes in the Liberty Seated series from 1840 to 1873 have just three stripes, as do Proofs of all years (including 1844). The fourth or extra stripe, to the right side of the normal three, is in all cases more lightly defined than the other three and is somewhat irregular. The feature is considered to be a doubled die. A few other elements of die doubling are present, including a doubling of the pointed top to the shield and the presence of three border lines (instead of the normal two) on the right edge of the shield. The feature of four elements to each stripe is unique in the series.

1844, Proof • Mintage: 10 to 15.

Commentary and Availability: Approximately eight examples have been certified, of which at least two are lightly circulated.

	Cert	Avg	%MS	PF-60	PF-63	PF-64	PF-65
1844, Proof	8	63.9		$12,500	$30,000	$55,000	$90,000

1845 Liberty Seated Dollar

1845 • **Mintage:** 24,500.

Availability in Mint State: In Mint State the 1845 is the rarest of all Liberty Seated dollars of the 1840s. *MS-60 to 62:* 3 to 5. *MS-63:* 2 to 4. *MS-64:* 1 or 2. *MS-65 or better:* 0 or 1.

Availability in circulated grades: *F-12 to AU-58:* 900 to 1,400.

Characteristics of striking: This issue is usually well struck, but there are exceptions.

Notes: Depositor requests for dollars remained small. Only two deliveries of silver dollars were made during the year. Silver coins of all denominations were scarce in circulation.

	Cert	Avg	%MS	VG-8	F-12	VF-20	EF-40	AU-50	MS-60	MS-63	MS-64	MS-65
1845	193	49.7	10%	$450	$500	$575	$800	$1,500	$9,000	$25,000	$55,000	$150,000

1845, Proof • **Mintage:** 10 to 15.

Commentary and Availability: The date is doubled. Approximately 11 examples have been certified.

	Cert	Avg	%MS	PF-60	PF-63	PF-64	PF-65
1845, Proof	11	63.8		$12,500	$30,000	$40,000	$70,000

1846 Liberty Seated Dollar

1846 • **Mintage:** 110,600.

Availability in Mint State: *MS-60 to 62:* 25 to 32. *MS-63:* 9 to 12. *MS-64:* 5 to 7. *MS-65 or better:* 3 to 5.

Availability in circulated grades: *F-12 to AU-58:* 2,000+ to 3,000.

Characteristics of striking: This issue is usually very well struck and very pleasing in appearance.

	Cert	Avg	%MS	VG-8	F-12	VF-20	EF-40	AU-50	MS-60	MS-63	MS-64	MS-65
1846	550	49.7	15%	$425	$450	$500	$600	$900	$2,500	$5,500	$10,000	$90,000

1846, Proof • Mintage: 10 to 15.

Commentary and Availability: More Proofs than normal appear to have been made this year. The reason is unknown. The date is repunched over an earlier 1846 that was too low. This variety was formerly called 1846/1845 (per the Lorin G. Parmelee Collection Sale, 1890) and, more often, 1846/1844 (per the 1945 F.C.C. Boyd "World's Greatest Collection" Sale and others). Approximately 14 examples have been certified.

	Cert	Avg	%MS	PF-60	PF-63	PF-64	PF-65
1846, Proof	14	62.9		$12,500	$30,000	$35,000	$105,000

1846-O Liberty Seated Dollar

1846-O • Mintage: 59,000.

Availability in Mint State: In Mint State the 1846-O is very rare; just how rare is not known with certainty. Some of the specimens seen have been so deeply toned that it is impossible for anyone (including a certification service) to determine, for example, whether they are AU-58 or Mint State. *MS-60 to 62:* 10 to 13. *MS-63:* 3 to 5. *MS-64:* 1 or 2. *MS-65 or better:* 1.

Availability in circulated grades: These were extensively circulated in the Mississippi River Basin. *VG-8 to AU-58:* 1,000 to 1,500, most of which are below Extremely Fine.

Characteristics of striking: This issue has an average strike showing weakness, particularly on the obverse stars, head, and horizontal shield stripes and on the reverse the eagle's head and claws.

Notes: Although the New Orleans Mint opened for business in 1838 it struck no silver dollars until 1846. The mintage was accomplished in June. This was the first of only four dates of Liberty Seated dollars from this mint: 1846-O, 1850-O, 1859-O, and 1860-O.

Most 1846-O dollars were exported, serving the purpose for which they were made (see introductory material in this chapter). Some have the reverse die rotated about 45 degrees clockwise from the normal position.

	Cert	Avg	%MS	VG-8	F-12	VF-20	EF-40	AU-50	MS-60	MS-63	MS-64	MS-65
1846-O	199	44.9	11%	$450	$500	$575	$800	$1,400	$7,250	$17,000	$40,000	$100,000

1847 Liberty Seated Dollar

1847 • Mintage: 140,750.

Availability in Mint State: This issue is available in Mint State, and when seen is apt to be very frosty. From the beginning of the series to 1847, it is the date most often seen MS-60 or above. *MS-60 to 62:* 20 to 25. *MS-63:* 25 to 32. *MS-64:* 15 to 20. *MS-65 or better:* 3 to 5.

Availability in circulated grades: The 1847 is one of the most available of all Liberty Seated dollars of the 1840–1865 No Motto type. In 1963 when the author was sorting through quantities of unattributed worn Liberty Seated dollars from the great Treasury release, he found more of this date than of any other early issue. *F-12 to AU-58:* 3,000 to 5,000.

Characteristics of striking: This issue is usually well struck.

Notes: The Philadelphia Mint was busy this year and turned out large numbers of silver coins of all denominations. However, as is true of other years, silver dollars were only struck to the order of bullion depositors specifically requesting them. Most were exported to England and the Chinese port of Canton.

	Cert	Avg	%MS	VG-8	F-12	VF-20	EF-40	AU-50	MS-60	MS-63	MS-64	MS-65
1847	573	49.9	14%	$425	$475	$550	$575	$800	$2,700	$5,500	$8,500	$90,000

1847, Proof • Mintage: 10 to 15.

Commentary and Availability: Approximately 16 examples have been certified.

	Cert	Avg	%MS	PF-60
1847, Proof	16	63.9		$12,500

1848 Liberty Seated Dollar

1848 • Mintage: 15,000.

Availability in Mint State: *MS-60 to 62:* 15 to 20. *MS-63:* 4 to 6. *MS-64:* 2 or 3. *MS-65 or better:* 1 or 2.

Availability in circulated grades: *F-12 to AU-58:* 600 to 1,000.

Characteristics of striking: This issue is usually well struck.

Notes: The Philadelphia Mint produced only 15,000 silver dollars, the lowest production of the 1840–1850 span.

Commentary and Availability: Approximately ten examples have been certified. One of these shows light wear.

	Cert	Avg	%MS	VG-8	F-12	VF-20	EF-40	AU-50	MS-60	MS-63	MS-64	MS-65
1848	106	48.4	9%	$450	$650	$750	$1,400	$1,900	$4,750	$13,000	$50,000	$90,000

1848, Proof • **Mintage:** 25 to 35.

Commentary and Availability: A great rarity, the 1848 Proof dollar is only slightly less rare than the 1847. In this entire series we are dealing with the rarest of the rare, and, as noted, comments concerning exactly *how* rare such coins are can be highly conjectural. In general, owners and catalogers opt for greater rarity, whereas objective analysts tend to have a broader view.

	Cert	Avg	%MS	PF-60	PF-63	PF-64	PF-65
1848, Proof	9	64.2		$12,500	$30,000	$40,000	$65,000

1849 Liberty Seated Dollar

1849 • **Mintage:** 62,600.

Availability in Mint State: *MS-60 to 62:* 30 to 40. *MS-63:* 10 to 15. *MS-64:* 5 to 7. *MS-65 or better:* 3 or 4.

Availability in circulated grades: *F-12 to AU-58:* 1,400 to 1,800.

Characteristics of striking: Striking of this issue varies; some are well struck and others show local weakness (particularly at the eagle's neck immediately above the shield, at the eagle's leg to the left, and/or at the stars on the right obverse). Some circulation strikes, even those with areas of light striking, have knife-rims, partial on the obverse, nearly full on the reverse and prooflike surface on both sides.

	Cert	Avg	%MS	VG-8	F-12	VF-20	EF-40	AU-50	MS-60	MS-63	MS-64	MS-65
1849	317	53.0	25%	$450	$500	$575	$700	$1,200	$2,600	$6,750	$13,000	$90,000

1849, Proof • **Mintage:** 10 to 15.

Commentary and Availability: The obverse has the date high and close to base. Extensive die-finish marks can be seen under the chin of Liberty. Approximately nine examples have been certified.

	Cert	Avg	%MS	PF-60	PF-63	PF-64	PF-65
1849, Proof	8	63.8		$13,500	$34,000	$40,000	$65,000

1850 Liberty Seated Dollar

1850 • **Mintage:** 7,500.

Availability in Mint State: Mint State coins, when seen, are apt to be nearly fully prooflike and are often mistaken for Proofs. Indeed, they were struck from dies also used to coin Proofs. Such coins are rare at all Mint State grade levels but are extremely so in MS-63 or better. *MS-60 to 62:* 10 to 15. *MS-63:* 2 to 4. *MS-64:* 1 or 2. *MS-65 or better:* 0 or 1.

Availability in circulated grades: *F-12 to AU-58:* 350 to 500.

Characteristics of striking: This issue is usually well struck and is always prooflike.

Notes: The 1850 dollar begins a decade of rare Liberty Seated dollar issues with nearly all exported.

	Cert	Avg	%MS	VG-8	F-12	VF-20	EF-40	AU-50	MS-60	MS-63	MS-64	MS-65
1850	116	53.7	28%	$600	$800	$1,250	$1,800	$2,500	$6,500	$14,000	$35,000	$90,000

1850, Proof • **Mintage:** 20 to 30.

Commentary and Availability: Approximately 16 examples have been certified.

	Cert	Avg	%MS	PF-60	PF-63	PF-64	PF-65
1850, Proof	16	63.9		$12,500	$25,000	$30,000	$50,000

1850-O Liberty Seated Dollar

1850-O • **Mintage:** 40,000.

Availability in Mint State: *MS-60 to 62:* 7 to 10. *MS-63:* 1 or 2. *MS-64:* 1 or 2. *MS-65 or better:* 0 or 1.

Availability in circulated grades: *VG-8 to AU-58:* 800 to 1,200.

Worn examples of the 1850-O dollar are fairly plentiful today up through and including the Very Fine level. Extremely Fine pieces are scarce, and About Uncirculated specimens are fairly rare.

Characteristics of striking: This issue has an average strike for most, though some have weakness on Liberty's head and/or on the eagle's head and claws.

Notes: Most if not all of the metal for this coinage was from melted-down Mexican dollars.

	Cert	Avg	%MS	VG-8	F-12	VF-20	EF-40	AU-50	MS-60	MS-63	MS-64	MS-65
1850-O	157	42.1	10%	$450	$500	$750	$1,450	$3,200	$11,500	$25,000	$75,000	$120,000

1851 Liberty Seated Dollar

1851, Original, High Date •

Mintage: 1,300.

Availability in Mint State: *MS-60 to 62:* 5 to 8. *MS-63:* 5 to 8. *MS-64:* 4 to 6. *MS-65 or better:* 2 or 3.

Availability in circulated grades: *VF-20 to AU-58:* 10 to 15, most of which are Extremely Fine or About Uncirculated. PCGS has graded a VG-8 and a VG-10.

Characteristics of striking: Stars on the right obverse are usually flat, otherwise, the coins are average strikes. Frosty circulation-strike coins have numerous die striae. The dies clashed at an early time, and to remove most traces the obverse die was relapped, giving it a highly prooflike surface. On all examples seen there is a clash mark in the field near Liberty's elbow drapery.

Notes: No originals are known in Proof format. Some called such have been prooflike circulation strikes.

	Cert	Avg	%MS	VG-8	F-12	VF-20	EF-40	AU-50	MS-60	MS-63	MS-64	MS-65
1851, Original, High Date	27	60.9	70%	$16,500	$19,500	$22,000	$25,000	$27,500	$32,500	$55,000	$85,000	$140,000

1851, Proof, Restrike, Date Centered • **Mintage:** 35 to 50.

Commentary and Availability: Proofs of this issue were struck for the numismatic trade. The date is centered, making restrikes easily identifiable.

Notes: It is not known when restrikes first appeared on the market. Probably many if not most were sold through William K. Idler, the Philadelphia dealer who had close private connections with Mint officials.

Two die pairs are known for restrikes, which are distinguished by having the date lower and better centered than on the originals. These may have been from a die made but not used in 1851, or a completely new die could have been made circa 1859. The date logotype is identical to that of the original obverse; Mint regulations did not even mention old logotypes, let alone mandate their destruction.

Over a long period of years into the early 1900s most auction offerings of Proof 1851 dollars omitted mentioning they were restrikes.

	Cert	Avg	%MS	PF-60	PF-63	PF-64	PF-65
1851, Proof, Restrike, Date Centered	19	62.8		$20,000	$30,000	$35,000	$75,000

1852 Liberty Seated Dollar

1852 • **Mintage:** 1,100.

Availability in Mint State: Mint State coins have satiny, lustrous surfaces with minute die striations. Perhaps the Mint saved a few of these for trading purposes at the time of issue. In high grades the 1852 seems to be slightly rarer than the 1851, but the population is so small that no unequivocal conclusions can be drawn. *MS-60 to 62:* 5 to 8. *MS-63:* 2 to 4. *MS-64:* 2 to 4. *MS-65 or better:* 1 or 2.

Availability in circulated grades: *F-12 to AU-58:* 30 to 40.

Characteristics of striking: This issue is usually sharp except for weakness at several stars to the right, especially 9 through 13.

	Cert	Avg	%MS	VG-8	F-12	VF-20	EF-40	AU-50	MS-60	MS-63	MS-64	MS-65
1852	19	59.8	68%	$15,000	$18,000	$20,000	$24,000	$27,500	$40,000	$65,000	$90,000	$140,000

1852, Proof, Original • **Mintage:** 20 to 30.

Proof originals: An estimated two to four are known. These were coined using the reverse die used on Proofs of the 1840s.

	Cert	Avg	%MS	PF-60	PF-63	PF-64	PF-65
1852, Proof, Original	16	63.5		$27,500	$43,500	$45,000	$75,000

1852, Proof, Restrike •

Mintage: 20 to 30.

Proof restrikes: Approximately 15 examples have been certified.

The restrikes are thought to have been made beginning in 1859. All are sharply struck. These were sold privately by Mint officials. There are several minute differences on the reverse, indicating several periods of striking.

	Cert	Avg	%MS	PF-60	PF-63	PF-64	PF-65
1852, Proof, Restrike	0	n/a		$17,500	$30,000	$45,000	$70,000

1853 Liberty Seated Dollar

1853 • **Mintage:** 46,110.

Availability in Mint State: It seems likely that somewhere a small hoard of Mint State pieces of this particular date came to light in the 1970s or early 1980s. Prior to that time, Uncirculated 1853 dollars were very rare. Most Mint State coins are brilliant or are lightly golden toned and are very frosty (rather than prooflike in areas), and seem to have come from a common source (in contrast to pieces from different sources, which have a wide variety of toning, handling marks, etc.). In any event, the 1853 is the only readily available Mint State Liberty Seated dollar of its immediate time frame. *MS-60 to 62:* 100 to 200. *MS-63:* 35 to 50. *MS-64:* 10 to 13. *MS-65 or better:* 2 to 4.

Availability in circulated grades: *F-12 to AU-58:* 700 to 1,000. Most coins of this issue are in higher grades.

Characteristics of striking: This issue is usually well struck, however there are exceptions and some have weak stars, especially stars 9 through 13. "Chin whiskers" or die-finish lines are seen below Liberty's chin on most circulation strikes.

	Cert	Avg	%MS	VG-8	F-12	VF-20	EF-40	AU-50	MS-60	MS-63	MS-64	MS-65
1853	156	57.5	55%	$350	$450	$650	$1,100	$1,300	$3,200	$7,250	$11,000	$85,000

1853, Proof, Restrike •

Mintage: 15 to 20.

Proof restrikes: It is thought that no Proofs were minted in 1853. As early as 1860, George F. Jones noted that no original Proof dollars were struck in 1853. This was rather frustrating, for a number of collectors desired to have complete sets of Proof dollars from 1840 onward. Accordingly, the traditional view held by numismatists for many years is that a number of Proof 1853 dollars were prepared at the Mint circa 1862. It has been repeated in numismatic literature that only 12 Proof 1853 pieces were made, and indeed, over the years 1853 Proof dollars have appeared on the market at infrequent intervals. Approximately six examples have been certified.

	Cert	Avg	%MS	PF-60	PF-63	PF-64	PF-65
1853, Proof, Restrike	6	63.7		$20,000	$37,000	$55,000	$110,000

1854 Liberty Seated Dollar

1854 • **Mintage:** 33,140.

Availability in Mint State: Some coins of this issue are from a group of five that surfaced in the 1970s. Population data can be misleading due to resubmissions. *MS-60 to 62:* 8 to 12. *MS-63:* 5 to 8. *MS-64:* 12 to 18. *MS-65 or better:* 5 to 8.

Availability in circulated grades: This may be the rarest Philadelphia Mint Liberty Seated dollar after 1851–1852. In fact, dollars of this date were considered rare by Montroville W. Dickeson in his *American Numismatical Manual* in 1859, just five years after they were minted! Writing in 1880, Ebenezer Locke Mason considered the 1854 to be the rarest circulation-strike silver dollar dated after 1852 (he did not consider mintmarks, as these were not collected at the time). *VF-20 to AU-58:* 130 to 170.

Characteristics of striking: Some coins of this issue are sharply struck, but others are lightly defined in areas, including the head of Liberty and the eagle's wings and claws. The top of the date is not bold in the die, a characteristic of all specimens, as the date logotype was punched more deeply into the die at the bottom.

Notes: These and other dollars of the era were made as bullion coins. Nearly all were exported to England and China and later melted. Walter H. Breen comments in his *Encyclopedia of U.S. and Colonial Coins* that 10,000 silver dollars dated 1854 were shipped from Philadelphia to San Francisco on November 11, 1854. Likely these were sent to China as well, as merchants of that city were in need of silver coins for export.

	Cert	Avg	%MS	VG-8	F-12	VF-20	EF-40	AU-50	MS-60	MS-63	MS-64	MS-65
1854	47	55.5	43%	$1,500	$2,500	$4,000	$5,000	$6,000	$9,000	$13,000	$20,000	$95,000

1854, Proof • Mintage: 40 to 60.

Commentary and Availability: Beginning in this year, Proofs were issued with vigor, and apparently at least 60 to 80 Liberty Seated dollars reached collectors. The dollar, though rare, is considerably less rare than Proof three-cent pieces, half dimes, dimes, quarters, and half dollars of the same year. Approximately 17 examples have been certified.

	Cert	Avg	%MS	PF-60	PF-63	PF-64	PF-65
1854, Proof	17	63.6		$12,500	$16,500	$23,500	$45,000

1855 Liberty Seated Dollar

1855 • Mintage: 26,000.

Availability in Mint State: Mint State coins tend to have somewhat dullish luster. The "fifty scruffy Uncs" in a 1975 Superior Galleries auction, mentioned by John Dannreuther in John Highfill's *Comprehensive U.S. Silver Dollar Encyclopedia*, may represent a hoard, but it is not known if any would presently qualify as Mint State. Mint State 1855 dollars are extremely rare, and even large collections are apt to lack a Mint State example, or to have a Proof instead. *MS-60 to 62:* 8 to 12. *MS-63:* 2 or 3. *MS-64:* 1 or 2. *MS-65 or better:* 0 or 1.

Availability in circulated grades: Circulated examples of the 1855 Liberty Seated dollar are few and far between, and finding an acceptable specimen of this date has never been an easy task. However, in comparison to many other areas under the numismatic rainbow (Morgan dollars being an obvious instance), 1855 silver dollars are relatively inexpensive in proportion to their rarity. *F-12 to AU-58:* 175 to 250.

Characteristics of striking: Striking of this issue varies. They are sometimes seen with weakness on the head of Liberty and the stars (particularly 9 through 13) on the obverse and the top of the eagle's wings and on the leg on the left side of the reverse.

Notes: About Uncirculated and better circulation strikes tend to be somewhat prooflike, and have often been cataloged as "Proofs" in the past, possibly causing a misconception of true Proof rarity in auction catalogs and other literature.

	Cert	Avg	%MS	VG-8	F-12	VF-20	EF-40	AU-50	MS-60	MS-63	MS-64	MS-65
1855	53	53.2	28%	$1,250	$2,500	$4,000	$5,000	$6,500	$8,000	$30,000	$150,000	—

1855, Proof • Mintage: 40 to 60.

Commentary and Availability: 1855 Proofs are rarer than those dated 1854 for some unknown reason. These were made from a single 1855 obverse die combined with two reverses (one of them the same used for 1854 Proofs). Approximately 21 examples have been certified.

	Cert	Avg	%MS	PF-60	PF-63	PF-64	PF-65
1855, Proof	17	63.9		$12,500	$16,000	$25,000	$40,000

1856 Liberty Seated Dollar

1856 • Mintage: 63,500.

Availability in Mint State: Although the 1856 dollar is an extreme rarity in Mint State, the appreciation of it by advanced collectors, and, to an extent, its market price, have been dimmed slightly by the availability of Proofs of this date. Proofs, although rarities in their own right, have served to absorb some of the demand for top-grade coins. Mint State 1856 dollars are few and far between. *MS-60 to 62:* 8 to 12. *MS-63:* 2 or 3. *MS-64:* 2 or 3. *MS-65 or better:* 0 or 1.

Availability in circulated grades: *F-12 to AU-58:* 200 to 300.

Characteristics of striking: This issue is usually weakly struck, typically with Liberty's head and stars eight through ten flat. On the reverse, the eagle's leg on the left is often weak.

Notes: Although most silver dollars sent to China were melted, money brokers in Shanghai held quantities of them. According to accounts, the accuracy of which is questionable, at one particular time 150 American dollars could be exchanged for 100 Mexican dollars.

	Cert	Avg	%MS	VG-8	F-12	VF-20	EF-40	AU-50	MS-60	MS-63	MS-64	MS-65
1856	53	52.6	28%	$600	$800	$1,100	$2,750	$4,000	$5,000	$15,000	$17,500	$85,000

1856, Proof • **Mintage:** 40 to 60.

Commentary and Availability: Approximately 37 examples have been certified.

	Cert	Avg	%MS	PF-60	PF-63	PF-64	PF-65
1856, Proof	38	63.7		$5,500	$13,000	$16,000	$30,000

1857 Liberty Seated Dollar

1857 • **Mintage:** 94,000.

Availability in Mint State: At this level the 1857 dollar is quite rare, but is still one of the most readily available (with 1853) Philadelphia Mint issues of the 1850s up to this point. When seen, Mint State coins almost always have a prooflike surface and are nearly always lightly struck, particularly at the upper part of the obverse. *MS-60 to 62:* 30 to 40. *MS-63:* 20 to 25. *MS-64:* 15 to 20. *MS-65 or better:* 2 to 4.

Availability in circulated grades: The 1857 is very rare, somewhat approaching the 1854 and 1855 in this regard, but not quite in the same league with them. *F-12 to AU-58:* 175 to 250.

Characteristics of striking: This issue is nearly always weakly struck at top of the obverse (Liberty's head and stars five through ten). Some coins are almost flat in this area and *very* flat on the eagle's wing to the left and on the eagle's head. Other coins are weak on the obverse but quite well struck on the reverse. Nearly all were made with prooflike surfaces. Only one needle-sharp example has been seen by the author, that with a frosty surface with no trace of being prooflike.

	Cert	Avg	%MS	VG-8	F-12	VF-20	EF-40	AU-50	MS-60	MS-63	MS-64	MS-65
1857	90	58.7	69%	$525	$650	$900	$2,500	$3,000	$3,500	$9,500	$15,000	$85,000

1857, Proof • **Mintage:** 50 to 70.

Commentary and Availability: The same reverse die was used to strike Proof silver dollars of 1856 and 1858. The Proof 1857 dollar is thought to be more readily available than the 1855 Proof but scarcer than the 1856 Proof. Approximately 28 examples have been certified.

	Cert	Avg	%MS	PF-60	PF-63	PF-64	PF-65
1857, Proof	28	64.0		$7,000	$13,500	$17,000	$30,000

1858 Liberty Seated Dollar

1858, Proof • **Mintage:** 300 estimated.

Commentary and Availability: This issue had 210 coins or so made for inclusion in silver Proof sets. Possibly others were struck as well. Many seeking a run of Proof Liberty Seated dollars start their sets with this year. Approximately 72 examples have been certified.

Notes: As the solitary Proof-only coin in the series the 1858 has been famous for a long time. The mintage was not recorded. Apparently, there was no call for export coins of this denomination. However, the Mint made large quantities of lower-denomination silver coins throughout the year for circulation.

	Cert	Avg	%MS	PF-60	PF-63	PF-64	PF-65
1858, Proof	77	62.3		$10,000	$14,000	$19,000	$35,000

1859 Liberty Seated Dollar

1859 • **Mintage:** 255,700.

Availability in Mint State: *MS-60 to 62:* 20 to 25. *MS-63:* 15 to 20. *MS-64:* 12 to 18. *MS-65 or better:* 2 to 4.

Availability in circulated grades: *F-12 to AU-58:* 350 to 500.

Characteristics of striking: Many coins of this issue are weakly struck at one or both of these areas: stars (irregularly weak striking, with stars one and four sharp and the others, especially eight and nine, weak) and the head of Liberty.

	Cert	Avg	%MS	VG-8	F-12	VF-20	EF-40	AU-50	MS-60	MS-63	MS-64	MS-65
1859	86	54.5	43%	$400	$425	$525	$750	$1,225	$2,500	$6,000	$10,000	$85,000

1859, Proof • **Mintage:** 800.

Commentary and Availability: These are readily available, mostly in lower-grade levels. Apparently, many Proofs were made this year in the hope that the public, which was becoming increasingly interested in numismatics, would buy them. Although 800 were struck, probably fewer than 450 were distributed. **PF-60 to 62:** 150 to 250. **PF-63:** 70 to 90. **PF-64:** 40 to 55. **PF-65 or better:** 35 to 50.

	Cert	Avg	%MS	PF-60	PF-63	PF-64	PF-65
1859, Proof	159	63.8		$2,400	$4,750	$6,500	$12,000

1859-O Liberty Seated Dollar

1859-O • **Mintage:** 360,000.

Availability in Mint State: During the 1962–1964 Treasury release of backdated silver dollars, it is believed that up to three Mint-sealed bags of 1,000 Uncirculated coins were distributed. Almost without exception, the coins from these bags are heavily bagmarked and scarred, the result of careless storage, handling, and shipping procedures over the years. The average grade today is MS-60 or just slightly better. Mint State coins from other sources tend to be in higher grades. *MS-60 to 62:* 2,250 to 2,750. *MS-63:* 40 to 80+. *MS-64:* 3 to 5. *MS-65 or better:* 2 to 4.

Availability in circulated grades: *F-12 to AU-58:* 2,000 to 3,000.

Characteristics of striking: Striking of this issue varies. The stars are often weak, beginning at stars eight and nine and, depending upon the coin, to the left or right as well. These are satiny rather than having a deeply frosty luster. The fields are usually prooflike.

Notes: Most of the 1859-O and 1860-O dollars were made for the China export trade.

	Cert	Avg	%MS	VG-8	F-12	VF-20	EF-40	AU-50	MS-60	MS-63	MS-64	MS-65
1859-O	721	51.3	44%	$350	$400	$450	$500	$775	$1,800	$5,000	$7,500	$65,000

1859-S Liberty Seated Dollar

1859-S • **Mintage:** 20,000.

Availability in Mint State: In true Mint State the 1859-S is a formidable rarity. Many if not most offered at this level are darkly toned or overgraded. Very few lustrous pieces with beautiful eye appeal exist. *MS-60 to 62:* 5 to 8. *MS-63:* 1 or 2. *MS-64:* 0 or 1. *MS-65 or better:* 1.

Availability in circulated grades: *VG-8 to AU-58:* 500 to 750.

Characteristics of striking: This issue is usually well struck.

Notes: A total of 15,000 silver dollars were struck at the San Francisco Mint in 1859 specifically for export on May 11 of that year. A further 5,000 were coined in July. Some were distributed on the West Coast, where they remained in circulation for many years.

	Cert	Avg	%MS	VG-8	F-12	VF-20	EF-40	AU-50	MS-60	MS-63
1859-S	155	44.6	14%	$600	$850	$1,100	$1,600	$3,350	$13,000	$29,000

1860 Liberty Seated Dollar

1860 • **Mintage:** 217,600.

Availability in Mint State: These are very scarce. When seen, examples often have a partially prooflike surface. The mint frost on typical specimens is apt to be satiny rather than deeply coruscating and frosty. *MS-60 to 62:* 40 to 75. *MS-63:* 20 to 25. *MS-64:* 20 to 25. *MS-65 or better:* 10 to 15.

Availability in circulated grades: *F-12 to AU-58:* 500 to 750.

Characteristics of striking: This issue is usually well struck. Many higher-grade coins show prooflike surfaces.

	Cert	Avg	%MS	VG-8	F-12	VF-20	EF-40	AU-50	MS-60	MS-63	MS-64	MS-65
1860	126	56.2	50%	$450	$500	$575	$700	$900	$2,100	$5,000	$7,500	$75,000

1860, Proof • Mintage: 1,330.

Commentary and Availability: This mintage is the largest Proof figure in the entire Liberty Seated series. Only 527 were eventually sold, and the rest were consigned to the melting pot. It seems that among those sold, some were spent or lost. *PF-60 to 62:* 125 to 225. *PF-63:* 60 to 90. *PF-64:* 35 to 50. *PF-65 or better:* 30 to 45.

	Cert	Avg	%MS	PF-60	PF-63	PF-64	PF-65
1860, Proof	150	63.7		$2,400	$4,750	$6,500	$12,000

1860-O Liberty Seated Dollar

1860-O • **Mintage:** 515,000.

Availability in Mint State: An estimated 5,000 were released in the Treasury dispersal that began in November 1862. The 1860-O is the most plentiful Liberty Seated dollar in Mint State. *MS-60 to 62:* 5,250 to 5,750; most are in the MS-60 category and are heavily bagmarked. *MS-63:* 90 to 120. *MS-64:* 20 to 25. *MS-65 or better:* 3 to 5.

Availability in circulated grades: *F-12 to AU-58:* 2,500 to 3,500.

Characteristics of striking: This issue is usually fairly well struck. Coins of this issue have a satiny rather than deeply frosty luster. The fields are usually prooflike, especially on non-hoard coins.

Notes: Most of these were made for export to China.

	Cert	Avg	%MS	VG-8	F-12	VF-20	EF 40	AU-50	MS-60	MS-63	MS-64	MS-65
1860-O	1,004	53.1	49%	$350	$400	$450	$500	$775	$1,800	$3,750	$5,000	$60,000

1861 Liberty Seated Dollar

1861 • Mintage: 77,500.

Availability in Mint State: High-grade coins typically show striations from incomplete polishing of the obverse die in particular. *MS-60 to 62:* 15 to 20. *MS-63:* 15 to 20. *MS-64:* 15 to 20. *MS-65 or better:* 4 to 6.

Availability in circulated grades: *F-12 to AU-58:* 200 to 300.

Characteristics of striking: Many 1861 circulation-strike dollars show areas of light striking, especially on Liberty's head. Indeed, this is a hallmark of this particular date.

Notes: A new reverse die with claws and arrowheads slightly more delicate than earlier years was first employed in 1861; however, the differences between the old and new dies are very subtle.

Dies were shipped to New Orleans for an 1861-O coinage of silver dollars, but they never went into use, so far as anyone knows. The 1861 *Mint Report* stated that the current price the Mint charged for silver dollars was $1.08. The buyers were agents of or those engaged in the export trade.

Beginning in 1859 there was a glut of silver in the state from production in Nevada. Much of this was sent to Philadelphia and coined into dollars. In 1859, 1860, and 1861 more than 1,250,000 of these dollars were shipped to China, where they were received at bullion value. They were not as popular as the slightly heavier Spanish-American dollars that took precedence there.

	Cert	Avg	%MS	VG-8	F-12	VF-20	EF-40	AU-50	MS-60	MS-63	MS-64	MS-65
1861	79	55.4	57%	$850	$1,200	$1,800	$3,000	$3,250	$4,000	$5,850	$10,000	$65,000

1861, Proof • Mintage: 1,000.

Commentary and Availability: It is thought that only a few hundred were distributed. The others were melted in 1862, per printed comments, or were placed into circulation. This is the rarest Proof date in the 1860s by far. *PF-60 to 62:* 100 to 120. *PF-63:* 110 to 150. *PF-64:* 40 to 55. *PF-65 or better:* 30 to 40.

	Cert	Avg	%MS	PF-60	PF-63	PF-64	PF-65
1861, Proof	101	63.4		$2,400	$4,750	$6,500	$12,000

1862 Liberty Seated Dollar

1862 • Mintage: 11,540.

Availability in Mint State: High-grade coins typically have extensive die striae, as struck, on the obverse and reverse, making it appear to the uninitiated as if the coin had been cleaned or brushed. This characteristic is similar to that seen on dollars of 1864. *MS-60 to 62:* 25 to 40. *MS-63:* 10 to 13. *MS-64:* 5 to 8. *MS-65 or better:* 3 to 5.

Availability in circulated grades: *F-12 to AU-58:* 200 to 300.

Characteristics of striking: Most coins of this issue are well struck.

	Cert	Avg	%MS	VG-8	F-12	VF-20	EF-40	AU-50	MS-60	MS-63	MS-64	MS-65
1862	95	55.2	62%	$900	$1,300	$1,900	$3,000	$3,750	$5,500	$9,000	$12,500	$65,000

1862, Proof • Mintage: 550.

Commentary and Availability: *PF-60 to 62:* 180 to 220. *PF-63:* 70 to 90. *PF-64:* 40 to 50. *PF-65 or better:* 20 to 30.

	Cert	Avg	%MS	PF-60	PF-63	PF-64	PF-65
1862, Proof	170	63.0		$2,400	$4,750	$6,500	$11,500

1863 Liberty Seated Dollar

1863 • Mintage: 27,200.

Availability in Mint State: There are fewer than 75 of these, most of which are at lower levels. High-grade coins always show striations from incomplete polishing of the obverse die in particular, but not as strong as 1862 and 1864. *MS-60 to 62:* 15 to 20. *MS-63:* 7 to 10. *MS-64:* 20 to 25. *MS-65 or better:* 5 to 7.

Availability in circulated grades: *F-12 to AU-58:* 125 to 175.

Characteristics of striking: Most coins of this issue are well struck.

	Cert	Avg	%MS	VG-8	F-12	VF-20	EF-40	AU-50	MS-60	MS-63	MS-64	MS-65
1863	82	54.8	57%	$900	$1,300	$2,000	$2,500	$2,800	$3,575	$7,000	$10,000	$50,000

1863, Proof • Mintage: 460.

Commentary and Availability: *PF-60 to 62:* 170 to 210. *PF-63:* 60 to 80. *PF-64:* 40 to 55. *PF-65 or better:* 18 to 25.

	Cert	Avg	%MS	PF-60	PF-63	PF-64	PF-65
1863, Proof	142	63.7		$2,400	$4,750	$7,500	$11,500

1864 Liberty Seated Dollar

1864 • **Mintage:** 30,700.

Availability in Mint State: Mint State 1864 dollars are very rare, with fewer than 50 estimated to exist—but when they do appear they are apt to be in higher levels, an unusual situation. High-grade coins typically have extensive die striae, as struck, on the obverse and reverse, making it appear to the uninitiated as if the coin had been cleaned or brushed. This characteristic is similar to that seen on dollars of 1862. *MS-60 to 62:* 8 to 12. *MS-63:* 4 to 6. *MS-64:* 10 to 13. *MS-65 or better:* 8 to 12.

Availability in circulated grades: *F-12 to AU-58:* 300 to 400.

Characteristics of striking: Most coins of this issue are very well struck.

	Cert	Avg	%MS	VG-8	F-12	VF-20	EF-40	AU-50	MS-60	MS-63	MS-64	MS-65
1864	93	45.7	22%	$500	$650	$1,000	$1,400	$2,100	$3,575	$7,500	$15,000	$60,000

1864, Proof • **Mintage:** 470.

Commentary and Availability: Three different obverse dies were used for the Proof coinage. *PF-60 to 62:* 200 to 230. *PF-63:* 80 to 100. *PF-64:* 45 to 60. *PF-65 or better:* 25 to 35.

	Cert	Avg	%MS	PF-60	PF-63	PF-64	PF-65
1864, Proof	159	63.4		$2,400	$4,750	$6,500	$11,500

1865 Liberty Seated Dollar

1865 • **Mintage:** 46,500.

Availability in Mint State: *MS-60 to 62:* 20 to 25. *MS-63:* 7 to 10. *MS-64:* 20 to 25. *MS-65 or better:* 1 or 2.

Availability in circulated grades: *F-12 to AU-58:* 250 to 325.

Characteristics of striking: Many coins of this issue show areas of light striking, often including the head, the stars, and the eagle's leg on the left.

	Cert	Avg	%MS	VG-8	F-12	VF-20	EF-40	AU-50	MS-60	MS-63	MS-64	MS-65
1865	83	49.3	28%	$500	$625	$1,000	$1,800	$2,400	$3,575	$7,500	$13,000	$80,000

1865, Proof • Mintage: 500.

Commentary and Availability: *PF-60 to 62:* 210 to 240. *PF-63:* 90 to 110. *PF-64:* 50 to 65. *PF-65 or better:* 30 to 40.

	Cert	Avg	%MS	PF-60	PF-63	PF-64	PF-65
1865, Proof	193	63.8		$2,400	$4,750	$6,500	$11,500

1866, No Motto, Liberty Seated Dollar

1866, No Motto, Proof • Mintage: 2.

Commentary and Availability: Two are known to exist. One is in the National Numismatic Collection at the Smithsonian Institution in Washington, D.C., a gift of the DuPont family.

1866, With Motto, Liberty Seated Dollar

1866, With Motto • Mintage: 48,900.

Availability in Mint State: *MS-60 to 62:* 20 to 25. *MS-63:* 20 to 25. *MS-64:* 15 to 20. *MS-65 or better:* 8 to 11.

Availability in circulated grades: *F-12 to AU-58:* 400 to 500.

Characteristics of striking: Striking of this issue varies, but there is often lightness on the head.

	Cert	Avg	%MS	VG-8	F-12	VF-20	EF-40	AU-50	MS-60	MS-63	MS-64	MS-65
1866, With Motto	130	51.5	38%	$425	$450	$600	$1,100	$1,400	$2,300	$5,500	$12,500	$65,000

1866, With Motto, Proof • Mintage: 725.

Commentary and Availability: Three different obverse dies were prepared for the Proof coinage. *PF-60 to 62:* 230 to 260. *PF-63:* 110 to 130. *PF-64:* 70 to 90. *PF-65 or better:* 45 to 60.

	Cert	Avg	%MS	PF-60	PF-63	PF-64	PF-65
1866, With Motto, Proof	232	63.5		$2,100	$3,800	$5,750	$10,000

1867 Liberty Seated Dollar

1867 • Mintage: 46,900.

Availability in Mint State: *MS-60 to 62:* 20 to 25. *MS-63:* 10 to 13. *MS-64:* 7 to 10. *MS-65 or better:* 2 to 4.

Availability in circulated grades: *F-12 to AU-58:* 450 to 600.

Characteristics of striking: Striking of this issue varies, but some have slight weakness at stars eight and nine.

	Cert	Avg	%MS	VG-8	F-12	VF-20	EF-40	AU-50	MS-60	MS-63	MS-64	MS-65
1867	78	49.5	36%	$425	$450	$600	$1,000	$1,200	$2,200	$5,300	$14,000	$70,000

VARIETY: *1867, Large Date Over Small Date.* Breen-5478. Apparently, a logotype for a half dollar was erroneously applied to the blank die, high and slanting down to the right, after which the regular dollar logotype was punched in the correct position. The early state (rarest) shows much of the small date while later states (slightly less rare) show less, and finally only traces.

1867, Proof • Mintage: 625.

Commentary and Availability: *PF-60 to 62:* 100 to 150. *PF-63:* 200 to 250. *PF-64:* 80 to 125. *PF-65 or better:* 35 to 50.

	Cert	Avg	%MS	PF-60	PF-63	PF-64	PF-65
1867, Proof	225	63.3		$2,100	$3,900	$5,750	$10,000

1868 Liberty Seated Dollar

1868 • Mintage: 162,100.

Availability in Mint State: Some high-grade pieces have unfinished areas within the lower right area of the shield. Most high-grade coins are prooflike. *MS-60 to 62:* 30 to 40. *MS-63:* 4 to 6. *MS-64:* 3 to 5. *MS-65 or better:* 3 or 4.

Availability in circulated grades: *F-12 to AU-58:* 300 to 400.

Characteristics of striking: Most coins of this issue are well struck.

	Cert	Avg	%MS	VG-8	F-12	VF-20	EF-40	AU-50	MS-60	MS-63	MS-64	MS-65
1868	122	47.1	15%	$425	$450	$500	$825	$1,200	$2,400	$7,000	$19,500	$65,000

1868, Proof • **Mintage:** 600.

Commentary and Availability: *PF-60 to 62:* 210 to 240. *PF-63:* 90 to 110. *PF-64:* 45 to 60. *PF-65 or better:* 30 to 40.

	Cert	Avg	%MS	PF-60	PF-63	PF-64	PF-65
1868, Proof	199	63.6		$2,100	$3,800	$5,750	$10,000

1869 Liberty Seated Dollar

1869 • **Mintage:** 423,700.

Availability in Mint State: Most high-grade coins are prooflike. *MS-60 to 62:* 15 to 20. *MS-63:* 12 to 18. *MS-64:* 8 to 12. *MS-65 or better:* 4 to 6.

Availability in circulated grades: *F-12 to AU-58:* 250 to 350.

Characteristics of striking: Striking of this issue varies, but the obverse is often sharp and the reverse often has slight weakness at top of the shield and top of the eagle's wing on the left.

	Cert	Avg	%MS	VG-8	F-12	VF-20	EF-40	AU-50	MS-60	MS-63	MS-64	MS-65
1869	146	50.0	32%	$425	$450	$500	$800	$1,150	$2,300	$5,250	$13,000	$65,000

1869, Proof • **Mintage:** 600.

Commentary and Availability: *PF-60 to 62:* 210 to 240. *PF-63:* 90 to 110. *PF-64:* 45 to 60. *PF-65 or better:* 30 to 40.

	Cert	Avg	%MS	PF-60	PF-63	PF-64	PF-65
1869, Proof	208	63.4		$2,100	$3,800	$5,750	$10,000

1870 Liberty Seated Dollar

1870 • **Mintage:** 415,000.

Availability in Mint State: *MS-60 to 62:* 50 to 75. *MS-63:* 20 to 25. *MS-64:* 15 to 20. *MS-65 or better:* 3 or 4.

Availability in circulated grades: Numerous worn coins came to light in the Treasury release of 1962–1964, but even before that they were easy to find. *F-12 to AU-58:* 1,200 to 1,800.

Characteristics of striking: Striking of this issue varies, but some have a curious pattern of weakness, with stars 10 through 13 weak, but eight, nine, and other stars more sharply defined. On many, the reverse appears to be a grade or two sharper than the obverse.

Notes: Exports continued apace in 1870, including to Bombay, India. For the first time since the 1840s, quantities of a Philadelphia Mint dollar remained within the borders of the United States. All coins were paid out to depositors at the time of coining and were worth a premium at the time. Any 1870 dollars found in Treasury vaults in later years were coins returned to the government, possibly in the mid-1870s.

	Cert	Avg	%MS	VG-8	F-12	VF-20	EF-40	AU-50	MS-60	MS-63	MS-64	MS-65
1870	275	47.6	24%	$425	$450	$525	$600	$950	$2,100	$4,750	$6,500	$55,000

1870, Proof • Mintage: 1,000.

Commentary and Availability: Proofs were carelessly made and are often weak on the leg to the left and on the eagle's neck feathers. *PF-60 to 62:* 200 to 230. *PF-63:* 85 to 105. *PF-64:* 50 to 65. *PF-65 or better:* 25 to 35.

	Cert	Avg	%MS	PF-60	PF-63	PF-64	PF-65
1870, Proof	214	63.2		$2,100	$3,800	$5,750	$10,000

1870-CC Liberty Seated Dollar

1870-CC • Mintage: 11,758.

Availability in Mint State: *MS-60 to 62:* 10 to 15. *MS-63:* 7 to 10. *MS-64:* 2 to 4. *MS-65 or better:* 0 or 1.

Availability in circulated grades: *VG-8 to F-15:* 150-250. *F-12 to AU-58:* 260 to 350.

Characteristics of striking: This issue is usually well struck, a general characteristic of most varieties of Carson City dollars over the years; this is especially true of the reverse. However, as is the case with other Carson City Mint Liberty Seated dollars, the word LIBERTY on the shield is not as prominent as on Philadelphia coins and tended to wear away especially quickly once the coins saw circulation. Most if not all were struck with prooflike surfaces that are visible today on coins in higher grades.

Notes: Nine varieties are known. These consist of four obverse dies combined with six reverse dies.

	Cert	Avg	%MS	VG-8	F-12	VF-20	EF-40	AU-50	MS-60	MS-63	MS-64	MS-65
1870-CC	245	39.9	7%	$1,000	$1,350	$2,100	$4,250	$5,500	$25,000	$42,500	$125,000	—

1870-S Liberty Seated Dollar

1870-S • **Mintage:** *300 or fewer.*

Availability in Mint State: Two or three are known in Mint State.

Availability in circulated grades: Nine are known in circulated grades.

Characteristics of striking: This issue had an average strike, but some have slight traces of prooflike surfaces.

Notes: Mint records omit this coinage. A reverse die with a Small S mintmark was shipped to San Francisco, but no record has been found for the obverse die. It could have been obtained from the Carson City Mint, or perhaps Mint Superintendent O.H. LaGrange got one when he visited the Philadelphia Mint in December 1869.

	Cert	Avg	%MS	VG-8	F-12	VF-20	EF-40	AU-50	MS-60	MS-63	MS-64	MS-65
1870-S	4	47.0	0%	$200,000	$250,000	$400,000	$525,000	$800,000	$1,750,000	—	—	—

1871 Liberty Seated Dollar

1871 • **Mintage:** 1,073,800.

Availability in Mint State: This date is the most readily available Philadelphia Mint coin in the series. It is possible that several hundred Mint State 1871 dollars were released by the Treasury from 1962 to 1964, probably mixed in with other coins.

Walter H. Breen in his *Encyclopedia* claimed to know of two bags of the issue. **MS-60 to 62:** 250 to 350+. **MS-63:** 50 to 80. **MS-64:** 15 to 20. **MS-65 or better:** 5 to 7.

Availability in circulated grades: *F-12 to AU-58:* 4,000 to 6,000.

Characteristics of striking: Striking quality of this issue varies, but some show weakness. According to a 2015 communication from Larry Briggs, "Many coins have a two-grade difference between the obverse and reverse, such as a VF-35 obverse and an AU-50 reverse!"

	Cert	Avg	%MS	VG-8	F-12	VF-20	EF-40	AU-50	MS-60	MS-63	MS-64	MS-65
1871	929	44.3	18%	$350	$410	$450	$500	$900	$2,100	$4,650	$6,500	$50,000

1871, Proof • **Mintage:** 960.

Commentary and Availability: *PF-60 to 62:* 210 to 240. *PF-63:* 90 to 110. *PF-64:* 40 to 55. *PF-65 or better:* 30 to 40.

	Cert	Avg	%MS	PF-60	PF-63	PF-64	PF-65
1871, Proof	205	62.9		$2,100	$3,800	$5,750	$10,000

1871-CC Liberty Seated Dollar

1871-CC • **Mintage:** 1,376.

Availability in Mint State: *MS-60 to 62:* 3 or 4. *MS-63:* 0. *MS-64:* 1. *MS-65 or better:* 0 or 1.

Availability in circulated grades: *VG-8 to F-15:* 15 to 20. *F-12 to AU-58:* 60 to 100.

Characteristics of striking: This issue is usually sharply struck. Some have lightness at stars 12 and 13. As is the case with other Carson City Mint Liberty Seated dollars, the word LIBERTY on the shield is not as prominent as on Philadelphia coins, and it tended to wear away especially quickly once the coins saw circulation.

Notes: The 1871-CC has the lowest mintage of any Carson City Mint coin of this design. However, examples today are more readily available than those of the higher-mintage 1873-CC, for many of the latter presumably were melted.

	Cert	Avg	%MS	VG-8	F-12	VF-20	EF-40	AU-50	MS-60	MS-63	MS-64	MS-65
1871-CC	49	41.8	8%	$3,750	$5,000	$6,500	$12,000	$17,500	$75,000	$175,000	$300,000	—

1872 Liberty Seated Dollar

1872 • **Mintage:** 1,105,500.

Availability in Mint State: Most of these are from the Treasury release of the 1960s. *MS-60 to 62:* 75 to 125+. *MS-63:* 25 to 32. *MS-64:* 20 to 25. *MS-65 or better:* 3 to 5.

Availability in circulated grades: *F-12 to AU-58:* 3,000 to 5,000.

Characteristics of striking: Striking of this issue varies. Some are flat from star 4 through 13, or others. Liberty's head is often lightly struck. Check the reverse as well, but it is usually sharper than the obverse.

Notes: The 1872 Liberty Seated dollar was coined in larger quantities than any other issue of the design. One interesting variety has an errant 2 punched into the rock on which Liberty is seated. Most were exported. This led to a call for a specific coin to be called a *commercial trade dollar*, a name later changed to *trade dollar*. Such trade dollars were first made in 1873 and are the subject of their own chapter.

	Cert	Avg	%MS	VG-8	F-12	VF-20	EF-40	AU-50	MS-60	MS-63	MS-64	MS-65
1872	678	42.2	15%	$350	$410	$450	$500	$900	$2,050	$4,700	$6,000	$50,000

1872, Proof • **Mintage:** 950.

Commentary and Availability: *PF-60 to 62:* 200 to 230. *PF-63:* 80 to 100. *PF-64:* 40 to 55. *PF-65 or better:* 25 to 35.

	Cert	Avg	%MS	PF-60	PF-63	PF-64	PF-65
1872, Proof	183	63.0		$2,100	$3,800	$5,750	$10,000

1872-CC Liberty Seated Dollar

1872-CC • **Mintage:** 3,150.

Availability in Mint State: *MS-60 to 62:* 5 to 8. *MS-63:* 1 or 2. *MS-64:* 2. *MS-65 or better:* 2.

Availability in circulated grades: *VG-8 to F-15:* 40 to 55. *F-12 to AU-58:* 100 to 150.

Characteristics of striking: This issue is usually seen well struck on the reverse with an average strike on the obverse. As is the case with other Carson City Mint Liberty Seated dollars, the word LIBERTY on the shield is not as prominent as on Philadelphia coins and tended to wear away especially quickly once the coins saw circulation.

	Cert	Avg	%MS	VG-8	F-12	VF-20	EF-40	AU-50	MS-60	MS-63	MS-64	MS-65
1872-CC	92	40.7	15%	$2,500	$3,250	$4,000	$5,750	$9,000	$28,000	$100,000	$150,000	$300,000

1872-S Liberty Seated Dollar

1872-S • **Mintage:** 9,000.

Availability in Mint State: *MS-60 to 62:* 1 to 4. *MS-63:* 1 or 2. *MS-64:* 1 or 2. *MS-65 or better:* 1.

Availability in circulated grades: *F-12 to AU-58:* 300 to 400.

Characteristics of striking: Striking of this issue varies. They often have slight weakness on Liberty's head and stars eight and nine on the obverse; and on the reverse, on the leg to the right and the talons. These often have semi-prooflike surface.

Notes: From *Banker's Magazine*, November 1872: "U.S. Coin in China. The new silver dollar recently struck in the San Francisco Mint is said to be adapted for general circulation in China, where the want of silver coin has been much felt. It is worth six percent more than the old dollar, and will be received in China on the same terms as the old Mexican dollar, which has hitherto been at a premium of five to eight percent." The dollars were sold at a premium for this purpose and were not placed into circulation.

	Cert	Avg	%MS	VG-8	F-12	VF-20	EF-40	AU-50	MS-60	MS-63	MS-64
1872-S	123	42.5	10%	$650	$800	$1,000	$1,750	$3,000	$12,000	$37,500	$150,000

1873 Liberty Seated Dollar

1873 • **Mintage:** 293,000.

Availability in Mint State: *MS-60 to 62:* 50 to 75. *MS-63:* 20 to 25. *MS-64:* 30 to 45. *MS-65 or better:* 4 to 6.

Availability in circulated grades: *F-12 to AU-58:* 250 to 350. These are much scarcer than the mintage might suggest.

Characteristics of striking: Striking of this issue varies, but some have lightly struck details on Liberty's head and light strike on the stars, especially eight through ten. Some Mint State coins have satiny surfaces while others are partially prooflike.

Notes: All 1873 Liberty Seated dollars have the Close 3 date logotype where the knobs of 3 are large and close together.

	Cert	Avg	%MS	VG-8	F-12	VF-20	EF-40	AU-50	MS-60	MS-63	MS-64	MS-65
1873	199	51.3	38%	$475	$500	$550	$650	$975	$2,100	$4,850	$7,000	$55,000

1873, Proof • Mintage: 600.

Commentary and Availability: *PF-60 to 62:* 200 to 230. *PF-63:* 80 to 100. *PF-64:* 40 to 55. *PF-65 or better:* 25 to 35.

	Cert	Avg	%MS	PF-60	PF-63	PF-64	PF-65
1873, Proof	184	63.3		$2,100	$3,800	$5,750	$10,000

1873-CC Liberty Seated Dollar

1873-CC • Mintage: 2,300.

Availability in Mint State: *MS-60 to 62:* 1 or 2. *MS-63:* 0. *MS-64:* 0. *MS-65 or better:* 1.

Availability in circulated grades: *VG-8 to F-15:* 10 to 15. *F-12 to AU-58:* 50 to 70.

Characteristics of striking: The 1873-CC is usually of above-average sharpness. However, some examples show weakness on Liberty's head and chest and/or on the reverse. As is the case with other Carson City Mint Liberty Seated dollars, the word LIBERTY on the shield is not as prominent as on Philadelphia coins, and tended to wear away especially quickly once the coins saw circulation.

	Cert	Avg	%MS	VG-8	F-12	VF-20	EF-40	AU-50	MS-60	MS-63	MS-64	MS-65
1873-CC	29	44.0	17%	$10,000	$13,000	$17,000	$27,500	$40,000	$115,000	$190,000	$300,000	$500,000

1873-S Liberty Seated Dollar

1873-S • Mintage: 700.

Notes: Although 700 coins were reported as minted, no example has ever been located. Six pairs of dies were shipped from Philadelphia in November 1872, indicating a possibility for a large mintage that never materialized. Probably the entire mintage of 700 coins was from a single pair.

MORGAN DOLLARS (1878–1921)

Designer: *George T. Morgan.* **Weight:** *26.73 grams.* **Composition:** *.900 silver, .100 copper (net weight .77344 oz. pure silver).* **Diameter:** *38.1 mm.* **Edge:** *Reeded.* **Mints:** *Philadelphia, New Orleans, Carson City, Denver, and San Francisco.*

Mintmark location is on the reverse, below the bow.

Circulation Strike

Proof

BACKGROUND

The Morgan silver dollar, named for English-born designer George T. Morgan, was struck every year from 1878 to 1904, and again in 1921. Far and away the most widely collected of the "classic" U.S. coins, Morgan dollars were produced to the extent of hundreds of millions of pieces, far more than were needed in circulation or for any aspect of commerce of the era.

They were called into being as a result of the Bland-Allison Act of 1878, one of the greatest political boondoggles of all time (at least from a numismatic viewpoint). They existed simply to provide a market for western and other silver-mining interests. At the time, the international price of silver had been dropping sharply, and Uncle Sam was asked to provide a price support. The result is the vast panorama of coins available to collectors today.

In the early years, 1878 through 1904, four different mints were used to strike Morgan dollars: Philadelphia (1878–1904), Carson City (1878–1885 and 1889–1893), New Orleans (1879–1904), and San Francisco (1878–1904). Each of these mints has its own history, its own aspect of interest, and its own excitement. Philadelphia, of course, was the "mother mint," the place where all dies were made—sometimes not quite correctly, with punching, mintmarks at crazy angles, and more. While technically reflecting

Gambling in Nevada, with silver dollars on the table. In the West, silver dollars were the coins of choice for a long time, and in some mountain states scarcely a paper dollar was ever used.

the loss of quality control, these errors created a garden of delightful varieties for collectors. Philadelphia also turned out a brilliant cascade of sparkling silver dollars by the millions. In addition, Proofs with mirrored surfaces were made there each year for collectors and sold at a premium. In 1895, the most desired year from a collector's viewpoint, there were 880 Proofs made, and today a choice example will bring tens of thousands of dollars.

The Carson City Mint evokes images of the Wild West, gambling in the mining districts, and more—part of American tradition and drama, of course, but at the same time quite true. Today, many collectors focus on and enjoy these CC-mintmarked dollars, often available in sparkling, lustrous Mint State.

The San Francisco Mint has its own story. The impressive new Mint building, made of granite, was opened in 1874. During the earthquake and fire of April 1906 it was the only structure in its district to remain intact. The coin presses in that facility struck many millions of Morgan dollars, most being very carefully made, with excellent sharpness of details.

The New Orleans Mint was close to the levee that guarded the city from the ravages of the Mississippi River. Coinage techniques were a bit different from those at San Francisco; minting was done in haste, and today this is evidenced by New Orleans dollars' often being weak at the centers—perhaps from sloppy workmanship, hurry, or both.

While millions of Morgan silver dollars were paid out during the period of their manufacture and used in circulation, particularly in the mountainous areas of the West, a far larger part, amounting to hundreds of millions, remained stored in 1,000-coin bags in vaults. These were deep within the various mints, and when that space was exhausted, in other places as well. For example, the Philadelphia Post Office and the Treasury Building in Washington, D.C., had storage areas stuffed with dollars.

Production of Morgan dollars ceased in 1904, then was revived in 1921. At the Treasury secretary's order, the original hubs for Morgan dollars were destroyed in 1910, along with other archival materials, to clear storage space. The Morgan dollars of 1921 were struck from shallow-relief dies, making them different from Morgans of 1878 to 1904. An actual silver dollar of 1878 was used to create models, and then, by adjustment and the changing of some details and the lowering of relief, new hubs for the 1921 dollars were made. The design and lettering were the same, but the overall result was coins of a shallow and flatly struck appearance.

From time to time after 1921, the Treasury paid out long-stored Morgan dollars when pieces were called for by banks in the West, by casinos in Nevada (prime users), and, in December, for use as holiday gifts. Every once in a while collectors would be delighted to find that a previously rare variety was now available at or near face value—and yet, because of the high face value of Morgan dollars and the general availability of certain varieties, such as the virtually impossible 1903-O (most leading dealers never even saw one in Mint State, let alone owned one), collecting such dollars was not popular.

All of this changed beginning in the 1950s, when several dealers began specializing in Morgan dollars, occasionally acquiring pieces stored in the San Francisco Mint, the Treasury Department, or elsewhere. Pages of the *Numismatic Scrapbook Magazine* contained many offerings of single coins and rolls. And yet, Morgan dollars were still second fiddle to series that were more plentiful, such as Indian Head and Lincoln cents, Buffalo nickels, and the like.

In November 1962 this changed. Bags of long-stored 1903-O dollars, considered to be the foremost rarity in the series, were brought out from a vault within the Philadelphia Mint that had been sealed in 1929, after bags of dollars had been shipped there from storage in the long-defunct New Orleans Mint.

Word spread about these fabulous dollars' availability, and banks across the nation sent requests to the Federal Reserve system, which in turn tapped coins stored at the various mints and elsewhere. During the next year, hundreds of millions of coins were paid out, singly, in small groups, and in sealed 1,000-coin bags to those who ordered them. In Washington at the Treasury Building, the cash window, so-called, paid out dollars to those interested, some of whom arrived with large bundles of cash to buy dollars, and wheelbarrows to cart them off! Occasionally a bonanza would be encountered with scarce or rare dates, for these coins had been stored there for decades, and no one had checked to see what dates and mints were involved.

By March 1964, the Treasury called a halt to the distribution, by which time only about three million silver dollars were left, as hundreds of millions were gone. Those three million, mostly stored in the Treasury Building in Washington, largely consisted of Carson City dollars, some of them quite remarkable—notably the 1884-CC, of which 1,136,000 were minted, and of which about 85% of the original coinage remained on hand at the Treasury, in Uncirculated grade, in the original bags. For collectors it was like finding long-lost treasure, or going in a time machine back to the wild and woolly days of the West, to Carson City in an earlier era.

Circa 1903 photo of one small part of one vault in the Treasury's basement in Washington, D.C. Shown are many bags of silver dollars, 1,000 coins per bag, each bag weighing about 57 pounds.

The 1921 Silver Dollar Coin Anniversary Act, signed into law January 5, 2021, requires the Treasury Department "to mint and issue coins in honor of the 100th anniversary of the completion of coinage of the Morgan dollar." See appendix I for more information.

Note: Values of common-date silver coins have been based on the current bullion price of silver, $27.50 per ounce, and may vary with the prevailing spot price.

GEORGE T. MORGAN, ENGRAVER

In 1877, Mint Director Henry R. Linderman (a medical doctor and numismatist, among other aspects) felt that Chief Engraver William Barber's work was below par and sought to hire a more talented artist. Through correspondence with Charles W. Fremantle, deputy master of the Royal Mint in London, he secured the services of young George T. Morgan, who had studied engraving with the Wyon family, highly accomplished as die cutters for coins and medals. Morgan came to the United States in 1876 and was hired as an assistant engraver. The arrangement was resisted by William Barber and his son Charles (who had been recruited by his father as an assistant in 1869). The surroundings were made uncomfortable for Morgan, who for a time worked away from the Mint premises.

Morgan also turned out a series of pattern coins, some of them very beautiful, his half dollars of 1877 being particularly notable in that regard. In 1878 his design for the new silver dollars was chosen over the motif created by Chief Engraver Barber. Thus the "Morgan dollar" was created, first known as the "Bland dollar" (from Richard Bland, co-author of the legislative act that enabled it).

George T. Morgan, as depicted in a directory, circa 1904. Designer of the 1878 "Bland dollar," today called the "Morgan dollar," he came to America from England in 1876 to work as an assistant engraver at the Philadelphia Mint.

In August 1879 William Barber vacationed at the seashore in New Jersey. On one particular day he became severely chilled in the surf, developed pulmonary congestion, and went back to Philadelphia, where he died on August 31. After Barber's passing, the selection of the next chief engraver was an open question. George T. Morgan was the obvious choice, but the position was made on a political basis, with artistic talent being a distant secondary consideration. Months passed without action, and then toward the end of the year Charles E. Barber was chosen. By that time, under his father's watch, he had created the 1879 Flowing Hair pattern $4 gold stella. Morgan remained as an assistant and had also created another version of the $4 gold coin, but Morgan's work was hidden from view, and only a few were made. Today it is known as the Coiled Hair style. Morgan died in 1918.

PROOF MORGAN DOLLARS

Each year at the Philadelphia Mint, 1878 through 1904, Proof strikings were made for sale to collectors and other interested buyers. A few additional Proofs may have been made in 1878 for ceremonial purposes. In each instance, Proofs were sold as part of silver coin sets, the contents of which varied according to the other denominations being made at the time.

An 1878 silver Proof set contained a dime, twenty-cent piece, quarter dollar, half dollar, silver dollar, and trade dollar. A 1904 silver Proof set contained a dime, quarter dollar, half dollar, and silver dollar.

No record has been found of Proofs' having been deliberately struck at Philadelphia in 1921, although it is believed that a few may have been made to the order of local dealer Henry Chapman, these being called Chapman Proofs today. Indeed, in 1921, Chapman advertised Proofs in *The Numismatist*. In addition, some pieces with slight prooflike surfaces, struck from dies with many minute striations, have been marketed as Zerbe Proofs, but it is unlikely that such were made as Proofs, as they are not deeply mirror-like, and Farran Zerbe, a leading numismatist of the era, would hardly have accepted them as such. Saul Teichman stated that the "Zerbe Proof" nomenclature is probably from the imagination of the late Walter Breen, who was fond of creating historical scenarios, often with fascinating details, when facts were scarce.

Proofs were struck from deeply polished dies, at slow speed on a special press, using specially prepared planchets. Most are cameos with frosted designs and lettering set against the mirrored field, but all of 1902 to 1904 were made from dies in which the portrait of Miss Liberty was polished in the die—perhaps by an employee unfamiliar with the process. In any event, such pieces lack contrast.

The striking of Proof coins was supposed to be needle-sharp, for such coins were sold at a premium and represented the finest impressions of their kind. However, some were made with the dies spaced slightly too far apart, showing some flatness near Miss Liberty's ear and on the eagle's breast. The individual Proof listings year by year in this book explain such variables.

BRANCH-MINT PROOFS

Were any Proof coins ever struck at the branch mints? Wayne Miller, in his highly important 1982 study, *The Morgan and Peace Dollar Textbook*, says, "Of all the specialized areas of numismatics none is more rife with misinformation, speculation, hyperbole, controversy, etc., than branch-mint Proof Morgan dollars."

The difficulty is this: If a branch-mint Morgan dollar has fully deep mirrorlike fields, excellent contrast against frosty or satiny devices, and a reasonably decent rim (not nicked or showing mishandling), is it a Proof? Many different date and mintmark varieties were struck with deep mirror prooflike (DMPL) surfaces in the ordinary course of business, simply because highly polished dies were employed to strike them.

Nonetheless, ever since the 1880s, some branch-mint dollars have been called Proofs. Again, from Miller: "The most extensive discussion thus far . . . is in Walter Breen's book on Proof coinage. Breen discusses the possibility of no fewer than 12 different dates of branch-mint Proof Morgans. He also provides detailed information regarding the events which occasioned their striking; estimates of total mintages; locations of known specimens; etc. However, much of Breen's information is based on conjecture. . . . Of the specimens which he himself has examined, none are described in detail."

In the absence of facts, many have elected to designate branch-mint coins with Proof characteristics as specimen strikings or simply as DMPL. However, the certification services have labeled a few as

Proofs. For the sake of simplicity, this edition of *Mega Red* calls them Proofs, but the reader should be aware of the complexities of the term with respect to branch-mint Morgan dollars.

MORGAN DOLLARS (1878–1921): GUIDE TO COLLECTING

For numismatists, the Treasury release of 1962 through 1964 was a godsend, a bonanza the effects of which are still felt today by anyone who collects Morgan dollars.

Today approximately 100 different date and mintmark varieties are considered to constitute a basic set from 1878 to 1921, and of these, more than half are readily available in Mint State for less than $100 per coin, many for *much less* than that. Only a handful are sufficiently rare as to cost more than $1,000 for a low-level Mint State specimen.

Accordingly, with little effort, dozens and dozens of Morgan dollars from the various mints—Philadelphia, Carson City, San Francisco, and New Orleans—from the early years plus the 1921-D (the Denver Mint struck Morgan dollars only in this year) can be acquired and enjoyed for a nominal cost, numismatically speaking.

Remarkably, choice and gem Mint State Morgan dollars of the 19th century are much more readily available than are the basic coins of the realm, Indian Head cents, made during the same era, as Indian Head cents were not saved in quantity in Mint State. Accordingly, anyone endeavoring to collect Indian Head cents by date sequence (such pieces were first made in 1859 and last in 1909) has to buy them one at a time, and not easily. In the annals of modern numismatics there is no such thing as a Mint-sealed bag of Indian Head cents, and there were no Treasury hoards. In contrast, there are enough Morgan silver dollars around that dozens of different dealers specialize in them, while only a handful make a point of featuring Indian Head cents.

BEING A SMART BUYER

On coins of 1878 to 1900, check the hair above Miss Liberty's ear and, on the reverse, the breast feathers of the eagle. These are weak on many issues, particularly those of the New Orleans Mint. From 1900 to 1904 a new reverse hub was used, and breast feathers, while discernible, are not as sharp. In 1921 new dies were made in lower relief, with certain areas indistinct. Many Morgan dollars have partially or fully prooflike surfaces. These are designated as Prooflike (PL), Deep Prooflike (DPL), or Deep Mirror Prooflike (DMPL). Certification practices can be erratic, and some DMPL-certified coins are not fully mirrored. All prooflike coins tend to emphasize contact marks, with the result that lower Mint State levels can be unattractive.

Proofs were struck from 1878 to 1904, with those of 1878 to 1901 generally having cameo contrast, and 1902 to 1904 having the portrait lightly polished in the die. Some are lightly struck; check the hair above Liberty's ear (in particular) and the eagle's breast feathers. In 1921 many so-called Zerbe Proofs (named after numismatic entrepreneur Farran Zerbe), with many microscopic die-finish lines, were made. A very few deeply mirrored 1921 coins were also struck, called Chapman Proofs (after coin dealer Henry Chapman, who started marketing them shortly after their production). Zerbe Proofs are not mirrored; some have been miscertified as Chapman Proofs. For a short time in 1964 the Mint considered issuing additional Morgan dollars to fill a shortage of coins in Nevada gambling casinos and elsewhere. Some tools such as dies and hubs were made, after which the idea was abandoned.

AVAILABILITY

All dates and mints of Morgan dollars from 1878 to 1904 are available in grades from well-worn to Mint State. Well-worn 1921 dollars are not often seen, as they did not remain in use for as long as the earlier dates. Some issues such as certain Carson City coins are rare if worn and common in Mint State. Others such as the 1901 Philadelphia coins are common if worn and are rarities if MS-65 or higher. The 1889-CC and 1893-S, and the Proof 1895, are considered to be the key issues. Varieties listed herein are some of those most significant to collectors. Numerous other variations exist, studied in the *Cherrypickers' Guide to Rare Die Varieties* and other specialized texts. Values shown herein are for the most common pieces. Values of varieties not listed in this guide depend on collector interest and demand.

MORGAN DOLLARS (1878–1921)

GRADING STANDARDS

MS-60 to 70 (Mint State). *Obverse:* At MS-60, some abrasion and contact marks are evident, most noticeably on the cheek and on the hair above the ear. The left field also shows such marks. Luster is present, but may be dull or lifeless. At MS-63, contact marks are extensive but not distracting. Abrasion still is evident, but less than at lower levels. Indeed, the cheek of Miss Liberty showcases abrasion. An MS-65 coin may have minor

1895-O. Graded MS-61.

abrasion, but contact marks are so minute as to require magnification. Luster should be full and rich. Coins with prooflike surfaces such as PL, DPL, and DMPL display abrasion and contact marks much more noticeably than coins with frosty surfaces; in grades below MS-64 many are unattractive. With today's loose and sometimes contradictory interpretations, many at MS-64 appear to have extensive marks as well. *Reverse:* Comments apply as for the obverse, except that in lower Mint State grades abrasion and contact marks are most noticeable on the eagle's breast. At MS-65 or higher there are no marks visible to the unaided eye. The field is mainly protected by design elements, so the reverse often appears to grade a point or two higher than the obverse. A Morgan dollar can have an MS-63 obverse and an MS-65 reverse, as was indeed the nomenclature used prior to the single-number system. A careful cataloger may want to describe each side separately for a particularly valuable or rare Morgan dollar. An example with an MS-63 obverse and an MS-65 reverse should have an overall grade of MS-63, as the obverse is traditionally given prominence.

AU-50, 53, 55, 58 (About Uncirculated). *Obverse:* Light wear is seen on the cheek and, to a lesser extent, on the hair below the coronet. Generally, the hair details mask friction and wear and it is not as easy to notice as on the cheek and in the fields. At AU-58, the luster is extensive, but incomplete, especially on the higher parts and in the left field. At AU-50 and 53, luster is less, but still is present. PL, DPL, and DMPL coins are not widely desired

1889-CC. Graded AU-58.

at these levels, as the marks are too distracting. *Reverse:* Wear is evident on the head, breast, wing tips, and, to a lesser extent, in the field. An AU-58 coin (as determined by the obverse) can have a reverse that appears to be full Mint State. (Incidentally, this is also true of Barber quarter dollars and half dollars.)

EF-40, 45 (Extremely Fine). *Obverse:* Further wear is seen on the cheek in particular. The hair near the forehead and temple has flatness in areas, most noticeable above the ear. Some luster can be seen in protected areas on many coins, but is not needed to define the EF-40 and 45 grades. *Reverse:* Further wear is seen on the breast of the eagle (most noticeably), the wing tips, and the leaves.

1879-CC. Graded EF-40.

VF-20, 30 (Very Fine). *Obverse:* The head shows more wear, now with most of the detail gone in the areas adjacent to the forehead and temple. The lower area has most hair fused into large strands. *Reverse:* Wear is more extensive on the breast and on the feathers in the upper area of the wings, especially the right wing, and on the legs. The high area of the leaves has no detail.

1889-CC. Graded VF-20.

F-12, 15 (Fine). *Obverse:* The head shows more wear, with most hair detail gone, and with a large flat area above the ear. Less detail is seen in the lower curls. *Reverse:* More wear is seen on the reverse, with the eagle's breast and legs flat and about a third of the feather detail gone, mostly near the tops of the wings.

1893-S. Graded F-15.

VG-8, 10 (Very Good). *Obverse:* More hair details are gone, especially from the area from the top of the head down to the ear. The details of the lower part of the cap are gone. The rim is weak in areas, and some denticles are worn away. *Reverse:* Further wear has smoothed more than half of the feathers in the wing. The leaves are flat except for the lowest areas. The rim is weak in areas.

1892-CC. Graded VG-8.

G-4, 6 (Good). *Obverse:* The head is in outline form, with most details gone. LIBERTY still is readable. The eye position and lips are discernible. Most of the rim is worn away. *Reverse:* The eagle shows some feathers near the bottom of the wings, but nearly all others are gone. The leaves are seen in outline form. The rim is mostly worn away. Some letters have details toward the border worn away.

1893-S. Graded G-4.

Morgan dollars are seldom collected in grades lower than G-4.

PF-60 to 70 (Proof). *Obverse and Reverse:* Dull, grainy Proofs, or extensively cleaned ones with many hairlines, are lower level (PF-60 to 62). Only the 1895 is desirable at such low grades. Those with medium hairlines and good reflectivity may grade at about PF-64, and with relatively few hairlines, Gem PF-65. Hairlines are most easily seen in the obverse field. Horizontal slide marks on Miss Liberty's cheek, caused by clear slides on some coin

1898. Graded PF-64.

albums, are common. PF-66 may have hairlines so delicate that magnification is needed to see them. Above that, a Proof should be free of such lines, including slide marks.

1878 Morgan Dollar

1878, 8 Tail Feathers •
Mintage: 750,000 estimated.

Key to Collecting: The 1878, 8 Tail Feathers, dollar begins the series. It is commonly called the "Type I" or "First Reverse" among the 1878 varieties. This is the only year and mint of the style with 8 Tail Feathers and thus is highly important, although

not rare. Many were distributed in and soon after 1878, but enough remained in Treasury holdings that today there is an ample supply of Mint State coins from which to choose. Most pieces are well struck and have excellent luster. All have the eagle with flat or shallow breast, per the early die standard, although the feathers on the eagle's breast can be well defined. Proofs are rare and are in special demand to illustrate this one-year reverse style.

Surface Quality: Examples are typically quite well struck. The eagle's breast is shallow, not well rounded, this being characteristic of all reverses used in 1878. They usually have excellent luster, the frost being deep. Often one side is lustrous and the other is prooflike.

	Cert	Avg	%MS	VF-20	EF-40	AU-50	MS-60	MS-63	MS-64	MS-64DMPL	MS-65	MS-65DMPL
1878, 8 Tail Feathers	14,329	61.6	92%	$85	$100	$120	$250	$350	$600	$4,000	$1,100	$21,000

VARIETY: *1878, 8 Tail Feathers, Obverse Die Gouge (FS-S1-1878-014.11).* Two spikes protrude from the front of Liberty's eye. According to the *Cherrypickers' Guide to Rare Die Varieties*, vol. II (sixth edition), "Fewer than a dozen specimens are known of this Top 100 variety and any sale is a landmark event."

	Cert	Avg	%MS	VF-20	EF-40	AU-50	MS-60	MS-63	MS-64
1878, 8 Tail Feathers, Obverse Die Gouge	8	60.4	75%	$3,000	$5,000	$8,500	$15,000	$18,000	$23,500

1878, 8 Tail Feathers, Proof •

Mintage: 500 (estimated).

Key to Collecting: Minimal cameo contrast is the rule. The demand for Proofs is especially strong, not as much from Proof specialists as from those who seek an example for a type set. Per usual for Proofs, low-grade examples usually lack eye appeal.

	Cert	Avg	%MS	PF-60	PF-63	PF-64	PF-65
1878, 8 Tail Feathers, Proof	139	64.1		$1,500	$3,500	$5,000	$11,500

1878, Doubled Tail Feathers •

Mintage: 500,000 (estimated).

Key to Collecting: When it was decided to change the standard tail feather count from eight to seven, the reverse dies already on hand with eight tail feathers were adapted by impression of the master die for the seven tail feather motif. The impression did not obliterate certain tips of the first eight tail feathers, and today various dies show some of the earlier tail feathers still visible. As a handy rule of thumb, to command a market premium the number of vestigial tips visible under the seven tail feathers should be at least four, with the more the better, some having as many as seven showing. This

FS-S1-1878-032.

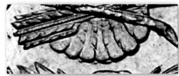

Detail of the
Doubled Tail Feathers.

used to be called 7 Over 8 Tail Feathers, a good description of the die-making process, but not reflective of the number of tail feathers that can be seen. Today, "Doubled Tail Feathers" is preferred.

Surface Quality: Usually seen with sharp strike on both sides. Check to be sure that the eagle's breast feathers are well defined. Certified examples of this reverse variety have been classified by the services as "weak" or "strong." ("Strong" refers to coins with tips of four or more underfeathers easily visible, not to the striking quality during the coining process.) Typically seen with satiny luster, although many are below average and some are dull, gray, and lifeless. Search for quality.

Prooflike coins (one or both sides) are sometimes encountered, but not with deep mirror surfaces against frosty motifs.

	Cert	Avg	%MS	VF-20	EF-40	AU-50	MS-60	MS-63	MS-64	MS-64DMPL	MS-65	MS-65DMPL
1878, Doubled Tail Feathers	5,319	62.4	95%	$50	$55	$75	$200	$275	$600	$5,200	$1,500	$16,000

VARIETY: *1878, Doubled Tail Feathers, Tripled Leaves (FS-S1-1878-044; VAM-44).* The bottom edges of the leaves and cotton bolls in Liberty's head-dress are tripled. The reverse is the same as VAM-33 with doubled legs and an extra five small tail feathers, this per the description in *The Top 100 Morgan Dollar Varieties*, which also notes that this may be the single most sought-after specialized variety in the series. Indeed, it is called the "King of VAMs" (Van Allen / Mallis varieties).

	Cert	Avg	%MS	VF-20	EF-40	AU-50	MS-60	MS-63
1878, Doubled Tail Feathers, Tripled Leaves	27	51.4	22%	$1,000	$2,500	$4,500	$14,000	$21,000

1878, 7 Tail Feathers, Reverse of 1878 (Parallel Arrow Feather) •

Mintage: 7,850,000.

Key to Collecting: The 7 Tail Feathers reverse occurs in two varieties:

- the Reverse of 1878 ("Second" or "Type 2" Reverse), with the arrow feathers parallel and the eagle's breast flat (sometimes called "Concave Breast")
- the Reverse of 1879 ("Third" or "Type 3" Reverse"), with a slanted top arrow feather and the eagle's breast rounded ("Round Breast")

First Reverse	**Second Reverse**	**Third Reverse**
Eight tail feathers.	*Parallel top arrow feather, concave breast.*	*Slanted top arrow feather, convex breast.*

These were struck in large quantity, being the design of choice after the brief 8 Tail Feathers coinage and the overstamping of many of those 8 Tail Feathers dies with this 7 Tail Feathers hub, creating the "Doubled Tail Feathers." The present listing is for "pure" 7 Tail Feathers coins. These were made in large quantity and comprise most of the mintage of 1878.

Surface Quality: Most circulation strikes have excellent detail, but some show weakness on the eagle's talons and below. The eagle's breast is flat, rather than rounded. At first glance, a well-struck 1878, 7 Tail Feathers, may appear to be weak. However, close examination will reveal excellent breast feather detail on most. Usually seen with satiny luster, sometimes lifeless and rather dull on the obverse, while frosty on the reverse. Some are prooflike, but without sharp contrast between field and motifs.

Prooflike coins are plentiful, but often with little contrast.

	Cert	Avg	%MS	VF-20	EF-40	AU-50	MS-60	MS-63	MS-64	MS-64DMPL	MS-65	MS-65DMPL
1878, 7 Tail Feathers, Reverse of 1878 (Parallel Arrow Feather)	16,946	62.2	94%	$45	$48	$60	$100	$150	$250	$2,200	$900	$11,000

1878, 7 Tail Feathers, Reverse of 1878 (Parallel Arrow Feather), Proof • Mintage: 250 (estimated).

Key to Collecting: Striking is sometimes light above the ear, and the surface has medium to low cameo contrast. This variety is a challenge—not only to find one in the first place, but beyond that, to get one with good eye appeal.

	Cert	Avg	%MS	PF-60	PF-63	PF-64	PF-65
1878, 7 Tail Feathers, Reverse of 1878 (Parallel Arrow Feather), Proof	94	63.6		$2,750	$3,750	$7,500	$12,500

1878, 7 Tail Feathers, Reverse of 1879 (Slanted Arrow Feather) •

Mintage: 1,500,000 (estimated).

Key to Collecting: The two different basic reverse styles with 7 Tail Feathers, Reverse of 1878 (Parallel Arrow Feather) and Reverse of 1879 (Slanted Arrow Feather, as here), were not always widely known. Nor are there any official mintage figures for either. Significant interest did not develop until the 1980s. Not all Morgan dollar collectors are aware of the varieties, but both are eminently worth owning. Even today, the price of the 1878 with Reverse of 1879, although considerably higher than that of the earlier style, does not reflect the true differential in rarity.

Surface Quality: These are usually fairly well struck, but needle-sharp examples are elusive. Patience may be required to find a keeper. Certification-service labels do not mention the quality of strike, and, accordingly, most buyers are not aware that there can be a difference. The breast of the eagle is rounded, characteristic of the Type 3 Reverse (Reverse of 1879). Excellent luster is seen on most, but there are exceptions, and cherrypicking is advised.

Some are from prooflike dies, sometimes on one side only, and show good contrast between the fields and motifs, a cameo appearance.

	Cert	Avg	%MS	VF-20	EF-40	AU-50	MS-60	MS-63	MS-64	MS-64DMPL	MS-65	MS-65DMPL
1878, 7 Tail Feathers, Reverse of 1879 (Slanted Arrow Feather)	6,110	61.1	88%	$45	$48	$50	$110	$280	$475	$5,500	$1,750	$23,000

1878, 7 Tail Feathers, Reverse of 1879 (Slanted Arrow Feather), Proof • Mintage: 25 to 50 (estimated).

Key to Collecting: The strike is decent, and the coins have a degree of cameo contrast. This is the Holy Grail among early Morgan dollar Proofs.

	Cert	Avg	%MS	PF-60	PF-63	PF-64	PF-65
1878, 7 Tail Feathers, Reverse of 1879 (Slanted Arrow Feather), Proof	5	62.4		$16,500	$85,000	$115,000	$200,000

1878-CC Morgan Dollar

1878-CC • **Mintage:** 2,212,000.

Key to Collecting: Only the Reverse of 1878 (with parallel top arrow feather) was used to produce 1878-CC dollars, and all have seven tail feathers. Most examples are in Mint State and are usually attractive.

Surface Quality: Striking quality varies. All have a flat breast on the eagle, according to the design, but most have sharply defined feathers. Some show parallel planchet lines, particularly on the cheek and jaw of Miss Liberty, where these features, on the original planchet, were not flattened out by the striking process. Some have lightness of detail in the lower part of the eagle and below. In 1982, Wayne Miller noted that this is "one of the most consistently well struck of all Morgan dollars."[6] The luster is very pleasing on the 1878-CC dollar, usually satiny.

Some dies are prooflike, but these are in the distinct minority. However, in absolute terms enough exist that there is no difficulty finding one.

	Cert	Avg	%MS	VF-20	EF-40	AU-50	MS-60	MS-63	MS-64	MS-64DMPL	MS-65	MS-65DMPL
1878-CC	30,266	59.9	87%	$150	$175	$280	$450	$500	$600	$2,900	$1,250	$10,000

1878-S Morgan Dollar

1878-S • **Mintage:** 9,774,000.

Key to Collecting: The 1878-S dollar is plentiful in Mint State, with the typical example being MS-62 to MS-64 and with decent luster, more satiny than deeply frosty. The 1878-S comes only with the Reverse of 1878 (flat eagle's breast, seven tail feathers, parallel top arrow feather).

Surface Quality: Usually fairly well struck; however, some pieces show planchet striations on the face of Miss Liberty and show some weakness at the lower part of the eagle and below. As all are of the Type 2 Reverse (flat eagle's breast, parallel top arrow feather), at first glance the reverse may appear to be weakly struck. However, upon close examination most have well-defined feathers. Usually lustrous and very attractive, satiny or frosty (but not deeply frosty), is the rule.

Some are struck from highly prooflike dies, many on just one side, although these are but a tiny fraction of the existing population.

	Cert	Avg	%MS	VF-20	EF-40	AU-50	MS-60	MS-63	MS-64	MS-64DMPL	MS-65	MS-65DMPL
1878-S	54,973	63.0	98%	$45	$47	$50	$75	$100	$150	$2,000	$295	$9,500

1879 Morgan Dollar

1879 • Mintage: 14,806,000.

Key to Collecting: The 1879 dollar is very plentiful in all grades, as you might expect from the mintage figure. Mint State coins abound, but the quality of strike and luster can vary widely.

Surface Quality: Most examples are fairly well struck. Many have lightness of center details particularly noticeable above the ear of Miss Liberty, this being typical for nearly all of the series from this point forward. The extra metal needed to flow into the rounded breast of the eagle on the Type 3 (Reverse of 1879) dies took away from metal available to fill the high points on the obverse, resulting in some loss of detail. Usually seen lustrous, sometimes grainy if a particular die has been used for a long period of time.

Prooflike coins exist, including some with high contrast. Many are one-sided prooflikes. Prooflike coins are scarce in comparison to frosty, lustrous examples.

	Cert	Avg	%MS	VF-20	EF-40	AU-50	MS-60	MS-63	MS-64	MS-64DMPL	MS-65	MS-65DMPL
1879	14,430	62.3	93%	$35	$38	$55	$75	$100	$140	$2,100	$450	$15,000

1879, Proof • Mintage: 1,100.

Key to Collecting: Most are of low contrast. Striking quality is average. Although the mintage is high, the challenge for quality is high as well.

	Cert	Avg	%MS	PF-60	PF-63	PF-64	PF-65
1879, Proof	328	64.1		$1,300	$3,200	$4,000	$5,500

1879-CC Morgan Dollar

1879-CC, Large CC • Mintage: 756,000.

Key to Collecting: Among basic date and mintmark issues, the 1879-CC is the first key or rare variety in the Morgan dollar series and is the second rarest (after 1889-CC) of all Carson City Morgans. Although thousands of Mint State coins exist, gems (MS-65 or better) are very difficult to find. There are two basic styles: the "perfect" or Large CC variety listed here and the "Large CC Over Small CC," on which, at the Mint, there was an attempt to tool away the small CC, so that larger CC letters could be stamped in that area. The Large CC variety is the more readily available of the two but is also more popular than the Large CC Over Small CC.

Surface Quality: Most 1879-CC dollars are quite well struck on obverse and reverse. The 1879-CC is typically encountered with attractive luster, although some are frostier than others, and still others are dull and lifeless. Not much searching is needed to find a "nice" coin, as such pieces are the rule.

Some are prooflike on one side or the other, this not being particularly unusual. The prooflike surface is often hazy or "gray," not deeply mirrorlike.

	Cert	Avg	%MS	VF-20	EF-40	AU-50	MS-60	MS-63	MS-64	MS-64DMPL	MS-65	MS-65DMPL
1879-CC, Large CC	4,197	46.4	54%	$375	$900	$2,400	$4,500	$6,750	$8,700	$22,000	$22,500	$42,500

1879-CC, Large CC Over Small CC •
Mintage: 756,000.

Key to Collecting: At the Mint, an attempt to tool away the small CC so that larger CC letters could be stamped in that area created this variety. The Large CC Over Small CC variety is less readily available than the Large CC, but the latter is more popular and is priced accordingly.

Surface Quality: See the surface-quality comments in the preceding listing.

Detail of the Overmintmark.

	Cert	Avg	%MS	VF-20	EF-40	AU-50	MS-60	MS-63	MS-64	MS-64DMPL	MS-65	MS-65DMPL
1879-CC, Large CC Over Small CC	2,334	46.3	47%	$310	$775	$1,950	$4,000	$6,000	$7,750	$42,000	$42,500	$60,000

1879-O Morgan Dollar

1879-O • **Mintage:** 2,887,000.

Key to Collecting: The 1879-O dollar is plentiful in lower Mint State levels from 60 through 63. MS-64 coins are scarce, and in proportion to the demand for them, MS-65 pieces are rare. A good choice for value is an MS-63 or MS-64, but hand-picked for quality; that is, without too many bagmarks. Coins in About Uncirculated grade, once called "slider Uncirculated," abound.

Surface Quality: Striking varies from sharp to average or below average, the last having weakness at the centers, in the hair strands above Miss Liberty's ear and the breast feathers of the eagle. Luster is typically frosty and attractive. Bagmarks are a huge problem.

Some dies are prooflike, scarce as such, and DMPL are scarcer yet.

	Cert	Avg	%MS	VF-20	EF-40	AU-50	MS-60	MS-63	MS-64	MS-64DMPL	MS-65	MS-65DMPL
1879-O	10,455	61.0	81%	$42	$45	$47	$120	$300	$510	$4,700	$2,450	$22,000

1879-O, Proof • Mintage: 12.

Key to Collecting: Branch-mint Proofs
are great rarities among the Morgan dollars,
and many numismatists will go a lifetime
without ever seeing one. For the advanced
collector they are extremely tantalizing. Four
different branch-mint Morgan dollar Proofs are
considered to be "Class I" by numismatist Wayne
Miller, meaning that documentation confirms the coins were authorized and issued by the Mint. The
1879-O Proof is one of the four; the other three are the 1883-O Proof, the 1893-CC Proof, and the
1921-S Zerbe Proof. Some numismatists classify these as Deep Mirror Prooflike circulation strikes,
rather than as Proofs

Of these, the 1879-O is the best known. Twelve examples were struck on February 20, 1879, to commemorate the reopening of the New Orleans Mint, which had ceased activity when the Civil War broke
out in 1861. Four of those examples are known to exist; one is held by the Smithsonian.

	Cert	Avg	%MS	PF-60	PF-63	PF-64	PF-65
1879-O, Proof	5	64.4				$200,000	$275,000

1879-S Morgan Dollar

1879-S, Reverse of 1878 (Parallel Arrow Feather) • Mintage: 500,000 estimated.

Key to Collecting: Like the 1878, the
1879-S comes in two varieties. The Reverse
of 1878 ("Second" or "Type 2" Reverse),
with flat eagle's breast and parallel top arrow
feather, is quite elusive, and the variety with the
Reverse of 1879 ("Third" or "Type 3" Reverse) is very common. The former, very rare variety was
hardly known even to the most active dealers and collectors until recent decades. Amazingly, it was found
that even well-worn pieces were very rare.

Surface Quality: Examples are usually seen well struck, but as with all Type 2 Reverse dollars, the eagle
can appear to be weak, due to the flat breast. However, the individual feathers in the breast are usually
well struck. Examples are usually seen with attractive, frosty luster. Some have areas of die polish interrupting the frost.

Semi-prooflike coins are seen with frequency in the context of the variety. Prooflike coins exist but
are in the distinct minority. DMPL coins are very rare.

	Cert	Avg	%MS	VF-20	EF-40	AU-50	MS-60	MS-63	MS-64	MS-64DMPL	MS-65	MS-65DMPL
1879-S, Reverse of 1878 (Parallel Arrow Feather)	2/11	59.4	74%	$75	$100	$200	$350	$1,300	$2,400	$6,500	$4,500	$15,000

1879-S, Reverse of 1879 (Slanted Arrow Feather) • Mintage: 8,600,000 estimated.

Key to Collecting: The 1879-S with Reverse of 1879 (Slanted Arrow Feather) is one of the most plentiful of all Morgan dollars in the early (1878–1904) date range. The majority of pieces are in Mint State and have excellent eye appeal.

Surface Quality: Examples are usually very well struck on both obverse and reverse. They are typically very brilliant and very lustrous, the usual piece having come from a bag in the Treasury release of 1962 through 1964.

Prooflike coins are common, sometimes on one side only. However, many two-sided prooflike coins exist, including in higher grades.

	Cert	Avg	%MS	VF-20	EF-40	AU-50	MS-60	MS-63	MS-64	MS-64DMPL	MS-65	MS-65DMPL
1879-S, Reverse of 1879 (Slanted Arrow Feather)	0	n/a		$35	$38	$40	$65	$75	$100	$1,000	$150	$3,500

1880 Morgan Dollar

1880 • **Mintage:** 12,600,000.

Key to Collecting: The 1880 dollars were made in enormous quantities and from many different dies, and strike quality varies from sharp to weak. However, there are so many available today that finding a choice one will be no problem. Many 1880 dollars show traces of overdating, but these require significant magnification to discern, and most collectors ignore them. More Proofs than usual are in very high grades, on the long side of PF-65.

Surface Quality: Striking varies from sharp to average; many pieces show lightness in the hair strands over the ear of Miss Liberty. The luster is usually very good. Some coins struck from worn dies have metal flow and graininess and are to be avoided.

Some are from prooflike dies, obverse or reverse, or both. DMPL coins were rare, until, per Wayne Miller, a Mint bag of 1,000 prooflike coins came onto the market in 1971.

	Cert	Avg	%MS	VF-20	EF-40	AU-50	MS-60	MS-63	MS-64	MS-64DMPL	MS-65	MS-65DMPL
1880	16,120	62.6	96%	$40	$42	$48	$65	$100	$125	$1,450	$525	$6,000

1880, 80 Over 79, Spikes •
Mintage: Part of 12,600,000.

Key to Collecting: Spikes can be seen above the second 8 in the date. The remains of a 7 in the underdate appear as an incomplete crossbar inside the 8. This is one of the easiest 1880 overdates to collect—that is, in circulated grades. Mint State coins are more of a challenge. FS-S1-1880-006; VAM-6.

Detail of the Overdate and Spikes.

	Cert	Avg	%MS	VF-20	EF-40	AU-50	MS-60	MS-63	MS-64
1880, 80 Over 79, Spikes	174	49.1	16%	$60	$100	$300	$550	$875	$7,000

1880, Proof • **Mintage:** 1,355.

Key to Collecting: The strike on the coins is good, and they usually have deep cameo contrast. The majority of coins have been cleaned.

	Cert	Avg	%MS	PF-60	PF-63	PF-64	PF-65
1880, Proof	427	64.8		$1,300	$3,000	$3,750	$5,500

1880-CC Morgan Dollar
1880-CC, Reverse of 1878, 80 Over 79 • **Mintage:** Part of 125,000 estimated.

Key to Collecting: Like the 1878 and 1879 issues, the 1880-CC exists in two varieties: the Reverse of 1878 (with flat breast and parallel top arrow feather), and the more commonly seen Reverse of 1879. The Reverse of 1878 is several times scarcer, but in the aggregate enough exist that the premium differential is not great. The 1880-CC dollars of both reverse types tend to be "baggy," with many contact marks. Even so, finding a choice one will not be difficult, as enough examples exist in the marketplace.

Detail of the Overdate.

Most if not all 1880-CC obverses were overdated, and some can be called 1880-CC, 80 Over 79, with traces of the 79 showing within the last two digits. These varieties were first published widely in *Coin World* and elsewhere in the 1960s, which created a sensation, after which studies were done, including by Van Allen and Mallis, and various rarities sorted out. On examples of the present listing, with Reverse of 1878 and 80 Over 79, the top crossbar and diagonal stem of an underlying 79 are clearly seen within the 8. Extensive polishing marks are visible within the 0. FS-S1-1880CC-004; VAM-4.

Surface Quality: The strike is usually quite good. On the obverse there may be some slight weakness of hair strands near the ear. The eagle's breast is flat, per the reverse style, but the individual feathers are usually well defined. Typically with attractive frosty surfaces.

Coins with significant prooflike surface are very rare. Note that certification data are confused for the 1880-CC. Most have been certified without mention of the reverse style; moreover, some have been certified as having overdate traces, and still others with overdate traces omit this mention.

	Cert	Avg	%MS	VF-20	EF-40	AU-50	MS-60	MS-63	MS-64	MS-64DMPL	MS-65	MS-65DMPL
1880-CC, Reverse of 1878, 80 Over 79	1,786	62.8	99%	$275	$300	$400	$600	$900	$1,500	$5,000	$2,000	$10,000

1880-CC, Reverse of 1878, 8 Over 7 • Mintage: Part of 125,000 estimated.

Key to Collecting: A dash appears under the last 8 of this variety. It is one of only two 1880-CC varieties with the Reverse of 1878 (with flat breast on the eagle). All known 1880 dies used at the Carson City Mint were overdates; thus, despite the lack of decisive overdate markings within the last 8 in the date, this is considered an overdate.

Surface Quality: See the surface-quality notes in the previous listing.

Detail of the Overdate.

	Cert	Avg	%MS	VF-20	EF-40	AU-50	MS-60	MS-63	MS-64	MS-64DMPL	MS-65	MS-65DMPL
1880-CC, Reverse of 1878, 8 Over 7	2,977	61.3	95%	$250	$285	$350	$575	$975	$1,250	$4,500	$2,000	$10,000

1880-CC, Reverse of 1879 (Slanted Arrow Feather) • Mintage: 466,000 estimated.

Key to Collecting: This variety, the Reverse of 1879 with slanted top arrow feather, is several times more plentiful (some would say many times more plentiful) than the Reverse of 1878 (with parallel top arrow feather). However, as many are extensively bagmarked, searching is needed to locate an example with good eye appeal. The 1880-CC is ever popular due to the magic of the CC mintmark.

Surface Quality: Strike varies from sharp in all areas to weak at the centers, examples of the last showing lack of definition in the hair strands near Miss Liberty's ear and on the breast feathers of the eagle. The luster on a typical 1880-CC is quite nice. Some pieces have planchet striations from the strip preparation process, these in the form of tiny parallel lines on the highest central points of the coin (which were the deepest areas of the dies, and thus not all characteristics of the original planchet were removed in the striking process).

Many partially prooflike or semi-prooflike pieces exist and can be very attractive. Significantly mirrored prooflike coins are apt to be lightly struck at the centers. Note that certification data are confused for the 1880-CC. Most have been certified without mention of the reverse style; moreover, some have been certified as having overdate traces, and still others with overdate traces omit this mention.

	Cert	Avg	%MS	VF-20	EF-40	AU-50	MS-60	MS-63	MS-64	MS-64DMPL	MS-65	MS-65DMPL
1880-CC, Reverse of 1879 (Slanted Arrow Feather)	0	n/a		$225	$260	$325	$500	$575	$700	$2,450	$1,000	$9,000

VARIETY: *1880-CC, Reverse of 1879, 8 Over High 7 (FS-S1-1880CC-005; VAM-5).* A nearly complete 7 can be seen inside the last 8 of the date, and the top edge of the 7 touches the top inside of the last 8 in the date.

	Cert	Avg	%MS	VF-20	EF-40	AU-50	MS-60	MS-63	MS-64	MS-64DMPL	MS-65	MS-65DMPL
1880-CC, Reverse of 1879, 8 Over High 7	697	63.5	100%	$250	$275	$350	$575	$700	$1,250	$3,000	$1,550	$9,000

VARIETY: *1880-CC, Reverse of 1879, 8 Over Low 7 (FS-S1-1880CC-006; VAM-6).* A complete 7 is visible inside the last of the date, the crossbar in the top loop and the diagonal in the lower loop. The fact that the 7 was set lower in the date than on VAM-5 explains its greater visibility.

	Cert	Avg	%MS	VF-20	EF-40	AU-50	MS-60	MS-63	MS-64	MS-64DMPL	MS-65	MS-65DMPL
1880-CC, Reverse of 1879, 8 Over Low 7	572	63.6	100%	$250	$275	$325	$525	$700	$850	$2,750	$1,550	$9,000

1880-O Morgan Dollar

1880-O • **Mintage:** 5,305,000.

Key to Collecting: All 1880-O dollars are from the reverse of 1879 with rounded eagle's breast and slanted top arrow feathers. A number of dies were overdated and show small traces of earlier digits. These have not created much attention in the marketplace, save for dyed-in-the-wool specialists. Certification reports are unreliable regarding overdates, as many coins were graded without checking for this feature. Since the 1970s and 1980s, the swing has been to certification for higher-grade Morgan dollars, and "sliders" are mostly called AU-55 or AU-58 now.

Surface Quality: Striking varies from strong to soft, but most are above average. Again, points to check are the hair above Miss Liberty's ear and the feathers on the eagle's breast. Cherry-picking is recommended. Luster varies from satiny to "greasy," but is generally satisfactory.

Some dies are prooflike; such coins are usually quite attractive if relatively free from bagmarks. Those with DMPL surfaces are elusive.

	Cert	Avg	%MS	VF-20	EF-40	AU-50	MS-60	MS-63	MS-64	MS-64DMPL	MS-65	MS-65DMPL
1880-O	11,267	60.3	73%	$45	$48	$65	$145	$450	$1,250	$7,500	$15,000	$62,500

VARIETY: *1880-O, 80 Over 79 (FS-S1-1880o-004; VAM-4).* The crossbar of an underlying 7 is evident within the upper loop of the last 8 of the date. The 1 and the first 8 are slightly doubled to the right. A micro-O mintmark is also present, but it has no effect on the variety's value.

	Cert	Avg	%MS	VF-20	EF-40	AU-50	MS-60	MS-63	MS-64	MS-64DMPL	MS-65	MS-65DMPL
1880-O, 80 Over 79	275	59.7	67%	$50	$70	$200	$275	$550	$2,650	$4,500	$16,000	$37,500

VARIETY: *1880-O, Die Gouge, "Hangnail" (FS-S1-1880o-049; VAM-49).* On the reverse, a die gouge runs from the bottom of the arrow feather, across the feathers, and out the eagle's rightmost tail feather. On the obverse the top left of the second 8 has a spike. (Another variety, VAM-48, does not have a spiked 8; that variety is worth less.)

	Cert	Avg	%MS	VF-20	EF-40	AU-50	MS-60	MS-63
1880-O, Die Gouge, "Hangnail"	43	49.8	2%	$200	$350	$500	$1,000	$1,750

1880-S Morgan Dollar

1880-S • **Mintage:** 8,900,000.

Key to Collecting: The 1880-S is a delightful Morgan dollar, usually combining excellent strike and luster with a plentiful supply of pieces in the marketplace. Indeed, among Morgan dollars of the early (1878–1904) years, the 1880-S is second only to the 1881-S in terms of availability. The majority of Mint State pieces in existence today were released during the dispersal of the Treasury hoard from 1962 through 1964.

Surface Quality: The 1880-S is usually seen quite well struck. Only a small percentage of pieces have weak striking and these can be easily enough avoided by the discriminating buyer. As is true of other Morgan dollar dates, certification services do not take striking into consideration. Most 1880-S dollars have deep, frosty luster of great beauty. Prooflike coins are not unusual.

	Cert	Avg	%MS	VF-20	EF-40	AU-50	MS-60	MS-63	MS-64	MS-64DMPL	MS-65	MS-65DMPL
1880-S	169,494	64.1	100%	$35	$38	$45	$60	$80	$110	$450	$195	$850

VARIETY: *1880-S, 80 Over 79 (VAM-8 and VAM-9).* Much is taking place on the obverse of these varieties, which share an obverse die. The 18 and 0 in the date are slightly doubled. The second 8 displays raised metal in the upper loop resulting from the punching of an 80 over a 79; it also has diagonal polishing lines along with a faint spike outside the upper loop to the left. A small bit of raised metal is visible inside the loop at upper right. VAM-9 also has a repunched S mintmark.

	Cert	Avg	%MS	VF-20	EF-40	AU-50	MS-60	MS-63	MS-64	MS-64DMPL	MS-65	MS-65DMPL
1880-S, 80 Over 79	972	63.8	99%	$40	$70	$85	$100	$175	$200	$450	$500	

VARIETY: *1880-S, 0 Over 9 (VAM-11).* On this "Hot 50" VAM variety, metal die-polishing marks are visible inside the upper right of the 0, where a 9 was polished away. Dots of metal are visible to the right outside the top loop of the second 8, and doubling is visible on the 1.

	Cert	Avg	%MS	VF-20	EF-40	AU-50	MS-60	MS-63	MS-64	MS-64DMPL	MS-65	MS-65DMPL
1880-S, 0 Over 9	1,325	63.6	100%	$45	$85	$95	$150	$250	$325	$600	$600	

1881 Morgan Dollar

1881 • **Mintage:** 9,163,000.

Key to Collecting: The 1881 dollar was struck in large quantities. The sharpness of striking varies widely on coins seen today, as does the quality of the luster. However, there is no shortage of "average" pieces in the marketplace. Sharply struck, lustrous coins with superb eye appeal are hard to find and mount a challenge for the serious collector.

Surface Quality: Most 1881 dollars are well struck on obverse and reverse, although below-average pieces are seen on occasion, these with light definition at the centers. The luster of the 1881 varies from grainy or "greasy" to lustrous and frosty.

Some dies are with prooflike surface and are in the distinct minority.

	Cert	Avg	%MS	VF-20	EF-40	AU-50	MS-60	MS-63	MS-64	MS-64DMPL	MS-65	MS-65DMPL
1881	13,037	63.0	97%	$35	$38	$45	$53	$80	$135	$1,250	$450	$12,500

1881, Proof • **Mintage:** 984.

Key to Collecting: Excellent strike and deep cameo contrast go together on most pieces.

	Cert	Avg	%MS	PF-60	PF-63	PF-64	PF-65
1881, Proof	269	64.1		$1,300	$3,000	$3,750	$5,500

1881-CC Morgan Dollar

1881-CC • **Mintage:** 296,000.

Key to Collecting: The 1881-CC dollar is easy to find in Mint State, often with deep luster and good strike. The low mintage of this issue and the popular Carson City mintmark contribute to the desirability. In worn grades this is one of the rarest dollars in the series.

Surface Quality: The strike is usually excellent on the 1881-CC, with good definition of the hair details and the eagle's breast feathers. Wayne Miller suggested that the 1881-CC is the nicest Morgan dollar struck at Carson City. The luster is typically deep and frosty, yielding a very attractive coin.

Many 1881-CC examples have semi-prooflike surfaces and can be attractive if they are not heavily bagmarked.

	Cert	Avg	%MS	VF-20	EF-40	AU-50	MS-60	MS-63	MS-64	MS-64DMPL	MS-65	MS-65DMPL
1881-CC	25,111	63.0	98%	$400	$425	$440	$500	$550	$600	$1,400	$750	$2,650

1881-O Morgan Dollar

1881-O • **Mintage:** 5,708,000.

Key to Collecting: The 1881-O is very common in About Uncirculated grade, once called "slider Uncirculated." Wayne Miller theorized that such coins were paid out into circulation in the greater New Orleans area, became redundant to commercial needs, and were brought back to the mint. To find a high-quality 1881-O will take some doing, but there are enough around that within a few months or so you should be successful.

Surface Quality: Strike is usually fairly sharp, but there are exceptions. Luster varies from frosty and attractive, these being in the distinct minority, to somewhat grainy and dull.

Many 1881-O dollars have one or both dies with prooflike surface. However, bagmarks are endemic among these coins, and finding a truly choice example can be a real challenge.

	Cert	Avg	%MS	VF-20	EF-40	AU-50	MS-60	MS-63	MS-64	MS-64DMPL	MS-65	MS-65DMPL
1881-O	20,535	62.4	94%	$40	$42	$45	$55	$95	$150	$975	$800	$12,000

VARIETY: *1881-O, Repunched Mintmark (VAM-5).* The repunched mintmark tilts slightly to the left, such that the upper serif on the underlying S is visible at the center of the upper loop.

	Cert	Avg	%MS	AU-50	MS-60	MS-63
1881-O, Repunched Mintmark	112	62.0	99%	$100	$225	$300

VARIETY: *1881-O, Doubled Die Obverse (VAM-27).* Doubling is visible on the first and last 1's and the first 8, while a spike appears inside the upper loop of the first 8.

	Cert	Avg	%MS	AU-50	MS-60	MS-63
1881-O, Doubled Die Obverse	37	57.1	32%	$175	$400	$2,500

1881-S Morgan Dollar

1881-S • **Mintage:** 12,760,000.

Key to Collecting: The 1881-S is far and away the most readily available Mint State Morgan dollar of 1878–1904. It is likely that at least half the original mintage remains in grades from MS-60 onward, which equals 6,000,000 or more coins. This makes it an ideal candidate to represent the Morgan series in a type set.

Surface Quality: Examples are usually very sharply struck on all points, which is remarkable in view of the huge mintage figure of 12,760,000. In general, the San Francisco Mint earned high marks for quality, while the New Orleans Mint earned a demerit. Luster is typically satiny, and often slightly prooflike.

Many are from prooflike dies, often prooflike on just one side, such as having a frosty and lustrous obverse and a DMPL reverse.

	Cert	Avg	%MS	VF-20	EF-40	AU-50	MS-60	MS-63	MS-64	MS-64DMPL	MS-65	MS-65DMPL
1881-S	277,206	64.0	100%	$35	$38	$45	$60	$80	$110	$450	$195	$850

1882 Morgan Dollar

1882 • Mintage: 11,100,000.

Key to Collecting: The 1882 dollar is the next in the continuing series of high-mintage Philadelphia issues. The quality of pieces varies from sharply struck and very attractive to weakly struck and unprepossessing. Many coins are heavily bagmarked. Cherrypicking is advised to track down a piece that is just right, and enough are in the marketplace that you will be crowned with success with relatively little effort.

Surface Quality: Strike varies from excellent to weak. Cherrypicking is recommended. Again, certification services pay no attention, so you need to search on your own or employ a trustworthy dealer on your behalf. The luster ranges from frosty to somewhat dull, suggesting that time spent searching for quality can be advantageous. However, most coins, regardless of strike, are quite lustrous.

Prooflike pieces exist and are in the distinct minority despite the high mintage for this date. Semi-prooflike or low-contrast prooflike coins are the rule.

	Cert	Avg	%MS	VF-20	EF-40	AU-50	MS-60	MS-63	MS-64	MS-64DMPL	MS-65	MS-65DMPL
1882	23,046	63.1	98%	$35	$38	$45	$55	$85	$125	$1,100	$350	$5,000

1882, Proof • Mintage: 1,100.

Key to Collecting: Another good vintage year for Proofs—what with excellent strike and deep cameo contrast being the rule. Still, the majority have been cleaned—and those deep mirror fields make hairlines pop out at you.

Die Varieties: Many varieties from 58 obverse and 60 reverse dies made, but perhaps not all were used. No varieties are dramatic.

	Cert	Avg	%MS	PF-60	PF-63	PF-64	PF-65
1882, Proof	363	64.4		$1,300	$3,000	$3,750	$5,500

1882-CC Morgan Dollar

1882-CC • Mintage: 1,133,000.

Key to Collecting: The 1882-CC and the two successive Carson City issues, 1883-CC and 1884-CC, constitute the most widely available Carson City silver dollars. In 1964 the Treasury Department held back vast quantities of these issues, later distributing them to collectors and others. Today, beautiful pieces can be obtained for a reasonable price.

Surface Quality: Examples are usually seen well struck, typically with beautiful, deep, frosty luster.

Prooflike pieces are encountered with some frequency, and some have deep mirror surfaces with sharp contrast, quite resembling Philadelphia Mint Proofs. Some coins are prooflike, even DMPL, in most areas of the field, except for satiny luster close to Miss Liberty's head and, on the reverse, surrounding the eagle's head.

	Cert	Avg	%MS	VF-20	EF-40	AU-50	MS-60	MS-63	MS-64	MS-64DMPL	MS-65	MS-65DMPL
1882-CC	48,661	63.1	99%	$165	$175	$190	$265	$275	$290	$650	$400	$2,100

1882-O Morgan Dollar

1882-O • **Mintage:** 6,090,000.

Key to Collecting: The 1882-O pieces seem to have been produced with relatively little care. As a handy rule, New Orleans pieces are more difficult to find with good strike and luster than are those from the other mints. If a palm were to be given for excellence in this regard, it would go to San Francisco, but Carson City pieces are usually well struck, and many Philadelphia pieces are as well.

Surface Quality: Strike varies from fairly decent to weak, but is usually above average. The luster is often dull and insipid, "greasy," or grainy. Finding a deeply frosty 1882-O can be a challenge.

Strikings from prooflike dies are seen with some frequency and are most attractive in higher grades.

	Cert	Avg	%MS	VF-20	EF-40	AU-50	MS-60	MS-63	MS-64	MS-64DMPL	MS-65	MS-65DMPL
1882-O	26,357	61.6	86%	$40	$42	$45	$65	$80	$135	$1,000	$600	$3,000

1882-O, O Over S Recessed •

Mintage: Small part of 6,090,000.

FS-S1-1882o-004.

Key to Collecting: The 1882-O, O Over S, is a worthwhile addition to any collection, with a reasonable grade goal being MS-63 or MS-64—not because of price, but because pieces at higher levels are virtually impossible to find. Beyond that, the overmintmark should be distinct under a good 4x glass. On some the under-S is weak, and these should be avoided. Traces of die rust are normal and are not a negative factor. FS-S1-1882o-004, VAM-4.

Detail of the Overdate.

Surface Quality: Striking varies from sharp to weak. On all known examples there is graininess in some areas, due to tiny raised dots from light rust pits in the dies. A few DMPL coins have been certified in low Mint State grades.

	Cert	Avg	%MS	VF-20	EF-40	AU-50	MS-60	MS-63	MS-64	MS-64DMPL	MS-65	MS-65DMPL
1882-O, O Over S Recessed	630	55.2	31%	$50	$55	$70	$150	$475	$1,500		$50,000	

1882-S Morgan Dollar

1882-S • **Mintage:** 9,250,000.

Key to Collecting: The 1882-S exists in large quantities in Mint State, so examples can be obtained easily. Most are fairly attractive. Many 1882-S dollars are heavily bagmarked, these fitting into the grade categories from MS-60 to MS-62. Many 1882-S dollars are prooflike, but just a small percentage of Mint State coins are in existence. However, in absolute terms there are enough to supply the demand.

Surface Quality: Striking ranges from sharp to somewhat weak, with most being above average. The luster is typically deeply frosty and very attractive, similar to that on 1881-S.

Prooflike pieces exist with some frequency, some of which are prooflike on just one side. Generally, the contrast between the mirrored fields and the devices is not great.

	Cert	Avg	%MS	VF-20	EF-40	AU-50	MS-60	MS-63	MS-64	MS-64DMPL	MS-65	MS-65DMPL
1882-S	87,631	64.2	100%	$35	$38	$45	$60	$80	$110	$900	$195	$3,000

1883 Morgan Dollar

1883 • **Mintage:** 12,290,000.

Key to Collecting: Among Morgan dollars of the 1880s, the 1883 Philadelphia Mint issue is among the most widely available. Produced in quantity, such pieces were often struck in haste, and some care needs to be exercised to find attractive pieces. Regardless of striking quality—sharp or weak—most pieces have satiny mint luster.

Surface Quality: The majority of 1883 Morgan dollars range from average strikes to sharp, but some weakly impressed examples exist here and there. Cherrypicking is recommended, as always. The 1883 is usually lustrous and frosty, although some pieces can be slightly dull.

Many are from prooflike dies, one side or the other, or both. Some DMPL coins exist with excellent cameo contrast and are rare, but no doubt the market for such is diminished by the availability of Proof strikings.

	Cert	Avg	%MS	VF-20	EF-40	AU-50	MS-60	MS-63	MS-64	MS-64DMPL	MS-65	MS-65DMPL
1883	26,677	63.5	98%	$35	$38	$45	$60	$80	$110	$550	$195	$1,300

1883, Proof • Mintage: 1,039.

Key to Collecting: Examples are usually well struck. Good cameo contrast is seen between the design and the mirrored fields, but it is not as dramatic as on the Proofs of recent years. Finding a nice one may require some searching. If higher grades are in the budget, the best way to start is to inspect pieces that have been certified as PF-64 or finer, then go from there to determine quality.

	Cert	Avg	%MS	PF-60	PF-63	PF-64	PF-65
1883, Proof	292	64.0		$1,300	$3,000	$3,750	$5,500

1883-CC Morgan Dollar

1883-CC • **Mintage:** 1,204,000.

Key to Collecting: The 1883-CC joins the 1882-CC and 1884-CC as one of a trio of very plentiful Carson City dollars in Mint State. There is a great pride of possession for such a piece as nearly all are well struck and very attractive, this in combination with a reasonable market price.

Surface Quality: The 1883-CC is typically seen well struck and with deep, frosty luster, bright and attractive.

Some dies are prooflike, often deeply mirrored and with cameo or frosted devices, quite like a Philadelphia Mint Proof except for certain aspects of the edge treatment. Some have DMPL fields, but with auras of satiny frost close to the outline of Miss Liberty's portrait and the edges of the eagle.

	Cert	Avg	%MS	VF-20	EF-40	AU-50	MS-60	MS-63	MS-64	MS-64DMPL	MS-65	MS-65DMPL
1883-CC	63,962	63.4	99%	$165	$175	$190	$310	$335	$350	$600	$450	$1,250

1883-O Morgan Dollar

1883-O • **Mintage:** 8,725,000.

Key to Collecting: Produced in quantity, the typical 1883-O coin seen today is apt to have unsatisfactory luster and a typical strike. Cherrypicking will make all the difference between a high-quality collection and the ordinary quality of most others.

Surface Quality: Striking varies all over the place for the 1883-O, with some quite flat at the centers, and others needle sharp, the latter being in the distinct minority. Careful selection is advised. The 1883-O is common in Mint State, and thus there are many opportunities to view candidates for a collection. The luster ranges from medium frosty to somewhat dull and grainy. Some were made from worn-out dies past retirement age, and these have granularity and metal flow lines. Cherrypicking is again advised, this in combination with seeking a sharp strike.

Prooflike coins are plentiful, but the majority show poor contrast between the fields and the devices, or are heavily bagmarked, or both. A DMPL coin with cameo contrast is a joy to behold.

	Cert	Avg	%MS	VF-20	EF-40	AU-50	MS-60	MS-63	MS-64	MS-64DMPL	MS-65	MS-65DMPL
1883-O	150,612	63.4	100%	$35	$38	$45	$60	$80	$115	$425	$195	$1,250

1883-O, Proof • Mintage: 12.

Key to Collecting: A numismatic tradition exists, dating back well over a century, that 12 full Proofs were struck of the 1883-O Morgan dollar. And, they may have been, although the differentiation between a cameo DMPL and a "branch-mint Proof" would be difficult to explain. Proofs have been certified on at least two instances.

   Four different branch-mint Morgan dollar Proofs are considered to be "Class I," meaning there is documentation confirming the coins were authorized and issued by the Mint. The 1883-O Proof is one of the four; the other three are the 1879-O Proof, the 1893-CC Proof, and the 1921-S Zerbe Proof.

	Cert	Avg	%MS	PF-60	PF-63	PF-64	PF-65
1883-O, Proof	2	64.0			$100,000	$125,000	$200,000

1883-S Morgan Dollar

1883-S • Mintage: 6,250,000.

Key to Collecting: Following the run of numismatically available San Francisco coins from 1878 through 1882, now with the 1883-S we encounter a key issue. In contrast with the earlier dates, the 1883-S is very difficult to find, especially at higher Mint State levels. Among 1883-S dollars, bagmarks are a significant problem. These must have been stored and handled roughly.

Surface Quality: The 1883-S usually is seen with above-average to quite sharp strike. The luster ranges from medium frosty to deep and is generally pleasing to the eye.

   Some dies are prooflike, but not necessarily deeply mirrored. Among 1883-S dollars in Mint State, these are encountered with regularity, that is, when Mint State pieces themselves are found—for all 1883-S dollars are elusive at that grade level. DMPL coins are exceedingly rare.

	Cert	Avg	%MS	VF-20	EF-40	AU-50	MS-60	MS-63	MS-64	MS-64DMPL	MS-65	MS-65DMPL
1883-S	6,322	55.1	31%	$35	$55	$125	$1,050	$2,300	$4,500	$90,000	$30,000	

1884 Morgan Dollar

1884 • Mintage: 14,070,000.

Key to Collecting: The 1884 Philadelphia Mint dollar is readily available in Mint State and has been for many years, even before the Treasury releases of the early 1960s. Quality varies all over the place, from sharp and lustrous to rather insipid. Today, while the 1884 remains plentiful in terms of single coins, quantities are seldom encountered.

Surface Quality: The striking varies but is usually average or above average. The luster varies from deeply frosty (and desirable as such) to rather grainy and insipid.

Some prooflike pieces exist and are in the distinct minority.

	Cert	Avg	%MS	VF-20	EF-40	AU-50	MS-60	MS-63	MS-64	MS-64DMPL	MS-65	MS-65DMPL
1884	21,083	63.1	97%	$35	$38	$45	$60	$80	$115	$950	$285	$3,500

VARIETY: *1884, Large Dot (FS-S1-1884-003, VAM-3).* A relatively large dot is visible after the designer's initial (relative in comparison to the dot on VAM-4, that is). It is thought that the dots on VAM-3 and 4 were used as some type of identifier.

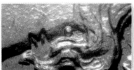 

	Cert	Avg	%MS	VF-20	EF-40	AU-50	MS-60	MS-63	MS-64
1884, Large Dot	107	55.0	42%	$45	$60	$75	$125	$150	$500

VARIETY: *1884, Small Dot (FS S1-1884-004, VAM-4).* A small dot is visible after the designer's initial. It is thought that the dots on VAM-3 and 4 were used as some type of identifier.

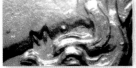 

	Cert	Avg	%MS	VF-20	EF-40	AU-50	MS-60	MS-63	MS-64
1884, Small Dot	257	61.9	91%	$45	$60	$75	$150	$175	$1,400

1884, Proof • Mintage: 875.

Key to Collecting: Examples of the 1884 Proof show good strike and deep cameo contrast.

	Cert	Avg	%MS	PF-60	PF-63	PF-64	PF-65
1884, Proof	0	n/a		$1,300	$3,000	$3,750	$5,500

1884-CC Morgan Dollar

1884-CC • **Mintage:** 1,136,000.

Key to Collecting: The 1884-CC is another Carson City Mint variety that exists in numismatic abundance. After the coins were struck, virtually all were inadvertently saved for generations of numismatists yet unborn, to come to light in 1964 and to be distributed into the market. Today, while worn

1884-CC dollars are understandably rare, Mint State coins abound. Accordingly, the market price is very reasonable, and examples are within the reach of all.

Surface Quality: The strike is typically average to above average, even sharp, but some pieces are weak at the centers. Cherrypicking is advised but will not be a great effort. The luster of some is deeply frosty.

Some are from prooflike dies, including DMPL pieces, and are seen with some frequency in view of the numbers in the Treasury hoard. Cameo contrast is the rule, not the exception, with 1884-CC.

	Cert	Avg	%MS	VF-20	EF-40	AU-50	MS-60	MS-63	MS-64	MS-64DMPL	MS-65	MS-65DMPL
1884-CC	73,432	63.6	100%	$155	$175	$190	$310	$335	$350	$550	$450	$1,300

1884-O Morgan Dollar

1884-O • Mintage: 9,730,000.

Key to Collecting: The 1884-O was minted in quantity, and examples are readily available today in all Mint State grades from MS-60 to 65 and beyond. Wayne Miller considered the 1884-O to be the most common Mint State Morgan dollar except for 1921, if all Mint State levels are considered.

Surface Quality: Striking ranges from poor (no hair detail above Miss Liberty's ear, little definition of breast feathers on the eagle) to very sharp, but is typically average or a bit above. Cherrypicking is advised. The luster ranges from grainy or insipid to frosty, but generally fails to dazzle.

There are many prooflike coins in existence, one-sided as well as two-sided examples. However, most show little contrast and are the antithesis of cameo, and most are heavily bagmarked.

	Cert	Avg	%MS	VF-20	EF-40	AU-50	MS-60	MS-63	MS-64	MS-64DMPL	MS-65	MS-65DMPL
1884-O	239,887	63.5	100%	$35	$38	$45	$60	$80	$115	$450	$195	$1,000

1884-S Morgan Dollar

1884-S • Mintage: 3,200,000.

Key to Collecting: Large quantities of 1884-S dollars were released into circulation in the 19th century. Accordingly, worn examples are fairly plentiful today and are available for a nominal price. Mint State coins are elusive at any and all levels and are keys in the series. Not much attention was paid to the 1884-S in Mint State until after the coin boom of the late 1930s (ignited by the commemorative craze). Afterward, the coin took its place as one of the more difficult S Mint varieties to acquire.

Surface Quality: The striking is usually average. However, some have light striking at the center of the reverse. The luster on the 1884-S is generally of a satiny nature, often dull, not deeply frosty, although some of the latter exist.

A few prooflike pieces are known with unremarkable luster and contrast. DMPL coins are unknown, a Holy Grail in the Morgan series.

	Cert	Avg	%MS	VF-20	EF-40	AU-50	MS-60	MS-63	MS-64	MS-64DMPL	MS-65	MS-65DMPL
1884-S	8,918	52.1	5%	$45	$100	$250	$7,500	$35,000	$125,000	$135,000	$225,000	

1885 Morgan Dollar

1885 • **Mintage:** 17,787,000.

Key to Collecting: The 1885 Philadelphia Mint Morgan dollar has been common for a long time, far before the Treasury releases of the early 1960s. Made in quantity, these pieces are seen today in varying degrees of eye appeal. Apart from the need to be selective as to quality, this will be an easy date to find.

Surface Quality: The striking is usually above average, but some hunting may be needed to find a particularly sharp piece. The luster is usually frosty, although many grainy pieces exist.

Some dies are prooflike and are most attractive in the higher grades.

	Cert	Avg	%MS	VF-20	EF-40	AU-50	MS-60	MS-63	MS-64	MS-64DMPL	MS-65	MS-65DMPL
1885	89,233	63.6	99%	$35	$38	$45	$60	$80	$115	$500	$195	$1,200

VARIETY: *1885, Die Chip (FS-S1-1885-022, VAM-22).* A large, raised die chip is evident below the second 8.

	Cert	Avg	%MS	VF-20	EF-40	AU-50	MS-60	MS-63	MS-64
1885, Die Chip	18	62.5	94%	$50	$60	$75	$100	$175	$300

1885, Proof • Mintage: 930.

Key to Collecting: Proofs are usually well struck. Medium cameo contrast. More than just a few of this date have been dipped so many times that the mirror surfaces are dull gray. Such coins are not for you.

Die Varieties: At least 89 obverse and 88 reverse dies were used. In 1982 the VAM text described 20 combinations. None have dramatically different characteristics.

	Cert	Avg	%MS	PF-60	PF-63	PF-64	PF-65
1885, Proof	253	64.2		$1,300	$3,000	$3,750	$5,500

1885-CC Morgan Dollar

1885-CC • **Mintage:** 228,000.

Key to Collecting: The 1885-CC exists by the hundreds of thousands of pieces, as more than half of the original mintage survived and was distributed in the late 20th century. Most examples are brilliant, lustrous, and attractive to the eye. Ironically, the 1885-CC is the rarest of all Morgan dollars in circulated grades, eclipsing the 1889-CC, 1893-S, and all other contenders (not counting the Proof-only 1895); but there are so many Mint State coins around that worn pieces are generally unappreciated.

Surface Quality: Striking ranges from somewhat weak to very sharp, but most are above average. Most are well struck with brilliant, frosty luster.

Some are struck from prooflike dies. DMPL coins with good cameo contrast exist and are highly sought.

	Cert	Avg	%MS	VF-20	EF-40	AU-50	MS-60	MS-63	MS-64	MS-64DMPL	MS-65	MS-65DMPL
1885-CC	25,111	63.4	99%	$540	$550	$565	$650	$675	$750	$1,500	$1,000	$2,250

1885-O Morgan Dollar

1885-O • Mintage: 9,815,000.

Key to Collecting: The 1885-O dollars were among the bonanza delights of the 1962 through 1964 Treasury releases, after which bags were common, all filled with bright, sparkling coins—but not necessarily well struck or with deep luster. Today, cherrypicking is the order of the day, but with so many coins from which to choose, the exercise will not take much time.

Surface Quality: The strike can range from flat at the centers to fairly sharp, the same general rule being applicable to other New Orleans pieces of the era. Luster ranges from frosty to grainy or dull. Cherrypicking is advised.

Some are seen with prooflike dies, but usually not with great contrast against the devices.

	Cert	Avg	%MS	VF-20	EF-40	AU-50	MS-60	MS-63	MS-64	MS-64DMPL	MS-65	MS-65DMPL
1885-O	234,830	63.7	100%	$35	$38	$45	$60	$80	$115	$375	$195	$850

1885-S Morgan Dollar

1885-S • Mintage: 1,497,000.

Key to Collecting: The 1885-S dollar fits into the medium-scarce category, neither common nor rare. There are enough around that for a reasonable price you can easily own an MS-63 or MS-64, but not so easy for an MS-65. Many are softly struck, more like a typical New Orleans dollar than one from San Francisco, so you will need to spend some time searching.

Surface Quality: Most have some flatness at the center of the obverse and the center of the reverse, in contrast to most earlier-dated San Francisco coins, which are well struck. Some excellent strikes exist of 1885-S, but searching is needed to find them. Most are with attractive luster.

Some are from prooflike dies, sometimes on one side only. DMPLs exist and are very rare.

	Cert	Avg	%MS	VF-20	EF-40	AU-50	MS-60	MS-63	MS-64	MS-64DMPL	MS-65	MS-65DMPL
1885-S	7,077	60.5	80%	$45	$60	$95	$280	$400	$625	$5,250	$1,500	$41,000

1886 Morgan Dollar

1886 • **Mintage:** 19,963,000.

Key to Collecting: Dollars of 1886 are very common, but often dies were used until they wore out. As a result, more than a few surviving Mint States coins are grainy and show metal flow lines. Cherrypicking is recommended. Worn 1886 dollars are common, and without doubt huge numbers of them went into refinery furnaces during the run-up of silver bullion prices in the 1980s, as few numismatists wanted them.

Surface Quality: The strike varies, but most are fairly sharp. As a rule of thumb the luster on the 1886 is rather dull, often grainy, as dies seem to have been used for a long time. Cherrypicking is needed to find one with deep mint frost.

Prooflike coins are occasionally seen, usually with low contrast. DMPL coins with cameo contrast are very elusive.

	Cert	Avg	%MS	VF-20	EF-40	AU-50	MS-60	MS-63	MS-64	MS-64DMPL	MS-65	MS-65DMPL
1886	151,347	63.7	99%	$35	$38	$45	$60	$80	$115	$375	$195	$850

VARIETY: *1886, Repunched Date (FS-S1-1886-020, VAM-20).* Repunching is especially evident in the base of the 1 and the lower loop of the 6.

	Cert	Avg	%MS	VF-20	EF-40	AU-50	MS-60	MS-63	MS-64
1886, Repunched Date	13	61.5	85%	$750	$1,500	$2,500	$3,500	$7,500	$8,500

1886, Proof • **Mintage:** 886.

Key to Collecting: Strike is usually decent, and contrast medium to low. Nice 1886 Proof dollars exist, but they are harder to find than certain other dates mentioned thus far.

	Cert	Avg	%MS	PF-60	PF-63	PF-64	PF-65
1886, Proof	248	63.9		$1,300	$3,000	$3,750	$5,500

1886-O Morgan Dollar

1886-O • **Mintage:** 10,710,000.

Key to Collecting: The 1886-O dollars are very common in worn grades today and exceedingly rare in choice to gem Mint State. Most all were released in the 19th century or melted in 1918, and few were ever saved for numismatic purposes.

Surface Quality: Striking varies from flat at the centers to fairly sharp, with most being quite decent. Cherrypicking is advised, to the extent that it can be done among Mint State coins, which are not often encountered. The luster on the 1886-O ranges from flat, grainy, and lifeless to fairly frosty, the last being in the distinct minority. Again, careful buying is advised, but this must be done over a period of time, as one certainly does not have the opportunity to view a significant number of 1886-O dollars side by side.

The 1886-O is rare with prooflike surface on one side or the other. DMPL coins exist and are exceedingly rare and desirable if in high grades with good eye appeal.

	Cert	Avg	%MS	VF-20	EF-40	AU-50	MS-60	MS-63	MS-64	MS-64DMPL	MS-65	MS-65DMPL
1886-O	6,991	55.2	27%	$45	$55	$85	$900	$2,600	$8,000	$70,000	$150,000	

VARIETY: *1886-O, Clashed Die (FS-S1-1886o-001a, VAM-1A):* Among varieties, VAM-1A is significant. Raised E prominent below the eagle's tail feathers, above the upper left of the ribbon bow.

	Cert	Avg	%MS	VF-20	EF-40	AU-50	MS-60	MS-63	MS-64
1886-O, Clashed Die	268	49.4	8%	$60	$125	$250	$1,250	$6,500	—

1886-S Morgan Dollar

1886-S • Mintage: 750,000.

Key to Collecting: Nearly all examples have excellent eye appeal, but some searching is needed to find a sharp strike. MS-63 and 64 are grades that are eminently affordable to most advanced numismatists, and MS-65 coins are, of course, even more worthwhile. However, for most grades the 1886-S is rarer than the 1885-S.

Surface Quality: Above-average strike is the rule for 1886-S, although very sharp strikes require some searching to find. The luster on the 1886-S is typically of high quality. This issue is reminiscent of certain San Francisco dollars earlier in the decade, when sharp strike and quality were the rule, not the exception.

Prooflike coins are seen with some frequency, perhaps 20% or more coins having some prooflike characteristics. DMPL coins are seen occasionally.

	Cert	Avg	%MS	VF-20	EF-40	AU-50	MS-60	MS-63	MS-64	MS-64DMPL	MS-65	MS-65DMPL
1886-S	5,334	59.4	71%	$80	$115	$140	$350	$450	$600	$8,000	$1,600	$27,000

1887 Morgan Dollar

1887 • Mintage: 19,940,000.

Key to Collecting: The 1887 is as common as can be. Today, examples remain plentiful, but as most are weakly struck in one area or another, or have poor luster, or are afflicted with both negatives, being fussy is the order of the day when buying one. Proofs are rarities in proportion to their mintage.

Surface Quality: Striking varies from flat at the centers, as usual, to fairly decent. Cherrypicking is advised. The 1887 is a plentiful date, so many opportunities will exist. The luster is typically dull and somewhat "greasy," at a low level of quality. Cherrypicking is needed to find a deeply lustrous example. Apparently, this large-mintage issue was produced in haste.

Many prooflike coins exist, as do many DMPLs, but relatively few have cameo contrast.

	Cert	Avg	%MS	VF-20	EF-40	AU-50	MS-60	MS-63	MS-64	MS-64DMPL	MS-65	MS-65DMPL
1887	218,387	63.7	100%	$35	$38	$45	$60	$80	$115	$450	$195	$850

1887, 7 Over 6 • **Mintage:** 350,000.

Key to Collecting: There is a significant demand for the 1887, 7 Over 6, and examples are elusive in all grades. While grade-for-grade the overdate is rare in comparison to the regular 1887 issue, enough MS-64 and 65 coins exist that the connoisseur can locate an example. This variety is not everyone's numismatic cup of tea. As the overdate is not easily seen without magnification, some have chosen not to include it in their collections. The prices of examples have fluctuated as popularity and availability have both varied over the years. FS-S1-1887-002, VAM-2.

FS-S1-1887-002.

Detail of the Overdate.

Surface Quality: Examples are average, but usually with deep mint frost.

Prooflike coins are occasionally seen, usually with low contrast. Some DMPL coins have been certified and are rare.

	Cert	Avg	%MS	VF-20	EF-40	AU-50	MS-60	MS-63	MS-64	MS-64DMPL	MS-65	MS-65DMPL
1887, 7 Over 6	1,078	62.5	94%	$50	$80	$150	$300	$425	$750		$2,500	

1887, Proof • **Mintage:** 710.

Key to Collecting: Examples usually show a decent strike with medium to low contrast. Diminished mintage quantities of this and other dates of this era add to the challenge of finding high-quality pieces. Incidentally, the majority of the PF-66–PF-68 or finer pieces represent coins certified in recent years. Earlier, many would have been called PF-65.

	Cert	Avg	%MS	PF-60	PF-63	PF-64	PF-65
1887, Proof	230	64.3		$1,300	$3,000	$3,750	$5,500

1887-O Morgan Dollar

1887-O • **Mintage:** 11,350,000.

Key to Collecting: Although the 1887-O is hardly in the common-date category, enough exist that a nice MS-63 coin can be found with little effort. However, among these only a fraction have a combination of sharp strike and attractive luster—yielding a great opportunity for cherrypicking. When you find one, the cost will not be any more than what others are paying for pieces with poor eye appeal. Check any and all examples for the overdate feature (see the next listing).

Surface Quality: The striking of the 1887-O is usually average or below average, and sometimes quite poor. Sharp pieces do exist but searching is needed to find them. At the New Orleans Mint during this era many dies were spaced too far apart, perhaps facilitating the coining process, but resulting in pieces that hardly deserve numismatic prizes. The luster on the 1887-O ranges from grainy and dull to frosty, but is usually subpar. A nice one can be found, however, with some effort.

Prooflike dies were used extensively, and pieces with a degree of prooflike surface, sometimes deep and accentuated with cameo devices, are elusive, but not great rarities. However, most are lightly struck at the center.

	Cert	Avg	%MS	VF-20	EF-40	AU-50	MS-60	MS-63	MS-64	MS-64DMPL	MS-65	MS-65DMPL
1887-O	11,839	61.7	92%	$35	$38	$45	$100	$165	$350	$1,500	$1,650	$2,500

1887-O, 7 Over 6 •

Mintage: 200,000 estimated.

FS-S1-1887o-003.

Key to Collecting: The 1887-O, 7 Over 6, overdate is very scarce in all grades. It can be a cherrypicker's delight, for although in recent years the certification services have been alert to the existence of this overdate, there are many "raw" pieces that have never been studied for this feature. All known Mint State coins are in lower grades, seemingly indicating potential for finding some higher ones by carefully studying "regular" 1887-O dollars, some of which are gems (numerically, not necessarily from aspects of strike or luster). FS-S1-1887o-003, VAM-3.

Detail of the Overdate.

Surface Quality: Examples are lightly struck at the center, and some are very lightly struck. Luster ranges from dull to average, not deeply frosty.

No prooflike examples have been seen or reported.

	Cert	Avg	%MS	VF-20	EF-40	AU-50	MS-60	MS-63	MS-64	MS-64DMPL	MS-65	MS-65DMPL
1887-O, 7 Over 6	609	60.3	82%	$55	$85	$160	$700	$1,500	$3,750		$17,500	

1887-S Morgan Dollar

1887-S • **Mintage:** 1,771,000.

Key to Collecting: The 1887-S dollar is a delight to own, as a coin selected with care will be well struck and very attractive. This date and mint is somewhat scarce in the series, but hardly a "stopper." A grade such as MS-63 offers a lot of coin for the money.

Surface Quality: Examples are usually seen well struck, and with few exceptions this is a no-problem issue. However, some are light at the centers, most noticeably on the eagle's breast. The 1887-S is usually seen with attractive frosty luster.

Prooflike coins are occasionally encountered. Nicks and marks can be a problem due to storage and repeated handling in bags. Several hundred were in the Redfield hoard dispersed after 1976.

	Cert	Avg	%MS	VF-20	EF-40	AU-50	MS-60	MS-63	MS-64	MS-64DMPL	MS-65	MS-65DMPL
1887-S	7,929	61.0	78%	$35	$38	$50	$175	$250	$550	$7,200	$1,500	$28,500

1888 Morgan Dollar

1888 • **Mintage:** 19,183,100.

Key to Collecting: The 1888 rates as a common date in the Morgan series, although the quality of individual specimens can vary dramatically. Extended die use caused granularity and metal flow lines on some. On the other hand, more than just a few 1888 dollars are attractive and prooflike.

Surface Quality: The strike varies from poor to decent. Truly sharp pieces are in the distinct minority and require cherrypicking to find. Luster ranges from grainy to good. Again, careful buying is recommended, but is not as difficult as with, for example, the Philadelphia Mint dollars of 1886 and 1887.

Prooflike coins are often seen, usually with low contrast.

	Cert	Avg	%MS	VF-20	EF-40	AU-50	MS-60	MS-63	MS-64	MS-64DMPL	MS-65	MS-65DMPL
1888	55,001	63.6	99%	$35	$38	$45	$60	$85	$115	$500	$200	$2,000

1888, Proof • **Mintage:** 833.

Key to Collecting: Examples are lightly struck at the centers and have low contrast. About this time the Mint became sloppy in the making of Proofs, and not long afterward dealer Harlan P. Smith filed a formal complaint. Proofs of the era beginning about now are not on a visual par with those earlier in the decade.

	Cert	Avg	%MS	PF-60	PF-63	PF-64	PF-65
1888, Proof	200	63.8		$1,300	$3,000	$3,750	$5,500

1888-O Morgan Dollar

1888-O • **Mintage:** 12,150,000.

Key to Collecting: The 1888-O is plentiful in Mint State, mostly from Treasury hoard dispersals, but most are at lower Mint State levels, and striking and luster are often far below par. However, with some searching it is possible to find an attractive example.

Surface Quality: The strike varies all over the place, from flat to sharp, but most show weakness at the center obverse and center reverse—really subpar. Dedicated cherrypicking is needed to find a sharp coin. The luster varies from grainy and rather dull to frosty and attractive.

Prooflike coins are easily enough found.

	Cert	Avg	%MS	VF-20	EF-40	AU-50	MS-60	MS-63	MS-64	MS-64DMPL	MS-65	MS-65DMPL
1888-O	30,470	62.0	95%	$35	$38	$50	$65	$95	$115	$600	$350	$2,500

VARIETY: *1888-O, Die Crack, "Scarface" (FS-S1-1888o-001b, VAM-1B):* A major die crack on the obverse runs from the rim between the E and the P, through the field, and all the way across Liberty's face and neck. This variety is nicknamed "Scarface."

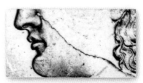

	Cert	Avg	%MS	AU-50	MS-60	MS-63	MS-64
1888-O, Die Crack, "Scarface"	96	61.6	96%	$1,500	$5,000	$9,000	$22,500

VARIETY: *1888-O, Doubled Die Obverse, "Hot Lips" (FS-S1-1888o-004, VAM-4):* Doubling is visible on the lips (especially), nose, eye, chin, entire profile, and part of the hair. This variety is nicknamed "Hot Lips."

	Cert	Avg	%MS	VF-20	EF-40	AU-50	MS-60	MS-63	MS-64
1888-O, Doubled Die Obverse	984	31.9	1%	$225	$300	$750	$8,700		—

1888-S Morgan Dollar

1888-S • **Mintage:** 657,000.

Key to Collecting: The 1888-S is scarce in Mint State in the context of Morgan dollars, but enough exist that there is no difficulty tracking down an example in MS-63 or MS-64. While many if not most San Francisco Morgan dollars are sharply struck, the 1888-S is an exception.

Surface Quality: The strike varies from poor to sharp, with sharp pieces being in the minority. Careful cherrypicking is recommended. The luster of the 1888-S is usually attractive, although there are some exceptions.

Prooflike coins, one-sided as well as two-sided, were plentiful a couple decades ago, but are widely scattered now. These can be very attractive. The Redfield hoard yielded some marvelous DMPL examples.

	Cert	Avg	%MS	VF-20	EF-40	AU-50	MS-60	MS-63	MS-64	MS-64DMPL	MS-65	MS-65DMPL
1888-S	5,995	58.3	67%	$125	$140	$150	$315	$425	$750	$2,750	$2,000	$15,500

1889 Morgan Dollar

1889 • **Mintage:** 21,726,000.

Key to Collecting: The mintage figure of 21,726,000 for the 1889 dollar sweeps away any other total in the early (1878–1904) Morgan series. Most 1889 dollars in any grade are indifferently struck and have miserable luster, sort of grayish, dull, and numismatically forgettable. As grading services will make no mention of sharpness of strike or quality of luster, so you have the opportunity, at least in theory, to land a gem for a "regular" price.

Surface Quality: Strike ranges from poor to sharp, mostly average or below average. The luster on the 1889 is often dull and insipid. Finding a deeply frosty coin in combination with a sharp strike can be a first-class challenge!

Some prooflike coins exist but are not common.

	Cert	Avg	%MS	VF-20	EF-40	AU-50	MS-60	MS-63	MS-64	MS-64DMPL	MS-65	MS-65DMPL
1889	59,107	63.1	98%	$35	$38	$45	$60	$80	$115	$1,000	$240	$3,250

VARIETY: *1889, Die Break, "Bar Wing" (FS-S1-1889-019a, VAM-19A).* A die break is visible on the top of the eagle's right wing, hence this variety's nickname, the "Bar Wing." Different obverse die pairings exist.

	Cert	Avg	%MS	VF-20	EF-40	AU-50	MS-60	MS-63	MS-64	MS-65
1889, Die Break, "Bar Wing"	162	59.1	62%	$60	$75	$90	$150	$330	$400	$550

1889, Proof • **Mintage:** 811.

Key to Collecting: Examples show average strike, usually flat at the centers, with medium to low cameo contrast. Lack of sharpness is hardly ever mentioned in price lists or catalogs, although it is visible in the photos.

	Cert	Avg	%MS	PF-60	PF-63	PF-64	PF-65
1889, Proof	193	64.1		$1,300	$3,000	$3,750	$5,500

1889-CC Morgan Dollar

1889-CC • **Mintage:** 350,000.

Key to Collecting: The 1889-CC dollar is one of the great keys in the Morgan series, and among Carson City issues it is far and away the most elusive. In comparison to the demand for them, examples are rare in all grades. However, for those who can afford one, attractive MS-63, 64, and 65 coins appear on the market with regularity, and gorgeous DMPL specimens are sometimes offered.

Surface Quality: Usually examples display an average strike at best, often below average. The luster varies from rather shallow and satin-like to frosty, but usually not deeply frosty.

Many 1889-CC dollars are semi-prooflike, more than 25% of the survivors it would seem. Some DMPL pieces exist and have cameo contrast.

	Cert	Avg	%MS	VF-20	EF-40	AU-50	MS-60	MS-63	MS-64	MS-64DMPL	MS-65	MS-65DMPL
1889-CC	5,479	31.1	10%	$1,250	$2,500	$6,500	$22,000	$36,000	$70,000	$95,000	$300,000	

1889-O Morgan Dollar

1889-O • **Mintage:** 11,875,000.

Key to Collecting: The 1889-O was struck in prodigious quantities, many of which were released into circulation in the 19th century and others of which were part of later Treasury holdings. Today Mint State coins are very common, but sharply struck gems with beautiful luster are rare. Gems exist and can be found.

Surface Quality: Examples are usually lightly struck at the centers and not very satisfactory. Aggressive searching is needed to find a sharp one. Luster ranges from dull to somewhat frosty.

Prooflike coins are seen with frequency, often having cameo contrast.

	Cert	Avg	%MS	VF-20	EF-40	AU-50	MS-60	MS-63	MS-64	MS-64DMPL	MS-65	MS-65DMPL
1889-O	5,357	59.2	78%	$35	$38	$60	$265	$385	$750	$6,750	$3,450	$55,000

VARIETY: *1889-O, Clashed Die (FS-1889o-001a, VAM-1A).* This variety shows a raised letter E between the eagle's tail and the upper left of the ribbon, similar to a variety of 1886-O, but from a different reverse die. Such pieces are very scarce, and unknown above MS-61.

	Cert	Avg	%MS	VF-20	EF-40	AU-50	MS-60	MS-63	MS-64
1889-O, Clashed Die	47	38.7	2%	$125	$350	$750	$1,000	—	—

1889-S Morgan Dollar

1889-S • Mintage: 700,000.

Key to Collecting: There are not many
Morgan dollars with a total mintage of less
than a million, and this is one of them.
Examples are desirable in all grades, but
enough exist in Mint State that serious
collectors can be satisfied easily.

Surface Quality: This coin is usually seen fairly well struck, typically with excellent luster.
Many have prooflike surfaces. DMPL specimens usually have good contrast.

	Cert	Avg	%MS	VF-20	EF-40	AU-50	MS-60	MS-63	MS-64	MS-64DMPL	MS-65	MS-65DMPL
1889-S	7,386	60.6	74%	$65	$85	$100	$275	$375	$550	$5,000	$1,350	$32,500

1890 Morgan Dollar

1890 • Mintage: 16,802,000.

Key to Collecting: The 1890 dollar is a very
common coin in Mint State, and circulated
pieces are likewise plentiful. Nearly all are
lightly or even poorly struck and with dull,
unattractive luster. Some show graininess
and metal flow. As is so often the case with
"common dates," most exist in lower Mint State
levels, and for MS-65 and higher grades the supply drops off logarithmically.

Surface Quality: Striking varies from weak to not so weak, but is seldom sharp. The typical 1890 is
average or below average, with flatness over the ear. As a rule of thumb, the luster on the 1890 is rather
dull and often grainy, as the dies seem to have been used for a long time.

Some are prooflike, and are also usually of low contrast. However, some DMPLs exist with cameo
contrast and are worth a premium over the others.

	Cert	Avg	%MS	VF-20	EF-40	AU-50	MS-60	MS-63	MS-64	MS-64DMPL	MS-65	MS-65DMPL
1890	22,308	62.7	97%	$35	$38	$45	$65	$100	$140	$1,750	$750	$15,000

1890, Proof • Mintage: 590.

Key to Collecting: Above-average strikes
are seen on some, flat centers on others, with
medium to low contrast. The workmanship
is better than in 1889, if only slightly.

	Cert	Avg	%MS	PF-60	PF-63	PF-64	PF-65
1890, Proof	240	64.9		$1,300	$3,000	$3,750	$5,500

1890-CC Morgan Dollar

1890-CC • Mintage: 2,309,041.

Key to Collecting: The mintage figure for
the 1890-CC dollar, far and away the largest
in the Carson City series, does not translate
to pieces being common in Mint State today.
Most probably, quantities were placed into
circulation in the 19th century, and perhaps
many bags were melted under the provisions
of the 1918 Pittman Act. By the time the supply on hand in the Treasury Building was checked, in 1964,
there were fewer than 4,000 pieces in sight. Today, many if not most 1890-CC dollars are decently
struck, and most have attractive luster. However, more than just a few are very "baggy." Certification
quantities fall off a cliff past MS-64.

Surface Quality: Striking varies from weak at the centers to fairly sharp, the last being the general rule.
Usually seen with attractive mint luster.

Prooflike coins are seen with frequency, but even a few bagmarks can make such pieces unattractive.
Prooflikes are often lightly struck above the ear.

	Cert	Avg	%MS	VF-20	EF-40	AU-50	MS-60	MS-63	MS-64	MS-64DMPL	MS-65	MS-65DMPL
1890-CC	10,116	53.4	69%	$125	$175	$250	$550	$1,000	$1,250	$3,400	$3,000	$13,750

VARIETY: *1890-CC, Die Gouge, "Tailbar" (FS-S1-1890CC-004, VAM-4).*
A heavy die gouge extends from between the eagle's first tail feather and the
lowest arrow feather to the leaves in the wreath below. From the *Cherrypick-*
ers' Guide to Rare Die Varieties, vol. II (sixth edition): "This is an extremely
popular and highly marketable variety, especially in Mint State." This variety
is nicknamed the "Tailbar."

	Cert	Avg	%MS	VF-20	EF-40	AU-50	MS-60	MS-63	MS-64	MS-65
1890-CC, Die Gouge, "Tailbar"	496	45.3	45%	$250	$400	$800	$1,300	$4,800	$4,500	$27,500

1890-O Morgan Dollar

1890-O • Mintage: 10,701,000.

Key to Collecting: The 1890-O is plentiful
enough in Mint State, "raw" and also in
"slabs," but the majority are lightly struck
in one area or another. Some were struck
from dies that should have been retired, and
flow lines and granularity tell the tale today.
However, enough sharp pieces exist that getting
one will be no problem. MS-65 coins are much more elusive than are MS-64s.

Surface Quality: The typical 1890-O shows areas of light striking in the center. A few sharp pieces exist
but require searching. As always, certification services do not make a distinction, thereby giving the
cherrypicker an advantage. The luster is usually attractive and rich on the 1890-O.

Some dies are prooflike and can be attractive in higher grades. However, among prooflike coins, striking is often soft. Some selected DMPL coins are gorgeous to behold.

	Cert	Avg	%MS	VF-20	EF-40	AU-50	MS-60	MS-63	MS-64	MS-64DMPL	MS-65	MS-65DMPL
1890-O	11,051	62.1	95%	$35	$38	$55	$100	$165	$275	$1,375	$1,100	$8,000

VARIETY: *1890-O, Die Gouges, "Comet" (FS-S1-1890o-010, VAM-10).* Die gouges are evident to the right of the date. This variety is nicknamed the "Comet."

	Cert	Avg	%MS	VF-20	EF-40	AU-50	MS-60	MS-63	MS-64	MS-65
1890-O, Die Gouges, "Comet"	138	61.6	90%	$50	$65	$140	$175	$375	$425	$1,750

1890-S Morgan Dollar

1890-S • **Mintage:** 8,230,373.

Key to Collecting: With the 1890-S, the San Francisco Mint again turned out coins that for the most part are well struck, lustrous, and very attractive, this at a time when workmanship at New Orleans was often downright sloppy. While the 1890-S is by no means a common date, choice and gem examples are well within the reach of most readers of this book.

Surface Quality: Examples are usually seen well struck, and exceptions should not be purchased. The 1890-S is normally encountered with attractive luster. The VAM text mentions that cloudy spots are sometimes seen on the surface, these due to dampness after striking.

Quite a few prooflike coins exist, but not many have the combination of deep mirror quality (DMPL) plus freedom from bagmarks.

	Cert	Avg	%MS	VF-20	EF-40	AU-50	MS-60	MS-63	MS-64	MS-64DMPL	MS-65	MS-65DMPL
1890-S	11,542	62.1	90%	$35	$38	$45	$100	$150	$275	$3,000	$750	$9,500

1891 Morgan Dollar

1891 • **Mintage:** 8,693,556.

Key to Collecting: The 1891 is a high-mintage dollar usually seen in low quality, which translates to opportunity for the buyer.

Surface Quality: The strike is usually average or below, not often sharp. Careful selection is suggested. The luster is often insipid and grainy, not at all attractive. Deeply lustrous, sharply struck pieces require cherrypicking to find.

Prooflike coins are sometimes seen, sometimes lightly struck. Gorgeous DMPL coins exist and are memorable, but the availability of somewhat similar-appearing Proofs probably dampens the market somewhat.

	Cert	Avg	%MS	VF-20	EF-40	AU-50	MS-60	MS-63	MS-64	MS-64DMPL	MS-65	MS-65DMPL
1891	8,783	61.5	90%	$35	$38	$45	$95	$185	$500	$5,000	$2,250	$25,000

1891, Proof • Mintage: 650.

Key to Collecting: Striking can be weak at the centers. Medium cameo contrast is seen. Given the low mintage, the possibility of a weak strike, and so many cleaned and dipped coins on the market, the 1891 Proof adds up to a challenge. However, many have been certified at PF-65 or higher.

	Cert	Avg	%MS	PF-60	PF-63	PF-64	PF-65
1891, Proof	238	64.2		$1,300	$3,000	$3,750	$5,500

1891-CC Morgan Dollar

1891-CC • **Mintage:** 1,618,000.

Key to Collecting: The 1891-CC is a "must have" coin because it is from Carson City and is usually available in Uncirculated state. However, although the mintage figure is generous for a CC dollar, today the coin is not in the "common" class. Still, enough are around, especially MS-63 and 64, that you can find a choice one. Virtually all are lustrous and have superb eye appeal, but not all are sharply struck. Patience is recommended.

Surface Quality: The striking varies from poor to sharp, but is usually average or finer. Cherrypicking is advised, but in this case it will not involve a great deal of effort. The luster is typically deeply frosty and beautiful.

Partially and fully prooflike coins exist, but usually have low contrast in relation to the design features, and, accordingly, the demand for them is not great.

	Cert	Avg	%MS	VF-20	EF-40	AU-50	MS-60	MS-63	MS-64	MS-64DMPL	MS-65	MS-65DMPL
1891-CC	12,770	58.7	81%	$130	$150	$250	$550	$775	$1,200	$4,500	$2,500	$30,000

1891-O Morgan Dollar

1891-O • **Mintage:** 7,954,529.

Key to Collecting: The 1891-O dollar is famous as an example of poor to casual striking sharpness, although some sharp ones can be found. In view of the paucity of MS-65 coins and the high prices (justifiably, if the striking is nice), coins at the MS-63 and 64 levels are recommended. The 1891-O had a bad reputation years ago for being less than lovely, but the advent of slabbing has helped.

Surface Quality: This coin is usually seen weak at the center. Some were made from tired dies and show granularity and flow lines. Some are also weakly struck at the date. A few sharp strikes do exist. Luster usually ranges from satiny to grainy or dull, not deep and frosty.

Quite a few prooflike and partially prooflike coins exist, many of which are well struck (an exception to the general rule for 1891-O). DMPL coins exist, some well struck, others not.

	Cert	Avg	%MS	VF-20	EF-40	AU-50	MS-60	MS-63	MS-64	MS-64DMPL	MS-65	MS-65DMPL
1891-O	5,436	59.7	84%	$35	$38	$45	$250	$450	$675	$7,000	$4,250	$35,000

VARIETY: *1891-O, Clashed Die (FS-S1-1891o-001a, VAM-1A).* The evidence of a clashed die is visible below the eagle's tail feathers and slightly left of the bow, where the E in LIBERTY has been transferred from the obverse die.

	Cert	Avg	%MS	VF-20	EF-40	AU-50	MS-60	MS-63	MS-64
1891-O, Clashed Die	188	35.7	1%	$100	$150	$300	$600	$1,000	—

VARIETY: *1891-O, Pitted Reverse Die (FS-S1-1891o-001b, VAM-1B).* Pitting on the reverse is visible around the ONE and on the bottom of the wreath above and between ONE and DOLLAR. This variety is rare in circulated grades, and unknown in Mint State.

	Cert	Avg	%MS	VF-20	EF-40	AU-50	MS-60	MS-63	MS-64
1891-O, Pitted Reverse Die	10	50.7	0%	$150	$250	$400	$800	—	—

1891-S Morgan Dollar

1891-S • **Mintage:** 5,296,000.

Key to Collecting: The 1891-S is usually seen well struck, lustrous, and with a generous measure of eye appeal—a Morgan dollar as a Morgan dollar should be. Many beautiful MS-63 and 64 coins are on the market, and there are enough in higher grades for those who can afford them, although the prices are reasonable across the board.

Surface Quality: Examples are usually seen well struck, and this is a no-problem issue, with few exceptions. Examples are usually lustrous, but some are spotted due to moisture on the surfaces after striking.

Prooflike coins are sometimes encountered and are attractive. Contrast varies and, as always, bagmarks can be a problem.

	Cert	Avg	%MS	VF-20	EF-40	AU-50	MS-60	MS-63	MS-64	MS-64DMPL	MS-65	MS-65DMPL
1891-S	7,664	62.1	90%	$35	$38	$50	$125	$200	$475	$3,200	$1,000	$18,500

1892 Morgan Dollar

1892 • **Mintage:** 1,036,000.

Key to Collecting: The 1892 Morgan dollar is scarce in Mint State. Most are in lower grade ranges, MS-60 to 62, and poorly struck. Really choice MS-64 and gem MS-65 or finer coins are very hard to find. Proofs exist in proportion to the mintage figure. Among surviving Proofs, many are choice or gem quality.

Surface Quality: Varies from weak to sharp, but usually average to below average. Some hunting is recommended to find a sharp one. Luster varies from dull and poor to lustrous and "flashy."

Semi-prooflike coins are seen on occasion, but gems are very elusive and sharply struck DMPLs are rarer yet.

	Cert	Avg	%MS	VF-20	EF-40	AU-50	MS-60	MS-63	MS-64	MS-64DMPL	MS-65	MS-65DMPL
1892	5,326	59.4	69%	$50	$65	$100	$300	$450	$850	$3,500	$2,300	$18,000

1892, Proof • Mintage: 1,245.

Key to Collecting: Striking is sometimes below average.

	Cert	Avg	%MS	PF-60	PF-63	PF-64	PF-65
1892, Proof	372	64.2		$1,300	$3,000	$3,750	$5,500

1892-CC Morgan Dollar

1892-CC • Mintage: 1,352,000.

Key to Collecting: Although the 1892-CC has a generous mintage figure for a Carson City dollar, survivors from the Treasury hoard were in the tens of thousands, not in the hundreds of thousands, and all but one coin were gone by the time of the General Services Administration sales. Most 1892-CC dollars are well struck and attractive, although there are some exceptions to be avoided. Year in and year out this coin has been in great demand. MS-63 and 64 offer excellent acquisition possibilities, or even higher grades if your budget permits.

Surface Quality: Striking varies from weak to sharp, with most being above average. Examples are usually lustrous and attractive.

Prooflike coins exist but are in the minority. Most of these have excellently mirrored surfaces. DMPLs are seen occasionally and are beautiful if not overly bagmarked.

	Cert	Avg	%MS	VF-20	EF-40	AU-50	MS-60	MS-63	MS-64	MS-64DMPL	MS-65	MS-65DMPL
1892-CC	6,781	53.4	67%	$250	$450	$700	$1,500	$1,950	$2,350	$9,500	$5,500	$36,000

1892-O Morgan Dollar

1892-O • Mintage: 2,744,000.

Key to Collecting: Somewhat similar to the scenario for 1891-O, the 1892-O is usually seen poorly struck and with subpar eye appeal. However, in 1977 a bag of 1,000 coins turned up with many fully struck gem pieces. From this marvelous find may come most of the gems now in collections. Enough

1892-O dollars exist that there are many purchase opportunities for grades such as MS-63 and 64, but careful examination is highly recommended.

Surface Quality: "This is probably the most consistently flat struck date of the entire Morgan series," the VAM text notes, going on to state, "A small number of full strikes exist, however." In terms of shallow definition this is a dandy rival for the 1891-O. Wayne Miller (1982) joined the thumbs-down chorus. Accordingly, cherrypicking is strongly recommended. Luster is often grainy and unattractive.

Prooflike coins are seldom encountered, and when they are, quality is often lacking. All have some flatness of strike.

	Cert	Avg	%MS	VF-20	EF-40	AU-50	MS-60	MS-63	MS-64	MS-64DMPL	MS-65	MS-65DMPL
1892-O	5,863	60.0	81%	$50	$65	$100	$300	$425	$775	$23,500	$2,600	$50,000

1892-S Morgan Dollar

1892-S • **Mintage:** 1,200,000.

Key to Collecting: Years ago, worn 1892-S dollars were common in dealers' stocks, and little attention was paid to them. Then, after the 1962 through 1964 Treasury releases were analyzed, and no cascade of Mint State 1892-S dollars had been found, a great demand arose for circulated pieces to supply the date and mintmark. The few Uncirculated coins that did exist mounted to ever-higher market levels, while more than just a few About Uncirculated pieces were sold as being in Mint State (casting a pall on the market for this rarity). Today, most collectors will opt for an inexpensive Very Fine or an affordable Extremely Fine, the 1892-S often being one of the few Morgan dollars in a set that is not Mint State.

Surface Quality: Examples are usually above average and quite good, and are typically seen with satiny luster or somewhat prooflike.

Among high-grade 1892-S dollars, many are somewhat prooflike (not at all DMPL), perhaps half of the population.

	Cert	Avg	%MS	VF-20	EF-40	AU-50	MS-60	MS-63	MS-64	MS-64DMPL	MS-65	MS-65DMPL
1892-S	4,520	39.3	1%	$150	$275	$1,450	$44,000	$95,000	$175,000		$225,000	

1893 Morgan Dollar

1893 • **Mintage:** 378,000.

Key to Collecting: In Mint State, the dollars of 1893 are elusive in comparison to the demand for them. MS-63 and 64 are worthwhile grades for value. Although many coins are lightly struck, there are quite a few sharp ones. Worn examples are scarce in their own right and offer an economical alternative for anyone not wanting to buy a Mint State coin.

Surface Quality: Circulation-strike examples are usually above average. Proof strikings of the 1893 are usually lightly struck at the centers, "and are the most poorly struck Morgan Proofs," per Van Allen and Mallis. Usually frosty and attractive.

Prooflike coins are elusive and have little contrast.

	Cert	Avg	%MS	VF-20	EF-40	AU-50	MS-60	MS-63	MS-64	MS-64DMPL	MS-65	MS-65DMPL
1893	5,816	50.7	41%	$225	$250	$375	$1,050	$1,500	$2,250	$32,500	$4,250	$67,500

1893, Proof • Mintage: 792.

Key to Collecting: Examples display indifferent striking as a result of poor workmanship—the dies were spaced too far apart. Good cameo contrast is often evident.

	Cert	Avg	%MS	PF-60	PF-63	PF-64	PF-65
1893, Proof	252	64.0		$1,300	$3,000	$3,750	$5,500

1893-CC Morgan Dollar

1893-CC • **Mintage:** 677,000.

Key to Collecting: The 1893-CC is, sadly, the last of the Carson City dollars—ending a romantic numismatic era. Today, surviving pieces are much loved, much desired by numismatists. Mint State 1893-CC dollars are well known for being extensively bagmarked, some actually appearing quite abused. Accordingly, the majority of Mint State pieces are in lower Mint State grades. A piece MS-63 or finer, with minimum bagmarks, is a numismatic find and is very special. Discount poor strikes and "baggy" coins, and you'll find that remaining pieces in the marketplace are few and far between. A really choice 1893-CC in any grade from MS-63 upward will be a find. Many attractive circulated coins exist and for many buyers will neatly fill the 1893-CC space.

Surface Quality: The appearance is average or below average, sometimes the lightness on the reverse not only being at on the eagle's breast (as expected) but also on the extremities of the wings. Luster is often satiny and attractive, although there are exceptions. Excessive bagmarks often negate any appeal luster might have.

Prooflike pieces are elusive and are usually lightly struck at the centers.

	Cert	Avg	%MS	VF-20	EF-40	AU-50	MS-60	MS-63	MS-64	MS-64DMPL	MS-65	MS-65DMPL
1893-CC	4,927	37.8	37%	$625	$1,250	$2,500	$4,500	$6,000	$12,500	$47,500	$90,000	$125,000

1893-CC, Proof • Mintage: 12.

Key to Collecting: The closing of the Carson City Mint in 1893 may have occasioned the striking of a special Proof coin. It is uncertain how many of the 1893-CC Proofs survive. The combined PCGS and NGC certification figures total more than 20, due to recertifications. Experts tend to agree that most of those struck—that is, 10 to 12—survive today. Some numismatists classify these as DMPL circulation strikes, rather than as Proofs.

Four different branch-mint Morgan dollar Proofs are considered to be "Class I," meaning there is documentation confirming the coins were authorized and issued by the Mint. The 1893-CC Proof is one of the four; the other three are the 1879-O and 1883-O Proofs and the 1921-S Zerbe Proof.

	Cert	Avg	%MS	PF-60	PF-63	PF-64	PF-65
1893-CC, Proof	10	63.8				$140,000	$200,000

1893-O Morgan Dollar

1893-O • Mintage: 300,000.

Key to Collecting: If you like a challenge, the 1893-O presents one. Many are peppered with bagmarks. Mint State coins are very elusive in both an absolute and a relative (to the demand) sense. Choice MS-64 coins are rare and MS-65 coins are of sufficient fame that an auction house might showcase one in a news release. Worn 1893-O dollars are fairly scarce, as the low mintage (the smallest figure of any New Orleans Mint dollar of type) might suggest, and are a worthwhile buy for anyone not wanting to pay for a Mint State coin.

Surface Quality: Striking is usually below average, but sometimes sharp on the reverse and, on the same coin, light at the center of the obverse. Searching is required to locate an overall sharp example. Luster often fails to impress, but there are exceptions to be found.

Prooflike coins are seldom encountered, and when they are, quality is often lacking.

	Cert	Avg	%MS	VF-20	EF-40	AU-50	MS-60	MS-63	MS-64	MS-64DMPL	MS-65	MS-65DMPL
1893-O	4,032	40.4	18%	$350	$475	$775	$3,650	$7,000	$16,500	$100,000	$175,000	$275,000

1893-S Morgan Dollar

1893-S • Mintage: 100,000.

Key to Collecting: The 1893-S is the object of great desire in the Morgan dollar series, and is ranked in the *100 Greatest U.S. Coins* (fifth edition). No single issue has greater popularity across the board. The majority of known pieces, into the thousands, are in the single grade category of Very Fine. Not Good or Very Good, not Extremely Fine or About Uncirculated, but Very Fine. Most such pieces circulated in the American West, and for an appropriate but apparently restricted time, to bring them to this grade. Mint State coins exist. However, among the great Treasury release coins of 1962 through 1964, no bag or even small group was found, although many stray pieces were identified, nearly all in the aforementioned Very Fine grade. Many fake 1893-S dollars exist. Absolutely and positively do not buy any "1893-S" dollar that has not been certified by a leading service, and avoid like the plague offerings of uncertified coins "from an old estate" or "from my grandfather's collection" offered on the Internet. While few will be able to afford a Mint State 1893-S, enough attractive Very Fine coins exist that out there somewhere is one just right for you.

Surface Quality: Examples are usually seen well struck, and even worn pieces are apt to have good detail. The luster is usually deep and rich on Mint State specimens, when they can be found. Prooflikes are in the minority.

About half of the known Mint State coins have a degree of prooflike character.

	Cert	Avg	%MS	VF-20	EF-40	AU-50	MS-60	MS-63	MS-64	MS-64DMPL	MS-65	MS-65DMPL
1893-S	3,391	19.5	1%	$5,500	$8,750	$20,000	$170,000	$325,000	$375,000		$600,000	

1894 Morgan Dollar

1894 • Mintage: 110,000.

Key to Collecting: The 1894 is the first true key date in the Philadelphia Mint lineup of Morgan dollars. This year the mintage dropped to just 110,000, or less than a third of 1893, itself a low figure, indeed the smallest circulation-strike figure in the series except for the 1893-S. Examples are elusive in all grades, from well-worn on up. Mint State coins are mostly in lower ranges, through MS-62, then falling off in availability through MS-63, more so for MS-64, and emerging as a rarity in MS-65. Proofs are readily available, and an amazing number are gems. A nice Proof furnishes an alternative for an impossible-to-find, or nearly impossible, gem Mint State coin. Circulated examples are rare as well. Beware of altered or otherwise fraudulent mintmarks.

Surface Quality: This issue is usually above average in striking sharpness. Proofs are usually well struck and very attractive, sometimes white and "creamy," rather than deeply lustrous and flashy.

A few prooflike coins exist, including a handful of DMPLs, and are rare and desirable in high grades.

	Cert	Avg	%MS	VF-20	EF-40	AU-50	MS-60	MS-63	MS-64	MS-64DMPL	MS-65	MS-65DMPL
1894	4,112	45.2	24%	$800	$1,000	$1,250	$3,100	$4,700	$7,500	$65,000	$35,000	

1894, Proof • Mintage: 972.

Key to Collecting: Proof examples are usually well struck with good cameo contrast. These offer a good value.

	Cert	Avg	%MS	PF-60	PF-63	PF-64	PF-65
1894, Proof	365	63.9		$2,500	$3,500	$4,750	$6,500

1894-O Morgan Dollar

1894-O • **Mintage:** 1,723,000.

Key to Collecting: Mint State examples of the 1894-O dollar are often wretched in appearance. A great deal of searching will be needed to find an example that is decent or above average (but not sharp) in striking details and with attractive luster—a cherrypicker's challenge and delight. Probably the best way is to view coins certified as MS-63 and 64, with patience, and see what happens. The luster is often nice on higher-grade pieces.

Surface Quality: The strike is usually below average. Diligent searching is needed to ferret out a piece with excellent detail. Luster is typically satiny and attractive on higher-grade pieces (which are elusive), dull on lower-grade ones.

Prooflike coins are elusive, and when encountered are apt to be of low contrast, bagmarked, and unattractive.

	Cert	Avg	%MS	VF-20	EF-40	AU-50	MS-60	MS-63	MS-64	MS-64DMPL	MS-65	MS-65DMPL
1894-O	5,705	49.9	19%	$65	$100	$175	$1,550	$4,000	$7,500	$29,000	$50,000	$65,000

1894-S Morgan Dollar

1894-S • **Mintage:** 1,260,000.

Key to Collecting: The 1894-S dollar is a numismatic delight. Most are well struck, lustrous, and pleasing to the eye. In MS-63 and MS-64 grades, examples will fit well into a high-quality collection. MS-65 coins are difficult to find and justifiably more expensive.

Surface Quality: The 1894-S is usually seen well struck, the only date and mintmark of this year for which this can be said. Examples typically have excellent luster. Some have distracting die-polishing lines in the field, consisting of minute raised lines that to the uninitiated can make a coin appear as if it has been cleaned.

Prooflike pieces are scarce, but Van Allen and Mallis say that they are more readily available than the other prooflike issues of the year span 1893 to 1895.

	Cert	Avg	%MS	VF-20	EF-40	AU-50	MS-60	MS-63	MS-64	MS-64DMPL	MS-65	MS-65DMPL
1894-S	3,778	54.4	59%	$100	$185	$475	$850	$1,400	$2,300	$22,000	$4,700	$35,000

1895 Morgan Dollar

1895, Proof • **Mintage:** 880.

Key to Collecting: In 1895, at the Philadelphia Mint, there was no coinage of silver dollars for circulation. (Mint records indicate that 12,000 Morgan dollars of 1895 were struck for circulation; however, none have ever been seen.) Striking was limited to Proofs, of which only 880 were made. Early in

1896, when samples of the previous year's precious metal coinage were submitted to the Assay Commission for review, the dollar was represented by a single Proof. Today, most of the Proofs remain and are cherished by numismatists, and the coin is ranked in the *100 Greatest U.S. Coins* (fifth edition). With the low production figure, the 1895 is far and away the rarest date in the series. In order to complete their collections, date-by-date collectors are forced to acquire one of the 880 Proofs struck that year, causing much competition for this, "The King of the Morgan Dollars."

As to their appearance, Proof 1895 dollars are well struck. The contrast between the devices and the mirrored fields is medium, sort of satiny on the high spots, not deep cameo. As might be expected, the majority of these and other Proof Morgan dollars have been dipped or cleaned, although quite a few have remained in grades of PF-65 or finer. Excellent strike with good contrast is the rule.

	Cert	Avg	%MS	PF-60	PF-63	PF-64	PF-65
1895, Proof	377	61.6		$45,000	$50,000	$60,000	$75,000

1895-O Morgan Dollar

1895-O • **Mintage:** 450,000.

Key to Collecting: The 1895-O is often seen in circulated grades, and among higher-level pieces, About Uncirculated examples are encountered with frequency. There are many high Extremely Fine and About Uncirculated coins around, indicating that many 1895-O dollars must have been in circulation for only a short time, "Mint State" coins do exist, including some that should be designated About Uncirculated. To obtain a decent one, look at the MS-63 grade, at least, and be prepared to spend a lot of money. No matter the grade, most are casually if not lightly struck and have dull, insipid luster. The 1895-O emerged as the single circulation-strike variety that is not known to have been a part of any Treasury releases via bags.

Surface Quality: Striking is usually below average to average, not often sharp. Cherrypicking is encouraged, not easy to do with 1895-O as Mint State pieces are quite elusive. High-grade pieces usually show attractive, satiny luster.

Among Mint State coins, many are prooflike or partially so, with decent contrast.

	Cert	Avg	%MS	VF-20	EF-40	AU-50	MS-60	MS-63	MS-64	MS-64DMPL	MS-65	MS-65DMPL
1895-O	6,461	38.3	2%	$325	$450	$1,100	$16,000	$52,500	$90,000	$140,000	$210,000	

1895-O, Proof • **Mintage:** 880.

Key to Collecting: As recently as the mid-1990s, no branch-mint Proof from New Orleans was known for 1895. Today at least five have been certified. Some numismatists classify these as DMPL circulation strikes, rather than as Proofs, and indeed the 1895-O—like other branch-mint Proofs—were clearly struck from known circulation dies, but with exceptional care.

	Cert	Avg	%MS	PF-60	PF-63	PF-64	PF-65
1895-O, Proof	3	64.7				—	

1895-S Morgan Dollar

1895-S • **Mintage:** 400,000.

Key to Collecting: Mint State 1895-S dollars are well known for being extensively bagmarked, some actually appearing quite abused. Accordingly, the majority of Mint State pieces are in lower Mint State grades. A piece MS-63 or finer, with minimum bagmarks, is a numismatic find and is very special. Circulated specimens are elusive, as the mintage might indicate, but an attractive example can be a reasonable financial as well as aesthetic alternative to a baggy MS-60.

Surface Quality: The strike is typically excellent. Rich luster is seen on high-grade specimens.

Prooflike coins exist and are desirable if in high grades, but the contrast is not strong.

	Cert	Avg	%MS	VF-20	EF-40	AU-50	MS-60	MS-63	MS-64	MS-64DMPL	MS-65	MS-65DMPL
1895-S	3,492	34.5	23%	$575	$950	$1,650	$4,500	$6,500	$8,250	$18,000	$20,000	$40,000

1896 Morgan Dollar

1896 • **Mintage:** 9,976,000.

Key to Collecting: The 1896 is the first Philadelphia Mint dollar of the 1890s to be common in Mint State. Examples abound, including choice MS-63 and 64 pieces as well as gem MS-65 or finer. Luster varies but is usually above average.

Surface Quality: The strike is typically above average. The luster ranges from satiny to frosty. Some cherrypicking is advised to find one with deep luster.

Prooflike pieces are seen with some occasion but are usually not with deep contrast.

	Cert	Avg	%MS	VF-20	EF-40	AU-50	MS-60	MS-63	MS-64	MS-64DMPL	MS-65	MS-65DMPL
1896	64,540	63.4	98%	$35	$38	$45	$60	$80	$115	$450	$195	$1,000

1896, Proof • **Mintage:** 762.

Key to Collecting: Good strike and deep cameo contrast are frequently seen—the years of weak striking, beginning in 1888, appear to be in the past.

	Cert	Avg	%MS	PF-60	PF-63	PF-64	PF-65
1896, Proof	288	64.8		$1,300	$3,000	$3,750	$5,500

1896-O Morgan Dollar

1896-O • **Mintage:** 4,900,000.

Key to Collecting: The 1896-O is a marvelous coin for study. "No other Morgan dollar is as consistently deficient in luster, strike, and degree of surface abrasions as the 1896-O," Wayne Miller wrote. "In my opinion the 1896-O is the rarest of all Morgan dollars (even more than 1901) in truly gem condition." Of course, those who are edged out of buying a gem Mint State 1901 can wink twice and buy a Proof quickly, but the collector seeking an 1896-O has no such fallback possibility. Most of the mintage must have been released into circulation, as well-worn coins are common today and worth little premium. On the other hand, About Uncirculated coins, of which there are thousands around, do have value and are a reasonable option for an example of this date, in view of the paucity of choice higher-grade pieces.

Surface Quality: Striking is usually below average, insipid, and unattractive. This will be a problem and a challenge, as very few exceptions can be found. The luster is typically dull and lifeless. Again, cherry-icking is needed, in combination with strike, making the challenge even greater.

Prooflike examples occur and are very rare, even well struck, but with dullish surfaces rendering most of them unattractive.

	Cert	Avg	%MS	VF-20	EF-40	AU-50	MS-60	MS-63	MS-64	MS-64DMPL	MS-65	MS-65DMPL
1896-O	7,343	53.8	19%	$42	$45	$125	$1,700	$4,500	$34,000	$60,000	$160,000	

1896-S Morgan Dollar

1896-S • **Mintage:** 5,000,000.

Key to Collecting: Although the mintage of 5,000,000 would suggest plenitude in the numismatic market today, such is not the case. Years ago the 1896-S was a key issue in all grades, and today, despite some turned loose in the Treasury releases, the 1896-S is still high on the most-wanted list. Striking varies, but is usually soft. Luster is average or somewhat shallow, not deeply frosty. Bagmarks are a problem. Accordingly, connoisseurship is needed to find a just-right example, an exception to the general rule that San Francisco Mint coins offer few problems. Mint State coins, especially MS-64 or higher grades, are rare. Circulated examples are scarce, but not rare. Likely, most of this generous issue went to the melting pot.

Surface Quality: Strike is usually average or a bit below, but sharp pieces can be found with searching. Examples are usually somewhat subdued, unlike most other San Francisco Mint dollars of the era.

Prooflike strikes are rare but win no awards for beauty. This feature was caused by the basining process, and many raised die-swirl lines are usually seen.

	Cert	Avg	%MS	VF-20	EF-40	AU-50	MS-60	MS-63	MS-64	MS-64DMPL	MS-65	MS-65DMPL
1896-S	2,052	46.3	37%	$75	$250	$875	$2,600	$3,750	$4,500	$57,500	$9,500	$100,000

1897 Morgan Dollar

1897 • Mintage: 2,822,000.

Key to Collecting: The 1897 Morgan dollar in Mint State is usually well struck and has nice luster, the paradigm of a common date. About Uncirculated coins can be very lustrous and attractive, and years ago many were sold as "slider Uncirculated" or, curiously, as "commercial Uncirculated." Bagmarks, while not endemic among 1897 dollars, can be unsightly on lower-grade Mint State pieces. What is available or even common in a later era of Morgan dollar collecting could have been rare earlier. Such is the case with 1897, examples of which were hardly ever seen in circulation as late as 1925, a quarter century after their release.

Surface Quality: Usually the strike is above average, with lustrous and frosty surfaces.
  Prooflike coins are seen, but are only a fraction of the overall population.

	Cert	Avg	%MS	VF-20	EF-40	AU-50	MS-60	MS-63	MS-64	MS-64DMPL	MS-65	MS-65DMPL
1897	20,790	63.3	97%	$35	$38	$45	$60	$80	$115	$550	$250	$2,500

1897, Proof • **Mintage:** 731.

Key to Collecting: Examples are well struck with deep cameo contrast.

	Cert	Avg	%MS	PF-60	PF-63	PF-64	PF-65
1897, Proof	224	64.4		$1,300	$3,000	$3,750	$5,500

1897-O Morgan Dollar

1897-O • Mintage: 4,004,000.

Key to Collecting: The 1897-O is a cherrypicker's dream. Most are poorly or lightly struck, and on most the luster is below par as well. However, there are exceptions. While others buy certified coins of mediocre quality, the patient collector can track down a nice one—say, a hand-picked MS-63. A choice MS-64 or a gem MS-65 is expensive, and not easily ordered just anywhere. The 1897-O is not a key date and not much attention is paid to it by the average collector.

Surface Quality: Strike ranges from poor to below average, not a good sign, but enough sharp pieces exist that with searching one can be found. The luster on 1897-O usually is dull and lifeless, mounting a challenge to be combined with searching for a sharp strike.
  Prooflike coins are rare, and when seen are usually extensively bagmarked.

	Cert	Avg	%MS	VF-20	EF-40	AU-50	MS-60	MS-63	MS-64	MS-64DMPL	MS-65	MS-65DMPL
1897-O	7,261	55.0	22%	$35	$55	$95	$1,200	$4,000	$11,000	$37,500	$60,000	$75,000

1897-S Morgan Dollar

1897-S • Mintage: 5,825,000.

Key to Collecting: the 1897-S is a really top-notch dollar in terms of availability, strike, luster, and all else good. One can be had on just about any budget. The entire situation of 1897-S is reminiscent of the memorable-quality, but inexpensive, S-Mint coins of the early years of the series.

Surface Quality: Examples are usually seen well struck, with decent strikes being the rule, not the exception, for San Francisco coins of this era—in contrast to those of New Orleans. Surfaces are usually lustrous and attractive.

Prooflike coins are fairly plentiful, but are often lightly struck and with little eye appeal. However, sharp and attractive coins can be found here and there.

	Cert	Avg	%MS	VF-20	EF-40	AU-50	MS-60	MS-63	MS-64	MS-64DMPL	MS-65	MS-65DMPL
1897-S	9,632	62.6	91%	$35	$38	$55	$100	$175	$250	$1,100	$500	$2,500

1898 Morgan Dollar

1898 • Mintage: 5,884,000.

Key to Collecting: The 1898 Morgan dollar is plentiful in any and all grades, from worn (though usually in Very Fine or Extremely Fine, toned gray) to gem Mint State. Most are well struck and have good luster. Many Proofs exist in remarkably high grades. Perhaps due to the semi-moribund state of the coin hobby at the time, not as many people were cleaning coins.

Surface Quality: Examples are usually well struck with attractive mint frost.

Many prooflike coins exist, one sided as well as two sided, but are not deeply mirrored. DMPL coins with cameo contrast are rare indeed.

	Cert	Avg	%MS	VF-20	EF-40	AU-50	MS-60	MS-63	MS-64	MS-64DMPL	MS-65	MS-65DMPL
1898	26,357	63.4	98%	$35	$38	$45	$60	$80	$115	$450	$225	$1,250

1898, Proof • **Mintage:** 735.

Key to Collecting: Proofs typically have nice cameo contrast, and in recent years the certification services have been noting such on their labels. In addition, they are well struck. Michael Fuljenz believes the 1898 was likely the best made in the entire series.

	Cert	Avg	%MS	PF-60	PF-63	PF-64	PF-65
1898, Proof	261	64.7		$1,300	$3,000	$3,750	$5,500

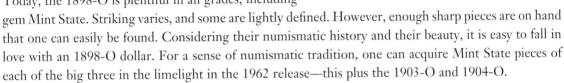

1898-O Morgan Dollar

1898-O • **Mintage:** 4,440,000.

Key to Collecting: The 1898-O is the first of the "big three" rarities released from a long-sealed vault in November 1962 to ignite the great Treasury-release treasure hunt. Previously, in Mint State the 1898-O was a rarity. Today, the 1898-O is plentiful in all grades, including gem Mint State. Striking varies, and some are lightly defined. However, enough sharp pieces are on hand that one can easily be found. Considering their numismatic history and their beauty, it is easy to fall in love with an 1898-O dollar. For a sense of numismatic tradition, one can acquire Mint State pieces of each of the big three in the limelight in the 1962 release—this plus the 1903-O and 1904-O.

Surface Quality: Striking of the 1898-O ranges from poor to sharp, but is usually above average. Surfaces are usually lustrous and attractive. Prooflike pieces are seen on occasion.

Prooflike coins range from "semi" to full and are not rare. DMPL coins with good cameo contrast are also fairly plentiful and are popular, but become harder to find as the years slip by.

	Cert	Avg	%MS	VF-20	EF-40	AU-50	MS-60	MS-63	MS-64	MS-64DMPL	MS-65	MS-65DMPL
1898-O	81,828	63.9	100%	$35	$38	$45	$60	$80	$115	$500	$200	$1,150

1898-S Morgan Dollar

1898-S • **Mintage:** 4,102,000.

Key to Collecting: The 1898-S is sometimes seen softly struck, so some searching is needed to find a choice one. Luster is subtle, even satiny. There are enough 1898-S dollars around that an MS-63 is easily enough found, and an MS-64 coin is within reach. Gem MS-65 and higher pieces are in the minority, but are not rarities.

Surface Quality: Examples are usually well struck, but there are exceptions. As always, a good eye helps form a good collection. Surfaces are typically lustrous and attractive.

Some are prooflike, but they usually have low contrast.

	Cert	Avg	%MS	VF-20	EF-40	AU-50	MS-60	MS-63	MS-64	MS-64DMPL	MS-65	MS-65DMPL
1898-S	3,865	58.9	63%	$45	$50	$95	$295	$600	$775	$3,250	$1,400	$15,000

1899 Morgan Dollar

1899 • **Mintage:** 330,000.

Key to Collecting: Despite its low mintage, the 1899 Morgan dollar is rather plentiful on the market, causing several well-known authorities to doubt the mintage total. Circulated coins are scarce, but the demand for them is muted by the wide availability of Mint State coins. Apparently, few 1899 Morgan dollars were released into circulation at that time, for years later in 1925 a serious specialist could not find one, despite a lot of searching through quantities of dollar coins.

Surface Quality: The striking varies from below average to sharp, usually average or above. The luster is usually satiny and attractive.

Prooflike coins are in the distinct minority, and when seen they usually have low contrast.

	Cert	Avg	%MS	VF-20	EF-40	AU-50	MS-60	MS-63	MS-64	MS-64DMPL	MS-65	MS-65DMPL
1899	11,642	61.0	86%	$175	$185	$195	$275	$300	$350	$1,350	$700	$2,600

1899, Proof • Mintage: 846.

Key to Collecting: Proof dollars of 1899 are fairly good contrast but not as "cameo" as certain immediately preceding years. There is no universally accepted definition of *cameo* in the trade, and opinions vary, as do labels affixed to holders.

	Cert	Avg	%MS	PF-60	PF-63	PF-64	PF-65
1899, Proof	232	64.1		$1,300	$3,000	$3,750	$5,500

1899-O Morgan Dollar

1899-O • **Mintage:** 12,290,000.

Key to Collecting: The 1899-O was another star in the great Treasury release of autumn 1962, but not of the fame of the 1898-O, 1903-O, and 1904-O, those three being acknowledged as rarities before the deluge. Although the striking quality varies, sharp pieces can be found without much problem among the large numbers on the market. The usual 1899-O is sparkling and beautiful to behold.

Surface Quality: Striking varies from below average to sharp, but is generally above average. Still, discrimination is advised when buying a specimen. Most 1899-O dollars are lustrous and attractive.

Prooflike coins are scarce. DMPLs with cameo contrast can be of stunning beauty in high grades.

	Cert	Avg	%MS	VF-20	EF-40	AU-50	MS-60	MS-63	MS-64	MS-64DMPL	MS-65	MS-65DMPL
1899-O	65,947	63.3	98%	$35	$38	$45	$60	$80	$115	$600	$200	$1,500

VARIETY: *1899-O, Micro O Mintmark (FS-S1-1899o-501; VAM-4, 5, 6, 31, and 32).* The O mintmark is smaller than normal; its punch was probably intended for a Barber half dollar. Five different dies are known, all scarce. Although some Mint State coins exist, they sell for a sharp premium if identified. MS-65 coins have sold for more than $20,000.

	Cert	Avg	%MS	VF-20	EF-40	AU-50	MS-60	MS-63	MS-64	MS-64DMPL	MS-65	MS-65DMPL
1899-O, Micro O	480	38.4	3%	$100	$200	$450	$3,000	$15,000	$30,000		$35,000	

1899-S Morgan Dollar

1899-S • **Mintage:** 2,562,000.

Key to Collecting: The 1899-S is of medium scarcity. The typical Mint State coin is well struck and has excellent luster. Bagmarks are slight and not a problem with most 1899-S dollars, a pleasant aspect. Most coins in the MS-63 to 65 range are attractive indeed. Circulated coins, while not among the commonest, attract little market interest.

Surface Quality: Usually seen quite well struck. Finding an example will be no problem at all. Usually with rich, frosty luster.

Often seen prooflike, but not with high contrast.

	Cert	Avg	%MS	VF-20	EF-40	AU-50	MS-60	MS-63	MS-64	MS-64DMPL	MS-65	MS-65DMPL
1899-S	3,496	59.4	71%	$55	$75	$100	$425	$625	$775	$4,000	$1,850	$20,000

1900 Morgan Dollar

1900 • **Mintage:** 8,830,000.

Key to Collecting: A new reverse hub was introduced this year. Coins struck from dies made from this hub have less definition to the eagle's breast feathers, introducing another aspect into grading techniques—as now a coin can be a full strike but lack full feathers. However, some old reverse dies continued in use in the next several years, alongside the new ones. Dollars of the 1900 date range from well struck to poorly defined, and from lustrous and frosty to dull and insipid. They are common enough, and although some discrimination is needed when buying, opportunities will abound.

Surface Quality: Striking is usually below average. Sharp pieces can be found but require some searching. Luster varies from dull and unattractive to somewhat pleasing. Again, cherrypicking is advised. More than just a few have raised die striae (tiny parallel raised lines) in the fields, from the basining process, probably using too large a grit size.

Occasionally prooflike pieces are seen, but the contrast is not sharp.

	Cert	Avg	%MS	VF-20	EF-40	AU-50	MS-60	MS-63	MS-64	MS-64DMPL	MS-65	MS-65DMPL
1900	38,168	63.5	98%	$35	$38	$45	$60	$80	$115	$18,000	$200	$50,000

1900, Proof • **Mintage:** 912.

Key to Collecting: Examples usually display a decent strike. Contrast varies from average to cameo. Most are cameos, and, increasingly, many are being certified as such.

	Cert	Avg	%MS	PF-60	PF-63	PF-64	PF-65
1900, Proof	285	64.3		$1,300	$3,000	$3,750	$5,500

1900-O Morgan Dollar

1900-O • Mintage: 11,390,000 estimated.

Key to Collecting: 1900-O dollars are plentiful in Mint State. However, the striking quality can vary widely, and it will pay to do some picking and choosing. The luster is usually excellent, but quite a few have prominent planchet striations—from the drawing-bench process before planchets were punched out. Avoid these.

Surface Quality: The strike varies from weak to quite sharp, but enough sharp pieces exist that the search will not be long. All New Orleans dollars this year are from the old-style die with well-defined breast feathers (which may or may not be sharply struck on a given coin). The mint luster is typically frosty and attractive.

Prooflike coins are for the most part unattractive, and deeply prooflike coins are rare. Many have raised die swirls from the basining process. Few have cameo contrast.

	Cert	Avg	%MS	VF-20	EF-40	AU-50	MS-60	MS-63	MS-64	MS-64DMPL	MS-65	MS-65DMPL
1900-O	50,745	63.5	99%	$35	$38	$45	$60	$80	$115	$1,100	$200	$5,000

VARIETY: *1900-O, Obverse Die Crack (FS-S1-1900o-029a, VAM-29A).* A die break is visible from the rim through the date to just below the lower point of the bust. This variety is very rare in Mint State.

	Cert	Avg	%MS	VF-20	EF-40	AU-50	MS-60	MS-63	MS-64
1900-O, Obverse Die Crack	76	28.7	5%	$130	$250	$400	$1,000	—	—

1900-O, O Over CC •

FS-S1-1900o-501.

Mintage: 1,200,000 estimated.

Key to Collecting: The 1900-O, O Over CC, is one of the more fascinating varieties in the series. Most are decently struck and have good luster. Even though the variety had been known since the 1920s, there was little demand for it, and thus the market premium was small. Then came a greatly expanded interest in Morgan dollars, along with reference guides and listings in the *Red Book*, and, in time, this became a "must have" variety. FS-S1-1900o-501, VAM: various.

Detail of the Overmintmark.

Surface Quality: The strike is usually average, but sharp ones can be found. The sharpness of the under-CC depends more on the die and its state (period of its use, sharper on earlier impressions, less distinct on later ones) than on striking. The luster is good, indeed usually excellent.

Although some have prooflike surface, no DMPL pieces have been reported.

	Cert	Avg	%MS	VF-20	EF-40	AU-50	MS-60	MS-63	MS-64	MS-64DMPL	MS-65	MS-65DMPL
1900-O, O Over CC	3,753	58.6	79%	$100	$150	$215	$350	$750	$1,050		$1,850	

1900-S Morgan Dollar

1900-S • **Mintage:** 3,540,000.

Key to Collecting: The 1900-S dollar is readily available in Mint State, although it is hardly a common date. Most are very lustrous. Actual striking sharpness ranges from flat to quite good, but perceived sharpness is affected on this and many other dollars from now through 1904, from the use of the new hub with lightly defined breast feathers.

Surface Quality: The strike varies from weak to sharp, with most being above average. The element of new hub use now needs to be factored into evaluating die sharpness versus striking sharpness, this general rule holding for coins of the next several years from the three mints. The luster is usually frosty and rich.

Prooflike pieces are occasionally seen and have low contrast.

	Cert	Avg	%MS	VF-20	EF-40	AU-50	MS-60	MS-63	MS-64	MS-64DMPL	MS-65	MS-65DMPL
1900-S	4,499	60.2	72%	$50	$65	$100	$300	$500	$625	$19,000	$1,250	$30,000

1901 Morgan Dollar

1901 • **Mintage:** 6,962,000.

Key to Collecting: Among circulation-strike coins in the Morgan series, the 1901 is second only to the 1896-O in terms of absolute rarity at the gem level. Among 1901 dollars, lower-grade Mint State coins exist with some frequency. Circulated coins are as common as can be and are worth only a slight premium. Proofs beckon to fill the void created by the paucity of top-grade circulation strikes. Beware of a fraudulently removed mintmark intended to make a less valuable 1901-O or 1901-S appear to be a 1901 dollar.

Surface Quality: The year 1901 was transitional, and coins from the earlier-style hub, called the C3 reverse by Van Allen and Mallis, are typically decently struck, although there are exceptions. The later pieces with the C4 are usually lightly struck. Numismatists seeking but a single 1901—and here, indeed, is a rarity in Mint State—would do well to go with the earlier, sharply struck variety.

Prooflike coins are very rare. No DMPL coins have been reported at the MS-65 level.

	Cert	Avg	%MS	VF-20	EF-40	AU-50	MS-60	MS-63	MS-64	MS-64DMPL	MS-65	MS-65DMPL
1901	5,528	53.0	14%	$65	$100	$225	$3,500	$9,000	$55,000		$350,000	

VARIETY: *1901, Doubled Die Reverse, "Shifted Eagle (FS-S1-1901-003, VAM-3).* Doubling is visible on the eagle's tail feathers, and also on IN GOD WE TRUST, as well as on the arrows, wreath, and bow. This variety, nicknamed the "Shifted Eagle," is very rare in Mint State.

	Cert	Avg	%MS	VF-20	EF-40	AU-50	MS-60	MS-63
1901, Doubled Die Reverse	130	41.1	2%	$200	$1,250	$2,000	$12,000	$40,000

1901, Proof • **Mintage:** 813.

Key to Collecting: Strike is usually good. Some from the new hub over the old one show slight doubling. Contrast is medium cameo, not deeply frosty.

	Cert	Avg	%MS	PF-60	PF-63	PF-64	PF-65
1901, Proof	287	63.7		$1,600	$3,000	$3,750	$5,500

1901-O Morgan Dollar

1901-O • **Mintage:** 13,320,000.

Key to Collecting: The 1901-O dollar is typical for a New Orleans product—quality varies all over the place. The issue was released in immense quantities in the early 1960s, giving the collector ample opportunity to choose.

Surface Quality: Most are below average or average, with sharp pieces being the distinct minority. However, with some searching a decent strike can be found. The luster is generally satiny and quite attractive.

Prooflike coins are known and do not have great contrast.

	Cert	Avg	%MS	VF-20	EF-40	AU-50	MS-60	MS-63	MS-64	MS-64DMPL	MS-65	MS-65DMPL
1901-O	43,527	63.6	99%	$45	$50	$55	$60	$80	$115	$1,350	$200	$8,500

1901-S Morgan Dollar

1901-S • **Mintage:** 2,284,000.

Key to Collecting: The 1901-S is quite scarce in the context of the series, the most elusive San Francisco Mint dollar since 1896, although it is hardly as rare as the 1896-S. Striking varies from poor to quite good, but the luster is usually satisfactory. MS-63 and 64 coins, if carefully selected,

offer good values on the market. MS-65 coins are, of course, nicer yet, but the price is substantially more—due to true rarity and also from demand by investors who have been conditioned to believe that "investment grade" begins at MS-65 (but who are often clueless on matters of striking and luster). There is a reflected glory on the 1901-S in that, in other silver series, especially the 1901-S Barber quarter, this is a key date.

Surface Quality: Examples are usually lightly struck or of medium sharpness, and seldom well detailed. Weak pieces often show parallel planchet striations from the drawing-bench process, these often on the face of Miss Liberty. Those from the new hub reverse are usually struck better than those from the old hub—the opposite of what might be expected. The luster is usually satisfactory.

Some prooflikes exist but the fields are not sharply contrasted with the designs.

	Cert	Avg	%MS	VF-20	EF-40	AU-50	MS-60	MS-63	MS-64	MS-64DMPL	MS-65	MS-65DMPL
1901-S	3,045	57.8	65%	$50	$70	$200	$475	$850	$1,250	$21,000	$2,150	$25,000

1902 Morgan Dollar

1902 • **Mintage:** 7,994,000.

Key to Collecting: The 1902 Philadelphia Mint dollar, while not in the common-date category, is still quite plentiful. Striking is apt to be indifferent or downright poor, but fairly sharp examples exist. Luster is subdued and satiny, not at all deeply frosty, probably due as much to die preparation procedures as to striking.

Surface Quality: The strike is usually above average, but as all are from the new hub, the feather detail is not what it was in the years prior to 1900. The luster can be satiny or somewhat dull, not deeply frosty.

Some prooflikes exist but are of low contrast.

	Cert	Avg	%MS	VF-20	EF-40	AU-50	MS-60	MS-63	MS-64	MS-64DMPL	MS-65	MS-65DMPL
1902	6,979	62.8	94%	$45	$55	$65	$100	$210	$250	$13,000	$350	$17,500

1902, Proof • **Mintage:** 777.

Key to Collecting: The strike is usually average at best, but some employee, perhaps new on the job, decided this year to polish the portraits on the various Proof dies, and to really polish them in 1903—doing away with cameo contrast.

	Cert	Avg	%MS	PF-60	PF-63	PF-64	PF-65
1902, Proof	239	64.2		$1,300	$3,000	$3,750	$5,500

1902-O Morgan Dollar

1902-O • **Mintage:** 8,636,000.

Key to Collecting: Some Mint State pieces are lustrous and attractive, but there is no reason to alter what Wayne Miller wrote in 1982: "Typically among the poorest struck of the late New Orleans dollars. Most are flatly struck with horrible luster." Cherrypicking can be done to great advantage. The 1902-O came out of the floodgates during the great Treasury release of November 1962 and later, and virtually countless pieces are in the marketplace.

Surface Quality: Generally the 1902-O is lightly struck at the centers. Some concentrated effort is needed to find sharp pieces, but, again, the advantage is that certification services take no notice, and such can be had for the finding. Some Mint State piece are lustrous and attractive, but most are not.

Some prooflikes exist but are not of high contrast, although there are exceptions.

	Cert	Avg	%MS	VF-20	EF-40	AU-50	MS-60	MS-63	MS-64	MS-64DMPL	MS-65	MS-65DMPL
1902-O	78,879	63.6	100%	$40	$45	$50	$55	$80	$115	$2,800	$200	$14,500

1902-S Morgan Dollar

1902-S • **Mintage:** 1,530,000.

Key to Collecting: The 1902-S is plentiful enough in Mint State to give the collector plenty to choose from, but most are lightly struck, and some also have parallel die striations located on Miss Liberty's face. Luster is usually satiny, sometimes dull, and nearly always without much life. Most from the Treasury releases are in grades MS-60 to 62, often baggy, sometimes MS-63, but not often MS-64 or finer.

Surface Quality: Examples are typically shallowly struck or of medium sharpness, seldom sharp. One can examine several hundred pieces and not find a single sharp specimen. Cherrypicking is the order of the day, and will take extensive effort. The luster of the 1902-S is typically quite good, somewhat satiny.

Some dies are prooflike but have little contrast. DMPL coins are very rare, are known only in low grades, and win no awards or even favorable mentions for eye appeal.

	Cert	Avg	%MS	VF-20	EF-40	AU-50	MS-60	MS-63	MS-64	MS-64DMPL	MS-65	MS-65DMPL
1902-S	4,013	56.7	67%	$150	$200	$250	$350	$650	$775	$8,000	$1,750	$14,000

1903 Morgan Dollar

1903 • **Mintage:** 4,652,000.

Key to Collecting: The 1903 Philadelphia Mint silver dollars were well made, with nice striking quality and bright luster, although more with a satiny sheen, sort of "greasy" (but attractive), than with a deep frost. Many choice and gem coins are in the marketplace.

Surface Quality: The 1903 dollars are usually fairly well struck, but there are exceptions. Surfaces are satiny and brilliant, but not deeply frosty. Raised die striae are seen on many coins, from the die-preparation process.

Prooflike pieces are seen at widely scattered intervals and do not have high contrast.

	Cert	Avg	%MS	VF-20	EF-40	AU-50	MS-60	MS-63	MS-64	MS-64DMPL	MS-65	MS-65DMPL
1903	14,708	63.3	95%	$50	$60	$65	$85	$115	$150	$7,500	$225	$22,500

1903, Proof • **Mintage:** 755.

Key to Collecting: Medium to subpar striking is the norm, plus no cameo contrast. The portraits and certain other recessed parts of the die were polished—what student of the series Michael Fuljenz calls "the chrome look."

	Cert	Avg	%MS	PF-60	PF-63	PF-64	PF-65
1903, Proof	269	64.1		$1,300	$3,000	$3,750	$5,500

1903-O Morgan Dollar

1903-O • **Mintage:** 4,450,000.

Key to Collecting: By 1962 the 1903-O was viewed as being the great rarity among Mint State Morgan dollars, valued at 10 times the price of an 1889-CC. No matter; even at the $1,500 listing none were available. Then in November 1962 a storage vault in the Philadelphia Mint, sealed since 1929, was opened to gain access to some dollars for holiday distribution. They turned out to be mint-fresh 1903-O issues—hundreds of thousands of them. The numismatic world has not been the same since. Today, there are many 1903-O dollars around, usually well struck and nearly always with brilliance and luster.

Surface Quality: Examples are usually fairly well struck, and are typically brilliant and lustrous.

Some prooflike pieces exist, are of light contrast, and are fairly elusive.

	Cert	Avg	%MS	VF-20	EF-40	AU-50	MS-60	MS-63	MS-64	MS-64DMPL	MS-65	MS-65DMPL
1903-O	9,050	62.8	98%	$410	$420	$430	$475	$500	$525	$1,800	$700	$6,000

1903-S Morgan Dollar

1903-S • **Mintage:** 1,241,000.

Key to Collecting: The 1903-S remains a rare issue in the Morgan dollar series, and Mint State coins are desirable at all levels. Most are well struck and very attractive, and bagmarks are often minimal. If you can afford it, an MS-63 coin, hand-picked for quality, is well worth owning. For many collectors the 1903-S will be one of those varieties for which a nice Very Fine or Extremely Fine coin is acquired, requiring some effort to find one of nice quality.

Surface Quality: Examples are usually well struck, lustrous, and attractive.

Prooflike coins are hardly ever seen, and on those blue-moon occasions it will be noticed that contrast is low.

	Cert	Avg	%MS	VF-20	EF-40	AU-50	MS-60	MS-63	MS-64	MS-64DMPL	MS-65	MS-65DMPL
1903-S	3,251	31.9	9%	$225	$350	$1,650	$5,250	$7,500	$8,250	$18,000	$11,000	

VARIETY: *1903-S, Small S Mintmark (FS-S1-1903S-002, VAM-2):* The S mintmark on this rare variety is smaller than normal, and possibly was intended for a Barber half dollar or quarter dollar die. Examples are usually in worn grades when seen at all.

	Cert	Avg	%MS	VF-20	EF-40	AU-50	MS-60	MS-63
1903-S, Small S	173	23.1	1%	$350	$1,300	$4,000	$28,000	$72,000

1904 Morgan Dollar

1904 • **Mintage:** 2,788,000.

Key to Collecting: Most coins seen today are poorly to indifferently struck and with poor luster—all in all, rather sorry looking. If quality is desired, some intense cherrypicking is called for. Nice coins do exist, but if choice or gem and well struck they can be expensive. Most such coins are from old-time collections or holdings and are lightly, often attractively, toned. The Treasury-release coins are usually subpar.

Surface Quality: The strike varies and is usually of only medium quality. According to Wayne Miller, "Most 1904 dollars give the appearance of being poorly struck. It is hard to believe that the same mint that produced the very beautiful 1903 dollar could, one year later, produce such an inferior dollars as the 1904." Sharp pieces can be found, but some searching is required. The luster is usually fairly shallow, not at all deep or flashy. To find a deeply lustrous, sharp 1904 will be a challenge.

Some prooflikes exist but are not of high contrast.

	Cert	Avg	%MS	VF-20	EF-40	AU-50	MS-60	MS-63	MS-64	MS-64DMPL	MS-65	MS-65DMPL
1904	5,223	61.5	86%	$40	$47	$50	$120	$300	$475	$42,500	$1,400	$65,000

1904, Proof • **Mintage:** 650.

Key to Collecting: Some lightness is present at the centers, and the motifs have an undesirable chrome look.

	Cert	Avg	%MS	PF-60	PF-63	PF-64	PF-65
1904, Proof	294	63.8		$1,300	$3,000	$3,750	$5,500

1904-O Morgan Dollar

1904-O • **Mintage:** 3,720,000.

Key to Collecting: The 1904-O is the last and also the most plentiful today of the big-three former New Orleans Mint rarities that launched the Treasury release and resultant pandemonium in November 1962, the others being the 1898-O and the marvelous and ultra-rare 1903-O. Today, many 1904-O dollars exist, usually very brilliant and very attractive. Striking sharpness is another matter entirely.

Surface Quality: The strike is usually average or a bit below average, although with some searching sharp pieces can be found. The luster is usually attractive—in fact, especially so.

Prooflike coins, some deeply mirrored, are abundant. The contrast is usually low and there is usually some light striking at the centers.

	Cert	Avg	%MS	VF-20	EF-40	AU-50	MS-60	MS-63	MS-64	MS-64DMPL	MS-65	MS-65DMPL
1904-O	152,211	63.7	100%	$45	$50	$55	$60	$80	$115	$450	$200	$1,150

1904-S Morgan Dollar

1904-S • **Mintage:** 2,304,000.

Key to Collecting: The 1904-S dollar is one of the key issues in the series, and in comparison to the demand for them, Mint State pieces are elusive. When found, the strike is apt to be shallow and the luster average or poor. In contrast, price-wise, there are many nice Very Fine and Extremely Fine pieces around, also requiring careful selection, that can be just right for those who do not want to invest in Mint State coins.

Surface Quality: The strike is typically about average. Sharp pieces exist but must be sought out, which is not particularly easy to do as Mint State pieces are somewhat elusive. Most Mint State pieces are usually below average in this respect, but there are some notable exceptions.

Prooflike coins exist but have low contrast. DMPL coins are very rare.

	Cert	Avg	%MS	VF-20	EF-40	AU-50	MS-60	MS-63	MS-64	MS-64DMPL	MS-65	MS-65DMPL
1904-S	2,532	44.4	27%	$80	$240	$600	$2,850	$4,250	$4,750	$17,000	$7,000	

1921 Morgan Dollar

1921 • **Mintage:** 44,690,000.

Key to Collecting: The 1921 Morgan dollar is far and away—by a country mile—more plentiful than any other coin in the entire series. Many millions exist in Mint State. However, finding one with eye appeal can be a challenge. Made from different hubs with shallow relief, 1921 dollars of all mints are different in appearance from those of the years 1878 through 1904.

Surface Quality: The nature of the dies is that even the best 1921 Morgan dollars are apt to be somewhat shallow. That said, on most there is additional weakness, due to striking, on the reverse among the lower wreath leaves. Examples with this feature sharp are in the minority. The die faces are "plane," not basined, on all 1921 Morgan dollars from the several mints. Luster is typically satiny rather than deeply frosty, but quite a few are grainy or dull.

Prooflike pieces are seen on occasion, and have a mirrorlike quality to the fields, which are not completely "plane" but show distortions in the mirror surface near the lettering and other features. Such pieces can have a very nice strike (for a 1921 dollar).

	Cert	Avg	%MS	VF-20	EF-40	AU-50	MS-60	MS-63	MS-64	MS-64DMPL	MS-65	MS-65DMPL
1921	133,313	63.3	99%	$35	$40	$42	$45	$50	$85	$7,750	$150	$11,500

1921, Zerbe Proof • Mintage: 200.

Key to Collecting: Struck at the behest (allegedly) of numismatist Farran Zerbe, so-called "Zerbe Proofs" are simply circulation strikes with a semi-prooflike character, not as nice as on the earlier-noted prooflike pieces, struck on circulation-quality planchets from dies that were slightly polished, but that retained countless minute striae and preparation lines. It seems highly unlikely that these were produced as Proofs for collectors. If indeed they were furnished to Farran Zerbe, a leading numismatic entrepreneur of the era, it is likely that they were simply regular production pieces. Zerbe had a fine collection and certainly knew what a brilliant Proof should look like; he never would have accepted such pieces as mirror Proofs. (See the 1921-S, Zerbe Proof, listing for more information.)

About 150 to 200 of these special-strike coins are believed to exist today.

	Cert	Avg	%MS	PF-60	PF-63	PF-64	PF-65
1921, Zerbe Proof	52	64.1		$4,000	$5,500	$8,500	$15,000

1921, Chapman Proof •

Mintage: 25 to30 estimated.

Key to Collecting: Q. David Bowers, in his *Silver Dollars and Trade Dollars of the United States*, relates: In 1921, [Philadelphia coin dealer] Henry Chapman went to the Mint and had some mirror-surface Proofs struck to his order. This was done clandestinely by or for George T. Morgan, chief engraver, who had a little "rare coin business" going on the side. Walter H. Breen reported that he has seen "the bill of sale for 10 Proofs, Morgan to Chapman." The original production of mirror-type Proofs must have been very small, perhaps just 15 in all (10 to Chapman, five to Ambrose Swasey). They were not officially sold by the Mint, nor were any Proof sets made that year.

Chapman advertised the coins for sale within a few months of their production.

Surface Quality: Most are nearly of the same highly polished deep mirror surfaces characteristic of 19th-century Proof Morgan dollars, but sometimes with slight tinges of graininess near the rims. Contrast is average.

	Cert	Avg	%MS	PF-60	PF-63	PF-64	PF-65
1921, Chapman Proof	22	64.1		$20,000	$35,000	$45,000	$75,000

1921-D Morgan Dollar

1921-D • **Mintage:** 20,345,000.

Key to Collecting: Dollars of the 1921-D variety are common in Mint State today (although not nearly as plentiful as Philadelphia pieces), but some searching is needed to find an example with good eye appeal. Prooflike coins exist, and DMPL pieces are rare; these coins have little eye appeal. All have a tiny or "micro" D mintmark.

Surface Quality: The 1921-D, from shallow dies to begin with, usually is lightly struck on the wreath leaves. Sharply struck pieces are in the distinct minority and will require extensive cherrypicking to find. The luster ranges from dull to somewhat frosty, with frosty pieces being plentiful.

Prooflike coins exist but are very elusive. Such pieces are nearly always weakly struck and with poor eye appeal.

	Cert	Avg	%MS	VF-20	EF-40	AU-50	MS-60	MS-63	MS-64	MS-64DMPL	MS-65	MS-65DMPL
1921-D	21,090	62.8	93%	$38	$42	$45	$55	$85	$185	$7,500	$250	$11,500

1921-S Morgan Dollar

1921-S • **Mintage:** 21,695,000.

Key to Collecting: Following suit with the other varieties of this year, the 1921-S Morgan is common in all grades including Mint State. Most are poorly struck, again, providing opportunity for connoisseurship. The 1921-S, although plentiful, is seen less often than its Philadelphia and Denver counterparts. All have a tiny or "micro" S mintmark.

Surface Quality: Most are somewhat shallowly struck on Miss Liberty's hair and on the reverse. "A fully struck piece with good luster is very rare," note Van Allen and Mallis, and raises a challenge for the collector who, in the word of the late Frank Archer, is in any way "particular." The strike varies, but is often unattractive.

Prooflike coins are very rare. As none of the 1921 dies of this or the other two mints were basined (a process that in the 1878–1904 era often imparted prooflike character to the dies), this feature is seldom seen.

	Cert	Avg	%MS	VF-20	EF-40	AU-50	MS-60	MS-63	MS-64	MS-64DMPL	MS-65	MS-65DMPL
1921-S	15,879	62.5	94%	$38	$42	$45	$55	$95	$200	$12,000	$575	

1921-S, Zerbe Proof •

Mintage: 24 estimated.

Key to Collecting: In *The Numismatist*, July 1955, Stuart Mosher (the Smithsonian's curator of numismatics at the time) relates the following:

> About 10 years ago [i.e., circa 1945], Farran Zerbe, father of the Peace dollar and our first American numismatic missionary, told me an intriguing story regarding a branch mint Morgan dollar issued in Proof.
>
> In 1921 he was in California awaiting the arrival of the dies that were to be used to strike the first Peace dollars at the San Francisco Mint. The Mint phoned him that the dies had arrived and he hastened there to see them put into operation. The new 1921 dies had arrived all right but they turned out to be dies for the old Morgan design, which had not been coined since 1904, and not the dies for the Peace dollar which he had worked so hard and long to promote.
>
> Mr. Zerbe . . . suggested to the chagrined Mint officials that they could assuage his disappointment somewhat if they would strike off a few Morgan dollars from the new 1921 dies in Proof condition. They were happy to oblige and manufactured about two dozen, which he bought and later handed out to his various coin collecting friends throughout the country. While I have never seen one of these Proofs it is logical to suppose some of them are extant.

Dollar coinage commenced at the San Francisco Mint on May 9, 1921, which is likely the day the Morgan Proofs were struck. Five surviving examples are known.

	Cert	Avg	%MS	PF-60	PF-63	PF-64	PF-65
1921-S, Zerbe Proof	0	n/a				$90,000	$140,000

PEACE DOLLARS (1921–1935)

Designer: *Anthony de Francisci.* **Weight:** *26.73 grams.*
Composition: *.900 silver, .100 copper (net weight .77344 oz. pure silver).*
Diameter: *38.1 mm.* **Edge:** *Reeded.* **Mints:** *Philadelphia, Denver, and San Francisco.*

Mintmark location is on the reverse, to the left of the tail feathers.

Circulation Strike

Proof

BACKGROUND

The Peace dollar of 1921–1935 is remarkable for many reasons, one of which is that *numismatists* played a key role in the coin's creation. In April 1918 the Pittman Act had authorized the Treasury to melt up to 350 million silver dollars for the war effort. (Some 270 million were ultimately melted; a relatively small portion of the bullion was used for U.S. domestic coinage, while the rest went to the British for use in the mints in India.) Congress had stipulated that the melted dollars had to be replaced using newly produced metal from American mines—and that the Treasury had to buy this silver at $1 per troy ounce, regardless of the market price.

After the end of the war in 1918 silver rose suddenly to more than $1 per ounce, and the Treasury did not make the required purchases at once. By May 1920 the price of silver fell to 70 cents per ounce or less, and purchases began at $1 per ounce, provided the seller could prove that the silver had been freshly mined. The inflated price was a boon for U.S. silver mine interests. In March 1921 the market hit a postwar low of 53 cents per ounce. Silver dollar coinage resumed, in the old (1878–1904) Morgan style, in May 1921. Millions of Morgan dollars dated 1921 were minted.

A NEW DESIGN

At the annual American Numismatic Association convention in 1920, coin dealer and numismatic promoter Farran Zerbe made an impassioned plea for a new silver dollar, one whose design would commemorate the signing of the peace treaties ending the Great War. (Zerbe was not the first to come up with the "peace coin" idea—*The Numismatist* editor Frank Duffield, for one, had suggested in 1918 that a "victory coin" be issued—but Zerbe is traditionally credited with promoting it the most.)

Zerbe's speech struck a chord among many numismatists, including two influential congressmen: William A. Ashbrook of Ohio (Ashbrook, a numismatist, was a member of the ANA) and Albert Vestal of Indiana. They attempted to obtain a unanimous resolution in Congress, but this failed and other methods had to be pursued.

On July 28, 1921, President Warren G. Harding issued an executive order assigning to the Commission of Fine Arts the right to pass on all coinage designs. It was not to have a veto power, but its influence would still be very great on the final designs.

Charles Moore, chairman of the commission, was soon in close consultation with Mint director Raymond T. Baker. Together they tackled the problem of obtaining a peace dollar. Treasury secretary Andrew Mellon joined the cause, and the process toward the new coin was at last off and running.

On November 23, 1921, eight prominent artists (Victor D. Brenner, Hermon MacNeil, Chester Beach, Henry Hering, Robert Aitken, Robert Tait McKenzie, John Flanagan, and Anthony de Francisci) were asked to participate in an extremely last-minute design contest—the winning obverse and reverse designs would be announced on December 19. De Francisci was judged a clear winner (President Harding personally approved the drawings) and was asked to submit plaster models as soon as possible. The artist did so, but in the meantime a political storm blew up over the reverse.

Representatives of veterans' groups had reviewed a copy of the drawing for the reverse, which featured an eagle grasping a broken sword in its talons. Veterans and others saw this as suggesting America had been broken or defeated, but that was certainly not the intent of the artist. He had, after all, included the olive branch—symbol of peace—in the design, to make the meaning of the imagery clear. The White House was deluged with telegrams demanding that the design be changed, and fearing negative public opinion, the administration gave in. President Harding communicated instructions to Treasury Secretary Mellon, who dropped the problem into the lap of chief engraver George T. Morgan to be solved.

Morgan apparently executed a plaster model based on an alternate design by de Francisci showing an eagle gazing out to sea at the rising sun with the word PEACE below. The eagle was clearly looking to the east (and Europe), where the peace treaties had been signed. Due to the shortness of time, de Francisci had little real input into the new reverse.

De Francisci's obverse, also hurriedly done, was loosely based on the Augustus Saint-Gaudens head for the gold eagle of 1907 and certain other works by the same artist. De Francisci's wife, Teresa Cafarelli de Francisci, served as a model. The obverse, too, was subject to "improvements" beyond the artist's control. President Harding apparently disliked the faint dimple present on an early version of Liberty's chin—somehow, it "did not exactly express peace," so the subtle touch had to go.

Both de Francisci's design of the Peace dollar and Morgan's work on the revision have generated strong feelings. With respect to the original design, many numismatists believe that both obverse and reverse are artistic masterpieces well worthy of the country. Hurried execution notwithstanding, the Morgan / de Francisci reverse is a work of genuine quality that well reflected the mood of the American people with respect to the end of the war. The eagle serenely gazes toward a scene of victory and renewal, and its perch atop a mountain symbolizes strength and a determination to watch out for those who would destroy the hard-won peace.

Others disliked the design intensely. Numismatic author and art historian Cornelius Vermeule used words like "empty" and "vapid" to describe the portrait of Liberty. As writer Ted Schwartz reports in a November 1975 article in *The Numismatist* ("The Morgan and Peace Silver Dollars"):

> A Syracuse paper [commented roughly] on the coin. A reporter wrote: "The old dollar had a solemn and serious look. The new one seems sissified by comparison. One has dignity, the other has prettiness, and if one wanted to be critical it might be added that while the old dollar had sentiment the new one has sentimentality.
>
> "The two leading differences are in the eagle, and the Goddess of Liberty. The old eagle was a scrapper. He looked as if he were on the alert to start something any time, and between whiles, to scream to his heart's content. The 1922 version of the American bird of freedom looks anything but free. He looks out of luck. He has wings furled and is sitting, gazing into vacancy with the cheerless and pepless attitude of a wet barnyard fowl waiting for the weather to clear. There are some who say that he even wears pants, but that is an illusion, The real eagle does have thick foliage on his legs. all the way to his claws, which, when in a standing position gives something of a trousered effect."

Others, including Vermeule, have found fault with the resemblance between de Francisci's Liberty and the goddess on Saint-Gaudens's Indian Head $10 gold coin; and between de Francisci's reverse eagle and Bela Lyon Pratt's eagle on the $5 gold coin. But as Schwartz notes:

> Whether the similarities are by design or chance is hard to say, the sculptors were all influenced by similar concepts and teachers. After all, Saint-Gaudens' pupils, Weinman and Fraser, were among de Francisci's teachers and they were all impressed by the ancient Greek and Roman sculpture they had studied. But whatever the influence, the final execution was uniquely that of de Francisci. Perhaps he learned from others and followed a classic approach, but the end result succeeds on its own merits.

Some viewers mistakenly thought the reverse design with the eagle holding a broken sword in its talons (right) symbolized defeat. The sword was summarily removed (center).

Anthony de Francisci's portrait of Liberty was modeled mostly after his wife, Teresa Cafarelli (bottom left), but the influence of works by Augustus Saint-Gaudens—like his head of Nike (top left) and his obverse portrait on the Indian Head gold eagle (top right)—is evident.

A STRIKING PROBLEM

The rushed production process left scant time to troubleshoot for problems, and the Peace dollars of 1921, all struck in the last week of the year, certainly had them. The centers, especially on the obverse, struck up badly. The 1,006,473 struck in 1921 and distributed early in 1922 got generally favorable remarks, except for the quality of striking.

Die breakage was reported (though not officially recorded) to be very high for the 1921 Peace dollar. On January 3, 1922, Morgan wrote to de Francisci:

> Today by American Express I send to you 50 of the Peace dollars. I know you will be disappointed, but the pressure necessary to bring up the work was so destructive to the dies that we got tired of putting new dies in.
>
> In changing the date to 1922 I took the opportunity of making a slight change in the curvature of the ground. I anticipate at least 20 tons less pressure will be required to bring up the design. This could double the life of the die. I send you an early strike of the 1922.

In a 1992 note to the Q. David Bowers, numismatic researcher Thomas K. DeLorey said, "I have only seen one 1921 Peace dollar with a die break, yet they are common on 1921 PDS Morgan, 1922 PDS Peace, and 1923 PDS dollars. I suspect that the reports of excess die breakage are a tale created to justify the change in design, and not a real reason."

Whatever the real reason, Morgan made a number of changes to the dies for 1922 in an effort to correct the problem. Regular coinage commenced but was soon stopped because the dies were getting only a few thousand coins per pair, and the breakage was nearly as bad as it was said to have been the year before. The Engraving Department at the Mint predicted thousands of dies would be needed for the new Peace coinage, and a conference was held at the Mint to figure out what to do next. It was decided, apparently with no input from de Francisci, that the relief of the design would have to be radically lowered.

Morgan now reduced the height of the designs on both sides, likely reducing them on the Mint's new Janvier machine (which could, among other things, alter the relief of the image). De Francisci was called to the Mint in late January 1922, ostensibly to supervise the reduction of the new models on the Janvier machine, but the real work had already been done. Coinage resumed within a matter of days; de Francisci was not pleased. Ted Schwartz's 1975 article continues the story:

> In a letter written to the secretary of the Commission of Fine Arts, de Francisci controlled his temper as he stated, "I would suggest and with emphasis, that if possible, to forbid the Mint engravers from touching in anyway the dies or hubs of said coins. A letter from Mr. Morgan which I enclose herewith states his intentions to do more changes small in mechanical gain but very damaging to artistic values. That is regrettable because unnecessary. The Mint's chief complaint is the height of the relief of the liberty head. Mr. Fraser and I have agreed that in order to overcome that mechanical hindrance to reduce the general relief of the coins by machine—a very simple process—a new hub would have to be made but the result, surely pleasing, would justify my work and the ideals and prestige of the American Fine Arts Commission."
>
> The retraction of the changes was not to be. Morgan had learned from the great master of artistic mediocrity, Charles Barber. Despite the artistic merits of his own coin, Morgan blindly slaughtered the relief of the de Francisci Peace dollar.

By November 1924 all of the required Pittman Act silver had been purchased, but it was not until the spring of 1928 that the last bullion was coined into dollars. Denver struck no dollars in that year. All of them were coined at the Philadelphia and San Francisco Mints by June 30. The 1928 Philadelphia coinage is perhaps the only scarce issue after 1921, with only 360,000 struck.

In 1964, Congress authorized 45 million new silver dollars, in part to meet the demands of the casinos in Nevada. The Denver Mint struck 316,076 of the coins, dated 1965, but concerns that the program was meant to serve special interests caused the order to be rescinded. All pieces were supposedly recalled and melted. However, according to Roger Burdette, "The absence of open, forthright disclosure by the Mint and Treasury in 1965, and the lack of a per-piece count of the coins, has created considerable suspicion among coin collectors. Rumors and assertions about the existence of 1964-D Peace dollars are commonplace, with a number of notable collectors and dealers claiming to have seen or been offered examples." (Burdette devotes an entire chapter to an investigation of this mysterious issue in *A Guide Book of Peace Dollars*.)

Until very recently, this was the end of the story of the Peace dollar.

ANTHONY DE FRANCISCI

Anthony de Francisci was born in Palermo, Sicily, Italy, on June 13, 1887. At age 18 he emigrated to the United States, embarking from Naples in November 1905 on the *Sicilia* and arriving in New York City on December 1.

His father, Benedetto de Francisci, had taught him marble cutting when he was a child, and young Anthony studied at the Palermo Institute of Fine Art. Once in America he studied at the Cooper Union and the National Academy of Design in New York. He studied under and/or worked with sculptors whose names numismatists will find familiar: Adolph Weinman, Hermon MacNeil, James Earle Fraser, and Augustus Saint-Gaudens.

In February 1911, de Francisci sought formal citizenship in the United States. On his "Declaration of Intention," signed on February 4, he describes himself as a sculptor, 5 feet 2 inches tall, and 104 pounds, with brown hair and brown eyes. (He also renounces all allegiance to Victor Emmanuel III, King of Italy, and swears that he is neither an anarchist nor a polygamist.) In 1917, now a U.S. citizen, he registered for the draft. He is described on his draft card as being "short" and "slender." He was not called up to serve; whether his slight stature or some other factor played a part in this is unknown. He would register again for the draft in the run-up to World War II, when he was 54, although only men aged 21 to 45 were required to do so.

A December 31, 1921, image by the National Photo Company shows Mint director Raymond T. Baker (right) and Anthony de Francisci examining a plaster model of the new Peace dollar, scheduled for release within days of the photo.

De Francisci's 1915 portrait plaque depicting his mentor, Adolph A. Weinman.

De Francisci married Mary Teresa Cafarelli in Manhattan in April 1920, when he was 33 years old and she was 21. Teresa's background was very similar to Anthony's. She was born May 4, 1898, near Naples, Italy. Around the time she was born, her father, Donato Cafarelli, emigrated with her older brother, Domenico, to the United States, and opened a grocery store in Clinton, Massachusetts. Baby Teresa and her mother, Rose Emma, traveled steerage class to from Naples to New York in 1900, reuniting the family in their new country after two years apart.

When the Mint issued its invitation to compete in a design competition in November 1921, the de Franciscis were living in Manhattan Assembly District 7, where Anthony was enjoying success as a sculptor. He had previously designed a portrait plaque of Adolph Weinman and had been selected to sculpt the 1920 Maine Centennial commemorative half dollar (from a design by Harry Cochrane), and the Mint was impressed enough with his work to include him in the august company of Victor David Brenner, Hermon MacNeil, John Flanagan, and the other invitees.

In his 1975 *Numismatist* article Ted Schwartz writes, "The least likely contestant, at least in his mind, was Anthony de Francisci."

> De Francisci had recently married when the design contest was held. His wife, the former Teresa Cafarelli, was born in a remote village 50 miles from Naples, and had been three years old when brought to the United States by her family. Teresa's brother, an art student who knew de Francisci, had introduced his sister to him. The couple found that they had mutual interests, a fact which brought them increasingly close together. Teresa was 21 when the couple were married, and her new husband entered the design contest.
>
> "My husband didn't think he had a chance in the competition going up against all those famous sculptors. But they were paying $100 for the designs, and I guess he figured we could use the money— so he went ahead and did it."
>
> In order to insure quality submissions the government authorized that $100 be given each of the men who submitted a design. A prize of $1,000 would be given to the person whose design was accepted for the coin.

De Francisci had a light-hearted attitude towards the contest. He bet his friends one dollar each that his creation would not prove acceptable. When he actually did win, he had to use the 50 early strike silver dollars the government gave him to pay off his bets.

The newlywed artist decided to use his ideal of womanhood as the model for Liberty. Teresa was asked to pose for the coin. His Liberty head was to be quite different from the almost matronly head of the Morgan coin. De Francisci wanted his design to reflect youth and vitality, he wanted a Liberty that was young, alive and strong.

Teresa normally wore her hair up but her husband made it more casual by opening a window so a breeze could give it a slightly wind-blown appearance. "You will see that the Liberty is not a photograph of Mrs. de Francisci," the artist mentioned in an interview with a reporter for the *Duluth Minneapolis Tribune* the year following the coin's introduction. "It is a composite face and in that way typifies something of America. I did not try to execute an 'American type' or a picture of any woman. I wanted the Liberty to express something of the spirit of the country—the intellectual speed and vigor and virility America has, as well as its youth. I had nothing of the magazine cover idea."

Teresa de Francisci's October 20, 1990, obituary in the *New York Times* quotes her as saying, "I was just an accessory. . . . And really, my husband wasn't making a portrait of me. He wanted to make an idealized portrait of what freedom represented to him, so it really wasn't a portrait of me at all."

The news that the high relief of the coins was causing trouble with the dies was apparently not well received. Schwartz writes, "The couple's initial euphoria was shattered by [the] letter de Francisci was sent by George Morgan, who had risen to the post of chief engraver for the Mint. . . . De Francisci was enraged: The beauty of the design was, in part, created by the unusually high relief. To arbitrarily reduce that relief was unthinkable."

The artist's strong objections notwithstanding, Morgan pressed forward with the changes. Teresa de Francisci later said that they never saved any of the Peace dollars, but it would be an error to assume that was from bitterness. "Anthony was content to do the creating and let others do the collecting," she said, and indeed her husband gave away the 50 coins he was given, well before there was any controversy over the relief of the design. Although it was relatively early in what would be a long career, he would have had experience with the whims of clients and the hazards involved in doing creative work for hire.

The Peace dollar also helped elevate de Francisci's status considerably, and he went on to enjoy a long career as a sculptor and medalist, with a particular talent for portraits. After the Peace dollar, his most famous work may be the World War II Honorable Service lapel pin and lozenge, awarded by the Department of Defense from 1939 to 1946 to military service members receiving honorable discharges during World War II. (This came to be known, unkindly, as the "Ruptured Duck" because of its design, which is said to resemble a duck more than an eagle.)

De Francisci was a prolific creator of awards and medals, including the 12th annual issue of the prestigious Society of Medalists; the ANS's 45th medallic issue, the Paul Revere medal; the Congressional Gold Medal for Gen. John J. Pershing; the inaugural medal for the 1964–1965 New York World's Fair; and many portrait plaques and medals of worthies such as Bernard Baruch, executives of the United Parcel Service, Ford Motor Company, the Winchester Repeating Arms Company, and U.S. Steel; and many others.

One of de Francisci's best-known works, in addition to the design of the Peace dollar, is the design for the Department of Defense's World War II Honorable Discharge insignia.

Anthony de Francisci died in the Bronx, New York City, on August 20, 1964. He was 77 years old. Teresa remained gracious to numismatists her entire life, and frequently obliged when asked to attend shows and conferences. She passed away on October 20, 1990, at the age of 92. Her obituary reports that a group of numismatists gave her a plaque on the 50th anniversary of the Peace dollar. The plaque was inscribed, "To a Lady of Peace."

PROOF PEACE DOLLARS

Production of Peace dollars from 1921 through 1935 and again in 1964 was limited to circulation strikes, but a very few Proofs were struck. In 1921, high-relief Proofs in two finishes, Satin and Sandblast, were produced; and in 1922, high-relief Sandblast Proofs and low-relief Proofs in both Sandblast and Satin finishes were struck. A high-relief Satin Proof may have been made in 1922 as well.

The 1970s saw a wave of chicanery with Mint State circulation-strike 1921 and 1922 Peace dollars (the 1922 issues being of the low-relief style). Pieces with exceptionally satiny surfaces were sold to investors as so-called presentation Proofs. Some of these investors wisely submitted the coins to the American Numismatic Association Certification Service for checking. ANACS staff sometimes saw as many as a half-dozen such submissions a month, not one of which they deemed to be a true Proof.

"Matte Proof" 1921 Peace dollars can be created from a decently struck example by having a machinist carefully and evenly remove metal from the obverse and reverse rims; this gives each a flat appearance (instead of the normal, slightly rounded shape). The reeding can be coated with wax to protect it from the acid bath into which the abused coin is then dunked. (Sandblasting is another method.) The result is a fairly passable "Matte Proof" or "Sandblast Proof" dollar. Domestic and, more recently, Chinese counterfeits abound; *never* buy a Proof Peace dollar without having it certified and guaranteed.

LATER YEARS

In June 1934 President Franklin D. Roosevelt, as part of his ongoing efforts to end the Depression, pushed through Congress a bill mandating the purchase of newly mined silver at a price (later raised) above the market—exactly the same principle that had operated in 1919–1924 for the Pittman silver bullion.

Chief engraver John Sinnock slightly modified the die style of 1922, and around seven million Peace dollars were struck from this slightly altered design in 1934 and 1935.

During World War II, 50 million silver dollars were melted for the war effort. In a terrible bit of irony, some of the silver was used to make conductors for the Manhattan Project to build the atomic bomb; it is not known how many of the affected coins were Peace dollars.

In 1964, Congress authorized 45 million new silver dollars, in part to meet the demands of the casinos in Nevada. The Denver Mint struck 316,076 of the coins, dated 1965, but the program was rescinded, in part because of concerns that the program was meant to serve special interests. All pieces were supposedly recalled and melted. However, according to Roger Burdette, "The absence of open, forthright disclosure by the Mint and Treasury in 1965, and the lack of a per-piece count of the coins, has created considerable suspicion among coin collectors. Rumors and assertions about the existence of 1964-D Peace dollars are commonplace, with a number of notable collectors and dealers claiming to have seen or been offered examples." (Burdette devotes an entire chapter to an investigation of this mysterious issue in *A Guide Book of Peace Dollars*.)

The abortive 1965 coinage, using the 1964 date, was a fitting end to a silver coinage whose beginning in 1794 had been steeped in secrecy. The illegal standard of 1794 was counterbalanced by a coin that might or might not exist, struck years later in 1965 but bearing the wrong date (1964). Alexander Hamilton's 1791 recommendation of 371.25 grains of pure silver in each dollar struck for circulation was no more.

THE CENTENNIAL OF THE PEACE DOLLAR

There is one final grace note to the story of the Peace dollar: On January 5, 2021, the 1921 Silver Dollar Coin Anniversary Act was signed into law. It requires the Treasury Department "to mint and issue coins in honor of the . . . 100th anniversary of the commencement of coinage of the Peace dollar." See appendix I for more information.

Note: Values of common-date silver coins have been based on a silver spot price of $27.50 per ounce, and may vary with the prevailing spot price.

PEACE DOLLARS (1921–1935): GUIDE TO COLLECTING

BEING A SMART BUYER

Since this is a relatively small series, and most Peace silver dollars exist in large quantities, the collector should have no problem building a complete set. In general, the 24 different dates and mintmarks are easily enough obtained, including in Mint State; the most elusive is the 1934-S.

Peace silver dollars can be collected as a single type, but one can also view the first year of issue, 1921, as a separate type, as the design is in high relief. Although the 1921 is plentiful in Mint State, it rarely comes sharply struck, for reasons described earlier. The later, low-relief Peace dollars abound in choice and gem preservation, although striking can still be a problem.

There are no extreme rarities in the series; however, 1928-P and 1934-S are key dates, commanding a good price even in circulated grades. The San Francisco issues, especially 1924-S, 1927-S, 1928-S, and 1934-S, tend to be hard to find in higher uncirculated grades, and are often "baggy."

Those who are new to collecting silver dollars would do well to go hesitantly into the Peace series, perhaps buying at first the Philadelphia Mint issues of 1922 through 1925. These four Philadelphia coins of the early and mid-1920s are inexpensive, easy to obtain, and commonly available in higher grades. From this point, one can branch out to pick up half a dozen or a dozen other coins at the lower end of the expense spectrum—and from that point proceed to the rarer ones.

HAIRLINES

Many Peace silver dollars graded in various Mint State categories have fine hairlines, as if they were wiped with a silver-polishing cloth. This undesirable feature is not always readily apparent. Bill Fivaz has recommended to classes at the ANA Summer Seminars that they carefully hold a coin they are considering under a pinpoint source of light, rotating it so that reflection occurs from all angles. If wear or hairlines are present, this process will reveal them. The key element is *rotating* the coin, for if it is held at only one angle to the light, hairlines going in a single direction might not be noticed. (The late Alan Herbert, a technical columnist for *Numismatic News*, took his diagnostic advice a step further: "Doctored coins hide the hairlines, mandating examination under a 20x to 40x stereo microscope to detect them.")

When paying a good price for a high-grade Peace dollar, you would be wise to check it carefully. Buying certified Peace dollars helps avoid doctored coins and counterfeit coins. You will still be on your own when it comes to selecting pieces of high aesthetic quality, however.

CONTACT MARKS

Many Peace silver dollars, even high-grade Mint State coins, show contact marks on the reverse on the higher-relief areas of the eagle. Such contact marks are often numerous even when there are few if any marks in the fields or elsewhere on the coin. (This situation is also seen elsewhere in numismatics, on the skirt of Miss Liberty on certain Liberty Walking half dollars, on the centers of Carver-Washington commemorative half dollars, etc.)

How could this happen? The explanation is that these marks weren't made after striking, during the bagging and transportation process, but were on the original planchets used to make the coins. As the higher areas of the eagle did not strike up fully, the original planchet contact marks remained intact and were visible as "bagmarks" on the finished coin, even if the finished coin never touched another after it was made.

Bill Fivaz, in a 1988 letter to Q. David Bowers,, agreed with this explanation:

> We point this out to our Grading Course students each summer at the American Numismatic Association Seminar and ask them to closely examine those marks, under a stereoscope if possible, to see that the edges of those marks are rather rounded, not sharp as would be the case if they were contact marks. The strike obliterates most of the planchet abrasions (as I prefer to call them), but those that are deep enough to remain, primarily where the deepest area of the die(s) strike, are not eliminated and present themselves precisely as you have said.
>
> We also point out to the Seminar students that the marks that were on the planchet prior to striking and which were not obliterated at the time of strike also have the original planchet frost on them. They are not shiny as if they have been hit by another (metal) coin.

Interestingly, true bagmarks on Peace dollars tend to be more common on the reverse than on the obverse. In the same letter Bill Fivaz offered an opinion on this phenomenon as well:

> The Buffalo 5c, Mercury 10c and Peace $1 all had the reverse die as the upper or hammer die. . . . This being the case, my theory is that when the struck coins came off the dies, down the chute and into the collection hopper, most fell reverse side up. Following coins falling on top of them had a better change to nick and mark the reverse as that was the exposed side of the coins in the bin. It's just a theory, but one that makes some sense, I believe.

ASPECTS OF STRIKING

While many coins are lightly struck on the reverse—the San Francisco issues of the 1920s being particularly egregious in this regard—the most notorious issue is the 1921 Peace dollar. The vast majority of these lack details in the hair at the center of the obverse, and most lack feather details on the reverse. The size of these flat areas can vary. Moreover, even a nicely struck example showing feather details on the reverse is apt to be struck lightly on the obverse. A sharply struck 1921 showing full hair detail at the center of the obverse and full feather detail in the reverse is a rare coin indeed, and worth a premium.

Certification services consider striking as just one of several factors. When buying a slabbed 1921 Peace dollar, the grade on the label says nothing about whether the coin was well struck. Chances are that it was not. This is to the buyer's benefit, because a little patience might turn up a more nicely struck coin for a relatively small extra premium. A sharply struck 1921 Peace dollar might cost only half again as much as an ordinary one, or even twice as much, even though it is dozens of times rarer—indeed, probably 100 times rarer.

Among other Peace dollars, striking varies, as noted in the individual descriptions of date-and-mintmark issues herein. If a certain issue nearly always comes weakly struck, you may have to settle for this or risk never completing your collection. However, you can still concentrate on other positive qualities: nice luster, brilliant surfaces, and so on.

Speaking of surface quality: Although choice Uncirculated specimens of 1934 and 1935 dollars of various dates are seen with some frequency and often have very attractive surfaces, in general the earlier issues, particularly those of branch mints, are relatively difficult to find. The broad, empty fields in the design of the Peace dollar seem to invite contact marks. In comparison to Morgan silver dollars, choice Uncirculated Peace dollars are very elusive. Grading them is a challenge, and experts often disagree on precisely what constitutes an MS-60 as opposed to an MS-63 or an MS-65.

Differences in striking quality: (a) original bronze model; (b) very well-struck
circulation coin; (c) above-average strike; (d) typical strike; (e) below-average strike;
(f) weak strike. Compare the detail of the hair next to Liberty's cheek and over her ear.
An average to above-average strike must have the two locks of hair at Liberty's cheek
separate and distinct. No Peace dollars, including the Proofs, maintain the full detail
of the artist's original. (As illustrated in *A Guide Book of Peace Dollars*, fourth edition.)

If the dies in a coining press were spaced even slightly too far apart, the Peace dollars minted in that press would not strike up fully at the center. This is most evident on the obverse and, in particular, on the body of the eagle at the center of the reverse. A coin can be fully lustrous and frosty in the fields, with very few bagmarks, and yet the body of the eagle can appear nicked, dull, and otherwise scruffy, due to not being fully struck up. As noted earlier, the explanation is that the surface on the eagle's body is the relatively untouched surface of the original planchet. As that part of the planchet has not been forced into the deepest recesses of the die, the nicks, marks, etc., on the original planchet before coining are still visible.

Peace dollar die pairs had an average working life of 500,000 coins. As a result, some coins struck toward the end of a die's use are apt to show graininess in the fields, indistinct features near the rims (the area of greatest metal movement as the planchet is struck), evidence of resurfacing (grinding or polishing marks, bright patches in the fields, etc.), and/or die breaks.

Luster varies from issue to issue and can be deeply frosty, or—in the instance of Philadelphia Mint coins of 1928, 1934, and 1935—satiny or "creamy."

Numerous Peace dollars have tiny white "milk spots" left over from when they were struck; these are not as desirable in the marketplace as unspotted coins. Sharply struck Uncirculated pieces with full luster and with a minimum of marks are quite scarce.

Sandblast Proofs of 1922 have a peculiar whitish surface in most instances, sometimes interrupted by small dark flecks or spots. There are a number of impostors among certified "Proofs."

Prooflike Peace dollars are extremely rare. These are believed to have originated when dies were polished, in part or the whole, to remove defects or clash marks. They were not produced consistently, and are often apt to be prooflike in one area of the coin and not another. Prooflike Peace dollars are not widely sought after today, nor are they necessarily more desirable than coins with frosty finishes.

PEACE DOLLARS (1921–1935)

GRADING STANDARDS

MS-60 to 70 (Mint State). *Obverse:* At MS-60, some abrasion and contact marks are evident, most noticeably on the cheek and on the hair to the right of the face and forehead. Luster is present, but may be dull or lifeless. At MS-63, contact marks are extensive but not distracting. Abrasion still is evident, but less than at lower levels. MS-64 coins are slightly finer. Some Peace dollars have whitish "milk spots" in the field; while these are

1921. Graded MS-64.

not caused by handling, but seem to have been from liquid at the mint or in storage, coins with these spots are rarely graded higher than MS-63 or 64. An MS-65 coin may have minor abrasion, but contact marks are so minute as to require magnification. Luster should be full and rich on earlier issues, and either frosty or satiny on later issues, depending on the date and mint. *Reverse:* At MS-60 some abrasion and contact marks are evident, most noticeably on the eagle's shoulder and nearby. Otherwise, comments apply as for the obverse.

AU-50, 53, 55, 58 (About Uncirculated). *Obverse:* Light wear is seen on the cheek and the highest-relief areas of the hair. The neck truncation edge also shows wear. At AU-58, the luster is extensive, but incomplete. At AU-50 and 53, luster is less but still present. *Reverse:* Wear is evident on the eagle's shoulder and back. Otherwise, comments apply as for the obverse.

1934-S. Graded AU-53.

EF-40, 45 (Extremely Fine). *Obverse:* Further wear is seen on the highest-relief areas of the hair, with many strands now blended together. Some luster can usually be seen in protected areas on many coins, but is not needed to define the EF-40 and 45 grades. *Reverse:* Further wear is seen on the eagle, and the upper 60% of the feathers have most detail gone, except for the delineation of the edges of rows of feathers. PEACE shows light wear.

1928. Graded EF-40.

VF-20, 30 (Very Fine). *Obverse:* More wear shows on the hair, with more tiny strands now blended into heavy strands. *Reverse:* Further wear has resulted in very little feather detail except on the neck and tail. The rock shows wear. PEACE is slightly weak.

1934-D. Graded VF-30.

F-12, 15 (Fine). *Obverse:* Most of the hair is worn flat, with thick strands blended together, interrupted by fewer divisions than on higher grades. The rim is full. *Reverse:* Fewer feather details show. Most of the eagle, except for the tail feathers and some traces of feathers at the neck, is in outline only. The rays between the left side of the eagle and PEACE are weak and some details are worn away.

1921. Graded F-12.

Peace dollars are seldom collected in grades lower than F-12.

PF-60 to 70 (Proof). *Obverse and Reverse:* Proofs of both types usually display very few handling marks or defects. To qualify as Satin PF-65 or Sandblast PF-65 or finer, contact marks must be microscopic.

1921. Satin Finish Proof.

1921 Peace Dollar

1921, High Relief • Mintage: 1,006,473.

Availability in Mint State: *MS-60 to MS-62:* 30,000 to 60,000. *MS-63:* 10,000 to 20,000. *MS-64:* 3,000 to 6,000. *MS-65 or better:* 1,000 to 2,000.

Availability in Circulated Grades: *VF-20 to AU-58:* 50,000 to 90,000.

Key to Collecting: It is not necessary to count the 1921 Peace dollar as a separate type, but it *is* worthwhile. The obverse and reverse are both in high relief, quite unlike the later issue, and thus even at quick glance justify classification as a separate type. Circulated coins are found easily enough, but a low-grade Mint State example may be a better option. Most pieces have deep, rich luster. Typical grades are up through and including MS-63 and 64, with finer pieces being elusive.

Some rare examples have the reverse die rotated 20 degrees counterclockwise from the normal orientation.

Per Roger Burdette, "[Proof] obverses have two roughly parallel lines within the truncation of the bust beginning just right of the 9 in the date. . . . The circulation strikes have remnants of these lines and lumps but also have many extra tool marks as if someone attempted to remove the two original lines from the master die or hub after the Proofs were made."

Aspects of Striking and Appearance: All examples seen have some lightness of strike at the hair details at the center of the obverse, in the portion of the hair that covers the ear. Sometimes the outlines of the neck truncation can be irregular or lightly struck as well. On the reverse, the details of the eagle, particularly the areas in the higher relief just behind the eagle's neck, are often indistinct.

	Cert	Avg	%MS	VF-20	EF-40	AU-50	MS-60	MS-63	MS-64	MS-65	MS-66
1921, High Relief	16,435	58.7	73%	$125	$150	$200	$300	$500	$850	$1,750	$6,500

VARIETY: *1921, High Relief, Line Through L (FS-S1-1921-003, VAM-3).* A ray runs through the first L in DOLLAR, instead of behind it. Varieties of Peace dollars are not usually noted on certified holders and are not widely collected. This is an advantage for those who are interested, as scarce and rare varieties are often available in the marketplace at no additional premium.

	Cert	Avg	%MS	AU-50	MS-60	MS-63	MS-64	MS-65
1921, High Relief, Line Through L	59	60.7	78%	$225	$315	$500	$1,000	$2,500

1921, High Relief, Satin Finish, Proof • Mintage: 10–20 (estimated).

Key to Collecting: Grading services sometimes refer to this as a "Matte" Finish Proof. Walter H. Breen believed that at least the first 20 Proofs made were Satin Finish (and, for what it's worth, an example in a 1987 auction, described as a "Satin Proof," came with a card that read, "20th dollar coined in Philadelphia Mint 1921 new Peace dollar"). About 10 are known today. These are sharply struck; the central hair on the obverse and the wing and leg feathers on the reverse are better than on circulation strikes.

Per Roger Burdette: "All obverses have two roughly parallel lines within the truncation of the bust beginning just right of the 9 in the date. There are also two small lumps within these lines."

Note: Be very cautious with any special Proof striking like "Satin Finish," "Matte Finish," etc., even if the coin comes with some kind of documentation from an "expert." Fakes abound; most of these have papers from before the late 1980s. Per Roger Burdette (emphasis added):

> Most Proof coins have a partial knife rim due to a mismatch between design relief and planchet milling (upsetting of the rim). All Proof specimens were struck on a medal press and with higher-than-normal pressure. Be cautious, though—Proof dies were used to make circulation coins in addition to the Proofs. This is very likely for 1921 due to the problems with short die life and the need to produce new coins as quickly as possible. **Be wary of any coin that matches Proof diagnostics, yet lacks exceptional sharpness and sandblast or satin surfaces. Careful third-party authentication is recommended for any Peace dollar described as a "Proof."**

	Cert	Avg	%MS	PF-60	PF-63	PF-64	PF-65
1921, High Relief, Satin Finish, Proof	20	63.6	100%	$15,000	$30,000	$50,000	$75,000

1921, High Relief, Sandblast Finish, Proof • Mintage: 5–8 (estimated).

Key to Collecting: A handful of 1921 High Relief Sandblast Proofs were made. If contemplating a purchase, consult with a trusted professional numismatist.

	Cert	Avg	%MS	PF-64	PF-65
1921, High Relief, Sandblast Finish, Proof	3	64.0		$60,000	$85,000

1922 Peace Dollar

1922, High Relief • Mintage: 35,401.

Notes: Between January 5 and January 23, 1922, a little more than 35,000 high-relief circulation-strike coins were made, using four obverse and nine reverse dies. As noted earlier, the die breakage was simply too great—the obverse dies could handle fewer than 9,000 strikes each, and the reverse dies, only about 4,000. For the 1921 coinage the obverse dies alone managed nearly 25,000 strikes each. (Even that is a low figure. Some Morgan dollar dies of 1878–1921 struck more than 400,000 pieces before being retired.)

The coins were melted, and the 1922 *Annual Report of the Director of the Mint* makes no mention of them, which was common practice for coins that were consigned to the melting pot after they were struck. As a result, the existence of the coins was unknown until Robert W. Julian identified the production. A lone example of a 1922 High Relief Peace dollar with non-Proof finish, identified by David W. Lange in 2007, is known to exist.

An experimental medium-relief coin was discovered in 2001. It has been argued that this is merely a Proof coin that made it into circulation and became worn, Roger Burdette points to definitive evidence that this was not struck from the Proof dies. In general, overlays of this coin and the Proof version shows different positions of the numbers in the date and other design elements.

	Cert	Avg	%MS	AU-50
1922, High Relief	0	n/a		—

1922, Normal Relief •

Mintage: 51,737,000.

Availability in Mint State: *MS-60 to MS-62:* 2,000,000 to 4,000,000. *MS-63:* 300,000 to 600,000. *MS-64:* 30,000 to 60,000. *MS-65 or better:* 10,000 to 20,000.

Availability in Circulated Grades: *VF-20 to AU-58:* 10,000,000 to 15,000,000.

Key to Collecting: In worn grades (VF-20 and higher), 1922 Peace dollars are exceedingly common—indeed, they are considered to be the most plentiful issue of the entire series. In Mint State the 1922 is exceedingly common as well, across all grades up to MS-65 and beyond. Whether it is *absolutely* the most common Peace dollar in grades MS-60 through 63 will probably never be known. Most rarity information in print for Uncirculated Peace dollars is based on population data from the certification services. However, such Peace dollar dates as 1922, 1923, 1924, and 1925 are so inexpensive in these lower grades that only a tiny fraction have ever been slabbed, because certification costs too much in proportion to the value of the coins. Certainly, in MS-63 either the 1922 or the 1923 is the most plentiful. The distinction is moot, for vast quantities exist of each.

In MS-64 grade, the 1922 is common, but not as common as the 1923 (the most common) and 1925; ditto for the MS-65 grade. These three dates plus 1924 represent an excellent nucleus around which to form a set of Peace dollars.

Most higher-grade Uncirculated 1922 dollars, slabbed at MS-63 or better, are attractive and lustrous. Many if not most 1922 Peace dollars are bagmarked, sometimes extensively—the result of having been moved around in storage many times. Wayne Miller wrote that one Mint State bag he examined carefully did not hold a single gem coin.

Unfortunately, the detail on this and other, later Peace dollars is often unsatisfactory due to the low relief of the design and dies. Stained and spotted coins are for the most part not submitted for certification, at least not in the lower grades. However, even at the MS-65 and better grades there can be seen a number of truly ugly Peace dollars, coins with dull gray, brown, or brown-black surfaces. They may be technically MS-65 or better, but who would want to own them?

Some Peace dollars of this era have white "milk spots" on them that cannot be effectively removed. Wayne Miller says:

> The most plausible explanation for these blotches is that the planchets were improperly washed and dried after they had emerged from the annealing ovens and subsequent acid bath. Also, an increase in the concentration of sulphuric acid and water solution used during this cleaning and polishing operation could have lightly etched the surface of the planchet in some places.

Notes: Beginning in 1922, Peace dollars were coined in fantastic quantities. At the Philadelphia Mint that year, more than 51 million were produced—an all-time record for a U.S. silver dollar. From this time onward, Peace dollars began to pile up in Mint vaults and other Treasury facilities.

	Cert	Avg	%MS	VF-20	EF-40	AU-50	MS-60	MS-63	MS-64	MS-65	MS-66
1922, Normal Relief	215,741	63.5	99%	$25	$27	$28	$30	$50	$60	$110	$350

VARIETY: *1922, Die Break in Field (FS-S1-1922-001f, VAM-1F)*. A die break is visible in the field above DOLLAR. From the *Cherrypickers' Guide to Rare Die Varieties*, vol. II (sixth edition): "This variety has turned out to be much rarer than previously thought, and is very scarce in grades above EF."

	Cert	Avg	%MS	AU-50	MS-60	MS-63
1922, Die Break in Field	63	55.9	29%	$400	$800	$2,500

VARIETY: *1922, Die Break at Ear (FS-S1-1922-002a, VAM-2A)*. A major die break near Liberty's ear, dangling down to her neck, gives this variety its nickname, the "Earring." Several die states are known.

	Cert	Avg	%MS	AU-50	MS-60	MS-63
1922, Die Break at Ear	70	58.8	54%	$290	$650	$2,300

VARIETY: *1922, Die Break in Hair (FS-S1-1922-002c, VAM-2C)*. An irregular line of raised metal runs along the back of Liberty's hair. This is called the "Extra Hair" variety. Several die states are known.

	Cert	Avg	%MS	AU-50	MS-60	MS-63
1922, Die Break in Hair	248	57.4	52%	$90	$180	$385

VARIETY: *1922, Die Break on Cheek (FS-S1-1922-005a, VAM-5A)*. Liberty's cheek has a raised, almost triangular chunk of metal along a vertical die break. Also, the reverse is lightly tripled. This variety, called the "Scar Cheek," is very scarce in Mint State.

	Cert	Avg	%MS	AU-50	MS-60
1922, Die Break on Cheek	43	59.5	63%	$190	$400

VARIETY: *1922, Die Break at Nose (FS-S1-1922-012a, VAM-12A)*. A die break is visible running from Liberty's nose along the top of her lip. This is known as the "Moustache" variety.

	Cert	Avg	%MS	AU-50	MS-60	MS-63	MS-64
1922, Die Break at Nose	160	58.4	45%	$90	$200	$500	$975

1922, High Relief, Sandblast Finish, Proof • **Mintage:** 10–15 (estimated).

Notes: According to Roger Burdette, "All [1922 High Relief Proofs] have the point of the bust sharply overlaying the 9 in the date." As for the reverse, "All have a small defect in the area between the eagle's talon and leg and the olive branch; the rays are rounded."

	Cert	Avg	%MS	PF-64	PF-65
1922, High Relief, Sandblast Finish, Proof	11	65.0		$100,000	$200,000

1922, Low Relief, Sandblast Finish, Proof • **Mintage:** 3–6 (estimated).

Notes: Of the 1922 Low Relief Proofs, Roger Burdette writes, "All have ghost rays at the sides of many of the tiara's rays; these are less pronounced than on the trial strikes. The rays are also thinner than on any of the trial or circulation pieces; upper surfaces of the rays are rounded rather than flattened, as on the trial strikes. The ray tips are pointed." Concerning the reverse, "The rays are broad and flat at the base and become narrow and rounded toward the tip; olive branch does not touch eagle's claw. A very well struck trial coin could mimic a Proof, provided it had flawless surfaces, very sharp features, indistinct cutting parallel to the rays, and complete sandblast or satin finish."

	Cert	Avg	%MS	PF-64	PF-65
1922, Low Relief, Sandblast Finish, Proof	2	65.0		$100,000	—

1922, Low Relief, Satin Finish, Proof • **Mintage:** 3–6 (estimated).

Notes: Refer to the notes under the preceding listing.

	Cert	Avg	%MS	PF-64	PF-65
1922, Low Relief, Satin Finish, Proof	1	63.0		$100,000	$150,000

1922-D Peace Dollar

1922-D • **Mintage:** 15,063,000.

Availability in Mint State: *MS-60 to MS-62:* 80,000 to 140,000. *MS-63:* 15,000 to 25,000. *MS-64:* 6,000 to 12,000. *MS-65 or better:* 2,500 to 4,500.

Availability in Circulated Grades: *VF-20 to AU-58:* 2,000,000 to 4,000,000.

Key to Collecting: Most examples of the 1922-D must have been released into circulation soon after they were minted, because the issue is readily available in worn grades up to and including About Uncirculated. Among worn Peace dollars in VF-20 to AU-58 grades, the 1922-D is the commonest branch-mint issue.

Uncirculated pieces are common, but mostly in lower grade levels. Bagmarks are plentiful on typical coins in these grades. MS-64 and MS-65 pieces are harder to find but still constitute the commonest branch-mint Peace dollars at these grade levels.

Some coins have an orange-peel texture to the surface, possibly due to die resurfacing with a wire brush, or possibly to die wear. Some dies were employed beyond their useful life; coins struck from these show extensive die breaks, particularly on the obverse. Striking is usually satisfactory on the obverse, but the reverse is often weak at the center, especially the high parts of the eagle. This was due to the dies being spaced too widely apart, and the metal not completely filling the deepest recesses. As a result, frosty fields can coexist with nicks on the eagle, held over from original planchet marks. Some 1922-D dollars are lightly struck at the bottom of the obverse, including the bottom of the date and the rim area.

Despite its common status, truly aesthetically pleasing, sharply struck 1922-D coins in MS-65 are hard to find, and cherrypicking will pay dividends.

Notes: The first Peace dollar struck at the Denver Mint, the 1922-D also had the highest Denver mintage of any date of the design. At the time, the Denver Mint had excellent facilities. It was closer to newly mined silver than Philadelphia, and was thus the logical choice to produce large quantities of the denomination.

	Cert	Avg	%MS	VF-20	EF-40	AU-50	MS-60	MS-63	MS-64	MS-65	MS-66
1922-D	8,439	62.7	92%	$28	$30	$33	$55	$80	$125	$500	$1,400

1922-S Peace Dollar

1922-S • Mintage: 17,475,000.

Availability in Mint State: *MS-60 to MS-62:* 25,000 to 50,000. *MS-63:* 6,000 to 12,000. *MS-64:* 2,000 to 3,000. *MS-65 or better:* 400 to 800.

Availability in Circulated Grades: *VF-20 to AU-58:* 1,500,000 to 2,500,000.

Key to Collecting: The 1922-S Peace dollar is very common in sheer numbers, but in high Mint State levels, and sharply struck, this issue is a major rarity. Although Mint State coins are very common, most are graded MS-60 to 62. MS-63 pieces are somewhat scarce, but are still among the easiest San Francisco Mint Peace dollars to obtain. MS-64 specimens appear with regularity, but are far from common. After this point, the rarity increases exponentially, and an MS-65 is at least several times rarer than an MS-64. John Highfill has written that they are *25 times* more elusive.

The 1922-S dollars win no awards for striking. Examples are shabby in appearance, with incomplete luster and/or raised lines in the field from abrasions acquired by the die during the surfacing process. In the left obverse field, IN GOD WE is often weakly struck. The center of the reverse is usually poorly struck and is often dull on the higher points of the eagle, where marks acquired by the original planchet can often be seen. As if this were not enough, the rims are often indistinct in areas—what Wayne Miller and John Highfill call "fade-away rims." Bagmarks are also a problem, and most coins have plenty.

All of these issues can be turned into an advantage for the careful buyer. Patience is needed, and a willingness to look through many dozens of pieces, a very few sharply struck coins are out there for the finding, and they can be bought at prices little if any higher than regular pieces.

Notes: The 1922-S had the second-highest (1923-S is highest) mintage of any San Francisco Mint coin of the Peace dollar type. As was the case with so many early Peace dollars, there was little commercial demand for them, so millions were stored for years in vaults of the San Francisco Mint.

	Cert	Avg	%MS	VF-20	EF-40	AU-50	MS-60	MS-63	MS-64	MS-65	MS-66
1922-S	7,402	61.8	89%	$28	$30	$33	$55	$90	$225	$1,250	$32,500

1923 Peace Dollar

1923 • **Mintage:** 30,800,000.

Availability in Mint State: *MS-60 to MS-62:* 2,500,000 to 5,000,000. *MS-63:* 300,000 to 500,000. *MS-64:* 60,000 to 120,000. *MS-65 or better:* 30,000 to 50,000.

Availability in Circulated Grades: *VF-20 to AU-58:* 5,000,000 to 8,000,000.

Key to Collecting: The 1923 Peace dollar is extremely common in VF-20 to AU-58 grades. With the 1922, 1924, and 1925, it is one of the most plentiful of all Philadelphia Mint Peace issues. It is also quite plentiful in Mint State, in all grades from MS-60 through MS-65 or even higher. It may well be the commonest of all Uncirculated Peace dollars.

Many 1923 Peace dollars, like those dated 1922 (along with certain other coins of the era), are often seen with milky-white spots that are virtually impossible to remove. These are believed to be the residue from dilute sulfuric acid used at the Mint. Some examples have yellowish stains, particularly around the rims.

The typical 1923 Peace dollar is well struck and has nice, frosty luster. No cherrypicking is needed to find an aesthetically pleasing specimen of this date, and as a bonus, it is one of the least expensive dates, both factors making it a good starter-coin for a collection. Many coins are bagmarked and/or stained, but enough others exist, that such impaired pieces can be ignored. Leave them for investors!

Notes: The 1923 Peace dollar mintage is the second-largest in the series, after the record-breaking 1922. Dollars were unpopular in commerce in the East so there was little need for more of them; thus, most of the 1923 Philadelphia production went into storage. In early 1945 the issue was thought to be the rarest of all Peace dollars in Mint State, but today it is known to be the commonest.

Van Allen and Mallis note that some 1923 dollars exist with the reverse rotated 25% to 100% clockwise from the normal alignment.

	Cert	Avg	%MS	VF-20	EF-40	AU-50	MS-60	MS-63	MS-64	MS-65	MS-66
1923	329,174	63.7	100%	$25	$27	$28	$30	$50	$60	$110	$350

VARIETY: *1923, Die Break at Jaw (FS-S1-1923-001a, VAM-1A).* A die break bridges Liberty's cheek and jaw. This is the "Whisker Jaw" variety.

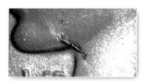

	Cert	Avg	%MS	AU-50	MS-60	MS-63	MS-64	MS-65	MS-66
1923, Die Break at Jaw	227	61.7	83%	$80	$125	$265	$550		$1,250

VARIETY: *1923, Die Break in Hair (FS-S1-1923-001b, VAM-1B).* A significant die break runs diagonally across the strands of Liberty's hair; die breaks may also be visible toward the back of her hair. This variety is nicknamed the 1923 "Extra Hair."

	Cert	Avg	%MS	AU-50	MS-60	MS-63	MS-64
1923, Die Break in Hair	91	61.8	88%	$125	$200	$400	$600

VARIETY: *1923, Die Break on O (FS-S1-1923-001c, VAM-1C).* A die break trails from the O of DOLLAR. This variety, called the "Tail on O," is very rare in any grade.

	Cert	Avg	%MS	AU-50	MS-60	MS-63
1923, Die Break on O	69	58.8	71%	$275	$650	$1,800

VARIETY: *1923, Die Break on Cheek (FS-S1-1923-001d, VAM-1D).* A die break runs down Liberty's cheek toward the junction of the chin and neck. This is the "Whisker Cheek" variety.

	Cert	Avg	%MS	AU-50	MS-60	MS-63	MS-64
1923, Die Break on Cheek	107	60.4	67%	$165	$250	$475	$875

VARIETY: *1923, Doubled Die Obverse (FS-S1-1923-002, VAM-2).* Doubling is most evident in the wide spread on the rays of Liberty's tiara, especially those under the BER of LIBERTY. This is the "Double Tiara" variety.

	Cert	Avg	%MS	AU-50	MS-60	MS-63	MS-64
1923, Doubled Die Obverse	82	61.8	80%	$58	$75	$160	$375

1923-D Peace Dollar

1923-D • **Mintage:** 6,811,000.

Availability in Mint State: *MS-60 to MS-62:* 25,000 to 50,000. *MS-63:* 5,000 to 10,000. *MS-64:* 2,500 to 5,000. *MS-65 or better:* 500 to 1,000.

Availability in Circulated Grades: *VF-20 to AU-58:* 500,000 to 1,000,000.

Key to Collecting: More 1923-D dollars were minted than were needed for commerce, and most were sent to storage vaults, not to be released for circulation until the 1940s. Thus, 1923-D is among the commonest mintmarked Peace dollars in VF-20 to AU-58 grades. In Extremely Fine and About Uncirculated condition, it is very plentiful indeed.

It is also quite plentiful in Mint State, especially in the lower ranges: severak tens of thousands around MS-60 to 62, 5,000 to 10,000 in MS-63, and 2,500 to 5,000 in MS-64. Yet compared to the number of collectors desiring Peace dollars for their collections, these numbers are small. Probably fewer than 1,000 survive at the MS-65 level.

Most Mint State 1923-D dollars are well struck and lustrous on the obverse. The reverse is often lightly struck at the center, due to the excessively wide spacing of the dies. Some are weakly struck on the rims and at the date. (Careless minting was endemic at Denver in the mid-1920s, and Buffalo nickels and Lincoln cents of the era were often poorly struck as well.)

As most Mint State dollars were shuffled hither and yon in storage vaults for years before being released, the typical 1923-D dollar is apt to show bagmarks—sometimes severe ones. Cherrypickers can profit by searching patiently for high-grade, well-struck, bagmark-free examples of this date. These are very beautiful, but also very rare.

It is not unusual to see 1923-D dollars with multiple fine die cracks on the obverse, the result of dies having been employed beyond their normal useful life.

	Cert	Avg	%MS	VF-20	EF-40	AU-50	MS-60	MS-63	MS-64	MS-65	MS-66
1923-D	4,350	61.9	87%	$28	$30	$40	$75	$170	$350	$850	$3,000

1923-S Peace Dollar

1923-S • **Mintage:** 19,020,000.

Availability in Mint State: *MS-60 to MS-62:* 25,000 to 50,000. *MS-63:* 6,500 to 13,000. *MS-64:* 2,000 to 3,000. *MS-65 or better:* 200 to 400.

Availability in Circulated Grades: *VF-20 to AU-58:* 1,500,000 to 2,500,000.

Key to Collecting: For all that the 1923 Philadelphia Peace dollars get high marks for good striking and a nice appearance, the 1923 San Francisco coins get terrible marks on both counts. The dies were simply too far apart for most of the production run, and coins are often seen with light striking on both the obverse and reverse.

The collector shopping for a 1923-S Peace dollar will have to make the best of a bad situation. Uncirculated coins are plentiful for an S-Mint issue, particularly in lower grade levels, but nearly all are aesthetically unappealing. A fully struck gem in a high grade such as MS-65 is a distinct rarity. Typical examples are weak and dull at the center of the reverse, and luster ranges from poor and dull to just average. Bagmarks on some coins are light; on others, heavy. If possible, cherrypick an MS-63 or 64 with nice luster, few bagmarks, and an above-average (i.e., only *somewhat* weakly struck) reverse.

Notes: The mintage of 19,020,000 constitutes a record for any San Francisco Mint Peace dollar. Many were placed into circulation at or near the time of striking, but millions remained in storage and were paid out in the 1940s and 1950s.

	Cert	Avg	%MS	VF-20	EF-40	AU-50	MS-60	MS-63	MS-64	MS-65	MS-66
1923-S	8,343	61.6	88%	$28	$30	$36	$50	$90	$300	$1,850	$30,000

VARIETY: *1923-S, Pitted Reverse (FS-S1-1923S-001c, VAM-1C).* From the *Cherrypickers' Guide to Rare Die Varieties,* vol. II (sixth edition): "Pitting runs from the eagle's back tail-feathers, just to the right of the mintmark, upward to the N in ONE. This is the most important Pitted Reverse variety in the Peace dollar series." That comment noted, still most are found by cherrypicking and not paying a premium.

	Cert	Avg	%MS	AU-50	MS-60	MS-63	MS-64
1923-S, Pitted Reverse	40	58.2	53%	$125	$250	$450	$975

1924 Peace Dollar

1924 • **Mintage:** 11,811,000.

Availability in Mint State: *MS-60 to MS-62:* 500,000 to 900,000. *MS-63:* 150,000 to 250,000. *MS-64:* 20,000 to 40,000. *MS-65 or better:* 7,500 to 15,000.

Availability in Circulated Grades: *VF-20 to AU-58:* 2,500,000 to 4,500,000.

Key to Collecting: Millions exist in circulated condition. This issue is among the most common Peace dollars in high grades and one of the least expensive. However, it is several orders rarer than the 1923, to which it is sometimes compared.

Many 1924 Peace dollars are above average in striking quality and have attractive, satiny luster. There are numerous exceptions, including high-grade coins with spotting from old moisture, or with pebbly-bright surfaces due to wire-brushing of the dies and/or excessive die wear. White "milk spots," thought to be from the use of dilute sulfuric acid at the Mint, are known on some Mint State coins. Still others are known from dies with pitted or pebbly matte surfaces. Perhaps the dies were pickled in acid in order to remove finishing marks, or were lightly rusted. The resultant coins have an irregular matte surface showing many tiny projections under high magnification.

Cherrypicking is advised, but in this instance it will not be difficult to find a really nice specimen in a grade such as MS-63, 64, or 65.

Notes: The nearly 12 million coins minted at Philadelphia in 1924 were not needed in commerce, and many bags went into storage and remained there for decades. The 1922–1925 Philadelphia Mint issues constitute the four most common Peace silver dollars, although in Mint State the 1924 is somewhat scarcer than the other three.

	Cert	Avg	%MS	VF-20	EF-40	AU-50	MS-60	MS-63	MS-64	MS-65	MS-66
1924	52,251	63.7	99%	$25	$28	$29	$35	$50	$60	$115	$350

VARIETY: *1924, Die Break on Wing (FS-S1-1924-005a, VAM-5A).* A dramatic die break runs down and across the entire width of the eagle's back. This is the "Broken Wing" variety. Fivaz-Stanton describe this variety thusly: "This die break is incredible to behold. Most would consider it one of the premier Peace dollar varieties. It is listed in the *Official Guide to the Top 50 Peace Dollar Varieties.*"

	Cert	Avg	%MS	AU-50	MS-60	MS-63
1924, Die Break on Wing	61	61.6	82%	$130	$200	$475

1924-S Peace Dollar

1924-S • **Mintage:** 1,728,000.

Availability in Mint State: *MS-60 to MS-62:* 10,000 to 20,000. *MS-63:* 3,000 to 5,000. *MS-64:* 1,500 to 2,500. *MS-65 or better:* 150 to 300.

Availability in Circulated Grades: *VF-20 to AU-58:* 40,000 to 70,000.

Key to Collecting: Circulated 1924-S dollars can be found but are relatively scarce. Most are in higher grades such as Extremely Fine and About Uncirculated; quantities may have slipped into circulation as late as the 1940s and 1950s, under the noses of numismatists.

In Mint State this is the third rarest issue, behind the 1928-S and 1934-S. Eye appeal can vary widely, and cherrypicking for quality is urged. Gems with good eye appeal are seldom encountered. However, MS-63 and 64 coins are often found.

Most examples are lightly struck, especially on the reverse. Well-struck coins are apt to be expensive, and deservedly so. Luster is usually average to frosty. Some pieces have a matte-like surface, possibly due to the use of acid on the surface of the dies to remove polish marks. Bagmarks can be a problem, and some coins have many.

Notes: By 1924, Peace dollars were redundant, and no specimens were struck at Denver. Production at the San Francisco Mint was just 1,728,000—a fraction of the earlier dollar mintages at the same facility.

Quantities of 1924-S dollars seem to have been paid out only occasionally. A few 1,000-coin bags were released in the late 1950s and were quickly absorbed at prices of about double face value, a high premium at the time. The Redfield estate is said to have had a few hundred Uncirculated coins, but no bags.

The low mintage and the relative unavailability of mint-sealed bags combine to make this one of the scarcest issues of the early part of the Peace dollar series, and the rarest S-Mint coin up to this point in time.

	Cert	Avg	%MS	VF-20	EF-40	AU-50	MS-60	MS-63	MS-64	MS-65	MS-66
1924-S	4,841	60.1	68%	$28	$40	$70	$235	$450	$850	$5,750	$50,000

1925 Peace Dollar

1925 • Mintage: 10,198,000.

Availability in Mint State: *MS-60 to MS-62:* 650,000 to 1,000,000. ***MS-63:*** 200,000 to 350,000. ***MS-64:*** 40,000 to 65,000. ***MS-65 or better:*** 20,000 to 35,000.

Availability in Circulated Grades: *VF-20 to AU-58:* 1,750,000 to 3,500,000.

Key to Collecting: The 1925 is one of the most common date and mintmark issues in the Peace dollar series, and in fact its mintage was the last to cross the 10 million mark. Circulated coins are common but not much in demand because Uncirculated examples are extremely plentiful.

The typical 1925 is everything a Peace dollar should be, but usually isn't. Uncirculated coins are typically very bright and lustrous with above-average striking, including at the center of the reverse. MS-63 and 64 coins are readily available, and MS-65 coins are frequently encountered as well, all of which qualifies the 1925 as a nice coin for a type set.

However, there are exceptions. Many have light, milky spots, possibly from dilute sulfuric acid used during the coining process at the Mint. Whatever their cause, the spots are lightly etched into the metal surface and cannot be effectively removed.

Bagmarks, when found on 1925 Peace dollars, are apt to be light and not at all disfiguring, although Walter H. Breen stated that many of the pieces released in the 1940s were heavily marked.

	Cert	Avg	%MS	VF-20	EF-40	AU-50	MS-60	MS-63	MS-64	MS-65	MS-66
1925	57,963	63.9	99%	$25	$28	$29	$35	$50	$60	$115	$350

VARIETY: *1925, Missing Ray (FS-S1-1925-005, VAM-5)*. This variety is the result of a reverse die polished with too much gusto. The partially effaced remains of bold clash marks are evident, but the topmost internal ray is missing.

	Cert	Avg	%MS	AU-50	MS-60	MS-63	MS-64	MS-65
1925, Missing Ray	117	62.7	91%	$65	$85	$145	$250	$400

1925-S Peace Dollar

1925-S • Mintage: 1,610,000.

Availability in Mint State: *MS-60 to MS-62:* 15,000 to 25,000. *MS-63:* 5,000 to 10,000. *MS-64:* 2,000 to 4,000. *MS-65 or better:* 125 to 225.

Availability in Circulated Grades: *VF-20 to AU-58:* 160,000 to 275,000.

Key to Collecting: Like the 1924-S, the 1925-S dollar was made in relatively small quantities. The majority were probably released into circulation in the 1920s. Worn pieces in VF-20 to AU-58 grades are common today but are far from the commonest in the series.

Uncirculated 1925-S dollars are much more plentiful than are Uncirculated 1924-S coins, despite having a lower mintage. However, in MS-65 grade, the 1925-S is surprisingly rare. Indeed, it and the 1928-S are the two toughest varieties to find in this grade in the entire Peace dollar series.

Striking on the typical 1925-S dollar is unlikely to be satisfactory, with weakness on the reverse, particularly on the high points of the eagle. Luster is only average, and bagmarks can be a problem. Cherry-picking is advised and will be difficult, although not as hard as for 1924-S. Be careful when buying coins in higher grades, for a tiny difference in grade can make big difference in price—especially on the border between MS-64 and MS-65.

Notes: The 1925-S is one of the key issues in the Peace dollar series. Twin aspects of low mintage and poor striking detail combine to make MS-65 and finer coins with good eye appeal very rare. Truly gem pieces are few and far between in the marketplace—quite similar in many respects to the 1928-S. Cherry-picking comes to the forefront if you are a connoisseur. A nice aspect is that most buyers concentrate on grading numbers alone, allowing buyers with an eye for quality to acquire gems with little extra premium.

	Cert	Avg	%MS	VF-20	EF-40	AU-50	MS-60	MS-63	MS-64	MS-65	MS-66
1925-S	6,541	61.5	84%	$28	$32	$45	$90	$250	$600	$25,000	$70,000

1926 Peace Dollar

1926 • Mintage: 1,939,000.

Availability in Mint State: *MS-60 to MS-62:* 32,500 to 65,000. *MS-63:* 15,000 to 30,000. *MS-64:* 7,000 to 14,000. *MS-65 or better:* 2,500 to 4,500.

Availability in Circulated Grades: *VF-20 to AU-58:* 150,000 to 300,000.

Key to Collecting: Examples are common in worn grades, up to and including About Uncirculated. The mintage for the 1926 Philadelphia Mint Peace dollar is the lowest for that facility since 1921, yet many seem to be in the higher grade ranges, suggesting they were not put into circulation until the 1940s or early 1950s. The 1926 is quite common in Mint State, including at the gem level. Most are in grades from MS-60 to 63, but MS-64 coins are not rare, and MS-65 pieces can be located easily. The typical example is well struck with nice luster. Bagmarks, when present, are apt to be light. Cherrypicking is worth doing, but you will not have to look long or hard to find a quality piece.

Notes: All lettering on Peace dollars has poorly defined vertical edges and easily blur into the fields. This contributes to the coins' dull, poorly defined appearance. However, Roger Burdette notes that the motto IN GOD WE TRUST became progressively weaker in 1924 and 1925. By the time it was necessary to produce 1926 master dies, the word IN was very weak, and it is possible that GOD was as well.

No records indicate why what occurred next was done, or at whose behest. One theory is that John R. Sinnock tried to correct the problem on the master die in the autumn of 1925 by using fine engraving tools to recut and strengthen the motto, beginning with the middle word simply because it was convenient. If this was the case, after retouching GOD he seems to have done no further work. IN and WE are flat, almost blending into the field, giving added prominence to the single altered word. The workmanship is completely different from that on the balance of the coin, and the cutting is irregular, especially on the O.

	Cert	Avg	%MS	VF-20	EF-40	AU-50	MS-60	MS-63	MS-64	MS-65	MS-66
1926	11,399	63.1	96%	$28	$32	$37	$55	$100	$170	$325	$1,250

1926-D Peace Dollar

1926-D • Mintage: 2,348,700.

Availability in Mint State: *MS-60 to MS-62:* 12,000 to 20,000. *MS-63:* 5,000 to 8,000. *MS-64:* 2,500 to 5,000. *MS-65 or better:* 1,500 to 2,500.

Availability in Circulated Grades: *VF-20 to AU-58:* 150,000 to 250,000.

Key to Collecting: Examples of 1926-D dollars are common in VF-20 to AU-58 grades, testimony to the fact that many were used in circulation. The issue is also readily available in Mint State. Most are in lower grade ranges, but enough MS-64 and even MS-65 coins have been certified that finding one will not be difficult. Many specimens have a rich, satiny luster, but striking can be a problem—not only at the center of the reverse (the usual spot for light striking when it occurs on Peace dollars), but also on the rims and at the date. In spite of this, there are enough well-struck coins around that locating a well-struck, lustrous, and appealing example will present no difficulty.

Most examples were struck from dies without cracks or problems, but some pieces show a tracery of die breaks on the obverse. As with the other issues of this year the word GOD was manually strengthened in the die.

	Cert	Avg	%MS	VF-20	EF-40	AU-50	MS-60	MS-63	MS-64	MS-65	MS-66
1926-D	4,222	61.9	84%	$28	$32	$44	$100	$225	$375	$750	$1,800

1926-S Peace Dollar

1926-S • **Mintage:** 6,980,000.

Availability in Mint State: *MS-60 to MS-62:* 35,000 to 60,000. *MS-63:* 12,000 to 20,000. *MS-64:* 4,000 to 5,000. *MS-65 or better:* 1,000 to 2,000.

Availability in Circulated Grades: *VF-20 to AU-58:* 300,000 to 600,000.

Key to Collecting: The 1926-S, similar to its Denver counterpart, is readily available in circulated grades up through and including About Uncirculated, indicating that many were placed into the channels of commerce. Some of these may have come from vast quantities of 1926-S dollars shipped to Nevada casinos in the 1950s.

Mint State 1926-S dollars are readily available. The typical piece encountered is fairly well struck, especially on the obverse, and overall is of better quality than such issues as 1924-S, 1925-S, and 1927-S. While reverse of the typical 1926-S may not be sharp at the center, it is usually frosty and lustrous. In contrast, other San Francisco Mint dollars of the era are apt to be dull on the eagle's feathers.

Choice and gem Uncirculated 1926-S dollars are very attractive, with lustrous, bright surfaces and plenty of sparkle. Bagmarks, when present, are apt to be light but numerous, often in the form of tiny slide marks or superficial nicks rather than the deep marks seen on some other issues. The typical MS-63 or MS-64 coin has a good deal of eye appeal. True MS-65 or better coins are on the rare side; probably only one or two thousand survive.

	Cert	Avg	%MS	VF-20	EF-40	AU-50	MS-60	MS-63	MS-64	MS-65	MS-66
1926-S	7,238	61.8	86%	$28	$32	$38	$60	$100	$240	$550	$2,600

VARIETY: *1926-S, Reverse Dot (FS-S1-1926S-004, VAM-4).* On the reverse, a raised, circular dot of metal is visible to the left of the bottom olive leaf. This is nicknamed the "Extra Berry" variety.

	Cert	Avg	%MS	AU-50	MS-60	MS-63	MS-64
1926-S, Reverse Dot	52	57.1	52%	$55	$90	$200	$360

1927 Peace Dollar

1927 • **Mintage:** 848,000.

Availability in Mint State: *MS-60 to MS-62:* 10,000 to 20,000. *MS-63:* 3,000 to 5,000. *MS-64:* 1,750 to 2,500. *MS-65 or better:* 300 to 500.

Availability in Circulated Grades: *VF-20 to AU-58:* 30,000 to 60,000.

Key to Collecting: Circulated 1927 Peace dollars are scarce in comparison to many other issues in the series. Roger Burdette has found that the 1927 is the rarest Philadelphia-minted coin in Uncirculated condition, although the 1928 is often given this honor because of its very low total mintage. However, there are enough around that there has never been a shortage of any kind.

The 1927 is widely available in Uncirculated grade. Most examples are in the lower ranges, MS-60 through 63, but enough MS-64 coins exist that finding one will not be a problem for the specialist. MS-65 coins are in the rare category, and only a few hundred are estimated to have survived.

The typical Uncirculated 1927 is very attractive and well struck, with lustrous, satiny surfaces—a numismatic gem to behold. There are exceptions (as there always seem to be among Peace silver dollars), and some are average strikes and/or are noticeably bagmarked.

Notes: As is true of many circulated Peace dollars, quantities probably went to the melting pot in the late 1970s, when the Hunt brothers tried to corner the silver bullion market and, foolishly, chased the price up to nearly $50 per ounce at a point, virtually bankrupting themselves in the process.

	Cert	Avg	%MS	VF-20	EF-40	AU-50	MS-60	MS-63	MS-64	MS-65	MS-66
1927	6,895	61.8	86%	$39	$42	$50	$80	$190	$410	$1,300	$22,500

1927-D Peace Dollar

1927-D • **Mintage:** 1,268,900.

Availability in Mint State: *MS-60 to MS-62:* 5,000 to 10,000. *MS-63:* 2,500 to 4,500. *MS-64:* 1,400 to 2,300. *MS-65 or better:* 200 to 300.

Availability in Circulated Grades: *VF-20 to AU-58:* 35,000 to 65,000.

Key to Collecting: The 1927-D is the second-rarest Peace dollar in Mint State. Roger Burdette: "This is not widely known, as some of the San Francisco issues such as the 1924-S and 1925-S are generally thought be rarer due to dealer promotion." Most are well struck and have excellent eye appeal. As there is a big jump in prices between MS-64 and MS-65, a good strategy is to review MS-64 coins to find a high-end example. Grading is a matter of opinion, and some certified 64 coins are actually in a higher grade than some 65s.

	Cert	Avg	%MS	VF-20	EF-40	AU-50	MS-60	MS-63	MS-64	MS-65	MS-66
1927-D	3,928	60.2	72%	$39	$45	$90	$200	$385	$900	$3,300	$25,000

1927-S Peace Dollar

1927-S • **Mintage:** 866,000.

Availability in Mint State: *MS-60 to MS-62:* 10,000 to 20,000. *MS-63:* 4,500 to 8,000. *MS-64:* 2,000 to 3,000. *MS-65 or better:* 150 to 250.

Availability in Circulated Grades: *VF-20 to AU-58:* 65,000 to 120,000.

Key to Collecting: The 1927-S Peace dollar is one of the key issues in Mint State. Grading is something of a problem, for even higher-level pieces are nearly always weakly struck. The eagle on the reverse is often dull, with poor detail on the feathers and with marks and nicks from the original planchet retained on the weak areas. True bagmarks are seldom a problem, and most are light. The rims are sometimes weak.

Luster on 1927-S dollars ranges from irregular to satiny. Cherrypicking for quality is advised. Compared to 1926-S dollars, which are usually attractive, the 1927-S dollars are generally unsatisfactory.

Notes: Prior to the find of the LeVere Redfield estate coins in Nevada in 1976, examples were very rare. Yet even though several thousand Redfield coins were added to the population, the 1927-S remains elusive. Striking sharpness is often lacking, making the issue a prime candidate for cherrypicking, as certified holders do not consider the strike.

	Cert	Avg	%MS	VF-20	EF-40	AU-50	MS-60	MS-63	MS-64	MS-65	MS-66
1927-S	4,402	60.7	77%	$39	$45	$75	$200	$500	$850	$5,750	$45,000

1928 Peace Dollar

1928 • Mintage: 360,649.

Availability in Mint State: *MS-60 to MS-62:* 5,000 to 9,000. *MS-63:* 3,500 to 6,500. *MS-64:* 1,600 to 2,750. *MS-65 or better:* 300 to 600.

Availability in Circulated Grades: *VF-20 to AU-58:* 12,500 to 25,000.

Key to Collecting: The 1928 is usually found in About Uncirculated or Mint State. Well-worn coins are rare. In Mint State the 1928 is second only to the 1934-S in availability. Its low mintage figure has always made this date attractive. The reverse rim is beveled on this issue, making it the one Peace dollar that is recognizable at sight by viewing only the reverse side. (Besides the 1935-S variety with four sun rays under ONE as opposed to the usual three.) David W. Lange has published that the motto was reinforced on the master die for this year and that the results are seen on coins from both the Philadelphia and San Francisco Mints. Decades ago, quite a few 1923 dollars were altered to the 1928 date, but buyers have become more sophisticated since then, and such coins are no longer a threat.

Notes: Among Peace dollars of the earlier years, the traditional rarity is the 1928 Philadelphia issue, since only 360,649 were made. At the very outset it was considered scarce, especially when the Treasury Department stated that these coins were minted just for cornerstone laying and other ceremonial purposes. Today, while the 1928 issue remains one of the most expensive Peace dollars in worn grades, several others have passed it by in terms of high-level Uncirculated valuation.

	Cert	Avg	%MS	VF-20	EF-40	AU-50	MS-60	MS-63	MS-64	MS-65	MS-66
1928	8,795	58.6	65%	$275	$300	$320	$400	$575	$725	$2,500	$30,000

1928-S Peace Dollar

1928-S • Mintage: 1,632,000.

Availability in Mint State: *MS-60 to MS-62:* 8,000 to 14,000. *MS-63:* 4,000 to 8,000. *MS-64:* 2,000 to 3,000. *MS-65 or better:* 125 to 200.

Availability in Circulated Grades: *VF-20 to AU-58:* 90,000 to 150,000.

Key to Collecting: Mint State coins are commonplace, but most are not choice and are poorly struck, especially at the center of the reverse. Most 1928-S Peace dollars seen today are in the MS-60 to MS-63 range. MS-64 pieces are scarce, and MS-65 coins is the rarest Peace dollar at the MS-65 level, and rarer still if sharply struck. Heavy bagmarks are common. Cherrypicking is needed to find a high-quality coin.

Note: According to John Kamin, unscrupulous sellers in the 1960s and 1970s would shave the mintmark off of 1928-S dollars, because the Philadelphia Mint coins were about six times more valuable. Later, as collecting preferences changed and the value differential swung the other way, the practice was to affix fake S mintmarks to Philadelphia coins. Be sure to scrutinize the mintmark area very carefully on 1928 and 1928-S examples!

	Cert	Avg	%MS	VF-20	EF-40	AU-50	MS-60	MS-63	MS-64	MS-65	MS-66
1928-S	6,251	60.1	71%	$39	$48	$70	$185	$375	$750	$12,500	$60,000

1934 Peace Dollar

1934 • Mintage: 954,057.

Availability in Mint State: *MS-60 to MS-62:* 15,000 to 25,000. *MS-63:* 7,000 to 16,000. *MS-64:* 4,500 to 7,500. *MS-65 or better:* 600 to 1,000.

Availability in Circulated Grades: *VF-20 to AU-58:* 20,000 to 40,000.

Key to Collecting: Uncirculated coins are plentiful in numismatic channels. You will have no trouble finding a 1934 to suit your requirements, whether it be MS-60 or MS-65, although the latter can be pricey. Most are well struck and have nice luster.

Sometimes it can be difficult to distinguish a high-grade About Uncirculated from a low-grade Mint State coin. The best place to look is on Miss Liberty's cheek, rotating the coin under a pinpoint light source to detect friction.

Some pieces, if not dipped, have a brownish or yellowish cast to the surface, perhaps from sulfur in the cloth bags in which these were once stored.

Notes: There was no need to increase the supply of silver dollars in 1934, as millions from earlier years remained in Treasury vaults. However, the Treasury wanted to increase the money supply, and the issuing of paper Silver Certificates backed by coins was an easy way to do it. Although the mintage of the 1934 dollar is relatively low, most survivors are in Mint State today, as these did not circulate widely. In the marketplace, coins with good eye appeal are the norm.

	Cert	Avg	%MS	VF-20	EF-40	AU-50	MS-60	MS-63	MS-64	MS-65	MS-66
1934	6,441	62.0	85%	$44	$45	$55	$130	$195	$300	$575	$2,000

1934-D Peace Dollar

1934-D • Mintage: 1,569,500.

Availability in Mint State: *MS-60 to MS-62:* 11,000 to 16,000. *MS-63:* 5,000 to 9,000. *MS-64:* 2,500 to 4,000. *MS-65 or better:* 500 to 800.

Availability in Circulated Grades: *VF-20 to AU-58:* 90,000 to 150,000.

Key to Collecting: The typical 1934-D is Mint State with silky, lustrous surfaces (as opposed to sharply contrasting mint luster). Uncirculated coins are readily available but are somewhat unappreciated in comparison to certain other issues in the series. Most coins are in lower grades from MS-60 through 63 or even 64. MS-65 pieces are surprisingly rare, considering the late date position of the issue in the series.

	Cert	Avg	%MS	VF-20	EF-40	AU-50	MS-60	MS-63	MS-64	MS-65	MS-66
1934-D	6,042	60.3	73%	$44	$45	$50	$130	$300	$425	$1,250	$3,000

VARIETY: *1934-D, Doubled Die Obverse, Small D (FS-S1-1934D-004, VAM-4).* The obverse shows strong doubling on most letters of IN GOD WE TRUST, the rays on the right, and especially on Liberty's profile. The mintmark is a small D, shaped much like that of the 1920s-era D punches. A 1934-D, Doubled Die Obverse, Medium D, exists as well, but the Small D is quite rare and in high demand among specialists.

	Cert	Avg	%MS	VF-20	EF-40	AU-50	MS-60	MS-63
1934-D, Doubled Die Obverse, Small D	39	53.1	26%	$115	$185	$375	$750	$1,650

1934-S Peace Dollar

1934-S • **Mintage:** 1,011,000.

Availability in Mint State: *MS-60 to MS-62:* 2,000 to 3,000. *MS-63:* 1,600 to 3,200. *MS-64:* 800 to 1,500. *MS-65 or better:* 300 to 600.

Availability in Circulated Grades: *VF-20 to AU-58:* 30,000 to 40,000.

Key to Collecting: The appeal of the 1934-S is everlasting, and the issue is key to the series. Considering all levels from MS-60 upward, the 1934-S is the rarest Peace silver dollar, although several other San Francisco varieties are harder to find at the gem level. Examples are readily available in higher Mint State grades such as MS-63, 64, and 65.

Typical 1934-S coins are covered with a golden patina; some are light and attractive, but many are dark and unsightly. The luster can be very strong, but many have surfaces that are hidden by the patina. Typically for coins struck at the San Francisco Mint, the 1934-S usually exhibits flatness in Liberty's hair just above her ear and also lacks detail in the feathers on the eagle's breast on the reverse. Bagmarks are usually minimal, a general rule that applies to the various Peace dollar issues of 1934 and 1935. The striking quality is usually decent as well.

Notes: Today, the 1934-S Peace dollar is considered to be the rarest variety in Mint State grades up through MS-64, but it was not always so. In the early 1940s, the 1925 Philadelphia dollar, for example, was priced higher, was considered to be rarer, and was in greater demand than the 1934-S. Dealers in the 1940s likely believed that hundreds of thousands were still stored in San Francisco or in banks, and that the 1934-S was common. Later, they found out that many if not most 1934-S dollars had been paid out at face value in the 1930s, went into circulation, and became worn; and that, as a result, Mint State coins were rare. Precisely the same situation existed with 1936-D Washington quarters; everyone thought they were common, but years later, when dealers and collectors began to search for them, few could be located.

A few forgeries of the 1934-S have been made by affixing S mintmarks from other dollars onto genuine 1934 Philadelphia coins. To detect these, use 20x or higher magnification to study the junction of mintmark and field. Ideally, examine the coin with a binocular microscope: tilt the coin nearly upright and focus on the junction. An added S will show a split or seam all the way around; a genuine S will show flow lines continuous with surrounding field.

	Cert	Avg	%MS	VF-20	EF-40	AU-50	MS-60	MS-63	MS-64	MS-65	MS-66
1934-S	4,358	49.6	31%	$80	$175	$500	$2,400	$4,250	$5,750	$8,000	$27,500

1935 Peace Dollar

1935 • **Mintage:** 1,576,000.

Availability in Mint State: *MS-60 to MS-62:* 20,000 to 35,000. *MS-63:* 10,000 to 18,000. *MS-64:* 5,000 to 10,000. *MS-65 or better:* 1,200 to 1,900.

Availability in Circulated Grades: *VF-20 to AU-58:* 75,000 to 125,000.

Key to Collecting: The 1935 is one of the more common Peace silver dollars after the mid-1920s and is readily available in Uncirculated grade. Most are found in MS-60 through 63 or even 64. MS-65 pieces are scarcer but can still be found with ease.

Since most from this issue were stored in Treasury vaults, well-worn coins are seldom seen. Some pieces show abrasions, often prominent on the face of Miss Liberty. It is not unusual for a 1934, 1935, or 1935-S to have frosty fields with few bagmarks, but to have the face nicked up, the latter possibly being from marks on the original planchet.

Luster, when present, is often satiny, rather than deeply frosty. Examples can be found with decent striking, including on the center of the reverse. Cherrypicking for quality is recommended.

	Cert	Avg	%MS	VF-20	EF-40	AU-50	MS-60	MS-63	MS-64	MS-65	MS-66
1935	8,383	62.3	88%	$44	$45	$65	$80	$130	$250	$575	$1,900

1935-S Peace Dollar

1935-S • **Mintage:** 1,964,000.

Availability in Mint State: *MS-60 to MS-62:* 12,000 to 17,000. *MS-63:* 6,000 to 10,000. *MS-64:* 4,000 to 6,500. *MS-65 or better:* 1,250 to 2,000.

Availability in Circulated Grades: *VF-20 to AU-58:* 60,000 to 100,000.

Key to Collecting: Most Mint State pieces are well struck, have a satiny luster, and are very attractive. There are enough around that anyone can own one.

Varieties: Varieties exist with either three or four rays below ONE on the reverse. VAM-1 has three rays and a Micro S mintmark; VAM-3 has four rays and a Micro S mintmark that is sometimes filled in. The difference in rarity between this and the next is not known, but they probably exist in about equal numbers. The four-rays style appears only on 1935-S and no other Peace dollar. The two styles are valued equally in the marketplace, and both are popular and widely collected.

	Cert	Avg	%MS	VF-20	EF-40	AU-50	MS-60	MS-63	MS-64	MS-65	MS-66
1935-S	4,043	60.2	75%	$44	$50	$90	$250	$415	$550	$1,050	$2,650

1964-D Peace Dollar

1964-D • **Mintage:** 316,076.

Notes: On August 3, 1964, President Lyndon B. Johnson signed legislation authorizing the first striking of silver dollars since 1935. This was ostensibly done to relieve a shortage of silver dollars in the American west, where they still circulated thanks to heavy use of the coins at

Dies, models, and hubs for the 1964-dated Peace dollar coinage have been discovered in the archives of the Philadelphia Mint . . . but no coins. (Pictured: the reversed image of a die.)

the gaming tables in Nevada. To prevent hoarding, the coins would be struck only in the region where they were actively used—in other words, they'd be struck only at the Denver Mint—and would be distributed only by commercial banks and only at face value. These efforts might have ended up being for naught, as there was great anticipation of the coins. It was reported that speculators were paying $120 for 100-coin rolls months before any were even struck.

As the remaining months of 1964 elapsed, the Mint's efforts were diverted to producing other coins to relieve a national shortage. As time passed and the silver were not produced, numismatists began to doubt that they would ever materialize. Then, in May 1965, President Johnson said in a statement that the supply of small coins in commerce had at last caught up to the demand, and he ordered 45 million silver dollars to be struck by June 30. More than 316,000 of coins dated 1964 were struck at Denver before it was realized that the small-coin shortage was not really over. The Coinage Act of 1965, enacted on July 23, forbade the minting of any standard silver dollars for a further five-year period. Because of this and also because of the continuing coin shortage, the freshly minted 1964 Peace dollars were ordered destroyed. No specimens were officially saved, not even pieces for the National Numismatic Collection in the Smithsonian Institution.

Several highly reputable numismatists have stated that they or someone the trusted were present when Fern Miller, superintendent of the Denver Mint at the time, permitted Mint employees to acquire examples of the 1964 Peace dollar for face value, as was often the custom when new coins were struck. In a 1992 letter to Q. David Bowers,, Thomas K. DeLorey recalled a situation which took place when he was senior authenticator at the American Numismatic Association Certification Service at ANA Headquarters in Colorado Springs:

> While I was at ANACS I talked with a visitor who saw the balance scale in the ANA Headquarters rotunda (where the scale was in the days before the addition was put on the building) and said that he used to use one of them up at the Denver Mint. I asked him if he had worked there when the 1964 Peace dollars were struck, and if it were true that employees were allowed to buy them on the day they were struck.
>
> He said he had, and that he remembered that the word was passed that any employee who wished could buy two of them from the cashier on the way out. He didn't bother, but several people did. The next day as he was coming in, all employees were told that anybody who had bought them and didn't return them would be fired. Many did, but one guy he knew said he had spent them in a bar on the way home the night before, and did not lose his job. The man was retired when I spoke to him, and had no reason to lie.

Another reputable source told Bowers that Mint director Eva Adams told her in person that President Johnson had been given one of the coins in 1965, and that it was probably somewhere among the Johnson papers.

With such stories making the rounds, it is no wonder the believe persists in numismatic circles that, one day, a genuine 1964-D Peace dollar will surface. To date, however, no examples have been confirmed to exist, although deceptive reproductions continue to find their way onto the market.

Modern Dollars
1971 to Date

AN OVERVIEW OF
MODERN DOLLARS

Silver dollars were a standard part of numismatics from the late 1800s through the early 1960s. When it came to the Morgan and Peace dollars, banks typically kept a few thousand coins or many 1,000-coin bags in their vaults—often with unsorted miscellaneous dates and mintmarks. For collectors who visited banks to look through what was on hand, most dates and mintmarks could be found for face value, although Carson City varieties in particular were scarce. Grades ranged from well-worn to Mint State.

Silver dollars of these two types rarely circulated in most regions of the country. The exception was Nevada, where silver dollars were in wide use on gaming tables; by the 1940s, Nevada casinos were the main users of such coins. They saw limited circulation in Montana, Idaho, and certain nearby areas. In the meantime, many collectors endeavored to build collections of Morgan and Peace dollars by date and mintmark. The *Guide Book of United States Coins*, the first edition of which was released in 1946, became the standard source for market values.

In November 1962 a long-sealed (since 1929) vault at the Philadelphia Mint was opened in order to tap reserves of silver dollars, which were popular for banks to pay out during the holiday season. The coins had been put there from a shipment from a vault in the inactive (since 1909) New Orleans Mint. A few hundred 1,000-coin bags of sparkling new 1903-O Morgan dollars were casually given out. At the time this date/mintmark was the rarest and most famous of all coins in the series—so rare that it was estimated that no more than a dozen or two dozen Mint State coins existed! The *Red Book* listed the

Nevada casinos were the main users of dollar coins: (left) stacks of silver dollars at a Las Vegas craps table in 1944; (right) paying the tab in a Vegas restaurant with a Morgan dollar.

1903-O for $1,500, the top price level for any Morgan dollar. This was like finding money in the streets, a nationwide silver rush occurred, and several hundred million silver dollars of various dates and mintmarks were paid out from Treasury and bank vaults.

THE END OF SILVER DOLLARS

By 1964 it was clear that the price of silver on international markets was set to rise above the $1.2727 melt value of the silver contained in 90% silver coins. This sharply accelerated the rush to buy silver dollars from banks and from the Treasury Department. There was nothing for an individual buyer to lose: a silver dollar would still be worth a dollar and could potentially be worth more in silver value.

In March 1964, Treasury secretary Douglas Dillon declared that Silver Certificates could no longer be redeemed for silver dollars, and that no more dollar coins would be paid out. This brought a hard stop to the great silver dollar rush. The Treasury took stock of its remaining pieces and found about 3,000,000 Carson City dollars on hand—Mint State, low-mintage issues that the Department would later auction over time.

Meanwhile, other silver coins continued to be made, including the new Kennedy half dollar. By year's end the Philadelphia Mint had struck 273,304,004 of the new half dollars for circulation, and the Denver Mint had struck an additional 156,205,446. All or nearly all disappeared into the hands of the public and speculators, and it was widely reported that no one had received even a single coin in pocket change. In the autumn Secretary Dillon stated that the Treasury was investigating alternative metals for striking coins from dimes to half dollars.

In the spring and early summer of 1964 there was a strong call for more silver dollars by the public and also by Nevada casinos. None of the coins had been minted for circulation since 1935. Legislation passed on August 4, 1964, provided for the coinage of 45 million silver dollars. At the Philadelphia Mint, hubs, dies, and models dated 1964 were made for the possibility of the Morgan design being revived. In 1965 at the Denver Mint 316,076 Peace-design coins were struck with D mintmarks. They were held back from being released into circulation and melted, although some accounts stated that Mint employees were allowed to buy them. No example has ever been publicized.

New silver dollars were not to be, at least for the time being. However, the scenario had encouraged tens of thousands of people to discover numismatics and become serious collectors, while hundreds of thousands more developed a casual interest.

Obverse and reverse dies for the 1964 Morgan dollars, which were not to be. Galvanos, hubs, and master dies were discovered in the Philadelphia Mint's archives by a team of researchers including John Dannreuther and Whitman Publishing's publisher, Dennis Tucker; David Sundman; and the author, Q. David Bowers.

Thus was set the scenario for modern metallic dollars commencing with the Dwight D. Eisenhower coins in 1971. The new coin was the size of the 20th century's earlier silver dollars, but made in copper-nickel for circulation (and, in much smaller quantities, in .400 fine silver for collectors). Its motifs honor the late President Dwight D. Eisenhower, and the Apollo 11 spaceflight that had landed the first men on the Moon in 1969.

The Eisenhower dollar was minted from 1971 to 1978, with those made in 1975 and 1976 being dual-dated 1776–1976 for the national bicentennial. In 1979 the "Ike" dollar was replaced by a smaller-format coin, the Susan B. Anthony dollar, honoring the famous women's-rights leader. Its reverse design shows an eagle landing on the Moon, similar to that of its predecessor. The Anthony dollar was struck in 1979, 1980, and 1981; then, in 1999, an additional final mintage of more than 40 million coins was produced, purportedly to meet the needs of the vending-machine industry until distribution of the next year's new-design dollars could begin.

The year 2000 marked the debut of the first of several types of "golden" dollars, so called for the lustrous color of their manganese-brass surfaces. First came the Sacagawea dollar, minted from 2000 to 2008, with its conceptualized portrait of the young Shoshone Native American interpreter and guide who assisted the Lewis and Clark expedition of the early 1800s. A series of Native American dollars, each celebrating a different aspect of Native culture and historical importance, which began in 2009 and is ongoing today, is an offshoot of the Sacagawea dollar. Since 2007, the golden-dollar format has been the canvas for a series of presidential portrait dollars honoring the nation's chief executives. And in 2018 a new series of American Innovation dollars commenced, symbolizing "quintessentially American traits—the willingness to explore, to discover, and to create one's own destiny."

FOR THE COLLECTOR AND INVESTOR: MODERN DOLLARS AS A SPECIALTY

The panorama of dollars from the first 1971 Eisenhower issues up to the latest Sacagawea, Native American, Presidential, and American Innovation coins comprises more than 350 dates and mintmarks—more than all of the 1836 to 1935 Liberty Seated, Morgan, and Peace dollar varieties listed in the *Red Book* combined. A set of these early dollars in MS–63 to 65 and PF–65 grades would cost several million dollars, with one (the 1870-S) being unknown at this level. A full set of *Red Book*–listed Eisenhower, Anthony, Sacagawea, Native American, Presidential, and American Innovation dollars costs a few thousand dollars!

Eisenhower dollars, Susan B. Anthony dollars, and the golden dollars of various types are all easily found in today's marketplace. A local coin show or coin shop is a good place to get started. Most have a nice variety of coins and albums. There are also many offerings on eBay and in other Internet auctions. Dealers often have an abundance on hand of every date and mintmark, and most of the varieties. Banks sometimes have small quantities of Eisenhower or Anthony dollars. The current series are available directly from the U.S. Mint in collector formats and in rolls and bags of circulation strikes.

EISENHOWER DOLLARS

First minted in 1971, Eisenhower dollars were hailed on several fronts. Nevada casinos, which had been using metal tokens and composition chips since 1965, could at last return to having dollar coins on their tables. The use of Ike dollars (as they were nicknamed) lasted for an unexpectedly short time, after which casinos went back to using colorful chips imprinted with their names.

Another expected bonus of the Eisenhower coins, especially in Treasury Department circles, was that metal dollars could last close to 20 years or even more in circulation, thus replacing paper dollar bills that had a life of only about 18 months. This change did not happen, as the Crane Paper Co., longtime supplier to the Bureau of Engraving and Printing, had deep and seemingly sacred political connections. In time, Canada, Great Britain, and other countries replaced their lowest-denomination paper currency with coins, but despite many attempts, paper dollars are still here, whereas metal dollars hardly ever circulate. Further casting a shadow on the use of metal dollars in American commerce anytime soon has been the development of new paper of improved strength and endurance.

Another factor at the launch of the Eisenhower dollar was numismatic interest. Although the design was not a favorite of everyone, there was a strong collector demand for the varieties issued from the Philadelphia, Denver, and San Francisco Mints. This was particularly true in the first several years. During the over-promoted 1776–1976 Bicentennial and afterward, interest slumped and new collectors were fewer. All along the way, the discoveries of interesting die varieties, some differing only minutely, was continually covered by *Coin World* and *Numismatic News*, the two weekly publications, plus other media. In time, several reference books on Eisenhower dollars were published, the Internet added information, and the Ike Group website was formed by Rob Ezerman as a forum for specialists.

Today, Eisenhower dollars are very widely and enthusiastically collected. They are readily found in choice Mint State, although some of the coins made for circulation, especially of the earlier years, tend to be blemished with contact marks from jostling other coins during minting, transportation, and storage. Gems can be elusive, but most of the major varieties can be collected in gem (MS-65) or finer grade and PF-65 or finer, for relatively little expense. Certain variations in the dies, especially for 1971 and 1972, including the charmingly named 1971-D Friendly Eagle, can be added to a basic collection for reasonable cost.

The Mint issued many options for collectors, including Proofs and .400 fine silver issues. Specialists look for die varieties including modified features, doubled dies, changes in depth of relief in the design, and other popular anomalies and variations that increase the challenge of building an extensive collection in what is otherwise a fairly short coinage series. Some Denver Mint dollars of 1974 and 1977 are also known to be struck in silver clad composition rather than the intended copper-nickel.

SUSAN B. ANTHONY DOLLARS

Forming a collection of Susan B. Anthony dollars, of 1979 to 1981 and then with a jump to 1999, can be done "quick as a wink." There is but one (sort of) scarce variety, the 1979, Wide Rim, issue. The border on early strikes, called the Narrow Rim issue, was thin, with a large gap between it and the date. It was widened on later coins, making it closer to the date. Because of this visual cue, these two varieties are sometimes referred to as Near Date and Far Date, although the date did not change location.

The 1999 coins came as a surprise to numismatists, especially as tens of millions or even more Anthony dollars were still languishing in Treasury vaults. The official story was that demand for dollars was increasing rapidly through use in public transit and vending machines.

A collection of modern dollars would be incomplete without the members of this brief series, which is easy to assemble into a complete, high-grade collection of dates and mintmarks. Specialists can focus on both varieties of 1979-P (Narrow Rim and Wide Rim) and on varieties of S-mintmark styles among the Proofs. Even these are common enough to easily acquire. Those seeking a harder challenge can search for the elusive 1980-S, Repunched Mintmark, Proof.

SACAGAWEA DOLLARS

The Susan B. Anthony mini-dollar, as it was often called, never became popular in commerce and never replaced the paper dollar. It taught some valuable lessons, however, and an essentially new group of legislators—different from those who conceived the SBA dollars years earlier—jumped on the idea that a small-diameter dollar, if configured differently, would replace the paper dollar bill. This time around it would not be likely to be confused with the quarter as it was a new coin format with a golden-color surface and a plain edge.

Sacagawea, the Native American interpreter who traveled as an interpreter (not a guide, as per popular wisdom) with the Lewis and Clark Expedition in the upper reaches of the Missouri River and Northwest, was the hands-on favorite for the obverse motif, and an American eagle in flight served well on the other side.

The story of the first year of the Sacagawea dollar is almost a book in itself. In 2000, enough coins were made to furnish three for every man, woman, and child in America. The expectation was that purses and pockets would soon be jingling and jangling with them. In one sense, the Sacagawea dollar was a win-win product for the U.S. Mint and the financial statements of the Treasury Department, as each one yielded a large profit over the cost of metal and striking. The only problem was that they weren't being used in commerce, and countless millions piled up in Treasury vaults. A stop was put to this in 2002, and from that year onward production was limited to numismatic strikes sold at a premium. By 2008, when the last pieces left the coining presses, a nice series had been created—one that was and still is dear to collectors. Today a basic run of Sacagawea dollar dates and mintmarks from 2000 to 2008 in gem Mint State and Proof preservation costs less than $300. There is room for such a display in every collection.

The Sacagawea dollar series includes several uncommon varieties that make an otherwise easy-to-collect type more challenging. The 2000-P coins include popular die varieties as detailed herein. Later dates were struck in smaller quantities and not issued for circulation, but still are readily available in high grades in the numismatic marketplace.

Native American Dollars

Launched in 2009, the Native American dollars preserved the popular Sacagawea obverse motif. Unfortunately for numismatists, Congress mandated that the Mint place the date and mintmark on the edge—where it cannot be seen in an album or in most holders. The idea was that it would be cheaper not to make dated and mintmarked dies each year. The same had been done in 2008 with the Presidential dollars. This move was a major deterrent to collectors' ability enjoy such coins and organize them at a glance.

Each year the reverse has a new design that portrays an aspect of the life, activities, or experience of various Native American tribes and individuals. The result has been a series that is interesting and attractive to contemplate on both sides. The Mint created a rarity, relatively speaking, when in 2015 it issued a 2015-W coin, the first ever "golden dollar" struck at the West Point Mint and intended for sale. The Mint produced only 90,000 of these coins, which had a special Enhanced Uncirculated finish, making it about 30 times rarer than earlier coins with mintages of 3 million so. This fact was not much ballyhooed by the Mint, with the result that most collectors did not learn about these coins until after they were sold out. Subsequent low-mintage, Enhanced Uncirculated coins were produced at the Philadelphia and San Francisco Mints. Although they are keys or semi-keys to the series, each can be had for about $20 to about $25 in gem condition.

A full set of standard dates and mintmarks from 2009 to date, graded MS-63 to 65 or so, costs less than $100, to which can be added the five Enhanced Uncirculated strikes for about another $75, and all the Proofs in PF-65 for less than $150. There is a lot to like with these coins, a continuation in a way of the Sacagawea dollar series, and there is room for a set of Native American dollars in every collection

Presidential Dollars

The Presidential dollars series began in 2007 with the George Washington coin, followed in the same year by those with portraits of John Adams, Thomas Jefferson, and James Madison. The series ran into 2016 at the rate of four coins per year. To be honored on a coin, a president had to have been dead for two years. That left three candidates for the last year of regular production—Richard M. Nixon, Gerald Ford, and Ronald Reagan. Not eligible were the living past presidents Jimmy Carter, George H.W.

Bush, George W. Bush, and Bill Clinton, or the then-current president, Barack Obama. George H.W. Bush passed away in 2018, and new legislation authorized a coin in his honor in 2020.

Each Presidential dollar has a standard reverse: a view of the Statue of Liberty, by Don Everhart. As it was noted at the time, it would have been nice to have each coin depict a scene from the honored president's administration. Had the numismatic community—people constituting by far the greatest demand for such coins—been considered, the situation might have been different.

The obverse features a portrait of each president—many of them adaptations of the images used on various presidential medals issued by the Mint in past years. The dates and mintmarks are on the edges, making quick identification a challenge, a slip-up in logic, it would seem.

A complete set of Mint State and Proof coins is inexpensive, if you ignore a few special strikings made in 2015 and 2016, but even those are quite affordable to most buyers.

The Presidential dollar series includes some error varieties with plain edges, instead of the normal lettered edge. These can be added to a date-and-mintmark collection for reasonable premiums.

Otherwise the entire series is readily collectible from the secondary market and, for the current year of issue, in quantity directly from the U.S. Mint.

AMERICAN INNOVATION DOLLARS

In 2018, the U.S. Mint issued the first coin in a new, 15-year series: the American Innovation $1 Coin Program. Authorized by Public Law 115-197, each of the golden dollars in the program features a reverse design that "symbolizes quintessentially American traits—the willingness to explore, to discover, and to create one's own destiny." Each year from 2019 through 2032, four new designs, in Uncirculated and Proof finishes, are issued—one for each state, in the order in which the states ratified the Constitution or were admitted to the Union, and then for the District of Columbia and each of the five U.S. territories. They are issued for numismatic sales only; none are distributed for circulation.

The common obverse depicts a left-facing profile of the Statue of Liberty, as designed by Justin Kunz and sculpted by Phebe Hemphill. Below the motto on coins from 2019 onward is a gear-like privy mark that changes each year. The reverse designs are selected by a process similar to that of other modern series, with various groups including the U.S. Commission of Fine Arts and the Citizens Coinage Advisory Committee making design recommendations to the secretary of the Treasury.

The required inscriptions are: on the obverse, IN GOD WE TRUST and the denomination; on the reverse, the name of the state, the District of Columbia, or territory (as appropriate), along with UNITED STATES OF AMERICA; and incused into the edge, the date, the mintmark, and the inscription E PLURIBUS UNUM.

The striking on American Innovation dollars is sharp, and they are readily found in gem Mint State condition for a modest price. Both Proof and Reverse Proof formats are produced.

CERTIFIED COINS

In recent times some collectors of modern dollars and other coins have felt that unless a coin is certified it is not worth owning. Advertisements have fostered this feeling. To old-timers this attitude seems strange and takes away from the basic enjoyment of building sets.

The fact is that all standard dates and mintmarks of dollars from the 1971 Eisenhower coins to the latest issues are very common in Mint State. Coins offered as MS-65 or finer can vary widely in eye appeal, with examples in which coins certified as MS-63 have nicer strike and eye appeal than do those labeled MS-65. Cherrypicking for quality is highly recommended. Most buyers consider only the label, and really choice coins are apt to cost no more, except in the effort of hunting them down.

Proof Eisenhowers are on the long side of PF-65 unless they have been cleaned. Proof Susan B. Anthony and later coins are easy to find in high Proof grades. Certain holders have been marketed with promotional comments such as "First Strike," "Early Strike," and the like, which generally add little or nothing to their resale value. The U.S. Mint has stated on a number of occasions that it keeps no track of which coins were struck first or earliest in the shipments it makes.

While it is wise to pursue certified coins for early issues such as Liberty Seated, Morgan, and Peace dollars (which are frequently counterfeited), such is not necessarily the case with dollars from Eisenhower to date. While there are, on many occasions, beautiful coins in high-grade holders, there are so many risks involved with paying today's going rates for *conditionally* rare modern coins.

Unless one means to build a registry set with PCGS or NGC, where numbers and not eye appeal count, a better option is to form beautiful sets in a group of albums with pages, which makes them easy to store, carry, and enjoy.

EISENHOWER DOLLARS (1971–1978)

Designer: *Frank Gasparro.* **Weight:** *Silver issue—24.59 grams; copper-nickel issue—22.68 grams.*
Composition: *Silver issue—40% silver, 60% copper, consisting of outer layers of .800 silver,*
.200 copper bonded to inner core of .209 silver, .791 copper (net weight .3161 oz. pure silver);
copper-nickel issue—outer layers of .750 copper, .250 nickel bonded to inner core of pure copper.
Diameter: *38.1 mm.* **Edge:** *Reeded.* **Mints:** *Philadelphia, Denver, and San Francisco.*

Circulation
Strike

Proof

Mintmark location is
on the obverse, between
the bust and the date.

Bicentennial variety: **Designers:** *Frank Gasparro and Dennis R. Williams.* **Weight:** *Silver issue—*
24.59 grams; copper-nickel issue—22.68 grams. **Composition:** *Silver issue—outer layers of .800 silver,*
.200 copper bonded to inner core of .209 silver, .791 copper (net weight .3161 oz. pure silver);
copper-nickel issue—outer layers of .750 copper, .250 nickel bonded to inner core of pure copper.
Diameter: *38.1 mm.* **Edge:** *Reeded.* **Mints:** *Philadelphia, Denver, and San Francisco.*

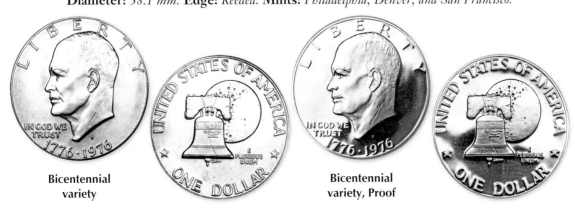

Bicentennial
variety

Bicentennial
variety, Proof

*Note: Values of common-date silver coins listed in the seventh edition of **Mega Red** have been based on a silver bullion price of $27.50 per ounce, and may vary with the prevailing spot price. To determine the intrinsic value of common silver coins, see page 1415.*

BACKGROUND

This dollar coin, honoring both President Dwight D. Eisenhower and the first landing of man on the Moon, is the work of Chief Engraver Frank Gasparro, whose initials are on the truncation of the president's neck and below the eagle. The reverse is an adaptation of the official Apollo 11 insignia. Collectors' coins were struck in 40 percent silver composition and sold by the Mint at a premium, and the circulation issue (for years a staple of the casino trade) was made in copper-nickel.

The dies for the Eisenhower dollar were modified several times by changing the relief, strengthening the design, and making Earth (above the eagle) more clearly defined.

Low-relief (Variety 1) dies, with a flattened Earth and three islands off the coast of Florida, were used for all copper-nickel issues of 1971, Uncirculated silver coins of 1971, and most copper-nickel coins of 1972.

High-relief (Variety 2) dies, with a round Earth and weak or indistinct islands, were used for all Proofs of 1971, all silver issues of 1972, and the reverse of some exceptional and scarce Philadelphia copper-nickel coins of 1972.

Improved high-relief reverse dies (Variety 3) were used for late-1972 Philadelphia copper-nickel coins and for all subsequent issues. Modified high-relief dies were also used on all issues beginning in 1973.

A few 1974-D and 1977-D dollars were made, in error, in silver clad composition.

A special reverse design was selected for the nation's Bicentennial. Nearly a thousand entries were submitted after the Treasury announced an open competition in October 1973. After the field was narrowed down to 12 semifinalists, the judges chose a rendition of the Liberty Bell superimposed on the Moon to appear on the dollar coins. The obverse remained essentially unchanged except for the dual date 1776–1976, which appeared on all dollars made during 1975 and 1976. These dual-dated coins were included in the various offerings of Proof and Uncirculated coins made by the Mint. They were also struck for general circulation.

HISTORY OF THE EISENHOWER DOLLAR

After more than a thirty-year hiatus in production of dollar coins, in 1969 Mint Director Mary Brooks advocated resuming their mintage, perhaps in a silver-clad composition (outer layers of silver-and-copper alloy bonded to an inner core of lower-grade silver alloy) as used for the Kennedy half dollars minted from 1965 up to that point. There was some demand for dollar coins from the casinos in Nevada, and there was also a sense that history and tradition required the denomination not be abandoned. To sell the concept to the budget-conscious Congress, Brooks noted that a paper dollar lasted about 18 months in circulation, while a dollar *coin* would be expected to survive nearly 20 years. The House Committee on Banking and Currency, chaired by Representative Wright Patman (D–Texas), was not convinced of the need for a dollar coin, and the idea failed to gain traction.

Official presidential portrait of Dwight D. Eisenhower.

This changed after March 28, 1969, when Dwight D. Eisenhower passed away. Many proposals were advanced to honor the widely popular former president, including more than two dozen bills presented to Congress. Among the numismatic ideas were replacing George Washington with Ike on the quarter dollar or on the dollar bill. Representative Florence Dwyer (R–New Jersey) suggested a new coin to honor the late president. She and Representative Leonor Sullivan (D–Missouri) agreed that a dollar coin would be a fitting tribute to the Republican president, balancing the representation of Democratic president John F. Kennedy on the half dollar. On April 29, 1969, Representative Robert R. Casey (D–Texas) introduced legislation that would authorize a new dollar coin with Eisenhower on the obverse and a motif relating to the Apollo 11 Moon mission on the reverse.

On October 3, 1969, the House Banking Committee agreed to support legislation to create an Eisenhower dollar without silver content, to be of cupro-nickel–clad copper (outer layers of 75 percent copper and 25 percent nickel bonded to an inner core of pure copper; sometimes called "copper-nickel clad"). This had been the composition of dimes and quarters since 1965. Supporters hoped that the House of Representatives and the Senate would both pass the bill on October 14, Eisenhower's birthday.

All of the nation's preceding dollar coins had been made of silver, and some legislators disliked the idea of a base-metal coinage. Senator Peter Dominick (R–Colorado) suggested that it be made with 40 percent silver content and supported his position with a letter from the late president's widow, Mamie Eisenhower, stating that her husband often tracked down silver dollars of his birth year, 1890, to give as gifts. The bill was amended to include silver coins in addition to cupro-nickel dollars and was passed by both houses of Congress on the desired date.

Chairman Wright Patman was still opposed to the use of silver. An amended bill was added as a rider to a bill favored by Patman relating to bank holding companies, to allow both silver-content and cupronickel coins, to eliminate silver in the current clad outer coating of half dollars, and to transfer several million long-stored nineteenth-century Morgan silver dollars, mostly from the Carson City Mint, then in a vault in the Treasury Building in Washington, to the General Services Administration to sell. President Richard M. Nixon signed the bill in the evening of December 31, New Year's Eve, just before the legislation was set to die.

THE APOLLO 11 REVERSE DESIGN

On October 29, 1969, Representative Robert Casey, who had introduced the original legislation for the dollar, proposed another bill to define the reverse as a tribute to the Apollo 11 Moon landing, one of America's proudest technological achievements. The two motifs had a connection: Eisenhower as president had signed the 1958 legislation that created NASA. Casey was inspired by the mission's insignia. The Mint advised him that his suggested inscription, WE CAME IN PEACE FOR ALL MANKIND, was too long, in view of the other lettering required by law.

Chief Engraver Frank Gasparro, who had prepared sketches earlier, went to work to create two reverse motifs—one with an eagle landing on the Moon and another with a heraldic stance for the national bird.

Congress mandated that the mission patch for Apollo 11 be used. The eagle depicted on the surface of the Moon was symbolic of the *Eagle* Lunar Module (LM), as it was called. The first iteration of the patch had the eagle holding an olive branch in its beak. In the final version the branch is on the surface of the Moon and the eagle is perched atop it.

The Apollo 11 insignia.

DESIGNING THE NEW DOLLARS

Chief Engraver Frank Gasparro wrote this reminiscence for Q. David Bowers's *Silver Dollars and Trade Dollars of the United States:*

> The happiest and most rewarding experience in my Mint career was the day I was commissioned to design the Eisenhower dollar. It was like training daily for an athletic event. I was ready. Only I had to wait twenty-five years. This is my story.
>
> I remember that happy day in 1945 when I made every effort to take off from my Mint work to go to New York City from Philadelphia. I was to see the "D" Day–World War II victory parade down Broadway to honor our hero, General Eisenhower. I admired him greatly. I stood with the rest of the bystanders to celebrate Eisenhower's welcome home. Everyone shouted and waved.
>
> Amidst all the rousing enthusiasm, I stepped back from the crowd and made a quick pencil profile sketch of our hero. I was pleased with my efforts. Then I took the train home to Philadelphia, and went back to work the next day.
>
> In my off hours, I modeled in wax and then cast in plaster a life-size portrait of Eisenhower from memory and sketches, in the round. Meanwhile, I also started to chisel and engrave in soft steel, three inches in diameter a profile portrait of him. It took a long time; as you know steel is hard to move. Meanwhile, time moved on. Late in 1970 (after twenty-five years), the director of the Mint, Mary T. Brooks, phoned me in Philadelphia from Washington (I was then chief engraver). She informed me that the Eisenhower dollar bill passed in Congress.
>
> In my capacity, I was requested to design and produce working dies for the Eisenhower dollar, fast. I knew in my bones I could make it. Time was tight and there was no time for a national competition. So, I had to work hard and long hours. This was the Thanksgiving weekend, I started. The new dollar had to be struck January 2nd, 1971 (six weeks in planning).
>
> I was ready; I had my Eisenhower early profile in hand. The dollar reverse had to portray the Apollo XI eagle insignia, as requested by the congressional bill. In this area I was fortunate, having pursued, for many years, research of the American eagle. Luckily my sketches were approved, with no changes. The rest is history.

Mint Director Mary Brooks requested of Gasparro a "peaceful eagle" and the chief engraver described his rendition as "pleasant looking." A Treasury circular described Mamie Eisenhower as being especially pleased with the portrait of her late husband.

On New Year's Day 1971 two of the galvanos used to make the pattern die hubs (the positive-image punches used to impress coin designs into dies for coinage) were presented to Mrs. Eisenhower. By January 2, 1971, hubs and working dies were ready.

TRIAL STRIKES

On January 25 the first two "official" trial or pattern strikings were made. The Mint noted the care being taken in the preparation of official master dies and hubs, including "the painstaking removal of every tiny defect and the sharpening up of each design detail." At the suggestion of Frank Gasparro the minute details in the Moon's craters had been reduced and smoothed, lest they catch dirt on the finished coins. The features of the Earth were changed (though without geographical accuracy). "Several trial working dies of the obverse and reverse of the Eisenhower dollar coin have been prepared by the Mint's engraver," read a circular distributed to the press. "Because dies of identical design may vary in height of relief and shape of the basin (background), a succession of preliminary strikes is necessary to determine the best combination of dies to use to produce the best coin within the limitations of coining press equipment and die tools. For example, too high relief or improper shape of the basin would result in

FRANK GASPARRO
216 WESTWOOD PARK DRIVE
HAVERTOWN, PENNSYLVANIA 19083

January 16, 1971

Mr. Kenneth E. Bressett
Manager, Whitman Coin Supply
              Division
Western Publishing Co., Inc.
1220 Mound Ave.
Racine, Wis. 53404

Dear Ken:

Since you are a distinguished authority on coins
I am very glad to have your comments on the Eisenhower Dollar. Thank you for writing and for the
fine compliments you have given this work.

As to the eagle, I have always been fascinated by
this beautiful bird and as a young art student I
spent many hours sketching the eagles in their
aerie at the Philadelphia Zoo. I had great pleasure
in designing this one.

As to the Eisenhower portrait, after a great deal
of study and experimentation I decided on a profile
because it seemed to lend itself best to my interpretation of him both as to appearance and character
and as I wished him to be remembered by posterity.
Of course, I kept in mind that my portrait would be
used on a coin and not a medal and I treated it differently.

You can probably appreciate the effort I put into
my designs and I hope this coin will be accepted
as graciously by others as you have accepted it.

Thank you again for your comments and interest in
my work.

Sincerely,

Frank

Frank Gasparro

A January 1971 letter written by Frank Gasparro to Kenneth Bressett, coordinating
editor of the *Guide Book of United States Coins,* regarding the Eisenhower dollar.

improper flow of the metal in the blanks and consequent damage to the dies or the coining press itself. (Too much pressure would be required to bring up all of the design elements.)"

The two January 25 coins, struck in the presence of the Mint director's Trial Strike Committee and members of the press, were examined and then destroyed in accordance with regulations. Q. David Bowers notes, "Then and now there was no policy in place to save examples of pattern and experimental coins for archiving or display in the National Numismatic Collection in the Smithsonian Institution, although in the past some have been given on an irregular and inconsistent basis."

Galvanos made in 1970 for the impending coinage of Eisenhower dollars, version 1. Note the eagle's breast feathers. The Earth is not round at the upper left. The reverse, with minutely detailed craters, was never used on regular circulation-strike or Proof coins but is likely the type or one of the types used for experimental strikes in January 1971. The Dwight D. Eisenhower Library in Abilene, Kansas, possesses similar galvanos, but of silver color.

Galvanos made in 1970, version 2. On the obverse the hair details are softer and the ear is slightly different. On the reverse the features have been softened. The island below Florida is unlike that later used in coinage.

Obverse galvano for a 1971 Eisenhower dollar.

Obverse Hub Changes, 1970–1978

In 1970 and 1971 many changes were made to the designs, mostly on the reverse, but obverse variants were also made. Various plasters, galvanos, and struck coins show differences, often minute.

Type I (Low Relief): For the first Eisenhower coinage of 1971 two sets of galvanos— electrolytic transfers from Frank Gasparro's models—were made. The Type I or low relief was used to make hubs, master dies, and, eventually, working dies for circulation-strike dollars of that year.

On Type I the upright of the R in LIBERTY has flared serifs to the left and the right of its base with each ending in a point. The definitive feature is *the lower right or tail of the R ends in a curve*. The base of the upright is much closer to the head than is the base of the tail of the R.

Type I was used exclusively on circulation strikes of all 1971 dollars from the three mints and on 1972 dollars from Philadelphia and Denver.

These obverse hub types or varieties have not gained wide popularity in the general marketplace as all issues except 1971-S Proofs are of one type or another, and the 1971-S Type II and III are from the same hub and differ mainly in the letter R in LIBERTY.

Type II (High Relief): On Type II the upright of the R is distinctive with the lower-left serif having a sharp tip on the upper side and extending to the left. The right tail of the R is long, straight, and pointed (as it is in types III and IV). The letters in LIBERTY are thicker and the styling of the hair strands is different from types II to IV. Type II was used on most Proof 1971-S dollars and not elsewhere. It is a variation of Type I. The 1971-S Proofs can be found with Type II or Type III.

Mint Director Mary T. Brooks watches a transfer lathe reducing an obverse Eisenhower dollar galvano.

The transfer lathe.

A small-size hub made by the transfer lathe, an exact copy of the galvano.

Plaster of a prototype 1970 dollar with heavier letters than are known to have been used on trial strikes.

1971-D Eisenhower dollar obverse, Type I.

Type III (High Relief): On Type III the upright of the R has no serif or projection at the lower left and is slightly indented at that point. This has been nicknamed the "Peg Leg."

Type III was used on a minority of 1971-S Proofs and on all 1972-S circulation strikes and Proofs.

Type IV (Modified High Relief): Type IV is a close copy of Type II. The left serif is slightly differently styled. The bottom of the tail of the R is slightly lower than on Type II. Three furrows are visible on Eisenhower's forehead. Type IV was used on all circulation-strike and Proof coinage for 1973, 1974, 1977, and 1978.

1971-S Eisenhower dollar obverse, Type II.

PROTOTYPE REVERSES OF *1970* AND *1971*

Several different prototype reverses were made in 1970 and 1971 that are not known to have been used for production coinage, although in some instances pattern coins were made. Points of observation include the distant Earth (the designs never did achieve a fully accurate representation), the head and feathers of the eagle, and the craters on the surface of the Moon. Q. David Bowers photographed plasters and galvanos of numerous prototypes in the archives of the Philadelphia Mint; these are illustrated in chapter 4 of the *Guide Book of Modern United States Dollar Coins.*

Mint policy at the time was to destroy all such struck pieces, rather than transferring them to the National Numismatic Collection at the Smithsonian Institution.

In addition to the reverses of the 1970 and 1971 era, others were made for the 1776–1976 Bicentennial coinage.

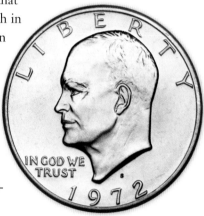

1972-S Eisenhower dollar obverse, Type III.

REGULAR REVERSES OF *1971* AND *1972*

In 1971 and 1972 the Mint produced several reverses for Eisenhower dollars, all of the standard design but with noticeable differences in the details of the Earth, the eagle, and the Moon craters. The outlines and geography of the Earth in particular permit easy attribution.

Reverse A: Low relief. *The State of Maine is huge and with a flat top.* Earth is flattened at the upper left. The north part of the Gulf of Mexico has a downward bulge. Mexico is a raised blob. The Florida peninsula can be raised overall or have a raised lump at the tip. The Eastern Seaboard is flat. Canada is almost non-existent. Below Florida is an island with another to its right and slightly lower. Beneath the first is a smaller island. South America has a prominent raised ridge at the lower right.

1973-D Eisenhower dollar obverse, Type IV.

The Ike Group identifies Reverse A as the Type 1 Reverse.

Reverse A was used on all cupro-nickel coins of 1971 of all three mints, on circulation-strike 1971-S silver coins, on a few Proof 1971-S dollars (not identified in this context until 2007), on many 1972 coins, and on all 1972-D coins. The details can vary depending on the strike and dies.

Reverse B: Earth is flattened at the upper left. *The northern part of the Gulf of Mexico is nearly round.* California, Oregon, and Washington are a raised lump, as is Mexico. The eagle has no eyebrow, giving the nickname "Friendly Eagle," sometimes listed as FEV (Friendly Eagle Variety); CONECA: RDV-006; FS-C1-1971D-901. In the Caribbean three islands slant down slightly to the right of the tip of Florida; these can appear to be joined or can be weak and almost invisible, depending on the impression. A smaller island below is in a line with the Florida peninsula.

Reverse B was used on the earlier strikings of 1971-D. Its coinage production was very small.

Eisenhower dollar regular Reverse A.

Reverse C: Aspects include a higher relief, round Earth, and continents redesigned to better match reality, but still in the same proportion. A very large low-relief amorphous island extends downward to the right, starting below the tip of Florida. The eagle's eye is different, and the breast feathers have been redone. The Moon craters are strengthened with higher rims.

Reverse C was used on most 1971-S Proofs.

Earth detail, regular Reverse A.

Reverse D: Round earth. The United States is represented as a flat country, with Maine and nearby states higher and slightly rounded. A large amorphous low-relief island(s) is seen to the lower right of Florida. South America is flat. Reverse D is identified by the Ike Group as 1972 Type 2.

Reverse D was used on some 1972 dollars.

Reverse E: Modified high relief. The Earth is round but the outline of North America has a very heavy ridge on the left; a prominent south coast; Florida raised and prominent; and a raised ridge along the coast from Florida to Maine. Canada is mostly absent. One large lumpy island is below Florida, a smaller lump is below the left side of the island, and a low-relief island more or less rectangular in shape is to the lower right of the first island. South America is outlined by a ridge, heaviest to the right. There is a hint of northwest Africa. The Ike Group identifies Reverse E as 1972 Type 3.

Eisenhower dollar Reverse B.

Eisenhower dollar Reverse C.

Eisenhower dollar Reverse D.

Earth detail, Reverse B.

Earth detail, Reverse C.

Earth detail, Reverse D.

Reverse E was introduced late in 1972 for most 1972-P cupro-nickel coins, and carried over into the next several years of production. It was used on some but not all 1972 coins, and was not used for the Bicentennial coins.

Eisenhower dollar Reverse E.

EISENHOWER DOLLARS COINED AND DISTRIBUTED

In early 1971 dies were sent to the Denver Mint and to the San Francisco Assay Office (which lost its "Mint" designation in 1962 because no coins had been struck there since 1955; the status would be restored in 1982). On February 3, 1971, the first production of circulation-strike Eisenhower dollars took place at the Denver Mint, apparently without a public ceremony.

On March 31, a first-strike ceremony was held at San Francisco. Mint Director Mary T. Brooks welcomed guests and invited everyone into a room where four old-style knuckle-action presses with Eisenhower dies were set up. The first coins struck on 40 percent silver planchets were reserved to be given to members of the Eisenhower family, President Richard Nixon, and select others. San Francisco superintendent John F. Breckle stated that an eight-hour shift on the presses could produce 240,000 coins.

Earth detail, Reverse E.

In the meantime, collectors eagerly awaited further news about methods of production, metallic content, and distribution policies for the coins. On June 18, according to an announcement, order forms for the new Eisenhower dollar coins would be made available. After that time approximately 53 million order blanks were sent to 84,000 distribution centers including 35,000 banks and branches and 44,000 post offices, and others to congressional offices, to the armed forces, and to customers on the Mint mailing list.

The order period opened on July 1, 1971, and orders were limited to five Proof and five Uncirculated coins per person. The initial cost of the 40 percent silver coins in the Proof format was $10, and the Uncirculated coins were offered at $3 each. None were included in the Treasury's offering of Mint sets for $3.50 per set, which held coins from the cent to the half dollar.

On July 27, 1971, President Nixon presented the first Proof Eisenhower dollar to Mrs. Eisenhower in a White House ceremony that included Mint Director Brooks and Secretary of the Treasury John Connally. In Abilene, Kansas, at 11:00 a.m. August 18, Director Brooks presented a pair of galvanos to Dr. John E. Wickman, director of the Dwight D. Eisenhower Library.

At the Post Office within the Treasury Building in Washington on Eisenhower's birthday, October 14, 1971, Assistant Secretary of the Treasury Eugene T. Rossides and Mint Director Brooks mailed the first order containing a Proof Eisenhower dollar. Uncirculated 1971-S 40 percent silver dollars were put up in bags of 1,000 coins and shipped from San Francisco to the New York Assay Office, where they were packaged and scheduled to be sent to buyers by registered mail.

President Richard M. Nixon presenting the first 1971-S Proof dollar to Mamie Eisenhower. Secretary of the Treasury John Connally and Mint Director Mary Brooks are to the left.

Circulation-strike Eisenhower dollars were released by the Federal Reserve System and distributed through banks beginning on November 1, 1971. The coins had attracted a lot of interest, and many people bought them. Contemporary news articles, including those sent out by the Mint, said little about the mints that produced them and rarely mentioned that certain coins had D or S mintmarks.

In 1972 the Mint introduced a new type of hardened steel that prolonged die life by 50 percent. As detailed above in the reverse-die descriptions, the circulation-strike 1971 coins were in lower relief with Reverse A, and the 1971-S Proofs were in higher relief with Reverse C. Other changes were made. In 1972 Reverse E was introduced; it was continued through to the end of the Eisenhower series in 1978, except for the 1776–1976 Bicentennial dollars, which had a special reverse. Sometimes circulation-strike dies toward the end of their service life showed certain features weakly, and in some instances the reverse details seem to have been touched up slightly. There were minor changes made in the obverse dies, not as distinctive as for the reverse dies.

EISENHOWER DOLLARS IN CIRCULATION

One welcome use of the Eisenhower dollars came from the Nevada casinos at Las Vegas, Reno, and Lake Tahoe, where hungry slot machines were to gobble millions of the coins during the next several years and had mechanisms to accommodate them. They were also familiar sights on roulette, blackjack, and other gaming tables. Most of these were Denver Mint coins. Silver dollars of like diameter had been last used in casinos in 1964, by which time most were Morgan dollars dated 1921 and Peace dollars from 1921 to 1935, nearly all in worn grades with none of numismatic value at the time. After then the casinos used metal tokens (many made by the Franklin Mint) and colored chips made of various material. Widespread use of Eisenhower dollars in the casinos proved to be short-lived, and did not continue past the early 1970s, although some stray pieces were seen on gaming tables as late as 1977. Colored chips made of composite material were the order of the day and took precedence. These also had an added advantage: many gamblers took chips home as souvenirs rather than cashing them in, yielding a profit to the issuers.

Although the Treasury hoped that Eisenhower dollars would circulate in everyday commerce, they did not. The public was used to paper dollars that were lighter and easier to carry, without caring that paper currency's life expectancy in circulation was short. The new dollars might have found use in vending machines, but that was unlikely, as by 1971 the largest coin of the realm in wide use was the quarter dollar. Half dollars were available in quantity in Treasury and other storage vaults, but they were hardly ever seen in pocket change. The last half dollars used in everyday transactions were Franklins, which started disappearing from circulation in 1964 and were mostly gone by late 1965. Silver-content Kennedy half dollars, launched in March 1964, were hoarded and never used in circulation.

Numismatists and their societies and journals were very supportive of the Eisenhower dollars, but, save for limited use in casinos during the first several years, the public did not take a fancy to them. A later study showed that cupro-nickel Eisenhower dollars paid out by banks, excepting those taken by casinos, were quickly returned and did not pass hand to hand. In contrast, cents, nickels, dimes, and quarters remained in circulation for years.

Merchants generally disliked the new coins as an inconvenience. As many cash drawers did not have a space for dollars, on the rare occasions they were received the cashiers would sometimes keep the Eisenhower coins in a separate box. The vast majority of vending machines, turnpike toll machines, and other devices would not accept them.

On July 31, 1972, Treasury vaults held 30.7 million Eisenhower dollars, and Federal Reserve Banks stored an additional 49.5 million. All official news releases proclaimed the Eisenhower dollar to be a great success, quite contrary to reality.

Uncirculated and Proof Packaging

The first Uncirculated silver-clad dollars were housed in Pliofilm packages in a navy-blue envelope, earning nicknames such as "blue Ikes" and "Blue Pack" Eisenhowers. These were released beginning on March 31, 1971. The Proof versions of the silver-content coins were housed in large, somewhat awkward plastic holders, and came in a brown wood-grain box with a gold embossed eagle design on the front, giving rise to "brown Ikes," "Brown Pack," and similar nicknames. The "blue" and "brown" nicknames were in use through the late twentieth century, but are seldom heard today as so many of the original holders have been replaced by third-party–certified slabs. In 1972 the Uncirculated and Proof silver-content dollars were each packaged in the same-style boxes.

The 1976 Bicentennial Celebration

The Advisory Panel on Coins and Medals of the American Revolution Bicentennial Commission (ARBC) held its first meeting in January 1970 in Washington, D.C. The field of numismatics was well represented by Margo Russell, editor of *Coin World*; Clifford Mishler, editor of *Numismatic News*; Herbert M. Bergen, president of the American Numismatic Association; and others.

The group proposed a sweeping program to change all of the coin designs from the cent to the dollar. In opposition, the Mint and Treasury Department officials were dead set against the idea of creating coins for collectors and other souvenir hunters. To back up their position, spokespeople recounted the irregular distribution, false marketing statements, and other ghosts from certain commemorative coin programs from 1935 to 1946. Abuses were many during that time as most coins were distributed by private individuals or groups without government or other oversight. For some exploitative issues few records were kept, false "sold out" information was given, profits disappeared, and there were other irregularities. Mint Director Mary T. Brooks stated that issuing commemoratives was counter to the Mint's business of producing regular coinage. Indeed, none had been made since 1954, when the Carver/Washington series of half dollars expired.

The Treasury thought that a line of Mint-made medals would be ideal to observe the Bicentennial, an idea opposed by the Medallic Art Company and the Franklin Mint, large producers in the private arena. Their argument was that the Mint could not market medals in quantity.

The Treasury's opposition to a Bicentennial coinage changed when Wright Patman (D–Texas), chairman of the House Banking Committee, wrote to ARBC chairman David J. Mahoney on October 1, 1970, stating that the Committee would be willing to give careful consideration to such an idea. At this time the Eisenhower dollar was not a reality yet, and it does not seem to have been proposed in any Bicentennial discussions.

Meetings of the ARBC continued, and on March 5, 1973, Treasury Secretary George Schultz sent the Nixon administration's proposal for a Bicentennial coinage to Capitol Hill. It was to consist of cupronickel–clad coins for general circulation and silver-content coins for sale to collectors and other buyers at a premium. Two denominations were proposed: the half dollar and dollar. In time the quarter denomination was added. After many meetings and discussions Public Law 93-127 authorizing the Bicentennial coinage was passed by both houses of Congress. President Nixon signed it into law on October 18, 1973.

Design Competition for Bicentennial Coins

Instead of using the many ideas proposed by the sculptor-engravers on the Mint staff, the Treasury Department invited citizens with artistic talent to submit ideas. These had to be emblematic of the 1776–1976 Bicentennial and had to include UNITED STATES OF AMERICA and E PLURIBUS UNUM as inscriptions. The rules stated that entries had to be from citizens of the United States; had to be accompanied by a black-and-white sketch or drawing within a 10-inch circle or a photograph of like diameter of a model, either to be mounted on an 11-by-14–inch illustration board; and had to be received by December 14, 1973. Semi-finalists would be required to submit a model not to exceed 8-1/2 inches in diameter and with the relief not to exceed 5/32 of an inch. "For coinability, areas of high relief on the obverse side should be opposite areas of low relief on the reverse."

Mint Director Brooks sent out notices to art schools and colleges to stir up interest. During the competition she went on a three-week trip around the United States to give television, radio, and newspaper interviews. These designs were to be of the people, by the people, and for the people—created by citizens.

The contest drew 884 qualified entries. These were forwarded to the Philadelphia Mint. Beginning at 11:00 a.m., January 9, 1974, these were reviewed by a panel of judges chaired by Robert Weinman, president of the National Sculpture Society. Interested media people were invited to watch the judging. The panel selected 12 semi-finalists, each of whom was invited to submit his or her design in the form of a plaster model, for which the Treasury Department would pay $750 each.

Finalists were to receive $5,000 each and to be announced after George Washington's birthday, February 22, 1974.

It was not until March 6 that Secretary of the Treasury George Shultz and Mint Director Mary Brooks announced the winners: Jack L. Ahr of Arlington Heights, Illinois, for the quarter, Seth G. Huntington of Minneapolis for the half dollar, and Dennis R. Williams of Columbus, Ohio, for the dollar. Later, chairman Weinberg commented, "I really don't think what we got was a great bargain. Nothing we selected was a real winner that I'd fight to the death for. In terms of what we had to work with, though, I think we did the best we could."

The news release included this about Williams:

> Dennis R. Williams . . . designed the Liberty Bell extending over the Moon that was selected for the back of the one dollar coin . . . He is 21 years old and in his junior year at the Columbus College of Art and Design in Columbus, Ohio, majoring in sculpture. His sculpture instructor assigned him the National Bicentennial Coin Design Competition as a design problem.
>
> Mr. Williams was born in Erie, Pennsylvania, October 26, 1952, but resides at 880 East Broad Street in Columbus while attending school. He says he would eventually like to teach sculpture at the college level and plans to use his $5,000 award to continue his education.

In the March 1974 issue of *The Numismatist*, American Numismatic Association president Virginia Culver included this as part of her monthly message:

> The upcoming bicentennial of our country's independence is drawing closer at hand and its celebration should affect every person in the United States. Coin collectors all over the world are going to be able to add specimens to their collections that will mark this commemoration.
>
> It was a rare privilege for me to be able to view the submitted entries for our coinage change at the Philadelphia Mint in January. History was being made as the five eminent judges reviewed the almost 1,000 entries. It was intriguing to see the varied submissions of the artists, knowing these were their interpretations of our country's birthday. In many, one could see the similarity of design that had been used before on either our coinage or on various tokens and medals. On some, one wondered just what connection the theme would have with our bicentennial.
>
> In choosing the semi-finalists, the judges not only had to consider the design, but if it would be effective when struck on the reverse of one of our coins. Our Mint Director, Mrs. Mary T. Brooks, is certainly to be commended for the interest she stimulated across this country for the almost 1,000 entries.

For the dollar a sketch for a *quarter* by Dennis R. Williams was selected—the Liberty Bell partly superimposed on the Moon. At the Mint the lettering was changed from QUARTER DOLLAR to ONE DOLLAR. E / PLURIBUS / UNUM was changed to three lines instead of two.

The original artwork for Dennis R. Williams's Bicentennial design entry for the *quarter dollar*. This image was distributed to the media in early 1974.

A plaster model for Williams's quarter dollar design.

Williams' artistically pockmarked Moon compared to the real Moon.

REVERSE VARIETIES 1 AND 2 OF 1976

The following images show the regular reverse varieties of 1976 as well as some pattern variants.

Galvano of the first reverse of the 1776–1976 dollar with block letters without serifs.

A plaster of the Bicentennial dollar reverse, Variety 1. The craters are not as prominent as on the final version.

Coin showing the adopted 1776–1976 Bicentennial dollar reverse Variety 1. These were struck in calendar-year 1975.

The new 1776–1976 Variety 2 reverse. The letters are lighter and have traces of serifs. The position of the E over the I in PLURIBUS is farther to the left.

Galvano of the 1776–1976 Bicentennial dollar reverse, Variety 2. Called *Light Letters* at the Mint.

Coin with the adopted 1976 Bicentennial dollar reverse, Variety 2, as used for coinage.

Variety 1: *Quick identifier:* The E is directly over the I in PLURIBUS. This is Dennis R. Williams's original design. Its heavy block letters are without serifs. The O in OF is thick with a smaller center than on the following.

The block letters on the Bicentennial reverse were viewed as being too harsh and modernistic, and late in 1975 a second variety was made, first with heavy letters and, finally, a version was made by Mint sculptor-engraver Philip Fowler featuring delicate lettering with light serifs.

Variety 2: *Quick identifier:* The E is directly over the RI in PLURIBUS. The letters are lighter and thinner, with small serifs on most. The O in OF is thin, with a larger center. This is a modification by Mint sculptor-engraver Philip Fowler. Called *Light Letters* at the Mint.

BICENTENNIAL COINS STRUCK AND RELEASED

At 11:00 a.m. August 12, 1974, the first-strike ceremony for the 1976 Bicentennial coins was held at the Philadelphia Mint with the three designers in attendance. Some of the coins and the galvanos were given to Mint Director Mary Brooks, who took them to the 83rd anniversary convention of the American Numismatic Association, on August 13, where they were displayed and admired.

In the White House on November 13, 1974, Mint Director Brooks presented President Gerald Ford with the first Bicentennial Proof set. An accompanying news release told of Bicentennial coins and order periods.

On November 15 the U.S. Mint began accepting orders for silver-content 1976-S coins. A three-coin Uncirculated set was priced at $9 and Proofs at $15 for the trio, with a limit of five sets per customer for each of the two options.

A dedication ceremony for the ANA Museum at its Colorado Springs headquarters was held on January 18, 1975. Director Brooks was on hand and presented a set of Bicentennial Proof coins. On January 19, 1975, the Mint announced a price reduction from $15 to $12 for 40% percent silver Bicentennial Proof sets and the removal of order limits. The same news release stated this:

> The new Automatic Proof Coin Handling System automates the feeding of blanks to a Proof coin press and places the finished coin into a color-coded coin tray providing faster inspection of the finished product. Minimal handling also results in fewer rejects due to accidental scratching.
>
> The prototype system is presently operational to handle dollar coins at the rate of 22 per minute and, by spring, will be further developed to handle 25 and 50 cent pieces.

In June 1975 the Treasury announced that as of July 7 the circulating Bicentennial coins would be available for face value at banks. This news was later revised to state that on the Monday, July 7, the 12 Federal Reserve Banks and their branches would begin shipping coins to their bank affiliates. Further changes were made in the schedule, and the dollars were expected to be released in September.

To the public this was very confusing. Citizens who expected to go to banks in early July and buy as many quarters, half dollars, and dollars as desired now did not know what to do. In July some collectors across the country reported receiving Proof sets. Confusion continued everywhere. Unsure of where the circulation-strike coins could be purchased, and when, the average American lost interest. There were no lines of waiting buyers at banks. There were no shortages except in a few isolated instances.

Not helping matters was the fact that reviews of the half dollar were often negative. At the First National Bank on Broad Street in Charleston, South Carolina, Mrs. Becky Thompson, head teller, told a reporter from the *Charleston News and Courier* that demand was light as people did not know which banks had the coins. Furthermore:

> One of the reasons the coin is not going at a faster pace, Mrs. Thompson said, it that "People just don't like half dollars. The Bicentennial quarter and dollar coins should go over better."

Sales of 40 percent silver circulation-strike Bicentennial coins were falling far behind the Treasury's predictions, while Treasury officials were scratching their heads in bewilderment. On September 11, 1975, Mint Director Brooks put into effect a new plan. Henceforth financial institutions such as banks and credit unions could take part in a bulk program to order silver sets in groups of 50. Eventually, more than 2.2 million sets were sold under this program.

THE LAUNCH AND DECLINE OF THE BICENTENNIAL DOLLAR

The launching of the Bicentennial dollar was a quiet affair. Monroe Kimbrel, president of the Federal Reserve Bank of Atlanta, invited Mint Director Brooks and designer Williams to a "ceremonial function" at the Monetary Museum at the bank at 10:30 a.m. on Monday, October 13. The event garnered hardly any nationwide interest or attention.

On the same day circulation strikes of the Bicentennial dollars were shipped to commercial banks. Distribution began on Tuesday the 14th.

As 1975 drew to a close the Bicentennial coins were no longer newsworthy on a national basis. Of the three denominations released, the dollar received only a tiny fraction of the coverage accorded to the half dollar and quarter. It was late at the gate. During 1976, sales of Bicentennial coins were satisfactory in terms of exceeding past annual sales of Proof sets and related collector coins. The last 40 percent silver coins were struck in a special ceremony in San Francisco on June 22, with Director Brooks on hand. The event was closed to the public due to unspecified security concerns.

On September 11 the Treasury stated that since the release of circulation strikes in 1975 "143 million Liberty Bell with Moon dollars" had been paid out, far exceeding comparable-period distribution of earlier regular-design Eisenhower dollars. This amounted to more than one coin for every family in America. In reality, few citizens ever saw one of the coins.

During the holiday season a push was made for sales by new packaging, "a scenic view of Independence Hall" on the Uncirculated silver sets, many of which were shipped from San Francisco to be offered at the shops in the Denver and San Francisco mints. Some banks and financial institutions continued offering Bicentennial coins in the two metal types. There was no particular rush to buy them, as they were old news by that time.

The high mintages anticipated by Mint Director Brooks did not come. According to later government statistics a nationwide recession began in November 1973 and lasted until March 1975, during which time the Gross Domestic Product lost 3.2 percent. No doubt this dramatically affected the public demand for Bicentennial coins, causing production figures to fall far short of their predictions.

After the Bicentennial celebration ended the Treasury Department came to the realization that Eisenhower dollars of either the old design or with the Bicentennial motif were never going to be popular in circulation. By that time the Nevada casinos had long since stopped ordering quantities.

Unrelated to numismatics and coinage there was wild speculation in the silver bullion market, and the use of this metal was discontinued for coinage of silver-content Eisenhower dollars for the numismatic market. Production was slowed, and in 1978 the last "Ikes" were coined. A core of collectors had kept the faith,

Advertisement No. 2 on sheets of ready-made notices for banks and other outlets to publicize sets of Uncirculated 1976-S silver-content coins. The Treasury Department had an overwhelming quantity of unsold sets.

however, and Proofs and circulation strikes remained popular until the end. In March 1985 the last Bicentennial silver Proof sets were sold. In fiscal-year 1986 28,379 Uncirculated silver sets were sold. The Mint stated that sales would end on December 31, after which any remaining coins would be melted.

EISENHOWER DOLLARS IN LATER YEARS

In January 1993 Joe Coyne, assistant to the board at the Office of Board Members, Federal Reserve Board Public Affairs Office, told Frank Van Valen, who was assisting Q. David Bowers in numismatic research, that the Federal Reserve had no stockpiles of Eisenhower dollars at any of the 12 Federal Reserve Banks. All had been dispersed to smaller banks throughout the system. In a visit to the vault in the San Francisco Federal Reserve Bank in April 2015, Bowers and Whitman publisher Dennis Tucker were informed that there were many twentieth-century dollars in storage there, but only a stray bag or two or three of Eisenhower or Anthony dollars, if any at all. No numismatically useful records were on hand.

SPECIAL COINS FOR THE SMITHSONIAN

In 1962 Eva Adams, then director of the Mint, the predecessor of Mary Brooks, directed the Denver Mint to make special strikings of current coins for the Smithsonian Institution. These pieces were especially carefully made with satiny "Special Mint Set"–type finishes, likely first strikes carefully made from new dies. Later, during the Eisenhower dollar era, at least two each of the following varieties were made, as evidenced by examples held by the Smithsonian today: 1971-D, 1973-D, 1776–1976-D, and 1977-D. These were in the National Numismatic Collection but not tagged or recognized until 2013, when professional numismatist Jeff Garrett came across them while doing other research under the aegis of NNC curator Dr. Richard Doty. Nothing about them had ever been mentioned in Mint reports or publicity, nor had such special strikings been made available to collectors.

Specimen strike of a 1973-D Eisenhower dollar in the National Numismatic Collection in the Smithsonian Institution.

A REMARKABLE HOARD

In 2011 the Big Sky Hoard was announced by Littleton Coin Company:

> After thirty years in a Montana bank vault, a previously unknown hoard of over 220,000 Eisenhower dollars was discovered in 2011. Put away for years by a prominent Montana family, most of the coins in this remarkable hoard were still in original mint-sewn bags and were untouched by the wear and tear of general circulation. Shipped from the Denver Mint right to a Federal Reserve Bank branch in Montana, the coins missed the traditional movement between the mint and local banks, and escaped the widespread use of "Ike" dollars in western casinos.

A small part of the Big Sky Hoard.

The majority of these were 1974-D and 1977-D and of above-average Mint State quality. These were offered to Littleton customers, and brisk sales resulted.

EISENHOWER DOLLARS (1971–1978): GUIDE TO COLLECTING

BEING A SMART BUYER

Striking on Eisenhower dollars generally is very good. For circulation strikes, on the obverse check the high parts of the portrait, and on the reverse, the details of the eagle. Nearly all Proofs are well struck and of high quality.

The popularity of Eisenhower dollars has varied over the years. As noted above, during the time of their production there was a steady numismatic demand, particularly from 1971 until the Bicentennial confusion, but nothing special. After a spike in sales for the 1971 coins, including Proofs, demand fell. In later years fewer Ike Proof dollars were made than of the other denominations, cents to half dollars, sold in sets.

In *The Numismatist* in April 1974 a brilliant landmark article by Herbert P. Hicks, "Eisenhower Dollar Varieties," explored in depth the differences he noted on dies. This set the standard for later research and descriptions by others. The lack of excitement for the 1976 Bicentennial designs dampened collector enthusiasm with the result that the issues of 1977 and 1978 did not garner much notice. By that time news concerning the development of a reduced-diameter "mini-dollar" attracted a lot of attention.

When the Susan B. Anthony mini-dollars were launched in 1979, the Eisenhower dollars became history. Many numismatists had completed basic sets of dates, mintmarks, and the two metal compositions. Excepting for dedicated specialists who followed the 1974 Hicks article, the obverse and reverse die varieties were generally ignored until the publication of *Walter Breen's Complete Encyclopedia of U.S. and Colonial Coins* in 1988. That book created a sensation. In its first year Q. David Bowers reported selling more than 10,000 copies. Bowers recalls the hobby environment for Eisenhower dollars in the late 1980s:

> A complete set of basic dates and mintmarks was inexpensive at the time, and many dealers offered them in albums. Write a check, and a few minutes later you owned a complete set. It was my feeling that in the future these coins would be widely collected. By way of analogy, I recall that when I first started my coin business on a part-time basis in 1953, hardly anyone liked Franklin half dollars—the main exceptions being investors who bought bank-wrapped rolls of all coins and never looked at them. Sure enough, by the early 1990s Franklin half dollars had not been made for a long time—since 1963—and they were very popular and enjoyed a strong market as they continue to do today. This happened with Eisenhower dollars. By the late 1990s they were in great demand, and a subculture had arisen of enthusiasts who examined coins under magnification to find doubled dies, to take notice of the variations in the depiction of Earth, and to otherwise note what differences they could find. The best-selling book by Bill Fivaz and J.T. Stanton, the *Cherrypickers' Guide to Rare Die Varieties*, created a dramatic spurt in interest in the 1990s as did the popular CONECA group (Combined Organizations of Numismatic Error Collectors of America). More specific and with more varieties is a book by John Wexler, *The Authoritative Reference on Eisenhower Dollars*, published in 1998, succeeded in 2007 by a book of the same title, now with additional coauthors. Appendix I of that book, "Important Letters and Documents," includes extensive correspondence to and from Herbert P. Hicks and is a valuable resource. In more recent times the Ike Group has maintained an information-filled Web site at www.ikegroup.info. To this Robert Ezerman, lead author of the 2011 book *Collectible Ike Varieties—Facts, Photos and Theories*, has been a prime contributor. The site includes the Designated Ike Variety Attribution section listing varieties thought to be of interest to specialists. Also included is an illustrated section on fantasy Eisenhower dollars dated 1970 and 1975 made by Daniel Carr, who operates the Moonlight Mint in Colorado.
>
> CONECA has a marvelous Web site, www.varietyvista.com, that lists and describes doubled dies and mintmark variations and gives much other information, much of which has been provided by Dr.

James Wiles from his careful and pioneering studies. Today the formation of a set of Eisenhower dollars of the basic dates and mintmarks, circulation strikes as well as Proofs, is an interesting and affordable pursuit. There are no "impossible" rarities. The more popular and publicized obverse and reverse die varieties range from common to slightly scarce, but all are affordable. Many can be found by cherry-picking at numismatic conventions and in coin shops.

Uncirculated Eisenhower dollars of the various years 1971 to 1978 vary in sharpness from issue to issue. Most Eisenhower dollars that have circulated, such as those used in the Nevada casinos, are dull in appearance and unattractive. More attractive Mint State coins are readily available and inexpensive. For the most part, the best specimens are represented by Proofs or by hand-selected high-grade Mint State coins.

Bowers advises: "A degree of connoisseurship is required to build a high-quality set. Eisenhower dollars produced for collectors—including Proofs and those sold in Mint sets—tend to be available in better grades, virtually as issued, which for Proof means PF-65 or much finer. However, circulation-strike coins taken from bags are apt to be a different story and are often heavily marked and fairly unattractive, this being particularly true of coins from the first two years."

AVAILABILITY

Eisenhower dollars are easily obtained in choice Mint State, although some of the coins made for circulation, especially of the earlier years, tend to be blemished with contact marks from jostling other coins during minting, transportation, and storage. Gems can be elusive. The Mint issued many options for collectors, including Proofs and .400 fine silver issues. Specialists look for die varieties including modified features, doubled dies, changes in depth of relief in the design, and other popular anomalies and variations that increase the challenge of building an extensive collection in what is otherwise a fairly short coinage series. Some Denver Mint dollars of 1974 and 1977 are also known to be struck in error, in silver clad composition rather than the intended copper-nickel. Mint State coins are common in the marketplace, although several early varieties are elusive at MS-65 or higher grades. Lower grades are not widely collected. Proofs were made of the various issues (both copper-nickel clad and silver clad from 1971 to 1976; copper-nickel only in 1977 and 1978).

Putting together a nicely matched MS-65 and PF-65 set can be a challenge, at least with respect to MS-65 coins of certain dates. As the individual date descriptions in this book indicate, there are some truly scarce issues, particularly among those that were not specifically sold to collectors, such as 1971 (scarcest), 1971-D Variety 1 reverse (second scarcest), 1972 Variety 2 reverse (slightly scarce, once considered a rarity), and 1972-D. The circulation-strike 1776–1976 Bicentennial dollars tend to have a lot of bagmarks, but such coins are plentiful in the marketplace and inexpensive, so tracking down an MS-65 or better example will not be difficult.

Due to the demand for registry sets (in which a set with the highest cumulative total of grading numbers wins), some buyers have paid tremendous premiums for certain Eisenhower dollars finer than MS-65. Use caution in this scenario. Grading is a matter of opinion, and there are many MS-66 coins in the marketplace that are not as attractive overall as hand-selected MS-64 or 65 coins. Bowers gives an example: "In December 2015 I purchased a certified MS-62 1971-D dollar that was nicer overall than a clearly photographed eBay offering of a certified MS-65 coin." In *CoinWeek*, March 21, 2012, Charles Morgan commented:

> I stand in defense of Eisenhower dollars because of their endless complexity. It stands today as the greatest achievement in clad coinage in U.S. history. It was the most technically challenging coin ever attempted. Sorry, Saint-Gaudens; your 1907 double eagle was spectacular, but try to churn out eighty million Eisenhower dollars on [old] presses leading to a number of modifications and revisions, some of which are only now being identified by experts—and it is a series like this that calls into question how much experts really know about modern coinage.

Researching the Eisenhower dollar is vital for numismatic historians who want to understand what the post-silver era was like. The Eisenhower dollar was a noble failure. In this respect, it truly is a perfect collectible coin.

EISENHOWER (1971–1978)

GRADING STANDARDS

MS-60 to 70 (Mint State). *Obverse:* At MS-60, some abrasion and contact marks are evident, most noticeably on the cheek, jaw, and temple. Luster is present, but may be dull or lifeless. At MS-63, contact marks are extensive but not distracting. Abrasion still is evident, but less than at lower levels. MS-64 coins are slightly finer. An MS-65 coin may have minor abrasion, but contact marks are so minute as to require magnification. Luster should be full and rich.

1971-S. Graded MS-65.

Reverse: At MS-60, some abrasion and contact marks are evident, most noticeably on the eagle's breast, head, and talons. Otherwise, the same comments apply as for the obverse.

AU-50, 53, 55, 58 (About Uncirculated). *Obverse:* Light wear is seen on the higher-relief areas of the portrait. At AU-58, the luster is extensive, but incomplete. At AU–50 and 53, luster is less but still present. *Reverse:* Further wear is evident on the eagle, particularly the head, breast, talons, and tops of the wings. Otherwise, the same comments apply as for the obverse.

1972. Graded AU-50.

Eisenhower dollars are seldom collected in grades lower than AU-50.

PF-60 to 70 (Proof). *Obverse and Reverse:* Proofs that are extensively cleaned and have many hairlines, or that are dull and grainy, are lower level, such as PF-60 to 62. There are not many of these in the marketplace. With medium hairlines and good reflectivity, assigned grades of PF–63 or 64 are appropriate. With relatively few hairlines a rating of PF-65 can be given. PF-66 may have hairlines so delicate that magnification is needed

1776–1976-S, Bicentennial. Graded PF-68.

to see them. Above that, a Proof should be free of any hairlines or other problems.

1971 Eisenhower Dollar

1971, Copper-Nickel Clad •
Mintage: 47,799,000.

Availability in Mint State: Among the regular-issue dates and mintmarks in the Eisenhower series the 1971 is the third most elusive, after the 1972, Variety 2, and the 1971-D Reverse B. At the MS-66 or higher level they are hard to find in relation to demand. In terms of basic date and mintmark issues this is the key to a set of high-grade Eisenhower dollars. There are enough MS-65 coins in the marketplace that finding one will be no problem at all, although some are certainly nicer than others. Early-die-state examples with flashy luster are elusive. MS-64 coins are very common and cost a fraction of the price of MS-65.

Availability in circulated grades: This issue is very common in circulated grades. The Treasury made vigorous efforts to put these into circulation. As a general statement, circulated Eisenhower dollars are rarely collected, as Mint State coins are readily available.

Characteristics of striking: These are of average striking quality. They are frequently seen with some obverse design weakness. Charles Morgan observed in the *Guide Book of Modern United States Dollar Coins:* "Philadelphia began minting the 1971 Ike dollar within days of the coin going into production in Denver. The large-format cupro-nickel–clad dollar coin was struck up on World War II–era presses; the results were less than complimentary to Frank Gasparro's design. Evidence of striking weakness can often be noted in the prevalence of annealing chatter (the star field of crisscross cuts on a planchet that are imparted on the coin during the planchet making process). Even on the most desirable Ike dollars, these marks will be visible to the naked eye on Eisenhower's jawline and cheek. Another feature of Ike dollars struck in 1971 and 1972 is die sink, which renders the far left portion of IN GOD WE TRUST flat and lifeless."

Notes: No circulation-strike 1971 Eisenhower dollars from any mint were included in 1971 Mint sets offered for sale for $3.50 to collectors. Acquisition was by a catch-as-catch-can basis, although dealers in modern coins stocked many. The Mint sold dollars separately for $3 each. None had been handled with particular care at the mints, so that most showed handling and bagmarks and graded MS-63 or lower.

About 478 obverse dies and 239 reverses were made for this coinage, and most were probably used.

	Cert	Avg	%MS	EF-40	MS-63	MS-65	MS-66
1971, Copper-Nickel Clad, Reverse A	1,930	63.9	97%	$3	$6	$85	$600

1971-D Eisenhower Dollar

1971-D, Copper-Nickel Clad, Variety 1 (Reverse A) • Mintage:
Most of 68,587,424.

Availability in Mint State: The 1971-D Variety 1 is slightly scarce in grades MS-66 and above. It is relatively common, as far as clad circulation-strike Eisenhower dollars go, in MS-65 or below. Flashy luster is common for this issue. Some examples may even exhibit a prooflike, "polished" appearance.

Availability in circulated grades: Very common. The Treasury made vigorous efforts to put these into circulation. Many were used in Nevada casinos.

Characteristics of striking: These are usually sharp, although weakly struck examples are numerous. Sharp strikes can be located with regularity. The overall quality of this issue is above average. Charles Morgan observed in the *Guide Book of Modern United States Dollar Coins:* "Throughout the entire run of the Eisenhower dollar series, the Denver Mint bettered the Philadelphia Mint in the quality of coins it struck for circulation. This holds true for all series of coins, from the Lincoln cent through to the Ike dollar. Of all of the D-Mint coins in the Ike series, the 1971-D and the 1976-D [Reverse A] are by far the nicest coins struck for circulation. The die-sink issue that plagues the 1971 also affects the 1971-D, however, it is possible to find exceptional Ike dollars from this issue in high numerical grades and very few if any detracting marks with die sink. Several PCGS-graded MS-67 coins exhibit this feature."

Notes: Despite not being included in the 1971 Annual Mint Set, the 1971-D is more common in Mint State than the 1971, likely due to its larger mintage. Unknown to collectors at the time of issue, the Denver Mint produced two dollar varieties in 1971. The more common Variety 1 shares a reverse with the 1971-P, while the scarcer Variety 2, known as the "Friendly Eagle," was probably struck in early 1971. That reverse design has several notable features that differ from the standard 1971 reverse.

Note that the grading services do not always differentiate the two reverses on the label or in their census reports, which gives the collector an opportunity for cherrypicking.

The National Numismatic Collection has two "Special Mint Set" finish coins.

Approximately 686 obverse dies and 343 reverses were prepared for this coinage.

	Cert	Avg	%MS	EF-40	MS-63	MS-65	MS-66
1971-D, Copper-Nickel Clad, Variety 1, Reverse A	3,448	64.6	97%	$3.50	$15	$50	$450

VARIETY: *1971-D, Copper-Nickel Clad, Variety 1, Peg Leg:* Some circulation strikes lack the serifs on the upright of the R in LIBERTY. "Peg Leg" varieties occur for a number of other Eisenhower dollar dates and mintmarks as well. It is one of six Peg Leg dollars listed and priced on the Ike Group Web site.

1971-D, Copper-Nickel Clad, Variety 2 (Reverse B) • Mintage: Small part of 68,587,424.

Availability in Mint State: The Reverse B in Mint State is very scarce and is the second most elusive of the *Red Book*–listed Eisenhower dollars. Although it had been popular with series specialists for years, the variety was not recognized by PCGS or NGC until the *Red Book* listed it in 2015. Before then, only ANACS recognized the significance of the Friendly Eagle variety, which is quite obviously different from the more plentiful regular reverse. Many Eisenhower dollar collectors learned of the Friendly Eagle through the efforts of the Ike Group and other specialists. It is so popular that Rob Ezerman devotes the entire first chapter of *Collectible Die Varieties: Facts, Photos, and Theories* to it.

Availability in circulated grades: Examples of this coin are scarce in the context of the series; probably fewer than 100,000 are in existence. These sell at a modest premium in coin shops and on eBay, but are not valuable enough to be listed in cataloged auctions.

Notes: These have been listed in the *Red Book* as 1971-D Variety 1, beginning with the 2016 edition. With this publicity the elusive issue will likely increase in popularity.

This reverse is different from all others in the Eisenhower series. Nicknamed the "Friendly Eagle," because there is no brow line over the eye of the national bird, the variety is most easily distinguished by the more nearly round shape of the northern Gulf of Mexico. Also, the Earth is rounder and the islands below Florida are shaped differently. James Sego has estimated that about 1 in 32 1971-D Ikes is of this variety, which gives an estimated mintage of about 2,000,000 coins out of the total given. Other estimates range from about 500,000 coins upward. Fivaz-Stanton-C1-1971D-901; CONECA: 1971-D, RDV-006.

Rob Ezerman comments, "Evaluating this variety seems to be especially difficult for third-party graders. The dies seemed to deteriorate rapidly so many Friendly Eagle varieties (FEVs) have strange features. Also, the Friendly Eagle dollars seem to have had a tendency to bond with whatever planchet and die cleaning fluids were in use on the old presses that stamped out the FEVs (my theory, no proof) so a substantial minority of FEVs look frankly corroded, except it's not corrosion, it's a bonded chemical toning that looks like corrosion."

	Cert	Avg	%MS	EF-40	MS-63	MS-65	MS-66
1971-D, Copper-Nickel Clad, Variety 2, Reverse B	(a)			$2	$5	$18	$60

a. Included in certified population figures for 1971-D, Copper-Nickel Clad, Variety I.

VARIETY: *1971-D, Copper-Nickel Clad, Variety 2, Peg Leg:* Some circulation strikes lack the serifs on the upright of the R in LIBERTY. "Peg Leg" varieties occur for a number of other Eisenhower dollar dates and mintmarks as well. It is one of six Peg Leg dollars listed and priced on the Ike Group Web site.

1971-S Eisenhower Dollar
1971-S, Silver Clad (Reverse A) •
Mintage: 6,868,530.

Availability: These are very common in lower Mint State levels, as they were sold at a premium to collectors and others, and most still exist today. Most surviving coins are in this category and have many bag marks. Very little care was taken at the Mint during the minting and packaging stage and many coins were left marked and unattractive. This did not sit well with the collectors who paid a premium for these pieces. MS-65 and higher coins are scarce in relation to demand.

Characteristics of striking: The Reverse A is usually seen with problems. It is possibly the most poorly struck issue in the series.

Notes: For the entirety of 1971-S Eisenhower dollar coinage, there were approximately 69 obverse circulation-strike dies prepared and 35 for the reverse.

Charles Morgan commented in the *Guide Book of Modern United States Dollar Coins,* "The 1971-S circulation-strike Ikes were shipped in bags from the San Francisco Mint to a processing facility for packaging. They typically come in grades MS-64 or below, spotted and ugly. I believe that the Mint included a card in the 'Blue Packs' of this year to explain to the collectors who paid a premium for the coin that it was struck up just as a circulation strike would have been, warts and all. This and the 1969 Philadelphia quarter dollar stand as two of the worst coin issues struck by the U.S. Mint in the clad era. An indeterminate amount of these Ike dollars have been melted for their silver. I doubt that as many as three million survive, but that is speculation. The 1971-S remains plentiful. This is the toughest silver Mint State Ike to find in high grade." In the same book, James Sego remarked: "There is a wide variance of quality even for graded specimens in

MS-65 and above. True Superb Gems (MS-67) are very scarce in the marketplace even though the populations are relatively high. The grading services seem to be one-half point more lenient on this issue."

What has been called a possible prototype 1971-S dollar is described on the Ike Group Web site and in the 2011 book, *Collectible Die Varieties: Facts, Photos, and Theories.* There are some slight variations from the usually seen 1971-S, especially on the obverse.

	Cert	Avg	%MS	EF-40	MS-63	MS-65	MS-66
1971-S, Silver Clad, Reverse A	4,996	65.3	100%		$14	$20	$35

VARIETY: *1971-S, Reverse A, Doubled Die Obverse:* Several varieties of 1971-S coins are known with IN GOD WE TRUST doubled.

VARIETY: *1971-S, Reverse A, Repunched Mintmark (FS-S1-1971S-501; CONECA RPM-001):* A secondary S is visible protruding northwest of the primary S. From the *Cherrypickers' Guide to Rare Die Varieties*: "This is one of fewer than a half dozen RPMs known for the entire series."

	Cert	Avg	%MS	EF-40	MS-63	MS-65	MS-66
1971-S, Silver Clad, Repunched Mintmark	0	n/a				$225	$350

VARIETY: *1971-S, Reverse C, Peg Leg (FS-S1-1971S-401; CONECA: ODV-002):* Those with Type III or the "Peg Leg" polished-die obverse are in the minority, perhaps 30. James Sego observes: "This variety typically comes slightly prooflike on the obverse with typical Mint State surfaces on the reverse. It is a very difficult coin to find in high grades of MS-66 and above."

	Cert	Avg	%MS	EF-40	MS-63	MS-65	MS-66
1971-S, Silver Clad, Polished Die, "Peg Leg"	10	67.1	100%			$125	$250

1971-S, Silver Clad (Reverses A and C), Proof • Mintage: 4,265,234.

Availability: Reverse C Proof coins are common; most can be found at PF-65 and higher. Reverse A Proofs have the low relief and are very rare. This variety was discovered by Andy Oskam in a rare wood-grain box with a golden Presidential Seal and a facsimile of President Richard M. Nixon's signature on the cover. It was publicized in 2007, by which time two other examples had been found. Since then several others have been located, but the variety remains rare.

Notes: Proofs had approximately 1,706 obverse dies prepared and 1,219 for the reverse. Charles Morgan notes in the *Guide Book of Modern United States Dollar Coins*: "In 2013, a 1971-S Proof Eisenhower dollar appeared on eBay in a brown box that was very different from the typical Brown Pack Ike box. This box had a large seal of the President of the United States and a facsimile signature of President Richard Nixon in gilt. The coin was apparently packaged for VIPs, although I have found no record to confirm this. The seller claimed the coin was presented at a ceremony honoring Mamie Eisenhower. The coin inside was unusual as it was a Proof 1971-S with a circulation-strike die used for the reverse. It sold for $140. This muling of a Proof obverse and a circulation-strike reverse is extremely rare."

	Cert	Avg	%MS	PF-65	PF-67Cam	PF-67DC	PF-68DC
1971-S, Silver Clad, Proof, Reverse A	5,148	68.1		$15	$16	$20	$25

VARIETY: *1971-S, Silver Clad, Reverse C, Proof, Doubled-Die Obverse; (FS-S1-1971S-103; FS-S1-1971S-106):* Strong doubling is visible on IN GOD WE TRUST, the date, and LIBER of LIBERTY. There are at least two doubled-die obverses for this date (valued similarly). This obverse is also paired with a minor doubled-die reverse.

	Cert	Avg	%MS	PF-65	PF-67Cam	PF-67DC	PF-68DC
1971-S, Silver Clad, Doubled Die Obverse, Proof	18	67.8		$90	$150		

1972 Eisenhower Dollar

1972, Copper-Nickel Clad, Variety 1 (Reverse A) • Mintage: Most of 75,890,000.

Availability in Mint State: This variety is very common, nearly but not quite as much so as Reverse E. MS-63 and MS-64 are the typical grades.

Availability in circulated grades: Reverse A coins are very common in circulated grades. Most are found with unimpressive luster.

Characteristics of striking: Striking of this issue varies, with many being mushily struck, but sharp coins can be found.

Notes: The second year of cupro-nickel–clad Eisenhower dollar coinage saw tens of millions more coins issued from the Philadelphia Mint. In fact, the "mother mint" produced nearly twice as many this year than in the first year of the series. 1972 Mint sets, sold by the Treasury for $3.50 per set, did not contain Eisenhower dollars. In the East, Eisenhower dollars were available at banks, but were rarely seen in everyday circulation. For the entirety of 1972 Philadelphia Ike coinage approximately 759 circulation-strike obverse dies were prepared and 380 for the reverse.

	Cert	Avg	%MS	EF-40	MS-63	MS-65	MS-66
1972, Copper-Nickel Clad, Variety 1, Reverse A	1,363	64.0	98%	$2	$5	$95	$2,500

1972, Copper-Nickel Clad, Variety 2 (Reverse D) • Mintage: Part of 75,890,000.

Availability in Mint State: This is the scarcest of the three 1972 varieties, about twice as scarce as the other two, and key to the circulation-strike Eisenhower dollar series. Most are found in lower Mint State levels with bagmarks. Many certified MS-65 coins are "low end" in quality. Herbert P. Hicks, who discovered the variety, stated the following: "In researching the matter further, I received a letter from a prominent numismatist quoting a Mint official who should know, saying 'Proof dies were accidentally sent to the coining room in Philadelphia.' Also, this official speculated on how long it would take collectors to discover this since the strikes were 'considerably different.' Please note the use of the plural 'dies' and the use of the term 'considerably different.'" Most were distributed in and around eastern Pennsylvania and Delaware. This was not an issue included in Mint sets. Simply stated, this is a rare issue in conservatively graded MS-65 or higher with good eye appeal.

Availability in circulated grades: Reverse D coins are scarcer than their Reverse E counterparts. These and other circulated coins are not widely collected due to the inexpensive nature of lower-range Mint State pieces.

Characteristics of striking: Striking on this issue varies, but sharp coins can be found.

Notes: Rob Ezerman observes, "In my quest for clashed Ikes and other varieties, recognized and not yet recognized, in years past I searched maybe twenty bags of circulated Ikes gathering dust in brick-and-mortar coin shops on local and East Coast trips. These bags were the dumping grounds for all the useless Ikes coin dealers often have to purchase from eager customers. The bags were uniformly grungy, black with dirt and whatever else. In those bags I found about 20 1972 Reverse D Ikes, half of which looked like possible MS-64s per PCGS grading standards. Understand that the average Reverse D may appear dull in spite of having no markers of sufficient wear to drop it into circulated grades. I sent in the best twelve to PCGS over time and received six MS-63s and six MS-64s, nicely sealed and labeled in their pristine plastic holders in spite of their humble and definitely circulated origins. I sold them all for $100–$200 each and helped fund my coin research."

	Cert	Avg	%MS	EF-40	MS-63	MS-65	MS-66
1972, Copper-Nickel Clad, Variety 2, Reverse D	803	62.5	88%	$10	$110	$1,500	$9,000

1972, Copper-Nickel Clad, Variety 3 (Reverse E) • Mintage: Part of 75,890,000.

Availability in Mint State: In lower Mint State grades this is the most common of the three varieties of this year and mint. This is the general style reverse used in later years except for the Bicentennial coins. Most have many bagmarks, as no effort was made to preserve them for collectors. Enough MS-65 coins exist, however, that finding one will be no problem. James Sego says that this is the second hardest variety to find in MS-65 or finer grade.

Availability in circulated grades: These are very common in circulated grades of VF-20 to AU-58. The Treasury made strong efforts to put them into circulation.

Characteristics of striking: Striking of this issue varies, but sharp coins can be found.

	Cert	Avg	%MS	EF-40	MS-63	MS-65	MS-66
1972, Copper-Nickel Clad, Variety 3, Reverse E	1,224	64.2	98%	$2.50	$5	$95	$1,500

1972-D Eisenhower Dollar

1972-D, Copper-Nickel Clad (Reverse A) • Mintage: 92,548,511.

Availability in Mint State: This issue in Mint State is common overall. Most are in lower Mint State grades, although thousands exist in MS-65 and finer. Occasionally a 1,000-coin bag turns up, but such events are now few and far between. MS-67 and finer coins are rare, as is true for other early circulation-strike years. This is the last issue of the Eisenhower dollar not sold in Mint sets by the government, thus they are scarcer than they would have been if they had been sold directly to collectors.

Availability in circulated grades: These are very common in circulated grades of VF-20 to AU-58. The Treasury made vigorous efforts to circulate the coins. Many were used in Nevada casinos.

Characteristics of striking: The 1972-D is usually found well struck and is unusual in this respect, in comparison to the Philadelphia coins.

Notes: The Treasury, in a further attempt to circulate the Eisenhower dollar, had nearly 100 million coins struck at Denver this year. Many did circulate for a time, particularly in the Western gambling halls, but most eventually disappeared into bank vaults or the hands of the public. Approximately 926 obverse dies and 463 reverses were prepared.

Rob Ezerman comments, "Mike Lantz, the Denver die setter who went on to lower-level management in the Ike era, is fond of saying that Denver always pushed harder to make quotas and with better-looking Ikes than Philadelphia. However, at the same time Denver had to stretch the dies shipped to them by the Philadelphia die shop by erasing clashed dies as best they could. Philadelphia seemed to pull and discard problematic dies sooner than Denver with their in-house die shop, assuming Philadelphia had as many clash episodes. Philadelphia was more attentive to spotting errors, possibly because Gasparro lived there and they had more politically important visitors than Denver."

	Cert	Avg	%MS	EF-40	MS-63	MS-65	MS-66
1972-D, Copper-Nickel Clad, Reverse A	2,168	64.5	97%	$2	$5	$10	$100

VARIETY: *1972-D, Doubled Die (CONECA: DDO-001/DDR-001):* This variety has doubling on the 1 in 1972, on the G in GOD, and all around the rim.

VARIETY: *1972-D, struck in silver (error planchet):* Thomas K. DeLorey observes, "The Denver Mint silver strikes happened when the San Francisco Assay Office shipped rejected cupro-nickel–clad Proof planchets to Denver to be coined as circulation strikes, and some silver planchets got in by mistake. The Assay Office had never used cupro-nickel–clad dollar planchets before 1973."

1972-S, Silver Clad (Reverse D) •

Mintage: 2,193,056.

Availability: A sharply struck MS-65 or finer example of this date can be readily located by the interested collector without too much difficulty. This is one of the few dates in the early range of the series this can be said for. James Sego identifies this as the most common Eisenhower dollar to find in high grades.

Characteristics of striking: Usually very well stuck. Many have a beautiful satin finish.

Notes: All 1972-S dollars are Peg Leg by design. Six varieties are listed and priced on the Ike Group Web site. Approximately 22 obverse circulation-strike dies were prepared and 11 for the reverse.

The second year of 40 percent silver Eisenhower dollar production saw a smaller mintage of Uncirculated and Proof coins. The mintage figure of the Uncirculated version dropped nearly 4.7 million coins.

Rob Ezerman comments, "After the debacle of shipping the 1971-S, silver-clad Specimen Ikes to San Francisco by rail in 1,000-coin bags, the Mint shipped the 1972-S, silver-clad Specimen Ikes in 20-coin plastic tubes. That plus better handling at the Mint resulted in the highest-quality silver clad Ikes of the series. For anyone looking for a single high-quality Ike for a type collection, look through 1972 'Blue Ike envelopes' at shows (you may have to ask the dealer) and you have a decent shot at finding a handsome MS-67 Ike for a low price."

Charles Morgan observes: "Most of the coins of this issue were struck with a beautiful satin finish—a tacit acknowledgement of the subpar effort from the year before."

	Cert	Avg	%MS	EF-40	MS-63	MS-65	MS-66
1972-S, Silver Clad	5,306	66.5	100%		$14	$20	$35

1972-S, Silver Clad (Reverse D), Proof • Mintage: 1,811,631.

Availability in Proof format: Proof coins with Reverse D are easily enough found.

Notes: About 725 obverse Proof dies were prepared and 518 for the reverse. The year's Proof mintage figure dropped by almost 2.5 million coins compared to the previous year. As before, Proofs were sold separately from the regular Proof sets. Clearly, Eisenhower dollars were no longer a novelty.

	Cert	Avg	%MS	PF-65	PF-67Cam	PF-67DC	PF-68DC
1972-S, Silver Clad, Proof	3,872	68.3		$15	$16	$20	$25

VARIETY: *1972-S, Proof, Doubled Die Obverse (FS-S1-1972S-101; CONECA: Unknown):* A medium spread of doubling is evident on IN GOD WE TRUST, LIBERTY, and slightly on the date. Nearly all are gems. This is an obvious (valuable) candidate for cherrypicking.

	Cert	Avg	%MS	PF-65	PF-67Cam	PF-67DC	PF-68DC
1972-S, Silver Clad, Doubled Die Obverse, Proof	26	68.0					—

1973 Eisenhower, Eagle Reverse, Dollar

1973, Copper-Nickel Clad •
Mintage: 2,000,056.

Availability in Mint State: No effort at the Mint was made to handle these carefully, and nearly all have bagmarks, from light to extensive, including those sold in mint sets. As a result only a small percentage (numbering in the hundreds and low thousands, rather than many thousands) are MS-65 or higher. (A note regarding all Eisenhower dollars: only a tiny percentage of each mintage has ever been submitted to PCGS or NGC for certification.)

Availability in circulated grades: These are quite rare in circulated grades, but there is only a limited market as most buyers seek Mint State coins.

Characteristics of striking: This issue is usually well struck and is seen with excellent luster.

Notes: The total mintage is given as 2,000,056, but 230,798 unsold pieces were reportedly melted, leaving a net total of 1,769,258. The 1973 cupro-nickel Eisenhower dollars from the Philadelphia Mint were not made for general circulation, and were intended to be included only in this year's Mint sets (which had all coins from the cent to the dollar and sold for $6). The Mint was overly optimistic concerning the number it would sell, and 230,798 unsold pieces were later recycled, per a Mint statement, but some were released into commercial channels. In the early 2000s collector Brian Vaile found a mint bag of 1,000 coins put into circulation from which a dealer had removed a hundred or so.

Approximately 20 obverse dies and 10 reverses were prepared.

Rob Ezerman comments, "Ikes have more than their share of dings, nicks, and scratches, but more than that some planchets seemed to have had an annealing problem: the best (or worst) examples are the 1973-P and 1976-P Type 1 Ikes whose annealing drum-planchet damage was not struck out in the coin press as is usually the case. These Ikes look like they received significant post-mint damage but that's not the case—the damage is mostly from transiting the annealing chamber."

1973 and 1973-D copper-nickel clad Eisenhower dollars are ranked in the *100 Greatest U.S. Modern Coins* (fourth edition), as a single entry.

	Cert	Avg	%MS	EF-40	MS-63	MS-65	MS-66
1973, Copper-Nickel Clad	1,289	64.5	100%		$13	$40	$400

1973-D, Copper-Nickel Clad •

Mintage: 2,000,000.

Availability in Mint State: Many thousands exist, including enough in MS-65 or slightly finer grades to satisfy numismatic demand. 1973 Eisenhower dollars from Denver are usually found in higher grades than are their Philadelphia Mint counterparts.

Availability in circulated grades: These are scarce in circulated grades, but the lower-grade coins are not sought by collectors.

Characteristics of striking: The striking of this issue is usually good. They are nearly always more attractive than Philadelphia Mint dollars of this year and the mint luster is usually well above average.

Notes: The total mintage was 2,000,000, of which 1,769,258 were sold as part of sets, and the balance was destroyed. By this time casinos had enough Eisenhower dollars because they were going out of use and were being replaced by colored chips. About 20 obverse dies and 10 reverses were prepared.

The National Numismatic Collection in the Smithsonian Institution has two "Special Mint Set"–finish coins. 1973 and 1973-D copper-nickel clad Eisenhower dollars are ranked in the *100 Greatest U.S. Modern Coins* (fourth edition), as a single entry.

	Cert	Avg	%MS	EF-40	MS-63	MS-65	MS-66
1973-D, Copper-Nickel Clad	1,277	64.6	100%		$13	$25	$235

1973-S Eisenhower Dollar

1973-S, Silver Clad • **Mintage:** 1,883,140.

Availability in Mint State: This coin is readily available even in higher Uncirculated grades.

Notes: The 1973-S, 40 percent silver circulation strikes have the lowest mintage figure of all the circulation-strike silver Eisenhower dollars. Charles Morgan comments:

"This is a tricky date for high grades. Many have a finish that lacks the desirability of the 1972 and the 1974. These coins physically do not resemble those two dates when seen in hand. Spotting is common on these coins. MS-66 and MS-67 coins are plentiful; attractive MS-68 coins are not."

	Cert	Avg	%MS	EF-40	MS-63	MS-65	MS-66
1973-S, Silver Clad	3,956	66.5	100%		$16	$22	$40

1973-S, Copper-Nickel Clad, Proof •

Mintage: 2,760,339.

Availability: Cupro-nickel–clad Proofs can be found easily enough.

Notes: For the entirety of 1973-S Ike coinage, there were approximately 1,104 obverse dies prepared and 789 for the reverse.

Charles Morgan observes: "Many of these coins have been certified as PF-69 Deep Cameo (DCAM). By late 2015 many earned the once-thought-impossible PF-70 grade, indicating that interpretations of the standards for 70s in the series have been relaxed in recent years. Further, the frosting on the reverse areas in relief—the Moon surface and the distant Earth—is usually unsatisfactory."

There are a small number (perhaps three coins) known of 1973-S Eisenhower dollars minted on regular circulation-strike planchets. One sold for $19,925 in June 2013. James Sego notes: "These errors look like silver coins at first glance, and even the edges look like silver. Weighing these coins is key to their authentication."

	Cert	Avg	%MS	PF-65	PF-67Cam	PF-67DC	PF-68DC
1973-S, Copper-Nickel Clad, Proof	1,764	68.2		$14	$16	$22	$30

1973-S, Silver Clad, Proof •

Mintage: 1,013,646.

Availability: Proof coins are readily available in high grades. Although the mintage is low in the Eisenhower dollar context, more than enough are available on the market to satisfy numismatic demand.

Notes: The 1973-S, 40 percent silver Proof has the lowest mintage figures of all the silver Eisenhower dollars. Because of this, it is generally regarded as the key date in the series.

	Cert	Avg	%MS	PF-65	PF-67Cam	PF-67DC	PF-68DC
1973-S, Silver Clad, Proof	3,321	68.2		$35	$37	$40	$50

VARIETY: *1973-S, Proof, Doubled Die Obverse (FS-S1-1973S-101):* A medium spread of doubling is evident on IN GOD WE TRUST, LIBERTY, and slightly on the date. Nearly all are gems. This is an obvious (valuable) candidate for cherrypicking.

	Cert	Avg	%MS	PF-65	PF-67Cam	PF-67DC	PF-68DC
1973-S, Silver Clad, Doubled Die Obverse, Proof	47	67.9					—

1974 Eisenhower Dollar

1974, Copper-Nickel Clad •

Mintage: 27,366,000.

Availability in Mint State: This issue is very common in Mint State, mostly in grades below MS-65. MS-65 coins, while in the minority, are readily available in comparison to demand. Carefully graded MS-66 and higher coins are somewhat scarce.

Availability in circulated grades: Circulated examples aren't seen often, but they are not rare.

Characteristics of striking: The striking on this issue is usually good and with excellent mint luster.

Notes: Mint sets sold at $6.00 each contained one each of all circulation-strike issues, cent through the Eisenhower dollar; 1,975,981 sets were sold for 1974.

Approximately 274 obverse dies and 137 reverses were prepared for this coinage.

	Cert	Avg	%MS	EF-40	MS-63	MS-65	MS-66
1974, Copper-Nickel Clad	1,561	64.5	99%	$2	$6	$25	$200

1974-D Eisenhower Dollar

1974-D, Copper-Nickel Clad •

Mintage: 45,517,000.

Availability in Mint State: This issue is very common in Mint State. Most are less fine than MS-65, although enough in the latter grade exist that they are readily available. Tens of thousands were in the Big Sky Hoard marketed by Littleton Coin Company beginning in 2011. Across the board, grade for grade, Denver's Eisenhower dollars have better eye appeal than do the Philadelphia issues.

Availability in circulated grades: These are common and of little interest to today's collectors.

Characteristics of striking: The striking on this issue is usually good and with nice mint luster.

Notes: Some of the 1974-D coins were minted in calendar-year 1975, technically making them restrikes. However, in recent decades the Mint has sometimes paid little attention to the nicety of dating coins in the year in which they were made. Numerous issues, especially commemoratives and other collector issues, have been "pre-struck" or restruck.

Approximately 456 obverse dies and 228 reverses were prepared for this coinage.

	Cert	Avg	%MS	EF-40	MS-63	MS-65	MS-66
1974-D, Copper-Nickel Clad	8,079	65.0	100%	$2	$6	$16	$70

VARIETY: *1974-D, Struck in Silver (error planchet):* The first example of this wrong-metal error is said to have been discovered by a croupier at a Las Vegas blackjack table. James Sego observes: "Today about 25 to 30 coins of this variety are known. These are almost always in lower grades with average sharpness at best."

VARIETY: *1974-D, Peg Leg:* Some circulation strikes lack the serifs on the upright of the R in LIBERTY. It is one of six Peg Leg dollars listed and priced on the Ike Group Web site.

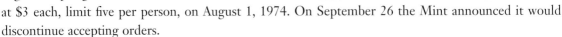

1974-S Eisenhower Dollar

1974-S, Silver Clad • Mintage: 1,900,156.

Availability: These are common as all were purchased by buyers who paid a premium and kept them. However, superb gems of good overall quality are elusive.

Notes: The U.S. Mint office in San Francisco began accepting orders for Uncirculated dollars at $3 each, limit five per person, on August 1, 1974. On September 26 the Mint announced it would discontinue accepting orders.

The 1974-S Eisenhower dollar is the last date in the series that features the original reverse design (commemorating the landing of Apollo 11) in the 40 percent silver format. There were no Eisenhower dollars dated 1975, and the 1776–1976 double-dated Bicentennial issue features a rendition of the Liberty Bell superimposed on the Moon. By the time the original reverse design was resumed in 1977, the silver format was discontinued. Approximately 19 obverse circulation-strike dies were prepared and 10 for the reverse.

Charles Morgan observes, "This is the second nicest Blue Pack Ike in the series, behind the 1972-S, referring to color of the circular labels in the original containers, of which many were discarded."

	Cert	Avg	%MS	EF-40	MS-63	MS-65	MS-66
1974-S, Silver Clad	5,123	66.6	100%		$15	$21	$35

1974-S, Copper-Nickel Clad, Proof •

Mintage: 2,612,568.

Availability: Cupro-nickel–clad Proof coins are readily available.

Notes: Approximately 1,045 obverse dies and 747 reverses were prepared for this coinage. The frosting on the areas on the reverse is often unsatisfactory, including on coins in high grades.

	Cert	Avg	%MS	PF-65	PF-67Cam	PF-67DC	PF-68DC
1974-S, Copper-Nickel Clad, Proof	1,527	68.2		$7	$10	$15	$20

1974-S, Silver Clad, Proof •

Mintage: 1,306,579.

Availability: Today these are common.

Notes: Order cards for Proof dollars were mailed by the U.S. Mint on April 22, 1974, and orders were accepted beginning on May 1, 1974. The price per coin was $10, with a limit of five per person. On June 20 the Mint announced it would not accept any further orders after June 28.

Charles Morgan notes, "1974-S Brown Packs tend to develop colorful toning due to a trace chemical found in the red velvet packaging. This chemical does not appear to be present on the 1971–1973 issues."

About 523 obverse dies and 373 reverses were prepared for this Proof coinage.

	Cert	Avg	%MS	PF-65	PF-67Cam	PF-67DC	PF-68DC
1974-S, Silver Clad, Proof	3,372	68.3		$16	$17	$25	$30

1776–1976 Eisenhower, Bicentennial Variety, Dollar

1776–1976, Copper-Nickel Clad, Variety 1 • Mintage: 4,019,000.

Availability in Mint State: Variety 1 is by far the scarcer of the two varieties in a relative sense. All known Mint sets sold to collectors had Variety 1 coins. However, as more than four million were struck, they are common today in just about any grade desired through MS-66 (but see caveats in the commentary below). Most coins are in lower grades and are bagmarked, often heavily.

Availability in circulated grades: Variety 1 coins are common in circulated grades.

Characteristics of striking: Striking on this issue varies, but is usually good. They are typically seen with good luster.

Notes: Approximately 41 obverse dies and 21 reverses were prepared for this coinage. Variety 1 dollars are thought to have been struck in calendar year 1975. (In total, approximately 1,134 obverse dies and 567 reverses were prepared for all Philadelphia coins of this year.)

This date has the distinction of the largest mintage in the Eisenhower dollar series—the only one with production above one hundred million pieces, Still, hardly any ever went into the channels of commerce.

Charles Morgan notes, "The Variety 1 is scarce in conservatively graded MS-65 and rare in MS-66. Loosely graded MS-65 coins are easily available as are MS-66s, often overgraded by a point or two. Be super careful." Similarly, James Sego warns: "This issue, in my opinion, is the most difficult to find in superb gem condition—well struck, free of marks, and with rich luster. Many of the certified MS-66 coins, I estimate 20 percent of the total, are misattributed Variety 1 coins, thus artificially inflating the population reports."

Rob Ezerman remarks, "Ikes have more than their share of dings, nicks, and scratches, but more than that some planchets seemed to have had an annealing problem: the best (or worst) examples are the 1973-P and 1976-P Type 1 Ikes whose annealing drum-planchet damage was not struck out in the coin press as is usually the case. These Ikes look like they received significant post-mint damage but that's not the case—the damage is mostly from transiting the annealing chamber."

	Cert	Avg	%MS	EF-40	MS-63	MS-65	MS-66
1776–1976, Copper-Nickel Clad, Variety 1	1,229	64.1	100%	$2	$8	$160	$1,500

1776–1976, Copper-Nickel Clad, Variety 2 • Mintage: 113,318,000.

Availability in Mint State: Variety 2 coins are very common, including in any grade desired through MS-66.

Availability in circulated grades: These coins are common in circulated grades.

Characteristics of striking: Strike quality varies, but usually is good. They are typically seen with nice luster.

Notes: Charles Morgan observes, "The typical Variety 2 is an all-round nicer coin than a Variety 1. MS-66 coins, while not common, are often seen. Obverse designs of the Variety 1 and Variety 2 are slightly different. This is a fact that usually goes unnoticed in published descriptions of the coins."

	Cert	Avg	%MS	EF-40	MS-63	MS-65	MS-66
1776–1976, Copper-Nickel Clad, Variety 2	4,549	64.0	99%	$2	$5	$30	$125

1776–1976-D Eisenhower, Bicentennial Variety, Dollar

1776–1976-D, Copper-Nickel Clad, Variety 1 • Mintage: 21,048,710.

Availability in Mint State: Variety 1 coins are very common due to the large number struck.

Availability in circulated grades: This issue is very common in circulated grades.

Characteristics of striking: These are usually seen with problems and are considered by some to be the poorest-looking coins in the Eisenhower series. Well-struck MS-65 or finer coins are on the scarce side.

Notes: Variety 1 dollars are thought to have been struck in calendar year 1975. Approximately 211 obverse dies and 106 reverses were prepared. James Sego notes: "In gem Mint State grades this is the most common of the Bicentennial dollars. It is pursued not only by Ike collectors, but is a favorite with type-set enthusiasts as well." Although Mint State examples are common and readily found, most are bagmarked.

	Cert	Avg	%MS	EF-40	MS-63	MS-65	MS-66
1776–1976-D, Copper-Nickel Clad, Variety 1	2,405	64.8	99%	$2	$5	$50	$185

1776–1976-D, Copper-Nickel Clad, Variety 2 • Mintage: 82,179,564.

Availability in Mint State: These are even more plentiful than the very common Variety 1. MS-66 and finer coins are readily available in relation to collector demand.

Availability in circulated grades: Variety 2 coins are very common.

Characteristics of striking: Many of these coins have striking problems.

Notes: Approximately 822 obverse dies and 411 reverses were prepared for this coinage. Some 1776–1976-D dollars were shipped in 1,000-coin cloth bags imprinted "1975-D." The Smithsonian's National Numismatic Collection has two "Special Mint Set"–finish coins.

	Cert	Avg	%MS	EF-40	MS-63	MS-65	MS-66
1776–1976-D, Copper-Nickel Clad, Variety 2	5,814	65.0	100%	$2	$5	$28	$60

VARIETY: *1976-D, Variety 2, Struck in Silver (error planchet):* This off-metal error is exceedingly rare, possibly unique.

VARIETY: *1976-D, Variety 2, Peg Leg:* Some circulation strikes lack the serifs on the upright of the R in LIBERTY. It is one of six Peg Leg dollars listed and priced on the Ike Group Web site.

1776–1976-S Eisenhower, Bicentennial Variety, Dollar

1776–1976-S, Copper-Nickel Clad, Variety 1, Proof • Mintage: 2,845,450.

Availability: These are common in high grades as all were bought at a premium by collectors and saved.

Notes: Variety 1 dollars were included in 1975 Proof sets. Approximately 1,138 obverse dies and 813 reverses were prepared for both varieties.

	Cert	Avg	%MS	PF-65	PF-67Cam	PF-67DC	PF-68DC
1776–1976-S, Copper-Nickel Clad, Variety 1, Proof	1,915	68.0		$12	$15	$20	$30

1776–1976-S, Copper-Nickel Clad, Variety 2, Proof • Mintage: 4,149,730.

Availability: Variety 2 coins are common in high grades as all were bought at a premium and saved.

Notes: Variety 2 dollars were included in the Proof sets that were actually minted in 1976, along with cents, nickels, and dimes dated 1976, and quarters and half dollars that bore the dual date 1776–1976. A variety of Proof-only coins with thin, tall, oval letter O's was issued in regular six-piece Proof sets of 1976. The release for this set ended July 22, 1976.

	Cert	Avg	%MS	PF-65	PF-67Cam	PF-67DC	PF-68DC
1776–1976-S, Copper-Nickel Clad, Variety 2, Proof	2,282	68.2		$8	$12	$15	$30

1776–1976-S, Silver Clad, Variety 1 • Mintage: *11,000,000.*

Availability: These were sold only as part of Mint Sets. The mintage was an incredible 11,000,000, of which 4,294,081 were distributed. The coins are readily available today. James Sego observes: "This is a very tough coin to find in ultra-high Mint State levels."

Notes: Approximately 43 circulation-strike obverse dies and 43 reverses were prepared. The open areas and shallow relief of the reverse made the Bicentennial dollars more susceptible to gaining nicks and contact marks. The 40 percent silver Eisenhower dollar made its final appearance this year as a regular-issue coinage, with Uncirculated and Proof specimens available to collectors in three-coin Bicentennial sets. The authorizing law required the Mint to finish striking the silver Bicentennials by July 4, 1976. Up through mid-June or so they were struck in small quantities and packaged immediately to avoid handling and/or spotting. With time running out and sales poor, the Mint decided to coin the last 7 million or so Uncirculated sets on high-speed presses and bag the coins against unlikely future sales. However, sales of unsold stored coins jumped in 1979 when silver shot up and the .53792 troy oz. of silver in one set became worth more than the bulk-sale price, and packaging resumed. The 40 percent silver dollars of this year are all of the Variety 1 style. Beginning the next year, 1977, the silver would disappear once more from

America's coinage, not to reappear until the commemorative issues of the early 1980s. Coinage was overly optimistic, and it is believed that many were melted, although exact figures are not known.

	Cert	Avg	%MS	EF-40	MS-63	MS-65	MS-66
1776–1976-S, Silver Clad, Variety 1	3,496	66.2	100%		$18	$22	$30

VARIETY: *1776–1976-S, Silver Clad, Variety 1, No Mintmark:* Certain sets of silver-clad Bicentennial coins, perhaps three in number, were made without an S mintmark. No such sets are known today. In 1977 Thomas DeLorey, then on the staff of *Coin World*, viewed a mintmarkless silver-content dollar found earlier that year in a cash register in a Woodward & Lathrop Department Store in Washington, D.C. James Sego informed Q. David Bowers for the *Guide Book of Modern United States Dollar Coins:* "This coin is currently in a PF-64 (PCGS) holder. I was able to examine the coin in the early 1990s and study it carefully before it was placed in a holder. It has a Variety 1 reverse."

1776–1976-S, Silver Clad, Variety 1, Proof • Mintage: *4,000,000.*

Availability in Proof format: Variety 1 Proofs are common in high grades as all were bought at a premium and saved.

Notes: On January 19, 1975, the Mint announced a price reduction from $15 to $12 for 40 percent silver Bicentennial Proof sets, and the removal of order limits. The silver Eisenhower dollar made its final appearance this year as a regular-issue coinage, with Uncirculated and Proof specimens made available to collectors in the three-piece Bicentennial sets. Approximately 1,305 obverse dies and 933 reverses were prepared for this coinage.

	Cert	Avg	%MS	PF-65	PF-67Cam	PF-67DC	PF-68DC
1776–1976-S, Silver Clad, Variety 1, Proof	6,490	68.2		$20	$21	$25	$35

VARIETY: *1776–1976-S, Silver Clad, Proof, Variety 2, No Mintmark:* One coin is known to exist in Proof format, silver clad, but is lacking the S mintmark typically seen on Proofs of this year. Presumably, it was struck at the Philadelphia Mint where all of the Bicentennial dies were made. Q. David Bowers reports seeing in 1976 a mintmarkless Proof obverse and an accompanying reverse-up coin (presumably without mintmark) at a Mint ceremony, but where these are today is unknown. From www.uspatterns.com: "The piece is unique and, according to the *Coin World Comprehensive Catalog & Encyclopedia*, was discovered in a cash register at Woodward and Lothrop Department store in Washington, D.C. in mid-1977. It is said to weigh 383.25 grains instead of 350 grains, thus it was struck on a 40% silver planchet. Only the single example is known and it was offered in Superior's February 1997 and Bowers and Merena's September 2002 sales."

1977 Eisenhower Dollar

1977, Copper-Nickel Clad •
Mintage: *12,596,000.*

Availability in Mint State: The 1977 issue is readily available in Mint State; MS-65 and finer coins are only a small percentage of the mintage.

Availability in circulated grades: These are common in circulated grades.

Characteristics of striking: This issue is usually well struck.

Notes: With the passing of the Bicentennial celebration, the original reverse design was restored to the Eisenhower dollar and would remain in use through the end of the series in 1978. From this point forward, the series would be struck in cupro-nickel–clad metal. Mint sets sold for $7.00 contained one each of all circulation-strike issues, cent through the Eisenhower dollar; 2,006,869 sets were sold.

Approximately 126 obverse dies and 63 reverses were prepared for this coinage.

Most 1977 Philadelphia Eisenhower dollars are bagmarked. James Sego observes: "These are usually seen with good luster. The number of superb gems graded is misleading, as three or four bags were submitted for grading [in a few years preceding 2016]. The quality of those pieces is lacking, even though the assigned grades are high. Be very careful when purchasing a high-grade specimen as the holders say nothing about overall desirability."

	Cert	Avg	%MS	EF-40	MS-63	MS-65	MS-66
1977, Copper-Nickel Clad	2,880	65.0	100%	$2	$6	$35	$85

1977-D Eisenhower Dollar

1977-D, Copper-Nickel Clad •

Mintage: 32,983,006.

Availability in Mint State: The 1977-D is readily available in Mint State. Most coins found from various sources are in grades below MS-65 and are bagmarked. The exceptions to this general rule are the tens of thousands of Eisenhower dollars in the Big Sky Hoard marketed by Littleton Coin Company beginning in 2011.

Availability in circulated grades: These are common in circulated grades.

Characteristics of striking: This issue is usually well struck.

Notes: Approximately 330 obverse dies and 165 reverses were prepared for this coinage. The Smithsonian's National Numismatic Collection has two "Special Mint Set"–finish coins.

	Cert	Avg	%MS	EF-40	MS-63	MS-65	MS-66
1977-D, Copper-Nickel Clad	15,695	65.1	100%	$2	$6	$35	$85

VARIETY: *1977-D, Struck in Silver (error planchet):* The February 22, 1978, issue of *Coin World* reported the finding of several 1977-D dollars struck on 40 percent silver planchets. Subsequently, more were located. These were on rejected blanks intended for S-mint Bicentennials, mistakenly included among copper-nickel–clad blanks shipped from San Francisco to the Denver Mint. About 20 examples are known. This off-metal error ranks as no. 65 in *100 Greatest U.S. Modern Coins.*

1977-S Eisenhower Dollar

1977-S, Copper-Nickel Clad, Proof •

Mintage: 3,251,152.

Availability: These are common; nearly all are in grades from PF-65 upward.

Notes: Approximately 1,300 obverse dies and 929 reverses were prepared for this coinage.

	Cert	Avg	%MS	PF-65	PF-67Cam	PF-67DC	PF-68DC
1977-S, Copper-Nickel Clad, Proof	2,444	68.5		$5	$7	$8	$15

1978 Eisenhower, Eagle Reverse, Dollar

1978, Copper-Nickel Clad •
Mintage: 25,702,000.

Availability in Mint State: These are very common due to the large number struck. Most examples grade MS-64 or lower and have bagmarks. However, enough MS-65 and higher coins survive to supply collector demand, though minimally bagmarked coins are scarce.

Availability in circulated grades: This issue is common in circulated grades.

Characteristics of striking: Most coins of this issue are well struck.

Notes: Approximately 257 obverse dies and 129 reverses were prepared for this coinage. Certain chrome-plated–reverse dies used to make Proofs were placed into service for making circulation strikes after being retired from Proof production.

	Cert	Avg	%MS	EF-40	MS-63	MS-65	MS-66
1978, Copper-Nickel Clad	1,397	64.9	100%	$2	$6	$45	$100

1978-D Eisenhower Dollar

1978-D, Copper-Nickel Clad •
Mintage: 33,012,890.

Availability in Mint State: This issue is common in Mint State. Most are MS-64 or below and are bagmarked. Attractive MS-65 and finer coins are in the minority.

Availability in circulated grades: These are common in circulated grades.

Characteristics of striking: This issue usually is well struck.

Notes: Approximately 331 obverse dies and 166 reverses were prepared for this coinage. James Sego notes: "Of all of the 1977 and 1978 varieties this is the most difficult to find in superb gem grade. As I write these words [in 2015] only one coin exists in certified MS-67, a PCGS coin. I have seen it, and it is of superior quality."

	Cert	Avg	%MS	EF-40	MS-63	MS-65	MS-66
1978-D, Copper-Nickel Clad	5,204	65.0	100%	$2	$5.50	$40	$115

VARIETY: *1978-D, Peg Leg:* Some circulation strikes lack the serifs on the upright of the R in LIBERTY. This is one of six Peg Leg dollars listed and priced on the Ike Group Web site.

1978-S Eisenhower Dollar

1978-S, Copper-Nickel Clad, Proof •
Mintage: 3,127,781.

Availability: Nearly all coins are in grades from PF-67 upward. These are common enough and are readily available.

Notes: Approximately 1,251 obverse dies and 894 reverses were prepared for this coinage. Charles Morgan comments: "The Mint changed its procedure of creating cameo finish this year, with the result that nearly all have deep frost on the relief areas. A side-by-side comparison of a 1978-S with any other date of clad Eisenhower dollar will easily demonstrate this."

	Cert	Avg	%MS	PF-65	PF-67Cam	PF-67DC	PF-68DC
1978-S, Copper-Nickel Clad, Proof	2,816	68.6		$5	$7	$8	$15

SUSAN B. ANTHONY (1979–1999)

Designer: *Frank Gasparro.* **Weight:** *8.1 grams.*
Composition: *Outer layers of copper-nickel (.750 copper, .250 nickel) bonded to inner core of pure copper.* **Diameter:** *26.5 mm.*
Edge: *Reeded.* **Mints:** *Philadelphia, Denver, and San Francisco.*

Circulation Strike — Mintmark location is on the obverse, above the left tip of the bust. — **Proof**

The Susan B. Anthony dollar was designed by Frank Gasparro, chief engraver of the U.S. Mint, following a congressional mandate. It features a portrait of the famous suffragette, along with an eagle-and-Moon motif reduced from the coin's larger predecessor, the Eisenhower dollar. Legislators hoped that these so-called mini-dollars would be an efficient substitute for paper dollars, which wear out much more quickly in circulation. A large mintage in 1979 was followed by smaller quantities in 1980 and 1981, and then a hiatus of almost 20 years. The coins were not popular in circulation, with some members of the public complaining that they were too easily confused with the similarly sized quarter dollar. A final coinage of Anthony dollars was struck in 1999—a stopgap measure to ensure the Treasury's supply of dollar coins before the Sacagawea dollar was launched in 2000.

HISTORY OF THE SUSAN B. ANTHONY DOLLAR

On May 12, 1975, while the Eisenhower dollar was several years into production, the Treasury Department commissioned the Research Triangle Institute, a highly accomplished North Carolina nonprofit study facility, to examine the panorama of American coinage and make recommendations for the future. The findings, released in early 1976, took 18 months to complete and cost $116,000.

Recommendations covered wide territory and included the eventual discontinuation of the cent (to be replaced by a two-cent piece), the abolishment of mintmarks on coins, and the introduction of "a coin larger than the current 25-cent piece but smaller than the 50-cent piece."

In August 1976 the Treasury issued a report, "New Small Dollar Coin—Technical Considerations." This was widely circulated and spawned many articles. The Washington Star Service, a news syndicate, issued a story in the same month, stating in part:

> The current $1 coin, the Eisenhower dollar, is "too big and bulky; it just doesn't circulate," says James Parker, a spokesman for the U.S. Mint.
>
> Leading the cheers for the new coin are the makers and operators of vending machines, since a 30-cent sandwich or 60-cent pack of cigarettes could be purchased with less fumbling.
>
> "I think a new coin would be good for the whole country as well as our industry," said G. Richard Schreiber of the National Automatic Merchandising Association. "So many things are at a point today where a dollar coin makes sense," he added.
>
> "We've done studies that have proven conclusively that a single-coin purchase will outsell a two-coin purchase, that a two-coin purchase will outsell one requiring three coins, and so on. The new coin would certainly help sales."

On September 15, 1976, the Treasury Department, citing increased coinage costs, announced it might do away with the penny and the half dollar and replace the dollar coin with a lighter version.

LIBERTY CAP DESIGN PROPOSED

The subject of a mini-dollar caught the nation's fancy, and many articles appeared concerning the Mint's own ideas and the Research Triangle Institute study. Mint Director Mary T. Brooks urged caution, stating that if changes were made they should come slowly.

Realizing that a new small-diameter dollar might become a reality, Chief Engraver Frank Gasparro created a prototype design featuring the head of Miss Liberty with a pole and cap, loosely adapted from the copper half cent and cent of the 1790s. Inside the rim on a later version was an 11-sided border to help distinguish it from the quarter. The reverse showed a soaring eagle. The motifs were approved by the U.S. Commission of Fine Arts, an advisory group that reviewed U.S. coins and medals in addition to monumental sculpture and other federal projects.

On December 31, 1976, Secretary of the Treasury William E. Simon submitted to Congress a report, "The State of the United States Coinage," based in part on the Research Triangle Institute study. It recommended a 26.5 mm dollar coin, smaller than the then-standard 38.1 mm.

On April 7, 1977, Secretary of the Treasury W. Michael Blumenthal, Simon's successor in that office, wrote to the chairman of the House Committee on Banking, Finance, and Urban Affairs, noting in part, "The Treasury recommends that the present dollar coin be replaced with a smaller, more conveniently-sized dollar and that the 50-cent piece be eliminated."

Kennedy half dollars, including newer issues without silver content, were not seen in circulation at the time. Except for use in Nevada casinos during the early 1970s, Eisenhower dollars did not circulate. Large quantities remained in Treasury vaults.

On April 17, 1978, the administration of President Jimmy Carter submitted a recommendation to Congress to adopt the small dollar. On May 1, this proposal was introduced to the House of Representatives by Walter E. Fauntroy (District of Columbia delegate to the House) and was referred to the House Committee on Banking, Finance, and Urban Affairs. A Liberty Head motif was proposed.

This was followed on May 3 by bill S. 3036, calling for suffragette Susan B. Anthony to be portrayed on the coin. It was introduced into the Senate by William Proxmire (D–Wisconsin), who was well known at the time for his campaign to cut costs and his satirical but often realistic "Golden Fleece Award" for abuses of spending.

Frank Gasparro with an early version
of his 1977 Liberty Head mini-dollar
and a sketch of his reverse design.

1977 "Liberty Head experimental
dollar coin," as illustrated in *The Annual
Report of the Director of the Mint,* 1978.

An early galvano, dated
1977, of Gasparro's
design for the proposed
small-diameter dollar
with a "recessed
border," per a notation
on the galvano.

A gilded plaster cast,
large diameter, dated
1977, of Frank
Gasparro's design
for the proposed
small-diameter dollar.
Note the addition of an
11-sided interior border.

One proposal within
the Mint was to adapt
the Eisenhower portrait
for use on the mini-
dollar. Trial pieces
were struck but later
all were destroyed.

A galvano, dated 1978, of
Frank Gasparro's design for the
proposed small-diameter dollar.

A galvano, dated 1979,
of Gasparro's design for the
proposed small-diameter dollar.

H.R. 12728, introduced on May 15, 1978, by Mary Rose Oakar for herself and for Patricia Schroeder, similarly called for the portrait of Anthony to be used.

The Anthony proposal did not sit well with the numismatic community. On May 17, Margo Russell, editor of *Coin World*, addressed the House Banking, Finance, and Urban Affairs Subcommittee on Historic Preservation and Coinage, praising the earlier recommendation: "We commend the Mint for its selection of the Liberty-Eagle personification on the coin, and we hope this beautiful allegorical design will be selected for the coin, should it become reality." On the same day Mint Director Stella B. Hackel addressed the same committee, noting in part:

> The new dollar would be distinguishable from the quarter by touch as well as by sight. The design proposed would have an eleven-side inner border on both sides of the coin within the outer circular configuration. This design element would provide for tactile recognition by the visually handicapped. . . .
>
> Many materials—including several copper alloys, titanium, and other clad combinations—were tested to determine the most suitable composition for the new coin. The results of the studies indicates that the best overall material is a 75% copper / 25% nickel alloy clad on a 100% copper core. . . .
>
> The recommended design for the obverse is a modern or stylized female Liberty Head. This historic design appeared on the first U.S. coins minted in 1793, and appeared in various forms on almost all denominations of coins through modern times. The female Liberty Head is symbolic of and honors all women rather than any particular individual. It is accompanied by the Phrygian cap which has been a symbol of freedom for over 2,500 years and has repeatedly appeared on our coins. It is most appropriate that such a historic American design once again return to an American coin.
>
> The recommended design for the reverse is a Soaring or Volant Eagle. The eagle has appeared on the reverse of every dollar coin since 1794, with the exception of the gold coins. The recommended design, which is similar to the 1916 quarter-dollar eagle, is a more vivid rendition emphasizing the independence and spirit which characterizes this national symbol.

Later in May, other proposals were introduced into Congress, one suggesting dual portraits of Harriet Tubman and Susan B. Anthony (H.R. 12872, May 25), but most calling for Anthony alone. In June there were more proposals, including for the images of Abigail Adams, Georgia Neese Clarke Gray, and Elizabeth Pole. Within the engraving department at the Mint some ideas were translated into plasters and galvanos, but most were not.

THE ANTHONY PORTRAIT

In June 1978 the Treasury Department, influenced by Congress's social progress, discarded the highly praised Liberty Head motif and directed Frank Gasparro to depict Anthony on the obverse, as it seemed a certainty that the civil-rights icon would be the dollar coin's subject. For the reverse Congress and the Treasury wanted a reduced version of the Apollo 11 motif used in the Eisenhower dollar. The engraver gathered many different Anthony portraits adapted from prints, engravings, and photographs, all reproduced to be about the same size, and at one time had them on display in his office.

The following commentary by Frank Gasparro was written at the request of Q. David Bowers on November 4, 1991, and gives his view of the creation of the Anthony dollar:

> The important question for me, that stood out in designing the Susan B. Anthony dollar was how the public would accept my interpretation of the great suffragist. My first plaster, June 1st, 1978, showed Susan B. Anthony's portrait at the age of twenty-eight. Considering the few photographs available, I chose this one. This was followed by a rejection by Susan B. Anthony, 2nd, a grandniece, then living. She stated that I portrayed her as "too pretty." So, I had to go back to the "drawing board." Then, the

only other photograph I could obtain was showing her in her very old age. I had to "'toughen" the features of my present plaster model.

Eventually, after much effort, I ended up with a portrait showing Susan B. Anthony in her fifties, at the height of her career. I had to sharpen her features giving her strength of character. I kept in mind, to make the coin artistic and still prove acceptable to the public.

What followed is history. There was trouble with the coin size.

The next hurdle was to experiment with giving the coin a gold or brass finish and still keep the same size.

This proved too late. There were already 450 million of the small dollars deposited in the Federal Reserve vaults and they could not move. Meanwhile, this experiment was picked up and pursued by European countries to give the higher denomination small coin a gold or brass finish. This proved very successful.

For America, the future will see a small size dollar with a gold or brass plate or finish that may prove acceptable, favorably, by the public.

Susan B. Anthony portrait from a steel engraving published in 1881 by G.E. Perine & Co. as part of the six-volume *History of Woman Suffrage.*

On July 17, Mint Director Hackel appeared before the Senate Committee on Banking, Housing, and Urban Affairs and reiterated her stance on using a Liberty Head, noting that more than 100 different women from history had been proposed. She urged that S. 3036 requiring Anthony's portrait not be passed. The legislators listened politely and then ignored what she said.

The Liberty Head idea remained alive a while longer. A poll of *Coin World* readers published on August 3, 1978, showed that Gasparro's preferred design gained 1,056 votes, with Anthony showing in seventh place with only 78 votes.

On August 22 the Senate approved S. 3036. *The Annual Report of the Director of the Mint*, 1978, illustrated the Anthony coin, but also showed the Gasparro Liberty Head as an "experimental coin."

On September 26, 1978, the Commission of Fine Arts recommended approval of the Gasparro designs featuring Anthony. Often in history the Commission's recommendations have been ignored by the bodies it advises (including the Treasury Department), but not in this instance.

A plaster showing a head-and-neck portrait of Susan B. Anthony, with light letters.

Another plaster, showing a head-and-neck portrait of Anthony, with slightly heavier letters.

A galvano made in 1978
for a proposed reverse,
signed FG at the lower right.

A galvano for an
unadopted reverse
for the 1979 dollar. The
initials FG are below the 1.

A galvano for another
unadopted reverse for
the 1979 dollar, a variation
of the preceding. This has
an 11-sided interior border.

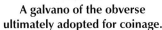

A galvano of the obverse
ultimately adopted for coinage.

Galvanos with an unadopted obverse showing slightly
different features (note the position of the second star at the
left) and a reverse with slight differences from that adopted.

THE DOLLAR BECOMES A REALITY

Representative Mary Rose Oakar (D–Ohio), who had been particularly active in the program, acted on behalf of the Carter administration and introduced the required legislation into Congress. It was passed on September 26, 1978. A descendant of the portrait subject, Susan B. Anthony III, was on hand with an enlarged model of the coin's obverse. President Carter signed the bill as Public Law 95-447 on October 10, 1978.

The legislation also provided for, as of December 31, 1978, the discontinuation of the Eisenhower dollar.

On December 13, 1978, a test run of about one million coins was made at the Philadelphia Mint, using 1979-dated dies. The event was opened to government officials and invited guests from the media and public sector. At 11:25 a.m. four presses were started simultaneously with two dignitaries attending each. Mint Director Stella B. Hackel and Philadelphia Mint Superintendent Shallie M. Bey were at Press No. 4.

On January 9, 1979, Colorado state officials, members of Congress, Treasury officials, and other government people took part in a reception at the Denver Mint to learn about the new dollar and to see the new coins, already in production.

LAUNCHING THE ANTHONY DOLLAR

The Mint held a ceremony to commemorate the production striking of both the circulating and Proof Susan B. Anthony dollar coins on February 2, 1979. Guests, media, and Treasury officials (including Secretary Blumenthal) gathered at the San Francisco Assay Office that morning for a ceremonial striking of the coins.

Blumenthal told of the new Anthony dollar and the government's expectations. It would, he said, present great efficiencies, for the coins would last longer in circulation than paper dollars and would be of a form easily handled by the public. It was expected this would bring a savings of $4.5 million a year, an important factor in an administration that was trying to cut costs. Blumenthal remarked on the social significance of the new dollar:

Frank Gasparro holding one of the new dollars the day of the ceremonial striking.

It's time the United States portrayed a woman on a coin, for we are one of the few countries which until now had no real female likeness represented on any of our coinage. Perhaps that is why the dollar was in some trouble. When Susan used to crusade from town to town to advocate women's rights she was backed by her father's money. Now we need Susan to back our money.

When President Carter signed the new coin act he said, "This new coin will be a constant reminder of the continuing struggle for the equality of all Americans."

It reminds me too of our constant struggle to stabilize the dollar. Susan Anthony, I sure hope you can help us now.

At the ceremony the Treasury distributed an information packet. Included was a sheet, "Advantages / Comparisons," which began:

The current [Eisenhower] cupro-nickel dollar does not circulate due primarily to its cumbersome size and weight. The recommended design for the $1 coin specifically addresses this problem of convenience. The $1 coin is only 9% greater in diameter than a quarter and only 43% heavier. Compared to the current $1 coin it is approximately 2/3 the diameter and 1/3 the weight.

The current $1 coin costs about 8 cents each to produce as compared to the cost for the new coin which will be 3 cents each. This is a savings of greater than 60% per coin compared to the existing coin! Based on production figures for Fiscal Year 1978 the new coin would save about $4.5 million per year.

Demand for one-dollar notes has been increasing steadily at the Bureau of Engraving and Printing. Current figures show that dollar notes represent 60% of currency production. A practical $1 note which circulates will displace $1 notes.

One dollar notes wear out and must be replaced in approximately 18 months at a cost of 1.8 cents each. Since each coin will last at least 15 years, the coin has, at minimum, a tenfold service life advantage. Considering the cost of the coin compared to the note, each coin would save over 80% of the production costs for the notes displaced. With nearly 3 billion Federal Reserve Notes in circulation today, only modest displacement by $1 coins could result in savings of many millions of dollars in costs.

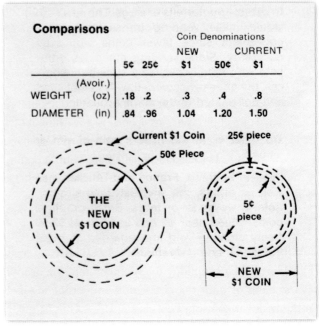

Comparisons			Coin Denominations			
				NEW		CURRENT
		5¢	25¢	$1	50¢	$1
WEIGHT (Avoir.) (oz)		.18	.2	.3	.4	.8
DIAMETER (in)		.84	.96	1.04	1.20	1.50

"Comparisons" issued by the Treasury Department, showing the size of the Susan B. Anthony dollar and other coins.

THE ANTHONY DOLLAR IN CIRCULATION

The Treasury Department stated that before the first coins could be released to the general public, anticipated to happen in July 1979, it wanted to have 300 to 500 million on hand so that there would be enough to meet demand. On target, July 2 saw the official release. A ceremony was held in Rochester, New York, the city where Susan B. Anthony made her home. Among those in attendance was Mint Director Stella Hackel. Various philatelic/numismatic first-day covers were made privately, these typically enclosing an Anthony dollar obtained on July 2 and put in an envelope and postmarked.

The initial production at the Philadelphia Mint amounted to a prodigious 360,222,000 coins, a figure that challenged the entire mintage of Morgan dollars from 1878 to 1904!

Although certain representatives of the vending-machine industry expressed approval of the mini-dollar, it turned out that vendors took a wait-and-see attitude to assure that the public would be as eager to use them as the Treasury hoped. None of the Nevada gambling casinos showed any interest, as by that time they were all using their own chips. By year's end, more than 757,000,000 dollars had been struck, or more than two for every man, woman, and child in America.

Although the new dollars were available at banks, and some citizens obtained them as curiosities, they did not flow into circulation. If the Treasury would pay the several hundred million dollars needed to make new coin acceptors for vending machines, the Anthony might circulate, officials were advised, but the Treasury had no budget for such an expense. The matter was at a standstill, and only a few vending machines could use the coins.

CONGRESSIONAL TESTIMONY

In diametric opposition to what the numismatic community and press had observed, Under Secretary of the Treasury Bette B. Anderson included this in September 25, 1979, testimony to the Subcommittee on Consumer Affairs of the House Committee on Banking, Finance, and Urban Affairs:

The initial reaction of the general public to the new coin has been essentially what the Department, and indeed the congressional committees, had anticipated. On the one hand there has been a favorable reception by many for this coin, which for the first time in our history, bears the image of an outstanding American woman.

Beyond that, a number of nationwide retailers and local stores in various areas, which realized the advantages of using the new coin in commercial transactions, promptly began using and promoting the acceptance of the coin. Many communities and citizens' organizations have promoted use of the coin as well.

Anderson went on to say:

Perhaps the strongest objection we have heard is that, because of its size and color, the Anthony dollar coin can be mistaken for the quarter. During the past several months we have received suggestions for making the coin more distinct—there have been recommendations to increase the diameter, change the color or shape, or punch a hole in the middle of the coin.

She stated that all of these ideas had been considered earlier and had been rejected. It takes time for citizens to get used to a new coin. To help things along the Appropriations Committee had approved $300,000 "for the Mint to conduct an educational circulation program." By the time of her speech nearly 400,000 kits had been distributed. It was only a matter of time, she suggested, before the Anthony dollar would save the Federal Reserve System $50 million yearly by replacing $1 bills in commerce.

Congressman Frank Annunzio (D–Illinois), who shepherded many coinage proposals of the era, commented: "The new dollar coin may well go down in history as the only coin that more people wanted before it was released than after it was released."

The preface to *The Annual Report of the Director of the Mint*, 1979, closed with this remark:

Let me relate a piece of advice Susan Anthony received from an uncle. He said to her, "If you want to be a real success you have to make the world notice you." She replied, "I'll make them stare." Little did she know that the whole world would one day be staring at her likeness on a $1 coin.

There was an attempt, late in 1979, to use the smaller dollars to pay military personnel in Europe, but complaints forced an end to the practice. The coins could be used only on U.S. military bases because European banks discounted them heavily when making exchanges for local currency. In 1980 the Department of Defense did its best to work with the Treasury Department to circulate SBA dollars as well as generally unwanted $2 bills on military bases. While many coins and bills were used this way, they did not migrate into broader commerce outside of the military installations.

TREASURY EFFORTS CONTINUE

Even the United States Postal Service was enlisted in another vain attempt (February 1 to March 14, 1980) to distribute the coins. Signs were posted in 35,000 locations, and the coins were given out in change. This idea crashed after patrons made it clear to postal clerks that they did not want the "Susies" under any conditions. The New York Port Authority was persuaded to put up red-lettered signs at its tunnel and bridge toll booths on roads in and out of Manhattan advising that attendants would accept Anthony dollars, but few riders had such coins in their pockets. In time more than 9,000 stamp-vending machines in post offices accepted Anthony dollars, and in most instances the clerks supplied the coins. This did not seem to make much sense as most people in such offices bought stamps over the counter.

History repeated itself, and echoing what happened with the twenty-cent pieces more than a century earlier in 1875, the public in 1979 confused the Susan B. Anthony dollars with the somewhat similarly sized quarters.

Frank Gasparro said that at the Philadelphia Mint cafeteria he tendered a new dollar for a small purchase, and the cashier gave him change thinking that a quarter had been paid. From the outset Gasparro had held the coin could confuse people, but no one paid attention to him.

In addition, there was a political aspect to the pieces. In times of double-digit inflation, President Jimmy Carter's novel new dollar was sometimes referred to as a "J.C. penny" or a "Carter quarter."

CIRCULATION CAMPAIGN

In July 1980 the Mint mounted its "Anthony Dollar Circulation Campaign" with brochures, kits, posters, and informational materials. A four-page letter was arranged by topics giving information and telling of past efforts. The following entries are the letter's headings and a synopsis of the information under each:

Why a re-sized dollar coin?

The Eisenhower dollar was cumbersome and inconvenient. The new dollar is more convenient. It will also save up to $50 million per year by replacing dollar bills. In addition a 20% displacement of one-dollar bills with one-dollar coins would indefinitely delay the need to build a new Bureau of Engraving & Printing at a cost of $100 million.

How was the size of the new dollar determined?

A Mint survey of world coins indicated that in order to provide a $1 coin that would circulate, the weight would have to be less than nine grams. In order to distinguish it from the 24.2 mm quarter the new coin would have to be from 26.0 to 28.0 mm. The size of the Anthony dollar is 26.5 mm in diameter. This size was selected so that the dollar coin could be distinguished from low-value foreign coins by automated counting, sorting, and vending machines.

Why wasn't the dollar made a different color?

Extensive testing was done on brass-colored materials bonded to a copper core. After months of handling the alloys deviated from their original brass color to various shades of yellow-green. The silver-colored cupro-nickel metal was found to be ideal.

Why wasn't the dollar multi-sided?

Testing of multi-sided coins was conducted by Bell Laboratories and several other discriminator [coin-detecting device] manufacturers as well as the Bureau of the Mint. It was found that this would require many changes in coin devices and would be easier to slug [fraudulently pay with a fake coin] than a round coin.

Why not put a hole in the dollar?

Mechanisms would find it to be hard to discriminate from washers used as slugs. It would also affect the "electrical response" of vending machines.

How can the visually impaired distinguish the dollar from the quarter?

The high relief of the top of the eagle's head and wings on the reverse of the coin is tactilely distinguishable. No comparable area of high relief exists on either side of the quarter. This feature together with the difference in diameter and weight should enable the visually impaired to distinguish the new dollar from the quarter.

Why does the new dollar have an eleven-sided inner border?

This permits it to be easily distinguished from other coins. More than eleven sides would appear to be nearly circular and would defeat the idea.

Why not take the reeding off the coin?

The reeded edge acts as a deterrent to anyone who may attempt to pass slugs to the visually handicapped. Without reeds it is easier to manufacture slugs the size and weight of any coin.

What about the additional weight of carrying dollar coins?

The Anthony dollar weights 0.3 ounce. This is approximately one-third as much as four quarters. Using the Anthony dollar would reduce the number of coins the average person carries, and therefore the weight of the change as well.

How many dollar coins were made and where can I get them?

The Mint produced 648.4 million Susan B. Anthony dollars in fiscal year 1979 [ended September 30, 1979]. Production of the dollars was divided between the Philadelphia Mint which produced 47%, the Denver Mint which produced 38%, and the San Francisco Assay Office which produced 15%. Production as of April 1980 totaled 845 million, and 462 million have been released into the Federal Reserve System. Dollars are available from commercial banks.

Is the Treasury planning to withdraw the $1 bill?

A study by the Treasury recommended a plan to replace dollar bills with dollar coins and to increase the use of the two dollar bill. These recommendations have not been adopted or endorsed by the Treasury Department. It is up to Congress to make changes.

How much was spent on promoting the $1 coin?

$300,000 was spent by the Mint and another $300,000 was allocated by the Federal Reserve Board. Part of the last was spent with a public relations firm.

In 1980 the production dropped to 89,660,708 coins, but it might as well have been zero, as hundreds of millions of 1979-dated dollars were still in storage. The Treasury threw in the towel in 1981 and made coins only for collectors. The game was over, or so it seemed.

THE NEW SUSAN B. ANTHONY SALES PROGRAM

On January 30, 1985, Donna Pope, who had been Mint director since 1982, announced a new program to distribute Anthony dollars. "Since most banks do not inventory the coins because of their limited use in commerce, we have devised a system whereby collectors and the general public can buy them directly from the Mint."

Although nothing was said about dollars dated 1981, quantities of 1979 and 1980 dollars from all three mints were available. Offered were:

Option #1: A complete set of six coins, one from each of the mints, for both production years. The coins are sealed in Mylar and sell for $10.00 per set.

Option #2: A bag of 100 coins from a specific mint and year. Customers must specify what date and mintmark they desire. This bag is a smaller variety of the bag normally used to ship the coins to the Federal Reserve Banks. The mint and year of mintage is stamped on each bag. This bag will sell for $110.00.

Option #3: An original bag of 2,000 coins direct from the Mint's vaults. Customers must specify what date and mintmark they desire. This bag sells for $2,050.00.

Mint Director Pope emphasizes that this is not an attempt to promote the dollar coin, but that these procedures have been established as a service to the general public. There are no plans to produce any additional SBA dollars.

Prices included shipping. There was no limit to the number of coins that could be ordered. Subsequent issues of *The Annual Report of the Director of the Mint* for fiscal years ending on September 30 showed these sales figures:

1985: Option 1: 20,442 • Option 2: 4,099 • Option 3: 173

1986: Option 1: 101,050 • Option 2: 12,473 • Option 3: 14910

1987: Option 1: 102,207 • Option 2: 13,899 • Option 3: 226.

1988: Option 1: 83,101 • Option 2: 11,736 • Option 3: 510

1989: Option 1: 87,862 • Option 2: 15,854 • Option 3: 164

1990: Option 1: 26,172 • Option 2: 5,811 • Option 3: 5411

1991: Option 1: 36,755 • Option 2: 6,249 • Option 3: 84

1992: Option 1: 14,790 • 1979 sets of 3 coins, 1980 sets of 3 coins: 14,322 sold totally. Options 2 and 3 were not reported.

1993: Option 1: 36,176 • 3-coin 1979 sets: 7,784 • 3-coin 1980 sets: 5,932 • Sales of $100 bags: 1979-P 158; 1979-D 98; 1979-S 132; 1980-P 90; 1980-D 108; 1980-S144 • Sales of $2000 bags: 1979-P 76; 1979-D 38; 1979-S 42; 1980-P 43; 1980-D12; 1980-S 31 • Total revenue from sales of SBA dollars: $968,974. Last year of reports.

WHERE THEY WENT

In January 1993, Lauren Vaughan, United States Mint Office of Public Affairs, sent this information to Q. David Bowers, who was researching the distribution of Susan B. Anthony dollars:

Calendar year 1979 production, all mints: 757.8 million.

Calendar year 1980 production, all mints: 89.7 million.

Calendar year 1981 production, all mints: 9.7 million.

Total production: 857.2 million paid out since 1979: 470.1 million.

Government inventory as of December 25, 1992:

Stored at the Philadelphia Mint: 111.2 million.

Stored at the Denver Mint: 14.2 million.

Stored at the San Francisco Mint: 55.2 million.

Total stored at all mints: 122.2 million.

Stored by Denver Federal Reserve Bank: 122.2 million.

Stored by other Federal Reserve Banks: 84.3 million.

Total stored by government: 387.1 million.

Bowers notes that the quantity stored by the Denver Federal Reserve Bank might include some coins earlier designated for use in 1981 Mint sets. The Mint Office was not sure. If this is the case, some low-mintage 1981 coins could have still been in government hands.

A LATER IDEA FOR A DOLLAR COIN

The hope that a small-size dollar coin would eliminate the need for dollar bills did not go away. In the late 1990s some experimental coins were made to suggest that a coin with two metallic elements would not be confused with quarter dollars, and that Braille inscriptions would aid the blind. These bimetallic test pieces were struck in 1997 or 1998 by Schuler in their Michigan offices as demonstration pieces for the U.S. Mint and for exhibition at congressional hearings. The test pieces had two purposes: to demonstrate the addition of Braille elements to coinage in response to concerns of the Alliance for the Blind; and to promote their own technology to produce bimetallic coins as the U.S. Mint was investigating ideas for a new dollar coin. It is believed that approximately 20 pieces were struck.

CHANGES OF THE LATE **1990s**

Gradually, as new mechanisms were being made for vending machines, transit-system coin acceptors, and the like, provision was made to accommodate Anthony dollars. The idea of retrofitting existing mechanisms had not been successful.

This demand resulted in a steady outflow of Anthony dollars from Treasury storage. The coins reached limited use, and relatively few were seen in everyday commerce.

On May 20, 1999, *Mint News*, an occasional Treasury newsletter, contained this:

U.S. Mint to Strike 1999 Susan B. Anthony Dollar Coins

Washington, D.C.—The U.S. Mint today announced plans to strike 1999-dated Susan B. Anthony dollar coins (SBAs) to ensure the availability of dollar coins until the introduction of the new [Sacagawea] dollar coin in early 2000. The Mint will announce the start date for 1999-dated production in the near future.

"Demand for dollar coins is growing as more mass transit authorities and vending operations convert to using the dollar coin," said Mint Director Philip N. Diehl. "As a result, we're likely to exhaust our current supply of SBA dollars before the new dollar coin is available in January. We're committed to providing an uninterrupted supply of dollar coins through this transaction. We also want to let collectors know that our annual Fall Catalog this year will feature a Proof version of the coin and a two-coin Uncirculated set including both P and D mintmark 1999-dated Susan B. Anthony dollar coins. We'll announce prices and estimated production levels for the sets when the catalog is released in the fall."

A total of 847.5 million Susan B. Anthony dollar coins were minted for circulation in 1979 and 1980 and 9.7 million for numismatic sets only in 1981. Because demand has increased for a dollar coin in commerce in recent years, the government's supply of SBA dollars is nearly exhausted. The increase in demand is attributable to a growing recognition in the vending industry of the efficiencies of using dollar coins, including the convenience that comes from more rapid transactions.

For the 1999 Anthony dollars the dies were modified very slightly. On the obverse the 1999 coins have minor different spacing of the distances from the stars and the W in WE to the portrait, and slightly different spacing of IN GOD WE TRUST, among other slight changes visible only upon close inspection. On the reverse the lettering and features were adjusted after multiple efforts at modifying the craters and the Earth.

Plasters for the 1999 Anthony dollar. Multiple ideas were tried for the reverse. On the illustrated plaster the Earth, which presented a continuing problem with regard to geographical accuracy, is outlined in ink (see detail). The craters also have strengthened vertical lines from their rims.

Another 1999 reverse plaster and Earth detail. The craters have minimal vertical lines. The islands below Florida are particularly extensive. Baja California is prominent.

A 1999 reverse plaster and Earth detail. The crater rims are mostly smooth. A small island is below Florida. A line seems to indicate the Mississippi River. Baja California is differently shaped than on the preceding.

Earth as modified on a circulation-strike 1999-D Anthony dollar.

Plaster for the adopted obverse of the 1999-P Anthony dollar.

What might have been, but wasn't. At the Philadelphia Mint plasters were prepared in case there was a further call for 2000-dated Susan B. Anthony dollars.

This is noticeable, for example, in the relation of the stars and the A in STATES and AM in AMERICA. On the final reverse made for circulating coinage the Earth was changed noticeably from its appearance on the 1979, 1980, and 1981 coins. The 1999 reverse has no islands below Florida, and Mexico and Central America appear as a thin line.

Minting proceeded in due course. By the close of the fiscal year on September 30 the Philadelphia Mint had struck 13,750,000 of the new dollars, but none had been made yet in Denver. In October the first shipments were made to the Federal Reserve Banks. The use of SBA dollars had been increasing slowly, particularly within Midwest and Western transit systems, but the there was no danger of running short.

In the meantime there had been a lot of excitement about the upcoming mini-dollar of golden color with a new design (which would become a reality with the Sacagawea dollar of 2000).

In a private interview in 2015, a highly placed Treasury official told Q. David Bowers and Whitman publisher Dennis Tucker that, essentially, much of the official Mint explanation for the 1999 coinage (of the growing demand for dollar coins in 1999, and the desire to ensure enough supply to transition smoothly to the 2000 Sacagawea coins) was a cover. The cover explanation was the Treasury's idea, not the Mint's, and it seems that Mint officials were not advised at the time that there was no real coin short-age. The real reason the coins were minted was the Y2K scare—a dread of the chaos that might accompany the arrival of the year 2000. The fear was that many computer systems that dropped the first two digits of a twentieth-century year (using, for example, *99* instead of *1999*) would be thrown into disarray once the year flipped over to 2000. The abbreviation of 00 would imply that data was from 1900, not 2000.

Fear that bank deposits would be lost, vital records would disappear, and government and business information would be destroyed gave the news media the opportunity to instill concern, even panic, across the country. The Treasury Department realized that there might be a great rush by the public to get hard-metal coins. Making more Anthony dollars was done as a precaution. This was the *only* reason for making them, as otherwise Treasury supplies were already sufficient to take care of regular demand until the Sacagawea dollars were generally available.

Forewarned, just about everyone with data missing the 19 part of the year date adjusted their com-puter systems. The stroke of midnight, December 31, 1999, came, and on New Year's Day, January 1, 2000, all remained just fine with computers, data storage, and the like. The rush for coins that the Trea-sury had feared did not take place. Some citizens who had withdrawn bank savings as cash, nearly all in easy-to-handle high-denomination bills, returned it soon thereafter.

A LATER PROPOSAL

The Treasury held large stocks of 1999 SBA dollars after they were minted, hesitating to put quantities into circulation and thereby interfere with the promotion of the new Sacagawea "golden dollar." On September 20, 2011, Representative David Schweikert (R–Arizona) introduced H.R. 2977, the Currency Optimization, Innovation, and National Savings Act—the COINS Act. Steve Roach in *Coin World*, October 10, 2011, reported:

> The bill calls for the sequestering of Susan B. Anthony dollars within six months of the bill's enactment. After one year the remaining quantities of Anthony dollars would be declared obsolete coins. The bill calls for the Federal Reserve to improve the circulation of dollar coins and conduct outreach and edu-cation programs to help businesses with the transition. It would require Federal Reserve Banks to stop issuing dollar notes four years after the enactment of the legislation or when circulation of dollar coins exceeds 600 million annually, whichever comes first.

By this time Sacagawea and other dollars had been coined since 2000, but reserves of Anthony coins were still on hand. The bill did not become law. No specific accounting of later quantities of SBA dollars in government vaults has been located.

After the final mintage of 1999 coins, the Susan B. Anthony dollar again entered the realm of obsolete U.S. coins—collector items, rather than day-to-day circulating cash.

SUSAN B. ANTHONY (1979–1999): GUIDE TO COLLECTING

BEING A SMART BUYER

Most Susan B. Anthony dollars are well struck, but check the highest areas of both sides. On the obverse the highest part of Anthony's cheek often has contact marks or, in the case of coins not fully struck up, stray marks from the original planchet surface. The eagle's talons on the reverse of some coins are weakly defined. On the www.smalldollars.com web site in January 2006 an article ("What are Full Talons?") by Robert Ezerman and David R Golan called attention to this area of sometime weakness. On the reverse of the 1999-P issues it is not unusual to find the entire branch on the reverse without details. As these aspects have not gained much publicity in the marketplace, anyone interested in obtaining sharply struck coins with minimal marks can do so by cherrypicking at regular prices.

Proof SBA dollars approach perfection, with such grades as 69 and 70 being common. The registry-set specialty—trying to find coins with the highest grading numbers, for submission to audited competitions—was initiated a generation ago by David Hall of the Professional Coin Grading Service (PCGS). Numismatic Guaranty Corporation (NGC) has a registry-set program as well. In 2021 there are thousands of participants assembling various sets from half cents to double eagles as well as other specialties. Collectors building SBA sets have accounted for some of the lofty prices for early circulation-strike issues in unusually high grades.

AVAILABILITY

Susan B. Anthony dollars are readily available in Mint State, although those of 1981 are less common than those of 1979 and 1980. Circulated coins are not widely sought by collectors. Proofs were made of all issues and are readily available today.

Collectors recognize the good news and bad news about building a set of Susan B. Anthony dollars. The good news is that there are no rarities and that a full set in MS-65 and Proof-65 or finer grade is easy and inexpensive to assemble. All are of cupro-nickel composition (no silver strikings). The bad news: the series is short; except for the Wide Rim 1979-P, there are no significant varieties; and it is difficult to make SBA dollars an in-depth specialty.

In general, circulation issues in MS-65 and 66 are easy to find and are inexpensive, the 1981-S being an exception as the average grade is lower. If they are in certified holders they are more costly, and the expense of such holders is often more than the value of the coins they contain. At the MS-67 or higher levels many are scarce in terms of certified coins, although this "scarcity" shouldn't be taken out of context; the vast majority have never been submitted for commercial grading. Auction records for certain early coins in ultra-high grades have run into four figures.

Q. David Bowers observes: "My own collection of Susan B. Anthony coins is mounted in a bookshelf-type album with clear sides to permit me to easily study and enjoy them. I selected the Mint State coins to include those MS-65 or finer, keeping an eye out for sharpness, and the Proofs were automatically of high quality, probably grading 69 or 70 if I were to submit them for certification. I have one of each date and mintmark, plus the added 1979-P Wide Rim variety. I have not collected the S-mintmark 'types,' so called, of 1979-S and 1981-S, as to me they are not very distinctive. They are widely listed, popular, and inexpensive. If you want them, they are easy to find." Bowers advises, "Unless you are building a competitive registry set, collecting a hand-selected MS-65 and PF-67 or 68 set is a nice way to go. The cost is very modest."

SUSAN B. ANTHONY (1979–1999)

GRADING STANDARDS

MS-60 to 70 (Mint State). *Obverse:* At MS-60, some abrasion and contact marks are evident, most noticeably on the cheek and upper center of the hair. Luster is present, but may be dull or lifeless. At MS-63, contact marks are extensive but not distracting. Abrasion still is evident, but less than at lower levels. MS-64 coins are slightly finer. An MS-65 coin may have minor abrasion, but contact marks are so minute as to require magnification. Luster should be full and rich. *Reverse:* At MS-60, some abrasion and contact marks are evident, most notice-ably on the eagle's breast, head, and talons. Otherwise, the same comments apply as for the obverse.

1980-D. Graded MS-65.

AU-50, 53, 55, 58 (About Uncirculated). *Obverse:* Light wear is seen on the higher-relief areas of the portrait. At AU-58, the luster is extensive but incomplete. At AU-50 and 53, luster is less but still present. *Reverse:* Further wear is evident on the eagle, particularly the head, breast, talons, and tops of the wings. Otherwise, the same comments apply as for the obverse.

Susan B. Anthony dollars are seldom collected in grades lower than AU-50.

1979-D. Graded AU-50.

PF-60 to 70 (Proof). *Obverse and Reverse:* Proofs that are extensively cleaned and have many hairlines, or that are dull and grainy, are lower level, such as PF-60 to 62. This comment is more theoretical than practical, as nearly all Proofs have been well kept. With medium hairlines and good reflectivity, assigned grades of PF-63 or 64 are appropriate.

With relatively few hairlines a rating of PF-65 can be given. PF-66 may have hair-

1979-S, Type 2. Graded PF-70 Deep Cameo.

lines so delicate that magnification is needed to see them. Above that, all the way to PF-70, a Proof should be free of any hairlines or other problems under strong magnification.

1979 Susan B. Anthony Dollar

1979-P, Narrow Rim •

Mintage: Most of 360,222,000.

Availability in Mint State: This issue is common and probably 15 percent or so of survivors grade MS-65 or better. Among certified coins, enough MS-66 coins exist to satisfy collector demand. MS-67 and finer coins are scarce. (But note that only a tiny fraction of the mintage has ever been submitted for certification.)

Availability in circulated grades: Narrow Rim coins are common in circulated grades.

Detail of the Narrow Rim.

Characteristics of striking: The striking of this issue varies.

Notes: This design was launched with a narrow rim on the obverse. Most of the Philadelphia coins and all of the Denver and San Francisco coins have this feature. To help alleviate the numerous complaints that these coins could be confused with quarters, the Mint widened the obverse rim. These new "Wide Rim" dollars were first coined in July 1979.

2,526,000 Uncirculated each of the 1979-P and 1979-D Anthony dollars were included in Mint sets sold by the Treasury to collectors. These sets contained the 1979-P and D dollars only (not the S), plus other denominations cent through half dollar—total face value, $3.82; issue price of set: $8.00.

	Cert	Avg	%MS	EF-40	MS-63	MS-64	MS-65	MS-66
1979-P, Narrow Rim	1,165	64.8	97%	$2	$6	$8	$14.50	$22

1979-P, Wide Rim •

Mintage: Part of 360,222,000.

Availability in Mint State: Only a small percentage of coins are of this variety. They are rare in comparison to the Narrow Rim, but enough exist overall that finding one will be no problem. Most are in grades of MS-64 or less. Several thousand have been certified MS-65 (mostly) or better by PCGS and NGC. James Sego notes: "In truly superb gem grade with excellent overall quality this is a very difficult variety to find." FS-1-1979P-301; CONECA: ODV-002.

Detail of the Wide Rim.

Availability in circulated grades: These are scarce in comparison to the Narrow Rim, but demand is low as nearly all buyers want Mint State coins. Still, they sell for a premium.

Characteristics of striking: The striking of the Wide Rim coins varies.

Notes: To address complaints that the new small-sized dollar could be confused with a quarter, the Mint ordered a widening of the obverse rim. Coinage of the "Wide Rim" versions started in July 1979. George W. Maschke, a New York collector, was the first numismatist to report the change. The numismatic community learned of this in an article by Herbert P. Hicks, "S.B.A. Dollar Varieties," in *Error-Variety News*, May 1980. Soon, theories abounded—such as this being the result of a worn hub—and opinions ran the gamut from the variety not being real, to its being a significant discovery. A detailed follow-up article appeared in *Error-Variety News* in September 1981. "The 1979P Type 2 Dollars," by John A. Wexler, quoted Dr. Alan J. Goldman, deputy director of the Mint, who confirmed there had been a die change.

George F. Hunter, assistant director for process and quality control at the Mint, stated that 643 working dies of the Wide Rim variety had been made, indicating an estimated mintage of 160,750,000 coins, which does not square with the variety being very scarce. Hunter's comment has been widely questioned by numismatists.

In 1993 David M. Sundman, president of Littleton Coin Company, wrote to Q. David Bowers:

> Apparently, the Near Date [Wide Rim] variety was only produced for a very short time in the Susan B. Anthony production. Since our company has sold over one million sets of 1979-P-D-S Susan B. Anthonys and only found 1,600 pieces of the "Near Date" variety, we assume the production of this variety was very small. In the past year, I have sold more than half of what we found at $30 a coin. You still can find good coins today, if you are lucky. There is nothing remarkable about any of the other coins in the Susan Anthony dollar set from our point of view. I actually think that the "Near Date" variety is far more important and more noticeable than the Type II 1979-S Proof and the Type II 1981-S Proof mintmark varieties. The Near Date variety was really a design change.

Theories regarding the rarity of the Wide Rim coins have varied. The Mint may have prepared a large number of dies, but only used a few. Large quantities of Narrow Rim dollars had already been minted and were ready for release into circulation in early July. Coins struck in July or later, which would include the Wide Rim dollars, were not needed for circulation and may have been bagged and stored.

The 1979-P Wide Rim dollar is ranked in the *100 Greatest U.S. Modern Coins* (fourth edition).

	Cert	Avg	%MS	EF-40	MS-63	MS-64	MS-65	MS-66
1979-P, Wide Rim	1,732	64.6	96%	$8	$38	$40	$45	$90

1979-D Susan B. Anthony Dollar

1979-D • Mintage: 288,015,744.

Availability in Mint State: This issue is very common, including in MS-65 and higher. For these and others, ultra-high grades exist and often sell for lofty prices to those who are building registry sets.

Availability in circulated grades: These coins are very common in circulated grades.

Characteristics of striking: The striking of this issue varies.

Notes: All 1979-D coins are with a Narrow Rim (the date farther from the inner edge of the border).

	Cert	Avg	%MS	EF-40	MS-63	MS-64	MS-65	MS-66
1979-D	1,301	65.2	98%	$2	$7	$9	$10	$18

1979-S Susan B. Anthony Dollar

1979-S • Mintage: 109,576,000.

Availability: These are readily available through MS-65 and slightly higher grades.

Characteristics of striking: Striking of this issue varies, but they are usually sharp.

Notes: All 1979-S coins are with a Narrow Rim (the date farther from the inner edge of the border).

	Cert	Avg	%MS	EF-40	MS-63	MS-64	MS-65	MS-66
1979-S	1,099	65.4	99%	$2	$6	$8	$10	$15

1979-S, Proof, Type 1 (Filled S) •

Mintage: Majority of 3,677,175.

Notes: The "Filled S" is the usually seen *variety* (the "type" designation is wrong, but has achieved popular use), with interior spaces of the S mintmark appearing to be filled. It was created from the use of a worn mintmark punch. Their production took place from July to October (according to Alan Herbert, quoted by Walter H. Breen in his 1988 *Encyclopedia*). Probably about 80 to 85 percent of the mintage consisted of this style mintmark. One variety is from an over-polished die and has the third star too small.

All 1979-S coins are with a Narrow Rim, the date farther from the inner edge of the border.

Detail of the
Type 1 Mintmark.

	Cert	Avg	%MS	PF-65	PF-67Cam	PF-68DC	PF-69DC
1979-S, Proof, Type 1 (Filled S)	4,682	69.0		$7	$8	$10	$20

1979-S, Proof, Type 2 (Clear S) •

Mintage: Part of 3,677,175.

Notes: The "Clear S" variety has the interior spaces of the S mintmark open. They are much scarcer than the Filled S. It is believed that these were minted in November and December. Probably about 15 to 20 percent of the mintage consisted of this style mintmark.

All 1979-S coins are with a Narrow Rim, the date farther from the inner edge of the border.

Detail of the
Type 2 Mintmark.

	Cert	Avg	%MS	PF-65	PF-67Cam	PF-68DC	PF-69DC
1979-S, Proof, Type 2 (Clear S)	3,799	68.9		$45	$55	$60	$70

1980-P Susan B. Anthony Dollar

1980-P • Mintage: 27,610,000.

Availability in Mint State: These are mostly seen in grades below MS-65, but enough have been certified MS-65 (mostly) to MS-67 to make them readily available.

Availability in circulated grades: Coins in circulated grades are common, but are not widely desired by collectors.

Characteristics of striking: The striking of this issue varies. For any Susan B. Anthony dollar, cherrypicking is advised. Oftentimes the lower center of the reverse has some weakness.

Notes: By 1980 it was evident that the Philadelphia Mint had struck enough coins to meet public demand. Production was scaled back sharply, but not stopped completely.

2,815,066 Uncirculated 1980-P Anthony dollars were included in Mint sets sold by the Treasury to collectors; these sets contained the 1980-P, D, and S dollars, plus other denominations cent through half dollar—total face value, $4.82; issue price, $9.00.

	Cert	Avg	%MS	EF-40	MS-63	MS-64	MS-65	MS-66
1980-P	1,414	65.8	100%	$3	$5	$8	$12	$18.50

1980-D Susan B. Anthony Dollar

1980-D • Mintage: 41,628,708.

Availability in Mint State: These are common in Mint State. Most coins grade below MS-65 but, similar to 1980-P, many are available in MS-65 and a couple grades higher.

Availability in circulated grades: This issue is common in circulated grades, but they are not widely sought by collectors.

Characteristics of striking: The striking of this issue varies.

	Cert	Avg	%MS	EF-40	MS-63	MS-64	MS-65	MS-66
1980-D	1,292	65.7	100%	$3	$5	$8	$13	$22

1980-S Susan B. Anthony Dollar

1980-S • Mintage: 20,422,000.

Availability: Similar comments as for 1980-P and D, but these are slightly scarcer. They are easy enough to find.

Characteristics of striking: The striking of this issue varies.

	Cert	Avg	%MS	EF-40	MS-63	MS-64	MS-65	MS-66
1980-S	1,230	65.2	100%	$3	$10	$12	$15	$35

1980-S, Proof • Mintage: 3,554,806.

Notes: Proofs were sold in sets, cent through dollar, to collectors. All Proofs of this issue are of the same variety. They have the Open S mintmark, of the style made in November and December of 1979. Despite occasional rumors to the contrary, none of the old-style, Filled S mintmark variety have been reported.

	Cert	Avg	%MS	PF-65	PF-67Cam	PF-68DC	PF-69DC
1980-S, Proof	4,332	68.9		$6	$8	$10	$20

VARIETY: *1980-S, Proof, Repunched Mintmark (FS-C1-1980S-501).* The *Cherrypickers' Guide to Rare Die Varieties* describes the remnants of a previously punched S appearing to the left of the primary S mintmark. Very few specimens of this variety have surfaced, and enough are available to meet collector demand.

	Cert	Avg	%MS	PF-65	PF-67Cam	PF-68DC
1980-S, Proof, Repunched Mintmark	0	n/a		—	—	—

1981-P Susan B. Anthony Dollar

1981-P • Mintage: 3,000,000.

Availability in Mint State: This issue is common in Mint State. They are mostly found in grades MS-63 to 65, although MS-66 coins are readily available.

Availability in circulated grades: These are very scarce in grades less than MS-60, as these did not circulate, but circulated examples are not numismatically in demand.

Characteristics of striking: The striking of this issue varies, but they usually are fairly sharp.

Notes: By 1981, the Anthony dollar was recognized as a failure as a circulating coin. To the incoming presidential administration of Ronald Reagan, the Anthony dollar was a relic of President Jimmy Carter's failed economic policies. With hundreds of millions of undistributed Anthony dollars piled up in government vaults, there was no reason to mint more for circulation. Three million were made for sale in Mint sets to collectors. Apparently, over 90,000 sets did not find buyers and remained undistributed by year's end.

	Cert	Avg	%MS	EF-40	MS-63	MS-64	MS-65	MS-66
1981-P	1,059	65.6	100%	$7	$12	$15	$17.50	$35

1981-D Susan B. Anthony Dollar

1981-D • Mintage: 3,250,000.

Availability in Mint State: This issue is common in Mint State. They are mostly found in grades MS-63 to 65, although MS-66 coins are readily available.

Availability in circulated grades: These coins are very scarce in circulated grades—simply because they did not circulate—but they are not in demand from collectors.

Characteristics of striking: The striking of this issue varies, but they usually are fairly sharp.

Notes: The 1981-D has the second lowest mintage (after 1981-P) of any Susan B. Anthony dollar. 2,908,145 Uncirculated 1981-D Anthony dollars were included in Mint sets sold by the Treasury to collectors; these sets contained the 1981-P, D, and S dollars, plus other denominations, cent through half dollar—total face value, $4.82; issue price, $11.00 (an increase of $2 from the price of the previous year's set).

Q. David Bowers poses "A burning question: What happened to the several hundred thousand 1981-D dollars not sold with the sets? In 1982 and 1983 I tried to find this out, also about the San Francisco coins, and was directed to the Federal Reserve System, after which I made several calls to individuals in Denver and elsewhere who were said to be familiar with the storage facilities. No one provided any useful information. I tried again in 1992 with no success at all."

	Cert	Avg	%MS	EF-40	MS-63	MS-64	MS-65	MS-66
1981-D	1,226	65.7	100%	$7	$10	$12	$15	$50

1981-S Susan B. Anthony Dollar

1981-S • Mintage: 3,492,000.

Availability in Mint State: This issue is common in Mint State. They are mostly seen in lower grades, MS-62 to 64. This is the scarcest of the circulation strikes of the era to find MS-65 or higher. However, enough higher-grade coins exist to easily fill collector demand, except at ultra-high levels.

Availability in circulated grades: These are very scarce in grades less than MS-60, as these did not circulate, but collector demand for circulated examples is low.

Characteristics of striking: Striking of this issue varies, but they are usually fairly sharp.

Notes: All 1981-S Anthony dollars, circulation strikes as well as Proofs, were minted especially for sale to collectors. Q David Bowers asks, "What happened to the more than 500,000 1981-S Uncirculated dollars not sold with the Mint sets?" James Sego observes: "This issue is by far the most difficult to find in superb gem grade with excellent overall quality. One would think with the high mintage this would not be the case."

	Cert	Avg	%MS	EF-40	MS-63	MS-64	MS-65	MS-66
1981-S	822	64.6	100%	$7	$20	$25	$35	$220

1981-S, Proof, Type 1 (Filled S) •

Mintage: Majority of 4,063,083.

Notes: There are two mintmark styles this year, both very similar to those of 1979. This year's Type 1 appears to be a worn version of 1979's Type 2, while the 1981-S Type 2 is a new style, very open in the loops, and distinctly different from the Type 1 and Type 2 pieces of 1979, and the Type 2 issue of 1981.

The Filled S and Clear S mintmark varieties are very similar in appearance, and study under magnification is needed to differentiate them. The Filled S sometimes, but not always, appears as a blob under low magnification.

Although these are popularly called "types," they are varieties, not representing a change in design.

Detail of the
Type 1 Mintmark.

	Cert	Avg	%MS	PF-65	PF-67Cam	PF-68DC	PF-69DC
1981-S, Proof, Type 1 (Filled S)	5,422	68.9		$6	$8	$10	$20

1981-S, Proof, Type 2 (Clear S) •

Mintage: Part of 4,063,083.

Notes: Type 2 (Clear S) coins constitute the minority of the Proofs of 1981-S, with a mintage of perhaps one-tenth that of the Filled S. (See "Notes" under the previous listing.)

The Filled S and Clear S mintmark varieties are very similar in appearance, and must be studied under magnification to differentiate them.

This variety is ranked in the *100 Greatest U.S. Modern Coins* (fourth edition).

Detail of the
Type 2 Mintmark.

	Cert	Avg	%MS	PF-65	PF-67Cam	PF-68DC	PF-69DC
1981-S, Proof, Type 2 (Clear S)	3,162	68.8		$125	$135	$145	$165

1999-P Susan B. Anthony Dollar

1999-P • Mintage: 29,592,000.

Availability in Mint State: These are common in Mint State, but most are weakly struck.

Availability in circulated grades: This issue is common in circulated grades, but not in numismatic demand due to the ready availability of Mint State coins.

Characteristics of striking: These are usually seen with weakness at the centers, most noticeably on the branch on the reverse. This is the poorest-struck coin in the series.

	Cert	Avg	%MS	MS-63	MS-64	MS-65	MS-66
1999-P	902	66.2	100%	$3	$5	$10	$22

1999-P, Proof •

Mintage: 750,000 estimated.

Notes: Proofs of this issue are easily available and all are in very high grades. The authorized mintage was 750,000. This was the second American Proof coin to bear a P mintmark, the earlier one being the 1942-P Jefferson nickel in silver-content "wartime" alloy.

	Cert	Avg	%MS	PF-65	PF-67Cam	PF-68DC	PF-69DC
1999-P, Proof	5,471	69.3		$22	$24	$27.50	$32

ERROR: *1999-P Susan B. Anthony dollar struck on a Sacagawea dollar planchet.* In late 1999 the Mint was producing both Anthony and Sacagawea dollars. Some "golden" planchets intended for Sacagawea dollars were inadvertently used for Susan B. Anthony dollars. More than a dozen examples are known. Conversely, some 2000-P Sacagawea dollars were struck on copper-nickel Anthony planchets.

1999-D Susan B. Anthony Dollar

1999-D • **Mintage:** 11,776,000.

Availability in Mint State: This issue is common in Mint State.

Availability in circulated grades: These are common, but are of no numismatic demand due to the ready availability of Mint State coins.

Characteristics of striking: This issue is often seen with weakness at the centers, most noticeably on the olive branch on the reverse.

	Cert	Avg	%MS	MS-63	MS-64	MS-65	MS-66
1999-D	1,109	66.5	100%	$3	$5	$10	$22

ERROR: *1999-D, Susan B. Anthony dollar struck on a Sacagawea dollar planchet.* A few 1999-D Susan B. Anthony dollars were struck on manganese-brass Sacagawea planchets.

SACAGAWEA DOLLARS (2000–2008)

Designers: *Glenna Goodacre (obverse), Thomas D. Rogers Sr. (reverse).*
Weight: *8.1 grams.* **Composition:** *Pure copper core with outer layer
of manganese brass (.770 copper, .120 zinc, .070 manganese, and .040 nickel).*
Diameter: *26.5 mm.* **Edge:** *Plain.* **Mints:** *Philadelphia, Denver, and San Francisco;
22-karat gold experimental specimens dated 2000-W were struck at West Point in 1999.*

Mintmark location
is on the obverse,
below the date.

Circulation Strike   **Proof**

BACKGROUND

The Sacagawea dollar was launched in 2000, with a distinctive golden color and a plain edge to distinguish it from other denominations or coins of similar size. (This followed complaints that the Susan B. Anthony dollar too closely resembled the quarter dollar; both were silvery, with reeded edges, and with only about two millimeters' difference in diameter.) A new coinage alloy and the change in appearance were mandated by the United States Dollar Coin Act of 1997. The core of the coin is pure copper, and the golden outer layer is of manganese brass. The obverse shows a modern artist's conception of Sacagawea, the Shoshone Indian who assisted the Lewis and Clark expedition, and her infant son, Jean Baptiste. (No known contemporary portraits of them exist.) The reverse shows an eagle in flight.

In 1999, about a dozen Sacagawea dollars were struck in 22-karat gold at the West Point Mint, as experimental or presentation pieces. These featured a prototype reverse design with boldly detailed tail feathers on the eagle. The following year, a small number of early circulation strikes from the Philadelphia Mint also featured that same prototype design. These are popularly called "Cheerio" dollars, as the coins were packaged as a promotion in boxes of Cheerios cereal. Their unusual nature was not recognized at the time, but today collectors seek them as rare and desirable varieties.

In addition to the regular Uncirculated or Mint State coins produced in large quantities, smaller numbers of Satin Finish dollars were made from 2005 to 2008 at the Philadelphia and Denver mints. Sold at an additional premium, most of these exist today in grades of MS-67 and upward and are designated SP (Specimen) or SMS (Special Mint Set) by the commercial grading services.

Several distinct finishes can be identified on the Sacagawea dollars as a result of the Mint's attempts to adjust the dies, blanks, strikes, or finishing to produce coins with minimal spotting and better surface color. One group of 5,000 pieces, dated 2000 and with a special finish, was presented to artist Glenna Goodacre in payment for the obverse design. These have since entered the numismatic market and command a significant premium.

Another peculiarity in the Sacagawea series is a numismatic mule (a coin made from mismatched dies)—the combination of an undated State quarter obverse and a Sacagawea dollar reverse. Examples of this error are extremely rare.

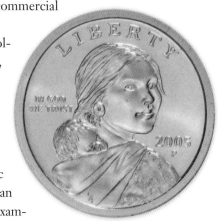

2005-P, Satin Finish.

HISTORY OF THE SACAGAWEA DOLLAR

In 1997 several bills were introduced in Congress to mint more small-diameter dollars, but of a different appearance than the Susan B. Anthony coins. The Treasury Department still had large stocks of the latter on hand. Those coins were never popular with the public and few were seen in circulation. The Mint reported, however, that the Anthony dollars had been finding increasing use in public transportation and in vending machines.

On March 20, Representative Jim Kolbe (R–Arizona) forwarded the first bill for a further dollar coinage, but of a different appearance. He stated that Canada had been very successful with its brass dollar nicknamed the "Loonie," featuring a loon, despite early opposition to the coin. The Canadian paper dollar was discontinued, and the coin became widely accepted in trade. Kolbe pointed out that the Anthony dollar had failed because it "looked and felt like the quarter" and also faced simultaneous circulation of paper dollar bills. The dollar bill should be phased out, he held. Representative Thomas M. Davis (R–Virginia) countered by saying that the public preferred dollar bills (which certainly had been the case during the Susan B. Anthony coin era) and, in any event, should not be told what type of money to use; furthermore, the American currency system was antiquated, and many universities, business, and people were switching to credit cards and other systems.

Theodore E. Allison, an assistant to the board of governors of the Federal Reserve System, recalled that before the Anthony dollars were introduced, focus groups and retailers expressed reservation about a coin that could be confused with the quarter and would necessitate large costs to retrofit vending and amusement machines. Debate continued, pro and con.

On December 1, 1997, President Bill Clinton signed the 50 States Commemorative Coin Program Act, Public Law 105-124. Section 4, the United States $1 Coin Act of 1997, made the dollar a reality. The new coin was to be "golden in color, to have a distinctive edge, and have tactile and visual features that made the denomination of the coin readily discernible."

SEEKING A NEW DESIGN

Secretary of the Treasury Robert Rubin, by virtue of his office, had the final say in the design of the new coin. He appointed a Dollar Coin Design Advisory Committee with nine members charged to follow his instructions that it should show one or more women and not a living person. Members included Mint Director Philip N. Diehl, Representative Michael Castle (R–Delaware), Undersecretary of the Smithsonian Institution Constance Berry Newman, vice chair of the President's Committee on the Arts and Humanities Peggy Cooper Cafritz, president of the American Numismatic Society Arthur Houghton, architect Hilario Candela, sculptor Edward Vega, executive director of Business and Professional Women U.S.A. Gail Shaffer, and president of Trinity College Patricia McGuire.

With the exception of Diehl, Castle, and Houghton these names were unfamiliar to nearly all the numismatists who read the official Mint news release and only Houghton was a longtime numismatist.

Suggestions varied widely, from abstractions such as "Liberty" and "Peace" to individuals in history such as Eleanor Roosevelt, abolitionist Sojourner Truth, African-American aviatrix Bessie Coleman, and, of course, *Liberty Enlightening the World* (the Statue of Liberty).

On June 9, 1998, the committee, having reviewed the submissions, selected Sacagawea, the Shoshone interpreter for the Corps of Discovery, popularly known as the Lewis and Clark Expedition, which explored westward of the upper reaches of the Missouri River.

Michael Castle, who had a powerful influence in the House of Representatives and was also well known to the numismatic community, protested the choice and reiterated that the Statue of Liberty would be ideal as it was popular and recognizable and would facilitate the coin's use. At Castle's suggestion the General Accountability Office conducted a poll of citizens. The Statue of Liberty was preferred by 65 percent, Sacagawea by 27 percent, 5 percent said that either was acceptable, 3 percent liked neither, and 3 percent had no opinion. This effort came to naught, for Secretary Rubin chose Sacagawea.

Q. David Bowers has commented: "This was a poster example of an often-repeated scenario in American coinage history: polls, the Commission of Fine Arts, the Citizens Coinage Advisory Committee, numismatic groups, and others often favor or recommend designs, such sometimes being dismissed by the secretary of the Treasury. In this instance, however, after the coin became a reality nearly all in the numismatic community admired it greatly."

Invitations were sent to 23 artists to submit their interpretation of a design featuring Sacagawea on the obverse and on the reverse an eagle representing peace and freedom, their work to arrive at the Mint on or before October 28, 1998. The Mint's instructions were that Sacagawea was to have the appearance of a Native American, not simply a generic woman. In November and December 1998 the Mint invited comments from government officials, numismatists, Native Americans, and others to review the designs submitted. This resulted in six obverse and seven reverse designs being named as semi-finalists. The creators of these were to receive $1,000 each, Mint employees excepted, and the designers for the final coin $5,000 each.

THE FINAL DESIGN

Using the Internet and other media the Mint also invited citizens to share their thoughts. The designs were then submitted to the U.S. Commission of Fine Arts for review. Chosen for recommendation to the Treasury secretary on December 17, 1998, was a representation of Sacagawea with her infant son Jean Baptiste Charbonneau, as submitted by sculptor Glenna Goodacre, who had a studio in Santa Fe, New Mexico. The reverse chosen was the work of Mint sculptor-engraver Thomas D. Rogers Sr., depicting a soaring eagle. To the satisfaction of almost everyone, the secretary of the Treasury agreed.

As there are no contemporary portraits or other illustrations of Sacagawea, Goodacre had gone to the nearby American Indian Arts Museum in Santa Fe to see if she could find an appropriate model. She chose Randy'L He-dow Teton, daughter of a museum employee and a student at the University of New Mexico. Born in 1976, she is a Shoshone-Bannock-Cree woman from the Lincoln Creek District within the Fort Hall Reservation in Idaho. Selection as the coin's model has brought her a degree of fame, and she has been a featured guest at numismatic events, the first-ever living model for circulating coinage to appear at such gatherings.

OBVERSE DESIGNER GLENNA GOODACRE

New Mexico artist Goodacre was a creator of monumental sculptures including the Vietnam Women's Memorial (part of the national Vietnam Veterans Memorial), situated on the National Mall in Washington, D.C., which was dedicated in 1993. Her Irish Memorial (2003), installed at Penn's Landing in Philadelphia, is a massive monument of 35 life-size sculptures dedicated to America's millions of Irish immigrants. Her delightful and energetic sculpture *The Puddle Jumpers* is in Montgomery, Alabama. The Smithsonian Art Inventory describes it:

> Six running children, three boys and three girls, are preparing to jump into a puddle. The children are holding hands and are in various states of motion. Three of the figures are anchored to the ground, though all have the appearance of being suspended in air. The figures wear play clothes and are all smiling and laughing.

Goodacre's portraiture included a bronze statue of Ronald Reagan, *After the Ride*, displayed at his Presidential Library in California. She created a full-length figure of ragtime composer Scott Joplin, a striding depiction of General Dwight D. Eisenhower, and many other impressive sculptural portraits.

Goodacre achieved fame within the numismatic community as the designer of the Sacagawea dollar. She died of natural causes at the age of 80, passing away at her home in Santa Fe on the evening of Monday, April 13, 2020. Robin Salmon, Brookgreen Gardens's vice president of Art and Historical Collections and curator of Sculpture, and a member of the Citizens Coinage Advisory Committee, described Goodacre as "a remarkable woman and a good friend who never met a stranger. Her artwork continues on as powerful testimony to her love of family and the beauty of the human spirit."

REVERSE DESIGNER THOMAS D. ROGERS SR.

Tom Rogers is a medallic artist originally from Wingdale, New York. He worked as a sculptor/engraver for the United States Mint from October 1991 to January 2001, designing and sculpting medals and coins including commemoratives, bullion, and several State quarters. His soaring eagle motif for the Sacagawea dollar, graceful and artfully balanced among the coin's inscriptions, has earned its place among the most attractive modern coinage designs.

Rogers's Smithsonian American Art Museum biography describes his work:

> After serving in the Navy for four years, Rogers earned an associate's degree in commercial art, and in the 1970s worked for the Medallic Art Company, where he developed his technique for carving directly into a plaster mold. The process gives him more control over details, helps him work quickly, and allows him to forgo the plasteline modeling clay favored by many medallic sculptors. In 1990, he spent a year at Medalcraft Mint, in Wisconsin, and from 1991 to 2001 worked as an engraver for the United States Mint, designing the reverse sides of the U.S. gold dollar coin (the Sacagawea dollar), and the Maryland, Massachusetts, and South Carolina state quarters. Over the years, Rogers has won numerous prestigious competitions and commissions, including the Gerald and Betty Ford Congressional medal, the Smithsonian Institution 150th anniversary coin, the 100th anniversary medal for the American Numismatic Association, and two commemorative coins celebrating the Library of Congress bicentennial in 2000. Rogers lives and works in Oregon as a freelance sculptor and medalist.

SACAGAWEA AND THE EXPEDITION

The historical Sacagawea, a Lemhi Shoshone woman, was born in May 1788. Her early life was mostly unfortunate. In 1800 she and some other girls were kidnapped by a group of Hidatsas. While captive at a Hidatsa village near present-day Washburn, North Dakota, in 1804, she was acquired as a wife by Toussaint Charbonneau, a Quebecois trapper who had resided there. She joined another Shoshone woman as Charbonneau's second wife. Facts are uncertain, but he may have "won" both women by gambling.

When the Lewis and Clark Expedition arrived at the Hidatsa settlement to stay the winter of 1804–1805 and build Fort Mandan, they hired Charbonneau as their interpreter. They learned that his captive wife spoke fluent Shoshone, providing an opportunity for her to join the group in their anticipated travels through Shoshone territory. Husband and wife both traveled with the adventurers. Their son Jean Baptiste was born on February 11, 1805.

Sacagawea's main occupation with the travelers was as an interpreter, not as the guide mentioned in popular histories. The presence of a Native American woman in the group also reassured other natives along the trip that their intent was peaceful, for a woman would not have been part of an invading force. Along the way Sacagawea negotiated the purchase of horses and at one time rescued the expedition's journal after a canoe accident. Several years later, in 1809, Sacagawea and her husband accepted William Clark's invitation to relocate to St. Louis, where their child, nicknamed "Pomp" by the explorers, became enrolled into the St. Louis Academy boarding school. In the next year or shortly afterward, Sacagawea gave birth to a daughter, Lizette. She grew homesick and returned to the Northwest, leaving her two children behind for adoption. She died of "putrid fever" on December 20, 1812. As Bowers has observed, "It cannot be said that her life was a happy one, but we can hope she enjoyed at least part of it."

PROS AND CONS OF THE UPCOMING COINS

News about the forthcoming Sacagawea dollar engendered much controversy, some of which was played out in the daily papers. The Mount Vernon Ladies' Association strongly opposed the possible replacement of the familiar dollar bill, which featured George Washington's portrait. Other observers stated that the elimination of the paper dollar would cost 600 to 1,000 jobs at the Bureau of Engraving and Printing as about 40 percent of the Crane & Co. paper contract of $65 million per year was for dollar bills.

Standing to benefit from the coins was the vending-machine industry of about $40 billion revenue per year. It would not cost much to configure coin mechanisms to take dollar coins, replacing bill changers that cost $400 each. Beyond vending machines billions of dollars in coins, usually quarters, went through non-vending devices such as parking meters, washing machines, airport luggage carts, and even vibrating beds in motel rooms. The new coins replacing the paper dollar would result in increased employment at the various mints, offsetting to an unknown degree the job losses at the Bureau of Engraving and Printing (both entities are part of the Treasury Department). The seigniorage or profit made on each coin would be a benefit as well.

SACAGAWEA COIN NEWS

On May 20, 1999, *Mint News*, an occasional Treasury newsletter, contained information about striking more Susan B. Anthony dollars, with a 1999 date, and concluded with this information:

> Authorized by the United States $1 Coin Act of 1997, the new dollar coin's Sacagawea obverse design and Eagle reverse design were unveiled at a White House ceremony on May 4.
>
> Although the new dollar coin will be the same diameter as the Susan B. Anthony dollar coin it will have some new features to ensure it is easily discernible for both the sighted and the seeing-impaired. The new dollar will be golden in color, with a smooth edge—in contrast to the reeded edge of the Susan B. Anthony dollar coin—and have a wider border than current U.S. coinage. The Mint is currently completing research to develop an alloy to meet the requirements of the legislation, including mechanical and chemical simulated wear and tarnish testing.

Photographs of the White House event showed First Lady Hillary Rodham Clinton standing with Randy'L Teton, model of the coin, in front of a large cut-out of the new dollar. "Sacagawea played an unforgettable role in the history of our nation," Mrs. Clinton said. "Every day this coin will remind us we are a nation of many cultures."

The *Annual Report of the Director of the Mint* for the fiscal year ending September 30, 1999, included this:

> At year end we finalized the alloy for the Sacagawea dollar—or as we call it, the golden dollar—after almost two years of experimentation and coordination with business stakeholders.
>
> We'll produce more than 100 million golden dollars for release in February, when our consumer awareness and business education campaign ramps up. We're readying a national print and TV consumer campaign, and our business-to-business outreach team is finalizing materials, interactive displays, and schedules of appearances. We've met repeatedly with banking and retail organizations and tested public perception of the new coin.

PROMOTION BY MINT DIRECTOR JAY JOHNSON

In August 1999 President Bill Clinton appointed Jay Johnson as director of the Mint, succeeding Philip Diehl. Johnson had served earlier in various government offices and at one time was a representative to Congress from Wisconsin. He had spent 36 years in media, including radio and television broadcasting. Confirmed by the Senate in May 2000, he served as Mint director until August 2001 when in the change of administration President George W. Bush appointed Henrietta Holsman Fore as director.

Q. David Bowers fondly remembers Johnson (who passed away in 2009): "He embraced his post with passion and enthusiasm rarely seen. He helped create innovative advertising for the 'golden dollars.' One television spot featured George Washington holding one of the coins. Kermit the Mint Spokesfrog was on the screen as well, mainly promoting State quarters. Similar to what Mary T. Brooks had done during her tenure, Johnson was always available to the numismatic community, appeared at many events, and answered questions."

A GREAT SUCCESS?

As planned, in 1999 and 2000 the Mint promoted the Sacagawea dollars with advertisements on radio and television as well as with print announcements. Kits were supplied to those interested and included a "Use the golden dollar here" decal that could be affixed to a glass entry door. The official view was that the launch was a spectacular success, per this in the *Annual Report of the Director of the Mint*, 2000:

> Formally introduced in January 2000 and propelled by full-scale outreach campaigns, the Mint's Sacagawea Golden Dollar has achieved overwhelming success in record time. In its first nine months, demand triggered the production and shipment of 979 million Golden Dollars—it took 14 years for the Susan B. Anthony dollars to reach demand at that level!
>
> By year's end, the billionth Golden Dollar rolled off our presses. Hundreds of millions of Americans are using the coins and collecting them. This enormous popularity resulted in a profit of over $800 million and was a major component of the Mint's record-breaking total revenues for the year. The Golden Dollar's clearly successful introduction underscores the value of the Mint's vigorous market orientation. We were able to harness all of the marketing, partnering, and educational tools available to create, rather than merely respond to, demand—and in a single year have made the Golden Dollar a fixture in American coinage.
>
> A high-profile national multi-media campaign, featuring a contemporary George Washington as spokesperson, reached 92% of urban/suburban adults 15–18 times during the promotional period. Additional awareness came from media coverage, including appearances on the Today Show, on prime-time programs, and at the National Press Club.
>
> The business-to-business element of the U.S. Mint's marketing campaign involves targeting its resources and message. It identified eight sectors to focus its efforts to get more Golden dollars in customers' hands and circulating in commerce: financial institutions, retailers, the entertainment industry, grocery stores, fast food restaurants, government agencies, the vending industry, and transit authorities.
>
> Seventeen of the top 20 metro transit networks in the U.S. distribute and accept the Golden Dollar, including the country's two largest: New York and Chicago. Marketing materials sent to small financial institutions promoted the public's use of the Golden Dollar. A special direct-ship program assured their sufficient supply. Partnering with the Mint, Allfirst Financial, a 261-branch mid-Atlantic bank, launched a promotion that includes routinely paying Golden Dollars in change to customers.

THE REST OF THE STORY

The above excerpt of the Mint director's Annual Report included a good dose of marketing spin. In reality, in most areas of America the only Sacagawea dollars to be seen were at bank counters, available if anybody asked for them, but not seen in day-to-day pocket change—this despite the huge mintage that equaled about three coins for every man, woman, and child in the United States.

Q. David Bowers offers this anecdotal analysis of the situation:

> At the time I carefully studied the distribution of the new dollar coins. Then and at no later time did I ever receive even a single one in change. The banks I surveyed often reported that the dollars they paid out were soon returned by merchant customers who hesitated to pass them on to general circulation.

At the congressional and Treasury level, there was no action at all to reduce the production of $1 notes, which could have made the Sacagawea dollars successful, similar to Canada's acceptance of its new dollar coin. Then came the recession of 2008: banks cut back, and within a few years hardly any banks made it known that they could order new coins for customers. Person-to-person interaction between tellers and customers was costly, and banks continued to try to minimize it.

At the same time, within the numismatic community the Sacagawea coins were warmly and enthusiastically admired.

Changes at the Mint—and Ecuador

The alloy used to make Sacagawea dollars was chemically active, causing many coins to become stained or spotted in circulation. The Mint tried several rinse compounds in an effort to prevent this. One, which was used on about 2,500 coins in 2001, imparted a distinctive pale patina. Faced with many complaints, mainly from collectors rather than the general public, the Mint issued this announcement:

> The different hues of the Golden Dollars now circulating are the result of the manganese-brass contained in the outer layer of the new coins. Like any brass, its color will eventually become darker, giving your coins an antique finish. As the coins are handled frequently, the darker "patina" may wear off the high points of the coin, leaving golden-colored highlights that accent the darker background around the border, lettering and other less exposed areas. The brighter, brass highlights, in contrast with the darker background, accentuate the profile and add a dimension of depth to the depiction of Sacagawea and her child.

In 2001 production dropped to about one-tenth of the previous year's mintage. Beginning in 2002 the Mint limited the mintage to coins and sets sold to collectors. Uncirculated coins dated back to 2000 were available in rolls of 25 and in bags of 2,000. In 2005 the 2,000-coin bag was replaced by a 250-coin bag, bowing to the wishes of Mint customers, according to Mint spokesman Michael White.

By December 2009 the Federal Reserve System had 857 million Sacagawea dollars in storage. In early 2010 the Mint announced that 2000-P and D dollars that had been in storage for nine years were now part of its Direct Ship Program and could be ordered in any quantity desired. The Direct Ship Program was intended to promote circulation of the coins by offering rolls of the coins at face value with free shipping.

Meanwhile, in Ecuador the Sacagawea dollar was quite popular. The U.S. government shipped hundreds of millions of the coins there, for use as circulating currency. Monica Martinez, general manager of a Quito-based retail operation, was quoted in a May 31, 2004, *Coin World* article: "The woman on the coin, she could be an Indian woman from the mountains selling hand woven rugs or artistic clay pots to tourists. Some people thought it was very nice for the U.S. to put an Ecuadorian Indian woman on these American coins they made especially for us!" The attractive design and the fact that the U.S. dollar has been Ecuador's official currency since 2000 have made the Sacagawea dollar a mainstay of pocket change in the South American nation.

SACAGAWEA DOLLARS (2000–2008): GUIDE TO COLLECTING

Being a Smart Buyer

Most Sacagawea dollars made for circulation are very well struck. Weakness sometimes is evident on the higher design points. Special numismatic issues are uniformly sharply struck.

A collector can assemble a basic set of dates and mintmarks of Sacagawea dollars with ease. Most circulation strikes can be readily found in Mint State. In the past, coins of "gem Uncirculated" (MS-65) grade were pleasing to nearly all numismatists, including the most discriminating. That changed somewhat in the 1990s when certified coins became popular, and collectors became more attuned to grades of MS-66, MS-67, and finer conditions. The hunt for rarefied ultra-high grades increased early in the present century when PCGS and NGC registry-set competition became popular. This has caused modern coins—dollars and other denominations—that are very common in circulation-strike format to be recognized as relative rarities if in a grade such as MS-68, 69, or 70. The result: a common coin that is worth slightly more than face value in MS-65 can be remarkably expensive in higher grades. A discerning collector should be aware of this situation.

Proofs with S mintmarks are typically found in PF-69 or 70 grades, although many uninformed buyers do not realize this and view these high grades as "rare."

Beyond the basic dates and mintmarks, there are three well-known Sacagawea dollar varieties of special interest:

1. The 2000-P "Cheerios" dollar with a prototype reverse.
2. The Glenna Goodacre presentation coins, which are slightly scarce, typically sell into mid- to high three figures, and are readily found in the marketplace.
3. Satin Finish Sacagawea dollars made from 2005 to 2008 at the Philadelphia and Denver mints, which were included in Mint sets and have a special satiny surface. Many of these have surface marks from careless handling at the mints, but among them are some in very high grades. The difference between the Satin Finish coins and the regular Uncirculated coins is not sufficiently distinctive to inspire many collectors to desire one of each finish for a given date and mint. Certain varieties such as 2005-P, 2006-D, and 2008-D are rare in MS-65 grade but common in Satin Finish-65.

The 2000-D Millennial coins that seem to have been burnished after striking are interesting, but no great demand exists for them.

Paul Gilkes, in "Experimental washes, special strikings challenge to collect. Sacagawea dollar collections can include VIP strikings, toned pieces," *Coin World*, March 3, 2010, pointed out that due to experimental rinses, efforts to prevent tarnish, and other situations the mints turned out coins with varying surfaces:

> In 2006, Sacagawea dollars from the Denver and Philadelphia Mints appeared with discolored surfaces similar to the surfaces on the 2001-P strikes, although the discoloration did not necessarily cover the entire coin. The discoloration on the 2006 dollars was the result of a failure to properly rinse an anti-tarnishing agent used by the U.S. Mint, an agent that had originally been developed as a wood preservative. Although the 2006 issues were circulation strikes, the coins came from special Mint-wrapped circulation strikes offered to collectors as a numismatic product.

Because of uncertainties as well as toning and other home-made treatments added outside of the Mint, such coins have a limited popularity, and great caution should be used if you are considering such a purchase. Professional third-party certification is your best protection.

In a slightly different category are dollars struck from planchets improperly annealed during the heat-treating process. In the early 2010s certain certification services began calling these *sintered*. This term is metallurgically incorrect as sintering refers to compacting metal powder under great pressure to form a solid. *Mis-annealed* would be an accurate description, agreed to by error-coin expert Fred W. Weinberg.

AVAILABILITY

These coins are common in high grades, and are usually collected in Mint State and Proof.

SACAGAWEA (2000–2008)

GRADING STANDARDS

MS-60 to 70 (Mint State). *Obverse:* At MS-60, some abrasion and contact marks are evident, most noticeably on the cheekbone and the drapery near the baby's head. Luster is present, but may be dull or lifeless. At MS-63, contact marks are extensive but not distracting. Abrasion still is evident, but less than at lower levels. MS-64 coins are slightly finer. An MS-65 coin may have minor abrasion, but contact marks are so minute as to require mag-

2006-D. Graded MS-65.

nification. Luster should be full and rich. *Reverse:* At MS-60, some abrasion and contact marks are evident, most noticeably on the eagle's breast. Otherwise, the same comments apply as for the obverse.

AU-50, 53, 55, 58 (About Uncirculated). *Obverse:* Light wear is seen on cheekbone, drapery, and elsewhere. At AU-58, the luster is extensive, but incomplete. At AU-50 and 53, luster is less but still present. *Reverse:* Further wear is evident on the eagle. Otherwise, the same comments apply as for the obverse.

2000-P. Graded AU-55.

Sacagawea dollars are seldom collected in grades lower than AU-50.

PF-60 to 70 (Proof). *Obverse and Reverse:* Proofs that are extensively cleaned and have many hairlines, or that are dull and grainy, are lower level, such as PF-60 to 62. This comment is more theoretical than practical, as nearly all Proofs have been well kept. With medium hairlines and good reflectivity, assigned grades of PF-63 or 64 are appropriate. With relatively few hairlines a rating of PF-65 can be given. PF-66 may have hair-

2002-S. Graded PF-69.

lines so delicate that magnification is needed to see them. Above that, all the way to PF-70, a Proof should be free of any hairlines or other problems evident under strong magnification.

2000-P Sacagawea Dollar

2000-P • **Mintage:** 767,140,000.

Availability: So many of these were struck that today they are extremely common. Typical examples are in MS-63 and 64, but enough higher-grade MS coins exist that they are common in relation to the demand for them. For these and all other Sacagawea dollars it is important to remember that only a tiny proportion of the mintage has ever been sent to the certification services for grading. A coin that may appear to be rare in population-report figures may actually be common.

Detail of the Normal Tail Feathers.

Notes: Some 2000-P Sacagawea dollars were struck in error on clad planchets intended for 1999-P Susan B. Anthony dollars. Over a dozen are known.

More double-struck and other mint error coins are known of 2000-P than of any other date and mint issue.

Several hundred million 2000-P and D dollars were shipped to Ecuador, where they saw use in everyday commerce.

On November 18, 1999, a first-strike ceremony was held at the Philadelphia Mint. Invited dignitaries and guests were on hand, and some were allowed to push a button to have a coin struck. A medal (not high-speed circulation-strike) press was used. These coins had a special finish, lightly polished in appearance. It is thought that fewer than 600 were struck. Some of these were later packaged and sent to those in attendance at the ceremony. The special characteristics of these have not been well defined in numismatic literature. Coins privately polished outside of the Mint have confused the matter.

	Cert	Avg	%MS	MS-64	MS-65	MS-66
2000-P	6,206	66.6	100%	$2.50	$5	$12

VARIETY: *2000-P, Reverse Die Aberrations (FS-C1-2000P-901).* Two spike-like die aberrations appear through the breast of the eagle. This variety is nicknamed the "Speared Eagle."

	Cert	Avg	%MS	MS-64	MS-65	MS-66
2000-P, Reverse Die Aberrations	99	65.4	99%		$700	$1,250

2000-P, Boldly Detailed Tail Feathers ("Cheerios" Variety) •

Mintage: 5,500.

Notes: The most famous standard variety in the Sacagawea series is an early-release coin with the tail feathers showing prominent diagonal veins. This was the first type of die in use and had also been employed in making the 2000-W 22-karat gold coins. The eagle was subsequently modified to the "regular" reverse style, showing the tail feathers in parallel lines.

Detail of the Boldly Detailed Tail Feathers.

The Mint was eager to promote public interest and acceptance of the new dollar. It arranged with General Mills, Inc., the Minneapolis manufacturer of cereals and other foods, to supply 5,500 coins struck in late summer or early autumn 1999 with a 2000-P obverse and the prototype reverse. The difference in the reverse details was not noticed at the time. General Mills advertised a "treasure hunt." Every marked box of Cheerios that year included a 2000-dated Lincoln cent. One in every 2,000 boxes would contain a new Sacagawea dollar, not yet in general release, as well as a Lincoln cent. During the month of January, General Mills noted, "The only place to get either coin is in a box of Cheerios." In addition, one box in every 4,400 had a certificate redeemable for 100 dollar coins (finders who redeemed them received the dollars with the later-type reverse).

These coins were struck in advance of the regular production run that started on November 19, 1999. The Cheerios dollars were indeed special for the recipients, as coins for general distribution were not released to the Federal Reserve Banks until January 26, 2000. Walmart had an early supply of 100,000,000 coins, of the regular-reverse style, which it agreed not to release as change to its customers until January 30, so as not to eclipse the General Mills promotion.

Remarkably, it was not until February 2005, or over five years later, that the special prototype variety was recognized by numismatists. One was sent by California collector Pat Braddick to NGC. By that time the Cheerios dollars had been widely dispersed, many had been spent, and those saved by chance were hard to track down.

In *100 Greatest U.S. Modern Coins*, in which the Cheerios dollar is highly ranked, Scott Schechter and Jeff Garrett note:

> Two factors account for the late discovery of such an important coin. For one, the coin was mounted obverse-up in the holder, and the reverse with the extra tail-feather detail is not visible. Secondly, these coins were distributed in non-numismatic circles—to buyers of Cheerios—and few went to coin dealers. For years, no one wanted to remove them from their holders, thinking that it was the holder that imparted a small premium.

After the variety was discovered and publicized, coins appeared on eBay and other auctions, some selling for several thousand dollars and with one bringing a much higher price. Typical grades were MS-65 to 67.

Per Bill Gibbs in "Cheerios dollars soften," *Coin World*, June 29, 2009: "Prices falling from 2008 levels. When a new subtype or variety is discovered there is initial excitement, when over the next several years the market adjusts as the coin does (or doesn't) enter 'mainstream' collecting. A year ago an example of the 'Cheerios' dollar sold at auction for nearly $35,000! However, the initial excitement that accompanied its discovery has waned, and savvy collectors can now acquire an example for a fraction of its price at its market apex."

Ten years after the variety's revelation, PCGS had certified 1 as MS-64, 1 as MS-65, 8 as MS-66, 33 as MS-67, and 31 as MS-68, for a total of 74 certification occasions (though some probably were resubmissions). NGC had certified 2, both MS-64. This would seem to indicate that fewer than 100 coins were in numismatic hands.

Prices on the market for grades of MS-66 and 67 vary widely, some being double or more than the price of others.

	Cert	Avg	%MS	MS-64	MS-65	MS-66
2000-P, Boldly Detailed Tail Feathers	3	64.3	100%	$2,750	$3,000	$4,500

2000-P, Goodacre Presentation Finish • Mintage: 5,000.

Notes: Glenna Goodacre received her $5,000 payment for her obverse design in the form of as many Sacagawea dollars—not regular strikes, but each with a specially burnished and treated surface. This was unexpected by her and unannounced in advance. The special surface treatment was part of the Mint's experimentation to control discoloring in circulation.

The coins were delivered to Goodacre's Santa Fe, New Mexico, studio by Mint Director Philip Diehl accompanied by two Mint police officers. A special ceremony was held there on April 5, 2000. Seeking to preserve them from rough handling, the artist had the Independent Coin Graders (ICG) encapsulate the coins (without grades being assigned to each) beginning on August 8. Goodacre kept 2,000 coins for herself. Most of the others were sold for $200 each. The label on each read:

> 2000-P / Sacagawea $1
> Presented to obverse sculptor
> Glenna Goodacre
> By the U.S. Mint
> ICG Certified [number here] of 5000 coins

Many of the coins were broken out of their ICG holders and certified by PCGS and NGC, called "specimens," such as SP-65. At least 126 of the coins were found to have regular (not burnished) surfaces. These were referred to as Type 1 and the burnished coins as Type 2.

From *Coin World*, April 11, 2011, reported by Paul Gilkes:

> Nearly 2,000 of the remaining specially produced 2000-P Sacagawea dollars from among the 5,000 that sculptor Glenna Goodacre was presented as compensation for her adopted Sacagawea dollar obverse design were acquired in 2010 by Kentucky dealer Jeff Garrett, owner of Mid-American Rare Coin Galleries in Lexington. He had the coins removed from the Independent Coin Grading holders originally encapsulating them and had them resealed in Professional Coin Grading Service holders with grading inserts pedigreeing the coins to Goodacre. Garrett has since dispersed the PCGS-encapsulated coins into the market through dealers, except for a small number he retained for his personal collection.

Some regular 2000-P dollars have been privately burnished, creating deceptive pieces. Caution is advised when buying any coin not clearly certified and attributed to the Goodacre holding.

The Goodacre presentation dollars are ranked among the *100 Greatest U.S. Modern Coins.*

	Cert	Avg	%MS	MS-64	MS-65	MS-66
2000-P, Goodacre Presentation Finish	44	67.1	100%	$400	$500	$650

2000, Dollar/Quarter Muling •

Mintage: Unknown.

Availability: Slightly more than a dozen examples have been identified, all in Mint State.

Notes: At the Philadelphia Mint an undated Washington quarter obverse (used to strike State quarters) was combined with a Sacagawea dollar reverse with the soaring eagle, also undated. The first example was found in May 2000 by Frank Wallis, a Mountain Home, Arkansas, collector, in a group of dollars obtained from the First National Bank & Trust Company in that town. It was brought to Bowers and Merena Galleries and auctioned in the 2000 ANA Convention Sale for $29,900. Additional pieces came to light, each with publicity and each attracting attention, and along the way two press operators from the Philadelphia Mint were arrested. James Watkins and Raymond Jackson were charged with disposing of some of the coins, and were indicted on June 13, 2002. Jackson pleaded guilty, and Watkins became a fugitive for more than two years before being captured and sentenced.

For a time the numismatic community feared that certain of the coins would be seized, but this did not happen.

Careful examination revealed that three different die pairs were used to make them, indicating three different striking occasions and, perhaps, that they were deliberately snuck out of the Mint. Some coins were recovered from a bin at the Mint and others at a wrapping facility and are thought to have been destroyed. The quantity made is not known, and the situation remains wrapped in mystery.

Tommy Bolack, a numismatist, rancher, and museum owner in Farmington, New Mexico, took a special fancy to these and has acquired several pieces. The PCGS Web site devotes a page to these and lists past prices, all below $100,000, except for one that was sold in the 2012 ANA Sale by Stack's Bowers Galleries for $155,250.

The mule striking is ranked among the *100 Greatest U.S. Modern Coins.*

2000-D Sacagawea Dollar

2000-D • Mintage: 518,916,000.

Availability: Typical coins of this issue are MS–63 to 65. Certified ultra-high-grade Mint State coins are elusive in proportion, but are much less frequently seen than are those of 2001-P.

Notes: Large quantities were sent to Ecuador for use as legal tender in commerce.

	Cert	Avg	%MS	MS-64	MS-65	MS-66
2000-D	1,449	66.1	100%	$4	$8	$15

VARIETY: *2000-D from burnished millennium sets.* As a special promotion in its 2000 Holiday Catalog the U.S. Mint offered the United States Millennium Coin and Currency Set, which contained a $1 Federal Reserve Note with the serial number starting with 2000, a 2000 American Silver Eagle bullion coin, and a 2000-D Sacagawea dollar. Also included was a booklet with information about each coin plus historical notes, including the tale about Benjamin Franklin preferring a wild turkey to a bald eagle as the national bird. These sets were offered at $39 each.

Soon, keen-eyed collectors noticed that the dollar was partially prooflike or burnished, reminiscent of the special coins given to Glenna Goodacre, and of a deeper golden color. PCGS and ICG graders contended that the burnishing was post-strike. NGC graders had mixed opinions.

These coins became collectible varieties in their own right, selling at a premium if submitted for certification with original Mint packaging (so as to screen out home-burnished coins). PCGS and NGC certified such dollars with a "Millennial Set" notation and DPL suffix for "Deep Mirror Prooflike." The degree of the prooflike surface can vary, and some small percentage of sets contained dollars that were not prooflike. Care is advised when contemplating a purchase.

VARIETY: *VIP strikes.* On February 25, 2000, a first-strike ceremony was held at the Denver Mint. Invited dignitaries and guests were on hand, and some were allowed to push a button to have a coin struck. A medal (not high-speed circulation-strike) press was used. These coins had a special finish, lightly polished in appearance. The mintage was just 120 pieces.

2000-S Sacagawea Dollar

2000-S, Proof • **Mintage:** 4,047,904.

Availability: Nearly all of these coins are gem Proofs approaching perfection.

Notes: 3,082,572 were sold as part of the 10-piece "clad" Proof sets; 965,421 were sold as part of the 10-piece "silver" Proof sets. This was the high-water mark in terms of the number of Proofs minted.

	Cert	Avg	%MS	PF-65	PF-69DC
2000-S, Proof	16,323	69.2		$6	$15

2000-W Sacagawea Dollar

2000-W, Gold •
Mintage: 39; all but 12 melted.

Notes: In June 1999 Mint Director Philip N. Diehl made the surprise announcement that 32 Sacagawea dollars, dated 2000 and with a W mintmark, had been struck in 22-karat gold. (Although they bore a W mintmark they were struck in Philadelphia, later research revealed.) Diehl stated that more would be struck and these would be offered for sale. This caused quite a stir, the director was accused of exceeding his authority, and on August 12 he announced that all but 12 would be melted. Those surviving had been carried aboard the *Columbia* space shuttle launched on July 23, 1999, on a five-day mission under the command of Eileen Collins. On December 1, 1999, two more gold strikes were made.

In March 2000 Congress placed an indefinite moratorium on the striking of Sacagawea coinage in gold after lawmakers questioned whether the Mint had the legal authority to produce the coins in precious metal. The 12 Proof Sacagawea gold dollars sent into space were transferred to the Mint's gold-bullion depository at Fort Knox, Kentucky. The 12 coins were put on public display for the first time as a group during the American Numismatic Association's World's Fair of Money in Milwaukee in August. The remaining 27 Proof Sacagawea gold dollars struck were destroyed, according to U.S. Mint officials.

2000-W, Sacagawea $5 patterns: In February and March 2000 the Philadelphia Mint struck 40 experimental circulation-strike and Proof $5 coins in gold. These had the higher denomination lettered on the reverse and bore W mintmarks. The tail feathers on the eagle were straight (the second style). Fifteen pairs of dies were prepared, the reverses denominated FIVE DOLLARS. It was thought that these might be a nice addition to the Mint's

Plasters of the 2000-W five-dollar patterns.

gold-bullion program. The idea was abandoned and all of the coins, hubs, and dies were destroyed. One reason was the fear that circulation-strike Sacagawea dollars could be gold plated and passed as $5 coins.

2001-P Sacagawea Dollar

2001-P • **Mintage:** 62,468,000.

Availability: This issue is abundantly available. Typical coins are MS-63 to MS-65. Ultra-high grade Mint State coins are elusive in proportion, but many exist due to the large quantities minted.

Notes: Many 2001 and 2002-P and D dollar coins were sent to Ecuador for use as legal tender in commerce.

2001-P	Cert	Avg	%MS	MS-64	MS-65	MS-66
2001-P	693	67.1	100%	$2	$4	$6

VARIETY: *Experimental rinse.* Spotting and staining was a problem with Sacagawea dollars in 2000, extending into 2001. Various rinses were tried in an effort to prevent this. One compound used on about 2,500 coins imparted a distinctive pale patina. Many of these were identified before being widely distributed and were sold into the numismatic market. Some were placed in holders by the Sovereign Entities Grading Service (SEGS) and labeled: "2001-P EXPERIMENTAL RINSE SAC $1 / EXPERIMENTAL RINSE BY U.S. MINT TO PREVENT SPOTS." (Also see 2006-D.)

2001-D Sacagawea Dollar

2001-D • **Mintage:** 70,939,500.

Availability: This coin is readily available. Typical coins are MS-63 to MS-64. In terms of certified coins, relatively few have been graded MS-68 or higher.

Notes: Certified examples graded MS-68 and higher sell at sharp premiums, with registry-set collectors increasing demand and driving the prices up.

	Cert	Avg	%MS	MS-64	MS-65	MS-66
2001-D	414	65.9	100%	$2	$4	$6

VARIETY: *2001-D muling with South Carolina quarter reverse.* At the Denver Mint in 2001 there were two scenarios where one or more coin-press operators intentionally created two mulings: (1) A 2001-D cent obverse with a Roosevelt dime reverse, struck on copper-plated–zinc planchets, and (2) A 2001-D Sacagawea dollar obverse mated with the reverse of a South Carolina State quarter. Investigators discovered these coins and are thought to have found and destroyed them all, but the matter was not certain. No examples have been reported on the coin market.

2001-S Sacagawea Dollar

2001-S, Proof • **Mintage:** 3,183,740.

Availability: Nearly all of these coins are gem Proofs approaching perfection.

Notes: 2,294,909 were sold as part of the 10-piece "clad" Proof sets; 889,967 were sold as part of the 10-piece "silver" Proof sets. Numismatist Charles Morgan observes: "Once thought of as the 'key date' to the series, a lower mintage later occurred in 2008. Promoters pumped certified PF-70DC versions of this coin into the stratosphere with many selling for thousands of dollars. The open-market price for a PF-70DCAM was about $60 in 2015."

	Cert	Avg	%MS	PF-65	PF-69DC
2001-S, Proof	11,810	69.2		$10	$20

2002-P Sacagawea Dollar

2002-P • **Mintage:** 3,865,610.

Availability: Readily available. Typical grades are MS-64 to MS-66.

Notes: From this year forward, Sacagawea dollar coins were only sold at a premium in Mint sets, rolls, and bags, and were not available for general circulation.

In terms of certified coins, MS-68 and finer examples are elusive and command strong premiums thanks in large part to competition from registry-set collectors.

	Cert	Avg	%MS	MS-64	MS-65	MS-66
2002-P	400	67.1	100%	$2	$4	$10

2002-D Sacagawea Dollar

2002-D • Mintage: 3,732,000.

Availability: Typical grades are MS-62 to MS-64. Many if not most of these coins have bagmarks. In terms of certified coins, MS-68 and finer examples are elusive.

Notes: Ultra-high-grade coins command strong premiums.

	Cert	Avg	%MS	MS-64	MS-65	MS-66
2002-D	373	66.3	100%	$2	$4	$8

2002-S Sacagawea Dollar

2002-S, Proof • Mintage: 3,211,995.

Availability: This mintage is readily available. Nearly all are gem Proofs approaching perfection.

Notes: 2,319,766 were sold as part of the 10-piece "clad" Proof sets; 892,229 were sold as part of the 10-piece "silver" Proof sets.

	Cert	Avg	%MS	PF-65	PF-69DC
2002-S, Proof	9,813	69.3		$6	$15

2003-P Sacagawea Dollar

2003-P • Mintage: 3,080,000.

Availability: These coins are easily available. Typical grades are MS-64 to MS-66. Higher grades are available, and in MS-68 and finer grades this is one of the more easily found circulation strikes of the era.

	Cert	Avg	%MS	MS-64	MS-65	MS-66
2003-P	707	66.7	100%	$3	$5	$8

2003-D Sacagawea Dollar

2003-D • Mintage: 3,080,000.

Availability: This issue is readily available. Typical grades are MS-63 to MS-64 or 65. In terms of certified coins, MS-68 and finer examples are elusive.

Notes: Ultra-high-grade examples command strong premiums.

	Cert	Avg	%MS	MS-64	MS-65	MS-66
2003-D	621	66.1	100%	$3	$5	$8

2003-S Sacagawea Dollar

2003-S, Proof • **Mintage:** 3,298,439.

Availability: This Proof mintage is easily available. Nearly all are gem Proofs approaching perfection.

Notes: 2,172,684 were sold as part of the 10-piece "clad" Proof sets; 1,125,755 were sold as part of the 10-piece "silver" Proof sets.

	Cert	Avg	%MS	PF-65	PF-69DC
2003-S, Proof	13,248	69.2		$6	$15

2004-P Sacagawea Dollar

2004-P • **Mintage:** 2,660,000.

Availability: This production is common. Typical grades are MS-63 to MS-65. In terms of certified coins, MS-68 and finer examples are elusive.

Notes: Coins of ultra-high grades (MS-68 and higher) command strong premiums, which is unusual for a Philadelphia issue.

	Cert	Avg	%MS	MS-64	MS-65	MS-66
2004-P	591	66.8	100%	$2	$4	$8

2004-D Sacagawea Dollar

2004-D • **Mintage:** 2,660,000.

Availability: Denver's Sacagawea dollars of 2004 are readily available. Typical grades are MS-64 to MS-66. Higher-grade coins are seen with frequency, but are scarcer.

	Cert	Avg	%MS	MS-64	MS-65	MS-66
2004-D	718	66.6	100%	$2	$4	$8

2004-S Sacagawea Dollar

2004-S, Proof • **Mintage:** 2,965,422.

Availability: These are easy to find in the market. Nearly all are gem Proofs approaching perfection.

Notes: 1,804,396 were sold as part of the 11-piece "clad" Proof sets; 1,187,673 were sold as part of the 11-piece "silver" Proof sets.

In *Coin World*, June 5, 2006, a market analyst gave multiple examples of essentially the same coins selling for widely differing prices. An example: "I found two 2004-S Sacagawea dollars graded PF-70DC by PCGS that sold for $230 and $345, while three coins of that same issue and graded PF-70UC by NGC (the two firms use slightly different terms for the 'same' grade), brought $138, $184, and $218.50. NGC's census lists a whopping 893 it has graded, while PCGS has graded just 184, according to its census. This compares to about 5,700 to 5,800 graded PF-69 deep or ultra cameo by each of these two services."

	Cert	Avg	%MS	PF-65	PF-69DC
2004-S, Proof	12,503	69.2		$6	$15

2005-P Sacagawea Dollar

2005-P • Mintage: 2,520,000.

Availability: Enough MS-65 coins exist that finding one will be no problem, although mark-free examples are in the distinct minority.

Notes: This issue typically has many bagmarks. Collector demand is diluted by the ready availability of Satin Finish coins.

	Cert	Avg	%MS	MS-64	MS-65	MS-66
2005-P	4,401	66.9	100%	$7	$10	$20

2005-P, Satin Finish • **Mintage:** 1,160,000.

Notes: Coins sold in Mint sets have a Satin Finish, which is slightly different from the regular Uncirculated finish. This finish was started in 2005 and continued through the end of the Sacagawea series in 2008. PCGS gives these a SP (Specimen) prefix and lists them separately in its population report. NGC designates these as SMS (Special Mint Set) and also lists them separately. According to NGC's David W. Lange: "The finish is similar to that on modern commemoratives that the U.S. Mint markets as Uncirculated."

These are typically graded 65 to 68, but select coins are finer.

	Cert	Avg	%MS	MS-64	MS-65	MS-66
2005-P, Satin Finish	4,044	67.0	100%		$5	$12

2005-D Sacagawea Dollar

2005-D • Mintage: 2,520,000.

Availability: Enough MS-65 coins exist that finding one will be no problem, although mark-free examples are in the distinct minority.

Notes: This issue typically has many bagmarks. Collector demand is diluted by the ready availability of Satin Finish coins.

	Cert	Avg	%MS	MS-64	MS-65	MS-66
2005-D	4,310	66.6	100%	$7	$10	$20

2005-D, Satin Finish • Mintage: 1,160,000.

Notes: These are typically graded 65 to 68, but select coins are found in higher grades. They are separately certified with an SP prefix by PCGS and with an SMS prefix by NGC.

	Cert	Avg	%MS	MS-64	MS-65	MS-66
2005-D, Satin Finish	3,714	66.6	100%		$5	$12

2005-S Sacagawea Dollar

2005-S, Proof • Mintage: 3,344,679.

Availability: These are readily available. Nearly all are gem Proofs approaching perfection.

Notes: 2,275,000 were sold as part of the 11-piece "clad" Proof sets; 998,000 were sold as part of the 11-piece "silver" Proof sets.

	Cert	Avg	%MS	PF-65	PF-69DC
2005-S, Proof	17,866	69.2		$6	$15

2006-P Sacagawea Dollar

2006-P • Mintage: 4,900,000.

Availability: Finding an MS-64 coin is easy, but MS-65 and finer coins certified in PCGS and NGC holders are scarce.

Notes: As is true of all of the later limited-issue circulation strikes, the vast majority have not been submitted to certification services.

	Cert	Avg	%MS	MS-64	MS-65	MS-66
2006-P	1,949	66.7	100%	$2	$4	$8

2006-P, Satin Finish • Mintage: 847,631.

Availability: These are typically graded 65 to 68, but select coins can be found in even finer grades.

Notes: These are separately certified with an SP prefix by PCGS and with an SMS prefix by NGC.

	Cert	Avg	%MS	MS-64	MS-65	MS-66
2006-P, Satin Finish	1,570	66.9	100%		$5	$12

2006-D Sacagawea Dollar

2006-D • Mintage: 2,800,000.

Availability: MS-62 and 63 coins are easily available, but are slightly scarce. Coins certified MS-65 or higher are very rare.

Notes: For regular Mint State coins (not Satin Finish), this is the key to the Sacagawea series dated after 2000. Demand for them is uncertain, as Satin Finish coins are easy to find.

Experimental rinse: An experimental rinse (see 2001-P) was also used on some 2006-D coins and gave them a distinctive hue. This discovery was made by Russ Flourney, whose coin was certified by PCGS with a special description.

	Cert	Avg	%MS	MS-64	MS-65	MS-66
2006-D	2,095	66.6	100%	$2	$4	$8

2006-D, Satin Finish • Mintage: 847,631.

Availability: These are readily available in the marketplace. They are typically graded 65 to 68, but select coins are higher.

Notes: These are separately certified with an SP prefix by PCGS and with an SMS prefix by NGC.

	Cert	Avg	%MS	MS-64	MS-65	MS-66
2006-D, Satin Finish	1,510	66.9	100%		$5	$12

2006-S Sacagawea Dollar
2006-S, Proof • Mintage: 3,054,436.

Availability: These are readily available to collectors. Nearly all are gem Proofs approaching perfection.

	Cert	Avg	%MS	PF-65	PF-69DC
2006-S, Proof	9,012	69.3		$6	$15

2007-P Sacagawea Dollar
2007-P • Mintage: 3,640,000.

Availability: MS-65 and 66 coins are readily available. MS-68 and higher coins constitute a tiny percentage of the series.

	Cert	Avg	%MS	MS-64	MS-65	MS-66
2007-P	1,160	66.9	100%	$3	$5	$8

2007-P, Satin Finish • Mintage: 895,628.

Availability: These are easy to find in the market, typically graded 65 to 68, with select coins certified higher.

Notes: These are separately certified with an SP prefix by PCGS and with an SMS prefix by NGC.

	Cert	Avg	%MS	MS-64	MS-65	MS-66
2007-P, Satin Finish	588	67.0	100%		$5	$12

2007-D Sacagawea Dollar

2007-D • **Mintage:** 3,920,000.

Availability: Certified MS-65 or higher coins are very scarce.

	Cert	Avg	%MS	MS-64	MS-65	MS-66
2007-D	1,178	66.5	100%	$3	$5	$8

VARIETY: *Lettered Edge.* The edge on these coins is lettered in error, as on a Presidential dollar. The first genuine specimen was found by Andrew Moores of Lakewood, New Jersey. Others were found later. The variety remains scarce. Many fake lettered-edge dollars have lettering fraudulently applied outside of the Mint.

2007-D, Satin Finish • **Mintage:** 895,628.

Availability: These are readily available, typically graded 65 to 68, but some grade even higher.

Notes: These are separately certified with an SP prefix by PCGS and with an SMS prefix by NGC.

	Cert	Avg	%MS	MS-64	MS-65	MS-66
2007-D, Satin Finish	642	66.9	100%		$5	$12

2007-S Sacagawea Dollar

2007-S, Proof • **Mintage:** 2,577,166.

Availability: Nearly all of this readily available mintage are gem Proofs approaching perfection.

	Cert	Avg	%MS	PF-65	PF-69DC
2007-S, Proof	9,042	69.2		$6	$15

2008-P Sacagawea Dollar

2008-P • **Mintage:** 1,820,000.

Availability: These are plentiful in MS-63 and 64 grades, but are scarce to rare at higher levels.

	Cert	Avg	%MS	MS-64	MS-65	MS-66
2008-P	575	66.9	100%	$3	$5	$8

2008-P, Satin Finish • Mintage: 745,464.

Availability: These are easily available in the collector market, typically certified 65 to 68, but select coins are graded higher.

Notes: They are separately certified with an SP prefix by PCGS and with an SMS prefix by NGC.

	Cert	Avg	%MS	MS-64	MS-65	MS-66
2008-P, Satin Finish	325	67.2	100%		$5	$12

2008-D Sacagawea Dollar

2008-D • Mintage: 1,820,000.

Availability: MS-62 and 63 coins are easily available, but are slightly scarce. Coins certified MS-65 or higher are very rare.

Notes: For regular Mint State coins (not Satin Finish) this is a key to the post-2000 Sacagawea series, second after the 2006-D. Demand for them is uncertain as attractive Satin Finish coins are easy to find.

	Cert	Avg	%MS	MS-64	MS-65	MS-66
2008-D	793	66.8	100%	$3	$5	$8

2008-D, Satin Finish • Mintage: 745,464.

Availability: These are readily available, typically graded 65 to 68, but select coins are higher.

Notes: Satin Finish coins are separately certified with an SP prefix by PCGS and with an SMS prefix by NGC.

	Cert	Avg	%MS	MS-64	MS-65	MS-66
2008-D, Satin Finish	413	67.3	100%		$5	$12

2008-S Sacagawea Dollar

2008-S, Proof • Mintage: 2,169,561.

Availability: Easily available to collectors, nearly all are gem Proofs approaching perfection.

Notes: Q. David Bowers opines: "With its lower mintage this may be a potential 'dark horse' issue."

	Cert	Avg	%MS	PF-65	PF-69DC
2008-S, Proof	6,496	69.2		$6	$15

PRESIDENTIAL DOLLARS (2007–2020)

Designers: *See image captions for obverse designers; Don Everhart (reverse).*
Weight: *8.1 grams.* **Composition:** *Pure copper core with outer layers
of manganese brass (.770 copper, .120 zinc, .070 manganese, and .040 nickel).*
Diameter: *26.5 mm.* **Edge:** *Lettered.* **Mints:** *Philadelphia, Denver, and San Francisco.*

**Obverse Style,
2007–2008,
Circulation Strike**
No motto on obverse.

**Obverse Style,
2009–2020,
Circulation Strike**
Motto beneath portrait.

**Common Reverse,
Circulation Strike**

**Date, Mintmark, and
Mottos Incused on Edge**
*IN GOD WE TRUST
moved to obverse in 2009.*

Proof

BACKGROUND

Presidential dollars debuted in 2007 and were issued at the rate of four designs per year through 2015, with three coins issued in 2016, followed by one in 2020. The series started with George Washington and continued in order of office. Living presidents are ineligible, so the program's final entry, as of mid-2021, is George H.W. Bush. Each coin has a common reverse, designed and sculpted by Don Everhart, showing the Statue of Liberty. The series began with the date, mintmark, and mottos IN GOD WE TRUST and E PLURIBUS UNUM incused on the edge of the coins; in 2009 IN GOD WE TRUST was moved from the edge to the obverse after some public criticism of the "Godless dollars."

In December 2011, Secretary of the Treasury Timothy Geithner directed that the U.S. Mint suspend minting and issuing Presidential dollars for circulation. "Regular circulating demand for the coins will be met through the Federal Reserve Bank's existing inventory of circulating coins minted prior to 2012," the Mint announced. Collector formats, however, continued to be issued.

In addition to the regular Uncirculated or Mint State coins produced in large quantities, smaller numbers of Satin Finish dollars were made of the 2007 to 2010 years, at the Philadelphia and Denver mints. These coins were sold at an additional premium, and today most of them exist in grades of MS-67 and upward and are designated SP (Specimen) or SMS (Special Mint Set) by the commercial grading services.

Catching collectors, dealers, and others by surprise, the Coin and Chronicles sets of Presidential dollars were introduced in 2015. A small number of additional (to the regular Uncirculated) coins were made with Reverse Proof finish and sold at a sharp premium as part of Coin and Chronicles sets, which also included a brochure and other collectibles including medals. Most collectors desired only the dollar. The Eisenhower and Truman sets, the first offered, sold out quickly, leaving many Mint clients disappointed. Letters of protest filled the columns of *Coin World* and *Numismatic News* when the only option to secure them seemed to be paying double or triple the issue price on eBay and other venues. The coins themselves were carefully produced, and nearly all grade MS–68 to 70.

In 2020 the original program was expanded by Congress to include George H.W. Bush, who died in 2018. Legislation currently pending in Congress (as of mid-2021) would grant the Treasury Department authority to mint additional coins, without requiring individual new acts of Congress, as presidents pass away.

HISTORY OF THE PRESIDENTIAL DOLLARS

Coin World editor Beth Deisher in the issue of May 17, 2004, wrote this (excerpted):

> Mistakes made in creating the small-sized circulating dollar coin a quarter century ago still haunt us today. And they will continue to impede the circulation of any dollar coin regardless of design or color unless and until someone in government figures out a way to remove all Susan B. Anthony dollar coins from circulation. . . .
>
> That's the dilemma two expert witnesses pointed out during a congressional hearing April 28. The hearing was a precursor to launching legislatively yet another plan to create yet another new small-sized dollar coin (Presidential series) that lawmakers are hoping beyond hope will be embraced and used by the public.

Coin programs then, earlier, and today are passed by Congress. Input from the Treasury Department and the Federal Reserve System is invited, officials from such organizations attend hearings (but their experience and wisdom are often discarded), the public is occasionally able to weigh in, and the Citizens Coinage Advisory Committee offers advice. But ultimately Congress does what it will. The result in the late twentieth and early twenty-first centuries is that there have been many commemorative coins that have fallen below expectations, Kennedy half dollars piling up in Treasury storage, and, of course, hundreds of millions of unused small-diameter dollars.

On December 13, 2005, the House of Representatives passed one of the mostly widely sweeping pieces of coinage legislation in history. For the bicentennial of Abraham Lincoln's birth in 2009 the Mint was to create four special reverse designs for the cent, new $10 denomination .9999 fine gold bullion coins for the First Spouse series were authorized, a .9999 fine $50 one-ounce gold bullion coin with James Earle Fraser's buffalo (bison) design used on the 1913 nickel was authorized, and, among other things, the new Presidential series of manganese-brass dollars was legislated. These were to be issued at the rate of four per year and feature the chief executives in chronological order from George Washington onward until the last deceased president had been honored in 2016.

It was hoped the Presidential dollar would reverse the bad luck of its Susan B. Anthony and Sacagawea dollar predecessors. The primary advocate of the new Presidential dollar was Michael Castle (R–Delaware), who for many years had taken a deep interest in coinage. It was his thought that if Sacagawea dollars were not popular with the public, ones featuring American presidents would be. He pointed to the fantastic success of the State quarter dollars launched in 1999 and minted at the rate of four per year since then. These had been widely accepted, and hundreds of millions of each issue reached circulation and stayed there. Banks stocked them in response to customer demand. Castle envisioned that bank customers would request them in quantity, and to promote goodwill various banks would gladly have them available.

In 2000 Mint Director Jay Johnson had stated that there were 140 million coin collectors in the United States. He was not referring to numismatists (researchers, curators, and the like, and active hobbyists who, for example, belonged to the American Numismatic Association or other groups, attended coin shows, and subscribed to hobby publications). Rather, he meant the number of people he estimated were saving as souvenirs one or more of the State quarters. In congressional discussions in 2005 this was brought up in a different context: there would be 140 million people who would desire one each of the Presidential dollars. Somehow, this would engender an enthusiasm for the long-neglected Sacagawea dollars.

Another proposal was that Sacagawea dollars should be minted in a quantity equal to 30 percent of the expected hundreds of millions of Presidential dollars each year. In 2004 just 2,600,000 Sacagawea dollars had been minted in circulation-strike format each at the two mints making these—Philadelphia and Denver. These went to numismatists. It was in 2002 that Sacagawea dollars were last coined in quantity for intended general circulation.

THE PRESIDENTIAL DOLLAR DESIGNS

Plans moved forward to create the Presidential dollars under the Presidential Coin Act of 2005, Public Law 109-145. Mint engravers were instructed to create a portrait of each president, using images from the bronze presidential medals that the Mint had been offering for sale for many years as inspiration, but to add their own interpretations. As a nod to Representative Michael Castle, the standard reverse was to feature the Statue of Liberty, a motif that in 1999 he strongly recommended for what became the Sacagawea dollar.

In January 2005 six variations in obverse inscriptions and ornamentation were made and were in time shown to the U.S. Commission of Fine Arts and, separately, the Citizens Coinage Advisory Committee for their review. They varied in typeface, ornamentations, and positioning of various standard design elements (the president's numerical rank, year of inauguration, etc.). A template was developed for the lettering and inscriptions, to give the coins a uniform canvas with different portraits in the center.

APPLYING THE EDGE LETTERING, AND IN GOD WE TRUST

The Mint revealed that for circulation strikes the edge lettering was applied after the coins were struck. Paul Gilkes of *Coin World* describes the process:

> For circulating and Uncirculated Mint set coins, after coins are struck on coinage presses, the struck coins are transported from the coin presses to the edge lettering equipment. The coins are fed in the lettering equipment horizontally at the rate of up to 1,000 coins per minute.
>
> The coins pass through an edge-lettering segment or die bearing the raised lettering that is imparted incuse on the finished coin. A vertical wheel spinning counterclockwise grips the struck coin's plain edge on one side while the point of contact on the opposite side of the edge of the coin is directed through the edge segment bearing the raised inscriptions. The groove in the edge lettering segment resembles the bottom half of a compressed circle.
>
> The orientation of the edge lettering to the obverse or reverse is random, as is the position in the edge where the lettering begins and ends.

For Proofs the edge lettering was applied with a three-part segmented collar during the striking process. As a result, all Proof coin lettering is upright in relation to the obverse.

Some Presidential dollars, especially those of 2007, were accidentally made without edge lettering, giving them a plain edge. Plain-edge issues are highly collectible, but market values remain erratic. These were called "godless" dollars by some, and the Mint received complaints. On March 7, 2007, "A Statement from the United States Mint" included this:

Plasters of the Presidential dollars for James Garfield and Gerald Ford, in the studio of Phebe Hemphill at the Philadelphia Mint.

A close-up of a plaster of the reverse design used on all Presidential dollars, showing the initials of Mint sculptor-engraver Don Everhart.

The United States Mint has struck more than 300 million George Washington Presidential $1 coins. We have recently learned that an unspecified quantity of these coins inadvertently left the United States Mint at Philadelphia without edge lettering on them. . . .

The United States Mint understands the importance of the inscriptions "In God We Trust" and "E Pluribus Unum" as well as the mintmark and year on U.S. coinage. We take this matter seriously. We also consider quality control a high priority. The agency is looking into the matter to determine a possible cause in the manufacturing process.

Production of the Presidential $1 coin, with its unique edge lettering, is a new, complex, high volume manufacturing system, and the United States Mint is determined to make technical adjustments to perfect the process. . . .

Beginning in 2009 the motto IN GOD WE TRUST was moved near the lower rim on the obverse of each coin.

OVERVIEW OF EDGES ON PRESIDENTIAL DOLLARS

Dollars minted in 2007 have the edge lettered with the date, mintmark, and mottoes as:

2007 D E PLURIBUS UNUM • IN GOD WE TRUST •

Dollars of 2008 have a period after the mintmark, as:

2008 D • E PLURIBUS UNUM • IN GOD WE TRUST •

Dollars were made with the lettering oriented upright with regard to the obverse (known variously as Type B, Type 2, or Position A) or inverted (Type A, Type 1, or Position A). There is no differentiation in numismatic market value, but this has caused some collectors to seek two examples of each Presidential dollar to show each edge orientation.

Some Presidential dollars were inadvertently struck with the edge lettering missing. A 2009-D, John Tyler, variety has the wrong date, 2010, on the edge.

RELATED GOLD BULLION COINS AND BRONZE MEDALS

In *American Gold and Silver: U.S. Mint Collector and Investor Coins and Medals, Bicentennial to Date*, Dennis Tucker describes the nation's gold bullion programs at the start of the Presidential dollar series:

By 2007 the United States was more than 20 years into its successful modern gold-bullion program. Collectors and investors were buying hundreds of thousands of ounces of American Gold Eagles annually. The American Buffalo 24-karat coins had been introduced the year before and were off to a galloping start. Next in the lineup was a gold-coinage series designed as a companion to the Mint's soon-to-roll-out Presidential dollars. The new bullion program's 24-karat coins would honor and commemorate the nation's First Ladies.

The Presidential $1 Coin Act of 2005, which authorized the Presidential dollars, also authorized the Mint's First Spouse gold bullion coins. "First Spouses have not generally been recognized on American coinage," the legislation observed. It ordered that, starting in 2007 to coincide with the debut of the Presidential dollar coins, "the Secretary shall issue bullion coins . . . that are emblematic of the spouse of [each] President." The coins would be the same diameter as the Presidential dollars (26.5 mm); they would weigh 1/2 ounce each; and they would contain 99.99 percent pure gold.

Tucker noted:

The legislation's focus on *First Spouses* rather than *First Ladies* avoided any confusion over cases where a president was widowed or unmarried and the usual ceremonial functions of First Lady were carried out by a daughter or other relative; or if he was married but someone other than his wife performed some or all of the duties typically assigned to the First Lady (as was the case when various presidential wives were too sick or frail).

In cases where a president served without a spouse, the act ordered that "the image on the obverse of the bullion coin corresponding to the $1 coin relating to such President shall be an image emblematic of the concept of 'Liberty'" [as represented on a coin issued during the president's tenure].

The Mint has also issued a series of bronze medals with designs based on those of the First Spouse gold bullion coins. Design-wise, because these are not legal-tender coins, they lack a denomination and certain legislated inscriptions. Otherwise they follow the motifs of the related gold coins.

MINT PUBLICITY

Although the Mint had little to do with the Presidential dollar legislation, it and the Treasury Department of which it was a part were charged with the task of making the new dollars a success. A news release of January 20, 2005, included this:

> The United States Mint has produced presidential medals from the earliest days of the republic. Most of these medals were designed during the terms of the presidents with input from the administration and sometimes family of the president. The design process approvals originally came from the secretary of war.
>
> We'd like to think that this is how the presidents, themselves, would like to be portrayed. In most cases, these designs are classic when viewed today. But they are contemporary to the president's own lifetime and offer a historic window through which the public can view the time line of our nation. These are classic, beautiful designs, often from periods when sculpture and medallic design were regularly employed for the production of official United States Mint coins and medals.
>
> From the terms of Thomas Jefferson through Benjamin Harrison, a period of nearly 100 years, the presidential medals were used by the United States government in conjunction with official treaty negotiations.

CRITICISMS OF THE DESIGN PROCESS

Q. David Bowers recalls discussing the Mint's design approach with other numismatists: "It was not pleasing to any with whom I discussed the matter at the time. Few people ordered bronze Mint medals." In *Coin World*, February 6, 2006, editor Beth Deisher spoke for many of her readers, saying "Apparently there's not an ounce of creativity left" and "Mint officials are retreating to the Treasury bureaucracy mindset so pervasive 20 years ago. At that time Treasury officials opposed any suggestion of changing designs on our circulating coins, stating that the presidential portraits in use had been 'time honored.'"

Deisher quoted Representative Castle, who earlier had said:

> In order to revitalize the design of United States coinage and return circulating coinage to its position as not only a necessary means of exchange in commerce, but also as an object of aesthetic beauty in its own right, it is appropriate to move many of the mottos and emblems, the inscription of the year, and the so-called "mint marks" that currently appear on the 2 faces of each circulating coin to the edge of the coin, which would allow larger and more dramatic artwork on the coins reminiscent of the so-called "Golden Age of Coinage" in the United States, at the beginning of the twentieth century, initiated by President Theodore Roosevelt, with the assistance of noted sculptors and medallic artists James Earle Fraser and Augustus Saint-Gaudens. . . .

She then stated that the Mint and its artists were up to the task of injecting new life into American coinage, and didn't need to dust off old designs:

An advertisement from the U.S. Mint emotionally connects
the Presidential dollars to the popular State quarter program.

The repository of presidential likenesses is plentiful, and today's sculptor-engravers and artists are fully capable of rendering new and exciting designs for our coins, if U.S. Mint officials would only give them a chance. The Presidential dollar series is too important to simply rush through, just to be going through the motions. The justifications for using the Presidential medal portraits Mint officials espouse are merely excuses. Secretary of the Treasury John Snow should send the Mint back to the drawing boards and ask for great, memorable artistic treatment of our nation's leaders. Settling for anything less would reduce the eminence of our new dollar coins.

Q. David Bowers opined that "The only unfortunate part of Representative Castle's proposal was accepted: moving the date and mintmark to the edge. As to the IN GOD WE TRUST and E PLURI-BUS UNUM, few collectors cared. The latter had been lettered on edges before, such as on the Saint-Gaudens double eagles beginning in 1907. IN GOD WE TRUST had been on most coins, but not all (for example it was not on the Barber dime of 1892 to 1916, nor the Buffalo nickel of 1913 to 1938). Putting the date and mintmark where it could not be seen if coins were in holders was heresy." This "heresy" would continue with the future programs of Native American and American Innovation dollar coins.

MINT DIRECTOR EDMUND C. MOY

On September 5, 2006, Edmund C. Moy took the oath of office to become the 38th director of the U.S. Mint, succeeding Henrietta Holsman Fore. He inherited the responsibility of launching the Presidential dollars. In an October 3 interview with Paul Gilkes of *Coin World* he included these remarks:

**Mint Director Ed Moy and "George Washington"
launch the first Presidential dollar.**

"We're looking at strategies over the long term, but there are things we have to do really, really well right now, and one of them is implementation of the Presidential $1 Coin Act. I realize that regardless of what people think of the Mint, what its past history and accomplishments are, people are going to judge the Mint on the basis of how well this rollout is going to be. We've put a lot of attention into its being done right."

Moy says the enabling legislation for the Presidential dollar coin program requires the Mint to not only educate the public about the coins, but also to stage forums to receive input from the vending machine industry, the U.S. Postal Service, banks and other end-users to ensure the failure of the past are not repeated.

"It's a well-written bill that gives us a lot of tools that we didn't have before, so it gives me optimism that we are going to have a more successful rollout with this than we did in the past. We'll also have more long-term interest in this program. Our idea is that Americans will be interested in this program just as they are with the 50 State Quarters Program. Because it's a series instead of a 'one-off' like the Sacagawea dollar, hopefully that interest can be maintained over a longer period of time."

Karen Springen in *Newsweek*, November 27, 2006, remarked on the government's $5 billion seigniorage "profit" (the difference between face value and production cost) from the State quarters program, and reported on Director Moy's enthusiasm for those coins and the millions of Americans who collected them. She quoted the pessimism of *Coin Dealer Newsletter* publisher Shane Downing ("It's going to be like the Sacagawea dollar—nobody uses it in everyday commerce") and the optimism of Citizens Coinage Advisory Committee chairman Mitch Sanders, who predicted many fans, including "the tooth fairy."

DISTRIBUTION OF PRESIDENTIAL DOLLARS

The first coin in the series depicted George Washington and was launched on February 16, 2007. Quantities of Washington and other dollars were available to collectors before their general release to the public. The Mint put rolls and bags of the coins on sale on January 29.

On February 15 Mint Director Moy put the first coin "officially" into circulation. Dressed as George Washington, he dropped one in a parking meter. On this day more than 68,000 of the coins were distributed to the public.

Release date for the John Adams dollar was May 18; for Thomas Jefferson, August 17; and for James Madison, November 16.

The Mint announced that banks could order supplies from the Federal Reserve System two weeks prior to each launch and could continue requesting them for four months afterward. A huge demand was predicted, and to be sure that all citizens could have an adequate supply, more than 100,000,000 coins were made at each of the three mints. Proof set for collectors, containing the year's four coin designs and with 2007 and S on their edges, were made available at Mint stores and through the mail beginning on June 21, 2007.

Editor David C. Harper of *Numismatic News* did not envision much excitement. In the issue of February 13, 2007, he wrote, "The hope is that collectors and souvenir hunters will ask for them and collect the whole set. They will indeed ask for them, but that act will not make the coin a successful circulating coin . . . The first few of these will have higher mintages than the issues that come afterward, but the new coins will not circulate." Harper's prediction proved prescient. Although well over 800 million circulation strikes of Presidential dollars were made in 2007, few circulated. Most remained stored in Treasury vaults. Mintages were lowered in 2008.

A Gradual Tarnishing

In June 2008 the Treasury Department announced the $1 Coin Direct Ship Program, whereby the Mint would ship up to $500 face value in rolls to financial and commercial entities as well as to individuals and would pay the postage. This was done in another effort to get the coins into circulation.

In 2009 mintages declined further, but still hundreds of millions of circulation-strike Presidential dollars were made—only to go into storage. A severe national recession was underway. Many banks and financial institutions were experiencing losses, and some failed. Banks tried to reduce expenses. For many, no longer were supplies of new dollar coins offered and paid out. Promotional signs and placards were taken down.

In 2010 the Federal Reserve changed its ordering policies for Presidential dollars. Financial institutions could place their requests three weeks before the public launch date, instead of two as previously. The post-release ordering time was shortened from four weeks to two. The minimum quantity was 1,000 coins, with additional increments to be in the same quantity. These were put up in boxes of 40 25-coin rolls.

In circulation, many "golden dollars" became discolored, a problem dating back to the early days of testing the Sacagawea dollars before their release in 2000. In 2008 an independent scientific laboratory analyzed a tarnished 2008-P and found that manganese, one of four metals in the alloy, was the culprit as under certain conditions it could oxidize rapidly. In 2009 the Mint revealed that for three years it had been using CarboShield BT, made by Lonza Inc., Allendale, New Jersey, a division of a Swiss firm. This product, originally developed as a wood preserver, was used to ameliorate the tarnish problem. "The CarboShield BT agent is applied during the burnishing process before the planchets are transferred to the coinage presses for striking into coins."

Slowing Down the Presses—And Weighing the Costs

In 2011 the Federal Reserve Banks and storage facilities held 1.4 *billion* Presidential dollars—enough, the Mint projected, to meet demand for a decade. Acknowledging this, on December 13, 2011, Secretary of the Treasury Timothy F. Geithner issued a directive suspending the production of all Presidential dollars intended for general circulation. Thenceforth, mintage was to be limited to expected numismatic demand. Geithner estimated that this would save $50 to $75 million annually in production costs (or, as economic reporter Jeffrey Sparshott remarked in a December 14 *Wall Street Journal* article, "about 15 minutes' worth of the federal deficit").

On the other side of the fence was a group who thought the hundreds of millions of dollars in profit made in seigniorage of unwanted dollars was a good idea. The Dollar Coin Alliance, a coalition of small businesses, budget watchdogs, transit agencies, and labor groups, stated that the suspension of production of Presidential dollar coins for circulation would cost taxpayers billions over time. The alliance cited the U.S. Mint's 2010 Annual Report, which stated the dollar coin program made a net profit of $283 million.

The alliance also asserted that the best way to achieve real savings would be to replace the Federal Reserve Note paper dollar with dollar coins, which the Government Accountability Office reported in March 2011 would save the government an average of $184 million per year and approximately $5.5 billion over 30 years.

Year after year different government offices and different surveys came up with widely differing "facts" on metal dollars versus paper dollars. In early 2012, for the fifth time in 22 years, the GAO offered an opinion on whether the dollar bill should replace the dollar coin. Contrary to previous recommendations, this time the GAO stated that the government would lose money in the first six years if it began to replace the dollar bill with dollar coins. While there still was anticipated savings over a 30-year time span, over 10 years the change would be unprofitable. One factor in the new scenario is that the GAO used an average life span for the bills of 56 months (per the Federal Reserve) as opposed to the Bureau of Engraving and Printing's previous estimate (quoted over the past 40 years) of about an 18-month life span.

LAUNCH CEREMONIES SUSPENDED

In early 2012 the Mint announced that as part of a program of cost savings it would no longer sponsor launch or related ceremonies for Presidential golden dollars.

Coin World editor Beth Deisher called the decision "a penny-wise, dollar-foolish reaction to the manic political atmosphere prevalent in Washington." She noted a Mint official's report that the average cost of earlier Presidential dollar coin-launch events had been about $10,000: "The direct costs have included travel expenses for two to three Mint staff members coordinating and speaking at the event, background materials for the media, and a free coin given to each child under the age of 18 attending the event." Deisher noted the audiences, of all ages, attracted to the events, the publicity they brought to presidential homes and other historic sites and their communities, and the headlines that resulted, which regular press releases couldn't bring. "Were the Mint a private enterprise," Deisher wrote, "the $40,000 spent yearly on the launch events would be looked upon as marketing and advertising expenses, a rather modest sum for introducing and creating interest in four new products."

The Mint's suspension made the previous year's James Garfield launch ceremony, November 17, 2011, the last of its kind. That event was held in Mentor, Ohio, at the James A. Garfield National Historic Site, the president's family home, two days before the 180th anniversary of his birth. "The Presidential dollar coin series connects Americans to inspiring life stories like President Garfield's," said Marc Landry, the Mint's acting associate director for Manufacturing. "He was the last President born in a log cabin, fatherless by the age of two, drove canal boat teams to earn money for college, became a classics professor and college president, rose to brigadier general in the Civil War, and enjoyed a long, distinguished career in the U.S. Congress." Other speakers at the launch included Rudolph Garfield (a great-grandson), and Dr. Allan Peskin, Garfield biographer and professor emeritus of history at Cleveland State University.

In April 2012 the Chester A. Arthur dollar was launched, the first in the Presidential series to have a sharply reduced mintage aimed primarily at collectors. As expected, there was no launch ceremony.

Director Moy hands new Thomas Jefferson dollars to young collectors at the coin's launch at the Jefferson Memorial, Washington, D.C., August 15, 2007.

THE COIN AND CHRONICLES PROGRAM

In 2015 the Mint introduced the Coin and Chronicles program pairing a *Reverse Proof* Philadelphia Mint Presidential dollar with a silver medal and other collectibles for $57.95. The sets were issued for Truman, Eisenhower, Kennedy, and Johnson. The autumn 2015 Mint gift catalog included this description for the Johnson issue:

> The 2015 Coin and Chronicles Set—Lyndon B. Johnson features a Presidential $1 Reverse Proof coin (found only in this set!) and a Johnson Presidential silver medal. Also included is a U.S. postage stamp issued in 1973 to pay tribute to President Johnson. The set is perfect for the coin collector, history buff or as a special gift!
>
> The coin, medal and stamp are displayed in a grey folder covered in a soft–touch material with a handsome textured look that is very gift-worthy.
>
> The set includes:
>
> One Reverse Proof Finish 2015 Lyndon B. Johnson Presidential $1 coin
> One Lyndon B. Johnson Presidential Medal struck in .999 fine silver
> One Lyndon B. Johnson U.S. postage stamp issued in 1973
> One booklet including images from Johnson's life, military career and presidency

To the dismay of many potential buyers, the Coin and Chronicles sets were offered in limited numbers, with the result that the first two—the Truman and Eisenhower issues—sold out quickly, within hours. Many if not most went to speculators rather than to longtime collectors loyal to the Mint. On eBay and elsewhere these were soon offered at figures that were multiples of the issue price. Complaints poured into the Mint as well as to *Coin World*, *Numismatic News*, and other numismatic media—collectors were not happy. Later issues were made in slightly larger numbers and were sold with less controversy.

EXTENSION OF THE PRESIDENTIAL DOLLARS

Originally the Presidential dollar program was expected to run from George Washington in 2007 to Ronald Reagan in 2016. At the start of the program, former presidents Jimmy Carter, George H.W. Bush, and Bill Clinton were still alive; George W. Bush was in the White House; and Barack Obama, Donald Trump, and Joe Biden were yet to be elected.

Bush Sr. passed away at the age of 94 on November 30, 2018, two years after the Presidential dollar program officially ended under its original legislation. In order to accommodate President Bush within the coinage program, Congress passed Public Law 116-112, the "President George H.W. Bush and First Spouse Barbara Bush Coin Act." This directed that President Bush be added to the Presidential dollar program, and First Lady Barbara Bush be added to the First Spouse gold bullion coin program, and to the Mint's accompanying bronze First Spouse medals.

President Trump signed the act into law in January 2020. On March 10, 2020, the Citizens Coinage Advisory Committee met to review and discuss 23 candidate designs for the Barbara Bush coins and medals. The following month the CCAC met to review 11 design candidates for the George H.W. Bush Presidential dollar. The Committee's recommendations were sent to the secretary of the Treasury, and soon the coins and medals were in production.

In early 2021, there is legislation being developed that would give the Treasury Department discretion to add presidents and their spouses to the coin and medal programs. If passed, this would negate the need for individual special bills every time a president passes away.

PRESIDENTIAL DOLLARS (2007–2020): GUIDE TO COLLECTING

BEING A SMART BUYER

Presidential dollars usually are well struck, but check the higher-relief parts of each side. Special numismatic issues are uniformly sharp. "First Strike" and other notations on holders add little or nothing to the resale value of these and other modern coins.

AVAILABILITY

Presidential dollars are very common in Mint State. Most have from a few to many bagmarks, with true MS-65 and better coins in the minority.

NOTABLE DIE VARIETIES AND ERRORS

Washington, 2007, plain-edge error: This variety is also called "missing edge lettering." Many of these coins were inadvertently issued without edge lettering and thus lack the date and mintmark. The 2007 Washington issues, not identifiable to a particular mint, are readily found in the marketplace today. Tens of thousands have been certified—more than all other plain-edge Presidential dollars combined. It is thought that 200,000 or more were minted. These are ranked among the *100 Greatest U.S. Modern Coins*.

George Washington, 2007-S, out-of-sequence edge lettering error: Normally the motto IN GOD WE TRUST is followed by the date and mintmark, but on some Proofs the lettering was out of normal sequence and the date and mintmark are found after E PLURIBUS UNUM.

John Adams, 2007, plain-edge error: Perhaps 10,000 or so were inadvertently issued without edge lettering and thus lack the date and mintmark. The 2007 Adams issues are not identifiable to a particular mint.

John Adams, 2007-P, doubled-edge lettering error: After they were struck these coins were run through the edge-lettering machine twice, giving IN GOD WE TRUST, E PLURIBUS UNUM, and 2007-P two impressions, off-register. It is thought that as many as 50,000 were made. These are ranked in the *100 Greatest U.S. Modern Coins.* (Also see 2007-D.)

John Adams, 2007-D, doubled-edge lettering error: After they were struck these coins were run through the edge-lettering machine twice, double impressions of the inscriptions, as was done for 2007-P. The mintage of these errors is estimated at fewer than 1,000 pieces. Some inscriptions are overlapped, while on others one inscription is inverted.

Thomas Jefferson, 2007, plain-edge error: Several thousand coins were inadvertently issued without edge lettering and thus lack the date and mintmark. The 2007 Jefferson issues are not identifiable to a particular mint.

Jefferson, 2007-S, out-of-sequence edge lettering error: Some 2007-S Proofs have the edge lettering out of sequence. Error coins have IN GOD WE TRUST followed immediately by E PLURIBUS UNUM. As many as 100,000 may have been produced thus.

James Madison, 2007, plain-edge error: More than 1,000 coins were inadvertently issued without edge lettering and thus lack the date and mintmark. The 2007 Madison issues are not identifiable to a particular mint.

James Monroe, 2008, plain-edge error: Hundreds of these coins were inadvertently issued without edge lettering and thus lack the date and mintmark. Not identifiable as to mint. They are rare today.

John Quincy Adams, 2008, plain-edge error: More than 1,000 of these coins were inadvertently issued without edge lettering and thus lack the date and mintmark. The 2008 Adams issues, not identifiable as to mint, are scarce today.

Andrew Jackson, 2008, plain-edge error: Hundreds of these coins were inadvertently issued without edge lettering and thus lack the date and mintmark. The 2008 Jackson issues, not identifiable as to mint, are scarce today.

Martin Van Buren, 2008, plain-edge error: Several thousands of these coins were inadvertently issued without edge lettering and thus lack the date and mintmark. The 2008 Van Buren issues are not identifiable to a particular mint.

William Henry Harrison, 2009, plain-edge error: Several thousands of these coins were inadvertently issued without edge lettering and thus lack the date and mintmark. These are not identifiable as to mint.

John Tyler, 2009, plain-edge error: More than a thousand Tyler dollars were inadvertently issued without edge lettering and thus lack the date and mintmark. These are not identifiable to a particular mint.

John Tyler, 2009-D, with 2010 edge date error: This error coin is exceedingly rare.

James K. Polk, 2009, plain-edge error: More than 1,000 Polk coins were inadvertently issued without edge lettering and thus lack the date and mintmark. These are not identifiable to a particular mint.

Zachary Taylor, 2009, plain-edge error: Several thousand Zachary Taylor coins were inadvertently issued without edge lettering and thus lack the date and mintmark. These are not identifiable to a particular mint.

Zachary Taylor, 2009-D, with 2010 edge date error: In early 2010 a Zachary Taylor dollar was found by Gary D. Laird in a roll of 2010-D Native American dollars, with the 2010 date on the edge. It was certified by NGC. The Mint announced that 700,000 coins already shipped to the Federal Reserve would be recalled so the edges could be checked. A "hold" was placed on coins in the position of Coin Wrap, Inc., the Pennsylvania contractor who made shipments to various buyers.

Millard Fillmore, 2010, plain-edge error: Several thousand Fillmore coins were inadvertently issued without edge lettering and thus lack the date and mintmark. These are not identifiable to a particular mint.

Franklin Pierce, 2010, plain-edge error: More than a thousand Franklin Pierce coins were inadvertently issued without edge lettering and thus lack the date and mintmark. These are not identifiable to a particular mint.

James Buchanan, 2010, plain-edge error: Several thousand James Buchanan dollars were inadvertently issued without edge lettering and thus lack the date and mintmark. These are not identifiable to a particular mint.

Chester Alan Arthur, 2012, plain-edge error: A few coins were inadvertently issued without edge lettering and thus lack the date and mintmark. These are not identifiable to a particular mint and are great rarities today.

Grover Cleveland (first term), 2012, plain-edge error: Dozens of these coins were inadvertently issued without edge lettering and thus lack the date and mintmark. These are not identifiable to a particular mint and are rare today.

Grover Cleveland (second term), 2012, plain-edge error: A few coins were inadvertently issued without edge lettering and thus lack the date and mintmark. These are not identifiable to a particular mint and are great rarities today.

Calvin Coolidge, 2014, plain-edge error: A few Coolidge coins were inadvertently issued without edge lettering and thus lack the date and mintmark. These are not identifiable to a particular mint and are great rarities today.

Dwight D. Eisenhower, 2015, plain-edge error: A small number of Eisenhower Presidential dollars was made without edge lettering. These are not identifiable to a particular mint.

PRESIDENTIAL (2007–2020)

GRADING STANDARDS

MS-60 to 70 (Mint State). *Obverse:* At MS-60, some abrasion and contact marks are evident, most noticeably on the highest-relief areas of the portrait, the exact location varying with the president depicted. Luster is present, but may be dull or lifeless. At MS-63, contact marks are extensive but not distracting. Abrasion still is evident, but less than at lower levels.

2007-P, Washington. Graded MS-68.

MS-64 coins are slightly finer. An MS-65 coin may have minor abrasion, but contact marks are so minute as to require magnification. Luster should be full and rich. *Reverse:* At MS-60, some abrasion and contact marks are evident, most noticeably on the cheek and arm. Otherwise, the same comments apply as for the obverse.

AU-50, 53, 55, 58 (About Uncirculated). *Obverse:* Light wear is seen on the portrait, most prominently on the higher-relief areas. At AU-58, the luster is extensive, but incomplete. At AU-50 and 53, luster is less, but still is present. *Reverse:* Further wear is evident on statue. Otherwise, the same comments apply as for the obverse.

2007-P, Madison. Graded AU-53.

Presidential dollars are seldom collected in grades lower than AU-50.

PF-60 to 70 (Proof). *Obverse and Reverse:* Proofs that are extensively cleaned and have many hairlines, or that are dull and grainy, are lower level, such as PF-60 to 62. This comment is more theoretical than practical, as nearly all Proofs have been well kept. With medium hairlines and good reflectivity, assigned grades of PF-63 or 64 are appropriate. With relatively few hairlines a rating of PF-65 can be given. PF-66 may have hair-

2007-S, Madison. Graded PF-65.

lines so delicate that magnification is needed to see them. Above that, all the way to PF-70, a Proof should be free of any hairlines or other problems under strong magnification.

A GALLERY OF PRESIDENTIAL DOLLARS (2007–2020)

The following pages show an example of a circulation strike coin and a Proof strike coin for all the Presidential dollars, as the only difference between Philadelphia and Denver strikes appears on the rim.

Circulation Strike.   Proof Strike.   Circulation Strike.   Proof Strike.
2007, George Washington.   2007, John Adams.
(Obverse designer: Joseph Menna)   *(Obverse designer: Joel Iskowitz)*

Circulation Strike.   Proof Strike.   Circulation Strike.   Proof Strike.
2007, Thomas Jefferson.   2007, James Madison.
(Obverse designer: Joseph Menna)   *(Obverse designer: Joel Iskowitz)*

Circulation Strike.   Proof Strike.   Circulation Strike.   Proof Strike.
2008, James Monroe.   2008, John Quincy Adams.
(Obverse designer: Joseph Menna)   *(Obverse designer: Don Everhart)*

Circulation Strike.   Proof Strike.   Circulation Strike.   Proof Strike.
2008, Andrew Jackson.   2008, Martin Van Buren.
(Obverse designer: Joel Iskowitz)   *(Obverse designer: Joel Iskowitz)*

Circulation Strike.	Proof Strike.	Circulation Strike.	Proof Strike.

2009, William Henry Harrison.
(Obverse designer: Joseph Menna)

2009, John Tyler.
(Obverse designer: Phebe Hemphill)

Circulation Strike.	Proof Strike.	Circulation Strike.	Proof Strike.

2009, James K. Polk.
(Obverse designer: Susan Gamble)

2009, Zachary Taylor.
(Obverse designer: Don Everhart)

Circulation Strike.	Proof Strike.	Circulation Strike.	Proof Strike.

2010, Millard Fillmore.
(Obverse designer: Don Everhart)

2010, Franklin Pierce.
(Obverse designer: Susan Gamble)

  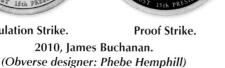  

Circulation Strike.	Proof Strike.	Circulation Strike.	Proof Strike.

2010, James Buchanan.
(Obverse designer: Phebe Hemphill)

2010, Abraham Lincoln.
(Obverse designer: Don Everhart)

Circulation Strike.   Proof Strike.   Circulation Strike.   Proof Strike.

2011, Andrew Johnson.   2011, Ulysses S. Grant.

(Obverse designer: Don Everhart)   *(Obverse designer: Don Everhart)*

Circulation Strike.   Proof Strike.   Circulation Strike.   Proof Strike.

2011, Rutheford B. Hayes.   2011, James Garfield.

(Obverse designer: Don Everhart)   *(Obverse designer: Phebe Hemphill)*

Circulation Strike.   Proof Strike.   Circulation Strike.   Proof Strike.

2012, Chester Arthur.   2012, Grover Cleveland, First Term.

(Obverse designer: Don Everhart)   *(Obverse designer: Don Everhart)*

Circulation Strike.   Proof Strike.   Circulation Strike.   Proof Strike.

2012, Benjamin Harrison.   2012, Grover Cleveland, Second Term.

(Obverse designer: Phebe Hemphill)   *(Obverse designer: Don Everhart)*

Circulation Strike.   Proof Strike.
2013, William McKinley.
(Obverse designer: Phebe Hemphill)

Circulation Strike.   Proof Strike.
2013, Theodore Roosevelt.
(Obverse designer: Joseph Menna)

Circulation Strike.   Proof Strike.
2013, William Howard Taft.
(Obverse designer: Barbara Fox)

Circulation Strike.   Proof Strike.
2013, Woodrow Wilson.
(Obverse designer: Don Everhart)

Circulation Strike.   Proof Strike.
2014, Warren G. Harding.
(Obverse designer: Michael Gaudioso)

Circulation Strike.   Proof Strike.
2014, Calvin Coolidge.
(Obverse designer: Phebe Hemphill)

Circulation Strike.   Proof Strike.
2014, Herbert Hoover.
(Obverse designer: Phebe Hemphill)

Circulation Strike.   Proof Strike.
2014, Franklin D. Roosevelt.
(Obverse designer: Joseph Menna)

Circulation Strike.   Proof Strike.   Circulation Strike.   Proof Strike.
2015, Harry S. Truman.   2015, Dwight D. Eisenhower.
(Obverse designer: Don Everhart)   *(Obverse designer: Joseph Menna)*

Circulation Strike.   Proof Strike.   Circulation Strike.   Proof Strike.
2015, John F. Kennedy.   2015, Lyndon B. Johnson.
(Obverse designer: Don Everhart)   *(Obverse designer: Michael Gaudioso)*

Circulation Strike.   Proof Strike.   Circulation Strike.   Proof Strike.
2016, Richard M. Nixon.   2016, Gerald R. Ford.
(Obverse designer: Don Everhart)   *(Obverse designer: Phebe Hemphill)*

Circulation Strike.   Proof Strike.   Circulation Strike.   Proof Strike.
2016, Ronald Reagan.   2020, George H.W. Bush.
(Obverse designer: Richard Masters)   *(Obverse designer: Elana Hagler)*

	Mintage	Cert	Avg	%MS	MS-64	MS-65 / PF-65	MS-66 / PF-69DC
2007-P, Washington	176,680,000	18,378	65.1	100%	$2	$3.50	$7
2007-P, Washington, Satin Finish (a)	895,628	769	66.3	100%		$5	$12
2007-P, Washington, Plain Edge †† (b)	(c)	43,498	64.7	100%	$30	$40	$65
2007-D, Washington	163,680,000	15,500	65.2	100%	$2	$3.50	$7
2007-D, Washington, Satin Finish (a)	895,628	938	66.9	100%		$5	$12
2007-S, Washington, Proof	3,965,989	45,341	69.2		$4	$15	
2007-P, J. Adams	112,420,000	20,730	64.7	100%	$2	$3.50	$7
2007-P, J. Adams, Satin Finish (a)	895,628	830	66.4	100%		$5	$12
2007-D, J. Adams	112,140,000	6,775	65.3	100%	$2	$3.50	$7
2007-D, J. Adams, Satin Finish (a)	895,628	920	67.0	100%		$5	$12
2007-S, J. Adams, Proof	3,965,989	45,098	69.2		$4	$15	
2007-P, Jefferson	100,800,000	5,582	65.4	100%	$2	$3.50	$7
2007-P, Jefferson, Satin Finish (a)	895,628	901	66.5	100%		$5	$12
2007-D, Jefferson	102,810,000	6,592	65.6	100%	$2	$3.50	$7
2007-D, Jefferson, Satin Finish (a)	895,628	926	67.0	100%		$5	$12
2007-S, Jefferson, Proof	3,965,989	45,189	69.2		$4	$15	
2007-P, Madison	84,560,000	3,268	65.5	100%	$2	$3.50	$7
2007-P, Madison, Satin Finish (a)	895,628	873	66.6	100%		$5	$12
2007-D, Madison	87,780,000	3,905	65.8	100%	$2	$3.50	$7
2007-D, Madison, Satin Finish (a)	87,780,000	888	66.9	100%		$5	$12
2007-S, Madison, Proof	3,965,989	45,452	69.2		$4	$15	
2008-P, Monroe	64,260,000	2,423	65.6	100%	$2	$3.50	$8
2008-P, Monroe, Satin Finish (a)	745,464	441	67.0	100%		$5	$12
2008-D, Monroe	60,230,000	2,229	65.7	100%	$2	$3.50	$8
2008-D, Monroe, Satin Finish (a)	745,464	428	67.1	100%		$5	$12
2008-S, Monroe, Proof	3,083,940	24,510	69.2		$4	$15	
2008-P, J.Q. Adams	57,540,000	2,781	65.9	100%	$2	$3.50	$8
2008-P, J.Q. Adams, Satin Finish (a)	745,464	464	67.0	100%		$5	$12
2008-D, J.Q. Adams	57,720,000	2,488	66.0	100%	$2	$3.50	$8
2008-D, J.Q. Adams, Satin Finish (a)	745,464	429	67.2	100%		$5	$12
2008-S, J.Q. Adams, Proof	3,083,940	24,518	69.3		$4	$15	
2008-P, Jackson	61,180,000	3,168	65.7	100%	$2	$3.50	$8
2008-P, Jackson, Satin Finish (a)	745,464	417	67.1	100%		$5	$12
2008-D, Jackson	61,070,000	2,361	65.6	100%	$2	$3.50	$8
2008-D, Jackson, Satin Finish (a)	745,464	427	67.3	100%		$5	$12
2008-S, Jackson, Proof	3,083,940	24,489	69.2		$4	$15	
2008-P, Van Buren	51,520,000	1,611	65.9	100%	$2	$3.50	$8
2008-P, Van Buren, Satin Finish (a)	745,464	431	66.8	100%		$5	$12
2008-D, Van Buren	50,960,000	1,326	65.7	100%	$2	$3.50	$8
2008-D, Van Buren, Satin Finish (a)	745,464	393	67.0	100%		$5	$12
2008-S, Van Buren, Proof	3,083,940	24,551	69.3		$4	$15	
2009-P, W.H. Harrison	43,260,000	1,627	66.0	100%	$2	$3.50	$8
2009-P, W.H. Harrison, Satin Finish (a)	784,614	503	67.3	100%		$5	$12
2009-D, W.H. Harrison	55,160,000	1,619	65.8	100%	$2	$3.50	$8
2009-D, W.H. Harrison, Satin Finish (a)	784,614	464	67.5	100%		$5	$12
2009-S, W.H. Harrison, Proof	2,809,452	18,015	69.2		$4	$15	
2009-P, Tyler	43,540,000	1,373	65.8	100%	$2	$3.50	$8
2009-P, Tyler, Satin Finish (a)	784,614	352	67.1	100%		$5	$12
2009-D, Tyler	43,540,000	1,290	65.6	100%	$2	$3.50	$8
2009-D, Tyler, 2010 Edge	(d)	0	n/a		—	—	—

†† Ranked in the *100 Greatest U.S. Modern Coins* (fourth edition). **a.** Not issued for circulation. **b.** Some circulation-strike Washington dollars are known without the normal edge lettering (date, mintmark, IN GOD WE TRUST, and E PLURIBUS UNUM). **c.** Included in 2007-P, Washington, mintage figure. **d.** Included in 2009-D, Tyler, mintage figure.

	Mintage	Cert	Avg	%MS	MS-64	MS-65 / PF-65	MS-66 / PF-69DC
2009-D, Tyler, Satin Finish (a)	784,614	286	67.0	100%		$5	$12
2009-S, Tyler, Proof	2,809,452	17,983	69.2		$4	$15	
2009-P, Polk	46,620,000	1,451	66.4	100%	$2	$3.50	$8
2009-P, Polk, Satin Finish (a)	784,614	415	67.3	100%		$5	$12
2009-D, Polk	41,720,000	1,152	66.0	100%	$2	$3.50	$8
2009-D, Polk, Satin Finish (a)	784,614	380	67.3	100%		$5	$12
2009-S, Polk, Proof	2,809,452	17,990	69.2		$4	$15	
2009-P, Taylor	41,580,000	1,270	66.4	100%	$2	$3.50	$8
2009-P, Taylor, Satin Finish (a)	784,614	489	67.6	100%		$5	$12
2009-D, Taylor	36,680,000	1,212	66.2	100%	$2	$3.50	$8
2009-D, Taylor, Satin Finish (a)	784,614	427	67.4	100%		$5	$12
2009-S, Taylor, Proof	2,809,452	18,148	69.3		$4	$15	
2010-P, Fillmore	37,520,000	1,703	66.5	100%	$2	$3.50	$9
2010-P, Fillmore, Satin Finish (a)	583,897	133	65.1	100%		$5	$12
2010-D, Fillmore	36,960,000	1,040	66.5	100%	$2	$3.50	$9
2010-D, Fillmore, Satin Finish (a)	583,897	569	67.5	100%		$5	$12
2010-S, Fillmore, Proof	2,224,827	15,330	69.2		$6	$15	
2010-P, Pierce	38,220,000	1,196	66.2	100%	$2	$3.50	$9
2010-P, Pierce, Satin Finish (a)	583,897	436	67.4	100%		$5	$12
2010-D, Pierce	38,360,000	1,279	66.4	100%	$2	$3.50	$9
2010-D, Pierce, Satin Finish (a)	583,897	585	67.6	100%		$5	$12
2010-S, Pierce, Proof	2,224,827	15,280	69.2		$6	$15	
2010-P, Buchanan	36,820,000	790	66.5	100%	$2	$3.50	$9
2010-P, Buchanan, Satin Finish (a)	583,897	435	67.2	100%		$5	$12
2010-D, Buchanan	36,540,000	1,062	66.5	100%	$2	$3.50	$9
2010-D, Buchanan, Satin Finish (a)	583,897	564	67.5	100%		$5	$12
2010-S, Buchanan, Proof	2,224,827	15,353	69.2		$6	$15	
2010-P, Lincoln	49,000,000	1,412	66.3	100%	$2	$3.50	$9
2010-P, Lincoln, Satin Finish (a)	583,897	685	67.1	100%		$5	$12
2010-D, Lincoln	48,020,000	1,323	66.7	100%	$2	$3.50	$9
2010-D, Lincoln, Satin Finish (a)	583,897	926	67.4	100%		$5	$12
2010-S, Lincoln, Proof	2,224,827	16,061	69.2		$6	$15	
2011-P, A. Johnson	35,560,000	393	66.7	100%	$2	$11	$15
2011-D, A. Johnson	37,100,000	379	67.0	100%	$2	$11	$15
2011-S, A. Johnson, Proof	1,972,863	8,129	69.2		$8	$15	
2011-P, Grant	38,080,000	431	66.8	100%	$2	$11	$15
2011-D, Grant	37,940,000	397	67.0	100%	$2	$11	$15
2011-S, Grant, Proof	1,972,863	8,193	69.2		$8	$15	
2011-P, Hayes	37,660,000	391	66.5	100%	$2	$11	$15
2011-D, Hayes	36,820,000	398	67.1	100%	$2	$11	$15
2011-S, Hayes, Proof	1,972,863	8,271	69.3		$8	$15	
2011-P, Garfield	37,100,000	342	66.4	100%	$2	$11	$15
2011-D, Garfield	37,100,000	351	67.0	100%	$2	$11	$15
2011-S, Garfield, Proof	1,972,863	8,260	69.2		$8	$15	
2012-P, Arthur (a)	6,020,000	306	66.9	100%	$3	$5	$12
2012-D, Arthur (a)	4,060,000	285	67.1	100%	$3	$5	$12
2012-S, Arthur, Proof	1,438,743	5,525	69.3		$17	$35	
2012-P, Cleveland, First Term (a)	5,460,000	294	66.7	100%	$3	$5	$12
2012-D, Cleveland, First Term (a)	4,060,000	255	66.9	100%	$3	$5	$12
2012-S, Cleveland, First Term, Proof	1,438,743	5,564	69.3		$17	$35	

a. Not issued for circulation.

	Mintage	Cert	Avg	%MS	MS-64	MS-65	MS-66
						PF-65	PF-69DC
2012-P, B. Harrison (a)	5,640,001	264	66.7	100%	$3	$5	$12
2012-D, B. Harrison (a)	4,200,000	254	67.1	100%	$3	$5	$12
2012-S, B. Harrison, Proof	1,438,743	5,519	69.3		$17	$35	
2012-P, Cleveland, Second Term (a)	10,680,000	285	66.9	100%	$3	$5	$12
2012-D, Cleveland, Second Term (a)	3,920,000	261	67.1	100%	$3	$5	$12
2012-S, Cleveland, Second Term, Proof	1,438,743	5,485	69.3		$17	$35	
2013-P, McKinley (a)	4,760,000	383	67.1	100%	$2.50	$4.50	$12
2013-D, McKinley (a)	3,365,100	175	67.0	100%	$2.50	$4.50	$12
2013-S, McKinley, Proof	1,488,798	5,144	69.5		$7	$16	
2013-P, T. Roosevelt (a)	5,310,700	554	66.9	100%	$2.50	$4.50	$12
2013-D, T. Roosevelt (a)	3,920,000	331	66.7	100%	$2.50	$4.50	$12
2013-S, T. Roosevelt, Proof	1,503,943	5,210	69.5		$7	$16	
2013-P, Taft (a)	4,760,000	404	67.0	100%	$2.50	$4.50	$12
2013-D, Taft (a)	3,360,000	223	67.0	100%	$2.50	$4.50	$12
2013-S, Taft, Proof	1,488,798	5,101	69.5		$7	$16	
2013-P, Wilson (a)	4,620,000	450	67.2	100%	$2.50	$4.50	$12
2013-D, Wilson (a)	3,360,000	209	67.2	100%	$2.50	$4.50	$12
2013-S, Wilson, Proof	1,488,798	5,100	69.5		$7	$16	
2014-P, Harding (a)	6,160,000	117	66.6	100%	$3.50	$8	$15
2014-D, Harding (a)	3,780,000	224	67.0	100%	$3.50	$8	$15
2014-S, Harding, Proof	1,373,569	4,241	69.5		$7	$16	
2014-P, Coolidge (a)	4,480,000	142	67.1	100%	$3.50	$8	$15
2014-D, Coolidge (a)	3,780,000	199	67.2	100%	$3.50	$8	$15
2014-S, Coolidge, Proof	1,373,569	4,261	69.5		$7	$16	
2014-P, Hoover (a)	4,480,000	100	66.9	100%	$3.50	$8	$15
2014-D, Hoover (a)	3,780,000	207	67.1	100%	$3.50	$8	$15
2014-S, Hoover, Proof	1,373,569	4,243	69.4		$7	$16	
2014-P, F.D. Roosevelt (a)	4,760,000	134	66.9	100%	$3.50	$8	$15
2014-D, F.D. Roosevelt (a)	3,920,000	166	67.2	100%	$3.50	$8	$15
2014-S, F.D. Roosevelt, Proof	1,392,619	4,290	69.5		$7	$16	
2015-P, Truman (a)	4,900,000	72	66.5	100%	$3	$7	$14
2015-P, Truman, Reverse Proof ††	16,812	1,514	69.0		$175	$225	
2015-D, Truman (a)	3,500,000	74	66.8	100%	$3	$7	$14
2015-S, Truman, Proof	1,272,232	4,186	69.4		$6	$15	
2015-P, Eisenhower (a)	4,900,000	59	65.7	100%	$3	$7	$14
2015-P, Eisenhower, Reverse Proof ††	16,744	1,230	68.9		$150	$180	
2015-D, Eisenhower (a)	3,645,998	78	66.8	100%	$3	$7	$14
2015-S, Eisenhower, Proof	1,272,232	4,194	69.4		$6	$15	
2015-P, Kennedy (a)	6,160,000	84	66.2	100%	$3	$7	$14
2015-P, Kennedy, Reverse Proof	49,501	2,791	69.0		$80	$125	
2015-D, Kennedy (a)	5,180,000	102	66.8	100%	$3	$7	$14
2015-S, Kennedy, Proof	1,272,232	4,305	69.4		$6	$15	
2015-P, L.B. Johnson (a)	7,840,000	177	66.5	100%	$3	$7	$14
2015-P, L.B. Johnson, Reverse Proof	23,905	1,374	68.8		$75	$90	
2015-D, L.B. Johnson (a)	4,200,000	76	66.7	100%	$3	$7	$14
2015-S, L.B. Johnson, Proof	1,272,232	4,192	69.4		$6	$15	
2016-P, Richard M. Nixon (a)	5,460,000	153	66.8	100%	$3	$8	$16
2016-D, Richard M. Nixon (a)	4,340,000	304	67.0	100%	$3	$8	$16
2016-S, Richard M. Nixon, Proof	1,163,415	3,643	69.5		$9	$17	

†† Ranked in the *100 Greatest U.S. Modern Coins* (fourth edition). **a.** Not issued for circulation.

	Mintage	Cert	Avg	%MS	MS-64	MS-65	MS-66
						PF-65	PF-69DC
2016-P, Gerald Ford (a)	5,460,000	133	66.5	100%	$3	$10	$22
2016-D, Gerald Ford (a)	5,040,000	299	66.8	100%	$3	$10	$22
2016-S, Gerald Ford, Proof	1,163,415	3,635	69.5		$9	$17	
2016-P, Ronald Reagan (a)	7,140,000	229	66.8	100%	$3	$10	$22
2016-D, Ronald Reagan (a)	5,880,000	301	67.0	100%	$3	$10	$22
2016-S, Ronald Reagan, Proof	1,163,415	3,681	69.5		$9	$17	
2016-P, Ronald Reagan, Reverse Proof	47,447	1,101	69.1		$60	$80	
2020-P, George H.W. Bush (a)		0	n/a			$10	$22
2020-D, George H.W. Bush (a)		0	n/a			$10	$22
2020-S, George H.W. Bush, Proof		0	n/a			$9	$20

a. Not issued for circulation.

NATIVE AMERICAN DOLLARS (2009 TO DATE)

Designers: *Glenna Goodacre (obverse); see image captions for reverse designers.*
Weight: *8.1 grams.* **Composition:** *Pure copper core with outer layers of manganese brass (.770 copper, .120 zinc, .070 manganese, and .040 nickel).* **Diameter:** *26.5 mm.*
Edge: *Lettered.* **Mints:** *Philadelphia, Denver, San Francisco, and West Point.*

| Circulation Strike | Mintmark location is on the rim. | Proof |

BACKGROUND

Since 2009, a series of golden dollars has featured annually changing reverse designs that memorialize Native Americans and, in the words of the authorizing legislation, "the important contributions made by Indian tribes and individual Native Americans to the development [and history] of the United States." The Native American $1 Coin Act, which authorized the coins, also specified that at least 20 percent of the total mintage of dollar coins in any given year will be Native American dollars.

Production of all dollar coins minted after 2011 has been limited to numismatic sales (Proofs and other collector formats, and circulation strikes in rolls and bags available directly from the U.S. Mint); none are issued for circulation, as they have proven unpopular in commerce and the Treasury and Federal Reserve have large quantities in storage.

The obverse of the Native American dollar coin is a modified version of the Sacagawea dollar, featuring that coin's central portraits (of Sacagawea and Jean Baptiste), and the legends LIBERTY and IN GOD WE TRUST. The date and mintmark are on the coin's edge. Each new reverse design is chosen by the secretary of the Treasury following consultation with the Senate Committee on Indian Affairs, the Congressional Native American Caucus of the House of Representatives, the U.S. Commission of Fine Arts, and the National Congress of American Indians. Design proposals are reviewed and recommendations given to the Treasury secretary by the Citizens Coinage Advisory Committee.

In addition to the regular Uncirculated or Mint State coins produced in large quantities, smaller numbers of Satin Finish dollars were made of the 2009-P, 2009-D, 2010-P, and 2010-D issues. Sold at an additional premium, most of these exist today in grades of MS-67 and upward and are designated SP (Specimen) or SMS (Special Mint Set) by the commercial grading services. In various years, coins have been made with Enhanced Uncirculated finish and sold at an extra premium. Most of these grade MS-68 to 70. In 2015 at the West Point Mint nearly 90,000 2015-W dollars were struck with Enhanced Uncirculated finish. These are unique up to this time as the only collectible West Point dollars in any of the four "golden dollar" series (Sacagawea, Native American, Presidential, and American Innovation). Nearly all are in grades of MS-68 to 70.

2019-P, Enhanced Uncirculated.

The Native American dollars have developed into an impressive well-designed collection of coins with richly diverse subjects.

Some error coins have been discovered without edge lettering.

NATIVE AMERICAN DOLLARS (2009 TO DATE): GUIDE TO COLLECTING

BEING A SMART BUYER

Most Native American dollar coins are very well struck. Check the higher points of the design. Special issues are uniformly sharply struck.

AVAILABILITY

Native American dollars are common and readily available in high grades. Collectors usually seek Mint State and Proof examples; only the first two years of coinage were intended for circulation, and even those saw little hand-to-hand commerce. Distribution for public circulation was slow despite Mint efforts such as the $1 Coin Direct Ship program (intended "to make $1 coins readily available to the public, at no additional cost [including shipping], so they can be easily introduced into circulation—particularly by using them for retail transactions, vending, and mass transit"). Proofs have been made each year and are readily available. Other special formats have been minted for collectors, as well.

NATIVE AMERICAN (2009 TO DATE)

GRADING STANDARDS

MS-60 to 70 (Mint State). *Obverse:* At MS-60, some abrasion and contact marks are evident, most noticeably on the cheekbone and the drapery near the baby's head. Luster is present, but may be dull or lifeless. At MS-63, contact marks are extensive but not distracting. Abrasion still is evident, but less than at lower levels. MS-64 coins are slightly finer. An MS-65 coin may have minor abrasion, but contact marks are so minute as to require magnification. Luster should be full and rich. *Reverse:* At MS-60, some abrasion and contact marks are evident. Otherwise, the same comments apply as for the obverse.

2009-P, Three Sisters. Graded MS-68.

Native American dollars are seldom collected in grades lower than MS-60.

PF-60 to 70 (Proof). *Obverse and Reverse:* Proofs that are extensively cleaned and have many hairlines, or that are dull and grainy, are lower level, such as PF-60 to 62. This comment is more theoretical than practical, as nearly all Proofs have been well kept. With medium hairlines and good reflectivity, assigned grades of PF-63 or 64 are appropriate. With relatively few hairlines a rating of PF-65 can be given. PF-66 may have hairlines so delicate that magnification is needed to see them. Above that, all the way to PF-70, a Proof should be free of any hairlines or other problems under strong magnification.

2009-S, Three Sisters. Graded PF-70 Deep Cameo.

Note: The listings that follow show an example of a representative circulation-strike coin and a Proof strike coin for all the Native American dollars, as the only difference between Philadelphia and Denver strikes appears on the rim.

2009-P Native American Dollar

2009-P, Three Sisters •
Mintage: 39,200,000.

Availability: MS-65 coins are common enough, but in terms of certified coins grading MS-68 and higher this issue is scarce.

Notes: The reverse design features a Native American woman planting seeds in a field of corn (maize), beans, and squash.

Reverse designer: Norman E. Nemeth.

Maize was domesticated in central Mexico and spread from the southwest through North America, along with symbiotic farming of the "Three Sisters," in which growing corn, beans, and squash in the same mound enhanced the productivity of each plant. Native American agricultural skill provided the margin of survival for early European colonists, through trade and from direct sharing of expertise. Before long, agricultural products native to the Americas became staples throughout Europe.

These coins were released to the public on January 2, 2009, having been pre-struck in 2008. Purchases could be made of $25 bank-wrapped rolls in quantities of 250 or 500 coins, with shipping and handling paid by the Mint. This policy was changed on January 15, after which time they could be ordered in 25-coin rolls for $35.95, plus postage.

On January 17 in the Potomac Atrium of the Smithsonian Institution's National Museum of the American Indian a ceremonial "pour" of dollars from a hand-made Indian basket was made by Mint Director Edmund C. Moy and the Indian museum's director, Kevin Gover. Free coins were given to attendees 18 years old and younger, and nearby the Mint's "Real Change Exchange Truck" employees sold coins to the public for face value.

	Cert	Avg	%MS	MS-64	MS-65	MS-66
2009-P, Three Sisters	959	66.9	100%	$3	$5	$8

VARIETY: *Three Sisters, 2009, plain-edge error.* Many coins were inadvertently issued without edge lettering and thus lack the date and mintmark. These are not identifiable to a particular mint. Probably close to 10,000 error coins have been identified by collectors and dealers.

2009-P, Three Sisters, Satin Finish • Mintage: 784,614.

Availability: These are typically graded 65 to 68, but selected coins are higher.

Notes: These are separately certified with an SP prefix by PCGS and with an SMS prefix by NGC.

	Cert	Avg	%MS	MS-64	MS-65	MS-66
2009-P, Three Sisters, Satin Finish	607	67.3	100%		$5	$12

2009-D Native American Dollar

2009-D, Three Sisters • Mintage: 35,700,000.

Availability: MS-65 coins are common enough to easily meet collector demand, but in terms of certified coins grading MS-68 and higher, this issue is scarce.

Notes: The concept of the Three Sisters relates to an efficient planting method wherein corn stalks provide support for bean vines, which add nitrogen to the soil. Squash provide ground cover, which discourages weeds. Productivity is as much as 30 percent higher for the three crops grown together compared to each grown separately.

"Agriculture has always been an important subject in Native American culture," the Mint explained in its descriptions of the Three Sisters coin. "It emphasizes living with the land and understanding the surrounding natural resources. . . . Native Americans practiced crop rotation, round cropping, hybridizations, seed development, irrigation methods, and many other agricultural techniques that are still used today."

Mint sculptor-engraver Norman Nemeth designed this coin and sculpted it.

	Cert	Avg	%MS	MS-64	MS-65	MS-66
2009-D, Three Sisters	728	66.5	100%	$3	$5	$8

2009-D, Three Sisters, Satin Finish • Mintage: 784,614.

Availability: Three Sisters dollars are typically graded 65 to 68, but selected coins are higher.

Note: These are separately certified with an SP prefix by PCGS and with an SMS prefix by NGC.

	Cert	Avg	%MS	MS-64	MS-65	MS-66
2009-D, Three Sisters, Satin Finish	452	67.2	100%		$5	$12

2009-S Native American Dollar

2009-S, Three Sisters, Proof •
Mintage: 2,179,867.

Availability: Nearly all of these coins, readily available, are gem Proofs approaching perfection.

	Cert	Avg	%MS	PF-65	PF-69DC
2009-S, Three Sisters, Proof	10,024	69.3		$8	$15

2010-P Native American Dollar

2010-P, Great Law of Peace •

Mintage: 32,060,000.

Availability: MS-65 coins are readily available. Certified coins grading MS-68 and higher are scarce.

Notes: The Great Law of Peace design features as its central motif an image of the Hiawatha Belt with five arrows bound together.

Reverse designer: Thomas Cleveland.

   The Haudenosaunee Confederation, also known as the Iroquois Confederacy of upstate New York, was founded by two historic figures: the Peacemaker and his Onondaga spokesman, Hiawatha, who spent years preaching the need for a league. To symbolically confirm the treaty, The Peacemaker buried weapons at the foot of a Great White Pine, or Great Tree of Peace. Its five-needle clusters represented the original five nations: Mohawk, Oneida, Onondaga, Cayuga, and Seneca.

   The Hiawatha Belt is a visual record of the creation of the Haudenosaunee dating back to the early 1400s. Upon the belt, five symbols represent the five original nations. The Haudenosaunee symbol, the Great White Pine, is the central figure. It also represents the Onondaga Nation. The four square symbols represent the Mohawk, Oneida, Cayuga, and Seneca nations. The bundle of five arrows symbolizes strength in unity for the Iroquois Confederacy.

   The Great Law of Peace reverse was designed by Thomas L. Cleveland of the Mint's Artistic Infusion Program and was engraved by Mint sculptor-engraver Charles L. Vickers. The Artistic Infusion Program, begun in 2004, added outside creative talent to that already possessed by the staff of highly accomplished artists and engravers headquartered at the Philadelphia Mint.

   The new dollars were made available to the public on January 4, 2010. The Mint's Direct Ship Program offered boxes of ten 25-coin bank-wrapped rolls for face value, delivered. A maximum of 20 boxes per household was set. On January 22 the Mint began offering 25-coin rolls in special wrappers for $35.95 per roll, plus shipping and handling, with no limit as to the quantity that could be ordered. Purchasers had their choice of Philadelphia or Denver coins.

   On January 25, 2010, the official launch ceremony for the 2010 coins was conducted in the National Museum of the American Indian facility at the George Gustav Heye Center in the Alexander Hamilton U.S. Custom House in New York City. On hand were Mint Director Edmund C. Moy and John Haworth, director of the Heye Center.

	Cert	Avg	%MS	MS-64	MS-65	MS-66
2010-P, Great Law of Peace	775	66.5	100%	$3	$5	$8

VARIETY: *2010, Great Law of Peace, plain-edge error.* Several hundred coins were inadvertently issued without edge lettering and thus lack the date and mintmark. These are not identifiable to a particular mint.

2010-P, Great Law of Peace, Satin Finish • Mintage: 583,897.

Availability: These coins are typically graded 65 to 68, but some select examples are higher. All are available enough to meet collector demand.

Notes: These are separately certified with an SP prefix by PCGS and with an SMS prefix by NGC.

	Cert	Avg	%MS	MS-64	MS-65	MS-66
2010-P, Great Law of Peace, Satin Finish	307	67.4	100%		$5	$12

2010-D Native American Dollar

2010-D, Great Law of Peace • Mintage: 48,720,000.

Availability: MS-65 coins are common, but this issue is scarce in certified grades of MS-68 and higher.

Notes: The Mint's explanatory documentation describes the Great Law of Peace coin: "Northern European settlers from France, England, and the Netherlands interacted with the Haudenosaunee as a separate diplomatic power. The success of the confederation showed the colonists that the Greek confederacies they had read about in the histories of Polybius were a viable political alternative to monarchy. The symbolism of the Great Tree of Peace and eagle sitting on its top were adopted as national icons during the American Revolutionary government.

Some early narratives by explorers and missionaries introduced Europe to Native American societies which practiced equality and democratic self-government. These narratives quickly found their way into classics of European thought, including Sir Thomas More's *Utopia* and Montaigne's *Essays*. John Locke cited the Huron election of its chiefs in his refutation of the Divine Right of Kings (the idea that a monarch is subject to no earthly authority because they derive their right to rule directly from the will of God).

When the newly independent Americans devised a continental government they may have seen in these native societies living examples of the successful confederacies that they admired in the ancient Greek histories. Many tribal groups established confederations often based on linguistic affinity. One of the most famous and powerful of these Native leagues was the Iroquois Confederacy, known to its members as the Haudenosaunee ('People of the Longhouse'), or the Six Nations."

The Great Law of Peace dollar was designed by Artistic Infusion Program Master Designer Thomas Cleveland, and engraved by Mint artist Charles Vickers in Philadelphia.

	Cert	Avg	%MS	MS-64	MS-65	MS-66
2010-D, Great Law of Peace	749	66.6	100%	$3	$5	$8

2010-D, Great Law of Peace, Satin Finish • Mintage: 583,897.

Availability: These coins are readily available, and are typically graded 65 to 68, but a number of them are even finer.

Notes: They are separately certified with an SP prefix by PCGS and with an SMS prefix by NGC.

	Cert	Avg	%MS	MS-64	MS-65	MS-66
2010-D, Great Law of Peace, Satin Finish	379	67.5	100%		$5	$12

2010-S Native American Dollar

2010-S, Great Law of Peace, Proof •
Mintage: 1,689,216.

Availability: These Proofs are readily available, and nearly all are gems approaching perfection.

	Cert	Avg	%MS	PF-65	PF-69DC
2010-S, Great Law of Peace, Proof	6,342	69.3		$8	$15

2011-P Native American Dollar

2011-P, Wampanoag Treaty •

Mintage: 29,400,000.

Availability: Examples are readily available in almost any Mint State grade desired, although most are below MS-65.

Reverse designer: Richard Masters.

Notes: The theme for the 2011 Native American dollar coin is "Supreme Sachem Ousamequin, Massasoit of the Great Wampanoag Nation, Creates Alliance with Settlers at Plymouth Bay (1621)." The design features hands of the Supreme Sachem Ousamequin Massasoit and Governor John Carver, exchanging the ceremonial peace pipe after the first formal written peace alliance between the Wampanoag tribe and the European settlers. It includes the inscription WAMPANOAG TREATY 1621.

The Mint's educational materials observed: "Within Native American culture, the ability to make peace was historically as highly prized as leadership in war and was often conducted by a separate peace chief who stepped in when the time for the warriors had passed. For centuries, tribes created alliances with each other that spanned hundreds of miles. One of the first treaties for a mutual alliance with settlers in what became the United States of America occurred between the Puritan settlers at Plymouth and the Massasoit (a title meaning 'head chief') of the Pokanoket Wampanoag in 1621. Historians credit the alliance with the Massasoit with ensuring survival of the Plymouth colony."

The reverse of the Wampanoag Treaty dollar was designed by Richard Masters of the Artistic Infusion Program and engraved by Joseph Menna, who would later be named chief engraver of the Mint.

In April 2011 almost 500 people witnessed the launch ceremony for the coin, held at Plimoth Plantation in Plymouth, Massachusetts.

	Cert	Avg	%MS	MS-64	MS-65	MS-66
2011-P, Wampanoag Treaty	382	66.7	100%	$3	$5	$8

VARIETY: *2011, Wampanoag Treaty, weak edge lettering.* A number of coins were issued with the edge lettering weakly defined.

VARIETY: *2011, Wampanoag Treaty, plain-edge error.* A few coins were inadvertently issued without edge lettering and thus lack the date and mintmark, making them a great rarity.

2011-D Native American Dollar

2011-D, Wampanoag Treaty • **Mintage:** 48,160,000.

Availability: Examples are readily available in almost any Mint State grade desired, although most are below MS-65. Only a tiny percentage of the mintage has ever been certified.

Notes: The Supreme Sachem Ousamequin Massasoit promised to defend the Plymouth settlers against hostile tribes in return for their intervention if his people were attacked. His intermediaries—Tisquantum, Samoset, and Hobbamack—gave the settlers invaluable tips on survival.

The Plymouth settlers honored the Wampanoag treaty in the summer of 1621 by coming to Massasoit's rescue when they thought he had been captured by enemies. In mid-October, Massasoit and 90 of his tribesmen celebrated a harvest feast at Plymouth for three days (a traditional English folk celebration). The 1621 feast inspired the legend of the first Thanksgiving, as it was called 220 years later. The treaty at Patuxet lasted more than 50 years.

The United States made some 370 treaties with American Indian tribes from the Declaration of Independence in 1776 until 1868, when Congress suspended formal treaty-making. Since then, government-to-government relations between the United States and sovereign tribes have taken a variety of other legal forms. Current U.S. policy states that federal relations with recognized tribes are conducted on a government-to-government basis.

	Cert	Avg	%MS	MS-64	MS-65	MS-66
2011-D, Wampanoag Treaty	423	67.0	100%	$3	$5	$8

2011-S Native American Dollar

2011-S, Wampanoag Treaty, Proof •
Mintage: 1,673,010.

Availability: Collectors will find this issue in sufficient abundance. Nearly all are gem Proofs approaching perfection.

	Cert	Avg	%MS	PF-65	PF-69DC
2011-S, Wampanoag Treaty, Proof	7,868	69.2		$8	$15

2012-P Native American Dollar

2012-P, Trade Routes in the 17th Century • Mintage: 2,800,000.

Availability: Typical grades for these coins are MS-64 to 66, although many higher-grade examples exist. This was the first year of restricted mintages. All dollar coins from this point onward exist in lower quantities than those of earlier times. Still, there are more than enough to satisfy numismatic demand.

Reverse designer: Thomas Cleveland.

Notes: The theme for the 2012 Native American dollar is "Trade Routes in the 17th century." The design features an American Indian in profile with a companion horse, and with other horses running in the background. Their presence embodies the historical spread of trade routes and the importance of the horse in opening and strengthening commerce.

The Mint noted: "American Indians maintained widespread trans-continental, inter-tribal trade for more than a millennium. The Native American trade infrastructure became the channel by which exploration, settlement, and economic development in the colonial period—and later of the young republic—ultimately thrived. When early European traders ventured from eastern city centers into the interior lands, they followed trading routes still in use, often in the company of Native American guides and traders who had used them for generations. By taking these routes they encountered an ecosystem and Native American culture already being transformed by European goods that had moved along the routes long before Europeans themselves arrived in the interior regions.

These routes showed the way to European explorers and traders and marked the corridors for future east-west travel. The Lewis and Clark Expedition in 1803 followed parts of this trail. This cross-continental trade infrastructure culminated in the construction of the modern-day interstate highway system. Trading routes centered on Zuni Pueblo in the Four Corners region of the southwest and the Mojave bead route to the California coast were incorporated into the Old Spanish Trail (now a National Park Service historic trail). The Old Snake Trade Route connected the pueblos of New Mexico north to the Mandan villages in the present-day Dakotas, branching to the west in present-day Wyoming and reaching the Columbia River at The Dalles in Oregon."

The reverse of the Trade Routes dollar was designed by Thomas Cleveland, a member of the Mint's Artistic Infusion Program. In the studio of the Philadelphia Mint it was engraved by sculptor-engraver Phebe Hemphill.

Beginning in 2012, the Mint discontinued launch events and special ceremonies for Native American dollars, citing the expense involved.

	Cert	Avg	%MS	MS-64	MS-65	MS-66
2012-P, Trade Routes in the 17th Century	231	67.1	100%	$5	$8	$15

2012-D Native American Dollar

2012-D, Trade Routes in the 17th Century • Mintage: 3,080,000.

Availability: The typical grades for these coins are MS-64 to 66. Many higher-grade coins exist for collectors who seek perfection.

Notes: Describing this coin's design, the Mint noted that the horse, spread by Indian tribes through Native American trade routes, was perhaps the most significant of all the goods exchanged throughout the continent. "Thanks to inter-tribal trade, horses had crossed the Rio Grande by 1600. This trade received a massive infusion in 1680, when the Pueblo Revolt released thousands of horses from the mission herds into Native American hands. The horse became perhaps the most sought-after commodity in inter-tribal trade. The horse's spread in Native American hands was so prodigious that it became the primary means of transportation and the nucleus of the ranching economy already underway in the western territories. In the south, the Caddo trade center became a major entry point for the horse. Trade up the Old Snake Route brought horses as far north as the Mandan in North Dakota, who supplied them to the Lakota and Blackfeet. A parallel inter-mountain route brought horses to the northwest. By the time Lewis and Clark wintered with the Mandan in 1803, they encountered a well-established horse culture. These long-established Native American trade routes also provided the path for this primary means of transportation—a significant contribution to opening up the continental interior to the developing nation."

	Cert	Avg	%MS	MS-64	MS-65	MS-66
2012-D, Trade Routes in the 17th Century	844	67.4	100%	$5	$8	$15

2012-S Native American Dollar

2012-S, Trade Routes in the 17th Century, Proof • Mintage: 1,189,445.

Availability: Nearly all are gem Proofs approaching perfection, and they are readily available.

	Cert	Avg	%MS	PF-65	PF-69DC
2012-S, Trade Routes in the 17th Century, Proof	5,647	69.3		$15	$20

2013-P Native American Dollar

2013-P, Treaty With the Delawares •
Mintage: 1,820,000.

Availability: Coins of this issue are readily
available. Typical grades are MS-64 to 66,
although many higher-grade coins exist.

Notes: The 2013 Native American dollar coin
commemorates the Delaware Treaty of 1778.
Its design features a turkey, a howling wolf, and a

Reverse designer: Susan Gamble.

turkey—all symbols of the clans of the Delaware Tribe. Around them is a circle of 13 stars to represent
Britain's American colonies that originally formed the Union.

The Mint described the treaty thus: "When the American Revolution established a new sovereign
government on the North American continent, its founders acknowledged the significance of Indian
tribes as the new United States of America dealt with tribes government-to-government, making peace
and winning allies through a series of treaties. The new Constitution in 1789 reserved the regulation of
commerce with the tribes to the federal government—specifically in Article I, section 8, clause 3—putting them on the same footing as foreign governments. The First Congress affirmed this principle in
major legislation on trade and land deals with Indians—laws that are still in effect. Treaty-making with
the United States was the foundation for tribal relations with the new American government, but the
legal theory underlying that relationship was sharply contested until Chief Justice John Marshall's pivotal
1832 decision in *Cherokee Nation v. Georgia*. In declaring tribes to be dependent nations, he started the
process by which tribes were recognized under the American federal system, equal in status with state
governments as the third leg of sovereign membership, but also diminished in stature under this system."

The design of the Treaty With the Delawares coin was by Susan Gamble of the Mint's Artistic Infusion Program. Mint sculptor-engraver Phebe Hemphill engraved it for coinage.

	Cert	Avg	%MS	MS-64	MS-65	MS-66
2013-P, Treaty With the Delawares	335	67.0	100%	$3	$5	$11

2013-D Native American Dollar

2013-D, Treaty With the Delawares • **Mintage:** 1,820,000.

Availability: This issue is readily available on the collector market. Typical grades are MS-64 to 66,
although many higher-grade coins exist.

Notes: The United States signed its first formal treaty with an Indian tribe, the Delaware, at Fort Pitt
(now Pittsburgh, Pennsylvania) on September 17, 1778. With this mutual-defense treaty, American
troops could pass through the Delaware Tribe's land to attack the British fort at Detroit, Michigan.
"Under the treaty," the Mint said in its publicity for the 2013 dollar, "the United States recognized the
Delaware Nation's sovereignty. The treaty also offered significant insight into the later process of incorporating tribes into the federal system. Article VI of the treaty gave the Delaware Nation the option of
joining other tribes in the Ohio region to form a state with the Delaware Tribe at the head to become
part of the U.S. confederation with representation in Congress. Although the statehood option was
never taken up, it foreshadowed the later acknowledgment of tribes as partners in the federal system."

	Cert	Avg	%MS	MS-64	MS-65	MS-66
2013-D, Treaty With the Delawares	711	67.0	100%	$3	$5	$11

2013-S Native American Dollar

2013-S, Treaty With the Delawares, Proof • Mintage: 1,222,180.

Availability: These Proofs are readily available. Nearly all are gem Proofs approaching perfection.

	Cert	Avg	%MS	PF-65	PF-69DC
2013-S, Treaty With the Delawares, Proof	4,219	69.5		$8	$15

2014-P Native American Dollar

2014-P, Native Hospitality • Mintage: 3,080,000.

Availability: More than enough coins exist to meet collector demand. Typical grades are MS-64 to 66, although many higher-grade coins exist.

Notes: The 2014 Native American dollar celebrates the Native American hospitality that

Reverse designer: Chris Costello.

ensured the success of the Lewis and Clark Expedition. Its reverse design depicts a Native American man offering a pipe while his wife offers provisions of fish, corn, roots, and gourds. In the background is a stylized image of the face of William Clark's compass highlighting "NW," the continental region that was the expedition's goal.

"When the Lewis and Clark Expedition crossed the Continental Divide the nature of its mission fundamentally changed," noted the Mint's historical literature regarding this coin. "Up to that point, the mission had been exploring territory that European powers would recognize as belonging to the United States through the Louisiana Purchase. Once past the headwaters of the Missouri River, the expedition was securing the American claim to a new accession of territory, the Pacific Northwest. More than ever before, success of the mission depended on help from the Indian tribes who might not have understood the long-term consequences of their hospitality. For every step of their way through the Rocky Mountains to the Pacific Coast, Lewis and Clark depended on the friendship, supplies, and logistical support of the tribes on their route. They camped in the midst of the Mandan and Hidatsa tribes in the winter of 1804–1805 and the Clatsop in 1806, and their cooperation was essential to the resounding success of this mission."

The reverse of the Native Hospitality dollar was designed by Chris Costello of the Mint's Artistic Infusion Program. It was engraved by Joseph Menna, who would later be appointed chief engraver of the Mint.

	Cert	Avg	%MS	MS-64	MS-65	MS-66
2014-P, Native Hospitality	217	67.0	100%	$3	$6	$9

2014-D Native American Dollar

2014-D, Native Hospitality • Mintage: 2,800,000.

Availability: This coin is readily available to meet collector demand; typical grades range from MS-64 to 66, although many higher-grade pieces exist.

Notes: The Mint described how the Mandan and Hidatsa tribes of the Missouri River, located in present-day North Dakota, welcomed Lewis and Clark and their Corps of Discovery to their unique dome-shaped earthen-lodge villages, often sitting and talking by the campfire when meeting with Black Cat, the Mandan chief. "Their village was the central marketplace for the northern plains. Lewis expressed the highest respect for Black Cat (Posecopsahe) and walked miles out of his way to smoke a pipe with him on the day of his departure. The expedition group traded for corn and gathered every scrap of intelligence they could about the route ahead. During the winter at Fort Mandan, the expedition blacksmith forged somewhat eccentric ax heads to trade for corn. Eighteen months later, the expedition found that some of the same ax heads had already been traded to the Nez Perce, which the expedition relied on to supply horses from their famous herd. Down the length of the Columbia River, the Americans traded with the Chinook and other tribes for provisions.

The Clatsop Indians were flourishing people who enjoyed plentiful amounts of fish and fur and occupied three villages on the southern side of the Columbia River. They were located in what is now known as Oregon. Some Clatsop tribesmen complained about the expedition's stinginess with gifts. Coboway, chief of one of the villages, visited the expedition group at its fort, which was still under construction. He exchanged some goods, including a sea otter pelt, for fishhooks and a small bag of Shoshone tobacco. Over the rest of the winter, Coboway would be a frequent and welcome visitor to this area they named Fort Clatsop. The Clatsop also aided the expedition both in preparing for, and dealing with, the northwest winter, and informed Lewis and Clark that there was a good amount of elk on the south side of the Columbia, information that influenced the location of Fort Clatsop. When the expedition's food supplies were running low, the Clatsop informed the corps that a whale had washed ashore some miles to the south.

At the expedition's departure from Fort Clatsop, Lewis wrote in his journal that Coboway 'has been much more kind an[d] hospitable to us than any other Indian in this neighbourhood.' Lewis committed the expedition's one act of pilferage, appropriating a Native canoe for the voyage up the river. (He later encountered a Lumhi Indian who claimed ownership of the vessel and paid him off with an elk skin.) This misdeed remained on the historical record, and late in 2011, the family of William Clark presented a replica of the original canoe to the Chinook tribe in recompense."

	Cert	Avg	%MS	MS-64	MS-65	MS-66
2014-D, Native Hospitality	363	67.2	100%	$3	$6	$9

2014-D, Native Hospitality, Enhanced Uncirculated • Mintage: 50,000.

Availability: Nearly all are in higher grades, since this issue was made especially for collectors and never circulated. This coinage is ranked among the *100 Greatest U.S. Modern Coins* (fourth edition).

Notes: The U.S. Mint on November 20, 2014, put on sale a "Native American $1 Coin and Currency Set" for $13.95. It included one Enhanced Uncirculated 2014 Native American dollar from Denver and one 2013 $1 note from the Bureau of Engraving and Printing. "The enhanced finish coin is only available as part of the set and will not be sold individually," the Mint announced. "The base finish on the obverse and reverse was wire brushed, giving the coins a bright finish without appearing polished liked Proof coins. The obverse and reverse artwork was then frosted with different finishes." In December the maximum authorized total of 50,000 sets had been reached, and distribution ceased.

	Cert	Avg	%MS	MS-64	MS-65	MS-66
2014-D, Native Hospitality, Enhanced Uncirculated	5,194	68.9	100%		$10	$15

VARIETY: *2014-D, Native Hospitality, plain-edge error.* This variety is also called "missing edge lettering." In January 2015 ANACS reported that it had certified about 1,000 Enhanced Uncirculated coins and, of those, just one was missing the edge inscriptions. It was certified as MS-69.

2014-S Native American Dollar

2014-S, Native Hospitality, Proof •
Mintage: 1,144,154.

Availability: This issue is readily available. Nearly all examples are gem Proofs approaching perfection.

	Cert	Avg	%MS	PF-65	PF-69DC
2014-S, Native Hospitality, Proof	6,372	69.3		$8	$15

2015-P Native American Dollar

2015-P, Mohawk Ironworkers •
Mintage: 2,800,000.

Availability: This coin is abundantly available for collectors. Most are in very high Mint State grades.

Reverse designer: Ronald D. Sanders.

Notes: The 2015 Native American dollar honors the contributions Kahnawake Mohawk and Mohawk Akwesasne communities made in "high-iron"–construction work and the building of New York City skyscrapers. The design shows a Mohawk ironworker reaching for an I-beam swinging into position. Rivets are on the left and right side of the border, and a high elevation view of the city skyline is in the background. The design includes the inscription MOHAWK IRONWORKERS.

The Mint described the coin thus: "American Indians have become legendary figures in hazardous occupations. Tribes take great pride in the bravery of their people, whether displayed in high-iron–construction work on the tallest skyscrapers or fire jumping and brake-cutting in the face of the West's raging wildfires. These occupations receive the honor given to warriors in days past, and they carry on the ancient ethic of putting one's life on the line to protect the welfare and safety of the people. Just as the ancient warriors devoted themselves to preserving all the people of the tribe, the modern risk-takers see their occupations as a contribution to the public good.

The tradition of Mohawk high-iron working dates to 1886, when the Dominion Bridge Company started a bridge from the Kahnawake Mohawk community across the St. Lawrence River. Mohawks were first employed as day laborers, but they insisted on working on the bridge itself, and supervisors were amazed at their ability to handle heights. The danger of the work became evident in 1907 at the Quebec Bridge project, designed to be the largest cantilevered bridge in the world. On August 29, the structure failed and the bridge collapsed into the river, killing 33 Mohawk workers. Four family names were wiped out. After the disaster the Kahnawake Clan Mothers ruled that large numbers of Mohawk men could not work on the same project at the same time."

The Mohawk Ironworkers dollar was designed by Ronald D. Sanders of the Artistic Infusion Program. Phebe Hemphill, sculptor-engraver at the Philadelphia Mint, engraved it from Sanders's design.

	Cert	Avg	%MS	MS-64	MS-65	MS-66
2015-P, Mohawk Ironworkers	110	66.2	100%	$3	$5	$8

2015-D Native American Dollar

2015-D, Mohawk Ironworkers • Mintage: 2,240,000.

Availability: The Mohawk Ironworkers dollar coins minted at Denver are readily available in MS-65 and nearby grades.

Notes: "Native ironworkers were in increasing demand in the twentieth century," the Mint's historical narrative explained, "as skyscrapers, tall bridges, and other high-elevation projects began to go up around North America. Crews from Kahnawake and the Mohawk Akwesasne communities in upstate New York and Canada made the trek to New York City to build its skyline, including the Empire State Building, the Chrysler Building, and work above the 80th floor on the World Trade Center twin towers. At one point, one in four men at Akwesasne worked in high-rise construction.

The tradition entered a new and poignant phase after the September 11, 2001, attacks on the World Trade Center, witnessed at close hand by a Mohawk construction crew on a nearby building. Dozens of Mohawk ironworkers volunteered for the dangerous job of removing debris. The venerated '9-11' flag displayed at the 2004 Winter Olympics was recovered from the lobby of Six World Trade Center by a Mohawk worker from Akwesasne on the day after the attack. The St. Regis Reservation Tribal Council—the government for the U.S. side of the Mohawk Akwesasne community that straddles the Canada/U.S. border—and the iron workers local union collected respirators to donate to the New York Fire Department for the recovery effort."

	Cert	Avg	%MS	MS-64	MS-65	MS-66
2015-D, Mohawk Ironworkers	164	66.6	100%	$3	$5	$8

2015-S Native American Dollar

2015-S, Mohawk Ironworkers, Proof • Mintage: 1,050,164.

Availability: These coins are easily available for today's collectors. Nearly all are gem Proofs approaching perfection.

	Cert	Avg	%MS	PF-65	PF-69DC
2015-S, Mohawk Ironworkers, Proof	4,048	69.4		$8	$15

2015-W Native American Dollar

2015-W, Mohawk Ironworkers, Enhanced Uncirculated • Mintage: 88,805.

Availability: These coins are easily available in superb gem preservation, as made.

Notes: The 2015-W dollar was made available only in Enhanced Uncirculated form as part of the 2015 American $1 Coin and Currency Set. This set also included a Series 2013 Federal Reserve Bank of New York $1 note with a serial number starting with 911, in memory of the 9/11 World Trade Center disaster. The sets were priced at $14.95 each and went on sale on August 24, 2015. The production was limited to 90,000 sets with an initial household limit of five sets. The sets were packaged at the San Francisco Mint.

On August 25 the Mint announced that sales for the first day amounted to 44,344 sets. By the end of the second day the total was up to 48,272. Some collectors, probably in the distinct minority, experienced difficulties and delays in accessing the Mint's website and sent letters of complaint to *Coin World.* Unsold sets remained on hand. At noon Eastern Standard Time on Monday, December 1, the limit of sets that could be sent to any given household was raised to 100, then not long afterward the household limit was lifted completely, but with a limit of 1,500 sets per day to any address. As of the sales report on the morning of December 4 the Mint had sold 77,416 sets. On the evening of December 5 at about 10:30 the Mint website posted a "no longer available" notice.

Q. David Bowers remarks: "Little publicity was given to the fact—the seemingly superb selling point—that these were the only collectible twenty-first-century coins struck at the West Point Mint." The coins are very similar to a Reverse Proof but with the portrait and other features not quite as deeply polished. The three-panel fold-out holder for the coin and note includes a printed "Certificate of Authenticity."

The combination of the unique W mintmark and the relatively low price for a limited-issue dollar has made these exceptionally popular.

Edge style: In contrast with earlier *Uncirculated finish* issues of "golden dollars" (Sacagawea and Presidential), which were struck with plain edges and later had the edge lettering with random orientation added by another machine, the 2015-W coins had the lettering applied by a three-part segmented collar at the same time they were struck. As a result all 2015-W coins have the edge lettering oriented vertically in relation to the obverse, as do Proofs from the San Francisco Mint.

	Cert	Avg	%MS	MS-64	MS-65	MS-66
2015-W, Mohawk Ironworkers, Enhanced Uncirculated	4,381	69.5	100%		$22	$32

2016-P Native American Dollar

2016-P, Code Talkers •

Mintage: 2,800,000.

Availability: These coins are readily available, and of gem Mint State quality.

Reverse designer: Thomas D. Rogers Sr.

Notes: The 2016 Native American $1 coin commemorates the Code Talkers from both World War I and World War II (1917–1945). The reverse design features two helmets with the inscriptions "WWI" and "WWII," and two feathers that form a "V," symbolizing victory, unity, and the important role that these Native Americans played.

The Mint's literature described the significance of the Code Talkers: "It is estimated that more than 12,000 Native Americans served in the U.S. military during World War I. In World War II, more than 44,000 Native Americans, out of a total Native American population of less than 350,000, served with distinction in both the European and Pacific theaters. Hundreds played a vital communications role in both world wars. This select group of Native Americans was asked to develop and use secret battle codes using their native languages to communicate troop movements and enemy positions. Their efforts saved many lives because America's enemies were unable to decode their messages."

The Code Talkers reverse was designed by Thomas D. Rogers Sr., retired Mint sculptor-engraver (who had developed the Flying Eagle reverse design of the 2000–2008 Sacagawea dollar). It was sculpted by Mint Medallic Artist Renata Gordon.

	Cert	Avg	%MS	MS-64	MS-65	MS-66
2016-P, Code Talkers	110	65.6	100%	$3	$5	$12

2016-D Native American Dollar

2016-D, Code Talkers • **Mintage:** 2,100,000.

Commentary: The Denver issue of Code Talkers dollars is readily available, with most coins being of gem Mint quality.

Notes: "Native languages came to play an increasingly vital role in the U.S. war effort in both World War I and II," noted the Mint's literature describing these coins. "Several tribes provided Native American speakers for telephone squads on the French battlefields in World War I. Additional tribes sent soldiers to join the Code Talkers of World War II, serving in North Africa, Italy, France, and the Pacific. The languages used by American Indians greatly assisted their fellow American soldiers in the heat of battle by transmitting messages in unbreakable battle codes. The Navajo Code Talkers from the World War II Pacific Theater were the most famous group, numbering approximately 420 by the end of the war."

	Cert	Avg	%MS	MS-64	MS-65	MS-66
2016-D, Code Talkers	249	66.4	100%	$3	$5	$12

2016-S Native American Dollar

2016-S, Code Talkers, Enhanced Uncirculated • **Mintage:** 50,737 (estimated).

Availability: These are available, though among the lower-mintage of the Enhanced Uncirculated dollars; practically all of the coins are of the Mint's usual high quality.

	Cert	Avg	%MS	MS-64	MS-65	MS-66
2016-S, Code Talkers, Enhanced Uncirculated	796	69.6	100%		$25	$35

2016-S, Code Talkers, Proof •

Mintage: 931,866.

Availability: Proofs of the Code Talker dollars are easy to find in the numismatic market, and are of the consistently high quality that collectors expect from the United States Mint.

	Cert	Avg	%MS	PF-65	PF-69DC
2016-S, Code Talkers, Proof	1,326	69.5		$8	$15

2017-P Native American Dollar

2017-P, Sequoyah •
Mintage: 1,820,000.

Availability: These dollars are readily available to meet collector demand. Nearly all are in gem Mint State.

Notes: The 2017 Native American dollar coin commemorates Sequoyah, inventor of the Cherokee Syllabary. He adapted writing, previously unknown to

Reverse designer: Chris Costello.

the Cherokee language, by devising symbols for each syllable. The Mint, in its unveiling of the new coin design, noted that Sequoyah's achievement was one of a handful of examples in world history of the development of an original writing system. "After 12 years of work, Sequoyah unveiled the alphabet in a demonstration with his daughter Ah-yo-ka. News spread quickly and Cherokees flocked to learn the system. In 1821, the Cherokee Nation adopted it as its own. Within months, thousands of Cherokee became literate."

The Sequoyah dollar reverse was designed by Artistic Infusion Program artist Chris Costello, and engraved for coinage by Charles Vickers.

	Cert	Avg	%MS	MS-64	MS-65	MS-66
2017-P, Sequoyah	221	66.8	100%	$3	$5	$8

2017-D Native American Dollar

2017-D, Sequoyah • **Mintage:** 1,540,000.

Availability: These dollars are readily available to meet collector demand. Nearly all are in gem Mint State.

Notes: The Mint described how the Cherokee Syllabary gave birth to Native American journalism: "The first American Indian newspaper, the *Cherokee Phoenix*, included editorials which embodied the Cherokees' determination to retain their lands, news on activities of the Cherokee government, as well as relations with the federal and state governments. This written language helped create a dialogue between Cherokee Nation and the United States Government, and assisted in the preservation of interests, hopes and struggles of individuals during a unique time in our history."

	Cert	Avg	%MS	MS-64	MS-65	MS-66
2017-D, Sequoyah	310	67.0	100%	$3	$5	$8

2017-S Native American Dollar

2017-S, Sequoyah, Enhanced Uncirculated • **Mintage:** 210,419.

Availability: These coins are readily available to meet collector demand. Nearly all are in gem condition.

				MS-64	MS-65	MS-66
2017-S, Sequoyah, Enhanced Uncirculated	0	n/a			$10	$15

2017-S, Sequoyah, Proof •

Mintage: 926,774.

Availability: Proof Sequoyah dollars are readily available in the numismatic marketplace, and in the Mint's usual sterling high quality.

	Cert	Avg	%MS	PF-65	PF-69DC
2017-S, Sequoyah, Proof	999	69.6		$8	$15

2018-P Native American Dollar

2018-P, Jim Thorpe •

Mintage: 1,400,000.

Availability: Jim Thorpe dollars are readily available to meet collector demand. Nearly all are in gem Mint State.

Notes: James Francis "Jim" Thorpe (1888–1953) was born near Prague, Oklahoma, in what at the time was Indian Territory. He was raised in the Sac and Fox tribe and given the native name Wa-Tho-Huk, meaning "Bright Path."

Reverse designer: Michael Gaudioso.

"Jim Thorpe became possibly the most versatile natural athlete of the early twentieth century," the Mint said in its descriptive narrative of the coin. "After a difficult youth, running away from school after several family crises, Thorpe came into his own at the Carlisle Indian Industrial School in Carlisle, Pennsylvania. Although the residential Indian school had a mixed reputation, Carlisle then had the services of one of the great early football coaches, Glenn Scobey 'Pop' Warner, and it fielded a national championship football team, led by Thorpe. At the time Thorpe was the core of the school's track and field team, also coached by Warner, and the story is that Warner was reluctant to let his track star run the risk of playing football.

Thorpe was named to the All-American first team in 1911 and 1912. In 1911, Carlisle upset Harvard 18-15, as Thorpe scored all its points, four field goals and a touchdown. In 1912, Carlisle won the national collegiate championship. It beat Army 27-6; a cadet named Dwight D. Eisenhower injured his knee trying to tackle Thorpe."

Michael Gaudioso, a medallic artist on the Mint staff in Philadelphia, designed the Jim Thorpe dollar's reverse and engraved it for coinage.

	Cert	Avg	%MS	MS-64	MS-65	MS-66
2018-P, Jim Thorpe	200	66.9	100%	$3	$5	$10

2018-D Native American Dollar

2018-D, Jim Thorpe • **Mintage:** 1,400,000.

Availability: These dollars are readily available to meet collector demand. Nearly all are in gem Mint State.

Notes: In 1912 Jim Thorpe represented the United States at the Summer Olympics in Stockholm, Sweden, competing in the new pentathlon and decathlon as well as two field events. "He easily won both multi-event medals, finishing first in eight of the combined 15 events," the Mint reported in its description of the 2018 Jim Thorpe dollar. "His point record stood for two decades. In an often-told story,

King Gustav V of Sweden, presenting Thorpe a special decathlon award, told him, 'You are the greatest athlete in the world,' and Thorpe replied, 'Thanks, King.'

Thorpe then embarked on an incredibly varied career with the public flocking to his professional appearances in football, baseball, and basketball. He played for six teams in what later became the National Football League. In 1922, he became the first president of the American Professional Football Association, precursor of the NFL. In baseball, he played for the New York Giants, the Cincinnati Reds, and the Boston Braves. He also organized an all-Indian football team, reuniting some Carlisle players. Today, sports writers rank him at the top of their lists of greatest athletes of the twentieth century."

	Cert	Avg	%MS	MS-64	MS-65	MS-66
2018-D, Jim Thorpe	293	66.8	100%	$3	$5	$10

2018-S Native American Dollar

2018-S, Jim Thorpe, Proof •

Mintage: 799,413.

Availability: Proof Jim Thorpe dollars are easily available in today's market, and in beautiful high quality.

	Cert	Avg	%MS	PF-65	PF-69DC
2018-S, Jim Thorpe, Proof	1,694	69.6		$8	$15

2018-S Native American Dollar

2018-S, Jim Thorpe, Reverse Proof •

Mintage: 199,116.

Availability: To mark the 50th anniversary of the San Francisco Mint's first production of Proof coins, the Mint released a special Reverse Proof set, which included a 2018-S Jim Thorpe dollar. The complete sets in their original government packaging are readily available for around $80 to $100. Beautiful, pristine Reverse Proof dollars are easy to find separately, both graded and ungraded.

	Cert	Avg	%MS	PF-65	PF-69DC
2018-S, Jim Thorpe, Reverse Proof	0	n/a		$25	$30

2019-P Native American Dollar

2019-P, American Indians in Space •

Mintage: 1,400,000 (estimated).

Availability: These dollars are readily available to meet collector demand. Nearly all are in gem Mint State.

Notes: The theme of the 2019 Native American $1 Coin design is American Indians in the Space Program. "Native Americans have been on the modern frontier of space flight since the beginning of NASA," the Mint observed. "Their contributions to the U.S. space program culminated in the space walks of John Herrington (Chickasaw Nation) on the International

Reverse designer: Emily Damstra.

Space Station in 2002. This and other pioneering achievements date back to the work of Mary Golda Ross (Cherokee Nation). Considered the first Native American engineer in the U.S. space program, Ross helped develop the Agena spacecraft for the Gemini and Apollo space programs."

The reverse of the American Indians in Space dollar was designed by Artistic Infusion Program artist Emily Damstra, and sculpted by Joseph Menna, who was named chief engraver of the U.S. Mint the year it was issued.

	Cert	Avg	%MS	MS-64	MS-65	MS-66
2019-P, American Indians in Space	249	66.6	100%	$3	$5	$10

2019-D Native American Dollar

2019-D, American Indians in Space • **Mintage:** 1,540,000 (estimated).

Availability: The Denver coinage of American Indians in Space dollars is readily available for today's collectors. Nearly all are in gem Mint State.

	Cert	Avg	%MS	MS-64	MS-65	MS-66
2019-D, American Indians in Space	1,535	67.5	100%	$3	$5	$10

2019-S Native American Dollar

2019-S, American Indians in Space, Proof • **Mintage:** 1,091,213 (estimated).

Availability: These Proof dollars are easy to obtain, even in the finest of quality.

	Cert	Avg	%MS	PF-65	PF-69DC
2019-S, American Indians in Space, Proof	7,803	69.9		$8	$15

2020-P Native American Dollar

2020-P, Elizabeth Peratrovich and Alaska's Anti-Discrimination Law • **Mintage:** To be determined.

Availability: These dollars are readily available for today's collectors. Nearly all are in gem Mint State.

Reverse designer: Phebe Hemphill.

Notes: The focus of the 2020 Native American $1 dollar is Elizabeth Peratrovich and Alaska's Anti-Discrimination Law. The coin's reverse was designed and engraved by Mint Medallic Sculptor Phebe Hemphill.

Alaska's territorial government in 1945 passed the first anti-discrimination law in the United States, prohibiting discrimination in access to public accommodations. Elizabeth Peratrovich (Tlingit nation) advocated for Alaskan Natives with her husband Roy, giving an impassioned speech in the Alaskan Senate in support of the legislation. Her efforts are widely credited with getting the law passed.

On January 22, 2020, Alaska's state legislature passed a joint resolution requesting that the Peratrovich dollar coins be made available at face value to financial institutions in the state. (Normally the Mint sells the coins to collectors in rolls and bags at a premium of 15 to 40 percent over face value, plus shipping.) To accommodate this request, the United States Mint designed a special program to sell the coins to Alaskan banks for $1 each plus shipping costs. The program started that summer, with banks able to order the coins in rolls of 25, bags of 100, and boxes of 250, with a minimum order of 1,000 coins. "This special program does not replace or circumvent financial institutions' normal Federal Reserve order process," the Mint noted, and "Financial institutions will be responsible for shipping costs."

	Cert	Avg	%MS	MS-64	MS-65	MS-66
2020-P, Elizabeth Peratrovich and Alaska's Anti-Discrimination Law	105	66.4	100%	$3	$5	$10

2020-D Native American Dollar

2020-D, Elizabeth Peratrovich and Alaska's Anti-Discrimination Law • Mintage: To be determined.

Availability: The Denver-minted Elizabeth Peratrovich coins are readily available to collectors. Nearly all are in gem Mint State.

Notes: The year of this coin's issue, 2020, marked the 75th anniversary of Elizabeth Peratrovich's famous testimony in support of the nation's first anti-discrimination law.

Alaska State Legislature House Joint Resolution 9, sponsored by state representative DeLena Johnson (R–Palmer), originally requested not fewer than 5 million of the coins be made available at face value to Alaska banks, to promote their circulation. The Alaska Native Sisterhood, state 4-H groups, the Peratrovich family, and other supporters presented the idea as a way to promote the history and culture embodied in the dollar coins. The resolution enjoyed widespread and bipartisan support. The Mint developed a Bulk Purchase program that waived the normal premiums charged for the coins, making them available to Alaskan banks (in 1,000-coin minimum orders) at face value plus transportation costs.

	Cert	Avg	%MS	MS-64	MS-65	MS-66
2020-D, Elizabeth Peratrovich and Alaska's Anti-Discrimination Law	118	67.0	100%	$3	$5	$10

2020-S Native American Dollar

2020-S, Elizabeth Peratrovich and Alaska's Anti-Discrimination Law, Proof • Mintage: To be determined.

Availability: These Proof coins are readily available in the numismatic marketplace, in superb condition.

	Cert	Avg	%MS	PF-65	PF-69DC
2020-S, Elizabeth Peratrovich and Alaska's Anti-Discrimination Law, Proof	3,917	69.8		$8	$15

2021-P Native American Dollar

2021-P, American Indians in the U.S. Military, Proof •

Mintage: To be determined.

Availability: These coins are readily available in numismatic channels.

Notes: The theme of the 2021 Native American dollar is Native Americans in the United States military.

Reverse designer: Donna Weaver.

Native Americans have served in the nation's armed forces in every military conflict beginning with the Revolutionary War. The Mint, in its literature describing the 2021 dollar, noted that "They have served at a higher rate in proportion to their population than any other ethnic group. During World War I, Native Americans volunteered to fight in astonishing numbers although most were ineligible for the draft."

Donna Weaver, an artist in the Mint's Artistic Infusion Program, designed the reverse of this dollar, and it was sculpted for coinage by Chief Engraver Joseph Menna.

	Cert	Avg	%MS	MS-64	MS-65	MS-66
2021-P, American Indians in the U.S. Military				$3	$5	$10

2021-D Native American Dollar

2021-D, American Indians in the U.S. Military • **Mintage:** To be determined.

Availability: The Denver-minted dollar coins are easy to find, and in gem condition.

Notes: The Mint observed of Native American volunteering during World War I: "Of the 10,000 Native Americans who served in the Army and the 2,000 who served in the Navy, three out of four were volunteers. Native Americans have received recognition for their service, including five Medals of Honor during World War II. Their exemplary record of military service continues to this day."

	Cert	Avg	%MS	MS-64	MS-65	MS-66
2021-D, American Indians in the U.S. Military				$3	$5	$10

2021-S Native American Dollar

2021-S, American Indians in the U.S. Military, Proof •

Mintage: To be determined.

Availability: These Proof coins are readily acquirable in high states of preservation.

	Cert	Avg	%MS	PF-65	PF-69DC
2021-S, American Indians in the U.S. Military, Proof				$8	$15

AMERICAN INNOVATION DOLLARS (2018–2032)

Designers: *Justin Kunz (obverse); see image captions for reverse designers.*
Weight: *8.1 grams.* **Composition:** *Pure copper core with outer layers of manganese brass (.770 copper, .120 zinc, .070 manganese, and .040 nickel).*
Diameter: *26.5 mm.* **Edge:** *Lettered.* **Mints:** *Philadelphia, Denver, and San Francisco.*

Circulation Strike

Mintmark location is on the rim, along with other inscriptions.

Proof

BACKGROUND

In 2018, the United States Mint issued the first coin in a new, 15-year series: the American Innovation $1 Coin Program. Authorized by Public Law 115-197, each of the golden dollars in the program features a reverse design that "symbolizes quintessentially American traits—the willingness to explore, to discover, and to create one's own destiny." Four new designs, in various formats including regular circulation-quality strikes as well as Proofs, are being issued each year from 2019 through 2032—one for each state, in the order in which the states ratified the Constitution or were admitted to the Union, and then for the District of Columbia and each of the five U.S. territories (Puerto Rico, Guam, American Samoa, the U.S. Virgin Islands, and the Northern Mariana Islands). Like all dollar coins minted after 2011, they are issued for numismatic sales only; none are distributed for circulation through the Federal Reserve and normal banking channels.

Design concepts that showcase "an innovation, innovator or group of innovators from each State or Territory" are submitted to the Mint by official state/territorial liaisons. The secretary of the Treasury selects the concepts deemed most appropriate for dollar coin designs, and the Mint—working in concert with its artists, the state liaisons, the U.S. Commission of Fine Arts (CFA), the Citizens Coinage Advisory Committee (CCAC), and technical and historical consultants (as needed)—produces the final design candidates. The Treasury secretary makes the final selection from the resulting designs.

Coins in the series bear the following required inscriptions: on the obverse, IN GOD WE TRUST and the denomination; on the reverse, the name of the state, the District of Columbia, or territory (as appropriate), along with UNITED STATES OF AMERICA; and incused into the edge, the date, the mintmark, and the inscription E PLURIBUS UNUM. The common obverse depicts a left-facing profile of the Statue of Liberty, as designed by Justin Kunz and sculpted by Phebe Hemphill. Each year's designs share an obverse privy mark unique to that year (except 2018, which had no privy mark).

While each issue from 2019 through 2032 represents an individual state, district, or territory, the 2018 inaugural issue (designed by Donna Weaver and sculpted by Renata Gordon) represents the program in general.

Mint Director David Ryder, at the program's ceremonial launch in Washington in December 2018, expressed his belief that the symbols of innovation chosen by the states and territories will have unifying and educational value. "The very nature of this program," he said, "provides an opportunity for us to become better connected with each other by learning more about this vast land that we call home."

THE CITIZENS COINAGE ADVISORY COMMITTEE

One of the two groups that formally advises the secretary of the Treasury on coin designs is the congressionally created Citizens Coinage Advisory Committee. The CCAC met on July 31, 2018, to review and discuss design candidates for the program's first year. There was a sense of urgency; this was just 11 days after the bill authorizing the coins was signed into law, and the first coin was scheduled for production and distribution before year's end. The Committee's minutes reflect the members' frustration with the rushed timeline:

> An animated discussion of the reverse designs followed, with the Committee members universally expressing dissatisfaction with the options presented.
>
> Mike Moran noted that the Committee was presented with only a single obverse for the next 15 years of the program and that was unacceptable, although the design itself [based on the common reverse of the Presidential dollar series] had been created by Don Everhart, retired Lead Sculptor-Engraver for the US Mint in Philadelphia. The single design underscored the short time frame allowed to strike the 2018 coin, which would then carry through the series.

The CCAC passed a unanimous motion to decline to discuss the presented reverse designs "due to quality of design and the pressures from a tight deadline."

A few weeks later, on September 27, the CCAC met again and was presented by the Mint with a new portfolio of multiple design candidates for the obverse, and a new set of design candidates for the reverse. After robust discussion, the Committee recommended Justin Kunz's obverse motif, praising it as "a bold design." The meeting minutes noted: "The negative space surrounding Liberty will make a distinctive and easily identifiable obverse. This design received 18 of 30 possible votes, and was also the preference of the Commission of Fine Arts." The reverse design recommended by the CCAC for the 2018 coin was the one ultimately chosen by the Treasury secretary.

In later meetings the Committee wrestled with the best approach for the new coinage series—whether it should focus on tangible, patentable innovations (e.g., scientific, medical, technological, and industrial inventions), or whether it should take a broader approach and include artistic, cultural, social, and other, not necessarily physical, innovations. So far the program's coins, as chosen by the secretaries of the Treasury, have included a mix of both.

JUSTIN KUNZ, OBVERSE DESIGNER

The Statue of Liberty motif on the obverse was designed by Utah-based Justin Kunz, an artist in the Artistic Infusion Program. The Mint's biography of Kunz describes him as a painter, concept artist, illustrator, and teacher. His Master of Fine Arts in Painting is from Laguna College of Art and Design (2011) and his BFA in Illustration is from Brigham Young University (1999). Currently an assistant professor in the Department of Visual Arts at Brigham Young, he worked for more than 11 years in game-development studios including Disney Interactive and Blizzard Entertainment, helping design environments in *World of Warcraft* expansions from *The Burning Crusade* to *Mists of Pandaria*.

Clients for Kunz's art also include LEGO, ATeam, Upper Deck, Novell, Brigham Young University, the Church of Jesus Christ of Latter-day Saints, and private collectors. His traditional paintings are included in exhibitions throughout the United States.

AMERICAN INNOVATION DOLLARS (2018–2032): GUIDE TO COLLECTING

BEING A SMART BUYER

Most examples of these coins are very well struck. Check the higher points of the design for sharpness.

AVAILABILITY

American Innovation dollars are common in high grades, and are collected in Mint State and Proof (including the Reverse Proof format). All are readily available in the marketplace. The coins can be purchased directly from the Mint in rolls and bags, for a premium over face value, plus shipping. They are also packaged in the Mint's annual collector sets.

AMERICAN INNOVATION (2018–2032)

GRADING STANDARDS

MS-60 to 70 (Mint State). *Obverse:* At MS-60, some abrasion and contact marks are evident, most noticeably on Liberty's cheek and in the wide, empty field. Luster is present but may be dull or lifeless. At MS-63, contact marks are extensive but not distracting. Abrasion still is evident, but less than at lower levels. MS-64 coins are slightly finer. An MS-65 coin may have minor abrasion, but contact marks are so minute as to require magnification. Luster should be full and rich. *Reverse:* At MS-60, some abrasion and contact marks are evident. Otherwise, the same comments apply as for the obverse.

American Innovation dollars are seldom collected in grades lower than MS-60.

PF-60 to 70 (Proof). *Obverse and Reverse:* With medium hairlines and good reflectivity, assigned grades of PF-63 or 64 are appropriate. With relatively few hairlines a rating of PF-65 can be given. PF-66 may have hairlines so delicate that magnification is needed to see them. Above that, all the way to PF-70, a Proof should be free of any hairlines or other problems under strong magnification.

Note: The listings that follow show an example of a representative circulation strike coin, a Proof strike coin, and where appropriate, a Reverse Proof strike coin for all the American Innovation dollars, as the only difference between Philadelphia and Denver strikes appears on the rim.

2018 American Innovation Dollar

2018-P, American Innovators •
Mintage: 750,875 (estimated).

Notes: The Mint opened sales of the new 2018 American Innovation dollar coins on December 14. Products offered included rolls of 25 coins (at $32.95 plus shipping), 100-coin bags (at $111.95 plus shipping), and Proof formats.

No Privy Mark
Reverse designer: Donna Weaver.

The reverse of the 2018 "introductory coin" (as the Mint termed it) features a representation of George Washington's signature on the first-ever U.S. patent, which was issued July 31, 1790, and the inscription AMERICAN INNOVATORS. The stylized gears represent industry and innovation. "The gears remind me of how the many contributions, thoughts, and ideas of Americans continuously mesh together to propel our nation forward," Director Ryder said at the program's launch ceremony in December 2018. On a cartouche at the right, an eagle crouches on an angled shield, its wings spread behind it, with tools representing innovation (hammer, plow, wheel, etc.) below it.

The inaugural reverse design of the series was created by Artistic Infusion Program member Donna Weaver and engraved by Mint Medallic Sculptor Renata Gordon.

	Cert	Avg	%MS	MS-64	MS-65	MS-66
2018-P, American Innovators	712	66.0	100%	$3	$8	$12

2018-D, American Innovators • **Mintage:** 724,475 (estimated).

Notes: The 2018 American Innovation dollar coins were officially presented to the public on December 14, in a ceremonial ribbon-cutting with Mint Director David Ryder and Marc Landry, acting associate director of the Mint's Numismatic and Bullion Directorate. Following the ceremony (held at the Mint Store on 9th Street in Washington, D.C.), products containing the introductory coin were available for purchase. Ryder autographed packaging, certificates of authenticity, and other Mint items.

The mintage level for the year's Denver coins nearly rivaled that of Philadelphia.

	Cert	Avg	%MS	MS-64	MS-65	MS-66
2018-D, American Innovators	1,052	66.5	100%	$3	$8	$12

2018-S, American Innovators, Proof •

Mintage: 224,553 (estimated).

Notes: The San Francisco Mint so far has been the source of Proof coinage for the American Innovation dollar series. Each Proof coin is packaged along with a certificate of authenticity. "Like all Proof coins, it has sharp relief with a mirror-like background," the Mint noted. The original issue price was $6.95.

	Cert	Avg	%MS	PF-65	PF-69DC
2018-S, American Innovators, Proof	6,208	69.7		$12	$15

2018-S, American Innovators, Reverse Proof • **Mintage:** 74,720 (estimated).

Notes: Reverse Proofs were minted at San Francisco, as were the year's regular Proofs. So far the inaugural 2018 issue has had the highest Reverse Proof mintage.

	Cert	Avg	%MS	PF-65	PF-69DC
2018-S, American Innovators, Reverse Proof	9,956	70.0		$32	$38

2019 American Innovation Dollar

2019-P, Delaware: Classifying the Stars • **Mintage:** 410,300 (estimated).

Notes: Mint Artistic Infusion Program artist Donna Weaver designed Delaware's entry in the American Innovation dollar series, and Chief Engraver Joseph Menna sculpted it for coinage. The motif recognizes astronomer Annie Jump Cannon, born in Delaware in 1843. She developed a system for the classification of stars. Ms. Cannon is shown silhouetted against the night sky, with a constellation of stars visible.

Reverse designer: Donna Weaver.

Detail of the 2019 privy mark.

	Cert	Avg	%MS	MS-64	MS-65	MS-66
2019-P, Delaware: Classifying the Stars	236	65.6	100%	$3	$6	$10

2019-D, Delaware: Classifying the Stars • Mintage: 421,375 (estimated).

Notes: The United States Mint began accepting orders for rolls and bags of the Delaware coins starting September 19, 2019. They were the first of the year's four American Innovation dollars. The rolls and bags contained Uncirculated coins from the Mint facilities at Philadelphia and Denver. 25-coin rolls were priced at $32.95, and 100-coin bags at $111.95—all prices plus shipping.

	Cert	Avg	%MS	MS-64	MS-65	MS-66
2019-D, Delaware: Classifying the Stars	284	66.0	100%	$3	$6	$10

2019-S, Delaware: Classifying the Stars, Proof • Mintage: 114,414 (estimated).

Notes: The Mint conducted a sales-launch event for the 2019 American Innovation $1 Coin Proof Set on Friday, October 11, 2019, at the public tour entrance of the Philadelphia Mint, 151 North Independence Mall East. Mint Director David J. Ryder delivered remarks and signed certificates of authenticity. The four-coin Proof sets were issued at $20.95.

The Proof mintage of the first "regular" coinage of the series was about half that of 2018's introductory coin.

	Cert	Avg	%MS	PF-65	PF-69DC
2019-S, Delaware: Classifying the Stars, Proof	2,074	69.3		$12	$15

2019-S, Delaware: Classifying the Stars, Reverse Proof • Mintage: 62,257 (estimated).

Notes: The San Francisco Mint produced nearly half as many Reverse Proofs as regular Proofs for the Annie Jump Cannon dollar coin. "The coin has a frosted background, and a brilliant, mirror-like finish," the Mint's sales literature noted. "Its reverse (tails) design features a silhouette of Dover native Annie Jump Cannon against the night sky, with a number of stars visible in the sky."

The Mint capped production of the Reverse Proof coin at 75,000 units, and limited orders to five per household for the first 24 hours of sales (starting November 7, 2019). After 24 hours, the household order limit was rescinded.

	Cert	Avg	%MS	PF-65	PF-69DC
2019-S, Delaware: Classifying the Stars, Reverse Proof	3,170	69.8		$15	$20

2019-P, Pennsylvania: Polio
Vaccine • **Mintage:** 423,000 (estimated).

Notes: The 2019 American Innovations coin for Pennsylvania was designed by the Artistic Infusion Program's Richard Masters, and sculpted by Chief Engraver Joseph Menna. The coin shows a conception of the poliovirus at three different levels of magnification, along with the silhouette of a period microscope, representing the extensive research conducted to develop a cure for polio.

Reverse designer: Richard Masters.

The discovery of the polio vaccine changed the very experience of growing up and living in America. Before its invention, the nation was gripped with fear about the debilitating and deadly ravages of polio. The vaccine's discovery was hailed by the American Medical Association as "one of the greatest events in the history of medicine."

	Cert	Avg	%MS	MS-64	MS-65	MS-66
2019-P, Pennsylvania: Polio Vaccine	280	65.9	100%	$3	$6	$10

2019-D, Pennsylvania: Polio Vaccine • **Mintage:** 390,850 (estimated).

Notes: The Pennsylvania American Innovation dollar honors the discovery of the polio vaccine in 1953 by Dr. Jonas Salk and his team at the University of Pittsburgh School of Medicine.

Uncirculated Polio Vaccine dollars went on sale October 24, 2019, about two weeks after packaged Proof sets of all the year's American Innovation coins were launched. Rolls and bags were available with coins from the Philadelphia and Denver mints. The price of a 25-coin roll was $32.95, and for a 100-coin bag $111.95—all prices plus shipping.

	Cert	Avg	%MS	MS-64	MS-65	MS-66
2019-D, Pennsylvania: Polio Vaccine	457	65.9	100%	$3	$6	$10

2019-S, Pennsylvania: Polio
Vaccine, Proof • **Mintage:** 114,414 (estimated).

Notes: Sales of the 2019 American Innovation $1 Coin Proof Set started October 11, 2019, at 12 noon Eastern. In Washington, D.C., Philadelphia, and Denver, the sets were available over the counter at the United States Mint's sales centers. Issue price was $20.95 for the four Proof coins. They could also be purchased by phone (including a TTY-equipment–enabled ordering system for hearing- and speech-impaired customers) and online at usmint.gov.

	Cert	Avg	%MS	PF-65	PF-69DC
2019-S, Pennsylvania: Polio Vaccine, Proof	1,844	69.2		$12	$15

2019-S, Pennsylvania: Polio Vaccine, Reverse Proof •

Mintage: 46,461 (estimated).

Notes: For the Polio Vaccine dollar—the second in the regular program—Reverse Proofs were minted in less than half the quantity of Proofs. "An informational four-panel envelope houses the coin," the Mint's sales literature noted. "The Certificate of Authenticity is embedded in the packaging." The coins went on sale December 5, 2019, with mintage limited to 75,000.

	Cert	Avg	%MS	PF-65	PF-69DC
2019-S, Pennsylvania: Polio Vaccine, Reverse Proof	1,485	69.9		$15	$20

2019-P, New Jersey: Light Bulb •

Mintage: 436,200 (estimated).

Notes: Paul C. Balan, an artist with the Mint's Artistic Infusion Program, designed New Jersey's dollar coin in the American Innovation series. His vision was sculpted by Mint Sculptor-Engraver Phebe Hemphill. The design features an Edison light bulb against an ornate background.

Reverse designer: Paul C. Balan.

The invention of commercially manufactured electric light bulbs, as developed by Thomas Edison and his team of researchers in New Jersey, gave Americans easy control over light in their homes and businesses. This innovation dramatically changed the nation's infrastructure, business, and society by allowing work and social activities to proceed no matter the time of day.

	Cert	Avg	%MS	MS-64	MS-65	MS-66
2019-P, New Jersey: Light Bulb	321	65.7	100%	$3	$6	$10

2019-D, New Jersey: Light Bulb • **Mintage:** 400,900 (estimated).

Notes: New Jersey's Light Bulb dollar coin honors the development of a lightbulb with a filament that could last 1,200 hours. Rolls and bags of Uncirculated coins went on sale November 21, 2019, with the coins sold at a premium as numismatic collectibles (priced at $32.95 for a 25-coin roll, or $111.95 for a 100-coin bag, plus shipping). Collectors could choose Philadelphia or Denver coins in either quantity.

	Cert	Avg	%MS	MS-64	MS-65	MS-66
2019-D, New Jersey: Light Bulb	370	65.8	100%	$3	$6	$10

2019-S, New Jersey: Light Bulb, Proof • Mintage: 114,414 (estimated).

Notes: October 11, 2019, at 12 noon Eastern, was the official start of sales for the 2019 American Innovation $1 Coin Proof Set. If you lived in Washington, D.C., Philadelphia, or Denver (or were visiting any of those cities), you could purchase the set over the counter at the United States Mint's sales centers there. The set of four Proof coins sold for $20.95. It was also available at catalog.usmint.gov and by calling 1-800-USA-MINT (872-6468).

	Cert	Avg	%MS	PF-65	PF-69DC
2019-S, New Jersey: Light Bulb, Proof	1,911	69.3		$12	$15

2019-S, New Jersey: Light Bulb, Reverse Proof • Mintage: 41,883 (estimated).

Notes: Reverse Proof dollars of the Light Bulb type went on sale January 7, 2020, by phone, online, and at the Mint's sales centers in Washington, D.C., Denver, and Philadelphia. Production was limited to 75,000 coins, of which more than half have been purchased. The issue price was $11.50.

	Cert	Avg	%MS	PF-65	PF-69DC
2019-S, New Jersey: Light Bulb, Reverse Proof	1,414	69.7		$12	$20

2019-P, Georgia: Trustees' Garden • Mintage: 397,150 (estimated).

Notes: Emily Damstra was the Artistic Infusion Program artist who designed Georgia's entry in the American Innovation coinage program. Her dollar recognizes the Trustees' Garden, established in the 1730s by James Oglethorpe. This was the first agricultural experimental garden in America. The design shows

Reverse designer: Emily Damstra.

a hand planting seeds in the U of the words TRUSTEES' GARDEN, with a variety of plant species seen in growth—an orange seedling, sassafras, grapes, white mulberry, flax, peaches, olive, and a young shoot.

The Trustees' Garden, a 10-acre plot of land in Savannah, reflected the scientific and commercial aspirations of Georgia's trustees and their backers in England. The trustees hoped to grow grapes for wine production and mulberry trees to feed silk worms essential for silk production. They also imported plants from around the world to determine the best crops for the Georgia climate.

	Cert	Avg	%MS	MS-64	MS-65	MS-66
2019-P, Georgia: Trustees' Garden	229	66.1	100%	$3	$6	$10

2019-D, Georgia: Trustees' Garden • Mintage: 371,225 (estimated).

Notes: Georgia's trustees at first believed their New World climate to be subtropical, and botanists attempted to grow such plants as flax, hemp, indigo, olives, capers, and oranges. Temperature fluctuations, however, caused many plants to fail. The experimental garden did enjoy two notable successes: the peach tree and the cotton plant.

The Mint began accepting orders for Georgia's Trustees' Garden dollars on December 19, 2019. Collectors could order coins from the Philadelphia Mint and the Denver Mint, at a premium price of $32.95 for a 25-coin roll, or $111.95 for a 100-coin bag (plus shipping).

	Cert	Avg	%MS	MS-64	MS-65	MS-66
2019-D, Georgia: Trustees' Garden	548	66.1	100%	$3	$6	$10

2019-S, Georgia: Trustees' Garden, Proof • Mintage: 114,414 (estimated).

Notes: It was from Georgia's Trustees' Garden that cotton was spread throughout the colony and across the South. Peach trees were also distributed from the garden, and today, nearly 300 years later, the peach remains Georgia's signature crop.

The San Francisco Mint was the source of Proof coins for the Georgia Trustees' Garden dollars.

On October 11, 2019, at the Philadelphia Mint, United States Mint Director David J. Ryder delivered remarks and sold the year's ceremonial first American Innovation $1 Coin Proof Set, which included the Trustees' Garden dollar. Philadelphia Mint Superintendent Robert Kurzyna began the event by welcoming the assembled guests and speaking about the Mint's rich history in Philadelphia. Director Ryder thanked the Mint employees whose combined efforts brought the coin set to market and stated that in producing it "the men and women of the United States Mint demonstrated the commitment to service, quality, and integrity that they apply to every coin and medal we produce." The Proof set of four coins sold for $20.95.

	Cert	Avg	%MS	PF-65	PF-69DC
2019-S, Georgia: Trustees' Garden, Proof	2,005	69.4		$12	$15

2019-S, Georgia: Trustees' Garden, Reverse Proof • Mintage: 38,363 (estimated).

Notes: A quantity of a little more than half of the Reverse Proof's mintage limit (of 75,000 coins) has so far been sold—about one-third the production of regular Proofs for the Trustees' Garden coin, which was the last in the series for 2019. Sales started February 11, 2020, at $11.50 per coin.

	Cert	Avg	%MS	PF-65	PF-69DC
2019-S, Georgia: Trustees' Garden, Reverse Proof	1,118	69.8		$12	$20

2020 American Innovation Dollar

2020-P, Connecticut: Gerber
Variable Scale • **Mintage:** To be determined.

Notes: The United States Mint officially announced the designs for the 2020 American Innovation dollar coins on June 30, 2020. Chief Engraver Joseph Menna designed and sculpted the Maryland coin; Artistic Infusion Program artists created the designs of the year's other coins (including the first released, that of Connecticut), which were sculpted by the Mint's medallic artists.

Reverse designer: Richard Masters.

Detail of the 2020 privy mark.

Connecticut's dollar was designed by Richard Masters and sculpted by Renata Gordon. It recognizes the significance of the Gerber Variable Scale, showing the innovative device being used to increase a geometric shape (resembling the state of Connecticut) by 200 percent. Before the invention of the graphing calculator, scientists needed a clear, quick, and simple solution to understand and solve problems of scale. The invention of the Gerber Variable Scale was that solution.

Orders for the Gerber Variable Scale coins started on September 29, 2020, with the Mint announcing, "To reduce the risk of employee exposure to COVID-19 in the workplace, the Mint's sales centers are closed until further notice. Additionally, due to operational adjustments in response to COVID-19, our customer service representatives are available to assist with any questions you may have, but are unable to accept credit card information or place your order over the phone. Please use our website for all order placements at this time."

	Cert	Avg	%MS	MS-64	MS-65	MS-66
2020-P, Connecticut: Gerber Variable Scale	63	65.7	100%	$3	$6	$10

2020-D, Connecticut: Gerber Variable Scale • **Mintage:** To be determined.

Notes: The subject of Connecticut's American Innovation dollar, the Gerber Variable Scale, has been called the most revolutionary engineering tool since the slide rule.

The Mint's literature describes it: "Heinz Joseph Gerber (1924–1996) invented the device while studying aeronautical engineering at Rensselaer Polytechnic Institute in 1945, a few years after escaping Nazi-controlled Austria with his mother. The earliest version of the variable scale had been fashioned from an elastic band removed from a pair of pajamas. Gerber created a rubber rule and scale that could flow with a curve, expand, contract, and turn a corner. It allowed for the direct numerical reading of curves, graphs, and graphical representations."

The Mint opened sales for the Gerber Variable Scale coins in collectible rolls and bags on September 29, 2020. Uncirculated coins from the Philadelphia and Denver mints were available, priced slightly higher than the previous year—$34.50 for a 25-coin roll, or $117.50 for a 100-coin bag, plus shipping.

	Cert	Avg	%MS	MS-64	MS-65	MS-66
2020-D, Connecticut: Gerber Variable Scale	73	66.0	100%	$3	$6	$10

2020-S, Connecticut: Gerber Variable Scale, Proof •

Mintage: To be determined.

Notes: This coin's "American Innovation," the Gerber Variable Scale, was a huge success because of its ease of use and quick solutions. By the 1950s it was considered the universally accepted tool for engineers and architects all over the world.

Sales of the Proof Gerber Variable Scale dollar started on October 8, 2020, in a four-coin set priced at $24 (for one of each design for the year). This was a price increase of $3.05 over the 2019 Proof set. The Proof set was available only online; the Mint's sales centers were closed to reduce the risk of the ongoing COVID-19 pandemic in the workplace.

	Cert	Avg	%MS	PF-65	PF-69DC
2020-S, Connecticut: Gerber Variable Scale, Proof	0	n/a		$12	$15

2020-S, Connecticut: Gerber Variable Scale, Reverse Proof •

Mintage: To be determined.

Notes: The Mint began accepting orders for the Gerber Variable Scale Reverse Proof dollars on July 21, 2020. The coins were produced at the San Francisco Mint with a frosted background and a brilliant, mirror-like finish. They were offered only online. Due to the impact of the COVID-19 pandemic, the Mint's sales centers were closed. Mintage was limited to 50,000 coins, with household orders capped at five coins for the first 24 hours of sales. The issue price was $11.50.

	Cert	Avg	%MS	PF-65	PF-69DC
2020-S, Connecticut: Gerber Variable Scale, Reverse Proof	955	69.6		$15	$20

2020-P, Massachusetts: Telephone •

Mintage: To be determined.

Notes: The Massachusetts dollar for the American Innovation program was designed by Emily Damstra and engraved for coinage by Eric David Custer. It features the dial of an early rotary telephone.

Reverse designer: Emily Damstra.

The first patent for an "apparatus for transmitting vocal or other sounds telegraphically" was issued to scientist, inventor, and innovator Alexander Graham Bell on March 7, 1876. He called his device the "tele-phone." Bell and his assistant, Thomas Watson, made the first successfully transmitted message three days after his patent was issued. With the receiver pressed to his ear, Watson heard Bell's message: "Mr. Watson, come here, I want to see you."

	Cert	Avg	%MS	MS-64	MS-65	MS-66
2020-P, Massachusetts: Telephone	0	n/a		$3	$6	$10

2020-D, Massachusetts: Telephone • **Mintage:** To be determined.

Notes: Alexander Graham Bell's large box telephone was one of two he used in a demonstration conducted between Boston and Salem, Massachusetts, on November 26, 1876. The Mint described Bell's invention: "It featured an iron diaphragm, two electromagnets, and a horseshoe permanent magnet. When used as a transmitter, sound waves at the mouthpiece caused the diaphragm to move, inducing a fluctuating current in the electromagnets. This current was conducted over wires to a similar instrument acting as a receiver. There, the fluctuating current in the electromagnets caused the diaphragm to move, producing air vibrations that could be heard."

The Mint started accepting orders for rolls and bags of Uncirculated Telephone dollars on October 29, 2020. Issue prices were increased slightly over those of 2019: a 25-coin roll cost $34.50, and a 100-coin bag $117.50. Collectors could choose between coins from the Philadelphia Mint or the Denver Mint.

	Cert	Avg	%MS	MS-64	MS-65	MS-66
2020-D, Massachusetts: Telephone	0	n/a		$3	$6	$10

2020-S, Massachusetts: Telephone, Proof • **Mintage:** To be determined.

Notes: The Telephone dollar Proofs went on sale October 8, 2020, as part of the four-coin Proof set of dollars priced at $24 (an increase over the previous year's $20.95). The Mint limited ordering to online sales, announcing, "To reduce the risk of employee exposure to COVID-19 in the workplace, the Mint's sales centers are closed until further notice. Additionally, due to operational adjustments in response to COVID-19, our customer service representatives are available to assist with any questions you may have, but are unable to accept credit card information or place your order over the phone. Please use our website for all order placements at this time."

	Cert	Avg	%MS	PF-65	PF-69DC
2020-S, Massachusetts: Telephone, Proof	877	69.6		$12	$15

2020-S, Massachusetts: Telephone, Reverse Proof • **Mintage:** To be determined.

Notes: The Reverse Proof version of the Massachusetts entry in the American Innovation series, the Telephone dollar, went on sale November 23, 2020, with an issue price of $11.50. The Mint described it as "A beautiful Reverse Proof coin featuring an inverted Proof finish. The background is frosted, while all design elements are polished to the same mirror-like finish."

	Cert	Avg	%MS	PF-65	PF-69DC
2020-S, Massachusetts: Telephone, Reverse Proof				$15	$20

2020-P, Maryland: Hubble Space Telescope • **Mintage:** To be determined.

Reverse designer: Joseph Menna.

Notes: Maryland's American Innovation dollar pays homage to the Hubble Space Telescope, one of the largest and most versatile space telescopes, with a depiction of it orbiting the Earth surrounded by a field of stars. It was both designed and sculpted by Mint Chief Engraver Joseph Menna. The Mint noted that "Menna's work was inspired by his life-long passion for space, an interest that started in childhood."

Sales of the coins officially opened on December 14, 2020, with a launch celebrated by Mint Director David J. Ryder and Maryland governor Larry Hogan. Issue prices were slightly higher than those of 2019: a 25-coin roll cost $34.50, and a 100-coin bag $117.50, plus shipping. Collectors could choose between coins from the Philadelphia Mint or the Denver Mint.

"I'm pleased to celebrate the release of the Maryland American Innovation $1 Coin with Governor Hogan," Director Ryder said in advance of the launch. "The Hubble Space Telescope is an important research tool that provides critical information about the universe, which has led to many scientific discoveries. Data transmitted by Hubble has helped refine estimates of the age of the universe, trace the growth of galaxies, identify and study planets, identify black holes, and observe stars."

	Cert	Avg	%MS	MS-64	MS-65	MS-66
2020-P, Maryland: Hubble Space Telescope	0	n/a		$3	$6	$10

2020-D, Maryland: Hubble Space Telescope • **Mintage:** To be determined.

Notes: The Hubble Space Telescope is managed by teams at the National Aeronautics and Space Administration's Goddard Space Flight Center and the Space Telescope Science Institute, both located in Maryland. Governor Larry Hogan remarked at the official launch of coin sales on December 14: "We are proud to share this new $1 coin with our fellow Marylanders and the nation, highlighting our state's contributions to expanding our knowledge of the universe. As Maryland scientists are in the spotlight once again in the race toward a COVID-19 vaccine, this coin is a reminder of our state's incredible spirit of innovation and perseverance in the face of unprecedented challenges."

Issue prices were increased slightly over those of 2019: a 25-coin roll cost $34.50, and a 100-coin bag $117.50. Shipping was extra. Collectors could choose between coins from the Philadelphia Mint or the Denver Mint.

	Cert	Avg	%MS	MS-64	MS-65	MS-66
2020-D, Maryland: Hubble Space Telescope	0	n/a		$3	$6	$10

2020-S, Maryland: Hubble Space Telescope, Proof • **Mintage:** To be determined.

Notes: The Hubble Space Telescope, named in honor of American astronomer Edwin P. Hubble, was developed by NASA and launched on April 24, 1990. It is the first telescope designed to be serviced in space by astronauts. Teams at NASA's Goddard Space Flight Center and the Space Telescope Science Institute, both located in Maryland, manage the telescope.

Proofs of the Hubble Space Telescope dollar went on sale October 8, 2020, as part of the year's four-coin Proof set. It was priced at $24 (an increase over the previous year's $20.95) for the four coins. The Mint limited ordering to online sales, announcing that its sales centers were closed to reduce the risk of employee exposure to COVID-19 in the workplace.

	Cert	Avg	%MS	PF-65	PF-69DC
2020-S, Maryland: Hubble Space Telescope, Proof	954	69.6		$12	$15

2020-S, Maryland: Hubble Space Telescope, Reverse Proof •

Mintage: To be determined.

Notes: The Mint began sales of Reverse Proof strikes of the Hubble Space Telescope dollar on December 30, 2020. The coins were priced at $11.50 each, with a limit of five coins per household during the first 24 hours of sale. Production was limited to 50,000 coins. Sales are ongoing as of the time of this publication.

	Cert	Avg	%MS	PF-65	PF-69DC
2020-S, Maryland: Hubble Space Telescope, Reverse Proof				$15	$20

2020-P, South Carolina: Septima Clark • Mintage: To be determined.

Notes: South Carolina's entry in the American Innovation dollar program was designed by Justin Kunz and engraved for coinage by Sculptor-Engraver Phebe Hemphill. It recognizes educator and civil-rights activist Septima Poinsette Clark, which was the preference of the Office of the Governor of

Reverse designer: Justin Kunz.

South Carolina. Septima Clark has been called the "Mother of the Civil Rights Movement." Born May 3, 1898, in Charleston, South Carolina, she was a social innovator and pioneer who shined the spotlight on the crucial link between education and political organizing aimed at gaining the right to vote.

The design shows Clark marching with three young African American students who carry books and an American flag. It highlights the idea that education and literacy among oppressed people are necessary for their empowerment and enjoyment of civil rights.

	Cert	Avg	%MS	MS-64	MS-65	MS-66
2020-P, South Carolina: Septima Clark	0	n/a		$3	$6	$10

2020-D, South Carolina: Septima Clark • Mintage: To be determined.

Notes: Septima Clark in her youth attended Charleston's Avery Normal Institute, a private school for African Americans. After she earned her Bachelor's degree at Benedict College and a Master's degree at Hampton Institute, Clark obtained a teaching license—but local laws at the time prohibited African Americans from teaching in public schools. As an alternative she moved and became an instructor on South Carolina's Johns Island. Later she returned to Charleston to teach at Avery, and she joined the National Association for the Advancement of Colored People (NAACP).

The Mint started selling its Septima Clark dollars—the final entry in the American Innovation program for 2020—on January 19, 2021. Issue prices were increased slightly over those of 2019: a roll of 25 Uncirculated coins cost $34.50, and a bag of 100 coins was $117.50. Collectors could choose between coins from the Philadelphia Mint or the Denver Mint.

	Cert	Avg	%MS	MS-64	MS-65	MS-66
2020-D, South Carolina: Septima Clark	0	n/a		$3	$6	$10

2020-S, South Carolina: Septima Clark, Proof • Mintage: To be determined.

Notes: Septima Clark did eventually become a teacher in the Charleston City Schools, but she was fired for her activism in the NAACP. She later worked at the Highlander Folk School in Tennessee, directing its citizenship school program focused on basic literacy and math skills in communities of need. Thanks to Clark's efforts, more voters registered at a time when many states still used inherently unfair literacy tests as a way to disenfranchise African Americans. In 1961 the Southern Christian Leadership Conference took over Clark's important education project, maintaining her as its director of education and teaching. Under her sustained leadership, more than 800 citizenship schools were established.

Septima Clark coins in Proof format went on sale October 8, 2020, as part of the year's American Innovation Proof set, priced at $24 for all four coins. This was an increase over the previous year's issue price of $20.95. Ordering was limited to online sales, with the Mint announcing that its sales centers were closed to reduce the risk of employee exposure to COVID-19 in the workplace.

	Cert	Avg	%MS	PF-65	PF-69DC
2020-S, South Carolina: Septima Clark, Proof	954	69.6		$12	$15

2020-S, South Carolina: Septima Clark, Reverse Proof • Mintage: To be determined.

Notes: The Reverse Proof version of the Septima Clark dollar went on sale February 1, 2021. The coins were priced at $11.50 each, with a limit of five coins per household during the first 24 hours of sale. Production was capped at 50,000 coins. Their packaging was described by the Mint: "Stylish and informational four-panel envelope packaging with imbedded Certificate of Authenticity and protective outer sleeve."

	Cert	Avg	%MS	PF-65	PF-69DC
2020-S, South Carolina: Septima Clark, Reverse Proof				$15	$20

2021 American Innovation Dollar

2021-P, New Hampshire: Ralph Baer •
Mintage: To be determined.

Notes: The United States Mint announced its 2021 designs for the American Innovation dollar program on April 8, 2021, noting that "The Mint works with the Governor's offices of each state along with subject matter experts to determine design concepts emblematic of innovation significant and meaningful to their jurisdiction and/or its role in the nation. After designs are developed and reviewed, the Secretary of the Treasury selects the final design for each coin."

Reverse designer: Christina Hess.

New Hampshire's dollar honors Ralph Baer and the first home video game. It was designed by Artistic Infusion Program artist Christina Hess and sculpted by sculptor-engraver Eric David Custer. It recognizes Ralph Baer and his creation of the

Detail of the 2021 privy mark.

first home video-game console. The design shows Baer's brown box game "Handball" on the right side of the coin. IN HOME VIDEO GAME SYSTEM and RALPH BAER encircle the perimeter of the coin in a typeface that pays homage to Baer's "Odyssey" game. The design of the coin is also deliberately reminiscent of a vintage arcade token.

This design received the strong recommendation of the Citizens Coinage Advisory Committee.

The Mint set June 15, 2021, as the start date of sales for its Uncirculated rolls and bags of Ralph Baer dollars.

	Cert	Avg	%MS	MS-64	MS-65	MS-66
2021-P, New Hampshire: Home Video Game System						

2021-D, New Hampshire: Ralph Baer • Mintage: To be determined.

Notes: "The New Hampshire series of the 2021 American Innovation coin is a fitting tribute to both Ralph Baer, the Father of Video Games, and the pioneering, innovative spirit that each Granite Stater carries with them," New Hampshire governor Chris Sununu said when the coins were announced. "Modern technology as we know it—stretching far beyond just video games—exists thanks to the advancements first imagined and made by Ralph Baer."

June 15, 2021, was set as the launch date for sales of 25-coin rolls and 100-coin bags of Uncirculated Ralph Baer dollars, from both the Philadelphia and Denver mints.

	Cert	Avg	%MS	MS-64	MS-65	MS-66
2021-D, New Hampshire: Home Video Game System						

2021-S, New Hampshire: Ralph Baer, Proof • Mintage: To be determined.

Notes: The Mint has not announced the sale date of the Ralph Baer Proof dollar, as of this edition's press date.

	Cert	Avg	%MS	PF-65	PF-69DC
2021-S, New Hampshire: Home Video Game System, Proof					

2021-S, New Hampshire: Ralph Baer, Reverse Proof • Mintage: To be determined.

Notes: The Mint has not announced the sale date of the Ralph Baer Reverse Proof dollar, as of this edition's press date.

	Cert	Avg	%MS	PF-65	PF-69DC
2021-S, New Hampshire: Home Video Game System, Reverse Proof					

2021-P, Virginia: Chesapeake Bay Bridge-Tunnel • Mintage: To be determined.

Notes: Artistic Infusion Program artist Matt Swaim designed Virginia's Chesapeake Bay Bridge-Tunnel dollar, which was sculpted for coinage by Mint sculptor-engraver John P. McGraw. The design shows a cross-section cutaway view of the Chesapeake Bay Bridge-Tunnel, illustrating the ingenuity involved in its construction.

Reverse designer: Matt Swaim.

July 27, 2021, was set by the Mint as the start of Uncirculated coin sales for the Chesapeake Bay Bridge-Tunnel dollar. As with earlier issues, the coins are available in 100-coin bags and 25-coin rolls, from both Philadelphia and Denver, at a premium price over face value, plus shipping.

	Cert	Avg	%MS	MS-64	MS-65	MS-66
2021-P, Virginia: Chesapeake Bay Bridge–Tunnel						

2021-D, Virginia: Chesapeake Bay Bridge-Tunnel • Mintage: To be determined.

Notes: "I grew up just a few miles from one of the world's great engineering achievements, and it makes me proud to see the U.S. Mint honor the Chesapeake Bay Bridge-Tunnel on this Virginia coin," said Governor Ralph S. Northam when the Mint unveiled the design.

The Mint announced July 27, 2021, as the first day of sales for rolls and bags of the coins in Uncirculated condition, available from both the Denver Mint and the Philadelphia Mint.

	Cert	Avg	%MS	MS-64	MS-65	MS-66
2021-D, Virginia: Chesapeake Bay Bridge–Tunnel						

2021-S, Virginia: Chesapeake Bay Bridge-Tunnel, Proof • Mintage:

To be determined.

Notes: As of press date for this edition of *Mega Red*, the Mint has not announced the start of sales of the Chesapeake Bay Bridge-Tunnel Proof dollar.

	Cert	Avg	%MS	PF-65	PF-69DC
2021-S, Virginia: Chesapeake Bay Bridge–Tunnel, Proof					

2021-S, Virginia: Chesapeake Bay Bridge-Tunnel, Reverse Proof •

Mintage: To be determined.

Notes: The Mint has not announced the sale date of the Chesapeake Bay Bridge-Tunnel Reverse Proof dollar, as of this edition's press date.

	Cert	Avg	%MS	PF-65	PF-69DC
2021-S, Virginia: Chesapeake Bay Bridge–Tunnel, Reverse Proof					

2021-P, New York: Erie Canal •

Mintage: To be determined.

Notes: Ronald D. Sanders of the Mint's Artistic Infusion Program designed New York State's American Innovation dollar, which pays homage to the engineering marvel of the Erie Canal. His design, sculpted by Mint sculptor-engraver Phebe Hemphill, shows a packet boat being pulled from a city in the East toward the country areas in Western New York.

Reverse designer: Ronald D. Sanders.

The Citizens Coinage Advisory Committee recommended to the secretary of the Treasury that the inscription ERIE CANAL and, if possible, the date 1825 be added to the design in order to provide more context to the scene. This recommendation was not carried through to the final design.

The Mint announced August 31, 2021, as the beginning of sales for the Erie Canal dollar in rolls of 25 Uncirculated coins and bags of 100 coins, from both the Denver and Philadelphia mints. The coins are sold directly from the Mint at a premium over face value, plus shipping.

	Cert	Avg	%MS	MS-64	MS-65	MS-66
2021-P, New York: Erie Canal						

2021-D, New York: Erie Canal • Mintage: To be determined.

Notes: "Built in the nineteenth century, the 363-mile Erie Canal forever changed the trajectory of commercial and agricultural development and set both New York and the nation on a path towards prosperity," said New York governor Andrew Cuomo when the design was unveiled. "I want to thank the United States Mint for New York's American Innovation coin, which celebrates the Erie Canal's rich history and recognizes the Empire State's innovative spirit and legacy of ingenuity."

August 31, 2021, was scheduled as the start of sales for the Erie Canal dollar in rolls of 25 Uncirculated coins and bags of 100 coins, from both the Denver and Philadelphia mints. The coins are sold directly by the Mint at a premium over face value, plus shipping.

	Cert	Avg	%MS	MS-64	MS-65	MS-66
2021-D, New York: Erie Canal						

2021-S, New York: Erie Canal, Proof • Mintage: To be determined.

Notes: The Mint has not announced the start of sales of the Erie Canal Proof dollar, as of this edition of *Mega Red*'s press deadline.

	Cert	Avg	%MS	PF-65	PF-69DC
2021-S, New York: Erie Canal, Proof					

2021-S, New York: Erie Canal, Reverse Proof • Mintage: To be determined.

Notes: As of press date for this edition of *Mega Red*, no sales date has been announced for the Erie Canal Reverse Proof dollar.

	Cert	Avg	%MS	PF-65	PF-69DC
2021-S, New York: Erie Canal, Reverse Proof					

2021-P, North Carolina: Higher Learning • Mintage: To be determined.

Notes: The North Carolina entry in the American Innovation dollar series was designed by Ronald D. Sanders, and sculpted by Chief Engraver Joseph Menna. Its motif acknowledges the first public institution of higher learning in the United States—the University of North Carolina at Chapel

Reverse designer: Ronald D. Sanders.

Hill opened its doors in 1795 and was the only American public institution to confer degrees in the seventeenth century. The dollar coin features a stack of three textbooks with "First Public University" on the spine of the middle book. A lamp of knowledge is perched atop, and olive branches curve around the edge of the design.

As of press deadline for this edition of *Mega Red*, the Mint has announced "Fall 2021" as the beginning of sales for rolls and bags of the Higher Learning dollar.

	Cert	Avg	%MS	MS-64	MS-65	MS-66
2021-P, North Carolina: First Public University						

2021-D, North Carolina: Higher Learning • Mintage: To be determined.

Notes: "North Carolina is proud of its legacy of innovation in creating and supporting opportunities for all students to pursue higher education," North Carolina governor Roy Cooper said when the state's Higher Learning dollar design was unveiled.

As of press date for this edition of *Mega Red*, no specific date has been set for the rollout of Uncirculated quantities of the Higher Learning dollars. The Mint has announced only that sales will start in the fall of 2021.

	Cert	Avg	%MS	MS-64	MS-65	MS-66
2021-D, North Carolina: First Public University						

2021-S, North Carolina: Higher Learning, Proof • Mintage: To be determined.

Notes: The Mint has not announced the beginning of sales of the Higher Learning Proof dollar, as of this edition of *Mega Red*'s press deadline.

	Cert	Avg	%MS	PF-65	PF-69DC
2021-S, North Carolina: First Public University, Proof					

2021-S, North Carolina: Higher Learning, Reverse Proof • Mintage: To be determined.

Notes: As of press date for this edition of *Mega Red*, no sales date has been announced for the Higher Learning Reverse Proof dollar.

	Cert	Avg	%MS	PF-65	PF-69DC
2021-S, North Carolina: First Public University, Reverse Proof					

Trade Dollars
1873–1885

Designer: *William Barber.* **Weight:** *27.22 grams.*
Composition: *.900 silver, .100 copper (net weight .7874 oz. pure silver).*
Diameter: *38.1 mm.* **Edge:** *Reeded.* **Mints:** *Philadelphia, Carson City, and San Francisco.*

Mintmark location is on the reverse, below the fineness.

Circulation Strike

Proof

HISTORY AND BACKGROUND

The idea for a commercial or trade dollar arose in 1870, when John Jay Knox, comptroller of the currency, was visiting Louis A. Garnett and others of influence in San Francisco. The port relied heavily on the China trade, in which Mexican dollars were preferred. Merchants had to pay a premium above the silver value to obtain them as the supply was nearly always short of the demand. It was thought that having the San Francisco Mint coin quantities of Liberty Seated dollars for the export trade would be ideal. In 1859 merchants in San Francisco suggested that the Mint do this; silver dollars had not been struck there before. Some 20,000 1859-S Liberty Seated dollars were produced, were sent to Eastern Asia, and were very successful for their intended purpose. However, California was distant from the seat of government in Washington, D.C., and the needs of merchants there were not particularly important to most politicians.

Despite the availability of Liberty Seated silver dollars minted in the United States and shipped in large quantities to Eastern Asia beginning in 1842, most Chinese merchants preferred the silver content of Mexican and other Spanish-American 8-reales coins, which were slightly heavier. Even accounts in inland China were often reckoned in this medium. Chinese bankers and other businessmen agreed to accept U.S. silver dollars only at a discount in comparison to the Spanish-American coins. In order to compete effectively, many commercial interests had to buy Mexican pesos at a premium of 10% to 15%

in order to have a supply for trade with the Chinese. The Mexican coins weighed slightly more than 417 grains, were .902 fine silver, and had slightly more than 377 grains of pure silver, in comparison to the Liberty Seated dollar, weighing 412.5 grains with 371.25 grains of silver. Thus, Congress, whose members were encouraged by silver-mining interests in the West, came to believe that a special "trade" dollar, at first called a commercial dollar, of slightly extra weight, would facilitate commerce on the other side of the Pacific Ocean. The California legislature requested that the federal government produce a new coin of 420 grains and .900 fine, which would about equal the Spanish-American dollar, and thus be competitive with it. Knox, following on this request and his research, was in favor of the idea and envisioned it as a coin to be used strictly in the export trade and not domestically.

This set the scene for an extensive series of commercial dollar and trade dollar patterns produced from 1871 through 1873. In the latter year the denomination became official with the Coinage Act of 1873.

Designed by Chief Engraver William Barber, the trade dollar incorporates motifs not used earlier on circulating coinage. Beginning in 1871, before the denomination was authorized, patterns were made and were called commercial dollars per the inscription on the reverse. The motifs for circulation were finalized in 1873.

The obverse portrays a female figure of Liberty holding a ribbon inscribed LIBERTY, seated on a bale of cotton tied with ropes (slightly odd, as most cotton exports went to Europe, not Asia). On another ribbon below the bale is the motto IN GOD WE TRUST. Liberty faces left, looking westward toward the Pacific Ocean and China. She wears a beaded coronet reminiscent of that on the double eagle. In her extended right hand is a laurel branch, symbolizing peace. Behind her is a sheaf of wheat. Around are 13 stars, spaced four, two, and seven, and the date is below. The overall configuration has been called the Liberty Seated type, although the design is not related to that created by Christian Gobrecht for use on standard silver dollars.

The reverse of the trade dollar depicts an eagle perched, holding three arrows in his right (observer's left) claw and a laurel branch in his left (observer's right) claw, an error from a heraldic viewpoint. Above and around the border appears UNITED STATES OF AMERICA, with TRADE DOLLAR at the bottom border. In the field above the eagle is E PLURIBUS UNUM on a ribbon, and below the arrows and laurel branch is the inscription 420 GRAINS, 900 FINE. A somewhat similar eagle was used later (1875–1878) on the 20-cent piece and on certain pattern coins.

The edge of the coin is reeded. The metallic composition is .900 silver and .100 copper. The weight of the trade dollar is 420 grains, which includes 378 troy grains of pure silver (the balance of the 420 grains' weight being copper, as noted). The standard diameter is 38.1 mm.

Counterfeits and underweight coins were a problem in Eastern commerce, so every silver coin was carefully tested; if a coin was deemed genuine, it was punched with the merchant's or banker's special mark, or *chop*. Chops are considered damage and can lower the value of common-date coins considerably—a perk for chopmark collectors. A few coins are so rare with chops, the marks actually increase their value. Caveat emptor: Just as trade dollars can be counterfeited, so can chopmarks.

HUB CHANGES IN 1875: REVERSE TYPES 1 AND 2

In 1875 Chief Engraver Barber redesigned the reverse master hub, following complaints by Chief Coiner Archibald Loudon Snowden to Superintendent James Pollock about imperfect striking quality of several high points of the design, especially the reverse. The most noticeable differences were at the claws and berries, but the topology of the reverse lettering in relation to the eagle was also altered. Barber sent working dies from the new hub to the coiners at all three mints, but notified only Snowden.

The old and new reverses (Types 1 and 2) are easily identifiable, as follows. (It would be more correct to call these *varieties* rather than *types*, but the "type" nomenclature has become common for varieties created from redesigned hubs.)

| Type 1 reverse detail. | Type 2 reverse detail. |

Type 1 Reverse: Used from 1873 through 1876, this type has a berry under the eagle's claw, narrow berries, and broad leaves.

Type 2 Reverse: Used from 1875 through 1885, this type has no berry under the claw, has larger round berries elsewhere, and narrow leaves.

Both reverses occur on 1875 and 1876 coins from all three mints. These can be further categorized into at least four subvarieties:

Type 2: This is the regular type, with a comma after GRAINS; the rightmost leaf tip in the branch is blunt. It is seen on 1875, Obverse 1, Reverse 2; 1876, Obverse 2, Reverse 2; 1877; 1877-CC; 1877-S; 1878-CC; and 1878-S.

Type 2a: This anomaly has a large period after GRAINS (much larger than the comma on 2a); the rightmost leaf tip is pointed. It is seen on the 1876-S, Obverse 2, Reverse 2, and the 1877-CC.

Type 2b: This anomaly has a large period after GRAINS and a tiny, almost subliminal tail to the bottom of the period (not quite giving it the appearance of a comma); the rightmost leaf is blunt. It is seen on the 1876-S, Obverse 1, Reverse 2.

Type 2c: Another anomaly, 2c has a comma after GRAINS; the leaf tip is pointed. It is seen on the 1875-CC, Obverse 1, Reverse 2.

These anomalies do not represent an alteration of the basic design, as all of the letters, inscriptions, designs, and so forth are in the same spatial relationship to each other and to the border denticles. They probably represent alterations to working hubs or dies. Type 2a is very distinctive; Types 2b and 2c are less so.

Hub Changes of 1876: Obverse Types 1 and 2

In 1876 Barber redesigned the obverse master hub of the trade dollar and sent new working dies to the coiners of all three mints. The coiners at Philadelphia and San Francisco received at least one Type 2 obverse dated 1876, while the Carson City Mint apparently received only the Type 2 dies for 1877 and 1878. If the Type 2 obverse is one of the two new hubs for fiscal year 1877 mentioned in a Mint report of July 7, 1877, cited by R.W. Julian, then it must date to after July 1, 1876, excluding the possibility that 1875-dated coins exist of Type 2/1 or 2/2.

| Type 1 obverse details. | Type 2 obverse details. |

Type 1. John W. McCloskey, in his article "Obverse Varieties of the U.S. Trade Dollar" in the *Gobrecht Journal* (July 1978), first described in print the two obverse types. The Type 1, he noted: "has both ribbon tails (the ribbon on which LIBERTY is imprinted) pointing sharply to the left. Three fingers on Liberty's right hand are below the laurel branch (her index finger is missing). Both RT of LIBERTY and ST of TRUST touch."

Type 1 Transitional. In 2005, in the *E-Gobrecht*, Dr. Gene Bruder published a new variety—an obverse die resembling Type 1 with the ribbon ends pointing left, but with four fingers and a thumb on Liberty's right hand, as used on Type 2. This enigmatic issue was researched by Dan Huntsinger and has been found with the fabric of both Proof and circulation-strike formats and with different reed counts (193 and 194). They are very scarce in Proof format. Many of the circulation-strike examples are low grade and/or weakly struck and often chopmarked.

Type 2: In the article noted above, McCloskey described the distinguishing features of the Type 2 obverse, which, he stated, "displays open ribbon ends, the right tail pointing down between the words WE and TRUST. Four fingers on Liberty's right hand are below the laurel branch. Both RT and ST are apart."

1875 and 1876 coins are known with these combinations:

- 1875 Circulation strikes: 1/1 and 1/2. *Proofs:* 1/1 and 1/2.
- 1875-CC 1/1 and 1/2.
- 1875-S 1/1 and 1/2.
- 1875-S/CC 1/1.
- 1876 Circulation strikes: 1/1, 1/2, and 2/2. *Proofs:* 1/1, 1/2, and 2/2; and transitional obverse 1.5.
- 1876-CC 1/1 and 1/2.
- 1876-S 1/1, 1/2, and 2/2.

RELEASE AND DISTRIBUTION

Trade dollars shipped to China were received with favor, and the new denomination was a resounding success from the start. The demand continued nonstop afterward.

In 1875 Superintendent Oscar H. LaGrange of the San Francisco Mint wrote:

> At no time since the commencement of the present calendar year has the mint been able to accumulate a surplus of trade dollars, and the public demand has not been fully met. The limited capacity of the Mint and the unusually large coinage of gold, which is given precedence over silver, has materially abridged the supply of this international coin at San Francisco, but the favorable introduction of the trade dollar into China has most effectually destroyed the use of the Mexican silver dollar as the medium of exchange between this city and the ports in the Chinese Empire. The city banks report an excessive demand for trade dollar exchange. The coinage capacity of the new Mint, shortly to be occupied, will, it is hoped, fully meet the requirements for all gold and silver coins. Great care has been given in the manufacture of the trade dollar to reach the closest approximate perfection in assay value, weight, and execution.

Many trade dollars struck at the San Francisco Mint and elsewhere were made to the order of Louis McLane, president of the Nevada Bank of San Francisco, who made this statement on August 31, 1877 (reproduced in the *Annual Report of the Director of the Mint*, 1877):

> The benefit of coining trade dollars is that it gives a better market for silver than fine bars would produce. This bank has had coined and sold in the last twenty-two months over six millions of trade dollars, and their sale has netted more than the average of our sales of silver to the government. Returns of trade dollars from the Mint have uniformly been made with honesty and fairness. I only remember one case in which the loss by melting was unusually large; but that was afterward explained. Our sales of silver to the government were made direct, through the director of the Mint, mostly by telegraph, except when he was present in person, and were, as specially agreed, free of all commissions or brokerages. In our dealings with the government no commission or brokerage or reward, or any other consideration, has ever been given, in any way, shape, or form, to any officer of the government, or to anyone else. It will happen in seasons of low sterling exchange that silver will rule lower in New York than the equivalent of the London market; but this is quite exceptional. The silver sold the government has been delivered at the mints in San Francisco, Carson, and Philadelphia, in sums as required by the director of the Mint.

McLane's enthusiasm notwithstanding, in 1876, when the price of silver had fallen and trade dollars were demonetized, the coins had begun to cause problems in domestic commerce. The trade dollar was reported as "fast becoming a drag on the market" in 1876. The *San Francisco Chronicle* noted:

> Our banks and money broker offices are becoming glutted with them. Their greater intrinsic value as well as their novelty threatened for a while to crowd the familiar half dollar and the handy quarter out of sight. Chinamen remitting their hard-earned savings to their far distant land would have nothing but trade dollars. Oriental commerce was, and still is to a large extent, conducted on the solid basis of this bright, new, and ringing silver representation of value. But the Orient, like San Francisco, is beginning to find that it is possible to be surfeited with even so much coveted a treasure as the trade dollar. The result is that a reaction has set in against the coin on this market and, it no longer enjoys a preference over other silver.
>
> On the contrary, although a trade dollar is intrinsically worth eight cents more than two half dollars, the two halves will sell in the street from a half to three quarters of a cent more than the dollar. The reason for this is primarily because of the superabundance of the latter. However, there is another reason which is not generally understood. Halves and quarters of the coinage of the United States are legal tender for all debts up to a certain amount; the trade dollar is not legal tender at all for any amount. It is merely a stamped ingot, having a certain value, like an ounce of gold, diamond, or a bushel of wheat. It is a commodity, the value of which fluctuates according to the supply and demand.

ASPECTS OF STRIKING

Striking varies from issue to issue and is discussed under the various issues below. Many show weakness on the obverse head of Liberty and on some of the stars. On the reverse, weakness is often seen on the eagle's leg and talons to the right.

Cherrypicking can pay good dividends as sharply defined coins cost no more than do those casually struck.

PROOF TRADE DOLLARS

The official Mint issue price for Proof trade dollars from 1878 to 1883 was $1.025 each, according to one account, because the coin had been demonetized; most other sources give the figure as $1.25 each, a figure with which numismatic researcher R.W. Julian agrees. Earlier, when the coins were worth $1 face value each, 1873 Proofs were sold for $1.75 each in paper money or $1.50 each in silver.

Trade dollars were in no particular favor with collectors, as many considered them to be outside of the regular circulating series (never mind that they were legal tender until their status was rescinded on July 22, 1876). Many of the Proofs of 1873 and 1874 in particular seem to have been spent. Survivors are at a lower percentage than the mintages would indicate and are usually in lower grades. True choice and gem coins are hard to find. Most often encountered are the Proof-only years of 1878 through 1883. A few 1884 and 1885 Proofs were struck secretly and are great rarities.

Proofs are often mishandled as noted above, and some of the later dates are weakly struck on the head. Others are dark or have questionable toning. With some patience it is possible to assemble a date run from 1873 to 1883, with the keys being the 1873 and 1874.

TRADE DOLLARS (1873–1885): GUIDE TO COLLECTING

Circulation strikes often have areas of weakness as mentioned above. Luster is sometimes dull or flat. Eye appeal can vary as well. My recommendation is to proceed slowly. If you are building a collection of circulated issues, pick better strikes. If you are opting for a Mint State set the challenges will be strike, luster, and eye appeal. For some varieties this will mean reviewing a half dozen or more offers before finding one that is just right. Proofs, also as noted above, often have problems.

The obverse and reverse types of 1875 and 1876 include rare issues. As these are not widely noticed, rarities can often be found by paying no more. In recent years the circulation strikes (but not the Proofs) have been delineated in the *Guide Book of United States Coins*, but at more or less generic prices not reflecting their rarity—simply because they have not been showcased in the marketplace. In time this may change. The 1876-CC with Doubled-Die Reverse and the 1876-S with Doubled-Die Obverse are two of the most spectacular blunders in the American series and are worth special attention.

As is the case for other denominations, quality varies widely among trade dollars. Nearly all buyers look only at the label on a certified coin, when in actuality there are *three* factors a connoisseur should consider:

1. The certified grade does have importance. In general, the higher the number the more desirable the coin.
2. For most issues, even including some Proofs, the quality of strike differs. It pays to seek a sharp example, as these can be found.
3. Eye appeal is *very* important. In the author's opinion, a sharply struck MS-63 or 64 coin with a beautiful appearance is far more desirable than a much more expensive MS-65 or 66 that is dull or unattractive (and such coins abound). The unswerving quest for high numbers without regard to other factors has been driven by the popularity of building Registry Sets, where only numbers count.

TRADE DOLLAR (1873–1885)

GRADING STANDARDS

MS-60 to 70 (Mint State). *Obverse:* At MS-60, some abrasion and contact marks are evident, most noticeably on the left breast, left arm, and left knee. Luster is present, but may be dull or lifeless. Many of these coins are light in color or even brilliant, having been repatriated from China, and have been cleaned to remove sediment and discoloration. At MS-63, contact marks are very few, and abrasion is minimal. An MS-65 coin has no abrasion in

1875-S, Reverse 1. Graded MS-61.

the fields (but may have a hint on the higher parts of the seated figure), and contact marks are trivial. Luster should be full and rich. *Reverse:* Comments apply as for the obverse, except that in lower Mint State grades abrasion and contact marks are most noticeable on the eagle's head, the claws, and the top of the wings. At MS-65 or higher there are no marks visible to the unaided eye. The field is mainly protected by design elements and does not show abrasion as much as does the obverse on a given coin.

AU-50, 53, 55, 58 (About Uncirculated). *Obverse:* Light wear is seen on the knees, bosom, and head. At AU-58, the luster is extensive but incomplete. At AU-50 and 53, luster is less. *Reverse:* Wear is visible on the eagle's head, the claws, and the top of the wings. An AU-58 coin will have nearly full luster. At AU-50 and 53, there still are traces of luster.

1876, Reverse 2. Graded AU-53.

EF-40, 45 (Extremely Fine). *Obverse:* Further wear is seen on all areas, especially the head, the left breast, the left arm, the left leg, and the bale on which Miss Liberty is seated. Little or no luster is seen on most coins. From this grade downward, strike sharpness on the stars and the head does not matter to connoisseurs. *Reverse:* Further wear is evident on the eagle's head, legs, claws, and wings, although on well-struck coins nearly all feather details on the wings are sharp.

1876-CC, Reverse 1. Graded EF-40.

VF-20, 30 (Very Fine). *Obverse:* Further wear is seen on the seated figure, although more than half the details of her dress are visible. Details of the wheat sheaf are mostly intact. IN GOD WE TRUST and LIBERTY are clear. *Reverse:* Wear is more extensive; some feathers are blended together, with two-thirds or more still visible.

1877-S. Graded VF-30.

F-12, 15 (Fine). *Obverse:* The seated figure is further worn, with fewer details of the dress visible. Most details in the wheat sheaf are clear. Both mottos are readable, but some letters may be weak. *Reverse:* Wear is extensive, with about half to nearly two-thirds of the feathers flat or blended with others. The eagle's left leg is mostly flat. Wear is seen on the raised E PLURIBUS UNUM, and one or two letters may be missing.

1873-CC. Graded F-12.

Trade dollars are seldom collected in grades lower than F-12.

PF-60 to 70 (Proof). *Obverse and Reverse:* Proofs that are extensively cleaned and have many hairlines, or that are dull and grainy, are lower level, such as PF-60 to 62. These are not widely desired. With medium hairlines and good reflectivity, an assigned grade of PF-64 is appropriate, and with relatively few hairlines, gem PF-65. In various grades hairlines are most easily seen in the obverse field. PF-66 may have hairlines so delicate that magnification is needed to see them. Above that, a Proof should be free of such lines.

1882. Graded PF-62.

Chopmarked Trade Dollar

Examples of chopmarks.

1873 Trade Dollar

1873 • **Mintage:** 396,900.

Availability in Mint State: *MS-60 to 62:* 150 to 250. *MS-63:* 60 to 100. *MS-64:* 50 to 75. *MS-65 or better:* 10 to 15.

Availability in circulated grades: *VF-20 to AU-58:* 1,250 to 2,000. With Chinese chopmarks these are rare. In a 2015 communication

Larry Briggs stated, "I have handled dozens of 1873 trade dollars over a span of many years and have seen only two or three with chopmarks."

Characteristics of striking: Many are well struck, though some have light definition on Liberty's head and on the eagle's leg on the right and talons. Some have slight lightness of strike near the bottom of the obverse—an unusual situation among trade dollars. The luster on Mint State coins is often more of a satiny or "greasy" appearance than deeply frosty.

Notes: Unlike the situation for other Liberty Seated denominations for which examples of many issues exist in lower-grade ranges, very few trade dollars grade lower than VF-20. Accordingly, in this chapter the grade ranges for circulated coins are VF-20 to AU-58.

Trade dollars first reached China in October 1873, and met a good reception. Nearly all of the 1873 trade dollars went there.

	Cert	Avg	%MS	VG-8	F-12	VF-20	EF-40	AU-50	MS-60	MS-63	MS-64	MS-65
1873	201	56.4	61%	$150	$185	$225	$300	$550	$1,100	$2,850	$3,800	$9,000

1873, Proof • Mintage: 600.

Availability in Proof State: *PF-60 to 62:* 200 to 300. *PF-63:* 60 to 100. *PF-64:* 40 to 55. *PF-64 or better:* 20 to 30. Nearly all Proofs of this issue are in lower grades. This is true of 1874 Proofs as well.

	Cert	Avg	%MS	PF-60	PF-63	PF-65
1873, Proof	172	63.0		$1,500	$3,000	$7,000

1873-CC Trade Dollar

1873-CC • Mintage: 124,500.

Availability in Mint State: *MS-60 to 62:* 40 to 60. *MS-63:* 2 to 4. *MS-64:* 2 or 3. *MS-65 or better:* 0 or 1.

Availability in circulated grades: *VF-20 to AU-58:* 1,000 to 1,500. With Chinese chopmarks these are somewhat rare.

Characteristics of striking: Some coins of this issue have slight weakness of striking on the eagle's leg to the right and on the eagle's claws.

Notes: The Carson City Mint received four pairs of trade-dollar dies, made in Philadelphia (where all dies for all mints were made), on July 22, 1873. It is not known if all dies were used; probably most were, as they did not last long, averaging only about 15,000 impressions per die pair. Coinage began immediately. The following day, 4,500 pieces were ready for shipment, and 2,580 coins were paid out to local depositors, this being the first circulation of the denomination in the West.

Mintmark varieties include Micro CC with widely spaced (1.2 mm) letters using the same reverse die that was used for 1874-CC and 1876-CC Type 1/1.

	Cert	Avg	%MS	VG-8	F-12	VF-20	EF-40	AU-50	MS-60	MS-63	MS-64	MS-65
1873-CC	144	51.2	26%	$400	$625	$900	$1,650	$2,750	$7,000	$25,000	$45,000	$110,000

1873-S Trade Dollar

1873-S • Mintage: 703,000.

Availability in Mint State: *MS-60 to 62:* 100 to 160. *MS-63:* 30 to 45. *MS-64:* 25 to 32. *MS-65 or better:* 4 to 6.

Availability in circulated grades: *VF-20 to AU-58:* 3,000 to 5,000. With Chinese chopmarks these are available in sufficient numbers to satisfy the numismatic demand, but are notable as the scarcest San Francisco chopmarked variety.

Characteristics of striking: Some coins of this issue have slight weakness on the eagle's leg on the right and on the eagle's claws.

	Cert	Avg	%MS	VG-8	F-12	VF-20	EF-40	AU-50	MS-60	MS-63	MS-64	MS-65
1873-S	110	59.4	68%	$175	$200	$300	$450	$600	$1,450	$3,800	$4,250	$22,500

1874 Trade Dollar

1874 • **Mintage:** 987,100.

Availability in Mint State: *MS-60 to 62:* 150 to 250. *MS-63:* 60 to 100. *MS-65 or better:* 6 to 10.

Availability in circulated grades: *VF-20 to AU-58:* 2,500 to 3,500. With Chinese chopmarks these are the most common chopmarked Philadelphia Mint trade dollar, as well as one of the most common of all chopmarked trade dollars. It is scarce, however, in relation to the mintage.

Characteristics of striking: Some coins of this issue have weakness on the obverse on Liberty's head and at stars six and seven while on others the weakness extends to the stars left and right of these. Some have light striking on eagle's leg on the right.

Notes: In this year a number of Philadelphia Mint 1874 quarters, half dollars, and trade dollars were counterstamped with the advertisement SAGE'S / CANDY / COIN. Today these are known in circulated grades and are rare. The trade dollar is especially elusive.

A rare counterstamp advertising SAGE'S CANDY COIN.

	Cert	Avg	%MS	VG-8	F-12	VF-20	EF-40	AU-50	MS-60	MS-63	MS-64	MS-65
1874	153	56.9	58%	$170	$185	$225	$350	$500	$1,200	$2,400	$3,900	$13,000

1874, Proof • **Mintage:** 700.

Availability in Proof State: *PF-60 to 62:* 225 to 325. *PF-63:* 70 to 110. *PF-64:* 45 to 65. *PF-64 or better:* 25 to 35. Nearly all are in lower grades. This is true of 1873 Proofs as well.

	Cert	Avg	%MS	PF-60	PF-63	PF-65
1874, Proof	212	63.2		$1,500	$3,000	$6,500

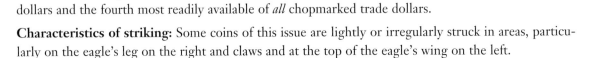

1874-CC Trade Dollar

1874-CC • Mintage: 1,373,200.

Availability in Mint State: *MS-60 to 62:* 150 to 250. *MS-63:* 30 to 45. *MS-64:* 10 to 15. *MS-65 or better:* 0 or 1.

Availability in circulated grades: *VF-20 to AU-58:* 2,500 to 4,000. With Chinese chopmarks this issue ranks as the most readily available of all chopmarked Carson City trade dollars and the fourth most readily available of *all* chopmarked trade dollars.

Characteristics of striking: Some coins of this issue are lightly or irregularly struck in areas, particularly on the eagle's leg on the right and claws and at the top of the eagle's wing on the left.

Notes: Mintmark varieties include the Micro CC with widely spaced (1.2 mm) letters using the same reverse die that was used for 1873-CC and 1876-CC Type 1/1.

Dangerous modern counterfeits have come on the market since the early 2000s.

	Cert	Avg	%MS	VG-8	F-12	VF-20	EF-40	AU-50	MS-60	MS-63	MS-64	MS-65
1874-CC	265	57.3	59%	$325	$425	$550	$750	$950	$2,500	$5,000	$16,500	$35,000

1874-S Trade Dollar

1874-S • Mintage: 2,549,000.

Availability in Mint State: *MS-60 to 62:* 400 to 600. *MS-63:* 30 to 45. *MS-64:* 20 to 25. MS-65: 2 or 3.

Availability in circulated grades: *VF-20 to AU-58:* 2,500 to 4,000. This is the third most common variety existing with chopmarks.

Characteristics of striking: Many if not most coins of this issue show some weakness at the top of the obverse and/or on the reverse at the eagle's claws on the right.

Notes: Some of these have the reverse rotated about 15° counterclockwise.

	Cert	Avg	%MS	VG-8	F-12	VF-20	EF-40	AU-50	MS-60	MS-63	MS-64	MS-65
1874-S	341	59.4	66%	$170	$185	$200	$250	$325	$900	$2,000	$3,250	$15,000

1875 Trade Dollar

1875, Obverse 1, Reverse 1 •
Mintage: Small portion of 218,200.

Points for identification: *Obverse:* The ribbon ends point left. *Reverse:* The berry is below the claw. The 1875 has the lowest circulation strike mintage of any trade dollar from this mint. All have a reed count of 190.

Rarity (% of date and mint, Borckardt study): *Circulation strike:* 10%. *Proof:* 34%.

Availability in Mint State: These are very rare. *MS-60 to 62:* 2 to 4. *MS-63:* 0. *MS-64:* 0. *MS-65 or better:* 0.

Availability in circulated grades: *VF-20 to AU-58:* These are very rare. An estimated 25 to 35 are known. With Chinese chopmarks these are very rare.

Characteristics of striking: This issue is usually well struck.

	Cert	Avg	%MS	VG-8	F-12	VF-20	EF-40	AU-50	MS-60	MS-63	MS-64	MS-65
1875, Obverse 1, Reverse 1	116	57.4	66%	$375	$450	$650	$1,000	$1,350	$2,500	$4,500	$7,500	$15,000

1875, Obverse 1, Reverse 1, Proof •

Mintage: Small portion of 700.

Availability in Proof State: *PF-60 to 62:* 60 to 80. *PF-63:* 60 to 80. *PF-64:* 30 to 45. *PF-64 or better:* 15 to 20.

  Some 1/1 Proofs have the reverse with a long arc scratch, the die first used 1873, but now with the scratch partly worn off. The last of these show die failure at the eagle's leg and claws above 900. Other Proofs have a different reverse.

	Cert	Avg	%MS	PF-60	PF-63	PF-65
1875, Obverse 1, Reverse 1, Proof	238	63.2		$1,500	$3,000	$8,500

1875, Obverse 1, Reverse 2 •

Mintage: Large portion of 218,200.

Points for identification: *Obverse:* The ribbon ends point left. *Reverse:* There is no berry below the claw.

Rarity (% of date and mint, Borckardt study): *Circulation strike:* 90%. *Proof:* 66%.

Availability in Mint State: *MS-60 to 62:* 150 to 175. *MS-63:* 55 to 75. *MS-64:* 25 to 32. *MS-65 or better:* 10 to 15.

Availability in circulated grades: *VF-20 to AU-58:* 25 to 35. With Chinese chopmarks these are extremely rare.

Characteristics of striking: This issue is usually well struck.

	Cert	Avg	%MS	VG-8	F-12	VF-20	EF-40	AU-50	MS-60	MS-63	MS-64	MS-65
1875, Obverse 1, Reverse 2	1	64.0	100%	$240	$375	$525	$750	$1,250	$2,600	$4,650	$9,000	$21,000

1875, Obverse 1, Reverse 2, Proof •

Mintage: Large portion of 700.

Availability in Proof State: *PF-60 to 62:* 90 to 120. *PF-63:* 100 to 130. *PF-64:* 75 to 95. *PF-64 or better:* 30 to 40.

	Cert	Avg	%MS	PF-60	PF-63	PF-65
1875, Obverse 1, Reverse 2, Proof	0	n/a		$1,750	$3,300	$8,500

1875-CC Trade Dollar

1875-CC, Obverse 1, Reverse 1 •

Mintage: Large portion of 1,573,700.

Points for identification: *Obverse:* The ribbon ends point left. *Reverse:* The berry is below the claw.

Rarity (% of date and mint, Borckardt study): 88%.

Availability in Mint State: *MS-60 to 62:* 300 to 450. *MS-60 to 62:* 300 to 450. *MS-63:* 75 to 125. *MS-64:* 5 to 8. *MS-65 or better:* 4 to 6.

Availability in circulated grades: *VF-20 to AU-58:* 4,000 to 6,000. With Chinese chopmarks these are very common.

Characteristics of striking: This issue is usually seen well struck.

Notes: With a total production quantity of 1,573,700 coins, the 1875-CC was produced in larger numbers than any other trade dollar from this mint.

The vast majority of known 1875-CC trade dollars are Type 1/1. Taken as a whole, the 1875-CC is the most widely available Carson City trade dollar, although in MS-64 or better grade it is a great rarity. A variety formerly known as Doubled-Reverse die is now discredited and is the result of strike doubling.

	Cert	Avg	%MS	VG-8	F-12	VF-20	EF-40	AU-50	MS-60	MS-63	MS-64	MS-65
1875-CC, Obverse 1, Reverse 1	345	54.2	46%	$325	$400	$475	$575	$850	$2,250	$4,500	$10,000	$33,500

1875-CC, Obverse 1, Reverse 2 •

Mintage: Small portion of 1,573,700.

Points for identification: *Obverse:* The ribbon ends point left. *Reverse:* There is no berry below the claw.

Rarity (% of date and mint, Borckardt study): 12%.

Availability in Mint State: *MS-60 to 62:* 30 to 45. *MS-60 to 62:* 30 to 45. *MS-63:* 8 to 12. *MS-64:* 1 or 2. *MS-65 or better:* 0 or 1.

Availability in circulated grades: *VF-20 to AU-58:* 400 to 600. With Chinese chopmarks these are elusive.

Characteristics of striking: Most coins of this issue exhibit weakness on the reverse, mainly on the top of the eagle's wing to the left.

	Cert	Avg	%MS	VG-8	F-12	VF-20	EF-40	AU-50	MS-60	MS-63	MS-64	MS-65
1875-CC, Obverse 1, Reverse 2	0	n/a		$275	$375	$475	$650	$925	$2,500	$5,500	$12,000	$33,500

1875-S Trade Dollar

1875-S, Obverse 1, Reverse 1 •

Mintage: Large portion of 4,487,000.

Points for identification: *Obverse:* The ribbon ends point left. *Reverse:* The berry is below the claw.

Rarity (% of date and mint, Borckardt study): 86%.

Availability in Mint State: *MS-60 to 62:* 1,250 to 2,000. *MS-63:* 400 to 600. *MS-64:* 150 to 250. *MS-65 or better:* 60 to 100.

Availability in circulated grades: *VF-20 to AU-58:* 20,000+. With Chinese chopmarks these are very common.

Characteristics of striking: This issue is usually seen with some lightness on the head of Liberty.

Notes: The 1875-S Type 1/1 exists with Medium S and Large S mintmarks.

The production quantity of trade dollars at the San Francisco Mint in 1875 was immense and set the record for the series. Some 80 to 90 percent are Type 1/1, and the rest are 1/2.

	Cert	Avg	%MS	VG-8	F-12	VF-20	EF-40	AU-50	MS-60	MS-63	MS-64	MS-65
1875-S, Obverse 1, Reverse 1	1,029	59.8	75%	$165	$185	$225	$300	$350	$900	$1,600	$2,500	$7,500

1875-S, Obverse 1, Reverse 2 •

Mintage: Small portion of 4,487,000.

Points for identification: *Obverse:* The ribbon ends point left. *Reverse:* There is no berry below the claw.

Rarity (% of date and mint, Borckardt study): 14%.

Availability in Mint State: *MS-60 to 62:* 200 to 300+. *MS-63:* 100 to 200. *MS-64:* 20 to 25. *MS-65 or better:* 15 to 20.

Availability in circulated grades: *VF-20 to AU-58:* 250 to 400. With Chinese chopmarks these are scarce.

Characteristics of striking: Striking of this issue varies.

Notes: The 1875-S Type 1/2 exists with Tall S as well as with Micro S mintmarks, the latter being rare.

	Cert	Avg	%MS	VG-8	F-12	VF-20	EF-40	AU-50	MS-60	MS-63	MS-64	MS-65
1875-S, Obverse 1, Reverse 2	0	n/a		$165	$185	$200	$325	$400	$1,175	$2,350	$3,400	$11,000

VARIETY: *1875-S, Obverse 1, Reverse 1, S Over CC (FS-T1-1876CC-501 and 502):* For some reason at least two Carson City reverse dies of the Type 1 style, with tall CC letters, had the CC mintmark partially effaced and overpunched with an S mintmark. On the variety most often seen the CC mintmark is more or less centered below the S. All examined coins are from an extensively cracked die. The variety with CC *far to the right* of the S is much rarer than the coins with the CC centered. These have a differently cracked reverse die. Several dozen or more are known with Chinese chopmarks. All are Type 1/1. Rarity is a small percent of that above. This variety is known in different die states up to and including extensively cracked.

	Cert	Avg	%MS	VG-8	F-12	VF-20	EF-40	AU-50	MS-60	MS-63	MS-64	MS-65
1875-S, Obverse 1, Reverse 1, S Over CC	54	58.1	44%	$400	$450	$550	$1,000	$1,650	$5,000	$14,500	$25,000	$45,000

1876 Trade Dollar

1876, Obverse 1, Reverse 1 •

Mintage: Small portion of 455,000.

Points for identification: *Obverse:* The ribbon ends point left. *Reverse:* The berry is below the claw.

Rarity (% of date and mint, Borckardt study): Circulation strike: 14%. Proof: 3%.

Availability in Mint State: Many Uncirculated coins seen in collections today have deep gray or even black toning. This toning may represent specimens having been saved by the public as a souvenir of the 1876 centennial year, or perhaps there is another explanation. *MS-60 to 62:* 150 to 200. *MS-63:* 40 to 55. *MS-64:* 25 to 35. *MS-65 or better:* 15 to 20.

Availability in circulated grades: *VF-20 to AU-58:* 500 to 700. Coins with Chinese chopmarks are seen more often than coins without chopmarks.

Characteristics of striking: Many coins of this issue are well struck, but many others are lightly struck on the eagle's claws to the left.

	Cert	Avg	%MS	VG-8	F-12	VF-20	EF-40	AU-50	MS-60	MS-63	MS-64	MS-65
1876, Obverse 1, Reverse 1	481	58.8	73%	$165	$185	$200	$300	$335	$900	$1,450	$2,250	$7,500

VARIETY: *1876 Type 1 Transitional 1.5/2:* In 2005 in the *E-Gobrecht* Dr. Gene Bruder published a new variety—an obverse die resembling Type 1 with the ribbon ends pointing left, but with four fingers and a thumb on Liberty's right hand, as used on Type 2. This enigmatic issue was researched by Dan Huntsinger and has been found in both Proof and circulation-strike formats and with different reed counts (193 and 194). They are very scarce in Proof format. Many of the circulation-strike examples are low grade and/ or weakly struck and often chopmarked. Only a few have been discovered since.

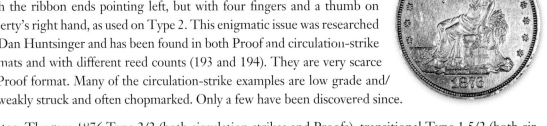

Notes: The rare 1876 Type 2/2 (both circulation strikes and Proofs), transitional Type 1.5/2 (both circulation strikes and Proofs), and one circulation-strike Type 1/2, all share the same reverse as noted by a unique die chip in the E PLURIBUS UNUM banner.

Director of the Mint Dr. Henry R. Linderman proposed that a special commemorative reverse be made for 1876 trade dollars, to honor the 100th anniversary of American independence. Had this come to pass—which it didn't—it would have been the first U.S. silver commemorative coin.

1876, Obverse 1, Reverse 1, Proof •

Mintage: Small portion of 1,150.

Availability in Proof State: For the variety specialist this is far and away the rarest Proof of 1876. *PF-60 to 62:* 25 to 35. *PF-63:* 8 to 10. *PF-64:* 3 to 5. *PF-64 or better:* 2 or 3.

	Cert	Avg	%MS	PF-60	PF-63	PF-65
1876, Obverse 1, Reverse 1, Proof	1	64.0		$1,750	$3,100	$8,500

1876, Obverse 1, Reverse 2 •

Mintage: Large portion of 455,000.

Points for identification: *Obverse:* The ribbon ends point left. *Reverse:* There is no berry below the claw.

Rarity (% of date and mint, Borckardt study): Circulation strike: 63%. Proof: 88%.

Availability in Mint State: *MS-60 to 62:* 650 to 800. *MS-63:* 140 to 160. *MS-64:* 90 to 120. *MS-65 or better:* 55 to 70.

Availability in circulated grades: These are common and are readily available with Chinese chopmarks.

Characteristics of striking: Many coins of this issue are well struck, but many others are lightly struck on the eagle's claws to the left.

	Cert	Avg	%MS	VG-8	F-12	VF-20	EF-40	AU-50	MS-60	MS-63	MS-64	MS-65
1876, Obverse 1, Reverse 2	0	n/a		$165	$185	$225	$300	$335	$900	$2,000	$3,200	$10,000

1876, Obverse 1, Reverse 2, Proof •

Mintage: Large portion of 1,150.

Availability in Proof State: *PF-60 to 62:* 150 to 200. *PF-63:* 80 to 120. *PF-64:* 40 to 55. *PF-64 or better:* 20 to 30. Of the differing die varieties, this is the variety nearly always seen. Although the mintage quantity was large, it is likely that many were sold to visitors to the Centennial Exhibition in Philadelphia and were not preserved.

	Cert	Avg	%MS	PF-60	PF-63	PF-65
1876, Obverse 1, Reverse 2, Proof	1	64.0		$1,500	$3,000	$6,500

1876, Obverse 2, Reverse 2 •

Mintage: Small portion of 455,000.

Points for identification: *Obverse:* The ribbon ends point down. *Reverse:* There is no berry below the claw.

Rarity (% of date and mint, Borckardt study): Circulation strike: 1% (the great rarity among these varieties). Proof: 9%.

Availability in Mint State: These are very rare. *MS-60 to 62:* 8 to 12. *MS-63:* 3 to 5. *MS-64:* 2 or 3. *MS-65 or better:* 1 or 2.

Availability in circulated grades: *VF-20 to AU-58:* 40 to 60. With Chinese chopmarks these are exceedingly rare.

Characteristics of striking: Striking of this issue varies.

	Cert	Avg	%MS	MS-60
1876, Obverse 2, Reverse 2	0	n/a		—

1876, Obverse 2, Reverse 2, Proof •

Mintage: Small portion of 1,150.

Availability in Proof State: *PF-60 to 62:* 18 to 25. *PF-63:* 10 to 13. *PF-64:* 5 to 8. *PF-64 or better:* 3 to 5.

	Cert	Avg	%MS
1876, Obverse 2, Reverse 2, Proof	0	n/a	

1876-CC Trade Dollar

1876-CC, Obverse 1, Reverse 1 •

Mintage: Portion of 509,000.

Points for identification: *Obverse:* The ribbon ends point left. *Reverse:* The berry is below the claw.

Rarity (% of date and mint, Borckardt study): 46%. About three out of four are of the Doubled-Die Reverse.

Availability in Mint State: *MS-60 to 62:* 30 to 40. *MS-63:* 5 to 8. *MS-64:* 2 to 4. *MS-65 or better:* 0.

Availability in circulated grades: *VF-20 to AU-58:* 1,350 to 2,000. Only a small percentage of this issue has Chinese chopmarks.

Characteristics of striking: Striking of this issue varies.

Notes: Mintmark varieties for this issue include the Micro CC with widely spaced (1.2 mm) letters using the same reverse die that was used for 1873-CC and 1874-CC Type 1/1, Medium CC, and Large CC.

	Cert	Avg	%MS	VG-8	F-12	VF-20	EF-40	AU-50	MS-60	MS-63	MS-64	MS-65
1876-CC, Obverse 1, Reverse 1	1	53.0	0%	$400	$450	$525	$650	$2,150	$7,250	$25,000	$40,000	$95,000

VARIETY: *1876-CC, Obverse 1, Reverse 1, Doubled-Die Reverse (FS-T1-1876CC-801):* Of all of the various die repunching, doublings, etc., in the entire American coin series, the 1876-CC 1/1 with doubled reverse die stands high as a Mint gaffe—but the 1876-S 2/2 with doubled obverse die is not far behind it. In a 1991 letter to the author, Bill Fivaz wrote, "This is probably the strongest and most widely spaced doubled die known in *any*

series. The reverse die shows dramatic doubling on the eagle's left wing (on the right side of the coin), the branches, berries, leaves, and much of the lettering. While not exceedingly rare, once you've found one, this scarce variety is very marketable due to the strength of the doubling." Illustrated is a detail showing doubling of the branch. Dangerous modern counterfeits exist, having come on the market beginning in the early 2000s. Many such fakes can be identified by a dent or depression on top of Liberty's ankle.

	Cert	Avg	%MS	VG-8	F-12	VF-20	EF-40	AU-50	MS-60	MS-63
1876-CC, Obverse 1, Reverse 1, Doubled Die Reverse	35	53.5	23%	$450	$550	$750	$1,200	$1,900	$9,000	$22,500

1876-CC, Obverse 1, Reverse 2 •

Mintage: Portion of 509,000.

Points for identification: *Obverse:* The ribbon ends point left. *Reverse:* There is no berry below the claw.

Rarity (% of date and mint, Borckardt study): 54%.

Availability in Mint State: *MS-60 to 62:* 35 to 45. *MS-63:* 7 to 10. *MS-64:* 3 to 5. *MS-65 or better:* 0 or 1.

Availability in circulated grades: *VF-20 to AU-58:* 1,500 to 2,250. Most coins of this issue have Chinese chopmarks, however they are slightly scarce.

Characteristics of striking: This issue is usually well struck. A few have prooflike surfaces.

	Cert	Avg	%MS	VG-8	F-12	VF-20	EF-40	AU-50	MS-60	MS-63	MS-64	MS-65
1876-CC, Obverse 1, Reverse 2	187	53.6	34%	$375	$525	$650	$1,000	$1,750	$5,500	$21,500	$37,500	$80,000

1876-S Trade Dollar

1876-S, Obverse 1, Reverse 1 •

Mintage: Large portion of 5,227,000.

Points for identification: *Obverse:* The ribbon ends point left. *Reverse:* The berry is below the claw.

Rarity (% of date and mint, Borckardt study): 62%.

Availability in Mint State: *MS-60 to 62:* 900 to 1,200. *MS-63:* 125 to 200. *MS-64:* 60 to 100. *MS-65 or better:* 15 to 25.

Availability in circulated grades: *VF-20 to AU-58:* These are very common. They are also common with Chinese chopmarks.

Characteristics of striking: Striking of this issue varies, but some are sharp.

Notes: This issue has both Medium S (rare) and Large S (common) mintmark varieties.

	Cert	Avg	%MS	VG-8	F-12	VF-20	EF-40	AU-50	MS-60	MS-63	MS-64	MS-65
1876-S, Obverse 1, Reverse 1	969	56.4	54%	$165	$185	$200	$300	$350	$900	$1,600	$2,500	$10,000

1876-S, Obverse 1, Reverse 2 •

Mintage: Small portion of 5,227,000.

Points for identification: *Obverse:* The ribbon ends point left. *Reverse:* There is no berry below the claw.

Rarity (% of date and mint, Borckardt study): 19%.

Availability in Mint State: *MS-60 to 62:* 300 to 450. *MS-63:* 50 to 70. *MS-64:* 30 to 40. *MS-65 or better:* 8 to 10.

Availability in circulated grades: *VF-20 to AU-58:* These are very common. They are also common with Chinese chopmarks, but are seen less often than the issues without.

Characteristics of striking: Striking of this issue varies, but some are sharp.

Notes: These are known with both the Micro S and Large S (scarce) mintmarks, the last thought to have been used for 1875-S as well.

	Cert	Avg	%MS	VG-8	F-12	VF-20	EF-40	AU-50	MS-60	MS-63	MS-64	MS-65
1876-S, Obverse 1, Reverse 2	4	51.5	0%	$165	$185	$200	$300	$350	$900	$1,950	$3,000	$10,000

1876-S, Obverse 2, Reverse 2 •

Mintage: Small portion of 5,227,000.

Points for identification: *Obverse:* The ribbon ends point down. *Reverse:* There is no berry below the claw.

Rarity (% of date and mint, Borckardt study): 19%.

Availability in Mint State: *MS-60 to 62:* 300 to 450. *MS-63:* 50 to 70. *MS-64:* 30 to 40. *MS-65 or better:* 8 to 10.

Availability in circulated grades: *VF-20 to AU-58:* These are very common. They are also common with Chinese chopmarks, but they are the least often seen of the three different die combinations.

Characteristics of striking: Striking of this issue varies, but some are sharp.

Notes: They are known with both the Micro S and Large S (very rare) mintmarks.

	Cert	Avg	%MS	VG-8	F-12	VF-20	EF-40	AU-50	MS-60	MS-63	MS-64	MS-65
1876-S, Obverse 2, Reverse 2	2	59.5	50%	$165	$200	$300	$500	$850	$1,500	$2,650	$3,700	$13,500

VARIETY: *1876-S, Obverse 2, Reverse 2, Doubled-Die Obverse (FS-T1-1876S-101):* "Doubling is evident on Liberty's hand, laurel branch, and left foot. Possibly first reported around 1973." Five to eight are estimated to be known.

	Cert	Avg	%MS	EF-40	AU-50	MS-60
1876-S, Obverse 1, Reverse 1, Doubled Die Obverse	0	n/a		$1,400	$1,750	$2,200

1877 Trade Dollar

1877 • **Mintage:** 3,039,000.

Availability in Mint State: *MS-60 to 62:* 450 to 700. *MS-63:* 150 to 250. *MS-64:* 60 to 100. *MS-65 or better:* 10 to 15.

Availability in circulated grades: *VF-20 to AU-58:* 20,000+. With Chinese chopmarks these are scarcer than the large mintage for this year would suggest, but enough are around that finding one will be no problem.

Characteristics of striking: Many coins of this issue are weakly struck on Liberty's head and certain obverse stars.

	Cert	Avg	%MS	VG-8	F-12	VF-20	EF-40	AU-50	MS-60	MS-63	MS-64	MS-65
1877	776	50.3	39%	$165	$200	$225	$300	$350	$900	$1,600	$3,000	$10,000

VARIETY: *1877, Doubled-Die Obverse, (FS-T1-1877-101):* Doubling on this rare variety is evident on the wheat stalks, LIBERTY, IN GOD WE TRUST, and stars 11, 12, and 13.

	Cert	Avg	%MS	EF-40	AU-50	MS-60
1877, Doubled Die Obverse	4	61.0	50%	$300	$400	$1,250

1877, Proof • **Mintage:** 510.

Availability in Proof State: *PF-60 to 62:* 90 to 120. *PF-63:* 90 to 120. *PF-64:* 65 to 90. *PF-64 or better:* 25 to 45. The mintage may have been 710 (or 510, according to Mint figures).

	Cert	Avg	%MS	PF-60	PF-63	PF-65
1877, Proof	201	63.5		$1,650	$3,500	$7,000

1877-CC Trade Dollar

1877-CC • **Mintage:** 534,000.

Availability in Mint State: Mint State coins are sometimes seen with a "greasy" rather than deeply frosty luster. *MS-63:* 15 to 20. *MS-64:* 5 to 8. *MS-65 or better:* 0 or 1.

Availability in circulated grades: *VF-20 to AU-58:* 400 to 700. With Chinese chopmarks these are scarce, but they are more often seen than those without chopmarks.

Characteristics of striking: Striking of this issue varies, but sharp examples can be found.

	Cert	Avg	%MS	VG-8	F-12	VF-20	EF-40	AU-50	MS-60	MS-63	MS-64	MS-65
1877-CC	140	54.4	53%	$350	$525	$700	$1,150	$1,400	$4,750	$8,750	$21,500	$75,000

1877-S Trade Dollar

1877-S • **Mintage:** 9,519,000.

Availability in Mint State: *MS-60 to 62:* 2,000 to 3,000. *MS-63:* 350 to 500. *MS-64:* 200 to 300. *MS-65 or better:* 6 to 80.

Availability in circulated grades: *VF-20 to AU-58:* 50,000+. These are the most common in the series with Chinese chopmarks.

Characteristics of striking: Striking of this issue varies, but sharp coins can be found.

Notes: This issue is known to have the Micro S (slightly scarce), Medium S, and Large S mintmark varieties.

The mintage of the 1877-S trade dollar broke all previous records, and no later mintage was ever to equal it, with the result that the production of 9,519,000 pieces stands as the high point of the denomination. In fact, the mintage of 1877-S alone was greater than all combined trade dollar mintages of the Philadelphia and Carson City Mints from the first year of circulation-strike production, 1873, until the last, 1878.

Although some coins were distributed within the United States to brokers who bought them at a discount from face value and sold them to industrialists and others, by far the greatest amount of 1877-S trade dollars went to China, where they were plentiful for decades afterward.

	Cert	Avg	%MS	VG-8	F-12	VF-20	EF-40	AU-50	MS-60	MS-63	MS-64	MS-65
1877-S	1,755	53.7	47%	$165	$185	$200	$300	$325	$900	$1,450	$2,250	$7,000

VARIETY: *1877-S, Repunched Date (FS-T1-1877S-301):* A secondary 7 protrudes prominently south of the last 7. This is probably the most prominent repunched date in the series.

	Cert	Avg	%MS	EF-40	AU-50	MS-60
1877-S, Repunched Date	0	n/a		$550	$800	$1,600

VARIETY: *1877-S, Doubled-Die Reverse (FS-T1-1877S-801):* Doubling on this rare variety is visible on E PLURIBUS UNUM, the ribbon, and UNITED STATES OF AMERICA. From the *Cherrypickers' Guide to Rare Die Varieties*, Vol. 2 (sixth edition): "Considered a highlight of the trade dollar varieties."

	Cert	Avg	%MS	EF-40	AU-50	MS-60
1877-S, Doubled Die Reverse, FS-T1-1887S-801	2	55.5	0%	$300	$425	$1,300

VARIETY: *1877-S, Doubled-Die Reverse (FS-T1-1877S-802):* Minor doubling is visible on nearly all reverse lettering, especially on 420 GRAINS. This reverse doubled die is more common than the preceding.

	Cert	Avg	%MS	EF-40	AU-50	MS-60
1877-S, Doubled Die Reverse, FS-T1-1887S-802	8	54.0	50%	$300	$400	$1,200

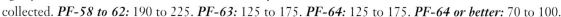

1878 Trade Dollar

1878, Proof • **Mintage:** 900.

Characteristics of striking: This issue is usually sharp, but there is sometimes slight weakness above Liberty's ear.

Availability in Proof State: Beginning with this year, figures start with PF-58, as many lightly circulated Proofs are known and are avidly collected. *PF-58 to 62:* 190 to 225. *PF-63:* 125 to 175. *PF-64:* 125 to 175. *PF-64 or better:* 70 to 100.

Notes: On February 22, 1878, Secretary of the Treasury John Sherman, a foe of the trade dollar denomination, mandated that coinage cease. By this time Philadelphia had produced no circulation strikes and made none later, only Proofs. Carson City had made some, production was halted there, and many extant coins were melted. San Francisco ended its coinage, but not immediately, as it wanted to take care of pending business and deposits.

	Cert	Avg	%MS	PF-60	PF-63	PF-65
1878, Proof	350	63.6		$1,500	$3,000	$7,000

1878-CC Trade Dollar

1878-CC • **Mintage:** 97,000.

Net after melting: 52,852.

Availability in Mint State: *MS-60 to 62:* 10 to 15. *MS-63:* 15 to 20. *MS-64:* 10 to 15. *MS-65 or better:* 5 to 8.

Availability in circulated grades: *VF-20 to AU-58:* 125 to 225. With Chinese chopmarks these are extremely rare.

Characteristics of striking: This issue is usually well struck.

Notes: Secretary of the Treasury John Sherman, who disliked trade dollars intensely (even though the director of the Mint, Dr. Henry Linderman, believed they were an excellent, useful coin), mandated on February 22, 1878, that no trade dollars would be paid out for deposits of bullion made prior to the order for discontinuance when received at Carson City. When this order reached Carson City, this branch mint had already struck 97,000 pieces; 56,000 in January and 41,000 in February—the smallest circulation strike quantity of the denomination. Thus, a rarity was created.

Apparently, relatively few were sent to China, and most probably remained in the United States. On July 19, 1878, some 44,148 undistributed trade dollars went to the melting pot. All must have been dated 1878-CC, many from the 41,000 delivered in February. This left a net mintage for distribution of only 52,852 coins.

	Cert	Avg	%MS	VG-8	F-12	VF-20	EF-40	AU-50	MS-60	MS-63	MS-64	MS-65
1878-CC	100	46.5	26%	$850	$1,250	$2,250	$3,750	$5,000	$13,500	$35,000	$80,000	$175,000

1878-S Trade Dollar

1878-S • **Mintage:** 4,162,000.

Availability in Mint State: In 2015 the Eugene H. Gardner Sale featured an example of this coin in MS-66. *MS-60 to 62:* 1,500 to 2,000. *MS-63:* 300 to 40. *MS-64:* 175 to 250. *MS-65 or better:* 70 to 100.

Availability in circulated grades: *VF-20 to AU-58:* 30,000+. Chopmarked coins are plentiful and are the second most common issue (after 1877-S).

Characteristics of striking: Striking of this issue varies.

Notes: By February 22, 1878, when Secretary of the Treasury John Sherman halted trade dollar mintage, the San Francisco Mint has already made 1,695,819 pieces. This branch did not end production until early April and by then the total was 4,162,000—nearly a record production (the fourth highest in the series).

By the time that the last 1878-S trade dollar fell from the dies, coins of this denomination face-valued at more than $36 million had been produced, a staggering sum, and an amount more than four times greater than all of the silver dollars that had been coined from 1794 until the denomination was suspended in 1873.

	Cert	Avg	%MS	VG-8	F-12	VF-20	EF-40	AU-50	MS-60	MS-63	MS-64	MS-65
1878-S	1,325	50.6	35%	$165	$185	$200	$275	$350	$800	$1,450	$2,000	$7,000

VARIETY: *1878-S, Doubled-Die Reverse (FS-T1-1878S-801):* Strong doubling is visible on the entire lower left of the reverse, on the arrow points and shafts, and on 420 GRAINS; slight doubling is evident on the motto. Rare in About Uncirculated and higher grades. There are at least two doubled-die reverses for this date.

	Cert	Avg	%MS	EF-40	AU-50	MS-60
1878-S, Doubled Die Reverse	15	52.7	33%	$450	$550	$1,300

1879 Trade Dollar

1879, Proof • **Mintage:** 1,541.

Availability in Proof State: *PF-58 to 62:* 300 to 450. *PF-63:* 250 to 400. *PF-64:* 225 to 300. *PF-64 or better:* 125 to 175.

Notes: There arose in 1879, and continued into 1880, a popular numismatic speculation (later extended to the general public). Word spread that certain coins were of low mintage and would become rare. The "best" condition was considered to be Proofs (circulation strikes were generally ignored and, in any event, were not available in the trade dollar series after 1878). There was also widespread investment interest in the low-mintage dimes, quarters, and half dollars of this year.

The fever to squirrel away Proof trade dollars was very short-lived (reminiscent of some fads today), extending only from December 1879 through the early part of 1880.

On December 16, 1878, the Engraving Department of the Philadelphia Mint, acting on the orders of Director Horatio Burchard (who seemingly anticipated there would be a coinage of 1879-S trade dollars even though they had been discontinued), shipped five obverse dies dated 1879 to San Francisco; however, no coinage materialized.

	Cert	Avg	%MS	PF-40	PF-60	PF-63	PF-65
1879, Proof	567	63.6		$1,250	$1,500	$3,000	$6,500

1880 Trade Dollar

1880, Proof • **Mintage:** 1,987.

Availability in Proof State: *PF-60 to 62:* 400 to 600. *PF-63:* 350 to 500. *PF-64:* 250 to 325. *PF-64 or better:* 150 to 200.

Notes: As in all years from 1879 to 1885, the only trade dollars struck in 1880 were Proofs. This year set a record for Proof trade dollar mintage. The popular speculation in Proof-only trade dollars continued and peaked in March 1880. By year's end some 1,987 Proofs had left the coining press, a record for the denomination and, for that matter, for any Proof silver coin before 1936!

From *Mason's Coin Collectors' Herald*, June 1880:

> Trade dollars of this year are still in demand, in Proof condition, at $2. While Proof sets remain at Mint prices the half dollars, quarters and dimes of this year, for general circulation, have not yet been coined, and we shall probably have a repetition of the speculative excitement which attended the distribution of the halves, quarters, and dimes of 1879, in the latter part of the present year.

	Cert	Avg	%MS	PF-40	PF-60	PF-63	PF-65
1880, Proof	722	63.4		$1,250	$1,500	$3,000	$6,500

1881 Trade Dollar

1881, Proof • **Mintage:** 960.

Availability in Proof State: *PF-60 to 62:* 150 to 250. *PF-63:* 200 to 300. *PF-64:* 150 to 225. *PF-64 or better:* 100 to 150.

Notes: Reflecting the dwindling fad, mintage of 1881 Proof trade dollars was once again nearly equal to the number of silver Proof sets minted (960 trade dollars versus 975 of other silver denominations).

Most of the Proofs of this year were poorly struck and exhibit flatness in areas, particularly on the head of Liberty and on the upper stars. This was due to incorrect die setting in the press. Poor striking continued to be a problem into 1883.

	Cert	Avg	%MS	PF-40	PF-60	PF-63	PF-65
1881, Proof	424	63.6		$1,250	$1,500	$3,000	$6,500

1882 Trade Dollar

1882, Proof • **Mintage:** 1,097.

Availability in Proof State: *PF-60 to 62:* 150 to 225. *PF-63:* 200 to 275. *PF-64:* 150 to 200. *PF-64 or better:* 90 to 125.

Notes: For the fifth year in a row, the only trade dollars minted at Philadelphia were Proofs. The mintage figure of 1,097 was nearly equal to the number of silver Proof sets (1,100) made of other denominations from the dime to the Morgan dollar.

   By year's end 1,097 Proofs had been struck, the third highest Proof mintage in the series, and one of just three Proof production quantities to break the 1,000 mark. Some may have been melted. Many Proofs are lightly struck.

	Cert	Avg	%MS	PF-40	PF-60	PF-63	PF-65
1882, Proof	527	63.8		$1,250	$1,500	$3,000	$6,500

1883 Trade Dollar

1883, Proof • **Mintage:** 979.

Availability in Proof State: *PF-60 to 62:* 100 to 150. *PF-63:* 200 to 300. *PF-64:* 140 to 175. *PF-64 or better:* 75 to 110.

Notes: In this final year of public sales of trade dollars, only Proofs were made. The figure of 979 Proof trade dollars fell short of the 1,039 Proofs made of other silver denominations. It is likely that many were melted as 1883 is rarer than the mintage would indicate.

	Cert	Avg	%MS	PF-40	PF-60	PF-63	PF-65
1883, Proof	485	63.6		$1,250	$1,500	$3,000	$6,500

1884 Trade Dollar

1884, Proof • **Mintage:** 10.

Notes: The trade dollars of 1884 and 1885 furnish a separate situation apart from Mint-authorized trade dollar issues. For many years, reference books, catalogs, and articles have claimed that just ten specimens were struck dated 1884 and just five dated 1885. These are believed to have been produced secretly at the Mint and were not included in any of the official reports. In fact, the very existence of these coins was not publicized to numismatists until 1908 when Captain John W. Haseltine (in partnership with Stephen K. Nagy), a Philadelphia coin dealer with close connections to the Mint, startled the hobby by announcing they had been found among coins in 1884 and 1885 Proof sets owned by his father-in-law, William K. Idler. However, the year before, Haseltine's partner, Nagy, had sold one to Virgil M. Brand in an unannounced transaction.

Farran Zerbe, editor of *The Numismatist*, wrote an article on the subject of 1884 trade dollars and noted that seven of the ten known pieces had been sold within a few months by a single dealer at prices ranging from $150 to $400. It was not revealed by Zerbe, if indeed he knew it, that Virgil Brand was the main buyer.

No one can be sure exactly how many 1884 and 1885 trade dollars were struck, absent official records. What we can be sure of is that only ten 1884s and only five 1885s *are now known.*

Today the 1884 and 1885 trade dollars are recognized as prime rarities, and the appearance of a single example on the market is cause for excited publicity. Several "pattern" strikings in copper are known, at least two of which have been silver plated, a deception not discovered until the coins were weighed. One of these was in a well-known collection auctioned in the 1960s. Another was discovered by Larry Briggs when evaluating a Michigan collection. It would seem wise to weigh *all* "silver" 1884 trade dollars.

The 1884 Proof trade dollar is ranked in the *100 Greatest U.S. Coins* (fifth edition).

	Cert	Avg	%MS	PF-40	PF-60	PF-63	PF-64	PF-65
1884, Proof	7	64.0		$1,250		$400,000	$550,000	$750,000

1885 Trade Dollar

1885, Proof • **Mintage:** 5.

Notes: Trade dollars dated 1885 first became known to the numismatic fraternity when five pieces came on the market in 1908, echoing the scenario of the 1884 coins. These had been "discovered" in 1906 in the estate of William K. Idler as it was being examined by his son-in-law John W. Haseltine. Both were "rascals" in that they were the primary outlet for Mint officials to funnel secret strikes of patterns, restrikes, etc., into the marketplace.

Most likely 1885 Proof trade dollars were struck early in that year, after the January 2, 1885, destruction of the 1884 obverse and reverse die (for the 1885 is from a different reverse than used in 1884), but before Colonel A. Loudon Snowden, superintendent of the Philadelphia Mint since 1879, turned in his resignation in June 1885. His successor as superintendent, Daniel M. Fox, was very circumspect and proper, and no hint of making "fancy pieces" ever surfaced during his administration.

On all five of the known coins the reverse die is doubled.

No Proof 1885 trade dollars are listed in Mint reports or records, and it is supposed that the coinage was unofficial. Today, specimens are highly prized as great rarities and are among the most famous and desirable of all U.S. silver coins.

The 1885 Proof trade dollar is ranked in the *100 Greatest U.S. Coins* (fifth edition).

	Cert	Avg	%MS	PF-63	PF-64	PF-65
1885, Proof	3	63.3		1,250,000	$1,500,000	$2,000,000

Gold Dollars
1849–1889

AN OVERVIEW OF GOLD DOLLARS

Coinage of the gold dollar was authorized by the Act of March 3, 1849, after the start of the California Gold Rush.

Although a case could be made for designating the Small Head, Open Wreath, gold dollar as a separate type, it is not generally collected as such. Instead, pieces dated from 1849 through 1854 (whether Open Wreath or Close Wreath) are collectively designated as Type 1. Examples today are readily available in all grades, although truly choice and gem Mint State pieces are in the minority.

In contrast, the Type 2 design, produced at the Philadelphia Mint in part of 1854, and at the Philadelphia, Charlotte, Dahlonega, and New Orleans mints in 1855, and only at the San Francisco Mint in 1856, is a great challenge. Examples are scarcer in all grades than are those of types 1 and 3. Choice and gem coins are especially rare. Striking is a great problem, and while some sharp pieces exist, probably 80% or more have areas of weakness, typically at the 85 (center two digits) of the date, but also often on the headdress and elsewhere. Further, the borders are sometimes imperfect.

Type 3 gold dollars, made from 1856 through 1889, are easier to acquire in nearly any grade desired, including choice and gem Mint State. Most are well struck and in Mint State have excellent eye appeal. Among Type 3 gold dollars the dates from 1879 through 1889 inclusive are most often seen, as these were widely saved by coin dealers and collectors at the time and did not circulate to any appreciable extent. Gold dollar coins also were popular as Christmas gifts in the late 1800s. Some of these have very low mintage figures, making them very appealing to today's collectors.

North Carolina Representative James Iver McKay was among the proponents for the introduction of a gold dollar coin. He introduced a bill to authorize the denomination into the House of Representatives on February 20, 1849.

FOR THE COLLECTOR AND INVESTOR: GOLD DOLLARS AS A SPECIALTY

Forming a specialized collection of gold dollars is a fascinating pursuit, one that has drawn the attention of many numismatists over the years. A complete run of date-and-mintmark issues from 1849 through 1889 includes no impossible rarities, although the 1875, with just 20 Proofs and 400 circulation strikes made, is the key date and can challenge collectors. While the dollars of 1879 through 1889 often have remarkably low mintages, they were saved in quantity, and certain of these dates are easily obtainable (although not necessarily inexpensive).

The branch-mint gold dollars of the early years present a special challenge. Among the Charlotte Mint varieties the 1849 comes with an Open Wreath (of which just five are presently known, with a rumor of a sixth) and with a Close Wreath, the latter being scarce but available. Later Charlotte gold dollars, extending through 1859, range from scarce to rare. The 1857-C is notorious for its poor striking.

Gold dollars were struck at the Dahlonega Mint from 1849 through 1861. In the latter year the facility was under the control of the Confederate States of America, and thus the 1861-D gold dollars, rare in any event, are even more desirable as true Confederate coins. The New Orleans Mint also produced gold dollars, which in general are better struck than those of the Charlotte and Dahlonega mints. From 1854 intermittently to 1860, and then in 1870, gold dollars were struck in San Francisco. These Western issues are usually sharply defined and range from scarce to rare. In particular, choice and gem Mint State pieces are elusive.

LIBERTY HEAD (1849–1854)

Designer: *James B. Longacre.* **Weight:** *1.672 grams.*
Composition: *.900 gold, .100 copper (net weight .04837 oz. pure gold).*
Diameter: *13 mm.* **Edge:** *Reeded.* **Mints:** *Philadelphia,*
Charlotte, Dahlonega, New Orleans, and San Francisco.

**Open Wreath
Reverse**

**Close Wreath
Reverse**

Proof

*Mintmark location
is on the reverse,
below the wreath.*

History. U.S. Mint chief engraver James Barton Longacre designed the nation's gold dollars. This first type measured 13 mm in diameter, which proved to be inconvenient, and the two later types were enlarged to 15 mm.

Striking and Sharpness. As a rule, Type 1 gold dollars struck in Philadelphia are sharper than those of the Charlotte and Dahlonega mints. On the obverse, check the highest areas of the hair below the coronet. On the reverse, check the wreath and the central two figures in the date. On both sides check the denticles, which can be mushy or indistinct (particularly on Charlotte and Dahlonega coins, which often have planchet roughness as well).

Availability. All dates and mintmarks are readily collectible, save for the 1849-C, Open Wreath, variety. MS coins often are found for the Philadelphia issues but can be elusive for the branch mints. Charlotte and Dahlonega coins often have striking problems. The few gold dollars of this type that are less than VF in grade usually are damaged or have problems. Although a few Proofs were coined in the early years, they are for all practical purposes unobtainable. Only about a dozen are known.

GRADING STANDARDS

MS-60 to 70 (Mint State). *Obverse:* At MS–60 to 62, there is abrasion on the hair below the coronet (an area that can be weakly struck as well) and on the cheeks. Marks may be seen. At MS-63, there may be slight abrasion. Luster is irregular. At MS-64, abrasion is less. Luster is rich on most coins, less so on Charlotte and Dahlonega varieties. At MS-65 and above, luster is deep and frosty. At MS-66 and higher, no marks at all are visible

1854, Close Wreath. Graded MS-62.

without magnification. *Reverse:* On MS–60 to 62 coins, there is abrasion on the 1, the highest parts of the leaves, and the ribbon. Otherwise, the same comments apply as for the obverse.

Illustrated coin: Some friction is visible on the portrait and in the fields.

AU-50, 53, 55, 58 (About Uncirculated). *Obverse:* Light wear on the hair below the coronet and the cheek is very noticeable at AU-50, and progressively less at higher levels to AU-58. Luster is minimal at AU-50 and scattered and incomplete at AU-58. Some tiny nicks and contact marks are to be expected and should be mentioned if they are distracting. *Reverse:* Light wear on the 1, the wreath, and the ribbon characterize an AU-50 coin,

1853-D. Graded AU-58.

progressively less at higher levels to AU-58. Otherwise, the same comments apply as for the obverse.

Illustrated coin: Much of the luster remains, especially in protected areas.

EF-40, 45 (Extremely Fine). *Obverse:* Medium wear is seen on the hair below the coronet, extending to near the bun, and on the curls below. Detail is partially gone on the hair to the right of the coronet. Luster is gone on most coins. *Reverse:* Light wear is seen overall, and the highest parts of the leaves are flat. Luster is gone.

1849-C, Close Wreath. Graded EF-45.

VF-20, 30 (Very Fine). *Obverse:* Most hair detail is gone, except in the lower-relief areas and on the lower curls. Star centers are flat. *Reverse:* The wreath and other areas show more wear. Most detail is gone on the higher-relief leaves.

Liberty Head gold dollars are seldom collected in grades lower than VF-20.

1851-D. Graded VF-25.

PF-60 to 70 (Proof). *Obverse and Reverse:* PF–60 to 62 coins have extensive hairlines and may have nicks and contact marks. At PF-63, hairlines are prominent, but the mirror surface is very reflective. PF-64 coins have fewer hairlines. At PF-65, hairlines should be minimal and mostly seen only under magnification. One cannot be "choosy" with Proofs of this type, as only a few exist.

1849, Open Wreath. Proof.

1849, With L   1849, No L

	Mintage	Cert	Avg	%MS	VF-20	EF-40	AU-50	AU-55	AU-58	MS-60	MS-63	MS-64	MS-65 / PF-60
1849, Open Wreath, So-Called Small Head, With L (a)	688,567	1,041	60.5	70%	$245	$275	$300	$325	$340	$450	$1,250	$1,750	$4,000
Auctions: $1,763, MS-64, June 2015; $705, MS-62, January 2015; $188, AU-58, January 2015; $235, AU-50, July 2015													
1849, Open Wreath, So-Called Small Head, No L (a)	(b)	407	62.1	85%	$245	$285	$350	$375	$475	$800	$1,600	$2,150	$4,750
Auctions: $4,935, MS-65, July 2015; $1,293, MS-63, January 2015; $881, MS-61, February 2015; $823, MS-60, October 2015													
1849, Open Wreath, So-Called Large Head (a)	(b)	0	n/a		$245	$275	$300	$325	$350	$450	$1,300	$1,750	$4,000
Auctions: $3,760, MS-65, January 2015; $1,495, MS-64, April 2012													
1849, Close Wreath	(b)	508	61.4	78%	$245	$275	$300	$325	$400	$650	$1,500	$2,200	$6,250
Auctions: $25,850, MS-66, August 2015; $705, MS-62, August 2015; $376, AU-58, August 2015; $329, AU-50, March 2015													
1849, Open Wreath, So-Called Small Head, No L, Proof (c)	unknown	3	62.7										—
Auctions: No auction records available.													
1849-C, Open Wreath † (d)	(b)	2	32.5	0%	$200,000	$225,000			$365,000		$650,000		
Auctions: $3,220, AU-58, April 2012													
1849-C, Close Wreath	11,634	98	55.8	33%	$1,300	$1,800	$2,650	$4,250	$6,750	$9,250	$17,500	$45,000	
Auctions: $49,350, MS-64, August 2015; $10,281, MS-62, September 2013; $1,058, AU-50, January 2015; $2,820, EF-45, July 2014													
1849-D, Open Wreath	21,588	318	57.0	37%	$1,500	$2,100	$2,600	$3,000	$3,800	$5,500	$14,000	$22,500	$55,000
Auctions: $22,325, MS-64, April 2013; $4,465, MS-62, January 2015; $3,760, MS-61, January 2015; $2,585, AU-55, September 2014													
1849-O, Open Wreath	215,000	791	57.8	45%	$275	$325	$400	$500	$600	$1,000	$3,500	$6,500	$13,500
Auctions: $11,750, MS-65, March 2015; $999, MS-61, September 2015; $423, AU-58, June 2015; $259, EF-45, November 2015													

† Ranked in the *100 Greatest U.S. Coins* (fifth edition). **a.** It is now well known that the so-called Small Head and Large Head coins are from the same punch. **b.** Included in 1849, Open Wreath, So-Called Small Head, With L, mintage figure. **c.** 2 to 3 examples are known. **d.** This coin is extremely rare.

	Mintage	Cert	Avg	%MS	VF-20	EF-40	AU-50	AU-55	AU-58	MS-60	MS-63	MS-64	MS-65
													PF-60
1850	481,953	595	59.5	62%	$245	$275	$285	$295	$315	$425	$775	$1,250	$4,000
	Auctions: $32,900, MS-67, August 2015; $2,585, MS-64, October 2015; $447, MS-61, June 2015; $235, AU-55, January 2015												
1850, Proof (e)	*unknown*	0	n/a										$100,000
	Auctions: No auction records available.												
1850-C	6,966	95	54.7	24%	$1,650	$2,150	$3,000	$4,000	$4,750	$6,000	$23,500		
	Auctions: $24,675, MS-63, February 2015; $19,975, MS-63, January 2014; $17,625, MS-63, November 2014; $11,163, MS-61, September 2016												
1850-D	8,382	102	54.6	23%	$1,650	$2,350	$3,400	$5,000	$6,500	$10,500	$30,000	$45,000	
	Auctions: $3,290, AU-55, January 2015; $3,204, AU-50, July 2014												
1850-O	14,000	192	58.1	42%	$350	$675	$900	$1,150	$2,000	$3,150	$6,000	$15,000	
	Auctions: $2,532, MS-61, April 2012												
1851	3,317,671	4,848	60.8	77%	$240	$250	$260	$270	$285	$325	$500	$700	$1,850
	Auctions: $3,995, MS-66, July 2015; $329, MS-61, January 2015; $229, AU-55, April 2015; $1,528, EF-45, September 2015												
1851-C	41,267	424	57.3	33%	$1,350	$1,650	$2,000	$2,250	$2,550	$3,200	$6,250	$13,500	$25,000
	Auctions: $5,376, MS-63, January 2015; $3,525, MS-62, June 2015; $2,468, AU-58, March 2015; $2,056, AU-55, January 2015												
1851-D	9,882	143	57.9	38%	$1,500	$2,000	$2,750	$3,250	$3,850	$5,000	$14,500	$22,500	$45,000
	Auctions: $14,688, MS-64, October 2014; $7,638, MS-62, February 2015; $4,113, AU-58, October 2014; $2,233, AU-50, March 2015												
1851-O	290,000	919	58.2	43%	$245	$275	$325	$425	$450	$750	$1,900	$4,000	$9,500
	Auctions: $12,925, MS-65, August 2015; $764, MS-61, January 2015; $270, AU-55, November 2015; $194, EF-45, January 2015												
1852	2,045,351	4,312	61.0	78%	$240	$250	$260	$270	$285	$325	$500	$700	$1,850
	Auctions: $4,700, MS-66, July 2015; $470, MS-63, August 2015; $259, AU-58, May 2015; $235, AU-55, August 2015												
1852-C	9,434	155	57.0	40%	$1,400	$1,750	$2,250	$2,750	$3,500	$4,600	$10,500	$16,500	$30,000
	Auctions: $15,863, MS-64, February 2013; $2,128, AU-55, October 2014; $2,585, AU-53, July 2014; $1,880, EF-40, July 2015												
1852-D	6,360	108	56.5	31%	$1,500	$2,250	$2,850	$3,750	$5,500	$8,250	$30,000		
	Auctions: $4,230, AU-58, February 2015; $4,994, AU-55, July 2014; $4,230, EF-45, January 2015												
1852-O	140,000	519	56.5	30%	$245	$275	$400	$600	$750	$1,300	$4,200	$12,500	$35,000
	Auctions: $37,600, MS-65, August 2015; $2,497, MS-63, January 2015; $541, AU-58, January 2015; $237, AU-53, June 2015												
1853	4,076,051	11,277	61.1	79%	$240	$250	$260	$270	$285	$325	$500	$700	$1,850
	Auctions: $20,575, MS-67, August 2015; $881, MS-64, February 2015; $353, MS-61, August 2015; $235, AU-55, November 2015												
1853-C	11,515	139	56.6	32%	$1,350	$1,600	$2,100	$2,600	$3,500	$4,750	$13,000	$22,000	$45,000
	Auctions: $14,100, MS-64, January 2014; $4,406, MS-62, August 2014; $9,988, MS-62, October 2014; $1,593, EF-40, July 2014												
1853-D	6,583	130	57.4	28%	$1,500	$2,000	$2,500	$3,750	$5,000	$8,000	$22,000	$33,500	$50,000
	Auctions: $17,038, MS-63, June 2015; $8,225, MS-62, June 2015; $6,933, MS-61, January 2015; $3,055, AU-55, October 2014												
1853-O	290,000	1,373	59.4	54%	$245	$275	$335	$425	$450	$700	$1,800	$2,750	$8,000
	Auctions: $23,500, MS-66, August 2015; $1,058, MS-62, January 2015; $259, AU-55, June 2015; $212, AU-50, February 2015												
1854	855,502	3,966	61.4	85%	$240	$250	$260	$270	$285	$325	$500	$700	$1,900
	Auctions: $19,975, MS-67, August 2015; $5,170, MS-66, August 2015; $376, MS-62, November 2015; $282, AU-55, October 2015												
1854, Proof	*unknown*	0	n/a										—
	Auctions: No auction records available.												
1854-D	2,935	77	56.6	35%	$2,000	$2,500	$5,250	$6,500	$7,750	$11,000	$35,000	$65,000	
	Auctions: $7,638, MS-61, October 2015; $6,465, AU-58, July 2015; $5,640, AU-58, January 2015; $4,465, EF-45, September 2016												
1854-S	14,632	149	58.5	39%	$450	$650	$1,000	$1,400	$2,000	$2,600	$6,500	$16,000	$37,500
	Auctions: $56,400, MS-65, August 2015; $2,820, MS-62, January 2015; $1,528, AU-58, January 2015; $1,058, AU-53, February 2015												

e. 2 examples are known.

INDIAN PRINCESS HEAD, SMALL HEAD (1854–1856)

Designer: *James B. Longacre.* **Weight:** *1.672 grams.*
Composition: *.900 gold, .100 copper (net weight .04837 oz. pure gold).* **Diameter:** *15 mm.*
Edge: *Reeded.* **Mints:** *Philadelphia, Charlotte, Dahlonega, New Orleans, San Francisco.*

Circulation Strike   *Mintmark location is on the reverse, below the wreath.*   **Proof**

History. The Type 2 gold dollar, with the diameter increased from 13 mm to 15 mm, was first made in 1854. The headdress is decorated with *ostrich* plumes, which would not have been used in any genuine Native American headgear. The design proved difficult to strike, leading to its modification in 1856.

Striking and Sharpness. On the obverse, check the highest area of the hair below the coronet and the tips of the feathers. Check the letters. On the reverse, check the ribbon bow knot and in particular the two central digits of the dates. Examine the digits on both sides. Nearly all have problems. This type is often softly struck in the centers, with weak hair detail and the numerals 85 in the date sometimes faint—this should not be confused with wear. The 1855-C and 1855-D coins are often poorly struck and on rough planchets.

Availability. All Type 2 gold dollars are collectible, but the Charlotte and Dahlonega coins are rare. With patience, Full Details coins are available of 1854, 1855, and 1856-S, but virtually impossible to find for the branch-mint issues of 1855. The few gold dollars of this type that are less than VF in grade usually are damaged or have problems. Proofs exist of the 1854 and 1855 issues, but were made in very small quantities.

GRADING STANDARDS

MS-60 to 70 (Mint State). *Obverse:* At MS–60 to 62, there is abrasion on the hair below the band lettered LIBERTY (an area that can be weakly struck as well), on the tips of the feather plumes, and throughout the field. Contact marks may also be seen. At MS-63, there should be only slight abrasions. Luster is irregular. At MS-64, abrasions and marks are less. Luster is rich on most coins, less so on Charlotte and Dahlonega issues. At

1854. Graded MS-61.

MS-65 and above, luster is deep and frosty, with no marks at all visible without magnification at MS-66 and higher. *Reverse:* At MS–60 to 62, there may be abrasions on the 1, on the highest parts of the leaves, on the ribbon knot, and in the field. Otherwise, the same comments apply as for the obverse.

Illustrated coin: Some loss of luster is evident in the fields, but strong luster remains among the letters and in other protected areas. Good eye appeal is elusive for this type.

AU-50, 53, 55, 58 (About Uncirculated). *Obverse:* Light wear on the hair below the coronet, the cheek, and the tips of the feather plumes is very noticeable at AU-50, progressively less at higher levels to AU-58. Luster is minimal at AU-50 and scattered and incomplete at AU-58. Some tiny nicks and contact marks are to be expected and should be mentioned if they are distracting. *Reverse:* Light wear on the 1, the wreath, and the ribbon

1855. Graded AU-55.

knot characterize an AU-50 coin, progressively less at higher levels to AU-58. Otherwise, the same comments apply as for the obverse.

Illustrated coin: This coin was lightly struck at the center. Clash marks appear on both sides, most prominent within the wreath on the reverse.

EF-40, 45 (Extremely Fine). *Obverse:* Medium wear is seen on the hair below the coronet and on the feather plume tips. Detail is partially gone on the hair, although the usual light striking may make this moot. Luster is gone on most coins. *Reverse:* Light wear is seen overall, and the highest parts of the leaves are flat. Luster is gone on most coins.

Illustrated coin: This coin was lightly struck at the centers, but overall has extraordinary quality.

1855-C. Graded EF-40.

VF-20, 30 (Very Fine). *Obverse:* Most hair detail is gone, except at the back of the lower curls. The feather plume ends are flat. *Reverse:* The wreath and other areas show more wear. Most detail is gone on the higher-relief leaves.

Illustrated coin: This coin is well worn, but has an exceptionally bold date, indicating that it must have been a very sharp strike.

Indian Princess Head, Small Head, gold dollars are seldom collected in grades lower than VF-20.

1854. Graded VF-25.

PF-60 to 70 (Proof). *Obverse and Reverse:* PF–60 to 62 coins have extensive hairlines and may have nicks and contact marks. At PF-63, hairlines are prominent, but the mirror surface is very reflective. PF-64 coins have fewer hairlines. At PF-65, hairlines should be minimal and mostly seen only under magnification. There should be no nicks or marks. PF-66 and higher coins have no marks or hairlines visible to the unaided eye.

1854. Graded PF-66.

1854, Doubled Die Obverse
FS-G1-1854-1101.

	Mintage	Cert	Avg	%MS	VF-20	EF-40	AU-50	AU-55	MS-60	MS-62	MS-63	MS-64	MS-65
											PF-63	PF-64	PF-65
1854	783,943	6,076	57.2	27%	$325	$425	$500	$625	$1,250	$2,000	$4,500	$7,500	$25,000
	Auctions: $51,700, MS-66, August 2015; $1,880, MS-62, January 2015; $402, AU-53, October 2015; $329, EF-40, August 2015												
1854, Doubled Die Obverse (a)	**(b)**	18	56.2	6%				$2,500	$5,500	$7,500	$12,500		
	Auctions: $3,738, MS-62, December 2011												
1854, Proof †	*4 known*	5	64.6								$200,000	$300,000	$400,000
	Auctions: $218,500, PF-64DCam, March 2009												
1855	758,269	5,584	57.1	27%	$325	$425	$500	$625	$1,250	$2,000	$4,500	$7,500	$25,000
	Auctions: $54,050, MS-66, August 2015; $4,230, MS-63, January 2015; $640, AU-58, February 2015; $529, EF-40, April 2015												
1855, Proof †	*unknown*	6	64.8								$165,000	$225,000	$325,000
	Auctions: $397,800, PF, September 2013												
1855-C	9,803	193	51.6	9%	$2,350	$4,750	$6,000	$9,000	$22,500	$35,000			
	Auctions: $24,675, MS-61, January 2015; $7,638, AU-55, June 2015; $5,611, AU-50, June 2015; $4,230, EF-40, June 2015												
1855-D	1,811	42	54.5	12%	$15,000	$25,000	$37,500	$45,000	$60,000	$70,000	$100,000	$175,000	
	Auctions: $164,500, MS-64, August 2015; $28,200, AU-55, September 2016; $8,225, AU-50, July 2015; $52,875, EF-45, July 2014												
1855-O	55,000	534	54.8	13%	$775	$1,200	$1,750	$2,650	$8,000	$14,000	$30,000	$45,000	
	Auctions: $3,525, AU-58, June 2015; $2,585, AU-55, January 2015; $1,998, AU-50, July 2015; $705, VF-25, January 2015												
1856-S	24,600	234	54.5	14%	$850	$1,500	$2,250	$3,500	$8,000	$16,000	$26,000	$45,000	
	Auctions: $52,875, MS-64, February 2013; $5,640, AU-58, January 2015; $3,290, AU-58, January 2015; $282, VF-20, August 2015												

† 1854 and 1855 Proof Indian Princess Head, Large Head Gold Dollars are ranked in the *100 Greatest U.S. Coins* (fifth edition), as a single entry. **a.** Check for strong doubling on UNITED STATES OF AMERICA, the beads in the headdress, the feathers, and portions of LIBERTY. **b.** Included in circulation-strike 1854 mintage figure.

INDIAN PRINCESS HEAD, LARGE HEAD (1856–1889)

Designer: *James B. Longacre.* **Weight:** *1.672 grams.*
Composition: *.900 gold, .100 copper (net weight .04837 oz. pure gold).* **Diameter:** *15 mm.*
Edge: *Reeded.* **Mints:** *Philadelphia, Charlotte, Dahlonega, and San Francisco.*

Circulation Strike   Proof

History. The design of the Indian Princess Head was modified in 1856. The new Type 3 portrait is larger and in shallower relief. After this change, most (but not all) gold dollars were struck with strong detail. Gold dollars of this type did not circulate extensively after 1861, except in the West. As they did not see heavy use, today most pieces are EF or better. MS coins are readily available, particularly of the dates 1879 through 1889 (during those years the coins were popular among investors and speculators, and many were saved). These gold dollars were very popular with jewelers, who would purchase them at a price of $1.50 for use in a variety of ornaments.

Striking and Sharpness. These dollars usually are well struck, but many exceptions exist. Charlotte and Dahlonega coins are usually weak in areas and can have planchet problems. On all coins, check the hair details on the obverse. The word LIBERTY may be only partially present or missing completely, as the dies were made this way for some issues, particularly in the 1870s; this does not affect their desirability. On the reverse, check the ribbon knot and the two central date numerals. Check the denticles on both sides. Copper stains are sometimes seen on issues of the 1880s due to incomplete mixing of the alloy. Many coins of the 1860s onward have highly prooflike surfaces.

Availability. All Type 3 gold dollars are collectible, but many issues are scarce. Most MS-65 or finer coins are dated from 1879 to 1889. The few gold dollars of this type that are less than VF usually are damaged or have problems. Proofs were made of all years. Most range from rare to very rare, some dates in the 1880s being exceptions. Some later dates have high Proof mintages, but likely many of these coins were sold to the jewelry trade (as the Mint was reluctant to release circulation strikes to this market sector). Such coins were incorporated into jewelry and no longer exist as collectible coins.

GRADING STANDARDS

MS-60 to 70 (Mint State). *Obverse:* At MS-60 to 62, there is abrasion on the hair below the band lettered LIBERTY (an area that can be weakly struck as well), on the tips of the feather plumes, and throughout the field. Contact marks may also be seen. At MS-63, there should be only slight abrasions. Luster is irregular. At MS-64, abrasions and marks are less. Luster is rich on most coins, less so on Charlotte and Dahlonega issues. At

1878. Graded MS-67.

MS-65 and above, luster is deep and frosty, with no marks at all visible without magnification at MS-66 and higher. *Reverse:* At MS–60 to 62, there may be abrasions on the 1, on the highest parts of the leaves, on the ribbon knot, and in the field. Otherwise, the same comments apply as for the obverse.

Illustrated coin: This exceptionally high-grade coin has superb eye appeal.

AU-50, 53, 55, 58 (About Uncirculated). *Obverse:* Light wear on the hair below the coronet, the cheek, and the tips of the feather plumes is very noticeable at AU-50, progressively less at higher levels to AU-58. Luster is minimal at AU-50 and scattered and incomplete at AU-58. Some tiny nicks and contact marks are to be expected and should be mentioned if they are distracting. *Reverse:* Light wear on the 1, the wreath, and the ribbon

1857-C. Graded AU-58.

knot characterize an AU-50 coin, progressively less at higher levels to AU-58. Otherwise, the same comments apply as for the obverse.

Illustrated coin: The obverse field is slightly bulged. This coin is lightly struck at the center, unusual for most Type 3 gold dollars, but sometimes seen on Charlotte and Dahlonega varieties. Among 1857-C gold dollars this coin is exceptional. Most have poor striking and/or planchet problems.

EF-40, 45 (Extremely Fine). *Obverse:* Medium wear is seen on the hair below the coronet and on the feather plume tips. Detail is partially gone on the hair, although the usual light striking may make this moot. Luster is gone on most coins. *Reverse:* Light wear is seen overall, and the highest parts of the leaves are flat. Luster is gone on most coins.

1859-S. Graded EF-40.

VF-20, 30 (Very Fine). *Obverse:* Most hair detail is gone, except at the back of the lower curls. The feather plume ends are flat. *Reverse:* The wreath and other areas show more wear. Most detail is gone on the higher-relief leaves.

Illustrated coin: This coin is lightly struck at the center obverse, as well as at the U and IC in the border lettering. It is lightly struck at the center of the reverse.

1859-D. Graded VF-20.

Indian Princess Head, Large Head, gold dollars are seldom collected in grades lower than VF-20.

PF-60 to 70 (Proof). *Obverse and Reverse:* PF-60 to 62 coins have extensive hairlines and may have nicks and contact marks. At PF-63, hairlines are prominent, but the mirror surface is very reflective. PF-64 coins have fewer hairlines. At PF-65, hairlines should be minimal and mostly seen only under magnification. There should be no nicks or marks. PF-66 and higher coins have no marks or hairlines visible to the unaided eye.

1884. Graded PF-68.

Illustrated coin: This splendid cameo Proof is one of the finest graded.

	Mintage	Cert	Avg	%MS	VF-20	EF-40	AU-50	AU-55	MS-60	MS-62	MS-63 PF-63	MS-64 PF-64	MS-65 PF-65
1856, All kinds	1,762,936												
1856, Upright 5		381	58.7	45%	$285	$315	$375	$450	$650	$850	$1,500	$2,100	$9,500
	Auctions: $16,450, MS-66, July 2015; $1,998, MS-64, September 2015; $447, MS-61, September 2015; $259, AU-55, September 2015												
1856, Slant 5		1,666	59.1	51%	$265	$275	$285	$295	$475	$525	$750	$1,100	$2,500
	Auctions: $42,300, MS-68, August 2015; $400, MS-62, January 2015; $306, AU-58, June 2015; $212, AU-50, November 2015												
1856, Slant 5, Proof	*unknown*	4	66.3								$30,000	$35,000	$65,000
	Auctions: $30,550, PF, January 2013												
1856-D	1,460	36	55.6	11%	$5,500	$8,000	$9,500	$12,000	$27,500	$45,000	$80,000		
	Auctions: $15,275, AU-58, September 2016; $11,750, AU-58, September 2013; $8,225, AU-50, September 2016; $7,050, EF-45, July 2014												

1862, Doubled Die Obverse
FS-G1-1862-101.

	Mintage	Cert	Avg	%MS	VF-20	EF-40	AU-50	AU-55	MS-60	MS-62	MS-63 PF-63	MS-64 PF-64	MS-65 PF-65
1857	774,789	1,417	59.9	61%	$265	$275	$285	$295	$475	$525	$750	$1,100	$3,000
Auctions: $51,700, MS-68, August 2015; $823, MS-64, October 2015; $353, MS-61, September 2015; $329, AU-50, October 2015													
1857, Proof	unknown	7	64.6								$20,000	$24,000	$40,000
Auctions: $16,100, PF-63Cam, June 2008													
1857-C	13,280	156	53.7	8%	$1,350	$1,750	$3,250	$5,000	$10,000	$16,500			
Auctions: $8,813, MS-61, January 2015; $3,290, AU-55, March 2015; $3,102, AU-55, January 2015; $3,055, EF-45, January 2015													
1857-D	3,533	98	55.6	21%	$1,500	$2,400	$3,750	$5,000	$10,500	$17,500			
Auctions: $5,581, AU-58, April 2013; $3,525, AU-53, October 2014; $2,238, EF-45, July 2014													
1857-S	10,000	119	54.1	15%	$450	$750	$1,250	$2,000	$5,250	$8,000	$20,000	$35,000	
Auctions: $3,995, MS-61, January 2015; $3,775, MS-61, June 2015; $2,350, AU-55, July 2014; $999, AU-53, January 2015													
1858	117,995	268	59.9	59%	$265	$275	$285	$295	$400	$650	$1,050	$1,500	$4,750
Auctions: $51,700, MS-68, August 2015; $1,410, MS-63, September 2015; $282, AU-55, July 2015; $235, AU-53, January 2015													
1858, Proof	unknown	14	64.6								$13,500	$15,000	$30,000
Auctions: $32,900, PF-66Cam+, November 2014; $79,313, PF, March 2014													
1858-D	3,477	116	55.5	28%	$1,500	$2,250	$3,250	$4,250	$7,750	$11,500	$21,500	$37,500	$60,000
Auctions: $7,638, MS-61, December 2013; $4,230, AU-58, February 2015; $1,439, AU-50, September 2014; $1,998, EF-45, July 2014													
1858-S	10,000	104	54.2	13%	$425	$750	$1,200	$1,600	$5,250	$8,500	$15,000	$25,000	$40,000
Auctions: $25,850, MS-64, August 2015; $7,050, MS-62, June 2015; $4,348, MS-61, August 2015; $852, AU-50, January 2015													
1859	168,244	440	60.4	70%	$265	$275	$285	$295	$400	$525	$800	$1,100	$2,250
Auctions: $37,600, MS-68, August 2015; $1,998, MS-65, August 2015; $376, MS-61, August 2015; $282, AU-58, January 2015													
1859, Proof	80	12	65.0								$10,000	$14,000	$22,500
Auctions: $22,325, PF-64, August 2013													
1859-C	5,235	90	56.8	27%	$2,000	$3,250	$4,000	$5,000	$7,000	$13,500	$25,000		
Auctions: $15,275, MS-63, June 2015; $5,640, AU-58, June 2015; $4,465, AU-55, July 2015; $2,585, AU-50, August 2015													
1859-D	4,952	126	57.0	24%	$1,600	$2,250	$3,250	$5,000	$8,750	$12,500	$21,500	$32,500	$55,000
Auctions: $11,750, MS-62, June 2013; $3,290, AU-55, July 2014; $3,055, AU-53, February 2015; $911, AU-50, November 2014													
1859-S	15,000	158	52.3	10%	$300	$575	$1,250	$1,900	$4,750	$8,000	$14,500	$24,000	
Auctions: $6,169, MS-62, February 2013; $3,760, MS-61, January 2015; $1,469, AU-58, June 2015; $306, EF-40, September 2015													
1860	36,514	170	61.1	81%	$265	$275	$285	$295	$525	$675	$1,250	$2,250	$7,500
Auctions: $10,869, MS-65, August 2015; $881, MS-63, September 2015; $646, MS-61, August 2015; $329, AU-55, February 2015													
1860, Proof	154	17	64.6								$8,000	$10,000	$20,000
Auctions: $27,600, PF-66, January 2012													
1860-D	1,566	63	55.2	22%	$3,750	$6,500	$10,000	$12,000	$20,000	$30,000	$50,000	$65,000	
Auctions: $42,300, MS-64, February 2013; $11,750, AU-50, June 2015; $6,463, EF-40, July 2014													
1860-S	13,000	152	56.1	26%	$350	$500	$775	$1,100	$2,650	$4,000	$6,000	$11,000	$30,000
Auctions: $31,725, MS-65, August 2015; $1,998, MS-61, January 2015; $1,116, AU-55, January 2015; $317, AU-50, October 2015													
1861	527,150	1,554	61.2	83%	$265	$275	$285	$295	$575	$675	$800	$1,500	$3,000
Auctions: $32,900, MS-67, August 2015; $2,585, MS-65, September 2015; $494, MS-61, January 2015; $212, EF-45, January 2015													
1861, Proof	349	14	65.0								$8,000	$11,000	$20,000
Auctions: $17,625, PF-65Cam, October 2014													
1861-D †	1,250	26	58.2	38%	$25,000	$32,500	$40,000	$57,500	$75,000	$90,000	$125,000	$160,000	$200,000
Auctions: $111,625, MS-63, June 2013; $70,500, MS-61, January 2015; $30,550, EF-45, July 2014													
1862	1,361,355	3,241	61.6	87%	$265	$275	$285	$295	$485	$525	$750	$875	$1,900
Auctions: $25,850, MS-67, August 2015; $4,230, MS-66, August 2015; $353, MS-61, April 2015; $223, AU-55, January 2015													
1862, DblDie Obv (a)	(b)	22	61.9	86%	$750	$1,500	$2,000	$2,500	$4,000	$4,750	$5,750		
Auctions: $675, MS-62, February 2011; $447, AU-50, April 2015													

† Ranked in the *100 Greatest U.S. Coins* (fifth edition). **a.** Doubling, visible on the entire obverse, is most evident on the tops of the hair curls and the feathers. **b.** Included in circulation-strike 1862 mintage figure.

	Mintage	Cert	Avg	%MS	VF-20	EF-40	AU-50	AU-55	MS-60	MS-62	MS-63 / PF-63	MS-64 / PF-64	MS-65 / PF-65
1862, Proof	35	17	64.9								$8,000	$11,000	$20,000
Auctions: $7,475, PF-63UCam, April 2008; $28,850, PF-65, April 2018													
1863	6,200	36	61.5	75%	$1,600	$2,300	$3,750	$4,750	$6,750	$9,000	$12,000	$15,000	$25,000
Auctions: $193,875, MS-68, August 2015; $10,575, MS-64, October 2014; $8,813, MS-63, April 2013; $5,434, AU-55, July 2014													
1863, Proof	50	17	65.2								$10,000	$17,500	$25,000
Auctions: $58,750, PF, February 2013													
1864	5,900	73	61.3	77%	$650	$850	$1,250	$1,300	$1,500	$2,500	$3,750	$6,500	$8,750
Auctions: $70,500, MS-68, August 2015; $705, MS-60, October 2014; $1,293, AU-55, July 2014; $235, AU-50, March 2015													
1864, Proof	50	13	64.2								$10,000	$17,500	$25,000
Auctions: $32,200, PF-66UCam, October 2011													
1865	3,700	35	62.0	83%	$750	$1,000	$1,100	$1,350	$2,000	$2,750	$5,000	$7,500	$12,000
Auctions: $15,275, MS-66, August 2015; $12,925, MS-65, July 2015; $3,055, MS-61, October 2014; $1,116, EF-45, July 2014													
1865, Proof	25	12	65.2								$10,000	$17,500	$25,000
Auctions: $25,300, PF-65, August 2011													
1866	7,100	72	62.2	83%	$450	$600	$750	$825	$1,250	$1,450	$2,500	$3,500	$5,750
Auctions: $23,500, MS-67, August 2015; $4,700, MS-66, January 2015; $1,175, MS-62, January 2015; $646, AU-55, January 2015													
1866, Proof	30	19	65.4								$10,000	$17,500	$25,000
Auctions: $27,600, PF-67UCam, August 2007													
1867	5,200	81	61.7	74%	$450	$625	$750	$850	$1,200	$1,500	$2,250	$3,000	$6,500
Auctions: $9,400, MS-66, August 2015; $1,763, MS-63, January 2015; $1,058, MS-61, January 2015; $823, MS-60, February 2015													
1867, Proof	50	12	63.5								$10,000	$17,500	$25,000
Auctions: $19,975, PF-66Cam, August 2014													
1868	10,500	128	60.9	78%	$450	$600	$700	$800	$1,000	$1,500	$2,000	$3,000	$6,500
Auctions: $35,250, MS-68, August 2015; $5,940, MS-66, June 2015; $881, MS-61, October 2015; $329, MS-60, May 2015													
1868, Proof	25	9	64.4								$10,000	$17,500	$25,000
Auctions: $29,900, PF-66UCam+, August 2011													
1869	5,900	87	61.7	83%	$450	$600	$700	$800	$1,150	$1,600	$2,000	$2,500	$5,500
Auctions: $42,300, MS-68, August 2015; $2,115, MS-64, January 2015; $1,293, MS-62, September 2015; $940, AU-58, January 2015													
1869, Proof	25	9	63.9								$10,000	$17,500	$25,000
Auctions: $19,975, PF-65Cam, April 2014													
1870	6,300	123	61.5	76%	$450	$600	$700	$800	$1,000	$1,500	$2,000	$2,750	$4,500
Auctions: $18,800, MS-67, August 2015; $1,410, MS-63, January 2015; $676, MS-61, July 2015; $588, AU-58, September 2015													
1870, Proof	35	8	62.1	88%							$10,000	$17,500	$25,000
Auctions: $17,625, PF-64, January 2014													
1870-S	3,000	53	60.1	64%	$700	$875	$1,250	$1,750	$2,750	$4,000	$8,250	$13,000	$35,000
Auctions: $35,250, MS-68, August 2015; $3,878, MS-62, January 2015; $3,525, AU-58, September 2015; $1,293, AU-50, January 2015													
1871	3,900	131	62.1	88%	$350	$450	$575	$675	$900	$1,100	$1,600	$2,250	$4,250
Auctions: $35,250, MS-68, August 2015; $823, MS-61, October 2014; $412, MS-60, September 2014; $852, AU-58, July 2014													
1871, Proof	30	4	65.5								$10,000	$17,500	$25,000
Auctions: $27,600, PF-65DCam, November 2011													
1872	3,500	74	60.6	72%	$350	$425	$575	$700	$1,000	$1,250	$2,250	$3,000	$5,500
Auctions: $14,100, MS-67, August 2015; $1,528, MS-63, October 2015; $764, AU-58, January 2015; $517, AU-55, June 2015													
1872, Proof	30	15	64.0								$10,000	$17,500	$25,000
Auctions: $4,888, PF-61, March 2011													
1873, Close 3	1,800	122	60.3	70%	$425	$750	$1,100	$1,150	$1,700	$2,500	$4,000	$8,000	$15,000
Auctions: $1,529, MS-62, August 2015; $1,293, MS-61, April 2015; $1,183, MS-61, September 2015; $832, AU-58, June 2015													
1873, Open 3	123,300	2,385	61.7	91%	$265	$275	$285	$295	$350	$450	$575	$800	$1,500
Auctions: $35,250, MS-68, August 2015; $1,410, MS-64, January 2015; $541, MS-63, August 2015; $353, MS-60, June 2015													
1873, Close 3, Proof	25	5	62.6								$15,000	$22,500	$35,000
Auctions: $30,550, PF-65, August 2014													
1874	198,800	4,150	62.1	93%	$265	$275	$285	$295	$350	$425	$550	$750	$1,000
Auctions: $10,575, MS-68, October 2015; $940, MS-65, January 2015; $341, MS-61, June 2015; $259, AU-53, June 2015													

	Mintage	Cert	Avg	%MS	VF-20	EF-40	AU-50	AU-55	MS-60	MS-62	MS-63	MS-64	MS-65
											PF-63	PF-64	PF-65
1874, Proof	20	7	64.1								$12,000	$15,000	$27,500
Auctions: $12,650, PF-64UC+, August 2010													
1875	400	30	61.6	83%	$3,500	$5,000	$6,000	$6,500	$10,000	$12,000	$16,000	$25,000	$42,500
Auctions: $76,375, MS-66, August 2015; $22,325, MS-64, April 2013; $2,820, MS-60, October 2014; $5,875, AU-53, July 2014													
1875, Proof	20	9	63.7								$18,500	$30,000	$45,000
Auctions: $55,813, PF-66DCam, November 2013													
1876	3,200	159	61.6	80%	$325	$375	$500	$600	$750	$1,000	$1,350	$1,750	$4,250
Auctions: $28,200, MS-67, October 2015; $940, MS-62, July 2014; $588, AU-55, September 2014; $646, AU-50, October 2014													
1876, Proof	45	13	65.3								$7,000	$14,000	$20,000
Auctions: $34,075, PF-66DCam, June 2013; $16,450, PF-65DCam, September 2014													
1877	3,900	196	62.1	85%	$300	$375	$525	$600	$800	$1,000	$1,400	$1,700	$3,500
Auctions: $12,338, MS-67, August 2015; $541, AU-58, June 2015; $423, AU-55, August 2015; $329, AU-55, January 2015													
1877, Proof	20	13	64.8								$8,000	$14,000	$20,000
Auctions: $7,638, PF, February 2014													
1878	3,000	163	61.7	87%	$300	$350	$400	$500	$775	$1,000	$1,500	$1,750	$4,750
Auctions: $32,900, MS-67, August 2015; $2,849, MS-65, August 2015; $1,175, MS-62, October 2014; $764, MS-61, July 2014													
1878, Proof	20	10	64.0								$7,500	$14,000	$20,000
Auctions: $19,550, PF-65DCam, January 2012													
1879	3,000	215	63.2	92%	$285	$325	$350	$365	$650	$800	$1,150	$1,300	$2,750
Auctions: $5,640, MS-67, July 2015; $4,113, MS-66, August 2015; $1,175, MS-64, January 2015; $270, AU-55, January 2015													
1879, Proof	30	7	64.3								$6,500	$14,000	$20,000
Auctions: $8,225, PF, August 2013													
1880	1,600	299	65.5	99%	$285	$325	$350	$365	$575	$700	$1,000	$1,050	$2,350
Auctions: $8,813, MS-68, January 2015; $7,050, MS-68, June 2015; $2,849, MS-67, August 2015; $2,585, MS-66, January 2015													
1880, Proof	36	27	64.3								$5,500	$10,500	$12,000
Auctions: $18,800, PF-65DCam, February 2013													
1881	7,620	400	64.7	97%	$285	$325	$350	$365	$575	$700	$900	$1,050	$1,800
Auctions: $12,925, MS-68, August 2015; $2,644, MS-67, October 2015; $1,645, MS-66, October 2015; $517, MS-63, March 2015													
1881, Proof	87	26	64.5								$5,000	$8,500	$12,500
Auctions: $2,820, PF-60, September 2014; $19,975, PF, March 2014													
1882	5,000	235	64.1	97%	$285	$325	$350	$365	$575	$700	$900	$1,050	$1,500
Auctions: $16,450, MS-68, August 2015; $1,998, MS-66, September 2015; $1,645, MS-66, August 2015; $646, MS-62, July 2014													
1882, Proof	125	33	65.3								$5,000	$8,500	$11,500
Auctions: $20,563, PF-67UCam, January 2015; $8,813, PF-64DCam, November 2014; $15,275, PF, August 2013; $5,760, PF-64, January 2018													
1883	10,800	497	63.9	96%	$285	$325	$350	$365	$575	$700	$900	$1,050	$1,500
Auctions: $18,800, MS-68, August 2015; $4,230, MS-67, September 2015; $3,055, MS-64, January 2015; $564, MS-62, January 2015													
1883, Proof	207	47	65.1								$5,000	$8,000	$11,500
Auctions: $9,400, PF-65Cam, February 2013													
1884	5,230	245	63.3	97%	$285	$325	$350	$365	$575	$700	$900	$1,050	$1,500
Auctions: $8,225, MS-68, July 2015; $3,995, MS-67, June 2015; $705, MS-64, January 2015; $588, MS-62, June 2015													
1884, Proof	1,006	56	65.3								$5,000	$7,000	$10,500
Auctions: $29,250, PF, September 2013; $10,200, PF-65, January 2018													
1885	11,156	472	63.6	96%	$285	$325	$350	$365	$575	$700	$900	$1,050	$1,500
Auctions: $7,638, MS-68, June 2015; $1,763, MS-66, June 2015; $1,175, MS-65, October 2015; $235, AU-55, January 2015													
1885, Proof	1,105	109	64.9								$5,000	$7,000	$10,500
Auctions: $16,450, PF-66, August 2015; $9,400, PF-65Cam, July 2014; $28,200, PF, August 2013													
1886	5,000	325	63.1	97%	$285	$325	$350	$365	$575	$700	$900	$1,050	$1,500
Auctions: $4,113, MS-67, January 2015; $1,645, MS-65, February 2015; $470, MS-61, July 2015; $282, AU-50, January 2015													
1886, Proof	1,016	71	64.4								$5,000	$7,000	$10,500
Auctions: $18,800, PF-67Cam, August 2014; $13,513, PF-67Cam, January 2015; $14,100, PF-66Cam, January 2015; $12,925, PF-66Cam, November 2014													

	Mintage	Cert	Avg	%MS	VF-20	EF-40	AU-50	AU-55	MS-60	MS-62	MS-63 / PF-63	MS-64 / PF-64	MS-65 / PF-65
1887	7,500	500	63.6	98%	$285	$325	$350	$365	$575	$675	$900	$1,050	$1,500
	Auctions: $35,250, MS-68, August 2015; $1,645, MS-66, October 2015; $494, MS-63, January 2015; $306, MS-60, November 2015												
1887, Proof	1,043	66	64.7								$5,000	$7,000	$10,500
	Auctions: $10,575, PF-65DCam, September 2013; $10,288, PF-65Cam+, October 2014; $4,700, PF-64Cam, January 2015												
1888	15,501	759	63.7	97%	$265	$300	$335	$345	$575	$600	$650	$800	$1,200
	Auctions: $15,275, MS-68, August 2015; $2,961, MS-67, July 2015; $1,645, MS-66, January 2015; $881, MS-64, February 2015												
1888, Proof	1,079	94	64.5								$5,000	$7,000	$10,500
	Auctions: $18,800, PF-66DCam, April 2013; $7,814, PF-65, April 2018												
1889	28,950	2,054	64.1	98%	$250	$265	$275	$285	$425	$475	$550	$700	$1,000
	Auctions: $8,225, MS-68, August 2015; $3,055, MS-67, July 2015; $764, MS-64, January 2015; $400, MS-62, October 2015												
1889, Proof	1,779	35	64.2								$5,000	$7,000	$10,500
	Auctions: $12,925, PF-66Cam, April 2013												

Gold Quarter Eagles ($2.50)
1796–1929

AN OVERVIEW OF GOLD QUARTER EAGLES

The quarter eagle, denominated at one-fourth of an eagle, or $2.50, was authorized by the Act of April 2, 1792. Early types in the series range from rare to very rare. The first, the 1796 without stars on the obverse, Heraldic Eagle motif on the reverse, is a classic, one of the most desired of all pieces needed for a type set, and accordingly expensive. Most examples are in such grades as EF and AU.

Quarter eagles with stars on the obverse and with the Heraldic Eagle reverse were produced from 1796 intermittently through 1807. Today they exist in modest numbers, particularly in grades such as EF and AU, but on an absolute basis are fairly rare.

The standalone 1808 Draped Bust type, by John Reich, of which only 2,710 were minted, is the rarest single type coin in the entire American copper, nickel, silver, and gold series, possibly excepting the 1839 Gobrecht dollar (in a different category, as Proof restrikes were made). Examples of the 1808 can be found in various grades from VF through AU, and only rarely higher.

The next style of quarter eagle, from 1821 through 1827, is scarce, but when seen is usually in grades such as EF, AU, or even the low levels of Mint State. The same can be said for the modified quarter eagle of 1829 through early 1834.

Finally, with the advent of the Classic Head in late 1834, continuing through 1839, quarter eagles become more readily available. Examples can be found in nearly any grade from VF into the lower levels of Mint State. Then come the Liberty Head quarter eagles, minted continuously from 1840 through 1907, in sufficient numbers and for such a long time that it is not difficult to obtain an example to illustrate the type, with choice and gem Mint State coins being plentiful for the dates of the early 20th century.

The last quarter eagles are of the Indian Head type, minted from 1908 through 1929. These pieces are plentiful today, but grading can be difficult, as they were struck in sunken relief and the highest part on the coin is the field (this area was immediately subject to contact marks and wear). Although many opportunities exist in the marketplace, a collector should approach a purchase with care, seeking an example that has frosty, lustrous fields.

FOR THE COLLECTOR AND INVESTOR: GOLD QUARTER EAGLES AS A SPECIALTY

Collecting quarter eagles by dates, mintmarks, and major varieties is a very appealing pursuit. Although many are scarce and rare—this description applies to any variety from 1796 through early 1834—none are truly impossible to obtain. Among the Classic Head issues of 1834–1839, branch-mint coins are especially scarce in higher grades.

Liberty Head quarter eagles, produced continuously from 1840 through 1907, include a number of key issues, such as the famous 1854-S (usually seen in well-circulated grades), the Proof-only 1863 (of which only 30 were struck), and a number of elusive mintmarks. Of particular interest is the 1848 coin with CAL. counterstamped on the reverse, signifying that the coin was made from gold bullion brought to the Philadelphia Mint in a special shipment from California.

CAPPED BUST TO RIGHT (1796–1807)

Designer: *Robert Scot.* **Weight:** *4.37 grams.* **Composition:** *.9167 gold, .0833 silver and copper.* **Diameter:** *Approximately 20 mm.* **Edge:** *Reeded.* **Mint:** *Philadelphia.*

No Stars on Obverse (1796)
Bass-Dannreuther–2.

Stars on Obverse (1796–1807)
Bass-Dannreuther–3.

History. The first quarter eagles were struck intermittently during the late 1790s and early 1800s, with consistently small mintages. The earliest issues of 1796 lack obverse stars. They likely circulated domestically, rather than being exported in international trade.

Striking and Sharpness. Most have light striking in one area or another. On the obverse, check the hair details and the stars. On the reverse, check the shield, stars, and clouds. Examine the denticles on both sides. Planchet adjustment marks (from a coin's overweight planchet being filed down to correct specifications) are seen on many coins and are not noted by the certification services. On high-grade coins the luster usually is very attractive. Certain reverse dies of this type were also used to make dimes of the era, which were almost exactly the same diameter.

Availability. Most Capped Bust to Right quarter eagles in the marketplace are EF or AU. MS coins are elusive; when seen, they usually are of later dates.

GRADING STANDARDS

MS-60 to 70 (Mint State). *Obverse:* At MS-60, some abrasion and contact marks are evident, most noticeably on the hair to the left of Miss Liberty's forehead and on the higher-relief areas of the cap. On the No Stars quarter eagles, there is some abrasion in the field—more so than the With Stars coins, on which the field is more protected. Luster is present, but may be dull or lifeless, and

1802, 2 Over 1. Graded MS-61.

interrupted in patches. At MS-63, contact marks are few, and abrasion is very light. An MS-65 coin will have hardly any abrasion, and contact marks are so minute as to require magnification. Luster should be full and rich. Coins grading above MS-65 exist more in theory than in reality for this type—but they do exist, and are defined by having fewer marks as perfection is approached. *Reverse:* Comments apply as for the obverse, except that abrasion and contact marks are most noticeable on the upper part of the eagle and the clouds. The field area is complex; there is not much open space, with stars above the eagle, the arrows and olive branch, and other features. Accordingly, marks are not as noticeable as on the obverse.

Illustrated coin: Some friction appears on the higher areas of this example, but the fields retain nearly full luster, and the coin overall has nice eye appeal.

AU-50, 53, 55, 58 (About Uncirculated). *Obverse:* Light wear is seen on the cheek, the hair immediately to the left of the face, and the cap, more so at AU-50 than at AU–53 or 55. An AU-58 coin has minimal traces of wear. An AU-50 coin has luster in protected areas among the stars and letters, with little in the open fields or on the portrait. At AU-58 most luster is present in the fields, but is worn away on the highest parts of the motifs. The

1796, No Stars; BD-2. Graded AU-58.

1796 No Stars type has less luster in any given grade. *Reverse:* Comments as for Mint State, except that the eagle's neck, the tips and top of the wings, the clouds, and the tail now show noticeable wear, as do other features. Luster ranges from perhaps 40% remaining in protected areas at AU-50 to nearly full mint bloom at AU-58. Often the reverse of this type retains much more luster than does the obverse.

EF-40, 45 (Extremely Fine). *Obverse:* Wear is evident all over the portrait, with some loss of detail in the hair to the left of Miss Liberty's face. Excellent detail remains in low-relief areas of the hair, such as the front curl and the back of the head. The stars show wear, as do the date and letters. Luster, if present at all, is minimal and in protected areas. *Reverse:* Wear is greater than at the About Uncirculated level. The neck lacks feather detail on its

1802; BD-1. Graded EF-45.

highest points. Feathers have lost some detail near the edges of the wings, and some areas of the horizontal lines in the shield may be blended together. Some traces of luster may be seen, more so at EF-45 than at EF-40. Overall, the reverse appears to be in a slightly higher grade than the obverse.

VF-20, 30 (Very Fine). *Obverse:* The higher-relief areas of hair are well worn at VF-20, less so at VF-30. The stars are flat at their centers. *Reverse:* Wear is greater, including on the shield and wing feathers. The star centers are flat. Other areas have lost detail as well. E PLURIBUS UNUM is easy to read.

Capped Bust to Right quarter eagles are seldom collected in grades lower than VF-20.

1796, With Stars; BD-3. Graded VF-30.

	Mintage	Cert	Avg	%MS	F-12	VF-20	EF-40	AU-50	AU-55	AU-58	MS-60	MS-63	MS-64
1796, No Stars on Obverse †	963	38	56.0	29%	$60,000	$77,500	$95,000	$130,000	$165,000	$200,000	$260,000	$850,000	$1,000,000 (a)
	Auctions: $352,500, MS-61, October 2015; $123,375, AU-58, February 2016; $82,250, EF-40, October 2015; $94,000, VF-30, December 2013												
1796, Stars on Obverse	432	22	58.4	50%	$52,500	$65,000	$95,000	$115,000	$135,000	$170,000	$200,000	$450,000	$650,000
	Auctions: $111,625, AU-58, February 2016; $102,813, AU-58, March 2014; $223,250, AU-58, November 2014												
1797	427	13	47.3	0%	$13,500	$20,000	$40,000	$65,000	$115,000	$165,000	$185,000	$350,000	$500,000
	Auctions: $105,750, AU-53, April 2013												

† Ranked in the *100 Greatest U.S. Coins* (fifth edition). **a.** Value in MS-65 is $2,000,000.

1798, Close Date

1798, Wide Date

1804, 13-Star Reverse

1804, 14-Star Reverse

	Mintage	Cert	Avg	%MS	F-12	VF-20	EF-40	AU-50	AU-55	AU-58	MS-60	MS-63	MS-64
1798, All kinds	1,094												
1798, Close Date		23	56.7	26%				$28,500	$40,000	$60,000	$75,000	$130,000	
Auctions: $18,800, AU-50, August 2014													
1798, Wide Date		**(b)**						$27,500	$35,000	$50,000	$65,000	$125,000	
Auctions: $70,500, AU-58, November 2014; $44,063, AU-50, June 2014													
1802	3,035	69	56.4	33%	$5,000	$8,500	$16,500	$20,000	$22,500	$25,500	$32,500	$70,000	$200,000
Auctions: $20,563, AU-58, August 2014; $21,150, AU-58, March 2013; $16,450, AU-50, August 2014; $15,275, EF-45, August 2014													
1804, 13-Star Reverse †	**(c)**	2	47.5	0%	$60,000	$95,000	$150,000	$185,000	$350,000	$500,000			
Auctions: $322,000, AU-58, July 2009													
1804, 14-Star Reverse	3,327	67	52.7	16%	$6,750	$9,000	$14,000	$17,000	$22,500	$30,000	$32,500	$165,000	
Auctions: $44,063, MS-62, April 2014; $70,501, MS-62, November 2014; $21,738, AU-58, November 2014; $19,975, AU-55, August 2014													
1805	1,781	55	54.7	27%	$5,000	$8,000	$13,000	$16,500	$20,000	$25,000	$35,000	$135,000	
Auctions: $32,900, MS-60, March 2015; $20,563, AU-58, August 2014; $23,500, AU-55, November 2014; $14,100, AU-53, October 2014													
1806, 6 Over 4, 8 Stars Left, 5 Right	1,136	23	53.3	35%	$5,000	$8,250	$14,000	$18,000	$25,000	$29,500	$37,000	$150,000	
Auctions: $30,550, MS-61, June 2014; $22,325, AU-58, August 2014; $21,150, AU-58, August 2014; $20,563, AU-58, October 2014													
1806, 6 Over 5, 7 Stars Left, 6 Right	480	13	56.5	38%	$7,500	$11,500	$20,000	$35,000	$50,000	$60,000	$90,000	$300,000	
Auctions: $67,563, AU-About Uncirculated, February 2014													
1807	6,812	120	55.4	34%	$5,000	$7,500	$13,000	$17,500	$23,500	$25,000	$31,500	$85,000	$200,000
Auctions: $44,063, MS-62, March 2014; $24,675, AU-58, March 2015; $17,625, AU-55, August 2014; $11,750, AU-50, November 2014													

† Ranked in the *100 Greatest U.S. Coins* (fifth edition). **b.** Included in certified population for 1798, Close Date. **c.** Included in 1804, 14-Star Reverse, mintage figure.

DRAPED BUST TO LEFT, LARGE SIZE (1808)

Designer: *John Reich.* **Weight:** *4.37 grams.* **Composition:** *.9167 gold, .0833 silver and copper.* **Diameter:** *Approximately 20 mm.* **Edge:** *Reeded.*

History. John Reich's Draped Bust was an adaptation of the design introduced in 1807 on the half dollar. On the quarter eagle it was used for a single year only, with fewer than 3,000 coins struck, making it the rarest of the major gold coin types (indeed, the rarest of any U.S. coin type).

Striking and Sharpness. All examples are lightly struck on one area or another, particularly the stars and rims. The rims are low and sometimes missing or nearly so (on the obverse), causing quarter eagles of this type to wear more quickly than otherwise might be the case. Sharpness of strike is overlooked by most buyers.

Availability. Examples are rare in any grade. Typical grades are EF and AU. Lower grades are seldom seen, as the coins did not circulate to any great extent. Gold coins of this era were not seen in circulation after 1821, so they did not get a chance to acquire significant wear.

GRADING STANDARDS

MS-60 to 70 (Mint State). *Obverse:* At MS-60, some abrasion and contact marks are seen on the cheek, on the hair below the LIBERTY inscription, and on the highest-relief folds of the cap. Luster is present, but may be dull or lifeless, and interrupted in patches. At MS-63, contact marks are few, and abrasion is very light. Abrasion is even less at MS-64. (Discussion of such high grades in these early coins starts to enter the realm of

1808; BD-1. Graded MS-63.

theory.) Quarter eagles of this type are almost, but not quite, non-existent in a combination of high grade and nice eye appeal. *Reverse:* Comments apply as for the obverse, except that abrasion is most noticeable on the eagle's neck and highest area of the wings.

Illustrated coin: Superbly struck, this coin is a "poster example" with few peers.

AU-50, 53, 55, 58 (About Uncirculated). *Obverse:* Light wear is seen on the cheek and higher-relief areas of the hair and cap. Friction and scattered marks are in the field, ranging from extensive at AU-50 to minimal at AU-58. The low rim affords little protection to the field of this coin, but the stars in relief help. Luster may be seen in protected areas, minimal at AU-50, but less so at AU-58. At AU-58 the field retains some lus-

1808. Graded AU-50.

ter as well. *Reverse:* Comments are as for a Mint State coin, except that the eagle's neck, the top of the wings, the leaves, and the arrowheads now show noticeable wear, as do other features. Luster ranges from perhaps 40% remaining in protected areas at AU-50 to nearly full mint bloom at AU-58. Often the reverse of this type retains much more luster than does the obverse, as on this type the motto, eagle, and lettering protect the surrounding flat areas.

Illustrated coin: Note some lightness of strike.

EF-40, 45 (Extremely Fine). *Obverse:* More wear is seen on the portrait, the hair, the cap, and the drapery near the clasp. Luster is likely to be absent on the obverse due to the low rim. *Reverse:* Wear is more extensive on the eagle, including the top of the wings, the head, the top of the shield, and the claws. Some traces of luster may be seen in protected areas, more so at EF-45 than at EF-40.

1808. Graded EF-40.

VF-20, 30 (Very Fine). *Obverse:* Wear on the portrait has reduced the hair detail, especially to the right of the face and the top of the head, but much can still be seen. *Reverse:* Wear on the eagle is greater, and details of feathers near the shield and near the top of the wings are weak or missing. All other features show wear, but most are fairly sharp. Generally, Draped Bust gold coins at this grade level lack eye appeal.

1808. Graded VF-20.

Illustrated coin: This is a nice, problem-free example of a lower but very desirable grade for this rare issue.

Draped Bust to Left, Large Size, quarter eagles are seldom collected in grades lower than VF-20.

	Mintage	Cert	Avg	%MS	F-12	VF-20	EF-40	AU-50	AU-55	AU-58	MS-60	MS-62	MS-63	MS-65
1808 †	2,710	47	54.6	30%	$30,000	$42,500	$72,500	$100,000	$110,000	$135,000	$180,000	$260,000	$500,000	$2,500,000
	Auctions: $223,250, MS-61, March 2016; $126,900, MS-60, January 2013; $80,781, AU-55, August 2014													

† Ranked in the *100 Greatest U.S. Coins* (fifth edition).

CAPPED HEAD TO LEFT (1821–1834)

Designer: *John Reich.* **Weight:** *4.37 grams.* **Composition:** *.9167 gold, .0833 silver and copper.* **Diameter:** *1821–1827—18.5 mm; 1829–1834—approximately 18.2 mm.* **Edge:** *Reeded.* **Mint:** *Philadelphia.*

Large Diameter, Circulation Strike BD-1.   **Large Diameter, Proof**

Small Diameter, Circulation Strike BD-1.   **Small Diameter, Proof**

History. Capped Head to Left quarter eagles dated 1821 through 1827 have a larger diameter and larger letters, dates, and stars than those of 1829 to 1834. The same grading standards apply to both. Gold coins of this type did not circulate in commerce, because their face value was lower than their bullion value. Many legislators, who had the option to draw their pay in specie (silver and gold coinage), took advantage of this fact to sell their salaries at a premium for paper money. Most wear was due to use as pocket pieces, or from minor handling.

Striking and Sharpness. Most Capped Head to Left quarter eagles are well struck. On the obverse, check the hair details (which on the Large Diameter style can be light in areas) and the stars. On the reverse, check the eagle. On both sides inspect the denticles. Fields are often semi-prooflike on higher grades.

Availability. All Capped Head to Left quarter eagles are rare. Grades typically range from EF to MS, with choice examples in the latter category being scarce, and gems being very rare. Proof coins were made on a limited basis for presentation and for sale to numismatists. All Proof examples are exceedingly rare today, and are usually encountered only when great collections are dispersed.

GRADING STANDARDS

MS-60 to 70 (Mint State). *Obverse:* At MS-60, some abrasion and contact marks are seen on the cheek, on the hair below the LIBERTY inscription, and on the highest-relief folds of the cap. Luster is present, but may be dull or lifeless, and interrupted in patches. At MS-63, contact marks are few, and abrasion is very light. Abrasion is even less at MS-64. (Discussion of such high grades in these early coins starts to enter the realm of theory.) Quarter eagles of this type are almost, but not quite, non-existent in a combination of high grade and nice eye appeal. *Reverse:* Comments apply as for the obverse, except that abrasion is most noticeable on the eagle's neck and highest area of the wings.

1827, BD-1. Graded MS-65.

Illustrated coin: This is a well-struck lustrous gem.

AU-50, 53, 55, 58 (About Uncirculated). *Obverse:* Light wear is seen on the cheek and higher-relief areas of the hair and cap. Friction and scattered marks are in the field, ranging from extensive at AU-50 to minimal at AU-58. The low rim affords little protection to the field of this coin, but the stars in relief help. Luster may be seen in protected areas, minimal at AU-50, but less so at AU-58. At AU-58 the field retains some luster as well.

1833; BD-1. Graded AU-53.

Reverse: Comments are as for a Mint State coin, except that the eagle's neck, the top of the wings, the leaves, and the arrowheads now show noticeable wear, as do other features. Luster ranges from perhaps 40% remaining in protected areas at AU-50 to nearly full mint bloom at AU-58. Often the reverse of this type retains much more luster than does the obverse, as on this type the motto, eagle, and lettering protect the surrounding flat areas.

EF-40, 45 (Extremely Fine). *Obverse:* More wear is seen on the portrait, the hair, the cap, and the drapery near the clasp. Luster is likely to be absent on the obverse due to the low rim. *Reverse:* Wear is more extensive on the eagle, including the top of the wings, the head, the top of the shield, and the claws. Some traces of luster may be seen in protected areas, more so at EF-45 than at EF-40.

1821; BD-1. Graded EF-40.

Capped Head to Left quarter eagles are seldom collected in grades lower than EF-40.

PF–60 to 70 (Proof). *Obverse and Reverse:* PF–60 to 62 coins have extensive hairlines and may have nicks and contact marks. At PF–63, hairlines are prominent, but the mirror surface is very reflective. PF–64 coins have fewer hairlines. At PF–65, hairlines should be minimal and mostly seen only under magnification. There should be no nicks or marks. PF–66 and higher coins should have no marks or hairlines visible to the unaided eye.

1824, 4 Over 1. Proof.

	Mintage	Cert	Avg	%MS	F-12	VF-20	EF-40	AU-50	AU-55	AU-58	MS-60	MS-63 / PF-63	MS-65 / PF-64
1821	6,448	18	57.3	39%	$6,250	$9,000	$14,500	$16,000	$17,500	$23,500	$35,000	$85,000	
	Auctions: $44,063, MS-62, March 2014												
1821, Proof	*3–5*	3	64.7									$275,000	$400,000
	Auctions: $241,500, PF-64Cam, January 2007												
1824, 4 Over 1	2,600	26	56.1	35%	$6,250	$9,500	$14,000	$16,500	$18,750	$25,000	$32,500	$80,000	
	Auctions: $18,800, AU-58, August 2013												
1824, 4 Over 1, Proof	*3–5*	0	n/a		*(unique, in the Smithsonian's National Numismatic Collection)*								
	Auctions: No auction records available.												
1825	4,434	52	59.1	60%	$6,250	$7,750	$14,000	$16,500	$17,500	$23,500	$30,000	$65,000	
	Auctions: $141,000, MS-65, November 2014; $105,750, MS-64, March 2014; $38,188, MS-62, July 2014; $32,900, MS-61, August 2014												
1825, Proof (a)	*unknown*	0	n/a										
	Auctions: No auction records available.												
1826, 6 Over 6	760	9	56.0	11%	$10,000	$12,500	$16,500	$25,000	$35,000	$47,500	$62,500		
	Auctions: $44,063, AU-58, August 2014; $27,025, AU-55, November 2014; $45,531, AU-55, September 2013												
1826, 6 Over 5, Proof (b)	*unknown*	0	n/a										
	Auctions: No auction records available.												
1827	2,800	24	57.6	58%	$6,500	$9,000	$13,100	$17,500	$19,500	$27,500	$35,000	$65,000	
	Auctions: $58,750, MS-63, September 2014; $21,150, AU-58, August 2014; $28,200, AU-55, February 2013												
1827, Proof (c)	*unknown*	0	n/a										
	Auctions: No auction records available.												
1829	3,403	45	60.2	64%	$6,000	$7,250	$9,500	$14,000	$17,500	$19,250	$22,500	$35,000	$115,000
	Auctions: $41,125, MS-63, June 2013; $12,925, AU-55, August 2014												
1829, Proof	*2–4*	0	n/a		*(extremely rare; 2–3 known)*								
	Auctions: No auction records available.												
1830	4,540	49	59.8	49%	$6,000	$7,250	$9,500	$14,000	$17,500	$19,250	$22,500	$35,000	$90,000
	Auctions: $29,375, MS-63, November 2013; $24,675, MS-62, November 2014; $22,913, MS-62, November 2014												
1830, Proof (d)	*unknown*	0	n/a										
	Auctions: No auction records available.												
1831	4,520	64	60.3	66%	$6,000	$7,250	$9,500	$14,000	$17,500	$19,250	$22,500	$35,000	$90,000
	Auctions: $28,200, MS-63, September 2014; $18,800, AU-58, February 2013; $15,863, AU-58, August 2014												
1831, Proof	*6–10*	2	64.5									$100,000	$150,000
	Auctions: $30,550, PF-60, September 2013												
1832	4,400	44	57.3	39%	$6,000	$7,250	$9,500	$14,000	$17,500	$19,250	$22,500	$37,500	
	Auctions: $21,150, MS-61, March 2014; $22,913, MS-61, August 2014; $15,275, AU-58, August 2014; $12,338, AU-55, August 2014												
1832, Proof	*2–4*	0	n/a		*(unique; in the Bass Foundation Collection)*								
	Auctions: No auction records available.												

a. The 1825 quarter eagle might not exist in Proof; see the *Encyclopedia of U.S. Gold Coins, 1795–1933* (second edition). **b.** Proofs have been reported, but none have been authenticated. **c.** Proof 1827 quarter eagles almost certainly were made, but none are known to exist. **d.** Examples identified as Proofs are extremely rare, many are impaired, and none have been certified.

	Mintage	Cert	Avg	%MS	F-12	VF-20	EF-40	AU-50	AU-55	AU-58	MS-60	MS-63	MS-65
												PF-63	PF-64
1833	4,160	45	58.7	49%	$6,000	$7,250	$9,500	$14,000	$17,500	$19,250	$22,500	$35,000	$100,000
Auctions: $41,125, MS-63, August 2013; $15,275, AU-58, August 2014													
1833, Proof	2–4	0	n/a		*(extremely rare; 3–4 known)*								
Auctions: No auction records available.													
1834, With Motto	4,000	8	54.4	13%	$22,500	$30,000	$55,000	$90,000	$135,000	$145,000	$200,000	$275,000	
Auctions: $19,975, AU-50, November 2014													
1834, With Motto, Proof	4–8	0	n/a		*(extremely rare; 4–5 known)*								
Auctions: No auction records available.													

CLASSIC HEAD, NO MOTTO ON REVERSE (1834–1839)

Designer: *William Kneass.* **Weight:** *4.18 grams.*
Composition: *.8992 gold, .1008 silver and copper (changed to .900 gold in 1837).*
Diameter: *18.2 mm.* **Edge:** *Reeded.* **Mints:** *Philadelphia, Charlotte, Dahlonega, and New Orleans.*

Circulation Strike
Breen-6143.

Mintmark location
is on the obverse,
above the date.

Proof

History. Gold quarter eagles had not circulated at face value in the United States since 1821, as the price of bullion necessitated more than $2.50 worth of gold to produce a single coin. Accordingly, they traded at their bullion value. The Act of June 28, 1834, provided lower weights for gold coins, after which the issues (of new designs to differentiate them from the old) circulated effectively. The Classic Head design by William Kneass is an adaptation of the head created by John Reich for the cent of 1808. The reverse illustrates a perched eagle. The motto E PLURIBUS UNUM, seen on earlier gold coins, no longer is present. These coins circulated widely until mid-1861 (for this reason, many show extensive wear). After that, they were hoarded by the public because of financial uncertainty during the Civil War.

Striking and Sharpness. Weakness is often seen on the higher areas of the hair curls. Also check the star centers. On the reverse, check the rims. The denticles usually are well struck.

Availability. Most coins range from VF to AU or lower ranges of MS. Most MS coins are of the first three years. MS-63 to 65 examples are rare. Good eye appeal can be elusive. Proofs were made in small quantities, and today probably only a couple dozen or so survive, most bearing the 1834 date.

GRADING STANDARDS

MS-60 to 70 (Mint State). *Obverse:* At MS-60, some abrasion and contact marks are seen on the portrait, most noticeably on the cheek, as the hair details are complex on this type. Luster is present, but may be dull or lifeless, and interrupted in patches. Many low-level Mint State coins have grainy surfaces. At MS-63, contact marks are few, and abrasion is very light. Abrasion is even less at MS-64. An MS-65 coin has hardly any abrasion, and contact marks are minute. Luster should be full and rich and is often more intense on the

1834. Graded MS-65.

obverse. Grades above MS-65 are defined by having fewer marks as perfection is approached. *Reverse:* Comments apply as for the obverse, except that abrasion is most noticeable on the eagle's neck and the highest area of the wings.

Illustrated coin: This coin is especially well struck.

AU-50, 53, 55, 58 (About Uncirculated). *Obverse:* Friction is seen on the higher parts, particularly the cheek and hair (under magnification) of Miss Liberty. Friction and scattered marks are in the field, ranging from extensive at AU-50 to minimal at AU-58. Luster may be seen in protected areas, minimal at AU-50 but more visible at AU-58. On an AU-58 coin the field retains some luster as well. *Reverse:* Comments as for Mint State,

1837. Graded AU-55.

except that the eagle's neck, the top of the wings, the leaves, and the arrowheads now show noticeable wear, as do other features. Luster ranges from perhaps 40% remaining in protected areas at AU-50 to nearly full mint bloom at AU-58. Often the reverse of this type retains much more luster than does the obverse.

Illustrated coin: The coin has light wear overall, but traces of luster can be seen here and there.

EF-40, 45 (Extremely Fine). *Obverse:* Wear is seen on the portrait overall, with reduction or elimination of some separation of hair strands, especially in the area close to the face. The cheek shows light wear. Luster is minimal or nonexistent at EF-40, and may survive in among the letters of LIBERTY at EF-45. *Reverse:* Wear is greater than on an About Uncirculated coin. On most (but not all) coins the eagle's neck lacks some feather detail on its highest points. Feathers have lost some detail near the edges and tips of the wings. Some areas of the horizontal lines in the shield may be blended together. Some traces of luster may be seen, more so at EF-45 than at EF-40.

1834. Graded EF-40.

Illustrated coin: This coin is well struck.

VF-20, 30 (Very Fine). *Obverse:* Wear on the portrait has reduced the hair detail, especially to the right of the face and the top of the head, but much can still be seen. *Reverse:* Wear is greater, including on the shield and wing feathers. Generally, Classic Head gold at this grade level lacks eye appeal.

Illustrated coin: This coin was lightly cleaned. It is lightly struck at the centers, although at this grade level that is not important.

1836. Graded VF-30.

Classic Head quarter eagles are seldom collected in grades lower than VF-20.

PF-60 to 70 (Proof). *Obverse and Reverse:* PF–60 to 62 coins have extensive hairlines and may have nicks and contact marks. At PF-63, hairlines are prominent, but the mirror surface is very reflective. PF-64 coins have fewer hairlines. At PF-65, hairlines should be minimal and mostly seen only under magnification. There should be no nicks or marks. PF-66 and higher coins should have no marks or hairlines visible to the unaided eye.

1836. Graded PF-65 Cameo.

1836, Script 8	1836, Block 8

	Mintage	Cert	Avg	%MS	F-12	VF-20	EF-40	AU-50	AU-55	AU-58	MS-60	MS-63	MS-65
											PF-60	PF-63	PF-65
1834, No Motto	112,234	1,084	56.1	31%	$425	$600	$800	$1,250	$1,650	$2,000	$3,100	$7,000	$50,000
Auctions: $3,525, MS-61, February 2015; $1,645, AU-58, June 2015; $1,293, AU-50, June 2015; $794, EF-40, January 2015													
1834, No Motto, Proof	15–25	6	64.3								$35,000	$100,000	$275,000
Auctions: $138,000, PF-64Cam, January 2011													
1835	131,402	335	54.3	29%	$425	$600	$800	$1,250	$1,650	$2,000	$3,100	$8,500	$50,000
Auctions: $7,050, MS-63, January 2015; $1,770, AU-58, August 2015; $1,528, AU-55, June 2015; $1,116, AU-53, July 2015													
1835, Proof	5–8	1	65.0								$35,000	$100,000	$300,000
Auctions: No auction records available.													
1836, All kinds	547,986												
1836, Script 8 (a)		602	51.2	18%	$425	$600	$800	$1,250	$1,650	$2,000	$3,100	$7,000	$42,500
Auctions: $7,638, MS-63, September 2015; $3,055, MS-61, October 2015; $1,424, AU-50, June 2015; $423, VF-30, January 2015													
1836, Block 8		528	49.7	16%	$425	$600	$800	$1,250	$1,650	$2,000	$3,100	$7,000	$42,500
Auctions: $9,400, MS-64, January 2015; $3,290, MS-61, September 2015; $999, AU-50, October 2015; $764, EF-45, January 2015													
1836, Proof	5–8	7	65.0	100%							$35,000	$115,000	$300,000
Auctions: $195,500, PF-64Cam, April 2012													
1837	45,080	279	52.0	16%	$450	$750	$1,200	$1,750	$2,000	$2,500	$4,500	$13,500	$55,000
Auctions: $11,750, MS-63, January 2014; $2,585, MS-60, August 2014; $3,055, AU-58, November 2014; $1,528, AU-50, October 2014													
1837, Proof (b)	3–5	2	64.5								$32,500	$125,000	$350,000
Auctions: No auction records available.													
1838	47,030	315	52.9	21%	$425	$625	$1,000	$1,500	$1,750	$2,600	$4,250	$11,500	$50,000
Auctions: $2,468, AU-58, August 2015; $1,469, AU-55, August 2015; $1,058, AU-50, January 2015; $541, VF-35, January 2015													
1838, Proof	2–4	0	n/a		*(extremely rare)*								
Auctions: No auction records available.													
1838-C	7,880	80	55.0	15%	$3,000	$4,500	$7,500	$10,000	$13,500	$18,500	$27,000	$50,000	
Auctions: $8,225, AU-53, October 2016; $3,055, AU-50, June 2015; $6,463, EF-45, August 2016; $6,756, EF-40, January 2015													

Note: So-called 9 Over 8 varieties for Philadelphia, Charlotte, and Denver mints were made from defective punches. **a.** Also known as the "Head of 1835." **b.** Two Proofs of 1837 are known; one is in the Smithsonian's National Numismatic Collection. A third example has been rumored, but its existence is not verified.

	Mintage	Cert	Avg	%MS	F-12	VF-20	EF-40	AU-50	AU-55	AU-58	MS-60 / PF-60	MS-63 / PF-63	MS-65 / PF-65
1839	27,021	103	52.9	15%	$650	$1,000	$1,650	$3,000	$4,000	$6,000	$9,500	$35,000	
	Auctions: $28,200, MS-61, August 2013; $4,700, AU-58, January 2015; $3,701, AU-58, January 2015; $1,116, AU-50, June 2015												
1839, Proof (c)	4–6	0	n/a				*(extremely rare)*						
	Auctions: $136,679, PF-62, August 2006												
1839-C	18,140	218	52.5	7%	$2,500	$4,250	$5,500	$9,000	$10,000	$15,000	$25,000	$65,000	
	Auctions: $44,063, MS-62, September 2015; $21,150, MS-61, August 2016; $7,403, MS-60, January 2015; $7,050, AU-55, June 2015												
1839-D	13,674	143	48.3	10%	$2,750	$4,500	$6,750	$9,000	$14,000	$20,000	$30,000	$55,000	
	Auctions: $105,750, MS-64, January 2013; $19,975, AU-58, November 2014; $18,800, AU-58, August 2015; $9,988, AU-55, July 2015												
1839-O	17,781	344	52.6	17%	$1,000	$1,650	$3,000	$4,250	$7,000	$9,000	$11,000	$30,000	
	Auctions: $32,900, MS-64, September 2015; $11,163, AU-58, August 2015; $3,995, AU-53, July 2015; $2,350, EF-45, August 2015												

c. Three Proofs of 1839 are reported to exist; only two are presently accounted for.

LIBERTY HEAD (1840–1907)

Designer: *Christian Gobrecht.* **Weight:** *4.18 grams.*
Composition: *.900 gold, .100 copper (net weight .12094 oz. pure gold).* **Diameter:** *18 mm.*
Edge: *Reeded.* **Mints:** *Philadelphia, Charlotte, Dahlonega, New Orleans, and San Francisco.*

Circulation Strike

Mintmark location is on the reverse, above the denomination.

Proof

History. The Liberty Head quarter eagle debuted in 1840 and was a workhorse of American commerce for decades, being minted until 1907. Christian Gobrecht's design closely follows those used on half eagles and eagles of the same era.

In 1848, about 230 ounces of gold were sent to Secretary of War William L. Marcy by Colonel R.B. Mason, military governor of California. The gold was turned over to the Philadelphia Mint and made into quarter eagles. The distinguishing mark CAL. was punched above the eagle on the reverse of these coins, while they were in the die. Several pieces with prooflike surfaces are known.

A modified reverse design (with smaller letters and arrowheads) was used on Philadelphia quarter eagles from 1859 through 1907, and on San Francisco issues of 1877, 1878, and 1879. A few Philadelphia Mint pieces were made in 1859, 1860, and 1861 with the old Large Letters reverse design.

Striking and Sharpness. On the obverse, check the highest points of the hair, and the star centers. On the reverse, check the eagle's neck, and the area to the lower left of the shield and the lower part of the eagle. Examine the denticles on both sides. Branch-mint coins struck before the Civil War often are lightly struck in areas and have weak denticles. Often, a certified EF coin from the Dahlonega or Charlotte mint will not appear any sharper than a VF coin from Philadelphia. There are exceptions, and some C and D coins are sharp. The careful study of photographs is useful in acquainting you with the peculiarities of a given date or mint. Most quarter eagles from the 1880s to 1907 are sharp in all areas. Tiny copper staining spots (from improperly mixed alloy) can be a problem. Cameo contrast is the rule for Proofs prior to 1902, when the portrait was polished in the die (a few years later cameo-contrast coins were again made).

Availability. Early dates and mintmarks are generally scarce to rare in MS and very rare in MS–63 to 65 or finer, with only a few exceptions. Coins of Charlotte and Dahlonega (all of which are especially avidly collected) are usually EF or AU, or overgraded low MS. Rarities for the type include 1841, 1854-S, and 1875. Coins of the 1860s onward generally are seen with sharper striking and in higher average grades. Typically, San Francisco quarter eagles are in lower average grades than are those from the Philadelphia Mint, as Philadelphia coins did not circulate at par in the East and Midwest from late December 1861 until December 1878, and thus did not acquire as much wear. MS coins are readily available for the early-1900s years, and usually have outstanding eye appeal. Proofs exist relative to their original mintages; all prior to the 1890s are rare.

Note: Values of common-date gold coins have been based on the current bullion price of gold, $2,000 per ounce, and may vary with the prevailing spot price.

GRADING STANDARDS

MS-60 to 70 (Mint State). *Obverse:* At MS-60, some abrasion and contact marks are evident, most noticeably on the hair to the right of Miss Liberty's forehead, and on the jaw. Luster is present, but may be dull or lifeless, and interrupted in patches. At MS-63, contact marks are few, and abrasion is very light. An MS-65 coin has hardly any abrasion, and contact marks are so minute as to require magnification. Luster should be full and rich.

1859-S. Graded MS-65.

Grades above MS-65 are usually found late in the series and are defined by having fewer marks as perfection is approached. *Reverse:* Comments apply as for the obverse, except that abrasion and contact marks are most noticeable on the eagle's neck and to the lower left of the shield.

Illustrated coin: Sharply struck, bright, and with abundant luster and great eye appeal, this is a "just right" coin for the connoisseur.

AU-50, 53, 55, 58 (About Uncirculated). *Obverse:* Light wear is seen on the face, the hair to the right of the face, and the highest area of the hair bun, more so at AU-50 than at AU–53 or 55. An AU-58 coin has minimal traces of wear. An AU-50 coin has luster in protected areas among the stars and letters, with little in the open fields or on the portrait. At AU-58, most luster is present in the fields, but is worn away on the highest parts

1855-D. Graded AU-55.

of the motifs. *Reverse:* Comments apply as for the preceding, except that the eagle shows wear in all of the higher areas, as well as the leaves and arrowheads. Luster ranges from perhaps 40% remaining in protected areas at AU-50 to nearly full mint bloom at AU-58. Often the reverse of this type retains more luster than the obverse.

Illustrated coin: The example has the bold rims often seen on Dahlonega Mint coins of this denomination.

EF-40, 45 (Extremely Fine). *Obverse:* Wear is evident on all high areas of the portrait, including the hair to the right of the forehead, the tip of the coronet, and the hair bun. The stars show light wear at their centers. Luster, if present at all, is minimal and in protected areas such as between the star points. *Reverse:* Wear is greater than on an AU coin. The eagle's neck is nearly smooth, much detail is lost on the right wing, and there is flatness at

1860-C. Graded EF-40.

the lower left of the shield, and on the leaves and arrowheads. Traces of luster may be seen, more so at EF-45 than at EF-40. Overall, the reverse appears to be in a slightly higher grade than the obverse.

Illustrated coin: This is an attractive coin with medium wear.

VF-20, 30 (Very Fine). *Obverse:* The higher-relief areas of hair are worn flat at VF-20, less so at VF-30. The hair to the right of the coronet is merged into heavy strands. The stars are flat at their centers. *Reverse:* Much of the eagle is flat, with less than 50% of the feather detail remaining. The vertical shield stripes, being deeply recessed, remain bold.

Liberty Head quarter eagles are seldom collected in grades lower than VF-20.

1843-O, Small Date, Crosslet 4. Graded VF-20.

PF-60 to 70 (Proof). *Obverse and Reverse:* PF–60 to 62 coins have extensive hairlines and may have nicks and contact marks. At PF-63, hairlines are prominent, but the mirror surface is very reflective. PF-64 coins have fewer hairlines; PF-65, minimal hairlines mostly seen only under magnification, and no nicks or marks. PF-66 and higher coins should have no marks or hairlines visible to the unaided eye.

1895. Graded PF-66.

Illustrated coin: This is an exceptional gem in rich yellow-orange gold.

	Mintage	Cert	Avg	%MS	VF-20	EF-40	AU-50	AU-55	AU-58	MS-60	MS-62	MS-63
												PF-63
1840	18,859	110	50.0	11%	$850	$1,250	$2,500	$3,250	$4,250	$6,500	$8,000	$16,500 (a)
	Auctions: $2,468, AU-58, April 2013; $1,777, AU-53, October 2014; $564, AU-50, July 2015; $999, VF-30, June 2015; $1,440, EF-45, January 2018											
1840, Proof	3–6	0	n/a		*(extremely rare; 3 known)*							
	Auctions: No auction records available.											
1840-C	12,822	160	52.5	11%	$1,750	$3,250	$4,250	$5,750	$7,500	$10,000	$16,500	$27,500
	Auctions: $3,525, AU-58, March 2015; $1,087, AU-50, February 2015; $2,115, EF-45, October 2014; $1,645, VF-25, June 2015											
1840-D	3,532	42	48.6	7%	$3,250	$8,500	$11,000	$18,000	$25,000	$35,000	$75,000	
	Auctions: $28,200, MS-60, August 2016; $11,163, AU-55, November 2016											
1840-O	33,580	114	51.5	12%	$500	$1,250	$2,100	$3,250	$5,000	$9,000	$16,000	$28,000
	Auctions: $14,100, MS-62, April 2014; $7,344, MS-61, October 2014; $4,113, AU-58, July 2015; $270, VF-20, August 2014											

a. Value in MS-64 is $30,000.

1843-C, Small Date, Crosslet 4	1843-C, Large Date, Plain 4	1843-O, Small Date, Crosslet 4	1843-O, Large Date, Plain 4

	Mintage	Cert	Avg	%MS	VF-20	EF-40	AU-50	AU-55	AU-58	MS-60	MS-62	MS-63
												PF-63
1841 † (b)	unknown	0	n/a		$100,000	$125,000	$150,000	$160,000	$175,000	$225,000		
	Auctions: $149,500, PF-55, April 2012											
1841, Proof †	15–20	3	58.3									$250,000
	Auctions: $149,500, PF-55, April 2012											
1841-C	10,281	110	51.4	5%	$1,650	$2,350	$4,750	$6,500	$10,000	$16,500	$26,500	
	Auctions: $28,200, MS-62, March 2014; $5,875, AU-58, November 2014; $3,055, AU-50, June 2015; $2,468, EF-45, January 2015											
1841-D	4,164	52	46.7	6%	$3,000	$4,750	$9,000	$12,000	$15,000	$26,500	$40,000	$55,000
	Auctions: $23,500, MS-60, August 2015; $10,575, AU-55, September 2016; $8,225, AU-55, October 2015; $7,638, AU-55, April 2013											
1842	2,823	23	49.7	4%	$1,850	$3,250	$6,750	$13,000	$15,000	$19,500	$35,000	
	Auctions: $15,275, MS-60, January 2014; $7,931, AU-55, August 2015; $7,050, AU-55, July 2014; $3,819, EF-40, November 2014											
1842, Proof	2–3	0	n/a		*(unique, in the Smithsonian's National Numismatic Collection)*							
	Auctions: No auction records available.											
1842-C	6,729	66	47.4	6%	$2,000	$3,250	$7,000	$10,000	$15,000	$23,500	$37,500	
	Auctions: $8,813, AU-55, September 2014; $5,581, AU, February 2014; $3,760, EF-45, January 2015; $1,645, VF-20, January 2015											
1842-D	4,643	66	48.7	6%	$2,650	$5,500	$8,500	$11,000	$18,500	$32,500	$60,000	
	Auctions: $25,850, AU-58, August 2015; $15,275, AU-58, August 2015; $13,513, AU-58, September 2015; $9,400, AU-55, June 2015											
1842-O	19,800	166	48.6	8%	$650	$1,350	$2,250	$4,500	$6,500	$8,500	$15,000	$30,000
	Auctions: $7,638, MS-61, August 2015; $3,760, AU-58, October 2015; $1,293, EF-45, September 2015; $259, F-12, November 2015											
1843, Large Date	100,546	216	54.0	11%	$350	$450	$700	$900	$1,250	$2,500	$4,000	$6,500
	Auctions: $3,231, MS-62, January 2015; $764, AU-58, January 2015; $470, AU-53, July 2015; $376, AU-50, January 2015											
1843, Proof	4–8	1	63.0		*(extremely rare; 5–6 known)*							$75,000
	Auctions: No auction records available.											
1843-C, Small Date, Crosslet 4	2,988	55	52.0	11%	$2,750	$5,500	$7,500	$10,000	$12,500	$22,500	$32,500	
	Auctions: $4,406, MS-63, August 2014; $499, MS-60, July 2014; $646, AU-55, July 2014; $441, AU-55, October 2014											
1843-C, Large Date, Plain 4	23,076	217	48.1	7%	$1,500	$2,300	$3,250	$4,250	$5,500	$8,000	$12,500	$21,000
	Auctions: $4,230, AU-58, August 2015; $3,525, AU-53, January 2015; $2,115, EF-45, January 2015; $764, VF-20, January 2015											
1843-D, Small Date, Crosslet 4	36,209	7	53.9	14%	$2,000	$2,400	$3,250	$4,500	$5,500	$6,500	$15,000	$30,000
	Auctions: $4,406, MS-63, August 2014; $499, MS-60, July 2014; $646, AU-55, July 2014; $441, AU-55, October 2014											
1843-O, Small Date, Crosslet 4	288,002	598	52.6	15%	$400	$425	$500	$750	$1,000	$1,750	$3,250	$7,000
	Auctions: $4,465, MS-63, June 2015; $764, AU-58, September 2015; $317, AU-50, October 2015; $259, F-15, August 2015											
1843-O, Large Date, Plain 4	76,000	140	53.4	13%	$450	$600	$1,750	$2,750	$4,500	$6,000	$15,000	$25,000
	Auctions: $15,275, MS-62, February 2014; $5,875, MS-61, June 2015; $3,525, AU-55, August 2015; $4,320, AU-58, January 2018											
1844	6,784	61	51.8	8%	$600	$1,000	$2,250	$3,000	$6,000	$8,500	$18,000	$22,500
	Auctions: $15,275, MS-61, January 2014											
1844, Proof	3–6	1	66.0		*(extremely rare; 4–5 known)*							
	Auctions: No auction records available.											
1844-C	11,622	123	48.6	10%	$1,650	$2,750	$5,500	$6,500	$8,500	$15,000	$25,000	$40,000
	Auctions: $14,100, MS-61, January 2014; $6,756, AU-58, July 2015; $2,350, AU-50, August 2014; $3,055, VF-30, June 2015											
1844-D	17,332	166	52.5	13%	$1,850	$2,500	$3,250	$4,500	$5,500	$8,000	$12,500	$25,000
	Auctions: $17,038, MS-63, April 2014; $1,645, AU-50, January 2015; $2,585, EF-45, August 2014											

† Both varieties of 1841 Liberty Head Quarter Eagles are ranked in the *100 Greatest U.S. Coins* (fifth edition). **b.** Values are for circulated Proofs; existence of circulation strikes is unclear.

	Mintage	Cert	Avg	%MS	VF-20	EF-40	AU-50	AU-55	AU-58	MS-60	MS-62	MS-63 / PF-63
1845	91,051	269	55.3	26%	$400	$450	$500	$600	$625	$1,250	$2,500	$5,000 (c)
Auctions: $18,800, MS-65, January 2014; $14,100, MS-65, October 2014; $1,410, MS-61, March 2015; $235, AU-50, May 2015											
1845, Proof	4–8	2	67.0		*(extremely rare; 4–5 known)*							$55,000
Auctions: No auction records available.											
1845-D	19,460	167	51.5	5%	$1,750	$2,350	$3,250	$4,250	$7,000	$10,000	$22,500	$40,000
Auctions: $35,250, MS-63, January 2014											
1845-O	4,000	64	50.8	3%	$1,350	$2,500	$6,500	$9,000	$12,000	$26,500	$35,000	$55,000
Auctions: $5,875, AU-50, January 2014; $10,800, AU-58, February 2018											
1846	21,598	139	55.5	17%	$400	$550	$900	$1,000	$2,250	$5,000	$13,500	$20,000
Auctions: $3,760, MS-61, August 2015; $1,293, AU-58, July 2015; $734, AU-53, October 2015; $646, AU-50, January 2015											
1846, Proof	4–8	1	64.0		*(extremely rare; 4–5 known)*							$55,000
Auctions: $106,375, PF-64Cam, January 2011											
1846-C	4,808	72	51.2	10%	$1,700	$3,250	$6,000	$8,500	$11,500	$16,000	$25,000	$37,500
Auctions: $15,275, MS-62, April 2014; $4,084, AU-58, February 2018											
1846-D	19,303	184	51.6	9%	$1,850	$2,750	$3,750	$4,650	$6,250	$9,500	$13,500	$28,500
Auctions: $7,638, MS-61, June 2013; $1,528, AU-50, August 2014; $3,055, EF-45, February 2015; $3,408, EF-40, July 2015											
1846-D, D Over D	(d)	4	52.0	0%			$2,850	$4,250	$5,750	$7,500	$15,000	
Auctions: $5,175, AU-55, November 2011; $4,800, AU-53, January 2018											
1846-O	62,000	322	51.5	9%	$425	$525	$1,100	$1,900	$3,200	$5,500	$10,000	$18,500
Auctions: $4,700, MS-61, February 2013; $423, AU-50, August 2015; $552, EF-45, June 2015; $400, EF-40, June 2015											
1847	29,814	133	54.8	16%	$400	$450	$850	$1,200	$1,750	$3,000	$5,000	$10,000
Auctions: $3,055, MS-61, November 2014; $1,175, AU-58, June 2013											
1847, Proof	2–3	0	n/a		*(unique, in the Smithsonian's National Numismatic Collection)*							
Auctions: No auction records available.											
1847-C	23,226	266	52.3	13%	$1,500	$2,250	$3,000	$3,500	$4,500	$5,750	$8,000	$15,000
Auctions: $3,525, AU-58, August 2015; $2,820, AU-50, July 2015; $2,364, AU-50, September 2015; $1,821, AU-50, January 2015											
1847-D	15,784	168	52.3	11%	$1,650	$2,500	$3,250	$4,500	$5,500	$8,750	$13,500	$24,000
Auctions: $9,404, MS, February 2014; $2,820, AU-53, August 2014; $2,350, AU-50, January 2015; $3,000, AU-55, February 2018											
1847-O	124,000	347	50.0	10%	$400	$450	$1,000	$1,650	$2,750	$4,500	$10,000	$16,000
Auctions: $1,645, AU-55, January 2015; $764, AU-53, February 2015; $376, EF-40, May 2015; $259, VF-20, January 2015											

c. Value in MS-64 is $8,000. **d.** Included in 1846-D mintage figure.

1848, CAL. Above Eagle

	Mintage	Cert	Avg	%MS	VF-20	EF-40	AU-50	AU-55	MS-60	MS-62	MS-63 / PF-60	MS-64 / PF-63	MS-65 / PF-65
1848	6,500	101	55.4	34%	$550	$1,100	$2,250	$3,650	$5,500	$8,500	$15,000	$25,000	
Auctions: $5,640, AU-55, September 2015; $2,585, AU-50, February 2014; $823, AU-50, July 2014												
1848, CAL. Above Eagle †	1,389	44	56.5	43%	$40,000	$50,000	$60,000	$65,000	$90,000	$115,000	$150,000	$200,000	$250,000
Auctions: $55,813, AU-58, October 2015; $32,900, VF-25, September 2016												
1848, Proof	3–6	0	n/a								$40,000	$55,000	$150,000
Auctions: $96,600, PF-64, January 2008												
1848-C	16,788	163	50.2	9%	$1,500	$2,850	$3,500	$4,500	$11,500	$20,000	$32,500		
Auctions: $15,275, MS-62, March 2014; $3,120, AU-55, January 2018												
1848-D	13,771	150	53.5	11%	$1,650	$2,650	$3,750	$4,250	$8,000	$12,500	$28,000		
Auctions: $25,850, MS-63, April 2014												

† Ranked in the *100 Greatest U.S. Coins* (fifth edition).

	Mintage	Cert	Avg	%MS	VF-20	EF-40	AU-50	AU-55	MS-60	MS-62	MS-63	MS-64	MS-65
											PF-60	PF-63	PF-65
1849	23,294	135	55.0	16%	$450	$700	$950	$1,250	$2,750	$4,000	$7,500	$14,000	
Auctions: $3,525, MS-62, March 2014; $3,055, MS-62, January 2015; $999, AU-55, July 2014; $764, AU-55, October 2015												
1849-C	10,220	106	51.1	9%	$1,650	$3,000	$5,000	$7,500	$13,500	$20,000			
Auctions: $15,275, MS-62, August 2015; $15,275,MS-61,January 2014; $12,338, MS-60, September 2016; $6,463, AU-58, November 2016												
1849-D	10,945	147	52.4	6%	$2,000	$2,750	$3,750	$5,500	$14,000	$25,000	—		
Auctions: $4,348, AU-55, September 2016; $2,820, AU-50, November 2016; $2,468, EF-40, August 2016; $1,800, VF-30, April 2018												
1850	252,923	513	56.2	24%	$400	$425	$450	$500	$1,000	$2,500	$3,750	$7,500	$25,000
Auctions: $940, MS-61, January 2015; $423, AU-58, September 2015; $376, AU-53, May 2015; $259, EF-40, July 2015												
1850, Proof	2–4	0	n/a		*(extremely rare; 1–2 known)*								
Auctions: $41,250, PF-62, June 1995												
1850-C	9,148	139	51.1	13%	$1,500	$2,500	$3,500	$5,000	$12,500	$20,000	$35,000		
Auctions: $8,879, MS-61, August 2014; $8,813, MS-61, October 2014; $12,925, MS-60, March 2014; $881, EF-40, January 2015												
1850-D	12,148	150	52.6	11%	$1,600	$2,750	$3,750	$5,500	$12,500	$22,500	$40,000		
Auctions: $23,500, MS-62, April 2014; $18,800, MS-62, March 2016; $10,575, MS-61, January 2015; $5,434, AU-55, August 2015												
1850-O	84,000	357	50.8	4%	$425	$550	$1,000	$1,500	$4,000	$8,500	$17,500	$45,000	
Auctions: $1,645, AU-58, March 2015; $1,410, AU-58, June 2015; $764, EF-45, August 2015; $447, EF-45, February 2015; $990, AU-55, March 2018												
1851	1,372,748	924	58.6	51%	$400	$410	$425	$435	$550	$750	$1,100	$2,000	$5,500
Auctions: $9,400, MS-66, February 2015; $376, MS-61, October 2015; $400, AU-58, March 2015; $266, AU-53, May 2015												
1851-C	14,923	116	50.9	15%	$1,500	$2,450	$3,750	$4,500	$8,500	$15,000	$35,000		
Auctions: $5,640, MS-61, September 2015; $3,290, AU-53, January 2015; $2,820, AU-53, January 2015; $2,115, EF-40, July 2015												
1851-D	11,264	88	51.5	6%	$1,650	$2,500	$4,000	$5,500	$11,500	$20,000	$32,500	$50,000	$75,000
Auctions: $7,638, AU-58, December 2013; $2,115, AU-50, September 2014; $5,520, AU-58, January 2018												
1851-O	148,000	491	53.5	10%	$425	$450	$800	$1,500	$4,500	$7,000	$11,500	$23,500	
Auctions: $3,539, MS-61, February 2015; $2,143, AU-58, January 2015; $823, AU-55, October 2015; $646, AU-50, January 2015												
1852	1,159,681	1,108	59.4	56%	$400	$410	$425	$435	$550	$800	$1,100	$2,250	$5,500
Auctions: $4,818, MS-65, June 2015; $1,998, MS-64, February 2015; $588, MS-62, June 2015; $329, AU-58, July 2015												
1852-C	9,772	102	52.7	11%	$1,500	$2,500	$4,000	$5,750	$11,000	$21,000	$32,500		
Auctions: $6,463, AU-58, August 2015; $4,465, AU-55, July 2015; $3,525, AU-53, October 2015; $4,935, AU-50, February 2015												
1852-D	4,078	53	53.5	6%	$1,850	$3,250	$6,000	$8,000	$16,500	$30,000	$42,500	$65,000	
Auctions: $8,813, AU-53, August 2013; $6,300, AU-58, April 2018												
1852-O	140,000	545	52.4	6%	$425	$450	$850	$1,000	$4,750	$7,000	$11,000		
Auctions: $4,465, MS-61, August 2015; $1,410, AU-58, July 2015; $764, AU-55, January 2015; $617, AU-53, July 2015; $3,240, MS-60, March 2018												
1853	1,404,668	1,618	59.5	56%	$400	$410	$425	$435	$475	$600	$1,000	$1,500	$5,000
Auctions: $9,988, MS-66, June 2015; $676, MS-62, March 2015; $306, AU-58, June 2015; $247, AU-50, January 2015												
1853-D	3,178	49	52.9	14%	$2,000	$3,500	$5,500	$6,500	$15,000	$35,000	$50,000		
Auctions: $25,850, MS-62, January 2014; $12,338, MS-61, October 2014; $13,513, MS-61, November 2014; $4,113, AU-50, July 2014												
1854	596,258	781	58.9	48%	$400	$410	$425	$435	$550	$700	$1,250	$2,500	$6,000
Auctions: $4,230, MS-65, January 2015; $470, MS-61, January 2015; $294, AU-55, August 2015; $376, AU-50, February 2015												
1854, Proof	2–4	0	n/a		*(unique; in the Bass Foundation Collection)*								
Auctions: No auction records available.												
1854-C	7,295	110	54.1	19%	$2,000	$3,000	$4,250	$6,500	$10,000	$20,000	$37,500		
Auctions: $9,988, MS-61, June 2013; $4,994, AU-58, August 2014; $4,230, AU-53, August 2015; $3,525, EF-45, January 2015												
1854-D	1,760	23	48.9	17%	$3,500	$7,500	$10,000	$13,500	$27,500	$40,000	$65,000	$85,000	
Auctions: $5,405, EF-40, November 2016; $2,938, VF-30, September 2016; $84,000, MS-64, April 2018												
1854-O	153,000	553	53.7	8%	$425	$450	$575	$700	$1,500	$4,500	$9,000	$15,000	
Auctions: $2,585, MS-61, February 2015; $435, MS-60, September 2015; $329, AU-53, January 2015; $329, EF-45, October 2015												
1854-S †	246	6	35.3	0%	$200,000	$300,000	$450,000						
Auctions: $202,000, EF-35, October 2013; $264,000, VF-35, April 2018												
1855	235,480	449	59.3	52%	$400	$410	$425	$435	$550	$1,100	$1,650	$3,250	$8,500
Auctions: $2,585, MS-64, October 2015; $764, MS-62, July 2015; $447, MS-61, July 2015; $329, AU-58, April 2015												

† Ranked in the *100 Greatest U.S. Coins* (fifth edition).

Old Reverse (Pre-1859)   **New Reverse**

	Mintage	Cert	Avg	%MS	VF-'20	EF-40	AU-50	AU-55	MS-60	MS-62	MS-63 / PF-60	MS-64 / PF-63	MS-65 / PF-65
1855-C	3,677	73	54.4	22%	$2,250	$4,250	$6,000	$7,500	$20,000	$27,500	$42,500	$65,000	$100,000
Auctions: $23,500, MS-62, January 2014; $81,000, MS-65, April 2018													
1855-D	1,123	26	53.7	12%	$4,500	$8,000	$13,500	$20,000	$50,000		$100,000		
Auctions: $25,850, AU-55, July 2014; $8,225, EF-45, March 2015													
1856	384,240	686	59.2	53%	$400	$410	$425	$435	$500	$850	$1,250	$3,000	$5,500
Auctions: $3,995, MS-65, July 2015; $1,234, MS-63, July 2015; $376, AU-58, March 2015; $282, AU-53, May 2015													
1856, Proof	6–8	0	n/a								$35,000	$55,000	$145,000
Auctions: No auction records available.													
1856-C	7,913	98	52.5	16%	$1,650	$2,750	$4,000	$6,000	$11,500	$20,000	$25,000		
Auctions: $6,463, AU-58, April 2013; $4,465, AU-58, August 2015; $4,230, AU-55, August 2015; $1,410, AU-50, October 2014													
1856-D	874	17	52.7	24%	$10,000	$15,000	$30,000	$37,500	$75,000				
Auctions: $55,813, AU-58, March 2014													
1856-O	21,100	155	53.8	10%	$450	$800	$1,650	$2,250	$8,250	$40,000			
Auctions: $7,050, MS-61, August 2013; $1,320, AU-55, January 2018													
1856-S	72,120	224	51.6	14%	$450	$500	$850	$1,250	$5,000	$8,000	$12,000	$13,500	$32,500
Auctions: $2,585, AU-58, September 2015; $1,821, AU-58, September 2015; $1,410, AU-58, June 2015; $1,058, AU-50, January 2015													
1857	214,130	496	59.5	56%	$400	$410	$425	$435	$550	$850	$1,250	$2,500	$6,500
Auctions: $5,904, MS-65, July 2015; $423, MS-61, January 2015; $282, MS-60, November 2015; $282, AU-55, May 2015													
1857, Proof	6–8	0	n/a								$35,000	$57,500	$125,000
Auctions: No auction records available.													
1857-D	2,364	66	56.7	29%	$1,750	$2,800	$4,000	$6,500	$12,000	$22,000	$35,000	$50,000	
Auctions: $18,800, MS-62, April 2014; $4,935, AU-55, June 2015; $1,586, AU-50, January 2015; $1,528, AU-50, July 2014													
1857-O	34,000	290	55.1	19%	$425	$500	$1,250	$1,700	$4,250	$8,000	$14,500	$22,500	
Auctions: $6,463, MS-62, April 2014; $4,113, MS-61, November 2014; $1,998, AU-58, January 2015; $823, AU-53, January 2015													
1857-S	69,200	193	51.1	10%	$425	$475	$1,200	$1,650	$5,500	$7,500	$13,500	$30,000	
Auctions: $5,875, MS-61, June 2015; $1,775, AU-58, July 2015; $1,293, AU-55, January 2015; $317, VF-35, July 2014													
1858	47,377	207	58.2	36%	$425	$450	$475	$500	$1,100	$1,850	$3,000	$6,000	$13,500
Auctions: $999, MS-61, January 2015; $564, AU-58, October 2015; $376, AU-55, February 2015; $353, AU-53, May 2015													
1858, Proof	6–8	3	65.3								$25,000	$45,000	$115,000
Auctions: $82,250, PF, March 2014													
1858-C	9,056	145	54.5	25%	$1,500	$2,250	$3,500	$4,250	$8,000	$13,500	$25,000		
Auctions: $11,163, MS-62, January 2014; $4,113, AU-58, November 2014; $3,525, AU-58, November 2014													
1859, Old Reverse	39,364	141	57.7	30%	$450	$550	$850	$1,000	$2,000	$3,500	$6,000	$10,000	
Auctions: $1,102, AU, February 2014; $456, AU-50, November 2014; $411, EF-40, August 2014													
1859, New Reverse	(a)	53	58.0	21%	$400	$425	$500	$650	$1,200	$1,750	$3,000	$7,250	$11,000
Auctions: $3,290, MS-63, October 2014; $3,055, MS-63, August 2015; $1,998, MS-62, November 2014; $2,879, MS, January 2014													
1859, Old Reverse Proof (b)	80	8	64.9								$15,000	$30,000	$75,000
Auctions: No auction records available.													
1859, New Reverse Proof (b)	(c)	(c)	64.0										—
Auctions: $80,500, PF-66, July 2005													

a. Included in circulation-strike 1859, Old Reverse, mintage figure. **b.** Nearly all 1859 Proofs are of the Old Reverse style. **c.** Included in figures for 1859, Old Reverse, Proof.

| 1862, 2 Over 1 | 1873, Close 3 | 1873, Open 3 |

	Mintage	Cert	Avg	%MS	VF-20	EF-40	AU-50	AU-55	MS-60	MS-62	MS-63 / PF-60	MS-64 / PF-63	MS-65 / PF-65
1859-D	2,244	94	54.9	14%	$2,200	$3,250	$4,250	$5,750	$17,500	$37,500			
Auctions: $44,063, MS-62, August 2015; $24,675, MS-62, August 2015; $13,513, MS-60, September 2015; $14,100, AU-58, September 2016
1859-S	15,200	108	47.3	8%	$475	$1,000	$2,000	$2,750	$5,500	$9,000	$17,500	$30,000	
Auctions: $4,994, MS-61, April 2014; $4,847, MS-61, August 2014; $3,290, AU-58, October 2014; $2,585, AU-58, July 2014
1860, Old Reverse	22,563	33	57.5	33%	$1,250	$2,000	$2,750	$4,000	$5,000	$6,000	$10,000	$12,500	
Auctions: $6,463, MS-62, April 2013
1860, New Reverse	(d)	59	58.2	42%	$400	$450	$500	$600	$1,100	$1,850	$3,000	$7,500	$12,500
Auctions: $1,763, MS-60, August 2013
1860, Proof (e)	112	9	64.0								$14,000	$22,500	$40,000
Auctions: $11,550, PF-64Cam, October 1993
1860-C	7,469	119	51.5	10%	$1,850	$2,500	$3,250	$6,000	$12,500	$20,000	$30,000		
Auctions: $25,850, MS-63, January 2014; $14,100, MS-61, June 2015; $12,925, MS-61, August 2015; $8,813, AU-58, September 2015
1860-S	35,600	127	46.9	8%	$500	$675	$1,250	$1,750	$3,750	$7,500	$20,000	$30,000	
Auctions: $6,756, MS-62, August 2013; $317, EF-40, November 2014
1861, Old Reverse	1,283,788	142	58.0	36%	$525	$1,000	$1,500	$1,850	$3,750	$5,500	$7,500	$10,000	$20,000
Auctions: $11,163, MS-64, October 2015; $8,225, MS-63, August 2016; $3,760, MS-61, September 2016; $2,849, MS-61, July 2016
1861, New Reverse	(f)	1,664	59.3	53%	$400	$410	$425	$435	$700	$1,000	$1,750	$2,500	$4,500
Auctions: $9,400, MS-66, January 2015; $646, MS-61, July 2015; $353, AU-55, September 2015; $329, AU-50, September 2015
1861, Proof (g)	90	3	65.3								$12,000	$20,000	$40,000
Auctions: $44,850, PF-65DCam, September 2005
1861-S	24,000	107	46.1	7%	$550	$1,000	$3,250	$4,750	$12,500	$25,000			
Auctions: $5,875, AU-58, April 2013
1862, 2 Over 1	(h)	56	54.3	13%	$1,000	$1,850	$3,000	$4,750	$8,500	$15,000	$32,500		
Auctions: $9,400, MS-61, January 2014; $558, AU-50, July 2014; $10,800, MS-61, January 2018
1862	98,508	223	56.3	29%	$450	$600	$1,350	$2,250	$4,750	$6,500	$11,000	$30,000	
Auctions: $8,225, MS-63, August 2015; $4,700, MS-62, October 2015; $2,381, AU-58, January 2015; $1,116, AU-50, January 2015
1862, Proof	35	11	64.7								$12,000	$20,000	$40,000
Auctions: $46,000, PF-65UCam, February 2007
1862-S	8,000	55	46.0	7%	$1,750	$2,500	$4,250	$6,000	$16,000	$25,000	$45,000		
Auctions: $23,500, MS-62, January 2014
1863, Proof † (i)	30	6	64.0								$50,000	$75,000	$125,000
Auctions: $45,531, PF-58, April 2014; $78,000, PF-63, January 2018
1863-S	10,800	79	46.3	10%	$1,250	$2,500	$4,500	$6,500	$15,000	$20,000		$75,000	
Auctions: $3,290, EF-45, March 2013
1864	2,824	7	52.7	29%	$15,000	$35,000	$55,000	$65,000	$100,000				
Auctions: $48,469, AU-55, March 2014
1864, Proof	50	14	64.8								$12,000	$25,000	$55,000
Auctions: $30,550, PF-64Cam, April 2014; $78,000, PF-65, January 2018
1865	1,520	18	53.4	0%	$4,500	$10,000	$20,000	$27,500			$100,000		
Auctions: $15,891, AU-55, June 2013; $16,450, AU-50, November 2016; $11,163, EF-45, August 2015; $4,113, VF-20, November 2014
1865, Proof	25	13	63.9								$13,500	$20,000	$55,000
Auctions: $48,875, PF-65UCam, January 2012
1865-S	23,376	111	44.5	4%	$750	$1,300	$2,000	$2,500	$4,500	$12,500	$17,500	$27,500	
Auctions: $1,998, AU-53, March 2014

† Ranked in the *100 Greatest U.S. Coins* (fifth edition). **d.** Included in 1860, Old Reverse, mintage figure. **e.** All known 1860 Proofs are of the New Reverse style. **f.** Included in 1861, Old Reverse, mintage figure. **g.** All 1861 Proofs were struck in the New Reverse style. **h.** Included in circulation-strike 1862 mintage figure. **i.** Proof only.

	Mintage	Cert	Avg	%MS	VF-20	EF-40	AU-50	AU-55	MS-60	MS-62	MS-63 / PF-60	MS-64 / PF-63	MS-65 / PF-65
1866	3,080	37	51.4	14%	$1,150	$3,500	$5,250	$7,500	$12,500	$20,000	$27,500	$35,000	
	Auctions: $7,050, AU-58, February 2013												
1866, Proof	30	14	64.0								$10,000	$17,500	$45,000
	Auctions: $23,500, PF-64Cam, April 2014												
1866-S	38,960	209	46.5	4%	$450	$750	$1,250	$2,000	$6,500	$12,500	$22,500		
	Auctions: $7,050, MS-61, August 2015; $1,880, AU-58, July 2015; $470, EF-45, January 2015; $376, VF-25, January 2015												
1867	3,200	38	55.0	24%	$500	$1,000	$1,500	$3,000	$8,000	$13,000	$23,000	$25,000	$35,000
	Auctions: $1,544, AU-55, July 2014; $1,645, AU-55, May 2013												
1867, Proof	50	11	64.1								$10,000	$16,000	$35,000
	Auctions: $35,250, PF-65DCam, October 2015; $18,800, PF-64DCam, October 2014; $99,875, PF, August 2013; $21,600, PF-64, April 2018												
1867-S	28,000	179	46.8	6%	$415	$650	$1,250	$1,600	$4,000	$8,000	$15,000	$20,000	
	Auctions: $1,163, AU-50, September 2015; $940, EF-45, August 2015; $541, EF-45, January 2015; $306, VF-30, November 2015												
1868	3,600	156	56.9	22%	$415	$450	$700	$850	$2,250	$5,000	$8,000	$14,500	
	Auctions: $3,290, MS-61, August 2014; $1,998, MS-61, November 2014; $1,880, AU-58, July 2015; $881, AU-58, February 2015												
1868, Proof	25	5	63.4								$9,500	$16,500	$45,000
	Auctions: $43,700, PF-65Cam, January 2009												
1868-S	34,000	256	51.7	7%	$415	$450	$700	$1,000	$3,000	$5,500	$8,500	$13,500	
	Auctions: $2,820, AU-58, August 2015; $999, AU-55, January 2015; $529, AU-50, July 2015; $447, EF-45, June 2015; $1,140, AU-58, January 2018												
1869	4,320	162	56.8	25%	$425	$500	$800	$1,150	$3,000	$5,000	$10,000	$22,500	
	Auctions: $19,975, MS-64, August 2014; $1,058, AU-58, January 2015; $881, AU-55, July 2015; $940, AU-50, June 2015												
1869, Proof	25	18	64.3								$8,500	$15,000	$40,000
	Auctions: $12,650, PF-63, October 2011												
1869-S	29,500	239	51.4	9%	$415	$475	$700	$1,350	$3,500	$5,500	$9,250	$13,000	
	Auctions: $3,525, MS-62, October 2015; $1,645, AU-58, January 2015; $1,528, AU-58, August 2015; $1,528, AU-58, June 2015												
1870	4,520	94	57.0	19%	$450	$500	$750	$1,250	$3,250	$5,000	$8,000		$25,000
	Auctions: $4,994, MS-61, January 2014; $3,525, MS-61, January 2015; $3,760, MS-60, August 2015; $1,645, AU-58, August 2015												
1870, Proof	35	5	63.8								$8,500	$15,000	$40,000
	Auctions: $70,500, PF-66DCam, January 2014												
1870-S	16,000	146	50.7	8%	$425	$500	$900	$1,500	$4,000	$8,500	$12,500	$20,000	
	Auctions: $8,225, MS-62, January 2014; $1,528, AU-58, July 2014; $1,645, AU-50, October 2015; $447, AU-50, September 2015												
1871	5,320	128	56.5	24%	$450	$500	$750	$1,000	$2,000	$2,750	$4,500	$10,000	$35,000
	Auctions: $999, AU-58, July 2015; $705, AU-55, October 2015; $646, AU-55, July 2015; $306, AU-50, January 2015												
1871, Proof	30	10	64.0								$8,500	$15,000	$40,000
	Auctions: $19,975, PF-64DCam, August 2014; $14,400, PF-63, April 2018												
1871-S	22,000	232	52.6	11%	$425	$500	$550	$1,000	$2,000	$3,000	$4,350	$9,000	$17,500
	Auctions: $1,087, AU-55, August 2015; $517, AU-53, June 2015; $423, AU-53, February 2015; $282, VF-30, November 2015												
1872	3,000	67	55.9	15%	$450	$850	$1,500	$2,000	$4,350	$10,000	$15,000	$30,000	
	Auctions: $2,596, AU-58, March 2014												
1872, Proof	30	8	64.6								$8,500	$15,000	$37,500
	Auctions: $34,075, PF-65Cam, March 2013												
1872-S	18,000	199	50.8	8%	$425	$500	$950	$1,250	$4,000	$6,000	$10,500	$13,500	
	Auctions: $3,594, MS-61, April 2012												
1873, Close 3	55,200	651	59.9	63%	$425	$435	$450	$465	$525	$650	$1,250	$1,750	$4,500
	Auctions: $3,525, MS-65, June 2015; $1,763, MS-64, June 2015; $1,293, MS-64, September 2015; $705, MS-63, July 2015												
1873, Open 3	122,800	562	60.7	73%	$400	$415	$425	$430	$500	$600	$825	$1,250	$4,250
	Auctions: $11,750, MS-66, July 2015; $1,116, MS-64, October 2015; $400, MS-62, August 2015; $329, AU-58, July 2015												
1873, Close 3, Proof	25	11	62.7								$8,500	$15,000	$40,000
	Auctions: $23,500, PF-63Cam, August 2014; $19,388, PF, August 2013												
1873-S	27,000	259	50.0	7%	$425	$500	$975	$1,000	$2,000	$4,000	$6,500	$13,500	$25,000
	Auctions: $11,750, MS-64, August 2015; $3,525, MS-62, October 2015; $620, AU-55, February 2015; $447, EF-45, May 2015												

	Mintage	Cert	Avg	%MS	VF-20	EF-40	AU-50	AU-55	MS-60	MS-62	MS-63	MS-64	MS-65
											PF-60	PF-63	PF-65
1874	3,920	126	57.1	27%	$425	$500	$650	$1,050	$2,000	$4,000	$6,000	$9,500	$25,000
	Auctions: $3,525, MS-62, August 2013; $2,280, MS-61, April 2018												
1874, Proof	20	10	64.4								$8,500	$17,500	$50,000
	Auctions: $38,188, PF-64DCam, August 2014												
1875	400	26	56.9	19%	$5,500	$8,000	$12,500	$15,000	$27,500	$40,000			
	Auctions: $25,850, MS-61, January 2015; $25,850, MS-61, August 2013; $28,200, MS-60, October 2016; $15,275, AU-58, October 2014												
1875, Proof	20	10	63.5								$25,000	$50,000	$125,000
	Auctions: $94,000, PF, October 2013												
1875-S	11,600	196	54.0	17%	$425	$500	$650	$1,100	$3,500	$5,000	$7,250	$12,000	$25,000
	Auctions: $5,581, MS-63, October 2014; $1,087, AU-58, July 2015; $999, AU-58, June 2015; $676, AU-53, August 2014												
1876	4,176	140	53.7	14%	$500	$675	$1,000	$1,750	$3,250	$5,500	$7,500	$12,000	
	Auctions: $5,581, MS-62, March 2014; $3,055, MS-61, September 2015; $2,350, MS-60, October 2015; $823, AU-53, October 2015												
1876, Proof	45	15	64.3								$7,500	$15,000	$40,000
	Auctions: $39,950, PF, January 2013												
1876-S	5,000	145	54.2	16%	$450	$550	$1,000	$1,350	$3,000	$4,000	$8,500		
	Auctions: $8,225, MS-63, January 2014; $2,820, MS-61, August 2014; $1,880, AU-58, November 2015; $734, AU-53, June 2015												
1877	1,632	106	56.7	29%	$500	$900	$1,250	$1,500	$3,000	$4,750	$9,500	$15,000	
	Auctions: $4,406, MS-62, April 2014; $3,055, MS-61, August 2014; $1,763, AU-58, June 2015; $884, AU-50, March 2015												
1877, Proof	20	5	63.4								$7,500	$15,000	$40,000
	Auctions: $8,050, PF-55, November 2011												
1877-S	35,400	426	58.7	45%	$415	$425	$435	$450	$650	$1,250	$2,350	$4,000	$10,000
	Auctions: $376, AU-58, June 2015; $259, AU-58, January 2015; $282, AU-53, May 2015; $329, AU-50, May 2015; $1,140, MS-62, January 2018												
1878	286,240	2,532	60.7	73%	$400	$415	$425	$430	$450	$500	$700	$1,000	$2,000
	Auctions: $12,925, MS-67, July 2015; $999, MS-64, August 2015; $541, MS-62, February 2015; $329, AU-58, June 2015												
1878, Proof	20	11	64.4								$7,500	$15,000	$40,000
	Auctions: $50,313, PF-65DCam, April 2012; $52,800, PF-65, April 2018												
1878-S	178,000	791	59.1	51%	$400	$415	$425	$435	$500	$850	$1,500	$3,500	$12,000
	Auctions: $12,925, MS-66, January 2015; $423, MS-61, June 2015; $353, AU-58, October 2015; $353, AU-53, September 2015												
1879	88,960	1,029	60.6	72%	$400	$415	$425	$435	$525	$550	$800	$1,000	$3,000
	Auctions: $7,638, MS-66, September 2015; $940, MS-64, January 2015; $423, MS-61, October 2015; $282, AU-58, May 2015												
1879, Proof	30	7	65.1								$7,500	$13,000	$35,000
	Auctions: $40,250, PF-67Cam, January 2011; $37,200, PF-65, April 2018												
1879-S	43,500	248	54.3	9%	$400	$415	$550	$850	$1,750	$3,500	$4,500	$17,500	
	Auctions: $423, MS-60, January 2015; $400, MS-60, February 2015; $617, AU-58, July 2015; $259, EF-45, January 2015												
1880	2,960	156	58.6	46%	$450	$500	$650	$800	$1,500	$2,150	$3,750	$6,000	$12,500
	Auctions: $2,820, MS-62, October 2013; $1,410, MS-61, February 2015; $1,410, AU-58, November 2014; $999, AU-58, January 2015												
1880, Proof	36	14	62.8								$6,500	$12,500	$35,000
	Auctions: $3,244, PF-55, January 2011; $13,214, PF-63, April 2018												
1881	640	79	57.0	30%	$2,000	$3,000	$5,000	$6,000	$10,000	$15,000	$20,000	$30,000	
	Auctions: $12,925, MS-61, November 2016; $11,750, MS-61, August 2016; $7,931, MS-60, June 2013; $5,875, AU-58, August 2014												
1881, Proof	51	22	64.2								$6,500	$13,500	$30,000
	Auctions: $34,075, PF-65DCam, August 2013; $14,100, PF-64DCam, July 2014												
1882	4,000	177	59.5	53%	$450	$500	$550	$700	$1,250	$2,000	$2,750	$5,500	$12,500
	Auctions: $9,400, MS-66, November 2014; $1,058, AU-58, July 2015; $282, AU-50, July 2015; $259, AU-50, July 2015; $1,148, MS-61, March 2018												
1882, Proof	67	14	65.4								$4,500	$9,500	$25,000
	Auctions: $9,487, PF-64, May 2006												
1883	1,920	57	58.1	35%	$1,000	$1,750	$2,750	$4,500	$6,000	$10,000	$12,500	$15,000	
	Auctions: $4,994, MS-61, June 2014; $5,040, AU-58, January 2018												
1883, Proof	82	23	64.7								$4,500	$9,500	$25,000
	Auctions: $28,200, PF, March 2014												

1891, Doubled Die Reverse
FS-G2.5-1891-801.

	Mintage	Cert	Avg	%MS	VF-20	EF-40	AU-50	AU-55	MS-60	MS-62	MS-63 PF-60	MS-64 PF-63	MS-65 PF-65
1884	1,950	128	60.0	63%	$450	$500	$800	$1,000	$2,000	$2,500	$3,500	$6,500	$25,000
Auctions: $18,800, MS-65, June 2015; $2,468, MS-62, June 2014; $1,645, MS-61, June 2015; $1,058, AU-58, August 2014													
1884, Proof	73	24	64.0								$4,500	$9,500	$25,000
Auctions: $82,250, PF, August 2013													
1885	800	50	58.4	42%	$950	$2,000	$2,750	$3,250	$5,500	$7,000	$10,000	$16,500	$35,000
Auctions: $13,513, MS-63, March 2014; $1,423, AU-50, July 2014													
1885, Proof	87	22	64.2								$5,000	$9,000	$27,500
Auctions: $56,160, PF, September 2013													
1886	4,000	159	59.6	56%	$450	$500	$550	$600	$1,250	$2,000	$3,500	$6,750	$11,000
Auctions: $1,528, MS-62, July 2014; $823, AU-58, September 2015; $823, AU-58, July 2015; $518, AU-53, June 2015													
1886, Proof	88	30	64.3								$4,500	$9,500	$25,000
Auctions: $40,538, PF, August 2013													
1887	6,160	214	60.0	65%	$450	$500	$525	$550	$800	$1,250	$1,500	$4,000	$15,000
Auctions: $15,275, MS-65, August 2015; $881, MS-62, February 2015; $764, AU-58, January 2015; $329, AU-50, October 2015													
1887, Proof	122	27	64.0								$4,500	$9,500	$30,000
Auctions: $58,750, PF, August 2013; $26,400, PF-64, April 2018													
1888	16,001	485	61.9	88%	$400	$415	$425	$435	$500	$650	$900	$1,850	$4,500
Auctions: $8,225, MS-66, August 2015; $1,234, MS-64, January 2015; $541, MS-62, January 2015; $376, MS-61, August 2015													
1888, Proof	97	30	64.3								$4,500	$8,500	$25,000
Auctions: $25,850, PF-65Cam, February 2013; $6,463, PF-63, November 2014; $5,288, PF-62, August 2014													
1889	17,600	422	61.4	85%	$400	$415	$425	$435	$500	$650	$950	$1,650	$5,500
Auctions: $6,463, MS-65, July 2014; $441, MS-61, August 2014; $341, AU-58, October 2014; $329, AU-58, July 2015													
1889, Proof	48	18	64.8								$4,500	$8,500	$25,000
Auctions: $31,792, PF-65DCam, August 2014													
1890	8,720	253	60.8	69%	$400	$415	$425	$435	$650	$800	$1,500	$3,250	$9,000
Auctions: $9,400, MS-65, July 2015; $940, MS-62, August 2015; $646, AU-58, May 2015; $400, AU-55, June 2015													
1890, Proof	93	50	64.7								$4,500	$8,500	$20,000
Auctions: $19,388, PF-65DCam, June 2014; $29,458, PF-65, October 2014													
1891	10,960	0	n/a		$400	$415	$425	$435	$550	$700	$1,450	$1,850	$6,000
Auctions: $2,233, MS-64, November 2014; $1,645, MS-64, June 2015; $447, MS-61, February 2015; $411, AU-58, May 2015													
1891, Doubled Die Reverse	(j)	343	60.8	74%				$550	$950	$1,600	$2,650	$3,250	$5,750
Auctions: $823, MS-63, November 2014													
1891, Proof	80	24	65.6								$4,500	$8,000	$20,000
Auctions: $30,550, PF, April 2013; $8,419, PF-63, April 2018													
1892	2,440	146	61.0	81%	$400	$415	$475	$525	$900	$1,100	$2,500	$4,500	$8,000
Auctions: $21,150, MS-67, November 2013; $8,527, MS-66, August 2014; $7,931, MS-66, November 2014; $1,998, MS-63, October 2014													
1892, Proof	105	33	64.7								$4,500	$8,000	$20,000
Auctions: $111,625, PF, February 2013; $24,000, PF-65, April 2018													
1893	30,000	955	62.2	91%	$400	$415	$425	$435	$550	$800	$1,250	$1,350	$1,750
Auctions: $7,050, MS-67, January 2015; $3,290, MS-66, January 2015; $494, MS-62, April 2015; $259, MS-60, January 2015													
1893, Proof	106	42	65.3								$4,500	$7,500	$20,000
Auctions: $21,150, PF-66DCam, September 2014; $44,063, PF, August 2013; $10,800, PF-64+, February 2018													

j. Included in circulation-strike 1891 mintage figure.

	Mintage	Cert	Avg	%MS	VF-20	EF-40	AU-50	AU-55	MS-60	MS-62	MS-63	MS-64	MS-65
											PF-60	PF-63	PF-65
1894	4,000	242	61.8	86%	$400	$425	$435	$475	$750	$900	$1,450	$2,000	$5,500
	Auctions: $3,525, MS-65, January 2015; $1,410, MS-62, July 2015; $833, MS-61, January 2015; $823, MS-61, August 2015												
1894, Proof	122	64	64.5								$4,500	$7,500	$20,000
	Auctions: $21,150, PF-66DCam, September 2014; $44,063, PF, August 2013; $20,400, PF-65, January 2018												
1895	6,000	281	62.4	92%	$400	$415	$425	$450	$575	$725	$1,100	$1,650	$3,750
	Auctions: $8,519, MS-66, March 2013												
1895, Proof	119	73	65.0								$4,500	$7,500	$20,000
	Auctions: $23,500, PF-66DCam, January 2014; $28,200, PF-66DCam, August 2014; $9,400, PF-64DCam, January 2015												
1896	19,070	739	62.5	94%	$400	$405	$410	$450	$500	$600	$800	$1,000	$2,000
	Auctions: $7,344, MS-67, March 2014; $1,998, MS-65, September 2014; $940, MS-64, March 2015; $306, AU-58, July 2015												
1896, Proof	132	67	64.8								$4,500	$7,500	$20,000
	Auctions: $3,819, PF-62, March 2015; $3,055, PF-62, November 2014; $21,150, PF, October 2013; $3,480, PF-61, April 2018												
1897	29,768	1,091	62.7	95%	$400	$405	$410	$415	$500	$525	$700	$900	$1,750
	Auctions: $7,638, MS-67, January 2015; $3,055, MS-66, July 2015; $881, MS-64, October 2015; $447, MS-62, January 2015												
1897, Proof	136	86	64.8								$4,500	$7,500	$20,000
	Auctions: $27,025, PF, March 2014; $38,400, PF-68, January 2018												
1898	24,000	817	63.1	96%	$400	$405	$410	$415	$475	$485	$675	$800	$1,500
	Auctions: $7,638, MS-67, January 2015; $2,879, MS-66, August 2015; $364, MS-61, September 2015; $294, MS-60, April 2015												
1898, Proof	165	110	64.3								$4,500	$7,500	$20,000
	Auctions: $25,850, PF-66DCam, September 2014; $25,850, PF-66DCam, September 2014; $5,941, PF-64Cam, June 2015												
1899	27,200	843	62.8	97%	$400	$405	$410	$415	$475	$485	$575	$625	$1,650
	Auctions: $2,585, MS-66, June 2015; $1,998, MS-65, July 2015; $1,414, MS-65, June 2015; $969, MS-64, June 2015												
1899, Proof	150	141	64.4								$4,500	$7,500	$20,000
	Auctions: $36,425, PF, August 2013												
1900	67,000	2,100	63.0	96%	$400	$405	$410	$415	$475	$485	$525	$600	$850
	Auctions: $3,290, MS-67, June 2015; $940, MS-65, January 2015; $705, MS-64, October 2015; $541, MS-62, July 2015												
1900, Proof	205	204	63.9								$4,500	$7,500	$17,500
	Auctions: $56,400, PF-68DCam+, October 2015; $37,600, PF-68UCam, June 2015; $64,625, PF-68DCam, November 2014												
1901	91,100	2,450	62.9	96%	$400	$405	$410	$415	$475	$485	$525	$600	$850
	Auctions: $4,700, MS-67, August 2014; $1,351, MS-65, January 2015; $541, MS-63, January 2015; $447, MS-62, January 2015												
1901, Proof	223	132	64.1								$4,500	$7,500	$17,500
	Auctions: $28,200, PF-67DCam, October 2014; $16,450, PF-66Cam+, June 2015; $11,750, PF-64Cam, September 2014												
1902	133,540	3,574	63.0	97%	$400	$405	$410	$415	$475	$485	$525	$600	$850
	Auctions: $5,405, MS-67, January 2015; $646, MS-64, August 2015; $329, MS-61, April 2015; $282, MS-60, January 2015												
1902, Proof	193	109	63.9								$4,500	$7,500	$17,500
	Auctions: $5,640, PF-64, June 2015; $3,290, PF-62, June 2015; $2,585, PF-61, January 2015; $1,528, PF-50, August 2015												
1903	201,060	6,366	63.0	96%	$400	$405	$410	$415	$475	$485	$525	$600	$850
	Auctions: $9,400, MS-68, January 2015; $2,350, MS-67, January 2015; $376, MS-62, February 2015; $235, MS-60, June 2015												
1903, Proof	197	121	63.0								$4,500	$7,500	$17,500
	Auctions: $12,925, PF-65, January 2015; $7,050, PF-64, August 2014; $3,173, PF-62, November 2014; $3,055, PF-62, March 2015												
1904	160,790	4,865	63.0	96%	$400	$405	$410	$415	$475	$485	$525	$600	$850
	Auctions: $28,200, MS-68, January 2013; $3,290, MS-67, July 2015; $2,585, MS-67, November 2014; $1,351, MS-66, November 2014												
1904, Proof	170	111	64.2								$4,500	$7,500	$17,500
	Auctions: $4,700, PF-63, January 2015; $1,293, MS-66, October 2015; $270, MS-60, January 2015; $259, AU-55, January 2015												
1905 (k)	217,800	6,770	63.0	96%	$400	$405	$410	$415	$475	$485	$525	$600	$850
	Auctions: $3,995, MS-67, August 2015; $1,528, MS-66, August 2015; $329, MS-62, July 2015; $282, AU-58, February 2015												
1905, Proof	144	119	63.6								$4,500	$7,500	$17,500
	Auctions: $8,225, PF-64, October 2014; $6,463, PF-64, July 2015; $6,463, PF-64, February 2015; $1,058, PF, March 2015												

k. Pieces dated 1905-S are counterfeit.

	Mintage	Cert	Avg	%MS	VF-20	EF-40	AU-50	AU-55	MS-60	MS-62	MS-63	MS-64	MS-65
											PF-60	PF-63	PF-65
1906	176,330	5,673	63.0	97%	$400	$405	$410	$415	$475	$485	$525	$600	$850
	Auctions: $21,150, MS-68, October 2015; $1,528, MS-66, January 2015; $353, MS-61, June 2015; $306, AU-58, June 2015												
1906, Proof	160	141	64.5								$4,500	$7,500	$17,500
	Auctions: $7,638, PF-64Cam, August 2014; $8,225, PF-64Cam, September 2014; $44,063, PF, August 2013; $7,200, PF-64, February 2018												
1907	336,294	9,550	63.1	97%	$400	$405	$410	$415	$475	$485	$525	$600	$850
	Auctions: $12,925, MS-68, January 2015; $1,351, MS-66, June 2015; $494, MS-62, January 2015; $282, MS-60, June 2015												
1907, Proof	154	111	64.5								$4,500	$7,500	$17,500
	Auctions: $32,900, PF-68, April 2013; $21,738, PF-65+, January 2015; $4,700, PF-63Cam, September 2014; $31,200, PF-67, January 2018												

INDIAN HEAD (1908–1929)

Designer: *Bela Lyon Pratt.* **Weight:** *4.18 grams.*
Composition: *.900 gold, .100 copper (net weight .12094 oz. pure gold).*
Diameter: *18 mm.* **Edge:** *Reeded.* **Mints:** *Philadelphia and Denver.*

Circulation Strike | *Mintmark is on the reverse, to the left of arrows.* | **Sandblast Finish Proof** | **Satin Finish Proof**

History. The Indian Head design—used on both the quarter eagle and the half eagle—is unusual in that the lettering and motifs are in sunken relief. (The design sometimes is erroneously described as incuse.) The designer, sculptor Bela Lyon Pratt, was chosen by President Theodore Roosevelt after Augustus Saint-Gaudens died before beginning his own design. Pratt modeled the head on Chief Hollow Horn Bear of the Lakota. The "standing eagle" reverse design was based on the reverse of Saint-Gaudens's Indian Head $10 gold coin of 1907; Pratt was a pupil of the famous sculptor.

Some Americans worried that the sunken designs of the Indian Head quarter eagle would accumulate dirt and germs—an unfounded fear. As the smallest gold denomination of the era, these coins were popular for use as souvenirs and gifts, but they did not circulate as money except in the West.

Striking and Sharpness. The striking quality of Indian Head quarter eagles varies. On many early issues the rims are flat, while on others, including most of the 1920s, they are slightly raised. Some have traces of a wire rim, usually on the reverse. Look for weakness on the high parts of the Indian's bonnet (particularly the garland of flowers) and in the feather details in the headdress. On the reverse, check the feathers on the highest area of the wing, the top of the shoulder. On some issues of the 1911-D, the D mintmark can be weak.

Availability. This design was not popular with collectors, and they saved relatively few of the coins. However, many coins were given as gifts and preserved in high quality. The survival of MS-63 and better coins is a matter of chance, especially for the issues dated from 1909 to 1915. The only scarce issue is 1911-D. Luster can range from deeply frosty to grainy. As the fields are the highest areas of the coin, luster diminished quickly as examples were circulated or jostled with others in bags. The Indian Head quarter eagle is one of the most challenging series for professional graders, and opinions can vary widely.

Proofs. Sandblast (also called Matte) Proofs were made in 1908 and 1911 to 1915, while Satin (also called Roman Finish) Proofs were made in 1909 and 1910. The Sandblast issues are usually somewhat dull, while the Satin Proofs are usually of a light-yellow gold. In their time the Proofs of both styles, made for all gold series, were not popular with numismatists. Today, they are in strong demand. As a class these are significantly more readily available than half eagles of the same date and style of finish.

Most are in grades from PF-63 upward. At lower levels coins can show light contact marks. Some microscopic bright flecks may have been caused by the sandblasting process and, although they do not represent handling, usually result in a coin being assigned a slightly lower grade.

Note: Values of common-date gold coins have been based on the current bullion price of gold, $2,000 per ounce, and may vary with the prevailing spot price.

GRADING STANDARDS

MS-60 to 70 (Mint State). *Obverse:* On MS–60 to 62 coins there is abrasion in the field, this representing the highest part of the coin. Abrasion is also evident on the headdress. Marks and, occasionally, a microscopic pin scratch may be seen. At MS-63, there may be some abrasion and some tiny marks. Luster is irregular. At MS-64, abrasion is less. Luster is rich. At MS-65 and above, luster is deep and frosty. No marks at all are visible

1911-D. Graded MS-64.

without magnification at MS-66 and higher. *Reverse:* At MS–60 to 62, there is abrasion in the field, this representing the highest part of the coin. Abrasion is also evident on the eagle's wing. Otherwise, the same comments apply as for the obverse.

Illustrated coin: This lustrous example has excellent eye appeal.

AU-50, 53, 55, 58 (About Uncirculated). *Obverse:* Friction on the cheek is very noticeable at AU-50, progressively less at higher levels to AU-58. The headdress shows light wear, most evident on the ribbon above the forehead and on the garland. Luster is minimal at AU-50 and scattered and incomplete at AU-58. Nicks and contact marks are to be expected. *Reverse:* Friction on the wing and neck is very noticeable at AU-50, increasingly

1911-D. Graded AU-55.

less at higher levels to AU-58. Otherwise, the same comments apply as for the obverse.

Illustrated coin: Much of the original luster remains in the incuse areas but not in the fields, which are the highest points on this design.

EF-40, 45 (Extremely Fine). *Obverse:* Light wear characterizes the portrait and headdress. Luster is gone. Marks and tiny scratches are to be expected, but not distracting. *Reverse:* Light wear is most evident on the eagle's head and wing, although other areas are lightly worn as well. Luster is gone. Marks and tiny scratches are to be expected, but not distracting.

1911-D. Graded EF-40.

VF-20, 30 (Very Fine). *Obverse:* Many details of the ribbon above the forehead and the garland are worn away. Many feather vanes are blended together. The field is dull and has contact marks. *Reverse:* The neck and the upper part of the wing show extensive wear, other areas less so. The field is dull and has contact marks.

Indian Head quarter eagles are seldom collected in grades lower than VF-20.

PF-60 to 70 (Proof). *Obverse and Reverse:* At PF–60 to 63, there is light abrasion and some contact marks; the lower the grade, the higher the quantity. On Sandblast Proofs these show up as visually unappealing bright spots. At PF-64 and higher levels, marks are fewer, with magnification needed to see any at PF-65. At PF-66, there should be none at all.

Illustrated coin: This is a Sandblast Proof of exceptionally high quality.

1912. Graded VF-20.

1913, Sandblast Finish. Graded PF-66.

	Mintage	Cert	Avg	%MS	VF-20	EF-40	AU-50	MS-60	MS-62	MS-63	MS-64	MS-65
										PF-60	PF-63	PF-65
1908	564,821	10,084	61.4	82%	$375	$385	$400	$450	$550	$750	$1,150	$2,500
Auctions: $7,931, MS-66, August 2015; $1,645, MS-64, July 2015; $353, MS-61, February 2015; $235, AU-50, August 2015											
1908, Sandblast Finish Proof	236	136	65.3							$4,500	$10,250	$28,000
Auctions: $49,938, PF-68, April 2014; $70,500, PF-67, January 2015; $38,188, PF-66, August 2014; $5,170, PF-58, February 2015											
1909	441,760	7,978	61.1	78%	$375	$385	$400	$475	$550	$1,100	$1,850	$3,600
Auctions: $11,750, MS-66, October 2015; $2,115, MS-64, January 2015; $317, MS-60, August 2015; $282, AU-58, January 2015											
1909, Satin Finish Proof	139	46	64.4							$4,000	$11,500	$38,500
Auctions: $57,500, PF-67, January 2011											
1910	492,000	9,238	61.3	83%	$375	$385	$400	$475	$500	$850	$1,200	$3,250
Auctions: $2,938, MS-65, August 2015; $1,293, MS-64, June 2015; $376, MS-62, July 2015; $282, AU-58, March 2015											
1910, Satin Finish Proof	682	113	65.2							$4,000	$10,000	$28,500
Auctions: $64,625, PF-67, January 2015; $23,500, PF-65, July 2015; $27,600, PF-64+, September 2011											
1910, Sandblast Finish Proof (a)	unknown	0	n/a					(unique)					
Auctions: $47,000, PF-66, August 2014											
1911	704,000	13,759	61.0	80%	$375	$385	$400	$475	$500	$625	$1,200	$3,500
Auctions: $3,525, MS-65, January 2015; $470, MS-62, June 2015; $423, AU-58, March 2015; $306, AU-55, June 2015											
1911, Sandblast Finish Proof	191	100	65.8							$4,500	$11,000	$28,500
Auctions: $27,025, PF-66, January 2014											
1911-D (b)	55,680	5,427	59.5	54%	$2,600	$3,300	$4,100	$7,000	$8,500	$11,000	$15,000	$55,000
Auctions: $52,875, MS-65, August 2015; $37,600, MS-65, February 2016; $3,525, MS-65, January 2015; $25,850, MS-64, October 2016											
1911-D, Weak D	(c)	242	54.0	3%	$1,000	$1,500	$2,100	$3,750				
Auctions: $2,645, AU-55, April 2012											

a. The sole known example is part of a complete 1910 Sandblast Finish Proof gold set. Other examples may exist, but have not yet been confirmed. **b.** Beware of counterfeit and altered pieces. **c.** Included in 1911-D mintage figure.

	Mintage	Cert	Avg	%MS	VF-20	EF-40	AU-50	MS-60	MS-62	MS-63 / PF-60	MS-64 / PF-63	MS-65 / PF-65
1912	616,000	9,797	60.6	73%	$375	$385	$400	$475	$525	$1,150	$1,950	$10,000
	Auctions: $14,100, MS-65, October 2015; $2,350, MS-64, September 2015; $400, MS-61, July 2015; $282, AU-55, February 2015											
1912, Sandblast Finish Proof	197	48	65.8							$4,500	$11,000	$29,000
	Auctions: $35,250, PF-66, October 2014; $41,125, PF-66, September 2013											
1913	722,000	13,214	61.0	79%	$375	$385	$400	$450	$475	$625	$1,000	$4,500
	Auctions: $3,290, MS-65, January 2015; $499, MS-62, February 2015; $264, AU-58, February 2015; $259, AU-50, February 2015											
1913, Sandblast Finish Proof	165	55	65.9							$4,500	$11,500	$30,000
	Auctions: $31,050, PF-67, January 2012											
1914	240,000	8,061	60.6	73%	$375	$400	$450	$550	$1,100	$1,850	$3,750	$15,000
	Auctions: $24,675, MS-65,January 2015; $23,500, MS-65, December 2015; $18,800, MS-65, August 2016; $16,450, MS-65, August 2015											
1914, Sandblast Finish Proof	117	76	65.2							$4,500	$11,750	$28,500
	Auctions: $12,650, PF-64, April 2012											
1914-D	448,000	11,247	61.0	78%	$375	$385	$400	$455	$550	$900	$2,000	$13,000
	Auctions: $15,275, MS-65, August 2015; $2,233, MS-64, June 2015; $376, MS-61, September 2015; $282, AU-55, November 2015											
1915	606,000	12,584	61.2	81%	$375	$385	$400	$450	$475	$600	$1,250	$3,000
	Auctions: $25,850, MS-66, October 2015; $1,058, MS-64, January 2015; $376, AU-58, March 2015; $259, AU-50, June 2015											
1915, Sandblast Finish Proof	100	42	65.2							$6,000	$12,000	$35,000
	Auctions: $41,688, PF-66, January 2012											
1925-D	578,000	21,841	62.2	93%	$375	$385	$400	$450	$465	$550	$725	$1,500
	Auctions: $6,500, MS-66, January 2015; $881, MS-64, January 2015; $329, MS-61, June 2015; $376, AU-58, March 2015											
1926	446,000	19,566	62.3	94%	$375	$385	$400	$450	$465	$550	$725	$1,500
	Auctions: $5,875, MS-66, January 2015; $705, MS-64, January 2015; $329, MS-61, January 2015; $259, MS-60, June 2015											
1927	388,000	16,120	62.3	95%	$375	$385	$400	$450	$465	$550	$725	$1,500
	Auctions: $14,688, MS-66, October 2015; $447, MS-63, November 2015; $306, MS-61, March 2015; $311, AU-58, July 2015											
1928	416,000	17,475	62.4	97%	$375	$385	$400	$450	$465	$550	$725	$1,500
	Auctions: $8,225, MS-66, September 2015; $764, MS-64, July 2015; $376, MS-62, March 2015; $247, AU-50, March 2015											
1929	532,000	21,410	62.3	98%	$375	$385	$400	$450	$465	$550	$725	$2,750
	Auctions: $7,638, MS-65, October 2015; $764, MS-64, August 2015; $376, MS-62, August 2015; $353, MS-60, October 2015											

Three-Dollar Gold Pieces
1854–1889

AN OVERVIEW OF THREE-DOLLAR GOLD PIECES

The three-dollar gold coin denomination was conceived in 1853 and first produced for circulation in 1854. Although there were high hopes for it at the outset, and mintages were generous, the value was redundant given the $2.50 quarter eagle then in circulation. Mintages declined, and although pieces were struck each year through 1889, very few actually circulated after the 1850s.

Although many different three-dollar dates are available at reasonable prices, most numismatists opt to acquire either a circulated or Mint State 1854 (significant as the first year of issue; also, in this year the word DOLLARS is in smaller letters than on later issues) or a Mint State coin from the low-mintage era of 1879–1889. Similar to the situation for gold dollars, although the mintages of these later pieces were low, they were popularly saved at the time, and many more have survived in high quality than might otherwise be the case.

Some numismatists have observed that $3 gold pieces might have been commonly used to purchase sheets of 100 3¢ stamps.

FOR THE COLLECTOR AND INVESTOR:
THREE-DOLLAR GOLD PIECES AS A SPECIALTY

Collecting three-dollar pieces by date and mint would at first seem to be daunting, but it is less challenging than expected, outside of a handful of pieces. The 1870-S is unique (in the Harry W. Bass Jr. Collection on loan to the American Numismatic Association), the 1875 and 1876 were made only in Proof format to the extent of 20 and 45 pieces respectively, and the 1873 is quite rare. Beyond that, examples of coins in grades such as EF and AU (including some varieties with very low mintages) can be purchased for reasonable prices.

Choice examples can be elusive, this being particularly true of branch-mint issues of the 1854–1860 years. Generally, Mint State Philadelphia pieces are rare after 1855, but then come on the market with frequency for 1861 and later, with dates in the 1860s being scarcer than later issues. Coins of the years 1878 and 1879 were made in larger quantities, with the 1878 in particular being easy to find today, although examples usually are quite bag-marked. The low-mintage three-dollar pieces of 1879 through 1889 were popular at the time of issue, many were saved, and today Mint State pieces exist to a greater extent than would otherwise be the case.

INDIAN PRINCESS HEAD (1854–1889)

Designer: *James B. Longacre.* **Weight:** *5.015 grams.*
Composition: *.900 gold, .100 copper (net weight .14512 oz. pure gold).* **Diameter:** *20.5 mm.*
Edge: *Reeded.* **Mints:** *Philadelphia, Dahlonega, New Orleans, and San Francisco.*

Circulation Strike

Mintmark location is on the reverse, below the wreath.

Proof

History. The three-dollar gold coin was designed by U.S. Mint chief engraver James B. Longacre, and first struck in 1854. The quarter eagle and half eagle had already been in use for a long time, and the reason for the creation of this odd new denomination is uncertain, although some numismatists note it could have been used to buy a sheet of current 3¢ postage stamps or a group of 100 silver trimes. After a large initial mintage in 1854, the coins were struck in smaller annual quantities. These coins were more popular on the West Coast, but, even in that region, use of this denomination dropped off sharply by the 1870s.

Striking and Sharpness. Points to observe on the obverse include the tips of the feathers in the headdress, and the hair details below the band inscribed LIBERTY. Focal points on the reverse are the wreath details (especially the vertical division in the ribbon knot), and the two central date numerals. Many of the later issues—particularly those of the early 1880s—are prooflike.

Availability. In circulated grades the issues of 1854 to 1860 survive in approximate proportion to their mintages. MS coins are plentiful for the first-year Philadelphia issue, 1854, but are scarce to rare for other years and for all branch-mint issues. For the 1860s and 1870s most are in grades such as EF, AU, and low MS, except for 1874 and in particular 1878, easily found in MS. Dates from 1879 to 1889 have a higher survival ratio and are mostly in MS, often at MS-65.

Proofs. Proofs were struck of all years. All prior to the 1880s are very rare today, with issues of the 1850s being exceedingly so. Coins of 1875 and 1876 were made only in Proof format, with no related circulation strikes. Most often seen in the marketplace are the higher-mintage Proofs of the 1880s. Some have patches of graininess or hints of non-Proof surface on the obverse, or an aura or "ghosting" near the portrait, an artifact of striking.

GRADING STANDARDS

MS-60 to 70 (Mint State). *Obverse:* On MS–60 to 62 coins there is abrasion on the hair below the band lettered LIBERTY (an area that can be weakly struck as well) and on tips of the feather plumes. At MS-63, there may be slight abrasion. Luster can be irregular. At MS-64, abrasion is less. Luster is rich on most coins, less so on the 1854-D (which is often overgraded). At MS-65 and above,

1879. Graded MS-64.

luster is deep and frosty, with no marks at all visible without magnification at MS-66 and higher. *Reverse:* On MS–60 to 62 coins there is abrasion on the 1, the highest parts of the leaves, and the ribbon knot. Otherwise, the same comments apply as for the obverse.

Illustrated coin: Satiny luster and partial mirror surfaces yield excellent eye appeal.

AU-50, 53, 55, 58 (About Uncirculated). *Obverse:* Light wear on the hair below the coronet, the cheek, and the tips of the feather plumes is very noticeable at AU-50, increasingly less at higher levels to AU-58. Luster is minimal at AU-50 and scattered and incomplete at AU-58. Some tiny nicks and contact marks are to be expected and should be mentioned if they are distracting. *Reverse:* Light wear on the 1, the wreath, and the ribbon knot characterize an AU-50 coin, increasingly less at higher levels to AU-58. Otherwise, the same comments apply as for the obverse.

1854. Graded AU-55.

Illustrated coin: Most of the original luster is gone, but perhaps 15% remains in the protected areas.

EF-40, 45 (Extremely Fine). *Obverse:* Medium wear is seen on the hair below the coronet and on the feather plume tips. Detail is partially gone on the hair. Luster is gone on most coins. *Reverse:* Light wear is seen overall, and the highest parts of the leaves are flat, but detail remains elsewhere. Luster is gone on most coins.

1854-D. Graded EF-40.

Illustrated coin: Note the mushy denticles (as seen on all but one specimen of this, the only Dahlonega variety in the series).

VF-20, 30 (Very Fine). *Obverse:* Most hair detail is gone, except at the back of the lower curls. The feather plume ends are flat. *Reverse:* The wreath and other areas show more wear. Most detail is gone on the higher-relief leaves.

Three-dollar gold pieces are seldom collected in grades lower than VF-20.

1874. Graded VF-20.

PF-60 to 70 (Proof). *Obverse and Reverse:* PF–60 to 62 coins have extensive hairlines and may have nicks and contact marks. At PF-63, hairlines are prominent, but the mirror surface is very reflective. PF-64 coins have fewer hairlines. At PF-65, hairlines should be minimal and mostly seen only under magnification. There should be no nicks or marks. PF-66 and higher coins should have no marks or hairlines visible to the unaided eye.

1876. Graded PF-61.

Illustrated coin: Extensive friction is visible in the fields, but the mirror surface can be seen in protected areas. This is still a desirable example of a date of which only 45 were minted.

	Mintage	Cert	Avg	%MS	VF-20	EF-40	AU-50	AU-55	MS-60	MS-62 / PF-63	MS-63 / PF-64	MS-65 / PF-65
1854	138,618	4,353	55.2	21%	$850	$1,000	$1,100	$1,250	$1,800	$2,200	$3,500	$12,500
Auctions: $17,050, MS-66, January 2015; $1,293, AU-58, January 2015; $999, EF-45, January 2015; $18,000, MS-65, April 2018												
1854, Proof	*15–20*	7	62.0							$75,000	$160,000	
Auctions: $164,500, PF-64Cam, November 2013; $30,550, PF-61, January 2015												
1854-D	1,120	92	51.3	10%	$18,250	$34,000	$46,000	$57,500	$85,000	$215,000		
Auctions: $188,000, MS-62, February 2016; $39,950, AU-53, September 2016; $52,875, EF-35, March 2013; $52,801, AU-55, April 2018												
1854-O	24,000	882	49.6	3%	$2,250	$2,750	$3,750	$6,500	$43,500	$77,500	$100,000	
Auctions: $76,375, MS-62; $58,750, MS-62, March 2016; $23,500, AU-58, March 2016; $12,338, AU-55, September 2016; $8,225, AU-55, July 2015												
1855	50,555	1,328	54.0	18%	$850	$950	$1,150	$1,300	$2,200	$3,000	$4,500	$30,000
Auctions: $5,170, MS-63, July 2015; $1,645, AU-58, October 2015; $794, EF-40, January 2015; $541, VF-20, June 2015												
1855, Proof	*4–8*	0								$130,000	$210,000	$375,000
Auctions: $75,900, PF-64Cam, November 2003												
1855-S	6,600	170	42.6	2%	$2,000	$3,000	$5,750	$11,000	$36,000	$57,500	$87,500	
Auctions: $55,225, MS-62, February 2016; $17,625, AU-58, November 2013; $2,820, EF-45, August 2015; $1,763, EF-40, March 2015												
1855-S, Proof	*unknown*	1	64.0								$1,450,000	
Auctions: $1,322,500, PF-64Cam, August 2011												
1856	26,010	839	54.8	18%	$850	$1,000	$1,100	$1,350	$2,850	$4,000	$6,750	$40,000
Auctions: $1,645, AU-58, August 2015; $999, AU-50, June 2015; $823, EF-45, October 2015; $494, VG-10, September 2015												
1856, Proof	*8–10*	2	63.5							$45,000	$70,000	$135,000
Auctions: $28,750, PF-62Cam, March 2011												
1856-S (a)	34,500	583	44.8	4%	$1,000	$1,500	$2,250	$3,500	$12,500	$18,500	$30,000	
Auctions: $2,115, AU-55, October 2015; $1,116, AU-50, July 2015; $1,175, EF-40, July 2015; $552, VF-20, July 2015												
1857	20,891	676	54.6	17%	$850	$1,100	$1,350	$1,500	$3,250	$4,250	$6,000	$36,000
Auctions: $14,100, MS-64, August 2015; $7,050, MS-63, June 2015; $1,175, AU-50, June 2015; $617, EF-40, October 2015												
1857, Proof	*8–12*	1	64.0							$37,500	$70,000	$135,000
Auctions: No auction records available.												
1857-S	14,000	207	42.6	1%	$1,500	$2,250	$5,000	$8,000	$22,500	$47,500	$60,000	$120,000
Auctions: $12,925, AU-58, November 2014; $6,463, AU-55, April 2013; $2,115, EF-45, January 2015; $999, VF-25, October 2015												
1858	2,133	119	52.3	8%	$1,500	$2,250	$3,500	$5,500	$10,500	$16,000	$23,000	$60,000
Auctions: $7,931, AU-58, August 2013												
1858, Proof	*8–12*	3	65.3							$30,000	$65,000	$110,000
Auctions: $85,188, PF-65Cam, April 2013; $94,000, PF-65, October 2014; $91,063, PF-65, January 2015												
1859	15,558	613	55.4	21%	$1,000	$1,250	$1,350	$1,750	$3,100	$4,000	$6,500	$25,000
Auctions: $38,188, MS-66, June 2013; $10,575, MS-64, July 2014; $9,988, MS-64, August 2014; $9,400, MS-64, September 2014												
1859, Proof	80	10	64.3							$18,000	$32,500	$65,000
Auctions: $59,925, PF-65DCam, April 2014												
1860	7,036	344	55.3	22%	$1,000	$1,300	$1,800	$1,950	$3,500	$6,000	$7,000	$37,500
Auctions: $5,875, MS-63, January 2015; $1,645, MS-60, October 2015; $1,763, AU-53, January 2015; $940, AU-50, June 2015												
1860, Proof	119	14	64.6							$17,500	$30,000	$65,000
Auctions: $88,125, PF-67Cam, September 2014; $67,563, PF-66Cam, August 2013												
1860-S	7,000	150	41.7	2%	$1,500	$3,500	$6,500	$11,500	$26,000	$52,500		
Auctions: $25,850, MS-61, February 2016; $21,150, AU-58, August 2015; $2,938, EF-45, March 2016; $999, F-15, October 2015												
1861	5,959	280	54.9	21%	$1,500	$2,500	$3,750	$4,500	$8,500	$11,000	$14,000	$32,500
Auctions: $17,625, MS-64, September 2015; $6,169, AU-58, January 2015; $2,115, AU-50, August 2014; $2,585, VF-35, September 2015												
1861, Proof	113	5	64.8							$17,500	$30,000	$65,000
Auctions: $37,375, PF-64Cam, January 2011												
1862	5,750	219	54.9	21%	$1,650	$2,750	$4,250	$4,750	$8,500	$11,000	$14,000	$40,000
Auctions: $6,463, AU-58, August 2015; $4,230, AU-53, October 2015; $1,293, AU-50, January 2015; $423, VG-8, July 2015												
1862, Proof	35	9	64.9							$17,500	$32,500	$65,000
Auctions: $74,750, PF-66UCam, August 2009												

a. Collectors recognize three mintmark sizes: Large (very rare), Medium (common), and Small (rare).

	Mintage	Cert	Avg	%MS	VF-20	EF-40	AU-50	AU-55	MS-60	MS-62 / PF-63	MS-63 / PF-64	MS-65 / PF-65
1863	5,000	256	55.4	21%	$1,500	$2,500	$4,000	$4,500	$8,500	$12,500	$15,000	$35,000
Auctions: $61,700, MS-67, July 2015; $28,200, MS-66, August 2015; $8,225, MS-61, June 2015; $3,055, AU-50, October 2015												
1863, Proof	39	8	62.8							$17,500	$30,000	$65,000
Auctions: $80,500, PF-66UCam, March 2011												
1864	2,630	171	56.3	28%	$1,650	$3,000	$4,750	$6,000	$8,000	$13,000	$15,000	$45,000
Auctions: $5,584, AU-58, June 2015; $4,935, AU-55, January 2015; $3,560, EF-45, October 2015; $588, VF-20, July 2015												
1864, Proof	50	19	62.7							$17,500	$30,000	$65,000
Auctions: $48,875, PF-64DCam, April 2012												
1865	1,140	79	56.2	37%	$2,750	$4,500	$7,500	$9,500	$16,500	$21,500	$26,500	$60,000
Auctions: $70,500, MS-66, January 2014; $3,290, VF-25, November 2014; $14,400, MS-61, January 2018												
1865, Proof	25	8	63.1							$20,000	$32,500	$67,500
Auctions: $46,000, PF-64Cam, March 2006												
1865, Proof Restrike (b)	5	0										
Auctions: No auction records available.												
1866	4,000	184	55.8	24%	$1,150	$1,350	$2,250	$2,500	$4,500	$7,250	$10,000	$37,000
Auctions: $12,925, MS-64, June 2015; $7,638, MS-63, November 2014; $2,115, AU-55, October 2015; $1,116, AU-50, August 2015												
1866, Proof	30	9	63.7							$17,500	$30,000	$65,000
Auctions: $46,000, PF-64DCam, April 2011												
1867	2,600	131	56.4	22%	$1,300	$1,650	$2,500	$3,250	$5,500	$10,000	$15,000	$37,000
Auctions: $141,000, MS-67, January 2014												
1867, Proof	50	11	62.6							$17,500	$30,000	$65,000
Auctions: $19,388, PF-63DCam, October 2014; $52,875, PF-66Cam, August 2014; $64,625, PF-66Cam, August 2013												
1868 (c)	4,850	379	56.6	25%	$1,150	$1,350	$2,000	$2,500	$4,000	$6,000	$10,000	$34,000
Auctions: $6,463, MS-63, January 2015; $3,290, AU-55, September 2015; $940, AU-50, August 2015; $823, VF-20, October 2015												
1868, Proof	25	9	64.3							$17,500	$30,000	$65,000
Auctions: $57,500, PF-65Cam, January 2011												
1869 (c)	2,500	189	54.5	16%	$1,150	$1,400	$2,200	$2,800	$4,300	$9,000	$13,500	$50,000
Auctions: $9,988, MS-63, August 2014; $3,525, MS-61, January 2015; $2,350, AU-55, March 2015; $1,763, AU-53, October 2015												
1869, Proof	25	3	64.3							$17,500	$30,000	$65,000
Auctions: $57,500, PF-65UCam, February 2009												
1870	3,500	290	54.4	12%	$1,150	$1,550	$2,250	$2,750	$4,300	$10,000	$15,000	$52,500
Auctions: $51,700, MS-65, January 2015; $2,820, AU-58, June 2015; $1,293, AU-50, January 2015; $823, EF-40, July 2015												
1870, Proof	35	10	62.9							$17,500	$30,000	$65,000
Auctions: $55,813, PF-64Cam, January 2014												
1870-S † (d)	0	n/a			$5,000,000							
Auctions: $687,500, EF-40, October 1982												
1871	1,300	201	56.3	21%	$1,150	$1,650	$2,250	$3,000	$4,500	$8,000	$10,000	$37,500
Auctions: $9,400, MS-63, November 2014; $6,463, MS-62, October 2014; $3,055, AU-58, October 2015; $1,880, AU-53, September 2015												
1871, Proof	30	6	61.5							$17,500	$30,000	$65,000
Auctions: $19,550, PF-63Cam, September 2007												
1872	2,000	210	56.4	27%	$1,150	$1,650	$2,500	$3,000	$4,750	$7,250	$12,500	$45,000
Auctions: $7,638, MS-62, August 2014; $7,050, MS-62, November 2014; $4,700, MS-62, February 2015; $3,290, AU-58, January 2015												
1872, Proof	30	23	62.9							$17,500	$30,000	$65,000
Auctions: $9,400, MS-62, November 2013; $7,638, AU-58, July 2014; $5,581, AU-58, November 2014; $2,115, AU-50, August 2014												

† Ranked in the *100 Greatest U.S. Coins* (fifth edition). **b.** Sometime around 1873, the Mint restruck a small number of 1865 three-dollar pieces using an obverse die of 1872 and a newly created reverse with the date slanting up to the right (previously listed in *United States Pattern Coins* as Judd-440). Two examples are known in gold. Versions were also made in copper (Judd-441) for interested collectors. **c.** Varieties showing traces of possible overdating include 1868, 8 Over 7; 1869, 9 Over 8; and 1878, 8 Over 7. **d.** A second example of the 1870-S is rumored to exist in the cornerstone of the San Francisco Mint, but the precise location of the cornerstone has long been unknown.

	Mintage	Cert	Avg	%MS	VF-20	EF-40	AU-50	AU-55	MS-60	MS-62 / PF-63	MS-63 / PF-64	MS-65 / PF-65
1873, Close 3	(e)	55	56.5	20%	$5,500	$9,500	$13,500	$18,000	$30,000	$42,500	$55,000	
Auctions: $51,700, MS-64, February 2016; $24,675, MS-61, May 2015												
1873, Open 3 (Original), Proof (f)	25	7	64.3							$55,000 (g)	$87,500	$150,000
Auctions: $212,750, PF-65DCam, September 2008; $164,500, PF-65, February 2016												
1873, Close 3, Proof	(h)	0								$55,000	$80,000	$140,000
Auctions: $37,375, PF-61, January 2011												
1874	41,800	3,093	56.3	26%	$850	$1,000	$1,050	$1,150	$1,850	$2,500	$3,650	$12,000
Auctions: $14,100, MS-66, October 2015; $1,998, MS-61, June 2015; $705, AU-50, July 2015; $564, F-15, September 2015												
1874, Proof	20	9	64.3							$25,000	$35,000	$67,500
Auctions: $54,625, PF-65Cam, January 2012												
1875, Proof † (i)	20	8	62.8							$150,000 (j)	$200,000	$275,000
Auctions: $329,000, PF-65, February 2016; $164,500, PF-64, January 2015												
1876, Proof (i)	45	29	64.0							$52,500 (k)	$72,500	$87,500
Auctions: $76,375, PF-65Cam, June 2013												
1877	1,468	39	57.0	26%	$4,500	$7,500	$11,000	$15,000	$30,000	$35,000	$50,000	
Auctions: $70,500, MS-64, February 2016; $22,325, MS-61, August 2013; $18,800, AU-58, September 2015; $18,000, AU-58, January 2018												
1877, Proof	20	14	63.1							$27,500	$40,000	$65,000
Auctions: $64,400, PF-65DCam, November 2011												
1878 (c)	82,304	5,622	59.2	56%	$850	$1,000	$1,050	$1,150	$1,850	$2,250	$3,250	$8,750
Auctions: $23,500, MS-66, January 2015; $999, AU-55, February 2015; $646, EF-40, September 2015; $423, AG-3, February 2015												
1878, Proof	20	8	64.4							$27,500	$40,000	$65,000
Auctions: $877, PF, June 2014												
1879	3,000	428	60.7	66%	$1,000	$1,300	$2,000	$2,750	$3,500	$4,500	$6,000	$14,000
Auctions: $19,975, MS-66, February 2015; $4,935, MS-64, July 2015; $2,233, AU-58, October 2015; $881, AU-50, September 2015												
1879, Proof	30	13	64.4							$17,500	$30,000	$47,500
Auctions: $14,375, PF-63Cam, October 2011												
1880	1,000	124	62.0	86%	$1,450	$2,000	$3,500	$3,750	$5,000	$6,000	$8,000	$17,500
Auctions: $16,450, MS-65, January 2015; $5,875, MS-62, June 2015; $3,995, MS-62, October 2015; $2,820, MS-60, October 2015												
1880, Proof	36	16	64.0							$17,000	$25,000	$37,500
Auctions: $51,113, PF, August 2013												
1881	500	109	57.7	38%	$3,000	$5,000	$8,000	$9,500	$14,000	$16,500	$22,500	$60,000
Auctions: $35,250, MS-64, September 2014; $14,100, MS-62, February 2015; $6,463, AU-55, January 2015; $3,290, EF-40, January 2015												
1881, Proof	54	27	64.1							$15,000	$25,000	$37,500
Auctions: $32,200, PF-64Cam, January 2011; $66,000, PF-66Cam, March 2018												
1882	1,500	278	58.9	55%	$1,250	$1,750	$2,500	$3,000	$4,000	$5,750	$8,500	$25,000
Auctions: $22,325, MS-65, August 2015; $3,643, MS-61, August 2015; $2,950, AU-58, September 2015; $705, AU-50, June 2015												
1882, Proof	76	32	63.1							$14,000	$18,000	$32,500
Auctions: $38,188, PF-65DCam, September 2014; $28,200, PF-64DCam, March 2014												
1883	900	145	58.5	55%	$1,500	$2,500	$3,000	$3,500	$4,500	$6,000	$8,500	$25,000
Auctions: $21,150, MS-65, June 2015; $3,760, MS-61, February 2015; $4,465, MS-60, July 2015; $2,820, AU-53, January 2015												
1883, Proof	89	37	64.3							$14,000	$17,500	$32,500
Auctions: $70,500, PF-66Cam+, November 2014; $38,188, PF-65Cam, April 2013												
1884	1,000	55	60.6	67%	$1,750	$2,500	$3,500	$4,000	$5,000	$7,500	$10,000	$25,000
Auctions: $7,931, MS-62, August 2013												
1884, Proof	106	42	64.0							$14,000	$17,500	$32,500
Auctions: $30,550, PF-65DCam, September 2014; $23,500, PF-64DCam, August 2013												

† Ranked in the *100 Greatest U.S. Coins* (fifth edition). **c.** Varieties showing traces of possible overdating include 1868, 8 Over 7; 1869, 9 Over 8; and 1878, 8 Over 7. **e.** The mintage figure for the 1873, Close 3, coins is unknown. Research suggests that only Proofs may have been struck (none for circulation), and those perhaps as late as 1879. **f.** Mint records report 25 Proof coins (with no reference to the style, Open or Close, of the number 3 in the date). The actual mintage may be as high as 100 to 1,000 coins. **g.** Value in PF-40, $20,500; in PF-50, $25,000. **h.** Included in 1873, Open 3 (Original), Proof, mintage figure. **i.** Proof only. **j.** Value in PF-50, $100,000. **k.** Value in PF-50, $30,000.

	Mintage	Cert	Avg	%MS	VF-20	EF-40	AU-50	AU-55	MS-60	MS-62 / PF-63	MS-63 / PF-64	MS-65 / PF-65
1885	800	158	59.4	56%	$1,650	$2,500	$3,750	$4,500	$6,000	$9,000	$12,000	$24,500
	Auctions: $27,025, MS-65, January 2015; $7,638, MS-62+, August 2014; $4,700, AU-58, January 2015; $3,995, AU-58, October 2015											
1885, Proof	110	55	63.4							$14,000	$17,500	$32,500
	Auctions: $10,281, PF-63, November 2014; $8,813, PF-62, October 2014; $76,050, PF, September 2013											
1886	1,000	172	57.8	44%	$1,500	$1,950	$2,750	$3,750	$5,000	$6,500	$12,000	$45,000
	Auctions: $11,163, MS-63, January 2015; $4,465, MS-61, September 2015; $2,233, MS-60, August 2015; $1,293, AU-50, January 2015											
1886, Proof	142	70	64.0							$14,000	$17,500	$32,500
	Auctions: $38,188, PF-65DCam, April 2013											
1887	6,000	229	60.4	66%	$1,000	$1,350	$2,000	$2,250	$3,000	$4,250	$5,500	$13,500
	Auctions: $11,750, MS-65, August 2015; $3,995, MS-63, January 2015; $1,410, AU-53, October 2015; $953, AU-50, September 2015											
1887, Proof	160	70	63.8							$14,000	$17,500	$32,500
	Auctions: $64,625, PF-67Cam, August 2013; $40,800, PF-66DC, January 2018											
1888	5,000	529	60.6	70%	$950	$1,250	$1,750	$1,850	$3,000	$4,250	$4,500	$12,000
	Auctions: $7,638, MS-65, October 2015; $4,935, MS-64, January 2015; $3,599, MS-63, January 2015; $3,055, MS-61, October 2015											
1888, Proof	291	94	64.0							$14,000	$17,250	$32,000
	Auctions: $38,188, PF-66Cam, November 2013; $15,863, PF-64Cam+, November 2014; $9,988, PF-63Cam, October 2015											
1889	2,300	327	60.4	66%	$850	$1,150	$1,450	$1,650	$3,000	$4,250	$4,500	$12,000
	Auctions: $15,275, MS-65, February 2015; $5,170, MS-63, January 2015; $3,760, MS-60, October 2015; $2,350, AU-58, October 2015											
1889, Proof	129	52	63.8							$14,000	$17,250	$32,000
	Auctions: $25,850, PF-65Cam, January 2014; $7,050, PF-62, November 2014											

Four-Dollar Gold Pieces
1879–1880

AN OVERVIEW OF FOUR-DOLLAR GOLD PIECES

The four-dollar pattern gold coin, or Stella, is not widely collected, simply because of its rarity. For type-set purposes some numismatists opt to acquire a single example of the only issue readily available, Charles Barber's 1879 Flowing Hair, although these are expensive. However, the Coiled Hair style is a different type, much rarer, and a collector with the means might acquire an example of that design as well.

FOR THE COLLECTOR AND INVESTOR: FOUR-DOLLAR GOLD PIECES AS A SPECIALTY

Over the past century perhaps two dozen numismatists have put together complete sets of one of each gold striking of the 1879 and 1880 Flowing Hair and Coiled Hair Stella, this being made possible by collections being dispersed and sold to others, as it is unlikely that even as many as 20 complete sets could exist at one time.

John A. Kasson, a former Iowa congressman, originally proposed the four-dollar gold piece, or "Stella."

STELLA, FLOWING HAIR AND COILED HAIR (1879–1880)

Designers: *Charles E. Barber (Flowing Hair, and common reverse); George T. Morgan (Coiled Hair).*
Weight: *7.0 grams.* **Composition:** *Approximately .857 gold, .042 silver, .100 copper.*
Diameter: *22 mm.* **Edge:** *Reeded.* **Mint:** *Philadelphia.*

Flowing Hair   Coiled Hair

History. The four-dollar gold Stellas of 1879 and 1880 are Proof-only patterns, not regular issues. However, as they have been listed in popular references for decades, collectors have adopted them into the regular gold series. The obverse inscription notes the coins' metallic content in proportions of gold, silver, and copper in the metric system, intended to facilitate their use in foreign countries, where the value could be quickly determined. The Stella was proposed by John A. Kasson (formerly a U.S. representative from Iowa and chairman of the House Committee on Coinage, Weights, and Measures; in 1879 serving as envoy extraordinary and minister plenipotentiary to Austria-Hungary). It is believed that Charles E. Barber designed the Flowing Hair type (as well as the reverse common to both types), and George T. Morgan designed the Coiled Hair. Those dated 1879 were struck for congressional examination; popular testimony of the era suggests that the Flowing Hair Stella became a favorite gift for congressmen's lovers in the Washington demimonde. The only issue produced in quantity was the 1879, Flowing Hair. The others were made in secret and sold privately by Mint officers and employees. The Coiled Hair Stella was not generally known to the numismatic community until they were illustrated in *The Numismatist* in the early 20th century. Stellas are cataloged by their Judd numbers, assigned in the standard reference, *United States Pattern Coins*.

Striking and Sharpness. On nearly all examples the high parts of the hair are flat, often with striations. The other areas of the coin are typically well struck. Tiny planchet irregularities are common.

Availability. The 1879 Flowing Hair is often available on the market—usually in PF–61 to 64, although higher-condition examples come on the market with regularity (as do lightly handled and impaired coins). The 1880 Flowing Hair is typically found in PF–63 or higher. Both years of Coiled Hair Stellas are great rarities; typical grades are PF–63 to 65, with a flat strike on the head and with some tiny planchet flaws.

GRADING STANDARDS

PF-60 to 70 (Proof). *Obverse and Reverse:* PF–60 to 62 coins have extensive hairlines and may have nicks and contact marks. At PF–63, hairlines are prominent, but the mirror surface is very reflective. PF–64 coins have fewer hairlines. At PF–65, hairlines should be minimal and mostly seen only under magnification. There should be no nicks or marks. PF–66 and higher coins should have no marks or hairlines visible to the unaided eye.

1879, Flowing Hair; J-1657. Graded PF-62.

Illustrated coin: A nick above the head and some light friction define the grade, but the coin has nice eye appeal overall.

PF-60 to 70 (Proof). *Obverse and Reverse:* PF–60 to 62 coins have extensive hairlines and may have nicks and contact marks. At PF-63, hairlines are prominent, but the mirror surface is very reflective. PF-64 coins have fewer hairlines. At PF-65, hairlines should be minimal and mostly seen only under magnification. There should be no nicks or marks. PF-66 and higher coins should have no marks or hairlines visible to the unaided eye.

1879, Coiled Hair; J-1660. Graded PF-65.

	Mintage	Cert	Avg	%MS	PF-40	PF-50	PF-60	PF-63	PF-64	PF-65	PF-66	PF-67
1879, Flowing Hair, Proof †	425+	240	63.7		$90,000	$95,000	$120,000	$165,000	$180,000	$225,000	$275,000	$350,000
	Auctions: $199,750, MS-65, August 2015; $312,000, PF-67Cam, January 2018; $168,000, PF-64, August 2019											
1879, Coiled Hair, Proof †	12–15 known	13	65.3				$300,000	$450,000	$550,000	$800,000	$1,100,000	$1,250,000
	Auctions: $1,041,300, PF, September 2013; $1,050,000, PF-66Cam, January 2018											
1880, Flowing Hair, Proof †	17–20 known	20	65.0				$175,000	$325,000	$350,000	$450,000	$550,000	$750,000
	Auctions: $417,125, MS-65, June 2015; $352,500, MS-65, August 2016; $959,400, PF, September 2013; $750,000, PF-67Cam, January 2018											
1880, Coiled Hair, Proof †	8–10 known	13	64.6				$650,000	$775,000	$875,000	$1,250,000	$1,750,000	$2,000,000
	Auctions: $1,860,000, PF-67Cam, February 2021; $2,574,000, PF, September 2013; $1,116,250, PF-65, June 2015											

Note: Many individual high-value rare coins are submitted for certification and grading multiple times over the years, which can inflate the number of certifications above the number of coins actually minted. † All Stella Four Dollar Gold pieces are ranked in the *100 Greatest U.S. Coins* (fifth edition), as a single entry.

Gold Half Eagles ($5)
1795–1929

AN OVERVIEW OF GOLD HALF EAGLES

The half eagle was the first gold coin actually struck for the United States. The five-dollar gold piece was authorized by the Act of April 2, 1792, and the first batch was minted in 1795.

Forming a type set of half eagles is a daunting but achievable challenge—if a collector has the finances and some determination. Examples of the first type, with Capped Bust to Right (conical cap obverse), and with an eagle on a palm branch on the reverse, regularly come up on the market, usually of the date 1795. Typical grades range from EF to lower Mint State levels. Such pieces are scarce, and the demand for them is strong. The next type, the Heraldic Eagle motif, first struck in 1798, but also known from a 1795-dated die used later, was produced through 1807, and is easily enough obtained today. Again, typical grades range from EF to Mint State. MS-63 and better coins are available, but are in the distinct minority.

The short-lived Capped Bust to Left style, 1807–1812, can be found in similar grades, although such pieces did not circulate as extensively, and AU and Mint State levels are the rule, with VF pieces being unusual. Then follows the era of rarities. The Capped Head to Left, stars surrounding head, large diameter, 1813–1829 style is available largely courtesy of the first date of issue, 1813. This is the only date seen with some frequency. When available, examples tend to be choice. The later stretch of this series includes some formidable rarities, among which are the famous 1815 and the even rarer 1822, along with a whole string of other seldom-seen varieties in the 1820s. The same style, but of reduced diameter, 1829–1834, also is rare; examples of the 1830s turn up with some regularity, but these often lack eye appeal. For some reason, half eagles of the early 1830s are often heavily marked and abraded, which is not true at all for coins of the 1820s.

Classic Head half eagles, capless and without the motto E PLURIBUS UNUM, first minted in August 1834, are easily enough obtained. Those seen in today's marketplace are usually of the first several dates, and less frequently of 1837 or 1838.

William Woodin, secretary of the Treasury under Franklin D. Roosevelt, built upon the findings of J. Colvin Randall in his research of half eagle die varieties.

Grades range from VF upward, reflecting their extensive use in circulation. Mint State coins can be found on occasion and are scarce. Choice and gem pieces are rare.

With just a few exceptions, Liberty Head half eagles of the 1839–1866 type without the motto IN GOD WE TRUST are very plentiful in worn grades, including certain of the higher-mintage issues from the popular Charlotte and Dahlonega mints (permitting interesting varieties to be added to a type set). Mint State coins are scarce, and when seen are usually in lower levels such as MS–60 and 62. Gems of any date are rare. Then follow the Liberty Head pieces with the motto IN GOD WE TRUST on the reverse, 1866 through 1908; the earlier years are mostly encountered in worn grades, the later ones are easy enough to find in Mint State. Proofs were made of all Liberty Head half eagle dates, and today they are generally collectible from about 1860 onward.

With two exceptions (1909-O and 1929), the Indian Head half eagles of 1908 to 1929 are common enough in worn grades as well as low Mint State levels, but true gems, accurately graded and with lustrous, frosty surfaces, are quite rare. The field is the highest area of the coin and thus is quite susceptible to scuffs and marks. Probably the most readily available dates in higher grades are 1908 and 1909, with the 1909-D being plentiful due to a hoard that came on the market a generation ago.

FOR THE COLLECTOR AND INVESTOR: GOLD HALF EAGLES AS A SPECIALTY

While in the annals of American numismatics dozens of old-time numismatists collected half eagles by date (or, less often, by date *and* mint), today rarities are so widely scattered and are so expensive that few collectors can rise to the challenge.

Early half eagles can be collected by dates and basic varieties, and also by die varieties. The year 1795 in particular is rich in the latter, and years ago several scholars described such varieties, beginning with J. Colvin Randall in the 1870s, continuing to William H. Woodin in the early 1900s, then Edgar H. Adams, Thomas Ollive Mabbott, and Walter Breen. In more recent times Robert Miller, Harry W. Bass Jr., John Dannreuther, and others have added their research to the literature.

Among early half eagles there are two unique varieties: the 1797 with a 16-star obverse, and the 1797 with a 15-star obverse, both with the Heraldic Eagle reverse, likely struck in 1798. Of the later 1822, just three are known, two of which are in the National Numismatic Collection at the Smithsonian Institution. Of all early half eagles the 1815 was far and away the most famous during the 19th century. (In the 1880s a publication on the Mint Collection stated that the two highlights there were the 1815 half eagle and the unique 1849 double eagle.) At the time the rarer 1822 was not recognized for its elusive nature. Today an estimated 11 examples of the 1815 half eagles exist, mostly in higher circulated grades, including those in museums. There are only two known of the 1825, 5 Over 4, overdate, but it is not at all famous, probably because it is an overdate variety, not a single date on its own. Half eagles of 1826 through 1829 all are rare, with the 1829 being particularly well known. The latter date includes early pieces with regular diameter and later ones with the diameter reduced. Generally, all half eagles from 1815 through 1834 are scarce, some of them particularly so.

Classic Head half eagles of 1834 to 1838 include the scarce 1838-C and 1838-D, the first of the Charlotte and Dahlonega mints respectively; none are prohibitively rare. Generally, the higher-grade pieces are found toward the beginning of the Classic Head series, especially bearing the date 1834.

Liberty Head half eagles are readily available of most dates and mints from 1839 to 1908, save for the one great rarity, the 1854-S, of which just three are known (one is in the Smithsonian). There is a vast panorama of Charlotte and Dahlonega issues through 1861, most of which were made in fairly large quantities, as this was the highest denomination ever struck at each of these mints (larger-capacity presses were not on hand). Accordingly, they are highly collectible today. Some varieties are scarce, but none are completely out of reach. Typical grades range from VF to EF and AU, occasionally Mint State, though not often MS-63 or higher.

Among San Francisco half eagles most of the early issues are scarce, as such pieces circulated extensively and there was no thought to saving numismatic examples. However, there are not many specialists in the field, and for some varieties it can be said that collectors are harder to find than are the coins themselves, yielding the opportunity to purchase truly rare pieces for significantly less than would otherwise be the case. Carson City half eagles were minted beginning in 1870 and continuing intermittently through 1893. Most of the early issues range from scarce to rare, the 1870-CC being particularly well known in this regard. Proofs of the Liberty Head type are generally collectible from the 1860s onward, with most on the market being of the higher-mintage issues of the 1890s and 1900s.

Among Indian Head half eagles, 1908 to 1929, the 1909-O is the rarest of the early coins, and when seen is usually worn. A choice or gem Mint State 1909-O is an incredible rarity. However, enough worn 1909-O half eagles exist, including many brought from overseas hoards in recent decades, that a piece in VF or so grade presents no problem. Half eagles of 1929, of which just 662,000 were minted, were mostly melted, it seems. A couple hundred or so exist today, nearly all of which are Mint State, but nicked and with bagmarks, MS–60 to 62 or 63. Truly high-quality gems are exceedingly rare.

CAPPED BUST TO RIGHT, SMALL EAGLE REVERSE (1795–1798)

Designer: *Robert Scot.* **Weight:** *8.75 grams.*
Composition: *.9167 gold, .0833 silver and copper.*
Diameter: *Approximately 25 mm.* **Edge:** *Reeded.* **Mint:** *Philadelphia.*

Bass-Dannreuther–6.

History. Half eagles of this style, the first federal gold coins, were introduced in July 1795. The obverse features Miss Liberty wearing a conical cap, a design generally called Capped Bust to Right. The reverse depicts a "small" eagle perched on a palm branch. The same motif was used on contemporary $10 gold coins. No Proofs or presentation strikes were made of this type.

Striking and Sharpness. On the obverse, check the star centers and the hair details. On the reverse, check the feathers of the eagle, particularly on the breast. Examine the denticles on both sides. Adjustment marks (from Mint workers filing down overweight planchets to acceptable standards) often are visible, but are not explicitly noted by the grading services.

Availability. Typical grades range from EF to AU and low MS. MS-63 and better coins are rare; when seen, they usually are of the 1795 date (of which many different die varieties exist). Certain varieties are rare, most famously the 1798 with Small Eagle reverse.

GRADING STANDARDS

MS-60 to 70 (Mint State). *Obverse:* At MS-60, some abrasion and contact marks are evident, most noticeably on the hair to the left of Miss Liberty's forehead and on the higher-relief areas of the cap. Luster is present, but may be dull or lifeless, and interrupted in patches. At MS-63, contact marks are few, and abrasion is very light. An MS-65 coin has hardly any abrasion, and contact marks are so minute as to require magnifica-

1795, S Over D in STATES; BD-6. Graded MS-63.

tion. Luster should be full and rich. Grades above MS-65 for this type are more often theoretical than actual—but they do exist and are defined by having fewer marks as perfection is approached. *Reverse:* Comments apply as for the obverse, except that abrasion and contact marks are most noticeable on the breast and head of the eagle. The field area is mainly protected by the eagle, branch, and lettering.

   Illustrated coin: This is the error die with the second S over an erroneous D in STATES (which originally read as STATED).

AU-50, 53, 55, 58 (About Uncirculated). *Obverse:* Light wear is seen on the cheek, the hair immediately to the left of the face, and the cap, more at AU-50 than at AU–53 or 55. An AU-58 coin has minimal traces of wear. An AU-50 coin has luster in protected areas among the stars and letters, with little in the open fields or on the portrait. At AU-58, most luster is present in the fields but is worn away on the highest parts of the motifs.

1795; BD-7. Graded AU-58.

Reverse: Comments as preceding, except that the eagle shows light wear on the breast and head in particular, but also at the tip of the wing on the left and elsewhere. Luster ranges from perhaps 40% remaining in protected areas (at AU-50) to nearly full mint bloom (at AU-58).

EF-40, 45 (Extremely Fine). *Obverse:* Wear is evident all over the portrait, with some loss of detail in the hair to the left of Miss Liberty's face. Excellent detail remains in low-relief areas of the hair, such as the front curl and at the back of her head. The stars show wear, as do the date and letters. Luster, if present at all, is minimal and in protected areas. *Reverse:* Wear is greater than on an About Uncirculated coin. The breast, neck, and legs of the

1795; BD-4. Graded EF-40.

eagle lack nearly all feather detail. More wear is seen on the edges of the wing. Some traces of luster may be seen, more so at EF-45 than at EF-40.

VF-20, 30 (Very Fine). *Obverse:* The higher-relief areas of hair are well worn at VF-20, less so at VF-30. The stars are flat at their centers. *Reverse:* Wear is greater, the eagle is flat in most areas, and about 40% to 60% of the wing feathers can be seen.

Illustrated coin: While exhibiting typical wear for a VF-20 coin, this specimen also shows rim damage from having been mounted as jewelry at some point in time.

1795. Graded VF-20.

Capped Bust to Right, Small Eagle Reverse, half eagles are seldom collected in grades lower than VF-20.

| **1796, 6 Over 5** | **1797, 15-Star Obverse** | **1797, 16-Star Obverse** |

	Mintage	Cert	Avg	%MS	F-12	VF-20	EF-40	AU-50	AU-55	MS-60	MS-62	MS-63	MS-64
1795	8,707	233	55.2	31%	$20,000	$25,000	$32,500	$45,000	$55,000	$80,000	$135,000	$165,000	$325,000 (a)
Auctions: $587,500, MS-66H, January 2015; $64,625, MS-61, February 2013; $64,625, AU-58, August 2014; $52,875, AU-58, August 2014													
1795, S Over D in STATES (b)	(c)	2	51.5	0%				$47,500	$60,000	$85,000			
Auctions: $345,000, MS-65PL, July 2009													
1796, 6 Over 5	6,196	36	56.4	42%	$22,500	$30,000	$40,000	$55,000	$70,000	$105,000	$165,000	$250,000	$350,000
Auctions: $67,563, AU-58, February 2014; $45,531, AU-55, October 2014; $52,875, AU-53, August 2014													
1797, All kinds	3,609												
1797, 15-Star Obverse		5	55.8	20%	$27,500	$40,000	$70,000	$125,000	$185,000	$325,000			
Auctions: $235,000, AU-58, August 2015: $152,750, AU-53, January 2014													
1797, 16-Star Obverse †		6	58.0	33%	$27,500	$40,000	$65,000	$120,000	$145,000	$240,000			
Auctions: $411,250, MS-61, August 2013													
1798, Small Eagle † (d)	*unknown*	1	55.0	0%				$500,000	$750,000	$1,250,000	—		
Auctions: $1,175,000, AU-55, September 2015													

† Ranked in the *100 Greatest U.S. Coins* (fifth edition). **a.** Value in MS-65 is $325,000. **b.** The final S in STATES is punched over an erroneous D. **c.** Included in 1795, Small Eagle, mintage figure. **d.** The reverse of the 1798, Small Eagle, was from a 1795 die. The obverse has an arched die crack or flaw beneath the date. 7 examples are known, and the finest is an AU-55 from the collection of King Farouk of Egypt.

CAPPED BUST TO RIGHT, HERALDIC EAGLE REVERSE (1795–1807)

Designer: *Robert Scot.* **Weight:** *8.75 grams.*
Composition: *.9167 gold, .0833 silver and copper.*
Diameter: *Approximately 25 mm.* **Edge:** *Reeded.* **Mint:** *Philadelphia.*

BD-15.

History. For this type, the obverse design is the same as that of the preceding. The reverse features a heraldic eagle, as used on other silver and gold coins of the era. Some half eagles of the Heraldic Eagle Reverse design are dated 1795, but these were actually struck in 1798, from a leftover obverse coinage die. The *Encyclopedia of U.S. Gold Coins, 1795–1933* (second edition) notes that "No Proofs were made, but one 1795 half eagle with a Heraldic Eagle reverse has been certified as a Specimen."

Striking and Sharpness. On the obverse, check the star centers and the hair details. On the reverse, check the upper part of the shield, the lower part of the eagle's neck, the eagle's wing, the stars above the eagle, and the clouds. Inspect the denticles on both sides. Adjustment marks (from overweight planchets being filed down to correct standards by Mint workers) can be an aesthetic problem and are not explicitly identified by the grading services.

Availability. Although there are many rare die varieties, as a type this half eagle is plentiful. Typical grades are EF to lower MS. MS-63 and higher coins are seen with some frequency and usually are dated from 1802 to 1807. Sharply struck coins without adjustment marks are in the minority.

GRADING STANDARDS

MS-60 to 70 (Mint State). *Obverse:* At MS-60, some abrasion and contact marks are evident, most noticeably on the hair to the left of Miss Liberty's forehead and on the higher-relief areas of the cap. Luster is present, but may be dull or lifeless, and interrupted in patches. At MS-63, contact marks are few, and abrasion is very light. An MS-65 coin has hardly any abrasion, and contact marks are so minute as to require magnifica-

1802, 2 Over 1. Graded MS-62.

tion. Luster should be full and rich. Grades above MS-65 are not often seen but are defined by having fewer marks as perfection is approached. *Reverse:* Comments apply as for the obverse, except that abrasion and contact marks are most noticeable on the upper part of the eagle and the clouds. The field area is complex, with not much open space, given the stars above the eagle, the arrows and olive branch, and other features. Accordingly, marks are not as noticeable as on the obverse.

Illustrated coin: This is an attractive coin with rich luster. Some friction is visible on the higher points and in the obverse field.

AU-50, 53, 55, 58 (About Uncirculated). *Obverse:* Light wear is seen on the cheek, the hair immediately to the left of the face, and the cap, more at AU-50 than at AU–53 or 55. An AU-58 coin has minimal traces of wear. An AU-50 coin has luster in protected areas among the stars and letters, with little in the open fields or on the portrait. At AU-58, most luster is present in the fields, but is worn away on the highest parts of the motifs.

1804. Graded AU-58.

Reverse: Comments as preceding, except that the eagle's neck, the tips and top of the wings, the clouds, and the tail now show noticeable wear, as do other features. Luster ranges from perhaps 40% remaining in protected areas (at AU-50) to nearly full mint bloom (at AU-58). Often the reverse of this type retains much more luster than the obverse.

   Illustrated coin: An abrasion in the left obverse field keeps this otherwise lustrous and attractive coin below the Mint State level.

EF-40, 45 (Extremely Fine). *Obverse:* Wear is evident all over the portrait, with some loss of detail in the hair to the left of Miss Liberty's face. Excellent detail remains in low-relief areas of the hair, such as the front curl and at the back of her head. The stars show wear, as do the date and letters. Luster, if present at all, is minimal and in protected areas. *Reverse:* Wear is greater than on an About Uncirculated coin. The neck lacks feather detail on its

1804, Small 8 Over Large 8; BD-7. Graded EF-45.

highest points. Feathers have lost some detail near the edges of the wings, and some areas of the horizontal lines in the shield may be blended together. Some traces of luster may be seen, more so at EF-45 than at EF-40. Overall, the reverse appears to be in a slightly higher grade than the obverse.

VF-20, 30 (Very Fine). *Obverse:* The higher-relief areas of hair are well worn at VF-20, less so at VF-30. The stars are flat at their centers. *Reverse:* Wear is greater, including on the shield and wing feathers. The star centers are flat. Other areas have lost detail as well. E PLURIBUS UNUM may be light or worn away in areas.

Capped Bust to Right, Heraldic Eagle Reverse, half eagles are seldom collected in grades lower than VF-20.

1798, Large 8, 13-Star Reverse; BD-4. Graded VF-20.

1797, 16-Star Obverse   1797, 15-Star Obverse

1797, 7 Over 5   1798, Small 8   1798, Large 8

1798, 13-Star Reverse   1798, 14-Star Reverse   1799, Small Reverse Stars   1799, Large Reverse Stars

	Mintage	Cert	Avg	%MS	F-12	VF-20	EF-40	AU-50	AU-55	MS-60	MS-62	MS-63	MS-64
1795	(a)	20	59.7	60%	$15,000	$23,000	$35,000	$60,000	$85,000	$115,000	$165,000	$250,000	$300,000
Auctions: No auction records available.													
1797, 7 Over 5	(a)	3	60.0	67%	$25,000	$32,500	$45,000	$80,000	$135,000	$200,000			
Auctions: $126,500, AU-58, September 2005													
1797, 16-Star Obverse	(a)	0	n/a				—						
Auctions: No auction records available.													
1797, 15-Star Obverse	(a)	0	n/a				—						
Auctions: No auction records available.													
1798, All kinds	24,867												
1798, Small 8		24	55.9	21%	$5,500	$6,500	$12,500	$18,500	$22,000	$32,500	$50,000	$77,500	
Auctions: $18,800, AU-53, April 2014													
1798, Large 8, 13-Star Reverse		77	53.7	22%	$5,000	$6,000	$10,000	$16,000	$20,000	$30,000	$40,000	$60,000	
Auctions: $21,150, AU-55, August 2014; $19,975, AU-55, November 2014; $16,450, AU-53, August 2014; $12,925, AU-50, January 2014													
1798, Large 8, 14-Star Reverse		20	53.6	5%	$5,500	$6,500	$15,000	$22,500	$35,000	$115,000			
Auctions: $32,900, AU-55, August 2014; $25,850, AU-55, October 2014; $25,850, AU, February 2014													
1799, All kinds	7,451												
1799, Small Reverse Stars		13	59.2	46%	$5,000	$5,750	$8,500	$13,000	$18,000	$27,500	$37,500	$65,000	$100,000
Auctions: $47,000, MS-62, February 2013; $19,975, AU-58, August 2014; $13,513, AU-55, September 2014; $4,711, EF-40, August 2014													
1799, Large Reverse Stars		17	57.9	53%	$5,250	$6,000	$10,000	$15,000	$20,000	$27,500	$37,500	$65,000	$100,000
Auctions: $70,500, MS-63, January 2014; $16,450, AU-55, August 2014; $11,750, AU-53, August 2014													

a. The 1795 and 1797 Heraldic Eagle half eagles are thought to have been struck in 1798 and are included in that year's mintage figure of 24,867.

1800, Pointed 1

1800, Blunt 1

1800, 8 Arrows

1800, 9 Arrows

1802, 2 Over 1
FS-G5-1802/1-301.

1803, 3 Over 2

1804, Small 8

1804, Small 8
Over Large 8

1806, Pointed-Top 6,
Stars 8 and 5

Closeup of
Pointed-Top 6

1806, Round-Top 6,
Stars 7 and 6

Closeup of
Round-Top 6

	Mintage	Cert	Avg	%MS	F-12	VF-20	EF-40	AU-50	AU-55	MS-60	MS-62	MS-63	MS-64
1800	37,628	271	56.6	38%	$4,500	$5,500	$7,500	$10,000	$12,000	$17,500	$22,500	$40,000	$85,000
	Auctions: $16,100, MS-62, April 2012; $11,750, AU-55, January 2015; $8,425, AU-53, March 2018												
1802, 2 Over 1	53,176	278	57.5	39%	$4,500	$5,000	$7,000	$10,000	$11,500	$16,000	$20,000	$33,500	$57,500 **(b)**
	Auctions: $58,750, MS-64, January 2014; $16,450, MS-62, October 2014; $11,750, AU-58, September 2014; $5,141, AU, March 2015												
1803, 3 Over 2	33,506	339	57.3	43%	$4,500	$5,000	$7,000	$10,000	$12,500	$17,500	$19,000	$30,000	$55,000 **(c)**
	Auctions: $12,925, MS-62, October 2014; $14,100, MS-62, November 2014; $20,563, MS-62, October 2013; $10,575, AU-58, August 2014												
1804, All kinds	30,475												
1804, Small 8		45	58.6	58%	$4,500	$5,000	$7,500	$10,000	$11,500	$16,500	$20,000	$35,000	$60,000
	Auctions: $18,800, MS-62, January 2014; $10,575, AU-58, August 2014; $12,925, AU-55, August 2014; $5,875, AU-50, August 2014												
1804, Small 8 Over Large 8 (d)		71	58.6	58%	$4,500	$5,000	$7,500	$10,500	$12,500	$19,000	$25,000	$42,500	$85,000
	Auctions: $32,900, MS-63, January 2014; $8,813, AU-53, August 2014; $8,813, AU-53, November 2014; $5,581, AU-50, September 2014												
1805	33,183	186	59.3	57%	$4,500	$5,500	$7,750	$10,500	$12,500	$16,000	$19,000	$32,500	$45,000 **(e)**
	Auctions: $15,275, MS-62, August 2014; $14,688, MS-61, November 2014; $16,450, MS, February 2014; $12,925, AU-58, November 2014												
1806, Pointed-Top 6	9,676	82	56.1	43%	$4,500	$4,750	$7,000	$10,000	$12,000	$16,500	$19,000	$34,500	$45,000
	Auctions: $15,275, MS-61, August 2014; $15,275, MS-60, August 2014; $12,925, MS-60, February 2016; $4,406, AU, March 2015												
1806, Rounded-Top 6	54,417	198	58.0	47%	$4,500	$4,750	$7,000	$10,000	$11,500	$15,500	$18,000	$30,000	$45,000 **(f)**
	Auctions: $111,625, MS-65, March 2013; $48,469, MS-64, August 2014; $19,388, MS-62, August 2014; $4,440, VF-30, February 2018												

b. Value in MS-65 is $135,000. **c.** Value in MS-65 is $145,000. **d.** Created when the engraver mistakenly used an 8 punch intended for $10 gold coins, then corrected the error by overpunching with a much smaller 8. **e.** Value in MS-65 is $165,000. **f.** Value in MS-65 is $125,000.

1807, Small Reverse Stars

1807, Large Reverse Stars

	Mintage	Cert	Avg	%MS	F-12	VF-20	EF-40	AU-50	AU-55	MS-60	MS-62	MS-63	MS-64
1807, All kinds	32,488												
1807, Small Reverse Stars		0	n/a		$4,500	$5,500	$7,500	$10,000	$11,500	$15,500	$17,000	$25,000	$35,000
Auctions: $44,563, MS-64, January 2012													
1807, Large Reverse Stars		2	53.0	50%	$4,500	$5,500	$7,500	$10,000	$11,500	$15,500	$17,000	$25,000	$35,000
Auctions: $21,850, MS-63, January 2012; $1,880, F-12, October 2015													

DRAPED BUST TO LEFT (1807–1812)

Designer: *John Reich.* **Weight:** *8.75 grams.*
Composition: *.9167 gold, .0833 silver and copper.*
Diameter: *Approximately 25 mm.* **Edge:** *Reeded.* **Mint:** *Philadelphia.*

BD-8.

History. This half eagle motif, designed by John Reich and stylistically related to his Capped Bust half dollar of 1807, was used for several years in the early 1800s. Quantities minted were high, and the coins saw wide circulation. No Proof examples were made of this type.

Striking and Sharpness. The striking usually is quite good and is significantly better than on earlier half eagle types. Adjustment marks (from overweight planchets being filed down to acceptable weight) are seen only occasionally. On the obverse, check the star centers and the hair details. On the reverse, check the eagle, particularity at the shield and the lower left. Examine the denticles on both sides.

Availability. After 1821 gold coins of this standard no longer circulated, as their bullion value exceeded their face value. Accordingly, they never sustained extensive wear, and nearly all examples are in EF or higher grades (coins used as pocket pieces or incorporated into jewelry are exceptions). As a type this issue is readily available in grades up to MS-63, although MS–64 and 65 coins are seen on occasion. Most have excellent eye appeal.

GRADING STANDARDS

MS-60 to 70 (Mint State). *Obverse:* At MS-60, some abrasion and contact marks are seen on the cheek, the hair below the LIBERTY inscription, and the highest-relief folds of the cap. Luster is present, but may be dull or lifeless, and interrupted in patches. At MS-63, contact marks are few, and abrasion is very light. At MS-64, abrasion is even less. An MS-65 coin has hardly any abrasion, and contact marks are minute. Luster should be

1808. Graded MS-60.

full and rich and is often more intense on the obverse. Grades above MS-65 are defined by having fewer marks as perfection is approached. *Reverse:* Comments apply as for the obverse, except that abrasion is most noticeable on the eagle's neck and the highest area of the wings.

   Illustrated coin: This attractive Draped Bust to Left half eagle has nice luster.

AU-50, 53, 55, 58 (About Uncirculated). *Obverse:* Light wear is seen on the cheek and the higher-relief areas of the hair and cap. Friction and scattered marks are in the field, ranging from extensive at AU-50 to minimal at AU-58. Luster may be seen in protected areas, minimal at AU-50 but more evident at AU-58. On an AU-58 coin the field retains some luster as well. *Reverse:* Comments as preceding, except that the eagle's neck, the

1811, Tall 5. Graded AU-58.

top of the wings, the leaves, and the arrowheads now show noticeable wear, as do other features. Luster ranges from perhaps 40% remaining in protected areas (at AU-50) to nearly full mint bloom (at AU-58). Often the reverse of this type retains much more luster than the obverse, as the motto, eagle, and lettering protect the surrounding flat areas.

   Illustrated coin: This lustrous example is well struck.

EF-40, 45 (Extremely Fine). *Obverse:* More wear is seen on the portrait, the hair, the cap, and the drapery near the clasp. Luster is minimal or nonexistent at EF-40, and may be slight at EF-45. *Reverse:* Wear is more extensive on the eagle, including the top of the wings, the head, the top of the shield, and the claws. Some traces of luster may be seen, more so at EF-45 than at EF-40.

1807; BD-8. Graded EF-40.

VF-20, 30 (Very Fine). *Obverse:* Wear on the portrait has reduced the hair detail, especially to the right of the face and the top of the head, but much can still be seen. *Reverse:* Wear on the eagle is greater, and details of feathers near the shield and near the top of the wings are weak or missing. All other features show wear, but most are fairly sharp. Generally, Draped Bust gold coins at this grade level lack eye appeal.

1807; BD-8. Graded VF-20.

Draped Bust to Left half eagles are seldom collected in grades lower than VF-20.

1808, 8 Over 7

1809, 9 Over 8

1808, Normal Date

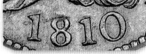

1810, Small Date

1810, Large Date

Small 5

Large 5

Tall 5

	Mintage	Cert	Avg	%MS	F-12	VF-20	EF-40	AU-50	AU-55	MS-60	MS-62	MS-63	MS-64
1807	51,605	259	58.4	51%	$3,250	$4,750	$5,750	$8,000	$9,750	$14,000	$15,000	$24,500	$36,500 (a)
Auctions: $76,375, MS-65, April 2013; $19,975, MS-63, October 2014; $11,750, MS-62, August 2014; $12,338, MS-62, November 2014													
1808, All kinds	55,578												
1808, 8 Over 7		45	58.3	51%	$3,250	$4,750	$6,500	$8,500	$11,500	$18,500	$25,000	$35,000	$65,000
Auctions: $24,675, MS-62, August 2014; $19,388, MS-61, June 2014; $6,463, EF-45, November 2015													
1808		187	57.6	50%	$3,000	$4,250	$5,750	$8,000	$9,500	$13,500	$16,000	$27,500	$45,000 (b)
Auctions: $25,850, MS-63, March 2013; $12,925, MS-60, October 2014; $4,113, MS, March 2015; $7,638, AU-58, November 2014													
1809, 9 Over 8	33,875	181	58.4	54%	$3,000	$4,250	$5,750	$8,000	$10,500	$14,000	$16,000	$28,500	$56,000
Auctions: $51,406, MS-64, January 2014; $11,750, MS-61, August 2014; $8,001, AU-53, August 2014													
1810, All kinds	100,287												
1810, Small Date, Small 5		4	53.0	25%			$45,000	$65,000	$85,000	$100,000	$150,000		
Auctions: $19,388, 88, November 2015; $18,800, AU-50, January 2014													
1810, Small Date, Tall 5		78	57.5	50%	$3,000	$4,250	$5,500	$8,000	$9,500	$14,000	$15,000	$29,000	$57,500
Auctions: $58,750, MS-64, August 2016; $12,925, MS-62, January 2014; $12,925, MS-62, August 2014; $12,925, AU-58, September 2014													
1810, Large Date, Small 5	(4–5 known)	0	n/a				$75,000	$110,000	$150,000				
Auctions: No auction records available.													
1810, Large Date, Large 5		262	59.0	61%	$3,000	$4,250	$5,500	$8,000	$9,500	$13,000	$14,500	$22,500	$32,500 (c)
Auctions: $32,900, MS-64, January 2014; $11,750, MS-62, November 2014; $8,813, AU-58, August 2014; $9,988, AU-55, March 2015													

a. Value in MS-65 is $125,000. **b.** Value in MS-65 is $95,000. **c.** Value in MS-65 is $115,000.

	Mintage	Cert	Avg	%MS	F-12	VF-20	EF-40	AU-50	AU-55	MS-60	MS-62	MS-63	MS-64
1811, All kinds	99,581												
1811, Small 5		36	55.3	44%	$3,000	$4,250	$5,500	$8,000	$9,500	$13,000	$14,500	$22,500	$32,500 **(d)**
	Auctions: $64,625, MS-64, August 2013; $10,575, MS-61, July 2014; $4,994, MS-60, October 2014; $3,836, AU-50, September 2014												
1811, Tall 5		51	59.5	57%	$3,000	$4,250	$5,500	$8,000	$9,500	$13,000	$18,500	$30,000	$43,500 **(d)**
	Auctions: $76,375, MS-65, August 2013; $9,400, AU-58, August 2014; $1,880, EF-40, July 2014; $3,055, EF-40, September 2014												
1812	58,087	237	58.8	62%	$3,000	$4,250	$5,500	$8,000	$9,500	$13,000	$14,500	$25,000	$42,500
	Auctions: $30,550, MS-64, November 2014; $61,688, MS-64, August 2013; $4,465, MS-60, August 2015												

d. Value in MS-65 is $115,000.

CAPPED HEAD TO LEFT (1813–1834)

Designer: *John Reich (design modified by William Kneass in 1829).*
Weight: *8.75 grams.* **Composition:** *.9167 gold, .0833 silver and copper.*
Diameter: *25 mm (reduced to 23.8 mm in 1829).* **Edge:** *Reeded.* **Mint:** *Philadelphia.*

Circulation Strike
BD-1.

Proof
BD-3.

History. Half eagles of the Capped Head to Left design are divided into issues of 1813 to 1829 (with a larger diameter), and issues of 1829 to 1834 (with a smaller diameter, and smaller letters, dates, and stars). Those dated 1813 to 1815 are in bold relief and sometimes collected as a separate variety.

Striking and Sharpness. On the obverse, check the star centers and the hair details (these details are usually less distinct on the 1829–1834 smaller-diameter coins). On the reverse, check the eagle. Most examples are well struck. Adjustment marks (from overweight planchets being filed down to acceptable specifications at the mint) are not often encountered. Proof coins were struck on a limited basis for inclusion in sets and for numismatists. Over the years some prooflike Mint State pieces have been classified as Proofs.

Availability. The 1813 and 1814, 4 Over 3, are seen with some frequency and constitute the main supply available for assembling type sets. Other dates range from very rare to extremely rare, with the 1822 topping the list (just three are known, two of which are in the Smithsonian Institution). As gold coins did not circulate after 1821, issues of 1813 to 1820 are usually seen in high-level AU or in MS, and those of the 1820s in MS. The half eagles of the early 1830s are exceptions; these usually show light wear and are much rarer in high-level MS. All Proofs are exceedingly rare.

GRADING STANDARDS

MS-60 to 70 (Mint State). *Obverse:* At MS-60, some abrasion and contact marks are seen on the cheek, the hair below the LIBERTY inscription, and the highest-relief folds of the cap. Luster is present, but may be dull or lifeless, and interrupted in patches. At MS-63, contact marks are few, and abrasion is very light. At MS-64, abrasion is even less. An MS-65 coin has hardly any abrasion, and

1832, 13 Obverse Stars; BD-1. Graded MS-63.

contact marks are minute. Luster should be full and rich and is often more intense on the obverse. Grades above MS-65 are defined by having fewer marks as perfection is approached. *Reverse:* Comments apply as for the obverse, except that abrasion is most noticeable on the eagle's neck and the highest area of the wings.

AU-50, 53, 55, 58 (About Uncirculated). *Obverse:* Light wear is seen on the cheek and the higher-relief areas of the hair and cap. Friction and scattered marks are in the field, ranging from extensive at AU-50 to minimal at AU-58. Luster may be seen in protected areas, minimal at AU-50 but more evident at AU-58. On an AU-58 coin the field retains some luster as well. *Reverse:* Comments as preceding, except that the eagle's neck, the

1813; BD-1. Graded AU-50.

top of the wings, the leaves, and the arrowheads now show noticeable wear, as do other features. Luster ranges from perhaps 40% remaining in protected areas (at AU-50) to nearly full mint bloom (at AU-58). Often the reverse of this type retains much more luster than the obverse, as the motto, eagle, and lettering protect the surrounding flat areas.

EF-40, 45 (Extremely Fine). *Obverse:* More wear is seen on the portrait, the hair, the cap, and the drapery near the clasp. Luster is minimal or nonexistent at EF-40, and may be slight at EF-45. *Reverse:* Wear is more extensive on the eagle, including the top of the wings, the head, the top of the shield, and the claws. Some traces of luster may be seen, more so at EF-45 than at EF-40.

1813; BD-1. Graded EF-45.

Capped Head half eagles are seldom collected in grades lower than EF-40.

PF-60 to 70 (Proof). *Obverse and Reverse:* PF–60 to 62 coins have extensive hairlines and may have nicks and contact marks. At PF-63, hairlines are prominent, but the mirror surface is very reflective. PF-64 coins have fewer hairlines. At PF-65, hairlines should be minimal and mostly seen only under magnification. There should be no nicks or marks. PF-66 and higher coins should have no marks or hairlines visible to the unaided eye.

1829, Small Date, Reduced Diameter; BD-2. Proof.

1820, Curved-Base 2	1820, Square-Base 2	1820, Small Letters	1820, Large Letters

	Mintage	Cert	Avg	%MS	F-12	VF-20	EF-40	AU-50	AU-55	MS-60	MS-62 PF-63	MS-63 PF-64	MS-64 PF-65
1813	95,428	302	58.6	55%	$4,750	$5,750	$7,000	$9,500	$11,000	$15,000	$17,500	$26,500	$50,000 (a)
	Auctions: $49,350, MS-64, January 2013; $15,863, MS-62, August 2014; $6,463, MS-60, September 2014; $9,400, AU-55, October 2014												
1814, 4 Over 3	15,454	60	59.4	60%	$4,750	$6,000	$8,000	$10,000	$13,000	$20,000	$27,500	$40,000	$55,000
	Auctions: $14,688, AU-58, January 2014; $11,764, AU-55, November 2014												
1815 † (b)	635	3	55.7	33%			$200,000	$275,000	$325,000	$400,000	$500,000	$600,000	
	Auctions: $822,500, MS-65, February 2016; $460,000, MS-64, January 2009												
1818, All kinds	48,588												
1818		81	60.0	67%	$4,750	$6,000	$7,000	$13,500	$16,500	$25,000	$27,500	$45,000	$60,000 (c)
	Auctions: $38,188, MS-62, November 2014; $19,388, MS-62, November 2014; $15,863, AU-50, September 2013												
1818, STATESOF one word		40	60.3	70%	$5,500	$7,000	$9,000	$15,000	$17,000	$22,500	$30,000	$45,000	$65,000
	Auctions: $23,500, MS-62, January 2014; $4,994, AU-50, September 2014												
1818, I Over O		6	62.2	100%	$5,000	$6,500	$8,000	$13,500	$15,000	$30,000	$35,000	$50,000	$65,000 (d)
	Auctions: $135,125, MS-65, January 2014												
1819, All kinds †	51,723												
1819 †		7	54.9	14%			$55,000	$70,000	$95,000	$135,000	$175,000		
	Auctions: $38,188, AU-50, August 2014												
1819, I Over O †		5	57.8	20%			$50,000	$65,000	$80,000	$125,000	$180,000	$225,000	
	Auctions: $67,563, AU-55, January 2014												
1820, All kinds	263,806												
1820, Curved-Base 2, Small Letters		1	62.0	100%	$5,250	$7,000	$11,000	$20,000	$25,000	$40,000	$60,000	$85,000	$170,000
	Auctions: $172,500, MS-64, January 2012												
1820, Curved-Base 2, Large Letters		1	64.0	100%	$5,000	$6,750	$8,500	$12,500	$17,500	$25,000	$27,500	$60,000	$95,000
	Auctions: $19,975, MS-60, January 2014; $11,750, MS-60, September 2014												
1820, Square-Base 2		5	62.2	100%	$5,500	$7,000	$11,000	$16,000	$20,000	$27,500	$32,500	$45,000	$65,000
	Auctions: $31,725, MS-63, January 2014												
1820, Square-Base 2, Proof (e)	2–3	0	n/a		*(unique, in the Bass Foundation Collection)*								
	Auctions: No auction records available.												
1821	34,641	6	54.5	33%	$25,000	$40,000	$60,000	$100,000	$150,000	$215,000	$265,000	$400,000	
	Auctions: $540,000, MS-63+, January 2015; $141,000, AU-55, January 2014												
1821, Proof (f)	3–5	0	n/a		*(extremely rare)*								
	Auctions: No auction records available.												
1822 † (g)	17,796	0	n/a						$6,000,000				
	Auctions: No auction records available.												
1822, Proof (h)	unknown	0	n/a		*(extremely rare)*								
	Auctions: No auction records available.												

† Ranked in the *100 Greatest U.S. Coins* (fifth edition); both 1819 Capped Bust Half Eagle varieties as a single entry. **a.** Value in MS-65 is $105,000. **b.** 11 examples are known. **c.** Value in MS-65 is $135,000. **d.** Value in MS-65 is $140,000. **e.** Some experts have questioned the Proof status of this unique piece; the surface of the coin is reflective, but it is not as convincing as other true Proofs of the type. Prior claims that as many as four Proofs exist of this date have not been substantiated. **f.** 2 examples are known. One is in the Harry W. Bass Jr. Foundation Collection, and another is in the Smithsonian's National Numismatic Collection. **g.** 3 examples are known. **h.** 3 examples are known, though the Proof status of these pieces has been questioned.

1825, 5 Over Partial 4

1825, 5 Over 4

1828, 8 Over 7

1829, Large Date
BD-1.

1829, Small Date
BD-2.

	Mintage	Cert	Avg	%MS	F-12	VF-20	EF-40	AU-50	AU-55	MS-60	MS-62	MS-63	MS-64
											PF-63	PF-64	PF-65
1823	14,485	23	56.6	43%	$8,500	$10,000	$15,000	$20,000	$25,000	$30,000	$37,500	$50,000	$75,000
	Auctions: $82,250, MS-64, January 2014; $29,375, MS-62, August 2014												
1823, Proof (i)	*unknown*	0	n/a										
	Auctions: No auction records available.												
1824	17,340	14	59.9	57%	$14,000	$20,000	$30,000	$37,500	$45,000	$57,500	$75,000	$125,000	$145,000 (j)
	Auctions: $199,750, MS-65, January 2014												
1824, Proof (k)	*unknown*	0	n/a										
	Auctions: No auction records available.												
1825, 5 Over Partial 4 † (l)	29,060	7	58.6	71%	$14,000	$20,000	$30,000	$37,500	$47,500	$75,000	$100,000	$130,000	$150,000
	Auctions: $99,875, MS-61, January 2014												
1825, 5 Over 4 † (m)	(n)	1	50.0	0%			$500,000	$700,000					$1,000,000
	Auctions: $940,000, MS-64, May 2016; $690,000, AU-50, July 2008												
1825, 5 Over Partial 4, Proof † (o)	*1–2*	0	n/a		*(unique, in the Smithsonian's National Numismatic Collection)*								
	Auctions: No auction records available.												
1826	18,069	6	63.8	100%	$10,000	$15,000	$20,000	$30,000	$40,000	$70,000	$80,000	$115,000	$140,000
	Auctions: $546,000, MS-66, January 2015; $763,750, MS-66, January 2014												
1826, Proof	*2–4*	0	n/a		*(unique, in the Smithsonian's National Numismatic Collection)*								
	Auctions: No auction records available.												
1827	24,913	11	62.6	91%				$45,000	$50,000	$65,000	$75,000	$125,000	$150,000
	Auctions: $141,000, MS-64, January 2014												
1827, Proof (p)	*unknown*	0	n/a										
	Auctions: No auction records available.												
1828, 8 Over 7 (q)	(r)	2	63.5	100%					$175,000			$350,000	$700,000
	Auctions: $632,500, MS-64, January 2012												
1828	28,029	4	61.0	75%				$80,000	$100,000	$200,000	$225,000	$325,000	$450,000
	Auctions: $499,375, MS-64, April 2013												
1828, Proof	*1–2*	0	n/a		*(unique, in the Smithsonian's National Numismatic Collection)*								
	Auctions: No auction records available.												
1829, Large Date †	57,442	1	66.0	100%			—	—		$225,000	$300,000	$425,000	$600,000
	Auctions: $763,750, MS-66+, May 2016												
1829, Large Date, Proof †	*2–4*	0	n/a										
	Auctions: $1,380,000, PF-64, January 2012												

† Ranked in the *100 Greatest U.S. Coins* (fifth edition); all 1825, 5 Over 4 Capped Bust Half Eagle varieties are a single entry, as are all 1829 Capped Bust Half Eagle varieties. **i.** The only auction references for a Proof 1823 half eagle are from 1885 and 1962. Neither coin (assuming they are not the same specimen) has been examined by today's standards to confirm its Proof status. **j.** Value in MS-65 is $150,000. **k.** No 1824 Proof half eagles are known to exist, despite previous claims that the Smithsonian's Mint collection specimen (actually an MS-62 circulation strike) is a Proof. **l.** Sometimes called 1825, 5 Over 1. **m.** 2 examples are known. **n.** Included in circulation-strike 1825, 5 Over Partial 4, mintage figure. **o.** The Smithsonian's example is a PF-67 with a mirrored obverse and frosty reverse. A second example, reported to have resided in King Farouk's collection, has not been confirmed. **p.** Two purported 1827 Proofs have been revealed to be circulation strikes: the Smithsonian's example is an MS-64, and the Bass example is prooflike. **q.** 5 examples are known. **r.** Included in circulation-strike 1828 mintage figure.

Small 5 D.	Large 5 D.	1832, Curved-Base 2, 12-Star Obverse	1832, Square-Base 2, 13-Star Obverse

1833, Large Date	1833, Small Date	1834, Plain 4	1834, Crosslet 4

	Mintage	Cert	Avg	%MS	F-12	VF-20	EF-40	AU-50	AU-55	MS-60 / PF-63	MS-62 / PF-64	MS-63 / PF-65
1829, Sm Dt, Reduced Diameter †	(a)	2	61.5	100%					$250,000	$375,000	$450,000	$500,000
Auctions: $881,250, MS-65+, May 2016; $431,250, MS-61, January 2012												
1829, Small Date, Proof † (b)	2–4	0	n/a			*(extremely rare)*				$1,400,000		
Auctions: $881,250, MS-65, May 2016												
1830, Small or Large 5 D. (c)	126,351	19	59.8	74%	$20,000	$27,500	$40,000	$45,000	$52,500	$75,000	$85,000	$100,000
Auctions: $73,438, MS-63, January 2014; $47,000, AU-58, August 2014; $41,125, AU-58, October 2014												
1830, Proof (d)	2–4	2	63.5			*(extremely rare)*				$450,000	$750,000	
Auctions: No auction records available.												
1831, Small or Large 5 D. (e)	140,594	8	59.5	50%	$20,000	$27,500	$40,000	$45,000	$52,500	$75,000	$85,000	$100,000
Auctions: $82,250, MS-61, January 2014												
1832, Curved-Base 2, 12 Stars † (f)	(g)	1	58.0	0%	$300,000	$350,000	$400,000	$450,000				$850,000
Auctions: $822,500, MS-63, May 2016												
1832, Square-Base 2, 13 Stars	157,487	10	62.0	80%	$20,000	$27,500	$40,000	$45,000	$55,000	$80,000	$95,000	$110,000 (h)
Auctions: $176,250, MS-65, January 2014												
1832, Square-Base 2, 13 Stars, Proof	2–3	0	n/a			*(extremely rare)*				$750,000		
Auctions: No auction records available.												
1833, Large Date	196,630	2	59.5	50%	$20,000	$27,500	$40,000	$45,000	$52,500	$65,000	$85,000	$115,000 (i)
Auctions: $29,375, AU-50, April 2014												
1833, Small Date (j)	(k)	2	63.0	100%	$20,000	$27,500	$40,000	$45,000	$52,500	$70,000	$100,000	$125,000 (l)
Auctions: $126,500, MS-63 PQ, May 2006												
1833, Proof † (m)	4–6	4	61.3			*(extremely rare)*				$500,000	$750,000	
Auctions: $977,500, PF-67, January 2005												
1834, All kinds	50,141											
1834, Plain 4		19	58.6	58%	$20,000	$27,500	$40,000	$45,000	$52,500	$75,000	$80,000	$100,000
Auctions: $143,750, MS-65, August 2011												
1834, Crosslet 4		8	59.8	63%	$21,500	$30,000	$40,000	$47,500	$57,000	$85,000	$100,000	$140,000
Auctions: $49,350, MS-63, May 2016: $45,531, AU-55, January 2014												

† Ranked in the *100 Greatest U.S. Coins* (fifth edition); all 1829 Capped Bust Half Eagle varieties are a single entry. **a.** Included in circulation-strike 1829, Large Date, mintage figure (see chart on page 1040). **b.** 2 examples are known. One is in the Harry W. Bass Jr. Foundation Collection, and another of equal quality (PF-66) is in the Smithsonian's National Numismatic Collection. **c.** The 1830, Small 5 D. is slightly rarer than the Large 5 D. Certified population reports are unclear, and auction-lot catalogers typically do not differentiate between the two varieties. **d.** 2 examples are known. One is in the Byron Reed collection at the Durham Museum, Omaha, Nebraska. **e.** The 1831, Small 5 D. is estimated to be three to four times rarer than the Large 5 D. Both are extremely rare. **f.** 5 examples are known. **g.** Included in circulation-strike 1832, Square-Base 2, 13 Stars, mintage figure. **h.** Value in MS-64 is $130,000. **i.** Value in MS-64 is $140,000. **j.** The 1833 Small Date is slightly scarcer than the Large Date. **k.** Included in 1833, Large Date, mintage figure. **l.** Value in MS-64 is $175,000. **m.** 4 or 5 examples are known.

CLASSIC HEAD, NO MOTTO ON REVERSE (1834–1838)

Designer: *William Kneass.* **Weight:** *8.36 grams.*
Composition: *(1834–1836) .8992 gold, .1008 silver and copper; (1837–1838) .900 gold.*
Diameter: *22.5 mm.* **Edge:** *Reeded.* **Mints:** *Philadelphia, Charlotte, and Dahlonega.*

Circulation Strike	Mintmark location is on the	Proof
McCloskey-2.	obverse, above the date.	McCloskey-5.

History. U.S. Mint chief engraver William Kneass based the half eagle's Classic Head design on John Reich's cent of 1808. Minted under the Act of June 28, 1834, the coins' reduced size and weight encouraged circulation over melting or export, and they served American commerce until hoarding became extensive during the Civil War. Accordingly, many show considerable wear.

Striking and Sharpness. On the obverse, weakness is often seen on the higher areas of the hair curls. Also check the star centers. On the reverse, check the rims. The denticles are usually well struck.

Availability. Most coins range from VF to AU or lower grades of MS. Most MS coins are dated 1834. MS-63 and better examples are rare. Good eye appeal can be elusive. Proofs of the Classic Head type were made in small quantities, and today probably only a couple dozen or so survive, most bearing the 1834 date.

GRADING STANDARDS

MS-60 to 70 (Mint State). *Obverse:* At MS-60, some abrasion and contact marks are seen on the portrait, most noticeably on the cheek, as the hair details are complex on this type. Luster is present, but may be dull or lifeless, and interrupted in patches. Many low-level Mint State coins have grainy surfaces. At MS-63, contact marks are few, and abrasion is very light. Abrasion is even less at MS-64. An MS-65 coin will have hardly any

1834, Plain 4. Graded MS-65.

abrasion, and contact marks are minute. Luster should be full and rich and is often more intense on the obverse. Grades above MS-65 are defined by having fewer marks as perfection is approached. *Reverse:* Comments apply as for the obverse, except that abrasion is most noticeable in the field, on the eagle's neck, and on the highest area of the wings. Most Mint State coins in the marketplace are graded liberally, with slight abrasion on both sides of MS-65 coins.

Illustrated coin: This well-struck coin has some light abrasion, most evident in the reverse field.

AU-50, 53, 55, 58 (About Uncirculated). *Obverse:* Friction is seen on the higher parts, particularly the cheek and the hair (under magnification) of Miss Liberty. Friction and scattered marks are in the field, ranging from extensive at AU-50 to minimal at AU-58. Luster may be seen in protected areas, minimal at AU-50, more evident at AU-58. On an AU-58 coin the field retains some luster as well. *Reverse:* Comments as preceding, except

1834, Crosslet 4. Graded AU-50.

that the eagle's neck, the top of the wings, the leaves, and the arrowheads now show noticeable wear, as do other features. Luster ranges from perhaps 40% remaining in protected areas (at AU-50) to nearly full mint bloom (at AU-58). Often the reverse of this type retains much more luster than the obverse.

EF-40, 45 (Extremely Fine). *Obverse:* Wear is seen on the portrait overall, with reduction or elimination of some separation of hair strands, especially in the area close to the face. The cheek shows light wear. Luster is minimal or nonexistent at EF-40, and may survive in among the letters of LIBERTY at EF-45. *Reverse:* Wear is greater than on an About Uncirculated coin. On most (but not all) coins the neck lacks some feather detail

1837, Script 8. Graded EF-40.

on its highest points. Feathers have lost some detail near the edges and tips of the wings, and some areas of the horizontal lines in the shield may be blended together. Some traces of luster may be seen, more so at EF-45 than at EF-40.

VF-20, 30 (Very Fine). *Obverse:* Wear on the portrait has reduced the hair detail, especially to the right of the face and the top of the head, but much can still be seen. *Reverse:* Wear is greater, including on the shield and the wing feathers. Generally, Classic Head gold at this grade level lacks eye appeal.

Classic Head half eagles are seldom collected in grades lower than VF-20.

1835, Block 8. Graded VF-30.

PF-60 to 70 (Proof). *Obverse and Reverse:* PF–60 to 62 coins have extensive hairlines and may have nicks and contact marks. At PF-63, hairlines are prominent, but the mirror surface is very reflective. PF-64 coins have fewer hairlines. At PF-65, hairlines should be minimal and mostly seen only under magnification. There should be no nicks or marks. PF-66 and higher coins should have no marks or hairlines visible to the unaided eye.

1834, Plain 4. Graded PF-65.

| 1834, Plain 4 | 1834, Crosslet 4 |

	Mintage	Cert	Avg	%MS	VF-20	EF-40	AU-50	AU-55	MS-60	MS-62 / PF-63	MS-63 / PF-64	MS-64 / PF-65
1834, Plain 4 (a)	657,460	2299	51.1	13%	$650	$750	$1,250	$1,750	$3,500	$6,000	$8,500	$20,000
Auctions: $4,230, MS-61, February 2015; $1,704, AU-55, September 2015; $824, EF-45, July 2015; $447, VF-20, May 2015												
1834, Crosslet 4	(b)	95	46.6	9%	$2,100	$3,750	$6,000	$9,500	$23,500	$27,500	$50,000	$80,000
Auctions: $14,688, MS-61, January 2015; $6,463, AU-55, January 2015; $5,581, AU-50, January 2015; $3,995, EF-45, September 2015												
1834, Plain 4, Proof †	8–12	4	63.3							$100,000	$150,000	$225,000
Auctions: $109,250, PF-63Cam, January 2011												
1835 (a)	371,534	768	51.1	14%	$650	$775	$1,250	$1,800	$3,500	$6,500	$11,000	$25,000
Auctions: $9,988, MS-63, September 2015; $2,115, AU-58, September 2015; $1,058, AU-53, August 2015; $517, F-12, November 2015												
1835, Proof † (c)	4–6	0	n/a							$125,000	$175,000	$275,000
Auctions: $690,000, PF-67, January 2005												
1836 (a)	553,147	1,301	49.7	11%	$650	$775	$1,250	$1,900	$3,500	$6,500	$11,000	$25,000
Auctions: $3,353, MS-61, January 2015; $1,175, AU-55, October 2015; $631, EF-40, March 2015; $588, VF-30, August 2015												
1836, Proof † (d)	4–6	2	67.0							$125,000	$175,000	
Auctions: No auction records available.												
1837 (a)	207,121	468	50.6	12%	$700	$850	$1,550	$2,100	$5,500	$8,500	$20,000	$35,000
Auctions: $21,738, MS-63, October 2013; $3,525, MS-61, October 2015; $1,763, AU-55, August 2014; $999, EF-45, January 2015												
1837, Proof †	4–6	0	n/a		*(unique, in the Smithsonian's National Numismatic Collection)*							
Auctions: No auction records available.												
1838	286,588	736	51.7	13%	$700	$850	$1,500	$2,050	$4,250	$8,500	$11,500	$35,000
Auctions: $2,233, AU-58, August 2015; $1,645, AU-55, January 2015; $940, EF-45, June 2015; $447, EF-40, January 2015												
1838, Proof	2–3	1	65.0		*(unique, in the Bass Foundation Collection)*							
Auctions: No auction records available.												
1838-C	17,179	111	43.9	4%	$6,000	$10,000	$15,000	$22,500	$75,000	$125,000	$250,000	
Auctions: $235,000, MS-63, May 2016; $8,813, EF-45, September 2016; $10,575, EF-40, August 2013; $5,405, EF-40, June 2015												
1838-D	20,583	140	49.4	8%	$6,500	$8,500	$12,500	$20,000	$35,000	$50,000	$95,000	
Auctions: $94,000, MS-63, May 2016; $21,150, MS-60, January 2014; $21,150, AU-58, October 2016; $21,738, AU-55, August 2014												

† All Classic Head Half Eagle Proof strikes from 1834–1837 are ranked in the *100 Greatest U.S. Coins* (fifth edition), as a single entry. **a.** Varieties have either a script 8 or block-style 8 in the date. (See illustrations of similar quarter eagles on page 990.) **b.** Included in circulation-strike, 1838, Plain 4, mintage figure. **c.** 3 or 4 examples are known. **d.** 3 or 4 examples are known.

LIBERTY HEAD (1839–1908)

Designer: *Christian Gobrecht.* **Weight:** *8.359 grams.*
Composition: *.900 gold, .100 copper (net weight .24187 oz. pure gold).*
Diameter: *(1839–1840) 22.5 mm; (1840–1908) 21.6 mm.* **Edge:** *Reeded.*
Mints: *Philadelphia, Charlotte, Dahlonega, Denver, New Orleans, San Francisco, and Carson City.*

Large Diameter, Without Motto, Circulation Strike (1839–1840)
McCloskey–1-A.

Mintmark location, 1839, is on the obverse, above the date.

Large Diameter, Without Motto, Proof

Reduced Diameter, Without Motto, Circulation Strike (1840–1865)

Reduced Diameter, Without Motto, Proof

Mintmark location, 1840–1908, is on the reverse, below the eagle.

With Motto, Circulation Strike (1866–1908)

With Motto, Proof

History. Christian Gobrecht's Liberty Head half eagle design was introduced in 1839. The mintmark (for branch-mint coins) in that year was located on the obverse; for all later issues it was relocated to the reverse. The motto IN GOD WE TRUST was added to the reverse in 1866.

Striking and Sharpness. On the obverse, check the highest points of the hair and the star centers; the reverse, the eagle's neck, the area to the lower left of the shield, and the lower part of the eagle. Generally, the eagle on the $5 coins is better struck than on quarter eagles. Examine the denticles on both sides. Branch-mint coins struck before the Civil War are often lightly struck in areas. San Francisco half eagles are in lower average grades than are those from the Philadelphia Mint, as Philadelphia coins did not circulate at par in the East and Midwest from late December 1861 until December 1878, thus acquiring less wear. Most late 19th- and early 20th-century coins are sharp in all areas; for these issues, tiny copper staining spots (from improperly mixed coinage alloy) can be a problem. Cameo contrast is the rule for Proofs prior to 1902. Beginning that year the portrait was polished in the die, although a few years later cameo-contrast coins were again made.

Availability. Early dates and mintmarks are typically scarce to rare in MS, very rare in MS–63 to 65. Charlotte and Dahlonega coins are usually EF or AU, or overgraded as low MS, as seen with quarter eagles. The 1854-S and several varieties in the 1860s and 1870s are rare. Coins from 1880 onward are seen in higher than average grades. Proof coins exist in relation to their original mintages; issues prior to the 1890s are rare.

Note: Values of common-date gold coins have been based on the current bullion price of gold, $2,000 per ounce, and may vary with the prevailing spot price.

GRADING STANDARDS

MS-60 to 70 (Mint State). *Obverse:* At MS-60, some abrasion and contact marks are evident, most noticeably on the hair to the right of Miss Liberty's forehead and on the jaw. Luster is present, but may be dull or life-less, and interrupted in patches. At MS-63, contact marks are few, and abrasion is very light. An MS-65 coin has only slight abrasion, and contact marks are so minute as to require

1848-C. Graded MS-63.

magnification. Luster should be full and rich. Grades above MS-65 are defined by having fewer marks as perfection is approached. *Reverse:* Comments apply as for the obverse, except that abrasion and contact marks are most noticeable on the eagle's neck and to the lower left of the shield.

Illustrated coin: Friction is seen in the obverse fields amid luster; on the reverse, luster is nearly complete.

AU-50, 53, 55, 58 (About Uncirculated). *Obverse:* Light wear is seen on the face, the hair to the right of the face, and the highest area of the hair bun, more so at AU-50 than at AU–53 or 55. An AU-58 coin has minimal traces of wear. An AU-50 coin has luster in protected areas among the stars and letters, with little in the open fields or on the portrait. At AU-58, most luster is present in the fields, but is worn away on the highest parts

1840. Graded AU-55.

of the motifs. Striking must be taken into consideration, for a lightly struck coin can be About Uncirculated, but be weak in the central areas. *Reverse:* Comments as preceding, except that the eagle shows wear in all of the higher areas, as well as the leaves and arrowheads. From 1866 to 1908 the motto IN GOD WE TRUST helped protect the field, with the result that luster is more extensive on this side in comparison to the obverse. Luster ranges from perhaps 50% remaining in protected areas (at AU-50) to nearly full mint bloom (at AU-58).

EF-40, 45 (Extremely Fine). *Obverse:* Wear is evident on all high areas of the portrait, including the hair to the right of the forehead, the tip of the coronet, the back of the head, and the hair bun. The stars show light wear at their centers (unless protected by a high rim). Luster, if present at all, is minimal and in protected areas such as between the star points. *Reverse:* Wear is greater than on an About Uncirculated coin, and flatness is

1844. Graded EF-40.

seen on the feather ends, the leaves, and elsewhere. Some traces of luster may be seen, more so at EF-45 than at EF-40. Overall, the reverse appears to be in a slightly higher grade than the obverse on coins from 1866 to 1908 (With Motto).

Illustrated coin: This coin is well struck on both sides.

VF-20, 30 (Very Fine). *Obverse:* The higher-relief areas of hair are worn flat at VF-20, less so at VF-30. The hair to the right of the coronet is merged into heavy strands. The stars are flat at their centers. *Reverse:* Feather detail is mostly worn away on the neck and legs, less so on the wings. The vertical shield stripes, being deeply recessed, remain bold.

Liberty Head half eagles are seldom collected in grades lower than VF-20.

PF-60 to 70 (Proof). *Obverse and Reverse:* PF–60 to 62 coins have extensive hairlines and may have nicks and contact marks. At PF-63, hairlines are prominent, but the mirror surface is very reflective. PF-64 coins have fewer hairlines. At PF-65, hairlines should be minimal and mostly seen only under magnification. There should be no nicks or marks. PF-66 and higher coins should have no marks or hairlines visible to the unaided eye.

1858-C. Graded VF-20.

1872. Graded PF-55.

	Mintage	Cert	Avg	%MS	VF-20	EF-40	AU-50	AU-55	MS-60	MS-63	MS-64	MS-65
										PF-63	PF-64	PF-65
1839	118,143	256	50.9	13%	$700	$1,150	$1,800	$2,500	$7,000	$27,500	$50,000	
	Auctions: $11,764, MS-62, January 2015; $3,760, AU-58, August 2015; $1,528, AU-55, January 2015; $1,410, AU-50, September 2015											
1839, Proof (a)	2–3	1	61.0		*(extremely rare)*							
	Auctions: $184,000, PF-61, January 2010											
1839-C	17,205	89	48.9	17%	$2,750	$5,000	$10,000	$14,500	$25,000	$65,000	$135,000	
	Auctions: $111,625, MS-64, May 2016; $42,300, MS-63, March 2016: $23,500, MS-61, January 2014; $16,450, MS-60, January 2015											
1839-D	18,939	119	46.0	5%	$3,250	$5,750	$10,000	$17,500	$30,000			
	Auctions: $9,400, AU-53, September 2013; $4,700, AU-50, July 2015; $4,700, EF-45, February 2015; $2,350, EF-40, November 2014											
1840 (b)	137,382	348	51.2	9%	$650	$800	$1,000	$1,350	$3,250	$9,000	$25,000	$50,000
	Auctions: $2,585, AU-58, October 2015; $2,115, AU-58, June 2015; $999, AU-53, January 2015; $646, EF-45, January 2015											
1840, Proof	2–3	0	n/a		*(unique, in the Smithsonian's National Numismatic Collection)*							
	Auctions: No auction records available.											
1840-C	18,992	90	47.4	11%	$2,000	$4,000	$6,000	$7,000	$20,000	$50,000	$70,000	
	Auctions: $28,200, MS-62, January 2014; $5,581, AU-55, February 2015; $4,700, AU-50, August 2015; $1,645, VF-20, August 2014											
1840-D	22,896	80	50.8	18%	$2,250	$3,500	$6,000	$7,500	$14,000	$45,000		
	Auctions: $14,100, MS-61, December 2013; $881, F-12, August 2014											
1840-O (b)	40,120	161	51.6	12%	$700	$1,200	$2,250	$3,000	$9,500	$40,000		
	Auctions: $5,405, AU-58, June 2015; $2,350, AU-55, October 2015; $1,763, AU-55, January 2015; $764, AU-50, January 2015											
1841	15,833	69	52.7	25%	$650	$1,000	$1,600	$1,850	$4,500	$12,000	$18,500	$37,500
	Auctions: $1,763, AU-55, December 2013											
1841, Proof (c)	2–3	1	63.0		*(extremely rare)*							
	Auctions: No auction records available.											
1841-C	21,467	98	48.6	7%	$1,850	$2,500	$5,000	$6,000	$15,000	$35,000	$55,000	
	Auctions: $5,581, AU-58, January 2014; $4,230, AU-55, September 2015; $1,939, EF-40, January 2015; $1,705, VF-35, August 2014											

a. 2 or 3 examples are known. **b.** Scarce varieties of the 1840 coins have the fine edge-reeding and wide rims of the 1839 issues. This is referred to as the broad-mill variety. **c.** 2 examples are known. One is in the Smithsonian's National Numismatic Collection; the other is ex Eliasberg Collection.

| **Small Letters** | **Large Letters** | **Small Date** | **Large Date** |

	Mintage	Cert	Avg	%MS	VF-20	EF-40	AU-50	AU-55	MS-60	MS-63	MS-64	MS-65
										PF-63	PF-64	PF-65
1841-D	27,492	109	49.7	21%	$2,250	$3,000	$4,500	$5,250	$12,500	$22,000	$45,000	
Auctions: $9,988, MS-61, January 2014; $8,578, MS-60, August 2014												
1841-O (d)	50	0	n/a									
Auctions: No auction records available.												
1842, All kinds	27,578											
1842, Small Letters		32	52.7	13%	$725	$1,250	$2,500	$6,000	$11,000			$60,000
Auctions: $15,275, MS-62, January 2014												
1842, Large Letters		20	48.8	0%	$850	$1,750	$3,750	$6,500	$11,500	$25,000		
Auctions: $4,113, AU-55, April 2014; $4,700, AU-55, August 2014												
1842, Small Letters, Proof (e)	4–6	0	n/a		*(extremely rare)*							
Auctions: $172,500, PF-64CamH, January 2009												
1842-C, All kinds	27,432											
1842-C, Small Date		24	49.5	21%	$9,000	$18,500	$26,000	$35,000	$75,000	$150,000		
Auctions: $111,625, MS-63, January 2015; $49,938, AU-58, July 2014; $20,563, AU-53, January 2015; $16,450, EF-45, August 2016												
1842-C, Large Date		101	50.4	14%	$2,000	$2,550	$4,000	$5,000	$12,500	$30,000	$50,000	
Auctions: $25,850, MS-63, September 2013; $11,750, MS-61, November 2014												
1842-D, All kinds	59,608											
1842-D, Small Date		165	45.8	5%	$2,000	$2,600	$4,250	$5,000	$13,500	$30,000		
Auctions: $16,450, MS-62, April 2014; $3,995, AU-55, October 2015; $2,350, EF-45, July 2014; $764, F-12, January 2015												
1842-D, Large Date		25	44.2	8%	$3,750	$7,500	$11,500	$20,000	$45,000			
Auctions: $7,050, MS-60, January 2014; $16,200, AU-55, April 2018												
1842-O	16,400	48	45.0	4%	$2,500	$4,000	$9,500	$12,500	$25,000			
Auctions: $7,638, AU-53, January 2014; $734, VF-20, January 2015; $646, VF-20, August 2014; $823, F-12, January 2015												
1843	611,205	611	53.5	15%	$650	$700	$800	$850	$1,400	$9,500	$20,000	$37,500
Auctions: $1,410, MS-61, January 2015; $1,175, MS-60, September 2015; $535, AU-55, January 2015; $447, EF-45, September 2015												
1843, Proof (f)	4–8	2	63.0		*(extremely rare)*							
Auctions: $34,500, PF-58, August 2009												
1843-C	44,277	163	44.8	9%	$1,800	$2,500	$3,750	$4,500	$9,500	$27,500	$50,000	
Auctions: $8,813, MS-61, October 2015; $3,084, AU-53, February 2015; $2,838, AU-50, November 2014; $2,233, EF-45, January 2015												
1843-D	98,452	251	46.1	8%	$2,000	$2,500	$3,500	$4,250	$10,500	$28,500	$50,000	
Auctions: $19,975, MS-63, April 2013; $4,406, MS-60, November 2014; $5,434, AU-58, September 2014; $1,998, AU-50, August 2015												
1843-D, Proof (g)	unknown	1	65.0									
Auctions: No auction records available.												
1843-O, Small Letters	19,075	77	47.2	8%	$850	$1,650	$2,250	$4,500	$17,500	$38,000	$55,000	$65,000
Auctions: $5,940, AU-58, January 2015; $2,585, AU-50, October 2014; $3,760, EF-45, September 2015; $1,116, EF-40, November 2014												
1843-O, Large Letters	82,000	126	49.6	19%	$700	$1,250	$2,000	$3,500	$10,000	$30,000	$40,000	
Auctions: $19,975, MS-62, January 2014; $5,875, AU-58, March 2015; $5,170, AU-58, July 2015; $797, EF-40, August 2014												

d. Official Mint records report 8,350 coins struck at the New Orleans Mint in 1841. However, most—if not all—were actually dated 1840. No 1841-O half eagle has ever appeared on the market. **e.** Of the examples known today, one is in the Smithsonian's National Numismatic Collection, and another is ex Pittman Collection. **f.** 4 or 5 examples are known. **g.** One non-circulation example of the 1843-D half eagle, probably a presentation strike of some sort, has been certified by NGC as a Specimen (rated Specimen-65).

1846-D, High
Second D Over D

	Mintage	Cert	Avg	%MS	VF-20	EF-40	AU-50	AU-55	MS-60	MS-63 PF-63	MS-64 PF-64	MS-65 PF-65
1844	340,330	365	53.1	10%	$600	$700	$800	$900	$1,950	$10,000	$18,000	$55,000
Auctions: $3,525, MS-62, October 2015; $564, AU-53, June 2015; $494, AU-50, January 2015; $12,000, MS-63, April 2018											
1844, Proof (h)	3–5	1	64.0				*(unique)*					
Auctions: No auction records available.											
1844-C	23,631	90	45.3	7%	$2,250	$3,250	$5,000	$7,000	$14,000	$35,000		
Auctions: $4,230, AU-55, January 2015; $3,290, AU-55, January 2015; $2,957, VF-35, March 2015; $999, G-6, October 2015											
1844-D	88,982	256	46.7	8%	$2,000	$2,750	$3,750	$4,250	$8,500	$25,000	$50,000	
Auctions: $7,638, MS-61, June 2015; $6,000, MS-60, January 2015; $5,405, EF-40, July 2015; $1,763, VF-35, September 2015											
1844-O	364,600	720	50.4	9%	$700	$800	$1,000	$1,350	$4,500	$16,000	$27,000	$45,000
Auctions: $1,880, AU-58, June 2015; $646, EF-45, July 2015; $494, EF-45, September 2015; $400, EF-40, October 2015											
1844-O, Proof † (i)	1	0	n/a									
Auctions: No auction records available.											
1845	417,099	411	53.4	13%	$650	$700	$800	$900	$2,000	$8,000	$15,000	
Auctions: $12,925, MS-64, July 2015; $1,235, AU-58, July 2015; $447, AU-53, January 2015; $470, EF-45, July 2015											
1845, Proof (j)	5–8	3	64.7				*(extremely rare)*					
Auctions: $149,500, PF-66UCam, August 2004											
1845-D	90,629	289	49.6	7%	$2,000	$2,500	$3,500	$4,500	$9,000	$22,500	$40,000	$85,000
Auctions: $7,050, MS-61, June 2015; $4,230, AU-58, January 2015; $2,056, EF-45, January 2015; $1,058, VG-8, October 2015											
1845-O	41,000	148	50.7	12%	$750	$1,200	$2,500	$4,500	$10,000	$27,500		
Auctions: $6,463, AU-58, December 2013											
1846, All kinds	395,942											
1846, Large Date		240	53.0	11%	$600	$700	$800	$850	$2,000	$13,000	$18,500	
Auctions: $16,450, MS-63, January 2015; $11,456, MS-63, September 2015; $1,058, MS-60, September 2015; $400, EF-45, June 2015											
1846, Small Date		102	54.3	15%	$650	$700	$900	$1,100	$3,500	$13,500	$20,000	
Auctions: $3,055, MS-61, October 2015; $2,585, MS-60, January 2015; $1,528, AU-58, July 2014; $388, EF-40, July 2014											
1846, Proof (k)	6–10	0	n/a				*(extremely rare)*					
Auctions: $161,000, PF-64Cam, January 2011											
1846-C	12,995	74	49.6	9%	$2,000	$3,750	$5,000	$7,000	$16,000	$50,000	$65,000	
Auctions: $12,925, MS-60, October 2015: $10,575, MS-60, January 2014											
1846-D, All kinds	80,294											
1846-D (l)		270	48.8	5%	$2,000	$2,750	$3,750	$4,750	$12,000			
Auctions: $3,055, AU-53, August 2014; $5,640, AU-50, July 2015; $2,350, EF-45, September 2015; $1,058, EF-40, August 2014											
1846-D, High Second D Over D		139	49.8	6%	$2,250	$2,500	$4,000	$5,000	$11,000	$27,500		
Auctions: $21,150, MS-63, January 2014; $2,115, EF-45, August 2014; $2,115, EF-40, January 2015; $1,763, VF-25, January 2015											
1846-O	58,000	151	49.2	6%	$700	$1,000	$3,250	$4,750	$11,000			
Auctions: $9,400, MS-61, January 2014; $4,230, AU-55, October 2015; $1,528, EF-45, July 2015; $881, EF-40, July 2014											

† Ranked in the *100 Greatest U.S. Coins* (fifth edition), grouped with 1844-O Proof Liberty Head Eagles, as a single entry. **h.** 2 examples are known. One is in the Smithsonian's National Numismatic Collection; the other is ex Pittman Collection. **i.** This unique coin first sold in 1890; pedigree is ex Seavy, Parmelee, Woodin, Newcomer, Farouk, Kosoff; current location unknown. **j.** 4 or 5 examples are known. **k.** 4 or 5 examples are known. Of the 20 or so Proof sets made in 1846, experts believe only 4 or 5 contained the year's gold coinage. **l.** The 1846-D half eagle with a normal mintmark actually is rarer than the variety with a boldly repunched D Over D mintmark.

| 1847, Top of Extra 7 Very Low at Border FS-G5-1847-301. | 1848-D, D Over D | 1850-C, Normal C | 1850-C, Weak C |

	Mintage	Cert	Avg	%MS	VF-20	EF-40	AU-50	AU-55	MS-60 PF-63	MS-63 PF-64	MS-64 PF-65	MS-65
1847, All kinds	915,981											
1847		1,072	54.3	16%	$600	$700	$800	$850	$1,650	$6,000	$11,000	$35,000
Auctions: $2,820, MS-62, June 2015; $940, AU-58, September 2015; $517, AU-53, September 2015; $388, EF-45, January 2015												
1847, Top of Extra 7 Very Low at Border		200	54.7	14%	$650	$750	$850	$1,250	$2,350	$9,000	$12,500	$45,000
Auctions: $3,173, MS-62, October 2013; $1,998, MS-61, November 2014; $705, AU-53, October 2015												
1847, Proof	2–3	0	n/a		(unique, in the Smithsonian's National Numismatic Collection)							
Auctions: No auction records available.												
1847-C	84,151	277	45.4	5%	$2,000	$2,350	$3,500	$4,500	$9,500	$28,500	$37,500	$75,000
Auctions: $4,406, AU-58, April 2014; $3,525, AU-55, October 2015; $2,350, EF-45, July 2014; $1,763, EF-40, August 2014												
1847-D	64,405	166	48.4	9%	$2,000	$2,500	$3,500	$5,000	$8,500	$20,000		
Auctions: $3,995, AU-55, October 2015; $3,995, AU-55, January 2015; $4,261, AU-50, January 2015; $2,056, EF-45, January 2015												
1847-O	12,000	48	43.6	4%	$3,000	$7,500	$11,500	$15,000	$47,500			
Auctions: $14,100, AU-53, January 2014; $11,163, AU-53, January 2015; $4,113, AU-50, August 2014												
1848	260,775	369	53.3	11%	$600	$700	$800	$850	$1,750	$9,500	$25,000	$35,000
Auctions: $1,058, MS-60, April 2013; $705, AU-58, August 2015; $564, AU-53, September 2015; $515, EF-45, July 2014												
1848, Proof (m)	6–10	0	n/a		(extremely rare)							
Auctions: No auction records available.												
1848-C	64,472	204	46.4	3%	$2,000	$2,500	$3,500	$5,500	$15,000	$40,000	$65,000	
Auctions: $3,055, AU-53, January 2015; $2,115, AU-50, June 2015; $1,880, AU-50, June 2015; $1,586, VF-30, January 2015												
1848-D	47,465	123	48.6	6%	$1,850	$2,750	$3,500	$5,500	$12,500	$25,000		
Auctions: $5,640, AU-58, February 2015; $4,113, AU-55, April 2014; $2,241, EF-45, August 2014; $2,115, EF-40, July 2014												
1848-D, D Over D	(n)	1	58.0	0%				$15,000				
Auctions: $29,900, MS-62, May 2008												
1849	133,070	219	52.6	15%	$600	$650	$750	$1,000	$2,750	$10,000	$15,000	
Auctions: $2,585, MS-61, August 2014; $5,288, MS-61, April 2013; $911, AU-55, August 2014; $705, AU-53, November 2014												
1849-C	64,823	240	49.7	10%	$2,000	$2,500	$3,250	$4,750	$8,500	$26,000	$40,000	
Auctions: $4,230, AU-55, September 2015; $2,585, AU-53, February 2015; $1,645, AU-50, February 2015; $2,233, EF-45, August 2015												
1849-D	39,036	151	48.7	4%	$2,000	$2,750	$3,500	$4,500	$11,500	$35,000		
Auctions: $5,288, AU-58, April 2013; $2,233, AU-50, September 2015; $2,585, EF-45, August 2014												
1850	64,491	151	50.1	5%	$600	$750	$975	$1,250	$3,000	$12,500	$32,000	$75,000
Auctions: $1,293, AU-58, October 2014; $1,028, AU-55, April 2014; $705, AU-50, October 2015; $499, EF-40, August 2014												
1850-C	63,591	222	48.4	10%	$2,000	$2,350	$3,250	$4,250	$10,000	$19,000	$40,000	
Auctions: $8,813, MS-61, February 2013; $3,995, AU-50, January 2015; $2,056, AU-50, August 2015; $1,763, VF-35, August 2015												
1850-C, Weak C (o)	(p)	51	49.9	8%	$1,200	$1,500	$2,000	$2,500	$4,500			
Auctions: $3,819, MS-61, August 2014; $1,293, EF-45, July 2014; $1,116, EF-45, October 2015; $1,058, VF-35, January 2015												
1850-D	43,984	145	47.8	3%	$2,000	$2,750	$3,950	$5,000	$23,500			
Auctions: $5,640, AU-58, October 2015; $5,170, AU-53, February 2015; $1,293, AU-50, August 2015; $2,115, EF-45, August 2014												

m. 2 examples are known. One is in the Smithsonian's National Numismatic Collection; the other is ex Pittman Collection. **n.** Included in 1848-D mintage figure **o.** Several branch-mint half eagles of the early 1850s can exhibit weak (sometimes very weak or almost invisible) mintmarks; such coins generally trade at deep discounts. **p.** Included in 1850-C mintage figure.

1851-D, Normal D

1851-D, Weak D

1854, Doubled Die Obverse
FS-G5-1854-101.

1854-C, Normal C

1854-C, Weak C

1854-D, Normal D

1854-D, Weak D

| | Mintage | Cert | Avg | %MS | VF-20 | EF-40 | AU-50 | AU-55 | MS-60 | MS-63 | MS-64 | MS-65 |
									PF-63	PF-64	PF-65	
1851	377,505	439	54.5	15%	$600	$725	$800	$850	$2,500	$8,500	$22,500	
Auctions: $2,820, MS-61, February 2015; $705, AU-55, June 2015; $447, AU-53, February 2015; $353, EF-40, July 2015												
1851-C	49,176	147	48.2	10%	$2,000	$2,500	$3,500	$4,500	$11,000	$37,500	$55,000	
Auctions: $30,550, MS-63, April 2013; $3,760, AU-55, January 2015; $2,820, AU-53, February 2015; $2,468, AU-50, September 2016												
1851-D	62,710	138	50.0	9%	$2,000	$2,500	$3,750	$5,500	$12,000	$25,000	$45,000	
Auctions: $16,450, MS-62, January 2014												
1851-D, Weak D (o)	(q)	12	56.0	33%	$1,200	$1,500	$2,000	$2,500				
Auctions: $2,185, AU-50, July 2009												
1851-O	41,000	145	47.2	2%	$900	$1,500	$4,500	$6,000	$10,000	$25,000	$65,000	
Auctions: $11,163, MS-61, October 2014; $6,463, AU-58, June 2013; $3,055, AU-50, July 2014; $447, EF-40, January 2015												
1852	573,901	786	54.8	14%	$600	$700	$800	$850	$1,500	$6,500	$12,500	$27,500
Auctions: $9,400, MS-64, January 2015; $3,055, MS-62, August 2015; $646, AU-55, October 2015; $477, AU-55, May 2015												
1852-C	72,574	254	49.3	16%	$2,000	$2,500	$3,500	$4,250	$6,000	$20,000	$27,500	
Auctions: $28,200, MS-64, August 2013; $9,694, MS-62, January 2015; $2,585, MS-60, November 2014; $2,468, EF-45, January 2015												
1852-D	91,584	281	48.8	9%	$2,000	$2,600	$3,750	$5,000	$9,500	$25,000		
Auctions: $3,290, AU-55, June 2015; $3,290, AU-53, August 2015; $2,233, EF-45, June 2015; $1,645, VF-25, January 2015												
1853	305,770	581	54.2	14%	$600	$700	$800	$850	$1,500	$6,000	$16,000	$60,000
Auctions: $15,863, MS-64, October 2015; $2,115, MS-62, March 2015; $1,528, MS-61, June 2015; $423, EF-40, January 2015												
1853-C	65,571	186	49.3	11%	$2,000	$2,500	$3,500	$4,250	$6,750	$21,500	$65,000	
Auctions: $8,225, MS-62, January 2015; $1,998, MS-60, January 2015; $4,406, AU-58, August 2014; $852, VF-20, February 2015												
1853-D	89,678	376	50.8	11%	$2,000	$2,400	$3,400	$4,500	$6,750	$15,000	$55,000	
Auctions: $13,513, MS-63, October 2015; $6,463, MS-61, January 2015; $3,290, AU-55, June 2015; $2,233, EF-45, October 2015												
1854	160,675	406	54.6	13%	$600	$700	$800	$850	$2,000	$8,500	$15,000	
Auctions: $764, AU-58, August 2015; $530, AU-55, June 2015; $470, AU-50, June 2015; $423, AU-50, April 2015												
1854, Doubled Die Obverse	(r)	51	54.5	12%					$1,550	$2,750		
Auctions: $1,998, AU-55, October 2014												
1854, Proof (s)	unknown	0	n/a									
Auctions: No auction records available.												
1854-C	39,283	102	49.0	8%	$2,000	$2,500	$4,000	$5,000	$12,000	$37,500	$55,000	
Auctions: $35,250, MS-63, April 2014; $3,819, AU-50, March 2015; $1,998, AU-50, January 2015; $2,115, EF-40, January 2015												
1854-C, Weak C (o)	(t)	44	47.9	11%	$1,200	$1,500	$1,750	$2,250	$5,750	$12,000		
Auctions: $12,338, MS-63, January 2014; $4,584, MS-60, September 2014												
1854-D	56,413	245	53.0	20%	$2,000	$2,500	$3,750	$4,500	$8,000	$23,500	$42,500	$75,000
Auctions: $8,813, MS-62, June 2013; $3,825, AU-55, March 2015; $3,055, EF-45, January 2015; $940, VF-30, January 2015												
1854-D, Weak D (o)	(u)	18	50.0	6%	$1,200	$1,500	$1,750	$2,500	$4,500			
Auctions: $5,581, MS-61, September 2014; $1,998, AU-55, April 2014												

o. Several branch-mint half eagles of the early 1850s can exhibit weak (sometimes very weak or almost invisible) mintmarks; such coins generally trade at deep discounts. **q.** Included in 1851-D mintage figure. **r.** Included in circulation-strike 1854 mintage figure **s.** According to Walter Breen, a complete 1854 Proof set was presented to dignitaries of the sovereign German city of Bremen who visited the Philadelphia Mint. The set resided in Bremen until it disappeared almost 100 years later, during World War II. **t.** Included in 1854-C mintage figure. **u.** Included in 1854-D mintage figure.

	Mintage	Cert	Avg	%MS	VF-20	EF-40	AU-50	AU-55	MS-60	MS-63 PF-63	MS-64 PF-64	MS-65 PF-65
1854-O	46,000	190	51.3	6%	$700	$850	$1,350	$2,250	$8,000	$22,500		
Auctions: $2,585, AU-58, October 2015; $1,234, AU-53, June 2015; $764, EF-40, January 2015; $494, VF-30, January 2015											
1854-S † (v)	268	1	45.0	0%	$2,500,000							
Auctions: No auction records available.											
1855	117,098	280	53.8	11%	$600	$700	$800	$850	$1,650	$7,500	$16,500	
Auctions: $2,115, MS-61, October 2015; $588, AU-58, October 2015; $470, AU-53, August 2014; $388, AU-53, November 2014											
1855-C	39,788	153	50.1	9%	$2,250	$2,500	$3,600	$5,000	$12,500	$45,000	$65,000	
Auctions: $11,163, MS-61, August 2016; $9,694, MS-61, April 2013; $7,638, AU-58, January 2015; $1,763, AU-50, January 2015											
1855-D	22,432	81	49.8	7%	$2,000	$2,750	$3,500	$5,000	$13,500	$35,000		
Auctions: $15,275, MS-61, January 2014; $3,819, MS-60, August 2014; $2,820, EF-45, July 2014; $5,640, VF-30, July 2015											
1855-O	11,100	55	49.6	4%	$1,350	$3,000	$5,000	$7,000	$20,000			
Auctions: $8,225, AU-58, January 2015; $4,700, AU-50, September 2014; $3,290, AU-50, November 2014; $3,525, EF-40, January 2015											
1855-S	61,000	113	48.7	4%	$800	$1,250	$2,250	$4,000	$12,500			
Auctions: $3,055, AU-58, September 2015; $2,115, AU-53, July 2014; $940, AU-50, August 2014; $1,351, EF-45, July 2014											
1856	197,990	434	54.0	11%	$600	$700	$800	$900	$1,750	$8,000	$17,000	$55,000
Auctions: $6,182, MS-63, October 2015; $2,115, MS-61, September 2015; $470, AU-55, August 2015; $317, AU-50, June 2015											
1856-C	28,457	156	51.2	9%	$2,000	$2,500	$3,750	$5,000	$13,500	$45,000		
Auctions: $17,625, MS-62, January 2014; $3,055, AU-50, September 2015; $2,820, AU-50, February 2015; $1,351, AU-50, January 2015											
1856-D	19,786	99	49.1	10%	$2,000	$2,500	$3,750	$5,500	$8,500	$27,500	$55,000	
Auctions: $12,925, MS-62, January 2014; $3,878, AU-53, August 2015; $3,878, AU-53, January 2015; $1,880, VF-25, July 2014											
1856-O	10,000	46	49.0	9%	$1,000	$1,850	$4,250	$6,500	$12,500			
Auctions: $10,575, MS-60, April 2014											
1856-S	105,100	158	46.8	3%	$700	$750	$1,250	$2,250	$7,500	$25,000	$40,000	
Auctions: $4,700, AU-58, January 2014; $1,763, AU-55, January 2015; $1,116, AU-55, November 2014; $951, AU-53, July 2014											
1857	98,188	323	55.4	14%	$600	$700	$800	$900	$1,850	$6,000	$15,000	
Auctions: $5,170, MS-63, January 2015; $1,528, MS-61, January 2015; $1,293, MS-61, September 2015; $705, AU-58, October 2015											
1857, Proof (w)	3–6	1	65.0									
Auctions: $230,000, PF-65Cam, January 2007											
1857-C	31,360	179	53.2	17%	$2,000	$2,500	$3,500	$4,250	$7,500	$27,500		$75,000
Auctions: $22,325, MS-63, January 2014; $8,813, MS-61, August 2015; $6,756, AU-55, July 2015; $2,115, EF-45, July 2014											
1857-D	17,046	105	52.0	12%	$2,000	$2,600	$3,750	$5,000	$10,000	$40,000		
Auctions: $9,988, MS-61, January 2014; $5,581, AU-58, October 2014; $5,405, AU-58, January 2015; $1,586, VF-25, August 2014											
1857-O	13,000	82	48.8	4%	$1,000	$2,000	$4,000	$5,750	$13,500	$50,000		
Auctions: $41,125, MS-63, April 2014; $3,672, AU-53, October 2014											
1857-S	87,000	133	47.0	6%	$700	$850	$1,100	$2,000	$10,500	$30,000		
Auctions: $2,820, AU-58, September 2015; $2,350, AU-58, September 2015; $881, AU-55, August 2014; $1,528, AU-55, September 2014											
1858	15,136	80	53.1	14%	$600	$700	$900	$1,250	$3,250	$8,000	$12,500	$50,000
Auctions: $14,100, MS-64, June 2015; $4,935, MS-62, August 2015; $1,410, AU-55, August 2014; $881, EF-40, August 2015											
1858, Proof (x)	4–6	5	65.6							$75,000	$100,000	$150,000
Auctions: $195,500, PF-66UCamH, March 2006											
1858-C	38,856	197	51.6	12%	$2,000	$2,500	$3,750	$4,500	$9,000	$30,000	$55,000	
Auctions: $9,400, MS-61, August 2013; $3,055, AU-55, August 2014; $2,585, EF-40, January 2015; $1,175, EF-40, August 2015											
1858-D	15,362	114	50.7	8%	$2,000	$2,500	$3,750	$4,750	$10,500	$32,500	$45,000	$85,000
Auctions: $17,625, MS-61, June 2013; $9,988, MS-61, February 2015; $7,638, MS-61, August 2014; $3,525, AU-55, June 2015											
1858-S	18,600	62	46.8	2%	$1,500	$3,000	$5,250	$9,000	$25,000			
Auctions: $7,050, AU-55, March 2014											

† Ranked in the *100 Greatest U.S. Coins* (fifth edition). **v.** 3 examples are known. **w.** 2 examples are known. **x.** 4 or 5 examples are known today. One resides in the Smithsonian's National Numismatic Collection, another in the collection of the American Numismatic Society. In recent decades the collections of Eliasberg, Trompeter, and Bass have included examples.

	Mintage	Cert	Avg	%MS	VF-20	EF-40	AU-50	AU-55	MS-60	MS-63 / PF-63	MS-64 / PF-64	MS-65 / PF-65
1859	16,734	99	50.6	8%	$700	$950	$1,650	$2,000	$6,000	$18,000	$40,000	
	Auctions: $17,625, MS-63 Prooflike, June 2014; $21,150, MS-62, April 2015; $2,585, AU-58, August 2015; $2,115, AU-55, October 2015											
1859, Proof	80	5	63.8							$45,000	$85,000	$125,000
	Auctions: $158,625, PF-66UCam, August 2015											
1859-C	31,847	164	50.9	8%	$2,000	$2,500	$3,500	$5,000	$10,500	$35,000		
	Auctions: $8,225, MS-61, January 2014; $4,113, AU-55, August 2014; $1,645, AU-50, July 2014; $1,469, VF-25, August 2014											
1859-D	10,366	113	50.9	12%	$2,000	$2,750	$3,750	$5,000	$10,000	$35,000		
	Auctions: $19,975, MS-62, January 2014; $2,938, MS-60, July 2014; $7,050, AU-58, June 2015; $2,115, AU-50, January 2015											
1859-S	13,220	31	46.5	3%	$1,500	$3,500	$5,000	$6,500	$25,000			
	Auctions: $8,695, AU-58, October 2013; $6,463, AU-53, August 2014; $4,230, EF-45, October 2015											
1860	19,763	126	52.5	6%	$700	$1,000	$1,500	$2,000	$3,750	$17,500	$25,000	
	Auctions: $4,700, AU-58, January 2014; $2,233, AU-58, August 2014; $646, AU-50, July 2014											
1860, Proof	62	4	64.3							$37,500	$75,000	$115,000
	Auctions: $103,500, PF-66CamH, January 2012											
1860-C	14,813	127	53.2	17%	$2,000	$2,750	$4,250	$6,500	$11,000	$25,000	$50,000	
	Auctions: $20,124, MS-63, April 2013; $4,113, AU-50, August 2014; $3,525, AU-50, June 2015; $2,585, EF-40, October 2014											
1860-D	14,635	130	51.1	12%	$2,250	$3,500	$4,500	$6,000	$13,000	$40,000	$65,000	
	Auctions: $14,100, MS-62, March 2014; $5,405, AU-58, June 2015; $3,760, AU-53, February 2015; $3,760, EF-45, September 2015											
1860-S	21,200	58	45.8	2%	$2,000	$3,500	$6,500	$9,500	$29,500			
	Auctions: $19,975, AU-58, April 2014; $4,994, AU-53, October 2014; $2,585, EF-45, September 2014											
1861	688,084	1,982	55.5	15%	$600	$700	$800	$850	$1,750	$5,500	$10,500	$35,000
	Auctions: $32,900, MS-65, January 2015; $2,820, MS-62, January 2015; $1,528, AU-55, January 2015; $376, EF-40, June 2015											
1861, Proof	66	2	65.0							$35,000	$75,000	$115,000
	Auctions: $117,500, PF-66Cam, August 2015											
1861-C	6,879	82	51.4	9%	$6,000	$9,500	$14,000	$17,000	$30,000	$100,000		
	Auctions: $25,850, MS-61, January 2014; $6,463, AU-50, January 2015; $3,290, AU-50, August 2014; $9,694, EF-45, January 2015											
1861-D	1,597	38	52.6	11%	$25,000	$40,000	$45,000	$60,000	$90,000	$200,000		
	Auctions: $99,875, MS-62, January 2014; $42,314, AU-53, August 2016; $42,300, AU-50, September 2016; $51,002, AU-55, April 2018											
1861-S	18,000	46	41.9	0%	$3,250	$6,500	$8,500	$12,500				
	Auctions: $11,163, AU-53, March 2014; $9,988, AU-53, January 2015; $8,813, AU-53, January 2015; $4,259, VF-35, August 2014											
1862	4,430	43	52.4	5%	$2,500	$5,000	$8,500	$13,500	$25,000			
	Auctions: $14,702, AU-58, August 2014; $17,625, AU-55, April 2013											
1862, Proof	35	8	64.5							$35,000	$75,000	$115,000
	Auctions: $92,000, PF-65UCam, August 2011											
1862-S	9,500	39	40.8	5%	$4,250	$8,500	$12,500	$17,500	$50,000			
	Auctions: $15,275, AU-53, March 2014; $4,406, VF-25, August 2014											
1863	2,442	18	52.7	6%	$3,500	$8,500	$18,500	$27,500	$50,000			
	Auctions: $35,250, AU-58, September 2016; $32,900, AU-58, August 2016: $30,550, AU-58, January 2014; $15,275, AU-50, March 2016											
1863, Proof	30	3	65.3							$35,000	$75,000	$115,000
	Auctions: $69,000, PF-64DCam, November 2005											
1863-S	17,000	58	41.4	0%	$3,500	$5,000	$16,000	$22,500	$50,000			
	Auctions: $16,450, AU-55, March 2014											
1864	4,170	57	51.0	7%	$2,500	$4,000	$8,500	$14,000	$22,500			
	Auctions: $12,925, AU-55, January 2014; $10,575, AU-55, June 2015; $10,281, AU-55, October 2015											
1864, Proof	50	19	64.6							$35,000	$75,000	$115,000
	Auctions: $103,500, PF-65UCam, October 2011											
1864-S	3,888	9	39.3	0%	$20,000	$45,000	$75,000	$85,000	$125,000			
	Auctions: $79,313, EF-45, March 2014											

	Mintage	Cert	Avg	%MS	VF-20	EF-40	AU-50	AU-55	MS-60	MS-63	MS-64	MS-65
										PF-63	PF-64	PF-65
1865	1,270	25	53.1	12%	$7,500	$12,000	$20,000	$25,000	$35,000			
Auctions: $17,626, AU-55, August 2014; $18,800, AU-53, January 2014; $17,625, AU-53, August 2015												
1865, Proof	25	13	64.5							$35,000	$75,000	$115,000
Auctions: $86,250, PF-65UCam, April 2012												
1865-S	27,612	89	43.4	6%	$2,750	$4,250	$7,000	$8,000	$14,500		$70,000	
Auctions: $8,813, AU-55, March 2014; $5,875, EF-45, August 2014												
1866-S, No Motto	9,000	54	36.4	0%	$2,250	$5,000	$8,500	$11,500	$30,000			
Auctions: $14,688, AU-58, March 2014; $14,100, AU-58, January 2015; $5,581, AU-50, August 2014; $2,350, VF-20, August 2014												
1866, Motto Above Eagle	6,700	47	53.8	13%	$1,000	$2,000	$3,000	$5,000	$12,000	$40,000		
Auctions: $34,075, MS-63, February 2013; $12,338, MS-61, January 2015; $3,290, AU-55, August 2014; $3,055, EF-40, September 2015												
1866, Motto Above Eagle, Proof	30	6	61.8							$25,000	$40,000	$65,000
Auctions: $80,500, PF-66UCamH, August 2010												
1866-S, Motto Above Eagle	34,920	52	37.7	0%	$1,250	$2,750	$7,000	$11,000	$25,000			
Auctions: $4,994, AU-50, June 2013; $2,585, EF-45, August 2014; $1,469, VF-30, October 2014												
1867	6,870	61	50.3	5%	$1,000	$1,750	$3,000	$5,000	$10,000			
Auctions: $16,450, MS-61, September 2014; $8,813, MS-60, January 2014; $881, AU-50, August 2014												
1867, Proof	50	4	63.3							$25,000	$40,000	$60,000
Auctions: $21,150, PF-63Cam, August 2014												
1867-S	29,000	79	38.2	0%	$1,100	$2,000	$5,500	$10,000				
Auctions: $1,351, EF-40, January 2015; $1,293, VF-30, October 2015; $1,058, VF-20, June 2015; $458, F-12, January 2015												
1868	5,700	58	51.6	5%	$600	$1,000	$2,500	$4,750	$10,000			
Auctions: $16,450, MS-61, April 2013; $5,405, AU-58, October 2015; $4,935, AU-55, July 2015; $2,233, AU-50, August 2014												
1868, Proof	25	3	64.7							$25,000	$40,000	$60,000
Auctions: $69,000, PF-64DCam, June 2008												
1868-S	52,000	118	42.4	1%	$600	$1,250	$3,000	$4,500	$20,000			
Auctions: $18,213, MS-61, June 2015; $23,500, MS-60, March 2014; $1,645, AU-53, October 2014; $1,827, AU-50, July 2014												
1869	1,760	38	52.6	8%	$1,100	$2,750	$5,000	$8,000	$15,000	$30,000	$40,000	
Auctions: $9,400, AU-55, April 2014; $4,700, AU-53, February 2015; $4,700, EF-45, September 2016; $2,267, EF-40, August 2014												
1869, Proof	25	5	64.0							$25,000	$40,000	$60,000
Auctions: $69,000, PF-65Cam, April 2012												
1869-S	31,000	113	40.4	3%	$650	$1,500	$3,000	$5,000	$16,000			
Auctions: $17,625, MS-61, July 2014; $2,233, AU-50, September 2015; $1,998, EF-45, August 2014												
1870	4,000	47	48.9	2%	$900	$2,000	$3,250	$5,000	$15,000			
Auctions: $7,640, AU-58, September 2014; $8,225, AU-55, January 2014; $2,180, VF-30, October 2015; $1,410, VF-30, October 2014												
1870, Proof	35	2	64.0							$25,000	$40,000	$75,000
Auctions: $82,250, PF-64, January 2014												
1870-CC	7,675	44	34.4	2%	$22,500	$35,000	$55,000	$70,000	$110,000			
Auctions: $47,000, AU-53, January 2014												
1870-S	17,000	97	40.0	0%	$1,000	$2,350	$5,500	$8,500	$25,000			
Auctions: $12,925, AU-58, August 2014; $1,763, AU-50, September 2015; $2,115, EF-40, July 2014; $1,116, VF-25, August 2014												
1871	3,200	46	54.1	7%	$1,200	$1,600	$2,650	$4,500	$10,000			
Auctions: $15,275, MS-61, September 2013; $3,525, AU-55, August 2014; $2,820, AU-53, August 2014												
1871, Proof	30	6	60.8							$25,000	$40,000	$60,000
Auctions: $73,438, PF-66Cam, August 2015; $70,500, PF-65Cam, September 2014												
1871-CC	20,770	92	37.5	2%	$5,000	$10,000	$15,000	$25,000	$55,000	$80,000		
Auctions: $48,469, MS-61, April 2013; $2,115, EF-40, July 2014; $5,288, EF-40, September 2014; $3,173, VF-30, August 2014												
1871-S	25,000	105	45.5	2%	$700	$1,100	$2,500	$4,000	$13,500	$35,000		
Auctions: $35,250, MS-63, August 2014; $25,850, MS-61, March 2014; $2,364, AU-50, August 2015; $2,585, VF-25, August 2014												

1873, Close 3 **1873, Open 3**

	Mintage	Cert	Avg	%MS	VF-20	EF-40	AU-50	AU-55	MS-60	MS-63 PF-63	MS-64 PF-64	MS-65 PF-65
1872	1,660	28	54.3	14%	$1,000	$2,000	$4,500	$5,500	$10,500	$20,000	$25,000	
	Auctions: $5,434, AU-58, April 2014											
1872, Proof	30	6	62.7							$22,500	$40,000	$60,000
	Auctions: $7,188, PF-55, March 2012											
1872-CC	16,980	71	34.7	0%	$4,000	$8,500	$16,000	$26,500				
	Auctions: $28,200, AU-58, March 2014; $11,764, AU-50, August 2014; $1,175, F-12, November 2014											
1872-S	36,400	120	42.3	2%	$800	$1,100	$2,750	$4,000	$12,000			
	Auctions: $3,055, AU-55, October 2014; $2,233, AU-50, August 2015; $1,998, AU-50, February 2015; $1,880, AU-50, October 2015											
1873, Close 3	112,480	313	55.6	23%	$600	$605	$610	$615	$1,000	$4,000	$7,500	$17,500
	Auctions: $5,875, MS-64, December 2013; $3,055, MS-63, July 2015; $852, MS-61, September 2014; $470, AU-58, August 2014											
1873, Open 3	112,505	348	55.8	24%	$600	$605	$610	$615	$1,000	$3,500	$8,000	$20,000
	Auctions: $5,875, MS-64, September 2013; $2,703, MS-63, May 2015; $363, AU-58, August 2015; $317, EF-40, October 2014											
1873, Close 3, Proof	25	9	64.3							$22,500	$40,000	$60,000
	Auctions: $24,675, PF-63Cam, August 2014; $12,338, PF-58, January 2014											
1873-CC	7,416	40	34.8	3%	$7,500	$15,000	$27,000	$38,000	$75,000			
	Auctions: $11,750, AU-50, August 2014; $21,150, AU-50, January 2013; $14,688, EF-45, September 2016; $5,581, F-12, August 2014											
1873-S	31,000	112	41.2	1%	$600	$1,100	$2,000	$3,500	$18,500			
	Auctions: $2,233, AU-55, August 2014; $3,173, AU-53, January 2014; $823, VF-35, January 2015; $376, VF-20, November 2015											
1874	3,488	57	50.3	7%	$850	$1,400	$2,250	$3,000	$10,000	$22,500		
	Auctions: $4,700, AU-58, January 2014; $3,290, AU-55, August 2014											
1874, Proof	20	3	66.0							$27,500	$50,000	$75,000
	Auctions: $54,625, PF-65CamH, August 2011											
1874-CC	21,198	126	37.2	2%	$3,000	$4,750	$12,000	$17,000	$35,000	$125,000		
	Auctions: $21,738, AU-58, August 2014; $14,100, AU-55, August 2015; $4,348, VF-35, February 2015; $734, F, March 2015											
1874-S	16,000	92	41.9	0%	$800	$1,650	$3,000	$4,750				
	Auctions: $3,760, AU-55, August 2015; $2,820, AU-55, January 2015; $2,820, AU-53, September 2015; $1,645, EF-45, October 2015											
1875	200	3	50.0	0%	$85,000	$100,000	$150,000	$250,000				
	Auctions: $211,500, AU-55, April 2014											
1875, Proof (y)	20	5	60.4							$150,000	$175,000	$250,000
	Auctions: $176,250, PF-65Cam, January 2014											
1875-CC	11,828	94	36.8	0%	$4,000	$8,000	$16,000	$25,000	$45,000			
	Auctions: $17,625, AU-58, January 2014											
1875-S	9,000	66	42.5	3%	$1,250	$2,500	$4,250	$7,500	$18,500			
	Auctions: $8,813, AU-58, August 2014; $3,819, AU-55, August 2014; $2,585, AU-50, August 2014; $3,055, AU-50, August 2013											
1876	1,432	25	55.4	16%	$1,750	$4,500	$5,500	$7,500	$14,000	$25,000	$32,500	$45,000
	Auctions: $19,975, MS-63, March 2013											
1876, Proof	45	18	64.0							$20,000	$25,000	$47,500
	Auctions: $48,469, PF-65Cam, February 2013											
1876-CC	6,887	80	38.3	3%	$4,500	$8,000	$14,000	$19,000	$50,000			
	Auctions: $21,150, AU-58, March 2014; $4,113, VF-25, July 2014											
1876-S	4,000	24	40.3	4%	$3,250	$5,500	$10,000	$12,500	$30,000			
	Auctions: $18,800, AU-58, March 2014											

y. The mintages of only 200 circulation strikes and 20 Proofs for the year 1875 combine to make the Proof a high-demand coin; hence its strong market value.

1881, Final 1 Over 0
FS-G5-1881-301.

1881, Recut 1881 Over 1881
FS-G5-1881-303.

	Mintage	Cert	Avg	%MS	VF-20	EF-40	AU-50	AU-55	MS-60	MS-63 / PF-63	MS-64 / PF-64	MS-65 / PF-65
1877	1,132	49	54.1	22%	$2,250	$3,750	$5,500	$6,000	$12,500			
Auctions: $7,638, AU-58, April 2014; $1,645, AU-50, June 2015; $1,469, AU-50, August 2015; $3,525, EF-45, July 2014												
1877, Proof	20	2	65.5							$22,500	$32,500	$57,500
Auctions: $51,750, PF-63, June 2005												
1877-CC	8,680	100	39.8	0%	$3,500	$6,000	$13,000	$21,500	$50,000			
Auctions: $14,688, AU-55, November 2014; $11,163, AU-53, July 2014; $8,871, AU-50, January 2015; $3,760, AU-50, August 2015												
1877-S	26,700	136	45.1	1%	$650	$800	$1,500	$3,000	$8,500	$20,000	$30,000	
Auctions: $1,645, AU-55, February 2015; $1,293, AU-53, August 2014; $1,175, EF-45, August 2014; $411, EF-40, June 2015												
1878	131,720	443	58.9	52%	$550	$560	$570	$580	$625	$1,750	$4,000	$8,500
Auctions: $8,813, MS-65, January 2015; $8,225, MS-65, September 2015; $3,525, MS-64, August 2014; $400, AU-58, March 2015												
1878, Proof	20	7	64.3							$22,500	$32,500	$57,500
Auctions: $31,725, PF-63DCam, June 2014												
1878-CC	9,054	51	43.9	4%	$5,500	$11,000	$17,500	$32,000				
Auctions: $47,000, AU-58, March 2014; $7,344, VF-25, September 2016												
1878-S	144,700	509	56.2	22%	$550	$560	$570	$580	$675	$4,000	$7,000	$20,000
Auctions: $423, AU-58, August 2015; $400, AU-55, March 2015; $323, AU-50, September 2015; $341, EF-45, August 2015												
1879	301,920	744	59.0	54%	$550	$560	$570	$580	$600	$1,500	$3,600	$8,500
Auctions: $6,463, MS-65, September 2014; $4,406, MS-64, September 2014; $2,115, MS-64, March 2015; $458, MS-60, February 2015												
1879, Proof	30	6	64.2							$22,500	$30,000	$55,000
Auctions: $63,250, PF-65Cam, April 2012												
1879-CC	17,281	171	44.2	5%	$1,750	$2,750	$4,000	$7,500	$25,000			
Auctions: $21,150, MS-60, March 2014; $8,813, AU-58, August 2014; $1,116, VG-8, June 2015; $764, G-6, July 2014												
1879-S	426,200	769	57.0	25%	$550	$560	$570	$580	$650	$1,750	$6,000	$25,000
Auctions: $1,058, MS-63, January 2015; $541, MS-61, February 2015; $376, AU-58, January 2015; $282, AU-50, July 2015												
1880	3,166,400	3,226	59.7	71%	$550	$560	$570	$580	$600	$800	$1,000	$1,850
Auctions: $10,575, MS-66, October 2015; $4,348, MS-65, August 2015; $705, MS-63, July 2015; $376, EF-40, February 2015												
1880, Proof	36	7	65.7							$17,500	$30,000	$52,500
Auctions: $72,702, PF-67Cam, August 2006												
1880-CC	51,017	330	44.9	3%	$1,250	$1,500	$2,000	$4,750	$12,500	$45,000		
Auctions: $14,100, MS-61, September 2016: $11,750, MS-61, January 2014; $705, VF-20, January 2015; $1,058, F-15, January 2015												
1880-S	1,348,900	2,393	60.9	83%	$550	$560	$570	$580	$600	$800	$1,100	$8,500
Auctions: $1,410, MS-64, January 2015; $940, MS-64, January 2015; $400, MS-62, January 2015; $329, AU-55, February 2015												
1881, Final 1 Over 0 (z)	(aa)	117	58.4	52%	$600	$650	$675	$750	$1,350	$2,500	$8,000	
Auctions: $2,233, MS-63, January 2014; $646, AU-55, August 2014; $499, EF-40, July 2014												
1881, Recut 1881 Over 1881	(aa)	8	57.4	38%				$750	$950	$1,450		
Auctions: $705, MS-63, August 2014; $1,528, MS-62, April 2014												
1881	5,708,760	18,240	61.4	91%	$550	$560	$570	$580	$600	$750	$925	$1,750
Auctions: $1,058, MS-64, June 2015; $435, MS-62, March 2015; $423, MS-61, July 2015; $329, AU-55, July 2015												
1881, Proof	42	11	65.6							$16,500	$25,000	$40,000
Auctions: $37,375, PF-65Cam, January 2011												
1881-CC	13,886	87	45.7	10%	$1,750	$3,500	$7,000	$10,500	$25,000	$55,000		
Auctions: $32,900, MS-62, May 2013; $11,750, AU-58, September 2016; $3,055, EF-40, August 2014; $1,763, VF-30, July 2014												
1881-S	969,000	2,024	61.2	88%	$550	$560	$570	$580	$600	$750	$1,250	$3,250
Auctions: $1,058, MS-64, January 2015; $969, MS-64, February 2015; $687, MS-63, January 2015; $494, MS-62, January 2015												

z. The last digit of the date is repunched over the remnants of a zero; this is easily visible with the naked eye, making the 1 Over 0 a popular variety. **aa.** Included in circulation-strike 1881 mintage figure.

	Mintage	Cert	Avg	%MS	VF-20	EF-40	AU-50	AU-55	MS-60	MS-63 / PF-63	MS-64 / PF-64	MS-65 / PF-65
1882	2,514,520	8,578	61.5	91%	$550	$560	$570	$580	$600	$750	$925	$3,500
	Auctions: $2,468, MS-65, May 2015; $999, MS-64, August 2015; $588, MS-63, August 2015; $454, MS-62, February 2015											
1882, Proof	48	11	64.3							$15,500	$25,000	$40,000
	Auctions: $9,085, PF-63Cam, February 2010											
1882-CC	82,817	609	50.5	5%	$1,000	$1,500	$2,000	$4,000	$11,500	$35,000		
	Auctions: $18,800, MS-62, February 2015; $1,175, AU-50, February 2015; $1,116, AU-50, January 2015; $734, EF-40, February 2015											
1882-S	969,000	2,537	61.5	92%	$550	$560	$570	$580	$600	$750	$925	$2,500
	Auctions: $3,408, MS-65, January 2015; $999, MS-64, January 2015; $823, MS-64, January 2015; $447, MS-62, January 2015											
1883	233,400	507	60.2	71%	$550	$560	$570	$580	$600	$1,250	$2,250	$12,500
	Auctions: $17,625, MS-67, February 2013; $1,410, MS-64, September 2015; $1,116, MS-63, June 2015; $411, AU-58, August 2014											
1883, Proof	61	9	64.0							$15,500	$25,000	$40,000
	Auctions: $5,288, PF-55, September 2014											
1883-CC	12,598	134	49.6	7%	$2,000	$3,000	$4,500	$6,750	$18,500	$50,000		
	Auctions: $18,213, MS-61, August 2014; $7,638, AU-58, August 2015; $5,875, AU-55, January 2015; $3,305, AU-50, September 2016											
1883-S	83,200	253	58.3	53%	$550	$560	$570	$580	$700	$1,650	$7,000	
	Auctions: $7,050, MS-64, August 2013; $706, MS-61, July 2015; $382, AU-58, January 2015; $1,058, AU-53, August 2014											
1884	191,030	492	59.1	58%	$550	$560	$570	$580	$600	$1,650	$2,750	$9,000
	Auctions: $2,468, MS-64, February 2013; $881, MS-62, July 2015; $588, MS-62, November 2015; $588, MS-61, August 2015											
1884, Proof	48	5	64.4							$15,500	$25,000	$40,000
	Auctions: $39,100, PF-66UCam, November 2010											
1884-CC	16,402	185	49.5	4%	$1,250	$2,750	$5,000	$7,500	$22,500			
	Auctions: $8,225, AU-58, January 2014; $8,519, AU-58, October 2014; $4,994, AU-55, August 2014											
1884-S	177,000	477	59.7	67%	$550	$560	$570	$580	$600	$1,150	$3,500	$9,500
	Auctions: $999, MS-63, August 2015; $940, MS-63, June 2015; $588, MS-62, October 2015; $541, MS-62, August 2015											
1885	601,440	1,496	61.1	83%	$550	$560	$570	$580	$600	$750	$1,250	$4,500
	Auctions: $1,528, MS-64, July 2015; $676, MS-63, July 2015; $517, MS-62, May 2015; $400, AU-53, February 2015											
1885, Proof	66	19	64.6							$15,500	$25,000	$40,000
	Auctions: $70,500, PF-67UCam, August 2015; $56,400, PF-66UCam, January 2015; $31,725, PF-65DCam, August 2014											
1885-S	1,211,500	4,589	61.9	94%	$550	$560	$570	$580	$600	$750	$925	$2,000
	Auctions: $5,170, MS-66, January 2015; $705, MS-63, August 2015; $458, MS-61, January 2015; $376, AU-55, July 2015											
1886	388,360	806	60.1	70%	$550	$560	$570	$580	$600	$700	$2,500	$5,500
	Auctions: $5,288, MS-65, June 2013; $573, MS-63, August 2014; $499, MS-61, July 2014											
1886, Proof	72	9	64.2							$15,500	$25,000	$40,000
	Auctions: $57,281, PF, March 2014											
1886-S	3,268,000	9,054	61.4	92%	$550	$560	$570	$580	$600	$750	$925	$1,750
	Auctions: $2,350, MS-65, January 2015; $823, MS-64, October 2015; $458, MS-62, January 2015; $400, MS-60, October 2015											
1887, Proof (bb)	87	18	62.6							$65,000	$80,000	$115,000
	Auctions: $54,050, PF, August 2013											
1887-S	1,912,000	3,631	61.1	90%	$550	$560	$570	$580	$600	$750	$1,100	$4,000
	Auctions: $1,410, MS-64, January 2015; $940, MS-64, July 2015; $881, MS-64, July 2015; $470, MS-62, June 2015											
1888	18,201	173	59.8	68%	$550	$560	$570	$580	$650	$1,750	$3,000	$12,500
	Auctions: $1,775, MS-63, January 2014; $764, MS-61, January 2015; $588, MS-60, August 2014											
1888, Proof	95	18	64.7							$13,500	$20,000	$32,500
	Auctions: $34,500, PF-65DCam, October 2008											
1888-S	293,900	352	55.0	23%	$550	$560	$570	$580	$1,000	$3,500		
	Auctions: $2,350, MS-64, August 2013; $1,116, MS-63, October 2014; $470, AU-53, July 2014; $368, EF-40, August 2014											
1889	7,520	159	58.1	43%	$575	$600	$700	$950	$1,250	$4,500	$6,000	
	Auctions: $4,406, MS-63, June 2014; $1,763, MS-62, September 2015; $1,058, AU-55, July 2015; $1,175, AU-53, August 2014											
1889, Proof	45	11	64.3							$14,000	$22,500	$35,000
	Auctions: $29,900, PF-65Cam, January 2011											

bb. Proof only.

	Mintage	Cert	Avg	%MS	VF-20	EF-40	AU-50	AU-55	MS-60	MS-63	MS-64	MS-65
										PF-63	PF-64	PF-65
1890	4,240	80	55.8	28%	$650	$850	$950	$1,250	$2,250	$6,000	$10,000	$15,000
	Auctions: $5,581, MS-62, June 2014; $1,000, AU-55, July 2014; $823, AU-50, August 2014											
1890, Proof	88	30	64.8							$14,000	$22,500	$35,000
	Auctions: $24,675, PF-64DCam, January 2014											
1890-CC	53,800	658	56.8	45%	$800	$1,000	$1,100	$1,500	$2,250	$8,500	$15,000	$45,000
	Auctions: $11,750, MS-64, June 2015; $9,400, MS-63, October 2015; $5,640, MS-63, March 2016; $2,820, MS-62, June 2015											
1891	61,360	399	60.5	78%	$550	$560	$570	$580	$600	$1,250	$3,250	$12,000
	Auctions: $4,700, MS-64, February 2013; $499, MS-61, August 2014; $400, AU-58, August 2015; $353, AU-53, September 2015											
1891, Proof	53	13	65.0							$13,500	$20,000	$32,500
	Auctions: $19,550, PF-64DCam, January 2010											
1891-CC	208,000	2,207	57.8	51%	$850	$1,000	$1,150	$1,450	$2,000	$4,500	$7,500	$32,500
	Auctions: $5,875, MS-64, January 2015; $1,175, AU-58, June 2015; $823, EF-45, July 2015; $764, VF-30, October 2015											
1892	753,480	2,213	61.5	92%	$550	$560	$570	$580	$600	$750	$1,100	$2,000
	Auctions: $3,760, MS-66, July 2015; $2,585, MS-65, September 2015; $823, MS-63, January 2015; $329, AU-50, September 2015											
1892, Proof	92	19	63.9							$13,500	$18,000	$32,500
	Auctions: $6,325, PF-62Cam, December 2011											
1892-CC	82,968	807	53.8	19%	$750	$1,000	$1,100	$1,350	$2,500	$9,000	$22,500	$42,500
	Auctions: $2,511, MS-61, February 2015; $1,058, AU-55, January 2015; $881, EF-45, January 2015; $541, VG-8, January 2015											
1892-O	10,000	42	57.3	36%	$1,800	$2,250	$2,650	$3,000	$5,000	$18,500		
	Auctions: $8,225, MS-62, December 2013; $3,290, AU-58, July 2014; $3,290, AU-58, August 2014											
1892-S	298,400	476	57.7	45%	$550	$560	$570	$580	$600	$1,800	$4,250	$7,500
	Auctions: $4,230, MS-64, January 2015; $2,350, MS-63, April 2013; $823, MS-62, August 2015; $400, MS-60, October 2015											
1893	1,528,120	9,415	62.0	97%	$550	$560	$570	$580	$600	$750	$925	$2,000
	Auctions: $4,230, MS-66, June 2015; $3,995, MS-66, January 2015; $940, MS-64, September 2015; $852, MS-64, January 2015											
1893, Proof	77	22	64.2							$13,500	$18,000	$32,500
	Auctions: $70,500, PF, August 2013											
1893-CC	60,000	716	55.6	26%	$850	$1,100	$1,300	$1,800	$3,000	$10,000	$22,500	$30,000
	Auctions: $24,675, MS-64, August 2015; $2,115, AU-58, June 2015; $1,410, AU-53, July 2015; $969, EF-40, February 2015											
1893-O	110,000	477	58.8	49%	$575	$585	$600	$625	$1,000	$5,000	$9,500	
	Auctions: $7,638, MS-64, January 2014; $1,880, MS-62, July 2015; $541, MS-60, August 2015; $529, AU-58, August 2014											
1893-S	224,000	1,104	60.9	84%	$550	$560	$570	$580	$600	$750	$1,750	$8,500
	Auctions: $1,645, MS-64, October 2015; $999, MS-64, July 2015; $482, MS-62, October 2015; $447, MS-61, October 2015											
1894	957,880	3,765	61.8	96%	$550	$560	$570	$580	$600	$750	$900	$3,300
	Auctions: $3,760, MS-65, January 2015; $1,058, MS-64, June 2015; $458, MS-62, August 2015; $329, MS-60, July 2015											
1894, Proof	75	24	64.1							$13,500	$18,500	$32,500
	Auctions: $58,750, PF-67DCam, October 2014; $37,600, PF-66UCam, August 2015; $29,375, PF-64UCam, August 2015											
1894-O	16,600	357	57.7	35%	$575	$585	$600	$800	$2,000	$8,500		
	Auctions: $3,525, MS-62, June 2014; $1,888, MS-61, July 2014; $1,175, AU-58, September 2015; $823, AU-55, November 2014											
1894-S	55,900	232	53.2	12%	$575	$600	$650	$750	$2,500	$9,000	$16,000	
	Auctions: $3,819, MS-62, March 2015; $2,938, MS-62, July 2015; $2,350, MS-60, February 2015; $881, AU-58, August 2014											
1895	1,345,855	9,118	61.8	95%	$550	$560	$570	$580	$600	$750	$900	$1,675
	Auctions: $19,975, MS-67, January 2015; $7,931, MS-66, February 2015; $564, MS-63, July 2015; $423, MS-61, May 2015											
1895, Proof	81	27	64.9							$12,500	$18,000	$30,000
	Auctions: $6,233, PF-60, February 2014											
1895-S	112,000	322	53.5	8%	$550	$560	$570	$650	$1,500	$5,000	$8,000	$18,500
	Auctions: $2,350, MS-62, September 2015; $1,645, MS-61, September 2015; $1,586, MS-61, June 2015; $447, AU-53, October 2015											
1896	58,960	522	61.7	93%	$550	$560	$570	$580	$600	$750	$1,500	$7,500
	Auctions: $1,410, MS-64, August 2015; $1,293, MS-64, June 2015; $1,293, MS-64, January 2015; $382, AU-55, August 2014											
1896, Proof	103	24	65.1							$12,500	$18,000	$30,000
	Auctions: $35,250, PF-65DCam, September 2014											
1896-S	155,400	407	54.5	19%	$550	$560	$570	$580	$1,100	$5,500	$8,500	$20,000
	Auctions: $7,064, MS-64, January 2015; $4,230, MS-63, July 2015; $3,525, MS-63, August 2015; $2,233, MS-62, January 2015											

1901-S, Final 1 Over 0
FS-G5-1901S-301.

	Mintage	Cert	Avg	%MS	VF-20	EF-40	AU-50	AU-55	MS-60	MS-63	MS-64	MS-65
										PF-63	PF-64	PF-65
1897	867,800	4,530	61.6	92%	$550	$560	$570	$580	$600	$750	$900	$1,800
	Auctions: $8,225, MS-66, January 2015; $1,175, MS-64, August 2015; $505, MS-62, July 2015; $388, AU-58, July 2015											
1897, Proof	83	27	64.6							$12,500	$18,000	$30,000
	Auctions: $9,988, PF-63, June 2014											
1897-S	354,000	444	56.1	25%	$550	$560	$570	$580	$800	$4,000	$5,000	$8,500
	Auctions: $15,275, MS-66, March 2015; $1,645, MS-62, July 2014; $499, MS-61, August 2014; $388, AU-58, November 2015											
1898	633,420	2,652	61.5	93%	$550	$560	$570	$580	$600	$750	$1,500	$3,000
	Auctions: $8,225, MS-66, June 2015; $3,643, MS-65, June 2015; $1,028, MS-64, June 2015; $447, MS-62, August 2015											
1898, Proof	75	35	64.8							$12,500	$18,000	$30,000
	Auctions: $105,750, PF-67UCam, August 2015; $29,375, PF-65DCam, September 2014; $18,800, PF-64DCam+, August 2015											
1898-S	1,397,400	731	59.1	66%	$550	$560	$570	$580	$600	$1,100	$2,750	$6,500
	Auctions: $70,500, MS-68, June 2015; $5,434, MS-65, June 2014; $7,050, MS-65, October 2014; $4,406, MS-64, August 2014											
1899	1,710,630	13,768	62.5	98%	$550	$560	$570	$580	$600	$750	$900	$1,675
	Auctions: $2,938, MS-66, June 2015; $2,585, MS-65, January 2015; $447, MS-62, January 2015; $388, AU-55, June 2015											
1899, Proof	99	30	64.5							$12,500	$18,000	$30,000
	Auctions: $134,550, PF, September 2013											
1899-S	1,545,000	1,047	59.2	68%	$550	$560	$570	$580	$600	$1,100	$1,950	$6,500
	Auctions: $1,410, MS-64, January 2015; $764, MS-63, January 2015; $734, MS-62, August 2015; $447, MS-62, March 2015											
1900	1,405,500	17,531	62.1	96%	$550	$560	$570	$580	$600	$750	$900	$1,650
	Auctions: $5,875, MS-66, January 2015; $2,820, MS-65, September 2015; $423, MS-62, July 2015; $329, MS-60, July 2015											
1900, Proof	230	63	64.3							$12,500	$18,000	$30,000
	Auctions: $35,250, PF-65DCam, September 2013											
1900-S	329,000	547	60.2	69%	$550	$560	$570	$580	$600	$850	$1,000	$7,000
	Auctions: $1,293, MS-64, March 2013; $940, MS-64, January 2015; $705, MS-63, August 2014; $529, MS-62, August 2014											
1901	615,900	5,659	61.8	93%	$550	$560	$570	$580	$600	$750	$900	$1,650
	Auctions: $16,450, MS-67, January 2015; $881, MS-64, July 2015; $823, MS-64, June 2015; $423, MS-62, May 2015											
1901, Proof	140	44	64.0							$12,500	$18,000	$30,000
	Auctions: $28,200, PF-65DCam, August 2014											
1901-S, All kinds	3,648,000											
1901-S, Final 1 Over 0		394	60.4	68%	$550	$560	$570	$600	$650	$1,250	$1,500	$3,000
	Auctions: $1,645, MS-64, January 2015; $1,116, MS-63, August 2014; $470, MS-62, October 2014; $401, AU-55, March 2015											
1901-S		8,207	61.9	90%	$550	$560	$570	$580	$600	$750	$900	$1,650
	Auctions: $2,585, MS-66, January 2015; $999, MS-64, June 2015; $705, MS-64, June 2015; $564, MS-63, August 2015											
1902	172,400	1,587	61.8	94%	$550	$560	$570	$580	$600	$750	$900	$1,850
	Auctions: $18,800, MS-67, October 2015; $2,820, MS-65, August 2015; $646, MS-63, June 2015; $535, MS-63, August 2015											
1902, Proof	162	27	63.1							$12,500	$18,000	$30,000
	Auctions: $12,925, PF-64, April 2013											
1902-S	939,000	2,713	62.0	91%	$550	$560	$570	$580	$600	$750	$900	$1,650
	Auctions: $23,500, MS-67, January 2014; $1,998, MS-65, January 2015; $588, MS-63, July 2015; $436, MS-62, March 2015											
1903	226,870	1,947	61.6	92%	$550	$560	$570	$580	$600	$750	$900	$1,650
	Auctions: $3,290, MS-66, July 2014; $3,819, MS-65, February 2014; $2,820, MS-65, September 2015; $423, MS-62, August 2015											
1903, Proof	154	54	63.7							$12,500	$18,000	$30,000
	Auctions: $32,900, PF-65, October 2014; $30,550, PF-65, August 2015; $66,975, PF, March 2014											
1903-S	1,855,000	4,562	62.0	91%	$550	$560	$570	$580	$600	$750	$900	$1,650
	Auctions: $2,585, MS-66, June 2015; $1,763, MS-65, January 2015; $764, MS-64, February 2015; $881, MS-63, September 2015											

	Mintage	Cert	Avg	%MS	VF-20	EF-40	AU-50	AU-55	MS-60	MS-63	MS-64	MS-65
										PF-63	PF-64	PF-65
1904	392,000	4,225	62.0	94%	$550	$560	$570	$580	$600	$750	$900	$1,650
Auctions: $5,170, MS-66, August 2015; $2,128, MS-65, July 2015; $482, MS-63, October 2015; $353, AU-58, June 2015												
1904, Proof	136	54	63.9							$12,500	$18,000	$30,000
Auctions: $31,725, PF-66Cam, June 2013												
1904-S	97,000	295	57.4	35%	$550	$560	$570	$600	$800	$3,000	$4,500	$8,500
Auctions: $4,113, MS-64, April 2013; $2,056, MS-63, January 2015; $423, AU-58, August 2015; $470, AU-55, October 2015												
1905	302,200	2,891	61.9	94%	$550	$560	$570	$580	$600	$750	$900	$1,650
Auctions: $2,350, MS-65, July 2015; $1,880, MS-65, February 2015; $999, MS-64, January 2015; $793, MS-64, June 2015												
1905, Proof	108	37	62.7							$12,500	$18,000	$30,000
Auctions: $23,000, PF-65Cam, October 2010												
1905-S	880,700	1,021	57.2	31%	$550	$560	$570	$600	$700	$1,500	$3,250	$6,500
Auctions: $764, MS-62, July 2015; $411, MS-61, March 2015; $347, AU-58, April 2015; $341, AU-53, March 2015												
1906	348,735	3,046	61.8	92%	$550	$560	$570	$580	$600	$750	$900	$1,650
Auctions: $7,050, MS-66, January 2015; $1,293, MS-64, September 2015; $517, MS-61, June 2015; $447, AU-55, January 2015												
1906, Proof	85	57	63.8							$12,500	$18,000	$30,000
Auctions: $64,625, PF-66Cam, August 2013												
1906-D	320,000	2,812	62.0	93%	$550	$560	$570	$580	$600	$750	$900	$1,650
Auctions: $4,935, MS-66, January 2015; $940, MS-64, August 2015; $823, MS-64, August 2015; $423, MS-60, February 2015												
1906-S	598,000	749	59.9	70%	$550	$560	$570	$580	$600	$1,000	$1,650	$4,500
Auctions: $793, MS-63, January 2015; $646, MS-63, February 2015; $470, MS-62, January 2015; $517, MS-61, June 2015												
1907	626,100	9,509	62.1	96%	$550	$560	$570	$580	$600	$750	$900	$1,650
Auctions: $7,638, MS-67, June 2015; $4,230, MS-66, August 2015; $1,175, MS-64, August 2015; $1,058, MS-64, August 2015												
1907, Proof	92	40	63.9							$12,500	$18,000	$30,000
Auctions: $24,675, PF-65Cam, April 2014												
1907-D	888,000	4,732	62.0	93%	$550	$560	$570	$580	$600	$750	$900	$1,650
Auctions: $1,704, MS-65, February 2015; $1,410, MS-64, September 2015; $423, MS-62, February 2015; $396, MS-61, July 2015												
1908	421,874	6,732	62.4	96%	$550	$560	$570	$580	$600	$750	$900	$1,650
Auctions: $4,465, MS-66, January 2015; $2,585, MS-65, August 2015; $999, MS-64, January 2015; $617, MS-63, January 2015												

INDIAN HEAD (1908–1929)

Designer: *Bela Lyon Pratt.* **Weight:** *8.359 grams.*
Composition: *.900 gold, .100 copper (net weight .24187 oz. pure gold).* **Diameter:** *21.6 mm.*
Edge: *Reeded.* **Mints:** *Philadelphia, Denver, New Orleans, and San Francisco.*

Circulation Strike   **Sandblast Finish Proof**   **Satin Finish Proof**

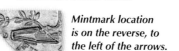

Mintmark location is on the reverse, to the left of the arrows.

History. The Indian Head half eagle made its first appearance in 1908; it was minted continuously through 1916, and again in 1929. Its design elements arc in sunken relief (sometimes imprecisely called "incuse"), like those of the similar quarter eagle; the mintmark is raised. On most examples the rims are flat, while on others they are slightly raised. These coins saw limited circulation in the West, and were rarely encountered elsewhere.

Striking and Sharpness. Striking quality of Indian Head half eagles varies. Look for weakness on the high parts of the Indian's bonnet and in the feather details in the headdress. On the reverse, check the feathers on the highest area of the wing.

Proofs. Sandblast (also called Matte) Proofs were made in 1908 and from 1911 to 1915, while Satin (also called Roman Finish) Proofs were made in 1909 and 1910. At lower levels, these coins can show light contact marks. Some microscopic bright flecks may be caused by the sandblasting process and, although they do not represent handling, usually result in a coin being assigned a slightly lower grade.

Availability. Indian Head half eagles were not popular with numismatists of the time, who saved very few. Rare issues include the 1909-O, which usually is seen with evidence of circulation (often extensive) and the 1929, most of which are in MS. Luster can range from deeply frosty to grainy. Because the fields are the highest areas of the coin, luster diminished quickly as the coins were circulated or jostled with others in bags. When Proof examples are seen, they are usually in higher Proof grades, PF-64 and above. As a class these half eagles are rarer than quarter eagles of the same date and style of finish.

Note: Values of common-date gold coins have been based on the current bullion price of gold, $2,000 per ounce, and may vary with the prevailing spot price.

GRADING STANDARDS

MS-60 to 70 (Mint State). *Obverse:* At MS–60 to 62, there is abrasion in the field, this representing the highest part of the coin. Abrasion is also evident on the headdress. Marks and, occasionally, a microscopic pin scratch may be seen. At MS-63, there may be some abrasion and some tiny marks. Luster is irregular. At MS-64, abrasion is less. Luster is rich. At MS-65 and above, luster is deep and frosty, with no marks at all visible with-

1911-D. Graded MS-62.

out magnification at MS-66 and higher. *Reverse:* At MS–60 to 62 there is abrasion in the field, this representing the highest part of the coin. Abrasion is also evident on the eagle's wing. Otherwise, the same comments apply as for the obverse.

    Illustrated coin: This example is lustrous and attractive. Most of the luster in the fields (the highest-relief area of this unusual design) is still intact.

AU-50, 53, 55, 58 (About Uncirculated). *Obverse:* Friction on the cheek is very noticeable at AU-50, increasingly less at higher levels to AU-58. The headdress shows light wear, most evident on the ribbon above the forehead and on the garland. Luster is minimal at AU-50 and scattered and incomplete at AU-58. Nicks and contact marks are to be expected. *Reverse:* Friction on the wing and neck is very noticeable at AU-50, increasingly

1911. Graded AU-50.

less noticeable at higher levels to AU-58. Otherwise, the same comments apply as for the obverse.

EF-40, 45 (Extremely Fine). *Obverse:* Light wear will characterize the portrait and head-dress. Luster is gone. Marks and tiny scratches are to be expected, but not distracting. *Reverse:* Light wear is most evident on the eagle's head and wing, although other areas are lightly worn as well. Luster is gone. Marks and tiny scratches are to be expected, but not distracting.

1909-O. Graded EF-40.

VF-20, 30 (Very Fine). *Obverse:* Many details of the garland and of the ribbon above the forehead are worn away. Many feather vanes are blended together. The field is dull and has contact marks. *Reverse:* The neck and the upper part of the wing show extensive wear, other areas less so. The field is dull and has contact marks.

  Illustrated coin: Some bumps are seen on the top obverse rim and should be mentioned in a description.

1909. Graded VF-25.

Indian Head half eagles are seldom collected in grades lower than VF-20.

PF-60 to 70 (Proof). *Obverse and Reverse:* At PF–60 to 63, there is light abrasion and some contact marks (the lower the grade, the higher the quantity). On Sandblast Proofs these show up as visually unappealing bright spots. At PF-64 and higher levels, marks are fewer, with magnification needed to see any at PF-65. At PF-66, there should be none at all.

  Illustrated coin: This is a particularly nice example.

1911, Sandblast Finish. Graded PF-67.

	Mintage	Cert	Avg	%MS	VF-20	EF-40	AU-50	AU-55	AU-58	MS-60	MS-62	MS-63	MS-65
											PF-63	PF-64	PF-65
1908	577,845	7,814	61.3	84%	$575	$600	$650	$670	$675	$750	$850	$1,100	$7,500
	Auctions: $51,700, MS-67, January 2015; $911, MS-62, August 2015; $558, AU-58, February 2015; $376, AU-55, March 2015												
1908, Sandblast Finish Proof	167	81	65.4								$15,000	$25,000	$50,000
	Auctions: $152,750, PF, August 2013												
1908-D	148,000	2,817	62.3	94%	$575	$600	$650	$670	$675	$750	$850	$1,100	$25,000
	Auctions: $3,290, MS-64, September 2015; $1,351, MS-63, June 2015; $705, MS-61, August 2015; $470, AU-58, July 2015												
1908-S	82,000	587	57.6	41%	$650	$750	$1,000	$1,350	$2,250	$3,000	$6,000	$9,000	$15,000
	Auctions: $47,000, MS-67, August 2014; $17,625, MS-65, January 2015; $7,344, MS-63, January 2015; $1,175, AU-55, July 2015												

	Mintage	Cert	Avg	%MS	VF-20	EF-40	AU-50	AU-55	AU-58	MS-60	MS-62 / PF-63	MS-63 / PF-64	MS-65 / PF-65
1909	627,060	7,093	60.9	81%	$575	$600	$650	$670	$675	$750	$850	$1,250	$7,500
Auctions: $7,638, MS-65, February 2015; $2,115, MS-64, October 2015; $676, MS-62, October 2015; $764, MS-61, July 2015												
1909, Satin Finish Proof	78	39	65.4								$16,750	$27,500	$55,000
Auctions: $82,250, PF-67, August 2014; $55,813, PF-66, August 2014; $99,875, PF-66, February 2013												
1909, Sandblast Finish Proof (a)	unknown	1	67.0										
Auctions: No auction records available.												
1909-D	3,423,560	32,862	61.5	86%	$575	$600	$650	$670	$675	$750	$850	$1,100	$7,000
Auctions: $2,350, MS-64, March 2015; $764, MS-62, June 2015; $552, MS-61, September 2015; $353, EF-40, April 2015												
1909-O (b)	34,200	997	55.6	16%	$4,750	$7,500	$9,500	$11,500	$17,500	$22,500	$45,000	$85,000	$400,000
Auctions: $56,400, MS-62, December 2015: $35,250, MS-61, August 2015; $32,900, MS-61, March 2016												
1909-S	297,200	759	56.4	27%	$575	$600	$675	$700	$725	$2,100	$6,000	$10,000	$47,500
Auctions: $5,640, MS-62, January 2015; $3,410, MS-61, January 2015; $529, AU-55, March 2015; $400, EF-40, February 2015												
1910	604,000	7,220	60.8	79%	$575	$600	$650	$670	$675	$750	$850	$1,200	$8,500
Auctions: $17,625, MS-65, August 2015; $1,998, MS-64, February 2015; $999, MS-63, October 2015; $447, MS-60, May 2015												
1910, Satin Finish Proof	250	47	65.4								$16,500	$25,000	$55,000
Auctions: $146,250, PF, September 2013												
1910, Sandblast Finish Proof (c)	unknown	0	n/a										
Auctions: No auction records available.												
1910-D	193,600	1,191	60.2	73%	$575	$600	$650	$670	$675	$750	$1,200	$2,300	$26,000
Auctions: $7,050, MS-64, January 2015; $1,029, MS-62, January 2015; $617, MS-61, June 2015; $400, AU-55, May 2015												
1910-S	770,200	1,586	56.8	26%	$575	$600	$650	$670	$800	$1,250	$2,800	$9,000	$75,000
Auctions: $3,290, MS-62, March 2015; $2,056, MS-61, January 2015; $676, AU-58, August 2015; $517, AU-55, August 2015												
1911	915,000	11,107	60.6	76%	$575	$600	$650	$670	$675	$750	$850	$1,200	$8,250
Auctions: $8,225, MS-65, January 2015; $1,880, MS-64, January 2015; $529, MS-61, September 2015												
1911, Sandblast Finish Proof	139	55	65.5								$15,500	$25,000	$47,500
Auctions: $99,875, PF-67, April 2013												
1911-D	72,500	1,521	55.9	16%	$750	$1,000	$1,600	$2,750	$4,250	$7,750	$17,500	$35,000	$225,000
Auctions: $36,425, MS-63, December 2015: $12,925, MS-62, August 2015; $8,813, MS-61, January 2015												
1911-S	1,416,000	2,862	57.0	34%	$575	$600	$650	$670	$675	$825	$1,750	$3,500	$37,500
Auctions: $12,925, MS-64, January 2015; $1,175, MS-61, July 2015; $494, AU-55, June 2015; $376, EF-45, March 2015												
1912	790,000	10,566	60.9	80%	$575	$600	$650	$670	$675	$750	$850	$1,100	$7,500
Auctions: $7,050, MS-65, January 2015; $2,820, MS-64, June 2015; $447, MS-61, October 2015; $482, AU-58, July 2015												
1912, Sandblast Finish Proof	144	38	66.4								$15,500	$25,000	$47,500
Auctions: $58,750, PF-66, September 2013												
1912-S	392,000	1,622	56.0	17%	$575	$600	$650	$670	$850	$1,500	$4,800	$14,000	$180,000
Auctions: $5,405, MS-62, August 2015; $2,820, MS-61, October 2015; $1,293, AU-58, August 2015; $449, AU-53, March 2015												
1913	915,901	12,171	60.9	81%	$575	$600	$650	$670	$675	$750	$850	$1,100	$7,500
Auctions: $2,585, MS-64, March 2015; $1,058, MS-63, October 2015; $764, MS-61, June 2015; $423, AU-58, July 2015												
1913, Sandblast Finish Proof	99	27	66.3								$16,000	$25,000	$50,000
Auctions: $51,750, PF-67, July 2011												
1913-S	408,000	1,969	56.3	22%	$600	$675	$750	$800	$825	$2,000	$4,500	$12,500	$120,000
Auctions: $4,600, MS-62, January 2015; $823, AU-58, July 2015; $470, AU-53, February 2015; $340, EF-40, February 2015												
1914	247,000	2,888	60.7	76%	$575	$600	$650	$670	$675	$750	$850	$1,550	$10,000
Auctions: $9,400, MS-65, January 2015; $5,170, MS-64, August 2015; $1,028, MS-62, June 2015; $541, MS-61, March 2015												
1914, Sandblast Finish Proof	125	31	65.7								$16,500	$25,000	$50,000
Auctions: $93,600, PF, September 2013												
1914-D	247,000	2,655	60.4	71%	$575	$600	$650	$670	$675	$750	$850	$2,000	$20,000
Auctions: $3,760, MS-64, October 2015; $1,880, MS-63, July 2015; $1,058, MS-61, February 2015; $470, AU-58, February 2015												
1914-S	263,000	1,537	57.7	34%	$575	$600	$650	$685	$850	$1,650	$4,000	$7,700	$125,000
Auctions: $16,450, MS-63, August 2015; $2,115, AU-58, September 2015; $470, AU-53, May 2015; $382, VF-35, June 2015												

a. This unique coin is certified by NGC as PF-67. **b.** Beware spurious "O" mintmark. **c.** This unique coin is part of the unique complete 1910 Sandblast Finish Proof gold set.

	Mintage	Cert	Avg	%MS	VF-20	EF-40	AU-50	AU-55	AU-58	MS-60	MS-62	MS-63	MS-65
											PF-63	PF-64	PF-65
1915 (d)	588,000	6,586	60.7	75%	$575	$600	$650	$670	$675	$750	$850	$1,050	$7,500
Auctions: $9,988, MS-65, August 2015; $3,760, MS-64, September 2015; $764, MS-62, August 2015; $646, MS-61, June 2015													
1915, Sandblast Finish Proof	75	24	65.1								$17,000	$27,500	$60,000
Auctions: $47,000, PF-66, June 2014													
1915-S	164,000	1,388	56.2	21%	$575	$600	$650	$750	$1,250	$2,300	$6,500	$10,500	$130,000
Auctions: $5,640, MS-62, January 2015; $3,525, MS-61, January 2015; $1,116, AU-58, October 2015; $364, AU-50, March 2015													
1916-S	240,000	2,173	58.8	46%	$600	$650	$675	$700	$850	$1,150	$2,150	$3,500	$31,000
Auctions: $41,126, MS-65, August 2015; $1,410, MS-61, October 2015; $400, AU-55, March 2015; $376, AU-50, October 2015													
1929	662,000	226	62.3	90%	$18,500	$20,000	$23,500	$25,000	$29,000	$32,500	$35,000	$37,500	$115,000
Auctions: $66,000, MS-64, January 2018; $44,650, April 2017; $37,200, MS-63, April 2018; $32,900, MS-62, January 2017													

d. Pieces dated 1915-D are counterfeit.

Gold
Eagles ($10)
1795–1933

AN OVERVIEW OF GOLD EAGLES

The ten-dollar gold coin, or *eagle*, was first produced in 1795. Coinage authority for the denomination, including its weight and fineness, had been specified by the Act of April 2, 1792.

The Capped Bust to Right with Small Eagle reverse is the rarest of the early ten-dollar coin types. However, when seen they tend to be in higher grades such as EF, AU, or low levels of Mint State. The Heraldic Eagle reverse issues from 1797 through 1804 are much more readily available and in slightly higher average grade.

The Liberty Head eagles without the motto IN GOD WE TRUST, minted from 1838 through 1865, are elusive in any Mint State grade, although VF and EF pieces are plentiful, and there are enough AU coins to easily satisfy collector demands. Some collectors have considered the 1838 and 1839, 9 Over 8, with the head of Miss Liberty tilted forward in relation to the date, to be a separate type. Eagles with IN GOD WE TRUST on the reverse, produced from 1866 to 1907, are plentiful in high grades, including choice and gem Mint State. Some of these were repatriated from overseas bank vaults beginning in the second half of the 20th century.

The Saint-Gaudens eagles of 1907, of the style with periods between and flanking the words E PLURIBUS UNUM, exist in the Wire Rim and Rounded Rim varieties. These can be collected as a distinct type, or not. Most readily available is the Wire Rim style, of which somewhat more than 400 are likely to exist today, nearly all in Mint State, often choice or gem. These coins were made as regular issues but soon became numismatic delicacies for Treasury officials to distribute as they saw fit. Some were to have gone to museums, but in reality most were secretly filtered out through favored coin dealers. Then comes the 1907–1908 style, without periods, easily available in EF, AU, and lower Mint State levels, although gems are elusive.

The final eagle type, the 1908–1933 style with IN GOD WE TRUST on the reverse, is readily obtained in grades from EF through MS-63. Higher-grade pieces are elusive, and

This pattern eagle of 1878, struck in copper and designated J-1580, was designed by George Morgan and strongly resembles the silver dollar design that bears his name.

when seen are often dated 1932, a year in which 4,463,000 were struck—more than any other coin in the history of the denomination.

FOR THE COLLECTOR AND INVESTOR: GOLD EAGLES AS A SPECIALTY

Collecting ten-dollar gold coins by die varieties is unusual, as the series includes so many scarce and rare coins. However, unlike other denominations, none is in the "impossible" category, and with some patience a full set of significant varieties, as listed in this book, can be obtained.

The early issues with a Small Eagle reverse, minted from 1795 through 1797, and those with the Heraldic Eagle reverse of 1797 through 1804, can be collected and studied by die varieties, with *United States Ten Dollar Gold Eagles 1795–1804,* by Anthony Teraskza, being one useful guide. *Early U.S. Gold Coin Varieties: A Study of Die States, 1795–1834,* by John W. Dannreuther and Harry W. Bass Jr., offers an abundance of information and enlarged photographs for study. In addition to the regular issues, a few 1804 restrike ten-dollar pieces exist from 1804-dated dies newly created in 1834.

Liberty Head eagles from 1838 through 1866 (without the motto IN GOD WE TRUST) comprise many scarce dates and mintmarks. Years ago the 1858, of which only 2,521 were minted, was highly acclaimed as a landmark issue, but since then the publicity has faded. In any event, although certain date-and-mintmark varieties are rare, the number of numismatists collecting them by date sequence is very small, and thus opportunities exist to acquire very elusive pieces at a much smaller proportionate premium than would be possible in, say, the gold dollar series. No full set of Mint State early eagles has ever been formed; probably none ever will be. EF and AU are typically the grades of choice, with Mint State pieces added when available.

Later Liberty Head eagles of the 1866–1907 style (with the motto IN GOD WE TRUST) include some low-mintage issues, but again these are not impossible to collect. The most famous is the 1875 Philadelphia coin, of which just 100 circulation strikes were made. Although smaller numbers exist for Proof-only mintages, in terms of those made for commerce the 1875 sets a record. The low-mintage 1879-O (1,500 made) and 1883-O (800) also have attracted much attention. Again, these pieces, while rare, are available to the specialist, as there is not a great deal of competition.

Among Indian Head eagles the 1907, With Periods, Wire Rim, is famous, popular, and rare. Examples come on the market with regularity but are expensive due to the demand they attract. The Rounded Rim style is much rarer and when seen is usually in choice Mint State.

The regular without-periods 1907 and 1908 eagles are easy enough to obtain in Mint State, although gems are elusive. The varieties from 1908 through 1916 include no great rarities, although some are scarcer than others. Not many such pieces were saved at the time they were issued, and, accordingly, gems are elusive. However, grades such as AU and low Mint State will present no problem. Among later eagles, the 1920-S, 1930-S, and 1933 are rarities. In particular the 1920-S is difficult to find in choice and gem Mint State. The 1933 eagle is usually found in Mint State, but is expensive due to the publicity given to it. Readily available at reasonable prices are the 1926 and 1932.

CAPPED BUST TO RIGHT, SMALL EAGLE REVERSE (1795–1797)

Designer: *Robert Scot.* **Weight:** *17.50 grams.*
Composition: *.9167 gold, .0833 silver and copper.*
Diameter: *Approximately 33 mm.* **Edge:** *Reeded.* **Mint:** *Philadelphia.*

Bass-Dannreuther–1.

History. Eagles of this style, the first in the denomination, debuted in the autumn of 1795. The obverse features Miss Liberty dressed in a conical cap. The reverse shows a "small" eagle perched on a palm branch and holding a laurel in his beak. The same motif was used on contemporary gold half eagles.

Striking and Sharpness. On the obverse, check the star centers and the hair details. On the reverse, check the feathers of the eagle. In particular, the breast feathers often are weakly struck. Examine the denticles on both sides. Adjustment marks (from a Mint worker filing an overweight planchet down to the correct weight) often are visible, but are not noted by the grading services.

Availability. Typical grades range from EF to AU and low MS. MS-63 and higher coins are rare; when seen, they usually are of the 1795 or 1796 dates. Certain varieties are rare. While no Proofs of this type were made, certain eagles of 1796 have prooflike surfaces and are particularly attractive if in high grades.

GRADING STANDARDS

MS-60 to 70 (Mint State). *Obverse:* At MS-60, some abrasion and contact marks are evident, most noticeably on the hair to the left of Miss Liberty's forehead and on the higher-relief areas of the cap. Luster is present, but may be dull or lifeless, and interrupted in patches. At MS-63, contact marks are few, and abrasion is very light. An MS-65 coin has hardly any abrasion, and contact marks are so minute as to require magnifica-

1795, 13 Leaves; BD-5. Graded MS-63.

tion. Luster should be full and rich. On prooflike coins in any Mint State grade, abrasion and surface marks are much more noticeable. Coins above MS-65 exist more in theory than in reality for this type—but they do exist, and are defined by having fewer marks as perfection is approached. ***Reverse:*** Comments apply as for the obverse, except that abrasion and contact marks are most noticeable on the breast and head of the eagle. The field area is mainly protected by the eagle, branch, and lettering.

AU-50, 53, 55, 58 (About Uncirculated). *Obverse:* Light wear is seen on the cheek, the hair immediately to the left of the face, and the cap, more so at AU-50 than at AU–53 or 55. An AU-58 coin has minimal traces of wear. An AU-50 coin has luster in protected areas among the stars and letters, with little in the open fields or on the portrait. At AU-58, most luster is present in the fields, but is worn away on the highest parts of the motifs.

1796. Graded AU-58.

Reverse: Comments as preceding, except that the eagle shows light wear on the breast and head in particular, but also at the tip of the wing on the left and elsewhere. Luster ranges from perhaps 40% remaining in protected areas (at AU-50) to nearly full mint bloom (at AU-58).

    Illustrated coin: This example shows light wear overall, with hints of original luster in protected areas.

EF-40, 45 (Extremely Fine). *Obverse:* Wear is evident all over the portrait, with some loss of detail in the hair to the left of Miss Liberty's face. Excellent detail remains in low-relief areas of the hair, such as the front curl and at the back of her head. The stars show wear, as do the date and letters. Luster, if present at all, is minimal and in protected areas. *Reverse:* Wear is greater than on an About Uncirculated coin. The breast, neck, and legs of the

1795, 9 Leaves; BD-3. Graded EF-45.

eagle lack nearly all feather detail. More wear is seen on the edges of the wing. Some traces of luster may be seen, more so at EF-45 than at EF-40.

VF-20, 30 (Very Fine). *Obverse:* The higher-relief areas of hair are well worn at VF-20, less so at VF-30. The stars are flat at their centers. *Reverse:* Wear is greater, the eagle is flat in most areas, and about 40% to 60% of the wing feathers can be seen.

Capped Bust to Right, Small Eagle Reverse, eagles are seldom collected in grades lower than VF-20.

1795, 13 Leaves; BD-2. Graded VF-30.

1795, 13 Leaves   **1795, 9 Leaves**

	Mintage	Cert	Avg	%MS	F-12	VF-20	EF-40	AU-50	AU-55	MS-60	MS-62	MS-63
1795, 13 Leaves Below Eagle	5,583	69	54.8	23%	$27,500	$35,000	$50,000	$55,000	$67,500	$105,000	$150,000	$275,000 (a)
	Auctions: $2,585,000, MS-66+, September 2015; $822,500, MS-64+, March 2019; $152,750, MS-62, November 2014											
1795, 9 Leaves Below Eagle †	(b)	14	56.4	14%	$57,500	$75,000	$90,000	$130,000	$175,000	$250,000	$350,000	$700,000
	Auctions: $1,057,500, MS-63+, September 2015; $146,875, EF-45, August 2014; $47,000, EF-40, January 2014											
1796	4,146	66	56.8	27%	$28,500	$35,000	$50,000	$57,500	$70,000	$115,000	$205,000	$425,000
	Auctions: $164,500, MS-62, April 2014; $82,250, AU-55, August 2014											
1797, Small Eagle	3,615	23	55.5	35%	$40,000	$55,000	$70,000	$105,000	$125,000	$225,000	$325,000	$450,000
	Auctions: $164,500, AU-58, August 2014; $91,063, EF-45, August 2016; $47,000, EF-40, August 2014											

† Ranked in the *100 Greatest U.S. Coins* (fifth edition). **a.** Value in MS-64 is $475,000. **b.** Included in 1795, 13 Leaves Below Eagle, mintage figure.

CAPPED BUST TO RIGHT, HERALDIC EAGLE REVERSE (1797–1804)

Designer: *Robert Scot.* **Weight:** *17.50 grams.*
Composition: *.9167 gold, .0833 silver and copper.*
Diameter: *Approximately 33 mm.* **Edge:** *Reeded.* **Mint:** *Philadelphia.*

Circulation Strike   **Proof**
BD-2.

History. Gold eagles of this type combine the previous obverse style with the Heraldic Eagle—a modification of the Great Seal of the United States—as used on other silver and gold coins of the era. Regarding the Proofs dated 1804: There were no Proofs coined in the era in which this type was issued, and all eagle and silver dollar production was suspended by President Thomas Jefferson in 1804. Years later, in 1834, the Mint made up new dies with the 1804 date (this time featuring a Plain 4 rather than a Crosslet 4) and struck a number of Proofs (the quantity unknown today, but perhaps a dozen or so) for inclusion in presentation Proof sets for foreign dignitaries.

Striking and Sharpness. On the obverse, check the star centers and the hair details. On the reverse, check the upper part of the shield, the lower part of the eagle's neck, the eagle's wing, the stars above the eagle, and the clouds. Inspect the denticles on both sides. Adjustment marks (from where an overweight planchet was filed down to correct specifications) can be problematic; these are not identified by the grading services.

Availability. Mintages of this type were erratic. Eagles of 1797 appear in the market with some regularity, while those of 1798 are rare. Usually seen are the issues of 1799 through 1803. Typical grades range from EF to lower MS. MS-62 and higher coins are seen with some frequency and usually are dated 1799 and later. The 1804 circulation strike is rare in true MS. Sharply struck coins without planchet adjustment marks are in the minority. Only a handful of the aforementioned 1804 Proofs survive today.

GRADING STANDARDS

MS-60 to 70 (Mint State). *Obverse:* At MS-60, some abrasion and contact marks are evident, most noticeably on the hair to the left of Miss Liberty's forehead and on the higher-relief areas of the cap. Luster is present, but may be dull or lifeless, and interrupted in patches. At MS-63, contact marks are few, and abrasion is very light. An MS-65 coin has even less abrasion (most observable in the right field), and contact marks are so minute as to require magnification. Luster should be full and rich. Coins graded above MS-65 are more

1799, Large Stars; BD-10. Graded MS-65.

theoretical than actual for this type—but they do exist, and are defined by having fewer marks as perfection is approached. Large-size eagles are usually graded with slightly less strictness than the lower gold denominations of this type. *Reverse:* Comments apply as for the obverse, except that abrasion and contact marks are most noticeable on the upper part of the eagle and the clouds. The field area is complex, without much open space, given the stars above the eagle, the arrows and olive branch, and other features. Accordingly, marks are not as noticeable as on the obverse.

Illustrated coin: This coin has an exceptionally sharp strike overall, but with some lightness on the eagle's dexter (viewer's left) talon. Note some trivial abrasion in the right obverse field.

AU-50, 53, 55, 58 (About Uncirculated). *Obverse:* Light wear is seen on the cheek, the hair immediately to the left of the face, and the cap, more so at AU-50 than at AU–53 or 55. An AU-58 coin has minimal traces of wear. An AU-50 coin has luster in protected areas among the stars and letters, with little in the open fields or on the portrait. At AU-58, most luster is present in the fields, but is worn away on the highest parts of the

1799, Small Stars; BD-7. Graded AU-50.

motifs. *Reverse:* Comments as preceding, except that the eagle's neck, the tips and top of the wings, the clouds, and the tail now show noticeable wear, as do other features. Luster ranges from perhaps 40% remaining in protected areas (at AU-50) to nearly full mint bloom (at AU-58). Often the reverse of this type retains much more luster than the obverse.

Illustrated coin: Note some lightness of strike at the center of the obverse. Significant luster remains.

EF-40, 45 (Extremely Fine). *Obverse:* Wear is evident all over the portrait, with some loss of detail in the hair to the left of Miss Liberty's face. Excellent detail remains in low-relief areas of the hair, such as the front curl and at the back of her head. The stars show wear as do the date and letters. Luster, if present at all, is minimal and in protected areas. *Reverse:* Wear is greater than on the preceding. The neck lacks some feather detail on its highest

1801; BD-2. Graded EF-45.

points. Feathers have lost some detail near the edges of the wings, and some areas of the horizontal lines in the shield may be blended together. Some traces of luster may be seen, more so at EF-45 than at EF-40. Overall, the reverse appears to be in a slightly higher grade than the obverse.

VF-20, 30 (Very Fine). *Obverse:* The higher-relief areas of hair are well worn at VF-20, less so at VF-30. *Reverse:* Wear is greater, including on the shield and wing feathers. The star centers are flat. Other areas have lost detail as well. E PLURIBUS UNUM may be faint in areas, but is usually sharp.

Capped Bust to Right, Heraldic Eagle Reverse, eagles are seldom collected in grades lower than VF-20.

1799, Small Stars; BD-7. Graded VF-30.

PF-60 to 70 (Proof). *Obverse and Reverse:* PF-60 to 62 coins have extensive hairlines and may have nicks and contact marks. At PF-63, hairlines are prominent, but the mirror surface is very reflective. PF-64 coins have fewer hairlines. At PF-65, hairlines should be minimal and mostly seen only under magnification. There should be no nicks or marks.

1804, Plain 4; BD-2. Proof.

1798, 8 Over 7,
9 Stars Left, 4 Right

1798, 8 Over 7,
7 Stars Left, 6 Right

1799, Small
Obverse Stars

1799, Large
Obverse Stars

1803, Small
Reverse Stars

1803, Large
Reverse Stars

	Mintage	Cert	Avg	%MS	F-12	VF-20	EF-40	AU-50	AU-55	MS-60	MS-62	MS-63	MS-64
											PF-63	PF-64	PF-65
1797	10,940	168	55.5	29%	$11,000	$15,000	$20,000	$32,500	$40,000	$52,500	$100,000	$150,000	$225,000
	Auctions: $117,500, MS-63, April 2014; $44,063, MS-61, November 2014; $41,125, AU-58, August 2014; $34,075, AU-58, August 2014												
1798, 8 Over 7, 9 Stars Left, 4 Stars Right †	900	25	56.2	24%	$22,500	$26,500	$38,000	$52,500	$75,000	$120,000	$225,000	$325,000	
	Auctions: $176,250, MS-62, April 2014; $76,375, AU-55, August 2016												
1798, 8 Over 7, 7 Stars Left, 6 Stars Right †	842	3	50.0	0%	$45,000	$65,000	$105,000	$185,000	$275,000	$475,000	$700,000		
	Auctions: $352,500, AU-58, August 2016; $161,000, AU-55, January 2005; $176,250, AU-50, August 2014												
1799, Small Obverse Stars	37,449	51	57.4	43%	$9,000	$12,500	$15,000	$18,500	$20,500	$32,500	$42,500	$72,500	$135,000
	Auctions: $9,988, AU-58, September 2014; $25,850, AU-58, August 2014; $24,675, AU-55, January 2014; $15,275, AU-50, August 2014												
1799, Large Obverse Stars	(a)	47	58.4	57%	$9,000	$12,500	$15,000	$18,500	$20,500	$32,500	$42,500	$72,500	$130,000
	Auctions: $32,900, MS-62, October 2014; $19,975, AU-58, August 2014; $16,450, AU-53, November 2014; $9,400, AU, March 2015												
1800	5,999	108	56.9	40%	$9,500	$13,000	$15,500	$19,000	$21,500	$32,500	$45,000	$87,500	$165,000
	Auctions: $117,500, MS-64, January 2014; $32,900, MS-61, August 2014; $15,275, AU-50, August 2014; $7,638, AU-50, July 2014												
1801	44,344	419	58.5	51%	$9,000	$11,000	$15,000	$18,000	$19,500	$28,500	$38,500	$60,000	$125,000
	Auctions: $88,125, MS-64, March 2013; $48,763, MS-63, August 2014; $45,535, MS-63, August 2014; $29,375, MS-61, October 2014												
1803, Small Reverse Stars	15,017	49	58.4	55%	$9,500	$12,000	$15,500	$20,000	$22,500	$35,000	$50,000	$65,000	$135,000
	Auctions: $28,200, MS-61, January 2014; $15,875, AU-55, November 2014; $17,625, AU-55, August 2014; $13,513, AU-55, August 2014												
1803, Large Reverse Stars (b)	(c)	46	60.1	65%	$9,500	$12,000	$15,500	$20,000	$22,500	$35,000	$50,000	$65,000	$135,000
	Auctions: $99,875, MS-64, January 2014; $42,594, MS-62, August 2014; $24,675, AU-53, August 2014												
1804, Crosslet 4	3,757	51	58.7	49%	$20,000	$23,500	$35,000	$50,000	$65,000	$85,000	$100,000	$185,000	
	Auctions: $73,438, MS-61, January 2014; $64,625, MS-60, August 2014; $58,750, AU-58, August 2014												
1804, Plain 4, Proof † (d)	5–8	1	65.0								$4,000,000	$4,500,000	$5,000,000
	Auctions: $73,438, MS-61, January 2014												

† Ranked in the *100 Greatest U.S. Coins* (fifth edition); both 1798, 8 Over 7 Capped Bust to Right, Heraldic Eagle Reverse Eagle varieties as a single entry. **a.** Included in 1799, Small Obverse Stars, mintage figure. **b.** A variety without the tiny 14th star in the cloud is very rare; 6 or 7 examples are known. It does not command a significant premium. **c.** Included in 1803, Small Reverse Stars, mintage figure. **d.** These coins were minted in 1834 (from newly created dies with the date 1804) for presentation sets for foreign dignitaries. 3 or four 4 are known today.

LIBERTY HEAD (1838–1907)

Designer: *Christian Gobrecht.* **Weight:** *16.718 grams.*
Composition: *.900 gold, .100 copper (net weight: .48375 oz. pure gold).* **Diameter:** *27 mm.*
Edge: *Reeded.* **Mints:** *Philadelphia, Carson City, Denver, New Orleans, and San Francisco.*

No Motto Above Eagle (1838–1866)   **No Motto Above Eagle, Proof**

Motto Above Eagle (1866–1907)   **Motto Above Eagle, Proof**

History. Production of the gold eagle, suspended after 1804, started up again in 1838 with the Liberty Head design. The coin's weight and diameter was reduced from the specifications of the earlier type. For the first time in the denomination's history, its value, TEN D., was shown. Midway through 1839 the style was modified slightly, including in the letters (made smaller) and in the tilt of Miss Liberty's portrait. In 1866 the motto IN GOD WE TRUST was placed on a banner above the eagle's head.

Striking and Sharpness. On the obverse, check the highest points of the hair and the star centers. On the reverse, check the eagle's neck, and the area to the lower left of the shield and the lower part of the eagle. Examine the denticles on both sides. Branch-mint coins issued before the Civil War often are lightly struck in areas, and some Carson City coins of the early 1870s can have areas of lightness. Most late 19th-century and early 20th-century coins are sharp in all areas. Tiny copper staining spots (from improperly mixed alloy) can be a problem for those issues. Cameo contrast is the rule for Proofs prior to 1902. Beginning that year the portrait was polished in the die, imparting a mirror finish across the entire design, although a few years later cameo-contrast coins were again made.

Availability. Early dates and mintmarks are generally scarce to rare in MS and very rare in MS-63 and better grades, with only a few exceptions. These were workhorse coins in commerce; VF and EF grades are the rule for dates through the 1870s, and for some dates the finest known grade can be AU. In MS, Liberty Head eagles as a type are rarer than either quarter eagles or half eagles of the same design. Indeed, the majority of Mint State examples were only discovered in recent decades, resting in European banks, and some varieties are not known to exist at this level. Eagles of the 1880s onward generally are seen in higher average grades. Proof coins exist in relation to their original mintages, with all issues prior to the 1890s being very rare.

Note: Values of common-date gold coins have been based on the current bullion price of gold, $2,000 per ounce, and may vary with the prevailing spot price.

GRADING STANDARDS

MS-60 to 70 (Mint State). *Obverse:* At MS-60, some abrasion and contact marks are evident, most noticeably on the hair to the right of Miss Liberty's forehead and on the jaw. Luster is present, but may be dull or lifeless, and interrupted in patches. At MS-63, contact marks are few, and abrasion is very light. An MS-65 coin has hardly any abrasion, and contact marks are so minute as to require magnification. Luster should be full and rich.

1880. Graded MS-63.

For most dates, coins graded above MS-65 exist more in theory than in actuality—but they do exist, and are defined by having fewer marks as perfection is approached. *Reverse:* Comments apply as for the obverse, except that abrasion and contact marks are most noticeable on the eagle's neck and to the lower left of the shield.

Illustrated coin: This coin is brilliant and lustrous with scattered marks in the field, as is typical for this grade.

AU-50, 53, 55, 58 (About Uncirculated). *Obverse:* Light wear is seen on the face, the hair to the right of the face, and the highest area of the hair bun, more so at AU-50 than at AU–53 or 55. An AU-58 coin has minimal traces of wear. An AU-50 coin has luster in protected areas among the stars and letters, with little in the open fields or on the portrait. At AU-58 most luster is present in the fields, but is worn away on the highest parts

1839, Large Letters, 9 Over 8. Graded AU-53.

of the motifs. *Reverse:* Comments as preceding, except that the eagle shows wear in all of the higher areas, as well as the leaves and arrowheads. Luster ranges from perhaps 40% remaining in protected areas (at AU-50) to nearly full mint bloom (at AU-58). Often the reverse of this type retains more luster than the obverse.

EF-40, 45 (Extremely Fine). *Obverse:* Wear is evident on all high areas of the portrait, including the hair to the right of the forehead, the tip of the coronet, and the hair bun. The stars show light wear at their centers. Luster, if present at all, is minimal and in protected areas such as between the star points. *Reverse:* Wear is greater than on an About Uncirculated coin. On the $10 coins (in contrast to the $2.50 and $5 of the same design), most of the details on

1868. Graded EF-40.

the eagle are sharp. There is flatness on the leaves and arrowheads. Some traces of luster may be seen, more so at EF-45 than at EF-40.

Illustrated coin: Note the many contact marks on both sides.

VF-20, 30 (Very Fine). *Obverse:* The higher-relief areas of hair are worn flat at VF-20, less so at VF-30. The hair to the right of the coronet is merged into heavy strands. The stars are flat at their centers. *Reverse:* The eagle is worn further, with most neck feathers gone and with the feathers in the wing having flat tips. The branch leaves have little or no detail. The vertical shield stripes, being deeply recessed, remain bold.

1838. Graded VF-25.

Liberty Head eagles are seldom collected in grades lower than VF-20.

PF-60 to 70 (Proof). *Obverse and Reverse:* PF–60 to 62 coins have extensive hairlines and may have nicks and contact marks. At PF-63, hairlines are prominent, but the mirror surface is very reflective. PF-64 coins have fewer hairlines. At PF-65, hairlines should be minimal and mostly seen only under magnification. There should be no nicks or marks. PF-66 and higher coins should have no marks or hairlines visible to the unaided eye.

1862. Graded PF-65.

Illustrated coin: This is a museum-quality gem, with cameo-contrast motifs and mirror fields.

1839, Large Letters	1839, Small Letters
(Type of 1838)	(Type of 1840)

	Mintage	Cert	Avg	%MS	VF-20	EF-40	AU-50	AU-55	AU-58	MS-60 / PF-63	MS-63 / PF-64	MS-65 / PF-65
1838	7,200	62	48.5	2%	$3,500	$9,000	$17,500	$25,000	$60,000	$62,500	$125,000	
Auctions: $105,750, MS-63, May 2016; $64,625, AU-58, August 2016: $41,125, AU-58, August 2014; $7,638, EF-40, August 2015												
1838, Proof † (a)	4–6	1	65.0		(extremely rare)							
Auctions: $500,000, ChPF, May 1998												
1839, Large Letters (b)	25,801	179	50.5	8%	$2,000	$5,000	$6,500	$11,500	$15,000	$30,000	$85,000	
Auctions: $10,575, AU-58, September 2015; $9,694, AU-55, August 2015; $9,400, AU-55, August 2016; $4,759, AU-50, August 2015												
1839, Small Letters	12,447	41	47.1	2%	$3,500	$12,000	$16,500	$25,000	$35,000	$65,000		
Auctions: $47,000, AU-58, February 2014; $9,988, AU-50, September 2015; $3,995, 35, September 2016												
1839, Large Letters, Proof (c)	4–6	1	67.0		(extremely rare)							
Auctions: $1,610,000, PF-67UCam, January 2007												

† Ranked in the *100 Greatest U.S. Coins* (fifth edition). **a.** 3 examples are known. **b.** The Large Letters style is also known as the "Type of 1838," because of the distinct style of the 1838 Liberty Head motif. The Small Letters style (or "Type of 1840") was used on subsequent issues. **c.** 3 examples are known.

| | 1842, Small Date | | 1842, Large Date | | | | | | | | | |

	Mintage	Cert	Avg	%MS	VF-20	EF-40	AU-50	AU-55	AU-58	MS-60 PF-63	MS-63 PF-64	MS-65 PF-65
1840	47,338	182	49.5	3%	$1,200	$1,500	$1,850	$2,750	$6,000	$11,500		
	Auctions: $35,250, MS-62, August 2014; $15,275, MS-61, June 2015; $1,528, AU-53, June 2015; $1,645, EF-40, September 2015											
1840, Proof (d)	1–2	0	n/a		*(unique, in the Smithsonian's National Numismatic Collection)*							
	Auctions: No auction records available.											
1841	63,131	219	50.1	7%	$1,150	$1,200	$1,450	$2,500	$5,000	$11,000	$45,000	
	Auctions: $9,400, MS-61, February 2014; $4,230, AU-58, August 2015; $1,645, AU-55, February 2015; $1,116, AU-53, June 2015											
1841, Proof (e)	4–6	1	61.0		*(extremely rare)*							
	Auctions: No auction records available.											
1841-O	2,500	48	44.8	0%	$7,500	$13,500	$30,000	$75,000	$85,000			
	Auctions: $25,850, AU-53, January 2014; $21,150, AU-50, September 2016; $14,688, AU-50, October 2014											
1842, Small Date	18,623	116	51.4	6%	$1,100	$1,150	$1,650	$2,750	$4,500	$12,500	$65,000	
	Auctions: $12,925, MS-61, June 2015; $2,115, AU-55, January 2015; $1,175, AU-50, February 2015; $940, AU-50, January 2015											
1842, Large Date	62,884	127	51.5	4%	$1,100	$1,150	$1,650	$2,500	$5,000	$15,000	$45,000	
	Auctions: $2,233, MS-60, January 2014											
1842, Small Date, Proof (f)	2	0	n/a		*(extremely rare)*							
	Auctions: No auction records available.											
1842-O	27,400	273	48.1	2%	$1,250	$1,650	$3,500	$7,500	$17,500	$65,000	$250,000	
	Auctions: $8,825, AU-55, March 2014; $4,230, AU-53, August 2015; $2,115, AU-50, July 2016; $999, AU-50, July 2015											
1843	75,462	214	49.8	2%	$1,100	$1,150	$1,850	$4,000	$8,500	$20,000		
	Auctions: $3,055, AU-55, October 2015; $1,763, AU-50, August 2015; $1,058, EF-40, January 2015; $1,011, VF-30, March 2015											
1843, Doubled Die	(g)	0	n/a									
	Auctions: No auction records available.											
1843, Proof (h)	6–8	1	61.0		*(extremely rare)*							
	Auctions: No auction records available.											
1843-O	175,162	442	49.5	2%	$1,150	$1,200	$1,800	$3,500	$5,500	$14,000	$55,000	
	Auctions: $7,050, AU-58, February 2015; $2,585, AU-53, July 2015; $1,175, AU-50, January 2015; $1,058, VF-35, January 2015											
1844	6,361	39	49.5	8%	$2,500	$4,500	$6,500	$16,000	$22,500	$27,500	$85,000	
	Auctions: $24,170, AU-55, January 2014											
1844, Proof (i)	6–8	1	63.0									
	Auctions: No auction records available.											
1844-O	118,700	392	50.9	5%	$1,150	$1,350	$1,850	$3,750	$7,000	$12,500		
	Auctions: $7,931, AU-58, June 2013; $2,585, AU-53, July 2015; $2,585, AU-53, March 2015; $1,293, EF-45, November 2014											
1844-O, Proof †	1	1	65.0		*(extremely rare)*							
	Auctions: No auction records available.											
1845	26,153	120	49.1	3%	$1,100	$1,450	$2,750	$5,500	$8,500	$18,500		
	Auctions: $4,994, AU-55, April 2013											
1845, Proof (j)	6–8	1	65.0		*(extremely rare)*							
	Auctions: $120,750, PF-64, August 1999											
1845-O	47,500	240	49.9	4%	$1,150	$1,650	$3,250	$7,500	$11,000	$18,000		
	Auctions: $2,820, AU-53, November 2014; $881, AU-50, October 2014; $3,819, AU, March 2014; $764, EF-40, January 2015											

† Ranked in the *100 Greatest U.S. Coins* (fifth edition), grouped with 1844-O Proof Liberty Head Half Eagles, as a single entry. **d.** While there is only one example known of this coin, it is possible that other 1840 Proof eagles were made, given that duplicates are known of the quarter eagle and half eagle denominations. **e.** 3 examples are known. **f.** 2 examples are known. **g.** Included in circulation-strike 1843 mintage figure. **h.** 5 examples are known. **i.** 3 or 4 examples are known. **j.** 4 or 5 examples are known.

1846-O, 6 Over 5

1850, Large Date   **1850, Small Date**

	Mintage	Cert	Avg	%MS	VF-20	EF-40	AU-50	AU-55	AU-58	MS-60	MS-63	MS-65
										PF-63	PF-64	PF-65
1846	20,095	100	48.0	6%	$1,350	$1,650	$4,500	$7,000	$10,000	$30,000		
	Auctions: $4,994, AU-55, September 2014; $4,406, AU-55, September 2014; $8,225, AU-55, January 2014; $3,760, AU-50, June 2015											
1846, Proof (k)	6–8	2	59.5		*(extremely rare)*							
	Auctions: $161,000, PF-64Cam, January 2011											
1846-O	81,780	281	47.6	1%	$1,250	$2,000	$3,500	$6,000	$9,000	$20,000		
	Auctions: $2,820, AU-50, January 2014											
1847	862,258	1,456	52.3	5%	$1,100	$1,150	$1,175	$1,200	$1,650	$3,500	$21,500	
	Auctions: $894, AU-55, June 2015; $823, AU-53, February 2015; $764, AU-50, January 2015; $881, EF-40, July 2015											
1847, Proof	1–2	0	n/a		*(unique, in the Smithsonian's National Numismatic Collection)*							
	Auctions: No auction records available.											
1847-O	571,500	1,159	50.1	2%	$1,100	$1,150	$1,175	$1,600	$2,500	$6,000	$30,000	
	Auctions: $2,056, AU-58, August 2015; $1,528, AU-55, October 2015; $1,058, AU-50, July 2015; $881, VF-30, January 2015											
1848	145,484	427	51.9	6%	$1,100	$1,150	$1,175	$1,350	$1,750	$6,000	$28,500	
	Auctions: $64,625, MS-64, October 2014; $3,760, MS-60, June 2015; $940, AU-53, June 2015; $881, EF-45, January 2015											
1848, Proof (l)	3–5	1	64.0		*(extremely rare)*							
	Auctions: No auction records available.											
1848-O	35,850	187	49.2	4%	$1,650	$3,500	$4,000	$6,500	$11,000	$15,000	$50,000	$100,000
	Auctions: $51,700, MS-64, January 2015; $2,820, MS-60, October 2014; $3,525, AU-50, September 2015; $2,820, AU-50, June 2015											
1849	653,618	1,322	50.6	4%	$1,100	$1,150	$1,300	$1,400	$1,850	$3,250	$18,000	
	Auctions: $4,467, MS-61, June 2015; $999, AU-55, August 2015; $1,058, EF-45, August 2015; $676, VF-25, October 2015											
1849, Recut 1849 Over 849	(m)	42	50.3	10%				$4,000	$6,000			
	Auctions: $978, EF-40, May 2011											
1849-O	23,900	105	47.6	1%	$1,750	$3,500	$5,500	$9,500	$13,500	$30,000		
	Auctions: $5,875, AU-53, October 2013											
1850, All kinds	291,451											
1850, Large Date		558	50.8	4%	$1,100	$1,150	$1,175	$1,250	$1,650	$4,500		
	Auctions: $3,525, MS-60, September 2015; $1,116, AU-55, February 2015; $1,058, AU-53, August 2015; $940, AU-50, October 2015											
1850, Small Date		165	49.3	4%	$1,150	$1,250	$1,850	$2,750	$4,500	$8,000		
	Auctions: $10,575, MS-61, August 2015; $1,528, AU-53, October 2015; $1,058, EF-45, July 2015; $999, EF-40, February 2015											
1850-O	57,500	229	46.8	1%	$1,350	$2,000	$3,500	$6,500	$11,000	$25,000		
	Auctions: $6,169, AU-58, November 2014; $3,967, AU-55, March 2015; $1,293, VF-35, January 2015; $1,293, VF-30, September 2015											
1851	176,328	362	52.3	6%	$1,100	$1,150	$1,175	$1,250	$1,850	$4,250	$32,500	
	Auctions: $852, AU-50, September 2014; $881, AU-50, August 2014; $3,819, MS-61, September 2013; $734, VF-30, October 2014											
1851-O	263,000	1,108	50.9	2%	$1,150	$1,200	$1,750	$2,750	$6,500	$9,500	$40,000	
	Auctions: $18,800, MS-61, January 2015; $2,820, AU-55, January 2015; $1,293, EF-45, August 2015; $705, VF-20, January 2015											
1852	263,106	803	52.9	6%	$1,100	$1,150	$1,175	$1,250	$1,650	$3,750	$25,000	
	Auctions: $3,995, MS-61, July 2015; $1,146, AU-55, July 2015; $940, AU-50, July 2015; $823, VF-35, February 2015											
1852-O	18,000	108	49.9	2%	$1,650	$2,500	$6,000	$11,000	$27,500	$85,000		
	Auctions: $7,638, AU-55, August 2015; $3,290, AU-53, November 2014; $18,800, AU, February 2014; $12,925, AU-50, November 2016											

k. 4 examples are known. **l.** 2 examples are known. **m.** Included in circulation-strike 1849 mintage figure.

| **1853, 3 Over 2** | **1854-O, Large Date** | **1854-O, Small Date** |

	Mintage	Cert	Avg	%MS	VF-20	EF-40	AU-50	AU-55	AU-58	MS-60 / PF-63	MS-63 / PF-64	MS-65 / PF-65
1853, All kinds	201,253											
1853, 3 Over 2		189	52.6	2%	$1,200	$1,500	$2,000	$3,250	$6,000	$13,000		
	Auctions: $14,688, MS-61, June 2015; $11,779, MS-60, August 2015; $5,875, AU-58, October 2014; $2,350, AU-55, June 2015											
1853		871	53.9	6%	$1,100	$1,150	$1,175	$1,200	$1,650	$3,200	$17,000	
	Auctions: $34,075, MS-64, October 2014; $3,819, MS-61, November 2014; $999, AU-55, January 2015; $793, AU-53, January 2015											
1853-O	$51,000	278	51.4	3%	$1,350	$1,600	$2,250	$4,750	$10,000	$15,000		
	Auctions: $16,450, MS-61, November 2014; $9,400, MS-60, June 2015; $6,463, AU-58, October 2014; $881, AU-50, January 2015											
1853-O, Proof (n)	1	1	61.0									
	Auctions: No auction records available.											
1854	54,250	289	52.5	4%	$1,100	$1,150	$1,250	$1,650	$2,750	$6,500	$27,500	
	Auctions: $2,350, AU-58, September 2015; $2,115, AU-58, August 2015; $1,410, AU-55, June 2015; $1,293, AU-55, May 2015											
1854, Proof (o)	unknown	1	61.0									
	Auctions: No auction records available.											
1854-O, Large Date (p)	52,500	169	53.6	8%	$1,250	$1,350	$2,000	$3,250	$6,000	$12,000		
	Auctions: $10,869, MS-60, August 2013; $1,998, AU-53, November 2014; $2,585, EF-40, September 2015											
1854-O, Small Date (q)	(r)	124	52.8	1%	$1,250	$1,500	$2,250	$3,500	$4,750	$15,000		
	Auctions: $1,821, AU-55, August 2013											
1854-S	123,826	522	50.5	2%	$1,250	$1,400	$2,000	$2,850	$6,500	$12,500		
	Auctions: $4,935, AU-58, June 2015; $3,290, AU-55, June 2015; $1,998, AU-53, January 2015; $1,293, AU-50, August 2015											
1855	121,701	670	54.3	11%	$1,100	$1,150	$1,200	$1,350	$1,850	$4,750	$17,500	
	Auctions: $7,115, MS-62, September 2015; $2,233, AU-58, August 2015; $1,058, AU-53, August 2015; $881, EF-45, January 2015											
1855, Proof (s)	unknown	0	n/a									
	Auctions: No auction records available.											
1855-O	18,000	115	49.6	0%	$1,350	$3,500	$5,500	$10,000	$25,000			
	Auctions: $17,625, AU-58, January 2014											
1855-S	9,000	33	48.3	0%	$3,000	$4,000	$7,000	$15,000	$27,500			
	Auctions: $17,625, AU-58, March 2014											
1856	60,490	390	54.0	11%	$1,100	$1,150	$1,175	$1,250	$1,500	$4,000	$15,000	
	Auctions: $3,995, MS-61, January 2015; $2,242, AU-58, January 2015; $881, AU-53, February 2015; $793, EF-45, February 2015											
1856, Proof (s)	unknown											
	Auctions: No auction records available.											
1856-O	14,500	121	50.4	3%	$1,350	$2,500	$4,500	$7,000	$12,500	$35,000		
	Auctions: $10,869, AU-58, September 2016: $4,406, AU-55, January 2014; $4,700, AU-53, August 2016											
1856-S	68,000	298	50.5	2%	$1,100	$1,150	$1,500	$2,750	$4,750	$11,500		
	Auctions: $9,988, MS-61, April 2014; $3,290, AU-58, November 2014; $1,763, AU-55, October 2015; $1,116, AU-53, June 2015											

n. The 1853-O Proof listed here is not a Proof from a technical standpoint. This unique coin has in the past been called a presentation piece and a branch-mint Proof. "Although the piece does not have the same convincing texture as the 1844-O Proof eagle, it is clearly different from the regular-issue eagles found for the year and mint" (*Encyclopedia of U.S. Gold Coins, 1795–1933*, second edition). **o.** According to Walter Breen, in July 1854 a set of Proof coins was given by the United States to representatives of the sovereign German city of Bremen. Various Proof 1854 gold dollars, quarter eagles, and three-dollar gold pieces have come to light, along with a single gold eagle. **p.** The Large Date variety was made in error, when the diesinker used a date punch for a silver dollar on the much smaller ten-dollar die. **q.** The Small Date variety is scarce in AU. Only 3 or 4 MS examples are known, none finer than MS-60. **r.** Included in 1854-O, Large Date, mintage figure. **s.** No Proof 1855 or 1856 eagles have been confirmed, but Wayte Raymond claimed to have seen one of each some time prior to 1949.

	Mintage	Cert	Avg	%MS	VF-20	EF-40	AU-50	AU-55	AU-58	MS-60	MS-63	MS-65
										PF-63	PF-64	PF-65
1857	16,606	134	51.6	6%	$1,100	$1,150	$1,650	$3,000	$5,500	$16,000		
	Auctions: $4,406, AU-58, April 2014; $1,293, EF-45, September 2014											
1857, Proof	2–3	1	66.0									
	Auctions: No auction records available.											
1857-O	5,500	61	51.8	0%	$2,500	$4,500	$8,500	$12,500	$20,000	—		
	Auctions: $22,325, AU-58, August 2014; $8,225, AU-55, February 2014											
1857-S	26,000	76	48.1	4%	$1,350	$1,850	$2,500	$4,500	$7,500	$11,000		
	Auctions: $8,225, AU-58, July 2014; $5,875, AU-55, January 2015; $3,378, EF-45, August 2014; $4,465, EF-40, September 2015											
1858 (t)	2,521	36	48.9	8%	$5,500	$7,500	$11,500	$17,500	$25,000	$35,000		
	Auctions: $15,275, AU-53, February 2014											
1858, Proof (u)	4–6	1	64.0		*(extremely rare)*							
	Auctions: No auction records available.											
1858-O	20,000	206	51.6	4%	$1,250	$1,600	$2,750	$3,750	$7,000	$11,000	$40,000	
	Auctions: $6,463, AU-58, January 2015; $2,585, AU-55, January 2015; $1,293, AU-50, October 2015; $1,645, EF-45, January 2015											
1858-S	11,800	51	51.1	0%	$1,600	$3,850	$7,000	$15,000	$25,000			
	Auctions: $15,275, AU-58, April 2013; $3,055, EF-45, November 2014; $2,820, EF-40, October 2015; $2,115, EF-40, November 2014											
1859	16,013	174	51.1	6%	$1,200	$1,350	$1,500	$2,250	$4,000	$17,500	$70,000	
	Auctions: $41,125, MS-62, November 2014; $47,000, MS-62, April 2014; $1,175, EF-45, July 2015; $734, VF-20, January 2015											
1859, Proof	80	5	63.6							$75,000	$150,000	$200,000
	Auctions: No auction records available.											
1859-O	2,300	23	50.3	4%	$6,000	$15,000	$27,500	$40,000	$60,000			
	Auctions: $28,200, AU-50, December 2013											
1859-S	7,000	39	43.5	3%	$3,000	$8,000	$20,000	$30,000	$35,000			
	Auctions: $14,100, AU-53, October 2014; $3,525, AU-50, June 2015; $6,463, EF-45, October 2015; $3,290, EF-40, August 2014											
1860	15,055	154	51.8	8%	$1,100	$1,200	$1,750	$2,500	$3,000	$7,500	$25,000	
	Auctions: $70,500, MS-64, February 2013; $14,100, MS-62, June 2015; $1,645, AU-50, September 2014; $1,293, EF-45, January 2015											
1860, Proof	50	5	63.6							$50,000	$100,000	$135,000
	Auctions: $142,175, PF-64DCam, April 2014											
1860-O	11,100	138	51.6	5%	$1,450	$2,750	$4,000	$6,000	$8,000	$17,500		
	Auctions: $8,814, AU-About Uncirculated, March 2014											
1860-S	5,000	26	49.4	8%	$5,500	$12,500	$17,500	$27,500	$35,000	$65,000		
	Auctions: $28,200, AU-55, March 2014; $25,850, AU-55, May 2016; $9,400, VF-35, August 2016; $7,050, VF-30, September 2016											
1861	113,164	829	54.6	11%	$1,100	$1,150	$1,500	$2,500	$3,500	$6,500	$20,000	
	Auctions: $8,225, MS-62, August 2015; $7,652, MS-62, January 2015; $4,113, AU-58, July 2014; $940, AU-50, January 2015											
1861, Proof	69	6	64.2							$45,000	$85,000	$125,000
	Auctions: $129,250, PF-64Cam, March 2013											
1861-S	15,500	76	50.1	1%	$4,000	$8,500	$12,500	$17,500	$25,000	$65,000		
	Auctions: $25,850, AU-58, March 2014; $9,400, AU-53, August 2015; $7,638, AU-53, September 2014; $6,463, EF-40, June 2015											
1862	10,960	93	51.5	12%	$3,000	$4,500	$5,500	$6,500	$12,000	$18,500		
	Auctions: $18,800, MS-61, October 2015; $7,050, AU-55, January 2015; $6,169, AU-53, July 2015; $4,935, AU-50, September 2015											
1862, Proof	35	5	64.4							$42,500	$85,000	$125,000
	Auctions: $152,750, PF-65DCam, August 2013											
1862-S	12,500	47	45.3	0%	$2,500	$5,000	$10,000	$22,500	$35,000	$85,000		
	Auctions: $21,150, AU-58, October 2014; $5,581, EF-35, February 2014											
1863	1,218	16	52.0	19%	$15,000	$32,500	$50,000	$70,000			—	
	Auctions: $49,938, AU-53, January 2014; $42,300, EF-45, September 2016; $35,250, EF-45, August 2016											
1863, Proof	30	12	64.2							$42,500	$85,000	$125,000
	Auctions: $299,000, PF-65DCam, August 2011											
1863-S	10,000	38	47.0	3%	$6,000	$13,500	$20,000	$35,000	$55,000			
	Auctions: $32,900, AU-53, February 2014; $12,925, AU-50, October 2015; $15,275, EF-45, October 2014; $5,875, F-12, November 2014											

t. Beware of fraudulently removed mintmark. **u.** 4 or 5 examples are known.

1865-S, 865
Over Inverted 186

	Mintage	Cert	Avg	%MS	VF-20	EF-40	AU-50	AU-55	AU-58	MS-60	MS-63	MS-65
										PF-63	PF-64	PF-65
1864	3,530	24	50.4	21%	$6,500	$10,000	$22,500	$35,000	$50,000	$75,000		
	Auctions: $41,125, AU-55, October 2014; $28,200, AU-55, January 2014											
1864, Proof	50	17	63.8							$42,500	$85,000	$125,000
	Auctions: $138,000, PF-64UCam, October 2011											
1864-S	2,500	7	42.9	0%	$45,000	$100,000	$150,000	$195,000				
	Auctions: $146,875, AU-53, March 2014; $114,000, EF-40, February 2018											
1865	3,980	32	51.3	9%	$4,500	$6,750	$15,000	$20,000	$27,500	$65,000		
	Auctions: $15,275, AU-53, October 2014; $18,800, AU-53, January 2014; $13,513, AU-50, October 2014; $12,925, AU-50, August 2015											
1865, Proof	25	13	64.1							$42,500	$85,000	$125,000
	Auctions: $528,750, PF, August 2013											
1865-S, All kinds	16,700											
1865-S		32	40.3	6%	$6,500	$12,500	$19,500	$27,500	$45,000	$95,000		
	Auctions: $5,170, VF-25, September 2016; $4,230, VF-20, September 2016: $6,756, F-12, February 2013											
1865-S, 865 Over Inverted 186		41	43.8	2%	$6,750	$10,000	$17,500	$25,000	$35,000	$45,000		
	Auctions: $20,563, AU-55, January 2015; $27,025, AU-53, March 2014; $9,400, EF-45, October 2015; $1,880, VG-8, August 2014											
1866-S, No Motto	8,500	35	47.6	3%	$5,000	$15,000	$20,000	$25,000	$30,000	$60,000		
	Auctions: $14,950, EF-45, August 2011											
1866, With Motto	3,750	51	49.9	12%	$1,500	$3,000	$4,750	$10,000	$25,000	$42,500		
	Auctions: $32,900, MS-61, January 2015; $14,100, AU-55, September 2013; $4,054, AU-50, August 2015; $1,763, EF-40, January 2015											
1866, Proof	30	9	64.1							$35,000	$55,000	$85,000
	Auctions: $66,125, PF-64UCam+H, January 2012											
1866-S, With Motto	11,500	40	48.6	0%	$2,500	$4,500	$7,250	$10,000	$17,500			
	Auctions: $15,275, AU-58, March 2014; $9,988, AU-55, August 2014; $4,230, EF-45, July 2015; $4,230, VF-35, January 2015											
1867	3,090	59	49.2	5%	$2,000	$3,200	$6,500	$11,500	$22,500	$40,000		
	Auctions: $30,550, AU-58, August 2013											
1867, Proof	50	4	64.8							$35,000	$55,000	$85,000
	Auctions: $64,625, PF-65Cam, August 2014; $64,625, PF-64Cam+, February 2015; $54,344, PF-64Cam, October 2014											
1867-S	9,000	32	48.2	0%	$4,000	$6,500	$9,000	$20,000	$40,000			
	Auctions: $12,925, AU-55, July 2016;$9,988, AU-53, June 2013; $6,463, AU-50, September 2016											
1868	10,630	151	50.5	7%	$1,250	$1,400	$1,900	$3,500	$8,000	$17,500		
	Auctions: $5,875, AU-58, February 2015; $4,700, AU-58, July 2015; $1,645, AU-50, January 2015; $2,350, EF-45, September 2015											
1868, Proof	25	4	64.8							$35,000	$55,000	$85,000
	Auctions: $24,150, PF-62Cam, June 2005											
1868-S	13,500	69	47.9	0%	$1,850	$2,500	$4,000	$7,000	$17,500			
	Auctions: $5,875, AU-58, August 2014; $4,700, AU-55, July 2015; $1,469, AU-50, August 2015; $2,115, EF-40, August 2014											
1869	1,830	41	50.8	7%	$1,650	$4,000	$5,750	$11,500	$18,500	$35,000		
	Auctions: $14,100, AU-58, August 2013											
1869, Proof	25	8	63.8							$35,000	$55,000	$80,000
	Auctions: $161,000, PF-67UCam+H, February 2012											
1869-S	6,430	40	46.9	3%	$2,200	$3,500	$6,250	$11,000	$20,000	$35,000		
	Auctions: $16,450, AU-58, January 2015; $11,163, AU-55, August 2015; $7,638, AU-55, January 2015; $1,528, EF-40, October 2015											

	Mintage	Cert	Avg	%MS	VF-20	EF-40	AU-50	AU-55	AU-58	MS-60 / PF-63	MS-63 / PF-64	MS-65 / PF-65
1870	3,990	70	49.2	1%	$1,750	$2,000	$3,000	$9,500	$15,000	$35,000		
	Auctions: $10,575, AU-55, January 2014											
1870, Proof	35	4	64.5							$35,000	$55,000	$80,000
	Auctions: $97,750, PF-65UCam, January 2010											
1870-CC	5,908	33	42.2	0%	$40,000	$60,000	$85,000	$150,000				
	Auctions: $135,125, AU-55, March 2014; $82,250, AU-50, January 2017; $66,000, VF-35, February 2018; $32,900, VG-10, September 2016											
1870-S	8,000	63	41.9	0%	$1,650	$4,000	$5,500	$11,000	$18,500			
	Auctions: $12,925, AU-58, March 2014											
1871	1,790	60	51.8	0%	$1,500	$3,000	$5,500	$8,500	$15,000			
	Auctions: $15,275, AU-58, September 2013; $9,400, AU-55, March 2015; $4,583, AU-50, July 2015; $3,290, EF-40, August 2014											
1871, Proof	30	5	63.2							$35,000	$55,000	$80,000
	Auctions: $76,375, PF-64DCam, August 2013											
1871-CC	8,085	74	46.8	3%	$5,500	$15,000	$22,500	$29,500	$45,000			
	Auctions: $35,250, AU-58, October 2014; $14,100, AU-53, January 2015; $5,170, AU-50, June 2015; $19,975, EF-45, August 2016											
1871-S	16,500	77	42.2	0%	$1,500	$2,250	$4,500	$8,250	$12,500			
	Auctions: $10,281, AU-58, March 2014; $2,115, AU-50, July 2014; $1,116, AU-50, October 2015; $2,231, EF-45, February 2015											
1872	1,620	23	51.4	4%	$3,500	$5,500	$9,500	$15,000	$22,500	$28,500		
	Auctions: $38,188, AU-58, August 2014; $16,450, AU-55, August 2015; $16,450, AU-55, February 2015; $6,169, EF-45, July 2015											
1872, Proof	30	8	64.3							$35,000	$55,000	$80,000
	Auctions: $48,875, PF-64DCam, June 2012											
1872-CC	4,600	51	43.1	2%	$8,500	$13,500	$27,500	$42,500	$62,500			
	Auctions: $47,000, AU, February 2014, $9,988, EF-40, August 2014											
1872-S	17,300	143	47.3	3%	$1,100	$1,600	$2,500	$4,000	$8,500	$25,000		
	Auctions: $8,225, AU-58, October 2014; $7,050, AU-58, March 2014; $5,640, AU-58, January 2015; $1,645, EF-45, July 2015											
1873	800	20	50.4	0%	$10,000	$20,000	$35,000	$47,500	$65,000	$75,000		
	Auctions: $64,625, AU-58, May 2016: $55,813, AU-55, January 2014; $30,550, AU-53, September 2016; $21,738, AU-53, January 2015											
1873, Proof	25	8	63.5							$37,500	$65,000	$85,000
	Auctions: $74,750, PF-65Cam+, February 2012											
1873-CC	4,543	38	40.8	0%	$12,500	$25,000	$52,500	$75,000	$100,000			
	Auctions: $58,750, AU-53, March 2014; $44,650, AU-50, August 2016											
1873-S	12,000	80	42.8	0%	$1,250	$2,750	$4,250	$7,000	$13,500	$30,000		
	Auctions: $4,700, AU-53, March 2013											
1874	53,140	359	55.9	19%	$1,050	$1,060	$1,065	$1,100	$1,150	$1,500	$10,000	$45,000
	Auctions: $1,410, MS-61, September 2014; $1,058, AU-58, August 2015; $940, AU-58, September 2015; $999, AU-50, October 2014											
1874, Proof	20	1	62.0							$35,000	$65,000	$85,000
	Auctions: $29,500, PF-64Cam, September 2006											
1874-CC	16,767	155	41.4	1%	$3,250	$5,500	$10,500	$22,500	$40,000	$70,000	$200,000	
	Auctions: $30,550, AU-58, May 2013; $3,643, VF-35, June 2015; $2,585, F-15, January 2015; $1,410, VG-8, February 2015											
1874-S	10,000	105	43.2	0%	$1,400	$2,250	$4,500	$8,000	$17,500			
	Auctions: $12,338, AU-58, July 2014; $2,644, EF-45, August 2014; $940, VF-20, February 2015											
1875	100	7	45.4	0%	$150,000	$200,000	$350,000	$450,000				
	Auctions: $211,500, AU-50, February 2014											
1875, Proof	20	4	64.5							$165,000	$200,000	$275,000
	Auctions: $372,000, AU-50, February 2018											
1875-CC	7,715	77	38.3	3%	$5,500	$10,000	$17,500	$45,000	$75,000	$100,000	$185,000	
	Auctions: $8,225, EF-45, February 2014											

	Mintage	Cert	Avg	%MS	VF-20	EF-40	AU-50	AU-55	AU-58	MS-60 PF-63	MS-63 PF-64	MS-65 PF-65
1876	687	19	51.6	5%	$5,000	$9,500	$27,500	$35,000	$55,000	$100,000		
	Auctions: $70,500, AU-58, January 2015; $28,200, AU-55, June 2015; $22,325, AU-53, August 2015; $18,800, AU-53, July 2014											
1876, Proof	45	14	63.7							$32,500	$45,000	$75,000
	Auctions: $100,625, PF-65Cam, April 2011											
1876-CC	4,696	95	41.9	0%	$5,500	$13,500	$22,500	$37,500	$65,000			
	Auctions: $14,100, AU-50, October 2013											
1876-S	5,000	51	45.9	0%	$2,150	$5,000	$10,000	$25,000	$35,000			
	Auctions: $22,325, AU-55, October 2013											
1877	797	32	54.3	3%	$4,500	$7,000	$11,500	$15,000	$20,000	$65,000		
	Auctions: $64,625, MS-61, March 2015; $11,163, AU-55, July 2014; $11,163, AU-55, January 2014; $3,290, EF-40, February 2015											
1877, Proof	20	2	64.5							$35,000	$45,000	$75,000
	Auctions: $39,100, PF-64Cam, April 2002											
1877-CC	3,332	49	41.6	0%	$8,500	$12,500	$25,000	$50,000	$100,000			
	Auctions: $10,575, EF-45, April 2014											
1877-S	17,000	167	47.1	2%	$1,050	$1,350	$2,000	$4,750	$11,000	$30,000		
	Auctions: $3,290, AU-55, September 2015; $881, AU-50, September 2015; $1,116, EF-45, September 2015; $1,116, EF-45, June 2015											
1878	73,780	383	57.9	43%	$1,050	$1,060	$1,065	$1,070	$1,075	$1,080	$4,500	
	Auctions: $1,410, MS-62, July 2015; $881, MS-61, September 2015; $852, MS-61, September 2015; $823, MS-61, January 2015											
1878, Proof	20	4	63.8							$27,500	$45,000	$75,000
	Auctions: $25,300, PF-63, August 2011											
1878-CC	3,244	43	47.1	2%	$7,500	$20,000	$40,000	$65,000	$100,000	$135,000		
	Auctions: $64,625, AU-55, September 2016: $28,200, AU-55, March 2014; $19,388, AU-50, August 2016											
1878-S	26,100	215	47.6	2%	$1,050	$1,060	$1,350	$2,000	$3,500	$11,500	$27,500	
	Auctions: $2,938, AU-58, October 2015; $1,410, AU-55, February 2015; $1,293, AU-50, October 2015; $646, EF-40, September 2014											
1879	384,740	962	58.8	53%	$1,050	$1,060	$1,065	$1,070	$1,075	$1,080	$3,000	
	Auctions: $2,585, MS-63, July 2015; $940, MS-61, August 2015; $711, MS-60, October 2015; $646, AU-58, January 2015											
1879, Proof	30	6	63.2							$25,000	$37,500	$65,000
	Auctions: $52,875, PF-65Cam, February 2013											
1879-CC	1,762	39	42.7	3%	$15,000	$22,500	$40,000	$55,000	$75,000			
	Auctions: $41,125, AU-50, March 2014											
1879-O	1,500	46	49.5	4%	$10,000	$17,500	$25,000	$35,000	$60,000	$85,000		
	Auctions: $88,125, MS-61, June 2014; $23,500, EF-45, August 2016; $14,688, VF-30, September 2016											
1879-S	224,000	521	57.1	28%	$1,050	$1,060	$1,065	$1,070	$1,075	$1,200	$6,000	
	Auctions: $1,410, MS-62, January 2015; $881, MS-60, June 2015; $999, AU-58, August 2015; $705, AU-55, October 2015											
1880	1,644,840	2,272	59.9	81%	$1,050	$1,060	$1,065	$1,070	$1,075	$1,080	$1,500	
	Auctions: $19,975, MS-65, August 2013; $764, MS-61, June 2015; $705, VF-35, February 2015; $646, AG-3, January 2015											
1880, Proof	36	5	64.2							$22,500	$35,000	$60,000
	Auctions: $32,200, PF-64, October 1999											
1880-CC	11,190	198	50.3	7%	$2,000	$2,750	$4,000	$6,500	$11,000	$37,500		
	Auctions: $2,761, AU-53, August 2013; $1,175, EF-40, July 2014											
1880-O	9,200	183	51.8	5%	$1,600	$2,500	$4,250	$5,500	$8,500	$20,000		
	Auctions: $3,760, AU-55, August 2015; $4,230, AU-50, September 2015; $2,233, AU-50, August 2015; $4,113, EF-40, June 2014											
1880-S	506,250	1,103	60.2	78%	$1,050	$1,060	$1,065	$1,070	$1,075	$1,080	$2,000	
	Auctions: $4,465, MS-64, October 2015; $1,293, MS-63, July 2015; $1,175, MS-62, August 2015; $764, MS-61, September 2015											
1881	3,877,220	13,463	60.9	94%	$1,050	$1,060	$1,065	$1,070	$1,075	$1,080	$1,200	$15,000
	Auctions: $2,115, MS-64, February 2015; $999, MS-63, January 2015; $705, MS-62, October 2014; $676, MS-61, January 2015											
1881, Proof	40	4	65.5							$22,500	$32,500	$55,000
	Auctions: $56,063, PF-65, October 2011											
1881-CC	24,015	361	52.2	13%	$1,750	$2,500	$3,250	$4,500	$5,000	$8,500		
	Auctions: $12,925, MS-62, April 2013; $4,113, AU-58, January 2015; $1,116, AU-50, July 2014; $1,763, EF-40, January 2015											
1881-O	8,350	170	52.2	9%	$1,350	$1,850	$2,850	$5,000	$7,000	$15,000		
	Auctions: $12,338, MS-60, January 2014											
1881-S	970,000	2,644	60.7	91%	$1,050	$1,060	$1,065	$1,070	$1,075	$1,080	$1,500	
	Auctions: $2,585, MS-63, January 2015; $1,763, MS-63, October 2015; $764, MS-62, January 2015; $734, MS-62, June 2015											

	Mintage	Cert	Avg	%MS	VF-20	EF-40	AU-50	AU-55	AU-58	MS-60 / PF-63	MS-63 / PF-64	MS-65 / PF-65
1882	2,324,440	14,996	61.2	96%	$1,050	$1,060	$1,065	$1,070	$1,075	$1,080	$1,200	
	Auctions: $1,175, MS-63, August 2015; $823, MS-62, August 2015; $881, MS-61, June 2015; $777, MS-61, September 2015											
1882, Proof	40	9	64.2							$20,000	$32,500	$55,000
	Auctions: $43,125, PF-65Cam, October 2009											
1882-CC	6,764	152	52.7	3%	$2,000	$3,500	$5,500	$11,500	$18,500	$32,500		
	Auctions: $25,850, MS-60, July 2014; $7,344, AU-55, February 2015; $4,935, EF-45, July 2015; $1,645, EF-40, January 2015											
1882-O	10,820	188	52.7	11%	$1,250	$1,500	$2,000	$4,500	$7,500	$12,500	$45,000	
	Auctions: $30,550, MS-62, January 2014; $2,389, AU-53, September 2014; $1,410, VF-35, September 2015											
1882-S	132,000	357	60.6	86%	$1,050	$1,060	$1,065	$1,070	$1,075	$1,080	$2,500	
	Auctions: $1,880, MS-63, January 2015; $1,293, MS-62, October 2015; $1,234, MS-62, August 2015; $1,087, MS-62, October 2015											
1883	208,700	1,479	61.2	95%	$1,050	$1,060	$1,065	$1,070	$1,075	$1,080	$1,350	
	Auctions: $3,995, MS-64, January 2015; $1,880, MS-63, October 2015; $1,293, MS-63, August 2015; $881, MS-62, July 2015											
1883, Proof	40	8	64.4							$20,000	$32,500	$55,000
	Auctions: $8,813, PF-60, July 2014											
1883-CC	12,000	177	47.7	3%	$1,850	$2,750	$4,500	$8,500	$16,500	$37,500		
	Auctions: $41,125, MS-61, October 2014; $3,055, AU-50, October 2015; $2,820, EF-40, June 2015; $1,586, VF-20, January 2015											
1883-O	800	20	51.6	5%	$20,000	$35,000	$65,000	$80,000	$125,000	$150,000		
	Auctions: $82,250, AU-58, August 2014; $70,500, AU-58, January 2015; $70,500, AU-55, February 2014; $47,000, AU-50, October 2014											
1883-S	38,000	143	56.2	42%	$1,050	$1,060	$1,065	$1,070	$1,075	$1,150	$8,500	
	Auctions: $11,163, MS-63, February 2013; $2,056, MS-62, January 2015; $1,293, MS-61, August 2015; $823, AU-58, November 2014											
1884	76,860	359	58.3	44%	$1,050	$1,060	$1,065	$1,070	$1,075	$1,080	$4,250	
	Auctions: $846, MS-61, July 2014; $823, AU-55, February 2014											
1884, Proof	45	6	64.7							$20,000	$32,500	$55,000
	Auctions: $37,375, PF-64DCam, March 2012											
1884-CC	9,925	178	51.0	5%	$1,750	$3,000	$5,500	$7,500	$13,500	$17,500	$65,000	
	Auctions: $17,625, AU-58, September 2016: $17,625, AU-58, February 2014; $9,988, AU-58, August 2016; $3,760, AU-55, August 2015											
1884-S	124,250	571	59.3	67%	$1,050	$1,060	$1,065	$1,070	$1,075	$1,080	$4,500	
	Auctions: $4,994, MS-63, July 2014; $1,175, MS-62, September 2015; $1,116, MS-62, September 2015; $1,175, MS-61, October 2015											
1885	253,462	670	60.5	82%	$1,050	$1,060	$1,065	$1,070	$1,075	$1,080	$2,000	$20,000
	Auctions: $1,880, MS-63, October 2013; $1,528, MS-63, November 2014; $1,410, MS-63, July 2015; $823, MS-60, August 2014											
1885, Proof	65	11	63.5							$20,000	$32,500	$52,500
	Auctions: $57,500, PF-66UCam, January 2012											
1885-S	228,000	874	60.7	87%	$1,050	$1,060	$1,065	$1,070	$1,075	$1,080	$1,250	
	Auctions: $5,875, MS-64, August 2014; $4,406, MS-63, August 2013; $705, MS-62, October 2014; $881, MS-62, July 2014											
1886	236,100	660	59.3	64%	$1,050	$1,060	$1,065	$1,070	$1,075	$1,080	$2,000	
	Auctions: $1,998, MS-63, June 2015; $764, MS-61, October 2015; $823, AU-58, June 2015; $564, VF-30, October 2015											
1886, Proof	60	7	64.7							$18,500	$32,500	$52,500
	Auctions: $39,656, PF-64DCam, April 2014											
1886-S	826,000	3,149	61.3	95%	$1,050	$1,060	$1,065	$1,070	$1,075	$1,080	$1,250	
	Auctions: $1,116, MS-63, January 2015; $999, MS-63, January 2015; $969, MS-63, May 2015; $852, MS-63, July 2015											
1887	53,600	290	57.8	43%	$1,050	$1,060	$1,065	$1,070	$1,075	$1,080	$4,500	
	Auctions: $4,465, MS-63, June 2015; $1,351, MS-62, February 2015; $881, MS-61, January 2015; $999, AU-58, August 2015											
1887, Proof	80	16	64.2							$18,500	$32,500	$52,500
	Auctions: $64,625, PF-65DCam, April 2014											
1887-S	817,000	1,606	60.8	90%	$1,050	$1,060	$1,065	$1,070	$1,075	$1,080	$1,500	
	Auctions: $3,819, MS-64, January 2015; $1,293, MS-63, January 2015; $1,234, MS-63, February 2015; $1,116, MS-63, January 2015											
1888	132,921	487	58.8	57%	$1,050	$1,060	$1,065	$1,070	$1,075	$1,080	$3,250	
	Auctions: $2,820, MS-63, January 2015; $1,175, MS-62, February 2015; $1,028, MS-62, August 2015; $940, MS-61, September 2015											
1888, Proof	75	11	63.8							$18,500	$32,500	$52,500
	Auctions: $17,250, PF-63DCam, February 2009											
1888-O	21,335	688	60.1	80%	$1,050	$1,060	$1,065	$1,070	$1,100	$1,250	$7,500	
	Auctions: $21,150, MS-64, August 2013; $999, MS-62, October 2014; $1,293, MS-61, July 2014; $734, MS-60, January 2015											
1888-S	648,700	1,965	60.8	90%	$1,050	$1,060	$1,065	$1,070	$1,075	$1,080	$1,350	
	Auctions: $1,763, MS-63, August 2015; $1,528, MS-63, July 2015; $881, MS-62, January 2015; $764, AU-58, January 2015											

1889-S, Repunched Mintmark
FS-G10-1889S-501.

	Mintage	Cert	Avg	%MS	VF-20	EF-40	AU-50	AU-55	AU-58	MS-60 / PF-63	MS-63 / PF-64	MS-65 / PF-65
1889	4,440	118	58.7	54%	$1,050	$1,060	$1,065	$1,150	$2,500	$4,250	$10,000	
Auctions: $4,935, MS-62, June 2015; $3,995, MS-61, August 2015; $1,998, AU-58, June 2015; $1,528, AU-50, January 2015												
1889, Proof	45	4	64.3							$18,000	$32,500	$52,500
Auctions: $23,500, PF-64Cam, August 2014; $4,994, PF-60, April 2013												
1889-S	425,400	1,391	60.9	89%	$1,050	$1,060	$1,065	$1,070	$1,075	$1,080	$1,350	
Auctions: $999, MS-63, January 2015; $764, MS-62, February 2015; $823, MS-61, July 2015; $676, AU-55, June 2015												
1889-S, Repunched Mintmark	(v)	2	53.5	50%				$1,150	$1,250	$1,350	$1,850	
Auctions: $1,035, MS-63, August 2006												
1890	57,980	458	59.0	63%	$1,050	$1,060	$1,065	$1,070	$1,075	$1,080	$3,500	$15,000
Auctions: $2,820, MS-63, July 2014; $1,058, MS-62, November 2014; $1,116, MS-62, September 2014; $764, MS-60, October 2015												
1890, Proof	63	23	63.8							$16,500	$25,000	$50,000
Auctions: $29,900, PF-64UCam, January 2012												
1890-CC	17,500	400	56.9	39%	$1,250	$1,550	$2,250	$2,750	$3,750	$4,500	$20,000	
Auctions: $15,863, MS-63, August 2016; $9,400, MS-62, August 2016: $7,050, MS-62, August 2015; $4,935, MS-61, June 2015												
1891	91,820	732	61.1	95%	$1,050	$1,060	$1,065	$1,070	$1,075	$1,080	$2,500	
Auctions: $7,344, MS-64, November 2013; $1,998, MS-63, August 2014; $1,410, MS-62, July 2014; $716, MS-62, October 2015												
1891, Proof	48	19	64.3							$16,500	$25,000	$50,000
Auctions: $54,625, PF-65Cam, February 2012												
1891-CC	103,732	2,631	58.4	57%	$1,250	$1,500	$1,650	$2,150	$2,650	$2,850	$8,500	
Auctions: $14,688, MS-64, June 2015; $2,115, MS-61, July 2015; $1,763, AU-55, August 2015; $1,410, AU-50, August 2015												
1892	797,480	9,101	61.4	98%	$1,050	$1,060	$1,065	$1,070	$1,075	$1,080	$1,150	$7,500
Auctions: $6,756, MS-65, October 2013; $1,028, MS-63, July 2014; $652, MS-62, October 2014; $852, MS-62, August 2014												
1892, Proof	72	14	63.6							$16,500	$25,000	$50,000
Auctions: $4,406, PF-55, January 2014												
1892-CC	40,000	577	52.7	7%	$1,250	$1,500	$2,000	$2,750	$3,500	$5,500	$35,000	
Auctions: $1,763, AU-53, August 2014; $1,528, EF-45, February 2015; $823, EF-40, October 2015; $1,528, VF-35, January 2015												
1892-O	28,688	739	60.1	78%	$1,050	$1,060	$1,065	$1,070	$1,075	$1,300	$8,000	
Auctions: $1,998, MS-62, August 2015; $1,763, MS-62, September 2015; $1,410, MS-60, July 2015; $764, AU-55, January 2015												
1892-S	115,500	339	59.1	65%	$1,050	$1,060	$1,065	$1,070	$1,075	$1,080	$2,000	
Auctions: $940, MS-62, July 2015; $852, MS-62, January 2015; $764, MS-61, January 2015; $764, AU-58, January 2015												
1893	1,840,840	37,644	61.8	99%	$1,050	$1,060	$1,065	$1,070	$1,075	$1,080	$1,150	$6,500
Auctions: $1,645, MS-64, August 2015; $1,528, MS-63, July 2015; $734, MS-62, August 2015; $705, MS-61, June 2015												
1893, Proof	55	16	63.2							$16,500	$25,000	$50,000
Auctions: $30,550, PF-64DCam, August 2014; $58,750, PF, March 2014												
1893-CC	14,000	257	52.4	8%	$1,650	$2,150	$3,500	$5,500	$9,500	$20,000	—	
Auctions: $18,800, MS-61, January 2014; $6,463, AU-58, July 2015; $4,465, AU-55, September 2015; $4,465, AU-55, July 2015												
1893-O	17,000	474	59.6	68%	$1,075	$1,085	$1,090	$1,095	$1,100	$1,350	$5,000	
Auctions: $4,465, MS-63, June 2015; $1,293, MS-61, September 2014; $4,406, AU-58, September 2013; $823, AU-53, January 2015												
1893-S	141,350	649	60.2	80%	$1,050	$1,060	$1,065	$1,070	$1,075	$1,080	$2,000	
Auctions: $999, MS-62, July 2015; $940, MS-62, July 2015; $881, MS-62, February 2015; $823, MS-62, March 2015												

v. Included in 1889-S mintage figure.

	Mintage	Cert	Avg	%MS	VF-20	EF-40	AU-50	AU-55	AU-58	MS-60 / PF-63	MS-63 / PF-64	MS-65 / PF-65
1894	2,470,735	39,548	61.7	99%	$1,050	$1,060	$1,065	$1,070	$1,075	$1,080	$1,150	$10,000
Auctions: $5,942, MS-65, October 2015; $1,528, MS-64, October 2015; $705, MS-62, June 2015; $650, MS-60, January 2015												
1894, Proof	43	11	64.1							$16,500	$25,000	$50,000
Auctions: $105,750, PF-65, January 2014												
1894-O	107,500	1,021	57.4	35%	$1,075	$1,085	$1,090	$1,095	$1,100	$1,250	$5,500	
Auctions: $1,410, MS-61, July 2015; $940, AU-58, August 2015; $823, AU-53, June 2015; $705, AU-50, January 2015												
1894-S	25,000	170	53.6	13%	$1,075	$1,085	$1,090	$1,150	$1,800	$3,500		
Auctions: $9,988, MS-61, March 2014; $1,058, AU-55, September 2014; $1,293, AU-50, September 2015												
1895	567,770	12,129	61.7	99%	$1,050	$1,060	$1,065	$1,070	$1,075	$1,080	$1,150	$11,000
Auctions: $9,400, MS-65, June 2015; $1,410, MS-64, January 2015; $1,058, MS-63, November 2015; $764, AU-58, June 2015												
1895, Proof	56	21	63.8							$16,000	$25,000	$47,500
Auctions: $51,750, PF-65UCam, January 2012												
1895-O	98,000	834	58.8	50%	$1,075	$1,085	$1,090	$1,100	$1,125	$1,225	$6,500	
Auctions: $9,400, MS-63, February 2013; $940, AU-55, July 2015; $764, AU-55, January 2015; $705, EF-45, January 2015												
1895-S	49,000	236	52.8	9%	$1,075	$1,085	$1,090	$1,100	$1,150	$2,000	$8,000	
Auctions: $5,875, MS-62, October 2014; $4,700, MS-62, November 2014; $966, AU-55, May 2015; $846, AU-55, September 2014												
1896	76,270	1,504	61.7	98%	$1,050	$1,060	$1,065	$1,070	$1,075	$1,080	$1,200	$12,000
Auctions: $1,293, MS-63, July 2015; $911, MS-63, May 2015; $881, MS-62, July 2015; $823, MS-62, October 2015												
1896, Proof	78	19	63.6							$16,000	$25,000	$47,500
Auctions: $89,125, PF-66DCam, April 2012; $70,500, PF-66, September 2014												
1896-S	123,750	467	54.1	14%	$1,050	$1,060	$1,065	$1,070	$1,075	$1,850	$8,000	
Auctions: $2,233, MS-62, January 2015; $823, AU-55, September 2015; $617, AU-50, October 2015; $705, EF-45, June 2015												
1897	1,000,090	10,584	61.6	97%	$1,050	$1,060	$1,065	$1,070	$1,075	$1,080	$1,150	$4,000
Auctions: $5,875, MS-65, August 2015; $2,233, MS-64, September 2015; $1,528, MS-64, October 2015; $764, MS-62, February 2015												
1897, Proof	69	13	64.0							$16,000	$25,000	$47,500
Auctions: $19,975, PF, August 2013												
1897-O	42,500	457	58.8	47%	$1,075	$1,085	$1,090	$1,100	$1,150	$1,500	$6,500	$27,500
Auctions: $6,169, MS-63, March 2013; $2,350, MS-62, June 2015; $1,880, AU-58, July 2014; $999, AU-55, January 2015												
1897-S	234,750	370	57.2	35%	$1,050	$1,060	$1,065	$1,070	$1,075	$1,080	$5,500	$25,000
Auctions: $1,058, MS-62, February 2015; $823, MS-61, July 2015; $823, MS-60, October 2015; $734, AU-55, September 2015												
1898	812,130	4,321	61.3	94%	$1,050	$1,060	$1,065	$1,070	$1,075	$1,080	$1,150	$6,500
Auctions: $5,599, MS-65, August 2015; $2,056, MS-64, August 2015; $1,293, MS-63, February 2015; $999, MS-63, January 2015												
1898, Proof	67	29	65.2							$16,000	$25,000	$47,500
Auctions: $58,750, PF-66DCam, September 2014; $85,188, PF-66DCam, April 2013												
1898-S	473,600	465	60.1	84%	$1,050	$1,060	$1,065	$1,070	$1,075	$1,080	$2,000	$15,000
Auctions: $3,290, MS-63, January 2014; $1,116, MS-62, October 2015; $870, MS-61, July 2014; $764, MS-61, October 2015												
1899	1,262,219	22,309	62.1	98%	$1,050	$1,060	$1,065	$1,070	$1,075	$1,080	$1,150	$2,750
Auctions: $25,850, MS-67, June 2015; $17,625, MS-66, January 2015; $1,175, MS-63, September 2015; $764, MS-62, October 2015												
1899, Proof	86	38	64.1							$15,000	$25,000	$45,000
Auctions: $76,375, PF-67DCam, September 2014; $56,400, PF, March 2014												
1899-O	37,047	260	58.9	48%	$1,075	$1,085	$1,090	$1,100	$1,150	$1,450	$7,500	
Auctions: $7,638, MS-63, October 2015; $2,115, MS-62, July 2015; $1,763, MS-62, January 2015; $940, AU-55, July 2014												
1899-S	841,000	691	60.0	78%	$1,050	$1,060	$1,065	$1,070	$1,075	$1,080	$1,750	$15,000
Auctions: $3,525, MS-64, January 2015; $1,293, MS-63, May 2015; $1,028, MS-63, July 2015; $764, EF-40, July 2015												
1900	293,840	6,921	62.1	99%	$1,050	$1,060	$1,065	$1,070	$1,075	$1,080	$1,150	$3,500
Auctions: $3,643, MS-65, January 2015; $2,500, MS-65, January 2015; $1,351, MS-64, July 2015; $940, MS-63, August 2014												
1900, Proof	120	54	64.2							$15,000	$25,000	$45,000
Auctions: $1,880, PF, February 2014												
1900-S	81,000	192	58.0	39%	$1,050	$1,060	$1,065	$1,070	$1,075	$1,100	$5,500	$20,000
Auctions: $6,169, MS-63, September 2013; $658, AU-58, November 2014; $705, AU-58, July 2014												

	Mintage	Cert	Avg	%MS	VF-20	EF-40	AU-50	AU-55	AU-58	MS-60 / PF-63	MS-63 / PF-64	MS-65 / PF-65
1901	1,718,740	29,649	62.6	98%	$1,050	$1,060	$1,065	$1,070	$1,075	$1,080	$1,150	$2,500
	Auctions: $7,931, MS-66, October 2015; $3,200, MS-65, January 2015; $999, MS-63, January 2015; $940, MS-62, June 2015											
1901, Proof	85	52	63.6							$15,000	$25,000	$45,000
	Auctions: $48,875, PF-66Cam, January 2012											
1901-O	72,041	578	59.8	65%	$1,075	$1,085	$1,090	$1,100	$1,150	$1,250	$3,250	$15,000
	Auctions: $6,169, MS-64, June 2014											
1901-S	2,812,750	20,855	62.9	99%	$1,050	$1,060	$1,065	$1,070	$1,075	$1,080	$1,150	$2,500
	Auctions: $19,975, MS-67, January 2015; $3,290, MS-65, August 2015; $1,146, MS-64, March 2015; $1,251, MS-63, August 2015											
1902	82,400	760	61.1	89%	$1,050	$1,060	$1,065	$1,070	$1,075	$1,080	$1,300	$9,000
	Auctions: $1,528, MS-63, June 2015; $1,293, MS-63, September 2015; $1,645, MS-62, August 2015; $712, AU-58, February 2015											
1902, Proof	113	27	63.7							$15,000	$25,000	$45,000
	Auctions: $61,688, PF-67, February 2013											
1902-S	469,500	3,325	62.9	99%	$1,050	$1,060	$1,065	$1,070	$1,075	$1,080	$1,150	$2,500
	Auctions: $8,519, MS-66, February 2014; $1,058, MS-63, September 2014; $1,058, MS-63, August 2014											
1903	125,830	1,124	61.3	91%	$1,050	$1,060	$1,065	$1,070	$1,075	$1,080	$1,150	$7,000
	Auctions: $1,116, MS-64, October 2014; $6,463, MS-65, January 2014; $1,058, MS-63, October 2014; $1,058, MS-63, August 2014											
1903, Proof	96	43	64.3							$15,000	$25,000	$45,000
	Auctions: $39,950, PF, October 2013											
1903-O	112,771	1,374	60.1	71%	$1,075	$1,085	$1,090	$1,100	$1,150	$1,200	$2,500	$17,500
	Auctions: $1,645, MS-62, September 2016: $1,175, MS-62, January 2015; $999, MS-61, January 2015; $940, AU-58, September 2015											
1903-S	538,000	1,010	62.2	92%	$1,050	$1,060	$1,065	$1,070	$1,075	$1,080	$1,150	$2,500
	Auctions: $9,106, MS-66, September 2015; $4,935, MS-66, July 2015; $4,935, MS-65, January 2015; $2,350, MS-64, June 2015											
1904	161,930	1,228	61.3	92%	$1,050	$1,060	$1,065	$1,070	$1,075	$1,080	$1,500	$8,500
	Auctions: $1,763, MS-64, October 2015; $1,293, MS-64, July 2015; $999, MS-63, June 2015; $999, MS-63, April 2015											
1904, Proof	108	35	63.2							$15,000	$25,000	$45,000
	Auctions: $64,625, PF-66Cam, June 2013											
1904-O	108,950	726	60.0	67%	$1,075	$1,085	$1,090	$1,100	$1,150	$1,200	$3,000	$20,000
	Auctions: $19,975, MS-65, January 2015; $1,410, MS-62, July 2015; $734, AU-58, January 2015; $764, AU-55, February 2015											
1905	200,992	2,369	61.6	94%	$1,050	$1,060	$1,065	$1,070	$1,075	$1,080	$1,250	$5,500
	Auctions: $24,675, MS-67, September 2015; $1,880, MS-64, June 2015; $1,880, MS-64, February 2015; $1,528, MS-64, June 2015											
1905, Proof	86	36	63.2							$15,000	$25,000	$45,000
	Auctions: $76,050, PF, September 2013											
1905-S	369,250	597	57.0	27%	$1,050	$1,060	$1,065	$1,070	$1,075	$1,080	$3,500	$30,000
	Auctions: $1,645, MS-62, July 2015; $940, MS-61, July 2015; $705, AU-58, January 2015; $617, AU-55, October 2015											
1906	165,420	1,600	61.2	91%	$1,050	$1,060	$1,065	$1,070	$1,075	$1,080	$1,250	$8,000
	Auctions: $1,998, MS-64, July 2015; $1,058, MS-63, July 2015; $1,058, MS-63, December 2014; $652, MS-61, October 2014											
1906, Proof	77	34	64.2							$15,000	$25,000	$45,000
	Auctions: $41,125, PF, February 2013											
1906-D	981,000	4,037	61.4	90%	$1,050	$1,060	$1,065	$1,070	$1,075	$1,080	$1,150	$6,500
	Auctions: $2,938, MS-64, June 2015; $1,058, MS-63, August 2015; $881, MS-62, September 2015; $764, MS-61, January 2015											
1906-O	86,895	504	60.0	65%	$1,075	$1,085	$1,090	$1,100	$1,125	$1,150	$4,750	$20,000
	Auctions: $21,150, MS-65, October 2014; $5,875, MS-64, August 2014; $1,645, MS-62, January 2015; $1,175, MS-62, October 2014											
1906-S	457,000	600	58.1	45%	$1,050	$1,060	$1,065	$1,070	$1,075	$1,080	$2,500	$16,500
	Auctions: $12,925, MS-64, February 2015; $1,998, MS-63, January 2015; $1,880, MS-63, January 2015; $1,528, MS-63, June 2015											
1907	1,203,899	28,826	62.1	98%	$1,050	$1,060	$1,065	$1,070	$1,075	$1,080	$1,150	$2,500
	Auctions: $3,525, MS-65, October 2015; $1,645, MS-64, October 2015; $764, MS-62, June 2015; $913, MS-61, July 2015											
1907, Proof	74	52	63.9							$15,000	$25,000	$45,000
	Auctions: $54,050, PF 65Cam, January 2015; $33,638, PF-65Cam, March 2012; $29,375, PF-64Cam, August 2014											
1907-D	1,030,000	574	61.3	88%	$1,050	$1,060	$1,065	$1,070	$1,075	$1,080	$1,650	$13,500
	Auctions: $2,585, MS-64, August 2015; $2,233, MS-64, January 2015; $1,821, MS-63, November 2014; $823, MS-61, August 2014											
1907-S	210,500	384	58.8	54%	$1,050	$1,060	$1,065	$1,070	$1,075	$1,080	$3,500	$22,500
	Auctions: $1,880, MS-62, September 2015; $969, MS-62, August 2015; $881, MS-61, January 2015; $823, MS-61, February 2015											

INDIAN HEAD (1907–1933)

Designer: *Augustus Saint-Gaudens.* **Weight:** *16.718 grams.*
Composition: *.900 gold, .100 copper (net weight: .48375 oz. pure gold).*
Diameter: *27 mm.* **Edge:** *1907–1911—46 raised stars; 1912–1933—48 raised stars.*
Mints: *Philadelphia, Denver, and San Francisco.*

No Motto (1907–1908)

Mintmark location, 1908-D (No Motto), is on the reverse, at the tip of the branch.

Mintmark location, 1908 (With Motto)–1930, is on the reverse, to the left of the arrows.

With Motto (1908–1933)

With Motto, Sandblast Finish Proof   **With Motto, Satin Finish Proof**

History. The Indian Head eagle, designed by sculptor Augustus Saint-Gaudens and championed by President Theodore Roosevelt, was struck from 1907 to 1916, and again in intermittent issues through the 1920s and early 1930s. Saint-Gaudens's original design proved impractical to strike and thus was modified slightly by Charles Barber before any large quantities were produced. Not long after (in July 1908), the motto IN GOD WE TRUST was added to the reverse, where it remained to the end of the series. These coins were widely used until 1918, in circulation in the American West and for export.

Striking and Sharpness. On the obverse, check the hair details and the vanes in the feathers. On the reverse, check the shoulder of the eagle. As well-struck coins are available for all varieties, avoid those that are weakly struck. Some examples may exhibit a pink-green color or rust-red "copper spots." Luster varies, but is often deeply frosty. On other coins, particularly from 1910 to 1916, it may be grainy.

Proofs. Sandblast (also called Matte) Proofs were made each year from 1907 through 1915. These have dull surfaces, much like fine-grained sandpaper. Satin (also called Roman Finish) Proofs were made in 1908, 1909, and 1910; they have satiny surfaces and are bright yellow.

Availability. Key rarities in this series are the rolled (or round) rim and wire rim 1907 coins, and the 1920-S, 1930-S, and 1933. Others are generally more readily available. MS-63 and higher coins are generally scarce to rare for the mintmarked issues. The Indian Head eagle is a very popular series. Most such coins in collectors' hands were exported in their time, then brought back to America after World War II. All of the Proofs are rare today.

Note: Values of common-date gold coins have been based on the current bullion price of gold, $2,000 per ounce, and may vary with the prevailing spot price.

GRADING STANDARDS

MS-60 to 70 (Mint State). *Obverse:* At MS-60, some abrasion and contact marks are evident, most noticeably on the hair to the left of Miss Liberty's forehead and in the left field. Luster is present, but may be dull or lifeless, and interrupted in patches. At MS-63, contact marks are few, and abrasion is very light. An MS-65 coin has hardly any abrasion, and contact marks are minute. Luster should be full and rich. Grades above MS-65 are defined by

1907. Graded MS-62.

having fewer marks as perfection is approached. *Reverse:* Comments apply as for the obverse, except that abrasion and contact marks are most noticeable on the front of the left wing and in the left field.

Illustrated coin: This is a brilliant and lustrous example.

AU-50, 53, 55, 58 (About Uncirculated). *Obverse:* Light wear is seen on the cheek, the hair to the right of the face, and the headdress, more so at AU-50 coin than at AU–53 or 55. An AU-58 coin has minimal traces of wear. An AU-50 coin has luster in protected areas among the stars and in the small field area to the right. At AU-58, most luster is present in the fields but is worn away on the highest parts of the Indian. *Reverse:* Com-

1908-D. Graded AU-58.

ments as preceding, except that the eagle's left wing, left leg, neck, and leg show light wear. Luster ranges from perhaps 40% (at AU-50) to nearly full mint bloom (at AU-58).

Illustrated coin: With nearly full original luster, this coin has remarkable eye appeal.

EF-40, 45 (Extremely Fine). *Obverse:* More wear is evident on the hair to the right of the face, and the feather vanes lack some details, although most are present. Luster, if present at all, is minimal. *Reverse:* Wear is greater than on the preceding. The front edge of the left wing is worn and blends into the top of the left leg. Some traces of luster may be seen, more so at EF-45 than at EF-40.

1907. Graded EF-40.

VF-20, 30 (Very Fine). *Obverse:* The Indian's forehead blends into the hair to the right. Feather-vane detail is gone except in the lower areas. *Reverse:* Wear is greater on the eagle, with only a few details remaining on the back of the left wing and the tail.

Indian Head eagles are seldom collected in grades lower than VF-20.

1908-S. Graded VF-25.

PF-60 to 70 (Proof). *Obverse and Reverse:* At PF–60 to 63, there is light abrasion and some contact marks (the lower the grade, the higher the quantity). On Sandblast Proofs these show up as visually unappealing bright spots. At PF-64 and higher levels, marks are fewer, with magnification needed to see any at PF-65. At PF-66, there should be none at all.

1915. Sandblast Finish. Graded PF-65.

No Periods	Periods

	Mintage	Cert	Avg	%MS	VF-20	EF-40	AU-50	AU-55	MS-60 / PF-63	MS-62 / PF-64	MS-63 / PF-65	MS-65
1907, Wire Rim, Periods	500	173	63.4	92%		$25,000	$27,500	$29,500	$35,000	$40,000	$45,000	$75,000
	Auctions: $82,250, MS-65, August 2016; $67,563, MS-65, October 2015; $58,750, MS-65, August 2015; $56,400, MS-65, May 2016											
1907, Rounded Rim, Periods Before and After •E•PLURIBUS•UNUM• † (a)	50	28	62.7	82%		$60,000	$65,000	$70,000	$85,000	$105,000	$150,000	$300,000
	Auctions: $470,000, MS-67, August 2013											
1907, No Periods	239,406	8,046	61.6	84%	$1,050	$1,060	$1,065	$1,070	$1,125	$1,500	$1,800	$6,000
	Auctions: $35,250, MS-67, August 2015; $5,170, MS-64, June 2015; $1,293, AU-58, January 2015; $999, AU-50, February 2015											
1907, Wire Rim, Periods, Plain Edge, Proof (b)	unknown	0	n/a									
	Auctions: $359,375, PF-62, August 2010											
1907, Rounded Rim, Periods, Satin Finish Proof	unknown	0	n/a		*(extremely rare)*							
	Auctions: $2,185,000, PF-67, January 2011											
1907, Sandblast Finish Proof (c)	unknown	0	n/a		*(extremely rare)*							
	Auctions: No auction records available.											

† Ranked in the *100 Greatest U.S. Coins* (fifth edition). **a.** All but 50 of the 31,500 coins were melted at the mint. **b.** According to the *Encyclopedia of U.S. Gold Coins, 1795–1933* (second edition), the only confirmed example may be from the Captain North set of 1907 and 1908 gold coins sold by Stack's in the 1970s. **c.** 2 or 3 examples are known.

	Mintage	Cert	Avg	%MS	VF-20	EF-40	AU-50	AU-55	MS-60	MS-62 / PF-63	MS-63 / PF-64	MS-65 / PF-65
1908, No Motto	33,500	877	60.9	77%	$1,050	$1,060	$1,065	$1,070	$1,400	$2,600	$4,000	$14,000
Auctions: $19,975, MS-66, October 2015; $7,050, MS-64, January 2015; $3,055, MS-62, October 2015; $1,763, AU-58, June 2015											
1908-D, No Motto	210,000	1,099	59.3	51%	$1,050	$1,060	$1,065	$1,070	$1,250	$2,500	$4,500	$45,000
Auctions: $13,513, MS-64, January 2015; $2,233, MS-61, February 2015; $1,234, AU-58, August 2015; $734, EF-45, October 2015											
1908, With Motto	341,370	4,898	60.7	78%	$1,050	$1,060	$1,065	$1,070	$1,100	$1,150	$1,300	$4,600
Auctions: $32,900, MS-66, October 2015; $1,998, MS-63, March 2015; $1,058, AU-58, August 2015; $764, EF-45, February 2015											
1908, With Motto, Sandblast Finish Proof	116	51	65.2							$20,000	$35,000	$60,000
Auctions: $69,000, PF-66, January 2012; $79,313, PF-65, August 2014; $61,688, PF-65, January 2015											
1908, With Motto, Satin Finish Proof (d)	(e)				*(extremely rare)*						
Auctions: No auction records available.											
1908-D, With Motto	836,500	899	58.9	52%	$1,050	$1,060	$1,065	$1,070	$1,100	$2,250	$4,000	$25,000
Auctions: $5,640, MS-63, January 2015; $3,525, MS-62, October 2015; $1,293, MS-61, January 2015; $999, AU-58, August 2015											
1908-S	59,850	881	54.4	19%	$1,150	$1,250	$1,350	$1,500	$4,500	$8,500	$13,000	$25,000
Auctions: $35,251, MS-66, October 2015; $14,100, MS-64, March 2015; $4,113, AU-58, September 2015; $999, EF-45, February 2015											
1909	184,789	2,222	60.4	73%	$1,050	$1,060	$1,065	$1,070	$1,100	$1,150	$1,500	$17,500
Auctions: $5,640, MS-64, June 2015; $3,290, MS-63, January 2015; $1,058, MS-62, March 2015; $940, MS-61, June 2015											
1909, Satin Finish Proof	74	43	65.1							$22,500	$35,000	$75,000
Auctions: $48,875, PF-65, July 2011											
1909, Sandblast Finish Proof (f)	(g)	0			*(extremely rare)*						
Auctions: No auction records available.											
1909-D	121,540	1,109	59.4	55%	$1,050	$1,060	$1,065	$1,070	$1,250	$2,000	$3,000	$30,000
Auctions: $4,113, MS-63, January 2015; $2,115, MS-62, March 2015; $999, AU-58, August 2015; $940, AU-55, August 2015											
1909-S	292,350	944	57.2	33%	$1,050	$1,060	$1,065	$1,100	$1,500	$2,500	$4,250	$17,500
Auctions: $7,638, MS-64, October 2015; $1,880, MS-61, September 2015; $1,116, AU-58, June 2015; $800, AU-53, August 2015											
1910	318,500	6,715	61.5	88%	$1,050	$1,060	$1,065	$1,070	$1,100	$1,150	$1,250	$5,500
Auctions: $17,625, MS-66, January 2015; $1,645, MS-64, January 2015; $940, MS-61, September 2015; $676, MS-60, October 2015											
1910, Satin Finish Proof	204	26	65.4							$20,000	$35,000	$75,000
Auctions: $80,500, PF-67, January 2012											
1910, Sandblast Finish Proof (h)	(i)											
Auctions: No auction records available.											
1910-D	2,356,640	14,158	61.6	90%	$1,050	$1,060	$1,065	$1,070	$1,100	$1,150	$1,250	$5,500
Auctions: $13,513, MS-66, October 2015; $1,998, MS-64, January 2015; $837, MS-60, June 2015; $705, AU-58, October 2015											
1910-S	811,000	1,998	57.0	32%	$1,050	$1,060	$1,065	$1,085	$1,150	$1,750	$5,000	$45,000
Auctions: $12,925, MS-64, January 2015; $1,645, MS-61, August 2015; $1,410, AU-58, January 2015; $823, AU-58, August 2015											
1911	505,500	10,769	61.5	86%	$1,050	$1,060	$1,065	$1,070	$1,100	$1,150	$1,250	$5,500
Auctions: $30,550, MS-67, August 2015; $9,988, MS-66, September 2015; $1,293, MS-63, February 2015; $705, AU-55, August 2015											
1911, Sandblast Finish Proof	95	23	66.4							$20,000	$35,000	$70,000
Auctions: $152,750, PF-67, November 2013; $76,375, PF-66, August 2015; $74,025, PF-66, October 2014											
1911-D	30,100	969	54.7	17%	$1,350	$1,750	$2,750	$3,500	$11,500	$14,500	$30,000	$250,000
Auctions: $23,500, MS-63, October 2015; $22,325, MS-63, August 2016; $30,550, MS-62, January 2015; $6,169, AU-58, January 2015											
1911-S	51,000	423	56.7	27%	$1,050	$1,060	$1,075	$1,150	$3,000	$6,500	$11,000	$25,000
Auctions: $24,793, MS-65, October 2015; $3,525, MS-61, October 2015; $2,820, AU-58, September 2015; $1,645, AU-50, February 2015											

d. 3 or 4 examples are known. **e.** Included in 1908, With Motto, Matte Proof, mintage figure. **f.** 2 or 3 examples are known. **g.** Included in 1909, Satin Finish Proof, mintage figure. **h.** The only example known is part of the unique complete 1910 Matte Proof gold set. **i.** Included in 1910, Satin Finish Proof, mintage figure.

	Mintage	Cert	Avg	%MS	VF-20	EF-40	AU-50	AU-55	MS-60	MS-62	MS-63	MS-65
										PF-63	PF-64	PF-65
1912	405,000	7,377	61.3	86%	$1,050	$1,060	$1,065	$1,070	$1,100	$1,150	$1,250	$7,500
	Auctions: $54,050, MS-67, January 2015; $3,290, MS-64, January 2015; $881, MS-61, September 2015; $705, AU-55, August 2015											
1912, Sandblast Finish Proof	83	21	65.7							$20,000	$35,000	$70,000
	Auctions: $99,875, PF, March 2014											
1912-S	300,000	1,229	57.1	27%	$1,050	$1,060	$1,075	$1,085	$1,250	$2,000	$4,750	$35,000
	Auctions: $12,402, MS-64, October 2015; $1,116, AU-58, August 2015; $734, AU-50, February 2015; $705, EF-45, January 2015											
1913	442,000	6,569	61.1	83%	$1,050	$1,060	$1,065	$1,070	$1,100	$1,150	$1,250	$5,000
	Auctions: $14,100, MS-66, January 2015; $3,408, MS-64, February 2015; $881, MS-62, June 2015; $705, AU-58, July 2015											
1913, Sandblast Finish Proof	71	27	65.5							$20,000	$32,500	$75,000
	Auctions: $63,250, PF-66, January 2012											
1913-S	66,000	983	54.9	13%	$1,100	$1,200	$1,350	$2,250	$6,000	$12,500	$21,000	$165,000
	Auctions: $22,325, MS-63, January 2015; $4,243, AU-58, February 2015; $1,528, AU-53, June 2015; $852, EF-40, January 2015											
1914	151,000	2,475	61.1	82%	$1,050	$1,060	$1,065	$1,070	$1,100	$1,150	$1,500	$7,750
	Auctions: $10,869, MS-65, October 2015; $2,832, MS-64, January 2015; $1,998, MS-63, January 2015; $881, MS-62, May 2015											
1914, Sandblast Finish Proof	50	33	65.7							$20,000	$40,000	$80,000
	Auctions: $96,938, PF, October 2013											
1914-D	343,500	3,049	60.6	74%	$1,050	$1,060	$1,065	$1,070	$1,100	$1,150	$1,400	$8,000
	Auctions: $9,988, MS-65, October 2015; $1,998, MS-63, January 2015; $887, MS-61, June 2015; $764, AU-55, October 2015											
1914-S	208,000	1,159	58.2	38%	$1,050	$1,060	$1,065	$1,085	$1,750	$3,000	$4,500	$37,500
	Auctions: $16,450, MS-64, October 2015; $1,645, AU-58, January 2015; $705, AU-53, August 2015; $709, EF-45, August 2015											
1915	351,000	4,747	61.0	79%	$1,050	$1,060	$1,065	$1,070	$1,100	$1,150	$1,300	$6,500
	Auctions: $6,463, MS-65, January 2015; $2,350, MS-63, January 2015; $823, MS-60, September 2015; $823, AU-58, September 2015											
1915, Sandblast Finish Proof	75	19	65.8							$25,000	$40,000	$80,000
	Auctions: $94,000, PF, August 2013											
1915-S	59,000	462	57.3	26%	$1,100	$1,200	$1,500	$2,250	$6,000	$12,500	$20,000	$65,000
	Auctions: $19,975, MS-62, September 2015; $6,611, MS-61, August 2015; $3,408, AU-58, January 2015; $1,058, AU-50, January 2015											
1916-S	138,500	977	58.9	48%	$1,150	$1,200	$1,250	$1,350	$1,500	$2,750	$5,750	$25,000
	Auctions: $7,050, MS-63, August 2015; $1,763, MS-61, October 2015; $1,528, AU-58, August 2015; $764, AU-50, September 2015											
1920-S	126,500	52	59.6	58%	$22,500	$25,000	$32,500	$40,000	$60,000	$75,000	$105,000	$225,000
	Auctions: $75,000, MS-62, January 2018; $70,500, MS-61, June 2015; $64,625, MS-61, October 2015; $42,300, AU-58, August 2016											
1926	1,014,000	42,852	62.5	99%	$1,050	$1,060	$1,065	$1,070	$1,100	$1,125	$1,250	$2,750
	Auctions: $7,638, MS-66, October 2015; $1,469, MS-64, October 2015; $823, MS-61, June 2015; $646, MS-60, July 2015											
1930-S	96,000	59	63.7	97%	$20,000	$22,500	$25,000	$30,000	$40,000	$45,000	$55,000	$100,000
	Auctions: $85,188, MS-65, September 2014; $69,000, MS-64, January 2018; $17,625, MS-60, January 2015											
1932	4,463,000	70,711	62.9	100%	$1,050	$1,060	$1,065	$1,070	$1,100	$1,125	$1,250	$2,750
	Auctions: $10,869, MS-66, January 2015; $2,482, MS-65, March 2015; $1,528, MS-63, August 2015; $793, MS-60, July 2015											
1933 † (j)	312,500	11	64.4	100%					$300,000	$325,000	$400,000	$750,000
	Auctions: $587,500, MS-65, June 2015: $367,188, MS-64, August 2013											

† Ranked in the *100 Greatest U.S. Coins* (fifth edition). **j.** Nearly all were melted at the mint.

Gold Double Eagles ($20)
1850–1933

AN OVERVIEW OF GOLD DOUBLE EAGLES

Congress authorized the double eagle, or twenty-dollar coin—the largest denomination of all regular U.S. coinage issues—by the Act of March 3, 1849, in response to the huge amounts of gold coming from California.

Double eagles are at once large and impressive to own. Many gold collectors form a type set of the six major double eagle designs (with the 1861 Paquet added as a sub-type if desired). Thanks to overseas hoards repatriated since the 1950s, finding choice and gem Mint State examples is no problem at all for the later types.

The first double eagle type, the Liberty Head of 1850 to 1866 without the motto IN GOD WE TRUST, is generally available in grades from VF up. Mint State pieces were elusive prior to the 1990s, but the market supply was augmented by more than 5,000 pieces—including some gems—found in the discovery of the long-lost treasure ship SS *Central America*. The SS *Brother Jonathan*, lost at sea in 1865, was recovered in the 1990s and yielded hundreds of Mint State 1865-S double eagles, along with some dated 1864 and a few earlier. The wreck of the SS *Republic*, lost in 1865 while on a voyage from New York City to New Orleans and salvaged in 2003, also yielded some very attractive Mint State double eagles of this first Liberty Head type.

The Liberty Head type from 1866 through 1876, with the motto IN GOD WE TRUST above the eagle and with the denomination expressed as TWENTY D., is the rarest in MS-63 and higher grades. Many EF and AU coins have been repatriated from overseas holdings, as have quite a few in such grades as MS–60 through 62. However, true gems are hardly ever seen.

Liberty Head double eagles of the 1877–1907 type with the IN GOD WE TRUST motto and with the denomination spelled out as TWENTY DOLLARS are exceedingly plentiful in just about any grade desired, with gems being readily available of certain issues of the early 20th century. While it is easy to obtain a gem of a common date, some collectors of type coins have opted to acquire a coin of special historical interest, such as a Carson City issue.

The famous Saint-Gaudens MCMVII High Relief double eagle of 1907 was saved in quantity by the general public as well as by numismatists, and today it is likely that at least 5,000 to 6,000 exist, representing about half of the mintage. Most of these are in varying degrees of Mint State, with quite a few graded as MS–64 and 65. Those in lower grades such as VF and EF often were used for jewelry or were polished, or have other problems. This particular design is a great favorite with collectors, and although the coins are not rarities, they are hardly inexpensive.

The so-called Arabic Numerals 1907–1908 Saint-Gaudens design is available in nearly any grade desired, with MS-60 through MS-63 or MS-64 pieces being plentiful and inexpensive. Double eagles of the final type, 1908–1933, are abundant in any grade desired, with choice and gem coins being plentiful.

FOR THE COLLECTOR AND INVESTOR: GOLD DOUBLE EAGLES AS A SPECIALTY

Collecting double eagles by date and mint is more popular than one might think. Offhand, one might assume that these high denominations, laden with a number of rare dates, would attract few enthusiasts. However, over a long period of years more collectors have specialized in double eagles than have specialized in five-dollar or ten-dollar pieces.

Two particularly notable collections of double eagles by date and mint, from the earliest times to the latest, were formed by Louis E. Eliasberg of Baltimore, and Jeff Browning of Dallas. Both have been dispersed across the auction block. The first was cataloged by Bowers and Ruddy in 1982, and the second was offered by Stack's and Sotheby's in 2001. In addition, dozens of other collections over the years have had large numbers of double eagles, some specializing in the Liberty Head types of 1850–1907, others only with the Saint-Gaudens types from 1907 onward, and others addressing the entire range.

Among rarities in the double eagle series are the 1854-O and 1856-O, each known only to the extent of a few dozen pieces; the 1861 Philadelphia Mint coins with Paquet reverse (two known); the Proof-only issues of 1883, 1884, and 1887; several other low-mintage varieties of this era; the famous Carson City issue of 1870-CC; and various issues from 1920 onward, including 1920-S, 1921, mintmarked coins after 1923, and all dates after 1928. Punctuating these rarities is a number of readily available pieces, including the very common Philadelphia issues from 1922 through 1928 inclusive.

LIBERTY HEAD (1849–1907)

Designer: *James B. Longacre.* **Weight:** *33.436 grams.*
Composition: *.900 gold, .100 copper (net weight: .96750 oz. pure gold).* **Diameter** *34 mm.*
Edge: *Reeded.* **Mints:** *Philadelphia, Carson City, Denver, New Orleans, and San Francisco.*

No Motto (1849–1866)   **No Motto, Proof**

*Mintmark location is on
the reverse, below the eagle.*

With Motto (1866–1907)   **With Motto, Proof**

History. The twenty-dollar denomination was introduced to circulation in 1850 (after a unique pattern, which currently resides in the Smithsonian's National Numismatic Collection, was minted in 1849). The large new coin was ideal for converting the flood of California gold rush bullion into federal legal tender. U.S. Mint chief engraver James B. Longacre designed the coin. A different reverse, designed by Anthony Paquet with taller letters than Longacre's design, was tested in 1861 but ultimately not used past that date. In 1866 the motto IN GOD WE TRUST was added to the reverse. In 1877 the denomination on the reverse, formerly given as TWENTY D., was changed to TWENTY DOLLARS. The double eagle denomination proved to be very popular, especially for export. By 1933, more than 75 percent of the American gold used to strike coins from the 1850s onward had been used to make double eagles. Oddly, some of the coins of 1850 to 1858 appear to have the word LIBERTY misspelled as LLBERTY.

Striking and Sharpness. On the obverse, check the star centers and the hair details. As made, the hair details are less distinct on many coins of 1859 (when a slight modification was made) through the 1890s, and knowledge of this is important. Later issues usually have exquisite detail. The reverse usually is well struck, but check the eagle and other features. The denticles are sharp on nearly all coins, but should be checked. Proofs were made in all years from 1858 to 1907, and a few were made before then. Proofs of 1902 onward, particularly 1903, have the portrait polished in the die, imparting a mirror finish across the design, and lack the cameo contrast of earlier dates.

Availability. Basic dates and mintmarks are available in proportion to their mintages. Key issues include the 1854-O, 1856-O, 1861 Paquet Reverse, 1861-S Paquet Reverse, 1866 No Motto, 1870-CC, 1879-O, and several Philadelphia Mint dates of the 1880s The vast majority of others are readily collectible. Among early coins, MS examples from about 1854 to 1857 are available, most notably the 1857-S and certain varieties of the 1860s. Most varieties of the 1880s onward, and particularly of the 1890s and 1900s, are easily available in MS, due to the repatriation of millions of coins that had been exported overseas. Proofs dated through the 1870s are all very rare today; those of the 1880s are less so; and those of the 1890s and 1900s are scarce. Many Proofs have been mishandled. Dates that are Proof-only (and those that are very rare in circulation-strike form) are in demand even if impaired. These include 1883, 1884, 1885, 1886, and 1887.

Note: Values of common-date gold coins have been based on the current bullion price of gold, $2,000 per ounce, and may vary with the prevailing spot price.

GRADING STANDARDS

MS-60 to 70 (Mint State). *Obverse:* At MS-60, some abrasion and contact marks are evident, most noticeably on the hair to the right of Miss Liberty's forehead and on the cheek. Luster is present, but may be dull or lifeless, and interrupted in patches. At MS-63, contact marks are few, and abrasion is light. An MS-65 coin has little abrasion, and contact marks are minute. Luster should be full and rich. Grades above MS-65 are defined by

1876-S. Graded MS-64.

having fewer marks as perfection is approached. *Reverse:* Comments apply as for the obverse, except that abrasion and contact marks are most noticeable on eagle's neck, wingtips, and tail.

AU-50, 53, 55, 58 (About Uncirculated). *Obverse:* Light wear is seen on the face, the hair to the right of the face, and the highest area of the hair behind the coronet, more so at AU-50 than at AU–53 or 55. An AU-58 coin has minimal traces of wear. An AU-50 coin has luster in protected areas among the stars and letters, with little in the open fields or on the portrait. At AU-58 most luster is present in the fields, but is worn away on the

1856-S. Graded AU-53.

highest parts of the motifs. *Reverse:* Comments as preceding, except that the eagle and ornaments show wear in all of the higher areas. Luster ranges from perhaps 40% remaining in protected areas (at AU-50) to nearly full mint bloom (at AU-58). Often the reverse of this type retains more luster than the obverse.

Illustrated coin: Much of the original luster still remains at this grade level, especially on the reverse.

EF-40, 45 (Extremely Fine). *Obverse:* Wear is evident on all high areas of the portrait, including the hair to the right of the forehead, the tip of the coronet, and hair behind the coronet. The curl to the right of the neck is flat on its highest-relief area. Luster, if present at all, is minimal and in protected areas such as between the star points. *Reverse:* Wear is greater than on an About Uncirculated coin. The eagle's neck and wingtips

1855-S. Graded EF-45.

show wear, as do the ornaments and rays. Some traces of luster may be seen, more so at EF-45 than at EF-40. Overall, the reverse appears to be in a slightly higher grade than the obverse.

VF-20, 30 (Very Fine). *Obverse:* The higher-relief areas of hair are worn flat at VF-20, less so at VF-30. The hair to the right of the coronet is merged into heavy strands and is flat at the back, as is part of the bow. The curl to the right of the neck is flat. *Reverse:* The eagle shows further wear on the head, the tops of the wings, and the tail. The ornament has flat spots.

1857-S. Graded VF-20.

Illustrated coin: Note the small test cut or mark on the top rim.

Liberty Head double eagles are seldom collected in grades lower than VF-20.

PF-60 to 70 (Proof). *Obverse and Reverse:* PF–60 to 62 coins have extensive hairlines and may have nicks and contact marks. At PF-63, hairlines are prominent, but the mirror surface is very reflective. PF-64 coins have fewer hairlines. At PF-65, hairlines should be relatively few. These large and heavy coins reveal hairlines more readily than do the lower denominations, mostly seen only under magnification. PF-66 and higher coins should have no marks or hairlines visible to the unaided eye.

1903. Graded PF-64.

Illustrated coin: A beautiful Proof, this is just a few hairlines away from a higher level.

Value TWENTY D. (1849–1876)	Value TWENTY DOLLARS (1877–1907)	1853, So-called 3 Over 2 Note rust under LIBERTY. FS-G20-1853-301.

	Mintage	Cert	Avg	%MS	VF-20	EF-40	AU-50	AU-55	MS-60	MS-62 / PF-63	MS-63 / PF-64	MS-65 / PF-65
1849, Proof † (a)	1	0	n/a		(unique; in the Smithsonian's National Numismatic Collection)							
	Auctions: No auction records available.											
1850	1,170,261	1,649	50.5	5%	$2,350	$2,850	$3,500	$5,850	$12,500	$40,000	$60,000	$175,000
	Auctions: $42,300, MS-62, August 2015; $7,344, AU-55, August 2015; $4,465, AU-50, June 2015; $2,585, EF-40, January 2015											
1850, Proof (b)	1–2	0	n/a									
	Auctions: No auction records available.											
1850-O	141,000	380	47.5	2%	$4,500	$6,500	$10,000	$22,500	$60,000			
	Auctions: $58,750, MS-61, January 2015; $21,150, AU-55, January 2015; $9,400, EF-45, August 2015; $4,465, VF-25, August 2015											
1851	2,087,155	1,200	51.4	8%	$2,150	$2,250	$2,450	$2,850	$5,250	$12,500	$25,000	
	Auctions: $14,100, MS-62, July 2015; $5,170, AU-55, August 2015; $1,645, EF-40, January 2015; $1,772, VF-35, June 2015											
1851-O	315,000	802	50.0	2%	$2,750	$4,250	$5,250	$7,500	$30,000	$65,000	$115,000	
	Auctions: $13,513, AU-58, August 2015; $7,638, AU-53, October 2015; $6,463, AU-50, January 2015; $4,818, EF-45, October 2015											
1852	2,053,026	2,577	51.5	5%	$2,100	$2,150	$2,300	$3,100	$5,000	$12,500	$22,500	
	Auctions: $10,600, MS-62, October 2015; $3,819, AU-58, March 2015; $1,704, AU-50, January 2015; $1,998, EF-40, January 2015											
1852-O	190,000	614	51.4	4%	$2,500	$4,000	$6,500	$10,000	$37,500	$75,000	$135,000	$350,000
	Auctions: $27,061, AU-58, August 2015; $5,640, AU-50, September 2015; $3,408, EF-40, July 2015; $2,291, VF-20, August 2015											
1853, All kinds	1,261,326											
1853, So-called 3 Over 2 (c)		212	52.4	3%	$3,000	$3,750	$5,500	$10,000	$15,000	$50,000		
	Auctions: $28,200, AU-58, August 2014; $28,200, AU-58, October 2014: $17,625, AU-58, April 2014											
1853		1,922	52.5	4%	$2,150	$2,250	$2,600	$3,000	$5,750	$15,000	$30,000	
	Auctions: $7,638, MS-61, February 2015; $6,169, AU-58, January 2015; $2,848, AU-53, January 2015; $1,880, EF-40, August 2015											
1853-O	71,000	249	49.9	3%	$3,000	$7,000	$10,000	$15,000	$37,500			
	Auctions: $14,100, AU-55, August 2015; $11,750, AU-55, January 2015; $10,575, AU-50, January 2015; $7,638, EF-45, August 2015											

† Ranked in the *100 Greatest U.S. Coins* (fifth edition). **a.** An unknown quantity of Proof 1849 double eagles was struck as patterns; all but two were melted. One (current location unknown) was sent to Treasury secretary W.M. Meredith; the other was placed in the Mint collection in Philadelphia, and transferred with that collection to the Smithsonian in 1923. **b.** Although no examples currently are known, it is likely that a small number of Proof 1850 double eagles were struck. For the years 1851 to 1857, no Proofs are known. **c.** Although overlaid photographs indicate this is not a true overdate, what appear to be remnants of a numeral are visible beneath the 3 in the date. This variety also shows a rust spot underneath the R of LIBERTY.

1854, Small Date **1854, Large Date**

	Mintage	Cert	Avg	%MS	VF-20	EF-40	AU-50	AU-55	MS-60	MS-62 / PF-63	MS-63 / PF-64	MS-65 / PF-65
1854, All kinds	757,899											
1854, Small Date		662	52.1	4%	$2,150	$2,250	$2,500	$3,500	$7,500	$15,000	$35,000	
	Auctions: $11,163, MS-61, January 2015; $4,714, AU-55, January 2015; $2,233, EF-45, October 2015; $1,645, VF-30, August 2015											
1854, Large Date		142	52.8	6%	$3,500	$4,250	$8,500	$12,500	$37,500	$45,000	$65,000	
	Auctions: $55,813, MS-61, August 2014; $19,975, AU-58, October 2014; $9,988, AU-53, September 2015; $9,400, AU-50, August 2015											
1854-O † (d)	3,250	17	52.8	0%	$160,000	$240,000	$335,000	$400,000	—			
	Auctions: $440,625, AU-55, April 2014; $340,750, AU-55, August 2015; $329,000, AU-50, August 2014; $204,000, EF-45, March 2018											
1854-S	141,468	233	52.5	22%	$3,000	$4,250	$11,000	$17,500	$30,000	$40,000	$50,000	$90,000
	Auctions: $16,450, AU-55, August 2015; $16,450, AU-55, September 2016; $21,738, AU-53, February 2015; $14,688, AU-53, July 2015											
1854-S, Proof † (e)	*unknown*				*(unique, in the Smithsonian's National Numismatic Collection)*							
	Auctions: No auction records available.											
1855	364,666	451	53.1	5%	$2,150	$2,250	$2,750	$3,750	$10,000	$18,500	$60,000	
	Auctions: $5,170, AU-58, September 2015; $3,878, AU-55, February 2015; $2,820, AU-53, August 2015; $2,350, AU-50, January 2015											
1855-O	8,000	51	50.4	8%	$13,500	$38,500	$48,000	$62,500	$125,000			
	Auctions: $141,000, MS-61, January 2014; $70,500, AU-58, August 2015; $58,750, AU-55, August 2014; $28,200, AU-50, October 2014											
1855-S	879,675	1,171	51.7	3%	$2,090	$2,100	$2,300	$3,350	$7,000	$16,000	$25,000	
	Auctions: $11,163, MS-61, July 2015; $3,819, AU-58, March 2015; $1,704, EF-40, June 2015; $1,528, VF-20, August 2015											
1856	329,878	398	52.7	6%	$2,150	$2,250	$2,850	$3,750	$7,500	$21,500	$35,000	
	Auctions: $7,050, AU-58, October 2015; $4,465, AU-55, June 2015; $3,290, AU-53, January 2015; $3,995, AU-50, August 2015											
1856-O † (f)	2,250	10	51.2	0%	$170,000	$240,000	$385,000	$400,000				
	Auctions: $340,750, AU-55, August 2015; $425,938, AU-53, August 2014; $164,500, AU-50, August 2014; $235,000, EF-45, January 2016											
1856-O, Proof † (g)	*unknown*	1	63.0									
	Auctions: $1,437,500, SP-63, May 2009											
1856-S	1,189,750	1,265	51.5	4%	$2,150	$2,200	$2,500	$3,000	$5,000	$12,500	$18,750	$45,000
	Auctions: $7,344, MS-61, June 2015; $4,935, AU-58, September 2015; $5,170, AU-53, January 2015; $2,115, EF-40, September 2015											
1857	439,375	558	53.5	10%	$2,150	$2,250	$2,500	$3,000	$5,500	$15,000	$40,000	
	Auctions: $5,875, MS-60, January 2015; $3,760, AU-58, January 2015; $2,350, AU-53, September 2015; $2,585, EF-45, January 2015											
1857-O	30,000	150	52.2	6%	$5,000	$8,500	$12,500	$16,000	$75,000	$175,000	$250,000	
	Auctions: $21,150, AU-53, August 2015; $11,163, AU-50, January 2015; $7,050, EF-40, October 2015; $2,585, VF-20, September 2015											
1857-S † (h)	970,500	1,530	54.5	26%	$2,100	$2,150	$2,300	$2,750	$4,500	$7,000	$8,500	$14,500
	Auctions: $15,863, MS-65, September 2015; $5,405, AU-58, August 2015; $2,233, AU-53, July 2015; $2,233, EF-40, January 2015											
1858	211,714	474	52.4	7%	$2,150	$2,500	$3,000	$4,000	$9,000	$26,500	$45,000	
	Auctions: $19,975, MS-62, January 2015; $4,935, AU-58, October 2015; $2,820, AU-53, October 2015; $3,055, EF-45, August 2015											
1858, Proof (i)	*unknown*	0	n/a		*(extremely rare)*							
	Auctions: No auction records available.											
1858-O	35,250	146	51.7	8%	$5,000	$9,500	$19,750	$28,500	$60,000	$70,000	$165,000	
	Auctions: $164,500, MS-63, January 2015; AU-58, August 2015; $9,988, AU-50, August 2015; $7,050, AU-50, January 2015											
1858-S	846,710	1,248	51.2	3%	$2,150	$2,250	$2,600	$3,000	$8,000	$16,500	$45,000	
	Auctions: $8,225, MS-60, October 2015; $7,638, AU-58, January 2015; $2,879, AU-53, June 2015; $1,528, EF-40, January 2015											

† Ranked in the *100 Greatest U.S. Coins* (fifth edition); both 1856-O Liberty Head Double Eagles are listed as a single entry. **d.** Probably fewer than 35 exist, most in VF and EF. **e.** This unique coin, perhaps more accurately described as a presentation strike than a Proof, was sent to the Mint collection in Philadelphia by San Francisco Mint superintendent Lewis A. Birdsall. It may have been the first coin struck for the year, set aside to recognize the opening of the San Francisco Mint. **f.** Probably fewer than 25 exist, most in VF and EF. **g.** This prooflike presentation strike is unique. **h.** The treasure of the shipwrecked SS *Central America* included thousands of 1857-S double eagles in high grades. Different size mintmark varieties exist; the Large S variety is rarest. **i.** 3 or 4 examples are known.

1861-S, Normal Reverse

1861-S, Normal Reverse

1861-S, Paquet Reverse, with taller letters

1861-S, Paquet Reverse

	Mintage	Cert	Avg	%MS	VF-20	EF-40	AU-50	AU-55	MS-60	MS-62 / PF-63	MS-63 / PF-64	MS-65 / PF-65
1859	43,597	135	51.6	5%	$3,250	$6,500	$11,000	$18,500	$32,150	$47,500		
	Auctions: $17,625, AU-55, August 2015; $12,925, AU-50, August 2015; $3,290, AU-50, August 2014; $7,050, EF-40, October 2015											
1859, Proof (j)	80	5	62.2							$250,000	$400,000	$500,000
	Auctions: $210,600, PF, June 2014											
1859-O	9,100	63	50.3	2%	$14,500	$26,000	$47,500	$60,000	$165,000			
	Auctions: $28,200, MS-60, August 2014: $105,750, AU-58, September 2016; $76,375, AU-58, August 2014											
1859-S	636,445	971	50.9	3%	$2,100	$2,150	$2,500	$3,500	$10,000	$25,000	$57,500	
	Auctions: $9,400, AU-58, August 2015; $3,995, AU-55, July 2015; $2,820, AU-53, October 2015; $2,585, EF-45, September 2015											
1860	577,611	1,187	52.7	9%	$2,100	$2,200	$2,350	$2,750	$4,500	$12,000	$21,500	
	Auctions: $10,575, MS-61, August 2015; $3,301, AU-58, January 2015; $2,644, AU-55, June 2015; $2,585, AU-53, January 2015											
1860, Proof (k)	59	8	64.4							$125,000	$250,000	$400,000
	Auctions: $367,188, PF-66Cam, August 2014											
1860-O	6,600	64	51.7	6%	$12,500	$37,500	$55,000	$67,500	$135,000			
	Auctions: $64,625, AU-58, August 2015; $55,813, AU-53, August 2014; $30,550, EF-40, January 2015											
1860-S	544,950	948	51.0	3%	$2,150	$2,250	$2,500	$3,500	$8,000	$21,500	$35,000	
	Auctions: $7,050, AU-58, January 2015; $3,673, AU-55, January 2015; $3,760, AU-53, August 2015; $1,528, VF-20, February 2015											
1861	2,976,387	4,380	54.0	13%	$2,100	$2,150	$2,300	$2,650	$4,500	$6,750	$18,500	$57,500
	Auctions: $8,813, MS-62, July 2015; $4,465, AU-58, February 2015; $1,998, AU-50, July 2015; $2,115, EF-40, January 2015											
1861, Proof (l)	66	2	64.0							$125,000	$250,000	$375,000
	Auctions: $44,850, PF-65DCam, September 2005											
1861-O	17,741	115	48.6	5%	$17,500	$35,000	$55,000	$65,000	$250,000			
	Auctions: $51,406, AU-50, March 2015; $44,650, AU-50, August 2015; $16,450, AU, March 2015; $11,163, AU-50, January 2015											
1861-S	768,000	974	50.5	3%	$2,150	$2,250	$2,750	$4,000	$15,000	$32,500	$47,500	
	Auctions: $3,525, MS-60, October 2015; $4,935, AU-58, January 2015; $2,350, AU-50, July 2015; $2,115, EF-45, August 2015											
1861, Paquet Rev (Tall Ltrs) † (m)	*unknown*	1	67.0						$2,150,000			
	Auctions: $1,645,000, MS-61, August 2014											
1861-S, Paquet Rev (Tall Ltrs) † (n)	19,250	78	48.8	0%	$30,000	$65,000	$87,500	$105,000				
	Auctions: $223,250, AU-58, April 2014; $164,500, AU-58, August 2015; $152,750, AU-58, August 2015; $105,750, August 2016											
1862	92,098	106	51.5	13%	$4,500	$12,150	$15,000	$21,500	$40,000	$60,000	$70,000	
	Auctions: $70,500, MS-62, August 2014; $49,938, MS-62, August 2014; $28,200, AU-58, August 2015											
1862, Proof (o)	35	6	64.2							$125,000	$250,000	$375,000
	Auctions: $381,875, PF-65Cam, April 2014											
1862-S	854,173	1,240	51.2	4%	$2,150	$2,500	$3,000	$4,000	$12,150	$30,000	$50,000	
	Auctions: $9,400, AU-58, January 2015; $3,995, AU-55, October 2015; $2,470, AU-50, August 2015; $2,585, EF-45, February 2015											

† Ranked in the *100 Greatest U.S. Coins* (fifth edition). **j.** 7 or 8 examples are known. **k.** Fewer than 10 examples are known. **l.** 5 or 6 examples are known. **m.** Once thought to be a pattern; now known to have been intended for circulation. 2 examples are known. **n.** Approximately 100 examples are known, most in VF and EF. **o.** Approximately 12 examples are known.

	Mintage	Cert	Avg	%MS	VF-20	EF-40	AU-50	AU-55	MS-60	MS-62 / PF-63	MS-63 / PF-64	MS-65 / PF-65
1863	142,760	220	52.7	11%	$3,000	$5,500	$11,500	$15,000	$32,500	$55,000	$85,000	
	Auctions: $85,188, MS-63, January 2015; $21,150, AU-58, September 2015; $20,563, AU-58, January 2015; $17,625, AU-55, August 2015											
1863, Proof (p)	30	8	64.3							$125,000	$250,000	$375,000
	Auctions: $381,875, PF-66Cam, August 2014; $345,150, PF, September 2013											
1863-S	966,570	1,822	51.8	7%	$2,150	$2,500	$3,000	$4,000	$8,000	$21,000	$35,000	
	Auctions: $5,405, AU-58, August 2015; $4,230, AU-55, August 2015; $2,115, EF-45, August 2015; $1,880, VF-30, January 2015											
1864	204,235	318	52.3	8%	$3,250	$5,500	$9,000	$11,000	$25,000	$47,500	$75,000	$275,000
	Auctions: $282,000, MS-65, April 2014; $8,813, AU-53, August 2015; $4,230, EF-40, August 2015; $3,760, EF-40, January 2015											
1864, Proof (q)	50	10	64.5							$125,000	$250,000	$375,000
	Auctions: $199,750, PF-64Cam, April 2014											
1864-S	793,660	1,153	51.4	11%	$2,150	$2,250	$2,500	$3,250	$8,000	$21,500	$45,000	$110,000
	Auctions: $19,975, MS-62, August 2015; $4,935, AU-53, February 2015; $1,998, EF-45, August 2015; $1,763, VF-35, July 2015											
1865	351,175	799	56.8	42%	$2,250	$2,750	$3,000	$3,750	$7,250	$14,500	$22,500	$57,500
	Auctions: $45,825, MS-65, October 2015; $3,290, AU-55, March 2015; $2,350, AU-50, January 2015; $2,115, EF-45, August 2015											
1865, Proof (r)	25	7	64.9							$125,000	$250,000	$375,000
	Auctions: $440,625, PF-66DCam, April 2014											
1865-S	1,042,500	1,470	53.6	33%	$2,150	$2,250	$2,500	$3,000	$6,750	$10,000	$15,000	$30,000
	Auctions: $25,850, MS-65, September 2015; $10,588, MS-62, August 2015; $2,233, AU-53, January 2015; $2,350, EF-45, August 2015											
1866-S, No Motto	120,000	169	48.1	5%	$9,500	$22,500	$30,000	$57,500	$155,000	$250,000		
	Auctions: $30,550, AU-50, October 2015; $28,200, AU-50, July 2015; $35,250, EF-45, August 2015; $8,225, VF-20, October 2015											

p. Approximately 12 examples are known. **q.** 12 to 15 examples are known. **r.** Fewer than 10 examples are known.

**1866, With Motto,
Doubled Die Reverse**
FS-G20-1866-801.

	Mintage	Cert	Avg	%MS	VF-20	EF-40	AU-50	AU-55	MS-60	MS-62 / PF-63	MS-63 / PF-64	MS-64 / PF-65
1866, With Motto	698,745	629	53.4	7%	$2,000	$2,400	$3,500	$5,000	$9,000	$30,000	$65,000	$145,000
	Auctions: $25,850, MS-61, January 2015; $9,400, AU-58, August 2015; $3,995, AU-55, January 2015; $3,055, AU-50, September 2015											
1866, With Motto, Doubled Die Reverse	(a)	0	n/a				$4,000	$6,000				
	Auctions: $12,650, MS-61, August 2010											
1866, With Motto, Proof (b)	30	9	63.6							$57,500	$125,000	$275,000
	Auctions: $126,500, PF-64, May 2007											
1866-S, With Motto	842,250	918	50.0	3%	$2,050	$2,250	$3,500	$7,500	$15,000	$35,000		
	Auctions: $15,275, AU-58, August 2015; $9,400, AU-55, February 2015; $3,760, AU-50, January 2015; $2,820, EF-40, August 2015											
1867	251,015	392	56.9	41%	$2,000	$2,025	$2,250	$3,250	$5,000	$8,500	$26,500	
	Auctions: $258,500, MS-66, November 2014; $9,400, MS-61, August 2015; $7,638, MS-61, August 2015; $6,492, AU-58, August 2015											
1867, Proof (c)	50	4	65.0							$57,500	$125,000	$225,000
	Auctions: $129,250, PF-64DCam, January 2015; $129,250, PF-64DCam, August 2014; $38,188, PF-61Cam, August 2014											
1867-S	920,750	1,306	51.0	2%	$2,000	$2,025	$2,050	$4,000	$10,000	$32,500		
	Auctions: $17,038, MS-61, January 2015; $8,225, AU-58, July 2015; $2,115, AU-53, January 2015; $1,763, EF-45, August 2015											

a. Included in circulation-strike 1866 mintage figure. **b.** Approximately 15 examples are known. **c.** 10 to 12 examples are known.

Open 3

Close 3

	Mintage	Cert	Avg	%MS	VF-20	EF-40	AU-50	AU-55	MS-60	MS-62 / PF-63	MS-63 / PF-64	MS-64 / PF-65
1868	98,575	210	51.7	5%	$2,150	$2,500	$4,250	$9,500	$20,000	$45,000	$70,000	
	Auctions: $44,063, MS-62, August 2014; $18,800, AU-58, August 2015; $8,813, AU-53, June 2015; $4,113, EF-45, August 2014											
1868, Proof (d)	25	6	64.2							$65,000	$125,000	$225,000
	Auctions: $149,500, PF-64DCam Plus, August 2011											
1868-S	837,500	1,772	51.7	2%	$2,000	$1,920	$1,950	$2,250	$6,000	$40,000		
	Auctions: $16,450, MS-61, January 2015; $7,050, AU-58, January 2015; $1,645, AU-50, February 2015; $1,410, EF-45, January 2015											
1869	175,130	356	53.0	3%	$2,000	$2,025	$2,250	$3,500	$10,500	$21,500	$40,000	$87,500
	Auctions: $108,688, MS-64, January 2014; $9,988, MS-60, January 2015; $2,115, AU-53, February 2015; $3,290, AU-50, August 2015											
1869, Proof (e)	25	7	65.0							$65,000	$125,000	$225,000
	Auctions: $106,375, PF-64DCam, February 2009											
1869-S	686,750	1,511	52.4	6%	$2,000	$2,025	$2,050	$2,500	$5,000	$22,500	$35,000	$70,000
	Auctions: $37,600, MS-62, August 2015; $7,638, AU-58, June 2015; $2,705, AU-55, February 2015; $1,880, AU-53, July 2015											
1870	155,150	275	54.0	15%	$2,000	$2,150	$2,850	$4,850	$11,950	$32,500	$57,500	
	Auctions: $22,325, MS-61, June 2015; $14,688, MS-60, June 2015; $7,638, AU-58, August 2015; $6,463, AU-55, August 2015											
1870, Proof (f)	35	4	65.5							$65,000	$175,000	$275,000
	Auctions: $503,100, PF, September 2013											
1870-CC † (g)	3,789	33	40.6	0%	$185,000	$265,000	$325,000	$500,000				
	Auctions: $411,250, AU-53, March 2014; $300,000, EF-45, January 2018; $188,000, VF-30, October 2014; $182,125, VF-30, August 2015											
1870-S	982,000	1,662	52.7	5%	$2,000	$2,025	$2,050	$2,100	$5,000	$22,500	$57,500	
	Auctions: $10,869, MS-61, September 2015; $2,000, AU-55, January 2015; $1,528, AU-50, January 2015; $1,410, EF-40, September 2015											
1871	80,120	289	53.2	6%	$2,000	$2,025	$3,000	$5,000	$8,500	$30,000	$50,000	$70,000
	Auctions: $4,935, AU-58, January 2015; $4,848, AU-55, August 2015; $2,585, AU-50, September 2015; $2,820, EF-45, July 2015											
1871, Proof (h)	30	6	63.8							$65,000	$125,000	$225,000
	Auctions: $26,450, PF-62Cam, August 2004											
1871-CC	17,387	178	48.8	2%	$27,500	$42,500	$57,500	$75,000	$130,000			$450,000
	Auctions: $111,625, MS-60, August 2015; $64,625, AU-55, October 2016; $55,200, AU-53, January 2018; $30,550, AU-50, September 2015											
1871-S	928,000	2,024	54.2	10%	$2,000	$2,025	$1,975	$2,025	$3,500	$11,500	$22,500	$55,000
	Auctions: $10,575, MS-62, August 2015; $6,463, MS-61, March 2016; $3,525, MS-60, March 2016; $2,471, AU-58, July 2015											
1872	251,850	734	55.2	12%	$2,000	$2,025	$2,050	$2,200	$3,750	$12,500	$25,000	$65,000
	Auctions: $28,200, MS-63, January 2015; $2,820, AU-58, October 2015; $2,291, AU-53, January 2015; $1,528, EF-40, October 2015											
1872, Proof (i)	30	5	61.8							$65,000	$125,000	$225,000
	Auctions: $135,125, PF-64, October 2014											
1872-CC	26,900	426	49.7	3%	$5,500	$10,500	$18,750	$22,500	$65,000	$150,000		
	Auctions: $94,000, MS-61, August 2015; $54,050, AU-58, January 2015; $13,513, AU-50, August 2015; $7,050, EF-40, January 2015											
1872-S	780,000	1,750	54.6	11%	$2,000	$2,025	$2,050	$2,100	$3,000	$13,500	$30,000	$50,000
	Auctions: $25,850, MS-63, February 2015; $4,700, MS-61, March 2015; $1,880, AU-55, August 2015; $1,645, EF-45, August 2015											
1873, Close 3	1,709,800	401	54.5	11%	$2,000	$2,025	$2,050	$2,250	$4,250	$12,500		
	Auctions: $3,525, MS-60, July 2015; $2,115, AU-55, January 2015; $1,880, AU-55, August 2015; $1,586, AU-55, October 2015											
1873, Open 3	(j)	8,973	58.8	56%	$2,000	$2,025	$2,050	$2,100	$2,175	$2,250	$5,500	$30,000
	Auctions: $6,463, MS-63, January 2015; $1,645, AU-58, August 2015; $1,322, AU-53, September 2015; $1,234, EF-45, May 2015											
1873, Close 3, Proof (k)	25	7	63.6							$65,000	$125,000	$225,000
	Auctions: $230,000, PF-65UCam, April 2011											

† Ranked in the *100 Greatest U.S. Coins* (fifth edition). **d.** Approximately 12 examples are known. **e.** Approximately 12 examples are known. **f.** Approximately 12 examples are known. **g.** An estimated 35 to 50 examples are believed to exist; most are in VF with extensive abrasions. **h.** Fewer than 10 examples are known. **i.** Fewer than 12 examples are known. **j.** Included in circulation-strike 1873, Close 3, mintage figure. **k.** 10 to 12 examples are known.

	Mintage	Cert	Avg	%MS	VF-20	EF-40	AU-50	AU-55	MS-60	MS-62 / PF-63	MS-63 / PF-64	MS-64 / PF-65
1873-CC, Close 3	22,410	399	52.2	4%	$4,250	$8,500	$17,500	$24,500	$52,500	$85,000	$145,000	
Auctions: $25,850, AU-55, August 2015; $18,800, AU-55, January 2015; $15,863, AU-53, August 2015; $7,050, EF-40, October 2015												
1873-S, Close 3	1,040,600	1,856	55.1	17%	$2,000	$2,025	$2,050	$2,100	$2,400	$7,500	$21,500	
Auctions: $7,638, MS-61, August 2015; $2,115, AU-58, February 2015; $1,410, AU-53, October 2015; $1,528, EF-45, September 2015												
1873-S, Open 3	(l)	947	54.7	11%	$2,000	$2,025	$2,050	$2,150	$5,000	$20,000		
Auctions: $14,100, MS-61, September 2015; $4,230, AU-58, August 2015; $1,528, AU-53, June 2015; $1,293, EF-45, September 2015												
1874	366,780	1,230	57.1	30%	$2,000	$2,025	$2,050	$2,100	$2,250	$8,500	$22,500	$50,000
Auctions: $39,950, MS-64, August 2015; $3,760, MS-60, January 2015; $2,585, AU-55, August 2015; $1,351, AU-50, January 2015												
1874, Proof (m)	20	6	63.3							$75,000	$135,000	$275,000
Auctions: $218,500, PF-64UCamH, January 2012												
1874-CC	115,085	1,543	49.1	1%	$2,850	$3,500	$4,500	$8,750	$25,500	$80,000		
Auctions: $21,150, AU-58, August 2015; $5,640, AU-53, October 2015; $3,760, EF-45, July 2015; $2,350, VF-30, January 2015												
1874-S	1,214,000	3,845	56.2	22%	$2,000	$2,025	$2,050	$2,100	$2,175	$4,500	$28,500	
Auctions: $7,050, MS-62, June 2015; $1,998, MS-60, January 2015; $1,645, AU-55, February 2015; $1,293, EF-45, January 2015												
1875	295,720	1,541	59.2	60%	$2,000	$2,025	$2,050	$2,100	$2,175	$2,750	$6,500	$40,000
Auctions: $8,225, MS-63, September 2015; $2,585, MS-60, August 2015; $1,528, AU-58, January 2015; $1,351, AU-55, January 2015												
1875, Proof (n)	20	4	63.8							$100,000	$175,000	$350,000
Auctions: $94,300, PF-63Cam, August 2009												
1875-CC	111,151	1,949	53.0	26%	$2,850	$3,250	$4,000	$5,750	$9,500	$18,500	$37,500	$75,000
Auctions: $28,200, MS-63, January 2015; $7,344, AU-58, July 2015; $2,585, AU-50, January 2015; $2,820, EF-45, March 2015												
1875-S	1,230,000	4,676	57.0	30%	$2,000	$2,025	$2,050	$2,100	$2,175	$2,750	$8,500	$30,000
Auctions: $16,450, MS-63, July 2015; $1,645, AU-58, August 2015; $1,410, AU-53, October 2015; $1,293, VF-35, January 2015												
1876	583,860	2,944	58.0	42%	$2,000	$2,025	$2,050	$2,100	$2,175	$2,750	$7,000	$45,000
Auctions: $3,995, MS-62, January 2015; $1,410, AU-55, September 2015; $1,351, AU-53, January 2015; $1,528, EF-40, September 2015												
1876, Proof (o)	45	13	63.8							$55,000	$75,000	$135,000
Auctions: $152,750, PF-64DCam, February 2013												
1876-CC	138,441	2,148	52.1	12%	$2,750	$3,250	$3,750	$5,500	$8,500	$22,500	$40,000	
Auctions: $12,925, MS-60, October 2015; $8,813, AU-58, August 2015; $3,995, AU-50, October 2015; $2,585, VF-20, August 2015												
1876-S	1,597,000	7,587	57.0	32%	$2,000	$2,025	$2,050	$2,100	$2,175	$2,250	$5,000	$35,000
Auctions: $42,300, MS-64, August 2015; $2,291, MS-61, August 2015; $1,528, AU-55, September 2015; $1,528, AU-50, October 2015												

l. Included in 1873-S, Close 3, mintage figure. m. Fewer than 10 examples are known. n. 10 to 12 examples are known. o. Approximately 15 examples are known.

	Mintage	Cert	Avg	%MS	VF-20	EF-40	AU-50	AU-55	MS-60	MS-62 / PF-63	MS-63 / PF-64	MS-65 / PF-65
1877	397,650	1,184	59.4	67%	$2,000	$2,005	$2,010	$2,015	$2,100	$4,500	$13,500	
Auctions: $3,995, MS-62, January 2015; $3,055, MS-61, August 2015; $2,000, MS-61, January 2015; $1,880, MS-61, July 2015												
1877, Proof (a)	20	7	63.3							$40,000	$75,000	$135,000
Auctions: $21,150, PF-58, February 2013												
1877-CC	42,565	956	49.1	3%	$3,000	$3,500	$6,750	$11,000	$30,000	$70,000		
Auctions: $24,675, AU-58, September 2015; $9,400, AU-55, August 2015; $4,700, AU-50, August 2015; $3,525, EF-40, January 2015												
1877-S	1,735,000	2,721	59.1	64%	$2,000	$2,005	$2,010	$2,015	$2,050	$4,750	$15,000	$45,000
Auctions: $5,170, MS-62, February 2015; $1,998, MS-61, December 2015; $1,528, MS-60, February 2015; $1,645, AU-58, August 2015												
1878	543,625	1,737	59.8	70%	$2,000	$2,005	$2,010	$2,015	$2,050	$3,750	$11,000	
Auctions: $9,400, MS-63, September 2015; $1,998, MS-61, July 2015; $1,645, AU-58, August 2015; $1,645, AU-55, August 2015												
1878, Proof (b)	20	8	64.5							$40,000	$65,000	$135,000
Auctions: $69,000, PF-64Cam, April 2011												
1878-CC	13,180	347	47.4	2%	$5,750	$9,000	$16,500	$26,500	$50,000	$75,000		
Auctions: $19,975, AU-55, August 2015; $9,400, EF-45, August 2015; $7,638, EF-40, July 2015; $6,169, VF-35, January 2015												
1878-S	1,739,000	1,752	58.2	56%	$2,000	$2,005	$2,010	$2,015	$2,050	$5,500	$15,000	
Auctions: $6,169, MS-62, September 2015; $1,763, MS-60, August 2015; $1,763, AU-58, July 2015; $1,351, AU-55, January 2015												

a. 10 to 12 examples are known. b. Fewer than 10 examples are known.

	Mintage	Cert	Avg	%MS	VF-20	EF-40	AU-50	AU-55	MS-60	MS-62 / PF-63	MS-63 / PF-64	MS-65 / PF-65
1879	207,600	634	58.3	46%	$2,000	$2,005	$2,010	$2,015	$2,150	$6,500	$17,500	$45,000
Auctions: $3,290, MS-61, September 2015; $2,585, MS-61, February 2015; $2,350, MS-60, August 2015; $2,115, AU-58, September 2015												
1879, Proof (c)	30	4	64.0							$40,000	$65,000	$135,000
Auctions: $57,500, PF-64, July 2009												
1879-CC	10,708	332	49.8	3%	$6,500	$11,500	$18,750	$28,500	$55,000	$85,000		
Auctions: $28,200, AU-55, July 2015; $4,230, AU-50, August 2015; $11,899, EF-45, January 2015; $3,055, EF-40, October 2015												
1879-O	2,325	88	49.5	11%	$30,000	$55,000	$60,000	$75,000	$140,000	$175,000		
Auctions: $135,125, MS-60, January 2014; $70,514, AU-58, April 2017; $57,600, AU-50, November 2017; $36,000, VF-35, January 2018												
1879-S	1,223,800	1,422	57.3	31%	$2,000	$2,005	$2,010	$2,015	$2,250	$18,750	$35,000	
Auctions: $4,714, MS-61, January 2015; $2,585, AU-58, July 2015; $1,316, AU-55, January 2015; $1,539, AU-53, August 2015												
1880	51,420	415	55.1	15%	$2,000	$2,005	$2,010	$2,015	$8,500	$25,000	$32,500	
Auctions: $15,275, MS-61, August 2015; $3,525, AU-58, February 2015; $3,760, AU-55, August 2015; $2,820, AU-53, September 2015												
1880, Proof (d)	36	3	64.7							$40,000	$65,000	$135,000
Auctions: $217,375, PF-65DCam, August 2014; $235,000, PF, March 2014												
1880-S	836,000	969	57.9	39%	$2,000	$2,005	$2,010	$2,015	$2,050	$8,500	$18,500	$100,000
Auctions: $5,405, MS-62, January 2015; $4,700, MS-61, August 2015; $1,645, AU-58, June 2015; $1,645, AU-53, August 2015												
1881	2,199	42	53.9	14%	$18,500	$32,500	$45,000	$67,500	$125,000			
Auctions: $141,000, MS-61, August 2015; $141,000, MS-61, January 2015; $82,290, AU-58, September 2016; $56,400, AU-58, August 2015												
1881, Proof (e)	61	6	63.8							$40,000	$75,000	$135,000
Auctions: $172,500, PF-65Cam, January 2011												
1881-S	727,000	853	58.6	55%	$2,000	$2,005	$2,010	$2,015	$2,150	$6,500	$20,000	
Auctions: $10,575, MS-62, January 2015; $1,998, MS-61, February 2015; $2,233, AU-58, August 2015; $3,055, AU-55, September 2015												
1882	571	14	55.9	14%	$30,000	$55,000	$90,000	$105,000	$135,000	$175,000	$250,000	
Auctions: $94,000, AU-58, January 2014; $129,250, AU-55, August 2014; $79,325, AU-53, January 2016												
1882, Proof (f)	59	7	63.9							$40,000	$75,000	$125,000
Auctions: $161,000, PF-64Cam, January 2011												
1882-CC	39,140	1,007	53.2	7%	$2,850	$3,500	$4,500	$6,000	$9,500	$32,500	$100,000	
Auctions: $12,925, AU-58, July 2015; $7,050, AU-55, January 2015; $5,288, AU-53, September 2015; $3,055, EF-45, February 2015												
1882-S	1,125,000	1,513	58.9	60%	$2,000	$2,005	$2,010	$2,015	$2,050	$3,500	$11,500	
Auctions: $12,925, MS-63, June 2015; $3,995, MS-62, September 2015; $1,528, MS-60, July 2015; $1,552, AU-58, October 2015												
1883, Proof (g)	92	12	63.2							$115,000	$150,000	$275,000
Auctions: $282,000, PF-65DCam, January 2014; $158,625, PF-64DCam, August 2014												
1883-CC	59,962	1,355	52.5	8%	$2,850	$3,250	$4,000	$5,500	$10,000	$26,500	$45,000	
Auctions: $19,975, MS-61, January 2015; $11,750, AU-58, June 2015; $5,875, AU-53, August 2015; $2,820, EF-45, February 2015												
1883-S	1,189,000	2,325	59.7	72%	$2,000	$2,005	$2,010	$2,015	$2,050	$2,250	$5,500	
Auctions: $14,100, MS-64, June 2015; $1,528, MS-61, March 2015; $1,469, AU-55, January 2015; $1,293, EF-45, January 2015												
1884, Proof (h)	71	9	63.0							$110,000	$150,000	$275,000
Auctions: $246,750, PF-65DCam, January 2015; $235,000, PF-65DCam, August 2014; $246,750, PF-66Cam, April 2014												
1884-CC	81,139	1,790	54.1	17%	$2,850	$3,250	$3,750	$5,500	$9,000	$18,750	$45,000	
Auctions: $28,200, MS-62, June 2015; $5,244, AU-55, August 2015; $3,290, EF-40, July 2015; $3,525, VG-10, August 2015												
1884-S	916,000	2,768	60.5	82%	$2,000	$2,005	$2,010	$2,015	$2,050	$2,150	$4,000	$45,000
Auctions: $3,761, MS-63, January 2015; $1,998, MS-61, August 2015; $1,396, MS-60, January 2015; $1,351, AU-58, January 2015												
1885	751	55	55.9	33%	$22,500	$32,500	$50,000	$65,000	$85,000	$105,000	$135,000	
Auctions: $82,250, MS-62, October 2014; $14,100, MS-60, November 2014; $58,750, AU-58, January 2014												
1885, Proof (i)	77	10	63.9							$50,000	$100,000	$135,000
Auctions: $35,250, PF-61DCam, September 2014												
1885-CC	9,450	306	50.7	7%	$6,500	$12,500	$17,500	$25,000	$42,500	$75,000	$125,000	
Auctions: $61,688, MS-62, March 2015; $37,600, MS-61, January 2015; $23,500, AU-55, August 2015; $3,055, AU-50, June 2015												
1885-S	683,500	2,415	60.0	86%	$2,000	$2,005	$2,010	$2,015	$2,050	$2,250	$3,250	
Auctions: $3,995, MS-63, January 2015; $1,998, MS-62, August 2015; $1,998, MS-61, August 2015; $1,528, AU-58, August 2015												

c. 10 to 12 examples are known. d. 10 to 12 examples are known. e. Fewer than 20 examples are known. f. 12 to 15 examples are known. g. Proof only. Approximately 20 examples are known. h. Proof only. Approximately 20 examples are known. i. 15 to 20 examples are known.

1888, Doubled Die Reverse
FS-G20-1888-801.

	Mintage	Cert	Avg	%MS	VF-20	EF-40	AU-50	AU-55	MS-60	MS-62 / PF-63	MS-63 / PF-64	MS-65 / PF-65
1886	1,000	27	54.8	7%	$40,000	$80,000	$95,000	$115,000	$135,000	$145,000	$165,000	
	Auctions: $129,250, MS-60, January 2014; $111,625, AU-58, August 2014; $76,375, AU-53, August 2015; $73,438, EF-45, August 2015											
1886, Proof (j)	106	17	64.4							$45,000	$75,000	$115,000
	Auctions: $19,975, PF-60, January 2014											
1887, Proof (k)	121	9	64.9							$67,500	$85,000	$125,000
	Auctions: $258,500, PF-66, January 2014; $123,375, PF-65Cam, August 2014; $117,500, PF-65Cam, August 2015											
1887-S	283,000	945	60.0	72%	$2,000	$2,005	$2,010	$2,015	$2,050	$4,750	$10,000	$45,000
	Auctions: $9,694, MS-63, January 2015; $4,935, MS-62, January 2015; $4,700, MS-62, August 2015; $2,585, MS-61, October 2015											
1888	226,161	1,143	60.0	73%	$2,000	$2,005	$2,010	$2,015	$2,100	$3,000	$10,000	$30,000
	Auctions: $4,465, MS-62, June 2015; $2,115, MS-61, September 2015; $1,763, MS-60, August 2015; $1,469, AU-55, January 2015											
1888, Doubled Die Reverse	(l)	29	60.2	83%					$3,000	$3,750		
	Auctions: $3,819, MS-62, April 2013											
1888, Proof (m)	105	19	64.3							$32,500	$50,000	$85,000
	Auctions: $126,500, PF-65DCam, April 2012											
1888-S	859,600	2,710	60.7	84%	$2,000	$2,005	$2,010	$2,015	$2,050	$2,100	$4,000	$35,000
	Auctions: $5,640, MS-63, August 2015; $2,291, MS-62, February 2015; $1,998, MS-61, August 2015; $1,557, AU-58, August 2015											
1889	44,070	538	60.4	81%	$2,000	$2,005	$2,010	$2,015	$2,150	$4,250	$15,000	
	Auctions: $5,405, MS-62, August 2015; $2,585, MS-61, February 2015; $1,880, AU-55, August 2015; $1,645, AU-50, September 2015											
1889, Proof (n)	41	11	63.8							$32,500	$50,000	$85,000
	Auctions: $352,500, PF-65, January 2014											
1889-CC	30,945	919	52.6	7%	$3,000	$3,250	$4,500	$6,500	$11,500	$27,500	$45,000	
	Auctions: $16,450, MS-61, January 2015; $14,688, MS-60, June 2015; $7,638, AU-55, August 2015; $5,699, AU-53, August 2015											
1889-S	774,700	2,117	60.6	83%	$2,000	$2,005	$2,010	$2,015	$2,050	$2,500	$3,250	$22,500
	Auctions: $21,150, MS-65, January 2015; $2,115, MS-62, July 2015; $1,998, MS-61, September 2015; $1,410, AU-50, January 2015											
1890	75,940	658	60.5	81%	$2,000	$2,005	$2,010	$2,015	$2,050	$3,250	$8,500	$35,000
	Auctions: $7,931, MS-63, January 2015; $2,820, MS-62, October 2015; $2,115, AU-58, August 2015; $2,115, AU-50, September 2015											
1890, Proof (o)	55	13	64.6							$32,500	$50,000	$85,000
	Auctions: $92,000, PF-65UCam, August 2011											
1890-CC	91,209	2,336	52.9	9%	$2,750	$3,250	$3,500	$5,000	$9,500	$18,750	$45,000	
	Auctions: $25,850, MS-62, June 2015; $10,575, AU-58, August 2015; $5,875, AU-50, February 2015; $3,055, EF-40, October 2015											
1890-S	802,750	1,857	60.0	73%	$2,000	$2,005	$2,010	$2,015	$2,050	$2,150	$4,000	
	Auctions: $21,150, MS-65, January 2015; $3,995, MS-63, June 2015; $2,056, MS-62, June 2015; $1,586, MS-61, September 2015											
1891	1,390	39	54.8	8%	$15,000	$22,500	$40,000	$50,000	$85,000	$100,000	$135,000	
	Auctions: $82,250, MS-61, January 2014; $52,889, AU-58, November 2016; $52,875, AU-58, August 2014											
1891, Proof (p)	52	24	63.5							$32,500	$50,000	$85,000
	Auctions: $655,200, PF, September 2013											
1891-CC	5,000	257	54.1	14%	$8,500	$18,500	$24,500	$30,000	$47,500	$70,000	$100,000	
	Auctions: $41,125, MS-61, March 2015; $38,775, MS-60, January 2015; $28,200, AU-55, October 2016; $23,500, AU-55, July 2015											
1891-S	1,288,125	5,938	61.2	91%	$2,000	$2,005	$2,010	$2,015	$2,050	$2,075	$2,750	
	Auctions: $4,935, MS-64, July 2015; $2,468, MS-63, January 2015; $1,998, MS-62, July 2015; $1,880, MS-62, August 2015											

j. 20 to 25 examples are known. **k.** Proof only. More than 30 examples are known. **l.** Included in circulation-strike 1888 mintage figure. **m.** 20 to 30 examples are known. **n.** 10 to 12 examples are known. **o.** Approximately 15 examples are known. **p.** 20 to 25 examples are known.

	Mintage	Cert	Avg	%MS	VF-20	EF-40	AU-50	AU-55	MS-60	MS-62	MS-63	MS-65
										PF-63	PF-64	PF-65
1892	4,430	125	56.0	30%	$4,500	$7,000	$10,000	$14,500	$22,500	$35,000	$40,000	$85,000
Auctions: $32,900, MS-62, August 2015; $23,500, MS-61, March 2016; $5,640, MS-60, July 2015; $11,788, AU-55, August 2014												
1892, Proof (q)	93	14	64.5							$32,500	$50,000	$85,000
Auctions: $188,000, PF-66DCam, January 2014												
1892-CC	27,265	893	54.4	22%	$2,750	$3,500	$4,500	$5,500	$12,500	$30,000	$57,500	
Auctions: $35,250, MS-63, August 2015; $28,200, MS-62, February 2016; $9,988, AU-58, July 2015; $4,465, AU-53, July 2015												
1892-S	930,150	4,662	61.1	90%	$2,000	$2,005	$2,010	$2,015	$2,050	$2,075	$2,500	$22,500
Auctions: $17,625, MS-65, January 2015; $8,225, MS-64, August 2015; $1,592, MS-62, August 2015; $1,351, AU-55, January 2015												
1893	344,280	8,143	61.8	98%	$2,000	$2,005	$2,010	$2,015	$2,050	$2,075	$2,500	
Auctions: $3,643, MS-63, February 2015; $2,826, MS-63, October 2015; $1,998, MS-62, August 2015; $1,410, MS-60, October 2015												
1893, Proof (r)	59	5	63.4							$32,500	$50,000	$85,000
Auctions: $15,525, PF-60Cam, August 2011												
1893-CC	18,402	794	57.6	48%	$2,850	$5,000	$6,000	$8,000	$12,150	$21,500	$50,000	
Auctions: $19,975, MS-62, August 2015; $17,625, MS-62, July 2015; $28,200, MS-61, September 2016; $14,688, MS-61, June 2015												
1893-S	996,175	6,045	61.1	93%	$2,000	$2,005	$2,010	$2,015	$2,050	$2,075	$3,250	$35,000
Auctions: $3,290, MS-63, February 2015; $2,820, MS-63, January 2015; $1,763, MS-62, August 2015; $1,645, MS-62, July 2015												
1894	1,368,940	16,003	61.5	97%	$2,000	$2,005	$2,010	$2,015	$2,050	$2,075	$2,150	$25,000
Auctions: $22,325, MS-65, January 2015; $4,700, MS-64, February 2015; $1,645, MS-62, September 2015; $1,351, AU-55, January 2015												
1894, Proof (s)	50	13	63.8							$32,500	$50,000	$85,000
Auctions: $54,625, PF-64Cam, January 2005												
1894-S	1,048,550	5,936	61.2	93%	$2,000	$2,005	$2,010	$2,015	$2,050	$2,075	$2,750	$23,000
Auctions: $4,935, MS-64, January 2015; $2,585, MS-63, February 2015; $1,763, MS-62, August 2015; $1,351, MS-61, January 2015												
1895	1,114,605	23,229	61.8	98%	$2,000	$2,005	$2,010	$2,015	$2,050	$2,075	$2,100	$21,500
Auctions: $3,055, MS-64, January 2015; $1,880, MS-63, August 2015; $1,528, MS-62, August 2015; $1,293, AU-58, February 2015												
1895, Proof	51	10	64.2							$32,500	$50,000	$85,000
Auctions: $82,250, PF-65Cam, September 2014												
1895-S	1,143,500	7,736	61.3	93%	$2,000	$2,005	$2,010	$2,015	$2,050	$2,075	$2,150	$12,500
Auctions: $9,583, MS-65, January 2015; $3,878, MS-64, February 2015; $1,763, MS-62, October 2015; $1,293, MS-60, June 2015												
1896	792,535	10,795	61.7	97%	$2,000	$2,005	$2,010	$2,015	$2,050	$2,075	$2,150	$18,000
Auctions: $3,290, MS-64, September 2015; $2,056, MS-63, January 2015; $1,763, MS-62, July 2015; $1,704, MS-62, September 2015												
1896, Proof (t)	128	37	63.9							$32,500	$50,000	$85,000
Auctions: $97,750, PF-65DCam, April 2012												
1896-S	1,403,925	9,761	61.3	94%	$2,000	$2,005	$2,010	$2,015	$2,050	$2,075	$2,150	$25,000
Auctions: $3,055, MS-63, January 2015; $2,468, MS-63, February 2015; $1,645, MS-62, September 2015; $1,528, MS-61, January 2015												
1897	1,383,175	19,341	61.7	98%	$2,000	$2,005	$2,010	$2,015	$2,050	$2,075	$2,150	$21,500
Auctions: $2,585, MS-64, January 2015; $2,115, MS-63, August 2015; $1,763, MS-62, September 2015; $1,351, MS-61, January 2015												
1897, Proof (u)	86	23	64.1							$32,500	$50,000	$85,000
Auctions: $73,438, PF-64Cam, August 2014; $30,550, PF-62Cam, April 2013												
1897-S	1,470,250	14,333	61.6	95%	$2,000	$2,005	$2,010	$2,015	$2,050	$2,075	$2,250	$18,000
Auctions: $16,450, MS-65, January 2015; $3,643, MS-64, June 2015; $1,763, MS-62, August 2015; $1,351, MS-61, January 2015												
1898	170,395	1,819	61.2	90%	$2,000	$2,005	$2,010	$2,015	$2,150	$2,250	$3,250	
Auctions: $4,818, MS-63, October 2015; $2,585, MS-62, August 2015; $1,410, MS-61, January 2015; $1,410, AU-58, January 2015												
1898, Proof (v)	75	34	64.1							$32,500	$50,000	$85,000
Auctions: $52,875, PF-64DCam, September 2014; $117,500, PF-65Cam, April 2013												
1898-S	2,575,175	24,497	61.7	96%	$2,000	$2,005	$2,010	$2,015	$2,050	$2,075	$2,150	$8,500
Auctions: $9,400, MS-65, June 2015; $1,645, MS-62, September 2015; $1,351, AU-58, January 2015; $1,351, AU-55, January 2015												

q. Approximately 25 examples are known. **r.** 15 to 20 examples are known. **s.** 15 to 20 examples are known. **t.** 45 to 50 examples are known. **u.** 20 to 25 examples are known. **v.** 35 to 40 examples are known.

	Mintage	Cert	Avg	%MS	VF-20	EF-40	AU-50	AU-55	MS-60	MS-62 / PF-63	MS-63 / PF-64	MS-65 / PF-65
1899	1,669,300	27,533	62.1	98%	$2,000	$2,005	$2,010	$2,015	$2,050	$2,075	$2,100	$8,500
Auctions: $7,638, MS-65, September 2015; $4,113, MS-64, June 2015; $1,410, MS-61, October 2015; $1,528, AU-58, August 2015												
1899, Proof (w)	84	34	62.9							$32,500	$50,000	$85,000
Auctions: $76,375, PF, March 2014												
1899-S	2,010,300	9,922	61.3	91%	$2,000	$2,005	$2,010	$2,015	$2,050	$2,075	$2,500	$21,500
Auctions: $2,291, MS-63, September 2015; $1,939, MS-63, February 2015; $1,763, MS-62, August 2015; $1,645, MS-62, August 2015												
1900	1,874,460	62,214	62.5	99%	$2,000	$2,005	$2,010	$2,015	$2,050	$2,075	$2,100	$5,500
Auctions: $7,344, MS-65, August 2015; $2,820, MS-64, August 2015; $1,821, MS-62, June 2015; $1,293, MS-60, July 2015												
1900, Proof (x)	124	29	64.2							$30,000	$45,000	$85,000
Auctions: $88,125, PF, March 2014												
1900-S	2,459,500	8,034	61.1	92%	$2,000	$2,005	$2,010	$2,015	$2,050	$2,075	$2,250	$22,500
Auctions: $3,055, MS-63, August 2015; $1,763, MS-62, August 2015; $1,422, MS-60, August 2015; $1,410, AU-58, October 2015												
1901	111,430	6,680	62.9	99%	$2,000	$2,005	$2,010	$2,015	$2,050	$2,075	$2,100	$2,850
Auctions: $3,290, MS-65, January 2015; $2,115, MS-64, August 2015; $1,880, MS-63, February 2015; $1,645, MS-62, August 2015												
1901, Proof (y)	96	45	62.6							$30,000	$45,000	$85,000
Auctions: $68,150, PF, February 2013												
1901-S	1,596,000	3,204	61.0	92%	$2,000	$2,005	$2,010	$2,015	$2,050	$2,075	$3,750	$22,500
Auctions: $3,525, MS-63, February 2015; $2,938, MS-63, September 2015; $2,115, MS-62, August 2015; $2,350, MS-61, August 2015												
1902	31,140	513	59.8	66%	$2,000	$2,005	$2,010	$2,015	$2,500	$6,000	$10,000	
Auctions: $4,700, MS-62, July 2015; $3,995, MS-61, August 2015; $2,350, MS-61, January 2015; $2,820, AU-58, August 2015												
1902, Proof (z)	114	28	62.9							$30,000	$45,000	$85,000
Auctions: $9,400, PF-50, January 2014												
1902-S	1,753,625	4,605	61.0	93%	$2,000	$2,005	$2,010	$2,015	$2,050	$2,075	$3,250	$30,000
Auctions: $28,200, MS-65, October 2015; $3,525, MS-63, January 2015; $1,410, MS-60, January 2015; $1,351, AU-58, June 2015												
1903	287,270	13,178	62.9	100%	$2,000	$2,005	$2,010	$2,015	$2,050	$2,075	$2,100	$3,000
Auctions: $3,290, MS-65, January 2015; $2,585, MS-64, August 2015; $1,645, MS-63, August 2015; $1,410, MS-61, January 2015												
1903, Proof (aa)	158	37	62.9							$30,000	$45,000	$85,000
Auctions: $63,450, PF, March 2014												
1903-S	954,000	6,627	61.8	97%	$2,000	$2,005	$2,010	$2,015	$2,050	$2,075	$2,250	$14,500
Auctions: $3,290, MS-64, September 2015; $2,174, MS-63, June 2015; $1,481, MS-62, August 2015; $1,422, AU-55, August 2015												
1904	6,256,699	239,071	62.6	100%	$2,000	$2,005	$2,010	$2,015	$2,050	$2,075	$2,100	$2,750
Auctions: $5,875, MS-66, October 2015; $4,818, MS-65, March 2015; $1,528, MS-62, August 2015; $1,351, MS-60, June 2015												
1904, Proof (bb)	98	42	63.5							$30,000	$45,000	$85,000
Auctions: $146,875, PF-67Cam, August 2013												
1904-S	5,134,175	25,112	62.4	98%	$2,000	$2,005	$2,010	$2,015	$2,050	$2,075	$2,100	$2,750
Auctions: $4,465, MS-65, January 2015; $2,350, MS-64, January 2015; $1,645, MS-62, August 2015; $1,293, AU-58, January 2015												
1905	58,919	804	59.3	59%	$2,000	$2,005	$2,010	$2,015	$2,500	$6,500	$15,000	$85,000
Auctions: $6,463, MS-62, August 2015; $5,405, MS-62, July 2015; $1,763, AU-58, June 2015; $1,763, AU-53, August 2015												
1905, Proof (cc)	92	27	62.7							$30,000	$45,000	$85,000
Auctions: $10,005, PF-58, January 2012												
1905-S	1,813,000	2,385	61.1	88%	$2,000	$2,005	$2,010	$2,015	$2,050	$2,075	$3,500	$21,500
Auctions: $4,935, MS-64, July 2015; $3,525, MS-63, January 2015; $2,468, MS-62, August 2015; $1,645, MS-61, September 2015												

w. Fewer than 30 examples are known. **x.** Approximately 50 examples are known. **y.** 40 to 50 examples are known. **z.** Fewer than 50 examples are known. **aa.** 40 to 50 examples are known. **bb.** Approximately 50 examples are known. **cc.** 30 to 40 examples are known.

	Mintage	Cert	Avg	%MS	VF-20	EF-40	AU-50	AU-55	MS-60	MS-62	MS-63	MS-65
										PF-63	PF-64	PF-65
1906	69,596	703	60.3	75%	$2,000	$2,005	$2,010	$2,015	$2,050	$5,000	$8,500	$32,500
	Auctions: $14,361, MS-64, August 2015; $4,230, MS-62, August 2015; $3,760, MS-61, August 2015; $3,055, AU-58, August 2015											
1906, Proof (dd)	94	47	63.3							$30,000	$45,000	$85,000
	Auctions: $85,188, PF, August 2013											
1906-D	620,250	1,916	61.8	96%	$2,000	$2,005	$2,010	$2,015	$2,050	$2,075	$4,000	$21,500
	Auctions: $10,575, MS-64, August 2015; $3,525, MS-63, January 2015; $3,760, MS-62, August 2015; $1,410, MS-61, January 2015											
1906-D, Proof (ee)	6	0	n/a		*(extremely rare)*							
	Auctions: No auction records available.											
1906-S	2,065,750	4,654	61.4	95%	$2,000	$2,005	$2,010	$2,015	$2,050	$2,075	$2,250	$25,000
	Auctions: $25,850, MS-65, January 2015; $4,935, MS-64, October 2015; $1,645, MS-62, August 2015; $1,645, EF-45, August 2015											
1907	1,451,786	35,126	62.0	99%	$2,000	$2,005	$2,010	$2,015	$2,050	$2,075	$2,100	$7,500
	Auctions: $2,820, MS-64, July 2015; $1,471, MS-62, August 2015; $1,351, MS-60, January 2015; $1,351, AU-55, January 2015											
1907, Proof (ff)	78	46	63.5							$30,000	$45,000	$85,000
	Auctions: $40,250, PF-64Cam, January 2012											
1907-D	842,250	2,336	62.3	96%	$2,000	$2,005	$2,010	$2,015	$2,050	$2,075	$3,500	$8,500
	Auctions: $8,813, MS-65, March 2015; $4,230, MS-64, January 2015; $1,998, MS-62, September 2015; $1,528, MS-61, January 2015											
1907-D, Proof (gg)	*unknown*	2	62.0									
	Auctions: $71,875, PF-62, January 2004											
1907-S	2,165,800	3,573	61.8	95%	$2,000	$2,005	$2,010	$2,015	$2,050	$2,075	$3,000	$22,500
	Auctions: $17,625, MS-65, June 2015; $5,875, MS-64, March 2015; $2,820, MS-63, August 2015; $1,410, MS-61, January 2015											

dd. 45 to 50 examples are known. **ee.** Six 1906-D presentation strikes were made to commemorate the first coinage of double eagles at the Denver Mint. The coins were well documented at the time; however, at present only two are accounted for. **ff.** 25 to 50 examples are known. **gg.** Believed to have once been part of the collection of King Farouk of Egypt; cleaned.

SAINT-GAUDENS, HIGH RELIEF AND ULTRA HIGH RELIEF, MCMVII (1907)

Designer: *Augustus Saint-Gaudens.* **Weight:** *33.436 grams.*
Composition: *.900 gold, .100 copper (net weight: .96750 oz. pure gold).*
Diameter *34 mm.* **Edge:** *E PLURIBUS UNUM with words divided by stars*
(one specimen of the high-relief variety with plain edge is known). **Mint:** *Philadelphia.*

Circulation Strike   Proof, Ultra High Relief Pattern

History. Created by famous artist Augustus Saint-Gaudens under a commission arranged by President Theodore Roosevelt, this double eagle was first made (in pattern form) with ultra high relief, sculptural in its effect, on both sides and the date in Roman numerals. The story of its production is well known and has been described in several books, notably *Renaissance of American Coinage, 1905–1908* (Burdette) and *Striking Change: The Great Artistic Collaboration of Theodore Roosevelt and August Saint-Gaudens* (Moran). After the Ultra High Relief patterns of 1907, a modified High Relief version was developed to facilitate production. Each coin required three blows of the press to strike up properly. Most featured a flat rim (now known as the Flat Rim variety), but planchet metal would occasionally be squeezed up between the collar and the die, resulting in the Wire Rim variety; this can exist around part of or the entire circumference of the coin. The coins were made on a medal press in December 1907 and January 1908, to the extent of fewer than 13,000 pieces. In the meantime, production was under way for low-relief coins, easier to mint in quantities sufficient for commerce—these dated 1907 rather than MCMVII. Today the MCMVII double eagle is a favorite among collectors, and when surveys are taken of beautiful and popular designs (as in *100 Greatest U.S. Coins*, by Garrett and Guth), it always ranks near the top.

Striking and Sharpness. The striking usually is good. Check the left knee of Miss Liberty, which sometimes shows lightness of strike and, most often, shows flatness or wear (sometimes concealed by post-mint etching or clever tooling). Check the Capitol at the lower left. On the reverse, check the high points at the top of the eagle. The surface on all is a delicate matte texture, grainy rather than deeply frosty. Under examination the fields show myriad tiny raised curlicues and other die-finish marks. There is no record of any MCMVII double eagles being made as *Proofs*, nor is there any early numismatic record of any being sold as Proofs. Walter Breen in the 1960s made up some guidelines for Proofs, which some graders have adopted. Some homemade "Proofs" have been made by pickling or sandblasting the surface of regular coins—*caveat emptor*.

Availability. Half or more of the original mintage still exist today, as many were saved, and these grade mostly from AU-50 to MS-62. Circulated examples often have been cleaned, polished, or used in jewelry. Higher-grade coins are seen with some frequency, up to MS-65. Overgrading is common.

GRADING STANDARDS

MS-60 to 70 (Mint State). *Obverse:* At MS-60, some abrasion and contact marks are seen on Liberty's chest. The left knee is flat on lower Mint State coins and all circulated coins. Scattered marks and abrasion are in the field. Satiny luster is present, but may be dull or lifeless, and interrupted in patches. Many coins at this level have been cleaned. At MS-63, contact marks are fewer, and abrasion is light, but the knee still has a flat spot. An MS-65 coin

MCMVII (1907), High Relief. Graded MS-63.

has little abrasion and few marks. Grades above MS-65 are defined by having fewer marks as perfection is approached. *Reverse:* Comments apply as for the obverse, except that abrasion and contact marks are most noticeable on the side of the eagle's body and the top of the left wing.

   Illustrated coin: This is a splendid choice striking.

AU-50, 53, 55, 58 (About Uncirculated). *Obverse:* Light wear is seen on the chest, the left leg, and the field, more so at AU-50 than at AU–53 or 55. An AU-58 coin has fewer traces of wear. An AU-50 coin has satiny luster in protected areas among the rays, with little in the open field above. At AU-58, most luster is present. *Reverse:* Comments as preceding, except that the side of the eagle below the front of the wing, the top of the wing, and the field

MCMVII (1907), High Relief. Graded AU-55.

show light wear. Satiny luster ranges from perhaps 40% (at AU-50) to nearly full mint bloom (at AU-58).

EF-40, 45 (Extremely Fine). *Obverse:* Wear is seen on all the higher-relief areas of the standing figure and on the rock at the lower right. Luster is minimal, if present at all. Eye appeal is apt to be lacking. Nearly all Extremely Fine coins have been cleaned. *Reverse:* The eagle shows more wear overall, especially at the bottom and on the tops of the wings.

MCMVII (1907), High Relief. Graded EF-45.

VF-20, 30 (Very Fine). *Obverse:* Most details of the standing figure are flat, her face is incomplete, and the tips of the rays are weak. Eye appeal is usually poor. As these coins did not circulate to any extent, a Very Fine coin was likely carried as a pocket piece. *Reverse:* Wear is greater overall, but most evident on the eagle. Detail is good at the center of the left wing, but worn away in most other areas of the bird.

MCMVII (1907), High Relief. Graded VF-30.

MCMVII (1907) High Relief double eagles are seldom collected in grades lower than VF-20.

	Mintage	Cert	Avg	%MS	VF-20	EF-40	AU-50	AU-55	MS-60 PF-63	MS-62 PF-64	MS-63 PF-65	MS-65 PF-67
1907, High Relief, MCMVII, Wire Rim † (a)	12,367	1,443	62.1	89%	$8,500	$9,500	$10,500	$11,000	$13,000	$14,000	$16,000	$35,000
Auctions: $660,000, MS-69, September 2020; $71,675, MS-66, October 2015; $44,650, MS-65, November 2016												
1907, High Relief, MCMVII, Flat Rim †	(b)	594	62.2	86%	$8,500	$9,500	$10,500	$11,000	$13,000	$14,000	$16,000	$36,500
Auctions: $117,500, MS-67, January 2015; $70,500, MS-66, August 2016; $16,450, AU-58, September 2015												
1907, High Relief, MCMVII, Wire or Flat Rim, Proof	unknown	280	63.8						$30,000	$42,500	$75,000	
Auctions: $32,900, PF-64, February 2013												
1907, Ultra High Relief, Plain Edge, Proof	(c)	1,778	62.2	89%								
Auctions: No auction records available.												
1907, Ultra High Relief, Inverted Edge, Proof	(c)	0	n/a									
Auctions: No auction records available.												
1907, Ultra High Relief, Lettered Edge, Proof †	16–22	3	67.3								$2,250,000	$2,500,000
Auctions: $2,115,000, PF-68, January 2015; $1,840,000, PF-68, January 2007												

† Ranked in the *100 Greatest U.S. Coins* (fifth edition); the 1907 High Relief and 1907 Ultra High Relief Saint-Gaudens Roman Numeral Double Eagles are listed as separate entries. **a.** The Wire Rim and Flat Rim varieties were the result of different collars used in the minting process. The Flat Rim is considered slightly scarcer, but this has not led to large value differentials, as both varieties are very popular among collectors. **b.** Included in 1907, High Relief, MCMVII, Wire Rim, mintage figure. **c.** Included in 1907, Ultra High Relief, Lettered Edge, Proof, mintage figure.

SAINT-GAUDENS, FLAT RELIEF, ARABIC NUMERALS (1907–1933)

Designer: *Augustus Saint-Gaudens.* **Weight:** *33.436 grams.*
Composition: *.900 gold, .100 copper (net weight: .96750 oz. pure gold).*
Diameter: *34 mm.* **Edge:** *E PLURIBUS UNUM with words divided by stars.*
Mints: *Philadelphia, Denver, and San Francisco.*

No Motto (1907–1908)

Mintmark location is on the obverse, above the date.

With Motto (1908–1933)

With Motto, Proof

History. In autumn 1907 U.S. Mint chief engraver Charles E. Barber modified Augustus Saint-Gaudens's design by lowering its relief and substituting Arabic (not Roman) numerals. Coins of this type were struck in large quantities from 1907 to 1916 and again from 1920 to 1933. In July 1908 the motto IN GOD WE TRUST was added to the reverse. Coins dated 1907 to 1911 have 46 stars on the obverse; coins of 1912 to 1933 have 48 stars. Sandblast (also called Matte) Proofs were made in 1908 and from 1911 to 1915; Satin (also called Roman Finish) Proofs were made in 1909 and 1910.

The vast majority of these coins were exported. Since World War II millions have been repatriated, supplying most of those in numismatic hands today.

Striking and Sharpness. The details are often light on the obverse. Check the bosom of Miss Liberty, the covering of which tends to be weak on 1907 and, especially, 1908 No Motto coins. Check the Capitol building and its immediate area at the lower left. The reverse usually is well struck, but check the feathers on the eagle and the top of the wings. The Matte Proofs have dull surfaces, much like fine-grained sandpaper, while the Satin Proofs have satiny surfaces and are bright yellow.

Availability. Most dates and mintmarks range from very common to slightly scarce, punctuated with scarce to very rare issues such as 1908-S, 1920-S, 1921, mintmarked coins from 1924 to 1927, and all issues of 1929 to 1933. From their initial mintages, most of the double eagles of the 1920s were returned to the Mint and melted in the 1930s. Some, however, were unofficially saved by Treasury employees. Estimates of the quantities saved range from a few dozen to several hundred thousand, depending on the date; this explains the high values for coins that, judged only by their initial mintages, should otherwise be more common. Probably a million or more MS coins exist of certain dates, most notably 1908 No Motto, 1924, 1925, 1926, and 1928 (especially common). Quality varies, as many have contact marks.

Philadelphia Mint coins from 1922 onward usually are seen with excellent eye appeal. Common varieties are not usually collected in grades below MS. All of the Proofs are rare today.

Note: Values of common-date gold coins have been based on the current bullion price of gold, $2,000 per ounce, and may vary with the prevailing spot price.

GRADING STANDARDS

MS-60 to 70 (Mint State). *Obverse:* At MS-60, some abrasion and contact marks are seen on Liberty's chest and left knee, and scattered marks and abrasion are in the field. Luster is present, but may be dull or lifeless, and interrupted in patches. At MS-63, contact marks are fewer, and abrasion is light. An MS-65 coin has little abrasion and few marks, although quality among certified coins can vary. On a conservatively graded coin the lus-

1924. Graded MS-65.

ter should be full and rich. Grades above MS-65 are defined by having fewer marks as perfection is approached. Generally, Mint State coins of 1922 onward are choicer and more attractive than the earlier issues. *Reverse:* Comments apply as for the obverse, except that abrasion and contact marks are most noticeable on the eagle's left wing.

AU-50, 53, 55, 58 (About Uncirculated). *Obverse:* Light wear is seen on the chest, the left knee, the midriff, and across the field, more so at AU-50 than at AU–53 or 55. An AU-58 coin has minimal traces of wear. An AU-50 coin has luster in protected areas among the rays, with little in the open field above. At AU-58, most luster is present. *Reverse:* Comments as preceding, except that the side of the eagle below the front of the wing, the top of

1909, 9 Over 8. Graded AU-50.

the wing, and the field show light wear. Luster ranges from perhaps 40% (at AU-50) to nearly full mint bloom (at AU-58).

EF-40, 45 (Extremely Fine). *Obverse:* Wear is seen on all the higher-relief areas of the standing figure and on the rock at the lower right. Luster is minimal, if present at all. Eye appeal is apt to be lacking. *Reverse:* The eagle shows more wear overall, especially at the bottom and on the tops of the wings.

1908-S. Graded EF-40.

VF-20, 30 (Very Fine). *Obverse:* Most details of the standing figure are flat, her face is incomplete, and the tips of the rays are weak. Eye appeal is usually poor. *Reverse:* Wear is greater overall, but most evident on the eagle. Detail is good at the center of the left wing, but worn away in most other areas of the bird.

Saint-Gaudens double eagles are seldom collected in grades lower than VF-20.

1914. Graded VF-20.

PF-60 to 70 (Proof). *Obverse and Reverse:* At PF–60 to 63, there is light abrasion and some contact marks (the lower the grade, the higher the quantity). On Sandblast Proofs these show up as visually unappealing bright spots. At PF-64 and higher levels, marks are fewer, with magnification needed to see any at PF-65. At PF-66, there should be none at all.

1909, Satin Finish. Graded PF-66.

	Mintage	Cert	Avg	%MS	VF-20	EF-40	AU-50	AU-55	MS-60	MS-62 PF-63	MS-63 PF-64	MS-65 PF-65
1907, Arabic Numerals	361,667	11,276	62.7	97%	$2,000	$2,005	$2,010	$2,015	$2,130	$2,150	$2,180	$3,750
	Auctions: $5,170, MS-66, January 2015; $4,113, MS-65, January 2015; $2,585, MS-64, August 2015; $1,645, MS-62, February 2015											
1907, Proof (a)	*unknown*								*(extremely rare)*			
	Auctions: $70,500, MS-64, January 2015; $47,000, MS-64, August 2015											
1908, No Motto	4,271,551	151,073	63.3	100%	$2,000	$2,005	$2,010	$2,015	$2,130	$2,150	$2,180	$2,550
	Auctions: $6,463, MS-67, June 2015; $4,700, MS-66, February 2015; $1,763, MS-63, September 2015; $1,469, MS-61, September 2015											
1908-D, No Motto	663,750	4,420	62.3	97%	$2,000	$2,005	$2,010	$2,015	$2,130	$2,150	$2,200	$5,500
	Auctions: $9,400, MS-65, August 2015; $2,820, MS-64, August 2015; $1,586, MS-63, February 2015; $1,528, MS-62, September 2015											
1908, With Motto	156,258	2,269	62.1	95%	$2,000	$2,005	$2,010	$2,015	$2,150	$2,250	$2,350	$11,000
	Auctions: $5,170, MS-64, January 2015; $2,233, MS-63, March 2015; $1,645, MS-62, October 2015; $1,645, MS-60, July 2015											
1908, With Motto, Sandblast Finish Proof	101	69	65.3							$30,000	$50,000	$75,000
	Auctions: $57,500, PF-66+, June 2012											
1908, With Motto, Satin Finish Proof (b)	*unknown*	0	n/a						*(extremely rare)*			
	Auctions: $152,750, PF, August 2013											
1908-D, With Motto	349,500	2,324	62.5	93%	$2,000	$2,005	$2,010	$2,015	$2,130	$2,180	$2,250	$4,500
	Auctions: $21,150, MS-66, June 2015; $7,050, MS-65, January 2015; $3,525, MS-64, October 2015; $1,880, MS-62, July 2015											
1908-S, With Motto	22,000	529	56.0	31%	$2,550	$3,150	$4,500	$4,850	$10,500	$12,000	$20,000	$40,000
	Auctions: $21,150, MS-63, August 2015; $4,935, AU-53, July 2015; $3,878, EF-45, February 2015; $3,055, VF-35, August 2015											

a. 2 or 3 examples are known. **b.** 3 or 4 examples are known.

1909, 9 Over 8

	Mintage	Cert	Avg	%MS	VF-20	EF-40	AU-50	AU-55	MS-60	MS-62	MS-63	MS-65
										PF-63	PF-64	PF-65
1909, All kinds	161,282											
1909, 9 Over 8 (c)		1,691	59.1	55%	$2,000	$2,005	$2,010	$2,015	$2,200	$2,500	$3,400	$30,000
Auctions: $14,153, MS-64, July 2015; $4,700, MS-63, January 2015; $1,880, AU-58, September 2015; $1,645, AU-50, August 2015												
1909		3,058	59.8	64%	$2,000	$2,005	$2,010	$2,015	$2,150	$2,200	$2,450	$30,000
Auctions: $35,250, MS-65, June 2015; $1,586, MS-61, April 2015; $1,469, AU-58, January 2015; $1,593, AU-53, July 2015												
1909, Satin Finish Proof	67	29	65.5							$32,500	$60,000	$95,000
Auctions: $184,860, PF, September 2013												
1909-D	52,500	506	59.7	59%	$2,000	$2,005	$2,010	$2,015	$2,750	$3,750	$5,250	$30,000
Auctions: $11,750, MS-64, July 2015; $5,640, MS-63, February 2015; $2,820, AU-58, September 2015; $1,528, AU-50, July 2015												
1909-S	2,774,925	5,908	62.5	96%	$2,000	$2,005	$2,010	$2,015	$2,150	$2,180	$2,300	$4,500
Auctions: $22,913, MS-66, July 2015; $2,938, MS-64, January 2015; $1,763, MS-63, June 2015; $1,645, MS-62, January 2015												
1910	482,000	8,799	62.3	98%	$2,000	$2,005	$2,010	$2,015	$2,130	$2,180	$2,200	$6,000
Auctions: $6,463, MS-65, September 2015; $3,055, MS-64, January 2015; $1,704, MS-63, August 2015; $1,704, MS-62, January 2015												
1910, Satin Finish Proof	167	1	66.0							$32,500	$60,000	$95,000
Auctions: $76,375, PF-65, August 2014; $56,063, PF-65, June 2012												
1910, Sandblast Finish Proof (d)	*unknown*	36	65.6					*(unique)*				
Auctions: No auction records available.												
1910-D	429,000	7,115	62.8	97%	$2,000	$2,005	$2,010	$2,015	$2,130	$2,150	$2,200	$2,850
Auctions: $9,400, MS-66, January 2015; $2,350, MS-65, July 2015; $1,763, MS-64, October 2015; $1,469, MS-62, September 2015												
1910-S	2,128,250	4,564	61.7	89%	$2,000	$2,005	$2,010	$2,015	$2,130	$2,150	$2,200	$5,250
Auctions: $88,125, MS-67, January 2015; $3,760, MS-64, January 2015; $1,998, MS-63, August 2015; $1,528, MS-62, October 2015												
1911	197,250	2,795	61.9	90%	$2,000	$2,005	$2,010	$2,015	$2,130	$2,150	$2,200	$10,000
Auctions: $17,038, MS-66, January 2015; $4,935, MS-64, June 2015; $1,763, MS-62, August 2015; $1,528, EF-45, September 2015												
1911, Sandblast Finish Proof	100	45	66.1							$30,000	$50,000	$80,000
Auctions: $157,950, PF, September 2013												
1911-D	846,500	13,529	63.5	98%	$2,000	$2,005	$2,010	$2,015	$2,130	$2,150	$2,200	$2,750
Auctions: $3,760, MS-66, January 2015; $2,644, MS-64, August 2015; $1,586, MS-63, July 2015; $1,469, MS-62, September 2015												
1911-S	775,750	5,567	62.8	97%	$2,000	$2,005	$2,010	$2,015	$2,130	$2,150	$2,200	$3,000
Auctions: $11,221, MS-66, October 2015; $5,758, MS-65, January 2015; $1,880, MS-63, February 2015; $1,469, MS-62, September 2015												
1912	149,750	2,482	61.4	88%	$2,000	$2,005	$2,010	$2,015	$2,130	$2,150	$2,200	$22,500
Auctions: $19,975, MS-65, September 2015; $5,640, MS-64, January 2015; $1,528, MS-61, February 2015; $1,469, AU-58, January 2015												
1912, Sandblast Finish Proof	74	53	66.0							$30,000	$50,000	$80,000
Auctions: $211,500, PF-67, August 2013												
1913	168,780	2,730	61.4	89%	$2,000	$2,005	$2,010	$2,015	$2,130	$2,150	$2,200	$40,000
Auctions: $11,750, MS-64, January 2015; $1,763, MS-62, July 2015; $1,645, MS-61, October 2015; $1,410, AU-58, January 2015												
1913, Sandblast Finish Proof	58	51	65.4							$30,000	$50,000	$80,000
Auctions: $79,313, PF, August 2013												
1913-D	393,500	4,105	62.5	95%	$2,000	$2,005	$2,010	$2,015	$2,130	$2,150	$2,200	$4,500
Auctions: $22,325, MS-66, February 2015; $6,463, MS-65, August 2015; $2,585, MS-64, October 2015; $2,350, MS-63, September 2015												
1913-S	34,000	1,169	61.6	86%	$2,000	$2,005	$2,010	$2,015	$2,250	$2,750	$3,250	$27,500
Auctions: $9,400, MS-64, January 2015; $3,055, MS-62, January 2015; $2,233, MS-61, July 2015; $2,585, AU-58, September 2015												

c. This is one of the few Saint-Gaudens double eagle die varieties that commands a premium over the regular coin. d. Part of the unique complete 1910 Sandblast Finish Proof gold set.

1922, Doubled Die Reverse

	Mintage	Cert	Avg	%MS	VF-20	EF-40	AU-50	AU-55	MS-60	MS-62 / PF-63	MS-63 / PF-64	MS-65 / PF-65
1914	95,250	1,748	62.0	90%	$2,000	$2,005	$2,010	$2,015	$2,130	$2,150	$2,200	$17,500
Auctions: $7,638, MS-64, January 2015; $7,050, MS-64, January 2015; $2,585, MS-63, August 2015; $2,115, MS-62, July 2015												
1914, Sandblast Finish Proof	70	28	65.5							$30,000	$55,000	$80,000
Auctions: $60,375, PF-66, June 2012												
1914-D	453,000	7,127	63.0	97%	$2,000	$2,005	$2,010	$2,015	$2,130	$2,150	$2,200	$2,650
Auctions: $3,055, MS-65, August 2015; $2,140, MS-64, September 2015; $1,788, MS-64, January 2015; $1,645, MS-63, October 2015												
1914-S	1,498,000	22,203	63.1	99%	$2,000	$2,005	$2,010	$2,015	$2,130	$2,150	$2,200	$2,650
Auctions: $4,583, MS-66, December 2015; $1,763, MS-64, September 2015; $1,410, MS-61, September 2015; $1,293, MS-60, June 2015												
1915	152,000	2,320	61.7	88%	$2,000	$2,005	$2,010	$2,015	$2,150	$2,175	$2,200	$15,000
Auctions: $5,170, MS-64, January 2015; $3,055, MS-63, September 2015; $1,586, MS-61, July 2015; $1,410, AU-55, January 2015												
1915, Sandblast Finish Proof	50	41	64.8							$45,000	$75,000	$125,000
Auctions: $63,250, PF-66, August 2011												
1915-S	567,500	16,464	63.3	99%	$2,000	$2,005	$2,010	$2,015	$2,130	$2,150	$2,200	$2,650
Auctions: $4,700, MS-66, June 2015; $1,528, MS-64, October 2015; $1,528, MS-63, June 2015; $1,410, MS-62, September 2015												
1916-S	796,000	4,341	63.4	96%	$2,000	$2,005	$2,010	$2,015	$2,130	$2,150	$2,250	$2,750
Auctions: $4,935, MS-66, January 2015; $2,233, MS-64, January 2015; $1,763, MS-63, September 2015; $1,469, AU-58, January 2015												
1920	228,250	7,051	62.1	99%	$2,000	$2,005	$2,010	$2,015	$2,130	$2,150	$2,250	$50,000
Auctions: $5,170, MS-64, January 2015; $4,348, MS-64, August 2015; $2,233, MS-63, January 2015; $1,528, MS-62, September 2015												
1920-S	558,000	73	60.8	73%		$17,000	$27,000	$30,000	$42,500	$60,000	$75,000	$325,000
Auctions: $517,000, MS-65, November 2016; $99,875, MS-64, January 2015; $70,500, MS-63, January 2015; $44,650, AU-58, May 2016												
1921	528,500	72	59.2	58%		$35,000	$50,000	$60,000	$85,000	$105,000	$200,000	$550,000
Auctions: $199,750, MS-63, August 2016; $164,500, MS-63, January 2014; $91,063, MS-62, January 2017; $88,125, MS-62, June 2017												
1921, Proof † (e)	unknown	1	64.0		*(extremely rare)*							
Auctions: $1,495,000, PF-64+, 2006; $203,500, PF, 2000												
1922	1,375,500	59,155	62.6	100%	$2,000	$2,005	$2,010	$2,015	$2,130	$2,150	$2,200	$3,250
Auctions: $11,750, MS-66, August 2015; $3,290, MS-65, January 2015; $2,585, MS-64, August 2015; $1,351, MS-61, September 2015												
1922, DblDie Rev	(f)	17	63.7				$2,000	$2,200	$2,500	$2,750	$3,500	
Auctions: $2,115, MS-64, December 2013												
1922-S	2,658,000	899	62.6	96%	$2,080	$2,090	$2,100	$2,150	$2,350	$2,800	$3,250	$35,000
Auctions: $9,988, MS-64, July 2015; $3,408, MS-63, January 2015; $3,290, MS-62, January 2015; $3,290, MS-61, July 2015												
1923	566,000	32,175	62.5	100%	$2,000	$2,005	$2,010	$2,015	$2,130	$2,150	$2,200	$3,500
Auctions: $3,760, MS-65, January 2015; $2,350, MS-64, August 2015; $2,115, MS-64, June 2015; $1,528, MS-63, July 2015												
1923-D	1,702,250	6,107	64.3	100%	$2,000	$2,005	$2,010	$2,015	$2,130	$2,150	$2,200	$2,750
Auctions: $11,750, MS-67, February 2015; $2,585, MS-66, October 2015; $2,350, MS-65, February 2015; $1,469, MS-62, March 2015												
1924	4,323,500	328,444	63.4	100%	$2,000	$2,005	$2,010	$2,015	$2,130	$2,150	$2,200	$2,600
Auctions: $6,463, MS-67, January 2015; $3,760, MS-66, June 2015; $1,528, MS-62, October 2015; $1,293, MS-60, February 2015												
1924-D	3,049,500	445	62.0	90%	$2,080	$2,100	$2,200	$2,250	$3,750	$5,000	$6,000	$55,000
Auctions: $12,925, MS-64, August 2015; $3,290, MS-60, July 2015; $1,998, AU-53, August 2015; $1,763, AU-50, January 2015												
1924-S	2,927,500	485	62.5	93%	$2,080	$2,100	$2,300	$2,600	$4,250	$6,000	$9,000	$85,000
Auctions: $16,450, MS-64, January 2015; $9,106, MS-63, January 2015; $3,173, MS-60, January 2015; $2,233, MS-60, January 2015												

† Ranked in the *100 Greatest U.S. Coins* (fifth edition). **e.** Prior to the first public auction of a 1921 presentation-strike double eagle (a lightly cleaned specimen) in summer 2000, this variety was unknown to the numismatic community at large. That example reportedly was struck in 1921 to celebrate the birth of Joseph Baker, nephew of U.S. Mint director Raymond T. Baker. In 2006 a second example (this one with original, uncleaned surfaces) was discovered and subsequently auctioned. **f.** Included in 1922 mintage figure.

1925, Doubled Die Reverse   **1933 Saint-Gaudens Double Eagle**

	Mintage	Cert	Avg	%MS	VF-20	EF-40	AU-50	AU-55	MS-60 / PF-63	MS-62 / PF-64	MS-63 / PF-65	MS-65
1925	2,831,750	56,180	63.2	100%	$2,000	$2,005	$2,010	$2,015	$2,130	$2,150	$2,200	$2,600
Auctions: $4,230, MS-66, August 2015; $1,528, MS-64, June 2015; $1,293, MS-62, June 2015; $1,421, MS-60, October 2015												
1925, Doubled Die Reverse (g)	(h)	26	64.0				$2,000	$2,500	$2,750	$3,000	$3,500	
Auctions: $3,055, MS-65, December 2013												
1925-D	2,938,500	305	62.6	99%	$2,500	$3,000	$3,500	$4,000	$5,000	$6,500	$9,500	$90,000
Auctions: $64,625, MS-65, June 2015; $12,925, MS-64, August 2014; $7,638, MS-62, June 2015; $4,465, MS-61, August 2015												
1925-S	3,776,500	411	59.5	59%	$2,500	$3,000	$3,750	$5,000	$8,000	$9,000	$12,500	$225,000
Auctions: $11,456, MS-63, August 2015; $8,225, MS-61, January 2015; $5,170, AU-58, January 2015; $5,405, AU-55, August 2015												
1926	816,750	24,834	63.6	100%	$2,000	$2,005	$2,010	$2,015	$2,130	$2,150	$2,200	$2,600
Auctions: $1,821, MS-65, August 2015; $1,645, MS-64, June 2015; $1,528, MS-64, October 2015; $1,469, MS-63, March 2015												
1926-D	481,000	108	61.3	89%		$8,500	$10,500	$14,000	$15,000	$16,000	$17,500	$240,000
Auctions: $47,000, MS-64, March 2014; $22,325, MS-63, June 2015; $14,100, MS-62, September 2015; $11,163, AU-58, September 2015												
1926-S	2,041,500	656	63.1	97%		$2,250	$2,350	$2,750	$3,500	$4,000	$6,000	$25,000
Auctions: $18,277, MS-65, October 2015; $8,226, MS-64, June 2015; $5,170, MS-63, February 2015; $2,115, MS-60, January 2015												
1927	2,946,750	150,343	63.5	100%	$2,000	$2,005	$2,010	$2,015	$2,130	$2,150	$2,200	$2,600
Auctions: $3,525, MS-66, September 2015; $2,585, MS-65, June 2015; $1,351, MS-61, September 2015; $1,410, MS-60, October 2015												
1927-D †	180,000	5	64.0	80%					$1,100,000	$1,200,000	$1,400,000	$2,000,000
Auctions: $1,997,500, MS-66, January 2014												
1927-S	3,107,000	123	61.1	75%			$15,000	$18,000	$25,000	$35,000	$42,500	$135,000
Auctions: $105,750, MS-65, March 2014; $42,300, MS-63, August 2016; $25,850, MS-62, June 2015; $17,625, AU-55, January 2015												
1928	8,816,000	55,374	63.4	100%	$2,000	$2,005	$2,010	$2,015	$2,130	$2,150	$2,200	$2,600
Auctions: $18,800, MS-67, August 2015; $4,818, MS-66, September 2015; $1,998, MS-64, June 2015; $1,379, MS-60, August 2015												
1929	1,779,750	128	63.1	95%				$12,500	$24,000	$29,000	$35,000	$60,000
Auctions: $57,281, MS-65, August 2014; $37,600, MS-64, January 2015; $32,900, MS-63, September 2015; $15,863, MS-60, August 2014												
1930-S	74,000	22	64.0						$60,000	$65,000	$100,000	$170,000
Auctions: $176,382, MS-65, March 2014; $164,500, MS-65, September 2014; $146,875, MS-64, November 2016; $164,500, MS-63, August 2014												
1931	2,938,250	31	64.3						$32,500	$45,000	$60,000	$105,000
Auctions: $105,751, MS-65, September 2014; $105,750, MS-65, August 2016; $76,375, MS-65, March 2014; $64,625, MS-64, August 2014												
1931-D	106,500	39	63.3	97%					$37,500	$52,500	$62,500	$120,000
Auctions: $129,250, MS-65, September 2014; $99,875, MS-64, January 2014; $94,000, MS-64, November 2016; $64,625, MS-62, August 2014												
1932	1,101,750	67	63.9						$50,000	$55,000	$70,000	$100,000
Auctions: $108,688, MS-66, March 2014; $99,875, MS-66, August 2014; $94,000, MS-64, August 2014												
1933 † (i)	445,500	0	n/a		*(extremely rare)*	—						
Auctions: $7,590,000, Gem BU, July 2002												

† Ranked in the *100 Greatest U.S. Coins* (fifth edition). **g.** Doubling is evident on the eagle's feathers, the rays, and IN GOD WE TRUST. **h.** Included in 1925 mintage figure. **i.** All but a few 1933 double eagles were to have been melted at the mint. Today 13 examples are known to have survived. Only one, said to have previously been in the collection of King Farouk of Egypt, has ever been sold at auction. The federal government has ruled that others are illegal to own privately.

U.S. Commemoratives
1892–1954 and 1982 to Date

AN OVERVIEW OF CLASSIC COMMEMORATIVES

Commemorative coins have been popular since the time of ancient Greece and Rome. In the beginning they recorded and honored important events and passed along the news of the day. Today commemorative coins, which are highly esteemed by collectors, have been issued by many modern nations—none of which has surpassed the United States when it comes to these impressive mementoes.

The unique position occupied by commemoratives in the United States coinage is largely due to the fact that, with few exceptions, all commemorative coins have real historical significance. The progress and advance of people in the New World are presented in an interesting and instructive manner on our commemorative coins. Such a record of history artistically presented on U.S. gold, silver, and other memorial issues appeals strongly to the collector who favors the romantic, storytelling side of numismatics. It is the historical features of our commemoratives, in fact, that create interest among many people who would otherwise have little interest in coins, and would not otherwise consider themselves collectors.

Proposed coin programs are considered by two congressional committees: the Senate Committee on Banking, Housing, and Urban Affairs; and the House Financial Services Committee. Once a program is approved by Congress, the independent Citizens Coinage Advisory Committee (ccac.gov) and the U.S. Commission of Fine Arts (cfa.gov) advise the secretary of the Treasury on its coin designs.

These special coins are usually issued either to commemorate events or to help pay for monuments, programs, or celebrations that commemorate historical persons, places, or things. Pre-1982 commemorative coins were offered in most instances by a commission in charge of the event to be commemorated and sold at a premium over face value.

Commemorative coins are popularly collected either by major types or in sets with mintmark varieties. The pieces covered in this section of the *Guide Book of United States Coins, Deluxe Edition*, are those of the "classic" era of U.S. commemoratives, 1892 to 1954. All commemoratives are of the standard weight and fineness of their regular-issue 20th-century gold and silver counterparts, and all are legal tender.

A note about mintages and distribution numbers: Unless otherwise stated, the coinage figures given in each "Distribution" column represent the total released mintage: the total mintage (including assay coins), minus the quantity of unsold coins. In many cases, larger quantities were minted but not all were sold. Unsold coins usually were returned to the mint and melted, although sometimes quantities were placed in circulation at face value. A limited number of Proof strikings or presentation pieces were made for some of the classic commemorative issues.

A note about price performance: It has mostly been in recent decades that the general public has learned about commemorative coins. They have long been popular with coin collectors who enjoy the artistry and history associated with them, as well as the profit to be made from owning these rare pieces. Very few of them ever reached circulation because they were all originally sold above face value, and because they are all so rare. Most of the early issues were of the half dollar denomination, often made in quantities of fewer than 20,000 pieces. This is minuscule when compared to the regular half dollar coins that are made by the millions each year, and still rarely seen in circulation.

At the beginning of 1988, prices of classic commemoratives in MS-65 condition had risen so high that most collectors had to content themselves with pieces in lower grades. Investors continued to apply pressure to the high-quality pieces, driving prices even higher, while the collector community went after coins in grades from AU to MS-63. For several months the pressure from both influences caused prices to rise very rapidly (for all issues and grades) without even taking the price-adjustment breather that usually goes along with such activity.

By 1990, prices dropped to the point that several of the commemoratives began to look like bargains once again. Many of the MS-65 pieces held firm at price levels above the $3,000 mark, but others were still available at under $500 even for coins of similar mintage. Coins in MS–63 or 64 were priced at but a fraction of the MS-65 prices, which would seem to make them reasonably priced because the demand for these pieces is universal, and not keyed simply to grade, rarity, or speculator pressure.

Historically, the entire series of commemorative coins has frequently undergone a roller-coaster cycle of price adjustments. These cycles have usually been of short duration, lasting from months to years, with prices always recovering and eventually exceeding previous levels.

See pages 1168 and 1169 for discussion of modern commemorative coins of 1982 to date, pages 1275–1280 for pricing of government commemorative sets, and page 1499 for an alphabetical cross-reference list of all commemoratives.

WORLD'S COLUMBIAN EXPOSITION HALF DOLLAR (1892–1893)

Designers: *Charles E. Barber (obverse), George T. Morgan (reverse).* **Weight:** *12.50 grams.*
Composition: *.900 silver, .100 copper (net weight .3617 oz. pure silver).*
Diameter: *30.6 mm.* **Edge:** *Reeded.* **Mint:** *Philadelphia.*

The first U.S. commemorative coin was the Columbian half dollar sold at the World's Columbian Exposition—also known as the Chicago World's Fair—during 1893. The event celebrated the 400th anniversary of Christopher Columbus's arrival in the New World. A great many of the coins remained unsold and a substantial quantity was later released for circulation at face value or melted.

Designs. *Obverse:* Charles Barber's conception of Christopher Columbus, derived from a plaster model by Olin Levi Warner, taken from the explorer's portrait on an 1892 Spanish medal. The medal's portrait was inspired by a statue by Jeronimo Suñel, which itself was from an imagined likeness by Charles Legrand. *Reverse:* A sailing ship atop two globes representing the Old World and the New World. The vessel is from a plaster model by Olin Levi Warner, taken from a model made in Spain of Columbus's flagship, the *Santa Maria.*

Mintage and Melting Data. *Maximum authorized*—5,000,000 (both years combined). *Number minted*—1892: 950,000 (including an unknown number of assay coins; approximately 100 Proofs were struck as well); 1893: 4,052,105 (including 2,105 assay coins). *Number melted*—1893: 2,501,700. *Net distribution*—1892: 950,000; 1893: 1,550,405.

Original Cost and Issuer. Sale price $1. Issued by the Exposition.

Key to Collecting. Both dates are common in all grades through MS-65, and are often available in MS-66 and higher. The typical high-grade coin is lustrous and frosty; some have attractive, original light-blue or iridescent toning. Well-worn examples are very common, as the Treasury Department eventually released large quantities into circulation at face value. Striking usually is good. Some coins can be weak at the center—on the higher areas of the portrait and, on the reverse, in the details of the ship's sails. Most have contact marks from handling and distribution. High-grade 1892 coins typically are better struck than those of 1893. Approximately 100 brilliant Proofs were struck for each date; they vary widely in quality and eye appeal.

First Points of Wear. *Obverse:* The eyebrow, the cheek, and the hair at the back of the forehead. (The hair area sometimes is flatly struck.) *Reverse:* The top of the rear sail, and the right side of the Eastern Hemisphere.

	Distribution	Cert	Avg	%MS	AU-50	MS-60	MS-62	MS-63	MS-64 / PF-63	MS-65 / PF-64	MS-66 / PF-65
1892	950,000	6,015	63.1	94%	$20	$27	$45	$70	$100	$275	$625
	Auctions: $2,350, MS-67, August 2016; $1,410, MS-66, September 2016										
1892, Proof	*100*	42	64.1						$5,750	$7,000	$13,000
	Auctions: $8,225, PF-65, November 2013										
1893	1,550,405	6,550	62.1	87%	$20	$27	$45	$70	$100	$275	$650
	Auctions: $8,229, MS-67, June 2015; $1,293, MS-66, July 2015; $400, MS-65, January 2015; $118, MS-64, August 2015										
1893, Proof	*3–5*	2	63.0								
	Auctions: $15,275, PF-66, January 2014; $5,830, PF-64, September 1993										

Note: Various repunched dates exist for both dates; these command little or no premium in the marketplace. For more information, see the *Cherrypickers' Guide to Rare Die Varieties, Vol. II* (sixth edition).

WORLD'S COLUMBIAN EXPOSITION ISABELLA QUARTER (1893)

Designer: *Charles E. Barber.* **Weight:** *6.25 grams.* **Composition:** *.900 silver, .100 copper (net weight .18084 oz. pure silver).* **Diameter:** *24.3 mm.* **Edge:** *Reeded.* **Mint:** *Philadelphia.*

In 1893 the Board of Lady Managers of the World's Columbian Exposition (also known as the Chicago World's Fair) petitioned for a souvenir quarter dollar. Authority was granted March 3, 1893, for the coin, which is known as the *Isabella quarter*.

Designs. *Obverse:* Crowned profile portrait of Spain's Queen Isabella, who sponsored Christopher Columbus's voyages to the New World. *Reverse:* A lady kneeling with a distaff and spindle, symbolic of the industry of American women.

Mintage and Melting Data. Authorized on March 3, 1893. *Maximum authorized*—40,000. *Number minted*—40,023 (including 23 assay coins). *Number melted*—15,809. *Net distribution*—24,214.

Original Cost and Issuer. Sale price $1. Issued by the Board of Lady Managers, World's Columbian Exposition.

Key to Collecting. Most examples in the marketplace are in Mint State, including many choice and gem pieces. Most are well struck and show full details, with richly lustrous fields. Connoisseurs avoid darkly toned, stained, and recolored coins. Many lower-grade Mint State examples have marks on Isabella's cheek and on the higher parts of the reverse design. The left obverse field often has marks made from contact with other coins during minting, storage, and distribution. The certification services have classified some coins with mirrored fields as Proofs, although no official records exist for the production of such.

First Points of Wear. *Obverse:* Isabella's cheekbone, and the center of the lower part of the crown. *Reverse:* The strand of wool at the lower-left thigh.

	Distribution	Cert	Avg	%MS	AU-50	MS-60	MS-62	MS-63	MS-64 / PF-63	MS-65 / PF-64	MS-66 / PF-65
1893	24,214	3,942	62.3	88%	$300	$325	$400	$450	$925	$1,400	$2,100
	Auctions: $17,625, MS-67, January 2015; $329, AU-58, February 2015; $306, EF-40, July 2015; $235, VF-30, February 2015										
1893, Proof	*100–105*	50	63.9						$4,750	$7,750	$13,000
	Auctions: $6,463, PF-64, July 2015; $5,640, PF-64, June 2015; $5,288, PF-64, October 2014										

LAFAYETTE DOLLAR (1900)

Designer: *Charles E. Barber.* **Weight:** *26.73 grams.* **Composition:** *.900 silver, .100 copper (net weight .7736 oz. pure silver).* **Diameter:** *38.1 mm.* **Edge:** *Reeded.* **Mint:** *Philadelphia.*

This issue—which was the first commemorative coin of one-dollar denomination, as well as the first authorized U.S. coin to bear a portrait of a U.S. president—commemorated the erection of a statue of Marquis de Lafayette in Paris in connection with the 1900 Paris Exposition (Exposition Universelle).

Designs. *Obverse:* Conjoined portraits of the marquis de Lafayette and George Washington. *Reverse:* Side view of the equestrian statue erected by the youth of the United States in honor of Lafayette. This view was based on an early model of the statue; the final version that was erected in Paris is slightly different.

Mintage and Melting Data. Authorized on March 3, 1899. *Maximum authorized*—50,000. *Number minted*— 50,026 (including 26 assay coins). *Number melted*—14,000. *Net distribution*—36,026.

Original Cost and Issuer. Sale price $2. Issued by the Lafayette Memorial Commission through the American Trust & Savings Bank of Chicago.

Key to Collecting. Most surviving examples show evidence of circulation or other mishandling. The typical grade is AU. In Mint State, most are MS–60 to 63, and many are dull or unattractive, having been dipped or cleaned multiple times. Many have marks and dings. Properly graded MS-64 coins are very scarce, and MS-65 or higher gems are very rare, especially if with good eye appeal. Several die varieties exist and are collected by specialists.

Varieties. *Obverse varieties:* (1) Small point on the bust of Washington. The tip of Lafayette's bust is over the top of the L in DOLLAR. The AT in STATES is cut high. (2) The left foot of the final A in AMERICA is recut, and the A in STATES is high. The second S in STATES is repunched (this is diagnostic). (3) The AT in STATES is recut and the final S is low. The letter F in OF and in LAFAYETTE is broken from the lower tip of the crossbar and to the right base extension, and AMERICA is spaced A ME RI C A. The period after OF is close to the A of AMERICA. The tip of Lafayette's vest falls to the right of the top of the first L in DOLLAR. (4) The C in AMERICA is repunched at the inside top (this is diagnostic). The CA in AMERICA is spaced differently from the obverses previously described. *Reverse varieties:* (A) There are 14 long leaves and a long stem. The tip of the lowest leaf is over the 1 in 1900. (B) There are 14 shorter leaves and a short stem. The tip of the lowest leaf is over the space between the 1 and 9 in 1900. (C) There are 14 medium leaves and a short, bent stem. The tip of the lowest leaf is over the 9 in 1900. (D) There are 15 long leaves and a short, bent stem. The tip of the lowest leaf is over the 9 in 1900. (E) The tip of the lowest leaf is over the space to the left of the 1 in 1900.

First Points of Wear. *Obverse:* Washington's cheekbone, and Lafayette's lower hair curl. *Reverse:* The fringe of Lafayette's epaulet, and the horse's blinder and left rear leg bone.

	Distribution	Cert	Avg	%MS	AU-50	MS-60	MS-62	MS-63	MS-64	MS-65	MS-66
1900	36,026	2,605	61.7	86%	$450	$775	$1,200	$1,300	$2,750	$5,000	$10,000

Auctions: $73,438, MS-67, January 2015; $25,850, MS-67, April 2017; $4,320, MS-65, April 2018; $2,040, MS-64, January 2018

LOUISIANA PURCHASE EXPOSITION JEFFERSON GOLD DOLLAR (1903)

Designer: *Charles E. Barber (assisted by George T. Morgan).* **Weight:** *1.672 grams.*
Composition: *.900 gold, .100 copper (net weight .04837 oz. pure gold).*
Diameter: *15 mm.* **Edge:** *Reeded.* **Mint:** *Philadelphia.*

The first commemorative U.S. gold coins were authorized for the Louisiana Purchase Exposition, held in St. Louis in 1904. The event commemorated the 100th anniversary of the United States' purchase of the Louisiana Territory from France, an acquisition overseen by President Thomas Jefferson.

Designs. *Obverse:* Bewigged profile portrait of Thomas Jefferson, inspired by an early-1800s medal by John Reich, after Jean-Antoine Houdon's bust. *Reverse:* Inscription and branch.

Mintage and Melting Data. Authorized on June 28, 1902. *Maximum authorized*—250,000 (both types combined). *Number minted*—250,258 (125,000 of each type; including 258 assay coins comprising both types). *Number melted*—215,250 (total for both types; no account was kept of the portraits; 250 assay coins were melted). *Net distribution*—35,000 (estimated at 17,500 of each type).

Original Cost and Issuer. Sale price $3. Issued by the Louisiana Purchase Exposition Company, St. Louis, Missouri (sales through Farran Zerbe). Some were sold as mounted in spoons, brooches, and stick pins; 100 certified Proofs of each design were made, mounted in an opening in a rectangular piece of imprinted cardboard.

Key to Collecting. Market demand is strong, from collectors and investors alike, as most surviving examples are in choice or gem Mint State, with strong eye appeal. Most specimens are very lustrous and frosty. An occasional coin is prooflike. Avoid any with copper stains (from improper mixing of the gold/copper alloy). Proofs enter the market rarely and garner much publicity.

First Points of Wear. *Obverse:* Portrait's cheekbone and sideburn. *Reverse:* Date and denomination.

| | Distribution | Cert | Avg | %MS | AU-50 | MS-60 | MS-62 | MS-63 | MS-64 | MS-65 | MS-66 |
									PF-63	PF-64	PF-65
1903	17,500	2,312	63.8	93%	$500	$600	$650	$700	$925	$1,000	$1,500
	Auctions: $5,993, MS-67, July 2015; $1,293, MS-64, July 2015; $470, AU-58, January 2015; $329, AU-50, January 2015										
1903, Proof (a)	100	36	65.0								
	Auctions: $37,375, PF-67UCamH, January 2012										

a. The first 100 Jefferson gold dollars were struck in brilliant Proof format. True Proofs exhibit deeply mirrored fields and are sharply struck. Many also have frosted devices, giving them a cameo appearance. "Although many of the coins seen today have been certified and lack original packaging, they were originally housed in cardboard holders certifying each coin as having been one of the first 100 impressions from the dies. The original holders are quite interesting, with the coin covered by a small piece of wax paper and a piece of string sealed by dark red wax. The coins are difficult to see behind the wax paper, and the author has seen holders with a circulation-strike example substituted for the Proof piece. Caution should be used when purchasing an example of this extreme rarity" (*Encyclopedia of U.S. Gold Coins, 1795–1933*, second edition).

LOUISIANA PURCHASE EXPOSITION MCKINLEY GOLD DOLLAR (1903)

Designer: *Charles E. Barber (assisted by George T. Morgan).* **Weight:** *1.672 grams.*
Composition: *.900 gold, .100 copper (net weight .04837 oz. pure gold).*
Diameter: *15 mm.* **Edge:** *Reeded.* **Mint:** *Philadelphia.*

President William McKinley—who had been assassinated while in office two years before the Louisiana Purchase Exposition—was remembered on a gold dollar issued alongside the aforementioned coin featuring Thomas Jefferson. Like Jefferson, McKinley oversaw expansion of U.S. territory, with the acquisition of Puerto Rico, Guam, and the Philippines, as well as the annexation of Hawaii.

Designs. *Obverse:* Bareheaded profile portrait of William McKinley, derived from his presidential medal (designed, like this coin, by Charles Barber). *Reverse:* Inscriptions and branch.

Mintage and Melting Data. Authorized on June 28, 1902. *Maximum authorized*—250,000 (both types combined). *Number minted*—250,258 (125,000 of each type; including 258 assay coins comprising both types). *Number melted*—215,250 (total for both types; no account was kept of the portraits; 250 assay coins were melted). *Net distribution*—35,000 (estimated at 17,500 of each type).

Original Cost and Issuer. Sale price $3. Issued by the Louisiana Purchase Exposition Company, St. Louis, Missouri (sales through Farran Zerbe). Some were sold as mounted in spoons, brooches, and stick pins; 100 certified Proofs of each design were made, mounted in an opening in a rectangular piece of imprinted cardboard.

Key to Collecting. Market demand is strong, from collectors and investors alike, as most surviving examples are in choice or gem Mint State, with strong eye appeal. Most specimens are very lustrous and frosty. An occasional coin is prooflike. Avoid any with copper stains (from improper mixing of the gold/copper alloy). Proofs enter the market rarely and garner much publicity.

First Points of Wear. *Obverse:* Portrait's cheekbone and sideburn. *Reverse:* Date and denomination.

	Distribution	Cert	Avg	%MS	AU-50	MS-60	MS-62	MS-63	MS-64	MS-65	MS-66
									PF-63	PF-64	PF-65
1903	17,500	2,177	63.9	95%	$500	$575	$625	$650	$850	$900	$1,200
	Auctions: $8,813, MS-68, January 2015; $1,763, MS-66, January 2015; $517, MS-63, January 2015; $376, AU-58, August 2015										
1903, Proof (a)	100	28	64.5								
	Auctions: $14,950, PF-65Cam, April 2012										

a. Like the Jefferson issue, the first 100 McKinley gold dollars were struck as Proofs, and packaged as such. "Prooflike circulation strikes are quite common for the issue, and true Proofs can be distinguished by deeply mirrored surfaces and cameo devices. Certification is highly recommended" (*Encyclopedia of U.S. Gold Coins, 1795–1933*, second edition).

LEWIS AND CLARK EXPOSITION GOLD DOLLAR (1904–1905)

Designer: *Charles E. Barber.* **Weight:** *1.672 grams.* **Composition:** *.900 gold, .100 copper (net weight .04837 oz. pure gold).* **Diameter:** *15 mm.* **Edge:** *Reeded.* **Mint:** *Philadelphia.*

A souvenir issue of gold dollars was struck to mark the Lewis and Clark Centennial Exposition, held in Portland, Oregon, in 1905. The sale of these coins financed the erection of a bronze memorial of the Shoshone Indian guide Sacagawea, who assisted in the famous expedition.

Designs. *Obverse:* Bareheaded profile portrait of Meriwether Lewis. *Reverse:* Bareheaded profile portrait of William Clark. These portraits were inspired by works of Charles Willson Peale.

Mintage and Melting Data. Authorized on April 13, 1904. *Maximum authorized*—250,000 (both years combined). *Number minted*—1904: 25,028 (including 28 assay coins); 1905: 35,041 (including 41 assay coins). *Number melted*—1904: 15,003; 1905: 25,000. *Net distribution*—1904: 10,025; 1905: 10,041.

Original Cost and Issuer. Sales price $2 (some at $2.50); many were probably discounted further. Issued by the Lewis and Clark Centennial and American Pacific Exposition and Oriental Fair Company, Portland, Oregon (sales through Farran Zerbe and others).

Key to Collecting. Most surviving examples show evidence of handling. Some exhibit die problems (a rough raised area of irregularity at the denticles). Most range from AU–50 to 58, with an occasional MS–60 to 63. MS-64 coins are scarce, and MS-65 rare. Pristine examples are very rare. Most MS coins have areas of prooflike finish; some are deeply lustrous and frosty. The 1905-dated issue is noticeably scarcer than the 1904.

First Points of Wear. *Obverse:* Lewis's temple. *Reverse:* Clark's temple.

	Distribution	Cert	Avg	%MS	AU-50	MS-60	MS-62	MS-63	MS-64	MS-65	MS-66
									PF-63	PF-64	PF-65
1904	10,025	1,284	63.4	94%	$750	$900	$950	$1,000	$2,150	$3,000	$6,000
	Auctions: $15,275, MS-67, January 2015; $6,580, MS-66, January 2015; $734, MS-61, February 2015; $400, AU-50, May 2015										
1904, Proof	2–3	3	63.3								
	Auctions: $30,550, PF-64, August 2015										
1905	10,041	1,274	62.8	92%	$750	$900	$1,100	$1,150	$2,875	$4,000	$9,000
	Auctions: $35,250, MS-67, January 2015; $19,388, MS-66, January 2015; $1,880, MS-63, January 2015; $705, MS-60, June 2015										

PANAMA-PACIFIC INTERNATIONAL EXPOSITION HALF DOLLAR (1915)

Designers: *Charles E. Barber (obverse), George T. Morgan (assisting Barber on reverse).*
Weight: *12.50 grams.* **Composition:** *.900 silver, .100 copper (net weight .3617 oz. pure silver).*
Diameter: *30.6 mm.* **Edge:** *Reeded.* **Mint:** *San Francisco.*

The Panama-Pacific International Exposition held in San Francisco in 1915 celebrated the opening of the Panama Canal, as well as the revival of the Bay Area following the 1906 earthquake and fire. Five commemorative coins in four different denominations, including a half dollar, were issued in conjunction with the event.

Designs. *Obverse:* Columbia scattering flowers, alongside a child holding a cornucopia, representing the bounty of the American West; the Golden Gate in the background. *Reverse:* A spread-winged eagle perched on a shield, with branches of oak and olive.

Mintage and Melting Data. Authorized by the Act of January 16, 1915. *Maximum authorized*—200,000. *Number minted*—60,030 (including 30 assay coins). *Number melted*—32,896 (including the 30 assay coins; 29,876 were melted on September 7, 1916 and the balance on October 30, 1916). *Net distribution*—27,134.

Original Cost and Issuer. Sale price $1. Issued by the Coin and Medal Department (Farran Zerbe), Panama-Pacific International Exposition, San Francisco, California (combination offers included a set of four coins, including the buyer's choice of one $50, in a leather case, for $100; and a set of five coins in a copper frame for $200).

Key to Collecting. The half dollar does not have the typical deep mint frost associated with earlier silver issues. Most are satiny in appearance with the high parts in particular having a microscopically grainy finish. Many pieces have an inner line around the perimeter near the rim, a die characteristic. On the reverse of all known coins, the eagle's breast feathers are indistinct, which sometimes gives MS coins the appearance of having light wear. Most surviving coins grade from AU-50 to MS-63.

First Points of Wear. *Obverse:* Columbia's left shoulder. *Reverse:* The eagle's breast.

	Distribution	Cert	Avg	%MS	AU-50	MS-60	MS-62	MS-63	MS-64	MS-65	MS-66
1915-S	27,134	2,832	63.2	92%	$375	$500	$650	$700	$925	$1,325	$2,000

Auctions: $13,513, MS-67, August 2015; $646, MS-61, October 2015; $247, AU-50, July 2015; $165, VF-25, February 2015

PANAMA-PACIFIC INTERNATIONAL EXPOSITION GOLD DOLLAR (1915)

Designer: *Charles Keck.* **Weight:** *1.672 grams.* **Composition:** *.900 gold, .100 copper (net weight .04837 oz. pure gold).* **Diameter:** *15 mm.* **Edge:** *Reeded.* **Mint:** *San Francisco.*

Coin dealer and entrepreneur Farran Zerbe conceived of a program of five different commemorative coins across four denominations (including the gold dollar) in conjunction with the Panama-Pacific International Exposition in 1915. The event was held in what eventually constituted a miniature city, whose sculptures and impressive architecture were intended to remind one of Rome or some other distant and romantic place, but which at night was more apt to resemble Coney Island.

Designs. *Obverse:* Capped profile portrait of a Panama Canal laborer. *Reverse:* Two dolphins, symbolizing the Atlantic and Pacific oceans, and legends.

Mintage and Melting Data. Authorized by the Act of January 16, 1915. *Maximum authorized*—25,000. *Number minted*—25,034 (including 34 assay coins). *Number melted*—10,034 (including the 34 assay coins; melted at the San Francisco Mint on October 30, 1916). *Net distribution*—15,000.

Original Cost and Issuer. Sale price $2 (and a few at $2.25). Issued by the Coin and Medal Department (Farran Zerbe), Panama-Pacific International Exposition, San Francisco, California (combination offers included, among others, a set of four coins, with the buyer's choice of one fifty-dollar coin, in a leather case, for $100; and a set of five coins in a copper frame for $200).

Key to Collecting. Most examples are in Mint State. Many exhibit deep mint frost. Friction is common, especially on the obverse.

First Points of Wear. *Obverse:* The peak of the laborer's cap. *Reverse:* The heads of the dolphins, and the denomination.

	Distribution	Cert	Avg	%MS	AU-50	MS-60	MS-62	MS-63	MS-64	MS-65	MS-66
1915-S	15,000	3,879	63.5	93%	$450	$550	$615	$625	$825	$1,000	$1,400

Auctions: $3,538, MS-67, January 2015; $1,733, MS-64, August 2015; $441, AU-55, April 2015; $329, EF-40, April 2015

PANAMA-PACIFIC INTERNATIONAL EXPOSITION QUARTER EAGLE (1915)

Designer: *Charles E. Barber (obverse), George T. Morgan (reverse).* **Weight:** *4.18 grams.* **Composition:** *.900 gold, .100 copper (net weight .12094 oz. pure gold).* **Diameter:** *18 mm.* **Edge:** *Reeded.* **Mint:** *San Francisco.*

The 1915 Panama-Pacific International Exposition—a name chosen to reflect the recently completed Panama Canal, as well as Pacific Ocean commerce—was planned to be the ultimate world's fair. Foreign countries, domestic manufacturers, artists, concessionaires, and others were invited to the 10-month event, which drew an estimated 19 million visitors. This quarter eagle was among the five coins issued to commemorate the celebration.

Designs. *Obverse:* Columbia seated on a hippocampus, holding a caduceus, symbolic of Medicine's triumph over yellow fever in Panama during the canal's construction. *Reverse:* An eagle, standing on a plaque inscribed E PLURIBUS UNUM, with raised wings.

Mintage and Melting Data. Authorized by the Act of January 16, 1915. *Maximum authorized*—10,000. *Number minted*—10,017 (including 17 assay coins). *Number melted*—3,268 (including the 17 assay coins; melted at the San Francisco Mint on October 30, 1916). *Net distribution*—6,749.

Original Cost and Issuer. Sale price $4. Issued by the Coin and Medal Department (Farran Zerbe), Panama-Pacific International Exposition, San Francisco, California (combination offers included, among others, a set of four coins, with the buyer's choice of one fifty-dollar coin, in a leather case, for $100; and a set of five coins in a copper frame for $200).

Key to Collecting. Most grade from AU-55 to MS-63. MS-64 coins are elusive, and MS-65 rare. Most MS pieces show a satiny, sometimes grainy luster.

First Points of Wear. *Obverse:* Columbia's head, breast, and knee. *Reverse:* The torch band and the eagle's leg.

| | Distribution | Cert | Avg | %MS | AU-50 | MS-60 | MS-62 | MS-63 | MS-64 | MS-65 | MS-66 |
									PF-63	PF-64	PF-65
1915-S	6,749	2,017	64.4	96%	$1,550	$2,000	$2,850	$3,000	$3,500	$4,000	$4,500
	Auctions: $12,925, MS-67, January 2015; $6,463, MS-66, February 2015; $5,405, MS-64, January 2015; $2,233, AU-50, August 2015										
1915-S, Proof (a)	*unique*	0	n/a								
	Auctions: No auction records available.										

a. This unique Satin Finish Proof resides in the National Numismatic Collection of the Smithsonian Institution.

PANAMA-PACIFIC INTERNATIONAL EXPOSITION FIFTY-DOLLAR GOLD PIECE (1915)

Designer: *Robert Aitken.* **Weight:** *83.59 grams.* **Composition:** *.900 gold, .100 copper (net weight 2.4186 oz. pure gold).* **Diameter:** *43 mm (round), 44.9 mm (octagonal, measured point to point).* **Edge:** *Reeded.* **Mint:** *San Francisco.*

Both round and octagonal $50 gold pieces were struck as part of the series commemorating the Panama-Pacific International Exposition in 1915. These coins, along with the half dollars in the same series, were the first U.S. commemoratives to feature the motto IN GOD WE TRUST.

Designs. Round: *Obverse:* Helmeted profile portrait of Minerva, with shield and armor. *Reverse:* An owl, symbolic of wisdom, vigilant on a pine branch, with pinecones. Octagonal: *Obverse and reverse:* Same as the round coin, but with dolphins in the eight angled exergues on obverse and reverse.

Mintage and Melting Data. Authorized by the Act of January 16, 1915. Round: *Maximum authorized*—Round: 1,500; Octagonal:

1,500. *Number minted* (including 10 assay coins)—Round: 1,510 (including 10 assay coins); Octagonal: 1,509 (including 9 assay coins). *Number melted*—Round: 1,027; Octagonal: 864. *Net distribution*—Round: 483; Octagonal: 645.

Original Cost and Issuer. Round and octagonal: Sale price, each, $100. Coin and Medal Department (Farran Zerbe), Panama-Pacific International Exposition, San Francisco, California. Combination offers included a set of four coins (buyer's choice of one fifty-dollar coin) in a leather case for $100, and a set of five coins in a copper frame for $200, this issued after the Exposition closed.

Key to Collecting. Because such small quantities were issued, these hefty gold commemoratives today are rare in any grade. The round coins trade hands slightly less frequently than the octagonal. Typical grades are MS–63 or 64 for coins kept in an original box or frame over the years, or AU-58 to MS-63 if removed. Coins that have been cleaned or lightly polished exhibit a multitude of tiny hairlines; such pieces are avoided by connoisseurs.

First Points of Wear. *Obverse:* Minerva's cheek. *Reverse:* The owl's upper breast.

	Distribution	Cert	Avg	%MS	AU-50	MS-60	MS-62	MS-63	MS-64	MS-65	MS-66
1915-S, Round †	483	421	63.4	95%	$55,000	$70,000	$80,000	$95,000	$120,000	$190,000	$255,000
	Auctions: $176,250, MS-65, August 2015; $79,313, MS-63, January 2015; $64,625, MS-61, July 2015; $51,700, MS-60, January 2015										
1915-S, Octagonal †	645	460	63.1	95%	$55,000	$67,500	$77,500	$90,000	$110,000	$190,000	$265,000
	Auction: $288,000, MS-66, January 2018; $138,000, MS-65, January 2018; $78,000, MS-63, August 2019; $87,000, MS-62, January 2018										

† Both 1915 Panama-Pacific $50 Gold Pieces are ranked in the *100 Greatest U.S. Coins* (fifth edition), as a single entry.

McKinley Memorial Gold Dollar (1916–1917)

Designers: *Charles E. Barber (obverse) and George T. Morgan (reverse).* **Weight:** *1.672 grams.*
Composition: *.900 gold, .100 copper (net weight .04837 oz. pure gold).*
Diameter: *15 mm.* **Edge:** *Reeded.* **Mint:** *Philadelphia.*

The sale of the William McKinley dollars aided in paying for a memorial building at Niles, Ohio, the martyred president's birthplace.

Designs. *Obverse:* Bareheaded profile portrait of William McKinley. *Reverse:* Artist's rendition of the proposed McKinley Birthplace Memorial intended to be erected in Niles, Ohio.

Mintage and Melting Data. Authorized on February 23, 1916. *Maximum authorized*—100,000 (both years combined). *Number minted*—1916: 20,026 (including 26 assay coins); 1917: 10,014 (including 14 assay coins). *Number melted*—1916: 5,000 (estimated); 1917: 5,000 (estimated). *Net distribution*—1916: 15,000 (estimated); 1917: 5,000 (estimated).

Original Cost and Issuer. Sale price $3. Issued by the National McKinley Birthplace Memorial Association, Youngstown, Ohio.

Key to Collecting. The obverse of the 1916 issue often displays friction while its reverse can appear as choice Mint State. Prooflike fields are common. Some are highly prooflike on both sides. The 1917 issue is much harder to find than the 1916; examples usually are in higher grades with rich luster on both sides, and often exhibit a pale yellow color.

First Points of Wear. *Obverse:* McKinley's temple area, and the hair above his ear. *Reverse:* The pillar above the second 1 in the date; and the bottom of the flagpole.

	Distribution	Cert	Avg	%MS	AU-50	MS-60	MS-62	MS-63	MS-64	MS-65	MS-66
									PF-63	PF-64	PF-65
1916	15,000	2,671	63.7	96%	$450	$500	$550	$575	$685	$850	$1,000
	Auctions: $4,465, MS-67, August 2015; $1,528, MS-66, July 2015; $376, MS-61, January 2015; $447, AU-58, October 2015										
1916, Proof	3–6	2	63.0								
	Auctions: $37,375, PF-63, January 2012										
1917	5,000	1,558	63.6	94%	$500	$550	$575	$600	$950	$1,000	$1,450
	Auctions: $7,344, MS-67, January 2015; $2,585, MS-66, July 2015; $541, MS-62, October 2015; $306, MS-60, May 2015										

ILLINOIS CENTENNIAL HALF DOLLAR (1918)

Designers: *George T. Morgan (obverse) and John R. Sinnock (reverse).* **Weight:** *12.50 grams.*
Composition: *.900 silver, .100 copper (net weight .3617 oz. pure silver).*
Diameter: *30.6 mm.* **Edge:** *Reeded.* **Mint:** *Philadelphia.*

This coin was authorized to commemorate the 100th anniversary of the admission of Illinois into the Union, and was the first souvenir piece for such an event. The head of Abraham Lincoln on the obverse was based on that of a statue of the celebrated president by Andrew O'Connor in Springfield, Illinois.

Designs. *Obverse:* Bareheaded, beardless profile portrait of Abraham Lincoln, facing right.
Reverse: A fierce eagle atop a crag, clutching a shield and carrying a banner; from the Illinois state seal.

Mintage Data. Authorized on June 1, 1918. *Maximum authorized*—100,000. *Number minted*—100,000 (plus 58 assay coins).

Original Cost and Issuer. Sale price $1. Issued by the Illinois Centennial Commission, through various outlets.

Key to Collecting. Examples were struck with deep, frosty finishes, giving Mint State pieces an unusually attractive appearance. The obverse typically shows contact marks or friction on Lincoln's cheek and on other high parts of his portrait. The field typically shows contact marks. The reverse usually grades from one to three points higher than the obverse, due to the protective nature of its complicated design. Most examples are lustrous and frosty, although a few are seen with partially prooflike fields.

First Points of Wear. *Obverse:* The hair above Lincoln's ear. *Reverse:* The eagle's breast. (Note that the breast was sometimes flatly struck; look for differences in texture or color of the metal.)

	Distribution	Cert	Avg	%MS	AU-50	MS-60	MS-62	MS-63	MS-64	MS-65	MS-66
1918	100,058	4,545	63.8	97%	$130	$150	$160	$170	$225	$325	$600
	Auctions: $5,640, MS-67, January 2015; $823, MS-66, January 2015; $212, MS-64, February 2015; $84, AU-55, February 2015										

MAINE CENTENNIAL HALF DOLLAR (1920)

Designer: *Anthony de Francisci.* **Weight:** *12.50 grams.* **Composition:** *.900 silver, .100 copper (net weight .3617 oz. pure silver).* **Diameter:** *30.6 mm.* **Edge:** *Reeded.* **Mint:** *Philadelphia.*

Congress authorized the Maine Centennial half dollar on May 10, 1920, to be sold at the centennial celebration at Portland. They were received too late for this event and were sold by the state treasurer for many years.

Designs. *Obverse:* Arms of the state of Maine, with the Latin word DIRIGO ("I Direct"). *Reverse:* The centennial inscription enclosed by a wreath.

Mintage Data. Authorized on May 10, 1920. *Maximum authorized*—100,000. *Number minted*—50,028 (including 28 assay coins).

Original Cost and Issuer. Sale price $1. Issued by the Maine Centennial Commission.

Key to Collecting. Relatively few Maine half dollars were sold to the hobby community; the majority of coins distributed saw careless handling by the general public. Most examples show friction or handling marks on the center of the shield on the obverse. The fields were not completely finished in the dies and always show tiny raised lines or die-finishing marks; at first glance these may appear to be hairlines or scratches, but they have no effect on the grade. Appealing examples in higher Mint State levels are much more elusive than the high mintage might suggest.

First Points of Wear. *Obverse:* The left hand of the scythe holder; the right hand of the anchor holder. (Note that the moose and the pine tree are weakly struck.) *Reverse:* The bow knot.

	Distribution	Cert	Avg	%MS	AU-50	MS-60	MS-62	MS-63	MS-64	MS-65	MS-66
1920	50,028	3,050	64.1	98%	$120	$140	$155	$160	$200	$325	$525
	Auctions: $10,575, MS-68, January 2015; $3,290, MS-67, September 2015; $200, MS-64, January 2015; $74, EF-40, September 2015										

PILGRIM TERCENTENARY HALF DOLLAR (1920–1921)

Designer: *Cyrus E. Dallin.* **Weight:** *12.50 grams.* **Composition:** *.900 silver, .100 copper (net weight .3617 oz. pure silver).* **Diameter:** *30.6 mm.* **Edge:** *Reeded.* **Mint:** *Philadelphia.*

To commemorate the landing of the Pilgrims at Plymouth, Massachusetts, in 1620, Congress authorized a special half dollar on May 12, 1920. The first issue had no date on the obverse. The coins struck in 1921 show that date in addition to 1620–1920.

Designs. *Obverse:* Artist's conception of a partial standing portrait of Governor William Bradford holding a book. *Reverse:* The *Mayflower* in full sail.

Mintage and Melting Data. Authorized on May 12, 1920. *Maximum authorized*—300,000 (both years combined). *Number minted*—1920: 200,112 (including 112 assay coins); 1921: 100,053 (including 53 assay coins). *Number melted*—1920: 48,000; 1921: 80,000. *Net distribution*—1920: 152,112; 1921: 20,053.

Original Cost and Issuer. Sale price $1. Issued by the Pilgrim Tercentenary Commission.

Key to Collecting. The 1920 issue is common, and the 1921 slightly scarce. Coins grading MS-64 and higher usually have excellent eye appeal, though many exceptions exist. Most coins have scattered contact marks, particularly on the obverse. Nearly all 1921 coins are this way. Many coins (particularly coins which are early impressions from the dies) show tiny raised lines in the obverse field, representing die finish marks; these are not to be confused with hairlines or other evidences of friction (which are recessed).

First Points of Wear. *Obverse:* Cheekbone, hair over ear, and the high areas of Governor Bradford's hat. *Reverse:* The ship's rigging and stern, the crow's nest, and the rim.

	Distribution	Cert	Avg	%MS	AU-50	MS-60	MS-62	MS-63	MS-64	MS-65	MS-66
1920	152,112	5,135	63.7	97%	$80	$90	$95	$100	$125	$175	$375
	Auctions: $6,756, MS-67, September 2015; $543, MS-66, October 2015; $153, MS-64, September 2015; $80, MS-62, September 2015										
1921, With Added Date	20,053	2,196	64.2	98%	$165	$180	$185	$195	$215	$275	$600
	Auctions: $5,876, MS-67, January 2015; $1,880, MS-66, July 2015; $447, MS-64, February 2015; $141, AU-58, March 2015										

MISSOURI CENTENNIAL HALF DOLLAR (1921)

Designer: *Robert Aitken.* **Weight:** *12.50 grams.* **Composition:** *.900 silver, .100 copper (net weight .3617 oz. pure silver).* **Diameter:** *30.6 mm.* **Edge:** *Reeded.* **Mint:** *Philadelphia.*

The 100th anniversary of the admission of Missouri to the Union was celebrated in the city of Sedalia during August 1921. To mark the occasion, Congress authorized the coinage of a fifty-cent piece.

Designs. *Obverse:* Coonskin-capped profile portrait of a frontiersman. One variety has 2★4 in the field; the other is plain. *Reverse:* Standing figures of a frontiersman and an Indian looking westward, against a starry field; SEDALIA (the location of the Missouri centennial exposition) incused below.

Mintage and Melting Data. Authorized on March 4, 1921. *Maximum authorized*—250,000 (both varieties combined). *Number minted*—50,028 (both varieties combined; including 28 assay coins). *Number melted*—29,600. *Net distribution*—20,428 (estimated; 9,400 for 1921 2★4 and 11,400 for 1921 Plain).

Original Cost and Issuer. Sale price $1. Issued by the Missouri Centennial Committee, through the Sedalia Trust Company.

Key to Collecting. Most grade from AU-55 to MS-63; have friction and contact marks on the higher areas of the design; and are lightly struck at the center of the portrait of Boone on the obverse, and at the torsos of the two figures on the reverse. MS-65 and higher coins with sharply struck centers are rarities.

First Points of Wear. *Obverse:* The hair in back of the ear. *Reverse:* The frontiersman's arm and shoulder.

	Distribution	Cert	Avg	%MS	AU-50	MS-60	MS-62	MS-63	MS-64	MS-65	MS-66
									PF-63	PF-64	PF-65
1921, "2★4" in Field	9,400	1,634	63.7	97%	$575	$625	$850	$950	$1,100	$1,800	$5,400
	Auctions: $6,169, MS-66, January 2015; $2,291, MS-65, August 2015; $705, MS-62, September 2015; $646, AU-58, September 2015										
1921, "2★4" in Field, Matte Proof	1–2	0	n/a								
	Auctions: No auction records available.										
1921, Plain	11,400	2,024	63.2	94%	$400	$525	$650	$675	$900	$1,500	$4,250
	Auctions: $5,640, MS-66, September 2015; $2,468, MS-65, January 2015; $353, AU-58, January 2015; $259, AU-50, November 2015										

ALABAMA CENTENNIAL HALF DOLLAR (1921)

Designer: *Laura Gardin Fraser.* **Weight:** *12.50 grams.* **Composition:** *.900 silver, .100 copper (net weight .3617 oz. pure silver).* **Diameter:** *30.6 mm.* **Edge:** *Reeded.* **Mint:** *Philadelphia.*

The Alabama half dollars were authorized in 1920 and struck until 1921 for the statehood centennial, which was celebrated in 1919. The coins were offered first during President Warren Harding's visit to Birmingham, October 26, 1921. T.E. Kilby's likeness on the obverse was first instance of a living person's portrait on a United States coin.

Designs. *Obverse:* Conjoined bareheaded profile portraits of William Wyatt Bibb, the first governor of Alabama, and Thomas Kilby, governor at the time of the centennial. *Reverse:* A dynamic eagle perched on a shield, clutching arrows and holding a banner; from the Alabama state seal.

Mintage and Melting Data. Authorized on May 10, 1920. *Maximum authorized*—100,000. *Number minted*—70,044 (including 44 assay coins). *Number melted*—5,000. *Net distribution*—2X2: estimated as 30,000; Plain: estimated as 35,000.

Original Cost and Issuer. Sale price $1. Issued by the Alabama Centennial Commission.

Key to Collecting. Most of these coins were sold to citizens of Alabama, and of those, few were acquired by numismatists. Many are in circulated grades (typical being EF or AU), with most surviving pieces grading MS-63 or less. Those grading MS-65 or finer are rare. Nearly all show friction or contact marks on Governor Kilby's cheek on the obverse, and many are flatly struck on the eagle's left leg and talons on the reverse. These coins were produced carelessly, and many lack sharpness and luster (sharply struck examples are very rare). Nicks and marks from the original planchets are often found on the areas of light striking. The eagle's upper leg is often lightly struck, particularly on the plain variety. The 2X2 coins usually are better struck than the plain variety.

First Points of Wear. *Obverse:* Kirby's forehead and the area to the left of his earlobe. *Reverse:* The eagle's lower neck and the top of its wings.

	Distribution	Cert	Avg	%MS	AU-50	MS-60	MS-62	MS-63	MS-64	MS-65	MS-66
1921, "2X2" in Field	6,006	1,772	63.3	94%	$250	$325	$375	$400	$550	$1,000	$2,000
	Auctions: $11,750, MS-67, August 2015; $3,525, MS-66, July 2015; $411, MS-63, September 2015; $188, AU-50, February 2015										
1921, Plain	16,014	2,070	62.4	88%	$160	$200	$300	$385	$460	$850	$1,500
	Auctions: $19,975, MS-67, January 2015; $5,405, MS-66, January 2015; $235, MS-62, March 2015; $141, AU-58, August 2015										

GRANT MEMORIAL HALF DOLLAR (1922)

Designer: *Laura Gardin Fraser.* **Weight:** *12.50 grams.* **Composition:** *.900 silver, .100 copper (net weight .3617 oz. pure silver).* **Diameter:** *30.6 mm.* **Edge:** *Reeded.* **Mint:** *Philadelphia.*

This half dollar (along with the Grant Memorial gold dollar) was struck during 1922 as a centenary souvenir of Ulysses S. Grant's birth. The Ulysses S. Grant Centenary Memorial Association originally planned celebrations in Clermont County, Ohio; the construction of community buildings in Georgetown and Bethel; and the laying of a five-mile highway from New Richmond to Point Pleasant in addition to the coins, but the buildings and highway never came to fruition.

Designs. *Obverse:* Bareheaded profile portrait of Ulysses S. Grant in a military coat. One variety has a star above GRANT. *Reverse:* View of the house Grant was born in (Point Pleasant, Ohio), amidst a wooded setting.

Mintage Data. Authorized on February 2, 1922. *Number minted*—With Star: 5,016 (including 16 assay coins); No Star: 5,000. *Net distribution*—10,016 (both varieties combined).

Original Cost and Issuer. Sale price $3 for either variety. Issued by the U.S. Grant Centenary Memorial Commission (mail orders were serviced by Hugh L. Nichols, chairman, Batavia, Ohio).

Key to Collecting. Almost all known specimens are MS-63 to 65 or better. MS–66 and 67 examples are easy to find. Some lower-grade coins show friction on Grant's cheek and hair. Some specimens have dull surfaces; these are avoided by connoisseurs.

First Points of Wear. *Obverse:* Grant's cheekbone and hair. *Reverse:* The leaves of the tree under the U in TRUST.

	Distribution	Cert	Avg	%MS	AU-50	MS-60	MS-62	MS-63	MS-64	MS-65	MS-66
1922, Star in Obverse Field	4,256	1,302	63.5	96%	$900	$1,200	$1,450	$1,675	$2,675	$4,500	$6,000
	Auctions: $37,600, MS-67, January 2015; $12,926, MS-66, July 2015; $764, AU-53, August 2015; $646, EF-40, August 2015										
1922, No Star in Obverse Field	67,405	3,733	63.6	96%	$110	$120	$135	$150	$250	$525	$800
	Auctions: $3,760, MS-67, September 2015; $2,115, MS-66, August 2015; $165, MS-61, February 2015; $60, AU-58, February 2015										

GRANT MEMORIAL GOLD DOLLAR (1922)

Designer: *Laura Gardin Fraser.* **Weight:** *1.672 grams.* **Composition:** *.900 gold, .100 copper (net weight .04837 oz. pure gold).* **Diameter:** *15 mm.* **Edge:** *Reeded.* **Mint:** *Philadelphia.*

The Ulysses S. Grant Centenary Memorial Association, incorporated in 1921, marked the 100th birth anniversary of the Civil War general and U.S. president with this gold dollar (as well as a commemorative half dollar).

Designs. *Obverse:* Bareheaded profile portrait of Ulysses S. Grant in a military coat. One variety has a star above GRANT. *Reverse:* View of the house Grant was born in (Point Pleasant, Ohio), amidst a wooded setting.

Mintage Data. Authorized on February 2, 1922. *Number minted*—With Star: 5,016 (including 16 assay coins); No Star: 5,000. *Net distribution*—10,016 (both varieties combined).

Original Cost and Issuer. Sale price $3 for either type. Issued by the U.S. Grant Centenary Memorial Commission (mail orders were serviced by Hugh L. Nichols, chairman, Batavia, Ohio).

Key to Collecting. Almost all known specimens are MS–63 to 65 or better. MS–66 and 67 examples are easy to find. Some lower-grade coins show friction on Grant's cheek and hair. Some specimens have dull surfaces; these are avoided by connoisseurs.

First Points of Wear. *Obverse:* Grant's cheekbone and hair. *Reverse:* The leaves of the tree under the U in TRUST.

	Distribution	Cert	Avg	%MS	AU-50	MS-60	MS-62	MS-63	MS-64	MS-65	MS-66
1922, With Star	5,016	1,345	64.8	99%	$950	$1,000	$1,075	$1,100	$1,300	$1,500	$1,800
	Auctions: $12,925, MS-68, January 2015; $6,463, MS-67, June 2015; $1,410, MS-64, October 2015; $646, AU-50, May 2015										
1922, No Star	5,016	1,241	64.4	96%	$1,000	$1,050	$1,100	$1,200	$1,375	$1,500	$1,800
	Auctions: $3,760, MS-67, August 2015; $3,055, MS-66, July 2015; $1,586, MS-64, February 2015; $764, MS-60, October 2015										

MONROE DOCTRINE CENTENNIAL HALF DOLLAR (1923)

Designer: *Chester Beach.* **Weight:** *12.50 grams.* **Composition:** *.900 silver, .100 copper (net weight .3617 oz. pure silver).* **Diameter:** *30.6 mm.* **Edge:** *Reeded.* **Mint:** *San Francisco.*

The California film industry promoted this issue in conjunction with a motion-picture exposition held in June 1923. The coin purportedly commemorated the 100th anniversary of the Monroe Doctrine, which warned that European countries that interfered with countries in the Western Hemisphere or established new colonies there would be met with disapproval or worse from the U.S. government.

Designs. *Obverse:* Conjoined bareheaded profile portraits of presidents James Monroe and John Quincy Adams. *Reverse:* Stylized depiction of the continents of North and South America as female figures in the outlines of the two land masses.

Mintage Data. Authorized on January 24, 1923. *Maximum authorized*—300,000. *Number minted*—274,077 (including 77 assay coins). *Net distribution*—274,077.

Original Cost and Issuer. Sale price $1. Issued by the Los Angeles Clearing House, representing backers of the First Annual American Historical Revue and Motion Picture Industry Exposition.

Key to Collecting. Most examples show friction or wear. MS coins are common. Evaluating the numerical grade of MS–60 to 63 coins is difficult because of the design's weak definition. Low-magnification inspection usually shows nicks and graininess at the highest point of the obverse center; these flaws are from the original planchets. Many examples of this coin have been doctored and artificially toned in attempts to earn higher grades upon certification; these are avoided by connoisseurs.

First Points of Wear. *Obverse:* Adams's cheekbone. *Reverse:* The upper figure, underneath the CT in DOCTRINE.

	Distribution	Cert	Avg	%MS	AU-50	MS-60	MS-62	MS-63	MS-64	MS-65	MS-66
1923-S	274,077	3,806	62.9	94%	$50	$75	$100	$120	$225	$700	$1,350
	Auctions: $11,163, MS-67, August 2015; $5,640, MS-66, January 2015; $1,645, MS-65, January 2015; $84, MS-62, July 2015										

HUGUENOT-WALLOON TERCENTENARY HALF DOLLAR (1924)

Designer: *George T. Morgan (with model modifications by James Earle Fraser).*
Weight: *12.50 grams.* **Composition:** *.900 silver, .100 copper (net weight .3617 oz. pure silver).*
Diameter: *30.6 mm.* **Edge:** *Reeded.* **Mint:** *Philadelphia.*

Settling of the Huguenots and Walloons in the New World was the occasion commemorated by this issue. New Netherland, now New York, was founded in 1624 by this group of Dutch colonists. Interestingly, the persons represented on the obverse were not directly concerned with the occasion; both Admiral Gaspard de Coligny and Prince William the Silent were dead long before the settlement.

Designs. *Obverse:* Hat-clad profile portraits representing Admiral Gaspard de Coligny and Prince William the Silent, first stadtholder of the Netherlands. *Reverse:* The ship *Nieuw Nederland* in full sail.

Mintage Data. Authorized on February 26, 1923. *Maximum authorized—300,000. Number minted—142,080 (including 80 assay coins). Net distribution—142,080.*

Original Cost and Issuer. Sale price $1. Issued by the Huguenot-Walloon New Netherland Commission, Inc., and designated outlets.

Key to Collecting. This coin is readily available on the market, with most examples in MS–60 to 63. Those grading MS–64 and 65 are also found quite often; MS–66 coins are scarcer. Relatively few worn pieces exist. Friction and contact marks are sometimes seen on the cheek of Admiral Coligny on the obverse, and on the masts and ship's rigging on the reverse. Many coins have been cleaned or repeatedly dipped. Connoisseurs avoid deeply toned or stained coins, even those certified with high numerical grades. MS coins usually have satiny (rather than deeply lustrous or frosty) surfaces, and may have a gray appearance. High in the reverse field of most coins is a "bright" spot interrupting the luster, from a touch of polish in the die.

First Points of Wear. *Obverse:* Coligny's cheekbone. *Reverse:* The rim near the F in FOUNDING and over the RY in TERCENTENARY; the lower part of the highest sail; the center of the ship's stern.

	Distribution	Cert	Avg	%MS	AU-50	MS-60	MS-62	MS-63	MS-64	MS-65	MS-66
1924	142,080	3,441	64.1	98%	$125	$130	$140	$160	$175	$240	$525
	Auctions: $15,275, MS-68, August 2015; $6,756, MS-67, September 2015; $100, MS-60, January 2015; $89, AU-58, January 2015										

LEXINGTON-CONCORD SESQUICENTENNIAL HALF DOLLAR (1925)

Designer: *Chester Beach.* **Weight:** *12.50 grams.* **Composition:** *.900 silver, .100 copper (net weight .3617 oz. pure silver).* **Diameter:** *30.6 mm.* **Edge:** *Reeded.* **Mint:** *Philadelphia.*

The Battle of Lexington and Concord—fought in 1775 just one day after Paul Revere's famous ride—is commemorated on this coin. Sculptor James Earle Fraser of the Commission of Fine Arts approved Beach's designs, but protested that the local committees had made a poor choice of subject matter.

Designs. *Obverse:* A view of *The Concord Minute Man of 1775* statue, by Daniel Chester French, located in Concord, Massachusetts. *Reverse:* Lexington's Old Belfry, whose tolling bell roused the Minute Men to action in 1775.

Mintage and Melting Data. Authorized on January 14, 1925. *Maximum authorized—300,000. Number minted—162,099 (including 99 assay coins). Number melted—86. Net distribution—162,013.*

Original Cost and Issuer. Sale price $1. Issued by the U.S. Lexington-Concord Sesquicentennial Commission, through local banks.

Key to Collecting. Examples are easily found in all grades, with most being in high AU or low MS grades, although eye appeal can vary widely. MS-65 coins are scarce in comparison to those in MS–60 through 64. Some specimens are deeply frosty and lustrous, whereas others have partially prooflike fields.

First Points of Wear. *Obverse:* The thighs of the Minuteman. *Reverse:* The top edge of the belfry.

	Distribution	Cert	Avg	%MS	AU-50	MS-60	MS-62	MS-63	MS-64	MS-65	MS-66
1925	162,013	4,374	63.6	96%	$75	$85	$90	$100	$135	$300	$500

Auctions: $6,463, MS-67, July 2015; $1,645, MS-66, January 2015; $106, MS-63, June 2015; $69, AU-58, October 2015

STONE MOUNTAIN MEMORIAL HALF DOLLAR (1925)

Designer: *Gutzon Borglum.* **Weight:** *12.50 grams.* **Composition:** *.900 silver, .100 copper (net weight .3617 oz. pure silver).* **Diameter:** *30.6 mm.* **Edge:** *Reeded.* **Mint:** *Philadelphia.*

The first of these half dollars were struck at Philadelphia on January 21, 1925, Confederate general Stonewall Jackson's birthday. Funds received from the sale of this large issue were devoted to the expense of carving figures of Confederate leaders and soldiers on Stone Mountain in Georgia. The coin's designer, Gutzon Borglum, was the original sculptor for that project, but left due to differences with the Stone Mountain Confederate Monumental Association. Augustus Lukeman took over in his stead, and the carving was completed and dedicated in 1970; Borglum would meanwhile go on to create the presidents' heads at Mount Rushmore.

Designs. *Obverse:* Equestrian portraits of Civil War generals Robert E. Lee and Thomas "Stonewall" Jackson. *Reverse:* An eagle perched on a cliff with wings in mid-spread.

Mintage and Melting Data. *Maximum authorized*—5,000,000. *Number minted*—2,314,709 (including 4,709 assay coins). *Number melted*—1,000,000. *Net distribution*—1,314,709.

Original Cost and Issuer. Sale price $1. Issued by the Stone Mountain Confederate Monumental Association through many outlets, including promotions involving pieces counterstamped with abbreviations for Southern states.

Key to Collecting. This is the most plentiful commemorative from the 1920s. Examples are easily found in grades ranging from lightly worn through gem Mint State (many with outstanding eye appeal). Circulated coins are also found, as well as those that were counterstamped for special fundraising sales. The typical coin has very lustrous and frosty surfaces, although the reverse field may be somewhat satiny.

First Points of Wear. *Obverse:* Lee's elbow and leg. *Reverse:* The eagle's breast.

	Distribution	Cert	Avg	%MS	AU-50	MS-60	MS-62	MS-63	MS-64	MS-65	MS-66
1925	1,314,709	9,327	63.8	96%	$55	$65	$70	$80	$135	$175	$250

Auctions: $3,055, MS-67, January 2015; $564, MS-66, August 2015; $182, MS-64, March 2015; $50, AU-58, September 2015

CALIFORNIA DIAMOND JUBILEE HALF DOLLAR (1925)

Designer: *Jo Mora.* **Weight:** *12.50 grams.* **Composition:** *.900 silver, .100 copper (net weight .3617 oz. pure silver).* **Diameter:** *30.6 mm.* **Edge:** *Reeded.* **Mint:** *San Francisco.*

The celebration for which these coins were struck marked the 75th anniversary of the admission of California into the Union. Notably, James Earle Fraser of the Commission of Fine Arts criticized Jo Mora's designs at the time. Art historian Cornelius Vermeule, however, called the coin "one of America's greatest works of numismatic art" in his book *Numismatic Art in America.*

Designs. *Obverse:* A rustic miner, squatting to pan for gold. *Reverse:* A grizzly bear, as taken from the California state flag.

Mintage and Melting Data. Authorized on February 24, 1925, part of the act also providing for the 1925 Fort Vancouver and 1927 Vermont half dollars. *Maximum authorized*—300,000. *Number minted*—150,200 (including 200 assay coins). *Number melted*—63,606. *Net distribution*—86,594.

Original Cost and Issuer. Sale price $1. Issued by the San Francisco Citizens' Committee through the San Francisco Clearing House Association and the Los Angeles Clearing House.

Key to Collecting. This coin's design is such that even a small amount of handling produces friction on the shoulder and high parts of the bear, in particular. As a result, most grade in the AU-55 to MS-62 range, and higher-level MS examples are rare. This issue exists in two finishes: frosty/lustrous, and the rarer "chrome-like" or prooflike. The frosty-finish pieces display some lack of die definition of the details. The prooflike pieces have heavily brushed and highly polished dies. Many specimens certified in high grades are toned, sometimes deeply, which can mask evidence of friction. Coins with no traces of friction are rarities.

First Points of Wear. *Obverse:* The folds of the miner's shirt sleeve. *Reverse:* The shoulder of the bear.

	Distribution	Cert	Avg	%MS	AU-50	MS-60	MS-62	MS-63	MS-64 / PF-63	MS-65 / PF-64	MS-66 / PF-65
1925-S	86,594	4,389	63.8	95%	$185	$200	$205	$210	$375	$450	$675
	Auctions: $12,925, MS-68, January 2015; $4,465, MS-67, September 2015; $165, MS-62, October 2015; $129, AU-55, March 2015										
1925-S, Matte Proof	*1–2*	2	65.5								
	Auctions: No auction records available.										

FORT VANCOUVER CENTENNIAL HALF DOLLAR (1925)

Designer: *Laura Gardin Fraser.* **Weight:** *12.50 grams.* **Composition:** *.900 silver, .100 copper (net weight .3617 oz. pure silver).* **Diameter:** *30.6 mm.* **Edge:** *Reeded.* **Mint:** *San Francisco.*

The sale of these half dollars at $1 each helped to finance the pageant staged for the celebration of the 100th anniversary of the construction of Fort Vancouver. As part of the publicity, pilot Oakley G. Kelly made a round-trip flight from Vancouver to San Francisco and back again to pick up and deliver the entire issue—which weighed 1,462 pounds.

Designs. *Obverse:* Bareheaded profile portrait of Dr. John McLoughlin, who built Fort Vancouver (Washington) on the Columbia River in 1825. *Reverse:* A pioneer in buckskin with a musket in his hands, with Fort Vancouver in the background.

Mintage and Melting Data. Authorized on February 24, 1925. *Maximum authorized*—300,000. *Number minted* (including 28 assay coins)—50,028. *Number melted*—35,034. *Net distribution*—14,994.

Original Cost and Issuer. Sale price $1. The Fort Vancouver Centennial Corporation, Vancouver, Washington.

Key to Collecting. This coin's design is such that even a small amount of handling produced friction on the higher spots. As a result, higher-level MS examples are rare.

First Points of Wear. *Obverse:* McLoughlin's temple area. *Reverse:* The pioneer's right knee.

	Distribution	Cert	Avg	%MS	AU-50	MS-60	MS-62	MS-63	MS-64 / PF-63	MS-65 / PF-64	MS-66 / PF-65
1925	14,994	2,349	63.9	96%	$300	$325	$350	$375	$450	$600	$900
	Auctions: $4,772, MS-67, September 2015; $2,115, MS-66, September 2015; $212, AU-53, March 2015; $129, EF-40, September 2015										
1925, Matte Proof	2–3	0	n/a								
	Auctions: $188,000, PF-66, April 2015										

SESQUICENTENNIAL OF AMERICAN INDEPENDENCE HALF DOLLAR (1926)

Designer: *John R. Sinnock.* **Weight:** *12.50 grams.* **Composition:** *.900 silver, .100 copper (net weight .3617 oz. pure silver).* **Diameter:** *30.6 mm.* **Edge:** *Reeded.* **Mint:** *Philadelphia.*

The 150th anniversary of the signing of the Declaration of Independence was the occasion for an international fair held in Philadelphia in 1926. To help raise funds for financing the fair, special issues of half dollars (as well as quarter eagles, below) were authorized by Congress. The use of Calvin Coolidge's likeness marked the first time a portrait of a president appeared on a coin struck during his own lifetime.

Designs. *Obverse:* Conjoined profile portraits of bewigged George Washington and bareheaded Calvin Coolidge. *Reverse:* The Liberty Bell.

Mintage and Melting Data. Authorized on March 23, 1925. *Maximum authorized*—1,000,000. *Number minted*—1,000,528 (including 528 assay coins). *Number melted*—859,408. *Net distribution*—141,120.

Original Cost and Issuer. Sale price $1. Issued by the National Sesquicentennial Exhibition Association.

Key to Collecting. Accurate grading can be problematic for this coin. Many examples certified at high grades have mottled or deeply toned surfaces that obfuscate examination, and others have been recolored. Most have graininess—marks from the original planchet—on the highest part of the portrait.

First Points of Wear. *Obverse:* Washington's cheekbone. *Reverse:* The area below the lower inscription on the Liberty Bell.

	Distribution	Cert	Avg	%MS	AU-50	MS-60	MS-62	MS-63	MS-64	MS-65	MS-66
1926	141,120	4,607	62.9	95%	$75	$90	$100	$130	$225	$1,250	$20,000
	Auctions: $5,288, MS-66, July 2015; $1,880, MS-65, January 2015; $112, MS-62, February 2015; $84, AU-55, July 2015										

SESQUICENTENNIAL OF AMERICAN INDEPENDENCE QUARTER EAGLE (1926)

Designer: *John R. Sinnock.* **Weight:** *4.18 grams.* **Composition:** *.900 gold, .100 copper (net weight .12094 oz. pure gold).* **Diameter:** *18 mm.* **Edge:** *Reeded.* **Mint:** *Philadelphia.*

This quarter eagle, along with a related half dollar, was sold to finance the National Sesquicentennial Exposition in Philadelphia (which marked the 150th anniversary of the signing of the Declaration of Independence). Note that though the issuer was known as the National Sesquicentennial *Exhibition* Association, the event was primarily billed with *Exposition* in its name.

Designs. *Obverse:* Miss Liberty standing, holding in one hand a scroll representing the Declaration of Independence and in the other, the Torch of Freedom. *Reverse:* A front view of Independence Hall in Philadelphia.

Mintage and Melting Data. Authorized on March 23, 1925. *Maximum authorized*—200,000. *Number minted*—200,226 (including 226 assay coins). *Number melted*—154,207. *Net distribution*—46,019.

Original Cost and Issuer. Sale price $4. National Sesquicentennial Exhibition Association.

Key to Collecting. Nearly all examples show evidence of handling and contact from careless production at the Mint, and from later indifference by their buyers. Most coins range from AU-55 to MS-62 in grade, and have scattered marks in the fields. MS-65 examples are rare. Well-struck coins are seldom seen. Some pieces show copper stains; connoisseurs avoid these.

First Points of Wear. *Obverse:* The bottom of the scroll held by Liberty. *Reverse:* The area below the top of the tower; and the central portion above the roof.

	Distribution	Cert	Avg	%MS	AU-50	MS-60	MS-62	MS-63	MS-64 / PF-63	MS-65 / PF-64	MS-66 / PF-65
1926	46,019	7,689	62.9	92%	$400	$450	$525	$550	$875	$1,350	$4,000
	Auctions: $25,850, MS-67, January 2015; $6,463, MS-66, January 2015; $494, MS-62, January 2015; $282, AU-55, September 2015										
1926, Matte Proof (a)	*unique*	1	65.0								
	Auctions: No auction records available.										

a. "The coin is unique and displays a matte surface similar to the Proof gold coins of 1908 to 1915. The coin was reportedly from the estate of the designer, John R. Sinnock, who is best known for his Roosevelt dime and Franklin half dollar designs. The piece was in the possession of coin dealer David Bullowa in the 1950s. Another example is rumored by Breen, but the whereabouts or existence of the coin is unknown" (*Encyclopedia of U.S. Gold Coins, 1795–1933*, second edition).

OREGON TRAIL MEMORIAL HALF DOLLAR (1926–1939)

Designers: *James Earle Fraser and Laura Gardin Fraser.* **Weight:** *12.50 grams.*
Composition: *.900 silver, .100 copper (net weight .3617 oz. pure silver).*
Diameter: *30.6 mm.* **Edge:** *Reeded.* **Mints:** *Philadelphia, San Francisco, and Denver.*

These coins—the longest-running series of commemoratives—were struck in commemoration of the Oregon Trail and in memory of the pioneers, many of whom lie buried along the famous 2,000-mile highway of history. This was the first commemorative to be struck at more than one Mint facility, and also the first commemorative to be struck at the Denver Mint.

Designs. *Obverse:* A pioneer family in a Conestoga wagon, heading west into the sunset. *Reverse:* A standing Indian with a bow, arm outstretched, and a map of the United States in the background.

Mintage and Melting Data. *Maximum authorized*—6,000,000 (for the entire series from 1926 onward). *Number minted*—1926: 48,030 (including 30 assay coins); 1926-S: 100,055 (including 55 assay coins); 1928: 50,028 (including 28 assay coins); 1933-D: 5,250 (including an unrecorded number of assay coins); 1934-D: 7,006 (including 6 assay coins); 1936: 10,006 (including 6 assay coins); 1936-S: 5,006 (including 6 assay coins); 1937-D: 12,008 (including 8 assay coins); 1938-P: 6,006 (including 6 assay coins); 1938-D: 6,005 (including 5 assay coins); 1938-S: 6,006 (including 6 assay coins). *Number melted*—1926: 75 (defective coins); 1926-S: 17,000; 1928: 44,000; 1933-D: 242 (probably defective coins). *Net distribution*—1926: 47,955; 1926-S: 83,055; 1928: 6,028; 1933-D: 5,008; 1934-D: 7,006; 1936: 10,006; 1936-S: 5,006; 1937-D: 12,008; 1938-P: 6,006; 1938-D: 6,005; 1938-S: 6,006.

Original Cost and Issuer. Sale price $1; later raised. Issued by the Oregon Trail Memorial Association, Inc.; some sold through Scott Stamp & Coin Co., Inc., and some sold through Whitman Centennial, Inc., Walla Walla, Washington. From 1937 onward, distributed solely by the Oregon Trail Memorial Association, Inc.

Key to Collecting. Although most of the later issues have low mintages, they are not rare in the marketplace, because the majority were originally sold to coin collectors and dealers. As a result, most surviving coins are in MS. The quality of the surface finish varies, with earlier issues tending to be frosty and lustrous and later issues (particularly those dated 1938 and 1939) having somewhat grainy or satiny fields. Grading requires care. Look for friction or contact marks on the high points of the Indian and the Conestoga wagon, but, more importantly, check both surfaces carefully for scattered cuts and marks. All three mints had difficulty in striking up the rims properly, causing many rejections. Those deemed acceptable and shipped out usually had full rims, but it is best to check when buying.

First Points of Wear. *Obverse:* The hip of the ox, and high points of the wagon (note that the top rear of the wagon was weakly struck in some years). *Reverse:* The Indian's left thumb and fingers (note that some pieces show flatness on the thumb and first finger, due to a weak strike).

	Distribution	Cert	Avg	%MS	AU-50	MS-60	MS-62	MS-63	MS-64 PF-63	MS-65 PF-64	MS-66 PF-65
1926	47,955	2,303	64.4	98%	$135	$160	$170	$190	$210	$250	$325
	Auctions: $999, MS-67, June 2015; $412, MS-66, November 2015; $235, MS-63, May 2015; $112, MS-61, February 2015										
1926, Matte Proof	1–2	2	65.0								
	Auctions: No auction records available.										
1926-S	83,055	3,196	64.5	97%	$135	$160	$170	$190	$210	$260	$350
	Auctions: $14,100, MS-68, January 2015; $1,998, MS-67, January 2015; $247, MS-65, June 2015; $129, MS-60, May 2015										
1928 (same as 1926)	6,028	1,341	65.3	100%	$160	$180	$185	$200	$240	$300	$435
	Auctions: $1,410, MS-67, September 2015; $400, MS-66, September 2015; $306, MS-65, February 2015; $223, MS-64, January 2015										
1933-D	5,008	1,069	65.0	100%	$350	$370	$375	$400	$425	$450	$550
	Auctions: $1,880, MS-67, June 2015; $564, MS-66, January 2015; $329, MS-65, August 2015; $329, MS-64, May 2015										
1934-D	7,006	1,368	64.8	100%	$190	$200	$205	$210	$215	$300	$450
	Auctions: $1,175, MS-67, September 2015; $376, MS-66, August 2015; $212, MS-65, August 2015; $188, MS-63, October 2015										
1936	10,006	1,684	65.3	100%	$160	$180	$190	$200	$220	$260	$280
	Auctions: $11,163, MS-68, September 2015; $1,293, MS-67, July 2015; $341, MS-66, February 2015; $200, MS-64, February 2015										
1936-S	5,006	1,163	65.5	100%	$170	$180	$190	$200	$225	$260	$335
	Auctions: $1,763, MS-68, November 2014; $10,575, MS-68, January 2013; $670, MS-67+, October 2014; $425, MS-67, November 2014										
1937-D	12,008	2,428	65.9	100%	$165	$180	$185	$195	$225	$250	$325
	Auctions: $4,935, MS-68, January 2015; $1,116, MS-67, September 2015; $353, MS-66, February 2015; $200, MS-64, February 2015										
1938 (same as 1926)	6,006	1,287	65.4	100%	$135	$160	$180	$190	$225	$250	$325
	Auctions: $1,410, MS-67, January 2015; $306, MS-66, June 2015; $259, MS-65, February 2015; $153, MS-63, May 2015										
1938-D	6,005	1,466	65.8	100%	$135	$160	$180	$190	$225	$250	$325
	Auctions: $5,405, MS-68, January 2015; $764, MS-67, August 2015; $306, MS-66, October 2015; $129, MS-63, May 2015										
1938-S	6,006	1,335	65.5	100%	$135	$160	$180	$190	$225	$250	$325
	Auctions: $6,933, MS-68, March 2015; $1,293, MS-67, January 2015; $306, MS-66, January 2015; $182, MS-64, September 2015										
Set of 1938 P-D-S					$575	$585	$600	$675	$850	$1,100	
	Auctions: $2,070, MS-67/67/67, February 2012; $617, MS-64/64/64, March 2015										
1939	3,004	789	65.5	100%	$135	$160	$180	$190	$225	$250	$325
	Auctions: $2,350, MS-67, January 2015; $823, MS-66, January 2015; $564, MS-65, January 2015; $494, MS-64, October 2015										
1939-D	3,004	813	65.8	100%	$135	$160	$180	$190	$225	$250	$325
	Auctions: $9,400, MS-68, January 2015; $1,880, MS-67, January 2015; $541, MS-65, January 2015; $353, AU-50, September 2015										
1939-S	3,005	801	65.5	100%	$135	$160	$180	$190	$225	$250	$325
	Auctions: $4,230, MS-68, January 2015; $1,410, MS-67, August 2015; $881, MS-66, January 2015; $588, MS-64, October 2015										
Set of 1939 P-D-S					$1,450	$1,500	$1,550	$1,625	$1,800	$2,000	
	Auctions: $5,175, MS-67/67/67, January 2012; $1,528, MS-65/65/65, March 2015										

VERMONT SESQUICENTENNIAL HALF DOLLAR (1927)

Designer: *Charles Keck.* **Weight:** *12.50 grams.* **Composition:** *.900 silver, .100 copper (net weight .3617 oz. pure silver).* **Diameter:** *30.6 mm.* **Edge:** *Reeded.* **Mint:** *Philadelphia.*

This souvenir issue commemorates the 150th anniversary of the Battle of Bennington and the independence of Vermont. Authorized in 1925, it was not coined until 1927. The Vermont Sesquicentennial Commission intended that funds derived would benefit the study of history.

Designs. *Obverse:* Profile portrait of a bewigged Ira Allen. *Reverse:* A catamount walking left.

Mintage and Melting Data. Authorized by the Act of February 24, 1925. *Maximum authorized*—40,000. *Number minted*—40,034 (including 34 assay coins). *Number melted*—11,892. *Net distribution*—28,142.

Original Cost and Issuer. Sale price $1. Issued by the Vermont Sesquicentennial Commission (Bennington Battle Monument and Historical Association).

Key to Collecting. The Vermont half dollar was struck with the highest relief of any commemorative issue to that date. Despite the depth of the work in the dies, nearly all of the coins were struck up properly and show excellent detail. Unfortunately, the height of the obverse portrait encourages evidence of contact at the central points, and nearly all coins show some friction on Allen's cheek. Most are in grades of MS–62 to 64 and are deeply lustrous and frosty. Cleaned examples are often seen—and are avoided by connoisseurs.

First Points of Wear. *Obverse:* Allen's cheek, and the hair above his ear and in the temple area. *Reverse:* The catamount's upper shoulder.

	Distribution	Cert	Avg	%MS	AU-50	MS-60	MS-62	MS-63	MS-64	MS-65	MS-66
1927	28,142	3,251	63.9	97%	$250	$265	$270	$275	$325	$460	$650
	Auctions: $3,290, MS-67, August 2015; $1,293, MS-66, January 2015; $282, MS-64, February 2015; $176, AU-53, January 2015										

HAWAIIAN SESQUICENTENNIAL HALF DOLLAR (1928)

Designer: *Juliette M. Fraser.* **Weight:** *12.50 grams.* **Composition:** *.900 silver, .100 copper (net weight .3617 oz. pure silver).* **Diameter:** *30.6 mm.* **Edge:** *Reeded.* **Mint:** *Philadelphia.*

This issue was struck to commemorate the 150th anniversary of the arrival on the Hawaiian Islands of Captain James Cook in 1778. The coin's $2 price was the highest ever for a commemorative half dollar up to that point.

Designs. *Obverse:* Portrait of Captain James Cook. *Reverse:* A Hawaiian chieftain standing with arm outstretched and holding a spear.

Mintage Data. Authorized on March 7, 1928. *Maximum authorized*—10,000. *Number minted*—10,008 (including 8 assay coins and 50 Sandblast Proofs). *Net distribution*—10,008.

Original Cost and Issuer. Sale price $2. Issued by the Captain Cook Sesquicentennial Commission, through the Bank of Hawaii, Ltd.

Key to Collecting. This is the scarcest of classic U.S. commemorative coins. It is elusive in all grades, and highly prized. Most are AU-55 to MS-62 or slightly finer; those grading MS-65 or above are especially difficult to find. Most examples show contact or friction on the higher design areas. Some coins have a somewhat satiny surface, whereas others are lustrous and frosty. Many undipped pieces have a yellowish tint. Beware of coins which have been repeatedly dipped or cleaned. Problem-free examples are rarer even than the low mintage would suggest. Fake "Sandblast Proofs" exist; these are coins dipped in acid.

First Points of Wear. *Obverse:* Cook's cheekbone. *Reverse:* The chieftain's legs; his fingers and the hand holding the spear.

	Distribution	Cert	Avg	%MS	AU-50	MS-60	MS-62	MS-63	MS-64	MS-65	MS-66
									PF-63	PF-64	PF-65
1928	10,008	1,728	63.7	98%	$1,700	$2,100	$2,200	$2,475	$2,875	$3,500	$5,250
	Auctions: $39,950, MS-67, January 2017; $14,100, MS-66, April 2016; $4,440, MS-66, April 2018; $2,880, MS-65, April 2018										
1928, Proof (a)	*50*	28	64.2						$20,000	$50,000	—
	Auctions: $25,300, PF-64, August 2004; $33,350, PF-64, January 2012; $21,850, PF-64, February 2000; $13,225, PF-63, January 2004										

a. Sandblast Proof presentation pieces. "Of the production figure, 50 were Sandblast Proofs, made by a special process which imparted a dull, grainy finish to the pieces, similar to that used on certain Mint medals of the era as well as on gold Proof coins circa 1908–1915" *(Guide Book of United States Commemorative Coins).*

MARYLAND TERCENTENARY HALF DOLLAR (1934)

Designer: *Hans Schuler.* **Weight:** *12.50 grams.* **Composition:** *.900 silver, .100 copper (net weight .3617 oz. pure silver).* **Diameter:** *30.6 mm.* **Edge:** *Reeded.* **Mint:** *Philadelphia.*

The 300th anniversary of the founding of the Maryland Colony by Cecil Calvert (known as Lord Baltimore) was the occasion for this special coin. The profits from the sale of this issue were used to finance the celebration in Baltimore during 1934. John Work Garrett, distinguished American diplomat and well-known numismatist, was among the citizens of Maryland who endorsed the commemorative half dollar proposal on behalf of the Maryland Tercentenary Commission of Baltimore.

Designs. *Obverse:* Three-quarter portrait of Cecil Calvert, Lord Baltimore. *Reverse:* The state seal and motto of Maryland.

Mintage Data. Authorized on May 9, 1934. *Maximum authorized—25,000. Number minted—25,015* (including 15 assay coins). *Net distribution—25,015.*

Original Cost and Issuer. Sale price $1. Issued by the Maryland Tercentenary Commission, through various outlets.

Key to Collecting. The coin's field has an unusual "rippled" appearance, similar to a sculptured plaque, so nicks and other marks that would be visible on a coin with flat fields are not as readily noticed. Most examples grade MS–62 to 64. Finer pieces, strictly graded, are elusive. This issue was not handled with care at the time of mintage and distribution, and nearly all show scattered contact marks. Some exist struck from a reverse die broken from the right side of the shield to a point opposite the upper right of the 4 in the date 1634.

First Points of Wear. *Obverse:* Lord Baltimore's nose (the nose usually appears flatly struck; also check the reverse for wear). *Reverse:* The top of the coronet on top of the shield, and the tops of the draperies.

	Distribution	Cert	Avg	%MS	AU-50	MS-60	MS-62	MS-63	MS-64	MS-65	MS-66
									PF-63	PF-64	PF-65
1934	25,015	3,578	64.7	100%	$130	$140	$150	$165	$175	$185	$275
	Auctions: $2,115, MS-67, January 2015; $447, MS-66, August 2015; $212, MS-65, January 2015; $119, MS-60, February 2015										
1934, Matte Proof	*2–4*	4	63.3								
	Auctions: $109,250, PF-64, March 2012										

TEXAS INDEPENDENCE CENTENNIAL HALF DOLLAR (1934–1938)

Designer: *Pompeo Coppini.* **Weight:** *12.50 grams.*
Composition: *.900 silver, .100 copper (net weight .3617 oz. pure silver).*
Diameter: *30.6 mm.* **Edge:** *Reeded.* **Mints:** *Philadelphia, Denver, and San Francisco.*

This issue commemorated the independence of Texas in 1836. Proceeds from the sale of the coin were intended to finance the Centennial Exposition, which was eventually held in Dallas. Sales were lower than expected, but the event was still held and attracted about 7 million visitors.

Designs. *Obverse:* A perched eagle with a large five-pointed star in the background.
Reverse: The goddess Victory kneeling, with medallions and portraits of General Sam Houston and Stephen Austin, founders of the republic and state of Texas, along with other Texan icons.

Mintage and Melting Data. Authorized on June 15, 1933. *Maximum authorized*—1,500,000 (for the entire series 1934 onward). 1934: *Number minted*—1934: 205,113 (including 113 assay coins); 1935-P: 10,008 (including 8 assay coins); 1935-D: 10,007 (including 7 assay coins); 1935-S: 10,008 (including 8 assay coins); 1936-P: 10,008 (including 8 assay coins); 1936-D: 10,007 (including 7 assay coins); 1936-S: 10,008 (including 8 assay coins); 1937-P: 8,005 (including 5 assay coins); 1937-D: 8,006 (including 6 assay coins); 1937-S: 8,007 (including 7 assay coins); 1938-P: 5,005 (including 5 assay coins); 1938-D: 5,005 (including 5 assay coins); 1938-S: 5,006 (including 6 assay coins). *Number melted*—1934: 143,650; 1935-P: 12 (probably defective coins); 1936-P: 12 (probably defective coins); 1937-P: 1,434; 1937-D: 1,401; 1937-S: 1,370; 1938-P: 1,225; 1938-D: 1,230; 1938-S: 1,192. *Net distribution*—1934: 61,463; 1935-P: 9,996; 1935-D: 10,007; 1935-S: 10,008; 1936-P: 9,996; 1936-D: 10,007; 1936-S: 10,008; 1937-P: 6,571; 1937-D: 6,605; 1937-S: 6,637; 1938-P: 3,780; 1938-D: 3,775; 1938-S: 3,814.

Original Cost and Issuer. Sale price $1; later raised. Issued by the American Legion Texas Centennial Committee, Austin, Texas, from 1934 through 1936; issued by the Texas Memorial Museum Centennial Coin Campaign in 1937 and 1938.

Key to Collecting. The typical example grades MS–64 or 65. Early issues are very lustrous and frosty; those produced toward the end of the series are more satiny.

First Points of Wear. *Obverse:* The eagle's upper breast and upper leg. *Reverse:* The forehead and knee of Victory.

	Distribution	Cert	Avg	%MS	AU-50	MS-60	MS-62	MS-63	MS-64	MS-65	MS-66
1934	61,463	2,696	64.4	98%	$130	$140	$145	$150	$165	$200	$300
	Auctions: $1,293, MS-67, July 2015; $306, MS-66, January 2015; $129, MS-64, September 2015; $100, MS-60, June 2015										
1935 (same as 1934)	9,996	1,655	65.6	100%	$130	$140	$145	$150	$160	$200	$300
	Auctions: $3,525, MS-68, January 2015; $1,998, MS-67, August 2015; $188, MS-65, September 2015; $106, MS-60, May 2015										
1935-D	10,007	1,659	65.5	100%	$130	$140	$145	$150	$160	$200	$300
	Auctions: $3,290, MS-68, September 2015; $1,410, MS-67, June 2015; $235, MS-66, May 2015; $153, MS-60, May 2015										
1935-S	10,008	1,412	65.2	100%	$130	$140	$145	$150	$160	$200	$300
	Auctions: $705, MS-67, January 2015; $259, MS-66, May 2015; $212, MS-65, August 2015; $129, MS-63, October 2015										
Set of 1935 P-D-S						$425	$450	$465	$500	$600	$900
	Auctions: $940, MS-67/67/67, March 2015; $871, MS-66/66/66, December 2011; $470, MS-65/65/65, April 2015										

	Distribution	Cert	Avg	%MS	AU-50	MS-60	MS-62	MS-63	MS-64	MS-65	MS-66
1936 (same as 1934)	8,911	1,500	65.4	100%	$120	$130	$140	$150	$180	$200	$300
Auctions: $14,100, MS-68, July 2015; $823, MS-67, June 2015; $382, MS-66, January 2015; $141, MS-64, January 2015											
1936-D	9,039	1,687	65.7	100%	$120	$130	$140	$150	$190	$200	$300
Auctions: $2,820, MS-68, July 2015; $705, MS-67, August 2015; $329, MS-66, March 2015; $123, MS-64, May 2015											
1936-S	9,055	1,389	65.3	100%	$120	$130	$140	$150	$190	$200	$300
Auctions: $1,058, MS-67, October 2015; $282, MS-66, September 2015; $176, MS-65, September 2015; $123, MS-64, March 2015											
Set of 1936 P-D-S						$450	$475	$525	$575	$725	$875
Auctions: $863, MS-66/66/66, December 2011; $705, MS-65/65/65, March 2015											
1937 (same as 1934)	6,571	1,234	65.2	100%	$120	$130	$140	$150	$175	$200	$300
Auctions: $12,925, MS-68, August 2015; $2,585, MS-67, August 2015; $200, MS-65, April 2015; $147, MS-63, October 2015											
1937-D	6,605	1,257	65.4	100%	$120	$130	$140	$150	$175	$200	$300
Auctions: $3,760, MS-68, January 2015; $1,175, MS-67, September 2015; $129, MS-62, October 2015; $89, MS-60, January 2015											
1937-S	6,637	1,266	65.3	100%	$120	$130	$140	$150	$175	$200	$300
Auctions: $1,880, MS-67, February 2015; $329, MS-66, February 2015; $259, MS-66, September 2015; $200, MS-65, October 2015											
Set of 1937 P-D-S						$450	$500	$550	$600	$800	$1,000
Auctions: $625, MS-66/66/66, April 2012; $617, MS-66/66/66, March 2015; $541, MS-65/65/65, September 2015											
1938 (same as 1934)	3,780	862	65.1	100%	$130	$140	$145	$150	$175	$200	$300
Auctions: $1,645, MS-67, January 2015; $823, MS-66, January 2015; $400, MS-65, July 2015; $176, MS-63, October 2015											
1938-D	3,775	904	65.4	100%	$130	$140	$145	$150	$175	$200	$300
Auctions: $1,880, MS-67, August 2015; $447, MS-66, January 2015; $447, MS-66, January 2015; $294, MS-64, October 2015											
1938-S	3,814	914	65.4	100%	$130	$140	$145	$150	$175	$200	$300
Auctions: $2,233, MS-67, January 2015; $646, MS-66, January 2015; $329, MS-65, October 2015; $176, MS-63, October 2015											
Set of 1938 P-D-S						$800	$850	$900	$1,125	$1,200	$1,800
Auctions: $604, MS-64/65/64, June 2012											

DANIEL BOONE BICENTENNIAL HALF DOLLAR (1934–1938)

Designer: *Augustus Lukeman.* **Weight:** *12.50 grams.*
Composition: *.900 silver, .100 copper (net weight .3617 oz. pure silver).*
Diameter: *30.6 mm.* **Edge:** *Reeded.* **Mints:** *Philadelphia, Denver, and San Francisco.*

This coin type, which was minted for five years, was first struck in 1934 to commemorate the 200th anniversary of the birth of Daniel Boone, famous frontiersman, trapper, and explorer. Coinage covered several years, similar to the schedule for the Texas issues; 1934 coins are the only examples with true bicentennial status.

Designs. *Obverse:* Artist's conception of Daniel Boone in a profile portrait. *Reverse:* Standing figures of Boone and Blackfish, war chief of the Chillicothe band of the Shawnee tribe. (In 1935 the date 1934 was added to the reverse design.)

Mintage and Melting Data. Authorized on May 26, 1934 and, with "1934" added to modify the design, on August 26, 1935. *Maximum authorized*—600,000 (for the entire series from 1934 onward). *Number minted*—1934: 10,007 (including 7 assay coins); 1935-P: 10,010 (including 10 assay coins); 1935-D: 5,005 (including 5 assay coins); 1935-S: 5,005 (including 5 assay coins); 1935-P, "Small 1934": 10,008 (including 8 assay coins); 1935-D, "Small 1934": 2,003; 1935-S, "Small 1934": 2,004; 1936-P: 12,012 (including 12 assay coins); 1936-D: 5,005 (including 5 assay coins); 1936-S: 5,006 (including 6 assay coins); 1937-P: 15,010 (including 10 assay coins); 1937-D: 7,506 (including 6 assay coins); 1937-S: 5,006 (including 6 assay coins); 1938-P: 5,005 (including 5 assay coins); 1938-D: 5,005 (including 5 assay coins); 1938-S: 5,006 (including 6 assay coins). *Number melted*—1937-P: 5,200; 1937-D: 5,000; 1937-S: 2,500; 1938-P: 2,905; 1938-D: 2,905; 1938-S: 2,906. *Net distribution*—1934: 10,007; 1935-P: 10,010; 1935-D: 5,005; 1935-S: 5,005; 1935-P, "Small 1934": 10,008 (including 8 assay coins); 1935-D, "Small 1934": 2,003; 1935-S, "Small 1934": 2,004; 1936-P: 12,012; 1936-D: 5,005; 1936-S: 5,006; 1937-P: 9,810; 1937-D: 2,506; 1937-S: 2,506; 1938-P: 2,100; 1938-D: 2,100; 1938-S: 2,100.

Original Cost and Issuer. Sale prices varied by mintmark, from a low of $1.10 per 1935-P coin to a high of $5.15 per 1937-S coin. Issued by Daniel Boone Bicentennial Commission (and its division, the Pioneer National Monument Association), Phoenix Hotel, Lexington, Kentucky (C. Frank Dunn, "sole distributor").

Key to Collecting. Most collectors desire just a single coin to represent the type, but there are enough specialists who want one of each date and mintmark to ensure a ready market whenever the scarcer sets come up for sale. Most surviving coins are in MS, with MS–64 to 66 pieces readily available for most issues. Early issues in the series are characterized by deep frosty mint luster, whereas issues toward the end of the run, particularly 1937 and 1938, often are seen with a satin finish and relatively little luster (because of the methods of die preparation and striking). The 1937-S is very often seen with prooflike surfaces, and the 1938-S occasionally so. In general, the Boone commemoratives were handled carefully at the time of minting and distribution, but scattered contact marks are often visible.

First Points of Wear. *Obverse:* The hair behind Boone's ear. *Reverse:* The left shoulder of the Indian.

	Distribution	Cert	Avg	%MS	AU-50	MS-60	MS-62	MS-63	MS-64	MS-65	MS-66
1934	10,007	1,084	64.8	100%	$130	$135	$140	$150	$160	$180	$275
	Auctions: $1,528, MS-67, January 2015; $569, MS-66, January 2015; $165, MS-65, September 2015; $94, MS-60, January 2015										
1935	10,010	1,244	64.7	100%	$130	$135	$140	$150	$175	$180	$275
	Auctions: $1,175, MS-67, January 2015; $200, MS-66, January 2015; $176, MS-65, January 2015; $94, MS-62, February 2015										
1935-D	5,005	710	64.6	100%	$130	$135	$140	$150	$165	$180	$275
	Auctions: $2,115, MS-67, January 2015; $201, MS-65, October 2015; $175, MS-65, March 2015; $153, MS-64, January 2015										
1935-S	5,005	886	65.0	100%	$130	$135	$140	$150	$175	$180	$275
	Auctions: $1,116, MS-67, October 2015; $376, MS-66, January 2015; $176, MS-65, February 2015; $106, MS-60, July 2015										
Set of 1935 P-D-S					$405	$420	$450	$525	$625	$875	
	Auctions: $380, MS-64/64/64, December 2011										
1935, With Small 1934	10,008	1,319	64.9	100%	$130	$135	$145	$150	$160	$180	$275
	Auctions: $1,528, MS-67, July 2015; $282, MS-66, January 2015; $188, MS-65, April 2015; $106, MS-60, May 2015										
1935-D, Same type	2,003	505	65.2	100%	$130	$135	$145	$150	$170	$180	$275
	Auctions: $6,463, MS-68, January 2015; $881, MS-66, January 2015; $646, MS-65, January 2015; $306, MS-64, January 2015										
1935-S, Same type	2,004	492	64.8	100%	$130	$135	$145	$150	$170	$180	$275
	Auctions: $4,230, MS-67, January 2015; $1,528, MS-66, September 2015; $541, MS-65, January 2015; $248, MS-64, April 2015										
Set of 1935 P-D-S, With Added Date					$675	$700	$800	$1,025	$1,550	$1,950	
	Auctions: $925, MS-65/63/64, May 2012										
1936	12,012	1,583	64.8	100%	$130	$135	$140	$150	$170	$180	$275
	Auctions: $7,050, MS-68, October 2015; $940, MS-67, January 2015; $306, MS-66, January 2015; $100, MS-63, February 2015										
1936-D	5,005	886	65.0	100%	$130	$135	$140	$150	$170	$180	$275
	Auctions: $1,293, MS-67, June 2015; $235, MS-66, September 2015; $188, MS-65, July 2015; $100, MS-63, February 2015										
1936-S	5,006	915	65.1	100%	$130	$135	$140	$150	$170	$180	$275
	Auctions: $11,163, MS-68, January 2015; $705, MS-67, August 2015; $353, MS-66, September 2015; $102, MS-63, August 2015										
Set of 1936 P-D-S					$415	$425	$450	$525	$650	$875	
	Auctions: $920, MS-66/66/66 Plus, November 2011										

	Distribution	Cert	Avg	%MS	AU-50	MS-60	MS-62	MS-63	MS-64	MS-65	MS-66
1937	9,810	1,456	64.9	100%	$130	$135	$140	$150	$170	$180	$275
	Auctions: $2,585, MS-67, October 2015; $376, MS-66, March 2015; $200, MS-65, February 2015; $100, MS-60, September 2015										
1937-D	2,506	572	64.9	100%	$130	$135	$140	$150	$170	$180	$275
	Auctions: $1,528, MS-67, October 2015; $376, MS-66, April 2015; $294, MS-65, January 2015; $212, MS-64, January 2015										
1937-S	2,506	684	65.0	100%	$130	$135	$140	$150	$170	$180	$275
	Auctions: $1,645, MS-67, January 2015; $470, MS-66, May 2015; $353, MS-65, January 2015; $118, MS-63, August 2015										
Set of 1937 P-D-S					$410	$425	$450	$525	$650	$950
	Auctions: $564, MS-66/65/64, November 2011										
1938	2,100	469	64.8	100%	$130	$135	$145	$150	$165	$180	$275
	Auctions: $2,585, MS-67, July 2015; $946, MS-66, January 2015; $306, MS-65, September 2015; $236, MS-63, February 2015										
1938-D	2,100	492	65.1	100%	$130	$135	$145	$150	$165	$180	$275
	Auctions: $7,050, MS-67, January 2015; $823, MS-66, January 2015; $423, MS-65, February 2015; $259, MS-63, February 2015										
1938-S	2,100	501	64.9	100%	$130	$135	$145	$150	$165	$180	$275
	Auctions: $1,410, MS-67, August 2015; $1,087, MS-66, January 2015; $235, MS-63, July 2015; $188, AU-50, November 2015										
Set of 1938 P-D-S					$800	$900	$1,000	$1,150	$1,400	$2,000
	Auctions: $4,312, MS-66/66/65, September 2011										

CONNECTICUT TERCENTENARY HALF DOLLAR (1935)

Designer: *Henry Kreis.* **Weight:** *12.50 grams.* **Composition:** *.900 silver, .100 copper (net weight .3617 oz. pure silver).* **Diameter:** *30.6 mm.* **Edge:** *Reeded.* **Mint:** *Philadelphia.*

In commemoration of the 300th anniversary of the founding of the colony of Connecticut, a souvenir half dollar was struck. According to legend, the Royal Charter of the colony was secreted in the Charter Tree (seen on the coin's reverse) during the reign of King James II, who wished to revoke it. The charter was produced after the king's overthrow in 1688, and the colony continued under its protection.

Designs. *Obverse:* A modernistic eagle, standing. *Reverse:* The Charter Oak.

Mintage Data. Authorized on June 21, 1934. *Maximum authorized*—25,000. *Number minted*—25,018 (including 18 assay coins). *Net distribution*—25,018.

Original Cost and Issuer. Sale price $1. Issued by the Connecticut Tercentenary Commission.

Key to Collecting. Most examples survive in upper AU and lower MS grades. Higher-grade coins such as MS-65 are elusive. Friction and/or marks are often obvious on the broad expanse of wing on the obverse, and, in particular, at the ground or baseline of the oak tree on the reverse. Examples that are otherwise lustrous, frosty, and very attractive, often have friction on the wing.

First Points of Wear. *Obverse:* The top of the eagle's wing. *Reverse:* The ground above ON and TI in CONNECTICUT.

	Distribution	Cert	Avg	%MS	AU-50	MS-60	MS-62	MS-63	MS-64	MS-65	MS-66
									PF-63	PF-64	PF-65
1935	25,018	3,621	64.5	99%	$215	$220	$225	$235	$250	$375	$550
	Auctions: $2,350, MS-67, January 2015; $823, MS-66, October 2015; $376, MS-65, January 2015; $188, MS-60, July 2015										
1935, Matte Proof	*1–2*	2	65.0								
	Auctions: No auction records available.										

ARKANSAS CENTENNIAL HALF DOLLAR (1935–1939)

Designer: *Edward E. Burr.* **Weight:** *12.50 grams.*
Composition: *.900 silver, .100 copper (net weight .3617 oz. pure silver).*
Diameter: *30.6 mm.* **Edge:** *Reeded.* **Mints:** *Philadelphia, Denver, and San Francisco.*

This souvenir issue marked the 100th anniversary of the admission of Arkansas into the Union. The 1936 through 1939 issues were the same as those of 1935 except for the dates. The coin's four-year lifespan was intended to maximize profits, and sluggish sales contributed to the crash of the commemorative market and subsequent suspension of commemorative coinage in 1939.

Designs. *Obverse:* An eagle with outstretched wings, stars, and other elements of the Arkansas state seal. *Reverse:* Portraits of a Liberty in a Phrygian cap and an Indian chief of 1836.

Mintage and Melting Data. Authorized on May 14, 1934. *Maximum authorized*—500,000 (for the entire series from 1935 onward). *Number minted* (including 5, 5, and 6 assay coins)—1935-P: 13,012 (including 5 assay coins); 1935-D: 5,505 (including 5 assay coins); 1935-S: 5,506 (including 6 assay coins); 1936-P: 10,010 (including 10 assay coins); 1936-D: 10,010 (including 10 assay coins); 1936-S: 10,012 (including 12 assay coins); 1937-P: 5,505 (including 5 assay coins); 1937-D: 5,505 (including 5 assay coins); 1937-S: 5,506 (including 6 assay coins); 1938-P: 6,006 (including 6 assay coins); 1938-D: 6,005 (including 5 assay coins); 1938-S: 6,006 (including 6 assay coins); 1939-P: 2,140 (including 4 assay coins); 1939-D: 2,104 (including 4 assay coins); 1939-S: 2,105 (including 5 assay coins). *Number melted*—1936-P: 350; 1936-D: 350; 1936-S: 350; 1938-P: 2,850; 1938-D: 2,850; 1938-S: 2,850. *Net distribution*—1935-P: 13,012; 1935-D: 5,505; 1935-S: 5,506; 1936-P: 9,660; 1936-D: 9,660; 1936-S: 9,662; 1937-P: 5,505; 1937-D: 5,505; 1937-S: 5,506; 1938-P: 3,156; 1938-D: 3,155; 1938-S: 3,156; 1939-P: 2,104; 1939-D: 2,104; 1939-S: 2,105.

Original Cost and Issuer. Sale prices varied by mintmark, from a low of $1 per coin to $12 for a set of three. Issued by the Arkansas Centennial Commission in 1935, 1936, 1938, and 1939 (note that dealer B. Max Mehl bought quantities and retailed them at higher prices in 1935). Issued by Stack's of New York City in 1937.

Key to Collecting. The coin sets were produced with a satiny, almost "greasy" finish; even freshly minted coins appeared as if they had been dipped or repeatedly cleaned. Issues of 1937 to 1939 are usually more satisfactory but still are not deeply lustrous. The prominence of the girl's portrait on the center of the obverse renders that part of the coin prone to receiving bagmarks, scuffs, and other evidence of handling. As a result, relatively few pieces have great eye appeal. The obverse area where the ribbon crosses the eagle's breast is often very weak. Some examples are lightly struck on the eagle just behind its head.

First Points of Wear. *Obverse:* The eagle's head and the top of the left wing. *Reverse:* The band of the girl's cap, behind her eye.

	Distribution	Cert	Avg	%MS	AU-50	MS-60	MS-62	MS-63	MS-64	MS-65	MS-66
									PF-63	PF-64	PF-65
1935	13,012	1,240	64.4	100%	$110	$120	$130	$140	$165	$200	$350
Auctions: $1,116, MS-67, September 2014; $1,528, MS-67 Plus, July 2014; $400, MS-66, December 2014; $558, MS-66, October 2014											
1935-D	5,505	885	64.7	100%	$110	$120	$130	$140	$165	$200	$350
Auctions: $1,880, MS-67, January 2015; $400, MS-66, August 2015; $153, MS-65, January 2015; $100, MS-64, September 2015											
1935-S	5,506	889	64.6	100%	$110	$120	$130	$140	$165	$200	$350
Auctions: $1,939, MS-67, January 2015; $705, MS-66, September 2015; $100, MS-64, January 2015; $74, MS-62, February 2015											
Set of 1935 P-D-S						$300	$315	$330	$360	$525	$1,400
Auctions: $322, MS-64/64/64 Plus, April 2012											
1936	9,660	1,049	64.2	100%	$110	$120	$130	$140	$165	$200	$350
Auctions: $1,998, MS-67, September 2015; $1,116, MS-66, July 2015; $120, MS-64, September 2015; $79, MS-60, August 2015											
1936-D	9,660	1,025	64.5	100%	$110	$120	$130	$140	$165	$200	$350
Auctions: $2,585, MS-67, January 2015; $353, MS-66, January 2015; $259, MS-65, July 2015; $100, MS-63, January 2015											
1936-S	9,662	1,048	64.4	100%	$110	$120	$130	$140	$165	$200	$350
Auctions: $1,528, MS-67, January 2015; $282, MS-66, September 2015; $153, MS-65, September 2015; $94, MS-63, October 2015											
Set of 1936 P-D-S						$285	$315	$330	$360	$475	$1,900
Auctions: $300, MS-64/64/65, December 2011											
1937	5,505	778	64.3	100%	$110	$120	$120	$125	$130	$200	$350
Auctions: $2,585, MS-67, June 2015; $541, MS-66, January 2015; $129, MS-64, January 2015; $118, MS-63, August 2015											
1937-D	5,505	818	64.6	100%	$110	$120	$120	$125	$130	$200	$350
Auctions: $2,233, MS-67, January 2015; $494, MS-66, January 2015; $165, MS-64, September 2015; $79, MS-63, April 2015											
1937-S	5,506	670	64.2	100%	$110	$120	$120	$125	$130	$200	$350
Auctions: $999, MS-66, September 2015; $940, MS-66, September 2015; $200, MS-65, May 2015; $79, MS-63, January 2015											
Set of 1937 P-D-S						$345	$360	$375	$400	$725	$1,875
Auctions: $600, MS-65/65/65, January 2012											
1938	3,156	553	64.4	100%	$110	$120	$130	$140	$175	$200	$350
Auctions: $3,290, MS-67, August 2015; $705, MS-66, January 2015; $306, MS-65, February 2015; $106, MS-63, April 2015											
1938-D	3,155	578	64.4	100%	$110	$120	$130	$140	$175	$200	$350
Auctions: $3,055, MS-67, January 2015; $881, MS-66, January 2015; $259, MS-64, June 2015; $123, MS-63, February 2015											
1938-S	3,156	511	64.3	100%	$110	$120	$135	$140	$175	$200	$350
Auctions: $1,058, MS-66, July 2015; $999, MS-66, September 2015; $282, MS-65, January 2015; $153, MS-64, April 2015											
Set of 1938 P-D-S						$435	$450	$500	$650	$1,075	$2,800
Auctions: $2,900, MS-66/66/66, April 2012; $411, MS-63/63/63, October 2015											
Set of 1938 P-D-S, Matte Proof	1–2										
Auctions: No auction records available.											
1939	2,104	473	64.2	100%	$110	$120	$130	$140	$170	$200	$350
Auctions: $1,880, MS-66, June 2015; $1,763, MS-66, July 2015; $610, MS-65, January 2015; $306, MS-64, September 2015											
1939-D	2,104	472	64.4	100%	$110	$120	$130	$140	$170	$200	$350
Auctions: $3,995, MS-67, August 2015; $1,146, MS-66, January 2015; $470, MS-65, January 2015; $270, MS-63, March 2015											
1939-S	2,105	528	64.5	100%	$110	$120	$130	$140	$170	$200	$350
Auctions: $3,760, MS-67, August 2015; $1,939, MS-66, January 2015; $764, MS-65, January 2015; $294, MS-64, April 2015											
Set of 1939 P-D-S						$725	$750	$800	$900	$2,200	$4,500
Auctions: $1,610, MS-65/65/65, February 2012											

ARKANSAS CENTENNIAL—ROBINSON HALF DOLLAR (1936)

Designers: *Henry Kreis (obverse) and Edward E. Burr (reverse).* **Weight:** *12.50 grams (net weight .3617 oz. pure silver).* **Composition:** *.900 silver, .100 copper.* **Diameter:** *30.6 mm.* **Edge:** *Reeded.* **Mints:** *Philadelphia, Denver, San Francisco.*

A new reverse design for the Arkansas Centennial coin (see preceding coin) was authorized by the Act of June 26, 1936. Senator Joseph T. Robinson was still living at the time his portrait was used. Note that though it is normally true that portraits appear on the obverse of coins, the side bearing Robinson's likeness is indeed technically the reverse of this coin.

Designs. *Obverse:* An eagle with outstretched wings, stars, and other elements of the Arkansas state seal. *Reverse:* Bareheaded profile portrait of Senator Joseph T. Robinson.

Mintage Data. Authorized on June 26, 1936. *Maximum authorized*—50,000 (minimum 25,000). *Number minted*—25,265 (including 15 assay coins). *Net distribution*—25,265.

Original Cost and Issuer. Sale price $1.85. Issued by Stack's of New York City.

Key to Collecting. Most known coins are in MS, as most or all were originally sold to collectors and coin dealers. Examples are plentiful in the marketplace, usually grading MS–62 to 64. The coins were not handled with care during production, so many have contact marks on Robinson's portrait and elsewhere. Some examples are lightly struck on the eagle, just behind the head.

First Points of Wear. *Obverse:* The eagle's head and the top of the left wing. *Reverse:* Robinson's cheekbone.

	Distribution	Cert	Avg	%MS	AU-50	MS-60	MS-62	MS-63	MS-64	MS-65	MS-66
1936	25,265	2,738	64.3	100%	$105	$125	$130	$135	$160	$200	$330

Auctions: $3,290, MS-67, August 2015; $617, MS-66, January 2015; $212, MS-65, February 2015; $112, MS-63, January 2015

HUDSON, NEW YORK, SESQUICENTENNIAL HALF DOLLAR (1935)

Designer: *Chester Beach.* **Weight:** *12.50 grams.* **Composition:** *.900 silver, .100 copper (net weight .3617 oz. pure silver).* **Diameter:** *30.6 mm.* **Edge:** *Reeded.* **Mint:** *Philadelphia.*

This souvenir half dollar marked the 150th anniversary of the founding of Hudson, New York, which was named after the explorer Henry Hudson. The area was actually settled in 1662, but not given its permanent name and formally incorporated until 1785. The distribution of these coins was widely criticized, as certain dealers were allowed to purchase large quantities at $1 or less and then resold them at dramatically inflated prices.

Designs. *Obverse:* The ship *Half Moon*, captained by Henry Hudson, in full sail. *Reverse:* The ocean god Neptune seated backward on a whale (derived from the seal of the city of Hudson); in the background, a mermaid blowing a shell.

Mintage Data. Approved May 2, 1935. *Maximum authorized*—10,000. *Number minted*—10,008 (including 8 assay coins). *Net distribution*—10,008.

Original Cost and Issuer. Sale price $1. Issued by the Hudson Sesquicentennial Committee, through the First National Bank & Trust Company of Hudson.

Key to Collecting. Examples are readily available in the marketplace. Note that deep or artificial toning, which can make close inspection impossible, has led some certified coins to certified grades that are higher than they should be. True gems are very rare. These coins were struck at high speed and with little care to preserve their quality; by the time they were originally distributed most pieces showed nicks, contact marks, and other evidence of handling. Most are lustrous and frosty (except on the central devices), and grade in the lower MS levels. MS–62 to 64 are typical. Carefully graded MS-65 coins are scarce, and anything higher is very rare.

First Points of Wear. *Obverse:* The center of the lower middle sail. *Reverse:* The motto on the ribbon, and the figure of Neptune (both of which may also be lightly struck).

	Distribution	Cert	Avg	%MS	AU-50	MS-60	MS-62	MS-63	MS-64	MS-65	MS-66
1935	10,008	2,050	64.1	98%	$650	$700	$765	$800	$900	$1,000	$1,250
	Auctions: $8,519, MS-67, July 2015; $2,350, MS-66, September 2015; $1,087, MS-65, September 2015; $588, MS-60, January 2015										

CALIFORNIA PACIFIC INTERNATIONAL EXPOSITION HALF DOLLAR (1935–1936)

Designer: *Robert Aitken.* **Weight:** *12.50 grams.* **Composition:** *.900 silver, .100 copper (net weight .3617 oz. pure silver).* **Diameter:** *30.6 mm.* **Edge:** *Reeded.* **Mints:** *San Francisco and Denver.*

Congress approved the coinage of souvenir half dollars for the California Pacific International Exposition on May 3, 1935. The event—held in San Diego's Balboa Park—was attended by only 4 million people, and interest in the coin was not particularly strong.

Designs. *Obverse:* Minerva seated, holding a spear and shield, with a grizzly bear to her right (from California's state seal). *Reverse:* The Chapel of St. Francis and the California Tower, at the California Pacific International Exposition in San Diego.

Mintage and Melting Data. Originally authorized on May 3, 1935; 1936-D issues authorized on May 6, 1936 (for recoinage of melted 1935-S issues). *Maximum authorized*—1935-S: 250,000; 1936-D: 180,000. *Number minted*—1935-S: 250,132 (including 132 assay coins); 1936-D: 180,092 (including 92 assay coins). *Number melted*—1935-S: 180,000; 1936-D: 150,000. *Net distribution*—1935-S: 70,132; 1936-D: 30,092.

Original Cost and Issuer. Sale prices $1 (1935-S; increased to $3 in 1937; dropped to $2 in 1938) and $1.50 (1936-D; increased to $3 in 1937; reduced to $1 in 1938). Issued by the California Pacific International Exposition Company.

Key to Collecting. Both the 1935-S and 1936-D issues were coined with deeply frosty and lustrous surfaces. The eye appeal usually is excellent. The design made these coins susceptible to bagmarks, and most survivors, even in higher MS grades, show evidence of handling. Minerva, in particular, usually displays some graininess or contact marks, even on coins given high numerical grades. Most coins are deeply lustrous and frosty. On the 1935 San Francisco coins the S mintmark usually is flat, and on the Denver coins the California Tower is often lightly struck at the top.

First Points of Wear. *Obverse:* The bosom and knees of Minerva. *Reverse:* The top right edge of the tower. (The 1936-D was flatly struck in this area; examine the texture of the surface to determine if actual wear exists.)

	Distribution	Cert	Avg	%MS	AU-50	MS-60	MS-62	MS-63	MS-64	MS-65	MS-66
1935-S	70,132	4,999	64.8	100%	$100	$105	$110	$115	$120	$135	$160
	Auctions: $2,115, MS-67, September 2015; $223, MS-66, September 2015; $153, MS-65, August 2015; $106, MS-60, February 2015										
1936-D	30,092	2,871	64.9	100%	$100	$105	$110	$115	$120	$140	$200
	Auctions: $1,528, MS-67, January 2015; $188, MS-66, September 2015; $176, MS-65, February 2015; $106, MS-64, September 2015										

OLD SPANISH TRAIL HALF DOLLAR (1935)

Designer: *L.W. Hoffecker.* **Weight:** *12.50 grams.* **Composition:** *.900 silver, .100 copper (net weight .3617 oz. pure silver).* **Diameter:** *30.6 mm.* **Edge:** *Reeded.* **Mint:** *Philadelphia.*

This coin commemorated the 400th anniversary of the overland trek of the Alvar Nuñez Cabeza de Vaca Expedition through the Gulf states in 1535. The coin's designer and distributor, L.W. Hoffecker, is known to have had his hands in many of this era's commemoratives (and the exploitative practices surrounding them).

Designs. *Obverse:* The head of a steer, inspired by the explorer's last name: Cabeza de Vaca translates to "head of cow." *Reverse:* A map of the Southeastern states and a yucca tree.

Mintage Data. Authorized on June 5, 1935. *Maximum authorized—10,000. Number minted—10,008.*

Original Cost and Issuer. Sale price $2. Issued by L.W. Hoffecker, trading as the El Paso Museum Coin Committee.

Key to Collecting. These coins were handled with care during their production and shipping—still, most show scattered contact marks. The typical grade is MS-65 and higher. The fields are usually somewhat satiny and gray, not deeply lustrous and frosty.

First Points of Wear. *Obverse:* The top of the cow's head. *Reverse:* The lettering at the top.

	Distribution	Cert	Avg	%MS	AU-50	MS-60	MS-62	MS-63	MS-64	MS-65	MS-66
1935	10,008	1,970	65.0	100%	$1,050	$1,100	$1,125	$1,150	$1,225	$1,275	$1,450
	Auctions: $2,468, MS-67, September 2015; $1,763, MS-66, January 2015; $1,410, MS-65, January 2015; $764, MS-60, June 2015										

PROVIDENCE, RHODE ISLAND, TERCENTENARY HALF DOLLAR (1936)

Designers: *Arthur G. Carey and John H. Benson.* **Weight:** *12.50 grams.*
Composition: *.900 silver, .100 copper (net weight .3617 oz. pure silver).*
Diameter: *30.6 mm.* **Edge:** *Reeded.* **Mints:** *Philadelphia, Denver, and San Francisco.*

The 300th anniversary of Roger Williams's founding of Providence was the occasion for this special half dollar in 1936. Interestingly, no mention of Providence is to be found on the coin. The distribution of this coin, like that of many other commemoratives of the 1930s, was wrapped in controversy—phony news releases reported that the coin was sold out when it was indeed not, and certain dealers procured large amounts at low prices only to resell for tidy profits.

Designs. *Obverse:* Roger Williams, the founder of Rhode Island, being welcomed by an Indian. *Reverse:* Elements from the Rhode Island state seal, including the anchor of Hope and a shield.

Mintage Data. Authorized on May 2, 1935. *Maximum authorized*—50,000. *Number minted*—1936-P: 20,013 (including 13 assay coins); 1936-D: 15,010 (including 10 assay coins); 1936-S: 15,011 (including 11 assay coins). *Net distribution*—1936-P: 20,013; 1936-D: 15,010; 1936-S: 15,011.

Original Cost and Issuer. Sale price $1. Issued by the Rhode Island and Providence Plantations Tercentenary Committee, Inc.

Key to Collecting. These coins are readily available singly and in sets, with typical grades being MS–63 to 65. Contact marks are common. Higher-level coins, such as MS–66 and 67, are not hard to find, but are elusive in comparison to the lesser-condition pieces. The 1936 (in particular) and 1936-S are sometimes found with prooflike surfaces. Most specimens have a combination of satiny/frosty surface. Many are light gray in color.

First Points of Wear. *Obverse:* The prow of the canoe, and the Indian's right shoulder. *Reverse:* The center of the anchor, and surrounding areas.

	Distribution	Cert	Avg	%MS	AU-50	MS-60	MS-62	MS-63	MS-64	MS-65	MS-66
1936	20,013	2,524	64.8	100%	$95	$105	$110	$120	$130	$150	$210
	Auctions: $823, MS-67, July 2015; $165, MS-66, August 2015; $212, MS-65, May 2015; $79, MS-60, February 2015										
1936-D	15,010	1,853	64.7	100%	$95	$105	$110	$120	$130	$150	$210
	Auctions: $969, MS-67, November 2015; $435, MS-66, January 2015; $176, MS-65, August 2015; $100, MS-64, May 2015										
1936-S	15,011	1,588	64.6	100%	$95	$105	$110	$120	$135	$150	$210
	Auctions: $2,820, MS-67, January 2015; $470, MS-66, November 2015; $112, MS-64, May 2015; $69, EF-45, September 2015										
Set of 1936 P-D-S							$300	$360	$410	$500	$675
	Auctions: $2,185, MS-66/66/66, January 2012										

CLEVELAND CENTENNIAL / GREAT LAKES EXPOSITION HALF DOLLAR (1936)

Designer: *Brenda Putnam.* **Weight:** *12.50 grams.* **Composition:** *.900 silver, .100 copper (net weight .3617 oz. pure silver).* **Diameter:** *30.6 mm.* **Edge:** *Reeded.* **Mint:** *Philadelphia.*

A special coinage of fifty-cent pieces was authorized in commemoration of the centennial celebration of Cleveland, Ohio, on the occasion of the Great Lakes Exposition held there in 1936. Numismatic entrepreneur Thomas G. Melish was behind the coins' production and distribution—though he served as the Cleveland Centennial Commemorative Coin Association's treasurer while based in Cincinnati.

Designs. *Obverse:* Bewigged profile portrait of Moses Cleaveland. *Reverse:* A map of the Great Lakes region with nine stars marking various cities, and a compass point at the city of Cleveland.

Mintage Data. Authorized on May 5, 1936. *Maximum authorized*—50,000 (minimum 25,000). *Number minted*—50,030 (including 30 assay coins). *Net distribution*—50,030.

Original Cost and Issuer. Sale prices: one coin for $1.65; two for $1.60 each; three for $1.58 each; five for $1.56 each; ten for $1.55 each; twenty for $1.54 each; fifty for $1.53 each; one hundred for $1.52 each. Issued by the Cleveland Centennial Commemorative Coin Association (Thomas G. Melish, Cincinnati).

Key to Collecting. The Cleveland half dollar is the most readily available issue from 1936—a bumper-crop year for U.S. commemoratives. Nearly all coins are in Mint State, typically from MS–63 to 65, and most are very lustrous and frosty. This issue was not handled with care at the Mint, and scattered contact marks are typically found on both obverse and reverse.

First Points of Wear. *Obverse:* The hair behind Cleaveland's ear. *Reverse:* The top of the compass, and the land (non-lake) areas of the map.

	Distribution	Cert	Avg	%MS	AU-50	MS-60	MS-62	MS-63	MS-64	MS-65	MS-66
1936	50,030	5,069	64.6	100%	$100	$110	$120	$130	$135	$150	$200
	Auctions: $3,995, MS-68, June 2015; $1,293, MS-67, September 2015; $247, MS-66, November 2015; $65, MS-62, March 2015										

WISCONSIN TERRITORIAL CENTENNIAL HALF DOLLAR (1936)

Designer: *David Parsons.* **Weight:** *12.50 grams.* **Composition:** *.900 silver, .100 copper (net weight .3617 oz. pure silver).* **Diameter:** *30.6 mm.* **Edge:** *Reeded.* **Mint:** *Philadelphia.*

The 100th anniversary of the Wisconsin territorial government was the occasion for this issue. Benjamin Hawkins, a New York artist, made changes to the original designs by University of Wisconsin student David Parsons so that the piece conformed to technical requirements.

Designs. *Obverse:* A badger on a log, from the state emblem; and arrows representing the Black Hawk War of the 1830s. *Reverse:* A miner's arm holding a pickaxe over a mound of lead ore, derived from Wisconsin's territorial seal.

Mintage Data. Authorized on May 15, 1936. *Minimum authorized*—25,000 (unlimited maximum). *Number minted*—25,015 (including 15 assay coins). *Net distribution*—25,015.

Original Cost and Issuer. Sale price $1.50 plus 7¢ postage for the first coin, 2¢ postage for each additional coin (later sold for $1.25 each in lots of 10 coins, and still later sold for $3 per coin). Issued by the Wisconsin Centennial Coin Committee (also known as the Coinage Committee of the Wisconsin Centennial Commission). Unsold remainders were distributed, into the 1950s, by the State Historical Society.

Key to Collecting. Examples are readily available in the marketplace. Most grade MS–62 to 64—although higher grades are not rare—and are very lustrous and frosty, except for the higher areas of the design (which often have a slightly polished appearance).

First Points of Wear. *Obverse:* The flank and shoulder of the badger. *Reverse:* The miner's hand.

	Distribution	Cert	Avg	%MS	AU-50	MS-60	MS-62	MS-63	MS-64	MS-65	MS-66
1936	25,015	3,969	65.3	100%	$175	$180	$185	$195	$210	$230	$250

Auctions: $3,055, MS-68, January 2015; $881, MS-67, January 2015; $235, MS-65, August 2015; $129, MS-60, November 2015

CINCINNATI MUSIC CENTER HALF DOLLAR (1936)

Designer: *Constance Ortmayer.* **Weight:** *12.50 grams.*
Composition: *.900 silver, .100 copper (net weight .3617 oz. pure silver).*
Diameter: *30.6 mm.* **Edge:** *Reeded.* **Mints:** *Philadelphia, Denver, and San Francisco.*

Although the head of Stephen Foster, "America's Troubadour," dominates the obverse of this special issue, the anniversary celebrated bears little to no relation to him. Foster did live in Cincinnati for a time, but never worked in music while there. The coins were supposedly struck to commemorate the 50th anniversary in 1936 of Cincinnati as a center of music, but the issue was really a personal project of numismatist Thomas G. Melish.

Designs. *Obverse:* Bareheaded profile portrait of Stephen Foster, "America's Troubadour." *Reverse:* A woman playing a lyre, personifying Music.

Mintage Data. Authorized on March 31, 1936. *Maximum authorized*—15,000. *Number minted*—1936-P: 5,005 (including 5 assay coins); 1936-D: 5,005 (including 5 assay coins); 1936-S: 5,006 (including 6 assay coins). *Net distribution*—1936-P: 5,005; 1936-D: 5,005; 1936-S: 5,006.

Original Cost and Issuer. Sale price $7.75 per set of three (actually $7.50 plus 25¢ for the display container with cellophane slide front). Issued by the Cincinnati Musical Center Commemorative Coin Association, Ohio (Thomas G. Melish).

Key to Collecting. Nearly all sets of these coins were bought by collectors and investors, thus most still exist in Mint State, primarily MS–63 to 65. Conservatively graded MS-65 and finer pieces are rare. Most coins were carelessly handled at the mints, and nearly all show scattered contact marks. This issue has a somewhat satiny or "greasy" surface, instead of fields with deep luster and frost. Denver Mint coins are typically found in slightly higher grades than their Philadelphia and San Francisco Mint companions.

First Points of Wear. *Obverse:* The hair at Foster's temple. *Reverse:* The left breast, and the skirt, of the female figure.

	Distribution	Cert	Avg	%MS	AU-50	MS-60	MS-62	MS-63	MS-64	MS-65	MS-66
1936	5,005	912	64.4	100%	$285	$300	$325	$360	$385	$450	$650
	Auctions: $4,700, MS-67, January 2015; $2,115, MS-66, January 2015; $423, MS-65, September 2015; $329, MS-64, January 2015										
1936-D	5,005	1,272	64.9	100%	$285	$300	$325	$360	$385	$450	$650
	Auctions: $3,290, MS-67, September 2015; $940, MS-66, January 2015; $705, MS-65, January 2015; $188, MS-60, November 2015										
1936-S	5,006	936	64.1	100%	$285	$300	$325	$360	$385	$450	$650
	Auctions: $3,055, MS-66, January 2015; $470, MS-65, January 2015; $329, MS-64, January 2015; $306, MS-63, January 2015										
Set of 1935 P-D-S						$900	$975	$1,100	$1,125	$1,375	$2,500
	Auctions: $4,198, MS-66/66/66, February 2012										

LONG ISLAND TERCENTENARY HALF DOLLAR (1936)

Designer: *Howard K. Weinman.* **Weight:** *12.50 grams.* **Composition:** *.900 silver, .100 copper (net weight .3617 oz. pure silver).* **Diameter:** *30.6 mm.* **Edge:** *Reeded.* **Mint:** *Philadelphia.*

This souvenir issue was authorized to commemorate the 300th anniversary of the first white settlement on Long Island, which was made at Jamaica Bay by Dutch colonists. This was the first issue for which a date was specified (1936) irrespective of the year minted or issued, as a safeguard against extending the coinage over a period of years. This measure proved effective in preventing many of the profiteering problems that arose with other commemorative issues of the era.

Designs. *Obverse:* Conjoined profile portraits of a Dutch settler and an Algonquin Indian. *Reverse:* A Dutch vessel with full-blown sails.

Mintage and Melting Data. Authorized on April 13, 1936. *Maximum authorized*—100,000. *Number minted*—100,053 (including 53 assay coins). *Number melted*—18,227. *Net distribution*—81,826.

Original Cost and Issuer. Sale price $1. Issued by the Long Island Tercentenary Committee, through various banks and other outlets.

Key to Collecting. These are among the most plentiful survivors from the commemorative issues of the 1930s, and examples grading MS–64 to 66 are readily obtainable. The coins were minted and handled carelessly, and at the time of distribution most showed nicks, bagmarks, and other evidence of contact; these grade from AU-50 to MS-60. Most coins have, as struck, a satiny or slightly "greasy" luster and are not deeply frosty.

First Points of Wear. *Obverse:* The hair and the cheekbone of the Dutch settler. *Reverse:* The center of the lower middle sail.

	Distribution	Cert	Avg	%MS	AU-50	MS-60	MS-62	MS-63	MS-64	MS-65	MS-66
1936	81,826	4,841	64.2	99%	$85	$95	$100	$110	$115	$195	$350
	Auctions: $9,988, MS-67, September 2015; $1,293, MS-66, January 2015; $129, MS-64, February 2015; $52, EF-40, July 2015										

YORK COUNTY, MAINE, TERCENTENARY HALF DOLLAR (1936)

Designer: *Walter H. Rich.* **Weight:** *12.50 grams.* **Composition:** *.900 silver, .100 copper (net weight .3617 oz. pure silver).* **Diameter:** *30.6 mm.* **Edge:** *Reeded.* **Mint:** *Philadelphia.*

A souvenir half dollar was authorized by Congress upon the 300th anniversary of the founding of York County, Maine. While the commemorated event was considered somewhat obscure, the proposing and distributing group—the York County Tercentenary Commemorative Coin Commission, led by ardent numismatist Walter P. Nichols—was lauded for its diligence and proper handling of the release.

Designs. *Obverse:* Brown's Garrison, on the Saco River (site of the original settlement in York County in 1636). *Reverse:* An adaptation of the seal of York County.

Mintage Data. *Maximum authorized*—30,000. *Number minted*—25,015 (including 15 assay coins).

Original Cost and Issuer. Sale price $1.50 ($1.65 postpaid by mail to out-of-state buyers). Issued by the York County Tercentenary Commemorative Coin Commission, York National Bank, Saco, Maine.

Key to Collecting. This issue was well handled at the Mint and in distribution, so most examples are in higher grades and are relatively free of marks. On the reverse, the top of the shield is a key point. Some coins have been brushed and have a myriad of fine hairlines; these can be detected by examining the coin at various angles to the light. MS–64 and 65 coins are readily found in the marketplace.

First Points of Wear. *Obverse:* The mounted sentry near the corner of the fort; the stockade; and the rim of the coin. *Reverse:* The pine tree in the shield; the top-right area of the shield; and the rim.

	Distribution	Cert	Avg	%MS	AU-50	MS-60	MS-62	MS-63	MS-64	MS-65	MS-66
1936	25,015	3,651	65.4	100%	$150	$165	$170	$180	$195	$200	$220

Auctions: $1,763, MS-68, August 2015; $881, MS-67, September 2015; $259, MS-66, January 2015; $121, MS-60, January 2015

BRIDGEPORT, CONNECTICUT, CENTENNIAL HALF DOLLAR (1936)

Designer: *Henry Kreis.* **Weight:** *12.50 grams.* **Composition:** *.900 silver, .100 copper (net weight .3617 oz. pure silver).* **Diameter:** *30.6 mm.* **Edge:** *Reeded.* **Mint:** *Philadelphia.*

In commemoration of the 100th anniversary of the incorporation of the city of Bridgeport, a special fifty-cent piece was authorized on May 15, 1936. The city—actually originally founded in 1639—served as an important center in the 17th and 18th centuries.

Designs. *Obverse:* Bareheaded profile portrait of P.T. Barnum, Bridgeport's most famous citizen. *Reverse:* An art deco eagle, standing.

Mintage Data. Authorized on May 15, 1936. *Minimum authorized*—25,000 (unlimited maximum). *Number minted*—25,015 (including 15 assay coins). *Net distribution*—25,015.

Original Cost and Issuer. Sale price $2. Issued by Bridgeport Centennial, Inc., through the First National Bank and Trust Co. and other banks.

Key to Collecting. These coins are readily available in the marketplace. Most grade from MS–62 to 64. Many have been cleaned or lightly polished, but pristine MS-65 pieces are readily available. Obvious friction rub and/or marks are often seen. Some coins were struck from dies with lightly polished fields and have a prooflike or partially prooflike appearance in those areas.

First Points of Wear. *Obverse:* Barnum's cheek. *Reverse:* The eagle's wing.

	Distribution	Cert	Avg	%MS	AU-50	MS-60	MS-62	MS-63	MS-64	MS-65	MS-66
1936	25,015	3,240	64.6	100%	$120	$125	$130	$135	$145	$180	$300
	Auctions: $1,880, MS-67, September 2015; $353, MS-66, February 2015; $235, MS-65, August 2015; $106, MS-60, May 2015										

LYNCHBURG, VIRGINIA, SESQUICENTENNIAL HALF DOLLAR (1936)

Designer: *Charles Keck.* **Weight:** *12.50 grams.* **Composition:** *.900 silver, .100 copper (net weight .3617 oz. pure silver).* **Diameter:** *30.6 mm.* **Edge:** *Reeded.* **Mint:** *Philadelphia.*

The issuance of a charter to the city of Lynchburg in 1786 was commemorated in 1936 by a special coinage of half dollars. Interestingly, Lynchburg native Senator Carter Glass objected to the use of portraits of living persons on coins, but was featured on the issue anyway. It was considered that a portrait of John Lynch—for whom the city was named—would be used, but no such likeness existed.

Designs. *Obverse:* Bareheaded profile portrait of Senator Carter Glass, a native of Lynchburg and former secretary of the Treasury. *Reverse:* A figure of Miss Liberty standing before the old Lynchburg courthouse.

Mintage Data. Authorized on May 28, 1936. *Maximum authorized*—20,000. *Number minted*—20,013 (including 13 assay coins). *Net distribution*—20,013.

Original Cost and Issuer. Sale price $1. Issued by the Lynchburg Sesqui-Centennial Association.

Key to Collecting. Most of these half dollars are in higher grades; MS–65 and 66 examples are readily available in the marketplace. Some show graininess (from striking) on the high areas of the obverse portrait and on the bosom and skirt of Miss Liberty, or show evidences of handling or contact in the same areas. Surfaces are often somewhat satiny, instead of deeply lustrous and frosty. Often the reverse field is semi-prooflike. This issue must have been handled with particular care at the Mint.

First Points of Wear. *Obverse:* The hair above Glass's ear. *Reverse:* The hair of Miss Liberty, the folds of her gown, and her bosom.

	Distribution	Cert	Avg	%MS	AU-50	MS-60	MS-62	MS-63	MS-64	MS-65	MS-66
1936	20,013	2,719	64.8	100%	$220	$230	$235	$240	$260	$270	$325
	Auctions: $2,820, MS-67, January 2015; $294, MS-66, June 2015; $170, MS-63, October 2015; $118, AU-58, August 2015										

ELGIN, ILLINOIS, CENTENNIAL HALF DOLLAR (1936)

Designer: *Trygve Rovelstad.* **Weight:** *12.50 grams.* **Composition:** *.900 silver, .100 copper (net weight .3617 oz. pure silver).* **Diameter:** *30.6 mm.* **Edge:** *Reeded.* **Mint:** *Philadelphia.*

The 100th anniversary of the founding of Elgin, Illinois, was marked by a special issue of half dollars in 1936. The year 1673 (seen on the obverse) bears no relation to the event but refers to the year in which Louis Joliet and Jacques Marquette entered Illinois Territory.

Designs. *Obverse:* The fur-capped profile of a bearded pioneer (a close-up view of the statue depicted on the reverse). *Reverse:* The Pioneer Memorial statuary group, whose creation was financed by the sale of these coins.

Mintage and Melting Data. Authorized on June 16, 1936. *Maximum authorized*—25,000. *Number minted*—25,015 (including 15 assay coins). *Number melted*—5,000. *Net distribution*—20,015.

Original Cost and Issuer. Sale price $1.50. Issued by the Elgin Centennial Monumental Committee, El Paso, Texas (L.W. Hoffecker in charge), through banks in and near Elgin, including the First National Bank of Elgin, the Elgin National Bank, and the Union National Bank.

Key to Collecting. Elgin half dollars are fairly plentiful in today's marketplace. They seem to have been handled with particular care at the time of minting, as most have fewer bagmarks than many other commemoratives of the same era. Typical coins grade MS–64 to 66. The surfaces often have a matte-like appearance (seemingly a combination of a lustrous circulation strike and a Matte Proof) quite different from other commemorative issues of 1936. Some coins are fairly frosty. On many a bright spot is evident on the reverse below the A of AMERICA, the result of an inadvertent polishing on a small area of the die. Chief Engraver John Sinnock made a few Matte Proofs, perhaps as many as 10, by pickling coins in acid at the Mint.

First Points of Wear. *Obverse:* The cheek of the pioneer. *Reverse:* The rifleman's left shoulder. (Note that a lack of detailed facial features is the result of striking, not wear, and that the infant is always weakly struck.)

	Distribution	Cert	Avg	%MS	AU-50	MS-60	MS-62	MS-63	MS-64	MS-65	MS-66
1936	20,015	3,452	65.0	100%	$150	$160	$170	$180	$190	$200	$225

Auctions: $3,995, MS-68, January 2015; $1,880, MS-67, September 2015; $200, MS-65, April 2015; $165, MS-60, February 2015

ALBANY, NEW YORK, CHARTER HALF DOLLAR (1936)

Designer: *Gertrude K. Lathrop.* **Weight:** *12.50 grams.* **Composition:** *.900 silver, .100 copper (net weight .3617 oz. pure silver).* **Diameter:** *30.6 mm.* **Edge:** *Reeded.* **Mint:** *Philadelphia.*

The 250th anniversary of the granting of a charter to the city of Albany—an event of strictly local significance—was the occasion for this commemorative half dollar. Amusingly, designer Gertrude K. Lathrop kept a live beaver in her studio (courtesy of the state Conservation Department) during her work.

Designs. *Obverse:* A plump beaver gnawing on a maple branch—fauna and flora evocative of Albany and New York State, respectively. *Reverse:* A scene with Albany's first mayor, Peter Schuyler, and his secretary, Robert Livingston, accepting the city's charter in 1686 from Governor Thomas Dongan of New York.

Mintage and Melting Data. Authorized on June 16, 1936. *Maximum authorized*—25,000. *Number minted*—25,013 (including 13 assay coins). *Number melted*—7,342. *Net distribution*—17,671.

Original Cost and Issuer. Sale price $1. Issued by the Albany Dongan Charter Coin Committee.

Key to Collecting. This issue was fairly carefully handled during production and distribution, and most examples are relatively free of marks in the fields. Most specimens are lustrous and frosty, although the frost has satiny aspects. Albany half dollars are readily available on the market. The typical example grades from MS–63 to 65 and has at least minor friction and marks.

First Points of Wear. *Obverse:* The hip of the beaver (nearly all coins show at least minor evidence of contact here). *Reverse:* The sleeve of Dongan (the figure at left).

	Distribution	Cert	Avg	%MS	AU-50	MS-60	MS-62	MS-63	MS-64	MS-65	MS-66
1936	17,671	3,114	64.9	100%	$210	$230	$235	$240	$250	$275	$350
	Auctions: $1,293, MS-67, September 2015; $470, MS-66, February 2015; $282, MS-65, June 2015; $176, MS-60, September 2015										

SAN FRANCISCO–OAKLAND BAY BRIDGE OPENING HALF DOLLAR (1936)

Designer: *Jacques Schnier.* **Weight:** *12.50 grams.* **Composition:** *.900 silver, .100 copper (net weight .3617 oz. pure silver).* **Diameter:** *30.6 mm.* **Edge:** *Reeded.* **Mint:** *San Francisco.*

The opening of the San Francisco Bay Bridge was the occasion for a special souvenir fifty-cent piece. The bear depicted on the obverse was a composite of animals in local zoos.

Designs. *Obverse:* A stylized grizzly bear standing on all fours and facing the viewer. *Reverse:* A fading-to-the-horizon view of the San Francisco–Oakland Bay Bridge and part of San Francisco.

Mintage and Melting Data. Authorized on June 26, 1936. *Maximum authorized*—200,000. *Number minted*—100,055 (including 55 assay coins). *Number melted*—28,631. *Net distribution*—71,424.

Original Cost and Issuer. Sale price $1.50. Issued by the Coin Committee of the San Francisco–Oakland Bay Bridge Celebration.

Key to Collecting. These coins are readily available in today's marketplace, with most grading MS–62 to 64, typically with contact marks on the grizzly bear. The reverse design, being complex with many protective devices, normally appears free of marks, unless viewed at an angle under a strong light. The grade of the reverse for a given coin often is a point or two higher than that of the obverse. The fields of this coin often have a "greasy" appearance, rather than being deeply lustrous and frosty.

First Points of Wear. *Obverse:* The bear's body, in particular the left shoulder. *Reverse:* The clouds.

	Distribution	Cert	Avg	%MS	AU-50	MS-60	MS-62	MS-63	MS-64	MS-65	MS-66
1936-S	71,424	3,956	64.6	99%	$145	$150	$160	$175	$185	$200	$300
	Auctions: $1,763, MS-67, January 2015; $764, MS-66, September 2015; $153, MS-64, January 2015; $129, AU-58, January 2015										

COLUMBIA, SOUTH CAROLINA, SESQUICENTENNIAL HALF DOLLAR (1936)

Designer: *A. Wolfe Davidson.* **Weight:** *12.50 grams.*
Composition: *.900 silver, .100 copper (net weight .3617 oz. pure silver).*
Diameter: *30.6 mm.* **Edge:** *Reeded.* **Mints:** *Philadelphia, Denver, and San Francisco.*

Souvenir half dollars were authorized to help finance the extensive celebrations marking the sesquicentennial of the founding of Columbia, South Carolina, in 1786. The pieces had not been minted by the time of the actual celebrations, which took place in late March 1936, and only reached collectors (which the Columbia Sesqui-Centennial Commission expressed desire to sell to instead of to dealers) in December.

Designs. *Obverse:* Justice, with sword and scales, standing before the state capitol of 1786 and the capitol of 1936. *Reverse:* A palmetto tree, the state emblem, with stars encircling.

Mintage Data. Authorized on March 18, 1936. *Maximum authorized*—25,000. *Number minted*—1936-P: 9,007; 1936-D: 8,009; 1936-S: 8,007. *Net distribution*—1936-P: 9,007; 1936-D: 8,009; 1936-S: 8,007.

Original Cost and Issuer. Sale price $6.45 per set of three (single coins $2.15 each). Issued by the Columbia Sesqui-Centennial Commission.

Key to Collecting. These coins were widely distributed at the time of issue, and examples are readily obtainable today. Most grade from MS–63 to 65. They were treated carefully in their minting and distribution, so most coins exhibit lustrous surfaces with very few handling marks. Nearly all, however, show friction on the bosom of Justice and, to a lesser extent, on the high areas of the palmetto-tree foliage on the reverse.

First Points of Wear. *Obverse:* The right breast of Justice. *Reverse:* The top of the palmetto tree.

	Distribution	Cert	Avg	%MS	AU-50	MS-60	MS-62	MS-63	MS-64	MS-65	MS-66
1936	9,007	1,632	65.2	100%	$180	$215	$220	$225	$230	$245	$300
	Auctions: $2,585, MS-68, June 2015; $705, MS-67, May 2015; $235, MS-64, July 2015; $376, MS-62, October 2015										
1936-D	8,009	1,651	65.6	100%	$180	$215	$220	$225	$230	$245	$300
	Auctions: $705, MS-67, June 2015; $294, MS-66, February 2015; $212, MS-65, August 2015; $194, MS-63, July 2015										
1936-S	8,007	1,598	65.4	100%	$180	$215	$220	$225	$230	$245	$300
	Auctions: $7,638, MS-68, August 2015; $999, MS-67, September 2015; $306, MS-66, January 2015; $165, MS-63, October 2015										
Set of 1936 P-D-S						$650	$660	$675	$700	$750	$875
	Auctions: $690, MS-65/66/65, February 2012										

DELAWARE TERCENTENARY HALF DOLLAR (1936)

Designer: *Carl L. Schmitz.* **Weight:** *12.50 grams.* **Composition:** *.900 silver, .100 copper (net weight .3617 oz. pure silver).* **Diameter:** *30.6 mm.* **Edge:** *Reeded.* **Mint:** *Philadelphia.*

The 300th anniversary of the landing of the Swedes in Delaware was the occasion for a souvenir issue of half dollars—as well as a two-krona coin issued in Sweden. The colonists landed on the spot that is now Wilmington and established a church, which is the oldest Protestant church in the United States still used for worship. Carl L. Schmitz's designs were chosen through a competition. These coins were authorized in 1936 and struck in 1937, but not released until 1938, as the Swedes' arrival was actually in 1638.

Designs. *Obverse:* Old Swedes Church. *Reverse:* The ship *Kalmar Nyckel.*

Mintage and Melting Data. Authorized on May 15, 1936. *Minimum authorized*—25,000 (unlimited maximum). *Number minted*—25,015 (including 15 assay coins). *Number melted*—4,022. *Net distribution*—20,993.

Original Cost and Issuer. Sale price $1.75. Issued by the Delaware Swedish Tercentenary Commission, through the Equitable Trust Company of Wilmington.

Key to Collecting. Most examples in today's marketplace grade MS–64 or 65, though they typically exhibit numerous original planchet nicks and marks. Most coins are very lustrous and frosty.

First Points of Wear. *Obverse:* The roof above the church entrance. (Note that the triangular section at the top of the entrance is weakly struck, giving an appearance of wear.) *Reverse:* The center of the lower middle sail (also often shows graininess and nicks from the original planchet).

	Distribution	Cert	Avg	%MS	AU-50	MS-60	MS-62	MS-63	MS-64	MS-65	MS-66
1936	20,993	3,107	64.8	100%	$195	$200	$220	$230	$240	$250	$300

Auctions: $881, MS-67, January 2015; $541, MS-66, October 2015; $188, MS-63, September 2015; $176, MS-60, August 2015

BATTLE OF GETTYSBURG ANNIVERSARY HALF DOLLAR (1936)

Designer: *Frank Vittor.* **weight:** *12.50 grams.* **Composition:** *.900 silver, .100 copper (net weight .3617 oz. pure silver).* **Diameter:** *30.6 mm.* **Edge:** *Reeded.* **Mint:** *Philadelphia.*

On June 16, 1936, Congress authorized a coinage of fifty-cent pieces in commemoration of the 75th anniversary of the 1863 Battle of Gettysburg. Similar to the previously mentioned Delaware Tercentenary coins, the coins were authorized two years before the event commemorated, and were minted a year early as well (in 1937). Paul L. Roy, secretary of the Pennsylvania State Commission, desired for the pieces to be struck at multiple mints—so as to sell more expensive sets of three coins, rather than just Philadelphia issues—but no coins were struck in Denver or San Francisco in the end.

Designs. *Obverse:* Uniformed profile portraits of a Union soldier and a Confederate soldier. *Reverse:* Union and Confederate shields separated by a fasces.

Mintage and Melting Data. Authorized on June 16, 1936. *Maximum authorized—50,000. Number minted—50,028 (including 28 assay coins). Number melted—23,100. Net distribution—26,928.*

Original Cost and Issuer. Sale price $1.65. Issued by the Pennsylvania State Commission, Hotel Gettysburg, Gettysburg. The price was later raised to $2.65 for coins offered by the American Legion, Department of Pennsylvania.

Key to Collecting. Examples are fairly plentiful in the marketplace. The typical coin grades from MS–63 to 65, is deeply frosty and lustrous, and shows scattered contact marks, which are most evident on the cheeks of the soldiers on the obverse and, on the reverse, on the two shields (particularly at the top of the Union shield on the left side of the coin).

First Points of Wear. *Obverse:* The cheekbones of each soldier. *Reverse:* The three ribbons on the fasces, and the top of the Union shield.

	Distribution	Cert	Avg	%MS	AU-50	MS-60	MS-62	MS-63	MS-64	MS-65	MS-66
1936	26,928	3,567	64.4	99%	$470	$480	$480	$500	$600	$750	$950

Auctions: $2,703, MS-67, January 2015; $1,763, MS-66, July 2015; $541, MS-64, September 2015; $423, AU-55, September 2015

NORFOLK, VIRGINIA, BICENTENNIAL HALF DOLLAR (1936)

Designers: *William M. and Marjorie E. Simpson.* **Weight:** *12.50 grams.*
Composition: *.900 silver, .100 copper (net weight .3617 oz. pure silver).*
Diameter: *30.6 mm.* **Edge:** *Reeded.* **Mint:** *Philadelphia.*

To provide funds for the celebration of Norfolk's anniversary of its growth from a township in 1682 to a royal borough in 1736, Congress first passed a law for the striking of medals. The proponents, however, being dissatisfied, finally succeeded in winning authority for half dollars commemorating the 300th anniversary of the original Norfolk land grant and the 200th anniversary of the establish-

ment of the borough. In a strange twist, none of the five dates on these coins actually reflects the year of the coins' actual striking (1937).

Designs. *Obverse:* The seal of the city of Norfolk, Virginia, with a three-masted ship at center. *Reverse:* The city's royal mace, presented by Lieutenant Governor Robert Dinwiddie in 1753.

Mintage and Melting Data. Authorized on June 28, 1937. *Maximum authorized—25,000. Number minted—25,013 (including 13 assay coins). Number melted—8,077. Net distribution—16,936.*

Original Cost and Issuer. Sale price $1.50 locally ($1.65 by mail for the first coin, $1.55 for each additional). Issued by the Norfolk Advertising Board, Norfolk Association of Commerce.

Key to Collecting. Examples are fairly plentiful in today's marketplace, with most in high MS grades. The cluttered nature of the design had a positive effect: all of the lettering served to protect the fields and devices from nicks and marks, with the result that MS–65 and 66 coins are plentiful.

First Points of Wear. *Obverse:* The sails of the ship, especially the lower rear sail. *Reverse:* The area below the crown on the royal mace.

	Distribution	Cert	Avg	%MS	AU-50	MS-60	MS-62	MS-63	MS-64	MS-65	MS-66
1936	16,936	2,935	65.9	100%	$250	$280	$290	$300	$315	$340	$350

Auctions: $1,175, MS-68, September 2015; $482, MS-67, August 2015; $388, MS-66, May 2015; $306, MS-64, August 2015

ROANOKE ISLAND, NORTH CAROLINA, 350TH ANNIVERSARY HALF DOLLAR (1937)

Designer: *William M. Simpson.* **Weight:** *12.50 grams.* **Composition:** *.900 silver, .100 copper (net weight .3617 oz. pure silver).* **Diameter:** *30.6 mm.* **Edge:** *Reeded.* **Mint:** *Philadelphia.*

A celebration was held in Old Fort Raleigh in 1937 to commemorate the 350th anniversary of Sir Walter Raleigh's "Lost Colony" and the birth of Virginia Dare, the first white child born in British North America. Interestingly, Raleigh himself never actually visited America, but only sent ships of colonists who eventually founded a city in his name.

Designs. *Obverse:* Profile portrait of Sir Walter Raleigh in plumed hat and fancy collar. *Reverse:* Ellinor Dare and her baby, Virginia, the first white child born in the Americas to English parents.

Mintage and Melting Data. *Minimum authorized*—25,000 (unlimited maximum). *Number minted*—50,030 (including 30 assay coins). *Number melted*—21,000. *Net distribution*—29,030.

Original Cost and Issuer. Sale price $1.65. Issued by the Roanoke Colony Memorial Association of Manteo.

Key to Collecting. Most of these coins were handled with care during their minting, and today are in high grades. MS-65 pieces are plentiful. Most coins are lustrous and frosty. Partially prooflike pieces are occasionally seen (sometimes offered as "presentation pieces" or "prooflike presentation pieces").

First Points of Wear. *Obverse:* Raleigh's cheek and the brim of his hat. *Reverse:* The head of Ellinor Dare.

	Distribution	Cert	Avg	%MS	AU-50	MS-60	MS-62	MS-63	MS-64	MS-65	MS-66
1937	29,030	4,113	65.1	100%	$165	$175	$185	$195	$215	$230	$250
	Auctions: $5,170, MS-68, October 2015; $940, MS-67, August 2015; $188, MS-64, September 2015; $112, AU-50, November 2015										

BATTLE OF ANTIETAM ANNIVERSARY HALF DOLLAR (1937)

Designer: *William M. Simpson.* **Weight:** *12.50 grams.* **Composition:** *.900 silver, .100 copper (net weight .3617 oz. pure silver).* **Diameter:** *30.6 mm.* **Edge:** *Reeded.* **Mint:** *Philadelphia.*

A souvenir half dollar was struck in 1937 to commemorate the 75th anniversary of the famous Civil War battle to thwart Robert E. Lee's invasion of Maryland. The Battle of Antietam, which took place on September 17, 1862, was one of the bloodiest single-day battles of the war, with more than 23,000 men killed, wounded, or missing.

Designs. *Obverse:* Uniformed profile portraits of generals Robert E. Lee and George B. McClellan, opponent commanders during the Battle of Antietam. *Reverse:* Burnside Bridge, an important tactical objective of the battle.

Mintage and Melting Data. Authorized on June 24, 1937. *Maximum authorized*—50,000. *Number minted*—50,028 (including 28 assay coins). *Number melted*—32,000. *Net distribution*—18,028.

Original Cost and Issuer. Sale price $1.65. Issued by the Washington County Historical Society, Hagerstown, Maryland.

Key to Collecting. Antietam half dollars were handled with care during production. More often seen are scattered small marks, particularly on the upper part of the obverse. Most examples are very lustrous and frosty. MS-65 and finer coins are plentiful in the marketplace.

First Points of Wear. *Obverse:* Lee's cheekbone. *Reverse:* The leaves of the trees; the bridge; and the rim of the coin.

	Distribution	Cert	Avg	%MS	AU-50	MS-60	MS-62	MS-63	MS-64	MS-65	MS-66
1937	18,028	2,897	65.1	99%	$510	$525	$545	$550	$575	$600	$650
	Auctions: $4,935, MS-68, January 2015; $1,411, MS-67, February 2015; $705, MS-65, September 2015; $447, AU-50, January 2015										

NEW ROCHELLE, NEW YORK, 250TH ANNIVERSARY HALF DOLLAR (1938)

Designer: *Gertrude K. Lathrop.* **Weight:** *12.50 grams.* **Composition:** *.900 silver, .100 copper (net weight .3617 oz. pure silver).* **Diameter:** *30.6 mm.* **Edge:** *Reeded.* **Mint:** *Philadelphia.*

To observe the founding of New Rochelle in 1688 by French Huguenots, a special half dollar was issued in 1938. The title to the land that the Huguenots purchased from John Pell provided that a fattened calf be given away every year on June 20; this is represented the obverse of the coin.

Designs. *Obverse:* John Pell, who sold the French Huguenots the land for New Rochelle, and a fatted calf, an annual provision of the sale. *Reverse:* A fleur-de-lis, adapted from the seal of the city.

Mintage and Melting Data. Authorized on May 5, 1936. *Maximum authorized—25,000. Number minted—25,015 (including 15 assay coins). Number melted—9,749. Net distribution—15,266.*

Original Cost and Issuer. Sale price $2. Issued by the New Rochelle Commemorative Coin Committee, through the First National Bank of New Rochelle, New Rochelle, New York.

Key to Collecting. These half dollars received better-than-average care and handling during the minting and distribution process. The typical coin grades MS-64 or higher. Some examples show very light handling marks, but most are relatively problem-free. Some show areas of graininess or light striking on the high spots of the calf on the obverse, and on the highest area of the iris on the reverse. The majority of pieces have lustrous, frosty surfaces, and a few are prooflike (the latter are sometimes offered as "presentation pieces"). A total of 50 Specimen strikings were given to important people in New Rochelle, as well as to the Coinage Committee and some members of the Westchester County Coin Club.

First Points of Wear. *Obverse:* The hip of the calf. *Reverse:* The bulbous part of the fleur-de-lis. (Note that on the central petal the midrib is flatly struck.)

	Distribution	Cert	Avg	%MS	AU-50	MS-60	MS-62	MS-63	MS-64 PF-63	MS-65 PF-64	MS-66 PF-65
1938	15,266	2,684	65.0	100%	$295	$300	$315	$325	$360	$375	$400
	Auctions: $1,410, MS-67, July 2015; $494, MS-66, September 2015; $400, MS-65, January 2015; $317, MS-64, January 2015										
1938, Proof	1–2	3	61.0								
	Auctions: No auction records available.										

Iowa Centennial Half Dollar (1946)

Designer: *Adam Pietz.* **Weight:** *12.50 grams.* **Composition:** *.900 silver, .100 copper (net weight .3617 oz. pure silver).* **Diameter:** *30.6 mm.* **Edge:** *Reeded.* **Mint:** *Philadelphia.*

This half dollar, commemorating the 100th anniversary of Iowa's statehood, was sold first to the residents of Iowa and only a small remainder to others. Numismatists of the time, having largely forgotten the deceptions and hucksterism of the 1930s (and also seen the values of previously issued commemoratives rebound from a low point in 1941), were excited to see the first commemorative coin struck in some years. Nearly all of the issue was disposed of quickly, except for 500 that were held back to be distributed in 1996, and another 500 slated for 2046.

Designs. *Obverse:* The Old Stone Capitol building at Iowa City. *Reverse:* An eagle with wings spreading, adapted from the Iowa state seal.

Mintage Data. Authorized on August 7, 1946. *Maximum authorized*—100,000. *Number minted*—100,057 (including 57 assay coins).

Original Cost and Issuer. Sale price $2.50 to in-state buyers, $3 to those out of state. Issued by the Iowa Centennial Committee, Des Moines, Iowa.

Key to Collecting. Most coins are in varying degrees of Mint State, and are lustrous and frosty. MS–63 to 66 are typical grades. The nature of the design, without open field areas, is such that a slight amount of friction and contact is usually not noticeable.

First Points of Wear. *Obverse:* The clouds above the Capitol, and the shafts of the building near the upper-left and upper-right windows. *Reverse:* The back of the eagle's head and neck. (Note that the head sometimes is flatly struck.)

	Distribution	Cert	Avg	%MS	AU-50	MS-60	MS-62	MS-63	MS-64	MS-65	MS-66
1946	100,057	6,369	65.5	100%	$85	$90	$95	$100	$105	$110	$130

Auctions: $4,700, MS-68, January 2015; $270, MS-67, August 2015; $212, MS-66, October 2015; $84, MS-63, August 2015

Booker T. Washington Memorial Half Dollar (1946–1951)

Designer: *Isaac S. Hathaway.* **Weight:** *12.50 grams.*
Composition: *.900 silver, .100 copper (net weight .3617 oz. pure silver).*
Diameter: *30.6 mm.* **Edge:** *Reeded.* **Mints:** *Philadelphia, Denver, and San Francisco.*

This commemorative coin was issued to perpetuate the ideals and teachings of African-American educator and presidential advisor Booker T. Washington and to construct memorials to his memory. Issued from all mints, it received wide distribution from the start. Unfortunately, the provision that the coins could be minted over several years led to many of the same problems seen with the Arkansas, Boone, Oregon Trail, and Texas pieces from the prior decade.

Designs. *Obverse:* Bareheaded three-quarters profile portrait of Booker T. Washington. *Reverse:* The Hall of Fame at New York University and a slave cabin.

Mintage Data. Authorized on August 7, 1946. *Maximum authorized*—5,000,000 (for the entire series 1946 onward). *Number minted*—1946-P: 1,000,546 (including 546 assay coins); 1946-D: 200,113 (including 113 assay coins); 1946-S: 500,279 (including 279 assay coins); 1947-P: 100,017 (including 17 assay coins); 1947-D: 100,017 (including 17 assay coins); 1947-S: 100,017 (including 17 assay coins); 1948-P: 20,005 (including 5 assay coins); 1948-D: 20,005 (including 5 assay coins); 1948-S: 20,005 (including 5 assay coins); 1949-P: 12,004 (including 4 assay coins); 1949-D: 12,004 (including 4 assay coins); 1949-S: 12,004 (including 4 assay coins); 1950-P: 12,004 (including 4 assay coins); 1950-D: 12,004 (including 4 assay coins); 1950-S: 512,091 (including 91 assay coins); 1951-P: 510,082 (including 82 assay coins); 1951-D: 12,004 (including 4 assay coins); 1951-S: 12,004 (including 4 assay coins). *Net distribution*—1946-P: 700,546 (estimated); 1946-D: 50,000 (estimated); 1946-S: 500,279 (estimated); 1947-P: 6,000 (estimated); 1947-D: 6,000 (estimated); 1947-S: 6,000 (estimated); 1948-P: 8,005; 1948-D: 8,005; 1948-S: 8,005; 1949-P: 6,004; 1949-D: 6,004; 1949-S: 6,004; 1950-P: 6,004; 1950-D: 6,004; 1950-S: 62,091 (estimated); 1951-P: 210,082 (estimated); 1951-D: 7,004; 1951-S: 7,004.

Original Cost and Issuer. Original sale price $1 per coin for Philadelphia and San Francisco, $1.50 for Denver, plus 10¢ postage per coin. In 1946, issued by the Booker T. Washington Birthplace Memorial Commission, Inc., Rocky Mount, Virginia (Dr. S.J. Phillips in charge); Stack's of New York City; and Bebee Stamp & Coin Company (a.k.a. Bebee's). For later issues, costs and distributors varied.

Key to Collecting. Of all commemorative half dollar issues produced up to this point, the Booker T. Washington half dollars were made with the least amount of care during the coining process at the mints. At the time of release, nearly all were poorly struck on the obverse and were marked with abrasions and nicks. Many have graininess and marks on Washington's cheek, from the original planchet surface that did not strike up fully. Many coins grade from MS–60 to (liberally graded) 65. Some have natural or artificial toning that masks the true condition and facilitates gem certification. Prooflike coins are sometimes seen, including for 1947-S (in particular), 1948-S, 1949, and 1951-S. These are not at all mirrorlike, but still have surfaces different from the normal mint frost.

First Points of Wear. *Obverse:* Washington's cheekbone. *Reverse:* The center lettering (FROM SLAVE CABIN TO HALL OF FAME, etc.).

	Distribution	Cert	Avg	%MS	AU-50	MS-60	MS-62	MS-63	MS-64	MS-65	MS-66
1946	700,546	3,309	64.6	99%	$18	$20	$21	$25	$35	$60	$100
Auctions: $1,293, MS-67, January 2015; $705, MS-67, March 2015; $141, MS-66, June 2015; $60, MS-65, March 2015											
1946-D	50,000	1,866	64.8	100%	$18	$20	$22	$25	$30	$60	$100
Auctions: $5,405, MS-68, July 2015; $1,410, MS-67, August 2015; $286, MS-66, October 2015; $32, MS-64, April 2015											
1946-S	500,279	2,762	64.8	99%	$18	$20	$22	$25	$30	$60	$100
Auctions: $4,113, MS-68, March 2015; $1,645, MS-67, August 2015; $123, MS-66, March 2015; $259, MS-64, November 2015											
Set of 1946 P-D-S						$60	$70	$75	$100	$180	$425
Auctions: $110, MS-65/65/65, May 2012											
1947	6,000	931	64.9	100%	$15	$18	$20	$25	$45	$60	$100
Auctions: $3,525, MS-67, July 2015; $400, MS-66, January 2015; $259, MS-66, February 2015; $54, MS-65, January 2015											
1947-D	6,000	745	64.9	100%	$15	$18	$20	$25	$45	$60	$100
Auctions: $1,645, MS-67, June 2015; $494, MS-66, January 2015; $329, MS-66, August 2015; $84, MS-65, September 2015											
1947-S	6,000	971	65.1	100%	$15	$18	$20	$25	$45	$60	$100
Auctions: $2,585, MS-67, January 2015; $176, MS-66, November 2015; $64, MS-65, April 2015; $69, MS-64, January 2015											
Set of 1947 P-D-S						$85	$120	$165	$180	$225	$700
Auctions: $196, MS-65/65/65, January 2012											

	Distribution	Cert	Avg	%MS	AU-50	MS-60	MS-62	MS-63	MS-64	MS-65	MS-66
1948	8,005	836	65.2	100%	$15	$18	$20	$25	$40	$60	$100
Auctions: $999, MS-67, June 2015; $282, MS-66, September 2015; $235, MS-66, February 2015; $79, MS-65, February 2015											
1948-D	8,005	873	65.2	100%	$15	$18	$20	$25	$40	$60	$100
Auctions: $1,028, MS-67, February 2015; $176, MS-66, November 2015; $94, MS-65, January 2015; $36, MS-64, April 2015											
1948-S	8,005	990	65.4	100%	$15	$18	$20	$25	$40	$60	$100
Auctions: $1,293, MS-67, February 2015; $212, MS-66, February 2015; $70, MS-65, February 2015; $38, MS-64, April 2015											
Set of 1948 P-D-S					$85	$150	$185	$215	$250	$525	
Auctions: $220, MS-66/65/65, June 2012											
1949	6,004	854	65.2	100%	$18	$20	$21	$25	$35	$60	$100
Auctions: $2,233, MS-67, January 2015; $400, MS-66, February 2015; $141, MS-65, April 2015; $84, MS-64, January 2015											
1949-D	6,004	808	65.2	100%	$18	$20	$21	$25	$35	$60	$100
Auctions: $1,058, MS-67, October 2015; $165, MS-66, April 2015; $112, MS-65, April 2015; $74, MS-64, January 2015											
1949-S	6,004	883	65.5	100%	$18	$20	$21	$25	$35	$60	$100
Auctions: $940, MS-67, October 2015; $212, MS-66, September 2015; $188, MS-65, September 2015; $79, MS-64, February 2015											
Set of 1949 P-D-S					$60	$63	$75	$105	$400	$525	
Auctions: $320, MS-65/66/66, May 2012											
1950	6,004	661	65.2	100%	$18	$20	$21	$25	$35	$60	$100
Auctions: $541, MS-67, October 2015; $300, MS-66, May 2015; $200, MS-66, October 2015; $74, MS-65, May 2015											
1950-D	6,004	636	65.1	100%	$18	$20	$21	$25	$35	$60	$100
Auctions: $1,763, MS-67, February 2015; $282, MS-66, August 2015; $212, MS-66, September 2015; $84, MS-65, January 2015											
1950-S	62,091	1,405	65.2	100%	$18	$20	$21	$25	$35	$60	$100
Auctions: $940, MS-67, January 2015; $764, MS-67, August 2015; $141, MS-66, August 2015; $34, MS-65, April 2015											
Set of 1950 P-D-S					$60	$65	$75	$135	$300	$500	
Auctions: $725, MS-66/66/66, April 2012											
1951	210,082	1,582	64.6	99%	$15	$18	$20	$25	$50	$60	$100
Auctions: $1,528, MS-67, June 2015; $376, MS-66, January 2015; $147, MS-65, March 2015; $40, MS-64, April 2015											
1951-D	7,004	718	65.3	100%	$15	$18	$20	$25	$40	$60	$100
Auctions: $764, MS-67, January 2015; $259, MS-66, September 2015; $141, MS-65, January 2015; $56, MS-63, April 2015											
1951-S	7,004	812	65.6	100%	$15	$18	$20	$25	$40	$60	$100
Auctions: $764, MS-67, September 2015; $646, MS-67, September 2015; $170, MS-66, July 2015; $165, MS-66, November 2015											
Set of 1951 P-D-S					$95	$120	$160	$200	$275	$450	
Auctions: $475, MS-66/66/66, May 2012; $153, MS-66/66/66, March 2015											

CARVER / WASHINGTON COMMEMORATIVE HALF DOLLAR (1951–1954)

Designer: *Isaac S. Hathaway.* **Weight:** *12.50 grams.*
Composition: *.900 silver, .100 copper (net weight .3617 oz. pure silver).*
Diameter: *30.6 mm.* **Edge:** *Reeded.* **Mints:** *Philadelphia, Denver, and San Francisco.*

Designed by Isaac Scott Hathaway, this coin portrays the conjoined busts of two prominent black Americans. Booker T. Washington was a lecturer, educator, and principal of Tuskegee Institute. He urged training to advance independence and efficiency for his race. George Washington Carver was an agricultural chemist who worked to improve the economy of the American South. He spent part of his life teaching crop improvement and new uses for soybeans, peanuts, sweet potatoes, and cotton waste. Controversy erupted when it came to light that money obtained from the sale of these commemoratives was to be used "to oppose the spread of communism among Negroes in the interest of national defense."

Designs. *Obverse:* Conjoined bareheaded profile portraits of George Washington Carver and Booker T. Washington. *Reverse:* A map of the United States, with legends.

Mintage Data. Signed into law by President Harry S Truman on September 21, 1951. *Maximum authorized*—3,415,631 (total for all issues 1951 onward; consisting of 1,581,631 undistributed Booker T. Washington coins which could be converted into Carver-Washington coins, plus the unused 1,834,000 earlier authorization for Booker T. Washington coins). The following include author's estimates: 1951-P-D-S: *Number minted* (including 18, 4, and 4 assay coins)—110,018; 10,004; 10,004. *Net distribution*—20,018 (estimated); 10,004 (estimated); 10,004 (estimated). 1952-P-D-S: *Number minted* (including 292, 6, and 6 assay coins)—2,006,292; 8,006; 8,006. *Net distribution*—1,106,292 (estimated); 8,006 (estimated); 8,006 (estimated). 1953-P-D-S: *Number minted* (including 3, 3, and 20 assay coins)—8,003; 8,003; 108,020. *Net distribution*—8,003 (estimated); 8,003 (estimated); 88,020 (estimated). 1954-P-D-S: *Number minted* (including 6, 6, and 24 assay coins)—12,006; 12,006; 122,024. *Net distribution*—12,006 (estimated); 12,006 (estimated); 42,024 (estimated).

Original Cost and Issuer. 1951-P-D-S: $10 per set. 1952-P-D-S: $10 per set; many Philadelphia coins were sold at or near face value through banks. 1953-P-D-S: $10 per set; some 1953-S coins were distributed at or near face value (Bebee's prices $9 until January 15, 1952, $10 after that date). 1954-P-D-S: Official sale price: $10 per set; some 1954-S coins were paid out at face value (Bebee's prices for sets $9 until January 20, 1954, $12 after that date). Issued mainly by the Carver-Washington Coin Commission acting for the Booker T. Washington Birthplace Memorial Foundation (Booker Washington Birthplace, Virginia) and the George Washington Carver National Monument Foundation (Diamond, Missouri). Also, for some issues, these dealers: Stack's, Bebee Stamp & Coin Company, Sol Kaplan, and R. Green.

Key to Collecting. Nearly all coins of this issue were handled casually at the mints and also during the distribution process. Most were not fully struck up, with the result that under magnification many tiny nicks and marks can be seen on the higher parts, originating from planchet marks that were not obliterated during the striking process. Many MS examples are available on the market.

First Points of Wear. *Obverse:* Carver's cheekbone. (Note that some pieces were struck poorly in this area; check the reverse also for wear.) *Reverse:* The lettering U.S.A. on the map.

	Distribution	Cert	Avg	%MS	AU-50	MS-60	MS-62	MS-63	MS-64	MS-65	MS-66
1951	20,018	1,104	64.1	99%	$20	$25	$27	$30	$45	$60	$150
Auctions: $940, MS-66, August 2015; $705, MS-66, January 2015; $141, MS-65, August 2015; $36, MS-64, April 2015											
1951-D	10,004	713	64.7	100%	$15	$20	$25	$30	$45	$60	$150
Auctions: $376, MS-66, February 2015; $89, MS-65, January 2015; $84, MS-65, January 2015; $79, MS-65, August 2015											
1951-S	10,004	878	65.1	100%	$15	$20	$25	$30	$55	$60	$150
Auctions: $1,763, MS-67, August 2015; $400, MS-66, August 2015; $275, MS-66, November 2015; $112, MS-65, August 2015											
Set of 1951 P-D-S					$70	$85	$110	$160	$350	$1,150	
Auctions: $140, MS-64/64/64, June 2012											
1952	1,106,292	4,572	64.2	98%	$20	$25	$26	$30	$30	$60	$150
Auctions: $2,820, MS-67, January 2015; $1,880, MS-67, August 2015; $306, MS-66, September 2015; $26, MS-60, August 2015											
1952-D	8,006	547	64.5	100%	$15	$20	$25	$30	$45	$60	$150
Auctions: $764, MS-66, January 2015; $517, MS-66, September 2015; $106, MS-65, August 2015; $30, MS-64, April 2015											
1952-S	8,006	732	65.1	100%	$15	$20	$25	$30	$50	$60	$150
Auctions: $3,200, MS-67, January 2015; $282, MS-66, September 2015; $84, MS-65, August 2015; $50, MS-64, August 2015											
Set of 1952 P-D-S					$85	$100	$115	$150	$285	$1,025	
Auctions: $230, MS-65/65/65, March 2012											

	Distribution	Cert	Avg	%MS	AU-50	MS-60	MS-62	MS-63	MS-64	MS-65	MS-66
1953	8,003	610	64.7	100%	$15	$20	$25	$30	$50	$60	$150
	Auctions: $259, MS-66, January 2015; $94, MS-65, September 2015; $89, MS-65, October 2015; $36, MS-64, May 2015										
1953-D	8,003	514	64.4	100%	$18	$20	$25	$30	$55	$60	$150
	Auctions: $376, MS-65, July 2015; $84, MS-65, May 2015; $48, MS-64, August 2015; $30, MS-64, August 2015										
1953-S	88,020	1,432	64.7	100%	$20	$25	$28	$30	$45	$60	$150
	Auctions: $3,290, MS-67, August 2015; $3,055, MS-67, March 2015; $282, MS-66, October 2015; $170, MS-65, May 2015										
Set of 1953 P-D-S					$95	$110	$120	$150	$270	$1,500	
	Auctions: $300, MS-65/65/65, May 2012										
1954	12,006	869	64.6	100%	$20	$25	$27	$30	$40	$60	$150
	Auctions: $282, MS-66, November 2015; $94, MS-65, July 2015; $79, MS-65, February 2015; $46, MS-64, April 2015										
1954-D	12,006	752	64.4	100%	$15	$20	$25	$30	$45	$60	$150
	Auctions: $676, MS-66, February 2015; $423, MS-66, August 2015; $100, MS-65, August 2015; $82, MS-65, January 2015										
1954-S	42,024	1,345	64.6	100%	$20	$25	$27	$30	$40	$60	$150
	Auctions: $1,998, MS-67, June 2015; $306, MS-66, August 2015; $84, MS-65, August 2015; $34, MS-64, August 2015										
Set of 1954 P-D-S					$80	$90	$100	$125	$210	$1,350	
	Auctions: $316, MS-65/65/65, March 2012										

AN OVERVIEW OF MODERN COMMEMORATIVES

No commemorative coins were made by the U.S. Mint from 1955 through 1981. As the years went by, the numismatic community missed having new commemoratives to collect, and many endorsements for events and subjects worthy of the honor were made through letters to congressmen and other officials, which were often reprinted in pages of *The Numismatist*, the *Numismatic Scrapbook Magazine*, *Numismatic News*, and *Coin World*.

Finally, in 1982, the Treasury Department issued the first commemorative coin since 1954—a silver half dollar celebrating the 250th anniversary of the birth of George Washington. This time around, distribution was placed in the hands of the Bureau of the Mint (today called the U.S. Mint) rather than with a commission or private individuals. The profits accrued to the Treasury Department and the U.S. government. The issue was well received in the numismatic community, with more than seven million of the half dollars sold nationwide.

Then came the 1983 and 1984 Los Angeles Olympiad coins, minted in the subject years for the Los Angeles Olympiad held in 1984. These comprised a diverse and somewhat experimental series, with dollars of two different designs and, for the first time, a commemorative ten-dollar gold coin. Sales were satisfactory, and the supply easily met the demand from collectors and investors.

The concept of a surcharge, or built-in fee, was introduced, with a certain amount per coin going to a congressionally designated beneficiary—in the instance of the Olympic coins, the Los Angeles Olympic Organizing Committee. These and related surcharges became controversial with collectors, some of whom resented making involuntary donations when they bought coins. Today the practice continues, though without as much controversy. Surcharges are the spark that has ignited most commemorative programs, as potential recipients of the earmarked profits launch intense lobbying campaigns in Congress.

In 1986 the 100th anniversary of the completion of the Statue of Liberty was commemorated by the issuance of a copper-nickel–clad half dollar (first of its kind in the commemorative series), a silver dollar, and a five-dollar gold coin, with varied motifs, each depicting on the obverse the Statue of Liberty or an element therefrom. Unprecedented millions of coins were sold.

Then followed a lull in commemorative purchases, although the Mint continued to issue coins celebrating more Olympic Games, various national anniversaries, and significant people, places, events, and other subjects. Some years saw four or five or more individual commemorative programs. Some were well received by the hobby community, but sales of most fell far short of projections. In certain cases these low sales would eventually prove beneficial for collectors who placed orders from the Mint. An example is the 1995 five-dollar commemorative honoring baseball star and Civil Rights hero Jackie Robinson. Only 5,174 Uncirculated pieces were sold, creating a modern rarity.

Most modern commemorative coins have seen only modest secondary-market appreciation, if any. Beyond their retail values, however, the coins will always have significant historical, cultural, and sentimental value. The 2001 American Buffalo silver dollar created a sensation with its bold design harkening back to the classic Buffalo nickel of 1913 to 1938; the issue sold out quickly and soon was commanding high premiums in the collector market. It remains popular and valuable today. In 2014, the National Baseball Hall of Fame commemoratives (a three-coin suite in copper-nickel, silver, and gold) captured mainstream-media headlines and national TV news coverage. Other modern commemoratives have honored American inventors and explorers, branches of the U.S. military, Boy Scouts and Girl Scouts, the Civil Rights Act of 1964, and other important themes, continuing a tradition of special coinage dating back to 1892 and giving today's collectors a broad spectrum of issues to study and cherish.

See pages 1275–1280 for pricing of government commemorative sets and page 1499 for an alphabetical cross-reference list of all commemoratives.

GEORGE WASHINGTON 250TH ANNIVERSARY OF BIRTH HALF DOLLAR (1982)

Designer: *Elizabeth Jones.* **Weight:** *12.50 grams.*
Composition: *.900 silver, .100 copper (net weight .3617 oz. pure silver).*
Diameter: *30.6 mm.* **Edge:** *Reeded.* **Mints:** *Denver (Uncirculated) and San Francisco (Proof).*

This coin, the first commemorative half dollar issued since 1954, celebrated the 250th anniversary of the birth of George Washington. It was also the first 90% silver coin produced by the U.S. Mint since 1964.

Designs. *Obverse:* George Washington on horseback. *Reverse:* Mount Vernon.

Mintage Data. Authorized by Public Law 97-014, signed by President Ronald Reagan on December 23, 1981. *Maximum authorized*—10,000,000. *Number minted*—1982-D: 478,716; 1982-S: 868,326. *Net distribution*—1982-D: 2,210,458 Uncirculated; 1982-S: 4,894,044 Proof.

Original Cost. Sale prices originally $8.50 (Uncirculated) and $10.50 (Proof), later raised to $10 and $12, respectively.

Key to Collecting. Today, Uncirculated 1982-D and Proof 1982-S Washington half dollars are plentiful on the market and are readily available in as-issued condition. They are popular and highly regarded as part of the modern commemorative series.

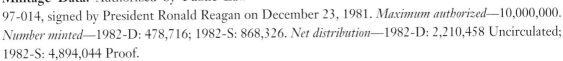

	Distribution	Cert	Avg	%MS	MS-67		
					PF-67		
1982-D ††	2,210,458	4,592	66.9	100%	$11		
Auctions: $123, MS-69, June 2014							
1982-S, Proof	4,894,044	10,013	69.0		$11		
Auctions: $110, PF-70, June 2014; $106, PF-70, September 2015; $106, PF-70, November 2014; $74, PF-70UCam, June 2015							

†† Ranked in the *100 Greatest U.S. Modern Coins* (fourth edition).

Los Angeles Olympiad Discus Thrower Silver Dollar (1983)

Designer: *Elizabeth Jones.* **Weight:** *26.73 grams.* **Composition:** *.900 silver, .100 copper (net weight .7736 oz. pure silver).* **Diameter:** *38.1 mm.* **Edge:** *Reeded.* **Mints:** *Philadelphia and Denver (Uncirculated), San Francisco (Uncirculated and Proof).*

Three distinctive coins were issued to commemorate the 1984 Los Angeles Summer Olympic Games. The 1983 Discus Thrower dollar was the first commemorative silver dollar since the 1900 Lafayette issue.

Designs. *Obverse:* Representation of the traditional Greek discus thrower inspired by the ancient work of the sculptor Myron. *Reverse:* The head and upper body of an American eagle.

Mintage Data. Authorized by Public Law 97-220, signed by President Ronald Reagan on July 22, 1982. *Maximum authorized*—50,000,000 totally for 1983 and 1984. *Number minted*—1983-P: 294,543 Uncirculated; 1983-D: 174,014 Uncirculated; 1983-S: 174,014 Uncirculated and 1,577,025 Proof.

Original Cost. Sale prices $28 (Uncirculated) and $24.95 (Proof, ordered in advance); Proof raised later to $29, and still later to $32. Part of the $10 surcharge per coin went to the U.S. Olympic Committee and the Los Angeles Olympic Organizing Committee.

Key to Collecting. These pieces in both Uncirculated and Proof format can be found today for prices near their issue cost. The vast quantities issued (never mind that 52 million were not sold) made them common. Nearly all surviving coins are in superb gem preservation. Today the aftermarket is supported by coin collectors, not by Olympic sports enthusiasts.

	Distribution	Cert	Avg	%MS	MS-67		
					PF-67		
1983-P	294,543	2,555	69.0	100%	$22		
Auctions: $499, MS-70, September 2014							
1983-D	174,014	1,880	69.0	100%	$22		
Auctions: $7,638, MS-70, April 2013							
1983-S	174,014	1,965	69.0	100%	$22		
Auctions: $8,813, MS-70, April 2013							
1983-S, Proof	1,577,025	5,329	69.0		$22		
Auctions: $1,175, PF-70DCam, April 2014							

LOS ANGELES OLYMPIAD OLYMPIC COLISEUM SILVER DOLLAR (1984)

Designer: *John Mercanti.* **Weight:** *26.73 grams.* **Composition:** *.900 silver, .100 copper (net weight .7736 oz. pure silver).* **Diameter:** *38.1 mm.* **Edge:** *Reeded.*
Mints: *Philadelphia and Denver (Uncirculated), San Francisco (Uncirculated and Proof).*

This coin became a reality at the insistence of the Los Angeles Olympic Organizing Committee. The semi-nude figures on the obverse created some controversy.

Designs. *Obverse:* Robert Graham's headless torso sculptures at the entrance of the Los Angeles Memorial Coliseum. *Reverse:* Perched eagle looking back over its left wing.

Mintage Data. Authorized by Public Law 97-220, signed by President Ronald Reagan on July 22, 1982. *Maximum authorized*—50,000,000 totally for 1983 and 1984. *Number minted*—1984-P: 217,954 Uncirculated; 1984-D: 116,675 Uncirculated; 1984-S: 116,675 Uncirculated and 1,801,210 Proof.

Original Cost. Sales prices $28 (Uncirculated) and $32 (Proof); Proof later raised to $35. Part of the $10 surcharge per coin went to the U.S. Olympic Committee and the Los Angeles Olympic Organizing Committee.

Key to Collecting. These pieces in both Uncirculated and Proof format can be found today for close to what they cost at the time of issue. The vast quantities issued (never mind that 52 million were not sold) made them common. Nearly all surviving coins are in superb gem preservation. Today, the aftermarket is supported by coin collectors, not by Olympic sports enthusiasts.

	Distribution	Cert	Avg	%MS	MS-67 PF-67
1984-P	217,954	1,937	69.0	100%	$22
	Auctions: $705, MS-70, September 2013; $456, MS-70, September 2014; $447, MS-70, August 2015				
1984-D	116,675	1,397	69.0	100%	$23
	Auctions: $4,994, MS-70, April 2013				
1984-S	116,675	1,404	68.9	100%	$23
	Auctions: $9,400, MS-70, April 2013				
1984-S, Proof	1,801,210	4,676	68.9		$24
	Auctions: $411, PF-70DCam, September 2014; $558, PF-70DCam, April 2013				

Los Angeles Olympiad $10 Gold Coin (1984)

Designer: *John Mercanti.* **Weight:** *16.718 grams.* **Composition:** *.900 gold, .100 copper (net weight .4837 oz. pure gold).* **Diameter:** *27 mm.* **Edge:** *Reeded.*

Mints: *Philadelphia, Denver, and San Francisco (Proof); West Point (Uncirculated and Proof).*

This ten-dollar coin was the first commemorative to be struck in gold since the 1926 Sesquicentennial $2.50 gold pieces. Mint engraver John Mercanti based the obverse design on a sketch by James Peed of the Bureau of the Mint's Washington office.

Designs. *Obverse:* Two runners holding aloft the Olympic torch. *Reverse:* Adaptation of the Great Seal of the United States.

Mintage Data. Authorized by Public Law 97-220, signed by President Ronald Reagan on July 22, 1982. *Maximum authorized*—2,000,000. *Number minted*—1984-P: 33,309 Proof; 1984-D: 34,533 Proof; 1984-S: 48,551 Proof; 1984-W: 75,886 Uncirculated and 381,085 Proof.

Original Cost. Sales prices $339 (Uncirculated) and $353 (Proof). Part of the $35 surcharge per coin went to the U.S. Olympic Committee and the Los Angeles Olympic Organizing Committee.

Key to Collecting. These coins are necessarily expensive due to their gold content, but are still quite reasonable. Nearly all surviving coins are in superb gem preservation. Today, the aftermarket is supported by coin collectors, not by Olympic sports enthusiasts.

	Distribution	Cert	Avg	%MS	MS-67
					PF-67
1984-P, Proof	33,309	1,887	69.0		$1,000
Auctions: $764, MS-70, September 2014; $893, MS-70, April 2013; $611, MS-69, October 2014					
1984-D, Proof	34,533	1,972	69.1		$1,000
Auctions: $1,763, PF-70DCam, April 2013; $823, PF-70DCam, September 2014; $624, PF-69DCam, October 2014; $588, PF-69, June 2015					
1984-S, Proof	48,551	1,865	69.2		$1,000
Auctions: $1,116, PF-70DCam, April 2013; $617, PF-69DCam, October 2014; $611, PF-69DCam, October 2014; $564, PF-69, June 2015					
1984-W ††	75,886	1,682	69.3	100%	$1,000
Auctions: $823, PF-70DCam, April 2013; $618, PF-69DCam, October 2014; $588, PF-69, June 2015					
1984-W, Proof ††	381,085	6,075	69.1		$1,000
Auctions: $646, PF-70UCam, January 2015; $646, PF-70UCam, July 2015; $646, PF-70UCam, July 2015; $588, PF-69, June 2015					

†† Both 1984-W Los Angeles Olympiad $10 Gold Coins are ranked in the *100 Greatest U.S. Modern Coins* (fourth edition), as a single entry.

Statue of Liberty Centennial Half Dollar (1986)

Designer: *Edgar Z. Steever IV (obverse), Sherl Winter (reverse).* **Weight:** *11.34 grams.* **Composition:** *.9167 copper, .0833 nickel.* **Diameter:** *30.61 mm.*

Edge: *Reeded.* **Mints:** *Denver (Uncirculated) and San Francisco (Proof).*

The 100th anniversary of the dedication of the Statue of Liberty in New York City harbor in 1886 furnished the occasion for the issuance of three different commemorative coins in 1986. The clad half dollar was the first U.S. commemorative issued in copper-nickel format.

Designs. *Obverse:* Ship of immigrants steaming into New York harbor, with the Statue of Liberty greeting them in the foreground and the New York skyline in the distance. *Reverse:* Scene of an immigrant family with their belongings on the threshold of America.

Mintage Data. Authorized by the Act of July 9, 1985. *Maximum authorized*—25,000,000. *Number minted*—1986-D: 928,008 Uncirculated; 1986-S: 6,925,627 Proof.

Original Cost. Sale prices $5 (Uncirculated, pre-order) and $6.50 (Proof, pre-order); Uncirculated later raised to $6, and Proof later raised to $7.50.

Key to Collecting. So many 1986 Statue of Liberty half dollars were issued that the aftermarket affords the possibility of purchasing the coins not much above the original offering price. Nearly all are superb gems.

	Distribution	Cert	Avg	%MS	MS-67
					PF-67
1986-D	928,008	2,916	69.0	100%	$5
	Auctions: $411, MS-70, April 2013				
1986-S, Proof ††	6,925,627	11,932	69.0		$5
	Auctions: $84, PF-69DCam, January 2015; $129, PF-67, October 2015				

†† Ranked in the *100 Greatest U.S. Modern Coins* (fourth edition).

STATUE OF LIBERTY CENTENNIAL SILVER DOLLAR (1986)

Designer: *John Mercanti.* **Weight:** *26.73 grams.* **Composition:** *.900 silver, .100 copper (net weight .7736 oz. pure silver).* **Diameter:** *38.1 mm.* **Edge:** *Reeded.*
Mints: *Philadelphia (Uncirculated) and San Francisco (Proof).*

These coins, which are also known as Ellis Island silver dollars, feature an excerpt from Emma Lazarus's poem, *The New Colossus.*

Designs. *Obverse:* Statue of Liberty in the foreground, with the Ellis Island immigration center behind her. *Reverse:* Liberty's torch, along with the words GIVE ME YOUR TIRED, YOUR POOR, YOUR HUDDLED MASSES YEARNING TO BREATHE FREE.

Mintage Data. Authorized by the Act of July 9, 1985. *Maximum authorized*—10,000,000. *Number minted*—1986-P: 723,635 Uncirculated; 1986-S: 6,414,638 Proof.

Original Cost. Sale prices $20.50 (Uncirculated, pre-order) and $22.50 (Proof, pre-order); Uncirculated later raised to $22, and Proof later raised to $24.

Key to Collecting. Nearly all coins of this issue are superb gems.

	Distribution	Cert	Avg	%MS	MS-67
					PF-67
1986-P	723,635	4,161	69.1	100%	$24
	Auctions: $170, MS-70, January 2013; $27, MS-69, August 2014				
1986-S, Proof	6,414,638	13,670	69.0		$24
	Auctions: $141, PF-70DCam, April 2014; $106, PF-70DCam, April 2013; $70, PF-69DCam, August 2014; $188, PF-69DCam, November 2014				

STATUE OF LIBERTY CENTENNIAL $5 GOLD COIN (1986)

Designer: *Elizabeth Jones.* **Weight:** *8.359 grams.* **Composition:** *.900 gold, .100 copper (net weight .242 oz. pure gold).* **Diameter:** *21.6 mm.* **Edge:** *Reeded.* **Mint:** *West Point.*

The designs on these five-dollar gold coins created a sensation in the numismatic community and were widely discussed, and the coin received Krause Publications' Coin of the Year Award. The entire authorization of a half million coins was spoken for—the only complete sellout of any commemorative coin of the 1980s.

Designs. *Obverse:* Face and crown of the Statue of Liberty. *Reverse:* American eagle in flight.

Mintage Data. Authorized by the Act of July 9, 1985. *Maximum authorized*—500,000. *Number minted*—95,248 Uncirculated and 404,013 Proof.

Original Cost. Sale prices $160 (Uncirculated, pre-order) and $170 (Proof, pre-order); Uncirculated later raised to $165, and Proof later raised to $175.

Key to Collecting. So many 1986 Statue of Liberty commemoratives were issued that the aftermarket affords the possibility of purchasing the coins at prices near bullion value. Nearly all coins of this issue are superb gems.

	Distribution	Cert	Avg	%MS	MS-67
					PF-67
1986-W	95,248	3,898	69.5	100%	$500
	Auctions: $353, MS-70, August 2014; $329, MS-70, September 2014; $329, MS-70, November 2014; $441, MS-70, February 2013				
1986-W, Proof	404,013	10,958	69.3		$500
	Auctions: $306, PF-70, September 2015; $306, MS-70, April 2015; $282, PF-70, October 2015; $329, PF-69DCam, October 2014				

CONSTITUTION BICENTENNIAL SILVER DOLLAR (1987)

Designer: *Patricia Lewis Verani.* **Weight:** *26.73 grams.*
Composition: *.900 silver, .100 copper (net weight .7736 oz. pure silver).*
Diameter: *38.1 mm.* **Edge:** *Reeded.* **Mints:** *Philadelphia (Uncirculated) and San Francisco (Proof).*

In connection with the 200th anniversary of the U.S. Constitution, observed in 1987, Congress held a competition to design both a silver dollar and a five-dollar gold coin.

Designs. *Obverse:* Quill pen, a sheaf of parchment, and the words WE THE PEOPLE. *Reverse:* Cross-section of Americans from various periods representing various lifestyles.

Mintage Data. Authorized by Public Law 99-582, signed by President Ronald Reagan on October 29, 1986. *Maximum authorized*—1,000,000. *Number minted*—1987-P: 451,629 Uncirculated; 1987-S: 2,747,116 Proof.

Original Cost. Sale prices $22.50 (Uncirculated, pre-issue) and $24 (Proof, pre-issue); Uncirculated later raised to $26, and Proof later raised to $28. A $7 surcharge per coin went toward reducing the national debt.

Key to Collecting. Today, these coins remain inexpensive. Nearly all are superb gems.

	Distribution	Cert	Avg	%MS	MS-67 PF-67
1987-P	451,629	3,632	69.1	100%	$22
	Auctions: $90, MS-70, January 2013				
1987-S, Proof	2,747,116	6,787	68.9		$22
	Auctions: $115, PF-70DCam, April 2013				

CONSTITUTION BICENTENNIAL $5 GOLD COIN (1987)

Designer: *Marcel Jovine.* **Weight:** *8.359 grams.* **Composition:** *.900 gold, .100 copper (net weight .242 oz. pure gold).* **Diameter:** *21.6 mm.* **Edge:** *Reeded.* **Mint:** *West Point.*

A modernistic design by Marcel Jovine was selected for the five-dollar gold coin honoring the bicentennial of the U.S. Constitution.

Designs. *Obverse:* Stylized eagle holding a massive quill pen. *Reverse:* Large quill pen with nine stars to the left (symbolizing the first colonies to ratify the Constitution) and four to the right (representing the remaining original states).

Mintage Data. Authorized by Public Law 99-582, signed by President Ronald Reagan on October 29, 1986. *Maximum authorized*—1,000,000. *Number minted*—214,225 Uncirculated and 651,659 Proof.

Original Cost. Sale prices $195 (Uncirculated, pre-issue) and $200 (Proof, pre-issue); Uncirculated later raised to $215, and Proof later raised to $225.

Key to Collecting. Nearly all coins of this issue are superb gems.

	Distribution	Cert	Avg	%MS	MS-67 PF-67
1987-W	214,225	7,537	69.7	100%	$500
	Auctions: $353, MS-70, August 2015; $317, MS-70, August 2015; $306, MS-70, August 2015; $300, MS-70, September 2015				
1987-W, Proof	651,659	16,604	69.5		$500
	Auctions: $376, PF-70UCam, September 2015; $353, PF-70UCam, January 2015; $329, PF-70UCam, October 2015				

SEOUL OLYMPIAD SILVER DOLLAR (1988)

Designer: *Patricia Lewis Verani (obverse), Sherl Winter (reverse).* **Weight:** *26.73 grams.*
Composition: *.900 silver, .100 copper (net weight .7736 oz. pure silver).*
Diameter: *38.1 mm.* **Edge:** *Reeded.* **Mints:** *Denver (Uncirculated) and San Francisco (Proof).*

The holding of the 1988 Summer Olympic Games in Seoul, Republic of South Korea, furnished the opportunity for the issuance of this silver dollar (as well as a five-dollar gold coin; see next entry).

Designs. *Obverse:* One hand holding an Olympic torch as another hand holds another torch to ignite it. *Reverse:* Olympic rings surrounded by a wreath.

Mintage Data. Authorized by Public Law 100-141, signed by President Ronald Reagan on October 28, 1987. *Maximum authorized*—10,000,000. *Number minted*—1988-D: 191,368 Uncirculated; 1988-S: 1,359,366 Proof.

Original Cost. Sale prices $22 (Uncirculated, pre-issue) and $23 (Proof, pre-issue); Uncirculated later raised to $27, and Proof later raised to $29. The surcharge of $7 per coin went to the U.S. Olympic Committee.

Key to Collecting. These coins are inexpensive. The numismatic market, representing actual buyers and sellers, is not extensive enough to maintain large premiums over the price of hundreds of thousands of coins purchased by the non-numismatic public and then later sold when their novelty passed. Nearly all coins are superb gems.

	Distribution	Cert	Avg	%MS	MS-67 PF-67
1988-D	191,368	2,184	69.0	100%	$22
	Auctions: $247, MS-70, September 2014				
1988-S, Proof	1,359,366	4,956	68.9		$22
	Auctions: $135, PF-70DCam, September 2014; $141, PF-70DCam, April 2013				

SEOUL OLYMPIAD $5 GOLD COIN (1988)

Designer: *Elizabeth Jones (obverse), Marcel Jovine (reverse).* **Weight:** *8.359 grams.*
Composition: *.900 gold, .100 copper (net weight .242 oz. pure gold).*
Diameter: *21.6 mm.* **Edge:** *Reeded.* **Mint:** *West Point.*

Elizabeth Jones's five-dollar obverse design is considered by many to be the high point of commemorative coinage art of the late 20th century. Some observers suggested that, because the event was not held in the United States, the Seoul Olympics were not an appropriate subject for American coinage; regardless, the gold coin was praised to the skies.

Designs. *Obverse:* Nike, goddess of Victory, wearing a crown of olive leaves. *Reverse:* Stylized Olympic flame.

Mintage Data. Authorized by Public Law 100-141, signed by President Ronald Reagan on October 28, 1987. *Maximum authorized*—1,000,000. *Number minted*—62,913 Uncirculated and 281,465 Proof.

Original Cost. Sale prices $200 (Uncirculated, pre-issue) and $205 (Proof, pre-issue); Uncirculated later raised to $225, and Proof later raised to $235. The surcharge of $35 per coin went to the U.S. Olympic Committee.

Key to Collecting. Examples are readily available today.

	Distribution	Cert	Avg	%MS	MS-67
					PF-67
1988-W	62,913	2,398	69.5	100%	$500
	Auctions: $306, MS-69, August 2014; $423, MS-69, March 2013				
1988-W, Proof	281,465	9,684	69.4		$500
	Auctions: $447, PF-70UCam, March 2015; $376, PF-70UCam, March 2015; $353, PF-70UCam, October 2015; $317, PF-70UCam, April 2015				

Congress Bicentennial Half Dollar (1989)

Designer: *Patricia Lewis Verani (obverse), William Woodward (reverse).*
Weight: *11.34 grams.* **Composition:** *.9167 copper, .0833 nickel.* **Diameter:** *30.61 mm.*
Edge: *Reeded.* **Mints:** *Denver (Uncirculated) and San Francisco (Proof).*

The 200th anniversary of the operation of Congress under the U.S. Constitution was observed in 1989, and a suite of commemorative coins was authorized to observe the bicentennial, among them this copper-nickel half dollar.

Designs. *Obverse:* The head of the *Freedom* statue (erected on top of the Capitol dome in 1863) is shown at the center, with inscriptions around, including LIBERTY in oversize letters at the bottom border. *Reverse:* A distant front view of the Capital is shown, with arcs of stars above and below, with appropriate lettering.

Mintage Data. Authorized by Public Law 100-673, signed by President Ronald Reagan on November 17, 1988. The coins were to be dated 1989 and could be minted through June 30, 1990. *Maximum authorized*—4,000,000. *Number minted*—1989-D: 163,753 Uncirculated; 1989-S: 767,897 Proof.

Original Cost. Sale prices $5 (Uncirculated, pre-issue) and $7 (Proof, pre-issue); Uncirculated later raised to $6, and Proof later raised to $8. The surcharge of $1 per coin went to the Capitol Preservation Fund.

Key to Collecting. Not popular with numismatists in 1989, these coins still languish in the marketplace. Exceptions are coins certified in ultra-high grades. The Uncirculated 1989-D half dollar exists with a misaligned reverse, oriented in the same direction as the obverse, instead of the usual 180 degree separation. These are rare and valuable, but are not widely known. Likely, some remain undiscovered in buyers' hands.

	Distribution	Cert	Avg	%MS	MS-67
					PF-67
1989-D	163,753	1,241	69.0	100%	$8
	Auctions: $4,113, MS-70, April 2013				
1989-S, Proof	767,897	3,269	69.0		$8
	Auctions: $382, PF-70, September 2014				

CONGRESS BICENTENNIAL SILVER DOLLAR (1989)

Designer: *William Woodward.* **Weight:** *26.73 grams.*
Composition: *.900 silver, .100 copper (net weight .7736 oz. pure silver).*
Diameter: *38.1 mm.* **Edge:** *Reeded.* **Mints:** *Denver (Uncirculated) and San Francisco (Proof).*

To inaugurate the Congress Bicentennial coins, four coining presses weighing seven tons each were brought from the Philadelphia Mint to the east front of the Capitol building, where in a special ceremony on June 14, 1989, the first silver dollars and five-dollar gold coins were struck (but no half dollars).

Designs. *Obverse:* The statue of *Freedom* full length, with a cloud and rays of glory behind. Lettering around the border. *Reverse:* The mace of the House of Representatives, which is in the House Chamber when that body is in session.

Mintage Data. Authorized by Public Law 100-673, signed by President Ronald Reagan on November 17, 1988. The coins were to be dated 1989 and could be minted through June 30, 1990. *Maximum authorized—3,000,000. Number minted—*1989-D: 135,203 Uncirculated; 1989-S: 762,198 Proof.

Original Cost. Sale prices $23 (Uncirculated, pre-issue) and $25 (Proof, pre-issue): Uncirculated later raised to $26, and Proof later raised to $29. Surcharge of $7 per coin went to the Capitol Preservation Fund.

Key to Collecting. Not popular with numismatists in 1989, these coins today can be found for prices close to bullion value. Exceptions are coins certified in ultra-high grades.

	Distribution	Cert	Avg	%MS	MS-67
					PF-67
1989-D	135,203	2,538	69.0	100%	$22
	Auctions: $646, MS-70, September 2014; $940, MS-70, April 2013				
1989-S, Proof	762,198	4,196	68.9		$24
	Auctions: $457, PF-70DCam, May 2013; $42, PF-69DCam, July 2014; $106, PF-69DCam, November 2014; $940, PF-70, March 2013				

CONGRESS BICENTENNIAL $5 GOLD COIN (1989)

Designer: *John Mercanti.* **Weight:** *8.359 grams.* **Composition:** *.900 gold, .100 copper (net weight .242 oz. pure gold).* **Diameter:** *21.6 mm.* **Edge:** *Reeded.* **Mint:** *West Point.*

To diversify the motifs of the three Congress Bicentennial commemorative coins, 11 artists from the private sector were invited to submit designs, as were members of the Mint's Engraving Department staff. The designs for this five-dollar gold coin were praised in the *Annual Report of the Director of the Mint*, 1989, which stated that the obverse displayed "a spectacular rendition of the Capitol dome," while the reverse "center[ed] around a dramatic portrait of the majestic eagle atop the canopy overlooking the Old Senate Chamber."

Designs. *Obverse:* The dome of the Capitol is shown, with lettering around. *Reverse:* The eagle in the old Senate chamber is depicted, with lettering surrounding.

Mintage Data. Authorized by Public Law 100-673, signed by President Ronald Reagan on November 17, 1988. The coins were to be dated 1989 and could be minted through June 30, 1990. *Maximum authorized*—1,000,000. *Number minted*—46,899 Uncirculated and 164,690 Proof.

Original Cost. Sale prices $185 (Uncirculated, pre-issue) and $195 (Proof, pre-issue); Uncirculated later raised to $200, and Proof later raised to $215. Surcharge of $35 per coin went to the Capitol Preservation Fund.

Key to Collecting. Not popular with numismatists in 1989, these coins today can be purchased in the secondary marketplace for prices close to their bullion value. Exceptions are coins certified in ultra-high grades.

	Distribution	Cert	Avg	%MS	MS-67
					PF-67
1989-W	46,899	2,267	69.5	100%	$500
Auctions: $646, MS-70, September 2014; $376, MS-70, May 2015; $400, MS-69, April 2013					
1989-W, Proof	164,690	5,577	69.4		$500
Auctions: $341, PF-70UCam, October 2015; $341, PF-70, July 2015; $323, PF-70DCam, April 2015; $306, PF-70DCam, January 2015					

EISENHOWER CENTENNIAL SILVER DOLLAR (1990)

Designer: *John Mercanti (obverse), Marcel Jovine (reverse).* **Weight:** *26.73 grams.*
Composition: *.900 silver, .100 copper (net weight .7736 oz. pure silver).* **Diameter:** *38.1 mm.*
Edge: *Reeded.* **Mints:** *West Point (Uncirculated) and Philadelphia (Proof).*

Five outside artists as well as the artists on the Mint Engraving Department staff were invited to submit designs for this silver dollar. In August 1989, secretary of the Treasury Nicholas F. Brady made the final selections.

This is the only U.S. coin to feature two portraits of the same person on the same side. The reverse shows Eisenhower's retirement residence, identified as EISENHOWER HOME.

Designs. *Obverse:* Profile of President Eisenhower facing right, superimposed over his own left-facing profile as a five-star general. *Reverse:* Eisenhower retirement home at Gettysburg, a national historic site.

Mintage Data. Authorized by Public Law 100-467, signed by President Ronald Reagan on October 3, 1988. *Maximum authorized*—4,000,000. *Number minted*—1990-W: 241,669 Uncirculated; 1990-P: 1,144,461 Proof.

Original Cost. Sale prices $23 (Uncirculated, pre-issue) and $25 (Proof, pre-issue; Uncirculated later raised to $26, and Proof later raised to $29. Surcharge of $7 per coin went to reduce public debt.

Key to Collecting. Eisenhower Centennial dollars are appreciated as a fine addition to the commemorative series. Examples are plentiful and inexpensive in the marketplace. Nearly all are superb gems.

	Distribution	Cert	Avg	%MS	MS-67
					PF-67
1990-W	241,669	2,283	69.1	100%	$27
Auctions: $206, MS-70, March 2013					
1990-P, Proof	1,144,461	4,970	69.0		$25
Auctions: $135, PF-70DCam, September 2014; $201, PF-70DCam, March 2013; $42, PF-69DCam, July 2014; $165, PF-68DCam, March 2015					

KOREAN WAR MEMORIAL SILVER DOLLAR (1991)

Designer: *John Mercanti (obverse), James Ferrell (reverse).* **Weight:** *26.73 grams.*
Composition: *.900 silver, .100 copper (net weight .7736 oz. pure silver).*
Diameter: *38.1 mm.* **Edge:** *Reeded.* **Mints:** *Denver (Uncirculated) and Philadelphia (Proof).*

In the annals of commemoratives, one of the more curious entries is the 1991 silver dollar observing the 38th anniversary of the end of the Korean War, struck to honor those who served there. The 38th anniversary was chosen—rather than the 50th or some other typical anniversary—because, during that war, the 38th degree of latitude on the map defined the division between North and South Korea.

Buyers reacted favorably to the coin, and more than 800,000 were produced.

Designs. *Obverse:* Two F-86 Sabrejet fighter aircraft flying to the right, a helmeted soldier carrying a backpack climbing a hill, and the inscriptions: THIRTY EIGHTH / ANNIVERSARY / COMMEM-ORATIVE / KOREA / IN GOD WE TRUST / 1953 / 1991. At the bottom of the coin are five Navy ships above the word LIBERTY. *Reverse:* Outline map of North and South Korea, divided. An eagle's head (representing the United States) is depicted to the right. Near the bottom is the symbol of Korea.

Mintage Data. Authorized by Public Law 101-495 of October 31, 1990. *Maximum authorized*—1,000,000. *Number minted*—1991-D: 213,049 Uncirculated; 1991-P: 618,488 Proof.

Original Cost. Sale prices $23 (Uncirculated, pre-issue) and $28 (Proof, pre-issue); Uncirculated later raised to $26, and Proof later raised to $31. A surcharge of $7 went to fund the Korean War Veterans Memorial.

Key to Collecting. Gem Uncirculated and Proof coins are readily available in the marketplace.

	Distribution	Cert	Avg	%MS	MS-67
					PF-67
1991-D	213,049	2,474	69.1	100%	$30
Auctions: $76, MS-70, July 2014; $106, MS-70, January 2013; $69, MS-70, May 2015					
1991-P, Proof	618,488	3,659	69.0		$25
Auctions: $382, PF-70DCam, September 2014; $505, PF-70DCam, March 2013					

MOUNT RUSHMORE GOLDEN ANNIVERSARY HALF DOLLAR (1991)

Designer: *Marcel Jovine (obverse), T. James Ferrell (reverse).* **Weight:** *11.34 grams.*
Composition: *.9167 copper, .0833 nickel.* **Diameter:** *30.61 mm.* **Edge:** *Reeded.*
Mints: *Denver (Uncirculated) and San Francisco (Proof).*

This half dollar was part of a trio of coins struck to mark the Mount Rushmore National Memorial's 50th anniversary. Surcharges from their sale were divided between the Treasury Department and the Mount Rushmore National Memorial Society of Black Hills, North Dakota, with money going toward restoration work on the landmark.

Designs. *Obverse:* View of Mount Rushmore with rays of the sun behind. *Reverse:* An American bison with the words GOLDEN ANNIVERSARY.

Mintage Data. Authorized by the Mount Rushmore National Memorial Coin Act (Public Law 101-332, July 16, 1990). *Maximum authorized*—2,500,000. *Number minted*—1991-D: 172,754 Uncirculated; 1991-S: 753,257 Proof.

Original Cost. Sale prices $6 (Uncirculated) and $8.50 (Proof); Uncirculated later raised to $7, and Proof later raised to $9.50. Fifty percent of the surcharge of $1 per coin went to the Mount Rushmore National Memorial Society of Black Hills; the balance went to the U.S. Treasury.

Key to Collecting. Examples are easily available today. The coins were carefully struck, with the result that nearly all are superb gems.

	Distribution	Cert	Avg	%MS	MS-67
					PF-67
1991-D	172,754	2,087	69.1	100%	$13
	Auctions: $306, MS-70, September 2014; $823, MS-70, March 2013				
1991-S, Proof	753,257	3,356	69.1		$10
	Auctions: No auction records available.				

Mount Rushmore Golden Anniversary Silver Dollar (1991)

Designer: *Marika Somogyi (obverse), Frank Gasparro (reverse).* **Weight:** *26.73 grams.*
Composition: *.900 silver, .100 copper (net weight .7736 oz. pure silver).* **Diameter:** *38.1 mm.*
Edge: *Reeded.* **Mints:** *Philadelphia (Uncirculated) and San Francisco (Proof).*

The Mount Rushmore silver dollar displays the traditional portraits of presidents George Washington, Thomas Jefferson, Theodore Roosevelt, and Abraham Lincoln as sculpted on the mountain by Gutzon Borglum. The reverse was by former chief sculptor-engraver of the U.S. Mint Frank Gasparro.

Designs. *Obverse:* View of Mount Rushmore with an olive wreath prominently below.
Reverse: The Great Seal of the United States, surrounded by a sunburst, above an outline map of the continental part of the United States inscribed SHRINE OF / DEMOCRACY.

Mintage Data. Authorized by the Mount Rushmore National Memorial Coin Act (Public Law 101-332, July 16, 1990). *Maximum authorized*—2,500,000. *Number minted*—1991-P: 133,139 Uncirculated; 1991-S: 738,419 Proof.

Original Cost. Sale prices $23 (Uncirculated, pre-issue) and $28 (Proof, pre-issue); Uncirculated later raised to $28, and Proof later raised to $31. Fifty percent of the surcharge of $7 per coin went to the Mount Rushmore National Memorial Society of Black Hills; the balance went to the U.S. Treasury.

Key to Collecting. Examples are easily available today. The coins were carefully struck, with the result that nearly all are superb gems.

	Distribution	Cert	Avg	%MS	MS-67
					PF-67
1991-P	133,139	1,908	69.3	100%	$28
	Auctions: $80, MS-70, July 2014; $92, MS-70, January 2013				
1991-S, Proof	738,419	3,941	69.0		$25
	Auctions: $194, PF-70DCam, September 2014; $176, PF-70DCam, June 2013; $174, PF-70DCam, February 2013; $53, PF-69DCam, July 2014				

MOUNT RUSHMORE GOLDEN ANNIVERSARY $5 GOLD COIN (1991)

Designer: *John Mercanti (obverse), William Lamb (reverse).* **Weight:** *8.359 grams.*
Composition: *.900 gold, .100 copper (net weight .242 oz. pure gold).*
Diameter: *21.6 mm.* **Edge:** *Reeded.* **Mint:** *West Point.*

The reverse of the five-dollar Mount Rushmore coin consisted solely of lettering, with no emblems or motifs, the first such instance in the history of U.S. commemorative coins.

Designs. *Obverse:* An American eagle flying above the monument with LIBERTY and date in the field. *Reverse:* MOUNT RUSHMORE NATIONAL MEMORIAL in script type.

Mintage Data. Authorized by the Mount Rushmore National Memorial Coin Act (Public Law 101-332, July 16, 1990). *Maximum authorized—500,000. Number minted—31,959 Uncirculated and 111,991 Proof.*

Original Cost. Sale prices $185 (Uncirculated, pre-issue) and $195 (Proof, pre-issue); Uncirculated later raised to $210, and Proof later raised to $225. Fifty percent of the surcharge of $35 per coin went to the Mount Rushmore National Memorial Society of Black Hills; the balance went to the U.S. Treasury.

Key to Collecting. Examples are easily available today. The coins were carefully struck, with the result that nearly all are superb gems.

	Distribution	Cert	Avg	%MS	MS-67 PF-67
1991-W	31,959	1,642	69.6	100%	$500
	Auctions: $653, MS-70, September 2014; $573, MS-70, November 2014; $353, MS-70, May 2015; $353, MS-70, April 2015				
1991-W, Proof	111,991	4,162	69.4		$500
	Auctions: $456, PF-70DCam, February 2013; $423, PF-70DCam, May 2015; $306, PF-69DCam, October 2014				

UNITED SERVICE ORGANIZATIONS SILVER DOLLAR (1991)

Designer: *Robert Lamb (obverse), John Mercanti (reverse).* **Weight:** *26.73 grams.*
Composition: *.900 silver, .100 copper (net weight .7736 oz. pure silver).*
Diameter: *38.1 mm.* **Edge:** *Reeded.* **Mints:** *Denver (Uncirculated) and San Francisco (Proof).*

The United Service Organizations is a congressionally chartered nonprofit group that provides services, programs, and live entertainment to U.S. military troops and their families. The 50th anniversary of the USO was commemorated with this silver dollar in 1991.

Designs. *Obverse:* Consists entirely of lettering, except for a banner upon which appears USO. Inscriptions include IN GOD WE TRUST, 50th ANNIVERSARY (in script), USO (on a banner, as noted; with three stars to each side), and LIBERTY 1991. *Reverse:* Illustrates an eagle, facing right, with a ribbon inscribed USO in its beak, perched atop a world globe. An arc of 11 stars is in the space below the globe. The legends include FIFTY YEARS / SERVICE (on the left side of the coin), TO SERVICE / PEOPLE (on the right side of the coin).

Mintage Data. Authorized by Public Law 101-404, October 2, 1990. *Maximum authorized*—1,000,000. *Number minted*—1991-D: 124,958 Uncirculated; 1991-S: 321,275 Proof.

Original Cost. Sale prices $23 (Uncirculated, pre-issue) and $28 (Proof, pre-issue); Uncirculated later raised to $26, and Proof later raised to $31. Fifty percent of the surcharge of $7 per coin went to the USO; the balance went toward reducing the national debt.

Key to Collecting. Mintages were low compared to other recent commemorative silver dollars. Today these coins can be purchased for slightly more than their bullion value.

	Distribution	Cert	Avg	%MS	MS-67 PF-67
1991-D	124,958	2,242	69.2	100%	$30
	Auctions: $92, MS-70, March 2013; $86, MS-70, July 2014; $66, MS-70, May 2015				
1991-S, Proof	321,275	2,558	69.0		$23
	Auctions: $881, PF-70DCam, September 2014; $235, PF-70DCam, September 2014; $382, PF-70DCam, April 2013				

CHRISTOPHER COLUMBUS QUINCENTENARY HALF DOLLAR (1992)

Designer: *T. James Ferrell.* **Weight:** *11.34 grams.* **Composition:** *.9167 copper, .0833 nickel.* **Diameter:** *30.61 mm.* **Edge:** *Reeded.* **Mints:** *Denver (Uncirculated) and San Francisco (Proof).*

The 500th anniversary of Christopher Columbus's first trip to the new world was observed in 1992 by a suite of commemoratives, including this clad half dollar. The numismatic tradition fit in nicely with the World's Columbian Exposition coins of a century earlier—the first commemorative half dollars issued in 1892 and 1893.

Designs. *Obverse:* A full-length figure of Columbus walking ashore, with a rowboat and the flagship *Santa Maria* in the background. *Reverse:* The reverse shows Columbus's three ships—the *Nina, Pinta,* and *Santa Maria.*

Mintage Data. Authorized by Public Law 102-281, signed by President George H.W. Bush on May 13, 1992. *Maximum authorized*—6,000,000. *Number minted*—1992-D: 135,702 Uncirculated; 1992-S: 390,154 Proof.

Original Cost. Sale prices $6.50 (Uncirculated, pre-issue) and $8.50 (Proof, pre-issue); Uncirculated later raised to $7.50, and Proof later raised to $9.50. A surcharge of $1 per coin went to the Christopher Columbus Quincentenary Coins and Fellowship Foundation.

Key to Collecting. Examples in the marketplace remain reasonably priced. Nearly all are superb gems.

	Distribution	Cert	Avg	%MS	MS-67 PF-67
1992-D	135,702	978	69.2	100%	$12
	Auctions: $86, MS-70, April 2013				
1992-S, Proof	390,154	2,769	69.2		$12
	Auctions: No auction records available.				

CHRISTOPHER COLUMBUS QUINCENTENARY SILVER DOLLAR (1992)

Designer: *John Mercanti (obverse), Thomas D. Rogers Sr. (reverse).* **Weight:** *26.73 grams.*
Composition: *.900 silver, .100 copper (net weight .7736 oz. pure silver).*
Diameter: *38.1 mm.* **Edge:** *Reeded.* **Mints:** *Denver (Uncirculated) and Philadelphia (Proof).*

Representative Frank Annunzio, a Democrat from Illinois who was prominent in coin legislation for some time, introduced the bill that led to these commemoratives. Interestingly, on the approved sketch for this silver dollar's obverse design, Columbus was depicted holding a telescope—but after it was pointed out that such instrument had not been invented yet in 1492, it was changed to a scroll on the final coin.

Designs. *Obverse:* Columbus standing, holding a flag in his right hand, with a scroll in his left hand, and with a globe on a stand. Three ships are shown in the distance, in a panel at the top border. *Reverse:* A split image is shown, depicting exploration in 1492 at the left, with half of a sailing vessel, and in 1992 at the right, with most of a space shuttle shown in a vertical position, with the earth in the distance.

Mintage Data. Authorized by Public Law 102-281, signed by President George H.W. Bush on May 13, 1992. *Maximum authorized*—4,000,000. *Number minted*—1992-D: 106,949 Uncirculated; 1992-P: 385,241 Proof.

Original Cost. Sale prices $23 (Uncirculated, pre-issue) and $27 (Proof, pre-issue); Uncirculated later raised to $28, and Proof later raised to $31. A surcharge of $7 per coin went to the Christopher Columbus Quincentenary Coins and Fellowship Foundation.

Key to Collecting. Examples in the marketplace remain reasonably priced. Nearly all are superb gems.

	Distribution	Cert	Avg	%MS	MS-67
					PF-67
1992-D	106,949	1,856	69.2	100%	$35
	Auctions: $135, MS-70, March 2013; $86, MS-70, July 2014; $62, MS-70, September 2015				
1992-P, Proof	385,241	3,229	69.0		$25
	Auctions: $441, PF-70DCam, September 2014; $418, PF-70DCam, June 2013; $96, PF-70DCam, April 2013				

CHRISTOPHER COLUMBUS QUINCENTENARY $5 GOLD COIN (1992)

Designer: *T. James Ferrell (obverse), Thomas D. Rogers Sr. (reverse).* **Weight:** *8.359 grams.*
Composition: *.900 gold, .100 copper (net weight .242 oz. pure gold).*
Diameter: *21.6 mm.* **Edge:** *Reeded.* **Mint:** *West Point.*

No portrait from the life of Christopher Columbus is known to exist, so the five-dollar gold commemorative features T. James Ferrell's artistic imagining of the explorer's profile.

Designs. *Obverse:* The artist's conception of Columbus's face is shown gazing to the left toward an outline map of the New World. *Reverse:* The crest of the Admiral of the Ocean Sea and a chart dated 1492 are depicted.

Mintage Data. Authorized by Public Law 102-281, signed by President George H.W. Bush on May 13, 1992. *Maximum authorized*—1,000,000. *Number minted*—24,329 Uncirculated and 79,730 Proof.

Original Cost. Sale prices $180 (Uncirculated, pre-issue) and $190 (Proof, pre-issue); Uncirculated later raised to $210, and Proof later raised to $225. A surcharge of $35 per coin went to the Christopher Columbus Quincentenary Coins and Fellowship Foundation.

Key to Collecting. Examples in the marketplace remain reasonably priced. Nearly all are superb gems.

	Distribution	Cert	Avg	%MS	MS-67
					PF-67
1992-W	24,329	1,344	69.6	100%	$500
	Auctions: $447, MS-70, June 2014; $646, MS-70, September 2014; $317, MS-69, August 2014; $306, MS-69, August 2014				
1992-W, Proof	79,730	2,873	69.5		$500
	Auctions: $353, PF-70DCam, May 2015; $329, PF-70DCam, May 2015; $435, PF-69DCam, April 2013; $306, PF-69DCam, August 2014				

XXV OLYMPIC GAMES HALF DOLLAR (1992)

Designer: *William Cousins (obverse), Steven M. Bieda (reverse).*
Weight: *11.34 grams.* **Composition:** *.9167 copper, .0833 nickel.* **Diameter:** *30.61 mm.*
Edge: *Reeded.* **Mints:** *Philadelphia (Uncirculated) and San Francisco (Proof).*

In 1992 the XXV Winter Olympic Games were held in Albertville and Savoie, France, while the Summer Games took place in Barcelona, Spain. Although the events did not take place in the United States, the rationale for a commemorative coin issue was, in part, to raise money to train American athletes. The same line of reasoning had been used for the coins made in connection with the 1988 Olympic Games held in Seoul, South Korea.

Designs. *Obverse:* A pony-tailed female gymnast doing the stretch against a background of stars and stripes. *Reverse:* The Olympic torch and an olive branch, with CITIUS / ALTIUS / FORTIUS nearby in three lines, Latin for "faster, higher, stronger."

Mintage Data. Authorized by the 1992 Olympic Commemorative Coin Act, Public Law 101-406, signed by President George H.W. Bush on October 3, 1990. *Maximum authorized*—6,000,000. *Number minted*—1992-P: 161,607 Uncirculated; 1992-S: 519,645 Proof.

Original Cost. Sale prices $6 (Uncirculated, pre-issue) and $8.50 (Proof, pre-issue); Uncirculated later raised to $7.50, and Proof later raised to $9.50. The surcharge of $1 per coin went to the U.S. Olympic Committee.

Key to Collecting. Examples are easily available today. Nearly all are gems.

	Distribution	Cert	Avg	%MS	MS-67
					PF-67
1992-P	161,607	1,155	69.3	100%	$8
	Auctions: $59, MS-70, January 2013				
1992-S, Proof	519,645	2,773	69.2		$7
	Auctions: No auction records available.				

XXV Olympic Games Silver Dollar (1992)

Designer: *John R. Deecken (obverse), Marcel Jovine (reverse).* **Weight:** *26.73 grams.*
Composition: *.900 silver, .100 copper (net weight .7736 oz. pure silver).* **Diameter:** *38.1 mm.*
Edge: *Lettered (Uncirculated), reeded (Proof).* **Mints:** *Denver (Uncirculated) and San Francisco (Proof).*

The image on this coin's obverse fit closely that of Fleer's card showing popular baseball player Nolan Ryan, of the Texas Rangers, but the designer denied there was any connection when queried on the subject by the Treasury Department. The Denver Mint Uncirculated dollars have XXV OLYMPIAD incuse four times around the edge, alternately inverted, on a reeded background; these are the first lettered-edge U.S. coins since the 1933 double eagle.

Designs. *Obverse:* A pitcher is shown about to throw a ball to a batter. *Reverse:* A shield, intertwined Olympic rings, and olive branches make up the main design.

Mintage Data. Authorized by the 1992 Olympic Commemorative Coin Act, Public Law 101-406, signed by President George H.W. Bush on October 3, 1990. *Maximum authorized*—4,000,000. *Number minted*—1992-D: 187,552 Uncirculated; 1992-S: 504,505 Proof.

Original Cost. Sale prices $24 (Uncirculated, pre-issue) and $28 (Proof, pre-issue); Uncirculated later raised to $28, and Proof later raised to $32. The surcharge of $1 per coin went to the U.S. Olympic Committee.

Key to Collecting. Examples are easily available today. Nearly all are gems.

	Distribution	Cert	Avg	%MS	MS-67
					PF-67
1992-D ††	187,552	3,812	69.0	100%	$25
	Auctions: $247, MS-70, April 2013				
1992-S, Proof	504,505	3,181	69.0		$23
	Auctions: $588, PF-70DCam, September 2013; $84, PF-70, February 2013; $30, PF-69UCam, January 2015				

†† Ranked in the *100 Greatest U.S. Modern Coins* (fourth edition).

XXV Olympic Games $5 Gold Coin (1992)

Designer: *James Sharpe (obverse), James Peed (reverse).* **Weight:** *8.359 grams.*
Composition: *.900 gold, .100 copper (net weight .242 oz. pure gold).*
Diameter: *21.6 mm.* **Edge:** *Reeded.* **Mint:** *West Point.*

The five-dollar entry in the XXV commemorative coin program features a dynamic sprinter against a backdrop of the U.S. flag. Sales were relatively low compared to other recent gold commemoratives.

Designs. *Obverse:* A sprinter running forward with a vertical U.S. flag in the background. *Reverse:* A heraldic eagle with five Olympic rings and USA above.

Mintage Data. Authorized by the 1992 Olympic Commemorative Coin Act, Public Law 101-406, signed by President George H.W. Bush on October 3, 1990. *Maximum authorized*—500,000. *Number minted*—27,732 Uncirculated and 77,313 Proof.

Original Cost. Sale prices $185 (Uncirculated, pre-issue) and $195 (Proof, pre-issue); Uncirculated later raised to $215, and Proof later raised to $230. The surcharge of $35 per coin went to the U.S. Olympic Committee.

Key to Collecting. Examples are easily available today. Nearly all are gems.

	Distribution	Cert	Avg	%MS	MS-67 PF-67
1992-W	27,732	1,582	69.7	100%	$500
	Auctions: $376, MS-70, May 2015; $364, MS-70, May 2015; $350, MS-70, April 2015; $329, MS-70, June 2015				
1992-W, Proof	77,313	3,154	69.5		$500
	Auctions: $423, PF-70UCam, March 2015; $364, PF-70UCam, April 2015; $358, PF-70UCam, March 2015; $333, PF-70UCam, May 2015				

WHITE HOUSE 200TH ANNIVERSARY SILVER DOLLAR (1992)

Designer: *Edgar Z. Steever IV (obverse), Chester Y. Martin (reverse).* **Weight:** *26.73 grams.*
Composition: *.900 silver, .100 copper (net weight .7736 oz. pure silver).*
Diameter: *38.1 mm.* **Edge:** *Reeded.* **Mints:** *Denver (Uncirculated) and West Point (Proof).*

This coin is one of few depicting Washington buildings that sold out its full authorized limit. Foliage, two trees, and a fountain were in the original sketch, but were removed at the suggestion of the Fine Arts Commission, yielding a clean and crisp design.

Designs. *Obverse:* The north portico of the White House is shown in a plan view, without out shrubbery or background. *Reverse:* James Hoban, architect of the first White House, in a half-length portrait with the original entrance door.

Mintage Data. Authorized by Public Law 102-281, signed by President George H.W. Bush on May 13, 1992. *Maximum authorized*—500,000. *Number minted*—1992-D: 123,803 Uncirculated; 1992-W: 375,851 Proof.

Original Cost. Sale prices (pre-issue only) $23 (Uncirculated) and $28 (Proof). The surcharge of $10 per coin went towards the preservation of public rooms within the White House.

Key to Collecting. The White House dollar has remained popular ever since its issuance. Examples are readily available today and are nearly always found in superb gem preservation, as issued.

	Distribution	Cert	Avg	%MS	MS-67 PF-67
1992-D	123,803	2,076	69.2	100%	$25
	Auctions: $108, MS-70, January 2013				
1992-W, Proof	375,851	3,049	69.0		$23
	Auctions: $194, PF-70DCam, April 2013				

BILL OF RIGHTS HALF DOLLAR (1993)

Designer: *T. James Ferrell (obverse), Dean McMullen (reverse).* **Weight:** *12.5 grams.*
Composition: *.900 silver, .100 copper.* **Diameter:** *30.6 mm.* **Edge:** *Reeded.*
Mints: *West Point (Uncirculated) and San Francisco (Proof).*

This silver half dollar, as well as the silver dollar and five-dollar gold coin issued alongside it, honored James Madison and the Bill of Rights, added to the Constitution in 1789 and intended to give basic rights and freedoms to all Americans. These were the first half dollars to be composed of 90% silver since the George Washington 250th Anniversary of Birth coins in 1982.

Designs. *Obverse:* James Madison seated at a desk, penning the Bill of Rights. Montpelier, Madison's Virginia home, is shown in the distance. *Reverse:* A hand holds a flaming torch, with inscriptions to each side.

Mintage Data. Authorized by Public Law 101-281, part of the White House Commemorative Coin Act, on May 13, 1992. *Maximum authorized*—1,000,000. *Number minted*—1993-W: 193,346 Uncirculated; 1993-S: 586,315 Proof.

Original Cost. Sale prices $9.75 (Uncirculated, pre-issue) and $12.50 (Proof, pre-issue); Uncirculated later increased in $11.50, and Proof later increased to $13.50. The surcharge went to the James Madison Memorial Scholarship Trust Fund.

Key to Collecting. Following the pattern of other commemoratives of the early 1990s, these coins are readily available on the market, typically in superb gem preservation.

	Distribution	Cert	Avg	%MS	MS-67 PF-67
1993-W	193,346	1,217	69.2	100%	$18
	Auctions: $82, MS-70, April 2013				
1993-S, Proof	586,315	2,943	69.0		$15
	Auctions: $441, PF-70DCam, April 2013; $382, PF-70DCam, April 2013				

BILL OF RIGHTS SILVER DOLLAR (1993)

Designer: *William Krawczewicz (obverse), Dean McMullen (reverse).* **Weight:** *26.73 grams.*
Composition: *.900 silver, .100 copper (net weight .7736 oz. pure silver).*
Diameter: *38.1 mm.* **Edge:** *Reeded.* **Mints:** *Denver (Uncirculated) and San Francisco (Proof).*

On June 1, 1992, U.S. Treasurer Catalina Vasquez Villalpando announced a nationwide competition seeking designs for the James Madison / Bill of Rights Commemorative Coin Program, with all entries to be received by August 31. Secretary of the Treasury Nicholas F. Brady selected his favorite motifs from 815 submissions, which were then sent to the Commission of Fine Arts for review.

Many changes were suggested, including simplifying the appearance of Madison's residence, Montpelier.

Designs. *Obverse:* Portrait of James Madison facing right and slightly forward. *Reverse:* Montpelier.

Mintage Data. Authorized by Public Law 101-281, part of the White House Commemorative Coin Act, on May 13, 1992. *Maximum authorized*—900,000. *Number minted*—1993-D: 98,383 Uncirculated; 1993-S: 534,001 Proof.

Original Cost. Sale prices $22 (Uncirculated, pre-issue) and $25 (Proof, pre-issue); Uncirculated later raised to $27, and Proof later raised to $29. The surcharge went to the James Madison Memorial Scholarship Trust Fund.

Key to Collecting. Following the pattern of other commemoratives of the early 1990s, these coins are readily available on the market, typically in superb gem preservation.

	Distribution	Cert	Avg	%MS	MS-67
					PF-67
1993-D	98,383	1,438	69.1	100%	$30
	Auctions: $182, MS-70, January 2013				
1993-S, Proof	534,001	3,045	69.0		$25
	Auctions: No auction records available.				

BILL OF RIGHTS $5 GOLD COIN (1993)

Designer: *Scott R. Blazek (obverse), Joseph D. Peña (reverse).* **Weight:** *8.359 grams.*
Composition: *.900 gold, .100 copper (net weight .242 oz. pure gold).*
Diameter: *21.6 mm.* **Edge:** *Reeded.* **Mint:** *West Point.*

The coin project that resulted in this five-dollar gold coin (and the related half dollar and silver dollar) was encouraged by the Madison Foundation.

Designs. *Obverse:* Portrait of Madison, waist up, reading the Bill of Rights. *Reverse:* Quotation by Madison with an eagle above and small torch and laurel branch at the border below.

Mintage Data. Authorized by Public Law 101-281, part of the White House Commemorative Coin Act, on May 13, 1992. *Maximum authorized*—300,000. *Number minted*—23,266 Uncirculated and 78,651 Proof.

Original Cost. Sale prices $175 (Uncirculated, pre-issue) and $185 (Proof, pre-issue); Uncirculated later raised to $205, and Proof later raised to $220. The surcharge of $10 per coin went to the James Madison Memorial Scholarship Trust Fund.

Key to Collecting. Following the pattern of other commemoratives of the early 1990s, these coins are readily available on the market, typically in superb gem preservation.

	Distribution	Cert	Avg	%MS	MS-67
					PF-67
1993-W	23,266	1,359	69.6	100%	$500
	Auctions: $329, MS-70, August 2014; $652, MS-70, September 2014; $400, MS-69, March 2013				
1993-W, Proof	78,651	3,301	69.4		$500
	Auctions: $306, PF-70DCam, November 2014; $435, PF-70DCam, March 2013; $317, PF-69DCam, August 2014; $329, PF-69DCam, October 2014				

50TH ANNIVERSARY OF WORLD WAR II, 1991–1995, HALF DOLLAR (1993)

Designer: *George Klauba (obverse), Bill J. Leftwich (reverse).* **Weight:** *11.34 grams.*
Composition: *.9167 copper, .0833 nickel.* **Diameter:** *30.61 mm.* **Edge:** *Reeded.* **Mint:** *Philadelphia.*

These half dollars and the other World War II 50th-anniversary coins were issued in 1993 and dated 1991–1995. Despite the importance of the war commemorated, the coins met with a lukewarm response by purchasers.

Designs. *Obverse:* The heads of a soldier, sailor, and airman are shown superimposed on a V (for victory), with a B-17 bomber flying overhead. *Reverse:* An American Marine is shown in action during the takeover of a Japanese-held island in the South Pacific. A carrier-based fighter plane flies overhead.

Mintage Data. Authorized by Public Law 102-414, signed by President William J. Clinton on October 14, 1992. *Maximum authorized*—2,000,000. *Number minted*—197,072 Uncirculated and 317,396 Proof.

Original Cost. Sale prices $8 (Uncirculated, pre-issue) and $9 (Proof, pre-issue); Uncirculated later raised to $9, and Proof later raised to $10. The surcharge of $2 per coin was split between the American Battle Monuments Commission (to aid in the construction of the World War II Monument in the nation's capital) and the Battle of Normandy Foundation (to assist in the erection of a monument in France).

Key to Collecting. Examples are easily enough found in the marketplace today and are nearly always of superb gem quality.

	Distribution	Cert	Avg	%MS	MS-67
					PF-67
1991–1995 (1993-P)	197,072	1,275	69.1	100%	$15
Auctions: $165, MS-70Cam, September 2014; $529, MS-70Cam, April 2013; $153, MS-70, June 2013					
1991–1995 (1993-P), Proof	317,396	2,547	69.0		$15
Auctions: No auction records available.					

50TH ANNIVERSARY OF WORLD WAR II, 1991–1995, SILVER DOLLAR (1993)

Designer: *Thomas D. Rogers Sr.* **Weight:** *26.73 grams.*
Composition: *.900 silver, .100 copper (net weight .7736 oz. pure silver).*
Diameter: *38.1 mm.* **Edge:** *Reeded.* **Mints:** *Denver (Uncirculated) and West Point (Proof).*

The designs for these silver dollars and the related half dollars and five-dollar gold coins were the result of a competition. The works of five artists were selected (only one of them, Thomas D. Rogers Sr., being from the Mint staff). It was mandated that the dollar use the Battle of Normandy as a theme.

Designs. *Obverse:* An American soldier is shown as he runs ashore on the beach in Normandy during the D-Day invasion on June 6, 1944, which launched from England to liberate France.

Reverse: The reverse illustrates the shoulder patch used on a uniform of Dwight D. Eisenhower's Supreme Headquarters Allied Expeditionary Force, with a quotation from Eisenhower.

Mintage Data. Authorized by Public Law 102-414, signed by President William J. Clinton on October 14, 1992. *Maximum authorized*—1,000,000. *Number minted*—1993-D: 107,240 Uncirculated; 1993-W: 342,041 Proof.

Original Cost. Sale prices $23 (Uncirculated, pre-issue) and $27 (Proof, pre-issue); Uncirculated later raised to $28, and Proof later raised to $31. The surcharge of $2 per coin was split between the American Battle Monuments Commission (to aid in the construction of the World War II Monument in the nation's capital) and the Battle of Normandy Foundation (to assist in the erection of a monument in France).

Key to Collecting. Examples are easily enough found in the marketplace today and are nearly always of superb gem quality.

	Distribution	Cert	Avg	%MS	MS-67 / PF-67
1991–1995 (1993-D)	107,240	2,048	69.3	100%	$35
Auctions: $118, MS-70, January 2013; $86, MS-70, July 2014; $74, MS-70, August 2015; $74, MS-70, May 2015					
1991–1995 (1993-W), Proof	342,041	3,426	69.0		$35
Auctions: $206, PF-70DCam, September 2014					

50TH ANNIVERSARY OF WORLD WAR II, 1991–1995, $5 GOLD COIN (1993)

Designer: *Charles J. Madsen (obverse), Edward Southworth Fisher (reverse).*
Weight: *8.359 grams.* **Composition:** *.900 gold, .100 copper (net weight .242 oz. pure gold).*
Diameter: *21.6 mm.* **Edge:** *Reeded.* **Mint:** *West Point.*

The approval of the American Legion, Veterans of Foreign Wars of the United States, American Veterans of World War, Korea and Vietnam (AMVETS), and the Disabled American Veterans, was required for the designs of all three 50th Anniversary of World War II commemoratives. The five-dollar coin was mandated to reflect the Allied victory in the war.

Designs. *Obverse:* An American soldier holds his rifle and raises his arm to indicate victory. *Reverse:* A large V (for victory) is at the center, with three dots and a dash over it, the Morse code for that letter. Branches are to each side.

Mintage Data. Authorized by Public Law 102-414, signed by President William J. Clinton on October 14, 1992. *Maximum authorized*—300,000. *Number minted*—23,672 Uncirculated and 67,026 Proof.

Original Cost. Sale prices $170 (Uncirculated, pre-issue) and $185 (Proof, pre-issue); Uncirculated later raised to $185, and Proof later raised to $220. The surcharge of $35 per coin was split between the American Battle Monuments Commission (to aid in the construction of the World War II Monument in the nation's capital) and the Battle of Normandy Foundation (to assist in the erection of a monument in France).

Key to Collecting. Examples are easily enough found in the marketplace today and are nearly always of superb gem quality.

	Distribution	Cert	Avg	%MS	MS-67 PF-67
1991–1995 (1993-W)	23,672	1,446	69.6	100%	$500
Auctions: $646, MS-70, September 2014; $411, MS-70, April 2013; $353, MS-69, August 2014					
1991–1995 (1993-W), Proof	67,026	2,593	69.3		$500
Auctions: $458, PF-70DCam, April 2013; $382, PF-70DCam, April 2013; $333, PF-69DCam, August 2014					

THOMAS JEFFERSON 250TH ANNIVERSARY OF BIRTH, 1993, SILVER DOLLAR (1994)

Designer: *T. James Ferrell.* **Weight:** *26.73 grams.*
Composition: *.900 silver, .100 copper (net weight .7736 oz. pure silver).*
Diameter: *38.1 mm.* **Edge:** *Reeded.* **Mints:** *Philadelphia (Uncirculated) and San Francisco (Proof).*

The 250th anniversary in 1993 of the birth of Thomas Jefferson in 1743 furnished the occasion for a commemorative silver dollar. The obverse portrait was based on an 1805 painting by Gilbert Stuart.

Designs. *Obverse:* Profile bust of President Thomas Jefferson. *Reverse:* Monticello, Jefferson's home.

Mintage Data. Authorized under Public Law 103-186, signed by President William J. Clinton on December 14, 1993. *Maximum authorized*—600,000. *Number minted*—1993-P: 266,927 Uncirculated; 1993-S: 332,891 Proof.

Original Cost. Sale prices $27 (Uncirculated, pre-issue) and $31 (Proof, pre-issue); Uncirculated later raised to $32, and Proof later raised to $35. The surcharge of $10 per coin went to the Jefferson Endowment Fund.

Key to Collecting. Although the Jefferson dollar was a popular sellout in its time, examples are easily found in the numismatic marketplace and are nearly always of superb gem quality. Most in demand, from the enthusiasm of five-cent piece collectors, are the special sets issued with the frosty Uncirculated 1994-P Jefferson nickel.

	Distribution	Cert	Avg	%MS	MS-67 PF-67
1993-P	266,927	3,545	69.2	100%	$25
Auctions: $86, MS-70, January 2013					
1993-S, Proof	332,891	2,792	69.0		$23
Auctions: $400, PF-70DCam, March 2013					

U.S. Capitol Bicentennial Silver Dollar (1994)

Designer: *William Cousins (obverse), John Mercanti (reverse).* **Weight:** *26.73 grams.*
Composition: *.900 silver, .100 copper (net weight .7736 oz. pure silver).*
Diameter: *38.1 mm.* **Edge:** *Reeded.* **Mints:** *Denver (Uncirculated) and San Francisco (Proof).*

These silver dollars commemorated the 200th anniversary of the U.S. Capitol in Washington, D.C. Although the Federal City, as it was called, was laid out in the 1790s, it was not until 1800 that the federal government relocated there from Philadelphia. In honor of the recently deceased first president, the name was changed to Washington City, or, in popular use, Washington. The Capitol building design represented the work of several architects and artists, among them Benjamin Latrobe, Charles Bulfinch, and Constantino Brumidi.

Designs. *Obverse:* Dome of the Capitol with stars surrounding the *Freedom* statue. *Reverse:* Shield with four American flags, branches, and surmounted by an eagle, a motif based on the center area of a stained-glass window near the House and Senate grand staircases (produced by J. & G. Gibson, of Philadelphia, in 1859 and 1860).

Mintage Data. Authorized by Public Law 103-186, signed by President William J. Clinton on December 14, 1993. *Maximum authorized*—500,000. *Number minted*—1994-D: 68,332 Uncirculated; 1994-S: 279,579 Proof.

Original Cost. Sale prices $32 (Uncirculated, pre-issue) and $36 (Proof, pre-issue; Uncirculated later raised to $37, and Proof later raised to $40. The surcharge of $15 per coin went to the United States Capitol Preservation Commission. A Mint announcement noted that this was to go "for the construction of the Capitol Visitor Center" (itself the subject of a 2001 commemorative dollar).

Key to Collecting. Superb gem Mint State and Proof coins are easily available.

	Distribution	Cert	Avg	%MS	MS-67 / PF-67
1994-D	68,332	1,608	69.4	100%	$30
	Auctions: $101, MS-70, January 2013; $100, MS-70, August 2015; $80, MS-70, July 2014				
1994-S, Proof	279,579	2,198	69.0		$30
	Auctions: $294, PF-70DCam, April 2013; $270, PF-70DCam, September 2014; $217, PF-70DCam, August 2014				

U.S. PRISONER OF WAR MEMORIAL SILVER DOLLAR (1994)

Designer: *Tom Nielsen (obverse), Edgar Z. Steever IV (reverse).* **Weight:** *26.73 grams.*
Composition: *.900 silver, .100 copper (net weight .7736 oz. pure silver).*
Diameter: *38.1 mm.* **Edge:** *Reeded.* **Mints:** *West Point (Uncirculated) and Philadelphia (Proof).*

The proposed National Prisoner of War
Museum set the stage for the issuance of a
silver dollar observing the tribulations of
prisoners held by foreign military powers.
The obverse designer, Nielsen, was a decorated former prisoner of war employed by the
Bureau of Veterans Affairs.

Designs. *Obverse:* An eagle with a chain on
one leg flies through a circle of barbed wire,
representing flight to freedom. *Reverse:* Plan view, with landscaping, of the proposed National Prisoner
of War Museum.

Mintage Data. Authorized by Public Law 103-186, signed by President William J. Clinton on December 14, 1993. *Maximum authorized*—500,000. *Number minted*—1994-W: 54,893 Uncirculated; 1994-P:
224,449 Proof.

Original Cost. Sale prices $27 (Uncirculated, pre-issue) and $31 (Proof, pre-issue); Uncirculated later
raised to $32, and Proof later raised to $35. The surcharge of $10 per coin went toward the construction
of the museum.

Key to Collecting. The 1994-W dollar is in special demand due to its relatively low mintage. Both
varieties are seen with frequency in the marketplace and are nearly always superb gems.

	Distribution	Cert	Avg	%MS	MS-67
					PF-67
1994-W	54,893	1,997	69.4	100%	$50
	Auctions: $129, MS-70, January 2014; $100, MS-70, February 2015; $94, MS-70, January 2015; $87, MS-70, May 2015				
1994-P, Proof	224,449	2,851	68.9		$55
	Auctions: $1,116, PF-70DCam, September 2014; $999, PF-70DCam, September 2014; $1,763, PF-70DCam, January 2013				

WOMEN IN MILITARY SERVICE MEMORIAL SILVER DOLLAR (1994)

Designer: *T. James Ferrell.* **Weight:** *26.73 grams.*
Composition: *.900 silver, .100 copper (net weight .7736 oz. pure silver).*
Diameter: *38.1 mm.* **Edge:** *Reeded.* **Mints:** *West Point (Uncirculated) and Philadelphia (Proof).*

These coins were issued to honor women
in the military and help fund the Women in
Military Service for America Memorial at the
ceremonial entrance to Arlington National
Cemetery (which became a reality and opened
in October 1997 on a 4.2-acre site).

Designs. *Obverse:* Servicewomen from the
Army, Marine Corps, Navy, Air Force, and

Coast Guard, with the names of these branches around the border. *Reverse:* A diagonal view of the front of the proposed the Women in Military Service for America Memorial.

Mintage Data. Authorized by Public Law 103-186, signed by President William J. Clinton on December 14, 1993. *Maximum authorized*—500,000. *Number minted*—1994-W: 69,860 Uncirculated; 1994-P: 241,278 Proof.

Original Cost. Sale prices $27 (Uncirculated, pre-issue) and $31 (Proof, pre-issue); Uncirculated later raised to $32, and Proof later raised to $35. The surcharge of $10 per coin went towards the construction of the memorial.

Key to Collecting. Mirroring the situation for other commemoratives of the era, these are easily enough found on the market and are usually in superb gem grades.

	Distribution	Cert	Avg	%MS	MS-67 PF-67
1994-W	69,860	3,328	69.3	100%	$32
Auctions: $72, MS-70, April 2013					
1994-P, Proof	241,278	2,485	69.0		$38
Auctions: $646, PF-70DCam, April 2013					

Vietnam Veterans Memorial Silver Dollar (1994)

Designer: *John Mercanti (obverse), Thomas D. Rogers Sr. (reverse).* **Weight:** *26.73 grams.*
Composition: *.900 silver, .100 copper (net weight .7736 oz. pure silver).*
Diameter: *38.1 mm.* **Edge:** *Reeded.* **Mints:** *West Point (Uncirculated) and Philadelphia (Proof).*

In Washington, D.C., the Vietnam Veterans Memorial, often called the Memorial Wall, has been one of the city's prime attractions since it was dedicated in 1984.

Designs. *Obverse:* A hand touching the Wall. In the distance to the right is the Washington Monument. *Reverse:* Three military medals and ribbons surrounded with lettering.

Mintage Data. Authorized by Public Law 103-186, signed by President William J. Clinton on December 14, 1993. *Maximum authorized*—500,000. *Number minted*—1994-W: 57,290 Uncirculated; 1994-P: 227,671 Proof.

Original Cost. Sale prices $27 (Uncirculated) and $31 (Proof); Uncirculated later raised to $32, and Proof later raised to $35. The surcharge of $10 per coin went towards the construction of a visitor's center near the Memorial.

Key to Collecting. Gem specimens are easily available. The aftermarket price for this dollar is stronger than for most others of the early 1990s.

	Distribution	Cert	Avg	%MS	MS-67 PF-67
1994-W	57,290	1,942	69.3	100%	$50
Auctions: $141, MS-70, January 2013; $103, MS-70, July 2014; $84, MS-70, May 2015					
1994-P, Proof	227,671	3,269	68.9		$60
Auctions: $2,115, PF-70DCam, April 2013; $793, PF-70DCam, August 2015; $770, PF-70DCam, September 2014					

World Cup Tournament Half Dollar (1994)

Designer: *Richard T. LaRoche (obverse), Dean McMullen (reverse).* **Weight:** *11.34 grams.*
Composition: *.9167 copper, .0833 nickel.* **Diameter:** *30.61 mm.* **Edge:** *Reeded.*
Mints: *Denver (Uncirculated) and Philadelphia (Proof).*

The United States' hosting of the XV FIFA World Cup playoff—the culmination of soccer games among 141 nations—was commemorated with this copper-nickel half dollar, as well as a silver dollar and a five-dollar gold coin.

Designs. *Obverse:* A soccer player in action, on the run with a ball near his feet. *Reverse:* The World Cup USA logo at the center, flanked by branches.

Mintage Data. Authorized by Public Law 102-281, signed by President George H.W. Bush on May 13, 1992. *Maximum authorized*—5,000,000. *Number minted*—1994-D: 168,208 Uncirculated; 1994-P: 609,354 Proof.

Original Cost. Sale prices $8.75 (Uncirculated, pre-issue) and $9.75 (Proof, pre-issue); Uncirculated later raised to $9.50, and Proof later raised to $10.50. The surcharge of $1 per coin went to the World Cup Organizing Committee.

Key to Collecting. The World Cup coins are reasonably priced in the secondary market. Nearly all are superb gems.

	Distribution	Cert	Avg	%MS	MS-67
					PF-67
1994-D	168,208	1,029	69.1	100%	$8
Auctions: $212, MS-70, September 2014					
1994-P, Proof	609,354	3,190	69.0		$8
Auctions: $411, PF-70, September 2014; $558, PF-70, April 2013					

World Cup Tournament Silver Dollar (1994)

Designer: *Dean McMullen.* **Weight:** *26.73 grams.*
Composition: *.900 silver, .100 copper (net weight .7736 oz. pure silver).*
Diameter: *38.1 mm.* **Edge:** *Reeded.* **Mints:** *Denver (Uncirculated) and San Francisco (Proof).*

In terms of mintage goals, this program was one of the greatest failures in the history of American commemorative coinage. The U.S. Mint stated it lost $3.5 million in the effort, noting that there simply were too many commemorative programs in progress, each with excessive mintage expectations. The only winner in the World Cup scenario seemed to be the recipient of the surcharge.

Designs. *Obverse:* Two competing soccer players converge on a soccer ball in play. *Reverse:* The World Cup USA logo at the center, flanked by branches.

Mintage Data. Authorized by Public Law 102-281, signed by President George H.W. Bush on May 13, 1992. *Maximum authorized*—5,000,000. *Number minted*—1994-D: 81,524 Uncirculated; 1994-S: 577,090 Proof.

Original Cost. Sale prices $23 (Uncirculated, pre-issue) and $27 (Proof, pre-issue); Uncirculated later raised to $28, and Proof later raised to $31. The surcharge of $7 per coin went to the World Cup Organizing Committee.

Key to Collecting. The World Cup coins are reasonably priced in the secondary market. Nearly all are superb gems.

	Distribution	Cert	Avg	%MS	MS-67 / PF-67
1994-D	81,524	1,441	69.0	100%	$30
Auctions: $329, MS-70, September 2014; $764, MS-70, April 2013					
1994-S, Proof	577,090	3,113	69.0		$35
Auctions: $170, PF-70DCam, September 2014; $294, PF-70DCam, April 2013					

World Cup Tournament $5 Gold Coin (1994)

Designer: *William J. Krawczewicz (obverse), Dean McMullen (reverse).* **Weight:** *8.359 grams.*
Composition: *.900 gold, .100 copper (net weight .242 oz. pure gold).*
Diameter: *21.6 mm.* **Edge:** *Reeded.* **Mint:** *West Point.*

The U.S. Mint's many recent commemoratives had caused buyer fatigue by the time the World Cup Tournament coins came out. Collectors blamed the Mint for creating coins that few people wanted. The complaints should have gone to Congress instead. Faced with so many coins to produce, often with very short deadlines, the Mint simply had no time to call for designs to be submitted from leading artists.

Designs. *Obverse:* The World Cup trophy. *Reverse:* The World Cup USA logo at the center, flanked by branches.

Mintage Data. Authorized by Public Law 102-281, signed by President George H.W. Bush on May 13, 1992. *Maximum authorized*—750,000. *Number minted*—22,447 Uncirculated and 89,614 Proof.

Original Cost. Sale prices $170 (Uncirculated, pre-issue) and $185 (Proof, pre-issue); Uncirculated later raised to $200, and Proof later raised to $220. The surcharge of $35 per coin went to the World Cup Organizing Committee.

Key to Collecting. The World Cup coins are reasonably priced in the secondary market. Nearly all are superb gems.

	Distribution	Cert	Avg	%MS	MS-67 / PF-67
1994-W	22,447	1,095	69.5	100%	$500
Auctions: $382, MS-70, September 2014; $382, MS-70, November 2014; $448, MS-70, April 2013; $306, MS-69, November 2014					
1994-W, Proof	89,614	2,202	69.3		$500
Auctions: $470, PF-70DCam, June 2013; $295, PF-69DCam, October 2014; $306, PF-68DCam, February 2015					

(1995–1996) ATLANTA CENTENNIAL OLYMPIC GAMES
BASKETBALL HALF DOLLAR (1995)

Designer: *Clint Hansen (obverse), T. James Ferrell (reverse).* **Weight:** *11.34 grams.*
Composition: *.9167 copper, .0833 nickel.* **Diameter:** *30.61 mm.* **Edge:** *Reeded.* **Mint:** *San Francisco.*

Men's basketball has been an Olympic sport since the 1936 Summer Games in Berlin. The 1996 U.S. team, also known as "Dream Team III," won the gold medal at the Summer Games in Atlanta.

Designs. *Obverse:* Three basketball players. *Reverse:* Symbol of the Atlanta Committee for the Olympic Games superimposed over the Atlantic Ocean as viewed from space.

Mintage Data. Authorized by Public Law 102-390, signed by President George H.W. Bush on October 6, 1992. *Maximum authorized*—2,000,000. *Number minted*—171,001 Uncirculated and 169,655 Proof.

Original Cost. Sale prices $10.50 (Uncirculated, pre-issue) and $11.50 (Proof, pre-issue); Uncirculated later raised to $11.50, and Proof later raised to $12.50. The surcharge per coin went to the Atlanta Olympic Committee.

Key to Collecting. Enough 1995 and 1996 Olympics coins are on the aftermarket that finding designs of choice, or forming a set, will be no problem. The obverse designs are varied, and in total the collection is an excellent representation of this quadrennial worldwide competition.

	Distribution	Cert	Avg	%MS	MS-67
					PF-67
1995-S	171,001	1,460	69.3	100%	$18
	Auctions: $118, MS-70, July 2014; $76, MS-70, July 2013				
1995-S, Proof	169,655	2,058	69.1		$18
	Auctions: No auction records available.				

(1995–1996) ATLANTA CENTENNIAL OLYMPIC GAMES
BASEBALL HALF DOLLAR (1995)

Designer: *Edgar Z. Steever IV (obverse), T. James Ferrell (reverse).* **Weight:** *11.34 grams.*
Composition: *.9167 copper, .0833 nickel.* **Diameter:** *30.61 mm.* **Edge:** *Reeded.* **Mint:** *San Francisco.*

Baseball was an official Olympic sport at each Summer Games between 1992 and 2008, but was voted out of the 2012 London Olympics and will remain off the docket until at least 2024 following a 2013 International Olympic Committee vote. The team representing Cuba took home the gold medal at the 1996 Atlanta Olympics.

Designs. *Obverse:* Batter at the plate with catcher and umpire. *Reverse:* Symbol of the Atlanta Committee for the Olympic Games superimposed over the Atlantic Ocean as viewed from space.

Mintage Data. Authorized by Public Law 102-390, signed by President George H.W. Bush on October 6, 1992. *Maximum authorized*—2,000,000. *Number minted*—164,605 Uncirculated and 118,087 Proof.

Original Cost. Sale prices $10.50 (Uncirculated, pre-issue) and $11.50 (Proof, pre-issue); Uncirculated later raised to $11.50, and Proof later raised to $12.50. The surcharge per coin went to the Atlanta Olympic Committee.

Key to Collecting. Enough 1995 and 1996 Olympics coins are on the aftermarket that finding designs of choice, or forming a set, will be no problem. The obverse designs are varied, and in total the collection is an excellent representation of this quadrennial worldwide competition.

	Distribution	Cert	Avg	%MS	MS-67 PF-67
1995-S	164,605	1,111	69.3	100%	$16
Auctions: $130, MS-70, April 2013					
1995-S, Proof	118,087	1,631	69.1		$20
Auctions: $329, PF-70DCam, September 2014; $200, PF-70DCam, September 2014					

(1995–1996) ATLANTA CENTENNIAL OLYMPIC GAMES GYMNASTICS SILVER DOLLAR (1995)

Designer: *James C. Sharpe (obverse), William Krawczewicz (reverse).* **Weight:** *26.73 grams.*
Composition: *.900 silver, .100 copper (net weight .7736 oz. pure silver).*
Diameter: *38.1 mm.* **Edge:** *Reeded.* **Mints:** *Denver (Uncirculated) and Philadelphia (Proof).*

The men's gymnastics competition has been held at each Olympic Summer Games since the birth of the modern Olympic movement in 1896. Russia won the gold medal in the team all-around event at the 1996 Games in Atlanta.

Designs. *Obverse:* Men's gymnastics. *Reverse:* Clasped hands of two athletes with torch above.

Mintage Data. Authorized by Public Law 102-390, signed by President George H.W. Bush on October 6, 1992. *Maximum authorized*—750,000. *Number minted*—1995-D: 42,497 Uncirculated; 1995-P: 182,676 Proof.

Original Cost. Sale prices $27.95 (Uncirculated, pre-issue) and $30.95 (Proof, pre-issue); Uncirculated later raised to $31.95, and Proof later raised to $34.95. The surcharge per coin went to the Atlanta Olympic Committee.

Key to Collecting. Enough 1995 and 1996 Olympics coins are on the aftermarket that finding designs of choice, or forming a set, will be no problem. The obverse designs are varied, and in total the collection is an excellent representation of this quadrennial worldwide competition.

	Distribution	Cert	Avg	%MS	MS-67 PF-67
1995-D	42,497	1,592	69.2	100%	$35
Auctions: $90, MS-70, April 2013					
1995-P, Proof	182,676	2,370	69.0		$30
Auctions: No auction records available.					

(1995–1996) Atlanta Centennial Olympic Games
Track and Field Silver Dollar (1995)

Designer: *John Mercanti (obverse), William Krawczewicz (reverse).* **Weight:** *26.73 grams.*
Composition: *.900 silver, .100 copper (net weight .7736 oz. pure silver).*
Diameter: *38.1 mm.* **Edge:** *Reeded.* **Mints:** *Denver (Uncirculated) and Philadelphia (Proof).*

Track and field—grouped with road running and racewalking in the overarching "athletics" category—has been a part of the Olympics from the birth of the modern Games and traces its roots to the ancient Greek Olympics. At the 1996 Summer Games in Atlanta, the United States took home 13 gold medals between its men's and women's track and field teams, easily the most of any nation.

Designs. *Obverse:* Men competing in track and field. *Reverse:* Clasped hands of two athletes with torch above.

Mintage Data. Authorized by Public Law 102-390, signed by President George H.W. Bush on October 6, 1992. *Maximum authorized*—750,000. *Number minted*—1995-D: 24,976 Uncirculated; 1995-P: 136,935 Proof.

Original Cost. Sale prices $27.95 (Uncirculated, pre-issue) and $30.95 (Proof, pre-issue); Uncirculated later raised to $31.95, and Proof later raised to $34.95. The surcharge per coin went to the Atlanta Olympic Committee.

Key to Collecting. Enough 1995 and 1996 Olympics coins are on the aftermarket that finding designs of choice, or forming a set, will be no problem. The obverse designs are varied, and in total the collection is an excellent representation of this quadrennial worldwide competition.

	Distribution	Cert	Avg	%MS	MS-67
					PF-67
1995-D	24,976	879	69.3	100%	$65
	Auctions: $159, MS-70, July 2014				
1995-P, Proof	136,935	1,658	69.0		$35
	Auctions: $411, PF-70DCam, September 2014				

(1995–1996) Atlanta Centennial Olympic Games
Cycling Silver Dollar (1995)

Designer: *John Mercanti (obverse), William Krawczewicz (reverse).* **Weight:** *26.73 grams.*
Composition: *.900 silver, .100 copper (net weight .7736 oz. pure silver).*
Diameter: *38.1 mm.* **Edge:** *Reeded.* **Mints:** *Denver (Uncirculated) and Philadelphia (Proof).*

Part of the Summer Games from the inception of the modern Olympic movement in 1896, cycling has been expanded over the years to include more track races, mountain biking, and BMX racing. France dominated the podium at the 1996 Olympics in Atlanta, taking home the most gold medals (five) and total medals (nine).

Designs. *Obverse:* Men cycling. *Reverse:* Clasped hands of two athletes with torch above.

Mintage Data. Authorized by Public Law 102-390, signed by President George H.W. Bush on October 6, 1992. *Maximum authorized*—750,000. *Number minted*—1995-D: 19,662 Uncirculated; 1995-P: 118,795 Proof.

Original Cost. Sale prices $27.95 (Uncirculated, pre-issue) and $30.95 (Proof, pre-issue); Uncirculated later raised to $31.95, and Proof later raised to $34.95. The surcharge per coin went to the Atlanta Olympic Committee.

Key to Collecting. Enough 1995 and 1996 Olympics coins are on the aftermarket that finding designs of choice, or forming a set, will be no problem. The obverse designs are varied, and in total the collection is an excellent representation of this quadrennial worldwide competition.

	Distribution	Cert	Avg	%MS	MS-67
					PF-67
1995-D	19,662	968	69.3	100%	$75
	Auctions: $206, MS-70, July 2014; $200, MS-70, April 2013; $112, MS-69, November 2014				
1995-P, Proof	118,795	1,683	69.0		$38
	Auctions: $707, PF-70DCam, September 2014				

PARALYMPICS BLIND RUNNER SILVER DOLLAR (1995)

Designer: *James C. Sharpe (obverse), William Krawczewicz (reverse).* **Weight:** *26.73 grams.*
Composition: *.900 silver, .100 copper (net weight .7736 oz. pure silver).*
Diameter: *38.1 mm.* **Edge:** *Reeded.* **Mints:** *Denver (Uncirculated) and Philadelphia (Proof).*

Track and field events (under the umbrella of "athletics") have been a part of the Summer Paralympic Games since 1960. Spanish athletes took home a number of medals in the track events for visually impaired athletes at the 1996 Summer Paralympic Games, including the gold in two of the men's 100-meter dash events (Júlio Requena in the T-10 race, and Juan António Prieto in the T-11 race) and both of the women's 100-meter dash events (Purificación Santamarta in the T-10 race, and Beatríz Mendoza in the T-11 race).

Designs. *Obverse:* Blind runner tethered to a seeing companion in a race. *Reverse:* Clasped hands of two athletes with torch above.

Mintage Data. Authorized by Public Law 102-390, signed by President George H.W. Bush on October 6, 1992. *Maximum authorized*—750,000. *Number minted*—1995-D: 28,649 Uncirculated; 1995-P: 138,337 Proof.

Original Cost. Sale prices $27.95 (Uncirculated, pre-issue) and $30.95 (Proof, pre-issue); Uncirculated later raised to $31.95, and Proof later raised to $34.95. The surcharge per coin went to the Atlanta Olympic Committee.

Key to Collecting. Enough 1995 and 1996 Olympics coins are on the aftermarket that finding designs of choice, or forming a set, will be no problem. The obverse designs are varied, and in total the collection is an excellent representation of this quadrennial worldwide competition.

	Distribution	Cert	Avg	%MS	MS-67 / PF-67
1995-D	28,649	1,349	69.3	100%	$55
	Auctions: No auction records available.				
1995-P, Proof	138,337	1,878	69.0		$30
	Auctions: No auction records available.				

(1995–1996) ATLANTA CENTENNIAL OLYMPIC GAMES
TORCH RUNNER $5 GOLD COIN (1995)

Designer: *Frank Gasparro.* **Weight:** *8.359 grams.*
Composition: *.900 gold, .100 copper (net weight .242 oz. pure gold).*
Diameter: *21.6 mm.* **Edge:** *Reeded.* **Mint:** *West Point.*

Whereas the concept of the Olympic flame dates from the ancient Games of ancient Greece, the torch relay has only been a tradition since 1936, when Carl Diem introduced the concept for the Berlin Summer Games. The 1996 Olympic torch relay spanned 112 days, approximately 18,030 miles, and 13,267 torch bearers before ending in Atlanta on July 19, 1996.

Designs. *Obverse:* Olympic runner carrying a torch. *Reverse:* Bald eagle with a banner in its beak with the Olympic Centennial dates 1896–1996.

Mintage Data. Authorized by Public Law 102-390, signed by President George H.W. Bush on October 6, 1992. *Maximum authorized*—175,000. *Number minted*—14,675 Uncirculated and 57,442 Proof.

Original Cost. Sale prices $229 (Uncirculated, pre-issue) and $239 (Proof, pre-issue); Uncirculated later raised to $249, and Proof later raised to $259. The surcharge per coin went to the Atlanta Olympic Committee.

Key to Collecting. Enough 1995 and 1996 Olympics coins are on the aftermarket that finding designs of choice, or forming a set, will be no problem. The obverse designs are varied, and in total the collection is an excellent representation of this quadrennial worldwide competition.

	Distribution	Cert	Avg	%MS	MS-67 / PF-67
1995-W	14,675	1,060	69.7	100%	$500
	Auctions: $646, MS-70, February 2015; $447, MS-70, May 2015; $423, MS-70, May 2015; $353, MS-69, January 2015				
1995-W, Proof	57,442	1,874	69.3		$500
	Auctions: No auction records available.				

(1995–1996) ATLANTA CENTENNIAL OLYMPIC GAMES
STADIUM $5 GOLD COIN (1995)

Designer: *Marcel Jovine (obverse), Frank Gasparro (reverse).* **Weight:** *8.359 grams.*
Composition: *.900 gold, .100 copper (net weight .242 oz. pure gold).*
Diameter: *21.6 mm.* **Edge:** *Reeded.* **Mint:** *West Point.*

Centennial Olympic Stadium was constructed in Atlanta for the 1996 Summer Games. The 85,000-seat venue hosted the track and field events, as well as the closing ceremony, and then was reconstructed into Turner Field, home of Major League Baseball's Atlanta Braves for two decades.

Designs. *Obverse:* Aerial view of the Olympic Stadium from a distance to the side. *Reverse:* Same as described for the Olympic Torch Runner $5 gold coin.

Mintage Data. Authorized by Public Law 102-390, signed by President George H.W. Bush on October 6, 1992. *Maximum authorized*—175,000. *Number minted*—10,579 Uncirculated and 43,124 Proof.

Original Cost. Sale prices $229 (Uncirculated, pre-issue) and $239 (Proof, pre-issue); Uncirculated later raised to $249, and Proof later raised to $259. The surcharge per coin went to the Atlanta Olympic Committee.

Key to Collecting. Enough 1995 and 1996 Olympics coins are on the aftermarket that finding designs of choice, or forming a set, will be no problem. The obverse designs are varied, and in total the collection is an excellent representation of this quadrennial worldwide competition.

	Distribution	Cert	Avg	%MS	MS-67
					PF-67
1995-W	10,579	1,009	69.6	100%	$500
Auctions: $823, MS-70, February 2015; $764, MS-70, January 2015; $823, MS-69, February 2015; $646, MS-69, February 2015					
1995-W, Proof	43,124	1,857	69.4		$500
Auctions: $499, PF-70DCam, June 2014; $470, PF-70DCam, June 2014					

(1995–1996) ATLANTA CENTENNIAL OLYMPIC GAMES
SWIMMING HALF DOLLAR (1996)

Designer: *William Krawczewicz (obverse), Malcolm Farley (reverse).* **Weight:** *11.34 grams.*
Composition: *.9167 copper, .0833 nickel.* **Diameter:** *30.61 mm.* **Edge:** *Reeded.* **Mint:** *San Francisco.*

Swimming—an Olympic sport since the modern Games began in 1896—was dominated by U.S. athletes at the 1996 Summer Games in Atlanta. Americans took home a total of 26 medals (more than double the 12 each of Russia and Germany, which come next on the list), and swept all six relay events across the men's and women's competitions.

Designs. *Obverse:* Male swimmer. *Reverse:* Symbols of the Olympic games, including flame, torch, rings, Greek column, and 100 (the latter to observe the 100th anniversary of the modern Olympic games inaugurated with the 1896 Games in Athens).

Mintage Data. Authorized by Public Law 102-390, signed by President George H.W. Bush on October 6, 1992. *Maximum authorized*—3,000,000. *Number minted*—49,533 Uncirculated and 114,315 Proof.

Original Cost. Sale prices $10.50 (Uncirculated, pre-issue) and $11.50 (Proof, pre-issue); Uncirculated later raised to $11.50, and Proof later raised to $12.50. The surcharge per coin went to the Atlanta Olympic Committee.

Key to Collecting. Enough 1995 and 1996 Olympics coins are on the aftermarket that finding designs of choice, or forming a set, will be no problem. The obverse designs are varied, and in total the collection is an excellent representation of this quadrennial worldwide competition.

	Distribution	Cert	Avg	%MS	MS-67
					PF-67
1996-S ††	49,533	930	69.2	100%	$75
Auctions: $499, MS-70, September 2013					
1996-S, Proof	114,315	1,043	69.1		$25
Auctions: No auction records available.					

†† Ranked in the *100 Greatest U.S. Modern Coins* (fourth edition).

(1995–1996) ATLANTA CENTENNIAL OLYMPIC GAMES SOCCER HALF DOLLAR (1996)

Designer: *Clint Hansen (obverse), Malcolm Farley (reverse).* **Weight:** *11.34 grams.*
Composition: *.9167 copper, .0833 nickel.* **Diameter:** *30.61 mm.* **Edge:** *Reeded.* **Mint:** *San Francisco.*

Women's soccer debuted as an Olympic sport at the 1996 Summer Games in Atlanta. The host nation's team—featuring such names as Mia Hamm, Brandi Chastain, and Briana Scurry—was victorious in the gold medal game.

Designs. *Obverse:* Women playing soccer. *Reverse:* Symbols of the Olympic games, including flame, torch, rings, Greek column, and 100.

Mintage Data. Authorized by Public Law 102-390, signed by President George H.W. Bush on October 6, 1992. *Maximum authorized*—3,000,000. *Number minted*—52,836 Uncirculated and 112,412 Proof.

Original Cost. Sale prices $10.50 (Uncirculated, pre-issue) and $11.50 (Proof, pre-issue); Uncirculated later raised to $11.50, and Proof later raised to $12.50. The surcharge per coin went to the Atlanta Olympic Committee.

Key to Collecting. Enough 1995 and 1996 Olympics coins are on the aftermarket that finding designs of choice, or forming a set, will be no problem. The obverse designs are varied, and in total the collection is an excellent representation of this quadrennial worldwide competition.

	Distribution	Cert	Avg	%MS	MS-67
					PF-67
1996-S	52,836	650	69.3	100%	$50
	Auctions: $147, MS-70, July 2014; $170, MS-70, August 2013				
1996-S, Proof	112,412	1,035	69.1		$50
	Auctions: $294, PF-70DCam, September 2014				

(1995–1996) ATLANTA CENTENNIAL OLYMPIC GAMES TENNIS SILVER DOLLAR (1996)

Designer: *James C. Sharpe (obverse), Thomas D. Rogers Sr. (reverse).* **Weight:** *26.73 grams.* **Composition:** *.900 silver, .100 copper (net weight .7736 oz. pure silver).* **Diameter:** *38.1 mm.* **Edge:** *Reeded.* **Mints:** *Denver (Uncirculated) and Philadelphia (Proof).*

Women's tennis was first a part of the Olympics in 1900, and singles competition was regularly held for the Summer Games between 1908 and 1924. Subsequent disputes between the International Lawn Tennis Federation and the International Olympic Committee led to both men's and women's tennis being removed from the Games for more than 60 years, but the sport returned permanently in 1988. U.S. athletes took both the women's singles gold medal (Lindsay Davenport) and women's doubles gold medal (Gigi Fernandez and Mary Joe Fernandez) at the 1996 Games in Atlanta.

Designs. *Obverse:* Woman playing tennis. *Reverse:* Atlanta Committee for the Olympic Games logo with torch and flame.

Mintage Data. Authorized by Public Law 102-390, signed by President George H.W. Bush on October 6, 1992. *Maximum authorized*—1,000,000. *Number minted*—1996-D: 15,983 Uncirculated; 1996-P: 92,016 Proof.

Original Cost. Sale prices $27.95 (Uncirculated, pre-issue) and $30.95 (Proof, pre-issue); Uncirculated later raised to $31.95, and Proof later raised to $34.95. The surcharge per coin went to the Atlanta Olympic Committee.

Key to Collecting. Enough 1995 and 1996 Olympics coins are on the aftermarket that finding designs of choice, or forming a set, will be no problem. The obverse designs are varied, and in total the collection is an excellent representation of this quadrennial worldwide competition.

	Distribution	Cert	Avg	%MS	MS-67
					PF-67
1996-D ††	15,983	836	69.1	100%	$140
	Auctions: $206, MS-70, September 2014; $482, MS-70, April 2013; $170, MS-69, July 2014; $170, MS-69, November 2014				
1996-P, Proof	92,016	1,448	68.9		$65
	Auctions: $355, PF-69DCam, November 2014				

†† Ranked in the *100 Greatest U.S. Modern Coins* (fourth edition).

(1995–1996) ATLANTA CENTENNIAL OLYMPIC GAMES
ROWING SILVER DOLLAR (1996)

Designer: *Bart Forbes (obverse), Thomas D. Rogers Sr. (reverse).* **Weight:** *26.73 grams.*
Composition: *.900 silver, .100 copper (net weight .7736 oz. pure silver).*
Diameter: *38.1 mm.* **Edge:** *Reeded.* **Mints:** *Denver (Uncirculated) and Philadelphia (Proof).*

Rowing has been an official Olympic sport from the first modern Games in 1896, though coincidentally the competition was cancelled for that event due to weather concerns. At the 1996 Summer Olympics in Atlanta, Australia won the most medals (six, two gold).

Designs. *Obverse:* Men rowing. *Reverse:* Atlanta Committee for the Olympic Games logo with torch and flame.

Mintage Data. Authorized by Public Law 102-390, signed by President George H.W. Bush on October 6, 1992. *Maximum authorized*—1,000,000. *Number minted*—1996-D: 16,258 Uncirculated; 1996-P: 151,890 Proof.

Original Cost. Sale prices $27.95 (Uncirculated, pre-issue) and $30.95 (Proof, pre-issue); Uncirculated later raised to $31.95, and Proof later raised to $34.95. The surcharge per coin went to the Atlanta Olympic Committee.

Key to Collecting. Enough 1995 and 1996 Olympics coins are on the aftermarket that finding designs of choice, or forming a set, will be no problem. The obverse designs are varied, and in total the collection is an excellent representation of this quadrennial worldwide competition.

	Distribution	Cert	Avg	%MS	MS-67
					PF-67
1996-D	16,258	781	69.2	100%	$145
	Auctions: $382, MS-70, April 2013; $153, MS-69, November 2014; $147, MS-69, November 2014				
1996-P, Proof	151,890	1,476	68.9		$60
	Auctions: $6,169, PF-70DCam, September 2014				

(1995–1996) ATLANTA CENTENNIAL OLYMPIC GAMES
HIGH JUMP SILVER DOLLAR (1996)

Designer: *Calvin Massey (obverse), Thomas D. Rogers Sr. (reverse).* **Weight:** *26.73 grams.*
Composition: *.900 silver, .100 copper (net weight .7736 oz. pure silver).*
Diameter: *38.1 mm.* **Edge:** *Reeded.* **Mints:** *Denver (Uncirculated) and Philadelphia (Proof).*

High jump has been one of the Olympic track and field program's events since the inaugural modern Games in 1896. At the 1996 Atlanta Olympics, the United States' Charles Austin won the gold medal in the men's competition with a height cleared of 2.39 meters.

Designs. *Obverse:* Athlete doing the "Fosbury Flop" maneuver. *Reverse:* Atlanta Committee for the Olympic Games logo with torch and flame.

Mintage Data. Authorized by Public Law 102-390, signed by President George H.W. Bush on October 6, 1992. *Maximum authorized*—1,000,000. *Number minted*—1996-D: 15,697 Uncirculated; 1996-P: 124,502 Proof.

Original Cost. Sale prices $27.95 (Uncirculated, pre-issue) and $30.95 (Proof, pre-issue); Uncirculated later raised to $31.95, and Proof later raised to $34.95. The surcharge per coin went to the Atlanta Olympic Committee.

Key to Collecting. Enough 1995 and 1996 Olympics coins are on the aftermarket that finding designs of choice, or forming a set, will be no problem. The obverse designs are varied, and in total the collection is an excellent representation of this quadrennial worldwide competition.

	Distribution	Cert	Avg	%MS	MS-67
					PF-67
1996-D ††	15,697	784	69.1	100%	$150
	Auctions: $441, MS-70, April 2013; $147, MS-69, July 2014; $165, MS-69, November 2014				
1996-P, Proof	124,502	1,497	68.9		$45
	Auctions: No auction records available.				

†† Ranked in the *100 Greatest U.S. Modern Coins* (fourth edition).

PARALYMPICS WHEELCHAIR SILVER DOLLAR (1996)

Designer: *James C. Sharpe (obverse), Thomas D. Rogers Sr. (reverse).* **Weight:** *26.73 grams.*
Composition: *.900 silver, .100 copper (net weight .7736 oz. pure silver).*
Diameter: *38.1 mm.* **Edge:** *Reeded.* **Mints:** *Denver (Uncirculated) and Philadelphia (Proof).*

Wheelchair racing events have comprised part of the Paralympic track and field program since 1960. Several countries were represented on the podium, though the United States' Shawn Meredith (gold medals in the T-51 400-meter and 800-meter), France's Claude Issorat (gold medals in the T-53 200-meter and 800-meter), and Switzerland's Heinz Frei (gold medals in the T52-53 1,500-meter and 10,000-meter) had particularly strong showings.

Designs. *Obverse:* Athlete in a racing wheelchair competing in a track and field competition. *Reverse:* Atlanta Committee for the Olympic Games logo with torch and flame.

Mintage Data. Authorized by Public Law 102-390, signed by President George H.W. Bush on October 6, 1992. *Maximum authorized*—1,000,000. *Number minted*—1996-D: 14,497 Uncirculated; 1996-P: 84,280 Proof.

Original Cost. Sale prices $27.95 (Uncirculated, pre-issue) and $30.95 (Proof, pre-issue); Uncirculated later raised to $31.95, and Proof later raised to $34.95. The surcharge per coin went to the Atlanta Olympic Committee.

Key to Collecting. Enough 1995 and 1996 Olympics coins are on the aftermarket that finding designs of choice, or forming a set, will be no problem. The obverse designs are varied, and in total the collection is an excellent representation of this quadrennial worldwide competition.

	Distribution	Cert	Avg	%MS	MS-67 PF-67
1996-D	14,497	901	69.2	100%	$140
	Auctions: $499, MS-70, April 2013; $223, MS-70, June 2015; $153, MS-69, November 2014; $129, MS-69, November 2014				
1996-P, Proof	84,280	1,533	69.0		$35
	Auctions: No auction records available.				

(1995–1996) ATLANTA CENTENNIAL OLYMPIC GAMES FLAG BEARER $5 GOLD COIN (1996)

Designer: *Patricia Lewis Verani (obverse), William Krawczewicz (reverse).*
Weight: *8.359 grams.* **Composition:** *.900 gold, .100 copper (net weight .242 oz. pure gold).*
Diameter: *21.6 mm.* **Edge:** *Reeded.* **Mint:** *West Point.*

For the opening and closing ceremonies of each Olympic Games, each participating nation selects two flagbearers from among its athletes to lead its delegation in the Parade of Nations (opening) and Parade of Flags (closing). Wrestler Bruce Baumgartner served as the United States's flagbearer for the opening ceremony of the 1996 Summer Games, and show jumper Michael Matz was awarded the honor for the closing ceremony.

Designs. *Obverse:* Athlete with a flag followed by a crowd. *Reverse:* Atlanta Committee for the Olympic Games logo within laurel leaves.

Mintage Data. Authorized by Public Law 102-390, signed by President George H.W. Bush on October 6, 1992. *Maximum authorized*—300,000. *Number minted*—9,174 Uncirculated and 32,886 Proof.

Original Cost. Sale prices $229 (Uncirculated, pre-issue) and $239 (Proof, pre-issue); Uncirculated later raised to $249, and Proof later raised to $259. The surcharge per coin went to the Atlanta Olympic Committee.

Key to Collecting. Enough 1995 and 1996 Olympics coins are on the aftermarket that finding designs of choice, or forming a set, will be no problem. The obverse designs are varied, and in total the collection is an excellent representation of this quadrennial worldwide competition.

	Distribution	Cert	Avg	%MS	MS-67 PF-67
1996-W ††	9,174	754	69.5	100%	$500
	Auctions: $881, MS-70, October 2015; $881, MS-70, February 2015; $494, MS-69, January 2015; $329, MS-69, September 2015				
1996-W, Proof	32,886	1,338	69.3		$500
	Auctions: No auction records available.				

†† Ranked in the *100 Greatest U.S. Modern Coins* (fourth edition).

(1995–1996) ATLANTA CENTENNIAL OLYMPIC GAMES
CAULDRON $5 GOLD COIN (1996)

Designer: *Frank Gasparro (obverse), William Krawczewicz (reverse).*
Weight: *8.359 grams.* **Composition:** *.900 gold, .100 copper (net weight .242 oz. pure gold).*
Diameter: *21.6 mm.* **Edge:** *Reeded.* **Mint:** *West Point.*

The tradition of maintaining an Olympic flame hearkens to the ancient Greek Olympics, during which a fire was kept burning to represent the theft of fire from Zeus by Prometheus. The concept became part of the modern Games in 1928 and now serves as the culmination of the Olympic torch relay. At the 1996 Summer Games in Atlanta, boxing legend and American icon Muhammad Ali (himself a gold medalist at the 1960 Olympics) was the final torch bearer and lit the cauldron.

Designs. *Obverse:* Lighting of the Olympic flame. *Reverse:* Atlanta Committee for the Olympic Games logo within laurel leaves.

Mintage Data. Authorized by Public Law 102-390, signed by President George H.W. Bush on October 6, 1992. *Maximum authorized—*300,000. *Number minted—*9,210 Uncirculated and 38,555 Proof.

Original Cost. Sale prices $229 (Uncirculated, pre-issue) and $239 (Proof, pre-issue); Uncirculated later raised to $249, and Proof later raised to $259. The surcharge per coin went to the Atlanta Olympic Committee.

Key to Collecting. Enough 1995 and 1996 Olympics coins are on the aftermarket that finding designs of choice, or forming a set, will be no problem. The obverse designs are varied, and in total the collection is an excellent representation of this quadrennial worldwide competition.

	Distribution	Cert	Avg	%MS	MS-67 PF-67
1996-W	9,210	848	69.4	100%	$600
	Auctions: $1,116, MS-70, February 2015; $940, MS-70, October 2015; $823, MS-69, January 2015; $705, MS-69, November 2014				
1996-W, Proof	38,555	2,228	69.3		$500
	Auctions: $505, PF-70UCam, March 2015; $423, PF-70UCam, March 2015; $353, PF-70UCam, May 2015				

CIVIL WAR BATTLEFIELD PRESERVATION HALF DOLLAR (1995)

Designer: *Don Troiani (obverse), T. James Ferrell (reverse).* **Weight:** *11.34 grams.*
Composition: *.9167 copper, .0833 nickel.* **Diameter:** *30.61 mm.* **Edge:** *Reeded.* **Mint:** *San Francisco.*

Preserving battlefields associated with the Civil War (1861–1865) formed the topic for a suite of three commemorative coins, including this copper-nickel half dollar.

Designs. *Obverse:* Drummer standing. *Reverse:* Cannon overlooking battlefield with inscription above.

Mintage Data. Authorized by Public Law 102-379. *Maximum authorized*—2,000,000. *Number minted*—119,520 Uncirculated and 330,002 Proof.

Original Cost. Sale prices $9.50 (Uncirculated, pre-issue) and $10.75 (Proof, pre-issue); Uncirculated later raised to $10.25, and Proof later raised to $11.75. The surcharge of $2 per coin went to the Civil War Trust for the preservation of historically significant battlefields.

Key to Collecting. This coin, as well as those two issued alongside it, are readily available in the marketplace today. Most are superb gems.

	Distribution	Cert	Avg	%MS	MS-67
					PF-67
1995-S	119,520	1,073	69.4	100%	$25
	Auctions: $206, MS-70, May 2014; $153, MS-70, July 2014; $112, MS-70, June 2015				
1995-S, Proof	330,002	2,044	69.0		$25
	Auctions: $188, PF-68DCam, November 2014				

CIVIL WAR BATTLEFIELD PRESERVATION SILVER DOLLAR (1995)

Designer: *Don Troiani (obverse), John Mercanti (reverse).* **Weight:** *26.73 grams.*
Composition: *.900 silver, .100 copper (net weight .7736 oz. pure silver).*
Diameter: *38.1 mm.* **Edge:** *Reeded.* **Mints:** *Philadelphia (Uncirculated) and San Francisco (Proof).*

Civil War history attracts millions of followers, and books on the subject are always very popular. While total sales of the Civil War Battlefield Preservation silver dollar didn't approach the million coins authorized, sales of the Proof version were stronger than those of many recent silver dollars.

Designs. *Obverse:* Soldier offering canteen to a wounded comrade. *Reverse:* Gettysburg landscape with a quotation from Joshua Chamberlain, hero in that battle.

Mintage Data. Authorized by Public Law 102-379. *Maximum authorized*—1,000,000. *Number minted*— 1995-P: 45,866 Uncirculated; 1995-S: 437,114 Proof.

Original Cost. Sale prices $27 (Uncirculated, pre-issue) and $30 (Proof, pre-issue); Uncirculated later raised to $30, and Proof later raised to $34. The surcharge of $7 per coin went to the Civil War Trust for the preservation of historically significant battlefields.

Key to Collecting. This coin, as well as those two issued alongside it, are readily available in the marketplace today. Most are superb gems.

	Distribution	Cert	Avg	%MS	MS-67
					PF-67
1995-P	45,866	1,293	69.1	100%	$50
	Auctions: $247, MS-70, April 2013				
1995-S, Proof	437,114	3,532	69.0		$40
	Auctions: $435, PF-70DCam, March 2013; $306, PF-70DCam, April 2013				

CIVIL WAR BATTLEFIELD PRESERVATION $5 GOLD COIN (1995)

Designer: *Don Troiani (obverse), Alfred F. Maletsky (reverse).* **Weight:** *8.359 grams.*
Composition: *.900 gold, .100 copper.* **Diameter:** *21.6 mm.* **Edge:** *Reeded.* **Mint:** *West Point.*

Troiani, the designer of this coin's obverse as well as those of the other two Civil War Battlefield Preservation commemoratives, is an artist in the private sector well known for his depictions of battle scenes.

Designs. *Obverse:* Bugler on horseback sounding a call. *Reverse:* Eagle perched on a shield.

Mintage Data. Authorized by Public Law 102-379. *Maximum authorized*—300,000. *Number minted*—12,735 Uncirculated and 55,246 Proof.

Original Cost. Sale prices $180 (Uncirculated, pre-issue) and $195 (Proof, pre-issue); Uncirculated later raised to $190, and Proof later raised to $225. The surcharge of $35 per coin went to the Civil War Trust for the preservation of historically significant battlefields.

Key to Collecting. This coin, as well as those two issued alongside it, are readily available in the marketplace today. Most are superb gems.

	Distribution	Cert	Avg	%MS	MS-67
					PF-67
1995-W	12,735	840	69.7	100%	$500
	Auctions: $517, MS-70, January 2015; $494, MS-70, April 2015; $482, MS-70, January 2015; $329, MS-69, August 2015				
1995-W, Proof	55,246	1,975	69.3		$500
	Auctions: $482, PF-70DCam, July 2015; $306, PF-69UCam, October 2015; $329, PF-69DCam, October 2015; $306, PF-69DCam, August 2015				

SPECIAL OLYMPICS WORLD GAMES SILVER DOLLAR (1995)

Designer: *T. James Ferrell from a portrait by Jamie Wyeth (obverse), Thomas D. Rogers Sr. (reverse).*
Weight: *26.73 grams.* **Composition:** *.900 silver, .100 copper (net weight .7736 oz. pure silver).*
Diameter: *38.1 mm.* **Edge:** *Reeded.* **Mints:** *West Point (Uncirculated) and Philadelphia (Proof).*

This silver dollar's subject, Eunice Kennedy Shriver, was not only the first living female on U.S. coinage, but also the sister of former president John F. Kennedy and the aunt of Joseph F. Kennedy II, the House representative who sponsored the bill that created the coin. She is credited on the silver dollar as the founder of the Special Olympics.

Designs. *Obverse:* Portrait of Eunice Shriver.
Reverse: Representation of a Special Olympics medal, a rose, and a quotation by Shriver.

Mintage Data. Authorized by Public Law 103-328, signed by President William J. Clinton on September 29, 1994. *Maximum authorized*—800,000. *Number minted*—1995-W: 89,301 Uncirculated; 1995-P: 351,764 Proof.

Original Cost. Sale prices $30 (Uncirculated, pre-issue) and $33 (Proof, pre-issue); Uncirculated later raised to $32, and Proof later raised to $37. The surcharge of $10 per coin went to the Special Olympics to support the 1995 World Summer Games.

Key to Collecting. These coins are plentiful in the marketplace. Most are superb gems.

	Distribution	Cert	Avg	%MS	MS-67
					PF-67
1995-W	89,301	1,018	69.2	100%	$30
	Auctions: $135, MS-70, April 2013				
1995-P, Proof	351,764	1,732	69.0		$30
	Auctions: $360, PF-70DCam, March 2013				

NATIONAL COMMUNITY SERVICE SILVER DOLLAR (1996)

Designer: *Thomas D. Rogers Sr. from a medal by Augustus Saint-Gaudens (obverse),*
William C. Cousins (reverse). **Weight:** *26.73 grams.* **Composition:** *.900 silver, .100 copper*
(net weight .7736 oz. pure silver). **Diameter:** *38.1 mm.* **Edge:** *Reeded.* **Mint:** *San Francisco.*

In 1996 the National Community Service dollar was sponsored by Representative Joseph D. Kennedy of Massachusetts, who also sponsored the Special Olympics World Games dollar.

Designs. *Obverse:* Standing figure of Liberty. *Reverse:* SERVICE FOR AMERICA in three lines, with a wreath around, and other lettering at the border.

Mintage Data. Authorized by Public Law 103-328, signed by President William J. Clinton on September 29, 1994. *Maximum authorized*—500,000. *Number minted*—23,500 Uncirculated and 101,543 Proof.

Original Cost. Sale prices $30 (Uncirculated, pre-issue) and $33 (Proof, pre-issue); Uncirculated later raised to $32, and Proof later raised to $37. The surcharge of $10 per coin went to the National Community Service Trust.

Key to Collecting. Uncirculated examples are scarce by virtue of their low mintage, but demand is scarce as well, with the result that they can be purchased easily enough. Both formats are usually seen in superb gem preservation.

	Distribution	Cert	Avg	%MS	MS-67
					PF-67
1996-S ††	23,500	1,133	69.3	100%	$75
	Auctions: $153, MS-70, August 2014; $129, MS-70, June 2015; $88, MS-69, July 2014; $86, MS-69, November 2014				
1996-S, Proof	101,543	2,254	69.1		$35
	Auctions: $195, PF-70DCam, April 2013				

†† Ranked in the *100 Greatest U.S. Modern Coins* (fourth edition).

SMITHSONIAN INSTITUTION 150TH ANNIVERSARY SILVER DOLLAR (1996)

Designer: *Thomas D. Rogers Sr. (obverse), John Mercanti (reverse).* **Weight:** *26.73 grams.*
Composition: *.900 silver, .100 copper (net weight .7736 oz. pure silver).* **Diameter:** *38.1 mm.*
Edge: *Reeded.* **Mints:** *Denver (Uncirculated) and Philadelphia (Proof).*

This silver dollar, as well as a five-dollar gold coin, marked the 150th anniversary of Congress establishing the Smithsonian Institution in Washington, D.C., on August 10, 1846. Named for James Smithson—an English scientist whose will funded the entity—the institution quickly became America's national museum.

Designs. *Obverse:* The "Castle" building on the Mall in Washington, the original home of the Smithsonian Institution. Branches to each side. *Reverse:* Goddess of Knowledge sitting on top of a globe. In her left hand she holds a torch, in the right a scroll inscribed ART / HISTORY / SCIENCE. In the field to the right in several lines is FOR THE INCREASE AND DIFFUSION OF KNOWLEDGE.

Mintage Data. Authorized by Public Law 104-96, signed by President William J. Clinton on January 10, 1996. *Maximum authorized*—650,000. *Number minted*—1996-D: 31,320 Uncirculated; 1996-P: 129,152 Proof.

Original Cost. Sale prices $30 (Uncirculated, pre-issue) and $33 (Proof, pre-issue); Uncirculated later raised to $32, and Proof later raised to $37. The surcharge of $10 per coin went to the Smithsonian Board of Regents.

Key to Collecting. This silver dollar and the five-dollar gold coin issued alongside it have risen in value considerably since their release. Today examples can be found readily in the marketplace and are nearly always superb gems.

	Distribution	Cert	Avg	%MS	MS-67
					PF-67
1996-D	31,320	1,161	69.4	100%	$60
	Auctions: $119, MS-70, July 2014; $100, MS-70, February 2015; $89, MS-70, February 2015; $65, MS-69, October 2014				
1996-P, Proof	129,152	2,131	69.0		$40
	Auctions: $447, PF-70DCam, March 2013				

SMITHSONIAN INSTITUTION 150TH ANNIVERSARY $5 GOLD COIN (1996)

Designer: *Alfred F. Maletsky (obverse), T. James Ferrell (reverse).* **Weight:** *8.359 grams.*
Composition: *.900 gold, .100 copper (net weight .242 oz. pure gold).*
Diameter: *21.6 mm.* **Edge:** *Reeded.* **Mint:** *West Point.*

The U.S. Mint offered the two 1996 Smithsonian commemorative coins via several new options, including the 50,000-set Young Collectors Edition and incorporated in jewelry items.

Designs. *Obverse:* Bust of James Smithson facing left. *Reverse:* Sunburst with SMITHSONIAN below.

Mintage Data. Authorized by Public Law 104-96, signed by President William J. Clinton on January 10, 1996. *Maximum authorized—*100,000. *Number minted—*9,068 Uncirculated and 21,772 Proof.

Original Cost. Sale prices $180 (Uncirculated, pre-issue) and $195 (Proof, pre-issue); Uncirculated later raised to $205, and Proof later raised to $225. The surcharge of $10 per coin went to the Smithsonian Board of Regents.

Key to Collecting. Both Smithsonian Institution 150th Anniversary coins have risen in value considerably since their release. Today examples can be found readily in the marketplace and are nearly always superb gems.

	Distribution	Cert	Avg	%MS	MS-67
					PF-67
1996-W ††	9,068	871	69.4	100%	$500
	Auctions: $646, MS-70, September 2014; $541, MS-70, January 2015; $447, MS-70, April 2015; $382, MS-69, August 2014				
1996-W, Proof	21,772	1,323	69.2		$500
	Auctions: $706, PF-70DCam, April 2013; $588, PF-70DCam, September 2014; $529, PF-70DCam, September 2014				

†† Ranked in the *100 Greatest U.S. Modern Coins* (fourth edition).

U.S. BOTANIC GARDEN SILVER DOLLAR (1997)

Designer: *Edgar Z. Steever IV (obverse), William C. Cousins (reverse).* **Weight:** *26.73 grams.*
Composition: *Silver .900, copper .100 (net weight .7736 oz. pure silver).*
Diameter: *38.1 mm.* **Edge:** *Reeded.* **Mint:** *Philadelphia.*

These coins were purportedly struck to celebrate the 175th anniversary of the United States Botanic Garden (which would have been 1995), but they were dated on one side as 1997. The authorizing legislation that created the coins specified that the French façade of the U.S. Botanic Garden be shown on the obverse and a rose on the reverse.

Designs. *Obverse:* Façade of the United States Botanic Garden in plan view without landscaping. *Reverse:* A rose at the center with a garland of roses above. The inscription below includes the anniversary dates 1820–1995. Note that some listings designate the rose side as the obverse.

Mintage Data. Authorized by Public Law 103-328, signed by President William J. Clinton on September 29, 1994. *Maximum authorized*—500,000. *Number minted*—58,505 Uncirculated and 189,671 Proof.

Original Cost. Sale prices $30 (Uncirculated, pre-issue) and $33 (Proof, pre-issue); Uncirculated later raised to $33, and Proof later raised to $37. The surcharge of $10 per coin went to the National Fund for the Botanic Garden.

Key to Collecting. These coins are readily available on the market today. Nearly all are superb gems. Ironically, the most popular related item is the Mint package containing the 1997-P special-finish Jefferson nickel, the demand coming from collectors of five-cent pieces! Only 25,000 sets were sold. This is *déjà vu* of the 1993 Jefferson dollar offer.

	Distribution	Cert	Avg	%MS	MS-67
					PF-67
1997-P	58,505	1,761	69.1	100%	$30
	Auctions: $159, MS-70, July 2014; $170, MS-70, April 2013				
1997-P, Proof	189,671	1,574	69.0		$35
	Auctions: $441, PF-70DCam, April 2013; $306, PF-70UCam, February 2015; $306, PF-70DCam, September 2014				

NATIONAL LAW ENFORCEMENT OFFICERS MEMORIAL SILVER DOLLAR (1997)

Designer: *Alfred F. Maletsky (obverse from a photograph by Larry Ruggieri).* **Weight:** *26.73 grams.*
Composition: *.900 silver, .100 copper (net weight .7736 oz. pure silver).*
Diameter: *38.1 mm.* **Edge:** *Reeded.* **Mint:** *Philadelphia.*

The National Law Enforcement Officers Memorial at Judiciary Square in Washington, D.C., dedicated on October 15, 1991, was the subject of this commemorative. The monument honors more than 14,000 men and women who gave their lives in the line of duty.

Designs. *Obverse:* United States Park Police officers Robert Chelsey and Kelcy Stefansson making a rubbing of a fellow officer's name.
Reverse: Shield with a rose across it, evocative of the sacrifices made by officers.

Mintage Data. Authorized by Public Law 104-329, signed by President William J. Clinton on October 20, 1996. *Maximum authorized*—500,000. *Number minted*—28,575 Uncirculated and 110,428 Proof.

Original Cost. Sale prices $30 (Uncirculated, pre-issue) and $33 (Proof, pre-issue); Uncirculated later raised to $32, and Proof later raised to $37.

Key to Collecting. Once the distribution figures were published, the missed opportunity was realized—collectors saw that these coins would be a modern rarity. The market price rose to a sharp premium, where it remains today. Nearly all coins approach perfection in quality.

	Distribution	Cert	Avg	%MS	MS-67
					PF-67
1997-P ††	28,575	881	69.3	100%	$115
	Auctions: $259, MS-70, May 2013; $206, MS-70, August 2014; $84, MS-69, February 2015				
1997-P, Proof	110,428	1,841	69.0		$60
	Auctions: $353, PF-70DCam, April 2013; $243, PF-70DCam, September 2014; $60, PF-69DCam, January 2015				

†† Ranked in the *100 Greatest U.S. Modern Coins* (fourth edition).

JACKIE ROBINSON SILVER DOLLAR (1997)

Designer: *Alfred F. Maletsky (obverse), T. James Ferrell (reverse).* **Weight:** *26.73 grams.*
Composition: *.900 silver, .100 copper (net weight .7736 oz. pure silver).*
Diameter: *38.1 mm.* **Edge:** *Reeded.* **Mint:** *San Francisco.*

This silver dollar and a concurrently issued five-dollar gold coin commemorated the 50th anniversary of the first acceptance of a black player in a major league baseball game, Jack ("Jackie") Robinson being the hero. The watershed event took place at Ebbets Field on April 15, 1947.

Designs. *Obverse:* Robinson in game action stealing home plate, evocative of a 1955 World Series play in a contest between the New York Yankees and the Brooklyn Dodgers. *Reverse:* 50th anniversary logotype of the Jackie Robinson Foundation (a motif worn by all Major League Baseball players in the 1997 season) surrounded with lettering of two baseball accomplishments.

Mintage Data. Authorized on October 20, 1996, by Public Law 104-329, part of the United States Commemorative Coin Act of 1996, with a provision tied to Public Law 104-328 (for the Botanic Garden dollar). Coins could be minted for a full year beginning July 1, 1997. *Maximum authorized*—200,000. *Number minted*—30,180 Uncirculated and 110,002 Proof.

Original Cost. Sale prices $30 (Uncirculated, pre-issue) and $33 (Proof, pre-issue); Uncirculated later raised to $32, and Proof later raised to $37. The surcharge of $10 per coin went to the Jackie Robinson Foundation.

Key to Collecting. Although the Jackie Robinson coins were losers in the sales figures of the U.S. Mint, the small quantities issued made both coins winners in the return-on-investment sweepstakes. Today, each of these can be found without a problem, and nearly all are in superb gem preservation.

	Distribution	Cert	Avg	%MS	MS-67
					PF-67
1997-S	30,180	1,286	69.1	100%	$55
Auctions: $411, MS-70, October 2014; $682, MS-70, January 2013					
1997-S, Proof	110,002	2,455	69.0		$45
Auctions: $999, PF-70DCam, September 2014; $646, PF-70DCam, September 2013					

JACKIE ROBINSON $5 GOLD COIN (1997)

Designer: *William C. Cousins (obverse), James Peed (reverse).* **Weight:** *8.359 grams.*
Composition: *.900 gold, .100 copper (net weight .242 oz. pure gold).*
Diameter: *21.6 mm.* **Edge:** *Reeded.* **Mint:** *West Point.*

The U.S. Mint's marketing of the Jackie Robinson coins was innovative, as it had been in recent times. One promotion featured a reproduction of a rare baseball trading card, with the distinction of being the first such card ever issued by the U.S. government. But no matter how important Robinson's legacy was, buyers voted with their pocketbooks, and sales were low—making the Uncirculated gold coin a modern rarity.

Designs. *Obverse:* Portrait of Robinson in his later years as a civil-rights and political activist. *Reverse:* Detail of the seam on a baseball, Robinson's 1919–1972 life dates, and the inscription "Life of Courage."

Mintage Data. Authorized on October 20, 1996, by Public Law 104-329, part of the United States Commemorative Coin Act of 1996, with a provision tied to Public Law 104-328 (for the Botanic Garden dollar). Coins could be minted for a full year beginning July 1, 1997. *Maximum authorized*—100,000. *Number minted*—5,174 Uncirculated and 24,072 Proof.

Original Cost. Sale prices $180 (Uncirculated, pre-issue) and $195 (Proof, pre-issue); Uncirculated later raised to $205, and Proof later raised to $225. The surcharge of $35 per coin went to the Jackie Robinson Foundation.

Key to Collecting. The Jackie Robinson five-dollar gold coin takes top honors as the key issue among modern commemoratives. Especially rare and valuable is the Uncirculated version.

	Distribution	Cert	Avg	%MS	MS-67
					PF-67
1997-W ††	5,174	923	69.3	100%	$850
	Auctions: $3,290, MS-70, February 2015; $3,055, MS-70, June 2015; $1,763, MS-69, February 2015; $1,645, MS-69, February 2015				
1997-W, Proof	24,072	1,686	69.3		$500
	Auctions: $376, PF-69DCam, April 2015; $376, PF-69DCam, January 2015; $367, PF-69UCam, February 2015				

†† Ranked in the *100 Greatest U.S. Modern Coins* (fourth edition).

FRANKLIN D. ROOSEVELT $5 GOLD COIN (1997)

Designer: *T. James Ferrell (obverse), James Peed (reverse).* **Weight:** *8.359 grams.*
Composition: *.900 gold, .100 copper (net weight .242 oz. pure gold).*
Diameter: *21.6 mm.* **Edge:** *Reeded.* **Mint:** *West Point.*

Considering that newly inaugurated President Franklin D. Roosevelt suspended the mintage and paying out of U.S. gold coins in 1933, it was ironic that he should later have a gold coin commemorating his life. The year 1997 does not seem to have been a special anniversary date of any kind, as it was 115 years after his birth, 64 years after his inauguration, and 52 years after his death.

Designs. *Obverse:* Upper torso and head of Roosevelt facing right, based on one of the president's favorite photographs, taken when he was reviewing the U.S. Navy fleet in San Francisco Bay. *Reverse:* Presidential seal displayed at Roosevelt's 1933 inaugural.

Mintage Data. Authorized by Public Law 104-329, signed by President William J. Clinton on October 20, 1996. *Maximum authorized*—100,000. *Number minted*—11,894 Uncirculated and 29,474 Proof.

Original Cost. Sale prices $180 (Uncirculated, pre-issue) and $195 (Proof, pre-issue); Uncirculated later raised to $205, and Proof later raised to $225. A portion of the surcharge of $35 per coin went to the Franklin Delano Roosevelt Memorial Commission.

Key to Collecting. Since the mintages for both Uncirculated and Proof formats were low, their values rose substantially on the aftermarket. Examples are easily available today and are nearly always in superb gem preservation.

	Distribution	Cert	Avg	%MS	MS-67
					PF-67
1997-W	11,894	891	69.5	100%	$500
	Auctions: $705, MS-70, August 2014; $611, MS-70, August 2014; $541, MS-70, April 2015; $535, MS-70, April 2015				
1997-W, Proof	29,474	1,782	69.3		$500
	Auctions: $447, PF-69DCam, March 2013				

BLACK REVOLUTIONARY WAR PATRIOTS SILVER DOLLAR (1998)

Designer: *John Mercanti (obverse), Ed Dwight (reverse).* **Weight:** *26.73 grams.*
Composition: *.900 silver, .100 copper (net weight .7736 oz. pure silver).*
Diameter: *38.1 mm.* **Edge:** *Reeded.* **Mint:** *San Francisco.*

This coin commemorates black Revolutionary War patriots and the 275th anniversary of the birth of Crispus Attucks, the first patriot killed in the infamous Boston Massacre in 1770 (an event predating the Revolutionary War, one among many incidents that inflamed the pro-independence passions of Americans).

Designs. *Obverse:* U.S. Mint engraver John Mercanti's conception of Crispus Attucks.
Reverse: A black patriot family, a detail from the proposed Black Patriots Memorial.

Mintage Data. Authorized by Public Law 104-329, signed by President William J. Clinton on October 20, 1996. *Maximum authorized*—500,000. *Number minted*—37,210 Uncirculated and 75,070 Proof.

Original Cost. Sale prices $30 (Uncirculated, pre-issue) and $33 (Proof, pre-issue); Uncirculated later raised to $32, and Proof later raised to $37. A portion of the surcharge of $10 per coin went to the Black Revolutionary War Patriots Foundation to fund the construction of the Black Patriots Memorial in Washington, D.C.

Key to Collecting. These coins became highly desirable when the low mintage figures were published. Examples remain valuable today, and deservedly so. Nearly all are superb gems.

	Distribution	Cert	Avg	%MS	MS-67
					PF-67
1998-S	37,210	1,358	69.2	100%	$60
	Auctions: $176, MS-70, April 2013				
1998-S, Proof	75,070	1,538	69.0		$50
	Auctions: $353, PF-70DCam, April 2013				

ROBERT F. KENNEDY SILVER DOLLAR (1998)

Designer: *Thomas D. Rogers Sr.* **Weight:** *26.73 grams.*
Composition: *.900 silver, .100 copper (net weight .7736 oz. pure silver).*
Diameter: *38.1 mm.* **Edge:** *Reeded.* **Mint:** *San Francisco.*

These coins marked the 30th anniversary of the death of Robert F. Kennedy, attorney general of the United States appointed by his brother, President John F. Kennedy.

Designs. *Obverse:* Portrait of Robert F. Kennedy. *Reverse:* Eagle perched on a shield with JUSTICE above, Senate seal to lower left.

Mintage Data. Authorized by Public Law 103-328, signed by President William J. Clinton on September 29, 1994. *Maximum authorized*—500,000. *Number minted*—106,422 Uncirculated and 99,020 Proof.

Original Cost. Sale prices $30 (Uncirculated, pre-issue) and $33 (Proof, pre-issue); Uncirculated later raised to $32, and Proof later raised to $37. A portion of the surcharge of $10 per coin went to the Robert F. Kennedy Memorial.

Key to Collecting. Upon their publication the mintage figures were viewed as being attractively low from a numismatic viewpoint. Examples are easily found today and are usually superb gems.

	Distribution	Cert	Avg	%MS	MS-67
					PF-67
1998-S	106,422	3,332	69.3	100%	$30
	Auctions: $70, MS-70, July 2014; $129, MS-70, April 2013				
1998-S, Proof	99,020	1,623	69.0		$40
	Auctions: $282, PF-70DCam, September 2014; $270, PF-70DCam, September 2014				

DOLLEY MADISON SILVER DOLLAR (1999)

Designer: *Tiffany & Co.* **Weight:** *26.73 grams.*
Composition: *.900 silver, .100 copper (net weight .7736 oz. pure silver).*
Diameter: *38.1 mm.* **Edge:** *Reeded.* **Mint:** *Philadelphia.*

If the myth that Martha Washington was the subject for the 1792 silver half disme is discarded, Dolley Madison, wife of President James Madison, became the first of the first ladies to be depicted on a legal-tender U.S. coin with this silver dollar. The designs by Tiffany & Co. were modeled by T. James Ferrell (obverse) and Thomas D. Rogers Sr. (reverse). Note the T&Co. logo in a flower petal on the obverse and at the base of the trees to the right on the reverse.

Designs. *Obverse:* Portrait of Dolley Madison as depicted near the ice house (in the style of classic pergola) on the grounds of the family estate, Montpelier. A bouquet of cape jasmines is to the left. *Reverse:* Angular view of the front of Montpelier, complete with landscaping.

Mintage Data. Authorized by Public Law 104-329, signed by President William J. Clinton on October 20, 1996. *Maximum authorized*—500,000. *Number minted*—89,104 Uncirculated and 224,403 Proof.

Original Cost. Sale prices $30 (Uncirculated, pre-issue) and $33 (Proof, pre-issue); Uncirculated later raised to $32, and Proof later raised to $37. A portion of the surcharge of $10 per coin went to the National Trust for Historic Preservation.

Key to Collecting. The Dolley Madison dollars have been popular with collectors ever since they were first sold. Examples can be obtained with little effort and are usually superb gems.

	Distribution	Cert	Avg	%MS	MS-67
					PF-67
1999-P	89,104	2,271	69.4	100%	$30
	Auctions: $90, MS-70, April 2013				
1999-P, Proof	224,403	2,775	69.2		$30
	Auctions: $106, PF-70DCam, April 2013				

GEORGE WASHINGTON DEATH BICENTENNIAL $5 GOLD COIN (1999)

Designer: *Laura Garden Fraser.* **Weight:** *8.359 grams.*
Composition: *.900 gold, .100 copper (net weight .242 oz. pure gold).*
Diameter: *21.6 mm.* **Edge:** *Reeded.* **Mint:** *West Point.*

The 200th anniversary of George Washington's death was commemorated with this coin. In 1932 Laura Garden Fraser's proposed Washington portrait for the quarter dollar had been rejected in favor of the portrait design by John Flanagan, but it was resurrected for this commemorative gold coin.

Designs. *Obverse:* A portrait of Washington inspired by the bust modeled in 1785 for French sculptor Jean Antoine Houdon. *Reverse:* A perched eagle with feathers widely separated at left and right.

Mintage Data. Authorized on October 20, 1996, by Public Law 104-329, part of the United States Commemorative Coin Act of 1996. *Maximum authorized*—100,000 pieces (both formats combined). *Number minted*—22,511 Uncirculated and 41,693 Proof.

Original Cost. Sale prices $180 (Uncirculated, pre-issue) and $195 (Proof, pre-issue); Uncirculated later raised to $195, and Proof later raised to $225. A portion of the surcharge went to the Mount Vernon Ladies' Association, which cares for Washington's home today.

Key to Collecting. This coin is readily available in any high grade desired.

	Distribution	Cert	Avg	%MS	MS-67
					PF-67
1999-W	22,511	1,525	69.5	100%	$500
	Auctions: $423, MS-70, April 2015; $423, MS-70, April 2015; $400, MS-70, April 2015; $353, MS-70, April 2015				
1999-W, Proof	41,693	2,133	69.4		$500
	Auctions: $705, PF-70DCam, March 2013; $400, PF-70UCam, April 2015; $382, PF-69DCam, July 2014				

YELLOWSTONE NATIONAL PARK SILVER DOLLAR (1999)

Designer: *Edgar Z. Steever IV (obverse), William C. Cousins (reverse).* **Weight:** *26.73 grams.*
Composition: *.900 silver, .100 copper (net weight .7736 oz. pure silver).*
Diameter: *38.1 mm.* **Edge:** *Reeded.* **Mint:** *Philadelphia.*

This coin commemorated the 125th anniversary of the establishment of Yellowstone National Park. Technically, it came out and was dated two years later than it should have, as the park was founded in 1872 (and therefore the 125th anniversary would have been in 1997, not 1999).

Designs. *Obverse:* An unidentified geyser (not the famed Old Faithful, for the terrain is different) is shown in action. YELLOWSTONE is above, with other inscriptions to the left center and below, as illustrated. *Reverse:* A bison is shown, facing left. In the background is a mountain range with sun and resplendent rays (an adaptation of the seal of the Department of the Interior).

Mintage Data. Authorized on October 20, 1996, by Public Law 104-329, part of the United States Commemorative Coin Act of 1996. The catch-all legislation authorized seven commemoratives to be issued from 1997 to 1999. *Maximum authorized*—500,000 (both formats combined). *Number minted*—82,563 Uncirculated and 187,595 Proof.

Original Cost. Sale prices $30 (Uncirculated, pre-issue) and $33 (Proof, pre-issue); Uncirculated later raised to $32, and Proof later raised to $37.

Key to Collecting. Easily obtainable in the numismatic marketplace, nearly always in high grades. Investors are attracted to coins certified as MS-70 or PF-70, but few can tell the difference between these and coins at the 69 level. Only a tiny fraction of the mintage has ever been certified.

	Distribution	Cert	Avg	%MS	MS-67
					PF-67
1999-P	82,563	1,931	69.3	100%	$40
	Auctions: No auction records available.				
1999-P, Proof	187,595	2,280	69.0		$40
	Auctions: $282, PF-70UCam, July 2015				

LIBRARY OF CONGRESS BICENTENNIAL SILVER DOLLAR (2000)

Designer: *Thomas D. Rogers Sr. (obverse), John Mercanti (reverse).* **Weight:** *26.73 grams.*
Composition: *.900 silver, .100 copper (net weight .7736 oz. pure silver).*
Diameter: *38.1 mm.* **Edge:** *Reeded.* **Mint:** *Philadelphia.*

The Library of Congress, located across the street from the U.S. Capitol in Washington, celebrated its 200th anniversary on April 24, 2000; these silver dollars and a ten-dollar bimetallic coin were issued to honor the milestone.

Designs. *Obverse:* An open book, with its spine resting on a closed book, with the torch of the Library of Congress dome behind. *Reverse:* The dome part of the Library of Congress.

Mintage Data. Authorized by Public Law 105-268, signed by President William J. Clinton on October 19, 1996. *Maximum authorized—*500,000. *Number minted—*53,264 Uncirculated and 198,503 Proof.

Original Cost. Sale prices $25 (Uncirculated, pre-issue) and $28 (Proof, pre-issue); Uncirculated later raised to $27, and Proof later raised to $32. A portion of the surcharges went to the Library of Congress Trust Fund Board.

Key to Collecting. The Library of Congress silver dollar (as well as the ten-dollar bimetallic coin issued alongside it) is readily available in the marketplace today, nearly always of the superb gem quality, as issued.

	Distribution	Cert	Avg	%MS	MS-67 PF-67
2000-P	53,264	1,668	69.4	100%	$25
Auctions: $108, MS-70, April 2013; $76, MS-70, July 2014; $74, MS-70, October 2015					
2000-P, Proof	198,503	2,102	69.0		$25
Auctions: $188, PF-70DCam, September 2014; $635, PF-70DCam, April 2013					

LIBRARY OF CONGRESS BICENTENNIAL $10 BIMETALLIC COIN (2000)

Designer: *John Mercanti (obverse), Thomas D. Rogers Sr. (reverse).*
Weight: *16.259 grams.* **Composition:** *.480 gold, .480 platinum, .040 alloy.*
Diameter: *27 mm.* **Edge:** *Reeded.* **Mint:** *West Point.*

This coin was the U.S. Mint's first gold/ platinum bimetallic coin. The Library of Congress—the original location of which was burned by the British, but which was resurrected using Thomas Jefferson's personal book collection—is today a repository that includes 18 million books and more than 100 million other items, including periodicals, films, prints, photographs, and recordings.

Designs. *Obverse:* The torch of the Library of Congress dome. *Reverse:* An eagle surrounded by a wreath.

Mintage Data. Authorized by Public Law 105-268, signed by President William J. Clinton on October 19, 1996. *Maximum authorized—*200,000. *Number minted—*7,261 Uncirculated and 27,445 Proof.

Original Cost. Sale prices $380 (Uncirculated, pre-issue) and $395 (Proof, pre-issue); Uncirculated later raised to $405, and Proof later raised to $425. A portion of the surcharges went to the Library of Congress Trust Fund Board.

Key to Collecting. The Library of Congress ten-dollar bimetallic coin (as well as the silver dollar issued alongside it) is readily available in the marketplace today, nearly always of the superb gem quality as issued.

	Distribution	Cert	Avg	%MS	MS-67 PF-67
2000-W ††	7,261	1,637	69.7	100%	$1,200
Auctions: $2,115, MS-70, June 2015; $1,998, MS-70, August 2015; $1,293, MS-69, October 2015; $1,175, MS-69, June 2015					
2000-W, Proof ††	27,445	3,821	69.3		$1,000
Auctions: $2,115, PF-70DCam, September 2015; $1,763, PF-70UCam, October 2015; $823, PF-69UCam, October 2015					

†† Both 2000 Library of Congress $10 Bimetallic Coins are ranked in the *100 Greatest U.S. Modern Coins* (fourth edition), as a single entry.

LEIF ERICSON MILLENNIUM SILVER DOLLAR (2000)

Designer: *John Mercanti (obverse), T. James Ferrell (reverse).* **Weight:** *26.73 grams.*
Composition: *.900 silver, .100 copper (net weight .7736 oz. pure silver).*
Diameter: *38.1 mm.* **Edge:** *Reeded.* **Mint:** *Philadelphia.*

This silver dollar was issued in cooperation with a foreign government, the Republic of Iceland, which also sponsored its own coin, struck at the Philadelphia Mint (but with no mintmark), a silver 1,000 krónur. Both commemorated the millennium of the year 1000, the approximate departure date of Leif Ericson and his crew from Iceland to the New World.

Designs. *Obverse:* Portrait of Leif Ericson, an artist's conception, as no actual image survives—based on the image used on the Iceland 1 krónur coin. The helmeted head of the explorer is shown facing right. *Reverse:* A Viking long ship with high prow under full sail, FOUNDER OF THE NEW WORLD above, other inscriptions below.

Mintage Data. Authorized under Public Law 106-126. *Maximum authorized*—500,000. *Number minted*—28,150 Uncirculated and 144,748 Proof.

Original Cost. Sale prices $30 (Uncirculated, pre-issue) and $33 (Proof, pre-issue); Uncirculated later raised to $32, and Proof later raised to $37. The surcharge of $10 per coin went to the Leifur Eiriksson Foundation for funding student exchanges between the United States and Iceland.

Key to Collecting. These coins are readily available in the marketplace today.

	Distribution	Cert	Avg	%MS	MS-67
					PF-67
2000-P	28,150	1,383	69.4	100%	$65
	Auctions: $223, MS-70, June 2015; $212, MS-70, January 2013; $176, MS-70, July 2014				
2000-P, Proof	144,748	2,686	69.0		$55
	Auctions: $999, PF-70DCam, September 2014; $999, PF-70DCam, April 2013				

AMERICAN BUFFALO SILVER DOLLAR (2001)

Designer: *James Earle Fraser.* **Weight:** *26.73 grams.*
Composition: *.900 silver, .100 copper (net weight .7736 oz. pure silver).*
Diameter: *38.1 mm.* **Edge:** *Reeded.* **Mints:** *Denver (Uncirculated) and Philadelphia (Proof).*

James Earle Fraser's design, originally used on nickels from 1913 to 1938, was modified slightly by Mint engravers for this silver dollar. Commonly called the "American Buffalo Commemorative," the coin debuted at the groundbreaking for the Smithsonian Institution's National Museum of the American Indian and was very well received.

Designs. *Obverse:* Portrait of a Native American facing right. *Reverse:* An American bison standing, facing left.

Mintage Data. Authorized by Public Law 106-375, October 27, 2000. *Maximum authorized*—500,000. *Number minted*—2001-D: 227,131 Uncirculated; 2001-P: 272,869 Proof.

Original Cost. Sale prices (pre-issue only) $30 (Uncirculated) and $33 (Proof). The surcharge of $10 per coin went to the National Museum of the American Indian.

Key to Collecting. Both the Uncirculated and Proof of the 2001 American Buffalo were carefully produced to high standards of quality. Nearly all examples today grade at high levels, including MS-70 and PF-70, these ultra-grades commanding a sharp premium for investors. Coins grading 68 or 69 often have little or any real difference in quality and would seem to be the best buys.

	Distribution	Cert	Avg	%MS	MS-67
					PF-67
2001-D ††	227,131	16,797	69.1	100%	$125
	Auctions: $259, MS-70, February 2015; $235, MS-70, July 2015; $259, MS-69, June 2015; $165, MS-69, January 2015				
2001-P, Proof ††	272,869	18,088	69.1		$120
	Auctions: $376, PF-70DCam, February 2015; $353, PF-70DCam, January 2015; $153, PF-69DCam, June 2015; $141, PF-69DCam, June 2015				

†† Both 2001 American Buffalo Silver Dollar varieties are ranked in the *100 Greatest U.S. Modern Coins* (fourth edition), as a single entry.

U.S. CAPITOL VISITOR CENTER HALF DOLLAR (2001)

Designer: *Dean McMullen (obverse), Alex Shagin and Marcel Jovine (reverse).* **Weight:** *11.34 grams.* **Composition:** *.9167 copper, .0833 nickel.* **Diameter:** *30.61 mm.* **Edge:** *Reeded.* **Mint:** *Philadelphia.*

In 1991 Congress voted on a Visitor Center to be established near the U.S. Capitol building. This copper-nickel half dollar, as well as a silver dollar and a ten-dollar gold coin, were decided upon to provide the funds through sale surcharges. The center and the coins did not become a reality until more than a decade later, though.

Designs. *Obverse:* The north wing of the original U.S. Capitol (burned by the British in 1814) is shown superimposed on a plan view of the present building. *Reverse:* Within a circle of 16 stars are inscriptions referring to the first meeting of the Senate and House.

Mintage Data. Authorized by Public Law 106-126, signed by President William J. Clinton on December 6, 1999. *Maximum authorized*—750,000. *Number minted*—99,157 Uncirculated and 77,962 Proof.

Original Cost. Sale prices $7.75 (Uncirculated, pre-issue) and $10.75 (Proof, pre-issue); Uncirculated later raised to $8.50, and Proof later raised to $11.50. The $3 surcharge per coin went towards the construction of the Visitor Center.

Key to Collecting. Today, this half dollar is readily available on the market, nearly always in the same gem quality as issued.

	Distribution	Cert	Avg	%MS	MS-67
					PF-67
2001-P	99,157	3,436	69.5	100%	$16
	Auctions: $153, MS-70, August 2013				
2001-P, Proof	77,962	1,428	69.0		$20
	Auctions: No auction records available.				

U.S. CAPITOL VISITOR CENTER SILVER DOLLAR (2001)

Designer: *Marika Somogyi (obverse), John Mercanti (reverse).* **Weight:** *26.73 grams.*
Composition: *.900 silver, .100 copper (net weight .7736 oz. pure silver).*
Diameter: *38.1 mm.* **Edge:** *Reeded.* **Mint:** *Philadelphia.*

The U.S. Capitol Visitor Center, as first proposed, was to offer free exhibits and films, and it was believed that the center would eliminate lengthy waits to view the Capitol proper. However, presumably many would still want to visit the Capitol itself, and no further plan to eliminate waiting time was presented. After the September 11, 2001, terrorist attack on the World Trade Center in New York City and the Pentagon in the District of Columbia, security at the Capitol was heightened—and the concept of the Visitor Center became even more important.

Designs. *Obverse:* The original Capitol is shown with the date 1800, and a much smaller later Capitol, with the date 2001—a variation on the same theme as used on the half dollar. *Reverse:* An eagle reminiscent of Mint engraver John Mercanti's reverse for the 1986 silver bullion "Eagle" dollar. In the present incarnation, the national bird wears a ribbon lettered U.S. CAPITOL VISITOR CENTER.

Mintage Data. Authorized by Public Law 106-126, signed by President William J. Clinton on December 6, 1999. *Maximum authorized—*500,000. *Number minted—*35,380 Uncirculated and 143,793 Proof.

Original Cost. Sale prices $27 (Uncirculated, pre-issue) and $29 (Proof, pre-issue); Uncirculated later raised to $29, and Proof later raised to $33. The $10 surcharge per coin went towards the construction of the Visitor Center.

Key to Collecting. Today, this silver dollar is readily available on the market, nearly always in the same gem quality as issued.

	Distribution	Cert	Avg	%MS	MS-67 PF-67
2001-P	35,380	1,904	69.3	100%	$30
	Auctions: $129, MS-70, April 2013				
2001-P, Proof	143,793	2,242	69.0		$36
	Auctions: $294, PF-70DCam, February 2014; $4,113, PF-70DCam, April 2013				

U.S. CAPITOL VISITOR CENTER $5 GOLD COIN (2001)

Designer: *Elizabeth Jones.* **Weight:** *8.359 grams.* **Composition:** *.900 gold, .100 copper*
(net weight .242 oz. pure gold). **Diameter:** *21.6 mm.* **Edge:** *Reeded.* **Mint:** *West Point.*

If there was a potential highlight for what proved to be yet another underperforming commemorative issue—with sales far below projections—it was that Elizabeth Jones, former chief engraver at the Mint, was tapped to do the obverse of the $5 gold coin in the Capitol Visitor Center series. The result might not be a showcase for her remarkable talent, given the nature of the subject, but it rounds out the suite of three commemorative coins with detailed architectural motifs.

Designs. *Obverse:* Section of a Corinthian column. *Reverse:* The 1800 Capitol (interestingly, with slightly different architectural details and proportions than seen on the other coins).

Mintage Data. Authorized by Public Law 106-126, signed by President William J. Clinton on December 6, 1999. *Maximum authorized*—100,000. *Number minted*—6,761 Uncirculated and 27,652 Proof.

Original Cost. Sale prices $175 (Uncirculated, pre-issue) and $177 (Proof, pre-issue); Uncirculated later raised to $200, and Proof later raised to $207. The $35 surcharge per coin went towards the construction of the Visitor Center.

Key to Collecting. Of all the Capitol Visitor Center commemoratives, the Uncirculated five-dollar gold coin is least often seen. After the distribution figure of only 6,761 was released for that coin, buyers clamored to acquire them, and the price rose sharply. Today, it still sells at one of the greatest premiums of any modern commemorative.

	Distribution	Cert	Avg	%MS	MS-67
					PF-67
2001-W ††	6,761	2,100	69.6	100%	$550
	Auctions: $1,087, MS-70, July 2014; $1,058, MS-70, August 2014; $881, MS-70, January 2015; $764, MS-70, June 2015				
2001-W, Proof	27,652	1,897	69.4		$500
	Auctions: No auction records available.				

†† Ranked in the *100 Greatest U.S. Modern Coins* (fourth edition).

SALT LAKE CITY OLYMPIC WINTER GAMES SILVER DOLLAR (2002)

Designer: *John Mercanti (obverse), Donna Weaver (reverse).* **Weight:** *26.73 grams.*
Composition: *.900 silver, .100 copper (net weight .7736 oz. pure silver).*
Diameter: *38.1 mm.* **Edge:** *Reeded.* **Mint:** *Philadelphia.*

In February 2002, Salt Lake City, Utah, was the focal point for the XIX Olympic Winter Games, a quadrennial event. Congress authorized both this silver dollar and a five-dollar gold coin to commemorate the competition.

Designs. *Obverse:* A stylized geometric figure representing an ice crystal. Five interlocked Olympic rings and inscriptions complete the picture, including XIX OLYMPIC WINTER GAMES. *Reverse:* The skyline of Salt Lake City is shown with exaggerated dimensions, with the rugged Wasatch Mountains in the distance. XIX OLYMPIC GAMES is repeated on the reverse.

Mintage Data. Authorized by Public Law 106-435, the Salt Lake Olympic Winter Games Commemorative Coin Act, signed by President William J. Clinton on November 6, 2000. *Maximum authorized*—400,000. *Number minted*—40,257 Uncirculated and 166,864 Proof.

Original Cost. Sale prices $30 (Uncirculated, pre-issue) and $33 (Proof, pre-issue); Uncirculated were later raised to $32, and Proof were later raised to $37. The surcharge of $10 per coin went to the Salt Lake Organizing Committee for the Olympic Winter Games of 2002 and the United States Olympic Committee.

Key to Collecting. As might be expected, coins encapsulated as MS-70 and PF-70 sell for strong prices to investors and Registry Set compilers. Most collectors are nicely satisfied with 68 and 69 grades, or the normal issue quality, since the coins are little different in actual appearance.

	Distribution	Cert	Avg	%MS	MS-67
					PF-67
2002-P	40,257	1,588	69.5	100%	$35
	Auctions: $94, MS-70, January 2013				
2002-P, Proof	166,864	2,224	69.1		$30
	Auctions: $217, PF-70DCam, April 2013				

SALT LAKE CITY OLYMPIC WINTER GAMES $5 GOLD COIN (2002)

Designer: *Donna Weaver.* **Weight:** *8.359 grams.*
Composition: *.900 gold, .100 copper (net weight .242 oz. pure gold).*
Diameter: *21.6 mm.* **Edge:** *Reeded.* **Mint:** *West Point.*

The design of the 2002 Olympic Winter Games commemoratives attracted little favorable notice outside of advertising publicity, and, once again, sales were low—all the more surprising, for Olympic coins often attract international buyers.

Designs. *Obverse:* An ice crystal dominates, superimposed over a geometric creation representing "Rhythm of the Land," but not identified. Also appearing are the date and SALT LAKE. *Reverse:* The outline of the Olympic cauldron is shown, with geometric sails above representing flames.

Mintage Data. Authorized by Public Law 106-435, the Salt Lake Olympic Winter Games Commemorative Coin Act, signed by President William J. Clinton on November 6, 2000. *Maximum authorized*—80,000. *Number minted*—10,585 Uncirculated and 32,877 Proof.

Original Cost. Sale prices $180 (Uncirculated, pre-issue) and $195 (Proof, pre-issue); Uncirculated were later raised to $205, and Proof were later raised to $225. The surcharge of $10 per coin went to the Salt Lake Organizing Committee for the Olympic Winter Games of 2002 and the United States Olympic Committee.

Key to Collecting. Although the mintage of the Uncirculated $5 in particular was quite low, there was not much interest in the immediate aftermarket. Coins graded MS-70 and PF-70 sell for strong prices to investors and Registry Set compilers.

	Distribution	Cert	Avg	%MS	MS-67
					PF-67
2002-W	10,585	1,207	69.5	100%	$500
	Auctions: $499, MS-70, August 2013; $397, MS-70, September 2014; $353, MS-70, April 2015				
2002-W, Proof	32,877	1,246	69.5		$500
	Auctions: $400, PF-70UCam, May 2015; $376, PF-70UCam, April 2015; $108, PF-70DCam, April 2013; $33, PF-69DCam, August 2014				

WEST POINT (U.S. MILITARY ACADEMY) BICENTENNIAL SILVER DOLLAR (2002)

Designer: *T. James Ferrell (obverse), John Mercanti (reverse).* **Weight:** *26.73 grams.*
Composition: *.900 silver, .100 copper (net weight .7736 oz. pure silver).*
Diameter: *38.1 mm.* **Edge:** *Reeded.* **Mint:** *West Point.*

The 200th anniversary of the U.S. Military Academy at West Point, New York, was celebrated with this coin. The Cadet Chapel is shown on the obverse of the dollar.

Designs. *Obverse:* A fine depiction of the Academy color guard in a parade, with Washington Hall and the Cadet Chapel in the distance— and minimum intrusion of lettering—projects this to the forefront of commemorative designs of the era. *Reverse:* The West Point Bicentennial logotype is shown, an adaptation of the Academy seal, showing at the center an ancient Greek helmet with a sword and shield.

Mintage Data. Authorized several years earlier by Public Law 103-328, signed by President William J. Clinton on September 29, 1994. *Maximum authorized*—500,000. *Number minted*—103,201 Uncirculated and 288,293 Proof.

Original Cost. Sale prices $30 (Uncirculated, pre-issue) and $32 (Proof, pre-issue); Uncirculated later raised to $32, and Proof later raised to $37. The surcharge of $10 per coin went to the Association of Graduates.

Key to Collecting. The scenario is familiar: enough coins were struck to satisfy all comers during the period of issue, with the result that there was no unsatisfied demand. Coins certified at the MS-70 level appeal to a special group of buyers and command strong premiums.

	Distribution	Cert	Avg	%MS	MS-67
					PF-67
2002-W	103,201	4,526	69.5	100%	$25
	Auctions: No auction records available.				
2002-W, Proof	288,293	5,643	69.3		$35
	Auctions: No auction records available.				

FIRST FLIGHT CENTENNIAL HALF DOLLAR (2003)

Designer: *John Mercanti (obverse), Norman E. Nemeth (reverse).* **Weight:** *11.34 grams.*
Composition: *.9167 copper, .0833 nickel.* **Diameter:** *30.61 mm.* **Edge:** *Reeded.* **Mint:** *Philadelphia.*

To celebrate the 100th anniversary of powered aircraft flight by Orville and Wilbur Wright in 1903, Congress authorized a set of 2003-dated commemoratives, including this copper-nickel half dollar.

Designs. *Obverse:* Wright Monument at Kill Devil Hill on the North Carolina seashore. *Reverse:* Wright Flyer biplane in flight.

Mintage Data. Authorized by Public Law 105-124, as an amendment and tag-on to the 50 States Commemorative Coin Program Act (which authorized the State quarters), signed by President William J. Clinton on December 1, 1997. *Maximum authorized*—750,000. *Number minted*—57,122 Uncirculated and 109,710 Proof.

Original Cost. Sale prices $9.75 (Uncirculated, pre-issue) and $12.50 (Proof, pre-issue); Uncirculated later raised to $10.75, and Proof later raised to $13.50. The surcharge of $1 per coin went to the First Flight Centennial Foundation, a private nonprofit group founded in 1995.

Key to Collecting. Values fell after sales concluded. In time, they recovered. Today, all the coins in this set sell for a premium. Superb gems are easily enough found.

	Distribution	Cert	Avg	%MS	MS-67 PF-67
2003-P	57,122	2,203	69.5	100%	$16
	Auctions: $50, MS-70, April 2013				
2003-P, Proof	109,710	2,128	69.1		$18
	Auctions: No auction records available.				

FIRST FLIGHT CENTENNIAL SILVER DOLLAR (2003)

Designer: *T. James Ferrell (obverse), Norman E. Nemeth (reverse).* **Weight:** *26.73 grams.*
Composition: *.900 silver, .100 copper (net weight .7736 oz. pure silver).*
Diameter: *38.1 mm.* **Edge:** *Reeded.* **Mint:** *Philadelphia.*

The release of this coin and the two other First Flight Centennial commemoratives with it marked the third straight year that a coin featuring the Wrights' plane was featured on a U.S. coin. In 2001, the North Carolina State quarter had portrayed the Wright Flyer, and the Ohio State quarter did the same in 2002 (though an astronaut was also incorporated).

Designs. *Obverse:* Conjoined portraits of Orville and Wilbur Wright. *Reverse:* The Wright brothers' plane in flight.

Mintage Data. Authorized by Public Law 105-124, as an amendment and tag-on to the 50 States Commemorative Coin Program Act (which authorized the State quarters), signed by President William J. Clinton on December 1, 1997. *Maximum authorized*—500,000. *Number minted*—53,533 Uncirculated and 190,240 Proof.

Original Cost. Sale prices $31 (Uncirculated, pre-issue) and $33 (Proof, pre-issue); Uncirculated later raised to $33, and Proof later raised to $37. The surcharge of $1 per coin went to the First Flight Centennial Foundation, a private nonprofit group founded in 1995.

Key to Collecting. Values fell after sales concluded, but they did recover in time. Today, all the coins in this program sell for a premium. Superb gems are easily enough found.

	Distribution	Cert	Avg	%MS	MS-67 PF-67
2003-P	53,533	3,223	69.4	100%	$40
	Auctions: $94, MS-70, May 2013				
2003-P, Proof	190,240	3,187	69.0		$42
	Auctions: $423, PF-70DCam, March 2013; $141, PF-70DCam, April 2013				

FIRST FLIGHT CENTENNIAL $10 GOLD COIN (2003)

Designer: *Donna Weaver (obverse), Norman E. Nemeth (reverse).* **Weight:** *16.718 grams.*
Composition: *.900 gold, .100 copper (net weight .4837 oz. pure gold).*
Diameter: *27 mm.* **Edge:** *Reeded.* **Mint:** *West Point.*

None of the First Flight Centennial commemoratives sold particularly well. The redundancy of the motifs undoubtedly contributed to this: each had the same reverse motif of the Wright brothers' plane, and the two largest denominations each pictured the Wright brothers.

Designs. *Obverse:* Portraits of Orville and Wilbur Wright. *Reverse:* Wright Brothers' plane in flight with an eagle overhead.

Mintage Data. Authorized by Public Law 105-124, as an amendment and tag-on to the 50 States Commemorative Coin Program Act (which authorized the State quarters), signed by President William J. Clinton on December 1, 1997. *Maximum authorized*—100,000. *Number minted*—10,009 Uncirculated and 21,676 Proof.

Original Cost. Sale prices $340 (Uncirculated, pre-issue) and $350 (Proof, pre-issue); Uncirculated later raised to $365, and Proof later raised to $375. The surcharge of $1 per coin went to the First Flight Centennial Foundation, a private nonprofit group founded in 1995.

Key to Collecting. Values fell after sales concluded, but they did recover in time. Today, all the coins in this commemorative program sell for a premium. Superb gems are easily enough found.

	Distribution	Cert	Avg	%MS	MS-67
					PF-67
2003-W ††	10,009	1,919	69.8	100%	$1,000
	Auctions: $823, MS-70, July 2015; $793, MS-70, January 2015; $617, MS-69, July 2015; $588, MS-69, June 2015				
2003-W, Proof	21,676	1,666	69.3		$1,000
	Auctions: $823, PF-70DCam, July 2014; $1,293, PF-70DCam, April 2013				

†† Ranked in the *100 Greatest U.S. Modern Coins* (fourth edition).

THOMAS ALVA EDISON SILVER DOLLAR (2004)

Designer: *Donna Weaver (obverse), John Mercanti (reverse).* **Weight:** *26.73 grams.*
Composition: *.900 silver, .100 copper (net weight .7736 oz. pure silver).*
Diameter: *38.1 mm.* **Edge:** *Reeded.* **Mint:** *Philadelphia.*

The 125th anniversary of the October 21, 1879, demonstration by Thomas Edison of his first successful electric light bulb was the event commemorated with this silver dollar. Despite sales falling far short of the authorized amount, the Edison dollar was well received by collectors. Interestingly, several proposals had earlier been made for commemoratives to be issued in 1997 to observe the 150th anniversary of Edison's February 11, 1847, birth in Milan, Ohio.

Designs. *Obverse:* Waist-up portrait of Edison holding a light bulb in his right hand. *Reverse:* Light bulb of the 1879 style mounted on a base, with arcs surrounding.

Mintage Data. Authorized by Public Law 105-331, signed by President William J. Clinton on December 6, 1999. *Maximum authorized*—500,000. *Number minted*—92,510 Uncirculated and 211,055 Proof.

Original Cost. Sale prices $31 (Uncirculated, pre-issue) and $33 (Proof, pre-issue); Uncirculated later raised to $33, and Proof later raised to $37. The surcharge of $10 per coin was to be divided evenly among the Port Huron (Michigan) Museum of Arts and History, the Edison Birthplace Association, the National Park Service, the Edison Plaza Museum, the Edison Winter Home and Museum, the Edison Institute, the Edison Memorial Tower, and the Hall of Electrical History.

Key to Collecting. Examples are plentiful. Nearly all are superb gems. As was the situation for many other U.S. Mint issues of the period, promoters who had coins encased in certified holders marked MS-70 or PF-70 were able to persuade, or at least imply, to investors (but not to seasoned collectors) that coins of such quality were rarities, and obtained strong prices for them. Smart buyers simply purchased examples remaining in original Mint holders, of which many were just as nice as the "70" coins.

	Distribution	Cert	Avg	%MS	MS-67
					PF-67
2004-P	92,510	2,853	69.3	100%	$35
	Auctions: $90, MS-70, April 2013				
2004-P, Proof	211,055	3,551	69.1		$35
	Auctions: $78, PF-70DCam, July 2014; $141, PF-70DCam, March 2013				

LEWIS AND CLARK BICENTENNIAL SILVER DOLLAR (2004)

Designer: *Donna Weaver.* **Weight:** *26.73 grams.*
Composition: *.900 silver, .100 copper (net weight .7736 oz. pure silver).*
Diameter: *38.1 mm.* **Edge:** *Reeded.* **Mint:** *Philadelphia.*

This was one of the most successful commemorative programs, despite the fact that many events across the nation celebrating the bicentennial were flops. Note that the Lewis and Clark Expedition had previously been commemorated with gold dollars dated 1903 for the Louisiana Purchase Exposition (St. Louis World's Fair held in 1904) and those of 1904 and 1905 for the Lewis and Clark Exposition (Portland, Oregon, 1905).

Designs. *Obverse:* Meriwether Lewis and William Clark standing with a river and foliage in the distance as a separate motif. Lewis holds the barrel end of his rifle in one hand and a journal in the other and is looking at Clark, who is gazing to the distance in the opposite direction. *Reverse:* Copy of the reverse of the Jefferson Indian Peace medal designed by John Reich and presented to Indians on the expedition (the identical motif was also revived for use on one variety of the 2004 Jefferson nickel). Feathers are to the left and right, and 17 stars are above.

Mintage Data. Authorized by Public Law 106-136, signed by President William J. Clinton on December 6, 1999. *Maximum authorized*—500,000. *Number minted*—142,015 Uncirculated and 351,989 Proof.

Original Cost. Sale prices $33 (Uncirculated, pre-issue) and $35 (Proof, pre-issue); Uncirculated later raised to $35, and Proof later raised to $39. Two-thirds of the surcharge of $10 per coin went to the National Council of the Lewis and Clark Bicentennial, while one-third went to the National Park Service for the bicentennial celebration.

Key to Collecting. Superb gem coins are readily available.

	Distribution	Cert	Avg	%MS	MS-67
					PF-67
2004-P	142,015	4,271	69.4	100%	$35
Auctions: $90, MS-70, April 2013					
2004-P, Proof	351,989	5,925	69.1		$30
Auctions: $88, PF-70DCam, February 2013					

MARINE CORPS 230TH ANNIVERSARY SILVER DOLLAR (2005)

Designer: *Norman E. Nemeth (obverse), Charles L. Vickers (reverse).* **Weight:** *26.73 grams.*
Composition: *.900 silver, .100 copper (net weight .7736 oz. pure silver).*
Diameter: *38.1 mm.* **Edge:** *Reeded.* **Mint:** *Philadelphia.*

The widespread appreciation of the heritage of the Marine Corps plus the fame of the obverse design taken from Joe Rosenthal's photograph of the flag-raising at Iwo Jima, propelled this coin to remarkable success. For the first time in recent memory, pandemonium reigned in the coin market, as prices rose, buyers clamored to find all they could, and most dealers were sold out. Within a year, interest turned to other things, and the prices dropped, but not down to the issue levels.

Designs. *Obverse:* Marines raising the Stars and Stripes over Iwo Jima as shown on the famous photograph by Joe Rosenthal. *Reverse:* Eagle, globe, and anchor emblem of the Marine Corps.

Mintage Data. Authorized under Public Law 108-291, signed by President George W. Bush on August 6, 2004. *Maximum authorized*—500,000, later increased to 600,000. *Number minted*—49,671 Uncirculated and 548,810 Proof.

Original Cost. Sale prices $33 (Uncirculated, pre-issue) and $35 (Proof, pre-issue); Uncirculated later raised to $35, and Proof later raised to $39. The surcharge of $10 per coin went toward the construction of the Marine Corps Heritage Center at the base in Quantico, Virginia.

Key to Collecting. Superb gem coins are readily available.

	Distribution	Cert	Avg	%MS	MS-67
					PF-67
2005-P	49,671	13,578	69.6	100%	$45
Auctions: $89, MS-70, January 2015; $76, MS-70, July 2014; $62, MS-70, August 2014					
2005-P, Proof	548,810	14,358	69.2		$45
Auctions: $165, PF-70DCam, November 2013					

CHIEF JUSTICE JOHN MARSHALL SILVER DOLLAR (2005)

Designer: *John Mercanti (obverse), Donna Weaver (reverse).* **Weight:** *26.73 grams.*
Composition: *.900 silver, .100 copper (net weight .7736 oz. pure silver).*
Diameter: *38.1 mm.* **Edge:** *Reeded.* **Mint:** *Philadelphia.*

Chief Justice John Marshall, who served 34 years in that post in the U.S. Supreme Court, was the subject for this commemorative dollar. Mint engravers submitted designs for the coin, with six depictions of Marshall inspired by a painting by Saint-Mèmin, ten from an oil painting by Rembrandt Peale, and three from a statue by William W. Story. It was John Mercanti's interpretation of the Saint-Mèmin work that was selected.

Designs. *Obverse:* Portrait of Marshall, adapted from a painting made in March 1808 by Charles-Balthazar-Julien Fevret de Saint-Mèmin, of France. *Reverse:* The old Supreme Court Chamber within the Capitol.

Mintage Data. Authorized by Public Law 108-290, signed by President George W. Bush on August 9, 2004. *Maximum authorized*—400,000. *Number minted*—67,096 Uncirculated and 196,753 Proof.

Original Cost. Sale prices $33 (Uncirculated, pre-issue) and $35 (Proof, pre-issue); Uncirculated later raised to $35, and Proof later raised to $39. The surcharge of $10 per coin went to the Supreme Court Historical Society.

Key to Collecting. Superb gem coins are available in the marketplace.

	Distribution	Cert	Avg	%MS	MS-67 PF-67
2005-P	67,096	2,441	69.6	100%	$35
Auctions: $106, MS-70, January 2013					
2005-P, Proof	196,753	3,337	69.3		$35
Auctions: $86, PF-70DCam, July 2014; $92, PF-70DCam, March 2013					

BENJAMIN FRANKLIN TERCENTENARY SCIENTIST SILVER DOLLAR (2006)

Designer: *Norman E. Nemeth (obverse), Charles L. Vickers (reverse).* **Weight:** *26.73 grams.*
Composition: *.900 silver, .100 copper (net weight .7736 oz. pure silver).*
Diameter: *38.1 mm.* **Edge:** *Reeded.* **Mint:** *Philadelphia.*

Two silver dollars were issued to commemorate the 300th anniversary of Benjamin Franklin's birth. This version celebrated Franklin's scientific accomplishments, which included discoveries in fields from electricity to oceanography to demographics.

Designs. *Obverse:* Franklin standing with a kite on a string, evocative of his experiments with lightning in June 1752. *Reverse:* Franklin's political cartoon, featuring a snake cut apart, titled "Join, or Die," reflecting the sentiment that the colonies should unite during the French and Indian War (and which had nothing to do with perceived offenses by the British, at this early time). This appeared in Franklin's *Pennsylvania Gazette* on May 9, 1754.

Mintage Data. Authorized by Public Law 104-463, the Benjamin Franklin Tercentenary Act, and signed by President George W. Bush on December 21, 2004. *Maximum authorized—250,000. Number minted—58,000 Uncirculated, 142,000 Proof.*

Original Cost. Sale prices $33 (Uncirculated, pre-issue) and $35 (Proof, pre-issue); Uncirculated later raised to $35, and Proof later raised to $39. The surcharge of $10 per coin went to the Franklin Institute.

Key to Collecting. Superb gems are easily found in the marketplace.

	Distribution	Cert	Avg	%MS	MS-67
					PF-67
2006-P	58,000	7,781	69.7	100%	$32
Auctions: $76, MS-70, January 2013					
2006-P, Proof	142,000	9,910	69.4		$30
Auctions: No auction records available.					

BENJAMIN FRANKLIN TERCENTENARY
FOUNDING FATHER SILVER DOLLAR (2006)

Designer: *Don Everhart (obverse), Donna Weaver (reverse).* **Weight:** *26.73 grams.*
Composition: *.900 silver, .100 copper (net weight .7736 oz. pure silver).*
Diameter: *38.1 mm.* **Edge:** *Reeded.* **Mint:** *Philadelphia.*

The bill authorizing the issue of this silver dollar and its counterpart (see previous coin) took note of many of his accomplishments, stating he was "the only Founding Father to sign all of our Nation's organizational documents," who printed "official currency for the colonies of Pennsylvania, Delaware, New Jersey and Maryland," and helped design the Great Seal of the United States.

Designs. *Obverse:* Head and shoulders portrait of Franklin facing forward slightly to the viewer's right, with his signature reproduced below. *Reverse:* Copy of a 1776 Continental dollar within a frame of modern lettering. The mottoes on this coin were suggested by Franklin.

Mintage Data. Authorized by Public Law 104-463, the Benjamin Franklin Tercentenary Act, and signed by President George W. Bush on December 21, 2004. *Maximum authorized—250,000. Number minted—58,000 Uncirculated, 142,000 Proof.*

Original Cost. Sale prices $33 (Uncirculated, pre-issue) and $35 (Proof, pre-issue); Uncirculated later raised to $35, and Proof later raised to $39. The surcharge of $10 per coin went to the Franklin Institute.

Key to Collecting. Superb gems are easily found in the marketplace.

	Distribution	Cert	Avg	%MS	MS-67
					PF-67
2006-P	58,000	8,391	69.8	100%	$35
Auctions: $90, MS-70, April 2013					
2006-P, Proof	142,000	10,305	69.7		$35
Auctions: $96, PF-70DCam, January 2013; $103, PF-70DCam, April 2013					

SAN FRANCISCO OLD MINT CENTENNIAL SILVER DOLLAR (2006)

Designer: *Sherl J. Winter (obverse), Joseph Menna after George T. Morgan (reverse).*
Weight: *26.73 grams.* **Composition:** *.900 silver, .100 copper (net weight .7736 oz. pure silver).*
Diameter: *38.1 mm.* **Edge:** *Reeded.* **Mint:** *San Francisco.*

This coin and the five-dollar gold coin issued alongside it celebrated the 100th anniversary of the second San Francisco Mint surviving the 1906 Bay Area earthquake and fire.

Designs. *Obverse:* The Second San Francisco Mint as viewed from off the left front corner. *Reverse:* Copy of the reverse of a standard Morgan silver dollar of the era 1878–1921, said to have been taken from a 1904-S.

Mintage Data. Authorized by Public Law 109-230, the San Francisco Old Mint Commemorative Act, signed by President George W. Bush in June 2006. *Maximum authorized—500,000. Number minted—67,100 Uncirculated and 160,870 Proof.*

Original Cost. Sale prices $33 (Uncirculated, pre-issue) and $35 (Proof, pre-issue); Uncirculated later raised to $35, and Proof later raised to $39. The surcharge of $10 per coin went to the "San Francisco Museum and Historical Society for rehabilitating the Historic Old Mint as a city museum and an American Coin and Gold Rush Museum."

Key to Collecting. Superb gems are easily found in the marketplace.

	Distribution	Cert	Avg	%MS	MS-67
					PF-67
2006-S	67,100	2,807	69.7	100%	$37
Auctions: $94, MS-70, January 2013					
2006-S, Proof	160,870	3,904	69.5		$35
Auctions: No auction records available.					

SAN FRANCISCO OLD MINT CENTENNIAL $5 GOLD COIN (2006)

Designer: *Charles L. Vickers (obverse), Don Everhart after Christian Gobrecht (reverse).*
Weight: *8.359 grams.* **Composition:** *.900 gold, .100 copper (net weight .242 oz. pure gold).*
Diameter: *21.6 mm.* **Edge:** *Reeded.* **Mint:** *San Francisco.*

The designs of this coin and the corresponding silver dollar both had obverses showing the same subject (albeit from a different view), and reverses being copies of old coinage designs.

Designs. *Obverse:* Front view of the portico of the Second San Francisco Mint, with a portion of the building to each side. Modeled after an 1869 construction drawing by Supervising Architect A.B. Mullet. *Reverse:* Copy of the reverse of the Liberty Head half eagle with motto IN GOD WE TRUST, as regularly used from 1866 to 1907.

Mintage Data. Authorized by Public Law 109-230, the San Francisco Old Mint Commemorative Act, signed by President George W. Bush in June 2006. *Maximum authorized*—100,000. *Number minted*—17,500 Uncirculated and 44,174 Proof.

Original Cost. Sale prices $220 (Uncirculated, pre-issue) and $230 (Proof, pre-issue); Uncirculated later raised to $245, and Proof later raised to $255. The surcharge of $35 per coin went to the "San Francisco Museum and Historical Society for rehabilitating the Historic Old Mint as a city museum and an American Coin and Gold Rush Museum."

Key to Collecting. Superb gems are easily found in the marketplace.

	Distribution	Cert	Avg	%MS	MS-67 PF-67
2006-S	17,500	4,715	69.6	100%	$500
	Auctions: $329, MS-70, October 2014; $294, MS-70, July 2015; $306, MS-69, July 2015; $282, MS-69, October 2015				
2006-S, Proof	44,174	8,572	69.2		$500
	Auctions: $376, PF-70UCam, February 2015; $353, PF-70UCam, July 2015; $341, PF-70UCam, February 2015				

JAMESTOWN 400TH ANNIVERSARY SILVER DOLLAR (2007)

Designer: *Donna Weaver (obverse), Susan Gamble (reverse).* **Weight:** *26.73 grams.*
Composition: *.900 silver, .100 copper (net weight .7736 oz. pure silver).*
Diameter: *38.1 mm.* **Edge:** *Reeded.* **Mint:** *Philadelphia.*

Note that Jamestown was also honored on the 2000 Virginia State quarter.

Designs. *Obverse:* Captain John Smith is shown with an Indian man and woman. *Reverse:* Three sailing ships are shown, elements already seen from the 2000 State quarter, but differently arranged.

Mintage Data. Authorized by Public Law 108-289, the Jamestown 400th Anniversary Commemorative Coin Act, signed by President George W. Bush on August 6, 2004. *Maximum authorized*—500,000. *Number minted*—81,034 Uncirculated and 260,363 Proof.

Original Cost. Sale prices $33 (Uncirculated, pre-issue) and $35 (Proof, pre-issue); Uncirculated later raised to $35, and Proof later raised to $39. The surcharge of $20 per coin went to fund the public observance of the anniversary.

Key to Collecting. Superb gem coins are readily available.

	Distribution	Cert	Avg	%MS	MS-67 PF-67
2007-P	81,034	7,960	69.6	100%	$30
	Auctions: $90, MS-70, April 2013				
2007-P, Proof	260,363	11,051	69.5		$30
	Auctions: $100, PF-70DCam, April 2013				

JAMESTOWN 400TH ANNIVERSARY $5 GOLD COIN (2007)

Designer: *John Mercanti (obverse), Susan Gamble (reverse).* **Weight:** *8.359 grams.*
Composition: *.900 gold, .100 copper (net weight .242 oz. pure gold).*
Diameter: *21.6 mm.* **Edge:** *Reeded.* **Mint:** *West Point.*

Susan Gamble, who designed the reverse of both this coin and the silver dollar issued alongside it, was a participant in the Mint's Artistic Infusion Program, which was created to bring artists in from the private sector to upgrade the quality of coin designs.

Designs. *Obverse:* Captain John Smith is shown with Indian chief Powhatan, who holds a bag of corn. *Reverse:* Ruins of the old church at Jamestown.

Mintage Data. Authorized by Public Law 108-289, the Jamestown 400th Anniversary Commemorative Coin Act, signed by President George W. Bush on August 6, 2004. *Maximum authorized*—100,000. *Number minted*—18,623 Uncirculated and 47,123 Proof.

Original Cost. Sale prices $33 (Uncirculated, pre-issue) and $35 (Proof, pre-issue); Uncirculated later raised to $35, and Proof later raised to $39. The surcharge of $35 per coin went to fund the public observance of the anniversary.

Key to Collecting. Superb gem coins are readily available.

	Distribution	Cert	Avg	%MS	MS-67
					PF-67
2007-W	18,623	3,256	69.8	100%	$500
	Auctions: $353, MS-70, April 2015; $329, MS-70, November 2014; $306, MS-70, July 2015; $294, MS-70, July 2015				
2007-W, Proof	47,123	4,179	69.6		$500
	Auctions: $341, PF-70DCam, July 2014; $317, PF-70DCam, August 2014; $306, PF-70UCam, July 2015				

LITTLE ROCK CENTRAL HIGH SCHOOL DESEGREGATION SILVER DOLLAR (2007)

Designer: *Richard Masters (obverse), Don Everhart (reverse).* **Weight:** *26.73 grams.*
Composition: *.900 silver, .100 copper (net weight .7736 oz. pure silver).*
Diameter: *38.1 mm.* **Edge:** *Reeded.* **Mint:** *Philadelphia.*

This coin commemorated the 50th anniversary of the desegregation of Little Rock Central High School, which was the result of the landmark U.S. Supreme Court case *Brown v. the Board of Education.*

Designs. *Obverse:* The feet of the "Little Rock Nine" students are shown, escorted by a soldier. *Reverse:* Little Rock Central High School as it appeared in 1957.

Mintage Data. Authorized by Public Law 109-146, the Little Rock Central High School Desegregation 50th Anniversary Commemorative Coin Act, signed by President George W. Bush on December 22, 2005. *Maximum authorized*—500,000. *Number minted*—66,093 Uncirculated and 124,678 Proof.

Original Cost. Sale prices $33 (Uncirculated, pre-issue) and $35 (Proof, pre-issue); Uncirculated later raised to $35, and Proof later raised to $39. The surcharge of $10 per coin went toward improvements at the Little Rock Central High School National Historic Site.

Key to Collecting. Superb gem coins are readily available.

	Distribution	Cert	Avg	%MS	MS-67 PF-67
2007-P	66,093	2,842	69.7	100%	$30
Auctions: $79, MS-70, October 2014; $90, MS-70, April 2013					
2007-P, Proof	124,678	3,193	69.5		$25
Auctions: $80, PF-70DCam, July 2014; $113, PF-70DCam, April 2013					

BALD EAGLE RECOVERY AND NATIONAL EMBLEM HALF DOLLAR (2008)

Designer: *Susan Gamble (obverse), Donna Weaver (reverse).* **Weight:** *11.34 grams.*
Composition: *.9167 copper, .0833 nickel.* **Diameter:** *30.61 mm.* **Edge:** *Reeded.* **Mint:** *San Francisco.*

This copper-nickel half dollar, as well as the silver dollar and five-dollar gold coin issued alongside it, was issued to commemorate the recovery of the bald eagle species, the 35th anniversary of the Endangered Species Act of 1973, and the removal of the bald eagle from the Endangered Species List.

Designs. *Obverse:* Two eaglets and an egg in a bald eagle nest. *Reverse:* "Challenger," a non-releasable bald eagle in the care of the American Eagle Foundation and the first of his species to be trained to free-fly into major sporting events during the National Anthem.

Mintage Data. Authorized by Public Law 108-486, the Bald Eagle Commemorative Coin Act, signed by President George W. Bush on December 23, 2004. *Maximum authorized*—750,000. *Number minted*—120,180 Uncirculated and 220,577 Proof.

Original Cost. Sale prices $7.95 (Uncirculated, pre-issue) and $9.95 (Proof, pre-issue); Uncirculated later raised to $8.95, and Proof later raised to $10.95. The surcharge of $3 per coin went to the American Eagle Foundation of Tennessee for the purposes of continuing its work to save and protect bald eagles nationally.

Key to Collecting. Superb gem coins are readily available.

	Distribution	Cert	Avg	%MS	MS-67 PF-67
2008-S	120,180	6,832	69.8	100%	$15
Auctions: $30, MS-70, April 2013					
2008-S, Proof	220,577	8,875	69.7		$18
Auctions: No auction records available.					

BALD EAGLE RECOVERY AND NATIONAL EMBLEM SILVER DOLLAR (2008)

Designer: *Joel Iskowitz (obverse), Jim Licaretz (reverse).* **Weight:** *26.73 grams.*
Composition: *.900 silver, .100 copper (net weight .7736 oz. pure silver).*
Diameter: *38.1 mm.* **Edge:** *Reeded.* **Mint:** *Philadelphia.*

The bald eagle, selected in 1782 by the Second Continental Congress as the national emblem of the United States, was common at the time of the nation's establishment. Through the years, however, poaching, habitat destruction, pesticides, and food-source contamination reduced the number of nesting pairs from approximately 100,000 to just more than 400 in the early 1960s. Fortunately, conservationists have saved the species in the past five decades.

Designs. *Obverse:* Bald eagle in flight, mountains in background. *Reverse:* The Great Seal of the United States used from 1782 to 1841.

Mintage Data. Authorized by Public Law 108-486, the Bald Eagle Commemorative Coin Act, signed by President George W. Bush on December 23, 2004. *Maximum authorized*—500,000. *Number minted*—119,204 Uncirculated and 294,601 Proof.

Original Cost. Sale prices $35.95 (Uncirculated, pre-issue) and $39.95 (Proof, pre-issue); Uncirculated later raised to $37.95, and Proof later raised to $43.95. The surcharge of $10 per coin went to the American Eagle Foundation of Tennessee for the purposes of continuing its work to save and protect bald eagles nationally.

Key to Collecting. Superb gem coins are readily available.

	Distribution	Cert	Avg	%MS	MS-67 / PF-67
2008-P	119,204	9,261	69.7	100%	$30
	Auctions: $90, MS-70, April 2013				
2008-P, Proof	294,601	13,824	69.3		$25
	Auctions: $92, PF-70DCam, July 2014; $89, PF-70UCam, July 2015; $79, PF-70DCam, July 2014				

BALD EAGLE RECOVERY AND NATIONAL EMBLEM $5 GOLD COIN (2008)

Designer: *Susan Gamble (obverse), Don Everhart (reverse).* **Weight:** *8.359 grams.*
Composition: *.900 gold, .100 copper (net weight .242 oz. pure gold).*
Diameter: *21.6 grams.* **Edge:** *Reeded.* **Mint:** *West Point.*

Government entities, private organizations, and citizens were all part of the bald eagle's recovery from near-extinction in the middle of the 1900s. Bans on certain pesticides, protections granted under the Endangered Species Act of 1973, and captive-breeding and nest-watch programs have been crucial and have led to the removal of the national emblem from the Endangered Species List.

Designs. *Obverse:* Two bald eagles perched on a branch. *Reverse:* The current Great Seal of the United States.

Mintage Data. Authorized by Public Law 108-486, the Bald Eagle Commemorative Coin Act, signed by President George W. Bush on December 23, 2004. *Maximum authorized*—100,000. *Number minted*—15,009 Uncirculated and 59,269 Proof.

Original Cost. Sale prices $284.95 (Uncirculated, pre-issue) and $294.95 (Proof, pre-issue); Uncirculated later raised to $309.95, and Proof later raised to $319.95. The surcharge of $35 per coin went to the American Eagle Foundation of Tennessee for the purposes of continuing its work to save and protect bald eagles nationally.

Key to Collecting. Superb gem coins are readily available.

	Distribution	Cert	Avg	%MS	MS-67 PF-67
2008-W	15,009	1,113	69.9	100%	$500
	Auctions: $458, MS-70, January 2013				
2008-W, Proof	59,269	1,897	69.8		$500
	Auctions: $442, PF-70DCam, March 2014; $427, PF-70DCam, September 2014; $306, PF-70UCam, July 2015				

ABRAHAM LINCOLN BICENTENNIAL SILVER DOLLAR (2009)

Designer: *Justin Kunz (obverse), Phebe Hemphill (reverse).* **Weight:** *26.73 grams.*
Composition: *.900 silver, .100 copper (net weight .7736 oz. pure silver).*
Diameter: *38.1 mm.* **Edge:** *Reeded.* **Mint:** *Philadelphia.*

These coins, issued to mark the 200th anniversary of President Abraham Lincoln's birth, were extremely popular with collectors. The 450,000 pieces allocated to individual coin sales sold out after a month. Note that this anniversary was also commemorated with the release of four different reverse designs for the 2009 Lincoln cents.

Designs. *Obverse:* A portrait of Abraham Lincoln in three-quarter view. *Reverse:* The final 43 words of President Lincoln's Gettysburg Address, surrounded by a laurel wreath.

Mintage Data. Authorized Public Law 109-285, the Abraham Lincoln Commemorative Coin Act, signed by President George W. Bush on September 27, 2006. *Maximum authorized*—500,000. *Number minted*—125,000 Uncirculated and 325,000 Proof.

Original Cost. Sale prices $31.95 (Uncirculated, pre-issue) and $37.95 (Proof, pre-issue); Uncirculated later raised to $33.95, and Proof later raised to $41.95. The surcharge of $10 per coin went to the Abraham Lincoln Bicentennial Commission.

Key to Collecting. Superb gem coins are readily available.

	Distribution	Cert	Avg	%MS	MS-67 PF-67
2009-P	125,000	10,265	69.8	100%	$30
	Auctions: $96, MS-70, February 2014; $60, MS-70, June 2015; $56, MS-70, July 2014				
2009-P, Proof	325,000	18,355	69.4		$35
	Auctions: $353, PF-70DCam, November 2014; $90, PF-70DCam, August 2014; $74, PF-70DCam, June 2015				

LOUIS BRAILLE BICENTENNIAL SILVER DOLLAR (2009)

Designer: *Joel Iskowitz (obverse), Phebe Hemphill (reverse).* **Weight:** *26.73 grams.*
Composition: *.900 silver, .100 copper (net weight .7736 oz. pure silver).*
Diameter: *38.1 mm.* **Edge:** *Reeded.* **Mint:** *Philadelphia.*

The 200th anniversary of the birth of Louis Braille—the inventor of the eponymous system which is used by the blind to read and write—furnished the occasion for this commemorative. Fittingly, this was the first U.S. coin to feature readable Braille.

Designs. *Obverse:* A forward-facing portrait of Louis Braille. *Reverse:* The word Braille (in Braille code, abbreviated Brl) above a child reading a book in Braille.

Mintage Data. Authorized by Public Law 109-247, the Louis Braille Bicentennial–Braille Literacy Commemorative Coin Act, signed by President George W. Bush on July 27, 2006. *Maximum authorized*—400,000. *Number minted*—82,639 Uncirculated and 135,235 Proof.

Original Cost. Sale prices $31.95 (Uncirculated, pre-issue) and $37.95 (Proof, pre-issue); Uncirculated later raised to $33.95, and Proof later raised to $41.95. The surcharge of $10 per coin went to the National Federation of the Blind.

Key to Collecting. Superb gem coins are readily available.

	Distribution	Cert	Avg	%MS	MS-67 PF-67
2009-P	82,639	3,527	69.4	100%	$27
	Auctions: $90, MS-70, April 2013				
2009-P, Proof	135,235	4,463	69.1		$25
	Auctions: $94, PF-70DCam, July 2014; $94, PF-70DCam, April 2013				

AMERICAN VETERANS DISABLED FOR LIFE SILVER DOLLAR (2010)

Designer: *Don Everhart.* **Weight:** *26.73 grams.*
Composition: *.900 silver, .100 copper (net weight .7736 oz. pure silver).*
Diameter: *38.1 mm.* **Edge:** *Reeded.* **Mint:** *West Point.*

This coin honored those members of the U.S. Armed Forces who have made extraordinary personal sacrifices in defense of the country.

Designs. *Obverse:* The legs and boots of three veterans, one of whom is using a pair of crutches. *Reverse:* The words "Take This Moment to Honor Our Disabled Defenders of Freedom," surrounded by a laurel wreath with a forget-me-not (widely known as a symbol for those who fought and became disabled in World War I) at its base.

Mintage Data. Authorized by Public Law 110-277, the American Veterans Disabled for Life Commemorative Coin Act, signed by President George W. Bush on July 17, 2008. *Maximum authorized*—350,000. *Number minted*—78,301 Uncirculated and 202,770 Proof.

Original Cost. Sale prices $33.95 (Uncirculated, pre-issue) and $39.95 (Proof, pre-issue); Uncirculated later raised to $35.95, and Proof later raised to $43.95. The surcharge of $10 per coin went to the Disabled Veterans' LIFE Memorial Foundation for the purpose of constructing the American Veterans' Disabled for Life Memorial in Washington, D.C.

Key to Collecting. Superb gem coins are readily available.

	Distribution	Cert	Avg	%MS	MS-67 PF-67
2010-W	78,301	4,287	69.8	100%	$32
	Auctions: $70, MS-70, May 2013				
2010-W, Proof	202,770	5,185	69.7		$32
	Auctions: $78, PF-70DCam, May 2013; $42, PF-70DCam, September 2014				

BOY SCOUTS OF AMERICA CENTENNIAL SILVER DOLLAR (2010)

Designer: *Donna Weaver (obverse), Jim Licaretz from the universal logo of the Boy Scouts of America (reverse).*
Weight: *26.73 grams.* **Composition:** *.900 silver, .100 copper (net weight .7736 oz. pure silver).*
Diameter: *38.1 mm.* **Edge:** *Reeded.* **Mint:** *Philadelphia.*

The 100th anniversary of the establishment of the Boy Scouts of America was celebrated with this silver dollar. The design was somewhat controversial due to its inclusion of a female but was specifically requested by the organization itself so as to portray the evolution of the Boy Scouts over time to include all American youth.

Designs. *Obverse:* A Cub Scout, a female member of the Venturer Program, and a Boy Scout saluting. *Reverse:* The universal logo of the Boy Scouts of America, featuring an eagle bearing a shield on a fleur-de-lis.

Mintage Data. Authorized by Public Law 110-363, the Boy Scouts of America Centennial Commemorative Coin Act, signed by President George W. Bush on October 8, 2008. *Maximum authorized*—350,000. *Number minted*—105,020 Uncirculated and 244,693 Proof.

Original Cost. Sale prices $33.95 (Uncirculated, pre-issue) and $39.95 (Proof, pre-issue); Uncirculated later raised to $35.95, and Proof later raised to $43.95. The surcharge of $10 per coin went to the National Boy Scouts of America Foundation; the funds were then meant to be made available to local councils in the form of grants for the extension of Scouting in hard-to-serve areas.

Key to Collecting. Superb gem coins are readily available.

	Distribution	Cert	Avg	%MS	MS-67 PF-67
2010-P	105,020	7,495	69.8	100%	$27
	Auctions: $82, MS-70, March 2013				
2010-P, Proof	244,963	8,239	69.4		$30
	Auctions: $82, PF-70DCam, March 2013				

U.S. ARMY HALF DOLLAR (2011)

Designer: *Donna Weaver (obverse), Thomas Cleveland (reverse).* **Weight:** *11.34 grams.*
Composition: *.9167 copper, .0833 nickel.* **Diameter:** *30.61 mm.*
Edge: *Reeded.* **Mints:** *Denver (Uncirculated) and San Francisco (Proof).*

This copper-nickel half dollar was one of three commemoratives released in honor of the U.S. Army in 2011, by which time the entity had already defended the nation for 236 years. The reverse design was praised by the Citizens Coinage Advisory Committee (CCAC) and the Commission of Fine Arts.

Designs. *Obverse:* Three scenes split in a "storyboard" fashion (from left to right): a soldier surveying; two servicemen laying a flood wall; the Redstone Army rocket at takeoff. *Reverse:* A Continental with a musket, with 13 stars (representing the first states) in an arc above.

Mintage Data. Authorized by Public Law 110-450, the United States Army Commemorative Coin Act of 2008, signed by President George W. Bush on December 1, 2008. *Maximum authorized*—750,000. *Number minted*—2011-D: 39,442 Uncirculated; 2011-S: 68,332 Proof.

Original Cost. Sale prices $15.95 (Uncirculated, pre-issue) and $17.95 (Proof, pre-issue); Uncirculated later raised to $19.95, and Proof raised to $21.95. The surcharge of $5 went toward the yet-to-be-constructed National Museum of the United States Army.

Key to Collecting. Superb gem coins are readily available.

	Distribution	Cert	Avg	%MS	MS-67 PF-67
2011-D	39,442	2,586	69.0	100%	$30
	Auctions: No auction records available.				
2011-S, Proof	68,332	2,475	69.5		$50
	Auctions: No auction records available.				

U.S. ARMY SILVER DOLLAR (2011)

Designer: *Richard Masters (obverse), Susan Gamble (reverse).* **Weight:** *26.73 grams.*
Composition: *.900 silver, .100 copper (net weight .7736 oz. pure silver).* **Diameter:** *38.1 mm.*
Edge: *Reeded.* **Mints:** *San Francisco (Uncirculated) and Philadelphia (Proof).*

The act authorizing this silver dollar (as well as the related copper-nickel half dollar and five-dollar gold coin) called for the coins to be "emblematic of the traditions, history, and heritage of the U.S. Army and its role in American society from the Colonial period to today."

Designs. *Obverse:* A male and female soldier back-to-back in front of a globe. *Reverse:* The Great Seal of the United States (which appears on Army uniforms) inside a ring that bears the seven core values of the Army (Loyalty, Duty, Respect, Selfless Service, Honor, Integrity, and Personal Courage).

Mintage Data. Authorized by Public Law 110-450, the United States Army Commemorative Coin Act of 2008, signed by President George W. Bush on December 1, 2008. *Maximum authorized—500,000. Number minted*—2011-S: 43,512 Uncirculated; 2011-P: 119,829 Proof.

Original Cost. Sale prices $49.95 (Uncirculated, pre-issue) and $54.95 (Proof, pre-issue); Uncirculated later raised to $54.95, and Proof later raised to $59.95. The surcharge of $10 per coin went toward the yet-to-be-constructed National Museum of the United States Army.

Key to Collecting. Superb gem coins are readily available.

	Distribution	Cert	Avg	%MS	MS-67 PF-67
2011-S	43,512	2,427	69.7	100%	$42
Auctions: No auction records available.					
2011-P, Proof	119,829	3,923	69.5		$42
Auctions: $80, PF-70DCam, April 2013					

U.S. ARMY $5 GOLD COIN (2011)

Designer: *Joel Iskowitz (obverse), Joseph Menna from the U.S. Army emblem (reverse).*
Weight: *8.359 grams.* **Composition:** *.900 gold, .100 copper (net weight .242 oz. pure gold).*
Diameter: *21.6 mm.* **Edge:** *Reeded.* **Mints:** *Philadelphia (Uncirculated) and West Point (Proof).*

By depicting soldiers from five distinct eras in U.S. history, the obverse of this five-dollar gold coin symbolizes the "continuity of strength and readiness" of the Army.

Designs. *Obverse:* Five U.S. Army soldiers representing various eras (from left to right): Revolutionary War, Civil War, modern era, World War II, and World War I. *Reverse:* The U.S. Army emblem, which features various items representative of home life and war time and the phrase "This We'll Defend" on a banner.

Mintage Data. Authorized by Public Law 110-450, the United States Army Commemorative Coin Act of 2008, signed by President George W. Bush on December 1, 2008. *Maximum authorized—100,000. Number minted*—2011-P: 8,052 Uncirculated; 2011-W: 17,148 Proof.

Original Cost. Sale prices $439.95 (Uncirculated, pre-issue) and $449.95 (Proof, pre-issue); Uncirculated later raised to $444.95, and Proof later raised to $454.95. The surcharge of $35 per coin went toward the yet-to-be-constructed National Museum of the United States Army.

Key to Collecting. Superb gem coins are readily available.

	Distribution	Cert	Avg	%MS	MS-67 PF-67
2011-P	8,052	456	69.9	100%	$500
Auctions: $560, MS-70, September 2013					
2011-W, Proof	17,148	610	69.8		$500
Auctions: $353, PF-69DCam, May 2014					

MEDAL OF HONOR SILVER DOLLAR (2011)

Designer: *Jim Licaretz (obverse), Richard Masters (reverse).* **Weight:** *26.73 grams.*
Composition: *.900 silver, .100 copper (net weight .7736 oz. pure silver).*
Diameter: *38.1 mm.* **Edge:** *Reeded.* **Mints:** *San Francisco (Uncirculated) and Philadelphia (Proof).*

The 150th anniversary of the creation of the Medal of Honor—the highest award for valor in action in the U.S. Armed Forces—was the impetus for this commemorative silver dollar, as well as a five-dollar gold coin.

Designs. *Obverse:* From left to right, the Medals of Honor of the Army, Navy, and Air Force. *Reverse:* An infantry soldier carrying a wounded soldier to safety on his back.

Mintage Data. Authorized by Public Law 111-91, the Medal of Honor Commemorative Coin Act of 2009, signed by President Barack Obama on November 6, 2009. *Maximum authorized*—500,000. *Number minted*—2011-S: 44,752 Uncirculated; 2011-P: 112,833 Proof.

Original Cost. Sale prices $49.95 (Uncirculated, pre-issue) and $54.95 (Proof, pre-issue); Uncirculated later raised to $54.95, and Proof later raised to $59.95. The surcharge of $10 per coin went to the Congressional Medal of Honor Foundation to help finance its educational, scholarship, and outreach programs.

Key to Collecting. Superb gem coins are readily available.

	Distribution	Cert	Avg	%MS	MS-67
					PF-67
2011-S	44,752	2,897	69.6	100%	$45
	Auctions: $100, MS-70, April 2013				
2011-P, Proof	112,833	2,265	69.3		$45
	Auctions: $123, PF-70DCam, March 2013				

MEDAL OF HONOR $5 GOLD COIN (2011)

Designer: *Joseph Menna (obverse), Joel Iskowitz (reverse).* **Weight:** *8.359 grams.*
Composition: *.900 gold, .100 copper (net weight .242 oz. pure gold).* **Diameter:** *21.6 mm.*
Edge: *Reeded.* **Mints:** *Philadelphia (Uncirculated) and West Point (Proof).*

This coin and the silver dollar issued alongside it were created in recognition of the Medal of Honor, the Navy's greatest personal award, first authorized by Congress in 1861. Though counterparts are now given in the Army and Air Force as well, fewer than 3,500 Medals of Honor have ever been awarded to date.

Designs. *Obverse:* The original Medal of Honor, the Navy's highest individual decoration. *Reverse:* Minerva, holding a shield and the U.S. flag on a staff, in front of munitions and a Civil War–era cannon.

Mintage Data. Authorized by Public Law 111-91, the Medal of Honor Commemorative Coin Act of 2009, signed by President Barack Obama on November 6, 2009. *Maximum authorized*—100,000. *Number minted*—2011-P: 8,233 Uncirculated; 2011-W: 17,999 Proof.

Original Cost. Sale prices $439.95 (Uncirculated, pre-issue) and $449.95 (Proof, pre issue); Uncirculated later raised to $444.95, and Proof later raised to $454.95. The surcharge of $35 per coin went to the Congressional Medal of Honor Foundation to help finance its educational, scholarship, and outreach programs.

Key to Collecting. Superb gem coins are readily available.

	Distribution	Cert	Avg	%MS	MS-67 PF-67
2011-P	8,233	526	69.8	100%	$500
	Auctions: $470, MS-70, November 2014; $470, MS-70, August 2014; $400, MS-70, January 2015; $400, MS-69, January 2015				
2011-W, Proof	17,999	567	69.6		$500
	Auctions: $646, PF-70DCam, February 2015; $646, PF-70DCam, November 2014; $558, PF-70DCam, July 2014				

INFANTRY SOLDIER SILVER DOLLAR (2012)

Designer: *Joel Iskowitz (obverse), Ronald D. Sanders (reverse).* **Weight:** *26.73 grams.*
Composition: *.900 silver, .100 copper (net weight .7736 oz. pure silver).*
Diameter: *38.1 mm.* **Edge:** *Reeded.* **Mint:** *West Point.*

This coin recognizes the long history and crucial role of the U.S. Army Infantry. The infantry has accounted for more than half of all the Medals of Honor awarded, despite being just one of many branches of the Army.

Designs. *Obverse:* An infantry soldier advancing and motioning for others to follow. *Reverse:* The infantry insignia of two crossed rifles.

Mintage Data. Authorized by Public Law 110-357, the National Infantry Museum and Soldier Center Commemorative Coin Act, signed by President George W. Bush on October 8, 2008. *Maximum authorized*—350,000. *Number minted*—44,348 Uncirculated and 161,151 Proof.

Original Cost. Sale prices $44.95 (Uncirculated, pre-issue) and $49.95 (Proof, pre-issue); Uncirculated later raised to $49.95, and Proof later raised to $54.95. The surcharge of $10 per coin went to an endowment to support the maintenance of the National Infantry Museum and Solider Center in Columbus, Georgia.

Key to Collecting. Superb gem coins are readily available.

	Distribution	Cert	Avg	%MS	MS-67 PF-67
2012-W	44,348	2,117	69.8	100%	$40
	Auctions: $69, MS-70, April 2013				
2012-W, Proof	161,151	2,700	69.2		$50
	Auctions: $74, PF-70DCam, April 2013				

STAR-SPANGLED BANNER SILVER DOLLAR (2012)

Designer: *Joel Iskowitz (obverse), William C. Burgard II (reverse).* **Weight:** *26.73 grams.*
Composition: *.900 silver, .100 copper (net weight .7736 oz. pure silver).*
Diameter: *38.1 mm.* **Edge:** *Reeded.* **Mint:** *Philadelphia.*

The 200th anniversary of the War of 1812—particularly the Battle of Baltimore, which is recounted in the U.S. National Anthem—was commemorated with this silver dollar, as well as a five-dollar gold coin issued alongside it.

Designs. *Obverse:* Miss Liberty waving the 15-star version of the U.S. flag with Fort McHenry in the background. *Reverse:* A waving modern U.S. flag.

Mintage Data. Authorized by Public Law 111-232, the Star-Spangled Banner Commemorative Coin Act, signed by President Barack Obama on August 16, 2010. *Maximum authorized—500,000. Number minted—*41,686 Uncirculated and 169,065 Proof.

Original Cost. Sale prices $44.95 (Uncirculated, pre-issue) and $49.95 (Proof, pre-issue); Uncirculated later raised to $49.95, and Proof later raised to $54.95. The surcharge of $10 per coin went to the Maryland War of 1812 Bicentennial Commission for the purpose of supporting bicentennial activities, educational outreach activities, and preservation and improvement activities pertaining to the sites and structures relating to the War of 1812.

Key to Collecting. Superb gem coins are readily available.

	Distribution	Cert	Avg	%MS	MS-67 / PF-67
2012-P	41,686	2,092	69.8	100%	$40
	Auctions: $100, MS-70, April 2013; $94, MS-70, October 2014				
2012-P, Proof	169,065	3,277	69.4		$40
	Auctions: $94, PF-70DCam, April 2013; $153, PF-69DCam, November 2014				

STAR-SPANGLED BANNER $5 GOLD COIN (2012)

Designer: *Donna Weaver (obverse), Richard Masters (reverse).* **Weight:** *8.359 grams.*
Composition: *.900 gold, .100 copper (net weight .242 oz. pure gold).*
Diameter: *21.6 mm.* **Edge:** *Reeded.* **Mint:** *West Point.*

The reverse of this commemorative coin features the first five words of the Star-Spangled Banner in the handwriting of Francis Scott Key, the man who penned it. On September 7, 1814, Key visited the British fleet in the Chesapeake Bay to secure the release of his friend Dr. William Beanes. Key secured Beanes's release, but the two were held by the British during the bombardment of Fort McHenry. It was on the morning of September 14, 1814, that the shelling stopped and Key saw through the smoke the massive American flag, flying above the U.S. fort, that would inspire his song.

Designs. *Obverse:* A naval battle, with a U.S. ship in the foreground and a British vessel in the background. *Reverse:* The words "O say can you see" over an arrangement of 13 stripes and 15 stars, representing the U.S. flag.

Mintage Data. Authorized by Public Law 111-232, the Star-Spangled Banner Commemorative Coin Act, signed by President Barack Obama on August 16, 2010. *Maximum authorized*—100,000. *Number minted*—7,027 Uncirculated and 18,313 Proof.

Original Cost. Sale prices $519.30 (Uncirculated, pre-issue) and $529.30 (Proof, pre-issue); both prices later increased by a base of $5 plus the change in gold market value. The surcharge of $35 per coin went to the Maryland War of 1812 Bicentennial Commission for the purpose of supporting bicentennial activities, educational outreach activities, and preservation and improvement activities pertaining to the sites and structures relating to the War of 1812.

Key to Collecting. Superb gem coins are readily available.

	Distribution	Cert	Avg	%MS	MS-67 PF-67
2012-W	7,027	682	69.9	100%	$500
Auctions: $618, MS-70, September 2013					
2012-W, Proof	18,313	538	69.8		$500
Auctions: $470, PF-70DCam, April 2014					

GIRL SCOUTS OF THE U.S.A. CENTENNIAL SILVER DOLLAR (2013)

Designer: *Barbara Fox (obverse), Chris Costello (reverse).* **Weight:** *26.73 grams.*
Composition: *.900 silver, .100 copper (net weight .7736 oz. pure silver).*
Diameter: *38.1 mm.* **Edge:** *Reeded.* **Mint:** *West Point.*

This commemorative silver dollar was issued as part of the celebration of the Girl Scouts of the United States of America's 100th anniversary of establishment. The Citizens Coinage Advisory Committee was particularly enthusiastic about this beautiful design.

Designs. *Obverse:* Three Girl Scouts of varying ages and ethnicities. The three girls are meant to reflect the organization's diversity. *Reverse:* The iconic Girl Scouts trefoil symbol.

Mintage Data. Authorized by Public Law 111-86, the 2013 Girl Scouts of the USA Centennial Commemorative Coin Program, signed by President Barack Obama on October 29, 2009. *Maximum authorized*—350,000. *Number minted*—37,462 Uncirculated and 86,355 Proof.

Original Cost. Sale prices $50.95 (Uncirculated, pre-issue) and $54.95 (Proof, pre-issue); Uncirculated later raised to $55.95, and Proof later raised to $59.95. The surcharge of $10 per coin went to the Girl Scouts of the United States of America.

Key to Collecting. Superb gem coins are readily available.

	Distribution	Cert	Avg	%MS	MS-67
					PF-67
2013-W	37,462	1,040	69.9	100%	$40
	Auctions: No auction records available.				
2013-W, Proof	86,355	1,784	69.3		$45
	Auctions: No auction records available.				

5-STAR GENERALS HALF DOLLAR (2013)

Designer: *Phebe Hemphill.* **Weight:** *11.34 grams.* **Composition:** *.9167 copper, .0833 nickel.*
Diameter: *30.61 mm.* **Edge:** *Reeded.* **Mints:** *Denver (Uncirculated) and San Francisco (Proof).*

The 5-star generals of the U.S. Army—as well as the institution that they each graduated from, the U.S. Army Command and General Staff College—were commemorated with this half dollar, as well as a silver dollar and five-dollar gold coin issued as part of the program.

Designs. *Obverse:* Side-by-side portraits of General Henry "Hap" Arnold and General Omar N. Bradley, 5-star insignia at center.
Reverse: Heraldic crest of Fort Leavenworth, home of the U.S. Army Command and General Staff College.

Mintage Data. Authorized by Public Law 111-262, the 5-Star Generals Commemorative Coin Act, signed by President Barack Obama on October 8, 2010. *Maximum authorized—*750,000. *Number minted—*2013-D: 38,095 Uncirculated; 2013-S: 47,326 Proof.

Original Cost. Sale prices $16.95 (Uncirculated, pre-issue) and $17.95 (Proof, pre-issue); Uncirculated later raised to $20.95, and Proof later raised to $21.95. The surcharge of $5 per coin went to the Command and General Staff College Foundation.

Key to Collecting. Superb gem coins are readily available.

	Distribution	Cert	Avg	%MS	MS-67
					PF-67
2013-D	38,095	1,092	69.0	100%	$22
	Auctions: No auction records available.				
2013-S, Proof	47,326	2,330	69.4		$35
	Auctions: No auction records available.				

5-STAR GENERALS SILVER DOLLAR (2013)

Designer: *Richard Masters (obverse), Barbara Fox (reverse).* **Weight:** *26.73 grams.*
Composition: *.900 silver, .100 copper (net weight .7736 oz. pure silver).*
Diameter: *38.1 mm.* **Edge:** *Reeded.* **Mints:** *West Point (Uncirculated) and Philadelphia (Proof).*

Each of the 5-star generals was given one appearance across this series of three commemoratives. Note that Dwight Eisenhower, who is featured on this silver dollar along with George C. Marshall, had previously appeared on another commemorative silver dollar that marked the centennial of his birth in 1990.

Designs. *Obverse:* Side-by-side portraits of General George C. Marshall and General Dwight D. Eisenhower against a striped background, 5-star insignia at top center. *Reverse:* The Leavenworth Lamp, a symbol of the Command and General Staff College.

Mintage Data. Authorized by Public Law 111-262, the 5-Star Generals Commemorative Coin Act, signed by President Barack Obama on October 8, 2010. *Maximum authorized—500,000. Number minted—2013-W: 34,638 Uncirculated; 2013-P: 69,283 Proof.*

Original Cost. Sale prices $50.95 (Uncirculated, pre-issue) and $54.95 (Proof, pre-issue); Uncirculated later raised to $55.95, and Proof later raised to $59.95. The surcharge of $10 per coin went to the Command and General Staff College Foundation.

Key to Collecting. Superb gem coins are readily available.

	Distribution	Cert	Avg	%MS	MS-67
					PF-67
2013-W	34,638	1,706	69.9	100%	$55
	Auctions: No auction records available.				
2013-P, Proof	69,283	2,719	69.7		$55
	Auctions: No auction records available.				

5-STAR GENERALS $5 GOLD COIN (2013)

Designer: *Ronald D. Sanders (obverse), Barbara Fox (reverse).* **Weight:** *8.359 grams.*
Composition: *.900 gold, .100 copper (net weight .242 oz. pure gold).*
Diameter: *21.6 mm.* **Edge:** *Reeded.* **Mints:** *Philadelphia (Uncirculated) and West Point (Proof).*

The Leavenworth Lamp, seen on the reverse of this coin as well as that of the silver dollar in this series, is a symbol of the Command and General Staff College. The institution celebrated its 132nd anniversary in the year these coins were released.

Designs. *Obverse:* A portrait of General Douglas MacArthur and the 5-star insignia to the right. *Reverse:* The Leavenworth Lamp, a symbol of the Command and General Staff College.

Mintage Data. Authorized by Public Law 111-262, the 5-Star Generals Commemorative Coin Act, signed by President Barack Obama on October 8, 2010. *Maximum authorized—100,000. Number minted—2013-P: 5,667 Uncirculated; 2013-W: 15,844 Proof.*

Original Cost. Sale prices $480.50 (Uncirculated, pre-issue) and $485.50 (Proof, pre-issue); both prices later increased by a base of $5 plus the change in gold market value. The surcharge of $35 per coin went to the Command and General Staff College Foundation.

Key to Collecting. Superb gem coins are readily available.

	Distribution	Cert	Avg	%MS	MS-67
					PF-67
2013-P	5,667	553	69.9	100%	$500
	Auctions: No auction records available.				
2013-W, Proof	15,844	621	69.8		$500
	Auctions: $499, PF-70DCam, September 2014				

NATIONAL BASEBALL HALL OF FAME HALF DOLLAR (2014)

Designer: *Cassie McFarland (obverse), Don Everhart (reverse).* **Weight:** *11.34 grams.*
Composition: *.9167 copper, .0833 nickel.* **Diameter:** *30.61 mm.* **Edge:** *Reeded.*
Mints: *Denver (Uncirculated) and San Francisco (Proof).*

This half dollar and the silver dollar and five-dollar gold coin issued alongside it were the first "curved" coins to be produced by the U.S. Mint—that is, the obverse is concave, and the reverse is convex. The three commemorated the 75th anniversary of the National Baseball Hall of Fame in Cooperstown, New York.

Designs. *Obverse:* A baseball glove, concave. *Reverse:* A baseball, convex.

Mintage Data. Authorized by Public Law 112-152, the National Baseball Hall of Fame Commemorative Coin Act, signed by President Barack Obama on August 3, 2012. *Maximum authorized*—750,000. *Number minted*—2014-D: 142,405 Uncirculated; 2014-S: 249,049 Proof.

Original Cost. Sale prices $18.95 (Uncirculated, pre-issue) and $19.95 (Proof, pre-issue); Uncirculated later raised to $22.95, and Proof later raised to $23.95. The surcharge of $5 per coin went to the National Baseball Hall of Fame.

Key to Collecting. Superb gem coins are readily available.

	Distribution	Cert	Avg	%MS	MS-67 PF-67
2014-D ††	142,405	8,609	69.5	100%	$30
2014-S, Proof ††	249,049	10,556	69.6		$24

†† All 2014 National Baseball Hall of Fame Commemorative coins (in all denominations and finishes) are ranked in the *100 Greatest U.S. Modern Coins* (fourth edition), as a single entry.

NATIONAL BASEBALL HALL OF FAME SILVER DOLLAR (2014)

Designer: *Cassie McFarland (obverse), Don Everhart (reverse).* **Weight:** *26.73 grams.*
Composition: *.900 silver, .100 copper (net weight .7736 oz. pure silver).*
Diameter: *38.1 mm.* **Edge:** *Reeded.* **Mint:** *Philadelphia.*

Coins shaped like this silver dollar (as well as the corresponding half dollar and five-dollar gold coin) had previously been minted by Monnaie de Paris in commemoration of the 2009 International Year of Astronomy. The National Baseball Hall of Fame coins were the first curved issues for the U.S. Mint.

Designs. *Obverse:* A baseball glove, concave. *Reverse:* A baseball, convex.

Mintage Data. Authorized by Public Law 112-152, the National Baseball Hall of Fame Commemorative Coin Act, signed by President Barack Obama on August 3, 2012. *Maximum authorized*—400,000. *Number minted*—131,910 Uncirculated and 267,847 Proof.

Original Cost. Sale prices $47.95 (Uncirculated, pre-issue) and $51.95 (Proof, pre-issue); Uncirculated later raised to $52.95, and Proof later raised to $56.95. The surcharge of $10 per coin went to the National Baseball Hall of Fame.

Key to Collecting. Superb gem coins are readily available.

	Distribution	Cert	Avg	%MS	MS-67
					PF-67
2014-P ††	131,910	20,796	69.6	100%	$50
2014-P, Proof ††	267,847	26,632	69.6		$48

†† All 2014 National Baseball Hall of Fame Commemorative coins (in all denominations and finishes) are ranked in the *100 Greatest U.S. Modern Coins* (fourth edition), as a single entry.

NATIONAL BASEBALL HALL OF FAME $5 GOLD COIN (2014)

Designer: *Cassie McFarland (obverse), Don Everhart (reverse).* **Weight:** *8.359 grams.*
Composition: *.900 gold, .100 copper (net weight .242 oz. pure gold).*
Diameter: *21.6 mm.* **Edge:** *Reeded.* **Mint:** *West Point.*

The common obverse design for these coins was selected through a national competition, and the Department of the Treasury chose California artist Cassie McFarland's submission after input from the National Baseball Hall of Fame, the U.S. Commission of Fine Arts, and the Citizens Coinage Advisory Committee.

Designs. *Obverse:* A baseball glove, concave. *Reverse:* A baseball, convex.

Mintage Data. Authorized by Public Law 112-152, the National Baseball Hall of Fame Commemorative Coin Act, signed by President Barack Obama on August 3, 2012. *Maximum authorized*—50,000. *Number minted*—17,674 Uncirculated and 32,428 Proof.

Original Cost. Sale prices $431.90 (Uncirculated, pre-issue) and $436.90 (Proof, pre-issue); Uncirculated later raised to $436.90, and Proof later raised to $441.90. The surcharge of $35 per coin went to the National Baseball Hall of Fame.

Key to Collecting. Superb gem coins are readily available.

	Distribution	Cert	Avg	%MS	MS-67
					PF-67
2014-W ††	17,674	4,303	69.9	100%	$500
2014-W, Proof ††	32,428	4,606	69.9		$500

†† All 2014 National Baseball Hall of Fame Commemorative coins (in all denominations and finishes) are ranked in the *100 Greatest U.S. Modern Coins* (fourth edition), as a single entry.

CIVIL RIGHTS ACT OF 1964 SILVER DOLLAR (2014)

Designer: *Justin Kunz (obverse), Donna Weaver (reverse).* **Weight:** *26.73 grams.*
Composition: *.900 silver, .100 copper (net weight .7736 oz. pure silver).*
Diameter: *38.1 mm.* **Edge:** *Reeded.* **Mint:** *Philadelphia.*

This silver dollar commemorated the 50th anniversary of the Civil Rights Act of 1964, which greatly expanded American civil rights protections; outlawed racial segregation in public places and places of public accommodation; and funded federal programs.

Designs. *Obverse:* Three people holding hands at a Civil Rights march; man on left holding sign that reads WE SHALL OVERCOME. *Reverse:* Three intertwined flames representing freedom of education, freedom to vote, and freedom to control one's own destiny. Inspired by a quote by Dr. Martin Luther King Jr.

Mintage Data. Authorized by Public Law 110-451, the Civil Rights Act of 1964 Commemorative Coin Act, signed by President George W. Bush on December 2, 2008. *Maximum authorized*—350,000. *Number minted*—24,720 Uncirculated and 61,992 Proof.

Original Cost. Sale prices $44.95 (Uncirculated, pre-issue) and $49.95 (Proof, pre-issue); Uncirculated later raised to $49.95, and Proof later raised to $54.95. The surcharge of $10 per coin went to the United Negro College Fund, which has provided scholarships and internships for minority students for the past 70 years.

Key to Collecting. Superb gem coins are readily available.

	Distribution	Cert	Avg	%MS	MS-67
					PF-67
2014-P	24,720	950	69.6	100%	$50
2014-P, Proof	61,992	1,032	69.5		$55

U.S. MARSHALS SERVICE 225TH ANNIVERSARY HALF DOLLAR (2015)

Designer: *Joel Iskowitz (obverse), Susan Gamble (reverse).* **Weight:** *11.34 grams.*
Composition: *.9167 copper, .0833 nickel.* **Diameter:** *30.61 mm.*
Edge: *Reeded.* **Mints:** *Denver (Uncirculated) and San Francisco (Proof).*

The 225th anniversary of the establishment of the U.S. Marshals Service was commemorated with the release of a series including this half dollar as well as a silver dollar and five-dollar gold coin. The actual anniversary—September 24, 2014—was marked with a celebration in Washington, D.C., and the issuance of 35 special preview sets to employees of the Service.

Designs. *Obverse:* An Old West marshal and his horse at left, and a modern marshal in tactical gear at right. *Reverse:* Lady Justice holding scales and the U.S. Marshals Service star and standing over a copy of the Constitution, a stack of books, handcuffs, and a whiskey jug, each representing areas of responsibility of the Service in the past or present.

Mintage Data. Authorized by Public Law 112-104, the United States Marshals Service 225th Anniversary Commemorative Coin Act, signed into law by President Barack Obama on April 2, 2012. *Maximum authorized*—750,000. *Number minted*—2015-D: 30,231 Uncirculated; 2015-S: 76,549 Proof.

Original Cost. Sale prices $13.95 (Uncirculated, pre-issue) and $14.95 (Proof, pre-issue); Uncirculated later raised to $17.95, and Proof later raised to $18.95. The surcharge of $3 per coin went to the U.S. Marshals Museum.

Key to Collecting. Superb gem coins are readily available.

	Distribution	Cert	Avg	%MS	MS-67
					PF-67
2015-D	30,231	1,488	69.2	100%	$20
2015-S, Proof	76,549	2,062	69.2		$22

U.S. MARSHALS SERVICE 225TH ANNIVERSARY SILVER DOLLAR (2015)

Designer: *Richard Masters (obverse), Frank Morris (reverse).* **Weight:** *26.73 grams.*
Composition: *.900 silver, .100 copper (net weight .7736 oz. pure silver).*
Diameter: *38.1 mm.* **Edge:** *Reeded.* **Mint:** *Philadelphia.*

The first federal law-enforcement officers of the United States, the U.S. Marshals were created under section 27 of the Act of Congress entitled "Chapter XX—An Act to Establish the Judicial Courts of the United States." The original 13 men to serve were confirmed on September 26, 1789.

Designs. *Obverse:* U.S. marshals riding on horseback under the U.S. Marshals Service star. *Reverse:* A U.S. marshal of the frontier era holding a "wanted" poster.

Mintage Data. Authorized by Public Law 112-104, the United States Marshals Service 225th Anniversary Commemorative Coin Act, signed into law by President Barack Obama on April 2, 2012. *Maximum authorized*—500,000. *Number minted*—38,149 Uncirculated and 124,329 Proof.

Original Cost. Sale prices $43.95 (Uncirculated, pre-issue) and $46.95 (Proof, pre-issue): Uncirculated later raised to $48.95, and Proof later raised to $51.95. The surcharge of $10 went to the U.S. Marshals Museum.

Key to Collecting. Superb gem coins are readily available.

	Distribution	Cert	Avg	%MS	MS-67
					PF-67
2015-P	38,149	2,603	69.7	100%	$47
2015-P, Proof	124,329	3,834	69.1		$52

U.S. MARSHALS SERVICE 225TH ANNIVERSARY $5 GOLD COIN (2015)

Designer: *Donna Weaver (obverse), Paul C. Balan (reverse).* **Weight:** *8.359 grams.*
Composition: *.900 gold, .100 copper (net weight .242 oz. pure gold).*
Diameter: *21.6 mm.* **Edge:** *Reeded.* **Mint:** *West Point.*

The U.S. Marshals officially became the U.S. Marshals Service in 1969 by order of the Department of Justice. The Service achieved Bureau status in 1974 and today is the primary agency for fugitive operations, as well as protection of officers of the court and court buildings.

Designs. *Obverse:* The U.S. Marshals Service star superimposed on a mountain range. *Reverse:* An eagle, shield on chest, holding a banner and draped flag.

Mintage Data. Authorized by Public Law 112-104, the United States Marshals Service 225th Anniversary Commemorative Coin Act, signed into law by President Barack Obama on April 2, 2012. *Maximum authorized*—100,000. *Number minted*—6,743 Uncirculated and 24,959 Proof.

Original Cost. Sale prices $395.45 (Uncirculated, pre-issue) and $400.45 (Proof, pre-issue): Uncirculated later raised to $400.45, and Proof later raised to $405.45. The surcharge of $35 per coin went to the U.S. Marshals Museum.

Key to Collecting. Superb gem coins are readily available.

	Distribution	Cert	Avg	%MS	MS-67 PF-67
2015-W	6,743	634	69.9	100%	$500
2015-W, Proof	24,959	1,007	69.8		$500

March of Dimes 75th Anniversary Silver Dollar (2015)

Designer: *Paul C. Balan (obverse), Don Everhart (reverse).* **Weight:** *26.73 grams.*
Composition: *.900 silver, .100 copper (net weight .7736 oz. pure silver).*
Diameter: *38.1 mm.* **Edge:** *Reeded.* **Mints:** *Philadelphia (Uncirculated) and West Point (Proof).*

Inspired by his own struggle with polio, President Franklin Delano Roosevelt created the National Foundation for Infantile Paralysis, now known as the March of Dimes, on January 3, 1938. This coin celebrated the organization's 75th anniversary (despite coming out after the actual date of said event) and recognized its accomplishments, which included the funding of research which resulted in Dr. Jonas Salk and Dr. Albert Sabin's polio vaccines.

Designs. *Obverse:* A profile view of President Franklin Delano Roosevelt and Dr. Jonas Salk. *Reverse:* A sleeping baby cradled in its parent's hand.

Mintage Data. Authorized by Public Law 112-209, the March of Dimes Commemorative Coin Act of 2012, signed into law by President Barack Obama on December 18, 2012. *Maximum authorized*—500,000. *Number minted*—2015-D: 24,742 Uncirculated; 2015-W: 32,030 Proof.

Original Cost. Sale prices $43.95 (Uncirculated, pre-issue) and $46.95 (Proof, pre-issue): Uncirculated later raised to $48.95, and Proof later raised to $51.95. The surcharge of $10 per coin went to the March of Dimes to help finance research, education, and services aimed at improving the health of women, infants, and children.

Key to Collecting. Superb gem coins are readily available.

	Distribution	Cert	Avg	%MS	MS-67 PF-67
2015-P	24,742	1,200	69.7	100%	$50
2015-W, Proof	32,030	2,011	69.6		$40

MARK TWAIN SILVER DOLLAR (2016)

Designer: *Chris Costello (obverse), Patricia Lucas-Morris (reverse).* **Weight:** *26.73 grams.*
Composition: *.900 silver, .100 copper (net weight .7736 oz. pure silver).*
Diameter: *38.1 mm.* **Edge:** *Reeded.* **Mint:** *Philadelphia.*

Samuel Langhorne Clemens—better known by his pen name, Mark Twain—is among the most celebrated authors in U.S. history. His *Adventures of Huckleberry Finn*, originally published in 1885, is often referred to as "The Great American Novel."

Designs. *Obverse:* A portrait of Mark Twain holding a pipe, with the smoke forming a silhouette of Huck Finn and Jim on their raft.

Reverse: Depictions of several characters from Mark Twain's works, including the knight and horse from *A Connecticut Yankee in King Arthur's Court*, the frog from *The Celebrated Jumping Frog of Calaveras County*, and Huck and Jim from *Adventures of Huckleberry Finn*.

Mintage Data. Authorized by Public Law 112-201, the Mark Twain Commemorative Coin Act, signed into law by President Barack Obama on December 4, 2012. *Maximum authorized—350,000. Number minted—26,291 Uncirculated and 78,549 Proof.*

Original Cost. Sale prices $44.95 (Uncirculated, pre-issue) and $45.95 (Proof, pre-issue). Uncirculated later raised to $49.95, and Proof later raised to $50.95. The surcharge of $10 per coin was distributed evenly between the Mark Twain House & Museum in Hartford, Conn.; the University of California, Berkeley, for the benefit of the Mark Twain Project at the Bancroft Library; Elmira College in New York; and the Mark Twain Boyhood Home and Museum in Hannibal, Missouri.

Key to Collecting. Superb gem coins are readily available.

	Distribution	Cert	Avg	%MS	MS-67
					PF-67
2016-P	26,291	1,490	69.9	100%	$45
2016-P, Proof	78,549	2,330	69.8		$40

MARK TWAIN $5 GOLD COIN (2016)

Designer: *Benjamin Sowers (obverse), Ronald D. Sanders (reverse).* **Weight:** *8.359 grams.*
Composition: *.900 gold, .100 copper (net weight .242 oz. pure gold).*
Diameter: *21.6 mm.* **Edge:** *Reeded.* **Mint:** *West Point.*

The designs for the Mark Twain commemorative coins were unveiled two days before the 180th anniversary of his birth, November 30, 2015. Interestingly, Twain was born shortly after a visit by Halley's Comet, and he later predicted that he would "go out with it," too. He passed away two days after the comet returned.

Designs. *Obverse:* A portrait of Mark Twain. *Reverse:* A steamboat on the Mississippi River.

Mintage Data. Authorized by Public Law 112-201, the Mark Twain Commemorative Coin Act, signed into law by President Barack Obama on December 4, 2012. *Maximum authorized*—100,000. *Number minted*—5,701 Uncirculated and 13,271 Proof.

Original Cost. Sale prices $359 (Uncirculated, pre-issue) and $364 (Proof, pre-issue). Uncirculated later raised to $364, and Proof later raised to $369. The surcharge of $35 per coin was distributed evenly between the Mark Twain House & Museum in Hartford, Conn.; the University of California, Berkeley, for the benefit of the Mark Twain Project at the Bancroft Library; Elmira College in New York; and the Mark Twain Boyhood Home and Museum in Hannibal, Missouri.

Key to Collecting. Superb gem coins are readily available.

	Distribution	Cert	Avg	%MS	MS-67 PF-67
2016-W	5,701	342	69.9	100%	$500
2016-W, Proof	13,271	467	69.8		$500

NATIONAL PARK SERVICE 100TH ANNIVERSARY HALF DOLLAR (2016)

Designer: *Barbara Fox (obverse), Thomas Hipschen (reverse).* **Weight:** *11.34 grams.*
Composition: *.9167 copper, .0833 nickel.* **Diameter:** *30.61 mm.*
Edge: *Reeded.* **Mints:** *Denver (Uncirculated) and San Francisco (Proof).*

The National Park Service was created through the National Park Service Organic Act, signed into law by President Woodrow Wilson on August 25, 1916. Today the agency employs approximately 20,000 people and operates on a budget of nearly $3 billion.

Designs. *Obverse:* A hiker taking in a mountain landscape above a child observing a frog. *Reverse:* The National Park Service logo.

Mintage Data. Authorized by Public Law 113-291, signed into law by President Barack Obama on December 19, 2014. *Maximum authorized*—750,000. *Number minted*—2016-D: 21,335 Uncirculated; 2016-S: 54,962 Proof.

Original Cost. Sale prices $20.95 (Uncirculated, pre-issue) and $21.95 (Proof, pre-issue). Uncirculated later raised to $24.95, and Proof later raised to $25.95. The surcharge of $5 per coin was assigned to the National Park Foundation.

Key to Collecting. Superb gem coins are readily available.

	Distribution	Cert	Avg	%MS	MS-67 PF-67
2016-D	21,335	939	69.3	100%	$30
2016-S, Proof	54,962	708	69.6		$35

NATIONAL PARK SERVICE 100TH ANNIVERSARY SILVER DOLLAR (2016)

Designer: *Joseph Menna (obverse), Chris Costello (reverse).* **Weight:** *26.73 grams.*
Composition: *.900 silver, .100 copper (net weight .7736 oz. pure silver).*
Diameter: *38.1 mm.* **Edge:** *Reeded.* **Mint:** *Philadelphia.*

The United States' National Parks range from Alaska's Gates of the Arctic National Park—an expanse of pristine wilderness devoid of any actual park facilities—to American Samoa National Park, which features coral reefs, rainforests, and volcanic mountains.

Designs. *Obverse:* Yellowstone National Park's Old Faithful geyser with a bison in the foreground. *Reverse:* A Latina Folklórico dancer and the National Park Service logo.

Mintage Data. Authorized by Public Law 113-291, signed into law by President Barack Obama on December 19, 2014. *Maximum authorized*—500,000. *Number minted*—21,003 Uncirculated and 77,367 Proof.

Original Cost. Sale prices $44.95 (Uncirculated, pre-issue) and $45.95 (Proof, pre-issue). Uncirculated later raised to $49.95, and Proof later raised to $50.95. The surcharge of $10 per coin was assigned to the National Park Foundation.

Key to Collecting. Superb gem coins are readily available.

	Distribution	Cert	Avg	%MS	MS-67
					PF-67
2016-P	21,003	557	69.7	100%	$40
2016-P, Proof	77,367	1,529	69.4		$38

NATIONAL PARK SERVICE 100TH ANNIVERSARY $5 GOLD COIN (2016)

Designer: *Don Everhart.* **Weight:** *8.359 grams.* **Composition:** *.900 gold, .100 copper (net weight .242 oz. pure gold).* **Diameter:** *21.6 mm.* **Edge:** *Reeded.* **Mint:** *West Point.*

The National Park Service acts as the steward of 409 official "units," which includes the 59 National Parks as well as the country's National Monuments, National Preserves, National Historic Sites, and more.

Designs. *Obverse:* Profiles of John Muir and Theodore Roosevelt with Yosemite National Park's Half Dome in the background. *Reverse:* The National Park Service logo.

Mintage Data. Authorized by Public Law 113-291, signed into law by President Barack Obama on December 19, 2014. *Maximum authorized*—100,000. *Number minted*—5,201 Uncirculated and 19,510 Proof.

Original Cost. Sale prices $395.45 (Uncirculated, pre-issue) and $400.45 (Proof, pre-issue). Uncirculated later raised to $412.60 and Proof later raised to $417.60. The surcharge of $35 per coin was assigned to the National Park Foundation.

Key to Collecting. Superb gem coins are readily available.

	Distribution	Cert	Avg	%MS	MS-67
					PF-67
2016-W ††	5,201	533	70.0	100%	$500
2016-W, Proof	19,510	609	69.8		$500

†† Ranked in the *100 Greatest U.S. Modern Coins* (fourth edition).

LIONS CLUB INTERNATIONAL CENTURY OF SERVICE SILVER DOLLAR (2017)

Designer: *Joel Iskowitz (obverse), Patricia Lucas-Morris (reverse).* **Weight:** *26.73 grams.*
Composition: *.900 silver, .100 copper (net weight .7736 oz. pure silver).*
Diameter: *38.1 mm.* **Edge:** *Reeded.* **Mint:** *Philadelphia.*

In 1917, Melvin Jones founded the Lions Clubs International as a service club organization with the simple guiding principle of "We Serve." The organization empowers its volunteers to serve their communities, meet humanitarian needs, encourage peace, and promote international understanding. Services participated in include community, environmental, youth, health programs, and disaster relief work.

Designs. *Obverse:* The portrait of founder Melvin Jones is paired with the Lions Clubs International logo. *Reverse:* A male and female lion with a lion cub superimposed over a globe.

Mintage Data. Authorized by Public Law 112-181, the Lions Clubs International Century of Service Commemorative Coin Act, signed into law by President Barack Obama on October 5, 2012 to commemorate the organization's centennial in 2017. *Maximum authorized*—400,000. *Number minted*—17,247 Uncirculated and 68,519 Proof (as of press time).

Original Cost. Sale prices $46.95 (Uncirculated, pre-issue) and $47.95 (Proof, pre-issue): Uncirculated later raised to $51.95, and Proof later raised to $52.95. The surcharge of $10 per coin was paid to the Lions Clubs International Foundation to further its programs for the blind and visually impaired, invest in adaptive technologies for the disabled, and invest in youth and those affected by major disaster.

Key to Collecting. Superb gem coins are readily available.

	Distribution	Cert	Avg	%MS	MS-67
					PF-67
2017-P	17,247	596	69.8	100%	$50
2017-P, Proof	68,519	741	69.7		$50

BOYS TOWN CENTENNIAL HALF DOLLAR (2017)

Designer: *Chris Costello.* **Weight:** *11.34 grams.* **Composition:** *.9167 copper, .0833 nickel.*
Diameter: *30.61 mm.* **Edge:** *Reeded.* **Mints:** *San Francisco (Uncirculated) and Denver (Proof).*

Through its Boys Town National Hotline, Boys Town National Research Hospital, and other community services, Boys Town provides treatment for the behavioral, emotional, and physical problems of children and families in 11 regions across the country. Boys Town programs impact the lives of more than two million children and families each year.

Designs. *Obverse:* Two brothers from 1917 walk toward Father Flanagan's Boys Home and a pylon erected at the facility in the 1940s, symbolizing what the home would grow into. *Reverse:* A present-day Boys Town neighborhood of homes overlooked by the profiles of Boys Town graduates.

Mintage Data. Authorized by Public Law 114-30, the Boys Town Centennial Commemorative Coin Program Act of 2015, signed into law by President Barack Obama on July 6, 2015. *Maximum authorized*—300,000. *Number minted*—2017-S: 15,525 Uncirculated; 2017-D: 23,164 Proof (as of press time).

Original Cost. Sale prices $20.95 (Uncirculated, pre-issue) and $21.95 (Proof, pre-issue): Uncirculated later raised to $25.95, and Proof later raised to $26.95. The surcharge of $5 per coin went to Boys Town to carry out its cause of caring for and assisting children and families in underserved communities across America.

Key to Collecting. Superb gem coins are readily available.

	Distribution	Cert	Avg	%MS	MS-67
					PF-67
2017-S	*15,525*	488	69.5	100%	$32
2017-D, Proof	*23,164*	403	69.6		$40

BOYS TOWN CENTENNIAL SILVER DOLLAR (2017)

Designer: *Emily Damstra.* **Weight:** *26.73 grams.* **Composition:** *.900 silver, .100 copper (net weight .7736 oz. pure silver).* **Diameter:** *38.1 mm.* **Edge:** *Reeded.* **Mint:** *Philadelphia.*

Father Edward Flanagan, a young parish priest, founded Boys Town on the maxim: "Every child could be a productive citizen if given love, a home, an education, and a trade." From the beginning boys of all races and religions were welcomed, and eventually the institution grew to support girls and families as well.

Designs. *Obverse:* A young girl sitting under a tree alone, looking up plaintively. *Reverse:* A family holding hands and playing under the same tree with the same girl.

Mintage Data. Authorized by Public Law 114-30, the Boys Town Centennial Commemorative Coin Program Act of 2015, signed into law by President Barack Obama on July 6, 2015. *Maximum authorized*—350,000. *Number minted*—12,234 Uncirculated and 31,610 Proof (as of press time).

Original Cost. Sale prices $46.95 (Uncirculated, pre-issue) and $47.95 (Proof, pre-issue): Uncirculated later raised to $51.95, and Proof later raised to $52.95. The surcharge of $10 per coin went to Boys Town to carry out its cause of caring for and assisting children and families in underserved communities across America.

Key to Collecting. Superb gem coins are readily available.

	Distribution	Cert	Avg	%MS	MS-67
					PF-67
2017-P	12,234	744	69.7	100%	$45
2017-P, Proof	31,610	696	69.5		$45

Boys Town Centennial $5 Gold Coin (2017)

Designer: *Donna Weaver.* **Weight:** *8.359 grams.* **Composition:** *.900 gold, .060 silver, .040 copper (net weight .242 oz. pure gold).* **Diameter:** *21.6 mm.* **Edge:** *Reeded.* **Mint:** *West Point.*

Father Flanagan's Home for Boys, or "Boys Town" as it became known, was founded in rented a boarding house with $90 he had borrowed. It has grown exponentially since its founding in 1917. Today it is one of the largest non-profit organizations in the country, dedicated to serving at-risk children and families of all backgrounds and religions.

Designs. *Obverse:* A portrait of Father Flanagan. *Reverse:* An outstretched hand holding a sprouting acorn.

Mintage Data. Authorized by Public Law 114-30, the Boys Town Centennial Commemorative Coin Program Act of 2015, signed into law by President Barack Obama on July 6, 2015. *Maximum authorized*—50,000. *Number minted*—2,947 Uncirculated and 7,347 Proof.

Original Cost. Sale prices $395.45 (Uncirculated, pre-issue) and $400.45 (Proof, pre-issue): Uncirculated later raised to $412.60, and Proof later raised to $417.60. The surcharge of $35 per coin went to Boys Town to carry out its cause of caring for and assisting children and families in underserved communities across America.

Key to Collecting. Superb gem coins are readily available.

	Distribution	Cert	Avg	%MS	MS-67
					PF-67
2017-W	2,947	155	69.9	100%	$600
2017-W, Proof	7,347	178	69.8		$500

WORLD WAR I CENTENNIAL SILVER DOLLAR (2018)

Designer: *LeRoy Transfield (obverse and reverse).* **Weight:** *26.73 grams.*
Composition: *.900 silver, .100 copper (net weight .7736 oz. pure silver).*
Diameter: *38.1 mm.* **Edge:** *Reeded.* **Mint:** *Philadelphia.*

This silver dollar commemorates the centennial of America's involvement in World War I (April 1917 to November 1918) and honors the more than four million men and women from the United States who served during the war. In support of the coin program, the Mint created special companion silver medals honoring each of the five branches of the U.S. Armed Forces that were active during the war. Each set included a Proof silver dollar and a Proof medal.

Designs. *Obverse:* "Soldier's Charge" depicts a doughboy gripping a rifle, with twines of barbed wire in the lower right. *Reverse:* "Poppies in the Wire" features abstract poppies—symbols of war remembrance—mixed in with barbed wire continued from the obverse.

Mintage Data. Authorized by Public Law 113-212, the World War I American Veterans Centennial Commemorative Coin Act, and signed by President Barack Obama on December 16, 2014. *Maximum authorized*—350,000 total. *Number minted*—22,336 Uncirculated, 64,982 individual Proofs, 62,885 Proofs in coin-and-medal sets (mintages as of February 2018; not final).

Original Cost. Sale prices $48.95 (Uncirculated, introductory) and $51.95 (Proof, introductory); later raised to $53.95 and $56.95. A surcharge of $10 went to the United States Foundation for the Commemoration of the World Wars, a non-profit organization that supports the U.S. World War I Centennial Commission in public outreach and education about American involvement in the war. The surcharge is expected to be used to help create a new National World War I Memorial at Pershing Park, a block from the White House.

The coin and medal sets were limited to 100,000 units across all five options; their issue price was $99.95.

Key to Collecting. Superb gems are easily found in the marketplace.

	Distribution	Cert	Avg	%MS	MS-67
					PF-67
2018-P	22,336	1,045	69.8	100%	$50
2018-P, Proof	127,837	3,248	69.8		$55

BREAST CANCER AWARENESS HALF DOLLAR (2018)

Designer: *Emily Damstra.* **Weight:** *11.34 grams.* **Composition:** *.9167 copper, .0833 nickel.*
Diameter: *30.61 mm.* **Edge:** *Reeded.* **Mints:** *Denver (Uncirculated) and San Francisco (Proof).*

This suite of three coins commemorates the role of awareness and education in funding cancer research to improve outcomes and save lives. All three coins share the same designs.

Designs. *Obverse:* A butterfly flies above two women. The older woman has her hands on her chest and a relieved expression on her face. The younger, with a scarf on her head, holds one hand over her chest and the other raised in a fist as if she is ready to fight. *Reverse:* A tiger swallowtail butterfly in flight, symbolic of hope.

Mintage Data. Authorized by Public Law 114-148, the Breast Cancer Awareness Commemorative Coin Act, and signed by President Barack Obama on April 29, 2016. *Maximum authorized—*750,000 total. *Number minted—*2018-D: 11,301 Uncirculated; 2018-S, 22,392 Proof (as of press time).

Original Cost. Sale prices $25.95 (Uncirculated, pre-issue) and $27.95 (Proof, pre-issue): Uncirculated later raised to $30.95, and Proof later raised to $32.95. A surcharges of $5 was assigned to the Breast Cancer Research Foundation.

	Distribution	Cert	Avg	%MS	MS-67 PF-67
2018-D	11,301	390	69.6	100%	$22
2018-S, Proof	22,392	350	69.8		$22

BREAST CANCER AWARENESS SILVER DOLLAR (2018)

Designer: *Emily Damstra.* **Weight:** *26.73 grams.* **Composition:** *.900 silver, .100 copper (net weight .7736 oz. pure silver).* **Diameter:** *38.1 mm.* **Edge:** *Reeded.* **Mint:** *Philadelphia.*

This suite of three coins commemorates the role of awareness and education in funding cancer research to improve outcomes and save lives. All three coins share the same designs.

Designs. *Obverse:* A butterfly flies above two women. The older woman has her hands on her chest and a relieved expression on her face. The younger, with a scarf on her head, holds one hand over her chest and the other raised in a fist as if she is ready to fight. *Reverse:* A tiger swallowtail butterfly in flight, symbolic of hope.

Mintage Data. Authorized by Public Law 114-148, the Breast Cancer Awareness Commemorative Coin Act, and signed by President Barack Obama on April 29, 2016. *Maximum authorized—*400,000 total. *Number minted—*12,526 Uncirculated and 34,542 Proof (as of press time).

Original Cost. Sale prices $48.95 (Uncirculated, pre-issue) and $51.95 (Proof, pre-issue): Uncirculated later raised to $53.95, and Proof later raised to $56.95. A surcharges of $10 was assigned to the Breast Cancer Research Foundation.

	Distribution	Cert	Avg	%MS	MS-67
					PF-67
2018-P	12,526	686	69.6	100%	$50
2018-P, Proof	34,542	889	69.6		$50

BREAST CANCER AWARENESS $5 GOLD COIN (2017)

Designer: *Emily Damstra.* **Weight:** *8.359 grams.* **Composition:** *.900 gold, .060 silver,*
.040 copper (net weight .242 oz. pure gold). **Diameter:** *21.6 mm.* **Edge:** *Reeded.* **Mint:** *West Point.*

This suite of three coins commemorates the role of awareness and education in funding cancer research to improve outcomes and save lives. The $5 gold coin, with slightly more copper and zinc than the standard alloy, has a pink hue, symbolizing breast cancer awareness. All three coins share the same designs.

Designs. *Obverse:* A butterfly flies above two women. The older woman has her hands on her chest and a relieved expression on her face. The younger, with a scarf on her head, holds one hand over her chest and the other raised in a fist as if she is ready to fight. *Reverse:* A tiger swallowtail butterfly in flight, symbolic of hope.

Mintage Data. Authorized by Public Law 114-148, the Breast Cancer Awareness Commemorative Coin Act, and signed by President Barack Obama on April 29, 2016. *Maximum authorized*—50,000 total. *Number minted*—4,477 Uncirculated and 10,386 Proof (as of press time).

Original Cost. Sale prices $421.95 (Uncirculated, pre-issue) and $431.95 (Proof, pre-issue): Uncirculated later raised to $426, and Proof later raised to $436. A surcharges of $35 was assigned to the Breast Cancer Research Foundation.

	Distribution	Cert	Avg	%MS	MS-67
					PF-67
2018-W	4,477	582	69.9	100%	$500
2018-W, Proof	10,386	1,031	69.9		$500

APOLLO 11 50TH ANNIVERSARY HALF DOLLAR (2019)

Designer: *Gary Cooper.* **Weight:** *11.34 grams.* **Composition:** *.9167 copper, .0833 nickel.*
Diameter: *30.61 mm.* **Edge:** *Reeded.* **Mints:** *San Francisco (Uncirculated) and Denver (Proof).*

This program commemorates the historic Apollo 11 Moon landing on July 20, 1969. All three domed-format coins share common designs, which include, on the concave reverse, the words MERCURY, GEMINI, and APOLLO separated by moon-phase emblems, indicating the three NASA missions that culminated with the world's first manned Moon landing. The coins are "curved"—that is, the obverse is concave, and the reverse is convex, the second series struck in such a fashion by the U.S. Mint.

Designs. *Obverse:* The footprint of Neil Armstrong on the Moon, with the names of NASA missions MERCURY, GEMINI, and APOLLO above. *Reverse:* A close-up of the famous "Buzz Aldrin on the Moon" photo centered on the astronaut's visor, which reflects the landing scene.

Mintage Data. Authorized by the Apollo 11 50th Anniversary Commemorative Coin Act (P.L. 114-282), signed by President Barack Obama on December 16, 2016. *Maximum authorized—750,000. Number minted —2019-D: 41,738 Uncirculated; 2019-S: 181,811 Proof (as of press time).*

Original Cost. Sale prices $25.95 (Uncirculated, pre-issue) and $27.95 (Proof, pre-issue); Uncirculated later raised to $30.95 and Proof to $32.95. The surcharge of $5 went to the Smithsonian Institution's National Air and Space Museum's "Destination Moon" exhibit, the Astronauts Memorial Foundation, and the Astronaut Scholarship Foundation.

Key to Collecting. Superb gem coins are readily available.

	Distribution	Cert	Avg.	%MS	MS-67
					PF-67
2019-D	*41,738*	6,352	69.9	100%	$30
2019-S, Proof	*181,811*	2,573	69.7		$30

APOLLO 11 50TH ANNIVERSARY SILVER DOLLAR (2019)

Both Varieties: **Designer:** *Gary Cooper.* **Edge:** *Reeded.* **Mint:** *Philadelphia.* **Standard Issue:** **Diameter:** *38.1 mm.* **Weight:** *26.73 grams.* **Composition:** *.999 silver (net weight .8594 oz. pure silver).* **Five-Ounce Proof:** **Diameter:** *76.2 mm.* **Weight:** *155.52 grams.* **Composition:** *.999 silver (net weight 5 oz. pure silver).*

The common reverse depicts the footprint of Neil Armstrong on the Moon's surface, as photographed by the astronaut to demonstrate the depth to which his boot could penetrate the lunar soil.

The silver dollar was produced in two sizes: the normal 38.1 mm and a large, 5-ounce size measuring 76.2 mm in diameter (struck only in Proof format). Except for the size, the designs are identical in every respect.

The coins are "curved"—that is, the obverse is concave, and the reverse is convex, the second series struck in such a fashion by the U.S. Mint.

Designs. *Obverse:* The footprint of Neil Armstrong on the Moon, with the names of NASA missions MERCURY, GEMINI, and APOLLO above. *Reverse:* A close-up of the famous "Buzz Aldrin on the Moon" photo centered on the astronaut's visor, which reflects the landing scene.

Mintage Data. Authorized by the Apollo 11 50th Anniversary Commemorative Coin Act (P.L. 114-282), signed by President Barack Obama on December 16, 2016. *Maximum authorized—Standard size, 400,000; 5-ounce size, 100,000. Number minted—Standard size, 59,697 Uncirculated and 223,737 Proof; 5-ounce size, 68,259 (all figures as of press time).*

Original Cost. Normal size, sale prices $51.95 (Uncirculated, pre-issue) and $54.95 (Proof, pre-issue); Uncirculated later raised to $56.95 and Proof to $59.95. 5-ounce size, sale price $224.95 (pre-issue) later raised to $229.95. The surcharges of $10 (normal size) and $50 (5-ounce size) went to the Smithsonian Institution's National Air and Space Museum's "Destination Moon" exhibit, the Astronauts Memorial Foundation, and the Astronaut Scholarship Foundation.

Key to Collecting. Superb gem coins are readily available.

	Distribution	Cert	Avg	%MS	MS-67 PF-67
2019-P	59,697	6,984	69.9	100%	$55
2019-P, Proof	223,737	12,877	69.8		$55
2019-P, 5-oz. Proof	68,259	9,932	69.9		$250

APOLLO 11 50TH ANNIVERSARY $5 GOLD COIN (2019)

Designer: *Gary Cooper.* **Weight:** *8.359 grams.* **Composition:** *.900 gold, .060 silver, .040 copper (net weight .242 oz. pure gold).* **Diameter:** *21.6 mm.* **Edge:** *Reeded.* **Mint:** *West Point.*

The convex reverse depicts one of the most famous images in U.S. history—the helmet of astronaut Buzz Aldrin, its visor reflecting Aldrin's shadow; astronaut Neil Armstrong, holding the camera; the lunar module *Eagle*; and the American flag the mission placed on the Moon. The design was mandated by the authorizing legislation. The coins are "curved" —that is, the obverse is concave, and the reverse is convex, the second series struck in such a fashion by the U.S. Mint.

Designs. *Obverse:* The footprint of Neil Armstrong on the Moon, with the names of NASA missions MERCURY, GEMINI, and APOLLO above. *Reverse:* A close-up of the famous "Buzz Aldrin on the Moon" photo centered on the astronaut's visor, which reflects the landing scene.

Mintage Data. Authorized by the Apollo 11 50th Anniversary Commemorative Coin Act (P.L. 114-282), signed by President Barack Obama on December 16, 2016. *Maximum authorized—50,000. Number minted*—12,035 Uncirculated and 34,037 Proof.

Original Cost. Sale prices $421 (Uncirculated, pre-issue) and $431 (Proof, pre-issue); Uncirculated later raised to $426 and Proof to $436. The surcharge of $35 goes to the Smithsonian Institution's National Air and Space Museum's "Destination Moon" exhibit, the Astronauts Memorial Foundation, and the Astronaut Scholarship Foundation.

Key to Collecting. Superb gem coins are readily available.

	Distribution	Cert	Avg	%MS	MS-67 PF-67
2019-W	12,035	2,043	70.0	100%	$500
2019-W, Proof	34,037	2,505	69.9		$500

AMERICAN LEGION 100TH ANNIVERSARY HALF DOLLAR (2019)

Designer: *Richard Masters.* **Weight:** *11.34 grams.* **Composition:** *.9167 copper, .0833 nickel.*
Diameter: *30.61 mm.* **Edge:** *Reeded.* **Mints:** *Denver (Uncirculated) and San Francisco (Proof).*

With divisions ranging from the national to the local levels, the American Legion focuses on service to veterans, their families, and the community. Among other efforts, the Legion runs civic programs for both boys and girls, and has awarded millions of dollars in Child Welfare Foundation grants and college scholarships.

Designs. *Obverse:* Two children recite the Pledge of Allegiance with their hands over their hearts, the little girl wearing her grandfather's old American Legion hat. *Reverse:* A flag on a flagpole is depicted from a low angle, as if from a child's point of view, with the American Legion's emblem above.

Mintage Data. Authorized by the American Legion 100th Anniversary Commemorative Coin Act (P.L. 115-65), signed by President Donald Trump on October 6, 2017. *Maximum authorized*—750,000. *Number minted*—2019-D: 11,425 Uncirculated; 2019-S, 27,300 Proof.

Original Cost. Sale prices $25.95 (Uncirculated, pre-issue) and $27.95 (Proof, pre-issue); Uncirculated later raised to $30.95 and Proof to $32.95. The surcharge of $5 went to the American Legion for costs related to promoting the welfare of veterans and servicemembers, and to promoting patriotic values, strong families, and the importance of assistance for at-risk children.

Key to Collecting. Superb gem coins are readily available.

	Distribution	Cert	Avg	%MS	MS-67
					PF-67
2019-D	11,425	466	69.7	100%	$26
2019-S, Proof	27,300	396	69.6		$30

AMERICAN LEGION 100TH ANNIVERSARY SILVER DOLLAR (2019)

Designer: *Paul C. Balan (obverse), Patricia Lucas-Morris (reverse).* **Weight:** *26.73 grams.* **Composition:** *.999 silver (net weight .8594 oz. pure silver).* **Diameter:** *38.1 mm.* **Edge:** *Reeded.* **Mint:** *Philadelphia.*

Founded on March 15, 1919, in Paris, France, the American Legion was concerned with the welfare of U.S. soldiers and the communities they returned to after World War I. Today the Legion focuses on four areas: Veterans Affairs and Rehabilitation, Children and Youth, National Security, and Americanism— the "Four Pillars" of American Legion service.

Designs. *Obverse:* The emblem of the American Legion adorned by oak leaves and a lily, commemorating the Legion's founding in March 1919. *Reverse:* The founding of the American Legion in Paris, France, is represented by crossed U.S. and Legion flags below a fleur de lis and the legend 100 YEARS OF SERVICE.

Mintage Data. Authorized by the American Legion 100th Anniversary Commemorative Coin Act (P.L. 115-65), signed by President Donald Trump on October 6, 2017. *Maximum authorized*—400,000. *Number minted*—13,788 Uncirculated and 63,144 Proof (as of press time).

Original Cost. Sale prices $51.95 (Uncirculated, pre-issue) and $54.95 (Proof, pre-issue); Uncirculated later raised to $56.95 and Proof to $59.95. The surcharge of $10 went to the American Legion for costs related to promoting the welfare of veterans and servicemembers, and to promoting patriotic values, strong families, and the importance of assistance for at-risk children.

Key to Collecting. Superb gem coins are readily available.

	Distribution	Cert	Avg	%MS	MS-67
					PF-67
2019-P	13,788	569	69.9	100%	$52
2019-P, Proof	63,144	1,524	69.8		$55

AMERICAN LEGION 100TH ANNIVERSARY $5 GOLD COIN (2019)

Designer: *Chris Costello (obverse), Paul C. Balan (reverse).* **Weight:** *8.359 grams.*
Composition: *.900 gold, .060 silver, .040 copper (net weight .242 oz. pure gold).*
Diameter: *21.6 mm.* **Edge:** *Reeded.* **Mint:** *West Point.*

The non-partisan American Legion is the nation's largest veterans' group, with nearly two million members in more than 12,000 posts throughout the United States. Men and women of any ethnic background or religious affiliation may join. The GI Bill, which provides educational assistance to veterans, servicemembers, and their children, has been among the Legion's many efforts.

Designs. *Obverse:* A "V" for "Victory" is superimposed over the Eiffel Tower. *Reverse:* An eagle soars from right to left, with the emblem of the American Legion in the field.

Mintage Data. Authorized by the American Legion 100th Anniversary Commemorative Coin Act (P.L. 115-65), signed by President Donald Trump on October 6, 2017. *Maximum authorized*—50,000. *Number minted*—3,090 Uncirculated and 10,920 Proof (as of press time).

Original Cost. Sale prices $408.75 (Uncirculated, pre-issue) and $418.75 (Proof, pre-issue): Uncirculated later raised to $462.75, and Proof later raised to $472.75. The surcharge of $35 went to the American Legion for costs related to promoting the welfare of veterans and servicemembers, and to promoting patriotic values, strong families, and the importance of assistance for at-risk children.

Key to Collecting. Superb gem coins are readily available.

	Distribution	Cert	Avg	%MS	MS-67
					PF-67
2019-W	3,090	281	70.0	100%	$500
2019-W, Proof	10,920	615	69.9		$500

NAISMITH MEMORIAL BASKETBALL HALL OF FAME 60TH ANNIVERSARY HALF DOLLAR (2020)

Designer: *Justin Kuntz (obverse), Donna Weaver (reverse).* **Weight:** *11.34 grams.*
Composition: *.9167 copper, .0833 nickel.* **Diameter:** *30.61 mm.* **Edge:** *Reeded.*
Mints: *Denver (Uncirculated) and San Francisco (Enhanced Uncirculated and Proof).*

James Naismith, a Canadian-born physical-education instructor living in Massachusetts, invented the game of basketball for his class at Springfield College on December 21, 1891. Within a few years the new game was popularized and was being played in more than a dozen countries. In 1959 the Naismith Memorial Basketball Hall of Fame was founded in Springfield to celebrate the sport and honor its creator.

Designs. All coins in this program are dome-shaped with concave obverses and convex reverses. *Obverse:* Three basketball players reach for the ball, symbolizing how the sport unifies diverse people around the world through a shared athletic experience. *Reverse:* A basketball is about to pass through a net.

Mintage Data. Authorized by Public Law 115–343, the Naismith Memorial Basketball Hall of Fame Commemorative Coin Act, signed into law by President Donald J. Trump on December 21, 2018. *Maximum authorized*—750,000 (Uncirculated and Proof) and 75,000 (Enhanced Uncirculated). *Number minted*—2020-D: 13,635 Uncirculated; 2020-S: 22,538 Enhanced Uncirculated, 26,572 Proof, and 32,582 Proof, colorized (as of press time).

Original Cost. Sale prices $37 (Uncirculated, pre-issue), $45 (Enhanced Uncirculated), $39 (Proof, pre-issue), and $55 (Proof, colorized); Uncirculated later raised to $42, and Proof later raised to $44. The surcharge of $5 per half dollar went to the Naismith Memorial Basketball Hall of Fame to fund an endowment for increased operations and educational programming.

Key to Collecting. Superb gem examples are readily available.

	Distribution	Cert	Avg	%MS	MS-67 PF-67
2020-D	*13,635*	792	69.9	100%	$85
2020-S, Enhanced Uncirculated (a)	*22,538*	0	n/a		$28
2020-S, Proof	*26,572*	1,105	69.9		$85
2020-S, Proof, Colorized	*32,582*	1,282	70.0		$55

a. Released as part of the 2020 Basketball Hall of Fame Kids Set.

NAISMITH MEMORIAL BASKETBALL HALL OF FAME
60TH ANNIVERSARY SILVER DOLLAR (2020)

Designer: *Justin Kuntz (obverse), Donna Weaver (reverse).* **Weight:** *26.73 grams.* **Composition:** *.999 silver (net weight .8594 oz. pure silver).* **Diameter:** *38.1 mm.* **Edge:** *Reeded.* **Mint:** *Philadelphia.*

James Naismith, a physical-education instructor in Springfield, Massachusetts, invented basketball in 1891 as an indoor physical-activity game for New England's winter months. Soon the sport spread throughout the United States and the world. The Naismith Memorial Basketball Hall of Fame, created in Springfield in 1959, is recognized as the premier institution entrusted with recording and disseminating the history of the game of basketball, and recognizing and honoring the achievements of its greatest players, coaches, and contributors.

Designs. All coins in this program are dome-shaped with concave obverses and convex reverses. *Obverse:* Three basketball players strive for a ball in play, their arms slightly elongated to emphasize the full exertion of physical and mental energy required to excel in the sport. *Reverse:* A basketball is about to pass through the hoop.

Mintage Data. Authorized by Public Law 115–343, the Naismith Memorial Basketball Hall of Fame Commemorative Coin Act, signed into law by President Donald J. Trump on December 21, 2018. *Maximum authorized*—400,000. *Number minted*—21,318 Uncirculated, 68,759 Proof, and 25,721 Proof, colorized (as of press time).

Original Cost. Sale prices $64 (Uncirculated, pre-issue), $69 (Proof, pre-issue), and $95 (Proof, colorized); Uncirculated later raised to $69, and Proof later raised to $74. The surcharge of $10 per silver dollar went to the Naismith Memorial Basketball Hall of Fame to fund an endowment that increases the Hall of Fame's operations and educational programming.

Key to Collecting. Superb gem examples are readily available.

	Distribution	Cert	Avg	%MS	MS-67
					PF-67
2020-P	21,318	1,347	69.9	100%	$65
2020-P, Proof	68,759	2,866	69.9		$65
2020-P, Proof, Colorized	25,721	1,621	69.9		$95

Naismith Memorial Basketball Hall of Fame
60th Anniversary $5 Gold Coin (2020)

Designer: *Justin Kuntz (obverse), Donna Weaver (reverse).* **Weight:** *8.359 grams.* **Composition:** *.900 gold, .060 silver, .040 copper (net weight .242 oz. pure gold).* **Diameter:** *21.6 mm.* **Edge:** *Reeded.* **Mint:** *West Point.*

The game of "basket ball" was invented by physical-education instructor James Naismith in Springfield, Massachusetts, in 1891. He developed the game as an athletic distraction to keep his rowdy students occupied in the cold winter months that kept them indoors. The Naismith Memorial Basketball Hall of Fame, created in Springfield in 1959, records and disseminates the history of basketball, recognizing and honoring the achievements of the sport's greatest players, coaches, and contributors.

Designs. All coins in this program are dome-shaped with concave obverses and convex reverses. *Obverse:* Three basketball players strive for a ball in play, their arms slightly elongated to emphasize the full exertion of physical and mental energy required to excel in the sport. *Reverse:* A basketball is about to pass through the hoop.

Mintage Data. Authorized by Public Law 115–343, the Naismith Memorial Basketball Hall of Fame Commemorative Coin Act, signed into law by President Donald J. Trump on December 21, 2018. *Maximum authorized*—50,000. *Number minted*—3,261 Uncirculated and 8,072 Proof (as of press time).

Original Cost. Sale prices $634.50 (Uncirculated, pre-issue) and $644.50 (Proof, pre-issue); Uncirculated later raised to $639.50 and Proof later raised to $649.50. The surcharge of $35 per $5 gold coin went to the Naismith Memorial Basketball Hall of Fame to fund an endowment that increases its operations and educational programming.

Key to Collecting. Superb gem examples are readily available.

	Distribution	Cert	Avg	%MS	MS-67
					PF-67
2020-W	3,261	350	70.0	100%	$500
2020-W, Proof	8,072	518	69.9		$500

Women's Suffrage Centennial Silver Dollar (2020)

Designer: *Christina Hess.* **Weight:** *26.73 grams.* **Composition:** *.999 silver (net weight .8594 oz. pure silver).* **Diameter:** *38.1 mm.* **Edge:** *Reeded.* **Mint:** *Philadelphia.*

For more than 70 years after the first Women's Rights Convention, held in Seneca Falls, New York, in 1848, suffrage activists such as Sojourner Truth, Susan B. Anthony, and Ida B. Wells conducted hundreds of campaigns, often at great personal and physical cost, to win women the right to vote. Their aims were finally achieved on August 26, 1920, when the 19th Amendment to the Constitution (the "Susan B. Anthony Amendment") was ratified. It was the single largest extension of voting rights in United States history, enfranchising 27 million American women.

Designs. *Obverse:* The heads of three women overlap; each wears a different type of hat to symbolize the many decades spanned by the suffrage movement. The woman in front wears a cloche hat with an art deco pattern and a button imprinted with "1920," the year the 19th Amendment was ratified. *Reverse:* The year 2020 appears to be dropping into the slot on top of an art deco–style ballot box. A circle on the front of the box is inscribed VOTES FOR WOMEN. UNITED STATES OF AMERICA is on the lid of the box, and IN GOD WE TRUST is at the bottom.

Mintage Data. Authorized by Public Law 116–71, the Women's Suffrage Centennial Commemorative Coin Act, signed into law by President Donald J. Trump on November 25, 2019. *Maximum authorized—* 400,000. *Number minted—*12,601 Uncirculated, 33,441 Proofs sold individually, and 9,995 Proofs sold in sets (as of press time).

Original Cost. Sale prices $64 (Uncirculated, pre-issue) and $69 (Proof, pre-issue); Uncirculated later raised to $69, and Proof later raised to $74. The surcharge of $10 per silver dollar goes to the Smithsonian Institution's American Women's History Initiative to fund the study of women's contributions to various fields that have influenced the direction of the United States, and to create exhibitions and programs recognizing diverse perspectives on women's history and contributions.

Key to Collecting. Superb gem examples are readily available.

	Distribution	Cert	Avg	%MS	MS-67 / PF-67
2020-P	12,601	221	69.6	100%	$69
2020-P, Proof	43,436	285	69.7		$74

CHRISTA MCAULIFFE SILVER DOLLAR (2020)

Designer: *Laurie J. Musser.* **Weight:** *26.73 grams.* **Composition:** *.999 silver (net weight .8594 oz. pure silver).* **Diameter:** *38.1 mm.* **Edge:** *Reeded.* **Mint:** *Philadelphia.*

In 1985, Sharon Christa McAuliffe was chosen to be the first participant in the NASA Teacher in Space program. A teacher of social studies, history, English, civics, law, economics, and a course titled "The American Woman," she planned to teach two lessons from orbit. On January 28, 1986, McAuliffe and six astronauts were tragically killed when the space shuttle *Challenger* exploded one minute and 13 seconds after launch. McAuliffe was posthumously awarded the Congressional Space Medal of Honor, and scores of schools, programs, and awards now bear her name.

Designs. *Obverse:* A portrait of Christa McAuliffe. *Reverse:* McAuliffe as a teacher, smiling as she points forward and upward, symbolizing the future. Three high-school-age students look on with wonder. Seven stars in the field pay tribute to those who perished in the *Challenger* tragedy. Below them is the logo of the FIRST (For Inspiration and Recognition of Science and Technology) robotics program, the beneficiary of the surcharges.

Mintage Data. Authorized by Public Law 116-65, the Christa McAuliffe Commemorative Coin Act, signed into law by President Donald J. Trump on October 9, 2019. *Maximum authorized—*350,000. *Number minted—*To be determined.

Original Cost. Sale prices $69 (Uncirculated, pre-issue) and $74 (Proof, pre-issue); Uncirculated later raised to $74, and Proof later raised to $79. Surcharges in the amount of $10 for each silver dollar sold are authorized to be paid to the FIRST robotics program for the purpose of engaging and inspiring young people, through mentor-based programs, to become leaders in the fields of science, technology, engineering, and mathematics.

Key to Collecting. Superb gem examples are readily available.

	Distribution	Cert	Avg	%MS	MS-67
					PF-67
2020-P					
2020-P, Proof					

NATIONAL LAW ENFORCEMENT MEMORIAL AND MUSEUM HALF DOLLAR (2021)

Designer: *Ronald D. Sanders (obverse), Heidi Wastweet (reverse).* **Weight:** *11.34 grams.*
Composition: *.9167 copper, .0833 nickel.* **Diameter:** *30.61 mm.*
Edge: *Reeded.* **Mints:** *Denver (Uncirculated) and San Francisco (Proof).*

The National Law Enforcement Officers Memorial Fund was established in 1984 to inspire all citizens to value the law enforcement profession by telling the story of American law enforcement, honoring the fallen, and making it safer for those who serve. On October 15, 1991, the memorial was officially dedicated at Judiciary Square in Washington, D.C. On October 13, 2018, after a decade of planning, the adjacent National Law Enforcement Officers Museum opened. Housing historical and contemporary artifact collections, the museum educates through interactive exhibits and has space dedicated to research and educational programming.

Designs. *Obverse:* A sheriff's star, representing the community served by law enforcement officers and the important role they play. *Reverse:* An eye in a magnifying glass looking at a fingerprint, portraying the human side of justice, a reminder that law enforcement is not only officers on the street but many others behind the scenes. The emblem of the National Law Enforcement Officers Museum is below the main devices.

Mintage Data. Authorized as part of Public Law 116-94, the Further Consolidated Appropriations Act, signed into law by President Donald J. Trump on December 20, 2019. *Maximum authorized—750,000. Number minted—*To be determined.

Original Cost. Sale prices $33 (Uncirculated, pre-issue) and $35 (Proof, pre-issue); Uncirculated later raised to $38, and Proof later raised to $40. Surcharges in the amount of $5 for each half dollar sold are authorized to be paid to the National Law Enforcement Officers Memorial Fund, Inc., for educational and outreach programs and exhibits.

Key to Collecting. Superb gem examples are readily available.

	Distribution	Cert	Avg	%MS	MS-67
					PF-67
2021-D					
2021-S, Proof					

NATIONAL LAW ENFORCEMENT MEMORIAL AND MUSEUM SILVER DOLLAR (2021)

Designer: *Frank Morris (obverse), Ronald D. Sanders (reverse).* **Weight:** *26.73 grams.* **Composition:** *.999 silver (net weight .8594 oz. pure silver).* **Diameter:** *38.1 mm.* **Edge:** *Reeded.* **Mints:** *Philadelphia.*

The National Law Enforcement Officers Museum tells the story of American law enforcement through an interactive, "walk in the shoes" experience. Exhibits include a decision-making training simulator, a 9-1-1 emergency operations dispatch experience, an interactive web of law enforcement, and immersive forensics and evidence-gathering interactives. The museum's collections include more than 25,000 objects spanning more than three centuries of U.S. law-enforcement history: uniforms; badges; radios; handcuffs; documents; law-enforcement-themed books, comics, and games; and more. The museum's blog, "On the Beat," tells the stories of law-enforcement officers and historic events.

Designs. *Obverse:* A police officer kneeling next to a child, who is reading a book and sitting on a basketball, symbolizing service to the community and future generations. *Reverse:* A handshake between a law-enforcement officer and a member of the public, representing the work law-enforcement officers do within their communities to increase safety through trusting relationships.

Mintage Data. Authorized as part of Public Law 116-94, the Further Consolidated Appropriations Act, signed into law by President Donald J. Trump on December 20, 2019. *Maximum authorized*—400,000. *Number minted*—To be determined.

Original Cost. Sale prices $69 (Uncirculated, pre-issue) and $74 (Proof, pre-issue); Uncirculated later raised to $74, and Proof later raised to $79. Surcharges in the amount of $10 for each silver dollar sold are authorized to be paid to the National Law Enforcement Officers Memorial Fund, Inc., for educational and outreach programs and exhibits.

Key to Collecting. Superb gem examples are readily available.

	Distribution	Cert	Avg	%MS	MS-67
					PF-67
2021-P					
2021-P, Proof					

NATIONAL LAW ENFORCEMENT MEMORIAL AND MUSEUM $5 GOLD COIN (2021)

Designer: *Justin Kuntz (obverse), Donna Weaver (reverse).* **Weight:** *8.359 grams.*
Composition: *.900 gold, .060 silver, .040 copper (net weight .242 oz. pure gold).*
Diameter: *21.6 mm.* **Edge:** *Reeded.* **Mint:** *West Point.*

The National Law Enforcement Officers Memorial is a three-acre park with a reflecting pool and walkways, the walls of which are inscribed with the names of all federal, state, and local U.S. law enforcement officers who have died in the line of duty. At the time of its dedication ceremony in 1991, the walls bore more than 12,000 names; by the early 2020s, the number of names had increased to more than 20,000. The monument and adjacent museum were constructed and are maintained with private funds. This is the second commemorative program to benefit the organization; the first was the 1997 National Law Enforcement Officers Memorial silver dollar.

Designs. *Obverse:* Overlapping heads of a male and a female officer saluting. *Reverse:* A folded flag with three roses beneath, symbolizing remembrance.

Mintage Data. Authorized as part of Public Law 116-94, the Further Consolidated Appropriations Act, signed into law by President Donald J. Trump on December 20, 2019. *Maximum authorized*—50,000. *Number minted*—To be determined.

Original Cost. Sale prices $671.25 (Uncirculated, pre-issue) and $681.25 (Proof, pre-issue); Uncirculated later raised to $676.25, and Proof later raised to $686.25. Surcharges in the amount of $35 for each $5 gold coin sold are authorized to be paid to the National Law Enforcement Officers Memorial Fund, Inc., for educational and outreach programs and exhibits.

Key to Collecting. Superb gem examples are readily available.

	Distribution	Cert	Avg	%MS	MS-67
					PF-67
2020-W					
2020-W, Proof					

GOVERNMENT COMMEMORATIVE SETS

	Value
(1983–1984) LOS ANGELES OLYMPIAD	
1983 and 1984 Proof silver dollars	$50
1983 and 1984 6-coin set. One each of 1983 and 1984 silver dollars, both Proof and Uncirculated gold $10 (a)	$2,150
1983 3-piece collector set. 1983 P, D, and S Uncirculated silver dollars	$70
1984 3-piece collector set. 1984 P, D, and S Uncirculated silver dollars	$75
1983 and 1984 gold and silver Uncirculated set. One each of 1983 and 1984 Uncirculated silver dollars and one 1984 Uncirculated gold $10	$1,100
1983 and 1984 gold and silver Proof set. One each of 1983 and 1984 Proof silver dollars and one 1984 Proof gold $10	$1,100

a. Packaged in cherrywood box.

	Value
(1986) STATUE OF LIBERTY	
2-coin set. Proof silver dollar and clad half dollar	$30
3-coin set. Proof silver dollar, clad half dollar, and gold $5	$550
2-coin set. Uncirculated silver dollar and clad half dollar	$30
2-coin set. Uncirculated and Proof gold $5	$1,000
3-coin set. Uncirculated silver dollar, clad half dollar, and gold $5	$550
6-coin set. One each of Proof and Uncirculated half dollar, silver dollar, and gold $5 (a)	$1,150
(1987) CONSTITUTION	
2-coin set. Uncirculated silver dollar and gold $5	$525
2-coin set. Proof silver dollar and gold $5	$525
4-coin set. One each of Proof and Uncirculated silver dollar and gold $5 (a)	$1,050
(1988) SEOUL OLYMPIAD	
2-coin set. Uncirculated silver dollar and gold $5	$525
2-coin set. Proof silver dollar and gold $5	$525
4-coin set. One each of Proof and Uncirculated silver dollar and gold $5 (a)	$1,050
(1989) CONGRESS	
2-coin set. Proof clad half dollar and silver dollar	$32
3-coin set. Proof clad half dollar, silver dollar, and gold $5	$525
2-coin set. Uncirculated clad half dollar and silver dollar	$32
3-coin set. Uncirculated clad half dollar, silver dollar, and gold $5	$535
6-coin set. One each of Proof and Uncirculated clad half dollar, silver dollar, and gold $5 (a)	$1,070
(1991) MOUNT RUSHMORE	
2-coin set. Uncirculated clad half dollar and silver dollar	$45
2-coin set. Proof clad half dollar and silver dollar	$40
3-coin set. Uncirculated clad half dollar, silver dollar, and gold $5	$550
3-coin set. Proof clad half dollar, silver dollar, and gold $5	$550
6-coin set. One each of Proof and Uncirculated clad half dollar, silver dollar, and gold $5 (a)	$1,100
(1992) XXV OLYMPIAD	
2-coin set. Uncirculated clad half dollar and silver dollar	$40
2-coin set. Proof clad half dollar and silver dollar	$40
3-coin set. Uncirculated clad half dollar, silver dollar, and gold $5	$550
3-coin set. Proof half dollar, silver dollar, and gold $5	$550
6-coin set. One each of Proof and Uncirculated clad half dollar, silver dollar, and gold $5 (a)	$1,100
(1992) CHRISTOPHER COLUMBUS	
2-coin set. Uncirculated clad half dollar and silver dollar	$45
2-coin set. Proof clad half dollar and silver dollar	$40
3-coin set. Uncirculated clad half dollar, silver dollar, and gold $5	$550
3-coin set. Proof half dollar, silver dollar, and gold $5	$550
6-coin set. One each of Proof and Uncirculated clad half dollar, silver dollar, and gold $5 (a)	$1,100
(1993) BILL OF RIGHTS	
2-coin set. Uncirculated silver half dollar and silver dollar	$50
2-coin set. Proof clad half dollar and silver dollar	$40
3-coin set. Uncirculated silver half dollar, silver dollar, and gold $5	$550
3-coin set. Proof clad half dollar, silver dollar, and gold $5	$550
6-coin set. One each of Proof and Uncirculated silver half dollar, silver dollar, and gold $5 (a)	$1,100
"Young Collector" set. Silver half dollar	$35
Educational set. Silver half dollar and James Madison medal	$35
Proof silver half dollar and 25-cent stamp	$20

a. Packaged in cherrywood box.

	Value
(1993) WORLD WAR II	
2-coin set. Uncirculated clad half dollar and silver dollar	$50
2-coin set. Proof clad half dollar and silver dollar	$50
3-coin set. Uncirculated clad half dollar, silver dollar, and gold $5	$550
3-coin set. Proof clad half dollar, silver dollar, and gold $5	$550
6-coin set. One each of Proof and Uncirculated clad half dollar, silver dollar, and gold $5 (a)	$1,100
"Young Collector" set. Clad half dollar	$30
Victory Medal set. Uncirculated clad half dollar and reproduction medal	$40
(1993) THOMAS JEFFERSON	
"Coinage and Currency" set (issued in 1994). Silver dollar, "frosted" Uncirculated Jefferson nickel, and $2 note	$110
(1994) WORLD CUP SOCCER	
2-coin set. Uncirculated clad half dollar and silver dollar	$40
2-coin set. Proof clad half dollar and silver dollar	$40
3-coin set. Uncirculated clad half dollar, silver dollar, and gold $5	$550
3-coin set. Proof clad half dollar, silver dollar, and gold $5	$550
6-coin set. One each of Proof and Uncirculated clad half dollar, silver dollar, and gold $5 (a)	$1,100
"Young Collector" set. Uncirculated clad half dollar	$20
"Special Edition" set. Proof clad half dollar and silver dollar	$50
(1994) U.S. VETERANS	
3-coin set. Uncirculated POW, Vietnam, and Women in Military Service silver dollars	$150
3-coin set. Proof POW, Vietnam, and Women in Military Service silver dollars	$125
(1995) SPECIAL OLYMPICS	
2-coin set. Proof Special Olympics silver dollar, 1995-S Kennedy half dollar	$75
(1995) CIVIL WAR BATTLEFIELD PRESERVATION	
2-coin set. Uncirculated clad half dollar and silver dollar	$80
2-coin set. Proof clad half dollar and silver dollar	$80
3-coin set. Uncirculated clad half dollar, silver dollar, and gold $5	$600
3-coin set. Proof clad half dollar, silver dollar, and gold $5	$575
6-coin set. One each of Proof and Uncirculated clad half dollar, silver dollar, and gold $5 (a)	$1,150
"Young Collector" set. Uncirculated clad half dollar	$50
2-coin "Union" set. Clad half dollar and silver dollar	$125
3-coin "Union" set. Clad half dollar, silver dollar, and gold $5	$620
(1995–1996) ATLANTA CENTENNIAL OLYMPIC GAMES	
4-coin set #1. Uncirculated clad half dollar (Basketball), silver dollars (Gymnastics, Paralympics), gold $5 (Torch Bearer)	$725
4-coin set #2. Proof clad half dollar (Basketball), silver dollars (Gymnastics, Paralympics), gold $5 (Torch Bearer)	$675
4-coin set #3. Proof clad half dollar (Baseball), dollars (Cyclist, Track Runner), gold $5 (Olympic Stadium)	$675
2-coin set #1: Proof silver dollars (Gymnastics, Paralympics)	$70
"Young Collector" set. Uncirculated Basketball clad half dollar	$35
"Young Collector" set. Uncirculated Baseball clad half dollar	$35
"Young Collector" set. Uncirculated Swimming clad half dollar	$200
"Young Collector" set. Uncirculated Soccer clad half dollar	$175
1995–1996 16-coin Uncirculated set. One each of all Uncirculated coins (a)	$3,700
1995–1996 16-coin Proof set. One each of all Proof coins (a)	$3,100
1995–1996 8-coin Proof silver dollars set	$400
1995–1996 32-coin set. One each of all Uncirculated and Proof coins (a)	$6,800
(1996) NATIONAL COMMUNITY SERVICE	
Proof silver dollar and Saint-Gaudens stamp	$100
(1996) SMITHSONIAN INSTITUTION 150TH ANNIVERSARY	
2-coin set. Proof silver dollar and gold $5	$550
4-coin set. One each of Proof and Uncirculated silver dollar and gold $5 (a)	$1,100
"Young Collector" set. Proof silver dollar	$100

a. Packaged in cherrywood box.

	Value
(1997) U.S. BOTANIC GARDEN	
"Coinage and Currency" set. Uncirculated silver dollar, "frosted" Uncirculated Jefferson nickel, and $1 note	$200
(1997) JACKIE ROBINSON	
2-coin set. Proof silver dollar and gold $5	$550
4-coin set. One each of Proof and Uncirculated silver dollar and gold $5 (a)	$1,475
3-piece "Legacy" set. Baseball card, pin, and gold $5 (a)	$775
(1997) FRANKLIN D. ROOSEVELT	
2-coin set. One each of Proof and Uncirculated gold $5	$1,000
(1997) NATIONAL LAW ENFORCEMENT OFFICERS MEMORIAL	
Insignia set. Silver dollar, lapel pin, and patch	$200
(1998) ROBERT F. KENNEDY	
2-coin set. RFK silver dollar and JFK silver half dollar	$200
2-coin set. Proof and Uncirculated RFK silver dollars	$100
(1998) BLACK REVOLUTIONARY WAR PATRIOTS	
2-coin set. Proof and Uncirculated silver dollars	$125
"Young Collector" set. Uncirculated silver dollar	$125
Black Revolutionary War Patriots set. Silver dollar and four stamps	$150
(1999) DOLLEY MADISON	
2-coin set. Proof and Uncirculated silver dollars	$75
(1999) GEORGE WASHINGTON DEATH	
2-coin set. One each of Proof and Uncirculated gold $5	$1,000
(1999) YELLOWSTONE NATIONAL PARK	
2-coin set. One each of Proof and Uncirculated silver dollars	$100
(2000) LEIF ERICSON MILLENNIUM	
2-coin set. Proof silver dollar and Icelandic 1,000 kronur	$100
(2000) MILLENNIUM COIN AND CURRENCY SET	
3-piece set. Uncirculated 2000 Sacagawea dollar; Uncirculated 2000 Silver Eagle; George Washington $1 note, series 1999	$100
(2001) AMERICAN BUFFALO	
2-coin set. One each of Proof and Uncirculated silver dollars	$300
"Coinage and Currency" set. Uncirculated American Buffalo silver dollar, face reprint of 1899 $5 Indian Chief Silver Certificate, 1987 Chief Red Cloud 10¢ stamp, 2001 Bison 21¢ stamp	$200
(2001) U.S. CAPITOL VISITOR CENTER	
3-coin set. Proof clad half dollar, silver dollar, and gold $5	$560
(2002) SALT LAKE OLYMPIC GAMES	
2-coin set. Proof silver dollar and gold $5	$550
4-coin set. One each of Proof and Uncirculated silver dollar and gold $5	$1,100
(2003) FIRST FLIGHT CENTENNIAL	
3-coin set. Proof clad half dollar, silver dollar, and gold $10	$1,070
(2003) LEGACIES OF FREEDOM	
Uncirculated 2003 $1 American Eagle silver bullion coin and an Uncirculated 2002 £2 Silver Britannia coin	$75
(2004) THOMAS A. EDISON	
Edison set. Uncirculated silver dollar and light bulb	$85
(2004) LEWIS AND CLARK	
Coin and Pouch set. Proof silver dollar and beaded pouch	$200
"Coinage and Currency" set. Uncirculated silver dollar, Sacagawea golden dollar, two 2005 nickels, replica 1901 $10 Bison note, silver-plated Peace Medal replica, three stamps, two booklets	$100
(2004) WESTWARD JOURNEY NICKEL SERIES	
Westward Journey Nickel Series™ Coin and Medal set. Proof Sacagawea golden dollar, two 2004 Proof nickels, silver-plated Peace Medal replica	$60
(2005) WESTWARD JOURNEY NICKEL SERIES	
Westward Journey Nickel Series™ Coin and Medal set. Proof Sacagawea golden dollar, two 2005 Proof nickels, silver-plated Peace Medal replica	$40

a. Packaged in cherrywood box.

	Value
(2005) CHIEF JUSTICE JOHN MARSHALL	
"Coin and Chronicles" set. Uncirculated silver dollar, booklet, BEP intaglio portrait	$60
(2005) AMERICAN LEGACY	
American Legacy Collection. Proof Marine Corps silver dollar, Proof John Marshall silver dollar, 11-piece Proof set	$100
(2005) MARINE CORPS 230TH ANNIVERSARY	
Marine Corps Uncirculated silver dollar and stamp set	$100
(2006) BENJAMIN FRANKLIN	
"Coin and Chronicles" set. Uncirculated "Scientist" silver dollar, four stamps, *Poor Richard's Almanack* replica, intaglio print	$75
(2006) AMERICAN LEGACY	
American Legacy Collection. Proof 2006-P Benjamin Franklin, Founding Father silver dollar; Proof 2006-S San Francisco Old Mint silver dollar; Proof cent, nickel, dime, quarter, half dollar, and dollar	$90
(2007) AMERICAN LEGACY	
American Legacy Collection. 16 Proof coins for 2007: five state quarters; four Presidential dollars; Jamestown and Little Rock Central High School Desegregation silver dollars; Proof cent, nickel, dime, half dollar, and dollar	$140
(2007) LITTLE ROCK CENTRAL HIGH SCHOOL DESEGREGATION	
Little Rock Coin and Medal set. Uncirculated 2007-P silver dollar, bronze medal	$175
(2008) BALD EAGLE	
3-piece set. Proof clad half dollar, silver dollar, and gold $5	$550
Bald Eagle Coin and Medal Set. Uncirculated silver dollar, bronze medal	$70
"Young Collector" set. Uncirculated clad half dollar	$18
(2008) AMERICAN LEGACY	
American Legacy Collection. 15 Proof coins for 2008: cent, nickel, dime, half dollar, and dollar; five state quarters; four Presidential dollars; Bald Eagle silver dollar	$150
(2009) LOUIS BRAILLE	
Uncirculated silver dollar in tri-fold package	$50
(2009) ABRAHAM LINCOLN COIN AND CHRONICLES	
Four Proof 2009-S cents and Abraham Lincoln Proof silver dollar	$150
(2012) STAR-SPANGLED BANNER	
2-coin set. Proof silver dollar and gold $5	$550
(2013) 5-STAR GENERALS	
3-coin set. Proof clad half dollar, silver dollar, and gold $5	$675
Profile Collection. Uncirculated half dollar and silver dollar, replica of 1962 General MacArthur Congressional gold medal	$80
(2013) THEODORE ROOSEVELT COIN AND CHRONICLES	
Theodore Roosevelt Presidential dollar, silver Presidential medal, National Wildlife Refuge System Centennial bronze medal, and Roosevelt print	$60
(2013) GIRL SCOUTS OF THE U.S.A.	
"Young Collector" set. Uncirculated silver dollar	$60
(2014) FRANKLIN D. ROOSEVELT COIN AND CHRONICLES	
Franklin D. Roosevelt Proof dime and Presidential dollar, bronze Presidential medal, silver Presidential medal, four stamps, information booklet	$100
(2014) NATIONAL BASEBALL HALL OF FAME	
"Young Collector" set. Uncirculated silver dollar	$30
(2014) AMERICAN $1 COIN AND CURRENCY SET	
2014-D Native American—Native Hospitality Enhanced Uncirculated dollar and $1 Federal Reserve Note	$50
(2015) HARRY S. TRUMAN COIN AND CHRONICLES	
Harry S. Truman Reverse Proof Presidential dollar, silver Presidential medal, one stamp, information booklet	$300
(2015) DWIGHT D. EISENHOWER COIN AND CHRONICLES	
Dwight D. Eisenhower Reverse Proof Presidential dollar, silver Presidential medal, one stamp, information booklet	$150
(2015) JOHN F. KENNEDY COIN AND CHRONICLES	
John F. Kennedy Reverse Proof Presidential dollar, silver Presidential medal, one stamp, information booklet	$100
(2015) LYNDON B. JOHNSON COIN AND CHRONICLES	
Lyndon B. Johnson Reverse Proof Presidential dollar, silver Presidential medal, one stamp, information booklet	$100
(2015) MARCH OF DIMES SPECIAL SILVER SET	
Proof dime and March of Dimes silver dollar, Reverse Proof dime	$80

	Value
(2015) AMERICAN $1 COIN AND CURRENCY SET	
2015-W Native American—Mohawk Ironworkers Enhanced Uncirculated dollar and $1 Federal Reserve Note	$25
(2015) U.S. MARSHALS	
3-coin set. Proof clad half dollar, silver dollar, and gold $5	$475
(2016) NATIONAL PARK SERVICE 100TH ANNIVERSARY	
3-piece set. Proof clad half dollar, silver dollar, and gold $5	$625
(2016) RONALD REAGAN COIN AND CHRONICLES	
Ronald Reagan Reverse Proof Presidential dollar, 2016-W American Eagle silver Proof dollar, Ronald and Nancy Reagan bronze medal, engraved Ronald Reagan Presidential portrait, information booklet	$125
(2016) AMERICAN $1 COIN AND CURRENCY SET	
2016-S Native American—Code Talkers Enhanced Uncirculated dollar and $1 Federal Reserve Note	$25
(2017) BOYS TOWN CENTENNIAL	
3-piece set. Proof clad half dollar, silver dollar, and gold $5	$625
(2018) BREAST CANCER AWARENESS	
Coin and Stamp Set. Breast Cancer Awareness Proof clad half dollar and Breast Cancer Research stamp	$100
(2018) WORLD WAR I CENTENNIAL	
Silver Dollar and Air Service Medal Set. Proof World War I Centennial silver dollar and Proof silver Air Service medal	$100
Silver Dollar and Army Medal Set. Proof World War I Centennial silver dollar and Proof silver Army medal	$100
Silver Dollar and Coast Guard Medal Set. Proof World War I Centennial silver dollar and Proof silver Coast Guard medal	$100
Silver Dollar and Marine Corps Medal Set. Proof World War I Centennial silver dollar and Proof silver Marine Corps medal	$100
Silver Dollar and Navy Medal Set. Proof World War I Centennial silver dollar and Proof silver Navy medal	$100
(2019) APOLLO 11 50TH ANNIVERSARY	
2-coin set. Uncirculated and Proof clad half dollars	$55
(2019) AMERICAN LEGION 100TH ANNIVERSARY	
3-coin set. Proof clad half dollar, silver dollar, and gold $5	$600
Silver Dollar and Medal Set. American Legion 100th Anniversary Proof silver dollar and American Veterans medal	$100
(2019) AMERICAN $1 COIN AND CURRENCY SET	
2019-P Native American – American Indians in Space Enhanced Uncirculated dollar and $1 Federal Reserve Note	$75
(2019) YOUTH COIN AND CURRENCY SET	
Five Proof clad America the Beautiful™ quarters and $2 Federal Reserve Note	$30
(2020) NAISMITH MEMORIAL BASKETBALL HALL OF FAME 60TH ANNIVERSARY	
"Kids Set." 2020-S Proof clad half dollar	$45
(2020) WOMEN'S SUFFRAGE CENTENNIAL	
Silver Dollar and Medal Set. Women's Suffrage Centennial Proof silver dollar and medal	$120
(2021) NATIONAL LAW ENFORCEMENT MEMORIAL AND MUSEUM	
3-coin set. Proof clad half dollar, silver dollar, and gold $5	

Proof and Mint Sets
1936 to Date
AN OVERVIEW OF PROOF AND MINT SETS

PROOF COINS AND SETS

A Proof is a specimen coin struck for presentation, souvenir, exhibition, or numismatic purposes. Before 1968, Proofs were made only at the Philadelphia Mint, except in a few rare instances in which presentation pieces were struck at branch mints. Today Proofs are made at the San Francisco and West Point mints.

The term *Proof* refers not to the condition of a coin, but to its method of manufacture. Regular-production coins (struck for circulation) in Mint State have coruscating, frosty luster; soft details; and minor imperfections. A Proof coin can usually be distinguished by its sharpness of detail, high wire edge, and extremely brilliant, mirrorlike surface. All Proofs are originally sold by the Mint at a premium.

Very few Proof coins were made prior to 1856. Because of their rarity and infrequent sales, they are not all listed in the regular edition of the *Guide Book of United States Coins*. However, here, in the *Deluxe Edition*, you will find them listed individually within their respective denominations.

Frosted Proofs were issued prior to 1936 and starting again in the late 1970s. These have a brilliant, mirrorlike field with contrasting dull or frosted design.

Matte Proofs have a granular, "sandblast" surface instead of the mirror finish. Matte Proof cents, nickels, and gold coins were issued from 1908 to 1916; a few 1921 and 1922 silver dollars and a 1998-S half dollar were also struck in this manner.

Brilliant Proofs have been issued from 1936 to date. These have a uniformly brilliant, mirrorlike surface and sharp, high-relief details.

Reverse Proofs were first struck for bullion coins in 2006, and regularly denominated, silver-struck coins have also been made with this finish since 2014. As their name implies, the devices, not the field, have a brilliant, mirrorlike finish, while the field has a matte finish.

"Prooflike" coins are occasionally seen. These are examples struck from dies that were lightly polished, often inadvertently during the removal of lines, contact marks, and other marks in the fields. In other instances, such as with certain New Orleans gold coins of the 1850s, the dies were polished in the machine shop of the mint. They are not true Proofs, but may have most of the characteristics of a Proof coin and generally command a premium. Collectors should beware of coins that have been buffed to look like Proofs; magnification will reveal polishing lines and loss of detail.

After a lapse of some 20 years, Proof coins were struck at the Philadelphia Mint from 1936 to 1942, inclusive. During these years the Mint offered Proof coins to collectors for individual sale, rather than in officially packaged sets, as such.

In 1942, when the composition of the five-cent piece was changed from copper-nickel to copper-silver-manganese, there were two Proof types of this denomination available to collectors.

The striking of all Proof coins was temporarily suspended from 1943 through 1949, and again from 1965 through 1967; during the latter period, Special Mint Sets were struck (see pages 1283–1284). Proof sets were resumed in 1968.

Sets from 1936 through 1972 included the cent, nickel, dime, quarter, and half dollar; from 1973 through 1981 the dollar was also included, and again from 2000 on. Regular Proof sets issued from 1982 to 1998 contain the cent through the half dollar. Specially packaged Prestige sets containing commemorative coins were sold from 1983 through 1997 at an additional premium. From 1999 to 2009, sets contain five different Statehood or Territorial quarters, and from 2010 to 2021, different National Parks quarters. In 1999 Proof dollars were sold separately. Four-piece Presidential dollar sets have been issued since 2007.

As part of a memorial John F. Kennedy half dollar set released in 2014, Reverse Proofs struck in silver at West Point were introduced. The Philadelphia mint first struck Reverse Proofs in 2015, also in silver, for inclusion in the March of Dimes commemorative set. Additionally, Coin and Chronicles sets of 2015 include Philadelphia-struck Reverse Proofs of the Presidential dollars of the year.

With the recent State and Territorial quarters programs, as well as the ongoing National Park quarters and Presidential dollars programs, the U.S. Mint has offered Proof sets featuring each of the designs issued for a particular year.

From time to time the Mint issues special Proof sets. One recent example is the four-piece 2009-S Lincoln Bicentennial set, which included each of the special cent designs issued that year, but coined in 95% copper (the Lincoln cent's original 1909 alloy).

Collectors are encouraged to consult David W. Lange's *Guide Book of Modern United States Proof Coin Sets* for detailed coverage and illustrations of Proof sets from 1936 to date.

How Modern Proof Coins Are Made

Selected dies are inspected for perfection and are highly polished and cleaned. They are again wiped clean or polished after every 15 to 25 impressions and are replaced frequently to avoid imperfections from wear. Coinage blanks for Proof coins are polished and cleaned to ensure high quality in striking. They are then hand fed into the coinage press one at a time, each blank receiving two or more blows from the dies to bring up sharp, high-relief details. The coinage operation is done at slow speed with extra pressure. Finished Proofs are individually inspected and are handled with gloves or tongs. They also receive a final inspection by packers before being sonically sealed in special plastic cases.

Mint Sets

Official Uncirculated Mint sets are specially packaged by the government for sale to collectors. They contain Uncirculated examples of each year's coins for every denomination issued from each mint. Before 2005, the coins were the same as those normally intended for circulation and were not minted with any special consideration for quality. From 2005 to 2010, however, Mint sets were made with a satin finish rather than the traditional Uncirculated luster. As in the past, coins struck only as Proofs are not included.

Uncirculated Mint sets sold by the Treasury from 1947 through 1958 contained two examples of each regular-issue coin. These were packaged in cardboard holders that did not protect the coins from tarnish. Nicely preserved early sets generally command a 10 to 20% premium above average values. Since 1959, sets have been sealed in protective plastic envelopes.

Privately assembled Mint sets, and Souvenir sets produced for sale at the Philadelphia or Denver mints for special occasions, are valued according to the individual pieces they contain. Only the official, government-packaged full sets are included in the following list. No Mint Sets were produced in 1950, 1982, or 1983, though Souvenir sets were sold in the latter two years (see the final section of this overview).

From time to time the Mint issues special Mint sets. One recent example is the 1996-P-D Mint set, which also included a 1996-W dime (released only in those sets).

Special Mint Sets

In mid-1964 the Treasury department announced that the Mint would not offer Proof sets or Mint sets the following year. This was prompted by a nationwide shortage of circulating coins, which was wrongly blamed on coin collectors.

In 1966 the San Francisco Assay Office began striking coins dated 1965, for inclusion in so-called United States Special Mint Sets. These were issued in pliofilm packaging similar to that of recent Proof sets. The coins in early 1965 Special Mint Sets are semi-brilliant or satiny (distinctive, but not equal in quality to Proofs); the coins in later 1965 sets feature very brilliant fields (but again not reaching Proof brilliance).

The San Francisco Assay Office started striking 1966-dated coins in August of that year, and its Special Mint Sets were packaged in rigid, sonically sealed plastic holders. The coins were struck once on unpolished planchets, unlike Proof coins (which are struck at least twice on polished planchets). Also unlike Proofs, the SMS coins were allowed to come into contact with each other during their production, which accounts for minor contact marks and abrasions. To achieve a brilliant finish, Mint technicians overpolished the coinage dies. The result was a tradeoff: most of the coins have prooflike brilliance, but many are missing polished-off design details, such as Frank Gasparro's initials on the half dollar.

All 1967-dated coinage was struck in that calendar year. Nearly all SMS coins of 1967 have fully brilliant, prooflike finishes. This brilliance was achieved without overpolishing the dies, resulting in coins that approach the quality of true Proofs. Sales of the 1967 sets were lackluster, however. The popularity of coin collecting had dropped from its peak in 1964. Also, collectors and speculators did not anticipate much secondary-market profit from the sets, which had an issue price of $4.00, compared to $2.10 for a 1964 Proof set. As a result, fewer collectors bought multiples of the 1967 sets, and today they are generally worth more than those of 1965 and 1966.

Similar SMS coins dated 1964 exist as single pieces and in sets. Like the 1965 through 1967 SMS coins, they have a semi-brilliant or satiny finish but are not equal in quality to Proofs. They are referred to as SP (Special Strike) coins and command much higher prices than their regular SMS counterparts. In August 2019, a 1964-dated Special Strike Kennedy half dollar (listed in the *100 Greatest U.S. Modern Coins*) sold at auction for $156,000, setting a new record for a non-error modern U.S. coin.

SOUVENIR SETS

Uncirculated Souvenir sets were packaged and sold in gift shops at the Philadelphia and Denver mints in 1982 and 1983 in place of the "official Mint sets," which were not made in those years. A bronze Mint medal is packaged with each set. Similar sets were also made in other years.

1936 Proof Set
Liberty Walking half dollar, Washington quarter dollar, Mercury or Winged Liberty dime, Buffalo nickel, and Lincoln cent with Wheat Ears reverse.

1938 Proof Set
Buffalo nickel replaced with the new Jefferson nickel.

1950 Proof Set
There was a seven-year hiatus (1943–1949) before Proof sets were issued again after World War II. By 1950 the Liberty Walking half dollar had been replaced by the Franklin half dollar (introduced 1948), and the Mercury dime by the Roosevelt dime (introduced 1946).

1955 Proof Set
Issued in traditional individual envelopes, or in the new pliofilm package (pictured), with a Philadelphia Mint embossed paper seal with a metallic finish.

MODERN PROOF SETS (1936 TO DATE)

	Mintage	Issue Price	Face Value	Current Value
1936	3,837	$1.89	$0.91	$6,000
1937	5,542	$1.89	$0.91	$2,850
1938	8,045	$1.89	$0.91	$1,175
1939	8,795	$1.89	$0.91	$1,125
1940	11,246	$1.89	$0.91	$925
1941	15,287	$1.89	$0.91	$875
1942, Both nickels	21,120	$1.89	$0.91	$1,000
1942, One nickel	(a)	$1.89	$0.91	$850
1950	51,386	$2.10	$0.91	$535
1951	57,500	$2.10	$0.91	$485
1952	81,980	$2.10	$0.91	$250
1953	128,800	$2.10	$0.91	$200

a. Included in 1942, Both nickels, mintage figure.

	Mintage	Issue Price	Face Value	Current Value
1954	233,300	$2.10	$0.91	$100
1955, Box pack	378,200	$2.10	$0.91	$100
1955, Flat pack	(b)	$2.10	$0.91	$120
1956	669,384	$2.10	$0.91	$65
1957	1,247,952	$2.10	$0.91	$28
1958	875,652	$2.10	$0.91	$32
1959	1,149,291	$2.10	$0.91	$28
1960, With Large Date cent	1,691,602	$2.10	$0.91	$28
1960, With Small Date cent	(c)	$2.10	$0.91	$32
1961	3,028,244	$2.10	$0.91	$25
1962	3,218,019	$2.10	$0.91	$25
1963	3,075,645	$2.10	$0.91	$25
1964	3,950,762	$2.10	$0.91	$22
1968-S	3,041,506	$5	$0.91	$7
1968-S, With No S dime	(d)	$5	$0.91	$14,500
1969-S	2,934,631	$5	$0.91	$7
1970-S	2,632,810	$5	$0.91	$11
1970-S, With Small Date cent	(e)	$5	$0.91	$85
1970-S, With No S dime *(estimated mintage: 2,200)*	(e)	$5	$0.91	$900
1971-S	3,220,733	$5	$0.91	$4
1971-S, With No S nickel *(estimated mintage: 1,655)*	(f)	$5	$0.91	$1,200
1972-S	3,260,996	$5	$0.91	$5
1973-S	2,760,339	$7	$1.91	$8
1974-S	2,612,568	$7	$1.91	$10
1975-S, With 1976 quarter, half, and dollar	2,845,450	$7	$1.91	$9
1975-S, With No S dime	(g)	$7	$1.91	$350,000
1976-S	4,149,730	$7	$1.91	$9
1976-S, Silver clad, 3-piece set	3,998,621	$15	$1.75	$25
1977-S	3,251,152	$9	$1.91	$7
1978-S	3,127,781	$9	$1.91	$7
1979-S, Type 1	3,677,175	$9	$1.91	$8
1979-S, Type 2	(h)	$9	$1.91	$48
1980-S	3,554,806	$10	$1.91	$5
1981-S, Type 1	4,063,083	$11	$1.91	$5
1981-S, Type 2 (all six coins in set)	(i)	$11	$1.91	$280
1982-S	3,857,479	$11	$0.91	$5
1983-S	3,138,765	$11	$0.91	$5
1983-S, With No S dime	(j)	$11	$0.91	$700
1983-S, Prestige set (Olympic dollar)	140,361	$59	$1.91	$42
1984-S	2,748,430	$11	$0.91	$6
1984-S, Prestige set (Olympic dollar)	316,680	$59	$1.91	$27
1985-S	3,362,821	$11	$0.91	$4
1986-S	2,411,180	$11	$0.91	$6
1986-S, Prestige set (Statue of Liberty half, dollar)	599,317	$48.50	$2.41	$28
1987-S	3,792,233	$11	$0.91	$5
1987-S, Prestige set (Constitution dollar)	435,495	$45	$1.91	$28
1988-S	3,031,287	$11	$0.91	$5
1988-S, Prestige set (Olympic dollar)	231,661	$45	$1.91	$30
1989-S	3,009,107	$11	$0.91	$5

b. Included in 1955, Box pack, mintage figure. c. Included in 1960, With Large Date cent, mintage figure. d. Included in 1968-S mintage figure. e. Included in 1970-S mintage figure. f. Included in 1971-S mintage figure. g. Included in 1975-S, With 1976 quarter, half, and dollar, mintage figure. h. Included in 1979-S, Type 1, mintage figure. i. Included in 1981-S, Type 1, mintage figure. j. Included in 1983-S mintage figure.

	Mintage	Issue Price	Face Value	Current Value
1989-S, Prestige set (Congressional half, dollar)	211,807	$45	$2.41	$32
1990-S	2,793,433	$11	$0.91	$5
1990-S, With No S cent	3,555	$11	$0.91	$4,250
1990-S, Prestige set (Eisenhower dollar)	506,126	$45	$1.91	$30
1990-S, Prestige set (With No S cent)	(k)	$45	$1.91	$4,650
1991-S	2,610,833	$11	$0.91	$5
1991-S, Prestige set (Mt. Rushmore half, dollar)	256,954	$59	$2.41	$45
1992-S	2,675,618	$11	$0.91	$5
1992-S, Prestige set (Olympic half, dollar)	183,293	$56	$2.41	$46
1992-S, Silver	1,009,586	$11	$0.91	$20
1992-S, Silver Premier set	308,055	$37	$0.91	$24
1993-S	2,409,394	$12.50	$0.91	$6
1993-S, Prestige set (Bill of Rights half, dollar)	224,045	$57	$2.41	$35
1993-S, Silver	570,213	$21	$0.91	$28
1993-S, Silver Premier set	191,140	$37.50	$0.91	$35
1994-S	2,308,701	$12.50	$0.91	$5
1994-S, Prestige set (World Cup half, dollar)	175,893	$57	$2.41	$35
1994-S, Silver	636,009	$21	$0.91	$28
1994-S, Silver Premier set	149,320	$37.50	$0.91	$36
1995-S	2,010,384	$12.50	$0.91	$10
1995-S, Prestige set (Civil War half, dollar)	107,112	$57	$2.41	$80
1995-S, Silver	549,878	$21	$0.91	$52
1995-S, Silver Premier set	130,107	$37.50	$0.91	$52
1996-S	1,695,244	$12.50	$0.91	$8
1996-S, Prestige set (Olympic half, dollar)	55,000	$57	$2.41	$325
1996-S, Silver	623,655	$21	$0.91	$28
1996-S, Silver Premier set	151,366	$37.50	$0.91	$32
1997-S	1,975,000	$12.50	$0.91	$8
1997-S, Prestige set (Botanic dollar)	80,000	$57	$1.91	$60
1997-S, Silver	605,473	$21	$0.91	$34
1997-S, Silver Premier set	136,205	$37.50	$0.91	$38
1998-S	2,086,507	$12.50	$0.91	$10
1998-S, Silver	638,134	$21	$0.91	$24
1998-S, Silver Premier set	240,658	$37.50	$0.91	$28
1999-S, 9-piece set	2,543,401	$19.95	$1.91	$9
1999-S, 5-piece quarter set	1,169,958	$13.95	$1.25	$5
1999-S, Silver 9-piece set	804,565	$31.95	$1.91	$90
2000-S, 10-piece set	3,082,572	$19.95	$2.91	$7
2000-S, 5-piece quarter set	937,600	$13.95	$1.25	$5
2000-S, Silver 10-piece set	965,421	$31.95	$2.91	$40
2001-S, 10-piece set	2,294,909	$19.95	$2.91	$11
2001-S, 5-piece quarter set	799,231	$13.95	$1.25	$5
2001-S, Silver 10-piece set	889,697	$31.95	$2.91	$40
2002-S, 10-piece set	2,319,766	$19.95	$2.91	$8
2002-S, 5-piece quarter set	764,479	$13.95	$1.25	$5.50
2002-S, Silver 10-piece set	892,229	$31.95	$2.91	$40
2003-S, 10-piece set	2,172,684	$19.95	$2.91	$7
2003-S, 5-piece quarter set	1,235,832	$13.95	$1.25	$5
2003-S, Silver 10-piece set	1,125,755	$31.95	$2.91	$40
2004-S, 11-piece set	1,789,488	$22.95	$2.96	$11
2004-S, 5-piece quarter set	951,196	$15.95	$1.25	$5
2004-S, Silver 11-piece set	1,175,934	$37.95	$2.96	$40

k. Included in 1990-S, Prestige set (Eisenhower dollar), mintage figure.

	Mintage	Issue Price	Face Value	Current Value
2004-S, Silver 5-piece quarter set	593,852	$23.95	$1.25	$26
2005-S, 11-piece set	2,275,000	$22.95	$2.96	$5
2005-S, 5-piece quarter set	987,960	$15.95	$1.25	$5
2005-S, Silver 11-piece set	1,069,679	$37.95	$2.96	$38
2005-S, Silver 5-piece quarter set	608,970	$23.95	$1.25	$24
2006-S, 10-piece set	2,000,428	$22.95	$2.91	$8
2006-S, 5-piece quarter set	882,000	$15.95	$1.25	$5
2006-S, Silver 10-piece set	1,054,008	$37.95	$2.91	$36
2006-S, Silver 5-piece quarter set	531,000	$23.95	$1.25	$24
2007-S, 14-piece set	1,702,116	$26.95	$6.91	$18
2007-S, 5-piece quarter set	672,662	$13.95	$1.25	$7
2007-S, 4-piece Presidential set	1,285,972	$14.95	$4	$6
2007-S, Silver 14-piece set	875,050	$44.95	$6.91	$45
2007-S, Silver 5-piece quarter set	672,662	$25.95	$1.25	$26
2008-S, 14-piece set	1,405,674	$26.95	$6.91	$28
2008-S, 5-piece quarter set	672,438	$13.95	$1.25	$20
2008-S, 4-piece Presidential set	869,202	$14.95	$4	$12
2008-S, Silver 14-piece set	763,887	$44.95	$6.91	$45
2008-S, Silver 5-piece quarter set	429,021	$25.95	$1.25	$25
2009-S, 18-piece set	1,482,502	$29.95	$7.19	$25
2009-S, 6-piece quarter set	630,976	$14.95	$1.50	$6
2009-S, 4-piece Presidential set	629,585	$14.95	$4	$9
2009-S, Silver 18-piece set	697,365	$52.95	$7.19	$50
2009-S, Silver 6-piece quarter set	299,183	$29.95	$1.50	$30
2009-S, 4-piece Lincoln Bicentennial set	201,107	$7.95	$0.04	$10
2010-S, 14-piece set	1,103,815	$31.95	$6.91	$35
2010-S, 5-piece quarter set	276,296	$14.95	$1.25	$13
2010-S, 4-piece Presidential set	535,397	$15.95	$4	$15
2010-S, Silver 14-piece set	585,401	$56.95	$6.91	$52
2010-S, Silver 5-piece quarter set	274,034	$32.95	$1.25	$25
2011-S, 14-piece set	1,098,835	$31.95	$6.91	$36
2011-S, 5-piece quarter set	152,302	$14.95	$1.25	$14
2011-S, 4-piece Presidential set	299,853	$19.95	$4	$30
2011-S, Silver 14-piece set	574,175	$67.95	$6.91	$60
2011-S, Silver 5-piece quarter set	147,901	$39.95	$1.25	$28
2012-S, 14-piece set	794,002	$31.95	$6.91	$125
2012-S, 5-piece quarter set	148,498	$14.95	$1.25	$15
2012-S, 4-piece Presidential set	249,265	$18.95	$4	$65
2012-S, Silver 14-piece set	395,443	$67.95	$6.91	$200
2012-S, Silver 8-piece Limited Edition set	44,952	$149.95	$2.85	$235
2012-S, Silver 5-piece quarter set	162,448	$41.95	$1.25	$28
2013-S, 14-piece set	802,460	$31.95	$6.91	$35
2013-S, 5-piece quarter set	128,377	$14.95	$1.25	$14
2013-S, 4-piece Presidential set	266,677	$18.95	$4	$18
2013-S, Silver 14-piece set	419,720	$67.95	$6.91	$70
2013-S, Silver 8-piece Limited Edition set	47,791	$139.95	$2.85	$125
2013-S, Silver 5-piece quarter set	138,451	$41.95	$1.25	$28
2014-S, 14-piece set	680,977	$31.95	$6.91	$35
2014-S, 5-piece quarter set	109,423	$14.95	$1.25	$16
2014-S, 4-piece Presidential set	218,976	$18.95	$4	$18
2014-S, Silver 14-piece set	387,310	$67.95	$6.91	$57
2014-S, Silver 8-piece Limited Edition set	41,609	$139.95	$2.85	$160
2014-S, Silver 5-piece quarter set	103,311	$41.95	$1.25	$35

	Mintage	Issue Price	Face Value	Current Value
2015-S, 14-piece set	662,854	$32.95	$6.91	$38
2015-S, 5-piece quarter set	99,466	$14.95	$1.25	$14
2015-S, 4-piece Presidential set	222,068	$18.95	$4	$18
2015-S, Silver 14-piece set	387,310	$53.95	$6.91	$56
2015-S, Silver 5-piece quarter set	103,311	$31.95	$1.25	$32
2016-S, 13-piece set	575,183	$31.95	$5.91	$50
2016-S, 5-piece quarter set	91,674	$14.95	$1.25	$14
2016-S, 3-piece Presidential set	231,549	$17.95	$3	$18
2016-S, Silver 13-piece set	356,683	$52.95	$5.91	$65
2016-S, Silver 8-piece Limited Edition set, with 2016-W American silver eagle	95,709	$139.95	$2.85	$135
2016-S, Silver 5-piece quarter set	49,647	$31.95	$1.25	$28
2017-S, 10-piece set	568,678	$26.95	$2.91	$36
2017-S, 5-piece quarter set	88,909	$14.95	$1.25	$15
2017-S, Silver 10-piece set	358,085	$47.95	$2.91	$48
2017-S, Silver 5-piece quarter set	89,632	$31.95	$1.25	$34
2017-S, Silver 8-piece Limited Edition set	48,901	$139.95	$2.85	$185
2018-S, 10-piece set	516,843	$27.95	$2.91	$34
2018-S, 5-piece quarter set	86,669	$15.95	$1.25	$15
2018-S, Silver 10-piece set	331,883	$49.95	$2.91	$50
2018-S, Silver 5-piece quarter set	79,259	$33.95	$1.25	$33
2018-S, 50th Anniversary Silver 10-piece Reverse Proof set	199,116	$54.95	$2.91	$80
2018-S, Silver 8-piece Limited Edition set	49,473	$144.95	$2.85	$175
2019-S, 10-piece set, plus 2019-W Proof cent	593,978	$27.95	$2.92	$30
2019-S, 5-piece quarter set	74,035	$15.95	$1.25	$15
2019-S, 4-piece American Innovation dollar set	114,414	$20.95	$1	$20
2019-S, Silver 10-piece set, plus 2019-W Reverse Proof cent	412,609	$54.95	$2.92	$60
2019-S, Silver 5-piece quarter set	78,559	$36.95	$1.25	$38
2019-S, Silver 8-piece Limited Edition set	46,076	$149.95	$2.85	$130
2020-S, 10-piece set, plus 2020-W Proof nickel		$32	$2.96	$80
2020-S, 5-piece quarter set		$18.50	$1.25	$20
2020-S, 4-piece American Innovation dollar set		$24	$1	$25
2020-S, Silver 10-piece set, plus 2020-W Reverse Proof nickel		$63.25	$2.96	$125
2020-S, Silver 5-piece quarter set		$42.50	$1.25	$45
2020-S, Silver 8-piece Limited Edition set		$201	$2.85	$200
2021-S, 7-piece set				
2021-S, 4-piece American Innovation dollar set				
2021-S, Silver 7-piece set				
2021-S, Silver 5-piece Limited Edition set				

UNCIRCULATED MINT SETS (1947 TO DATE)

	Mintage	Issue Price	Face Value	Current Value		Mintage	Issue Price	Face Value	Current Value
1947 P-D-S	5,000	$4.87	$4.46	$1,500	1958 P-D	50,314	$4.43	$3.64	$275
1948 P-D-S	6,000	$4.92	$4.46	$1,100	1959 P-D	187,000	$2.40	$1.82	$52
1949 P-D-S	5,000	$5.45	$4.96	$1,225	1960 P-D	260,485	$2.40	$1.82	$40
1951 P-D-S	8,654	$6.75	$5.46	$950	1961 P-D	223,704	$2.40	$1.82	$40
1952 P-D-S	11,499	$6.14	$5.46	$900	1962 P-D	385,285	$2.40	$1.82	$40
1953 P-D-S	15,538	$6.14	$5.46	$775	1963 P-D	606,612	$2.40	$1.82	$40
1954 P-D-S	25,599	$6.19	$5.46	$425	1964 P-D	1,008,108	$2.40	$1.82	$40
1955 P-D-S	49,656	$3.57	$2.86	$360	1968 P-D-S	2,105,128	$2.50	$1.33	$7
1956 P-D	45,475	$3.34	$2.64	$360	1969 P-D-S	1,817,392	$2.50	$1.33	$7
1957 P-D	34,324	$4.40	$3.64	$360					

a. Included in 1970 P-D-S, With Large Date cent, mintage figure.

	Mintage	Issue Price	Face Value	Current Value		Mintage	Issue Price	Face Value	Current Value
1970 P-D-S, With Large Date cent	2,038,134	$2.50	$1.33	$20	1996 P-D, Plus 1996-W dime	1,457,949	$8	$1.92	$15
					1997 P-D	950,473	$8	$1.82	$6
1970 P-D-S, With Small Date cent	(a)	$2.50	$1.33	$50	1998 P-D	1,187,325	$8	$1.82	$5
					1999 P-D (18 pieces) (c)	1,243,867	$14.95	$3.82	$8
1971 P-D-S (no Ike dollar)	2,193,396	$3.50	$1.83	$5	2000 P-D (20 pieces)	1,490,160	$14.95	$5.82	$8
1972 P-D-S (no Ike dollar)	2,750,000	$3.50	$1.83	$5	2001 P-D (20 pieces)	1,116,915	$14.95	$5.82	$8
1973 P-D-S	1,767,691	$6	$3.83	$12	2002 P-D (20 pieces)	1,139,388	$14.95	$5.82	$8
1974 P-D-S	1,975,981	$6	$3.83	$6	2003 P-D (20 pieces)	1,001,532	$14.95	$5.82	$8
1975 P-D, With 1976 quarter, half, dollar	1,921,488	$6	$3.82	$9	2004 P-D (22 pieces)	842,507	$16.95	$5.92	$8
					2005 P-D (22 pieces)	1,160,000	$16.95	$5.92	$8
1976, Silver clad, 3-piece set	4,908,319	$9	$1.75	$19	2006 P-D (20 pieces)	847,361	$16.95	$5.82	$8
					2007 P-D (28 pieces)	895,628	$22.95	$13.82	$18
1976 P-D	1,892,513	$6	$3.82	$9	2008 P-D (28 pieces)	745,464	$22.95	$13.82	$30
1977 P-D	2,006,869	$7	$3.82	$6	2009 P-D (36 pieces)	784,614	$27.95	$14.38	$24
1978 P-D	2,162,609	$7	$3.82	$8	2010 P-D (28 pieces)	583,897	$31.95	$13.82	$24
1979 P-D (b)	2,526,000	$8	$3.82	$7	2011 P-D (28 pieces)	533,529	$31.95	$13.82	$24
1980 P-D-S	2,815,066	$9	$4.82	$8	2012 P-D (28 pieces)	392,224	$27.95	$13.82	$65
1981 P-D-S	2,908,145	$11	$4.82	$9	2013 P-D (28 pieces)	376,844	$27.95	$13.82	$24
1984 P-D	1,832,857	$7	$1.82	$5	2014 P-D (28 pieces)	327,969	$27.95	$13.82	$24
1985 P-D	1,710,571	$7	$1.82	$5	2015 P-D (28 pieces)	314,029	$28.95	$13.82	$25
1986 P-D	1,153,536	$7	$1.82	$8	2016 P-D (26 pieces)	296,582	$27.95	$11.82	$35
1987 P-D	2,890,758	$7	$1.82	$5	2017 P-D (20 pieces)	286,813	$20.95	$5.82	$35
1988 P-D	1,646,204	$7	$1.82	$5	2017-S, 225th Anniversary Enhanced Uncirculated set (10 pieces)	210,419	$29.95	$2.91	$40
1989 P-D	1,987,915	$7	$1.82	$5					
1990 P-D	1,809,184	$7	$1.82	$5					
1991 P-D	1,352,101	$7	$1.82	$5	2018 P-D (20 pieces)	257,424	$21.95	$5.82	$25
1992 P-D	1,500,143	$7	$1.82	$5	2019 P-D, plus 2019-W cent (21 pieces)	344,238	$21.95	$5.83	$25
1993 P-D	1,297,431	$8	$1.82	$6					
1994 P-D	1,234,813	$8	$1.82	$5	2020 P-D (20 pieces)			$5.87	$27
1995 P-D	1,038,787	$8	$1.82	$6	2021 P-D (14 pieces)				

b. S-mint dollar not included. c. Dollar not included.

SPECIAL MINT SETS (1965–1967)

	Mintage	Issue Price	Face Value	Current Value
1965 ††	2,360,000	$4	$0.91	$10
1966 ††	2,261,583	$4	$0.91	$10
1967 ††	1,863,344	$4	$0.91	$10

Note: See page 1283 for details on the similar 1964 Special Strike coins. Values for these coins are approximately $13,000 for each denomination. †† All 1965–1967 Special Mint Set coins graded Ultra Cameo are ranked in the *100 Greatest U.S. Modern Coins* (fourth edition), as a single entry.

SOUVENIR SETS (1982–1983)

	Issue Price	Face Value	Current Value
1982-P	$4	$0.91	$60
1982-D	$4	$0.91	$60
1983-P	$4	$0.91	$80
1983-D	$4	$0.91	$80

POPULAR DIE VARIETIES FROM MINT SETS

As noted in the *Cherrypickers' Guide to Rare Die Varieties*, "Beginning with those modern Mint sets from 1947 . . . there are many years of one or the other that are absent of a significant variety. Not all of the known varieties are significant." The following are some popular die varieties from Mint sets; for more information and additional examples, consult the *Cherrypickers' Guide*.

DIE VARIETIES IN MINT SETS

Year	Denomination	Variety	Year	Denomination	Variety
1949	5¢	D/S—over mintmark (**a**)	1970	50¢	D—doubled-die reverse (**d**)
1954	25¢	doubled-die reverse (**b**)	1971	5¢	D/D—repunched mintmark
1960	5¢	(P)—doubled-die obverse (**c**)	1971	10¢	D/D—repunched mintmark
1960	25¢	(P)—doubled-die obverse (**c**)	1971	10¢	D—doubled-die reverse
1961	50¢	D/D—repunched mintmark	1971	50¢	D—doubled-die obverse
1963	10¢	(P)—doubled-die obverse	1971	50¢	D—doubled-die reverse
1963	25¢	(P)—doubled-die obverse	1972	1¢	(P)—doubled-die obverse
1963	25¢	(P)—doubled-die reverse	1972	5¢	D—doubled-die reverse
1963	50¢	(P)—doubled-die obverse	1972	50¢	D—doubled-die reverse
1963	50¢	(P)—doubled-die reverse	1973	50¢	(P)—doubled-die obverse
1968	10¢	(P)—doubled-die obverse	1973	50¢	D—doubled-die obverse
1968	25¢	D—doubled-die reverse	1974	50¢	D—doubled-die obverse
1969	5¢	D/D—repunched mintmark	1981	5¢	D—doubled-die reverse
1969	10¢	D/D—repunched mintmark	1984	50¢	D/D—repunched mintmark
1969	25¢	D/D—repunched mintmark	1987	5¢	D/D—repunched mintmark
1969	50¢	D—doubled-die reverse	1987	10¢	D/D—repunched mintmark
1970	1¢	D/D—repunched mintmark	1989	5¢	D—doubled-die reverse
1970	1¢	D—doubled-die obverse	1989	10¢	P—doubled-die reverse
1970	10¢	D—doubled-die reverse	1989	50¢	D/D—repunched mintmark
1970	25¢	D—doubled-die reverse	1991	5¢	D—doubled-die obverse

a. Although known, most have already been removed from their Mint-packaged sets. **b.** Small Date. **c.** Found in sets labeled as Small Date. **d.** Small Date.

U.S. Mint Bullion Coins

AN OVERVIEW OF U.S. MINT BULLION COINS

The United States' bullion-coin program was launched in 1986. Since then, American Eagle and other silver, gold, platinum, and palladium coins have provided investors with convenient vehicles to add physical bullion to their portfolios. They also have value as numismatic collectibles.

In addition to regular investment-grade strikes, the U.S. Mint offers its bullion coins in various collectible formats. Proofs are created in a specialized minting process: a polished coin blank is manually fed into a press fitted with special dies; the blank is struck multiple times "so the softly frosted yet detailed images seem to float above a mirror-like field" (per Mint literature); a white-gloved inspector scrutinizes the coin; and it is then sealed in a protective plastic capsule and mounted in a satin-lined velvet presentation case along with a certificate of authenticity. Members of the public can purchase Proofs directly from the Mint, at fixed prices.

Burnished (called Uncirculated by the Mint) coins are also sold directly to the public. These coins have the same design as other bullion coins, but are distinguished from regular bullion strikes by a W mintmark (for West Point), and by their distinctive finish (the result of burnished coin blanks). Their blanks are individually fed by hand into specially adapted coining presses. After striking, each Burnished specimen is carefully inspected, encapsulated in plastic, and packaged in a satin-lined velvet presentation case, along with a certificate of authenticity.

In recent years the Mint has also broadened its collectible bullion offerings with Reverse Proof and Enhanced Uncirculated formats. Various bullion coins have been offered in collector sets, as well.

Since the inception of the bullion-coin program in 1986, the Mint has marked several anniversaries with special issues and sets.

Mint-authorized purchasers (wholesalers, brokerage companies, precious-metal firms, coin dealers, and participating banks) buy regular bullion-strike coins in bulk. These authorized purchasers in turn sell them to secondary retailers, who then make them available to the general public. Authorized purchasers are required to meet financial and professional criteria, attested to by an internationally accepted accounting firm. They must be an experienced and established market-maker in bullion coins; provide a liquid two-way market for the coins; be audited annually; have an established and broad retail-customer base for distribution; and have a tangible net worth of $5 million (for American Silver Eagles) or $25 million (for gold and platinum American Eagles). Authorized purchasers of gold, platinum, and palladium must have sold 100,000 or more ounces of those metals (bullion, or bullion coins) in any 12-month period since 1990. For gold, the initial order must be for at least 1,000 ounces, with reorders in increments of 500 ounces; for platinum/palladium, 100 ounces for both the initial order and reorders; and for silver, a minimum order of 25,000 ounces. For American Eagles, an authorized purchaser's cost is based on the market value of the bullion, plus a premium to cover minting, distribution, and other overhead expenses. For ASEs, the premium is $2 per coin. For gold, the premiums are 3% (for the one-ounce coin), 5% (1/2 ounce), 7% (1/4 ounce), and 9% (1/10 ounce). For platinum the premium is 4% for the one-ounce coin; for palladium, 6.25%.

Note that the U.S. Mint does not release bullion mintage data on a regular basis; the numbers given herein reflect the most recently available official data.

The listed values of uncertified, average Mint State coins have been based on bullion prices of silver ($27.50 per ounce), gold ($2,000), platinum ($950), and palladium ($2,250).

For more detailed coverage of these coins, readers are directed to *American Silver Eagles: A Guide to the U.S. Bullion Coin Program* (Mercanti), *American Gold and Platinum Eagles: A Guide to the U.S. Bullion Coin Programs* (Moy), and *American Gold and Silver: U.S. Mint Collector and Investor Coins and Medals, Bicentennial to Date* (Tucker).

AMERICAN SILVER EAGLES (1986 TO DATE)

Designers: *Adolph A. Weinman (obverse) and John Mercanti (reverse).*
Weight: *31.101 grams.* **Composition:** *.999 silver, .001 copper (net weight 1 oz. pure silver).*
Diameter: *40.6 mm.* **Edge:** *Reeded.* **Mints:** *Philadelphia, San Francisco, and West Point.*

Regular
Finish

Burnished
Finish

**Reverse Lettering
Style of 1986–2007**
*Note the lack of spur or
stem at bottom right of U.*

**Reverse Lettering Style
of 2008 to Date**
*Note the spur at
bottom right of U.*

Enhanced Uncirculated Finish
*This special format incorporates elements with a brilliant
mirrored finish, a light frosted finish, and a heavy frosted finish.*

Proof
Finish

Reverse
Proof Finish

History. The American Silver Eagle (face value $1, actual silver weight one ounce) is a legal-tender bullion coin with weight, content, and purity guaranteed by the federal government. It is one of the few silver coins allowed in individual retirement accounts (IRAs). The obverse design features Adolph A. Weinman's Liberty Walking, as used on the circulating half dollar of 1916 to 1947. Weinman's initials appear on the hem of Miss Liberty's gown. The reverse design, by John Mercanti, is a heraldic eagle.

From 1986 to 1999 all American Silver Eagles were struck at the Philadelphia and San Francisco mints (with the exception of the 1995 West Point Proof). In 2000 they were struck at both Philadelphia (Proofs) and the U.S. Mint's West Point facility (bullion strikes). From 2001 to 2010, West Point was their sole producer (with one exception in 2006), making regular bullion strikes (without mintmarks) and Proof and "Burnished" specimens (with mintmarks). (The exception is the 2006 Reverse Proof, which was struck in Philadelphia.) In 2011, for the 25th anniversary of the American Eagle bullion program, the mints at West Point, San Francisco, and Philadelphia were all put into production to make several collectible formats of the coins. Since 2012, West Point has been their main production mint, with Philadelphia and San Francisco helping when demand is high.

In addition to the individually listed coins, American Silver Eagles were issued in two 2006 "20th Anniversary" sets and in several other special bullion coin sets.

Striking and Sharpness. Striking is generally sharp. The key elements to check on the obverse are Miss Liberty's left hand, the higher parts and lines of her skirt, and her head. On the reverse, the eagle's breast is a main focal point.

Availability. The American Silver Eagle is one of the most popular silver-investment vehicles in the world. Between the bullion coins and various collectible formats, more than 400 million have been sold since 1986. The coins are readily available in the numismatic marketplace and from some banks, investment firms, and other non-numismatic channels.

MS-60 to 70 (Mint State). *Obverse and Reverse:* At MS-60, some abrasion and contact marks are evident on the higher design areas (Miss Liberty's left arm, her hand, and the areas of the skirt covering her left leg). Luster may be dull or lifeless at MS–60 to 62, but there should be deep frost at MS-63 and better, particularly in the lower-relief areas. At MS-65 and above, the luster should be full and rich. These guidelines are more academic than practical, as American Silver Eagles are not intended for circulation, and nearly all are in high Mint State grades.

PF-60 to 70 (Proof). *Obverse and Reverse:* Proofs that are extensively cleaned and have many hairlines are lower level, such as PF-60 to 62. Those with fewer hairlines or flaws are deemed PF–63 to 65. (These exist more in theory than actuality, as nearly all Proof ASEs have been maintained in their original high condition by collectors and investors.) Given the quality of modern U.S. Mint products, even PF–66 and 67 are unusually low levels for ASE Proofs.

AMERICAN SILVER EAGLES

| | Mintage | MS | MS-69 | MS-70 |
		PF	PF-69	PF-70
1986 †† (a,b)	5,393,005	$50	$65	$1,000
1986-S, Proof	1,446,778	$55	$90	$450
1987 (a,c)	11,442,335	$38	$47	$1,200
1987-S, Proof	904,732	$55	$85	$600
1988 (a,d)	5,004,646	$38	$47	$1,900
1988-S, Proof	557,370	$55	$85	$550
1989 (a)	5,203,327	$38	$85	$1,200
1989-S, Proof	617,694	$55	$85	$300
1990 (a)	5,840,210	$38	$47	$2,900
1990-S, Proof	695,510	$55	$85	$300
1991 (a,e)	7,191,066	$38	$47	$2,400
1991-S, Proof	511,925	$55	$85	$500
1992 (a,f)	5,540,068	$38	$47	$1,700
1992-S, Proof	498,654	$55	$85	$500
1993 (a,g)	6,763,762	$40	$50	$4,000
1993-P, Proof (h)	405,913	$95	$130	$1,200
1994 (a,i)	4,227,319	$50	$65	$5,000
1994-P, Proof †† (j)	372,168	$180	$195	$1,600
1995 (a)	4,672,051	$45	$55	$2,200
1995-P, Proof	438,511	$65	$90	$700
1995-W, Proof †† (k)	30,125	$3,500	$4,500	$16,000
1996 †† (a,l)	3,603,386	$85	$120	$5,500
1996-P, Proof	500,000	$50	$95	$600
1997 (a)	4,295,004	$40	$50	$1,500
1997-P, Proof	435,368	$50	$95	$700
1998 (a)	4,847,549	$38	$47	$1,900
1998-P, Proof	450,000	$50	$85	$300
1999 (a,m)	7,408,640	$50	$65	$14,000
1999-P, Proof	549,769	$50	$85	$400
2000 (n,o)	9,239,132	$38	$47	$3,700
2000-P, Proof	600,000	$50	$75	$400
2001 (n)	9,001,711	$38	$47	$800
2001-W, Proof	746,398	$50	$80	$200
2002 (n)	10,539,026	$38	$47	$250
2002-W, Proof	647,342	$50	$80	$175

| | Mintage | MS | MS-69 | MS-70 |
		PF	PF-69	PF-70
2003 (n)	8,495,008	$38	$47	$275
2003-W, Proof	747,831	$50	$80	$140
2004 (n)	8,882,754	$38	$47	$200
2004-W, Proof	801,602	$50	$80	$125
2005 (n)	8,891,025	$38	$47	$200
2005-W, Proof	816,663	$50	$80	$125
2006 (n)	10,676,522	$38	$47	$180
2006-W, Burnished †† (p)	468,020	$75	$85	$265
2006-W, Proof	1,092,477	$50	$80	$125
2006-P, Reverse Proof †† (q,r,s)	248,875	$160	$185	$325
2007 (n)	9,028,036	$38	$47	$125
2007-W, Burnished	621,333	$42	$47	$90
2007-W, Proof	821,759	$50	$80	$110
2008 (n)	20,583,000	$36	$45	$90
2008-W, Burnished	533,757	$48	$65	$100
2008-W, Burnished, Reverse of 2007 †† (t,u)	47,000	$450	$550	$1,400
2008-W, Proof	700,979	$55	$75	$90
2009 (n)	30,459,000	$36	$45	$90
2010 (n)	34,764,500	$36	$45	$80
2010-W, Proof (v)	849,861	$55	$75	$90
2011 (n,w)	40,020,000	$36	$45	$80
2011-W, Burnished	409,927	$45	$52	$90
2011-W, Proof	947,355	$60	$80	$100
2011-P, Reverse Proof †† (r,x)	99,882	$255	$280	$500
2011-S, Burnished †† (y)	99,882	$225	$275	$350
2012 (n,w)	33,121,500	$36	$45	$80
2012-W, Burnished	226,120	$55	$85	$140
2012-W, Proof	869,386	$70	$90	$120
2012-S, Proof	285,184	$75	$95	$165
2012-S, Reverse Proof †† (r)	224,981	$125	$175	$250
2013 (n,w)	42,675,000	$36	$45	$80

Note: For more information, consult Mercanti's *American Silver Eagles: A Guide to the U.S. Bullion Coin Program* (third edition). MS values are for uncertified Mint State coins of average quality, in their complete original U.S. Mint packaging. PF values are for uncertified Proof coins of average quality, in their complete original U.S. Mint packaging. †† Ranked in the *100 Greatest U.S. Modern Coins* (fourth edition). **a.** Minted at Philadelphia, without mintmark. **b.** Auction: $1,028, MS-70, September 2015. **c.** Auction: $999, MS-70, August 2015. **d.** Auction: $1,704, MS-70, August 2015. **e.** Auction: $3,760, MS-70, August 2015. **f.** Auction: $1,528, MS-70, June 2015. **g.** Auction: $3,760, MS-70, June 2015. **h.** Auction: $1,528, PF-70UCam, March 2015. **i.** Auction: $4,700, MS-70, June 2015. **j.** Auction: $1,293, PF-70DCam, September 2015. **k.** Auction: $14,100, PF-70UCam, June 2015. **l.** Auction: $5,640, MS-70, August 2015. **m.** Auction: $4,935, MS-70, June 2015. **n.** Minted at West Point, without mintmark. **o.** Auction: $1,293, MS-70, July 2015. **p.** In celebration of the 20th anniversary of the Bullion Coinage Program, in 2006 the W mintmark was used on bullion coins produced in sets at West Point. **q.** The 2006-P Reverse Proof coins were issued to mark the 20th anniversary of the Bullion Coinage Program. **r.** Reverse Proofs have brilliant devices, and their background fields are frosted (rather than the typical Proof format of frosted devices and mirror-like backgrounds). **s.** Auction: $329, PF-70, February 2015. **t.** Reverse dies of 2007 and earlier have a plain U in UNITED. Modified dies of 2008 and later have a small spur at the bottom right of the U. **u.** Auction: $940, MS-70, August 2015. **v.** The U.S. Mint did not strike any Proof American Silver Eagles in 2009. **w.** Minted at San Francisco, without mintmark. **x.** Auction: $376, PF-70, September 2015. **y.** Auction: $306, MS-70, October 2015.

	Mintage	MS / PF	MS-69 / PF-69	MS-70 / PF-70		Mintage	MS / PF	MS-69 / PF-69	MS-70 / PF-70
2013-W, Burnished	222,091	$50	$75	$125	2018-S, Proof	208,258	$75	$90	$120
2013-W, Enhanced Uncirculated ††	235,689	$90	$115	$150	2019 (n)	14,863,500	$36	$45	$85
					2019-W, Burnished	140,779	$65	$75	$100
2013-W, Proof	934,812	$60	$80	$95	2019-W, Proof	372,118	$70	$85	$115
2013-W, Reverse Proof	235,689	$115	$140	$160	2019-W, Enhanced Reverse Proof (bb)	99,675	$1,250		
2014 (n,w)	44,006,000	$36	$45	$80					
2014-W, Burnished	253,169	$50	$75	$100	2019-S, Proof	192,811	$75	$90	$120
2014-W, Proof	944,770	$70	$85	$100	2019-S, Enhanced Reverse Proof	29,909	$950	$1,100	$2,000
2015 (n,w)	47,000,000	$36	$45	$85					
2015-W, Burnished	201,188	$50	$75	$100	2020 (n,w)		$36	$45	$80
2015-W, Proof	707,518	$70	$85	$125	2020-W, Burnished		$70	$80	$150
2016 (n,w)	37,701,500	$36	$45	$85	2020-W, Proof		$75	$90	$110
2016-W, Burnished †† (z)	216,501	$55	$75	$125	2020-W, End of World War II 75th Anniversary, Proof (cc)	75,000	$500		
2016-W, Proof ††	651,453	$75	$90	$150					
2017 (n,w)	18,065,500	$36	$45	$85	2020-S, Proof		$80	$95	$125
2017-W, Burnished	176,739	$65	$75	$90	2021, Flying Eagle (n,w)		$38	$45	$85
2017-W, Proof	440,586	$70	$85	$115	2021-W, Flying Eagle, Burnished		$75	$90	$125
2017-S, Proof (aa)	123,799	$115	$150	$200					
2018 (n,w)	15,700,000	$36	$45	$85	2021-W, Flying Eagle, Proof		$80	$90	$130
2018-W, Burnished	138,947	$65	$75	$100	2021-S, Flying Eagle, Proof		$80	$90	$130
2018-W, Proof	411,397	$70	$85	$110	2021-W, Heraldic Eagle		$85	$95	$145

Note: For more information, consult Mercanti's *American Silver Eagles: A Guide to the U.S. Bullion Coin Program* (third edition). MS values are for uncertified Mint State coins of average quality, in their complete original U.S. Mint packaging. PF values are for uncertified Proof coins of average quality, in their complete original U.S. Mint packaging. †† Ranked in the *100 Greatest U.S. Modern Coins* (fourth edition). **n.** Minted at West Point, without mintmark. **w.** Minted at San Francisco, without mintmark. **z.** In celebration of the 30th anniversary of the Bullion Coinage Program, in 2016 special edge lettering was used on bullion coins sold directly to the public. **aa.** Issued in the 2017 Congratulations Set. **bb.** Included in the 2019 Pride of Two Nations set. **cc.** Struck with a "V75" privy mark. See page 533 for an illustration and description of the privy mark as used on 2020 quarters.

AMERICAN SILVER EAGLE COIN SETS

	Uncertified	69	70
1997 Impressions of Liberty set (a)	$4,000	$4,500	$6,800
2006 20th Anniversary Three-Coin Set. Silver dollars, Uncirculated, Proof, Reverse Proof	$285	$350	$700
2006 20th Anniversary 1-oz. Gold- and Silver-Dollar Set. Uncirculated	$2,350	$2,425	$2,500
2011 25th Anniversary Five-Coin Set	$600	$725	$1,100
2012 75th Anniversary of San Francisco Mint Two-Coin Set. Proof, Reverse Proof	$200	$270	$500
2013 75th Anniversary of West Point Depository Two-Coin Set. Reverse Proof, Enhanced Uncirculated	$175	$220	$250
2019 Pride of Two Nations Limited Edition Two-Coin Set. W-Mint Enhanced Reverse Proof and Royal Canadian Mint Silver Maple Leaf modified Proof	$145	$185	$225
2021 Reverse Proof Two-Coin Set. S-Mint and W-Mint Reverse Proof silver eagles			

Note: Uncertified values are for uncertified sets of average quality, in their complete original U.S. Mint packaging. **a.** This set contains a $100 platinum, $50 gold, and $1 silver piece.

AMERICA THE BEAUTIFUL 5-OUNCE
SILVER BULLION COINS (2010–2021)

Designers: *See image captions on pages 524–533 for designers.* **Weight:** *155.517 grams.* **Composition:** *.999 silver, .001 copper (net weight 5 oz. pure silver).* **Diameter:** *76.2 mm.* **Edge:** *Lettered.* **Mint:** *Philadelphia.*

Bullion Strike

Specimen Strike

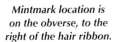

Mintmark location is on the obverse, to the right of the hair ribbon.

Details of the incused edge markings.

Details on 2014 Great Smoky Mountains National Park 5-ounce silver bullion coin (left) and quarter dollar (right). Note differences on window, cabin, and grass in foreground.

History. In conjunction with the National Park quarter dollars, the U.S. Mint issues silver-bullion coins based on each of the "America the Beautiful" program's circulation-strike coins. The coinage dies are cut on a CNC milling machine, bypassing a hubbing operation, which results in finer details than seen on the smaller quarter dollars. The bullion coins are made of .999 fine silver, have a diameter of three inches, weigh five ounces, and carry a face value of 25 cents. The fineness and weight are incused on each coin's edge. The Mint's German-made Gräbener press strikes 22 coins per minute, with two strikes per coin at 450 to 500 metric tons of pressure. In December 2010, the Mint announced it would produce Specimen versions (called *Uncirculated* by the Mint) for collectors. Detailed information on each issue is in *American Gold and Silver: U.S. Mint Collector and Investor Coins and Medals, Bicentennial to Date* (Tucker).

Striking and Sharpness. Striking is generally sharp.

Availability. The National Park silver bullion coins are distributed through commercial channels similar to those for the Mint's American Silver Eagle coins. Production of the 2010 coins was delayed (finally starting September 21) as the Mint worked out the technical details of striking such a large product. Production and distribution have been smoother since then.

MS-65 to 70 (Mint State). *Obverse and Reverse:* At MS-65, some abrasion and contact marks are evident on the higher design areas. Luster may be dull or lifeless at MS–65 to 66, but there should be deep frost at MS-67 and better, particularly in the lower-relief areas. At MS-68 and above, the luster should be full and rich. These guidelines are more academic than practical, as these coins are not intended for circulation, and nearly all are in high Mint State grades.

SP-68 to 70 (Specimen). *Obverse and Reverse:* These pieces should be nearly perfect and with full luster, in their original Mint packaging. Any with imperfections due to careless handling or environmental damage are valued lower.

The U.S. Mint produces the America the Beautiful™ 5-ounce silver coins in bullion and numismatic versions. The bullion version, which lacks the P mintmark, has a brilliant finish and is sold only through dealers. The numismatic version, with the mintmark, has a matte or burnished finish. These coins are designated "Specimens" (SP) by most collectors and grading services. They are sold directly to the public by the Mint.

25¢ AMERICA THE BEAUTIFUL 5-OUNCE SILVER BULLION COINS

	Mintage	MS	MS-69	MS-70
		SP	SP-69	SP-70
2010, Hot Springs National Park	33,000	$165	$250	—
2010-P, Hot Springs National Park, Specimen	26,788	$220	$240	$600
2010, Yellowstone National Park	33,000	$165	$190	—
2010-P, Yellowstone National Park, Specimen	26,711	$220	$245	$270
2010, Yosemite National Park	33,000	$175	$250	—
2010-P, Yosemite National Park, Specimen	26,716	$220	$245	$325
2010, Grand Canyon National Park	33,000	$165	$250	—
2010-P, Grand Canyon National Park, Specimen	25,967	$220	$245	$270
2010, Mt. Hood National Forest	33,000	$180	$250	—
2010-P, Mt. Hood National Forest, Specimen	26,637	$220	$245	$270
2011, Gettysburg National Military Park	126,700	$200	$275	—
2011-P, Gettysburg National Military Park, Specimen (a)	24,625	$255	$290	$650
2011, Glacier National Park	126,700	$165	$250	—
2011-P, Glacier National Park, Specimen (b)	20,856	$220	$245	$400
2011, Olympic National Park	104,900	$160	$250	—
2011-P, Olympic National Park, Specimen (c)	18,398	$220	$245	$400

Note: MS values are for uncertified Mint State coins of average quality, in their complete original U.S. Mint packaging. SP values are for uncertified Specimen coins of average quality, in their complete original U.S. Mint packaging. **a.** Auction: $341, SP-70, May 2015. **b.** Auction: $376, SP-70, September 2014. **c.** Auction: $188, SP-69, December 2015.

	Mintage	MS	MS-69	MS-70
		SP	SP-69	SP-70
2011, Vicksburg National Military Park	58,100	$160	$250	—
2011-P, Vicksburg National Military Park, Specimen (d)	18,594	$220	$245	$450
2011, Chickasaw National Recreational Area	48,700	$160	$250	—
2011-P, Chickasaw National Recreational Area, Specimen (e)	16,827	$215	$250	$500
2012, El Yunque National Forest	24,000	$260	$350	—
2012-P, El Yunque National Forest, Specimen (f)	17,314	$400	$435	$600
2012, Chaco Culture National Historical Park	24,400	$260	$285	—
2012-P, Chaco Culture National Historical Park, Specimen (g)	17,146	$355	$390	$600
2012, Acadia National Park	25,400	$375	$395	—
2012-P, Acadia National Park, Specimen (h)	14,978	$550	$585	$875
2012, Hawai'i Volcanoes National Park	20,000	$400	$850	—
2012-P, Hawai'i Volcanoes National Park, Specimen (i)	14,863	$650	$700	$1,500
2012, Denali National Park and Preserve	20,000	$260	$350	—
2012-P, Denali National Park and Preserve, Specimen	15,225	$475	$515	$700
2013, White Mountain National Forest	35,000	$160	$210	—
2013-P, White Mountain National Forest, Specimen	20,530	$220	$245	$270
2013, Perry's Victory and International Peace Memorial	30,000	$160	$210	—
2013-P, Perry's Victory and International Peace Memorial, Specimen	17,707	$220	$245	$270
2013, Great Basin National Park	30,000	$160	$210	—
2013-P, Great Basin National Park, Specimen	17,792	$220	$245	$270
2013, Ft. McHenry National Monument & Historic Shrine	30,000	$160	$210	—
2013-P, Ft. McHenry National Monument & Historic Shrine, Specimen	19,802	$220	$245	$270
2013, Mount Rushmore National Monument	35,000	$160	$210	—
2013-P, Mount Rushmore National Monument, Specimen	23,547	$220	$245	$270
2014, Great Smoky Mountains National Park	33,000	$165	$190	—
2014-P, Great Smoky Mountains National Park, Specimen	24,710	$200	$225	$250
2014, Shenandoah National Park	25,000	$165	$190	—
2014-P, Shenandoah National Park, Specimen	28,276	$200	$225	$250
2014, Arches National Park	22,000	$165	$190	—
2014-P, Arches National Park, Specimen	28,183	$200	$225	$250
2014, Great Sand Dunes National Park	22,000	$165	$190	—
2014-P, Great Sand Dunes National Park, Specimen	22,262	$200	$225	$250
2014, Everglades National Park	34,000	$165	$190	—
2014-P, Everglades National Park, Specimen	19,772	$200	$225	$250
2015, Homestead National Monument of America	35,000	$165	$190	—
2015-P, Homestead National Monument of America, Specimen	21,286	$200	$225	$250
2015, Kisatchie National Forest	42,000	$165	$190	—
2015-P, Kisatchie National Forest, Specimen	19,449	$200	$225	$250
2015, Blue Ridge Parkway	45,000	$165	$190	—
2015-P, Blue Ridge Parkway, Specimen	17,461	$200	$225	$250
2015, Bombay Hook National Wildlife Refuge	45,000	$165	$190	—
2015-P, Bombay Hook National Wildlife Refuge, Specimen	17,309	$200	$225	$250
2015, Saratoga National Historic Park	45,000	$165	$190	—
2015-P, Saratoga National Historic Park, Specimen	17,563	$200	$225	$250
2016, Shawnee National Forest	105,000	$165	$190	—
2016-P, Shawnee National Forest, Specimen	18,781	$200	$225	$250
2016, Cumberland Gap National Historical Park	75,000	$165	$190	—
2016-P, Cumberland Gap National Historical Park, Specimen	18,713	$200	$225	$250

Note: MS values are for uncertified Mint State coins of average quality, in their complete original U.S. Mint packaging. SP values are for uncertified Specimen coins of average quality, in their complete original U.S. Mint packaging. **d.** Auction: $212, SP-69, October 2014. **e.** Auction: $353, SP-70, September 2014. **f.** Auction: $206, SP-69, December 2015. **g.** Auction: $306, SP-70, December 2014. **h.** Auction: $529, SP-70, September 2014. **i.** Auction: $776, SP-70, December 2014.

	Mintage	MS / SP	MS-69 / SP-69	MS-70 / SP-70
2016, Harpers Ferry National Historical Park	75,000	$165	$190	—
2016-P, Harpers Ferry National Historical Park, Specimen	18,743	$200	$225	$250
2016, Theodore Roosevelt National Park	40,000	$165	$190	—
2016-P, Theodore Roosevelt National Park, Specimen	18,917	$200	$225	$250
2016, Fort Moultrie (Fort Sumter National Monument)	35,000	$165	$190	—
2016-P, Fort Moultrie (Fort Sumter National Monument), Specimen	17,882	$200	$225	$250
2017, Effigy Mounds National Monument	35,000	$165	$190	—
2017-P, Effigy Mounds National Monument, Specimen	17,251	$200	$225	$250
2017, Frederick Douglass National Historic Site	20,000	$165	$190	—
2017-P, Frederick Douglass National Historic Site, Specimen	17,678	$200	$225	$250
2017, Ozark National Scenic Riverways	20,000	$165	$190	—
2017-P, Ozark National Scenic Riverways, Specimen	17,694	$200	$225	$250
2017, Ellis Island (Statue of Liberty National Monument)	40,000	$165	$190	—
2017-P, Ellis Island (Statue of Liberty National Monument), Specimen	17,670	$200	$225	$250
2017, George Rogers Clark National Historical Park	35,000	$165	$190	—
2017-P, George Rogers Clark National Historical Park, Specimen	14,731	$200	$225	$250
2018, Pictured Rocks National Lakeshore	30,000	$165	$190	—
2018-P, Pictured Rocks National Lakeshore, Specimen	17,773	$200	$225	$250
2018, Apostle Islands National Lakeshore	30,000	$165	$190	—
2018-P, Apostle Islands National Lakeshore, Specimen	16,802	$200	$225	$250
2018, Voyageurs National Park	30,000	$165	$190	—
2018-P, Voyageurs National Park, Specimen	16,839	$200	$225	$250
2018, Cumberland Island National Seashore	52,500	$165	$190	—
2018-P, Cumberland Island National Seashore, Specimen	16,360	$200	$225	$250
2018, Block Island National Wildlife Refuge	80,000	$165	$190	—
2018-P, Block Island National Wildlife Refuge, Specimen	15,902	$200	$225	$250
2019, Lowell National Historical Park	80,000	$165	$190	—
2019-P, Lowell National Historical Park, Specimen	16,645	$200	$225	$250
2019, American Memorial Park	80,000	$165	$190	—
2019-P, American Memorial Park, Specimen	16,283	$230	$255	$275
2019, War in the Pacific National Historical Park	72,500	$165	$190	—
2019-P, War in the Pacific National Historical Park, Specimen	16,275	$230	$255	$275
2019, Frank Church River of No Return Wilderness	25,000	$165	$190	—
2019-P, Frank Church River of No Return Wilderness, Specimen	16,417	$230	$255	$275
2020, San Antonio Missions National Historical Park	55,200	$165	$190	—
2020-P, San Antonio Missions National Historical Park, Specimen	16,207	$230	$255	$275
2020, National Park of American Samoa		$165	$190	$210
2020-P, National Park of American Samoa, Specimen		$230	$255	$275
2020, Weir Farm National Historic Site		$165	$190	$210
2020-P, Weir Farm National Historic Site, Specimen		$230	$255	$275
2020, Salt River Bay National Historical Park and Ecological Preserve		$165	$190	$210
2020-P, Salt River Bay National Historical Park and Ecological Preserve, Specimen		$230	$255	$275
2020, Marsh-Billings-Rockefeller National Historical Park		$165	$190	$210
2020-P, Marsh-Billings-Rockefeller National Historical Park, Specimen		$230	$255	$275
2020, Tallgrass Prairie National Preserve		$165	$190	$210
2020-P, Tallgrass Prairie National Preserve, Specimen		$230	$255	$275
2021, Tuskegee Airmen National Historic Site		$165	$190	$210
2021-P, Tuskegee Airmen National Historic Site, Specimen		$230	$255	$275

Note: MS values are for uncertified Mint State coins of average quality, in their complete original U.S. Mint packaging. SP values are for uncertified Specimen coins of average quality, in their complete original U.S. Mint packaging.

AMERICAN GOLD EAGLES (1986 TO DATE)

Designers: *Augustus Saint-Gaudens (obverse) and Miley Busiek (reverse).* **Weight:** *$5 1/10 oz.—3.393 grams; $10 1/4 oz.—8.483 grams; $25 1/2 oz.—16.966 grams; $50 1 oz.—33.931 grams.* **Composition:** *.9167 gold, .03 silver, .0533 copper.* **Diameter:** *$5 1/10 oz.—16.5 mm; $10 1/4 oz.—22 mm; $25 1/2 oz.—27 mm; $50 1 oz.—32.7 mm.* **Edge:** *Reeded.* **Mints:** *Philadelphia and West Point.*

Regular Finish
Obverse design common to all denominations.

Burnished Finish

Mintmark location is on the obverse, below the date.

Proof Finish

Reverse Proof Finish

History. American Eagle gold bullion coins are made in four denominations: $5 (1/10 ounce pure gold), $10 (1/4 ounce), $25 (1/2 ounce), and $50 (1 ounce). Each shares the same obverse and reverse designs: a modified rendition of Augustus Saint-Gaudens's famous Liberty (as depicted on the double eagle of 1907 to 1933), and a "family of eagles" motif by sculptor Miley Tucker-Frost (nee Busiek). From 1986 to 1991 the obverse bore a Roman numeral date, similar to the first Saint-Gaudens double eagles of 1907; this was changed to Arabic dating in 1992. The coins are legal tender—with weight, content, and purity guaranteed by the federal government—and are produced from gold mined in the United States. Investors can include them in their individual retirement accounts.

"American Eagles use the durable 22-karat standard established for gold circulating coinage over 350 years ago," notes the U.S. Mint. "They contain their stated amount of pure gold, plus small amounts of alloy. This creates harder coins that resist scratching and marring, which can diminish resale value."

Since the Bullion Coin Program started in 1986, these gold pieces have been struck in Philadelphia and West Point, in various formats similar to those of the American Silver Eagles—regular bullion strikes, Burnished, Proof, and Reverse Proof. Unlike their silver counterparts, none of the American Gold Eagles have been struck at San Francisco.

In addition to the individual coins listed below, American Eagle gold bullion coins have been issued in various sets (see pages 1253–1254).

Striking and Sharpness. Striking is generally sharp. The key elements to check on the obverse are Liberty's chest and left knee, and the open fields.

Availability. American Gold Eagles are the most popular gold-coin investment vehicle in the United States. The coins are readily available in the numismatic marketplace as well as from participating banks, investment firms, and other non-numismatic channels.

MS-60 to 70 (Mint State). *Obverse and Reverse:* At MS-60, some abrasion and contact marks are evident on the higher design areas (in particular, Miss Liberty's chest and left knee) and the open fields. Luster may be dull or lifeless at MS–60 to 62, but there should be deep frost at MS-63 and better, particularly in the lower-relief areas. At MS-65 and above, the luster should be full and rich. Contact marks and abrasion are less and less evident at higher grades. These guidelines are more academic than practical, as these coins are not intended for circulation, and nearly all are in high Mint State grades.

PF-60 to 70 (Proof). *Obverse and Reverse:* Proofs that are extensively cleaned and have many hairlines are lower level, such as PF–60 to 62. Those with fewer hairlines or flaws are deemed PF-63 to 65. (These exist more in theory than actuality, as nearly all Proof American Eagle gold bullion coins have been maintained in their original high condition by collectors.) Given the quality of modern U.S. Mint products, even PF–66 and 67 are unusually low levels for these Proofs.

$5 1/10-OUNCE AMERICAN GOLD EAGLES

	Mintage	MS / PF	MS-69 / PF-69	MS-70 / PF-70		Mintage	MS / PF	MS-69 / PF-69	MS-70 / PF-70
$5 MCMLXXXVI (1986)	912,609	$265	$295	$700	$5 2000	569,153	$260	$280	$330
$5 MCMLXXXVII (1987)	580,266	$275	$290	$1,200	$5 2000-W, Proof	49,971	$280	$300	$400
$5 MCMLXXXVIII (1988) (a)	159,500	$270	$320	$7,000	$5 2001	269,147	$260	$280	$330
$5 MCMLXXXVIII (1988)-P, Proof	143,881	$300	$320	$375	$5 2001-W, Proof	37,530	$290	$310	$400
					$5 2002	230,027	$275	$295	$335
$5 MCMLXXXIX (1989) (b)	264,790	$275	$295	$2,600	$5 2002-W, Proof	40,864	$280	$310	$400
$5 MCMLXXXIX (1989)-P, Proof	84,647	$290	$305	$375	$5 2003	245,029	$260	$280	$330
$5 MCMXC (1990) (c)	210,210	$285	$315	$3,000	$5 2003-W, Proof	40,027	$280	$310	$345
$5 MCMXC (1990)-P, Proof	99,349	$290	$305	$375	$5 2004	250,016	$260	$280	$330
$5 MCMXCI (1991) (d)	165,200	$285	$315	$1,400	$5 2004-W, Proof	35,131	$280	$310	$350
$5 MCMXCI (1991)-P, Proof	70,334	$290	$305	$400	$5 2005	300,043	$250	$270	$320
$5 1992	209,300	$280	$295	$1,400	$5 2005-W, Proof	49,265	$280	$310	$350
$5 1992-P, Proof	64,874	$290	$310	$450	$5 2006	285,006	$250	$270	$320
$5 1993	210,709	$270	$290	$1,500	$5 2006-W, Burnished	20,643	$285	$305	$355
$5 1993-P, Proof	58,649	$290	$310	$450	$5 2006-W, Proof	47,277	$290	$310	$340
$5 1994	206,380	$270	$290	$1,200	$5 2007	190,010	$250	$270	$320
$5 1994-W, Proof	62,849	$280	$295	$350	$5 2007-W, Burnished	22,501	$290	$310	$355
$5 1995	223,025	$265	$290	$1,100	$5 2007-W, Proof	58,553	$290	$310	$340
$5 1995-W, Proof	62,667	$280	$295	$450	$5 2008	305,000	$250	$270	$320
$5 1996	401,964	$260	$290	$600	$5 2008-W, Burnished (g)	12,657	$370	$395	$445
$5 1996-W, Proof	57,047	$280	$295	$450	$5 2008-W, Proof	28,116	$290	$310	$340
$5 1997	528,266	$250	$280	$450	$5 2009	270,000	$250	$270	$320
$5 1997-W, Proof	34,977	$300	$320	$550	$5 2010	435,000	$250	$270	$320
$5 1998	1,344,520	$265	$290	$350	$5 2010-W, Proof	54,285	$290	$315	$350
$5 1998-W, Proof	39,395	$280	$295	$450	$5 2011	350,000	$250	$270	$320
$5 1999	2,750,338	$260	$280	$330	$5 2011-W, Proof	42,697	$290	$315	$340
$5 1999-W, Unc made from unpolished Proof dies †† (e,f)	14,500	$895	$1,095	$4,000	$5 2012	290,000	$250	$270	$320
					$5 2012-W, Proof	20,637	$290	$315	$340
$5 1999-W, Proof	48,428	$280	$295	$400	$5 2013	555,000	$250	$270	$320

Note: MS values are for uncertified Mint State coins of average quality, in their complete original U.S. Mint packaging. PF values are for uncertified Proof coins of average quality, in their complete original U.S. Mint packaging. †† Ranked in the *100 Greatest U.S. Modern Coins* (fourth edition). **a.** Auction: $159, MS-69, October 2014. **b.** Auction: $141, MS-69, October 2014. **c.** Auction: $141, MS-69, October 2014. **d.** Auction: $2,115, MS-70, January 2016. **e.** Unpolished Proof dies were used to mint some 1999 $5 gold coins, resulting in a regular bullion-strike issue bearing a W mintmark (usually reserved for Proofs). A similar error exists in the $10 (1/4-ounce) series. The mintage listed is an estimate. Other estimates range from 6,000 to 30,000 pieces. **f.** Auction: $764, MS-69, July 2015. **g.** Auction: $352, MS-70, November 2014.

	Mintage	MS / PF	MS-69 / PF-69	MS-70 / PF-70
$5 2013-W, Proof	21,738	$290	$315	$340
$5 2014	545,000	$250	$270	$320
$5 2014-W, Proof	22,725	$300	$315	$340
$5 2015	980,000	$250	$270	$320
$5 2015, Narrow Reeding	(h)			
$5 2015-W, Proof	26,769	$300	$325	$350
$5 2016	925,000	$250	$270	$320
$5 2016-W, Proof	37,312	$290	$315	$340
$5 2017	395,000	$250	$270	$320
$5 2017-W, Proof	20,969	$290	$315	$340
$5 2018	230,000	$250	$270	$320

	Mintage	MS / PF	MS-69 / PF-69	MS-70 / PF-70
$5 2018-W, Proof	22,155	$290	$315	$340
$5 2019	195,000	$250	$270	$320
$5 2019-W, Proof	17,504	$290	$315	$340
$5 2020		$250	$270	$320
$5 2020-W, Proof		$290	$315	$340
$5 2021, Family of Eagles		$250	$270	$320
$5 2021-W, Family of Eagles, Proof		$290	$315	$340
$5 2021, Head of Eagle		$250	$270	$320
$5 2021-W, Head of Eagle, Proof		$290	$315	$340

Note: MS values are for uncertified Mint State coins of average quality, in their complete original U.S. Mint packaging. PF values are for uncertified Proof coins of average quality, in their complete original U.S. Mint packaging. **h.** Included in mintage for $5 2015.

$10 1/4-OUNCE
AMERICAN GOLD EAGLES

	Mintage	MS / PF	MS-69 / PF-69	MS-70 / PF-70
$10 MCMLXXXVI (1986) (a)	726,031	$675	$725	$1,550
$10 MCMLXXXVII (1987) (b)	269,255	$675	$775	—
$10 MCMLXXXVIII (1988) (c)	49,000	$875	$925	$1,700
$10 MCMLXXXVIII (1988)-P, Proof	98,028	$645	$675	$1,100
$10 MCMLXXXIX (1989) (d)	81,789	$825	$900	$1,900
$10 MCMLXXXIX (1989)-P, Proof	54,170	$645	$675	$1,050
$10 MCMXC (1990) (e)	41,000	$975	$1,025	$4,000
$10 MCMXC (1990)-P, Proof	62,674	$645	$675	$800
$10 MCMXCI (1991) (f)	36,100	$950	$1,000	$2,400
$10 MCMXCI (1991)-P, Proof	50,839	$645	$675	$900
$10 1992 (g)	59,546	$775	$825	$2,000
$10 1992-P, Proof	46,269	$645	$675	$950
$10 1993 (h)	71,864	$775	$825	$2,400
$10 1993-P, Proof	46,464	$645	$675	$950
$10 1994 (i)	72,650	$775	$825	$2,700
$10 1994-W, Proof	48,172	$645	$675	$900
$10 1995 (j)	83,752	$775	$825	$3,700
$10 1995-W, Proof	47,526	$645	$675	$900
$10 1996 (k)	60,318	$775	$825	$1,900
$10 1996-W, Proof	38,219	$645	$675	$775
$10 1997	108,805	$625	$650	$3,700
$10 1997-W, Proof	29,805	$645	$675	$900
$10 1998	309,829	$625	$650	$2,700
$10 1998-W, Proof	29,503	$645	$675	$1,100

	Mintage	MS / PF	MS-69 / PF-69	MS-70 / PF-70
$10 1999	564,232	$625	$650	$1,800
$10 1999-W, Unc made from unpolished Proof dies †† (l,m)	10,000	$1,800	$2,000	$10,000
$10 1999-W, Proof	34,417	$645	$675	$950
$10 2000	128,964	$650	$700	$1,100
$10 2000-W, Proof	36,036	$645	$675	$950
$10 2001	71,280	$775	$825	$900
$10 2001-W, Proof	25,613	$645	$675	$950
$10 2002	62,027	$775	$825	$900
$10 2002-W, Proof	29,242	$645	$675	$800
$10 2003	74,029	$625	$675	$800
$10 2003-W, Proof	30,292	$645	$675	$800
$10 2004	72,014	$590	$615	$700
$10 2004-W, Proof	28,839	$645	$675	$825
$10 2005	72,015	$590	$615	$700
$10 2005-W, Proof	37,207	$645	$675	$775
$10 2006	60,004	$590	$615	$700
$10 2006-W, Burnished (n)	15,188	$875	$900	$950
$10 2006-W, Proof	36,127	$645	$675	$775
$10 2007	34,004	$775	$825	$1,000
$10 2007-W, Burnished (o)	12,766	$925	$975	$1,025
$10 2007-W, Proof	46,189	$645	$675	$825
$10 2008	70,000	$590	$615	$665
$10 2008-W, Burnished (p)	8,883	$1,100	$1,200	$1,900

Note: MS values are for uncertified Mint State coins of average quality, in their complete original U.S. Mint packaging. PF values are for uncertified Proof coins of average quality, in their complete original U.S. Mint packaging. †† Ranked in the *100 Greatest U.S. Modern Coins* (fourth edition). **a.** Auction: $1,058, MS-70, January 2016. **b.** Auction: $306, MS-68, November 2015. **c.** Auction: $3,290, MS-70, August 2014. **d.** Auction: $3,290, MS-70, October 2015. **e.** Auction: $16,450, MS-70, October 2015. **f.** Auction: $1,293, MS-70, October 2014. **g.** Auction: $9,400, MS-70, September 2015. **h.** Auction: $3,055, MS-70, June 2014. **i.** Auction: $5,640, MS-70, February 2015. **j.** Auction: $505, MS-69, March 2014. **k.** Auction: $306, MS-68, October 2015. **l.** Unpolished Proof dies were used to mint some 1999 $10 gold coins, resulting in a regular bullion-strike issue bearing a W mintmark (usually reserved for Proofs). A similar error exists in the $5 (1/10-ounce) series. The mintage listed is an estimate. Other estimates range from 6,000 to 30,000 pieces. **m.** Auction: $1,763, MS-69, July 2015. **n.** Auction: $646, MS-70, October 2015. **o.** Auction: $376, MS-70, October 2015. **p.** Auction: $1,528, MS-70, July 2015.

	Mintage	MS	MS-69	MS-70
		PF	PF-69	PF-70
$10 2008-W, Proof	18,877	$725	$755	$925
$10 2009	110,000	$590	$615	$680
$10 2010	86,000	$590	$615	$680
$10 2010-W, Proof	44,507	$675	$725	$775
$10 2011	80,000	$590	$615	$665
$10 2011-W, Proof	28,782	$675	$725	$775
$10 2012	90,000	$590	$615	$680
$10 2012-W, Proof	13,926	$675	$725	$775
$10 2013	114,500	$590	$615	$680
$10 2013-W, Proof	12,782	$675	$725	$775
$10 2014	90,000	$590	$615	$680
$10 2014-W, Proof	14,790	$675	$725	$775
$10 2015	158,000	$590	$615	$680
$10 2015-W, Proof	15,775	$675	$725	$775

	Mintage	MS	MS-69	MS-70
		PF	PF-69	PF-70
$10 2016	152,000	$590	$615	$680
$10 2016-W, Proof	22,828	$675	$725	$775
$10 2017	64,000	$590	$615	$680
$10 2017-W, Proof	14,513	$675	$725	$775
$10 2018	62,000	$590	$615	$680
$10 2018-W, Proof	12,769	$675	$725	$775
$10 2019	38,000	$590	$615	$680
$10 2019-W, Proof	10,596	$675	$725	$775
$10 2020		$590	$615	$680
$10 2020-W, Proof		$675	$725	$775
$10 2021, Family of Eagles		$590	$615	$680
$10 2021-W, Family of Eagles, Proof		$675	$725	$775
$10 2021, Head of Eagle		$590	$615	$680
$10 2021-W, Head of Eagle, Proof		$675	$725	$775

Note: MS values are for uncertified Mint State coins of average quality, in their complete original U.S. Mint packaging. PF values are for uncertified Proof coins of average quality, in their complete original U.S. Mint packaging.

$25 1/2-OUNCE
AMERICAN GOLD EAGLES

	Mintage	MS	MS-69	MS-70
		PF	PF-69	PF-70
$25 MCMLXXXVI (1986) (a)	599,566	$1,100	$1,150	$2,000
$25 MCMLXXXVII (1987) (b)	131,255	$1,100	$1,150	$6,500
$25 MCMLXXXVII (1987)-P, Proof	143,398	$1,300	$1,335	$1,700
$25 MCMLXXXVIII (1988) (c)	45,000	$1,500	$1,800	$3,200
$25 MCMLXXXVIII (1988)-P, Proof	76,528	$1,300	$1,335	$1,600
$25 MCMLXXXIX (1989) (d)	44,829	$1,500	$1,800	$5,500
$25 MCMLXXXIX (1989)-P, Proof	44,798	$1,300	$1,335	—
$25 MCMXC (1990) (e)	31,000	$1,800	$2,200	$10,000
$25 MCMXC (1990)-P, Proof	51,636	$1,300	$1,335	—
$25 MCMXCI (1991) †† (f)	24,100	$2,750	$3,000	—
$25 MCMXCI (1991)-P, Proof	53,125	$1,300	$1,335	$1,500
$25 1992 (g)	54,404	$1,075	$1,250	$5,500
$25 1992-P, Proof	40,976	$1,300	$1,335	$1,500
$25 1993 (h)	73,324	$1,075	$1,150	$2,800
$25 1993-P, Proof	43,819	$1,300	$1,335	—
$25 1994 (i)	62,400	$1,075	$1,150	$2,000
$25 1994-W, Proof	44,584	$1,300	$1,335	$1,500
$25 1995 (j)	53,474	$1,075	$1,350	$2,300
$25 1995-W, Proof	45,388	$1,300	$1,335	$1,500
$25 1996 (k)	39,287	$1,350	$1,500	$3,800
$25 1996-W, Proof	35,058	$1,300	$1,335	$1,500

	Mintage	MS	MS-69	MS-70
		PF	PF-69	PF-70
$25 1997 (l)	79,605	$1,075	$1,150	$2,800
$25 1997-W, Proof	26,344	$1,300	$1,335	$1,500
$25 1998	169,029	$1,075	$1,150	—
$25 1998-W, Proof	25,374	$1,300	$1,335	$1,500
$25 1999 (m)	263,013	$1,075	$1,150	$3,000
$25 1999-W, Proof	30,427	$1,300	$1,335	$1,500
$25 2000	79,287	$1,075	$1,150	—
$25 2000-W, Proof	32,028	$1,300	$1,335	$1,500
$25 2001 (n)	48,047	$1,250	$1,500	$1,800
$25 2001-W, Proof	23,240	$1,300	$1,335	$1,500
$25 2002	70,027	$1,075	$1,150	—
$25 2002-W, Proof	26,646	$1,300	$1,335	$1,500
$25 2003	79,029	$1,075	$1,100	$1,200
$25 2003-W, Proof	28,270	$1,300	$1,335	$1,500
$25 2004	98,040	$1,075	$1,100	$1,200
$25 2004-W, Proof	27,330	$1,300	$1,335	$1,500
$25 2005	80,023	$1,075	$1,100	$1,200
$25 2005-W, Proof	34,311	$1,300	$1,335	$1,500
$25 2006	66,005	$1,075	$1,100	$1,200
$25 2006-W, Burnished (o)	15,164	$1,075	$1,150	$1,250
$25 2006-W, Proof	34,322	$1,300	$1,335	$1,500

Note: MS values are for uncertified Mint State coins of average quality, in their complete original U.S. Mint packaging. PF values are for uncertified Proof coins of average quality, in their complete original U.S. Mint packaging. †† Ranked in the *100 Greatest U.S. Modern Coins* (fourth edition) **a.** Auction: $646, MS-68, October 2015. **b.** Auction: $999, MS-69, January 2016. **c.** Auction: $1,528, MS-69, October 2015. **d.** Auction: $9,400, MS-70, September 2015. **e.** Auction: $9,694, MS-70, September 2015. **f.** Auction: $2,820, MS-69, October 2015. **g.** Auction: $3,966, MS-70, July 2014. **h.** Auction: $4,964, MS-70, January 2015. **i.** Auction: $705, MS-68, October 2015. **j.** Auction: $5,875, MS-70, August 2015. **k.** Auction: $1,293, MS-69, September 2015. **l.** Auction: $1,293, MS-69, September 2015. **m.** Auction: $646, MS-69, November 2014. **n.** Auction: $1,763, MS-69, July 2014. **o.** Auction: $705, MS-70, October 2015.

| | Mintage | MS | MS-69 | MS-70 |
		PF	PF-69	PF-70
$25 2007	47,002	$1,075	$1,100	$1,200
$25 2007-W, Burnished †† (p)	11,455	$1,100	$1,200	$1,700
$25 2007-W, Proof	44,025	$1,300	$1,335	$1,500
$25 2008	61,000	$1,075	$1,100	$1,200
$25 2008-W, Burnished (q)	15,682	$1,150	$1,250	$1,300
$25 2008-W, Proof	22,602	$1,300	$1,335	$1,400
$25 2009	110,000	$1,075	$1,100	$1,200
$25 2010	81,000	$1,075	$1,100	$1,200
$25 2010-W, Proof	44,527	$1,300	$1,335	$1,400
$25 2011	70,000	$1,075	$1,100	$1,200
$25 2011-W, Proof	26,781	$1,300	$1,335	$1,400
$25 2012	43,000	$1,075	$1,100	$1,200
$25 2012-W, Proof	12,809	$1,300	$1,335	$1,400
$25 2013	57,000	$1,075	$1,100	$1,200
$25 2013-W, Proof	12,570	$1,300	$1,335	$1,400
$25 2014	35,000	$1,075	$1,100	$1,200
$25 2014-W, Proof	17,760	$1,300	$1,335	$1,400

| | Mintage | MS | MS-69 | MS-70 |
		PF	PF-69	PF-70
$25 2015	78,000	$1,075	$1,100	$1,200
$25 2015-W, Proof	15,820	$1,300	$1,335	$1,400
$25 2016	71,000	$1,075	$1,100	$1,200
$25 2016-W, Proof	22,001	$1,300	$1,335	$1,400
$25 2017	37,000	$1,075	$1,100	$1,200
$25 2017-W, Proof	12,715	$1,300	$1,335	$1,400
$25 2018	32,000	$1,100	$1,150	$2,500
$25 2018-W, Proof	9,961	$1,300	$1,335	$1,400
$25 2019	30,000	$1,075	$1,100	$1,200
$25 2019-W, Proof	9,479	$1,300	$1,335	$1,400
$25 2020		$1,075	$1,100	$1,200
$25 2020-W, Proof		$1,300	$1,335	$1,400
$25 2021, Family of Eagles		$1,075	$1,100	$1,200
$25 2021-W, Family of Eagles, Proof		$1,300	$1,335	$1,400
$25 2021, Head of Eagle		$1,075	$1,100	$1,200
$25 2021-W, Head of Eagle, Proof		$1,300	$1,335	$1,400

Note: MS values are for uncertified Mint State coins of average quality, in their complete original U.S. Mint packaging. PF values are for uncertified Proof coins of average quality, in their complete original U.S. Mint packaging. †† Ranked in the *100 Greatest U.S. Modern Coins* (fourth edition). **p.** Auction: $646, MS-69, October 2015. **q.** Auction: $1,175, MS-70, November 2015.

$50 1-Ounce American Gold Eagles

| | Mintage | MS | MS-69 | MS-70 |
		PF	PF-69	PF-70
$50 MCMLXXXVI (1986) (a)	1,362,650	$2,200	$2,250	$5,500
$50 MCMLXXXVI (1986)-W, Proof	446,290	$2,600	$2,700	$2,800
$50 MCMLXXXVII (1987) (b)	1,045,500	$2,200	$2,250	$5,000
$50 MCMLXXXVII (1987)-W, Proof	147,498	$2,600	$2,700	$2,800
$50 MCMLXXXVIII (1988) (c)	465,000	$2,200	$2,250	$11,000
$50 MCMLXXXVIII (1988)-W, Proof	87,133	$2,600	$2,700	$2,800
$50 MCMLXXXIX (1989)	415,790	$2,200	$2,250	—
$50 MCMLXXXIX (1989)-W, Proof	54,570	$2,600	$2,700	$2,800
$50 MCMXC (1990) (d)	373,210	$2,200	$2,250	$5,500
$50 MCMXC (1990)-W, Proof	62,401	$2,600	$2,700	$2,800
$50 MCMXCI (1991) (e)	243,100	$2,200	$2,250	$5,500
$50 MCMXCI (1991)-W, Proof	50,411	$2,600	$2,700	$2,800
$50 1992	275,000	$2,200	$2,250	$2,400
$50 1992-W, Proof (f)	44,826	$2,600	$2,650	$3,000
$50 1993	480,192	$2,200	$2,250	$2,600
$50 1993-W, Proof (g)	34,369	$2,600	$2,650	$3,500
$50 1994 (h)	221,633	$2,200	$2,250	$6,500

| | Mintage | MS | MS-69 | MS-70 |
		PF	PF-69	PF-70
$50 1994-W, Proof	46,674	$2,600	$2,650	$2,800
$50 1995	200,636	$2,200	$2,250	—
$50 1995-W, Proof	46,368	$2,600	$2,650	$2,800
$50 1996	189,148	$2,200	$2,250	—
$50 1996-W, Proof	36,153	$2,600	$2,650	$2,800
$50 1997 (i)	664,508	$2,200	$2,250	$5,000
$50 1997-W, Proof	32,999	$2,600	$2,650	$2,800
$50 1998	1,468,530	$2,200	$2,250	$2,300
$50 1998-W, Proof (j)	25,886	$2,600	$2,650	$4,000
$50 1999	1,505,026	$2,200	$2,250	$2,300
$50 1999-W, Proof	31,427	$2,600	$2,650	$3,000
$50 2000	433,319	$2,200	$2,250	$2,500
$50 2000-W, Proof	33,007	$2,600	$2,650	$2,800
$50 2001 (k)	143,605	$2,200	$2,250	$3,000
$50 2001-W, Proof †† (l)	24,555	$2,600	$2,650	$5,000
$50 2002	222,029	$2,200	$2,250	$2,800
$50 2002-W, Proof	27,499	$2,600	$2,650	$2,800

Note: MS values are for uncertified Mint State coins of average quality, in their complete original U.S. Mint packaging. PF values are for uncertified Proof coins of average quality, in their complete original U.S. Mint packaging. **a.** Auction: $2,585, MS-70, June 2015. **b.** Auction: $1,351, MS-68, August 2014. **c.** Auction: $1,303, MS-68, December 2013. **d.** Auction: $1,469, MS-69, March 2014. **e.** Auction: $1,293, MS-69, July 2015. **f.** Auction: $2,056, PF-70UCam, July 2015. **g.** Auction: $2,233, PF-70UCam, June 2015. **h.** Auction: $2,820, MS-69, April 2014. **i.** Auction: $1,645, MS-69, April 2014. **j.** $2,233, PF-70UCam, September 2015. **k.** Auction: $1,351, MS-69, October 2014. **l.** Auction: $2,820, PF-70UCam, January 2015.

	Mintage	MS / PF	MS-69 / PF-69	MS-70 / PF-70
$50 2003	416,032	$2,200	$2,250	$2,500
$50 2003-W, Proof	28,344	$2,600	$2,650	$2,800
$50 2004	417,019	$2,200	$2,250	$2,500
$50 2004-W, Proof	28,215	$2,600	$2,650	$2,800
$50 2005	356,555	$2,200	$2,250	$2,350
$50 2005-W, Proof	35,246	$2,600	$2,650	$2,800
$50 2006	237,510	$2,200	$2,250	$2,350
$50 2006-W, Burnished	45,053	$2,250	$2,300	$2,400
$50 2006-W, Proof	47,092	$2,600	$2,650	$2,800
$50 2006-W, Reverse Proof †† (m,n)	9,996	$2,650	$2,800	$3,400
$50 2007	140,016	$2,200	$2,250	$2,350
$50 2007-W, Burnished	18,066	$2,250	$2,300	$2,400
$50 2007-W, Proof	51,810	$2,600	$2,650	$2,800
$50 2008	710,000	$2,200	$2,250	$2,350
$50 2008-W, Burnished (o)	11,908	$2,250	$2,300	$2,400
$50 2008-W, Proof	30,237	$2,600	$2,650	$2,800
$50 2009	1,493,000	$2,200	$2,250	$2,350
$50 2010	1,125,000	$2,200	$2,250	$2,350
$50 2010-W, Proof	59,480	$2,600	$2,650	$2,800
$50 2011	857,000	$2,200	$2,250	$2,350
$50 2011-W, Burnished (p)	8,729	$2,250	$2,300	$2,400
$50 2011-W, Proof	48,306	$2,600	$2,650	$2,800
$50 2012	675,000	$2,200	$2,250	$2,350
$50 2012-W, Burnished (q)	6,118	$2,250	$2,300	$2,400
$50 2012-W, Proof	23,630	$2,600	$2,650	$2,800
$50 2013	758,500	$2,200	$2,250	$2,350
$50 2013-W, Burnished	7,293	$2,250	$2,300	$2,400
$50 2013-W, Proof	24,710	$2,600	$2,650	$2,800
$50 2014	425,000	$2,200	$2,250	$2,350
$50 2014-W, Burnished	7,902	$2,250	$2,300	$2,400
$50 2014-W, Proof	28,703	$2,600	$2,650	$2,800
$50 2015	594,000	$2,200	$2,250	$2,350
$50 2015-W, Burnished	6,533	$2,250	$2,300	$2,400
$50 2015-W, Proof	32,652	$2,600	$2,650	$2,800
$50 2016	817,500	$2,200	$2,250	$2,350
$50 2016-W, Burnished	6,887	$2,250	$2,300	$2,800
$50 2016-W, Proof	40,044	$2,600	$2,650	$2,800
$50 2017	228,500	$2,200	$2,250	$2,350
$50 2017-W, Burnished	5,800	$2,750	$2,900	$3,500
$50 2017-W, Proof	19,056	$2,600	$2,650	$2,800
$50 2018	191,000	$2,200	$2,250	$2,350
$50 2018-W, Burnished	8,518	$2,550	$2,600	$3,000
$50 2018-W, Proof	15,570	$2,600	$2,650	$2,800
$50 2019	108,000	$2,200	$2,250	$2,350
$50 2019-W, Burnished	5,741	$2,550	$2,600	$3,000
$50 2019-W, Proof	13,480	$2,600	$2,650	$2,800
$50 2020		$2,550	$2,600	$3,000
$50 2020-W, Burnished	7,000	$2,150	$2,200	$2,300
$50 2020-W, Proof		$2,500	$2,600	$2,750
$50 2020-W, End of World War II 75th Anniversary, Proof (r)	1,945	$2,500	$2,600	$3,000
$50 2021, Family of Eagles		$10,000	$12,500	$16,500
$50 2021-W, Family of Eagles, Proof		$2,500	$2,600	$3,000
$50 2021, Head of Eagle		$2,150	$2,200	$2,300
$50 2021-W, Head of Eagle, Proof		$2,500	$2,600	$3,000

Note: MS values are for uncertified Mint State coins of average quality, in their complete original U.S. Mint packaging. PF values are for uncertified Proof coins of average quality, in their complete original U.S. Mint packaging. †† Ranked in the 100 Greatest U.S. Modern Coins (fourth edition). m. The 2006-W Reverse Proof coins were issued to mark the 20th anniversary of the Bullion Coinage Program. They have brilliant devices, and their background fields are frosted (rather than the typical Proof format of frosted devices and mirror-like backgrounds). n. Auction: $4,935, PF-70, September 2015. o. Auction: $1,293, MS-69, July 2015. p. Auction: $1,998, MS-70, June 2015. q. Auction: $2,585, MS-70, February 2015. r. Struck with a "V75" privy mark. See page 533 for an illustration and description of the privy mark as used on 2020 quarters.

AMERICAN GOLD EAGLE PROOF COIN SETS

	PF	PF-69	PF-70
1987 Gold Set. $50, $25	$4,000	$4,400	$5,200
1988 Gold Set. $50, $25, $10, $5	$5,020	$5,400	$6,150
1989 Gold Set. $50, $25, $10, $5	$5,000	$5,450	$6,500
1990 Gold Set. $50, $25, $10, $5	$5,000	$5,400	$6,650
1991 Gold Set. $50, $25, $10, $5	$5,000	$5,550	$7,050
1992 Gold Set. $50, $25, $10, $5	$4,900	$5,400	$6,500
1993 Gold Set. $50, $25, $10, $5	$4,900	$5,400	—
1993 Bicentennial Gold Set. $25, $10, $5, Silver Eagle, and medal (a)	$1,400	$2,300	—
1994 Gold Set. $50, $25, $10, $5	$4,900	$5,400	$6,000
1995 Gold Set. $50, $25, $10, $5	$4,900	$5,400	$6,500
1995 Anniversary Gold Set. $50, $25, $10, $5, and Silver Eagle (b)	$8,000	$8,500	—
1996 Gold Set. $50, $25, $10, $5	$4,900	$5,400	$6,000
1997 Gold Set. $50, $25, $10, $5	$4,900	$5,400	$6,000
1997 Impressions of Liberty Set. $100 platinum, $50 gold, Silver Eagle (c)	$4,000	$4,500	$6,800
1998 Gold Set. $50, $25, $10, $5	$4,900	$5,000	$7,500
1999 Gold Set. $50, $25, $10, $5	$4,900	$5,000	$6,500
2000 Gold Set. $50, $25, $10, $5	$4,900	$5,400	$6,000
2001 Gold Set. $50, $25, $10, $5	$4,900	$5,400	$8,000
2002 Gold Set. $50, $25, $10, $5	$4,900	$5,400	$6,000
2003 Gold Set. $50, $25, $10, $5	$4,900	$5,400	$6,000
2004 Gold Set. $50, $25, $10, $5	$4,900	$5,400	$6,000
2005 Gold Set. $50, $25, $10, $5	$4,900	$5,000	$5,500

Note: PF values are for uncertified Proof sets of average quality, in their complete original U.S. Mint packaging. a. The 1993 set was issued to commemorate the bicentennial of the first coins struck by the U.S. Mint in Philadelphia. b. The 1995 set marked the 10th anniversary of the passage of the Liberty Coin Act, which authorized the nation's new bullion coinage program. c. The Impressions of Liberty set was issued in the first year that platinum coins were added to the Mint's bullion offerings.

	PF	PF-69	PF-70		PF	PF-69	PF-70
2006 Gold Set. $50, $25, $10, $5	$4,900	$5,000	$5,500	2017 Gold Set. $50, $25, $10, $5	$4,900	$5,000	$5,500
2007 Gold Set. $50, $25, $10, $5	$4,900	$5,000	$5,500	2018 Gold Set. $50, $25, $10, $5	$4,900	$5,000	$5,500
2008 Gold Set. $50, $25, $10, $5	$4,900	$5,400	$6,000	2019 Gold Set. $50, $25, $10, $5	$4,900	$5,000	$5,500
2010 Gold Set. $50, $25, $10, $5 (d)	$4,900	$5,000	$5,500	2020 Gold Set. $50, $25, $10, $5	$4,900	$5,000	$5,500
2011 Gold Set. $50, $25, $10, $5	$4,900	$5,000	$5,500	2021 Gold Set, Family of Eagles. $50, $25, $10, $5	$4,900	$5,000	$5,500
2012 Gold Set. $50, $25, $10, $5	$4,900	$5,000	$5,500				
2013 Gold Set. $50, $25, $10, $5	$4,900	$5,000	$5,500	2021 Gold Set, Head of Eagle. $50, $25, $10, $5	$4,900	$5,000	$5,500
2014 Gold Set. $50, $25, $10, $5	$4,900	$5,000	$5,500				
2015 Gold Set. $50, $25, $10, $5	$4,900	$5,000	$5,500	2021-W 1/10-oz. Gold Proof Two-Coin Set			
2016 Gold Set. $50, $25, $10, $5	$4,900	$5,000	$5,500				

Note: PF values are for uncertified Proof sets of average quality, in their complete original U.S. Mint packaging. **d.** The U.S. Mint did not issue a 2009 gold set.

2006 AMERICAN GOLD EAGLE 20TH-ANNIVERSARY COIN SETS

	Uncertified	69	70
2006-W $50 Gold Set. Uncirculated, Proof, and Reverse Proof	$7,500	$7,800	$8,500
2006-W 1-oz. Gold- and Silver-Dollar Set. Uncirculated	$2,350	$2,425	$2,500

Note: Uncertified values are for uncertified sets of average quality, in their complete original U.S. Mint packaging.

GOLD BULLION BURNISHED SETS

	Uncertified	69	70
2006-W Burnished Gold Set. $50, $25, $10, $5	$4,500	$4,650	$4,950
2007-W Burnished Gold Set. $50, $25, $10, $5 ††	$4,550	$4,700	$5,500
2008-W Burnished Gold Set. $50, $25, $10, $5	$4,800	$5,400	$7,000

Note: Uncertified values are for uncertified sets of average quality, in their complete original U.S. Mint packaging. †† Ranked in the *100 Greatest U.S. Modern Coins* (fourth edition).

AMERICAN BUFFALO .9999 FINE GOLD BULLION COINS (2006 TO DATE)

Designer: *James Earle Fraser.* **Weight:** *$5 1/10 oz.—3.393 grams; $10 1/4 oz.—8.483 grams; $25 1/2 oz.— 16.966 grams; $50 1 oz.—31.108 grams.* **Composition:** *.9999 gold.* **Diameter:** *$5 1/10 oz.—16.5 mm; $10 1/4 oz.—22 mm; $25 1/2 oz.—27 mm; $50 1 oz.—32.7 mm.* **Edge:** *Reeded.* **Mint:** *West Point.*

Regular Finish

Burnished Finish

Proof Finish

Mintmark location is on the obverse, behind the neck.

Reverse Proof Finish

History. American Buffalo gold bullion coins, authorized by Congress in 2005 and produced since 2006, are the first 24-karat (.9999 fine) gold coins made by the U.S. Mint. They are coined, by mandate, of gold derived from newly mined sources in America. They feature an adaptation of James Earle Fraser's iconic Indian Head / Buffalo design, first used on circulating five-cent pieces of 1913 to 1938.

Only 1-ounce ($50 face value) coins were struck in the American Buffalo program's first two years, 2006 and 2007. For 2008, the Mint expanded the coinage to include fractional pieces of 1/2 ounce ($25), 1/4 ounce ($10), and 1/10-ounce ($5), in various finishes, individually and in sets.

The coins are legal tender, with weight, content, and purity guaranteed by the federal government. Investors can include them in some individual retirement accounts. Proofs and Burnished (*Uncirculated*, in the Mint's wording) pieces undergo special production processes, similar to the American Eagle gold-bullion coinage, and can be purchased directly from the Mint. As with other products in the Mint's bullion program, regular bullion-strike pieces are distributed through a network of authorized distributors.

All American Buffalo gold bullion coins (Proofs, Burnished, and regular bullion pieces) are struck at the U.S. Mint's West Point facility.

Striking and Sharpness. Striking is generally sharp.

Availability. American Buffalo .9999 fine gold bullion coins are a popular way to buy and sell 24-karat gold. The coins are readily available in the numismatic marketplace as well as from participating banks, investment firms, and other non-numismatic channels.

MS-60 to 70 (Mint State). *Obverse and reverse:* At MS-60, some abrasion and contact marks are evident on the higher design areas and the open areas of the design. Luster may be dull or lifeless at MS–60 to 62, but there should be deep frost at MS-63 and better, particularly in the lower-relief areas. At MS-65 and above, the luster should be full and rich. Contact marks and abrasion are less and less evident at higher grades. These guidelines are more academic than practical, as these coins are not intended for circulation, and nearly all are in high Mint State grades, as struck.

PF-60 to 70 (Proof). *Obverse and reverse:* Proofs that are extensively cleaned and have many hairlines are lower level, such as PF–60 to 62. Those with fewer hairlines or flaws are deemed PF–63 to 65. (These exist more in theory than actuality, as nearly all Proof American Buffalo gold coins have been maintained in their original high condition by collectors.) Given the quality of modern U.S. Mint products, even PF–66 and 67 are unusually low levels for these Proofs.

AMERICAN BUFFALO *.9999 FINE GOLD BULLION COINS*

$5 1/10-oz. $10 1/4-oz. $25 1/2-oz. $50 1-oz.

	Mintage	MS / PF	MS-69 / PF-69	MS-70 / PF-70
$5 2008-W, Burnished (a)	17,429	$500	$535	$600
$5 2008-W, Proof (b)	18,884	$500	$535	$600
$10 2008-W, Burnished †† (c)	9,949	$1,000	$1,100	$1,400
$10 2008-W, Proof (d)	13,125	$1,000	$1,200	$1,500
$25 2008-W, Burnished (e)	16,908	$1,500	$1,600	$1,750
$25 2008-W, Proof (f)	12,169	$1,500	$1,650	$2,000
$50 2006	337,012	$2,200	$2,250	$2,400
$50 2006-W, Proof	246,267	$2,350	$2,400	$2,500
$50 2007	136,503	$2,200	$2,250	$2,400
$50 2007-W, Proof	58,998	$2,350	$2,400	$2,500
$50 2008	214,058 (g)	$2,200	$2,250	$2,400
$50 2008-W, Burnished (h)	9,074	$2,600	$2,700	$3,400
$50 2008-W, Proof †† (i)	18,863	$2,800	$2,900	$3,800
$50 2009	200,000	$2,200	$2,250	$2,400
$50 2009-W, Proof	49,306	$2,350	$2,400	$2,500
$50 2010	209,000	$2,200	$2,250	$2,400
$50 2010-W, Proof	49,263	$2,350	$2,400	$2,500
$50 2011	250,000	$2,200	$2,250	$2,400
$50 2011-W, Proof	28,693	$2,450	$2,500	$2,600
$50 2012	100,000	$2,200	$2,250	$2,400

	Mintage	MS / PF	MS-69 / PF-69	MS-70 / PF-70
$50 2012-W, Proof	19,765	$2,550	$2,600	$2,800
$50 2013	198,500	$2,200	$2,250	$2,400
$50 2013-W, Proof	18,594	$2,550	$2,600	$2,800
$50 2013-W, Reverse Proof ††	47,836	$2,650	$2,700	$2,900
$50 2014	180,500	$2,200	$2,250	$2,400
$50 2014-W, Proof	20,557	$2,550	$2,600	$2,800
$50 2015	223,500	$2,200	$2,250	$2,400
$50 2015-W, Proof	16,591	$2,550	$2,600	$2,800
$50 2016	*219,500*	$2,200	$2,250	$2,400
$50 2016-W, Proof	21,878	$2,550	$2,600	$2,800
$50 2017	*99,500*	$2,200	$2,250	$2,400
$50 2017-W, Proof	*15,810*	$2,650	$2,700	$2,900
$50 2018	*121,500*	$2,200	$2,250	$2,400
$50 2018-W, Proof	*15,756*	$2,650	$2,700	$3,400
$50 2019	*61,500*	$2,200	$2,250	$2,400
$50 2019-W, Proof	*14,836*	$2,650	$2,700	$3,700
$50 2020		$2,200	$2,250	$2,400
$50 2020-W, Proof		$2,800	$2,900	$4,700
$50 2021		$2,200	$2,250	$2,400
$50 2021-W, Proof		$2,800	$2,900	$4,700

Note: MS values are for uncertified Mint State coins of average quality, in their complete original U.S. Mint packaging. PF values are for uncertified Proof coins of average quality, in their complete original U.S. Mint packaging. †† Ranked in the *100 Greatest U.S. Modern Coins* (fourth edition). **a.** Auction: $447, MS-70, September 2015. **b.** Auction: $705, PF-70DCam, June 2015. **c.** Auction: $1,116, MS-70, August 2015. **d.** Auction: $823, PF-70DCam, January 2015. **e.** Auction: $764, MS-69, November 2015. **f.** Auction: $1,528, PF-70UCam, August 2015. **g.** Includes 24,558 sold as Lunar New Year Celebration coins. **h.** Auction: $2,703, MS-70, June 2015. **i.** Auction: $3,525, PF-70DCam, July 2015.

AMERICAN BUFFALO .9999 FINE GOLD BULLION COIN SETS

	Uncertified	MS-69 / PF-69	MS-70 / PF-70
2008-W Four-coin set ($5, $10, $25, $50), Proof	$5,800	$6,100	$7,500
2008-W Four-coin set ($5, $10, $25, $50), Burnished	$5,600	$6,000	$7,000
2008-W Double Prosperity set (Unc. $25 American Buffalo gold and $25 American Gold Eagle coins)	$2,600	$2,700	$3,100

Note: Uncertified values are for uncertified sets of average quality, in their complete original U.S. Mint packaging.

FIRST SPOUSE $10 GOLD BULLION COINS
(2007–2016)

Designers: *See image captions for designers.* **Weight:** *8.483 grams.*
Composition: *.9999 gold.* **Diameter:** *26.5 mm.* **Edge:** *Reeded.* **Mint:** *West Point.*

Burnished Finish
The first coin in the series,
featuring Martha Washington.

Mintmark location is on the
obverse, below the date.

Proof Finish

History. The U.S. Mint's First Spouse bullion coins were struck in .9999 fine (24-karat) gold. Each weighs one-half ounce and bears a face value of $10. The coins honor the nation's first spouses and were struck on the same schedule as the Mint's Presidential dollars program. Each features a portrait on the obverse, and on the reverse a unique design symbolic of the spouse's life and work. In cases where a president held office widowed or unmarried, the coin bears "an obverse image emblematic of Liberty as depicted on a circulating coin of that era and a reverse image emblematic of themes of that president's life." All First Spouse gold bullion coins (Proofs and Burnished pieces) were struck at the U.S. Mint's West Point facility.

Note that the Mint does not release bullion mintage data on a regular basis; the numbers given herein reflect the most recently available official data.

Striking and Sharpness. Striking is generally sharp.

Availability. These coins are readily available in the numismatic marketplace. They could be purchased by the public, in both Burnished and Proof formats, directly from the U.S. Mint. Sales of later issues were low, leading to some issues being ranked among the 100 Greatest U.S. Modern Coins.

MS-60 to 70 (Mint State). *Obverse and Reverse:* At MS-60, some abrasion and contact marks are evident on the higher design areas and the open areas of the design. Luster may be dull or lifeless at MS–60 to 62, but there should be deep frost at MS-63 and better, particularly in the lower-relief areas. At MS-65 and above, the luster should be full and rich. Contact marks and abrasion are less and less evident at higher grades. These guidelines are more academic than practical, as these coins are not intended for circulation, and nearly all are in high Mint State grades, as struck.

PF-60 to 70 (Proof). *Obverse and Reverse:* Proofs that are extensively cleaned and have many hairlines are lower level, such as PF–60 to 62. Those with fewer hairlines or flaws are deemed PF–63 to 65. (These exist more in theory than actuality, as nearly all Proof First Spouse gold coins have been maintained in their original high condition by collectors.) Given the quality of modern U.S. Mint products, even PF–66 and 67 are unusually low levels for these Proofs.

First Spouse $10 Gold Bullion Coins

Martha Washington
Designers:
obverse—Joseph Menna;
reverse—Susan Gamble.

Abigail Adams
Designers:
obverse—Joseph Menna;
reverse—Thomas Cleveland.

Jefferson's Liberty
Designers: obverse—
Robert Scot / Phebe Hemphill;
reverse—Charles Vickers.

Dolley Madison
Designers:
obverse—Don Everhart;
reverse—Joel Iskowitz.

	Mintage	MS	MS-69	MS-70
		PF	PF-69	PF-70
$10 2007-W, M. Washington	17,661	$1,050	$1,075	$1,100
$10 2007-W, M. Washington, Proof	19,167	$1,050	$1,075	$1,100
$10 2007-W, A. Adams	17,142	$1,050	$1,075	$1,100
$10 2007-W, A. Adams, Proof	17,149	$1,050	$1,075	$1,100
$10 2007-W, Jefferson's Liberty ††	19,823	$1,050	$1,075	$1,100
$10 2007-W, Jefferson's Liberty, Proof ††	19,815	$1,050	$1,075	$1,100
$10 2007-W, D. Madison	12,340	$1,050	$1,075	$1,100
$10 2007-W, D. Madison, Proof	17,943	$1,050	$1,075	$1,100

Note: MS values are for uncertified Mint State coins of average quality, in their complete original U.S. Mint packaging. PF values are for uncertified Proof coins of average quality, in their complete original U.S. Mint packaging. †† All First Spouse Gold Bullion with "Liberty" Designs, in all finishes, are ranked in the *100 Greatest U.S. Modern Coins* (fourth edition), as a single entry.

Elizabeth Monroe
Designers:
obverse—Joel Iskowitz;
reverse—Donna Weaver.

Louisa Adams
Designers:
obverse—Susan Gamble;
reverse—Donna Weaver.

Jackson's Liberty
Designers:
obverse—John Reich;
reverse—Justin Kunz.

Van Buren's Liberty
Designers:
obverse—Christian Gobrecht;
reverse—Thomas Cleveland.

	Mintage	MS	MS-69	MS-70
		PF	PF-69	PF-70
$10 2008-W, E. Monroe	4,462	$1,050	$1,075	$1,250
$10 2008-W, E. Monroe, Proof	7,800	$1,050	$1,500	$1,600
$10 2008-W, L. Adams	3,885	$1,050	$1,075	$1,250
$10 2008-W, L. Adams, Proof	6,581	$1,100	$1,500	$1,600

Note: MS values are for uncertified Mint State coins of average quality, in their complete original U.S. Mint packaging. PF values are for uncertified Proof coins of average quality, in their complete original U.S. Mint packaging.

	Mintage	MS	MS-69	MS-70
		PF	PF-69	PF-70
$10 2008-W, Jackson's Liberty †† (a)	4,609	$1,100	$1,650	$1,750
$10 2008-W, Jackson's Liberty, Proof ††	7,684	$1,150	$1,500	$1,650
$10 2008-W, Van Buren's Liberty ††	3,826	$1,100	$1,550	$1,600
$10 2008-W, Van Buren's Liberty, Proof †† (b)	6,807	$1,250	$1,400	$1,750

Note: MS values are for uncertified Mint State coins of average quality, in their complete original U.S. Mint packaging. PF values are for uncertified Proof coins of average quality, in their complete original U.S. Mint packaging. †† All First Spouse Gold Bullion with "Liberty" Designs, in all finishes, are ranked in the *100 Greatest U.S. Modern Coins* (fourth edition), as a single entry. **a.** Auction: $999, MS-69, February 2015. **b.** Auction: $1,058, PF-70DCam, January 2015.

Anna Harrison
Designers:
obverse—Donna Weaver;
reverse—Thomas Cleveland.

Letitia Tyler
Designers:
obverse—Phebe Hemphill;
reverse—Susan Gamble.

Julia Tyler
Designer:
obverse and reverse—
Joel Iskowitz.

Sarah Polk
Designer: obverse and
reverse—Phebe Hemphill.

Margaret Taylor
Designers: obverse—Phebe Hemphill;
reverse—Mary Beth Zeitz.

	Mintage	MS	MS-69	MS-70
		PF	PF-69	PF-70
$10 2009-W, A. Harrison	3,645	$1,050	$1,100	$1,550
$10 2009-W, A. Harrison, Proof (c)	6,251	$1,150	$1,200	$1,450
$10 2009-W, L. Tyler	3,240	$1,150	$1,200	$1,700
$10 2009-W, L. Tyler, Proof (d)	5,296	$1,250	$1,300	$1,450
$10 2009-W, J. Tyler (e)	3,143	$1,150	$1,200	$1,750
$10 2009-W, J. Tyler, Proof (f)	4,844	$1,250	$1,300	$1,450
$10 2009-W, S. Polk	3,489	$1,175	$1,225	$1,500
$10 2009-W, S. Polk, Proof	5,151	$1,050	$1,100	$1,250
$10 2009-W, M. Taylor	3,627	$1,050	$1,075	$1,275
$10 2009-W, M. Taylor, Proof	4,936	$1,050	$1,075	$1,300

Note: MS values are for uncertified Mint State coins of average quality, in their complete original U.S. Mint packaging. PF values are for uncertified Proof coins of average quality, in their complete original U.S. Mint packaging. **c.** Auction: $646, PF-69DCam, June 2015. **d.** Auction: $881, PF-70DCam, June 2015. **e.** Auction: $1,293, MS-70, June 2015. **f.** Auction: $764, PF-69DCam, June 2015.

Abigail Fillmore
Designers:
obverse—Phebe Hemphill;
reverse—Susan Gamble.

Jane Pierce
Designer:
obverse and reverse—
Donna Weaver.

Buchanan's Liberty
Designers:
obverse—Christian Gobrecht;
reverse—David Westwood.

Mary Lincoln
Designers:
obverse—Phebe Hemphill;
reverse—Joel Iskowitz.

	Mintage	MS	MS-69	MS-70
		PF	PF-69	PF-70
$10 2010-W, A. Fillmore	3,482	$1,050	$1,075	$1,350
$10 2010-W, A. Fillmore, Proof	6,130	$1,150	$1,200	$1,300
$10 2010-W, J. Pierce	3,338	$1,050	$1,075	$1,350
$10 2010-W, J. Pierce, Proof	4,775	$1,200	$1,250	$1,600
$10 2010-W, Buchanan's Liberty ††	5,162	$1,050	$1,100	$1,300
$10 2010-W, Buchanan's Liberty, Proof ††	7,110	$1,150	$1,200	$1,300
$10 2010-W, M. Lincoln	3,695	$1,050	$1,100	$1,350
$10 2010-W, M. Lincoln, Proof	6,861	$1,150	$1,200	$1,500

Note: MS values are for uncertified Mint State coins of average quality, in their complete original U.S. Mint packaging. PF values are for uncertified Proof coins of average quality, in their complete original U.S. Mint packaging. †† All First Spouse Gold Bullion with "Liberty" Designs, in all finishes, are ranked in the *100 Greatest U.S. Modern Coins* (fourth edition), as a single entry.

Eliza Johnson
Designers:
obverse—Joel Iskowitz;
reverse—Gary Whitley.

Julia Grant
Designers:
obverse—Donna Weaver;
reverse—Richard Masters.

Lucy Hayes
Designers:
obverse—Susan Gamble;
reverse—Barbara Fox.

Lucretia Garfield
Designers:
obverse—Barbara Fox;
reverse—Michael Gaudioso.

	Mintage	MS	MS-69	MS-70
		PF	PF-69	PF-70
$10 2011-W, E. Johnson	2,905	$1,050	$1,100	$1,550
$10 2011-W, E. Johnson, Proof	3,887	$1,200	$1,250	$1,350
$10 2011-W, J. Grant	2,892	$1,050	$1,100	$1,400
$10 2011-W, J. Grant, Proof	3,943	$1,200	$1,250	$1,450
$10 2011-W, L. Hayes (g)	2,196	$1,200	$1,250	$1,850

Note: MS values are for uncertified Mint State coins of average quality, in their complete original U.S. Mint packaging. PF values are for uncertified Proof coins of average quality, in their complete original U.S. Mint packaging. **g.** Auction: $1,763, MS-70, January 2015.

	Mintage	MS	MS-69	MS-70
		PF	PF-69	PF-70
$10 2011-W, L. Hayes, Proof	3,868	$1,150	$1,400	$1,750
$10 2011-W, L. Garfield	2,168	$1,200	$1,250	$1,850
$10 2011-W, L. Garfield, Proof	3,653	$1,150	$1,200	$1,550

Note: MS values are for uncertified Mint State coins of average quality, in their complete original U.S. Mint packaging. PF values are for uncertified Proof coins of average quality, in their complete original U.S. Mint packaging.

Alice Paul
Designers:
obverse—Susan Gamble;
reverse—Phebe Hemphill.

Frances Cleveland (Type 1)
Designers:
obverse—Joel Iskowitz;
reverse—Barbara Fox.

Caroline Harrison
Designers:
obverse—Frank Morris;
reverse—Donna Weaver.

Frances Cleveland (Type 2)
Designers:
obverse—Barbara Fox;
reverse—Joseph Menna.

	Mintage	MS	MS-69	MS-70
		PF	PF-69	PF-70
$10 2012-W, Alice Paul	2,798	$1,100	$1,150	$1,350
$10 2012-W, Alice Paul, Proof	3,505	$1,125	$1,175	$1,600
$10 2012-W, Frances Cleveland, Variety 1	2,454	$1,100	$1,150	$1,200
$10 2012-W, Frances Cleveland, Variety 1, Proof	3,158	$1,175	$1,225	$1,350
$10 2012-W, Caroline Harrison	2,436	$1,100	$1,150	$1,350
$10 2012-W, Caroline Harrison, Proof	3,046	$1,175	$1,225	$1,400
$10 2012-W, Frances Cleveland, Variety 2	2,425	$1,100	$1,150	$1,200
$10 2012-W, Frances Cleveland, Variety 2, Proof	3,104	$1,175	$1,225	$1,400

Note: MS values are for uncertified Mint State coins of average quality, in their complete original U.S. Mint packaging. PF values are for uncertified Proof coins of average quality, in their complete original U.S. Mint packaging.

Ida McKinley
Designers:
obverse—Susan Gamble;
reverse—Donna Weaver.

Edith Roosevelt
Designers:
obverse—Joel Iskowitz;
reverse—Chris Costello.

Helen Taft
Designers:
obverse—William C. Burgard;
reverse—Richard Masters.

Ellen Wilson
Designers: obverse—Frank Morris;
reverse—Don Everhart.

Edith Wilson
Designers: obverse—David Westwood;
reverse—Joseph Menna.

| | Mintage | MS | MS-69 | MS-70 |
		PF	PF-69	PF-70
$10 2013-W, I. McKinley	2,008	$1,075	$1,125	$1,200
$10 2013-W, I. McKinley, Proof	2,724	$1,150	$1,200	$1,550
$10 2013-W, E. Roosevelt	2,027	$1,075	$1,125	$1,200
$10 2013-W, E. Roosevelt, Proof	2,840	$1,150	$1,200	$1,300
$10 2013-W, H. Taft	1,993	$1,075	$1,125	$1,200
$10 2013-W, H. Taft, Proof	2,598	$1,150	$1,200	$1,300
$10 2013-W, Ellen Wilson	1,980	$1,075	$1,125	$1,200
$10 2013-W, Ellen Wilson, Proof	2,511	$1,150	$1,200	$1,300
$10 2013-W, Edith Wilson	1,974	$1,075	$1,125	$1,200
$10 2013-W, Edith Wilson, Proof	2,464	$1,150	$1,200	$1,300

Note: MS values are for uncertified Mint State coins of average quality, in their complete original U.S. Mint packaging. PF values are for uncertified Proof coins of average quality, in their complete original U.S. Mint packaging.

Florence Harding
Designer:
obverse and reverse—
Thomas Cleveland.

Grace Coolidge
Designers:
obverse—Joel Iskowitz;
reverse—Frank Morris.

Lou Hoover
Designers:
obverse—Susan Gamble;
reverse—Richard Masters.

Eleanor Roosevelt
Designer:
obverse and reverse—
Chris Costello.

| | Mintage | MS | MS-69 | MS-70 |
		PF	PF-69	PF-70
$10 2014-W, F. Harding	1,944	$1,075	$1,125	$1,200
$10 2014-W, F. Harding, Proof	2,372	$1,125	$1,175	$1,500
$10 2014-W, G. Coolidge	1,949	$1,075	$1,125	$1,200
$10 2014-W, G. Coolidge, Proof	2,315	$1,150	$1,200	$1,750
$10 2014-W, L. Hoover	1,936	$1,075	$1,125	$1,200
$10 2014-W, L. Hoover, Proof	2,392	$1,150	$1,200	$1,850
$10 2014-W, E. Roosevelt	1,886	$1,850	$1,950	$2,450
$10 2014-W, E. Roosevelt, Proof	2,377	$1,650	$1,750	$2,650

Note: MS values are for uncertified Mint State coins of average quality, in their complete original U.S. Mint packaging. PF values are for uncertified Proof coins of average quality, in their complete original U.S. Mint packaging.

Bess Truman
*Designer:
obverse and reverse—
Joel Iskowitz.*

Mamie Eisenhower
*Designers:
obverse—Richard Masters;
reverse—Barbara Fox.*

Jacqueline Kennedy
*Designers:
obverse—Susan Gamble;
reverse—Benjamin Sowards.*

Claudia "Lady Bird" Johnson
*Designers:
obverse—Linda Fox;
reverse—Chris Costello.*

	Mintage	MS	MS-69	MS-70
		PF	PF-69	PF-70
$10 2015-W, E. Truman	1,946	$1,075	$1,100	$1,200
$10 2015-W, E. Truman, Proof	2,747	$1,150	$1,175	$1,250
$10 2015-W, M. Eisenhower	2,102	$1,075	$1,100	$1,200
$10 2015-W, M. Eisenhower, Proof	2,704	$1,150	$1,175	$1,250
$10 2015-W, J. Kennedy	6,439	$1,075	$1,100	$1,200
$10 2015-W, J. Kennedy, Proof	11,222	$1,150	$1,175	$1,250
$10 2015-W, Lady Bird Johnson	1,927	$1,075	$1,100	$1,200
$10 2015-W, Lady Bird Johnson, Proof	2,611	$1,150	$1,175	$1,250

Note: MS values are for uncertified Mint State coins of average quality, in their complete original U.S. Mint packaging. PF values are for uncertified Proof coins of average quality, in their complete original U.S. Mint packaging.

Patricia Nixon
*Designer:
obverse and reverse—
Richard Masters.*

Betty Ford
*Designers:
obverse—Barbara Fox;
reverse—Chris Costello.*

Nancy Reagan
*Designers: obverse—
Benjamin Sowards;
reverse—Joel Iskowitz.*

Barbara Bush
*Designers: obverse—
Benjamin Sowards;
reverse—Barbara Fox.*

	Mintage	MS	MS-69	MS-70
		PF	PF-69	PF-70
$10 2016-W, P. Nixon	1,839	$1,200	$1,350	$1,450
$10 2016-W, P. Nixon, Proof	2,646	$1,200	$1,300	$1,400
$10 2016-W, B. Ford	1,824	$1,350	$1,450	$1,650
$10 2016-W, B. Ford, Proof	2,471	$1,300	$1,400	$1,550
$10 2016-W, N. Reagan	2,009	$1,100	$1,200	$1,250
$10 2016-W, N. Reagan, Proof	3,548	$1,150	$1,250	$1,300
$10 2020-W, B. Bush		$1,275	$1,375	$1,650
$10 2020-W, B. Bush, Proof		$1,300	$1,400	$1,700

Note: MS values are for uncertified Mint State coins of average quality, in their complete original U.S. Mint packaging. PF values are for uncertified Proof coins of average quality, in their complete original U.S. Mint packaging.

AMERICAN PLATINUM EAGLES
(1997 TO DATE)

Designers: *John M. Mercanti (obverse), Thomas D. Rogers Sr. (original reverse)*
(see image captions for other reverse designers). **Weight:** *$10 1/10 oz.—3.112 grams;*
$25 1/4 oz.—7.780 grams; $50 1/2 oz.—15.560 grams; $100 1 oz.—31.120 grams.
Composition: *.9995 platinum.* **Diameter:** *$10 1/10 oz.—16.5 mm; $25 1/4 oz.—22 mm;*
$50 1/2 oz.—27 mm; $100 1 oz.—32.7 mm. **Edge:** *Reeded.* **Mints:** *Philadelphia and West Point.*

Regular Finish

Burnished Finish
*Burnished coins of all denominations feature the year's
Proof reverse design. Mintmark location varies by design.*

Proof Finish
*First-year Proof coins featured the original
reverse design, which is still in use on bullion
strikes. See pages 1267–1269 for illustrations
of Proof reverse designs from 1998 to date.*

Reverse Proof Finish
*Reverse Proofs were only struck in 2007,
and only in the $50 1/2-oz. denomination.*

 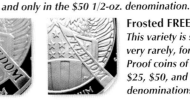

Frosted FREEDOM
*This variety is seen,
very rarely, for 2007
Proof coins of the
$25, $50, and $100
denominations.*

History. Platinum American Eagles (face values of $10 to $100) are legal-tender bullion coins with weight, content, and purity guaranteed by the federal government. They were added to the U.S. Mint's program of silver and gold bullion coinage in 1997.

In their debut year, Proofs had the same reverse design as regular bullion strikes. Since then, the regular strikes have continued with the 1997 reverse, while the Proofs have featured new reverse designs each year. From 1998 through 2002, these special Proof designs comprised a "Vistas of Liberty" subset, with eagles flying through various American scenes. Since 2003, they have featured patriotic allegories and symbolism. From 2006 to 2008 the reverse designs honored "The Foundations of Democracy"—the nation's legislative branch (2006), executive branch (2007), and judicial branch (2008). In 2009 the Mint introduced a new six-year program of reverse designs, exploring the core concepts of American democracy as embodied in the preamble to the Constitution. The designs—which were based on narratives by John Roberts, chief justice of the United States—began with *To Form a More Perfect Union* (2009), which features four faces representing the nation's diversity, with the hair and clothing interweaving symbolically. The tiny eagle privy mark is from an original coin punch from the Philadelphia Mint's archives. This design is followed by *To Establish*

Justice (2010), *To Insure Domestic Tranquility* (2011), *To Provide for the Common Defence* (2012), *To Promote the General Welfare* (2013), and *To Secure the Blessings of Liberty to Ourselves and Our Posterity* (2014). In 2015, the Mint issued the first of a two-year series of new reverse designs emblematic of the core values of liberty and freedom called *Liberty Nurtures Freedom*. In 2017 the Proof reverse returned to the original 1997 design for the program's 20th anniversary. One-ounce Proofs of 2018 through 2020 feature new obverse designs in the theme of Life, Liberty, and the Pursuit of Happiness, and also share a new common reverse design. Beginning in 2021 the Mint will issue a new five-year series of one-ounce Proofs, for the five freedoms guaranteed under the First Amendment of the U.S. Constitution.

The Philadelphia Mint strikes regular bullion issues, which are sold to the public by a network of Mint-authorized precious-metal firms, coin dealers, banks, and brokerages. The West Point facility strikes Burnished pieces (called *Uncirculated* by the Mint, and featuring the reverse design of the Proof coins), which are sold directly to collectors. Proofs are also struck at West Point and, like the Burnished coins, are sold by the Mint to the public, without middlemen. Similar to their gold-bullion cousins, the platinum Proofs and Burnished coins bear a W mintmark and are specially packaged in plastic capsules and fancy presentation cases.

In addition to the individual coins listed below, platinum American Eagles were issued in the 1997 "Impressions of Liberty" bullion coin set; in 2007 "10th Anniversary" sets; and in annual platinum-coin sets.

Striking and Sharpness. Striking is generally sharp.

Availability. The platinum American Eagle is one of the most popular platinum-investment vehicles in the world. The coins are readily available in the numismatic marketplace and through some banks, investment firms, and other non-numismatic channels.

MS-60 to 70 (Mint State). *Obverse and Reverse:* At MS-60, some abrasion and contact marks are evident on the higher design areas. Luster may be dull or lifeless at MS–60 to 62, but there should be deep frost at MS-63 and better, particularly in the lower-relief areas. At MS-65 and above, the luster should be full and rich. These guidelines are more academic than practical, as platinum American Eagles are not intended for circulation, and nearly all are in high Mint State grades.

PF-60 to 70 (Proof). *Obverse and Reverse:* Proofs that are extensively cleaned and have many hairlines are lower level, such as PF-60 to 62. Those with fewer hairlines or flaws are deemed PF–63 to 65. (These exist more in theory than actuality, as nearly all Proof American Eagle platinum bullion coins have been maintained in their original high condition by collectors.) Given the quality of modern U.S. Mint products, even PF–66 and 67 are unusually low levels for these Proofs.

$10 1/10-OUNCE
AMERICAN PLATINUM EAGLES

	Mintage	MS	MS-69	MS-70		Mintage	MS	MS-69	MS-70
		PF	PF-69	PF-70			PF	PF-69	PF-70
$10 1997 (a)	70,250	$210	$245	$1,300	$10 2000	34,027	$210	$245	$600
$10 1997-W, Proof	36,993	$230	$265	$290	$10 2000-W, Proof (c)	15,651	$230	$265	$400
$10 1998 (b)	39,525	$210	$245	$1,450	$10 2001	52,017	$210	$245	$375
$10 1998-W, Proof (c)	19,847	$230	$275	$550	$10 2001-W, Proof (c)	12,174	$230	$265	$425
$10 1999 (d)	55,955	$210	$245	$800	$10 2002	23,005	$210	$245	$300
$10 1999-W, Proof (c)	19,133	$230	$265	$300	$10 2002-W, Proof (c)	12,365	$230	$265	$400

Note: MS values are for uncertified Mint State coins of average quality, in their complete original U.S. Mint packaging. PF values are for uncertified Proof coins of average quality, in their complete original U.S. Mint packaging. **a.** Auction: $4,230, MS-70, January 2015. **b.** Auction: $223, MS-69, January 2013. **c.** Burnished and Proof coins since 1998 featured the designs illustrated on pages 1267–1269. **d.** Auction: $170, MS-69, August 2014.

	Mintage	MS / PF	MS-69 / PF-69	MS-70 / PF-70		Mintage	MS / PF	MS-69 / PF-69	MS-70 / PF-70
$10 2003	22,007	$210	$245	$300	**$10 2006-W, Proof** (c)	10,205	$230	$265	$350
$10 2003-W, Proof (c,e)	9,534	$230	$265	$290	**$10 2007** (i)	13,003	$215	$250	$325
$10 2004	15,010	$210	$245	$300	**$10 2007-W, Burnished** (c,j)	5,556	$290	$325	$650
$10 2004-W, Proof (c,f)	7,161	$295	$375	$490					
$10 2005	14,013	$210	$245	$300	**$10 2007-W, Proof** (c)	8,176	$230	$265	$350
$10 2005-W, Proof (c,g)	8,104	$230	$265	$375	**$10 2008**	17,000	$210	$245	$300
$10 2006	11,001	$210	$245	$300	**$10 2008-W, Burnished** (c,k)	3,706	$425	$460	$675
$10 2006-W, Burnished (c,h)	3,544	$500	$535	$700	**$10 2008-W, Proof** (c,l)	5,138	$365	$400	$450

Note: MS values are for uncertified Mint State coins of average quality, in their complete original U.S. Mint packaging. PF values are for uncertified Proof coins of average quality, in their complete original U.S. Mint packaging. **c.** Burnished and Proof coins since 1998 featured the designs illustrated on pages 1267–1269. **e.** Auction: $176, PF-69DCam, December 2014. **f.** Auction: $447, PF-69DCam, February 2015. **g.** Auction: $212, PF-70UCam, February 2015. **h.** Auction: $441, MS-70, June 2013. **i.** Auction: $153, MS-70, September 2015. **j.** Auction: $364, MS-70, May 2015. **k.** Auction: $282, MS-69, September 2015. **l.** $376, PF-70UCam, January 2015.

$25 1/4-Ounce
American Platinum Eagles

	Mintage	MS / PF	MS-69 / PF-69	MS-70 / PF-70		Mintage	MS / PF	MS-69 / PF-69	MS-70 / PF-70
$25 1997 (a)	27,100	$360	$400	$3,000	**$25 2005**	12,013	$360	$425	$600
$25 1997-W, Proof	18,628	$380	$475	$575	**$25 2005-W, Proof** (b,f)	6,592	$385	$600	$950
$25 1998	38,887	$360	$400	$1,400	**$25 2006**	12,001	$360	$425	$600
$25 1998-W, Proof (b)	14,873	$380	$475	$700	**$25 2006-W, Burnished** (b,g)	2,676	$650	$700	$800
$25 1999 (c)	39,734	$360	$400	$2,750					
$25 1999-W, Proof (b)	13,507	$380	$475	$700	**$25 2006-W, Proof** (b)	7,813	$380	$475	$750
$25 2000	20,054	$360	$400	$800	**$25 2007**	8,402	$360	$430	$650
$25 2000-W, Proof (b)	11,995	$380	$475	$700	**$25 2007-W, Burnished** (b,h)	3,690	$600	$650	$750
$25 2001 (d)	21,815	$360	$400	$2,300					
$25 2001-W, Proof (b)	8,847	$380	$475	$750	**$25 2007-W, Proof** (b)	6,017	$380	$475	$750
$25 2002	27,405	$360	$400	$575	**$25 2007-W, Frosted FREEDOM, Proof ††** (b)	21	—		
$25 2002-W, Proof (b)	9,282	$380	$475	$750					
$25 2003	25,207	$360	$400	$550	**$25 2008**	22,800	$360	$400	$575
$25 2003-W, Proof (b)	7,044	$380	$475	$750	**$25 2008-W, Burnished** (b,i)	2,481	$810	$960	$1,250
$25 2004	18,010	$360	$400	$550					
$25 2004-W, Proof (b,e)	5,193	$560	$900	$1,250	**$25 2008-W, Proof** (b,j)	4,153	$610	$810	$1,000

Note: MS values are for uncertified Mint State coins of average quality, in their complete original U.S. Mint packaging. PF values are for uncertified Proof coins of average quality, in their complete original U.S. Mint packaging. †† All Proof 2007-W Platinum Eagles with Frosted FREEDOM, in all denominations, are ranked in the *100 Greatest U.S. Modern Coins* (fourth edition), as a single entry. **a.** Auction: $7,638, MS-70, January 2015. **b.** Burnished and Proof coins since 1998 featured the designs illustrated on pages 1267–1269. **c.** Auction: $411, MS-68, October 2012. **d.** Auction: $374, MS-68, June 2012. **e.** Auction: $764, PF-70DCam, July 2015. **f.** Auction: $564, PF-70DCam, January 2015. **g.** Auction: $306, MS-69, November 2015. **h.** Auction: $598, MS-70, August 2014. **i.** Auction: $764, MS-70, September 2015. **j.** Auction: $470, PF-70UCam, June 2015.

$50 1/2-Ounce
American Platinum Eagles

	Mintage	MS / PF	MS-69 / PF-69	MS-70 / PF-70		Mintage	MS / PF	MS-69 / PF-69	MS-70 / PF-70
$50 1997 (a)	20,500	$700	$775	$4,000	$50 2005-W, Proof (c,h)	5,942	$750	$1,100	$1,400
$50 1997-W, Proof	15,431	$750	$850	$1,000	$50 2006	9,602	$700	$850	$1,000
$50 1998 (b)	32,415	$700	$775	$4,500	$50 2006-W, Burnished (c)	2,577	$950	$1,100	$1,400
$50 1998-W, Proof (c)	13,836	$750	$850	$1,000					
$50 1999 (d)	32,309	$700	$775	$4,000	$50 2006-W, Proof (c)	7,649	$750	$850	$1,250
$50 1999-W, Proof (c)	11,103	$750	$850	$1,000	$50 2007	7,001	$750	$850	$1,000
$50 2000 (e)	18,892	$700	$775	$4,000	$50 2007-W, Burnished (c)	3,635	$1,000	$1,200	$1,500
$50 2000-W, Proof (c)	11,049	$750	$850	$1,000					
$50 2001 (f)	12,815	$700	$775	$3,750	$50 2007-W, Proof (c)	25,519	$750	$850	$1,000
$50 2001-W, Proof (c)	8,254	$750	$850	$1,000	$50 2007-W, Reverse Proof (c)	19,583	$900	$950	$1,100
$50 2002	24,005	$700	$775	$1,700					
$50 2002-W, Proof (c)	8,772	$750	$850	$1,000	$50 2007-W, Frosted FREEDOM, Proof †† (c)	21	—		
$50 2003	17,409	$700	$775	$1,100					
$50 2003-W, Proof (c)	7,131	$750	$850	$1,000	$50 2008	14,000	$700	$775	$1,000
$50 2004	13,236	$700	$775	$1,100	$50 2008-W, Burnished †† (c,i)	2,253	$1,000	$1,400	$2,500
$50 2004-W, Proof (c,g)	5,063	$750	$1,250	$1,550					
$50 2005	9,013	$700	$825	$1,100	$50 2008-W, Proof ‡ (c,j)	4,020	$1,050	$1,350	$1,600

Note: MS values are for uncertified Mint State coins of average quality, in their complete original U.S. Mint packaging. PF values are for uncertified Proof coins of average quality, in their complete original U.S. Mint packaging. †† Ranked in the *100 Greatest U.S. Modern Coins* (fourth edition); all Proof 2007-W Platinum Eagles with Frosted FREEDOM, in all denominations, are listed as a single entry. **a.** Auction: $870, MS-69, July 2014. **b.** Auction: $881, MS-68, October 2012. **c.** Burnished and Proof coins from 1998 on featured the designs illustrated on pages 1267–1269. **d.** Auction: $823, MS-69, April 2014. **e.** Auction: $823, MS-69, November 2012. **f.** Auction: $796, MS-69, July 2014. **g.** Auction: $1,058, PF-70DCam, July 2015. **h.** Auction: $705, PF-70UCam, February 2015. **i.** Auction: $1,528, MS-70, October 2015. **j.** Auction: $1,234, PF-70UCam. October 2015.

$100 1-OUNCE AMERICAN PLATINUM EAGLES

Proof Reverse, 1998: Eagle Over New England.
Vistas of Liberty series. Designer: John Mercanti.

Proof Reverse, 1999: Eagle Above Southeastern Wetlands.
Vistas of Liberty series. Designer: John Mercanti.

Proof Reverse, 2000: Eagle Above America's Heartland.
Vistas of Liberty series. Designer: Alfred Maletsky.

Proof Reverse, 2001: Eagle Above America's Southwest.
Vistas of Liberty series. Designer: Thomas D. Rogers Sr.

Proof Reverse, 2002: Eagle Fishing in America's Northwest.
Vistas of Liberty series. Designer: Alfred Maletsky.

Proof Reverse, 2003.
Designer: Alfred Maletsky.

Proof Reverse, 2004.
Designer: Donna Weaver.

Proof Reverse, 2005.
Designer: Donna Weaver.

Proof Reverse, 2006:
Legislative Branch.
Foundations of
Democracy series.
Designer: Joel Iskowitz.

Proof Reverse, 2007:
Executive Branch.
Foundations of
Democracy series.
Designer: Thomas Cleveland.

Proof Reverse, 2008:
Judicial Branch.
Foundations of
Democracy series.
Designer: Joel Iskowitz.

Proof Reverse, 2009:
"To Form a More
Perfect Union."
Preamble to the
Constitution series.
Designer: Susan Gamble.

Proof Reverse, 2010:
"To Establish Justice."
Preamble to the
Constitution series.
Designer: Donna Weaver.

Proof Reverse, 2011:
"To Insure Domestic
Tranquility."
Preamble to the
Constitution series.
Designer: Joel Iskowitz.

Proof Reverse, 2012:
"To Provide for the
Common Defence."
Preamble to the
Constitution series.
Designer: Barbara Fox.

Proof Reverse, 2013:
"To Promote the
General Welfare."
Preamble to the
Constitution series.
Designer: Joel Iskowitz.

Proof Reverse, 2014:
"To Secure the Blessings
of Liberty to Ourselves
and Our Posterity."
Preamble to the
Constitution series.
Designer: Susan Gamble.

Proof Reverse, 2015:
Liberty Nurtures
Freedom.
Designer: Joel Iskowitz.

Proof Reverse, 2016:
Portrait of Liberty.
Designer: John Mercanti.

Common Reverse,
2018 to date.
Designer: Patricia Lucas-Morris.

Proof Obverse, 2018:
"Life."
Preamble to the Declaration
of Independence series.
Designer: Justin Kunz.

Proof Obverse, 2019:
"Liberty."
Preamble to the Declaration
of Independence series.
Designer: Justin Kunz.

Proof Obverse, 2020:
"Happiness."
Preamble to the Declaration
of Independence series.
Designer: Justin Kunz.

Proof Obverse, 2021:
"Freedom of Religion."
First Amendment to the
U.S. Constitution series.
Designer: Patricia Lucas-Morris.

	Mintage	MS / PF	MS-69 / PF-69	MS-70 / PF-70
$100 1997 (a)	56,000	$1,250	$1,350	$25,000
$100 1997-W, Proof	20,851	$1,350	$1,500	$2,900
$100 1998 (b)	133,002	$1,250	$1,350	$25,000
$100 1998-W, Proof	14,912	$1,350	$1,500	$2,800
$100 1999 (c)	56,707	$1,250	$1,350	$35,000
$100 1999-W, Proof (d)	12,363	$1,350	$1,500	$3,750
$100 2000 (e)	10,003	$1,250	$1,350	—
$100 2000-W, Proof (f)	12,453	$1,350	$1,500	$2,300
$100 2001 (g)	14,070	$1,250	$1,350	—
$100 2001-W, Proof	8,969	$1,350	$1,500	$3,900
$100 2002 (h)	11,502	$1,250	$1,350	—
$100 2002-W, Proof (i)	9,834	$1,350	$1,500	$3,900
$100 2003	8,007	$1,250	$1,350	$3,750
$100 2003-W, Proof (j)	8,246	$1,350	$1,500	$3,900
$100 2004	7,009	$1,250	$1,350	$2,500
$100 2004-W, Proof (k)	6,007	$1,350	$2,150	$3,400
$100 2005	6,310	$1,250	$1,350	$2,500
$100 2005-W, Proof (l)	6,602	$1,350	$2,350	$3,000
$100 2006	6,000	$1,250	$1,350	$2,200
$100 2006-W, Burnished †† (m)	3,068	$2,100	$2,200	$2,400
$100 2006-W, Proof	9,152	$1,350	$1,500	$2,000
$100 2007	7,202	$1,250	$1,350	$2,100
$100 2007-W, Burnished	4,177	$1,900	$2,000	$2,200
$100 2007-W, Proof	8,363	$1,350	$1,500	$2,500
$100 2007-W, Frosted FREEDOM, Proof ††	12	—		

	Mintage	MS / PF	MS-69 / PF-69	MS-70 / PF-70
$100 2008	21,800	$1,250	$1,350	$1,950
$100 2008-W, Burnished (n)	2,876	$2,200	$2,300	$2,500
$100 2008-W, Proof (o)	4,769	$1,900	$2,150	$3,500
$100 2009-W, Proof ††	7,945	$1,300	$1,850	$2,000
$100 2010-W, Proof	14,790	$1,300	$1,850	$2,000
$100 2011-W, Proof	14,835	$1,300	$1,600	$1,750
$100 2012-W, Proof	9,081	$1,300	$1,600	$1,750
$100 2013-W, Proof	5,763	$2,000	$2,200	$2,600
$100 2014	16,900	$1,200	$1,350	$1,800
$100 2014-W, Proof	4,596	$2,300	$2,450	$3,000
$100 2015	20,000	$1,200	$1,350	$1,800
$100 2015-W, Proof	3,881	$2,500	$2,600	$3,250
$100 2016	20,000	$1,250	$1,300	$1,400
$100 2016-W, Proof	9,151	$1,400	$1,550	$1,700
$100 2017	20,000	$1,250	$1,300	$1,400
$100 2017-W, Proof	8,890	$1,500	$1,650	$1,850
$100 2018	30,000	$1,250	$1,300	$1,400
$100 2018-W, Proof	14,499	$1,500	$1,650	$1,850
$100 2019	40,000	$1,250	$1,300	$1,400
$100 2019-W, Proof	10,928	$1,500	$1,650	$1,850
$100 2020		$1,250	$1,300	$1,400
$100 2020-W, Proof		$1,500	$1,650	$1,850
$100 2021		$1,250	$1,300	$1,400
$100 2021-W, Proof		$1,500	$1,650	$1,850

Note: MS values are for uncertified Mint State coins of average quality, in their complete original U.S. Mint packaging. PF values are for uncertified Proof coins of average quality, in their complete original U.S. Mint packaging. †† Ranked in the *100 Greatest U.S. Modern Coins* (fourth edition); all Proof 2007-W Platinum Eagles with Frosted FREEDOM, in all denominations, are listed as a single entry. **a.** Auction: $1,821, MS-69, July 2014. **b.** Auction: $1,704, MS-68, October 2012. **c.** Auction: $1,660, MS-69, November 2012. **d.** Auction: $1,645, PF69-UCam, March 2015. **e.** Auction: $1,553, MS-69, June 2012. **f.** Auction: $1,410, PF-70UCam, April 2015. **g.** Auction: $4,994, MS-69, April 2014. **h.** Auction: $1,645, MS-69, September 2012. **i.** Auction: $1,880, PF-70DCam, February 2015. **j.** Auction: $1,880, PF-70DCam, April 2015. **k.** Auction: $2,291, PF-70UCam, January 2015. **l.** Auction: $1,998, PF-70UCam, October 2015. **m.** Auction: $1,351, MS-69, November 2015. **n.** Auction: $1,880, MS-70, October 2015. **o.** Auction: $2,291, PF-70UCam, October 2015.

AMERICAN PLATINUM EAGLE BULLION COIN SETS

	MS	MS-69	MS-70		MS	MS-69	MS-70
1997 Platinum Set. $100, $50, $25, $10	$2,500	$2,750	—	2000 Platinum Set. $100, $50, $25, $10	$2,500	$2,750	—
1998 Platinum Set. $100, $50, $25, $10	$2,500	$2,750	—	2001 Platinum Set. $100, $50, $25, $10	$2,500	$2,750	—
1999 Platinum Set. $100, $50, $25, $10	$2,500	$2,750	—	2002 Platinum Set. $100, $50, $25, $10	$2,500	$2,750	—

Note: MS values are for uncertified Mint State sets of average quality, in their complete original U.S. Mint packaging.

	MS	MS-69	MS-70		MS	MS-69	MS-70
2003 Platinum Set. $100, $50, $25, $10	$2,500	$2,750	$5,700	2007 Platinum Set. $100, $50, $25, $10	$2,500	$2,750	$3,900
2004 Platinum Set. $100, $50, $25, $10	$2,500	$2,750	$4,450	2007-W Platinum Burnished Set. $100, $50, $25, $10	$3,700	$4,100	$5,000
2005 Platinum Set. $100, $50, $25, $10	$2,500	$2,750	$4,450				
2006 Platinum Set. $100, $50, $25, $10	$2,500	$2,750	$4,100	2008 Platinum Set. $100, $50, $25, $10	$2,500	$2,750	$3,800
2006-W Platinum Burnished Set. $100, $50, $25, $10	$3,800	$4,200	$4,900	2008-W Platinum Burnished Set. $100, $50, $25, $10	$3,900	$4,800	$7,000

Note: MS values are for uncertified Mint State sets of average quality, in their complete original U.S. Mint packaging.

AMERICAN PLATINUM EAGLE PROOF COIN SETS

	PF	PF-69	PF-70		PF	PF-69	PF-70
1997-W Platinum Set. $100, $50, $25, $10	$2,700	$3,000	$4,700	2003-W Platinum Set. $100, $50, $25, $10	$2,700	$3,100	$5,900
1998-W Platinum Set. $100, $50, $25, $10	$2,700	$3,000	$5,000	2004-W Platinum Set. $100, $50, $25, $10	$2,900	$4,600	$6,500
1999-W Platinum Set. $100, $50, $25, $10	$2,700	$3,100	$5,700	2005-W Platinum Set. $100, $50, $25, $10	$2,700	$4,300	$5,700
2000-W Platinum Set. $100, $50, $25, $10	$2,700	$3,100	$4,400	2006-W Platinum Set. $100, $50, $25, $10	$2,700	$3,000	$4,350
2001-W Platinum Set. $100, $50, $25, $10	$2,700	$3,100	$6,000	2007-W Platinum Set. $100, $50, $25, $10	$2,700	$3,000	$4,500
2002-W Platinum Set. $100, $50, $25, $10	$2,700	$3,100	$6,000	2008-W Platinum Set. $100, $50, $25, $10	$3,900	$4,500	$6,500

Note: PF values are for uncertified Proof sets of average quality, in their complete original U.S. Mint packaging. The Proof $100 American Platinum Eagle of 1997 is also included in the 1997 Impressions of Liberty set, listed on pages 1243 and 1253.

2007 AMERICAN PLATINUM EAGLE 10TH-ANNIVERSARY PROOF COIN SETS

	PF	PF-69	PF-70
2007 Two-Coin Set (a)	$1,800	$2,100	$2,500

a. This two-coin set, housed in a mahogany-finish hardwood box, includes one half-ounce Proof (with the standard cameo-finish background and frosted design elements) and one half-ounce Reverse Proof (with frosted background fields and mirrored raised elements) dated 2007-W.

AMERICAN PALLADIUM EAGLES
(2017 TO DATE)

Designer: *Adolph A. Weinman.* **Weight:** *31.120 grams (1 oz. pure palladium).* **Composition:** *.9995 palladium.* **Diameter:** *32.7 mm.* **Edge:** *Reeded.* **Mints:** *Philadelphia and West Point.*

A side view showing the coin's high relief.

History. In 2017 palladium was added to the U.S. Mint's American Eagle bullion programs, becoming the fourth precious metal in the lineup.

The American Palladium Bullion Act of 2010 (Public Law 111-303) required the secretary of the Treasury to mint and issue .9995 fine palladium bullion coins weighing one troy ounce and with a face value of $25, "in such quantities as the secretary determines appropriate to meet demand." Only coins in the one-ounce size are permitted; fractional sizes are not authorized. Title 31 U.S.C. Section 5112(v) authorizes the secretary to mint and issue Proof and Burnished ("Uncirculated") versions for collectors.

The American Palladium Eagle's designs were mandated by law. The obverse is a high-relief allegorical portrait derived from artist Adolph Weinman's Winged Liberty dime of 1916 to 1945. The reverse is a high-relief version of Weinman's 1907 American Institute of Architects gold medal reverse, showing an eagle grasping a branch. To develop the coin, the Mint was able to use the original reverse plaster of the AIA gold medal.

Although largely symbolic, the palladium coin's denomination of $25 provides proof of its authenticity as official U.S. coinage.

Bullion-strike coins are minted in Philadelphia on an annual basis, and distributed through the Mint's network of authorized purchasers. Proof and Reverse Proof numismatic versions struck at the West Point Mint are sold by the Mint directly to collectors.

Striking and Sharpness. Striking is generally sharp.

Availability. The American Palladium Eagle is a readily available bullion and collector coin. The coins are easily acquired in the numismatic marketplace and through some banks, investment firms, and other non-numismatic channels.

MS-60 to 70 (Mint State). *Obverse and Reverse:* Grading guidelines are more academic than practical for this program, since American Palladium Eagles are not intended for circulation, and nearly all are in high Mint State grades.

PF-60 to 70 (Proof). *Obverse and Reverse:* Impaired, cleaned, and otherwise low-level Proofs exist more in theory than in actuality for this series, as nearly all Proof American Palladium Eagle coins have been maintained in their original high condition by collectors. Given the quality of modern U.S. Mint products, even PF-66 or 67 would be unusually low for these Proofs.

	Mintage	Value
2017	15,000	$3,000
2018-W, Proof	14,986	$3,500
2019-W, Reverse Proof	18,115	$3,150
2020-W		$3,500
2021-W, Proof		$3,500

Significant U.S. Patterns

Pattern coins are a fascinating part of numismatics that encompass thousands of designs and experimental pieces made by the U.S. Mint to test new motifs, alloys, coin sizes, and other variables. Most were official creations—products of the research-and-development process that takes a coin from congressionally authorized concept to finished pocket change. Some were made in secret, outside the normal day-to-day work of the Mint. The book *United States Pattern Coins*, by J. Hewitt Judd, gives extensive details of the history and characteristics of more than 2,000 different pattern varieties from 1792 to the present era.

Patterns provide students and collectors a chronology of the continuing efforts of engravers and artists to present their work for approval. Throughout the 220-plus years of federal coinage production, concepts meant to improve various aspects of circulating coins have been proposed and given physical form in patterns. In some instances, changes have been prompted by an outcry for higher aesthetics, a call for a more convenient denomination, or a need to overcome striking deficiencies. In many other instances, workers or officials at the Mint simply created special coins for the numismatic trade—often controversial in their time, but enthusiastically collected today. Certain patterns, bearing particular proposed designs or innovations, provided tangible examples for Mint and Treasury Department officials or members of Congress to review and evaluate. If approved and adopted, the pattern design became a familiar regular-issue motif; those that were rejected have become part of American numismatic history.

The patterns listed and illustrated in this section are samples from a much larger group. Such pieces generally include die and hub trials, off-metal Proof strikings of regular issues, and various combinations of dies that were sometimes struck at a later date. Certain well-known members of this extended pattern family historically have been included with regular issues in many popular, general-circulation numismatic reference books. The four-dollar gold Stellas of 1879 and 1880; certain Gobrecht dollars of 1836, 1838, and 1839; the transitional half dimes and dimes of 1859 and 1860; and the Flying Eagle cents of 1856 are examples. No official mintage figures of patterns and related pieces were recorded in most instances, and the number extant of each can usually only be estimated from auction appearances and from those found in museum holdings and important private collections. Although most patterns are very rare, the 2,000-plus distinct varieties make them unexpectedly collectible—not by one of each, but by selected available examples from favorite types or categories. Curiously, the most common of all patterns is the highly sought and expensive 1856 Flying Eagle cent!

Unlike regular coin issues that were emitted through the usual channels of commerce, and Proofs of regular issues that were struck expressly for sale to collectors, patterns were not intended to be officially sold. Yet as a matter of Mint practice, often against stated policy and law, countless patterns were secretly and unofficially sold and traded to favorite dealers (most notably William K. Idler and his son-in-law John W. Haseltine) and collectors, disseminated to government officials, and occasionally made available to numismatic societies. Not until mid-1885 did an incoming new director of the Mint enforce stringent regulations prohibiting their sale and distribution, although there had been many misleading statements to this effect earlier. In succeeding decades the Mint, while not making patterns available to numismatists, did place certain examples in the Mint Collection, now called the National Numismatic Collection, in the Smithsonian Institution. On other occasions, selected patterns were obtained by Mint and Treasury officials, or otherwise spared from destruction. Today, with the exception of certain cents and five-cent pieces of 1896, all pattern coins dated after 1885 are extremely rare.

The private possession of patterns has not been without its controversy. Most significant was the 1910 seizure by government agents of a parcel containing some 23 pattern pieces belonging to John W. Haseltine, a leading Philadelphia coin dealer with undisclosed private ties to Mint officials. The government asserted that the patterns had been removed from the Mint without authority, and that they remained the property of the United States. Haseltine's attorney successfully used the Mint's pre-1887 policies in his defense, and recovered the patterns a year after their confiscation. This set precedent for ownership, at least for the patterns minted prior to 1887, as all of the pieces in question predated that year. Today pattern coins can be legally held, and, in fact, they were inadvertently made legal tender (as was the earlier demonetized silver trade dollar) by the Coinage Act of 1965.

Among the grandest impressions ever produced at the U.S. Mint are the two varieties of pattern fifty-dollar gold pieces of 1877. Officially titled half unions, these large patterns were created at the request of certain politicians with interests tied to the gold-producing state of California. Specimens were struck in copper, and one of each variety was struck in gold. Both of the gold pieces were purchased around 1908 by numismatist William H. Woodin (who, years later, in 1933, served as President Franklin D. Roosevelt's first secretary of the Treasury). The sellers were John W. Haseltine and Stephen K. Nagy, well known for handling many rarities that few others could obtain from the Mint. The Mint desired to re-obtain the pieces for its own collection, and through a complex trade deal for quantities of other patterns, did so, adding them to the Mint Collection. Now preserved in the Smithsonian Institution, these half unions are regarded as national treasures.

The following resources are recommended for additional information, descriptions, and complete listings:

> *United States Pattern Coins*, 10th edition, J. Hewitt Judd, edited by Q. David Bowers, 2009.
>
> *United States Patterns and Related Issues*, Andrew W. Pollock III, 1994. (Out of print)
>
> www.harrybassfoundation.org
>
> www.uspatterns.com

Judd-52

J-67

	PF-60	PF-63	PF-65
1836 Two-cent piece (J-52, billon) (a)	$3,000	$5,000	$8,500
Auctions: $8,625, PF-65, January 2009			
1836 Gold dollar (J-67, gold) (b)	$7,500	$12,500	$30,000
Auctions: $24,725, PF-65, November 2010			

a. This proposal for a two-cent coin is one of the earliest collectible patterns. It was designed by Christian Gobrecht. An estimated 21 to 30 examples are known. b. Gobrecht styled the first gold dollar pattern after the familiar "Cap and Rays" design used on Mexican coins, which at the time were legal tender in the United States. An estimated 31 to 75 pieces are known.

J-164   **J-177**

	PF-60	PF-63	PF-65
1854 Cent (J-164, bronze) (a)	$1,750	$3,500	$7,500
Auctions: $16,100, PF-67BN, March 2005			
1856 Half cent (J-177, copper-nickel) (b)	$2,500	$4,500	$5,500
Auctions: $6,038, PF-64, January 2006			

a. Beginning in 1850, the Mint produced patterns for a reduced-weight cent. Among the designs were ring-style, Liberty Head, and Flying Eagle motifs. These experiments culminated with the 1856 Flying Eagle cent. An estimated 31 to 75 examples of J-164 are known. Those with red mint luster are worth more than the values listed here. **b.** Before producing copper-nickel small-size cents in 1856, the Mint experimented with that alloy using half-cent dies. An estimated 31 to 75 examples are known.

J-204   **J-239**   **J-305**

	PF-60	PF-63	PF-65
1858 Cent (J-204, copper-nickel) (a)	$1,600	$2,500	$4,000
1859 Half dollar (J-239, silver) (b)	$1,500	$2,000	$3,750
1863 Washington two-cent piece (J-305, copper) (c)	$1,500	$2,250	$4,000

a. This pattern cent's flying eagle differs from the one adopted for regular coinage of the one-cent piece. An estimated 31 to 75 pieces are known. **b.** This design proposal for a new half dollar features James Longacre's French Liberty Head design. An estimated 76 to 200 pieces are known. **a.** Before the two-cent coin was introduced to circulation, two basic designs were considered. If this George Washington portrait design had been adopted, it would have been the first to depict a historical figure. An estimated 76 to 200 pieces are known.

J-349   **J-407**   **J-470**

	PF-60	PF-63	PF-65
1863 Eagle (J-349, gold) (a)		$450,000	
1865 Bimetallic two-cent piece (J-407, silver and copper) (b)	$6,000	$11,000	$19,500
1866 Five-cent piece (J-470, nickel) (c)	$1,650	$2,500	$4,500

a. This unique gold eagle features IN GOD WE TRUST on a scroll on the reverse. This feature would not appear on regular eagle coinage until 1866. The obverse is from the regular 1863 die. **b.** This experimental piece is the first "clad" coin. It consists of an irregular and streaky layer of silver fused to copper. The experiment was unsuccessful. An estimated 4 to 6 pieces are known.
c. Another of George Washington's early pattern appearances was on five-cent pieces of 1866. An estimated 21 to 30 are known.

J-486   **J-611**

	PF-60	PF-63	PF-65
1866 Lincoln five-cent piece (J-486, nickel) (a)	$5,000	$11,000	$25,000
1868 Cent (J-611, copper) (b)	$17,500	$30,000	$36,000
Auctions: $36,800, PF-66BN, March 2005			

a. A number of pattern nickels were produced in 1866, including one designed to depict the recently assassinated President Abraham Lincoln. An estimated 7 to 12 examples are known. **b.** There is no known reason for the minting of this unusual piece, which mimics the original large cents that had last been made in 1857. There was no intent to resume the coinage of old-style copper "large" cents in 1868. Accordingly, this variety is regarded as a rarity created for collectors. Fewer than 15 examples are believed to exist.

J-1195   **J-1235**

	PF-60	PF-63	PF-65
1872 Amazonian quarter (J-1195, silver) (a)	$17,500	$30,000	$65,000
Auctions: $80,500, PF-66Cam, January 2009			
1872 Amazonian gold $3 (J-1235, gold) † (b)	—	—	$1,250,000

† All 1872 Amazonian Gold Patterns are ranked in the *100 Greatest U.S. Coins* (fifth edition), as a single entry. **a.** Many of the most popular patterns have been given colorful nicknames by collectors in appreciation of their artistry. This design is by Chief Engraver William Barber. An estimated 7 to 12 examples are known. **b.** This unique piece was contained in the Mint's only uniform gold set using the same design from the gold dollar to the double eagle.

J-1373

	PF-60	PF-63	PF-65
1874 Bickford eagle (J-1373, gold) † (a)	—	$550,000	$1,500,000

† Ranked in the *100 Greatest U.S. Coins* (fifth edition). **a.** Dana Bickford, a New York City manufacturer, proposed a ten-dollar gold coin that would be exchangeable at set rates with other world currencies. Patterns were made, but the idea proved impractical. 2 examples are known.

	PF-60	PF-63	PF-65
1877 Morgan half dollar (J-1507, copper) (a)	$18,000	$29,000	$50,000
1877 Morgan half dollar (J-1512, silver) (b)	$15,000	$28,000	$45,000
1877 Half dollar (J-1528, silver) (c)	$17,000	$33,000	$50,000

a. A year before his famous and eponymous dollar design was adopted for regular coinage, engraver George Morgan's Liberty Head appeared on several varieties of pattern half dollars, all of which are rare today. J-1507 pairs the well-known obverse with an indented shield design. 2 examples are known. b. The half dollar pattern cataloged as J-1512 pairs Morgan's "silver dollar style" obverse with a dramatic "Defiant Eagle" reverse. 6 examples are known. c. This is one of several 1877 pattern half dollars by Chief Engraver William Barber. 4 are known.

J-1549

	PF-60	PF-63	PF-65
1877 Half union (J-1549, copper) (a)	$115,000	$215,000	$350,000
Auctions: $575,000, PF-67BN, January 2009			

a. This famous fifty-dollar pattern by Chief Engraver William Barber would have been the highest denomination ever issued by the Mint up to that time. The gold impression (J-1548) is unique and resides in the Smithsonian's National Numismatic Collection, but copper specimens (J-1549, which are priced here and are sometimes gilt) occasionally come to the market. Varieties exist with a somewhat larger or smaller head. The gold impression is ranked in the *100 Greatest U.S. Coins* (fifth edition).

J-1590

	PF-60	PF-63	PF-65
1879 Quarter dollar (J-1590, silver) (a)	$4,500	$8,000	$16,500
Auctions: $34,500, PF-68, January 2007			

a. Referred to as the "Washlady" design, this was Charles Barber's first attempt at a uniform silver design. An estimated 13 to 20 examples are known.

J-1609

	PF-60	PF-63	PF-65
1879 Dollar (J-1609, copper) (a)	$12,500	$17,500	$45,000
Auctions: $74,750, PF-66RB, September 2006			

a. The "Schoolgirl" design by George T. Morgan is a widespread favorite among pattern collectors. Examples are rare, with only 7 to 12 known.

J-1643

	PF-60	PF-63	PF-65
1879 Metric double eagle (J-1643, gold) (a)	$325,000	$600,000	$1,000,000

a. James Longacre's Liberty Head design was the same as that used on regular-issue double eagles, but with an added inscription indicating the coin's specifications in metric units. 5 are known.

J-1667   **J-1669**   **J-1673**

	PF-60	PF-63	PF-65
1881 One-cent piece (J-1667, aluminum) (a)	$2,025	$3,780	$6,440
1881 Three-cent piece (J-1669, copper) (a)	$2,000	$3,750	$6,000
1881 Five-cent piece (J-1673, aluminum) (a)	$2,300	$4,800	$9,000

a. These patterns by Chief Engraver Charles Barber represent an attempt at a uniform set of minor coins; if adopted, they would have been struck in nickel for circulation. An estimated 7 to 20 examples are known of each of the illustrated patterns.

J-1698

	PF-60	PF-63	PF-65
1882 Quarter dollar (J-1698, silver) (a)	$17,500	$34,000	$55,000

a. George Morgan's "Shield Earring" design was made in patterns of quarter, half, and dollar denominations. 7 to 12 of the quarter dollar patterns are known.

J-1761　　　　　　　　　　　J-1770

	PF-60	PF-63	PF-65
1891 Barber quarter (J-1761, silver) (a)	—	—	—
1896 Shield nickel (J-1770, nickel) (b)	$1,500	$2,750	$4,000

a. Charles Barber prepared various pattern dimes, quarters, and half dollars in 1891. The quarter illustrated is similar to the design adopted for regular coinage in 1892. Two pieces are known, both in the Smithsonian's National Numismatic Collection. b. In 1896 the Mint struck experimental cents and nickels with similar designs, by Charles Barber. 21 to 30 examples of J-1770 are known.

J-1905

	PF-60	PF-63	PF-65
MCMVII (1907) Indian Head double eagle (J-1905, gold) † (a)			$15,000,000

† Ranked in the *100 Greatest U.S. Coins* (fifth edition). a. Designed by Augustus Saint-Gaudens, this pattern is unique and extremely valuable. A variation of the reverse of this design was used on the double eagles struck for circulation from 1907 through 1933.

J-1992

	PF-60	PF-63	PF-65
1916 Liberty Walking half dollar (J-1992, silver) (a)	$25,000	$50,000	$100,000
Auctions: $115,000, PF-65, July 2008			

a. Various pattern Mercury dimes, Standing Liberty quarters, and Liberty Walking half dollars were struck, all dated 1916. All are extremely rare, but a few found their way into circulation.

J-2063

	PF-60	PF-63	PF-65
1942 Experimental cent (J-2051 through J-2069, several metallic and other compositions) (a)	$1,500	$2,750	$4,500

a. Before settling on the zinc-coated steel composition used for the Lincoln cents of 1943, the Mint considered various alternative compositions, including plastics. Most were struck by outside contractors using specially prepared dies provided by the Mint. An estimated 7 to 12 examples are known of most types and colors.

Private and Territorial Gold

The expression *private gold*, used with reference to coins struck outside the United States Mint, is a general term. In the sense that no state or territory had authority to coin money, *private gold* simply refers to those necessity pieces of various shapes, denominations, and degrees of intrinsic worth that were coined by facilities other than official U.S. mints and circulated in isolated areas of the United States by assayers, bankers, and other private individuals and organizations. Some numismatists use the terms *territorial gold* and *state gold* to cover certain issues because they were coined and circulated in a territory or state. While the state of California properly sanctioned the ingots stamped by F.D. Kohler as state assayer, in no instance (except for the Mormon issues of Salt Lake City) were any of the gold pieces struck by authority of any of the territorial governments.

The stamped fifty-dollar and other gold coins, sometimes called *ingots*, but in coin form, were made by Augustus Humbert, the United States Assayer of Gold, but were not receivable at face value for government payments, despite the fact that Humbert was an official agent selected by the Treasury Department. However, such pieces circulated widely in commerce.

Usually, private coins were circulated due to a shortage of regular federal coinage. In the Western states particularly, official money became so scarce that gold itself—the very commodity the pioneers had come so far to acquire—was converted into a local medium of exchange.

Ephraim Brasher's New York doubloons of 1786 and 1787 are also private American gold issues and are described on pages 154–155.

TEMPLETON REID

GEORGIA GOLD, 1830

The first private gold coinage in the 19th century was struck by Templeton Reid, a jeweler and gunsmith, in Milledgeville, Georgia, in July 1830. To be closer to the mines he moved some 120 miles northwest to Gainesville, where most of his coins were made. Although their weights were accurate, Reid's assays were not and his coins were slightly short of their claimed value. He was severely attacked in the newspapers by a determined adversary, and soon lost the public's confidence. He closed his mint before the end of October in 1830; his output had amounted to only about 1,600 coins. Denominations struck were $2.50, $5, and $10. All are great rarities today.

	VF	EF	AU	Unc.
1830 $2.50	$160,000	$220,000	$350,000	$450,000
1830 $5 (a)	$400,000	$575,000	$725,000	

a. 7 examples are known.

	VF	EF
1830 TEN DOLLARS (a)	$700,000	$975,000
(No Date) TEN DOLLARS (b)	—	

a. 6 examples are known. **b.** 3 examples are known.

CALIFORNIA GOLD, 1849

The enigmatic later issues of Templeton Reid, dated 1849 and marked CALIFORNIA GOLD, were probably made from California gold late in that year when bullion from California arrived in quantity in the East. Reid, who never went to California, was by then a cotton-gin maker in Columbus, Georgia (some 160 miles southwest of his former location of Gainesville), where he would die in 1851. The coins were in denominations of ten and twenty-five dollars. Struck copies of both exist in various metals.

The only example known of the twenty-five–dollar piece was stolen from the cabinet of the U.S. Mint on August 16, 1858. It was never recovered.

1849 TEN DOLLAR CALIFORNIA GOLD	*(unique, in Smithsonian collection)*
1849 TWENTY-FIVE DOLLARS CALIFORNIA GOLD	*(unknown)*

THE BECHTLERS, RUTHERFORD COUNTY, NORTH CAROLINA, 1831–1852

A skilled German metallurgist, Christopher Bechtler, assisted by his son August and his nephew, also named Christopher, operated a private mint in Rutherford County, North Carolina. Rutherford County and other areas in the Piedmont region of North Carolina and Georgia (from the coastal plain to the mountains of north Georgia) were the principal sources of the nation's gold supply from the early 1800s until the California gold strikes in 1848.

The coins minted by the Bechtlers were of only three denominations, but they covered a wide variety of weights and sizes. Rotated dies are common throughout the series. In 1831, the Bechtlers produced the first gold dollar in the United States. (The Philadelphia Mint made patterns in 1836 and struck its first circulating gold dollar in 1849.) Bechtler coins were well accepted by the public and circulated widely in the Southeast without interference from the government.

The legend AUGUST 1. 1834 on several varieties of five-dollar pieces has a special significance. The secretary of the Treasury recommended to the director of the U.S. Mint that gold coins of the reduced weight introduced in 1834 bear the authorization date. This ultimately was not done on federal gold coinage, but the elder Christopher Bechtler evidently acted on the recommendation to avoid potential difficulty with Treasury authorities.

CHRISTOPHER BECHTLER

	VF	EF	AU	Unc.
ONE GOLD DOLLAR N. CAROLINA, 30.G., Star	$3,000	$4,500	$7,000	$15,000
ONE GOLD DOLLAR N. CAROLINA, 28.G Centered, No Star	$5,000	$6,000	$11,500	$26,000
ONE GOLD DOLLAR N. CAROLINA, 28.G High, No Star	$9,000	$15,000	$23,000	$35,000

	VF	EF	AU	Unc.
ONE DOLLAR CAROLINA, 28.G, N Reversed	$2,600	$3,200	$4,750	$8,250
2.50 NORTH CAROLINA, 20 C. Without 75 G.	$28,000	$38,500	$57,500	$120,000

	VF	EF	AU	Unc.
2.50 NORTH CAROLINA, 75 G., 20 C. RUTHERFORD in a Circle. Border of Large Beads	$26,000	$36,000	$52,500	$115,000
2.50 NORTH CAROLINA, 20 C. Without 75 G., CAROLINA above 250 instead of GOLD (a)				—
2.50 NORTH CAROLINA, 20 C. on Obverse, 75 G. and Star on Reverse. Border Finely Serrated	—	—	—	

a. This piece is unique.

	VF	EF	AU	Unc.
2.50 CAROLINA, 67 G., 21 CARATS	$8,750	$12,500	$17,000	$33,000
2.50 GEORGIA, 64 G., 22 CARATS (Uneven "22")	$7,500	$12,500	$16,500	$32,000
2.50 GEORGIA, 64 G., 22 CARATS (Even "22")	$9,000	$15,000	$20,000	$40,000
2.50 CAROLINA, 70 G., 20 CARATS	$7,500	$12,500	$16,500	$32,000

	VF	EF	AU	Unc.
5 DOLLARS NORTH CAROLINA GOLD, 150 G., 20.CARATS	$28,000	$40,000	$72,000	$120,000
Similar, Without 150.G. (a)		—	—	

a. 1 or 2 examples are known.

CHRISTOPHER BECHTLER, CAROLINA

	VF	EF	AU	Unc.	PF
5 DOLLARS CAROLINA, RUTHERFORD, 140 G., 20 CARATS, Plain Edge	$6,000	$8,500	$12,500	$26,000	
5 DOLLARS CAROLINA, RUTHERFORD, 140 G., 20 CARATS, Reeded Edge	$20,000	$30,000	$45,000	$70,000	
5 DOLLARS CAROLINA GOLD, RUTHERF., 140 G., 20 CARATS, AUGUST 1, 1834	$11,000	$18,000	$30,000	$50,000	
Similar, but "20" Distant From CARATS	$6,500	$10,000	$15,000	$27,500	
5 DOLLARS CAROLINA GOLD, 134 G., 21 CARATS, With Star	$6,000	$8,000	$12,000	$24,000	
5 DOLLARS CAROLINA GOLD, 134 G., 21 CARATS, Restrike					$32,500

CHRISTOPHER BECHTLER, GEORGIA

	VF	EF	AU	Unc.
5 DOLLARS GEORGIA GOLD, RUTHERFORD, 128 G., 22 CARATS	$8,500	$12,000	$16,500	$33,000
5 DOLLARS GEORGIA GOLD, RUTHERFORD, 128 G:, 22 CARATS, With Colon After G	$16,000	$26,000	$38,500	
5 DOLLARS GEORGIA GOLD, RUTHERF., 128 G., 22 CARATS	$8,000	$11,500	$15,000	$32,000

AUGUST BECHTLER, CAROLINA

	VF	EF	AU	Unc.	PF
5 DOLLARS, CAROLINA GOLD, 128.G., 22 CARATS	$1,900	$2,500	$3,350	$5,500	
5 DOLLARS, CAROLINA GOLD, 141.G., 20 CARATS	$6,000	$8,750	$15,000	$36,000	
5 DOLLARS, CAROLINA GOLD, 134 G:, 21 CARATS, Reverse of C. Bechtler as Shown Above	—	—			
Same as above, Restrike					$32,500

	VF	EF	AU	Unc.	Proof
5 DOLLARS, CAROLINA GOLD, 128.G., 22 CARATS	$15,000	$18,000	$27,500	$45,000	
5 DOLLARS, CAROLINA GOLD, 141.G., 20 CARATS	$12,500	$17,000	$25,000	$40,000	
5 DOLLARS, CAROLINA GOLD, 141.G., 20 CARATS, Restrike					$35,000

Note: Restrikes in "Proof" of this type using original dies were made about 1920.

NORRIS, GREGG & NORRIS, SAN FRANCISCO, 1849

Collectors consider this piece the first of the California private gold coins. A newspaper account dated May 31, 1849, described a five-dollar gold coin, struck at Benicia City, though with the imprint of San Francisco. It mentioned the private stamp of Norris, Gregg & Norris, the California branch of a New York City plumbing and hardware firm.

	F	VF	EF	AU	Unc.
1849 Half Eagle, Plain Edge	$5,000	$7,000	$12,000	$17,000	$37,000
1849 Half Eagle, Reeded Edge	$5,000	$7,000	$12,000	$17,000	$37,000
1850 Half Eagle, With STOCKTON Beneath Date (a)		—			

a. This unique piece is housed in the Smithsonian's National Numismatic Collection.

MOFFAT & CO., SAN FRANCISCO, 1849–1853

The firm of Moffat & Co. (principals John Little Moffat, Joseph R. Curtis, Philo H. Perry, and Samuel H. Ward) was the most important of the California private coiners. The assay office they conducted became semi-official in character starting in 1851. The successors to this firm, Curtis, Perry, and Ward, later sold their coining facility to the Treasury Department, which in March 1854 reopened it as the branch mint of San Francisco.

In June or July 1849, Moffat & Co. began to issue small, rectangular ingots of gold in response to lack of coin in the locality, in values from $9.43 to $264. The $9.43, $14.25, and $16.00 varieties are the only types known today.

$9.43 Ingot (a)	—
$14.25 Ingot (a)	—
$16.00 Ingot	$235,000

a. This unique piece is housed in the Smithsonian's National Numismatic Collection.

The dies for the five-dollar and ten-dollar Moffat & Co. pieces were cut by a Bavarian engraver, Albrecht Küner, who had moved to the United States in October 1848. On the coronet of Miss Liberty appear the words MOFFAT & CO., instead of the word LIBERTY as in regular U.S. issues.

	F	VF	EF	AU	Unc.
1849 FIVE DOL. (a)	$2,300	$3,300	$4,700	$7,000	$15,000
1850 FIVE DOL. (a)	$2,300	$3,500	$5,000	$7,500	$17,500
1849 TEN DOL.	$4,000	$6,500	$12,500	$22,500	$38,000
1849 TEN D.	$5,000	$7,000	$13,500	$25,000	$45,000

a. Multiple varieties exist.

UNITED STATES ASSAY OFFICE

Augustus Humbert, United States Assayer of Gold, 1851

Augustus Humbert, a New York watchcase maker, was appointed United States assayer by the Treasury Department in 1850 and arrived in California in early 1851. He placed his name and the government stamp on the ingots of gold issued by Moffat & Co., but without the Moffat imprint. The assay office, a provisional government mint, was a temporary expedient to accommodate the Californians until the establishment of a permanent federal branch mint.

The fifty-dollar gold piece was accepted by most banks and merchants as legal tender on a par with standard U.S. gold coins and was known variously as a *slug*, *quintuple eagle*, *five-eagle piece*, or *adobe* (the latter a type of construction brick). It was officially termed an *ingot*.

Lettered-Edge Varieties

	F	VF	EF	AU	Unc.
1851 50 D C 880 THOUS., No 50 on Reverse. Sunk in Edge: AUGUSTUS HUMBERT UNITED STATES ASSAYER OF GOLD, CALIFORNIA 1851 †	$26,500	$40,000	$60,000	$90,000	$200,000
Auctions: $546,250, MS-63, August 2010					
1851 50 D C 880 THOUS., Similar to Last Variety, but 50 on Reverse †	$50,000	$60,000	$90,000	$160,000	$300,000
1851 50 D C, 887 THOUS., With 50 on Reverse †	$35,000	$50,000	$75,000	$115,000	$250,000

† All U.S. Assay Office $50 Gold Slugs are ranked in the *100 Greatest U.S. Coins* (fifth edition), as a single entry.

Reeded-Edge Varieties

	F	VF	EF	AU	Unc.
1851 FIFTY DOLLS, 880 THOUS., "Target" Reverse †	$17,500	$27,500	$40,000	$55,000	$150,000
Auctions: $460,000, MS-65, September 2008					
1851 FIFTY DOLLS, 887 THOUS., "Target" Reverse †	$17,500	$27,500	$40,000	$55,000	$150,000
1852 FIFTY DOLLS, 887 THOUS., "Target" Reverse †	$18,500	$30,000	$50,000	$95,000	$200,000

† All U.S. Assay Office $50 Gold Slugs are ranked in the *100 Greatest U.S. Coins* (fifth edition), as a single entry.

MOFFAT-HUMBERT

In 1851, certain issues of the Miners' Bank, Baldwin, Pacific Company, and others were discredited, some unfairly, by newspaper accounts stating they were of reduced gold value. This provided an enhanced opportunity for Moffat and the U.S. Assay Office of Gold. Supplementing privately struck gold pieces and federal issues, coins of almost every nation were being pressed into service by the Californians, but the supply was too small to help to any extent. Moffat & Co. proceeded in January 1852 to issue a new ten-dollar gold piece bearing the stamp MOFFAT & CO.

Close Date   **Wide Date**

	F	VF	EF	AU	Unc.
1852 TEN D. MOFFAT & CO., Close Date	$4,200	$7,000	$25,000	$65,000	
1852 TEN D. MOFFAT & CO., Wide Date	$4,200	$7,000	$15,000	$35,000	$77,500
Auctions: $940,000, SP-63, January 2014					

1852, Normal Date   **1852, 2 Over 1**

	F	VF	EF	AU	Unc.
1852 TEN DOLS.	$3,000	$4,250	$7,500	$12,000	$27,500
Auctions: $1,057,500, MS-68, April 2013					
1852 TEN DOLS. 1852, 2 Over 1	$3,250	$5,250	$9,500	$20,000	$50,000

	F	VF	EF	AU	Unc.
1852 TWENTY DOLS., 1852, 2 Over 1	$9,000	$15,000	$27,500	$45,000	$140,000
Auctions: $211,500, MS-64, April 2014					

UNITED STATES ASSAY OFFICE OF GOLD, 1852

The firm of Moffat & Co. was dissolved in 1852 and a newly reorganized company known as the United States Assay Office of Gold took over the contract. Principals in the firm were Joseph Curtis, Philo Perry, and Samuel Ward.

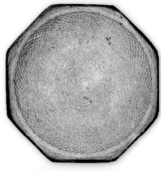

	F	VF	EF	AU	Unc.
1852 FIFTY DOLLS., 887 THOUS.	$17,500	$25,000	$40,000	$65,000	$150,000
1852 FIFTY DOLLS., 900 THOUS.	$18,500	$27,000	$42,000	$55,000	$125,000

	F	VF	EF	AU	Unc.
1852 TEN DOLS., 884 THOUS.	$2,750	$3,500	$5,500	$10,000	$22,500
1853 TEN D., 884 THOUS.	$10,000	$20,000	$30,000	$45,000	$125,000
1853 TEN D., 900 THOUS.	$4,500	$6,500	$10,000	$16,000	$25,000

	F	VF	EF	AU	Unc.
1853 TWENTY D., 884 THOUS.	$7,800	$11,500	$19,000	$32,000	$75,000

	F	VF	EF	AU	Unc.
1853 TWENTY D., 900 THOUS.	$2,500	$3,500	$5,000	$8,000	$13,000

Note: Modern prooflike forgeries exist.

MOFFAT & CO. GOLD, 1853

The last Moffat & Co. issue, an 1853 twenty-dollar piece, is very similar to the U.S. double eagle of that period. It was struck after John L. Moffat retired from the Assay Office. The circumstances of its issue are unclear, but many were coined.

	F	VF	EF	AU	Unc.
1853 TWENTY D.	$5,000	$7,250	$12,500	$20,000	$65,000

J.H. BOWIE, 1849

Joseph H. Bowie joined his cousins in San Francisco in 1849 and possibly produced a limited coinage of gold pieces. A trial piece of the dollar denomination is known in copper, but may never have reached the coinage stage. Little is known about the company or the reason for considering these pieces.

1849 1 DOL., copper pattern	—

CINCINNATI MINING & TRADING CO., 1849

The origin and location of this company are unknown.

	EF	Unc.
1849 FIVE DOLLARS (a)		
1849 TEN DOLLARS (b)	$825,000	—

Note: Beware of spurious specimens cast in base metal with the word TRACING in place of TRADING. **a.** This piece is unique. **b.** 5 examples are known.

MASSACHUSETTS AND CALIFORNIA COMPANY, 1849

This company was organized in Northampton, Massachusetts, in May 1849. Years later fantasy and copy dies were made and coins struck in various metals including gold. Pieces with the denomination spelled as 5D are not genuine.

	VF	EF
1849 FIVE D. (a)	$325,000	$475,000

a. 2 to 3 examples are known.

MINERS' BANK, SAN FRANCISCO, 1849

The institution of Wright & Co., exchange brokers located in Portsmouth Square, San Francisco, was known as the Miners' Bank. The firm issued a ten-dollar gold piece in the autumn of 1849, and it saw wide use in commerce. However, the firm's coinage was ephemeral, and it was dissolved on January 14, 1850. Unlike the gold in most California issues, the gold in these coins was alloyed with copper.

	VF	EF	AU	Unc.
(1849) TEN D.	$25,000	$35,000	$50,000	$110,000

J.S. ORMSBY, SACRAMENTO, 1849

The initials J.S.O., which appear on certain issues of California privately coined gold pieces, represent the firm of J.S. Ormsby & Co., located in Sacramento. They struck five- and ten-dollar denominations, all undated.

	VF
(1849) 5 DOLLS, Plain Edge (a)	—
(1849) 5 DOLLS, Reeded Edge (b)	—
(1849) 10 DOLLS (c)	$675,000

a. This piece may be unique. **b.** This unique piece is housed in the Smithsonian's National Numismatic Collection. **c.** 5 examples are known.

PACIFIC COMPANY, SAN FRANCISCO, 1849

The origin of the Pacific Company is very uncertain. All data regarding the firm are based on conjecture.

Edgar H. Adams wrote that he believed that the coins bearing the stamp of the Pacific Company were produced by the coining firm of Broderick and Kohler. The coins were probably hand struck with the aid of a sledgehammer. Trial pieces exist in silver. All are rarities today.

	EF	AU	Unc.
1849 1 DOLLAR (a)			$300,000
1849 5 DOLLARS (b)	$550,000	$775,000	
Auctions: $763,750, AU-58, April 2014			
1849 10 DOLLARS (b)			$1,000,000

a. 2 examples are known. **b.** 4 examples are known.

F.D. KOHLER, CALIFORNIA STATE ASSAYER, 1850

The State Assay Office was authorized on April 12, 1850. That year, Governor Peter Burnett appointed to the position of state assayer Frederick D. Kohler, who thereupon sold his assaying business to Baldwin & Co. Kohler served at both the San Francisco and Sacramento offices. The State Assay Offices were discontinued at the time the U.S. Assay Office was established, on February 1, 1851.

Ingots issued ranged from $36.55 to $150. An Extremely Fine specimen sold in the Garrett Sale, 1980, for $200,000. Each is unique.

$36.55 Sacramento	—
$37.31 San Francisco	—
$40.07 San Francisco	—
$45.34 San Francisco	—
$50.00 San Francisco	—
$54.00 San Francisco	—

Note: A $40.07 ingot was stolen from the Mint Cabinet in 1858 and never recovered.

DUBOSQ & COMPANY, SAN FRANCISCO, 1850

Theodore Dubosq Sr., a Philadelphia jeweler, took melting and coining equipment to San Francisco in 1849 and minted five-dollar gold pieces.

	VF
1850 FIVE D. (a)	—
1850 TEN D. (b)	$325,000
Auctions: $329,000, MS-60, April 2014	

a. 3 to 5 examples are known. **b.** 8 to 10 examples are known.

BALDWIN & CO., SAN FRANCISCO, 1850–1851

George C. Baldwin and Thomas S. Holman were in the jewelry business in San Francisco and were known as Baldwin & Co. They were the successors to F.D. Kohler & Co., taking over its machinery and other equipment in May 1850. The firm ceased minting coins in early 1851, at which time newspaper accounts stated that its coins fell short of their stated gold value. The 1850 Vaquero or Horseman ten-dollar design is one of the most famous of the California gold issues.

The Baldwin & Co. twenty-dollar piece was the first of that denomination issued in California. Baldwin coins are believed to have contained about 2% copper alloy.

	F	VF	EF	AU	Unc.
1850, FIVE DOL.	$7,500	$13,000	$25,000	$35,000	$75,000
1850 TEN DOLLARS, Horseman Type	$50,000	$80,000	$125,000	$175,000	$350,000

	F	VF	EF	AU	Unc.
1851 TEN D.	$16,000	$34,000	$50,000	$85,000	$225,000
1851 TWENTY D. (a)			$650,000		—
		Auctions: $646,250, EF-45, April 2014			

a. 4 to 6 examples are known.

SCHULTZ & COMPANY, SAN FRANCISCO, 1851

The firm of Schultz & Co., a brass foundry, was operated by Judge G.W. Schultz and William T. Garratt. The surname is misspelled as SHULTZ on the coins.

	F	VF	EF	AU	Unc.
1851 FIVE D.	—	$80,000	$130,000	$235,000	$350,000

DUNBAR & COMPANY, SAN FRANCISCO, 1851

Edward E. Dunbar operated the California Bank in San Francisco. He later returned to New York City and organized the famous Continental Bank Note Co.

	VF	EF	Unc.
1851 FIVE D. (a)	$425,000	$575,000	$750,000

a. 4 to 6 examples are known.

WASS, MOLITOR & CO., SAN FRANCISCO, 1852–1855

The gold-smelting and assaying plant of Wass, Molitor & Co. was operated by two Hungarian patriots exiled after the Revolution of 1848, Count Samu Wass and A.P. Molitor. They maintained an excellent laboratory and complete apparatus for analysis and coinage of gold.

The company struck five-, ten-, twenty-, and fifty-dollar coins. In 1852 they produced a ten-dollar piece similar in design to the five-dollar denomination. The difference is in the reverse legend, which reads: S.M.V. [Standard Mint Value] CALIFORNIA GOLD TEN D.

No pieces were coined in 1853 or 1854, but they brought out the twenty- and fifty-dollar pieces in 1855. A considerable number of the fifty-dollar coins were made. There was a ten-dollar piece issued in 1855 also, with the Liberty Head design and small close date.

Small Head, Rounded Bust

Large Head, Pointed Bust

	F	VF	EF	AU	Unc.
1852 FIVE DOLLARS, Small Head, With Rounded Bust	$5,500	$11,000	$22,500	$40,000	$80,000
1852 FIVE DOLLARS, Large Head, With Pointed Bust	$5,000	$10,000	$20,000	$36,000	$70,000

Large Head		**Small Head**		**Small Date**		**1855**

	F	VF	EF	AU	Unc.
1852 TEN D., Large Head	$2,750	$4,750	$8,250	$14,500	$32,500
1852 TEN D., Small Head	$6,200	$8,000	$19,000	$32,000	$80,000
1852 TEN D., Small Close Date	$12,500	$28,000	$47,000	$90,000	
1855 TEN D.	$9,500	$16,000	$22,000	$29,000	$52,500

Large Head   **Small Head**

	F	VF	EF	AU	Unc.
1855 TWENTY DOL., Large Head (a)	—	—	$550,000	$675,000	—
Auctions: $558,125, AU-53, April 2014					
1855 TWENTY DOL., Small Head	$13,500	$25,000	$35,000	$75,000	$165,000

a. 4 to 6 examples are known. A unique piece with the Large Head obverse and the reverse used on the Small Head coins (which differs in the position of the eagle's left wing) also exists.

	F	VF	EF	AU	Unc.
1855 50 DOLLARS	$27,500	$40,000	$60,000	$90,000	$180,000

KELLOGG & CO., SAN FRANCISCO, 1854–1855

John G. Kellogg went to San Francisco on October 12, 1849, from Auburn, New York. At first he was employed by Moffat & Co., and remained with that organization when control passed to Curtis, Perry, and Ward. When the U.S. Assay Office was discontinued, December 14, 1853, Kellogg became associated with George F. Richter, who had been an assayer in the U.S. Assay Office of Gold. These two set up business as Kellogg & Richter on December 19, 1853.

When the U.S. Assay Office ceased operations, a period ensued during which no private firm was striking gold. The new San Francisco branch mint did not produce coins for some months after Curtis & Perry took the contract for the government (Ward having died). The lack of coin was again keenly felt by businessmen, who petitioned Kellogg & Richter to "supply the vacuum" by issuing private coin. Their plea was soon answered: on February 9, 1854, Kellogg & Co. placed their first twenty-dollar piece in circulation.

The firm dissolved late in 1854 and reorganized as Kellogg & Humbert. The latter partner was Augustus Humbert, for some time identified as U.S. assayer of gold in California. Regardless of the fact that the San Francisco branch mint was then producing coins, Kellogg & Humbert issued twenty-dollar coins in 1855 in a quantity greater than before. On September 12, 1857, hundreds of the firm's rectangular gold ingots in transit to New York City were lost in the sinking of the SS *Central America*. They were the most plentiful of bars aboard the ill-fated ship from several different assayers.

The 1855 Kellogg & Co. twenty-dollar piece is similar to that of 1854. The letters on the reverse are larger and the arrows longer on one 1854 variety. There are die varieties of both.

	F	VF	EF	AU	Unc.
1854 TWENTY D.	$3,500	$5,000	$6,500	$10,000	$25,000
1855 TWENTY D.	$3,750	$5,250	$7,000	$12,000	$27,500

In 1855, Ferdinand Grüner cut the dies for a round-format fifty-dollar gold coin for Kellogg & Co., but coinage seems to have been limited to presentation pieces in Proof format. Only 10 to 12 pieces are known to exist. A "commemorative restrike" was made in 2001 using transfer dies made from the original and gold recovered from the SS *Central America*. These pieces have the inscription S.S. CENTRAL AMERICA GOLD, C.H.S. on the reverse ribbon.

	PF
1855 FIFTY DOLLS. (a)	$600,000
Auctions: $763,750, PF-64Cam, April 2014; $747,500, PF-64, January 2007	

a. 13 to 15 examples are known.

OREGON EXCHANGE COMPANY, OREGON CITY, 1849
THE BEAVER COINS OF OREGON

Upon the discovery of gold in California, a great exodus of Oregonians joined in the hunt for the precious metal. Soon, gold seekers returned with their gold dust, which became an accepted medium of exchange. As in other Western areas at that time, the uncertain qualities of the gold and weighing devices tended to irk tradespeople, and petitions were made to the legislature for a standard gold coin issue.

On February 16, 1849, the territorial legislature passed an act providing for a mint and specified five- and ten-dollar gold coins without alloy. Oregon City, the largest city in the territory with a population of about 1,000, was designated as the location for the mint. At the time this act was passed, Oregon had been brought into the United States as a territory by act of Congress. When the new governor arrived on March 2, he declared the coinage act unconstitutional.

The public-spirited people, however, continued to work for a convenient medium of exchange and soon took matters into their own hands by starting a private mint. Eight men of affairs, whose names were Kilborne, Magruder, Taylor, Abernethy, Willson, Rector, Campbell, and Smith, set up the Oregon Exchange Company.

The coins struck were of virgin gold as specified in the original act. Ten-dollar dies were made slightly later.

	F	VF	EF	AU	Unc.
1849 5 D.	$36,500	$50,000	$75,000	$150,000	$275,000

	F	VF	EF	AU	Unc.
1849 TEN.D.	$92,500	$175,000	$300,000	$385,000	—

MORMON GOLD PIECES,
SALT LAKE CITY, UTAH, 1849–1860

The first name given to the organized Mormon Territory was the "State of Deseret," the last word meaning "honeybee" in the Book of Mormon. The beehive, which is shown on the reverse of the five-dollar 1860 piece, was a favorite device of the followers of Joseph Smith and Brigham Young. The clasped hands appear on most Mormon coins and exemplify strength in unity. HOLINESS TO THE LORD was an inscription frequently used.

Brigham Young was the instigator of the coinage system and personally supervised the mint, which was housed in a little adobe building in Salt Lake City. The mint was inaugurated late in 1848 as a public convenience and to make a profit for the church. Each coin had substantially less gold than the face value stated.

	F	VF	EF	AU	Unc.
1849 TWO.AND.HALF.DO.	$15,000	$25,000	$37,500	$60,000	$90,000
1849 FIVE.DOLLARS	$11,000	$18,500	$30,000	$40,000	$75,000

	F	VF	EF	AU
1849 TEN.DOLLARS	$375,000	$550,000	$750,000	$850,000
	Auctions: $705,000, AU-58, April 2014			

	F	VF	EF	AU	Unc.
1849 TWENTY.DOLLARS (a)	$95,000	$175,000	$275,000	$375,000	$525,000
Auctions: $558,125, MS-62, April 2014					

a. The first coin of the twenty-dollar denomination to be struck in the United States.

	F	VF	EF	AU	Unc.
1850 FIVE DOLLARS	$14,000	$25,000	$34,000	$47,500	$85,000

	F	VF	EF	AU	Unc.
1860 5.D.	$23,500	$32,000	$42,000	$65,000	$90,000

COLORADO GOLD PIECES

CLARK, GRUBER & CO., DENVER, 1860–1861

Clark, Gruber & Co. was a well-known private minting firm in Denver, Colorado, in 1860 and 1861, formed by bankers from Leavenworth, Kansas Territory. In 1862 their operation was purchased by the Treasury Department and thenceforth operated as an assay office.

	F	VF	EF	AU	Unc.
1860 2 1/2 D.	$2,100	$3,000	$4,200	$5,700	$13,500
1860 FIVE D.	$2,300	$3,000	$4,500	$6,250	$14,500

	F	VF	EF	AU	Unc.
1860 TEN D.	$10,000	$15,000	$21,000	$30,000	$55,000
1860 TWENTY D.	$75,000	$135,000	$250,000	$385,000	$650,000
Auctions: $690,000, MS-64, January 2006					

The $2.50 and $5 pieces of 1861 follow closely the designs of the 1860 issues. The main difference is found in the legends. The reverse side now has CLARK GRUBER & CO. DENVER. On the obverse, PIKES PEAK now appears on the coronet of Miss Liberty.

	F	VF	EF	AU	Unc.
1861 2 1/2 D.	$2,000	$3,000	$4,500	$7,500	$14,000
1861 FIVE D.	$2,400	$3,700	$6,000	$11,500	$37,500
1861 TEN D.	$2,500	$4,200	$7,000	$11,500	$28,500

	F	VF	EF	AU	Unc.
1861 TWENTY D.	$22,500	$40,000	$60,000	$100,000	$235,000

JOHN PARSONS & COMPANY, TARRYALL MINES, COLORADO, 1861

Very little is known regarding the mint of John Parsons and Co., although it is reasonably certain that it operated in the South Park section of Park County, Colorado, near the original town of Tarryall, in the summer of 1861.

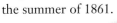

	VF	EF
(1861) Undated 2 1/2 D. (a)	$325,000	$425,000
(1861) Undated FIVE D. (b)	$450,000	$650,000

a. 6 to 8 examples are known. b. 5 or 6 examples are known.

J.J. CONWAY & CO., GEORGIA GULCH, COLORADO, 1861

Records show that the Conway mint operated for a short while in 1861. As in all gold-mining areas the value of gold dust caused disagreement among the merchants and the miners. The firm of J.J. Conway & Co. solved this difficulty by bringing out its gold pieces in August 1861.

	VF	EF	AU
(1861) Undated 2 1/2 DOLL'S (a)		$475,000	$675,000
(1861) Undated FIVE DOLLARS (b)	$500,000	$675,000	

a. 8 to 12 examples are known. b. 5 to 8 examples are known.

(1861) Undated TEN DOLLARS (a)	—

a. 3 examples are known.

CALIFORNIA SMALL-DENOMINATION GOLD

There was a scarcity of small coins during the California gold rush. Starting in 1852, quarter, half, and dollar coins were privately minted from native gold to alleviate the shortage. Period 1 California fractional gold coins were issued between 1852 and 1857 as Liberty Head denominations of 25 cents, 50 cents, and one dollar, in both octagonal and round formats. There is much credible evidence available to conclude these were used in daily commerce during the early stages of the gold rush. Beginning in 1859, various private entities continued to make them, but more as souvenirs, as charms, or for barter. These are called Period 2 California fractional gold coins and were issued up to 1882. Period 2 has both the Liberty Head and Indian Head designs and the coins are often prooflike. Most have a wreath on the reverse, but some have original designs.

Early coins contained up to 85% of face value in gold. The amount and quality of gold in the coins soon decreased, and some are merely gold plated.

The Coinage Act of April 22, 1864, made private coinage illegal, but the law was not fully enforced until 1883. In compliance with the law, non-denominated tokens were made, and from 1872 until 1883 both coins and tokens were produced. After 1883, most of the production was tokens. To circumvent the law, and to make them more acceptable, some pieces made after 1881 were backdated to the 1850s or 1860s.

About 35,000 pieces are believed to exist. More than 570 different varieties have been identified, many of them very rare. The quality of strike and edge treatment is inconsistent. Many bear their makers' initials: D, DERI, DERIB, DN, FD, G, GG, GL, H, L, N, or NR. Major denominated coins are listed below; values are for the most common variety of each type. Non-denominated tokens are not included in these listings. They are much less valuable. ***Beware of extremely common modern replicas*** (often having a bear in the design), which have little numismatic value.

The values in the following charts are only for coins made before 1883 with the denomination on the reverse expressed as CENTS, DOL., DOLL., or DOLLAR.

QUARTER DOLLAR, OCTAGONAL

	AU	Unc.	Ch. Unc.	Gem BU
Period 1 (reverse 1/4 DOLLAR unless noted otherwise)				
Small Liberty Head / Circular Value and Date in Beaded Circle, 1853	$450	$900	$4,250	
Large Liberty Head / Circular Value and Date in Beaded Circle, 1853	$225	$300	$525	
Large Liberty Head / Value in Beaded Circle, Date Below, DOLLA, 1853	$12,500	$20,000	$30,000	
Large Liberty Head / Value and Date in Beaded Circle, 1854–1856	$225	$325	$450	
Small Liberty Head 1854 / Value in Wreath, DOL.	$225	$300	$450	
Small Liberty Head 1854 / Value in Wreath, DOLLAR	$275	$450	$650	
Small Liberty Head / Value and Date in Wreath, 1855–1856	$225	$350	$450	
Period 2				
Large Liberty Head / Value and Date in Wreath		$210	$300	$700
Washington Head 1872 / Value and CAL in Wreath		$1,250	$2,000	$3,750
Large Liberty Head and Date / Value and CAL in Wreath		$250	$300	$650
Small Liberty Head / Value and CAL in Wreath		$300	$450	—
Small Liberty Head, Initial G / Value in Shield, Date in Wreath		$300	$700	—
Small Indian Head / Value and CAL in Wreath		$225	$375	$850
Small Liberty Head / Value in Wreath, Date Below		$300	$500	$1,200
Large Indian Head / Value and CAL in Wreath		$225	$350	$1,100
Large Indian Head and Date / Value in Wreath		$230	$375	$700

QUARTER DOLLAR, ROUND

	AU	Unc.	Ch. Unc.	Gem BU
Period 1				
Small Liberty Head / 25 CENTS in Wreath, No Date (c. 1853)	$1,750	$3,250	$8,500	
Small Liberty Head / Value in Wreath, No Date (c. 1852–1854)	$225	$300	$425	
Small Liberty Head / Value in Wreath, Star Above, No Date (c. 1853)	$400	$625	$1,800	
Small Liberty Head / Value in Wreath, Star Below, No Date (c. 1853–1854)	$175	$255	$390	
Large Liberty Head / Value in Wreath, Star Above, No Date (c. 1853)	$275	$425	$900	
Large Liberty Head / Value and Date in Wreath, 1853–1854	$400	$700	$2,150	
Large Liberty Head, Initials FD / Value and Date in Wreath, 1853	$1,750	$3,000	$12,000	
Large Liberty Head, Initials GG / Value and Date in Wreath, 1853	$1,250	$2,000	$3,750	
Defiant Eagle and Date / 25 CENTS in Wreath, 1854	$20,000	$30,000	$75,000	
Small Liberty Head / Value and Date in Wreath, 1855–1856		$250	$450	
Period 2				
Large Liberty Head and Date / Value and CAL in Wreath		$220	$325	$675
Liberty Head / Value in Wreath		$200	$275	$600
Washington Head 1872 / Value and CAL in Wreath		$1,250	$2,000	$3,750
Small Liberty Head / Value in Shield, Date in Wreath		$340	$650	—
Small Liberty Head / Value and CAL in Wreath		$235	$400	$1,050
Small Indian Head / Value and CAL in Wreath		$210	$350	$1,200
Large Indian Head / Value and CAL in Wreath		$235	$350	$700
Large Indian Head and Date / Value in Wreath		$250	$375	$750

HALF DOLLAR, OCTAGONAL

	AU	Unc.	Ch. Unc.	Gem BU
Period 1 (reverse CALIFORNIA GOLD)				
Large Liberty Head and FD / Large Eagle with Raised Wings, FIFTY CENTS, 1853	$17,500	$32,500	—	
Large Liberty Head Date and FD/ Peacock with Rays, 50 CENTS, 1853	$1,500	$2,200	$4,500	
Large Liberty Head Date and FD / Value in Beaded Circle, 1853	$300	$500	$750	
Large Liberty Head Date / Value in Beaded Circle, 1854	$225	$350	$475	
Large Liberty Head Date / Value in Beaded Circle, Initials FD, 1854	$225	$325	$600	
Large Liberty Head / Value, Date, and Star in Beaded Circle, 1856	$275	$425	$1,300	
Small Liberty Head / Date within Wreath Value Below HALF DOL., Initial N., 1854–1856	$225	$325	$600	
Period 2				
Large Liberty Head / Value and Date in Wreath		$250	$400	$675
Small Liberty Head / Value and Date in Wreath		$275	$425	$3,000
Large Liberty Head / Value and CAL in Wreath		$275	$400	$950
Small Liberty Head and Date / Value and CAL in Wreath		$260	$375	$1,200
Small Indian Head and Date / Value and CAL in Wreath		$250	$400	$1,250
Large Indian Head and Date / Value in Wreath		$230	$400	$900
Large Indian Head and Date / Value and CAL in Wreath		$275	$450	$875

HALF DOLLAR, ROUND

	AU	Unc.	Ch. Unc.	Gem BU
Period 1 (reverse CALIFORNIA GOLD except on Eagle reverse issues)				
Small Liberty Head / Date and Value in Wreath, HALF DOL., 1852	$225	$400	$525	
Large Liberty Head / Small Eagle, No Rays, Date Below, 1853	—	—	$35,000	
Large Liberty Head, Initials FD / Value and Date in Wreath, 1854–1855	$400	$650	$1,250	
Small Liberty Head, Initials DN / Date in Wreath, Value Below, HALF DOL., 1852–1853	$225	$350	$650	
Small Liberty Head, Initials DN / Date in Wreath, Value Below, HALF D, 1853	$450	$700	$2,250	
Small Liberty Head, Initials GG / Small Eagle, No Rays, Date Below, 1853	$9,500	$15,000	$30,000	
Small Liberty Head, Initials GG / Value in Wreath, Date Below, 1853	$350	$550	$1,450	
Large Liberty Head / Date in Wreath, HALF D. 1853–1854	$225	$450	$1,000	
Liberty Head, Initial D / Date in Wreath, HALF D, 1853–1854	$175	$300	$495	
Large Liberty Head / Date in Wreath, HALF DOL, Initial D, 1854	$1,750	$3,500	$5,750	
Small Liberty Head / Date in Wreath, HALF DOL, 1852–1853	$175	$275	$500	
Small Liberty Head / Date Below HALF DOL, 1854	$275	$450	$1,200	
Large Liberty Head / Date in Wreath, HALF DOL, 1855	$200	$325	$450	
Large Liberty Head, Initial N. / Date in Wreath, HALF DOL, 1856	$175	$250	$650	
Arms of California / Small Eagle with Raised Wings, 1853	$6,500	$10,000	$13,000	
Liberty Head / Large Eagle with Raised Wings, 1854	—	—	$4,300	
Period 2				
Liberty Head / Value in Wreath		$230	$375	$650
Liberty Head and Date / Value and CAL in Wreath		$230	$400	$1,300
Liberty Head / CALIFORNIA GOLD around Wreath, HALF DOL		$250	$600	$2,000
Liberty Head / Value and Date in Wreath, *HALF DOLLAR		$260	$350	$1,350
Small Indian Head and Date / Value and CAL in Wreath		$275	$400	$1,250
Large Indian Head and Date / Value and CAL in Wreath		$250	$375	$1,200
Large Indian Head and Date / Value in Wreath		$275	$450	$1,200

DOLLAR, OCTAGONAL

	AU	Unc.	Ch. Unc.	Gem BU
Period 1 (reverse CALIFORNIA GOLD)				
Liberty Head / Large Eagle with Scroll, ONE. DOL., No Date	$3,250	$5,500	$14,500	
Liberty Head / Large Eagle with Scroll, ONE DOL, 1853	$2,500	$4,500	$7,800	
Liberty Head / Value and Date in Beaded Circle, Initials FD, 1853–1856	$800	$1,200	$2,150	
Liberty Head / Value and Date in Wreath, Initials GL, 1854 (about 3 known)	$875	$1,350	—	
Liberty Head, Initials DERI / Value and Date in Beaded Circle, 1853–1854		—	—	
Liberty Head, Initials DERIB / Value and Date in Beaded Circle, 1853–1854	$475	$875	$2,000	
Liberty Head / Value and Date in Beaded Circle, Initial N., 1853–1855	$550	$925	$1,500	
Liberty Head / Large Eagle, No Scroll, 1854	$7,500	$12,000	$17,500	
Period 2				
Liberty Head / Legend around Wreath		$800	$1,500	$2,000
Small Indian Head and Date / Value and CAL in Wreath		$825	$1,400	$2,000
Large Indian Head and Date / Value in Wreath		$750	$1,500	$2,000

DOLLAR, ROUND

	AU	Unc.	Ch. Unc.	Gem BU
Period 1				
Liberty Head / CALIFORNIA GOLD., Value and Date in Wreath, 1854, 1857	—	—	—	
Liberty Head, Initials FD / CALIFORNIA GOLD., Value and Date in Wreath, 1854	$8,500	$12,500	$20,000	
Liberty Head, Initials GG / Eagle Reverse, Date Below, 1853	$75,000	$120,000	—	
Period 2				
Liberty Head / Date Beneath Head		$2,700	$4,500	—
Indian Head / Date Beneath Head		$2,200	$3,200	$6,500

COINS OF THE GOLDEN WEST

Small souvenir California gold pieces were made by several manufacturers in the early 20th century. A series of 36 pieces, in the size of 25¢, 50¢, and $1 coins, was sold by the M.E. Hart Company of San Francisco to honor Alaska and various Western states. The Hart Company also marketed the official commemorative Panama-Pacific gold coins from the 1915 Exposition and manufactured plush copper cases for them. Similar cases were acquired by Farran Zerbe, who mounted 15 complete sets of what he termed "Coins of the Golden West." Intact, framed 36-piece sets are rare; individual specimens are among the most popular of all souvenir pieces of that era.

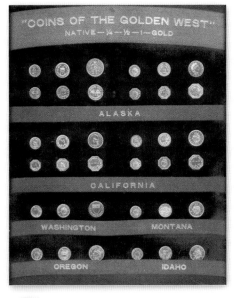

	AU	Unc.	Ch. Unc.
Alaska Pinch, 25¢, octagonal, 1902	$300	$550	
Alaska Pinch, 50¢, octagonal, 1900	$300	$600	
Alaska Pinch, $1, octagonal, 1898	$400	$750	
Alaska Pinch, 25¢, round, 1901	$300	$550	
Alaska Pinch, 50¢, round, 1899	$350	$600	
Alaska Pinch, $1, round, 1897	$400	$750	
Alaska Parka, 25¢, round, 1911	$1,200	$1,900	
Alaska Parka, 50¢, round, 1911	$1,300	$2,250	
Alaska Parka, $1, round, 1911	$1,500	$2,650	
Alaska AYPE, 25¢, round, 1909	$200	$300	
Alaska AYPE, 50¢, round, 1909	$225	$350	
Alaska AYPE, $1, round, 1909	$300	$450	
California Minerva, 25¢, octagonal, 1915	$200	$400	
California Minerva, 50¢, octagonal, 1915	$250	$400	
California Minerva, $1, octagonal, 1915	$300	$550	
California Minerva, 25¢, round, 1915	$250	$400	
California Minerva, 50¢, round, 1915	$250	$450	
California Minerva, $1, round, 1915	$300	$550	
California 25¢, octagonal, 1860 or 1902	$500	$1,200	
California 50¢, octagonal, 1900	$600	$1,350	
California $1, octagonal, 1898	$700	$1,600	
California 25¢, round, 1849, 1860, 1871, or 1901	$450	$1,250	
California 50¢, round, 1849 or 1899	$550	$1,500	
California $1, round, 1849	$700	$1,750	
Idaho, 25¢, round, 1914	$700	$1,250	
Idaho, 50¢, round, 1914	$800	$1,350	
Idaho, $1, round, 1914	$850	$1,550	
Montana, 25¢, round, 1914	$550	$1,050	
Montana, 50¢, round, 1914	$650	$1,150	
Montana, $1, round, 1914	$750	$1,400	
Oregon, 25¢, round, 1914	$500	$1,200	
Oregon, 50¢, round, 1914	$600	$1,250	
Oregon, $1, round, 1914	$700	$1,450	
Washington, 25¢, round, 1914	$500	$1,150	
Washington, 50¢, round, 1914	$600	$1,250	
Washington, $1, round, 1914	$700	$1,450	
36-Piece Gold Set: Coins of Alaska, California, Idaho, Montana, Oregon, Washington	—	—	$75,000

CALIFORNIA GOLD INGOT BARS

During the Gold Rush era, gold coins, ingots, and "dust" (actually flakes and nuggets) were sent by steamship from San Francisco to other ports, most importantly to New York City and London, where the gold was sold or, in some instances, sent to mints for conversion into coins. The typical procedure in the mid-1850s was to send the gold by steamship from San Francisco to Panama, where it was transported across 48 miles of territory by small water craft and pack animals from 1849 until the Panama Railroad opened in 1855, then loaded aboard another ship at the town of Aspinwall on the Atlantic side. On September 12, 1857, the SS *Central America*, en route from Aspinwall to New York City with more than 475 passengers, over 100 crew members, and an estimated $2.6 million in gold (in an era in which pure gold was valued at $20.67 per ounce) was lost at sea. Miraculously, more than 150 people, including all but one of the women and children, were rescued by passing ships. The *Central America* went to the bottom of the Atlantic Ocean off the Carolina coast.

In the 1980s a group of researchers secured financing to search for the long-lost ship. After much study and many explorations, they discovered the wreck of the *Central America* 7,200 feet below the surface. They used the robotic *Nemo*, a sophisticated device weighing several tons, to photograph the wreck and to carefully bring to the surface many artifacts. A king's ransom in gold ingots was found, along with more than 7,500 coins, the latter mostly consisting of Mint State 1857-S double eagles.

The 500-plus gold ingots furnished a unique opportunity to study specimens that, after conservation, were essentially in the same condition as they had been in 1857. These bore the imprints of five different California assayers, who operated seven offices. With few exceptions, each ingot bears individual stamps, indicating its maker, a serial number, the weight in ounces, the fineness (expressed in thousandths, e.g., .784 indicating 784/1000 pure gold), and the 1857 value in dollars. The smallest bar found was issued by Blake & Co., weighed 4.95 ounces, was .795 fine, and was stamped with a value of $81.34. The largest ingot, dubbed the "Eureka bar," bore the imprint of Kellogg & Humbert, and was stamped with a weight of 933.94 ounces, .903 fine, and a value of $17,433.57.

Blake & Co., Sacramento, California: From December 28, 1855, to May 1858, Blake & Co. was operated by Gorham Blake and W.R. Waters. • 34 ingots recovered. Serial numbers in the 5,100 and 5,200 series. Lowest weight and value: 4.95 ounces, $81.34. Highest weight and value: 157.40 ounces, $2,655.05. These bars have beveled or "dressed" edges and may have seen limited use in California commerce.

Harris, Marchand & Co., Sacramento and Marysville: This firm was founded in Sacramento in 1855 by Harvey Harris and Desiré Marchand, with Charles L. Farrington as the "& Co." The Marysville office was opened in January 1856. Serial numbers in the 6000 series are attributed to Sacramento, comprising 36 bars; a single bar in the 7000 series (7095) is attributed to Marysville. The Marchand bars each have a circular coin-style counterstamp on the face. Lowest weight and value (Sacramento): 9.87 ounces, $158.53. Highest weight and value (Sacramento): 295.20 ounces, $5,351.73. • Unique Marysville bar: 174.04 ounces, $3,389.06.

Henry Hentsch, San Francisco: Hentsch, a Swiss, was an entrepreneur involved in banking, real estate, assaying, and other ventures. In February 1856, he opened an assay office as an annex to his bank. It is likely that many of his ingots were exported to Europe, where he had extensive banking connections. • 33 ingots recovered. Lowest weight and value: 12.52 ounces, $251.82. Highest weight and value: 238.84 ounces, $4,458.35.

Justh & Hunter, San Francisco and Marysville: Emanuel Justh, a Hungarian, was a lithographer in San Francisco in the early 1850s. In 1854 and 1855 he worked as assistant assayer at the San Francisco Mint. Solomon Hillen Hunter came to California from Baltimore. The Justh & Hunter partnership was announced in May 1855. • Although study is continuing, the 60 ingots in the 4000 series are tentatively attributed to San Francisco, and the 26 ingots in the 9000 series are attributed to Marysville. • San Francisco—Lowest weight and value: 5.24 ounces, $92.18. Highest weight and value: 866.19 ounces, $15,971.93. • Marysville—Lowest weight and value: 19.34 ounces, $356.21. Highest weight and value: 464.65 ounces, $8,759.90.

Kellogg & Humbert, San Francisco: John Glover Kellogg and Augustus Humbert, two of the most famous names in the minting of California gold coins, formed the partnership of Kellogg & Humbert in spring 1855. The firm was one of the most active of all California assayers during the mid-1850s. • 346 ingots recovered, constituting the majority of those found. • Lowest weight and value: 5.71 ounces, $101.03. Highest weight and value: 933.94 ounces, $17,433.57.

A selection of gold ingots from the SS *Central America* treasure (with an 1857-S double eagle shown for scale, near lower left). (1) Harris, Marchand & Co., Marysville office, serial number 7095, 174.04 ounces, .942 fine, $3,389.06 (all values as stamped in 1857). (2) Henry Hentsch, San Francisco, serial number 3120, 61.93 ounces, .886 fine, $1,134.26. (3) Kellogg & Humbert, San Francisco, serial number 215, .944 fine, $1,045.96. (4) Blake & Co., Sacramento, 19.30 ounces, .946 fine, $297.42. (5) Another Blake & Co. ingot, serial number 5216, .915 fine, $266.12. (6) Justh & Hunter, Marysville office, serial number 9440, 41.79 ounces, $761.07. (7) Justh & Hunter, San Francisco office, serial number 4243, 51.98 ounces, .916 fine, $984.27. (8) Harris, Marchand & Co., Sacramento office, serial number 6514, 35.33 ounces, .807 fine, $589.38. (9) Harris, Marchand & Co., Sacramento office, serial number 6486, 12.64 ounces, .950 fine, $245.00.

Private Tokens

Privately issued tokens are by no means an American invention. They were common to most capitalist nations in the 1800s (and known even earlier), created and circulated by businessmen and others in periods of economic weakness or uncertainty, during financial panics, depressions, and times of war. Sometimes they were handed out as advertising trinkets or political propaganda pieces; more often they passed as makeshift currency when few real coins were available to make small change. Unlike real coins, which are government-issued as legal tender, tokens are minted by private citizens and companies. Commonly made of metal, usually round in shape, coins and tokens are very similar in appearance, but a token lacks a coin's official status as government-backed currency. Typically it would only have trade value, and then only in the vicinity in which it was issued (if, for example, a local merchant was prepared to redeem it in goods or services).

This section describes several of the more commonly encountered American tokens of the 1800s.

HARD TIMES TOKENS (1832–1844)

Hard Times tokens, as they are called, are pieces of Americana dating from the era of presidents Andrew Jackson and Martin Van Buren. They are mostly the size of a contemporary large copper cent. Privately minted from 1832 to 1844, they display diverse motifs reflecting political campaigns and satire of the era as well as carrying advertisements for merchants, products, and services. For many years these have been a popular specialty within numismatics, helped along with the publication of *Hard Times Tokens* by Lyman H. Low (1899; revised edition, 1906) and later works, continuing to the present day (see the *Guide Book of Hard Times Tokens*, 2015). In 1899 Low commented (adapted) that "the issues commonly called Hard Times tokens . . . had no semblance of authority behind them. They combine the character of political pieces with the catch-words of party cries; of satirical pieces with sarcastic allusions to the sentiments or speeches of the leaders of opposing parties; and in some degree also of necessity pieces, in a time when, to use one of the phrases of the day, 'money was a cash article,' hard to get for daily needs."

Although examples from the earlier 1830s are designated as Hard Times tokens, the true Hard Times period started in a serious way on May 10, 1837, when banks began suspending specie payments and would no longer exchange paper currency for coins. This date is memorialized on some of the token inscriptions. Difficult economic conditions continued through 1843; the first full year of recovery was 1844. From March 1837 to March 1841, President Martin Van Buren vowed to "follow in the steps of my illustrious predecessor," President Andrew Jackson, who had been in office from March 1829 until Van Buren's inauguration. Jackson was perhaps the most controversial president up to that time. His veto in 1832 of the impending (1836) recharter of the Bank of the United States set off a political firestorm, and the flames were fanned when his administration shifted deposits to favored institutions, derisively called "pet banks."

The Jackson era was one of unbridled prosperity. Due to sales of land in the West, the expansion of railroads, and a robust economy, so much money piled up in the Treasury that distributions were made in 1835 to all of the states. Seeking to end wild speculation, Jackson issued the "Specie Circular" on July 11, 1836, mandating that purchases of Western land, often made on credit, by paper money of uncertain worth, or by non-cash means, had to be paid in silver or gold coins. Almost immediately, the land boom settled and prices stabilized. A chill began to spread across the economy, which worsened in early 1837. Finally, many banks ran short of ready cash, causing the specie suspension.

After May 10, 1837, silver and gold coins completely disappeared from circulation. Copper cents remained, but were in short supply. Various diesinkers and others produced a flood of copper tokens. These were sold at discounts to merchants and banks, with $6 for 1,000 tokens being typical. Afterward, they were paid out in commerce and circulated for the value of one cent.

The actions of Jackson, the financial tribulations that many thought he precipitated, and the policies of Van Buren inspired motifs for a class of Hard Times tokens today known as "politicals." Several hundred other varieties were made with the advertisements of merchants, services, and products and are known as "store cards" or "merchants' tokens." Many of these were illustrated with elements such as a shoe, umbrella, comb, coal stove, storefront, hotel, or carriage.

One of the more famous issues depicts a slave kneeling in chains, with the motto "Am I Not a Woman & a Sister?" This token was issued in 1838, when abolition was a major rallying point for many Americans in the North. The curious small-size Feuchtwanger cents of 1837, made in Feuchtwanger's Composition (a type of German silver), were proposed to Congress as a cheap substitute for copper cents, but no congressional action was taken. Lewis Feuchtwanger produced large quantities on his own account and circulated them extensively (see page 1310).

As the political and commercial motifs of Hard Times tokens are so diverse, and reflect the American economy and political scene of their era, numismatists have found them fascinating to collect and study. Although there are major rarities in the series, most of the issues are very affordable. Expanded information concerning more than 500 varieties of Hard Times tokens can be found in Russell Rulau's *Standard Catalog of United States Tokens, 1700–1900* (fourth edition). Collectors and researchers are also encouraged to consult *A Guide Book of Hard Times Tokens* (Bowers). A representative selection is illustrated here.

L1, HT1   L57, HT76

L4, HT6   L56, HT75

	VF	EF	AU
L1, HT1. Andrew Jackson. Copper	$5,000	$8,500	—
L57, HT76. Van Buren, facing left. Brass	$2,200	$3,250	$4,250
L4, HT6. Jackson President of the U.S. Brass	$200	$325	$750
L56, HT75. Van Buren facing left. Copper	$80	$160	$375

L66, HT24

L54, HT81

L55, HT63

L31, HT46

L8, HT9

L18, HT32

L51, HT70

L47, HT66

L60, HT18

L44, HT69

L59, HT17

L65, HT23

	VF	EF	AU
L66, HT24. Agriculture. Copper	$225	$350	$650
L54, HT81. A Woman & A Sister. Copper ‡	$180	$275	$400
L55, HT63. Loco Foco, 1838. Copper ‡	$55	$160	$275
L31, HT46. Not One Cent, Motto. Copper ‡	$45	$60	$135
L8, HT9. My Victory / Jackson. Copper ‡	$40	$90	$125
L18, HT32. Executive Experiment. Copper ‡	$30	$65	$110
L51, HT70. Roman Firmness. Copper ‡	$35	$70	$125
L47, HT66. Phoenix / May Tenth. Copper ‡	$25	$65	$110
L60, HT18. Ship/Lightning. Copper ‡	$25	$65	$110
L44, HT69. Ship/Jackson. Copper ‡	$25	$70	$125
L59, HT17. Ship / Wreath Border. Copper	$25	$65	$110
L65, HT23. Ship / Liberty Head. Copper	$100	$200	$350

† Ranked in the *100 Greatest American Medals and Tokens*; L54, HT81 as its own entry, the other listings as a single entry for Satirical Hard Times Tokens.

FEUCHTWANGER TOKENS (1837–1864)

Lewis Feuchtwanger, a German-born chemist, moved to the United States in 1829 and settled in New York City. He produced a variety of German silver (an alloy of metals not including any actual silver) consisting of nickel, copper, and some zinc. Feuchtwanger suggested to Congress as early as 1837 that his metal be substituted for copper in U.S. coinage, and he made one-cent and three-cent trial pieces that circulated freely during the coin shortage of 1836 through 1844.

	VF	EF	AU	Unc.
1837 One Cent, Eagle ‡	$135	$210	$300	$550
1837 Three-Cent, New York Coat of Arms ‡	$750	$1,600	$2,750	$5,250
1837 Three-Cent, Eagle ‡	$1,700	$3,600	$5,500	$13,000
1864 Three-Cent, Eagle	$1,750	$2,800	$3,800	$7,500

‡ All 1837 Feuchtwanger Tokens are ranked in the *100 Greatest American Medals and Tokens*, as a single entry.

CIVIL WAR TOKENS (1860s)

Early Friday morning, April 12, 1861, the Confederate States Army fired shells from 10-inch siege mortars into the Union's Fort Sumter in Charleston Bay, South Carolina, touching off the American Civil War. The ensuing turmoil would bring many changes to America's financial and monetary systems, including a dramatic reworking of the banking structure, federalization of paper money, bold innovations in taxation, tariffs, and land grants, and radical government experiments in new kinds of currency. For the man on the street, one daily noticeable development of the war was the large-scale hoarding of coins, which began in late 1861 and early 1862—people squirreled away first their gold, then silver coins, and finally, as the war dragged on that summer, even small copper-nickel cents. This caused trouble for day-to-day commerce. There were no coins to buy a newspaper or a glass of soda, to get a haircut, or tip a doorman. The situation gave birth to the humble but ubiquitous Civil War token.

Tokens were a familiar sight on the American scene by the time the Civil War was ignited. In fact, Americans had been using tokens as monetary substitutes since the colonial era, during the early days of the new nation, and throughout the 1800s. Two main kinds of tokens entered into American commerce during the war: *patriotics*, so called for their political and nationalistic themes; and *store cards*, or merchant tokens. An estimated 50 million or more were issued—more than two for every man, woman, and child in the Union. Civil War tokens were mostly a Northern phenomenon; not surprising, considering that New York State alone produced four times as much manufacturing as the entire Confederacy at the start of the war. Southerners had to make do with weak government-backed paper money, which quickly depreciated in value; Yankee tradesmen had the industrial base and financial means to produce a hard-money substitute that at least *looked* like money, even if it was backed by nothing more substantial than a local grocery store's promise to accept it at the value of one cent.

Most Civil War tokens were made of copper, some were brass, and rare exceptions were struck in copper-nickel or white metal. In addition to patriotics and store cards, some issuers crafted *numismatic* tokens during the war. These were struck for collectors rather than for day-to-day commerce, and made in the typical alloys as well as (rarely) in silver and other metals. Some were overstruck on dimes or copper-nickel cents.

Many kinds of tokens and medals were issued during the war. This sometimes leads to the question, "What, exactly, counts as a *Civil War token?*" How about the small hard-rubber checks and tickets, in various shapes, of that era? Or encased postage stamps, another small-change substitute of the war years? Or sutler tokens, issued by registered vendors who supplied the Union Army and traveled with the troops? These and more are sometimes collected along with the main body of about 10,000 varieties of store cards and patriotics. There is a long tradition of collecting Civil War tokens, dating back to even before the end of the war, and the hobby community has developed various habits and traditions over the years. Ultimately what to include in a collection is up to the individual collector. The Civil War Token Society (www.cwtsociety.com), the preeminent club for today's collector, suggests that to be "officially" considered a Civil War token, a piece must be between 18 and 25 mm in diameter. (Most of the copper tokens issued to pass as currency during the war were 18 or 19 mm, the size of the federal government's relatively new Flying Eagle and Indian Head cents, introduced in the late 1850s.)

Civil War tokens can be collected by state and by city, by type of issuer (druggist, saloonkeeper, doctor, etc.), or by any number of designs and themes. If you live in New York City and would like to study store cards issued by local shops and businesses, you have hundreds to choose from. You might hail from a small town and still be able to find a Civil War token from where you grew up. In 1863 in Oswego, New York, M.L. Marshall—a general-store seller of the unlikely combination of toys, fancy goods, fishing tackle, and rare coins—issued a cent-sized copper token featuring a fish! Undertakers issued store cards with tiny coffins advertising their services. Booksellers, bootmakers, beer brewers, hat dealers, and hog butchers all pictured their products on small copper tokens. On the patriotic side, Civil War tokens show Abraham Lincoln, various wartime presidential candidates, national heroes, cannons at the ready, unfurled flags, defiant eagles, and soldiers on horseback. They shout out the slogans of the day, warning the South of the strength of THE ARMY & NAVY, urging Americans to STAND BY THE FLAG, and insisting that THE FEDERAL UNION MUST AND SHALL BE PRESERVED.

Many tokens were more or less faithful imitations of the federal copper-nickel Indian Head cent. A few of this type have the word NOT in small letters above the words ONE CENT. For a time the legal status of the Civil War tokens was uncertain. Mint Director James Pollock thought they were illegal; however, there was no law prohibiting the issue of tradesmen's tokens or of private coins not in imitation of U.S. coins. Finally a law was passed April 22, 1864, prohibiting the private issue of any one- or two-cent coins, tokens, or devices for use as money, and on June 8 another law was passed that abolished private coinage of every kind. By that summer the government's new bronze Indian Head cents, minted in the tens of millions, were plentiful in circulation.

Today, Civil War tokens as a class are very accessible for collectors. Store-card tokens of Illinois, Massachusetts, Michigan, New York, Ohio, Pennsylvania, and Wisconsin are among those most frequently seen. A collector seeking special challenges will hunt for tokens from Iowa, Kansas, Maryland, and Minnesota—and, on the Confederate side, from Alabama, Louisiana (a counterstamped Indian Head cent), and Tennessee.

Three pieces of advice will serve the beginning collector. First, read the standard reference books, including *Patriotic Civil War Tokens* and *U.S. Civil War Store Cards*, both classics by George and Melvin Fuld, and the *Guide Book of Civil War Tokens*, by Q. David Bowers. These books lay the foundation and offer inspiration for building your own collection. Second, join the Civil War Token Society. This will put you in touch with other collectors who offer mentoring, friendship, and information. Third, visit a coin show and start looking for Civil War tokens in the inventories of the dealers there. Above all, enjoy the hobby and the many paths and byways it can lead you on through this important and turbulent era of American history.

Values shown are for the most common tokens in each composition.

	F	VF	EF	MS-63
Copper or brass	$15	$25	$35	$125
Nickel or German silver	$55	$75	$130	$290
White metal	$80	$125	$150	$275
Copper-nickel	$75	$125	$175	$325
Silver	$200	$300	$500	$1,200

PATRIOTIC CIVIL WAR TOKENS

Patriotic Civil War tokens feature leaders such as Abraham Lincoln; military images such as cannons or ships; and sociopolitical themes popular in the North, such as flags and slogans. Thousands of varieties are known.

	F	VF	AU	MS-63
Lincoln ‡	$35	$70	$150	$300
Monitor ‡	$30	$50	$125	$225
"Wealth of the South" ‡ (a)	$200	$400	$600	$1,000
Various common types ‡	$15	$25	$45	$125

‡ Ranked in the *100 Greatest American Medals and Tokens*; "Wealth of the South" as its own entry, the other listings as a single entry for Patriotic Civil War Tokens. **a.** Dated 1860, but sometimes collected along with Civil War tokens.

CIVIL WAR STORE CARDS

Tradesmen's tokens of the Civil War era are often called store cards. These are typically collected by geographical location or by topic. The Fuld text (see bibliography) catalogs store cards by state, city, merchant, die combination, and metal. Values shown below are for the most common tokens for each state. Tokens from obscure towns or from merchants who issued only a few can be priced into the thousands of dollars and are widely sought.

	VG	VF	AU	MS-63
Alabama ‡	$1,500	$3,000	$4,000	$6,500
Connecticut ‡	$10	$25	$50	$125
Washington, D.C. ‡	—	$1,000	$1,400	$2,200
Idaho ‡	$400	$700	$1,300	—
Illinois ‡	$10	$25	$50	$125
Indiana ‡	$10	$30	$60	$135
Iowa ‡	$150	$450	$550	$1,250
Kansas ‡	$900	$2,500	$3,500	$5,500
Kentucky ‡	$50	$125	$200	$350
Louisiana ‡	$2,000	$3,500	$4,500	—

‡ Ranked in the *100 Greatest American Medals and Tokens*; Sutlers' Store Cards as its own entry, the other listings as a single entry for Civil War Store Cards.

	VG	VF	AU	MS-63
Maine ‡	$50	$100	$175	$300
Maryland ‡	$150	$350	$550	$1,000
Massachusetts ‡	$15	$35	$60	$140
Michigan ‡	$10	$25	$50	$125
Minnesota ‡	$150	$450	$550	$750
Missouri ‡	$40	$100	$150	$250
New Hampshire ‡	$80	$130	$175	$275
New Jersey ‡	$10	$25	$50	$135
New York ‡	$10	$25	$50	$125
Ohio ‡	$10	$25	$50	$125
Pennsylvania ‡	$10	$25	$50	$125
Rhode Island ‡	$10	$25	$50	$135
Tennessee ‡	$300	$650	$1,200	$1,750
Virginia ‡	$250	$500	$1,000	—
West Virginia ‡	$45	$100	$200	$450
Wisconsin ‡	$15	$30	$60	$130
Sutlers' ‡ (a)	$185	$375	$500	$700

‡ Ranked in the *100 Greatest American Medals and Tokens*; Sutlers' Store Cards as its own entry, the other listings as a single entry for Civil War Store Cards. **a.** Sutler tokens were issued by registered contractors who operated camp stores that traveled with the military. These were made by coiners who also produced Civil War tokens, including John Stanton, Shubael Childs, and Francis X. Koehler. Each had a denomination, typically 5 cents to 50 cents. Some used on one side a die also used on Civil War tokens.

DC500A-1h

IN190D-3a

	VG	VF	AU	MS-63
DC500a-1h. H.A. Hall, Washington, D.C.	—	$1,000	$1,400	$2,200
IN190D-3a. J.L. & G.F. Rowe, Corunna, IN, 1863	$15	$40	$75	$175

MI865A-1a

MN980A-1a

MO910A-2a

NY630AQ-4a

NY630Z-1a

OH165M-1a

NY630BJ-1a

WI510M-1a

PA750F-1a

WV890D-4a

	VG	VF	AU	MS-63
MI865A-1a, W. Darling, Saranac, MI, 1864	$7,500	$12,000	$15,000	—
MN980A-1a. C. Benson, Druggist, Winona, MN	$300	$700	$900	$1,500
MO910A-4a. Drovers Hotel, St. Louis, MO, 1863	$125	$300	$600	$1,250
NY630AQ-4a. Gustavus Lindenmueller, New York, 1863	$15	$25	$50	$125
NY630Z-1a. Fr. Freise, Undertaker, New York, 1863	$20	$35	$85	$150
OH165M-1a. B.P. Belknp., "Teeth Extracted Without Pain"	$125	$250	$400	$700
NY630BJ-1a. Sanitary Commission, New York, 1864	$400	$850	$1,100	$1,750
WI510M-1a. Goes & Falk Malt House & Brewery, Milwaukee, WI, 1863	$25	$65	$100	$200
PA750F-1a. M.C. Campbell's Dancing Academy, Philadelphia, PA	$20	$35	$50	$130
WV890D-4a. R.C. Graves, News Dealer, Wheeling, WV, 1863	$45	$100	$200	$450

LESHER REFERENDUM DOLLARS (1900–1901)

Distributed in 1900 and 1901 by Joseph Lesher of Victor, Colorado, these private tokens manufactured in Denver were used in trade to some extent, and stocked by various merchants who redeemed them in goods. Lesher was an Ohio-born Civil War veteran and, after the war, an early pioneer of Colorado's mining fields. His coins, octagonal in shape, were numbered and a blank space left at bottom of 1901 issues, in which were stamped names of businessmen who bought them. All are quite rare; many varieties are extremely rare. Their composition is .950 fine silver (alloyed with copper).

	VF	EF	AU	Unc.
1900 First type, no business name ‡	$2,750	$3,500	$4,200	$6,750
1900 A.B. Bumstead, with or without scrolls (Victor) ‡	$1,500	$2,400	$2,700	$4,000
1900 Bank type ‡	$15,000	$21,000	$34,000	—
1901 Imprint type, no name ‡	$1,700	$2,100	$3,200	$4,500
1901 Imprint type, Boyd Park. Denver ‡	$1,700	$2,100	$3,200	$4,500
1901 Imprint type, Slusher. Cripple Creek ‡	$2,000	$2,500	$3,500	$5,500
1901 Imprint type, Mullen. Victor ‡	$2,500	$3,700	$6,500	$11,000
1901 Imprint type, Cohen. Victor ‡	$5,000	$7,500	$11,000	$15,000
1901 Imprint type, Klein. Pueblo ‡	$7,000	$9,500	$14,000	$20,000
1901 Imprint type, Alexander. Salida ‡	$7,500	$10,000	$16,000	$23,000
1901 Imprint type, White. Grand Junction ‡	$13,000	$20,000	$30,000	—
1901 Imprint type, Goodspeeds. Colorado Springs ‡	$27,000	$37,000	$50,000	—
1901 Imprint type, Nelson. Holdrege, Nebraska ‡	$20,000	$30,000	$40,000	—
1901 Imprint type, A.W. Clark (Denver) ‡ (a)			$42,000	

‡ All Lesher Referendum Tokens are ranked in the *100 Greatest American Medals and Tokens*, as a single entry. **a.** This piece is unique.

Confederate Issues

The Confederate States of America proclaimed itself in February 1861, a few weeks after Abraham Lincoln was elected president of the United States in November 1860. The newly formed nation based its monetary system on the Confederate dollar. Its paper currency was backed not by hard assets (such as gold) but by the promise to pay the bearer after the war was over—assuming Southern victory and independence. In addition to paper money, the Confederacy also explored creating its own coinage for day-to-day circulation. While this goal never came to fruition, interesting relics remain as testaments to the effort.

CONFEDERATE CENTS

Facts about the creation of the original Confederate cents are shrouded in mystery. However, a plausible storyline has developed based on research and recollections, through telling and retelling over the years. An order to make cents for the Confederacy is said to have been placed with Robert Lovett Jr., an engraver and diesinker of Philadelphia, through Bailey & Co., a jewelry firm of that city. Fearing arrest by the United States government for assisting the enemy, Lovett decided instead to hide the coins and the dies in his cellar. Captain John W. Haseltine, well known for finding numismatic rarities unknown to others, claimed that a bartender had received one of the coins over the counter and sold it to him. Haseltine recognized it as the work of Lovett, called on him, learned that he had struck 12 of the coins, and bought the remaining 11 and the dies. In 1874 Haseltine made restrikes in copper, silver, and gold.

Circa 1961, the dies were copied and additional pieces made by New York City coin dealer Robert Bashlow. These show prominent die cracks and rust marks that distinguish them from earlier examples.

	Mintage	Unc. PF
1861 Cent, Original, Copper-Nickel, Unc.	13–16	$135,000
1861 Cent, Haseltine Restrike, Copper, Proof	55	$15,000
1861 Cent, Haseltine Restrike, Gold, Proof	7	$45,000
1861 Cent, Haseltine Restrike, Silver, Proof	12	$12,500

CONFEDERATE HALF DOLLARS

According to records, only four original Confederate half dollars were struck (on a hand press). Regular silver planchets were used, as well as a regular federal obverse die. One of the coins was given to Secretary of the Treasury Christopher G. Memminger, who passed it on to President Jefferson Davis for his approval. Another was given to Professor John L. Riddell of the University of Louisiana. Edward Ames of New Orleans received a third specimen. The last was kept by chief coiner Benjamin F. Taylor. Lack of bullion prevented the Confederacy from coining more pieces.

The Confederate half dollar was unknown to collectors until 1879, when a specimen and its reverse die were found in Taylor's possession in New Orleans. E. Mason Jr., of Philadelphia, purchased both and later sold them to J.W. Scott and Company of New York. J.W. Scott acquired 500 genuine 1861-O half dollars, routed or otherwise smoothed away the reverses, and then restamped them with the Confederate die. Known as restrikes, these usually have slightly flattened obverses. Scott also struck some medals in white metal using the Confederate reverse die and an obverse die bearing this inscription: 4 ORIGINALS STRUCK BY ORDER OF C.S.A. IN NEW ORLEANS 1861 / ******* / REV. SAME AS U.S. (FROM ORIGINAL DIE•SCOTT)

Confederate Reverse   **Scott Obverse**

	Mintage	VF-20	EF-40	Unc.
1861 HALF DOL. (a)		—	$1,000,000	—
	Auctions: $881,250, VF, January 2015			
1861 HALF DOL., Restrike	500	$6,500	$7,500	$15,000
1861 Scott Obverse, Confederate Reverse	500	$3,000	$4,000	$6,500

a. 4 examples are known.

Hawaiian and Puerto Rican Issues

Although the following issues of Hawaii and Puerto Rico were not circulating U.S. coins, they have political, artistic, and sentimental connections to the United States. Generations of American numismatists have sought them for their collections.

HAWAIIAN ISSUES

Five official coins were issued for the Kingdom of Hawaii. These include the 1847 cent issued by King Kamehameha III and the 1883 silver dimes, quarters, halves, and dollars of King Kalakaua I. The silver pieces were all designed by U.S. Mint chief engraver Charles E. Barber and struck at the San Francisco Mint. The 1883 eighth-dollar piece is a pattern. The 1881 five-cent piece is an unofficial issue.

The Hawaiian dollar was officially valued equal to the U.S. dollar. After Hawaii became a U.S. territory in 1900, the legal-tender status of these coins was removed and most were withdrawn from circulation and melted.

1847, One Cent

1883, Ten Cents

1883, Eighth Dollar

1881, Five Cents
Unofficial issue.

1883, Quarter Dollar

1883, Half Dollar

1883, Dollar

| | Mintage | F-12 | VF-20 | EF-40 | AU-50 | MS-60 | MS-63 |
							PF-63
1847 Cent (a)	100,000	$325	$425	$600	$800	$900	$1,800
	Auctions: $2,585, MS-64BN, August 2014; $3,056, MS-64BN, November 2014; $2,350, MS-63RB, August 2014						
1881 Five Cents		$7,000	$9,000	$10,000	$11,000	$14,000	$20,000
	Auctions: $14,688, MS-63, August 2014						
1881 Five Cents, Proof (b)							$7,000
	Auctions: $2,185, PF-62, June 2001						
1883 Ten Cents	249,974	$65	$100	$250	$350	$850	$1,750
	Auctions: $1,528, MS-63, July 2014; $823, MS-62, September 2014; $282, AU-55, September 2014; $206, EF-45, July 2014						
1883 Ten Cents, Proof	26						$15,000
	Auctions: $12,690, PF-64, August 2014; $11,750, PF-63, November 2014						
1883 Eighth Dollar, Proof	20						$40,000
	Auctions: $8,800, PF-50, July 1994						
1883 Quarter Dollar	499,974	$75	$100	$135	$165	$250	$400
	Auctions: $9,400, MS-67, July 2014; $1,293, MS-66, August 2014; $823, MS-65, August 2014; $646, MS-65, August 2014						
1883 Quarter Dollar, Proof	26						$15,000
	Auctions: $10,575, PF-62, January 2017						
1883 Half Dollar	699,974	$125	$175	$275	$425	$900	$1,750
	Auctions: $17,625, MS-66, August 2014; $5,875, MS-65, August 2014; $2,350, MS-64, August 2014; $2,115, MS-64, August 2014						
1883 Half Dollar, Proof	26						$20,000
	Auctions: $31,200, PF-64, April 2018; $14,100, PF-63, November 2014						
1883 Dollar	499,974	$350	$500	$750	$1,200	$3,500	$7,500
	Auctions: $10,575, MS-64, July 2014; $6,463, MS-63, August 2014; $1,087, AU-55, July 2014; $823, EF-45, August 2014						
1883 Dollar, Proof	26						$35,000
	Auctions: $22,325, PF-61, November 2014						

a. Values shown are for the most common of the six known varieties. **b.** All Proofs were made circa 1900.

PLANTATION TOKENS

During the 1800s, several private firms issued tokens for use as money in Hawaiian company stores. These are often referred to as Plantation tokens. The unusual denomination of 12-1/2 cents was equivalent to a day's wages in the sugar plantations, and was related to the fractional part of the Spanish eight-reales coin.

(1860) Undated, Waterhouse Token

(1871) Undated, Wailuku Plantation

1880, Wailuku Plantation

1882, Haiku Plantation

1891, Kahului Railroad

	F-12	VF-20	EF-40	AU-50
Waterhouse / Kamehameha IV, ca. 1860	$1,500	$2,750	$4,000	$6,500
Wailuku Plantation, 12-1/2 (cents), (1871), narrow starfish	$750	$2,000	$3,750	$6,200
Similar, broad starfish	$800	$2,300	$4,250	$7,250
Wailuku Plantation, VI (6-1/4 cents), (1871), narrow starfish	$1,800	$4,750	$7,000	$9,500
Similar, broad starfish	$2,000	$5,500	$7,500	$10,000
Thomas H. Hobron, 12-1/2 (cents), 1879 (a)	$600	$850	$1,100	$1,400
Similar, two stars on both sides	$1,600	$3,000	$6,000	$10,000
Thomas H. Hobron, 25 (cents), 1879 (b)			$55,000	$70,000
Wailuku Plantation, 1 Real, 1880	$750	$1,800	$3,500	$7,500
Wailuku Plantation, Half Real, 1880	$2,100	$5,000	$8,500	$11,500
Haiku Plantation, 1 Rial, 1882	$750	$1,250	$1,750	$2,250
Grove Ranch Plantation, 12-1/2 (cents), 1886	$1,500	$3,000	$5,000	$7,000
Grove Ranch Plantation, 12-1/2 (cents), 1887	$2,500	$4,500	$8,000	$10,500
Kahului Railroad, 10 cents, 1891	$3,000	$6,000	$11,000	$13,500
Kahului Railroad, 15 cents, 1891	$3,000	$6,000	$11,000	$13,500
Kahului Railroad, 20 cents, 1891	$3,000	$6,000	$11,000	$13,500
Kahului Railroad, 25 cents, 1891	$3,000	$6,000	$11,000	$13,500
Kahului Railroad, 35 cents, 1891	$3,000	$6,000	$11,000	$13,500
Kahului Railroad, 75 cents, 1891	$3,000	$6,000	$11,000	$13,500

a. Rare varieties exist. a. 3 examples are known.

PUERTO RICAN ISSUES

Puerto Rico, the farthest east of the Greater Antilles, lies about 1,000 miles southeast of Florida between the Atlantic Ocean and the Caribbean Sea. Settled by Spain in 1508, the island was ceded to the United States after the Spanish-American War in 1898. Puerto Ricans were granted U.S. citizenship in 1917. Today Puerto Rico is a self-governing territory of the United States with commonwealth status.

The Puerto Rican coins of 1895 and 1896 were minted at the Casa de Moneda de Madrid, in Spain. The peso was struck in .900 fine silver, and the others were .835 fine. The portrait is of King Alfonso XIII, and the arms are of the Bourbons, the royal house of Spain. These coins were in circulation at the time of the Spanish-American War of 1898, which ended with U.S. victory and with Spain's loss of sovereignty over Cuba (along with its cession of the Philippine Islands, Puerto Rico, and Guam to the United States for $20 million). Puerto Rico's Spanish coins continued to circulate after the war.

Collectors of United States coins often include Puerto Rican coins in their collections, even though they are not U.S. issues. After the Spanish-American War, exchange rates were set for these coins relative to the U.S. dollar, and the island transitioned to a dollar-based currency. Today in Puerto Rico the dollar is still popularly referred to as a "peso."

1896, 5 Centavos

1896, 10 Centavos

1895, 20 Centavos

1896, 40 Centavos

1895, One Peso

	Mintage	F-12	VF-20	EF-40	AU-50	Unc.
1896 5 Centavos	600,000	$30	$50	$100	$150	$200
	Auctions: $56, EF-45, September 2014					
1896 10 Centavos	700,000	$40	$85	$135	$200	$300
	Auctions: $170, AU-55, September 2014; $212, AU-55, January 2014					
1895 20 Centavos	3,350,000	$45	$100	$150	$250	$400
	Auctions: No auction records available.					
1896 40 Centavos	725,002	$180	$300	$900	$1,700	$2,900
	Auctions: $705, AU-55, January 2015; $352, EF-45, January 2015					
1895 1 Peso	8,500,021	$200	$400	$950	$2,000	$3,250
	Auctions: $3,819, MS-63, September 2014; $1,380, AU-55, June 2006					

Philippine Issues

In April 1899, control of the Philippine Islands was officially transferred from Spain to the United States, as a condition of the treaty ending the Spanish-American War. The U.S. military suppressed a Filipino insurgency through 1902, and partway through that struggle, in July 1901, the islands' military government was replaced with a civilian administration led by American judge William Howard Taft. One of its first tasks was to sponsor a new territorial coinage that was compatible with the old Spanish issues, but also legally exchangeable for American money at the rate of two Philippine pesos to the U.S. dollar. The resulting coins—which bear the legend UNITED STATES OF AMERICA but are otherwise quite different in design from regular U.S. coins—today can be found in many American coin collections, having been brought to the States as souvenirs by service members after World War II or otherwise saved. The unusual designs, combined with the legend, have sometimes caused them to be confused with standard federal United States coins.

The coins, introduced in 1903, were designed by Filipino silversmith, sculptor, engraver, and art professor Melecio Figueroa, who had earlier worked for the Spanish *Casa de Moneda*, in Manila. They are sometimes called "Conant coins" or "Conants," after Charles Arthur Conant, an influential American journalist and banking expert who served on the commission that brought about the Philippine Coinage Act of March 2, 1903. "Both in the artistic quality of the designs and in perfection of workmanship, they compare favorably with anything of the kind ever done in America," wrote Secretary of War Elihu Root in his annual report to President Theodore Roosevelt. Figueroa died of tuberculosis on July 30, 1903, age 61, shortly after seeing his coins enter circulation.

Following Spanish custom, the dollar-sized peso was decimally equivalent to 100 centavos. Silver fractions were minted in denominations of fifty, twenty, and ten centavos, and minor coins (in copper-nickel and bronze) included the five-centavo piece, the centavo, and the half centavo.

In addition to the name of the United States, the coins bear the Spanish name for the islands: FILIPINAS. The silver coins feature a female personification of the Philippines, holding in one hand a hammer that she strikes against an anvil, and in the other an olive branch, with the volcanic Mount Mayon (northeast of the capital city of Manila) visible in the background. The minor coinage shows a young Filipino man, bare-chested and seated at an anvil with a hammer, again with Mount Mayon seen in the distance. The first reverse design, shared across all denominations, shows a U.S. federal shield surmounted by an eagle with outstretched wings, clutching an olive branch in its right talon and a bundle of arrows in its left. This reverse design was changed in 1937 to a new shield emblem derived from the seal of the 1936 Commonwealth.

Dies for the coins were made at the Philadelphia Mint by the U.S. Mint's chief engraver, Charles F. Barber. Mintmarks were added to the dies, as needed, at the branch mints. From 1903 to 1908 the coins were struck at the Philadelphia Mint (with no mintmark) and the San Francisco Mint (with an S mintmark). From

1909 through 1919, they were struck only at San Francisco. In the first part of 1920, one-centavo coins were struck in San Francisco; later in the year a new mint facility, the Mint of the Philippine Islands, was opened in Manila, and from that point into the early 1940s Philippine coins of one, five, ten, twenty, and fifty centavos were struck there. The coins produced at the Manila Mint in 1920, 1921, and 1922 bore no mintmark. No Philippine coins were struck in 1923 or 1924. The Manila Mint reopened in 1925; from then through 1941 its coinage featured an M mintmark. The Denver and San Francisco mints would be used for Philippine coinage in the final years of World War II, when the islands were under Japanese occupation.

Rising silver prices forced reductions in the fineness and weight for each Philippine silver denomination beginning in 1907, and subsequent issues are smaller in diameter. The new, smaller twenty-centavo piece was very close in size to the five-centavo piece (20.0 mm compared to 20.5 mm), resulting in a mismatching of dies for these two denominations in 1918. A small number of error coins were minted from this accidental combination, with some finding their way into circulation (often with the edge crudely reeded to induce them to pass as twenty-centavo coins). A solution was found by reducing the diameter of the five-centavo piece beginning in 1930.

It should be noted that, in addition to normal coins and paper currency, special token money in the form of coins and printed currency was made for use in the Culion Leper Colony. The token coinage saw six issues from 1913 to 1930, some produced at the Manila Mint. The leper colony was set up in May 1906 on the small island of Culion, one of the more than 7,000 islands comprising the Philippines, and the coinage was intended to circulate only there.

In 1935 the United States, responding to popular momentum for independence, approved the establishment of the Commonwealth of the Philippines, with the understanding that full self-governing independence would be recognized after a ten-year transition period. In 1936 a three-piece set of silver commemorative coins was issued to mark the transfer of executive power.

An adaptation of the new commonwealth's seal, introduced on the 1936 commemorative coins, was used for the reverse design of all circulating Philippine issues beginning in 1937. For their obverses, the Commonwealth coins retained the same Figueroa designs as those struck from 1903 to 1936. (A final transitional issue of more than 17 million 1936-dated one-centavo coins was minted using the federal-shield reverse design, rather than the new Commonwealth shield.)

After the bombing of Pearl Harbor, Japanese military forces advanced on the Philippines in late 1941 and early 1942, prompting the civil government to remove much of the Philippine treasury's bullion to the United States. Nearly 16 million pesos' worth of silver remained, mostly in the form of one-peso pieces of 1907 through 1912. These coins were hastily crated and dumped into Manila's Caballo Bay to prevent their capture by Japan. The Japanese occupied the Philippines, learned of the hidden treasure, and managed to recover some of the sunken coins (probably fewer than half a million). After the war, over the course of several years, more than 10 million of the submerged silver pesos were retrieved under the direction of the U.S. Treasury and, later, the Central Bank of the Philippines. Most of them show evidence of prolonged salt-water immersion, with dark corrosion that resists cleaning. This damage to so many coins has added to the scarcity of high-grade pre-war silver pesos.

Later during World War II, in 1944 and 1945, the U.S. Mint struck coins for the Philippines at its Philadelphia, Denver, and San Francisco facilities. These coins were brought over and entered circulation as U.S. and Philippine military forces fought to retake the islands from the Japanese.

After the war, the Commonwealth of the Philippines became an independent republic, on July 4, 1946, as had been scheduled by the Constitution of 1935. Today the Philippine coins of 1903 to 1945, including the set of commemoratives issued in 1936, remain significant mementoes of a colorful and important chapter in U.S. history and numismatics. They are a testament to the close ties and special relationship between the United States of America and the Republic of the Philippines.

PHILIPPINES UNDER U.S. SOVEREIGNTY (1903–1936)

The Philippine Islands were governed under the sovereignty of the United States from 1899 until early 1935. (In the latter year a largely self-governing commonwealth was established, followed by full independence in 1946.) Coinage under U.S. sovereignty began in 1903. There was a final issue of centavos dated 1936, minted in the style of 1903–1934, after which the design of all circulating coins changed to the new Commonwealth style.

BRONZE COINAGE

HALF CENTAVO (1903–1908)

Designer: *Melecio Figueroa.* **Weight:** *2.35 grams.* **Composition:** *.950 copper, .050 tin and zinc.* **Diameter:** *17.5 mm.* **Edge:** *Plain.* **Mint:** *Philadelphia.*

History. In 1903 and 1904 the United States minted nearly 18 million half centavos for the Philippines. By March of the latter year, it was obvious that the half centavo was too small a denomination, unneeded in commerce despite the government's attempts to force it into circulation. The recommendation of Governor-General Luke Edward Wright—that the coin be discontinued permanently—was approved, and on April 18, 1904, a new contract was authorized to manufacture one-centavo blanks out of unused half-centavo blanks. In April 1908, Governor-General James Francis Smith received permission to ship 37,827 pesos' worth of stored half centavos (7,565,400 coins) to the San Francisco Mint to be re-coined into one-centavo pieces. Cleared from the Philippine Treasury's vaults, the coins were shipped to California in June 1908, and most of them were melted and made into 1908 centavos.

Striking and Sharpness. Half centavos typically are well struck, except for the 1903 issue, of which some coins may show weak numerals in the date. Reverses sometimes show light flattening of the eagle's wing tips.

Half Centavo, 1903–1908

High Points of Wear. *Obverse Checkpoints:* 1. Figure's left hand. 2. Figure's right hand. 3. Face and frontal hair just above ear. 4. Edge of anvil. *Reverse Checkpoints:* 1. Eagle's wing tips. 2. Eagle's breast feathers. 3. Upper points of shield. 4. Eagle's right leg.

Proofs. The Philadelphia Mint struck small quantities of Proof half centavos for collectors throughout the denomination's existence, for inclusion in Proof sets (except for 1907, when no Proof sets were issued).

	Mintage	EF	MS-60	MS-63
		PF-60	PF-63	PF-65
1903	12,084,000	$5	$15	$65
	Auctions: $138, MS-65RD, September 2012; $247, MS-65RB, September 2013; $103, MS-65RB, September 2012			
1903, Proof	2,558		$125	$175
	Auctions: $447, PF-67RB, October 2014; $282, PF-66RD, October 2014			
1904	5,654,000	$8	$20	$75
	Auctions: $270, MS-65RD, July 2013; $200, MS-65BN, January 2013; $65, MS-64RB, July 2013			
1904, Proof	1,355		$140	$200
	Auctions: $382, PF-66RB, November 2014			
1905, Proof (a)	471	$175	$300	$550
	Auctions: $253, PF-64RB, June 2007; $207, PF-62BN, January 2012			
1906, Proof (a)	500	$150	$250	$500
	Auctions: $323, PF-65BN, January 2012; $374, PF-64RB, June 2007			
1908, Proof (a)	500	$150	$250	$500
	Auctions: $282, PF-64RB, April 2014; $230, PF-64RB, January 2012			

Note: The half centavo was unpopular in circulation. More than 7,500,000 were withdrawn and melted to be recoined as one-centavo pieces in 1908. **a.** Proof only.

One Centavo (1903–1936)

Designer: *Melecio Figueroa.* **Weight:** *4.7 grams.* **Composition:** *.950 copper, .050 tin and zinc.* **Diameter:** *24 mm.* **Edge:** *Plain.* **Mints:** *Philadelphia, San Francisco, and Manila.*

Mintmark location is on the reverse, to the left of the date.

History. Unlike the half centavo, the bronze centavo was a popular workhorse of Philippine commerce from the start of its production. Nearly 38 million coins were minted in the denomination's first three years. In 1920 the centavo was struck for circulation by two different mints (the only year this was the case). San Francisco produced the coins during the first part of 1920; later in the year, the coins were struck at the Manila Mint, after that facility opened. From that point forward all centavos struck under U.S. sovereignty were products of the Manila Mint. Those dated 1920, 1921, and 1922 bear no mintmark identifying their origin. Manila produced no coins (of any denomination) in 1923 and 1924.

Coin collectors, notably educator, writer, and American Numismatic Association member Dr. Gilbert S. Perez, urged Manila Mint officials to include an M mark on their coinage—similar to the way that, for example, San Francisco coins were identified by an S—and this change was made starting with the coinage of 1925.

Coinage of the centavo continued through the late 1920s and early 1930s. U.S. sovereignty was significantly altered in 1935 with the establishment of the Commonwealth of the Philippines, and this change was reflected in all Philippine currency. A final mintage of 1936-dated centavos (17,455,463 pieces) was struck using the federal-shield reverse of the denomination's 1903–1934 coinage. The coin then switched over to the Commonwealth shield design in 1937.

Several centavo die varieties exist to give the specialist a challenge. Among them is the 1918-S, Large S, whose mintmark appears to be the same size and shape of that used on fifty-centavo pieces of the era.

Striking and Sharpness. On the obverse, the figure's right hand (holding the hammer) is almost always found flatly struck. The reverse, especially of later-date centavos, often shows flattening of the eagle's breast and of the left part of the shield. Issues of the Manila Mint, especially of 1920, often are lightly struck. Those of San Francisco typically are better struck, with only occasional light strikes. On centavos of 1929 to 1936, the M mintmark often is nearly unidentifiable as a letter.

One Centavo, 1903–1936

High Points of Wear. *Obverse Checkpoints:* 1. Figure's left hand. 2. Frontal hair just above ear. 3. Head of hammer. 4. Left part of anvil. *Reverse Checkpoints:* 1. Eagle's breast feathers. 2. Upper points of shield. 3. Eagle's right leg.

Proofs. One-centavo Proofs were struck at the Philadelphia Mint for annual Proof sets in 1903, 1904, 1905, 1906, and 1908. Proof centavos of 1908 bear a date with numerals noticeably larger than those of circulation-strike 1908-S coins.

1908-S, S Over S

	Mintage	VF	EF	MS-60	MS-63
				PF-60	PF-63
1903	10,790,000	$1.25	$5	$18	$65
Auctions: $247, MS-66BN, January 2014					
1903, Proof	2,558			$90	$175
Auctions: $408, PF-65RB, April 2010; $212, PF-65RB, October 2015					
1904	17,040,400	$1.25	$5	$20	$75
Auctions: $94, MS-65BN, July 2015					
1904, Proof	1,355			$95	$185
Auctions: $217, PF-65RD, August 2013; $141, PF-64RB, April 2014					
1905	10,000,000	$1.25	$5	$25	$75
Auctions: $76, MS-64BN, June 2014					
1905, Proof	471			$175	$325
Auctions: $441, PF-65RB, April 2014; $805, PF-65RB, April 2010; $235, PF-64RD, August 2013					
1906, Proof (a)	500			$150	$275
Auctions: $423, PF-64RD, February 2014					
1908, Proof (a)	500			$150	$275
Auctions: $411, PF-66RD, October 2014; $499, PF-65RB, January 2014; $400, PF-65RB, August 2015					
1908-S	2,187,000	$4	$8	$30	$95
Auctions: $141, MS-65RB, April 2014; $129, MS-65RB, February 2014; $84, MS-64RB, December 2015					
1908-S, S Over S	(b)	$40	$85	$150	$350
Auctions: $558, MS-64RB, January 2014					

a. Proof only. b. Included in 1908-S mintage figure.

1918-S, Normal S   **1918-S, Large S**

	Mintage	VF	EF	MS-60	MS-63
1909-S	1,737,612	$20	$35	$80	$180
	Auctions: $317, MS-65RB, August 2014; $153, MS-64RB, December 2015; $62, MS-64BN, March 2014				
1910-S	2,700,000	$4	$10	$20	$95
	Auctions: $881, MS-66RD, April 2015; $118, MS-65RB, April 2014; $80, MS-64RB, April 2014				
1911-S	4,803,000	$4	$10	$20	$100
	Auctions: $90, MS-65RB, April 2014; $64, MS-64RB, March 2014				
1912-S	3,001,000	$5	$12	$25	$120
	Auctions: $118, MS-65BN, March 2014; $90, MS-64BN, June 2014				
1913-S	5,000,000	$5	$12	$25	$110
	Auctions: $270, MS-65BN, November 2014; $79, MS-63BN, January 2014; $62, MS-63BN, April 2015				
1914-S	5,000,500	$4	$10	$20	$95
	Auctions: $84, MS-64BN, November 2014; $113, MS-64BN, May 2014				
1915-S	2,500,000	$45	$85	$400	$850
	Auctions: $805, MS-63BN, June 2011; $647, MS-62BN, January 2014				
1916-S	4,330,000	$8	$15	$80	$150
	Auctions: $135, MS-64BN, July 2014; $159, MS-63RB, June 2014				
1917-S	7,070,000	$5	$12	$60	$120
	Auctions: $176, MS-65RD, February 2014; $53, MS-62BN, September 2014				
1917-S, 7 Over 6	(c)	$80	$150	$300	$500
	Auctions: No auction records available.				
1918-S	11,660,000	$5	$12	$80	$125
	Auctions: $212, MS-65BN, January 2015; $229, MS-64RB, June 2014				
1918-S, Large S	(d)	$125	$250	$800	$2,000
	Auctions: $2,585, MS-62BN, January 2016; $306, EF-45, January 2014				
1919-S	4,540,000	$5	$15	$25	$120
	Auctions: $110, MS-64BN, June 2014; $128, MS-64BN, January 2014				
1920	3,552,259	$4	$12	$25	$120
	Auctions: $259, MS-65RB, January 2014; $353, MS-65BN, June 2014				
1920-S	2,500,000	$5	$18	$30	$135
	Auctions: $236, MS-64BN, January 2014; $90, MS-62BN, March 2014				
1921	7,282,673	$3	$8	$20	$85
	Auctions: $153, MS-65RB, January 2014				
1922	3,519,100	$3	$8	$20	$75
	Auctions: $223, MS-65RB, January 2014; $52, MS-64BN, March 2014				
1925-M	9,325,000	$3	$8	$20	$75
	Auctions: $68, MS-64BN, May 2014				
1926-M	9,000,000	$3	$8	$20	$70
	Auctions: $89, MS-65BN, January 2015; $30, MS-64RB, March 2014				
1927-M	9,279,000	$3	$8	$20	$70
	Auctions: $212, MS-66RD, April 2014; $165, MS-66RB, January 2014				
1928-M	9,150,000	$3	$8	$20	$70
	Auctions: $141, MS-65RD, October 2015; $75, MS-64RD, April 2014; $50, MS-64RB, May 2014				
1929-M	5,657,161	$3	$8	$20	$75
	Auctions: $141, MS-65RD, January 2014; $106, MS-65RB, October 2015; $43, MS-63BN, March 2014				

c. Included in 1917-S mintage figure. d. Included in 1918-S mintage figure.

	Mintage	VF	EF	MS-60	MS-63
1930-M	5,577,000	$3	$8	$20	$70
	Auctions: $69, MS-65BN, January 2014; $75, MS-64RD, August 2014				
1931-M	5,659,355	$3	$8	$20	$70
	Auctions: $100, MS-65RB, December 2015; $40, MS-65RB, March 2014; $89, MS-65RB, January 2014				
1932-M	4,000,000	$3	$10	$25	$80
	Auctions: $112, MS-65RD, April 2014; $95, MS-65RD, January 2014				
1933-M	8,392,692	$2	$5	$15	$60
	Auctions: $147, MS-66RD, January 2014; $80, MS-66RB, March 2014; $141, MS-65RB, December 2015				
1934-M	3,179,000	$3	$6	$20	$65
	Auctions: $200, MS-66RD, April 2014; $112, MS-65RB, January 2014				
1936-M	17,455,463	$3	$6	$20	$65
	Auctions: $37, MS-64BN, March 2014				

COPPER-NICKEL COINAGE

FIVE CENTAVOS (1903–1935)

Designer: *Melecio Figueroa.* **Weight:** *1903–1928, 5 grams; 1930–1935, 4.75 grams.*
Composition: *.750 copper, .250 nickel.* **Diameter:** *1903–1908, 20.5 mm; 1930–1935, 19 mm.*
Edge: *Plain.* **Mints:** *Philadelphia, San Francisco, and Manila.*

Five Centavos, Large Size
(1903–1928, 20.5 mm)

Mintmark location is on the reverse, to the left of the date.

Five Centavos, Reduced Size
(1930–1935, 19 mm)

History. Five-centavo coins were minted under U.S. sovereignty for the Philippines from 1903 to 1935, with several gaps in production over the years. Circulation strikes were made in Philadelphia in 1903 and 1904, then coinage resumed in 1916, this time at the San Francisco Mint. The newly inaugurated Manila Mint took over all five-centavo production starting in 1920, continuing through the end of direct U.S. administration, and under the Commonwealth government beginning in 1937.

The Manila Mint coins of 1920 and 1921 bore no mintmark indicating their producer, a situation noticed by coin collectors of the day. Gilbert S. Perez, superintendent of schools for Tayabas in the Philippines (and a member of the American Numismatic Association), wrote to Assistant Insular Treasurer Salvador Lagdameo in June 1922: "Several members of numismatic societies in Europe and America have made inquiries as to why the Manila mint has no distinctive mint mark. Some do not even know that there is a mint in the Philippine Islands and that the mint is operated by Filipinos." He recommended the letter M be used to identify Manila's coins. Lagdameo replied later that month, thanking Perez and informing him: "It is now being planned that the new dies to be ordered shall contain such mark, and it is hoped that the coins of 1923 and subsequent years will bear the distinctive mint mark suggested by you." Coinage would not resume at the Manila facility until 1925, but from that year forward the mintmark would grace the coins struck in the Philippines.

The diameter of the five-centavo coin was 20.5 mm diameter from 1903 to 1928. This was very close to the 20 mm diameter of the twenty-centavo coin of 1907 to 1929. By 1928 there had been two separate instances where a reverse die of one denomination was "muled" to an obverse of the other. In 1918 this occurred by accident when a small quantity of five-centavo pieces was struck in combination with the reverse die of the twenty centavos (identifiable by its wider shield and a smaller date, compared to the normal five-centavo reverse). This error was known to numismatists by 1922, by which time it was recognized as a scarce variety. The second instance of muling, in 1928, is discussed under twenty-centavo pieces. In 1930, to clearly differentiate the sizes of the coins, the diameter of the five-centavo piece was reduced from 20.5 to 19.0 mm.

Five-centavo coinage under U.S. sovereignty continued to 1935. From 1937 on, the Manila Mint's production of five-centavo coins would use the new Commonwealth shield design on the reverse.

Striking and Sharpness. The obverse of the 1918 and 1919 San Francisco Mint issues often is weakly struck, with considerable loss of detail. The Manila Mint started production in 1920, and many five-centavo coins from that year lack sharpness in the rims and have weak details overall.

Five Centavos, 1903–1928

High Points of Wear. *Obverse Checkpoints:* 1. Figure's right hand. 2. Frontal hair just above ear. 3. Figure's left hand. *Reverse Checkpoints:* 1. Eagle's breast feathers. 2. Eagle's wing tip (to viewer's right). 3. Upper points of shield.

Five Centavos, 1930–1935

High Points of Wear. *Obverse Checkpoints:* 1. Figure's right hand. 2. Frontal hair just above ear. 3. Edge of anvil. *Reverse Checkpoints:* 1. Eagle's breast feathers. 2. Eagle's wing tip (to viewer's right).

Proofs. Five-centavo Proofs were struck at the Philadelphia Mint for annual Proof sets in 1903, 1904, 1905, 1906, and 1908.

	Mintage	VF	EF	MS-60 / PF-60	MS-63 / PF-63
1903	8,910,000	$2	$8	$25	$65
	Auctions: $247, MS-66, July 2013; $200, MS-65, August 2013; $242, MS-65, December 2012; $123, MS-65, January 2015				
1903, Proof	2,558			$95	$180
	Auctions: $270, PF-66, August 2013; $223, PF-65, October 2015; $200, PF-65, November 2013				

	Mintage	VF	EF	MS-60	MS-63
				PF-60	PF-63
1904	1,075,000	$3	$10	$35	$85
	Auctions: $82, MS-64, June 2013; $76, MS-64, May 2013				
1904, Proof	1,355			$100	$185
	Auctions: $235, PF-65, August 2013; $153, PF-64, October 2014; $153, PF-64, August 2013				
1905, Proof (a)	471			$200	$400
	Auctions: $952, PF-67, August 2012; $476, PF-65, August 2013; $382, PF-64, August 2013				
1906, Proof (a)	500			$175	$300
	Auctions: $617, PF-66, October 2014; $670, PF-66, August 2013; $400, PF-65, August 2013				
1908, Proof (a)	500			$200	$300
	Auctions: $505, PF-66, October 2014; $969, PF-66, August 2013; $500, PF-66, August 2013				
1916-S	300,000	$100	$275	$800	$1,800
	Auctions: $4,465, MS-65, January 2016; 240, MS-62, January 2014; $235, MS-62, February 2014				
1917-S	2,300,000	$5	$12	$60	$180
	Auctions: $423, MS-65, April 2014; $447, MS-64, August 2014				
1918-S	2,780,000	$8	$15	$80	$200
	Auctions: $306, MS-63, August 2014; $188, MS-62, January 2014				
1918-S, S Over S	(b)	$20	$150	$600	$1,250
	Auctions: No auction records available.				
1918-S, Mule (c)	(b)	$500	$1,200	$2,500	$8,000
	Auctions: $14,100, MS-61, January 2016; $544, VF-30, April 2014				
1919-S	1,220,000	$15	$30	$200	$450
	Auctions: $588, MS-64, September 2014; $499, MS-63, January 2014				
1920	1,421,078	$8.50	$20	$175	$375
	Auctions: $141, MS-63, January 2014; $200, MS-63, July 2013				
1921	2,131,529	$9	$15	$125	$300
	Auctions: $212, MS-63, August 2013; $212, MS-63, July 2013; $153, MS-63, August 2014				
1925-M	1,000,000	$12	$30	$175	$300
	Auctions: $575, MS-64, November 2011; $423, MS-63, December 2015; $217, MS-63, January 2014				
1926-M	1,200,000	$5	$25	$140	$250
	Auctions: $112, MS-62, January 2014				
1927-M	1,000,000	$5	$10	$90	$150
	Auctions: $259, MS-65, January 2014; $129, MS-64, June 2014				
1928-M	1,000,000	$7	$14	$75	$150
	Auctions: $259, MS-65, January 2014; $259, MS-63, November 2015; $96, MS-63, June 2014				
1930-M	2,905,182	$2.50	$6	$50	$100
	Auctions: $353, MS-65, September 2014; $71, MS-64RD, July 2014; $153, MS-64, August 2013				
1931-M	3,476,790	$2.50	$6	$75	$150
	Auctions: $108, MS-64, June 2014; $74, MS-64, October 2015; $86, MS-63, June 2014				
1932-M	3,955,861	$2	$6	$50	$130
	Auctions: $143, MS-64, June 2014; $65, MS-62, January 2014				
1934-M	2,153,729	$3.50	$10	$100	$300
	Auctions: $306, MS-64, September 2014; $170, MS-63, June 2014; $88, MS-63, July 2013				
1934-M, Recut 1	(d)	$10	$35	$125	$300
	Auctions: No auction records available.				
1935-M	2,754,000	$2.50	$8	$85	$225
	Auctions: $282, MS-64, September 2014; $100, MS-63, January 2014				

a. Proof only. b. Included in 1918-S mintage figure. c. Small Date Reverse of twenty centavos. d. Included in 1934-M mintage figure.

SILVER COINAGE

TEN CENTAVOS (1903–1935)

Designer: *Melecio Figueroa.* **Weight:** *1903–1906, 2.7 grams (.0779 oz. ASW);*
1907–1935, 2 grams (.0482 oz. ASW). **Composition:** *1903–1906, .900 silver, .100 copper;*
1907–1935, .750 silver, .250 copper. **Diameter:** *1903–1906, 17.5 mm; 1907–1935, 16.5 mm.*
Edge: *Reeded.* **Mints:** *Philadelphia, San Francisco, and Manila.*

| Ten Centavos, Large Size (1903–1906, 17.5 mm) | Mintmark location is on the reverse, to the left of the date. | Ten Centavos, Reduced Size (1907–1935, 16.5 mm) |

History. The Philippine ten-centavo coin was minted from 1903 to 1935, in several facilities and with occasional interruptions in production.

In 1907 the silver ten-centavo coin's fineness was reduced from .900 to .750, and at the same time its diameter was decreased. This was in response to the rising price of silver, with the goal of discouraging exportation and melting of the silver coins. The net effect was nearly 40 percent less silver, by actual weight, in the new ten-centavo piece. The older coins continued to be removed from circulation, and by June 30, 1911, it was reported that only 35 percent of the ten-centavo pieces minted from 1903 to 1906 still remained in the Philippines.

The Manila Mint took over ten-centavo production from San Francisco in 1920. The ten-centavo coins of 1920 and 1921 bear no mintmark identifying them as products of Manila (this was the case for all Philippine coinage of those years, and of 1922). The efforts of Philippine numismatists, including American Numismatic Association member Gilbert S. Perez, encouraged mint officials to add the M mintmark when the facility reopened in 1925 after a two-year hiatus for all coinage.

Ten-centavo production after 1921 consisted of 1 million pieces struck in 1929 and just less than 1.3 million in 1935. The next ten-centavo mintage would be under the Commonwealth, not U.S. sovereignty.

Die varieties include a 1912-S with an S Over S mintmark, and date variations of the 1914-S.

Striking and Sharpness. The ten-centavo coins of 1903 to 1906 generally are well struck, although some show slight weakness of features. Those of 1907 to 1935 also are generally well struck; some obverses may have slight flattening of the hair just above the ear and on the upper part of the figure. On the reverse, check the eagle's breast feathers for flatness.

Ten Centavos, 1903–1906

High Points of Wear. *Obverse Checkpoints:* 1. Figure's left bosom. 2. Figure's right knee. 3. Figure's left knee. 4. Edge of anvil. *Reverse Checkpoints:* 1. Eagle's breast feathers. 2. Upper points of shield. 3. Eagle's wing tips. 4. Eagle's right leg.

Ten Centavos, 1907–1935

High Points of Wear. *Obverse Checkpoints:* 1. Figure's left thigh. 2. Figure's left bosom. 3. Figure's left hand. *Reverse Checkpoints:* 1. Eagle's breast feathers. 2. Upper points of shield. 3. Eagle's right leg.

Proofs. Ten-centavo Proofs were struck at the Philadelphia Mint for annual Proof sets in 1903, 1904, 1905, 1906, and 1908.

	Mintage	VF	EF	MS-60 / PF-60	MS-63 / PF-63
1903	5,102,658	$4	$5	$35	$75
	Auctions: $188, MS-65, January 2015; $100, MS-64, October 2014; $76, MS-64, July 2013				
1903, Proof	2,558			$100	$195
	Auctions: $270, PF-65, May 2014; $153, PF-63, September 2015; $70, PF-60, June 2013				
1903-S	1,200,000	$25	$45	$350	$1,200
	Auctions: $1,645, MS-62, January 2014				
1904	10,000	$30	$50	$120	$250
	Auctions: $397, MS-66, September 2014; $223, MS-65, July 2013; $100, MS-64, November 2014				
1904, Proof	1,355			$110	$220
	Auctions: $388, PF-66, October 2014; $259, PF-64, April 2015; $153, PF-64, October 2014; $88, PF-62, June 2014				
1904-S	5,040,000	$4	$9	$65	$120
	Auctions: $92, MS-64, June 2014; $59, MS-62, November 2014				
1905, Proof (a)	471			$225	$450
	Auctions: $259, PF-63, June 2004; $299, PF-62, April 2011				
1906, Proof (a)	500			$150	$375
	Auctions: $470, PF-65, April 2014; $212, PF-61, January 2014				
1907	1,500,781	$4	$8	$60	$135
	Auctions: $223, MS-65, April 2014; $188, MS-65, January 2014; $118, MS-65, August 2013				
1907-S	4,930,000	$2	$5	$40	$70
	Auctions: $170, MS-64, June 2014; $90, MS-63, May 2014				
1908, Proof (a)	500			$175	$325
	Auctions: $617, PF-66, October 2014; $353, PF-65, January 2014; $207, PF-63, January 2012				
1908-S	3,363,911	$2	$5	$40	$70
	Auctions: $306, MS-65, September 2014; $112, MS-64, January 2014				
1909-S	312,199	$30	$65	$450	$1,200
	Auctions: $2,350, MS-65, April 2015; $752, MS-62, May 2014; $382, MS-61, January 2014				
1911-S	1,000,505	$10	$15	$250	$600
	Auctions: $588, MS-63, January 2014				

a. Proof only.

| 1912-S, S Over S | 1914-S, Short Crossbar | 1914-S, Long Crossbar |

	Mintage	VF	EF	MS-60 / PF-60	MS-63 / PF-63
1912-S	1,010,000	$6	$12	$150	$300
	Auctions: $306, MS-63, April 2014				
1912-S, S Over S	(b)		$85	$200	$500
	Auctions: $646, MS-63, September 2014				
1913-S	1,360,693	$4.25	$13	$140	$250
	Auctions: $558, MS-65, September 2014, $270, MS-63, June 2014				
1914-S (c)	1,180,000	$6	$12	$175	$375
	Auctions: $411, MS-63, May 2014; $374, MS-63, April 2010				
1915-S	450,000	$25	$40	$350	$800
	Auctions: $1,234, MS-64, January 2014; $200, AU-58, January 2014				
1917-S	5,991,148	$2	$3	$20	$65
	Auctions: $247, MS-65, June 2014; $447, MS-64, July 2014; $129, MS-64, October 2015				
1918-S	8,420,000	$2	$3	$20	$75
	Auctions: $188, MS-65, December 2015; $129, MS-65, January 2013; $306, MS-63, July 2014				
1919-S	1,630,000	$2.50	$3.50	$30	$110
	Auctions: $182, MS-64, June 2014				
1920	520,000	$6	$16	$105	$300
	Auctions: $494, MS-64, June 2014				
1921	3,863,038	$2	$3	$25	$50
	Auctions: $182, MS-65, June 2014; $153, MS-63, July 2014				
1929-M	1,000,000	$2	$3	$25	$45
	Auctions: $176, MS-65, December 2015; $123, MS-65, June 2014				
1935-M	1,280,000	$2	$4	$30	$50
	Auctions: $182, MS-65, June 2014				

b. Included in 1912-S mintage figure. c. Varieties exist with a short or long crossbar in the 4 of 1914. The Long Crossbar is scarcer.

TWENTY CENTAVOS (1903–1929)

Designer: *Melecio Figueroa.* **Weight:** *1903–1906, 5.385 grams (.1558 oz. ASW);
1907–1929, 4 grams (.0964 oz. ASW).* **Composition:** *1903–1906, .900 silver, .100 copper;
1907–1929, .750 silver, .250 copper.* **Diameter:** *1903–1906, 23 mm; 1907–1929, 20 mm.*
Edge: *Reeded.* **Mints:** *Philadelphia, San Francisco, and Manila.*

| Twenty Centavos, Large Size (1903–1906, 23 mm) | *Mintmark location is on the reverse, to the left of the date.* | Twenty Centavos, Reduced Size (1907–1929, 20 mm) |

History. In the early 1900s the rising value of silver was encouraging exportation and melting of the Philippines' silver twenty-centavo coins. As was the case with the ten-centavo piece, in 1907 the diameter of the twenty-centavo coin was reduced and its silver fineness decreased from .900 to .750. The net effect was about 40 percent less silver, by actual weight, in the new smaller coins. Attrition continued to draw the older coins out of circulation and into the melting pot, as their silver value exceeded their face value. A report of June 30, 1911, held that only about 25 percent of the twenty-centavo coins minted from 1903 to 1906 still remained in the Philippines.

Circulation strikes were made at the Philadelphia and San Francisco mints through 1919. In July 1920, a new "Mint of the Philippine Islands," located in Manila, started production. Its output during the period of U.S. sovereignty included twenty-centavo pieces in 1920, 1921, 1928, and 1929. (Production of the coins later continued under the Commonwealth, with a slightly modified design.) The first two years of coinage did not feature a mintmark identifying Manila as the producer of the coins. This was noticed by collectors of Philippine coins; they protested the oversight, and later coinage dies had an M mintmark added.

In 1928 a rush order for twenty-centavo coins was received at the Manila Mint—by that time the only producer of the denomination. Manila had not minted the coins since 1921, and the Philadelphia Mint had not shipped any new reverse dies (which would have featured their 1928 date). Under pressure to produce the coins, workers at the Manila Mint married a regular twenty-centavo obverse die with the 1928-dated reverse die of the five-centavo denomination, which was only .5 mm larger. As a result, the entire mintage of 100,000 1928 twenty centavos consists of these "mule" (mismatched-die) coins. The reverse of the 1928 coins, compared with others of 1907 to 1929, has a narrower shield and a larger date.

Striking and Sharpness. Most twenty centavos of 1903 to 1906 are well struck. The 1904-S usually shows weak striking on the figure's left bosom, the frontal hair just above her ear, and her left hand. Most of the coins of 1907 to 1929 show flattening of the figure's hair, sometimes extending into the area of her left bosom and her left hand.

Twenty Centavos, 1903–1906

High Points of Wear. *Obverse Checkpoints:* 1. Figure's left thigh and knee. 2. Figure's left bosom. 3. Figure's left hand. *Reverse Checkpoints:* 1. Eagle's breast feathers. 2. Upper points of shield. 3. Eagle's right leg.

Twenty Centavos, 1907–1929

High Points of Wear. *Obverse Checkpoints:* 1. Figure's left thigh. 2. Edge of anvil. 3. Figure's left bosom. 4. Figure's left hand. *Reverse Checkpoints:* 1. Eagle's breast feathers. 2. Eagle's right leg. 3. Upper points of shield.

Proofs. Twenty-centavo Proofs were struck at the Philadelphia Mint for annual Proof sets in 1903, 1904, 1905, 1906, and 1908.

	Mintage	VF	EF	MS-60 / PF-60	MS-63 / PF-63
1903	5,350,231	$3.50	$15	$45	$100
	Auctions: $88, MS-64, July 2014; $86, AU-55, July 2014				
1903, Proof	2,558			$125	$200
	Auctions: $482, PF-66, October 2014; $129, PF-63, September 2014; $123, PF-63, September 2014				
1903-S	150,080	$25	$50	$600	$1,900
	Auctions: $447, AU-58, May 2014				
1904	10,000	$45	$60	$125	$250
	Auctions: $529, MS-66, June 2014; $194, MS-64, May 2014; $200, MS-63, January 2016; $188, MS-62, January 2015				
1904, Proof	1,355			$150	$225
	Auctions: $200, PF-65, July 2014; $153, PF-63, May 2014; $200, PF-61, January 2014				
1904-S	2,060,000	$7.50	$11	$110	$200
	Auctions: $223, MS-64, January 2015; $211, MS-64, March 2014; $411, MS-63, January 2014				
1905, Proof (a)	471			$250	$500
	Auctions: $470, PF-64, January 2013; $282, PF-61, January 2014				
1905-S	420,000	$20	$45	$425	$1,250
	Auctions: No auction records available.				
1906, Proof (a)	500			$225	$425
	Auctions: $541, PF-66, October 2014; $564, PF-64, April 2015; $329, PF-62, November 2014; $329, PF-62, October 2014				
1907	1,250,651	$6	$12	$200	$450
	Auctions: $881, MS-63, April 2015; $558, MS-63, September 2014				
1907-S	3,165,000	$4.50	$10	$75	$200
	Auctions: $3,525, MS-65, April 2015; $374, MS-63, January 2010; $247, MS-62, June 2014				
1908, Proof (a)	500			$200	$400
	Auctions: $397, PF-64, January 2014; $299, PF-63, January 2012				
1908-S	1,535,000	$3.50	$10	$100	$300
	Auctions: $1,880, MS-64, September 2015; $2,233, MS-63, September 2014				
1909-S	450,000	$12.50	$50	$600	$1,500
	Auctions: $5,640, MS-66, April 2015; $4,113, MS-64, April 2014; $1,528, MS-64, January 2013				
1910-S	500,259	$25	$60	$400	$1,200
	Auctions: $9,988, MS-66, April 2015; $3,450, MS-64, April 2012; $2,070, MS-63, April 2012				
1911-S	505,000	$25	$45	$400	$1,000
	Auctions: $2,350, MS-64, September 2013				
1912-S	750,000	$10	$30	$200	$400
	Auctions: $294, MS-63, July 2014				
1913-S	795,000	$10	$15	$175	$300
	Auctions: $235, MS-63, July 2014; $247, MS-62, June 2014				
1914-S	795,000	$12.50	$30	$300	$750
	Auctions: $353, MS-63, January 2014				
1915-S	655,000	$20	$50	$500	$1,800
	Auctions: $1,116, MS-63, January 2014; $270, AU-58, May 2014				
1916-S (b)	1,435,000	$10	$17.50	$225	$725
	Auctions: $373, AU-55, November 2013				
1917-S	3,150,655	$5	$8	$75	$200
	Auctions: $1,293, MS-66, September 2014; $646, MS-65, September 2014				
1918-S	5,560,000	$4	$6	$50	$125
	Auctions: $188, MS-64, January 2014; $66, MS-63, June 2014				
1919-S	850,000	$6	$15	$125	$225
	Auctions: $1,880, MS-66, January 2014; $106, MS-61, November 2014				

a. Proof only. b. Tilted 6 and Straight 6 varieties exist.

	Mintage	VF	EF	MS-60	MS-63
1920	1,045,415	$8	$20	$135	$225
	Auctions: $411, MS-63, September 2014				
1921	1,842,631	$2	$7	$50	$90
	Auctions: $79, MS-63, January 2014; $48, AU-58, May 2014				
1928-M, Mule (c)	100,000	$15	$50	$900	$1,800
	Auctions: $3,055, MS-65, April 2014; $3,525, MS-64, January 2016; $2,233, MS-64, January 2013				
1929-M	1,970,000	$3	$5	$40	$100
	Auctions: $92, MS-64, June 2014; $21, AU-55, May 2014				
1929-M, 2 Over 2 Over 2	(d)		$75	$250	$600
	Auctions: No auction records available.				

c. Reverse of 1928 five centavos. d. Included in 1929-M mintage figure.

FIFTY CENTAVOS (1903–1921)

Designer: *Melecio Figueroa.* **Weight:** *1903–1906, 13.48 grams (.3900 oz. ASW);
1907–1921, 10 grams (.2411 oz. ASW).* **Composition:** *1903–1906, .900 silver, .100 copper;
1907–1921, .750 silver, .250 copper.* **Diameter:** *1903–1906, 30 mm; 1907–1921, 27 mm.*
Edge: *Reeded.* **Mints:** *Philadelphia, San Francisco, and Manila.*

Fifty Centavos, Large Size
(1903–1906, 30 mm)

Mintmark location is
on the reverse, to
the left of the date.

Fifty Centavos, Reduced Size
(1907–1921, 27 mm)

History. After four years of fifty-centavo coinage, in 1907 the denomination's silver fineness was lowered from .900 to .750, and its diameter was reduced by ten percent. This action was in response to rising silver prices. The new smaller coins contained 38 percent less silver, by actual weight, than their 1903–1906 forebears, making them unprofitable to melt for their precious-metal content. Gresham's Law being what it is ("Bad money will drive out good"), the older, heavier silver coins were quickly pulled from circulation; by June 30, 1911, it was officially reported that more than 90 percent of the 1903–1906 coinage had disappeared from the Philippines.

The reduced-size coins of the U.S. sovereignty type were minted from 1907 to 1921. The Manila Mint took over their production from the Philadelphia and San Francisco mints in 1920, using coinage dies shipped from Philadelphia. The fifty centavos was the largest denomination produced at the Manila Mint. Neither the 1920 nor the 1921 coinage featured a mintmark identifying Manila as its producer.

Production of the fifty-centavo denomination would again take place, in 1944 and 1945, in San Francisco, using the Commonwealth design introduced for circulating coins in 1937.

Striking and Sharpness. On fifty-centavo coins of 1903 to 1906, many obverses show slight flattening of the frontal hair just above the figure's ear. The reverses sometimes show slight flattening of the eagle's breast feathers. On the reverse, a high spot on the shield is the result of an unevenness in striking. The coins of 1907 to 1921 often show notable flatness of strike in the figure's hair just above her ear, and sometimes on her left hand. A flat strike on the abdomen and left leg should not be mistaken for circulation wear. The reverses are quite unevenly struck; observe the top part of the shield, which has a depressed middle and raised sides. The right side is slightly higher than the left and may show some flattening.

Fifty Centavos, 1903–1906

High Points of Wear. *Obverse Checkpoints:* 1. Edge of anvil. 2. Figure's left thigh and knee. 3. Figure's right knee. 4. Figure's right bosom. *Reverse Checkpoints:* 1. Part of shield just to left of lower-right star. 2. Eagle's breast feathers. 3. Eagle's right leg and claws.

Fifty Centavos, 1907–1921

High Points of Wear. *Obverse Checkpoints:* 1. Figure's left thigh and lower leg. 2. Mid-drapery. 3. Figure's left bosom. 4. Edge of anvil. *Reverse Checkpoints:* 1. Eagle's breast feathers. 2. Eagle's right leg. 3. Part of shield just to left of lower-right star.

Proofs. Fifty-centavo Proofs were struck at the Philadelphia Mint for annual Proof sets in 1903, 1904, 1905, 1906, and 1908. Proofs of 1908 often are found with considerable flatness in the frontal hair above Miss Liberty's hair and sometimes with flatness in her left hand.

	Mintage	VF	EF	MS-60 / PF-60	MS-63 / PF-63
1903	3,099,061	$7.50	$10	$75	$120
	Auctions: $259, MS-64, May 2014; $165, MS-64, September 2013; $129, MS-62, January 2014				
1903, Proof	2,558			$150	$275
	Auctions: $1,140, PF-67, February 2018; $764, PF-66, January 2016; $734, PF-66, October 2014; $189, PF-64, September 2014				
1903-S (a)			$30,000		
	Auctions: No auction records available.				
1904	10,000	$50	$80	$150	$350
	Auctions: $1,234, MS-66+, June 2014; $329, MS-64, September 2015; $223, MS-63, November 2014; $247, MS-63, May 2014				
1904, Proof	1,355			$175	$350
	Auctions: $476, PF-65, September 2012; $470, PF-64, April 2015; $247, PF-63, February 2014				
1904-S	216,000	$15	$25	$125	$225
	Auctions: $881, MS-65, September 2014; $443, MS-64, May 2014				
1905, Proof (b)	471			$350	$625
	Auctions: $3,760, PF-65, January 2016; $764, PF-63, January 2015; $411, PF-63, April 2014				
1905-S	852,000	$20	$75	$700	$2,100
	Auctions: $1,058, MS-62, April 2014; $206, AU-55, June 2014				

a. 2 examples are known. **b.** Proof only.

	Mintage	VF	EF	MS-60 PF-60	MS-63 PF-63
1906, Proof (b)	500			$325	$575
Auctions: $2,820, PF-67, October 2014; $940, PF-65, April 2014; $353, PF-61, November 2014					
1907	1,200,625	$15	$40	$250	$475
Auctions: $1,763, MS-64, April 2014; $427, MS-62, September 2014					
1907-S	2,112,000	$12.50	$30	$225	$450
Auctions: $5,640, MS-66, August 2015; $499, MS-63, September 2014; $427, MS-62, September 2014					
1908, Proof (b)	500			$300	$525
Auctions: $1,645, PF-66, January 2016; $499, PF-64, April 2014; $499, PF-64, January 2014					
1908-S	1,601,000	$15	$40	$500	$1,800
Auctions: $2,820, MS-63, January 2014; $823, MS-62, September 2014					
1909-S	528,000	$17.50	$60	$450	$1,400
Auctions: $4,230, MS-65, April 2015; $1,645, MS-64, April 2014; $1,528, MS-63, January 2014					
1917-S	674,369	$15	$35	$200	$550
Auctions: $541, MS-63, December 2015; $294, MS-63, January 2014; $411, MS-62, September 2014					
1918-S	2,202,000	$7.50	$15	$125	$220
Auctions: $129, MS-62, June 2014; $176, MS-61, January 2014					
1918-S, S Over Inverted S	(c)	$7.50	$15	$185	$600
Auctions: No auction records available.					
1919-S	1,200,000	$7.50	$15	$100	$225
Auctions: $353, MS-64, July 2014; $129, MS-62, January 2015					
1920	420,000	$7.50	$12.50	$120	$200
Auctions: $211, MS-64, January 2014; $212, MS-62, July 2014					
1921	2,316,763	$5	$11	$70	$110
Auctions: $588, MS-65, January 2016; $62, MS-63, October 2014; $94, MS-63, July 2014; $82, MS-63, July 2013					

b. Proof only. c. Included in 1918-S mintage figure.

ONE PESO (1903–1912)

Designer: *Melecio Figueroa.* **Weight:** *1903–1906, 26.96 grams (.7800 oz. ASW); 1907–1912, 20 grams (.5144 oz. ASW).* **Composition:** *1903–1906, .900 silver, .100 copper; 1907–1912, .800 silver, .200 copper.* **Diameter:** *1903–1906, 38 mm; 1907–1912, 35 mm.* **Edge:** *Reeded.* **Mints:** *Philadelphia and San Francisco.*

Peso, Large Size
(1903–1906, 38 mm)

Peso, Reduced Size
(1907–1912, 35 mm)

Mintmark location is on the
reverse, to the left of the date.

History. The Philippine silver peso was struck under U.S. sovereignty from 1903 to 1912. The key date among those struck for circulation is the issue of 1906-S. Although the San Francisco Mint produced more than 200,000 of the coins that year, nearly all of them were held back from circulation. They were instead stored and then later sold as bullion.

By 1906 natural market forces were driving the Philippine silver pesos out of commerce and into the melting pot: the rising price of silver made the coins worth more as precious metal than as legal tender. In 1907 the U.S. Mint responded by lowering the denomination's silver fineness from .900 to .800 and reducing its diameter from 38 mm to 35. The resulting smaller coins had about one-third less silver, by actual weight, than those of 1903 to 1906, guaranteeing that they would stay in circulation. The older coins, meanwhile, were still profitable to pull aside and melt for their silver value. An official report of June 30, 1911, disclosed that less than ten percent of the heavier silver coins still remained in the Philippines.

The new smaller pesos were minted every year from 1907 to 1912, with the San Francisco Mint producing them for commerce and the Philadelphia Mint striking a small quantity of Proofs in 1907 and 1908. Millions of the coins were stored as backing for Silver Certificates (and, later, Treasury Certificates) in circulation in the Philippines. Although the Manila Mint started operations in 1920, the silver peso was never part of its production for circulation.

In December 1941, Imperial Japan, immediately after attacking Pearl Harbor, began a fierce assault on the Philippines. Manila fell on January 2, 1942, and General Douglas MacArthur, commander of U.S. Army Forces in the Far East, fell back to the Bataan Peninsula. In late February President Franklin Roosevelt ordered him to leave the Philippines for Australia, prompting the general's famous promise to the Philippine people: "I shall return!" Not long after the fighting erupted it had become apparent that the Japanese would overtake the islands, and early in 1942 the U.S. military dumped crates holding 15,700,000 silver pesos, mostly of 1907–1912 coinage, into the sea near Corregidor, to avoid their seizure. Many millions of these coins were salvaged by the U.S. Treasury and the Central Bank of the Philippines after the war, with all but about five million pieces being reclaimed by 1958. Today a great majority of the salvaged "war pesos" show clear evidence of their prolonged submersion in saltwater. A typical effect is a dark corrosion strongly resistant to any manner of cleaning or conservation.

Striking and Sharpness. The silver pesos of 1903 to 1906 generally have well-struck obverses, but occasionally with some flattening of the figure's frontal hair above her ear, and sometimes her left bosom and hand. On the reverse, the feathers on the eagle's breast are indistinctly cut, and the wing tips can sometimes be found slightly flatly struck. Of the silver pesos of 1907 to 1912, some but not all exhibit flattened frontal hair, and sometimes a flattened left hand. On the reverse, the eagle's breast feathers are not clearly defined. On some examples the reverses are quite unevenly struck; check the top part of the shield, which has a depressed middle and raised sides, and the right side, which is slightly higher than the left and may show some flattening.

One Peso, 1903–1906

High Points of Wear. *Obverse Checkpoints:* 1. Figure's upper-left leg and knee. 2. Figure's right knee. 3. Figure's left bosom. 4. Frontal hair just above ear. *Reverse Checkpoints:* 1. Eagle's breast feathers. 2. Eagle's right leg. 3. Eagle's wing tips.

One Peso, 1907–1912

High Points of Wear. *Obverse Checkpoints:* 1. Figure's upper-left leg and knee. 2. Figure's lower-left leg. 3. Figure's left hand. 4. Frontal hair just above ear. *Reverse Checkpoints:* 1. Eagle's breast feathers. 2. Eagle's right leg.

Proofs. Proof pesos were struck at the Philadelphia Mint for annual Proof sets in 1903, 1904, 1905, 1906, and 1908. Unlike the smaller denominations, Proof pesos of 1907 also are known—but only to the extent of two examples.

1905-S, Curved Serif on "1"   1905-S, Straight Serif on "1"

	Mintage	VF	EF	MS-60	MS-63
				PF-60	PF-63
1903	2,788,901	$50	$65	$250	$1,200
Auctions: $3,290, MS-64, January 2016; $552, MS-63, October 2014					
1903, Proof	2,558			$350	$1,000
Auctions: $3,525, PF-67, October 2014; $999, PF-65, January 2016; $200, PF-62, September 2014					
1903-S	11,361,000	$40	$50	$160	$600
Auctions: $690, MS-63, March 2011; $188, MS-60, January 2014; $129, AU-58, September 2015					
1904	11,355	$100	$180	$400	$1,000
Auctions: $3,995, MS-65, January 2016; $705, MS-64, January 2014; $329, MS-63, August 2013					
1904, Proof	1,355			$450	$1,200
Auctions: $7,050, PF-67, January 2016; $3,525, PF-67, October 2014; $3,290, PF-67, October 2014; $881, PF-64, September 2014					
1904-S	6,600,000	$40	$55	$180	$850
Auctions: $440, MS-63, September 2014; $282, MS-62, May 2015; $188, MS-62, January 2015					
1905, Proof (a)	471			$1,000	$2,500
Auctions: $11,163, PF-67, January 2013; $5,875, PF-65, January 2016; $911, PF-63, October 2014					
1905-S, Curved Serif on "1"	6,056,000	$75	$120	$450	$1,200
Auctions: $764, MS-61, January 2014					
1905-S, Straight Serif on "1"	(b)	$100	$150	$2,000	$6,000
Auctions: $3,819, MS-63, September 2014					
1906, Proof (a)	500			$900	$2,200
Auctions: $3,819, PF-67, October 2014; $3,525, PF-67, October 2014; $6,463, PF-66, January 2016; $1,880, PF-63, April 2014					
1906-S	201,000	$2,000	$4,500	$22,000	$50,000
Auctions: $7,050, AU-55, October 2014; $7,638, AU-55, April 2014					

Note: Philippine silver pesos of 1907–1912 that were corroded from submersion in Caballo Bay during World War II are worth considerably less than their problem-free counterparts, but are avidly collected for their historical value. **a.** Proof only. **b.** Included in 1905-S, Curved Serif on "1," mintage figure.

	Mintage	VF	EF	MS-60 PF-60	MS-63 PF-63
1907, Proof (a,c)					$160,000
	Auctions: $189,750, PF, June 2012				
1907-S	10,278,000	$20	$30	$200	$600
	Auctions: $940, MS-64, October 2014; $447, MS-63, March 2015; $188, MS-62, December 2014; $112, MS-60, January 2014				
1908, Proof (a)	500			$900	$1,800
	Auctions: $2,585, PF-66, January 2016; $1,763, PF-64, January 2015; $940, PF-64, August 2014; $999, PF-64, January 2014				
1908-S	20,954,944	$20	$30	$200	$550
	Auctions: $881, MS-64, January 2016; $852, MS-64, January 2015; $705, MS-64, September 2014				
1909-S	7,578,000	$25	$35	$275	$800
	Auctions: $4,935, MS-65, April 2015; $1,058, MS-64, October 2014; $235, MS-62, January 2014				
1909-S, S Over S	(d)	$100	$400	$1,200	
	Auctions: No auction records available.				
1910-S	3,153,559	$28	$55	$500	$1,200
	Auctions: $5,170, MS-65, April 2015; $489, MS-63, January 2010				
1911-S	463,000	$100	$160	$1,400	$5,000
	Auctions: $5,875, MS-62, January 2016				
1912-S	680,000	$140	$220	$4,000	$12,000
	Auctions: $14,100, MS-63, August 2017; $7,344, MS-61, August 2016; $999, AU-58, April 2014				

Note: Philippine silver pesos of 1907–1912 that were corroded from submersion in Caballo Bay during World War II are worth considerably less than their problem-free counterparts, but are avidly collected for their historical value. **a.** Proof only. **c.** 2 examples are known. **d.** Included in 1909-S mintage figure.

MANILA MINT OPENING MEDAL (1920)

Designer: *Clifford Hewitt.* **Composition:** *bronze; silver; gold.*
Diameter: *38 mm.* **Edge:** *Plain.* **Mint:** *Manila.*

Bronze

Silver

Gold

History. During U.S. sovereignty, much of the civilian government of the Philippines was administered by the Bureau of Insular Affairs, part of the War Department. Most heads or secretaries of Philippine government departments were appointed by the U.S. governor general, with the advice and consent of the Philippine Senate. In 1919, the chief of the Bureau of the Insular Treasury (part of the Department of Finance) was Insular Treasurer Albert P. Fitzsimmons, formerly a mayor of Tecumseh, Nebraska, and member of the municipal board of Manila. Fitzsimmons, a surgeon who had served in the U.S. Army Medical Corps in Cuba and the Philippines, was active in civil affairs, and had been in charge of U.S. government bond issues in the Philippines during the Great War. On May 20, 1919, he was named director ad interim of the Mint of the Philippine Islands, which was then being organized.

The genesis of this new mint started on February 8, 1918, when the Philippine Legislature passed an appropriations bill for construction of its machinery. The war in Europe was interfering with shipments from the San Francisco Mint, where Philippine coinage was produced, and a local mint was seen as more expedient and economical. In addition, a mint in Manila would serve the United States' goal of preparing the Philippines for its own governance and infrastructure.

The mint was built in Manila in the Intendencia Building, which also housed the offices and hall of the Senate, and the offices and vaults of the Philippine Treasury. Its machinery was designed and built in Philadelphia under the supervision of U.S. Mint chief mechanical engineer Clifford Hewitt, who also oversaw its installation in Manila. The facility was opened, with formalities and machine demonstrations, on July 15, 1920. The fanfare included the production of an official commemorative medal, the first example of which was struck by Speaker of the House of Representatives Sergio Osmeña.

The medal has since come to be popularly known as the "Wilson Dollar" (despite not being a legal-tender coin), because of its size and its bold profile portrait of Woodrow Wilson on the obverse, surrounded by the legend PRESIDENT OF THE UNITED STATES. The reverse features the ancient Roman goddess Juno Moneta guiding a youth—representing the fledgling mint staff of the Philippines—in the art of coining. She holds a pair of metallurgical scales. The reverse legend is TO COMMEMORATE THE OPENING OF THE MINT / MANILA P.I., along with the date, 1920. The medal was designed by Hewitt, the mint's supervising engineer from Philadelphia. Its dies were made by U.S. Mint chief engraver George T. Morgan, whose initial, M, appears on the obverse on President Wilson's breast and on the reverse above the goddess's sandal.

The issue was limited to 2,200 silver medals (2,000 of which were struck on the first day), sold to the public at $1 apiece; and 3,700 in bronze, sold for 50¢. In addition, at least five gold specimens were reportedly struck. These included one for presentation to President Wilson and one for U.S. Secretary of War Newton Baker. The other gold medals remained in the Philippines and were lost during World War II. Of the medals unsold and still held by the Treasury in the early 1940s, some or all were dumped into Caballo Bay in April 1942 along with millions of silver pesos, to keep them from the approaching Japanese forces. The invaders learned of the coins and in May attempted to recover the sunken silver coins using the labor of Filipino divers. Although skilled divers, the Filipinos were not experienced in deep-sea diving, and the coins were at the bottom of the bay, 120 feet below the surface. After three deaths the Filipinos refused to participate in further recovery efforts. The Japanese then forced U.S. prisoners of war who were experienced deep-sea divers to recover the coins and medals. The American divers conspired to salvage only small quantities of the sunken treasure. They repeatedly sabotaged the recovery process, and smuggled a significant number of recovered silver coins to the Philippine guerrillas. Only about 2 to 3 percent of the dumped coinage was recovered before the Japanese ceased recovery operations. Following the war the United States brought up much of the coinage that had been dumped into the sea. Many of the recovered silver and bronze Wilson dollars in grades VF through AU bear evidence of saltwater corrosion.

The Manila Mint Opening medal is popular with collectors of Philippine coins and of American medals. It is often cataloged as a *So-Called Dollar*, a classification of historic dollar-sized souvenir medals, some of which were struck by the U.S. Mint and some produced privately. The Manila Mint Opening medal is valued for its unique connections to the United States and to American numismatics.

	Mintage	VF-20	EF-40	AU-50	MS-60	MS-63	MS-65
Manila Mint medal, 1920, bronze	3,700	$50	$125	$235	$785	$1,350	$4,500
Manila Mint medal, 1920, silver	2,200	$100	$250	$350	$600	$2,000	$3,250

Note: VF, EF, and AU examples in bronze and silver often show signs of saltwater corrosion. The values above are for problem-free examples.

	Mintage	AU-55	MS-62
Manila Mint medal, 1920, gold	5	$45,000	$75,000

COMMONWEALTH ISSUES FOR CIRCULATION (1937–1945)

The Philippine Islands were largely self-governed, as a commonwealth of the United States, from 1935 until full independence was recognized in 1946. Coinage under the Commonwealth began with three commemorative coins in 1936 (see next section). Circulating issues were minted from 1937 to 1941 (in Manila) and in 1944 and 1945 (in Philadelphia, Denver, and San Francisco).

The Commonwealth coinage retained the obverse motifs designed by Melecio Figueroa and used on the coinage of 1903 to 1936. Its new reverse design featured a shield derived from the official seal of the government of the Philippines, with three stars symbolizing Luzon, Mindanao, and the Visayas, the islands' three main geographical regions. In the oval set in the shield's center is a modification of the colonial coat of arms of the City of Manila: a fortress tower above with a heraldic crowned *morse* or sea-lion (half dolphin, half lion) below. An eagle with outstretched wings surmounts the entirety of the shield design, and beneath is a scroll with the legend COMMONWEALTH OF THE PHILIPPINES.

World War II forced the Commonwealth government to operate in exile during the Japanese occupation of 1942 to 1945. A pro-Japan puppet government was set up in Manila in 1943; it issued no coins of its own, and in fact during the Japanese occupation many coins were gathered from circulation to be melted and remade into Japanese coins. Barter and low-denomination emergency paper money took their place in day-to-day commerce. (Much of the money used in the Philippines during World War II consisted of hastily printed "guerrilla" currency.) The United States military knew of the local need for circulating coins, and the U.S. and Philippine governments included new coinage in the plans to liberate the islands. The U.S. Treasury Department used its Philadelphia, San Francisco, and Denver mints to produce brass, copper-nickel-zinc, and silver coins in 1944 and 1945, to be shipped to the Philippines during and after the liberation.

Note that mintage figures given for 1938, 1939, 1940, and 1941 are estimates, as many Manila Mint records were lost during the war.

BRONZE AND BRASS COINAGE
ONE CENTAVO (1937–1944)
Designer: *Melecio Figueroa (obverse).* **Weight:** *5.3 grams.*
Composition: *.950 copper, .050 tin and zinc (except for 1944-S: .950 copper, .050 zinc).*
Diameter: *24 mm.* **Edge:** *Plain.* **Mints:** *Manila and San Francisco.*

Bronze Alloy (1937–1941)

Mintmark location is on the reverse, to the left of the date.

Brass Alloy (1944)

History. The Manila Mint struck one-centavo coins for the Commonwealth of the Philippines every year from 1937 through 1941. This production was brought to an end by the Japanese invasion that started in December 1941, immediately after the bombing of Pearl Harbor. Part of the United States–Commonwealth plan to retake the islands included the San Francisco Mint's 1944 striking of 58 million one-centavo coins—a quantity greater than all of Manila's centavo output since 1937. Like the federal Lincoln cents of 1944 to 1946, these coins were made of *brass* rather than bronze—their alloy was derived in part from recycled cartridge cases, and their composition included copper and zinc, but no tin (a vital war material). The coins were transported to the islands to enter circulation as U.S. and Philippine military forces fought back the Japanese invaders. This would be the final mintage of centavos until the Republic of the Philippines, created on July 4, 1946, resumed the denomination's production in 1958.

The centavo was a popular coin that saw widespread circulation. As a result, many of the coins today are found with signs of wear or damage, exacerbated by corrosion and toning encouraged by the islands' tropical climate.

Striking and Sharpness. Well-struck examples are uncommon. Obverses of the Commonwealth centavos usually have very flat or depressed strikes in the left shoulder of the seated figure, and part of the face and chest. His right hand is better struck than in the coins struck under U.S. sovereignty. The left side of the anvil's edge is slightly rounded. On the reverse, many Uncirculated coins have flatness on the lower and central sections of the coat of arms, and some or most of the words COMMONWEALTH OF THE PHILIPPINES are unreadable.

On a perfectly struck coin, the eagle surmounting the Commonwealth shield would have a pattern of feathers visible on its breast; this level of detail is rarely evident, with the breast instead appearing smooth or flat.

Many 1937-M centavos have a barely readable mintmark. Issues of 1938 to 1941 used a narrow M mintmark, rather than a square version of the letter, resulting in better legibility.

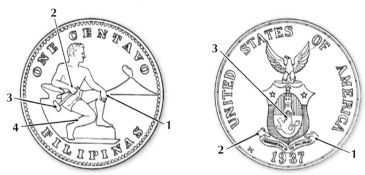

One Centavo, 1937–1944

High Points of Wear. *Obverse Checkpoints:* 1. Figure's left hand. 2. Figure's right hand. 3. Head of hammer. 4. Figure's right calf. *Reverse Checkpoints:* 1. Inner-right fold of ribbon. 2. Outer-left fold of ribbon. 3. Center of coat of arms.

	Mintage	VF	EF	MS-60	MS-63
1937-M	15,790,492	$3	$6	$18	$65
	Auctions: $153, MS-65RD, December 2015				
1938-M	10,000,000	$3	$6	$18	$60
	Auctions: $66, MS-65RB, March 2014; $94, MS-64RB, January 2014				
1939-M	6,500,000	$3	$6	$20	$65
	Auctions: $223, MS-66RD, April 2014				

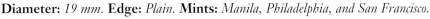

	Mintage	VF	EF	MS-60	MS-63
1940-M	*4,000,000*	$2	$5	$16	$60
	Auctions: $50, MS-65RB, May 2014; $30, MS-64RD, March 2014				
1941-M	*5,000,000*	$2	$5	$16	$60
	Auctions: $59, MS-65RD, March 2014				
1944-S	*58,000,000*	$0.50	$1	$4	$10
	Auctions: $32, MS-65RD, March 2014				

COPPER-NICKEL AND COPPER-NICKEL-ZINC COINAGE
FIVE CENTAVOS (1937–1945)

Designer: *Melecio Figueroa (obverse).* **Weight:** *1937–1941, 4.8 grams; 1944–1945, 4.92 grams.*
Composition: *1937–1941, .750 copper, .250 nickel; 1944–1945, .650 copper, .230 zinc, .120 nickel.*
Diameter: *19 mm.* **Edge:** *Plain.* **Mints:** *Manila, Philadelphia, and San Francisco.*

Copper-Nickel
(1937–1941)

*Mintmark location is on the reverse,
to the left of the date (Manila and San
Francisco issues only; Philadelphia
issues have no mintmark).*

Copper-Nickel-Zinc
(1944–1945)

*Manila mintmark style of 1937
and 1941 (wide, with midpoint
not extending to baseline).*

*Manila mintmark style of 1938
(narrow, with midpoint
extending to baseline).*

History. The Manila Mint switched its coinage of five-centavo pieces to the Commonwealth reverse design in 1937. Production of the coins increased in 1938, then skipped two years. The 1941 output would be Manila's last for the type; the Japanese invasion at year's end stopped all of its coinage.

Philippine commerce was starved for coins during the war. As part of the broader strategy for liberating the Philippines from Japanese occupation, the U.S. Treasury Department swung its mints into production of five-centavo coins in 1944 (Philadelphia and San Francisco) and 1945 (San Francisco alone). This effort dwarfed that of the Commonwealth's late-1930s coinage, producing in those two years more than ten times the combined output of 1937, 1938, and 1941. In order to help save copper and nickel for military use, the U.S. Mint reduced the proportions of those metals in the five-centavo coinage, making up for them with the addition of zinc. This substitution saved more than 4.2 million pounds of nickel and 3.2 million pounds of copper for the war effort. The Philadelphia and San Francisco coins were shipped to the islands during the combined American-Filipino military operations against Japan.

Striking and Sharpness. Most pre-war five-centavo coins are poorly struck. On the obverse, the seated figure's left hand is flat, and the left shoulder can be as well. The left side of the pedestal and the right side of Mount Mayon can be poorly detailed. The obverse rim typically lacks sharpness. On the reverse, the ribbon usually is flat, with its wording partially or completely illegible, and the coat of arms can lack detail especially at the top-left side. On a perfectly struck coin, the eagle surmounting the Commonwealth shield would have a pattern of feathers visible on its breast; this level of detail is rarely evident, with the breast instead appearing smooth or flat.

The mintmark style of 1937 and 1941—a wide M, with the middle point not descending to the letter's baseline—usually did not strike clearly, making it difficult to read. The mintmark style of 1938 was narrower, with the middle point descending to the base, and typically is more legible.

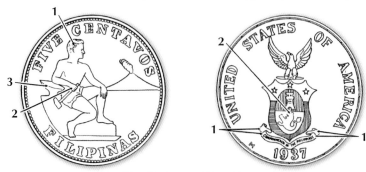

Five Centavos, 1937–1945

High Points of Wear. *Obverse Checkpoints:* 1. Frontal hair just above ear. 2. Figure's right hand. 3. Edge of anvil. *Reverse Checkpoints:* 1. Inner and outer folds of ribbon. 2. Center of coat of arms.

	Mintage	VF	EF	MS-60	MS-63
1937-M	2,493,872	$5	$7	$50	$75
	Auctions: $188, MS-65, September 2013				
1938-M	4,000,000	$1	$2.25	$25	$55
	Auctions: $92, MS-65, July 2014; $112, MS-65, September 2013				
1941-M	2,750,000	$4	$8	$55	$150
	Auctions: $282, MS-65, January 2014; $88, MS-64, September 2013				
1944 (a)	21,198,000	$0.50	$1	$3	$6
	Auctions: $46, MS-65, June 2013; $29, MS-64, April 2013				
1944-S (a)	14,040,000	$0.25	$0.50	$2	$5
	Auctions: $165, MS-67, September 2013; $200, MS-67, August 2013; $188, MS-67, August 2013				
1945-S (a)	72,796,000	$0.25	$0.50	$2	$5
	Auctions: No auction records available.				

a. Copper-nickel-zinc alloy.

SILVER COINAGE
TEN CENTAVOS (1937–1945)

Designer: *Melecio Figueroa.* **Weight:** *2 grams (.0482 oz. ASW).* **Composition:** *.750 silver, .250 copper.* **Diameter:** *16.5 mm.* **Edge:** *Reeded.* **Mints:** *Manila and Denver.*

Mintmark location is on the reverse, to the left of the date.

History. As with its production of other denominations, the Manila Mint under Commonwealth governance struck ten-centavo coins in 1937 and 1938, followed by a hiatus of two years, and a final coinage in 1941. Normal mint functions were interrupted in 1941 when Imperial Japan invaded the Philippines as part of its war with the United States. The Japanese puppet government of 1943–1945 would not produce any of its own coins, and the Manila Mint, damaged by bombing during the Japanese assault, was later used as part of the invaders' defensive fortifications on the Pasig River.

Japan's wartime exportation of Philippine coins resulted in scarcity of coinage in day-to-day commerce. The U.S. Treasury geared up the Denver Mint for a massive production of Philippine ten-centavo coins in 1944 and 1945, to be shipped overseas and enter circulation as American and Philippine troops liberated the islands. The 1945 coinage was particularly heavy: more than 130 million ten-centavo coins, compared to the Denver Mint's production of just over 40 million Mercury dimes that year. This large mintage of silver coins continued to circulate in the Philippines into the 1960s.

Striking and Sharpness. Well-struck examples of the Commonwealth ten-centavo coin are unusual. Part of the figure's bust is nearly always flatly struck, especially along the left side. The hair and left arm may also be poorly struck. On the reverse, the coat of arms usually lacks detail, and COMMONWEALTH OF THE PHILIPPINES, on the ribbon, often is only partly legible. On a perfectly struck coin, the eagle surmounting the Commonwealth shield would have a pattern of feathers visible on its breast; this level of detail is rarely evident, with the breast instead appearing smooth or flat.

The Denver coinage of 1944 and 1945 often is weakly struck on the obverse, with loss of detail. The reverse typically is weakly struck on the ribbon, with indistinct lettering.

The mintmark style of 1937 and 1941—a wide M, with the middle point not descending to the letter's baseline—usually did not strike clearly, making it difficult to read. The mintmark style of 1938 was narrower, with the middle point descending to the base, and typically is more legible.

Ten Centavos, 1937–1945

High Points of Wear. *Obverse Checkpoints:* 1. Figure's left leg. 2. Edge of anvil. 3. Mid-drapery area. *Reverse Checkpoints:* 1. Inner and outer folds of ribbon. 2. Center of coat of arms.

	Mintage	VF	EF	MS-60	MS-63
1937-M	3,500,000	$2.25	$3.50	$15	$45
	Auctions: $500, MS-67, January 2013				
1938-M	3,750,000	$1.75	$2.25	$12	$20
	Auctions: $36, MS-63, August 2009				
1941-M	2,500,000	$1.50	$2	$7	$12.50
	Auctions: $36, MS-65, August 2009				
1944-D	31,592,000	$1	$2	$2.50	$3.50
	Auctions: No auction records available.				
1945-D	137,208,000	$1	$2	$2.50	$3.50
	Auctions: No auction records available.				
1945-D, D Over D	(a)	$12	$35	$80	$160
	Auctions: $470, AU-50, April 2014				

a. Included in 1945-D mintage figure.

TWENTY CENTAVOS (1937–1945)

Designer: *Melecio Figueroa (obverse).* **Weight:** *4 grams (.0964 oz. ASW).*
Composition: *.750 silver, .250 copper.* **Diameter:** *20 mm.*
Edge: *Reeded.* **Mints:** *Manila and Denver.*

Mintmark location is on the
reverse, to the left of the date.

History. The twenty-centavo piece was the largest circulating coin struck by the Commonwealth of the Philippines at the Manila Mint. Production commenced in 1937 and 1938, followed by a hiatus of two years, and a final year of output in 1941 before Japan's December invasion put a halt to all coinage. During their occupation, the Japanese pulled many twenty-centavo pieces out of circulation and melted them as raw material for new imperial coins.

Anticipating driving the Japanese military out of the islands, the United States and Commonwealth governments planned an impressive production of coinage for the Philippines in 1944 and 1945. The Denver Mint was the source for twenty-centavo pieces, and its output was immense, in 1945 exceeding even the Philadelphia Mint's production of Washington quarters for domestic use. 111 million of the coins were shipped overseas to accompany the U.S. military as Americans and Filipinos fought to liberate the islands. The need was great, as legal-tender coins had largely disappeared from circulation. Most day-to-day commerce was transacted with small-denomination scrip notes and paper money issued by guerrilla military units, local governments, or anti-Japanese military and civilian currency boards.

Striking and Sharpness. Well-struck twenty-centavo Commonwealth coins are a challenge to locate. Nearly all obverses have flattened hair on the figure's head. On the reverse, the coat of arms usually lacks detail, and COMMONWEALTH OF THE PHILIPPINES, on the ribbon, often is only partly legible. The Denver coins typically lack sharp details on the obverse and have the same reverse weakness as earlier Manila issues.

On a perfectly struck coin, the eagle surmounting the Commonwealth shield would have a pattern of feathers visible on its breast; this level of detail is rarely evident, with the breast instead appearing smooth or flat.

The mintmark style of 1937 and 1941—a wide M, with the middle point not descending to the letter's baseline—usually did not strike clearly, making it difficult to read. The mintmark style of 1938 was narrower, with the middle point descending to the base, and typically is more legible.

Twenty Centavos, 1937–1945

High Points of Wear. *Obverse Checkpoints:* 1. Figure's left thigh and knee. 2. Figure's left hand. 3. Edge of anvil. *Reverse Checkpoints:* 1. Inner folds of ribbon. 2. Center of coat of arms.

1944-D, D Over S

	Mintage	VF	EF	MS-60	MS-63
1937-M	2,665,000	$3	$5	$35	$40
	Auctions: No auction records available.				
1938-M	3,000,000	$3	$5	$15	$20
	Auctions: $40, MS-64, August 2009; $32, MS-64, August 2009				
1941-M	1,500,000	$3	$3.50	$15	$20
	Auctions: No auction records available.				
1944-D	28,596,000	$2	$2.75	$3	$5
	Auctions: No auction records available.				
1944-D, D Over S	(a)	$15	$40	$95	$180
	Auctions: $403, MS-66, January 2010				
1945-D	82,804,000	$2	$2.75	$3	$5
	Auctions: No auction records available.				

a. Included in 1944-D mintage figure.

Fifty Centavos (1944–1945)

Designer: *Melecio Figueroa.* **Weight:** *10 grams (.2411 oz. ASW).*
Composition: *.750 silver, .250 copper.* **Diameter:** *27 mm.*
Edge: *Reeded.* **Mint:** *San Francisco.*

Mintmark location is on the
reverse, to the left of the date.

History. No fifty-centavo coins were struck at the Manila Mint for the Commonwealth of the Philippines. The denomination's first issue was a wartime production of the San Francisco Mint, in 1944, to the extent of some 19 million coins, or double that facility's production of Liberty Walking half dollars for the year. This was followed by a similar mintage in 1945. These coins were intended to enter circulation after being shipped overseas with the U.S. military during the liberation of the Philippines from Imperial Japan's 1942–1945 occupation. They were readily accepted in the coin-starved wartime economy and continued to circulate in the islands into the 1960s.

Striking and Sharpness. Many Commonwealth fifty-centavo coins are lightly struck, but they typically show flattening less severe than that of the 1907–1921 issues struck under U.S. sovereignty. On the reverse, the coat of arms usually is weakly struck, with COMMONWEALTH OF THE PHILIPPINES rarely completely legible. On a perfectly struck coin, the eagle surmounting the Commonwealth shield would have a pattern of feathers visible on its breast; this level of detail is rarely evident, with the breast instead appearing smooth or flat.

Fifty Centavos, 1944–1945

High Points of Wear. *Obverse Checkpoints:* 1. Figure's left thigh and lower leg. 2. Mid-drapery area. 3. Figure's left bosom. 4. Edge of anvil. *Reverse Checkpoints:* 1. Inner folds of ribbon. 2. Center of coat of arms.

1945-S, S Over S

	Mintage	VF	EF	MS-60	MS-63
1944-S	19,187,000	$5	$6	$8	$10
	Auctions: $94, MS-66, July 2015; $44, MS-64, March 2013				
1945-S	18,120,000	$5	$6	$8	$10
	Auctions: $100, MS-66, January 2014				
1945-S, S Over S	(a)	$20	$30	$80	$200
	Auctions: $306, MS-66, May 2014; $118, MS-62, October 2015				

a. Included in 1945-S mintage figure.

COMMONWEALTH COMMEMORATIVE ISSUES

The American territory of the Philippines was governed by the U.S. military from 1899 to mid-1901. Its executive branch was managed by the Bureau of Insular Affairs (part of the War Department) from mid-1901 to 1935. In the latter year the Philippines' status was changed to that of a commonwealth—a type of organized but unincorporated dependent territory, self-governed (except in defense and foreign policy) under a constitution of its own adoption, whose right of self-government would not be unilaterally withdrawn by Congress. This was a step in the direction of complete independence, scheduled to be recognized after an additional ten years of "nation building."

To celebrate this transfer of government, the Manila Mint in 1936 produced a set of three silver commemorative coins—one of the fifty-centavo denomination, and two of the one-peso. These were designed by Ambrosio Morales, professor of sculpture at the University of the Philippines School of Fine Arts.

The fifty-centavo coin and one of the set's pesos feature busts of Philippine president Manuel L. Quezon and the last U.S. governor-general, Frank Murphy, who served (largely ceremonially) as the first U.S. high commissioner to the Commonwealth of the Philippines. On the fifty-centavo piece the two men face each other with the rising sun between them; on the peso, they appear jugate (in conjoined profile portraits). The other peso has busts of Quezon and U.S. president Franklin D. Roosevelt. This was a rare instance of a living American president appearing on a coin, the only precedent being the 1926 Sesquicentennial commemorative half dollar, which showed President Calvin Coolidge.

On each of the three coins appears the date November 15, 1935, when the new commonwealth's government was inaugurated on the steps of the Legislative Building in Manila, witnessed by 300,000 people in attendance.

The set's issue price was $3.13, or about 2.5 times the coins' face value expressed in U.S. dollars. Commemorative coins were popular in the United States at the time, but still these sets sold poorly, and thousands remained within the Philippine Treasury at the onset of World War II. In early 1942 many if not all of the remainders were crated and thrown into Caballo Bay, to keep them (along with millions of older silver pesos) from being captured by the approaching forces of Imperial Japan. Today many of the coins are found with corrosion caused by their long exposure to saltwater before being salvaged.

FIFTY CENTAVOS (1936)

Designer: *Ambrosio Morales (obverse).* **Weight:** *10 grams (.2411 oz. ASW).*
Composition: *.750 silver, .250 copper.* **Diameter:** *27.5 mm.* **Edge:** *Reeded.* **Mint:** *Manila.*

Striking and Sharpness. This issue typically is found well struck.

	Mintage	VF	EF	MS-60	MS-63
1936-M, Silver fifty centavos	20,000	$35	$60	$125	$180
Auctions: $1,528, MS-66, January 2016; $206, MS-64, January 2014; $112, MS-63, December 2014					

ONE PESO (1936)

Designer: *Ambrosio Morales (obverse).* **Weight:** *20 grams (.5144 oz. ASW).*
Composition: *.800 silver, .200 copper.* **Diameter:** *35 mm.* **Edge:** *Reeded.* **Mint:** *Manila.*

One Peso, Busts of Murphy and Quezon   **One Peso, Busts of Roosevelt and Quezon**

Striking and Sharpness. Sharply struck gems of the Murphy/Quezon peso can be a challenge to locate. Weak strike is evident on the reverse in particular, where the sea-lion can be softly detailed. On some pieces, tiny bubbles resulting from improper fabrication of the planchet can be observed among the letters surrounding the rim.

The Roosevelt/Quezon peso typically is found well struck.

	Mintage	VF	EF	MS-60	MS-63
1936-M, Silver one peso, busts of Murphy and Quezon	10,000	$70	$85	$200	$325
Auctions: $940, MS-66, October 2014; $764, MS-66, October 2014; $176, MS, May 2015					
1936-M, Silver one peso, busts of Roosevelt and Quezon	10,000	$70	$85	$200	$300
Auctions: $823, MS-66, January 2016; $359, MS-65, August 2013; $329, MS-65, January 2013					

Alaska Tokens

ALASKA RURAL REHABILITATION CORPORATION TOKENS OF 1935

Before the Roosevelt Administration's dramatic New Deal response to the Great Depression, it was the states themselves, rather than the federal government, that organized and funded the relief of their citizens in need. This changed with the Federal Emergency Relief Act of 1933, by which Congress appropriated $250 million for states to use in their relief efforts, with the same amount funded for federal programs. Other relief acts would follow. The states were to use their 1933 FERA grant money "to aid in meeting the costs of furnishing relief and in relieving the hardship and suffering caused by unemployment in the form of money, service, materials, and/or commodities to provide the necessities of life to persons in need as a result of the present emergency, and/or their dependents, whether resident, transient, or homeless," as well as to "aid in assisting cooperative and self-help associations for the barter of goods and services."

Americans living in cities benefited from direct relief grants as well as employment in work-relief projects. Those in rural areas, however, had a stronger need for *rehabilitation* programs rather than relief as such. In April 1934 a special Rural Rehabilitation Division was set up. This helped establish rural camps where people made homeless by the Depression could find shelter and assistance until conditions improved. Nonprofits called *rural rehabilitation corporations* were devised to carry this effort forward. One function of the corporations was to buy large expanses of farmland to divide into 40- or 60-acre plots. These would be mortgaged to displaced farm families who agreed to develop and farm the land in exchange for low-interest loans and other assistance. One community developed under this plan was the Matanuska Valley Colony at Palmer, about 45 miles northeast of Anchorage, in the territory of Alaska. For the Alaska program some 203 families were recruited from Michigan, Minnesota, and Wisconsin. Those states were targeted not only because they had a very high percentage of displaced farmers on social-assistance relief, but also because their cold-weather climates were similar to Alaska's.

A suite of (undated) 1935 tokens was issued by the U.S. government for the use of the Midwesterners who relocated to the colonization project. These aluminum and brass tokens (nicknamed "bingles") would supply the settlers with much-needed federal aid, being paid out for work at the rate of 50¢ per hour. In theory this wage payment in tokens, rather than regular coinage, would also discourage the workers from spending their money unwisely, as the bingles were redeemable only at Alaska Rural Rehabilitation Corporation stores. In addition to use as wages, the tokens were issued based on immediate need and according to the size of the family. A family of two would receive a monthly allowance of $45; a family of three, $55; a family of four, $75; and a family of five, $85. The bingles were in use only about six months, during the winter of 1935 and 1936. The colony's managers were unable to restrict their use to the purchase of necessities in corporation-run stores—other merchants, including the local saloon, realized they could also accept them as currency. Eventually the tokens were recalled and redeemed for regular U.S. money. Practically all of the circulated tokens were destroyed after redemption.

Of the $23,000 face value minted, about $18,000 worth of tokens were issued in the months they were in active use. The unissued tokens were later made into souvenir sets for collectors. Some 250 complete sets were thus preserved in unused condition, in addition to about 100 "short" sets consisting of the one-cent, five-cent, and ten-cent pieces.

Each token is similar in size to the corresponding U.S. coin of the same denomination (one cent through ten dollars), with the exception of the one-cent piece, which is octagonal. The design is the same on both sides of each denomination.

Even after leaving hardship in the Midwest, and even with this federal aid, the Alaska colonists faced ongoing challenges. Potatoes and other crops were successfully grown, but the farming seasons were short, markets were far away, and the expense of shipping was high. More than half of the Alaska colonists left the Matanuska Valley within five years, and thirty years later only twenty of the original families were still farming there. Still, the New Deal colony helped the Matanuska Valley to slowly grow into Alaska's most productive agricultural region.

For more information on these and other Alaska-related coins and tokens, see *Alaska's Coinage Through the Years*, by Maurice Gould, Kenneth Bressett, and Kaye and Nancy Dethridge.

ALUMINUM

	Mintage	EF	Unc.
One Cent	5,000	$90	$160
Five Cents	5,000	$90	$160
Ten Cents	5,000	$90	$160
Twenty-Five Cents	3,000	$135	$265
Fifty Cents	2,500	$135	$265
One Dollar	2,500	$225	$265

BRASS

	Mintage	EF	Unc.
Five Dollars	1,000	$225	$350
Ten Dollars	1,000	$250	$400

APPENDIX A

Misstrikes and Errors

With the production of millions of coins each year, it is natural that a few abnormal pieces escape inspection and are inadvertently released for circulation, usually in original bags or rolls of new coins. These are not considered regular issues because they were not made intentionally. They are all eagerly sought by collectors for the information they shed on minting techniques, and as a variation from normal date and mint series collecting.

MISSTRUCK COINS AND ERROR PIECES

Nearly every misstruck or error coin is unique in some way, and prices may vary from coin to coin. They may all be classified in general groups related to the kinds of errors or manufacturing malfunctions involved. Collectors value these pieces according to the scarcity of each kind of error for each type of coin. Non-collectors usually view them as curios, and often believe that they must be worth much more than normal coins because they look so strange. In reality, the value assigned to various types of errors by collectors and dealers reflects both supply and demand, and is based on recurring transactions between willing buyers and sellers.

The following listings show current average values for the most frequently encountered kinds of error coins. In each case, the values shown are for coins that are unmarred by serious marks or scratches, and in Uncirculated condition for modern issues, and Extremely Fine condition for obsolete types. Exceptions are valued higher or lower. Error coins of rare-date issues generally do not command a premium beyond their normal values. In most cases each of these coins is unique in some respect and must be valued according to its individual appearance, quality, and eye appeal.

There are many other kinds of errors and misstruck coins beyond those listed in this guide book. Some are more valuable, and others less valuable, than the most popular pieces that are listed here as examples of what this interesting field contains. The pieces illustrated are general examples of the types described.

Early in 2002 the mints changed their production methods to a new system designed to eliminate deformed planchets, off-center strikes, and similar errors. They also changed the delivery system of bulk coinage, and no longer shipped loose coins in sewn bags to be counted and wrapped by banks or counting rooms, where error coins were often found and sold to collectors. Under the new system, coins are packaged in large quantities and go directly to automated counters that filter out deformed coins. The result has been that very few error coins have entered the market since late 2002, and almost none after that date. The values shown in these listings are for pre-2002 coins; those dated after that, with but a few exceptions, are valued considerably higher.

For additional details and information about these coins, the following books are recommended:

Margolis, Arnold, and Fred Weinberg. *The Error Coin Encyclopedia* (4th ed.). 2004.

Herbert, Alan. *Official Price Guide to Minting Varieties and Errors.* New York, 1991.

Fivaz, Bill, and J.T. Stanton. *The Cherrypickers' Guide to Rare Die Varieties.* Atlanta, GA, updated regularly.

The coins discussed in this section must not be confused with others that have been mutilated or damaged after leaving the mint. Examples of such pieces include coins that have been scratched, hammered, engraved, impressed, acid etched, or plated by individuals to simulate something other than a normal coin. Those pieces have no numismatic value, and can only be considered as altered coins not suitable for a collection.

TYPES OF ERROR COINS

***Clipped Planchet*—An incomplete coin, missing 10 to 25% of the metal.** Incomplete planchets result from accidents when the steel rods used to punch out blanks from the metal strip overlap a portion of the strip already punched. There are curved, straight, ragged, incomplete, and elliptical clips. Values may be greater or less depending on the nature and size of the clip. Coins with more than one clip usually command higher values.

***Multiple Strike*—A coin with at least one additional image from being struck again off center.** Value increases with the number of strikes. These minting errors occur when a finished coin goes back into the press and is struck again with the same dies. The presence of a date can bring a higher value.

No Rim   With Rim

***Blank or Planchet*—A blank disc of metal intended for coinage but not struck with dies.** In the process of preparation for coinage, the blanks are first punched from a strip of metal and then milled to upset the rim. In most instances, first-process pieces (blanks without upset rims) are slightly more valuable than the finished planchets. Values shown are for the most common pieces.

Defective Die—**A coin showing raised metal from a large die crack, or small rim break.** Coins that show evidence of light die cracks, polishing, or very minor die damage are generally of little or no value. Prices shown here are for coins with very noticeable, raised die-crack lines, or those for which the die broke away, producing an unstruck area known as a *cud*.

Off Center—**A coin that has been struck out of collar and incorrectly centered, with part of the design missing.** Values are for coins with approximately 10 to 20% of design missing from obsolete coins, or 20 to 60% missing from modern coins. These are misstruck coins that were made when the planchet did not enter the coinage press properly. Coins that are struck only slightly off center, with none of the design missing, are called broadstrikes (see the next category). Those with nearly all of the impression missing are generally worth more, but those with a readable date and mint are the most valuable.

Broadstrike—**A coin that was struck outside the retaining collar.** When coins are struck without being contained in the collar die, they spread out larger than normal pieces. All denominations have a plain edge.

Lamination—**A flaw whereby a fragment of metal has peeled off the coin's surface.** This defect occurs when a foreign substance, such as gas oxides or dirt, becomes trapped in the strip as it is rolled out to the proper thickness. Lamination flaws may be missing or still attached to the coin's surface. Minor flaws may only decrease a coin's value, while a clad coin that is missing the full surface of one or both sides is worth more than the values listed here.

Brockage—**A mirror image of the design impressed on the opposite side of the same coin.** These errors are caused when a struck coin remains on either die after striking, and impresses its image into the next blank planchet as it is struck, leaving a negative or mirror image. Off-center and partial brockage coins are worth less than those with full impression. Coins with negative impressions on both sides are usually mutilated pieces made outside the mint by the pressing together of coins.

Wrong Planchet—**A coin struck on a planchet intended for another denomination or of the wrong metal.** Examples of these are cents struck on dime planchets, nickels on cent planchets, or quarters on dime planchets. Values vary depending on the type of error involved. Those struck on coins of a different denomination that were previously struck normally are of much greater value. A similar kind of error occurs when a coin is struck on a planchet of the correct denomination but wrong metal. One famous example is the 1943 cent struck in bronze (pictured), rather than in that year's new steel composition. (Fewer than three dozen are thought to exist.) Such errors presumably occur when an older planchet is mixed in with the normal supply of planchets and goes through the minting process.

MINT-CANCELED COINS

In mid-2003, the U.S. Mint acquired machines to eliminate security concerns and the cost associated with providing Mint police escorts to private vendors for the melting of scrap, substandard struck coins, planchets, and blanks. Under high pressure, the rollers and blades of these machines cancel the coins and blanks in a manner similar in appearance to the surface of a waffle, and they are popularly known by that term. This process has effectively kept most misstruck coins produced after 2003 from becoming available to collectors. Waffled examples are known for all six 2003-dated coin denominations, from the Lincoln cent through the Sacagawea dollar. The Mint has not objected to these pieces' trading in the open market because they are not considered coins with legal tender status.

MISSTRUCK AND ERROR PIECES

	Clipped Planchet	Multiple Strike	Blank, No Raised Rim	Planchet, Raised Rim	Defective Die	Off Center	Broadstrike	Lamination	Brockage
Large Cent	$50	$1,000	$200	$275	$25	$600	$100	$25	$1,000
Indian Head 1¢	$15	$600	—	—	$25	$150	$50	$15	$400
Lincoln 1¢ (95% Copper)	$3	$50	$3	$3	$12	$10	$8	$3	$35
Steel 1¢	$18	$250	$55	$75	$15	$60	$35	$15	$250
Lincoln 1¢ (Zinc)	$4	$35	$2	$2	$15	$8	$5	$15	$35
Liberty 5¢	$20	$700	—	$250	$35	$250	$110	$20	$450
Buffalo 5¢	$15	$2,500	—	$600	$40	$500	$300	$30	$850
Jefferson 5¢	$3	$40	$12	$10	$15	$12	$10	$10	$40
Wartime 5¢	$8	$400	$400	$350	$25	$200	$70	$15	$200
Barber 10¢	$40	$750	—	—	$75	$300	$85	$12	$400
Mercury 10¢	$15	$800	—	—	$35	$175	$55	$15	$300
Roosevelt 10¢ (Silver)	$5	$250	$50	$40	$35	$150	$45	$12	$100
Roosevelt 10¢ (Clad)	$3	$50	$3	$4	$15	$12	$10	$16	$40

	Clipped Planchet	Multiple Strike	Blank, No Raised Rim	Planchet, Raised Rim	Defective Die	Off Center	Broadstrike	Lamination	Brockage
Washington 25¢ (Silver)	$15	$400	$175	$160	$25	$350	$200	$15	$300
Washington 25¢ (Clad)	$5	$150	$8	$7	$12	$70	$20	$25	$50
Bicentennial 25¢	$35	$350	—	—	$65	$150	$50	$50	$250
State 25¢	$20	$500	—	—	$25	$75	$35	$125	$325
Franklin 50¢	$35	$1,800	—	—	$150	$1,800	$500	$25	$750
Kennedy 50¢ (40% Silver)	$20	$1,000	$165	$150	$70	$450	$200	$40	$450
Kennedy 50¢ (Clad)	$15	$600	$125	$100	$50	$250	$75	$25	$300
Bicentennial 50¢	$40	$700	—	—	$90	$300	$95	$40	$550
Silver $1	$40	$5,000	$1,400	$1,200	$950	$2,200	$700	$50	$550
Eisenhower $1	$25	$1,000	$150	$100	$500	$600	$150	$50	$950
Bicentennial $1	$45	$1,500	$135	—	$750	$750	$200	$50	$950
Anthony $1	$25	$600	$175	$100	$100	$250	$75	$30	$300
Sacagawea $1	$85	$1,950	$200	$50	$50	$1,500	$275	$50	$450

WRONG PLANCHETS

	Zinc 1¢	Copper 1¢	Steel 1¢	5¢	Silver 10¢	Copper-Nickel Clad 10¢	Silver 25¢	Copper-Nickel Clad 25¢	Copper-Nickel Clad 50¢
Indian Head 1¢	(a)	—	(a)	(a)	$9,500	(a)	(a)	(a)	(a)
Lincoln 1¢	—	—	—	(a)	$1,000	$350	(a)	(a)	(a)
Buffalo 5¢	(a)	$4,000	(a)	—	$6,000	(a)	(a)	(a)	(a)
Jefferson 5¢	$300	$250	$2,750	—	$450	$350	(a)	(a)	(a)
Wartime 5¢	(a)	$2,500	$3,500	—	$2,000	(a)	(a)	(a)	(a)
Washington 25¢ (Silver)	(a)	$900	$7,000	$450	$1,500	—	—	—	(a)
Washington 25¢ (Clad)	—	$750	(a)	$225	—	$350	—	—	(a)
Bicentennial 25¢	(a)	$3,000	(a)	$2,500	—	$3,500	—	—	(a)
State 25¢ (b)	$4,500	(a)	(a)	$600	(a)	$4,000	(a)	—	(a)
Walking Liberty 50¢	(a)	—	—	—	—	(a)	$25,000	(a)	(a)
Franklin 50¢	(a)	$5,500	(a)	$5,000	$6,000	(a)	$1,500	(a)	(a)
Kennedy 50¢ (c)	(a)	$3,000	(a)	$1,250	—	$2,000	—	$650	—
Bicentennial 50¢	(a)	$3,800	(a)	$2,750	—	—	—	$1,200	—
Eisenhower $1	(a)	$10,000	(a)	$9,000	—	$10,000	—	$6,000	$2,500
Anthony $1	—	$3,500	(a)	$4,500	(a)	—	—	$1,000	(a)
Sacagawea $1	$10,000	(a)	(a)	$10,000	(a)	$10,000	(a)	$3,500	(a)

Note: Coins struck over other coins of different denominations are usually valued three to five times higher than these prices. Coins made from mismatched dies (State quarter obverse combined with Sacagawea dollar reverse) are extremely rare. **a.** Not possible. **b.** Values for State quarter errors vary with each type and state, and are generally much higher than for other quarters. **c.** The Kennedy fifty-cent piece struck on an Anthony one-dollar planchet is very rare.

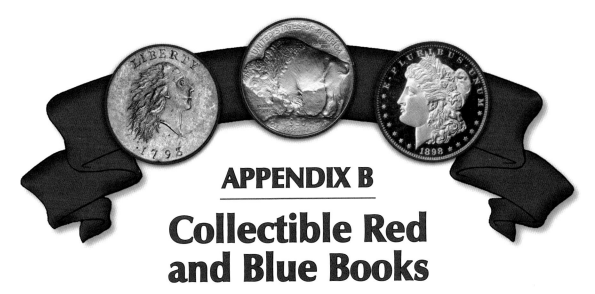

APPENDIX B

Collectible Red and Blue Books

The book you are reading is the *Deluxe Edition* of a classic hobby reference, the *Guide Book of United States Coins*, popularly known as the *Red Book*. More than 25 million copies of the *Red Book* have been sold since 1946, making it one of the best-selling nonfiction titles in American publishing history. By 1959 more than 100,000 copies were being printed annually. The 1965 (18th) edition, published in 1964, reached a peak of 1,200,000 copies. That year the *Red Book* was ranked fifth on the list of best-selling nonfiction—ahead of Dale Carnegie's classic *How to Win Friends and Influence People* (at number 6) and John F. Kennedy's *Profiles in Courage* (at number 9).

The idea for the *Red Book* started in the 1940s with R.S. Yeoman. Employed by Whitman Publishing Company (part of Western Publishing), Yeoman at first created the *Blue Book* (official title, the *Handbook of United States Coins With Premium List*), which gave hobbyists an overview of American coinage and a detailed guide to the prices that dealers were paying for collectible coins. The first edition was published in 1942. Yeoman saw that collectors wanted even more information, and he began compiling data and records for an expanded *retail* version of the *Blue Book* (showing how much a collector could expect to pay a dealer for coins). After World War II ended, Yeoman and his team introduced the new volume, the *Guide Book of United States Coins*, soon nicknamed the *Red Book* because of its distinctive cover color.

Numismatist Kenneth E. Bressett joined the *Red Book* in 1956 as a freelance editor. He has continued to work on the annually published book, and other Whitman projects, ever since. He took a full-time editorial position with Whitman Publishing in 1959, and assumed full editorship of the *Red Book* in 1975. Today Bressett serves as the *Red Book*'s editor emeritus, with Jeff Garrett as senior editor, Q. David Bowers as research editor, and a panel of more than 100 coin dealers, researchers, and other specialists.

THE *RED BOOK* AS A COLLECTIBLE

The *Guide Book of United States Coins* holds the record as the longest-running annual retail coin-price guide. It has passed its 65th anniversary, and collectors seem to be almost as interested in assembling sets of old *Red Book*s as of old coins. The demand for old *Red Book*s has created a solid market. Some who collect these old editions maintain reference libraries of all kinds of coin publications. To them, having one of each edition is essential, because that is the way old books are collected. Others are speculators who believe that the value of old editions will go up as interest and demand increase. Many people who save old *Red Book*s do so to maintain a record of coin prices going back further than any other source.

Following price trends in old *Red Books* is a good indicator of how well individual coins are doing in comparison to each other. The price information published in each year is an average of what collectors are paying for each coin. It is a valuable benchmark, showing how prices have gone up or down over the years. Information like this often gives investors an edge in predicting what the future may hold.

Old *Red Books* are also a handy resource on collecting trends. They show graphically how grading has changed over the years, what new coins have been discovered and added to the listings, and which areas are growing in popularity. Studying these old books can be educational as well as nostalgic. It's great fun to see what your favorite coins sold for 15 or 25 years ago or more—and a bit frustrating to realize what might have been if we had only bought the right coins at the right time in years past.

Many collectors have asked about the quantities printed of each edition. That information has never been published, and now no company records exist specifying how many were made. The original author, R.S. Yeoman, told inquirers that the first press run in November 1946 was for 9,000 copies. In February 1947 an additional 9,000 copies were printed to satisfy the unexpected demand.

There were several slight but noticeable differences that can be used to differentiate between the first and second printings. The wording in the first printing at the bottom of page 135 reads, "which probably accounts for the scarcity of *this* date." Those last few words were changed to "the scarcity of *1903 O*" in the second printing.

The second edition had a press run of 22,000. The printing of each edition thereafter gradually increased, with the highest number ever being reached with the 18th edition, dated 1965 and published in 1964. At the top of a booming coin market, a whopping 1,200,000 copies were produced. Since that time the numbers have decreased, but the *Red Book* still maintains a record of being the world's largest-selling coin publication each year.

In some years a very limited number of *Red Books* were made for use by price contributors. Those were interleaved with blank pages. No more than 50 copies were ever made for any one year. Perhaps fewer than 20 were made in the first few years. Three of these of the first edition, and one of the second edition, are currently known. Their value is now in four figures. Those made in the 1960s sell for about $300–$500 today.

There are other unusual *Red Books* that command exceptional prices. One of the most popular is the 1987 special edition that was made for, and distributed only to, people who attended the 1986 American Numismatic Association banquet in Milwaukee. Only 500 of those were printed with a special commemorative cover.

Error books are also popular with collectors. The most common is one with double-stamped printing on the cover. The second most frequently seen are those with an upside-down cover. Probably the best known of the error books is the 1963 16th edition with a missing page. For some uncanny reason, page 239 is duplicated in some of those books, and page 237 is missing. The error was corrected on most of the printing.

The terminology used to describe book condition differs from that utilized in grading coins. A "Very Fine" book is one that is nearly new, with minimal signs of use. Early editions of the *Red Book* are rarely if ever found in anything approaching "New" condition. Exceptionally well-preserved older editions command a substantial premium and are in great demand. Nice used copies that are still clean and in good shape, but slightly worn from use, are also desirable. Only the early editions are worth a premium in badly worn condition.

For a more detailed history and edition-by-edition study of the *Red Book*, see Frank J. Colletti's *A Guide Book of The Official Red Book of United States Coins* (Whitman, 2009).

See also *A Penny Saved: R.S. Yeoman and His Remarkable Red Book*, by Kenneth Bressett (Whitman, 2021). That volume is a history of Whitman Publishing and the *Red Book*, and a biography of Yeoman as well as an autobiography of Bressett.

VALUATION GUIDE FOR PAST EDITIONS OF THE *RED BOOK*
CLASSIC HARDCOVER BINDING
See page 1413 for special editions in the classic hardcover binding.

Year/Edition	Issue Price	VG	F	VF	New
1947 (1st ed.), 1st Printing	$1.50	$225	$425	$675	$1,350 (a)
1947 (1st ed.), 2nd Printing	$1.50	$175	$350	$600	$1,100 (a)
1948 (2nd ed.)	$1.50	$60	$125	$210	$475 (a)
1949 (3rd ed.)	$1.50	$60	$100	$210	$500 (a)
1951/52 (4th ed.)	$1.50	$50	$90	$175	$350 (a)
1952/53 (5th ed.)	$1.50	$85	$150	$375	$975 (a)
1953/54 (6th ed.)	$1.75	$30	$50	$65	$85
1954/55 (7th ed.)	$1.75	$30	$45	$60	$85
1955 (8th ed.)	$1.75	$30	$35	$55	$75
1956 (9th ed.)	$1.75	$20	$35	$45	$70
1957 (10th ed.)	$1.75	$10	$15	$35	$45
1958 (11th ed.)	$1.75		$8	$12	$20
1959 (12th ed.)	$1.75		$8	$10	$20
1960 (13th ed.)	$1.75		$7	$9	$20
1961 (14th ed.)	$1.75		$4	$6	$20
1962 (15th ed.)	$1.75		$4	$6	$15
1963 (16th ed.)	$1.75		$4	$6	$15
1964 (17th ed.)	$1.75		$3	$4	$10
1965 (18th ed.)	$1.75		$3	$4	$10
1966 (19th ed.)	$1.75		$3	$4	$10
1967 (20th ed.)	$1.75		$2	$3	$8
1968 (21st ed.)	$2		$2	$3	$8
1969 (22nd ed.)	$2		$2	$3	$8
1970 (23rd ed.)	$2.50		$2	$3	$8
1971 (24th ed.)	$2.50		$2	$3	$7
1972 (25th ed.)	$2.50		$2	$3	$7
1973 (26th ed.)	$2.50		$2	$3	$7
1974 (27th ed.)	$2.50		$2	$3	$7
1975 (28th ed.)	$3			$3	$6
1976 (29th ed.)	$3.95			$3	$6
1977 (30th ed.)	$3.95			$3	$6
1978 (31st ed.)	$3.95			$3	$6
1979 (32nd ed.)	$3.95			$3	$6
1980 (33rd ed.)	$3.95			$3	$6
1981 (34th ed.)	$4.95			$2	$5
1982 (35th ed.)	$4.95			$2	$5
1983 (36th ed.)	$5.95			$2	$5
1984 (37th ed.)	$5.95			$2	$5
1985 (38th ed.)	$5.95			$2	$5
1986 (39th ed.)	$5.95			$2	$5
1987 (40th ed.)	$6.95			$2	$5
1988 (41st ed.)	$6.95			$2	$5
1989 (42nd ed.)	$6.95			$2	$5
1990 (43rd ed.)	$7.95			$2	$5
1991 (44th ed.)	$8.95			$2	$5
1992 (45th ed.)	$8.95			$2	$5
1993 (46th ed.)	$9.95				$5

Note: Values are for unsigned books. Those signed by R.S. Yeoman are worth substantially more. **a.** Values are for books in Near Mint condition, as truly New copies are effectively nonexistent.

Year/Edition	Issue Price	VG	F	VF	New
1994 (47th ed.)	$9.95				$3
1995 (48th ed.)	$10.95				$3
1996 (49th ed.)	$10.95				$3
1997 (50th ed.)	$11.95				$3
1998 (51st ed.)	$11.95				$2
1999 (52nd ed.)	$11.95				$2
2000 (53rd ed.)	$12.95				$2
2001 (54th ed.)	$13.95				$2
2002 (55th ed.)	$14.95				$2
2003 (56th ed.)	$15.95				$2
2004 (57th ed.)	$15.95				$2
2005 (58th ed.)	$15.95				$2
2006 (59th ed.)	$16.95				$2
2007 (60th ed.)	$16.95				$2
2008 (61st ed.)	$16.95				$2
2009 (62nd ed.)	$16.95				$2
2010 (63rd ed.)	$16.95				$2
2011 (64th ed.)	$16.95				$2
2012 (65th ed.)	$16.95				$2
2013 (66th ed.)	$16.95				$2
2014 (67th ed.)	$16.95				$2
2015 (68th ed.)	$16.95				$2
2016 (69th ed.)	$16.95				$2
2017 (70th ed.)	$16.95				$2
2018 (71st ed.) (b)	$16.95				$2
2019 (72nd ed.) (c)	$17.95				$2
2020 (73rd ed.)	$17.95				$2
2021 (74th ed.)	$17.95				$2

Note: Values are for unsigned books. Those signed by R.S. Yeoman are worth substantially more. **b.** The 2018 hardcover features a back-cover gold-foil portrait of David Rittenhouse, first director of the United States Mint, in celebration of 225 years of U.S. coinage at Philadelphia. **c.** The 2019 *Red Book* (in every format) includes a 10-page illustrated tribute to Editor Emeritus Kenneth Bressett. The back of the hardcover features a gold-foil portrait of Bressett.

SOFTCOVERS (1993–2007)

The first softcover (trade paperback) *Red Book* was the 1993 (46th) edition. The softcover binding was offered (alongside other formats) in the 1993, 1994, 1995, and 1996 editions; again in the 1998 edition; and from 2003 through 2007. All are fairly common and easily collectible today. Values in New condition range from $2 up to $3–$4 for the earlier editions.

SPIRALBOUND SOFTCOVERS (1997 TO DATE)

The first spiralbound softcover *Red Book* was the 1997 (50th) edition. The spiralbound softcover format was next available in the 1999 edition, and it has been an annually offered format every edition since then. Today the spiralbound softcovers all are easily collectible. The 1997 edition is worth $4 in New condition, and later editions are valued around $2.

SPIRALBOUND HARDCOVERS (2008 TO DATE)

The first spiralbound hardcover *Red Book* was the 2008 (61st) edition. The format has been available (alongside other formats) every edition since. All spiralbound hardcovers are readily available to collectors, and are valued from $2 to $4.

JOURNAL EDITION (2009)

The large-sized Journal Edition, featuring a three-ring binder, color-coded tabbed dividers, and removable pages, was issued only for the 2009 (62nd) edition. Today it is valued at $5 in VF and $30 in New condition.

LARGE PRINT EDITIONS (2010 TO DATE)

The oversized Large Print format of the *Red Book* has been offered annually since the 2010 (63rd) edition. All editions are readily available to collectors and are valued at $5 in New condition.

ESSENTIAL EDITION (2013–2017)

A magazine-sized softcover version of the *Red Book*, called the *Essential Edition*, was published annually from 2013 to 2017. Aimed at mainstream readers, it featured large print and focused on the most popular federal coins. Copies are rarely seen on the secondary market; valued around $10.

LEATHER LIMITED EDITIONS (2005–2019)

	Print Run	Face Value	Current Value		Print Run	Face Value	Current Value
2005 (58th ed.)	3,000	$69.95	$70	2010 (63rd ed.)	1,500	$69.95	$75
2006 (59th ed.)	3,000	$69.95	$70	2011 (64th ed.)	1,500	$69.95	$75
2007 (60th ed.)	3,000	$69.95	$70	2012 (65th ed.)	1,000	$69.95	$75
2007 1947 Tribute Edition	500	$49.95	$100	2013 (66th ed.)	1,000	$69.95	$75
2008 (61st ed.)	3,000	$69.95	$70	2014 (67th ed.)	1,000	$69.95	$75
2008 (61st ed.), Numismatic Literary Guild (a)	135 (b)		$650	2015 (68th ed.)	500	$99.95	$100
				2016 (69th ed.)	500	$99.95	$100
2008 (61st ed.), American Numismatic Society (c)	250 (b)		$400	2017 (70th ed.)	500	$99.95	$100
				2018 (71st ed.)	500	$99.95	$100
2009 (62nd ed.)	3,000	$69.95	$75	2019 (72nd ed.)	500	$99.95	$100

a. One hundred thirty-five imprinted copies of the 2008 leather Limited Edition were created. Of these, 125 were distributed to members of the NLG at its 2007 literary awards ceremony; the remaining 10 were distributed from Whitman Publishing headquarters in Atlanta.
b. Included in total print-run quantity. c. Two hundred fifty copies of the 2008 leather Limited Edition were issued with a special bookplate honoring the 150th anniversary of the ANS. They were distributed to attendees of the January 2008 celebratory banquet in New York.

SPECIAL EDITIONS

Year/Edition	Print Run	Issue Price	VF	New
1987 (40th ed.), American Numismatic Association 95th Anniversary	500		$600	$750
1992 (45th ed.), American Numismatic Association 100th Anniversary	600		$120	$225
1997 (50th ed.), *Red Book* 50th Anniversary	1,200	$24.95	$50	$90
2002 (55th ed.), American Numismatic Association "Target 2001"	500	$100	$25	$40
2002 (55th ed.), SS *Central America*		$35	$20	$35
2005 (58th ed.), FUN (Florida United Numismatists) 50th Anniversary	1,100		$50	$90
2007 (60th ed.), American Numismatic Association 115th Anniversary	500		$50	$90
2007 (60th ed.), Michigan State Numismatic Society 50th Anniversary	500		$50	$90
2007 (1st ed.), 1947 Tribute Edition		$17.95	$5	$20
2008 (61st ed.), ANA Milwaukee World's Fair of Money	1,080		$25	$50
2008 (61st ed.), Stack's Rare Coins			$5	$15
2010 (63rd ed.), Hardcover, Philadelphia Expo (a)		$24.95	$20	$40
2011 (64th ed.), Boston Numismatic Society		$85	$45	$90
2012 (65th ed.), American Numismatic Association	800	$100	$30	$60
2013 (66th ed.), American Numismatic Society (b)	250		$100	$250
2015 (68th ed.), Central States Numismatic Society	500	$15	$25	$60
2016 (69th ed.), American Numismatic Association 125th Anniversary		$100	$40	$75
2018 (71st ed.), NGC 30th Anniversary			$60	$100
2020 (73rd ed.), Chicago Coin Club 100th Anniversary	250			$75
2021 (74th ed.), Philippine Collectors Forum / 100th Anniversary Manila Mint	250	$25		$90

a. Two thousand and nine copies of a special 2010 hardcover edition were made for distribution to dealers at the premiere Whitman Coin and Collectibles Philadelphia Expo (September 2009). Extra copies were sold at $50 apiece with proceeds benefiting the National Federation for the Blind. b. Two hundred fifty copies of the 2013 hardcover were issued with a special bookplate honoring ANS Trustees' Award recipient (and *Red Book* research contributor) Roger Siboni.

THE *BLUE BOOK* AS A COLLECTIBLE

The precursor to the *Red Book* was the *Handbook of United States Coins With Premium List*, popularly known as the *Blue Book*. Its mastermind was R.S. Yeoman, who had been hired by Western Publishing as a commercial artist in 1932. He distributed Western's Whitman line of "penny boards" to coin collectors, promoting them through department stores, along with children's books and games. He eventually arranged for Whitman to expand the line into other denominations, giving them the reputation of a numismatic endeavor rather than a "game" of filling holes with missing coins. He also developed these flat boards into a line of popular folders.

Yeoman began to compile coin-mintage data and market values to aid collectors. This research grew into the *Blue Book*: now collectors had a coin-by-coin guide to the average prices dealers would pay for U.S. coins. The first two editions were both published in 1942.

In the first edition of the *Red Book*, Whitman Publishing would describe the *Blue Book* as "a low-priced standard reference book of United States coins and kindred issues" for which there had been "a long-felt need among American collectors."

The *Blue Book* has been published annually (except in 1944 and 1950) since its debut. Past editions offer valuable information about the hobby of yesteryear as well as developments in numismatic research and the marketplace. Old *Blue Book*s are collectible; most editions after the 12th can be found for a few dollars in VF or better condition. Major variants were produced for the third, fourth, and ninth editions, including perhaps the only "overdate" books in American numismatic publishing. Either to conserve the previous years' covers or to correct an error in binding, the cloth on some third-edition covers was overstamped "Fourth Edition," and a number of eighth-edition covers were overstamped "Ninth Edition." The third edition was produced in several shades of blue ranging from light to dark. Some copies of the fourth edition were also produced in black cloth—the only time the *Blue Book* was bound in other than blue.

The history of the *Blue Book* is given by Kenneth Bressett in *A Penny Saved: R.S. Yeoman and His Remarkable Red Book* (Whitman, 2021). In that book, Bressett reveals recent archival research that shows there were two printings of the first edition of the *Blue Book*, with significant differences between them.

VALUATION GUIDE FOR SELECT PAST EDITIONS OF THE *BLUE BOOK*

Edition	Date (a)		VF	New
	Title Page	Copyright		
1st	1942	1942	$100	$225
2nd	1943	1942	$35	$55
3rd	1944	1943	$30	$50
4th	*none*	1945	$30	$45
5th	*none*	1946	$20	$45
6th	1948	1947	$15	$30
7th	1949	1948	$12	$25
8th	1950	1949	$10	$20
9th	1952	1951	$5	$10
10th	1953	1952	$5	$10

a. During its early years of production, the *Blue Book*'s date presentation was not standardized. Full information is given here to aid in precise identification of early editions.

APPENDIX C

Bullion Values

These charts show the bullion values of silver and gold U.S. coins. These are intrinsic values and do not reflect any numismatic premium a coin might have. The weight listed under each denomination is its actual silver weight (ASW) or actual gold weight (AGW).

In recent years, the bullion price of silver has fluctuated considerably. You can use the following chart to determine the approximate bullion value of many 19th- and 20th-century silver coins at various price levels—or you can calculate the approximate value by multiplying the current spot price of silver by the ASW for each coin, as indicated. Dealers generally purchase common silver coins at around 15% below bullion value, and sell them at around 15% above bullion value.

Nearly all U.S. gold coins have an additional premium value beyond their bullion content, and thus are not subject to minor bullion-price variations. The premium amount is not necessarily tied to the bullion price of gold, but is usually determined by supply and demand levels in the numismatic marketplace. Because these factors can vary significantly, there is no reliable formula for calculating "percentage below and above bullion" prices that would remain accurate over time. The gold chart lists bullion values based on AGW only; consult a coin dealer to ascertain current buy and sell prices.

BULLION VALUES OF SILVER COINS

Silver Price Per Ounce	Wartime Nickel (1942–1945) .05626 oz.	Dime (1892–1964) .07234 oz.	Quarter (1892–1964) .18084 oz.	Half Dollar (1892–1964 .36169 oz.	Silver Clad Half Dollar (1965–1970) .14792 oz.	90% Silver Dollar (1878–1935) .77344 oz.	40% Silver Dollar (1971–1976) .3161 oz.
$10	$0.56	$0.72	$1.81	$3.62	$1.48	$7.73	$3.16
$11	$0.62	$0.80	$1.99	$3.98	$1.63	$8.51	$3.48
$12	$0.68	$0.87	$2.17	$4.34	$1.78	$9.28	$3.79
$13	$0.73	$0.94	$2.35	$4.70	$1.92	$10.05	$4.11
$14	$0.79	$1.01	$2.53	$5.06	$2.07	$10.83	$4.43
$15	$0.84	$1.09	$2.71	$5.43	$2.22	$11.60	$4.74
$16	$0.90	$1.16	$2.89	$5.79	$2.37	$12.38	$5.06
$17	$0.96	$1.23	$3.07	$6.15	$2.51	$13.15	$5.37
$18	$1.01	$1.30	$3.26	$6.51	$2.66	$13.92	$5.69
$19	$1.07	$1.37	$3.44	$6.87	$2.81	$14.70	$6.01
$20	$1.13	$1.45	$3.62	$7.23	$2.96	$15.47	$6.32
$21	$1.18	$1.52	$3.80	$7.60	$3.11	$16.24	$6.64

Note: The U.S. bullion coins first issued in 1986 are unlike the older regular issues. They contain the following amounts of pure metal: silver $1, 1 oz.; gold $50, 1 oz.; gold $25, 1/2 oz.; gold $10, 1/4 oz.; gold $5, 1/10 oz.

Silver Price Per Ounce	Wartime Nickel (1942–1945) .05626 oz.	Dime (1892–1964) .07234 oz.	Quarter (1892–1964) .18084 oz.	Half Dollar (1892–1964) .36169 oz.	Silver Clad Half Dollar (1965–1970) .14792 oz.	90% Silver Dollar (1878–1935) .77344 oz.	40% Silver Dollar (1971–1976) .3161 oz.
$22	$1.24	$1.59	$3.98	$7.96	$3.25	$17.02	$6.95
$23	$1.29	$1.66	$4.16	$8.32	$3.40	$17.79	$7.27
$24	$1.35	$1.74	$4.34	$8.68	$3.55	$18.56	$7.59
$25	$1.41	$1.81	$4.52	$9.04	$3.70	$19.34	$7.90
$26	$1.46	$1.88	$4.70	$9.40	$3.85	$20.11	$8.22
$27	$1.52	$1.95	$4.88	$9.77	$3.99	$20.88	$8.53
$28	$1.58	$2.03	$5.06	$10.13	$4.14	$21.66	$8.85
$29	$1.63	$2.10	$5.24	$10.49	$4.29	$22.43	$9.17
$30	$1.69	$2.17	$5.43	$10.85	$4.44	$23.20	$9.48
$31	$1.74	$2.24	$5.61	$11.21	$4.59	$23.98	$9.80
$32	$1.80	$2.31	$5.79	$11.57	$4.73	$24.75	$10.12
$33	$1.86	$2.39	$5.97	$11.94	$4.88	$25.52	$10.43
$34	$1.91	$2.46	$6.15	$12.30	$5.03	$26.30	$10.75
$35	$1.97	$2.53	$6.33	$12.66	$5.18	$27.07	$11.06
$36	$2.03	$2.60	$6.51	$13.02	$5.33	$27.84	$11.38
$37	$2.08	$2.68	$6.69	$13.38	$5.47	$28.62	$11.70
$38	$2.14	$2.75	$6.87	$13.74	$5.62	$29.39	$12.01
$39	$2.19	$2.82	$7.05	$14.11	$5.77	$30.16	$12.33
$40	$2.25	$2.89	$7.23	$14.47	$5.92	$30.94	$12.64
$41	$2.31	$2.97	$7.41	$14.83	$6.06	$31.71	$12.96
$42	$2.36	$3.04	$7.60	$15.19	$6.21	$32.48	$13.28
$43	$2.42	$3.11	$7.78	$15.55	$6.36	$33.26	$13.59
$44	$2.48	$3.18	$7.96	$15.91	$6.51	$34.03	$13.91
$45	$2.53	$3.26	$8.14	$16.28	$6.66	$34.80	$14.22
$46	$2.59	$3.33	$8.32	$16.64	$6.80	$35.58	$14.54
$47	$2.64	$3.40	$8.50	$17.00	$6.95	$36.35	$14.86
$48	$2.70	$3.47	$8.68	$17.36	$7.10	$37.13	$15.17
$49	$2.76	$3.54	$8.86	$17.72	$7.25	$37.90	$15.49
$50	$2.81	$3.62	$9.04	$18.08	$7.40	$38.67	$15.81
$51	$2.87	$3.69	$9.22	$18.45	$7.54	$39.45	$16.12
$52	$2.93	$3.76	$9.40	$18.81	$7.69	$40.22	$16.44
$53	$2.98	$3.83	$9.58	$19.17	$7.84	$40.99	$16.75
$54	$3.04	$3.91	$9.77	$19.53	$7.99	$41.77	$17.07
$55	$3.09	$3.98	$9.95	$19.89	$8.14	$42.54	$17.39
$56	$3.15	$4.05	$10.13	$20.25	$8.28	$43.31	$17.70
$57	$3.21	$4.12	$10.31	$20.62	$8.43	$44.09	$18.02
$58	$3.26	$4.20	$10.49	$20.98	$8.58	$44.86	$18.33
$59	$3.32	$4.27	$10.67	$21.34	$8.73	$45.63	$18.65
$60	$3.38	$4.34	$10.85	$21.70	$8.88	$46.41	$18.97
$61	$3.43	$4.41	$11.03	$22.06	$9.02	$47.18	$19.28
$62	$3.49	$4.49	$11.21	$22.42	$9.17	$47.95	$19.60
$63	$3.54	$4.56	$11.39	$22.79	$9.32	$48.73	$19.91
$64	$3.60	$4.63	$11.57	$23.15	$9.47	$49.50	$20.23
$65	$3.66	$4.70	$11.75	$23.51	$9.61	$50.27	$20.55
$66	$3.71	$4.77	$11.94	$23.87	$9.76	$51.05	$20.86
$67	$3.77	$4.85	$12.12	$24.23	$9.91	$51.82	$21.18
$68	$3.83	$4.92	$12.30	$24.59	$10.06	$52.59	$21.49
$69	$3.88	$4.99	$12.48	$24.96	$10.21	$53.37	$21.81
$70	$3.94	$5.06	$12.66	$25.32	$10.35	$54.14	$22.13

Note: The U.S. bullion coins first issued in 1986 are unlike the older regular issues. They contain the following amounts of pure metal: silver $1, 1 oz.; gold $50, 1 oz.; gold $25, 1/2 oz.; gold $10, 1/4 oz.; gold $5, 1/10 oz.

BULLION VALUES OF GOLD COINS

Gold Price Per Ounce	$5.00 Liberty Head 1839–1908 Indian Head 1908–1929 .24187 oz.	$10.00 Liberty Head 1838–1907 Indian Head 1907–1933 .48375 oz.	$20.00 1849–1933 .96750 oz.
$850	$205.59	$411.19	$822.38
$875	$211.64	$423.28	$846.56
$900	$217.68	$435.38	$870.75
$925	$223.73	$447.47	$894.94
$950	$229.78	$459.56	$919.13
$975	$235.82	$471.66	$943.31
$1,000	$241.87	$483.75	$967.50
$1,025	$247.92	$495.84	$991.69
$1,050	$253.96	$507.94	$1,015.88
$1,075	$260.01	$520.03	$1,040.06
$1,100	$266.06	$532.13	$1,064.25
$1,125	$272.10	$544.22	$1,088.44
$1,150	$278.15	$556.31	$1,112.63
$1,175	$284.20	$568.41	$1,136.81
$1,200	$290.24	$580.50	$1,161
$1,225	$296.29	$592.59	$1,185.19
$1,250	$302.34	$604.69	$1,209.38
$1,275	$308.38	$616.78	$1,233.56
$1,300	$314.43	$628.88	$1,257.75
$1,325	$320.48	$640.97	$1,281.94
$1,350	$326.52	$653.06	$1,306.13
$1,375	$332.57	$665.16	$1,330.31
$1,400	$338.62	$677.25	$1,354.50
$1,425	$344.66	$689.34	$1,378.69
$1,450	$350.71	$701.44	$1,402.88
$1,475	$356.76	$713.53	$1,427.06
$1,500	$362.81	$725.63	$1,451.25
$1,525	$368.85	$737.72	$1,475.44
$1,550	$374.90	$749.81	$1,499.63
$1,575	$380.95	$761.91	$1,523.81
$1,600	$386.99	$774	$1,548
$1,625	$393.04	$786.09	$1,572.19
$1,650	$399.09	$798.19	$1,596.38
$1,675	$405.13	$810.28	$1,620.56
$1,700	$411.18	$822.38	$1,644.75
$1,725	$417.23	$834.47	$1,668.94
$1,750	$423.27	$846.56	$1,693.13
$1,775	$429.32	$858.66	$1,717.31
$1,800	$435.37	$870.75	$1,741.50
$1,825	$441.41	$882.84	$1,765.69
$1,850	$447.46	$894.94	$1,789.88
$1,875	$453.51	$907.03	$1,814.06
$1,900	$459.55	$919.13	$1,838.25
$1,925	$465.60	$931.22	$1,862.44
$1,950	$471.65	$943.31	$1,886.63
$1,975	$477.69	$955.41	$1,910.81
$2,000	$483.74	$967.50	$1,935

Note: The U.S. bullion coins first issued in 1986 are unlike the older regular issues. They contain the following amounts of pure metal: silver $1, 1 oz.; gold $50, 1 oz.; gold $25, 1/2 oz.; gold $10, 1/4 oz.; gold $5, 1/10 oz.

APPENDIX D

Top 250 U.S. Coin Prices Realized at Auction

Rank	Price	Coin	Grade	Firm	Date
1	$10,016,875	$1(s), 1794	PCGS SP-66	Stack's Bowers	Jan-13
2	$9,360,000	Prefed, 1787, Brasher dbln, EB on Wing (P)	NGC MS-65*	Heritage	Jan-21
3	$8,400,000	$5, 1822	AU-50	Stack's Bowers	Mar-21
4	$7,590,020	$20, 1933	Gem BU	Sotheby's/Stack's	Jul-02
5	$5,280,000	$10, 1804, Plain 4, BD-2	PCGS 65+ DCam	Heritage	Jan-21
6	$4,993,750	$1(s), 1794	PCGS MS-66+	Sotheby's / Stack's Bowers	Sep-15
7	$4,582,500	Prefed, 1787, Brasher dbln, EB on Wing	NGC MS-63	Hertage	Jan-14
8	$4,560,000	5¢, 1913, Liberty Head (U)	PCGS PF-66	Stack's Bowers	Aug-18
9	$4,140,000	$1(s), 1804, Class I	PCGS PF-68	B&M	Aug-99
10	$3,960,000	$1 Trade, 1885	NGC Pf-66	Heritage	Jan-19
11	$3,877,500	$1(s), 1804, Class I (V)	PCGS PF-62	Heritage	Aug-13
12	$3,737,500	5¢, 1913, Liberty Head (L)	NGC PF-64	Heritage	Jan-10
13	$3,737,500	$1(s), 1804, Class I (V)	NGC PF-62	Heritage	Apr-08
14	$3,360,000	$1(s), 1804, Class I (X)	PCGS PF-65	Stack's Bowers	Dec-20
15	$3,290,000	$1(s), 1804, Class I	PCGS PF-65	Sotheby's / Stack's Bowers	Mar-17
16	$3,290,000	5¢, 1913, Liberty Head (L)	NGC PF-64	Heritage	Jan-14
17	$3,172,500	5¢, 1913, Liberty Head	PCGS PF-63	Heritage	Apr-13
18	$2,990,000	$20, MCMVII, Ultra HR, LE (H)	PCGS PF-69	Heritage	Nov-05
19	$2,990,000	Prefed, 1787, Brasher dbln, EB on Breast	NGC EF-45	Heritage	Jan-05
20	$2,820,000	$1(s), 1794	PCGS MS-64	Stack's Bowers	Aug-17
21	$2,760,000	$20, MCMVII, Ultra HR, LE (H)	PCGS PF-69	Stack's Bowers	Jun-12
22	$2,640,000	$1(s), 1804, Class I (V)	PCGS PF-62	Heritage	Jun-18
23	$2,585,000	$10, 1795, 13 Leaves, BD-4	PCGS MS-66+	Sotheby's / Stack's Bowers	Sep-15
24	$2,585,000	Pattern 1¢, 1792 Birch, LE, J-4	NGC MS65* RB	Heritage	Jan-15
25	$2,574,000	$4, 1880, Coiled Hair (D)	NGC PF-67 Cam	Bonhams	Sep-13
26	$2,520,000	Pattern 1¢, 1792 Silver Center, J-1	PCGS SP-67 BN	Heritage	Jan-21
27	$2,415,000	Prefed, 1787, Brasher dbln, EB on Wing	NGC AU-55	Heritage	Jan-05
28	$2,350,000	$2.50, 1808	PCGS MS-65	Sotheby's / Stack's Bowers	May-15
29	$2,350,000	1¢, 1793, Chain AMERICA, S-4	PCGS MS-66 BN	Heritage	Jan-15
30	$2,300,000	$1(s), 1804, Class III	PCGS PF-58	Heritage	Apr-09
31	$2,232,500	Pattern 25¢, 1792, copper, J-12	NGC MS-63 BN	Heritage	Jan-15
32	$2,185,000	$10, 1907, Rounded Rim	NGC Satin PF-67	Herltage	Jan-11

Rank	Price	Coin	Grade	Firm	Date
33	$2,160,000	$20, 1927-D (W)	PCGS MS-65+	Heritage	Jan-20
34	$2,160,000	$5, 1854-S	NGC EF-45	Heritage	Aug-18
35	$2,115,000	$20, MCMVII, Ultra HR, LE	PCGS PF-68	Heritage	Jan-15
36	$2,100,000	Prefed, 1786, Brasher dbln, Lima style	NGC MS-61	Heritage	Jan-21
37	$2,100,000	$1 Trade, 1885 (Y)	PCGS PF-63+ Cam	Heritage	Jan-21
38	$1,997,500	10¢, 1894-S	PCGS PF-66	Heritage	Jan-16
39	$1,997,500	Pattern 1¢, 1792 Silver Center, J-1	PCGS MS-64 BN	Heritage	Aug-14
40	$1,997,500	$20, 1927-D (W)	NGC MS-66	Heritage	Jan-14
41	$1,920,000	$5, 1854-S	PCGS AU-58+	Stack's Bowers	Mar-20
42	$1,897,500	$20, 1927-D	PCGS MS-67	Heritage	Nov-05
43	$1,880,000	Pattern $20, 1879, Quintuple Stella, J-1643	PCGS PF-64 DCam	Legend	May-16
44	$1,880,000	$1(s), 1804, Class III	NGC PF-55	Stack's Bowers	Aug-14
45	$1,840,000	10¢, 1873-CC, No Arrows (K)	PCGS MS-65	Stack's Bowers	Aug-12
46	$1,840,000	5¢, 1913, Liberty Head	NGC PF-66	Superior	Mar-08
47	$1,840,000	$20, MCMVII, Ultra HR, LE	PCGS PF-68	Heritage	Jan-07
48	$1,840,000	$1(s), 1804, Class I (Q)	PCGS PF-64	Stack's	Oct-00
49	$1,821,250	$4, 1880, Coiled Hair	NGC PF-67	Heritage	Apr-15
50	$1,815,000	$1(s), 1804, Class I (X)	PF-63	B&M/Stack's	Apr-97
51	$1,740,000	Prefed, 1792, Washington $10, Large Eagle, M-31	NGC EF-45*	Heritage	Aug-18
52	$1,725,000	$2.50, 1796, No Stars (A)	PCGS MS-65	Heritage	Jan-08
53	$1,725,000	$10, 1920-S	PCGS MS-67	Heritage	Mar-07
54	$1,645,000	$20, 1861, Paquet Reverse (G)	PCGS MS-61	Heritage	Aug-14
55	$1,610,000	$10, 1839/8, Type of 1838, Lg Letters (F)	NGC PF-67 UCam	Heritage	Jan-07
56	$1,610,000	$20, 1861, Paquet Reverse (G)	PCGS MS-61	Heritage	Aug-06
57	$1,552,500	10¢, 1894-S	PCGS PF-64	Stack's	Oct-07
58	$1,527,500	25¢, 1796, B-2	PCGS MS-66	Sotheby's / Stack's Bowers	May-15
59	$1,527,500	50¢, 1797, O-101a	PCGS MS-66	Sotheby's / Stack's Bowers	May-15
60	$1,527,500	Prefed, 1776, Cont. $1, silver, N-3D	NGC MS-62	Heritage	Jan-15
61	$1,527,500	Prefed, 1776, Cont. $1, silver, N-1C	NGC EF-40	Heritage	Jan-15
62	$1,527,500	25¢, 1796, B-2	NGC MS-67+ *	Heritage	Nov-13
63	$1,500,000	10¢, 1894-S	NGC PF-66	Heritage	Sep-20
64	$1,500,000	1¢, 1793, Chain, S-1	PCGS MS-64+ BN	Heritage	Jan-19
65	$1,495,000	$20, 1927-D	PCGS MS-66	Heritage	Jan-10
66	$1,495,000	$20, 1921	PCGS MS-63	B&M	Aug-06
67	$1,485,000	5¢, 1913, Liberty Head (U)	Gem PF-66	B&M/Stack's	May-96
68	$1,440,000	10¢, 1894-S	NGC MS-65	Stack's Bowers	Dec-20
69	$1,440,000	$1(s), 1804, Class III	PCGS PF-55	Stack's Bowers	Mar-20
70	$1,437,500	$20, 1856-O	NGC SP-63	Heritage	May-09
71	$1,410,000	Prefed, 1776, Cont. $1, silver, N-3D	NGC MS-63	Heritage	May-14
72	$1,410,000	Pattern 1¢, 1792 Silver Center, J-1	NGC MS-63+ BN	Heritage	May-14
73	$1,410,000	Pattern half disme, 1792 half disme, J-7 (N)	PCGS SP-67	Heritage	Jan-13
74	$1,380,000	$2.50, 1796, Stars, Bass-3003, BD-3 (B)	PCGS MS-65	Heritage	Jan-21
75	$1,380,000	$5, 1829, Large Date	PCGS PF-64	Heritage	Jan-12
76	$1,380,000	1¢, 1793, Chain AMERICA, S-4 (T)	PCGS MS-65 BN	Heritage	Jan-12
77	$1,380,000	50¢, 1797, O-101a (M)	NGC MS-66	Stack's	Jul-08
78	$1,380,000	$2.50, 1796, No Stars (A)	PCGS MS-65	Stack's (ANR)	Jun-05
79	$1,351,250	$5, 1833, BD-1	PCGS PF-67	Sotheby's / Stack's Bowers	May-16
80	$1,322,500	$3, 1855-S	NGC PF-64 Cameo	Heritage	Aug-11
81	$1,322,500	Pattern half disme, 1792, J-7 (N)	PCGS SP-67	Heritage	Apr-06
82	$1,322,500	$20, 1927-D	NGC MS-65	Heritage	Jan-06
83	$1,322,500	10¢, 1894-S	NGC PF-66	DLRC	Mar-05
84	$1,320,000	$1 Trade, 1885	PCGS PF-64	Stack's Bowers	Mar-20

Rank	Price	Coin	Grade	Firm	Date
85	$1,320,000	10¢, 1894-S	PCGS PF-63	Stack's Bowers	Aug-19
86	$1,292,500	Pattern half disme, 1792, J-7 (N)	PCGS SP67	Heritage	Aug-14
87	$1,292,500	50¢, 1797, O-101a	PCGS MS-65+	Heritage	Aug-14
88	$1,265,000	Pattern $10, 1874, Bickford, J-1373	PCGS PF-65 DC	Heritage	Jan-10
89	$1,265,000	1¢, 1795, Reeded Edge, S-79	PCGS VG-10	Goldberg	Sep-09
90	$1,265,000	$1(s), 1795, Flowing Hair, B-7, BB-18	V Ch Gem MS	Bullowa	Dec-05
91	$1,210,000	$20, MCMVII, Ultra HR, LE (I)	PCGS PF-67	Goldberg	May-99
92	$1,207,500	$1(s), 1794	NGC MS-64	B&M	Aug-10
93	$1,207,500	$1(s), 1866, No Motto	NGC PF-63	Stack's (ANR)	Jan-05
94	$1,207,500	$1(s), 1804, Class III (R)	PCGS PF-58	B&M	Jul-03
95	$1,175,000	$5, 1798, Small Eagle, BD-1	PCGS AU-55	Sotheby's / Stack's Bowers	Sep-15
96	$1,175,000	Pattern 1¢, 1792, Birch, LE, J-4	PCGS AU-58	Stack's Bowers	Mar-15
97	$1,175,000	Prefed, 1783, Nova Constellatio quint, Type II	PCGS AU-53	Heritage	Apr-13
98	$1,175,000	$1(s), 1796, Small Date, Small Letters, B-2, BB-63	NGC MS-65	Heritage	Apr-13
99	$1,150,000	1/2¢, 1794, C-7 (S)	PCGS MS-67 RB	Goldberg	Jan-14
100	$1,150,000	Pattern 1¢, 1792, Silver Center, J-1	PCGS MS-61 BN	Heritage	Apr-12
101	$1,150,000	$1(s), 1794	NGC MS-64	Stack's (ANR)	Jun-05
102	$1,145,625	Pattern half disme, 1792 half disme, J-7	NGC MS-68	Stack's Bowers	Jan-13
103	$1,140,000	$1 Trade, 1884	NGC PF-66	Heritage	Jan-19
104	$1,121,250	1/2¢, 1811, C-1	PCGS MS-66 RB	Goldberg	Jan-14
105	$1,116,250	$4, 1880, Coiled Hair	PCGS PF-65	Heritage	Jun-15
106	$1,092,500	$20, 1921	PCGS MS-66	Heritage	Nov-05
107	$1,092,500	$1(s), 1870-S	BU PL	Stack's	May-03
108	$1,057,500	$1(s), 1795, Draped Bust, BB-51	PCGS SP-66	Sotheby's / Stack's Bowers	May-16
109	$1,057,500	$10, 1795, 9 Leaves, BD-3	PCGS MS-63+	Sotheby's / Stack's Bowers	Sep-15
110	$1,057,500	Pattern disme, 1792, copper, J-11	NGC MS-64 RB	Heritage	Jan-15
111	$1,057,500	Terr, 1852, Humbert $10, K-10	NGC MS-68	Heritage	Apr-13
112	$1,057,500	$20, MCMVII, Ultra HR, LE of '06	PCGS PF-58	Heritage	Aug-12
113	$1,050,000	$1(s), 1794	NGC MS-62	Stack's Bowers	Dec-20
114	$1,050,000	$4, 1879, Coiled Hair	NGC PF-66 Cam	Heritage	Jan-19
115	$1,041,300	$4, 1879, Coiled Hair (C)	NGC PF-67 Cam	Bonhams	Sep-13
116	$1,035,000	10¢, 1894-S	PCGS PF-65	Heritage	Jan-05
117	$1,012,000	$20, 1921	PCGS MS-65 PQ	Goldberg	Sep-07
118	$1,006,250	$2.50, 1796, Stars, Bass-3003, BD-3 (B)	NGC MS-65	Heritage	Jan-08
119	$1,006,250	$1 Trade, 1885	NGC PF-62	DLRC	Nov-04
120	$998,750	1/2¢, 1811, C-1	PCGS MS-66 RB	Sotheby's / Stack's Bowers	Mar-17
121	$998,750	Pattern disme, 1792, Silver, J-9	PCGS AU-50	Heritage	Apr-16
122	$998,750	1¢, 1793, Chain, S-3	PCGS MS-65 RB	Sotheby's / Stack's Bowers	Feb-16
123	$998,750	Pattern disme, 1792, J-9	NGC AU-50	Heritage	Jan-15
124	$998,750	$1 Trade, 1884	PCGS PF-65	Heritage	Jan-14
125	$998,750	1¢, 1793, Chain, S-2	PCGS MS-65 BN	Stack's Bowers	Jan-13
126	$990,000	1¢, 1793, Chain, AMERICA, S-4 (T)	PCGS MS-65 BN	Heritage	Jun-18
127	$990,000	$1(s), 1804, Class I (Q)	Choice Proof	Rarcoa	Jul-89
128	$977,500	1¢, 1799, S-189	NGC MS-62 BN	Goldberg	Sep-09
129	$977,500	$4, 1880, Coiled Hair (D)	NGC PF-66 Cam	Heritage	Jan-05
130	$977,500	$5, 1833, Large Date	PCGS PF-67	Heritage	Jan-05
131	$966,000	50¢, 1797, O-101a (M)	NGC MS-66	Stack's (ANR)	Mar-04
132	$962,500	5¢, 1913, Liberty Head	Proof	Stack's	Oct-93
133	$960,000	Confed, 1861, Original 50¢	NGC PF-40	Heritage	Nov-17
134	$959,400	$4, 1880, Flowing Hair	NGC PF-67*	Bonhams	Sep-13
135	$948,750	Terr, 1852, Moffat & Co. $10, Wide Date, K-9	PCGS SP-67	Stack's (ANR)	Aug-06
136	$940,000	1¢, 1793, Liberty Cap, S-13, B 20	PCGS AU-58	Sotheby's / Stack's Bowers	Mar-17

Rank	Price	Coin	Grade	Firm	Date
137	$940,000	$5, 1825, 5 Over 4, BD-2	PCGS MS-64	Sotheby's / Stack's Bowers	May-16
138	$940,000	1/2¢, 1794, C-7 **(S)**	PCGS MS-67 RB	Sotheby's / Stack's Bowers	Feb-16
139	$940,000	Terr, 1852, Moffat & Co. $10, Wide Date, K-9	PCGS SP-63	Heritage	Jan-14
140	$920,000	1/2¢, 1793, C-4	PCGS MS-66 BN	Goldberg	Jan-14
141	$920,000	$1(s), 1802, Restrike	PCGS PF-65 Cam	Heritage	Apr-08
142	$920,000	$20, 1907, Small Edge Letters	PCGS PF-68	Heritage	Nov-05
143	$920,000	$1 Trade, 1885 **(Y)**	NGC PF-61	Stack's	May-03
144	$910,625	$1(s), 1794	PCGS AU-58+	Stack's Bowers	Mar-17
145	$910,625	$1(s), 1795, Draped Bust, Off-Center, B-14, BB-51	NGC MS-66+*	Heritage	Nov-13
146	$907,500	$1 Trade, 1885	Gem PF-65	B&M/Stack's	Apr-97
147	$900,000	Pattern 1¢, 1792, silver Center, J-1	PCGS MS-61 BN	Stack's Bowers	Nov-17
148	$891,250	1/2¢, 1796, No Pole, C-1	PCGS MS-65 BN	Goldberg	Jan-14
149	$891,250	10¢, 1873-CC, No Arrows **(K)**	NGC MS-65	B&M	Jul-04
150	$881,250	$10, 1933	PCGS MS-66	Goldberg	Jun-16
151	$881,250	$5, 1829, Small Date, BD-2	PCGS MS-65+	Sotheby's / Stack's Bowers	May-16
152	$881,250	$4, 1879, Coiled Hair	PCGS PF-65	Heritage	Apr-15
153	$881,250	Confed, 1861, Original 50¢	NGC PF-30	Heritage	Jan-15
154	$881,250	25¢, 1796, B-1	PCGS SP-66	Heritage	Aug-14
155	$881,250	$10, 1795, BD-5	PCGS MS-65	Heritage	Aug-14
156	$881,250	10¢, 1796, JR-1	PCGS MS-67	Heritage	Jun-14
157	$881,250	$1(s), 1889-CC	PCGS MS-68	Stack's Bowers	Aug-13
158	$881,250	1¢, 1794, Head of '93, S-18b	PCGS MS-64 BN	Stack's Bowers	Jan-13
159	$874,000	$1(s), 1804, Class III **(R)**	PCGS PF-58	B&M	Nov-01
160	$870,000	50¢, 1794, O-101a **(J)**	PCGS MS-64+	Heritage	Jan-21
161	$862,500	1¢, 1793, Strawberry Leaf, NC-3	NGC F-12	Stack's	Jan-09
162	$862,500	Pattern $20, 1879, Quintuple Stella, J-1643, P-1843	PCGS PF-62	Heritage	Jan-07
163	$862,500	$2.50, 1796, Stars, Bass-3003, BD-3 **(B)**	NGC MS-65	Heritage	Jan-07
164	$851,875	$4, 1879, Coiled Hair	PCGS PF-66	Heritage	Jan-14
165	$851,875	$1(s), 1803, Restrike	PCGS PF-66	Heritage	Jan-13
166	$851,875	$1(s), 1802, Restrike	PCGS PF-65 Cam	Heritage	Aug-12
167	$840,000	1¢, 1943-D, Bronze Planchet	PCGS MS-64 BN	Heritage	Jan-21
168	$840,000	Terr, 1849, Mormon $10, K-3	PCGS AU-53	Stack's Bowers	Dec-20
169	$825,000	$20, MCMVII, Ultra HR, LE	Proof	Sotheby's	Dec-96
170	$824,850	Pattern half disme, 1792, copper, J-8	NGC AU-55	Heritage	Jan-15
171	$822,500	$10, 1797, Large Eagle 13 Leaves	PCGS MS-64+	Legend	Mar-19
172	$822,500	$5, 1815, BD-1	PCGS MS-65	Sotheby's / Stack's Bowers	Feb-16
173	$822,500	$5, 1832, 12 Stars, BD-12	PCGS MS-63	Sotheby's / Stack's Bowers	May-16
174	$822,500	$5, 1835, McM-5	PCGS PF-67+ DCam	Soth/S/B	May-16
175	$822,500	$1(s), 1795, Flowing Hair, B-7, BB-18	PCGS MS-66	Sotheby's / Stack's Bowers	Sep-15
176	$822,500	50¢, 1796, 16 Stars, O-102	PCGS MS-66	Sotheby's / Stack's Bowers	May-15
177	$822,500	$2.50, 1796, No Stars, BD-2	PCGS MS-62	Sotheby's / Stack's Bowers	May-15
178	$822,500	$10, 1933	PCGS MS-65	Heritage	Apr-15
179	$822,500	$1(s), 1795, Flowing HairB-2, BB-20	NGC SP-64	Stack's Bowers	Aug-14
180	$822,500	$1(s), 1799, B-5, BB-157	NGC MS-67	Heritage	Nov-13
181	$822,500	Pattern 1¢, 1792, Silver Center, J-1 **(O)**	NGC MS-61+ BN	Heritage	Apr-13
182	$805,000	$1(s), 1870-S	NGC EF-40	Heritage	Apr-08
183	$805,000	$20, 1921	PCGS MS-65	Heritage	Nov-05
184	$793,125	10¢, 1796, JR-6	PCGS MS-68	Heritage	Aug-14
185	$793,125	Pattern half disme, 1792, J-7	PCGS MS-66	Stack's Bowers	Aug-13
186	$780,000	1/2¢, 1796, No Pole, C-1 **(E)**	PCGS MS-67 RB	Heritage	Jan-21
187	$780,000	$1(s), 1886-O	PCGS MS-67 DMPL	Stack's Bowers	Nov-20
188	$780,000	$1(s), 1794	NGC AU-58	Heritage	Aug-18

Rank	Price	Coin	Grade	Firm	Date
189	$763,750	$1(s), 1795, Draped Bust, BB-51	PCGS MS-66	Sotheby's / Stack's Bowers	May-16
190	$763,750	$5, 1829, Large Date, BD-1	PCGS MS-66+	Sotheby's / Stack's Bowers	May-16
191	$763,750	1/2¢, 1796, No Pole, C-1 (E)	PCGS MS-67 RB	Sotheby's / Stack's Bowers	Feb-16
192	$763,750	50¢, 1794, O-101a (J)	PCGS MS-64	Sotheby's / Stack's Bowers	May-15
193	$763,750	$2.50, 1798, BD-1	PCGS MS-65	Sotheby's / Stack's Bowers	May-15
194	$763,750	Terr, 1849, Pacific Company $5, K-1	PCGS AU-58	Heritage	Apr-14
195	$763,750	Terr, 1855, Kellogg & Co. $50	PCGS PF-64 Cam	Heritage	Apr-14
196	$763,750	50¢, 1838-O	NGC PF-64	Heritage	Jan-14
197	$763,750	$1(s), 1870-S	PCGS EF-40	Heritage	Jan-14
198	$763,750	$5, 1826, BD-2	PCGS MS-66	Heritage	Jan-14
199	$750,000	$1(s), 1884-S	PCGS MS-68	Stack's Bowers	Nov-20
200	$750,000	10¢, 1796, JR-1	PCGS SP-67	Heritage	Sep-20
201	$750,000	Pattern 1¢, 1792, Silver Center, J-1	PCGS SP-58+ BN	Heritage	Jan-19
202	$750,000	$4, 1880, Flowing Hair	NGC PF-67 Cam	Heritage	Jan-18
203	$747,500	1¢, 1793, Chain, S-3	NGC MS-66 BN	Stack's Bowers	Aug-12
204	$747,500	$20, 1921	PCGS MS-66	Heritage	Jan-12
205	$747,500	Terr, 1855, Kellogg & Co. $50	PCGS PF-64	Heritage	Jan-07
206	$747,500	$1(s), 1794	NGC MS-61	Heritage	Jun-05
207	$734,375	50¢, 1838-O	PCGS PF-64	Heritage	Jan-13
208	$725,000	Prefed, 1787, Brasher dbln, EB on Wing (P)	MS-63	B&R	Nov-79
209	$720,000	Terr, 1849, Mormon $20, K-4	PCGS-62	Heritage	Jan-21
210	$720,000	$1(s), 1896-S	PCGS MS-69	Stack's Bowers	Nov-20
211	$718,750	1/2¢, 1793, C-3	PCGS MS-65 BN	Goldberg	Jan-14
212	$718,750	1/2¢, 1796, With Pole, C-2	PCGS MS-65+ RB	Goldberg	Jan-14
213	$718,750	$10, 1933	Unc	Stack's	Oct-04
214	$705,698	$1(s), 1870-S	VF-25	B&M	Feb-08
215	$705,000	$1(s), 1795, Bust, B-14, BB-51	PCGS MS-66	Legend	Oct-20
216	$705,000	$1(s), 1796, Bust, B-2, BB-63	PCGS MS-65	Legend	Oct-20
217	$705,000	1¢, 1796, Liberty Cap, S-84	PCGS MS-66+ RB	Sotheby's / Stack's Bowers	Mar-17
218	$705,000	Pattern disme, 1792, copper, RE, J-10	PCGS SP-64 BN	Heritage	Apr-16
219	$705,000	$1(s), 1795, Flowing Hair, B-7, BB-18	PCGS MS-65+	Sotheby's / Stack's Bowers	Sep-15
220	$705,000	$10, 1798/7, 7x6 Stars, BD-2	PCGS MS-61	Sotheby's / Stack's Bowers	Sep-15
221	$705,000	25¢, 1827, Original	PCGS PF-66+ Cam	Sotheby's / Stack's Bowers	May-15
222	$705,000	50¢, 1794, O-109	NGC VF-25	Heritage	Apr-15
223	$705,000	Pattern 1¢, 1792, Silver Center, J-1 (O)	NGC MS-61+ BN	Heritage	Sep-14
224	$705,000	Prefed, 1783, Nova Constellatio bit, PE, W-1820	NGC AU-55	Heritage	May-14
225	$705,000	Terr, 1849, Mormon $10, K-3	NGC AU-58	Heritage	Apr-14
226	$705,000	$1(s), 1803, Large 3, B-6, BB-255	NGC MS-65+	Heritage	Nov-13
227	$690,300	$5, 1836	NGC PF-67* UCam	Bonhams	Sep-13
228	$690,000	$5, 1909-O	PCGS MS-66	Heritage	Jan-11
229	$690,000	1¢, 1796, Liberty Cap, S-84	PCGS MS-66 RB	Goldberg	Sep-08
230	$690,000	Pattern disme, 1792, copper, RE, J-10	NGC PF-62 BN	Heritage	Jul-08
231	$690,000	$5, 1825, 5 Over 4	NGC AU-50	Heritage	Jul-08
232	$690,000	$20, MCMVII, Ultra HR, LE of '06	NGC PF-58	Stack's	Jul-08
233	$690,000	Terr, 1860, Clark, Gruber & Co. $20	NGC MS-64	Heritage	Jan-06
234	$690,000	Prefed, 1742 (1786), Brasher dbln, Lima style	NGC EF-40	Heritage	Jan-05
235	$690,000	$5, 1835	PCGS PF-67	Heritage	Jan-05
236	$690,000	$1(g), 1849-C, Open Wreath	NGC MS-63 PL	DLRC	Jul-04
237	$690,000	$20, MCMVII, Ultra HR, LE	Proof	Sotheby's/Stack's	Oct-01
238	$690,000	$10, 1839/8, Type of 1838, Lg Letters (F)	NGC PF-67	Goldberg	Sep-99
239	$687,500	$3, 1870-S	EF-40	B&R	Oct-82
240	$687,500	$5, 1822	VF-30/EF-40	B&R	Oct-82

Rank	Price	Coin	Grade	Firm	Date
241	$675,525	$10, 1795, BD-5	NGC MS-65	Heritage	Aug-13
242	$672,750	$1(s), 1803, Restrike	PF-66	B&M	Feb-07
243	$661,250	1¢, 1804, S-266c	PCGS MS-63 BN	Goldberg	Sep-09
244	$661,250	1/2 dime, 1870-S	NGC MS-63 PL	B&M	Jul-04
245	$660,000	$20, MCMVII, High Relief, Wire Rim	NGC MS-69	Heritage	Sep-20
246	$660,000	Pattern 1¢, 1792, Birch, PE, J-3	PCGS AU-58	Stack's Bowers	Oct-18
247	$660,000	$20, MCMVII, Ultra HR, LE **(I)**	PF-67	B&M	Jan-97
248	$660,000	$20, 1861, Paquet Reverse	MS-67	B&M	Nov-88
249	$655,500	$4, 1879, Coiled Hair **(C)**	NGC PF-67 Cam	Heritage	Jan-05
250	$655,200	$20, 1891	NGC PF-68* UCam	Bonhams	Sep-13

KEY

Price: The sale price of the coin, including the appropriate buyer's fee.

Coin: The denomination/classification, date, and description of the coin, along with pertinent catalog or reference numbers. B = Baker (for pre-federal), Bolender (for silver dollars), Breen (for gold), or Browning (for quarter dollars); BB = Bowers/Borckardt; BD = Bass-Dannreuther; Confed = Confederate States of America issue; dbln = doubloon; HR = High Relief; J = Judd; JR = John Reich Society; LE = Lettered Edge; N = Newman; NC = Non-Collectible; O = Overton; P = Pollock; Pattern = a pattern, experimental, or trial piece; Prefed = pre-federal issue; S = Sheldon; T = Taraskza; Terr = territorial issue. Letters in parentheses, **(A)** through **(T)**, denote instances in which multiple sales of the same coin rank within the Top 250.

Grade: The grade of the coin, plus the name of the grading firm (if independently graded). BM = branch mint; NGC = Numismatic Guaranty Corporation of America; PCGS = Professional Coin Grading Service; PQ = premium quality.

Firm: The auction firm (or firms) that sold the coin. ANR = American Numismatic Rarities; B&R = Bowers & Ruddy; DLRC = David Lawrence Rare Coins; Stack's Bowers = Stack's Bowers Galleries (name under which Stack's and B&M merged in 2010; also encompasses the merger of Stack's and ANR in 2006).

Date: The month and year of the auction.

Auction records compiled and edited by P. Scott Rubin.

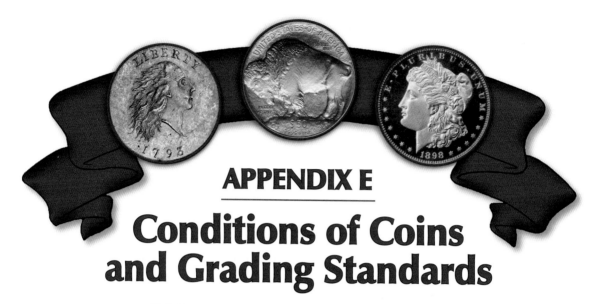

APPENDIX E

Conditions of Coins and Grading Standards

ESSENTIAL ELEMENTS OF THE AMERICAN NUMISMATIC ASSOCIATION GRADING STANDARDS

Proof—A specially made coin distinguished by sharpness of detail and usually with a brilliant, mirrorlike surface. *Proof* refers to the method of manufacture and is not a grade. The term implies superior condition unless otherwise noted.

Perfect Proof (PF-70)—The perfect coin, with strike and surface of the highest quality. No contact marks are visible under magnification. There are absolutely no hairlines, scuff marks, or defects.

Gem Proof (PF-65)—Surfaces are brilliant, with no noticeable blemishes or flaws. A few scattered, barely noticeable marks or hairlines.

Choice Proof (PF-63)—Surfaces are reflective, with only a few blemishes in secondary focal places. No major flaws.

Proof (PF-60)—Surfaces may have several contact marks, hairlines, or light rubs. Luster may be dull and eye appeal lacking.

Mint State—The terms *Mint State (MS)* and *Uncirculated (Unc.)* are interchangeable and refer to coins showing no trace of wear from circulation. Such coins may vary slightly because of minor surface imperfections, as described in the following subdivisions:

Perfect Uncirculated (MS-70)—Perfect new condition, showing no trace of wear. The finest quality possible, with no evidence of scratches, handling, or contact with other coins. Very few circulation-issue coins are ever found in this condition.

Gem Uncirculated (MS-65)—An above-average Uncirculated coin that may be brilliant or lightly toned and that has very few contact marks on the surface or rim.

Choice Uncirculated (MS-63)—A coin with some distracting contact marks or blemishes in prime focal areas. Luster may be impaired.

Uncirculated (MS-60)—A coin that has no trace of wear, but which may show a number of marks from contact with other coins during minting, storage, or transportation, and whose surface may be spotted or lack some luster.

Choice About Uncirculated (AU-55)—Evidence of friction on high points of design. Most of the mint luster remains.

About Uncirculated (AU-50)—Traces of light wear on many of the high points. At least half of the mint luster is still present.

Choice Extremely Fine (EF-45)—Light overall wear on the highest points. All design details are very sharp. Some of the mint luster is evident.

Extremely Fine (EF-40)—Light wear on the design throughout, but all features are sharp and well defined. Traces of luster may show.

Choice Very Fine (VF-30)—Light, even wear on the surface and highest parts of the design. All lettering and major features are sharp.

Very Fine (VF-20)—Moderate wear on design high points. All major details are clear.

Fine (F-12)—Moderate to considerable even wear. The entire design is bold with an overall pleasing appearance.

Very Good (VG-8)—Well worn with main features clear and bold, although rather flat.

Good (G-4)—Heavily worn, with the design visible but faint in areas. Many details are flat.

About Good (AG-3)—Very heavily worn with portions of the lettering, date, and legend worn smooth. The date may be barely readable.

A star, plus sign, or similar notation in the grade on a holder means the coin has exceptional quality or eye appeal.

Important: Undamaged coins are worth more than bent, corroded, scratched, holed, nicked, stained, or mutilated ones. Flawless Uncirculated coins are generally worth more than values quoted in this book. Slightly worn coins ("sliders") that have been cleaned and conditioned ("buffed") to simulate Uncirculated luster are worth considerably less than perfect pieces.

Unlike damage inflicted after striking, manufacturing defects do not always lessen values. Examples include colonial coins with planchet flaws or weakly struck designs; early silver or gold coins with weight-adjustment "file marks" (parallel cuts made on the planchet prior to striking); and coins with "lint marks" (surface marks due to the presence of dust or other foreign matter during striking).

Note that while grading *standards* strive to be precise, interpretations are subjective and can vary among collectors, dealers, and certification services.

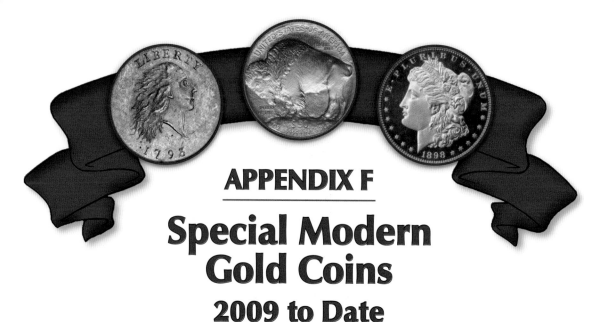

APPENDIX F
Special Modern Gold Coins
2009 to Date

AN OVERVIEW OF SPECIAL MODERN GOLD COINS

In recent years, the U.S. Mint has introduced several innovative new gold coins. These coins showcase the Mint's technological and creative abilities in impressive and often surprising ways.

Chapter 31, section 5112, of the United States Code gives the secretary of the Treasury considerable leeway in the specifics of the nation's gold bullion coins. Without needing to get congressional orders or approval, the secretary can change coinage designs, denominations, and other details in coins of that precious metal (similar changes in silver bullion coins would require Congress to get involved).

The Mint has used this authority to create such modern marvels as the MMIX Ultra High Relief gold double eagle (2009), a gold Kennedy half dollar (2014), and a series of American Liberty high-relief gold coins (2015 to date). Authority for 2016 gold coins struck with the designs of the Mercury dime, the Standing Liberty quarter, and the Liberty Walking half dollar, to celebrate the 100th anniversary of their debut, derives from the same legislation.

These gold coins are focused on collectors, using the U.S. Mint's 40 years of modern experience to determine what collectors and investors want (and don't want) in terms of gold. While these gold–collector coin programs would have been impossible for much of the 20th century under the gold laws legislated in the 1930s, it was made legal for private citizens to own gold again in 1974. The minting of the gold National Bicentennial Medals and the Colorado Centennial Medal was followed by the minting of the American Arts gold medallions of the early 1980s, which ramped up to the globally popular American Gold Eagles, and the subsequent American Buffalo and First Spouse bullion programs have also met with success. Special modern gold coins represent the culmination of the Mint's experience with each of these series, and at the same time they promise new innovations in the coming years.

The American Liberty gold coin's packaging.

MMIX ULTRA HIGH RELIEF $20 GOLD COIN (2009)

In 2009 the U.S. Mint produced a modern collector's version of the first Augustus Saint-Gaudens double eagle. When the original debuted in 1907, the Mint had been unable to strike large quantities for circulation—the ultra high relief design was artistic, but difficult to coin. (It was modified later in 1907 to a lower relief suitable for commercial production.) Just over 100 years later, the 2009 version was a showcase coin: a tangible demonstration of the Mint's 21st-century ability to combine artistry and technology to make an outstanding numismatic treasure.

Like its predecessor, the new coin was dated in Roman numerals (with 2009 as MMIX). The Mint digitally mapped Saint-Gaudens's original plasters and used the results in the die-making process. The date was changed, and four additional stars were inserted, to represent the nation's current 50 states. Augustus Saint-Gaudens's striding Liberty occupied the obverse. On the reverse was his flying eagle, with the addition of IN GOD WE TRUST, a motto not used in the original design. The 2009 version, struck in Philadelphia, was made in a smaller diameter (27 mm instead of 34), with a thickness of 4 mm, and composed of 24-karat (.9999 fine) gold, thus making it easier to strike and stay true to the ultra high-relief design. Its weight is one ounce.

As with other coins of the U.S. Mint, these are legal tender and their weight, content, and purity are guaranteed by the federal government. They were packaged in a fancy mahogany box and sold directly to the public, instead of through a network of distributors.

Note that the Mint does not release bullion mintage data on a regular basis; the number given here reflects the most recently available official data.

	Mintage	MS	MS-69	MS-70
MMIX (2009) Ultra High Relief $20 Gold Coin †† (a)	114,427	$2,500	$2,700	$3,200

Note: MS values are for uncertified Mint State coins of average quality, in their complete original U.S. Mint packaging. †† Ranked in the *100 Greatest U.S. Modern Coins* (fourth edition) **a.** Auction: $2,820, MS-70, October 2015.

KENNEDY 50TH ANNIVERSARY HALF DOLLAR GOLD COIN (2014)

Following the assassination of President John F. Kennedy on November 22, 1963, the Kennedy half dollar was authorized. The first coins were made available to the public on March 24, 1964. The new half dollars were immediately hoarded by the public who were eager to obtain a memento of the late president.

The 50th anniversary Kennedy gold half dollar was struck as a tribute to the original issue as part of a year-long numismatic celebration that included two other coin sets (one Uncirculated set and one silver set). The gold coin, struck at West Point, features a restored obverse portrait of President Kennedy, which brings out the original details of the coin, and it is dual dated as "1964–2014". On the reverse an indication of the precious metal weight and purity appears: .9999 gold weighing 3/4 of an ounce. Otherwise the specifications match those of a standard half dollar.

The release of this coin caused a collector frenzy, but prices and collector interest soon stabilized.

	Mintage	PF-65	PF-67Cam	PF-68DC
2014-W, Kennedy 50th Anniversary Half Dollar Gold Coin, Proof	73,772	$1,400	$1,650	$1,750

AMERICAN LIBERTY HIGH-RELIEF GOLD COINS

2018-W, Tenth-Ounce

2015-W   **1792–2017-W**   **2019-W**

The first American Liberty high-relief .9999-fine gold coin, with a weight of one troy ounce and a face value of $100, was minted at West Point in 2015. The coin was not congressionally mandated, instead being created under authority granted to the secretary of the Treasury by federal law—31 U.S.C. Section 5112 (i)(4)(C).

The design was strongly influenced by the Citizens Coinage Advisory Committee, who, according to a Mint spokesperson, "emphasized creating a 'modern' Liberty that reflects the nation's diversity." The U.S. Commission of Fine Arts also reviewed designs and made recommendations.

Of the 2015 American Liberty's eagle reverse the designer, Paul C. Balan, commented, "My reverse design for the American Liberty High Relief gold coin was created with inspiration from the Great Seal of the United States and its depiction of an American bald eagle clutching an olive branch. The soaring eagle is a symbol of strength, freedom and bravery, and the 13 olives on the branch represent the original 13 colonies, which epitomize the power and solidarity of our nation. I want people to feel a sense of pride and integrity as Americans when they see my design." Balan also shares that his design was initially submitted for the U.S. Marshals Service commemorative but was chosen for the American Liberty high-relief coin instead.

The designs for the American Liberty high-relief gold coins are created to take full advantage of the same high-relief techniques used to create the MMIX Ultra High Relief gold coin.

The design of the 2015 American Liberty high-relief gold coin was adapted for a silver medal in 2016, but in 2017 the Mint continued the series with a 1792–2017 American Liberty high-relief gold coin. The series is slated to continue biennially, with a new design being issued every two years. In the years between gold issues, silver medals featuring the same designs will be issued.

	Mintage	Unc.	PF
$100, 2015-W, 1 ounce	49,325	$2,400	
$100, 1792–2017-W, 1 ounce	32,612		$2,500
$10, 2018-W, 1/10 ounce	36,351		$275
$100, 2019-W, 1 ounce, Enhanced Finish	10,421	$2,500	
$100, 2021-W, 1 ounce		$2,500	

1916 CENTENNIAL GOLD COINS (2016)

In 2016 the Mint celebrated the 100th anniversary of the Mercury dime, Standing Liberty quarter, and Walking Liberty half dollar designs by issuing gold versions of the three classic coins, all struck at West Point. The gold coins are reduced in diameter from the original silver coins. They are composed of .9999-fine gold and weigh, respectively, 1/10 oz., 1/4 oz., and 1/2 oz. The dime was struck at 16.5 mm; the quarter, at 22 mm; and the half dollar, 27 mm. Some discussion at the Mint had centered around issuing similar commemorative coins in silver, but that would require congressional action. The gold Mercury dime sold out within 45 minutes of its release, but the two larger gold coins have seen much slower sales.

	Mintage	SP-67	SP-70
2016-W, Mercury Dime Centennial Gold Coin	124,885	$300	$350
2016-W, Standing Liberty Quarter Centennial Gold Coin	91,752	$500	$675
2016-W, Liberty Walking Half Dollar Centennial Gold Coin	65,509	$1,000	$1,150

MAYFLOWER LANDING 400TH ANNIVERSARY $10 GOLD COINS AND MEDAL (2020)

In 2020 the Mint is remembering the 400th anniversary of the 1620 *Mayflower* landing with a special gold coin. As the coin is not linked to any U.S. legislation, it is not a commemorative as such but is being struck under the Treasury secretary's legal authority to produce bullion gold coins and silver medals.

The coin will be 1/4 ounce of 24-karat gold and will have a denomination of $10. It will be accompanied by a 1-ounce silver medal whose fineness and size were not yet determined at press time. The mintages and finishes for both items had likewise not been chosen. It is possible the coin and medal will be issued in a joint program with the United Kingdom's Royal Mint, in a fashion similar to that of the 2019 Pride of Two Nations set produced jointly with the Royal Canadian Mint.

	Mintage	MS	MS-69	MS-70
2020-W, Mayflower Landing 400th Anniversary $10 Gold Coin	5,350	$750	$850	$1,150
2020-W, Mayflower Landing 400th Anniversary $10 Gold Coin, Reverse Proof	5,000	$900	$1,000	$1,250

END OF WORLD WAR II 75TH ANNIVERSARY $25 GOLD COIN AND MEDALS (2020)

The Mint will pay respect to the 75th anniversary of the end of World War II with a $25 gold coin along with medals in silver and bronze. The 1/2-ounce coin will be .9999 fine gold and the medal .999 fine silver; as of press time, Mint officials had not disclosed the intended finishes, diameters, or mintages.

	Mintage	MS	MS-69	MS-70
2020-W, End of World War II 75th Anniversary $25 Gold Coin	7,500	$1,350	$1,500	$1,750

APPENDIX G
So-Called Dollars

The contents of this section are based on the work and research of Jeff Shevlin.

AN OVERVIEW OF SO-CALLED DOLLARS

So-Called Dollars are U.S. medals approximately the size of a silver dollar that were struck to commemorate a historical subject. A collection of So-Called Dollars is strikingly different from a typical collection of U.S. coins assembled by date and mintmark, in that each piece in the collection has a uniquely different design. There are more than 750 different design types, and when different metal compositions are considered, there are more than 1,500 varieties to consider collecting. So-Called Dollars were struck in virtually every metal composition conceivable, including gold, silver, copper, bronze, brass, aluminum, nickel, white metal, German silver, gutta-percha, gold-plated, and silver-plated.

These collectibles were cataloged in the illustrated standard reference book *So-Called Dollars*, authored by Harold Hibler and Charles Kappen and published in 1963. This book, which is widely considered as the most definitive reference on So-Called Dollars, was revised and edited by Tom Hoffman, Dave Hayes, Jonathan Brecher, and John Dean in 2008.

So-Called Dollars were struck by the U.S. Mint as well as by private mints (and one was struck by the Manila Mint while the Philippines was an American territory). Many of the most famous engravers of U.S. coins also engraved So-Called Dollars, including William and Charles Barber, George T. Morgan, Augustus Saint-Gaudens, and others. Some of the designs and artwork on these pieces match or surpass these artists' other work in coin and medal design.

Historical medals come in all sizes. To be classified as a So-Called Dollar one must be approximately the size of a silver dollar, between 33 and 45 mm in diameter (a silver dollar is 38.1 mm), although collectors traditionally include a few specific exceptions such as the 1939 Charbneau medals

From national events and celebrations to local anniversaries, from great successes to major disasters, bits and pieces of the history of the United States are chronologically depicted on these fascinating historical medals.

About half of the So-Called Dollars are related to a Fair or Exposition with the other half commemorating important events in U.S. history. Expositions played a significant part in the development of the United States. Local communities, often with federal funding support, would begin to plan years ahead of time and build enormous halls and buildings for their expositions, which would last anywhere from a few months to a few years. Millions of people would travel to attend these grand events and see things they had never seen before, often visiting for days, sometimes weeks.

When the city of Chicago hosted the World's Columbian Exposition in 1893, its population was slightly greater than a million people. More than five years were spent in the exposition's planning and construction on a 700-acre site on the shore of Lake Michigan. President Benjamin Harrison invited all of the nations of the earth to take part by sending exhibits that most fully illustrated their resources, their industries, and their progress in civilization. Every state and territory of the United States and more than 50 foreign countries were represented, many erecting their own buildings. Exhibits exceeded 50,000, including one set up by the U.S. Mint. Attendance at the exposition was 27,500,000, and by the end of the 1890s Chicago's population had grown to 1,700,000, making it one of the fastest-growing cities in the history of mankind and the fifth or sixth largest city in the world. More than 100 So-Called Dollars were struck commemorating the World's Columbian Exposition, its events, and its structures—the last remaining of which, originally called the "Palace of Fine Arts," now serves as Chicago's Museum of Science and Industry.

When Philadelphia hosted the Centennial Exposition in 1876, the first United States International Exhibition of the arts, manufacturers, and products, the country was showing the world the progress it had made in the past 100 years. The United States was, for the first time being recognized as one of the leading nations in the world. Until then, the young nation had focused on material problems, with art playing a less significant part in American life. Approximately 10,000,000 people attended the exposition and were not only exposed to the latest machines, mechanical progress, and industrial expansion, but also electrified by displays of art by the world's greatest artists throughout time. After the exposition numerous art schools and societies were formed, and there was a rush of American students to art schools in Paris. The impact on the emphasis for the arts in American culture was dramatic and everlasting. There are close to 50 different So-Called Dollars related to the 1876 Centennial Exposition.

The U.S. Mint had a presence at many of the expositions, often setting up presses and striking souvenir medals to sell to the attendees. The medals produced by the Mint were always designated as the official exposition medal and were usually struck in a variety of metals including silver.

Outside of fairs and expositions, the other half of the series of So-Called Dollars covers a broad range of topics. From the completion of the Erie Canal in 1826 and the completion of the first Transcontinental Railroad in 1869 through the centennial of the Pony Express in 1961, So-Called Dollars celebrate and remember hundreds of national, regional, and local events.

FOR THE COLLECTOR AND INVESTOR: SO-CALLED DOLLARS AS A SPECIALTY

So-Called Dollars as a specialty can be exciting, fascinating, and controversial, and they are collected in hundreds of different ways. Some collectors aspire to collect the entire series, and some collect specific metal compositions. Many collectors have an interest in one or more of the major expositions or other significant events in U.S. history that are portrayed on these medals. Some collect medals from local or regional areas, while others have an interest in those with a U.S. Mint relationship, which includes a broad area of different designs. In addition to marking battles of the Revolutionary War and the Civil War, as well as other military events, So-Called Dollars were struck that address the gold-versus-silver political controversy of the late 1800s and early 1900s. Lesher dollars; silver Bryan dollars; Pedley-Ryan dollars; and others struck by professor Montroville Dickeson, coin dealer Thomas Elder, numismatic historian Q. David Bowers, and other famous personalities are all popular collector categories.

So-Called Dollars range in rarity from very common to exceptionally rare. For many types only one example or very few are known to exist; for others there are thousands. Many So-Called Dollars are considerably rarer than U.S. coins. One of the most common So-Called Dollars is the 1931 McCormick Reaper Centennial Dollar, of which there were possibly as many as 5,000 struck. Compare that to the 09-S V.D.B. Lincoln cent, of which 484,000 were minted. While the Lincoln cent in MS-63 would

Throngs of tourists entering the Electrical Building at the World's Columbian Exposition.

sell for $1,500, the McCormick Reaper in the same grade sells for around $20 despite being 100 times rarer. The following rarity scale is used for So-Called Dollars in this appendix:

R-1	More than 5000 known
R-2	2001–5000 known
R-3	501–2000 known
R-4	201–500 known
R-5	76–200 known
R-6	21–75 known
R-7	11–20 known
R-8	5–10 known
R-9	2–4 known
R-10	1 known (unique)

Hundreds of different So-Called Dollars in MS-63 can be purchased for less than $100. All of the major third-party grading firms, including NGC, PCGS, ANACS, and ICG, grade So-Called Dollars. Professional grading and slabbing of So-Called Dollars has had a significant impact on collector interest and prices realized when they appear in auction. Many of today's advanced collectors want the finer and higher-grade pieces, and if the medals are certified by a major grading firm, their confidence in the value goes up. Higher prices paid today for rare So-Called Dollars are a direct result of this increase in buyers' confidence.

So-Called Dollars have a broad appeal to today's collectors. Similar to most series of U.S. coinage, there are many interesting and historically significant pieces available to the beginning collector at relatively low introductory prices. There are literally hundreds of different types available in Uncirculated and Choice Uncirculated grades in the $25 to $75 range. There are also many highly desired rare varieties from the 1800s that are beautiful pieces of art, struck in bronze and with high relief, that the more advanced collectors appreciate. At the upper end of the So-Called Dollar market—those that sell for $1,000 or more—collectors are treated to exceptionally rare and significant pieces.

The following catalog illustrates and describes a number of So-Called Dollars issued to celebrate the 1876 centennial of American independence.

1876, Centennial Exposition Official

1876, Centennial Exposition Nevada

1876, Centennial Exposition Liberty Bell / Independence Hall

1876, Centennial Liberty Bell Rounded 6 / Independence Hall

	Rarity	SH#	HK#	VF-20	EF-40	AU-50	MS-60 PF-60	MS-63 PF-63	MS-65 PF-65
1876, Centennial Exposition Official Medal. Silver ‡	R-4	2-1 S	20	$65	$120	$145	$325	$750	$1,250
1876, Centennial Exposition Official Medal. Silver Proof	R-6	2-1 S PR	UNL				$450	$900	$1,500
1876, Centennial Exposition Official Medal. Bronze	R-4	2-1 BZ	21	$50	$85	$100	$210	$285	$375
1876, Centennial Exposition Official Medal. Bronze Proof	R-8	2-1 BZ PR	UNL				$275	$350	$575
1876, Centennial Exposition Official Medal. White Metal	R-9	2-1 WM	22a				—	$2,500	—
1876, Centennial Exposition Official Medal. Gold-Plated	R-4	2-1 GP	22	$25	$50	$70	$230	$300	$400
1876, Centennial Exposition Official Medal. Silver-Plated	R-7	2-1 SP	UNL	$90	$150	$225	—	—	—
1876, Centennial Nevada. Silver	R-4	2-2 S	19	$175	$300	$500	$550	$1,150	$1,500
1876, Centennial Nevada. Silver Proof	R-6	2-2 S PR	UNL				$600	$1,350	$1,650
1876, Centennial Nevada. Copper	R-9	2-2 CU	19a				—	$2,000	$2,500
1876, Centennial Liberty Bell / Independence Hall. Silver Proof	R-9	2-3 S PR	23				$3,500	$6,500	$9,500
1876, Centennial Liberty Bell / Independence Hall. Copper	R-6	2-3 CU	25	$25	$45	$75	$145	$230	$425
1876, Centennial Liberty Bell / Independence Hall. White Metal	R-5	2-3 WM	26	$20	$40	$80	$150	$325	$525
1876, Centennial Liberty Bell / Independence Hall. Gold-Plated	R-8	2-3 GP	UNL				$250	$500	—
1876, Centennial Liberty Bell Rounded 6 / Independence Hall. Copper	R-5	2-4 CU	UNL	$25	$45	$70	$130	$190	$375
1876, Centennial Liberty Bell Rounded 6 / Independence Hall. White Metal	R-4	2-4 WM	UNL	$20	$40	$65	$140	$200	$350
1876, Centennial Liberty Bell Rounded 6 / Independence Hall. Copper, no signature	R-7	2-4.1 CU	UNL				—	$425	—

UNL = Unlisted. ‡ Ranked in the *100 Greatest American Medals and Tokens*.

Centennial Exposition Official SCD (SH 2-1 / HK 20–22): This medal depicts a female (Liberty) as a symbol of the United States rising up and reaching for the stars, representing greatness. She is grasping a sword in her right hand, indicating that the U.S. will become a world power to be reckoned with. The dies were engraved by William Barber. **Centennial Nevada SCD (SH 2-2 / HK 19):** This medal is made of pure silver crushed from Nevada ores at the Nevada quartz mill located in the Centennial Exposition and later refined at the Philadelphia Mint. The medal was also struck at the Philadelphia Mint, and sold at the 1876 Centennial Exposition. The dies were engraved by William Barber. **Centennial Liberty Bell / Independence Hall SCD (SH 2-3 / HK 23–25):** The Liberty Bell was on display at the Centennial Exposition held in Philadelphia. The dates on this die variety have pointed 6s, and is found paired with several other centennial dies. The dies were engraved by William H. Key, assistant engraver to William Barber, 1864–1885; Key's signature is below Independence Hall. Both Frossard and Holland report these as being struck in copper, not bronze. **Centennial Liberty Bell Rounded 6 / Independence Hall SCD (SH 2-4 / HK Unl):** William H. Key engraved two different dies with the Liberty Bell design. Careful inspection reveals numerous differences between them, most noticeably in the digit 6 in the date. This variety has a rounded 6 on both the obverse and reverse; the other die variety (SH 2-3) has a pointed 6. These dies are not found paired with any other dies and are almost always holed.

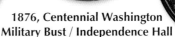

1876, Centennial Washington
Military Bust / Liberty Bell

1876, Centennial Washington
Military Bust / Independence Hall

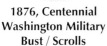

1876, Centennial
Washington Military
Bust / Scrolls

1876, Centennial
Independence Hall /
Chosen Friends

	Rarity	SH#	HK#	VF-20	EF-40	AU-50	MS-60 PF-60	MS-63 PF-63	MS-65 PF-65
1876, Centennial Washington Military Bust / Liberty Bell. Silver	R-9	2-5 S	30			$700	—	$2,500	—
1876, Centennial Washington Military Bust / Liberty Bell. Copper	R-9	2-5 CU	31				—	$900	—
1876, Centennial Washington Military Bust / Liberty Bell. White Metal	R-7	2-5 WM	32	$150	$200	$300	$500	$750	$1,250
1876, Centennial Washington Military Bust / Independence Hall. Silver	R-9	2-6 S	39			$975	—	$3,500	—
1876, Centennial Washington Military Bust / Independence Hall. Copper	R-8	2-6 CU	40	$150	$275	$475	$550	$750	$1,200
1876, Centennial Washington Military Bust / Independence Hall. White Metal	R-6	2-6 WM	41	$75	$115	$200	$400	$650	$900
1876, Centennial Washington Military Bust / Independence Hall. Gold-Plated	R-9	2-6 GP	40a				—	$850	—
1876, Centennial Washington Military Bust / Scrolls. Copper	R-9	2-7 CU	70c				—	$950	—
1876, Centennial Washington Military Bust / Scrolls. White Metal	R-9	2-7 WM	70b				—	$900	—
1876, Centennial Independence Hall / Chosen friends. Silver	R-9	2-8 S	46c				—	$2,500	—
1876, Centennial Independence Hall / Chosen friends. Copper	R-8	2-8 CU	46a				$550	$750	$1,200
1876, Centennial Independence Hall / Chosen friends. White Metal	R-8	2-8 WM	46				$550	$750	$1,200
1876, Centennial Independence Hall / Chosen friends. Gold-Plated	R-9	2-8 GP	46b				—	$800	—

UNL = Unlisted.

Centennial Washington Military Bust / Liberty Bell SCD (SH 2-5 / HK 30–32): The military bust of Washington is signed Key F. below the bust. Both dies were engraved by William H. Key, an assistant engraver to William Barber at the U.S. Mint in Philadelphia. **Centennial Washington Military Bust / Independence Hall SCD (SH 2-6 / HK 39–41):** Engraver William H. Key's signed military bust of Washington is combined with the large Independence Hall edifice also engraved by Key. J.H. Diehl of Philadelphia was offering for sale this medal as well as Key's Liberty Bell SH 2-3 and SH 2-4. **Centennial Washington Military Bust / Scrolls SCD (SH 2-7 / HK 70B–70C):** Key's signed military bust of Washington is paired with an unsigned arabesque scrolls reverse die. Apparently this was not a popular medal sold for the exposition, as there are very few known today. The scrolls reverse was possibly a stock die at the U.S. Mint, likely engraved by George B. Soley but possibly by Key. **Centennial Independence Hall / Chosen Friends SCD (SH 2-8 / HK 46–46C):** This medal was authorized by the Independent Order of Odd Fellows, a non-political and non-sectarian international fraternal organization. It is a benevolent and social society and and the new medal has been cataloged as a So-Called Dollar due to its historical relationship to the Centennial Exposition. This medal was engraved by Key.

1876, Centennial Liberty
Bell / G.A.R. Badge

1876, Centennial Liberty
Bell / Garland

1876, Centennial
Washington Large Bust /
Liberty Bell

1876, Centennial
Washington Large Bust /
Independence Hall

| | Rarity | SH# | HK# | VF-20 | EF-40 | AU-50 | MS-60 | MS-63 | MS-65 |
							PF-60	PF-63	PF-65
1876, Centennial Liberty Bell / G.A.R. Badge. Copper	R-9	2-9 CU	37				$600	$800	$1,300
1876, Centennial Liberty Bell / G.A.R. Badge. White Metal	R-8	2-9 WM	38			$250	$550	$750	$1,200
1876, Centennial Liberty Bell / G.A.R. Badge. Silver-Plated	R-8	2-9 SP	UNL			$250	—	$750	—
1876, Centennial Liberty Bell / Garland. Copper	R-9	2-10 CU	UNL				—	$650	—
1876, Centennial Washington Large Bust / Liberty Bell. Silver	R-9	2-11 S	UNL				—	$2,500	—
1876, Centennial Washington Large Bust / Liberty Bell. Copper	R-7	2-11 CU	32a				$550	$750	$1,200
1876, Centennial Washington Large Bust / Liberty Bell. White Metal	R-8	2-11 WM	UNL				$650	$850	$1,300
1876, Centennial Washington Large Bust / Independence Hall. Copper	R-8	2-12 CU	UNL				$650	$850	$1,300

UNL = Unlisted.

Centennial Liberty Bell / G.A.R. Badge SCD (SH 2-9 / HK 37–38): An argument could be made that, since the reverse die has a G.A.R Grand Army of the Republic badge, it is a fraternal medal and should not be included as a So-Called Dollar. Originally included by Hibler & Kappen in the 1963 edition, the authors opted to leave it in as well, considering it more a centennial celebration medal than a G.A.R. related event. The dies were engraved by Key. This particular medal has a clamp attached. **Centennial Liberty Bell / Garland SCD (SH 2-10 / HK Unl):** Key's Liberty Bell is paired with a plain reverse that has a circle of garland along the perimeter. Although the reverse could be engraved, it is not known engraved and the authors do not consider it to be an award medal and so have included it. **Centennial Washington Large Bust / Liberty Bell SCD (SH 2-11 / HK 32A):** The Washington bust design engraved by Soley is combined with the Liberty Bell design engraved by Key. Both dies are unsigned. This and the medal below are the only Soley & Key die pairs, except for the scrolls reverse (SH 2-7). H.W. Holland in the 1876 *American Journal of Numismatics*, "Centennial Medals," states that this was struck in silver, copper, and white metal, with no mention of bronze. **Centennial Washington Large Bust / Independence Hall SCD (SH 2-12 / HK Unl):** The Washington bust design engraved by Soley is combined with the Independence Hall design engraved by Key. This and the medal above are the only Soley & Key die pairs, except for the Scrolls reverse (SH 2-7). This medal is only known in low grade. The photo depicted is a composite image.

1876, Centennial Washington Large Bust / Small Independence Hall

1876, Centennial Washington Large Bust / Seated Liberty

1876, Centennial Washington Large Bust / American Colonies

1876, Centennial Washington Large Bust / Centennial Fountain

	Rarity	SH#	HK#	MS-60 PF-60	MS-63 PF-63	MS-65 PF-65
1876, Centennial Washington Large Bust / Small Independence Hall. Silver	R-9	2-13 S	42	—	$2,500	—
1876, Centennial Washington Large Bust / Small Independence Hall. Copper	R-7	2-13 CU	43	$650	$750	$1,200
1876, Centennial Washington Large Bust / Small Independence Hall. Bronze	R-8	2-13 BZ	UNL	$750	$900	$1,300
1876, Centennial Washington Large Bust / Small Independence Hall. Copper Nickel	R-9	2-13 CN	UNL	$750	$900	$1,300
1876, Centennial Washington Large Bust / Small Independence Hall. White Metal	R-6	2-13 WM	45	$400	$650	$900
1876, Centennial Washington Large Bust / Small Independence Hall. Gold-Plated	R-8	2-13 GP	44	$650	$750	$1,200
1876, Centennial Washington Large Bust / Seated Liberty. Silver	R-9	2-14 S	52	—	$2,500	—
1876, Centennial Washington Large Bust / Seated Liberty. Copper	R-8	2-14 CU	53	$800	$1,000	$1,350
1876, Centennial Washington Large Bust / Seated Liberty. Bronze	R-8	2-14 BZ	UNL	$850	$1,100	$1,400
1876, Centennial Washington Large Bust / Seated Liberty. White Metal	R-7	2-14 WM	55	$650	$750	$1,200
1876, Centennial Washington Large Bust / Seated Liberty. Gold-Plated	R-8	2-14 GP	54	$800	$1,000	$1,350
1876, Centennial Washington Large Bust / Seated Liberty. Silver-Plated	R-9	2-14 SP	UNL	$650	$750	$1,100
1876, Centennial Washington Large Bust / American Colonies. Silver	R-9	2-15 S	72b	—	$2,500	—
1876, Centennial Washington Large Bust / American Colonies. Copper	R-8	2-15 CU	UNL	$850	$1,100	$1,400
1876, Centennial Washington Large Bust / American Colonies. Bronze	R-8	2-15 BZ	71	$800	$1,000	$1,200
1876, Centennial Washington Large Bust / American Colonies. White Metal	R-8	2-15 WM	72a	$700	$800	$1,150
1876, Centennial Washington Large Bust / American Colonies. Gold-Plated	R-7	2-15 GP	72	$650	$750	$1,100
1876, Centennial Washington Large Bust / 1876, Centennial Fountain. Silver	R-9	2-16 S	65	—	$2,500	—
1876, Centennial Washington Large Bust / 1876, Centennial Fountain. Copper	R-8	2-16 CU	66	$850	$1,100	$1,400
1876, Centennial Washington Large Bust / 1876, Centennial Fountain. White Metal	R-7	2-16 WM	68	$650	$750	$1,200
1876, Centennial Washington Large Bust / 1876, Centennial Fountain. Gold-Plated	R-8	2-16 GP	67	$700	$800	$1,150
1876, Centennial Washington Large Bust / 1876, Centennial Fountain. Gold Plated, with comma	R-8	2-16.1 GP	UNL	$750	$850	$1,200

UNL = Unlisted.

Centennial Washington Large Bust / Small Independence Hall SCD (SH 2-13 / HK 42–45): Both dies were engraved by George B. Soley. Presidential Sale #58 cataloged lot 193 as copper-nickel. **Centennial Washington Large Bust / Seated Liberty SCD (SH 2-14 / HK 52–55):** Soley's Seated Liberty design, with Liberty sitting on a keystone, symbolizes the strength of America and our "keystone" principles of justice and righteousness, represented by the square and scales on the keystone. The dies were engraved by George B. Soley. **Centennial Washington Large Bust / American Colonies SCD (SH 2-15 / HK 71–72B):** Auction catalogs from 1878 and 1879 name the reverse die the "American Colonies," representing the fact that General Washington's troops were farmers during peace and soldiers when at war; this is truly an emotional design considering the fact that they were victorious over the well-trained British army. **Centennial Washington Large Bust / Centennial Fountain SCD (SH 2-16 / HK 65–68):** The Centennial Fountain was funded and built under the direction of the Catholic Church to "honor the Republic, express patriotism of the membership, and to promote the Irish-Catholic temperance societies." There is an excellent article about the Centennial Fountain authored by Donald Lannon and published by Greg Burns in the Summer 2019 edition of *The California Numismatist*. There is a reverse die variety with a "," following Fountain. The dies were engraved by Soley.

**1876, Centennial Washington
Large Bust / Scrolls**

**1876, Centennial Washington
Large Bust / Star**

**1876, Centennial Small
Independence Hall / Star**

**1876, Centennial
Seated Liberty / Star**

| | Rarity | SH# | HK# | AU-50 | MS-60 | MS-63 | MS-65 |
					PF-60	PF-63	PF-65
1876, Centennial Washington Large Bust / Scrolls. Silver	R-9	2-17 S	UNL		—	$2,500	—
1876, Centennial Washington Large Bust / Star. Silver	R-9	2-18 S	UNL		—	$3,500	—
1876, Centennial Washington Large Bust / Star. Copper	R-9	2-18 CU	70a		—	$2,800	$4,200
1876, Centennial Washington Large Bust / Star. Bronze	R-9	2-18 BZ	UNL		—	$2,800	$4,200
1876, Centennial Washington Large Bust / Star. Brass	R-9	2-18 BS	UNL		—	$2,800	$4,200
1876, Centennial Washington Large Bust / Star. White Metal	R-8	2-18 WM	UNL		—	$2,800	$4,200
1876, Centennial Small Independence Hall / Star. Silver	R-9	2-19 S	UNL		—	$3,500	—
1876, Centennial Small Independence Hall / Star. Copper	R-8	2-19 CU	47a		—	$2,800	$4,200
1876, Centennial Small Independence Hall / Star. Bronze	R-8	2-19 BZ	UNL		—	$2,800	$4,200
1876, Centennial Small Independence Hall / Star. Brass	R-9	2-19 BS	UNL		—	$2,800	$4,200
1876, Centennial Small Independence Hall / Star. White Metal	R-9	2-19 WM	47		—	$2,800	$4,200
1876, Centennial Seated Liberty / Star. Silver	R-9	2-20 S	UNL		—	$3,500	—
1876, Centennial Seated Liberty / Star. Copper	R-8	2-20 CU	60		—	$2,800	$4,200
1876, Centennial Seated Liberty / Star. Bronze	R-8	2-20 BZ	UNL		—	$2,800	$4,200
1876, Centennial Seated Liberty / Star. Brass	R-9	2-20 RS	UNL		—	$2,800	$4,200
1876, Centennial Seated Liberty / Star. White Metal	R-8	2-20 WM	61		—	$2,800	$4,200
1876, Centennial Seated Liberty / Star. White Metal, reverse signed Soley	R-9	2-20.1 WM	UNL		—	$3,300	—
1876, Centennial Seated Liberty / Star. Gold-Plated Copper, reverse signed Soley	R-9	2-20.1 GP	UNL		—	$3,300	—

UNL = Unlisted.

Centennial Washington Large Bust / Scrolls SCD (SH 2-17 / HK Unl): The obverse die is by Soley, and the reverse die with arabesque scrolls is likely done by Soley as well. It is noted by Baker in his Washington book that this medal exists. The H.W. Holland list of Centennial Medals published in the January 1876 *American Journal of Numismatics* reports this was struck in silver, but it was likely struck in other compositions as well. The photo depicted is a composite image. **Centennial Washington Large Bust / Star SCD (SH 2-18 / HK 70A):** Soley's white metal variety reverse die has a "No" for "number" engraved into the die below the date. The example pictured has a digit "1" counterpunched into the medal, indicating it is medal number one. Other than the "1," no other counterpunched numbers are known for any of the star reverses except for this variety in copper, which is known counterpunched with an upside down "8." **Centennial Small Independence Hall / Star SCD (SH 2-19 / HK 47 and 47A):** This medal depicts Soley's Independence Hall obverse die and his star reverse die, with a legend stating it was struck in the Centennial Building at the exposition. In 1875 Soley purchased the U.S. Mint's first steam coining press, refurbished it, and took it to the Centennial Exposition to strike medals. **Centennial Seated Liberty / Star SCD (SH 2-20 / HK 60–61):** Scott Stamp & Coin Company, in their October 27, 1879, auction, lot #689, sold a white metal example with a Soley signature. It was reported that two in white metal and two in gold-plated copper were struck and then the dies were altered, according to Holland. Soley's signature is replaced with a feathered pen and twig on the slightly more common unsigned varieties.

1876, Centennial American Colonies / Star

1876, Centennial Fountain / Star

1876, Centennial Fountain / Total Abstinence

1876, Centennial Fountain / Scrolls

	Rarity	SH#	HK#	EF-40	AU-50	MS-60 PF-60	MS-63 PF-63	MS-65 PF-65
1876, Centennial American Colonies / Star. Silver	R-9	2-21 S	UNL			—	$3,500	—
1876, Centennial American Colonies / Star. Copper	R-9	2-21 CU	72c			—	$2,800	$4,200
1876, Centennial American Colonies / Star. Bronze	R-9	2-21 BZ	UNL			—	$2,800	$4,200
1876, Centennial American Colonies / Star. Brass	R-9	2-21 BS	UNL			—	$2,800	$4,200
1876, Centennial American Colonies / Star. White Metal	R-9	2-21 WM	UNL			—	$2,800	$4,200
1876, Centennial Fountain / Star. Silver	R-9	2-22 S	UNL			—	$3,500	—
1876, Centennial Fountain / Star. Copper	R-9	2-22 CU	UNL			—	$2,800	$4,200
1876, Centennial Fountain / Star. Bronze	R-9	2-22 BZ	UNL			—	$2,800	$4,200
1876, Centennial Fountain / Star. Brass	R-9	2-22 BS	UNL			—	$2,800	$4,200
1876, Centennial Fountain / Star. White Metal	R-9	2-22 WM	UNL			—	$2,800	$4,200
1876, Centennial Fountain / Total Abstinence. Silver	R-9	2-23 S	69a			—	$4,500	—
1876, Centennial Fountain / Total Abstinence. Copper	R-7	2-23 CU	69b			—	$800	$1,100
1876, Centennial Fountain / Total Abstinence. White Metal	R-7	2-23 WM	70			—	$800	$1,100
1876, Centennial Fountain / Total Abstinence. Gold-Plated	R-6	2-23 GP	69			—	$600	$900
1876, Centennial Fountain / Total Abstinence. Gold-Plated, with comma	R-8	2-23.1 GP	UNL			—	$600	$900
1876, Centennial Fountain / Total Abstinence. White Metal, with comma	R-8	2-23.1 WM	UNL			—	$600	$900
1876, Centennial Fountain / Scrolls. Silver	R-9	2-24 S	62			—	$1,500	—

UNL = Unlisted.

Centennial American Colonies / Star SCD (SH 2-21 / HK 72C): Soley's star reverse was struck in five different metals and is found paired with five different obverse dies that he also engraved. Soley's star reverses were all struck with a reeded edge. All of Soley's and Key's other medals were struck with a smooth collar. **Centennial Fountain / Star SCD (SH 2-22 / HK Unl):** The Centennial Fountain die is found paired with Soley's Washington Large Bust, this Star reverse, the Scrolls reverse and the Total Abstinence die. The Centennial Fountain was constructed to be a source for clean drinking water, as an alternative to alcohol consumption. **Centennial Fountain / Total Abstinence SCD (SH 2-23 / HK 69–70):** The Centennial Fountain design is found in two varieties, with and without a comma following the word "Fountain" in the upper legend. All compositions are known without a comma and a few are also known with a comma. The Total Abstinence Union encouraged abstaining from alcohol. The dies were engraved by Soley. **Centennial Fountain / Scrolls SCD (SH 2-24 / HK 62):** In the January 1876 issue of the *American Journal of Numismatics* Henry W. Holland began his series "Centennial Medals"—a series that listed 206 different medals, in all compositions, relating to the Centennial when completed in October 1878. This medal was cataloged by Holland in silver and is photographed in Hibler & Kappen's *So-Called Dollar* book. No other compositions are known. The photo depicted is a composite image.

1876, Centennial Total Abstinence / Scrolls

**1876, Centennial Seated Liberty /
Small Independence Hall**

1876, Centennial Small Independence Hall / Scrolls

1876, Centennial Seated Liberty / American Colonies

	Rarity	SH#	HK#	VF-20	EF-40	AU-50	MS-60	MS-63	MS-65
							PF-60	PF-63	PF-65
1876, Centennial Total Abstinence / Scrolls. Silver	R-9	2-25 S	UNL				—	$2,500	—
1876, Centennial Seated Liberty / Small Independence Hall. Silver	R-9	2-26 S	48				—	$2,500	—
1876, Centennial Seated Liberty / Small Independence Hall. Copper	R-7	2-26 CU	49				$650	$750	$1,400
1876, Centennial Seated Liberty / Small Independence Hall. White Metal	R-7	2-26 WM	51				$600	$700	$1,300
1876, Centennial Seated Liberty / Small Independence Hall. Gold-Plated	R-7	2-26 GP	50				$500	$650	$1,200
1876, Centennial Small Independence Hall / Scrolls. Silver	R-9	2-27 S	UNL				—	$2,500	—
1876, Centennial Small Independence Hall / Scrolls. Copper	R-9	2-27 CU	UNL				$850	$1,100	$1,400
1876, Centennial Seated Liberty / American Colonies. Silver	R-9	2-28 S	56				—	$4,500	—
1876, Centennial Seated Liberty / American Colonies. Copper	R-9	2-28 CU	57				$850	$1,100	$1,400
1876, Centennial Seated Liberty / American Colonies. White metal	R-7	2-28 WM	59				$600	$700	$1,000
1876, Centennial Seated Liberty / American Colonies. Gold-Plated	R-6	2-28 GP	58				$400	$650	$900
1876, Centennial Seated Liberty / American Colonies. Silver-Plated	R-9	2-28 SP	UNL				$850	$1,100	$1,400

UNL = Unlisted.

Centennial Total Abstinence / Scrolls SCD (SH 2-25 / HK Unl): The H.W. Holland list of Centennial Medals published in the January 1876 *American Journal of Numismatics* reports this was struck in silver, but it was likely struck in other compositions as well. There is no other confirmation that it exists, although the authors believe it was very likely struck and so have included it. The photo depicted is a composite image. **Centennial Seated Liberty / Small Independence Hall SCD (SH 2-26 / HK 48–51):** This was engraved by George B. Soley, who was a diesinker and worked at the U.S. Mint in Philadelphia from 1859 until his death in 1908. A seated woman, similar to that on William Barber's 1873–1885 U.S. trade dollars, represents America. **Centennial Small Independence Hall / Scrolls SCD (SH 2-27 / HK Unl):** Soley's Small Independence Hall is paired with his Scrolls reverse. It is only known struck in copper and reported in silver according to Holland in 1876, but it was likely struck in other compositions. The photo depicted is a composite image, and its reverse has been colorized to appear copper. **Centennial Seated Liberty / American Colonies SCD (SH 2-28 / HK 56–59):** A seated woman, similar to that on William Barber's 1873–1885 U.S. trade dollars, represents America. The reverse depicts an interesting scene with a farmer and a Continental soldier preparing for battle. This medal was engraved by George B. Soley. Presidential Auctions sold a silver-plated variety in sale #58, lot #946.

1876, Centennial Seated Liberty / Scrolls

1876, Centennial American Colonies / Scrolls

1876, Centennial Washington Large Bust / Crossing the Delaware

1876, Centennial Washington Large Bust / New Jersey Seal

| | Rarity | SH# | HK# | VF-20 | EF-40 | AU-50 | MS-60 | MS-63 | MS-65 |
							PF-60	PF-63	PF-65
1876, Centennial Seated Liberty / Scrolls. Copper	R-9	2-29 CU	UNL				—	$1,300	—
1876, Centennial American Colonies / Scrolls. Silver	R-9	2-30 S	UNL				—	$2,500	—
1876, Centennial Washington Large Bust / Crossing the Delaware. White Metal	R-9	2-31 WM	UNL				—	$1,300	—
1876, Centennial Washington Large Bust / New Jersey Seal. White Metal	R-8	2-32 WM	UNL				—	$800	—

UNL = Unlisted. ‡ Ranked in the *100 Greatest American Medals and Tokens*.

Centennial Seated Liberty / Scrolls SCD (SH 2-29 / HK Unl): Soley's Seated Liberty design is paired with his Scrolls reverse. The Scrolls reverse is found paired with almost all of Soley's dies and only one of Key's dies. Scott Stamp & Coin Company, in their October 27, 1879, auction, lot #688, sold a copper version and reported that only two of these medals were struck. The photo depicted is a composite image. **Centennial American Colonies / Scrolls SCD (SH 2-30 / HK Unl):** The H.W. Holland list of Centennial medals published in the January 1876 *American Journal of Numismatics* reports this was struck in silver, but it was likely struck in other compositions as well. There is no other confirmation that it exists, although the authors believe it was very likely struck and so have included it. The photo depicted is a composite image. **Centennial Washington Large Bust / Crossing the Delaware SCD (SH 2-31 / HK Unl):** Soley's obverse of Washington's bust is paired with a die by an unknown engraver. The reverse die is found paired with other likely Morgan dies. However, it could have been engraved by any other then-current Mint employee including Soley, Key, or Barber, or privately struck. **Centennial Washington Large Bust / New Jersey Seal SCD (SH 2-32 / HK Unl):** Soley's obverse of Washington's bust is paired with a die by an unknown engraver. The reverse is the State Seal of New Jersey with slight variations.

1876, Centennial General George Washington / Crossing the Delaware

1876, Centennial Liberty Bell / Sunday School

1876, Centennial Liberty Bell / Siloam M.E. Church

1876, Centennial Liberty Bell / Cumberland M.E. Church

	Rarity	SH#	HK#	VF-20	EF-40	AU-50	MS-60 / PF-60	MS-63 / PF-63	MS-65 / PF-65
1876, Centennial General George Washington / Crossing the Delaware. Bronze	R-9	2-33 BZ	UNL				—	$950	—
1876, Centennial Liberty Bell / Sunday School. Silver	R-9	2-34 S	35a				—	$2,500	—
1876, Centennial Liberty Bell / Sunday School. Copper	R-8	2-34 CU	35				$650	$850	$1,350
1876, Centennial Liberty Bell / Sunday School. White Metal	R-9	2-34 WM	36				—	$900	—
1876, Centennial Liberty Bell / Siloam M.C. Church. Silver	R-9	2-35 S	33a				—	$2,500	—
1876, Centennial Liberty Bell / Siloam M.C. Church. Copper	R-9	2-35 CU	33				—	$900	—
1876, Centennial Liberty Bell / Siloam M.C. Church. Brass	R-9	2-35 BS	UNL				—	$900	—
1876, Centennial Liberty Bell / Siloam M.C. Church. White Metal	R-8	2-35 WM	33b				$650	$850	$1,350
1876, Centennial Liberty Bell / Cumberland M.C. Church. Silver	R-9	2-36 S	34a				—	$2,500	—
1876, Centennial Liberty Bell / Cumberland M.C. Church. Copper	R-9	2-36 CU	34				—	$900	—
1876, Centennial Liberty Bell / Cumberland M.C. Church. White Metal	R-9	2-36 WM	34b				—	$900	—
1876, Centennial Liberty Bell / Cumberland M.C. Church. Silver-Plated Copper	R-8	2-36 SP	UNL				—	$850	

UNL = Unlisted.

Centennial General George Washington / Crossing the Delaware SCD (SH 2-33 / HK Unl): The authors struggled with this medal as it was possibly engraved by George Morgan, and if so it would have most likely been done after 1876. However, it could have been engraved by any other then-current Mint employee including Soley, Key, or Barber, or privately struck. **Centennial Liberty Bell / Sunday School SCD (SH 2-34 / HK 35–36):** This was authorized to be struck by a church, so an argument could be made that this medal should be excluded. Many religious organizations did have medals struck to commemorate events in the United States history. Since this one is more historically themed and was included in the original H&K reference, the authors have decided to leave it in. It was engraved by Key. **Centennial Liberty Bell / Siloam M.E. Church SCD (SH 2-35 / HK 33–33B):** As with the previous So-Called Dollar, the authors could have opted to exclude this medal, which was included in Hibler & Kappen's original publication, but due to its connection with the Centennial Exposition we have decided it should be included. It was engraved by Key. **Centennial Liberty Bell / Cumberland M.E. Church SCD (SH 2-36 / HK 34–34B):** As with the two prior cataloged So-Called Dollars, the authors could have opted to exclude this medal, which was included in Hibler & Kappen's original publication, but due to its connection with the Centennial Exposition we have decided it should be included. It was engraved by Key.

1876, Centennial Liberty Bell / Children's HOP

1876, Centennial Main Building / Free People

1876, Centennial Horticultural Hall / Free People

1876, Centennial Art Gallery / Free People

	Rarity	SH#	HK#	VF-20	EF-40	AU-50	MS-60 PF-60	MS-63 PF-63	MS-65 PF-65
1876, Centennial Liberty Bell / Children's HOP. White Metal	R-8	2-37 WM	UNL				—	$900	—
1876, Centennial Main Building / Free People. Silver	R-8	2-38 S	81a				—	$5,800	—
1876, Centennial Main Building / Free People. Copper	R-6	2-38 CU	81			$150	$250	$500	$1,000
1876, Centennial Main Building / Free People. White Metal	R-6	2-38 WM	82				$150	$450	$800
1876, Centennial Main Building / Free People. Gold-Plated	R-8	2-38 GP	81b				—	$800	—
1876, Centennial Horticultural Hall / Free People. Silver	R-9	2-39 S	87a				—	$3,800	—
1876, Centennial Horticultural Hall / Free People. Copper	R-7	2-39 CU	87				$650	$850	$1,300
1876, Centennial Horticultural Hall / Free People. White Metal	R-6	2-39 WM	88				$500	$650	$900
1876, Centennial Horticultural Hall / Free People. Gold-Plated	R-9	2-39 GP	87b				—	$900	—
1876, Centennial Art Gallery / Free People. Silver	R-9	2-40 S	83a				—	$5,800	—
1876, Centennial Art Gallery / Free People. Copper	R-6	2-40 CU	83				$200	$400	$750
1876, Centennial Art Gallery / Free People. White Metal	R-6	2-40 WM	84				$175	$300	$550
1876, Centennial Art Gallery / Free People. Gold-Plated	R-8	2-40 GP	83b				$600	$700	$1,000
1876, Centennial Art Gallery / Free People. Gutta-Percha	R-7	2-40.1 GPR	86	$100	$300	$500	$850	$1,200

UNL = Unlisted.

Centennial Liberty Bell / Children's HOP SCD (SH 2-37 / HK Unl): This was authorized to be struck by a church, so an argument could be made that this medal should be excluded. Many religious organizations did have medals struck to commemorate events in the United States history. Since this one is more historically themed, the authors have decided to leave it in. It was engraved by Key. **Centennial Main Building / Free People SCD (SH 2-38 / HK 81–82):** The Main Exposition Building adorns the obverse, with the microscopic text "W.H. Key F" (William H. Key's signature with the abbreviation F representing the Latin translation of "made it") at the base of the building to the right. The reverse legend reads "1776 Illustrating the Growth and Prosperity of a Free People in a Hundred Years 1876." Also microscopic on the reverse is the text "PAT NOV 3 1874 H&L." **Centennial Horticultural Hall / Free People SCD (SH 2-39 / HK 87–88):** The Horticultural Hall is on the obverse. Key's signature is centered below the edifice. The reverse legend reads "1776 Illustrating the Growth and Prosperity of a Free People in a Hundred Years 1876." The text "PAT NOV 3 1874 H&L" is microscopic on the reverse. **Centennial Art Gallery / Free People SCD (SH 2-40 / HK 83–84):** The Edifice of the Art Gallery is on the obverse. Key's signature is below the edifice to the left. The reverse legend reads "1776 Illustrating the Growth and Prosperity of a Free People in a Hundred Years 1876." The text "PAT NOV 3 1874 H&L" is microscopic on the reverse.

1876, Centennial
Main Building /
Art Gallery

1876, Centennial
Main Building /
Horticultural Hall

1876, Centennial
Art Gallery /
Horticultural Hall

1876, Centennial
Grand Entrance /
Main Building

	Rarity	SH#	HK#	VF-20	EF-40	AU-50	MS-60	MS-63	MS-65
							PF-60	PF-63	PF-65
1876, Centennial Main Building / Art Gallery. Copper	R-9	2-41 CU	89e			$125	—	$800	—
1876, Centennial Main Building / Art Gallery. Brass	R-9	2-41 BS	UNL				—	$800	—
1876, Centennial Main Building / Art Gallery. White Metal	R-7	2-41 WM	89a				$600	$700	$1,000
1876, Centennial Main Building / Horticultural Hall. Copper	R-9	2-42 CU	UNL				—	$800	—
1876, Centennial Main Building / Horticultural Hall. Brass	R-9	2-42 BS	89c				—	$800	—
1876, Centennial Main Building / Horticultural Hall. White Metal	R-7	2-42 WM	89b				$600	$700	$1,000
1876, Centennial Main Building / Horticultural Hall. Gold-Plated	R-9	2-42 GP	89f				—	$800	—
1876, Centennial Art Gallery / Horticultural Hall. Copper	R-8	2-43 CU	89				$700	$1,100	—
1876, Centennial Art Gallery / Horticultural Hall. Brass	R-8	2-43 BS	89d				—	$800	—
1876, Centennial Art Gallery / Horticultural Hall. White Metal	R-9	2-43 WM	UNL				—	$800	—
1876, Centennial Grand Entrance / Main Building. Silver	R-9	2-44 S	UNL				—	$2,500	—
1876, Centennial Grand Entrance / Main Building. Bronze	R-9	2-44 BZ	UNL				—	$800	—
1876, Centennial Grand Entrance / Main Building. White Metal	R-6	2-44 WM	80				$300	$450	$700
1876, Centennial Grand Entrance / Main Building. Gold-Plated	R-8	2-44 GP	UNL				—	$800	—

UNL = Unlisted.

Centennial Main Building / Art Gallery SCD (SH 2-41 / HK 89A & 89E): Key's Main Exposition Building die and his Art Gallery die are paired on this So-Called Dollar. **Centennial Main Building / Horticultural Hall SCD (SH 2-42 / HK 89B, 89C, and 89F>):** Key's Main Exposition Building die and his Horticultural Hall die are paired on this So-Called Dollar. **Centennial Art Gallery / Horticultural Hall SCD (SH 2-43 / HK 89 & 89D):** Key's Art Gallery die and his Horticultural Hall die are paired on this So-Called Dollar. **Centennial Grand Entrance / Main Building SCD (SH 2-44 / HK 80):** This is the only exposition building die not engraved by Key; it is a George Hampden Lovett design and engraving of the Main Building, titled "Grand Entrance." Signed "U.S.M.Co.," Lovett produced the dies for this medal, which was sold by U.S. Medal Company. Both Key and Lovett produced Centennial Exposition dies for the U.S. Medal Company. This medal was struck in the four compositions listed, according to Frossard's 1876 listing.

1876, Centennial Small Liberty Bell with Star / Independence Hall with Trees

1876, Centennial Small Liberty Bell No Star / Independence Hall with Trees

1876, Centennial Declaration of Independence Demarest / Washington Ornamental Bust

1876, Centennial Declaration of Independence Demarest / John Hancock Signature

	Rarity	SH#	HK#	MS-60 / PF-60	MS-63 / PF-63	MS-65 / PF-65
1876, Centennial Small Liberty Bell with Star / Independence Hall with Trees. Silver	R-9	2-45 S	27b	—	$800	—
1876, Centennial Small Liberty Bell with Star / Independence Hall with Trees. Copper	R-6	2-45 CU	27	$350	$700	$950
1876, Centennial Small Liberty Bell with Star / Independence Hall with Trees. Brass	R-6	2-45 BS	28	$400	$800	$1,100
1876, Centennial Small Liberty Bell with Star / Independence Hall with Trees. White Metal	R-4	2-45 WM	29	$175	$375	$550
1876, Centennial Small Liberty Bell with Star / Independence Hall with Trees. Copper Piedfore	R-9	2-45.1 CU	UNL	—	—	—
1876, Centennial Small Liberty Bell No Star / Independence Hall with Trees. Copper	R-7	2-46 CU	27a		$600	$800
1876, Centennial Small Liberty Bell No Star / Independence Hall with Trees. White Metal	R-8	2-46 WM	29a	$250	$600	$850
1876, Centennial Small Liberty Bell No Star / Independence Hall with Trees. Copper Piedfore	R-9	2-46.1 CU	UNL	—	—	—
1876, Centennial Declaration of Independence Demarest / Washington Ornamental Bust. Silver	R-9	2-47 S	75a	—	$7,000	—
1876, Centennial Declaration of Independence Demarest / Washington Ornamental Bust. Copper	R-8	2-47 CU	75	—	$1,600	$2,600
1876, Centennial Declaration of Independence Demarest / Washington Ornamental Bust. White Metal	R-8	2-47 WM	76	—	—	$4,800
1876, Centennial Declaration of Independence Demarest / John Hancock Signature. Silver	R-9	2-48 S	UNL	—	$5,000	—
1876, Centennial Declaration of Independence Demarest / John Hancock Signature. Copper	R-9	2-48 CU	UNL	—	—	$4,200
1876, Centennial Declaration of Independence Demarest / John Hancock Signature. White Metal	R-8	2-48 WM	UNL	—	$900	—

UNL = Unlisted.

Centennial Small Liberty Bell with Star / Independence Hall with Trees SCD (SH 2-45 / HK 27–29): The smaller Liberty Bell design is found with and without a star at 6:00 in the lower legend. This is the more common with-star variety. There are other differences in the star and non-star dies, but the star is the main diagnostic indicator. It was issued by John W. Kline of Philadelphia. Both Frossard and Holland report these as being struck in copper, not bronze. **Centennial Small Liberty Bell No Star / Independence Hall with Trees SCD (SH 2-46 / HK 27A and 29A):** The smaller Liberty Bell no-star variety is considerably scarcer than the star variety. The varieties were struck from different but similar dies, and notably the no-star variety has hash marks along the perimeter whereas the star variety has a beaded border. The planchet thicknesses vary. Several different minor die varieties exist, most noticeably in the spacing between the letters in "ALL." It was issued by John W. Kline of Philadelphia. **Centennial Declaration of Independence Demarest / Washington Ornamental Bust SCD (SH 2-47 / HK 75, 75A, and 76):** The Declaration of Independence die has three different varieties that are found paired with the Washington Ornamental Bust. All of these medals have extensive die cracks on the obverse near the signature. **Centennial Declaration of Independence Demarest / John Hancock Signature SCD (SH 2-48 / HK Unl):** The Declaration of Independence die engraved by Demarest has four people seated and two standing to the right of the Committee of Five. It is signed "Demarest. SC." All of these medals have extensive die cracks on the obverse near the signature. The reverse features Demarest's John Hancock signature die.

1876, Centennial Declaration of Independence three seated one standing / John Hancock Signature

1876, Centennial Declaration of Independence four seated / Washington Ornamental Bust

	Rarity	SH#	HK#	VF-20	EF-40	AU-50	MS-60	MS-63	MS-65
							PF-60	PF-63	PF-65
1876, Centennial Declaration of Independence three seated one standing / John Hancock Signature. White Metal	R-8	2-49 WM	UNL				—	$900	—
1876, Centennial Declaration of Independence Demarest / Declaration of Independence four seated. White Metal	R-9	2-50 WM	UNL				—	$900	—
1876, Centennial Declaration of Independence four seated / Washington Ornamental Bust. Silver	R-9	2-51 S	79a				—	$7,000	—
1876, Centennial Declaration of Independence four seated / Washington Ornamental Bust. Copper	R-8	2-51 CU	78				$500	$1,000	$1,500
1876, Centennial Declaration of Independence four seated / Washington Ornamental Bust. Brass	R-9	2-51 BS	79b						
1876, Centennial Declaration of Independence four seated / Washington Ornamental Bust. White Metal	R-8	2-51 WM	79				$450	$900	$1,300
1876, Centennial Declaration of Independence three seated one standing / Washington Ornamental Bust. Silver	R-9	2-52 S	UNL				—	$7,000	—
1876, Centennial Declaration of Independence three seated one standing / Washington Ornamental Bust. Copper	R-8	2-52 CU	UNL				—	$1,000	—
1876, Centennial Declaration of Independence three seated one standing / Washington Ornamental Bust. Brass	R-9	2-52 BS	UNL				—	$1,000	—
1876, Centennial Declaration of Independence three seated one standing / Washington Ornamental Bust. White Metal	R-8	2-52 WM	UNL				—	$900	—

UNL = Unlisted.

Centennial Declaration of Independence three seated one standing / John Hancock Signature SCD (SH 2-49 / HK Unl): The Declaration of Independence obverse has three different varieties that are found paired with the Washington Ornamental Bust reverse. This variety, engraved by George Hampden Lovett but not signed, has three people seated and one standing to the right of the Committee of Five. The reverse is the John Hancock signature die. **Centennial Declaration of Independence Demarest / Declaration of Independence four seated SCD (SH 2-50 / HK Unl):** This medal features two Declaration of Independence dies muled together. One is signed by Demarest and the other is unsigned but believed to be a George Hampden Lovett engraving. The only example of this medal that the authors are aware of is in the American Numismatic Society collection. The photo depicted is a composite image. **Centennial Declaration of Independence four seated / Washington Ornamental Bust SCD (SH 2-51 / HK 78–79B):** The Declaration of Independence die has three different varieties that are found paired with the Washington Ornamental Bust. This variety, engraved by George Hampden Lovett, has only four people seated and none standing to the right of the Committee of Five. The die is not signed. The reverse, also engraved by Lovett, features a naked bust of George Washington with an ornamental border of Cavalry and Infantry. **Centennial Declaration of Independence three seated one standing / Washington Ornamental Bust SCD (SH 2-52 / HK Unl):** The Declaration of Independence obverse has three different varieties that are found paired with the Washington Ornamental Bust reverse. This variety, engraved by George Hampden Lovett, has three people seated and one standing to the right of the Committee of Five. The die is not signed. The reverse, also engraved by Lovett, features a naked bust of Washington with an ornamental border of Cavalry and Infantry.

1876, Centennial Declaration of Independence three seated one standing / Commemoration

1876, Centennial Washington Ornamental Bust / John Hancock Signature

	Rarity	SH#	HK#	MS-60 / PF-60	MS-63 / PF-63	MS-65 / PF-65
1876, Centennial Declaration of Independence three seated one standing / Commemoration. Copper	R-7	2-53 CU	74a	$350	$600	$800
1876, Centennial Declaration of Independence three seated one standing / Commemoration. Brass	R-9	2-53 BS	74b	—	$900	—
1876, Centennial Declaration of Independence three seated one standing / Commemoration. White Metal	R-5	2-53 WM	74	$175	$350	$500
1876, Centennial Declaration of Independence three seated one standing / Commemoration. Gold-Plated	R-8	2-53 GP	UNL	—	$900	—
1876, Centennial Washington Ornamental Bust / John Hancock Signature. Silver	R-9	2-54 S	UNL	—	$5,000	—
1876, Centennial Washington Ornamental Bust / John Hancock Signature. Copper	R-9	2-54 CU	UNL	—	$900	—
1876, Centennial Washington Ornamental Bust / John Hancock Signature. Brass	R-8	2-54 BS	UNL	—	$900	—
1876, Centennial Washington Ornamental Bust / John Hancock Signature. White Metal	R-7	2-54 WM	UNL	—	$900	—
1876, Centennial Washington Ornamental Bust / Commemoration. Silver	R-9	2-55 S	UNL	—	$5,000	—
1876, Centennial Washington Ornamental Bust / Commemoration. Copper	R-9	2-55 CU	UNL	—	$1,600	—
1876, Centennial Washington Ornamental Bust / Commemoration. White Metal	R-9	2-55 WM	UNL	—	$1,600	—
1876, Centennial Union Forever. Silver	R-8	2-56 S	UNL	—	$4,000	—
1876, Centennial Union Forever. Copper	R-6	2-56 CU	UNL	$350	$500	$800
1876, Centennial Union Forever. Brass	R-6	2-56 BS	UNL	$350	$500	$800
1876, Centennial Union Forever. White Metal	R-6	2-56 WM	UNL	$700	$1,100	—
1876, Centennial Union Forever. Silver-Plated	R-9	2-56 SP	UNL	$350	$500	$800

UNL = Unlisted.

Centennial Declaration of Independence three seated one standing / Commemoration SCD (SH 2-53 / HK 74–74B): The obverse, likely engraved by Lovett, features a copy of John Trumbull's painting of the 1776 Congress Committee of Five making its report on the Declaration of Independence. This variety has three people seated and one person standing to the right of the Committee of Five. The die is not signed. The reverse commemoration legend has a microscopic "Pat. Nov. 3 1874 H&L" below. **Centennial Washington Ornamental Bust / John Hancock Signature SCD (SH 2-54 / HK Unl):** The Washington die, engraved by George Hampden Lovett, features a naked bust of George Washington with an ornamental border of Cavalry and Infantry. The reverse is Demerest's John Hancock die, a simple design with a national impact. **Centennial Washington Ornamental Bust / Commemoration SCD (SH 2-55 / HK Unl):** The obverse, engraved by George Hampden Lovett, features a naked bust of George Washington with an ornamental border of Cavalry and Infantry. On the reverse is a commemoration legend with a microscopic "Pat. Nov. 3 1874 H&L" below. **Centennial Union Forever SCD (SH 2-56 / HK Unl):** A microscopic "Lovett," for George H. Lovett, is on Washington's bust truncation. Shaking hands are shown in the center of the reverse with "Union" above and "Forever" below. Often attributed to Robert Lovett Sr., the authors are crediting George H. Lovett for its production, using a Washington bust punch or hub likely created by Robert Lovett Sr.

1876, Centennial Lovett Battle of Moores Creek #1

1876, Centennial Lovett Battle of Sullivan's Island #2

1876, Centennial Lovett Battle of Long Island #3

1876, Centennial Lovett Battle of Harlem Plains #4

| | Rarity | SH# | HK# | VF-20 | EF-40 | AU-50 | MS-60 | MS-63 | MS-65 |
							PF-60	PF-63	PF-65
1876, Centennial Lovett Battle of Moores Creek #1. Silver	R-9	2-57 S	90	—	—	$1,900	$2,900	$4,500	$5,900
1876, Centennial Lovett Battle of Moores Creek #1. Bronze	R-8	2-57 BZ	91	$200	$400	$625	$1,000	$1,800	$2,500
1876, Centennial Lovett Battle of Moores Creek #1. White Metal	R-6	2-57 WM	92	$50	$100	$160	$275	$425	$700
1876, Centennial Lovett Battle of Moores Creek #1. Bronzed White Metal	R-8	2-57 BWM	UNL	—	—	—	$1,000	$1,800	$2,150
1876, Centennial Lovett Battle of Sullivan's Island #2. Silver	R-9	2-58 S	93	—	—	$1,900	$2,900	$4,500	$5,900
1876, Centennial Lovett Battle of Sullivan's Island #2. Bronze	R-8	2-58 BZ	94	$200	$400	$625	$1,000	$1,800	$2,500
1876, Centennial Lovett Battle of Sullivan's Island #2. White Metal	R-6	2-58 WM	95	$50	$100	$160	$275	$425	$700
1876, Centennial Lovett Battle of Sullivan's Island #2. Bronzed White Metal	R-8	2-58 BWM	UNL	—	—	—	$1,000	$1,800	$2,150
1876, Centennial Lovett Battle of Long Island #3. Silver	R-9	2-59 S	96	—	—	$1,900	$2,900	$4,500	$5,900
1876, Centennial Lovett Battle of Long Island #3. Bronze	R-8	2-59 BZ	97	$200	$400	$625	$1,000	$1,800	$2,500
1876, Centennial Lovett Battle of Long Island #3. White Metal	R-6	2-59 WM	98	$50	$100	$160	$275	$425	$700
1876, Centennial Lovett Battle of Long Island #3. Bronzed White Metal	R-8	2-59 BWM	UNL	—	—	—	$1,000	$1,800	$2,150
1876, Centennial Lovett Battle of Harlem Plains #4. Silver	R-9	2-60 S	99	—	—	$1,900	$2,900	$4,500	$5,900
1876, Centennial Lovett Battle of Harlem Plains #4. Bronze	R-8	2-60 BZ	100	$200	$400	$625	$1,000	$1,800	$2,500
1876, Centennial Lovett Battle of Harlem Plains #4. White Metal	R-6	2-60 WM	101	$50	$100	$160	$275	$425	$700
1876, Centennial Lovett Battle of Harlem Plains #4. Bronzed White Metal	R-8	2-60 BWM	UNL	—	—	—	$1,000	$1,800	$2,150

UNL = Unlisted.

Centennial Lovett Battle of Moores Creek #1 SCD (SH 2-57 / HK 90–92): This is the first in a series of eight medals with a large bust of Washington, engraved and issued by George Hampden Lovett to commemorate Washington's revolutionary battles of 1776. At the Battle of Moores Creek Bridge on February 27, 1776, the Americans' defeat of the British ended British authority in North Carolina and greatly boosted patriotic morale. In less than two months following the victory, North Carolina became the first colony to vote in favor of independence from Britain. **Centennial Lovett Battle of Sullivan's Island #2 SCD (SH 2-58 / HK 93–95):** This is the second in a series of eight medals with a large bust of Washington, engraved and issued by George Hampden Lovett to commemorate Washington's revolutionary battles of 1776. The Battle of Sullivan's Island, also known as the Battle of Fort Sullivan, which is located near Charleston, South Carolina, was the first British attempt to capture the city from American rebels. It was a land and sea battle. **Centennial Lovett Battle of Long Island #3 SCD (SH 2-59 / HK 96–98):** This is the third in a series of eight medals with a large bust of Washington, engraved and issued by George Hampden Lovett to commemorate Washington's revolutionary battles of 1776. Also known as the Battle of Brooklyn Heights, it was the first major battle in the American Revolutionary War and the first engagement of an army of the new United States, having declared itself a nation only a month before. **Centennial Lovett Battle of Harlem Plains #4 SCD (SH 2-60 / HK 99–101):** This is the fourth in a series of eight medals with a large bust of Washington, engraved and issued by George Hampden Lovett to commemorate Washington's revolutionary battles of 1776. Fighting took place in what is now Manhattan, New York. The Continentals, who were in an orderly retreat, were infuriated by the British sounding the "gone away" and galvanized to hold their ground. After flanking the British attackers, the Americans slowly pushed the British back and after the British withdrawal, Washington had his troops end the pursuit.

1876, Centennial Lovett Battle of Lake Champlain #5

1876, Centennial Lovett Battle of White Plains #6

1876, Centennial Lovett Battle of Fort Washington #7

1876, Centennial Lovett Battle of Trenton #8

	Rarity	SH#	HK#	VF-20	EF-40	AU-50	MS-60	MS-63	MS-65
							PF-60	PF-63	PF-65
1876, Centennial Lovett Battle of Lake Champlain #5. Silver	R-9	2-61 S	102	—	—	$1,900	$2,900	$4,500	$5,900
1876, Centennial Lovett Battle of Lake Champlain #5. Bronze	R-8	2-61 BZ	103	$200	$400	$625	$1,000	$1,800	$2,500
1876, Centennial Lovett Battle of Lake Champlain #5. White Metal	R-6	2-61 WM	104	$50	$100	$160	$275	$425	$700
1876, Centennial Lovett Battle of Lake Champlain #5. Bronzed White Metal	R-8	2-61 BWM	UNL	—	—	—	$1,000	$1,800	$2,150
1876, Centennial Lovett Battle of White Plains #6. Silver	R-9	2-62 S	105	—	—	$1,900	$2,900	$4,500	$5,900
1876, Centennial Lovett Battle of White Plains #6. Bronze	R-8	2-62 BZ	106	$200	$400	$625	$1,000	$1,800	$2,500
1876, Centennial Lovett Battle of White Plains #6. White Metal	R-6	2-62 WM	107	$50	$100	$160	$275	$425	$700
1876, Centennial Lovett Battle of White Plains #6. Bronzed White Metal	R-8	2-62 BWM	UNL	—	—	—	$1,000	$1,800	$2,150
1876, Centennial Lovett Battle of Fort Washington #7. Silver	R-9	2-63 S	108	—	—	$1,900	$2,900	$4,500	$5,900
1876, Centennial Lovett Battle of Fort Washington #7. Bronze	R-8	2-63 BZ	109	$200	$400	$625	$1,000	$1,800	$2,500
1876, Centennial Lovett Battle of Fort Washington #7. White Metal	R-6	2-63 WM	110	$50	$100	$160	$275	$425	$700
1876, Centennial Lovett Battle of Fort Washington #7. Bronzed White Metal	R-8	2-63 BWM	UNL	—	—	—	$1,000	$1,800	$2,150
1876, Centennial Lovett Battle of Trenton #8. Silver	R-9	2-64 S	111	—	—	$1,900	$2,900	$4,500	$5,900
1876, Centennial Lovett Battle of Trenton #8. Bronze	R-8	2-64 BZ	112	$200	$400	$625	$1,000	$1,800	$2,500
1876, Centennial Lovett Battle of Trenton #8. White Metal	R-6	2-64 WM	113	$50	$100	$160	$275	$425	$700
1876, Centennial Lovett Battle of Trenton #8. Bronzed White Metal	R-8	2-64 BWM	UNL	—	—	—	$1,000	$1,800	$2,150

UNL = Unlisted.

Centennial Lovett Battle of Lake Champlain #5 SCD (SH 2-61 / HK 102–104): This is the fifth in a series of eight medals with a large bust of Washington, engraved and issued by George Hampden Lovett to commemorate Washington's revolutionary battles of 1776. Also known as the Battle of Valcour Bay, it is generally regarded as the first battle fought by the United States Navy. Although the outcome of the battle was the destruction of most of the American ships, the overall campaign delayed the British attempt to cut the colonies in half and eventually led to the British military disaster at Saratoga the following year. **Centennial Lovett Battle of White Plains #6 SCD (SH 2-62 / HK 105–107):** This is the sixth in a series of eight medals with a large bust of Washington, engraved and issued by George Hampden Lovett to commemorate Washington's revolutionary battles of 1776. Pursuing the retreat of George Washington's Continental Army northward from New York City, British General William Howe landed troops further north, intending to cut off Washington's escape route. Alerted to this move, Washington retreated further, establishing a position in the village of White Plains. Unable to hold their position, Howe's troops forced Washington to retreat further north. **Centennial Lovett Battle of Fort Washington #7 SCD (SH 2-63 / HK 108–110):** This is the seventh in a series of eight medals with a large bust of Washington, engraved and issued by George Hampden Lovett to commemorate Washington's revolutionary battles of 1776. After defeating the Continental Army under the leadership of their commander-in-chief, George Washington, at the battle of White Plains, British General William Howe looked to capture the last American stronghold, Fort Washington, on Manhattan. The Battle of Fort Washington was a decisive British victory and the entire garrison of 3,000 men were forced to surrender. **Centennial Lovett Battle of Trenton #8 SCD (SH 2-64 / HK 111–113):** This is the eighth in a series of eight medals with a large bust of Washington, engraved and issued by George Hampden Lovett to commemorate Washington's revolutionary battles of 1776. The Battle of Trenton took place on December 26, 1776, after General George Washington's crossing of the Delaware River north of Trenton, New Jersey. The hazardous crossing in adverse weather made it possible for Washington to lead the main body of the Continental Army against Hessian soldiers. After a brief battle, nearly the entire Hessian force was captured with negligible losses to the Americans.

1876, Centennial Lovett Small Bust
Battle of Moores Creek #1

1876, Centennial Lovett Small
Bust Battle of Sullivan's Island #2

1876, Centennial Lovett Small Bust
Battle of Long Island #3

1876, Centennial Lovett Small Bust
Battle of Harlem Plains #4

	Rarity	SH#	HK#	VF-20	EF-40	AU-50	MS-60 / PF-60	MS-63 / PF-63	MS-65 / PF-65
1876, Centennial Lovett Small Bust Battle of Moores Creek #1. Silver	R-9	2-65 S	UNL	—	—	—	—	$4,100	—
1876, Centennial Lovett Small Bust Battle of Moores Creek #1. Bronze	R-8	2-65 BZ	UNL	—	—	—	$1,200	$2,200	$3,000
1876, Centennial Lovett Small Bust Battle of Moores Creek #1. White Metal	R-9	2-65 WM	UNL	—	—	—	$1,200	$2,200	$3,000
1876, Centennial Lovett Small Bust Battle of Sullivan's Island #2. Silver	R-9	2-66 S	UNL	—	—	—	—	$4,100	—
1876, Centennial Lovett Small Bust Battle of Sullivan's Island #2. Bronze	R-8	2-66 BZ	UNL	—	—	—	$1,200	$2,200	$3,000
1876, Centennial Lovett Small Bust Battle of Sullivan's Island #2. White Metal	R-9	2-66 WM	UNL	—	—	—	$1,200	$2,200	$3,000
1876, Centennial Lovett Small Bust Battle of Long Island #3. Silver	R-9	2-67 S	UNL	—	—	—	—	$4,100	—
1876, Centennial Lovett Small Bust Battle of Long Island #3. Bronze	R-8	2-67 BZ	UNL	—	—	—	$1,200	$2,200	$3,000
1876, Centennial Lovett Small Bust Battle of Long Island #3. White Metal	R-9	2-67 WM	UNL	—	—	—	$1,200	$2,200	$3,000
1876, Centennial Lovett Small Bust Battle of Harlem Plains #4. Silver	R-9	2-68 S	UNL	—	—	—	—	$4,100	—
1876, Centennial Lovett Small Bust Battle of Harlem Plains #4. Bronze	R-8	2-68 BZ	UNL	—	—	—	$1,200	$2,200	$3,000
1876, Centennial Lovett Small Bust Battle of Harlem Plains #4. White Metal	R-9	2-68 WM	UNL	—	—	—	$1,200	$2,200	$3,000

UNL = Unlisted.

Centennial Lovett Small Bust Battle of Moores Creek #1 SCD (SH 2-65 / HK Unl): This is the first in a series of eight medals with a smaller bust of Washington, engraved and issued by George Hampden Lovett to commemorate the revolutionary battles of 1776. They share the same eight reverses as the Lovett Battle Series and are considerably scarcer. **Centennial Lovett Small Bust Battle of Sullivan's Island #2 SCD (SH 2-66 / HK Unl):** This is the second in a series of eight medals with a smaller bust of Washington, engraved and issued by George Hampden Lovett to commemorate the revolutionary battles of 1776. They share the same eight reverses as the Lovett Battle Series and are considerably scarcer. **Centennial Lovett Small Bust Battle of Long Island #3 SCD (SH 2-67 / HK Unl):** This is the third in a series of eight medals with a smaller bust of Washington, engraved and issued by George Hampden Lovett to commemorate the revolutionary battles of 1776. They share the same eight reverses as the Lovett Battle Series and are considerably scarcer. **Centennial Lovett Small Bust Battle of Harlem Plains #4 SCD (SH 2-68 / HK Unl):** This is the fourth in a series of eight medals with a smaller bust of Washington, engraved and issued by George Hampden Lovett to commemorate the revolutionary battles of 1776. They share the same eight reverses as the Lovett Battle Series and are considerably scarcer.

**1876, Centennial Lovett Small Bust
Battle of Lake Champlain #5**

**1876, Centennial Lovett Small Bust
Battle of White Plains #6**

**1876, Centennial Lovett Small Bust
Battle of Fort Washington #7**

**1876, Centennial Lovett Small Bust
Battle of Trenton #8**

| | Rarity | SH# | HK# | VF-20 | EF-40 | AU-50 | MS-60 | MS-63 | MS-65 |
				PF-60	PF-63	PF-65	PF-60	PF-63	PF-65
1876, Centennial Lovett Small Bust Battle of Lake Champlain #5. Silver	R-9	2-69 S	UNL	—	—	—	—	$4,100	—
1876, Centennial Lovett Small Bust Battle of Lake Champlain #5. Bronze	R-8	2-69 BZ	UNL	—	—	—	$1,200	$2,200	$3,000
1876, Centennial Lovett Small Bust Battle of Lake Champlain #5. White Metal	R-6	2-69 WM	UNL	—	—	—	$1,200	$2,200	$3,000
1876, Centennial Lovett Small Bust Battle of White Plains #6. Silver	R-9	2-70 S	UNL	—	—	—	—	$4,100	—
1876, Centennial Lovett Small Bust Battle of White Plains #6. Bronze	R-8	2-70 BZ	UNL	—	—	—	$1,200	$2,200	$3,000
1876, Centennial Lovett Small Bust Battle of White Plains #6. White Metal	R-6	2-70 WM	UNL	—	—	—	$1,200	$2,200	$3,000
1876, Centennial Lovett Small Bust Battle of Fort Washington #7. Silver	R-9	2-71 S	UNL	—	—	—	—	$4,100	—
1876, Centennial Lovett Small Bust Battle of Fort Washington #7. Bronze	R-8	2-71 BZ	UNL	—	—	—	$1,200	$2,200	$3,000
1876, Centennial Lovett Small Bust Battle of Fort Washington #7. White Metal	R-6	2-71 WM	UNL	—	—	—	$1,200	$2,200	$3,000
1876, Centennial Lovett Small Bust Battle of Trenton #8. Silver	R-9	2-72 S	UNL	—	—	—	—	$4,100	—
1876, Centennial Lovett Small Bust Battle of Trenton #8. Bronze	R-8	2-72 BZ	UNL	—	—	—	$1,200	$2,200	$3,000
1876, Centennial Lovett Small Bust Battle of Trenton #8. White Metal	R-6	2-72 WM	UNL	—	—	—	$1,200	$2,200	$3,000

UNL = Unlisted.

Centennial Lovett Small Bust Battle of Lake Champlain #5 SCD (SH 2-69 / HK Unl): This is the fifth in a series of eight medals with a smaller bust of Washington, engraved and issued by George Hampden Lovett to commemorate the revolutionary battles of 1776. They share the same eight reverses as the Lovett Battle Series and are considerably scarcer. **Centennial Lovett Small Bust Battle of White Plains #6 SCD (SH 2-70 / HK Unl):** This is the sixth in a series of eight medals with a smaller bust of Washington, engraved and issued by George Hampden Lovett to commemorate the revolutionary battles of 1776. They share the same eight reverses as the Lovett Battle Series and are considerably scarcer. **Centennial Lovett Small Bust Battle of Fort Washington #7 SCD (SH 2-71 / HK Unl):** This is the seventh in a series of eight medals with a smaller bust of Washington, engraved and issued by George Hampden Lovett to commemorate the revolutionary battles of 1776. They share the same eight reverses as the Lovett Battle Series and are considerably scarcer. **Centennial Lovett Small Bust Battle of Trenton #8 SCD (SH 2-72 / HK Unl):** This is the eighth in a series of eight medals with a smaller bust of Washington, engraved and issued by George Hampden Lovett to commemorate the revolutionary battles of 1776. They share the same eight reverses as the Lovett Battle Series and are considerably scarcer.

1876, Centennial Lovett Large and Small Bust

1876, Centennial Children of America

1876, Centennial Delphos School

1876, Centennial Washington First in War

| | Rarity | SH# | HK# | VF-20 | EF-40 | AU-50 | MS-60 | MS-63 | MS-65 |
							PF-60	PF-63	PF-65
1876, Centennial Lovett Large & Small Bust. Silver	R-10	2-73 S	UNL				—	$4,500	—
1876, Centennial Lovett Large & Small Bust. Bronze	R-9	2-73 BZ	UNL				—	$2,500	—
1876, Centennial Children of America. Silver	R-9	2-74 S	115a				—	$3,800	—
1876, Centennial Children of America. Bronze	R-8	2-74 BZ	115				—	$550	—
1876, Centennial Children of America. Brass	R-9	2-74 BS	UNL				—	$550	—
1876, Centennial Children of America. White Metal	R-6	2-74 WM	117				$150	$300	$500
1876, Centennial Children of America. White Metal Proof	R-8	2-74 WMP	UNL				$250	$400	$600
1876, Centennial Delphos School. Bronze	R-6	2-75 BZ	UNL				—	$600	—
1876, Centennial Delphos School. White Metal	R-6	2-75 WM	UNL				$150	$450	$1,800
1876, Centennial Washington First in War. Silver	R-9	2-76 S	UNL				—	$3,000	—
1876, Centennial Washington First in War. White Metal	R-6	2-76 WM	UNL				$500	$750	—
1876, Centennial Washington First in War. Gold-Plated White Metal (also called brass)	R-8	2-76 GP	UNL				—	$750	—

UNL = Unlisted.

Centennial Lovett Large & Small Bust SCD (SH 2-73 / HK Unl): This is the Lovett Battle Series with large and small busts combined. Reportedly, one was struck in silver and two in bronze. **Centennial Children of America SCD (SH 2-74 / HK 115–117):** This is another Lovett design using the same central device with a small bust of Washington as on the Lovett Small Bust Battle series. **Centennial Delphos School SCD (SH 2-75 / HK Unl):** This is another Lovett design using the same central device with a small bust of Washington as on the Lovett Small Bust Battle series. **Centennial Washington First in War SCD (SH 2-76 / HK Unl):** This original Washington bust design was engraved by Mathias Nicole Marie Vivier around 1818 for the "Series Numismatica." In the early 1830s Charles Cushing Wright copied Vivier's portrait design and struck a series of medals. George H. Lovett copied the design for this Centennial medal. A microscopic "U.S.M. CO." for United States Medal Company is located below the bust. USMC had contracts with Lovett and Key, who produced dies on their behalf. The authors believe this is most likely a Lovett creation as it was marketed by USMC along with other medals that he engraved.

1876, Centennial Washington / Memorial Building

1876, Centennial Washington / Independence Hall

1876, Centennial Washington with Sword / Memorial Hall

| | Rarity | SH# | HK# | VF-20 | EF-40 | AU-50 | MS-60 | MS-63 | MS-65 |
							PF-60	PF-63	PF-65
1876, Centennial Washington Memorial Building. Brass	R-7	2-77 BS	UNL				—	$1,100	—
1876, Centennial Washington Memorial Building. White Metal	R-9	2-77 WM	UNL				—	$1,000	—
1876, Centennial Washington Memorial Building. Wood	R-7	2-77 WD	UNL				—	$200	—
1876, Centennial Washington Memorial Building Copyright. Brass	R-8	2-78 BS	UNL				—	$1,100	—
1876, Centennial Washington Independence Hall. Bronze	R-7	2-79 BZ	UNL				—	$400	—
1876, Centennial Washington Independence Hall. Brass	R-7	2-79 BS	UNL				—	$400	—
1876, Centennial Washington Independence Hall. White Metal	R-6	2-79 WM	UNL				—	$350	—
1876, Centennial Washington Independence Hall. Silver-Plated White Metal	R-7	2-79 SP	UNL				—	$350	—
1876, Centennial Washington with Sword. White Metal	R-8	2-80 WM	UNL				—	$1,700	$2,200
1876, Centennial Washington with Sword. Terracotta	R-8	2-80 TC	UNL				—	$250	—
1876, Centennial Washington with Sword. Leather	R-8	2-80 LR	UNL				—	$250	—
1876, Centennial Washington with Sword. Wood	R-8	2-80 WD	UNL				—	$250	—

UNL = Unlisted.

Centennial Washington / Memorial Building SCD (SH 2-77 / HK Unl): George Washington's bust is on the obverse and the Memorial Building is on the reverse. Neither die is signed. **Centennial Washington / Memorial Building Copyright SCD (SH 2-78 / HK Unl):** The obverse is similar to the preceding (SH 2-78) without the counterfoils on either side of the date and with denticles around the rim. The reverse has the date 1876 replaced with "Copyright Secured." The authors have not been able to obtain a photo of this variety. **Centennial Washington Independence Hall SCD (SH 2-79 / HK Unl):** The obverse features the bust of Washington in civilian dress, three-quarters facing left. Independence Hall is on the reverse. **Centennial Washington with Sword Memorial Hall SCD (SH 2-80 / HK Unl):** The obverse features a half-length view of Washington in civilian dress facing three-quarters to the right with a sword resting on his forearm. Memorial Hall is on the reverse. This medal is reported to be of German origin according to L. Bayard Smith, a prominent collector from the latter 1800s.

1876, Centennial
Washington
and Grant

1876, Centennial
Seventh
Regiment Visit

1876, Centennial
Eternal Vigilance

1876, Centennial
Abraham Lincoln

	Rarity	SH#	HK#	VF-20	EF-40	AU-50	MS-60 PF-60	MS-63 PF-63	MS-65 PF-65
1876, Centennial Washington and Grant. Silver	R-9	2-81 S	118a				—	$3,500	—
1876, Centennial Washington and Grant. Bronze	R-9	2-81 BZ	118b				—	$3,500	—
1876, Centennial Washington and Grant. White Metal	R-5	2-81 WM	118	$25	$65	$135	$250	$450	$1,200
1876, Centennial Seventh Regiment Visit. Silver	R-9	2-82 S	UNL				—	$3,500	—
1876, Centennial Seventh Regiment Visit. Bronze	R-8	2-82 BZ	UNL				—	—	$2,700
1876, Centennial Seventh Regiment Visit. White Metal	R-7	2-82 WM	UNL				—	$800	—
1876, Centennial Eternal Vigilance. Copper	R-8	2-83 CU	UNL	—	—	$400	—	—	—
1876, Centennial Abraham Lincoln. Silver	R-9	2-84 S	UNL				—	$6,500	—
1876, Centennial Abraham Lincoln. Bronze	R-8	2-84 BZ	UNL				—	$6,500	—
1876, Centennial Abraham Lincoln. White Metal	R-8	2-84 WM	73				—	—	$9,400

UNL = Unlisted.

Centennial Washington and Grant SCD (SH 2-81 / HK 118–118B): This design features the standing figures of Washington, who was 6 feet, 3 inches tall, and Grant, each with their hand on a large shield between them with an enormous eagle above the shield. A micro signature, "F X Koehler," is below the shield. Francis Xavier Koehler of Baltimore, Maryland, cut the dies. Approximately 75 percent of the white metal pieces are found holed. **Centennial Seventh Regiment Visit SCD (SH 2-82 / HK Unl):** This is signed by engraver Demarest SC. N.Y. for Abraham Demarest Sr. New York, with the signature located below the monument. It was struck by George H. Lovett. **Centennial Eternal Vigilance SCD (SH 2-83 / HK Unl):** A scene of Liberty holding a wreath over a kneeling figure represents the United States. Liberty's left hand rests on a bust of Washington, symbolizing that the United States is now a free country because of George Washington. The dies were engraved by Charles Stubenrauch. Stubenrauch also engraved the official So-Called Dollar for the 1853 New York Crystal Palace Exhibition (SH 1-1). **Centennial Abraham Lincoln SCD (SH 2-84 / HK 73):** An Abraham Lincoln bust is on the obverse. The reverse legend states, "Our Nations Freedom Achieved by Washington and Perpetuated by Lincoln." The dies were owned by Robert Sneider Co., New York. A bronze strike was reported in Frossard's 1876 listing.

1876, Centennial Ulysses S. Grant

1876, Centennial Washington See How We Prosper

1876, Centennial Catholic See How We Prosper

1876, Centennial England See How We Prosper

	Rarity	SH#	HK#	VF-20	EF-40	AU-50	MS-60 PF-60	MS-63 PF-63	MS-65 PF-65
1876, Centennial Ulysses S. Grant. White Metal	R-7	2-85 WM	UNL				—	$350	—
1876, Centennial Washington See How We Prosper. Silver	R-9	2-86 S	UNL				—	$2,000	—
1876, Centennial Washington See How We Prosper. Bronze	R-7	2-86 BZ	UNL				—	—	$800
1876, Centennial Washington See How We Prosper. White Metal	R-6	2-86 WM	UNL				$400	$1,300	$1,900
1876, Centennial Catholic See How We Prosper. Silver	R-9	2-87 S	UNL				—	$2,000	—
1876, Centennial Catholic See How We Prosper. Bronze	R-7	2-87 BZ	UNL				—	$350	—
1876, Centennial Catholic See How We Prosper. White Metal	R-6	2-87 WM	UNL				—	$200	—
1876, Centennial England See How We Prosper. Silver	R-9	2-88 S	UNL				—	$2,000	—
1876, Centennial England See How We Prosper. Bronze	R-7	2-88 BZ	UNL				—	$350	—
1876, Centennial England See How We Prosper. White Metal	R-6	2-88 WM	UNL				—	$200	—

UNL = Unlisted.

Centennial Ulysses S. Grant SCD (SH 2-85 / HK Unl): A bust of Ulysses S. Grant in uniform is on the obverse. An angel with wings flies above the exposition buildings on the reverse. **Centennial Washington See How We Prosper SCD (SH 2-86 / HK Unl):** The obverse bust of Washington was engraved by German-American engraver Rudolf Laubenheimer. It is one of five different obverse designs that share a common "See How We Prosper" reverse. According to Joe Levine of Presidential Auctions, 25 were struck in bronze and a smaller number in silver. The set of five medals was sold by U.S. Medallion Company and was designed and patented by jeweler S.J. Delon of New York, according to Frossard's 1876 listing. **Centennial Catholic See How We Prosper SCD (SH 2-87 / HK Unl):** This is the Catholic version, "In Honor of the Catholic Visitors to the International Exposition." It was designed by German-American engraver Rudolf Laubenheimer. It is one of five different obverse designs that share a common "See How We Prosper" reverse. The medal features the bust of Blessed Pope Pius IX. **Centennial England See How We Prosper SCD (SH 2-88 / HK Unl):** This is the English version, "In Honor of the English Visitors to the International Exposition." It was designed by German-American engraver Rudolf Laubenheimer. It is one of five different obverse designs that share a common "See How We Prosper" reverse. The medal features the bust of Queen Victoria.

1876, Centennial German See How We Prosper

1876, Centennial France See How We Prosper

1876, Centennial Washington and Liberty Bell on Shields

	Rarity	SH#	HK#	VF-20	EF-40	AU-50	MS-60 PF-60	MS-63 PF-63	MS-65 PF-65
1876, Centennial German See How We Prosper. Silver	R-9	2-89 S	UNL				—	$2,000	—
1876, Centennial German See How We Prosper. Bronze	R-7	2-89 BZ	UNL				—	$350	—
1876, Centennial German See How We Prosper. White Metal	R-6	2-89 WM	UNL				—	$200	—
1876, Centennial France See How We Prosper. Silver	R-9	2-90 S	UNL				—	$2,000	—
1876, Centennial France See How We Prosper. Bronze	R-7	2-90 BZ	UNL				—	$350	—
1876, Centennial France See How We Prosper. White Metal	R-6	2-90 WM	UNL				—	$200	—
1876, Centennial Washington & Liberty Bell on Shields. White Metal	R-8	2-91 WM	UNL	—	—	$250	—	—	—

UNL = Unlisted.

Centennial German See How We Prosper SCD (SH 2-89 / HK Unl): This is the German version, and in German the legend states "In Honor of the German Visitors to the International Exposition." It was designed by Laubenheimer. It is one of five different obverse designs that share a common "See How We Prosper" reverse. The design features the bust of Wilhelm I, later known as Wilhelm the Great, the first German emperor who unified modern Germany and established its Empire. His reign lasted from 1871 to 1888. **Centennial France See How We Prosper SCD (SH 2-90 / HK Unl):** This is the French version, and in French the legend states "In Honor of the French Visitors to the International Exposition." It was designed by Laubenheimer. It is one of five different obverse designs that share a common "See How We Prosper" reverse. The design features the bust of Marie Edme Patrice Maurice de Mac-Mahon, marshal of France. **Centennial Washington and Liberty Bell on Shields SCD (SH 2-91 / HK Unl):** The obverse features the bust of Washington superimposed on a shield with the date 1776 at the top. The reverse states, "Centennial 1776 1876 America," with the Liberty Bell superimposed on a shield.

APPENDIX H

Canceled Coin Dies of the 1995–1996 Atlanta Centennial Olympic Games

by Steve Bieda

In 1997, for the first and only time, the United States Mint—in perhaps one of the most novel offerings of any world mint—offered canceled coin dies that maintained most of their original surface detail to customers on its mailing list.

Steel coin dies, with separate dies bearing designs for the obverse and reverse designs, are used to strike coins. After the Mint has no further use for them, unwanted dies are usually defaced and securely destroyed.

One notable exception involved the U.S. Mint's unique sale of canceled coin dies from the 1995–1996 Atlanta Centennial Olympic Games commemorative coin program, with each die retaining full design details except for a large X cut into the die surface.

Dies formerly used to strike commemorative Olympic Proof silver dollars and Proof and Uncirculated $5 gold coins were included in a September 1997 Mint offering at $49.00 each. Buyers were retroactively limited to one die each, with no choice of denomination or design.

The entire offering, a total of 2,833 dies, including 367 examples of the $5 denomination and 2,466 of the $1 denomination, sold out within eight days.

The coin dies were defaced with the cutting of an X that split the design into quadrants but left a considerable amount of detail. The dies used for Proof coinage were re-plated with chrome prior to being sold, and the resulting dies showed little, if any, evidence of use. The mirrored surfaces of the Proof dies can be clearly distinguished from the matte gray surfaces on the dies used to strike the Uncirculated $5 gold coins.

Each die has a unique serial number inscribed on the die shaft and came with a certificate of authenticity bearing the serial number and information about the die, including service dates, number of strikes, and the reason for retirement of the die. The most common reason for retiring dies is the buildup of abrasive particles that etch the dies as they move in the direction of the metal flow during successive strikes, a phenomenon the Mint simply calls "starburst" because the result looks like a starburst gemstone. Other reasons for retirement include change of calendar year; scratched, reeded, cracked, or clashed dies; and over-polishing.

Packaging for the dies consisted of a simple black-velvet drawstring pouch with a removeable plastic cap that fit snugly over the head of the die, all contained within a foam insert inside a Priority Mail box.

Although the Atlanta Olympic commemorative coin program included four coins with the half dollar denomination, half dollar dies were not offered, reportedly because the half dollar denomination was still being issued for circulation, whereas the $1 and $5 denominations were used exclusively for collector issues.

The 1996 one-dollar reverse dies had the largest number of examples sold, with 632 sales recorded. The scarcest of the dollar dies is the 1996 Paralympics Wheelchair dollar, with 135 sold.

The 1995 Proof $5 Torch Runner is the rarest of all the dies offered, with only 8 sold. The 1996 $5 proof reverse dies claimed the largest number sold of that denomination, with 78 examples sold.

The 1997 offering of the dies from the 1995–1996 Olympic commemorative program is the only time the Mint has offered canceled coin dies with any detail remaining. Subsequent offerings of canceled coin dies from the Mint consisted of dies for circulating coins with all design details completely obliterated.

Date	Denomination	Design	Type	Number Sold	Current Pricing Trend
1995-P	$1	Paralympics–Blind Runner obverse	Proof	205	$800
1995-P	$1	Gymnastics obverse	Proof	186	$800
1995-P	$1	Cycling obverse	Proof	207	$800
1995-P	$1	Track and Field obverse	Proof	220	$800
1995	$1	Reverse	Proof	375	$600
1996-P	$1	Paralympics–Wheelchair obverse	Proof	135	$850
1996-P	$1	Tennis obverse	Proof	145	$850
1996-P	$1	Rowing obverse	Proof	143	$850
1996-P	$1	High Jump obverse	Proof	217	$800
1996	$1	Reverse	Proof	632	$550
1995-W	$5	Torch Runner obverse	Unc.	19	$2,100
1995-W	$5	Torch Runner obverse	Proof	8	$2,600
1995-W	$5	Stadium obverse	Unc.	17	$2,100
1995-W	$5	Stadium obverse	Proof	39	$1,900
1995	$5	Reverse	Unc.	33	$1,900
1995	$5	Reverse	Proof	39	$1,900
1996-W	$5	Cauldron obverse	Unc.	13	$2,100
1996-W	$5	Cauldron obverse	Proof	60	$1,700
1996-W	$5	Flag Bearer obverse	Unc.	13	$2,100
1996-W	$5	Flag Bearer obverse	Proof	30	$1,900
1996	$5	Reverse	Unc.	19	$2,100
1996	$5	Reverse	Proof	78	$1,700

Nearly all coin dies outside the Mint have been canceled in some form. A *defaced* die's design has been completely eradicated, as shown at top; such a die can be identified only by its serial number in conjunction with its certificate of authenticity, which lists the denomination. Some dies are only partially defaced, like these obverse dies for the Winged Liberty dime (middle image), defaced by grinding, and the Philippine 10 sentimos, defaced with a torch. Dies can be canceled without being defaced, as is the case with the 1995–1996 Olympic commemoratives.

1996-P Tennis $1 Proof
die, with velvet bag
and protective die cap.

Silver dollar reverse dies in
two finishes: a 1995-P Reverse
Proof (top) and a 1996-P Proof.

A 1996-P Tennis $1 Proof reverse die
(top) and a 1996-W $5 circulation-
strike die. The extra care taken
(cleaning and re-chroming)
with the Proof die is evident.

APPENDIX I

The 1921 Silver Dollar Coin Anniversary Act

When it comes to classic American coins, for several generations the Morgan silver dollar has ranked near the top of the popularity list—if not sitting comfortably in the #1 spot. Hobbyists collect them by date and mintmark. Specialists collect them by die variety. "Silver stackers" who accumulate precious metal as a hedge against inflation buy them by the roll or bag. There are folders, albums, display cases, and other ways to store and show off the hefty old coins. Entire books have been written about them. Even people who don't consider themselves coin collectors are familiar with, or at least vaguely aware of, the Morgan dollar. It's part of the national shared culture of the United States.

Like the Morgan dollar, its successor, the Peace dollar, also consistently ranks among the most popular and recognizable American coins. If Grandpa's cigar box of old-time pocket change or Grandma's purse had a silver dollar in it, chances are it was a 1922 or 1923 Peace dollar. More than 140 million of the coins were minted in those two years alone.

In 2021—the 100th anniversary of the last Morgan dollars and the first Peace dollars—the nation's awareness of these coins will take a sharp upward turn. The "1921 Silver Dollar Coin Anniversary Act" authorizes the production of new coins to mark the centennial of the last Morgan dollars and the first Peace dollars.

United States Mint model renderings of Morgan dollar and Peace dollar anniversary coins for 2021.

DECADES OF PRODIGIOUS PRODUCTION

The first Morgan dollars—named for their designer, English-born artist George T. Morgan, who worked for the U.S. Mint in Philadelphia—were produced in 1878. From that point they were minted annually through 1904. Every active Mint facility was involved in their production (Philadelphia, Denver, San Francisco, New Orleans, and Carson City). Every year, millions of the coins— and in some years, tens of millions—were added to the nation's reserves.

The *Guide Book of United States Coins* describes the fate of many of the Morgan dollars minted from 1878 to 1904:

> Although silver dollars were used in commerce in certain areas of the West, paper currency by and large served the needs of trade and exchange. As these hundreds of millions of newly minted dollars were not needed, most were put up in 1,000-coin canvas bags and stored in Treasury vaults.

The coins served as backing for paper-money Silver Certificates, which had been issued since 1878.

After 1904 there was a hiatus in minting; public demand for the silver dollar was low, and the government's bullion supply was exhausted. In 1918 Congress passed the Pittman Act, which was essentially a federal subsidy to the American silver-mining industry. Under the act, up to 350 million of the Treasury's stored silver dollars could be converted into bullion, to be sold or minted into smaller coins. It also directed the government to purchase domestically mined silver to be coined into a like number of new silver dollars. Under the Pittman Act, more than 270 million old silver dollars were taken out of storage and melted. The bullion of nearly 260 million of them was sold to Great Britain. More than 11 million were scheduled for recoining into smaller denominations. Between 1922 and 1933, the government purchased the same quantity of silver (some 209 million fine ounces) from domestic mines at a fixed price above the market rate.

A new silver dollar was planned for the freshly replenished bullion supply. In 1921 the Peace dollar was designed as a coin celebrating the end of the 1914–1918 Great War. Before minting began for the new coin, George Morgan's old designs were brought back for one final production—and a massive production it was. Nearly 87 million Morgan dollars were struck in 1921 at the Philadelphia, Denver, and San Francisco mints.

Coinage of the new Peace dollar started in December of 1921.

**A Morgan dollar struck at
the New Orleans Mint in 1904.**

**A Proof 1921
Peace dollar.**

In day-to-day commerce, the dollar coin continued to be an unpopular and largely unnecessary denomination. Peace dollars were minted in smaller quantities than their predecessor, but still in the millions. The Philadelphia, Denver, and San Francisco mints produced the coins from 1921 through 1928 (though not every mint in every year), then again in 1934 and 1935. Most of the coins continued to be bagged and stored in Treasury vaults, rather than being used in everyday transactions.

INTO THE VAULT, AND OUT AGAIN

Starting in the 1920s and 1930s, the Treasury Department would periodically release bags of earlier-dated silver dollars, especially around the Christmas season, when people often gave the coins as gifts. Sometimes these bags included rare dates, which would be absorbed into the hobby market.

In 1926 visitors to the American Numismatic Association convention in Washington, D.C., could buy Uncirculated 1882-S Morgan dollars at face value, from the Cash Room of the Treasury Building. In 1938 the Cash Room paid out at face value several bags of 1880-CC silver dollars (and about 50 more bags of the same in 1955). In 1942 dozens—possibly hundreds—of bags of 1879-S dollars were distributed from the San Francisco Mint. In 1952 there was a major release of 1883-O dollars. These and many other Morgan dollar dates and mintmarks were released in bag quantities into the 1950s, to varying degrees—some in a trickle, some in relative floods.

Peace dollars, too, were paid out by the bag, starting soon after they were first minted. In 1938 and again in 1942, the San Francisco Mint released many 1,000-coin bags of 1925-S Peace dollars at face value. In 1939 several bags of the relatively scarce 1927-D emerged in the Midwest, and were absorbed into the numismatic market. Bags of 1927-S dollars, of which only 866,000 were minted, entered the market in the 1930s, at various times in the 1940s, and into the 1950s. Dealers were careful not to flood the hobby, knowing that Peace dollars were not a popular series and saturation would depress the retail value even of scarce dates. Many of the 1927-S coins served as gambling cash in Nevada, and were worn down from Mint State as they shuffled around the casinos. Peace dollars of 1935-S were released by the San Francisco Mint in large quantities, in 1949 and 1950. Professional numismatist Q. David Bowers recalls being offered a bag of them, in gem Mint State, for $1,200 in 1955, and passing—"I couldn't figure out what to do with more than a few dozen pieces (what a mistake!)."

**A sculpture based on the Morgan silver dollar,
at U.S. Mint Headquarters in Washington, D.C.**

Morgan dollars started becoming more popular with coin collectors in the 1950s. In *Lost and Found Coin Hoards and Treasures*, Bowers describes the hobby situation:

> In time, numismatic passion for these pieces came to rest in a gray area. By 1962, the Morgan dollar market was a side branch of numismatics—hardly in the limelight, but not in the shadows either. There was a ready market for these, including in roll (20 coins) and bag quantities. However, they were not mainstream. Most numismatists sought Indian Head and Lincoln cents, Buffalo nickels, Mercury dimes, commemoratives, and other series of the 1800s and 1900s.

Then, something remarkable happened. In 1962, as the holiday season approached, bags of silver dollars that had been sealed in the Philadelphia Mint since 1929 were brought out of storage. They would meet the year-end demand from people who liked to give the fancy old-time coins as Christmas gifts. Soon it was discovered that the bags included sparkling brilliant Uncirculated 1903-O dollars—at the time, considered to be the rarest of them all, worth $1,500 apiece! In the treasure hunt that followed, hundreds of thousands of coins of that particular date/mintmark were discovered in beautiful Mint State. Previously experts had estimated only a dozen or so had survived the Pittman Act melt of 1918. Other prized Morgan dollar rarities emerged, as well, 1898-O and 1904-O coins among them, and a few bags of older circulated Liberty Seated silver dollars.

Through 1963 and up to March of 1964, speculators and collectors lined up at banks and the Treasury Building to get their hands on the bagged-up riches. Some people even came with wheelbarrows, traded paper currency for cold hard cash, and left with 1,000-coin canvas sacks to search through. Hundreds of millions of Morgan dollars were brought back into the light of day (and into hobby collections). Then, when there were about three million coins remaining—many of them from the Carson City Mint—the Treasury put a stop to the payouts at face value. The last few million coins were auctioned off by the General Services Administration from 1972 to 1979.

This flurry of activity, excitement, and competition cemented the popularity of the Morgan dollar in particular. Peace dollars remained not quite as popular, with fewer excited buyers. (Many of the 1,000-coin bags bought in the early 1960s were quickly searched through, with numismatically valuable coins saved and others then spent as legal tender, at face value.) Instead of permanently oversaturating the market, the hundreds of millions of coins actually increased the number of active collectors, and in time silver dollar values went up with the demand. In August 1967 trading in 1,000-coin bags of silver dollars commenced on the New York Mercantile Exchange. Bowers has observed, "In today's era of certified coins and wide distribution, it may be hard for modern readers to realize that in 1967 any well-funded person who wanted to put a few thousand *bags* of silver dollars in a vault would have had no trouble finding them!"

MORGAN AND PEACE DOLLARS TODAY

Today the Morgan dollar is among the most popular classic U.S. coins. The preface to the *Guide Book of Morgan Silver Dollars*, sixth edition, describes its popularity:

> Here at Whitman Publishing headquarters we clearly see its universal appeal. Hobbyists buy thousands and thousands of our folders, albums, and other holders to store and display their Morgan dollars. We get letters, emails, and phone calls about the hefty old coins. When we go to coin shows, collectors and investors are talking about them. As we work on each year's edition of the *Guide Book of United States Coins* (the "Red Book"), we hear plenty of Morgan dollar observations and market analysis from coin dealers around the country. Meanwhile, outside the realm of the active hobby community, this is one of the "rare coins" that even non-collectors are likely to know about. They saw one in Grandma's old purse, or offered in a Sunday-newspaper ad, or maybe tossed onto a bar in a Hollywood Western. The Morgan dollar is a coin that sparks the imagination. Once it entered the American consciousness it never left.

As Whitman Publishing prepared to release the fourth edition of the *Guide Book of Peace Dollars* in 2020, publisher Dennis Tucker informally polled 139 hobbyists for their opinions on the Peace dollar.

- 40 percent of those polled self-identified as casual collectors of Peace dollars—collecting them, but not as their primary hobby niche.

- 45 percent indicated that they own some Peace dollars, but don't consider them a carefully assembled collection.

- 5 percent considered themselves active collectors of the coins—e.g., constantly upgrading their sets, competing in registries, cherrypicking or collecting by die variety, and/or participating in the National Silver Dollar Roundtable, the Society of Silver Dollar Collectors, or other dedicated groups.

- 10 percent said that they don't collect them, and don't own any.

Tucker interpreted this feedback as showing a coin with broad presence in the hobby community, and "It also suggests a field primed for many casual collectors to ramp up to 'active collector' status."

Looking beyond the poll numbers—learning collectors' opinions, and the feelings inspired by the Peace dollar—is anecdotally informative. Medalist and sculptor Heidi Wastweet, formerly a member of the Treasury's Citizens Coinage Advisory Committee and now a member of the United States Mint's Artistic Infusion Program, identified the Peace dollar as "one of the most beautiful" U.S. coin designs. U.S. Mint medallic artist Phebe Hemphill, the sculptor-engraver behind many excellent coinage designs, said, "The 1921 High Relief Peace dollar is my favorite U.S. coin." That sentiment was echoed by artist and former CCAC chairman Gary Marks, who called the Peace dollar "my favorite among classic U.S. coins." One collector opined, "I do love the design and I am of the 'peaceful persuasion,' so they are sort of dear to me." Another called them "big, heavy, and easy on the eyes—that's why I don't collect dimes!"

MORGAN AND PEACE DOLLAR COINS OF THE FUTURE

For 100 years, collectors knew the 1921 Morgan dollar as the last of its breed. That changes in 2021. The 1921 Silver Dollar Coin Anniversary Act ordered the minting of new coins honoring both the Morgan dollar and the Peace dollar.

The act was signed into law on January 5, 2021. It "requires the Department of the Treasury to mint and issue coins in honor of the 100th anniversary of the completion of coinage of the Morgan dollar and the 100th anniversary of the commencement of coinage of the Peace dollar." The legislation was the brainchild of two members of the Citizens Coinage Advisory Committee, chairman Thomas Uram and Michael Moran. Both are longtime numismatists and published researchers active in the hobby community.

The CCAC convened by videoconference on January 19, 2021, to review designs for the Morgan and Peace dollar tribute coins. U.S. Mint Chief Engraver Joseph Menna and the Mint's manager of design and engraving, Ron Harrigal, discussed the process of creating the new coins. They will be an "homage" or "rendition" of the old silver dollars, crafted from a variety of Mint assets and records to "honor the original intent of the original artists as much as possible," as Menna said. Harrigal pointed out that the change from the historical .900 fineness to .999 fine silver would cause a minuscule reduction in planchet volume. Modern technology will bring improvements over what was available a century ago. CCAC members reviewed computer-generated illustrations of the new designs and were pleased with the outcome.

Historically, the Morgan dollar was struck at three Mint facilities that still are operational and two that are not. Philadelphia, Denver, and San Francisco will strike Morgan dollar tribute coins with either no mintmark (for Philadelphia) or a D (Denver) or S (San Francisco) mintmark. To represent the old Morgan dollars struck in Carson City and New Orleans, the Philadelphia Mint will produce tribute coins with "CC" and "O" privy marks.

In April 2021 the United States Mint announced the following formats of the 2021 coins, noting that "Each coin is packaged in an elegant black box, with a beautiful outer sleeve adorned with an image of the coin obverse and accompanied by a Certificate of Authenticity." Coins of other formats or packaging may be issued, as well—and the legislation does not mandate an end to the production, meaning that other Morgan and Peace dollar tribute coins could be issued in coming years.

Morgan 2021 Silver Dollar with "CC" Privy Mark

Mint: Philadelphia.
Pre-ordering window: May 24 at 12 noon Eastern to June 7 at 3 pm, or until inventory is depleted. Product shipments begin in October 2021.
Issue price: $85.00
Mintage Limit: —
Product Limit: 175,000
Household Order Limit: 25
Denomination: $1
Finish: Uncirculated
Composition: 99.9% Silver
Silver Weight: 0.858 troy oz.
Diameter: 1.500 inches (38.10 mm)
Edge: Reeded
Mint / Mintmark: Philadelphia / none

Morgan 2021 Silver Dollar with "O" Privy Mark

Mint: Philadelphia.
Pre-ordering window: May 24 at 12 noon Eastern to June 7 at 3 pm, or until inventory is depleted. Product shipments begin in October 2021.
Issue price: $85.00
Mintage Limit: —
Product Limit: 175,000
Household Order Limit: 25
Denomination: $1
Finish: Uncirculated
Composition: 99.9% Silver
Silver Weight: 0.858 troy oz.
Diameter: 1.500 inches (38.10 mm)
Edge: Reeded
Mint / Mintmark: Philadelphia / none

MORGAN 2021-D SILVER DOLLAR

Mint: Denver.

Pre-ordering window: June 1 at 12 noon Eastern to June 14 at 3 pm, or until inventory is depleted. Product shipments begin in October 2021.

Issue price: $85.00

Mintage Limit: —

Product Limit: 175,000

Household Order Limit: 25

Denomination: $1

Finish: Uncirculated

Composition: 99.9% Silver

Silver Weight: 0.858 troy oz.

Diameter: 1.500 inches (38.10 mm)

Edge: Reeded

Mint / Mintmark: Denver / D

MORGAN 2021 SILVER DOLLAR

Mint: Philadelphia.

Pre-ordering window: June 7 at 12 noon Eastern to June 21 at 3 pm, or until inventory is depleted. Product shipments begin in October 2021.

Issue price: $85.00

Mintage Limit: —

Product Limit: 175,000

Household Order Limit: 25

Denomination: $1

Finish: Uncirculated

Composition: 99.9% Silver

Silver Weight: 0.858 troy oz.

Diameter: 1.500 inches (38.10 mm)

Edge: Reeded

Mint / Mintmark: Philadelphia / none

MORGAN 2021-S SILVER DOLLAR

Mint: San Francisco.

Pre-ordering window: June 1 at 12 noon Eastern to June 14 at 3 pm, or until inventory is depleted. Product shipments begin in October 2021.

Issue price: $85.00

Mintage Limit: —

Product Limit: 175,000

Household Order Limit: 25

Denomination: $1

Finish: Uncirculated

Composition: 99.9% Silver

Silver Weight: 0.858 troy oz.

Diameter: 1.500 inches (38.10 mm)

Edge: Reeded

Mint / Mintmark: San Francisco / S

PEACE 2021 SILVER DOLLAR

Mint: Philadelphia.

Pre-ordering window: June 7 at 12 noon Eastern to June 21 at 3 pm, or until inventory is depleted. Product shipments begin in October 2021.

Issue price: $85.00

Mintage Limit: —

Product Limit: 175,000

Household Order Limit: 25

Denomination: $1

Finish: Uncirculated

Composition: 99.9% Silver

Silver Weight: 0.858 troy oz.

Diameter: 1.500 inches (38.10 mm)

Edge: Reeded

Mint / Mintmark: Philadelphia / none

APPENDIX J

Beware Fake 2021 Morgan and Peace Dollar Coins

by Beth Deisher

Silver dollars celebrating the Morgan and Peace designs, authorized by the 1921 Silver Dollar Coin Anniversary Act (Public Law 116-286) signed into law in January of 2021, present Chinese counterfeiters of U.S. coins a bonanza unlike any witnessed since the Internet became their primary vehicle for illicit trade in the early twenty-first century.

The Morgan dollar is the most widely collected classic U.S. series and has been a collector favorite since the U.S. Treasury opened its vaults in the early 1960s to sell the storied coins to the general public. Thus demand for the 2021 coins—initially in U.S. Mint sales and then in the secondary market—will likely surpass most modern U.S. commemoratives issued since 1982. Also predictable, secondary market premiums will skyrocket and likely remain high for the foreseeable future.

Since at least 2008 counterfeits of virtually every date and mintmark of the Morgan and Peace dollar series have been sold on Chinese websites such as Alibaba, AliExpress, and DHgate and have made their way onto the e-commerce platforms Amazon, eBay, and Craigslist as well as social media forums such as Facebook and Instagram.

The counterfeiters are readily acquainted with the vintage Morgan and Peace dollar series. Thus, U.S. Mint officials' desire to pay homage to the original sculptors' designs by scanning old hubs, plaster models, galvanos, and original coins to achieve the desired relief in order to recreate the original 1921 designs will in all likelihood facilitate the counterfeiters' ability to produce high-quality fakes. Chinese counterfeiters have high-tech capabilities in die-making and coining operations and have typically in recent years offered fakes of new U.S. commemorative coins within six weeks of the launch of U.S. Mint sales.

The 2021 Morgan and Peace dollar coins will be struck on .999 silver planchets, the same as those used for U.S. commemorative silver dollars since 2019. Original 1921 Morgan and Peace dollars were made of .900 silver and .100 copper. Using just visual inspection it is virtually impossible to distinguish between genuine .999 percent silver and genuine .900 percent silver coins. Likewise, it is extremely difficult to visually spot the silver-plated fakes sold by the counterfeiters that have the capability to produce both Uncirculated and Proof versions.

Thus, one will have to rely on coin specifications to detect the counterfeits.

Genuine 2021 silver dollars will have the same weight and diameter of the original genuine Morgan and Peace dollars struck in 1921: weight, 26.73 grams; diameter, 38.1 mm. Since the counterfeiters typically silver-plate steel, zinc, copper, or lead alloys used in the core of their fakes, the weights and diameters are often close to the genuine numbers, but are not exact. Remember, genuine U.S. coins are

Counterfeiters use .900 fine silver planchets to strike higher-quality fake Morgan dollars and offer a choice of colors in toned specimens. Note price at USD $49.73 for one coin, discounted to $43.74 per piece with a minimum order of 22.

produced to exacting standards. If either the weight or diameter vary or both the weight and diameter differ from the genuine standards, the coin in question is counterfeit. Note: Digital scales and a digital caliper (slide gauge) provide the most accurate measurements.

Be aware that if premiums go high enough in the secondary market, the counterfeiters may offer fakes struck on either .900 silver or .999 silver planchets. As has been their practice, many of the counterfeiters have offered fakes using .900 silver for a higher price. Both .900 and .999 silver strip is available on the world market. If it becomes economically viable for the counterfeiters to produce higher-priced fakes, don't be surprised to find them offered in venues frequented by the counterfeiters.

As noted, the physical difference between a genuine .900 silver dollar and genuine .999 silver dollar is virtually impossible to detect using the naked eye. So, too, it is difficult to discern the difference between a genuine silver coin and a silver-plated counterfeit. There is a minute difference in the thickness and the specific gravity of the .900 silver and .999 silver dollars, which each have a weight of 26.730 grams and a diameter 38.1 mm. However, the U.S. Mint has chosen not to make public the thickness or the specific gravity of the 2021 Morgan and Peace dollar coins. Lack of access to these key diagnostics of the new coins could prove problematic for individuals. Thus it may be prudent to insist upon authentication by a reputable third-party grading service before completing the purchase of a "raw" coin (one that has not been authenticated and encapsulated by a reputable third-party grading service).

The 2021 Morgan dollar coins will be struck at the Philadelphia, Denver, and San Francisco Mints. The Philadelphia strike will not bear a mintmark, the same as the 1921 issue did not have a mintmark. The 2021-D and 2021-S Morgan dollar coins will bear their mintmarks on their reverses below the eagle's tail feathers, just as the 1921 issues did.

Morgan dollars were struck at the Carson City Mint between 1878 and 1893 and at the New Orleans Mint between 1879 and 1904. The Philadelphia Mint will strike 2021 Morgan dollar coins to honor these historic mints. However, special privy marks rather than the historic CC and O mintmarks will be used on the 2021 coins.

The 2021 Peace dollar coin will be struck at the Philadelphia Mint, and, like the 1921 Peace dollar struck at Philadelphia, will not bear a mintmark.

Variety specialists have often relied on counterfeiters' use of incorrect style, size, and location of mintmarks to detect fakes. Such diagnostics are unlikely to prove beneficial for determining the authenticity of the 2021 issues because the counterfeiters have the capability to work from scans of high-definition images of genuine coins or specimens of the genuine coins to produce dies using EDM (electrical discharge machines) and CNC (computerized numerically controlled) equipment. In essence, counterfeiters will be able to replicate the placement, style, and size of the genuine mintmarks or privy marks.

There will be keen competition in purchasing these new issues directly from the U.S. Mint. For some collectors, the secondary market will be the only realistic way to obtain them. Thus, basic, common-sense precautions apply to purchasing these as well as all new issues in the secondary market.

- Be aware of current market premiums. Current values are reported in hobby publications and on the websites of the major grading services. If you are offered a coin at a price below the current market price, extra scrutiny should be exercised. Fakes are often priced below market values.
- Know with whom you are dealing. Many reputable coin dealers have websites as well as brick-and-mortar locations and set up at major coin shows throughout the nation. If you have never purchased a coin from the company/dealer or person offering the coin, complete your research of the vendor prior to completing a purchase. Use caution when responding to advertisements in classified pages, social media forums, and other sources.
- Does the coin meet each of the published specifications of metallic content, weight, and diameter?
- Are all of the key design elements present for both the obverse and reverse of the coin?
- Is the coin certified by a third-party grading service or guaranteed by the seller to be genuine?
- Be aware of the existence of sophisticated counterfeits of the major third-party grading services' holders or "slabs." Check the websites of the grading services to verify the genuineness of the holder and coin residing in it.

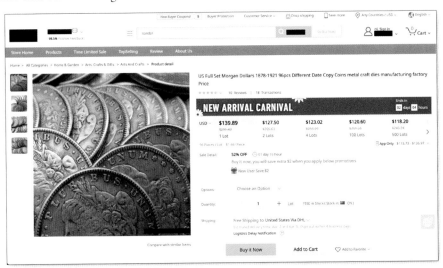

Complete sets (date and mintmark) of 96 fake silver-plated Morgan dollars can be purchased from counterfeiters in China starting at an average of USD $1.45 per coin. Buying 100 sets will reduce the per-piece price to $1.25. Competition is keen and often the counterfeiters will offer free shipping and delivery within 10 to 12 days.

Prices for fake Peace dollars decrease with quantity purchases. This counterfeiter in China sells counterfeit Peace dollars for USD 50¢ each with a minimum order of 50 pieces.

APPENDIX K

Pattern Dollars

or, What Might Have Been but Wasn't

From 1792, continuing into modern times, there have been many proposals for changes in circulating U.S. coins. Different metal compositions and different designs for the first century of coins, to 1892, comprised more than 1,000 different varieties known as patterns. Some were adopted, after which motifs in circulating coinage changed. Most, however, were similar to movie scenes on the cutting-room floor—created, but never shown in public.

Most patterns were of higher denominations. In silver series new designs were often tried out on half dollars and dollars, rarely on quarters, and hardly ever on dimes. In 1879 William Barber's "Washlady" obverse motif was made in the form of dimes, quarters, half dollars, and dollars, to create sets for numismatists. George T. Morgan's beautiful "Shield Earring" design of 1882 was used on quarters, half dollars, and dollars.

Often sets were made in multiple metals, again for collectors. Copper, silver, and, sometimes, aluminum were employed. To create numismatic rarities some sets of regular-design Proofs were made in off metals. Hence, for example, there are a number of different Liberty Seated coins that were struck in copper and aluminum. From spring 1859 until the summer of 1885, most patterns were secretly made, with few records kept, and were privately sold by Mint officials for their own profit. This practice accounts for an estimated 90 percent or more of the patterns in existence today.

In this appendix we offer a photographic gallery of selected pattern dollars, with the date and Judd catalog number for each, as described in *United States Pattern Coins*, by J. Hewitt Judd, edited by Q. David Bowers—a Whitman title that is the standard reference on the subject.

1794, Judd-18. The distinguishing feature of this copper pattern is the absence of stars around the perimeter. (Stars were used on the regular 1794-dated silver dollars.)

1863, Judd-348. This is a copper striking of the year's regular dollar designs.

1870, Judd-998. The year 1870 brought the first appearance of the dollar denomination in the Mint's experimental Standard Silver series. Note there is no mention of the country of origin in this die combination.

1870, Judd-1010. Q. David Bowers calls 1870 "the greatest pattern zoo of all time,"
with hundreds of varieties—including the Indian Princess design by James B. Longacre.

1872, Judd-1205. This pattern combines two designs by William Barber:
his classically inspired Amazonian Liberty, and a Standing Eagle.

1876, Judd-1458A. William Barber's portrait of Miss Liberty wearing a pearl-bordered coronet
is affectionately nicknamed the Sailor Head (for the ribbons hanging from her hair bow).

1879, Judd-1608. George T. Morgan's Schoolgirl is one
of the most famous and highly desired of all dollar patterns.

1880, Judd-1652. The goloid alloy and its related coinage proposals never excited much interest
in Congress or among the public. But it did give birth to many fascinating pattern coins.

1922, Judd-2020. This essai piece exhibits the design used on the high-relief Peace
dollar of 1921, but in medium relief and with minor differences in the date position, the
shape of the base of the 1, and a distorted S in TRUST. One example is confirmed to exist.

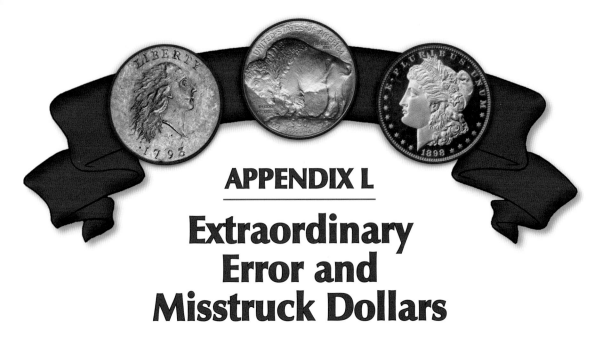

APPENDIX L

Extraordinary Error and Misstruck Dollars

This appendix is based on the work of
Nicholas P. Brown, David J. Camire, and Fred Weinberg.

"*Errare humanum est,*" wrote Richard G. Doty, curator of the Smithsonian's National Numismatic Collection, in his foreword to *100 Greatest U.S. Error Coins*. "To err is human. Errors on coins have been around as long as coinage itself. The reason is simple. Coinage is an industrial process, and coins were the first mass-produced objects in human history. Mass production of anything involves a number of simple, repetitive steps. During each of these steps, something can go wrong. Given the nature of human endeavor as summed up by Murphy's Law, something *will* go wrong, even if the manufacturing process is simple, requiring few steps for its completion. And the more sophisticated production becomes, the more individual steps it involves, the greater the potential for error. This is as true for coinage as it is for any other human product."

This appendix explores some of the most fascinating error and misstruck dollars. As outrageous as many of them seem, they are all real coins—each was personally examined by error-coin experts Nicholas Brown, David Camire, and Fred Weinberg as they wrote their book *100 Greatest U.S. Error Coins*. "In selecting the 100 greatest error coins for this book," they said, "we felt it was crucial to have each coin in our possession to be able to confirm that it actually exists, to ensure the authenticity of each error coin being considered, and to capture high-resolution photographs of the selected coins."

THE IMPORTANCE OF CERTIFICATION

With the advent of grading services like Professional Coin Grading Service (PCGS) and Numismatic Guaranty Corporation of America (NGC), even novice hobbyists can now easily collect error coins. This is because the grading services offer four valuable services: authentication of the coin; attribution (i.e., verification of its die characteristics); grading; and protection through encapsulation, ensuring safe long-term storage. This standardized assessment process has helped propel error coins to the mainstream market, attracting an even larger audience. After certification, the only variable the buyer needs to determine is how much to pay for the coin. Years ago, some seeming "error" coins were fabricated outside of the mint by private individuals; the only error was in buying them!

GRADING ERROR COINS

Grading mint errors is generally the same as grading normal coins, with a few exceptions. First, an extensive understanding of the minting process is a must. Grading a mint error has a lot to do with knowing how the coin was made. For instance, when an off-center coin is assessed, a grade is determined not only by the features of the portion of the coin that was struck but also by the area that was not struck. Why is that? Because such after-coining defects as scratches, wheel marks, post-strike mechanical damage, and environmental damage have to be taken into consideration—just as they must be on a normal coin. However, because mint errors occur from a malfunction in the minting process, there are times when there is "allowable damage" (although this is usually damage that occurred before striking). For instance, on an off-center Liberty Walking half dollar, a scratch on the planchet (pre-striking) that can still be seen after striking will generally not affect the grade of the coin. If the scratch occurred after the coin was struck, then it would matter.

Moreover, there are times when error coins can be attributed but not graded. One instance is blanks and planchets: since they were never struck, these items cannot be assessed a numerical grade. Another such example is die-adjustment strikes: since these pieces are used to adjust the amount of detail on a coin, many show very little detail. Again, no grade can be assigned to such coins.

Mint-error grading employs the same system, the Sheldon scale (which grades numerically from Poor-1 to MS-70), as does non-error grading. Most half dollars and other coins minted before the advent of the steam press show considerable wear, because in the early years of the Philadelphia Mint, economics dictated what went out the door—that is, nearly everything. For this reason, most mint errors from the late 1700s and early 1800s survive in a low state of preservation. In many cases they circulated as money. True Mint State *gems* of this era are genuinely rare and highly prized. In contrast, many mint errors from the 1980s to the present are found in brilliant Uncirculated condition.

PRICING ERROR COINS

It is challenging to price error coins, since many are considered to be unique and many trade privately. The factors in determining error-coin values are similar to those that determine the price for non-error coins, with some important distinctions.

- The first is referred to as the "wow" factor. How excited does someone get viewing the coin? Error coins are often dramatic. The more dramatic an error, the higher the price usually is for the coin. It bodes well when someone says, "I have never seen this coin before." Even better is when someone says, "I never knew a coin like this existed"—which leads us to the second variable:
- Rarity. How rare is the error? How many coins are known of its type and of the series? Is it the only known of that date? Does it even have a date? Is it the farthest off center? The list of qualities that can make an error coin unique is nearly endless. Rarity definitely plays a key role in determining the price.
- Third, what is the condition of the coin? How much detail can be seen, and how well preserved is it? This is no less important a consideration for an error coin than for a regular coin.
- The popularity of its series is also an important factor in determining the price of an error coin.

These four factors are just a few of the variables that determine an error coin's price. Brown, Camire, and Weinberg used auction records, fixed-price lists, known private transactions, and their experience as professional numismatists to determine the value of each error coin ranked in the 100 Greatest.

Until recently, a question many collectors asked was, "Which error coin will be the first to pass the $1,000,000 threshold?" Among non-error coins, it took quite a while for this barrier to be surmounted.

Once the threshold was breached, however—when Bowers and Merena Galleries sold the Eliasberg specimen 1913 Liberty Head nickel at auction for $1,485,000 on May 21, 1996—it suddenly became more common to hear of coins selling for this price or higher. The same is true for error coins, as bronze 1943 cents have crossed the $1,000,000 mark in recent years.

For error coins, values continue to rise as the market continues to mature. "Looking back, it is almost unbelievable that error-coin prices have reached these levels," wrote Brown, Camire, and Weinberg ten years ago. "In fact, when researching for the *100 Greatest U.S. Error Coins* we were amazed at the prices of mint errors in the 1980s. It was hard to find an error coin then that sold in the high four figures, never mind high five figures! Fast-forward to today, and it is a whole different story. Many major error coins are now trading in the high five figures, with some in the high six figures. Who would have guessed?"

A 2000-P state quarter muled with the reverse die of a Sacagawea dollar, on a manganese dollar planchet, struck at the Philadelphia Mint.

An undated low-relief Peace dollar that could have been struck only between 1922 and 1935, struck on a quarter dollar planchet.

A double-struck 1887 Morgan dollar.

Notes

THE HISTORY OF COINS IN AMERICA, 1607 TO DATE

1. Decades ago James F. Kelly, a leading Ohio dealer, demonstrated this to the editor. On June 24, 1922, Sanford Saltus, a well-to-do numismatist and benefactor of the American Numismatic Society, died while using cyanide to clean ancient silver coins (widely reported at the time).

2. Narrative by Q. David Bowers. Certain information and text provided by Kenneth E. Bressett, Dennis Tucker, Christopher McDowell, Ray Williams, and the late Dr. Richard Doty was particularly valuable in the compilation and editing of this narrative.

3. An example is provided by the ledgers of Henry Rust, who operated a general store in Wolfeboro, New Hampshire, and took in goods as pay as late as the 1840s.

4. *American Journal of Numismatics*, April 1874.

5. Per a comment from Edward D. Cogan in the *American Journal of Numismatics*, March 1868. Cogan had no firsthand knowledge of the activities of the Mint in the 1820s and 1830s, for he did not become involved in numismatics until the late 1850s.

6. The $285 figure is from R.W. Julian (letter, December 27, 1998); another source states $290. No doubt exchange rates varied from city to city and from broker to broker.

7. Certain commemorative information is adapted from the editor's "Joys of Collecting" column in *Coin World*.

8. Extensive details of all commemorative prices in 1989 and 1990 can be found in *Commemorative Coins of the United States: A Complete Encyclopedia*, Q. David Bowers, 1993.

9. As of August 2018 PCGS had certified 102 and NGC 43. Including resubmissions likely nets to about 100 different.

10. The 1976 convention in New York City was posted at over 20,000, but examination revealed that some attendees were counted twice (information from Edward C. Rochette).

11. Clifford Mishler stated he came up with a similar estimate years ago when he reviewed this comment (letter to the editor, August 30, 2018).

12. The PCGS Population Report of August 29, 2018, listed one coin, the same as years ago, but 93 in PF-69 DC and 273 in PF-68 DC.

13. An example is the story, "Limited Supply—How to Sell Coins and Frustrate People," by Tom DeLorey, *COINage*, May 2005.

14. *Coin World*, April 4, 2015.

15. Editorial in *Numismatic News*, April 26, 2005, and many other articles of the era.

16. David C. Harper editorial in *Numismatic News*, August 16, 2005; lengthy letter from collector R. Mittelbach, *Coin World*.

17. Details were given by Debbie Bradley in "Poor Quality Coin Designs Lamented," *Numismatic News*, June 3, 2010.

18. Ibid.

19. Partly adapted from Steve Roach, "Stickers and Plus Signs—Markets Multiply, Heads Spin," *Coin World*, July 12, 2010.

20. 2011 Annual Report to the Congress on the Presidential $1 Coin Program.

21. Paul Gilkes, *Coin World*, December 12, 2011.

22. Written by Clifford Mishler and Q. David Bowers at the request of the ANA.

23. Reports by Harry Miller in *Numismatic News*, September 13, 2011, and November 28, 2011.

24. The extensively detailed scenario was given by William T. Gibbs and Paul Gilkes in *Coin World*, August 25, 2014. When the ANA was asked if it would publish this information in *The Numismatist* or censure the arrangement, the "unofficial" comment was that the names were "too big" to criticize.

25. Connor Falk provided details in *Numismatic News*, October 14, 2014.

26. Proofs struck at the West Point Mint were offered in September 2018, in limited quantity. The offering was sold out in a matter of just a few minutes, to the disappointment of many loyal Mint customers who received "sold out" notices.

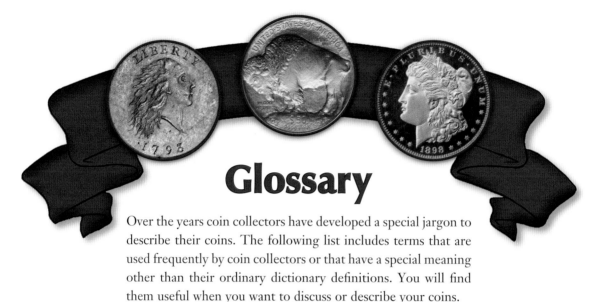

Glossary

Over the years coin collectors have developed a special jargon to describe their coins. The following list includes terms that are used frequently by coin collectors or that have a special meaning other than their ordinary dictionary definitions. You will find them useful when you want to discuss or describe your coins.

alloy—A combination of two or more metals.

altered date—A false date on a coin; a date altered to make a coin appear to be one of a rarer or more valuable issue.

bag mark—A surface mark, usually a small nick, acquired by a coin through contact with others in a mint bag.

billon—A low-grade alloy of silver (usually less than 50%) mixed with another metal, typically copper.

blank—The formed piece of metal on which a coin design will be stamped.

bronze—An alloy of copper, zinc, and tin.

bullion—Uncoined gold or silver in the form of bars, ingots, or plate.

cast coins—Coins that are made by pouring molten metal into a mold, instead of in the usual manner of striking blanks with dies.

cent—One one-hundredth of the standard monetary unit. Also known as a *centavo*, *centimo*, or *centesimo* in some Central American and South American countries; *centime* in France and various former colonies in Africa; and other variations.

certified coin—A coin that has been graded, authenticated, and encapsulated in plastic by an independent (neither buyer nor seller) grading service.

cherrypicker—A collector who finds scarce and unusual coins by carefully searching through unattributed items in old accumulations or dealers' stocks.

circulation strike—An Uncirculated coin intended for eventual use in commerce, as opposed to a Proof coin.

clad coinage—Issues of the United States dimes, quarters, halves, and some dollars made since 1965. Each coin has a center core of pure copper and a layer of copper-nickel or silver on both sides.

collar—The outer ring, or die chamber, that holds a blank in place in the coinage press while the coin is impressed by the obverse and reverse dies.

contact marks—Minor abrasions on an Uncirculated coin, made by contact with other coins in a bag or roll.

countermark—A stamp or mark impressed on a coin to verify its use by another government or to indicate revaluation.

crack-out—A coin that has been removed from a grading service holder.

crown—Any dollar-size coin (c. 38 mm in diameter) in general, often struck in silver; specifically, one from the United Kingdom and some Commonwealth countries.

cud—An area of raised metal at the rim of a coin where a portion of the die broke off, leaving a void in the design.

designer—The artist who creates a coin's design. An engraver is the person who cuts a design into a coinage die.

die—A piece of metal, usually hardened steel, with an incuse reverse image, engraved with a design and used for stamping coins.

die crack—A fine, raised line on a coin, caused by a broken die.

die defect—An imperfection on a coin, caused by a damaged die.

die variety—Any minor alteration in the basic design of a coin.

dipped, dipping—Refers to chemical cleaning of a coin to remove oxidation or foreign matter.

double eagle—The United States twenty-dollar gold coin.

doubled die—A die that has been given two misaligned impressions from a hub; also, a coin made from such a die.

doubloon—Popular name for a Spanish gold coin originally valued at $16.

eagle—A United States ten-dollar gold coin; also refers to U.S. silver, gold, and platinum bullion pieces made from 1986 to the present.

edge—Periphery of a coin, often with reeding, lettering, or other decoration.

electrotype—A reproduction of a coin or medal made by the electrodeposition process. Electrotypes are frequently used in museum displays.

electrum—A naturally occurring mixture of gold and silver. Some of the world's first coins were made of this alloy.

encapsulated coins—Coins that have been authenticated, graded, and sealed in plastic by a professional service.

engrailed edge—A coin edge marked with small curved notches.

engraver—The person who engraves or sculpts a model for use in translating to a coin die.

error—A mismade coin not intended for circulation.

exergue—That portion of a coin beneath the main design, often separated from it by a line, and typically bearing the date.

field—The background portion of a coin's surface not used for a design or inscription.

filler—A coin in worn condition but rare enough to be included in a collection.

fineness—The purity of gold, silver, or any other precious metal, expressed in terms of one thousand parts. A coin of 90% pure silver is expressed as .900 fine.

flan—A blank piece of metal in the size and shape of a coin; also called a *planchet*.

gem—A coin of exceptionally high quality, typically considered MS-65 or PF-65 or better.

gripped edge—An edge with irregularly spaced notches.

half eagle—The United States five-dollar gold coin minted from 1795 to 1929.

hub—A positive-image punch to impress the coin's design into a die for coinage.

incuse—The design of a coin that has been impressed below the coin's surface. A design raised above the coin's surface is in relief.

inscription—The legend or lettering on a coin.

intrinsic value—Bullion or "melt" value of the actual precious metal in a numismatic item.

investment grade—Promotional term; generally, a coin in grade MS-65 or better.

junk silver—Common-date silver coins taken from circulation; worth only bullion value.

key coin—One of the scarcer or more valuable coins in a series.

laureate—Head crowned with a laurel wreath.

legal tender—Money that is officially issued and recognized for redemption by an authorized agency or government.

legend—A principal inscription on a coin.

lettered edge—The edge of a coin bearing an inscription, found on some foreign and some older United States coins, modern Presidential dollars, and the MMIX Ultra High Relief gold coin.

luster—The brilliant or "frosty" surface quality of an Uncirculated (Mint State) coin.

milled edge—The raised rim around the outer surface of a coin, not to be confused with the reeded or serrated narrow edge of a coin.

mint error—Any mismade or defective coin produced by a mint.

mint luster—Shiny "frost" or brilliance on the surface of an Uncirculated or Mint State coin.

mintmark—A small letter or other mark on a coin, indicating the mint at which it was struck.

Mint set—A set of Uncirculated coins packaged and sold by the Mint. Each set contains one of each of the coins made for circulation at each of the mints that year.

motto—An inspirational word or phrase used on a coin.

mule—A coin struck from two dies not originally intended to be used together.

obverse—The front or face side of a coin.

overdate—Date made by superimposing one or more numerals on a previously dated die.

overgraded—A coin in poorer condition than stated.

overstrike—An impression made with new dies on a previously struck coin.

patina—The green or brown surface film found on ancient copper and bronze coins, caused by oxidation over a long period of time.

pattern—Experimental or trial coin, generally of a new design, denomination, or metal.

pedigree—The record of previous owners of a rare coin.

planchet—The blank piece of metal on which a coin design is stamped.

Proof—Coins struck for collectors by the Mint using specially polished dies and planchets.

Proof set—A set of each of the Proof coins made during a given year, packaged by the Mint and sold to collectors.

quarter eagle—The United States $2.50 gold coin.

raw—A coin that has not been encapsulated by an independent grading service.

reeded edge—The edge of a coin with grooved lines that run vertically around its perimeter, as seen on modern United States silver and clad coins.

regula—The bar separating the numerator and the denominator in a fraction.

relief—Any part of a coin's design that is raised above the coin's field is said to be in relief. The opposite of relief is incuse, meaning sunk into the field.

restrike—A coin struck from genuine dies at a later date than the original issue.

reverse—The back side of a coin.

rim—The raised portion of a coin that protects the design from wear.

round—A round one-ounce silver medal or bullion piece.

series—A set of one coin of each year of a specific design and denomination issued from each mint. For example, Lincoln cents from 1909 to 1959.

slab—A hard plastic case containing a coin that has been graded and encapsulated by a professional service.

spot price—The daily quoted market value of precious metals in bullion form.

token—A privately issued piece, typically with an exchange value for goods or services, but not an official government coin.

trade dollar—Silver dollar issued especially for trade with a foreign country. In the United States, trade dollars were first issued in 1873 to stimulate commerce with the Orient. Many other countries have also issued trade dollars.

truncation—The sharply cut-off bottom edge of a bust or portrait.

type—A series of coins defined by a shared distinguishing design, composition, denomination, and other elements. For example, Barber dimes or Franklin half dollars.

type set—A collection consisting of one representative coin of each type, of a particular series or period.

Uncirculated—A circulation-strike coin that has never been used in commerce, and has retained its original surface and luster; also called Mint State.

unique—An item of which only one specimen is known to exist.

variety—A coin's design that sets it apart from the normal issue of that type.

wheaties—Lincoln cents with the wheat ears reverse, issued from 1909 to 1958.

year set—A set of coins for any given year, consisting of one of each denomination issued that year.

Bibliography

A note from Q. David Bowers on the bibliography:

From the time that the first numismatically important book was published in America by Joseph B. Felt in 1839 to the present day, books have been the key to knowledge. A basic library of useful volumes is essential to the collecting and enjoyment of coins.

The following list includes the most important titles published over a long period of years. "Standard References" are ones that are essential today and include many updates of past writing and research. "References of Historical Interest" include titles from the past that for the most part have been made obsolete by later writing and research. Some of these remain valuable as a window into the state of the art years ago: they often contain anecdotal and narrative text not included in later works. Quality, usefulness, and desirability can vary widely, so before spending a large sum it is advisable to seek further information.

Beyond this listing, auction catalogs and price lists issued by various firms contain much interesting and valuable information. Countless articles in numismatic publications are valuable. The Numismatic Bibliomania Society (www.coinbooks.org) is the key to information on publications of the past and present. The Newman Numismatic Portal (www.nnp.wustl.edu) offers thousands of auction catalogs, magazine issues, and books free of charge; an incredible treasury for research and enjoyment.

The Whitman Publishing Web site (www.whitman.com) offers publications on coins, tokens, medals, and paper money currently available for purchase.

COLONIAL AND STATE COINAGE

STANDARD REFERENCES:

Bowers, Q. David. *Whitman Encyclopedia of Colonial and Early American Coins.* Second edition. Pelham, AL: 2019.

Breen, Walter. *Walter Breen's Complete Encyclopedia of U.S. and Colonial Coins.* New York, NY: 1988.

Carlotto, Tony. *The Copper Coins of Vermont.* Chelsea, MI: 1998.

Crosby, S.S. *The Early Coins of America.* Boston, MA: 1875 (reprinted 1945, 1965, 1974, 1983).

Demling, Michael. *New Jersey Coppers.* 2011.

Howes, Jack, James Rosen, and Gary Trudgen. *The History and Coinage of Machin's Mills.* Colonial Coin Collectors Club, 2020.

Maris, Edward. *A Historic Sketch of the Coins of New Jersey.* Philadelphia, PA: 1881 (reprinted 1965, 1974, 1987).

Martin, Sydney F. *The Hibernia Coinage of William Wood (1722–1724).* n.p., 2007.

——. *French Coinage Specifically for Colonial America.* Ann Arbor, MI: Colonial Coin Collectors Club, 2015.

——. *The Rosa Americana Coinage of William Wood.* Ann Arbor, MI: 2011.

——. *Saint Patrick Coinage for Ireland and New Jersey.* Ann Arbor, MI: 2019.

McDowell, Christopher. *Abel Buell and the History of the Connecticut and Fugio Coppers.* Ann Arbor, MI: 2015.

Miller, Henry C., and Hillyer C. Ryder. *The State Coinages of New England.* New York, NY: 1920.

Moore, Roger. *The Coins of Colonial Virginia.* Ann Arbor, MI: 2019.

Musante, Neil. *Medallic Washington* (2 vols.). London and Boston, MA: 2016.

Newman, Eric P. *Coinage for Colonial Virginia.* New York, NY: 1956.

——. *The United States Fugio Copper Coinage of 1787.* Ypsilanti, MI: 2007.

Newman, Eric P., and Richard G. Doty. *Studies on Money in Early America.* New York, NY: 1976.

Nipper, Will. *In Yankee Doodle's Pocket: The Myth, Magic, and Politics of Early America.* Conway, AR: 2008.

Noe, Sydney P. *The New England and Willow Tree Coinage of Massachusetts*. New York, NY: 1943.

——. *The Oak Tree Coinage of Massachusetts*. New York, NY: 1947.

——. *The Pine Tree Coinage of Massachusetts*. New York, NY: 1952.

——. *The Silver Coins of Massachusetts (Combined Reprint)*. New York, NY: 1973.

Rulau, Russell, and George Fuld. *Medallic Portraits of Washington*. Iola, WI: 1999.

Salmon, Christopher J. *The Silver Coins of Massachusetts*. New York, NY: 2010.

Siboni, Roger; John Howes; and A. Buell Ish. *New Jersey State Coppers. History. Description. Collecting*. New York, NY: 2013.

REFERENCES OF HISTORICAL INTEREST:

Anton, William T., Jr., and Bruce Kesse. *The Forgotten Coins of the North American Colonies*. Published by William T. Anton: 1990.

Atkins, James. *Coins and Tokens of the Possessions and Colonies of the British Empire*. London: 1889.

Baker, W.S. *American Engravers and Their Works*. Philadelphia, PA: 1875.

——. *The Engraved Portraits of Washington*. Philadelphia, PA: Lindsay & Baker, 1880.

——. *Medallic Portraits of Washington*. Philadelphia, PA: Robert M. Lindsay, 1885. An annotated reprint with updated information was prepared by George J. Fuld in 1965 and issued by Krause Publications.

Betts, C. Wyllys. *Counterfeit Half Pence Current in the American Colonies and Their Issue from the Mints of Connecticut and Vermont*. New York, NY: American Numismatic and Archaeological Society, 1886. Transcript of speech given to the Society.

Bressett, Kenneth E. "The Vermont Copper Coinage," part of *Studies on Money in Early America*. New York, NY: 1976.

Dalton, R., and S.H. Hamer. *English Provincial Token Coinage of the 18th Century*. London: 1910–1922. Issued in parts.

Douglas, Damon G. Manuscript notes on James Jarvis and Fugio coppers. Notes on New Jersey coppers. Excerpts published in *The Colonial Newsletter* and elsewhere. Loose copies made.

Felt, Joseph B. *An Historical Account of Massachusetts Currency*. Boston, MA: 1839.

Freidus, Daniel. "The History and Die Varieties of the Higley Coppers." *The Token: America's Other Money*. Coinage of the Americas Conference, 1994; New York, NY: 1995.

Guth, Ronald J. "The Copper Coinage of Vermont," *America's Copper Coinage 1783–1857*. Coinage of the Americas Conference, 1984; New York, NY: 1985.

Hull, John. "The Diaries of John Hull, Mint-Master and Treasurer of the Colony of Massachusetts Bay." *Archæologica Americana: Transactions and Collections of the American Antiquarian Society*. Vol. III. Cambridge, MA: 1850.

Jordan, Louis E., Robert H. Gore Jr., Numismatic Endowment, University of Notre Dame, Department of Special Collections, Website compiled maintained by Louis E. Jordan. Anthology of published information on various series.

Kenney, Richard D. *Struck Copies of Early American Coins*. New York, NY: 1952.

——. *Early American Medalists and Die-Sinkers Prior to the Civil War*. New York, NY: 1954.

Kessler, Alan. *The Fugio Cents*. Newtonville, MA: 1976.

Maris, Edward. *A Historical Sketch of the Coins of New Jersey*. Philadelphia, PA: 1881.

Mossman, Philip L. *Money of the American Colonies and Confederation: A Numismatic, Economic & Historical Correlation*. New York, NY: 1993.

——. "The American Confederation: The Times and Its Money." *Coinage of the American Confederation Period*. New York, NY: 1996.

——. *From Crime to Punishment: Counterfeit and Debased Currencies in Colonial and Pre-Federal America*. New York, NY: American Numismatic Society, 2013.

Musante, Neil E. *The Medallic Works of John Adams Bolen, Die Sinker &c*. Springfield, MA: 2002.

Nelson, Philip. *The Coinage of William Wood, 1722–1733*. London: 1959. Reprint.

Newman, Eric P. *The Secret of the Good Samaritan Shilling*. New York, NY: 1959.

Peck, C. Wilson. *English Copper, Tin and Bronze Coins in the British Museum 1558–1958*. London: 1960.

Prattent, Thomas, and M. Denton. *The Virtuoso's Companion and Coin Collector's Guide*. 8 volumes. London: 1795–1797.

Richardson, John M. "The Copper Coins of Vermont," published in *The Numismatist:* May 1947.

Ryder, Hillyer C. "The Colonial Coins of Vermont." Part of *State Coinages of New England*. New York, NY: 1920.

Slafter, Edmund F. "The Vermont Coinage." Essay in *Proceedings of the Vermont Historical Society*. Volume 1. Montpelier, VT: 1870.

Smith, Pete. "Vermont Coppers: *Coinage of an Independent Republic*." *Coinage of the American Confederation Period*. New York, NY: 1996.

Snelling, T. *A View of the Silver Coin and Coinage of England, From the Norman Conquest to the Present Time, Considered with Regard to Type, Legend, Sorts, Rarity, Weight, Fineness and Value, with Copper-Plates*. London: 1762.

Vlack, Robert A. *A. Catalog of Early American Coins*. Anaheim, CA: 1963.

——. *Early American Coins*. Johnson City, NY: Windsor Research Publications, Inc., 1965.

Williams, Malcolm E., Peter T. Sousa, and Edward C. Harris. *Coins of Bermuda 1616–1996*. Hamilton, Bermuda: 1997.

Wroth, Lawrence C. *Abel Buell of Connecticut: Silversmith, Type Founder & Engraver.* Middletown, CT: Acorn Club of Connecticut,1958.

HALF CENTS

STANDARD REFERENCES:

Bowers, Q. David. *A Guide Book of Half Cents and Large Cents.* Atlanta, GA: 2015.

Breen, Walter. *Walter Breen's Encyclopedia of United States Half Cents 1793–1857.* South Gate, CA: 1983.

Cohen, Roger S., Jr. *American Half Cents–The "Little Half Sisters."* Second edition. 1982.

Manley, Ronald P. *The Half Cent Die State Book, 1793–1857.* United States, 1998.

REFERENCES OF HISTORICAL INTEREST:

Frossard, Ed. *Monograph of United States Cents and Half Cents Issued Between the Years 1793 and 1857.* Irving-ton-on-Hudson, NY: 1879.

Gilbert, Ebenezer. *The United States Half Cents from the First Year of Issue, in 1793, to the Year When Discontin-ued.* New York, NY: 1916.

LARGE CENTS

STANDARD REFERENCES:

Bowers, Q. David. *A Guide Book of Half Cents and Large Cents.* Atlanta, GA: 2015.

Breen, Walter. *Walter Breen's Encyclopedia of Early United States Cents 1793–1814.* Wolfeboro, NH: 2001.

Grellman, J.R., Jr. *The Die Varieties of United States Large Cents 1840–1857.* Lake Mary, FL: 1991.

——. *Attribution Guide for United States Large Cents 1840–1857.* Third edition. Bloomington, MN: 2002.

Neiswinter, Jim. *The Aristocrat: The Story of the 1793 Sheldon 1.* Printed by the author, 2013.

Newcomb, H.R. *United States Copper Cents 1816–1857,* New York, NY: 1944 (reprinted 1983).

Noyes, William C. *United States Large Cents, 1793–1857.* Six volumes. Ypsilanti, MI: 2006–2015.

——. *United States Large Cents 1793–1814.* Bloomington, MN: 1991.

——. *United States Large Cents 1816–1839.* Bloomington, MN: 1991.

Penny-Wise, official publication of Early American Coppers, Inc.

Sheldon, William H. *Penny Whimsy (1793–1814),* New York, NY: 1958 (reprinted 1965, 1976).

Smith, Pete. *The Story of the Starred Reverse Cent.* Minneap-olis, MN: Printed by the author.

Wright, John D. *The Cent Book 1816–1839.* Bloomington, MN: 1992.

REFERENCES OF HISTORICAL INTEREST:

Adams, John W. (editor). *Monographs on Varieties of United States Large Cents, 1793–1794.* Lawrence, MA: 1976.

Chapman, S. Hudson. *The United States Cents of the Year 1794.* Second edition. Philadelphia, PA: 1926.

Clapp, George H. *The United States Cents of the Years 1798–1799.* Sewickley, PA: 1931.

——. *The United States Cents 1804–1814.* The Coin Collector Series Number Eight. New York, NY: 1941.

Clapp, George H., and Howard R. Newcomb. *The United States Cents of the Year 1795, 1796, 1797 and 1800.* New York, NY: The American Numismatic Society, 1947.

Crosby, Sylvester S. *The United States Coinage of 1793—— Cents and Half Cents.* Boston, MA: 1897.

Frossard, Ed. *Monograph of United States Cents and Half Cents Issued Between the Years 1793 and 1857.* Irvington-on-Hudson, NY: 1879.

Frossard, Ed., and W.W. Hays. *Varieties of United States Cents of the Year 1794: Described and Illustrated.* New York, NY: 1893.

Lapp, Warren A., and Herbert A. Silberman (editors). *United States Large Cents 1793–1857.* Lawrence, MA: 1975.

Loring, Denis W. (editor). *Monographs on Varieties of United States Large Cents, 1795–1803.* Lawrence, MA: 1976.

Maris, Edward. *Varieties of the Copper Issues of the United States Mint in the Year 1794.* Philadelphia, PA: 1869 and 1870.

McGirk, Charles E. "United States Cents and Die Varieties, 1793–1857," *The Numismatist,* October 1913 to December 1914.

Noyes, William C., Del Bland, and Dan Demeo. *The Official Condition Census for U.S. Large Cents 1793–1839.* 2005.

Sheldon, William H. *Early American Cents.* New York, NY: 1949.

Smith, Pete. *Names with Notes.* Minneapolis, MN: 1992.

SMALL CENTS

STANDARD REFERENCES:

Bowers, Q. David. *A Guide Book of Lincoln Cents.* Second edition. Atlanta, GA: 2016.

Lange, David W. *The Complete Guide to Lincoln Cents.* Wolfeboro, NH: 1996.

Schein, Allan. *The Gold Indians of Bela Lyon Pratt.* Published by the author, 2016.

Snow, Richard. *A Guide Book of Flying Eagle and Indian Head Cents.* Third edition. Atlanta, GA: 2016.

REFERENCES OF HISTORICAL INTEREST:

Anderson, Shane M. *The Complete Lincoln Cent Encyclope-dia.* Iola, WI: 1996.

Bowers, Q. David. *A Buyer's and Enthusiast's Guide to Flying Eagle and Indian Cents.* Wolfeboro, NH: 1996.

Daughtrey, Charles D. *Looking Through Lincoln Cents: Chronology of a Series.* Second edition. Irvine, CA: 2005.

Lange, David W. *The Complete Guide to Lincoln Cents.* Wolfeboro, NH: 1996.

Manley, Stephen G. *The Lincoln Cent.* Muscatine, IA: 1981.

Taylor, Sol. *The Standard Guide to the Lincoln Cents.* Fourth Edition. Anaheim, CA: 1999.

Tomaska, Rick Jerry, *Cameo and Brilliant Proof Coinage of the 1950 to 1970 Era.* Encinitas, CA: 1991.

TWO-CENT PIECES AND THREE-CENT PIECES

Bierly, William. *In God We Trust: The American Civil War, Money, Banking, and Religion.* Pelham, AL: 2019.

Bowers, Q. David. *United States Three-Cent and Five-Cent Pieces.* Wolfeboro, NH: 2005.

Kliman, Myron. *The Two Cent Piece and Varieties.* South Laguna, CA: 1977.

Leone, Frank. *Longacre's Two Cent Piece Die Varieties & Errors.* College Point, NY: 1991.

NICKEL FIVE-CENT PIECES
STANDARD REFERENCES:

Bowers, Q. David. *United States Three-Cent and Five-Cent Pieces.* Wolfeboro, NH: 2005.

——. *A Guide Book of Buffalo and Jefferson Nickels.* Atlanta, GA: 2007.

——. *A Guide Book of Shield and Liberty Head Nickels.* Atlanta, GA: 2006.

Fletcher, Edward L., Jr. *The Shield Five Cent Series.* Ormond Beach, FL: 1994.

Lange, David W. *The Complete Guide to Buffalo Nickels.* Virginia Beach, VA: 2006.

Nagengast, Bernard. *The Jefferson Nickel Analyst.* Second edition. Sidney, OH: 1979.

REFERENCES OF HISTORICAL INTEREST:

Montgomery, Paul, Mark Borckardt, and Ray Knight. *Million Dollar Nickels: Mysteries of the Illicit 1913 Liberty Head Nickels Revealed.* Irvine, CA: 2005.

Peters, Gloria, and Cynthia Mahon. *The Complete Guide to Shield and Liberty Head Nickels.* Virginia Beach, VA: 1995.

Spindel, Howard. "The Shield Nickel Viewer." Computerized reference on the series published by Howard Spindel, 2005. Information available at www.shieldnickels.net.

Wescott, Michael. *The United States Nickel Five-Cent Piece: A Date-by-Date Analysis and History.* Wolfeboro, NH: 1991.

Young, Richard G., and Wade J. Wilkin. *Racketeer Nickel and Its Many Mysteries.* Published by the authors, 2004.

HALF DIMES
STANDARD REFERENCES:

Bowers, Q. David. *A Guide Book of Liberty Seated Silver Coins.* Second edition. Pelham, AL: 2019.

Blythe, Al. *The Complete Guide to Liberty Seated Half Dimes.* Virginia Beach, VA: 1992.

Logan, Russell, and John McCloskey. *Federal Half Dimes 1792–1837.* Manchester, MI: 1998.

Smith, Pete, Joel J. Orosz, and Leonard Augsburger. *1792: Birth of a Nation's Coinage.* Dallas, TX: 2017.

REFERENCES OF HISTORICAL INTEREST:

Amato, Jon. *Numismatic Background and Census of 1802 Half Dimes.* Dallas, TX: 2017.

Breen, Walter. *United States Half Dimes: A Supplement.* New York, NY: 1958.

Newlin, H.P. *The Early Half-Dimes of the United States.* Philadelphia, PA: 1883 (reprinted 1933).

Valentine, D.W. *The United States Half Dimes.* New York, NY: 1931 (reprinted 1975).

DIMES AND TWENTY-CENT PIECES
STANDARD REFERENCES:

Bowers, Q. David. *A Guide Book of Barber Silver Coins.* Atlanta, GA: 2015.

——. *A Guide Book of Liberty Seated Silver Coins.* Second edition. Pelham, AL: 2019.

——. *A Guide Book of Mercury Dimes, Standing Liberty Quarters, and Liberty Walking Half Dollars.* Atlanta, GA: 2015.

Brunner, Lane J., and John M. Frost. *Double Dime: The United States Twenty-Cent Piece.* 2014.

Davis, David, Russell Logan, Allen Lovejoy, John McCloskey, and William Subjack. *Early United States Dimes 1796–1837.* Ypsilanti, MI: 1984.

Fortin, Gerry. *Liberty Seated Dimes Web-Book.* www.seateddimevarieties.com.

Greer, Brian. *The Complete Guide to Liberty Seated Dimes.* Virginia Beach, VA: 2005.

Lange, David W. *The Complete Guide to Mercury Dimes.* Second edition. Virginia Beach, VA: 2005.

Lawrence, David. *The Complete Guide to Barber Dimes.* Virginia Beach, VA: 1991.

REFERENCES OF HISTORICAL INTEREST:

Ahwash, Kamal M. *Encyclopedia of United States Liberty Seated Dimes 1837–1891.* Kamal Press, 1977.

Lawrence, David. *The Complete Guide to Barber Dimes.* Virginia Beach, VA: 1991.

QUARTER DOLLARS
STANDARD REFERENCES:

Bowers, Q. David. *A Guide Book of Barber Silver Coins.* Atlanta, GA: 2015.

——. *A Guide Book of Liberty Seated Silver Coins*. Second edition. Pelham, AL: 2019.

——. *A Guide Book of Mercury Dimes, Standing Liberty Quarters, and Liberty Walking Half Dollars*. Atlanta, GA: 2015.

——*A Guide Book of Washington Quarters*. Second edition. Pelham, AL: 2017.

Bressett, Kenneth. *The Official Whitman Statehood Quarters Collector's Handbook*. New York, NY: 2000.

Briggs, Larry. *The Comprehensive Encyclopedia of United States Seated Quarters*. Lima, OH: 1991.

Cline, J.H. *Standing Liberty Quarters*. Third edition. 1996.

Knauss, Robert H. *Standing Liberty Quarter Varieties & Errors*. Second edition. Published by the author, 2014.

Rea, Rory, Glenn Peterson, Bradley Karoleff, and John Kovach. *Early Quarter Dollars of the U.S. Mint, 1796–1838*. 2010.

Tompkins, Steve M. *Early United States Quarters, 1796–1838*. 2008.

REFERENCES OF HISTORICAL INTEREST:
Browning, A.W. *The Early Quarter Dollars of the United States 1796–1838*. New York, NY: 1925 (reprinted 1992).

Duphorne, R. *The Early Quarter Dollars of the United States*. 1975.

Haseltine. J.W. *Type Table of United States Dollars, Half Dollars and Quarter Dollars*. Philadelphia, PA: 1881 (reprinted 1927, 1968).

Lawrence, David. *The Complete Guide to Barber Quarters*. Virginia Beach, VA: 1989.

HALF DOLLARS
STANDARD REFERENCES:
Ambio, Jeff. *Collecting and Investing Strategies for Walking Liberty Half Dollars*. Irvine, CA: 2008.

Bowers, Q. David. *A Guide Book of Barber Silver Coins*. Atlanta, GA: 2015.

——. *A Guide Book of Liberty Seated Silver Coins*. Second edition. Pelham, AL: 2019.

——. *A Guide Book of Mercury Dimes, Standing Liberty Quarters, and Liberty Walking Half Dollars*. Atlanta, GA: 2015.

Overton, Al C. *Early Half Dollar Die Varieties 1794–1836*. Fifth edition. Murietta, CA: 2014.

Peterson, Glenn R. *The Ultimate Guide to Attributing Bust Half Dollars*. Rocky River, OH: 2000.

Tomaska, Rick. *A Guide Book of Franklin and Kennedy Half Dollars*. Second edition. Atlanta, GA: 2012.

Wiley, Randy, and Bill Bugert. *The Complete Guide to Liberty Seated Half Dollars*. Virginia Beach, VA: 1993.

REFERENCES OF HISTORICAL INTEREST:
Amato, Jon. *The Draped Bust Half Dollars of 1796–1797*. Dallas, TX: 2015.

Beistle, M.L. *A Register of Half Dollar Die Varieties and Sub-Varieties*. Shippensburg, PA: 1929.

Haseltine. J.W. *Type Table of United States Dollars, Half Dollars and Quarter Dollars*. Philadelphia, PA: 1881 (reprinted 1927, 1968).

Howe, Dean F. *Walking Liberty Half Dollars, an In-Depth Study*. Sandy, UT: 1989.

Lawrence, David. *The Complete Guide to Barber Halves*. Virginia Beach, VA: 1991.

Souders, Edgar. *Bust Half Fever*. Second edition. Money Tree Press, 2007.

Swiatek, Anthony. *Walking Liberty Half Dollars*. New York, NY: 1983.

SILVER AND RELATED DOLLARS
STANDARD REFERENCES:
Bolender, M.H. *The United States Early Silver Dollars From 1794 to 1803*. Fifth edition. Iola, WI: 1987.

Bowers, Q. David. *The Encyclopedia of United States Silver Dollars 1794–1804*. Wolfeboro, NH: 2013.

——. *A Guide Book of Liberty Seated Silver Coins*. Second edition. Pelham, AL: 2019.

——. *A Guide Book of Modern United States Dollar Coins*. Atlanta, GA: 2016.

——. *A Guide Book of Morgan Silver Dollars*. Sixth edition. Atlanta, GA: 2016.

——. *The Rare Silver Dollars Dated 1804*. Wolfeboro, NH: 1999.

——. *Silver Dollars and Trade Dollars of the United States: A Complete Encyclopedia*. Wolfeboro, NH: 1993.

Burdette, Roger W. *A Guide Book of Peace Dollars*. Fourth edition. Pelham, AL: 2019.

Crum, Adam, Selby Ungar, and Jeff Oxman. *Carson City Morgan Dollars*. Fourth edition. Pelham, AL: 2019.

Fey, Michael S., and Jeff Oxman. *The Top 100 Morgan Dollar Varieties*. Morris Planes, NJ: 1997.

Logies, Martin A. *The Flowing Hair Silver Dollars of 1794*. 2004.

Newman, Eric P., and Kenneth E. Bressett. *The Fantastic 1804 Dollar*, Racine, WI: 1962 (tribute edition 2009).

Standish, Michael "Miles," with John B. Love. *Morgan Dollar: America's Love Affair With a Legendary Coin*. Atlanta, GA: 2014.

Van Allen, Leroy C., and A. George Mallis. *Comprehensive Catalogue and Encyclopedia of U.S. Morgan and Peace Silver Dollars*. New York, NY: 1997.

REFERENCES OF HISTORICAL INTEREST:
Carter, Mike. *The 1921 Morgan Dollars: An In-Depth Study*. Beverly Hills, CA: 1986.

Coinage of Gold and Silver. Collection, amounting to 491 printed pages, of documents, testimonies, etc., before the House of Representatives, Committee on Coinage, Weights, and Measures, 1891. The silver question, the silver-gold ratio, international monetary situations, financial panics, and more are debated. Washington, D.C.: Government Printing Office, 1891.

Haseltine. J.W. *Type Table of United States Dollars, Half Dollars and Quarter Dollars.* Philadelphia, PA: 1881 (reprinted 1927, 1968).

Highfill, John W. *The Comprehensive U.S. Silver Dollar Encyclopedia.* Broken Arrow, OK: 1992.

Osburn, Dick, and Brian Cushing. *A Register of Liberty Seated Dollar Varieties.* www.seateddollarvarieties.com.

Willem, John M. *The United States Trade Dollar.* Second edition. Racine, WI: 1965.

GOLD COINS ($1 THROUGH $20)
STANDARD REFERENCES:
Akers, David W. *Gold Dollars (and Other Gold Denominations).* Englewood, OH: 1975–1982.

Bowers, Q. David. *United States Gold Coins: An Illustrated History.* Second edition. Wolfeboro, NH: 2011.

——. *Harry W. Bass, Jr. Museum Sylloge,* Wolfeboro, NH: 2002.

——. *A Guide Book of Gold Dollars.* Atlanta, GA: 2008.

——. *A Guide Book of Double Eagle Gold Coins.* Second edition. Pelham, AL: 2019.

——. *A Guide Book of Quarter Eagle and Half Eagle Gold Coins.* Pelham, AL: 2019.

——. *U.S. Liberty Head Double Eagles: The Gilded Age of Coinage.* Wolfeboro, NH: 2015.

Bowers, Q. David, and Douglas Winter, *The United States $3 Gold Pieces 1854–1889.* Wolfeboro, NH: 2005.

Dannreuther, John W., and Harry W. Bass Jr. *Early U.S. Gold Coin Varieties.* Atlanta, GA: 2006.

Fivaz, Bill. *United States Gold Counterfeit Detection Guide.* Atlanta, GA: 2005.

Garrett, Jeff, and Ron Guth. *Encyclopedia of U.S. Gold Coins, 1795–1933.* Second edition. Atlanta, GA: 2008.

Schein, Allan. *The $2 1/2 and $5 Gold Indians of Bela Lyon Pratt.* 2016.

Winter, Douglas. *Gold Coins of the Charlotte Mint, 1838–1861.* Wolfeboro, NH: 1987.

——. *New Orleans Mint Gold Coins.* Wolfeboro, NH: 1992.

——. *Gold Coins of the Dahlonega Mint 1838–1861.* Dallas, TX: 1997.

Winter, Douglas, and Lawrence E. Cutler, M.D., *Gold Coins of the Old West: The Carson City Mint 1870–1893.* Wolfeboro, NH: 1994.

REFERENCES OF HISTORICAL INTEREST:
Augsburger, Leonard D. *Treasure in the Cellar: A Tale of Gold in Depression-Era Baltimore.* Baltimore, MD: 2008.

Breen, Walter. *Major Varieties of U.S. Gold Dollars.* Chicago, IL: 1964.

Gilliland, Cory. *Sylloge of the United States Holdings in the National Numismatic Collection of the*

Smithsonian Institution. Volume 1: Gold Coins, 1785–1834. Washington, D.C.: 1992.

Miller, Robert W., Sr., *U.S. Half Eagle Gold Coins.* Elmwood Park, NJ: 1997.

Schein, Allan. *The Gold Indians of Bela Lyon Pratt.* 1997.

Taglione, Paul F. *Federal Gold Coinage: Volume I, An Introduction to Gold Coinage & the Gold Dollars.* Boston, MA: 1986.

——. *A Reference to United States Federal Gold Coinage: Volume II, The Quarter Eagles.* Boston, MA: 1986.

——. *A Reference to United States Federal Gold Coinage: Volume III, The Three Dollar Pieces.* Boston, MA: 1986.

——. *A Reference to United States Federal Gold Coinage: Volume IV, An Investment Philosophy for the Prudent Consumer.* Boston, MA: 1986.

Taraszka, Anthony J. *United States Ten Dollar Gold Eagles.* Portage, MI: 1999.

Tripp, David E. *Illegal Tender: Gold, Greed, and the Mystery of the Lost 1933 Double Eagle.* New York, NY: 2004.

COMMEMORATIVE COINS
STANDARD REFERENCES:
Bowers, Q. David. *A Guide Book of United States Commemorative Coins.* Second edition. Atlanta, GA: 2016.

Swiatek, Anthony J. *Encyclopedia of the Commemorative Coins of the United States.* Chicago, IL: 2012.

REFERENCES OF HISTORICAL INTEREST:
Bullowa, David M. *The Commemorative Coinage of the United States 1892–1938.* New York, NY: 1938.

Mosher, Stuart. *United States Commemorative Coins.* New York, NY: 1940.

Swiatek, Anthony and Walter H, Breen. *The Encyclopedia of United States Silver and Gold Commemorative Coins 1892–1954.* New York, NY: 1981.

Taxay, Don. *An Illustrated History of U.S. Commemorative Coinage.* New York, NY: 1967.

BULLION COINS
Mercanti, John M., with Michael Standish. *American Silver Eagles: A Guide to the U.S. Bullion Coin Program.* Third edition. Atlanta, GA: 2016 (reprint, Pelham, AL, 2018).

Moy, Edmund. *American Gold and Platinum Eagles: A Guide to the U.S. Bullion Coin Programs.* Atlanta, GA: 2013.

Tucker, Dennis. *American Gold and Silver: U.S. Mint Collector and Investor Coins and Medals, Bicentennial to Date.* Atlanta, GA: 2016.

Whitman Publishing. *Precious Metal: Investing and Collecting in Today's Silver, Gold, and Platinum Markets.* Second edition. Pelham, AL: 2019.

PATTERN COINS

STANDARD REFERENCES:

Judd, J. Hewitt. *United States Pattern Coins.* Tenth edition. Atlanta, GA: 2008. Updated by Q. David Bowers.

REFERENCES OF HISTORICAL INTEREST:

Adams, Edgar H., and William H. Woodin. *United States Pattern, Trial, and Experimental Pieces.* New York, NY: 1913.

Cassel, David. *United States Pattern Postage Currency.* Miami, FL: 2000.

Davis, Robert Coulton. "Pattern and Experimental Issues of the United States Mint." *The Coin Collector's Journal.* September 1885.

Pollock, Andrew W., III. *United States Patterns and Related Issues.* Wolfeboro, NH: 1994.

PRIVATE AND TERRITORIAL GOLD

STANDARD REFERENCES:

Adams, Edgar H. *Private Gold Coinage of California 1849–1855.* Brooklyn, NY: 1913.

Bowers, Q. David. *A California Gold Rush History Featuring Treasure from the S.S. Central America.* Wolfeboro, NH: 2001.

Breen, Walter H., and Ronald Gillio. *California Pioneer Fractional Gold.* Second edition. Santa Barbara, CA: 1983.

Kagin, Donald H. *Private Gold Coins and Patterns of the United States.* New York, NY: 1981.

Leonard, Robert D., Jr., *California Pioneer Fractional Gold.* Wolfeboro, NH: 2003.

Moulton, Karl. *John J. Ford, Jr. and the Franklin Hoard.* Congress, AZ: 2003.

Owens, Dan. *California Coiners and Assayers.* Wolfeboro, NH; and New York, NY: 2000.

REFERENCES OF HISTORICAL INTEREST:

Adams, Edgar H. *Official Premium Lists of Private and Territorial Gold Coins.* Brooklyn, NY: 1909.

——. *Private Gold Coinage of California 1849–1855.* Brooklyn, NY: 1913.

Conrad, Judy (editor). Preface by Barry Schatz. *Story of an American Tragedy. Survivors' Accounts of the Sinking of the Steamship Central America.* Columbus, OH: 1988.

Griffin, Clarence. *The Bechtlers and Bechtler Coinage and Gold Mining in North Carolina 1814–1830.* Spindale, NC: 1929.

Lee, Kenneth W. *California Gold—Dollars, Half Dollars, Quarter Dollars.* Santa Ana, CA: 1979.

TOKENS, MEDALS, AND EXONUMIA

STANDARD REFERENCES:

Betts, C. Wyllys. *American Colonial History Illustrated by Contemporary Medals.* New York, NY: 1894.

Bowers, Q. David. *A Guide Book of Civil War Tokens.* Second edition. Atlanta, GA: 2015.

——. *A Guide Book of Hard Times Tokens.* Atlanta, GA: 2015.

Brunk, Gregory G. *American and Canadian Countermarked Coins.* Rockford, IL: 1987.

Coffee, John M., and Harold V. Ford, *The Atwood-Coffee Catalogue of United States and Canadian Transportation Tokens.* Fifth edition. Boston, MA: 1996.

Fuld, George, and Melvin Fuld (edited by John Ostendorf, Q. David Bowers, Evelyn R. Mishkin, and Susan Trask). *U.S. Civil War Store Cards.* Third edition. Civil War Token Society, 2015.

Fuld, George, and Melvin Fuld (edited by John Mark Glazer, Q. David Bowers, and Susan Trask). *Patriotic Civil War Tokens.* Sixth edition. Civil War Token Society. 2016.

Hibler, Harold E., and Charles V. Kappen. *So-Called Dollars.* Second edition. Clifton, NJ: 2008.

Hodder, Michael, and Q. David Bowers. *The Standard Catalogue of Encased Postage Stamps.* Wolfeboro, NH: 1989.

Jaeger, Katherine. *A Guide Book of United States Tokens and Medals.* Atlanta, GA: 2008.

Jaeger, Katherine, and Q. David Bowers. *100 Greatest American Medals and Tokens.* Atlanta, GA: 2007.

Julian, R.W. *Medals of the United States Mint: The First Century 1792–1892.* El Cajon, CA: 1977.

Leonard, Robert D., Jr., Ken Hallenbeck, and Adna G. Wilde Jr. *Forgotten Colorado Silver: Joseph Lesher's Defiant Coins.* Charleston, SC: 2017.

Musante, Neil. *Medallic Washington* (2 volumes). London and Boston, MA: 2016.

Rulau, Russell. *Standard Catalog of U.S. Tokens 1700–1900.* Fourth edition. Iola, WI: 2004.

Schenkman, David E. *Civil War Sutler Tokens and Cardboard Scrip.* Bryans Road, MD: 1983.

Schuman, Robert A., M.D. *The True Hard Times Tokens.* M&G Publications, 2000.

Sullivan, Edmund. *American Political Badges & Medals.* Lawrence, MA: 1981.

REFERENCES OF HISTORICAL INTEREST:

Adams, Edgar H. *United States Store Cards.* New York, NY: Edgar H. Adams and Wayte Raymond, 1920.

Appleton, William Sumner, *Description of Medals of Washington in the Collection of W.S. Appleton.* Boston, MA: 1873.

Bushnell, Charles I. *An Arrangement of Tradesmen's Cards, Political Tokens, also Election Medals, Medalets, &c. Current in the United States of America for the Last Sixty Years, Described from the Originals, Chiefly in the Collection of the Author.* Published by the author, 1858.

Collett, Mark W., J. Ledyard Hodge, and Alfred B. Taylor. *Catalogue of American Store Cards & c.* Philadelphia, PA: 1859.

DeWitt, J. Doyle. *A Century of Campaign Buttons 1789–1889.* Hartford, CT: 1959.

Doty, Richard G. (editor), *The Token: America's Other Money.* New York, NY: American Numismatic Society and Coinage of the Americas Conference, 1994.

Loubat, J.F. *The Medallic History of the United States of America, 1776–1876.* New York, NY: 1878.

Low, Lyman H. *Hard Times Tokens.* New York, NY: 1899.

Miller, Donald M. *A Catalogue of U.S. Store Cards or Merchants' Tokens.* Indiana, PA: 1962.

Rulau, Russell. *Hard Times Tokens: A Complete Revision and Enlargement of Lyman H. Low's 1899 Classic Reference.* Iola, WI: Krause Publications, 1987.

Rulau Russell, and George Fuld, *Medallic Portraits of Washington.* Iola, WI: 1985 and later editions.

Satterlee, Alfred H. *An Arrangement of The Medals and Tokens Struck in Honor of the Presidents of the United States and of the Presidential Candidates From the Administration of John Adams to That of Abraham Lincoln, Inclusive.* New York, NY: Printed for the author, 1862.

Snowden, James Ross. *A Description of the Medals of Washington.* Philadelphia, PA: 1861.

Woodward, W. Elliot. *A List of Washington Memorial Medals.* Boston, MA: 1865.

GENERAL COVERING MULTIPLE AMERICAN COIN SERIES

STANDARD REFERENCES:

Bowers, Q. David. *The History of United States Coinage as Illustrated by the Garrett Collection.* Los First printing. Los Angeles, CA: Published for The Johns Hopkins University.

——. *American Coin Treasures and Hoards.* Wolfeboro, NH: 1997.

——. *The History of American Numismatics Before the Civil War, 1760–1860.* Wolfeboro, NH: 1998.

——. *A Guide Book of United States Type Coins.* Second edition. Atlanta, GA: 2008.

Breen, Walter H. *Walter Breen's Encyclopedia of U.S. and Colonial Proof Coins, 1792–1977.* Albertson, NY: 1977; updated, Wolfeboro, NH: 1989.

——"Secret History of the Gobrecht Coinages." *Coin Collectors Journal,* 157–158. New York, NY: Wayte Raymond, Inc., 1954.

——. *Walter Breen's Encyclopedia of U.S. and Colonial Proof Coins, 1792–1977.* Albertson, NY: FCI Press, 1977.

——. *Walter Breen's Complete Encyclopedia of U.S. and Colonial Coins.* New York, NY: 1988.

Burdette, Roger W. *The Renaissance of American Coinage 1905–1908.* Great Falls, VA: 2006.

——. *The Renaissance of American Coinage 1909–1915.* Great Falls, VA: 2007.

——. *The Renaissance of American Coinage 1916–1921.* Great Falls, VA: 2005.

Carothers, Neil. *Fractional Money.* New York, NY: John Wiley & Sons, Inc., 1930.

Fivaz, Bill, and J.T. Stanton. *The Cherrypickers' Guide to Rare Die Varieties.* Atlanta, GA: various editions and volumes.

Garrett, Jeff, and Ron Guth. *100 Greatest U.S. Coins.* Fourth edition. Atlanta, GA: 2014.

Guth, Ron, and Jeff Garrett. *United States Coinage: A Study by Type.* Atlanta, GA: 2005.

Lange, David W. *A Guide Book of Modern United States Proof Coin Sets.* Second edition. Atlanta, GA: 2010.

Tucker, Dennis. *American Gold and Silver: U.S. Mint Collector and Investor Coins and Medals, Bicentennial to Date.* Atlanta, GA: 2016.

REFERENCES OF HISTORICAL INTEREST:

Alexander, David T., Thomas K. DeLorey, and Brad Reed. *Coin World Comprehensive Catalog & Encyclopedia of United States Coins.* Sidney, OH: Coin World, 1995.

Eckfeldt, Jacob R., and William E. DuBois. *A Manual of Gold and Silver Coins of All Nations, Struck Within the Past Century.* Philadelphia, PA: Assay Office of the Mint, 1842.

Scott Stamp & Coin Co., Ltd., also Scott & Co. and J.W. Scott Co., Ltd. *Standard Catalogue* (various titles). 1878–1913.

Taxay, Don. *Counterfeit, Mis-Struck and Unofficial U.S. Coins.* New York, NY: 1963.

——. *U.S. Mint and Coinage.* New York, NY: Arco Publishing, 1966.

——. *Scott's Comprehensive Catalogue of United States Coinage.* New York, NY: Scott Publications, 1970 (cover date 1971).

Tomaska, Rick Jerry. *Cameo and Brilliant Proof Coinage of the 1950 to 1970 Era.* Encinitas, CA: 1991.

Vermeule, Cornelius. *Numismatic Art in America.* Cambridge, MA: 1971.

Witham, Stewart. *Johann Matthaus Reich, Also Known as John Reich.* Canton, OH: November 1993.

WORLD ISSUES RELATED TO THE UNITED STATES

Allen, Lyman L. *U.S. Philippine Coins.* Oakland Park, FL: 1998.

Medcalf, Donald, and Russell, Ronald. *Hawaiian Money Standard Catalog.* Second edition. Mill Creek, WA: 1991.

Schilke, Oscar G., and Raphael E. Solomon. *America's Foreign Coins: An Illustrated Standard Catalogue with Valuations of Foreign Coins with Legal Tender status in the United States, 1793–1857.* New York, NY: 1964.

Shafer, Neil. *United States Territorial Coinage for the Philippine Islands.* Racine, WI: 1961.

HISTORY OF THE U.S. MINTS AND THE MINT COLLECTION

STANDARD REFERENCES:

Augsburger, Leonard D., and Orosz, Joel J. *The Secret History of the First U.S. Mint*. Atlanta, GA: 2011.

Bierly, William. *In God We Trust*. Pelham, AL: 2019.

Bowers, Q. David. *Guide Book of the United States Mint*. Pelham, AL: 2016.

Goe, Rusty. *The Mint on Carson Street*. Reno, NV: 2003.

Lange, David W. *History of the United States Mint and Its Coinage*. Atlanta, GA: 2005.

Mishler, Clifford. *Coins: Questions and Answers*. Sixth edition. Pelham, AL: 2019.

Smith, Pete, Joel Orosz, and Leonard Augsburger. *1792: Birth of a Nation's Coinage*. Birmingham, UK: 2017.

Taxay, Don. *The United States Mint and Coinage*. New York, NY: 1966.

REFERENCES OF HISTORICAL INTEREST:

Comparette, T.L. *Catalogue of Coins, Tokens and Medals in the Numismatic Collection of the Mint of the United States at Philadelphia, Pa*. Washington, D.C.: 1914.

Dubois, William E. *Pledges of History: A Brief Account of the Collection of Coins Belonging to the Mint of the United States, More Particularly of the Antique Specimens*. First edition. Philadelphia, PA: C. Sherman, 1846; Second edition. New York, NY: George P. Putnam, 1851.

Evans, George. *Illustrated History of the U.S. Mint* (various eds.), Philadelphia, PA: 1885–1901.

Hickson, Howard. *Mint Mark CC: The Story of the United States Mint at Carson City, Nevada*. Carson City, NV: The Nevada State Museum, 1972 and 1990.

Johnston, Elizabeth B. *A Visit to the Cabinet of the United States Mint, at Philadelphia*. Philadelphia, PA: 1876.

McClure, R.A. *An Index to the Coins and Medals of the Mint of the United States at Philadelphia*. Philadelphia, PA: 1891.

Moulton, Karl. *Henry Voigt and Others Involved in Early American Coinage*. Congress, AZ: 2003.

Smith, A.M. *Illustrated History of the U.S. Mint*. Philadelphia, PA: 1881.

Snowden, James Ross. *A Description of Ancient and Modern Coins in the Cabinet of the Mint of the United States*. Philadelphia, PA: 1860. (Mostly researched and written by George Bull [then curator of the Mint Cabinet] and William Ewing Dubois.)

Stewart, Frank. *History of the First United States Mint, Its People and Its Operations*. 1924 (reprinted 1974).

Treasury Department, United States Mint, *et al. Annual Report of the Director of the Mint*. Philadelphia (later, Washington), 1795 onward.

Young, James Rankin. *The United States Mint at Philadelphia*. Philadelphia, PA: Capt. A.J. Andrews (agent, not publisher), 1903.

PUBLICATIONS ABOUT BOOKS, COINAGE, MONEY, AND NUMISMATICS

Burdette, Roger. *From Mine to Mint: American Coinage Operations and Technology, 1833 to 1837*. Great Falls, VA: 2013.

Coin Collector's Journal, The. New York City, NY: J.W. Scott & Co.,1870s and 1880s.

Coin World Almanac. Sidney, OH: Coin World, 1976 and later editions.

Coinage Laws of the United States 1792–1894. Modern foreword to reprint by David L. Ganz. Wolfeboro, NH: 1991.

Cooper, Denis R. *The Art and Craft of Coinmaking, A History of Minting Technology*. London, England: 1988.

Davis, Charles E. *American Numismatic Literature: An Annotated Survey of Auction Sales 1980–1991*. Lincoln, MA: 1992.

Del Mar, Alexander. *The History of Money in America from the Earliest Times to the Establishment of the Constitution*. Reprint. Hawthorne, CA: 1966.

Dickeson, Montroville W. *American Numismatical Manual*. Philadelphia, PA: J.B. Lippincott & Co., 1859, also editions of 1860 and 1866.

Doty, Richard G. *America's Money, America's Story*. Iola, WI: 1998.

Durst, Lorraine S. *United States Numismatic Auction Catalogs: A Bibliography*. New York, NY: 1981.

Eckfeldt, Jacob Reese, and William Ewing DuBois. *A Manual of Gold and Silver Coins of All Nations, Struck Within the Past Century*. Philadelphia, PA: 1842.

Gengerke, Martin. *American Numismatic Auctions*. Woodside, NY: printed by the author, 1990.

Groce, George C., and David H. Wallace. *New York Historical Society's Dictionary of Artists in America*. New Haven, CT: 1957.

Heaton, Augustus G. *A Treatise on the Coinage of the United States Branch Mints*. Washington, D.C.: Published by the author, 1893.

Hepburn, A. Barton. *A History of Currency in the United States*. New York, NY: 1915.

Hickcox, John H. *An Historical Account of American Coinage*. Albany, NY: 1858.

Hodder, Michael J., and Q. David Bowers. *The Norweb Collection: An American Legacy*. Wolfeboro, NH: 1987.

Jaeger, Katherine M., and Q. David Bowers. *The 100 Greatest American Medals and Tokens*. Atlanta, GA: 2007.

Jones, George F. *The Coin Collector's Manual: A Guide Book for Coin Collectors*. Philadelphia, PA: 1860.

Kenney, Richard D. *Early American Medalists and Die-Sinkers Prior to the Civil War*. New York, NY: 1954.

Kleeberg, John M. "The Shipwreck of the *Faithful Steward:* A 'Missing Link' in the Exports of British and Irish Halfpence." New York, NY: 1996.

Linderman, Henry R. *Money and Legal Tender.* New York, NY: G.P. Putnam's Sons, 1877.

Lupia, John N. III. *American Numismatic Auctions to 1875, Volume 1, 1738–1850.* 2013.

Moulton, Karl. *United States Numismatic Catalogues, 1990–2000.* Congress, AZ: 2001.

Orosz, Joel J. *The Eagle That Is Forgotten: Pierre Eugène Du Simitière, Founding Father of American Numismatics.* Wolfeboro, NH: 1988.

Prime, W.C. *Coins, Medals, and Seals.* New York, NY: 1861.

Raymond, Wayte. *Standard Catalogue of United States Coins and Paper Money* (titles vary). New York, NY: Scott Stamp & Coin Co. (and others), 1934 to 1957 editions.

Ruddy, James F. *Photograde.* Nineteenth edition. Racine, WI: Western Publishing Co., 1990.

Rulau, Russell. *Standard Catalogue of United States Tokens 1700–1900.* Fourth edition. Iola, WI: 2004.

Shippee, Robert W. *Pleasure & Profit: 100 Lessons for the Building and Selling of a Collection of Rare Coins.* Atlanta, GA: 2015.

Smith, A.M. *Coin Collectors' of the United States, Illustrated Guide.* Philadelphia, PA: January 1886.

Stauffer, David McNeely. *American Engravers Upon Copper and Steel.* New York, NY: 1907.

Sumner, William Graham. *A History of American Currency.* New York, NY: 1874.

Taxay, Don. *Counterfeit, Mis-Struck, and Unofficial U.S. Coins.* New York, NY: 1963.

——. *U.S. Mint and Coinage.* New York, NY: 1966.

——. *Scott's Comprehensive Catalogue of United States Coinage.* New York, NY.

Wright, Benjamin P. "The American Store or Business Cards." Published serially in *The Numismatist,* 1898–1901. Reprinted by the Token and Medal Society, 1963.

Image Credits

Note: Images are credited by page number and by location on the page, starting with number 1 at upper left and reading left to right. Obverse-reverse pairs are counted as a single image and are noted in italic type.

American Numismatic Rarities (ANR) contributed the following image: 1,354.*2x*.

Ken Bressett contributed the following image: 1,396.*5x*.

Heritage Auctions contributed the following images: 28.*2x*; 28.3; 28.6; 29.*3x*; 29.*4x*; 121.*1x*; 136.5; 139.*4x*; 139.*5x*; 141.*3x*; 145.5; 148.*1x*; 153.*1x*; 153.2; 153.3; 153.4; 164.*1x*; 166.*2x*; 166.*3x*; 175.*2x*; 176.*1x*; 176.*3x*; 178.*2x*; 179.2; 179.*5x*; 180.*4x*; 186.*1x*; 189.*1x*; 189.*2x*; 189.*3x*; 192.*1x*; 193.*1x*; 193.5; 194.*4x*; 195.*1x*; 196.*1x*; 197.*3x*; 201.*1x*; 201.*2x*; 201.*3x*; 203.6; 203.7; 204.1; 204.2; 205.*3x*; 207.*1x*; 211.*1x*; 212.*2x*; 212.*3x*; 214.*2x*; 215.*1x*; 217.*1x*; 217.*2x*; 217.*3x*; 220.*1x*; 220.*2x*; 220.*3x*; 221.*1x*; 221.3; 221.4; 222.2; 222.3; 226.*2x*; 227.1; 230.*1x*; 230.*2x*; 230.5; 232.*3x*; 233.*3x*; 233.*4x*; 236.*2x*; 247.*3x*; 255.*3x*; 256.*1x*; 256.*2x*; 258.*1x*; 262.*1x*; 277.1; 277.2; 284.*4x*; 284.*5x*; 284.*7x*; 286.*1x*; 292.1; 292.1; 292.2; 292.3; 292.4; 292.5; 292.6; 292.7; 292.8; 292.9; 293.*1x*; 294.*1x*; 295.*1x*; 295.*1x*; 295.*3x*; 296.*3x*; 297.*1x*; 297.*1x*; 297.*2x*; 300.*1x*; 301.*1x*; 301.*2x*; 301.*3x*; 301.*4x*; 302.*1x*; 308.*1x*; 309.*2x*; 313.*1x*; 314.*2x*; 319.*2x*; 320.*1x*; 320.*2x*; 322.*1x*; 322.*2x*; 326.*1x*; 326.*2x*; 327.*4x*; 355.*1x*; 360.*2x*; 361.*1x*; 361.*2x*; 361.*3x*; 362.*1x*; 362.*2x*; 364.*2x*; 366.*3x*; 367.*2x*; 369.*1x*; 371.3; 371.4; 371.5; 373.*2x*; 374.*1x*; 374.*3x*; 376.*3x*; 377.*2x*; 380.*3x*; 380.*4x*; 380.*5x*; 380.*6x*; 385.1; 385.2; 393.*1x*; 394.*2x*; 395.*1x*; 395.*2x*; 395.*3x*; 396.*1x*; 396.*2x*; 396.30; 396.40; 397.*1x*; 401.*8x*; 403.*2x*; 409.*1x*; 409.*2x*; 409.*5x*; 410.*8x*; 410.*9x*; 413.*3x*; 413.*4x*; 414.70; 418.*1x*; 420.30; 420.40; 421.10; 421.20; 424.*3x*; 440.*1x*; 440.*3x*; 440.*6x*; 441.*1x*; 457.*2x*; 458.*1x*; 458.*2x*; 458.*3x*; 459.*1x*; 459.*2x*; 459.*3x*; 461.*3x*; 462.*1x*; 462.*2x*; 462.*3x*; 463.*1x*; 463.2; 463.*4x*; 464.*2x*; 467.4; 467.5; 468.1; 468.2; 468.3; 468.4; 468.5; 468.6; 468.8; 468.9; 469.2; 469.3; 469.4; 469.5; 471.*2x*; 471.*3x*; 471.*4x*; 471.*5x*; 471.*7x*; 472.*1x*; 472.*2x*; 472.*4x*; 475.4; 475.5; 475.6; 476.1; 476.2; 478.1; 481.1; 481.2; 482.1; 483.*1x*; 483.*3x*; 485.*3x*; 487.1; 487.2; 491.*1x*; 491.2; 491.*3x*; 494.*4x*; 495.3; 495.4; 495.5; 512.*1x*; 512.*2x*; 513.*1x*; 513.2; 513.*3x*; 522.*1x*; 522.*2x*; 523.*1x*; 523.*2x*; 536.*1x*; 542.*1x*; 553.*4x*; 578.4; 578.*5x*; 585.*1x*; 585.2; 585.*3x*; 585.*4x*; 585.*5x*; 585.*6x*; 585.*7x*; 585.*9x*; 586.*1x*; 586.*2x*; 586.*3x*; 586.*4x*; 586.*5x*; 591.2; 591.3; 592.2; 592.3; 621.*2x*; 628.*1x*; 719.3; 719.4; 858.*4x*; 867.*2x*; 871.*1x*; 871.*3x*; 895.*1x*; 897.*2x*; 932.*1x*; 932.*1x*; 940.*1x*; 944.*3x*; 954.1; 956.1; 967.*1x*; 980.*1x*; 987.*1x*; 990.1; 990.2; 990.4; 992.3; 992.4; 995.2; 995.3; 996.*3x*; 996.*4x*; 996.*5x*; 996.*6x*; 996.*7x*; 999.1; 999.2; 1,001.4; 1,002.2; 1,020.*3x*; 1,023.1; 1,023.2; 1,023.3; 1,023.4; 1,024.*1x*; 1,024.*2x*; 1,024.*3x*; 1,024.*4x*; 1,026.3; 1,026.4; 1,044.*2x*; 1,083.*1x*; 1,168.*1x*; 1,270.*2x*; 1,274.*1x*; 1,274.*2x*; 1,274.3; 1,274.*4x*; 1,274.*5x*; 1,275.*1x*; 1,276.*1x*; 1,277.*1x*; 1,278.*1x*; 1,280.*1x*; 1,280.*2x*; 1,280.3; 1,280.*4x*; 1,280.*5x*; 1,281.*1x*; 1,281.*2x*; 1,281.*3x*; 1,283.*1x*; 1,283.2; 1,283.*3x*; 1,290.*1x*; 1,290.*2x*; 1,290.*3x*; 1,290.*4x*; 1,291.*1x*; 1,292.*1x*; 1,292.*2x*; 1,293.*1x*; 1,303.*1x*; 1,313.2; 1,313.*4x*; 1,313.5; 1,313.6; 1,313.*7x*; 1,352.2; 1,375.1; 1,407.*3x*; 1,409.*1x*.

Harry Miller contributed the following images: 29.*2x*; 29.*3x*.

Tom Mulvaney photographed the following images: 28.*3x*; 29.*1x*; 29.*2x*; 29.*3x*; 29.*4x*; 97.*1x*; 97.*2x*; 97.3; 97.4; 97.*5x*; 97.*6x*; 00.*2x*; 59.*2x*; 59.*3x*; 79.*3x*; 79.*4x*; 80.*2x*; 182.*2x*; 184.*1x*; 274.*3x*; 286.*2x*; 308.*3x*; 309.*1x*; 314.*3x*; 314.*4x*; 315.*1x*; 354.1; 483.2; 850.*1x*; 888.*1x*; 895.*1x*; 895.*2x*; 897.*1x*; 985.*3x*; 987.3; 987.5; 988.*1x*; 997.*3x*; 1,020.2; 1,029.1; 1,047.2; 1,047.3; 1,048.1; 1,051.1; 1,120.*1x*; 1,122.*1x*; 1,123.*2x*; 1,124.*1x*; 1,125.*1x*; 1,125.*2x*; 1,126.*1x*; 1,127.*1x*; 1,128.*1x*; 1,129.*1x*; 1,130.*1x*; 1,131.*1x*; 1,131.2; 1,132.*1x*; 1,133.*1x*; 1,133.2; 1,134.*1x*; 1,135.*1x*; 1,135.2; 1,137.*1x*; 1,137.2; 1,138.*1x*; 1,139.*1x*; 1,139.2; 1,140.*1x*; 1,141.*1x*; 1,141.2; 1,142.*1x*; 1,143.*1x*; 1,144.*1x*; 1,145.*1x*; 1,145.2; 1,146.*1x*; 1,147.*1x*; 1,147.2; 1,148.*1x*; 1,160.*2x*; 1,161.*1x*; 1,162.*1x*; 1,162.*2x*; 1,164.*1x*; 1,165.*1x*; 1,165.2; 1,166.*1x*; 1,167.*1x*; 1,167.2; 1,169.*1x*; 1,170.*1x*; 1,170.2; 1,171.*1x*; 1,172.*1x*; 1,172.2; 1,173.*1x*; 1,174.*1x*; 1,174.2; 1,175.*1x*; 1,176.*1x*; 1,176.2; 1,177.*1x*; 1,179.*1x*;

1,179.2x; 1,180.1x; 1,181.1x; 1,181.2x; 1,182.1x; 1,299.2x; 1,300.3x; 1,324.3x; 1,338.5x; 1,338.6x; 1,338.7x; 1,339.1x; 1,339.2x; 1,340.1x; 1,340.2x; 1,340.3x; 1,340.4x; 1,340.5x; 1,340.6x; 1,340.7x; 1,340.8x; 1,340.9x; 1,340.10x.

The **National Numismatic Collection** at the Smithsonian Institution contributed the following images: 957.3; 973.2x; 973.3x.

Ken Potter contributed the following image: 612.1.

Jeff Shevlin contributed the following images: 1,413.1x; 1,413.2x; 1,413.3x; 1,413.4x; 1,414.1x; 1,414.2x; 1,414.3x; 1,414.4x; 1,415.1x; 1,415.2x; 1,415.3x; 1,415.4x; 1,416.1x; 1,416.2x; 1,416.3x; 1,416.4x; 1,417.1x; 1,417.2x; 1,417.3x; 1,417.4x; 1,418.1x; 1,418.2x; 1,418.3x; 1,418.4x; 1,419.1x; 1,419.2x; 1,419.3x; 1,419.4x; 1,420.1x; 1,420.2x; 1,420.3x; 1,420.4x; 1,421.1x; 1,421.2x; 1,421.3x; 1,422.1x; 1,422.2x; 1,422.3x; 1,422.4x; 1,423.1x; 1,423.2x; 1,423.3x; 1,423.4x; 1,424.1x; 1,424.2x; 1,424.3x; 1,424.4x; 1,425.1x; 1,425.2x; 1,425.3x; 1,425.4x; 1,426.1x; 1,426.2x; 1,426.3x; 1,426.4x; 1,427.1x; 1,427.2x; 1,427.3x; 1,427.4x; 1,427.4x.

Roger Siboni contributed the following images: 123.3; 123.4; 124.3x; 158.3; 158.5; 158.6; 159.2; 159.3; 159.7; 159.8; 159.9; 160.3; 160.5; 161.9; 169.1x; 257.3; 257.4; 258.3x; 258.5x; 258.6x; 529.1x; 1,409.2x; 1,409.3x.

Stack's Bowers Galleries contributed the following images: 123.1x; 123.2x; 132.2; 138.5; 139.1x; 139.2; 139.3x; 140.2x; 140.4x; 140.5x; 141.1x; 141.2x; 142.3; 144.1x; 144.4x; 144.5x; 145.7; 160.1; 160.4; 163.1x; 170.2x; 171.3x; 180.2; 180.3; 181.4x; 182.3x; 186.2x; 187.1x; 187.2x; 188.1x; 188.2x; 188.3x; 191.1x; 191.2x; 191.3x; 192.2x; 192.3x; 193.2; 193.4; 194.1x; 195.2x; 196.2x; 196.3x; 197.1x; 197.2x; 198.6; 198.7; 199.8x; 199.9x; 200.1x; 200.2x; 201.4x; 202.1x; 202.2x; 202.3x; 204.3; 205.1x; 205.2x; 206.1x; 206.2x; 206.3x; 207.2x; 212.1x; 213.1x; 213.2x; 213.3x; 214.1x; 215.2x; 216.1x; 216.2x; 216.3x; 219.1x; 219.2x; 219.3x; 221.2x; 223.2x; 224.1x; 224.2x; 225.1x; 225.2x; 225.3x; 226.1x; 232.1x; 232.2x; 233.1x; 235.2x; 235.4x; 235.5x; 236.1x; 237.1x; 237.2x; 237.3x; 238.1x; 238.2; 240.2x; 245.2x; 246.1x; 246.2x; 247.1x; 247.2x; 247.4x; 252.1x; 253.2x; 254.1x; 254.2x; 255.1x; 255.2x; 255.4x; 256.3x; 258.2x; 258.4x; 260.1x; 260.2x; 260.3x; 261.1x; 261.2x; 261.3x; 261.4x; 262.2x; 270.1x; 270.2x; 270.3x; 270.4x; 270.5x; 272.1x; 272.2x; 272.3x; 273.1x; 273.2x; 273.3x; 273.4x; 274.1x; 274.2x; 283.1; 284.6x; 285.1x; 286.3x; 295.2x; 299.1x; 299.2x; 299.3x; 300.3x; 306.1x; 306.2x; 306.3x; 306.4x; 306.5x; 306.6x; 307.1x; 308.2x; 309.3x; 312.1x; 312.2x; 313.2x; 313.3x; 314.1x; 315.2x; 321.1x; 321.4x; 322.3x; 325.2x; 326.3x; 326.4x; 327.1x; 327.2x; 327.3x; 328.1x; 333.1x; 333.2x; 334.1x; 334.2x; 334.3x; 335.1x; 335.2x; 335.3x; 335.4x; 341.1x; 342.1x; 342.2x; 342.3x; 342.4x; 356.4x; 356.5x; 365.1x; 365.2x; 365.3x; 366.1x; 366.2x; 367.1x; 368.1x; 368.2x; 369.2x; 369.3x; 370.1x; 370.2x; 370.3x; 372.1x; 372.2x; 372.3x; 373.1x; 374.2x; 375.4x;

376.1x; 376.2x; 377.1x; 377.4x; 378.2x; 380.2x; 380.7x; 380.8x; 380.12x; 382.1x; 382.2x; 382.3x; 383.1x; 383.2x; 383.3x; 384.2x; 394.1x; 394.3x; 397.2x; 398.1x; 398.2x; 398.3x; 399.1x; 399.2x; 399.3x; 400.1x; 401.5x; 401.7x; 402.1x; 403.1x; 403.3x; 404.1x; 404.2x; 405.1x; 405.2x; 406.10; 406.20; 407.40; 407.50; 407.60; 410.2x; 410.5x; 411.1x; 412.1x; 412.2x; 412.3x; 413.1x; 413.2x; 414.1x; 415.40; 424.1x; 424.4x; 425.1x; 426.1x; 426.2x; 426.3x; 426.4x; 431.3x; 432.1x; 432.2x; 433.1x; 433.2x; 433.3x; 433.4x; 434.1x; 434.2x; 434.3x; 440.20; 440.50; 440.7x; 441.3x; 456.2x; 457.1x; 460.1x; 464.3x; 465.1x; 465.2x; 466.1x; 466.2x; 466.3x; 467.1x; 467.2x; 467.3x; 468.7; 470.1x; 470.2x; 473.1x; 473.2x; 473.3x; 473.4; 474.1x; 474.2x; 474.3x; 474.4x; 475.1x; 475.2x; 476.3; 477.1; 478.2; 484.1x; 484.2x; 485.1x; 485.2x; 485.4x; 486.1x; 486.2x; 486.3x; 492.1x; 493.1x; 493.2x; 493.3x; 494.1x; 494.2x; 494.3x; 495.2; 498.1x; 498.2x; 499.1x; 499.2x; 499.3x; 499.4x; 500.1x; 500.3x; 538.2x; 546.3x; 548.1x; 552.2; 557.1x; 557.2x; 563.2x; 580.1x; 580.2x; 584.1x; 586.6x; 594.1x; 597.1x; 597.2x; 599.3x; 599.4x; 602.1x; 602.2; 604.1x; 606.5; 606.6; 606.7; 606.8; 609.1x; 610.1x; 611.2x; 613.3x; 613.4; 616.1x; 617.1x; 618.1x; 619.2x; 623.2x; 624.3x; 626.1x; 626.2; 626.4x; 628.3x; 630.2x; 631.3x; 633.2x; 634.3x; 636.2x; 639.1x; 639.3x; 640.1x; 640.3x; 641.1x; 642.1x; 642.2; 642.3x; 644.2x; 645.2x; 646.2x; 646.3x; 647.1x; 647.2x; 648.1x; 648.2x; 650.1x; 651.2x; 653.1x; 653.1; 655.2x; 656.3x; 658.2x; 660.1x; 661.1x; 661.2; 661.3x; 662.1x; 663.2x; 665.1x; 665.2x; 666.1x; 666.3x; 667.1x; 667.3x; 668.1x; 668.2x; 669.1x; 669.3x; 670.2x; 671.1x; 671.2x; 671.3x; 672.2x; 672.3x; 672.3; 673.1x; 678.1x; 678.2x; 680.3x; 681.2x; 682.1x; 682.2; 684.1x; 685.2x; 686.2x; 688.1x; 689.2x; 691.2x; 693.1x; 694.2x; 696.1x; 697.2x; 699.1x; 700.2x; 702.1x; 703.2x; 705.2x; 707.2x; 709.2x; 711.1x; 712.1x; 713.3x; 715.1x; 716.2x; 717.3x; 719.2x; 728.1x; 730.2x; 738.3x; 739.1x; 739.2x; 739.3x; 755.1x; 840.2x; 858.1; 858.2; 864.1x; 906.1x; 926.1x; 926.2x; 940.2x; 956.2; 957.2; 962.3x; 962.4x; 963.1x; 963.1x; 967.3x; 967.4x; 968.1x; 968.4x; 974.1x; 978.1x; 980.3; 980.4; 981.1x; 981.2x; 982.1x; 982.2x; 984.1; 984.9; 984.11; 984.12; 986.1x; 986.2x; 993.1x; 993.3x; 996.1x; 997.1x; 997.2x; 998.2x; 1,002.5; 1,002.7; 1,011.2x; 1,011.3x; 1,012.1x; 1,019.1x; 1,025.1x; 1,025.2x; 1,026.2x; 1,038.1x; 1,038.4x; 1,038.5x; 1,038.6x; 1,039.1x; 1,039.2x; 1,044.1x; 1,044.4x; 1,044.5x; 1,045.1x; 1,046.1x; 1,047.1x; 1,049.1x; 1,057.1x; 1,057.2x; 1,058.1x; 1,067.1x; 1,068.1x; 1,069.1x; 1,070.1x; 1,071.1x; 1,072.1x; 1,074.1x; 1,074.2x; 1,075.1x; 1,075.2x; 1,078.2x; 1,079.1; 1,079.2x; 1,079.3; 1,080.1x; 1,080.2; 1,081.1x; 1,081.2; 1,082.1x; 1,082.2; 1,083.2x; 1,084.1x; 1,085.1x; 1,088.1x; 1,089.1x; 1,090.1x; 1,091.1x; 1,092.1x; 1,093.1x; 1,094.1x; 1,094.2; 1,096.1x; 1,097.1x; 1,099.1x; 1,099.2x; 1,100.1x; 1,101.1x; 1,102.1x; 1,103.1x; 1,103.2x; 1,104.1x; 1,105.1x; 1,106.1x; 1,106.2x; 1,107.1x; 1,108.1x; 1,108.2x; 1,109.1x; 1,110.1x; 1,111.1x; 1,111.2x; 1,113.1x; 1,113.2x; 1,114.1x; 1,115.1x; 1,115.2x; 1,117.1x; 1,129.2x. 1,270.1x; 1,313.1x; 1,313.3.

Index
General Index

Alphabetical Index of Dates for Commemoratives

* See also "Government Commemorative Sets" on page 1275.

* See also "Government Commemorative Sets" on page 1275.

They Say Rome Wasn't Built in a Day
CAC has been building confidence "coin upon coin" for 13 years

It takes time to build something great. Now in its 13th year, CAC continues to grow - chiseling and shaping impressive new milestones as it continues to hold coins to a higher standard. Formed by leading members of the numismatic community, CAC's sticker gives collectors confidence that a coin is solid for the grade. What's more, CAC stands behind its stickered coins as the biggest and most active market maker.

Coin upon coin, CAC continues to build and grow, passing new milestones along the way.

- ☑ **Over 1.3 Million Coins Evaluated** (insured value $6 billion, average value over $4,500.00)
- ☑ **Team of 4 Expert Graders** (each with decades of professional experience)
- ☑ **CAC is the premier market maker for its stickered coins** (nearly $625,000,000 in purchases)
- ☑ **CAC provides a FREE Independent Market Value Guide** powered by CDN Greysheet
- ☑ **CAC coins continue to bring a premium in the market**

CAC is Building Confidence Coin upon Coin!

CAC now has over 2,250 members

"Because Confidence is Priceless"

www.caccoin.com